Kurzban's Immigration Law Sourcebook

Eleventh Edition

AILA Titles of Interest

AILA's Occupational Guidebooks

Immigration Options for Artists and Entertainers

Immigration Options for Physicians

Immigration Options for Nurses & Allied Health Care Professionals

Immigration Options for Religious Workers

Immigration Options for Academics and Researchers

Immigration Options for Investors and Entrepreneurs

Statutes, Regulations, Agency Materials & Case Law

Immigration & Nationality Act (INA)

Immigration Regulations (CFR)

Agency Interpretations of Immigration Policy (Cables, Memos, and Liaison Minutes)

AILA's Immigration Case Summaries

Core Curriculum

Navigating the Fundamentals of Immigration Law

*Immigration Law for Paralegals**

AILA's Guide to Technology and Legal Research for the Immigration Lawyer

CD Products & Toolbox Series

AILA's Immigration Practice Toolbox

AILA's Litigation Toolbox

For Your Clients

Client Brochures (10 Titles)

*U.S. Tax Guides for Foreign Persons and Those Who Pay Them, 4 volumes— (H-1Bs, L-1s, J-1s, B-1s)**

Online Research Tools

AILA*Link* Online

AILA's Focus Series

EB-2 & EB-3 Degree Equivalency
by Ronald Wada

Waivers Under the INA
by Julie Ferguson

Private Bills & Pardons in Immigration
by Anna Gallagher

Treatises & Primers

Kurzban's Immigration Law Sourcebook
by Ira J. Kurzban

Professionals: A Matter of Degree
by Martin J. Lawler

AILA's Asylum Primer
by Regina Germain

Immigration Consequences of Criminal Activity
by Mary E. Kramer

Essentials of Removal and Relief
by Joseph A. Vail

Essentials of Immigration Law
by Richard A. Boswell

Litigating Immigration Cases in Federal Court
by Robert Pauw

Other Titles

AILA's Guide to Worksite Enforcement and Corporate Compliance

David Stanton Manual on Labor Certification

AILA's Global Immigration Guide: A Country-by-Country Survey

Immigration & Nationality Law Handbook

The Visa Processing Guide

Ethics in a Brave New World

Immigration Practice Under NAFTA and Other Free Trade Agreements

Government Reprints

BIA Practice Manual

Immigration Judge Benchbook

Citizenship Laws of the World

CBP Inspector's Field Manual

USCIS Adjudicator's Field Manual

EOIR Immigration Practice Manual

Tables of Contents and other information about these publications can be found at ***www.ailapubs.org***. Orders may be placed at that site or by calling 1-800-982-2839.

*An AILA-distributed title

KURZBAN'S

IMMIGRATION LAW SOURCEBOOK

Eleventh Edition

A Comprehensive Outline and Reference Tool

Ira J. Kurzban

AMERICAN IMMIGRATION LAW FOUNDATION

Obtaining Documents Posted on AILA's InfoNet

Citations in this book include references to documents published on the AILA InfoNet (*www.aila.org*), the website of the American Immigration Lawyers Association. Access to portions of that site is restricted. However, non–AILA members and government officials are allowed access to certain documents found on InfoNet. However, to obtain restricted-access documents, call AILA's Liaison and Information Department at (202) 507-7600. Charges may apply.

Website for Corrections and Updates

Corrections and other updates to AILA publications can be found on the Internet at ***www.aila.org/BookUpdates***. If you have any corrections or other updates to the information in this book, please let us know by sending a message to *books@aila.org*.

This publication is designed to provide accurate and authoritative information in regard to the subject matter covered. It is distributed with the understanding that the publisher is not engaged in rendering legal, accounting, or other professional service. If legal advice or other expert assistance is required, the services of a competent professional should be sought.

—from a Declaration of Principles Jointly Adopted by a Committee of the American Bar Association and a Committee of Publishers

Printed in the United States of America

ISBN 978-1-57370-238-6
Stock No. 52-38

This book is dedicated to the memory of my father, Benjamin Kurzban, an immigrant who taught me to love and appreciate my country and my family, and to the memory of my mother, Irene Kurzban, who taught all her children that the basic human condition requires self respect and the desire to help others. This book is also dedicated to the memory of Leonard B. Boudin, who showed me the reason to practice law, and to the memory of the Hon. Eugene P. Spellman, whose warmth and sense of justice lit up his courtroom and his community.

About AILA

The American Immigration Lawyers Association (*www.aila.org*) is the national bar association of more than 11,000 attorneys and law professors who practice and teach immigration law. AILA member attorneys represent tens of thousands of U.S. families who have applied for permanent residence for their spouses, children, and other close relatives to lawfully enter and reside in the United States. AILA members also represent thousands of U.S. businesses and industries who sponsor highly skilled foreign workers seeking to enter the United States in a temporary or—having proven the unavailability of U.S. workers—permanent basis. AILA members also represent foreign students, entertainers, athletes, and asylum-seekers, often on a pro bono basis. Founded in 1946, AILA is a nonpartisan, not-for-profit organization that provides its members with publications, continuing legal education, information, professional services, and expertise through its 36 chapters and over 50 national committees. AILA is an Affiliated Organization of the American Bar Association and is represented in the ABA House of Delegates.

About AILF

The American Immigration Law Foundation (*www.ailf.org)* was established in 1987 as a tax-exempt, nonprofit educational and service organization. The Foundation's mission is to promote understanding among the general public of immigration law and policy, through education, policy analysis, and support to litigators. AILF is governed by a board of directors and a board of trustees.

Working closely with leading immigration experts throughout the country, AILF has established four core program areas: the Legal Action Center, the Public Education Program, an Exchange Visitor Program, and the Immigration Policy Center (IPC). Through these programs, the Foundation sponsors numerous awards programs, publishes policy reports, engages in impact litigation, and provides policymakers and the public with complete and accurate information about the benefits of immigration.

In conjunction with these four core areas, many other activities of the Foundation are conducted. These include the E. Michael Berger Memorial Scholarships, awarded for continuing legal education to immigration attorneys; the Edward L. Dubroff Memorial Legal Writing Competition, an annual award presented to an outstanding law student's original paper on an immigration topic; the Michael Maggio Award, in recognition of outstanding efforts in providing pro bono representation to deserving aliens in the immigration field; and the annual Immigrant Achievement Awards and Benefit.

SUMMARY OF CONTENTS

PREFACE

This book is written for practitioners, government officials, judges, students, and everyone interested in a detailed knowledge of immigration law. It is designed to be a quick reference sourcebook to federal and administrative cases, regulations and statutes, and INS/DHS, DOS, and DOL rulings on significant issues in the field. The book represents my research over more than a 20-year period on topics and issues that are relevant to practicing lawyers and students of immigration law.

Although we are fortunate in the immigration field to have a number of outstanding treatises and in-depth reference materials, as a practitioner I was often frustrated by their lengthy explanations when I sought short citations to relevant cases and materials. This sourcebook does not attempt to compete with or be a substitute for any treatise; it is designed to be used to pinpoint the significant cases and references on a particular topic, or as a basis for further research on a particular issue. The book was intentionally written as a briefcase-size resource tool to carry to immigration court or to immigration interviews. (Keeping it briefcase-sized has indeed been a challenge.) In an effort to enhance usability, we have, in this edition, moved the detailed table of contents to the beginning of each chapter (with "bleed tabs" for quicker access), and added in a reference in the header to current part and section number.

The book also is valuable to law students when read in conjunction with an immigration and nationality course and case book. Each chapter previously has been used as a basis for lecture notes in a law school course on immigration and nationality law. The sourcebook contains references to all major cases cited in Aleinikoff, Martin & Motomura's *Immigration Process and Policy*; Richard Boswell's *Immigration and Nationality Law*: Cases and Materials; and Stephen Legomsky's, *Immigration Law and Policy* that are used in the teaching of immigration and nationality law. A student can use the text as an outline to the major areas of immigration law that are developed in his or her immigration law course.

As a guide to practitioners and students, the sourcebook contains the most recent cases and authorities in immigration law. The book will be updated biannually and will continue to contain the latest authorities. Be sure to also check AILA's Book Update Webpage at *www.aila.org/BookUpdates* for any corrections or further information. This eleventh edition has incorporated all available regulatory and case citations through April 2008.

References to INS and Attorney General

Readers will notice that the book still includes some references to the now-abolished INS and its officials (*e.g.*, Commissioner). This occurs primarily in historical discussions (*e.g.*, "a memo issued by INS," "INS has taken the position that…," etc.). A more difficult call was deciding when it was appropriate to write in the present tense about a DHS position or practice when the position or practice was established during the legacy INS days. This task was further complicated by still-existing references in the statutes and regulations to INS, Commissioner, etc. Similarly, many of the past practices (and current statutory/regulatory provisions) refer to the Attorney General for tasks that are now the responsibility of the Secretary of Homeland Security. I have, accordingly, attempted to balance the desire to accurately track legislative/regulative language with the desire to be as practicably useful as possibly. Inevitably, in the process, there probably remain some references to past government agencies or officials that might have been better off changed to their current counterparts. Readers should keep in mind, in any event, that §1517 of the 2002 Homeland Security Act provides that "[w]ith respect to any function transferred by or under this Act … and exercised on or after the effective date of this Act, reference in any other Federal law to any department, commission, or agency or any officer or office the functions of which are so transferred shall be deemed to refer to the Secretary, other official, or component of the Department to which such function is so transferred."

ACKNOWLEDGMENTS

Although this book bears my name, there are many people whose support, encouragement, and criticism contributed to the final work. This book never could have been written without the support and encouragement of my brother and partner, Marvin Kurzban, and my partner who is like a brother, Steven M. Weinger. Despite the substantial time and resources that my firm dedicated to the work on this book over a number of years, they never wavered in their support for it. They have encouraged me and indulged me, even though it meant additional burdens to them.

This book also could not have been written without the encouragement and support of my family. My wife, Magda Montiel Davis, who is the finest immigration lawyer I know, encouraged and ultimately convinced me that this book was worth publishing. My children, Kathryn, Paula, Maggie, Sadie, and Benjamin, were an inspiration to me during the long and seemingly endless nights that I drafted and redrafted this book. I am also blessed with four beautiful grandchildren who have enriched all of our lives. My brothers, Mitchell, Jerold, and Marvin, have always encouraged me in my work and that encouragement has always been appreciated.

This book had the benefit of being reviewed and critiqued by some of the best legal minds in the immigration field. None of my colleagues can be criticized, however, for any of the shortcomings of this book, but they deserve to share whatever praise the book may engender. I was fortunate to have my colleagues review various chapters of this book: James David Acoba, Matt Adams, Deborah Anker, Robert Aronson, Ahilan Arulanantham, Carmen Arce, -Peter Ashman, Lauren Aucoin, Roxana Bacon, Betsy Bedient, Naveen Rahman Bhora, Sylvia Boecker, Tanya Broder, Jan Brown, Matthew Carlson, Henry Chang, Steven A. Clark, Robert H. Cohen, Susan J. Cohen, Susan Compernolle, Brian Concannon, Kari Converse, Bill Cook, Anne Janet De Ases, Dyann DelVecchio, Goldie C. Domingue, Neil S. Dornbaum, Nancy Elkind, Beth Feinberg, James Feroli, Eugene Flynn, Robert Foley, Niels Frenzen, Avi Friedman, Lee Gelernt, Robert Gibbs, Jonathan Ginsburg, Mark Gardberg, Josie Gonzalez, Adam Green, Richard A. Gump, Jr., Lucas Guttentag, Bruce Hake, Denise Hammond, Terry Helbush, Barbara Hines, Geoffrey Hoffman, Thomas Hutchins, Mark Ivener, Sarah Ignatius, Benita Jain, Linton Joaquin, Robert Jobe, Harvey Kaplan, Mary Kenney, Dan Kesselbrenner, Ron Klasko, Martin Lawler, Daniel Levy, Jody LeWitter, Alexandra Lin, Donna Lipinski, Michael Maggio, Javier Maldonado, Hon. Stephen E. Mander, Cyrus Mehta, Matt Muller, R. Patrick Murphy, Amy Nice, Zachary Nightingale, George Newman, Amy Nice, Deborah Notkin, Maureen O'Sullivan, Hon. Juan Osuna, David Paruch, Robert Pauw, Eleanor Pelta, Gail Pendleton, Mary Pivec, John P. Pratt, Judy Rabinovitz, Thomas Ragland, Trina Realmuto, Catherine Reynolds, Arturo Rios, Helene Robertson, Linda Rose, Hon. Lory D. Rosenberg, Chuck Roth, Martin Rothstein, Edwin R. Rubin, Jay Ruby, Theodore Ruthizer, Denyse Sabagh, Hon. Paul W. Schmidt, Naomi Schorr, Heather Segal, Ilyce Shugall, Paula Singer, Daniel H. Smith, Martin M. Solomon, Melvin Solomon, Beth Stickney, Margaret Stock, Lincoln Stone, Andrew Strojny, Brian Tang, Hedi Tehbaz, Lee J. Teran, my partner, Helena Tetzeli, Stacy Tolchin, Roger Tsai, Marc Van Der Hout, Manuel D. Vargas, Abigail Walsh, Tony Weigel, Charles Wheeler, Crystal Williams, Bernard Wolfsdorf, Marianne Yang, Palma Yanni, Florence Zolin, and Paul Zulkie. Their comments were invaluable and their graciousness in extending their valuable time strengthened the book immeasurably.

I am also indebted to the members of the National Lawyers Guild Immigration Project for their cooperation and assistance in supporting and producing the book. I owe a special debt of gratitude to Dan Kesselbrenner and Sarah Ignatius for shepherding this book through the most critical stages of the publication process.

I also owe a special debt of gratitude to the University of Miami School of Law for their financial support in providing law students to work with me on the first draft of this book. The assistance of Barbara Kamali, and especially Mario Lovo, who checked and rechecked and commented on drafts of this work made the first edition possible. I am deeply appreciative of the work of my student, Raquel M. Chaviano, of Nova Southeastern Law School, who provided extensive help on the sixth edition of this book and to Matthew Carlson, Alejandra Arroyave, Elena Ionita, and Dr. Kathryn Davis for their assistance on the eighth edition. The ninth edition of the book has benefited greatly from the help of Catherine Reynolds who checked and rechecked every single citation in the book. This incredible undertaking was done by Catherine with good cheer and in the most professional and scholarly manner. I also could not have completed the ninth edition without the help of Alejandra Arroyave, Eric Nierenberg, Cristina Jimenez, David Kim, John Pratt, and Krista Teibel, who worked tirelessly in the daunting task of creating an index that was not computer generated. The tenth edition could not have been completed without the help of numerous comments from my colleagues around the country and from the work of the lawyers and law clerks in my office who worked day and night over holiday weekends to complete the book. Special thanks go to Professor Geoffrey Hoffman, John Pratt, Anne Janet De Asses, Mark Gardberg, Vanessa Paz, Andrea Martini, Lacy Brinson, Paul Schwartz, Michael Almonte, and Nicolas Chancy.

The Florida Bar and Matthew Bender also deserve recognition for their agreement to permit me to reprint, in a substantially expanded form for the first edition, chapters 4 and 10 respectively. In addition, the National Immigration Law Center was kind enough to permit me to copy their chart on Eligibility for Public Benefits, which has been incorporated as Appendix F. The last several editions also benefited greatly from the technical assistance of Ken Schleimer. Leslie Share of Packman, Newell & Rosenberg of Miami, has graciously allowed me to reprint a chart he created of countries that have tax treaties with the United States as Appendix G, and thanks also are due Carmen DiPlacido, of Arlington, VA, who prepared and updated the naturalization charts.

The eleventh edition is unique because I have now had the benefit of a brilliant young lawyer, Betsy Lawrence, who carefully edited virtually every chapter of the book. Our goal always has been to maintain the book in one volume, and Betsy's efforts, in the eleventh edition, made that possible. I also am particularly appreciative of all the lawyers at my firm, along with my other colleagues and law students, who were kind enough to pitch-in and work on the index.

I owe a special debt of gratitude to two colleagues who are good friends: Amy Novick and Randy Auerbach. Amy Novick worked on the first nine editions of this book and she is largely responsible for its success. Her literary and organizational skills are unrivaled and she is primarily responsible for the concept, design, and idea behind the sourcebook. Randy Auerbach is unique. His literary skills, his professionalism, his patience, his wit, and his command of the Queen's English never cease to amaze me. I am extremely fortunate to have him as an editor and friend. Thank you for making the book a professional work that is a source of pride to me and to all our readers. I also want to thank Tatia Gordon-Troy, my editor-in-chief, Mary Johnson, Becky Rice, and the professional staff of AILA who have spent countless hours reviewing, designing, promoting, and providing support for this book. Thank you all.

CHAPTER 1
BRIEF HISTORY OF IMMIGRATION LAWS

CHAPTER 1
BRIEF HISTORY OF IMMIGRATION LAWS

I. FIRST 100 YEARS: 1776–1875

A. ***Open Door Policy***—Unimpeded immigration.

B. ***Naturalization Act of 1790***—[1 Stat. 103]. Established process for becoming a naturalized citizen. Required 2 years residence. Amended in 1795 to increase residence period to 5 years [1 Stat. 414].

C. ***Alien and Sedition Acts of 1798***—A series of four acts, three of which were immigration-related:

1. *Naturalization Act*—[1 Stat. 566]. Increased residence period from 5 to 14 years. Later restored to 5 years by the Naturalization Act of 1802 [2 Stat. 153];
2. *Alien Act*—[1 Stat. 570]. Authorized the president to expel dangerous aliens; and
3. *Alien Enemies Act*—[1 Stat. 577]. Provided that whenever there is a declared war with another country, male nationals of that country, age 14 and up, may be detained or removed by proclamation of the President. Provision restricting the law to males was eliminated in 1918 [40 Stat. 531; 50 U.S.C. §21–24]. The law still exists today and is codified at 50 U.S.C. §§21–24.

D. ***Steerage Act of 1819***—[3 Stat. 488]. Limited the number of passengers and required the maintenance of passenger lists.

E. ***Act to Encourage Immigration of 1864***—[13 Stat. 385]. Made employment contracts binding in an effort to recruit foreign labor to work in factories during the Civil War. As some states sought to restrict immigration, the Supreme Court declared state laws regulating immigration unconstitutional. *Passenger Cases* (*Smith v. Turner*), 48 U.S. (7 How.) 283 (1849); *Henderson v. Mayor of New York*, 92 U.S. 259 (1875).

II. FIRST IMMIGRATION RESTRICTIONS: 1875–1917

A. ***Act of March 3, 1875***—[18 Stat. 477]. Provided for the exclusion of convicts and prostitutes.

B. ***Chinese Exclusion Act of 1882***—[22 Stat. 58]. Provided for the exclusion of persons from China. Repealed by the Act of Dec. 17, 1943 [57 Stat. 600].

C. ***Immigration Act of 1882***—[22 Stat. 214]. The first general federal immigration law. Included a head tax of 50¢, and excluded "idiots, lunatics, convicts and persons likely to become public charges."

D. ***Alien Contract Labor Laws of 1885 and 1888***—[23 Stat. 332; 25 Stat. 566]. Excluded cheap foreign workers where their employment would depress the labor market. The 1888 amendment provided for the deportation of persons entering in violation of contract labor laws. During this period, Congress also established the first immigration statute of limitations by permitting deported aliens to return after one year.

E. ***Immigration Act of 1891***—[26 Stat. 1084]. Established the Bureau of Immigration. Provided for medical and general inspection, and excludability based on contagious diseases, crimes involving moral turpitude, and status as a pauper or polygamist. Established one-year statute of limitations on illegal entry.

F. ***1903 Amendments***—[32 Stat. 1213]. Enacted in response to the McKinley assassination, provided for the exclusion of "epileptics, insane persons, professional beggars, and anarchists." Extended the statute of limitations to 3 years (2 years for public charge).

G. *Immigration Act of 1907*—[34 Stat. 898].

1. Established additional grounds of exclusion including: feeble minded persons, unaccompanied children, persons with tuberculosis, and persons with a physical or mental defect that might affect their ability to earn a living.
2. Established Dillingham Commission to study immigration policy in response to influx of over one million immigrants per year, mostly from southern and eastern Europe.

III. FIRST QUOTA SYSTEMS: 1917–1951

A. *Asiatic Barred Zone Act (Immigration Act of 1917)*—[39 Stat. 874]. Established a literacy requirement for admission and provided for the exclusion of all natives of the Asia-Pacific triangle. The Act passed over President Wilson's veto.

B. *Alien Enemies Act of 1918*—[40 Stat. 531; 50 U.S.C. §21–24]. Amended the *Alien Enemies Act of 1798* by striking the provision that restricted the application of the law to males.

C. *Passport Act of 1918*—[40 Stat. 559]. Authorized the President, in time of war or national emergency, to impose additional restrictions on aliens entering or leaving the U.S. Allowed the AG to deny admission to aliens whose entry would be prejudicial to the interests of the U.S. Provided for exclusion without a hearing where the exclusion is based on confidential information, the disclosure of which may be contrary to public interest.

D. *Quota Act of 1921*—[42 Stat. 5]. Enacted in response to post-WWI fears that southern and eastern Europeans would inundate the U.S. Established an annual national origin quota of 3% of the number of foreign born persons for each nationality (not including persons from the Western Hemisphere) enumerated in the 1910 census. Maintained the Asiatic Barred Zone.

E. *National Origin Quota Act (Immigration Act of 1924)*—[43 Stat. 153]. Established a permanent national origin quota system, which remained substantially unchanged until 1952.

1. Restricted immigration to 2% of the number of foreign-born persons for each nationality enumerated in the 1890 census (changed in 1927 to use 1920 census data). No hemispheric quotas.
2. Established a ceiling of 150,000 admissions per year.
3. Established a system for issuing visas abroad.

IV. 1952–1964

A. *McCarran Walter Act (Immigration and Nationality Act of 1952)*—[PL 82-414, 66 Stat. 163]. Preceded by a 2-year study conducted by the Senate Judiciary Committee and passed over President Truman's veto. Established the basic structure of present immigration law, codified at Title 8 of the U.S. Code.

1. Retained national origin quota system but decreased percentage to 1/6 of 1% of 1920 census.
2. Repealed the Asiatic Barred Zone provisions, but established racial quotas for Asians.
3. Established preferences within quotas for aliens with special skills (today's first, second, and third employment-based preferences).
4. Established deportation procedures and relief from deportation.
5. Established procedures and grounds for denaturalization.
6. Established political grounds for exclusion under former INA §212(a)(28), 8 U.S.C. §1182(a)(28).

V. 1965–1985

A. *1965 Amendments*—[PL 89-236, 79 Stat. 911].

1. Eliminated racial and national origin quotas, but established quotas for Western (120,000) and Eastern (170,000) Hemispheres.
2. Established a 20,000 cap per fiscal year on each Eastern Hemisphere country.

3. Changed priority status for skilled workers and family.
4. Established labor certification requirement and conditional refugee status under former INA §203(a)(7), 8 U.S.C. §1153(a)(7).

B. ***1976 Amendments***—[PL 94-571, 90 Stat. 2703]. Applied 20,000 per country limit to Western Hemisphere.

C. ***1978 Amendments***—[PL 95-412, 92 Stat. 907]. Eliminated hemispheric quota system and established worldwide quota of 290,000 visas.

D. ***Refugee Act of 1980***—[PL 96-212, 94 Stat. 102 (Mar. 17, 1980), 1980 S. 643].

1. Limited parole of refugees under INA §212(d)(5) and created an ideologically neutral procedure for applying for asylum in the U.S. based on the U.N. Convention Relating to the Status of Refugees.
2. Reduced worldwide quota to 270,000 and authorized the admission of an additional 50,000 refugees.
3. Allowed 5,000 eligible asylees per year to adjust status to lawful permanent resident.

E. ***1981 Amendments***—[PL 97-116, 95 Stat. 1611]. Established waiver of exclusion under INA §212(h), 8 U.S.C. §1182(h) for possession of 30 grams or less of marijuana.

VI. 1986–1995

A. ***Immigration Reform and Control Act of 1986 (IRCA)***—[PL 99-603, 100 Stat. 3359 (Nov. 6, 1986), 1986 S. 1200].

1. Established sanctions against employers for hiring aliens not authorized to work in the U.S.
2. Established provisions prohibiting discrimination based on citizenship/nationality.
3. Established legalization programs to grant amnesty and residency to qualified aliens:
   - 3.a. *General Legalization*—Cutoff: Jan. 1, 1982.
   - 3.b. *Cuban-Haitian Adjustment*—Cutoff: Jan. 1, 1982.
   - 3.c. *Registry*—Cutoff: Jan. 1, 1972.
   - 3.d. *Farmworkers*—Special Agricultural Workers (SAWS) and Replenishment Agricultural Workers (RAWS).
4. Permitted natural fathers to petition for illegitimate children.
5. Overcame *INS v. Phinpathya*, 464 U.S. 183 (1984), by giving a broader reading to the physical presence requirement for suspension of deportation.
6. Established a policy for expedited deportation of persons convicted of crimes.
7. Established the Systematic Alien Verification for Entitlements (SAVE) program to allow government agencies and licensing bureaus to obtain information on immigration status to determine eligibility for public benefits.

B. ***Immigration Marriage Fraud Amendments Act of 1986 (IMFA)***—[PL 99-639, 100 Stat. 3537 (Nov. 10, 1986), 1986 HR 3737].

1. Established conditional resident status based on marriage to a USC or LPR.
2. Prohibited adjustment for 2 years where marriage takes place while in deportation/exclusion proceedings.
3. Established 5-year bar to petition for new spouse where residency obtained through prior marriage unless the petitioner can prove that first marriage was *bona fide*. INA §204(a)(2), 8 U.S.C. §1154(a)(2).
4. Created greater restrictions for persons charged with material misrepresentations upon entry or application for immigration benefits under former INA §212(a)(19), 8 U.S.C. §1182(a)(19).

C. *Anti-Drug Abuse Act of 1986*—[PL 99-570, title I, subtitle M; 100 Stat. 3207 (Oct. 27, 1986) 1986 U.S.C.C.A.N. at 5649; HR Rep. 99-682(I) (July 16, 1986)]. Redefined drug categories to include all controlled substances for purposes of excludability under former INA §212(a)(23), 8 U.S.C. §1182(a)(23) and deportability under former INA §241(a)(11), 8 U.S.C. §1251(a)(11), and provided that the statute would be applied retroactively.

D. *Omnibus Anti-Drug Abuse Act of 1988*—[PL 100-690, title VII, subtitle J; 102 Stat. 4181 (Nov. 18, 1988; 1988 U.S.C.C.A.N. 5937].

1. Established ground of deportability for persons convicted of an aggravated felony (murder, trafficking in drugs or weapons) and expedited deportation of aggravated felons. INA §101(a)(43), former INA §241(a)(4)(B); 8 U.S.C. §1101(a)(43), former 8 U.S.C. §1251(a)(4)(B).
   - 1.a. Precluded aggravated felons from release from detention during proceedings. Former INA §242(a)(2), 8 U.S.C. §1252(a)(2).
   - 1.b. Precluded the grant of voluntary departure to aggravated felons.
   - 1.c. Required appeal to circuit court within 60 days. Former INA §106, 8 U.S.C. §1105a.
   - 1.d. Barred reentry of aggravated felons for 10 years.
2. Expanded former INA §241(a)(14), 8 U.S.C. §1251(a)(14) to provide for deportation for virtually all firearms offenses.
3. Provided for the revocation or nonissuance of passports to persons convicted of a federal or state drug charge where s/he used a U.S. passport or crossed an international border in the commission of a crime.

E. *Immigration Nursing Relief Act of 1989*—[PL 101-238, 103 Stat. 2099 (Dec. 18, 1989)].

1. Provided for adjustment of status of persons performing services as a registered nurse under an H-1 visa on Sept. 1, 1989 and who were employed as a registered nurse for at least 3 years.
2. Established H-1A nonimmigrant classification for nurses subject to a 5-year cap. Former INA §101(a)(15)(H)(i)(a). Established strict requirements for employers to demonstrate efforts to recruit USC and LPR workers and required attestations.
3. Established SAW provision permitting denial of permanent residency for fraud, misrepresentation or other ineligibility.

F. *Immigration Act of 1990 (IMMACT90)*—[PL 101-649, 104 Stat. 4978 (Nov. 29, 1990), 1990 S. 358].

1. Substantially altered preference system by establishing categories of employment-based immigration (including investors), placing an overall cap on immigration, redefining immediate relatives to include widows/widowers, and by establishing annual diversity visa lottery program.
2. Changed the definition of D, H-1B, H-3, E, and L-1 categories; placed a numerical cap on H-1Bs and H-2Bs; established O and P categories for athletes and entertainers, Q visas for international cultural exchange, and R visas for religious workers. Established attestation for Ds and H-1Bs.
3. Established temporary protected status (TPS) programs enabling the AG to designate nationals of certain countries suffering political or environmental upheaval to remain in the U.S. for increments of 18 months.
4. Established administrative naturalization.
5. Expanded the definition of aggravated felony; eliminated judicial recommendation against deportation (JRAD); eliminated INA §212(c) relief for aggravated felons incarcerated for 5 years or more; provided for bond for LPR aggravated felons.
6. Expanded provisions under the Unfair Immigration Employment Practices to include protection against employer retaliation, request for unnecessary documentation, and defenses based on failure to file declarations of intending citizenship.
7. Substantially raised existing fines and created a new category of fines for the use or acceptance of fraudulent or improper documents.

8. Expanded the ability of the immigration court to enter *in absentia* orders; expanded court authority to sanction attorneys for frivolous conduct; restricted rights to reopen proceedings; limited respondents' time to procure counsel.
9. Eliminated a number of medical and ideological grounds for exclusion; broadened the right to exclude on foreign policy and terrorist grounds; changed the requirements for INA §§212(h) and (i) waivers; heightened criminal-related grounds.
10. Amended the marriage fraud provisions to eliminate the need for good cause to obtain a waiver and the prohibition on adjustment for marriages during proceedings.
11. Extended the time period for temporary residents under legalization program to apply for permanent residency.

G. ***Armed Forces Immigration Adjustment Act of 1991***—[PL 102-110, 105 Stat. 555 (Oct. 1, 1991)]. Established special immigrant status for persons who served honorably in U.S. Armed Forces.

H. ***Miscellaneous and Technical Immigration and Naturalization Amendments of 1991***—[PL 102-232, 105 Stat. 1733 (Dec. 12, 1991)].

1. Reinstituted court administered ceremonies for naturalization upon court's request.
2. Revised O and P categories by eliminating numerical limitations (Ps), loosening requirements for international recognition, extraordinary ability, and one-year affiliation (Os).
3. Altered H-1B category to include certain doctors and fashion models and changed requirements for labor condition applications.
4. Amended provisions relating to TPS, Family Unity, deportation and exclusion; reinstated former standards for waiver under INA §212(h), 8 U.S.C. §1182(h).

I. ***Chinese Student Protection Act of 1992***—[PL 102-404, 106 Stat. 1969 (Oct. 9, 1992)]. Provided for adjustment of status of certain nationals of the PRC who arrived in the U.S. before Apr. 11, 1990, as described in Exec. Order No. 12,711.

J. ***Soviet Scientists Immigration Act of 1992***—[PL 102-509, 106 Stat. 3316 (Oct. 24, 1992)]. Permitted scientists and engineers from the former Soviet Union, with expertise in certain high technology fields, or who were working on defense projects to enter under the EB-2 category without a job offer. Remained in effect for 4 years and permitted no more than 750 beneficiaries (excluding family members) to enter. Revived by the *Foreign Relations Authorization Act of 2003* [PL 107-228, title XIII, §1304; 116 Stat. 1350, 1436 (Sept. 30, 2002)].

K. ***Adjustment of Status Provisions of State Department Authorization Act***—[PL 103-317, title V, §506; 108 Stat. 1724, 1765–66 (Aug. 26, 1994)]. Provided for adjustment of status for persons traditionally ineligible (EWI, O/S) upon payment of a heightened fee. Required IV applicants to be present in home country for 90 days if O/S in U.S.

L. ***Violent Crime Control and Law Enforcement Act of 1994***—[PL 103-322, 108 Stat. 1796 (Sept. 13, 1994); 1994 U.S.C.C.A.N. 1801; HR Rep. 103-324 (Nov. 3, 1993)].

1. Created protections for foreign nationals subjected to battery or extreme cruelty.
2. Established S visa for persons providing information to law enforcement authorities.
3. Established summary deportation for non-LPR aggravated felons who are ineligible for relief.

M. ***Immigration and Nationality Technical Corrections Act of 1994***—[PL 103-416, 108 Stat. 4305 (Oct. 25, 1994); 1994 HR 783].

1. Provided for equal treatment of women in conferring citizenship to children born abroad, and broadened category of people eligible for naturalization without the language and history test.
2. Established judicial deportation and provided changes to summary deportation.
3. Established provision to waive 2-year foreign residency requirement for physicians through state public health agencies.
4. Substantially broadened the definition of aggravated felony.

5. Ended carrier liability for maintaining custody over stowaways and provided for mitigation in fine proceedings.

6. Broadened visa waiver pilot program to include all countries meeting certain standards during a probationary period.

VII. 1996–2000

A. ***Anti-Terrorism and Effective Death Penalty Act of 1996 (AEDPA)***—[PL 104-132, title IV; 110 Stat. 1214, 1258–81 (Apr. 24, 1996)].

1. Established special deportation provisions for persons deemed to be terrorists.

2. Established summary exclusion proceedings for persons inadmissible under INA §212(a)(6)(C), 8 U.S.C. §1182(a)(6)(C) or INA §212(a)(7), 8 U.S.C. §1182(a)(7). Allowed limited screening of persons who articulate a credible fear of persecution, and severely restricted judicial and administrative review.

3. Expanded the criteria for crimes of moral turpitude by including crimes where a sentence of one year or more could be imposed.

4. Allowed for deportation of nonviolent offenders prior to completion of their sentence. Eliminated judicial review for persons convicted of most deportable crimes.

5. Reinstated provision requiring incarceration of noncitizens convicted of most deportable crimes, without bond.

6. Broadened the definition of aggravated felony.

7. Eliminated INA §212(c) relief for persons convicted of most crimes.

8. Broadened expedited and summary deportation provisions.

B. ***Personal Responsibility and Work Opportunity Reconciliation Act of 1996***—[PL 104-193, title IV; 110 Stat. 2105, 2260–77 (Aug. 22, 1996)].

1. Prevented future LPRs from receiving most means-tested benefits.

2. Strengthened and made enforceable the affidavit of support.

3. Contained "deeming" provision, requiring the sponsor's income to be counted when considering need.

C. ***Illegal Immigration Reform and Immigrant Responsibility Act of 1996 (IIRIRA)***—[PL 104-208, div. C; 110 Stat. 3009, 3009–46 to 724 (Sept. 30, 1996); HR Rep. 104-863 (Sept. 28, 1996), 104th Cong. 2d Sess,; HR Conf. Rep. No. 104-828, 104th Cong. 2d Sess. (Sept. 24, 1996); S. Rep.104-249, 104th Cong. 2d Sess. (Apr. 10, 1996); 142 Cong. Rec. S4730-01, §150 (May 6, 1996); 142 Cong. Rec. H2378-05, §309 (Mar. 19, 1996) at H10, 841–02].

1. *Enhanced enforcement*—Established automatic entry/exit control system to track NIV overstays; established biometric machine readable identifiers for border crossing cards; allowed the AG to contract with state and local law enforcement to investigate and apprehend undocumented persons; enhanced criminal penalties for smuggling, document fraud, unlawful reentry and unauthorized employment related to smuggling; established criminal penalties for anyone (including attorneys and notaries) who presents an application, affidavit or other document to INS/EOIR that fails to contain any reasonable basis in law or fact.

2. Replaced definition of "entry" with "lawful admission" and defined persons subject to inspection to include EWIs, thereby ending the distinction created by the entry doctrine. Restricted judicial interpretation of the *Fleuti* doctrine by defining when an LPR makes a new entry.

3. Established new and far-reaching grounds of inadmissibility including:

   3.a. Three-year bar to reentry for persons unlawfully present in the U.S. for more than 180 days but less than one year who voluntarily depart.

   3.b. Ten-year bar to reentry for persons unlawfully present in the U.S. for one year or more, who are removed or depart.

   - 3.c. Reentry or attempted reentry without inspection following an aggregate of more than one year of unlawful presence or after having been ordered removed.
   - 3.d. Presence in the U.S. without admission or parole or arrival at any time or place other than as designated by AG.
   - 3.e. Lack of vaccinations against certain diseases.
   - 3.f. Incitement to terrorism.
   - 3.g. Health care workers (other than physicians) who are not properly certified.
   - 3.h. False claim to U.S. citizenship or illegal voting.
   - 3.i. Five-year bar to reentry for students who violate status by transferring from private to public school.
   - 3.j. Family-based IV applicants who fail to meet affidavit of support requirements. Must have sponsor who earns and will support applicant with annual income at least 125% of poverty guidelines. Can have others accept joint and several liability.

4. Increased the one-year bar after exclusion to 5 years and the 5-year deportation bar to 10 years.
5. Established new grounds of deportation including:
   - 5.a. Conviction for high speed flight from an immigration checkpoint.
   - 5.b. Conviction for domestic violence, stalking, child abuse/neglect, or for violating a court protective order to prevent domestic violence.
   - 5.c. False claim to U.S. citizenship or illegal voting.
   - 5.d. Incitement to terrorism.
6. Replaced exclusion and deportation proceedings with four procedures:
   - 6.a. Summary removal for persons seeking entry (immigrants or nonimmigrants) without proper documents or by making a material misrepresentation. Does not apply to Cuban nationals or to persons who establish a credible fear of persecution.
   - 6.b. Special removal proceedings for persons arriving in the U.S. who are suspected terrorists or pose a threat to security or foreign policy.
   - 6.c. Removal of stowaways without a hearing unless they establish a credible fear of persecution.
   - 6.d. Removal proceedings for persons seeking entry (EWIs, all other excludables) and for persons in the U.S. The distinction between exclusion and deportation hearings is eliminated, although differences in burden of proof remain.
7. Altered relief from deportation and waivers of exclusion:
   - 7.a. Replaced INA §§212(c) and 244 suspension of deportation with cancellation of removal. LPRs must establish 7 years continuous residence, 5 in LPR status. Non-LPRs must establish 10 years continuous physical presence, good moral character and exceptional and extremely unusual hardship to a qualifying relative (not the applicant). Aggravated felons are barred from both provisions; persons committing most other crimes are barred from 10-year provision. Accrual of continuous residence stops upon service of NTA or commission of crime.
   - 7.b. INA §212(h) modified to preclude LPRs convicted of an aggravated felony or who have not lawfully resided in the U.S. for 7 years.
   - 7.c. INA §212(i) modified to require a showing of extreme hardship.
   - 7.d. Voluntary departure modified to permit a maximum of 120 days prior to completion of proceedings and 60 days at conclusion of proceedings. Bond required for voluntary departure granted at the conclusion of proceedings.
8. *Detention*—Provided for mandatory detention of persons who are removable due to certain criminal convictions or activity. Required minimum $1,500 bond and denial of work authorization for all persons subject to nonmandatory detention.

9. *Judicial Review*—No judicial review for persons convicted of certain crimes. No judicial review of discretionary relief except asylum in limited circumstances. No judicial review of discretionary bond or detention determinations. No judicial review of summary exclusion except in limited circumstances and then only in habeas. No class-wide injunctive relief except in U.S. Supreme Court if challenging the operation of removal proceedings. No judicial review over AG's actions to commence proceedings, adjudicate cases or execute removal orders. No automatic stays pending appeal. No appeal of amnesty cases in class action context unless person had applied within original deadline or was denied the right to file. Appeals are only in courts of appeal and only where IJ proceedings were held. Expedited schedule for appeal and briefing.

10. *Conviction and Sentencing Redefined*—Changed definition of "conviction" making it far more stringent than *Matter of Ozkok*, 19 I&N Dec. 546 (BIA 1988). Redefined term of imprisonment and sentence to include time ordered imprisoned or sentenced even if the imposition was withheld.

11. *Aggravated Felonies*—Redefined aggravated felony to include any crime of theft or violence for which a one-year sentence could be imposed.

12. *Judicial Deportation*—Allowed federal judges to order deportation as a condition of probation. Permitted stipulated orders as part of a plea. Extended judicial deportation to all cases not just aggravated felons.

13. *Employer Sanctions and Unfair Immigration Employment Practices*—Prohibited fines for technical paperwork violations without the opportunity to correct. Required proof of discriminatory intent to prevail in an unfair immigration employment practice claim.

14. *Parolees/Asylum*—Counted parolees who enter after FY1999 and remain for one year toward worldwide family quota. Barred asylum for failure to file an application within one year of entry unless s/he can show changed circumstances which affect eligibility or extraordinary circumstances justifying the delay. Expanded refugee definition to include within political opinion, forced abortion, sterilization and resistance to population control. Barred asylum to persons who can go to a third country under bilateral agreement with U.S. Permanent bar to admission for frivolous asylum applications.

15. *Nonimmigrants*—DOS given authority to establish new forms for each visa category. Visa Waiver Pilot Program made permanent. F-1 students may not attend public school, except for secondary school, and then only for 12 months if they reimburse the school for full cost of attending. NIVs automatically invalidated upon overstay and cannot be used to re-enter the U.S.; must return to home country to obtain new visa.

D. *Extension of Stay in the United States For Nurses Act*—[PL 104-302, 110 Stat. 3656 (Oct. 11, 1996); 142 Cong. Rec. H12,293-01 (Oct. 4, 1996)]. Extended the stay of certain H-1A nurses until Sept. 30, 1997 and made technical corrections to IIRIRA §309(c)(1).

E. *Nicaraguan Adjustment and Central American Relief Act (NACARA)*—[PL 105-100, title II; 111 Stat. 2160, 2193–201 (Nov. 19, 1997), *amended by* PL 105-139, 111 Stat. 2644 (Dec. 2, 1997)].

1. Provided for adjustment of status for all Nicaraguans and Cubans who were continuously present in the U.S. since Dec. 1, 1995, including spouses, children and unmarried sons and daughters.

2. Codified *Matter of N-J-B-*, 21 I&N Dec. 812 (BIA 1997), thereby eliminating suspension of deportation for persons served with an OSC within 7 years of entry. Established exceptions for:

   2.a. Salvadorans and Guatemalans who registered for *ABC* benefits, or applied for asylum before Apr. 1, 1990, including spouses, children and certain sons and daughters.

   2.b. Eastern Europeans who entered the U.S. before Dec. 31, 1990, and filed for asylum before Dec. 31, 1991.

3. Reduced other worker category and diversity visas by 5,000 visas each per year.

F. *INA §§245(i)/245(k) Legislation*—[PL 105-119, title I, §111; 111 Stat. 2440, 2458–59 (Nov. 26, 1997)].

1. Terminated adjustment under INA §245(i), but grandfathered persons who filed a visa petition, AOS application, or labor certification, on or before Jan. 14, 1998.

2. Eliminated INA §212(o), requiring people to remain outside the U.S. for 90 days.

3. Allowed certain EB visa applicants to adjust under §245(a) if they have not been out of status for an aggregate period exceeding 180 days. INA §245(k), 8 U.S.C. §1255(k).

G. *No Visas for Certain Haitian Nationals*—[PL 105-119, title VI, §621; 111 Stat. 2440, 2520–21 (Nov. 26, 1997)]. Instructed Secy. of State not to grant visas to certain Haitians who were "credibly alleged" to have been involved in political killings in Haiti, to members of the Haitian High Command involved in the coup, or to persons credibly alleged to have been a member of FRAPH.

H. *FY 1999 Omnibus Consolidated and Emergency Supplemental Appropriations Act*—[PL 105-277, 112 Stat. 2681, 105th Cong. 2d Sess. (Oct. 21, 1998)].

1. *Haitian Refugee Immigration Fairness Act of 1998 (HRIFA)*—[PL 105-277, div. A, title IX; 112 Stat. 2681-538 to 542].

   1.a. Provided for AOS for Haitians who: (1) filed for asylum before Dec. 31, 1995; (2) were paroled into U.S. prior to Dec. 31, 1995 due to credible fear of persecution, emergent or public interest reasons; *or* (3) were children as defined in the INA at the time of their arrival in the U.S. before Dec. 31, 1995 and (i) arrived and remained without parents; (ii) became orphaned after arrival; or (iii) were abandoned prior to Apr. 1, 1998, and remained abandoned.

   1.b. Required applicant to be physically present in U.S. since Dec. 31, 1995, while allowing up to 180 days absence in the aggregate.

   1.c. Allowed for AOS of spouse, children, unmarried sons/daughters who are Haitian nationals and are otherwise admissible, except for the sections waived. Must be physically present on the date of the application. Unmarried sons/daughters, must be physically present since Dec. 31, 1995, allowing an aggregate of 180 days absence.

2. *American Competitiveness and Workforce Improvement Act of 1998 (ACWIA)*—[PL 105-277, div. C, title IV; 112 Stat. 2681-641 to 658]. Imposed additional requirements on "H-1B dependent" employers. Increased H-1B cap to 115,000 for FY1999 and FY2000, and 107,000 for FY2001. Created special immigrant status for civilian NATO employees, similar to G status.

3. Created new grounds of inadmissibility for persons who aid or assist others in abducting children [div. G, title XXII, §2226; 112 Stat. 2681-820 to 821] and for those who misuse confidential business information [div. I, title I, §103; 112 Stat. 2681-865 to 866].

4. Implemented the United Nations Convention Against Torture (CAT) with a clear policy statement that the U.S. may not return or extradite a person to a place where s/he will be tortured. Restricted judicial review and directed the AG to implement regulations [div. G, subdiv. B, title XXII, §2242; 112 Stat. 2681-822 to 823].

5. Abolished USIA and required its operations to be transferred to DOS by Oct. 1, 1999 [div. G, subdiv. A, title XIII, ch. 2; 112 Stat. 2681-776 to 777].

6. Amended 18 U.S.C. §922 to prohibit most nonimmigrants from using or possessing firearms [div. A, title I, §121; 112 Stat. 2681-71 to 72].

I. *International Religious Freedom Act of 1998*—[PL 105-292, 112 Stat. 2787 (Oct. 27, 1998)]. Created INA §212(a)(2)(G), which provided that: a person who, while serving as a foreign government official, was responsible for or directly carried out, at any time during the preceding 24 month period, particularly severe violations of religious freedom, as defined in section 3 of the Act (22 U.S.C. §6402), is inadmissible. Spouses and children of violators were also inadmissible. Amended in 2004 by the *Intelligence Reform and Terrorism Prevention Act* [PL 108-458, 118 Stat. 3638 (Dec. 17, 2004)] to make violations carried out "at any time" grounds for inadmissibility and to remove provision regarding spouses and children.

J. *Irish Peace Process Cultural and Training Program Act of 1998*—[PL 105-319, 112 Stat. 3013 (Oct. 30, 1998); PL 108-449, 118 Stat. 3469 (Dec. 10, 2004)]; 65 Fed. Reg. 14764, 17768 (Mar. 17, 2000); 22 C.F.R. §139 *et seq.* Created Q-2 visa for persons seeking to enter the U.S. for no more than 24 months to participate in a cultural and training program for the purpose of providing practical training, employment and the experience of coexistence and conflict resolution in a diverse society. Must: (1) be a citizen of the UK or Republic of Ireland; (2) be between 21 and 35 years of age on the date of departure to the U.S.; (3) have continuously resided in Northern Ireland or the counties of Louth, Monaghan, Cavan, Leitrim, Sligo or Donegal in the Republic of Ireland for not less than 18 months before departure; (4) have been continuously unemployed for not less than 12 months before departure; (5) not have a degree from an institute of higher education. Q-2s are subject to a 2-year foreign residence requirement that may be waived upon a showing of exceptional hardship to a USC/LPR spouse or child, or if admission is in the public or national interest. INA §§212(t)[second](1) & (2), 8 U.S.C. §§1182(t)(1) & (2). Program operates through a private company (Northrop Grumman Information Technology, Inc) that serves as the private administrator for the program and includes identifying job opportunities for program participants, recommending employers, and reinstating participants if they alter employment. Neither the program administrator, nor the employers have tort or contract liability for erring in the grant or denial of the program. *Murray v. Northrop Grumman Information Technology, Inc.* 444 F.3d 169 (2d Cir. 2006) [the program administrator was absolutely immune from suit in conveying possible national security issues regarding the petitioners to DOS and DHS and the program participant had no implied-in-fact contract with the employer sponsor].

K. ***Nursing Relief for Disadvantaged Areas Act of 1999***—[PL 106-95, 113 Stat. 1312 (Nov. 12, 1999); 1994 HR 441].

1. Created H-1C visa for nurses working in Health Professional Shortage Areas (HPSAs) for a period of 3 years. No extensions. Hospital must file attestations. Program extended for 3 years by the *Nursing Relief for Disadvantaged Areas Reauthorization Act of 2005* [PL 109-423, 120 Stat. 2900 (Dec. 20, 2006)].
2. Provided for national interest waiver for physicians to work in medical shortage area or Veteran's facility. Must complete 5 years of qualifying employment before obtaining IV or AOS.
3. Allowed international management companies that split from international accounting firms but still retain their worldwide structure to petition for L-1 employees.

L. ***Amendment to Definition of Adopted Child***—[PL 106-139, 113 Stat. 1696 (Dec. 7, 1999); 1999 HR 2886]. Amended the age that a child may be adopted to 18, but only where the child is adopted at the same time or subsequent to a sibling who is adopted by the same family/person.

M. ***Intercountry Adoption Act***—[PL 106-279, 114 Stat 825 (Oct. 6, 2000); 146 Cong. Rec. 58866-8868 (Sept. 20, 2000). In anticipation of the Hague Convention on Protection of Children and Cooperation in Respect of Intercountry Adoption entering into force the Congress:

1. Designated the Department of State as the central U.S. authority to monitor overseas requests for adoption under the Hague Convention
2. Established a new definition for a Hague Convention adoption under INA §101(b)(1)(G), 8 U.S.C. §1101(b)(1)(G).

N. ***American Competitiveness in the 21st Century Act***—[PL 106-313, 114 Stat. 1251, 2000 S. 2045; PL 106-311, 114 Stat. 1247 (Oct. 17, 2000); 2000 HR 5362; 146 Cong. Rec. H9004-06 (Oct. 5, 2000)].

1. Increased H-1B fee from $500 to $1,000, as of Dec. 16, 2000. Exempted certain nonprofits, primary and secondary schools, institutions of higher education and governmental research organizations from paying the fee.
2. Increased H-1B cap to 195,000 for FY2001-2003.
   - 2.a. Visas obtained by fraud or misrepresentation are to be recaptured and restored to the cap.
   - 2.b. Individual H-1B holders may only be counted against the cap one time within their 6-year period, unless they would be eligible for a new 6-year period when the petition is filed (*i.e.*, out of the country for one year, seasonal or intermittent work).
   - 2.c. H-1Bs employed at institutions of higher education or related nonprofit entities, or nonprofit or governmental research organizations are not counted against the cap.
3. Allowed unused employment-based visas to be used for persons from oversubscribed countries (*e.g.*, India, China). INA §202(a)(5), 8 U.S.C. §1152(a)(5).

4. Allowed EB-1, EB-2 or EB-3 beneficiaries who are unable to obtain a visa due to per-country limitations to obtain H-1B extensions beyond 6 years until their AOS application is adjudicated.
5. Permitted H-1Bs with a pending I-140 or AOS application to extend their status in 1-year increments beyond 6 years, where 365 days or more have passed since the filing of a labor certification (if required) or the I-140 petition.
6. Allowed H-1Bs to accept new employment upon the *filing* of a nonfrivolous petition by the prospective employer. INA §214(n)(1), 8 U.S.C. §1184(n)(1). The employee must have been lawfully admitted to the U.S. and may not have been employed without authorization after entry. Applied to petitions filed on, before, or after Oct. 17, 2000.
7. Allowed EB-1, EB-2 or EB-3 beneficiaries, whose AOS applications have been pending 180 days or more to change employers without affecting their applications if the new job is in the "same or a similar occupational classification as the job for which the petition was filed." INA §§204(j); 8 U.S.C. §1154(j).
8. Permitted B visa holders to accept honorarium payment and incidental expenses for usual academic activity lasting no more than 9 days. May not have accepted payment or expenses from more than 5 institutions in previous 6 months. INA §212(q), 8 U.S.C. §1182(q).
9. Amended employment-creation (EB-5) law.

O. ***Syrian Adjustment Act***—[PL 106-378, 114 Stat. 1442 (Oct. 27, 2000); 2000 HR 4681]. Allowed 2,000 Syrian Jews who were previously granted asylum to obtain permanent residency independent of the annual statutory limit of 10,000 asylees. Must have arrived in the U.S. after Dec. 31, 1991, been physically present for at least one year after asylum grant, and not firmly resettled in a third country. Must file for AOS no later than Oct. 27, 2001 and must be physically present in the U.S. at the time of filing. Spouse, child or unmarried son/daughter may also apply.

P. ***Victims of Trafficking and Violence Protection Act of 2000***—[PL 106-386, 114 Stat. 1464 (Oct. 28, 2000); 2000 HR 3244].

1. Established T visa for victims of severe form of trafficking in persons (use of force, fraud, coercion for sex trafficking, involuntary servitude, peonage, debt bondage, or slavery).
2. Established U visa for victims of criminal activity who have suffered substantial physical or mental abuse, who have assisted or may assist in the investigation or prosecution of the crime.
3. Created a ground of inadmissibility for individuals (and their families) involved in severe trafficking of persons.
4. Amended VAWA provisions to allow self-petitions by certain divorcees or spouses who were not lawfully married due to their abuser's bigamy. Remarriage of a battered spouse does not invalidate an approved petition.
5. Permitted naturalization of battered spouse/child, even if spouse did not live with USC abuser for the requisite 3-year period.
6. Amended VAWA suspension/cancellation provisions to consider extreme hardship to applicant's parents. Eliminated IIRIRA's "stop-time" rule to VAWA cancellation cases. Motions to reopen for VAWA cancellation are not subject to 90-day limitation and may be filed within one year of a final order or longer if AG permits.
7. Waivers under INA §§212(g)–(i) and 237(a)(7) amended to include provision for battered spouse/child.
8. Created battered spouse/child exceptions in special adjustment acts such as the Cuban Refugee Adjustment Act, NACARA, and HRIFA. Amended INA §§245(a) & (c) to make all approved self-petitioners eligible for adjustment of status.

Q. ***Child Citizenship Act of 2000***—[PL 106-395, 114 Stat. 1631 (Oct. 30, 2000); 2000 HR 2883].

1. Allowed child of USC, born outside the U.S., but residing permanently in the U.S. in the legal and physical custody of the USC parent, to automatically acquire USC status. Allowed children residing outside the U.S. with the USC parent, who are lawfully admitted temporarily, to obtain certificates of citizenship.

2. Created exception to inadmissibility and deportability for false claim to U.S. citizenship or unlawful voting for persons who reasonably believed that they were a USC at the time of such violation.

R. ***International Patient Act of 2000***—[PL 106-406, 114 Stat. 1755 (Nov. 1, 2000); 2000 HR 2961]. Authorized a 3-year program to allow the AG to extend voluntary departure beyond the 120-day maximum for visa waiver entrants who require prolonged medical treatment. Up to 300 allowed per year. Included family members.

S. ***Vietnamese, Cambodian and Laotian Adjustment***—[PL 106-429, §586; 114 Stat. 1900, 1900A-57 to 58 (Nov. 1, 2000); 2000 HR 4811]. Provided for adjustment of status of 5,000 eligible Vietnamese, Cambodian and Laotian nationals who were physically present and paroled into the U.S. before Oct. 1, 1997.

T. ***Disability Waiver for Persons Seeking Naturalization***—[PL 106-448, 114 Stat. 1939 (Nov. 6, 2000); 2000 S. 2812]. Amended INA §337(a) to allow for a waiver of the oath of renunciation and allegiance for naturalization for persons who are unable to understand or communicate an understanding of the oath's meaning because of a physical or developmental disability or mental impairment.

U. ***Legal Immigration Family Equity Act (LIFE); LIFE Act Amendments***—[PL 106-553, title XI; 114 Stat. 2762, 2762A-142 to 149 (Dec. 21, 2000), HR Rep. 106-1005 at 185; 2000 HR 4942; PL 106-554, div. B, title XV; 114 Stat. 2763, 2763A-324 to 328 (Dec. 21, 2000), H. Conf. Rep. 106-1033; 146 Cong. Rec. S11850-02 (daily ed. Dec. 15, 2000-Senator's Joint Memorandum)].

1. Extended INA §245(i) to Apr. 30, 2001 for persons present in U.S. on Dec. 21, 2000.
2. Established V visa for spouses and children of LPRs where an I-130 petition was filed on or before Dec. 21, 2000, and at least 3 years have passed and the petition is still pending or the petition has been approved, but an IV is not immediately available or the IV/AOS application is still pending. Provided for employment authorization for 30 days after the denial of the I-130 or AOS. INA §212(a)(9)(B) does not apply. Persons in the U.S. may be "adjusted" to V status.
3. Established K-3 visa for spouses and children of USC who seek to enter the U.S. while awaiting approval of an I-130. K-3 status terminates 30 days after the denial of the I-130 or AOS.
4. Provided that the spouse of a USC who married abroad, is inadmissible if not in possession of a valid NIV issued by a consular officer in the foreign state where the marriage took place.
5. Provided for AOS of persons who filed for class membership in *CSS v. Meese, LULAC v. INS, or Zambrano v. INS* if they entered before Jan. 1, 1982 and meet certain residency requirements.
6. Made technical corrections to NACARA and HRIFA, permitting the AG to waive INA §§212(a)(9)(A) & (C) and nullifying the application of INA §241(a)(5) [reinstatement of removal] in both acts. Allowed NACARA and HRIFA applicants with final orders of removal, deportation or exclusion, to file one motion to reopen within 180 days of Dec. 21, 2000.

VIII. POST–SEPT. 11, 2001

A. ***USA PATRIOT Act (Uniting and Strengthening America by Providing Appropriate Tools Required to Intercept and Obstruct Terrorism Act of 2001)***—[PL 107-56, 115 Stat. 272 (Oct. 26, 2001); 2001 HR 3162].

1. Tripled the number of border patrol and inspectors at the northern border.
2. Permitted INS/DOS to receive information from FBI's National Crime Information Center Database (NCIC-II).
3. Required INS to develop an interagency system to conduct background checks and verify the identity of persons applying for a visa and/or entering the U.S. Required AG to develop biometric technology for the border.
4. Expanded the definition of terrorism to encompass groups whose public endorsement of terrorist acts undermines U.S. efforts to combat terrorism.
5. Provided that persons (and their spouses and children) will be deemed inadmissible for using their position of prominence to endorse terrorist activity or to persuade others to support terrorist activity that undermines U.S. efforts to combat terrorism.

6. Established grounds of inadmissibility for soliciting funds for terrorist groups or activities or commission of any act that one knows or should have known affords material support to terrorist groups or individuals.
7. Provided for retroactive application to persons in removal proceedings, except that a person is not responsible for providing material support to a group that was not designated a terrorist organization at the time.
8. Redefined terrorist organization to include a group of two or more individuals, whether organized or not, that engages in terrorist activities.
9. Allowed AG to detain persons for 7 days before deciding whether to charge them as terrorists if reasonable grounds support the belief that the person has engaged in terrorism or sought to overthrow the U.S. government. If charged, the person may be detained even after a final order of removal has been issued if s/he cannot be returned to his or her country. Detention reviewed every 6 months to determine whether release would threaten national security, community safety or another person. Habeas review permitted in any jurisdiction but must apply law of D.C. Circuit or Supreme Court. All appeals must be brought in D.C. Circuit.
10. Allowed DOS to share information in visa lookout database with foreign governments.
11. Required AG and Secy. of State to implement entry/exit data system for all land, sea and airports.
12. Expanded the Foreign Student Monitoring Program established by IIRIRA §641(a) to include flight, language and vocational schools, and required date and port of entry to be recorded.
13. Allowed certain family member of Sept. 11, 2001 victims to self-petition for special immigrant status. Extended certain deadlines for children who turned 21, persons granted voluntary departure, and persons who missed the DV lottery deadline as a result of the Sept. 11 attacks.
14. Established new ground of inadmissibility for persons who the consular officer or the AG have reason to believe engaged in money laundering [as described in 18 U.S.C. §§1956–57) or knowingly aided and abetted others in money laundering. Required the creation of a money laundering watchlist.

B. ***Work Authorization for Spouses of Treaty Traders and Treaty Investors***—[PL 107-124, 115 Stat. 2402 (Jan. 16, 2002); 2002 HR 2277]. Provided for employment authorization for spouses of E visa holders.

C. ***Work Authorization for Spouses of Intracompany Transferees***—[PL 107-125, 115 Stat. 2403 (Jan. 16, 2002); HR Rep. 107-188 (Aug. 2, 2001); 2002 HR 2278]. Provided for employment authorization for spouses of L visa holders. Reduced period of employment for L employee transferred under a blanket petition from one year to 6 months.

D. ***Family Sponsor Immigration Act of 2002***—[PL 107-150, 116 Stat. 74 (Mar. 13, 2002); 2002 HR 1892]. Permitted substitution of certain relatives or a legal guardian to meet the affidavit of support requirements under INA §213A(f)(5), where the petitioner has died and the AG decides not to revoke the approved I-130 on humanitarian grounds. Applied to deaths occurring before, on, or after Mar. 13, 2002, but if death occurred before Mar. 13, 2002, the beneficiary must seek reinstatement of the petition and demonstrate s/he is not a public charge.

E. ***Enhanced Border Security and Visa Entry Reform Act of 2002***—[PL 107-173, 116 Stat. 543 (May 14, 2002].

1. Established comprehensive law enforcement and intelligence sharing data base called Chimera.
2. Required Secy. of State to provide an electronic version of visa files for use by immigration inspectors at ports of entry.
3. Required visa waiver countries to issue machine-readable, tamper-resistant passports with biometric and document authentication identifiers to remain in the visa waiver program.
4. Prevented Secy. of State from issuing NIVs to persons from countries designated as a state sponsors of international terrorism without consulting with AG and other U.S. agencies to determine that such persons do not pose a threat to the safety or national security of the U.S.

5. Provided for immediate employment authorization for refugees upon arrival in the U.S. and for asylees upon grant of asylum.
6. Tightened requirements for common carriers to report information before passengers and crew arrive in the U.S.
7. Required DSOs to notify DHS of any student who does not report to school and enroll within 30 days of the school's registration deadline.

F. *Child Status Protection Act*—[PL 107-208, 116 Stat. 927 (Aug. 6, 2002); 2002 HR 1209]. Altered when and how children would be considered to have "aged-out" in the visa petition process. Applied to all pending or approved petitions as long as a final determination has not been made on the beneficiary's IV or AOS.

1. Child beneficiary of an immediate-relative (IR) petition, who was under 21 when the petition was filed will not "age-out."
2. Child beneficiary of a 2A petition who was under 21 on the date the LPR petitioner naturalizes will not "age-out" and will be treated as a child for purposes of an IR petition.
3. The date of divorce of a married son/daughter beneficiary of a 3rd preference petition determines whether the son/daughter will be treated as a child under an IR petition (divorced before 21) or an unmarried son/daughter under a 1st preference petition (divorced at 21 or older).
4. The age of the child on the date an asylum or refugee application is filed by the parent will be used to determine whether the child has aged-out for purposes of asylum, refugee status, and AOS.
5. A 2B petition (unmarried son/daughter of LPR) automatically becomes a 1st preference petition upon naturalization of the parent unless the son/daughter elects in writing not to convert the petition and the petition was properly filed. Original priority date remains irrespective of conversion.
6. For derivative and other children (such as 2A children of LPRs), the date a child will be considered to have "aged-out" is determined by the age of the child on the date an IV number becomes available reduced by the days the I-130, I-140, I-360, I-526 or DV petition has been pending, but only if the "child" applies for LPR status within one year of the approval of the petition.

G. *Foreign Relations Authorization Act, FY 2003*—[PL 107-228, title XIII, §1304; 116 Stat. 1350, 1436–37 (Sept. 30, 2002)]. Revived the *Soviet Scientists Immigration Act of 1992* by reopening the eligibility period for filing until Sept. 30, 2006 and raising the numerical limit from 750 to 950, while precluding any scientist previously admitted for LPR status from benefits under the Act.

H. *21st Century Department of Justice Appropriations Authorization Act*—[PL 107-273, div. C, title I, subtitle A, §11030, subtitle B §11031–37; 116 Stat. 1758, 1836–48 (Nov. 2, 2002)].

1. Allowed H-1B extensions beyond 6 years where a labor certification is pending one year or more.
2. Allowed USC grandparent or legal guardian to file for certificate of citizenship on behalf of a child whose USC parent died. Must file within 5 years of the parent's death.
3. Raised number of state J-1 ("Conrad") exemptions from 20 to 30 for each state through 2004.
4. Established new EB-5 (immigrant investor) law, providing new protections for persons who filed their I-526 between Jan. 1, 1995 and Aug. 31, 1998 and their I-829 (to remove conditional resident status) or their AOS/IV applications (to become conditional residents) before Nov. 2, 2002. Allowed persons who contribute to a partnership after its formation to be considered investors. Redefined full-time employment so that positions requiring 35 hours/week are considered full-time. INA §203(b)(5)(D), 8 U.S.C. §1153(b)(5)(D). Expanded certain aspects of regional centers.

I. *Homeland Security Act of 2002*—[PL 107-296, title IV, subtitle C-F; 116 Stat. 2135, 2177–2212 (Nov. 25, 2002); 2002 HR 5005].

1. Abolished INS and placed its functions within new Department of Homeland Security (DHS) and the Department of Health and Human Services (DHHS).
   - 1.a. Bureau of Citizenship and Immigration Services (now USCIS), under DHS, given jurisdiction over the adjudication of visa petitions, naturalization, asylum and refugee applications, and all

other adjudications. USCIS given its own legal advisor to provide advice and representation in visa petition appeals before EOIR.

1.b. Established ombudsman to assist individuals and employers in resolving problems with USCIS, to identify areas in which there are problems with USCIS, and to propose changes.

1.c. Bureau of Border Security given jurisdiction over border patrol, detention, removal, intelligence, investigations, and inspections. Created legal advisor's office to provide representation in all exclusion, deportation and removal proceedings before EOIR. The Bureau of Border Security was reorganized to comprise of (1) Immigration and Customs Enforcement (ICE) (immigration and customs special agents, detention and deportation officers, immigration litigation, Federal Protective Service employees, and the legal advisor's office); and (2) Customs and Border Protection (CBP) (border patrol and inspection, Customs and Plant Protection and Quarantine Bureau employees).

1.d. Established Director of Shared Services to coordinate information resources of USCIS, CBP and ICE.

1.e. Gave jurisdiction over the care of unaccompanied minor children to the Office of Refugee Resettlement under DHHS.

2. DHS Secretary given exclusive authority to issue regulations and administer/enforce the INA, but did not affect Secy. of State's authority to deny a visa or other authority as designated under INA §§101(a)(15)(A), 204(d)(2), 212(a)(3)(B)(i)(VI), 212(a)(3)(B)(vi)(II), 212(a)(3)(C), 212(a)(10)(C), 212(f), 219(a), 237(a)(4)(C), §401 of PL 104-114 (Cuban Liberty and Democratic Solidarity Act of 1996) and several other special acts.

2.a. Gave authority to DHS employees to review visa applications at consulates and provided for the possibility of their permanent assignment to consular posts. Required all visa applications in Saudi-Arabia to be reviewed by on-site DHS personnel prior to adjudication.

2.b. No private right of action regarding issuance or denial of visas.

2.c. In the case where a visa has been denied, provided that no subsequent visa or waiver shall be issued unless the consular officer reviews the information which resulted in the denial and states why the visa or waiver will be issued in spite of that information.

J. ***Homeland Security Act of 2002 Amendments Act***—[PL 108-7, div. L; 117 Stat. 11, 526–32 (Feb. 20, 2003)].

1. Preserved AG's controlling authority "with respect to all questions of law" in immigration matters.
2. Provided that DHS Secretary "shall be vested exclusively with all authorities to issue regulations with respect to, administer, and enforce the provisions" of the INA "relating to the functions of consular officers of the United States in connection with the granting or refusal of visas, and shall have the authority to refuse visas in accordance with law." 6 U.S.C. §236.

K. ***National Defense Authorization Act for Fiscal Year 2004 (Naturalization and Other Immigration Benefits for Military Personnel and Families)***—[PL 108-136, title XVII; 117 Stat. 1392, 1691–96 (Nov. 24, 2003)].

1. Reduced the period of required service in the Armed Forces to obtain naturalization from 3 years to one year under INA §328(a).
2. No fee for certificates of naturalization under INA §§328 or 329 after Oct. 1, 2004.
3. Provided for revocation of naturalization under INA §§328 or 329 if person is dishonorably separated from the Armed Forces before serving honorably for an aggregate of 5 years. Applied to citizenship granted after Nov. 24, 2003.
4. Gave high priority to Armed Forces members for emergency leave and transportation to finalize naturalization.
5. Allowed members of the Selected Reserve of the Ready Reserve to naturalize under INA §329.

6. Allowed spouse, parent or child of USC who served honorably in the Armed Forces and died as a result of injury or disease incurred in or aggravated by combat, to self-petition within 2 years of USC's death. Spouse cannot have been legally separated from USC at time of death and cannot remarry during the petitioning process. Child may apply even if s/he becomes 21 or marries after the USC's death. Parent is treated as IR even if USC child was under 21. Public charge is waived as a ground of inadmissibility.
7. Allowed spouse, parent, or child of an LPR who served honorably in the Armed Forces and died as a result of injury or disease incurred in or aggravated by combat and who posthumously became a USC, to self-petition as an IR within 2 years of LPR's death. Spouse, parent, or child is also eligible for deferred action, advance parole and work authorization. Public charge is waived as a ground of inadmissibility.
8. Allowed spouse, parent, or child of an LPR who served honorably in the armed forces and died as a result of injury or disease incurred in or aggravated by combat, and who posthumously became a USC, to adjust status to LPR if the AOS was filed prior to the LPR's death.
9. Waived residence and physical presence requirements under INA §319(d) for spouse of a posthumous USC who died in combat. Applied retroactively to all persons granted posthumous citizenship under INA §329A on or after Sept. 11, 2001. Added parents and children to those who could benefit from a waiver under INA §319(d) when the child or parent died in combat.
10. Established expedited process for granting posthumous citizenship for persons who died in combat.

L. ***Torture Victims Relief Reauthorization Act of 2003***—[PL 108-179, 117 Stat. 2643 (Dec. 15, 2003); HR Rep. 108-261(II)]. Provided funding to maintain and establish centers for the treatment of torture victims.

M. ***Trafficking Victims Protection Reauthorization Act of 2003***—[PL 108-193, 117 Stat. 2875 (Dec. 19, 2003); HR Rep. 108-264(II)].

1. Permitted trafficking victims to bring civil action against the perpetrator in U.S. district court for violating 18 U.S.C. §§1589–91 and allowed recovery for attorney's fees. 18 U.S.C. §1595.
2. Raised the age of cooperation with law enforcement authorities for T visa from 15 to 18.
3. Provided that unmarried siblings of the victim who are under 18 may obtain T status upon showing of extreme hardship. May also adjust status.
4. Siblings and children under 21 do not age-out if T application is filed before age 21. Principal who is under 21 will continue to be treated as such for purposes of accompaniment by family.
5. Permitted the use of statements from state and local law enforcement regarding the applicant's cooperation for T visa purposes.
6. Exempted public charge ground of inadmissibility for T applicants and AOS from T status.
7. Added new category of aggravated felony to include offenses described in 18 U.S.C. §§1581–85 or §§1588–91 (relating to peonage, slavery, involuntary servitude, and trafficking in persons).

N. ***Consolidated Appropriations Act, 2004***—[PL 108-199, 118 Stat. 3 (Jan. 23, 2004)].

1. Permitted denial of visas without prejudice under INA §221(g) if processing delayed more than 60 days due to a determination regarding inadmissibility on security, terrorism and related grounds [div. B, title IV, §406; 118 Stat. 86].
2. Provided for the denial of visas to persons who assist Colombian terrorists or commit gross human rights violations [div. D, title V, §564; 118 Stat. 194].

O. ***L-1 Visa and H-1B Visa Reform Act of 2004 (Omnibus Appropriations Act for FY 2005)***—[PL No. 108-447, div. J, title IV; 118 Stat. 2809, 3351 (Dec. 8, 2004)].

1. Created INA §214(c)(2)(F) which states that an employee who seeks to enter the U.S. to serve in a position involving specialized knowledge (L-1B), who will be "stationed primarily" at the worksite of an employer other than the petitioner, affiliate, subsidiary, or parent, is ineligible for L-1B status if (1) he will be controlled and supervised principally by that employer; *or* (2) the placement of the worker at the unaffiliated worksite is "essentially an arrangement to provide labor for

hire for the unaffiliated employer." Applied to all L-1B petitions, amendments and extensions filed on or after June 6, 2005.

2. Required blanket L-1 beneficiaries be employed abroad by the L entity for 12 months; eliminated the 6-month exception for blanket Ls. Applied to initial petitions filed on or after June 6, 2005.

3. Restored provisions and attestations for H-1B dependent employers.

4. Raised H-1B fee to $1,500 but allowed employers with not more than 25 full-time equivalent employees to pay half the required fee.

5. Provided that the prevailing wage for LCs, H-1Bs, and H-1B1s shall be 100% (up from 95%) of the wage determined.

6. Required the Secy. of Labor to establish prevailing wage surveys that provide at least 4 levels of wages based on experience, education, and supervision. Established a formula for adding 2 additional levels to surveys that currently only have 2 levels.

7. Allowed Secy. of Labor to investigate without the need for an outside credible source, if there is reasonable cause to believe the LCA process has been violated *and* the investigation is initiated for reasons "other than completeness and obvious inaccuracies by the employer in complying with" the LCA provisions. Provided for 60 days investigation, 120 days to initiate proceedings, and 120 days post-hearing to make a finding. INA §212(n)(2)(G)(viii), 8 U.S.C. §1182(n)(2)(G)(viii).

8. Established good-faith exception for technical or procedural failures to comply with LCA requirements. INA §212(n)(2)(H)(i), 8 U.S.C. §1182(n)(2)(H)(i).

9. Exempted up to 20,000 visas per year from the H-1B/H-1B1 cap, persons who have earned a master's or higher degree from a U.S. institution of higher education, as defined in 20 U.S.C. §1101(a). INA §214(g)(5)(C), 8 U.S.C. §1184(g)(5)(C).

10. Initiated a $500 fraud prevention fee for initial H-1B and L-1 petitions, including blanket L-1s seeking a visa abroad. No fee for dependents. INA §214(c)(12), 8 U.S.C. §1184(c)(12).

P. *Intelligence Reform and Terrorism Prevention Act of 2004*—[PL 108-458, title V; 118 Stat. 3638, 3732–42 (Dec. 17, 2004); HR Conf. Rep. 108-796].

1. Increased detention space and directed DHS to prioritize for detention, persons charged under security, terrorism, and related grounds pursuant to INA §§212(a)(3), 237(a)(4).

2. Authorized DHS Secretary to create regulations permitting comparison of passenger lists on international flights with the terrorist watchlist, and to correct misidentification and erroneous information.

3. Amended INA §222(h) to require all NIV applicants between 14 and 79 (with certain exceptions) to submit to an in person interview before a consular officer.

4. Eliminated judicial review by habeas, mandamus, or All Writs Act, of the revocation of an IV or NIV under INA §221(i) except in removal proceedings and only if the revocation provides the sole ground for removal under INA §237(a)(1)(B). Applied retroactively.

5. Established new grounds of removal: (1) persons whose NIV or other document authorizing temporary admission has been revoked under INA §221(i) [INA §237(a)(1)(B), 8 U.S.C. §1227(a)(1)(B)]; (2) persons who have received military-type training by a terrorist organization [INA §237(a)(4)(E)[first], 8 U.S.C. §1227(a)(4)(E)[first]]; and (3) persons who participated in the commission of severe violations of religious freedom [INA §237(a)(4)(E)[second], 8 U.S.C. §1227(a)(4)(E)[second]].

6. Amended and added new grounds of inadmissibility: (1) amended INA §212(a)(3)(E)(ii) by deleting references to International Convention on Genocide and determining inadmissibility based on whether a person "ordered, incited, assisted, or otherwise participated in conduct" considered genocide under 18 U.S.C. §1091(a); (2) added INA §212(a)(3)(E)(iii) for persons who have committed, ordered, incited, assisted or participated in torture or extrajudicial killing; and (3) amended INA §212(a)(2)(G) regarding violators of religious freedom by removing the 24-month time limitation on inadmissible acts. Also made these grounds of deportability under INA §§237(a)(4)(D) & (E).

7. Amended INA §§212(d)(5)(A) & (B) to bar NIV waivers for Nazis and persons who committed genocide.
8. Added new statutory bars to good moral character: persons who *at any time* engaged in conduct described in INA §212(a)(3)(E) [relating to Nazi persecution, genocide, torture or extrajudicial killings]; or INA §212(a)(2)(G) [relating to severe violations of religious freedom].
9. Eliminated notice requirement and penalty to DHS for failure to notify regarding the revocation of an approved visa petition under INA §205. Applied retroactively.
10. Added INA §274(a)(4) to enhance sentencing up to 10 years for alien smuggling, if the offense was part of an ongoing commercial enterprise, the aliens were transported in groups of 10 or more and the aliens were transported in a manner that endangered their lives, or the aliens presented a life-threatening risk to people in the U.S.
11. Established Office of Special Investigations within DOJ's criminal division to investigate whether persons designated under INA §212(a)(3)(E) [relating to Nazis, genocide, torture, extrajudicial killings] should be denaturalized, extradited, and/or prosecuted.
12. Required USCs and NIV holders to enter the U.S. with passports or other DHS designated alternatives by Jan. 1, 2008.

Q. *REAL ID Act of 2005*—[*Emergency Supplemental Appropriations for Defense, the Global War on Terror, and Tsunami Relief, 2005*, PL 109-13, div. B, 119 Stat. 231, 302–23 (May 11, 2005); HR Cong. Rep. 109-72 at 173–75, 151 Cong. Rec. H2813, 2386–77 (May 3, 2005)].

1. *Asylum* [§101(a); amending INA §208(b)(1)].
   - 1.a. Required applicants to establish that race, religion, nationality, membership in a particular social group, or political opinion "was or will be at least one central reason" for persecution. INA §208(b)(1)(B)(i), 8 U.S.C. §1158(b)(1)(B)(i).
   - 1.b. Corroboration unnecessary where trier of fact is satisfied that the "applicant's testimony is credible, is persuasive, and refers to specific facts sufficient to demonstrate that the applicant is a refugee." In determining whether applicant has met burden, the trier of fact may weigh the credible testimony along with other record evidence. Trier of fact may require corroboration of otherwise credible testimony unless the applicant does not have and cannot reasonably obtain the evidence. INA §208(b)(1)(B)(ii), 8 U.S.C. §1158(b)(1)(B)(ii).
   - 1.c. Credibility is determined by the "totality of the circumstances and all relevant factors," and may be based on demeanor, candor, or responsiveness, the inherent plausibility of the account, consistency between written and oral statements (whenever made, whether or not under oath, and considering circumstances under which the statements were made), internal consistency of statements, consistency of statements with other evidence of record (including DOS country-condition reports), and any inaccuracies or falsehoods in statements, without regard to whether an inconsistency, inaccuracy or falsehood goes to the heart of the applicant's claim, or any other relevant factor. No presumption of credibility, but applicant has a rebuttable presumption on appeal if no adverse credibility determination is explicitly made. INA §208(b)(1)(B)(iii), 8 U.S.C. §1158(b)(1)(B)(iii).
   - 1.d. Persons who fit the definition of a terrorist under certain subsections of INA §§212 or 237 are ineligible for asylum even if not removable or inadmissible under those sections. INA §208(b)(2)(A)(v), 8 U.S.C. §1158(b)(2)(A)(v).
   - 1.e. Removed 10,000 cap on asylee adjustment and 1,000 cap on persons resisting coercive population control. Effective May 11, 2005.
   - 1.f. Changes in burden and standards of proof apply to applications made on or after May 11, 2005.
2. *Withholding of Removal* [§101(c); amending INA §241(b)(3)]—Applied same corroboration and credibility requirements as asylum. Changes in burden and standards of proof apply to applications made on or after May 11, 2005.

3. *Burden of Proof in Other Forms of Relief* [§101(d); amending INA §240(c)]—Applicant for relief from removal has the burden to establish: (i) eligibility for relief; and (ii) s/he merits a favorable exercise of discretion (where required). INA §240(c)(4)(A), 8 U.S.C. §1229a(c)(4)(A).

   3.a. *Sustaining Burden of Proof/Corroborative Evidence*—Applicant must comply with applicable information or documentary requirements specified by law, regulation and application instructions. IJ must weigh the credible testimony with other evidence and can require corroboration unless the applicant does not have the evidence and cannot reasonably obtain it. INA §240(c)(4)(B), 8 U.S.C. §1229a(c)(4)(B).

   3.b. *Credibility*—Same totality of the circumstances test as asylum. INA §240(c)(4)(C), 8 U.S.C. §1229a(c)(4)(C).

   3.c. Changes in burden and standards of proof apply to applications made on or after May 11, 2005.

4. *Definition of Terrorism* [§103]—Broadened definition of terrorist activities to include military-type training under INA §212(a)(3)(B), shifted waivers to INA §212(d)(3)(B), and added waiver for endorsement of terrorism and affording material support. Broadened grounds of deportation to include any terrorist act under INA §212(a)(3)(B) *and* INA §212(a)(3)(F) [association with terrorists]. Applied to acts before, on or after May 11, 2005 and to proceedings instituted before, on or after May 11, 2005.

5. *Judicial Review* [§§101(e) & (f), 102, 106].

   5.a. Corroboration *Claims*—Can only reverse IJ/BIA's decision on the need for corroborative evidence if the court finds that "a reasonable trier of fact is compelled to conclude that such corroborating evidence is unavailable." INA §242(b)(4), 8 U.S.C. §1252(b)(4). Applied to all final orders issued before, on or after May 11, 2005.

   5.b. *Discretionary Decisions*—Amended INA §242(a)(2)(B), to preclude review of all discretionary decisions by DHS Secretary and AG "regardless of whether the judgment, decision, or action is made in removal proceedings." Applied to all cases pending before any court on or after May 11, 2005.

   5.c. *Habeas/Mandamus and All Writs Jurisdiction.*

      (1) Eliminated habeas, mandamus, and all writs jurisdiction from district courts regarding "an order of removal entered or issued under any provision of this Act," INA §242(a)(5), 8 U.S.C. §1252(a)(5), but preserved in court of appeals, review of constitutional claims and questions of law through petition for review. INA §242(a)(2)(D), 8 U.S.C. §1252(a)(2)(D). Applied to all final orders issued before, on, or after May 11, 2005.

      (2) CAT claims may only be reviewed in circuit courts. INA §242(a)(4), 8 U.S.C. §1252(a)(4).

      (3) Eliminated habeas, mandamus, and all writs jurisdiction in every other provision of the INA where judicial review is limited or eliminated. INA §242(a)(5), 8 U.S.C. §1252(a)(5).

      (4) Added the provision eliminating habeas, mandamus, and all writs jurisdiction to INA §242(b)(7), 8 U.S.C. §1252(b)(7) and INA §242(g), 8 U.S.C. §1252(g).

      (5) Transferred to circuit courts all habeas cases challenging a final order of removal, deportation, or exclusion pending in district court on May 11, 2005. Cases to be treated as petitions for review, without regard to the 30-day filing requirement.

      (6) Eliminated transitional rules by requiring a petition for review filed under former INA §106(a), pending on May 11, 2005, to be treated as a petition for review under INA §242.

6. *Driver's Licenses/Identification Documents* [title II, §201].

   6.a. Set standards for state issued driver's licenses and ID documents. Required digital photo, signature, security features, and common machine-readable technology. Applicant must show proof of lawful status to obtain license or ID. Required compliance by May 11, 2008.

6.b. Criminalized the use of false driver's licenses at airports. Amended 18 U.S.C. §1028(a)(8) to include actual authentication features on documents.

7. *H-2B Amendments* [§§401–07].

7.a. Provided that returning H-2B worker counted in cap within last 3 years prior to approved start date, will not be counted in the cap for the fiscal year in which a new petition is approved. Required to be implemented by May 25, 2005, effective as if enacted Oct. 1, 2004, expired Oct. 1, 2006.

7.b. Required H-2B petitions to include worker's full name, certification that s/he is a returning worker, and a fraud prevention fee of $150. Fee effective May 25, 2005.

7.c. Provided that no more than 33,000 H-2Bs subject to the cap may be issued in the first 6 months of the fiscal year to eliminate advantage of winter employees over summer employees. INA §214(g), 8 U.S.C. §1184(g).

7.d. Allowed DHS to impose, in addition to all other penalties and only after a hearing, penalties of $10,000 per violation for a "substantial failure" to meet the conditions of the H-2B petition or a willful misrepresentation of material fact. DHS may also refuse to grant petitions for 1–5 years. INA §214(c)(14)(A), 8 U.S.C. §1184(c)(14)(A). "Substantial failure" is defined at INA §214(c)(14)(D). Effective Oct. 1, 2005.

8. *Australian Special Occupation Visas* [§501]—Established E-3 category to allow 10,500 Australian nationals per year to enter the U.S. to perform services in a specialty occupation. Must file labor attestation. INA §212(t), 8 U.S.C. §1182(t).

9. *Visas for Nurses* [§502]—Recaptured unused EB visas for fiscal years 2001–04 (up to a maximum of 50,000) for use by Schedule A occupations (nurses, physical therapists and performing artists of exceptional ability).

R. *Violence Against Women and DOJ Reauthorization Act of 2005*—[PL 109-162, title VIII; 119 Stat. 2960, 3053–77 (Jan. 5, 2006); HR Rep. 109-233].

1. Amended T provisions to include: (a) state and local investigations along with federal investigations for trafficking; (b) investigations where trafficking is as least one central reason for the crime; and (c) family members without requiring extreme hardship. Amended INA §245(*l*) to allow adjustment of T applicants who have either accumulated 3 years of continuous presence since admission in T status or who have been continuously physically present during the investigation and prosecution of a trafficking case that in the AG's opinion is complete, whichever time period is less. Applied VAWA confidentiality provisions to T applicants. Limited T status to 4 years unless officials need T holder to assist an investigation or prosecution. Allowed change of status under INA §248 notwithstanding any of the bars enumerated in that section.

2. Amended U provisions to include family members without requiring extreme hardship or necessity for an investigation. Limited U status to 4 years unless officials need U holder to assist an investigation or prosecution. Allowed change of status under INA §248 notwithstanding any of the bars enumerated in that section.

3. Amended unlawful presence provisions to except victims of severe forms of trafficking. INA §212(a)(9)(B)(iii)(V), 8 U.S.C. §1182(a)(9)(B)(iii)(V).

4. Preserved original priority date of self-petitioning LPR or derivative subject to domestic violence (including child who may have lost his LPR status because abusive parent dies or terminates parent/child relationship) and who has now aged-out. INA §§201(f)(4), 203(h)(4), 204(a)(1)(D); 8 U.S.C. §§1151(f)(4), 1153(h)(4), 1154(a)(1)(D). Allowed children of USCs subject to abuse to petition until age 25 if they can demonstrate that the "abuse was at least one central reason for the filing delay." INA §204(a)(1)(D)(v), 8 U.S.C. §1154(a)(1)(D)(v).

5. Exempted battered children from the legal custody and 2-year residency requirement for adoption. INA §101(b)(1)(E)(i), 8 U.S.C. §1101(b)(1)(E)(i).

6. Defined VAWA self-petitioner under INA §101(a)(51), as an alien or child of an alien who qualifies for relief under: (1) INA §§204(a)(1)(A)(iii)–(v); (2) INA §§204(a)(1)(B)(ii) & (iii); (3) INA

§216(c)(4)(C); (4) the Cuban Adjustment Act as a battered child or spouse; (5) HRIFA §902(d)(1)(B); (6) NACARA §202(d)(1); and (7) IIRIRA §309.

7. Exempted VAWA self-petitioners from certain penalties for failure to voluntarily depart under INA §240B(d), if the extreme cruelty or battery was "at least one central reason for the alien's overstaying the grant of voluntary departure."
8. Defined "exceptional circumstances" for *in absentia* orders as including battery or extreme cruelty to the alien or any child or parent of the alien. Applied retroactively.
9. Provided that DHS, AG, and DOS should "particularly consider exercising their authority" to allow reapplication for admission after removal to VAWA 1994 cases, to T and U visa holders, and for battered spouses and children seeking special cancellation or suspension.
10. Provided for employment authorization for VAWA self-petitioners when the petition is approved. INA §204(b)(1), 8 U.S.C. §1154(b)(1).
11. Prohibited VAWA self-petitioners from filing a NIV or IV petition on behalf of the abuser. INA §204(a)(1)(L), 8 U.S.C. §1154(a)(1)(L).
12. Allowed VAWA self-petitions for parents of USCs or persons who were the parent of a USC who, within the past two years, lost or renounced U.S. citizenship related to an incident of domestic violence or died. The parent can apply if she is a person of good moral character, may be classified as an IR, resides or has resided with the USC son/daughter, and demonstrates that she has been battered or subject to extreme cruelty by the USC son/daughter. INA §204(a)(1)(A)(vii), 8 U.S.C. §1154(a)(1)(A)(vii).
13. Allowed abused spouse or child under NACARA to petition for 18 months after Jan. 5, 2006, even if qualifying spouse did not petition for NACARA. Allowed abused spouse or child under HRIFA to petition at any time, even if qualifying spouse did not petition for HRIFA.
14. Amended the Cuban Adjustment Act to permit a self-petition for 2 years after Cuban spouse dies as long as the non-Cuban resided with the Cuban spouse. Permitted self-petition for 2 years after termination of the marriage if marriage termination is connected to the battery or extreme cruelty by the Cuban spouse.
15. Required K-1 and K-2 *petitioners* to provide a criminal record, if any, prior to approval of the petition. INA §§214(d)(1), 212(r)(1); 8 U.S.C. §§1184(d)(1), 1182(r)(1). K-1 may not be approved if the petitioner previously filed two or more fiancée petitions and if the approved petition was filed within 2 years. DHS may waive this bar in its discretion, but a waiver shall not be granted if petitioner has a record of violent criminal offenses unless s/he can establish s/he has been battered or subjected to extreme cruelty and was not the primary perpetrator of the violence. INA §214(d)(2), 8 U.S.C. §1184(d)(2). Once a petitioner has had two fiancée or spousal petitions approved, if a subsequent petition is filed within 10 years of the date the first petition was filed, DHS must notify the petitioner and the beneficiary of the new petition. INA §214(r)(4)(B)(i), 8 U.S.C. §1184(r)(4)(B)(i).
16. Regulated international marriage brokers by: (a) prohibiting them from providing information on individuals under 18; (2) requiring them to obtain background information on U.S. clients, including any listing on the state or national sex offender public registry, and any federal, state, or local criminal records; (3) prohibiting them from disclosing personal contact information of any foreign client to a U.S. client until background checks have been performed and the results disclosed to the foreign national; and (4) prohibiting them from disclosing the personal contact information of any foreign national client to any person or entity other than the U.S. client. Provided for civil and criminal penalties for violations. 8 U.S.C. §1375a(d).

S. *National Defense Authorization Act for FY 2006*—[PL 109-163, 119 Stat. 3136 (Jan 6, 2006)].

1. Established special immigrant category for translators with the U.S. Armed Forces [title X, §1059, 119 Stat. 3136, 3443].
2. Provided that the uniform standards for the interrogation of persons under the U.S. Army Field Manual on Intelligence Interrogation do not apply to persons in the custody or under the effective control of the DOD pursuant to U.S. criminal or immigration law [title XIV, §1402, 119 Stat. 3136, 3475].

T. *Immigration Law Reforms to Prevent Sex Offenders from Abusing Children (Adam Walsh Child Protection and Safety Act of 2006)*—[PL 109-248, title IV; 120 Stat. 587, 622–23 (July 27, 2006)].

1. Established new ground of deportation for persons convicted under 18 U.S.C. §2250, for failing to register as sex offenders. INA §237(a)(2)(A), 8 U.S.C. §1227(a)(2)(A).
2. Prohibited USCs and LPRs who have been convicted of certain sexual offenses against a minor as defined in §111(7) of the Act from petitioning for family members, unless in the "unreviewable discretion" of the Secretary of DHS, the USC or LPR poses no risk to the beneficiary.
3. Prohibited the approval of a K petition if the petitioner has been convicted of certain sexual offenses against a minor as defined in §111(7) of the Act, unless in the "unreviewable discretion" of the Secretary of DHS, the K petitioner poses no risk to the beneficiary.

U. *Military Commissions Act of 2006*—[PL 109-366, 120 Stat. 2600 (Oct. 17, 2006)].

1. Established military commissions for the trial and appellate review of "alien unlawful enemy combatants." 10 U.S.C. §948b.
2. Prohibited the use of the Geneva Convention as a source of rights for such persons. 10 U.S.C. §948b(g).
3. Allowed the use of certain hearsay evidence and restricted the use of classified information. 10 U.S.C. §§949a(b)(2)(E), 949d(f).
4. Prohibited the invocation of the Geneva Convention in any habeas proceeding or other civil action.
5. Allowed the President, through Executive Order, to define what satisfies the Geneva Convention except for "grave breaches," and prohibited the use of foreign or international law to do so.
6. Prohibited any court from hearing or considering a writ of habeas corpus by an alien who has been determined by the U.S. to have been properly detained as an enemy combatant or is awaiting such determination. 28 U.S.C. §2241(e)(1). Prohibited judicial review of any aspect of the detention, transfer, treatment, trial or conditions of confinement of such persons. 28 U.S.C. §2241(e)(2).

V. *Secure Fence Act of 2006*—[PL 109-367, 120 Stat 2638 (Oct. 26, 2006); HR 6061]

1. Eighteen month deadline to take operations control over the "entire international land a maritime borders of the U.S. including: (1) systematic surveillance; (2) physical infrastructure enhancements. Operational control is defined as "the prevention of all unlawful entries into the United States…"
2. Establish reinforced fencing in certain areas of Texas, New Mexico and California
3. Northern Border study
4. Evaluation and Report relating to CBP's authority to stop fleeing vehicles.

W. *Creating Opportunities for Minor League Professionals, Entertainers, and Teams Through Legal Entry Act of 2006 (COMPETE Act of 2006)*—[PL 109-463, 120 Stat. 3477 (Dec. 22, 2006)]

1. Expands P-1 category to include: (1) an athlete, whether or not professional, who performs at an internationally recognized level of performance; (2) amateur athletes and coaches of sports teams in the U.S. that are members of a foreign league or association if (i) the foreign league or association is the highest level of amateur performance of that sport in that country; (ii) participation renders the athlete ineligible for U.S. scholarships or participation in college sports under NCAA rules; and (iii) a significant number of the players in the league are drafted into major league teams or minor teams affiliated with them; *or* (3) professional or amateur ice skater who performs individually or as part of a group theatrical production.
2. The athletes must seek entry with respect to a specific athletic competition and the ice skater with respect to a particular production or tour. Petitions for multiple athletes/entertainers are permitted.
3. Visas cannot be issued to a national of a country that is a state sponsor of international terrorism unless the Secretary of DOS in consultation with the Secretary of DHS and the heads of other appropriate U.S. agencies grants a waiver.

X. ***Consolidated Appropriations Act of 2008***—[P.L. 110-161, Div. J, Sec. 691, 121 Stat. 1844, 2364–65 (Dec. 26, 2007)]

1. Expands INA §212(d)(3)(B)(i) regarding the scope of the Secretaries of State and DHS in consultation with the AG to waive the terrorism ground of inadmissibility under INA §212(a)(3)(B) except for: (1) persons involved in terrorist activity on behalf of organizations designated under INA §219 (Foreign Terrorist Organization List) known as Tier I organizations or otherwise designated in the Federal Register (Terrorist Exclusion List) known as Tier II organizations; (2) members or representatives of Tier I or Tier II organization; (3) persons who have voluntarily and knowingly engaged in or endorsed or espoused or persuaded others to endorse or espouse or support terrorist activity on behalf of a Tier I or Tier II organization; (4) persons who have voluntarily and knowingly received military-type training from a Tier I or Tier II organization; and (5) any group (designated as Tier III organization pursuant to INA §212(a)(3)(B)(vi)(III)) that has engaged in terrorist activity against he U.S. or another democratic country or engaged in a pattern or practice of terrorist activity directed at civilians.
2. The waiver is in the "unreviewable discretion" of the Secretaries of DHS/DOS and is not subject to judicial review except through an order of removal and then only as to constitutional questions or questions of law under INA §242(a)(2)(D). The waiver authority may *not* be exercised by the Secretary of *State* while the person is in removal proceedings.
3. Exempts Hmong, Montagnard groups from being considered terrorist organizations for events occurring before Dec. 26, 2007.
4. Designates the Taliban as a terrorist organization.

Y. ***National Defense Authorization Act for FY 2008***—[PL 110-181 (HR 4986), 122 Stat 3 (Jan. 28, 2008)]

1. Iraqis Employed by the U.S. Government in Iraq—Title XII, Subtitle C §1243. Designates as refugees of special humanitarian concern, eligible for Priority 2 processing: (1) Iraqis who were or are employed by the U.S. government in Iraq; (2) Iraqis who establish to the Secy. of State that they are or were employed in Iraq by: (i) a media or NGO headquartered in the U.S. *or* (ii) an organization or entity closely associated with the U.S. mission in Iraq that received funding from the U.S.; (3) spouses, children, and parents of the Iraqis designated above whether or not accompanying or following to join as well as sons, daughters and siblings; and (4) Iraqis who are members of a religious or minority community that have been identified by the Secy. of State as a persecuted group and who have immediate relatives or family-preference relatives in the U.S. All groups are subject to the annual refugee admission quotas.
2. Iraqis Providing Faithful and Valuable Service to U.S., Title XII, Subtitle C §1244

   2.a. Provides that Iraqi citizens or nationals who: (1) were employed by or on behalf of the U.S. in Iraq after Mar. 20, 2003 for not less than one year; (2) provided faithful and valuable service to the U.S. which is documented in a positive recommendation or evaluation by the employees' senior supervisor and approved by the Chief of Mission; (3) have experienced or are experiencing ongoing serious threats as a consequence of employment by the U.S.; (4) are otherwise eligible to receive an IV; (5) are otherwise admissible except for public charge; and (6) submit an I-360 petition are eligible for residency as special immigrants.

   2.b. Spouse and children are included who accompany or follow to join. Also includes surviving spouse or children who had approved petitions that were revoked on the death of the principal if the petition would have been approved.

   2.c. 5000 visas per year.

   2.d. Existence of another IR or preference petition is not a basis to deny special immigrant status.
3. Motions to Reopen—Title XII, Subtitle C, §1247. Grants Iraqi citizens and nationals who have remained in the U.S. since the denial of their asylum or withholding claims the right to move to reopen their claims notwithstanding numerical or time limitations if asylum was denied on or after Mar. 1, 2003 solely, or in part, because of changed conditions in Iraq.
4. Broadening the Waiver of Sovereign Immunity Against Terrorist States—Title X, Subtitle F, §1083. Establishes a new section 1605A that waives sovereign immunity for any State previously

designated as a terrorist state (*e.g.,* Libya) who is no longer so designated as long as an action is brought no later than 10 years after the action arose. Expands the base of plaintiffs beyond U.S. citizens and nationals to U.S. government employees or U.S. government contractors. Expands the scope of damages to include foreseeable property loss, third party liability and loss claims under life and property insurance policies. Establishes a private right of action no longer requiring reliance on state causes of action. Also allows for the filing of a lis pendens upon real property or tangible personal property and allows for the enforcement of those liens.

5. Families of U.S. Military Personnel Stationed Abroad—Title VI, Subtitle G §§673, 674

5.a. A LPR spouse or child of a member of the Armed Forces stationed abroad will not be deemed to have abandoned his or her residency in the U.S. by accompanying and residing with the member abroad.

5.b. For purposes of naturalization under INA §§319 and §322 any time spent abroad accompanying and residing with a spouse or parent who is in the Armed Forces and stationed abroad shall be treated as physical presence in the U.S.

5.c. Spouse is eligible for naturalization overseas.

CHAPTER 2
FEDERAL AUTHORITY TO REGULATE IMMIGRATION AND THE RIGHTS OF ALIENS

CHAPTER 2
FEDERAL AUTHORITY TO REGULATE IMMIGRATION AND THE RIGHTS OF ALIENS

I. THE SOURCES OF FEDERAL POWER OVER IMMIGRATION

A. *Enumerated Constitutional Powers*

1. *The Commerce Clause*—Art. I, §8, cl. 3 of the Constitution authorizes Congress "to regulate commerce with foreign nations and among the several states." *Passenger Cases (Smith v. Turner)*, 48 U.S. (7 How.) 283 (1849) [invalidating taxes imposed on immigrants by NY and MA]; *Head Money Cases (Edye v. Robertson)*, 112 U.S. 580 (1884) [upholding federal tax on arriving aliens under the Commerce Clause]; *U.S. v. Hernandez-Guerrero*, 963 F.Supp. 933, 937 (S.D. Cal. 1997) [upholding constitutionality of INA §276 under the Commerce Clause].

2. *The Naturalization Clause*—Art. I, §8, cl. 4 of the Constitution empowers Congress to "establish a uniform Rule of Naturalization." The uniformity rule has been interpreted as referring to "geography only" in that rules of naturalization must apply uniformly to all of the states. *Kharaiti Ram Samras v. U.S.*, 125 F.2d 879 (9th Cir. 1945). *See also Nehme v. INS*, 252 F.3d 415, 427–29 (5th Cir. 2001) [discussing history of the uniformity requirement in the Naturalization Clause]; *Nemetz v. INS*, 647 F.2d 432 (4th Cir. 1981) [government's reliance on state law prohibiting consensual sodomy as bar to naturalization found improper as "overlook[ing] the constitutional mandate of uniformity in the area of naturalization"].

3. *The Migration and Importation Clause*—Art. I, §9, cl. 1 of the Constitution limits "the migration or importation of such persons as any of the States, now existing, shall think proper to admit," after 1808. While the Clause refers to the "importation" of slaves, it has been suggested that the word "migration" refers to other persons as well. *See Passenger Cases (Smith v. Turner)*, 48 U.S. (7 How.) 283 (1849). *But see People v. Compagnie Generale Transatlantique*, 107 U.S. 59, 62 (1883) [finding that the Migration and Importation Clause refers exclusively "to persons of the African race"].

4. *The War Power*—Art. I, §8, cl. 11 of the Constitution provides Congress with the power to declare war and permits the federal government to stop the entry of aliens and to expel them from the U.S. Pursuant to 50 U.S.C. §21, the President may apprehend, restrain, secure, and remove alien enemies.

B. *Implied Constitutional Powers*

1. *As an Incident of Sovereignty*—In *The Chinese Exclusion Case (Chae Chan Ping v. U.S.)*, 130 U.S. 581, 609 (1889), Justice Field found that the power to exclude foreigners is "an incident of sovereignty." In *Ekiu v. U.S.*, 142 U.S. 651, 659 (1892), Justice Gray held that "[i]t is an accepted maxim of international law, that every sovereign nation has the power, as inherent in sovereignty, and essential to self-preservation, to forbid the entrance of foreigners within its dominions, or to admit them only in such cases and upon such conditions as it may see fit to prescribe." In *Fong Yue Ting v. U.S.*, 149 U.S. 698, 711 (1893), the Court held that "the right to exclude or to expel all aliens [is] ... an inherent and inalienable right of every sovereign and independent nation...."

2. *As an Incident of Foreign Policy*—"The broad statement that the federal government can exercise no powers except those specifically enumerated in the Constitution, and such implied powers as are necessary and proper to carry into effect the enumerated powers, is categorically true only in respect of our internal affairs." *U.S. v. Curtis-Wright Export Co.*, 299 U.S. 304, 315–16 (1936). *Curtis-Wright* was applied in *Jean v. Nelson*, 727 F.2d 957, 963–65 (11th Cir. 1984) (en banc),

aff'd as to judgment to remand only, 472 U.S. 846 (1985), where the court discussed two sources of Executive authority over immigration: (1) power delegated by Congress; and (2) its inherent power arising from the Executive's plenary authority over foreign relations. *See also U.S. v. Hernandez-Guerrero*, 147 F.3d 1075, 1077 (9th Cir. 1998) ["[t]he immigration power, which was born out of a concern for 'our relations with foreign nations,' simply is not an 'internal affairs' power; consequently in exercising its immigration power, Congress is not subject to the rigid constraints that govern its authority in domestic contexts"].

II. THE LIMITATION OF FEDERAL POWER THROUGH THE ASSERTION OF ALIENS' RIGHTS

A. *Standard of Review; Levels of Scrutiny*—When a court reviews the constitutionality of a federal or state action, whether on due process or equal protection grounds, it will generally choose one of three standards of review: strict scrutiny, intermediate scrutiny or rational basis.

1. *Strict Scrutiny*—The government action or classification must be narrowly tailored to promote a compelling government interest. *Adarand Constructors v. Pena*, 515 U.S. 200, 227 (1995); *Toll v. Moreno,* 458 U.S. 1 (1982); *Graham v. Richardson,* 403 U.S. 365 (1971); *Torao Takahashi v. Fish and Game Commission,* 334 U.S. 410, 419 (1948). In *Toll*, the Court said: "Read together, *Takahashi* and *Graham* stand for the broad principle (footnote omitted) that 'state regulation not congressionally sanctioned that discriminates against aliens lawfully admitted to the country is impermissible if it imposes additional burdens not contemplated by Congress.' "

2. *Intermediate Scrutiny*—The government action or classification must serve important governmental objectives and the discriminatory means employed must be substantially related to the achievement of those objectives. *Nguyen v. INS*, 533 U.S. 53, (2001); *Plyler v. Doe*, 457 U.S. 202 (1982).

3. *Rational Basis Test*—The government action or classification must be rationally related to a legitimate government interest. The classification "must be reasonable, not arbitrary, and must rest upon some ground of difference having a fair and substantial relation to the object of the legislation, so that all persons similarly circumstanced shall be treated alike." *Royster Guano Co. v. Virginia*, 253 U.S. 412, 415 (1920). *See also Stanton v. Stanton*, 421 U.S. 7, 14 (1975). Where rational basis applies, the government "has no obligation to produce evidence" or "empirical data" to "sustain the rationality of a statutory classification," *Heller v. Doe*, 509 U.S. 312, 320 (1993) (quoting *FCC v. Beach Communications, Inc.*, 508 U.S. 307, 315 (1993)), can base its statutes on "rational speculation," and uphold legislation even where there is "an imperfect fit between means and ends." *Id.*

B. *Who Has Acted?*

1. *The Legislative Branch*—Congress has broad powers, both enumerated and implied, to regulate immigration. *The Chinese Exclusion Case (Chae Chan Ping v. U.S.)*, 130 U.S. 581 (1889) [power of Congress to regulate immigration is a function of national sovereignty]; *Kleindienst v. Mandel*, 408 U.S. 753, 766 (1972) [Congress has "plenary power" to make rules for the admission and exclusion of aliens]. "Congress regularly makes rules that would be unacceptable if applied to citizens." *Demore v. Kim*, 538 U.S. 510, 521 (2003). The "plenary power" doctrine also applies to substantive categories concerning deportation. *Harisiades v. Shaughnessy*, 342 U.S. 580 (1952) [upholding deportation of LPR because of prior communist membership]. *See also Reno v. American-Arab Anti-Discrimination Committee*, 525 U.S. 471 (1999) [undocumented aliens have no right to selective prosecution claim except in rare cases of outrageous conduct]; *Resendez-Alcaraz v. U.S. Att'y Gen.*, 383 F.3d 1262, 1271–72 (11th Cir. 2004) [finding that the plain language of INA §101(a)(48)(A) indicates that it applies to state expunged convictions]; *Acosta v. Ashcroft*, 341 F.3d 218 (3d Cir. 2003) [rejecting equal protection challenge to the distinction between FFOA and state equivalents which, under INA §101(a)(48)(A), are treated as convictions]; *Lukowski v. INS*, 279 F.3d 644 (8th Cir. 2002) [rejecting equal protection claim denying §212(h) eligibility to certain LPRs while granting it to nonresidents]; *Moore v. Ashcroft*, 251 F.3d 919, 923–25 (11th Cir. 2001) [same]; *Rodriguez-Silva v. INS*, 242 F.3d 243, 248 (5th Cir. 2001) [provision of benefits to certain nationalities under NACARA does not violate equal protection because the Fifth Amendment does not "in any way restrict Congress' authority to set admission and naturalization

criteria that are place of origin or nationality-sensitive"]; *Ram v. INS*, 243 F.3d 510, 516–17 (9th Cir. 2001) [upholding Congress's decision to favor aliens from specific war-torn countries for suspension of deportation as stemming from a rational diplomatic decision to encourage such aliens to remain in the U.S.]; *Pinho v. INS*, 249 F.3d 183 (3d Cir. 2001) [same]; *Bartoszewska-Zajac v. INS*, 237 F.3d 710 (6th Cir. 2001) [same]; *Appiah v. INS*, 202 F.3d 704 (4th Cir. 2000) [same]; *Tefel v. Reno*, 180 F.3d 1286 (11th Cir. 1999) [same]; *Cato v. INS*, 84 F.3d 597, 601–02 (2d Cir. 1996) [no equal protection violation to deny §212(c) relief to LPR with gun charge, as Congress has a "facially legitimate and bona fide reason" to treat weapons offenders and other offenders differently]; *Raya-Ledesma v. INS*, 55 F.3d 418 (9th Cir. 1995) [rejecting equal protection challenge to requirement that an applicant for §212(c) relief be an LPR for 7 years]; *Smith v. INS*, 684 F.Supp. 1113 (D. Mass. 1988) [upholding Marriage Fraud Amendments Act regarding separation of wife and husband for two years]. But even Congress must act in accordance with the Constitution. *INS v. Chadha*, 462 U.S. 919, 941 (1983) [Congress can exercise its plenary power over immigration only if it "does not offend some other constitutional restriction"]; *Fiallo v. Bell*, 430 U.S. 787, 793 n.5 (1977); *Almeida-Sanchez v. U.S.*, 413 U.S. 266, 272 (1973) [no act of Congress can authorize a violation of the Constitution]; *Wong Wing v. U.S.*, 163 U.S. 228 (1896) [Congress cannot criminally penalize aliens without due process].

2. *The Executive Branch*—Executive officers may act on immigration matters if such authority is expressly conferred upon them by Congress. *Ekiu v. U.S.*, 142 U.S. 651 (1892). The Executive may not depart from the channels of authority fixed by statute. *Gegiow v. Uhl*, 239 U.S. 3 (1915) [commissioner exceeded his authority by denying admission on public charge grounds, citing poor labor market in city of destination]; *Galvan v. Press*, 347 U.S. 522, 531 (1954) [executive must respect due process in enforcement of laws]; *Accardi v. Shaughnessy*, 347 U.S. 260 (1954) [AG cannot interfere with procedure established in regulations]; *Kleindienst v. Mandel*, 408 U.S. 753, 770 (1972) [AG must have "facially legitimate and bona fide" reason for exclusion]. *See also Zadvydas v. Davis*, 533 U.S. 678 694–97 (2001) [rejecting plenary powers doctrine in interpretation and enforcement of post-removal indefinite detention]; *Jean v. Nelson*, 472 U.S. 846, 857 (1985) [AG's broad parole power must be made without regard to race or national origin]; *Blake v. Carbone*, 489 F.3d 88 (2d Cir. 2007) [reaffirming *Francis* and applying equal protection principles to reject BIA comparable ground interpretation of former INA §212(c)]; *Salgado-Diaz v. Ashcroft*, 395 F.3d 1158, 1162–65 (9th Cir. 2005) [denial of an evidentiary hearing on the legality of petitioner's arrest and removal while he had a pending deportation hearing was a violation of due process]; *Tijani v. Willis*, 430 F.3d 1241 (9th Cir. 2005) [ordering bond hearing for LPR who had been detained for close to 3 years finding that "it is constitutionally doubtful that Congress may authorize imprisonment of this duration" for LPRs subject to removal]; *Ly v. Hansen*, 351 F.3d 263 (6th Cir. 2003) [finding violation of substantive due process to detain a person subject to removal for 1½ years when it is unlikely he can be physically removed]; *Servin-Espinoza v. Ashcroft*, 309 F.3d 1193 (9th Cir. 2002) [holding that INS policy of allowing excludable, but not deportable aliens to apply for §212(c) during the time period between *Fuentes-Campos* and *Estrada-Torres*, violated the petitioner's equal protection rights]; *Immigrant Assistance Project of the L.A. County Federation of Labor (AFL-CIO) v. INS*, 306 F.3d 842, 872–73 (9th Cir. 2002) [finding no "reasonable conceivable state of facts that could provide a rational basis" for determining that students who took insufficient credits were not in unlawful status for legalization purposes but students who overstayed were]; *Dillingham v. INS*, 267 F.3d 996, 1005–11 (9th Cir. 2001) [finding equal protection violation where INS refused to recognize the effects of an expungement on a foreign conviction that would have qualified for FFOA treatment]; *Singh v. Reno*, 182 F.3d 504 (7th Cir. 1999) [improper delay of deportation hearing by INS is a violation of due process]; *Yeung v. INS*, 76 F.3d 337 (11th Cir. 1995) [finding §212(h) waiver of excludability available in deportation proceedings, under *Francis* analysis]; *Gonzalez-Julio v. INS*, 34 F.3d 820 (9th Cir. 1994) [10-day BIA filing rule held unconstitutional for persons residing in Hawaii]; *Garberding v. INS*, 30 F.3d 1187 (9th Cir. 1994) [no rational basis for BIA treating state expungement, which is the exact counterpart of the FFOA, differently from federal expungement]; *Francis v. INS*, 532 F.2d 268, 272 (2d Cir. 1976) [striking distinction between deportable and excludable persons with respect to §212(c) relief as irrational]. *But see Klementanovsky v. Gonzales*, 501 F.3d 788 (7th Cir. 2007) [equal protection is not violated under a facially legitimate and bona fide standard by denying the use of a §212(h) waiver to defeat deportation while permitting it use to challenge inadmissibility; *Yeung* rejected];*Danso v. Gonzales*, 489 F.3d 709 (5th Cir. 2007)

[finding no equal protection violation in the BIA's refusal to equate a "spent" drug conviction under UK law with the FFOA and questioning whether the FFOA survived the statutory definition of conviction under 8 U.S.C. §1101(a)(48)(A)];*Elkins v. Comfort,* 392 F.3d 1159 (10th Cir. 2004) [equal protection not violated by refusal to extend FFOA treatment to foreign expunged conviction]; *Cervantes-Ascencio v. INS*, 326 F.3d 83, 86–87 (2d Cir. 2003) [requiring a respondent to waive appeal to obtain voluntary departure does not violate due process]; *Robledo-Gonzales v. Ashcroft*, 342 F.3d 667, 681–83 (7th Cir. 2003) [rejecting equal protection challenge to regulation barring persons who have reentered the U.S. illegally following an order of deportation from applying for §212(c) relief]; *Vieira Garcia v. INS*, 239 F.3d 409, 414–15 (1st Cir. 2001) [rejecting the argument that the Federal Juvenile Delinquency Act must be applied to avoid disparate treatment of juveniles in the immigration context and finding it entirely rational for the BIA to rely on the law of the convicting state to determine whether a juvenile has been convicted as an adult]; *Carr v. INS*, 86 F.3d 949 (9th Cir. 1996) [rejecting equal protection challenge on the finding that it is not wholly unconstitutional to distinguish between crimes that may be expunged and ones that may not]; *Yao v. INS*, 2 F.3d 317 (9th Cir. 1993) [upholding INS distinctions between SAW and other legalization applicants in the initiation of deportation proceedings under rational basis test]; *Berroteran-Melendez v. INS*, 955 F.2d 1251 (9th Cir. 1992) [rejecting equal protection challenge on the grounds that a person who was less qualified received asylum]; *Seven Star, Inc. v. U.S.*, 873 F.2d 225 (9th Cir. 1989) [INS may draw different distinctions in enforcement at different times without running afoul of the Fifth Amendment].

3. *Lower Level Government Officials*—The authority of lower-level government officials is more circumscribed than that of Congress or the Executive. Lower-level government officials may be given broad discretionary authority by Congress, but still must act within the statutory and regulatory framework. *Jean v. Nelson*, 472 U.S. 846 (1985) [INS district directors cannot invidiously discriminate in contravention of facially neutral parole statute]. When discretionary enforcement implicates a liberty interest, courts will hesitate to "impute to Congress [an intention] to give unbridled discretion." *Kent v. Dulles*, 357 U.S. 116, 128 (1958) [Secy. of State not authorized to deny passports to USCs "for any substantive reason he may choose"]; *Hampton v. Mow Sun Wong*, 426 U.S. 88 (1976) [while Congress and the President may have authority to bar aliens from federal civil service employment, the Civil Service Commission does not].

C. *What is the Issue?*

1. *Distinction Based on Race or National Origin*—Classifications by the federal government based solely on race or national origin, which implicate the rights of USCs, are subject to strict scrutiny. *Korematsu v. U.S.*, 323 U.S. 214, 216 (1944) [applying strict scrutiny and upholding internment of persons of Japanese descent, including USCs during WWII]; *Bolling v. Sharpe*, 347 U.S. 497 (1954) [finding the concepts of equal protection and due process "not mutually exclusive" and holding racial discrimination in Washington DC schools is a denial of due process].

2. *Distinction Based on Alienage*—"In the exercise of its broad power over naturalization and immigration, Congress regularly makes rules that would be unacceptable if applied to citizens." *Demore v. Kim*, 538 U.S. 510, 521 (2003); *Mathews v. Diaz*, 426 U.S. 67, 79–80 (1976). Congressional classifications based on alienage are generally subject to rational basis review. *U.S. v. Ferreira*, 275 F.3d 1020, 1024–28 (11th Cir. 2001) [applying rational basis test and upholding constitutionality of Hostage Taking Act which draws a distinction between USCs and aliens]; *U.S. v. Yian*, 905 F.Supp. 160, 166–68 (S.D.N.Y. 1995) [same]. Similarly, when confronted with statutes restricting economic benefits, courts will generally apply the rational basis test. *Lewis v. Thompson*, 252 F.3d 567 (2d Cir. 2001) [applying rational basis standard and upholding Welfare Reform Act provision precluding undocumented women from obtaining prenatal benefits under Medicaid]; *U.S. v. Lue*, 134 F.3d 79 (2d Cir. 1998) [same]; *Rodriguez v. U.S.*, 169 F.3d 1342 (11th Cir. 1999) [upholding on rational basis test Welfare Reform Act provisions, 8 U.S.C. §1612, denying most LPRs SSI and food stamp benefits]. *But see Hampton v. Mow Sun Wong*, 426 U.S. 88 (1976) [in absence of Presidential proclamation or congressional statute, refusal, by virtue of a civil service regulation, to employ LPRs in the federal government, is violative of Fifth Amendment]; *Gebin v. Mineta*, 231 F.Supp.2d 971 (C.D. Cal. 2002) [federal statute requiring all airport screeners to be USCs is subject to strict scrutiny because the job does not implicate a governmental function or require congressional deference].

3. *Distinction Based on Physical Location*—The effort of noncitizens to invoke statutory and constitutional protection against the U.S. government's actions outside the U.S. have achieved mixed results. In *U.S. v. Verdugo-Urquidez*, 494 U.S. 259 (1990), the Court held that the Fourth Amendment had no extraterritorial application to a DEA seizure in Mexico of property of a person who was paroled into the U.S. to stand trial, but who had no other sufficient connection to the U.S. *But see Xiao v. Reno*, 837 F.Supp. 1506, 1547–48 (N.D. Cal. 1993), *aff'd sub nom. Wang v. Reno*, 81 F.3d 808, 816–18 (9th Cir. 1996) [distinguishing *Verdugo-Urquidez*, and finding a two-year prosecutorial effort violated the Fifth Amendment due process rights of an alien who was brought to the U.S. and placed on witness stand, where he was forced to choose between committing perjury or telling the truth and facing torture upon being returned to the PRC]. In *U.S. v. Alvarez-Machain*, 504 U.S. 655 (1992), the Court ruled that an individual, forcibly abducted to the U.S. from a country with which it has an extradition treaty, may be tried in district court for violations of U.S. criminal law. In *Sale v. Haitian Centers Council, Inc.*, 509 U.S. 155 (1993), the Court held that neither INA §243(h) [now INA §241(b)(3)] nor the U.N. Convention and Protocol Relating to the Status of Refugees, applies outside the territorial U.S. to actions taken by the Coast Guard on the high seas in interdicting Haitian refugees. *See also Cuban American Bar Ass'n, Inc. v. Christopher*, 43 F.3d 1412 (11th Cir. 1995) [no First or Fifth Amendment rights of Cuban and Haitian refugees at Guantanamo Bay]; *Haitian Refugee Center, Inc. v. Baker*, 953 F.2d 1498 (11th Cir. 1992). More recently, in *Rasul v. Bush,* 542 U.S. 466 (2004), the Court found habeas jurisdiction to review the legality of the detention of foreign nationals held at Guantanamo Bay. The Court distinguished *Johnson v. Eisentrager*, 339 U.S. 763 (1950), and found that habeas jurisdiction extends to aliens held in a territory over which the U.S. exercises plenary and exclusive jurisdiction. The Court also found jurisdiction under 28 U.S.C. §1331 (general federal question jurisdiction) and §1350 (Alien Tort Claims Act) and noted that: "[t]he courts of the United States have traditionally been open to nonresident aliens." *Rasul,* 542 U.S. at 481. *See also Abu Ali v. Ashcroft,* 350 F.Supp.2d 28, 39–57 (D.D.C. 2004) [denying motion to dismiss habeas petition brought by USC held in Saudi Arabia at the direction of the U.S.]. Criminal immigration laws also apply extraterritorially. *U.S. v. Chen*, 2 F.3d 330, 333 (9th Cir. 1993) [holding INS agents did not exceed their statutory authority in conducting investigation of alien smuggling operation on high seas]; *U.S. v. Hsin-Yung*, 97 F.Supp.2d 24, 27 (D.D.C. 2000) [finding jurisdiction over indictment against persons engaged in alien smuggling operation on the high seas because the alleged criminal transaction would have had a direct effect in the U.S.].

4. *Distinctions Among Aliens in Immigration Matters*—In general, deference is given to the federal government when it draws distinctions among aliens in immigration matters, and such distinctions are subject to rational basis review. *See e.g., Granados-Oseguera v. Gonzales,* 464 F.3d 993, 996–97 (9th Cir. 2006) [applying rational basis test and finding equal protection is not violated where persons who do not seek VD have 90 days to reopen their case, but those who obtain VD from the IJ have only 30 or 60 days]; *Kandamar v. Gonzales,* 464 F.3d 65, 70–74 (1st Cir. 2006) [rejecting due process and equal protection challenge to NSEERS program on rational basis grounds]; *Camacho-Salinas v. U.S. Att'y Gen.*, 460 F.3d 1343, 1347–49 (11th Cir. 2006) [equal protection is not violated under rational basis test where an illegal alien is not required to have 7 years residence to qualify for a §212(h) waiver but an LPR is so required]; *Gonzalez v. Chertoff,* 454 F.3d 813, 818 (8th Cir. 2006) [rational basis test required the government to show only a facially legitimate and bona fide reason for giving the AG the choice to institute summary removal under INA §238(b) or proceedings before an IJ for nonresidents]; *Flores-Ledezma v. Gonzales,* 415 F.3d 375, 381–82 (5th Cir. 2005) [same]; *Elkins v. Comfort,* 392 F.3d 1159 (10th Cir. 2004) [equal protection not violated under rational basis test by refusal to extend FFOA treatment to foreign expunged conviction]; *U.S. v. Pollard*, 326 F.3d 397, 406–10 (3d Cir. 2003) [applying rational basis test and holding that the requirement of a checkpoint in the Virgin Islands but not in any state does not violate equal protection]. However, such deference is not absolute, particularly where issues of citizenship are involved. *Breyer v. Meissner,* 214 F.3d 416, 423–26 (3d Cir. 2000) [applying intermediate scrutiny and finding §1993 of Rev. Stat. of 1874, which granted derivative citizenship through USC fathers but not USC mothers, unconstitutional because it perpetuated gender discrimination]; *Wauchope v. DOS*, 985 F.2d 1407 (9th Cir. 1993) [same, but applying rational basis test]; *Elias v. DOS*, 721 F.Supp. 243 (N.D. Cal. 1989) [same]; *Lebrun v. Thornburgh*, 777 F.Supp. 1204 (D.N.J. 1991) [striking down citizenship retention requirements for illegitimate children born abroad as a violation of equal protection]. *But see Nguyen v. INS*, 533 U.S. 53 (2001) [apply-

ing the heightened standard in gender discrimination cases and finding that INA §309(a)(4), requiring USC fathers to acknowledge paternity of illegitimate children born abroad does not violate equal protection]; *Friend v. Reno*, 172 F.3d 638, 645–46 (9th Cir. 1999) [applying rational basis test and upholding §1933 of Rev. Stat. of 1874, which considered the U.S. territories of Hawaii and Puerto Rico, but not the Philippines, as part of the U.S. for naturalization purposes].

4.a. *Fundamental or Substantial Right Implicated*—Whether the matter implicates a fundamental or substantive right may not impact on court decisions where Congress has enacted legislation or where the AG has exercised his or her authority pursuant to congressional enactment. In *Demore v. Kim*, 538 U.S. 510, 521 (2003), the Court upheld the constitutionality of mandatory detention of LPRs pending their removal proceedings. *But see Zadvydas v. Davis*, 533 U.S. 678, 690 (2001) [finding indefinite detention of aliens in the U.S. a violation of due process as "[f]reedom from imprisonment—from government custody, detention or other forms of physical restraint—lies at the heart of the liberty that [the Due Process Clause] protects"]. With regard to parental rights, the Court in *Nguyen v. INS*, 533 U.S. 53 (2001), found that INA §309(a)(4), which requires fathers to acknowledge paternity, passes intermediate scrutiny and does not violate equal protection. *See also Fiallo v. Bell*, 430 U.S. 787 (1977) [upholding distinction in congressional enactment that refused to accord equal rights to USC fathers to petition for their illegitimate children]. *But see Breyer v. Meissner,* 214 F.3d 416 423–26 (3d Cir. 2000), *Wauchope v. DOS*, 985 F.2d 1407 (9th Cir. 1993), *Elias v. DOS*, 721 F.Supp. 243 (N.D. Cal. 1989) [striking down pre-1934 federal statute (§1993 of Rev. Stat. of 1874) that denied the right of USC mothers to confer citizenship at birth to children as violative of equal protection]. In *Bangura v. Hansen,* 434 F.3d 487, 494–96 & n.2 (6th Cir. 2006), the court rejected substantive and procedural due process challenges to INA §204(c) even though the statute interferes with the fundamental right to marry. *See also Smith v. INS*, 684 F.Supp. 1113 (D. Mass. 1988) [applying rational basis test and upholding provisions which required aliens who marry while in proceedings to depart the U.S. for 2 years, even though the statute impinged on the marital relationship]. *But see Manwani v. INS,* 736 F.Supp. 1367 (W.D.N.C. 1990). Furthermore, the Supreme Court has rejected the argument that the First Amendment interests of USCs outweigh the authority of the AG to deny entry to an inadmissible alien. *Kleindienst v. Mandel*, 408 U.S. 753, 770 (1972) [upholding the denial of a waiver for a self-described "revolutionary Marxist" who sought to come to the U.S. to speak at various university conferences].

4.b. *Race or National Origin*—As a result of Congress's broad powers to regulate immigration, distinctions among aliens that are based on race or national origin are generally subject to rational basis review. *Kandamar v. Gonzales,* 464 F.3d 65, 70–74 (1st Cir. 2006) [rejecting due process and equal protection challenge to NSEERS program on rational basis grounds]; *Masnauskas v. Gonzales,* 432 F.3d 1067 (9th Cir. 2005) [applying rational basis test and denying equal protection challenge by Lithuanian spouse to NACARA §202 which allows derivative adjustment only for Nicaraguan and Cuban spouses]; *Angel-Ramos v. Reno*, 227 F.3d 942, 949 (7th Cir. 2000) [distinction between nationalities in application of stop-time rule for suspension does not violate equal protection]; *Legal Assistance to Vietnamese Asylum Seekers v. DOS*, 104 F.3d 1349, 1353–54 (D.C. Cir. 1997) [upholding DOS policy requiring Vietnamese and Laotian migrants to process IV applications in their home country under the Comprehensive Plan of Action]; *Cuban American Bar Ass'n, Inc. v. Christopher*, 43 F.3d 1412, 1427–29 (11th Cir. 1995) [permitting distinctions based on nationality for parole under rational basis test]; *Narenji v. Civiletti*, 617 F.2d 745 (D.C. Cir. 1979) [upholding regulations that singled out Iranian nationals under rational basis test]; *Panas v. Reno*, 114 F.Supp.2d 283, 288 (S.D.N.Y. 2000) [regulation favoring Guatemalans and Salvadorans in special cancellation presumption does not violate equal protection principles because INS established a "facially legitimate and bona fide reason"]. *But see Jean v. Nelson*, 472 U.S. 846, 857 (1985) [finding discrimination on the basis of race or national origin would violate a facially neutral INS parole statute]; *Bertrand v. Sava*, 684 F.2d 204, 212 (2d Cir. 1982) [although no discrimination found, "discretion may not be exercised to discriminate invidiously against a particular race or group"].

4.c. *Gender*—*Nguyen v. INS*, 533 U.S. 53 (2001) [finding that INA §309(a)(4), requiring fathers to acknowledge paternity, does not violate equal protection as analyzed under the heightened standard applied to gender discrimination cases]; *Breyer v. Meissner,* 214 F.3d 416 423–26 (3d Cir. 2000) [applying intermediate scrutiny and holding §1993 of Rev. Stat. of 1874 which granted derivative citizenship through USC fathers but not USC mothers, unconstitutional because it perpetuates gender discrimination]; *Wauchope v. DOS*, 985 F.2d 1407 (9th Cir. 1993) [same, but applying rational basis test]; *Elias v. DOS*, 721 F.Supp. 243 (N.D. Cal. 1989) [same].

4.d. *Inadmissible vs. Deportable*

(1) *Inadmissible Aliens*

(a) *Pre-IIRIRA: Excludable Aliens*—Prior to the replacement of exclusion and deportation hearings with removal hearings, the traditional distinction was that excludable persons, unlike deportable persons, were generally not entitled to procedural due process protections and could not assert a liberty interest under the Constitution to be admitted into the U.S. or to be released from detention. *Shaughnessy v. Mezei*, 345 U.S. 206 (1953) [finding no right to release on parole for LPR held on Ellis Island because he had been ordered excluded]; *U.S. ex rel. Knauff v. Shaughnessy*, 338 U.S. 537, 544 (1950) ["[w]hatever the procedure authorized by Congress is, it is due process as far as an alien denied entry is concerned"]; *Alexis v. U.S. Att'y Gen.*, 431 F.3d 1291, 1294–96 (11th Cir. 2005) [finding no jurisdiction to hear HRIFA claimant's equal protection challenge because as an excludable alien, claimant cannot assert a constitutional right to admission]; *Alvarez-Garcia v. Ashcroft,* 378 F.3d 1094 (9th Cir. 2004) [under the "entry fiction" doctrine, a person seeking admission does not have an equal protection right to the same procedures for adjustment of status before the IJ as a deportable person]; *Barrera-Echavarria v. Rison*, 44 F.3d 1441 (9th Cir. 1995) (en banc) [upholding constitutionality of indefinite detention under former 8 U.S.C. §1227(a)(1), of excludable Mariel Cuban]; *Guzman v. Tippy*, 130 F.3d 64 (2d Cir. 1997) [same]. However, the Fifth Amendment applies to "persons" not to citizens, and excludable aliens were entitled to certain substantive due process protections, including criminal matters, *U.S. v. Henry*, 604 F.2d 908 (5th Cir. 1979), conditions of confinement, *Lynch v. Cannatella*, 810 F.2d 1363 (5th Cir. 1987); *Rodriguez-Fernandez v. Wilkinson*, 654 F.2d 1382 (10th Cir. 1981); *Haitian Centers Council v. Sale*, 823 F.Supp. 1028 (E.D.N.Y. 1993), deprivation of property, *Russian Volunteer Fleet v. U.S.*, 282 U.S. 481 (1931), deprivation of parental rights in asylum/departure control orders, *Polovchak v. Meese*, 774 F.2d 731 (7th Cir. 1985), or where government actions toward persons are wholly independent of the immigration laws. *Xiao v. Reno*, 837 F.Supp. 1506, 1548–50 (N.D. Cal. 1993), *aff'd sub nom. Wang v. Reno*, 81 F.3d 808 (9th Cir. 1996) [finding a violation of Fifth Amendment due process rights of an alien who was brought to the U.S. to testify in a criminal case and forced to choose between committing perjury or telling the truth and facing torture upon being returned to the PRC].

(b) *Post-IIRIRA: Inadmissible Aliens*—Under INA §101(a)(13), persons who entered the U.S. without inspection or who are deemed not to have entered lawfully, are now treated as persons seeking admission. Moreover, an alien who is paroled under INA §212(d)(5) is not considered to have been "admitted." INA §101(a)(13)(B); 8 C.F.R. §1.1(q). Despite the changes to the entry doctrine, inadmissible aliens remain entitled to certain Fifth Amendment substantive due process protections. *Clark v. Martinez,* 543 U.S. 371 (2005) [finding that *Zadvydas'* 6-month constitutional limitation on detention of deportable persons with final orders of removal applies equally to inadmissible persons as a matter of statutory construction under INA §241(a)(6)]; *Martinez-Aguero v. Gonzales,* 459 F.3d 618, 622–25 (5th Cir. 2006) [rejecting application of "entry fiction" to treatment of detained aliens in *Bivens* action for unlawful detention and excessive force]; *Kwai Fun Wong v. U.S.,* 373 F.3d 952, 968–75 (9th Cir. 2004) [finding that a *Bivens* claim for discrimination in the revocation of parole and denial of AOS were actionable because the "entry fiction" applies only to certain procedural rights and does not apply to all constitutional claims of unadmitted persons]; *Xi v. INS*, 298 F.3d 832 (9th Cir. 2002). In addition, some courts have rejected regulatory attempts to limit the rights of arriving persons, where Congress itself did not impose such limitations. *Scheerer v. U.S. Att'y Gen.,* 445 F.3d 1311, 1318–22 (11th Cir. 2006) [rejecting language in former 8 C.F.R. §1245.1(c)(8) precluding arriving persons from applying for adjustment of status]; *Bona v. Gonzales,* 425 F.3d 663 (9th Cir. 2005) [same]; *Zheng v. Gonzales,* 422 F.3d 98 (3d Cir. 2005) [same]; *Succar v. Ashcroft,* 394 F.3d 8 (1st Cir. 2005) [same]. However, the entry doctrine continues to limit the procedural due process rights of arriving aliens. *Gonzalez v. Reno*, 212 F.3d 1338, 1346 (11th Cir. 2000) [unadmitted minor seeking asylum has no due process rights with respect to an application for admission]; *AILA v. Reno*, 18 F.Supp.2d 38 (D.D.C. 1998) [persons subject to expedited removal have no due process rights with respect to their admission to the U.S.].

(c) *Returning LPRs*—Returning LPRs were historically entitled to constitutional due process protections. *Kwong Hai Chew v. Colding*, 344 U.S. 590 (1953). In *Landon v. Plasencia*, 459 U.S. 21 (1982), the Court found that returning LPRs have due process rights but did not decide the extent of such rights, including burden of proof, notice and the right to counsel in exclusion proceedings. In *Rafeedie v. INS*, 795 F.Supp. 13 (D.D.C. 1992) the district court held that the INS's use of secret evidence in its effort to exclude a returning LPR was a violation of due process, and also found that returning residents were accorded First Amendment rights. *See also Ramirez v. U.S.*, 81 F.Supp.2d 532, 536–37 (D.N.J. 2000) [returning LPRs are entitled to Fourth Amendment protection from unreasonable detention]; *Ekekhor v. Aljets*, 979 F.Supp. 640 (N.D. Ill. 1997) [finding INA §236(e), which bars judicial review of custody determinations, unconstitutional as applied to returning LPRs and detention of LPR without hearing violates due process]; *Hamaya v. McElroy*, 797 F.Supp. 186 (E.D.N.Y. 1992) [returning resident is entitled to post-incarceration evidentiary hearing to determine parole]. However, post-IIRIRA, certain returning LPRs are now treated as applicants for admission. INA §101(a)(13)(C). *De Fuentes v. Gonzales,* 462 F.3d 498, 503–05 (5th Cir. 2006) [returning LPR/arriving alien has no constitutional right to admission and equal protection is not violated under rational basis review where Congress treated certain LPRs as arriving aliens and not others]; *Tineo v. Ashcroft*, 350 F.3d 382 (3d Cir. 2003) [holding that IIRIRA repealed by implication that aspect of INA §101(a)(13), which permitted an inquiry into the innocent, casual and brief nature of an LPR's departure, also known as the *Fleuti* doctrine]; *Ferraras v. Ashcroft*, 160 F.Supp.2d 617, 623 (S.D.N.Y. 2001) [treating returning LPR as arriving alien for detention purposes is constitutional post-*Zadvydas*]. Whether the limitations placed on the rights of returning LPRs, who the government believes are inadmissible, conflicts with the liberty interest of returning to the U.S. and cases such as *Kwong Hai Chew* and *Landon*.

(d) *Applicants for AOS or Other Benefits*—The BIA has long recognized that persons seeking adjustment of status are "assimilated" to the position of someone seeking admission, because they are subject to all grounds of inadmissibility. *Jankowski-Burczyk v. INS*, 291 F.3d 172, 175 & n.3 (2d Cir. 2002); *Matter of Mendez-Moralez*, 21 I&N Dec. 296 (BIA 1996); *Matter of Rainford*, 20 I&N Dec. 598 (BIA 1992). But due process is applicable to such persons even if it would not be to persons seeking admission. *American-Arab Anti-Discrimination Comm. v. Reno*, 70 F.3d 1045, 1067–68 (9th Cir. 1995) [finding due process applies to persons in legalization process].

(e) *Right to a Fair Hearing*—All inadmissible aliens have the statutory and due process right to a fundamentally fair hearing. INA §240(b)(4); *Chin Yow v. U.S.*, 208 U.S. 8 (1908). This includes the right to present witnesses, *Najaf-Ali v. Meese*, 653 F.Supp. 833 (N.D. Cal. 1987), the right to adequate interpretation, *Augustin v. Sava*, 735 F.2d 32 (2d Cir. 1984), and the right to effective representation. *Dakane v. U.S. Att'y Gen.,* 399 F.3d 1269, n.6 (11th Cir. 2005).

(2) *Deportable/Removable Aliens*—In contrast to inadmissible aliens, deportable/removable aliens are accorded full due process and equal protection rights. *Zadvydas v. Davis*, 533 U.S. 678, 693 (2001) ["...the Due Process Clause applies to all 'persons' within the United States, including aliens, whether their presence here is lawful, unlawful, tempo-

rary, or permanent"]; Deportable aliens also enjoy First Amendment rights. *Bridges v. Wixon*, 326 U.S. 135, 161 (1945). In determining the constitutional sufficiency of INS procedures for deportable aliens, courts have relied on the tripartite test established in *Mathews v. Eldridge*, 424 U.S. 319 (1976). This test looks to: (1) the interest at stake for the individual; (2) the risk of an erroneous deprivation of the interest through the procedures used and the probable value of additional procedural safeguards; and (3) the government's interest in avoiding the potential burdens that the additional or substitute procedure would entail. *Id.* at 335. *See Flores-Chavez v. Ashcroft,* 362 F.3d 1150, 1160–62 (9th Cir. 2004) [applying *Mathews* analysis and finding that service of OSC and hearing notice to minor and not to custodian raises serious constitutional questions]; *Walters v. Reno*, 145 F.3d 1032, 1043–45 (9th Cir. 1998) [concluding that the notice form in document fraud cases under INA §274C does not comport with due process and requiring the government to alter it]; *Padilla-Agustin v. INS*, 21 F.3d 970 (9th Cir. 1994) [finding constitutionally deficient notice of the potential for summary dismissal as analyzed under *Mathews*]; *Hernandez v. Cremer*, 913 F.2d 230 (5th Cir. 1990) [INS procedures for denying person seeking admission as USC violate due process]; *Haitian Refugee Center v. Nelson*, 872 F.2d 1555 (11th Cir. 1989), *aff'd sub nom. McNary v. Haitian Refugee Center*, 498 U.S. 479 (1991) [finding INS procedures in determining SAW status constitutionally insufficient under *Mathews*]; *Chike v. INS*, 948 F.2d 961 (5th Cir. 1991) [failure to provide notice of BIA briefing schedule was a denial of due process]; *Orantes-Hernandez v. Smith*, 541 F.Supp. 351, 374–78 (C.D. Cal. 1982) and 685 F.Supp. 1488, *aff'd*, 919 F.2d 549, 554, 557 (9th Cir. 1990) [due process requires INS to inform Salvadoran detainees of their right to apply for asylum and right to counsel]. *But see Reno v. American-Arab Anti-Discrimination Committee*, 525 U.S. 421 (1999) [unlawful alien has no right to selective prosecution claim except in rare case of outrageous conduct].

D. *Relief from Removal: A Matter of Grace or a Matter of Right?*—In *Arevalo v. Ashcroft*, 344 F.3d 1, 14–15 (1st Cir. 2003), the court considered whether INA §241(a)(5) (reinstatement of prior removal order) may be applied retroactively to bar AOS filed prior to IIRIRA's effective date. In finding that the statute could not be applied retroactively, the court noted that applying for AOS was a vested right, even if the relief itself was discretionary. Citing *Accardi v. Shaughnessy*, 347 U.S. 260 (1954), and other cases, the court stated that "an alien is not precluded from having a vested right in a form of relief merely because the relief itself is ultimately at the discretion of the Executive Branch." *See also INS v. St. Cyr,* 533 U.S. 289, 307–08 (2001) ["[t]raditionally, courts recognized a distinction between eligibility for discretionary relief, on the one hand, and the favorable exercise of discretion, on the other hand. Eligibility that was 'governed by specific statutory standards' provided 'a right to a ruling on an applicant's eligibility,' even though the actual granting of relief was 'not a matter of right under any circumstances, but rather is in all cases a matter of grace.'"]; *U.S. v. Copeland,* 376 F.3d 61, 72 (2d Cir. 2004) [noting a distinction between "a right to seek relief and the right to that relief itself" and finding incorrect, the assumption that because the grant of §212(c) relief is discretionary, the denial of a §212(c) hearing cannot be a fundamental procedural error]. *But see U.S. v. Aguirre-Tello,* 353 F.3d 1199, 1205 (10th Cir. 2004) (*en banc*) [no due process problem in failing to advise an LPR about possible §212(c) eligibility, because noncitizen has no liberty interest in being able to apply for relief]; *Mejia Rodriguez v. Reno*, 178 F.3d 1139, 1146 (11th Cir. 1999) [rejecting ineffective-assistance-of-counsel claim, because noncitizen had no liberty interest in being able to apply for relief under former suspension of deportation provision]. *See also* "Constitutional Protection for Due Process Violations When Seeking Relief" in Ch. 8, section I.I (p.960), *infra*.

III. STATE EFFORTS TO LIMIT THE RIGHTS OF ALIENS

A. *State vs. Federal Government*—Because the power to regulate immigration is a function of the federal government, the authority of state governments to act in immigration-related matters is limited. *Compare Graham v. Richardson*, 403 U.S. 365 (1971) [invalidating AZ statute restricting welfare benefits to USCs or LPRs who have lived in the U.S. for a minimum of 15 years as unconstitutional] with *Mathews v. Diaz*, 426 U.S. 67 (1976) [upholding federal statute requiring LPRs to reside continuously in the U.S. for 5 years to qualify for medical benefits]. Therefore, state laws designed to regulate immigration are preempted by federal law. *Lozano v. City of Hazleton,* 496 F.Supp.2d 477, 517–29 (M.D. Pa. 2007) [local ordinance governing employment and leases by individuals and businesses to undocumented persons preempted by federal law and violates due process]; *Villas at Parkside Partners v. City of Farmers Branch,* 496 F.Supp.2d 757 (N.D. Tex. 2007) [same]; *Garrett v. City of Escondido,* 465 F.Supp.2d 1043, 1056–58 (S.D. Cal. 2006) [same]; *LULAC v. Wilson*, 997 F.Supp. 1244 (C.D. Cal. 1997) [striking down portions of CA Proposition 187]. Moreover, Congress has the authority to strike down state laws that interfere with immigration enforcement. *City of New York v. U.S.*, 179 F.3d 29 (2d Cir. 1999) [upholding IIRIRA §642, which invalidated state and local rules that prohibit government employees from voluntarily providing information about illegal aliens to the INS]. However, where state and federal authorities work jointly in an immigration-related area, state officials may be given the benefit of federal deference. *Isaraphanich v. Coughlin*, 716 F.Supp. 119 (S.D.N.Y. 1989) [upholding state's reliance on INS detainer to prohibit inmate participation in special programs].

1. *Preemption Issues*—The determination that a state law or local ordinance is preempted by federal law originates in the "Supremacy Clause" (U.S. Const. art. VI, cl.2) of the Untied States Constitution. Preemption may be express or implied. *Lozano v. City of Hazleton,* 496 F.Supp.2d 477, 517–29 (M.D. Pa. 2007) [striking down local ordinance that prohibits hiring undocumented persons because it is expressly preempted by IRCA and striking down the city's tenant registration provisions because they impliedly conflict with federal law]; *Villas at Parkside Partners v. City of Farmers Branch,* 496 F.Supp.2d 757 (N.D. Tex. 2007) [same as to ordinance requiring tenants to present evidence of citizenship or eligible immigration status]. Implied preemption arises where Congress has occupied the subject area to the preclusion of state or local laws because of the nature of the federal interest or the pervasiveness of the federal regulatory scheme. See *e.g., Hines v. Davidowitz,* 312 U.S. 52 (1941) or because the state or local law conflicts with federal law. "Conflict preemption" exists where the state or local law stands as an obstacle to the accomplishment and execution of the full purposes and objectives of Congress or if it is impossible for a party to comply with both state and federal law. *Lozano, supra* at 525–29. Where state law does not actually conflict with federal immigration law and where the area of law is not traditionally occupied by federal law, state law will be respected. *De Canas v. Bica,* 424 U.S. 351 (1976) [CA statute prohibiting employers from knowingly employing persons not authorized to work was not preempted prior to 1986 employer sanctions law]. In *De Canas* the Court adopted three tests to determine whether a state law relating to immigration is preempted by federal law. A state statute will be deemed preempted if (1) the state law is a regulation of immigration; (2) Congress intended to completely oust state power; or (3) the state law stands as "an obstacle" to the accomplishment of congressional objectives or conflicts with federal law, making compliance with both state and federal law impossible. *See Gao v. Jenifer*, 185 F.3d 548 (6th Cir. 1999) [permitting state court to declare undocumented minor a "dependent" so he could obtain special immigrant status while in custody of INS is not preempted]; *Equal Access Education v. Merten,* 305 F.Supp.2d 585, 601–11 (E.D. Va. 2004) [Virginia policy preventing undocumented students from enrolling in post-secondary institutions is not preempted under *De Canas* standards]; *John Doe No. 1 v. Georgia Dep't of Public Safety*, 147 F.Supp.2d 1369, 1375–76 (N.D. Ga. 2001) [Georgia statute denying undocumented persons a state driver's license is not preempted].
2. *Political Sovereignty*—In *Sugarman v. Dougall*, 413 U.S. 634 (1973), the Supreme Court recognized a viable state interest in "establishing its own form of government, and in limiting participation in that government to those who are within 'the basic conception of a political community.' " Therefore, state statutes that restrict employment in certain public positions may be given deference. *Cabell v. Chavez-Salido*, 454 U.S. 432 (1982) [state statute precluding LPRs from employment as peace officers is valid because the position "involves discretionary decision making, or execution of policy, which substantially affects members of the political community"]; *LeClerc v. Webb,* 419 F.3d 405 (5th Cir. 2005) [upholding constitutionality of Louisiana Bar rule prohibiting nonimmigrants from sitting for the bar in face of equal protection, due process, and preemption challenges]. *But see Bernal v. Fainter*, 467 U.S. 216 (1984) [state refusal to permit LPRs to become notaries held unconstitutional]; *Application of Griffiths*, 413 U.S. 717 (1973) [state law prohibiting LPRs from becoming lawyers held unconstitutional]; *City of Orlando v. Florida*, 751 F.Supp. 974 (M.D. Fla. 1990) [striking down in part, the state loyalty oath requiring attestation of U.S. citizenship].

B. *Immigration-Related Classifications and Issues*

1. *Alienage*—While congressional classifications based on alienage are subject to rational basis review, state classifications are generally subject to strict scrutiny. *See Nyquist v. Mauclet*, 432 U.S. 1 (1977)

[applying strict scrutiny and striking down NY statute restricting receipt of financial assistance for higher education by LPRs to those who have applied or intend to apply for citizenship]; *U.S. v. Ferreira*, 275 F.3d 1020 (11th Cir. 2001). However, undocumented persons are not considered a suspect class. *See e.g., John Doe No. 1 v. Georgia Dep't of Public Safety*, 147 F.Supp.2d 1369, 1375–76 (N.D. Ga. 2001) [applying rational basis review and denying equal protection challenge to state law denying undocumented persons a state driver's license]. *But see Plyler v. Doe*, 457 U.S. 202 (1982) [applying intermediate scrutiny to TX law depriving public education to undocumented minor children, in recognition that their presence in the U.S. is not the product of their own unlawful conduct]. Lawful temporary residents are also no considered a suspect class for purposes of strict scrutiny. *League of United Latin American Citizens (LULAC) v. Bredesen,* 500 F.3d 523, 530–34 (6th Cir. 2007) [equal protection and right to travel challenge by temporary residents to Tennessee law that granted them the issuance of a certificate of driving rather than a full driver's license was rejected because plaintiffs failed to demonstrate any harm and the law had a rational basis].

2. *Fundamental or Substantial Right Implicated—Plyler v. Doe*, 457 U.S. 202 (1982) [applying intermediate scrutiny to TX law depriving public education to undocumented minor children, noting that while public education is not a constitutional right, "education has a fundamental role in maintaining the fabric of our society"]; *Lozano v. City of Hazleton,* 496 F.Supp.2d 477, 533–38 (M.D. Pa. 2007) [local ordinance seeking to regulate employment and tenancy of undocumented persons violates due process because it fails to provide notice to the employee and tenant]; *Villas at Parkside Partners v. City of Farmers Branch,* 496 F.Supp.2d 757 (N.D. Tex. 2007) [same as to ordinance requiring tenants to present evidence of citizenship or eligible immigration status]; *John Doe No. 1 v. Georgia Dep't of Public Safety*, 147 F.Supp.2d 1369 (N.D. Ga. 2001) [applying rational basis test and denying equal protection challenge to undocumented persons deprived of state driver's license on theory that they have no fundamental right to travel].

3. *Race or National Origin—Yick Wo v. Hopkins*, 118 U.S. 356, 369 (1886) [the protections of the Constitution "are universal in their application to all persons within the territorial jurisdiction, without regard to any differences of race, of color or of nationality"]; *Castaneda v. Partida*, 430 U.S. 482 (1977), *Hernandez v. Texas*, 347 U.S. 475 (1954) [finding national origin discrimination against Mexican-Americans in grand jury selection impermissible]; *Oyama v. California*, 332 U.S. 633, 644–47 (1948) [restriction on transfer of agricultural property of Japanese LPR is a violation of equal protection].

CHAPTER 3
ADMISSION AND REMOVAL

CHAPTER 3
ADMISSION AND REMOVAL

I. LAWFUL ADMISSION AS THE DEFINING CONCEPT

A. ***Lawful Admission, Not Entry, is the Defining Concept***—The traditional distinction between exclusion and deportation historically turned upon the concept of entry into the United States. This distinction became far less important with the passage of the Illegal Immigration Reform and Immigrant Responsibility Act of 1996 (IIRIRA). The current law struck the definition of entry and replaced it with a definition for admission. Admission is now defined as the "lawful entry of the alien into the United States after inspection and authorization by an immigration officer." INA §101(a)(13)(A). The traditional test for entry—requiring (1) physical presence (a crossing into the territorial limits of the U.S.); (2) either (a) an inspection and admission by an immigration officer, or (b) actual and intentional evasion of inspection at the nearest inspection point, and (3) freedom from restraint—is of limited importance because it has been replaced by a statutory distinction drawn between people who are lawfully admitted into the U.S. and all other people. However, for cases that arose prior to Apr. 1, 1997, this definition, adopted by the BIA remains. *Matter of Patel,* 20 I&N Dec. 368, 370 (BIA 1991); *Mariscal-Sandoval v. Ashcroft,* 370 F.3d 851, 854–55 (9th Cir. 2004) [person paroled and released was not free from restraint because he was in exclusion proceedings the entire time and therefore did not enter the U.S.]; *But see Matter of Sanchez,* 17 I&N Dec. 218, 220 (BIA 1980).

Persons who are not lawfully admitted and entered without inspection are deemed to be inadmissible as if they had been detained at the border. INA §212(a)(6)(A)(i). 8 C.F.R. §235.1(d)(2) [an alien "present in the U.S. who has not been admitted or paroled, or an alien who seeks entry at other than an open, designated port of entry ... is subject to the provisions of INA §212(a)"]. Thus, the entry doctrine which spawned substantial litigation over when and under what circumstances a person entered the U.S., *see, e.g., Matter of Z,* 20 I&N Dec. 707 (BIA 1993); *Matter of Patel*, 20 I&N Dec. 368 (BIA 1991); *Matter of Pierre*, 14 I&N Dec. 467 (BIA 1973); *Sidhu v. Ashcroft,* 368 F.3d 1160 (9th Cir. 2004); *Yang v. Maugans*, 68 F.3d 1540 (3d Cir. 1995); *Zhang v. Slattery*, 55 F.3d 732, 756 (2d Cir. 1995), *cert. denied, Xin-Chang Zhang v. Slattery,* 516 U.S. 1176 (1996), is now far less significant for cases initiated after Apr. 1, 1997. However, even the definition of admission requires a "lawful entry," so entry remains an aspect of admission. And notwithstanding the determination that persons who are EWI are subject to inadmissibility, they are still considered to have made an "entry" for other purposes. *Heng Meng Lin v. Ashcroft,* 247 F.Supp.2d 679, 683–85 (E.D. Pa. 2003) [for purposes of due process right of release under *Zadvydas* and application of Service regulation 8 C.F.R. §241.13, person who entered EWI has entered and is entitled to due process notwithstanding treatment as an inadmissible person].

Because a person who enters without inspection (EWI) is now treated legally as an applicant for admission under INA §235(a)(1), 8 U.S.C. §1225(a)(1), who is inadmissible under INA §212(a)(6)(A)(i), 8 U.S.C. §1182(a)(6)(A)(i), s/he qualifies for parole into the U.S. under 8 U.S.C. §1182(d)(5)(A) even if s/he does not meet the definition of an "arriving alien" under 8 C.F.R. §1.1(q). Memo, Virtue, G.C. to Field (HQCOU 120/17-P) (Aug. 21, 1998), *reprinted in* 76, No. 26 *Interpreter Releases* 1067–70 (July 12, 1999).

B. ***Parole Is Not an Admission***—Historically, the parole of a person at the border or the parole of a person out of detention is not an admission into the U.S. *Leng May Ma v. Barber*, 357 U.S. 185 (1958); INA §212(d)(5), 8 U.S.C. §1182(d)(5). The Act specifically determines that a person granted parole, like a crewmember given permission to land temporarily, is not deemed to be admitted. INA §101(a)(13)(B). *Ibragimov v. Gonzales,* 476 F.3d 125, 132–38 (2d Cir. 2007) [an adjustment applicant reentering on an advance parole is an arriving alien under 8 C.F.R. §1.1(q) and if his adjustment application is denied he remains a parolee and does not revert to a person admitted as an overstay].

C. ***Applicants for Admission***—The question of admission prior to IIRIRA also turned on whether the person was an applicant for admission into the U.S. If the person was not an applicant for admission s/he could not be placed in an exclusion proceeding. *Matter of Badalamenti*, 19 I&N Dec. 623 (BIA 1988) [person extradited to U.S. and paroled until trial not applicant for admission]; *Schuldreich v. INS*, ___ F.Supp. ___, No. B-93-93 (FBV) (S.D. Tex. Aug. 9, 1993), *reported in* 70, No. 45 *Interpreter Releases* 1562–64 (Nov. 22, 1993) [same]. Similarly, a person involuntarily removed from the U.S. (other than through deportation) could not be considered to make a new admission upon his or her return. *Delgadillo v. Carmichael*, 332 U.S. 388, 390–91 (1947) [where ship torpedoed and person taken to Cuba to recuperate his return is not a new entry]. However, INA §235(a)(1), 8 U.S.C. §1225(a)(1), provides that a person "present in the United States who has not been admitted or who arrives in the United States (whether or not at a designated port of arrival and including an alien who is brought to the United States after having been interdicted in international or United States waters) shall be deemed for purposes of the Act "an applicant for admission." *See also* 8 C.F.R. §235.1(f)(3); 8 C.F.R. §1.1(q). The legacy INS has taken the position that anyone brought to the U.S. is an applicant for admission regardless of intent and that *Matter of Badalamenti* is no longer good law in light of INA §235(a)(1). Memo, Virtue, GC to Cronin, Asst. Comm. Inspections (HQCOU 70/6.2.17-P), *reprinted in* 76 *Interpreter Releases* 471, 474 (Mar. 22, 1999). The BIA has also held that someone who lawfully entered the U.S. but wishes to leave may be held for removal proceedings. *Matter of Ruiz-Massieu,* 22 I&N Dec. 833 (BIA 1999) [person seeking to leave U.S. within 24 hours of lawful entry held for removal proceeding for 4 years on grounds that Secretary of State determined his presence would have serious foreign policy consequences].

D. ***No Departure Means No New Admission***—The question of admission is also related to whether a person has "departed" the U.S. A person who leaves the U.S. but does not enter another country does not "enter" the U.S. upon his return. *Matter of T*, 6 I&N Dec. 638 (BIA 1955). Thus, a crew member, for example, would not be deemed to depart the U.S. simply by sailing out of U.S. waters if s/he does not enter a foreign nation. Letter, Cronin, Asst. Comm. Inspections (CO 235-C) (Feb. 7, 1992), *reprinted in* 69 No. 12 *Interpreter Releases* 384, 399 (Mar. 30, 1992). Similarly, a person who leaves the U.S. and is denied admission to Mexico at the border is deemed not to have departed the U.S. Memo, Puleo, Acting Exec. Assoc. Comm. (HQ 245-C) (Nov. 15, 1993), *reprinted in* 13 *AILA Monthly Mailing* 35–37 (Jan. 1994). *See also Handa v. Crawford,* 401 F.3d 1129 (9th Cir. 2005) [where person on visa waiver program was turned away at Canadian border, his drive into Canada to go around Canadian flagpole did not constitute a departure from the U.S. and, therefore, he was not an applicant for admission upon return]. *But see Matter of R-D-,* 24 I&N Dec. 221 (BIA 2007) [Guinean who left the U.S., applied for asylum, stayed in Canada for several years and then was denied departed the U.S. notwithstanding Reciprocal Agreement with Canada to return individuals to the U.S.]

E. ***The Constitutional Question***—The entry doctrine fiction has always been the basis for determining when and under what circumstances persons are accorded due process in proceedings. Although IIRIRA ended the traditional distinction between exclusion and deportation hearings *per se* and replaced them with removal hearings, the entry doctrine may have continuing vitality in regard to whether full constitutional rights are given to someone if they are in the U.S. even if they were not admitted. *Clark v. Martinez,* 543 U.S. 371 (2005) [avoiding constitutional question regarding the indefinite detention of inadmissible aliens and applying *Zadvydas* 6-month limitation on detention post-removal to inadmissible Cuban parolees as a statutory matter]. To the extent the distinction between inadmissible and deportable persons has continuing vitality the following discussion concerning distinctions drawn about entry has been retained.

F. ***Entry Defined***—Immigration decisions draw numerous distinctions concerning when and under what circumstances a person has made an entry into the U.S. For example, an alien who escaped from detention while awaiting an exclusion hearing did not make an entry into the U.S. *Matter of Lin*, 18 I&N Dec. 219 (BIA 1982). An alien in transit without a visa (TWOV) has not entered the U.S. *U.S. v. Kavazanjian*, 623 F.2d 730 (1st Cir. 1980); *U.S. v. Esperdy*, 210 F.Supp. 786 (S.D.N.Y. 1962). An alien who was placed in carrier custody and failed to appear for an INS interview to determine admissibility has not made an entry. *Vitale v. INS*, 463 F.2d 579 (7th Cir. 1972). An alien under surveillance before he enters may bar a claim to entry. *Zhang v. Slattery, supra* at 755 [continuous surveillance by INS can be sufficient to place alien under affirmative restraint].

An LPR who passed primary immigration inspection but was deferred for a customs inspection thereby never leaving the "customs enclosure" did not make an entry because he was not free from restraint. *Correa v. Thornburgh*, 901 F.2d 1166, 1171–72 (2d Cir. 1990); *Matter of Patel*, 20 I&N Dec. 368 (BIA 1991) [freedom from restraint need not be by INS officers]; *Zhang v. Slattery, supra* [same].

However, a detained stowaway who escapes while awaiting removal, *Matter of A-*, 9 I&N Dec. 356 (BIA 1961), or an alien who escapes after being refused admission, *Matter of Ching and Chen*, 19 I&N Dec. 203 (BIA 1984), or a person who comes ashore on land within federal jurisdiction but for reasons unrelated to immigration processing, *Matter of Z, supra*, has made an entry into the U.S.

The question of entry may often turn on whether the applicant is free from restraint. Eluding INS for a brief period of time after landing does not necessarily mean the applicant is free from restraint. *Yang v. Maugans*, 68 F.3d 1540, 1550 (3d Cir. 1995) [applicants who landed on beach and stayed there while it was teeming with law enforcement officers were not free from restraint].

An intention to evade inspection need not be established through the person's own words. It may be established through documentary evidence and the facts and circumstances of entry, even where INS provides rebuttal testimony. *Nyirenda v. INS,* 279 F.3d 620 (8th Cir. 2002) [evidence indicated person intended to evade inspection and her response was not credible]; *Matter of Z, supra*; *Zhang v. Slattery, supra* [same].

While the INS may establish that a person was not free from restraint because INS was constructively surveilling him or he was otherwise under constructive restraint, such restraint does not arise where a person makes a landing and is at liberty for some period of time. *Nyirenda v. INS,* 279 F.3d 620 (8th Cir. 2002) [persons free from restraint where they were driving out of site of INS officials while traveling on a highway for approx. 2 miles in U.S.]; *Matter of Z, supra.*

G. ***Territorial Waters and Admission***—The question of admission also turns in part on crossing into U.S. territory. In 1988, President Reagan issued a proclamation extending U.S. territorial waters to 12 miles. Proclamation 5928, 54 Fed. Reg. 777 (Jan. 9, 1989). This 12-mile limit has been incorporated in DHS regulations governing the external boundary for enforcement purposes. 8 C.F.R. §287.1(a)(1). This is consistent with U.S. obligations under the U.N. Convention on the Territorial Sea and the Contiguous Zone, Art. 24 (Apr. 29, 1958), 15 U.S.T. 1606, 1612. However, crossing into territorial waters may not be sufficient for an entry. *Yang v. Maugans*, 68 F.3d 1540, 1547–49 (3d Cir. 1995) [INA definition of U.S. does not include territorial waters]; *Zhang v. Slattery*, 55 F.3d 732, 754 (2d Cir. 1995), *cert. denied, Xin-Chang Zhang v. Slattery,* 516 U.S. 1176 (1996); *Chen Zhou Chih v. Carroll*, 48 F.3d 1331 (4th Cir. 1995); *Rodriguez v. Ridge,* 310 F.Supp.2d 1242, 1245–46 (S.D. Fla. 2004), [crossing into territorial waters in not an admission into U.S. unless government brings person to U.S.]; *Matter of G-*, 20 I&N Dec. 764, 770 n.5 (BIA 1993) [BIA never held that crossing into territorial waters is entry]; *Matter of Cenatice*, 16 I&N Dec. 163 (BIA 1977); Legal Opinion, Dellinger, Acting Asst. Atty. General, Memoranda on Immigration Consequences of Undocumented Aliens' Arrival in United States Territorial Waters (Oct. 13, 1993). *But see Lazarescu v. U.S.*, 199 F.2d 898, 900–01 (4th Cir. 1952) [entry into port and harbor of Baltimore is entry]; *Chung v. Reno*, 886 F.Supp. 1172 (M.D. Pa. 1995) [extensive discussion of the issue], *rev'd sub nom. Yang v. Maugans*, 68 F.3d 1540 (3d Cir. 1995).

H. ***Admission and Adjustment of Status***—The question of admission also arises in the context of an adjustment application. An AOS is not deemed an entry (even though the grounds of inadmissibility are applicable), *Matter of Adetiba*, 20 I&N Dec. 506 (BIA 1992); *Matter of Connelly*, 19 I&N Dec. 156 (BIA 1984). The plain language of INA §101(a)(13)(A) provides that admission requires a "lawful entry…into the United States after inspection and authorization by an immigration officer." Nevertheless, the BIA has held that adjustment is an admission. *Matter of Rodarte,* 23 I&N Dec. 905, 908 (BIA 2006) [the 10-year bar provision under INA §212(a)(9)(B)(i)(II) applies to adjustment of status because "the term 'admission' generally refers to adjustment of status within the United States as well as lawful entry at the border"]; *Matter of Rosas,* 22 I&N Dec. 616 (BIA 1999). *But see Martinez v. Mukasey,* 519 F.3d 532, 542-45 (5th Cir. 2008) [under the first prong of *Chevron* and under longstanding principles construing statutes in favor of persons facing removal, the court rejected *Matter of Rosas* in interpreting the exclusion provision of INA §212(h) and concluded that the term "admitted" as used in INA §212(h) does not bar LPRs who were convicted of aggravated felonies from obtaining relief if they were adjusted]; *Abdelqadar v. Gonzales,* 413 F.3d 668, 672–74 (7th Cir. 2005) [questioning and rejecting *Matter of Rosas* in the context of a commission of a crime of moral turpitude under §1227(a)(2)(A)(i) because the 5 years is correctly interpreted to be within 5 years of admission and not 5 years of adjustment]; *Aremu v. DHS,* 450 F.3d 578 (4the Cir. 2006) [same; reversing *Matter of Shanu,* 23 I&N Dec. 754, 756–59 (BIA 2005) and finding the plain language of §101(a)(13)(A) is contrary to BIA's interpretation because an adjustment clearly is not an admission when the person's original entry was lawful]; *Zhang v. Mukasey,* 509 F.3d 313 (6th Cir. 2007) [5 years is not measured from AOS for purposes of a CIMT committed within 5 years of admission, because AOS does not constitute an admission for purposes of calculating the time period]; *Shivaraman v. Ashcroft,* 360 F.3d 1142, 1146 (9th Cir. 2004). It may also arise in the context of relief. *Gomes v. Ashcroft,* 311 F.3d 43, 45–46 (1st Cir. 2002) [the term "admission" in IMMACT90 §511(b), which sets the date for the bar to INA §212(c) relief for a person who has been imprisoned for 5 years or more, applies not only to the person's original entry into the U.S., but also to the date of the application for INA §212(c) relief].

I. *Admission Flexibly Applied in Other Contexts*—Notwithstanding the statutory definition of admission under §101(a)(13)(A) as requiring an inspection, the courts and the BIA have interpreted the word "admitted" in other contexts to include persons already in the United States. In *Garcia-Quintero v. Gonzales,* 455 F.3d 1006, 1015–19 (9th Cir. 2006) the court determined that "admitted in any status" for purposes of cancellation for LPRs included persons who registered in the U.S. for family unity benefits despite the lack of inspection at the border. Similarly in *Matter of Rosas,* 22 I&N Dec. 616, 623 (BIA 1999) the Board held that a person who entered EWI was still admitted when he attained LPR status.

II. ADMISSION AND LAWFUL PERMANENT RESIDENTS

A. *Generally*—Traditionally, a lawful permanent resident was not deemed to make a new admission into the U.S. upon his or her return if the trip was "innocent, casual and brief" and not meant to be "meaningfully interruptive" of the LPR's status. *Rosenberg v. Fleuti*, 374 U.S. 449 (1963). The distinction is significant for an LPR who would not be subject to removal from the U.S. but who might be inadmissible if his or her presence at the border was considered a request for a new admission into the U.S. For example, in *Fleuti,* a homosexual LPR would have been inadmissible into the U.S. if his return was considered a request for a new admission under former INA §212(a)(4). However, the Court did not treat Fleuti's return as a request to be readmitted. Rather, it treated him as if he had never left the U.S. Thus, his homosexuality could not result in his removal from the U.S. because homosexuality, although at the time a basis for inadmissibility, was not a basis for removal. There have been numerous cases defining "brief, casual and innocent," for purposes of determining whether the LPR should be treated as making a new admission. *See, e.g., Selimi v. INS,* 312 F.3d 854, 859–60 (7th Cir. 2002) [where LPR was involved in smuggling his wife, children, and cousin it was not an innocent trip and the benefits of *Fleuti* are inapplicable]; *Carbajal-Gonzalez v. INS*, 78 F.3d 194 (5th Cir. 1996) [brief trip to Mexico for party with wife and student was innocent trip where student did not have proper documents]; *Castrejon-Garcia v. INS*, 60 F.3d 1359 (9th Cir. 1995) [trip for 8 days to obtain a visa did not interrupt stay in suspension case]; *Biggs v. INS*, 55 F.3d 1398 (9th Cir. 1995) [obtaining fraudulent residency was not an innocent trip under *Fleuti*]; *Rosendo-Ramirez v. INS*, 32 F.3d 1085, 1090–94 (7th Cir. 1994) [EWI is separate charge and *Fleuti* inapplicable]; *Leal-Rodriquez v. INS*, 990 F.2d 939, 943–48 (7th Cir. 1993) [EWI is meaningfully interruptive of status]; *Molina v. Sewell*, 983 F.2d 676, 678 (5th Cir. 1993) [temporary departure of LPR during deportation proceedings is not meaningfully interruptive of status]; *Hernandez-Luis v. INS*, 869 F.2d 496 (9th Cir. 1989) [voluntary departure is meaningfully interruptive of status]; *Jubilado v. INS*, 819 F.2d 210 (9th Cir. 1987) [3-month trip with family is not meaningfully interruptive of status]; *DeOliviera v. INS*, 873 F.Supp. 338 (C.D. Cal. 1994) [4 months out due to airline strike and pregnancy was not meaningfully interruptive of status]; *Hamaya v. McElroy*, 797 F.Supp. 186, 188 (E.D.N.Y. 1992) [10-month trip not brief trip].

Congress has now defined when an LPR will be regarded as seeking a new admission. INA §101(a)(13)(C). An LPR will not be regarded as seeking a new admission unless: (1) s/he abandoned or relinquished her LPR status; (2) s/he has been absent from the U.S. for a continuous period in excess of 180 days; (3) s/he has engaged in illegal activity after having departed the U.S.; (4) s/he has departed from the U.S. while under legal process seeking removal of the LPR from the U.S., including removal proceedings and extradition proceedings; (5) s/he has committed a criminal offense under INA §212(a)(2), unless s/he was granted INA §212(h) or INA §240A(a) (cancellation of removal) relief; or (6) s/he is attempting to enter EWI or has not been admitted. The question of whether *Fleuti* has now been overturned or modified by the enactment of INA §101(a)(13) and may no longer be relied upon has been addressed in a number of cases. *Matter of Collado-Munoz*, 21 I&N Dec. 1061 (BIA 1997) [finding in detention context *Fleuti* no longer requires the admission of an LPR whose trip was brief, casual and innocent but who had a conviction that would bar him under INA §212(a)(2)]; *De Vega v. Gonzales,* 503 F.3d 45, 48–49 (1st Cir. 2007) [the elements of the *Fleuti* doctrine are irrelevant to the legal determination under INA §101(a)(13)(C)]; *Camins v. Gonzales,* 500 F.3d 872 (9th Cir. 2007) [under *Chevron* deference following *Matter of Collado-Munoz*, the court determined that IIRIRA's passage of INA §101(a)(13)(C) abrogated the *Fleuti* doctrine]; *Malagon De Fuentes v. Gonzales,* 462 F.3d 498, 501–05 (5th Cir. 2006) [IIRIRA superseded the *Fleuti* doctrine and the decision cannot be read to create a constitutional right]; *Tineo v. Ashcroft,* 350 F.3d 382 (3d Cir. 2003) [determining that Congress did abolish the *Fleuti* doctrine in the passage of INA §101(a)(13)(C) for certain returning LPRs, and upholding *Matter of Collado-Munoz* on *Chevron* deference grounds]; *Ferraras v. Ashcroft,* 160 F.Supp.2d 617, 623 (S.D.N.Y. 2001) [treating returning LPR as arriving alien for detention purposes is constitutional post-*Zadvydas*].

Whether INA §101(a)(13)(C) abrogates *Fleuti,* it may not be applied retroactively to persons who were convicted or engaged in acts prior to IIRIRA that now affect their admissibility. *Camins v. Gonzales,* 500 F.3d 872, 880–85 (9th Cir. 2007) [INA §101(a)(13)(C) may not be applied retroactively to guilty pleas entered prior to its passage under IIRIRA]; *Olatunji v. Ashcroft,* 387 F.3d 383, 388–96 (4th Cir. 2004) [finding that "reliance, in any form, is irrelevant to the retroactivity inquiry" and holding that IIRIRA's change in the *Fleuti* doctrine could not be retroactively applied to a person who pled guilty prior to its enactment]. *See also generally Falek v. Gonzales,* 475 F.3d 285 (5th Cir. 2007) [failure to raise retroactivity of INA §101(a)(13)(C) before BIA barred federal review].

In regard to a returning LPR, DHS has the burden of proving inadmissibility. *Landon v. Plasencia,* 459 U.S. 21 (1982) [returning resident entitled to due process protections]; *Molina v. Sewell,* 983 F.3d 676, 678 (5th Cir. 1993); *Matter of Sosa*, 15 I&N Dec. 572 (BIA 1976). Post-IIRIRA and the passage of INA §101(a)(13)(C), however, there is a question as to whether the government must prove by "clear, convincing and unequivocal" evidence the application of INA §101(a)(13)(C). *Sandoval-Loffredo v. Gonzales,* 414 F.3d 892 (8th Cir. 2005) [addressing but not deciding who has the burden; IJ found that the government established by clear, convincing, and unequivocal evidence that the LPR engaged in unlawful activity under §101(a)(13)(C)(ii) in facilitating his brother's illegal entry]; *Molina v. Sewell,* 983 F.2d 676, 678 (5th Cir. 1993) [applicant bears the burden to prove he comes within the statutory definition of lawful admission (formerly the *Fleuti* exception)].

The application of INA §101(a)(13)(C)(v) may turn on whether the BIA makes a finding that a person committed a criminal act. *Toro-Romero v. Ashcroft,* 382 F.3d 930 (9th Cir. 2004) [whether a returning LPR can be found inadmissible for making a false claim to citizenship will turn on whether he committed a CIMT and is therefore inadmissible and subject to §101(a)(13)(C). Where BIA failed to make that finding, the court reversed].

Notwithstanding Congress's efforts to restrict *Fleuti*, a question remains whether *Fleuti* may be applied to persons who are not LPRs. *Aquilera-Medina v. INS,* 137 F.3d 1401 (9th Cir. 1998) [applying *Fleuti* to SAW temporary residents]; *Joshi v. INS*, 720 F.2d 799 (4th Cir. 1983); *Patel v. Landon*, 739 F.2d 1455 (9th Cir. 1984); *Siverts v. Craig*, 602 F.Supp. 50 (D. Hawaii 1985) [where returning to U.S. after advance parole (I-512) person entitled to deportation hearing]; *Flores-Salgado v. Caplinger*, 872 F.Supp. 1521 (E.D. La. 1995) [*Fleuti* applicable to conditional resident even if person traveled on I-512]; *Campos v. Smith*, 791 F.Supp. 262 (W.D. Wa. 1991) [applying *Fleuti* to legalization applicant]. DHS regulations may not bar a registry applicant who received advance parole from asserting a right to deportation proceedings. *Navarro-Aispura v. INS*, 53 F.3d 233 (9th Cir. 1995). The BIA, however, has declined to follow *Joshi*, *supra*, limiting the *Fleuti* doctrine pre-IIRIRA to LPRs. *Matter of Torres*, 19 I&N Dec. 371 (BIA 1986) [alien paroled on I-512 for adjustment in exclusion not deportation proceedings; adjustment determination independent of excludable status]; *Assa'ad v. U.S. Att'y General,* 332 F.3d 1321, 1332 (11th Cir. 2003) [limiting *Fleuti* to LPRs and finding that denied legalization applicant traveling on advance parole was properly placed in exclusion proceeding]; and INS regulations were subsequently changed, thereby nullifying *Joshi*. 8 C.F.R. §245.2(a)(4)(ii). *See also Ibragimov v. Gonzales,* 476 F.3d 125, 132–38 & n.18 (2d Cir. 2007) [finding *Joshi* and *Patel* no longer good law and determining that adjustment applicant reentering on an advance parole is an arriving alien under 8 C.F.R. §1.1(q)]; *Tapia v. Ashcroft,* 351 F.3d 795, 798–99 (7th Cir. 2003) [*Fleuti* doctrine cannot be relied upon post-IIRIRA to assist respondent who claims he had 7 years of physical presence that were not interrupted because his 6½-month trip abroad was brief, casual and innocent]; *Assa'ad,* 332 F.3d 1321 (11th Cir. 2003); *Balogun v. U.S. Att'y Gen.,* 304 F.3d 1303(11th Cir. 2002) [no constitutionally protected right to be advised of consequences of accepting advance parole]; *Dimenski v. INS,* 275 F.3d 574 (7th Cir. 2001) [adjustment applicant who received advance parole properly in exclusion proceeding and there is no requirement that the advance parole form warn person of consequences]; *Mendoza v. INS*, 16 F.3d 335 (9th Cir. 1994); *Kasbati v. District Director*, 805 F.Supp. 619 (N.D. Ill. 1992); *Matter of S-O-S-,* 22 I&N Dec. 107 (BIA 1998) [describing law in 9th Cir. regarding advance parole]; *Matter of G-A-C-,* 22 I&N Dec. 83 (BIA 1998) [asylum applicant returning on advance parole properly in exclusion; distinguished *Navarro-Aispura*]; *Matter of Singh*, 21 I&N Dec. 427 (BIA 1996) [a class member in *CSS* who is a returning applicant for legalization under INA §245A may not terminate exclusion proceedings based on *Fleuti*]; *Matter of Chavez-Calderon*, 20 I&N Dec. 744 (BIA 1993) [*Fleuti* inapplicable to lawful temporary residents under INA §210].

III. GROUNDS FOR INADMISSIBILITY, INA §212(a), 8 U.S.C. §1182(a)—CLASSES OF PERSONS INELIGIBLE FOR VISAS AND ADMISSION

A. *Health-Related Grounds*—INA §212(a)(1), 8 U.S.C. §1182(a)(1); 22 C.F.R. §40.11; AFM at 23.3, 41.3

1. *Communicable Disease of Public Health Significance*—INA §212(a)(1)(A)(i), 8 U.S.C. §1182(a)(1)(A)(i); 42 C.F.R. §34.2(b); 9 FAM 40.11 N.6.

   1.a. An alien who is determined (in accordance with HHS regulations) to have a communicable disease of public health significance.

      (1) HIV infection by statute is now considered a communicable disease of public health significance. Infectious tuberculosis is also listed by regulation. 42 C.F.R. §34.2(b); 9 FAM 40.11 N. 6. In *Haitian Centers Council v. Sale*, 817 F.Supp. 336 (E.D.N.Y. 1993), applicants for asylum who were HIV-infected successfully challenged their continued detention.

   1.b. Waiver Available—INA §212(g)(1), 8 U.S.C. §1182(g)(1). The AG may waive inadmissibility under INA §212(a)(1)(A)(i) if the alien is the spouse, unmarried son or daughter or the minor unmarried lawfully adopted child of a USC, LPR, or a person issued an immigrant visa, *or* the alien has a son or daughter who is a USC, LPR, or a person issued an IV. A VAWA self-petitioner is also covered. Service policy in regard to waiver explained in Memo, Aleinikoff, Exec. Assoc. Comm., HQ 212.3-P (Sept. 6, 1995), *reprinted in* 72 No. 38 *Interpreter Releases* 1347–54 (Oct. 2, 1995). The waiver procedure for IV cases for persons who are HIV-positive equally applies to K-3/K-4 and V-1/V-2 applicants. Memo, Yates, Assoc. Dir. Operations, USCIS, HQ 70/21.1.1, AD 04-05 (Nov. 2, 2004), *published on* AILA InfoNet at Doc. No. 04111862. DHS guidelines for waivers are at AFM at 41.3 and Memo, Williams, Ex. Assoc. Comm. Field Operations, HQ 70/21/1.1-P, AD 0103 (Oct. 17, 2002), *published on* AILA InfoNet at Doc. No. 03031763. For nonimmigrants, USCIS/DOS has granted blanket waivers for individuals who are HIV-positive to attend special conferences. *See e.g.,* Blanket Waiver for United Nations Special Session on HIV/AIDS, Cable, DOS, 08-State-048125 (May 6, 2008), *published on* AILA InfoNet at Doc. No. 08050831.

2. *Vaccinations*—INA §212(a)(1)(A)(ii), 8 U.S.C. §1182(a)(1)(A)(ii); 22 C.F.R. §40.11.

   2.a. A person who seeks an *immigrant visa* or *adjustment of status* and has failed to present documentation of having received vaccination against vaccino-preventable diseases (including, at least: mumps, measles, rubella, polio, tetanus and diphtheria, pertussis, influenza type R and hepatitis B, and any other vaccination recommended by the Advisory Committee for Immunization Practices (ACIP)) is inadmissible. The ACIP has also included varicella and pneumococcal. The section does *not* apply to NIVs. A K visa applicant is subject to an assessment of whether s/he has taken the proper vaccinations, but cannot be denied the visa for noncompliance because the requirement only applies to IVs. Nor are refugees, asylees, registry applicants, North American Indians born in Canada or children of returning residents required to comply with the requirements. Memo, Virtue, Acting Exec. Assoc. Comm. (Sept. 29, 1997), *reprinted in* 74 No. 42 *Interpreter Releases* 1682, 1687–90 (Nov. 3, 1997). Congress has also exempted internationally adopted children under 10. *See* PL 105-73. The Center for Disease Control has set forth technical instructions for the medical examinations.

CDC, *Addendum to the Technical Instruction for Medical Examination of Aliens in the United States*, April 1997, *reprinted in* 75 No. 13 *Interpreter Releases* 472, 481 (Apr. 6, 1998). The CDC information is also available online at *www.cdc.gov/ncidod/dq/technica.htm*. These instructions are changed from time to time. *See e.g.,* 2007 "CDC Immigration Requirements: Technical Instructions for Vaccination," *reprinted in* 85 No. 10 *Interpreter Releases* 661, 691 and 723–41 (Mar. 3, 2008).

2.b. Waiver—INA §212(g)(2), 8 U.S.C. §1182(g)(2). Waiver is available where: (1) person received vaccination but does not have documentation; (2) vaccination would not be medically appropriate; (3) regulations of AG do not require vaccination because of person's religious beliefs or moral convictions. The legislative history provides for a broad interpretation of the waiver to include its use where the person is: (A) "unable to receive a safe dosage or vaccine in the country of nationality"; (B) "a child who is required to complete a series of vaccinations over a course of time and has not had a reasonable opportunity to complete that course"; or (C) is an active member of a religious faith that notifies the AG that such vaccination would contradict the fundamental tenets of the religion. H.R. Conf. Rep. 828, 104th Cong., 2d Sess. at 226 (1996). To qualify for a religious objection waiver, the applicant must show: (1) s/he is opposed to vaccinations in any form; (2) the objection is based on religious belief or moral conviction; and (3) the belief or conviction is sincere. Memo, Virtue, Acting Exec. Assoc. Comm. (Sept. 29, 1997), *reprinted in* 74 No. 42 *Interpreter Releases* 1682, 1687–90 (Nov. 3, 1997). The religious waiver may also be filed for an adopted child. Cable, DOS, (98-State-083590), *reprinted in* 75 No. 19 *Interpreter Releases* 700 (May 18, 1998). An applicant may also receive a waiver because the vaccine is not medically appropriate due to: (1) age; (2) contraindication; (3) insufficient time interval; (4) seasonality of vaccination (*e.g.*, flu shot); or (5) unavailability. Memo, Yates, Deputy Exe. Assoc. Comm. Immigration Services Division, HQADN 70/21.1.1 (June 25, 2002), *published on* AILA InfoNet at Doc. No. 02070240; Cable, Albright, Secy. of State, 97-State-071637 (Apr. 17, 1997), *reprinted in* 74 No. 17 *Interpreter Releases* 749–56 (May 5, 1997); Memo, Virtue, Acting Exec. Comm. Programs, INS, HQ 5015.12, 96 Act. 027 (Apr. 10, 1997), *reprinted in* 74 No. 15 *Interpreter Releases* 639, 660–63 (Apr. 21, 1997). USCIS has granted to consular officers the right to grant the waivers in IV cases. *Id.* The waiver is submitted on an I-601 form. DHS guidelines for waivers are at AFM at 41.3 and Memo, Williams, Ex. Assoc. Comm. Field Operations, HQ 70/21/1.1-P, AD 0103 (Oct. 17, 2002), *published on* AILA InfoNet at Doc. No. 03031763.

2.c. Refugees and asylees are not required to comply with the vaccination requirements because refugees are not admitted as immigrants and asylees are in the U.S. However, when refugees or asylees seek to adjust, they are subject to the vaccination requirements. They are also eligible for a broader waiver under INA §209(c) than the vaccination waiver. Memo, Bednarz, Acting Assoc. Comm. Adjudications (HQ 70/21.1.1, 96 Act 074) (July 30, 1998), *reprinted in* 75 No. 33 *Interpreter Releases* 1193, 1203–07 (Aug. 31, 1998). Refugees and asylees seeking waivers under INA §209(c) or the religious waiver under INA §212(g)(2)(C) shall file them on Form I-602.

3. *Physical or Mental Disorder*—INA §212(a)(1)(A)(iii), 8 U.S.C. §1182(a)(1)(A)(iii); 42 C.F.R. §§34.2(d)(2), (*l*)(2); (n), (p).

3.a. An alien who is determined (in accordance with HHS regulations in consultation with the AG):

(1) To have a physical or mental disorder *and* behavior associated with the disorder that may pose, or has posed, a threat to the property, safety and welfare of the person or others; or

(2) Has had such disorder and associated behavior in the past *and* it is likely to recur or to lead to other harmful behavior.

(3) The presence of a physical or mental illness alone does not determine whether a person poses a significant risk, and where the mental shortcoming is due to ignorance or where the person is suffering from a condition attributable to remediable physical causes or of a temporary nature caused by toxin, medically prescribed drug, or disease, the medical examiner may not issue a class A notification. 42 C.F.R. §34.4(b).

(4) A history of institutionalization for a mental disorder, a criminal history such as assaults and domestic violence where alcohol or other psychoactive substance was a contributing factor,

other criminal arrests where there is a reasonable possibility of a mental disorder as a contributing factor, or DUI/DWI convictions and/or arrests under certain circumstances should require a mental status examination to determine admissibility. Memo, Yates, Assoc. Dir. Operations (Jan 16, 2004), *published on* AILA InfoNet at 04022362.

(5) This section has been interpreted to include an episode of DWI or other alcohol related human behavior. 12 *AILA Monthly Mailing* 385 (May 1993) [denied IV because of DWI conviction]. Although an alcoholic is not ineligible to receive a visa unless there is harmful behavior associated with the disorder, DHS has recognized that "alcohol abuse/dependence resulting in alcohol-impaired driving may serve as the basis for a determination that an alien has mental disorder with associated harmful behavior" resulting in inadmissibility under this section. Memo, Yates, Assoc. Dir. Operations (Jan 16, 2004), *published on* AILA InfoNet at 04022362. DOS also requires that an IV applicant who has " a single drunk driving arrest or conviction within the last three calendar years or two or more drunk driving arrests or convictions in any time period" be referred to a panel physician for additional evaluation. 9 FAM 40.11 N8.3.

3.b. Waiver Available—INA §212(g)(3), 8 U.S.C. §1182(g)(3)—The AG, under such terms as he, in consultation with the HHS Secretary, may prescribe, may waive inadmissibility under this section. DHS guidelines for waivers are at AFM at 41.3 and Memo, Williams, Ex. Assoc. Comm. Field Operations, HQ 70/21/1.1-P, AD 0103 (Oct. 17, 2002), *published on* AILA InfoNet at Doc. No. 03031763.

4. *Persons determined to be drug abuser or addict* (in accordance with HHS regulations)—INA §212(a)(1)(A)(iv), 9 FAM 40.11 N9.; *Matter of T-*, 8 I&N Dec. 523 (BIA 1960); *Matter of K.C.B.*, 6 I&N Dec. 374 (BIA 1954). Drug abuse is defined as the nonmedical use of a substance listed in §202 of the Controlled Substances Act that has not necessarily resulted in physical or psychological dependence. 42 C.F.R. §34.2(g). However, it does not include the experimentation with a substance (*e.g.*, single use of marijuana or amphetamines). Cable, DOS, 91-State-416180 (Dec. 24, 1991), *reprinted in* 69 No. 1 *Interpreter Releases* 5 (Jan. 6, 1992). 9 FAM 40.11 N. 9.1(c). A person is also not inadmissible as a drug addict or drug abuser if he is has not used a psychoactive substance within the last 3 years. 9 FAM 40.11 N.9.5. If it is not a controlled substance (*e.g.,* alcohol), the waiting period is 2 years. *Id.* The CDC will issue an advisory opinion to DOS where the applicant disagrees with the medical decision. AILA-DOS Liaison Committee Minutes (DOS clarification) (May 24, 2006), *published on* AILA InfoNet at Doc. No. 06052460. Unlike §§212(a)(1)(A)(i) & (ii), drug abusers or addicts have no waiver available to them under this section.

5. Person or guardian who accompanies an inadmissible alien who is certified to be helpless due to infancy, sickness, or physical or mental disability, and whose protection or guardianship is determined to be required by the person—A medical examining officer may certify this. INA §212(a)(10)(B), 8 U.S.C. §1182(a)(10)(B); 22 C.F.R. §40.102.

6. *Appeal*—A person given a class A certification leading to inadmissibility may appeal to DHS whereupon a medical board is convened and the applicant may bring his own medical experts to testify. 42 C.F.R. §34.8(a)(2).

7. *Burden of Proof*—If a medical officer, civil surgeon or board of medical officers certifies under INA §232(b) that a person has a disease, illness or addiction which makes her inadmissible under INA §212(a)(1), the IJ's decision shall be based solely on the certification. INA §240(c)(1)(B).

8. IMMACT90 substantially altered the former health-related grounds by eliminating as a ground of exclusion: mental retardation, *Matter of Azevedo*, 13 I&N Dec. 611 (Comm. 1970); insanity per se or one or more attacks of insanity per se, *Matter of W-*, 2 I&N Dec. 68 (BIA 1944); *Matter of M-*, 7 I&N Dec. 140 (BIA 1956); affliction with psychopathic personality, sexual deviation or mental defect, including homosexuality, *Boutilier v. INS*, 387 U.S. 118 (1967); *Matter of Hill*, 18 I&N Dec. 81 (BIA 1981), *rev'd*, *Hill v. INS*, 714 F.2d 1470 (9th Cir. 1983) [not excludable without Public Health Service determination]; *Matter of Longstaff*, 716 F.2d 1439 (5th Cir. 1983), *cert. denied*, *Longstaff v. INS*, 467 U.S. 1219 (1984) [PHS cannot thwart congressional definition]; and chronic alcoholism.

B. *Economic Grounds*

1. *Persons Likely to Become Public Charge*—INA §212(a)(4), 8 U.S.C. §1182(a)(4); 22 C.F.R. §40.41; 9 FAM 40.41 N1-13, PN 1-4; H.R. Conf. Rep. 104-828, 104th Cong., 2d Sess. 240–42. Prior case law has defined public charge as a person who "by reason of poverty, insanity, disease or disability would become a charge upon the public." *Gegiow v. Uhl*, 239 U.S. 3 (1915). "Poverty" is defined by the annually updated poverty guidelines. In 2008 the poverty guidelines for the 48 contiguous United States and D.C. (excluding Alaska and Hawaii, which are higher), are as follows: for one person ($10,400); 2 people ($14,000); 3 people ($17,600); 4 people ($21,200); 5 people ($24,800); 6 people ($28,400); 7 people ($32,000); and 8 people ($35,600,). For family units with more than 8 members, add $3,600 for each additional member. 73 Fed. Reg. 3791–92 (Jan. 23, 2008). For more information about the poverty guidelines go to *www.census.gov/hhes/www/poverty/poverty.html*. For USCIS purposes, the guidelines become effective on the second full month following their release, which would be March following their release in January. Memo, Aytes, Acting Dir. Domestic Operations, USCIS HQRPM 70/21.1.13 at 15, 18 (June 27, 2006), *published on* AILA InfoNet at Doc. No. 06063013. To determine public charge, INS traditionally has applied a "totality of the circumstances" approach, which includes whether alien has received public assistance, his or her age, capacity to earn a living, health, family situation, work history, affidavits of support and physical and mental condition. *Matter of A-*, 19 I&N Dec. 867 (Comm. 1988) [unemployed woman who is young and has no physical or mental impediments that would affect her ability to earn a living is not a public charge]. *See also Matter of Vindman*, 16 I&N Dec. 131 (R.C. 1977). Under IIRIRA §531(a), Congress mandated that the following factors be taken into account in deciding public charge: (1) age; (2) health; (3) family status; (4) assets, resources, and financial status; and (5) education and skills. DOS has instructed consular officers to review HIV cases in light of the public charge provisions. Cable, DOS, No. 92-State-093280 (Mar. 25, 1992), *reprinted in* 69 No. 16 *Interpreter Releases* 516–17 (Apr. 27, 1992). DOS has also determined that "a properly filed, nonfraudulent I-864 (affidavit of support) shall normally be considered sufficient to overcome the §212(a)(4) requirements." Cable, DOS (98-State-102426) (June 8, 1998), *reprinted in* 75 No. 24 *Interpreter Releases* 879 (June 29, 1998). However, DOS recognizes that public charge concerns may be appropriate even with a valid affidavit of support where there are identifiable personal characteristics of the applicant that would require considerable resources from either the sponsor or the public and the sponsor does not have such resources. These characteristics might include "chronic illness, physical or mental handicaps, extreme age or other serious conditions." Cable, 98-State-102426, *supra* at 880. *Accord* USCIS, 71 Fed. Reg. 35732, 35737–38 (June 21, 2006). As a general rule receipt of public benefits by a family member is not attributable to the applicant absent a showing that it is the sole means of support for the family. *See* INS field guidance on public charge. 64 Fed. Reg. 28689–93 (May 26, 1999), *reprinted in* 76 No. 21 *Interpreter Releases* 843, 873–77 (May 28, 1999). Public charge is defined by DOS as "likely to become primarily dependent on the government for subsistence, as demonstrated by either (1) the receipt of public cash assistance for income maintenance or (2) institutionalization for long-term care at government expense." 9 FAM 40.41 N1-2. However, DOS recognizes that the receipt of public cash assistance or institutionalization for long term care are only factors to be considered in the totality of the circumstances. Cable, Albright, DOS 99-State-095509 (May 24, 1999), *published on* AILA InfoNet at Doc. No. 99052491. Moreover, if a person has received public benefits, it is not the role of the consular officer to establish or address repayment in its assessment. *Id.* Public cash assistance is generally limited to SSI, Temporary Assistance for Need Families (TANF) and state General Assistance. The receipt of such things as Food Stamps, WIC, Medicaid, Children's Health Insurance Program (CHIP), Head Start, public housing, and others does not automatically determine that someone is a public charge. Nor does the receipt of cash or noncash welfare programs that are received by a person's children or other family members considered a public charge for the immigrant unless the cash welfare is the family's only means of support. *A Quick Guide to Public Charge and Receipt of Public Benefits* (Oct. 18, 1999), *reprinted in* 76 No. 43 *Interpreter Releases* 1613, 1637–38 (Nov. 8, 1999). If a person seeks to demonstrate future employment to refute any inference of public charge, he may submit an offer of employment. The submission of an offer of employment must be sworn to and subscribed before a notary and must contain the signatory's title. 22 C.F.R. §40.41(e).

1.a. Affidavit of Support (I-864)—8 C.F.R. §213a, 22 C.F.R. §40.41; AFM at 20.5; 71 Fed. Reg. 35732–57 (June 21, 2006); 62 Fed. Reg. 54346 (Oct. 20, 1997); Memo, Aytes, Acting Dir. Domestic Operations, USCIS HQRPM 70/21.1.13 (June 27, 2006), *published on* AILA InfoNet at Doc. No. 06063013. Each beneficiary, in order to obtain LPR status, must submit an affidavit of support (I-864) by a sponsor. The submission of customary affidavits of support (I-134) traditionally carried some weight in determining public charge, *Matter of Kohama*, 17 I&N Dec. 257 (A.C. 1978), but now the consular or DHS officer must, at a minimum, require the I-864 affidavits, when they are specified under INA §213A. The submission of a sufficient I-864 will generally overcome the public charge ground but not in every possible case. In a particular case there may be specific facts about the intending immigrant that warrant a finding of public charge under the factors specified in INA §212(a)(4)(B). 71 Fed. Reg. 35738 (June 21, 2006).

(1) Effective Date for I-864—The provisions governing the affidavits of support apply beginning Dec. 19, 1997; but they shall not apply to persons who applied for IVs (*i.e.,* signed an OF-230 in front of consular officer) before Dec. 19, 1997. Cable, DOS, 97-State-238374 (Dec. 22, 1997), *reprinted in* 75 No. 1 *Interpreter Releases* 3, 7–8 (Jan. 5, 1998).

(2) The Sponsor for the I-864—8 C.F.R. §213a.2(b). The sponsor for the affidavit in family-based petitions must be the petitioning family member. This sponsorship requirement includes persons seeking residency as orphans (unless she would become a USC upon entry under INA §320) and adjustment after admission on a K visa. 8 C.F.R. §213a.2(a)(2)(i)(A). Where more than one petition has been filed, the sponsor must be the petitioner on the petition used for residency. 8 C.F.R. §213a.2(b)(1). The requirement that an I-864 be filed and that a sponsor for the I-864 be found also applies to employment-based cases, but only where it is a relative that files the immigrant visa (I-140) petition or where the relative has a "significant ownership interest," in the entity that files the immigrant visa petition. A "relative" is defined as a husband, wife, father, mother, child, adult son or daughter, brother or sister. 8 C.F.R. §213a.1. A "significant ownership interest" means 5% or more. 8 C.F.R. §213a.1. However, if the relative who owns an interest in the company is not a USC or LPR, the affidavit is not required. 8 C.F.R. §213a.2(b)(2); Cable, DOS, 98-State-042068 (Mar. 12, 1998), *published on* AILA InfoNet at Doc. No. 98031291. An I-864 is also not required if the relative is a brother or sister who is not a USC. 8 C.F.R. §213a.2(a)(2)(i)(C). All sponsors must be 18 years of age, but if under 18 can cure the improper filing by signing the I-864 again on or after his 18th birthday before a decision on the intending immigrant's IV or AOS. 71 Fed. Reg. 35732, 35734 (June 21, 2006)

(3) Affidavit of Support (I-864) Does Not Apply to Certain Cases—The specialized affidavit does not apply to all other employment cases. Similarly, the I-864 Affidavit of Support is not required in cases involving: (1) diversity immigrants; (2) special immigrants; (3) self-petitioning immigrants (widows/widowers, spouses/children subjected to battery or extreme cruelty, and certain children, spouses and grandparents under the USA PATRIOT Act); (3) Refugees and asylees adjusting status; (4) Registrants under INA §249; and (5) persons who have already earned or can be credited with 40 quarters of coverage pursuant to SSA regulations. Memo, Aytes, Acting Dir. Domestic Operations, USCIS HQRPM 70/21.1.13 (June 27, 2006) at p.5, *published on* AILA InfoNet at Doc. No. 06063013 (June 27, 2006); Memo, Cronin, Acting Assoc. Comm. Office of Program (70/23.1) (Mar. 7, 2000), *published on* AILA InfoNet at Doc. No. 00032704. An affidavit also need not be filed in a family-based petition where the beneficiary will be immediately eligible to become a USC under INA §320(a), because the affidavit would be futile as its validity is extinguished as soon as s/he becomes a USC. 8 C.F.R. §213a.2(a)(2)(ii)(E); Memo, Cronin, Acting Ex. Assoc. Comm. Field Operations, HQ PGM 50/10 (May 17, 2001), *published on* AILA InfoNet at Doc. No. 01060821; Cable, DOS, 01-State-105806 (June 16, 2001), *published on* AILA InfoNet at Doc. No. 01061691 [children adopted abroad in IR-3 category do not require an I-864 affidavit]. An affidavit is also not required for a child admitted as an LPR under INA §211(a) and 8 C.F.R. §211.1(b)(1) when returning with her LPR/USC parent. 8 C.F.R. §213a.2(a)(2)(ii)(D). Also, derivative

beneficiaries of employment-based petitions and K-1 and K-3 applicants do not require affidavits of support. Finally, an affidavit of support is not required if, at the time the applicant seeks an IV or AOS, he has already worked *or* can be credited with working 40 qualifying quarters of coverage. 8 C.F.R. §213a.2(a)(2)(ii)(C); 71 Fed. Reg. 35732, 35733 (June 21, 2006); Memo, Cronin, Acting Ex. Assoc. Comm. Programs, HQPGM 70/21 (May 17, 2001), *published on* AILA InfoNet at Doc. No. 01060729. Working 40 quarters is calculated based on the amount of income earned during the course of the year, rather than the actual number of days worked within a given quarter. To prove 40 quarters of earnings an applicant may request certified earnings records from the Social Security Administration. Cable, DOS, 02-State-034687 (Feb. 22, 2002), *published on* AILA InfoNet at Doc. No. 02022233. A person may also be *credited* with quarters worked by his or her parent before s/he was 18. INA §213A(a)(3)(B)(i). Where the I-864 is not required, the I-864W must be filed.

(4) Household Wage-Earners (I-864A), Joint Sponsor, and Substitute Sponsors—In addition to the primary sponsor on the I-864, there may be circumstances where others are called upon to submit sponsoring affidavits. In order to meet the income requirements for the I-864, the sponsor needs to demonstrate that he or she has income that meets at least 125% of the poverty guidelines as described below. If the sponsor's income is insufficient to meet the minimum income requirements, s/he may seek to include a household wage-earner, who must sign an I-864A, or a joint or substitute sponsor, who must file his or her own I-864.

(a) Household Wage-Earner on I-864A—If the sponsor cannot rely entirely on his or her own income to meet the income requirements, s/he may include other household income as defined at 8 C.F.R. §213a.1. The household members who sign the I-864A must be at least 18 years of age, 8 C.F.R. §213a.1, and are not required to be USCs or LPRs. 8 C.F.R. §213a.2(c)(2)(i)(C)(1). "Household income" may include the income of the intending immigrant only if the intending immigrant is the sponsor's spouse or has the same principal residence as the sponsor, and the income is the result of "lawful employment in the United States" or from "some other lawful source" that will continue to be available to the intending immigrant after s/he acquires LPR status. 8 C.F.R. §213a.1. These household members would be required to file an I-864A, which is a written contract between the sponsor and them, providing that they would be jointly and severally liable for any reimbursement obligation that the sponsor may incur. Their income could then be counted toward the minimum income requirements. 8 C.F.R. §213a.2(c)(2)(i)(C)(1).

(b) Joint Sponsor—If the sponsor cannot meet the minimum-income requirements, s/he may also seek a joint sponsor. The joint sponsor must be 18 years of age, be a USC or LPR, and be domiciled in the U.S. 8 C.F.R. §213a.2(c)(1). The joint sponsor must file a separate I-864 and must meet the minimum income requirements separate and apart from the sponsor. 8 C.F.R. §213a.2(c)(1)(i). An intending immigrant may not have more than one joint sponsor. 71 Fed. Reg. 35732, 35734 (June 21, 2006). However, it is not necessary for all the derivative beneficiaries to have the same joint sponsor and a family may be divided so that there are joint sponsors for different members of the intending immigrant family. 8 C.F.R. §213a.2(c)(2)(iii)(C); 71 Fed. Reg. 35732, 35734–35 (June 21, 2006). There may not be more than two joint sponsors for any family group. 8 C.F.R. §213a.2(c)(2)(iii)(C). And the sponsor and joint sponsor cannot pool their incomes to obtain the appropriate amount needed. 71 Fed. Reg. 35732, 35734 (June 21, 2006).

(c) Substitute Sponsor—If the petitioner dies before the intending immigrant obtains his IV or AOS in a family sponsored case, a substitute sponsor, under certain conditions, is permitted. 8 C.F.R. §213a.2(c)(2)(iii)(D); 71 Fed. Reg. 35732, 35735 (June 21, 2006). *See also in this section* "Death of the Sponsor," ¶ (8) (p.64), *infra.*

(5) Documentary Requirements with Affidavit—The sponsor is required to submit with the affidavit: (i) Federal tax returns for the most recent year, including W-2 forms; (ii) evidence of current employment; (iii) evidence that sponsor's income is sufficient to meet

the income requirements and (iv) the current edition of the poverty guidelines (I-864P). INA §§213A(f)(6)(A) & (B); 8 C.F.R. §§213a.2(a)(1)(ii), 213a.2(c)(2)(i)(A). The sponsor, as well as the individual who has signed an I-864A, must provide documentation, including the submission of tax returns for the same year by the sponsor and individual. 8 C.F.R. §213a.2(c)(2)(i)(C)(4). The sponsor need not submit certified copies of tax return but may submit photocopies or IRS-generated transcripts. 71 Fed. Reg. 35732, 35738 (June 21, 2006). The sufficiency of the Form I-864 or I-864A should be based on the evidence submitted unless more than one year has passed between the filing and the examination. If it is more than one year, the adjudicator or IJ may request additional evidence. 8 C.F.R. §§213a.2(a)(1)(v)(A) & (B). The affidavit will normally be held sufficient unless there are specific facts, including a material change in employment or income history, to infer the sponsor may not be able to maintain his household income to meet his sponsorship obligations. 8 C.F.R. §213a.2(c)(2)(ii)(C). INA §213A(f)(6)(B) permits DHS and DOS to require the sponsor provide only the past year's tax return and not 3 years. USCIS has determined that *the past year's return is sufficient* and that a sponsor is no longer required to provide 3 years of returns. 8 C.F.R. §213a.2(c)(2)(i); DOS has agreed. Cable, DOS "Revised Requirements for Form I-864 Processing," 06-State-051172 (Mar. 30, 2006) ¶¶1–3, *published on* AILA InfoNet at Doc. No. 06040469 (Apr. 4. 2006).The sponsor's income must meet the 125% requirement of the poverty guidelines in effect at the time the I-864 was submitted. Memo, Aytes, Acting Dir. Operations, USCIS, HQOPRD 70/21.1.13 (Nov. 23, 2005), *published on* AILA InfoNet at Doc. No. 05120210; Cable, 06-State-051172, *supra* at ¶4. The sponsor need only submit tax returns in years s/he was obligated to file, but if she had no legal duty to file she must provide an explanation. 8 C.F.R. §213a.2(c)(2)(i)(B); Cable, DOS, 98-State-133584 (July 22, 1998), *published on* AILA InfoNet at Doc. No. 98072291. A DOS officer may request a tax summary prepared by IRS if, and only if, s/he has doubts about the validity of the tax returns. *Id.* Amended returns are permissible. In following-to-join cases, a person who meets the qualification of a sponsor may file the I-864 if the petitioning sponsor has died. *Id.* USCIS may accept a transcript of the taxpayer's income tax return where the taxpayer files an IRS 4506T. Because IRS issues this document, it is not necessary to ask the sponsor for a W-2 or 1099. Aytes Memo (Nov. 23, 2005), *supra.* Consular officers are also not to require an employment letter from the sponsor unless there is some reason to questions the veracity of the income stated. Cable, 06-State-051172, *supra* at ¶4; 9 FAM 40.41 N.5.4. An explanation of the 125% requirement, and the affidavit of support generally, can be found at *www.uscis.gov.*

Processing Delays and Documentation—The delay between the date of signing the I-864 and the date of the visa interview should not be a basis to request updated information. Cable, 06-State-051172, *supra* at ¶4. For additional consular procedural issues *see* 9 FAM 40.41 N5.1, N.5.4, PN2.10-2, PN3; 9 FAM 42.73 PN3.4; 9 FAM 40.41 Ex. 1. However, the regulations recognize that if it has been more than a year from the initial filing of the I-864, the consular or DHS officer or the IJ may make additional inquiry. 8 C.F.R. §213a.2(a)(1)(v)(B).

(6) Domicile Requirement—The affidavit *must* be from the petitioning relative and any other qualifying person under INA §213A(f). The affiant must be domiciled in the U.S. under DHS regulations, thereby precluding USCs who are domiciled abroad from complying with the affidavit requirement. 8 C.F.R. §213a.2(c)(1)(ii); Legal Opinion, G.C., INS, Legal Opinion No. 97-10 (July 8, 1997), *reprinted in* 75 No. 10 *Interpreter Releases* 380–83 (Mar. 16, 1998). Domicile is defined as the person's principal, actual dwelling place. 8 C.F.R. §213a.1. DOS defines it as the place where the person has a residence as defined in INA §101(a)(33). Cable, DOS, 97-State-235619 (Dec. 19, 1997), *published on* AILA InfoNet at Doc. No. 98010690. However, a person residing abroad may still have his domicile in U.S. if he went abroad pursuant to INA §§316(b), 317 or 319(b) relating to residency for naturalization purposes. 8 C.F.R. §213a.2(c)(1)(ii)(A); Memo, G.C., INS, supra; AFM §20.5. The DOS agrees. Cable, DOS 98-State-042068 (Mar. 12, 1998), *reprinted in* 75 No. 13 *Interpreter Releases* 468–70 (Apr. 6, 1998); Under DOS guidelines a person domiciled abroad who wishes to take up his residence again in the U.S. may do so and "[t]here is no requirement that the residence have been established for any length

of time... [T]he sponsor must have taken steps to make the U.S. his immediate principal place of abode. Such steps might include finding U.S. employment, locating a place to live, registering children in U.S. schools and other indices of residence. The sponsor should also have made arrangements to relinquish residence in the third country." Cable, 98-State-042068, *supra*. Under DHS guidelines, the sponsor domiciled abroad must establish by a preponderance of the evidence that s/he will establish a domicile in the U.S. "on or before the date of the principal intending immigrant's admission or adjustment of status." 8 C.F.R. §213a.2(c)(1)(ii)(B); 71 Fed. Reg. 35732, 35734 (June 21, 2006). If the sponsor enters the U.S. at the same time as the beneficiary of the petition with the intention of establishing her principal residence in the U.S., the sponsor shall be deemed to have established a domicile in the U.S. Memo, Aytes, Acting Dir. Domestic Operations, USCIS HQRPM 70/21.1.13 at 6 (June 27, 2006), *published on* AILA InfoNet at Doc. No. 06063013

(a) Change of Address—A sponsor who changes his address must file with USCIS a notice on Form I-865 within 30 days of the change. Failure to file the change results in monetary penalties above and beyond the payment for lost means-tested public benefits. INA §213A(d), 8 U.S.C. §1183a(d); 8 C.F.R. §213a.3; 71 Fed. Reg. 35732, 35740 (June 21, 2006).

(7) Age, Lawful Status, and Income Requirements—The sponsor must be a USC or LPR, 18 years of age, domiciled in U.S., have an income 125% above the federal poverty line, INA §213A(f)(1), and petitioning for the person's admission. The 125% guideline is determined in relationship to the household size. 8 C.F.R. §213a.2(c)(2)(ii)(C). The household size includes the sponsor, the sponsor's spouse, all of the sponsor's children unless the children are 18 and they were not claimed as dependents. Household size also includes: (1) any other person (whether or not related to the sponsor) whom the sponsor has claimed as a dependent in the most recent tax year, even if s/he does not reside with the sponsor; (2) all persons sponsored previously where the obligation has not terminated; and (3) all persons currently sponsored. A spouse or child of the intending immigrant will not be counted if she does not currently reside in the U.S. and does not seek to immigrate within six months or if they are residents or citizens. 8 C.F.R. §213a.1. The 4 categories, when added together, constitute the number of people in the household for purposes of the federal poverty guidelines. The 125% measurement based on 2008 poverty guidelines, except Alaska and Hawaii, which are higher, *see* I-864P, are as follows: for one person ($13,000); 2 people ($17,500); 3 people ($22,00); 4 people ($26,500); 5 people ($31,000); 6 people ($35,500); 7 people ($40,000); and 8 people ($44,500). After 8 household members add $4,500 for each additional person. 9 FAM 40.41 Exh. 1. The sponsor may count disability benefits and Social Security benefits (but not SSI) in computing his or her income. Cable, DOS (98-State-133584) (July 22, 1998), *published on* AILA InfoNet at Doc. No. 98072291.

If the petitioner is on active duty in the Armed Forces he need only meet 100% of the federal poverty guidelines if the intending immigrant is his spouse or child. 8 C.F.R. §213a.2(c)(2)(ii)(C).

If the petitioner cannot meet the 125% figure, then the sponsor (petitioner) may provide evidence of other assets that are readily available, including the beneficiaries assets and income. The sponsor may include the income of others in the household to meet the income eligibility requirements. Household income includes the income of the sponsor, the sponsor's spouse and any other person claimed as a dependent in the most recent tax year as long as s/he is 18 or older, whether or not s/he resides in the sponsor's household. The sponsor may also include relatives (father, mother, adult son, adult daughter, brother or sister) who have the same principal residence as the sponsor. Household income does not include the income of an intending immigrant unless it is the sponsor's spouse or unless the immigrant has the same principal residence as the sponsor and his income was through lawful employment or from some other lawful source. 8 C.F.R. §213a.1 (defining Household Income and Household Size). The household member must sign an I-864A affidavit making him or her jointly and severally liable.

Assets Other Than Salary—The sponsor may also include other assets in addition to salary and income. Evidence of assets include: (1) bank statements covering the last 12 months or statement from officer of bank/financial institution; (2) stocks, bonds and CDs and dates acquired; (3) other personal property; and (4) real estate. 8 C.F.R. §213a.2(c)(2)(iii)(B); Cable, DOS, 97-State-211673 (Nov. 8, 1997), *reprinted in* 74 No. 48 *Interpreter Releases* 1923–30 (Dec. 18, 1997). In determining whether assets are sufficient, the value of the assets less any offsetting liabilities must exceed by at least 5 times the poverty guidelines minus the sponsor's household income (*e.g.*, if poverty guidelines call for $10,600 for 2 and person earns $8,600 they must show 5 x $2,000 = $10,000 in assets). If the intending immigrant is the spouse or child of a USC and the child has reached her 18th birthday, the adjudicator may use 3 times the poverty guideline, rather than 5 times. 8 C.F.R. §213a(c)(2)(iii)(B)(1). Another method of meeting the affidavit of support requirement is to have one or more joint sponsors submit separate affidavits of support. INA §213A(f)(5), 8 C.F.R. §213a.2(c)(2)(iii)(C). Joint sponsors (unlike persons living in household) cannot combine their assets to reach the 125%. *Each joint sponsor must meet the full* 125% income requirement. Cable, DOS, 97-State-228462, *supra*. The joint sponsor *need not* be a relative by blood or marriage. *Id.*

The sponsor may rely on income that is not subject to taxation such as a housing allowance for clergy or military personnel. The sponsor may also count significant assets outside the U.S. as long as they are readily convertible to cash within 13 months. Cable, DOS, (98-State-112510) (June 23, 1998), *reprinted in* 75 No. 25 *Interpreter Releases* 913, 917 (July 6, 1998).

The sponsor's use of means-tested benefits does not disqualify him or her from being the sponsor. It simply means those benefits are not counted toward income. Memo, Cronin, Acting Assoc. Comm. Office of Program (70/23.1) (Mar. 7, 2000), *published on* AILA InfoNet at Doc. No. 00032704.

"Household income" may include the income of the intending immigrant only if the intending immigrant is the sponsor's spouse or has the same principal residence as the sponsor, and the income is the result of "lawful employment in the United States" or from "some other lawful source" that will continue to be available to the intending immigrant after s/he acquires LPR status. 8 C.F.R. §213a.1.

(8) Death of the sponsor—If sponsor dies after principal applicant has immigrated but before all qualified family members who are following to join have immigrated, another person may step in as a substitute sponsor. 8 C.F.R. §213a.2(c)(2)(iii)(D); 71 Fed. Reg. 35732, 35735 (June 21, 2006). Cable, DOS (98-State-112510) (June 23, 1998), *reprinted in* 75 No. 25 *Interpreter Releases* 913, 916 (July 6, 1998). Under the Family Sponsor Immigration Act of 2002, PL 107-150, 116 Stat. 74 (Mar. 13, 2002) Congress now permits the substitution of certain relatives to meet the affidavit of support requirements under INA §213A(f)(5) when the petitioning relative has died after approval of the petition and the AG, on humanitarian grounds, decides not to revoke the approved I-130 petition. Under the Act a spouse, parent, mother-in-law, father-in-law, sibling, child (if at least 18 years of age), son, daughter, son-in-law, daughter-in-law, sister-in-law, brother-in-law, grandparent, grandchild or legal guardian of the beneficiary qualifies to substitute for the deceased petitioner. The beneficiary of the I-130 must ask the AG to reinstate the petition and must demonstrate she has a substitute sponsor designated under the Act. 8 C.F.R. §§205.1(a)(3)(i)(C)(2), 1205.1(a)(3)(i)(C)(2). The Act applies with respect to deaths occurring before, on, or after the date of the enactment of the Act. Cable, DOS, 02-State-071485 (Apr. 15, 2002) at ¶4, *published on* AILA InfoNet at Doc. No. 02041732. A person who has had his case denied on the grounds that no substitute sponsor was permissible prior to the Family Sponsor Immigration Act may file a motion to reopen beyond the time limit and the new law should be considered a "sufficient reason" for filing the motion late. Memo, Williams, Ex. Assoc. Comm., Field Operations, HQADJ/70/21.1.13 (June 15, 2002), *published on* AILA InfoNet at Doc. No. 02120941.

(9) Affidavit as Enforceable Contract

(a) The affidavit of support is now an enforceable contract against the affiant. INA §213A(a), 8 U.S.C. §1183a(a). The sponsor and joint sponsor are "jointly and severally liable." 71 Fed. Reg. 35732, 35743 (June 21, 2006). Execution of the I-864 creates a contract but the obligation begins *after* the sponsored immigrant "acquires permanent residence." 8 C.F.R. §213a.2(d); 71 Fed. Reg. 35732, 35740 (June 21, 2006). The affidavit is enforceable by the sponsored person, the local, state or federal government, or any agency providing a means-tested public benefit against the affiant until the sponsored relative or employee is: (1) naturalized; (2) loses or relinquishes his LPR status; (3) obtains a new grant of AOS in a removal proceeding; (4) has earned or been credited with 40 qualifying quarters under Title II of the Social Security Act (approx. 10 years) without including periods s/he received means-tested benefits or (5) dies. 8 C.F.R. §213a.2(e)(2)(i). Qualifying quarters are attributed to the child (if under 18) or the spouse (if they remain married). An action need be brought no later than 10 years after the date the sponsored person received any means-tested public benefit. The contract is only enforceable if the government agency seeking enforcement published that the benefit is a means-tested public benefit prior to the date the benefit was first provided the immigrant. 71 Fed. Reg. 35732, 35742 (June 21, 2006). The affiant is now required to report his or her change of address or be subject to a fine which may range from $250 to $5,000. INA §213A(d).

Means-tested federal public benefits are: Supplemental Security Income (SSI); Medicaid; and Temporary Assistance to Needy Families (TANF). 62 Fed. Reg. 45256, 45284 (Aug. 26, 1997). It also includes state means-tested benefits. 8 C.F.R. §213a.4(b). The following benefits are exempt: emergency medical care; short term, noncash in-kind emergency disaster relief; benefits under National School Lunch Act and similar state and local programs; benefits under Food Stamps, Child Nutrition Act of 1966 and similar state/local programs; WIC (Supplemental Nutrition Program for Women, Infants, and Children) program; public assistance for immunizations and for testing and treatment of communicable diseases; Medicaid, Children's Health Insurance Program (CHIP), payment for foster care and adoption assistance; services, or assistance (such as soup kitchens, crisis counseling and intervention and short-term shelter) specified by the AG; student assistance under Titles IV, V, IX, and X of Higher Education Assistance Act of 1965 and Titles IV, VII and VIII of Public Health Service Act; benefits under Head Start Act; means-tested programs under the Elementary and Secondary Education Act of 1965; and benefits under Job Training Partnership Act. Cable, DOS, 97-State-228462 (Dec. 6, 1997), *reprinted in* 74 No. 47 *Interpreter Releases* 1,889–94 (Dec. 15, 1997). HUD programs are not considered to fall under the category of federal means-tested public benefits. 65 Fed. Reg. 49994 (Aug. 21, 2000).

(b) Affidavit Used To Claim Support—Congress "clearly intended to permit the sponsored immigrant to sue to enforce the support obligation, if necessary." 71 Fed. Reg. 35732, 35743 (June 21, 2006). In addition to the obligation to the U.S. government or the states to repay any means-tested public benefits, and in addition to any alimony payments, the sponsor or perhaps even the joint sponsor (and the household member who signs the I-864A) may have a continuing responsibility to support the immigrant and his or her family at 125% of the poverty guideline. INA §213A(a)(1)(A) ["[T]he sponsor agrees to provide support to maintain the sponsored alien at an annual income that is not less than 125 percent of the Federal poverty line during the period in which the affidavit is enforceable."] The instructions to the I-864 clearly state that: "By signing this form, you, the sponsor, agree to support the intending immigrant and any spouse and/or children immigrating with him or her..." Form I-864, p.1 (Sponsor's Obligation). Part 7 of the I-864 further states that: "I agree to provide the sponsored immigrant(s) whatever support is necessary to maintain the sponsored immigrant(s) at an income that is at least 125 percent of the Federal poverty guidelines. I understand that my obligation will continue until my death or the sponsored immigrant(s) have become U.S. citizens, can be credited with 40 quarters of work, depart the United States permanently, or die." The support obligation, however, begins when the immigration officer or IJ "grants" the immigrant's application for admission or her adjustment of status. 8 C.F.R. §213a.2(e); 71 Fed. Reg. 35732, 35740 (June 21, 2006). Based upon the I-864 some courts have found the document enforceable and ordered support payments to the former spouse. *Naik v. Naik,* No. A-6270-05T5 (N.J. Super. Apr. 14, 2008) [I-864EZ creates legally enforceable contract but there is a set-off for spousal and child support and equitable distribution]; *Cheshire v. Cheshire*, 2006 WL 1208010, No. 3:05-cv-00453-TJC-MCR (M.D. Fla. May 4, 2006) [based upon the language of INA §213a(a)(1), the sponsor's obligation under the I-864 to support his former wife is contractual and independent of reimbursement to the government or alimony]; *Stump v. Stump,* 2005 WL 2757329 (N.D. Ind. Oct. 25, 2005) [finding I-864 enforceable and ordering defendant to pay former spouse support related to defendant's obligation to maintain former spouse at 125% over the poverty guidelines]. *See also Moody v. Sorokina,* 40 A.D.3d 14 (N.Y. App. Div. 2007) [lower court erred in determining that defendant was not entitled to seek enforcement of the federal affidavit of support on the grounds that the statute was for public benefit only]; *Davis v. Davis,* 2004 WL 2924344 (Ohio App.6 Dist. Dec. 17, 2004) [reversing trial court's decision to declining jurisdiction to enforce I-864]. *But see Tornheim v. Kohn,* 2002 WL 482534 (E.D.N.Y. Mar. 26, 2002) [declining to enforce Form I-134 affidavit of support]. *See also Davis v. U.S.,* 499 F.3d 590 (6th Cir. 2007) [court dismissed declaratory judgment action by legally separated U.S. husband to determine amount owed to wife and step-sons under I-864 after wife obtained support ruling in state court]. The commentary to the regulations take no view on whether divorce does or does not affect support obligations under the affidavit. But the commentary notes that a sponsored immigrant, in a divorce settlement, can surrender his or her right to sue the sponsor to enforce the affidavit of support. 71 Fed. Reg. 35732, 35740 (June 21, 2006). The enforcement statute also includes other remedies such as "payment of legal fees and other costs of collection" 8 U.S.C. 1183(a)(c). *See Iannuzzelli v. Lovett,* __ So.2d ___ (Fla. App. 3d Dist. May 7, 2008) [legal fees limited to collecting on judgment obtained, not seeking, judgment].

(10) Forms I-864/I-864EZ/I-864W/I-134—The specialized affidavit of support under INA §213A is filed on Form I-864 by sponsors, joint sponsors, and substitute sponsors. The sponsor may submit a simplified version of the I-864 named an I-864EZ. 8 C.F.R. §213a.2(a)(1)(i)(A). Household wage-earners need to file an I-864A. Persons who are not required to file an I-864 because they have earned 40 quarters of coverage under the Social Security Act, are intending immigrant children who will become USCs by virtue of the Child Citizenship Act of 2000, or self-petitioning widows(ers) or battered spouses or children, must file an I-864W exemption form when filing an application for AOS. Persons required to meet the public charge ground but not required to submit an I-864 may use the I-134 affidavit of support if necessary.

(11) Procedure—The I-864 and all supporting documents are filed with the I-485 and all other AOS-required documents when seeking AOS. If the applicant is seeking an IV, the I-864 and supporting documents are sent to NVC. The I-864 should be filed within 6 months of being signed. However, DOS has stated that it may accept, on a case-by-case basis, affidavits signed as long as one year before the interview. Cable, DOS (99-State-220435) (Nov. 28, 1998), *reprinted in* 76 No. 6 *Interpreter Releases* 247 (Feb. 8, 1999). If the I-864 and I-864A (if needed) is properly signed only one original is needed. Family members can attach copies. Cable, DOS, 98-State-092491 (May 22, 1998), *published on* AILA InfoNet at Doc. No. 98060590.

(12) Criminal Issues—*U.S. v. Wu,* 419 F.3d 142 (2d Cir. 2005) [where I-864 contained false statements that were not material, government can still convict by showing that I-864 was part of the larger process of falsely petitioning, though the use of an I-130 petition, for relatives].

2. *Person Seeking Entry for Purpose of Performing Skilled or Unskilled Labor*—Persons are inadmissible under this category unless the Secy. of Labor certifies that there are not enough workers

who are able, willing, qualified, and available to perform such labor, and that the wages and working conditions of workers in the U.S. similarly employed will not be adversely affected. INA §212(a)(5)(A), 8 U.S.C. §1182(a)(5)(A). This category applies to the 2nd and 3rd preference categories of employment-based admissions. There is an elaborate procedure under DOL regulations to test the U.S. labor market to determine whether there are qualified U.S. workers who are able, willing, and available for the position before a labor certification for an alien can be issued. 20 C.F.R. §656. *See* "Labor Certification" in Ch. 7, part VIII (p.907), *infra*.

3. *Certain Medical Graduate of Nonapproved Schools*—Medical graduates of nonapproved schools are excludable if they have not passed the National Board of Medical Examiners (NBME) examination Part I and II (or an equivalent exam as determined by the Secy. of HHS) and are not competent in oral and written English, if they are immigrating principally to perform services as a member of the medical profession. INA §212(a)(5)(B), 8 U.S.C. §1182(a)(5)(B), 22 C.F.R. §40.52. *Matter of Sheikh*, 17 I&N Dec. 634 (R.C. 1980). The equivalency exam now given is the U.S. Medical Licensing Exam (USMLE) parts I, II, and III, which replaces the Foreign Medical Graduate Exam in the Medical Sciences (FMGEMS). Parts I and II of the USMLE are the equivalent of parts I and II of the NBME. The prohibition extends to teaching, research, and other activities that require a medical degree. Letter, Weinig, Asst. Comm. Adjudications, reprinted in 7 AILA Monthly Mailing 357 (Aug. 1988). This exclusion does not apply to physicians of national or international renown in the field of medicine. INA §§101(a)(41), 203(b)(1)(A), 8 U.S.C. §§1101(a)(41), 1153(b)(1)(A). Nor does it apply to doctors who wish to enter as family relatives, investors, or through the AA-1 program, as the ground of inadmissibility applies *only* to the new 2nd and 3rd employment-based preferences.

4. *Uncertified Foreign Health Care Workers*—INA §212(a)(5)(C), 8 U.S.C. §1182(a)(5)(C); 8 C.F.R. §§212.15, 1212.15; 68 Fed. Reg. 43901–21 (July 25, 2003), AFM at 30.12. A person seeking to enter as a health care worker (other than a physician) is inadmissible unless s/he presents a certificate from the appropriate accrediting agency verifying that: (1) the person's education, training, license, and experience are comparable with that required for an American health care worker of the same type; (2) the education, training, license, and experience are authentic and in the case of a license, unencumbered; (3) the education, training, license, and experience meet all applicable statutory and regulatory requirements for admission into the U.S. although the verification is not binding on the DHS; (4) the applicant has passed a predictor licensing or occupation examination recognized by a majority of states licensing the occupation or has passed the actual occupation licensing or certification examination; and (5) the applicant meets certain English language requirements by either graduating from a school in one of several English-speaking countries or by passing an English language test administered by ETS, TOEIC, or IELTS. 8 C.F.R. §§212.15(f), (g), 1215.12(f), (g). The English language examination is administered through either the Educational Testing Service (ETS) (which includes the TOEFL), the Test of English for International Communication Service International (TOEIC), or the International English Language Testing System (IELTS). 8 C.F.R. §§212.15(g)(3), 1212.15(g)(3). The organization affiliated with the Michigan English Language Assessment Battery (MELAB) has decided not to be designated any longer. 68 Fed. Reg. 43901, 43914 (July 25, 2003). Persons are exempt from the English language requirement if they attended college, university, or professional training school in Australia, Canada (except Quebec), Ireland, New Zealand, U.K., or the U.S. 8 C.F.R. §§212.15(g)(2), 1212.15(g)(2). Health care workers may also be exempt from an English language proficiency test (as well as a comparability review) if they meet the streamlined certification process in their occupation. 8 C.F.R. §§212.15(i).

The ground of inadmissibility applies even to persons who did their training in the U.S. 8 C.F.R. §212.15(c); 68 Fed. Reg. 43901, 43904–05 (July 25, 2003). The legislative history suggests that this section applies to persons seeking entry through NAFTA or any other treaty and includes nurses, physical therapists, occupational therapists, speech-language pathologists, medical technologists and technicians, physician assistants, and any others designated by regulation. H.R. Conf. Rep. 828, 104th Cong., 2d Sess. at 227 (1996); 68 Fed. Reg. 43901, 43904 (July 25, 2003). It also includes persons indirectly involved in health care work such as a supervisory nurse even if they do not engage in clinical work. 63 Fed. Reg. 5507 at 55009. DHS has interpreted the statute to apply at the present time only to those professions listed in the legislative history. 8 C.F.R. §212.15(c), 1212.15(c). However, the Conference Report did allow DHS to designate other categories and DHS will consult extensively with HHS regarding any future additions. 68 Fed. Reg. 43901, 43905–06 (July 25, 2003). The DOS has agreed and suggested the DOT as guidance for defining the professions. Cable, DOS, (98-State-079570), *reprinted in* 75 No. 19 *Interpreter Releases* 697 (May 18, 1998).

The statute does not include a number of people and professions such as: (1) physicians, (2) persons performing nonclinical health care such as medical teachers, medical researchers, and managers of health care facilities; (3) persons receiving training under F, J or H-3; (4) spouse and dependent children of an immigrant or NIV holder; and (5) persons obtaining AOS or IV under family-based petitions, employment-based petitions not involving direct medical care, refugee adjustment, registry, cancellation or legalization. 8 C.F.R. §§212.15(b), 1212.15(b), 68 Fed. Reg. 43901, 43904 (July 25, 2003). In addition, DHS has recognized that neither dentists nor physical therapist assistants are covered. Letter, Simmons, Branch Chief, Business and Trade Services (HQ 70/6.2.8) (Dec. 10, 1999), *reprinted in* 77 No. 6 *Interpreter Releases* 193 (Feb. 7, 2000). *But see* 22 C.F.R. §40.53(a) [suggesting that all foreign health care workers performing care except physicians need to obtain a CGFNS or another credentialing service's certification].

4.a. Procedures—The ground of inadmissibility applies each time the health care worker enters the U.S. S/he must present a certificate from a credentialing organization listed at 8 C.F.R. §§212.15(e), 1212.15(e) each time s/he enters. A nurse may present a certificate or a certified statement consistent with 8 C.F.R. §212.15(h) each time s/he enters the U.S. 68 Fed. Reg. 43901, 43906 (July 25, 2003). The certificate is only valid for a 5-year period. 8 C.F.R. §212.15(n)(4). The certification or certificate must also be presented to DHS each time the person applies for extension of stay or change of status. Memo, Yates, Assoc. Dir. Operations, USCIS (Sept. 22, 2003), *published on* AILA InfoNet at Doc. No. 03092641. The certificate must also be presented for LPR status at the interview for AOS or IV. 8 C.F.R. §212.15(n)(3). DOS has authorized consular officers to accept certificates issued consistent with DHS regulations. Cable, DOS, 01-State-48497, *reprinted in* 78 No. 19 *Interpreter Releases* 814–15 (May 14, 2001). DHS has also established procedures to accredit credentialing organizations, set standards for them, review their performance, and terminate their status. Applicants must apply on an I-905. 8 C.F.R. §§212.15(j)–(m), 1212.15(j)–(m); AFM at 30.12(g).

(1) Nurses—INA §212(r), 8 U.S.C. §1182(r), 8 C.F.R. §212.15(h). Applies a different standard and different criteria than INA §212(a)(5)(C). Must be certified through the Commission on Graduates of Foreign Nursing Schools (CGFNS). 8 C.F.R. §§212.15(e), 1212.15(e). Under the Nursing Relief for Disadvantaged Areas Act of 1999, PL 106-95 §4, CGFNS (or an equivalent approved independent credentialing organization) may issue a certified statement (instead of a certificate) if: (1) the individual has a valid unrestricted license as a nurse in a state where the individual is to be employed and the state has verified that any foreign licenses are authentic and unencumbered; (2) the nurse has passed the NCLEX; (3) the nurse is a graduate of an English-language nursing program; (4) the nursing program was located in Australia, Canada, Ireland, New Zealand, South Africa, the U.K., or the U.S. or in any other country designated by unanimous agreement of CGFNS (or another equivalent credentialing service) approved for certification of nurses; and (5) the nursing program was in operation on or before Nov. 12, 1999, or has been approved by unanimous agreement by CGFNS or another equivalent credentialing service. CGFNS has designated nursing programs. 8 C.F.R. §§212.15(h)(2), 1212.15(h)(2). If a certified statement is issued, the nurse need not comply with the certificate requirements or the English language requirements for certification in the regulations.

(a) Alternatively a nurse may obtain a certificate under the requirements of INA §212(a)(5)(C) as specified in 8 C.F.R. §212.15(f)–(g) and §1212.15(f)–(g). A nurse therefore may meet the requirements by taking a predictor examination as specified in 8 C.F.R. §§212.15(f)(1)(iv), 1212.15(f)(9) instead of the NCLEX. 68 Fed. Reg. 43901, 43914 (July 25, 2003). In addition, a nurse who has graduated from an entry level program accredited by the National League for Nursing Accreditation Commission (NLNAC) or the Commission on Collegiate Nursing Education (CCNE) is exempt from the educational comparability review and English language proficiency testing. If the nurse is not exempt from the English language exam either because of the streamlined certification or due to graduation in an English-speaking country,

8 C.F.R. §§212.15(g), (i), 1212.15(g), s/he must attain a certain score on the ETS (TOEFL), TOEIC or IELTS exam. 8 C.F.R. §§212.15(g)(4)(ii), 1212.15(g)(4)(ii). Includes licensed practical nurses, licensed vocational nurses, and registered nurses. 8 C.F.R. §§212.15(c)(1), 1212.15(c)(1).

(2) Occupational Therapist—Must be certified by the National Board for Certification in Occupational Therapy (NBCOT) or the CGFNS. The only acceptable English exam for occupational therapists is the ETS. 8 C.F.R. §§212.15(g)(4)(i); 1212.15(g)(4)(i).

(3) Physical Therapist—The Foreign Credentialing Commission on Physical Therapy or the CGFNS is authorized to certify physical therapists. The only acceptable English exam for physical therapy is the ETS. 8 C.F.R. §§212.15(g)(4)(i), 1212.15(g)(4)(i).

(4) Speech-language Pathologists and Audiologists, Medical Technologists (Clinical Laboratory Scientists), and Physicians Assistants—The CGFNS is authorized to issue certificates in these fields. The ETS, TOEIC, or IELTS administered tests can be used to satisfy the English language requirement.

(5) Medical Technicians (Clinical Laboratory Technicians)—The CGFNS is authorized to issue certificates in these fields. The ETS-, TOEIC-, or IELTS-administered tests can be used to satisfy the English language requirement.

5. *Former Citizen Who Renounced Citizenship for Tax Purposes*—INA §212(a)(10)(E), 8 U.S.C. §1182(a)(10)(E), 22 C.F.R. §40.105. Inadmissible if AG determines that person renounced citizenship for the purpose of avoiding taxation by the U.S. Applies to people who have renounced on or after Sept. 30, 1996. IIRIRA §352(b). To effectuate this provision, DOS will provide information to Treasury who will then coordinate with DHS.

6. IMMACT90 eliminated excludability based on a person being certified by an examining medical officer as having a physical defect, disease, or disability that may effect his or her ability to earn a living. *Rokiyi Tambara v. Weedin*, 299 F. 299 (9th Cir. 1924); *Wallis v. U.S.*, 273 F. 509 (2d Cir. 1921). It also eliminated excludability for persons who are paupers, professional beggars, or vagrants. *Matter of M*, 2 I&N Dec. 131 (BIA 1944).

C. *Criminal Grounds*

1. *Crimes of Moral Turpitude*—INA §212(a)(2)(A)(i)(I), 8 U.S.C. §1182(a)(2)(A)(i)(I)

1.a. Determining a Crime Involving Moral Turpitude (CIMT)

(1) Persons who have been convicted of a crime of moral turpitude, *Jordan v. De George*, 341 U.S. 223 (1951), who admit to a DHS/consular officer having committed such crime, or who admit committing acts that constitute the essential elements of such a crime, are inadmissible. INA §212(a)(2)(A)(i)(I), 8 U.S.C. §1182(a)(2)(A)(i)(I). It includes attempts and conspiracy to commit the crime. For a discussion of what constitutes a conviction, *see* Ch. 3, part VI (p.207), *infra*. In *Matter of K*, 7 I&N Dec. 594, 598 (BIA 1957), the BIA adopted a 3-part test for the acceptance of an admission: (1) the admitted conduct must constitute the essential elements of the crime; (2) the applicant must have been provided with a definition and the essential elements of the offense prior to his admission; and (3) the admission must be voluntary. The applicant must also admit all facts constituting the crime. *Matter of E-N-*, 7 I&N Dec. 153 (1956). *See also* 22 C.F.R. §40.21(a)(1); *Matter of G*, 1 I&N Dec. 225 (BIA 1942) [admission must be voluntary]; *Pazcoguin v. Radcliffe*, 292 F.3d 1209 (9th Cir. 2002) [beneficiary's admission to medical doctor during medical examination for IV in Philippines that he smoked marijuana for a number of years was used as the basis to deny visa upon entry to U.S. and to thereafter exclude him].

(2) Juvenile Crimes of Moral Turpitude—An alien may not be inadmissible if s/he committed the crime while under the age of 18 and if the crime was committed more than 5 years prior to the date of application for entry or for a visa to enter. If s/he was imprisoned, the alien must have been released more than 5 years prior to the application for admission, adjustment, or visa. INA §212(a)(2)(A)(ii)(I). Moreover, an act that would amount to juvenile delinquency is not a crime and therefore cannot be the basis for inad-

missibility. *Matter of Ramirez-Rivero,* 18 I&N Dec. 135 (BIA 1981); 22 C.F.R. §40.21(a)(2). The standards established in the Federal Juvenile Delinquency Act, 18 U.S.C. §5031–50, govern whether an offense by a young offender is to be considered an act of delinquency or a crime. *Matter of Devison,* 22 I&N Dec. 1362, 1366 (BIA 2000) [finding an adjudication under CPL Art. 720 of the New York youthful offender procedures to be equivalent to the FJDA and therefore not a conviction even though the procedures were only similar]. *But see Savchuck v. Mukasey,* 518 F.3d 119, 122–23 (2d Cir. 2008) [respondent's guilty plea prior to his 18th birthday, after being charged as adult, did not affect the conviction for immigration purposes, on theory that he would have been charged as a juvenile under the FJDA if it were a federal crime]; *Vargas-Hernandez v. Gonzales,* 497 F.3d 919, 922–23 (9th Cir. 2007) [sixteen-year-old tried as an adult for voluntary manslaughter is convicted under INA §101(a)(48)(A)]; *Uritsky v. Gonzales,* 399 F.3d 728 (6th Cir. 2005) [distinguishing *Devison*, the court determined that a sentence to probation under Michigan's youthful Trainee Act was a conviction]; *Vieira Garcia v. INS,* 239 F.3d 409, 414–15 (1st Cir. 2001) [upholding a BIA decision that 17-year-old tried as an adult under Rhode Island law was an aggravated felon, and finding that the failure to apply the Federal Juvenile Delinquency Act as a standard for all state convictions does not violate equal protection]. *But see* 22 C.F.R. §40.21(a)(2)(i)(A) [child under 15 will always be considered a juvenile for purposes of INA even where tried as adult].

(3) Petty Offense—Also, any alien (whether or not a minor) is not inadmissible if the CIMT conviction is for a petty offense. A conviction is considered a petty offense where "the maximum penalty *possible* for the crime of which the alien was convicted did not exceed imprisonment for one year *and* the alien was not sentenced to a term of imprisonment in excess of six months [regardless of the extent to which the sentence was ultimately executed]." INA §212(a)(2)(A)(ii)(II). An undesignated probationary sentence, unlike an indeterminate sentence, is not considered a felony punishable by more than one year imprisonment, where the court has designated it a misdemeanor punishable by a maximum term of imprisonment of 6 months. *Lafarga v. INS,* 170 F.3d 1213 (9th Cir. 1999) [although an indeterminate sentence under *Matter of D-* requires the BIA to look at the maximum possible sentence, an undesignated sentence does not]. *Accord Garcia-Lopez v. Ashcroft,* 334 F.3d 840 (9th Cir. 2003) [Cal. Penal Code §487.2 is considered a "wobbler" statute because offense can result in a range of punishment and where state judge designates it as a misdemeanor, the BIA is bound by that determination for purposes of the petty offense exception]. If there was no conviction but the person admits facts, the petty offense exception applies and the alien is not inadmissible so long as the maximum sentence that could have been imposed does not exceed one year under the law of the foreign country or jurisdiction. INA §212(a)(2)(A)(ii)(II). The petty offense exception is not applicable if more than one CIMT offense has been committed or admitted. *Matter of Jurado,* 24 I&N Dec. 29, 34–35 (BIA 2007) [where there was a second CIMT, the "stop-time" rule applied because the petty offense exception only applied to the first CIMT]. However, it remains effective where one of the two offenses was not for a CIMT. *Matter of Garcia-Hernandez,* 23 I&N Dec. 590, 594–95 (BIA 2003) [applicant who was convicted of a petty offense that was a CIMT and a second offense (battery) that was not a CIMT, he is not barred from cancellation, because he has not been convicted of an offense under §212(a)(2)]. It also remains effective for purposes of relief, where the second CIMT was not committed until after the residency requirement had accrued. *Matter of Deanda-Romo,* 23 I&N Dec. 597 (BIA 2003) [the "stop-time" rule barring cancellation for LPRs who did not accrue seven years of residence before committing a crime referred to in §212(a)(2) did not apply until after the second offense was committed, where the 7 years accrued before the second offense was committed and the first conviction was a petty offense]. DOS takes the position that the petty offense exception is not applicable to drug cases. Correspondence in March-May, 1989 of Odom, Chief of Advisory Opinions Division, DOS, *reprinted in* 66 No. 36 *Interpreter Releases* 1042–43, 1052–55 (Sept. 18, 1989). IMMACT90 appears to support that view. INA §212(a)(2)(A)(ii) refers to exceptions only for CIMTs. The determination of whether an offense comes within the petty offense exception is based upon the status of the

law at the time the alien sought entry and not at the time of the criminal acts. *Squires v. INS*, 689 F.2d 1276 (6th Cir. 1982).

(4) Political Offenses—Purely political offenses are not crimes for purpose of this section. INA §212(a)(2)(A)(i)(I). The Department of State recognizes that purely political offenses include ones which are "based on fabricated charges or predicated upon repressive measures against racial, religious or political minorities." 22 C.F.R. §40.21(a)(6). This view is consistent with the legislative history, Conf. Rep. No. 82-2096 (1952), *reprinted in* 1952 U.S.C.C.A.N. 1753, 1754, 1952 WL 3083 and case law interpreting earlier identical provisions. *See Matter of K-*, 4 I&N Dec. 108 (C.O. 1950); *Matter of B-*, 1 I&N Dec. 47 (BIA, A.G. 1941). The BIA more recently held that the offense must "be completely and totally 'political' in order to qualify for the CIMT exception" and therefore the balancing test for the serious nonpolitical crime exception for asylum/withholding was inapplicable. *Matter of O'Cealleagh,* 23 I&N Dec. 976, 981 (BIA 2006) [respondent's conviction for aiding and abetting the murder of two British corporals was not purely a political offense because it was not fabricated]. In *O'Cealleagh* the Board specified three types of political crimes: (1) Baseless, trumped-up, or fabricated charges; (2) acts directed against the State, such as treason, sedition, or espionage; and (3) a common offense such as murder, assault, or theft that is so connected with a political act that the offense is regarded as political. *Matter of O'Cealleagh,* 23 I&N Dec. 976, 980 (BIA 2006). At least one circuit court has upheld a BIA decision finding that the political offense exception does *not* apply as a defense to a deportation charge based solely on terrorist activity. *McAllister v. Att'y Gen. of the U.S.,* 444 F.3d 178, 188(3d Cir. 2006) [upheld under *Chevron*, a BIA determination that the political offense exception did not apply to a deportation charge under INA §237(a)(4)(B)]

(5) Defining a CIMT—A crime of moral turpitude (CIMT) "refers generally to conduct which is inherently base, vile, or depraved, *and* contrary to the accepted rules of morality and the duties owed between persons or to society in general ... Moral turpitude has been defined as an act which is per se morally reprehensible and intrinsically wrong, or *malum in se* so it is the nature of the act itself and not the statutory prohibition of it which renders a crime one of moral turpitude." *Matter of Franklin*, 20 I&N Dec. 867, 868 (BIA 1994), *aff'd*, 72 F.3d 571 (8th Cir. 1995) (emphasis added); *Matter of Flores,* 17 I&N Dec. 225, 227 (BIA 1980).

(6) Inherent Nature of Crime—In determining a CIMT, it is the "inherent nature of the crime as defined by statute and interpreted by the courts as limited and described by the record of conviction" and not the facts and circumstances of the particular person's case that determines whether it is a crime of moral turpitude. *Matter of Short*, 20 I&N Dec. 136 (BIA 1989); *Hyder v. Keisler,* 506 F.3d 388, 391–92 (5th Cir. 2007) [found that misuse of Social Security number is a CIMT notwithstanding petitioner's argument that he was misled by others and did not personally commit fraud]; *Navarro-Lopez v. Gonzales,* 502 F.3d 1063 (9th Cir. 2007) (*en banc*) [nothing in Cal. Penal Code §32 inherently makes accessory after the fact a CIMT]; *Omagah v. Ashcroft,* 288 F.3d 254, 260 (5th Cir. 2002); *Goldeshtein v. INS*, 8 F.3d 645 (9th Cir. 1993); *Okabe v. INS*, 671 F.2d 863 (5th Cir. 1982); *McKenzie v. Savoretti*, 200 F.2d 546, 548 (5th Cir. 1952); *Giglio v. Neeley*, 208 F.2d 337 (7th Cir. 1953); *Ablett v. Brownell*, 240 F.2d 625 (D.C. Cir. 1957). *See generally Taylor v. U.S.*, 495 U.S. 575 (1990) [focused on elements of the offense, not on details of criminal conduct in sentence enhancement]. Moreover, it is not "the seriousness of the offense nor the severity of the sentence imposed" that determines whether the crime involves moral turpitude. *Matter of Serna*, 20 I&N Dec. 579 (BIA 1992). Similarly, not all crimes involving injurious touching of another reflect moral depravity, "even though they may carry the label of assault, aggravated assault, or battery under the law." *Matter of Sanudo,* 23 I&N Dec. 968, 971 (BIA 2006) [domestic battery under Cal. Penal Code §§242 and 243(e)(1) is not a CIMT]. Rather, the crime must be one which is *per se* morally reprehensible and intrinsically wrong or *malum in se. Serna, supra; Beltran-Tirado v. INS*, 213 F.3d 1179, 1184 (9th Cir. 2000) [making a false attestation on an I-9 and using a false Social Security number are *malum prohibitum* but not *malum in se*]. The "violation of statutes which merely license or regulate and impose criminal li-

ability without regard to evil intent do not involve moral turpitude." *Matter of G-*, 7 I&N Dec. 114, 118 (BIA 1956). Moreover, simply because the statute requires evil intent, it "is not enough to convert a crime that is not serious into one of moral turpitude." *Rodriguez-Herrera v. INS*, 52 F.3d 238, 241 (9th Cir. 1995). Intent to commit a crime and evil intent are not the same. *Matter of Short, supra*; *Goldeshtein v. INS*, 8 F.3d 645, 648 (9th Cir. 1993). Nor is willfulness in the commission of a crime the equivalent to evil intent. *Notash v. Gonzales,* 427 F.3d 693, 698 (9th Cir. 2005) [willfully making a false statement does not equate to evil intent]. Although moral turpitude often involves evil intent, the BIA has stated that "such a specific intent is not a prerequisite" for such a crime. *Matter of Torres-Varela,* 23 I&N Dec. 78, 83–84 (BIA 2001); *Matter of Lopez-Meza,* 22 I&N Dec. 1188 (BIA 1999). *But see Matter of Khourn,* 21 I&N Dec. 1041, 1046 (BIA 1997) [holding that evil intent is a prerequisite for a CIMT]; *Matter of Flores,* 17 I&N Dec. 225, 227 (BIA 1980) [holding that evil intent is the essence of moral turpitude]; *Matter of Abreu-Semino,* 12 I&N Dec. 775, 777 (BIA 1968). And there may be rare instances when intent is not even required as in statutory rape. *Castle v. INS,* 541 F.2d 1064, 1066 (4th Cir. 1976); *Marciano v. INS,* 450 F.2d 1022 (8th Cir. 1971); *Matter of Dingena,* 11 I&N Dec. 723 (BIA 1966). Recklessness under some circumstances may be enough, *Knapik v. Ashcroft*, 384 F.3d 84, 88–90 (3d Cir. 2004) [under *Chevron* deference, court determined that BIA's longstanding position is that crimes involving recklessness may be CIMTs]; *Matter of Medina,* 15 I&N Dec. 611 (BIA 1976) [recklessness sufficient for CIMT under Illinois aggravated-assault statute]. *But see Reyes-Morales v. Gonzales,* 435 F.3d 937, 944–45 (8th Cir. 2006) [IJ erred in finding that Minn. Stat. §609.749, regarding harassing telephone calls, was a CIMT solely because it encompassed threatening behavior without determining whether there was malicious intent and a reckless state of mind without more is insufficient].

(7) Before one can be convicted of a CIMT, the statute in question by its terms, must necessarily involve moral turpitude, *Matter of L-V-C-,* 22 I&N Dec. 594, 603 (BIA 1999) [reversing *Matter of Goldeshtein* regarding structuring financial transactions because the "statutory provision ...encompasses at least some violations that do not involve moral turpitude."]; *Matter of Esfandiary*, 16 I&N Dec. 659 (BIA 1979); *Matter of Garcia,* 11 I&N Dec. 521 (BIA 1966); *Matter of C-*, 5 I&N Dec. 65 (BIA 1953), *Matter of B-*, 6 I&N Dec. 98, 106 (BIA 1954), *or* the courts must have interpreted the statute to require moral turpitude. *Matter of Bart*, 20 I&N Dec. 436 (BIA 1992) [even where language of statute did not require intent to defraud, bad check conviction under Georgia statute deemed to be a CIMT because of judicial interpretation requiring intent to defraud].

As a general rule, if a statute encompasses both acts that do and do not involve moral turpitude, deportability cannot be sustained. *Hernandez-Martinez v. Ashcroft,* 329 F.3d 1117 (9th Cir. 2003), *reh'g denied* 343 F.3d 1075 (9th Cir. 2003) [finding that Arizona Law §28-697(A)(1) for aggravated drunk driving cited as a CIMT in *Lopez-Meza* is *not* a CIMT because statute is divisible and a person can be convicted for sitting in one's own driveway with the key in the ignition and a bottle of beer in his hand and therefore does not commit an "inherently base, vile or depraved" act]; *Pichardo v. INS*, 104 F.3d 756, 760 n.6 (5th Cir. 1997); *Hamdan v. INS*, 98 F.3d 183, 187 (5th Cir. 1996); *Matter of Short*, 20 I&N Dec. 136 (BIA 1989). The court must also analyze "the elements of the crime that the government must prove before obtaining a conviction" to determine whether it is a CIMT. *Smalley v. Ashcroft,* 354 F.3d 332, 337 (5th Cir. 2003) [money laundering constitutes a CIMT].

Where the statute is divisible (broad or multi-sectional), *see, e.g., Matter of P-*, 6 I&N Dec. 193 (BIA 1954); *Neely v. U.S.*, 300 F.2d 67 (9th Cir. 1962), the court looks to the "record of conviction." *Matter of Ajami,* 22 I&N Dec. 949, 950 (BIA 1999) [look to indictment, plea, verdict, and sentence]; *Matter of Sanudo,* 23 I&N Dec. 968, 972–73 (BIA 2006) [BIA did not sustain claim that California domestic battery conviction was a CIMT where both the statute and the admissible portion of respondent's conviction did not reflect that the battery was injurious to the victim or that it involved anything more that nonviolent touching]; *Singh v. DHS,* 517 F.3d 638, 643–46 (2d Cir. 2008) [court found that DHS had established by clear and convincing evidence that petitioner was convicted of assault under N.Y.P.L §120.05(1) by upholding the admission of a Conditions of Probation document, a Certificate of Disposition, and a post-conviction rap sheet which individually would be insufficient but in combination proved the conviction]; ;*Chanmouny v. Ashcroft,* 376 F.3d 810, 813 (8th Cir. 2004) ["The record of conviction typically includes the indictment or information, plea, verdict or judgment, and sentence" and transcript of plea indicated purpose to terrorize rather than reckless disregard]; *Zaffarano v. Corsi,* 63 F.2d 757 (2d Cir. 1933) [look only at record of conviction—"charge (indictment), plea, verdict and sentence"—to determine if crime involves moral turpitude]; *Guarino v. Uhl,* 107 F.2d 399 (2d Cir. 1939); *U.S. v. Kiang,* 175 F.Supp.2d 942, 950 (E.D. Mich. 2001) [denaturalization case where court addressed divisibility issue and looked to record of conviction]. The record does not include the prosecutor's statement during sentencing. *Matter of Cassisi,* 10 I&N Dec. 136 (BIA 1963), nor an admission made by a respondent in removal proceedings, *Matter of Pichardo,* 21 I&N Dec. 330 (BIA 1996) [firearms offense], but does include "other documents admissible as evidence in proving a criminal conviction." *Matter of Sweetser,* 22 I&N Dec. 709, 714 (BIA 1999) [criminal negligent child abuse not aggravated felony]. In *Notash v. Gonzales,* 427 F.3d 693, 697 (9th Cir. 2005) the court relied upon the Supreme Court's decision in *Shepard v. U.S.,* 544 U.S. 13, 125 S.Ct. 1254 (2005), to reject the assertion that respondent was convicted of a crime of moral turpitude. In *Shepard,* 125 S.Ct. at 1257, the Court found that a narrow, specific set of documents comprised the record: "[the] charging document, written plea agreement, transcript of plea colloquy, and any explicit factual finding by the trial judge to which the defendant assented." *But see Ali v. Mukasey,* 521 F.3d 737 (7th Cir. 2008) [finding that *Shepard* only applies to establishing the fact of the conviction, not to whether it is a CIMT, and holding that the BIA may rely on the presentence investigative report or other documents, because "when deciding how to classify convictions under criteria that go beyond the criminal charge—such as the amount of the victim's loss, or whether the crime is one of 'moral turpitude' the agency has discretion to consider evidence beyond the charging papers and judgment of conviction"].

More recently, the courts and the BIA have described this approach as the same approach used in analyzing aggravated felonies: the categorical and modified categorical approach. *See e.g., Wala v. Mukasey,* 511 F.3d 102, 107–10 (2d Cir. 2007) [relying on *Shepard* and determining that the BIA may rely only on facts that the petitioner "necessarily pleaded" the court held that burglary with an intent to commit larceny was not necessarily a CIMT because petitioner did not plead to facts that would constitute an intent to permanent deprived the victim of his property]; *Cerezo v. Mukasey,* 512 F.3d 1165, 1167 (9th Cir. 2008) [the limitations on analysis under the categorical approach in *Gonzales v. Duenas-Alvarez,* 549 U.S. ____, 127 S.Ct. 815 (2007) are not applicable when the language of the statute is clear and "plainly and specifically criminalizes conduct outside the contours of the federal definition"]; *Quintero-Salazar v. Keisler,* 506 F.3d 688 (9th Cir. 2007) [relying on the categorical and modified categorical approach the court determined that Cal. Penal Code §261.5(d) involving intercourse between a person 21 or older with a minor under 16 is not categorically a CIMT and there was no proof in the record supporting the modified categorical approach]; *Amouzadeh v. Winfrey,* 467 F.3d 451, 455 (5th Cir. 2006) [when determining whether "a particular law meets the BIA's definition of 'moral turpitude,' we employ a categorical approach..." Found conviction for 8 U.S.C. §1425(a) unlawful procurement of naturalization as CIMT]; *Morales v. Gonzales,* 478 F.3d 972, 978 (9th Cir. 2007) [applied categorical approach to determine that communicating with a minor for immoral purposes is a CIMT]; *Galeana-Mendoza v. Gonzales,* 465 F.3d 1054, 1057–58 (9th Cir. 2006) [under the modified categorical approach, DHS failed to establish that a conviction under Cal. Penal Code §243(e) for domestic battery is a CIMT]; *Navarro-Lopez v. Gonzales,* 503 F.3d 1063 (9th Cir. 2007) (*en banc*) [relying on the categorical and modified categorical approach the court determined that nothing in Cal. Penal Code §32 makes an accessory after the fact inherently a CIMT]; *Hashish v. Gonzales,* 442 F.3d 572, 575–76 (7th Cir. 2006) [quoting *Padilla v. Gonzales,* 397 F.3d 1016 (7th Cir. 2005), for the use of the categorical approach toward determining moral turpitude]; *Vuksanovic v. U.S. Att'y Gen.,* 439 F.3d 1308, 1311 (11th Cir. 2006) [relied on categorical approach to find second degree arson under Florida law a CIMT]; *Cuevas-Gaspar v. Gonzales,* 430 F.3d 1013 (9th Cir. 2005) [finding that accomplice to residential burglary under Washington Revised Code §§9A.52.025(1) and 9A.08.020(3) was a CIMT under modified categorical approach]; *Notash v. Gonzales,* 427 F.3d 693, 696–97 (9th Cir. 2005) [finding that a conviction for attempted entry of goods by means of a false statement in violation of 18 U.S.C. §542 is not a CIMT under the categorical or modified categorical approach]; *Matter of Tejwani,* 24 I&N Dec. 97, 98 (BIA 2007) [in determining whether an respondent was convicted of a CIMT the Board stated "we use the categorical approach, focusing on the statute and the record of conviction rather than on the specific act committed by the alien"]; *Cf. Abdelqadar v. Gonzales,* 413 F.3d 668, 671–72 (7th Cir. 2005) [questioning whether the categorical approach looking at the elements of the crime instead of the alien's conduct should be used in the analysis of CIMTs, but using the categorical approach nevertheless]. For a more complete discussion of the categorical and modified categorical approach, *see in this chapter* ¶ V.G.4.f (p.192), *infra.*

One must also look at what criminal mental state is necessary for a conviction under the statute. *Matter of Fualaau,* 21 I&N Dec. 475 (BIA 1996); *Matter of Medina*, 15 I&N Dec. 611 (BIA 1976). Although evil intent signifies a CIMT, willfulness in the commission of the crime does not, by itself, suggest that it is a CIMT. *Goldeshtein v. INS*, 8 F.3d 645 (9th Cir. 1993). Under the statute, evil intent must be explicit or implicit given the nature of the crime. *Gonzalez-Alvarado v. INS*, 39 F.3d 245, 246 (9th Cir. 1994). Conspiracy for moral turpitude can only result in inadmissibility when the underlying offense is a crime of moral turpitude. *Matter of Short*, 20 I&N Dec. 136 (BIA 1989); *Matter of Flores*, 17 I&N Dec. 225 (BIA 1980); *Goldeshtein v. INS*, 8 F.3d 645 (9th Cir. 1993).

(8) The statute must also be legally coherent to support a CIMT. *Gill v. INS,* 420 F.3d 82, 89–91 (2d Cir. 2005) [attempted reckless assault under N.Y. Penal Law §120.05(4) is not a CIMT because, although reckless conduct may be enough for a CIMT, attempted recklessness is legally incoherent]; *Knapik v. Ashcroft,* 384 F.3d 84, 90–94 (3d Cir. 2004) [although reckless endangerment under N.Y. Penal Law §120.25 would be a CIMT, attempted reckless endangerment is a nonsensical crime and therefore could not be a CIMT because it requires intent to meet the "attempt" part but recklessness to do the crime].

(9) Burden of Proof. The DHS always bears the burden of proving that a crime is a CIMT by clear and convincing evidence. *See e.g., Matter of Tobar-Lobo,* 24 I&N Dec. 143, 144 (BIA 2007) [government met burden of proof in determining that failure to report as a sex offender is a CIMT]; *Cf. Singh v. DHS,* 517 F.3d 638, 643–46 (2d Cir. 2008) [court found that DHS had established by clear and convincing evidence that petitioner was convicted of assault under N.Y. Penal Law §120.05(1) by upholding the admission of a Conditions of Probation document, a Certificate of Disposition, and a post-conviction rap sheet which individually would be insufficient but in combination proved the conviction].

(10) A foreign conviction has no effect where it was conducted *in absentia.* 22 C.F.R. §40.21(a)(4). Conduct must also be deemed criminal by U.S. standards. *Matter of McNaughton*, 16 I&N Dec. 569 (BIA 1978); *Matter of De La Nues,* 18 I&N Dec. 140 (BIA 1981) [look to Title 18 of U.S. Code and if no equivalent to Title 22 of D.C. Code to determine whether foreign conviction constitutes juvenile delinquency]. And whether a crime is deemed to be a felony or misdemeanor is judged by looking to Title 18 of the U.S. Code and if there is no equivalent by looking to Title 22 of the D.C. Code. *Matter of Scarpulla,* 15 I&N Dec. 139, 141 (BIA 1974) (and cases cited therein). A foreign conviction, at the time U.S. law provided for a recommendation against deportation, could not be the basis to bar a person convicted in a foreign country when there was no provision and therefore no opportunity to apply for a recommendation against deportation. *Gubbels v. Hoy*, 261 F.2d 952 (9th Cir. 1958); *Matter of Gian*, 11 I&N Dec. 242 (BIA 1965). But the elimination of Judicial Recommendations Against Deportation (JRADs) under IMMACT90 may change the BIA and the Court's view. However, the same reasoning may apply to pardons. *But see Matter of Nolan*, 19 I&N Dec. 539 (BIA 1988).

(11) The determination of whether a crime is a CIMT is a matter of law and the court reviews the BIA's decision *de novo*. *Goldeshtein v. INS*, 8 F.3d 645 (9th Cir. 1993); *Hamdan v. INS*, 98 F.3d 183, 185 (5th Cir. 1996). *See also Franklin v. INS*, 72 F.3d 571, 573–606 (8th Cir. 1995) (Bennett, J. dissenting) for an exhaustive analysis of this and other issues concerning CIMTs.

1.b. Examples of CIMTs—Crimes of moral turpitude can be grouped into several categories:

(1) Crimes Against the Person

(a) Involving moral turpitude

i) **Assault**—Assault in the second degree, *Singh v. DHS*, 517 F.3d 638, 643–46 (2d Cir. 2008) [court found that DHS had established by clear and convincing evidence that petitioner was convicted of assault under N.Y. Penal Law §120.05(1), which petitioner conceded was a CIMT]; Assault with intent to rob or kill or to commit abortion or rape, *Clark v. Orabona*, 59 F.2d 187 (1st Cir.), *cert. denied*, 287 U.S. 629 (1932) [assault with intent to kill]; *Rizzio v. Kenney*, 50 F.2d 418 (D. Conn. 1931); *Matter of Beato*, 10 I&N Dec. 730 (BIA 1964). Assault with intent to cause serious physical injury. *Nguyen v. Reno,* 211 F.3d 692, 694–95 (1st Cir. 2000) [under Conn. Gen. Stat. §53a-60(a)(1) involving second degree assault]. Assault with a deadly weapon, *Matter of Logan*, 17 I&N Dec. 367 (BIA 1980). Aggravated assault, *Pichardo v. INS,* 104 F.3d 756, 759–61 (5th Cir. 1997); *U.S. v. Robelo,* 358 F.Supp.2d 400, 415–21 (D.N.J. 2005) [aggravated assault under N.J.S.A. §2C:12-1b.(5)(a), which includes simple assault on a law enforcement officer]; *Matter of Medina*, 15 I&N Dec. 611 (BIA 1976); *Matter of O*, 3 I&N Dec. 193 (BIA 1948); *Matter of J*, 2 I&N Dec. 477 (BIA 1946). Assault with a dangerous weapon. *Yousefi v. INS,* 260 F.3d 318, 326–27 (4th Cir. 2001) (In dicta, court determined that conviction under D.C. Code Ann. §22-502 is a CIMT]. Aggravated assault against a police officer, *Matter of Danesh*, 19 I&N Dec. 669 (BIA 1988). *But see Garcia-Meza v. Mukasey,* 516 F.3d 535 (7th Cir. 2008) [aggravated battery of a police officer under 720 Ill. Comp. Stat. 5/12-4(b)(6) is not a CIMT because unlike *Danesh* officer does not have to sustain bodily injury]; *Partyka v. Attorney General,* 417 F.3d 408, 411–17 (3d Cir. 2005) [aggravated assault on law enforcement officer under N.J. Stat. Ann. §2C:12-1b(5)(a) is not a CIMT because a person may be convicted for negligent conduct and record in the case did not reveal otherwise]; *Zaranska v. DHS,* 400 F.Supp.2d 500, 504–05 (E.D.N.Y. 2005) [assaulting a police officer pursuant to N.Y. Penal Law §120.15(3) was not a CIMT; *Danesh* distinguished]; *Matter of O*, 4 I&N Dec. 301 (BIA 1951) [assault on police officer is not a CIMT]. Indecent assault, *Solano-Chicas v. Gonzales,* 440 F.3d 1050, 1055–56 (8th Cir. 2006) [misdemeanor fifth-degree assault under Minnesota law, where plea indicated respondent fondled a 9- or 10-year old girl, was a CIMT]; *Maghsoudi v. INS*, 181 F.3d 8, 12–15 (1st Cir. 1999) [Mass. statute]; *Matter of S-*, 5 I&N Dec. 686 (BIA 1954) [Canadian statute]; Felony assault (3rd degree) but only if it requires intentional or reckless conduct for a conviction. *Matter of Perez-Contreras,* 20 I&N Dec. 615 (BIA 1992) [withdrawing from *Matter of Baker*, 15 I&N Dec. 50 (BIA 1974) to the extent it holds that assault is a CIMT without regard to the existence of intentional or reckless conduct and holding that there was no CIMT under the Washington state statute in the absence of intentional or reckless conduct]; *Matter of Solon,* 24 I&N Dec. 239 (BIA 2007) [assault in the third degree under N.Y. Penal Law §120.00(1), which requires both specific intent and physical injury is a CIMT—the presence of an *aggravating factor is not necessary*].

ii) **Assistance, Failure to Stop and Render Aid**—*Garcia-Maldonado v. Gonzales,* 491 F.3d 284 (5th Cir. 2007) [failure to stop and render aid after being involved in an automobile accident under Tex. Transp. Code Ann. §550.021 and §550.023 is CIMT where person intentionally left scene of accident where driver died]. *But see Cerezo v. Mukasey,* 512 F.3d 1163 (9th Cir. 2008) [leaving the scene of an accident resulting in bodily injury or death under California Vehicle Code §20001(a) is not categorically a CIMT].

iii) **Battery (aggravated)**—*Sosa-Martinez v. U.S. Att'y Gen.*, 420 F.3d 1338 (11th Cir. 2005) [aggravated battery under Fla. Stat. Ann. §784.045 is CIMT].

iv) **Carrying a concealed weapon with intent to use**—*Matter of S*, 8 I&N Dec. 344 (BIA 1959).

v) **Child/spousal abuse**—*Garcia v. Att'y Gen. of the U.S.*, 329 F.3d 1217, 1222 (11th Cir. 2003) [conviction for aggravated child abuse under Fla. Stat. §§827.03(1) and 784.045(1) is CIMT]; *Guerrero de Nodahl v. INS*, 407 F.2d 1405 (9th Cir. 1969); Child pornography, *Matter of Olquin,* 23 I&N Dec. 896 (BIA 2006); Communicating with a minor for immoral purposes, *Morales v. Gonzales,* 478 F.3d 972 (9th Cir. 2007) [Wash. Rev. Code §9.68A.090 regarding communicating with a minor for immoral purposes]; Delinquency of a minor, *Sheikh v. Gonzales,* 427 F.3d 1077, 1082 (8th Cir. 2005) [misdemeanor of contributing to the delinquency of a minor under North Dakota law]; Spousal abuse, *Grageda v. INS*, 12 F.3d 919 (9th Cir. 1993). Aggravated stalking (where threat is involved), *Matter of Ajami*, 22 I&N Dec. 949 (BIA 1999). Willful infliction of corporal injury on spouse, parent or perpetrator's child, or cohabitant under §273.5 of Cal. Penal Code, *Matter of Tran*, 21 I&N Dec. 291 (BIA 1996). Failure to support a child. *Matter of R-*, 4 I&N 192, 194 (BIA 1950) [willfully leaving a child destitute under Wisconsin law]; *Matter of S-*, 2 I&N Dec. 553 (BIA 1945) [same destitute crime under NY law]. *But see Matter of E-*, 2 I&N Dec. 134, 135 (BIA 1944) [Ohio nonsupport statute was not CIMT where violation could occur even if defendant believed he was acting in best interest of the child].

vi) **Disorderly conduct** (in certain limited circumstances)—*Hudson v. Esperdy*, 290 F.2d 879 (2d Cir.), *cert. denied*, 368 U.S. 918 (1961) [loitering for lewd purposes]; *Matter of Alfonso-Bermudez*, 12 I&N Dec. 225 (BIA 1967) [soliciting charge].

vii) **Driving under the influence** (aggravated)—*Marmolejo-Campos v. Gonzales,* 503 F.3d 922 (9th Cir. 2007) [conviction under Ariz. Rev. Stat. §28-697(A)(1) [now 28-1383(A)(1)] for aggravated drunk driving which includes driving drunk with knowledge that he is without a valid license is a CIMT; deferred to *Lopez-Meza* and distinguished *Hernandez-Martinez*]; *Matter of Lopez-Meza,* 22 I&N Dec. 1188 (BIA 1999) [aggravated DUI under Arizona law §28-697(A)(1) (now §1383(a)(1)) occurs where person commits DUI while knowingly driving on a suspended, canceled, or revoked license, or while under a restricted license owing to prior DUI]; *But see Matter of Torres-Varela,* 23 I&N Dec.78, 82–86 (BIA 2001) [distinguished *Lopez-Meza* because aggravated DUI under §28-697(A)(2) (now 1383(a)(2) of Arizona law did not require a culpable mental state as did the Arizona law section 28-697(A)(1) in *Lopez-Meza*]; *Hernandez-Martinez v. Ashcroft,* 329 F.3d 1117 (9th Cir. 2003), *reh'g denied* 343 F.3d 1075 (9th Cir. 2003) [finding that Ariz. Law §28-697(A)(1) in *Lopez-Meza* is *not* categorically a CIMT because statute is divisible and a person can be convicted for sitting in one's own driveway with the key in the ignition and a bottle of beer in his hand and therefore does not commit an "inherently base, vile or depraved" act].

viii) **Firearms Discharge** at occupied building or vehicle. *Recio-Prado v. Gonzales,* 456 F.3d 819 (8th Cir. 2006) [conviction for aiding and abetting the unlawful discharge of a firearm in a building in violation of Kansas Statute §21-4219(b)].

ix) **Kidnapping**—*Matter of Nakoi,* 14 I&N Dec. 208 (BIA 1972), *Matter of C-M-*, 9 I&N Dec. 487 (BIA 1961), *but see Hamdan v. INS*, 98 F.3d 183 (5th Cir. 1996) [attempted simple kidnapping under Louisiana law not CIMT].

x) **Mayhem**—*Matter of Santoro,* 11 I&N Dec. 607 (BIA 1966).

xi) **Murder and voluntary manslaughter**—*Carter v. INS*, 90 F.3d 14, 18 (1st Cir. 1996) [manslaughter stemming from assault and battery is CIMT]; *De Lucia v. Flagg*, 297 F.2d 58 (7th Cir. 1962), *cert. denied*, 369 U.S. 837 (1962); *Allessio* *v. Day*, 42 F.2d 217 (2d Cir. 1930); *Matter of Abi-Rached*, 10 I&N Dec. 551 (BIA 1964). Accessory after the fact to murder, *Cabral v. INS*, 15 F.3d 193 (1st Cir. 1994). Attempted murder, *Matter of Awaijane*, 14 I&N Dec. 117 (BIA 1972); Manslaughter (recklessness) *Matter of Jean,* 23 I&N Dec. 373, 375–76 (AG 2002) [although respondent did not contest her admissibility the AG asserted that her conviction for 2nd degree manslaughter under N.Y. Penal Law §124.15(1), which allows a conviction for recklessness is "indisputably" a CIMT].

xii) **Restraint**—*Sharpe v. Riley,* 271 F.Supp.2d 631, 635–36 (E.D. Pa. 2003) [unlawful restraint under 18 Pa. Cons. Stat. Ann. §2902 is a CIMT even though it is not a specific intent crime, because it is contrary to justice, honesty, and morality];

xiii) **Robbery**—*Matter of Martin,* 18 I&N Dec. 226 (BIA 1982); *Matter of GR,* 2 I&N Dec. 733 (BIA 1946); *Matter of F,* 2 I&N Dec. 517 (BIA 1946); *Brett v. INS,* 386 F.2d 439 (2d Cir. 1967) *But see U.S. ex rel. Fontan v. Uhl,* 16 F.Supp. 428 (S.D.N.Y. 1936).

xiv) **Threats; terrorist threats**—*Chanmouny v. Ashcroft,* 376 F.3d 810 (8th Cir. 2004) [terrorist threats under Minn. Stat. §609.713 was CIMT where respondent, based upon plea transcript, acted with a purpose to terrorize and not just recklessly].

(b) Not involving moral turpitude

i) **Assault**—Simple Assault. *Fernandez-Ruiz v. Gonzales,* 468 F.3d 1159, 1163–69 (9th Cir. 2006) [misdemeanor assault under Ariz. Rev. Stat. §13-1203(A)(1)–(3) and domestic violence under Ariz. Rev. Stat. §13-3601(A), which refers back to the reckless commission under the assault statute are not CIMTs under the categorical approach because they lack *willful conduct* and do not necessarily involve more than *insubstantial* injury].

ii) **Assault and battery (simple)**—*Griffo v. McCandless,* 28 F.2d 287 (E.D. Pa. 1928), *Matter of Sejas,* 24 I&N Dec. 236 (BIA 2007) [assault and battery against a family or household member under Va. Code §16.1-228 does not require the actual infliction of physical injury but merely offensive touching]; *Matter of S*, 9 I&N Dec. 688 (BIA 1962), *Matter of B*, 5 I&N Dec. 538 (BIA 1953), *Matter of E*, 1 I&N Dec. 505 (BIA 1943) [simple assault]; Assault/Aggravated Assault on a Law Enforcement Officer. *Garcia-Meza v. Mukasey,* 516 F.3d 535 (7th Cir. 2008) [aggravated battery of a police officer under Illinois statute 720 Ill. Comp. Stat. 5/12-4(b)(6) is not a CIMT because unlike *Danesh* officer does not have to sustain bodily injury]; *Partyka v. Attorney General,* 417 F.3d 408, 411–17 (3d Cir. 2005) [aggravated assault on law enforcement officer under N.J. Stat. Ann. §2C:12-1b(5)(a) is not a CIMT because a person may be convicted for negligent conduct and record in the case did not reveal otherwise]; *Zaffarano v. Corsi*, 63 F.2d 757 (2d Cir. 1933) [assault related to resisting arrest]; *Ciambelli v. Johnson*, 12 F.2d 465 (D. Mass. 1926) [assault on police]; *Zaranska v. DHS,* 400 F.Supp.2d 500, 504–05 (E.D.N.Y. 2005) [assaulting a police officer pursuant to N.Y. Penal Law §120.15(3) was not a CIMT; *Danesh* distinguished]; *Matter of O-*, 4 I&N Dec. 301 (BIA 1951) [same]. Assault with intent to commit a felony unless the felony is a CIMT, *Matter of Short*, 20 I&N Dec. 136 (BIA 1989). Assault based on negligence where reckless or intentional conduct is excluded from definition, *Matter of Perez-Contreras*, 20 I&N Dec. 615 (BIA 1992) [Washington State conviction for assault in 3rd degree]. Assault where recklessness could be an element but without serious bodily harm, *Matter of Fualaau,* 21 I&N Dec. 475 (BIA 1996) [Hawaii conviction for assault in 3rd degree]. Attempted assault where recklessness is an element. *Gill v. INS,* 420 F.3d 82, 89–91 (2d Cir. 2005) [attempted reckless assault under N.Y. Penal Law §120.05(4) is not a CIMT because, although reckless conduct may be enough for a CIMT, attempted recklessness is legally incoherent]. *But see Mazzillo v. Day,* 15 F.2d 391 (S.D.N.Y. 1926) [simple assault was a CIMT].

iii) **Battery**—*Matter of Sanudo,* 23 I&N Dec. 968, 970–73 (BIA 2006) [domestic battery under Cal. Penal Code §§242 and 243(e)(1) do not categorically qualify as CIMT and the BIA recognized that not all crimes involving injurious touching of another reflect moral depravity, "even though they may carry the label of assault, aggravated assault, or battery under the law"]; *Matter of Garcia-Hernandez,* 23 I&N Dec. 590, 594 (BIA 2003); *Galeana-Mendoza v. Gonzales,* 465 F.3d 1054, 1057–58 (9th Cir. 2006) [under the modified categorical approach, DHS failed to establish that a conviction under Cal. Penal Code §243(e) for domestic battery is a CIMT because domestic battery is not *per se* a CIMT as it does not necessarily involve violence or bodily harm];

iv) **Child Abandonment**—*Rodriguez-Castro v. Gonzales,* 427 F.3d 316, 321–24 (5th Cir. 2005) [conviction under Texas Penal Code §22.041(b) attempted misdemeanor child abandonment with intent to return is not a CIMT]; *Matter of E-,* 2 I&N Dec. 134, 135 (BIA 1944) [Ohio nonsupport statute was not a CIMT, where violation could occur even if defendant believed he was acting in best interest of the child].

v) **Domestic Violence**—*Fernandez-Ruiz v. Gonzales,* 468 F.3d 1159, 1163–69 (9th Cir. 2006) [domestic violence under Ariz. Rev. Stat. §13-3601(A), which refers back to the reckless commission of simple assault statute is not a CIMT under the categorical approach because it does not require *willful conduct* or more than *insubstantial* injury for a conviction].

vi) **DUI involving simple DUI**—*Matter of Lopez-Meza,* 22 I&N Dec. 1188, 1194 (BIA 1999); *Murillo-Salmeron v. INS,* 327 F.3d 898 (9th Cir. 2003) [waiver under INA §212(h) unnecessary where simple DUI is not a grounds of inadmissibility]. DUI that was aggravated but without culpable mental state is not a CIMT simply because there are multiple (simple) DUIs, *Matter of Torres-Varela,* 23 I&N Dec.78, 82–86 (BIA 2001) [distinguished *Lopez-Meza* because aggravated DUI under §28-697(A)(2) of Arizona law did not require a culpable mental state as did the Arizona law §28-697(A)(1) in *Lopez-Meza*]; DUI where statute is divisible and does not include crimes that are inherently base, vile, or depraved. *Hernandez-Martinez v. Ashcroft,* 329 F.3d 1117 (9th Cir. 2003), *reh'g denied* 343 F.3d 1075 (9th Cir. 2003) [Ariz. law §28-697(A)(1) (now §28-1383(A)(1)) found to be CIMT in *Lopez-Meza* is not categorically a CIMT].

vii) Other—**Leaving the Scene of an Accident.** *Cerezo v. Mukasey,* 512 F.3d 1163 (9th Cir. 2008) [leaving the scene of an accident resulting in bodily injury or death under Cal. Vehicle Code §20001(a) is not categorically a CIMT]; *but see Garcia-Maldonado v. Gonzales,* 491 F.3d 284 (5th Cir. 2007) [failure to stop and render aid after being involved in an automobile accident under Tex. Transp. Code Ann. §550.021 and §550.023 is CIMT where person intentionally left scene of accident where driver died]. **Harassing telephone calls**, *Reyes-Morales v. Gonzales,* 435 F.3d 937, 944–45 (8th Cir. 2006) [harassing phone calls under Minn. Stat. §609.749 is not a CIMT because it encompasses threatening behavior without intent]; **Kidnapping** (simple) (under La. law), *Hamdan v. INS*, 98 F.3d 183 (5th Cir. 1996); **Malicious mischief**, *Rodriguez-Herrera v. INS,* 52 F.3d 238 (9th Cir. 1995); **Manslaughter** (involuntary), *Matter of Lopez*, 13 I&N Dec. 725 (BIA 1971), *Mongiovi v. Karnuth*, 30 F.2d 825 (S.D.N.Y. 1929), *Tutrone v. Shaughnessy*, 160 F.Supp. 433 (S.D.N.Y. 1958). *But see Matter of Franklin*, 20 I&N Dec. 867 (BIA 1994), *aff'd, Franklin v. INS*, 72 F.3d 571 (8th Cir.), *cert. denied, Franklin v. INS*, 519 U.S. 834 (1996) [where statute requires conscious disregard of a substantial risk it is a CIMT]; **Reckless endangerment (attempted)** *Knapik v. Ashcroft,* 384 F.3d 84, 90–94 (3d Cir. 2004) [although reckless endangerment under N.Y. Penal Code §120.25 would be a CIMT, attempted reckless endangerment is a nonsensical crime and therefore could not be a CIMT because it requires intent to meet the "attempt" part but recklessness to do the crime]; **Weapons possession**, *Matter of Granados*, 16 I&N Dec. 726 (BIA 1979) [possession of sawed-off shotgun is not a CIMT].

(2) Sexual offenses

(a) Involving moral turpitude—**Adultery**, *Tourny v. Reimer*, 8 F.Supp. 91 (S.D.N.Y. 1934); *Matter of A-*, 3 I&N Dec. 168 (BIA 1948); **Bigamy**, *Matter of V-L-*, 3 I&N Dec. 10 (BIA 1947), *Matter of E-*, 2 I&N Dec. 328 (BIA 1945); *but see Matter of S,* 1 I&N Dec. 314 (BIA 1942) [bigamy not CIMT]; **Incest**, *Gonzalez-Alvarado v. INS*, 39 F.3d 245 (9th Cir. 1994), *Matter of Y*, 3 I&N Dec. 544 (CO 1949), *but see Matter of B*, 2 I&N Dec. 617 (BIA 1946); **Lewdness**, *Fitzgerald v. Landon*, 238 F.2d 864 (1st Cir. 1956); *Matter of M*, 7 I&N Dec. 144 (BIA 1956), *but see Matter of Mueller*, 11 I&N Dec. 268 (BIA 1965) [lewd and lascivious conduct not CIMT], *Matter of H*, 7 I&N Dec. 616 (BIA 1957) [lascivious conduct not CIMT]; **Oral sex**, *Matter of Leyva*, 16 I&N Dec. 118 (BIA 1977). **Prostitution**, *Lane v. Tillinghast*, 38 F.2d 231 (1st Cir. 1930), *Matter of Lambert*, 11 I&N Dec. 340 (BIA 1965). **Rape**, *Ng Sui Wing v. U.S.*, 46 F.2d 755 (7th Cir. 1931), *Matter of Beato*, 10 I&N Dec. 730 (BIA 1964) [attempted rape]. **Registration (failure to register) by Sex Offender.** *Matter of Tobar-Lobo,* 24 I&N Dec. 143 (BIA 2007) [failure to register as a sex offender in violation of Cal. Penal Code §290(g)(1)]; *but see Plasencia-Ayala v. Mukasey,* 516 F.3d 738, 746–49 (9th Cir. 2008) [failure to register under Nev. Rev. Stat. §179D.550 is a strict liability, regulatory crime and it does not involve a level of depravity or baseness contrary to moral law]; **Statutory rape**, *Castle v. INS,* 541 F.2d 1064, 1066 (4th Cir. 1976); *Marciano v. INS,* 450 F.2d 1022 (8th Cir. 1971); *Matter of Dingena,* 11 I&N Dec. 723 (BIA 1966).

(b) Not involving moral turpitude—**Bastardy**, *Matter of D*, 1 I&N Dec. 186 (BIA 1941); **Fornication or Mann Act violations** where compulsion was not inherent in crime, *Matter of R*, 6 I&N Dec. 444 (BIA 1954); **Indecency**, *Toutounjian v. INS*, 959 F.Supp. 598 (W.D.N.Y. 1997); *Matter of Mueller*, 11 I&N Dec. 268 (BIA 1965); *Matter of H-*, 7 I&N Dec. 301 (BIA 1956) [statute did not require specific intent], *Matter of Z-,* 2 I&N Dec. 316 (BIA 1945); *but see Matter of Z-*, 7 I&N Dec. 253 (BIA 1956) [indecent assault]; **Mailing obscene letter**, *Matter of D-*, 1 I&N Dec. 190 (BIA 1942). **Maintaining a nuisance**, *Matter of A-*, 3 I&N Dec. 168 (BIA 1948). **Minors, contributing to the delinquency of**, *Matter of P*, 2 I&N Dec. 117 (BIA 1944); *but see Castle v. INS*, 541 F.2d 1064 (4th Cir. 1976) [indecent liberties with minor is a CIMT], *Matter of Garcia*, 11 I&N Dec. 521 (BIA 1966) [same]; **Registration (failure to register) by Sex Offender.** *Plasencia-Ayala v. Mukasey,* 516 F.3d 738, 746–49 (9th Cir. 2008) [failure to register under Nev. Rev. Stat. §179D.550 is a strict liability, regulatory crime and it does not involve a level of depravity or baseness contrary to moral law]; *but see Matter of Tobar-Lobo,* 24 I&N Dec. 143 (BIA 2007) [failure to register as a sex offender in violation of Cal. Penal Code 290(g)(1)]; **Statutory rape,** *Quintero-Salazar v. Keisler,* 506 F.3d 688 (9th Cir. 2007) [Cal. Penal Code §261.5(d) involving intercourse between a person 21 or older with a minor under 16 is not categorically a CIMT]; **Vagrancy** (when charged in lieu of prostitution), *Matter of V-S-*, 2 I&N Dec. 703 (BIA 1946).

(3) Crimes against property

(a) Involving moral turpitude—**Arson**, *Vuksanovic v. U.S. Att'y Gen.*, 439 F.3d 1308, 1311 (11th Cir. 2006) [second degree arson under Fla. Stat. §806.01(2)]; *Matter of S*, 3 I&N Dec. 617 (BIA 1949). **Blackmail**, *Lehmann v. Carson*, 353 U.S. 685 (1957). **Burglary**, *Cuevas-Gaspar v. Gonzales,* 430 F.3d 1013 (9th Cir. 2005) [finding that accomplice to residential burglary under Wash. Rev. Code §§9A.52.025(1) and 9A.08.020(3) was a CIMT under modified categorical approach, because respondent had pled guilty to entering residence with intent to steal property]; *Matter of Frentescu*, 18 I&N Dec. 244 (BIA 1982) (burglary with intent to commit theft is CIMT), *Matter of R*, 1 I&N Dec. 540 (BIA 1940), *but see Matter of M,* 2 I&N Dec. 721 (BIA 1946) (breaking and entering without intent to commit larceny is not a CIMT). **Counterfeit Goods.** *Matter of Kochlani,* 24 I&N Dec. 128, 129–31 (BIA 2007) [trafficking in counterfeit goods under 18 U.S.C. §2320 is a CIMT even if intent to defraud is not an element]; *Tall v. Mukasey,* 517 F.3d 1115 (9th Cir. 2008) [counterfeit of a registered mark in violation of Cal. Penal Code §350(a)(2)]; **Embezzlement**, *Matter of Batten*, 11 I&N Dec. 271 (BIA 1965). **Extortion**, *Matter of F*, 3 I&N Dec. 361 (BIA 1949). Forgery, *Robinson v. Day*, 51 F.2d 1022 (2d Cir. 1931), *Abbenante v. Butterfield,* 112 F.Supp. 324 (E.D. Mich. 1953). **Food Stamp Fraud**, *Abdelqadar v. Gonzales,* 413 F.3d 668, 671–72 (7th Cir. 2005) [conviction under 720 Ill. Comp. Stat. 5/17B-5, where defendant admitted he purchased food stamps for cash at lower than face value and arranged to deceive the state by collecting the full value]; *Matter of Adetiba*, 20 I&N Dec. 506 (BIA 1992). **Illegal use of credit cards**, *Matter of Chouinard*, 11 I&N Dec. 839 (BIA 1966). **Larceny**, *Matter of Kim*, 17 I&N Dec. 144 (BIA 1979), *Matter of Grazley,* 14 I&N Dec. 330 (BIA 1973). Larceny (Petit) *Caesar v. Ashcroft,* 355 F.Supp.2d 693, 703 (S.D.N.Y. 2005). **Possession of stolen property** with the knowledge it is stolen, *Matter of Serna*, 20 I&N Dec. 579 (BIA 1992) at 11 n.10. **Receipt of stolen property**, *Smriko v. Ashcroft,* 387 F.3d 279, 282–83 (3d Cir. 2004) [followed *De Leon-Reynoso* and found a violation of 18 Pa. Cons. Stat. §3925(a) at CIMT]; *Aquino-Encarnacion v. INS,* 296 F.3d 56 (1st Cir. 2002) [receipt of stolen property worth over $250 under Mass. Gen. Laws ch. 266 §§60 and 28]; *De Leon-Reynoso v. Ashcroft,* 293 F.3d 633, 635–37 (3d Cir. 2002) [CIMT under 18 Pa. Cons. Stat. §3925(a) where person can be convicted of possessing stolen goods that s/he believes probably are stolen]; *Matter of Salvail*, 17 I&N Dec. 19 (BIA 1979), *Matter of Z,* 7 I&N Dec. 253 (BIA 1956), *Matter of R*, 6 I&N Dec. 772 (BIA 1955), *but see Matter of K,* 2 I&N Dec. 90 (BIA 1944) [where statute convicts if one knows "or must assume" that the property is stolen is not CIMT]. **Shoplifting**. *Da Rosa Silva v. INS,* 263 F.Supp.2d 1005, 1010–12 (E.D. Pa. 2003) [shoplifting in violation of N.J. Stat. Annot. §2C:20-11(b)(1) is a CIMT]. **Stealing cellular air time**, *U.S. v. Qadeer*, 953 F.Supp. 1570, 1580–81 (S.D. Ga. 1997). **Theft**, *Hashish v. Gonzales,* 442 F.3d 572, 576–77 (7th Cir. 2006) [theft of a recorded sound under former Ill. Crim. Code §38-16-1, and misdemeanor theft under 720 Ill. Comp. Stat. 5/16-1(a), involving knowingly obtaining or exerting unauthorized control over property of the owner are CIMTs under categorical approach]; *Okoro v. INS*, 125 F.3d 920, 926 (5th Cir. 1997) (Delaware law), *U.S. v. Esparza-Ponce*, 193 F.3d 1133, 1135–37 (9th Cir. 1999) [petty theft under California law]; *Rashtabadi v. INS,* 23 F.3d 1562, 1568 (9th Cir. 1994) [grand theft under Cal. statute]; *Deluca v. Ashcroft,* 203 F.Supp.2d 1276, 1279 (M.D. Ala. 2002) [theft of property in the 2nd degree under Alabama law is a CIMT]; *Matter of Kochlani,* 24 I&N Dec. 128, 129 (BIA 2007) [grand theft under Cal. Penal Code §487.1 is a CIMT]; *Matter of Jurado,* 24 I&N Dec. 29, 33–34 (BIA 2007) [retail theft under 18 Pa. Cons. Stat. §3929(a)(1) is a CIMT, because a conviction requires that the defendant take merchandise without paying and have the intention to deprive the store owner of goods even if temporarily]; *Matter of Alarcon*, 20 I&N Dec. 557 (BIA 1992) [grand theft]. **Securities fraud**, *Matter of McNaughton*, 16 I&N Dec. 569 (BIA 1978). **Trespass (malicious)**, *Matter of Esfandiary*, 16 I&N Dec. 659 (BIA 1979).

(b) Not involving moral turpitude—**Breaking and entering or unlawful entry** when no intent, *Matter of M-*, 2 I&N Dec. 721 (AG 1946), *Matter of G-*, 1 I&N Dec. 403 (BIA 1943), *but see Matter of Moore*, 13 I&N Dec. 711 (BIA 1971) [CIMT where intent to commit larceny is an element], *Tahir v. Lehmann.* 171 F.Supp. 589 (N.D. Ohio 1958), *aff'd,* 264 F.2d 892 (6th Cir.), *cert. denied,* 366 U.S. 905 (1961). **Burglary**, *Wala v. Mukasey,* 511 F.3d 102 (2d Cir. 2007) [third degree burglary under Conn. General Statute §53a-103 was not a CIMT because burglary with intent to commit larceny is not a CIMT where there was no intent to deprive the victim permanently of his property and under the modified categorical approach the petitioner did not plead to facts that constitute intent to deprive permanently]; *Cuevas-Gaspar v. Gonzales,* 430 F.3d 1013 (9th Cir. 2005) [finding that accomplice to residential burglary under Wash. Rev. Code §§9A.52.025(1) and 9A.08.020(3) was not a CIMT under categorical approach because one could be convicted without intent; however court found under modified categorical approach that it was a CIMT]; **Burglary (possession of tools to commit)** *Guarino v. Uhl,* 107 F.2d 399 (2d Cir. 1939), *Matter of S-,* 6 I&N Dec. 769 (BIA

1955); **Entry of goods by means of a false statement**, *Notash v. Gonzales,* 427 F.3d 693, 696–700 (9th Cir. 2005) [finding that a conviction for attempted entry of goods by means of a false statement in violation of 18 U.S.C. §542 is not a CIMT under the categorical approach and ICE failed to prove under the modified categorical approach that respondent was convicted under section 2 of the statute]; **Malicious destruction of property**, *Matter of M-,* 2 I&N Dec. 686 (BIA 1946), *Matter of C-,* 2 I&N Dec. 716 (BIA 1947), *Matter of B-,* 2 I&N Dec. 867 (BIA 1947); *but see Matter of M-*, 3 I&N Dec. 272 (BIA 1948); **Malicious mischief**, *Rodriguez-Herrera v. INS,* 52 F.3d 238 (9th Cir. 1995), *Matter of N-,* 8 I&N Dec. 466 (BIA 1956); **Passing bad checks** where intent is not a necessary element, *Matter of Zangwill*, 18 I&N Dec. 22, 28 (BIA 1981); *Matter of Balao*, 20 I&N Dec. 440 (BIA 1992) [passing a bad check], *Matter of Stasinski*, 11 I&N Dec. 202 (BIA 1965), *Matter of Bailie*, 10 I&N Dec. 679 (BIA 1964); *but see Matter of Khalik*, 17 I&N Dec. 518 (BIA 1980) [where intent is necessary element then the crime is of moral turpitude]; *Matter of Westman*, 17 I&N Dec. 50 (BIA 1979), *Matter of F*, 6 I&N Dec. 783 (BIA 1955), *Matter of Bart*, 20 I&N Dec. 436 (BIA 1992) [issuing a bad check]; **Possession of stolen property** where guilty knowledge not essential, *Matter of K-*, 2 I&N Dec. 90 (BIA 1944); **Joyriding**, *Matter of M-,* 2 I&N Dec. 686 (BIA 1946); **Rioting**, *Matter of O-,* 4 I&N Dec. 301 (BIA 1951); **Theft of services**, *Matter of G-,* 2 I&N Dec. 235 (BIA 1945); **Unauthorized use of a vehicle** under Tex. law, *Ramirez v. Ashcroft,* 361 F.Supp.2d 650, 657–59 (S.D. Tex. 2005).

(4) Crimes against government

(a) **Generally**. The Board has held that: "A crime that impairs and obstructs a function of a department of government by defeating its efficiency or destroying the value of its lawful operations by deceit, graft, trickery, or dishonest means is a crime involving moral turpitude." *Matter of Tejwani,* 24 I&N Dec. 97, 98 (BIA 2007) [quoting Board decisions in *Matter of Jurado,* 24 I&N Dec. 29, 35 (BIA 2006) and *Matter of Flores,* 17 I&N Dec. 225, 229 (BIA 1980 and finding that N.Y. Penal L. 470.10(1) involving money laundering is a CIMT]. It has also held that "[a]ffirmative acts to conceal criminal activity and impede law enforcement have been found to be crimes involving moral turpitude." *Id.* [citing *Matter of Robles,* 24 I&N Dec. 22, 25–26 (BIA 2006).

(b) Involving moral turpitude—**Bribery**, *Sollazzo v. Esperdy,* 285 F.2d 341 (2d Cir.), *cert. denied*, 366 U.S. 905 (1961); *Matter of H-,* 6 I&N Dec. 358 (BIA 1954); *Matter of V-,* 4 I&N Dec. 100 (BIA 1950) [attempted bribery], *Matter of Alarcon,* 20 I&N Dec. 557 (BIA 1992) [kickbacks on government contracts]. **Counterfeiting**, *Lozano-Giron v. INS,* 506 F.2d 1073 (7th Cir. 1974), *Matter of P-,* 6 I&N Dec. 795 (BIA 1955), *Matter of Lethbridge,* 11 I&N Dec. 444 (BIA 1965) [possession of counterfeit securities], *Matter of Fernandez,* 14 I&N Dec. 24 (BIA 1972) [transportation of forged securities]. **Driver's license**, *Montero-Ubri v. INS,* 229 F.3d 319 (1st Cir. 2000) [use of fraudulent license]; *Matter of Serna,* 20 I&N Dec. 579 (BIA 1992) [same]; *Zaitona v. INS,* 9 F.3d 432, 437–38 (6th Cir. 1993) [false statement to obtain license]. **False statements** on passport applications, *Rodriguez v. Gonzales,* 451 F.3d 60 (2d Cir. 2006) [making a false statement on a passport application under 18 U.S.C. §1542]; *Bisaillon v. Hogan,* 257 F.2d 435 (9th Cir.), *cert. den.* 358 U.S. 872 (1958), *Matter of Correa-Garces,* 20 I&N Dec. 451, 454 (BIA 1992)], on firearms applications [*Matter of Acosta,* 14 I&N Dec. 338 (BIA 1973)], to government authorities [*Matter of Jurado,* 24 I&N Dec. 29, 34–35 (BIA 2007) unsworn falsification to authorities under Title 18, section 4904(a) of the Pennsylvania Consolidated Statutes is a CIMT because it requires the intent to mislead a government official and a false statement, even if not material, that impairs or obstructs a function of government], under 18 U.S.C. §1546 (document fraud), *Calvo-Ahumada v. Rinaldi,* 435 F.2d 544 (3d Cir. 1970) and false representations regarding SSNs, *Matter of Adetiba,* 20 I&N Dec. 506 (BIA 1992); *but see Beltran-Tirado v. INS,* 213 F.3d 1179, 1183–85 (9th Cir. 2000) [using false Social Security card not CIMT]. **Fleeing (aggravated) a police officer**, *Mel v. Ashcroft,* 393 F.3d 737 (7th Cir. 2004) [aggravated fleeing from police officer in violation of Ill. statute 625 ILCS 5/11-204.1(a)(1)]. **Harboring a fugitive**, *Matter of Sloan,* 12 I&N Dec. 840 (AG 1968). **Immigration fraud** under 18 U.S.C. §1546, *Omagah v. Ashcroft,* 288 F.3d 254 (5th Cir. 2002) [conviction under 18 U.S.C. §371 for conspiracy to possess illegal immigration documents with the intent to defraud the government]; *Matter of Serna,* 20 I&N Dec. 579 (BIA 1992) [possession of document with knowledge that it was altered]. Impersonating a federal officer], *Matter of B-,* 3 I&N Dec. 270 (BIA 1948). **Mail (possession of stolen mail)**, *Okoroha v. INS,* 715 F.2d 380 (8th Cir. 1983). **Mail fraud**, *Nason v. INS,* 394 F.2d 223 (2d Cir. 1968), *cert. denied,* 393 U.S. 830 (1968), *Matter of Alarcon,* 20 I&N Dec. 557 (BIA 1992). **Money laundering**, *Smalley v. Ashcroft,* 354 F.3d 332, 335–40 (5th Cir. 2003) [conviction for Interstate Travel in Aid of a Racketeering Enterprise in violation of 18 U.S.C. §1952 to facilitate an unlawful activity namely money laundering in violation of 18 U.S.C. §1956(a)(3)(B)]; *Matter of Tejwani,* 24 I&N Dec. 97 (BIA 2007) [money laundering under N.Y. Penal L. 470.10(1) involving the intentional use of monetary instruments to conceal or disguise proceeds of any crime]. **Naturalization, unlawful procurement.** *Amouzadeh v. Winfrey,* 467 F.3d 451, 455 (5th Cir. 2006) [conviction for 8 U.S.C. §1425(a) for unlawful procurement of naturalization, because it requires proof of a culpable mind is a CIMT]; **Obstruction of justice**, *Padilla v. Gonzales,* 397 F.3d 1016, 1019–21 (7th Cir. 2005) [obstruction of justice under 720 Ill. Comp. Stat. 5/31-4(a) for knowingly furnishing false information with intent to prevent the apprehension or obstruct the prosecution or defense of any person]. **Pell Grant fraud**, *Izedonmwen v. INS*, 37 F.3d 416 (8th Cir. 1994). **Perjury**, *Matter of W-,* 5 I&N Dec. 759 (BIA 1954); *Matter of B-,* 5 I&N Dec. 405 (BIA 1953); *Matter of P-,* 4 I&N Dec. 373 (BIA 1951); *Matter of H-,* 1 I&N Dec. 581 (BIA 1943); *but see Matter of L-,* 1 I&N Dec. 324 (BIA 1942) [perjury under Canadian statute not CIMT]. **Social Security Misuse,** *Hyder v. Keisler,* 506 F.3d 388 (5th Cir. 2007) [misusing a Social Security number obtained by fraud in violation of 42 U.S.C. §408(a)(7)(A)]; *but see Beltran-Tirado v. INS,* 213 F.3d 1179 (9th Cir. 2000) [falsely representing a Social Security number in violation of 42 U.S.C. §408(g)(2) now recodified at §408(a)(7)(B) is not a CIMT]; **Stolen bus transfers**, *Michel v. INS,* 206 F.3d 253, 261–66 (2d Cir. 2000) [possession of stolen bus transfers is a CIMT where knowledge that property was stolen is an element]; **Tax evasion**, *Carty v. Ashcroft,* 395 F.3d 1081 (9th Cir. 2005) [intent to evade taxes under Cal. Rev. & Tax Code §19406 is CIMT because intent to defraud is implicit in the statute]; *Wittgenstein v. INS*, 124 F.3d 1244, 1246 (10th Cir. 1997) [willful tax evasion under state law]; *Khan v. Barber*, 253 F.2d 547 (9th Cir. 1958), *cert. denied*, 357 U.S. 920 (1958); *but see U.S. v. Carollo*, 30 F.Supp. 30 (D. Mo. 1939). **Transport (Unlawful)**, *Fuentes-Cruz v. Gonzales,* 489 F.3d 724 (5th Cir. 2007) [Texas Penal Code Sec. 20.05 is CIMT because it requires unlawful transportation for pecuniary gain in a manner designed to conceal the person from local, state, or federal law enforcement]. **Turnstile jumping** (going into subway without paying) *Santos-Gonzalez v. Reno,* 93 F.Supp.2d 286, 288 n.3 (E.D. N.Y. 2000); **Welfare fraud**, *Miller v. INS*, 762 F.2d 21 (3d Cir. 1985), *U.S. v. Concepcion*, 795 F.Supp. 1262, 1274–75 (E.D.N.Y. 1992) [theft and conversion of U.S. funds by obtaining welfare benefits fraudulently].

(c) Not involving moral turpitude—**Alien smuggling** under 8 U.S.C. §1324(a), *U.S. v. Sucki*, 748 F.Supp. 66 (E.D.N.Y. 1990), *Matter of Tiwari*, 19 I&N Dec. 875 (BIA 1989), *but see U.S. v. Raghunandan*, 587 F.Supp. 423 (S.D.N.Y. 1984). **Conspiracy to commit offenses against U.S.**, *Hirsch v. INS*, 308 F.2d 562 (9th Cir. 1962). **Contempt of Congress**, *Matter of P-,* 6 I&N Dec. 400 (BIA 1954). **False attestation on I-9**, *Beltran-Tirado v. INS*, 213 F.3d 1179, 1183–85 (9th Cir. 2000). **False identification to a police officer,** *Blanco v. Mukasey,* 518 F.3d 714, 718–20 (9th Cir. 2008) [Cal. Penal Code §148.9(a) is not categorically a CIMT because it does not require fraudulent intent]; **False statements** not amounting to perjury, *Matter of S,* 2 I&N Dec. 353 (BIA 1945), false Social Security card, *Beltran-Tirado v. INS,* 213 F.3d 1179, 1183–85 (9th Cir. 2000).; false statement under 18 U.S.C. §1001, *U.S. v. Hirsch*, 308 F.2d 562 (9th Cir. 1962), *Matter of G,* 8 I&N Dec. 315 (BIA 1959),

Matter of Marchena, 12 I&N Dec. 355 (BIA 1967); *Matter of Expinoza,* 10 I&N Dec. 98 (BIA 1962); *Matter of B-M-*, 6 I&N Dec. 806 (BIA 1955), *but see Omagah v. Ashcroft,* 288 F.3d 254 (5th Cir. 2002); *Kabongo v. INS*, 837 F.2d 753, 758 (6th Cir. 1988). **Military crimes**, desertion, *Matter of S-B-*, 4 I&N Dec. 682 (BIA 1952); failure to report for induction, *Matter of S*, 5 I&N Dec. 425 (BIA 1953), *but see Matter of R,* 5 I&N Dec. 29 (AG 1952). **Money laundering** (structuring financial transactions to avoid currency reporting under 31 U.S.C. §5324(a)(3)), *Goldeshtein v. INS*, 8 F.3d 645 (9th Cir. 1993); *Matter of L-V-C,* 22 I&N Dec. 594 (BIA 1999) [reversing *Matter of Goldeshtein*] *but see Smalley v. Ashcroft,* 354 F.3d 332, 335–40 (5th Cir. 2003) [conviction for Interstate Travel in Aid of a Racketeering Enterprise in violation of 18 U.S.C. §1952 to facilitate an unlawful activity namely money laundering in violation of 18 U.S.C. §1956(a)(3)(B)]; *Matter of Tejwani,* 24 I&N Dec. 97 (BIA 2007) [money laundering under N.Y. Penal L. 470.10(1) involving the intentional use of monetary instruments to conceal or disguise proceeds of any crime]. **Re-entry after deportation**, *Rodriguez v. Campbell,* 8 F.2d 983 (5th Cir. 1925); **Social Security Misuse,** *Beltran-Tirado v. INS,* 213 F.3d 1179 (9th Cir. 2000) [falsely representing a Social Security number in violation of 42 U.S.C. §408(g)(2) (now recodified at §408(a)(7)(B)) is not a CIMT]; *but see Hyder v. Keisler,* 506 F.3d 388 (5th Cir. 2007) [misusing a Social Security number obtained by fraud in violation of 42 U.S.C. §408(a)(7)(A)].

(5) Crimes Involving fraud—Any crime involving fraud is almost always a crime of moral turpitude, *see, e.g., Jordan v. DeGeorge,* 341 U.S. 223, 227–32 (1951); *Matter of Adetiba,* 20 I&N Dec. 506 (BIA 1992), whether against the government or individuals, except for false statements not amounting to perjury. However, a person may be deported even if the statute does not require an intent to defraud. *Matter of Kochlani,* 24 I&N Dec. 128, 129–31 (BIA 2007) [trafficking in counterfeit goods under 18 U.S.C. §2320 is a CIMT even if intent to defraud is not an element]. *But see also Navarro-Lopez v. Gonzales,* 503 F.3d 1063, 1069 (9th Cir. 2007) (*en banc*) (concurrence Pregerson) [in the context of finding that an accessory after the fact under Cal. Penal Code §32 is not a CIMT, Judge Pregerson noted that not all fraud crimes may be CIMTs because they may not be base, vile or depraved *and* contrary to accepted rules of morality such as the person who forges a welfare check to feed her children; the majority of the court disagreed *see* Reinhardt, J concurring].

(6) Misprision of Felony—At least one circuit has found that misprision of felony constitutes a crime of moral turpitude. *Itani v. Ashcroft,* 298 F.3d 1213 (11th Cir. 2002) [misprision of felony is CIMT where it arose in connection with a scheme to rent automobiles, report them stolen to local police, and export them to Kuwait]. The BIA now agrees. *Matter of Robles,* 24 I&N Dec. 22, 25–27 (BIA 2006) [overruling *Matter of Sloan* and finding that misprision of a felony in violation of 18 U.S.C. §4 is a CIMT].

(7) Accessory After the Fact—One circuit has found that accessory after the fact is not a CIMT. *Navarro-Lopez v. Gonzales,* 503 F.3d 1063 (9th Cir. 2007) (*en banc*) [nothing in Cal. Penal Code §32 under the categorical or modified categorical approach inherently makes accessory after the fact a CIMT].

(8) Violations of regulatory laws—Violations of regulatory laws generally are not CIMTs. *Plasencia-Ayala v. Mukasey,* 516 F.3d 738, 746–49 (9th Cir. 2008) [failure to register as a sex offender under Nev. Rev. Stat. §179D.550 is a strict liability, regulatory crime and it does not involve a level of depravity or baseness contrary to moral law]; *Goldeshtein v. INS*, 8 F.3d 645 (9th Cir. 1993) [structuring deposits to avoid reporting requirements under 31 U.S.C. §5324(a)(3) is not a CIMT]; *Matter of L-V-C-,* 22 I&N Dec. 594 (BIA 1999) [adopting *Goldeshtein* nationwide]; *U.S. v. Gloria,* 494 F.2d 477 (5th Cir.), *cert. denied,* 419 U.S. 955 (1974) [illegal re-entry not CIMT]; *Matter of G*, 1 I&N Dec. 73 (BIA 1941) [immigration laws]; *Rodriguez v. Campbell,* 8 F.2d 983 (5th Cir. 1925) [re-entry after deportation], *Matter of Gaglioti,* 10 I&N Dec. 719 (BIA 1964) [gambling not CIMT]. *Matter of Lopez-Meza,* 22 I&N Dec. 1188 (BIA 1999) [simple DUI is *not* a CIMT, but aggravated DUI is a CIMT].

(9) Drug Offenses—Generally, possessory offenses are not CIMTs. *Matter of Abreu-Semino*, 12 I&N Dec. 775 (BIA 1968) [possession of LSD not CIMT]. However, BIA has determined that possession with intent to distribute cocaine, where knowledge or intent is an element, is a CIMT. *Matter of Khourn*, 21 I&N Dec. 1041 (BIA 1997). The Second Circuit has held that solicitation to possess at least 4 pounds of marijuana for sale in violation of Ariz. Rev. Stat. §13-1002(A) & (B)(2) and §13-3405(A)(2) & (B)(6) is a CIMT. *Barragan-Lopez v. Mukasey,* 508 F.3d 899 (9th Cir. 2007).

(10) Weapons offenses

(a) Involving moral turpitude—Use of weapons in the course of other crimes may indicate moral turpitude, *Matter of Logan*, 17 I&N Dec. 367 (BIA 1980).

(b) Not involving moral turpitude—Carrying concealed weapon. *Matter of Granados*, 16 I&N Dec. 726 (BIA 1979). *But see Matter of S-*, 8 I&N Dec. 344 (BIA 1959).

2. *Drug Offenses*—INA §212(a)(2)(A)(i)(II), 8 U.S.C. §1182(a)(2)(A)(i)(II)

2.a. Persons who have been convicted, *or who admit* having committed, or who admit committing acts that constitute the essential elements of a violation of or conspiracy to violate any law or regulation of a state, the U.S., or a foreign country relating to a controlled substance as defined in 21 U.S.C. §802. 8 U.S.C. §1182(a)(2)(A)(i)(II). This includes an attempt or conspiracy to commit the crimes. This section also includes any drug listed in 21 U.S.C. §§802(23) and 812 and any drug designated by the AG in accordance with 21 U.S.C. §811. The list of designated drugs are found at Schedules I through V in 21 C.F.R. §1308.1. *See* Anti-Drug Abuse Act of 1986, PL 99-570, subtitle M; 8 C.F.R. §§212.11, 1212.11. Congress intended to expand the kinds of drugs under the Act. *Matter of Hernandez-Ponce*, 19 I&N Dec. 613 (BIA 1988) [BIA found language broad enough to include conviction for use of a drug (PCP) as sufficient], and to expand it to include virtually any drug related conviction. *Matter of Esqueda*, 20 I&N Dec. 850 (BIA 1994). But the crime must still be a violation of a law relating to a controlled substance under the appropriate law. *Argaw v. Ashcroft,* 395 F.3d 521 (4th Cir. 2005) [where "khat," a traditional herbal stimulant widely used in East Africa and the lower Arabian peninsula, is not listed as a controlled substance under 21 U.S.C. §812, 21 C.F.R. §1308.11-15, and it was not chemically analyzed to determine if its consistent elements, which may be on the list, contained a controlled substance, it cannot be a ground of inadmissibility as an admission or for "reason to believe"]; *Leyva-Licea v. INS,* 187 F.3d 1147 (9th Cir. 1999) [following *Coronado-Durazo*, solicitation to possess marijuana for sale is not a conviction under Controlled Substances Act]. *But see Al-Najar v. Mukasey,* 515 F.3d 708, 715 (6th Cir. 2008) [guilty plea where respondent possessed Khat which was not listed as a controlled substance under the CSA was, nevertheless, a drug conviction because respondent pleaded guilty to possession of a controlled substance in violation of Mich. Comp. Laws §333.7411 and therefore admitted that he possessed a controlled substance]; *Mizrahi v. Gonzales,* 492 F.3d 156 (2d Cir. 2007) [guilty plea to a misdemeanor fourth-degree criminal solicitation of the sale of drugs under N.Y. Penal Law §100.05(1) is a law relating to a controlled substance under 8 U.S.C. §1182(a)(2)(A)(i)(II)]; *Peters v. Ashcroft,* 383 F.3d 302 (5th Cir. 2004) [felony solicitation to transport marijuana for sale under Ariz. Rev. Stat. §13-1002 is a drug crime]. The petty offense exception under INA §212(a)(2)(A)(ii) does not appear to apply to waive petty drug offenses. This is consistent with DOS policy. Correspondence in March–May 1989 of Odom, Chief of Advisory Opinions, DOS, *reprinted in* 66 No. 36 *Interpreter Releases* 1042–43, 1052–55 (Sept. 18, 1989). However, DOS recognizes that a person shall not be ineligible for a visa based upon an admission or conviction relating to simple possession or use of a controlled substance, "if the acts ... occurred while the alien was under the age of eighteen." 9 FAM 40.21(b) N.2.1.

2.b. Drug Paraphernalia—*Alvarez Acosta v. U.S. Att'y Gen.,* ___ F.3d ___, 2008 WL 1733208 (11th Cir. Apr. 16, 2008) [conviction for drug paraphernalia is a crime relating to a controlled substance under INA §212(a)(2)(A)(i)(II)]; *Escobar Barraza v. Mukasey,* 519 F.3d 388 (7th Cir. 2008) [in removal proceeding regarding inadmissibility, the court rejected the argument that drug paraphernalia is not banned under 21 USC §863, but also held that in certain cases an INA §212(h) waiver would apply to drug paraphernalia]; *Luu-Le v. INS*, 224 F.3d 911 (9th

Cir. 2000) [possession of drug paraphernalia under §13-3415 of Ariz. Crim. Code is a drug conviction].

2.c. Admissions—A foreign conviction under this statute must include the requisite intent necessary for a criminal conviction. *Lennon v. INS*, 527 F.2d 187 (2d Cir. 1975). However, specific intent or *mens rea* is no longer required for a U.S. conviction given the broadening of the statute. *Matter of Esqueda, supra*. Under the Anti-Drug Abuse Act of 1986, the drugs included as controlled substances are expressly made retroactive, but affect only those persons who made an entry after the date of the Act. For a person to be inadmissible, the drug must be listed as a controlled substance on federal schedules. *See Matter of Paulus*, 11 I&N Dec. 274 (BIA 1965).

In *Matter of K,* 7 I&N Dec. 594, 598 (BIA 1957) the BIA adopted a 3-part test for the acceptance of an admission as a ground of inadmissibility: (1) the admitted conduct must constitute the essential elements of the crime; (2) the applicant must have been provided with a definition and the essential elements of the offense prior to his admission; and (3) the admission must be voluntary. The applicant must also admit all facts constituting the crime. *Matter of E-N-,* 7 I&N Dec. 153 (1956). *See also* 22 C.F.R. §40.21(a)(1); *Matter of G,* 1 I&N Dec. 225 (BIA 1942) [admission must be voluntary]; *Matter of C-,* 1 I&N Dec. 14 (BIA 1941); *Pazcoguin v. Radcliffe,* 292 F.3d 1209 (9th Cir. 2002) [beneficiary's admission to medical doctor during medical examination for IV in Philippines that he smoked marijuana for a number of years was used as the basis to deny visa upon entry to U.S. and to thereafter exclude him]. *See also* IFM at 17.17(a) ["An alien must admit violating a specific controlled substance statute, with reference to the specific statute and to the factual elements that would have to be proved to establish a conviction for the offense"].

At least one court has suggested that a person whose conviction is expunged under the Federal First Offender Act or its equivalent (including a foreign expungement) cannot be inadmissible for admitting facts that constitute a drug crime. *Dillingham v. INS,* 267 F.3d 996 (9th Cir. 2001) [finding that the BIA's decision to refuse to recognize a foreign expungement for first time offenders under the UK's Rehabilitation of Offenders Act of 1974 violated equal protection]. *But see Danso v. Gonzales,* 489 F.3d 709 (5th Cir. 2007) [finding no equal protection violation in the BIA's refusal to equate a "spent" drug conviction under UK law that automatically expunges a conviction after a number of years with the Federal First Offender Act and questioning whether the FFOA survived the statutory definition of conviction under 8 U.S.C. §1101(a)(48)(A)].

Legacy INS also adopted the view that an Agreement to Pay Monetary Penalty to Customs, where a person has a controlled substance in his possession at the time of his customs' inspection, is *not* considered an admission and the "Service may not seek an alien's exclusion as an alien who has admitted a controlled substance violation," based solely on the signed agreement to pay. Legal Memo, Aleinikoff, G.C. Op. No. 95-4, HQ 235-P (Jan. 20, 1995), *reprinted in* 1995 WL 1796311.

2.d. A related inadmissibility ground also includes a person that the U.S. knows or has reason to believe is a trafficker in any controlled substance or knows or has reason to believe is or has been a knowing assister, abettor, conspirator, or colluder with others in the illicit trafficking in any controlled substance as defined in 21 U.S.C. §802. INA §212(a)(2)(C)(i), 8 U.S.C. §1182(a)(2)(C)(i); 9 FAM 40.23 N.1-2. A conviction is unnecessary if DHS relies upon the part of the statute concerning "reason to believe" that the person is a trafficker. *Matter of Rico*, 16 I&N Dec. 181 (BIA 1977). Moreover, a vacation of a conviction in the view of some courts does not bar the use of the underlying facts to deny admission as a trafficker under this section. *Castano v. INS*, 956 F.2d 236 (11th Cir. 1992) [expungement under Federal Youth Corrections Act only bars the use of the conviction to deny admission, not the use of the underlying facts]; *Nunez-Payan v. INS*, 815 F.2d 384 (5th Cir. 1987) [where Texas deferred adjudication statute doesn't result in conviction, the plea can be used as admission to exclude]; *Matter of Faveloa,* 16 I&N Dec. 753, 755–57 (BIA 1979). However, a deportation charge based on inadmissibility at time of entry will not be sustained unless the "reason to believe" existed at the time of entry. *Matter of Rocha*, 20 I&N Dec. 944 (BIA 1995). The determination must be based on reasonable, substantial and probative evidence. *Alarcon-Serrano v. INS*, 220 F.3d 1116, 1119 (9th Cir. 2000) [affirming exclusion on reason to believe charge]. The respondent has a right to present evidence rebutting the charge. *Pronsivakulchai v. Gonzales,* 461 F.3d 903 (7th Cir. 2006) [reversed IJ's finding that respondent was ineligible for asylum on the grounds that there was reason to believe she had committed a drug trafficking crime in Thailand when she was deprived of the right to present evidence rebutting the government's evidence]. Further, drug trafficking requires remuneration for the sale or distribution of the drugs. *Steele v. Blackman,* 236 F.3d 130 (3d Cir. 2001) [distribution of less than 30 grams of marijuana without remuneration is not a drug trafficking crime]. *See also Matter of Davis,* 20 I&N Dec. 536, 541 (BIA 1992). The "reason to believe" charge in the context of a denial of a NIV may be difficult to challenge. *Bruno v. Albright,* 20 F.Supp.2d 51 (D.D.C. 1998) [no jurisdiction to review decision of consular officer on "reason to believe" grounds, but there may be review of DOS's advisory opinion]. The BIA in another context has equated "reason to believe" with "probable cause." *Matter of U-H-,* 23 I&N Dec. 355, 356 (BIA 2002) [addresses "reasonable ground to believe" that someone is engaged in terrorist activity].

Congress has now also made the spouse, son, or daughter of a person inadmissible for trafficking or assisting traffickers inadmissible if that spouse, son, or daughter, within the past 5 years, has obtained any financial or other benefit from the illicit activity and knew or reasonably should have known that the financial or other benefit was the product of such illicit activity. INA §212(a)(2)(C)(ii), 8 U.S.C. §1182(a)(2)(C)(ii).

2.e. A waiver specific to INA §212(a)(2)(A)(i)(II) is available, but only for simple possession of 30 grams or less of marijuana and under limited circumstances. INA §212(h), 8 U.S.C. §1182(h). The waiver may be limited. *Matter of Moncada,* 24 I&N Dec. 62, 65 & n.4 (BIA 2007) [narrowly interpreting the deportability exception for simple possession of 30 grams or less as not including a conviction for possession of 30 grams or less of marijuana in prison]; *Matter of Martinez-Zapata,* 24 I&N Dec. 424 (BIA 2007) [where conviction was enhanced by virtue of respondent's possession of marijuana in a "drug-free zone" the enhancement was an element of the crime and the conviction was therefore more than a conviction for simple possession of 30 grams of marijuana. Respondent was ineligible for INA §212(h) relief and *Matter of Rodriguez-Cortes*, 20 I&N Dec. 587 (BIA 1992) was superseded for *post-Apprendi* cases]. Cancellation of removal under INA §240A(a), 8 U.S.C. §1229b(a), may also be available for LPRs if the applicant meets the requirements.

2.f. The constitutionality of the reason to believe provision has been upheld. *Rojas-Garcia v. Ashcroft,* 339 F.3d 814, 822–24 (9th Cir. 2003) [rejecting void for vagueness challenge to "reason to believe" standard for someone deemed inadmissible as a drug trafficker and raising, but not deciding, whether a void for vagueness challenge may even be raised in regard to issues of admissibility]; *Correa v. Thornburgh*, 901 F.2d 1166, 1173 (2d Cir. 1990).

3. *Money Laundering*—INA §212(a)(2)(I), 8 U.S.C. §1182(a)(2)(I)

3.a. Alien who a consular officer or the AG knows, or has reason to believe has engaged, is engaging, or seeks to enter the U.S. to engage in an offense that is described in 18 U.S.C. §§1956 or 1957 (relating to laundering of monetary instruments) is inadmissible. The BIA in another context has equated "reason to believe" with "probable cause." *Matter of U-H-,* 23 I&N Dec. 355, 356 (BIA 2002) [addresses "reasonable ground to believe" that someone is engaged in terrorist activity]. At least one circuit has found money laundering to be a CIMT. *Smalley v. Ashcroft,* 354 F.3d 332, 335–40 (5th Cir. 2003) [conviction for Interstate Travel in Aid of a Racketeering Enterprise in violation of 18 U.S.C. §1952 to facilitate an unlawful activity namely money laundering in violation of 18 U.S.C. §1956(a)(3)(B)].

3.b. An alien who the consular officer or AG knows is, or has been a knowing aider, abettor, assister, conspirator, or colluder in regard to money laundering.

4. *Two or More Offenses*—INA §212(a)(2)(B), 8 U.S.C. §1182(a)(2)(B). Alien who has been convicted of 2 or more offenses (other than purely political offenses) whether or not moral turpitude, and whether or not it was a conviction in a single trial or whether the convictions form a single scheme, if the aggregate sentence of confinement actually imposed is 5 years or more, are inadmissible. INA §212(a)(2)(B), 8 U.S.C. §1182(a)(2)(B). To determine what sentence was actually imposed a party must look to what the court did, not how it may have characterized its actions. *Rodrigues v. INS*, 994 F.2d 32 (1st Cir. 1993) [vacated INS determination that person ineligible to adjust under this provision on grounds that the sentencing judge stated the person was sentenced

to 10 years and deemed to have served it by having served 1709 days]; *Matter of Esposito*, 21 I&N Dec. 1 (BIA 1995) [a sentence to confinement where the execution is subsequently suspended *is* a sentence actually imposed for purposes of this section]. Pursuant to INA §101(a)(48)(B) sentence is now defined as including any suspension or withholding of the sentence, including suspension of imposition of the sentence. *Matter of S-S*, 21 I&N Dec. 900 (BIA 1997).

5. *Prostitution*—Prostitutes or persons who have engaged in or sought to engage in prostitution or to procure prostitutes *within the past 10 years* or seek to enter the U.S. to engage in prostitution are inadmissible. INA §§212(a)(2)(D)(i)–(ii), 8 U.S.C. §1182(a)(2)(D)(i)–(ii); 22 C.F.R. §40.24. *Matter of R-M-*, 7 I&N Dec. 392 (BIA 1957); *Matter of C*, 7 I&N Dec. 432 (BIA 1957); *Matter of M*, 7 I&N Dec. 251 (BIA 1956); *Mirabal-Balon v. Esperdy*, 188 F.Supp. 317 (S.D.N.Y. 1960). A person may be barred even if prostitution is not illegal in his or her country. 22 C.F.R. §40.24(c). The BIA has held that to "engage in" prostitution, one must have engaged in a regular pattern of behavior or conduct. *See Matter of T*, 6 I&N Dec. 474 (BIA 1955) [a noncitizen who was twice convicted for committing acts of prostitution was not excludable; *Matter of R*, 2 I&N Dec. 50 (BIA 1944) [single act for gain under circumstances showing prostitution]. The DOS similarly defines prostitution as "engaging in promiscuous sexual intercourse for hire." 22 C.F.R. §40.24(b). Thus, where the statute criminalizes an isolated act that does not necessarily involved sexual intercourse, the person may not be deemed to have committed prostitution under the categorical or modified categorical approach. *Kepilino v. Gonzales*, 454 F.3d 1057 (9th Cir. 2006) [because Hawaii Rev. Stat. §712-1200 regarding prostitution includes conduct broader than engaging in sexual intercourse and because the record does not reveal the acts leading to the conviction, the charge of being inadmissible for prostitution can not be upheld under the categorical or modified categorical approach].

6. *Significant Traffickers in Persons*—INA §212(a)(2)(H), 8 U.S.C. §1182(a)(2)(H). Any foreign person the President publicly lists in a submission to Congress as playing a significant role in a severe form of trafficking in persons (*e.g.*, the use of force, fraud, or coercion for sex trafficking and/or involuntary servitude, peonage, debt bondage, or slavery) or materially assists in, or provides financial/technological support for such trafficking is inadmissible. A person is also inadmissible if a consular officer or the AG knows or has reason to believe that the person is or has been a knowing aider, abettor, assister, conspirator, or colluder with such a trafficker in severe forms of trafficking. The provision also includes the spouse and son or daughter of such a person who within the previous 5 years obtained any financial or other benefit from the illicit activity and knew or should have known that the financial or other benefit was the product of the illicit activity. However, it does not include a son or daughter who at the time s/he received a financial benefit was a child. The BIA in another context has equated "reason to believe" with "probable cause." *Matter of U-H-*, 23 I&N Dec. 355, 356 (BIA 2002) [addresses "reasonable ground to believe" that someone is engaged in terrorist activity].

7. *Diplomats or Others Involved in Serious Criminal Activity Who Have Been Granted Immunity from Prosecution*—INA §212(a)(2)(E), 8 U.S.C. §1182(a)(2)(E).

   7.a. Diplomats who have committed a serious crime as defined in INA §101(h) [any felony, any crime of violence as defined in Sec. 16 of Title 18 USC, or reckless driving/driving under the influence involving personal injury to another], who assert immunity, who depart the U.S., and who have not subsequently submitted fully to the jurisdiction of the U.S. courts.

   7.b. The section as written is not limited to diplomats, but may encompass anyone granted immunity from prosecution.

D. *Inadmissibility on Moral Grounds*

1. Persons coming to the U.S. to *practice* polygamy are excluded. INA §212(a)(10)(A), 8 U.S.C. §1182(a)(10)(A). *Matter of G*, 6 I&N Dec. 9 (BIA 1953). The prior law, excluding persons who had the status of a polygamist or who advocated polygamy, has been eliminated.

2. The former section relating to the exclusion of persons who were coming to the U.S. to engage in any immoral sexual acts, *Matter of B*, 5 I&N Dec. 185 (BIA 1953), has been eliminated.

E. *Violation of INA Laws Regarding Entry or Documentation*

1. Person who has been ordered removed (through expedited removal or through removal proceedings initiated at person's arrival in U.S.) after Apr. 1, 1997, and who seeks admission within 5 years (or 20 years if second or subsequent removal or at any time if convicted of an aggravated felony), unless prior permission has been granted. INA §212(a)(9)(A)(i), 8 U.S.C. §1182(a)(9)(A)(i). *See* 8 C.F.R. §§212.2, 1212.2; 22 C.F.R. §40.91(a).

2. Person who has been ordered removed after a deportation or removal hearing from the U.S. or who departed while an order of removal was outstanding and who seeks admission within 10 years (or within 20 years if it is after a second or subsequent removal or at any time if person convicted of an aggravated felony) from the date of such physical deportation or removal, unless the AG has given his consent for readmission. INA §212(a)(9)(A)(ii), 8 U.S.C. §1182(a)(9)(A)(ii). This provision applies to persons removed under INA §240, deported under former INA §242, excluded under former INA §236 and denied admission under VWPP and ordered removed. Cable, DOS, 98-State-060539 (Apr. 4, 1998) at ¶6, *published on* AILA InfoNet at Doc. No. 98040490. Thus, a person who would have been barred only for only one year because of an order of exclusion or 5 years for an order of deportation is now barred for 10 years. *See also in this chapter* ¶ III.E.4 (p.95), *infra*, for discussion on INA §212(a)(9)(C)(i)(II), which permanently bars (with no waiver available for 10 years) a person who enters without being admitted or attempts to enter without being admitted after being ordered removed.

   INA §212(a)(9)(A) applies only if the person has physically departed the U.S. or been physically removed subsequent to the issuance of an order. Memo, Crocetti, Assoc. Comm. INS, HQ 5015.12, 96 Act .034 (May 1, 1997), *reprinted in* 74 No. 18 *Interpreter Releases* 781, 791–94, 792 (May 12, 1997). The legislative history supports this view as it views the waiver as applying to persons "reapplying for admission." H.R. Conf. Rep. No. 828, 104th Cong., 2d Sess. at 207. Also the waiver language applies to persons re-embarking to a place outside the U.S. Nevertheless, the BIA has granted permission to reapply after the fact (*nunc pro tunc*), where to do so would resolve the case. *See Matter of Ducret*, 15 I&N Dec. 620 (BIA 1976); *Matter of Garcia Linares,* 21 I&N Dec. 254 (BIA 1996).

   I-212 Waiver for Reapplication for Admission—A person who is barred from admission under INA §§212(a)(9)(A)(i) or (ii) may apply for readmission prior to the period of inadmissibility by seeking an I-212 waiver. For procedures regarding application for a waiver (I-212), *see* 8 C.F.R. §§212.2, 1212.2 (if no waiver must prove out of U.S. for requisite time). I-212 regulations upheld. *Valdez-Gaona v. INS*, 817 F.2d 1164 (5th Cir. 1987); *Estrada-Figueroa v. Nelson*, 611 F.Supp. 576 (S.D. Cal. 1985). *See also Matter of Li*, 15 I&N Dec. 514 (BIA 1975); *Matter of Bunag*, 13 I&N Dec. 103 (D.D. 1967). In a limited number of circumstances, a person may apply for an I-212 waiver in adjustment proceeding or before the IJ. 8 C.F.R. §212.2(e); *Lopez-Flores v. DHS,* 376 F.3d 793, 795 n.2 (8th Cir. 2004). However, an I-212 waiver may not be applied to cure INA §212(a)(9)(C)(i)(II) unless the person is outside the U.S. for 10 years and applies outside the U.S. Thus, as a practical matter the waiver cannot be filed in the U.S. even to waive §§212(a)(9)(A)(i) or (ii) if the person re-enters EWI because s/he would be subject to the bar under §212(a)((9)(C)(i)(II) and that provision may not be waived without being outside the U.S. for 10 years and applying for the waiver outside of the U.S. *Matter of Torres-Garcia,* 23 I&N Dec. 866 (BIA 2006) [an I-212 waiver cannot retroactively waive inadmissibility under INA §212(a)(9)(C)(i)(II) because the applicant cannot seek admission under that section for 10 years after the date of his last departure from the U.S.; *Disagreed with Perez-Gonzalez*]; *Matter of Briones,* 24 I&N Dec. 355 (BIA 2007) [INA §245(i) adjustment is unavailable to someone who is subject to INA §212(a)(9)(C)(i)(I)]; *Ramirez-Canales v. Mukasey,* 517 F.3d 904, 907–10 (6th Cir. 2008 [followed *Briones* under *Chevron* but remanded for potential *nunc pro tunc* relief]; *Delgado v. Mukasey,* 516 F.3d 65 (2d Cir. 2008) [same, agreeing with *Torres-Garcia* and *Gonzales*]; *Gonzales v. DHS,* 508 F.3d 1227, 1234–42 (9th Cir. 2007) [reversed its prior decision in *Perez-Gonzales v. Ashcroft,* 379 F.3d 783 (9th Cir. 2004) and upheld on *Chevron* deference under *National Cable & Telecommunications Ass'n v. Brand X*, 545 U.S. 967 (2005) the BIA's decision in *Matter of Torres-Garcia*]; *Mortera-Cruz v. Gonzales,* 409 F.3d 246 (5th Cir. 2005) [*Chevron* deference granted to BIA's determination that a person inadmissible under INA §212(a)(9)(C)(i) may not adjust under INA §245(i)]; *Berrum-Garcia v. Comfort,* 390 F.3d 1158, 1166–68 (10th Cir. 2004) [applicant for §245(i) adjustment who re-enters after removal/deportation is *not* eligible to waive INA §212(a)(9)(C)(i)(II) with an I-212 without returning to his home country for 10 years. Disagreed with *Perez-Gonzalez*]. However, Congress indicated that at least as to persons covered under VAWA of 1994, U and T visas and battered persons eligible for the special provisions in cancellation or suspension, DHS, DOS, and the AG "should particularly consider exercising their authority" for reapplication for admission. Section 813(b) of the Violence Against Women and Department of Justice Reauthorization Act of 1005, PL 109-162, 119 Stat. 2960 (Jan. 5, 2006). Also Congress expressly provided for a waiver of INA §212(a)(9)(C)(i) for VAWA petitioners under INA §212(a)(9)(C)(iii). A person who is inadmissible under §212(a)(9)(A) and reenters may also be precluded from seeking any relief in light of INA §241(a)(5). *Fernandez-Vargas v. Gonzales,* 126 S.Ct. 2422, 2432–33 (2006) [found that INA §241(a)(5)—the provision regarding reentry after removal—retroactively bars relief; however the court did not decide whether the provision retroactivity bars relief with respect to persons who applied for relief and a waiver *before* the effective date of IIRIRA (Apr. 1, 1997)]; *Warner v. Ashcroft,* 381 F.3d 534, 539–40 (6th Cir. 2004) [found that INA §245(i) "has no effect upon §241(a)(5)'s preclusion of relief" and therefore no relief is available]; *Flores v. Ashcroft,* 354 F.3d 727, 730–31 (8th Cir. 2003) [reinstatement provision bars adjustment except in limited circumstances for persons seeking relief under NACARA or HRIFA]; *Padilla v. Ashcroft,* 334 F.3d 921 (9th Cir. 2003) [pending INA §245(i) application does not trump the reinstatement provision that bars relief].

In *Matter of Lee*, 17 I&N Dec. 275 (Comm. 1978), legacy INS established the criteria to be applied by the AG to determine readmission for the I-212 waiver. They include (a) moral character; (b) recency of deportation; (c) need for the applicant's services in the U.S.; (d) applicant's contention that s/he did not know s/he was deported; and (e) length of time applicant had been in the U.S. *See also Garay v. INS*, 620 F.Supp. 11 (N.D. Cal. 1985) [where alien had re-entered without inspection, existence of LPR wife insufficient to find AG abused his discretion in denying application]; *Jaimez-Revolla v. Bell*, 598 F.2d 243 (D.C. Cir. 1979) [upheld denial for alien who committed a series of INS violations including re-entry without permission]; *Matter of Tin,* 14 I&N Dec. 371 (Reg. Comm. 1973); AFM at 43.2. *But see Matter of* ___ (AAO Mar. 20, 2003), *reported in* 80 No. 32 *Interpreter Releases* 1165–67 (Aug. 14, 2003) [questioning whether *Lee* and *Tin* are still good law in light of various INA amendments including IIRIRA where persons who violate immigration laws are viewed unfavorably]. The waiver is written as an exception to the provisions. INA §212(a)(9)(A)(iii), 8 U.S.C. §1182(a)(9)(A)(iii).

3. *Persons Unlawfully Present in the U.S.*—INA §212(a)(9)(B), 8 U.S.C. §1182(a)(9)(B), 22 C.F.R. §40.92.

3.a. Beginning Apr. 1, 1997, a person who is unlawfully present in the U.S. for a period of more than 180 consecutive days but less than one year who voluntarily departs the U.S. *before* commencement of proceedings is barred from readmission for 3 years from the date of the person's departure or removal. INA §212(a)(9)(B)(i)(I), 8 U.S.C. §1182(a)(9)(B)(i)(I). Thus, if a person departs after or at the conclusion of commencement of proceedings (*e.g.,* issuance of an I-862) she is not subject to the 3-year bar. If a person is granted voluntary departure (VD) *after* proceedings are initiated s/he is *not* subject to 3-year bar. Cable, DOS, 98-State-060539 at ¶¶17–19 (Apr. 4, 1998), *published on* AILA InfoNet at Doc. No. 98040490. The distinction that allows persons to escape the 3-year bar but not the 10-year bar if they are granted VD after proceedings has been upheld. *Cervantes-Ascencio v. INS,* 326 F.3d 83, 85–86 (2d Cir. 2003) [statute making exception is clear on its face and agency interpretation of statute is reasonable under *Chevron*].

3.b. Beginning Apr. 1, 1997, a person who has been unlawfully present in the U.S. for one year or more consecutively and again seeks admission is barred for 10 years from the date of such person's departure or removal from the U.S. INA §212(a)(9)(B)(i)(II), 8 U.S.C. §1182(a)(9)(B)(i)(II). Note, the legislative history clearly provides that departure is necessary to trigger the effects of this section. H.R. Conf. Rep. 104-828, 104th Cong. 2d Sess. at 207. Consistent with the legislative history, DHS has also adopted the position that the statute requires departure to be effective because the bar only applies when someone is seeking admission which by definition must be from outside the U.S. Memo, Crocetti, (May 1, 1997) *supra. See also Matter of Rodarte,* 23 I&N Dec. 905 (BIA 2006) [departure triggers bar because purpose of statute is to punish recidivists and IJ erred in determining that one year of unlawful presence can bar adjustment of status even if person had not departed]. However, the departure need not be by a removal order or a grant of VD to trigger the provision. *Matter of Lemus,* 24 I&N Dec. 373, 376–77 (BIA 2007). Under one theory the section does not apply to AOS because admission is expressly defined in the statute as a lawful entry and traditionally AOS has not been considered to be a new entry. *But see Matter of Rodarte,* 23 I&N Dec. 905, 908 (BIA 2006) [statute does apply to AOS because AOS is an admission and statute applies to admission]. *See also Matter of Lemus,* 24 I&N Dec. 373 (BIA 2007) [adjustment of status under INA §245(i) is unavailable to person inadmissible under 10 year bar]. Unlike the 3-year bar, a person is subject to the 10-year bar whether or not s/he departs during or after proceedings.

3.c. The statute defines unlawful presence as being present in U.S. "after the expiration of the period of stay authorized by the Attorney General or is present in the United States without being admitted or paroled." INA §212(a)(9)(B)(ii), 8 U.S.C. §1182(a)(9)(B)(ii). However, no period of unlawful presence that accrued before Apr. 1, 1997, may be considered for inadmissibility under INA §212(a)(9)(B), *Matter of Rodarte,* 23 I&N Dec. 905 (BIA 2006). At least one court has made the distinction between unlawful presence and exceptions that bar counting time toward 3/10 year provisions. *Equal Access Education v. Merten,* 325 F.Supp.2d 655, 662–67 (E.D. Va. 2004) [although exceptions due to asylum or minor status may stop the running of time not authorized by AG, the minor is still in unlawful presence in the U.S. when he entered on a B-2 and remained in U.S. after I-94 expired]. This section has become the subject of the following interpretations by legacy INS:

(1) *EWI*—All time in EWI status (which includes being present without permission or parole)

(2) *Voluntary Departure*—It is considered a period of stay authorized by the AG "regardless of whether it is granted by USCIS prior to the commencement of proceedings, or by an IJ at the end of proceedings, or by the BIA after an appeal." If the party granted VD fails to depart, unlawful presence accrues as of the date VD expired. Memo, Virtue, Acting Exec. Assoc. Comm., INS, HQ IRT 5015.12, 96 Act. 058 (Sept. 19, 1997), *published on* AILA InfoNet at Doc. No. 97092240. Also, all unlawful presence that accrued before VD was granted still remains unlawful presence. Memo, Pearson, Exec. Assoc. Comm. Field Operations (HQADN 70/21.1.24-P, AD 00-07) (Mar. 3, 2000) at ¶5, *published on* AILA InfoNet at Doc. No. 00030774. Legacy INS took the position that a person who is granted VD *after* commencement of proceeding is *not* subject to the 3-year bar because of the language of §212(a)(9)(B)(i)(I), but if s/he was unlawfully present in U.S. for more than one year s/he would be subject to the 10-year bar. Letter, Chang, Branch Chief of Residence and Status Branch, INS, HQ 70/21.1.16 (Mar. 23, 1998), *published on* AILA InfoNet at Doc. No. 98032391. If the denial of VD is reversed on appeal, then the time from the denial to the reversal will be considered authorized time in U.S.

(3) *Nonimmigrants*—Unauthorized stay only includes periods of stay beyond the date specified on the I-94 or the I-797 (where an extension has been granted). It does not include acts (*e.g.*, criminal conduct or working without authorization) that might otherwise render someone subject to removal. It does not include persons with D/S (*e.g.,* A, F, G, M, J), until there is a determination by DHS that they are no longer in status. For NIVs seeking an E/S or C/S they will be considered to be in authorized stay until their applications are decided, so long as they did not work without authorization and did not file untimely or frivolous applications. Memo, Pearson, Exec. Assoc. Comm. Field Operations (HQADN 70/21.1.24-P, AD 00-07) (Mar. 3, 2000) at ¶4, *published on* AILA InfoNet at Doc. No. 00030774; Cable, DOS, No. 00-State-102274 (May 30, 2000), *published on* AILA InfoNet at Doc. No. 00060202. Even if the application is approved beyond 120 days, no unlawful presence accrues. If the C/S or E/S application is denied unlawful presence only accrues from the original expiration date on the I-94 if the application was frivolous, was denied as untimely filed, or because the applicant engaged in unlawful employment. If it was denied for any other reason unlawful presence only accrues from the time of the denial. The submission of untimely applications for E/S or C/S while a timely C/S or E/S is pending will *not* prolong the period of unlawful status if the original timely application is denied. Thus, unlawful presence will accrue from the time the first (timely) C/S or E/S is denied and not from the subsequently filed applications for E/S or C/S even if they are filed while the timely application is pending. Memo, Cook, Acting

Asst. Comm., Office of Adjudications HQBUSCIS 70/21.1.24-P (Apr. 2, 2003) and Memo, Podolny, Chief, Inspections Law Div., GC, HQCOU 90/15 (Mar. 27, 2003), *published on* AILA InfoNet at Doc. No. 03042140. For example, suppose that a person whose B-2 status expires April 1 on her I-94 files an extension of status on March 29. She then files, on April 15, a change of status to F-1 or H-1B. Then, on May 30, her (timely) March 29 E/S is denied. This person's unlawful presence accrues from May 30; her C/S filed on April 15 is treated as untimely.

An appeal to the AAO of a denial of C/S or E/S does not toll unlawful presence. Thus, unlawful presence begins to run from the time of the denied application. For example, a person who had his C/S or E/S of an I-129 (regarding an L-1) denied, and appeals that decision to the AAO, is accruing unlawful status during the entire appeal, unless his appeal is ultimately successful.

An NIV who departs during the pendency of the C/S or E/S will not be subject to the 3- or 10-year bar if he departs after the expiration of the I-94 unless the consular officer or DHS officer at the border determines that the C/S or E/S application was untimely, frivolous, or the person worked without authorization. The requirement that the application was timely filed may be established through the submission of evidence of the date the previously authorized stay expired together with a copy of a dated filing receipt, a canceled check payable to DHS or other credible evidence. A nonfrivolous application is one that must have an arguable basis in law and fact and not filed for an improper purpose. Memo, Pearson, Exec. Assoc. Comm. Field Operations (HQADN 70/21.1.24-P, AD 00-07) (Mar. 3, 2000) at ¶7, *published on* AILA InfoNet at Doc. No. 00030774. A person who departs during the E/S or C/S application and is in D/S is not subject to the 3/10 year bar on return.

(4) *Duration of Status (D/S)*—An F or J with D/S is not considered to be in an unauthorized stay until an IJ or USCIS has made a determination regarding his or her status. This may accrue (a) when IJ enters an *order* of exclusion, deportation, or removal in a proceeding, or (b) when USCIS makes a determination during the course of adjudicating a benefit. If it is an IJ determination, time accrues from IJ decision, not the final order. If a USCIS decision, the time accrues from the date the benefit is denied (*e.g.*, C/S or E/ S denied). Memo, Pearson, Exec. Assoc. Comm. Field Operations (HQADN 70/21.1.24-P, AD 00-07) (Mar. 3, 2000) at ¶2B, *published on* AILA InfoNet at Doc. No. 00030774.

(5) *Canadians at the Border*—DOS has indicated that legacy INS's position is that Canadians inspected at the border but not given an I-94 are treated as D/S similar to F and J visas. However, DHS itself has not opined on this issue in writing. Cable, DOS, *reprinted in* 76 No. 41 *Interpreter Releases* 1552–53 (Oct. 25, 1999).

(6) *In Proceedings*—Time in proceedings is not authorized stay as follows: (a) if EWI (including present without permission or parole), time accrues from date of entry; (b) if NIV time accrues when I-94 expires or IJ *orders* removal, whichever is earlier; (c) if a parolee, when parole expires or date parole is revoked or terminated, or if paroled in for a waiver, the date IJ enters removal order; (d) if person is successful in removal proceedings no time accrues unless her stay expired during the course of the proceedings, and then it would accrue from the date of the successful order; (e) if person obtains relief in the removal proceeding and DHS appeals, time accrues only from date BIA reverses IJ; (f) if VD, where denial of VD is reversed at BIA, no unlawful time accrues between improper denial and reversal. Memo, Virtue, Acting Exec. Assoc. Comm., INS, HQ IRT 5015.12, 96 Act. 058 (Sept. 19, 1997), *published on* AILA InfoNet at Doc. No. 97092240. The filing of a Notice to Appear (NTA) for a removal hearing has no effect on determining periods of unlawful presence. 8 C.F.R. §239.3. Proceedings, in some sense, are neutral. If the person was not considered to be in unlawful status at the time of the proceedings, then unlawful status would only begin to run from the court's decision. If someone was in unlawful status at the time of the proceedings, the current view of DHS is that the compulsion to appear at proceedings does not toll the unlawful time or turn that time into lawful time in the U.S.

(7) *Conditional Permanent Resident (CR)*—Time accrues from date CR fails to timely file I-751 (marriage) or I-829 (investor). If late filing is accepted by DHS or IJ, the CR's status is restored and CR is not considered to have accrued period of unlawful presence. If it is not accepted, time accrues from date CR *status expired*. If DHS seeks to revoke CR status, unlawful presence does not accrue until DHS successfully terminates status and unlawful presence runs then from date of termination. If DHS denies I-829 or I-751 and *terminates* status under 8 C.F.R. §216.3(a) unlawful status accrues from date of termination. Memo, Virtue, Acting Exec. Assoc. Comm., INS, HQ IRT 5015.12, 96 Act. 058 (Sept. 19, 1997), *published on* AILA InfoNet at Doc. No. 97092240; Cable, DOS, No. 98-State-060539 at ¶28 (Apr. 4, 1998), *published on* AILA InfoNet at Doc. No. 98040490.

(8) *Adjustment of Status*—Properly filed affirmative §245(a)/§245(i) AOS applications and affirmative registry applications under §249 toll any unauthorized time and are considered to be a period of stay authorized by the AG. Memo, Pearson, Exec. Assoc. Comm. Field Operations (HQADN 70/ 21.1.24-P, AD 00-07) (Mar. 3, 2000) at ¶3, *published on* AILA InfoNet at Doc. No. 00030774. An exception arises only if AOS application is filed *after* an NTA is served on the applicant. Memo, Virtue, Acting Exec. Assoc. Comm., HQ IRT 5015.12, 96 Act. 043 (June 17, 1997), *published on* AILA InfoNet at Doc. No. 97061790; Cable, DOS, No. 00-State-102272 (May 30, 2000), *published on* AILA InfoNet at Doc. No. 00060201. Time in unlawful status that accrued prior to the filing of an AOS or registry application also counts toward the 180-day / one-year periods. The period of authorized stay upon the filing of an AOS application, however, continues during the period in which the application is denied, renewed during the course of removal proceedings, through review by the BIA. Memo, Williams, Ex. Assoc. Comm., Field Operations, HQADN 70/21.1.24-P (June 12, 2002), *published on* AILA InfoNet at Doc. No. 02062040; Memo, Pearson, Exec. Assoc. Comm. Field Operations (HQADN 70/21.1.24-P, AD 00-07) (Mar. 3, 2000) at ¶3, *published on* AILA InfoNet at Doc. No. 00030774 (Mar. 7, 2000); Memo, Bach, Ex. Assoc. Comm. Off. Policy and Programs, (HQ 70/23.1-P, HQ 70/8-P) (Apr. 14, 1999), *reprinted in* 76 No. 16 *Interpreter Releases* 621, 652–58 (Apr. 26, 1999).

(9) *Asylum/Refugee Related*—Person admitted as refugee, granted asylum or withholding, granted withholding or deferral under UN Convention Against Torture. Memo, Williams, Ex. Assoc. Comm., Field Operations, HQADN 70/21.1.24-P (June 12, 2002), *published on* AILA InfoNet at Doc. No. 02062040.

(10) *TPS / DED / Cuban-Haitian Entrant*—A person granted DED by the President, or granted TPS or Cuban-Haitian Entrants is in authorized stay. Memo, Pearson, Exec. Assoc. Comm. Field Operations (HQADN 70/21.1.24-P, AD 00-07) (Mar. 3, 2000) at ¶3, *published on* AILA InfoNet at Doc. No. 00030774. For TPS the period of authorized stay begins on the date a prima facie TPS application is filed if it is ultimately approved. If TPS is denied or the application does not establish prima facie eligibility, the unlawful presence begins to run from the expiration of the previous stay. For DED the period of authorized stay takes effect beginning on the date specified in the Executive Order. When TPS or DED are no longer in effect unlawful presence resumes. Memo, Williams, Ex. Assoc. Comm., Field Operations, HQADN 70/21.1.24-P (June 12, 2002), *published on* AILA InfoNet at Doc. No. 02062040.

Deferred Action—The time a person is granted the status of deferred action is considered a time authorized by the AG. Memo, Williams, Ex. Assoc. Comm., Field Operations, HQADN 70/21.1.24-P (June 12, 2002), *published on* AILA InfoNet at Doc. No. 02062040. It covers only the period during which deferred action is in effect. It does not eliminate any unlawful presence accrued before the grant.

Cuban-Haitian Entrants—A Cuban-Haitian Entrant is defined under section 501(e)(1) of the Refugee Education Assistance Act of 1980, PL 96-422, as amended at 8 U.S.C. §1522 note and 8 C.F.R. §212.5(h).

(11) *Order of Supervision*—It is not considered a time authorized by the AG. Memo, Pearson, Exec. Assoc. Comm. Field Operations (HQADN 70/21.1.24-P, AD 00-07) (Mar. 3, 2000) at ¶3, *published on* AILA InfoNet at Doc. No. 00030774.

(12) *Federal Court Litigation*—Not considered stay authorized by AG. *Id.*

(13) *Advance Parole*—If adjustment applicant had 180 days / one year of unauthorized stay in U.S. *before* filing an AOS application, his or her return on an advance parole *will* trigger the 3/10 year bar. Memo, Virtue, Acting Exec. Comm., INS, HQ IRT 50/5.12, 96 Act. 068 (Nov. 26, 1997), *reprinted in* 74 No. 46 *Interpreter Releases* 1,842, 1,864–68 (Dec. 8, 1997).

(14) *Parole*—Persons who are paroled into the U.S. are considered authorized by the AG to be in the U.S. and do not accrue unlawful presence so long as they do not violate the terms of their parole. General Counsel Liaison Meeting with AILA, *published on* AILA InfoNet at Doc. No. 99122271.

(15) *Legalization/SAW*—Legalization and SAW applicants who have applications pending through an administrative appeal are in authorized stay. Memo, Pearson, Exec. Assoc. Comm. Field Operations (HQADN 70/21.1.24-P, AD 00-07) (Mar. 3, 2000) at ¶3, *published on* AILA InfoNet at Doc. No. 00030774.

(16) *Suspension and Cancellation*—A person granted suspension of deportation or cancellation of removal is in a status authorized by the AG. Memo, Pearson, Exec. Assoc. Comm. Field Operations (HQADN 70/21.1.24-P, AD 00-07) (Mar. 3, 2000) at ¶3, *published on* AILA InfoNet at Doc. No. 00030774. A person who is a conditional suspension or conditional cancellation of removal grantee is also in a status authorized by the AG. General Counsel Liaison Meeting with AILA, *published on* AILA InfoNet at Doc. No. 99122271.

3.d. The following exceptions to the unlawful presence statute apply, INA §212(a)(9)(B)(iii), 8 U.S.C. §1182(a)(9)(B)(iii):

(1) *Minors*—No time period under 18 taken into account.

(2) *Asylum Applicant Where Application Is Bona Fide* (unless the applicant worked without authorization)—The denial of an asylum claim is not determinative of whether it was *bona fide.* Memo, Cooper, G.C. (HQPGM 70/6.2.6) (June 8, 1999), *reprinted in* 76 No. 33 *Interpreter Releases* 1289, 1304–10 (Aug. 30, 1999). Includes all periods of time from initial affirmative filing through IJ hearing, BIA appeal and federal appeals. However, if applicant worked without authorization for one day only, the remainder of his or her status is not authorized and s/he is therefore deemed to be in unlawful presence in U.S. from that day forward under the current DHS interpretation. Also, a pending application for withholding is not a period of stay authorized by the AG. A person's asylum application would be considered "pending" for purposes of this section where a pre-reform (prior to Jan. 4, 1995) asylum application was denied but to bureaucratic mishap the person was not put in proceedings. Memo, Pearson, Exec. Assoc. Comm. (HQIAO 120/9) (Aug. 2, 1999), *reprinted in* 76 No. 33 *Interpreter Releases* 1289, 1309 (Aug. 30, 1999). Also a dependent child who aged-out of his parents' application will still be considered to have an asylum application pending if within a reasonable period of time he files his own application, which will be treated *nunc pro tunc* to date of parents' filing. Memo, Pearson (Aug. 2, 1999), *supra.*

(3) *Family unity*—No period of time in which the person is a beneficiary of family unity protection under IMMACT90 §301(b)(1)(B)(iii)(III). There is also a transitional provision that allows the AG to waive inadmissibility under INA §212(a)(9) for persons provided family unity benefits. IIRIRA §309(c)(6). Authorized stay pursuant to 8 C.F.R. §236.15(c) begins from the date Form I-817 is filed and continues through the time the applicant retains Family Unity Protection benefits unless it is terminated. Unlawful presence would begin from the denial of the I-817 and would be in addition to any unlawful presence accrued before the I-817 was filed. Memo, Williams, Ex. Assoc. Comm., Field Operations, HQADN 70/10.19 (Jan. 27, 2003), *published on* AILA InfoNet at Doc. No. 03013042.

(4) *Battered Women and Children*—The provision does not apply to spouses or children subjected to battery or extreme cruelty, if there is a relationship between the battery or cruelty and the violation of the term of the spouse or child's nonimmigrant stay. Those who "first arrived" in the U.S. before Apr. 1, 1997, are not required to show the domestic violence relationship. IIRIRA §301(c)(2).

(5) *Victims of Severe Form of Trafficking*—The provision does not apply if a severe form of trafficking as defined in 22 U.S.C. §7102 (the use of force, fraud, or coercion for sex trafficking and/or involuntary servitude, peonage, debt bondage, or slavery) was at least one central reason for the person's unlawful presence.

(6) *U status*—Where a person in U status was granted deferred action or parole while s/he is placed on a waiting list because the 10,000 cap per year has been reached, she does not accrue unlawful presence in the U.S. 8 C.F.R. §214.14(d)(3).

(7) *Burden of Proof*—The burden is on the applicant to prove the exception. Cable, DOS, No. 98-State-060539 at ¶26 (Apr. 4, 1998), *published on* AILA InfoNet at Doc. No. 98040490

3.e. Tolling for Good Cause—8 U.S.C. §1182(a)(9)(B)(iv). The time period of unlawful presence in regard to the *3-year bar* is tolled for 120 days if the person has been lawfully admitted or paroled, has filed a nonfrivolous application for a change or extension of status before the date of expiration of the period of stay authorized by the AG and has not been employed without authorization before or during the pendency of such application. Although this tolling period, by statute, does *not* apply to persons subject to the 10-year bar, the Service, by memo, has applied tolling in another manner to relieve the problem for persons filing E/S or C/S and neither the 3- nor 10-year bars accrue during the extension-of-status or change-of-status application period. And although the legislative history indicates that the application must be approved to toll the period, there is nothing in the statute to indicate that it is a requirement, H.R. Conf. Rep. 104-828, 104th Cong., 2d Sess. at 207, and the Service has interpreted the toll to apply when applications are filed, even if not subsequently approved. Memo, Pearson, Exec. Assoc. Comm. Field Operations (HQADN 70/21.1.24-P, AD 00-07) (Mar. 3, 2000) at ¶4, *published on* AILA InfoNet at Doc. No. 00030774; AFM at 30.1(d).

In light of the prolonged delays in adjudicating C/S and E/S applications, USCIS has determined that NIVs seeking an E/S or C/S will be considered to be in authorized stay until their applications are decided, so long as they did not work without authorization and did not file untimely or frivolous applications. Memo, Pearson, Exec. Assoc. Comm. Field Operations (HQADN 70/21.1.24-P, AD 00-07) (Mar. 3, 2000) at ¶4, *published on* AILA InfoNet at Doc. No. 00030774. Even if the application is denied (or approved) beyond 120 days, no unlawful presence accrues. If the C/S or E/S application is denied, unlawful presence accrues from the original expiration date on the I-94 only if the application was frivolous, was denied as untimely filed, or because the applicant engaged in unlawful employment. If it was for any other reason unlawful presence only accrues from the time of the denial. Similarly, unlawful status accrues in C/S or E/S applications for persons in D/S when the applications are denied even if they were filed untimely, were frivolous or were denied as a result of unauthorized employment. Memo, Pearson, Exec. Assoc. Comm. Field Operations (HQADN 70/21.1.24-P, AD 00-07) (Mar. 3, 2000), *published on* AILA InfoNet at Doc. No. 00030774.

3.f. The 180 days or one year are *not* counted in the aggregate. Thus, departure before the appropriate period breaks the 180 days / one year and re-entry starts the time period anew. Memo, Virtue, Acting Exec. Comm., INS, HQ IRT 50/5.12, 96 Act. 068 (Nov. 26, 1997), *reprinted in* 74 No. 46 *Interpreter Releases* 1,842, 1,864–68 (Dec. 8, 1997); Cable, DOS, No. 98-State-060539 (Apr. 4, 1998), *reprinted in* 75 No. 15 *Interpreter Releases* 543 (Apr. 20, 1998) at ¶27. Thus, a person who is unlawfully present in the U.S. for 5 months, leaves the U.S., returns, and has another 5 months unlawful presence is not subject to the 3-year bar. *Id.* As with the 3-year bar, periods of unlawful presence are not aggregated for the 10-year bar. Cable, DOS, No. 98-State-060539 (Apr. 4, 1998), *supra* at ¶33.

3.g. Embassy investigation—Consular officers "should not routinely undertake in-depth questioning of applicants concerning possible ineligibility under 9B unless ... in the normal course of processing a particular visa application, the possibility of a previous period of unlawful presence becomes apparent through otherwise routinely available information." Cable, DOS, No. 98-State-060539 (Apr. 4, 1998), *supra.*

3.h. Agency Reporting—Under IIRIRA §404 federal agencies are required to report to DHS four times a year any person the agency "knows" is not lawfully present in the U.S. A joint notice has been submitted by HHS, HUD, SSA, and DOL that defines an agency's knowledge of unlawful presence as: "when the unlawful presence is a finding of fact or conclusion of law that is made by the [agency] as part of a formal determination that is subject to administrative review on an alien's claim for any of the statutorily specified programs." The agencies further determined that the conclusion must be supported by EOIR or the DHS and that a negative hit on the SAVE program is insufficient. 65 Fed. Reg. 58301 (Sept. 28, 2000).

3.i. Waivers—8 U.S.C. §1182(a)(9)(B)(v). If the person is an immigrant and the spouse or son or daughter of a USC or LPR (but not the parent) and s/he can show extreme hardship to the spouse or parent (but not his child), inadmissibility can be waived. *Matter of* ___(AAO Oct 31, 2007) *reported in* 85 No. 12 *Interpreter Releases* 837, 856–57 (Mar. 18, 2008) [financial hardship to applicant's spouse who was requesting public benefits, receiving assistance from her parent, was unable to find employment and unable to read while her husband had an employment offer and emotional hardship to her because of her own condition and her children] *Matter of* __, (AAO Apr. 24, 2007) *reported in* 84 No. 21 *Interpreter Releases* 1117, 1139 (May 21, 2007) [USC husband documented history of family depression]; *Matter of* ___, (AAO Mar. 27, 2007) *reported in* 85 No. 4 *Interpreter Releases* 201-04 (Jan. 21, 2008) [granted waiver after considering how the medical hardship to the child would affect the hardship to the spouse]. There is no judicial review of the waiver provision. The waiver is filed on an I-601 form. If a person is seeking entry as an NIV s/he may apply for a waiver under INA §212(d)(3)(A).

4. *Person Unlawfully Present Who Enters or Seeks to Enter EWI*—INA §§212(a)(9)(C)(i)(I) & (II), 8 U.S.C. §§1182(a)(9)(C)(i)(I) & (II), 22 C.F.R. §40.93. A person who has been unlawfully present in U.S. for an aggregate period of more than one year *or* has been ordered removed under summary exclusion or removal, deportation, or exclusion provisions *and* who enters *or* attempts to enter without inspection is inadmissible. The one-year period is aggregated but no period of unlawful presence prior to Apr. 1, 1997 will be counted. Memo, Virtue, Acting Exec. Comm., INS, HQ IRT 50/5.12, 96 Act. 068 (Nov. 26, 1997). A person ineligible under this provision may not adjust under INA §245(i). *Matter of Briones,* 24 I&N Dec. 355 (BIA 2007) [INA §245(i) adjustment is unavailable to someone who is subject to INA §212(a)(9)(C)(i)(I)]; *Matter of Torres-Garcia,* 23 I&N Dec. 866 (BIA 2006) [an I-212 waiver cannot retroactively waive inadmissibility under INA §212(a)(9)(C)(i)(II) because the applicant cannot seek admission under that section for 10 years after the date of his last departure from the U.S.; *disagreed with Perez-Gonzalez*]; *Ramirez-Canales v. Mukasey,* 517 F.3d 904, 907–10 (6th Cir. 2008 [followed *Briones* under *Chevron* but remanded for potential *nunc pro tunc* relief]; *Delgado v. Mukasey,* 516 F.3d 65 (2d Cir. 2008) [same, agreeing with *Torres-Garcia* and *Gonzales*]; *Gonzales v. DHS,* 508 F.3d 1227, 1234–42 (9th Cir. 2007) [reversed its prior decision in *Perez-Gonzales v. Ashcroft,* 379 F.3d 783 (9th Cir. 2004) and upheld on *Chevron* deference under *National Cable & Telecommunications Ass'n v. Brand X,* 545 U.S. 967 (2005) the BIA's decision in *Matter of Torres-Garcia*]; *Mortera-Cruz v. Gonzales,* 409 F.3d 246 (5th Cir. 2005) [*Chevron* deference granted to BIA's determination that a person inadmissible under INA §212(a)(9)(C)(i) may not adjust under INA §245(i)]; *Berrum-Garcia v. Comfort,* 390 F.3d 1158, 1166–68 (10th Cir. 2004) [applicant for §245(i) adjustment who re-enters after removal/deportation is *not* eligible to waive INA §212(a)(9)(C)(i)(II) with an I-212 without returning to his home country for 10 years]; *but see Acosta v. Gonzales,* 439 F.3d 550, 552–56 (9th Cir. 2006) [following *Perez-Gonzales*, the court held that INA §245(i) also applies to persons inadmissible under INA §212(a)(9)(C)(i)(I), but that the waiver under INA §212(a)(9)(B)(v) for unlawful presence is not available]; *Padilla-Caldera v. Gonzales,* 453 F.3d 1237 (10th Cir. 2006) [applicant for INA §245(i) adjustment who is subject to inadmissibility under INA §212(a)(9)(C)(i)(I) because s/he has been unlawfully present in the U.S. for an aggregate period of more than one year and re-entered the country illegally may adjust status. *Berrum-Garcia* distinguished and Crocetti INS memo not given *Chevron* deference];

4.a. Limited Waivers Available—INA §§212(a)(9)(C)(ii) and (iii). DHS, under subsection (iii), may waive this ground of inadmissibility for a battered spouse/child who has been granted a classification as such, if there is a connection between the person having been battered and her removal, departure from the U.S., re-entry, or attempted re-entry into the U.S. A waiver is also available under subsection (ii) to a person "seeking admission more than 10 years after the date of [her] last departure from the United States" if DHS gives its approval. This latter provision may not be applied for less than 10 years after the last departure from the U.S. The BIA has suggested that because the authority for the waiver was changed from the AG to DHS under the Violence Against Women and Department of Justice Reauthorization Act—Technical Corrections, PL 109-271, §6(b), 120 Stat. 750, 762 (2006) that IJs may no longer have jurisdiction to grant these waivers. *Matter of Briones,* 24 I&N Dec. 355, 359 n.5 (BIA 2007).

5. *Person Present Without Admission or Parole*—INA §212(a)(6)(A), 8 U.S.C. §1182(a)(6)(A), 22 C.F.R. §40.61. A person present in the U.S. without having been admitted or paroled or who arrives at a place other than that designated by DHS is inadmissible. This section is inapplicable and does not bar adjustment under §245(i). Legal Opinion, Martin, General Counsel, CO 245(i) (Feb. 19, 1997), *published on* AILA InfoNet at Doc. No. 97021991. This section is also not applicable when a person seeks an immigrant visa at a U.S. consulate. The ground of inadmissibility applies only when the person is in the U.S. and therefore "does not apply to visa applicants outside the U.S." Memo, Virtue, Acting Exec. Assoc. Comm., HQ IRT 5015.12, 96 Act 026 (Mar. 31, 1997), *published on* AILA InfoNet at Doc. No. 97033190. It also does not apply to VAWA self-petitioners who entered before Apr. 1, 1997. In addition, VAWA adjustment applicants are no longer subject to this ground of inadmissibility based on USCIS's interpretation of section 1506 of Public Law 106-386 (2000), and are not required to show a "substantial connection" between the qualifying battery or extreme cruelty and the VAWA self-petitioner's "unlawful entry" under INA §212(a)(6)(ii). Memo, Aytes, Assoc. Director, Domestic Operations, USCIS, HQDOMO 70/23.1 (Apr. 11, 2008), *published on* AILA InfoNet at Doc. No. 08042161; also available from *www.NationalImmigrationProject.org*. A VAWA applicant whose application was previously denied based on INA §212(a)(6)(A)(i) may file a motion to reopen or reconsider without the payment of a filing fee. AFM at 23.5(k).

6. *Failure to Attend Removal Proceeding*—INA §212(a)(6)(B), 8 U.S.C. §1182(a)(6)(B), 22 C.F.R. §40.62. A person who without reasonable cause fails or refuses to attend or remain in attendance at her removal proceeding is inadmissible for 5 years from departure or removal. This section only applies if the person is physically removed or departs the U.S. and then seeks re-entry. Memo, Virtue, Acting Exec. Assoc. Comm., HQ IRT 50/51.2, 96 Act 043 (June 17, 1997), *published on* AILA InfoNet at Doc. No. 97061790. This section applies to persons placed in removal proceedings and does *not* apply to persons who fail to appear for exclusion/deportation cases. *Id.*

7. *Stowaways*—INA §212(a)(6)(D), 8 U.S.C. §1182(a)(6)(D). INA §101(a)(49), 8 U.S.C. §1101(a)(49), specifically defines stowaway as a person who obtains transportation without consent and through concealment. "A passenger who boards with a valid ticket is not to be considered a stowaway." *Id.*

8. *Smugglers*—Persons who at any time knowingly encourage, induce, assist and abet, or aid any other alien to try to enter the U.S. in violation of the law are inadmissible. INA §212(a)(6)(E)(i), 8 U.S.C. §1182(a)(6)(E)(i); 9 FAM 40.65. In DOS's view, this includes bringing in a minor child. Letter, Odom, Chief Advisory Opinions, Visa Services (Oct. 20, 1993), *reprinted in* 71 No. 10 *Interpreter Releases* 352, 375–78 (Mar. 14, 1994). At least one court has suggested that a person who has been convicted of illegally transporting undocumented aliens is not inadmissibile under this statute because the statute refers to aiding or abetting. *Rodriguez-Gutierrez v. INS,* 59 F.3d 504, 509 n.3 (5th Cir. 1995). *See also Matter of I-M-,* 7 I&N Dec. 389 (BIA 1957). A person cannot be deemed to "knowingly assist" an alien to illegally enter unless s/he engages in "an affirmative and illicit act of assistance in shepherding someone across the border." *Tapucu v. Gonzales,* 399 F.3d 736 (6th Cir. 2005) [reversed IJ determination of inadmissibility of LPR who shared driving with three friends, acknowledged that his friend was living illegally in U.S., but believed he could travel back and forth and that his family was applying for him for LPR status]. *See also Altamirano v. Gonzales,* 427 F.3d 586, 591–96 (9th Cir. 2005) [reversed IJ determination of inadmissibility because mere presence in a vehicle with knowledge that someone was hiding in the trunk is not assisting or abetting in alien smuggling]. *But see Chambers v. Office of Chief Counsel,* 494 F.3d 274 (2d Cir. 2007) [where re-

spondent made false statements at border about smuggled alien's permanent residency in the U.S., the record contained substantial evidence that respondent had the requisite knowledge]; *Covarrubias v Gonzales,* 487 F.3d 742, 748-49 (9th Cir. 2007) [statute covers any act that continues until the initial transporter ceases to transport, that is, until he drops them off on the U.S. side of the border, but here respondent was aware of illegal acts at time they occurred and therefore can be considered to have aided and abetted]; *Soriano v. Gonzales,* 484 F.3d 318 (5th Cir. 2007) [upheld removal where respondent did not assist undocumented persons on entry but drove them in friend's truck after entry]. *See generally U.S. v. Lopez,* 484 F.3d 1186 (9th Cir. 2007) (en banc)

The former statute required that the government establish that the violation was "for gain," *Matter of Tiwari*, 19 I&N Dec. 875 (BIA 1989); *Matter of Contreras*, 18 I&N Dec. 30 (BIA 1981); *Matter of Arthur*, 16 I&N Dec. 558 (BIA 1978); *Ribeiro v. INS*, 531 F.2d 179 (3d Cir. 1976); *Sanchez-Marquez v. INS*, 725 F.2d 341 (7th Cir. 1984) [actual receipt of money is unnecessary. Agreement to pay later is sufficient "gain"]; *Matter of B-G-*, 8 I&N Dec. 182 (BIA 1958) [same], has been *eliminated.*

Although the statute eliminated the "for gain" requirement, it added a special waiver under INA §212(d)(11), 8 U.S.C. §1182(d)(11). *See in this part* ¶ I.7 (p.122), *infra*.

9. *Document Fraud*—A person who is the subject of a final order (civil penalty) for violation of INA §274C, 8 U.S.C. §1324c (relating to civil fines for falsely making or using fraudulent documents under the INA or using someone else's lawfully issued document) is inadmissible. INA §212(a)(6)(F), 8 U.S.C. §1182(a)(6)(F), 22 C.F.R. §40.66. A waiver is authorized for humanitarian purposes or to assure family unity for a returning LPR or a person seeking an IV or AOS under the family-preference or immediate-relative categories if she has not been subjected to a previous civil money penalty under INA §274C and the offense was committed solely to assist and/or support his or her spouse or child (and no other person). INA §212(d)(12), 8 U.S.C. §1182(d)(12). There is no judicial review of the denial of the waiver. The Service should not institute INA §274C proceedings where there is an I-485 on file and an I-601 waiver to forgive fraud unless the applications are denied. Memo, Puleo, Acting Exec. Assoc. Comm. Operations (HQ 274C-C) (Mar. 25, 1993), *reprinted in* 12 *AILA Monthly Mailing* 922–23 (Dec. 1993); Memo, Rees, Gen. Counsel, INS (May 18, 1993). However, the BIA has held that an INA §212(i) waiver is unavailable to waive §212(a)(6)(F) arising from a final order under INA §274C. *Matter of Lazarte*, 21 I&N Dec. 214 (BIA 1996) [distinguishing INS view as exercise of prosecutorial discretion].

10. *Student Visa Abuse*—INA §212(a)(6)(G), 8 U.S.C. §1182(a)(6)(G), 22 C.F.R. §40.67. A student who enters the U.S. to study at a private institution and then switches to a public school in violation of INA §214(m)(2) is inadmissible for 5 years. This section only applies to students who obtain or extend their student status beginning 60 days after Sept. 30, 1996. IIRIRA §346(b).

F. *Most Common Violations*

1. Alien who, by fraud or willfully misrepresenting a material fact, seeks to procure or has sought to procure or has procured a visa, other documentation or entry into the U.S. or other benefit provided under the Act—INA §212(a)(6)(C), 8 U.S.C. §1182(a)(6)(C). *See* 22 C.F.R. §40.63, 9 FAM 40.63 N.1-10; *Matter of S-& B-C-*, 9 I&N Dec. 436 (BIA 1960) [the determination of materiality is a fact that would make alien excludable or shut off line of inquiry which may have resulted in exclusion]. *See also Kungys v. U.S.*, 485 U.S. 759 (1988) [materiality is a legal question of whether "misrepresentation or concealment was predictably capable of affecting, *i.e.*, had a natural tendency to affect the official decision."]; *U.S. v. Gaudin*, 115 S.Ct. 2310, 2319 (1995) [materiality is a mixed question of law and fact]. In *Kungys,* the Court established a 4-part analysis to determine judicial denaturalization proceedings: (1) the applicant must have misrepresented or concealed some fact; (2) the misrepresentation or concealment must have been willful; (3) the fact must have been material; and (4) the applicant must have procured the benefit. *Kungys v. U.S.,* 485 U.S. 759, 767 (1988). In order to establish the 4th part of the test, the government's finding of materiality establishes a presumption and shifts the burden to the applicant to establish that s/he was statutorily qualified for the benefit. *Id.* at 777. In *Monter v. Gonzales,* 430 F.3d 546 (2d Cir. 2005), the Second Circuit adopted the *Kungys* 4-part test in the context of an I-751 conditional residency application. The court found that respondent's failure to list a separate address for his wife on the I-751 was material but that the IJ's refusal to change venue deprived respondent of the opportunity to rebut the presumption that he procured his permanent residency by a material mis-

representation and to show he was nevertheless qualified to receive his permanent residency. The Ninth Circuit in *Forbes v. INS*, 48 F.3d 439, 443 (9th Cir. 1995), applying the *Kungys* analysis and particularly the concurring opinion of Justice Brennan that the government must "produce evidence sufficient to raise a fair inference that a statutory disqualifying fact actually existed," determined that the failure of an IV applicant to disclose an arrest that ultimately resulted in a dismissal was *not* material. *Solis-Muela v. INS*, 13 F.3d 372 (10th Cir. 1993) [read *Kungys* to result in material misrepresentation where applicant admitted arrest but failed to disclose conviction]. In the Eleventh Circuit, the court determined that materiality required disclosure that would make the inadmissibility "apparent" and "would have adversely affected [the] application for permanent residence." *Ali v. U.S. Att'y Gen.*, 443 F.3d 804, 812 (11th Cir. 2006) [found material misrepresentation where respondent answered "no" to a question whether he had ever been convicted, despite his conviction being vacated subsequent to the application]; *Suite v. INS*, 594 F.2d 972 (3d Cir. 1979); *Espinoza-Espinoza v. INS*, 554 F.2d 921 (9th Cir. 1977); *Matter of Healy and Goodchild*, 17 I&N Dec. 22 (BIA 1979). *But see U.S. v. Matsumaru,* 244 F.3d 1092, 1101–02 (9th Cir. 2001) [upheld conviction of immigration lawyer on theory that the government need not prove that the misrepresentation to be material actually affected the consular officer's decision but rather that it was "capable of affecting or influencing a governmental decision."]; *Mwongera v. INS,* 187 F.3d 323, 330–31 (3d Cir. 1999) [distinguishing *Kungys* as applying only to denaturalization cases and utilized standard regarding whether statements "shut off a line of inquiry"].

The issue of materiality relates to the person's state of mind. *Garcia v. INS*, 31 F.3d 441, 443 (7th Cir. 1994). The charge cannot be sustained in regard to someone subject to a primary inspection unless the fraud was practiced on a U.S. government official. *Matter of Y-G-*, 20 I&N Dec. 794 (BIA 1994) [when applicant with photo-switched passport came to U.S., he gave his real name, and stated that documents were invalid]; *Matter of D-L- & A-M-*, 20 I&N Dec. 409 (BIA 1991) [Cuban asylum seekers who boarded aircraft in Spain with photo-switch passports, but upon entry to U.S. did not seek to use passports and instead claimed asylum, did not violate section. *Shirdel* limited to TWOV cases]; *Matter of L-L-*, 9 I&N Dec. 324 (BIA 1961); *Matter of Areguillin*, 17 I&N Dec. 308 (BIA 1980). *But see Ymeri v. Ashcroft,* 387 F.3d 12, 18–20 (1st Cir. 2004) [sustained charge where Albanian TWOVs presented Greek passports but admitted immediately when questioned that their documents were fraudulent]; *Matter of Shirdel*, 19 I&N Dec. 33 (BIA 1984). An applicant's "silence or the failure to volunteer information does not in itself constitute a misrepresentation." 9 FAM 40.63 N.4.2. Moreover, "a timely retraction will serve to purge a misrepresentation and remove it from further consideration." 9 FAM 40.63 N.4.6.

Under the previous statute, if an alien "seeks to enter" by fraud, s/he is only barred on that occasion. However, under the Marriage Fraud Amendments Act of 1986, PL 99-639, all misrepresentations permanently bar entry. Moreover, INA §212(a)(6)(C) is also applicable to misrepresentations in procuring "other benefit[s] provided under the Act." The BIA has found that this includes a conviction for possession of a false Texas birth certificate with intent to defraud the U.S. by obtaining a U.S. passport. *Matter of Cervantes,* 22 I&N Dec. 560, 563 (BIA 1999), *aff'd, Cervantes-Gonzales v. INS,* 244 F.3d 1001 (9th Cir. 2001); *but see* Rosenberg dissent in 22 I&N Dec. 560, 575. DOS has also provided guidelines as to when a presumption arises as to a material misrepresentation in an employment context upon entry into the U.S. Where a person obtains a B-2 and/or enters on a B-2 claiming tourism and within 30 days of visa issuance or entry actively begins seeking unauthorized employment and subsequently is employed or accepts unauthorized employment and begins work, s/he "may be presumed to have misrepresented his or her intention in seeking a visa or entry." If it is between 30 and 60 days there is no presumption. If it is longer than 60 days, DOS will not entertain a recommendation that the person is inadmissible under INA §212(a)(6)(C). Cable, DOS, 91-State-187392 (June 7, 1991), *reprinted in* 68 No. 42 *Interpreter Releases* 1569–71 (Nov. 4, 1991).

A misrepresentation must also be willful. This element is satisfied by a finding that the misrepresentation was deliberate and voluntary. *Falaja v. Gonzales,* 418 F.3d 889, 897–99 (8th Cir. 2005) [where IJ/BIA found that inconsistencies in asylum application were the basis for an adverse credibility finding and were willfully made, court upheld denial of AOS based upon an employment petition because the applicant was ineligible under §212(a)(6)(C)(i)]; *Mwongera v. INS,* 187 F.3d 323, 330 (3d Cir. 1999) [does not need to show intent to deceive where person put on visa application that he stayed in U.S. for 6 months when it was 11 months]; *Witter v. INS*, 113 F.3d 549 (5th Cir. 1997); *Espinoza-Espinoza v. INS*, 554 F.2d 921 (9th Cir. 1977). Knowledge of the falsity is necessary. *Forbes v. INS*, 48 F.3d 439, 442 (9th Cir. 1995); *Garcia v. INS,* 31 F.3d 441 (7th Cir. 1994). In *Bryan v. U.S.*, 524 U.S. 184, 193, 118 S.Ct. 1939, 1946 (1998), the Court in the context of a criminal statute defined willfully as "the defendant acted with an evil-meaning mind, that is to say that he acted with knowledge that his conduct was unlawful." *See also U.S. v. Chowdhury,* 169 F.3d 402, 406–07 (6th Cir. 1999) [regarding criminal charge of marriage fraud].

Fraudulent conduct of a parent should not be attributed to the child. *Singh v. Gonzales,* 451 F.3d 400 (6th Cir. 2006) [the court distinguished *Matter of Aurelio,* 19 I&N Dec. 458 (BIA 1987) and *Senica v. INS,* 16 F.3d 1013 (9th Cir. 1994) and held that under the second prong of *Chevron* the imputation of fraudulent conduct to children is not a reasonable extension of caselaw].

For a detailed discussion regarding the government's burden of proof regarding materiality and willfulness, *see Matter of Tijam,* 22 I&N Dec. 408 (BIA 1998) (Rosenberg concurring and dissenting).

The relation-back doctrine generally cannot be used to cure fraud. The INS has recognized that a past marriage that is annulled *ab initio* may still result in a fraud charge. *Garcia v. INS*, 31 F.3d 441, 443–44 (7th Cir. 1994) [upheld deportation for material misrepresentation on entry where person obtained *ab initio* order that marriage was not valid and because such order should not be given effect to cover up a fraud, *i.e.*, obtaining 2nd preference visa when married]; *Hendrix v. INS*, 583 F.2d 1102 (9th Cir. 1978). Similarly, vacating an annulment to validate a marriage *ab initio* does not cure the fraud. *Witter v. INS*, 113 F.3d 549 (5th Cir. 1997). *But see Mayo v. Schiltgen*, 921 F.2d 177 (8th Cir. 1990).

"Negative credibility finding alone in an asylum case is not the equivalent of a finding of willful misrepresentation and the one does not necessarily lead to the other…" *Singh v. Gonzales,* 413 F.3d 156, 160–61 (1st Cir. 2005) [found person ineligible for INA §245(i) relief because of several intentional misrepresentations].

INA §212(a)(6)(C)(i) in lieu of INA §204(c)—Court upheld BIA's denial of employment-based AOS where it found that respondent's previous marriage constituted a fraudulent scheme to obtain an immigration benefit under INA §212(a)(6)(C)(i) without addressing INA §204(c). *Coelho v Gonzales,* 452 F.3d 104 (1st Cir. 2006)

INA §212(i) has traditionally been used to waive fraud or a material misrepresentation under INA §212(a)(6)(C). Previously, INA §212(i) provided for a more expansive waiver that included a statute of limitations. However, the 10-year statute of limitations on fraud or misrepresentation was removed from INA §212(i) by the passage of IIRIRA §349. Additionally, the right of a parent of a USC or LPR to seek the waiver has been removed and extreme hardship to the USC/LPR relative must be established. The waiver is available to a spouse or son or daughter of a USC/LPR who can show that his or her denial of LPR stratus would result in extreme hardship to the USC/LPR spouse or parent. The extreme hardship standard is the same as that applied in suspension. *Matter of Kao & Lin,* 23 I&N Dec. 45, 49 n.3 (BIA 2001). Applying the changes in §212(i) to pending cases is not a retroactive application of the statute. *Okpa v. INS,* 266 F.3d 313, 318–19 (4th Cir. 2001); *Cervantes-Gonzales v. INS,* 244 F.3d 1001, 1005–06 (9th Cir. 2001). The §212(i) waiver is also available to an approved VAWA self-petitioner if s/he demonstrates extreme hardship to herself or her USC/LPR parent or child.

A waiver under INA §237(a)(1)(H) may also be available in certain contexts to waive a material misrepresentation. *See* Ch. 8, section VII.A (p.1009), *infra*, for a more complete discussion of the waiver.

2. Intending immigrant not in possession of valid immigrant visa or other document needed for entry and a valid unexpired passport—INA §212(a)(7)(A), 8 U.S.C. §1182(a)(7)(A). Where a no-passport charge is linked to a visa fraud charge on the grounds of misrepresentation as to identity (*i.e.*, an alias was used on the passport and visa), the no-passport charge will fail if the visa is found to have been validly issued despite the existence of the misrepresentation as to identity. *Matter of Box*, 10 I&N Dec. 87 (BIA 1962). Failure of an individual to provide the biometric identification required at the border may result in a finding that the person is inadmissible under INA §212(a)(7). 8 C.F.R. §235.1(d)(1)(ii). A waiver may be available. INA §212(k). *Mayo v. Ashcroft,* 317 F.3d 867, 873–74 (8th Cir. 2003).

3. Nonimmigrant not in possession of a valid passport for 6 months or of a BCC or NIV—INA §212(a)(7)(B), 8 U.S.C. §1182(a)(7)(B).

   3.a. LIFE Act §1103(b)(2) provides that the spouse of a USC who marries the USC abroad is inadmissible into the U.S. as a person without a valid NIV if s/he is not in possession of a valid NIV issued by a consular officer in the foreign state in which s/he was married.

G. *Miscellaneous Grounds of Inadmissibility*

1. *Alien ineligible for citizenship, or alien who has evaded the draft*—INA §212(a)(8), 8 U.S.C. §1182(a)(8). This section applies to persons who are barred from naturalization as a result of their military service evasion and does *not* include persons who were convicted of aggravated felonies and are now therefore ineligible for citizenship. *Matter of Kanga,* 22 I&N Dec. 1206 (BIA 2000); *Espinoza-Castro v. INS,* 242 F.3d 1181 (9th Cir. 2001) [court found that there was not substantial evidence to support economic hardship as reason for desertion]. Evasion of military service during Vietnam war has been specifically pardoned. Proclamation 4483 (Jan. 24, 1977) implemented by Executive Order 11967. *See Rahman v. INS*, 429 U.S. 1084 (1977). IMMACT90 has amended INA §315 so that a person who obtained an exemption from U.S. military service pursuant to the exercise of rights under a treaty is no longer ineligible for citizenship if before exercising that right s/he served in the armed forces of the foreign country of which s/he was a national. 9 FAM 40.81 N.1.1. For cases concerning any ineligibility of citizenship by reason of claiming draft exemption, *see Ceballos y Arboleda v. Shaughnessy*, 352 U.S. 599 (1957); *McGrath v. Kristensen*, 340 U.S. 162 (1950). *See also Matter of Riva*, 13 I&N Dec. 268 (BIA 1969).

2. *Falsely claiming citizenship*—INA §212(a)(6)(C)(ii), 8 U.S.C. §1182(a)(6)(C)(ii). A person who falsely represents or has falsely represented he is USC to obtain a benefit under the INA or any other federal or state law. *Theodros v. Gonzales,* 490 F.3d 396 (5th Cir. 2007) [where respondent acknowledged he had worked without authorization by stating he was USC and DHS provided a document from one employer where he checked off box, similar to an I-9, that stated he was USC or LPR, there was sufficient evidence in the record to support finding and the fact that this false claim to citizenship was made to obtain private-sector employment is not a defense]; *Rodriguez v. Gonzales,* 451 F.3d 60, 65 (2d Cir. 2006) [where respondent was convicted under 18 U.S.C. §1542 for making a false statement on a passport where he obtained passport by representing himself as a USC, his adjustment of status application was barred]; *Jamieson v. Gonzales,* 424 F.3d 765 (8th Cir. 2005) [replying "U.S." to immigration officer's question at the border regarding citizenship or country is a false representation for the benefit of entry into the US]; *Pichardo v. INS,* 216 F.3d 1198 (9th Cir. 2000) [removal order upheld based upon plea to making a false claim of USC in violation of 18 U.S.C. §91]. This applies to any representation made on or after Sept. 30, 1996. IIRIRA §344(c); Memo, Greene, Acting Assoc. Comm., Programs. (96 Act #059, HQIRT 50/5.12) (Apr. 6, 1998), *published on* AILA InfoNet at Doc. No. 98040691. It may apply to a misrepresentation on an I-9 form. *Rodriguez v. Mukasey,* 519 F.3d 773, 776–78 (8th Cir. 2008) [A noncitizen who marks the "citizen or national of the United States" box on Form I-9 for the purpose of falsely representing himself as a citizen (as distinguished from a national) to secure private employment is inadmissible under §1182(a)(6)(C)(ii)(I)]; *Kechkar v. Gonzales,* 500 F.3d 1080 (10th Cir. 2007) [where the respondent checked off the box on the I-9 that stated he was a "citizen *or* national" the court upheld the BIA's determination that he falsely claimed citizenship and that doing so for private employment is not a defense because it was done for the purpose of evading the employer sanctions statute]; *Ateka v. Ashcroft,* 384 F.3d 954, 956–57 (8th Cir. 2004) [upheld on substantial evidence grounds IJ finding of ineligibility for AOS but declined to rule, due to failure to exhaust administrative remedies, on whether a false statement on an I-9 in private employment is a bar to residency]; *Njai v. U.S.,* 484 F.Supp.2d 1040, 1048 & n.11 (D. Ariz. 2007) [person pled to 18 U.S.C. §911 and then IJ asserted removability for signing I-9]. *But see U.S. v. Karaouni,* 379 F.3d 1139 (9th Cir. 2004) [where defendant checked off I-9 box that stated he was a citizen *or* national of the U.S., he could not be convicted under §911 that makes it a crime only to make a false claim to citizenship]. The waiver under §212(i) is *not* available to waive this form of fraud or material misrepresentation [*see* INA §212(i) waiving only the first paragraph of §212(a)(6)(C)]. This section does not apply to false claims made about another person's citizenship, for example, the citizenship of the person's child. Cable, Albright, 97-State-174342 (Sept. 17, 1997), *published on* AILA InfoNet at Doc. No. 97091791. Congress has also provided an exception; a person will not be inadmissible if his or her: (1) parents were or are USCs; (2) the per-

son permanently resided in the U.S. prior to 16; and (3) the person reasonably believed at the time of making such representations that he or she was a USC. INA §212(a)(6)(C)(ii)(II). The exception is applied retroactively as if included in IIRIRA and applies to representations made on or after Sept. 30, 1996. Section 201(b)(2) of the Child Citizenship Act of 2000, PL 106-395, 114 Stat. 1631 (Oct. 30, 2000). *See also* Memo, Yates, Deputy Exe. Assoc. Comm. Operations, USCIS, HQ 70/33 (May 7, 2002), *published on* AILA InfoNet at Doc. No. 05030768 [setting forth criteria for determining a false claim to USC and determining whether an exception or prosecutorial discretion applies].

3. *Unlawful voting*—INA §212(a)(10)(D), 8 U.S.C. §1182(a)(10)(D), 22 C.F.R. §40.104. A person who has voted in violation of any federal, state or local constitutional provision, statute, ordinance, or regulation is inadmissible. Applies to voting occurring before, on or after Sept. 30, 1996. IIRIRA §347(c). A consular officer can consider whether it was a knowing violation where a knowing violation was required. 63 Fed. Reg. 64626 (Nov. 23, 1998). Congress has provided an exception; a person will not be inadmissible if his or her: (1) parents were or are USCs; (2) the person permanently resided in the U.S. prior to 16; and (3) the person reasonably believed at the time of such violation that he or she was a USC. INA §212(a)(10)(D)(ii). The exception is applied retroactively as if included in IIRIRA and applies to voting occurring before, on, or after Sept. 30, 1996. Section 201(b)(1) of the Child Citizenship Act of 2000, PL 106-395, 114 Stat. 1631 (Oct. 30, 2000) added this exception. If the DHS places the person in a removal proceeding, it must prove, under the state or federal voting statute, that a violation occurred. Depending upon the federal, state, or local law that was violated, DHS may be required to prove under the *Woodby* standard (*Woodby v. INS*, 385 U.S. 276 (1966)) that the respondent acted knowingly or willfully. *McDonald v. Gonzales,* 400 F.3d 684 (9th Cir. 2005) [where the IJ applied a civil standard to a violation of the Hawaiian voting fraud statute, the court reversed the finding of removability and found the government failed to prove a knowingly violation of the state law]. To determine whether a respondent knowingly or willfully violated a voting statute adjudicating officers should determine: "(1) how, when and where the applicant registered to vote and/or voted; (2) the extent of the applicant's knowledge of the election laws; (3) whether the applicant received any instructions, or was questioned verbally about his or her eligibility to vote; (4) who provided the applicant with information about election laws or his or her eligibility to vote; (5) whether the election registration form and/or voting ballot: (a) contains a specific question asking if the applicant is a USC; (b) requires the applicant to declare under penalty of perjury that he or she is a USC; or (c) requires the applicant to be qualified to vote and lists specifically the requirement of U.S. citizenship elsewhere on the form." Memo, Yates, Deputy Exe. Assoc. Comm. Operations, USCIS, HQ 70/33 (May 7, 2002), *published on* AILA InfoNet at Doc. No. 05030768 [setting forth the criteria to be applied for a willful or knowingly violation where the federal, state, or local authority requires such a violation and permitting the exercise of prosecutorial discretion under the Commissioner's Nov. 17, 2000, memo].

4. *International child abduction*—INA §212(a)(10)(C), 8 U.S.C. §1182(a)(10)(C). If a U.S. court has granted custody of a USC child to a person, and the child is detained, retained or withheld outside the U.S. from the person granted custody, the person is inadmissible until the child is surrendered to the person granted custody. This provision now includes and makes inadmissible persons who assist, support, or provide safe haven to abductors or who are the spouse (other than the spouse who is the parent of the abducted child), child (other than the abducted child), parent, sibling, or agent of an abductor if designated by the Secretary of State. The grounds of inadmissibility do not apply to a child located in a country that is a signatory to the Hague Convention on the Civil Aspects of International Child Abduction.

5. *Illiteracy*—IMMACT90 eliminated illiteracy, *Matter of Gaglioti*, 14 I&N Dec. 677 (Comm. 1974), as a ground of inadmissibility. In addition, Congress eliminated the requirement that a person must remain in his or her home country for 90 days before obtaining an IV if s/he was in the U.S. in an unlawful status, at the same time it eliminated §245(i).

H. *Security and Related Grounds*

1. *Espionage, Sabotage, or Illegal Activity*—INA §212(a)(3)(A), 8 U.S.C. §1182(a)(3)(A). An alien whom the consular officer or AG knows or has reasonable ground to believe seeks to enter the U.S. to engage solely, principally, or incidentally in:

1.a. Espionage or sabotage (I), or a violation or evasion of any laws prohibiting export of goods, technology or sensitive information (II). INA §212(a)(3)(A)(i)(I)–(II), 8 U.S.C. §1182(a)(3)(A)(i)(I)–(II). *Beslic v. INS,* 265 F.3d 568 (7th Cir. 2001) [void for vagueness challenge rejected]. Export laws may be violated when goods, technology or sensitive information is transferred to NIV holders *in* the U.S. 15 C.F.R. §734.1(b)(1). *See generally* 15 C.F.R. §730 *et seq.* DOS has developed a Technology Alert List (TAL) to deny admission to a person who may engage in technology transfer. The TAL consists of a Critical Field List, which designates major fields of controlled goods and technologies that raise technological transfer concerns and the DOS list of state sponsors of terrorism. 9 FAM 40.31 Exh. I; Cable, DOS, 02-State-147566 (Aug. 2, 2001), *published on* AILA InfoNet at Doc. No. 03030449 (Mar. 4, 2002). DOS has developed a procedure to help consular officers to determine whether there is reason to believe that certain persons (including visiting students and scholars) might be ineligible under INA §212(a)(3)(A)(i)(II). Cable, DOS, 02-State-147566 (Aug. 2, 2002), *published on* AILA InfoNet at Doc. No. 03030449; Cable, DOS, 98-State-015652 (Jan. 28, 1998), *reprinted in* 75 No. 27 *Interpreter Releases* 980–84 (July 17, 1998). They also rely on a Visa Mantis cable process to verify the applicant's background. 9 FAM 40.31 Exh. I; Cable, DOS, 02-State-147566 (Aug. 2, 2002), *published on* AILA InfoNet at Doc. No. 03030449; Cable, DOS (99-State-158241) (Aug. 24, 1999), *published on* AILA InfoNet at Doc. No. 99120673. DOS procedures allows for a more expedited process to issue 12-month visas if the person is returning to same program or activity (whether U.S. government sponsored or not) and performing the same functions as previously authorized through Mantis, the post has evidence that a previous Mantis authorization was received and the post requests a post-check Visas Mantis process. Cable, DOS, 03-State-285912 (Oct. 7. 2003), *published on* AILA InfoNet at Doc. No. 03121143; Cable, DOS, 03-State-153587 (June 5, 2003), *published on* AILA InfoNet at Doc. No. 03061748. If a visa applicant has not been cleared within 90 days, s/he may request the status of his or her case by inquiring at *SAOInquiries@state.gov.*

(1) Export Administration Act violations—Under Export Control Act regulations, a person or employer may violate the Act if he "release[s] ... technology or software subject to the Export Administration Regulations to a foreign national in the United States." 15 C.F.R. §734.2(b)(1). This means that an employer bringing a "high-tech" employee into the U.S. may violate the Export Administration Act by disclosing or releasing to him or her software or technology that is restricted. The definition of release is very broad under a "deemed export" rule and includes: (1) visual inspection by foreign nationals of U.S. origin equipment and facilities; and (2) oral exchanges of information in the U.S. or abroad. 15 C.F.R. §734.2(b)(3). Thus, an employer may be liable criminally and/or civilly for obtaining an H-1 and bringing a person into the U.S.

1.b. Any other unlawful activity—INA §212(a)(3)(A)(ii), 8 U.S.C. §1182(a)(3)(A)(ii). DOS views this section as *not* changing the existing interpretation of the law, thereby limiting the scope of this ground of inadmissibility. Cable, DOS, 91-State-171906 (May 26, 1991), *reprinted in* 68 No. 23 *Interpreter Releases* 755–59 (June 24, 1991). DOS has normally interpreted the right to exclude persons who may be engaged in unlawful activities as limited to such matters as violation of foreign asset control regulations. It "cautions all consular officers that this enactment is not intended to result in new procedures, new lines of inquiry. It does not open new horizons ... The Department is strongly of the view that it is inappropriate to adjudicate [technical, regulatory crimes or violations] through the nonimmigrant visa application process." *Id.* INS has opined that the section may be used to deny visas and entry to persons who belong to organized crime groups operating in states that formerly belonged to the USSR, even if s/he has no conviction. Legal Opinion, Martin, General Counsel, HQ 235-P (Sept. 14, 1995), *reprinted in* 72 No. 40 *Interpreter Releases* 1420, 1430–32 (Oct. 16, 1995). DOS concurred in that view in February 1996. 9 FAM 40.31 N.4

1.c. Any activity, a purpose of which is the opposition, control or overthrow of the U.S. government by force, violence or other unlawful means—INA §212(a)(3)(A)(iii), 8 U.S.C. §1182(a)(3)(A)(iii).

2. *Terrorist Activity*—INA §212(a)(3)(B), 8 U.S.C. §1182(a)(3)(B).

2.a. Inadmissible under INA §212(a)(3)(B)(i) if the person:

(1) Has engaged in a terrorist activity;

(2) Is one whom a consular officer or AG or Secretary of DHS knows or has reasonable grounds to believe is engaged in or likely to engage in terrorist activity; the BIA has equated "reasonable grounds to believe" with "probable cause." *Matter of U-H-,* 23 I&N Dec. 355, 356 (BIA 2002) [found that the USA PATRIOT Act did not alter the "reasonable grounds to believe" standard].

(3) Has incited terrorist activity under circumstances indicating an intention to cause death or serious bodily harm;

(4) Is a representative of: (a) a foreign terrorist organization as designated by the Secy. of State under INA §219, or (b) a political, social, or other similar group that endorses or espouses terrorist activity;

(5) Is a member of a foreign terrorist organization as designated by the Secy. of State under §219 or otherwise designated by Secy. of State as a terrorist organization for engaging in terrorist activity as defined;

(6) Is a member of a group of two or more individuals, whether organized or not, which engages in or has a subgroup which engages in terrorist activity as defined unless s/he can demonstrate by clear and convincing evidence that s/he did not know, and should not reasonably have known, that the organization was a terrorist organization;

(7) Endorses or espouses terrorist activity, or persuades others to endorse or espouse terrorist activity or support a terrorist organization;

(8) Has received military-type training (as defined in 18 U.S.C. §2339D(c)(1)) from or on behalf of any organization that, at the time the training was received, was a terrorist organization as defined;

2.b. The spouse or child of a person who is inadmissible under this section is also inadmissible if the activity causing the person to be found inadmissible occurred within the last 5 years. However, with respect to inadmissibility of a person who espouses or supports terrorism, his or her child or spouse is not inadmissible if she did not know or should not reasonably have known of the spouse's activity or there are reasonable grounds to believe the spouse who is inadmissible has renounced the activity causing his or her inadmissibility.

2.c. "Terrorist activity" is defined as an act unlawful in a foreign country or if committed in the U.S. would be unlawful under U.S. law and involves:

(1) Hijacking or sabotage of any conveyance;

(2) The seizing or detaining or threatening to kill, injure, or continue to detain another individual to compel a third person to carry on or abstain from an act as an explicit or implicit condition for release;

(3) A violent attack on an internationally protected person under 18 U.S.C. §1116(b)(4) [head of state, foreign minister, representative, officer, employee or agent of a government];

(4) An assassination;

(5) The use of any biological or chemical agent or nuclear weapon/device or explosive, firearm, or other weapon or dangerous device (other than for mere personal monetary gain), with intent to endanger, directly or indirectly, the safety of one or more individuals or to cause substantial property damage;

(6) Any threat or attempt or conspiracy to commit the above acts.

The statute has been determined not to be unconstitutionally vague. *Hussain v. Mukasey,* 518 F.3d 534, 537-38 (7th Cir. 2008) [although statute stretches the definition of terrorism, it defines it—and in denying petitioner's request for cancellation, it is not relevant that the MQM-H in Pakistan did not have a political agenda and was not hostile to the U.S.]; *McAllister v.*

Att'y Gen. of the U.S., 444 F.3d 178, 185–89 (3d Cir. 2006) [upheld finding of deportation and rejected challenge that terrorist definition under §212(a)(3)(B)(iii)(V)(b) was unconstitutionally vague, that the definition of terrorist organization under §212(a)(3)(B)(iv) required that person must act on his own or with a terrorist organization as opposed to *any* organization and that political offense exception applied].

2.d. "Engaged in terrorist activity" means in an individual capacity or as a member of an organization:

(1) To commit or incite to commit a terrorist activity under circumstances indicating an intention to cause death or serious bodily injury;

(2) To prepare or plan a terrorist activity;

(3) To gather information on potential targets for terrorist activity;

(4) To solicit funds or other things of value for: (i) terrorist activity, (ii) a terrorist organization designated under §219 or otherwise designated by the Sec of State in consultation with the AG, or (iii) two or more individuals engaging in terrorist activities unless the solicitor can demonstrate, by clear and convincing evidence, that he did not know, and should not reasonably have known, that the organization was a terrorist organization. Prior to the REAL ID Act addition of the clear and convincing standard, the government's determination was rejected, *see Cheema v. Ashcroft,* 383 F.3d 848, 856–59 (9th Cir. 2004) [two donations by wife to unspecified widows and orphans in India with no evidence linking it to specific group is not a terrorist activity; BIA reversed under substantial evidence standard. However, husband's fundraising did reach terrorist organizations and unfavorable inferences can be drawn against him from his telephone calls to Sikh militants supporting BIA's findings].

The criminal statute (18 U.S.C. §2339B(a)) to avoid constitutional problems has been construed to require proof that a person charged under it "had knowledge of the organization's designation [as a terrorist organization] or knowledge of the unlawful activities that caused it to be so designated." *Humanitarian Law Project v. DOJ,* 352 F.3d 382, 385 (9th Cir. 2003). However, that standard has not been applied in the immigration context, and the INA still provides for removal based upon activity committed prior to an organization's designation as a terrorist organization.).

(5) To solicit individuals to engage in terrorist activity or for membership in terrorist organizations as stated above and under the same standards as this subsection. Pursuant to the REAL ID Act, a person may be removed under this ground even if the organization was not designated formally as a terrorist organization, unless the respondent can "demonstrate by clear and convincing evidence that he did not know, and should not reasonably have known, that the organization was a terrorist organization." REAL ID Act §103(b). Prior to the REAL ID Act, this section required that the organization be designated a terrorist organization at the time of the questionable activity. When the organization was not designated then the individual does not know or should not reasonably know that the solicitation furthered terrorist activity. *Daneshvar v. Ashcroft,* 355 F.3d 615, 625–29 (6th Cir. 2004) [reversed denial of motion to reopen for AOS by BIA, where the alleged Iranian terrorist organization, MEK, was not designated as such at the time the respondent engaged in conduct and where DHS failed to consider evidence regarding applicant's state of mind as a 16-year-old joining the MEK]. Although *Daneshvar* represents the pre–REAL ID Act law, it has continuing vitality because REAL ID applies only to removal proceedings, and, per the language of the Act, does not apply to deportation or exclusion proceedings.

(6) Material Support Provision, INA §212(a)(3)(B)(iv)(VI). To commit an act that the actor knows, or reasonably should know, affords material support, including a safe house, transportation, communications, funds, transfer of funds or other material financial benefit, false documentation or identification, weapons (including chemical, biological, or radiological weapons) explosives, or training: (i) for the commission of a terrorist activity; (ii) to any individual the actor knows, or reasonably should know, has committed or plans to commit a terrorist activity; (iii) to a terrorist organization designated under §219 or otherwise designated by the Secy. of State in consultation with the AG or to any member of such an organization; (iv) to a terrorist organization made up of 2 or more people

or to any member of such an organization, unless the actor can demonstrate, by clear and convincing evidence, that he did not know, and should not reasonably have known, that the organization was a terrorist organization.

(a) Challenging a Material Support Claim—An applicant for a benefit or a person facing removal for material support to a *nondesignated* terrorist organization [called a Tier III organization] may seek to prove that she "did not know, and should not reasonably have known that the [nondesignated] organization [as defined under INA §212(a)(3)(B)(vi)(III)] was a terrorist organization." INA §212(a)(3)(B)(iv)(VI)(dd).

i) Burden of Proof—The burden of proof is on the respondent or applicant who must establish by "clear and convincing evidence" that he did not know or have reason to know that the organization was a terrorist organization. INA §212(a)(3)(B)(iv)(VI)(dd); *Matter of S-K-* 23 I&N Dec. 936, 942 n.5 (BIA 2006) [finding that the Chin National Front that fights against repression of Chins by the illegitimate Burma military government is a terrorist organization, that contributions to the organization need not be demonstrated to be for terrorist purposes, and that a contribution of $685 over an 11month period was sufficient to establish "material" support for purposes of INA §212(a)(3)(B)(iv)(VI)]; *cf. Matter of S-K-,* 24 I&N Dec. 289 (AG 2007) [maintaining precedential value of BIA decision but remanding case to BIA in light of DHS decision to grant a waiver under INA §212(d)(3)(B)(i) and not to apply the "material support" bar on asylum to certain persons providing support to the CNF]; *Singh-Kaur v. Ashcroft*, 385 F.3d 293 (3d Cir. 2004) [the provision of food and shelter for terrorists is providing material support].

(b) Waiver Provision—In addition to establishing that the applicant did not know or have reason to know that the organization was a terrorist organization when it provided material support, an applicant may seek a waiver from the material support provision. Under INA §212(d)(3)(B)(i), the Secy. of State and the Secy. of DHS in consultation with each other and the AG can, in their "unreviewable discretion," issue waivers of the material support and most other terrorism grounds of inadmissibility as a result of the broad powers for waiver accorded them under the Consolidated Appropriations Act, 2008, PL 110-161, Div. J §691(a), 121 Stat. 1844, 2364–65 (Dec. 26, 2007). The waiver may be applied to applications for benefits or protection under the INA, including asylum, refugee status, AOS, and following to join petitions and may be based on a waiver involving a group or a waiver due to duress. Memo, Scharfen, Deputy Director, USCIS ¶ I. D (May 24, 2007), *published on* AILA InfoNet at Doc. No. 07070572; Memo, Langlois, Chief, Asylum Division, USCIS, HQASM 120/16.1 (June 1, 2007), *reprinted in* 12 No. 14 *Bender's Immigration Bulletin* 899, 974–79 (July 15, 2007) [providing field instructions for implementing the material support provisions in asylum cases]. The Secretary of *State* may not, however, grant a waiver during a removal proceeding, although the DHS Secretary may do so. The Act itself exempted certain groups, including Hmong and Montagnard groups and the CNF, that were the subject of the AG's decision in *Matter of S-K-*. In light of the Act, DHS granted the respondent in *Matter of S-K-* asylum and the BIA vacated its grant of deferral of removal and found no need to address withholding. *Matter of S-K-,* 24 I&N Dec. 475 (BIA 2008). To obtain either a group based exemption or a duress exemption an applicant must meet certain threshold requirements: (1) establish that s/he is otherwise eligible for the immigration benefit; (2) pass all background and security checks; (3) fully disclose all material support; and (4) establish s/he poses no danger to the safety or security of the U.S. Memo, Scharfen, Deputy Director, USCIS ¶ II (May 24, 2007), *published on* AILA InfoNet at Doc. No. 07070572.

i) Group Based Exemptions.

a) By Congressional Act—In the Consolidated Appropriations Act of 2008, PL 110-161, §691(b), *supra,* Congress designated certain organizations that do not pose a threat to the United States and therefore will not be considered terrorist organizations on the basis of any act or event that occurred before Dec. 26, 2007 the date of the Act's passage. The groups are the Karen National Union/Karen Liberation Army (KNU/KNLA), the Chin National Front/Chin National Army (CNF/CAN), the Chin National League for Democracy (CNLD) the Kayan New Land Party (KNLP), the Arakan Liberation Party (ALP), the Tibetan Mustangs, the Cuban Alzados de Armas, the Karenni National Progressive Party, and appropriate groups affiliated with the Hmong and the Montagnards. Notwithstanding the exemption afforded persons providing material support to these groups, DHS has identified circumstances where a person may still be found ineligible under terrorism grounds regarding these groups and has therefore stayed processing the cases: (1) if the terrorist activity involved something other than material support such as armed insurrection; (2) if the activity in regard to a Tier III organization was not under duress; (3) if the person was inadmissible under the terrorist related provisions, other than material support, based on any activity or association related to Tier I, II or III organizations even if the activity was under duress; (4) if the applicant voluntarily provided medical care to Tier I-III organization, to members of the organizations or to individuals who have engaged in terrorist activity; and (5) if the applicant is inadmissible because s/he is the spouse or child of someone in the above referenced categories. Memo, Scharfen, Deputy Dir., DHS (Mar. 26, 2008), *reprinted in* 85 No. 14 *Interpreter Releases* 993, 1046–49 (Mar. 31, 2008)

b) By the Secretary of State—The Secy. of State has exercised her authority to exempt the material support provision as follows: **2006** for Burmese Karen individuals living in refugee camps in Thailand who provided support for Karen National Union (KNU) or Karen National Liberation Army (KNLA); Chin refugees from Burma living in Malaysia, India or Thailand who provided support to Chin National Front (CNF) or Chin National Army (CNA); **2007** for refugee resettlement applicants to provide material support to: (1) KNU/KNLA; (2) Chin National Front/Chin National Army; (3) Chin National League for Democracy (CNLD); (4) Kayan New Land Party (KNLP); (5) Arakan Liberation Party (ALP); (6) Tibetan Mustangs; (7) Cuban Alzados en Armas; and (8) Karenni National Progressive Party (KNPP).

c) By the Secretary of DHS— By notices in the Federal Register the Secy. of DHS exempted the above eight groups from the application of the material support bar. 72 Fed. Reg. 9954–57 (Mar. 6, 2007). The National Liberation Army of Colombia (ELN) is also exempt, Memo [Authorization to USCIS], Rosenzweig, Deputy Asst. Sec., Policy, DHS (Dec. 18, 2007), *published on* AILA InfoNet at Doc. No. 08041772, as is the provision of material support under duress to the Revolutionary Armed Forces of Colombia (FARC), Memo, Scharfen, Deputy Director, USCIS (Sept. 6, 2007), *reprinted in* 12 No. 21 *Bender's Immigration Bulletin* 1527, 1593 (Nov. 1, 2007).

ii) Duress Exemption. The Secretary of DHS exercised his authority to exempt the "material support" provision for persons who provided support under "duress" to terrorist organizations (*e.g.,* asylees who were required to pay ransom or extortion money). Memo, Chertoff, Secy. of DHS, Exercise of Authority Under Sec. 212(d)(3)(B)(i) (Apr. 27, 2007), *published on* AILA InfoNet at Doc. No. 07050168; 72 Fed. Reg. 26138–39.

a) To establish duress the following factors are considered: (1) could person avoid giving material support; (2) the severity and type of harm inflicted or threatened and if threatened the likelihood of actual harm; and (3) to whom the harm was directed. DHS should consider the totality of the circumstances including also: (1) the amount, type, and frequency of material support provided, (2) the nature of the activities committed by the terrorist organization; (3) the applicant's awareness of those activities; (4) the passage of time since the material support; and (5) the applicant's conduct since that time. *See* Memo, Chertoff (Apr. 27, 2007), *supra.* The exemption shall apply if the person satisfies DHS that: (1) s/he is seeking a benefit or protection under the INA that she is deemed to be eligible for; (2) passed background and security checks; (3) fully disclosed all material support provided; and (4) posses not danger to the U.S. *See* Memo, Scharfen, Deputy Director, USCIS (May 24, 2007), *published on* AILA InfoNet at Doc. No. 07070572, at ¶ II for above threshold criteria and at ¶III B for additional criteria regarding the "totality of the circumstances".

b) The duress exemption does *not* apply to person who provides material support to Tier I and Tier II terrorist organizations as designated under INA §212(a)(3)(B)(vi)(I) [Foreign Terrorist Organization List] or INA §212(a)(3)(B)(vi)(II) [Terrorist Exclusion List]. Memo, Scharfen, Deputy Director, USCIS ¶ I C (May 24, 2007), *published on* AILA InfoNet at Doc. No. 07070572. It only applies to Tier III (undesignated terrorist organizations) under INA §212(a)(3)(B)(vi)(III).

iii) Limitation on Review. There is no judicial review of a decision to grant or deny of waiver except in the review of a final removal order and then only as to questions of law or constitutional questions under INA §242(a)(2)(D).

(c) Criminal Context. In criminal context the government must prove a "material support" charge by demonstrating that the defendant knowingly provided the support *and* that he knew that the organization he provided the support to was a designated foreign terrorist organization or engaged in terrorist activities. *U.S. v. Abdi,* 498 F.Supp.2d 1048, 1059–61 (S.D. Ohio 2007).

(d) Definition of Representatives. Representative for purposes of this section includes an officer, official, or spokesman of an organization, and any person who directs, counsels, commands, or induces an organization or its members to engage in terrorist activities.

2.e. Terrorist organization is defined as: (i) an organization designated under §219 by the Secy. of State; (ii) an organization, otherwise designated, upon publication by DOS in the Federal Register, as a terrorist organization after finding that the organization engages in terrorist activity including providing material support; (iii) a group of 2 or more individuals whether or not organized who engages in, or has a subgroup that engages in, terrorist activities, including providing material support. *McAllister v. Att'y Gen. of the U.S.,* 444 F.3d 178, 185–89 (3d Cir. 2006) [upheld finding of deportation and rejected challenge that terrorist definition under §212(a)(3)(B)(iii)(V)(b) was unconstitutionally vague, that the definition of terrorist organization under §212(a)(3)(B)(iv) required that person must act on his own or with a terrorist organization as opposed to *any* organization and that political offense exception applied]. Prior to the REAL ID Act, an organization that solely provided material support to a terrorist organization was not, itself, considered a "terrorist organization" under the former INA §212(a)(3)(B)(vi). This was changed by REAL ID.

2.f. Congress established a procedure for the Secretary of State, in consultation with Congress, to designate an organization as a foreign terrorist organization (FTO)

(1) Procedure for Designating FTOs—The Office of Coordinator for Counterterrorism at DOS is responsible for designating terrorist organizations. It not only looks at actual terrorist attacks that a group has carried out, but also whether the group has engaged in planning and preparations for possible future acts. The office then prepares a detailed administrative record that includes both classified and nonclassified information. If the Secretary of State, in consultation with the AG and Secretary of Treasury, decide to make the designation, Congress is notified. Memo, DOS, Foreign Terrorist Organization Designation (Apr. 22, 2004), *published in* 81 No. 21 *Interpreter Releases* 681, 687–90 (May 24, 2004). The Secretary of State designated 8 persons as terrorists and 29 organizations as terrorist on Mar. 19, 2002. 67 Fed. Reg. 12633–34 (Mar. 19, 2002). At the same time the Office of Foreign Assets Control issued blocking orders regarding property of terror-

ists and terrorist organizations. 67 Fed. Reg. 12644–46 (Mar. 19, 2002). A current list of the designated FTOs, as well as other related DOS information, can be found at *www.state.gov/s/ct/rls/fs/37191.htm*.

(2) Other Methods for Designating FTOs—INA §219(a) represents only one method for designating terrorist organizations. An organization may also be designated by the Secretary of State in consultation with or upon the request of the Attorney General or the Secretary of Homeland Security. INA §212(a)(3)(B)(iv)(II) [Terrorist Exclusion List]. An organization may also be designated as a terrorist organization by the Department of Treasury pursuant to the International Emergency Economic Powers Act (IEEPA), 50 U.S.C. §1701 *et seq*. This designation would fall under the terrorist organization provision of INA §212(a)(3)(B)(iv)(III). Neither of these designations requires that the organization be a *foreign* terrorist organization. Procedures for Challenging FTO Designation

(a) Generally—An organization may submit a petition for revocation of its §219 FTO status and provide evidence that the relevant circumstances are sufficiently different from the circumstances that were the basis for the designation. If no review has taken place within 5 years, the Secretary of State must review the designation to determine whether such designation should be revoked. INA §219(a)(4). There is limited judicial review under this section. INA §219(b). *People's Mujahedin Organization of Iran v. DOS,* 182 F.3d 17 (D.C. Cir.), *cert. denied,* 529 U.S. 1104 (2000) [unsuccessful challenge to DOS designation of two organizations]. One court has determined that in designating organizations as terrorist (which results in freezing their bank accounts, making their members inadmissible into the U.S., and preventing them from receiving donations), the Secretary violates due process by not affording the organizations notice of the impending designation and an opportunity to present contrary evidence. *National Council of Resistance of Iran v. DOS,* 251 F.3d 192 (D.C. Cir. 2001). For challenges to IEEPA designation, *see, e.g., Holy Land Foundation v. Ashcroft,* 333 F.3d 156 (D.C. Cir. 2003), *cert. denied* 124 S.Ct. 1506 (2004).

(b) Challenges During Removal Proceedings—INA §219(a)(8) provides that the validity of a §219 FTO designation cannot be raised as a defense or objection by a respondent in removal proceedings. This provision also applies to defendants in criminal prosecutions and has been upheld as constitutional. *See U.S. v. Afshari,* 426 F.3d 1150 (9th Cir. 2005). *Cf. National Council of Resistance of Iran v. DOS,* 251 F.3d 192, 196 (D.C. Cir. 2001).

2.g. Membership in a Terrorist Organization—The statute does not define membership for purposes of inadmissibility. DOS has taken the position that a person may be found inadmissible "without a finding of actual participation in terrorist activities." Membership should be determined from facts which include, but are not limited to:

(1) Acknowledgment of membership by the organization, by other members, or by the applicant;

(2) Actively working to further the organization's aims and methods in a way suggesting close affiliation constituting membership, *e.g.*, proposing legislation;

(3) Occupying a position of trust in the organization, past or present;

(4) Receiving financial support from the organization, *e.g.*, scholarships, salary, pension;

(5) Contributing money to the organization;

(6) Determination of membership by a competent court;

(7) Frequent association with other members;

(8) Participation in the organization's activities, even if lawful;

(9) Voluntarily displaying symbols of the organization; and

(10) Receiving honors or awards given by the organization.

Cable, DOS, 97-State-191813 (Oct. 9, 1997), *reprinted in* 75 No. 8 *Interpreter Releases* 294, 295–300 (Mar. 2, 1998). A person must be a current member. Past membership is *not* a basis for inadmissibility. However, if a person was a past member, current membership may be inferred absent a showing of current nonmembership. *Id.* Termination may be shown by changes in a person's attitudes, actions, associations, and activities over time. A single event "such as a self-serving resignation" would not usually establish that membership has ended. *Id.*

2.h. Know or Reason to Know—To be inadmissible for being a member or representative of a terrorist organization, the person must know or have reason to know that the organization is terrorist. This can be met by facts peculiar to the individual applicant, publication of organization in the Federal Register, and/or presentation of the names of the organizations to applicants at the Consular Offices. *Id.*

2.i. Waiver under INA §212(d)(3)(B)(i)—Consolidated Appropriations Act of 2008, PL 110-161, Sec. 691, Division J. The Secy. of State in consultation with the AG/DHS or the Secy. of DHS in consultation with the AG/DOS may waive the terrorism ground of inadmissibility under INA §212(a)(3)(B) except for: (1) persons involved in terrorist activity on behalf of organizations designated under INA §219 (Foreign Terrorist Organization List) known as Tier I organizations or otherwise designated in the Federal Register (Terrorist Exclusion List) known as Tier II organizations; (2) members or representatives of Tier I or Tier II organization; (3) persons who have voluntarily and knowingly engaged in or endorsed or espoused or persuaded others to endorse or espouse or support terrorist activity on behalf of a Tier I or Tier II organization; (4) persons who have voluntarily and knowingly received military-type training from a Tier I or Tier II organization; and (5) any group (designated as Tier III organization pursuant to INA §212(a)(3)(B)(vi)(III)) that has engaged in terrorist activity against he U.S. or another democratic country or engaged in a pattern or practice of terrorist activity directed at civilians. The waiver is in the "unreviewable discretion" of the Secretaries of DHS/DOS and is not subject to judicial review except through an order of removal and then only as to constitutional questions or questions of law under INA §242(a)(2)(D). The waiver authority may *not* be exercised by the Secretary of *State* (but can be exercised by the Secretary of DHS) while the person is in removal proceedings. *See in this section* "Waiver Provision," ¶ 2.d(6)(b) (p.105), *supra*.

2.j. Retroactive Application—The changes made to the definition of terrorist activity and terrorist organization in the USA PATRIOT Act apply retroactively to any action taken on, before or after Oct. 26, 2001. USA PATRIOT Act, PL 107-56, §411(c), 115 Stat. 272 (2001). An exception to retroactivity is provided if the group the person is linked to was not designated as a terrorist organization at the time. Further, the Secy. of State with the AG may decide not to apply the law retroactively to a person who committed acts outside the U.S. before Oct. 26, 2001, if a consular officer concludes that there is no reasonable grounds to believe that the person knew or reasonably should have known that his actions would further a terrorist activity. The changes made by the REAL ID Act, PL 109-13, 119 Stat. 231 (2005), Div. B, §103, apply to removal proceedings instituted before, on or after May 11, 2005, and apply to acts and conditions constituting a ground of inadmissibility or deportation existing before, on or after May 11, 2005.

2.k. Terrorist Screening Center/Terrorist Threat Integration Center (TTIC) Identities Database—Pursuant to the Homeland Security Presidential Directive 6 dated Sept. 16, 2003 titled "Integration and Use of Screening Information" to protect against terrorism, the Secretary of State, the Attorney General, the Secretary of Homeland Security and the Director of the Central Intelligence Agency entered into a Memorandum of Understanding On the Integration and Use of Screening Information To Protect Against Terrorism." Homeland Security Presidential Directive-6, Bush (Sept. 16, 2003), *reprinted in* 80 No. 36 *Interpreter Releases* 1305–06, 1322 (Sept. 22, 2003). The MOU establishes a Terrorist Screening Center that consolidates the government approach to terrorism. The Center is to maintain a consolidated database, ensure consistent application of the law, provide operation support to assist in the identification of persons screened and will be under a Director who will report to the AG through the Director of the FBI. The database established is called the Terrorist Threat Integration Center (TTIC) Identities Database and is designed to include all information the government possesses related to the identities of individuals "known or appropriately suspected to be or have been involved in activities constituting, in preparation for, in aid of, or related to terrorism." The Purely Domestic Terrorism Information database will continue to be maintained separately by the FBI. MOU, Powell, et al., Integration and Use of Screening Information to Protect Against Terrorism (Sept 16, 2003), *published on* AILA InfoNet at Doc. No. 03092540.

3. *Association with Terrorist Organizations*—INA §212(a)(3)(F), 8 U.S.C. §1182(a)(3)(F). Any person who the Secy. of State or the AG in consultation determines has been associated with a terrorist organization and intends while in the U.S. to engage solely, principally, or incidentally in activities that could endanger the welfare, safety, or security of the U.S. is inadmissible. This section is made retroactive to any acts taken before, on, or after Oct. 26, 2001. USA PATRIOT Act §411(c), 115 Stat. 272 (2001).

4. *Foreign Policy Grounds*—INA §212(a)(3)(C), 8 U.S.C. §1182(a)(3)(C): A person is inadmissible if the Secy. of State has reasonable grounds to believe that his or her entry or proposed activity in the U.S. "would have potentially serious adverse foreign policy consequences for the United States."

4.a. Exception for foreign officials—An alien who is an official of a government (or purported government) or who is a candidate for election to a foreign government office (immediately prior to the election) is not inadmissible for past conduct, statements, or beliefs that are lawful in the U.S.;

4.b. Exception for other persons—All other aliens are not inadmissible for statements and acts that would be legal in the U.S. unless the Secy. of State "personally determined that the ... admission would compromise a compelling United States foreign policy interest." If the Secretary does make the determination he must timely notify the Senate and House Judiciary and Foreign Relations Committee.

The Conference Report noted that: "It is the intent of the conference committee that this authority would be used sparingly and not merely because there is a likelihood that an alien will make certain remarks about the United States or its policies. Furthermore, the conferees intend that the 'compelling foreign policy interest' standard be interpreted as a significantly higher standard than the general 'potentially serious adverse foreign policy consequences standard....' The fact that the Secretary of State personally must inform the relevant Congressional Committees when a determination of excludability is made under this provision is further indication that the conferees intend that this provision be used only in unusual circumstances." H.R. Conf. Rep. No. 955 at 6794, 101st Cong., 2d Sess. at 129 (1990).

5. *Immigrant Membership in Totalitarian Party*—INA §212(a)(3)(D), 8 U.S.C. §1182(a)(3)(D)

5.a. Any *immigrant* who is or has been a member of or affiliated with the Communist or any other totalitarian party (or subdivision or affiliate), domestic or foreign, is inadmissible. Affiliate defined at 22 C.F.R. §40.34(a).

5.b. An *immigrant* is not inadmissible if:

(1) his or her membership is or was involuntary, solely under the age of 16, by operation of law or for the purpose of obtaining employment, food rations, or other essentials of living. A question of whether membership was voluntary or a "meaningful association" has been addressed by the courts and the Board. *Rowoldt v. Perfetto*, 355 U.S. 115 (1957); *Matter of Rusin*, 20 I&N Dec. 128 (BIA 1989). *See also* INA §§101(a)(2) and (e), 8 U.S.C. §§1101(a)(2) and (e); 22 C.F.R. §40.34.

(2) the membership or affiliation terminated at least 2 years before application for admission (or 5 years if a member of a party controlling the government), *and* s/he is not a threat to U.S. security; or

(3) the AG, in his discretion, grants a waiver to the parent, spouse, son, daughter, brother, or sister of a USC or a spouse, son or daughter of an LPR for "humanitarian purposes, to assure family unity or when it is otherwise in the public interest if [s/he] is not a threat to the security of the United States." INA §212(a)(3)(D)(iv), 8 U.S.C. §1182(a)(3)(D)(iv).

(4) IMMACT90 has substantially changed this area of the law by permitting persons who are members of Communist or anarchist parties to enter the U.S. as nonimmigrants. This issue had been actively litigated for many years. *Kleindienst v. Mandel*, 408 U.S. 753 (1972); *Abourezk v. Reagan*, 785 F.2d 1043 (D.C. Cir. 1986), *aff'd per curiam by an*

equally divided court, 108 S.Ct. 252 (1987); *Adams v. Baker*, 909 F.2d 643, 648–50 (1st Cir. 1990); *American-Arab Anti-Discrimination Comm. v. Nelson*, 940 F.2d 445 (9th Cir. 1991), *amended and superseded on denial of reh'g,* 970 F.2d 501 (9th Cir. 1991); *Rafeedie v. INS*, 795 F.Supp. 13, 21–23 (D.D.C. 1992); *Allende v. Schultz*, 605 F.Supp. 1220 (D. Mass. 1988); *Matter of Hajdu*, 16 I&N Dec. 497 (BIA 1978).

6. *Nazis, Persons Committing Genocide, Persons Committing Torture*—INA §212(a)(3)(E), 8 U.S.C. §1182(a)(3)(E): Nazis or former Nazis are inadmissible. INA §212(a)(3)(E)(i). For Nazis to be excludable at least one court has ruled that the individual must have personally engaged in persecution and was not involuntarily involved. *Petkiewytsch v. INS*, 945 F.2d 871 (6th Cir. 1991). *See also Laipenieks v. INS,* 750 F.2d 1427, 1431 (9th Cir. 1985) [deportability may only be sustained when the evidence establishes that the individual in question personally ordered, incited, assisted or otherwise participated in the persecution]. *But see Negele v. Ashcroft,* 368 F.3d 981, 983 (8th Cir. 2004) (and cases cited therein) [being an armed guard and dog-handler at concentration camp without proof of direct involvement in persecution is sufficient for removal] *Maikovskis v. INS*, 773 F.2d 435 (2d Cir. 1985), *cert. denied*, 476 U.S. 1182 (1986). Genocide for purposes of this section has been defined consistent with the International Convention on the Prevention and Punishment of Genocide to include any of the following acts committed with the intent to destroy, in whole or part, a national, ethnic, racial, or religious group by: (1) killing members of the group; (2) causing serious bodily or mental harm to members of the group; (3) deliberately inflicting on the group conditions of life calculated to bring about its physical destruction in whole or part; (4) imposing measures intended to prevent births within the group; and (5) forcibly transferring children of the group to another group. Memo, Pearson, Ex. Assoc. Comm., Field Operations (HQADN 70/21.1-12-P) (July 19, 1999), *published on* AILA InfoNet at Doc. No. 99071992.

   Genocide—Any person who ordered, incited, assisted, or otherwise participated in conduct outside the U.S. that would be genocide under 18 U.S.C. §1091(a) is inadmissible. INA §212(a)(3)(E)(ii), 8 U.S.C. §1182(a)(3)(E)(ii).

   Torture—Any person who outside the U.S. committed, ordered, incited, assisted, or otherwise participated in torture under 18 U.S.C. §2340 or, under color of law of any foreign nation, any extrajudicial killing as defined in section 3(a) of the Trafficking Victims Protection Act (TVPA) is inadmissible. INA §212(a)(3)(E)(iii), 8 U.S.C. §1182(a)(3)(E)(iii).

7. *Violators of Religious Freedom*—INA §212(a)(2)(G), 8 U.S.C. §1182(a)(2)(G). A person who while serving as a foreign government official was responsible for or carried out, at any time, severe violations of religious freedom as defined in Section 3 of the International Religious Freedom Act of 1998 (PL 105-292) is inadmissible. His spouse and children are also inadmissible. Violations of religious freedom under Section 3 of the Act include arbitrary prohibitions on, restrictions of, or punishment for religious assembly, religious speech, changing religious affiliation, possession and distribution of religious literature, and raising a child in the religious teachings of one's choice. It also includes detention, interrogation, forced religious conversion, forced labor and other acts because of a person's religious beliefs or practices. In determining whether someone is a foreign government official, DHS may look to the definition at 9 FAM 40.26 N3.3 and consult with the DOS. Memo, Pearson, Ex. Asst. Comm., Field Operations (HQADN 70/21.1.1-P) (July 9, 1999), *reprinted in* 76 No. 27 *Interpreter Releases* 1091, 1103–06 (July 19, 1999). The provision applies to all admissions after Oct. 27, 1998. *Id.*

8. *The Cuban Liberty and Democratic Solidarity Act of 1996* makes inadmissible and denies a visa to any person who the Secy. of State determines after Mar. 12, 1996, has confiscated property, traffics in confiscated property, or is a corporate officer, principal, or shareholder with a controlling interest in an entity which has been involved in the confiscation of property or trafficking in confiscated property in Cuba, where there is a claim of ownership by a U.S. national. This section also applies to the spouse, minor child, or agent of such person. The law permits an exemption for medical reasons or for purposes of litigation under this Act, and guidelines drafted by INS also exempt diplomats of foreign governments and representatives of international organizations. 61 Fed. Reg. 30655–56 (June 17, 1996).

9. *Confiscators of American Property*—The Secy. of State may deny a visa to any person who, through the abuse of position, including a governmental or political party position, converts or has converted for personal gain real property that has been confiscated or expropriated, where there is

a claim of ownership by a national of the U.S. It also includes those who are complicit with a confiscator or induce such action. Omnibus Consolidated Approp. Act, PL 105-277, Div. G (Foreign Affairs Reform and Restructuring Act of 1998) §2225, 112 Stat. 2681–819 (1998). 8 U.S.C. §1182d. The Asst. Secy. of State for Economic and Business Affairs makes the determinations under this section. A person subject to this provision will be sent *prior* notification that his name will be put in the appropriate lookout systems and will be given 45 days to respond. The provision does not apply to property in any country established by international mandate through the U.N. or to any territory recognized to be in dispute by the U.S. 64 Fed. Reg. 29731 (June 2, 1999).

10. *Persons Who Disclose Confidential Business Information*—The Secy. of State "shall deny a visa to, and the [AG] shall exclude" a person: (1) who previously served as, an officer or employee of the Organization for the Prohibition of Chemical Weapons and disclosed any U.S. confidential business information coming to him in the course of his employment or official duties that has resulted in financial loss or damages to a U.S. national; (2) who traffics in U.S. confidential business information, where there is a proven claim of ownership by a U.S. national; or (3) who is a corporate officer, principal, shareholder with a controlling interest of an entity which has been involved in the unauthorized disclosure. Includes spouses, minor children, or agents of a person who is inadmissible. Omnibus Consolidated Approp. Act, PL 105-277, Div. I (Chemical Weapons Convention Implementation Act of 1998), §103(f), 112 Stat. 2681–85 (1998).

11. *Certain Haitian nationals accused of human rights violations* are ineligible for visas. Department of Commerce, Justice and State, the Judiciary and Related Agencies and Appropriations and Emergency Supplement Act, 1998, PL 105-119, 111 Stat. 2440, Sec. 621 (Nov. 26, 1997), Omnibus Consolidated and Emergency Supplemental Appropriations Act of 1999, PL 105-277, 112 Stat. 2681 (Oct. 21, 1998) §616; Consolidated Appropriations Act, 2004, PL 108-199, 118 Stat. 3 (Jan. 23, 2004) Div. B, title VI, §616. These include persons who are credibly alleged to be involved in certain political killings, members of the Haitian High Command involved in the coup, persons credibly alleged to be members of FRAPH, persons involved in the execution of certain political figures including Antoine Izmery, Guy Malary, Father Jean-Marie Vincent, and Mireille Durocher Bertin, persons on a list provided to President Aristide by Tony Lake, and persons who the FBI sought to interview in connection with the execution of Mireille Durocher Bertin.

12. *Forced abortion or sterilization policies*—Consolidated Appropriations Act, 2000, PL 106-113, 113 Stat. 1501, Sec. 801 (Nov. 29, 1999). Any foreign national whom the Secretary of State finds, "based on credible and specific information, to have been directly involved in the establishment or enforcement of population control" by forced abortion or sterilization is inadmissible "unless the Secretary has substantial grounds for believing that the foreign national has discontinued his or her involvement with, and support for, such policies." 8 U.S.C. §1182e.

13. *Aiders or Abettors to Colombian Insurgent and Paramilitary Groups*—Consolidated Appropriations Act, 2004, PL 108-199, 118 Stat. 3 (Jan. 23, 2004), §564. Any person whom the Secy. of State determines, based on credible evidence, has: (1) willfully provided any support to the Revolutionary Armed Forces of Colombia (FARC), the National Liberation Army (ELN) or the United Colombian Self Defense organization (AUC) including taking or failing to take actions which allow, facilitate, or otherwise foster the activities of such group; or (2) committed, ordered, incited, assisted or otherwise participated in the commission of gross violations of human rights, including extra-judicial killings, in Colombia. The Secretary of State may waive this provision on a case-by-case basis for urgent humanitarian reasons or to support the peace process in Colombia.

14. *Persons Engaged in Coerced Organ or Bodily Tissue Transplantation*—PL 107-228, Div. A, title II §232 (Sept. 30, 2002), 116 Stat. 1372. The Secretary of State shall direct consular officers not to issue visas to person where there is "credible and specific information" that an applicant has been "directly involved with the coercive transplantation of human organs or bodily tissue" unless the foreign national has discontinued his involvement or support of such practices. This provision does not apply to heads of state, heads of government, or cabinet-level ministers. A waiver in the national interest is available. 8 U.S.C. §1182f.

15. The President also has used executive proclamations to suspend the admission of persons into the U.S., INA §212(f), 8 U.S.C. §1182(f). Proclamation 7750, 69 Fed. Reg. 2287–88 (Jan. 12, 2004) [suspending IVs and NIVs from entering if they are public officials or former public officials engaged in corruption having a serious adverse effect on U.S. national interest]; Proclamation 7524,

67 Fed. Reg. 8857–58 (Feb. 26, 2002) [suspension of IVs and NIVs of persons who undermine or injure Zimbabwe's democratic institutions]; Proclamation 7452, 66 Fed. Reg. 34775–76 (June 26, 2001) [suspending the entry of persons who seek to undermine peace, stability, reconciliation or democratic development in the Western Balkans]; Proclamation 7249, 64 Fed. Reg. 62561 (Nov. 12, 1999) [suspending immigrant and nonimmigrant entry into U.S. of Yugoslav officials responsible for repression in Kosovo]; Proclamation 7060, 62 Fed. Reg. 65987–88 (Dec. 12, 1997) [suspended senior officials of UNITA in Angola as well as adult members of their immediate families for IVs and NIVs]; Proclamation 6925, 61 Fed. Reg. 52233 (Oct. 3, 1996) [denying entry for NIVs and IVs and their immediate families from Burma who formulate, implement or benefit from policies that impede Burma's transition to democracy];. Proclamation 5377, 50 Fed. Reg. 41329 (Oct. 10, 1985) [suspending nonimmigrant entry of officers and employees of the Cuban Government or Cuban Communist Party], *see City of New York v. Baker*, 878 F.2d 507 (D.C. Cir. 1989); Proclamation 4865, 46 Fed. Reg. 48107 (Sept. 29, 1981); Executive Order 12324, 46 Fed. Reg. 48109 (Sept. 29, 1981); Executive Order 12807, 57 Fed. Reg. 23133–34 (May 24, 1992), to interdict Haitians seeking to enter the U.S. *Sale v. Haitian Centers Council*, 509 U.S. 155 (1993); *Haitian Refugee Center, Inc. v. Baker*, 953 F.2d 1498 (11th Cir.), *cert. denied*, 502 U.S. 1122 (1992); *Haitian Refugee Center, Inc. v. Baker*, 949 F.2d 1109 (11th Cir. 1991). This includes the power to suspend the entry of persons aboard commercial airlines who do not comply with regulations regarding document fraud. IIRIRA §124. The Secy. of State is also given the authority to order consular officers to discontinue issuing IVs and NIVs to a person from a country that does not accept back its citizens who are deported. INA §243(d). The AG is also given authority where she determines there is "an actual or imminent mass influx of aliens arriving on the coast of the United States or near a land border" that presents urgent circumstances requiring a federal response, to authorize state and local law enforcement officers with approval of appropriate authority of state or local level to perform DHS duties. 8 U.S.C. §1103(a)(8).

I. *Waivers of Inadmissibility*

1. INA §212(a) waivers—There are a number of waivers specifically written into sections of INA §212 discussed *supra.* For example, INA §212(a)(9)(B)(v) waives the 3/10 year bar under §212(a)(9)(B) and INA §§212(a)(9)(C)(ii) & (iii) waives inadmissibility for unlawful reentry after removal or remaining in the U.S. unlawful for more than one year under §212(a)(9)(C). These waivers are discussed *supra* in the respective sections relating to the ground of inadmissibility. The waivers may be obtained through CBP at a port of entry, field office, or admissibility review office, through USCIS or through a DOS consulate abroad. For a detailed procedural outline on how to obtain the waiver *see* Waiver of Inadmissibility Practice Guide (Mar. 13, 2007), *published on* AILA InfoNet at Doc. No. 07060774.

2. Cancellation of Removal for LPRs—INA §240A(a), 8 U.S.C. §1229b(a) [similar to former INA §212(c)]

   2.a. This section is similar to former INA §212(c) relief. Under IIRIRA §304, Congress eliminated INA §212(c) relief and replaced it with cancellation of removal for LPRs. In order to qualify an applicant must be lawfully admitted for permanent residence for not less than 5 years, be residing continuously in the U.S. for 7 years after having been admitted in any status; and not be convicted of any aggravated felony. The 7-year period of continuous residence can begin when a person is "admitted" in "any status" which includes admission as a nonimmigrant *Matter of Blancas,* 23 I&N Dec. 458 (BIA 2002) [Mexican admitted on a border crossing card] or temporary resident *Matter of Perez,* 22 I&N Dec. 689, 692 (BIA 1999), and may include persons not "admitted" at the border. *Garcia-Quintero v. Gonzales,* 455 F.3d 1006, 1015–19 (9th Cir. 2006) [admission into family unity program is sufficient to qualify as an admission for purposes of cancellation and LPR in removal proceeding had the necessary seven years based upon his acceptance into the family unity program while in the US]. But in the view of one court the person must be a lawful permanent resident not a temporary resident to qualify. *Bonhometre v. Ashcroft,* 414 F.3d 442, 448–50 (3d Cir. 2005) [relief not available to temporary resident]. The 7-year period is deemed to end when the person is served with a notice to appear or when the person has committed an offense referred to in INA §212(a)(2) that renders him or her inadmissible or removable under INA §§237(a)(2) or 237(a)(4). INA §240A(d)(1). *Briseno-Flores v. Att'y Gen. of the U.S.,* 492 F.3d 226, 229–31 (3d Cir. 2007) [respondent's conviction in 1985 stopped the time for calculating the seven years needed for suspension; nor did a new seven year period begin from that point; *Okeke distinguished*]; *Matter of Perez,* 22 I&N Dec. 689 (BIA 1999) [stop-time period begins with commission not conviction of a crime]. *But see Okeke v. Gonzales,* 407 F.3d 585 (3d Cir. 2005) [in case involving 10-year provision for cancellation for nonresidents, a conviction under §240A(d)(1) does not bar the clock from restarting so that applicant can accrue a new 10-year period of continuous residence where applicant left the U.S. and re-entered lawfully]. The clock for the 7-year residence requirement is not stopped by the commission of an offense that is not "referred to in Section 212(a)(2)." *Matter of Campos-Torres,* 22 I&N Dec. 1289 (BIA 2000) [firearms offense]. A person is ineligible for the waiver if s/he obtained her LPR status by fraud. *Matter of Koloamatangi*, 23 I&N Dec. 548 (BIA 2003). The standards to be applied in weighing the equities to obtain cancellation will follow those set forth in *Matter of Marin. Matter of C-V-T-,* 22 I&N Dec. 7 (BIA 1998). But a showing of outstanding and unusual equities need not be made. *Matter of Sotelo,* 23 I&N Dec. 201 (BIA 2001). For greater details concerning this now highly limited form of relief, *see* Chapter 8, Relief from Removal (p.957).

2.b. *Continuing availability of INA §212(c) waivers*—Under AEDPA, Congress precluded all LPRs who had a conviction that would make them deportable for certain specified grounds from applying for INA §212(c) relief. The effective date of AEDPA was Apr. 24, 1996. A question remained as to whether such relief would be available to persons who were already in deportation proceedings on Apr. 24, 1996 or whose criminal conduct or conviction took place before April 24. The AG, vacating the decision of the BIA, determined that AEDPA applied retroactively to bar any applications that were pending on Apr. 24, 1996. *Matter of Soriano*, 21 I&N Dec. 516 (AG 1997); *Matter of Gonzalez-Camarillo,* 21 I&N Dec. 937 (BIA 1997) [applying *Soriano* to application in conjunction with adjustment before IJ]. However, after years of litigation, the AG promulgated regulations that provided that persons in proceedings before AEDPA (Apr. 24, 1996) continue to be eligible for §212(c) relief. *See* 8 C.F.R. §§212.3(g), 1212.3(g). Then, with respect to those placed in proceedings after AEDPA, the Supreme Court, in *INS v. St. Cyr,* 533 U.S. 289, 324 (2001), held that neither IIRIRA §304, nor AEDPA §440(d), applied retroactively barring §212(c) and that INA "§212(c) relief remains available for aliens ... whose convictions were obtained through plea agreements and who, notwithstanding those convictions, would have been eligible for §212(c) relief at the time of their plea under the law then in effect." *Accord, Thaqi v. Jenifer,* 377 F.3d 500 (6th Cir. 2004) [*St. Cyr* retroactivity analysis applies where a person was deportable for the commission of two crimes and he pleaded guilty to the second crime prior to AEDPA]. The *St. Cyr* analysis extends to persons who enter a plea of guilt prior to AEDPA even if the judgment of conviction imposing sentence was entered after AEDPA's effective date. *Alvarez-Hernandez v. Acosta,* 401 F.3d 327, 332–34 (5th Cir. 2005). However, a person may not be covered if his conviction was entered after AEDPA and before IIRIRA, *Morgan v. Keisler,* 507 F.3d 1053 (6th Cir. 2007); *Cruz-Bucheli v. Gonzales* 463 F.3d 105 (1st Cir. 2006); or prior to AEDPA but it was subsequently vacated and he re-pleaded after IIRIRA, *Lawrence v. Gonzales,* 446 F.3d 221, 225 (1st Cir. 2006) [the court rejected petitioner's claim that his 1995 conviction should fix the pertinent date for INA §212 (c) and not the vacatur and superseding 1998 conviction which was done for strategic purposes to avoid the expanded aggravated felony definition]; or if he was criminally charged before IIRIRA but absconded and pled guilty after IIRIRA. *Cespedes-Acquino v. Att'y Gen. of the U.S.,* 498 F.3d 221 (3d Cir. 2007).

Post–*St. Cyr* Rules—DOJ subsequently adopted rules to comply with *St. Cyr* and the rules permit a person to apply for INA §212(c) relief if a plea agreement was made before (even if not entered until after) Apr. 24, 1996. 8 C.F.R. §§ 1003.44, 1212.3(f). It also covers persons who committed aggravated felonies and served five years if their plea agreements were made before Nov. 29, 1990. 8 C.F.R. §1212.3(f)(4)(ii). It does not cover person who were found guilty after trial or who served five years. *Alexandre v. U.S. Att'y Gen.,* 452 F.3d 1204, 1207 (11th Cir. 2006) [following 8 C.F.R. §§1003.44(a), 1212.3(f)(4)(ii), the court determined that a person was not eligible for INA §212(c) relief because of retroactivity concerns who was found guilty after trial in 1989 and who served 5 years before applying for relief in 1994]. If the plea was made after Apr. 24, 1996, but before Apr. 1, 1997 an applicant would be eligible if he complies with AEDPA §440(d). A person is ineligible for INA §212(c) relief if the plea was made after Apr. 1, 1997, the ground of deportation or removal does not have a statutory counterpart in §212, or the person is under INA §§212(a)(3)(A)–(C), (E) and (10)(C) inadmissible for security, terrorism. foreign policy, Nazism, or international child abduction grounds. 8 C.F.R. §§1212.3(f)(3)–(5), (h)(3). *Cyrus v. Keisler,* 505 F.3d 197, 201–02 (2d Cir. 2007) [respondent with gun conviction is not eligible for INA §212(c) relief and therefore not eligible to reopen under §1003.44]. The date of the plea agreement is the date it was agreed to by the parties. 8 C.F.R. §1212.3(h). The rules must be strictly adhered to if applicant seeks relief. *Akio Kawashima v. Gonzales,* 503 F.3d 997, 1004–05 (9th Cir. 2007) [court upheld BIA's denial of a motion to reopen for relief under the regulations because respondent failed to put the notation on the motion pursuant to 8 C.F.R. §1003.44 that it was a "special motion to seek section 212(c) relief" as the rule required].

Moreover, circuit cases not overruled by *St. Cyr* may provide even broader coverage extending INA §212(c) to persons who became eligible for the relief after their pleas under the law that existed prior to IIRIRA. For example, a person who did not obtain 7 years of LPR status until after his or her plea, but would have been eligible under prior law may still be protected. *Alvarez-Hernandez v. Acosta,* 401 F.3d 327, 329–32 (5th Cir. 2005) [under law prior to *St. Cyr,* 7 years could be accrued after the entry of the guilty plea]. The courts are also now free to allow for a *Gabryelsky* adjustment of status in conjunction with an INA §212(c) application where the criminal conviction occurred before passage of AEDPA and IIRIRA. *Matter of Azurin,* 23 I&N Dec. 695 (BIA 2005) [for convictions prior to AEDPA, the Board reaffirmed *Matter of Rainford*, 20 I&N Dec. 598 (BIA 1992) and *Matter of Gabryelsky*, 20 I&N Dec. 750 (BIA 1993) and determined a §212(c) waiver was available in conjunction with an application for adjustment even if the ground of deportation (gun charge) could not be waived because it did not have an equivalent ground of inadmissibility]; *Drax v. Reno,* 338 F.3d 98 (2d Cir. 2003) [court found that persons with drug conviction and attempted weapons conviction was eligible for *Gabryelsky* relief even where a visa was not immediately available because the IJ could have granted a continuance]; *Nolasco v. U.S.*, 358 F.Supp. 224, 230–31 (S.D.N.Y. 2004) [applied *St. Cyr* and *Drax* to order of deportation that was executed, and respondent physically removed from the U.S. but illegally re-entered, prior to either decision]. But if the conviction occurred after AEDPA or IIRIRA, a "*Gabryelsky* adjustment" is not permitted. *Ruiz-Almanzar v. Ridge,* 485 F.3d 193 (2d Cir. 2007).

Five-Year Incarceration Doesn't Necessarily Bar §212(c) Relief—Even persons who were barred post–*St. Cyr* because they were incarcerated for 5 years or more may be eligible for INA §212(c) relief if their conviction was based upon a plea that arose before IMMACT90 (Nov. 29, 1990). 8 C.F.R. §1212.3(f)(4)(ii) and 69 Fed. Reg. 57826, 57830–31 (Sept. 28, 2004) [adopting *Toia*]; *Toia v. Fasano,* 334 F.3d 917 (9th Cir. 2003) [IMMACT90 §511, which was enacted on Nov. 29, 1990, and barred INA §212(c) relief to persons who served a term of imprisonment of more than 5 years for an aggravated felony, may not be applied retroactively under *St. Cyr.* If the conviction arose before Nov. 29, 1990 such person is eligible for §212(c) relief]. *But see Singh v. Mukasey,* 520 F.3d 119 (2d Cir. 2008) [person who confessed to crime before Nov. 29, 1990, but pled guilty after was barred from INA §212(c) relief] *Alexandre v. U.S. Att'y Gen.,* 452 F.3d 1204, 1207 (11th Cir. 2006) [following 8 C.F.R. §§1003.44(a), 1212.3(f)(4)(ii), the court determined that a person was not eligible for INA §212(c) relief because he was found guilty after trial in 1989 and served 5 years before applying for relief in 1994]; *Reid v. Holmes,* 323 F.3d 187 (2d Cir. 2003) [rejected retroactivity argument regarding §511 for someone convicted before 1990]; *Torres-Rascon v. Heston,* 339 F.3d 633 (8th Cir. 2003) [determining that person who served 5 years after guilty plea was barred and branding as "absurd" respondent's argument that the 5 years in detention had to accrue at the time of the guilty plea and not after to bar INA §212(c) relief]; *Melo v. Ashcroft,* 364 F.Supp.2d 183 (D.R.I. 2005) [relying on *Barreiro* and finding that IMMACT90 applied retroactively to bar INA §212(c) relief and therefore respondent who had aggregate time in prison of 5 years where some time was before and some after IMMACT90 was barred]; *See also cases counting the five years: Saravia-Paguada v. Gonzales,* 488 F.3d 1122 (9th Cir. 2007) [time spent as recidivist counted toward 5 years and court rejected retroactivity argument because unlike *Toia* respondent was convicted after trial in 1988]; *Moreno-Cebrero v. Gonzales,* 485 F.3d 395 (7th Cir. 2007) [time spent in pretrial detention counted toward the 5-

year period]; *Spina v. DHS,* 470 F.3d 116, 125–30 (2d Cir. 2006) [time spent in pre-conviction detention when credited is counted toward the five years and the court rejected the idea that the time should only be accrued at the end of a person's sentence as a matter of fairness regarding INA §212(c) eligibility]; *Gordon v. Ashcroft,* 283 F.Supp.2d 435 (D. Mass. 2003) [pretrial detention period is included in the five years of imprisonment and respondent is therefore barred from relief]; *See also Romero-Rodriguez v Gonzales,* 488 F.3d 672 (5th Cir. 2007) [deferring to BIA's position pursuant to *Chevron* that the 5 year period runs from the date of the BIA's subsequent denial of an appeal following a prior reopening of the case but holding that the BIA, but not the court, may grant *nunc pro tunc* relief]; *Velez-Lotero v. Achim,* 414 F.3d 776 (7th Cir. 2005) [person who had served more than 5 years in prison after pleading guilty to a controlled substance violation in 1995 was properly denied INA §212(c) relief]; *Clavis v. Ashcroft,* 281 F.Supp.2d 490, 493–97 (E.D.N.Y. 2003) [rejected INA §212(c) argument for someone with greater than 5 years of incarceration without addressing retroactivity argument]; *Brzuszek.v. McElroy,* 275 F.Supp.2d 442, 448–52 (S.D.N.Y. 2003) [rejected retroactivity argument for persons who pleaded guilty after AEDPA on Apr. 24, 1996, but who committed the offenses prior to that date]. *Cf. Gomes v. Ashcroft,* 311 F.3d 43, 45–46 (1st Cir. 2002) [the term "admission" in IMMACT90 §511(b) applies not only to the original admission into the U.S. but to whenever applicant applies for INA §212(c) and therefore bar due to 5-year imprisonment is applicable]. At least one court has also found that pre-AEDPA aggravated felony convictions where a person cumulatively spent more than five years in jail would not bar INA §212(c) relief. *Paulino-Jimenez v. INS,* 279 F.Supp.2d 313, 317–19 (S.D.N.Y. 2003) [person who pled guilty to two aggravated felonies prior to AEDPA would be eligible for INA §212(c) relief as he served less than 5 years on each one]. Also, where 5 years accrued as a result of improperly determining that respondent was not eligible for INA §212(c) relief under *Matter of Soriano* the court held that §212(c) relief would be applied *nunc pro tunc* even where conviction arose after 1990. *Edwards v. INS,* 393 F.3d 299 (2d Cir. 2004) [the court rejected the idea that *nunc pro tunc* equitable relief could only be applied where there was a constitutional violation or where respondent could prove that he would definitively obtain the relief; respondents need only demonstrate they were erroneously denied the opportunity to apply when they were eligible]. *But see Spina v. DHS,* 470 F.3d 116, 125–30 (2d Cir. 2006) [petitioner not eligible for *nunc pro tunc* relief under *Edwards* because he had served more than 5 years at the time the IJ made the legal error in applying *Matter of* Soriano]; *Fernandes Pereira v. Gonzales,* 417 F.3d 38, 46–48 (1st Cir. 2005) [rejected *nunc pro tunc* relief as well as constitutional claim, where respondent was not statutorily eligible for §212(c) relief due to erroneous decisions by IJ/BIA on retroactivity later reversed by Supreme Court in *St. Cyr*].

Motion to Reopen for §212(c) Relief—The DHS also issued regulations permitting motions to reopen to apply for INA §212(c) relief in limited circumstances. 8 C.F.R. §1003.44, 69 Fed. Reg. 57826–35 (Sept. 28, 2004). In order to obtain the benefit under the regulation the applicant has to establish that s/he: (1) was an LPR and is now subject to a final order of deportation or removal; (2) agreed to plead guilty or *nolo contendere* pursuant to plea agreement made before Apr. 1, 1997; (3) had 7 consecutive years of lawful unrelinquished domicile in the U.S. prior to the date of the final deportation or removal order; and (4) is otherwise eligible to apply for §212(c) relief under standards in effect at time s/he made plea, regardless of when plea was entered by the court. 8 C.F.R. §1003.44(b). The motion to reopen must be made prior to Apr. 26, 2005. A person is eligible to file a special motion to reopen irrespective of the time and number limitations on motions to reopen, but may not reopen the case if a prior §212(c) motion was denied on discretionary grounds or under *St. Cyr.* An applicant must submit a completed Form I-191 with supporting documentation and the motion must contain a notation that says it is a "Special Motion to Seek Section 212(c) Relief." 8 C.F.R. §1003.44(f). The provision does not apply to persons who have departed the U.S., to persons who had final orders and illegally returned, or to persons who have not been admitted or paroled. 8 C.F.R. §1003.44(k). *Avila-Sanchez v. Mukasey,* 509 F.3d 1037, 1041 (9th Cir. 2007) [regulation does not violate equal protection or due process]; *Robledo-Gonzales v. Ashcroft,* 342 F.3d 667, 681–83 (7th Cir. 2003) [equal protection challenge rejected under rational basis test to regulation barring persons who have departed the U.S. from applying for INA §212(c) relief]. It also does not apply to persons who are ineligible because there is no comparable ground of inadmissibility. *Cyrus v. Keisler,* 505 F.3d 197, 201–02 (2d Cir. 2007) [respondent with gun conviction is not eligible for INA §212(c) relief and therefore not eligible to reopen under §1003.44].

Pre-AEDPA Convictions Do Not Bar §212(c) Relief—At least one court has ruled that a person eligible for INA §212(c) relief pursuant to *St. Cyr* remains eligible for the pre-AEDPA convictions even if he has subsequent convictions which would bar cancellation of removal for those post-AEDPA/IIRIRA convictions. *Da Rosa Silva v. INS,* 263 F.Supp.2d 1005, 1013–15 (E.D. Pa. 2003).

Person in Exclusion Proceeding Not Barred—The BIA has found that a person in exclusion proceedings is not barred from INA §212(c) relief even after Apr. 24, 1996. *Matter of Fuentes-Campos*, 21 I&N Dec. 905 (BIA 1997) [AEDPA bar to §212(c) is inapplicable to persons in exclusion proceedings].

Equal Protection Challenges Rejected—However, courts have found that INA §212(c) is not preserved under an equal protection analysis for persons in deportation proceedings convicted after Apr. 24, 1996. *Chuang v. U.S. Att'y Gen.,* 382 F.3d 1299, 1303–04 (11th Cir. 2004) [no equal protection violation because rational basis for distinction]; *Armendariz-Montoya v. Sonchik,* 291 F.3d 1116, 1122–23 (9th Cir. 2002) [no equal protection violation because excludable persons given right to apply for §212(c) relief]; *Domond v. INS,* 244 F.3d 81, 87–88 (2d Cir. 2001) [same]; *Mohammed v. Reno,* 309 F.3d 95, 102–03 (2d Cir. 2002) [affirmed holding in *Domond* post–*St. Cyr* in decision to deny stay pending appeal]; *Asad v. Reno,* 242 F.3d 702, 706–07 (6th Cir. 2001) [equal protection not violated]; *Almon v. Reno,* 192 F.3d 28 (1st Cir. 1999) [equal protection not violated and *Francis* distinguished]; *Requena-Rodriguez v. Pasquarell,* 190 F.3d 299, 308–09 (5th Cir. 1999) [same]; *DeSousa v. Reno,* 190 F.3d 175, 183–85 (3d Cir. 1999) [same]; *Jurado-Gutierrez v. Greene,* 190 F.3d 1135, 1152 (10th Cir. 1999) [no equal protection violation]; *Turkhan v. Perryman,* 188 F.3d 814, 828–29 (7th Cir. 1999) [same]; *LaGuerre v. Reno,* 164 F.3d 1035, 1041 (7th Cir. 1998), *cert. denied, LaGuerre v. Reno* 528 U.S. 1153 (2000) [in *dicta* discussed no equal protection violation]; *But see Servin-Espinoza v. Ashcroft,* 309 F.3d 1193 (9th Cir. 2002) [finding equal protection violation post *Fuentes-Campos* because of differing treatment; *Estrada-Torres* distinguished].

At least one court has rejected an equal protection challenge based upon the claim that persons who are convicted after trial before AEDPA/IIRIRA as distinguished from those who pled guilty as in *St. Cyr* before that time should not be denied INA §212(c) relief. *Brooks v. Ashcroft,* 283 F.3d 1268, 1274 (11th Cir. 2002).

Conviction After Trial May Bar §212(c) Relief—INA §212(c) may also not be preserved post–*St. Cyr* for persons who were convicted of criminal offenses after trial. 8 C.F.R. §1212.3(f) and 69 Fed. Reg. 27826, 27828 (May 17, 2004); *see Saravia-Paguada v. Gonzales,* 488 F.3d 1122, 1129–35 (9th Cir. 2007) [followed *Armendariz* and found that provision barring §212(c) relief to someone who was incarcerated for 5 years was not barred retroactively to a conviction prior to 1990 because the conviction was obtained after trial by jury and not through a plea]; *Mbea v. Gonzales,* 482 F.3d 276, 280–82 (4th Cir. 2007) [followed *Chambers* and found no impermissible retroactive effect where person went to trial]; *Alexandre v. U.S. Att'y Gen.,* 452 F.3d 1204, 1207 (11th Cir. 2006) [following 8 C.F.R. §§1003.44(a), 1212.3(f)(4)(ii), the court determined that a person was not eligible for INA §212(c) relief because of retroactivity concerns who was found guilty after trial in 1989 and who served 5 years before applying for relief in 1994]; *Hernandez-Castillo v. Moore,* 436 F.3d 516, 519–20 & n.3 (5th Cir. 2006) [followed *Rankine* and *Chambers* and rejected INA §212(c) relief to LPR who was found guilty in 1989 of felony indecency with a child after trial and who asserted he gave up plea agreement believing he had INA §212(c) relief available]; *Thom v. Ashcroft,* 369 F.3d 158, 161–64 (2d Cir. 2004) [following *Rankine*, court determined that trial in 1982 for second degree murder did not implicate *St. Cyr.* retroactivity even if it was before the definition of aggravated felonies and before the 5-year incarceration limitation on INA §212(c)]; *Rankine v. Reno,* 319 F.3d 93 (2d Cir. 2003) [*St. Cyr* and *Landgraf* analysis do not extend to a conviction after a trial]; *Armendariz-Montoya v. Sonchik,* 291 F.3d 1116, 1121–22 (9th Cir. 2002) [where LPR did not plead but was convicted of aggravated felony *St. Cyr* is inapplicable]; *Chambers v. Reno,* 307 F.3d 284 (4th Cir. 2002) [where 17-year-old was convicted of robbery with a deadly weapon and sentenced to 4 years, which was not an aggravated felony at the time, IIRIRA §304(b) applied retroactively to bar INA §212(c) relief notwithstanding *St. Cyr*]; *Brooks v. Ashcroft,* 283 F.3d 1268, 1274 (11th Cir. 2002) [rejected constitutional equal protection challenge on theory that persons who were convicted should not be treated differently than those who pled under *St. Cyr*; however the Court did not address the statutory retroactivity argument for want of jurisdiction]; *Montenegro v. INS,* 245 F.Supp.2d 936, 937–39 (C.D. Ill. 2003) [where aggravated felon did not plead guilty but was convicted after trial *St. Cyr* does not apply].

Conviction After Trial Not a Bar to §212(c) Relief—Walcott v. Chertoff, 517 F.3d 149 (2d Cir. 2008) [petitioner could make a *Restrepo* argument despite his jury conviction being on appeal after the passage of AEDPA because he could have waived appeal and applied for §212(c) relief before AEDPA]; *Atkinson v. Att'y Gen. of the U.S.,* 479 F.3d 222 (3d Cir. 2007) [a person convicted before AEDPA/IIRIRA did *not* have to demonstrate a *quid pro quo* to obtain §212(c) relief because personal reliance is not a factor; rather the issue is whether the enactment of a new law has created a new disability following *Landgraf, Hughes and Hadix*]; *Carranza-De Salinas v. Gonzales,* 477 F.3d 200 (5th Cir. 2007) [relying on the second circuit opinion in *Restrepo*, the court held that IIRIRA's abolition of §212(c) would not be applied retroactively if the respondent demonstrated actual reliance by choosing not to apply for §212(c) relief immediately after his trial and instead waiting until deportation proceedings were initiated to bolster his claim for rehabilitation]; *Hem v. Maurer,* 458 F.3d 1185 (10th Cir. 2006) [rejected subjective/actual reliance in favor of objective reasonable reliance of prior law, where respondent went to trial and did not appeal his conviction]; *Thaqi v. Jenifer,* 377 F.3d 500 (6th Cir. 2004) [*St. Cyr* retroactivity analysis applies where a person was deportable for the commission of two crimes when he was convicted after jury trial in the first trial but pleaded guilty to the second crime prior to AEDPA]; *Ponnapula v. Ashcroft,* 373 F.3d 480 (3d Cir. 2004) [where defendant went to trial prior to AEDPA/IIRIRA on reliance that he would still be eligible for INA §212(c) relief because he would not be sentenced to five years and was not, AEDPA/IIRIRA should not retroactively bar relief]; *Restrepo v. McElroy,* 369 F.3d 627, 632–40 (2d Cir. 2004) [distinguished *Rankine* and *Domond* and found that person who was convicted before AEDPA and gave up the right to apply *affirmatively* for INA §212(c) relief should not have statute abolishing relief applied against him under second prong of *Landgraf* concerning "fair notice, reasonable reliance and settled expectations"]; *See also Wilson v. Gonzales,* 471 F.3d 111, 117–23 (2d Cir. 2006) [followed *Rankine* and rejected the categorical approach for all persons who were found guilty after trial because the retroactivity analysis required an individualized showing of reliance]. *Cf. Perez v. Elwood,* 294 F.3d 552, 561–62 (3d Cir. 2002) [where person found guilty by jury in January 1997 but not sentenced until June 1997 he was ineligible for INA §212(c) relief which IIRIRA abolished on Apr. 1, 1997 because the "formal judgment of guilt" is defined by reference to Fed. R. Crim. P. 32(d)(1), which occurs at the time of sentence not jury adjudication]. *See also Hernandez de Anderson v. Gonzales,* 497 F.3d 927, 937–44 (9th Cir. 2007) [the BIA erred in impermissibly repealing suspension of deportation where person was convicted after trial and was placed in removal proceedings after seeking naturalization one year before the passage of IIRIRA that eliminated suspension].

Person who committed the crime prior to AEDPA/IIRIRA but pled afterwards may not be eligible for INA §212(c) under a retroactivity analysis. *James v. Riley,* 329 F.Supp.2d 570 (E.D. Pa. 2004) [rejected extension of *Ponnapula* to cover Jamaican who sold drugs before and therefore committed crimes before AEDPA/IIRIRA but pleaded afterwards].

However, 8 C.F.R. §§212.3(g), 1212.3(g) provides that persons in proceedings before AEDPA are eligible for INA §212(c) relief. *See Armendariz-Montoya v. Sonchik,* 291 F.3d 1116 (9th Cir. 2002).

Conviction After AEDPA But Before IIRIRA—Some courts have also found that a person convicted after AEDPA but before IIRIRA is also barred from relief. *Morgan v. Keisler,* 507 F.3d 1053 (6th Cir. 2007) [because AEDPA barred persons with aggravated felonies from receiving INA §212(c), and IIRIRA §321 made the definition of aggravated felonies retroactive, a person whose conviction became an aggravated felony retroactively under INA §321 is ineligible for INA §212(c) relief where his plea was entered after the passage of AEDPA on April 24, 1996 and before IIRIRA's effective date of April 1, 1997]; *Cruz-Bucheli v. Gonza-*

les 463 F.3d 105 (1st Cir. 2006) [respondent was not eligible for INA §212(c) relief because he pled guilty after the effective date of AEDPA and had no expectation following *St Cyr* that relief would still be available to him]; *Garcia-Echaverria v. U.S.,* 376 F.3d 507, 515–16 (6th Cir. 2004) [plea of guilty entered after AEDPA but before IIRIRA nevertheless means that there was no reliance]; *U.S. v. Velasco-Medina,* 305 F.3d 839 (9th Cir. 2002) [in criminal proceeding for re-entry Court rejected defense that IJ should have informed defendant of his eligibility for §212(c) relief where guilty plea taken after passage of AEDPA]; *Oguejiofor v. Attorney General,* 277 F.3d 1305, 1309–10 (11th Cir. 2002) [in *dicta* court found that guilty pleas taken after AEDPA barred retroactivity claim]; *Khan v. Ashcroft,* 352 F.3d 521 (2d Cir. 2003) [affirmed *Mohammed* and *Domond* and found no retroactivity issue in regard to respondent who committed a crime before AEDPA but pled guilty after AEDPA and before IIRIRA].

Reopening Barred If Person Not in U.S.—In addition, a person who left the country or was deported prior to the change in law may be barred from re-opening the case if s/he seeks to return or actually returns. *Avila-Sanchez v. Mukasey,* 509 F.3d 1037, 1041 (9th Cir. 2007) [former LPR who was deported and returned could not collaterally attack his first removal order because the BIA's original interpretation in *Matter of Soriano* barring §212(c) relief while erroneous did not make his removal order unlawful]; *Pena-Muriel v. Gonzales,* 489 F.3d 438 (1st Cir. 2007) [due process was not violated where the BIA refused to allow respondent, who was outside the United States, to reopen his deportation proceeding because his conviction was vacated]; *Patel v. U.S. Att'y Gen.,* 334 F.3d 1259 (11th Cir. 2003) [court of appeals lacked jurisdiction because of the criminal alien bar under INA §242(a)(2)(C) to review the denial of motion to reopen under 8 C.F.R. §1003.2(d) where the person was out of the country and the district court lacked habeas jurisdiction because the person was no longer in custody]; *Mansour v. Gonzales,* 470 F.3d 1194 (6th Cir. 2007) [when person departed for brief trip to Mexico he executed the order of removal and could not move to reopen it]; *Smith v. Ashcroft,* 295 F.3d 425, 429–31 (4th Cir. 2002) [no due process right to challenge reinstatement of order arising out of denial of INA §212(c) under AEDPA and IIRIRA because there is no property or liberty interest in discretionary statute]; *Alvarenga-Villalobos v. Ashcroft,* 271 F.3d 1169, 1172–73 (9th Cir. 2001) [rejected claim that person subject to INA §241(a)(5) should be allowed to reopen his case in light of the *Magana-Pizano* decision as that decision occurred subsequent to first deportation order]. *But see William v. Gonzales,* 499 F.3d 329 (4th Cir. 2007) [the prohibition in 8 C.F.R. §1003.2(d) to motions to reopen where the person is outside the U.S. is contrary to INA §240(c)(7)(A), 8 U.S.C. §1229a(c)(7)(A) permitting one motion to reopen without limitation and the regulation is therefore invalid]; *Mendez-Alcaraz v. Gonzales,* 464 F.3d 842, 844 (9th Cir. 2006) [court had jurisdiction to review denial of motion to reconsider filed 14 months after respondent's removal from the U.S.]; *Contreras-Rodriguez v. U.S. Att'y Gen.,* 462 F.3d 1314 (11th Cir. 2006) [although respondent was physically removed after *in absentia* order, he is not barred from filing a motion to reopen for lack of notice because §1003.23(b)(4)(ii) allows motion regarding lack of notice to be filed at "any time." *Patel* distinguished]; *Cardoso-Tlaseca v. Gonzales,* 460 F.3d 1102 (9th Cir. 2006) [where respondent's conviction is vacated after physical removal, court reversed BIA for denying motion to reopen because conviction was a "key part" of removal proceeding]; *Leitao v. Reno,* 311 F.3d 453 (1st Cir. 2002) [where person's denial of habeas was appealed and he was deported during pendency of appeal his claim is not moot because he may be permanently barred].

No Comparable Ground of Inadmissibility—A person may also be ineligible for INA §212(c) relief, if there is no ground of inadmissibility under INA §212(a) that is the statutory counterpart to the ground of removability that is the basis for removal. 8 C.F.R. §1212.3(f)(5); 69 Fed. Reg. 57826 (Sept. 28, 2004). Whether there is a statutory counterpart between the aggravated felony and a ground of inadmissibility will turn on whether Congress has employed similar language to describe substantially equivalent categories of offenses. The mere overlap between the aggravated felony and crimes of moral turpitude, for example, are insufficient to demonstrate that the provisions were statutory counterparts *Matter of Brieva,* 23 I&N Dec. 766, 770–73 (BIA 2005), *aff'd, Brieva-Perez v. Gonzales,* 482 F.3d 356 (5th Cir. 2007) [where respondent is subject to removal because the unauthorized use of a vehicle under Texas law is considered a crime of violence, he was ineligible for §212(c) relief because there is only an "incidental overlap" between INA §101(a)(43)(F) (crime of violence) and §212(a)(2)(A)(i)(I) (CIMT)]; *Matter of Blake,* 23 I&N Dec. 722 (2005), *rev'd, Blake v. Carbone,* 489 F.3d 88 (2d Cir. 2007) [the BIA's decision was that a person who the government seeks to remove because of his aggravated felony conviction for sexual abuse of a minor may not apply for INA §212(c) relief even if there is overlap with CIMT because there is no statutory counterpart that employed similar language in the grounds of inadmissibility. *Matter of Meza* distinguished]; *Zamora-Mallari v. Mukasey,* 514 F.3d 679, 689–93 (7th Cir. 2008) [in a case involving an aggravated felony for sexual abuse, the court rejected Eight Amendment, retroactivity, and equal protection challenges to *Matter of Blake* and 8 C.F.R. §1212.3(f)(5)]; *Vue v. Gonzales,* 496 F.3d 858 (8th Cir. 2007) [following its brief opinion in *Soriano v. Gonzales,* 489 F.3d 909 the court upheld the BIA's position in *Matter of Blake* and rejected an equal protection challenge to the denial of INA §212(c) to a person convicted of first degree assault where the ground of removal was both an aggravated felony and CIMT]; *Abebe v. Gonzales,* 493 F.3d 1092 (9th Cir. 2007), *petition for reh'g granted* [upheld *Blake/Brieva* in the face of equal protection, due process, retroactivity, and statutory challenges]; *Dalombo Fontes v. Gonzales,* 483 F.3d 115, 120–23 (1st Cir. 2007) [adopted BIA approach in *Blake* and *Brieva* in case involving sexual assault and rejected equal protection, regulatory and comparability arguments]; *Vo v. Gonzales,* 482 F.3d 363 (5th Cir. 2007) [same in context of Texas Unauthorized Use of a Motor Vehicle statute]; *Avilez-Granados v. Gonzales,* 481 F.3d 869, 871–72 (5th Cir. 2007) [followed *Vo* in context of sexual assault]; *Caroleo v. Gonzales,* 476 F.3d 158 (3d Cir. 2007) [respondent convicted in state court of attempted murder, burglary, and unlawful possession of a weapon for an unlawful purpose, he could not seek INA §212(c) relief, following *Brieva* and *Blake,* where his removal was sought as a "crime of violence" because there is a distinction between the underlying crime being a CIMT and a statutory counterpart for purposes of §212(c)]; *Valere v. Gonzales,* 473 F.3d 757 (7th Cir. 2007) [upheld *Blake* in the face of retroactivity and equal protection challenges]; *Kim v. Gonzales,* 468 F.3d 58 (1st Cir. 2006) [respondent convicted of manslaughter which was designated a COV and therefore no comparable §212(c) ground under *Brieva*]; *Sena v. Gonzales,* 428 F.3d 50, 53–54 (1st Cir. 2005) [person convicted of inducing and encouraging illegal alien to remain in U.S. is an aggravated felon under §101(a)(43)(N) subjecting respondent to removal, but there is no counterpart in inadmissibility permitting INA §212(c) relief because alien smuggling under §1182(a)(6)(E) does not apply to inducing or encouraging crime]. *See also Cyrus v. Keisler,* 505 F.3d 197, 201–02 (2d Cir. 2007) [respondent with gun conviction is not eligible for INA §212(c) relief and therefore not eligible to reopen under §1003.44]. *But see Blake v. Carbone,* 489 F.3d 88 (2d Cir. 2007) [reversed *Matter of Blake* and determined that it would violate equal protection to focus on the ground of deportation rather than the particular offense]; *Matter of Meza,* 20 I&N Dec. 257 (BIA 1991) [where aggravated felony of illicit trafficking in drugs had a counterpart in the grounds of inadmissibility for drug convictions, INA §212(c) was available].

Terrorism May Bar §212(c) Relief—At least one court has held that the bar to §212(c) relief may be retroactively applied to terrorist charges, because there is no reliance on legal status when committing the act. *Kelava v. Gonzales,* 434 F.3d 1120, 1124 (9th Cir. 2006) [applicant could not have relied on §212(c) in committing terrorist act].

2.c. Judicial Review—For a discussion of judicial review, *see* "Cancellation of Removal" in Ch. 8, Part IV (p.972); and "The Discretionary Decision Bars," Ch. 10, ¶ IV.A.3 (p. 1112).

2.d. Waiver submitted on Form EOIR-42 if before the IJ [I-191 if before the DD]—Must submit fee when filing in conjunction with removal proceeding. 8 C.F.R. §1240.20(a) can only file with IJ if NTA filed. 8 C.F.R. §1240.20(b).

3. *INA §209(c), 8 U.S.C. §1159(c),* waives most grounds of inadmissibility for persons seeking to AOS as refugees or asylees. It provides that public charge, labor certification, and lack of IV documents are inapplicable to persons seeking to adjust. It also allows a waiver "for humanitarian purposes, to assure family unity, or when it is in the public's interest" for all other grounds of inadmissibility, except if the DHS/DOS has reason to believe the person is a drug trafficker or inadmissible on security grounds (except membership in a totalitarian party). An IJ has original jurisdiction to adjudicate a person's request for a §209(c) waiver and need not wait for the initial denial of such a waiver by the DHS. *Matter of K-A-,* 23 I&N Dec. 661 (BIA 2004) [modified *Mat-*

ter of H-N-, finding that the IJ possessed original jurisdiction of an AOS and waiver, that the IJ had the authority but was not compelled to terminate asylee status because of applicant's aggravated felony conviction before adjudication of AOS, and that if respondent is an aggravated felon it is only in "those rare situations where (there are) compelling countervailing equities" that AOS and waiver should be granted]; *Matter of H-N-,* 22 I&N Dec. 1039 (BIA 1999); 8 C.F.R. §§209.2(c), 1209.2(c), 1240.11(a)(2). However, a waiver for serious ("violent or dangerous") crimes will almost never be granted absent extraordinary circumstances such as those involving national security or foreign policy considerations or where the denial would result in exceptional and extremely unusual hardship. *Matter of Jean,* 23 I&N Dec. 373, 381–84 (AG 2002) *affirmed Jean v. Gonzales,* 452 F.3d 392, 396–98 (5th Cir. 2006) [denying adjustment to person convicted of second degree manslaughter in the death of a baby and reversing BIA where the focus was on the family's hardship without considering the nature of the criminal offense; on appeal court rejected argument that AG's standard was *ultra vires*]; *Ali v. Achim,* 468 F.3d 462, 465–67 (7th Cir. 2006) *cert. dismissed* 128 S.Ct. 828 (2007) [AG did not exceed his authority when he articulated the heightened waiver standard in *Matter of Jean*]. *But see Rivas-Gomez v. Gonzales,* 441 F.3d 1072, 1074–79 (9th Cir. 2006) [reversing IJ for denying §209(c) waiver where respondent was convicted of an aggravated felony (statutory rape) and IJ determined there was insufficient hardship without first determining that the crime was a violent or dangerous felony].

4. *INA §212(d)(1), 8 U.S.C. §1182(d)(1)*—Waives inadmissibility under INA §212(a) (except Nazis) for S visas. The AG may grant waiver in the national interest. The grant does not prevent deportation for acts arising after admission or for information not disclosed before admission.

5. *INA §212(d)(3)(A), 8 U.S.C. §1182(d)(3)(A)*—General waiver for NIV. DHS follows 3 criteria established in *Matter of Hranka*, 16 I&N Dec. 491 (BIA 1978) to determine waiver: (1) the risk of harm to society if applicant admitted; (2) the seriousness of the applicant's criminal law or immigration law violation; and (3) the nature of the applicant's reason for seeking entry. *See also* 8 C.F.R. §§212.4, 1212.4; 9 FAM 40.301. Cannot obtain a waiver for political or security grounds under INA §212(a)(3)(A)(i)(I) [espionage or sabotage], §212(a)(3)(A)(ii) [any unlawful activity], §212(a)(3)(A)(iii) [overthrow the government by force], §212(a)(3)(C) [foreign policy grounds], and §§212(a)(3)(E)(i) & (ii) [Nazi and genocide]. A K visa holder may also be ineligible for a INA §212(d)(3) if s/he is otherwise inadmissible and her inadmissibility is not waivable. If the ground of inadmissibility is waivable, however, (*e.g.,* by a §212(h) waiver), then a K visa applicant may obtain the INA §212(d)(3) waiver. 9 FAM 41.81 N.9.1. Applicant needs the approval of the DHS and recommendation of the consular officer to obtain the waiver. Waiver request submitted on Form I-192 if submitted at port of entry. 8 C.F.R. §§212.4(b), 1212.4(b). If the application is submitted at the consulate neither an application or fee is required. 8 C.F.R. §212.4(a)(1). Where person with waiver in U.S. desires to change status his or her waiver may continue to be valid, but is subject to DHS scrutiny for continuing validity. Letter, Bednarz, Chief NIV Branch, Adjudications (HQ 212.42-C) (Mar. 17, 1994), *published on* AILA InfoNet at Doc. No. 94031791.

   In the past, when waivers for AIDS or persons testing positive for HIV were necessary, Service guidelines have provided that the applicant must meet the factors in *Matter of Hranka*, 16 I&N Dec. 491 (BIA 1978) *and* establish that (1) the danger to the public health of admission is minimal; (2) the danger of the spread of infection by admission is minimal; and (3) there will be no cost incurred by any government agency without the agency's prior approval. 66 No. 22 *Interpreter Releases* 624–27 (June 6 1989); 66 No. 15 *Interpreter Releases* 427–28 (Apr. 17, 1989). DOS took a more liberal view toward granting waivers for HIV. Cable, DOS 89-State-296666 (Sept. 15, 1989), *reprinted in* 66 No. 42 *Interpreter Releases* 1211–12 (Oct. 30, 1989). The INS/DHS more current practice permits HIV waiver decisions to be made by the DD. Criteria to be considered includes whether: (1) the person is currently afflicted with the symptoms of the disease; (2) s/he is coming for a short visit; (3) s/he has insurance or assets to pay for medical care; and (4) there is reason to believe that the person's trip poses a danger. Cable, INS (HQ 235-C) (Aug. 19, 1993), *reprinted in* 71 No. 19 *Interpreter Releases* 653 (May 16, 1994).

   There is a distinction between an INA §212(d)(3)(A)(i) waiver and an INA §212(d)(3)(A)(ii) waiver. The former is applied for at a consular office and requires the concurrence of DHS. The latter may be applied for at the border and does not require DOS approval. It only requires the approval of CBP. The (d)(3)(A)(ii) waiver is for someone who already has a valid entry document (*e.g.*, visa) but needs a waiver to enter. The application is submitted on an I-192 form. IFM at 17.5(d)(1)–(2); Memo, Williams, Ex. Assoc. Comm. Field Operations, HQINS 70/ 12.2.1 (Sept. 30, 2002), *published on* AILA InfoNet at Doc. No. 02111340; 8 C.F.R. §212.4(b). The Secretary of DHS has delegated the adjudication of INA §212(d)(3)(A) waivers at the border under (A)(ii), waivers requested from consular posts in Canada and "seat of government" recommendations made by DOS to CBP. But current regulations require requests for §212(d)(3)(A) waivers from other consular posts go to ICE Offices in Rome, Bangkok and Mexico City. Memo, Ahern, Asst. Comm. Field Operations, CBP "Interim Guidance: Jurisdiction and Authority for Waivers of Inadmissibility under Section 212(d)(3)," (Apr. 8, 2004), *published on* AILA InfoNet at Doc. No. 05040165.

Procedures to Obtain Waivers—The §212(d)(3)(A) waiver may be obtained through CBP at a port of entry, field office, or admissibility review office, through USCIS or through a DOS consulate abroad. For a detailed procedural outline to obtain this waiver *see* Waiver of Inadmissibility Practice Guide (Mar. 13, 2007), *published on* AILA InfoNet at Doc. No. 07060774.

INA §212(d)(3)(B), 8 U.S.C. §1182(d)(3)(B); 72 Fed. Reg. 9957 (Mar. 6, 2007); PL 110-161 at Div. J, §691(a), 121 Stat. 1844, 2364–65 (Dec. 26, 2007) Terrorism Waiver— Under INA §212(d)(3)(B)(i), the Secy. of State and the Secy. of DHS in consultation with each other and the AG can, in their "unreviewable discretion," issue waivers of the material support and most other terrorism grounds of inadmissibility as a result of the broad powers for waiver accorded them under the Consolidated Appropriations Act, 2008, PL 110-161, Div. J §691(a), 121 Stat. 1844, 2364–65 (Dec. 26, 2007). For a more complete discussion of the waiver and its exceptions, *see in this part* "Waiver Provision," ¶ H.2.d(6)(b) (p.105), *supra*.

6. *INA §212(d)(4), 8 U.S.C. §1182(d)(4)*—Alien not in possession of a valid NIV, BCC, or passport valid for six months or TWOV may be waived if unforeseen emergency, on the basis of reciprocity, or because there is a contract with the transportation line to permit TWOVs and the country is not prohibited from TWOV by 8 C.F.R. §212.1(f)(2). Waiver can now be granted directly by the DD without getting DOS's concurrence in cases of unforeseen emergencies. 8 C.F.R. §212.1(g), 22 C.F.R. §41.2(j). However, unforeseen emergencies are narrowly defined to include an alien arriving only: (1) for a medical emergency; (2) as an emergency or rescue worker in response to a catastrophe in the U.S.; (3) accompanying or following to join a person with a medical emergency; (4) visiting a spouse, child, parent, or sibling who became critically ill or died within the past 5 days; or (5) appearing without a passport or visa because they were lost or stolen within 48 hours of departing the last port of embarkation to the U.S. IFM at 17.5(d)(3)(i)–(ii). If the unforeseen emergency does not fall within one of these categories a waiver can still be granted with the express consent of the Field Officer Director, or the Assistant for CBP or USCIS and with an explanation as to why a reasonable person in the applicant's situation could not have anticipated the emergency. IFM at 17.5(d)(3)(iii)–(iv). A waiver under this section may also be granted to a person whose visa is cancelled at the border under INA §222(g). IFM at 15.15(k); Memo, Williams, Ex. Assoc. Comm. Field Operations, HQINS 70/12.2.1 (Sept. 30, 2002), *published on* AILA InfoNet at Doc. No. 02111340. In all other cases the waiver must be done by AG and Secy. of State acting jointly. An IJ can determine this waiver. *Matter of Kazemi*, 19 I&N Dec. 49 (BIA 1984), *overruling Matter of Le Floch*, 13 I&N Dec. 251 (BIA 1969).

7. *INA §212(d)(11), 8 U.S.C. §1182(d)(11)*—Under this section, the AG in his discretion for humanitarian purposes, to insure family unity, or when it is otherwise in the public interest, may grant a waiver of inadmissibility where the person smuggled into the U.S. was the "spouse, parent, son or daughter" of the inadmissible person. INA §212(d)(11), 8 U.S.C. §1182(d)(11). The waiver is available to LPRs who are returning from abroad and to persons who are seeking admission as an IR or under INA §§203(a)(1)–(3). IIRIRA §351 amended the statute to clarify that the applicant for the waiver had to have the family relationship at the time of the smuggling, thus overriding *Matter of Farias*, 21 I&N Dec. 269 (BIA 1996) *Moran v. Ashcroft,* 395 F.3d 1089 (9th Cir. 2005) [where applicant smuggled woman who later became his wife, the waiver for smuggling was inapplicable and he was therefore barred from good moral character for cancellation]. The requirement that an immediate family member is involved is applicable to LPRs as well as others seeking admission. *Matter of Compean*, 21 I&N Dec. 51 (BIA 1995); *Perez Suriel de Batista v. Gonzales,* 494 F.3d 67 (2d Cir. 2007) [rejected argument that nephew who was functional equivalent of a son could be basis for waiver and upheld BIA's construction of statute]; *Selimi v. INS,* 312 F.3d

854, 861–62 (7th Cir. 2002) [where LPR was involved in smuggling his wife, children, *and* cousin, waiver was unavailable]. *See also Lopez De Jesus v. INS,* 312 F.3d 155, 161–64 (5th Cir. 2002) [retroactive application of amendment constitutional]. At least one court has determined it lacks jurisdiction under INA §242(a)(2)(B)(ii), 8 U.S.C. §1252(a)(2)(B)(ii) to review the denial of the waiver on discretionary grounds. *Saloum v. USCIS,* 437 F.3d 238 (2d Cir. 2006) [*post*–REAL ID Act, no jurisdiction to review a denial of a INA §212(d)(11) waiver on discretionary grounds].

8. *INA §212(d)(12), 8 U.S.C. §1182(d)(12)*—Waiver for inadmissibility as a result of having a final INA §274C order. The waiver is available for humanitarian purposes or to ensure family unity if the person is a returning LPR or seeking an IV or AOS under the immediate-relative or family-preference categories where no previous civil money penalty was imposed under §274C and the offense was committed solely to assist and/ or support a spouse or child and no other persons. DOS believes relationship had to exist at time of fraud, not just at time of waiver application. Cable, DOS, 96-State-226596 (Oct. 31, 1996), *reprinted in* 73 No. 43 *Interpreter Releases* 1588–90 (Nov. 11, 1996). There is no judicial review of the denial of the waiver. The legislative history provides that this waiver also is applicable to persons who are employment-based immigrants. H.R. Conf. Rep. No. 828, 104th Cong., 2d Sess. at 227 (1996).

9. *INA §212(d)(13), 8 U.S.C. §1182(d)(13)*—The waiver for persons who are eligible for a T visa permits the AG, if he considers it to be in the national interest to do so, to waive health related and public charge grounds and any other ground of inadmissibility (except security and related grounds, international child abduction, and former citizen who renounced citizenship to avoid taxation) if the activities rendering the T visa applicant inadmissible were caused by, or were incident to, a severe form of trafficking in persons.

10. *INA §212(d)(14), 8 U.S.C. §1182(d)(14)*—8 C.F.R. §212.17. The waiver for U visa applicants is even broader than for T visas. All grounds of inadmissibility except for INA §212(a)(3)(E) are waivable by DHS if in the "public or national interest." INA §212(d)(14). Inadmissibility is not waived for Nazis, participants in genocide, or persons who committed, ordered, incited, assisted or otherwise participated in torture or extrajudicial killings under INA §212(a)(3)(E). If the applicant is inadmissible on criminal or related grounds, USCIS will consider the number and severity of the offenses. In cases involving violent or dangerous crimes or inadmissibility based on security or related grounds under INA §212(a)(3) USCIS will only exercise discretion in "extraordinary circumstances." 8 C.F.R. §212.17(b)(2). No appeal from the denial of the waiver.

11. *INA §212(e), 8 U.S.C. §1182(e)*—Allows for exchange student J waiver where there is: (a) exceptional hardship to USC or LPR spouse or child; (b) fear of persecution of applicant; (c) no objection from home country (not applicable to foreign doctors practicing medicine); (d) an interested U.S. governmental agency asserts/establishes that the admission is in the public interest; or (e) if a foreign physician where a state department of health requests it (maximum of 20 waivers per state). For a more extensive discussion, *see* Ch. 5, section VI.C (p.660), *infra.*

12. *INA §212(g), 8 U.S.C. §1182(g)*—This is a waiver where a person is determined to have a disease of public health significance or fails to obtain vaccination or has a physical or mental disorder under INA §212(a)(1)(A)(i), (ii), (iii). It does not waive drug abuse or drug addiction under INA §212(a)(1)(A)(iv). A waiver for a communicable disease under INA §212(a)(1)(A)(i) may be obtained in the case of an alien who is the spouse, unmarried son or daughter, or the minor unmarried lawfully adopted child of a USC or person issued an immigrant visa or who has a son or daughter who is a USC or LPR or been issued an immigrant visa. A VAWA self-petitioner is also covered. A waiver for failure to document vaccinations is available where (1) person actually had vaccination; (2) the vaccination is medically inappropriate; or (3) the AG promulgates regulations that exempt people on religious or moral grounds. To qualify for a religious objection waiver, the applicant must show: (1) s/he is opposed to vaccinations in any form; (2) the objection is based on religious belief or moral conviction; and (3) the belief or conviction is sincere. Memo, Virtue, Acting Exec. Assoc. Comm. (Sept. 29, 1997), *reprinted in* 74 No. 42 *Interpreter Releases* 1682, 1687–90 (Nov. 3, 1997). The religious waiver may also be filed for an adopted child. Cable, DOS (98-State-083590), *reprinted in* 75 No. 19 *Interpreter Releases* 700 (May 18, 1998). An applicant may also receive a waiver because the vaccine is not medically appropriate due to: (1) age; (2) contraindication; (3) insufficient time interval; (4) seasonality of vaccination (*e.g.*, flu shot); or (5) unavailability. Memo, Yates, Deputy Exe. Assoc. Comm. Immigration Services Division,

HQADN 70/21.1.1 (June 25, 2002), *published on* AILA InfoNet at Doc. No. 02070240; Cable, DOS, Albright, 97-State-071637 (Apr. 17, 1997), *published on* AILA InfoNet at Doc. No. 97041791; Memo, Virtue, Acting Exec. Comm. Programs, INS, HQ 5015.12, 96 Act. 027 (Apr. 10, 1997), *published on* AILA InfoNet at Doc. No. 97041091. The Service has granted to consular officers the right to grant the waivers in IV cases. Memo, Virtue (Apr. 10, 1997), *supra*. For a waiver of a physical or mental disorder under INA §212(a)(1)(A)(iii), no family relationship need exist. The AG in his discretion and after consultation with the Secy. of HHS may grant a waiver under such terms, conditions and controls if any, including the setting of a bond. A waiver application is filed on Form I-601 with the Center for Disease Control (CDC) in Atlanta. Cable, INS, HQ 212.25-P (June 3, 1993), *reprinted in* 70 No. 25 *Interpreter Releases* 873 (July 2, 1993). DHS guidelines for waivers on medical grounds are at AFM at 41.3 and Memo, Williams, Ex. Assoc. Comm. Field Operations, HQ 70/21/1.1-P, AD 0103 (Oct. 17, 2002), *published on* AILA InfoNet at Doc. No. 03031763.

13. *INA §212(h), 8 U.S.C. §1182(h)*—The statute allows waivers for (1) crimes of moral turpitude (except murder and torture); (2) commission of more than one crime; (3) prostitution; (4) diplomats who assert immunity; and (5) a single offense of simple possession of 30 grams or less of marijuana. The waiver may be obtained either by asserting extreme hardship or a 15-year statute of limitations period. *Matter of Alarcon*, 20 I&N Dec. 557 (BIA 1992). In the case of all categories except prostitution, the person needs to establish to the satisfaction of the AG: (1) that the activities occurred more than *15 years* before the date of application for visa, admission or adjustment; (2) that the admission would not be contrary to the national welfare, safety or security of the U.S.; (3) that the person has been rehabilitated; and (4) that s/ he meets all other terms, conditions, and procedures as established by regulation. Alternatively, a person may obtain an INA §212(h) waiver if s/he is the spouse, parent, son or daughter of a USC or LPR and that USC or LPR family member would suffer extreme hardship if the person is deported. Extreme hardship is interpreted narrowly by the BIA. *Matter of Ngai*, 19 I&N Dec. 245 (BIA 1984); *Shooshtary v. INS*, 39 F.3d 1049 (9th Cir. 1994); *Palmer v. INS*, 4 F.3d 482 (7th Cir. 1993). A VAWA self-petitioner is also covered. The grant of an INA §212(h)(1)(B) waiver requires balancing favorable and unfavorable factors embracing the standards used for the former INA §212(c) under *Matter of Marin*, but rejecting the analysis employed under INA §245 to determine adjustment. *Matter of Mendez-Moralez*, 21 I&N Dec. 296 (BIA 1996) [establishment of extreme hardship and eligibility for waiver still requires a separate discretionary determination]. The standard of review requires the BIA to consider all factors and is analogous to the extreme hardship review under INA §244. *Hassan v. INS*, 927 F.2d 465 (9th Cir. 1991). One court has found it permissible for the IJ to consider applicant's involvement in a crime despite the fact that the charges were dismissed. *Schroeck v. Gonzales,* 429 F.3d 947 (10th Cir. 2005) [IJ's consideration of a dismissed criminal case did not violate respondent's constitutional rights against double jeopardy or by requiring him to prove his innocence]. Notwithstanding the "extreme hardship" statutory standard, the AG has now promulgated a regulation pursuant to INA §212(h)(2) that on "discretionary grounds" permits the denial of a 212(h) waiver in cases involving violent or dangerous crimes unless there are "extraordinary circumstances." The regulation defines extraordinary circumstances as including "national security or foreign policy considerations" or where an applicant demonstrates "exceptional and extremely unusual hardship." The regulation notes that even a showing of extraordinary circumstances may be insufficient to warrant a favorable exercise of discretion. 8 C.F.R. §212.7(d). *Accord Mejia v. Gonzales,* 499 F.3d 991, 995–98 (9th Cir. 2007) [upholding validity of §212.7(d) under *Chevron* deference and applying it retroactively]; *Matter of Jean,* 23 I&N Dec. 373, 383 (AG 2002). The AG's standard under the regulation is also being applied to the adjudication of AOS applications. Memo, Yates, Acting Director of Operations, HQADN 70/23 (May 27, 2003), *published on* AILA InfoNet at Doc. No. 03080717.

At least one court has held that a person cannot use the waiver to cure statutory ineligibility for good moral character under INA §101(f). *Miller v. INS*, 762 F.2d 21 (3d Cir. 1985). Prior to IIRIRA the Eleventh Circuit found that it was unconstitutional to restrict the waiver solely to persons seeking admission while denying it to persons fighting deportation. *Yeung v. INS*, 76 F.3d 337 (11th Cir. 1995). *But see Klementanovsky v. Gonzales,* 501 F.3d 788 (7th Cir. 2007) [equal protection is not violated under a facially legitimate and bona fide standard by denying the use of a 212(h) waiver to defeat deportation while permitting it use to challenge inadmissibility; *Yeung* rejected]; *Moore v. Ashcroft,* 251 F.3d 919, 923–25 (11th Cir. 2001) [post-IIRIRA denying LPRs the right to apply for the waiver if they are aggravated felons does not violate equal protection]. Under the apparent eligibility standard, the IJ should inform a respondent if he is eligible for INA §212(h) relief. *U.S. v. Arrieta,* 224 F.3d 1076 (9th Cir. 2000) [IJ's failure to advise of apparent eligibility for INA §212(h) resulted in reversal of guilty plea for re-entering].

The waiver as it applies to marijuana convictions may be limited. *Matter of Moncada,* 24 I&N Dec. 62, 65 & n.4 (BIA 2007) [narrowly interpreting the deportability exception for simple possession of less than 30 grams as not including a conviction for possession of less than 30 grams of marijuana *in prison*]; *Matter of Martinez-Zapata,* 24 I&N Dec. 424 (BIA 2007) [where conviction was enhanced by virtue of respondent's possession of marijuana in a "drug-free zone" the enhancement was an element of the crime and the conviction was therefore more than a conviction for simple possession of 30 grams of marijuana. Respondent was ineligible for INA §212(h) relief and *Matter of Rodriguez-Cortes*, 20 I&N Dec. 587 (BIA 1992) was superseded for *post-Apprendi* cases]. But it may be used to waive a drug paraphernalia charge. *Escobar Barraza v. Mukasey,* 519 F.3d 388 (7th Cir. 2008) [found that if drug paraphernalia is a drug offense resulting in inadmissibility, then a §212(h) waiver may apply to drug paraphernalia where the amount involved with 30 grams or less of marijuana].

The waiver is unavailable to persons who have been convicted of or admit having committed murder or acts of torture or an attempt or conspiracy to commit murder or acts of torture.

The waiver is also unavailable to LPRs if since their admission they were convicted of an aggravated felony *or* they had not lawfully resided continuously for a period of 7 years immediately preceding the date of initiation of proceedings. However, this provision may only apply to person who were "admitted" as LPRs and therefore does not apply to LPRs who gained their residency through adjustment of status. *Martinez v. Mukasey,* 519 F.3d 532, 542–45 (5th Cir. 2008) [under the first prong of *Chevron* and under longstanding principles construing statutes in favor of persons facing removal, the court concluded that the term "admitted" as used in INA §212(h) does not bar LPRs who were convicted of aggravated felonies from obtaining relief if they obtained LPR status through adjustment because they were not "admitted"]. The courts, however, have rejected equal protection challenges to these bars to LPR eligibility for the waiver. *Malagon De Fuentes v. Gonzales,* 462 F.3d 498, 506–08 (5th Cir. 2006) [LPR who was ineligible for waiver because she returned from Mexico prior to reaching 7 years as LPR does not have an equal protection claim because she is not being treated differently than other LPRs who are out of the U.S. when they reach the 7 year period; she simply doesn't qualify]; *Camacho-Salinas v. U.S. Att'y Gen.,* 460 F.3d 1343, 1347–49 (11th Cir. 2006) [equal protection is not violated under rational basis test where an illegal alien is not required to have seven years residence to qualify for a INA §212(h) waiver but an LPR is so required]; *Latu v. Ashcroft,* 375 F.3d 1012, 1019–21 (10th Cir. 2004) [the §212(h) prohibition against granting LPRs the waiver if they are aggravated felons but allowing non-LPRs to apply has a rational basis that survives an equal protection challenge]; *Taniguchi v. Schultz,* 303 F.3d 950, 957–58 (9th Cir. 2002) [denying the INA §212(h) waiver to aggravated felon LPRs but not to other aliens does not violate equal protection because a rational basis for the distinction exists]; *De Leon-Reynoso v. Ashcroft,* 293 F.3d 633, 637–40 (3d Cir. 2002) [rejected equal protection challenge where LPR had not accrued the 7 years, whereas non-LPRs were free to apply]; *Jankowski-Burczyk v. INS,* 291 F.3d 172 (2d Cir. 2002) [rejected equal protection challenge regarding bar to 212(h) waiver if LPR (but not nonresidents) convicted of aggravated felony]; *Lukowski v. INS,* 279 F.3d 644 (8th Cir. 2002) [same]; *Moore v. Ashcroft,* 251 F.3d 919, 923–25 (11th Cir. 2001) [same]; *Lara-Ruiz v. INS,* 241 F.3d 934, 946–48 (7th Cir. 2001) [same]; *Matter of Yeung*, 21 I&N Dec. 610 (BIA 1996); *but see Roman v. Ashcroft,* 181 F.Supp.2d 808 (N.D. Ohio 2002) [distinction allowing §212(h) relief for nonresidents who are aggravated felons but not allowing the same relief to LPRs fails the rational basis test].

Courts have also rejected retroactivity challenges to the aggravated felony bar. *U.S. v. Gonzalez,* 429 F.3d 1252 (9th Cir. 2005 [the bar to INA §212(h) relief under 8 U.S.C. §1228(b)(5), which barred all discretionary relief for a person subject to expedited removal who was a non-LPR aggravated felon, could be retroactively applied]; *Guaylupo-Moya v. Gonzales,* 423 F.3d 121, 128–32 (2d Cir. 2005) [under step one of the *Landgraf* analysis Congress clearly intended that IIRIRA §321(a) regarding the retroactive definition of aggravated felonies and IIRIRA §§348(a) & (b) regarding the elimination of §212(h) for aggravated felons apply retroactively]; *Alvarez-Barajas v. Gonzales,* 418 F.3d 10150, 1054–55 (9th Cir. 2005) [IIRIRA §348(b) made the bar to §212(h) relief for LPRs who commit aggravated felons retroactive and IIRIRA §321 made respondent's plea to receipt of stolen property an aggravated felony retroactively]. One court has also rejected a retroactivity challenge to the AG's regulation under 8 C.F.R. §212.7(d) restricting the waiver for violent or dangerous crimes. *Mejia v. Gonzales,* 499 F.3d 991, 997–98 (9th Cir. 2007) [upholding validity of §212.7(d) under *Chevron* deference and applying it retroactively].

One court has also extended the bar for aggravated felons to temporary legal residents. *Bonhometre v. Ashcroft,* 414 F.3d 442, 449 (3d Cir. 2005) [no due process violation for failure to inform temporary resident of INA §212(h) because his aggravated felony barred him from relief].

An LPR who was "previously…admitted" in LPR status is also not eligible for 212(h) relief if he has not "lawfully resided continuously" for seven years "immediately preceding the date of initiation of proceedings." Previous admission includes admission even if obtained unlawfully or through misrepresentation. *Matter of Ayala,* 22 I&N Dec. 398 (BIA 1998) [An LPR is previously admitted under statute even if he made an unlawful entry or unlawfully obtained LPR status]; *Onwumaegbu v. Gonzales,* 470 F.3d 405, 408–09 (1st Cir. 2006) [applying *Ayala* where respondent had made a fraudulent misrepresentation in his application for LPR status but vacating the IJ order because the IJ failed to articulate why the respondent had not lawfully resided in U.S. for seven years].

These provisions apply to anyone in exclusion or deportation proceedings on Sept. 30, 1996, unless there is a final administrative order on that date. *Matter of Yeung*, 21 I&N Dec. 610 (BIA 1997). The restrictions also apply to someone who seeks to reopen proceedings after Sept. 30, 1996. *Matter of Pineda*, 21 I&N Dec. 1017 (BIA 1997). Based on the clear language of the statute, the bar does not apply to persons with aggravated felony convictions who are seeking the waiver in conjunction with an AOS application and who were never LPRs. *Matter of Michel*, 21 I&N Dec. 1101 (BIA 1998) [non-LPR allowed to AOS in removal proceeding notwithstanding aggravated felony conviction]. However, an adjustment of status application is not necessary in a removal case based upon inadmissibility where the person otherwise qualifies for 212(h). *Matter of Abosi,* 24 I&N Dec. 204 (2007) [a returning LPR, eligible for 212(h) who is treated as an arriving alien and therefore subject to inadmissibility may simply file a 212(h) waiver and need not file an adjustment application in conjunction with the waiver]. But it may not be used in a removal case based solely on deportation grounds where it is not used in conjunction with an AOS. *Klementanovsky v. Gonzales,* 501 F.3d 788 (7th Cir. 2007) [equal protection is not violated under a facially legitimate and bona fide standard by denying the use of a 212(h) waiver to defeat deportation while permitting it use to challenge inadmissibility; *Yeung* rejected].

Congress has sought to restrict judicial review of IJ decisions regarding waivers. INA §242(a)(2)(B)(i), 8 U.S.C. §1252(a)(2)(B)(i). *See, generally,* Chapter 10, "Federal Judicial Review" (p.1071), *infra*; *Compare Schroeck v. Gonzales,* 429 F.3d 947, 950–51 (10th Cir. 2005) [notwithstanding preclusion of review of §212(h) petitions under INA §242(a)(2)(B)(i), INA §242(a)(2)(D) permits jurisdiction to review respondent's constitutional claim that the IJ should not have heard and considered evidence regarding a dismissed criminal case], *with Bygayong v. INS,* 442 F.3d 67 (2d Cir. 2006) [INA §242(a)(2)(D) does not overcome the discretionary decision bar under §242(a)(2)(B)(i) for a §212(h) waiver, even if there was a finding of extreme hardship, because the ultimate decision to grant the waiver is discretionary].

14. *INA §212(i), 8 U.S.C. §1182(i)*—Waiver for violation of INA §212(a)(6)(C)(i), 8 U.S.C. §1182(a)(6)(C)(i) for fraudulent, or material misrepresentation, but only if the person is spouse or son or daughter of a USC/LPR and only if s/he can establish *extreme hardship* to the USC or LPR spouse or parent. Note that the right of a parent to seek the waiver has been removed and the provision regarding a waiver if the fraud occurred more than 10 years ago has also been removed. Circuit courts have determined that applying the changes in §212(i) to pending cases is not a retroactive application of the statute. *Patel v. Gonzales,* 432 F.3d 685, 689–92 (6th Cir. 2005); *Okpa v. INS,* 266 F.3d 313, 318–19 (4th Cir. 2001); *Cervantes-Gonzales v. INS,* 244 F.3d 1001, 1005–06 (9th Cir. 2001). But an IJ may have authority to grant a *nunc pro tunc* waiver under the prior (1993) version of INA §212(i) to waive fraud that occurred at that time. *Patel v. Gonzales,* 432 F.3d 685, 692–95 (6th Cir. 2005) [reversing IJ's determination that she did not have authority to grant *nunc pro tunc* waiver but finding that on the facts of the case respondent was not eligible].

    The waiver is also available to an approved VAWA self-petitioner if s/he demonstrates extreme hardship to herself or her USC/LPR parent or child.

The factors to be considered in determining extreme hardship to the USC/LPR relative include: (1) the presence of LPR or USC family ties to the U.S.; (2) the qualifying relative's family ties outside the U.S.; (3) the country conditions in the country of relocation and the qualifying relative's ties to that country; (4) the financial impact of departure from the U.S.; (5) significant health conditions, particularly when tied to unavailability of suitable medical care in the country of relocation. *Matter of Cervantes,* 22 I&N Dec. 560, 566 (BIA 1999), *aff'd Cervantes-Gonzales v. INS,* 244 F.3d 1001, 1005–06 (9th Cir. 2001) [applying extreme hardship and other requirements retroactively]. The extreme hardship standards are the same as those applied in suspension cases. *Matter of Kao & Lin,* 23 I&N Dec. 45, 49 n.3 (BIA 2001). Other factors that may be considered include the qualifying relative's family ties within and without the U.S. and the impact of separation; the economic and other conditions in the country to which she has to accompany her relative; the financial, emotional, cultural, and political conditions in that country; her ability to raise children and other quality of life factors in that country; as well as her age, length of residence in this country, health, technical skills, employability, and other factors. *Matter of Cervantes, supra.* at 583 (Rosenberg concurring). The IJ may also consider whether the USC/LPR married the applicant after removal proceedings began. *Cervantes, supra.* at 567. One of the central purposes of the waiver is to provide for the unification of families, *Matter of Lopez-Monzon*, 17 I&N Dec. 280 (Comm. 1979), and failure to weigh all family factors is reversible. *Delmundo v. INS*, 43 F.3d 436, 442–43 (9th Cir. 1994). However, there may be no review of the extreme hardship determination. *Zhang v. Gonzales,* 457 F.3d 172 (2d Cir. 2006) [post-REAL ID Act, INA §242(a)(2)(B)(i) bars review of the discretionary decision of extreme hardship under INA §212(i)].

In deciding INA §212(i) waivers, the fraud requiring the waiver *can* be used as an adverse factor in determining the case. *Matter of Cervantes,* 22 I&N Dec. 560, 569 (BIA 1999) [following the S.Ct. decision in *INS v. Yang,* 519 U.S. 26, 117 S.Ct. 350 (1996) and *Matter of Tijam*]. *But see Matter of Da Silva*, 17 I&N Dec. 288 (Comm. 1979); *Matter of Alonzo*, 17 I&N Dec. 292 (Comm. 1979) [pre-*Yang* cases by Commissioner]; *Delmundo v. INS*, 43 F.3d 436 (9th Cir. 1994) [in pre-*Yang* case BIA could not rely on applicant's fraudulent acts in applying for LPR status and obtaining a Social Security, voter's registration and driver's license because they were an extension of the fraudulent entry]. At least one court has also determined that INS may use criteria not stated in the statute to deny a waiver. *Esposito v. INS*, 936 F.2d 911 (7th Cir. 1991) [Board used *in absentia* criminal convictions pending charges and request by Italy for extradition as basis to deny waiver]. Congress has sought to restrict judicial review of the decision by the AG regarding the waiver.

An INA §212(i) waiver is unavailable to waive inadmissibility under INA §212(a)(6)(F) because of a final order for document fraud in violation of INA §274C. *Matter of Lazarte*, 21 I&N Dec. 214 (BIA 1996). It is also unavailable to waive a false claim to USC status under INA §212(a)(6)(C)(ii) as the waiver expressly covers only the first clause of §212(a)(6)(C).

The waiver is submitted on Form I-601, 8 C.F.R. §§212.7, 1212.7.

15. *INA §212(k), 8 U.S.C. §1182(k)*—Waiver for person with immigrant visa who is not in possession of a labor certification or valid immigrant visa or whose immigrant visa was not issued in compliance with law (and is therefore inadmissible under INA §212(a)(5)(A) or (7)(A)(i)) and who the AG is satisfied did not know, nor could have known by exercise of reasonable diligence, that she was inadmissible at time of entry; 8 C.F.R. §212.10. IJ can adjudicate INA §212(k) waiver even if USCIS has not made a determination on the application. *Matter of Aurelio*, 19 I&N Dec. 458 (BIA 1987); *Mayo v. Ashcroft,* 317 F.3d 867, 873–74 (8th Cir. 2003). The parent's knowledge as to inadmissibility is imputed to the child in the view of at least one court. *Senica v. INS*, 16 F.3d 1013 (9th Cir. 1994).

16. *INA §213, 8 U.S.C. §1183*—Can waive public charge provision, INA §212(a)(4), if bond posted. Waiver for permanent/temporary visa. *Matter of Ulloa,* 22 I&N Dec. 725 (BIA 1999) [waiver is available in deportation proceedings and IJ has obligation to inform person who is apparently eligible to apply]; 8 C.F.R. §213.1.

J. *Forms for Waiver*

1. I-601 for all grounds of inadmissibility—In seeking waivers of criminal grounds, applicant must supply fingerprints, G-325A, national police report from any country resided in, complete court

records, and where appropriate, evidence of rehabilitation. IMMACT90, Wire #57 (CO 1803-C), *reprinted in* 68 No. 22 *Interpreter Releases* 717 (June 17, 1991).

2. EOIR-42—Used for cancellation of removal before the IJ.

K. ***Consular Decision on Waiver***—Pursuant to the FAM, consular officers are not to recommend waivers of ineligibility for multiple entries for a person who: (a) has a mental or physical disorder; (b) is a narcotic drug addict or a narcotic trafficker; (c) is afflicted with a communicable disease; (d) was convicted for committing a serious CIMT and has not been rehabilitated and integrated into society for *at least five (5) years* since the date of conviction or release from confinement whichever is later in time; or (e) has engaged in prostitution or has procured or attempted to procure or import prostitutes or has received proceeds of prostitution within 10 years immediately preceding the visa application.

L. ***Fee Waivers***—Pursuant to 8 C.F.R. §§103.7(c), 1103.7(c), DHS may waive any fees for any petitions or applications. DHS has provided general guidance as to the grant of such a waiver. In determining whether someone can demonstrate "inability to pay" under the regulation DHS officers should consider: (1) whether person qualified for and received federal means-tested public benefits; (2) whether his or her household income is below the poverty guidelines; (3) whether the person is elderly (65 or over); (4) whether a person is disabled as determined by a federal agency; (5) the age and number of dependents in the person's household who are seeking derivative status or concurrent benefits; (6) humanitarian or compassionate reasons (*e.g.,* temporary destitution or in a nursing home). DHS should also take into consideration whether person is a self-petitioning abused spouse or child. DHS guidance on fee waivers is found at AFM at 10.9. *See also* Memo, Neufeld, Acting Assoc. Director, Domestic Operations, USCIS, HQ 70/5.5 (July 20, 2007), *published on* AILA InfoNet at Doc. No. 07072665.

M. ***Right to Notice of Denial of Visa***—INA §212(b), 8 U.S.C. §1182(b), provides that if a person's application for a visa, for admission or adjustment is denied by an immigration or consular officer because of a determination of inadmissibility, that officer *shall* provide the applicant a *timely* written notice that states the determination and lists the specific provisions of law under which the person is inadmissible or ineligible. However, this section may be waived by the Secy. of State with respect to a particular person or class of inadmissible persons and the section does not apply to persons deemed inadmissible under INA §212(a)(2) and (a)(3).

N. ***Effective Date***

1. Under IMMACT90—The exclusion provisions and waivers shall apply to individuals entering the U.S. on or after June 1, 1991.
2. Under IIRIRA—Provisions became effective on Apr. 1, 1997.

IV. PROCEDURES GOVERNING INADMISSIBILITY

A. *Preliminary Procedures Upon Arrival in the U.S.*

1. *Alien subject to inspection at border*—INA §235, 8 U.S.C. §1225, 8 C.F.R. §§235, 1235. Inspection includes medical (mental examination) as well as immigration inspection. INA §232, 8 U.S.C. §1222. Immigration inspectors are empowered to interrogate applicants and examine documents to determine whether the alien or LPR is admissible. INS officers previously consulted a "Lookout Book," has now been automated through a computerized lookout system or in remote areas through the use of the Portable Automated Lookout System (PALS), which uses CD or DVD technology. DHS maintains an interagency computerized lookout system called the Interagency Border Inspection System (IBIS) which compliments the State Department's Consular Lookout and Support System (CLASS), and TECS II (Treasury Enforcement Communications System). There are also other automated internal DHS systems such as NAILS (National Automated Immigration Lookout System), DACS (Deportable Alien Control System), NIIS (Nonimmigrant aliens), RAPS (Refugee, Asylum and Parole System) and TIPOFF (terrorist database). The overall system for arrivals and departures is the Arrival and Departure Information System (ADIS), which is a centralized database that reports each person's arrival and departure from the U.S. With the advent of US-VISIT, which will be part of ADIS, DHS will now utilize the automated biometric identification system (IDENT), which is the fingerprint database managed by CBP to check biometric identifiers (fingerprints/photographs) against other databases such as

CLASS. One goal of Congress and DHS is to link IDENT and US-VISIT with criminal history data contained in the FBI's Integrated Automated Fingerprint Identification System (IAFIS) so that a person entering the U.S. will have his or her criminal history reviewed electronically. CBP also maintains the Advanced Passenger Information System (APIS) which allows it to obtain information from carriers on persons entering and leaving the U.S. before the passengers enter or depart. 70 Fed. Reg. 17820 (Apr. 7, 2005).

2. *Money Laundering Watchlist*—Under the USA PATRIOT Act §1006(b), Congress authorized the executive to establish a special money laundering watchlist that identifies individuals worldwide who are known or suspected of money laundering.

3. *Disclosure of Lookout Information*—Federal courts have ordered the disclosure of certain information in the "Lookout Book." *Lawyers Comm. for Human Rights v. INS*, 721 F.Supp. 552 (S.D. N.Y. 1989). Under IMMACT90 §601(c), the AG and Secy. of State were required to develop "protocols and guidelines for updating lookout books and the automated visa lookout system and similar mechanisms for the screening of aliens applying for visas." These protocols and guidelines were required to be developed in such a manner as to remove an alien's name after a request and to inform the alien of the removal or that s/he continues to be inadmissible. In addition, the Foreign Relations Authorization Act, FY 1992, PL 102-138, 105 Stat. 647 (Oct. 1991), required DOS to establish a procedure to delete within 3 years the names of all persons who are not inadmissible from the "Lookout Book" except those listed for law enforcement persons. The computer system must clearly provide that those listed solely for law enforcement purposes are not excludable from the U.S. Consular officers are now mandated to certify that they have checked the relevant lookout system before issuing a visa. Foreign Relations Authorization Act, FY 1994 and 1995, PL 103-236, 108 Stat. 382.

4. *Disclosure of ADIS and ENFORCE/IDENT Records*—68 Fed. Reg. 69412–17 (Dec. 12, 2003). Records in the ADIS system may be disclosed to: (1) Appropriate law enforcement agencies and organizations; (2) An attorney or representative for individual in removal proceedings; (3) Court, grand jury or adjudicative body where DHS or employee of DHS is involved; (4) Member of Congress or staff; (5) GSA or NARA (National Archives and Records Administration) for inspections; (6) News media or public where there exists a legitimate public interest in the disclosure or where disclosure is necessary to preserve the integrity of DHS, unless it would constitute an unwarranted invasion of privacy; (7) Contractors and grantees; (8) Former DHS employee to respond to government or licensing request; and (9) Federal, state, tribal, local, or foreign government in regard to hiring or retaining an employee.

   Records in the ENFORCE/IDENT system (which includes US-VISIT) may be disclosed to: (1) Law Enforcement agencies where there is a facial violation of the law; (2) Other law enforcement where information is necessary to carry out DHS's functions and statutory mandates; (3) Government agency regarding employment or the issuance of a benefit; (4) Actual or potential party or his attorney for the purpose of negotiation or discussion on such matters as settlement of the case or discovery proceedings; (5) Government agency seeking to collect a loan/debts; (6) News media or public where there exists a legitimate public interest in the disclosure or where disclosure is necessary to preserve the integrity of DHS unless it would constitute an unwarranted invasion of privacy; (7) Member of Congress or staff; (8) Contractors and grantees; (9) Former DHS employee to respond to government or licensing request; (10) Former employee of DHS to respond to official inquiry, (11) Individuals who apply for any form of automated or other expedited inspection for verifying eligibility to cross the borders into the U.S.; and (12) individuals who are permitted access to the sterile areas of airports after undergoing screening, including an immigration check. 71 Fed. Reg. 13987 (Mar. 20, 2006)

5. *Challenging US-VISIT Records*—69 Fed. Reg. 2615 (Jan. 16, 2004). A person who believes the US-VISIT system contains inaccurate information about them needs to send the following information by mail or fax (202-298-5201) to US-VISIT Privacy Officer, US-VISIT Program, U.S. Department of Homeland Security, Washington, D.C. 20528: name, address, contact numbers, date and place of birth, date of arrival in and/or departure from the U.S., port of arrival and/or departure in U.S., name of airline or sea vessel and flight number or cruise line ticket number, passport number and country of issuance, and U.S. visa number. The requestor must sign the request *and the signature must be notarized or submitted under penalty of perjury* under 28 U.S.C. §1746.

The privacy officer may also be called. The position is currently held by Steve Yonkers at (202) 298-5200. 69 Fed. Reg. 2608 (Jan. 16, 2004); 71 Fed. Reg. 13987 (Mar. 20, 2006).

6. *Challenging the ADIS Records*—A USC or LPR can obtain the information contained in this database through the Privacy Act and can then contest or seek amendment of record entries should address their letter for ADIS to: ADIS Program Management Office, 1616 N. Fort Myer Drive, Arlington, VA 22209. Include in request the requestor's full name, current address, DOB, a copy of the record in question, and a detailed explanation of the change sought. If the matter cannot be resolved at this level the USC/LPR can appeal to the DHS Privacy Office. 68 Fed. Reg. at 69414 (Dec. 12, 2003)

7. *Challenging the ENFORCE/IDENT Records*—Subject to 5 U.S.C. §552a(j)(2) and (k)(2), a person may submit a FOIA request to the appropriate agency or to DHS at Chief, Information and Disclosure Mission Support, Office of Investigations, 425 "I" Street, NW, Washington DC 20536. If a record is contested and the party desires deletion or amendment to the record, s/he should direct her request to ENFORCE/IDENT Program Management Office, 1616 North Fort Myer Drive, Arlington, VA. 22209. 68 Fed. Reg. at 69417 (Dec. 12, 2003).

8. *Challenging a Lookout Determination*—If a person wishes to delete information from a computerized database regarding inadmissibility one place to contact is the U.S. Customs Service and ask that information in IBIS (Interagency Border Inspection System) be deleted. A person seeking deletion of derogatory information should write to: Director, Information Disclosure, FOIA/PA Group, Room 5.5-C, U.S. Customs and Border Protection, 1300 Pennsylvania Ave. NW, Washington, DC 20229 and provide all identifying information including date of birth, place of birth, full name, address, and passport number as well as the reasons the person was deemed inadmissible and why it is incorrect. These records may contain inaccurate information from NCIA which has recognized the limitations of its own records. 28 C.F.R. §§16.96(b)(6), (h)(5), and (k)(5).

9. *Removing Information from CLASS*—An LPR or USC seeking to remove their names from CLASS or correct information contained in CLASS should write to Chief, Systems Liaison and Procedures Division, Visa Office, U.S. Department of State, Washington, DC. 20522-0113. Those who are not USCs or LPRs must go back to the consular post that placed the information into the system and ask for a correction or deletion. If the post was not responsible for the information, the concerned person must write to the agency that placed in the information in the database. 9 FAM Part IV, Appendix D, 203.4.

10. *Representation*—At primary or secondary inspection, DHS policy is not to permit representation by counsel. 8 C.F.R. §292.5(b), 1292.5(b). *But see* 5 U.S.C. §555(b) [Administrative Procedures Act]. A CBP inspector may obtain his or her own interpreter for assistance under regulated conditions. *See* IFM at 17.18.

    The CBP inspector by statute may require an applicant for admission to provide a statement under oath. INA §235(a)(5). There is a serious question as to whether this provision violates the Fifth Amendment's prohibition against self-incrimination.

11. *Medical Grounds*—The DHS has guidelines for inspecting persons who may be inadmissible on medical grounds. The guidelines provide that an applicant for admission will not be asked in a primary inspection if s/he is inadmissible under any of the medical exclusion grounds. An applicant cannot be referred to secondary inspection regarding medical grounds based on literature s/he is carrying or on answers to questions concerning the purpose of the trip. Memo, McNary, Commissioner (CO 234-P) (Sept. 18, 1990), *reprinted in* 67 No. 37 *Interpreter Releases* 1084, 1100 (Oct. 1, 1990).

12. *Public Charge*—CBP officials may not inspect returning LPRs regarding public charge. Nor do inspectors have the authority to require LPRs or others to repay public benefits as part of inspection process. Memo, Virtue, Exec. Assoc. Comm., INS, HQ IRT 50/5.12, 96 Act. 044 (Dec. 16, 1997), *published on* AILA InfoNet at Doc. No. 97121691.

13. *Low Risk Border Travelers*—INS PORTPASS was developed as a system to designate certain low risk border crossers to allow expedited crossing. 8 C.F.R. §235.7 [containing eligibility requirements for program]. Low risk programs include NEXUS (between U.S. and Canada), SENTRI (between U.S. and Mexico), and INSPASS (for citizens of U.S., Canada, Bermuda,

and VWP countries who travel to the U.S. on business 3 or more times per year or diplomats, representatives of international organizations, or crew members from VWP countries). INSPASS is not available to anyone with a criminal record or who otherwise requires a waiver. Individuals may now be enrolled for 2 years in these programs. 8 C.F.R. §235.7(a)(4)(xi); 68 Fed. Reg. 10143–45 (Mar. 4, 2003) [describes various programs]. SENTRI has now established an on-line enrollment system. CBP Announces SENTRI Electronic Applications, 83 No. 43 *Interpreter Releases* 2361, 2396 (Nov. 6, 2006)

B. *Persons Subject to Inspection*—INA §235(a), 8 U.S.C. §1225(a), 8 C.F.R. §§235.1, 1235.1

1. Persons present in the U.S. who were not admitted;
2. Persons who arrive in the U.S. even if they are not at a designated port of entry;
3. Persons who are interdicted in international waters;
4. Stowaways; and
5. All persons who are applicants for admission, readmission or transit.

C. *Expedited Removal*—INA §235(b)(1), 8 U.S.C. §1225(b)(1)

1. Under IIRIRA, Congress mandated (beginning Apr. 1, 1997) a procedure for expedited removal of persons deemed inadmissible at the border under INA §212(a)(6)(C) (material misrepresentation) and INA §212(a)(7) (lack of IV or NIV documents). 8 C.F.R. §§235.3(b), 1235.3(b). The regulations implementing expedited removal have been upheld. *AILA v. Reno,* 199 F.3d 1352, 1356–57 (D.C. Cir. 2000) [determined that AILA lacked third-party standing on prudential grounds and that district court's dismissal of individual plaintiffs for failure to state cause of action was correct]. The AG may also apply expedited removal to persons not admitted or paroled who are unable to prove they have been in the U.S. continuously for 2 or more years. INA §235(b)(1)(A)(iii)(I)–(II). On Aug. 11, 2004, the DHS, pursuant to this provision, expanded expedited removal to include persons present in the U.S., without having been admitted or paroled, who are encountered within 100 miles of the border, and who cannot establish that they have been physically present in the U.S. continuously for the preceding 14 days. Notice Designating Aliens for Expedited Removal, 69 Fed. Reg. 48877 (Aug. 11, 2004). It was subsequently expanded to all borders including the Northern Border. Press Release, DHS (Jan. 30, 2006), *published on* AILA InfoNet at Doc. No. 06013018.The AG also previously announced that persons who arrive in the U.S. by sea (except Cubans) will be subject to expedited removal, unless they were in the U.S. for two years prior to the determination of inadmissibility. 67 Fed. Reg. 68924–26 (Nov. 13, 2002). Persons paroled prior to Apr. 1, 1997, will not be put in expedited removal proceedings. Also, persons re-entering the U.S. on advance parole, although arriving aliens, are not considered to be such for purposes of being subject to expedited removal. 8 C.F.R. §§1.1(q), 1001.1(q). Memo, Perryman, Exec. Assoc. Comm. INS, 501 12.1-P (June 30, 1997), *reprinted in* 74 No. 31 *Interpreter Releases* 1247, 1258–59 (Aug. 18, 1997). *See also Bona v. Gonzales,* 425 F.3d 663, 667–68 (9th Cir. 2005) [person granted advance parole not considered an arriving alien for purposes of expedited removal]; *American-Arab Anti-Discrimination Comm. v. Ashcroft,* 272 F.Supp.2d 650 (E.D. Mich. 2003) [where ICE placed person who was paroled on a fraudulent I-512 into expedited removal proceedings, the court found that persons paroled into U.S. are not "arriving aliens" under the statute or regulations]. If a person subject to inspection is not inadmissible under one of the two designated sections, then s/he would be subject to a removal proceeding under INA §240 for persons who are inadmissible (unless suspected of being a terrorist in which case INA §235(c) would apply). A record of the proceedings, including the facts of the case and the statements made by the applicant for admission, should be created on Form I-867AB. 8 C.F.R. §§235.3(b)(2)(i), 1235.3(b)(2)(i).
2. Exceptions

   2.a. Where the applicant states he is seeking asylum or fears persecution or torture and can establish to an asylum officer that he has a credible fear of persecution he will not be subject to expedited removal. 8 C.F.R. §§235.3(b)(4), 1235.3(b)(4). The credible fear interview process is governed by 8 C.F.R. §208.30. If he establishes a credible fear to the officer, his case is then referred for an asylum, withholding of removal, and/or Convention Against Torture determination and the applicant is given an INA §240 hearing before an IJ. 8 C.F.R. §§208.30, 235.3, 1208.30, 1235.3. If the asylum officer determines that the applicant does not have a credible fear, then the applicant may request review before the IJ and s/he is referred to the IJ by DHS issuing a Form I-863, which limits the IJ's jurisdiction to review of the negative credible fear determination. 8 C.F.R. §1208.30(g). Review by the IJ of a denial of the credible fear determination must be made within 7 days. The applicant must be detained until the credible fear determination is made, subject to narrow parole grounds for medical emergency or law enforcement purposes. 8 C.F.R. §§235.3(b)(4)(ii), 1235.3(b)(4)(ii). If the applicant is determined by the IJ to have a credible fear, the IJ, except if he is a stowaway, then places him in an INA §240 removal proceeding. If no credible fear is found the applicant must be detained until removed. INA §§235(b)(1)(B)(iii)(IV). An applicant can consult with counsel before the asylum officer interview. The consultation shall be at no expense to the government and shall not delay the proceedings. A person may obtain a second credible fear determination prior to removal, even if the first one was rejected by the AO and the IJ, where the Office of International Affairs determines that the applicant "has made a reasonable claim that compelling new information concerning the case exists and should be considered." Memo, Benson, Exec. Assoc. Comm. for Field Operations, INS (Dec. 30, 1997), *reprinted in* 75 No. 7 *Interpreter Releases* 255, 270–73 (Feb. 23, 1998). Credible fear is defined as: "A significant possibility...that the alien could establish eligibility for asylum under section 208." The definition of an asylum officer for purposes of expedited removal includes persons who receive comparable training to asylum officers or who are supervised by persons who have substantial experience adjudicating asylum claims and have receive comparable training.

2.b. A native or citizen of Cuba seeking entry at an airport is not subject to expedited removal.

2.c. LPRs or persons granted refugee or asylee status are not subject to expedited removal. 8 C.F.R. §§235.3(b)(5), 1235.3(b)(5).

2.d. Persons lawfully admitted are not subject to expedited removal. 8 C.F.R. §§235.3(b)(6), 1235.3(b)(6).

2.e. Minors—A minor should not be placed in summary removal proceedings unless (i) he has, in the presence of an DHS officer, engaged in criminal activity that would qualify as an aggravated felony; (ii) he has been convicted or adjudicated delinquent of an aggravated felony within the U.S. or another country and the inspecting officer has confirmation of the order; or (iii) he has previously been formally removed, excluded, or deported from the U.S. Memo, Virtue, Acting Exec. Comm., HQ 50/5.12, 96 Act. 054 (Aug. 21, 1997), *published on* AILA InfoNet at Doc. No. 97082191.

2.f. A person applying for admission under the Visa Waiver Program, even if inadmissible under §§212(a)(6)(C) or (7) is not subject to expedited removal if s/he seeks asylum. 8 C.F.R. §217.4(a) *Matter of Kanagasundram,* 22 I&N Dec. 963 (BIA 1999).

3. *Detention*—A person subject to expedited removal shall be detained pending removal, except where DHS paroles the applicant because "parole is required to meet a medical emergency or is necessary for a legitimate law enforcement objective." 8 C.F.R. §§235.3(b)(2)(iii), 1235.3(b)(2)(iii). The AG has determined that persons who come by sea (except Cubans) will be detained (with certain humanitarian exceptions) throughout the credible fear and asylum process before the IJ without the right to request a bond redetermination hearing. 67 Fed. Reg. 68924–26 (Nov. 13, 2002). If an applicant is determined by an asylum officer to have a credible fear or if the IJ determines that the person has a credible fear despite the asylum officer's negative determination, the applicant, unless a stowaway, is then put in an INA §240 proceeding. In that proceeding, s/he is now eligible for a bond hearing before the IJ if s/he is not an arriving alien or otherwise ineligible for a bond hearing before an IJ under 8 C.F.R. §1003.19(h)(2)(i). Thus, an applicant who was placed in expedited removal because s/he was picked up within 2 years of entry is eligible for bond. *Matter of X-K-*, 23 I&N Dec. 731 (BIA 2005) [holding that current DHS regulations do not bar the IJ from making custody determinations of person subject to expedite removal if they are determined to have a credible fear and placed in an INA §240 proceeding, and if a bond hearing is not otherwise precluded by 8 C.F.R. §1003.19(h)(2)(i). Legislative history at H.R. Conf. Rep. No. 104-828 at 209 (1996) supports this view]. DHS's criteria for parole of persons who pass the credible-fear interview are published. ICE Directive No. 7-1.0 (Nov. 6, 2007), *published on* AILA InfoNet at Doc. No. 07111263.

4. *Bar to Cancellation*—A person who departed the U.S. and was removed through expedited removal severs continuous residence for cancellation purposes. *Juarez-Ramos v. Gonzales,* 485 F.3d 509 (9th Cir. 2007).

5. *Administrative Review*—There is no administrative review of an expedited removal order except for a person who claims under penalty of perjury to have been lawfully admitted for permanent residence, to have been admitted as a refugee under INA §207 or to have been granted asylum under INA §208.

6. Judicial Review—INA §242(e)

   6.a. Declaratory, injunctive, or other equitable relief except as authorized below may no longer be authorized.

   6.b. No class action litigation.

   6.c. Habeas corpus review but only to determine whether: (1) petitioner is an alien; (2) petitioner was ordered removed under such section; *and* (3) petitioner is an LPR, or was granted refugee or asylum status. In determining whether the person has been ordered removed, the court's inquiry is limited to whether such an order was in fact issued and whether it relates to the petitioner. The court is precluded from reviewing whether the person is actually inadmissible or entitled to any relief from removal. *Brumme v. INS,* 275 F.3d 443 (5th Cir. 2001) [cannot review post–*St. Cyr* whether person subject to summary removal was admissible or entitled to relief]. *But see American-Arab Anti-Discrimination Comm. v. Ashcroft,* 272 F.Supp.2d 650 (E.D. Mich. 2003) [habeas jurisdiction exists to determine whether expedited removal statute was lawfully applied to the petitioner and where person was paroled into the U.S. it was inappropriate to apply summary removal].

   6.d. Judicial review may be brought as to whether any section of the expedited removal statute or regulation implementing the section is constitutional or whether any regulation or written policy, directive, or guideline written by or under the authority of DHS is consistent with the INA and not otherwise violative of law. Such an action may only be brought in the U.S. District Court for the District of Columbia and must be brought within 60 days of the implementation of the section, regulation, directive, or guideline that is being challenged. The action must be handled expeditiously by the circuit court and the Supreme Court and the Court's remedial power is limited exclusively to requiring that the person be given a hearing under INA §240.

   6.e. No Petition for Review—*Avendano-Ramirez v. Ashcroft,* 365 F.3d 813, 816–19 (9th Cir. 2004) [statute does not permit review of summary removal through a petition for review].

7. *Stay of Removal*—The AG has the authority to stay the removal of a person whose removal is not practicable or proper or who is needed as a witness in a prosecution. As part of that authority, the AG may release a witness on bond during the stay. INA §241(c)(2), 8 U.S.C. §1231(c)(2). *Zardui-Quintana v. Richard*, 768 F.2d 1213 (11th Cir. 1985) [DD, as distinguished from IJ, can grant stay].

D. ***Removal of Suspected Terrorists and Foreign Policy or Security Threats***—INA §235(c), 8 U.S.C. §1225(c), 8 C.F.R. §§235.8, 1235.8. If an immigration officer at the border or an IJ *suspects* that a person arriving in the U.S. is a terrorist or security or foreign policy threat under INA §212(a)(3)(A) (except section ii), (B), or (C), the IJ or IO shall order the person's removal without further inquiry and shall refer the case to the AG for review. The AG may order the person removed without a hearing if s/he is satisfied on the basis of confidential information and after checking with appropriate security agencies that the person is inadmissible on terrorist, security or foreign policy grounds. The person or his representative may only submit a written statement and additional information for consideration by the AG. According to the legislative history, this section merely restates existing law and is not designed to cover persons who are deemed inadmissible under INA §212(a)(6)(A) because they are in the U.S. without being inspected or paroled. H.R. Conf. Rep. 104-828, 104th Cong. 2d Sess. at 210. A returning LPR may not be subject to such summary removal even if DHS invokes security concerns. *Rafeedie v. INS,* 880 F.2d 506 (D.C. Cir. 1989); *Rafeedie v. INS,* 795 F.Supp. 13 (D.D.C. 1992). A person subject to a final order under INA §235(c) may nevertheless seek an interview before DHS on a claim under the Convention Against Torture. 8 C.F.R. §§208.18(d), 1208.18(d).

E. *Stowaways*—INA §235(a)(2), 8 U.S.C. §1225(a)(2). Stowaways are not eligible for admission or removal hearing under INA §240 and they shall be removed unless they claim asylum, withholding, or a Convention Against Torture claim. The claim is referred to an officer for a credible fear determination. 8 C.F.R. §§208.30, 1208.30.

F. *Other Removal Where Admissibility is Challenged at the Border*—INA §235(b)(2)(A), 8 U.S.C. §1225(b)(2)(A).

1. IIRIRA eliminated the traditional distinction between exclusion proceedings and deportation proceedings. Where someone does not fall under summary or expedited removal procedures s/he is entitled to a removal proceeding under INA §240. This statute procedurally treats applicants for admission and persons subject to deportation identical in many respects. However, it does continue to make a distinction between the burden of proof for someone who is an applicant for admission and someone who is subject to grounds of deportation. INA §240(c)(2). *Altamirano v. Gonzales,* 427 F.3d 586, 590–91 (9th Cir. 2005) [person paroled into U.S. under §212(d)(5)(A) whose admission was challenged at the border for alien smuggling had the burden to prove admissibility]. LPRs, however, if treated as applicants for admission, are still entitled to due process protections. *Landon v. Plasencia*, 459 U.S. 21 (1982).

2. If the person is arriving on land (whether or not at a designated port of arrival) from a foreign territory contiguous to the U.S., the AG may return the person to that territory pending a proceeding under INA §240.

G. *Deferred Inspection*—There are primary, secondary, and deferred inspections. Primary inspection is the initial inspection at an airport or seaport. Secondary inspection at an airport or seaport occurs when the person is pulled from the line for further questioning. Deferred inspection is a form of parole. 8 C.F.R. §§235.2, 1235.2.

1. Representation—DHS guidelines do not permit counsel at primary or secondary inspections, although a relative, friend, or representative may have access to the "inspection area to provide assistance when the situation warrants such action." IFM at 2.9. In a deferred inspection, the guidelines provide that "an attorney may be allowed to be present upon request if the supervisory inspector on duty deems it appropriate. The role of the attorney in such a situation is limited to that of observer and consultant to the applicant." IFM at 17.1(e). The guidelines also provide that in matters other than a primary or secondary inspection, an officer "should allow an alien to seek counsel to the extent that doing so does not hinder or unduly delay the adjudicative process." AFM at 12.1. Whether or not DHS permits a person at a deferred inspection to have counsel, general principles of due process always permit representation and current regulations or guidelines do not bar it. At a deferred inspection, as in a primary and secondary inspection, the officer may decide to admit the alien, to continue his parole, to permit him to withdraw his application for admission, or to detain him for removal. At any time during primary, secondary or deferred inspection any officer may challenge the decision of any other officer to admit a person. If such challenge occurs the person must appear before an IJ. INA §235(b)(3).

2. Criteria for Granting—The criteria used to determine whether to grant deferred inspection include: (a) the likelihood the applicant will establish admissibility; (b) the type of documents needs and the ability to obtain them; (c) the good faith effort of the applicant to obtain documents prior to arrival at the port-of-entry; (d) verification of applicant's identity and nationality; (e) age, health, and family ties of applicant; (f) other humanitarian considerations; (g) likelihood that applicant would appear at deferred inspection; (h) the nature of the ground of inadmissibility; and (i) the danger to society if applicant paroled. Memo, Williams, Ex. Assoc. Comm. Field Operations, HQINS 70/10.10 (May 18, 2002), *published on* AILA InfoNet at Doc. No. 02053134 (May 31, 2002); IFM at 17.1(a).

3. Failure to Appear—If the applicant fails to appear at a deferred inspection an NTA is issued to the address s/he provided and a lookout is posted on the NAILS system. IFM at 17.1(d).

H. *Parole*—The alien may be paroled into the U.S. for "urgent humanitarian reasons" or where a grant would result in a "significant public benefit." INA §212(d)(5)(A), 8 U.S.C. §1182(d)(5)(A). The standard prior to IIRIRA was for "emergent reasons" or "reasons deemed strictly in the public interest." An alien "shall be detained" if there is a question as to his admissibility. INA §235(b)(2), 8 U.S.C. §1225(b)(2). The "shall be detained" language does not require incarceration. *Louis v. Nelson*, 544

F.Supp. 973 (S.D. Fla. 1982). Similarly, the BIA traditionally interpreted the "shall be detained" language not as incarceration, but as the means to place someone in exclusion proceedings. *Matter of H*, 20 I&N Dec. 611 (BIA 1992). Because a person who enters EWI is now considered in law to be an applicant for admission under INA §235(a)(1), 8 U.S.C. §1225(a)(1) who is inadmissible under INA §212(a)(6)(A)(i), 8 U.S.C. §1182(a)(6)(A)(i), s/he may be paroled into the U.S. even if s/he does not meet the definition of an "arriving alien" under 8 C.F.R. §§1.1(q), 1001.1(q). Memo, Virtue, G.C. to Field (HQCOU 120/17-P) (Aug. 21, 1998), *published on* AILA InfoNet at Doc. No. 98082191. In the aftermath of Sept. 11, 2001, the Service issued directives that only DD, Deputy DD, or Asst. DD for Inspections or Examinations may parole someone into the U.S., parole for deferred inspection, or grant a waiver of documentary requirements and that their authority may not be delegated. Memo, Pearson, Ex. Assoc. Comm. Field Operations, HQINS 70/10.10 (Nov. 14, 2001), *reprinted in* 79 No. 2 *Interpreter Releases* 36, 59–60 (Jan 7, 2002). If a person is paroled into the U.S. he may be eligible for adjustment of status ("inspected and admitted or paroled" under INA §245(a)) unless he is otherwise ineligible (*e.g.*, o/s and worked without permission) or otherwise barred (*e.g.*, person with approved I-140 petition because she can only adjust under INA §245(c)(7) if entered in lawful nonimmigrant status and not parole].

I. *Withdrawal of Application*—Aliens are often encouraged to withdraw their applications for admission. The withdrawal of application is available at initial inspection, the deferred inspection, and even during or near the conclusion of a removal hearing to determine admissibility. INA §235(a)(4); 8 C.F.R. §§235.4, 1235.4 1240.1(d). Inspecting officers at the border however may not engage in a practice designed to extract waivers. *Hernandez v. Casillas*, 520 F.Supp. 389 (S.D. Tex. 1981).

1. Criteria for CBP officers at the border permitting withdrawal includes:

   1.a. Seriousness of the immigration violation;

   1.b. Previous findings of inadmissibility against the applicant;

   1.c. Intent of person to violate the law;

   1.d. Ability to overcome the ground of inadmissibility (*e.g.*, lack of documents);

   1.e. Age or poor health of applicant;

   1.f. Other humanitarian or public interest considerations;

   1.g. Visa invalid because of unknowing violation of §222(g).

   IFM at 17.2; Memo, Virtue, Exec. Assoc. Comm., INS (Dec. 22, 1997), *published on* AILA InfoNet at Doc. No. 98122291.

2. Withdrawal is not granted where there is an obvious, deliberate fraud. But if someone acted "innocently or through ignorance, misinformation or bad advice, obtained an inappropriate visa" withdrawal should be given.

3. If an applicant withdraws his application for admission, his or her NIV can be physically canceled by consular or immigration officer. 22 C.F.R. §41.122(h)(3). The *Inspector's Field Manual* requires cancellation and also requires a notification to the consular office issuing visa on Form I-275. IFM at 17.2.

J. *Detention of Inadmissible Persons*

1. *Overview*—In general, persons stopped at the border and found inadmissible are deemed to have no constitutional right to release. *Shaughnessy v. U.S. ex rel. Mezei,* 345 U.S. 206, 210 (1953) [no due process right to release of person deemed inadmissible]. Pursuant to statute, however, such individuals are eligible for release on parole. INA §212(d)(5). Historically, parole was exercised generously. But this changed in the 1980s in response to Haitian refugees arriving by boat. *Louis v. Nelson*, 544 F.Supp. 973 (S.D. Fla. 1982) (Finding the "shall be detained" language of former INA §235 to not require incarceration); *Matter of H,* 20 I&N Dec. 611 (BIA 1992).

   Prior to IIRIRA, "inadmissible" persons were generally deemed "excludable," were placed in special "exclusion" (as opposed to "deportation") proceedings, and were not eligible for release on bond, only parole. In addition, unlike persons in deportation proceedings, who were entitled to a bond hearing before an IJ, excludable persons were not entitled to review, before an IJ, of the district director's parole decision. IIRIRA §303 eliminated separate exclusion and deportation proceedings and created a single removal proceeding under INA §240 for both inadmissible and deportable individuals. In addition, IIRIRA created a "summary" or "expedited" removal proceeding under INA §235(b) that allows an immigration officer, at the border and in the absence of an immigration judge, to make a determination as to a person's admissibility. For those persons placed in an INA §240 removal proceeding (in contrast to the INA §235(b) expedited proceeding), the detention/bond statute, INA §236, no longer distinguishes between inadmissible and deportable persons in terms of eligibility for bond. This makes sense in that most persons who were traditionally detained as excludable will now be placed in expedited removal proceedings under INA §235(b) and will continue to be ineligible for bond and eligible for parole only under limited circumstances.

The government, however, has taken the position that, notwithstanding the fact that that INA §236 provides bond eligibility for both inadmissible and deportable persons, only those inadmissible persons who are apprehended in the U.S. are eligible for bond. Those inadmissible persons who are apprehended at the border (also described as "arriving aliens") are ineligible for bond even when they are subsequently place in a §240 proceeding. They may, nevertheless, be eligible for parole under INA §212(d)(5), but parole may only be granted by ICE, not an IJ. Moreover, DOJ regulations specifically divest the IJ of jurisdiction to hear any bond cases involving "arriving aliens. 8 C.F.R. §§1003.19(h)(2)(i)(B), 236.1(c)(11), 1236.1(c)(11); *Matter of Oseiwusu,* 22 I&N Dec. 19 (BIA 1998) [under Transition Period Custody Rules (TPCR)].

2. *Detention of Inadmissible Persons who are Arriving Aliens (including returning LPRs)*—An arriving alien, as defined under 8 C.F.R. §§1.1(q), 1001.1(q), includes persons apprehended at the border seeking admission even if paroled into the U.S., persons interdicted who are brought into the U.S. even if they are not seeking admission, and those returning LPRs who are considered to be seeking admission because of the statutory definition of "admission" or "admitted" under INA §101(a)(13)(C). Thus, under the regulations that divest IJs of authority to redetermine custody for "arriving aliens," returning LPRs, who are deemed to be seeking admission by virtue of INA §101(a)(13)(C), are not entitled to a bond hearing before an IJ. *See, e.g., Matter of Collado-Munoz,* 21 I&N Dec. 1061 (BIA 1997) [LPR is deemed to be seeking admission upon return because of old conviction, notwithstanding brief casual and innocent departure, and therefore is not entitled to IJ bond hearing; *Fleuti* doctrine deemed abandoned by IIRIRA]; *Tineo v. Ashcroft,* 350 F.3d 382 (3d Cir. 2003) [determining that Congress did abolish the *Fleuti* doctrine in the passage of INA §101(a)(13)(C) for certain returning LPRs, and upholding *Matter of Collado-Munoz* on *Chevron* deference grounds]; *Evangelista v. Ashcroft,* 204 F.Supp.2d 405, 409–10 (E.D.N.Y. 2002) [due process not violated because the decision to deny bail to a long-term LPR pending the outcome of his merits hearing was made by the DD and not an IJ]; *Ferraras v. Ashcroft,* 160 F.Supp.2d 617 (S.D.N.Y. 2001) [returning LPR not entitled to hearing before IJ and INS regulatory scheme allowing paper record before DD is not, post-*Zadvydas,* violative of due process or equal protection]. *Cf. Zubeda v. Elwood,* 265 F.Supp.2d 509 (E.D. Pa. 2003) [inadmissible person detained during removal proceeding had no due process right to a bond hearing before an IJ]. *But see Olatunji v. Ashcroft,* 387 F.3d 383, 388–96 (4th Cir. 2004) [holding that IIRIRA's change in the *Fleuti* doctrine could not be retroactively applied to a person who pled guilty prior to its enactment]; *Shahwan v. Chertoff,* Case No. C-05-4218 MMC (N.D. Cal. Dec. 12, 2005) [advance parolee treated as "arriving alien" could not be deprived of bond hearing without advance notice; court relied on *Navarro-Aispura v. INS,* 53 F.3d 233 (9th Cir. 1995) to find that deprivation of such a bond hearing without advance notice would violate due process); *Cabreja-Rojas v. Reno,* 999 F.Supp. 493 (S.D.N.Y. 1998) [returning LPRs entitled to a hearing before an independent IJ, not the INS]; *Ekekhor v. Aljets,* 979 F.Supp. 640 (N.D. Ill. 1997) (and cases cited therein) *St. John v. McElroy,* 917 F.Supp. 243 (S.D.N.Y. 1996).

Bail by the Circuit Court—At least one circuit court has also determined it has the inherent authority to grant bond while a petition for review is pending in the circuit court where petitioner has presented a substantial claim and there are extraordinary circumstances that make the grant of bail necessary to make the petition for review remedy effective. *Elkimya v. DHS,* 484 F.3d 151 (2d Cir. 2007) [finding court has inherent authority to grant bail pending resolution of a petition for review of returning LPR who has been out of the U.S. for 4 years, but concluding there were no extraordinary circumstances permitting bail); *Mapp v. Reno,* 241 F.3d 221 (2d Cir. 2001) [district courts have inherent authority to grant bail while habeas petition is pending where to do so is "necessary to make the habeas remedy effective"]; *but see Bolante v. Keisler,* 506 F.3d 618 (7th

Cir. 2007) [admitting a person to bail while challenging admission is contrary to the INA and the inherent authority to admit persons to bail does not extend to persons deemed inadmissible at the border].

Parole by ICE—Even if an arriving alien is ineligible for bond, s/he may seek release on parole before ICE, who maintains the right to consider parole for LPRs, CRs, or temporary residents who do not have convictions that subject them to the mandatory detention provisions, or persons who establish they have a credible fear of persecution. 8 C.F.R. §212.5. *See also* ICE Directive 7-1.0, Myers, Asst. Secy., (Nov. 6, 2007), *published on* AILA InfoNet at Doc. No. 07111264 [establishing the procedure and criteria for parole in credible fear cases]; Memo, Reed, Acting Ex. Assoc. Comm. Field Operations (Oct. 22, 1997), *published on* AILA InfoNet at Doc. No. 97103190. For a more detailed discussion of parole, *see in this section* "ICE Parole Generally," ¶ 10 (p.140), *infra.*

3. *Detention of Inadmissible Persons Who Are Not Considered "Arriving Aliens" and Who Are Not Subject to Mandatory Detention on Criminal Grounds or Terrorism*—For persons who are not considered arriving aliens or who have not committed any offense covered by INA §212(a)(2) or INA §212(a)(3)(B) the AG may grant bond pursuant to INA §236(a). Under IIRIRA, a person who enters EWI is now considered to be an applicant for admission under INA §235(a)(1), who is inadmissible under INA §212(a)(6)(A)(i) rather than deportable. Because EWIs are not apprehended at the border, however, they do not fall within the definition of "arriving aliens" under 8 C.F.R. §§1.1(q), 1001.1(1). Therefore, the regulations do not preclude an IJ from conducting a bond hearing in their cases. However, because they are inadmissible persons "seeking admission," the government still views their detention and release as governed by the parole statute. *See* Memo, Virtue, G.C. to Field (HQCOU 120/17-P) (Aug. 21, 1998), *reprinted in* 76 No. 26 *Interpreter Releases* 1050, 1067–70 (July 12, 1999) [justifying availability of IJ bond hearings for EWIs as an exercise of the statutory parole authority].

Pursuant to INA §236(a), the IJ may grant bond in the minimum amount of $1,500 but the person may not obtain work authorization unless he is an LPR or would have otherwise obtained an employment authorization. A bond hearing can be held even if charging documents have *not* been filed with the immigration court. 8 C.F.R. §1003.14(a). The AG may at any time revoke the bond, INA §236(b), although the setting and revocation of bond is subject to administrative review before the BIA. The DHS may also obtain an *automatic* stay of an IJ's bond order simply by filing an EOIR-43 where the DD denied bond or set bond at $10,000 or more and the IJ authorized release on bond. The EOIR-43 must be filed within one business day of the IJ's order. 8 C.F.R. §1003.19(i)(2). Thereafter, DHS must file a notice of appeal consistent with §1003.38 to the BIA within 10 days of the IJ's decision or the stay will lapse. The notice of appeal, to preserve the stay, must be accompanied by a certification from a senior legal official that certifies that s/he has approved the filing of the notice of appeal and is satisfied that the contentions justifying the continued detention have evidentiary support and that the legal arguments are warranted by existing law or by a nonfrivolous argument for extension of the law. 8 C.F.R. §1003.6(c)(1). Once the notice of appeal is filed the IJ has 5 days to issue a written bond decision but may, in exigent circumstances, obtain an additional 5 days. 8 C.F.R. §1003.6(c)(2). If the BIA has not acted on the custody appeal within 90 days the automatic stay "shall" lapse. However, if the BIA grants a motion by the detainee to enlarge the time for submitting his brief, the 90 days are tolled. 8 C.F.R. §1003.6(c)(4). In addition, if the stay will lapse, DHS may seek a discretionary stay. 8 C.F.R. §1003.6(c)(5). If the BIA ultimately rules against DHS in its bond appeal, the release order is automatically stayed for 5 days to allow DHS to seek AG review. 8 C.F.R. §103.6(d). *See also* Memo [Interim OPPM 06-03], Neal, Chief IJ (Oct. 31, 2006), *published on* AILA InfoNet at Doc. No. 06110264. The provision has been found to be unconstitutional, although these decisions were all prior to the regulation's revision in 2006 to include the 90-day lapse provision. *Uritsky v. Ridge,* 286 F.Supp.2d 842 (E.D. Mich. 2003); *Bezmen v. Ashcroft,* 245 F.Supp.2d 446 (D. Conn. 2003). *Accord Zabadi v. Chertoff,* 2005 WL 1514122 (N.D. Cal. June 17, 2005) and 2005 WL 3157377 (N.D. Cal. Nov. 22, 2005); *Zavala v. Ridge,* 310 F.Supp.2d 1071 (N.D. Cal. 2004); *Ashley v. Ridge,* 288 F.Supp.2d 662 (D.N.J. 2003) [automatic-stay provision violates substantive and procedural due process for person who is not subject to mandatory detention and not a national security threat]. *But see Pisciotta v. Ashcroft,* 311 F.Supp.2d 445, 453–56 (D.N.J. 2004) [the stay provision is not unconstitutional under *Demore*].

For the applicable law governing the standards for bond, *e.g.*, *Matter of Patel*, 15 I&N Dec. 666 (BIA 1976), *see in this chapter* "Detention," section X.K (p.291), *infra*.

The law also seeks to prohibit judicial review of the AG's discretionary decisions regarding bond and parole. INA §236(e). *See in this section* "Judicial Review of Detention Decisions," ¶ 12 (p. 141), *infra*.

4. *Detention of Inadmissible Persons Who Are Not "Arriving Aliens" But Who Are Placed in Expedite Removal*—Pursuant to its authority under INA §235(b)(1)(A)(iii)(II) DHS has begun applying expedited removal to persons who entered the United States without inspection (EWIs) and who have been present for less than 14 days. DHS has took the position that because these persons were placed in expedited removal proceedings, they were ineligible for IJ bond hearings even when they passed the credible fear screening and were referred for Section 240 removal proceedings. The BIA rejected this argument in *Matter of X-K-*, 23 I&N Dec. 731 (BIA 2005) [holding that current DHS regulations do not bar the IJ from making custody determinations of person subject to expedite removal if they are determined to have a credible fear and placed in an INA §240 proceeding, and if a bond hearing is not otherwise precluded by 8 C.F.R. §1003.19(h)(2)(i). Legislative history at H.R. Conf. Rep. No. 104-828 at 209(1996) supports this view].

5. Mandatory Detention of Persons Inadmissible on Criminal or Terrorism Grounds under INA §236(c)

5.a. Detention Laws from 1988 to 1996—Congress has legislated extensively as to when and under what circumstances persons convicted of crimes will be incarcerated pending immigration removal proceedings and after a final removal order. As a result of legislation in 1988 persons who were aggravated felons, including LPRs, were for the first time subject to mandatory detention pending removal proceedings without the possibility of release on bond. This mandatory detention provision was successfully challenged in many district courts. *Kellman v. District Director,* 750 F.Supp. 625 (S.D.N.Y. 1990); *Probert v. INS,* 750 F.Supp. 252 (E.D. Mich. 1990) *aff'd on other grounds,* 954 F.2d 1253 (6th Cir. 1992) [involving an NIV holder and finding the limitation on habeas authority under INA §242(a)(1) also unconstitutional]; *Paxton v. INS*, 745 F.Supp. 1261 (E.D. Mich. 1990), *dismissed as moot*, 925 F.2d 1465 (6th Cir. 1991); *Agunobi v. Thornburgh,* 745 F.Supp. 533 (N.D. Ill. 1990); *Leader v. Blackman,* 744 F.Supp. 500 (S.D.N.Y. 1990); *Davis v. Weiss,* 749 F.Supp. 47 (D. Conn. 1990); *Morrobel v. Thornburgh,* 744 F.Supp. 725 (E.D. Wa. 1990). Thereafter, amendments in IMMACT90 and the MTINA of 1991 restored bond hearings for those aggravated felons who had been lawfully admitted to the U.S., including LPRs. Those individuals were eligible for bond if they could affirmatively demonstrate that their release would pose neither a danger or flight risk. *See* former INA §242(a)(2)(B), 8 U.S.C. §1252(a)(2)(B) (1994). However, in 1996, Congress enacted new legislation that greatly expanded the reach of the mandatory detention statute while eliminating the release policy for "lawfully admitted" noncitizens. The first provision enacted, on Apr. 26, 1996, as part of AEDPA, barred aggravated felons and others who had committed criminal acts from release even if they were LPRs. These provisions were struck down by many district courts on retroactivity and constitutional grounds. *Lopez-Tellez v. INS,* __ F.Supp. __, Case No 96-1432-BTM (CGA) (S.D. Cal. Sept. 26, 1996) (Moskowitz, J); *Grodzki v. Reno*, 950 F.Supp. 339 (N.D. Ga. 1996); *Montero v. Cobb*, 937 F.Supp. 88, 92 (D. Mass. 1996); *Morales-Villagomez v. Smith*, 1996 WL 622451, Case No. C96-1141C (W.D. Wash. July 21, 1996) (Coughneour, J.); *Matter of Reyes*, Case No. B-94-80 (S.D. Tex. May 31, 1996) (Vela, J).

5.b. Thereafter, on Sept. 30, 1996, the President signed IIRIRA, which mandates detention, without release, for virtually all persons who have committed crimes (as well as persons removable on terrorist grounds). Under the IIRIRA amendments, codified at INA §236(c), 8 U.S.C. §1226(c), the only persons who are eligible for release if subject to mandatory detention are persons who are a part of the Witness Protection Program or whose release will protect other witnesses. IIRIRA, however, also provided for limited exceptions to mandatory detention over a 2-year period if the AG invoked the Transition Period Custody Rules (TPCR). IIRIRA §303(b). The TPCR was invoked for 2 years, from Oct. 9, 1996, to Oct. 9, 1998. While the TPCR mandated detention of virtually all noncitizens with criminal convictions, it permitted release of "lawfully admitted" noncitizens. Application of the TPCR was successfully challenged. *Pastor-Camarena v. Smith*, 977 F.Supp. 1415 (W.D. Wash. 1997) [finding that the "when release" language in TPCR limited the provision's application to persons with criminal convictions who had not yet been released from criminal incarceration].

5.c. The IIRIRA Provisions

(1) INA §236(c) provides that the AG shall detain and shall not release the following categories of persons who are subject to removal from the U.S.: (a) persons who are inadmissible by reason of having committed any offense covered under INA §212(a)(2), 8 U.S.C. §1182(a)(2); (b) persons who are deportable by reason of having committed 2 or more CIMTs, an aggravated felony, a drug offense, a firearm offense, *or* a miscellaneous crime as defined in INA §237(a)(2)(D), including espionage, sabotage, or treason for which a term of imprisonment of 5 years or more may be imposed, threatening the President in violation of 18 U.S.C. §871, violating the Neutrality Act under 18 U.S.C. §960, violating the Selective Service Act or Trading with the Enemies Act, committing travel control crimes under 8 U.S.C. §1185, or importing a person for an immoral purpose under 8 U.S.C. §1328, (c) persons who have committed a CIMT for which the sentence of imprisonment is at least one year; or (d) persons involved in terrorist activity. The AG shall take them into custody "when the alien is released on parole, supervised release, or probation, and without regard to whether the alien may be arrested or imprisoned again for the same offense." If the person is subject to mandatory detention, the AG may only release such person if s/he is involved in the Witness Protection Program or to protect another witness, and the AG is satisfied that the person will not pose a danger to the safety of other persons or property. A person need not be charged with the crime in the NTA to be subject to mandatory detention. *Matter of Kotliar,* 24 I&N Dec. 124 (BIA 2007) [person apprehended at home while on probation who was not charged in NTA with crime is still subject to mandatory detention for the crime].

(2) For a discussion of the application, effective dates, procedures, and constitutional and statutory challenges to mandatory detention, *see in this chapter* ¶ X.Q.3 (p.305), *infra.*

6. *Challenge by Returning LPRs to Mandatory or Nonmandatory Detention*—In light of *Demore v. Kim,* 538 U.S. 510 (2003), these challenges have become more difficult. For discussion setting forth pre- and post-*Demore* cases, *see in this chapter* ¶ X.Q.3 (p.305), *infra.* However, DHS's policy of detaining returning LPRs is typically the result of the AG/DHS refusing to exercise its parole authority—and the DHS regulation prohibiting IJ review of this decision—rather than, as in *Kim,* the result of a congressional determination to prohibit release (as reflected in legislation). In addition, the Supreme Court's decision in *Demore* has, itself, been limited by subsequent decisions refusing to apply it to cases of prolonged detention. For possible challenges to the detention *see Demore,* 538 U.S. at 531–33 (Justice Kennedy); *Tijani v. Willis,* 430 F.3d 1241 (9th Cir. 2005); *Ly v. Hansen,* 351 F.3d 263 (6th Cir. 2003); and *Uritsky v. Ridge,* 286 F.Supp.2d 842 (E.D. Mich. 2003) discussed above. Prior to *Demore v. Kim*, federal courts entertained constitutional claims of returning LPRs. *Cabreja- Rojas v. Reno,* 999 F.Supp. 493 (S.D.N.Y. 1998) [unconstitutional, under *Eldridge*, to deny returning LPRs under TPCR a hearing before an independent IJ]. *See also Ekekhor v. Aljets*, 979 F.Supp. 640 (N.D. Ill. 1997) (and cases cited therein); *St. John v. McElroy*, 917 F.Supp. 243 (S.D.N.Y. 1996); *Cruz-Taveras v. McElroy,* 1996 WL 455012, Case No. 96 C.V.5068 (M.M.) (S.D.N.Y. Aug. 12, 1996); *St. John v. McElroy*, 917 F.Supp. 243 (S.D.N.Y. 1996). *But see Tineo v. Ashcroft,* 350 F.3d 382 (3d Cir. 2003) [declining to address constitutional issue but determining that Congress did abolish the *Fleuti* doctrine in the passage of INA §101(a)(13)(C) for certain returning LPRs]; *Ferraras v. Ashcroft,* 160 F.Supp.2d 617 (S.D.N.Y. 2001) [returning LPR post-*Zadvydas* was not entitled under constitution to more than a paper record before DD to determine release].

7. *Mandatory Detention of Suspected Terrorists*—INA §236A, 8 U.S.C. §1226a; USA PATRIOT Act, §412. The AG/ICE is authorized to mandatorily detain any person he/it has certified as having reasonable grounds to believe is a person described under the inadmissibility provisions, INA §212(a)(3)(A)(i) [engage in espionage, sabotage, or export control], §212(a)(3)(A)(iii) [opposition by violence or overthrow of U.S. government] or §212(a)(3)(B) [terrorist activity]. For a more detailed discussion, *see in this chapter* "Mandatory Detention of Suspected Terrorists," section X.R (p.309), *infra.*

8. *Detention of Persons Subject to Expedited Removal*—8 C.F.R. §§235.3(b)(2)(iii), 1235.3(b)(2)(iii).

   8.a. A person subject to expedited removal shall be detained pending removal, except where DHS paroles the applicant because "parole is required to meet a medical emergency or is necessary for a legitimate law enforcement objection." *Id.* This stringent parole standard, however, does not apply to a person seeking asylum/CAT protection who is placed in expedited removal but then satisfies the credible fear standard. Such persons are eligible for parole under INA §212(d)(5). However, the AG established a policy of detention for persons (except Cubans) who arrive by sea. They will be detained, with certain humanitarian exceptions, throughout the credible fear and asylum process before the IJ. 67 Fed. Reg. 68924–26 (Nov. 12, 2002).

   8.b. "Arriving Aliens" vs. "Non–Arriving Aliens"—To the extent that expedited removal is applied to "arriving aliens" as defined at 8 C.F.R. §§1.1(q), 1001.1(1), DHS regulations deprive an IJ of authority to review the DHS custody determination. However, under expanded expedited removal (as applied to EWIs who have been present in the country for less than 14 days), the regulations do not prohibit an IJ from reviewing custody determinations of those asylum seekers who establish a credible fear of persecution and are referred to INA §240 removal proceedings. *See Matter of X-K-,* 23 I&N Dec. 731 (BIA 2005) [rejecting DHS position that IJ could not conduct bond hearings for EWIs placed in expanded expedited removal and later referred for §240 proceedings].

9. *Prolonged and Indefinite Detention of Inadmissible Persons Pending Removal Proceedings— Nadarajah v. Gonzales,* 443 F.3d 1069 (9th Cir. 2006) [applying reasoning of *Zadvydas* and *Martinez* to find that general detention provisions in the INA do not provide statutory authority for indefinite detention of inadmissible persons pending removal proceedings; petitioner an "arriving alien" who had been granted relief under CAT was detained for 4½ years pending completion of removal proceedings even though his ultimate removal to Sri Lanka was not reasonably foreseeable. Government argued unsuccessfully that INA §§235(b)(1)(B)(ii) and (b)(2)(A) permit indefinite detention].

10. *ICE Parole Generally*—Although DHS regulations, 8 C.F.R. §§236.1(c)(2), 1236.1(c)(2) (which appear contrary to INA §236), preclude IJs from considering bond for arriving aliens, 8 C.F.R. §§212.5(b), 235.1(d), 1235.1(d) permits DHS to grant parole. Because a person who enters EWI is now considered by law to be an applicant for admission under INA §235(a)(1), 8 U.S.C. §1225(a)(1), who is inadmissible under INA §212(a)(6)(A)(i), 8 U.S.C. §1182(a)(6)(A)(i), s/he may also be paroled into the U.S. even if s/he does not meet the definition of an "arriving alien" under 8 C.F.R. §§1.1(q), 1001.1(q). Memo, Virtue, G.C. to Field (HQCOU 120/17-P) (Aug. 21, 1998), *published on* AILA InfoNet at Doc. No. 98082191.

    A person may be paroled if:

    10.a. s/he has a "serious medical condition";

    10.b. she has been medically certified as pregnant;

    10.c. s/he is a juvenile;

    10.d. s/he has an immediate relative who is eligible to file and has filed an I-130 petition;

    10.e. s/he will be a witness in judicial, administrative, or legislative proceedings, *see Gutierrez v. Ilchert*, 682 F.Supp. 467 (N.D. Cal. 1988) [detainees should be paroled to present legalization application];

    10.f. his or her detention is not in the public interest as determined by the DD; *or*

    10.g. s/he was granted asylum, withholding, or CAT before IJ and case on appeal. Persons granted asylum, withholding, or CAT before the IJ may be released pending DHS appeal. Although under DHS regulations persons *granted* deferral of removal pursuant to CAT may remain in detention [8 C.F.R. §§208.17(b)(1)(ii), 1208.17(b)(1)(ii)], DHS has issued a memo providing that: "In general, it is ICE policy to favor release of aliens who have been granted protection relief by an immigration judge, absent exceptional concerns such as national security issues or danger to the community and absent any requirement under law to detain.... Arriving aliens should [also] be considered for parole." Memo, Garcia, Asst. Sec. DHS (Feb. 9, 2004), *published on* AILA InfoNet at Doc. No. 04022462. *But see* ICE Directive 7-1.0, Myers, Asst.

Secy. (Nov. 6, 2007), *published on* AILA InfoNet at Doc. No. 07111264 [establishing the procedure and criteria for parole in credible-fear cases, and expressly superseding prior Garcia Memo as applied to arriving aliens].

11. *ICE Parole for Persons Who Establish a Credible Fear of Persecution—See* ICE Directive 7-1.0, Myers, Asst. Secy. (Nov. 6, 2007), *published on* AILA InfoNet at Doc. No. 07111264 [setting guidelines and revoking all prior memos and directive on parole for persons who establish credible fear]. ICE parole decisions are to be made only on a case-by-case basis for "urgent humanitarian reasons" or "significant public benefit" and persons found to have a credible fear must fall within one of the five criteria of 8 C.F.R. §212.5(b): (1) persons with serious medical conditions or impairment; (2) women medically certified as pregnant; (3) juveniles; (4) witnesses in proceedings; and (5) persons whose continued detention is not in the public interest. ICE has set forth a two step process to determine parole:

11.a. Step One. ICE officer must make a threshold assessment if the person's request and supporting documents establish: (1) his identity; (2) that he does not pose a flight risk; and (3) that he is not a danger to the community. To establish identity he must produce valid government issued documents and if he cannot "reasonably provide" them he can submit third party affidavits but those people must have valid government issued documents. To establish lack of flight risk the officer should consider, but is not limited to: (1) family ties; (2) employment history; (3) manner of entry; (4) length and stability of residence in the U.S.; (5) record of appearance in immigration court and prior immigration history; (6) ability to post bond; (7) property ownership; and (8) possible relief. A bond must be in a sufficient for reasonable assurances that the person will appear and/or depart. To address danger to the community ICE officers must look at contrary evidence such as: (1) past criminal history in the U.S. and abroad; (2) national security interests; (3) public safety concerns; (4) prior immoral acts; (5) participation in subversive activities; and (6) evidence that he would be a harm to himself or others.

11.b. Step Two. ICE officer must determine, in an analysis separate from Step One, whether the potential parolee fits under one of the five categories for parole in 8 C.F.R. §212.5(b). If the person is claiming a serious medical condition or impairment the medical or psychological evaluation, diagnosis, treatment plan or other documentation by the medical professional must support the claim. If seeking release as a witness, the officer must consider: (1) whether the relevant law enforcement agent or entity made a formal request; (2) whether some other law enforcement agency will take custody; (3) whether the person's testimony could endanger him; and (4) whether he would be safer in the community-at-large than in a secure detention facility. The public interest parole "requires careful consideration," whether consistent with ICE's mission, a specific case is appropriate for parole. Because the term has no standard definition "parole on this basis must be documented by a well-reasoned justification." If the parole is considered based upon the public interest the officer "shall draft a full written justification for supervisory review."

11.c. Decision. If parole is denied a standardized written response is provided. If approved, the person gets a stamped I-94 that authorizes parole.

12. Judicial Review of Detention Decisions

12.a. INA §236(e), 8 U.S.C. §1226(e), provides that: "The Attorney General's discretionary judgment regarding the application of this section shall not be subjected to review. No court may set aside any action or decision by the Attorney General under this section regarding the detention or release of any alien or the grant, revocation or denial of bond or parole." To the extent that inadmissible persons are detained under the authority of INA §235 (or any other statute), rather than INA §236, this section is not applicable. However, to the extent that some inadmissible persons are detained under the authority of INA §236 as well *(e.g.*, EWIs and others referred for INA §240 removal proceedings), INA §236(e) bars review only of discretionary decisions regarding bond or parole. It does not bar review of statutory or constitutional challenges, which can be brought under the statutory writ of habeas corpus, 28 U.S.C. §2241. *Demore v. Kim,* 538 U.S. 510, 516–17 (2003) [INA §236(e) does not bar habeas jurisdiction in absence of specific provision barring habeas and because petitioner lodged a constitutional challenge to mandatory detention legislation]; *Gonzalez v. O'Connell,* 355 F.3d 1010, 1014–15 (7th Cir. 2004) [finding habeas jurisdiction to challenge mandatory detention even where the predicate issue to the constitutional claim was a statutory claim]; *Waffi v. Loiselle,* 527 F.Supp.2d 480, 483–85 (E.D. Va. 2007) [INA §236(e) does not bar habeas jurisdiction to determine statutory question whether person released from criminal custody can be subject to mandatory detention]; *Campbell v. Chadbourne,* 505 F.Supp.2d 191, 195–97 (D. Mass. 2007) [INA §236(e) does not bar constitutional challenge to detention where refugee claims he was detained for refusing to apply for AOS]; *Aguilar v. Lewis,* 50 F.Supp.2d 539, 542–43 (E.D. Va. 1999) [INA §236(e) bars discretionary decisions not statutory interpretation]; *Velasquez v. Reno,* 37 F.Supp.2d 663, 667–70 (D.N.J. 1999) [INA §236(e) barring review of detention decisions does not foreclose habeas challenge to application of statute]. *But see Hatami v. Chertoff,* 467 F.Supp.2d 637 (E.D. Va. 2006) [respondent's challenge that IJ failed to provide meaningful bond hearing was precluded by INA §§236(e), 242(a)(2)(B)(ii) and 242(b)(9)]; *Pisciotta v. Ashcroft,* 311 F.Supp.2d 445, 453 (D.N.J. 2004) [the decision by ICE to re-detain petitioner without bond or revoke his previous status because his removal hearing was re-opened, notwithstanding a previous $12,000 bond, is not reviewable].

12.b. *Other Preclusion Statutes Do Not Bar Review of Detention Decisions*—INA §242(g) does not bar review of detention decisions; nor does INA §242(b)(9) or INA §242(a)(2)(B)(ii). *Zadvydas v. Davis,* 533 U.S. 678, 686–89 (2001) [INA §§236(e), 242(a)(2)(B)(ii), 242(a)(2)(C), 242(g) did not bar habeas jurisdiction for challenge to post-removal detention]; *Sillah v. Davis,* 252 F.Supp.2d 589, 593–97 (W.D. Tenn. 2003) [INA §242(a)(2)(B)(ii) does not preclude habeas jurisdiction to challenge revocation of parole]; *Zhislin v. Reno,* 195 F.3d 810 (6th Cir. 1999) [INA §242(g) as interpreted by *Reno v. American-Arab Anti-Discrimination Comm.*, 119 S.Ct. 936, 943 (1999) does not bar review of challenge to indefinite detention]; *Parra v. Perryman,* 172 F.3d 954 (7th Cir. 1999) [in light of *American-Arab,* INA §242(g) does not bar habeas to review detention issue]; *Bouayad v. Holmes,* 74 F.Supp.2d 471, 473–74 (E.D. Pa. 1999) [government conceded that habeas jurisdiction existed to challenge mandatory detention and the court determined that neither INA §236(e) nor INA §242(b)(9) preclude jurisdiction over detention]; *Kiareldeen v. Reno,* 71 F.Supp.2d 402, 405–07 (D.N.J. 1999) [neither INA §236(e) nor §242(g) bars habeas jurisdiction to review detention based upon secret evidence]; *Alikhani v. Fasano,* 70 F.Supp.2d 1124, 1126–30 (S.D. Cal. 1999) [INA §§242(g), 242(b)(9) and 236(e) do not bar challenge to statutory and constitutional challenge to mandatory detention]; *But see Hatami v. Chertoff,* 467 F.Supp.2d 637 (E.D. Va. 2006) [respondent's challenge that IJ failed to provide meaningful bond hearing was precluded by INA §§236(e), 242(a)(2)(B)(ii) and 242(b)(9)]; *Loa-Herrera v. Trominski,* 231 F.3d 984, 990–91 (5th Cir. 2000) [no jurisdiction by district court to require DD to permit parole hearing for LPR stopped at the border].

12.c. *REAL ID Act and Judicial Review of Detention*—With the passage of the REAL ID Act of 2005, PL 109-13, 119 Stat. 231, Div. B §106 (May 11, 2005), Congress sought to eliminate habeas, mandamus, and All Writs jurisdiction in the district courts in regard to "judicial review of an order of removal entered or issued under any provision of this Act." INA §242(a)(5). The legislative history of the REAL ID Act, however, makes clear that it "will not preclude habeas review over challenges to detention that are independent of challenges to removal orders. Instead, the bill would eliminate habeas review only over challenges to removal orders." Joint Explanatory Statement of the Committee of Conference, H.R. Cong. Rep. No. 109-72 at 175, 151 Cong. Rec. H2836, 2873 (May 3, 2005). *See also Hernandez v. Gonzales,* 424 F.3d 42 (1st Cir. 2005) [remanding habeas detention challenge by Mariel Cuban back to district court because habeas may be brought post–REAL ID Act when it is a challenge to detention]; *Bonhometre v. Ashcroft,* 414 F.3d 442, 446 n.4 (3d Cir. 2005); *Moallin v. Cangemi,* 427 F.Supp.2d 908, 918–21 (D. Minn. 2006) [citing the REAL ID Act legislative history a Somalian detained subsequent to his removal order can challenge his custody as violative of the constitution]; *Abdulle v. Gonzales,* 422 F.Supp.2d 774, 776 (W.D. Tex. 2006) [REAL ID does not preclude habeas related to detention only]. *But see Deljevic v. Baker,* 463 F.Supp.2d 699 (E.D. Mich. 2006) [no habeas jurisdiction to review detention where there is final order of removal and detention is challenged on ground that final order was improper].

12.d. *Discretionary Decisions May Be Reviewed Where They Raise Constitutional Issues*—Courts have found jurisdiction to review even discretionary detention decisions, where the detention violates due process or exceeds statutory authority. *See U.S. v. Grand China, Inc.* 376 F.Supp.2d 1150 (D.N.M. 2005) [reviewing denial of bond by ICE but upholding denial]. *But see Pisciotta v. Ashcroft,* 311 F.Supp.2d 445, 453 (D.N.J. 2004) [the decision by ICE to re-detain petitioner without bond or revoke his previous status because his removal hearing was reopened, notwithstanding a previous $12,000 bond, is not reviewable]; *Loa-Herrera v. Trominski,* 231 F.3d 984, 990–91 (5th Cir. 2000) [pre-*Demore* decision finding that INA §236(e) barred district court from considering challenge to lack of parole hearing for LPR stopped at the border]; *Galvez v. Lewis,* 56 F.Supp.2d 637 (E.D. Va. 1999) [pre-*Demore* decision finding no jurisdiction to review IJ's decision to apply INA §236(c) and refuse bond hearing].

12.e. If there is jurisdiction, the standards for reviewing parole decisions are as follows:

(1) Abuse of discretion standard, *Jean v. Nelson*, 472 U.S. 846 (1985); *Marczak v. Greene*, 971 F.2d 510, 515–18 (10th Cir. 1992) [no practical difference between facially legitimate and abuse of discretion as both require reference to the record]; *Nadarajah v. Gonzales,* 443 F.3d 1069 (9th Cir. 2006) [finding no "facially legitimate and bona fide" reason for denial of parole, and, hence, abuse of discretion, where government's conclusions that petitioner's detention was in the public interest and that his release posed a security risk were "based on facially implausible evidence" that had already been rejected by the IJ]; *Moret v. Karn*, 746 F.2d 989 (3d Cir. 1984); *Palma v. Verdeyen*, 676 F.2d 100 (4th Cir. 1982); *Ahrens v. Rojas*, 292 F.2d 406 (5th Cir. 1961); *Sakthinesan v. Smith*, No. C90-529R (W.D. Wash. May 29, 1990), *reported in* 67 No. 30 *Interpreter Releases* 887 (Aug. 13, 1990) [finding DD abused his discretion by failing to release an asylum applicant under the "public interest provision" solely on the basis of false documents where he did not claim the applicant was a danger or likely to abscond]; *Soroa-Gonzalez v. Civiletti*, 515 F.Supp. 1049, 1056–57 (N.D. Ga. 1981); *Paktorovics v. Murff*, 260 F.2d 610 (2d Cir. 1958); *Conceiro v. Marks*, 360 F.Supp. 454, 456–57 (S.D.N.Y. 1973); *Kordic v. Esperdy*, 279 F.Supp. 880 (D.N.Y. 1967). Certain circuit courts have relied upon the even narrower standard of "facially legitimate and *bona fide*." *Garcia-Mir v. Smith*, 766 F.2d 1478, 1485 (11th Cir. 1985), *cert. denied sub nom. Marquez-Medina v. Meese,* 475 U.S. 1022 (1986) [rejects abuse of discretion standard for parole decisions]. *See also Bertrand v. Sava*, 684 F.2d 204 (2d Cir. 1982); *Mason v. Brooks*, 862 F.2d 190 (9th Cir. 1988) [applied facially legitimate standard to parole of applicant for citizenship who was outside U.S.]; *Sanchez v. Kindt*, 752 F.Supp. 1419 (S.D. Ind. 1990); *Pierre v. INS*, 793 F.Supp. 440 (E.D.N.Y. 1992) [application for habeas denied even where magistrate set bond in temporary resident's criminal case]; *Gutierrez v. Ilchert*, 702 F.Supp. 787 (N.D. Cal. 1988) [under "facially legitimate" standard reversed order denying parole to legalization applicant]. DD cannot use *post hoc* explanations to support his decision. *Gutierrez v. Ilchert*, 682 F.Supp. 467, 472 (N.D. Cal. 1988); *Moret, supra*. DD's decision will also be reversed even under the facially legitimate and *bona fide* standard where s/he fails to make a finding that the person's continued detention is in the public's interest and fails to provide adequate support for such a finding, *Li v. Greene*, 767 F.Supp. 1087 (D. Colo. 1991) [DD failed to address how person's detention serves the public's interest]; *Diaz v. Schiltgen*, 946 F.Supp. 762 (N.D. Cal. 1996), or where he relies on an undisclosed review process. *Noorani v. Smith*, 810 F.Supp. 280 (W.D. Wash. 1993).

(2) Can challenge ICE:

(a) For failure to exercise discretion—*Accardi v. Shaughnessy*, 347 U.S. 260 (1954);

(b) For violation of international law—U.N. Convention and Protocol Relating to the Status of Refugees (Art. 3, 32 §2), Universal Declaration of Human Rights, Art. 3 and 9, the American Convention on Human Rights, Part 1, Ch. II, Art. 7. *See Rodriguez-Fernandez v. Wilkinson*, 654 F.2d 1382, 1388 (10th Cir. 1981). *But see Barrera-Echavarria v. Rison*, 44 F.3d 1441 (9th Cir. 1995) (*en banc*) [international law not binding in the face of statute—§1226(e)—to the contrary]; *Gisbert v. U.S. Att'y Gen.*, 988 F.2d 1437, 1447–49 (5th Cir. 1993) [rejecting public international law and human rights claims regarding indefinite detention]; *Garcia-Mir v. Meese*, 788 F.2d 1446, 1453 (11th Cir. 1986), *cert. denied sub nom. Ferrer-Mazorra v. Meese,* 479 U.S. 889 (1986) [no international law right because there are controlling executive (AG) acts and judicial (*Jean v. Nelson*) decisions]; *Hernandez Nodarse v. U.S.,* 166 F.Supp.2d 538 (S.D. Tex. 2001) [post-*Zadvydas* finding that excludable Cuban not entitled to release]; *Sanchez v. Kindt*, 752 F.Supp. 1419, 1432 (S.D. Ind. 1990);

(c) For denial of counsel—*Raul-Chavez v. Turnage*, No. C-80-405J (W.D. Wash. 1980);

(d) For use of race or national origin in deciding parole—*Jean v. Nelson*, 472 U.S. 846 (1985); *but see Jeanty v. Bulger,* 204 F.Supp.2d 1366, 1373–75 (S.D. Fla. 2002), *aff'd sub nom. Moise v. Bulger,* 321 F.3d 1336 (11th Cir. 2003) [finding *Jean* did not foreclose denying parole to Haitians as a class]; *Cuban American Bar Ass'n, Inc. v. Christopher*, 43 F.3d 1412, 1427–29 (11th Cir. 1995). There may also be jurisdiction for a *Bivens* claim based upon discrimination. *Kwai Fun Wong v. U.S.,* 373 F.3d 952, 968–75 (9th Cir. 2004) [finding that a *Bivens* claim for discrimination regarding the revocation of parole and rejection of adjustment of status were actionable because the entry fiction applies to a narrow class of procedural rights and does not apply to all constitutional claims of nonadmitted persons, but granting qualified immunity]

(e) For due process or equal protection violations—For discussion regarding constitutionality of pre- and post-removal order review of detention of inadmissible persons, *see in this chapter* ¶ X.Q.3 (p.305) *infra*. Inadmissible persons who have entered the country (EWIs) are entitled to due process, as are returning LPRs, notwithstanding their classification as "arriving aliens." *Landon v. Plasencia* 459 U.S. 21 (1982). At least one court has distinguished between EWI for purposes of inadmissibility in a removal proceedings and whether the EWI entrant is eligible for due process protection under *Zadvydas. Heng Meng Lin v. Ashcroft,* 247 F.Supp.2d 679, 683–85 (E.D. Pa. 2003) [for purposes of due process right of release under *Zadvydas* and application of 8 C.F.R. §241.13, person who entered EWI has entered and is entitled to due process, notwithstanding treatment in removal proceeding as an inadmissible person];

(f) If person should be treated as deportable rather than inadmissible—*Appah v. Sava*, 636 F.Supp. 207 (S.D.N.Y. 1986) [where person charged as inadmissible but Court determined that he was deportable he had right to bond];

(g) For conditions of detention—*Haitian Centers Council v. Sale*, 823 F.Supp. 1028 (E.D.N.Y. 1993), but due process challenge may be unavailable for negligent treatment, *Ortega v. Rowe*, 796 F.2d 765 (5th Cir. 1986); *Al Najjar v. Ashcroft,* 186 F.Supp.2d 1235, 1242–44 (S.D. Fla. 2002) [standards applied to post–removal order detention are the same for pretrial detainees, and detention is only unconstitutional where it is meant to punish detainee], *but see Lynch v. Cannatella*, 810 F.2d 1363 (5th Cir. 1987);

(h) If detainee must appear before DHS in another proceeding such as legalization—*Gutierrez v. Ilchert*, 682 F.Supp. 467 (N.D. Cal. 1988);

(i) For relying upon impermissible criteria—*Mersereau v. Ingham*, 875 F.Supp. 148, 153 (W.D.N.Y. 1995) [DD's reliance on person's apparent excludability is not a facially legitimate and *bona fide* reason to deny parole]; *Li v. Greene*, 767 F.Supp. 1087 (D. Colo. 1991) [DD's reliance on likelihood of success on asylum application as criteria for release is illegitimate because it is not mentioned in the statute or regulations]; *Noorani v. Smith*, 810 F.Supp. 280 (W.D. Wash. 1993) [reliance on litigation section recommendation without disclosing basis is insufficient];

(j) Where relief has been granted in person's favor—*But see Clark v. Smith*, 967 F.2d 1329 (9th Cir. 1992);

(k) Where detainee is an LPR who has been denied a post-deprivation due process evidentiary hearing on parole—Prior to *Demore v. Kim* federal courts held that returning LPRs had a due process right to a custody hearing before an impartial adjudicator, such as an IJ. *Hamaya v. McElroy,* 797 F.Supp. 186 (E.D.N.Y. 1992); *Cabreja-Rojas v.*

Reno, 999 F.Supp. 493 (S.D.N.Y. 1998) [unconstitutional under *Eldridge* to deny returning LPRs under TPCR a hearing before an independent IJ,]. *See also Ekekhor v. Aljets*, 979 F.Supp. 640 (N.D. Ill. 1997) (and cases cited therein); *St. John v. McElroy*, 917 F.Supp. 243 (S.D.N.Y. 1996); *Cruz-Taveras v. McElroy*, Case No. 96 C.V.5068 (M.M.) (S.D.N.Y. Aug. 12, 1996). *But see Ferraras v. Ashcroft,* 160 F.Supp.2d 617 (S.D.N.Y. 2001) [returning LPR post-*Zadvydas* was not entitled under Constitution to more than a paper record before DD to determine release].

(l) Where Detention Is Prolonged and/or Indefinite—Post-*Demore*, some courts have placed limits on the time that the government can detain a person in a removal proceeding. *Tijani v. Willis,* 430 F.3d 1241 (9th Cir. 2005) [ordered bond hearing before IJ for LPR who has been imprisoned for two years and eight months duration finding that "it is constitutionally doubtful that Congress may authorize imprisonment of this duration for lawfully admitted resident aliens who are subject to removal"]; *Nadarajah v. Gonzales,* 443 F.3d 1069 (9th Cir. 2006) [finding no statutory authority for indefinite detention of inadmissible person pending completion of removal proceedings and ordering release of Sri Lankan torture survivor who had been detained for 4½ years and whose removal was not reasonably foreseeable in light of CAT grant]; *Ly v. Hansen,* 351 F.3d 263 (6th Cir. 2003) [post-*Demore* it is a violation of substantive due process to detain a person subject to deportation for 1½ years waiting for a final order of removal, particularly when it is unlikely he can be physically removed]; *Judulang v. Chertoff,* 535 F.Supp.2d 1129, 1132–33 (S.D. Cal. 2008) [detention lasting over 2½ years is unreasonable; district court ordered bond hearing before IJ over DHS objection that IJ lost jurisdiction over bond matters under 8 C.F.R. §1003.19(a) when administrative order became final, and that his detention became voluntary when he chose to petition to the circuit court]; *Madrane v. Hogan,* 520 F.Supp.2d 654 (M.D. Pa. 2007) [reading *Demore* narrowly and ordering non-LPR petitioner's release after more than three years in custody fighting his removal to Morocco]; *Martinez v. Gonzales,* 504 F.Supp.2d 887 (C.D. Cal. 2007) [5 year detention was excessive and unauthorized under INA §236 and his successful requests for stays of removal cannot be a basis to deny release]; *Moallin v. Cangemi,* 427 F.Supp.2d 908, 25–27 (D. Minn. 2006) [if detention is treated as pre-removal, then year period is a violation of due process under Kennedy opinion in *Demore*]; *Ovediji v. Ashcroft,* 332 F.Supp.2d 747 (M.D. Pa. 2004) [applying reasoning of *Zadvydas* to order release of LPR detained more than 4 years, where pending petition for review was unlikely to be decided in the reasonably foreseeable future]; *Lawson v. Gerlinski,* 332 F.Supp.2d 735, 744–46 (M.D. Pa. 2004) [long-term LPR who obtained stay of removal and remained in detention for 18 months was granted release pending evidentiary hearing on underlying substantive due process claim to remain in U.S.]; *Uritsky v. Ridge,* 286 F.Supp.2d 842 (E.D. Mich. 2003) [court in *Demore* operated on assumption that detention preremoval was for a short duration and would be less than 6 months as in *Zadvydas*, and therefore person in detention for over 11 months should be released notwithstanding mandatory detention provision]. *But see Hussain v. Mukasey,* 510 F.3d 739, 742–44 (7th Cir. 2007) [no jurisdiction to challenge pre-final order of detention because of INA §242(a)(2)(B)(ii) and court could not enter order releasing petitioner while merits appeal is pending but would have to remand release issue to district court; however, the court did not rule out a constitutional challenge for inordinate delay in certain circumstances]; *Soberanes v. Comfort,* 388 F.3d 1305, 1311 (10th Cir. 2004) [in case involving a non-LPR asylum seeker (and not involving mandatory detention), reading *Zadvydas* and *Demore* to permit detention while removal proceeding and review is ongoing, but recognizing that subsequent delays may warrant remedial action]; *Ali v. Achim*, 342 F.Supp.2d 769 (N.D. Ill. 2004) [reading *Demore* broadly and finding that non-LPR respondent in detention for 28 months during removal proceedings was not a violation of due process].

(m) Where reasons articulated by the DHS are unsupported by the record—*Bajrami v. Greene*, Case No. 94-S-1783 (D. Colo. June 2, 1995).

12.f. Questions concerning matters of parole or policies concerning incarceration are not "political questions" immune from judicial scrutiny. *Chiles v. Thornburgh*, 865 F.2d 1197, 1215–16 (11th Cir. 1988).

13. *Parole Revocation*—Traditionally, parole had to be revoked prior to proceedings. *Matter of O,* 16 I&N Dec. 344 (BIA 1997). Regulatory changes provide that revocation is automatic at expiration. Revocation has been judicially reviewable. *Moret v. Karn*, 746 F.2d 989 (3d Cir. 1984); *Soroa-Gonzalez v. Civiletti*, 515 F.Supp. 1049 (N.D. Ga. 1981).

14. *Cuban Review Plan*—DHS maintains separate parole procedures for Mariel Cubans who are detained with final orders. 8 C.F.R. §§212.12, 1212.12. However, following *Clark v. Martinez,* 543 U.S. 371 (2005) [following *Zadvydas*, and finding that as a matter of statutory construction of INA §241(a)(6), inadmissible persons must be released after 6 months], such persons are entitled to custody reviews under 8 C.F.R. §241.13, the regulation implementing *Zadvydas,* which requires that DHS release under conditions of supervision individuals whose removal is not reasonably foreseeable after expiration of the 6-month presumptively reasonable removal period; *Morales-Fernandez v. INS,* 418 F.3d 1116, 1122–25 (10th Cir. 2005) [post-*Clark* finding it impermissible to hold Cuban beyond 6-month period]; *Rosales-Garcia v. Holland,* 322 F.3d 386, 403–15 (6th Cir. 2003) [under *Zadvydas* and independently under the Fifth Amendment, the period of detention post-removal has an implicit reasonable-time limitation]; *Gallego v. INS*, 663 F.Supp. 517 (W.D. Wis. 1987) [the language of former INA §235(b) and INA §237(a)(1) supports only temporary detention of excludable aliens].

15. *Review Procedures for Non–Mariel Cuban and Other Indefinite Detainees—See in this chapter* ¶ X.U.9.a (p.415), *infra.*

16. Humanitarian Parole

16.a. This form of parole is also pursuant to INA §212(d)(5) and typically arises where someone is in another country and needs to enter the U.S. for a medical reason or a reason related to judicial proceedings. In requesting a humanitarian parole, all routine requests must be sent to DHS Headquarters Parole and Humanitarian Assistance Branch. The request for parole must contain information regarding the parolee as follows:

(1) Name, date and place of birth, occupation and current address of parolee;

(2) Relationship to sponsor;

(3) Length of time parole is sought;

(4) A fee for each prospective parolee;

(5) If parole is for medical reasons, results of a recent medical examination by a panel physician.

16.b. The request must also contain the following information:

(1) Name, address, place of birth, U.S. immigration status and occupation of sponsor;

(2) Statement of how and by when medical care, housing, transportation and other subsistence needs will be met for each parolee;

(3) Affidavit of support (I-134) for each parolee;

(4) Statement as to why U.S. visa or waiver cannot be obtained and steps taken to obtain each;

(5) Copies of approved visa petitions;

(6) Statement of emergent reasons for parole;

(7) Documentary support for all claims.

Checklist for Humanitarian Parole Requests, *reprinted in* 69 No. 34 *Interpreter Releases* 1099, 1111 (Sept. 4, 1992).

17. *Release During Stay Order*—INA §241(c)(2), 8 U.S.C. §1231(c)(2). The AG may release on bond any person who has been denied admissibility but whose removal is stayed because they are a witness in a prosecution.

18. *Detention and Release of Juveniles*—DHS rules governing detention and release of juveniles allow release to immediate family or, in unusual circumstances, to another adult with consent of DD or chief patrol agent. The regulations, however, permit detention of other juveniles with Juvenile Coordinator. 8 C.F.R. §§212.5(b)(3)(i), 236.3, 1236.3. A facial challenge to the regulations under former 8 C.F.R. §242.24 in regard to deportable juveniles was rejected by the Supreme Court. *Reno v. Flores*, 507 U.S. 292 (1993) [no facial violation of substantive or procedural due process, equal protection, or statute]. Routine strip searches of juveniles in detention was found unconstitutional. *Flores v. Meese*, 681 F.Supp. 665 (C.D. Cal. 1988). ICE also detains minors pursuant to their policy of family detention. In early Jan. 2008, following litigation and advocacy, ICE issued family detention standards (available on ICE website at *www.ice.gov/pi/familyresidential*).

19. *Employment while Detained*—INS policy of paying $1/day upheld as not violative of the FLSA. *Alvarado-Guevara v. INS*, 902 F.2d 394 (5th Cir. 1990). It also does not constitute involuntary servitude. *Channer v. Hall*, 112 F.3d 214 (5th Cir. 1997). Americans with Disabilities Act (ADA) claim regarding conditions also dismissed as not applicable to federal INS detention center under private management. *Hurtado v. Reno,* 34 F.Supp.2d 1261 (D. Colo. 1999).

20. *Force Feeding During Detention*—Neither the First Amendment nor the right to privacy may prevent DHS from engaging in force feeding of a person on a hunger strike. *In re Soliman,* 134 F.Supp.2d 1238, 1252–58 (N.D. Ala. 2001), *vacated as moot, Soliman v. U.S.* 296 F.3d 1237 (11th Cir. 2002) [under standards articulated in *Turner v. Safely,* 482 U.S. 78 (1987); *Washington v. Glucksberg,* 521 U.S. 702 (1997); and *Cruzan v. Director, Mo. Dep't of Health*, 497 U.S. 261 (1990), indefinite detainee could be forced feed without violating his First Amendment rights or right to privacy].

21. *Detention at Overseas Facilities (Guantanamo)*—Legacy INS believed it had no jurisdiction to detain or to manage detention facilities outside the U.S. such as the Guantanamo facility. Legal Opinion, Virtue, G.C. to Meissner, Comm. (HQCOU 90/15) (Sept. 1, 1998), *reprinted in* 76 No. 13 *Interpreter Releases* 529, 536–45 (Apr. 2, 1999).

22. *Release of Identity and Information Relating to Detainees*—State, local, and private detention facilities may not release information, including names, of DHS detainees being held in their facilities. Such information "shall be under the control of the Service and shall be subject to public disclosure only pursuant to the provisions of applicable federal laws, regulations and executive orders." 8 C.F.R. §§236.6, 1236.6; *Center for National Security Studies v. DOJ,* 331 F.3d 918 (D.C. Cir. 2003), *cert. denied,* 124 S.Ct. 1041 (2004) [the names, the attorneys' names, the dates of arrest and release, locations of arrest and detention and reasons for detention of post 9/11 detainees, including immigration, criminal and material witness detainees, are all exempt from disclosure under Exemption 7(A) of the FOIA regarding law enforcement proceedings]; *CEI Washington Bureau v. DOJ*, 404 F.Supp.2d 172 (D.D.C. 2005) [organization's request for personal information, such as alien numbers, in an electronic database regarding the administration of the State Criminal Alien Assistance Program was exempt under section 6 (privacy) and 7(C) (law enforcement purposes) of the FOIA]; *American Civil Liberties Union v. County of Hudson,* 799 A.2d 629 (N.J. Super. 2002) [8 C.F.R. §236.6 preempts state open-records laws]. The regulation, however, applies only to records relating to current detainees, and does not preempt release of information by state or local jails regarding former immigration detainees. *Badrawi v. Commissioner, State of Conn.,* Conn. Freedom of Information Commission, FIC #2007-136 (2008), *notice of appeal pending* [ordering release of all records regarding former immigration detainees].

23. *Conditions of Detention*—DHS has published a Detention Operations Manual, available at *www.ice.gov/partners/dro/opsmanual,* and *published on* AILA InfoNet at Doc. No. 07101669, which provides detailed standards to be applied in all ICE and contractor detention facilities including: access to legal materials, telephones and facility equipment, visitation, law libraries, free legal services, correspondence, mail, classification, grievance procedures, group presentation of legal rights, religious services, and educational opportunities. The manual also has a section on policies regarding requests to be married in prison. It is a violation of a person's fundamental right to marry to prohibit him or her from marrying while in detention. *Turner v. Safley,* 482 U.S. 78 (1987); *Theck v. Warden, INS,* 22 F.Supp.2d 1117 (C.D. Cal. 1998). Conditions of immigration detention are generally judged by the standards applicable to pretrial detainees under *Bell v. Wolfish,* 441 U.S. 520, 539 (1979). Thus, the petitioner must show that the government intended to punish him or her or that

their actions are arbitrary or purposeless and not reasonably related to legitimate government objectives. *Al Najjar v. Ashcroft,* 186 F.Supp.2d 1235, 1242–44 (S.D. Fla. 2002). *See also Ortega v. Rowe,* 796 F.2d 765 (5th Cir. 1986). *But see Lynch v. Cannatella,* 810 F.2d 1363 (5th Cir. 1987). *See also Jones v. Blanas,* 393 F.3d 918 (9th Cir. 2004) [suggesting more protective standard for civil detainees than "deliberate indifference" standard that applies to convicted prisoners].

23.a. If a detainee wishes to file a complaint he may do so with the Office of Inspector General and/or the Office of Internal Audit. The OIG generally deals with matters that may be criminal and includes investigating non-Service as well as Service employees. The OIG may be contacted at: *inspector.general@usdoj.gov.* The OIA deals exclusively with Service employees in noncriminal matters. A complaint may be filed on Form I-847, which may be obtained from DHS website.

K. ***Special Registration (NSEERS)***—National Security Entry-Exit Registration System (NSEERS), 8 C.F.R. §264.1; 67 Fed. Reg. 52584–93 (Aug. 12, 2002); 67 Fed. Reg. 61352–53 (Sept. 30, 2002); 67 Fed. Reg. 67766–68 (Nov. 6, 2002); 67 Fed. Reg. 70526–28 (Nov. 22, 2002); 67 Fed. Reg. 77136–38 (Dec. 16, 2002); 67 Fed. Reg. 77642–44 (Dec. 18, 2002); 68 Fed. Reg. 2363–65 (Jan. 16, 2003); 68 Fed. Reg. 2366–67 (Jan. 16, 2003); 68 Fed. Reg. 8046–48 (Feb. 19, 2003); 68 Fed. Reg. 8967; 68 Fed. Reg. 67578 (Dec. 2, 2003).

1. NSEERS was designed to establish a registration system, including interviewing, fingerprinting and photographing, for certain nonimmigrants entering, exiting, and remaining in the U.S. Under 8 C.F.R. §264.1(f)(2) the registration provisions apply to nonimmigrants males: (1) who are nationals or citizens of certain countries designated by the AG in consultation with the Secretary of State; (2) who a consular officer or inspecting officer has reason to believe are nationals or citizens of such countries; and (3) who meet profiles ("pre-existing criteria") or who the consular officer or inspecting officer has reason to believe meet such profiles or otherwise warrant registration for national security or law enforcement purposes irrespective of their country of nationality or citizenship. TWOVs and crewman are subject to registration at the port of entry. Persons not subject to NSEERS include "A" and "G" visa holders, members of the NATO armed forces seeking entry pursuant to 8 C.F.R. §235.1(c), transiting international-to-international passengers, women, children under 16 (although regulation provides for under 14), LPRs and asylum applicants and asylees. If an asylum applicant registered or a NIV registered first and then applied for asylum, s/he must continue to comply with the registration requirements. 8 C.F.R. §264.1(f)(1); 67 Fed. Reg. 67767; 67 Fed. Reg. 70527; 67 Fed. Reg. 77137; 68 Fed. Reg. 2365; Memo, Williams, Ex. Assoc. Comm. Field Operations, "Standard Operating Procedures for Alien Registration—IFM Update IN02-34, HQINS 70/28 (Sept. 5, 2002) at 1–2, 18, *published on* AILA InfoNet at Doc. No. 03043048. The profiles established by the AG will not be made public and the reason to believe standard is the same as that applied in other contexts in the INA relating to inadmissibility. 67 Fed. Reg. 52588–89.
2. *Criteria*—In order to determine whether a person from a nondesignated country should register an inspecting officer "may only consider" the following pre-existing criteria established by the AG: (1) the nonimmigrant alien has made an unexplained trip to Iran, Iraq, Libya, Sudan, Syria, North Korea, Cuba, Saudi Arabia, Afghanistan, Yemen, Egypt, Somalia, Pakistan, Indonesia, or Malaysia or the explanation lacks credibility; (2) s/he has engaged in other travel not well explained by his job or other legitimate circumstances; (3) s/he has previously overstayed in the U.S. on his or her NIV and monitoring is now appropriate in the interest of national security; (4) s/he meets characteristics established by current intelligence updates and advisories; (5) s/he is identified by local, state, or federal law enforcement as requiring monitoring in the interest of national security; (6) the nonimmigrant's behavior, demeanor, or answers indicate that s/he should be monitored in the interest of national security; and (7) the nonimmigrant provides information that causes the officer to reasonably determine that s/he requires monitoring in the interests of national security. The decision to require compliance with NSEERS must be concurred by a supervisor. Memo, Williams, Ex. Assoc. Comm. Field Operations, HQ/INS 70/28 (Sept. 30, 2002) at 2–3, *published on* AILA InfoNet at Doc. No. 03043053.
3. *Countries Designated Under NSEERS*—Afghanistan, Algeria, Bangladesh, Bahrain, Egypt, Eritrea, Indonesia, Iran, Iraq, Jordan, Kuwait, Lebanon, Libya, Morocco, North Korea, Oman, Pakistan, Qatar, Saudi Arabia Somalia, Sudan, Syria. Tunisia, United Arab Emirates, Yemen. A person

from a designated country must be a national or citizen of the country and is required to register even if he or she is a dual national of a nonregistrant country. *See, e.g.,* 67 Fed. Reg. 67766.

3.a. In determining whether an inspecting officer has reason to believe that someone is a citizen or national of a designated country the officer must base his decision on "articulable facts or evidence" and "[t]he fact that a nonimmigrant alien is born in a country designated in the [Federal Register] does not, in and of itself, constitute a reason to believe that the alien is a citizen or national of that country." Articulable facts include an additional valid passport or travel document form a designated country, an oral declaration or affirmation from the person that he is a citizen or national of a designated country or database lookouts or intelligence information. Memo, Williams, Ex. Assoc. Comm. Field Operations, HQ/INS 70/28 (Sept. 13, 2002) at 2, *published on* AILA InfoNet at Doc. No. 03043052.

3.b. Requiring registration of persons only from certain countries may not violate equal protection. *Kandamar v. Gonzales,* 464 F.3d 65, 70–74 (1st Cir. 2006) [rejected due process and equal protection challenge to NSEERS program on intermediate scrutiny and rational basis grounds];*Roudnahal v. Ridge,* 310 F.Supp.2d 884, 892 (N.D. Ohio 2003).

4. *Timing of Registration*—(1) At the port of entry (POE) upon each entry into the U.S.; (2) At designated immigration offices within 30–40 days of entering if remaining in the U.S. 30 days or more; (3) At the port of departure (POD) upon each departure from the U.S. except for crew members; (4) At designated immigration offices annually within 10 days of original registration; *and* (5) By mail on form AR-11 within 10 days of each change of address if registrant remains in the U.S. more than 30 days. 8 C.F.R. §§264.1(f)(3), (5), (6), (8); Memo, Williams (Sept. 5. 2002), *supra,* at 1. The provisions concerning registering with local offices within 30 days of entry and registering annually have now been suspended. 68 Fed. Reg. 67578 (Dec. 2, 2003). Persons departing the U.S. must still register each time they depart and, if required, must register each time upon entry. Any person subject to registration may apply to the DD in city which he resides for a waiver of these requirements. Waivers can be granted for up to one year. The DD's decision is final and not appealable. 8 C.F.R. §264.1(f)(7). A person subject to registration, even if granted a waiver, may not participate in any special inspection program such as SENTRI, NEXUS, INSPASS or I-68 small boat program. Memo, Williams (Sept. 5. 2002), *supra,* at 8–9. In addition to the waiver process, the Secretary of State may exempt individual nonimmigrants from special registration. Memo, Williams (Sept. 5, 2002), *supra,* at 9. Locations for PODs are listed at 81 No. 8 *Interpreter Releases* 248, 259–66 (Feb. 23, 2004) and 81 No. 9 *Interpreter Releases* 282, 292–301 (Mar. 1, 2004).

5. *Traveling on Advance Parole*—If asylum applicant travels on advance parole he does not have to register because he "would be a parolee and not a non-immigrant applicant." Memo, Williams, Ex. Assoc. Comm. Field Operations, "Standard Operating Procedures for Alien Registration—IFM Update IN02-34, HQINS 70/28 (Sept. 5, 2002) at 1–2, 18, *published on* AILA InfoNet at Doc. No. 03043048.

6. Consequences of Failure to Register

6.a. Failing to Register Upon Departure—If a designated person fails to register upon departure "without good cause" he shall "be presumed to be inadmissible [upon re-entry] under, but not limited to, section 212(a)(3)(A)(ii)" as a person the AG believes has engaged in "unlawful activity." The presumption may be overcome but only where the person, if previously required, registered upon entry and/or registered in the U.S. 8 C.F.R. §264.1(f)(8). The officer is instructed to "carefully consider the totality of the circumstances before applying this ground of inadmissibility" and to know or have reason to believe "that the alien seeks to enter the United States to engage in unlawful activity." Memo, Williams (Sept. 5, 2002), *supra*, at 5. In looking at all the circumstances the officer should examine, but is not limited to, "the type of visa, the duration of the prior and intended trip, the purpose of the trips, any documentary materials the registrant has in his possession, and any other verification that may be appropriate." Memo, Williams, Ex. Assoc. Comm. Field Operations, HQ/INS 70/28 (Dec. 23, 2002) at 5, *published on* AILA InfoNet at Doc. No. 03050140. The DOS appears to utilize a more forgiving standard in determining whether a person may overcome the presumption of engaging in unlawful activity. Under DOS standards consular officers do not look at whether an NSEERS violation has occurred but on whether there is reason to believe the NSEERS violator will, in the future, fail to comply with NSEERS if a visa is issued. Consular officers can issue visas to NSEERS violators if the applicant can demonstrate good cause for the violation and/or "reasonable assurances" that he will comply in the future. In addition to the factors cited by immigration for good cause, consular officers can consider whether the registrant was given "confusing or wrong instructions, or had an emergent need to travel." They can also look at whether the applicant can "credibly demonstrate" that he fully understands NSEERS and will comply in the future. Cable, DOS, 03-State-123678 (May 10, 2003), *published on* AILA InfoNet at Doc. No. 03051245 (May 12, 2003).

6.b. Failing to Comply After Admission—If a person from a designated country who has been admitted to the U.S. fails to comply with the registration requirements, he will be considered to have failed to maintain status under INA §237(a)(1)(C)(i) unless he can demonstrate that "the failure was reasonably excusable or was not willful." 67 Fed. Reg. 67766. The failure must be "knowing and voluntary" and where DHS has charged respondent with an NSEERS violation but believes that there is insufficient evidence that the violation was willful, they may move terminate proceedings. Memo, Cerda, Acting Principal Legal Advisor, ICE, (Jan. 8. 2004), *published on* AILA InfoNet at Doc. No. 06050512

6.c. Failure to Notify Concerning Change of Address—If a person fails to notify immigration authorities of a change of address he may be subject to criminal prosecution under INA §266(b) and deportable under INA §237(a)(3)(A). *See, e.g.,* 67 Fed. Reg. 67767. However, if a person subject to NSEERS is a student he does not have to separately notify DHS if he notifies DHS through the SEVIS program. 8 C.F.R. §264.1(f)(5).

6.d. Refusal to Register—If a person refuses to register upon entry he will be subject to expedited removal "but should be allowed to withdraw [his] application for admission in lieu of ER at the discretion of the Service." Memo, Williams (Sept. 5, 2002), *supra*, at 8.

6.e. Persons Encountered After Failing to Register—If a person is in lawful status and can demonstrate that his failure to register was not willful or was reasonably excusable, the officer, with concurrence of a supervisor, may forgo placing him in removal proceeding and simply initiate the registration process. If he is out-of-status the officer "will process the alien for removal." Examples of what would be considered a reasonable excuse for persons in status include hospitalization, being a patient in a nursing home or extended care facility where mobility was severely restricted or demonstrating that he was unaware of the registration process. Memo, Williams, Ex. Assoc. Comm. Field Operations, HQ/INS 70/28 (Nov. 21, 2002), *published on* AILA InfoNet at Doc. No. 02121241.

7. *Out-of-Status Registrants*—If an applicant for registration is out-of-status but has submitted an AOS application or otherwise has a benefit immediately available to him, an immigration officer, subject to the Nov. 17, 2000, guidelines on prosecutorial discretion [InfoNet Doc. No. 00112702], will decline to issue an NTA if the registrant appears to be immediately and prima facie eligible for the benefit and if no adverse or disqualifying information is developed through other sources. Memo, Williams, Ex. Assoc. Comm. Field Operations, HQOPS 50/5.11 (Jan 8, 2003) at 2–3, *published on* AILA InfoNet at Doc. No. 03050141. *But see Roudnahal v. Ridge,* 310 F.Supp.2d 884, 892–94 (N.D. Ohio 2003), [pending adjustment application does not prevent the initiation of removal proceedings]; *American-Arab Anti-Discrimination Comm. v. Ashcroft,* 241 F.Supp.2d 1111 (C.D. Cal. 2003) [denying injunction where registrants with adjustment applications were arrested and issued NTAs]. However, if a registrant is out-of-status, an NTA will be issued and a custody determination will normally be made if there is no relief available or if the applicant has a pending or approved labor certification or immigrant visa (but no benefit immediately available) even if he is eligible for INA §245(i) status. Memo, Williams (Jan. 8, 2003), *supra* at 2–4. The evidence resulting in the placement of an out-of-status NSEERS registrant in removal proceedings may not be suppressed even if NSEERS violates equal protection. *Ali v. Gonzales,* 440 F.3d 678, 681–82 (5th Cir. 2006)

8. *Petition Approval Notwithstanding NSEERS Violation*—A willful and unexcused failure to comply with NSEERS cannot support the denial of a visa petition. Memo, Divine, G.C., USCIS, HQOCC 70/6.22/04 (Oct. 14, 2004), *published on* AILA InfoNet at Doc. No. 04111566; *Matter of*

O-, 8 I&N Dec. 295 (BIA 1959); [under INA §204(b) a petition may not be denied based upon the conclusion that the beneficiary is inadmissible].

9. *End of NSEERS Processing*—As of Dec. 2, 2003, the special registration requirements announced in 2002 were modified. The provisions concerning registering with local offices within 30 days of entry and registering annually have now been suspended. 68 Fed. Reg. 67578 (Dec. 2, 2003). A person subject to NSEERS is still required to register upon departure from the U.S. and his failure to do so may result in the initiation of removal proceedings. Memo, Cerda, Acting Principal Legal Advisor, ICE, (Jan. 8. 2004), *published on* AILA InfoNet at Doc. No. 06050512. Although NSEERS has been supplanted by US-VISIT for all nonimmigrants entering the U.S., who are now subject to photograph and fingerprint requirements upon entry, DHS or a consular officer may still require registration upon entry and Canadian citizens or landed immigrants from Canada may still be subject to NSEERS because of birth in an NSEERS country even if they are not subject to US-VISIT. In addition, persons who previously violated NSEERS by failing to appear for registration, for annual re-registration, or 30-day follow-up interview before Dec. 1, 2003 may be placed in removal proceedings. Memo, Cerda (Jan. 8, 2004), *supra.*

10. *Waiver of the NSEERS Requirements*—A person seeking to waive the remaining NSEERS requirement or to remove his name from the NSEERS list because he has become an LPR needs to: (1) make the request in writing to Director, Field Operations, CBP having jurisdiction over the place of most frequent arrival; (2) provide two 1" x 1" photographs; and (3) submit supporting documentation. Memo, Ahern, Asst. Comm., Field Operations, CBP (INS 1:BSF:PO SK) (May 6, 2005), *published on* AILA InfoNet at Doc. No. 05051960 (May 19, 2005).

11. *Judicial Challenges. Iqbal Ali v. Gonzales,* 502 F.3d 659, 665 (7th Cir. 2007) [following *Hadayat* INA §242(g) bars jurisdiction to hear constitutional challenges to NSEERS]; *Zerrei v. Gonzales,* 471 F.3d 342, 347–48 (2d Cir. 2006) [rejected claims regarding NSEERS prejudicing respondent who was found excludable as an overstay where there was not evidence that DHS obtained his passport through NSEERS and nothing in the record substantiates his claim that he was singled out for removal]; *Kandamar v. Gonzales,* 464 F.3d 65, 70–74 (1st Cir. 2006) [denied respondent's motion to suppress statements taken at the NSEERS interview as well as the improper seizure of his passport, denied selective prosecution claim, and rejected due process and equal protection challenge to NSEERS program on intermediate scrutiny and rational basis grounds]; *Zafar v. U.S. Att'y Gen.,* 461 F.3d 1357, 1367 (11th Cir. 2006) *reh'g en banc denied* 473 F.3d 1350 (2007) [NSEERS did not infringe on respondent's equal protection by placing him in discretionary removal proceedings]; *Ahmed v. Gonzales,* 447 F.3d 433, 439–40 (5th Cir. 2006) [same];

L. *Removal Hearing for Persons Seeking Admission*

1. There is now one unified removal hearing for persons formerly subject to deportation and exclusion hearings. (For the procedures for the removal hearing, *see EOIR Immigration Court Practice Manual; see also in this chapter* section X.S (p.311), *infra.*) The burden of proof, however, remains different for non-LPRs seeking admission. INA §240(c)(2), 8 U.S.C. §1229a(c)(2), 8 C.F.R. §1240.8. *Altamirano v. Gonzales,* 427 F.3d 586, 590–91 (9th Cir. 2005) [person paroled into U.S. under §212(d)(5)(A) whose admission was challenged at the border for alien smuggling had the burden to prove admissibility]. With regard to returning LPRs, however, DHS has the burden of proving inadmissibility. *Landon v. Plasencia*, 459 U.S. 21 (1982) [due process applies]; *Molina v. Sewell,* 983 F.3d 676, 678 (5th Cir. 1993); *Matter of Sosa*, 15 I&N Dec. 572 (BIA 1976). Post-IIRIRA and the passage of INA §101(a)(13)(C), however, there is a question as to whether the government must prove by "clear, convincing and unequivocal" evidence the application of INA §101(a)(13)(C). *Sandoval-Loffredo v. Gonzales,* 414 F.3d 892 (8th Cir. 2005) [addressing but not deciding who has the burden; IJ found that government established by clear, convincing, and unequivocal evidence that LPR engaged in unlawful activity under §101(a)(13)(C)(ii) in facilitating his brother's illegal entry]; *Molina v. Sewell*, 983 F.2d 676, 678 (5th Cir. 1993) [applicant bears the burden to prove he comes within the statutory definition of lawful admission (formerly the *Fleuti* exception)].

2. Effective Date—IIRIRA §309(c). Proceedings under the new removal procedure went into effect on Apr. 1, 1997. If someone is in exclusion or deportation proceedings on April 1, the amendments to the Act do not apply and proceedings were to continue under pre-IIRIRA criteria.

IIRIRA §309(c)(1), 8 C.F.R. §1240.30 to .39. If the evidentiary hearing has not actually commenced before Apr. 1, 1997, the AG may proceed under the new procedures if he provides 30 days' notice. IIRIRA §309(c)(2). The AG may also elect to terminate proceedings and restart them under the new procedure after Apr. 1, 1997, if there is not a final administrative decision. IIRIRA §309(c)(3). IIRIRA applies in assessing whether persons detained after Apr. 1, 1997, are in violation of constitutional or statutory law. *Rosales-Garcia v. Holland,* 322 F.3d 386, 401–03 (6th Cir. 2003) [IIRIRA §309(c) does not preserve the former detention statute for excludable persons (§236(e)) as authority to detain inadmissible persons with pre-IIRIRA removal orders]; *Martinez-Vazquez v. INS,* 346 F.3d 903 (9th Cir. 2003) [same]; *Arango Marquez v. INS,* 346 F.3d 892, 897–902 (9th Cir. 2003) [same].

DOJ established regulations governing removal hearing post–Apr. 1, 1997, 8 C.F.R. §§1240.1 to .29, and exclusion hearings that were initiated prior to Apr. 1, 1997. 8 C.F.R. §§1240.30 to .39. The exclusion hearing will not be addressed here. See §1240.30 *et seq.*

3. Pre-Hearing Matters

3.a. Process is initiated by the filing of a notice to appear (NTA) with the immigration court. 8 C.F.R. §§239.1(a), 1239.1(a). INS may be required to translate the NTA. *Louis v. Meissner*, 530 F.Supp. 924 (S.D. Fla. 1981). If applicant was not provided proper notice, the IJ should terminate proceedings. *Matter of Lopez-Barrios*, 20 I&N Dec. 203 (BIA 1990). The IJ may require a prehearing conference and may require parties to submit pretrial statements and objections. 8 C.F.R. §1003.21. The DHS may exercise prosecutorial discretion not to initiate proceedings. *See in this chapter,* section X.S (p. 311), *infra.*

3.b. Change of Venue—Venue is normally at the DHS office having jurisdiction over the alien. The IJ has jurisdiction to change venue in removal hearings. *Matter of Dobere*, 20 I&N Dec. 188 (BIA 1990). 8 C.F.R. §1003.20(b).

3.c. Right to Counsel—INA §240(b)(4)(A), 8 U.S.C. §1229a(b)(4)(A). There is a right to counsel in removal proceedings for persons where inadmissibility is being challenged under INA §§239(b), 240(b)(4), 8 C.F.R. §§1240.3, 1292. Under former exclusion proceedings the applicant also had a right to counsel, although it was more qualified. *Ledesma-Valdes v. Sava*, 604 F.Supp. 675 (S.D.N.Y. 1985) [no denial of right to counsel where alien was transferred from N.Y. to Texas after counsel was retained in N.Y., but where no special personal or professional relationship was demonstrated and where there was no showing that counsel was unavailable in transferred area]; *Committee of Central American Refugees v. INS*, 795 F.2d 1434 (9th Cir. 1986), *modified*, 807 F.2d 769 (1986) [no statutory or constitutional right for deportable aliens where no attorney-client privilege established. Injunction not issued to prevent future transfers. In absence of statutory or constitutional right, prudential considerations prevent interference in AG's right to select detention sites]. *But see Orantes-Hernandez v. Thornburgh*, 919 F.2d 549, 554, 564–66 (9th Cir. 1990) [distinguishing *Committee of Central American Refugees*]; *Rios-Berrios v. INS*, 776 F.2d 859 (9th Cir. 1985) [deportation]; *Castro-O'Ryan v. INS*, 847 F.2d 1307 (9th Cir. 1987) (*en banc*) [legislative history confirms that Congress wanted to confer a right to counsel]; *Molaire v. Smith*, 743 F.Supp. 839 (S.D. Fla. 1990) [reversing exclusion order where person not informed of right to counsel and did not knowingly or voluntarily waive counsel]; *Louis v. Meissner*, 530 F.Supp. 924 (S.D. Fla. 1981) [excludable aliens deprived of counsel by virtue of transfer to remote areas]. There may also be a right to obtain appointed counsel in federal court under the Criminal Justice Act, *Saldina v. Thornburgh*, 775 F.Supp. 507 (D. Conn. 1991), *but see Perez-Perez v. Hanberry*, 781 F.2d 1477 (11th Cir. 1986), or under the *in forma pauperis* statute, 28 U.S.C. §1915(e). *Santana v. Chandler*, 961 F.2d 514 (5th Cir. 1992). Generally, DHS's position is that there is no right to counsel in primary, secondary, and deferred inspections, and that the right to counsel only attaches for removal proceedings.

4. Removal Hearing for Person Deemed Inadmissible

4.a. Applicant for admission has a right to a fundamentally fair hearing under DHS statutes and regulations. *Chin Yow v. U.S.*, 208 U.S. 8 (1908); *Xiang v. Cadman*, ___ F.Supp. ___, Case No. 93-640-Civ-Davis (S.D. Fla. Apr. 20, 1993) [where applicant medicated to point he was unable to effectively participate in hearing]; *Bajrami v. Greene*, __ F.Supp. __, Case No. 94-S-1783 (D. Colo. June 2, 1995) [procedures did not provide fair hearing consistent with due process where non–English-speaking applicant denied right to cross-examination and not provided any translation]; *Matter of G-*, 20 I&N Dec. 764 (BIA 1993) [administrative proceedings must conform to basic notions of fundamental fairness citing *Harisiades v. Shaughnessy*, 342 U.S. 580 (1952), but finding no prejudice from executive directive to expedite Golden Venture cases]. Procedures for removal hearing at INA §240(a), 8 U.S.C. §§1229 and 1229a. The unification of procedures for both inadmissible (formerly excludable) and deportable persons suggests greater rights for inadmissible persons in removal proceedings (*e.g.*, some forms of voluntary departure now available to all persons in removal proceedings). Former exclusion proceedings at INA §236, 8 U.S.C. §1226; 8 C.F.R. §1003.12, 8 C.F.R. §§236, 1236. Proceedings initiated when DHS files NTA before IJ. 8 C.F.R. §1003.14. Procedures include: (1) open hearing unless IJ decides otherwise, 8 C.F.R. §1240.10(b); (2) IJ identifies person served with I-122; (3) IJ advises alien of right to witnesses, cross-examination and counsel. 8 C.F.R. §1240.10. *Molaire, supra*; *Molina v. Sewell*, 983 F.2d 676, 680 (5th Cir. 1993) [IJ's failure to advise returning LPR that he could present evidence prejudiced LPR's right to demonstrate his brief departure did not result in new entry]; *Augustin v. Sava*, 735 F.2d 32 (2d Cir. 1984) [right to adequate translation]; *Najaf-Ali v. Meese*, 653 F.Supp. 833 (N.D. Cal. 1987) [right to present witnesses]. An application for admission is a continuing application and admissibility is determined on the basis of the law and facts existing at the time the application is finally considered before the IJ. *Matter of Kazemi*, 19 I&N Dec. 49, 51 (BIA 1984) (and cases cited therein).

4.b. Continuance granted only upon showing: (1) that inability to proceed occurred despite good-faith effort; (2) additional evidence sought is favorable and not cumulative; and (3) actual prejudice caused by denial. *Matter of Sibrun*, 18 I&N Dec. 354 (BIA 1983), 8 C.F.R. §§1003.29, 1240.6 [for good cause shown]. *See also in this chapter* "Continuances," ¶ X.S.5.f (p.326), *infra*. The IJ also must advise alien of availability of free legal counsel under INA §292, 8 U.S.C. §1362, and must ascertain on the record whether the respondent wants counsel. 8 C.F.R. §1240.10(a)(1); *Matter of Michel*, 21 I&N Dec. 1101 (BIA 1998); *Molaire, supra*. If DHS seeks to amend the charges during the hearing an applicant does not automatically get a continuance. *Matter of Salazar*, 17 I&N Dec. 167 (BIA 1979).

4.c. Burden of Proof—The burden of proof is now statutory. An applicant for admission in a removal proceeding must establish that s/he is "clearly and beyond doubt entitled to be admitted and is not inadmissible under section 212." INA §240(c)(2), 8 U.S.C. §1229a(c)(2), 8 C.F.R. §1240.8(b). *Altamirano v. Gonzales,* 427 F.3d 586, 590–91 (9th Cir. 2005) [person paroled into U.S. under §212(d)(5)(A) whose admission was challenged at the border for alien smuggling had the burden to prove admissibility]. For others who may be subject to charges of inadmissibility, even if they are *in* the U.S. (former EWI), the DHS must first establish alienage. 8 C.F.R. §1240.8(c). Once alienage is established, unless the respondent demonstrates by clear and convincing evidence that s/he is lawfully in U.S. pursuant to a prior admission, the respondent must prove that s/he is clearly and beyond a doubt entitled to be admitted to the U.S. and not inadmissible as charged. 8 C.F.R. §1240.8(c). In the latter case, the applicant "shall have access to the visa or other entry documents and any other records" pertaining to the applicant's admission or presence that are not confidential. INA §240(c)(2). If a consular post has issued a visa, it is prima facie evidence of admissibility sufficient to shift the burden of producing evidence to DHS at an exclusion hearing where admissibility is questioned. *Matter of Walsh & Pollard*, 20 I&N Dec. 60 (BIA 1988). In regard to a citizenship claim, if respondent claims citizenship, s/he bears the burden by a preponderance of the evidence that s/he possess derivative citizenship. *Leal Santos v. Mukasey,* 516 F.3d 1, 4 (1st Cir. 2008) [once DHS establishes that respondent was born abroad, burden then shifts to her to prove derivative citizenship]; *Matter of Tijerina-Villarreal,* 13 I&N Dec. 327, 330–31 (BIA 1969). But what happens if a person is inspected and admitted at the border through fraudulent means? Has he made a lawful admission? *Compare Matter of Areguillin*, 17 I&N Dec. 308 (BIA 1980) [Mexican citizen not questioned at border while riding in a car that was stopped was "inspected and admitted" even though she had no lawful basis to enter] *with* 8 C.F.R. §101.2 and INA §101(a)(13)(A) [defining admission as *lawful* entry] *and Orozco v. Mukasey,* 521 F.3d 1068 (9th Cir. 2008) [a person who is inspected and admitted at the border through the use of fraudulent documents is ineligible to adjust status because admission under

§101(a)(13)(A) now requires *lawful entry*. The court found that *Matter of Areguillin* is not longer good law in light of the passage of §101(a)(13)(A)].

In regard to a returning LPR, DHS has the burden of proving inadmissibility. *Landon v. Plasencia*, 459 U.S. 21 (1982); *Molina v. Sewell,* 983 F.3d 676, 678 (5th Cir. 1993); *Matter of Sosa*, 15 I&N Dec. 572 (BIA 1976). Post-IIRIRA and the passage of INA §101(a)(13)(C), however, there is a question as to whether the government must prove by "clear, convincing and unequivocal" evidence the application of INA §101(a)(13)(C). *Sandoval-Loffredo v. Gonzales,* 414 F.3d 892 (8th Cir. 2005) [addressing but not deciding who has the burden; IJ found that the government established by clear, convincing, and unequivocal evidence that the LPR engaged in unlawful activity under §101(a)(13)(C)(ii) in facilitating his brother's illegal entry]; *Molina v. Sewell*, 983 F.2d 676, 678 (5th Cir. 1993) [applicant bears the burden to prove he comes within the statutory definition of lawful admission (formerly the *Fleuti* exception)].

4.d. A returning resident in a removal proceeding is also entitled to full due process rights at his or her hearing. *Landon v. Plasencia*, 459 U.S. 21 (1982). A returning resident cannot be summarily excluded, even when DHS invokes security concerns. *Rafeedie v. INS*, 880 F.2d 506 (D.C. Cir. 1989); *Rafeedie v. INS*, 795 F.Supp. 13 (D.D.C. 1992). However, DHS can rely on national security information in the removal hearing. INA §240(b)(4)(B), 8 U.S.C. §1229a(b)(4)(B); *Ali v. Reno*, 829 F.Supp. 1415, 1434–36 (S.D.N.Y. 1993), *aff'd*, 22 F.3d 442 (2d Cir. 1994).

4.e. Under IIRIRA §304, an applicant for admission is now subject to removal *in absentia* as well as all other procedures applicable in removal proceedings. INA §240(b)(5), (b)(7). *See in this chapter* "Hearings *In Absentia,*" ¶ X.S.7.w (p.383), *infra*. Under former procedures for exclusion hearings, which remain in effect for all hearings initiated before Apr. 1, 1997 (unless the AG chooses otherwise), DHS could exclude applicants *in absentia,* even though there was no statutory provision for *in absentia* hearings in exclusion. *Matter of Nafi*, 19 I&N Dec. 430 (BIA 1987); 8 C.F.R. §1003.26. An *in absentia* hearing could proceed in exclusion if notice of the hearing was provided on the record at the prior hearing or by written notice to counsel or applicant. But applicant could move to reopen on showing of reasonable cause for failure to appear. 8 C.F.R. §1003.23(b)(4)(ii). *Matter of Haim*, 19 I&N Dec. 641 (BIA 1988). *But see Matter of S-A-*, 21 I&N Dec. 1050 (BIA 1997) [general assertion that applicant could not get to hearing on time due to heavy traffic does not meet reasonable cause standard]. And where the BIA misapplied *Matter of S-A-*, the court ordered that the case be reopened. *De Jimenez v. Ashcroft,* 370 F.3d 783 (8th Cir. 2004) [where respondent gave specific reasons for failing to appear and IJ's order mislead her into believing she should file an appeal to the BIA rather than a motion to reopen, the court granted her motion to reconsider]. Motions to reopen in exclusion hearings may be filed without regard to the time (90 day) or numerical (one motion) limitations. *Matter of N-B-,* 22 I&N Dec. 590 (BIA 1999). And reasonable cause is not needed to reopen where the applicant seeking asylum/withholding based on changed circumstances *Matter of A-N- & R-M-N-,* 22 I&N Dec. 953 (BIA 1999) [Afghan citizen did not have reasonable cause for failing to appear at exclusion hearing based on claim that lawyer had filed change of venue motion, nevertheless he could reopen *in absentia* order based on changed circumstances].

Prior to IIRIRA, the IJ had no jurisdiction to proceed *in absentia* where a person was neither detained nor paroled at the border, but simply sent back to his country (Mexico/Canada) to await a hearing. *Matter of Sanchez*, 21 I&N Dec. 444 (BIA 1996). This is changed under summary exclusion procedures which permit DHS to require persons to wait in border countries. If IJ believed notice was insufficient to proceed *in absentia*, case should have been terminated, not administratively closed, unless both parties agree. *Matter of Lopez-Barrios*, 20 I&N Dec. 203 (BIA 1990). *In absentia* determination reversed where INS's notice was not actually received by applicant but INS argued that applicant moved and did not provide a change of address. *Mohammad v. Slattery*, 842 F.Supp. 1553 (S.D.N.Y. 1994). A claim for ineffective assistance of counsel when *Matter of Lozada* is followed can be a basis to reopen *in absentia* hearings in exclusion. *Matter of N-K- & V-S-*, 21 I&N Dec. 879 (BIA 1977); *Lu v. Ashcroft,* 259 F.3d 127, 131–32 (3d Cir. 2001) [denied reopening for failure to comply with *Lozada* but finding right to challenge ineffective assistance by counsel]. *See also Twum v. INS,* 411 F.3d 54 (2d Cir. 2005) [where IJ misconstrued *in absentia* motion in exclusion as an ineffective assistance of counsel claim under *Lozada* rather than a claim that security guards barred his entry to the court, the circuit court reversed and remanded]. The *in absentia* provisions of former INA §242B do not govern exclusion proceedings. *Matter of Gonzalez*, 20 I&N Dec. 644 (BIA 1993).

An applicant who has an order of removal *in absentia* entered against him or her is ineligible for most forms of relief for a period of 10 years if s/he was provided oral notice in his or her native language or another language s/he understands of the time and place of the proceedings and the consequences of failing to appear. INA §240(b)(7).

4.f. The applicant has a right to accurate interpretation, but not simultaneous translation. DHS regulations establish form for document translations. 8 C.F.R. §1003.33. For a further discussion, *see in this chapter* "Interpretation," ¶ X.S.7.r (p.379), *infra*.

5. *Relief for Persons Deemed Inadmissible*—An applicant for admission may obtain any of the following avenues of relief in his or her removal hearing:

5.a. Admission, because the applicant has proven admissibility, because the ground for inadmissibility is not applicable to a given applicant or because the applicant is granted a waiver. Waivers are available under INA §240A(a), 8 U.S.C. §1229b(a) (formerly INA §212(c)) [*Matter of Marin*, 16 I&N Dec. 581 (BIA 1978)]; INA §212(g) [waives tuberculosis]; 8 U.S.C. §1182(h) [waives INA §§212(a)(2)(A)(i)(I), (a)(2)(B), (a)(2)(D), (a)(2)(E) and (a)(2)(A)(i)(II) if it relates to a single offense of marijuana possession of 30 grams or less]; INA §212(i) [waives visa fraud]. To get waiver must be spouse, parent (but not for §212(i) waiver) or son or daughter of USC or LPR, or as in INA §240A(a), be an LPR. Some waivers may require prior approval by other officials. INA §212(d)(3) and (e), 8 U.S.C. §§1182(d)(3) and (e). INA §212(d)(4), 8 U.S.C. §1182(d)(4) waiver can be decided by IJ *Matter of Kazemi*, 19 I&N Dec. 49 (BIA 1984). When IJ can decide, s/he can request alien to post maintenance of status and departure bond. For other waivers, *see in this chapter* section III.I (p.113), *supra*.

5.b. Asylum or Withholding of Deportation—INA §§208 and 241(b)(3); 8 C.F.R. §1240.11(c).

5.c. Adjustment of Status—As a result of regulatory changes arising from nationwide litigation, an applicant for admission may seek adjustment before the USCIS. *See* Ch. 6, ¶ XII.C.5 (p.851), *infra*.

5.d. Unconditional Withdrawal—*Matter of Lepofsky*, 14 I&N Dec. 718 (BIA 1974). Withdrawal discretionary, not a matter of right, but when justice may best be served. *Matter of Vargas-Molina*, 13 I&N Dec. 651 (BIA 1971). Can withdraw while case is on appeal. INA §235(a)(4) allowing withdrawal in discretion of AG at any time and 8 C.F.R. §1240.1(d) (expressly providing for withdrawal on appeal). Can only allow withdrawal where applicant: (1) demonstrates s/he possesses both the intent and means to depart immediately; and (2) establishes that factors directly relating to the issue of admissibility indicate that justice would be served. Once excludability is determined, IJ should ordinarily not grant permission to withdraw without concurrence of the Service. *Matter of Gutierrez*, 19 I&N Dec. 562 (BIA 1988); 8 C.F.R. §1240.1(d). In *Sharma v. Reno*, 902 F.Supp. at 1139–40, the court upheld denial of permission to withdraw application based on *Gutierrez* standard. However, the 9th Circuit has held that there is no jurisdiction to review an IJ's decision regarding the review of a decision concerning withdrawal of admission. *Avendano-Ramirez v. Ashcroft*, 365 F.3d 813, 819 (9th Cir. 2004).

5.e. Voluntary Departure—Pursuant to IIRIRA, VD is now available for all persons at a master calendar hearing, whether or not they are inadmissible (formerly excludable) persons. INA §240B(b), 8 U.S.C. §1229c(b). For further details, see Chapter 8, part III (p.964), *infra*.

5.f. May allow permission to reapply for admission *nunc pro tunc* if alien is inadmissible because of previous deportation, if otherwise admissible. 8 C.F.R. §§212.2(i), 1212.2(i); *Matter of Roman*, 19 I&N Dec. 855 (BIA 1988); *Matter of Ducret*, 15 I&N Dec. 620 (BIA 1976); *Matter of M-C-*, 9 I&N Dec. 280 (BIA 1961); *Matter of S-N-*, 6 I&N Dec. 73 (AG 1954). *But see Matter of Balao*, 20 I&N Dec. 440 (BIA 1992); *Matter of Alarcon*, 20 I&N Dec. 557 (BIA 1992); *Perez-Rodriguez v. INS*, 3 F.3d 1074, 1079–80 (7th Cir. 1993).

6. *Summary Decision*—IJ may enter summary decision where inadmissibility is determined on the pleadings and respondent does not make an application for relief, or if the IJ only grants VD. 8 C.F.R. §1240.12(b).

7. *Consequences of Removal for Inadmissibility*—A person found inadmissible in a removal proceeding is not admissible to the U.S. for 5 years from the date of removal, unless the AG consents in advance to readmission. INA §212(a)(9)(A)(i), 8 U.S.C. §1182(a)(9)(A)(i).

7.a. Adjustment—Alien who has been found inadmissible but not removed under former regulations could adjust status but only before DD if eligible. *Matter of C-H*, 9 I&N Dec. 265 (Asst. Comm. 1961) [not barred by former section INA §212(a)(16) unless also physically deported]; *Matter of Manneh*, 16 I&N Dec. 272 (BIA 1977); *Alvarez-Garcia v. Ashcroft,* 378 F.3d 1094 (9th Cir. 2004) [upholding limitation on adjustment before DD for excludable persons who were paroled into the U.S. because, under the "entry doctrine" fiction, a person seeking admission does not have an equal protection right to the same procedures for AOS before the IJ as a deportable person]. *But see* 8 C.F.R. §§1.1(p), 1001.1(p) and *Elkins v. Comfort,* 245 F.Supp.2d 1161, 1164–65 (D. Colo. 2003), *overruled on other grounds,* 392 F.3d 1159 (10th Cir. 2004) [claiming that *Matter of C-H-* was overruled by 8 C.F.R. §1.1(p)]. As a result of regulatory changes arising from nationwide litigation, *see e.g., Bona v. Gonzales,* 425 F.3d 663 (9th Cir. 2005) [agreeing with *Succar v. Ashcroft,* 394 F.3d 8 (1st Cir. 2005), and disagreeing with *Mouelle v. Gonzales,* 416 F.3d 923 (8th Cir. 2005) *vacated* 126 S.Ct. 2964 (2006), and finding that an arriving alien in removal proceeding may adjust status], "arriving aliens" are no longer barred from AOS before USCIS. They may seek to adjust status before the IJ only if they are returning on an advance parole, USCIS has denied their AOS, they are placed in removal proceedings, and they seek review of a previously filed AOS. 8 C.F.R. §§245.2(a)(1), 245.2(a)(5)(ii), 1240.11(a)(1), 1245.2(a)(1), 1245.2(a)(5)(ii); 71 Fed. Reg. 27585–92 (May 12, 2006) [withdrawing 8 C.F.R. §§245.1(c)(8), 1245.1(c)(8), which barred arriving aliens from adjusting status]; AFM at 23.2(b) [discussing jurisdiction of USCIS and IJ regarding arriving aliens seeks to adjust]; Memo, Aytes, Assoc. Dir. Domestic Operations, USCIS HQDOMO 70/23.1 (Jan. 12, 2007), *published on* AILA InfoNet at Doc. No. 07030661. *But see Chambers v. Mukasey,* 520 F.3d 445, 450–51 (5th Cir. 2008) [IJ had no jurisdiction to address an AOS application that was filed 3 years after advance parole and was not the original denied AOS application, because the regulation only permits IJ review of a previously filed application]. The regulation limiting adjustment of status to USCIS for arriving aliens has been upheld. *Scheerer v. U.S. Att'y Gen.,* 513 F.3d 1244 (11th Cir. 2008) [8 C.F.R. §1245.2(a)(1), limiting arriving aliens' adjustment in most cases solely to USCIS was valid under *Chevron* because it did not eliminate adjustment but merely limited the forum for it]; *Vakker v. Att'y Gen. of the U.S.,* 519 F.3d 143, 148-50 (3d Cir. 2008) [upholding denial of remand of AOS to IJ for arriving alien under new regulations that require application is filed with USCIS and not IJ]. *See also Matter of Artigas,* 23 I&N Dec. 99 (BIA 2001) [a Cuban adjustment applicant who is an arriving alien may adjust before the IJ because his application is under §1 of the Cuban Adjustment Act and not under INA §245]. *But see Jiang v. Gonzales,* 425 F.3d 649, 652–53 (9th Cir. 2005) [applicant who first entered U.S. under TWOV was arriving alien, even though he subsequently obtained an advance parole and therefore was ineligible to adjust before the IJ under the Chinese Student Protection Act]. Some courts have held, however, that it is an abuse of discretion for an IJ/BIA to deny a motion to reopen or motion to continue to allow the filing and processing of an adjustment application before USCIS. *Kalilu v. Mukasey,* 516 F.3d 777, 779–81 (9th Cir. 2008) [BIA abused its discretion by denying motion to reopen contrary to *Matter of Velarde-Pacheco* and on the grounds that only USCIS had jurisdiction because motion should have been granted to give USCIS the time to adjudicate the AOS]; *See also Shen Gao Ni v. BIA,* 520 F.3d 125 (2d Cir. 2008) [the BIA's recital in denying the motion to reopen because the IJ had no jurisdiction to adjust arriving aliens under the new regulation, "even if technically accurate," does not adequately discharge the BIA's duty to consider the record facts and offer an explanation, where respondents sought to reopen to terminate proceedings and go before USCIS].

7.b. SAW Program—If person adjusted through the SAW program s/he is still subject to removal. *Matter of Jimenez-Lopez*, 20 I&N Dec. 738 (BIA 1993) [distinguishing INA §245 adjustment].

8. *Physical Removal*—INA §§241(a) & (b), 8 U.S.C. §§1231(a) & (b). The AG "shall" remove person found inadmissible within 90 days of final order. INA §241(a)(1). However, if person is not removed within 90 days and there are no exceptions under INA §§241(a)(1)(B) & (C), the person should be released and placed under and order of supervision. The Supreme Court has ruled that pursuant to 8 U.S.C. §1231(a)(6), an inadmissible persons may not be incarcerated beyond a reasonable time after the 90-day period if his or her removal is not reasonably foreseeable. *Clark v. Martinez,* 543 U.S. 371 (2005) [following *Zadvydas* and finding that as a matter of statutory construction of 8 U.S.C. §1231(a)(6), inadmissible persons must be released within 6 months after it is determined that removal is not reasonably foreseeable]; *Morales-Fernandez v. INS,* 418 F.3d 1116, 1122–25 (10th Cir. 2005) [post-*Clark* finding it impermissible to hold Cuban beyond 6-month period]; *Rosales-Garcia v. Holland,* 322 F.3d 386, 403–15 (6th Cir. 2003) [under *Zadvydas* and independently under the Fifth Amendment the period of detention post-removal has an implicit reasonable time limitation]; *But see Carrera-Valdez v. Perryman,* 211 F.3d 1046 (7th Cir. 2000) [rejecting constitutional argument because of *Mezei*]. For a more detailed discussion of physical removal *see in this chapter* section X.U (p.409), *infra.*

   If applicant is removed, s/he should be removed to the country where s/he boarded the vessel or aircraft. INA §241(b)(1)(A), 8 U.S.C. §1231(b)(1)(A). However, if that is not possible s/he may be removed to any other location in the following order: (1) country of which person is citizen, subject or national; (2) country of birth; (3) country where person has residence; or (4) any other government that will accept person. INA §241(b)(1)(C), 8 U.S.C. §1231(b)(1)(C). If U.S. tries to deport alien to another willing country it must make prior inquiry and obtain written assurance from that country. *Amanullah v. Cobb*, 862 F.2d 362 (1st Cir. 1988). Where IJ has made determination that person only has minimal connection to a country and cannot obtain asylum, the IJ would be precluded from ordering that the respondent be removed to that country. *Shuaibu v. Gonzales,* 425 F.3d 1142, 1144–45 (8th Cir. 2005) [where IJ denied asylum and found respondent had no connection to Liberia he could not be deported there].

9. *Stay of Removal*—INA §241(c)(2), 8 U.S.C. §1231(c)(2). The AG may stay removal of a person on board a vessel or aircraft if it is not practical or proper or if the person is needed to testify in a prosecution. INA §241(c)(2)(A).

10. *Appeal*—A person can appeal even if physically removed from the country. *Matter of Keyte*, 20 I&N Dec. 158 (BIA 1990); *Matter of Kennedy*, 13 I&N Dec. 242 (BIA 1969). But cannot file motion to reconsider or reopen if excluded and deported. *Matter of Okoh*, 20 I&N Dec. 864 (BIA 1994); 8 C.F.R. §§1003.23(b)(1), 1003.2(d). *See also Aguilar v. Gonzales,* 475 F.3d 415, 417–18 (1st Cir. 2007) [respondent's voluntary departure effected a withdrawal of his motion to reopen]; *Gomez Chavez v. Perryman,* 308 F.3d 796, 801 (7th Cir. 2002) [finding that a departure divests the EOIR of jurisdiction over a motion to reopen]. *But see Contreras-Rodriguez v. U.S. Att'y Gen.,* 462 F.3d 1314 (11th Cir. 2006) [although respondent was physically removed after *in absentia* order, he is not barred from filing a motion to reopen for lack of notice because §1003.23(b)(4)(ii) allows motion regarding lack of notice to be filed at "any time." *Patel* distinguished]; *Cardoso-Tlaseca v. Gonzales,* 460 F.3d 1102 (9th Cir. 2006) [where respondent's conviction is vacated after physical removal, court reversed BIA for denying motion to reopen because conviction was a "key part" of removal proceeding].

V. DEPORTATION GROUNDS

A. *Inadmissible at Time of Entry*—INA §237(a)(1)(A), 8 U.S.C. §1227(a)(1)(A). Incorporates all grounds of inadmissibility including the most common, INA §§212(a)(2), (6)(C), and (7), 8 U.S.C. §§1182(a)(2), (6)(C), and (7). Inadmissibility must be at the time the person entered, not at the time of the removal hearing. *Francis v. Gonzales,* 442 F.3d 131, 139–41 (2d Cir. 2006) [court looked to the deportation statute for drugs at the time of entry (which did not include admission as a ground of inadmissibility), as well as the definition of conviction (which at the time was under the narrower *Matter of Ozkok* standard), to determine that respondent was not inadmissible when he sought entry]. Also, a charge based on the DHS officer's "reason to believe" that a person was a drug trafficker on entry will not be sustained where the officer did not know at the time of entry that the person was a trafficker even if the person acknowledged it after entry. *Matter of Rocha*, 20 I&N Dec. 944 (BIA 1995). A person who enters with a valid visa may be deported under this section for a previous conviction unless he can show conviction was waived. *Zavaleta-Gallegos v. INS,* 261 F.3d 951 (9th Cir. 2001) [admission as LPR does not bar removal proceedings under this section for prior crime absent a showing that a waiver for conviction was granted by the consulate]. Under this section a person must be admissible at the time of AOS as well, and the BIA's determination that adjustment occurs when the application is approved, not filed, was upheld. *Perez-Enriquez v. Ashcroft,* 411 F.3d 1079 (9th Cir. 2004) [upheld IJ decision that inadmissibility at time of adjustment under this section relates to time of approval of adjustment, not to time of filing].

B. *Other Status Violations*

1. *Present in U.S. in violation of INA or any other U.S. law, or with revoked NIV*—INA §237(a)(1)(B), 8 U.S.C. §1227(a)(1)(B), 8 C.F.R. §103.12 (defining lawfully present); *Matter of Ruis*, 18 I&N Dec. 320 (BIA 1982). Includes all violations related to status. For example, can include person who stays longer than s/he was given permission to on I-94. *Zerrei v Gonzales,* 471 F.3d 342, 346 (2d Cir. 2006) ["The Federal Rules of Evidence do not apply in removal proceedings" and where respondent's counsel did not object to admission of a copy of respondent's passport at trial, it alone was sufficient to establish deportability as an overstay]. *But see Matter of R-D-,* 24 I&N Dec. 221 (BIA 2007) [overstay charge dismissed where person went to Canada, applied for asylum, and after several years was returned to the U.S. under the U.S.-Canadian Reciprocal Agreement because he was arriving alien seeking admission upon return]. .Includes each entry (even if person subsequently enters with I-551). Includes EWI. *Farquharson v. U.S. Att'y Gen.,* 246 F.3d 1317, 1319–22 (11th Cir. 2001) [found drug smuggler whose plane crashed was EWI under former section]; Includes LPR who previously entered without inspection, deported, and re-entered through inspection checkpoint. *Gunaydin v. INS*, 742 F.2d 776 (3d Cir. 1984). EWI also includes a person who evades inspection by claiming s/ he is a USC. *Reid v. INS,* 420 U.S. 619, 624 (1975) (and cases cited therein) [a person who makes an entry into the country by falsely representing himself as a citizen is not only excludable under former §212(a)(19) but is deportable as one who has "entered the United States without inspection"]; *Ramsay v. INS*, 14 F.3d 206, 211 n.6 (4th Cir. 1994). However, after Sept. 30, 1996, a person who is EWI can be treated as an inadmissible person subject to summary removal from the U.S. if the person cannot show that s/he has continuously been in U.S. for 2 years. INA §235(b)(1)(A)(iii).

2. *Fails to maintain nonimmigrant status*—INA §237(a)(1)(C), 8 U.S.C. §1227(a)(1)(C). This section is now divided into two parts. The first part retains existing law making it a deportable offense for a person to fail to maintain his or her NIV status. INA §237(a)(1)(C)(i). The second part now makes it a deportable offense for a person to fail to comply with the terms, conditions, and controls imposed under INA §212(g), concerning waivers for persons with communicable diseases or physical or mental disorders. INA §237(a)(1)(C)(ii). This second part requires a certificate from HHS certifying that the person has failed to comply with the terms, conditions and controls.

   The first section regarding violations of NIV status includes all conditions needed to maintain status. For example, a student who has failed to maintain a full course of study or has transferred schools without permission or a temporary worker who has abandoned employment or changed jobs without authorization has failed to maintain status. Incarceration of a nonimmigrant visitor for conviction is deemed a breach of status (because status cannot be pursued in jail). *Matter of A*, 6 I&N Dec. 762 (BIA 1955). *See also Matter of Halabi*, 15 I&N Dec. 105 (BIA 1974); *Matter of Siffre*, 14 I&N Dec. 444 (BIA 1973); *Matter of Neely & Whylie*, 11 I&N Dec. 864 (BIA 1966). Conviction of a student that does not interrupt studies is not necessarily a violation. *Matter of C*, 9 I&N Dec. 100 (BIA 1960). *But see* 8 C.F.R. §§214.1(g), [making certain convictions violations of any nonimmigrant status].

   Persons who overstays the time granted to them on their entry are also subject to removal even if they overstay during the pendency of removal proceedings. *Matter of Halabi,* 15 I&N Dec. 105 (1974). *But see Westover v. Reno,* 202 F.3d 475, 481–82 (1st Cir. 2000) [noting concern that the practice of charging persons with overstaying when they remain in U.S. to defend themselves in removal proceedings could violate due process].

   Other regulatory grounds for asserting a failure to maintain nonimmigrant status include: (1) Willful failure to provide full and truthful information requested by the Service, even if not material. 8 C.F.R. §214.1(f), *but see Romero v. INS,* 39 F.3d 977 (9th Cir. 1994) [struck down regulation because it exceeded the AG's authority by including nonmaterial misrepresentations]; (2) Willful failure to comply with any register requirements, 8 C.F.R. §214.1(f), and failure to file a change-of-address form under INA §266(b); DHS takes the position that failure to provide biometric and other information upon departure may lead to a determination that the individual failed to maintain the terms of his or her immigration status. 69 Fed. Reg. 467, 470 (Jan. 5, 2004); (3) criminal activity where a person is involved in a crime of violence for which a sentence of one year or more is imposed, 8 C.F.R. §214.1(g); and (4) Unauthorized employment. 8 C.F.R. §214.1(e).

The submission of a timely filed but yet unapproved extension may not bar a INA §237(a)(1)(C) charge. *Matter of Teberen*, 15 I&N Dec. 689 (BIA 1976) [deportable as overstay even where application for extension timely filed but not yet adjudicated]. *But see Matter of Dacanay*, 16 I&N Dec. 238 (BIA 1977) [subsequently approved H-1 barred visa holder's deportation even where person worked without authorization for second employer before new H-1 petition was approved]. *See also* INA §212(a)(9)(B)(iv) [tolling of unlawful status for 120 days upon timely filing extension or C/S] and 8 C.F.R. §§274a.12(b)(20), 1274a.12(b)(20) [granting automatic extension of work authorization for 240 days while extension is pending].

The grant of indefinite voluntary departure pre-IIRIRA also did not bar deportation under this section, where VD was granted until immigrant visa was available and respondent failed to acquire visa when it was available. *Matter of Balao*, 20 I&N Dec. 440 (BIA 1992).

3. *Termination of Conditional Permanent Residence*—INA §237(a)(1)(D), 8 U.S.C. §1227(a)(1)(D). Applies to conditional residents under INA §216 (relating to spouses and children who are CRs) and INA §216A (relating to investors and their spouses and children who are CRs) who have had their status terminated.

4. *Encouraged, induced, assisted, abetted, or aided illegal immigration at the time of any entry or within 5 years of any entry*—INA §237(a)(1)(E), 8 U.S.C. §1227(a)(1)(E). *Hernandez-Guadarrama v. Ashcroft*, 394 F.3d 674, 678–83 (9th Cir. 2005) [alien smuggling is not limited solely to persons who participate in the physical border-crossing but removal order against person who allegedly transported aliens in U.S. was reversed because DHS failed to prove alien smuggling under *Woodby* standard where limited evidence was not subject to cross-examination and was insufficiently reliable]. Under the previous statute, the INS was required to establish that the smuggling was "for gain." *Hernandez-Garza v. INS*, 882 F.2d 945 (5th Cir. 1989) [where "for gain" not established by *Woodby v. INS*, 385 U.S. 276 (1966) standard deportation order reversed. Criminal conviction under 8 U.S.C. §1324(a) does not establish "for gain"]; *Pryce v. INS*, 568 F.2d 278 (2d Cir. 1978) [where gain could not be demonstrated no deportation]; *Ribeiro v. INS*, 531 F.2d 179 (3d Cir. 1976) [same]. Although the "for gain" requirement has been eliminated, there is a waiver if the person who was smuggled at the time they were smuggled was the spouse, parent, son, or daughter of the LPR subject to deportation. INA §237(a)(1)(E)(iii), 8 U.S.C. §1227(a)(1)(E)(iii). The "at the time of" language was added by IIRIRA §351. *Matter of Farias*, 21 I&N Dec. 269 (BIA 1996). The waiver does not apply where brothers or other close family members are smuggled into the U.S. *Perez-Oropeza v. INS*, 56 F.3d 43 (9th Cir. 1995) [rejected equal protection challenge to statute]. There is also a waiver for persons who are eligible immigrants under the family reunification provisions of IMMACT90 §301(b)(1). INA §237(a)(1)(E)(ii).

5. *Marriage Fraud*—INA §237(a)(1)(G), 8 U.S.C. §1227(a)(1)(G), repeals INA §241(c) [IMMACT90 §602(b)(1)], and retains as a grounds of deportation:

   5.a. The termination or annulment of a marriage, where the marriage was entered into less than 2 years prior to entry and terminated within 2 years after entry, unless the alien can establish that the marriage was not entered into for the purpose of evading the immigration laws; *Rodriguez v. INS*, 204 F.3d 25 (1st Cir. 2000) [state court judgment ending marriage that was specifically based upon a finding of fraudulent intent to evade the immigration laws was a "presumption plus" that was not sufficiently rebutted]; and

   5.b. The failure of the alien to fulfill his marital agreement. *Nakamoto v. Ashcroft*, 363 F.3d 874 (9th Cir. 2004) [court's jurisdiction was not precluded by INA §242(a)(2)(B)(ii) to review AG's decision to deport for marriage fraud under INA §237(a)(1)(G)(ii), but there was substantial evidence to support AG's decision].

C. *Economic Reasons*

1. Public Charge Provisions—INA §237(a)(5), 8 U.S.C. §1227(a)(5). A person is deportable if in the opinion of the AG s/he has, within 5 years after entry, become a public charge from causes not affirmatively shown to have arisen after entry. BIA defined public charge as requiring that a state imposes a charge for services, makes a demand for payment, and failure to pay. *Matter of V*, 2 I&N Dec. 78 (BIA 1944); *Matter of A-*, 19 I&N Dec. 867 (Comm. 1988) [discusses standards for public charge]. A person is not automatically a public charge by virtue of receiving a public benefit. *Matter of B,* 3 I&N Dec. 323 (BIA and AG 1948). The 3 requirements are that: (1) government agency must impose charge or fee for services that person legally obligated to repay; (2) demand must be made on person; and (3) person fails to repay. If there is no reimbursement requirement the person cannot be a public charge. The demand for repayment must be within the 5 years. *Matter of L,* 6 I&N Dec. 349 (BIA 1954). The INS has provided field guidance on public charge. 64 Fed. Reg. 28689–93 (May 26, 1999).

2. The former ground for deportation of a person who became institutionalized at public expense because of a mental disease, defect, or deficiency within 5 years after entry, *Matter of Kowalski*, 10 I&N Dec. 159 (BIA 1963), has been eliminated.

D. *Security/Political Related Grounds*—INA §237(a)(4), 8 U.S.C. §1227(a)(4).

1. *In general*—Under INA §237(a)(4)(A), 8 U.S.C. §1227(a)(4)(A), an alien is deportable if s/he has engaged, is engaged, or at any time after entry has engaged in:

   1.a. Any activity to violate any law of the U.S. relating to espionage, sabotage, or laws prohibiting export of goods, technology, or sensitive information from the U.S.; *Matter of Luis-Rodriguez,* 22 I&N Dec. 747 (BIA 1999) [broadly read former §241(a)(4)(A)(i) to include violation of 50 U.S.C. §851, where person did not engage in activity generally considered espionage because he did not procure sensitive national defense related information but instead spied on an anti-Castro paramilitary organization].

   1.b. Any other criminal activity that endangers public safety or national security; or

   1.c. Any activity, a purpose of which is to oppose, control, or overthrow the U.S. government by force, violence, or other unlawful means.

   The BIA in an unpublished opinion held that the public-safety provision under INA §237(a)(4)(A)(ii) should be read to mean activity contrary to national security, not simply criminal activity. *Matter of Javier-Camarena*, Case No. A91 996 032 (BIA Aug. 17, 1993) [rape of minor does not make a person deportable under the public safety provision].

2. *Terrorist activities*—Under INA §237(a)(4)(B), 8 U.S.C. §1227(a)(4)(B), any alien described in paragraphs INA §212(a)(3)(B) *or* §212(a)(3)(F) [association with terrorists] is deportable. The REAL ID Act of 2005, §105(a), broadened the grounds of deportation and made them retroactive, though only to persons in removal, as opposed to deportation, proceedings. The respondent's state of mind may always be an issue in these cases, *see Daneshvar v. Ashcroft,* 355 F.3d 615, 627–29 (6th Cir. 2004) [reversed BIA finding of deportability where it failed to consider the respondent's state of mind under the USA PATRIOT Act standard]. *But see McAllister v. Att'y Gen. of the U.S.,* 444 F.3d 178, 185–89 (3d Cir. 2006) [upheld finding of deportation and rejected challenge that terrorist definition under §212(a)(3)(B)(iii)V)(b) was unconstitutionally vague and that the definition of terrorist organization under §212(a)(3)(B)(iv) required that person must act on his own or with a terrorist organization as opposed to *any* organization]; *Matter of S-K-* 23 I&N Dec. 936, 942 n.5 (BIA 2006) [finding that the Chin National Front that fights against repression of Chins by the illegitimate Burma military government is a terrorist organization, that contributions to the organization need not be demonstrated to be for terrorist purposes, and that a contribution of $685 over an 11-month period was sufficient to establish "material" support for purposes of INA §212(a)(3)(B)(iv)(VI)]; *cf. Matter of S-K-,* 24 I&N Dec. 289 (AG 2007) [maintaining precedential value of BIA decision but remanding case to BIA in light of DHS decision to grant a waiver under INA §212(d)(3)(B)(i) and not to apply the "material support" bar on asylum to certain persons providing support to the CNF]. Subsequent to the AG's decision, the Secretary of DHS and the Secretary of State were given broader powers to waive the material support provision under the Consolidated Appropriations Act, 2008, PL 110-161 Div. J, §691(a), 121 Stat. 1844, 2364–65 and the Act itself exempted certain groups, including the CNF, that was the subject of the AG's deci-

sion in *Matter of S-K-*. In light of Congress' Act DHS granted the respondent asylum and the BIA vacated its grant of deferral of removal and found no need to address withholding. *Matter of S-K-*, 24 I&N Dec. 475 (BIA 2008).

3. *Foreign policy*—INA §237(a)(4)(C), 8 U.S.C. §1227(a)(4)(C), provides that an alien is deportable if the Secretary of State has reasonable grounds to believe that his or her presence or activities in the U.S. would have potentially serious adverse foreign policy consequences for the U.S.

3.a. An official of a foreign government or a purported government, or a candidate for election immediately preceding the election, cannot be deported solely because of his past, current or expected beliefs, statements, or association if such matters are lawful within the U.S.

3.b. All other persons also cannot be deported for such beliefs, statements, or associations unless the Secretary of State personally determines the alien's continued presence would compromise a compelling U.S. foreign policy interest. If the Secretary does make such determination, s/he must timely notify the Senate and House Judiciary and Foreign Relations Committees.

3.c. Speaking of this ground, the Conference Report accompanying IMMACT90 noted that:

> "It is the intent of the conference committee that this authority would be used sparingly and not merely because there is a likelihood that an alien will make certain remarks about the United States or its policies.
>
> "Furthermore, the conferees intend that the 'compelling foreign policy interest' standard be interpreted as a significantly higher standard than the general 'potentially serious adverse foreign policy consequences' standard.... The fact that the Secretary of State personally must inform the relevant Congressional committees when a determination of excludability is made under this provision is further indication that the conferees intend that this provision be used only in usual circumstances."

H.R. Conf. Rep. No. 955, 101st Cong., 2d Sess. 129 (1990).

The BIA has interpreted the statute to require only that the Secretary of State set forth "a facially reasonable and bona fide basis" for his determination that the person's presence would have an adverse foreign policy consequence. *Matter of Ruiz-Massieu,* 22 I&N Dec. 833 (BIA 1999). The Board regarded its role as "ministerial" as "neither the Attorney General nor her delegates have a role in that basic determination." *Id* at 12. The BIA also sought to limit discovery stating "there is no prejudice to the respondent if he is not allowed to cross-examine the Secretary regarding the contents of the letter" the Secretary submits. *Id.* at 16 n.13.

4. *Nazi, Genocide, or Commission of Any Act of Torture or Extrajudicial Killing.*—INA §237(a)(4)(D), 8 U.S.C. §1227(a)(4)(D). Nazi war criminals, persons who have engaged, assisted or otherwise participated in genocide or persecution of others, or committed acts of torture or extrajudicial killing as defined in INA §§212(a)(3)(E)(i)–(iii) are subject to removal. *Naujalis v. INS,* 240 F.3d 642 (7th Cir. 2001) [guarded railway facility under German direction as member of a battalion involved in execution of Jews and others]; *Hammer v. INS,* 195 F.3d 836 (6th Cir. 1999); *Kalejs v. INS*, 10 F.3d 441 (7th Cir. 1993). Fraud or misrepresentation is not an element that must be proven to deport under the Holtzman Amendment. *Tittjung v. Reno,* 199 F.3d 393, 397 (7th Cir. 1999). The courts have also upheld on collateral estoppel grounds removal based upon facts established in the denaturalization proceedings. *Szehinskyj v. Att'y Gen. of the U.S.,* 432 F.3d 253 (3d Cir. 2005) [former concentration camp guard and SS member who was denaturalized for illegal procurement was collaterally estopped from asserting he did assist in the persecution of others]; *Dailide v. U.S. Att'y Gen.,* 387 F.3d 1335, 1342–43 (11th Cir. 2004) [where Lithuanian was denaturalized for illegally procuring his citizenship because he did not qualify as a displaced person due to his persecution of Jews, the record of the denaturalization proceeding was admitted in immigration court and used to determine removal by collateral estoppel].

5. *Recipient of Military-Type Training*—INA §237(a)(4)(E), 8 U.S.C. §1227(a)(4)(E). A person who receives military-type training from or on behalf of an organization that at the time was a terrorist organization as defined in §§212(a)(3)(B)(vi)(I) & (II). Military-type training includes "training in means or methods that can cause death or serious bodily injury, destroy or damage property, or disrupt services to critical infrastructure, or training on the use, storage, production, or assembly

of any explosive, firearm, or other weapon, including any weapon of mass destruction" as defined in section 18 U.S.C. §2332a(c)(2).

6. *Severe Violation of Religious Freedom*—INA §237(a)(4)(E), 8 U.S.C. §1227(a)(4)(E). A person described in INA §212(a)(2)(G) [foreign government official who was responsible for or directly carried out, at any time, particularly severe violations of religious freedom] is deportable.

E. *Failure to Register and Falsification of Documents*—INA §237(a)(3), 8 U.S.C. §1227(a)(3)

1. *Change of Address*—INA §237(a)(3)(A), 8 U.S.C. §1227(a)(3)(A). Failure to comply with INA §265 is a deportable act unless the alien establishes that such failure was reasonably excusable or not willful. If person is in DHS custody, DHS has responsibility to notify the Immigration Court. 8 C.F.R. §1003.19(g); Memo, Hamilton, Assoc. Gen. Counsel, (HQCOU 50/10.2) (Apr. 13, 1998), *reprinted in* 75 No. 17 *Interpreter Releases* 627, 636 (May 4, 1998). DHS Form AR-11 or EOIR-33 (if in removal proceedings) should be used to notify the DHS or the AG of a change of address. It may now be done electronically at *www.uscis.gov/AR-11*.

2. *Failure to Register; Falsification of Documents*—INA §237(a)(3)(B). An alien is deportable if at any time s/he is convicted, regardless of the sentence imposed, for a violation of (a) INA §266(c) or of §36(c) of the Alien Registration Act; (b) the Foreign Agents Registration Act (22 U.S.C. §611 *et seq.*); or (c) 18 U.S.C. §1546 (relating to fraud and misuse of visas).

3. *Document Fraud*—Final administrative order for violating INA §274C (document fraud) subjects party to deportation. INA §237(a)(3)(C)(i), 8 U.S.C. §1227(a)(3)(C)(i). There is a waiver available for LPRs, if there was no previous civil monetary penalty under §274C and the offense was incurred solely to assist and/or support the LPR's spouse or child (and no other person). There is no jurisdiction to review the denial of the waiver. INA §237(a)(3)(C)(ii).

4. *False Claim to Citizenship*—INA §237(a)(3)(D), 8 U.S.C. §1227(a)(3)(D). A person who falsely represents or has falsely represented him- or herself to be USC to obtain benefit under INA, federal, or state law is removable. This section applies to representations made on or after Sept. 30, 1996. IIRIRA §344(c). Congress has provided an exception and a person will not be subject to deportation or removal if: (1) his or her parents were or are USCs; (2) s/he permanently resided in the U.S. prior to 16; and (3) s/he reasonably believed at the time of making such representations that s/he was a USC. INA §237(a)(3)(D)(ii). The exception is applied retroactively as if included in IIRIRA and applies to representations made on or after Sept. 30, 1996. Section 201(b)(2) of the Child Citizenship Act of 2000, PL 106-395, 114 Stat. 1631 added this exception. Section 201(b)(3) of the same Act provided the effective date language. *See also* Memo, Yates, Deputy Exe. Assoc. Comm. Operations, USCIS, HQ 70/33 (May 7, 2002), *published on* AILA InfoNet at Doc. No. 05030768 [setting forth criteria for determining a false claim to USC and determining whether an exception or prosecutorial discretion applies]. A false statement on an I-9 may be a basis to charge a false claim to U.S. citizenship to obtain a benefit. *Rodriguez v. Mukasey,* 519 F.3d 773, 776-78 (8th Cir. 2008) [A noncitizen who marks the "citizen or national of the United States" box on Form I-9 for the purpose of falsely representing himself as a citizen (as distinguished from a national) to secure private employment is inadmissible under INA §212(a)(6)(C)(ii)(I)]; *Kechkar v. Gonzales,* 500 F.3d 1080 (10th Cir. 2007) [where the respondent checked off the box on the I-9 that stated he was a "citizen *or* national" the court upheld the BIA's determination that he falsely claimed citizenship and that doing so for private employment is not a defense because it was done for the purpose of evading the employer sanctions statute]; *Ateka v. Ashcroft,* 384 F.3d 954, 956–57 (8th Cir. 2004) [upheld on substantial evidence grounds IJ finding of ineligibility for AOS but declined to rule, due to failure to exhaust administrative remedies, on whether a false statement on an I-9 in private employment is a bar to residency]; *Njai v. U.S.,* 484 F.Supp.2d 1040, 1048 & n.11 (D. Ariz. 2007) [person pled to 18 U.S.C. §911 and then IJ asserted removability for signing I-9]. The false claim may be made in private-sector employment and need not be in written form. *Theodros v. Gonzales,* 490 F.3d 396 (5th Cir. 2007) [where respondent acknowledged he had worked without authorization by stating he was USC and DHS provided a document from one employer where he checked off box, similar to an I-9, that stated he was USC or LPR, there was sufficient evidence in the record to support finding and the fact that this false claim to citizenship was made to obtain private-sector employment is not a defense]. *But see U.S. v. Karaouni,* 379 F.3d 1139 (9th Cir. 2004) [where defendant checked off I-9 box that stated he was a citizen *or* na-

tional of the U.S., he could not be convicted under §911 that makes it a crime only to make a false claim to citizenship].

F. *Unlawful Voting*—INA §237(a)(6), 8 U.S.C. §1227(a)(6). Any person who has voted in violation of any federal, state, or local constitutional provision, statute, ordinance, or regulation. A conviction is *not* required. This section shall apply to voting that occurred before, on or after Sept. 30, 1996. IIRIRA §347(c). Congress has provided an exception and a person will not be subject to deportation and removal if: (1) his or her parents were or are USCs; (2) s/he permanently resided in the U.S. prior to 16; and (3) s/he reasonably believed at the time of such violation that s/he was a USC. INA §237(a)(6)(B). The exception is applied retroactively as if included in IIRIRA and applies to voting occurring before, on, or after Sept. 30, 1996. Section 201(b)(1) of the Child Citizenship Act of 2000, PL 106-395, 114 Stat. 1631 added this exception. Sec. 201(b)(3) of the Child Citizenship Act provided the effective date language. Prior to putting a person in removal proceedings, a DHS agent is supposed to determine whether the individual acted knowingly or willfully including the extent of the applicant's knowledge of election laws. Depending upon the federal, state, or local law that was violated, DHS may be required to prove that the respondent acted knowingly or willfully. To determine whether a respondent knowingly or willfully violated a voting statute adjudicating officers should determine: "(1) how, when and where the applicant registered to vote and/or voted; (2) the extent of the applicant's knowledge of the election laws; (3) whether the applicant received any instructions, or was questioned verbally about his or her eligibility to vote; (4) who provided the applicant with information about election laws or his or her eligibility to vote; (5) whether the election registration form and/or voting ballot: (a) contains a specific question asking if the applicant is a U.S. citizen; (b) requires the applicant to declare under penalty of perjury that he or she is a U.S. citizen; or (c) requires the applicant to be qualified to vote and lists specifically the requirement of U.S. citizenship elsewhere on the form." Memo, Yates, Deputy Exe. Assoc. Comm. Operations, USCIS, HQ 70/33 (May 7, 2002), *published on* AILA InfoNet at Doc. No. 05030768 [setting forth the criteria to be applied for a willful or knowingly violation where the federal, state, or local authority requires such a violation and permitting the exercise of prosecutorial discretion under the Commissioner's Nov. 17, 2000, memo (InfoNet Doc. No. 00112702)]. If the DHS places the person in a removal proceeding, it must prove, by the *Woodby* standard, that a violation occurred under the federal or state statute. *McDonald v. Gonzales,* 400 F.3d 684 (9th Cir. 2005) [where the IJ applied a civil standard to a violation of the Hawaiian voting fraud statute, the court reversed the finding of removability and found the government failed to prove a knowingly violation of the state law].

G. *Criminal Grounds*

1. Defining Sentence and Term of Imprisonment for Criminal Grounds—Any reference to a term of imprisonment or sentence includes, by virtue of INA §101(a)(48)(B), the time of incarceration or confinement *ordered by a court*, even if the time is *suspended* or the execution is *withheld. U.S. v. Ayala-Gomez*, 255 F.3d 1314 (11th Cir. 2001) [sentence that was probated is considered suspended for purposes of statute and therefore full sentence must be considered]. Statute includes all sentences and convictions entered on, before or after Sept. 30, 1996, IIRIRA §322(c), and includes suspension of "imposition" of sentence. *Matter of S-S-*, 21 I&N Dec. 900 (BIA 1997). At least one court has found that the clear language of the statute results in the retroactive application of the new definition of sentence and conviction. *Moosa v. INS,* 171 F.3d 994, 1006–10 (5th Cir. 1999). However, if a sentence is vacated or modified *nunc pro tunc*, the new sentence will be determinative of whether the person is subject to removal even if it was vacated or modified solely for immigration purposes. *Matter of Cota,* 23 I&N Dec. 849 (BIA 2005) [where sentence was modified *nunc pro tunc* expressly to avoid deportation as an aggravated felon, IJ and BIA must recognize it. *Matter of Pickering* distinguished].

2. **Crimes of Moral Turpitude**—INA §§237(a)(2)(A)(i) & (ii), 8 U.S.C. §§1227(a)(2)(A)(i) & (ii)

   2.a. Under section INA §237(a)(2)(A)(i), an alien or LPR is deportable if s/he is (1) convicted; (2) of a crime involving moral turpitude; (3) committed within 5 years of admission (unless s/he adjusted under S visa, in which case it is within 10 years of admission); and is (4) convicted of a crime for which a sentence of one year or longer *may* be imposed.

      (1) This represents a change from the previous statute, which required a sentence or actual confinement of one year or more and thus now applies to individuals who receive a sen-

tence of less than a year as long as the offense carried a potential sentence of a year or longer. This provision and the change in subsection (a)(2)(A)(ii) applies to persons whose deportation proceedings are initiated after Apr. 24, 1996. AEDPA §435(b). *Matter of Fortiz,* 21 I&N Dec. 1199 (BIA 1998); *Aquino-Encarnacion v. INS,* 296 F.3d 56 (1st Cir. 2002) [where sentenced reduced to 11 months probation person still subject to deportation because changed statute only requires that a sentence of one year or longer may be imposed].

(2) Prior law required commission of the crime within 5 years of "entry," which meant any entry. *Matter of Sanchez*, 17 I&N Dec. 218 (BIA 1980). The *Fleuti* doctrine, *supra*, therefore was important to determine whether return to the U.S. after a trip abroad constituted a new "entry." *But see Matter of Collado-Munoz*, 21 I&N Dec. 1061 (BIA 1997) [finding *Fleuti* no longer applicable even to returning LPRs with conviction]; *Tineo v. Ashcroft,* 350 F.3d 382 (3d Cir. 2003) [determining that Congress did abolish the *Fleuti* doctrine in the passage of INA §101(a)(13)(C) for certain returning LPRs and upholding *Matter of Collado-Munoz* on *Chevron* deference grounds]. The current law however looks to whether the crime was committed within 5 years of *admission*, not entry. Admission is defined under INA §101(a)(13)(A). The unambiguous definition of admission under the statute means that the criminal act must occur within 5 years of the person's lawful entry into the U.S. and not within 5 years of his or her later adjustment of status. Thus, admission under INA §101(a)(13)(A) is *not* defined as including AOS but rather the prior "lawful entry of the alien into the United States after inspection and authorization by an immigration officer." *Shivaraman v. Ashcroft,* 360 F.3d 1142 (9th Cir. 2004) [rejecting interpretation of INA §237(a)(2)(A)(i) that would permit counting the 5 years from AOS instead of admission under INA §101(a)(13)(A)]. *Accord Zhang v. Mukasey,* 509 F.3d 313 (6th Cir. 2007) [5 years is not measured from AOS because AOS does not constitute an admission for purposes of calculating the time period]; *Abdelqadar v. Gonzales,* 413 F.3d 668, 672–74 (7th Cir. 2005) [questioning and rejecting *Matter of Rosas* in the context of a commission of a CIMT under §237(a)(2)(A)(i) within 5 years of admission where person entered more than 5 years but adjusted status within 5 years]; *Aremu v. DHS,* 450 F.3d 578 (4th Cir. 2006) [same; reversing *Matter of Shanu* and finding §101(a)(13)(A) is clear and that admission applies to lawful entry and not to AOS]. *But see Matter of Shanu,* 23 I&N Dec. 754, 756–59 (BIA 2005) *reversed Aremu v. DHS,* 450 F.3d 578 (4th Cir. 2006) [the term "date of admission" in 237(a)(2)(A)(i) includes the date of AOS and applies to *any* admission]; *Matter of Rosas,* 22 I&N Dec. 616 (BIA 1999); *Ocampo-Duran v. Ashcroft,* 254 F.3d 1133, 1135 (9th Cir. 2001) [concluding that the date of adjustment qualifies as "date of admission" when the individual has never been "admitted"]. Also "committed" within 5 years of admission applies to the time of the commission of the crime not the conviction. *Matter of Yanez-Jaquez,* 13 I&N Dec. 449, 451 (BIA 1970)

(3) Similarly, someone who has been committed for treatment has not been sentenced. *Matter of N*, 8 I&N Dec. 660 (BIA 1960); *Matter of K*, 3 I&N Dec. 48 (BIA 1947); and *Holzapfel v. Wyrsch*, 259 F.2d 890 (3d Cir. 1958). And the underlying criminal statutes, rather than recidivist sentencing statutes, should be utilized to determine whether a sentence of one year may be imposed. *Rusz v. Ashcroft,* 376 F.3d 1182 (9th Cir. 2004) [felony conviction for petty theft with a qualifying prior offense under Cal. Penal Code §§484, 488, and 666 is not a crime for which a sentence of one year or longer may be imposed]. Where the person has been sentenced but the execution is withheld (suspended), it is nevertheless considered a sentence for immigration purposes. INA §101(a)(48)(B); *see also Fonseca-Leite v. INS*, 961 F.2d 60, 62 (5th Cir. 1992). If the alien has been sentenced, actual confinement is not required. *Velez-Lozano v. INS*, 463 F.2d 1305 (D.C. Cir. 1972).

2.b. An LPR or an alien is deportable also under if (1) at any time after admission; (2) s/he is convicted of two crimes involving moral turpitude; (3) not arising out of a single scheme of criminal misconduct.

(1) *See Abdelqadar v. Gonzales,* 413 F.3d 668, 674–75 (7th Cir. 2005) [upheld *Matter of Adetiba* and found respondent subject to removal on the grounds that he has 2 convictions for food stamp fraud on 2 different days]; *Gonzalez-Sandoval v. INS*, 910 F.2d 614 (9th Cir.

1990) [two robberies occurring within 2 days of each other, at the same bank, and which were conceived and planned at same time, arise out of single scheme]; *Sawkow v. INS*, 314 F.2d 34 (3d Cir. 1963). The BIA takes a narrower view finding that the single scheme exception only applies where the crimes "were performed in furtherance of a single criminal episode, such as where one crime constitutes a lesser offense of another or where 2 crimes flow from and are the natural consequences of a single act of criminal misconduct." *Matter of Adetiba*, 20 I&N Dec. 506 (BIA 1992). *Accord Michel v. INS,* 206 F.3d 253, 259–61 (2d Cir. 2000) [under either the Court's prior decision in *Nason* or the BIA's narrower standard in *Adetiba*, 2 possession of stolen property offenses committed 2 months apart were not part of a single scheme in absence of other evidence]; *Okoro v. INS*, 125 F.3d 920, 926 (5th Cir. 1997) [where computer equipment ordered together and parts came 2 days apart and were paid for by 2 fraudulent checks, it was 2 crimes]; *Akindemowo v. INS*, 61 F.3d 282 (4th Cir. 1995) [grand larceny by passing two fraudulent checks at 2 different stores at the same mall on the same day considered separate crimes]; *Balogun v. INS*, 31 F.3d 8 (1st Cir. 1994) [mail fraud arising from same plan but plea to 3 counts involving 3 different insurance companies in separate locations with petitioner using different aliases were considered separate crimes]; *Nguyen v. INS*, 991 F.2d 621 (10th Cir. 1993) [respondent convicted of possession of stolen vehicle and shooting with intent to kill when stopped by police officer for speeding in stolen vehicle was considered, following *Matter of Adetiba*, to be convicted of 2 separate crimes warranting deportation]; *Iredia v. INS*, 981 F.2d 847 (5th Cir. 1993) [where person applied for 13 different credit cards under false names and was convicted at one trial, court upheld INS view that they were separate schemes]; *Leon-Hernandez v. INS*, 926 F.2d 902 (9th Cir. 1991) [conviction for 2 counts of oral copulation with the same person one month apart considered 2 crimes because there was no evidence of a conscious coherent plan or program of future action]; *Pacheco v. INS*, 546 F.2d 448 (lst Cir. 1976), *cert. denied,* 430 U.S. 985 (1977); *Nason v. INS*, 394 F.2d 223 (2d Cir.), *cert. denied*, 393 U.S. 830 (1968) [break-ins committed 2 days apart during drunken spree, sufficient for 2 crimes criteria for deportation]; *Jeronimo v. Murff*, 157 F.Supp. 808, 815 (S.D.N.Y. 1957). *See generally Fong Haw Tan v. Phelan*, 333 U.S. 6 (1948) [former statute read to resolve all doubts in favor of respondent so that person only deportable if a "repeater"—separate crimes and separate convictions].

(2) Under previous statute, the grant of INA §212(c) relief on the first conviction did not bar deportation under former INA §241(a)(2)(A)(ii) if a second CIMT was committed. 8 C.F.R. §§212.3(d), 1212.3(d); *Matter of Balderas*, 20 I&N Dec. 389 (BIA 1991); *Molina-Amezcua v. INS*, 6 F.3d 646 (9th Cir. 1993); *Molenda v. INS*, 998 F.2d 291 (5th Cir. 1993). *See also Amouzadeh v. Winfrey,* 467 F.3d 451, 458–59 (5th Cir. 2006) [where respondent had a drug conviction and a CIMT, a grant of INA §212(c) relief for the drug conviction still bars cancellation for the CIMT because respondent still has an aggravated felony conviction that bars cancellation even if §212(c) waives it].

(3) A person is subject to deportation:

(a) Even if there is no confinement, *Matter of O*, 7 I&N Dec. 539 (BIA 1957); *Matter of P*, 8 I&N Dec. 424 (BIA 1959);

(b) Even if s/he was convicted at a single trial, so long as s/he is charged with separate counts and the prosecution needs to prove separate facts for conviction, *Chanan Din Khan v. Barber*, 253 F.2d 547 (9th Cir. 1958); *Fitzgerald v. Landon*, 238 F.2d 864 (1st Cir. 1956).

(c) Even if second offense is a misdemeanor. *Matter of Tran*, 21 I&N Dec. 291 (BIA 1996).

(4) The government has the burden of proving that the two separate crimes were not part of a single scheme, *Sawkow v. INS,* 314 F.2d 34 (3d Cir. 1963); *Wood v. Hoy*, 266 F.2d 825 (9th Cir. 1959); *Matter of C*, 9 I&N Dec. 524 (BIA 1962), *rev'd on other grounds*, *Costello v. INS,* 376 U.S. 120 (1964). The government must prove that both crimes were CIMTs. *Hamdan v. INS*, 98 F.3d 183 (5th Cir. 1996) [person not deportable where one crime was not a CIMT].

2.c. Juvenile delinquency is not considered a crime unless the juvenile was tried as an adult. *Vargas-Hernandez v. Gonzales,* 497 F.3d 919, 922–23 (9th Cir. 2007) [sixteen (16) year old tried as an adult for voluntary manslaughter is convicted under INA §101(a)(48)(A)]. Foreign juvenile dispositions are evaluated under U.S. standards. *Matter of Ramirez-Rivero*, 18 I&N Dec. 135 (BIA 1981). *But see Matter of De La Nues*, 18 I&N Dec. 140 (BIA 1981). The standards established in the Federal Juvenile Delinquency Act, 18 U.S.C. §5031–50 govern whether an offense by a young offender is to be considered an act of delinquency or a crime. *Matter of Devison,* 22 I&N Dec. 1362, 1366 [finding an adjudication under CPL Art. 720 of the New York youthful offender procedures to be equivalent to the FJDA and therefore not a conviction even though the procedures were only similar]; *But see Savchuk v. Mukasey,* 518 F.3d 119 (2d Cir. 2008) [finding determinative state's treatment of petition as an adult]; *Vargas-Hernandez v. Gonzales,* 497 F.3d 919 (9th Cir. 2007); *Uritsky v. Gonzales,* 399 F.3d 728 (6th Cir. 2005) [distinguishing *Devison*, the court determined that a sentence to probation under Michigan's Youthful Trainee Act was a conviction]; *Vieira Garcia v. INS,* 239 F.3d 409, 414–15 (1st Cir. 2001) [upholding BIA decision that 17-year-old tried as adult under Rhode Island law was an aggravated felon and finding that the failure to apply the Federal Juvenile Delinquency Act as a standard for all state convictions does not violate equal protection].

2.d. A person cannot be deported for a foreign conviction because the crime had to be committed after admission.

3. **Aggravated Felonies**—INA §§101(a)(43), 237(a)(2)(A)(iii), 8 U.S.C. §§1101(a)(43), 1227(a)(2)(A)(iii); S. Rep. No. 55, 101st Cong. 2d Sess. (1990); 134 Cong. Rec. S17301, S17318 (1988); 136 Cong. Rec. at S17106, S17117; S17741 (Oct. 26–27, 1990); H.R. Rep. No. 681, 101st Cong. 2d Sess. 1990, *reprinted in* 1990 U.S.C.C.A.N. 6472, 6553; PL 103-416, Sec. 222, 140 Cong. Rec. at S14479-02, S14543 (1994), 140 Cong. Rec. at H11291-01, H11293 (1994); H.R. Rep. No. 104-22 (1995); 141 Cong. Rec. E330 (1995); H.R. Conf. Rep. No. 828, 104th Cong., 2d Sess. (1996) at 223.

An LPR or other alien is deportable if convicted of an aggravated felony at any time after admission. *Matter of Rosas,* 22 I&N Dec. 616 (BIA 1999) ["After admission" includes after AOS even if person never subsequently left the country and re-entered]; *Ocampo-Duran v. Ashcroft,* 254 F.3d 1133, 1134–35 (9th Cir. 2001) [same]. DHS must prove the conviction by clear and convincing evidence. *Cruz-Garza v. Ashcroft,* 396 F.3d 1125, 1128–29 (10th Cir. 2005) [DHS did not prove by clear and convincing evidence that reduced felony conviction was an aggravated felony because the reduction of respondent's conviction to a misdemeanor did not meet the *Roldan/Salazar* standards in light of the vagaries of the evidentiary record and the existence of a Utah statute permitting reduction, which could have occurred for other than rehabilitative purpose]. An aggravated felony is defined under INA §101(a)(43), 8 U.S.C. §1101(a)(43) as:

3.a. Murder, rape, or sexual abuse of a minor

(1) Sexual Abuse of a Minor—Includes persons charged with misdemeanor sexual abuse. *Matter of Small,* 23 I&N Dec. 448 (BIA 2002) [conviction for misdemeanor sexual abuse in the second degree, in violation of N.Y. Penal Law §130.60(2), is aggravated felony]; *Sharashidze v. Gonzales,* 480 F.3d 566 (7th Cir. 2007) [indecent solicitation of a sex act under 720 Ill. Comp Stat. 5/11-14.1 was divisible but complaint demonstrated act was against a child]; *Parrilla v. Gonzales,* 414 F.3d 1038 (9th Cir. 2005) [conviction under Wash. Rev. Code §9.68A.090 for communicating with a minor was a misdemeanor and although not abuse under the categorical approach it was a conviction under the modified categorical approach]. It also includes any child under 18, notwithstanding the federal definition that involves only children under 16. and which requires that the minor be at least 4 years younger than the perpetrator, 18 U.S.C. §2243(a)(1). *Matter of V-F-D-,* 23 I&N Dec. 859 (BIA 2006) [Fla. Stat. Ann. §794.05(1), concerning sexual activity by a person 24 years or older with a person 16 or 17 years of age where victim was actually 16 is abuse of a minor because a child includes any person under 18]; *Estrada-Expinoza v. Gonzales,* 498 F.3d 933 (9th Cir. 2007) [followed *Afridi* and found California statutory rape statute under §261.5(c) an aggravated felony]; *Afridi v. Gonzales,* 442 F.3d 1212, 1214–17 (9th Cir. 2006) [Cal. Penal Code §261.5(c), which punishes sexual intercourse with a minor who is more than 3 years younger than the perpetrator, is an aggravated felony even where minor was 17]. The term abuse of a minor does not require physical con-

tact. *Matter of Rodriguez-Rodriguez,* 22 I&N Dec. 991 (BIA 1999) [BIA addressed "indecency with a child by exposure" under Tex. Penal Code §21.11(a)(2), and relied on federal definition under 18 U.S.C. §3509(a) and *not* 18 U.S.C. §2242, 2243, and 2246, because §3509 did not require contact with the minor to obtain conviction]; *Hernandez-Alvarez v. Gonzales,* 432 F.3d 763 (7th Cir. 2005) [attempted indecent solicitation of a child under Illinois statute, 720 Ill. Comp. Stat. 5/11-6(a), where solicited person was a police officer]; *Gattem v. Gonzales,* 412 F.3d 758, (7th Cir. 2005) [solicitation of sexual contact of nonspouse under Illinois misdemeanor statute 720 Ill. Comp. Stat. 5/11-14.1(a) is aggravated felony]; *Taylor v. U.S.,* 396 F.3d 1322, 1328–39 (11th Cir. 2005) [soliciting a minor under Fla. Stat. §794.011(8)(a)]; *U.S. v. Padilla-Reyes,* 247 F.3d 1158 (11th Cir. 2001) [in sentencing enhancement case court found Fla. Stat. §800.04 involving acts that may not include physical contact to be within statute because abuse of a minor includes physical or nonphysical misuse or mistreatment]. The courts have read the statute broadly. *Espinoza-Franco v. Ashcroft,* 394 F.3d 461, 464–65 (7th Cir. 2005) [in finding that aggravated sexual abuse under Illinois law, 720 Ill. Comp. Stat. 5/12-16(b), was an aggravated felony, the court rejected a formal definition of sexual abuse of a minor and held that Congress intended the phrase to broadly incorporate all acts that fall with the "ordinary, contemporary and common meaning of the words"]; *Chuang v. U.S. Att'y Gen.,* 382 F.3d 1299, 1301–02 (11th Cir. 2004) [indecent assault of a child under 16 pursuant to Fla. Stat. §800.04 is an aggravated felony because both physical and nonphysical misuse or maltreatment for a purpose associated with sexual gratification is covered];

<u>Finding Sexual Abuse of a Minor</u>—*Vargas v. DHS,* 451 F.3d 1105 (10th Cir. 2006) [Colorado conviction for contributing to the delinquency of a minor under Colo. Rev. Stat. §18-6-701 is an aggravated felony for sexual abuse of a minor under the modified categorical approach where the criminal records indicated that the delinquency was unlawful sexual contact under Colo. Rev. Stat. §18-3-404(1)(a)]; *Santos v. Gonzales,* 436 F.3d 323 (2d Cir. 2006) [conviction under Conn. Gen. Stat. §53-21(a)(2), which criminalizes contact with the intimate parts of a child under 16, is an aggravated felony]; *Cedano-Viera v. Ashcroft,* 324 F.3d 1062, 1065–67 (9th Cir. 2003) [lewdness with a Child Under Fourteen Years of Age under Nev. Rev. Stat. §201.230 is an aggravated felony even if it is broader in scope than the federal offense of sexual abuse of a minor under 18 U.S.C. §2243(a)]; *Bahar v. Ashcroft,* 264 F.3d 1309 (11th Cir. 2001) [taking indecent liberties with a child under N.C. Gen. Stat. §14-202.1 even if it does not require physical contact is an aggravated felony]; *Mugalli v. Ashcroft,* 258 F.3d 52, 54–61 (2d Cir. 2001) [accepting BIA's broad definition in *Rodriguez-Rodriguez* pursuant to *Chevron* and determining that statutory rape under N.Y. Penal Law §130.25-2 is aggravated felony]; *Emile v. INS,* 244 F.3d 183 (1st Cir. 2001) [indecent assault and battery on a child under 14 under Mass. G.L. ch. 265 §13B is a crime involving abuse of a minor by relying on definitions at 18 U.S.C. §§2241–48]; *U.S. v. Marin-Navarette,* 244 F.3d 1284 (11th Cir. 2001) [although attempted child molestation in the third degree is a misdemeanor under Washington State law, it is an aggravated felony]; *Guerrero-Perez v. INS,* 242 F.3d 727 (7th Cir.) *reh'g denied,* 256 F.3d 546 (7th Cir. 2001) [a misdemeanor offense for sexual abuse of a minor under Illinois law, 720 Ill. Comp. Stat. 5/12-15(c), constituted an aggravated felony]; *U.S. v. Zavala-Sustaita,* 214 F.3d 601 (5th Cir. 2000) [finding same Texas statute as abuse of a minor for sentence enhancement]; *Lara-Ruiz v. INS,* 241 F.3d 934, 939–42 (7th Cir. 2001) [rejecting definitional limitations to 18 U.S.C. §2243 and finding a violation of Ill. Rev. Stat. 1991 ch. 38, §§12-13(a)(1)–(2) was abuse of a minor]; *U.S. v. Baron-Medina,* 187 F.3d 1144 (9th Cir. 1999) [Cal. Penal Code §288(a), prohibiting lewd or lascivious acts on children under age 14, is an aggravated felony]; *Pequeno-Martinez v. Trominski,* 281 F.Supp.2d 902, 914–17 (S.D.Tex. 2003) [read statute broader than federal statute finding that sexual assault of a child under Tex. Penal Code §21.11(a)(1) is not unconstitutionally vague, is "sexual abuse of a minor" under aggravated felony definition and that deferred adjudication did constitute an aggravated felony even if no time was specified]; *Santapaola v. Ashcroft,* 249 F.Supp.2d 181, 199–203 (D. Conn. 2003) [relying on plea transcript the court determined that a conviction under former Conn. Gen. Stat. §53-21 for injury to a minor, made the respondent removable for sexual abuse of a minor under divisible part of the statute].

Not Sexual Abuse of a Minor—*Rebilas v. Keisler,* 506 F.3d 1161 (9th Cir. 2007) [attempted public sexual indecency to a minor under Ariz. Rev. Stat. §13-1001, 13-1403(B) does not constitute sexual abuse of a minor under the generic federal definition because the minor does not have to be touched or even aware of the offending conduct for a conviction and the attempt statute is broader than the federal definition]; *Stubbs v. Att'y Gen. of the U.S.,* 452 F.3d 251 (3d Cir. 2006) [N.J. Stat. Ann. §2C:24–4(a), concerning "engag[ing] in sexual conduct which would impair or debauch the morals of the child," is not an aggravated felony because it does not necessarily require that a past act with a child actually occur as does 18 U.S.C. §3509(a)(8) addressed in *Matter of Rodriguez-Rodriguez*]; *Singh v. Ashcroft,* 383 F.3d 144 (3d Cir. 2004) [unlawful sexual conduct in the third degree under 11 Del. C. §767 is not sexual abuse of a minor because under the categorical approach the statute does not address minors]; *U.S. v. Pallares-Galan,* 359 F.3d 1088, 1099–103 (9th Cir. 2004) [a misdemeanor conviction under Cal. Penal Code §647.6(a) for Annoying or Molesting a Child Under 18 is not an aggravated felony]; *Gonzalez v. Ashcroft,* 369 F.Supp.2d 442, 447–54 (S.D.N.Y. 2005) [N.Y. Penal Law §263.05 regarding parents consenting to the participation of their child in a sexual performance has no *scienter* requirement]; *see also Gattem v. Gonzales,* 412 F.3d 758 (7th Cir. 2005) (Posner, J., dissenting) [an offense involving mere solicitation of a sexual act without knowledge that the person solicited is a minor is not "sexual abuse of a minor"].

(2) Rape—*Silva v. Gonzales,* 455 F.3d 26 (1st Cir. 2006) [statutory rape under Mass. Gen. Laws ch. 265 §23 is an aggravated felony]; *Rivas-Gomez v. Gonzales,* 441 F.3d 1072, 1074–79 (9th Cir. 2006) [Or. Rev. Stat. §163.355 (rape in the third degree), which criminalizes as a felony sexual intercourse with another person under 16 years of age, constitutes an aggravated felony as "rape"]; *Castro-Baez v. Reno,* 217 F.3d 1057 (9th Cir. 2000) [rape in violation of Cal. Penal Code §261(a)(3) is aggravated felony].

Felony Conviction Not Necessary—A person convicted of misdemeanor sexual abuse is an aggravated felon. *Matter of Small,* 23 I&N Dec. 448 (BIA 2002) [conviction for misdemeanor sexual abuse in the second degree, in violation of N.Y. Penal Law §130.60(2), is aggravated felony]; *Guerrero-Perez v. INS,* 242 F.3d 727 (7th Cir.), *reh'g denied* 256 F.3d 546 (7th Cir. 2001) [rejected analysis in *Matter of Crammond,* 23 I&N Dec. 9 (BIA 2001), *vacated on jurisdictional grounds*, 23 I&N Dec. 179 (BIA 2001), and found that a misdemeanor offense for sexual abuse of a minor under Illinois law constituted an aggravated felony]; *U.S. v. Marin-Navarette,* 244 F.3d 1284 (11th Cir. 2001) [although attempted child molestation in the third degree is a misdemeanor under Washington State law it is an aggravated felony].

3.b. *Illicit trafficking in controlled substance* (as defined in 21 U.S.C. §802), including drug trafficking crime as defined under 18 U.S.C. §924(c)

Under section 18 U.S.C. §924(c)(2) drug trafficking crimes include: "any felony punishable under the Controlled Substances Act (21 U.S.C. §801 *et seq.*), the Controlled Substance Import and Export Act (21 U.S.C. §921 *et seq.*), or the Maritime Drug Law Enforcement Act (46 U.S.C. §1901 *et seq.*)." The statute requires that the drug being sold is a controlled substance or otherwise falls under the federal law crimes. *Wilson v. Ashcroft,* 350 F.3d 377, 381–82 (3d Cir. 2003) [where it was unclear if the NJ statute for possession with intent to distribute fell within the exception to drug trafficking under 21 U.S.C. §841(b)(1)(D) regarding a small amount of marijuana for no remuneration, the court reversed the finding that it was an aggravated felony]; *Lara-Chacon v. Ashcroft,* 345 F.3d 1148, 1151–54 (9th Cir. 2003) [Arizona money laundering statute was not drug trafficking crime because the full range of conduct did not encompass drug trafficking and IJ could not rely on pre-sentence report to encompass drug trafficking]. *But see Salviejo-Fernandez v. Gonzales,* 455 F.3d 1063, 1066–68 (9th Cir. 2006) [Cal. Health & Safety Code §11366 penalizing every person who opens or maintains any place for the purpose of unlawfully selling, giving away, or using controlled substances is an aggravated felony]; *U.S. v. Palacios-Quinonez,* 431 F.3d 471 (5th Cir. 2005) [Cal. Health & Safety Code §11351, which includes "purchasing for purposes of sale" of a drug is an aggravated felony warranting a 16-level upward adjustment in sentencing]; *Ali v. Ashcroft,* 395 F.3d 722, 727–28 (7th Cir. 2005) [conviction for possession of 200 grams or less of THC with intent to deliver, in violation of Wis. Stat. §961.41(1m)(h)(1), is an aggravated felony]; *Gousse v. Ashcroft,* 339 F.3d 91 (2d Cir. 2003) [adopted categorical approach and found Conn. Gen. Stat. 21a-277(a) is an aggravated felony because the drug he hypothetically sold was a drug listed under federal law, although use of the categorical approach was complicated by respondent's *Alford* plea in which he did not admit the facts of a crime during the plea]; *Evola v. Carbone,* 365 F.Supp.2d 592 (D.N.J. 2005) [conviction for 21 U.S.C. §843(b) regarding the use of a communication device to facilitate a conspiracy to distribute and possess with intent to distribute a controlled substance is an aggravated felony].

In two cases the BIA has established a general approach to determine when a conviction will be determined to be a drug trafficking crime for purposes of this section. *See Matter of Barrett,* 20 I&N Dec. 171 (BIA 1990), *Matter of Davis,* 20 I&N Dec. 536 (BIA 1992). Under the *Davis/Barrett* approach there are two routes to determine a conviction under the statute: (1) whether the conviction involved "illicit trafficking in any controlled substance" or (2) whether the conviction is defined as a "drug trafficking crime (as defined in 924(c) of Title 18)." *Matter of Davis, supra.*

The BIA's approach in *Barrett* was confirmed by amendments made to the definition of the aggravated felony statute that added the term "any illicit trafficking in any controlled substance" to the definition of aggravated felony and determined that aggravated felonies encompassed offenses "whether in violation of Federal or State law." *See* §501 of IMMACT90, PL 101-649, 104 Stat. 4978, 5048, and §306(a)(1) MTINA, PL 102-232, 105 Stat. 1733, 1751 (1991); *See also* H.R. Rep. No. 681 (1990), *reprinted at* 1990 U.S.C.C.A.N. 6472 at 6553; *Paxton v. INS,* 745 F.Supp. 1261 (E.D. Mich. 1990); and *Leader v. Blackman,* 744 F.Supp. 500 (S.D.N.Y. 1990).

Under the first prong of the *Davis/Barrett* approach, a conviction for "illicit trafficking in a controlled substance" occurs if: (1) the offense is a felony under the law of the convicting sovereign whether state or federal and (2) the offense contains a "trafficking element" such that it involves "the unlawful trading or dealing of a controlled substance." *Matter of Davis,* 20 I&N Dec. 536 at 541 (BIA 1992). Thus, an offense that is not a felony and/or lacks a "sufficient nexus to the trade or dealing of controlled substances," *Id.,* is not a drug trafficking crime for purposes of the statute. *See, e.g., Steele v. Blackman,* 236 F.3d 130 (3d Cir. 2001) [finding that distribution of less than 30 grams of marijuana without remuneration is not a drug trafficking crime]; *Sandoval-Lua v. Gonzales,* 499 F.3d 1121 (9th Cir. 2007) [a conviction under Cal. Health & Safety Code §11379(a) contains a solicitation element, *e.g.,* "offer" to transport controlled substance, and therefore is broader than the generic drug trafficking crime defined under the Controlled Substances Act]; *U.S. v. Gonzales,* 484 F.3d 712, 714 (5th Cir.), *cert. denied,* 127 S.Ct. 3031 (2007) [holding that Texas offense covering offering to sell a controlled substance does not come within definition of drug trafficking offense under U.S.S.G. §2L1.2] *U.S. v. Aguilar-Ortiz,* 450 F.3d 1271 (11th Cir. 2006) [finding that solicitation to deliver cocaine under Fla. Stat. §777.04(2), when it involves a small quantity of drugs (and in an amount less than the trafficking definition Fla. Stat. §893.135(1)(b) of 28 grams or more), is in essence, under the categorical approach, attempted possession without intent to distribute and is therefore *not* a drug trafficking crime for purposes of sentence enhancement]. In determining whether the statute is for drug trafficking, it is necessary to look beyond the title of the statute to determine the actual charge and conviction. *Gerbier v. Holmes,* 280 F.3d 297, 313–14 (3d Cir. 2002) [respondent was convicted under a Delaware trafficking statute but he pled guilty only to possession of between 5 and 50 grams of cocaine, which is not a trafficking offense]; *Wilson v. Ashcroft,* 350 F.3d 377, 381–82 (3d Cir. 2003) [where it was unclear if the NJ statute for possession with intent to distribute fell within the exception to drug trafficking under 21 U.S.C. §841(b)(1)(D) regarding a small amount of marijuana for no remuneration, the court reversed the finding that it was an aggravated felony]; *U.S. v. Rivera-Sanchez,* 247 F.3d 905 (9th Cir. 2001) (*en banc*) [applied *Leyva-Licea* in the sentencing context to find that a state offense that includes "offers" to transport, import, sell, furnish, administer, or give away marijuana thus includes solicitation conduct not covered under the Controlled Substances Act and, thus, could not categorically be determined to be an aggravated felony]; *Leyva-Licea v. INS,* 187 F.3d 1147 (9th Cir. 1999) [solicitation to possess marijuana for sale under Arizona law is not an aggravated felony conviction because it is not a drug trafficking crime under the Controlled Substances Act as that act does not mention solicitation]. *Cf. Garcia v. Att'y Gen. of the U.S.,* 462 F.3d 287 (3d Cir. 2006) [respondent's conviction under 35 Pa. Stat. Ann §780-113(a)(30), where he pled guilty to delivery and possession with intent to deliver marijuana, contains a trafficking element under *Gerbier*]. *But see Rendon v. Mukasey*, __F.3d ___(9th Cir. Mar. 19, 2008) 2008 WL 726354 [under the categorical approach, Kan. Stat. Ann. §65-4163(a) was not an aggravated felony because it contained a solicitation component; however, under the modified categorical approach the conviction was clearly one of possession with intent to sell a controlled substance]; *Jeune v. Att'y Gen. of the U.S.*, 476 F.3d 199 (3d Cir. 2007) [respondent convicted under the same statute as in *Garcia* which may or may not be a drug trafficking crime under the categorical approach, but unlike *Garcia* there was insufficient evidence to indicate this was a trafficking offense when the permissible documents were reviewed, even though the sentencing was under a drug trafficking provision]. Telephone facilitation offense may be a drug trafficking crime. *U.S. v. Orihuela*, 320 F.3d 1302 (11th Cir. 2003) [telephone facilitation offense can constitute drug trafficking offense for purpose of sentence enhancement where underlying offense was felony and sentence imposed exceeded 13 months]; *U.S. v. Zuñiga-Guerrero*, 460 F.3d 733, 739 (6th Cir. 2006) [same following *Orihuela* and cases cited therein]; *Kayrouz v. Ashcroft*, 261 F.Supp.2d 760, 763–64 (E.D. Ky. 2003).

Under the second prong of the *Davis/Barrett* approach, a state drug conviction could be an aggravated felony under the INA if it is analogous to an offense punishable under one of the 3 federal acts specified in 18 U.S.C. §924(c)(2) and is a felony under federal law. *Matter of Davis*, 20 I&N Dec. at 543, *see also Matter of L-G-*, 21 I&N Dec. 89 (BIA1995) *reaff'd by Matter of K-V-D-*, 22 I&N Dec. 1163 (BIA 1999). Under this approach, some courts have held that it is not necessary that the conviction have a trafficking component. *Garcia-Echaverria v. U.S.*, 376 F.3d 507, 511–14 (6th Cir. 2004) [possession with intent to sell even without a trafficking component is an aggravated felony by virtue of 21 U.S.C. §§841(a)(1) and (b)(1)(D)]. The second requirement under *Matter of Davis* that the person must be convicted of a crime that is a felony under *federal* law has now been upheld by the Supreme Court in *Lopez v. Gonzales*, 549 U.S. ___, 127 S.Ct. 625 (2006). In *Lopez* the Court rejected the approach articulated in *Matter of Yanez-Garcia*, 23 I&N Dec. 390 (BIA 2002) that a state felony conviction is sufficient to be an aggravated felony under 18 U.S.C. §924(c)(2) even if it is not a felony under federal law. *Lopez* determined that a South Dakota conviction for aiding and abetting another person's possession of cocaine, while a felony under state law, could not be an aggravated felony that barred cancellation of removal because under federal law the conviction is treated as a misdemeanor. The Court held that "a state offense constitutes a 'felony punishable under the Controlled Substances Act' only if it proscribes conduct punishable as a felony under that federal law." 549 U.S. ___, ____, 127 S.Ct. 625, 633 (2006). In reaching it conclusion the Court noted that: (1) ordinarily "trafficking" "means some sort of commercial dealing" which was absent from the possession charge and that to "turn simple possession into trafficking [is] just what the English language tells us not to expect"; (2) there are a limited number of crimes where Congress has specifically defined possession crimes as trafficking, *see* 549 U.S. at ___ n.6, 127 S.Ct. 625, 630 n.6 (2006); (3) the language in the aggravated felony statute requiring that it be a "felony punishable under the [CSA]" means that it must be a felony under federal law and "using the phrase to cover even a misdemeanor punishable under the Act would be so much trickery, violating 'the cardinal rule that statutory language must be read in context'"; (4) the language in INA §101(a)(43) stating that aggravated felonies apply to an offense "whether in violation of Federal or State law" is limited to describing generic offenses, such as trafficking offenses, whether under state or federal law but that the crime must still be a felony under federal law; (5) the definition under 21 U.S.C. §802(13) does not apply in determining whether a conviction is a felony because it must be defined as a felony under the CSA, *see* 549 U.S. at ___n. 7, 127 S.Ct. 625, 631 n.7 (2006); (6) the government's reading of the cancellation provision barring relief for aggravated felons when states define conduct as felonies would undermine the federal scheme. *See also Arce-Vences v. Mukasey*, 512 F.3d 167, 170–71 (5th Cir. 2007) [simple possession of more than 50 pounds but less than 200 pounds under Texas Health and Safety Code §481.121(b)(5) is not an aggravated felony post-*Lopez*]; *Tostado v. Carlson*, 481 F.3d 1012 (8th Cir. 2007) [where *two* state law convictions for possession of cocaine and possession of cannabis would constitute misdemeanors if prosecuted under the CSA they do not constitute drug trafficking crimes for the aggravated felony statute]; *Gonzales-Gomez v. Achim*, 441 F.3d 532 (7th Cir. 2006) [rejected position that a state-law felony that would be punishable only as a misdemeanor under federal law is an aggravated felony]; *Gerbier v. Holmes,* 280 F.3d 297, 309–10 (3d Cir. 2002) [affirming BIA's former approach in *Matter of L-G-* and noting that despite the language in 21 U.S.C. §§802(13) & (44), which are sentence enhancement provisions, a state felony conviction cannot be counted as a felony for purposes of the aggravated felony statute]; *Aguirre v. INS,* 79 F.3d 315 (2d Cir. 1996) [relying on prior BIA decision but doing so in the context of deferring to BIA's interpretation at that time]. In *Cazarez-Gutierrez v. Ashcroft,* 382 F.3d 905 (9th Cir. 2004), the Ninth Circuit following *Gerbier* and *Aguirre* rejected *Yanez-Garcia* and held that "a state drug offense is not an aggravated felony for immigration purposes unless it is punishable as a felony under CSA or other federal drug laws named in the definition of 'drug trafficking crime,' or is a crime involving a trafficking element." *Cazarez-Gutierrez,* 382 F.3d at 919. *Accord, Gonzales-Gomez v. Achim,* 441 F.3d 532 (7th Cir. 2006) [rejected position that Illinois felony for possession of cocaine that would be punishable only as a misdemeanor under federal law is an aggravated felony]; *U.S. v. Palacios-Suarez,* 418 F.3d 692 (6th Cir. 2005) [finding that state simple possession felony not to be an aggravated felony in federal sentencing context because the offense would not be a felony under federal law and indicating that the rule is the same in the immigration context]; *Ferreira v. Ashcroft,* 382 F.3d 1045, 1050 (9th Cir. 2004) [possession of methamphetamine under Cal. Health & Safety Code §11377 would not be a felony under the CSA because the maximum sentence for possession of a scheduled drug under the CSA is one year. Conviction would also not be an aggravated felony even if state felonies would be considered because the sentence under the "wobbler" statute directed that the conviction be treated as a misdemeanor]; *U.S. v. Peralta-Espinoza,* 413 F.Supp.2d 970 (E.D. Wis. 2006) [in sentencing guideline case, an aggravated felony must be a felony punishable under the CSA].

Prior to the Supreme Court's decision is *Lopez,* the BIA had held that when a conviction is not a felony under state law, it will not be considered an aggravated felony. *Matter of Elgendi,* 23 I&N Dec. 515 (BIA 2002), *superseded by U.S. v. Simpson,* 319 F.3d 81 (2d Cir. 2002) [finding that two convictions of misdemeanor possession of marijuana in the fifth degree under N.Y. Penal Code §221.10 was not a felony conviction as defined under 21 U.S.C. §802(13) and therefore not an aggravated felony]; *Matter of Santos-Lopez,* 23 I&N Dec. 419 (BIA 2002) [because possession of marijuana under Tex. Penal Code §481.121 is classified as a misdemeanor, respondent is *not* convicted of an aggravated felony even though possession of marijuana is an offense punishable under the CSA, 21 U.S.C. §844(a)].

Under the federal felony standard, however, a state conviction may be an aggravated felony where it is a misdemeanor under state law but a felony under federal law. Thus, even if drug trafficking was not a felony under state law, it can still be under federal law. *Matter of Aruna,* 24 I&N Dec. 492 (BIA 2008) [conviction for conspiracy to distribute a controlled dangerous substance (marijuana) in violation of Maryland law, although a misdemeanor, is an aggravated felony under §§101(a)(43)(B) & (U) because under the categorical approach its elements correspond to the elements of the federal felony of conspiracy to distribute an indeterminate quantity of marijuana under 21 U.S.C. §§841(a)(1) & (b)(1)(D) and 846]; *Matter of Davis,* 20 I&N Dec. 536 (BIA 1992); *Matter of Ponce de Leon,* 21 I&N Dec. 154 (BIA 1996) [sale of marijuana even if not punished harshly under state law is aggravated felony if it is drug trafficking crime and felony under federal law]; *U.S. v. Graham,* 927 F.Supp. 619 (W.D.N.Y. 1996) [state law for criminal sale of marijuana, where misdemeanor under NY law, is felony under federal law and person is therefore aggravated felon]. *But see U.S. v. Gomez-Ortiz,* 62 F.Supp.2d 508 (D.R.I. 1999) [Mass. statute that was misdemeanor for first offense possession with intent to distribute was not aggravated felony under sentencing guidelines]. To determine whether the offense constitutes an aggravated felony under federal law, it is only necessary that there is a federal analogue under one of the 3 federal statutes and that it is punishable as a felony. However, a misdemeanor marijuana "sale" offense that might cover transfer of a small amount of marijuana for no compensation should not be considered an "illicit trafficking" aggravated felony if the offense might cover transfer of a small amount of marijuana for no compensation, by analogy to 21 U.S.C. §841(b)(4) [distributing a small amount of marijuana for no remuneration is treated as simple possession misdemeanor under 21 U.S.C. §844]. *See Wilson v. Ashcroft,* 350 F.3d 377 (3d Cir. 2003); *Steele v. Blackman,* 236 F.3d 130 (3d Cir. 2001). *See also U.S. v. Aguilar-Ortiz,* 450 F.3d 1271 (11th Cir. 2006) [finding that solicitation to deliver cocaine under Fla. Stat. §777.04(2), when it involves a small quantity of drugs (and in an amount less than the trafficking definition Fla. Stat. §893.135(1)(b) of 28 grams or more), is in essence, under the categorical approach, attempted possession without intent to distribute and is therefore *not* a drug trafficking crime for purposes of sentence enhancement].

Whether a substantive federal offense is a felony is controlled by 18 U.S.C. §3559, which defines a felony as an offense for which the term of imprisonment exceeds one year. In *Matter of Crammond*, 23 I&N Dec. 9 (BIA 2001), *vacated on jurisdictional grounds*, 23 I&N Dec. 179 (BIA 2001), the BIA determined that a felony is defined as a term of "more than 1 year" imprisonment pursuant to 18 U.S.C. §3559(a)(5) while a misdemeanor is defined as "one year or less" of imprisonment under 18 U.S.C. §§3559(a)(6)–(8). *See Lopez v. Gonzales*, 549 U.S. ___, 127 S.Ct. 625 (2006) [the Court held that "a state offense constitutes a 'felony punishable under the Controlled Substances Act' only if it proscribes conduct punishable as a felony under that federal law."]. *But see Guerrero-Perez v. INS*, 242 F.3d 727 (7th Cir.) *reh'g denied*, 256 F.3d 546 (7th Cir. 2001) [rejected analysis in *Crammond* and found that a misdemeanor offense for sexual abuse of a minor under Illinois law constituted an aggravated felony]; *U.S. v. Marin-Navarette*, 244 F.3d 1284 (11th Cir. 2001) [although attempted child molestation in the third degree is a misdemeanor under Washington State law it is an aggravated felony]; *cf. Francis v. Reno*, 269 F.3d 162, 167–71 (3d Cir. 2001) [rejected reliance on §3559 analysis for nondrug case (18 U.S.C. §16, regarding crime of violence) and found that state misdemeanor statute where person sentenced to over one year was not an aggravated felony].

Certain state misdemeanors may be aggravated felonies under federal law if they are defined as felonies under federal law. *See Lopez v. Gonzales*, 549 U.S.__,___ n.6, 127 S.Ct. 625, 630 n.6 (2006) [recognizing that despite the clear "English language" distinction between possession and trafficking, Congress has at times defined certain state possession offenses, such as possession of cocaine base or recidivist possession, as illicit trafficking]. Both the BIA and the courts have looked to 21 U.S.C. §844(a) as an analogous federal statute in determining whether the state crime is a federal felony for purposes of the aggravated felony provision. Under 21 U.S.C. §844(a), a person convicted for the first time of possession of more than five grams of crack (mixture which contains cocaine base) may be considered an aggravated felon because possession of such an amount of "crack" is treated as a felony under federal law even if it may be a misdemeanor possession charge under state law. Pursuant to §844(a) it is unlawful for "any person knowingly or intentionally to possess a controlled substance..." If there was a prior drug conviction, the sentence may be 2 years. Thus, a state possession charge may under certain circumstances be analogous to a felony under 21 U.S.C. §844(a) and therefore be an aggravated felony. Under this statute courts *prior to Lopez* have found that two state misdemeanor *possession* charges are an aggravated felony. *U.S. v. Sanchez-Villalobos*,412 F.3d 572 (5th Cir. 2005) [found second misdemeanor possession offense constituted an aggravated felony]; *U.S. v. Simpson*, 319 F.3d 81 (2d Cir. 2002) [found second misdemeanor possession offense to be aggravated felony in criminal illegal reentry sentencing context, but noting at fn. 9 that the Court declined to comment on whether such offense would also be an aggravated felony in the immigration context]; *U.S. v. Forbes*, 16 F.3d 1294, 1300–01 (1st Cir. 1994) [2 or more convictions under state law for simple possession is an aggravated felony]; *Amaral v. INS*, 977 F.2d 33, 35–36 (1st Cir. 1992) [same]; *U.S. v. Haggerty*, 886 F.Supp. 709 (D.S.D. 1995); *cf. Berhe v. Gonzales*, 464 F.3d 74, 85–87 (1st Cir. 2006) [adopting the analysis in *Amaral* that a state misdemeanor could be an aggravated felony if it is a felony under federal law, but finding that the failure to charge respondent with his prior drug possession conviction in obtaining his more recent drug possession conviction barred his current possession conviction from being an aggravated felony where the former conviction was not otherwise part of the record of conviction]. *But see Tostado v. Carlson*, 481 F.3d 1012 (8th Cir. 2007) [where *two* state law convictions for possession of cocaine and possession of cannabis would constitute misdemeanors if prosecuted under the CSA they do not constitute drug trafficking crimes for the aggravated felony statute]; *Smith v. Gonzales*, 468 F.3d 272 (5th Cir. 2006) [found state drug possession offense preceded by a prior drug conviction not to be an offense that would be a felony under federal law, because later offense was committed while the individual was still within the time to seek leave to appeal the prior conviction]; *U.S. v. Palacios-Suarez*, 418 F.3d 692 (6th Cir. 2005) [second state drug possession offense not a felony under federal law because later offense was committed while prior drug case was still pending in criminal court]; *Berhe v. Gonzales,* 464 F.3d 74 (1st Cir. 2006) ["Because Berhe's 1996 conviction is not part of the record of the 2003 conviction, the government did not establish that Berhe was convicted of hypothetical federal felony]; *Steele v. Blackman,* 236 F.3d 130 (3d Cir. 2001) [finding that three state convictions for possession do not amount to an aggravated felony because no determination was made in the second possession charge that the state sentence was based upon the prior possession conviction.]; *Wilson v. Ashcroft,* 350 F.3d 377, 381–82 (3d Cir. 2003) [where it was unclear if the NJ statute for possession with intent to distribute fell within the exception to drug trafficking under 21 U.S.C. §841(b)(1)(D) regarding a small amount of marijuana for no remuneration, the court reversed the finding that it was an aggravated felony]; *Gerbier v. Holmes,* 280 F.3d 297, 316–18 (3d Cir. 2002) [finding that "in order for a state drug conviction to constitute a hypothetical federal felony under §844(a) based on the prior drug conviction enhancement, we must be satisfied that the state adjudication possessed procedural safeguards equivalent to [those] that would have accompanied the enhancement in federal court."]. *See also Oliveira-Ferreira v. Ashcroft,* 382 F.3d 1045 (9th Cir. 2004) [second possession conviction should not be treated as punishable by more than one year's imprisonment and therefore not a felony by virtue of a recidivist sentence enhancement] *U.S. v. Ballesteros-Ruiz,* 319 F.3d 1101 (9th Cir. 2003) [in sentencing enhancement case the fact that a second or third possession offense may be punishable under federal law by a 2- or 3-year term for recidivism does not make them aggravated felonies]; *U.S. v. Arellano-Torres,* 303 F.3d 1173, 1178 (9th Cir. 2002) [same];

Recidivist Possession *Post–Lopez v. Gonzales*—In *Matter of Carachuri-Rosendo,* 24 I&N Dec. 382 (BIA 2007) and *Matter of Thomas,* 24 I&N Dec. 416 (BIA 2007), the BIA addressed whether the "recidivist possession" definition under 21 U.S.C. §844(a) (2000) would make two drug possession convictions an aggravated felony for purposes of that section. The Board determined that absent controlling authority a state conviction based upon recidivism will not be an aggravated felony unless the respondent's status as a recidivist drug offender was either admitted by her or determined by judge or jury in a state proceeding. The Board stated: "[W]e find it inappropriate to treat a series of misdemeanor possession offenses as 'trafficking' felonies unless we are confident that the State offense corresponds in a meaningful way to the essential requirements that must be met before a felony sentence can be imposed under Federal law on the basis of recidivism." *Matter of Carachuri-Rosendo,* 24 I&N Dec.382, 390 (BIA 2007) It is not necessary that the structure of the state law process be comparable to how recidivism is determined under the Controlled Substantive Act but it must provide comparable treatment by providing a defendant with notice and an opportunity to be heard on whether recidivist punishment is proper. *Id* at 391. In *Carachuri-Rosendo*, the Board however determined that it was bound by Fifth Circuit law in *U.S. v. Sanchez-Villalobos,* 412 F.3d 572 (5th Cir. 2005) *cert. denied,* 546 U.S. 1137 (2006) because the Fifth Circuit in that case held that the defendant was an aggravated felon by virtue of a second drug possession conviction solely because that conviction was for a felony. In *Matter of Thomas*, the Board, following the reasoning in *Matter of Carachuri-Rosendo*, found that a respondent's second conviction under Florida law for simple possession of marijuana is not for recidivist possession under 21 U.S.C. §844(a) because it did not arise from a state proceeding in which his status as a recidivist drug offender was either admitted or determined by a judge or jury. *But see U.S. v. Pacheco-Diaz,* 506 F.3d 545, 548–50 (7th Cir. 2007) *reh'g denied* 513 F.3d 776 (7th Cir. 2008) [in a post-*Lopez* Sentencing Guideline case, the court determined that two separate convictions for possession under Illinois law are an aggravated felony because had the defendant been charged in federal court he would have been subject to recidivist treatment].

Travel Act and telephone facilitation violations may be aggravated felonies. *U.S. v. Orihuela,* 320 F.3d 1302 (11th Cir. 2003) [telephone facilitation offense can constitute drug trafficking offense for purpose of sentence enhancement where underlying offense was felony and sentence imposed exceeded 13 months]; *U.S. v. Zuñiga-Guerrero,* 460 F.3d 733, 739 (6th Cir. 2006) [same following *Orihuela* and cases cited therein]; *Evola v. Carbone,* 365 F.Supp.2d 592 (D.N.J. 2005) [conviction for 21 U.S.C. §843(b) regarding the use of a communication device to facilitate a conspiracy to distribute and possess with intent to distribute a controlled substance is an aggravated felony]. One circuit court has found that a violation of the Travel Act is a violation of a law relating to aggravated felonies concerned with drug trafficking where respondent was transporting drugs in interstate commerce. *Urena-Ramirez v. Ashcroft,* 341 F.3d 51, 53–57 (1st Cir. 2003) [fact that Travel Act involves other criminal conduct does not mean it is not also a law relating to a controlled substance];

3.c. *Illicit trafficking in any firearms or destructive devices* as defined in 18 U.S.C. §921; or explosive materials as defined in 18 U.S.C. §841(c) (*see also* ¶ 3.e, *infra*).

Kuhali v. Reno, 266 F.3d 93, 107–10 (2d Cir. 2001) [conspiracy to export firearms and ammunition without a license under 22 U.S.C. §2778 is an aggravated felony because the BIA's interpretation, given *Chevron* deference, defines trafficking in "business and merchant" terms regarding "trading, selling or dealing in goods"]. *But see Joseph v. Att'y Gen. of the U.S.,* 445 F.3d 123 (3d Cir. 2006) [a conviction under 18 U.S.C. §922(a)(3) for transporting or receiving firearms purchased or otherwise obtained in another state is not a trafficking offense and therefore not an aggravated felony].

3.d. *Any offense related to laundering of monetary instruments* as described in 18 U.S.C. §§1956 or 1957, relating to engaging in monetary transactions in property derived from specific unlawful activity, if the amount of the funds exceeds $10,000

Chowdhury v. INS, 249 F.3d 970 (9th Cir. 2001) [reversed finding of deportability where the amount of funds involved was one check for $1,310 even though restitution was ordered in the amount of $967,753 because the statute relates to the amount of funds involved in the transaction and not the loss to the victim].

3.e. Explosives, firearms, arson

(1) Offenses described in 18 U.S.C. §842(h) relating to transportation or receipt of stolen explosives and 18 U.S.C. §842(i) barring certain categories of persons such as drug users and addicts and those under indictment for transporting or receiving any explosive.

Offenses described in 18 U.S.C. §844(d)–(i), including: transporting or receiving explosives to injure persons or destroy property [§844(d)]; using telephone or mail to threaten injury to persons or property [§844(e)]; using fire and explosives to damage or destroy or attempt to damage and destroy property of U.S. or any institution receiving federal financial assistance [§844(f)]; possessing explosives at an airport under certain circumstances [§844(g)]; using fire (arson) or an explosive to commit any felony or causing an explosion during the commission of any felony [§844(h)] damaging or destroying property or attempting to do so by fire (arson) or explosives [§844(i)].

(2) Offenses described in 18 U.S.C. §922(g)(1)–(5), (j), (n), (o), (p), or (r), barring certain categories of persons, including aliens illegally or unlawfully in the U.S. from possessing or receiving any firearms or ammunition [18 U.S.C. §922(g)], *Alvarado v. Gonzales,* 484 F.3d 535 (8th Cir. 2007) [conviction under §922(g)(3) was an aggravated felony even though sentencing noted weapons were used solely for lawful sporting purposes]; *U.S. v. Mendoza-Reyes,* 331 F.3d 1119 (9th Cir. 2003) [conviction under Wash. Rev. Code §9.41.040(1) regarding possession of a firearm by person who has been convicted of a serious crime is a categorical match to §922(g)(1)]; receiving, storing or selling stolen firearms or ammunition [§922(j)]; shipping or transporting firearms or ammunition if under indictment [§922(n)]; transferring or possessing a machine gun under certain circumstances [§922(o)] possessing, selling, or manufacturing parts of firearms that could go through airport and other metal detectors undetected [§922(p)]; assembling semiautomatic rifles or shotguns from foreign parts when the rifle or shotgun is prohibited from importation [§922(r)].*Matter of Vasquez-Muniz,* 23 I&N Dec. 207 (BIA 2002) [prior felon convicted under Cal. Penal Code §12021(a)(1) is convicted of an aggravated felony under INA §101(a)(43)(E)(ii) because it is an offense "described in" §922(g)(1)]; *Negrete-Rodriguez v. Mukasey,* 518 F.3d 497 (7th Cir. 2008) [same, regarding unlawful possession of a weapon by a felon in violation of 720 Ill. Comp Stat. 5/24-1.1(a)]; *U.S. v. Castillo-Rivera,* 244 F.3d 1020, 1025 (9th Cir. 2001) [same]. *But see U.S. v. Sandoval-Barajas,* 206 F.3d 853 (9th Cir. 2000) [possession of a firearm by noncitizen under Washington state law is not an aggravated felony]. NIV holders are also prohibited from possessing and/or transferring firearms and ammunition without a waiver. 27 C.F.R. pt. 478. And persons who are

EWI without parole status are prohibited from possessing weapons under ATF regulations. 27 C.F.R. §478.11. So are applicants for TPS, *U.S. v. Flores,* 404 F.3d 320 (5th Cir. 2005) [a person who *applies* for TPS who entered the U.S. illegally may be charged criminally as an alien illegally or unlawfully in the U.S. in possession of a firearm in violation of §922(g)(5)(A)]; or AOS applicants under LIFE Act, *U.S. v. Lucio,* 428 F.3d 519 (5th Cir. 2005) [adjustment under LIFE Act with employment authorization convicted under §922(g)(5)(A)] on the theory that the status does not constitute lawful presence. However, a person *granted* TPS is not an illegal alien or unlawfully in U.S. for purposes of §922(g)(5)(A). *U.S. v. Orellana,* 405 F.3d 360 (5th Cir. 2005) [applying rule of lenity given the ambiguity of §922(g)(5)(A) and the questionable interpretation of the ATF regulation, Congress did not intend to criminalize the possession of firearms by persons granted TPS]. Persons who have filed for AOS, if otherwise not lawful in the U.S., are also considered illegal for purposes of the statute even if they have temporary permission to remain while the AOS application is pending. *U.S. v. Latu,* 479 F.3d 1153 (9th Cir. 2007) and cases cited therein; 27 C.F.R. §478.11(b). *But see U.S. v. Bruno-Muzquiz,* 412 F.3d 1052, 1054 (9th Cir. 2005); *U.S. v. Hernandez,* 913 F.2d 1506, 1513–14 (10th Cir. 1990).

(3) Offenses under 18 U.S.C. §924(b) and (h) relating to: transporting or receiving firearms or ammunition with intent to commit an offense punishable by imprisonment of more than one year [18 U.S.C. §924(b)]; transferring a firearm knowing that it will be used to commit a crime of violence (*i.e.*, crime where element is use of force or substantial risk of force) or drug trafficking [18 U.S.C. §924(h)].

(4) Offenses under 26 U.S.C. §5861 relating to receipt, manufacture or possession of firearms without proper licenses or taxes.

3.f. **Crimes of Violence (COVs)**

An aggravated felony under INA §101(a)(43) includes any COV as defined in 18 U.S.C. §16 (not including a purely political offense) for which the term of imprisonment imposed (regardless of any suspension of imprisonment) is at least one year. Section 16 defines crime of violence as: §16(a) "any offense that has as an element the use or attempted use or threatened use of physical force against the person or property of another," or §16(b) "any other offense that is a felony and that, by its nature, involves a substantial risk that physical force against the person or property of another may be used in the course of committing the offense."

The BIA's definition of crime of violence includes any offense where either: (a) the elements of the offense must be such that the use, attempted use, or threatened use of physical force is an element, or (b) the nature of the crime—as evidenced by the generic elements of the offense—must be such that its commission ordinarily would present a risk that physical force would be used against the person or property of another irrespective of whether the risk develops or harm actually occurs. *Matter of Sweetser,* 22 I&N Dec. 709, 716 (BIA 1999) [criminal negligent child abuse does not by its nature involve substantial risk of physical force and distinguished sentencing guideline cases because they address risk of physical injury not risk of physical force]; *Matter of Palacios,* 22 I&N Dec. 434 (BIA 1998) (Arson in first degree under Alaska law does involve substantial risk); *Matter of Ramos,* 23 I&N Dec. 336, 342–46 (BIA 2002) [the language in 18 U.S.C. §16(b) regarding "may be used," "against," and "in the course of committing the offense" requires that an aggravated felony under this section involves a volitional not a negligent act and therefore an individual must act with at least recklessness or "recklessness plus"].

An offense will not be a COV if it lacks a *mens rea* requirement for a conviction or if a person may be convicted simply on a showing of negligence or less than intentional conduct. *Leocal v. Ashcroft,* 543 U.S. 1 (2004) [DUI causing serious bodily injury under Florida law was not a COV because the "use ... of physical force" under 16(a) or the "substantial risk that physical force ... may be used" under 16(b) are given an "identical construction requiring a higher *mens rea* than the merely accidental or negligent conduct involved in a DUI offense;"]. In *Leocal*, 125 S.Ct. 377 at 384 (2004), the Court expressly declined to decide whether more than negligent conduct, such as reckless conduct, would constitute an aggravated felony under 18 U.S.C. §16. *See U.S. v. Narvaez-Gomez,* 489 F.3d 970, 975–77 (9th Cir. 2007) [following *Fernandez-Ruiz* and holding that Cal. Penal Code §246 that criminalizes maliciously and willfully discharging a firearm at an inhabited dwelling was not categorically a COV because purely reckless conduct was sufficient for a conviction]; *Fernandez-Ruiz v. Gonzales,* 466 F.3d 1121 (9th Cir. 2006) (en banc) [misdemeanor domestic violence assault under Ariz. Rev. Stat. §§13-1203 and 13-3601 permit convictions for something short of intentional conduct including recklessness, gross negligence, and simple negligence and therefore cannot be a crime of violence post-*Leocal*]; *Malta-Espinoza v. Gonzales,* 478 F.3d 1080, 1084 (9th Cir. 2007) [reversing *Matter of Malta,* 23 I&N Dec. 656 (BIA 2004) and finding that stalking under Cal. Penal Code §646.9(b), where it involved reckless conduct, was insufficient to establish a COV]; *Garcia v. Gonzales,* 455 F.3d 465 (4th Cir. 2006) [reckless assault in the second degree under N.Y. Penal Law §120.05(4) is not an aggravated felony because reckless conduct cannot be a basis for crime of violence under §16(b)]; *Singh v. Gonzales,* 432 F.3d 533 (3d Cir. 2006) [recklessly endangering another person under Penn. Law is not a COV, because it requires no more than a *mens rea* of recklessness]; *Oyebanji v. Att'y Gen. of the U.S.,* 418 F.3d 260 (3d Cir. 2005) [reckless vehicular manslaughter is not a COV]; *Popal v. Gonzales,* 416 F.3d 249, 253–55 (3d Cir. 2005) [misdemeanor simple assault under 18 Pa. Cons. Stat. §2701(a)(1) is not a COV because it does not require a *mens rea* greater than recklessness for a conviction]; *Tran v. Gonzales,* 414 F.3d 464 (3d Cir. 2005) [conspiracy to commit reckless burning or exploding under 18 Pa. Cons. Stat. §3301(d)(2) regarding arson and related crimes is not a COV because recklessness will not suffice as the term "use" in §16(a) requires specific intent to use force and the crime by its nature does not involve a risk of intentionally using force under §16(b)]; *Bejarano-Urrutia v. Gonzales,* 413 F.3d 444 (4th Cir. 2005) [involuntary manslaughter is not a COV]; *Lara-Cazares v. Gonzales,* 408 F.3d 1217 (9th Cir. 2005) [gross vehicular manslaughter while intoxicated under Cal. Penal Code §191.5(a) is not a COV because under *Leocal* it is still negligent conduct (although gross negligence) and does not constitute the kind of active employment of force/intentional conduct necessary for a COV]; *Bazan-Reyes v. INS,* 256 F.3d 600, 605–12 (7th Cir. 2001) [homicide by intoxicated use of vehicle is not a COV under §§16(a) or (b)]; *U.S. v. Vargas-Duran,* 356 F.3d 598 (5th Cir. 2004) [Texas intoxication assault is not a COV under Sentencing Guideline similar to first prong of federal definition, because intentional use of force is not a necessary component of the offense]; *U.S. v. Lucio-Lucio,* 347 F.3d 1202 (10th Cir. 2003) [Texas DWI offense is not a COV under second prong of federal definition because it does not require intentional or close to intentional conduct]; *But see Blake v. Gonzales,* 481 F.3d 152 (2d Cir. 2007) [conviction under Mass. Gen. laws ch. 265 §13D for aggravated assault on a police officer is a COV under §16(b) despite the inclusion under Massachusetts common law of wanton or reckless conduct because such conduct must require violence and injury to obtain a conviction]; *Matter of Alcantar*, 20 I&N Dec. 801 (BIA 1994) [pre-*Leocal* involuntary manslaughter considered an aggravated felony].

A COV under §16(a) must also include a determination that the use of force is an "element" of the crime. *Szucz-Toldy v. Gonzales,* 400 F.3d 978 (7th Cir. 2005) [Illinois harassment by telephone is not a COV under §16(a)—the first prong of the federal definition—because the elements of the offense do not require the use, attempted use, or threatened use of physical force]; *Singh v. Ashcroft*, 386 F.3d 1228 (9th Cir. 2004) [harassment under Or. Rev. Stat. §166.065(1)(a)(A) is not a COV because it includes an offensive touching that is not aimed at creating physical injury and therefore does not have as an "element" the use of force].

A COV must also include a "risk that physical force ... may be used," not a "risk of physical injury" as defined under the Sentencing Guidelines §4B1.2(1)(ii). The courts distinguish between a risk of injury and a risk of the use of force, finding that only the latter is an aggravated felony. *Leocal v. Ashcroft,* 125 S.Ct. 377, 383 n.7 (2004) [distinguishing between risk of injury and risk of the use of force to determine that DUI causing serious bodily harm is not a COV]; *Jobson v. Ashcroft,* 326 F.3d 367, 373 (2d Cir. 2003) [finding that N.Y. involuntary manslaughter provision which may have resulted in death was not an aggravated felony because it is the risk of the use of force and not the risk of injury that is at issue and because the statute covered unintentional accidents caused by recklessness]; *Matter of Sweetser,* 22 I&N Dec. 709, 716 (BIA 1999) [criminal negligent child abuse does not by its nature involve substantial risk of physical force and distinguished sentencing guideline cases because they address risk of physical injury not risk of physical force].

The BIA looks only to whether the generic nature of the offense is an aggravated felony. *Matter of Ramos,* 23 I&N Dec. 336, 339 (BIA 2002); *Matter of Palacios, supra* at 436. In making that determination a federal standard must be applied and a conviction under a state statute cannot be presumed to be an equivalent federal crime for purposes of the aggravated felony statute. *Matter of Palacios, supra* at 438–57 (Rosenberg dissenting) citing *Taylor v. U.S.,* 495 U.S. 575, 579–82 (1990) and defining COV under federal law; *Szucz-Toldy v. Gonzales,* 400 F.3d 978, 981 (7th Cir. 2005) [court looks solely to the elements of the offense to determine whether it is a COV and court would only look beyond statute to person's record where a statute defines as a single felony some acts that constitute COV and some that do not]. *But see Xiong v. INS,* 173 F.3d 601, 605 (7th Cir. 1999) [the court may look beyond the record to the criminal complaint where it is not possible to determine the proper classification of the offense and where a hearing is not required to resolve contested factual issues].

When the conviction is under a statute that is divisible, it is necessary to look to the record of conviction (not the facts) "and to other documents admissible as evidence in proving a criminal conviction" to determine whether the specific offense will sustain an aggravated felony charge. *Matter of Sweetser, supra* at 714; *Santapaola v. Ashcroft*, 249 F.Supp.2d 181, 189–99 (D. Conn. 2003) [relying on plea transcript the court determined that a conviction under former Conn. Gen. Stat. §53-21 for injury to a minor, made the respondent removable as aggravated felon under divisible part]. *See in this section* "Categorical and Modified Categorical Approach," ¶ 4.f (p.192), *infra.*

(1) <u>"Crime of violence" under 18 U.S.C. §16 has been ruled to include</u>

Arson in the first degree, *Matter of Palacios,* 22 I&N Dec. 434 (BIA 1998) [under Alaska law]; *Mbea v. Gonzales,* 482 F.3d 276, 279–80 (4th Cir. 2007) [malicious burning of property in violation of D.C. Code §22-401]; **assault (simple)** *Singh v. Gonzales,* 432 F.3d 533, 538–40 (3d Cir. 2006) [simple assault under 18 Pa. Cons. Stat. Ann. §2701(a)(3), unlike §2701(a)(1), is an aggravated felony because it requires specific intent]; **assault in the second degree**, *U.S. v. Hermoso-Garcia,* 413 F.3d 1085, 1089 (9th Cir. 2005) [Wash. Rev. Code §9A.36.021(1)(a) required defendant to have recklessly inflicted substantial bodily harm]; **assault in the third degree**, *Matter of Martin,* 23 I&N Dec. 491 (BIA 2002) [Conn. Gen. Stat. §53a-61], *but see Flores v. Ashcroft,* 350 F.3d 666, 671 (7th Cir. 2003) [finding *Martin* not persuasive because it confuses intent to injure with any injury that occurs]; *Chrzanoski v. Ashcroft,* 327 F.3d 188 (2d Cir. 2003); **assault of public safety,** *Canada v. Gonzales,* 448 F.3d 560 (2d Cir. 2006) [assault on police officer with intent to prevent him from performing his duty under Conn. Gen. Stat. §53a-167c(a)(1) is COV under §16(b)]; **assault and battery,** *Ramirez v. Mukasey,* 520 F.3d 47 (1st Cir. 2008) [indecent assault and battery under Mass. Gen Laws ch. 265 §13H is a COV under §16(b)]; *Lopes v. Keisler,* 505 F.3d 58, 61–63 (1st Cir. 2007) [simple assault and battery under R.I. Gen. Laws §11-5-3 is COV under §16(a)]; *U.S. v. Earle,* 488 F.3d 537, 547–48 (1st Cir. 2007) [assault and battery under Mass. Gen. Laws ch. 265 §15A]; **assault and battery on a police officer,** *Blake v. Gonzales,* 481 F.3d 152 (2d Cir. 2007) [conviction under Mass. Gen. Laws ch. 265 §13D is a COV under §16(b)]; **battery, simple,** *Hernandez v. U.S. Att'y Gen.,* 513 F.3d 1336 (11th Cir. 2008) [simple battery under Ga. Code Ann. §16-5-23(a)(2) is a COV under §16(a)]; *U.S. v. Glover,* 431 F.3d 744 (11th Cir. 2005) [simple battery on a law enforcement officer is a COV]; **battery, aggravated,** *U.S. v. Llanos-Agostadero,* 486 F.3d 1194 (11th Cir. 2007) [aggravated battery on a pregnant woman was COV for purposes of sentence enhancement]; *U.S. v. Dominguez,* 479 F.3d 345 (5th Cir. 2007) [in sentencing case, aggravated battery under Fla. Stat. Ann. §784.045(1)(a)(1998) constitutes COV under §16(b)]; **burglary of a dwelling,** *U.S. v. Reina-Rodriguez,* 468 F.3d 1147 (9th Cir. 2006) [burglary of a dwelling, in violation of Utah Code §76-6-203, is a COV because it does require the entry into a building under *Taylor*]; **burglary of a habitation,** *U.S. v. Guadardo,* 40 F.3d 102, 103–04 (5th Cir. 1994); **burglary of a non-residential structure or vehicle,** *U.S. v. Ramos-Garcia,* 95 F.3d 369, 371 (5th Cir. 1996), *cert. denied,* 117 S.Ct. 751 (1997); **child abuse,** *U.S. v. Lopez-Patino,* 391 F.3d 1034, 1036–38 (9th Cir. 2004) [Arizona child abuse statute, Ariz. Rev. Stat. §13-2623(C) is not per se a COV, but under modified categorical approach defendant admitted a COV in the plea]; **child, lewd acts upon,** *U.S. v. Ortiz-Delgado,* 451 F.3d 752, 753–57 (11th Cir. 2006) [lewd acts upon a child in violation of Cal. Penal Code §288 is a crime of violence in sentencing context because sexual abuse of a minor is defined as a crime of violence under Sentencing Guideline §2L1.2(b)(1)(A)(ii)]; **child, risk of injury**, *Perez-Munoz v. Keisler,* 507 F.3d 357 (5th Cir. 2007) [injury to a child under Tex. Penal Code §22.04 is a COV under modified categorical approach]; *Hongsathirath v. Ashcroft,* 322 F.Supp.2d 203 (D. Conn. 2004) [risk of injury to a child in violation of Conn. Gen. Stat. §53-21(a)(2) is a COV]; **criminal contempt**, *Matter of Aldabesheh,* 22 I&N Dec. 983 (BIA 1999) [criminal contempt in the first degree under N.Y. Penal Code §215.51(b)(i)]; **domestic abuse under Massachusetts law** *Andrade v. Gonzales,* 459 F.3d 538, 544 (5th Cir. 2006) [finding that a conviction for a violation of a domestic abuse protective order was a crime of violence]; **firearm, aggravated discharge of**, *Quezada-Luna v. Gonzales,* 439 F.3d 403 (7th Cir. 2006) [aggravated discharge of a firearm under Ill. statute 720 Ill. Comp. Stat. 5/24-1.2]; **imprisonment** (unlawful imprisonment) *Dickson v. Ashcroft,* 346 F.3d 44, 48–55 (2d Cir. 2003) [unlawful imprisonment in first degree under N.Y. Penal Law §135.10 of an incompetent person or child is not COV, but unlawful imprisonment of an adult always is a COV]; **indecent assault and battery**, *Sutherland v. Reno,* 228 F.3d 171 (2d Cir. 2000) [for domestic violence Mass. Gen. Laws ch. 265 §13H pertaining to indecent assault and battery is a COV because nonconsent is a necessary element], *U.S. v. Lepore,* 304 F.Supp.2d 183, 186–89 (D. Mass. 2004) [same]; **indecency with a child**, *U.S. v. Velazquez-Overa,* 100 F.3d 418, 419 (5th Cir. 1996), *cert. denied,* 520 U.S. 1133 (1997) [sentencing case]; **injury (risk of) to a minor**, *Santapaola v. Ashcroft,* 249 F.Supp.2d 181, 189–99 (D. Conn. 2003) [relying on plea transcript the court determined that a conviction under former Conn. Gen. Stat. §53-21 for injury to a minor, made the respondent removable as aggravated felony under divisible part]; **use of interstate commerce facility in the commission of a murder-for-hire** under 18 U.S.C. §1958, *NG v. Att'y Gen. of the U.S.,* 436 F.3d 392 (3d Cir. 2006) [under categorical approach §1958, is a COV under §16(b)]; **kidnapping**, *Choeum v. INS,* 129 F.3d 29, 35 n.4 (1st Cir. 1997); **lewd assault** under Florida law (attempt), *Ramsey v. INS,* 55 F.3d 580 (11th Cir. 1995); **manslaughter in the first degree** (N.Y. Penal Law §125.20) *Matter of Vargas,* 23 I&N Dec. 651 (BIA 2004) *aff'd* 448 F.3d 159 (2d Cir. 2006) [distinguishing *Jobson* and finding the statute divisible but determining the respondent engaged in a COV]; manslaughter in the first degree (Conn. Gen. Stat. §53a-55(a)(1), *Benjamin v. Bureau of Customs,* 383 F.Supp.2d 344 (D. Conn. 2005) [distinguished *Chrzanoski* and *Jobson* and finding it is COV under §16(b)]; **mayhem** (under Cal. Penal Code §203), *Ruiz-Morales v. Ashcroft,* 361 F.3d 1219 (9th Cir. 2004); **menacing** (under N.Y. law), *U.S. v. Drummond,* 240 F.3d 1333, 1335 (11th Cir. 2001); **resisting arrest,** *Estrada-Rodriguez v. Mukasey,* 512 F.3d 517 (9th Cir. 2007) [resisting arrest under Ariz. Rev. Stat. §13-2508]; **robbery**, *Gomez v. Ashcroft,* 293 F.Supp.2d 162, 165–68 (D. Conn. 2003) [robbery in the third degree under Conn. Gen. Statute §53a-136 is a COV and his suspended sentence still qualified as a sentence of imprisonment]; **sexual abuse**, *Dos Santos v. Gonzales,* 440 F.3d 81 (2d Cir. 2006) [violation of Conn. Gen. Stat. §53-21(a)(2) makes it a class C felony for any person to have "contact with the intimate parts … of a child under the age of 16 years … in a sexual and indecent manner likely to impair the health or morals of such child"]; *Patel v. Ashcroft,* 401 F.3d 400, 407–11 (6th Cir. 2005) [following reasoning in *Chery* court found that aggravated sexual abuse under 720 Ill. Comp. Stat. §5/12-16 is a COV], *U.S. v. Reyes-Castro,* 13 F.3d 377 (10th Cir. 1993) [attempted sexual abuse of a child in the third degree]; **sexual assault**, *Aguiar v. Gonzales,* 438 F.3d 86 (1st Cir. 2006) [sexual assault under R.I. Gen. Laws §11-37-6, holding criminally liable a person over the age of 18 who engages in sexual penetration with another person over 14 and under 16, is a crime of violence]; *Chery v. Ashcroft,* 347 F.3d 404 (2d Cir. 2003) [sexual assault in the second degree in violation of Conn. Gen. Stat. §53a-71 is a COV because victim is unable to consent to sexual intercourse if under age 18], *Hongsathirath v. Ashcroft,* 322 F.Supp.2d 203 (D. Conn. 2004) [sexual assault on a minor in the fourth degree, which involves sexual contact, in violation of Conn. Gen. Stat. §53a-73a, is COV]; **sexual battery**, *Lisbey v. Gonzales,* 420 F.3d 930 (9th Cir. 2005) [sexual battery under Cal. Penal Code §243.4(a) is a COV under §16(b) but not §16(a)], *Wireko v. Reno,* 211 F.3d 833 (4th Cir. 2000) [sexual misdemeanor battery in violation of Va. Code §18.2-67.4 is a COV; person sentenced to one-year suspended sentence]; *Zaidi v. Ashcroft,* 374 F.3d 357, 359–61 (5th Cir. 2004) [sexual felony battery under Okla. Stat. Ann. Title 21, §1123(B) is a COV]; **spousal corporal injury** under Cal. Penal Code §273.5, *U.S. v. Gonzalez-Valerio,* 342 F.3d 1051, 1054–56 (9th Cir. 2003) [no prejudice from IJ's failure to inform applicant of INA §212(c) relief where aggravated felony conviction occurred after effective date of IIRIRA]; **statutory rape** under Maryland law, *Matter of B-*, 21 I&N Dec. 287 (BIA 1996) [statutory rape is a COV because there is a substantial risk of physical force]; **terrorism**, *Matter of S-S-*, 21 I&N Dec. 900 (BIA 1997); **terrorist threats**, *Bovkun v. Ashcroft,* 283 F.3d 166, 169–70 (3d Cir. 2002) [terrorist threats in violation of Penn. Crim. Code §2706 requires proof of a threat to commit a COV]; **threats,** *Rosales-Rosales v. Ashcroft,* 347 F.3d 714 (9th Cir. 2003) [conviction for willfully threatening to commit a crime which will result in death or great bodily injury pursuant to Cal. Penal Code §422 is a COV]; **criminal trespass** (under Colorado law), *U.S. v. Delgado-Enriquez,* 188 F.3d 592 (5th Cir. 1999) [sentencing case]; **vehicular homicide**, *Omar v. INS,* 298 F.3d 710, 715–20 (8th Cir. 2002) [using the categorical approach criminal vehicular homicide under Minn. Stat. §609.21, subd.1(4) is an aggravated felony]; **unauthorized use of a vehicle**, *De La Paz Sanchez v. Gonzales,* 473 F.3d 133 (5th Cir. 2006) [followed *Galvan-Rodriguez*]; *U.S. v. Galvan-Rodriguez,* 169 F.3d 217 (5th Cir. 1999) [sentencing case], *Ramirez v. Ashcroft,* 361 F.Supp.2d 650, 653–57 (S.D.Tx. 2005) [post-*Leocal* court maintained position that unauthorized use of a vehicle under Texas law is an aggravated felony], *Matter of Brieva,* 23 I&N Dec. 766 (BIA 2005) *aff'd Brieva-Perez v. Gonzales,* 482 F.3d 356 (5th Cir. 2007) [post-*Leocal* followed *Galvan-Rodriguez* in 5th Circuit]; **use of vehicle to facilitate intentional discharge of firearm**, *Nguyen v. Ashcroft,* 366 F.3d 386 (5th Cir. 2004) [violation of Okla. Stat., title 12, §652(b), relating to use of vehicle to facilitate intentional discharge of firearm is a COV]; **weapon** (exhibiting a deadly weapon with intent to evade arrest), *Reyes-Alcaraz v. Ashcroft,* 363 F.3d 937, 941 (9th Cir. 2004) [Cal. Penal Code §417.8 regarding exhibiting a deadly weapon with intent to evade arrest is an aggravated felony]; **weapon, possession with intent to use,** *Henry v. ICE,* 493 F.3d 303 (3d Cir. 2007) [N.Y. Penal Law §265.08 regarding possession of a weapon in the second degree, which includes intent to use, is a COV].

(2) Not Crimes of Violence—The following were found to *not* be COVs:

Arson by burning or creating an explosion recklessly, *Tran v. Gonzales,* 414 F.3d 464 (3d Cir. 2005) [conspiracy to commit reckless burning or exploding under 18 Pa. Cons. Stat. §3301(d)(2) regarding arson and related crimes is not a COV because recklessness will not suffice, as the term "use" in §16(a) requires specific intent to use force and the crime by its nature does not involve a risk of intentionally using force under §16(b); *Palacios* distinguished]; **setting a fire,** *Jordison v. Gonzales,* 501 F.3d 1134 (9th Cir. 2007) [setting a fire in violation of Cal. Penal Code §452(c) does not necessarily involve risk against the person or property of another under §16(b) because defendant can be convicted for setting fire to her own property]; **assault (simple)**, *Popal v. Gonzales,* 416 F.3d 249, 253–55 (3d Cir. 2005) [misdemeanor simple assault under 18 Pa. Cons. Stat. §2701(a)(1) is not a COV because it does not require a *mens rea* greater than recklessness for a conviction]; **assault in the fourth degree,** *Suazo Perez v. Mukasey,* 512 F.3d 1222 (9th Cir. 2008) [under Wash. Rev. Code §9A.36.041, a person may be convicted of assault for nonconsensual offensive touching which is not a COV and neither documents reviewed under *Shepard* nor police report established a COV]; **assault (intentional) in the third degree** under Conn. Gen. Stat. 53a-61, *Chrzanoski v. Ashcroft,* 327 F.3d 188 (2d Cir. 2003) [intentional causation of injury does not necessarily involve the risk of the use of force], *but see Matter of Martin,* 23 I&N Dec. 491 (BIA 2002); **assault (reckless) in the second degree** under N.Y. Penal Law §120.05(4), *Garcia v. Gonzales,* 455 F.3d 465 (4th Cir. 2006) [court's interpretation of *Leocal* forecloses reckless conduct as basis for crime of violence under §16(b)]; **assault in the second degree** under N.Y. Penal Law §120.05(6), *Persaud v. McElroy,* 225 F.Supp.2d 420 (S.D.N.Y. 2002) [conviction does not require use of physical force, nor a substantial risk that physical force may be used]; **assault and battery** under Mass. Gen. Laws Ch. 265, §13A, *Andrade v. Gonzales,* 459 F.3d 538, 544 (5th Cir. 2006) [finding that a conviction under §13A is not a per se aggravated felony] but noting that where one of the acts constituted a violation of a domestic abuse protective order the person was convicted of an aggravated felony]; **battery,** *Ortega-Mendez v. Gonzales,* 450 F.3d 1010 (9th Cir. 2006) [simple battery under Cal. Penal Code §242 as interpreted by California court requiring no violence is not a COV; *U.S. v. Robinson,* 967 F.2d 287 (9th Cir. 1992) distinguished]; *Flores v. Ashcroft,* 350 F.3d 666 (7th Cir. 2003) [finding *Martin* not persuasive and distinguishing between a statute requiring violent force and a statute, like the Indiana misdemeanor law, Ind. Code §35-42-2-1 (Class A misdemeanor), that requires only a touching and therefore does not necessarily require violence]; **battery, aggravated** *Larin-Ulloa v. Gonzales,* 462 F.3d 456 (5th Cir. 2006) [under modified categorical approach, a conviction under Kan. Stat. §21-3414(a)(1)(C) was not a COV, and the BIA erroneously referred to a special sentencing factor notation in the Kansas journal entry form to determine it was a COV]; **burglary,** *U.S. v. Gomez-Guerra,* 485 F.3d 301 (5th Cir. 2007) [in sentencing guideline case, burglary under Fla. Stat. §810.02(3) is not a COV because it includes burglary of a dwelling's cartilage]; **burglary, aggravated,** *U.S. v. Reina-Rodriguez,* 468 F.3d 1147 (9th Cir. 2006) [Utah attempted aggravated burglary Utah Code §76-6-203 is not COV because it does not require the entry into a building as *Taylor* requires and merely possessing a weapon is sufficient]; **burglary of a vehicle**, *Sareang Ye v. INS,* 214 F.3d 1128, 1133–34 (9th Cir. 2000) [Cal. Penal Code §459 conviction for entry of locked vehicle is not a COV], *Solorzano-Patlan v. INS*, 207 F.3d 869, 874–75 (7th Cir. 2000) [§720 Ill. Comp. Stat. 5/19-1(a) not a COV], *but see Santos v. Reno,* 228 F.3d 591, 597 n.13 (5th Cir. 2000) [Tex. Penal Code §30.04 is a COV but not a burglary offense under §101(a)(43)(G)]; **child endangerment**, *U.S. v. Calderon-Pena,* 383 F.3d 254 (5th Cir. 2004) [finding child endangerment under Tex. Penal Code §22.041(c) is not a COV]; **criminal negligent child abuse** (under Colorado law), *Matter of Sweetser*, 22 I&N Dec. 709 (BIA 1999) [nature of crime did not entail a substantial risk that violence would be used]; **Domestic battery,** *Matter of Sanudo,* 23 I&N Dec. 968, 974–75 (BIA 2006) [domestic battery under Cal. Penal Code §§242 and 243(e)(1) are not crimes of violence under modified categorical approach where record of conviction did not sustain anything but a nonviolent touching]; **Domestic Violence.** *Fernandez-Ruiz v. Gonzales,* 466 F.3d 1121 (9th Cir. 2006) (en banc) [misdemeanor domestic violence assault under Ariz. Rev. Stat. §§13-1203 and 13-3601 permit convictions for something short of intentional conduct including recklessness, gross negligence, and simple negligence and therefore cannot be a crime of violence post-*Leocal*]; **Driving under the influence (felony),** *Leocal v. Ashcroft,* 543 U.S. 1 (2004) [DUI causing serious bodily injury under Florida law was not a COV because the "use ... of physical force" under §16(a) or the "substantial risk that physical force ... may be used" under §16(b) are given an "identical construction requiring a higher *mens rea* than the merely accidental or negligent conduct involved in a DUI offense"], *Matter of Ramos,* 23 I&N Dec. 336 (BIA 2002) [enhanced penalty DUI conviction under Mass. law is not aggravated felony because COV must be volitional, and therefore at a minimum must require recklessness finding; overruled *Puente & Magallanes*], *Matter of Olivares,* 23 I&N Dec. 148 (BIA 2001) [in Fifth Circuit, the BIA will not apply *Puente* because of *Chapa-Garza*], *U.S. v. Lucio-Lucio,* 347 F.3d 1202 (10th Cir. 2003) [DWI under Tex. Penal Code Ann. §49.04 is not an aggravated felony where there is no injury to another], *Montiel-Barraza v. INS,* 275 F.3d 1178 (9th Cir. 2002) [DUI with injury to another]; *Dalton v. Ashcroft,* 257 F.3d 200 (2d Cir. 2001) [felony DUI under N.Y. Vehicle & Traffic Law §1192.3 is not aggravated felony using categorical approach because risk of injury is not the same as risk of use of physical force, and, under categorical approach, not all convictions involve intent], *Bazan-Reyes v. INS,* 256 F.3d 600, 605–12 (7th Cir. 2001) [aggravated drunk driving including homicide by the intoxicated use of a vehicle is not an aggravated felony under §§16(a) or (b) because the word "use" requires recklessness in the intentional use of force; court distinguishes *Rutherford* a sentencing guideline case], *U.S. v. Chapa-Garza,* 243 F.3d 921, 927 (5th Cir. 2001) [§16(b) requires recklessness in regard to intentional use, and Texas DWI is therefore not a COV]; **evading a police officer**, *Penuliar v. Ashcroft,* 435 F.3d 961, 967–69 (9th Cir. 2006) [conviction for evading an officer under Cal. Veh. Code §2800.2(a) is not a COV under categorical or modified categorical approach]; **harassment**, *Singh v. Ashcroft*, 386 F.3d 1228 (9th Cir. 2004) [harassment under Or. Rev. Stat. §166.065(1)(a)(A) is not a COV because it includes an offensive touching that is not aimed at creating physical injury and therefore does not have as an "element" the use of force]; **firearms, discharging,** *U.S. v. Narvaez-Gomez,* 489 F.3d 970, 975–77 (9th Cir. 2007) [following *Fernandez-Ruiz* and holding that Cal. Penal Code §246 that criminalizes maliciously and willfully discharging a firearm at an inhabited dwelling was not categorically a COV because purely reckless conduct was sufficient for a conviction]; **harassment-by-telephone**, *Szucz-Toldy v. Gonzales,* 400 F.3d 978 (7th Cir. 2005) [harassment-by-telephone under 720 Ill.

Comp. Stat. 135/1-1(2) is not a COV under generic terms of the statute, and respondent's acts are not relevant]; **imprisonment** (unlawful Imprisonment), *Dickson v. Ashcroft,* 346 F.3d 44, 48–55 (2d Cir. 2003) [unlawful imprisonment in first degree under N.Y. Penal Law §135.10 of an incompetent person or child is not a COV, but unlawful imprisonment of an adult always is a COV]; **manslaughter**, *U.S. v. Torress-Villalobos,* 487 F.3d 607, 613–17 (8th Cir. 2007) [Minn. Stat. §609.205 for manslaughter in the second degree is not a COV under §16(a) or §16(b)]; *Jobson v. Ashcroft,* 326 F.3d 367 (2d Cir. 2003) [no substantial risk of the use of force to obtain conviction for second degree manslaughter under N.Y. Penal Law §125.15(1)]. *But see Matter of Vargas,* 23 I&N Dec. 651 (BIA 2004) [distinguishing *Jobson* and finding *first* degree manslaughter under N.Y. Penal Law §125.20 is a COV] *aff'd* 448 F.3d 159 (2d Cir. 2006); **involuntary manslaughter**, *Bejarano-Urrutia v. Gonzales,* 413 F.3d 444 (4th Cir. 2005) [post-*Leocal* involuntary manslaughter under Va. Code Ann. §18.2-36 may intrinsically involve a substantial risk that the defendant's actions will cause physical harm, but does not intrinsically involve a substantial risk that force will be applied as a means to an end under §16(b)]; **reckless endangerment**, *Singh v. Gonzales,* 432 F.3d 533, 540–41 (3d Cir. 2006) [reckless endangering another person under 18 Pa. Cons. Stat. Ann. §2705 requires a *mens rea* no greater than recklessness and therefore is not an aggravated felony]; **sexual assault of a child** under Wis. Stat. §948.02(2), *Xiong v. INS,* 173 F.3d 601, 604–07 (7th Cir. 1999) [looked beyond record to criminal complaint to demonstrate it was consensual sex between 18-year-old boyfriend and 15-year-old girlfriend]; **sexual battery**, *U.S. v. Meraz-Enriguez,* 442 F.3d 331 (5th Cir. 2006) [aggravated sexual battery under Kan. Stat. Ann. §21-3518, concerning touching of 16-year-old or older without consent, is not an aggravated felony]; *U.S. v. Bonilla-Mungia,* 422 F.3d 316, 320–22 (5th Cir. 2005) [sexual battery under Cal. Penal Code §243.4 (1998) contain sections that are not COVs, so case remanded to obtain criminal records]; **sexual abuse of a child in the second degree** under N.Y. Penal Law §130.60, *Matter of Small,* 23 I&N Dec. 448, 449 n.1 (BIA 2002); **sexual intercourse with a minor**, *Valencia v. Gonzales,* 439 F.3d 1046 (9th Cir. 2006) [absent aggravating factors such as incest or a substantial age difference, sexual intercourse with a person under 18 who was more than 3 years younger than defendant under Cal. Penal Code §261.5(c) is not a COV]; **shooting into an occupied dwelling**, *U.S. v. Alfaro,* 408 F.3d 204, 207–09 (5th Cir. 2005) [shooting into an occupied dwelling under Va. Code. Ann. §18.2-279 does not implicate use of force against a person]; **stalking**, *Malta-Espinoza v. Gonzales,* 478 F.3d 1080 (9th Cir. 2007) [reversing *Matter of Malta,* 23 I&N Dec. 656 (BIA 2004) and finding that stalking under Cal. Penal Code §646.9(b) involving harassment does not involve a substantial risk of harm under the categorical or modified categorical approach]; **vehicular homicide**, *Oyebanji v. Gonzales,* 418 F.3d 260 (3d Cir. 2005) [post-*Leocal* vehicular homicide in violation of N.J. Stat. Ann. §2C:11-5(b)(1) is not COV under §16(b) because it encompasses reckless as well as intentional conduct], *Lara-Cazares v. Gonzales,* 408 F.3d 1217 (9th Cir. 2005) [gross vehicular manslaughter while intoxicated under Cal. Penal Code §191.5(a) is not a COV because under *Leocal* it is still negligent not intentional conduct], *Francis v. Reno,* 269 F.3d 162 (3d Cir. 2001) [homicide by vehicle under 75 Pa. Cons. Stat. Ann. §3732 is not felony and not COV where person was convicted for unintentional/negligent conduct], *U.S. v. Mojica-Linos,* 399 F.Supp.2d 1115, 1119–21 (W.D. Wash. 2005) [post-*Leocal,* vehicular homicide under Wash. Rev. Code §46.61.520(1)(a)–(b) is not an aggravated felony].

3.g. *A theft offense (including receipt of stolen property) or burglary offense for which the term of imprisonment imposed (regardless of any suspension of such imprisonment) is at least one year*

Jaafar v. INS, 77 F.Supp.2d 360, 364–65 (W.D.N.Y. 1999) [a sentence to a one-year term of imprisonment for petit larceny, although a misdemeanor under state law is an aggravated felony for purposes of INA §101(a)(43)(G)]. *Accord U.S. v. Graham,* 169 F.3d 787 (3d Cir.), *cert. denied,* 528 U.S. 845 (1999).

The Supreme Court in *Taylor v. U.S.,* 495 U.S. 575, 598–99 (1990), has determined that burglary has a uniform national definition as the "unlawful or unprivileged entry into, or remaining in, a building or structure, with intent to commit a crime." The BIA agrees. *Matter of Perez,* 22 I&N Dec. 1325 (BIA 2000) [burglary of a vehicle under 30.04(a) of Tex. Penal Code is not a burglary offense within definition of INA §101(a)(43)(G)].

The "generic approach" established by the Supreme Court in *Taylor* and *Gonzales v. Duenas-Alvarez,* 549 U.S. ____, 127 S.Ct. 815 (2007) has been adopted by the circuits. *See e.g., Ilchuk v. Att'y Gen. of the U.S.,* 434 F.3d 618, 622–23 (3d Cir. 2006) [citing *Taylor,* the court held that where the common law definition may not be in tune with more modern forms of theft that a contemporary or generic approach is more appropriate, and holding that Pennsylvania's Theft of Service statute, 18 Pa. Cons. Stat. Ann. §3926, which includes diversion of services, is an aggravated felony]. Relying on the "generic" approach in *Taylor*, the Seventh Circuit determined that "theft offense (including receipt of stolen property)" should be read broadly as one offense ("theft") that includes an example of theft ("receipt of stolen property"), and not as two separate offenses, so that the definition "is a taking of property or an exercise of control over property without consent with the criminal intent to deprive the owner of rights and benefits of ownership, even if such deprivation is less than total or permanent." *Hernandez-Mancilla v. INS,* 246 F.3d 1002, 1009 (7th Cir. 2001) [possession of a stolen motor vehicle under 625 ILCS 5/4-103(a)(1) is a theft offense]; *U.S. v. Corona-Sanchez,* 291 F.3d 1201, 1205 (9th Cir. 2002) (*en banc*) [adopting Seventh Circuit definition in context of petty theft of beer and cigarettes under Cal. Penal Code §484(a) but finding them not to be aggravated felonies]; *Randhawa v. Ashcroft,* 298 F.3d 1148, 1152–54 (9th Cir. 2002) [following *Taylor*, possession of stolen mail under 18 U.S.C. §1708 is theft offense]; *U.S. v. Vasquez-Flores,* 265 F.3d 1122 (10th Cir. 2001) [adopted Seventh Circuit definition in context of attempted receiving or transferring a stolen motor vehicle under Utah Code Ann. §41-1a-1316)].

The generic approach, following *Taylor,* also includes aiding and abetting under the theft statutes. *Gonzales v. Duenas-Alvarez,* 549 U.S. ____, 127 S.Ct. 815 (2007) [Cal. Veh. Code Ann. §10851(a) including aiding and abetting is an aggravated felony].

The BIA has broadly interpreted the theft provision finding that "a taking of property constitutes a 'theft' whenever there is a criminal intent to deprive the owner of the rights and benefits of ownership, even if such deprivation is less than total or permanent." *Matter of V-Z-S-*, 22 I&N Dec. 1338 (BIA 2000) [relying on *U.S. v. Turley* and the Model Penal Code §223 and finding that proving specific intent to permanently deprive the owner of property is not a requirement]. However, the BIA clarified *Matter of V-Z-S-* to distinguish theft crimes from fraud finding that theft crimes involve taking property without consent and fraud and deceit crimes under INA §101(a)(43)(M)(i) involve taking property *with* consent that has been fraudulently obtained. *Matter of Garcia-Madruga,* 24 I&N Dec. 436 (BIA 2008) [finding that IJ's determination that Rhode Island General Law 40-6-15 concerning welfare fraud was a theft crime was in error]. *See also Soliman v. Gonzales,* 419 F.3d 276 (4th Cir. 2005). Also when there is not necessarily an intent to deprive the owner of his property, as in a divisible statute, a theft statute may not be an aggravated felony if the government does not prove a conviction by clear and conviction evidence under the appropriate section. *Jaggernauth v. U.S. Att'y Gen.,* 432 F.3d 1346, 1352–56 (11th Cir. 2005) [grand theft under Fla. Stat. §812.014(1) is a divisible statute that includes under subsection (b) a temporary appropriation of the use of the property, and therefore not necessarily "theft" under the common law definition].

The BIA has also broadly interpreted the receipt of stolen property provision. In *Matter of Bahta,* 22 I&N Dec. 1381, 1390 (BIA 2000), the BIA found that the "receipt of stolen property" parenthetical in the theft provision was used in a generic sense to "include the category of offenses involving knowing receipt, possession or retention of property from its rightful owner." The BIA rejected the view that the statute should be limited to the definition contained in 18 U.S.C. §2315, and instead looked to a variety of state and federal statutes as well as the Model Penal Code §223.6. *Matter of Bahta* at 1386–90. *See Kendall v. Mooney,* 273 F.Supp.2d 216, 220–22 (E.D.N.Y. 2003) [following *Bahta* and *V-Z-S-* and finding criminal possession of stolen property in the fourth degree under N.Y. Penal Law §165.45 an aggravated felony].

Hybrid Crimes—One court has found that a theft offense that is also an offense involving fraud or deceit, is an aggravated felon only if the conviction qualifies under the definition of both. *Nugent v. Ashcroft,* 367 F.3d 162 (3d Cir. 2004) [where respondent convicted of theft by deception under 18 Pa. Cons. Stat. Ann. §3922(a) but amount was less than $10,000, he was not convicted of an aggravated felony]. It is important to analyze the statute to determine whether a fraud offense is a theft offense under the appropriate law. *Martinez v. Mukasey,* 519 F.3d 532, 538-41 (5th Cir. 2008) [court engaged in hybrid analysis but concluded that a conviction under 18 U.S.C. §1344 while a fraud crime was not a theft crime]; *Soliman v. Gonzales,* 419 F.3d 276, 284–86 (4th Cir. 2005) [under categorical and modified categorical approach, fraudulent use of a credit card under Va. Code §18.2-195, while a fraud offense, is not a theft offense]. The BIA clarified *Matter of V-Z-S-* to distinguish theft crimes from fraud finding that theft crimes involve taking property without consent and fraud and deceit crimes under INA §101(a)(43)(M)(i) involve taking property *with* consent that has been fraudulently obtained. *Matter of Garcia-Madruga,* 24 I&N Dec. 436 (BIA 2008) [finding that IJ's determination that R.I. Gen. Law §40-6-15, concerning welfare fraud, was a theft crime was in error].

(1) Theft Offenses as Aggravated Felonies

Attempted possession of stolen property, *Matter of Bahta,* 22 I&N Dec. 1381 (BIA 2000) [attempted possession of stolen property under Nev. Rev. Stat. §§193.330 & 205.275]; **attempted robbery**, *U.S. v. Fernandez-Antonia,* 278 F.3d 150, 161–63 (2d Cir. 2002) [attempted robbery in the third degree under N.Y. statute is an aggravated felony in sentencing enhancement context]; **larceny (theft of services)**, *Abimbola v. Ashcroft,* 378 F.3d 173, 175–80 (2d Cir. 2004) [third-degree larceny under Conn. Gen. Stat. §53a-124; court disagreed with Ninth Circuit analysis in *Corona-Sanchez*], *Plummer v. Ashcroft,* 258 F.Supp.2d 43, 46–47 (D. Conn. 2003) [larceny under Conn. Gen. Stat. §53a-123(a)(3) is aggravated felony where sentenced to 3 years suspended sentence]; **possession of stolen mail**, *Randhawa v. Ashcroft,* 298 F.3d 1148 (9th Cir. 2002) [possession of stolen mail in violation of 18 U.S.C. §1708]; **possession of stolen property,** *Burke v. Mukasey,* 509 F.3d 695 (5th Cir. 2007) [criminal possession of stolen property under N.Y. Penal Law §165.50 is an aggravated felony]; **theft**, *Fernandez-Ruiz v. Gonzales,* 468 F.3d 1159, 1169–70 (9th Cir. 2006) [Ariz. Rev. Stat. §§13-1802(A)(1) & (C) regarding controlling the property of another without lawful authority with the intent to deprive is an aggravated felony but this aspect of the case was remanded to determine if the one-year sentence was unlawful because it was designated a misdemeanor]; **theft of services**, *Ilchuk v. Att'y Gen. of the U.S.,* 434 F.3d 618, 622–23 (3d Cir. 2006) [Pennsylvania's Theft of Service statute, 18 Pa. Cons. Stat. Ann. §3926, which includes diversion of services, is an aggravated felony]; **petty theft with a prior jail term,** *Mutascu v. Gonzales,* 444 F.3d 710 (5th Cir. 2006) [conviction for petty theft with a prior jail term under Cal. Penal Code §666 was an aggravated felony even if the predicate offenses were petty thefts, because §666 carried a one-year sentence; *U.S. v. Corona-Sanchez* rejected]; **vehicle theft,** *Gonzales v. Duenas-Alvarez,* 549 U.S. ____, 127 S.Ct. 815 (2007) [Cal. Veh. Code §10851(a) including aiding and abetting under the statute]; *Matter of V-Z-S-,* 22 I&N Dec. 1338 (BIA 2000) [unlawful driving and taking of a vehicle in violation of Cal. Veh. Code §10851], *Arteaga v. Mukasey,* 511 F.3d 940, 946–48 (9th Cir. 2007) [vehicle theft/joyriding in violation of Cal. Veh. Code §10851(a) under the modified categorical approach because petitioner was not an accessory after the fact]; *U.S. v. Vasquez-Flores,* 265 F.3d 1122 (10th Cir. 2001) [attempted receiving or transferring a stolen motor vehicle under Utah Code Ann. §41-1a-1316]; *Hernandez-Mancilla v. INS,* 246 F.3d 1002 (7th Cir. 2001) [possession of a stolen motor vehicle under 625 Ill. Comp. Stat. 5/4-103(a)(1)].

(2) Offenses Ruled *Not* Aggravated Felonies

Credit card fraud, *Soliman v. Gonzales,* 419 F.3d 276, 284–86 (4th Cir. 2005) [under categorical and modified categorical approach fraudulent use of a credit card under Va. Code §18.2-195 is a fraud offense but is not a theft offense]; **grand theft**, *Jaggernauth v. U.S. Att'y Gen.,* 432 F.3d 1346, 1352–56 (11th Cir. 2005) [grand theft under Fla. Stat. §812.014(1) is a divisible statute that includes under subsection (b) a temporary appropriation of property, and therefore is not necessarily "theft" under the common law definition, which requires an intent to deprive the owner of rights and benefits of ownership], *Martinez-Perez v. Ashcroft,* 417 F.3d 1022 (9th Cir. 2005) [court relied on the modified categorical approach and found that grand theft under Cal. Penal Code §487(c) was not an aggravated felony because court could not rely on the "facts" of the information, where the plea was a different offense than the one charged in the information]; **petty theft,** *U.S. v. Corona-Sanchez,* 291 F.3d 1201 (9th Cir.

2002) (*en banc*) [petty theft under Cal. Penal Code §484(a) is not aggravated felony]; **possession of stolen vehicle**, *Huerta-Guevara v. Ashcroft,* 321 F.3d 883 (9th Cir. 2003) [respondent found not removable as aggravated felon for possession of stolen vehicle under Ariz. Stat. §13-1802, where statute encompasses acts that do not require criminal intent, and concessions in respondent's appellate brief were not necessarily elements she pled guilty to]; **vehicle theft**, *Nevarez-Martinez v. INS,* 326 F.3d 1053 (9th Cir. 2003) [theft of a means of transportation under Ariz. Rev. Stat. §13-1814 is not an aggravated felony because it is divisible and certain sections do not require intent to deprive]; **welfare fraud,** *Matter of Garcia-Madruga,* 24 I&N Dec. 436 (BIA 2008) [finding that Rhode Island General Law 40-6-15 concerning welfare fraud was not a theft crime].

(3) Non–Burglary Offenses

Sareang Ye v. INS, 214 F.3d 1128, 1131–33 (9th Cir. 2000) [vehicle burglary not an agg. felony because it is not a burglary]; *Lopez-Elias v. Reno,* 209 F.3d 788, 791–92 (5th Cir. 2000) [same but is crime of violence]; *Solorzano-Patlan v. INS,* 207 F.3d 869, 874–75 (7th Cir. 2000); *Matter of Perez,* 22 I&N Dec. 1325 (BIA 2000) [burglary of a vehicle under Tex. Penal Code §30.04(a) is not a burglary offense within definition of §101(a)(43)(G)]

3.h. Ransom offenses including: using interstate communications to demand ransom or threaten kidnap [18 U.S.C. §875); using mails to make threatening communication [18 U.S.C. §876]; making threatening communications from foreign countries [18 U.S.C. §877]; receiving, possessing, or disposing of ransom money or property [18 U.S.C. §1202]

3.i. Child pornography offenses including: employing, using, or coercing minors to engage in pornography [18 U.S.C. §2251]; selling or transferring custody of a child with knowledge that the child will be used for pornography [18 U.S.C. §2251A]; receiving or distributing child pornography [18 U.S.C. §2252]. *Gonzalez v. Ashcroft,* 369 F.Supp.2d 442, 447–54 (S.D.N.Y. 2005) [N.Y. Penal Law §263.05 regarding parents consenting to the participation of their child in a sexual performance has no scienter requirement and is therefore not an aggravated felony under this or sexual-abuse-of-minor section].

3.j. RICO offenses under 18 U.S.C. §1962, an offense described in §1084 (if it is a second or subsequent offense) or §1955 (relating to gambling offenses) for which a sentence of one-year imprisonment or more *may* be imposed

3.k. Prostitution and slavery offenses

(1) relating to owning, controlling, managing or supervising a prostitution business;

(2) relating to transportation for the purpose of prostitution if committed for commercial advantage under 18 U.S.C. §§2421, 2422 or 2423; or

(3) holding, selling or enticing persons into slavery or transporting, possessing, detaining or seizing slaves. 18 U.S.C. §§1581–85 or 1588–91.

3.l. National defense offenses, including:

(1) gathering, transmitting or losing defense information [18 U.S.C. §793]; disclosing classified information [18 U.S.C. §798]; injuring, destroying, contaminating or infecting war materials or premises [18 U.S.C. §2153]; treason [18 U.S.C. §2381]; and concealing and failing to disclose treason [18 U.S.C. §2382];

(2) Disclosing identity or information about covert intelligence agents [50 U.S.C. §421];

3.m. **INA §101(a)(43)(M)(i)**—Fraud or deceit crimes in which the loss to the victim or victims exceeds $10,000; and **§101(a)(43)(M)(ii)**—An offense described in 26 U.S.C. §7201 (relating to tax evasion) in which the loss to the government exceeds $10,000.

Aggravated Felonies under Subsection (M)(i)— *Martinez v. Mukasey,* 519 F.3d 532, 538-41 (5th Cir. 2008) [conviction for bank fraud under 18 U.S.C. §1344 is an aggravated felony]; *Eke v. Mukasey,* 512 F.3d 372, 378–81 (7th Cir. 2008) [convictions for identity theft under 730 Ill. Comp. Stat. 5/16G-15(a) and conspiracy to commit a financial crime under 720 Ill. Comp. Stat. 5/16H-45, where the intended loss exceeded $10,000, resulted in an aggravated felony under INA §101(a)(43)(U) (attempt or conspiracy to commit an offense described in INA §101(a)(43)); court found that intended loss can be used in conspiracy offenses]; *Marti-*

nez v. Mukasey, 508 F.3d 255 (5th Cir. 2007) [insurance fraud under Tex. Penal Code §35.02(a) where defendant paid only $5,733.68 of an $11,467.36 restitution order for which he was jointly and severally liable]; *Akio Kawashima v. Gonzales,* 503 F.3d 997, 1001–02 (9th Cir. 2007) [conviction under 26 U.S.C. §7206(1) for willfully making and subscribing to a false statement on a tax return where the loss was in excess of $10,000 even though other tax offenses are covered separately in 101(a)(43)(M)(ii)]; *Kharana v. Gonzales,* 487 F.3d 1280 (9th Cir. 2007) [where respondent pleaded guilty to violation of Cal. Penal Code §532 concerning fraud in an amount in excess of $10,000 but paid down the loss to victim post-plea, the loss to the victim is still in excess of $10,000 for purposes of the aggravated felony statute]; *Iysheh v. Gonzales,* 437 F.3d 613 (7th Cir. 2006) [the court relying on *Shepard* found that a person who had a corrected judgment identifying his offense as a non–aggravated felony, 18 U.S.C. §2313(a) (Sale or receipt of stolen vehicles) but who pled guilty to a count that included fraud (to defraud a financial institution) did commit an aggravated felony when the plea agreement, superseding indictment, and judgment were considered together]; *Ferreira v. Ashcroft,* 390 F.3d 1091 (9th Cir. 2004) [a conviction under Cal. Welfare & Institutions Code §10980(c)(2), for submitting false statements to obtain aid, is a fraud crime for purposes of the aggravated felony statute; the court, using the modified categorical approach, found that the amount stated as restitution in the plea agreement exceeded $10,000]; *Khalayleh v. INS,* 287 F.3d 978 (10th Cir. 2002) [in calculating $10,000 loss court considered not only count that respondent pled to for a $9,308 bad check but to losses from dismissed counts where they were part of the same fraudulent scheme because the count pled to included allegations of an entire scheme to defraud and because defendant was ordered to pay restitution of $24,000]; *Moore v. Ashcroft,* 251 F.3d 919, 923 (11th Cir. 2001) [conviction for misapplication of bank funds under 18 U.S.C. §656 is aggravated felony because it necessarily involves fraud or deceit]; *Beshli v. DHS,* 272 F.Supp.2d 514, 522–25 (E.D. Pa. 2003) [conviction for conspiracy under 18 U.S.C. §1029(b)(2) to traffic in and use unauthorized access devices under §1029(a) is an aggravated felony where he pled guilty to a count in the indictment for losses to the victims in excess of $10,000].

Not Aggravated Felonies Under Subsection M(i)—*Dulal-Whiteway v. DHS,* 501 F.3d 116, 123–34 (2d Cir. 2007) [in conviction for fraudulently trafficking in unauthorized access devices under 18 U.S.C. §1029(a)(2), the court cannot rely on PSR and restitution order to prove that loss to the victim was greater than $10,000]; *Knutsen v. Gonzales,* 429 F.3d 733 (7th Cir. 2005) [distinguished *Khalayleh* and cited *Chang*, holding that a person who pled guilty only to count one of an indictment involving a $7,350 loss where count two was a distinct offense, is not an aggravated felon simply because his plea agreement accepted restitution above $10,000 based upon "relevant conduct" for sentencing purposes that included the $12,930 lost from count 2]; *Omari v. Gonzales,* 419 F.3d 303 (5th Cir. 2005) [where respondent convicted of conspiracy under 18 U.S.C. §371 to violate 18 U.S.C. §2314, which is a divisible statute, the removal order was vacated because under the modified categorical approach the only documents in evidence were the indictment and conviction and they suggested a nonfraud crime of possession of illegal airline tickets]; *Li v. Ashcroft,* 389 F.3d 892 (9th Cir. 2004) [where amount of loss due to fraud was not an element of the crime but where indictment alleges that more than $10,000 was involved in the fraud, the government may not prove under the modified categorical approach that this was a fraud or attempted fraud in excess of $10,000 by simply putting into evidence the charging document and the judgment without a verdict form or jury instructions, because the government was not required to prove and the jury was not required to find a loss in excess of $10,000 in order to convict]; *Lee v. Ashcroft,* 368 F.3d 218 (3d Cir. 2004) [filing a false tax return in violation of 26 U.S.C. §7206(1) is not an aggravated felony, because Congress only specified one tax crime—§7201—as aggravated felony]; *Chang v. INS,* 307 F.3d 1185, 1189–92 (9th Cir. 2002) [distinguishing *Khalayleh* because it involved a scheme to defraud and not, as here, a discrete fraud based on the plea agreement to cashing a counterfeit $650.30 check]; *Valansi v. Ashcroft,* 278 F.3d 203 (3d Cir. 2002) [distinguishing *Moore* and finding that a conviction under 18 U.S.C. §656 for embezzlement is not necessarily a fraud or deceit crime because a person may be convicted if s/ he has the intent to *injure* or defraud the employer].

Amount of Loss—The amount of the loss that the defendant was *convicted of* and not the amount of restitution, or other losses, governs whether it is an aggravated felony. *Dulal-*

Whiteway v. DHS, 501 F.3d 116, 123–34 (2d Cir. 2007) [in conviction for fraudulently trafficking in unauthorized access devices under 18 U.S.C. §1029(a)(2), the court cannot rely on PSR and restitution order to prove loss to the victim as it can only rely upon facts to which the defendant actually pleaded to establish the offense or if tried upon facts found beyond a reasonable doubt by the jury]; *Obasohan v. U.S. Att'y Gen.,* 479 F.3d 785 (11th Cir. 2007) [requiring clear, unequivocal and convincing evidence that respondent was *convicted* of an aggravated felony including that the loss to the victim exceeded $10,000 and finding that the restitution order of $37,000 failed to demonstrate that respondent was convicted of loss to the victim because the restitution order was based upon other losses for which respondent was *not* charged or convicted]; *Alaka v. Att'y Gen. of the U.S.,* 456 F.3d 88, 104–09 (3d Cir. 2006) [conviction for bank fraud under 18 U.S.C. §1344 and aiding and abetting were not aggravated felonies because the loss for which she was *convicted* was not in excess of $10,000; the IJ erroneously considered the amount of intended loss for all of the charges rather than the single count for which respondent was convicted]; *Munroe v. Ashcroft,* 353 F.3d 225 (3d Cir. 2003) [if the amount of loss is unclear then the amount of restitution may be helpful; however when restitution is not based upon the amount of loss but is instead intended solely to affect the defendant's immigration status, it is not controlling]; *see also Akio Kawashima v. Gonzales,* 503 F.3d 997, 1002–04 (9th Cir. 2007) [aiding and assisting in the preparation of a false tax return under 26 U.S.C. §7206(2) may be an aggravated felony but here the documents only demonstrated failure to report income which does not equate to loss to the government]; *Chang,* 307 F.3d 1185 (9th Cir. 2002). The amount of loss must also be related to a plea to an aggravated felony and not a charge that was dropped. *Martin v. Gantner,* 443 F.Supp.2d 367, 371 (E.D.N.Y. 2006) [restitution was ordered for larceny that was charged but was not pled to because naturalization applicant only pled to falsification of business s records, which, unlike larceny, is not an aggravated felony]. The court, however, is not prohibited from relying on a restitution order to find the amount of loss in all cases. *Martinez v. Mukasey,* 508 F.3d 255, 259–60 (5th Cir. 2007) [the court is not prohibited from relying on a restitution order to find the amount of loss where the plea agreement states the defendant agrees to an amount in excess of $10,000 and recognizes it as a condition of probation, and it is irrelevant that the defendant paid only $5,733.68 of an $11,467.36 restitution order for which he was jointly and severally liable because it is the loss to the victim and not the payment of the defendant that counts];*De Vega v. Gonzales,* 503 F.3d 45, 49–50 (1st Cir. 2007) [where defendant appeared to have pleaded to both a fraud (false representation under Mass. Gen. Laws ch.18 §5B) and a larceny charge and nothing in the record suggested the loss was only for the larceny, the court found that the required restitution resulted in an aggravated felony]; *James v. Gonzales,* 464 F.3d 505, 510–14 (5th Cir. 2006) [where respondent pled guilty to one count of bank fraud resulting in a loss of $9,500 but the restitution amount exceeded $10,000, the court found it was an aggravated felony because the indictment alleged a scheme to defraud in excess of $10,000 and the PSR also found the intended loss was in excess of $10,000]; *Ferreira v. Ashcroft,* 390 F.3d 1091 (9th Cir. 2004) [a conviction under Cal. Welfare & Institutions Code §10980(c)(2), the court found that the amount stated as restitution in the plea agreement exceeded $10,000]. Loss can also include "intended loss" if the defendant is charged with attempt or conspiracy because aggravated felonies also encompass attempts and conspiracies of the substantive crime at INA §101(a)(43)(U). *Eke v. Mukasey,* 512 F.3d 372, 378–81 (7th Cir. 2008) [in identity theft case where petitioner conspired to obtain a car through identity theft, the intended loss was in excess of $10,000 and therefore actionable under INA §§101(a)(43)(M)(i) & (U)].

Proving the Amount of Loss—The BIA has held that the categorical and modified categorical approaches under *Taylor* and *Shepard* only apply to the elements of the prior State or Federal conviction and do *not* apply to matters that are not part of the elements of the prior crime, but are included in the immigration statute, such as loss to the victim. As these nonelements are not part of the categorical/modified categorical approach, their proof is not limited to the "record of conviction" as in *Shepard* but may include any documents or testimony allowed in immigration matters. *Matter of Babaisakov,* 24 I&N Dec. 306, 319–21 (BIA 2007) [holding that not only restitution orders, presentence reports, and admissions during plea colloquies may be used to prove loss but "any evidence, otherwise admissible in removal proceedings, including witness testimony" and "testimonial admissions of the respondent made during the removal hearing"]. *See also Nijhawan v. Att'y Gen.,* ___F.3d___ (3d Cir. May 2, 2008) [court held that the loss amount need not be specifically pled or found by jury, but, rather allows inquiry into facts underlying conviction, and is satisfied if this inquiry shows that the "amount of loss is sufficiently tethered to the fraud conviction"]; *See generally Ali v. Mukasey,* 521 F.3d 737 (7th Cir. 2008) [following *Matter of Babaisakov* and reinterpreting its own precedent post–*Brand X Internet Services,* the circuit court concluded the BIA could rely on the presentence investigation report to establish whether crime is a CIMT because "when deciding how to classify convictions under criteria that go beyond the criminal charge–such as the amount of the victim's loss, or whether the crime is one of 'moral turpitude' the agency has discretion to consider evidence beyond the charging papers and judgment of conviction"]. *But see e.g., Dulal-Whiteway v. DHS,* 501 F.3d 116, 123–34 (2d Cir. 2007) [cannot rely on PSR to prove loss to the victim as court can only rely upon facts to which the defendant actually pleaded to establish the offense or if tried upon facts found beyond a reasonable doubt by the jury].

Government as Victim—Some courts have rejected the idea that INA §101(a)(43)(M)(i) applies only to individuals and corporations but not to the government, rejecting the idea that the government cannot be a victim. *Akio Kawashima v. Gonzales,* 503 F.3d 997, 1001 (9th Cir. 2007) [followed *Balogun* and plain meaning to determine government is a victim of violations of 26 U.S.C. §§7206(1) & (2)]; *Balogun v. U.S. Att'y Gen.,* 425 F.3d 1356, 1360–61 (11th Cir. 2005) [*Chevron* deference given to interpretation that includes government within the definition of "victim"]. *But see Ki Se Lee v. Ashcroft,* 368 F.3d 218 (3d Cir. 2004).

Attempt Crimes—Actual loss of $10,000 not necessary because it can be viewed as an "attempt" crime under INA §101(a)(43)(U). *Matter of Onyido,* 22 I&N Dec. 552 (BIA 1999) [false claim with intent to defraud arising from unsuccessful scheme to obtain $15,000 from insurance company was "attempt" crime under INA §§101(a)(43)(M)(i) & (U), and therefore an aggravated felony]. *But see Sui v. INS,* 250 F.3d 105 (2d Cir. 2001) where the court adopted the 2-prong test for an attempt articulated in *Onyido* but found that respondent was not an aggravated felon based upon an attempt, because a conviction for possession of counterfeit securities with an intent to deceive does not necessarily constitute an attempt to pass those securities and cause a loss.

Aiding and Abetting—Although aiding and abetting is *not* included in the definition of an aggravated felony under INA §101(a)(43)(U), a least one circuit has held that aiding and abetting is an aggravated felony in the context of INA §101(a)(43)(M)(i) regarding bank fraud. *James v. Gonzales,* 464 F.3d 505, 508–10 (5th Cir. 2006) [respondent was found guilty of aiding and abetting bank fraud under 18 U.S.C. §§2 & 1344]. *See also Gonzales v. Duenas-Alvarez,* 549 U.S. ____, 127 S.Ct. 815 (2007) [Cal. Veh. Code §10851(a), a vehicle-theft statute, includes aiding and abetting under the "generic approach" first addressed in *Taylor* and is therefore considered an aggravated felony].

Hybrid Crimes—One court found that a theft offense that is also an offense involving fraud or deceit, is an aggravated felon only if the conviction qualifies under the definition of both. *Nugent v. Ashcroft,* 367 F.3d 162 (3d Cir. 2004) [where respondent convicted of theft by deception under 18 Pa. Cons. Stat. Ann. §3922(a) but amount was less than $10,000, he was not convicted of an aggravated felony]. *See also Martinez v. Mukasey,* 519 F.3d 532, 538-41 (5th Cir. 2008) [court engaged in hybrid analysis but concluded that a conviction under 18 U.S.C. §1344 while a fraud crime was not a theft crime]; *But see Bobb v. Att'y Gen. of the U.S.,* 458 F.3d 213 (3d Cir. 2006) [conviction under 18 U.S.C. §510(a)(2) for passing, uttering, and publishing a U.S. Treasury check in an amount of $13,277, for which defendant received only 4 months imprisonment, is a fraud aggravated felony under §101(a)(43)(M)(i) even if it is also, under §101(a)(43)(R), a crime related to forgery].

Fraud and Theft Crimes Distinguished—The BIA clarified *Matter of V-Z-S-* to distinguish theft crimes from fraud finding that theft crimes involve taking property without consent and fraud and deceit crimes under INA §101(a)(43)(M)(i) involve taking property *with* consent that has been fraudulently obtained. *Matter of Garcia-Madruga,* 24 I&N Dec. 436 (BIA 2008) [finding that IJ's determination that Rhode Island General Law 40-6-15 concerning welfare fraud was a theft crime was in error]. *See also Soliman v. Gonzales,* 419 F.3d 276 (4th Cir. 2005); *Nugent v. Ashcroft,* 367 F.3d 162 (3d Cir. 2004).

Crimes Under Subsection (M)(ii) [INA §101(a)(43)(M)(ii), for income tax evasion under IRC §7201 where the revenue loss to the government exceeds $10,000]: *Evangelista v. Ashcroft,* 359 F.3d 145, 149–53 (2d Cir. 2004) [conviction under §7201 where income evasion in excess of $300,000 is an aggravated felony whether conviction was for "defeating" or "evading" taxes under §7201]. *But see Lee v. Ashcroft,* 368 F.3d 218 (3d Cir. 2004) [filing a false tax return in violation of §7206(1) is not an aggravated felony because Congress only specified one tax crime—§7201—as aggravated felony].

3.n. Alien smuggling offenses under INA §274(a)(1)(A) or (a)(2), 8 U.S.C. §1324(a)(1)(A) or (a)(2), except in the case of a first offense for which the person has affirmatively shown that he committed the offense for the purpose of assisting, abetting or aiding a spouse, parent, or child to violate the Act. Congress intended to eliminate the "for gain" or commercial purposes requirement while allowing this exception. H.R. Conf. Rep. No. 828, 104th Cong., 2d Sess. at 223. *Matter of Alvarado-Alvina,* 22 I&N Dec. 718 (BIA 1999) [person not aggravated felon under INA §101(a)(43)(N) if convicted of alien smuggling under §275]. *Accord Rivera-Sanchez v. Reno,* 198 F.3d 545 (5th Cir. 1999). The definition includes misdemeanors as well as felonies *Biskupski v. Att'y Gen. of the U.S.,* 503 F.3d 274, 279–81 (3d Cir. 2007) [a conviction under 8 U.S.C. §1324(a)(2) for misdemeanor smuggling is an aggravated felony]. This provision also covers persons encouraging and inducing an alien to reside in U.S., *Sena v. Gonzales,* 428 F.3d 50, 51–53 (1st Cir. 2005), harboring *Patel v. Ashcroft,* 294 F.3d 465 (3d Cir. 2002); *Castro-Expinosa v. Ashcroft,* 257 F.3d 1130 (9th Cir. 2001) as well as transporting, *Matter of Ruiz-Romero,* 22 I&N Dec. 486 (BIA 1999) *aff'd Ruiz-Romero v. Reno,* 205 F.3d 837 (5th Cir. 2000) [conviction for transporting under §274(a)(1)(A)(ii)]; *Gavilan-Cuate v. Yetter,* 276 F.3d 418 (8th Cir. 2002) [conspiracy to transport and harbor]; *U.S. v. Galinda-Gallego,* 244 F.3d 728, 733 (9th Cir. 2001) and not solely smuggling. Although "mere employment" is a defense to harboring and smuggling charges, a least one court has found that it was not reversible error for the district court to deny a jury instruction on mere employment. *U.S. v. Khanani,* 502 F.3d 1281, 1285–89 (11th Cir. 2007) [failure to give mere employment jury instruction did not seriously impair the defendant's ability to conduct their defense because the instructions as given already required proof beyond mere employment].

3.o. An offense described in INA §§275(a) or 276 committed by a person who was previously deported for another aggravated felony conviction. *Matter of Alvarado-Alvina,* 22 I&N Dec. 718 (BIA 1999) [person convicted under §275(a) who was not previously deported is not an aggravated felon under INA §101(a)(43)(O)]; *Rivera-Sanchez v. Reno,* 198 F.3d 545 (5th Cir. 1999) [same].

3.p. Falsely making, forging, counterfeiting, mutilating, or altering a passport or instrument in violation of 18 U.S.C. §1543, or as described in the document fraud section under 18 U.S.C. §1546(a) *and* the term of imprisonment is at least 12 months, except if it is a first offense and the person affirmatively shows s/he committed the offense for the purpose of assisting, abetting, or aiding his or her spouse, child, or parent to violate the Act.

3.q. An offense relating to a failure to appear by a defendant for service of sentence, if the underlying offense is punishable by imprisonment for a term of 5 years or more.

3.r. An offense relating to commercial bribery, counterfeiting, forgery, or trafficking in vehicles with altered ID numbers, where the term of imprisonment is at least one year. *Young Wong Park v. Attorney General of the U.S.,* 472 F.3d 66, 71–73 (3d Cir. 2007) [a conviction for "knowingly using a counterfeit mark" and trafficking in good and services with a counterfeit mark in violation of 18 U.S.C. §2320 is a crime "relating to" counterfeiting]; *Morales-Alegria v. Gonzales,* 449 F.3d 1051 (9th Cir. 2006) [forgery under Cal. Penal Code §476 is consistent with the generic definition of the crime and therefore is an aggravated felony]; *Richards v. Ashcroft,* 400 F.3d 125, 127–30 (2d Cir. 2005) [second-degree forgery under Conn. Gen. Stat. §53a-139 is an offense "relating to" forgery even if it is broader than the federal or common law definition of forgery because it includes possession of forged instruments]; *Kamagate v. Ashcroft,* 385 F.3d 144, 151–56 (2d Cir. 2004) [a conviction under 18 U.S.C. §371 for conspiracy to violate 18 U.S.C. §513(a) for making, uttering, or possessing counterfeit securities intending to deceive others is a crime "related to" counterfeiting even though it includes possession; declined to construe "relating to" narrowly]; *Drakes v. Zimski,* 240 F.3d 246 (3d Cir. 2001) [forgery in the second degree under 11 Del. Code §861 is an offense "relating to" forgery as broadly defined]; *Albillo-Figueroa v. INS,* 221 F.3d 1070 (9th Cir. 2000) [possession of counterfeit obligations is a crime "relating to" counterfeiting and thus an aggravated felony]; *Matter of Aldabesheh,* 22 I&N Dec. 983 (BIA 1999) [forgery in second degree under N.Y. Penal Code §170.10(2)]. *But see Vizcarra-Ayala v. Mukasey,* 514 F.3d 870 (9th Cir. 2008) [forgery conviction under Cal. Penal Code §475(c) was not an aggravated felony on the categorical approach because it permits a conviction for the use of a genuine document fraudulently and there was no evidence in the record for the modified categorical approach to indicate otherwise]. At least one circuit has determined that even if a forgery crime is covered under this section, a person may be charged under the fraud section. *Bobb v. Att'y Gen. of the U.S.,* 458 F.3d 213 (3d Cir. 2006) [conviction under 18 U.S.C. §510(a)(2) for passing, uttering, and publishing a U.S. Treasury check in an amount of $13,277, for which defendant received only 4 months imprisonment, is a fraud aggravated felony under §101(a)(43)(M)(i) even if it is also, under §101(a)(43)(R), a crime related to forgery].

3.s. An offense relating to obstruction of justice, perjury, or subordination of perjury or bribery of a witness for which the term of imprisonment is at least one year—*Matter of Martinez-Recinos,* 23 I&N Dec. 175 (BIA 2001) [perjury in violation of Cal. Penal Code §118(a) is an aggravated felony because it is essentially the same as the federal perjury statute, 18 U.S.C. §1621]. A conviction for an accessory after the fact under 18 U.S.C. §3 is considered an offense related to obstruction. *Matter of Batista-Hernandez,* 21 I&N Dec. 955 (BIA 1997). One circuit has also determined that a conviction for criminal contempt under 18 U.S.C. §401(3), which punishes disobedience of a court order, is considered obstruction of justice and therefore an aggravated felony. *Alwan v. Ashcroft,* 388 F.3d 507, 513–15 (5th Cir. 2004) [finding18 U.S.C. §1503(a) applicable to define obstruction of justice]. However, a conviction for a misprision of a felony under 18 U.S.C. §4 is not. *Matter of Espinoza,* 22 I&N Dec. 889 (BIA 1999).

3.t. An offense relating to a failure to appear before a court pursuant to court order to answer or disprove a felony charge for which a sentence of 2 years imprisonment or more *may* be imposed—*Barnaby v. Reno,* 142 F.Supp.2d 277 (D. Conn. 2001) [conviction under Conn. Gen. Stat. §53a-172 is not an aggravated felony because it permits a conviction if a party fails to appear after being "legally called" and does not require that it be pursuant to "court order."].

3.u. Any *attempt* to commit any of the above offenses—*Matter of Onyido*, 22 I&N Dec. 552 (BIA 1999) [false claim with intent to defraud arising from unsuccessful scheme to obtain $15,000 from insurance company was "attempt" crime under INA §§101(a)(43)(M)(i) & (U)]; In *Sui v. INS,* 250 F.3d 105 (2d Cir. 2001), the court clarified the attempt provision as stated in *Onyido* to require the "presence of criminal intent and the completion of a substantial stop toward committing the crime" for an attempt to be an aggravated felon. *Sui,* 250 F.3d at 115. In *Sui,* the court found that conviction for possession of counterfeit securities with intent to deceive does not necessarily constitute an attempt to pass the securities and cause a loss in excess of $10,000, and the court vacated the order of removal. *U.S. v. Martinez-Garcia,* 268 F.3d 460, 465–66 (7th Cir. 2001), followed *Sui* in establishing a generic approach to "attempt" based on common law and the Model Penal Code and required both "intent" and "a substantial step toward completion of the crime" before finding that the defendant had committed attempted theft. However, in the view of one court, an impossibility defense is not permissible for an attempt crime. *Hernandez-Alvarez v. Gonzales,* 432 F.3d 763, 766 (7th Cir. 2005) [the impossibility of completing an attempted indecent solicitation of a minor, because the person solicited was actually a police officer, is not a defense]. Where the attempt statute under state law is broader than the federal definition, the respondent may also not be considered an aggravated felon. *Rebilas v. Keisler,* 506 F.3d 1161, 1164–65 (9th Cir. 2007) [where Arizona's definition of attempt under Ariz. Rev. Stat. §13-1001 regarding attempted public sexual indecency to a minor is broader than the federal definition because it includes "any step" in the commission of the offense and the federal statute requires a "substantial step," respondent is not an aggravated felon].

3.v. Any *conspiracy* to commit any of the above offenses—The conspiracy provision has been interpreted broadly in some circuits. *Conteh v. Gonzales,* 461 F.3d 45, 54–57 (1st Cir. 2006) [where the conviction was for conspiracy under 18 U.S.C. §371 the government was not required to demonstrate that the conspiracy involved every element of the substantive offense enumerated under the aggravated felony statute but was only required to show that the substantive crime that was the conspiratorial objective was an aggravated felony]; *Kamagate v. Ashcroft,* 385 F.3d 144, 151–56 (2d Cir. 2004) [a conviction under 18 U.S.C. §371 for conspiracy to violate 18 U.S.C. §513(a) for making, uttering, or possessing counterfeit securities intending to deceive others is a crime "related to" counterfeiting]. *But see Omari v. Gonzales,* 419 F.3d 303 (5th Cir. 2005) [where respondent convicted of conspiracy under 18 U.S.C. §371 to violate 18 U.S.C. §2314, which is a divisible statute, the removal order was vacated, because under the modified categorical approach, the only documents in evidence were the indictment and conviction, and they suggested a nonfraud crime of possession of illegal airline tickets]. The Board's position is that deportation under the conspiracy provision for aggravated felonies requires proof by clear and convincing evidence that respondent was: (1) convicted of engaging in a conspiracy within the meaning of INA §101(a)(43)(U) and that (2) at least one of the acts that was the object of the conspiracy was an offense involving the aggravated felony; and (3) any other aspect of the ground of deportation occurred or was contemplated *e.g.,* loss to the victim exceeded $10,000. *Matter of S-I-K-,* 24 I&N Dec. 324 (BIA 2007) [removal upheld where respondent was convicted of conspiracy and the object of the conspiracy was a fraud crime where the record demonstrated that the potential loss to the victim exceeded $10,000]. Loss can also include "intended loss" if the defendant is charged with conspiracy. *Eke v. Mukasey,* 512 F.3d 372, 378–81 (7th Cir. 2008) [in identity theft case where petitioner conspired to obtain a car through identity theft, the intended loss was in excess of $10,000 and therefore actionable under INA §§101(a)(43)(M)(i) & (U)].

3.w. Aiding and Abetting—Although aiding and abetting is *not* included in the definition of an aggravated felony under INA §101(a)(43)(U), the Supreme Court in *Gonzales v. Duenas-Alvarez,* 549 U.S. ____, 127 S.Ct. 815 (2007) recognized that "aiding and abetting" for a theft crime under the "generic approach" addressed in *Taylor* fell within the definition of the substantive crime because "every jurisdiction—all States and the Federal Government—has 'expressly abrogated the distinction' among principals and aiders and abettors" except for accessories after the fact. *Duenas-Alvarez,* 127 S.Ct. 815, ___ (2007). The Court reversed the Ninth Circuit and determined that a person convicted of aiding and abetting under the California vehicle theft statute, Cal. Veh. Code §10851(a), is an aggravated felon. *See also James v. Gonzales,* 464 F.3d 505, 508–10 (5th Cir. 2006) [respondent was found guilty of aiding and abetting bank fraud under 18 U.S.C. §§2 & 1344 and therefore was an aggravated felon pursuant to INA §101(a)(43)(M)(i)].

4. **Other Aggravated Felony Issues**

4.a. *Federal and State Law Apply*—INA §101(a)(43) also provides that the term "aggravated felony" applies to an offense described in the above paragraphs "whether in violation of federal or state law ..." *Matter of Ponce de Leon,* 21 I&N Dec. 154 (BIA 1996) [sale of marijuana even if not punished harshly under state law is aggravated felony if it is drug trafficking crime under federal law]; *Lopez-Elias v. Reno,* 209 F.3d 788, 792 n.6 (5th Cir. 2000) [how Texas characterizes offense does not control for immigration purposes]; *Blake v. Gonzales,* 481 F.3d 152, 160 (2d Cir. 2007) [although assault and battery on a police officer in chapter 265, section 13D is not a felony under Massachusetts law, it is a felony under federal law because the maximum term of imprisonment is more than one year];*Castro-Baez v. Reno,* 217 F.3d 1057, 1059 (9th Cir. 2000) [definition of rape under federal law has no bearing on conviction under California statute because state convictions constitute aggravated felonies]. *But see Francis v. Reno,* 269 F.3d 162 (3d Cir. 2001) [finding that a Pennsylvania misdemeanor offense could not be considered a COV under 18 U.S.C. §16(b), even though the offense was punishable by more than one year in prison, and therefore would have been deemed a felony under federal law].

4.b. *State Felonies as Aggravated Felonies*—Whether a state categorizes its crime as a felony or misdemeanor is no longer relevant, at least as to drug trafficking aggravated felonies, as the courts must look to whether the state offense is punishable as a felony under federal law. *Lopez v. Gonzales,* 549 U.S. ___, 127 S.Ct. 625 (2006). Prior to *Lopez v.* Gonzales, the BIA maintained the position that a state conviction that is a felony under state law but not a felony under federal law may be an aggravated felony in those circuits that agree with that position or have taken no position. *Matter of Yanez-Garcia,* 23 I&N Dec. 390 (BIA 2002) [reversed *Matter of K-V-D-* and modified *Matter of L-G-* and *Matter of Davis*, and held that a state felony for possession of cocaine can be an aggravated felony in those circuits that have not yet spoken on the issue or have adopted the view]. The BIA's position was squarely rejected by the Supreme Court with respect to drug possession offenses that are state felonies but not federal felonies. *Lopez v. Gonzales,* 549 U.S. ___, 127 S.Ct. 625 (2006) [the Court held that "a state offense constitutes a 'felony punishable under the Controlled Substances Act' only if it proscribes conduct punishable as a felony under that federal law."]. *Accord. Gonzales-Gomez v. Achim,* 441 F.3d 532 (7th Cir. 2006) [a felony in Illinois for possession of cocaine that would be punishable only as a misdemeanor under federal law is not an aggravated felony]; *Cazarez-Gutierrez v. Ashcroft,* 382 F.3d 905, 919 (9th Cir. 2004) [rejecting *Yanez-Garcia* and holding that "a state drug offense is not an aggravated felony for immigration purposes unless it is punishable as a felony under CSA or other federal drug laws named in the definition of 'drug trafficking crime,' or is a crime involving a trafficking element."]; *Gerbier v. Holmes,* 280 F.3d 297 (3d Cir. 2002); *U.S. v. Pornes-Garcia,* 171 F.3d 142, 147 (2d Cir.), *cert. denied*, 528 U.S. 880 (1999); *Aguirre v. INS*, 79 F.3d 315 (2d Cir. 1996); *U.S. v. Peralta-Espinoza,* 413 F.Supp.2d 970 (E.D. Wis. 2006) [in sentencing guideline case possession of 4 pounds of marijuana under Arizona law, although a felony, is not an aggravated felony because it is not a felony punishable under the CSA].

In *Matter of Crammond*, 23 I&N Dec. 9 (BIA 2001), *vacated on jurisdictional grounds*, 23 I&N Dec. 179 (BIA 2001), the BIA determined that a felony is defined as a term of "more than 1 year" imprisonment pursuant to 18 U.S.C. §3559(a)(5) while a misdemeanor is defined as "one year or less" of imprisonment under 18 U.S.C. §§3559(a)(6)–(8). *Blake v. Gonzales,* 481 F.3d 152, 160 (2d Cir. 2007) [although assault and battery on a police officer is not a felony under Mass. Gen Laws. ch. 265 §13D, it is a felony under federal law because the maximum term of imprisonment is more than one year]; *U.S. v. Cordova-Arevalo,* 456 F.3d 1229 (10th Cir. 2006) [although Colorado third-degree assault conviction is a misdemeanor under state law, it is a felony under the federal definition pursuant to 18 U.S.C. §3559(a) and therefore enhancement of sentence was appropriate]; *Bovkun v. Ashcroft,* 283 F.3d 166, 171 (3d Cir. 2002) [following *U.S. v. Graham,* found that a conviction for state misdemeanor may constitute a §16(a) crime of violence aggravated felony if the term of imprisonment is more than one year]. There must be proof that the state charge contains all the elements of a felony offense "for which an alien could be convicted and punished under the cited federal laws." *Matter of Barrett* at 174. *See also Steele v. Blackman,* 236 F.3d 130, 135–36 (3d Cir. 2001) for a detailed description of the BIA's analysis. *But see Matter of Yanez-Garcia, supra; Biskupski v. Att'y Gen. of the U.S.,* 503 F.3d 274, 279–81 (3d Cir. 2007) [a conviction under 8 U.S.C. §1324(a)(2) for misdemeanor smuggling is an aggravated felony because Congress defined it as an aggravated felony irrespective of its nonfelony status under federal law]; *Francis v. Reno,* 269 F.3d 162, 167–71 (3d Cir. 2001) [rejected reliance on §3559 analysis for 18 U.S.C. §16(a) regarding crime of violence, and found that state misdemeanor statute, punishable by more than one year imprisonment, is not a "felony"]; *Guerrero-Perez v. INS,* 242 F.3d 727 (7th Cir.), *reh'g denied* 256 F.3d 546 (7th Cir. 2001) [rejected analysis in *Crammond* and found that a misdemeanor offense for sexual abuse of a minor under Illinois law constituted an aggravated felony]; *U.S. v. Marin-Navarette,* 244 F.3d 1284 (11th Cir. 2001) [although attempted child molestation in the third degree is a misdemeanor under Washington State law it is an aggravated felony].

4.c. *"Described In" Language in Aggravated Felony Statutes*—In a number of aggravated felony provisions, *e.g.,* §§101(a)(43)(D), (E), and (H)–(O), Congress requires that the conviction be one which is "described in" the criminal section referred to. In *Matter of Vasquez-Muniz,* 22 I&N Dec. 1415 (BIA 2000), the BIA rejected INS's claim that "described in" simply meant "similar to" the federal statute. Rather it refers to "a matter *specifically* delineated" and therefore must contain all of the elements including federal jurisdictional elements to be an aggravated felony. *Matter of Vasquez-Muniz,* 22 I&N Dec. 1415, 1420–24 (BIA 2000) [prior felon convicted under Cal. Penal Code §12021(a)(1) is not convicted of an aggravated felony under

§101(a)(43)(E)(ii), because it was not an offense "described in" §922(g)(1), as that offense required federal jurisdiction by interstate commerce]. The BIA, however, subsequently reversed its view and reconsidered *Matter of Vasquez-Muniz,* at 23 I&N Dec. 207 (BIA 2002). In the latest decision it rejected the position that the federal jurisdictional element must be present to demonstrate that the statutes are similar and found that the California state statute was similar to the federal statute because it contained the other elements of knowing possession of a firearm by a person who has been convicted of a felony. *Id. See also Negrete-Rodriguez v. Mukasey,* 518 F.3d 497 (7th Cir. 2008) [unlawful possession of a weapon by a felon in violation of Illinois statute 720 ILCS 5/24-1.1(a) is an aggravated felony "described in" 18 U.S.C. §922(g)(1) as the only additional element in the federal crime is an "interstate commerce" requirement" where merely grants federal jurisdictional over the crime].

4.d. *"Relating To" Language*—At least one court has found that the "relating to" language in 101(a)(43)(R) signifies a broad construction and that "Congress evidenced an intent to define [the listed offenses] in [their] broadest sense…" *Young Wong Park v. Attorney General of the U.S.*, 472 F.3d 66, 72 (3d Cir. 2007) [quoting court's decision in *Drakes v. Zimski,* 240 F.3d 246, 249 (3d Cir. 2001) and finding that a conviction under 18 U.S.C. §2320 for knowing use of a counterfeit mark is a crime "relating to" counterfeiting within the meaning of 101(a)(43)(R)]

4.e. *Foreign Convictions*—The term "aggravated felony" also applies to foreign convictions for all of the above if the term of imprisonment was completed within the previous 15 years. The 15 year limitation applies to foreign convictions only, not to domestic convictions. *U.S. v. Maturin,* 499 F.3d 1243 (11th Cir. 2007) [plain language of 101(a)(43) limits provision to foreign convictions].

4.f. ***Categorical and Modified Categorical Approach***

In *Chang v. INS,* 307 F.3d 1185, 1189–92 (9th Cir. 2002) the Ninth Circuit discussed two approaches to determine whether a crime was an aggravated felony. The "categorical" approach looks solely to the structure of the statute that is the subject of the conviction, and not the "underlying circumstances" (what the person actually did), and determines whether a person convicted under that statute must be convicted of the designated aggravated felony. In *Chang*, for example, a person convicted of 18 U.S.C. §1344 did not necessarily commit an aggravated felony under INA §101(a)(43)(M)(i) because a conviction could be obtained under §1344 even if the amount was less than $10,000. If the statute of conviction is not a categorical match because it is divisible and contains elements that do and do not qualify as an aggravated felony, the court proceeds to the "modified categorical" approach. Some circuits have taken the position that in determining whether the conviction is an aggravated felony under the categorical approach the court must assume the least culpable conduct under the statute. *Jeune v. Att'y Gen. of the U.S.,* 476 F.3d 199, 204 (3d Cir. 2007); *Vargas-Sarmiento v. DOJ,* 448 F.3d 159 (2d Cir. 2006). Under the "modified categorical" inquiry, the court will conduct "a limited examination of documents in the record of conviction to determine if there is sufficient evidence to conclude that a defendant was convicted of the elements of the generically defined crime even though his or her statute of conviction was facially over inclusive." *Chang v. INS,* 307 F.3d at 1189. *See also Larin-Ulloa v. Gonzales,* 462 F.3d 456, 463–65 (5th Cir. 2006) [describing the categorical and modified categorical approach and finding that a conviction under a Kansas aggravated battery statute was not a crime of violence]. If the record is unclear the court may remand the case and order the government to supplement the record. *U.S. v. Bonilla-Mungia,* 422 F.3d 316, 320–22 (5th Cir. 2005) [where defendant was convicted of sexual battery under the 1998 version of Cal. Penal Code §243.4, which includes sections that may be crimes of violence and ones that are not, court remanded case to permit government to supplement record pursuant to *Shepard* to establish which elements were pled to by defendant]. But if the entire record demonstrates that all documents that may be considered do not establish an aggravated felony the court will reverse the BIA's contrary determination. *Sandoval-Lua v. Gonzales,* 499 F.3d 1121 (9th Cir. 2007) [a conviction under Cal. Health & Safety Code §11379(a) under modified categorical approach does not constitute an aggravated felony because the record is inconclusive]; *Larin-Ulloa v. Gonzales,* 462 F.3d 456, 463–65 (5th Cir. 2006). In addition, where the particular elements of the crime are *not broader* than the generic crime and the jury or judge are therefore not required to find all the elements of an underlying generic crime to obtain a conviction, the modified categorical approach is inappropriate. *Navarro-Lopez v. Gonzales,* 503 F.3d 1063, 1073 (9th Cir. 2007) (*en banc*) [to obtain a conviction under Cal. Penal Code §32 a finding that respondent committed a CIMT is unnecessary, because accessory after the fact lacks moral turpitude as an element for conviction, and therefore there is no need to conduct a modified categorical approach].

Supreme Court and Categorical Approach—The Supreme Court has accepted the categorical approach in *Leocal v. Ashcroft,* 543 U.S. 1, 125 S.Ct. 377, 381 (2004) where it "looked to the elements and the nature of the offense of conviction, rather than to the particular facts relating to the petitioner's crime." *See also Gonzales v. Duenas-Alvarez,* 549 U.S. ____, 127 S.Ct. 815 (2007); *Shepard v. U.S.,* 544 U.S. 13, 125 S.Ct. 1254, 1260 (2005); *Taylor v. U.S.,* 495 U.S. 575, 598–600 (1990). In *Shepard* the Court clarified the documents that may be considered when analyzing a 'generic' conviction under the modified categorical approach: "the charging document, written plea agreement, transcript of plea colloquy, and any explicit findings by the trial judge to which the defendant assented." *Shepard v. U.S.,* 125 S.Ct. at 1257.

Analyzing Crimes Under the BIA's Categorical Approach—The BIA's view of the categorical approach, at least in drug trafficking cases, is that the elements of the respondent's offense must correspond to the elements of an offense "that carries a maximum term of imprisonment of more than 1 year" and that any aggravating fact (other than a prior conviction) that increases the penalty for a crime is considered an element of the crime *only if* it must be submitted to a jury and proved beyond a reasonable doubt on the fewest facts necessary for a conviction. *Matter of Aruna,* 24 I&N Dec. 452, 455–57 (BIA 2008) Therefore, under the categorical approach you do not look at the offense that carries the *least penalty*, but rather the crime that may be proved on the *fewest facts*. *But see Jeune v. Att'y Gen. of the U.S.,* 476 F.3d 199, 205 (3d Cir. 2007); *Wilson v. Ashcroft,* 350 F.3d 377, 382 (3d Cir. 2003) and *Steele v. Blackman,* 236 F.3d 130, 137 (3d Cir. 2001) which look at factors regarding lowering the penalty including issues regarding remuneration as a basis for the categorical approach. Thus, according to the Board, the Third Circuit's error is to look to 21 U.S.C. §841(b)(4) because that statute addresses "mitigating factors" in lowering sentences and not establishing the element of the crime for categorical review purposes. *See generally Matter of Palacios,* 22 I&N Dec. 434 (BIA 1998) and *Matter of Alcantar,* 20 I&N Dec. 801 (BIA 1994) for the Board's treatment generally of aggravated-felony issues.

Documents to Prove Conviction—Efforts by the government to use documents other than those specified in *Shepard v. U.S.,* 544 U.S. 13, 125 S.Ct. 1254, 1260 (2005) have met resistance in the federal courts. Thus, (1) statements in a brief were insufficient *Huerta-Guevara v. Ashcroft,* 321 F.3d 883, 888 (9th Cir. 2003) [INS could not rely on statements in respondent's brief to support intent]; (2) as are Presentence Investigative Reports (PSI), *Dulal-Whiteway v. DHS,* 501 F.3d 116, 123–34 (2d Cir. 2007) [in conviction for fraudulently trafficking in unauthorized access devices under 18 U.S.C. §1029(a)(2), the court cannot rely on PSR and restitution order to prove loss to the victim]; *Hernandez-Martinez v. Ashcroft,* 343 F.3d 1075 (9th Cir. 2003) [affirming *Huerta-Guevara* and determining that a presentence report cannot be used to establish that a divisible statute is an aggravated felony]; *Conteh v. Gonzales,* 461 F.3d 45, 57–59 (1st Cir. 2006) [cannot rely on respondent's after-the-fact statements or the PSI report to establish the record of conviction]; *Dickson v. Ashcroft,* 346 F.3d 44, 53 n.1 (2d Cir. 2003) [where statute is divisible cannot use narrative facts in pre-sentence report to determine whether unlawful imprisonment under NYPL is a crime of violence]; *Lara-Chacon v. Ashcroft,* 345 F.3d 1148, 1151–54 (9th Cir. 2003) [under modified categorical approach could not use pre-sentence report to determine that conviction under Arizona money laundering statute was a drug trafficking crime]; *Chang v. INS,* 307 F.3d 1185 (9th Cir. 2002) [the plea agreement clearly demonstrated that the $10,000 threshold amount for an aggravated felony based upon fraud was not met and that the BIA could not use a presentence report to contradict the plea agreement]; (3) notations regarding special sentencing reasons or factors, *Larin-Ulloa v. Gonzales,* 462 F.3d 456, 468–69 (5th Cir. 2006) [BIA erroneously referred to a special sentencing factor notation in the Kansas journal entry form to determine under the modified categorical approach that respondent's conviction for aggravated battery was a crime of violence]; (4) police reports, *Matter of Sanudo,* 23 I&N Dec. 968, 974–75 (BIA 2006) [where the factual narrative of the police report was not incorporated into the charging document or the plea, it could not be considered in determining whether respondent may be removed as an aggravated felon for a conviction of a California domestic battery charge]; *Wala v. Mukasey,* 511 F.3d 102, 107–10 and n.5 (2d Cir. 2007) [relying on *Shepard* and determining that the BIA may rely only on facts that the petitioner "necessarily pleaded" the court held that the government could not rely on the police report to demonstrate that plea]; (5) abstract of judgment, *Sandoval-Lua v. Gonzales,* 499 F.3d 1121, 1130 n.8 (9th Cir. 2007) [abstract of judgment is not the judgment itself and is insufficient to establish elements of a crime]; or (6) the respondent's after-the-fact statements, *Conteh v. Gonzales,* 461 F.3d 45, 57–59 (1st Cir. 2006). *But see Suazo Perez v. Mukasey,* 512 F.3d 1222, 1226–27 (9th Cir. 2008) [police report could be utilized in modified categorical approach where defendant checked a box on his plea that stated he agreed that "the court may review the police reports and/or statement of probable cause supplied by the prosecution to establish a factual basis of the plea"]; *Lara-Ruiz v. INS,* 241 F.3d 934 (7th Cir. 2001) [allowing evidence outside of the record to establish age of victim]. Similarly, the IJ/BIA may not infer a conviction under the modified categorical approach from the charges when respondent pled to something different. *See e.g., Cisneros-Perez v. Gonzales,* 465 F.3d 386, 392–94 (9th Cir. 2006) [the court determined that under the modified categorical approach an inference could not be drawn from the charges concerning domestic violence when the respondent pled to simple battery and no other document identified the victim as respondent's wife]; *Martinez-Perez v. Ashcroft,* 417 F.3d 1022, 1028–29 (9th Cir. 2005) [the court, following the documents specified under *Shepard*, found that it could not determine that respondent's conviction for grand theft under Cal. Penal Code §487(c) was a theft offense as generically defined because it could not rely on the "facts" of the information, where the plea was a different offense than the one charged in the information.]; *Sareang Ye v. INS,* 214 F.3d 1128, 1133 (9th Cir. 2000) [when a statute reaches conduct that would or would not constitute an aggravated felony, "we look to charging paper and judgment of conviction to determine if the actual offense that defendant was convicted of qualifies as a crime of violence."]. *Cf. Parrilla v. Gonzales,* 414 F.3d 1038, 1042–44 (9th Cir. 2005) [the court, following *Shepard,* allowed the use of a certificate for determination of probable cause (CDPC) to establish that a conviction under Wash. Rev. Code §9.68A.090 for communicating with a minor was an aggravated felony under the modified categorical approach because the CDPC was expressly incorporated in respondent's guilty plea]; *Iysheh v. Gonzales,* 437 F.3d 613 (7th Cir. 2006), [the court also relying on *Shepard* found that a person who had a corrected judgment identifying his offense as a non–aggravated felony, but who pled guilty to a count that included fraud, did commit an aggravated felony]; *U.S. v. Lopez-Patino,* 391 F.3d 1034, 1036–38 (9th Cir. 2004) [Arizona child abuse statute, Ariz. Rev. Stat. §13-2623(C), is not *per se* a crime of violence, but under modified categorical approach defendant admitted a crime of violence in the plea]. The First Circuit has independently taken the position that the IJ/BIA may also rely on documents specified in 8 U.S.C. §1229a(c)(3)(B)(ii) [the plea, verdict and sentence] and §1229a(c)(3)(B)(iii) [docket entries from court records].

Documents After Trial—The modified categorical approach is also used where a person is convicted after a trial. If a person is convicted after trial (not by a plea) and there is no verdict form or jury instructions to demonstrate a finding regarding an element of the aggravated felony statute, the submission of an indictment and a judgment will *not* be sufficient. *Li v. Ashcroft,* 389 F.3d 892 (9th Cir. 2004) [where amount of loss due to fraud was not an element of the crime but where indictment alleges that more than $10,000 was involved in the fraud, the government may not prove under the modified categorical approach that this was a fraud or attempted fraud in excess of $10,000 by simply putting into evidence the charging document and the judgment without a verdict form or jury instructions because the government was not required to prove and the jury was not required to find a loss in excess of $10,000 in order to convict]. *U.S. v. Corona-Sanchez,* 291 F.3d 1201, 1211 (9th Cir. 2002) (en banc) [the court relied on *Taylor v. U.S.*, 495 U.S. 575, 602 to support a modified categorical approach but limited the documents to provide evidence of conviction as follows: "In the case of a jury trial, the charging document and jury instructions from the prior offense may demonstrate that the 'jury was actually required to find all the elements' of the generic crime. Similarly, if a defendant enters a guilty plea, the sentencing court may consider the charging documents in conjunction with the plea agreement, the transcript of a plea proceeding, or the judgment to determine whether the defendant pled guilty to the elements of the generic crime. Charging papers alone are never sufficient. However, charging papers may be considered in combination with a signed plea agreement."].

Documents to Prove Matters Other Than the Criminal Conviction—The BIA had determined that notwithstanding the categorical and modified categorical approach to evidence and document proof as expressed in *Shepard,* the IJs may rely on other evidence to prove elements of the offense regarding removal that are not part of the predicate crime. In *Matter of Gertsenshteyn,* 24 I&N Dec. 111 (BIA 2007) for example, the Board determined that when an aggravated felony includes a component that is neither an element of the underlying offense nor a basis for a sentence enhancement, the IJ may look outside the record of conviction to determine whether the immigration statutory definition of the aggravated felony has been met. In *Gertsenshteyn* the Board addressed whether respondent committed an aggravated felony under INA §101(a)(43)(K)(ii) which required a conviction under certain statutes "if committed for commercial advantage." The BIA determined that the limited documentary inquiry under *Shepard* and other cases was appropriate to determine whether a conviction had occurred, but that a broader inquiry, including the use of "the presentence report, the respondent's own admissions, and any other relevant evidence pertaining to aspects of the criminal conviction" could be used to determine the more general behavior associated with the criminal conduct which in the case included an inquiry into whether the crime was "committed for commercial advantage." Similarly, in *Matter of Babaisakov,* 24 I&N Dec. 306, 319–21 (BIA 2007) the Board held that to prove the amount of loss, where the charge of deportation is based upon a fraud conviction, where the loss to the victim exceeds $10,000, the IJ may not only rely on restitution orders, presentence reports, and admissions during plea colloquies but may also use "any evidence, otherwise admissible in removal proceedings, including witness testimony" and "testimonial admissions of the respondent made during the removal hearing" to prove the loss. *Accord. Nijhawan v. Att'y Gen.,* __F.3d ___ (3d Cir. May 2, 2008) [court held that the loss amount need not be specifically pled or found by jury but rather allows inquiry into facts underlying conviction and is satisfied if this inquiry shows that the "amount of loss is sufficiently tethered to the fraud conviction"]; *Ali v. Mukasey,* 521 F.3d 737 (7th Cir. 2008) [following *Matter of Babaisakov* and reinterpreting its own precedent post–*Brand X Internet Services,* the circuit court concluded the BIA could rely on the presentence investigation report to establish whether crime is a CIMT because "when deciding how to classify convictions under criteria that go beyond the criminal charge–such as the amount of the victim's loss, or whether the crime is one of 'moral turpitude' the agency has discretion to consider evidence beyond the charging papers and judgment of conviction"]. *But see e.g., Akio Kawashima v. Gonzales,* 503 F.3d 997, 1003 (9th Cir. 2007) [can only use the documents in *Taylor* and its progeny—charging document, a signed plea agreement, jury instructions, guilty pleas, transcripts of a plea proceeding and the judgment—and not sentencing guidelines to prove the loss]; *Obasohan v. U.S. Att'y Gen.,* 479 F.3d 785 (11th Cir. 2007) [requiring clear, unequivocal and convincing evidence that respondent was convicted of an aggravated felony including that the loss to the victim exceeded $10,000 and finding that the restitution order of $37,000 failed to demonstrate that respondent was convicted of loss to the victim because it was based upon other losses for which respondent was *not* convicted]. *See also Conteh v. Gonzales,* 461 F.3d 45 (1st Cir. 2006) and *Tokatly v. Ashcroft,* 371 F.3d 613 (9th Cir. 2004).

Standard of Proof—The modified categorical approach still requires the government to prove their case by clear and convincing evidence and it may rely only upon the record of conviction to do so. *Berhe v. Gonzales,* 464 F.3d 74, 85–87 (1st Cir. 2006) [DHS failed to put the first drug possession conviction in the record, and where the record of the second possession conviction did not indicate that the defendant was charged or pled to the first drug conviction as part of the second conviction, the government failed to prove that the second conviction was an aggravated felony by clear and convincing evidence]. However, when the applicant is seeking relief such as cancellation and must establish he has not been convicted of an aggravated felony the burden shifts to him by a preponderance of the evidence. The burden is met by establishing the crime does not fit under the categorical approach and it was *incon-*

clusive under the modified categorical approach. *Sandoval-Lua v. Gonzales,* 499 F.3d 1121, 1129–32 (9th Cir. 2007) [when respondent produced an *inconclusive* record of conviction on drug trafficking, he has met his burden that under the modified categorical approach he was not convicted of an aggravated felony].

(1) *Beyond a Reasonable Doubt Standard*—The First Circuit has distinguished its analysis from the Ninth Circuit finding that the modified categorical approach used by the Ninth Circuit ignores the distinction between criminal proceedings, where constitutional issues arise, and immigration proceedings and suggests that the government's burden is beyond a reasonable doubt rather than clear and convincing evidence. *Conteh v. Gonzales,* 461 F.3d 45, 54–57 (1st Cir. 2006) [where the conviction was for conspiracy under 18 U.S.C. §371 the government was not required to demonstrate that the conspiracy involved every element of the substantive offense enumerated under the aggravated felony statute but was only required to show that the substantive crime that was the conspiratorial objective was an aggravated felony]

Modification of the Categorical Approach—The Supreme Court in *Gonzales v. Duenas-Alvarez,* 549 U.S. ____, 127 S.Ct. 815 (2007) has added a wrinkle to the categorical/modified categorical approach. In *Duenas-Alvarez*, the Court addressed whether "aiding and abetting" under a vehicle theft statute in California was an aggravated felony and rejected the Ninth Circuit's determination that "aiding and abetting" a theft is not itself a crime that falls within the generic definition of theft. In so doing, the Court found that when a respondent seeks to create a new "subspecies" of a crime so that it falls outside of the generic definition of the aggravated felony then it has the burden to demonstrate that the statute was applied that way in his or her case or that it has been applied that way in other actual, not hypothetical, cases. The Court stated the following: "[I]n our view, to find that a state statute creates a crime outside the generic definition of a listed crime in a federal statute requires more than the application of legal imagination to a state statute's language. It requires a realistic probability, not a theoretical possibility, that the State would apply its statute to conduct that falls outside the generic definition of a crime. To show that realistic possibility, an offender, of course, may show that the statute was so applied in his own case. But he must at least point to his own case or other cases in which the state courts in fact did apply the statute in the special (non-generic) manner for which he argues." *Duenas-Alvarez,* 549 U.S. ___, 127 S. Ct. 815, 822 (2007). *See also James v. United States,* 127 S.Ct. 1586, 1597 (2007) [quoting above language in *Duenas-Alvarez* and suggesting a broad application]; *Rebilas v. Keisler,* 506 F.3d 1161, 1162–63 (9th Cir. 2007) [followed *Duenas-Alvarez* and *James* by reviewing actual decisions from the Arizona courts in concluding that attempted sexual indecency to a minor was not categorically an aggravated felony]. *Cf Navarro-Lopez v. Gonzales,* 503 F.3d 1063, 1072–73 (9th Cir. 2007) (*en banc*) [post-*Duenas Alvarez*, the court found that accessory after the fact was not a crime of moral turpitude and rejected the idea that the dissent could simply present a list of cases under *Duenas-Alvarez* where people were prosecuted and where the crime was moral turpitude because there was nothing inherent in the crime that made it a CIMT and the majority pointed to examples of prosecutions as an accessory for non-CIMTs]. *But see Cerezo v. Mukasey,* 512 F.3d 1165, 1167 (9th Cir. 2008) [*Duenas-Alvarez* is not applicable when the language of the statute is clear and "plainly and specifically criminalizes conduct outside the contours of the federal definition"]. Some courts have also adhered to the view that it is not necessary to analyze a statute in terms of the two-step categorical and then modified categorical approach when the documents that may be relied upon under *Shepard* clearly indicate the actual charge. Under this view the court may directly address the modified categorical approach to determine which subsection the person was convicted under and whether that subsection is an aggravated felony. *See e.g., Martinez v. Mukasey,* 508 F.3d 255, 259 (5th Cir. 2008) [court need not analyze whether any section of Tex. Penal Code §35.02 is an aggravated felony because the court could look at *Shepard* documents to determine that defendant was convicted under §35.02(a), and that it was an aggravated felony].

Following the Modified Categorical Approach—*Shepard v. U.S.,* 544 U.S. 13, 125 S.Ct. 1254, 1260 (2005) [establishing limitation on documents used in the modified categorical approach]; *Sandoval-Lua v. Gonzales,* 499 F.3d 1121, 1129–32 (9th Cir. 2007) [when respondent produced an *inconclusive* record of conviction, he has met his burden that under the modified categorical approach he was not convicted of an aggravated felony]; *Omari v. Gonzales,* 419 F.3d 303 (5th Cir. 2005) [where respondent convicted of conspiracy under 18 U.S.C. §371 to violate 18 U.S.C. §2314 which is a divisible statute, the removal order was vacated because under the modified categorical approach the only documents in evidence were the indictment and conviction and they suggested a nonfraud crime of possession of illegal airline tickets]; *Soliman v. Gonzales,* 419 F.3d 276, 284–86 (4th Cir. 2005) [under categorical and modified categorical approach fraudulent use of a credit card under Va. Code §18.2-195 is not a theft offense]; *Singh v. Ashcroft,* 383 F.3d 144 (3d Cir. 2004) [court analyzed categorical approach and determined that unlawful sexual conduct in the third degree under 11 Del. Code §767 is not categorically sexual abuse of a minor because under the categorical approach the statute does not address minors even if respondent's conduct was related to a child under 16]; *U.S. v. Pallares-Galan,* 359 F.3d 1088, 1099 (9th Cir. 2004) [explaining categorical and modified categorical approach in determining crime was not aggravated felony]; *U.S. v. Calderon-Pena,* 339 F.3d 320, 327–30 (5th Cir. 2003) [reviewing the indictment and determining that based upon indictment a conviction for child endangerment under Tex. Penal Code §22.041(c) is a crime of violence and an aggravated felony]; *Gousse v. Ashcroft,* 339 F.3d 91 (2d Cir. 2003) [adopted categorical approach and found Conn. Gen. Stat. 21a-277(a) is an aggravated felony, although use of categorical approach was complicated by respondent's *Alford* plea, in which he did not admit the facts of the plea]; *See also Matter of Sweetser,* 22 I&N Dec. 709 (BIA 1999) [BIA looks to elements of the offense not to the underlying facts]; *Matter of B-,* 21 I&N Dec. 287, 289 (BIA 1996) [BIA looks to the "statutory definition, not the underlying circumstances of the crime"].

4.g. *Definition of Term of Imprisonment*—Under INA §101(a)(48)(B), any term of imprisonment referenced to in the statute includes suspension of the imposition or execution of the sentence. *Drakes v. Zimski,* 240 F.3d 246, 251 (3d Cir. 2001) [suspended sentence of one year on each count is at least a one-year sentence]; *U.S. v. Maldonado-Ramirez,* 216 F.3d 940 (11th Cir. 2000) [ambiguity in term of imprisonment refers to sentence initially imposed and not time actually served]; *Gomez v. Ashcroft,* 293 F.Supp.2d 162 (D. Conn. 2003) [a suspended sentence is considered a sentence for defining aggravated felonies]. INA §101(a)(48)(B) applies to sentences entered before, on or after Sept. 30, 1996. IIRIRA §322(c). A term of imprisonment may be broadly construed to cover more than time spent in jail. *Ilchuk v. Att'y Gen. of the U.S.,* 434 F.3d 618, 623–24 (3d Cir. 2006) [house arrest with electronic monitoring is imprisonment]. A sentence to probation, however, has generally not been considered a sentence to imprisonment. *U.S. v. Gonzalez-Coronado,* 419 F.3d 1090, 1093–94 (10th Cir. 2005) [following *Martinez-Villalva* and holding that multiple-year sentence to probation is *not* a "term of imprisonment" under §101(a)(43)(F)]; *U.S. v. Martinez-Villalva,* 232 F.3d 1329, 1332–34 (10th Cir. 2000) [where government could not prove that sentence was a suspended sentence as opposed to a sentence to probation person not aggravated felon]; *U.S. v. Guzman-Bera,* 216 F.3d 1019 (11th Cir. 2000) [where person who was sentenced to probation violated the probation resulting in an 18-month incarceration, he was *not* sentenced to imprisonment and therefore was not aggravated felon]; *U.S. v. Banda-Zamora,* 178 F.3d 728, 730 (5th Cir. 1999) ["Thus, when a court does not order a period of incarceration and then suspends it, but instead imposes probation directly, the conviction is not an 'aggravated felony.' "]; *Matter of Martin,* 18 I&N Dec. 226, 227 (BIA 1982) [a sentence to probation is not considered a sentence to confinement]; *Matter of V-,* 7 I&N Dec. 577 (1957); *Matter of Eden,* 20 I&N Dec. 209 (BIA 1990). *But see Fernandez-Ruiz v. Gonzales,* 410 F.3d 585, 587–88 (9th Cir. 2005) [Ariz. Rev. Stat. §§13-1802(A)(1) & (C) regarding controlling the property of another without lawful authority with the intent to deprive is an aggravated felony notwithstanding the fact that the statute was a "wobbler" ultimately designated as a misdemeanor and that the one year was imposed because of a probation violation]; *Osses v. McElroy,* 287 F.Supp.2d 199, 205–06 (W.D.N.Y. 2003) [where sentence to probation was revoked and respondent was re-sentenced to time in prison, it was considered a sentence for purposes of an aggravated felony]; *Da Rosa Silva v. INS,* 263 F.Supp.2d 1005, 1010 (E.D. Pa. 2003) [sentence to probation as conditional sentence which was then revoked and four-year sentence imposed]. Also, at least one court has held that a person who has had a sentence imposed that is then, in part, probated is still considered sentenced to the full time. *U.S. v. Ayala-Gomez*, 255 F.3d 1314 (11th Cir. 2001) [sentence that was probated is considered suspended for purposes of statute and therefore full sentence must be considered].

An indeterminate sentence, is considered by the AG/BIA and some courts to be a sentence for the *maximum* term of imprisonment. *Matter of Jean,* 23 I&N Dec. 373, 386 n.14 (AG 2002) [interpreting N.Y. law]; *Matter of S-S-*, 21 I&N Dec. 900 (BIA 1997); *Pichardo v. INS,* 104 F.3d 756, 759 (5th Cir. 1997); *Nguyen v. INS*, 53 F.3d 310 (10th Cir. 1995) [following the sentencing guidelines definition]; *Matter of D-*, 20 I&N Dec. 827 (BIA 1994) [interpreting Mass. law]. An undesignated probationary sentence may not be considered a sentence for the maximum period. *Lafarga v. INS,* 170 F.3d 1213 (9th Cir. 1999). A concurrent sentence for purposes of determining an "aggregate term of imprisonment" under INA §241(b)(3) (withholding of removal) is equal in length of the longest concurrent sentence. *Matter of Aldabesheh,* 22 I&N Dec. 983 (BIA 1999) [rejects the addition of concurrent sentences as a basis for establishing an aggregate term of imprisonment]. When the sentence specifies a minimum and maximum sentence of imprisonment at least one court has held that the maximum sentence should be utilized in determining whether there is a one-year term of imprisonment. *Bovkun v. Ashcroft,* 283 F.3d 166, 170–71 (3d Cir. 2002).

The term of imprisonment refers to the actual sentence imposed by the judge and not the potential sentence that might be imposed under the statute. *Alberto-Gonzalez v. INS,* 215 F.3d 906, 909–10 (9th Cir. 2000); *U.S. v. Graham,* 169 F.3d 787, 789–90 (3d Cir.), *cert. denied,* 528 U.S. 845 (1999). However, 2 sections of the aggravated felony provisions, INA §101(a)(43)(J) and (T), suggest by the use of the term "may" that, in those cases, the sentence may be the statutory maximum penalty rather than the actual sentence imposed.

A term of imprisonment of 365 days is considered to be imprisonment for one year under the aggravated felony statutes. *Matsuk v. INS,* 247 F.3d 999, 1001–02 (9th Cir. 2001) [a person sentenced to 365 days is considered to have committed an aggravated felony under the crime of violence statute, which requires a term of imprisonment of "at least one year."]. If a person's sentence is reduced to less than 365 days by the vacation of his previous sentence and the institution of a new less-than-365-day sentence, s/he will not be considered to be convicted of an aggravated felony. *Matter of Song,* 23 I&N Dec. 173 (BIA 2001) [no aggravated felony where state judge vacated prior 365-day sentence *nunc pro tunc* and resentenced person to 360 days]. This is true even if the sentence is vacated or modified *nunc pro tunc* expressly to avoid immigration consequences. *Matter of Cota,* 23 I&N Dec. 849 (BIA 2005) [where sentence was modified *nunc pro tunc* expressly to avoid deportation as an aggravated felon, IJ and BIA must recognize it. *Matter of Pickering* distinguished].

A conviction for a petty offense, where the sentence could not be more than 6 months, but where the person was sentenced to 2 years under an enhancement provision, may now meet the one-year-sentence requirement to be a theft aggravated felony, as a result of the Supreme Court's decision in *U.S. v. Rodriguez,* ___ U.S. ___ (May 19, 2008) [reversing the Ninth Circuit analysis in *U.S. v. Corona-Sanchez,* 291 F.3d 1201, 1208–09 (9th Cir. 2002) (en banc) that, because "recidivism does not relate to the commission of the offense," the court would not consider petty theft as an aggravated felony where the maximum sentence was 6 months notwithstanding the 2-year sentence received by defendant due to an enhancement statute]. *U.S. v. Moreno-Hernandez,* 397 F.3d 1248 (9th Cir. 2005) [allowing consideration of sentence enhancement that relates to crime, and restricting *Corona-Sanchez* rule to sentencing factors based on defendant's legal history, such as recidivism]; *U.S. v. Marin-Navarette,* 244 F.3d 1284 (11th Cir. 2001) [although attempted child molestation in the third degree is a misdemeanor under Washington State law, it is an aggravated felony for sentencing enhancement]; *U.S. v. Christopher,* 239 F.3d 1191 (11th Cir. 2001), *cert. denied,* 122 S.Ct. 178 (2001) [theft by shoplifting although a misdemeanor under state law was aggravated felony where sentence imposed, although suspended, was one year]; *U.S. v. Pacheco,* 225 F.3d 148, 154 (2d Cir. 2000); *Wireko v. Reno,* 211 F.3d 833, 835 (4th Cir. 2000); *U.S. v. Graham,* 169 F.3d 787, 790–92 (3d Cir.), *cert. denied,* 528 U.S. 845 (1999).

If a sentence was unlawful it may not count as a sentence that meets the threshold for an aggravated felony. *Fernandez-Ruiz v. Gonzales,* 468 F.3d 1159, 1169–70 (9th Cir. 2006) [where respondent was convicted of a theft offense that was an aggravated felony but argued that his one year sentence was unlawful because Ariz. Rev. Stat. §13-802(A)(1) & (C) was a misdemeanor, the case was remanded].

4.h. *Effective Date*—Under the BIA's decision in *Matter of A-A-*, 20 I&N Dec. 492 (BIA 1992), there is a 2-part analysis for determining whether a person has committed an aggravated felony and its effect. The first question is whether the conviction is an aggravated felony. The second is what consequences result from the conclusion that a crime is an aggravated felony. *Lewis v. INS,* 194 F.3d 539, 542–43 n.5 (4th Cir. 1999); Legal Opinion, Martin, General Counsel, 96-16 (Dec. 3, 1996), *reprinted in* 74 No. 38 *Interpreter Releases* 1515, 1530–32 (Oct. 6, 1997).

The definition of aggravated felony applies to any conviction that occurred *before* the term was introduced to the INA in 1988, unless Congress designated otherwise. *Scheidemann v. INS*, 83 F.3d 1517, 1523–25 (3d Cir. 1996); *U.S. v. Kingston*, 966 F.Supp. 183 (S.D.N.Y. 1997). In IMMACT90, Congress added the crimes of money laundering, nonpolitical crimes of violence, and certain crimes in violation of foreign law to the definition of aggravated felony, but only made them aggravated felonies if "committed on or after the date of enactment." IMMACT90 §501(b). Similarly, all crimes added by the 1994 INTCA, including attempts and conspiracies were considered to apply only to convictions "entered on or after October 25, 1994." In addition, the changes to INA §§101(a)(43)(J), (K)(ii), (P), and (Q), as well as the addition of §§101(a)(43)(O), (R), (S), and (T), were considered to apply to convictions entered on or after Apr. 24, 1996, the date the AEDPA was signed into law, except the changes to INA §101(a)(43)(N) were considered to apply as if included in the 1994 Act, with an effective date of Oct. 24, 1994. The original aggravated felonies, *e.g.*, drug trafficking, arms trafficking, and murder, have been considered aggravated felonies even if committed *prior to* 1988. *Matter of A-A-*, 20 I&N Dec. 492, 498; *De Osorio v. INS*, 10 F.3d 1034 (4th Cir. 1993) [followed *Matter of A-A-*]. However, IIRIRA appears to have made the definition retroactive for all crimes committed on, *before,* or after Sept. 30, 1996. Under IIRIRA §321(b) the effective date of the definition of aggravated felony is retroactive covering all crimes within the definition irrespective of the date of commission ["notwithstanding any other provision of law (including any effective dates) the term applies regardless of whether the conviction was entered before, on or after the date of enactment" of this paragraph (*i.e.*, Sept. 30, 1996)]; *Chan v. Gantner,* 464 F.3d 289, 292–94 (2d Cir. 2006) [applying INA §§101(a)(43)(N) & (U) retroactively regarding a conviction for conspiracy to commit alien smuggling to bar citizenship because of lack of good moral character]; *Sena v. Gonzales,* 428 F.3d 50, 51–53 (1st Cir. 2005) [retroactive application of alien smuggling provisions under §101(a)(43)(N) has a rational basis and does not violated due process]; *Tran v. Gonzales,* 447 F.3d 937, 940–41 (6th Cir. 2006) [aggravated felony definition applies retroactively to permit removal even where the respondent was previously found not deportable under the CIMT provisions for the same convictions; res judicata not raised]; *Guaylupo-Moya v. Gonzales,* 423 F.3d 121, 128–32 (2d Cir. 2005) [Congress clearly intended under IIRIRA §321(a) that the expanded definition of aggravated felonies be applied retroactively to bar INA §212(h) relief]; *Alvarez-Barajas v. Gonzales,* 418 F.3d 1050, 1054 (9th Cir. 2005) [definitions apply retroactively to bar relief for conviction that was not an aggravated felony at the time of the plea]; *Brown v. Ashcroft,* 360 F.3d 346, 353–55 (2d Cir. 2004) [definition of aggravated felony applied retroactively to attempted robbery convictions to bar respondent's eligibility for INA §212(c) relief]; *Seale v. INS,* 323 F.3d 150, 157–60 (1st Cir. 2003) [followed *Sousa* on retroactivity and rejected respondent's *ex post facto* and double jeopardy arguments for assault with intent to murder conviction that arose before 1988]; *Kuhali v. Reno,* 266 F.3d 93, 110–11 (2d Cir. 2001) [Congress intended definitions to apply retroactively and no due process or *ex post facto* claims are raised in unlicensed firearms export under 22 U.S.C. §2778]; *Flores-Leon v. INS*, 272 F.3d 433, 438–39 (7th Cir. 2001) [Congress intended the amended definition of aggravated felony to apply retroactively and the retroactive application does not violate the Ex Post Facto Clause]; *Mohammed v. Ashcroft,* 261 F.3d 1244 (11th Cir. 2001) [statutory retroactivity and due process challenges to §321 are rejected in case involving a plea to 2 counts of stolen property]; *Sousa v. INS,* 226 F.3d 28, 32–35 (1st Cir. 2000) [person convicted of unarmed robbery in 1990 was aggravated felon even if he would not be under all pre-IIRIRA statutes because IIRIRA is explicitly retroactive]; *Aragon-Ayon v. INS,* 206 F.3d 847 (9th Cir. 2000) [aggravated felony definition was expressly made retroactive by Congress in INA §321(b) and therefore applies to a 1992 conviction]; *Matter of Truong,* 22 I&N Dec. 1090 (BIA 1999). *But see U.S. v. Ubaldo-Figueroa,* 364 F.3d 1042, 1050–56 (9th Cir. 2004) [retroactively applying the expanded definition of aggravated felony to encompass an attempted burglary conviction that arose prior to 1996 would plausibly violate due process]; *U.S. v. Saldivar-Vargas,* 290 F.Supp.2d 1210 (S.D. Cal. 2003) [followed *Ubaldo-Figueroa*].

An alternative, but not yet accepted interpretation of IIRIRA §321(b) is that the legislative history indicates that the retroactive provision may apply only to the amendments to the definition of aggravated felony in IIRIRA ["The amendment provides that the *amended* definition of 'aggravated felony' applies to offenses that occurred before, on or after the date of enactment." H.R. Conf. Rep. No. 828, 104th Cong., 2d Sess. at 223]. *But see Sango-Dema v. District Director, INS,* 122 F.Supp.2d 213, 218 (D. Mass. 2000) [1996 additions to aggravated felony definition apply to 1994 conviction].

For the amendments made by IIRIRA §321, the effective date of its application is that it "shall apply to actions taken on or after the date of enactment [Sept. 30, 1996] regardless of when the conviction occurred" and shall apply to §276(b) [criminal statute pertaining to reentry] only to violations occurring after Sept. 30, 1996. IIRIRA §321(c). The amendments were: (1) adding rape and sexual abuse of a minor to §101(a)(43)(A); (2) striking $100,000 and $200,000 and inserting $10,000 to §§101(a)(43)(D) and (M), respectively; (3) striking 5 years and replacing it with one year in §§101(a)(43)(F), (G), (J), (N), (P), (R), and (S); (4) adding requirement of commercial advantage to §§101(a)(43)(K)(ii); and (5) adding to §§101(a)(43)(N) and (P) the exception for family members. The BIA and the courts have interpreted "actions taken" to mean only orders and decisions issued against a respondent by the AG after the effective date. *Matter of Truong,* 22 I&N Dec. 1090, 1095–97 (BIA 1999) [removal proceedings are considered "actions taken"]; *Biskupski v. Att'y Gen. of the U.S.,* 503 F.3d 274, 281–84 (3d Cir. 2007) ["action taken" refers to orders and decisions of the IJ or BIA]; *Garrido-Morato v. Gonzales,* 485 F.3d 319, 323–24 (5th Cir. 2007) [court rejected argument that "actions taken" also includes pleading guilty and applying for relief which would thereby preclude the amendments in 321(b) from applying]; *Xiong v. INS,* 173 F.3d 601 (7th Cir. 1999); *Choeum v. INS*, 129 F.3d 29, 33–35 (1st Cir. 1997); *Valderrama-Fonseca v. INS,* 116 F.3d 853 (9th Cir. 1997); *Aragon-Ayon v. INS,* 206 F.3d 847, 852–53 (9th Cir. 2000) [applies to any action taken by the AG]; *But see Mendez-Morales v. INS*, 119 F.3d 738 (8th Cir. 1997) [judicial review is action taken making crime aggravated felony, thereby barring judicial review]. In *Matter of Yeung*, 21 I&N Dec. 610 (BIA 1996), the BIA suggested the law applied retroactively at least as to the amended provision of INA §101(a)(43)(F), reducing crimes of violence from 5 years to one year.

The second question as to the consequences of a retroactive definition are separate from the definition. Thus, the good moral character requirement under §101(f)(8), notwithstanding the retroactive definition of aggravated felony, does not bar an aggravated felon from good moral character if the conviction occurred prior to Nov. 29, 1990. 8 C.F.R. §316.10(b)(1)(ii), 8 C.F.R. §1240.56. Legal Opinion, Martin (Dec. 3, 1996), *supra*; *Lopez-Castellanos v. Gonzales,* 437 F.3d 848, 851 (9th Cir. 2006); *U.S. v. Hovsepian,* 359 F.3d 1144, 1165–69 (9th Cir. 2004) (*en banc*). In addition, whether or not the aggravated felony definition applies retroactively to persons with pre–AEDPA/IIRIRA convictions, those persons who pled guilty prior to AEDPA/IIRIRA remain eligible for §212(c) relief from removal because the aggravated felony bar on §212(c) relief may not be retroactively applied. *INS v. St. Cyr,* 121 S.Ct. 2271, 2293 (2001).

A person convicted of a crime that may, through retroactive application, be defined as an aggravated felony is subject to deportation, because the BIA read the deportation statute to encompass prior convictions. *Matter of Lettman,* 22 I&N Dec. 365 (BIA 1998), *aff'd, Lettman v. Reno,* 207 F.3d 1368 (11th Cir. 2000) [person convicted in 1987 is deportable as an aggravated felon pursuant to IMMACT90 §602(c), even though conviction occurred prior to the Anti-Drug Abuse Act of 1988, which first defined aggravated felonies and made them prospective. BIA relied on IMMACT90 §602]. *Accord Lewis v. INS,* 194 F.3d 539, 543–47 (4th Cir. 1999). *See also Gelman v. Ashcroft,* 372 F.3d 495 (2d Cir. 2004) [following *Bell v. Reno* and finding that post–*St. Cyr,* IMMACT90 §602(d) permits the definition of an aggravated felony to apply to convictions which arose before Nov. 18, 1988 where notice of proceeding was provided after Mar. 1, 1991]; *Bell v. Reno,* 218 F.3d 86 (2d Cir. 2000) [finding that IMMACT90 §602(c) could not be applied retroactively but that §602(d) does apply to allow for the retroactive application of aggravated felony provisions as long as proceedings were after Mar. 1, 1991.] The importance of the retroactivity of the definition relates not only to deportability but also to matters such as former INA §212(c) relief which may be unavailable to certain persons even if their convictions were prior to 1988. *Scheidemann v. INS*, 83 F.3d 1517, 1523–25 (3d Cir. 1996). *See also Reid v. Holmes,* 323 F.3d 187 (2d Cir. 2003) [rejected retroactivity argument regarding IMMACT90 §511 for someone convicted before 1990]. *Cf. Gomes v. Ashcroft,* 311 F.3d 43, 45–46 (1st Cir. 2002) [the term "admission" in IMMACT90 §511(b) applies not only to the original admission into the U.S. but to whenever applicant applies for INA §212(c) and therefore bar due to 5-year imprisonment is applicable]. *But see Toia v. Fasano,* 334 F.3d 917 (9th Cir. 2003) [IMMACT90 §511, which was enacted on Nov. 29, 1990, barring INA §212(c) relief to persons who served a term of imprisonment of more than five years for an aggravated felony, may not be applied retroactively under *St. Cyr* and if the conviction arose before Nov. 29, 1990, such person is eligible for §212(c) relief], *Compare Saravia-Paguada v. Gonzales,* 488 F.3d 1122 (9th Cir. 2007) [court rejected retroactivity argument because respondent was convicted after trial in 1988].

5. **High Speed Flight**—INA §237(a)(2)(A)(iv), 8 U.S.C. §1227(a)(2)(A)(iv). Any person convicted of a violation of 18 U.S.C. §758 relating to high speed flight from an immigration checkpoint.

6. **Drug-Related Offenses**—INA §237(a)(2)(B), 8 U.S.C. §1227(a)(2)(B). Under this section a LPR or alien is deportable if:

   6.a. Alien is, or at any time after admission has been a narcotic/drug addict or drug abuser (status), INA §237(a)(2)(B)(ii), 8 U.S.C. §1227(a)(2)(B)(ii); or

   6.b. At any time after admission, has been convicted of a violation of or conspiracy or attempt to violate any law or regulation of a state, the U.S., or a foreign country relating to a controlled substance as defined in 21 U.S.C. §802. INA §237(a)(2)(B)(i), 8 U.S.C. §1227(a)(2)(B)(i). Includes all drugs listed at 21 U.S.C. §812 and all drugs designated by the AG at 21 U.S.C. §811 and Schedules I through V in 21 C.F.R. §1308.1. BIA gives broad reading to the statute. *Matter of Esqueda*, 20 I&N Dec. 850 (BIA 1994) [includes conviction for being under the influence of a drug, including any conviction even if specific intent or mens rea is absent—superseding Second Circuit's reasoning in *Lennon*]; *Matter of Hernandez-Ponce*, 19 I&N Dec. 613 (BIA 1988). Some circuit courts have found that a violation of the Travel Act is a violation of a law relating to a controlled substance where respondent was transporting drugs in interstate commerce. *Urena-Ramirez v. Ashcroft,* 341 F.3d 51, 53–57 (1st Cir. 2003) [fact that Travel Act involves other criminal conduct does not mean it is not also a law relating to a controlled substance]; *Johnson v. INS*, 971 F.2d 340, 342–43 (9th Cir. 1992) [conviction was for traveling in interstate commerce to distribute drug proceeds]. Other broad interpretations of the statute have been sustained. *Al-Najar v. Mukasey,* 515 F.3d 708, 715 (6th Cir. 2008) [guilty plea where respondent possessed Khat which is not listed on the CSA was, nevertheless, a drug conviction because respondent pleaded guilty to possession of a controlled substance in violation of Mich. Comp. Laws §333.7411 and therefore admitted that he possessed a controlled substance]; *Mizrahi v. Gonzales,* 492 F.3d 156 (2d Cir. 2007) [guilty plea to a misdemeanor]; *Peters v. Ashcroft,* 383 F.3d 302 (5th Cir. 2004) [felony solicitation to transport marijuana for sale under Ariz. Rev. Stat. §13-1002 is a drug crime]; *Matter of Beltran*, 20 I&N Dec. 521 (BIA 1992) [conviction for solicitation to commit a crime renders person deportable as solicitation is like aiding or abetting]. *But see Argaw v. Ashcroft,* 395 F.3d 521 (4th Cir. 2005) [where "khat," a traditional herbal stimulant widely used in East Africa and the lower Arabian peninsula, is not listed as a controlled substance under 21 U.S.C. §812, 21 C.F.R. §1308.11-15, and it was not chemically analyzed to determine if its consistent elements, which may be on the list, contained a controlled substance, it cannot be a ground of inadmissibility as an admission or for "reason to believe"]; *Medina v. Ashcroft,* 393 F.3d 1063 (9th Cir. 2005) [a conviction under Nevada law for attempting to be under the influence of THC-carboxylic acid is a crime for a small amount of possession of marijuana and the fact that the statute involved the use of marijuana rather than possession was irrelevant]; *Lara-Chacon v. Ashcroft,* 345 F.3d 1148, 1154–56 (9th Cir. 2003) [Arizona money laundering statute is a distinct crime from underlying crime and therefore conviction does not necessarily "relate to" a controlled substance violation]; *Coronado-Durazo v. INS*, 123 F.3d 1322 (9th

Cir. 1997) [solicitation under Arizona statute is *not* a deportable offense. *Beltran* not followed]; *Leyva-Licea v. INS,* 187 F.3d 1147 (9th Cir. 1999) [following *Coronado-Durazo* solicitation to possess marijuana for sale under Arizona law is not a conviction under Controlled Substances Act]; *Castaneda de Esper v. INS*, 557 F.2d 79 (6th Cir. 1977) [misprision of a felony is not a drug crime under previous statute]; *Matter of Carrillo*, 16 I&N Dec. 625 (BIA 1978) [illegally carrying a firearm during commission of a felony not drug crime]; *Matter of Batista-Hernandez*, 21 I&N Dec. 955 (BIA 1997) [accessory after the fact under 18 U.S.C. §3 is not drug crime]. Attempted illicit possession may render alien deportable. *Abudu v. INS,* 802 F.2d 1096, 1099 (9th Cir. 1986), *rev'd on other grounds*, 485 U.S. 94 (1988). Facilitation of unlawful sale of cocaine may render alien deportable. *Matter of Del Risco*, 20 I&N Dec. 109 (BIA 1989) [conviction for facilitation under Arizona law is conviction].

6.c. It is *not* a deportable offense for someone to be convicted of "a single offense involving possession for one's own use of 30 grams or less of marijuana." INA §237(a)(2)(B)(i). The INS does not include hashish or other marijuana derivatives within this exception. Legal Opinion, Virtue, Deputy General Counsel, HQ 241(a)(2)(B)(i) (Aug. 19, 1992). Also, being under the influence of a drug other than marijuana even if a misdemeanor may be a deportable offense. *Flores-Arellano v. INS*, 5 F.3d 360 (9th Cir. 1993) [conviction for being under the influence of amphetamines is deportable offense]; *Matter of Esqueda, supra. But see Medina v. Ashcroft,* 393 F.3d 1063 (9th Cir. 2005) [a conviction under Nevada law for attempting to be under the influence of THC-carboxylic acid is a crime for a small amount of possession of marijuana and the fact that the statute involved the use of marijuana rather than possession was irrelevant]. The exception may be narrowly applied. *Matter of Moncada,* 24 I&N Dec. 62 (BIA 2007) [narrowly interpreting the deportability exception for simple possession of 30 grams or less of marijuana as not including a conviction for possession of 30 grams or less of marijuana in *prison* under section 4573.6 of the California penal Code]; *Matter of Martinez-Zapata,* 24 I&N Dec. 424 (BIA 2007) [where conviction was enhanced by virtue of respondent's possession of marijuana in a "drug-free zone" the enhancement was an element of the crime and the conviction was therefore more than a conviction for simple possession of 30 grams of marijuana. Respondent was ineligible for INA §212(h) relief and *Matter of Rodriguez-Cortes*, 20 I&N Dec. 587 (BIA 1992) was superseded for *post-Apprendi* cases].

6.d. The government must prove the drug charge by clear, convincing and unequivocal evidence. *Ruiz-Vidal v. Gonzales,* 473 F.3d 1072 (9th Cir. 2007) [criminal records proved a conviction for possession of a controlled substance but none of the documents demonstrated what drug was involved and therefore the government did not meet it burden of proof];

6.e. Under the Anti-Drug Abuse Act of 1986, PL 99-570, subtitle M, of the Narcotics Traffickers Deportation Act the provision is expressly made retroactive to cover all previous convictions.

6.f. Drug Paraphernalia Included—*Alvarez Acosta v. U.S. Att'y Gen.,* ___F.3d ___ (11th Cir. Apr. 16, 2008) 2008 WL 1733208 [conviction for drug paraphernalia was a conviction relating to a controlled substance under INA §212(a)(2)(A)(i)(II)]; *Escobar Barraza v. Mukasey,* 519 F.3d 388 (7th Cir. 2008) [in removal proceeding regarding inadmissibility, the court rejected the argument that drug paraphernalia is not banned under 21 USC §863, but also held that in certain cases a §212(h) waiver would apply to drug paraphernalia]; *Luu-Le v. INS*, 224 F.3d 911 (9th Cir. 2000) [possession of drug paraphernalia under Ariz. Crim. Code §13-3415 is a drug conviction].

7. **Firearms Violations**—INA §237(a)(2)(C), 8 U.S.C. §1227(a)(2)(C)—Under this section alien is deportable if any time after admission:

7.a. Person is convicted under any law of purchasing, selling, offering for sale, exchanging, using, owning, possessing or carrying in violation of any law, any weapon, part or accessory which is a firearm or destructive device as defined in 18 U.S.C. §921(a). It includes attempts and conspiracies to commit the crime. *Matter of St. John*, 21 I&N Dec. 593 (BIA 1996) [the amendment to the statute to include attempts by §203(b) of INTCA of 1994 is retroactive applying to convictions occurring "before, on or after" Oct. 25, 1994. *Matter of Hou* superseded]; *Drax v. Reno,* 338 F.3d 98, 108–10 (2d Cir. 2003) [same]. It includes convictions that include pure firearms offenses even if no other crime is committed. *Lemus-Rodriguez v. Ashcroft,* 350 F.3d 652, 655–56 (7th Cir. 2003) [conviction under Illinois law for reckless discharge of a rifle on New Years Eve was sufficient to bar cancellation]; *Valerio-Ochoa v. INS,* 241 F.3d 1092 (9th Cir. 2001) [subject to removal for conviction of negligently discharging a firearm under Cal. Penal Code §246.3). May include a conviction of a crime for which "possessing" or "carrying" a firearm is an *element* of the offense. *Kuhali v. Reno,* 266 F.3d 93, 101–07 (2d Cir. 2001) [conspiracy to export firearms and ammunition without a license under 22 U.S.C. §2778 is a firearms offense because unlicensed export entails constructive possession]. It includes misdemeanors. *Awad v. Gonzales,* 494 F.3d 723 (8th Cir. 2007) [misdemeanor citation and $100 fine for transportation of a loaded firearm in violation of Minn. Stat. §97B.045 where respondent was carrying hunting rife in all-terrain vehicle was a deportable offense notwithstanding the hunting rife exception under federal law]. Possession under the statute includes constructive possession. *Kuhali, supra; Aybar-Alejo v. INS,* 230 F.3d 487 (1st Cir. 2000) [conviction for possession or control of a firearm by an alien under R.I. Gen. Laws §11-47-7 is within INA statute because conviction for control of firearm is the same as constructive possession]. It also includes any enhancement provision, *e.g.*, where a sentence was enhanced because a gun was used during the commission of the crime, but only if it must be proved beyond a reasonable doubt or is admitted by the defendant, thus being an element of the crime. *Matter of Martinez-Zapata,* 24 I&N Dec. 424 (BIA 2008) [arising in a drug enhancement context but finding that *Matter of Rodriguez-Cortes,* 20 I&N Dec. 587 (BIA 1992) which held that enhancement of a sentence due to the use of a weapon in the commission of a crime was not a gun crime is superseded by virtue of *Apprendi v. New Jersey*, 530 U.S. 466 (2000) in *post-Apprendi* cases]. *See also Matter of K-L-*, 20 I&N Dec. 654 (BIA 1993) [distinguishing *Matter of Rodriguez-Cortes,* 20 I&N Dec. 587 (BIA1992) and finding a conviction under 18 U.S.C. §924(c)(1) as creating a distinct offense not simply a penalty enhancement provision]; *Matter of P-F-*, 20 I&N Dec. 661 (BIA 1993) [Fla. Stat. §§810.02, 812.13 armed burglary with a firearm not simply sentencing enhancement provision but requires use of firearm as an essential element of the crime]; *Matter of Lopez-Amaro*, 20 I&N Dec. 668 (BIA 1993), *aff'd*, *Lopez-Amaro v. INS*, 25 F.3d 986, 989–90 (11th Cir. 1994), *cert. denied*, 115 S.Ct. 1093 (1995) [same as to murder with a firearm under Fla. Stat. §775.087]. But where the use of a firearm is not an element of the crime, a conviction will not be considered a deportable offense as a gun charge. For example, a conviction for assault is not a firearms offense where the use of a firearm is not an element of the offense. *Matter of Perez-Contreras*, 20 I&N Dec. 615 (BIA 1992) [when assault in third degree in State of Washington was accomplished with a pistol of person not charged with use of pistol, no firearms offense]. *But see Vue v. INS*, 92 F.3d 696 (8th Cir. 1996) [finding a conviction for aggravated robbery with a weapon was sufficient where record of conviction demonstrated it was a firearm]; *Matter of Lopez-Amaro, supra* [conviction where firearms is an element or lesser included offense is firearms violation]. One court, reading the section broadly, has found that a false statement to a federally licensed dealer in connection with a firearms purchase under 18 U.S.C. §922(a)(6) is a firearms offense under this section. *Hall v. INS,* 167 F.3d 852 (4th Cir. 1999).

Former INA §241(a)(2)(C) applies to any convictions, including those which arose prior to IMMACT90. *Matter of Chow*, 20 I&N Dec. 647 (BIA) *aff'd*, *Chow v. INS*, 12 F.3d 34 (5th Cir. 1993); *Lopez-Amaro v. INS*, 25 F.3d 986, 988–89 (11th Cir. 1994) [same]. *See also Drax v. Reno*, 338 F.3d 98, 108–10 (2d Cir. 2003) [Congress intended the amendments to the firearms statute under INTCA §203 that included "attempts" to apply retroactively]. For a partial legislative history of the previous statute, *see Cabasug v. INS*, 847 F.2d 1321, 1322–25 (9th Cir. 1988).

Where a criminal statute encompassing offenses that may, but do not necessarily include firearm offenses, the determination of whether a person was convicted of a firearms offense can only occur, under a modified categorical approach, through the admission of the record of conviction or other documents admissible as evidence to prove a conviction under 8 C.F.R. §1003.41. *Dulal-Whiteway v. DHS,* 501 F.3d 116, 121–23 (2d Cir. 2007) [a conviction under 18 U.S.C. §922(a)(6) regarding making a fraudulent statement in connection with the acquisition or attempted acquisition of a firearm is not, under the categorical approach, a firearms offense because it includes acquisition of ammunition; however, it is a firearms conviction under the modified categorical approach because the judgment of conviction described the activity as acquisition of a firearm]. However, certain documents may not be used to prove a firearms conviction under the modified categorical approach. A police report, for example, cannot be used to prove a conviction. *Matter of Teixeira*, 21 I&N Dec. 316 (BIA 1996). *But see Emile v. INS,* 244 F.3d 183, 188 (1st Cir. 2001) [rejecting challenge to admission of police report on due process grounds]. Similarly, where the conviction offered into evidence to support a firearms conviction simply specifies a conviction for possession of a weapon deportability cannot be sustained, even where there was extrinsic evidence through respondent's testimony that he used a gun. *Matter of Pichardo*, 21 I&N Dec. 330 (BIA 1996). *But see Adefemi v. Ashcroft,* 386 F.3d 1022, 1030 n.11 (11th Cir. 2004) (*en banc*) [distinguishing *Pichardo* and finding that respondent's admission corroborating his conviction for a firearms offense was relevant evidence]; *Matter of Madrigal*, 21 I&N Dec. 323 (BIA 1996) [where admission that weapon was firearm was in transcript of plea and sentence that is part of record, deportability established]. *See also Francis v. Gonzales,* 442 F.3d 131, 141–45 (2d Cir. 2006) [documents other than those listed in §1003.41 may be submitted as evidence, but the court found a "rap sheet"/police report from Jamaica did not support a finding of a conviction under the *Woodby* standard even where there was some admission of guilt]; *Fequiere v. Ashcroft,* 279 F.3d 1325, 1327 (11th Cir. 2002) [recognizing that the statute permits other forms of proof].

INA §212(c) cannot waive a firearm offense ground of deportability because there is no comparable ground of inadmissibility. *Cyrus v. Keisler,* 505 F.3d 197, 201–02 (2d Cir. 2007) [respondent with gun conviction is not eligible for INA §212(c) relief and therefore not eligible to reopen under §1003.44].

The statute does not bar an adjustment of status in a deportation proceeding even if s/he would be deportable for a gun charge, because conviction of a gun charge is not a ground of inadmissibility. *Matter of Rainford*, 20 I&N Dec. 598 (BIA 1992).

8. **Miscellaneous Crimes**—INA §237(a)(2)(D), 8 U.S.C. §1227(a)(2)(D)

8.a. Person convicted of violating, conspiracy, or attempting to violate:

(1) Neutrality laws under 18 U.S.C. §960;

(2) Trading with the Enemy Act, 50 U.S.C. App. 1 *et seq.*;

(3) Selective Service laws;

(4) Importation of alien for immoral purpose, INA §278, 8 U.S.C. §1328;

(5) Travel restrictions during war or national emergency, INA §215, 8 U.S.C. §1185;

(6) Threatening the President under 18 U.S.C. §871;

(7) Espionage, sabotage and treason and sedition law violations under 18 U.S.C. chaps. 37, 105, or 115, for which a term of imprisonment of 5 years or more may be imposed.

9. **Domestic Violence, Stalking, Protective Order Violations, and Child Abuse**—INA §237(a)(2)(E), 8 U.S.C. §1227(a)(2)(E).

9.a. A conviction at any time after admission for domestic violence, stalking, child abuse, child neglect, or child abandonment. 8 U.S.C. §1227(a)(2)(E)(i).

(1) Domestic Violence. The statute defines domestic violence by reference to the definition of "crime of violence" under 18 U.S.C. §16 and includes acts by former as well as current spouse, by a person similarly situated to a spouse, or by any other individual against a person who is protected from that person's acts under federal, state, tribal or local governmental law. A crime constitutes domestic violence if: (1) it is a crime of violence as defined by 18 U.S.C. §16; and (2) the victim was a "protected person" within the meaning of 8 U.S.C. §1227(a)(2)(E)(i). *Fernandez-Ruiz v. Gonzales,* 410 F.3d 585, 587–88 (9th Cir. 2005) [Ariz. Rev. Stat. §§13-1203 and 13-3601, which are Class 2 misdemeanors are crimes of violence and domestic violence statutes]; *Sutherland v. Reno,* 228 F.3d 171 (2d Cir. 2000) [Mass. Gen. Laws ch. 265 §13H pertaining to indecent assault and battery is a domestic violence crime because nonconsent is a necessary element in regard to it being a crime of violence and because victim was a protected person as a household member]. *But see Cisneros-Perez v. Gonzales,* 465 F.3d 386 (9th Cir. 2006) [followed

Tokatly and found that conviction for simple battery where respondent was charged with domestic violence without more did not establish a domestic violence crime under the modified categorical approach]; *Singh v. Ashcroft*, 386 F.3d 1228 (9th Cir. 2004) [finding that harassment under Or. Rev. Stat. §166.065(1)(a)(A) is not a crime of violence because it is not a crime of violence as it includes offensive touching that is not aimed at creating physical injury and does not have as an "element" the use of force]; *Tokatly v. Ashcroft,* 371 F.3d 613, 619–24 (9th Cir. 2004) [the government must not only establish a crime of violence but one of domestic violence and it was impermissible for the IJ to rely on testimony of respondent or the victim to establish that he committed a crime of domestic violence as IJ may only look at record of conviction]; *Flores v. Ashcroft,* 350 F.3d 666 (7th Cir. 2003) [finding that battery under Ind. Code §35-42-2-1, which is a Class A misdemeanor was not a crime of violence even though factually respondent beat his wife. The court found *Matter of Martin,* 23 I&N Dec. 491 defining crime of violence as not persuasive and distinguished between a statute that requires that force is violent in nature and force, like the Indiana misdemeanor statute, that requires only a touching and therefore does not necessarily require violence]; *Matter of Sanudo,* 23 I&N Dec. 968, 974–75 (BIA 2006) [domestic battery under Cal. Penal Code §§242 and 243(e)(1) are not crimes of violence under the modified categorical approach where record of conviction did not sustain anything but a nonviolent touching and therefore the conviction is not a removable offense for domestic violence];

(2) Child Abuse. The term is broadly construed by the BIA "to mean any offense involving an international, knowing, reckless, or criminally negligent act or omission that constitutes maltreatment of a child or that impairs a child's physical or mental well-being, including sexual abuse or exploitation." *Matter of Velazquez-Herrera*, 24 I&N Dec. 503, 512 (BIA 2008) [finding that fourth-degree assault under Wash. RC §9A.44.083 was not child abuse under categorical approach]. In *Matter of Velazquez-Herrera* that child abuse encompasses slightly physical harm, mental or emotional harm, sexual abuse and exploitation, but refers only to offenses committed against an individual who has not reached 18. *Id. See also Matter of Rodriguez-Rodriguez*, 22 I&N Dec. 991, 996 (BIA 1999); *Velazquez-Herrera v. Gonzales*, 466 F.3d 781 (9th Cir. 2006) [prior remand to the BIA of *Velazquez-Herrera* to determine if it was child abuse]; *Lopez-Dominquez v. Gonzales*, 428 F.3d 1156 (8th Cir. 2005) [broadly construing section and finding malicious punishment of a child under Minn. Stat. §609.377 is child abuse].

9.b. Person found to have violated domestic violence injunction, whether issued by civil or criminal court. 8 U.S.C. §1227(a)(2)(E)(ii). The deportation ground is limited to a violation of the "portion of a protection order that involves protection against credible threats of violence, repeated harassment, or bodily injury…" INA §237(a)(2)(E)(ii).

9.c. Effective Date: Convictions or violations occurring after Sept. 30, 1996. IIRIRA §350(b). *Matter of Gonzalez-Silva*, 24 I&N Dec. 218 (BIA 2007) [a conviction which predated the effective date of INA §237(a)(2)(E) bars a finding but deportability and therefore does not but cancellation].

9.d. Waiver—INA §237(a)(7). The AG may grant a waiver to a person who has been battered or subjected to extreme cruelty and who is not and was not the primary perpetrator of violence in the relationship upon a determination that the respondent was acting in self defense, violated a protective order intended to protect her/him or was arrested for, convicted of, or pled guilty to committing a crime that did not result in serious bodily injury and there was a connection between the crime and being battered or subject to extreme cruelty.

10. **Sex Offender Who Fails to Register**—INA §237(a)(2)(A)(v), 8 U.S.C. §1227(a)(2)(A)(v). A conviction under 18 U.S.C. §2250 for failing to register as a sex offender is a deportable offense. Under 18 U.S.C. §2250 a person who knowingly fails to register or update a registration under the Sex Offender Registration and Notification Act and is required to register commits a crime if s/he: (1) is a sex offender as defined under the Sex Offender Registration and Notification Act due to a conviction under Federal law (including the Uniform Code of Military Justice), the law of the District of Columbia, Indian trial law, or the law of any territory or possession of the U.S. *or* (2) travels in interstate or foreign commerce, or enters or leaves, or resides in, Indian country.

11. The Immigration Act of 1990 eliminated as a grounds of deportation a person who became a prostitute or associated with prostitution subsequent to entry.

H. *Effective Date / Savings Provision*

1. Deportation grounds pursuant to IMMACT90 apply to persons who have been provided notice of their deportation proceedings on or after Mar. 1, 1991. IMMACT90 §602(d); *Matter of Esposito*, 21 I&N Dec. 2 n.1 (BIA 1995). This provision is effective under the BIA's decision even if the charge is excludable on entry based upon an entry prior to the Act's effective date. *Matter of Papayzan*, 20 I&N Dec. 568 (BIA 1992). If an OSC is issued, but not served before Mar. 1, 1991, INS must issue a new OSC reflecting the new section of the law. IMMACT90 Wire No. 40, Lempres, Executive Comm. (Feb. 27, 1991).

2. IMMACT90 supersedes earlier effective dates governing deportability for an aggravated felony conviction and therefore a person is deportable for an aggravated felony conviction that arose before Nov. 19, 1988. *Matter of Lettman,* 22 I&N Dec. 365 (BIA 1999), *aff'd, Lettman v. Reno,* 207 F.3d 1368 (11th Cir. 2000) [applying IMMACT90 §602(c) to permit retroactive application of agg. felony definitions]; *Lewis v. INS,* 194 F.3d 539 (4th Cir. 1999); *Lopez-Amaro v. INS,* 25 F.3d 986 (11th Cir. 1994) [applying same rationale to non–aggravated felony firearm conviction]. *See also Gelman v. Ashcroft,* 372 F.3d 495 (2d Cir. 2004) [following *Bell v. Reno* and finding that post–*St. Cyr,* IMMACT90 §602(d) permits the definition of an aggravated felony to apply to convictions which arose before Nov. 18, 1988 where notice of proceeding was provided after Mar. 1, 1991]; *Bell v. Reno,* 218 F.3d 86 (2d Cir. 2000) [finding that IMMACT90 §602(c) could not be applied retroactively but that §602(d) does apply to allow for the retroactive application of aggravated felony provisions, as long as proceedings were after Mar. 1, 1991]. *But see U.S. v. Ubaldo-Figueroa,* 364 F.3d 1042, 1050–56 (9th Cir. 2004) [retroactively applying the expanded definition of aggravated felony to encompass an attempted burglary conviction that arose prior to 1996 would plausibly violate due process].

3. An alien who was deportable because of a conviction before Nov. 29, 1990, of an offense referred to in former INA §241(a)(15), (16), (17), or (18), "shall be" considered to remain so deportable. The deportation provisions applies to all aliens even if they entered before Nov. 29, 1990, or the facts concerning the grounds of deportation arose before Nov. 29, 1990. IMMACT90 §602(c). *See Attul v. INS,* 42 F.3d 958 (5th Cir. 1995). Under IIRIRA, generally the effective date of all grounds of inadmissibility and removal is Apr. 1, 1997. IIRIRA §309(a). There are certain exceptions, *e.g.*, the change in INA §237(a)(2)(A)(i) applies to any deportation proceeding initiated after the date of enactment. The AG may opt to utilize new procedures if an evidentiary hearing is not held by Apr. 1, 1997, or s/he may terminate proceedings and begin anew. IIRIRA §§309(c)(2) & (3).

4. Transition Rules and Service of OSC—A person served with an OSC and a warrant of detainer may be considered to be in proceedings under pre–AEDPA/IIRIRA law so that a later served and filed NTA does not deprive him or her of relief under pre-IIRIRA standards. *Alanis-Bustamante v. Reno,* 201 F.3d 1303 (11th Cir. 2000) [AEDPA/IIRIRA does not bar §212(c) relief where person served with OSC and warrant of detainer, even if OSC not filed with the immigration court and even if INS subsequently issues and serves and NTA]; *Wallace v. Reno,* 194 F.3d 279 (1st Cir. 1999). Similarly a person served with an OSC would be considered under pre–AEDPA/IIRIRA proceedings even if s/he were not subject to a detainer, where immigration authorities never intended to place a detainer. *Cunningham v. U.S. Att'y Gen.,* 335 F.3d 1262 (11th Cir. 2003) [followed *Alanis-Bustamante* and allowed for filing of §212(c) and §212(h) relief, even where no detainer was lodged, when INS never intended to lodge detainer]. *But see Thom v. Ashcroft,* 369 F.3d 158, 164–65 (2d Cir. 2004) [legacy INS filing notice of detainer with prison but neither serving nor filing NTA until after Apr. 1, 1997, does not place person in proceedings before that date]; *Dipeppe v. Quarantillo,* 337 F.3d 326, 333–35 (3d Cir. 2003) [the delay between the service of the OSC in 1992 and the filing of the NTA in 2000 did not justify application of *St. Cyr* because the OSC was not filed and therefore proceeding commenced only with the filing in court of the NTA]; *Armendariz-Montoya v. Sonchik,* 291 F.3d 1116 (9th Cir. 2002) [rejecting both *Alanis-Bustamante* and *Wallace*]; *DeLeon-Holguin v. Ashcroft,* 253 F.3d 811 (5th Cir. 2001) [proceedings have not commenced where OSC is served but not filed, and thereafter INS serves and files NTA]; *Asad v. Reno,* 242 F.3d 702, 706 (6th Cir. 2001); *Morales-Ramirez v. Reno,* 209 F.3d 977 (7th Cir. 2000) [finding that a person served with an exclusion notice but not put into removal proceedings until after IIRIRA is barred from §212(c) because proceeding only commenced under 8 C.F.R. §§1003.14 and 1240.30 after INS filed the NTA with the court].

VI. A CONVICTION UNDER THE INA

A. *Definition*—A conviction exists where there has been a formal judgment of guilt entered by a court or if adjudication has been withheld, where all of the following elements are present: (1) a judge or jury has found alien guilty, or the person entered a plea of guilty or nolo contendere or has admitted sufficient facts to warrant a finding of guilt; *and* (2) the judge has ordered some form of punishment, penalty or restraint on the person's liberty to be imposed. INA §101(a)(48)(A). A conviction does not occur at the time the court accepts the guilty plea, but rather at the "date on which judgment is entered on the docket." *Puello v. Bureau of USCIS,* 511 F.3d 324, 331 (2d Cir. 2007) [applicant ineligible for naturalization due to lack of GMC because he was convicted "on or after" Nov. 29 1990 despite his guilty plea before that date].

1. The previous definition under *Matter of Ozkok*, 19 I&N Dec. 546 (BIA 1988), which required as a condition for a conviction that a judgment or adjudication of guilt may be entered if the person violates probation or court orders without any additional proceedings to determine guilt or innocence of the original charge, has been removed. IIRIRA §322. "The section deliberately broadened the scope of the definition of conviction." H.R. Conf. Rep. 828, 104th Cong., 2d Sess. at 223–24. The purpose of the change is to hold that "deferred adjudications" are still convictions. H.R. Conf. Rep., *supra* at 224. The new definition of conviction applies to convictions entered "before, on, or after" Sept. 30, 1996. IIRIRA §322(c). *Matter of Punu,* 22 I&N Dec. 224 (BIA 1998) [finding Texas deferred adjudication's statute a conviction because the third prong of *Ozkok* has been removed. New definition applied retroactively]; *Perez v. Elwood,* 294 F.3d 552, 561–62 (3d Cir. 2002) [IIRIRA §322(c) applies retroactively, and the term "formal judgment of guilt" is defined by reference to Fed. R. Crim. P. 32(d)(1), and occurs at the time of sentencing, not jury adjudication, thereby foreclosing INA §212(c) relief, as sentence was entered after Apr. 1, 1997, the repeal date of INA §212(c)].

2. The definition under §101(a)(48)(A) has been upheld. *De Vega v. Gonzales,* 503 F.3d 45, 48–49 (1st Cir. 2007) [relying on the definition under §101(a)(48)(A), the court determined that a continuation of defendant's case under Massachusetts law without a finding of guilt was a conviction where it was based upon an admission of facts sufficient for a finding of guilt and the payment of restitution, because the restitution order was punitive and the admission could ripen into a guilty plea];*Batrez Gradiz v. Gonzales,* 490 F.3d 1206, 1207–09 (10th Cir. 2007) [nolo plea and deferred sentence under Wyoming statute is conviction]; *Salazar-Regino v. Gonzales,* 415 F.3d 436, 448 (5th Cir. 2005) [BIA's decision in *Matter of Roldan* interpreting §101(a)(48)(A) should be accorded *Chevron* deference and person with deferred adjudication under Texas law §322(a) is convicted]; *Uritsky v. Gonzales,* 399 F.3d 728 (6th Cir. 2005) [relying on *Chevron* deference in the BIA's interpretation of §101(a)(48) and distinguishing *Matter of Devison,* 22 I&N Dec. 1362 (BIA 2000) as a juvenile delinquency case, the court determined that a sentence to probation under Michigan's Youthful Trainee Act was a conviction]; *Cruz-Garza v. Ashcroft,* 396 F.3d 1125, 1128–29 (10th Cir. 2005) [affirmed *Roldan/Salazar* standard but found that under that standard DHS did not prove by clear and convincing evidence that reduced felony conviction was an aggravated felony because the reduction of respondent's conviction to a misdemeanor in light of the vagaries of the evidentiary record and the existence of a Utah statute permitting reduction could have occurred for other than rehabilitative purpose]; *Resendez-Alcaraz v. U.S. Att'y Gen.,* 383 F.3d 1262 (11th Cir. 2004) [finding expunged state conviction for simple possession that is equivalent to FFOA remains a conviction under the clear language of §101(a)(48)(A) and BIA's interpretation in *Roldan*]; *Murillo-Espinoza v. INS,* 261 F.3d 771 (9th Cir. 2001) [where Ariz. Rev. Stat. §13-907(A) provided that a judgment of guilt would be set aside upon fulfillment of the conditions of probation or sentence it remained a conviction for immigration purposes under the BIA's interpretation in *Matter of Roldan*]; *Griffiths v. INS,* 243 F.3d 45, 49–55 (1st Cir. 2001) [finding Massachusetts "on file" procedure a conviction post-IIRIRA and distinguishing *Pino* because finality is no longer a consideration]; *Herrera-Inirio v. INS,* 208 F.3d 299 (1st Cir. 2000) [Puerto Rican rehabilitative programs that have the effect of vacating a conviction other than on the merits or a basis tied to violations of statutory or constitutional right in the underlying case are deemed convictions. Found INA definition of conviction constitutional in face of full faith and credit, substantive due process and 10th Amendment challenge]; *Moosa v. INS,* 171 F.3d 994, 1006–10 (5th Cir. 1999) [finding that a plea under Texas deferred adjudication statute is a conviction]; *Pequeno-Martinez v. Trominski,* 281 F.Supp.2d 902, 915 (S.D. Tex. 2003) [rejected argu-

ment that under deferred adjudication person was not sentenced to any term of imprisonment and therefore was not sentenced to a felony for purposes of aggravated felony statute].

3. The Board in *Matter of Roldan,* 22 I&N Dec. 512 at 528 (BIA 1999) read the new statutory definition broadly, finding that: "State rehabilitative actions which do not vacate a conviction on the merits or on any ground related to the violation of a statutory or constitutional right in the underlying criminal proceeding are of no effect in determining whether an alien is considered convicted for immigration purposes." *Roldan* was subsequently vacated *sub nom* in *Lujan-Armendariz v. INS,* 222 F.3d 728 (9th Cir. 2000) in cases involving state equivalents to the Federal First Offender Act (FFOA) under 18 U.S.C. §3607. However, the BIA reaffirmed its position that state equivalents of the FFOA are still convictions for immigration purposes for cases outside of the Ninth Circuit, *Matter of Salazar* 23 I&N Dec. 223 (BIA 2002). Some circuits have supported the Board's reasoning in *Roldan* and *Salazar. See De Jesus Melendez v. Gonzales,* 503 F.3d 1019 (9th Cir. 2007) [court distinguished *Lujan-Armendariz* and *Garberding* and held that equal protection was not violated because El Salvadoran with expunged 1999 conviction for possession under Cal. Penal Code §1203.4 was convicted for immigration purposes because the FFOA did not apply as respondent had a previous 1996 diversion program]; *Salazar-Regino v. Gonzales,* 415 F.3d 436, 448 (5th Cir. 2005) [BIA's decision in *Matter of Roldan* interpreting §101(a)(48)(A) should be accorded *Chevron* deference and person with deferred adjudication under Texas law §322(a) is convicted]; *Ramos v. Gonzales,* 414 F.3d 800, 806–07 (7th Cir. 2005) [following *Gill*, the court rejected an equal protection challenge to a Nebraska conviction vacated for rehabilitative purposes]; *Resendez-Alcaraz v. U.S. Att'y Gen.,* 383 F.3d 1262 (11th Cir. 2004) [finding expunged state conviction for simple possession that is equivalent to FFOA remains a conviction under the clear language of §101(a)(48)(A) and BIA's interpretation in *Roldan* and rejected equal protection and due process challenge]; *Madriz-Alvarado v. Ashcroft,* 383 F.3d 321 (5th Cir. 2004) [same]; *Acosta v. Ashcroft,* 341 F.3d 218 (3d Cir. 2003) [rejected equal protection challenge to distinction between FFOA and state equivalents and upheld, under *Chevron* deference standards, the BIA's interpretation in *Roldan* and *Salazar* that a state equivalent to FFOA is still a conviction under INA §101(a)(48)(A)]; *Gill v. Ashcroft,* 335 F.3d 574 (7th Cir. 2003) [finding FFOA only applies to federal and not state convictions]; *Fernandez-Bernal v. AG,* 257 F.3d 1304, 1311–17 (11th Cir. 2001) [rejecting an equal protection challenge to BIA decision following *Roldan* but found that it need not reach the issue because the respondent would not have qualified under the FFOA]; *Vasquez-Velezmoro v. INS,* 281 F.3d 693 (8th Cir. 2002) [agreed with *Fernandez Bernal*, finding no equal protection violation because state sentence to probation was longer than one year and, therefore, conviction not the same as under FFOA; but disagreed with reasoning in *Lujan-Armendariz*]; *Herrera-Inirio v. INS,* 208 F.3d 299, 305 (1st Cir. 2000).

4. Punishment under the Definition of Conviction—The statutory definition of a conviction under INA §101(a)(48)(A) requires that some form of penalty or punishment be imposed. The BIA determined that the imposition of costs and surcharges in a criminal sentence constitutes a form of penalty or punishment under the Act and therefore, is a conviction for immigration purposes. *Matter of Cabrera,* 24 I&N Dec. 459 (BIA 2008) [nolo plea to drug possession charge under Florida law, where defendant received a withhold of adjudication and was assessed costs and surcharges, resulted in defendant's conviction because the costs and surcharges were a punishment under federal law]. In *De Vega v. Gonzales,* 503 F.3d 45, 48–49 (1st Cir. 2007) the court determined that a continuation of defendant's case under Massachusetts law without a finding of guilt was a conviction where it was based upon an admission of facts sufficient for a finding of guilt and the payment of restitution because the restitution order was punitive and the admission could ripen into a guilty plea. *See also Uritsky v. Gonzales,* 399 F.3d 728 (6th Cir. 2005), *cert. denied,* 546 U.S. 823 (2005) [treating participation in Michigan's Youthful Offender Trainee Program as a penalty pursuant to the immigration definition of conviction]; *Gonzalez v. O'Connell,* 355 F.3d 1010 (7th Cir. 2004) [treating probation as a punishment for purposes of statutory definition of conviction].

5. The former definition under *Ozkok* was also upheld. *Wilson v. INS*, 43 F.3d 211 (5th Cir. 1995) [upheld *Ozkok* in context of Texas law allowing for dismissal of charges after completion of probation and found *Pino* not relevant, notwithstanding *Martinez-Montoya*]; *Yanez-Popp v. INS*, 998 F.2d 231 (4th Cir. 1993) [upheld *Ozkok* in context of Maryland's probation-without-judgment law]; *Molina v. INS*, 981 F.2d 14 (1st Cir. 1992) [applies *Ozkok* to Rhode Island conviction even if a conviction as defined by *Ozkok* "does not conform perfectly with the application of the same

word in Rhode Island's State law"]; *Chong v. INS*, 890 F.2d 284 (11th Cir. 1989) (per curiam) [withholding of adjudication under Florida law is conviction for immigration purposes under *Ozkok*]. Compare *Matter of M*, 19 I&N Dec. 861 (Comm. 1989) [more stringent standard than *Ozkok* applied to legalization applicants]. *But see Martinez-Montoya v. INS*, 904 F.2d 1018 (5th Cir. 1990) [rejecting *Matter of M* standard as contrary to finality requirement of *Pino v. Landon* and *Ozkok*]. *See also* 9 FAM 40.21(a) N.3, 26 ALR Fed. 709.

6. Court-Martial is a Conviction—*Matter of Rivera-Valencia,* 24 I&N Dec. 484 (BIA 2008) [court-martial is a conviction under INA §101(a)(48)(A) and cannot be collaterally attacked on grounds that defendant was not advised of rights under Art. 36 of the Vienna Convention]. *But see Gubbels v. Hoy,* 261 F.2d 952, 954 (9th Cir. 1958); *Matter of Gian,* 11 I&N Dec. 242 (BIA 1965).
7. Judgment of Guilt Not Necessarily a Conviction—Where a state procedure allows for the entry of a judgment of guilt under a standard less than "beyond a reasonable doubt" and the state need not provide counsel or a jury, a "criminal conviction" is not a conviction for immigration purposes under INA §101(a)(48)(A). *Matter of Eslamizar,* 23 I&N Dec. 684 (BIA 2004) [a finding of guilt of third-degree theft under Oregon law in a proceeding conducted under Or. Rev. Stat. §153.076 that allows for a conviction by preponderance of the evidence and no right to counsel or jury trial is not a judgment of guilt for purposes of establishing a conviction under the INA. *Matter of C-R-* overruled].
8. Pretrial Intervention May Not Be a Conviction—While the federal definition of what constitutes a conviction is controlling, a person will not be deemed convicted under the INA if there is no plea entered under state law. *Matter of Grullon*, 20 I&N Dec. 12 (BIA 1989) [Florida's pretrial intervention program, Fla. Stat. §944.025, not deemed to result in a conviction for immigration purposes]; *Matter of Sirhan*, 13 I&N Dec. 592 (BIA 1970) [state *coram nobis* proceeding vacating conviction means no conviction exists under former §241(a)(11)]; *Matter of O'Sullivan*, 10 I&N Dec. 320 (BIA 1963); 66 No. 19 *Interpreter Releases* 539–40 (May 15, 1989). Also, pretrial intervention where there's no plea at all may not be a conviction. *Cf. Pinho v. Gonzales,* 432 F.3d 193, 204–16 (3d Cir. 2005) [where conviction vacated for ineffective assistance of counsel and defendant repleaded to PTI, he was not considered convicted for immigration purposes].
9. Vacated Conviction May Not Be a Conviction—Similarly, a vacated conviction that is not vacated pursuant to a rehabilitative statute is not a conviction for immigration purposes. *Matter of Adamiak,* 23 I&N Dec. 878 (BIA 2006) [where the criminal court in Ohio failed to advise defendant of the immigration consequences of his plea pursuant to Ohio Rev. Code §2943.031, the subsequent *vacatur* is not a conviction for immigration purposes because the guilty plea has been vacated as a result of a "defect in the underlying criminal proceeding"]; *Matter of Rodriguez-Ruiz,* 22 I&N Dec. 1378 (BIA 2000) [distinguished *Roldan* and found conviction vacated under N.Y. Crim. Proc. Law Art. 440, notwithstanding INS's claim that it was vacated for immigration purposes]; *Cruz v. Att'y Gen. of the U.S.,* 452 F.3d 240, 246 & n.3 (3d Cir. 2006) [reversed denial of *sua sponte* reopening where respondent vacated conviction and then sought reopening which was denied by BIA as untimely despite numerous unpublished BIA decisions granting untimely reopening where convicted was vacated]; *Alim v. Gonzales,* 446 F.3d 1239, 1250–51 (11th Cir. 2006) [where respondent was not advised of the immigration consequences of his plea under Florida law and his conviction was vacated, the court looked to the *coram nobis* petition when the order was ambiguous to determine that the *vacatur* was on substantive grounds]; *Pinho v. Gonzales,* 432 F.3d 193, 204–16 (3d Cir. 2005) [where conviction vacated for ineffective assistance of counsel and defendant repleaded to PTI, he was not considered convicted for immigration purposes]; *Sandoval v. INS,* 240 F.3d 577 (7th Cir. 2001) [reversed deportation order where the vacatur of the conviction was on constitutional grounds, *Roldan* therefore did not apply, and the IJ improperly placed burden on respondent to prove vacatur was not proper]. *But see Pena-Muriel v. Gonzales,* 489 F.3d 438 (1st Cir. 2007) [due process was not violated where the BIA refused to allow respondent, who was outside the United States, to reopen his deportation proceeding because his conviction was vacated]; *Padilla v. Gonzales,* 470 F.3d 1209, 1212–15 (7th Cir. 2006) [where respondent vacated convictions after BIA appeal and counsel never sought *sua sponte* review from BIA after government refused to file joint motion, the court determined that counsel failed to exhaust administrative remedies and dismissed the petition for review]. *But see William v. Gonzales,* 499 F.3d 329 (4th Cir. 2007) [where petitioner vacated his conviction after departure, the court

distinguished *Pena-Muriel* and struck down the prohibition in 8 C.F.R. §1003.2(d) to motions to reopen where the person is outside the U.S. as contrary to INA §240(c)(7)(A), 8 U.S.C. §1229a(c)(7)(A)]; *Cardoso-Tlaseca v. Gonzales,* 460 F.3d 1102 (9th Cir. 2006) [permitting motion to reopen, where deportable conviction vacated after noncitizen departed under removal order notwithstanding language of 8 C.F.R. §1003.2]

9.a. *Matter of Pickering Exception*—However, the vacatur of the plea must be for a procedural or substantive defect in the underlying criminal proceeding and not for reasons solely related to post-conviction events such as rehabilitation or immigration hardship. *Matter of Pickering,* 23 I&N Dec. 621 (BIA 2003) *reversed on other grounds Pickering v. Gonzales,* 465 F.3d 263 (6th Cir. 2006) [if the court vacates a conviction for reasons unrelated to the merits of the underlying criminal proceedings the respondent remains convicted for immigration purposes]; *Saleh v. Gonzales,* 495 F.3d 17 (2d Cir. 2007) [affirmed *Pickering* under second step of *Chevron* analysis, rejected a full faith and credit argument under 28 U.S.C. §1738, and held that where stolen property conviction under Cal. Penal Code §496(a) was reduced to a petty offense for immigration purposes it remained a CIMT]; *Sanusi v. Gonzales*, 474 F.3d 341 (6th Cir. 2007) [where petitioner did not raise or argue any colorable legal basis for vacating his conviction but solely asked for mercy from the harsh immigration consequences of his plea, the *writ of coram nobis* did not vacate plea for immigration purposes]; *Ali v. U.S. Att'y Gen.,* 443 F.3d 804, 810–12 (11th Cir. 2006) [where the strongest inference supported by respondent's pleadings was that he sought vacatur because he previously thought a First Offender plea would not effect his immigration status, it was neither a substantive nor procedural vacatur and therefore remained a conviction]; *Ali v. Ashcroft,* 395 F.3d 722, 728–30 (7th Cir. 2005) [where parties stipulated to amend conviction from trafficking offense to simple misdemeanor possession of THC "simply to avoid deportation" and not for a procedural or substantive defect *Pickering* applied and respondent's conviction for trafficking remained]; *Bah v. Cangemi,* 489 F.Supp.2d 905, 912–14 (D. Minn. 207) [court had no jurisdiction to review AAO decision to withdraw Liberian's TPS on the grounds that his vacated conviction for second-degree criminal sexual conduct under *Matter of Pickering* was still a conviction and therefore he was ineligible for TPS]; *Pequeno-Martinez v. Trominski,* 281 F.Supp.2d 902, 926–27 (S.D. Tex. 2003) [where order vacating conviction stated it was "in the interest of justice and equity and to avoid a manifest injustice" court found that it was still a conviction under *Pickering* because there was no evidence conviction was withdrawn from legal defect]. The Fifth Circuit appears to have gone even further by finding that all vacated convictions may remain convictions for immigration purposes. *Renteria-Gonzalez v. INS*, 322 F.3d 804, 812–14 (5th Cir. 2002) [immigration definition of conviction read broadly to include virtually all vacated convictions including those vacated for equitable reasons]; *But see Larin-Ulloa v. Gonzales,* 462 F.3d 456, 461–63 (5th Cir. 2006) [distinguishing *Renteria-Gonzalez* and finding that a Kansas judgment vacated *nunc pro tunc* is the operative judgment]; *Discipio v. Ashcroft,* 417 F.3d 448 (5th Cir. 2005) [vacating prior decision that read *Renteria-Gonzalez* broadly to find a conviction for immigration purposes despite it being vacated on *criminal procedural grounds* where government announced it would terminate proceedings based upon *Matter of Pickering*].

9.b. Burden of Proof—To determine whether a person's conviction was vacated for substantive or procedural reasons, one circuit has set forth the following procedure: "The agency must first look to the order itself. If the order explains the court's reasons for vacating the conviction, the agency inquiry must end. If the order does not give a clear statement of reasons, the agency may look to the record before the court when the order was issued. No other evidence or reasons may be considered." *Pinho v. Gonzales,* 432 F.3d 193, 215 (3d Cir. 2005) [where conviction vacated for ineffective assistance of counsel and defendant repleaded to PTI, he was not considered convicted for immigration purposes]. *Accord Alim v. Gonzales*, 446 F.3d 1239, 1249–51 (11th Cir. 2006). *but see Sanusi v. Gonzales*, 474 F.3d 341 (6th Cir. 2007) [court distinguished *Pickering* and found that where petitioner did not raise or argue any colorable legal basis for vacating his conviction but solely asked for mercy from the harsh immigration consequences of his plea, the *writ of coram nobis* did not vacate plea for immigration purposes]; *Al-Najar v. Mukasey,* 515 F.3d 708, 715–16 (6th Cir. 2008) [followed *Sanusi* and found that the government met its burden of proof where petitioner filed a motion to vacate his conviction based upon the judgment having been satisfied, released or discharged]. There is a split in the circuits regarding who has the burden of proof that a vacated conviction was vacated for other than procedural or substantive reasons. In *Nath v. Gonzales,* 467 F.3d 1185, 1188–89 (9th Cir. 2006) and *Pickering v. Gonzales,* 465 F.3d 263, 269 n.4 (6th Cir. 2006) [notwithstanding the respondent's immigration motive as expressed in his moving papers to the Canadian court, the Canadian vacatur of his conviction without explanation but with citation to authority was sufficient to vacate the conviction for immigration purposes and DHS had burden to prove that vacatur was not for a substantive or procedural reason], the circuit courts have determined that the government bears the burden. *But see Matter of Chavez,* 24 I&N Dec. 272 (BIA 2007) [the Board held that for purposes of a motion to reopen the burden is on the respondent]; *Rumierz v. Gonzales,* 456 F.3d 31, 40–41 (1st Cir. 2006) [respondent has burden on motion to reopen to demonstrate compliance with the *Pickering* standard when the conviction is vacated or modified after a final order of removal have been entered].

10. Vacating a Sentence—Vacating a sentence is treated differently than vacating a conviction. A party may vacate a sentence for any reason, including immigration avoidance, and it must be given full faith and credit by the IJs and BIA. *Matter of Cota,* 23 I&N Dec. 849 (BIA 2005) [where sentence was modified *nunc pro tunc* expressly to avoid deportation as an aggravated felon, IJ and BIA must recognize it. *Matter of Pickering* distinguished].

11. Juvenile Proceedings Not a Conviction—Juvenile delinquency proceedings do not constitute a conviction for immigration purposes. *Matter of Devison,* 22 I&N Dec. 1362, 1365–66 (BIA 2000). Foreign juvenile dispositions are evaluated under U.S. standards. *Matter of Ramirez-Rivero*, 18 I&N Dec.135 (BIA 1981). *But see Matter of De La Nues*, 18 I&N Dec. 140 (BIA 1981). The standards established in the Federal Juvenile Delinquency Act, 18 U.S.C. §5031–50 govern whether an offense by a young offender is to be considered an act of delinquency or a crime. *Matter of Devison, supra* at 1366 [finding an adjudication under §720 of the New York youthful offender procedures to be equivalent to the FJDA and therefore not a conviction even though the procedures were only similar]; *But see Vargas-Hernandez v. Gonzales,* 497 F.3d 919, 922–23 (9th Cir. 2007) [sixteen-year-old tried as an adult for voluntary manslaughter is convicted under INA §101(a)(48)(A)]; *Uritsky v. Gonzales,* 399 F.3d 728 (6th Cir. 2005) [relying on *Chevron* deference in the BIA's interpretation of §101(a)(48) and distinguishing *Devison,* the court determined that a sentence to probation under Michigan's Youthful Trainee Act was a conviction]; *Vieira Garcia v. INS,* 239 F.3d 409, 414–15 (1st Cir. 2001) [upholding BIA decision that 17-year-old tried as adult under Rhode Island law was an aggravated felon and finding that the failure to apply the Federal Juvenile Delinquency Act as a standard for all state convictions does not violate equal protection].

12. Conviction Not Reviewed—If a person is convicted, the IJ will generally not look behind the conviction. *Matter of Rivera-Valencia,* 24 I&N Dec. 484, 491-92 (BIA 2008) [court-martial is a conviction under INA §101(a)(48)(A) and cannot be collaterally attacked on grounds that defendant was not advised of rights under Art. 36 of the Vienna Convention]; *Matter of Short*, 20 I&N Dec. 136 (BIA 1989); *Okabe v. INS*, 671 F.2d 863 (5th Cir. 1982); *Ablett v. Brownell*, 240 F.2d 625 (D.C. Cir. 1957). *But see Doe v. Gonzales,* 484 F.3d 445, 451–53 (7th Cir. 2007) [finding that the IJ erred in not questioning a conviction in an asylum proceeding that was "demonstrably … a travesty—a parody—of justice"]; *Martinez-Benitez v. INS*, 956 F.2d 1053 (11th Cir. 1992) [IJ cannot ignore evidence which contradicts the indictment]. However, where the conviction is vacated, the "vacatur affects the 'underlying lawfulness' of the original judgment." *Matter of Thomas,* 24 I&N Dec. 416, 420 n.5 (BIA 2007).

13. Enhancement of a Sentence as a Conviction—The BIA, interpreting *Apprendi v. New Jersey,* 530 U.S. 466 (2000), has found that a person can be considered convicted of an enhancement provision for immigration purposes where the enhancement provision is proved to a jury by beyond a reasonable doubt or admitted by the defendant thus becoming an element of the offense. *Matter of Martinez-Zapata,* 24 I&N Dec. 424 (BIA 2008) [where conviction was enhanced by virtue of respondent's possession of marijuana in a "drug-free zone" the enhancement was an element of the crime and the conviction was therefore more than a conviction for simple possession of 30 grams of marijuana. Respondent was ineligible for INA §212(h) relief and *Matter of Rodriguez-Cortes,* 20 I&N Dec. 587 (BIA 1992) was superseded for *post-Apprendi* cases].

14. Reason to Believe Even if Conviction Is Vacated—Even if there is no conviction, or conviction is vacated, a person may, under certain circumstances, still be inadmissible under INA §212(a)(2)(A)(i)(II) or (2)(C) as being deportable under INA §237(a)(1) where consular or INS officer has reason to believe person involved is trafficking, or as admission of commission of a drug crime. *Castano v. INS*, 956 F.2d 236 (11th Cir. 1992) [expungement under Federal Youth Corrections Act only bars the use of the conviction to deny admission, not the use of the underlying facts]; *Nunez-Payan v. INS*, 815 F.2d 384 (5th Cir. 1987) [use of plea as admission for former INA §212(a)(23) purposes where plea did not result in conviction]; *Matter of Favela*, 16 I&N Dec. 753 (BIA 1979). *See* Inspector's Field Manual §17.17(a).

B. *Finality of Conviction*

1. A conviction will be deemed effective for immigration purposes only when it is based on the finality of a state or federal court procedure. *Pino v. Landon*, 349 U.S. 901 (1955) [Massachusetts procedure to place conviction "on file" could not be considered a conviction under INA because it had not attained finality]; *Smith v. Gonzales,* 468 F.3d 272 (5th Cir. 2006) [for purposes of the CSA and 21 U.S.C. §§844(a) and 841(b)(1)(B) a drug conviction is not final under the CSA "until the time for seeking discretionary review of the conviction has elapsed"]; *Matter of Punu,* 22 I&N Dec. 224 (BIA 1998) (Rosenberg, concurring and dissenting) [finality a separate requirement from "conviction" for immigration purposes]. *But see Puello v. Bureau of USCIS,* 511 F.3d 324, 332 (2d Cir. 2007) [IIRIRA "eliminate[d] the requirement that all direct appeals be exhausted or waived before a conviction is considered final under the statute"]; *Montenegro v. Ashcroft,* 355 F.3d 1035, 1037 (7th Cir. 2004) [IIRIRA treats a person convicted once a court enters a formal judgment of guilt]; *Griffiths v. INS,* 243 F.3d 45, 49–55 (1st Cir. 2001) [distinguishing *Pino* in light of IIRIRA definition of conviction because "finality is no longer a requirement in cases where the adjudication of guilt has been withheld" but leaving open the issue whether under Massachusetts "on file" procedure the defendant had any punishment imposed]; *Moosa v. INS,* 171 F.3d 994, 1008–10 (5th Cir. 1999) [the new definition of conviction under IIRIRA eliminates finality requirement]. Similarly, an appealed judgment to first appellate court is not a final conviction for DHS purposes. *Will v. INS*, 447 F.2d 529 (7th Cir. 1971); *Marino v. INS*, 537 F.2d 686 (2d Cir. 1976); *Matter of Thomas*, 21 I&N Dec. 20, 21 n.1 (BIA 1995). *But see Garcia-Maldonado v. Gonzales,* 492 F.3d 284, 290–91 (5th Cir. 2007) [a pending appeal of a conviction does *not* affect the finality of the conviction and BIA did not err in treating a conviction on appeal as a final conviction for immigration purposes]. A conviction vacated, for nonimmigration reasons, or overturned on appeal is an appropriate basis for reopening deportation proceedings. *DeFaria v. INS*, 13 F.3d 422, 423 (1st Cir. 1993) [and cases cited therein].

2. Post-conviction remedies do not affect the finality of a conviction for immigration purposes while still pending (*e.g.*, *coram nobis* petition or habeas corpus petition while being pursued do not affect the finality of the conviction if DHS seeks to deport/exclude alien in interim). Similarly, an appeal not-of-right to a state's highest court or an appeal or petition for certiorari to the U.S. Supreme Court does not effect the finality of the conviction. *Morales-Alvarado v. INS*, 655 F.2d 172 (9th Cir. 1989). An untimely appeal to the first appellate court (direct appeal) will also be considered a conviction, even if the court has a procedure to accept appeals out of time. *Matter of Polanco*, 20 I&N Dec. 894 (BIA 1994).

3. Withholding execution of sentence does not affect finality of conviction

   3.a. When sentence imposed but execution is suspended it is still regarded as a final conviction; *Arrellano-Flores v. Hoy*, 262 F.2d 667 (9th Cir. 1958); *Wood v. Hoy*, 266 F.2d 825 (9th Cir. 1959). It is also regarded as a sentence for that period of time. INA §101(a)(48)(B). *Matter of Esposito*, 21 I&N Dec. 1 (BIA 1995).

   3.b. Parole after finding of guilt is a final conviction; *Gutierrez v. INS*, 323 F.2d 593 (9th Cir. 1963), *cert. denied*, 377 U.S. 910 (1964).

4. Collateral Attack of Conviction in EOIR Hearing or Challenge to IJ Hearing—A criminal conviction cannot be collaterally attacked in action challenging an EOIR removal proceeding. *Al-Najar v. Mukasey,* 515 F.3d 708, 714–15 (6th Cir. 2008) [cannot collaterally attack state court conviction that is the basis for removal in the review of the decision of the BIA in circuit court]; *Abiodun v. Gonzales,* 461 F.3d 1210, 1217 (10th Cir. 2006) [cannot collaterally attack state criminal convic-

tions in the removal proceeding]; *Resendiz v. Kovensky,* 416 F.3d 952, 960–61 (9th Cir. 2005) [post-AEDPA and post-IIRIRA respondent cannot collaterally attack, in an 28 U.S.C. §2241 habeas action, his state court conviction that forms the basis for his DHS custody]; *Taylor v. U.S.,* 396 F.3d 1322, 1330 (11th Cir. 2005) [barred collateral challenge to validity of state court conviction in habeas seeking review of removal order]; *Broomes v. Ashcroft,* 358 F.3d 1251, 1255 (10th Cir. 2004) [cannot collaterally attack state court expired conviction by resort to §2241]; *Drakes v. INS,* 330 F.3d 600 (3d Cir. 2003) [following Supreme Court decisions in *Coss* and *Daniels*, the court determined that petitioner could not challenge, by suing INS through §2241, the constitutionality of his state court conviction that resulted in his removal]; *Contreras v. Schiltgen*, 151 F.3d 906 (9th Cir. 1998) [cannot collaterally attack state court conviction in habeas proceeding against INS]; *Mansoori v. INS*, 32 F.3d 1020, 1023–24 n.4 (7th Cir. 1994) [and cases cited therein]; *Urbina-Mauricio v. INS*, 989 F.2d 1085, 1089 (9th Cir. 1993); *De La Cruz v. INS*, 951 F.2d 226, 228 (9th Cir. 1991) [IJ not authorized to consider the validity of the criminal conviction]; *Trench v. INS*, 783 F.2d 181 (10th Cir. 1986); *Zinnanti v. INS*, 651 F.2d 420 (5th Cir. 1981); *Martinez v. Lockyer,* 453 F.Supp.2d 1150 (C.D. Cal. 2006) [cannot collaterally attack a state conviction in a federal coram nobis proceeding challenging removal]; *Tinoco v. Ridge,* 359 F.Supp.2d 1042, 1053–54 (S.D.Cal. 2005) [cannot collaterally challenge state court conviction even if the sentence is still technically pending]; *Neyor v. INS,* 155 F.Supp.2d 127 (D.N.J. 2001) [following Supreme Court decisions in *Coss* and *Daniels,* court determined that petitioner could not challenge through §2254 or §2241 a state court conviction by suing INS]; *Matter of Rivera-Valencia,* 24 I&N Dec. 484, 491-92 (BIA 2008) [court-martial is a conviction under INA §101(a)(48)(A) and cannot be collaterally attacked on grounds that defendant was not advised of rights under Art. 36 of the Vienna Convention]. A foreign conviction may be more susceptible to a collateral attack. *Tahan v. Hodgson*, 662 F.2d 862 (D.C. Cir. 1981) [found prejudice contrary to public policy]. A person may collaterally attack his conviction, even if by plea, for illegal reentry when he was a derivative U.S. citizen. *Perez v. U.S.,* 502 F.Supp.2d 301 (N.D.N.Y. 2006) [procedural default rules were excused because maintaining conviction would be miscarriage of justice under *Murray v. Carrier,* 477 U.S. 478, 495 (1986)].

C. *Guilty Pleas*

1. A guilty plea coupled with a court-ordered restraint on liberty is a conviction for immigration purposes. But some states by statute or rule of procedure require the court to first advise defendant of the immigration consequences before s/he pleads, and if s/he is not advised the conviction may be vacated. [Arizona (Ariz. R. Crim. P. 17.2); California (Cal. Penal Code §1016.5); Connecticut (Conn. Gen. Stat. Ann. §54lj); District of Columbia (D.C. Code Ann. §16-713); Florida (Fla. R. Crim. P. 3.172(C)(8)]; Georgia (Ga. Code Ann. §17-7-93); Hawaii (Haw. Rev. Stat. §802E); Illinois (725 Ill. Comp. Stat. 5/113-8); Iowa (Iowa R. Crim P. 2.8(2)(b)); Maine (Me. R. Crim. P. 11(h)); Maryland (Md. Rule 4-242(e)); Massachusetts (Mass. Gen. Laws Ann. ch. 278 §29D); Minnesota (Minn. R. Crim. P. 15.01 ¶10(d) (felony cases) and Minn. R. Crim. P. 15.02 ¶2 (misdemeanor cases)); Montana (Mont. Code Ann. §46-12-204); Nebraska (Neb. Rev. Stat. §29-1819.02); New Mexico (N.M. Dist. Ct. R. Crim. P. 5-303 (E)(5)); New York (N.Y. Crim. Proc. Law §220.50(7)); North Carolina (N.C. Gen. Stat. §15A-1022(a)(7)); Ohio (Ohio Rev. Code §§2937.06, 2943.031)]; Oregon (Or. Rev. Stat. §135.385(2)(d)); Rhode Island (R.I. Gen. Laws 1956 §12-12-22); Texas (Tex. Code Crim. Proc. Art. 26.13); Vermont (Vt. Stat. Ann. Title 13 §6565); Washington (Wash. Rev. Code §10.40.200); and Wisconsin (Wis. Stat §971.08) *Machado v. State,* 839 A.2d 509 (R.I. 2003) [where R.I. statute requires judge to inform defendant of three potential immigration consequences of his plea and he provides only one, conviction was vacated]; *Commonwealth v. Hilaire,* 777 N.E. 2d 804 (Mass. 2002) [new trial ordered where judged failed to orally advise defendant during plea colloquy of possible immigration consequences]; *DeAbreu v. State*, 593 So.2d 233 (Fla. 1st DCA 1991) [reversed plea where judge failed to advise defendant pursuant to Florida regulation].

2. *Alford* Plea—At least one federal court has held that an *Alford* plea is a conviction for immigration purposes. *Abimbola v. Ashcroft,* 378 F.3d 173, 180–81 (2d Cir. 2004) [finding *Alford* plea to be a conviction under the INA].

3. Pleas may also be vacated where counsel ineffective. *U.S. v. Couto,* 311 F.3d 179 (2d Cir. 2002) [vacated guilty plea based on defendant's counsel's incorrect advice that the plea would not nec-

essarily lead to deportation]; *Downs-Morgan v. U.S.*, 765 F.2d 1534 n.15 (11th Cir. 1985) [where alien improperly advised and raised asylum claim because of fear of imprisonment and execution he is entitled to vacate plea]; *State v. Paredez,* 101 P.3d 799 (Ariz. 2004) [criminal defense attorneys are obligated to determine the immigration status of their clients and to advise them of the immigration consequences of a guilty, and failure to do so is ineffective assistance]; *U.S. v. Russell*, 686 F.2d 35, 39 (D.C. Cir. 1982); *State v. Sallato*, 519 So.2d 605 (Fla. 1988) [where attorney gave "positive misadvice" to alien, it could render plea involuntary]; *In re Resendiz,* 19 P.3d 1171, 105 Cal. Rptr.2d 431 (Cal. 2001) [affirmative misrepresentations or erroneous advice can, in certain circumstances, constitute ineffective assistance of counsel but defendant must demonstrate he would not have otherwise pled guilty]; *People v. Soriano*, 240 Cal. Rptr. 328 (1987); *Commonwealth v. Mahedo*, 397 Mass. 314 (1986); *People v. Guzman*, 172 Cal. Rptr. 34 (Ct. App. 1981); *People v. Correa*, 485 N.E.2d 307 (Ill. 1985); *Lyons v. Pearce*, 676 P.2d 905 (Or. App. 1984); *State v. Malik*, 680 P.2d 770 (Wash. 1984); *People v. Pozo*, 746 P.2d 523 (Colo. 1987) [where defense counsel is aware that client is alien, he has duty to investigate relevant immigration law]. *But see Resendiz v. Kovensky,* 416 F.3d 952, 956–58 (9th Cir. 2005) [immigration consequences post-AEDPA and post-IIRIRA remain collateral and failure of counsel to advise respondent properly of immigration consequences is not a Sixth Amendment violation]; *U.S. v. Del Rosario*, 902 F.2d 55 (D.C. Cir. 1990) [plea not vacated because information regarding immigration consequences is collateral]; *U.S. v. George*, 869 F.2d 333 (7th Cir. 1989) [same]; *U.S. v. Yearwood*, 863 F.2d 6 (4th Cir. 1988) [same]; *U.S. v. Campbell*, 778 F.2d 764 (11th Cir. 1985); *Garcia-Trigo v. U.S.*, 671 F.2d 147 (5th Cir. 1982); *Fruchtman v. Kenton*, 531 F.2d 946 (9th Cir. 1976); *U.S. v. Santelises*, 509 F.2d 703 (2d Cir. 1975); *U.S. v. Nagaro-Garbin*, 653 F.Supp. 586 (E.D. Mich. 1987); *Kentucky v. Fuartado,* 170 S.W.3d 384 (Ky. 2005); *People v. Huante*, 571 N.E.2d 736 (Ill. 1991); *Commonwealth v. Frometa*, 555 A.2d 92 (Pa. 1989); *Carson v. State*, 755 P.2d 242 (Wyo. 1988); *State v. Santos*, 401 N.W.2d 856 (Wis. App. 1987) [failure to inform of JRAD]; *Lyons v. Pearce* (Lyons II), 694 P.2d 969, 978 (Or. 1985); *State v. Ginebra*, 511 So.2d 960 (Fla. 1987) [disapproving of *Edwards v. State*, 393 So.2d 597 (3d DCA 1981) and holding that failure to advise is insufficient to invalidate plea]; *Bermudez v. State*, 603 So.2d 657 (Fla. App. 3 Dist.1992) [even where lawyer gives misadvice to client judge's colloquy informing person of immigration consequences vitiates any misadvice]; *Matter of Fortis*, 14 I&N Dec. 576 (BIA 1974). *See also in this chapter* "Motion to Withdraw Plea," section VII.H (p.222), *infra.*

4. A plea may be vacated where counsel was ineffective and made false promises to defendant. *Blackledge v. Allison,* 431 U.S. 63 (1977) [allowed defendant to proceed on habeas petition where he alleged that facially valid plea was invalid because it was based upon a false promise by his ineffective counsel].

5. A plea of guilt does "not constitute an admission that the petitioner possessed ... any particular amount of [the drug] ..." and an IJ cannot ignore any evidence that contradicts the indictment. *Martinez-Benitez v. INS*, 956 F.2d 1053 (11th Cir. 1992).

6. *Nolo contendere* plea together with a court-imposed restraint or punishment on defendant's liberty is a conviction for immigration purposes. INA §101(a)(48)(A). *See also Qureshi v. INS*, 519 F.2d 1174 (5th Cir. 1975).

7. Guilty plea or *nolo* plea is only conclusive for immigration purposes where conviction requires all elements for a deportable offense. *Soto-Hernandez v. INS*, 726 F.2d 1070 (5th Cir. 1984) [guilty plea to 8 U.S.C. §1325 was not conclusive for violation of former INA §241(a)(13), 8 U.S.C. §1251(a)(13), because "for gain" was not an element of the criminal conviction under 8 U.S.C. §1325].

8. Fast track pleas—A four-level downward departure in sentence is offered to defendants under §5K3.1 of Sentencing Guidelines who agree to the factual basis of the criminal charge and waive the right to file pretrial motions, appeals and collateral relief (except ineffective assistance of counsel). It applies to defendants charged under 8 U.S.C. §1326. Fast track pleas are legal even if not offered to every defendant and the U.S. is not under an obligation to offer it to every defendant. *U.S. v. Vargas,* 477 F.3d 94, 98–100 (3d Cir. 2007) [post-*Booker* sentencing under §3553(a)(6), although required to consider disparities in sentences, need not address disparity between fast-track and non–fast-track sentences and grant a downward departure because the disparity was mandated by Congress]; *U.S. v. Arevalo-Juarez,* 464 F.3d 1246 (11th Cir. 2006) [a sen-

tencing court may not rely solely on a sentencing disparity created by the "fast-track" provision to support a downward departure from the sentencing guideline range]; *U.S. v. Mejia,* 461 F.3d 158 (2d Cir. 2006) [post-*Booker* finding that disparity between districts on fast-track pleas does not violate 18 U.S.C. §3553(a)(6)]; *U.S. v. Anaya Castro,* 455 F.3d 1249, 1250–53 (11th Cir. 2006) [court rejected claim that defendant was entitled to downward adjustment of his sentence in reentry case because Northern District of Georgia did not offer fast track pleas and therefore a sentencing disparity existed]; *U.S. v. Hernandez-Fierros,* 453 F.3d 309 , 312–13 (6th Cir. 2006) [the existence of fast track pleas in certain districts does not require below-Guideline sentence to avoid disparate treatment]; *U.S. v. Martinez-Martinez,* 442 F.3d 539, 541–43 (7th Cir. 2006) [in light of congressional legislation permitting fast-track cases and recognizing possible discrepancies, a sentence is not unreasonable simply because it was imposed in a district that does not have a fast-track program]; *U.S. v. Estrada-Plata,* 57 F.3d 757 (9th Cir. 1995). However, a court may consider the disparities between fast-track and non–fast-track districts in calculating an appropriate sentence. *U.S. v. Montes-Pineda,* 445 F.3d 375, 379–80 (4th Cir. 2006). But a sentence is not unreasonable because a court fails or refuses to adjust a sentence to compensate for the disparities in sentences that arise because some districts are not fast-track districts. *U.S. v. Andújar-Arias,* 507 F.3d 734, 741–45 (1st Cir. 2007) (and cases cited therein) ["Because Congress has authorized fast-track programs with the understanding that the programs would create sentencing disparities, we find that such disparities are not unwarranted as a matter of law]; *U.S. v. Gonzalez-Alvarado,* 477 F.3d 648, 651–52 (8th Cir. 2007) [impermissible for district court to lower sentence based upon absence of fast rack]; *U.S. v. Galicia-Cardenas,* 443 F.3d 553 (7th Cir. 2006) [following *Martinez-Martinez* the court reversed a downward departure where the judge gave the departure because the person was not in a fast-track district and the failure to give the departure would result in sentencing disparities].

9. Where no conviction exists because plea withdrawn, then court will remand immigration case back to IJ. *Quedraogo v. INS*, 864 F.2d 376 (5th Cir. 1989).

D. *Foreign Convictions*—Generally, foreign convictions cannot be collaterally attacked. *Chiaramonte v. INS*, 626 F.2d 1093 (2d Cir. 1980) [violates comity to permit challenge]. *But see Lennon v. INS*, 527 F.2d 187 (2d Cir. 1975). Conviction analogized to Title 18 of U.S. Code or D.C. Code in determining its nature. Moreover, if foreign proceeding violates American public policy or reflects fraud or prejudice, it can be attacked. *Tahan v. Hodgson*, 662 F.2d 862 (D.C. Cir. 1981). Also expungement of person's foreign drug-related conviction pursuant to a foreign rehabilitation statute will not prevent a finding of deportability even if the expungement were equivalent to the federal first offender statute. *Matter of Dillingham*, 21 I&N Dec. 1001 (BIA 1997). The Board's decision in *Dillingham*, however, was reversed and is therefore not the law in the Ninth Circuit. *Dillingham v. INS,* 267 F.3d 996 (9th Cir. 2001) [finding that the BIA's decision to refuse to recognize a foreign expungement for first time offenders under Great Britain's Rehabilitation of Offenders Act of 1974 violated equal protection]. *But see Danso v. Gonzales,* 489 F.3d 709 (5th Cir. 2007) [finding no equal protection violation in the BIA's refusal to equate a "spent" drug conviction under UK with the FFOA and questioning whether the FFOA survived the statutory definition of conviction under 8 U.S.C. §1101(a)(48)(A)]; *Elkins v. Comfort,* 392 F.3d 1159 (10th Cir. 2004) [equal protection not violated by refusal to extend FFOA treatment to foreign expunged conviction].

E. *Misprision/Solicitation/Accessory*—The plea or determination of guilt to a crime such as solicitation or misprision may not be considered to be a conviction of a deportable offense. Thus, misprision of a felony may not, under certain circumstances, be considered a drug crime, *Castaneda de Esper v. INS*, 557 F.2d 79 (6th Cir. 1977); *Matter of Velasco,* 16 I&N Dec. 281 (BIA 1977) [BIA followed the Sixth Circuit's ruling in *Castaneda de Esper*], but solicitation is considered such a crime. *Matter of Beltran*, 20 I&N Dec. 521 (BIA 1992); *Barragan-Lopez v. Mukasey,* 508 F.3d 899 (9th Cir. 2007) [solicitation to possess at least four pounds of marijuana for sale in violation of Ariz. Rev. Stat. §13-1002(A) & (B)(2) and §13-3405(A)(2) & (B)(6) is a CIMT because an inchoate crime is a CIMT if the underlying offense is a CIMT]; *Mizrahi v. Gonzales,* 492 F.3d 156 (2d Cir. 2007) [guilty plea to a misdemeanor fourth-degree criminal solicitation of the sale of drugs under N.Y. Penal Law §100.05(1) is a law relating to a controlled substance under 8 U.S.C. §1182(a)(2)(A)(i)(II)]; *Peters v. Ashcroft,* 383 F.3d 302 (5th Cir. 2004) [felony solicitation to transport marijuana for sale under Ariz. Rev. Stat. §13-1002 is a drug crime]. *But see Sandoval-Lua v. Gonzales,* 499 F.3d 1121 (9th Cir. 2007) [a conviction under Cal. Health & Safety Code §11379(a) contains a solicitation element, *e.g.*, "offer" to transport controlled substance, and therefore is not an aggravated felony because it is broader than the generic drug trafficking crime defined under the Controlled Substances Act]; *Coronado-Durazo v. INS*, 123 F.3d 1322 (9th Cir. 1997) [*Beltran* not followed]; *U.S. v. Aguilar-Ortiz,* 450 F.3d 1271 (11th Cir. 2006) [finding that solicitation to deliver cocaine under Fla. Stat. §777.04(2), when it involves a small quantity of drugs (and in an amount less than the trafficking definition Fla. Stat. §893.135(1)(b) of 28 grams or more), is in essence, under the categorical approach, attempted possession without intent to distribute and is therefore *not* a drug trafficking crime for purposes of sentence enhancement].

F. Misprision is also not considered an aggravated felony under §101(a)(43)(S) relating to obstruction of justice. *Matter of Espinoza,* 22 I&N Dec. 889 (BIA 1999). *But see Patel v. Mukasey,* __F.3d __, 2008 WL 1874579 (5th Cir. 2008) [holding that misprision conviction is a fraud or deceit aggravated felony under §101(a)(43)(M) offense where the loss exceeds $10,000]. However, it is considered a CIMT. *Matter of Robles,* 24 I&N Dec. 22, 25–27 (BIA 2006) [overruling *Matter of Sloan* and finding that misprision of a felony in violation of 18 U.S.C. §4 is a CIMT]; *Itani v. Ashcroft,* 298 F.3d 1213 (11th Cir. 2002) [misprision of felony is a CIMT where it arose in connection with a scheme to rent automobiles, report them stolen to local police, and export them to Kuwait]. However, an accessory after the fact has been found not to be a crime of moral turpitude. *Navarro-Lopez v. Gonzales,* 503 F.3d 1063 (9th Cir. 2007) (*en banc*) [relying on the categorical and modified categorical approach and holding that nothing in Cal. Penal Code §32 inherently makes accessory after the fact a CIMT].

VII. RELIEF FROM CONVICTIONS

A. ***Judicial Recommendations Against Deportation (JRAD)***—JRAD, under former INA §241(b), 8 U.S.C. §1251(b) was *abolished.* IMMACT90 §602(b) repealed INA §241(b) in *its entirety*. The Service has interpreted this provision to relate to cases prospectively and it does not apply to JRADs "granted prior to date of enactment." IMMACT90 Wire No. 5, McNary, Comm. (Nov. 28, 1990); *Phong Thanh Nguyen v. Chertoff,* 501 F.3d 107 (2d Cir. 2007) [where JRAD was effective against both CIMTs and aggravated felonies, the respondent's conviction for rape of a 5 year old child under Mass. law, which at the time was a CIMT but later became, retroactively, an aggravated felony as well, could not be the basis for removal because JRAD was effective against aggravated felony charge as well]; *Renteria-Gonzalez v. INS,* 322 F.3d 804, 811 n.5 (5th Cir. 2002) [rejected government argument that JRAD issued before Nov. 29, 1990, was no longer effective]. However, JRADs granted on or after Nov. 29, 1990, or for a drug offense under former §241(a)(11) are not effective against a deportation charge. 8 C.F.R. §1240.10(d). The Ex Post Facto Clause, in the view of several courts, does not apply to a person whose crime occurred before the effective date of the repeal of JRADs, and a person who sought a JRAD after Nov. 29, 1990, was barred. *U.S. v. Koziel*, 954 F.2d 831 (2d Cir. 1992); *U.S. v. Bodre*, 948 F.2d 28 (1st Cir.), *cert. denied*, 503 U.S. 941 (1992). Moreover, at least one court has found that a JRAD will not bar deportation for a ground created after the bar. *U.S. v. Yacoubian*, 24 F.3d 1 (9th Cir. 1994) [rejecting retroactivity, separation of powers, *ex post facto*, and double jeopardy challenges].

1. Effect of prior granted recommendation in other proceedings.

   1.a. Bars use of conviction as basis for deportation. *Santarelli v. Hughes*, 116 F.2d 613 (3d Cir. 1940).

   1.b. Bars use of conviction to show lack of good moral character in adjustment of status proceedings. *Giambanco v. INS*, 531 F.2d 141 (3d Cir. 1976).

   1.c. Bars the use of the conviction by both DOS and DHS as a basis for future exclusion. *U.S. v. Castro*, 26 F.3d 557, 558 n.2 (5th Cir. 1994); *Rasmussen v. Robinson*, 163 F.2d 732 (3d Cir. 1947); *Matter of K*, 9 I&N Dec. 121 (BIA 1960); *Matter of C-*, 6 I&N Dec. 709 (BIA 1955).

   1.d. *But see Hassan v. INS*, 66 F.3d 266, 269 (10th Cir. 1995) [a conviction may be considered when evaluating discretionary relief, notwithstanding a JRAD]; *U.S. v. Yacoubian, supra* [allowed newly created deportation ground, notwithstanding JRAD]; *Oviawe v. INS*, 853 F.2d 1428 (7th Cir. 1988) [can use conviction of CIMT as adverse factor in determining motion to reopen for adjustment of status. JRAD also does not bar deportation proceeding on another ground (*e.g.*, overstay)]; *Delgado-Chavez v. INS*, 765 F.2d 868 (9th Cir. 1985) [recommendation does not preclude use of conviction at voluntary departure hearing]; *Matter of Parodi*, 17 I&N Dec. 608 (BIA 1980) [recommendation does not preclude use of conviction to deport for separate conviction, even if that conviction was based on same underlying facts as conviction where JRAD was obtained]; *Matter of Gonzalez*, 16 I&N Dec. 134 (BIA 1977) [BIA does not follow *Giambanco* in other circuits and takes position that crime can at least be considered an adverse factor]; *Matter of Y-M-*, 8 I&N Dec. 94 (BIA 1958) [overruled *Matter of C-* in part by finding that a person who received a JRAD before 1952 for a narcotics violation could be deported in light of 1952 changes].

2. Where counsel failed to advise client of relief from deportation, sentence set aside for ineffective assistance of counsel. *U.S. v. Castro*, 26 F.3d 557 (5th Cir. 1994) [failure to advise person of availability of JRAD]; *Lyons v. Pearce*, 298 Or. 554 (1985); *Janvier v. U.S.*, 793 F.2d 449 (2d Cir. 1986). *But see State v. Santos*, 401 N.W.2d 856 (Wis. App. 1987).

3. Where respondent's sentence was set aside solely to allow him to obtain a JRAD, the JRAD was deemed ineffective for deportation purposes. *Zaitona v. INS*, 9 F.3d 432 (6th Cir. 1993).

B. *Expungement of Conviction*

1. State court expungements under rehabilitative statutes are no longer considered to ameliorate the immigration consequences of a conviction. *Matter of Marroquin,* 23 I&N Dec. 705 (AG 2005) [vacating/setting aside or expunging a judgment as a result of a rehabilitative statute such as Cal. Penal Code §1203.4(a), like a deferred adjudication statute, is deemed to be a conviction under INA §101(a)(48) as a result of IIRIRA §322(a)]; *Matter of Luviano,* 23 I&N Dec. 718 (AG 2005) [firearms conviction expunged under Cal. Penal Code §1203.4 remains a conviction for immigration purposes]; *Matter of Roldan,* 22 I&N Dec. 512 (BIA 1999) *vacated sub nom. Lujan-Armendariz v. INS,* 222 F.3d 728 (9th Cir. 2000). *Accord De Jesus Melendez v. Gonzales,* 503 F.3d 1019 (9th Cir. 2007) [court distinguished *Lujan-Armendariz* and *Garberding* and held that equal protection was not violated because El Salvadoran with expunged 1999 conviction for possession under Cal. Penal Code §1203.4 was convicted for immigration purposes because the FFOA did not apply as respondent had a previous 1996 diversion program]; *Salazar-Regino v. Gonzales,* 415 F.3d 436, 448 (5th Cir. 2005) [BIA's decision in *Roldan* interpreting §101(a)(48)(A) should be accorded *Chevron* deference, and person with deferred adjudication under Texas law §322(a) is convicted]; *Resendez-Alcaraz v. U.S. Att'y Gen.,* 383 F.3d 1262 (11th Cir. 2004) [expunged state conviction for simple possession that is equivalent to FFOA remains a conviction under the clear language of §101(a)(48)(A) and BIA's interpretation in *Roldan*; equal protection and due process challenge rejected]; *Madriz-Alvarado v. Ashcroft,* 383 F.3d 321 (5th Cir. 2004) [same]; *Cedano-Viera v. Ashcroft,* 324 F.3d 1062, 1067 (9th Cir. 2003) [expunged lewdness charge still an aggravated felony]; *Ramirez-Castro v. INS,* 287 F.3d 1172 (9th Cir. 2002) [court recognized *Lujan-Armendariz* as a limited exception and found that expungement pursuant to Cal. Penal Code §1203.4 did not vacate a concealed weapons charge]; *Murillo-Espinoza v. INS,* 261 F.3d 771, 772 (9th Cir. 2001). In reaching this conclusion the BIA in *Roldan* reversed 40 years of immigration history based upon the majority's reading of the new definition of conviction under INA §101(a)(48). Prior to *Marroquin* and *Roldan* a state court expungement of an offense of moral turpitude meant that the conviction could not be used for immigration purposes. *Kolios v. INS,* 532 F.2d 786 (1st Cir.), *cert. denied,* 429 U.S. 884 (1976); *Matter of Ozkok,* 19 I&N Dec. 546 (BIA 1988); *Matter of G-,* 9 I&N Dec. 159 (AG 1961) [Cal. statute of expungement returns defendant to status as if he had not been convicted]; 9 FAM 40.21(a) N.3.2-2, 3.2-3. The AG in *Marroquin* and the BIA in *Roldan,* however have found that these and other similar decisions are no longer controlling. The Board's decision in *Roldan,* however, has no effect on a decision to reduce a sentence under Fed. R. Crim. P. 35. *Matter of Martin,* 18 I&N Dec. 226 (BIA 1982). Although, *Roldan* was vacated *sub nom.* in *Lujan-Armendariz v. INS,* 222 F.3d 728 (9th Cir. 2000), the Ninth Circuit's ruling was limited to state convictions that were the equivalent of convictions covered by FFOA, an issue also left open in the AG's decision in *Marroquin*, 23 I&N Dec. at 717. Subsequent to *Lujan-Armendariz*, however, the BIA reaffirmed its position that even state equivalents of convictions under the Federal First Offender Act are still convictions for immigration purposes for cases outside of the Ninth Circuit *Matter of Salazar,* 23 I&N Dec. 223 (BIA 2002). *Accord. Ramos v. Gonzales,* 414 F.3d 800, 806–07 (7th Cir. 2005) [following *Gill,* the court rejected an equal protection challenge to a Nebraska conviction vacated for rehabilitative purposes]; *Resendez-Alcaraz v. U.S. Att'y Gen.,* 383 F.3d 1262 (11th Cir. 2004) [finding expunged state conviction for simple possession that is equivalent to FFOA remains a conviction under the clear lan-

guage of §101(a)(48)(A) and BIA's interpretation in *Roldan* and rejected equal protection and due process challenge]; *Madriz-Alvarado v. Ashcroft,* 383 F.3d 321 (5th Cir. 2004) [same]; *Acosta v. Ashcroft,* 341 F.3d 218 (3d Cir. 2003) [rejected equal protection challenge to distinction between FFOA and state equivalents and upheld, under *Chevron* deference standards, the BIA's interpretation in *Roldan* and *Salazar* that a state equivalent to FFOA is still a conviction under INA §101(a)(48)(A)]; *Gill v. Ashcroft,* 335 F.3d 574 (7th Cir. 2003) [finding FFOA only applies to federal and not state convictions].

Even prior to *Roldan* at least one court took the view that if INS has facts proving offense, then an expungement could not bar deportation: *Sanchez-Marquez v. INS*, 725 F.2d 61 (7th Cir. 1984) [will not overturn deportation order where expungement obtained after deportation order on appeal and the facts of the transportation of illegal aliens were in record]. Similarly, one court determined that an expungement was not available for gun charges because only certain classes of crimes could be expunged. *Carr v. INS*, 86 F.3d 949 (9th Cir. 1996) [rejecting constitutional equal protection challenge].

In light of *Marroquin, Luviano*, and *Roldan,* the requirement that an IJ should defer proceeding for time to obtain an expungement certificate may no longer be appropriate. *Matter of Ozkok*, 19 I&N Dec. 546 (BIA 1988); *Matter of Tinajero*, 17 I&N Dec. 424 (BIA 1980); *Matter of Luviano*, 21 I&N Dec. 235 (BIA 1996) [approved IJ's decision not to continue proceeding awaiting expungement where there was issue as to whether expungement could affect outcome]. *Accord Chavez-Perez v. Ashcroft,* 386 F.3d 1284 (9th Cir. 2004) [upheld removal despite the fact that a person convicted of a first-time simple drug possession under Oregon law might be expunged sometime in the future in a manner similar to the FFOA].

2. An expungement did not wipe out a narcotics conviction for immigration purposes even prior to *Marroquin, Luviano,* and *Roldan. See Matter of Ozkok*, 19 I&N Dec. 546 (BIA 1988); *Matter of Moeller*, 16 I&N Dec. 65 (BIA 1976); *Matter of A-F-*, 8 I&N Dec. 429 (AG 1959) [AG held expungement of narcotic conviction under California law does not wipe out conviction for deportation purposes] *unless* the person received FFOA treatment or "would have been eligible for federal first offender treatment under the provisions of the FFOA had he been prosecuted under federal law." *Matter of Manrique,* 21 I&N Dec. 58 (BIA 1995). However, under *Roldan* and *Matter of Salazar,* 23 I&N Dec. 223 (BIA 2002) the BIA has reversed *Matter of Manrique* for cases outside of the Ninth Circuit, and has found that the statutory definition of a conviction under §101(a)(48)(A) bars state equivalents of the federal FFOA. Most circuits courts now agree, *see* "Federal First Offender Act," ¶ 4, *infra.*

3. Foreign expungements are not given effect. *Danso v. Gonzales,* 489 F.3d 709 (5th Cir. 2007) [finding no equal protection violation in the BIA's refusal to equate a "spent" drug conviction under UK with the FFOA and questioning whether the FFOA survived the statutory definition of conviction under 8 U.S.C. §1101(a)(48)(A)]; *Elkins v. Comfort,* 392 F.3d 1159 (10th Cir. 2004) [equal protection not violated by refusal to extend FFOA treatment to foreign expunged conviction]; *Zgodda v. Holland*, 184 F.Supp. 847 (E.D. Pa. 1960); *Matter of Dillingham*, 21 I&N Dec. 1001 (BIA 1997) [expungement not effective even where expungement would be the equivalent of the FFOA]; *Matter of Adamo*, 10 I&N Dec. 593 (BIA 1964). The Board's decision in *Dillingham*, however, was reversed and is therefore not the law in the Ninth Circuit. *Dillingham v. INS,* 267 F.3d 996 (9th Cir. 2001) [finding that the BIA's decision to refuse to recognize an expungement for first time offenders under Great Britain's Rehabilitation of Offenders Act of 1974 violated equal protection].

4. Federal First Offender Act—In 1987 Congress, as part of the Comprehensive Crime Control Act, established a new Federal First Offender provision. The new provision combines both the former Federal Youth Corrections Act, 18 U.S.C. §5005 *et seq.* and the former First Offenders Act, 21 U.S.C. §844(b)(1). The FFOA sections are now found at 18 U.S.C. §3607(a) and 18 U.S.C. §3607(c), respectively. Section 3607(a) is a dismissal statute. Section 3607(c) is an expungement provision. Thus, a person who falls within §3607(a) is arguably not deemed to be convicted for immigration purposes. The legislative history of 18 U.S.C. §3607 indicates congressional intent to retain the effect of the previous provisions, particularly 21 U.S.C. §844(b). H.R. Rep. No. 1030, 98th Cong., S. Rep. 225, p.133, 1984 U.S.C.C.A.N. 3182, 3316.

In *Matter of Roldan,* 22 I&N Dec. 512 (BIA 1999), *vacated sub nom. Lujan-Armendariz v. INS,* 222 F.3d 728 (9th Cir. 2000), however, the BIA determined that treatment under state rehabilitative statutes or state "first offender" equivalents would still be considered convictions for immigration purposes. A majority of the BIA stated: "We find no room in the present statutory scheme for recognizing state rehabilitative actions in the context of immigration proceedings, or otherwise applying a first offender exception to the definition of 'conviction' to an alien who has been subject of such an action." Under *Roldan* and *Matter of Salazar,* 23 I&N Dec. 223 (BIA 2002) the BIA has reversed *Matter of Manrique* for cases outside of the Ninth Circuit and has found that the statutory definition of a conviction under Section 1101(a)(48)(A) bars state equivalents of the Federal First Offender statute. Persons convicted under state equivalents will now be deemed to have a conviction for immigration purposes. The Ninth Circuit has taken a different view. In *Lujan-Armendariz v. INS*, 222 F.3d 728 (9th Cir. 2000), *rev'g Matter of Roldan*, the Ninth Circuit has determined that a conviction for a first-time simple possession of a drug offense if expunged under state law is not a conviction because IIRIRA did not repeal the Federal First Offender Act, which permits expungement for such first-time drug offenses. *See also Dillingham v. INS,* 267 F.3d 996 (9th Cir. 2001) [applying *Lujan-Armendariz* rule to foreign expungements that are equivalent to FFOA]. *Cf. De Jesus Melendez v. Gonzales,* 503 F.3d 1019 (9th Cir. 2007) [court distinguished *Lujan-Armendariz* and *Garberding* and held that equal protection was not violated because El Salvadoran with expunged 1999 conviction for possession under Cal. Penal Code §1203.4 was convicted for immigration purposes because the FFOA did not apply as respondent had a previous 1996 diversion program]; *Aguiluz-Arellano v. Gonzales,* 446 F.3d 980 (9th Cir. 2006) [FFOA is applicable but respondent did not qualify because he had a prior drug conviction]. *But see Danso v. Gonzales,* 489 F.3d 709 (5th Cir. 2007) [rejecting, the ninth circuit's decision in *Dillingham,* finding no equal protection violation regarding a "spent" drug conviction under UK law in regard to the FFOA, and questioning whether the FFOA survived the statutory definition of conviction under 8 U.S.C. §1101(a)(48)(A)];*Salazar-Regino v. Gonzales,* 415 F.3d 436, 441, 448 (5th Cir. 2005) [BIA's decision in *Matter of Roldan* interpreting §101(a)(48)(A) should be accorded *Chevron* deference and person with deferred adjudication under Texas law §322(a), who would have been considered a first offender for purposes of FFOA, is nevertheless convicted]; *Ramos v. Gonzales,* 414 F.3d 800, 806–07 (7th Cir. 2005) [following *Gill*, the court rejected an equal protection challenge to a Nebraska conviction vacated for rehabilitative purposes]; *Elkins v. Comfort,* 392 F.3d 1159 (10th Cir. 2004) [equal protection not violated by refusal to extend FFOA treatment to foreign expunged conviction]; *Resendez-Alcaraz v. U.S. Att'y Gen.,* 383 F.3d 1262 (11th Cir. 2004) [expunged state conviction for simple possession that is equivalent to FFOA remains a conviction under the clear language of §101(a)(48)(A) and BIA's interpretation in *Roldan*; equal protection and due process challenge rejected]; *Madriz-Alvarado v. Ashcroft,* 383 F.3d 321 (5th Cir. 2004) [same]; *Acosta v. Ashcroft,* 341 F.3d 218 (3d Cir. 2003) [rejected equal protection challenge to distinction between FFOA and state equivalents and upheld, under *Chevron* deference standards, the BIA's interpretation in *Roldan* and *Salazar* that a state equivalent to FFOA is still a conviction under INA §101(a)(48)(A)]; *Gill v. Ashcroft,* 335 F.3d 574 (7th Cir. 2003) [finding FFOA only applies to federal and not state convictions]. *Fernandez-Bernal v. AG,* 257 F.3d 1304, 1311–17 (11th Cir. 2001) [expungement under Cal. Penal Code §1203.4 deemed a conviction and no equal protection violation where *Manrique* standard not met because person sentenced to longer probation than permitted under the FFOA]; *Mugalli v. Ashcroft,* 258 F.3d 52, 61–62 (2d Cir. 2001) [a Certificate of Relief under N.Y. law does not alter a conviction for immigration purposes; *Rehman* is no longer valid].

In *Matter of Devison,* 22 I&N Dec. 1362 at 1372 (BIA 2000), the BIA stated that *Roldan* also applied to convictions under the Federal Youth Corrections Act and that proceedings under those statutes would also be considered convictions, thereby distinguishing them from proceedings under the Federal Juvenile Delinquency Act, which were not considered convictions under IIRIRA's new definition. Under *Roldan*, cases such as *Garberding v. INS*, 30 F.3d 1187 (9th Cir. 1994) [striking down *Matter of Deris* on equal protection grounds as irrational where actual charge was simple possession and person could have received FFOA relief] and *Paredes-Urrestarazu v. INS*, 36 F.3d 801, 815–16 (9th Cir. 1994) [limiting *Garberding* to cases where person could have received the benefit of the FFOA], might no longer be good law except that the Ninth Circuit reversed *Roldan* in *Lujan-Armendariz v. INS*, 222 F.3d 728 (9th Cir. 2000) and found that state equivalents to FFOA in regard to first-time simple drug possession charges if expunged may not be used as convictions under the INA. The Ninth Circuit extended the rule to foreign equivalents to the FFOA in *Dillingham v. INS,* 267 F.3d 996 (9th Cir. 2001), reversing the BIA's decision in *Matter of Dillingham.* In addition if a person was qualified for first offender treatment under federal law prior to IIRIRA, he may still qualify. *Cardenas-Uriarte v. INS,* 227 F.3d 1132, 1135–38 (9th Cir. 2000) [remanded to determine application of *Matter of Manrique* and first offender status for drug paraphernalia expungement under Arizona law]. *But see Danso v. Gonzales,* 489 F.3d 709 (5th Cir. 2007) [finding no equal protection violation in the BIA's refusal to equate a "spent" drug conviction under UK law with the FFOA and questioning whether the FFOA survived the statutory definition of conviction under 8 U.S.C. §1101(a)(48)(A)].

Whether an alien has a right to participate in a first offender program is open to question. A prosecutor's refusal to permit an alien to participate in a first offender treatment program was upheld in the face of an equal protection challenge. *Chavez v. U.S.*, 499 A.2d 813 (D.C. App. 1985).

C. *Pardon*—If there is a "full and unconditional" pardon by the President, governor of the state, or constitutionally recognized executive body, it will prevent deportation for CIMTs, multiple criminal convictions, *aggravated felonies*, and high-speed flight from DHS checkpoint. INA §237(a)(2)(A)(vi), 8 U.S.C. §1227(a)(2)(A)(vi). *See also Estrada-Rosales v. INS*, 645 F.2d 819 (9th Cir. 1981); *Matter of Nolan*, 19 I&N Dec. 539 (BIA 1988) [automatic pardon upon completion of sentence was a conditional pardon by legislature, not executive, and therefore insufficient]; *Matter of B-*, 3 I&N Dec. 551 (BIA 1949); *Matter of Tajer*, 15 I&N Dec. 125 (BIA 1974); *Matter of G-*, 3 I&N Dec. 808 (BIA 1949). A pardon is only available under Board law to prevent removal on those grounds specifically named in INA §237(a)(2)(A)(vi). *Matter of Suh,* 23 I&N Dec. 626 (BIA 2003). Thus a pardon is not available for someone convicted of a drug charge whose removal is sought under the controlled substance provision 8 U.S.C. §1227(a)(2)(B) even if he could not be removed as an aggravated felon, or for someone under the domestic violence provision for something that might otherwise be considered an aggravated felony. *Matter of Suh,* 23 I&N Dec. 626 (BIA 2003) [conviction for child abuse pardoned aggravated felony ground of removal but cannot pardon domestic violence ground of removal because the domestic violence section is not covered under former INA §237(a)(2)(A)(v)]; *Eskite v. District Director*, 901 F.Supp. 530, 536–37 (E.D.N.Y. 1995) [drug offense cannot be pardoned even if aggravated felony can]; *Mullen-Cofee v. INS*, 976 F.2d 1375, 1379 n.10 (11th Cir. 1992) *amended on denial of rehearing* 986 F.2d 1364 (11th Cir. 1993) [same]. An application for a pardon is also not sufficient to stay deportation proceedings. *U.S. v. Butterfield*, 223 F.2d 804 (6th Cir. 1955). *But see Ozkok* [suggesting continuance proper for expungement]. Foreign pardons unavailable to alleviate conviction. *Mullen-Cofee v. INS*, 976 F.2d 1375, 1379 (11th Cir. 1992) *amended on denial of rehearing* 986 F.2d 1364 (11th Cir. 1993) [Canadian pardon]; *Marino v. INS*, 537 F.2d 686, 691 (2d Cir. 1976); *Matter of F- y G-*, 4 I&N Dec. 717 (BIA 1952); 22 C.F.R. §40.21(a)(5). *See also Effects of a Presidential Pardon,* Memo. Office of Legal Counsel (June 19, 1995), at *www.usdoj.gov/olc/pardon3.19.htm* [opining that a full and unconditional presidential pardon precludes the exercise of the authority to deport a convicted noncitizen under criminal deportation grounds] Absence of a pardon provision does not effect whether an offense is a crime. *Matter of Nolan, supra* [even if there is no provision for a pardon, the validity of the conviction is a separate issue]. In the view of one circuit, the pardon provision only applies to persons subject to deportation and does not apply to respondents deemed inadmissible. *Balogun v. U.S. Att'y Gen.*, 425 F.3d 1356, 1362–63 (11th Cir. 2005) [person pardoned by Alabama legislature is still subject to removal as an inadmissible person because the pardon statute only applies to persons subject to deportation]. *But see Matter of H-*, 6 I&N Dec. 90 (BIA 1954) ["As long as there is a full and unconditional pardon granted by the President or by a Governor of a State covering the crime which forms the ground of deportability, whether in exclusion or expulsion, the immunizing feature of the pardon clause applies, and such a crime no longer forms a basis for deportability"]; 22 C.F.R. §§40.21, 40.22; 9 FAM 40.21(a) N.3.5. In filing evidence of a pardon, the movant must comply with 8 C.F.R. §287.6 or provide a compelling reason for the failure to do so. *Ali v. U.S. Att'y Gen.*, 443 F.3d 804, 812–13 (11th Cir. 2006) [BIA did not abuse its discretion in rejecting a photocopy of pardon that did not comply with the regulation, where respondent offered no compelling reason for his failure to obtain a properly certified copy].

D. *Writ of Error Coram Nobis*—State/federal and 28 U.S.C. §1651(a). To obtain a writ of *coram nobis* under federal law, a petitioner must demonstrate that: "(1) there are circumstances compelling such action to achieve justice; (2) sound reasons exist for failure to seek appropriate earlier relief, and (3) the petitioner continues to suffer legal consequences from his conviction that may be remedied by granting the writ." *Tocci v. U.S.,* 178 F.Supp.2d 176 (N.D.N.Y. 2001) [finding the 28 U.S.C. §§2241

& 2255 were unavailable but that the writ of *coram nobis* should issue because of errors in accepting a guilty plea for alien smuggling]; *Urbina v. U.S.,* 992 F.Supp. 641(S.D.N.Y. 1998); *U.S. v. Castro*, 26 F.3d 557, 559 (5th Cir. 1994) [must "demonstrate ... suffering civil disabilities as a consequence of the criminal conviction."]; *Hanan v. U.S.,* 402 F.Supp.2d 679, 687 (E.D. Va. 2005) [denied *coram nobis* where petitioner sought relief on basis he would suffer hardship if returned to Afghanistan because he was ineligible for cancellation as an aggravated felon]. Must have error of fact at time of original judgment and no knowledge of the fact in time to move for new trial. *U.S. v. Morgan*, 346 U.S. 502 (1954). If granted, vacates conviction *ab initio*. *Matter of C-*, 8 I&N Dec. 611 (BIA 1960); *Matter of Sirhan*, 13 I&N Dec. 592 (BIA 1970). Some states may place limitations on a writ of *coram nobis*. *State v. Green,* 944 So.2d 208 (Fla. 2006) [a motion under Fla. R. Crim. P. 3.850, rather than a writ of coram nobis, is the proper vehicle to withdraw plea, and petitioner only has a 2-year period to do so unless he could not have ascertained by due diligence that the plea would subject him to removal]. In the view of one court a *coram nobis* proceeding may not be brought in federal court to attach a state criminal judgment. *Chavez v. Superior Court of California,* 194 F.Supp.2d 1037, 1039 (C.D. Cal. 2002).

E. *Writ of Audita Querela*—Defined as the initial process in an action brought by a judgment defendant to obtain relief against the consequences of the judgment on account of some matter of defense or discharge arising since its rendition and which could not be taken advantage of otherwise. *Black's Law Dictionary*, 120 (5th ed. 1979). It has been applied where subsequent events would render continual existence of judgment and its consequences unjust. However, it has not been well received by the courts when seeking to overturn a conviction for immigration purposes. *U.S. v. Reyes*, 945 F.2d 862 (5th Cir. 1991) [*audita querela* not available to vacate an otherwise final criminal conviction on purely equitable grounds]; *U.S. v. Holder*, 936 F.2d 1 (1st Cir. 1991) [writ cannot provide a purely equitable basis for relief independent of any legal defect in the underlying conviction]. The writ of *audita querela* will also not necessarily eliminate a conviction for immigration purposes even if it is granted. *Beltran-Leon v. INS,* 134 F.3d 1379 (9th Cir. 1998) [dismissed for lack of jurisdiction an appeal from a decision by the BIA which refused to recognize a writ of *audita querela* as vacating a conviction]; *Doe v. INS,* 120 F.3d 200 (9th Cir. 1997) [the state of California's *audita querela* does not vacate a conviction for immigration purposes]; *U.S. v. Johnson,* 962 F.2d 579 (7th Cir. 1992) [writ available only to discharge legal defect in conviction or sentence, not because of equities or gross injustice].

F. *All Writs Act*—The All Writs Act, 28 U.S.C. §1651(a), has been used to vacate a criminal conviction in an immigration context where justice and equity would be served. *U.S. v. Javanmard,* 767 F.Supp. 1109, 111–12 (D. Kan. 1991) [vacated conviction to permit person to obtain amnesty]. *But see Renteria-Gonzalez v. INS,* 322 F.3d 804, 811–12 (5th Cir. 2002) [the All Writs Act does not confer an independent basis for subject-matter jurisdiction to vacate a conviction and the Court lacks equitable authority to do so]; *U.S. v. Bravo-Diaz,* 312 F.3d 995, 997–98 (9th Cir. 2002) [abrogating *U.S. v. Grajeda-Perez*, 727 F.Supp. 1374 (E.D. Wash. 1989) on grounds that courts do not have jurisdiction to vacate convictions on equitable grounds for immigration purposes]; *Tran v. U.S.,* 45 F.Supp.2d 157 (D.P.R. 1999).

G. *Habeas Corpus to Vacate or Set Aside Conviction; State Counterparts*—28 U.S.C. §§2254, 2255

1. Congress in AEDPA §101–06 has substantially reduced the ability to use 28 U.S.C. §§2254 and 2255 to attack state and federal convictions. There is now a one-year statute of limitations for filing a habeas petition in federal court attacking a state conviction, §2244(d)(1), or federal conviction, §2255. It also strengthened the presumption of correctness of the convictions and restricted successive petitions. However, petitions have been granted to vacate a conviction even under these rules where the court would not have accepted the plea had it been aware of the immigration consequences. *Urbina v. U.S.*, 992 F.Supp. 641 (S.D.N.Y.1998). Jurisdiction exists for petition even where alien released from incarceration. *U.S. v. Romero-Vilca*, 850 F.2d 177 (3d Cir. 1988). And at least one court has found that detention by DHS does not amount to being in custody for purposes of §2255. *Evola v. Carbone,* 365 F.Supp.2d 592, 597–98 (D.N.J. 2005) [being in the custody of ICE does not mean individual is "in custody" for purposes of §2255 and he thus avoiding the successive petition problem].
2. Certain states permit a vacatur of a plea only if filed within a limited time period. For example, Fla. R. Crim. P. 3.850 permits a party to vacate a plea only if it is filed within 2 years of the conviction. *State v. Green,* 944 So.2d 208 (Fla. 2006) [a motion under Fla. R. Crim. P. 3.850, rather than a

writ of coram nobis, is the proper vehicle to withdraw plea, and petitioner only has a 2-year period to do so unless he could not have ascertained by due diligence that the plea would subject him to removal]. The defendant must allege and prove that s/he would not have entered into the plea if informed of the possibility of removal. *Green.*

3. Vacation of a plea will vacate the conviction for immigration purposes as long as it was not pursuant to a rehabilitative statute or because of immigration hardship. *Matter of Adamiak,* 23 I&N Dec. 878 (BIA 2006) [where the criminal court in Ohio failed to advise defendant of the immigration consequences of his plea pursuant to Ohio Rev. Code §2943.031, the subsequent vacatur is not a conviction for immigration purposes because the guilty plea has been vacated as a result of a "defect in the underlying criminal proceeding" and not for a rehabilitative or immigration hardship purpose]; *Matter of Rodriguez-Ruiz,* 22 I&N Dec. 1378 (BIA 2000) [distinguished *Roldan* and accepted vacated plea under Article 440 of N.Y. Crim. Proc. Law over INS's argument that vacation was solely for immigration purposes]; *Matter of Marroquin*, 23 I&N Dec. 705, 713 (AG 2005) [distinguishing between a *vacatur* for rehabilitative purposes or "for reasons that are entirely unrelated to the legal propriety of the underlying judgment," which remains a conviction for immigration purposes, and reasons that go to "the factual basis for, or the procedural validity of, the conviction," which would bar the use of a vacated conviction]. The vacation of the plea must be for a procedural or substantive defect in the underlying criminal proceeding and not for reasons solely related to post-conviction events such as rehabilitation or immigration hardship. *Matter of Pickering,* 23 I&N Dec. 621 (BIA 2003) *reversed on other grounds Pickering v. Gonzales,* 465 F.3d 263 (6th Cir. 2006) [if the court vacates a conviction for reasons unrelated to the merits of the underlying criminal proceedings the respondent remains convicted for immigration purposes]; *Ali v. U.S. Att'y Gen.,* 443 F.3d 804, 809–10 (11th Cir. 2006) [where the strongest inference supported by respondent's pleadings was that he sought vacatur because he previously thought a First Offender plea would not effect his immigration status, it was neither a substantive nor procedural vacatur and therefore remained a conviction]; *Ali v. Ashcroft,* 395 F.3d 722, 728–30 (7th Cir. 2005) [where parties stipulated to amend conviction from trafficking offense to simple misdemeanor possession of THC "simply to avoid deportation" and not for a procedural or substantive defect *Pickering* applied and respondent's conviction for trafficking remained]. *Renteria-Gonzalez v. INS*, 322 F.3d 804, 812 (5th Cir. 2002) [vacated federal conviction to enforce purposes of JRAD remains a valid conviction notwithstanding the reason it was vacated]. *But see Discipio v. Ashcroft,* 417 F.3d 448, 450 (5th Cir. 2005). Vacation of a plea will vacate conviction for immigration purposes even in drug cases. Where conviction withdrawn not simply expunged, then it is effective, even in drug cases. *Matter of O'Sullivan*, 10 I&N Dec. 320 (BIA 1963) [BIA eliminated narcotics conviction for deportation purposes when court granted new trial and nolle prosequi conviction following completion of sentence]; *Matter of Gonzalez*, Case No. A35 294 664 (BIA Mar. 12, 1982) [BIA found alien not deported on drug charge 21 U.S.C. §841(a)(1), where Fed. P. Crim. P. 32(d) vacation of judgment granted by federal court]. The burden of proof that a vacated conviction was vacated for other than procedural or substantive reasons rests with the government and not the respondent. *Pickering v. Gonzales,* 465 F.3d 263, 269 n.4 (6th Cir. 2006) [notwithstanding the respondent's immigration motive as expressed in his moving papers to the Canadian court, the Canadian vacatur of his conviction without explanation but with citation to authority was sufficient to vacate the conviction for immigration purposes and DHS had burden to prove that vacatur was not for a substantive or procedural reason].

4. Vacation of Sentence—A respondent may also seek to vacate a sentence to relieve himself of the consequences of the sentence and if successful in doing so may avoid immigration consequences. *Matter of Song,* 23 I&N Dec. 173 (BIA 2001) [where respondent had 365-day sentence vacated *nunc pro tunc* to 360 days while case was pending before BIA, he avoided aggravated felony consequence]. A respondent may vacate a sentence for any reason, including immigration avoidance, and it must be given full faith and credit by the IJs and BIA. *Matter of Cota,* 23 I&N Dec. 849 (BIA 2005) [where sentence was modified *nunc pro tunc* expressly to avoid deportation as an aggravated felon, IJ and BIA must recognize it. *Matter of Pickering* distinguished].

H. *Motion to Withdraw Plea*—Rule 11 [requires inquiry by a court before taking plea that plea voluntarily and knowingly given]; Fed. R. Crim. P. 11(d) [permits withdrawal of plea in interest of justice or if there is a "fair and just reason for requesting the ... withdrawal." *See in this chapter* "Guilty Pleas," Section VI.C (p. 213), *supra*; *U.S. v. Ortega-Ascanio,* 376 F.3d 879 (9th Cir. 2004) [permitted withdrawal of plea before sentencing where defendant argued that intervening *St. Cyr* decision was basis to dismiss indictment for illegal re-entry because IJ, at removal hearing, failed to inform him of INA §212(c) relief even though he informed him of cancellation but only if he did not commit aggravated felony]; *U.S. v. Couto,* 311 F.3d 179 (2d Cir. 2002) [vacated guilty plea based on defendant's counsel's incorrect advice that the plea would not necessarily lead to deportation]; *McCarthy v. U.S.*, 394 U.S. 459 (1969); *Matter of Sirhan,* 13 I&N Dec. 592 (BIA 1970); *Matter of Kaneda*, 16 I&N Dec. 677 (BIA 1979); *U.S. v. Reyna-Tapia,* 328 F.3d 1114, 1117 (9th Cir. 2003) (en banc) [refused to allow defendant to withdraw plea in illegal re-entry case on grounds that he was still a resident despite being deported]; *U.S. v. Del Rosario*, 902 F.2d 55, 56–59 (D.C. Cir. 1990) [rejects effort to withdraw plea for ineffective assistance of counsel because failure of counsel to inform client of immigration consequences of plea is collateral]; *U.S. v. George*, 869 F.2d 333 (7th Cir. 1989) [same]; *U.S. v. Yearwood*, 863 F.2d 6 (4th Cir. 1988); *Downs-Morgan v. U.S.*, 765 F.2d 1534 (11th Cir. 1985) [Rule 11 does not require court to inform alien of immigration consequences of his guilty plea; however, counsel's affirmative misrepresentation under certain circumstances (*e.g.*, where person has sought asylum and fears persecution) will constitute ineffective assistance of counsel]; *U.S. v. Campbell*, 778 F.2d 764 (11th Cir. 1985) [Rule 11 does not require counsel to inform defendant of immigration consequences of guilty plea; Fed. P. Crim. P. 32(d) does not require withdrawal of plea. Under Rule 32(d) 3-part test: (1) strength of defendant's reasons for withdrawal including assertion of innocence; (2) prejudice to government's case if withdrawal of plea was granted; and (3) whether defendant's ignorance of immigration consequences was due to government misconduct. There was no ineffective assistance of counsel in the absence of affirmative misconduct]; *U.S. v. Shapiro*, 16 FRD 499 (E.D. Wis.), *dismissed*, 222 F.2d 836, 840 (7th Cir. 1955) [granted relief where defendant thought he was USC]; *Janvier v. U.S.*, 793 F.2d 449 (2d Cir. 1986) [ineffective assistance of counsel for failure to inform alien of former right to apply for recommendation against deportation or for failing to file recommendation under 8 U.S.C. §1251(b)]. *But see U.S. v. Sandoval,* 390 F.3d 1294 (10th Cir. 2004) [upheld district court's refusal to withdraw plea, where respondent could not demonstrate that it was reasonably likely that he would have received §212(c) waiver even if properly informed of it]. Under Supreme Court decisions, effective assistance of counsel standard addressed in *Strickland v. Washington*, 466 U.S. 668 (1984); *McMann v. Richardson*, 397 U.S. 759, 771 (1970). *See also Lozada v. Deeds,* 498 U.S. 430 (1991) (*per curiam)*; *Hill v. Lockhart*, 474 U.S. 52, 58 (1985).

A withdrawal of plea under Rule 32(d) vacates conviction (including drug conviction) *ab initio* for immigration purposes. *Matter of Gonzalez-Escalante*, Case No. A35 294 644 (BIA Mar. 12, 1982) [in drug case vacation under 32(d) has same effect as *coram nobis*].

I. ***Motion to Correct or Reduce Sentence***—Authority to correct or reduce a sentence under Fed. R. Crim. P. 35 is limited. A district court may modify a sentence after a federal appeals court remands a case pursuant to 18 U.S.C. §3742, because the original sentence was illegal or imposed in violation of the guidelines. Alternatively, a district court may correct a sentence within 7 days of sentencing where the erroneous sentence was the result of technical, arithmetical, or other clear error. The government may also file a Rule 35(b) motion where the defendant has provided "substantial" post-conviction assistance in the investigation or prosecution of another person. As the government is the only party who can move for a Rule 35(b) motion, a defendant can appeal on the basis that the government's refusal was in bad faith. *U.S. v. Treleaven*, 35 F.3d 458 (9th Cir. 1994). The correction of an illegal sentence is valid for immigration purposes. *Matter of Song,* 23 I&N Dec. 173 (BIA 2001) [where respondent had 365-day sentence vacated *nunc pro tunc* to 360 days while case was pending before BIA, he avoided aggravated felony consequences]; *Matter of Martin,* 18 I&N Dec. 226 (BIA 1982). [where sentence of confinement reduced to sentence of probation, it was valid to take person out of CIMT section]. A party may vacate a sentence for any reason, including immigration avoidance, and it must be given full faith and credit by the IJs and BIA. *Matter of Cota,* 23 I&N Dec. 849 (BIA 2005) [where sentence was modified *nunc pro tunc* expressly to avoid deportation as an aggravated felon, IJ and BIA must recognize it. *Matter of Pickering* distinguished].

J. ***Cancellation of Removal***—Not available for persons charged with aggravated felonies. For an extensive discussion of cancellation of removal, *see* Chapter 8, part IV (p.972), *infra*.

K. *Other Forms of Relief*

1. Asylum. INA §208.
2. Withholding of deportation for fear of persecution. INA §241(b)(3).
3. Deferred action status.
4. Adjustment of status. INA §245.
5. Asylum and cancellation of removal are not available to aggravated felons. Withholding is also unavailable if person incarcerated for 5 years or more. Adjustment of status is not available to LPRs who are aggravated felons if they will need an accompanying waiver under INA §212(h) for a criminal ground of inadmissibility.

VIII. CRIMINAL MATTERS RELATED TO REMOVAL

A. *Requirements Concerning Probation*

1. A sentence to probation is not considered a sentence to confinement or imprisonment. *U.S. v. Gonzalez-Coronado,* 419 F.3d 1090, 1093–94 (10th Cir. 2005) [following *Martinez-Villalva* and holding that multiple-year sentence to probation is *not* an aggravated felony under §101(a)(43)(F)]; *U.S. v. Martinez-Villalva,* 232 F.3d 1329, 1332–34 (10th Cir. 2000) [where government could not prove that sentence was a suspended sentence, as opposed to a sentence to probation, person not aggravated felon]; *U.S. v. Guzman-Bera,* 216 F.3d 1019 (11th Cir. 2000) [where person who was sentenced to probation violated the probation resulting in an 18-month incarceration, he was *not* sentenced to imprisonment and therefore was not aggravated felon]; *U.S. v. Banda-Zamora,* 178 F.3d 728, 730 (5th Cir. 1999) [sentence to probation unlike a suspended sentence is not a sentence to meet the definition of an aggravated felony]; *Matter of Martin,* 18 I&N Dec. 226, 227 (BIA 1982); *Matter of V-,* 7 I&N Dec. 577 (1957); *Matter of Eden,* 20 I&N Dec. 209 (BIA 1990). *But see Da Rosa Silva v. INS,* 263 F.Supp.2d 1005, 1010 (E.D. Pa. 2003) [sentenced to probation as conditional sentence that was revoked and 4-year sentence imposed is considered a sentence to confinement]. Also, at least one court has held that a person who has had a sentence imposed which is then, in part, probated is still considered sentenced to the full time. *U.S. v. Ayala-Gomez*, 255 F.3d 1314 (11th Cir. 2001) [sentence that was probated is considered suspended for purposes of statute and therefore full sentence must be considered].
2. Requirement that person must serve probation outside of U.S. invalid, *U.S. v. Mercedes-Mercedes*, 851 F.2d 529 (1st Cir. 1988); *U.S. v. Abushaar*, 761 F.2d 954 (3d Cir. 1985), or that sentence be suspended if he departs. *U.S. v. Jalilian*, 896 F.2d 447 (10th Cir. 1990); *Dear Wing Jung v. U.S.*, 312 F.2d 73, 75–76 (9th Cir. 1962); *U.S. v. Concepcion*, 795 F.Supp. 1262, 1273–75 (E.D.N.Y. 1992). Similarly a requirement that a person must forgo all defenses to removal is invalid. *U.S. v. Maldonado-Ramirez,* 216 F.3d 940, 944–45 (11th Cir. 2000). However, a person may agree to leave the country as part of a plea. *U.S. v. Janko*, 865 F.2d 1246 (11th Cir. 1989) [upheld negotiated special condition of probation that person leave U.S. and not return other than by lawful means].
3. Probation, parole, or supervised release are not grounds for deferral of deportation, INA §241(a)(4)(A), 8 U.S.C. §1231(a)(4)(A); *Walford v. INS*, 48 F.3d 477 (10th Cir. 1995), although the AG is now authorized to deport nonviolent offenders prior to completion of their sentences. INA §241(a)(4)(B). The federal district court may also order deportation as a condition of probation if the parties stipulate to it under INA §238(c)(5), 8 U.S.C. §1228(c)(5) or if, after notice and hearing, the AG establishes deportation by clear and convincing evidence. 18 U.S.C. §3563(b)(21).
4. Parole terms may continue even after person deported. *Guerrero-Guerrero v. Clark*, 687 F.Supp. 1022, 1027 (E.D. Va. 1988) [parole commission still had jurisdiction over special parole terms even after parolee deported].

B. *Conviction for Re-entry or Being Found in U.S. After Deportation*—8 U.S.C. §1326.

1. Re-Entry—Any person who has been denied admission, excluded, deported or removed or has departed the U.S. while an order of exclusion, deportation or removal is outstanding and thereafter enters, attempts to enter, or is found in the U.S. is subject to a 2-year penalty and $1,000 fine.

8 U.S.C. §1326(a). If exclusion, deportation, or removal was subsequent to commission of 3 or more misdemeanors involving drugs, crimes against the person, or both, or if it was subsequent to a non–aggravated felony, the maximum penalty is 10 years. 8 U.S.C. §1326(b)(1). If exclusion, deportation or removal was subsequent to a conviction for commission of an aggravated felony, the maximum penalty is 20 years. 8 U.S.C. §1326(b)(2). If deported, excluded or removed as an alien terrorist, there is a 10-year nonconcurrent penalty. 8 U.S.C. §1326(b)(3), (4). The Supreme Court has determined that under §1326(b)(2) the commission of an aggravated felony prior to the commission of the offense is a sentencing enhancement, not an element of a distinct offense. Since it does not create a separate crime, the government is not required to charge, in the indictment, the fact of the earlier conviction for the aggravated felony. *Almendarez-Torres v. U.S.*, 523 U.S. 224 (1999). *See also U.S. v. Martinez,* 434 F.3d 1318, 1323 (11th Cir. 2006) [Supreme Court decisions in *Apprendi, Blakely, Booker*, and *Shepard*, while casting doubt on *Almendarez*, have not overruled it, so uncharged prior convictions can be used to enhance defendant's sentence]; *U.S. v. Quintana-Quintana,* 383 F.3d 1052, 53 (9th Cir.) *reh'g and reh'g en banc denied,* 383 F.3d 1052 (9th Cir. 2004) *cert. denied,* 125 S.Ct. 1100 (2004) [*Blakely* did not alter *Almendarez-Torres*]; *U.S. v. Perez-Olalde,* 328 F.3d 222, 224 (6th Cir. 2003) [following *Almendarez-Torres*, enhancement need not be charged]; *U.S. v. Martinez-Villalva,* 232 F.3d 1329, 1331–32 (10th Cir. 2000). [following *Almendarez-Torres* and rejecting argument based on *Apprendi v. New Jersey,* 530 U.S. 466 (2000) that issue of sentence enhancement must go to jury]; *U.S. v. Rodriguez-Montelongo,* 263 F.3d 429, 434–35 (5th Cir. 2001) [same in regard to due process challenge based upon *Apprendi*]; *U.S. v. Gonzalez-Ruiz,* 369 F.Supp.2d 1151, 1153–54 (N.D. Cal. 2005) [the Supreme Court decision is *Shepard v. U.S.* does not alter *Almendarez-Torres*].

However, where the sentencing court bases enhancement on something other than a prior conviction, such as a subsequent removal, it does violate *Apprendi. U.S. v. Covian-Sandoval,* 462 F.3d 1090, 1096–98 (9th Cir. 2006) [where sentencing court relied on a removal order subsequent to a conviction that was not pleaded or proved, it violated *Apprendi* because *Almendarez-Torres* allowed the court to consider only a prior conviction in determining sentence enhancement as a prior conviction had procedural safeguards. The court however found that the error did not violate defendant's substantial rights]. Also, where the government does allege the conviction as a separate offense the conviction may be reversed unless the defendant was indicted, convicted and sentenced for one crime. *U.S. v. Rivera-Sanchez,* 222 F.3d 1057 (9th Cir. 2000). A felony for purposes of §§1326(b)(1) & (2) is defined by federal law under 18 U.S.C. §3559(a) and not by state law even if it was a state conviction. *U.S. v. Cordova-Arevalo,* 456 F.3d 1229 (10th Cir. 2006) [although Colorado third degree assault conviction is a misdemeanor under state law, it is defined as a felony under federal law and therefore enhancement of sentence was appropriate].

There is a split in the circuits as to whether "attempt" to enter is a specific intent crime. *Compare U.S. v. Rodriguez,* 416 F.3d 123, 125–27 (1st Cir. 2005) [specific intent not required for attempted illegal re-entry in light of language of §1326]; *U.S. v. Morales-Palacios,* 369 F.3d 442 (5th Cir. 2004) [specific intent is not required for attempted illegal re-entry because it is a regulatory crime]; *U.S. v. Peralt-Reyes*, 131 F.3d 956 (11th Cir. 1997) [specific intent not required] *Gilbert v. U.S.*, 489 F.Supp.2d 150, 153–54 (N.D.N.Y. 2006) [attempted entry is not specific intent crime and person who boarded train in Canada bound for NY was properly found guilty]; *with U.S. v. Gracidas-Ulibarry,* 231 F.3d 1188 (9th Cir. 2000) (en banc) [specific intent is required for attempt crime because "Congress intended to incorporate the well established common law meaning of 'attempt' into §1326" and the government must demonstrate that "the defendant had the purpose, *i.e.,* conscious desire, to re-enter the United States without the express consent of the Attorney General."].

The 4 elements of a re-entry crime generally are: (1) alienage; (2) a valid deportation/exclusion/removal order; (3) physical departure after deportation/removal; and (4) voluntary re-entry free from official restraint. *U.S. v. Contreras Palacios,* 492 F.3d 39 (1st Cir. 2007) [conviction upheld on challenge to alienage where government produced as proof only the "A" file which contained conflicting information]; *U.S. v. Garcia,* 452 F.3d 36 (1st Cir. 2006) [affidavit of defendant in his Alien Registration File coupled with fingerprint card and warrant of deportation were sufficient to establish prior deportation] *U.S. v. Bahena-Cardenas,* 411 F.3d 1067, 1072–73 (9th Cir. 2005) [finding evidence sufficient to sustain elements of the crime including submission of warrant of deportation as proof of physical removal notwithstanding *Crawford's* prohibition on testimonial evidence without cross-examination]; *U.S. v. Torres-Villalobos,* 487 F.3d 607, 612–13 (8th Cir. 2007) [conviction upheld against Crawford challenge to warrants of deportation]; *U.S. v. Bello-Bahena,* 411 F.3d 1083, 1088–91 (9th Cir. 2005) [reversed conviction where jury instruction on lack of freedom from official restraint was not granted]. The statute, to establish the crime of reentry, also requires that the government demonstrate that the person reentered the U.S. without the permission of the Attorney General. The defendant's belief that he need not have the AG's permission is irrelevant. *U.S. v. Rea-Beltran,* 457 F.3d 695, 702 (7th Cir. 2006).

The lawfulness of the prior deportation order is *not* an element of the offense. *U.S. v. Alvarado-Delgado,* 98 F.3d 492 (9th Cir. 1996) (*en banc*). But person physically removed from the U.S. while a stay order was in effect is not "deported" under the statute and cannot be tried for unlawful re-entry. *U.S. v. Fermin-Rodriguez,* 5 F.Supp.2d 157 (S.D.N.Y. 1998). A summary removal order under §1228(b) may serve as the basis for an illegal re-entry and found-in charge. *U.S. v. Calderon-Segura,* 512 F.3d 1104, 1107–08 (9th Cir. 2008) [use of expedited removal proceedings under 8 U.S.C. §1228(b) do not violate equal protection when used as the basis for a "found-in" charge after removal]; *U.S. v. Garcia-Martinez,* 228 F.3d 956 (9th Cir. 2000) [INS officers conducting both prosecutorial and adjudicative functions is not violative of due process]; *U.S. v. Benitez-Villafuerte,* 186 F.3d 651 (5th Cir. 1999) [reversed district court order that had considered deportation order under former §1228(b) on grounds that summary deportation meets minimum due process notice requirements and the commingling of prosecutorial and adjudicative functions is permissible]. For purposes of this statute, deportation also includes an agreement in which a person stipulates to removal, whether or not the stipulation is during a state or federal criminal trial. 8 U.S.C. §1326. Deportation for purposes of the statute means physical removal not the entry of the order. *U.S. v. Zelaya,* 293 F.3d 1294, 1298 (11th Cir. 2002) [conviction upheld where aggravated felony arose after deportation order but before physical deportation]. And a person cannot be charged under §1326 who was not physically deported. *U.S. v. Romo-Romo,* 246 F.3d 1272 (9th Cir. 2001) [where Mexican evaded removal after his deportation order, he cannot be charged with re-entry or attempted re-entry].

The making of a false claim to U.S. citizenship or lawful residency is not an element of the crime. *U.S. v. Barnes,* 244 F.3d 331 (2d Cir. 2001). Intent to enter the U.S. unlawfully is also not an element of the crime. *U.S. v. Carlos-Colmenares,* 253 F.3d 276 (7th Cir. 2001) [specific intent to enter without AG's consent is not required]; *U.S. v. Gonzalez-Chavez,* 122 F.3d 15 (8th Cir. 1997); *U.S. v. Henry,* 111 F.3d 111 (11th Cir. 1997) [specific intent is not required); *U.S. v. Guzman-Ocampo,* 236 F.3d 233 (5th Cir. 2000) [Section 1326 requires only general intent in context of "found-in" case]; *U.S. v. Meraz-Valeta,* 26 F.3d 992, 997 (10th Cir. 1994); *U.S. v. Champegnie,* 925 F.2d 54 (2d Cir. 1991) [person's subjective, good faith, but mistaken belief as to legality of entry is irrelevant]; *U.S. v. Espinoza-Leon,* 873 F.2d 743 (4th Cir. 1989) [only general intent required]; *Pena-Cabanillas v. U.S.,* 394 F.2d 785, 788–89 (9th Cir. 1968).

Where matters are an element of the offense, however, each must be stated in the indictment or the conviction is not valid. *U.S. v. Cabrera-Teran,* 168 F.3d 141 (5th Cir. 1999) [conviction under former version of statute reversed where government failed to list on the indictment that the person was previously *arrested* as well as deported]. *But see U.S. v. Landeros-Mendez,* 206 F.3d 1354 (10th Cir. 2000) [where deportation order not introduced jury could still infer from physical expulsion and officer's testimony that deportation occurred]; *U.S. v. Pena-Renovato,* 168 F.3d 163 (5th Cir. 1999) [where person removed but charged with being deported conviction stands because removal proceedings and deportation proceedings are the same]. *U.S. v. Nunez-Rodelo,* 378 F.3d 877 (9th Cir. 2004) [same]; *U.S. v. Lopez-Gonzalez,* 183 F.3d 933 (9th Cir. 1999) [same]. The government must also allege an overt act in seeking a conviction under §1326. *U.S. v. Resendiz-Ponce,* 425 F.3d 729 (9th Cir. 2005) [reversed conviction for attempted unlawful entry where no overt act was alleged in the indictment]. If all elements are not proven the conviction will also be reversed. *U.S. v. Bahena-Cardenas,* 70 F.3d 1071 (9th Cir. 1995) [where no warrant of arrest was served under former statute, defendant's self-deportation while case before BIA was not enough to trigger conviction]; *U.S. v. Morales-Tovar,* 37 F.Supp.2d 846 (W.D. Tex. 1999) [government failed to prove that defendant sought to re-enter or had specific intent to enter in violation of law where he simply presented himself at the border and asked how he could replace his green card].

1.a. Statutory language requires the AG's permission before re-entering—8 U.S.C. §1326(a)(2). Under the former INA §212(a)(6)(B) (now INA §212(a)(9)(A)(ii)), a person seeking to re-enter the U.S. 5/10 years after removal does not have to seek the AG's permission before entry. However, the courts, following the current statute generally do require the AG's permission before re-entry. *U.S. v. Marte,* 356 F.3d 1336, 1341–42 (11th Cir. 2004) [upheld conviction for attempted re-entry where applicant did not file I-212 seeking permission to re-apply]. At least one court has found that the government may prove that the AG did not give permission to re-enter by submitting a certificate of nonexistence of record of permission in the files of the INS. *U.S. v. Sanchez-Milam,* 305 F.3d 310 (5th Cir. 2002). The government is also not required to prove that the defendant did not have a visa. The government need only prove: (1) that the defendant is an alien who was previously arrested and deported; (2) that he re-entered the U.S. voluntarily; and (3) that he failed to secure the express permission of the AG. *U.S. v. Martus*, 138 F.3d 95 (2d Cir. 1998) [re-entry at checkpoint without being stopped by INS is not express permission of the AG]; *U.S. v. Joya-Martinez*, 947 F.2d 1141 (4th Cir. 1991) [proof as to whether person had visa is not an element of the crime and therefore burden is on defendant; Court also rejected selective prosecution claim]; *U.S. v. Mancebo-Santiago*, 875 F.Supp. 1030 (S.D.N.Y. 1995) [court rejected defense that person was admitted at the border where he did not inform border officials of previous deportation]; *U.S. v. Soto*, 106 F.3d 1040 (1st Cir. 1997) [person re-entering with visa but without AG's permission after deportation is culpable]; *U.S. v. Trevino-Martinez*, 86 F.3d 65, 68 (5th Cir. 1996) [same]; *U.S. v. Asibor*, 109 F.3d 1023, 1035–36 (5th Cir. 1997) [rejecting good faith defense based on approved I-130 petition]. The defendant's belief that he need not have the AG's permission is irrelevant. *U.S. v. Rea-Beltran,* 457 F.3d 695, 702 (7th Cir. 2006). Similarly, it is not a defense that subsequent to re-entry a person became a temporary resident. *U.S. v. Gutierrez-Alba*, 128 F.3d 1324, 1327–28 (9th Cir. 1997) [immigration amnesty subsequent to entry not a defense]. *But see U.S. v. Fermin-Rodriguez,* 5 F.Supp.2d 157 (S.D.N.Y. 1998) [where person unlawfully removed despite automatic stay while case on appeal to circuit court, he was not deported within meaning of statute]; *U.S. v. Idowu*, 105 F.3d 728 (D.C. Cir. 1997) [where defendant waited outside U.S. for 5 years and re-entered on green card, allowed to withdraw plea and defend on INA §212(a)(6)(B)]. *See also U.S. v. Smith-Baltiher,* 424 F.3d 913, 922–25 (9th Cir. 2005) [in certain circumstances there may be a *mens rea* defense that defendant's reasonable belief he was a U.S. citizen did not require the AG's consent to cross into U.S.].

1.b. Re-entry may extend beyond the 12-mile limit—*U.S. v. De Leon,* 270 F.3d 90 (1st Cir. 2001) [person stopped by Coast Guard in ship stopped beyond the 12-mile limit subject to prosecution notwithstanding the Convention on the Territorial Sea and the Contiguous Zone, Article 24].

1.c. Constitutionality of §1326 has been upheld—*U.S. v. Bahena-Cardenas,* 411 F.3d 1067, 1072–73 (9th Cir. 2005 [not unconstitutional under *Apprendi* on theory that prior deportation/removal hearing is an element of the offense and it requires a lower standard of proof and less procedural protections]; *U.S. v. Martinez,* 434 F.3d 1318, 1323 (11th Cir. 2006) [Supreme Court decisions in *Apprendi, Blakely, Booker*, and *Shepard*, while casting doubt on *Almendarez*, have not overruled it, so uncharged prior convictions can be used to enhance defendant's sentence]; *U.S. v. Hernandez-Guerrero,* 147 F.3d 1075 (9th Cir. 1998) [finding Congress has inherent powers to criminalize immigration matters].

1.d. Failure to establish entry and existence of official restraint as a defense—A conviction requires an entry under traditional standards which includes freedom from official restraint. *U.S. v. Lombera-Valdovinos,* 429 F.3d 927 (9th Cir. 2005) [where defendant was observed before he entered U.S. and upon seeking to enter went straight to a border patrol officer and said he wanted to go before an IJ and go to jail, he was never free from official restraint, and charge of attempted illegal entry could not be sustained]; *U.S. v. Bello-Bahena,* 411 F.3d 1083, 1088–91 (9th Cir. 2005) [reversed conviction where jury instruction on lack of freedom from official restraint was not granted]; *U.S. v. Gonzalez-Torres*, 309 F.3d 594, 597–99 (9th Cir. 2002) [where defendant was under observation before crossing the Mexican border his conviction was reversed because he had not made an entry]; *U.S. v. Castellanos-Garcia,* 270 F.3d 773, 775 (9th Cir. 2001) [person does not commit unlawful entry when s/he is under "constant observation by government authorities" from the time of physical entry until the time of arrest]. *But see U.S. v. Vela-Robles,* 397 F.3d 786 (9th Cir. 2005) [official restraint preventing occurrence of entry does not arise when defendant triggers sensor a border]; *U.S. v. Hernandez-Herrera,* 279 F.3d 1213, 1218–19 (9th Cir. 2001) [where there was tracking of defendant as he crossed the Mexican border but not continuous visual surveillance, he made an entry]; The crime of attempted entry may be charged even if the person makes an entry. *U.S. v. Rivera-Relle,* 333 F.3d 914 (9th Cir. 2003) [held that person may be convicted of attempt even if he has actually completed the crime]. Also, a person may be convicted of "attempted entry" even if he is under surveillance when he seeks to enter. *U.S. v. Leos-Maldonado,* 302 F.3d 1061 (9th Cir. 2002).

1.e. Justification as a defense—If person had no legal alternative to violating the law because, for example, he was fleeing persecution, s/he may have a justification defense. *U.S. v. Nwene,* 20 F.Supp.2d 716, 720–22 (D.N.J. 1998) [justification is an affirmative defense that requires a showing that there was no legal alternative to violating the law; that the harm to be prevented was imminent; and that there is a direct causal relationship between defendant's actions and the avoidance of harm]; *But see U.S. v. Castro-Cabrera,* 534 F.Supp.2d 1156, 1162 (C.D. Cal. 2008) [evidence that defendant sought to return because his mother was dying or his cultural assimilation in the U.S. are irrelevant to the charges and a motion *in limine* was granted]; *U.S. v. Grieveson,* 110 F.Supp.2d 880 (S.D. Ind. 2000) [person required by arrest warrant to appear in state court could not obtain jury instruction of a "reasonable belief" defense].

1.f. Duress as a defense—This defense requires a showing that there is: (1) an immediate threat of death or serous bodily injury; (2) a well-grounded fear that the threat will be carried out, and (3) no reasonable opportunity to escape the threatened harm. *U.S. v. Portillo-Vega,* 478 F.3d 1194, 1197–1202 (10th Cir. 2007) [where respondent was in the U.S. for over three months before reporting his circumstances and therefore did not surrender as soon as the claimed duress had lost its coercive force, the district court did not abuse its discretion in denying the defense].

1.g. Consent as defense—*U.S. v. Hermoso-Garcia,* 413 F.3d 1085, 1088–89 (9th Cir. 2005) [court entertained but rejected that approval of I-130 constituted consent to re-enter the U.S.].

1.h. Double Jeopardy as defense—*U.S. v. Castillo-Basa,* 483 F.3d 890 (9th Cir. 2007) [double jeopardy attaches so that a perjury charge arising out of first trial cannot go forward where jury, in order to acquit him of illegal reentry, had to have decided that testimony was truthful].

1.i. Citizenship as a defense—A person who derived U.S. citizenship cannot be charged with a crime under §1326, because alienage is an element of the crime. *U.S. v. Smith-Baltiher,* 424 F.3d 913, 920–22 (9th Cir. 2005) [reversed conviction where defendant was denied right to present evidence of acquisition of citizenship at birth]; *U.S. v. Gomez-Orozco,* 188 F.3d 422 (7th Cir. 1999) [withdrawal of guilty plea permissible where person discovered they may be derivative citizen]; *U.S. v. Castro-Cabrera,* 534 F.Supp.2d 1156, 1162 (C.D. Cal. 2008) [evidence that defendant sought to return because his mother was dying or his cultural assimilation in the U.S. are irrelevant to the charges and a motion *in limine* was granted but evidence that he may be a derivative citizen is relevant and admissible]; *But see U.S. v. Guerrier,* 428 F.3d 76 (1st Cir. 2005) [district judge did not err in granting motion *in limine* to strike defendant's derivative citizenship defense where he could not proffer facts that he qualified]; *U.S. v. Cervantes-Nava,* 281 F.3d 501 (5th Cir. 2002) [claim that derivative citizenship statute violated equal protection in his case does not assist defendant because even if statute was stricken as unconstitutional it would not result in defendant receiving citizenship].

1.j. Lacking *mens rea* as a defense—*U.S. v. Smith-Baltiher,* 424 F.3d 913, 923–25 (9th Cir. 2005) [in certain circumstances there may be a *mens rea* defense that defendant's reasonable belief he was a U.S. citizen did not require the AG's consent to cross into U.S.].

1.k. Suppression of evidence—The circuits are split as to whether a defendant's immigration file or identity can be suppressed. *U.S. v. Bowley,* 435 F.3d 426, 430–31 (3d Cir. 2006) (and cases cited therein) [defendant has no possessory interest or reasonable expectation of privacy in his immigration file kept by the government; absent egregious circumstances referred to in *Lopez Mendoza*, the file or identity will not be suppressed]. *See also U.S. v. Orozco- Gonzalez,* 60 F.Supp.2d 599 (W.D. Tex. 1999) [evidence of the defendant's unlawful status can not be suppressed in an illegal re-entry case]. *But see U.S. v. Guevara-Martinez,* 268 F.3d 751 (8th Cir. 2001) [suppressing fingerprints in an illegal re-entry case].

2. Found In—A person "found in" the United States after having been deported is subject to criminal penalties under 8 U.S.C. §1326(a)(2). The "found in" language refers to being found by federal not state officials, and a person, for statute of limitations purposes, is deemed to be found in the U.S. when the federal official either knows of or, "with the exercise of diligence typical of law enforcement authorities, could have discovered the illegality of the defendant's presence." *U.S. v. Clarke,* 312 F.3d 1343, 1346 (11th Cir. 2002); *U.S. v. Scott,* 447 F.3d 1365 (11th Cir. 2006); *But see U.S. v. Gordon,* 513 F.3d 659, 663–65 (7th Cir. 2008) [rejected "constructive knowledge" standard where person entered U.S. with "green card" that he knew was no longer valid and by doing did not put immigration on notice that he was illegal]; *U.S. v. Herrera-Ordones,* 190 F.3d 504, 510 (7th Cir. 1999) [found in requires that the DHS discover the deported person's physical presence in the U.S. and that they ascertain the person's identity (as illegal) and status (as one who re-entered after deportation)]. However, a person cannot be indicted for being "found in" the U.S. when he was not physically present in the U.S. at the time of his indictment. *U.S. v. Thomas,* 492 F.Supp.2d 405 (S.D.N.Y. 2007) [defendant who illegally reentered the U.S. after removal but left the U.S. from Dec. 1999 to Dec. 2006 when he was stopped in transit at LAX airport could not be indicted in September 2006 for being found in the U.S. because he was not in the U.S. at the time of the indictment]. To be convicted of a found-in crime, the government must prove beyond a reasonable doubt that the defendant entered the U.S. voluntarily and had knowledge that he was committing the underlying act that made his conduct illegal–entering or remaining in the United States after being deported. *U.S. v. Salazar-Gonzalez,* 458 F.3d 851, 855–58 (9th Cir. 2006) [district court erred, but conviction not reversed, where court failed to give instruction on voluntariness and knowledge]. *But see U.S. v. Hernandez-Hernandez,* 519 F.3d 1236 (10th Cir. 2008) [rejected intoxication and "blacked-out" defense because it does not make it any more or less likely that he was innocently carried across the border against his will]. A person stopped at the border of the U.S. or who did not make an entry into the U.S. because he was never free from official restraint cannot be charged under 8 U.S.C. §1326(a)(2) as a person "found in" the country, *U.S. v. Zavala-Mendez,* 411 F.3d 1116, 1118–21 (9th Cir. 2005) [where defendant presented himself at the Alaskan border station that was physically a short distance inside the U.S., his conviction was reversed]; *U.S. v. Gonzalez-Torres*, 309 F.3d 594, 597–99 (9th Cir. 2002) [where defendant was under observation before crossing the Mexican border his conviction, was reversed because he had not made an entry]; *U.S. v. Pacheco-Medina,* 212 F.3d 1162 (9th Cir. 2000) [where defendant was under surveillance and captured within seconds after he crossed the border and therefore within official restraint at all times he did not enter U.S. and therefore he was not "found in"]; *U.S. v. Ruiz-Lopez,* 234 F.3d 445 (9th Cir. 2001) [where one officer testified he encountered defendant at the border station and the arresting officer could not remember the arrest, the conviction was reversed for lack of sufficient evidence]; *U.S. v. Angeles-Mascote,* 206 F.3d 529 (5th Cir. 2000); *U.S. v. Canals-Jimenez*, 943 F.2d 1284 (11th Cir. 1991) [court also questioned whether "found in" provision is void for vagueness]; *U.S. v. Ayala-Ayala,* 470 F.Supp.2d 281 (W.D.N.Y. 2007) [person turned away at Canadian border and the presents himself to immigration at U.S. border cannot be charged with being "found in" U.S.]. *But see U.S. v. Cruz-Escoto,* 476 F.3d 1081, 1085–86 (9th Cir. 2007) [where defendant was caught running 100–150 yards inside the U.S. but before permanent post he did enter and conviction was upheld]; *U.S. v. Ramos-Godinez,* 273 F.3d 820 (9th Cir. 2001) [where defendant was out of sight for two significant periods while crossing Mexican border he made entry and therefore could be charged as "found in" U.S.]. Even if a person cannot be charged under the "found in" provision, s/he could be charged as a person who attempted re-entry. *U.S. v. Cardenas-Alvarez*, 987 F.2d 1129, 1132–33 (5th Cir. 1993) [person stopped at inspection station could be charged with attempted re-entry but not found in]. However, a person can be charged with being "found in" the U.S. even if s/he did not enter illegally and even if the government does not allege or prove entry. *U.S. v. Rivera-Sillas,* 417 F.3d 1014, 1019–20 (9th Cir. 2005) [government need not plead nor prove entry to convict on a "found-in" charge]; *U.S. v. Pina-Jaime,* 332 F.3d 609 (9th Cir. 2003) [previously deported defendant who was paroled into U.S. for one day to attend custody hearing violated the "found in" provision by staying beyond that day]; *U.S. v. Parga Rosas,* 238 F.3d 1209, 1213 (9th Cir. 2001) [limiting language in *Pacheco-Medina* and not requiring proof of entry for "found in" charge]; *U.S. v. Ortiz-Villegos*, 49 F.3d 1435 (9th Cir. 1995); *U.S. v. Gay*, 7 F.3d 200 (11th Cir. 1993). The "found in" language has been determined not to be void for vagueness. *U.S. v. Palacios-Casquete*, 55 F.3d 557, 560–61 (11th Cir. 1995); *U.S. v. Ortiz-Gutierrez*, 36 F.3d 80 (9th Cir. 1994); *U.S. v.*

Meraz-Valeta, 26 F.3d 992, 996–97 (10th Cir. 1994); *U.S. v. Whitaker*, 999 F.2d 38, 42–43 (2d Cir. 1993). However, the person's physical presence at the time he was "found in" the U.S. cannot be proven by judicial notice that he is at trial now. *U.S. v. Herrera-Ochoa,* 245 F.3d 495, 499–502 (5th Cir. 2001). The "found in" provision is "passive" and does not raise any issue of voluntariness. *U.S. v. Dixon,* 327 F.3d 257 (3d Cir. 2003) [found in police custody due to parole violation arising out of traffic violation]; *U.S. v. Salazar-Robles,* 207 F.3d 648, 650 (9th Cir. 2000). [person found in state prison]. No specific intent is required in the commission of the crime. *U.S. v. Berrios-Centeno,* 250 F.3d 294 (5th Cir. 2001) [statute only requires general intent]. Only general intent is required and that may be inferred from the fact that the defendant was previously deported and subsequently found in the U.S. *U.S. v. Rivera-Sillas,* 417 F.3d 1014, 1020–21 (9th Cir. 2005) [although §1326 is not a status or strict liability offense, involuntary presence in the U.S. is the rare exception not the rule, and an inference of voluntariness is raised where the person is found in the U.S. and has raised no evidence to the contrary]; *U.S. v. Berrios-Centeno,* 250 F.3d 294, 299 (5th Cir. 2001). The government does not have to allege in the indictment the exact date the person is found in the U.S. *U.S. v. Gondinez-Rabadan,* 289 F.3d 630, 633–34 (9th Cir. 2002). The provision has withstood an Eighth Amendment, cruel and unusual punishment challenge, and a due process challenge on the grounds that it punishes status and is a strict liability statute. *U.S. v. Tovias-Marroquin,* 218 F.3d 455, 456–57 (5th Cir. 2000) [found in is not a status crime]; *U.S. v. Cupa-Guillen,* 34 F.3d 860 (9th Cir. 1994) [statute requires intent to convict]. Venue arises where the DHS first discovers the deported person. *U.S. v. Hernandez,* 189 F.3d 785 (9th Cir. 1999) [dismissed indictment rejecting claim that person may be found in more than one district]. But because "found in" is a continuing offense it may begin with a non-DHS officer finding the deported person but must end when the DHS officer "finds" him or her. *U.S. v. Jimenez-Borja,* 378 F.3d 853 (9th Cir. 2004) [found in begins when deportee was found by local police and is a continuing offense that ends when he is found by DHS]; *U.S. v. Ruelas-Arreguin,* 219 F.3d 1056, 1060–62 (9th Cir. 2000) [court harmonizes *Hernandez* as prohibiting venue in post-crime venue and finds that venue was proper either where the illegal entry was made or where the crime was completed]; *U.S. v. Santana-Castellano*, 74 F.3d 593 (5th Cir. 1996) [found in is continuing offense and person in prison on state charge falls within statute]. *But see U.S. v. Rivera-Ventura*, 72 F.3d 277, 281–82 (2d Cir. 1995) [not a continuing offense]. A party who conceals his whereabouts knowing he is subject to criminal prosecution, however, tolls the statute of limitations. *Id.*

2.a. Venue as a defense—Under the Sixth Amendment, a defendant has the right to be tried in the district where the offense was committed. *See also* Article III, §2, cl. 3 of the U.S. Constitution; Fed. R. Crim. P. 18; *U.S. v. Cores,* 356 U.S. 405, 407, 78 S.Ct. 875 (1958). When ICE placed a detainer on a defendant incarcerated in a county jail, he was "found in" that district and it was error to try him in the district he was transferred to when formally placed in ICE custody. *U.S. v. Hernandez-Hernandez,* 291 F.Supp.2d 490 (W.D. Tex. 2003) [granted motion to dismiss for improper venue].

3. It is not a defense that DHS's original deportation letter incorrectly informed person of the severity of the penalty upon re-entry. *U.S. v. Meraz-Valeta*, 26 F.3d 992, 996 (10th Cir. 1994) [person informed re-entry caused a two-year penalty, when in fact it was a five-year penalty].

4. The 5-year statute of limitations (18 U.S.C. §3282) does not run on surreptitious or fraudulent "entry" or "attempted entry"; it runs from the time the person is apprehended. However, a "found in" violation begins when person is discovered by DHS *or* should have been discovered by reasonable diligence. *U.S. v. Gunera,* 479 F.3d 373 (5th Cir. 2007) [where defendant filed TPS application and used his correct name, date of birth and country of origin, DHS could not argue they did not have knowledge of his illegality where they had a positive hit in a NAILS search]; *U.S. v. Lennon,* 372 F3d 535, 541 (3d Cir. 2004) [illegal reentry begin when person presents himself non-surreptitiously at the port of entry even if immigration fails to react]; *U.S. v. Clarke,* 312 F.3d 1343, 1347 (11th Cir. 2002) [reasonable diligence standard]; *U.S. v. Santana-Castellano,* 74 F.3d 593, 598 (5th Cir. 1996) [should have know through reasonable diligence standard]; *U.S. v. Rivera-Ventura,* 72 F.3d 277, 281–82 (2d Cir. 1995) [standard is that the government knew or with the exercise of diligence typical of law enforcement authorities could have discovered the defendant's illegal presence]; *U.S. v. Gomez,* 38 F.3d 1031, 1037 (8th Cir. 1994) [standard is immigration could have discovered the violation using diligence typical of law enforcement officer]; *But see U.S. v. Gordon,* 513 F.3d 659, 663–65 (7th Cir. 2008) [rejected "constructive knowledge"

standard where person entered U.S. with "green card" that he knew was no longer valid but in doing so did not put immigration on notice that he was illegal]; *U.S. v. Deleon,* 444 F.3d 41, 51–53 (1st Cir. 2006) [where defendant hid his identity upon reentry he could not argue that DHS had constructive knowledge that he was in U.S. that would have triggered five year statute of limitations]; *See also U.S. v. Lopez-Flores,* 275 F.3d 661, 663 (7th Cir. 2001) (And cases cited therein); *U.S. v. Coeur,* 196 F.3d 1344 (11th Cir. 1999) [sentence enhancement case where person was "found in" U.S. while serving time for illegal re-entry]. The statute, however, may not be tolled simply because someone provides a false identity to local police. *U.S. v. Sotelo-Salgado,* 201 F.Supp.2d 957 (S.D. Iowa 2002) [where INS knew of person's presence and took no action to follow up or check his identity statute was not tolled]. *But see U.S. v. Clarke,* 312 F.3d 1343 (11th Cir. 2002) [for purposes of statute of limitations, the date of defendant's discovery by state officials cannot be imputed to INS officials]. But where person provides false identity on entry to DHS he is not "found in" the U.S. until actually discovered by DHS and therefore statute of limitations does not run until he is discovered. *U.S. v. Lennon,* 372 F.3d 535, 540–42 (3d Cir. 2004); *U.S. v. Acevedo,* 229 F.3d 350 (2d Cir. 2000) [regarding person who entered by fraud through use of green card and was subsequently found in the U.S.].

5. Double Jeopardy—Prosecution for improperly entering the U.S. under 8 U.S.C. §1325(a) does not bar prosecution under the double jeopardy clause for being found in U.S. illegally after deportation under 8 U.S.C. §1326(a). *U.S. v. Flores-Peraza*, 58 F.3d 164 (5th Cir. 1995). *But see U.S. v. Mendoza,* 390 F.Supp.2d 925 (N.D. Cal. 2005). Double jeopardy is not offended where criminal proceeding for illegal re-entry is brought because deportation is not a punishment. *U.S. v. Garay-Burgos*, 961 F.Supp. 1321 (D. Ariz. 1997).

6. Necessity Defense—The defense requires a reasonable jury to conclude: (1) that the defendant was faced with a choice of evils and chose the lesser evil; (2) that he acted to prevent imminent harm; (3) that he reasonably anticipated a causal relation between his conduct and the harm to be avoided; *and* (4) that there were no other legal alternatives to violating the law. *U.S. v. Cervantes-Flores,* 421 F.3d 825, 828–29 (9th Cir. 2005) [denied necessity defense where defendant was HIV positive and entered U.S. to see his children before he died on grounds that testing positive for HIV did not constitute imminent harm].

7. Entrapment by Estoppel—To obtain estoppel, government must actively mislead. *U.S. v. Ramirez-Valencia,* 202 F.3d 1106 (9th Cir. 2000) [where I-294 said "any person who returned within 5 years is guilty of a felony " the government has not affirmatively misled because they did not say person could lawfully come in after 5 years]; *U.S. v. Miranda-Ramirez,* 309 F.3d 1255, 1261–62 (10th Cir. 2002) [same]; *U.S. v. Aquino-Chacon,* 109 F.3d 936 (4th Cir. 1997) [same]; *U.S. v. Trevino-Martinez*, 86 F.3d 65, 69 (5th Cir. 1996).

8. Defense that Person Was Under Official Restraint Prior to Entry—Where person was under official restraint and never entered the U.S., s/he may not be convicted of being "found-in" the U.S. *U.S. v. Gonzalez-Torres*, 309 F.3d 594, 597–99 (9th Cir. 2002) [where defendant was under observation before crossing the Mexican border his conviction was reversed because he had not made an entry]; *U.S. v. Pacheco-Medina,* 212 F.3d 1162, 1163 (9th Cir. 2000) [a person who was under surveillance when he scaled fence at the border and dropped over on to U.S. soil and was quickly apprehended had not entered U.S.]; *U.S. v. Oscar,* 496 F.2d 492, 493 (9th Cir. 1974). *But see U.S. v. Rivera-Sillas,* 417 F.3d 1014, 1019–20 (9th Cir. 2005) [government need not plead nor prove entry to convict on a "found-in" charge]. Surveillance need not be by federal officials. *See U.S. v. Lombera-Valdovinos,* 429 F.3d 927, 929 (9th Cir. 2005).

9. Defense that Person Was Involuntarily in U.S.—The voluntariness of a defendant's re-entry "is an element of the crime and, as such, must be proved beyond a reasonable doubt by the prosecution." *U.S. v. Quintana-Torres,* 235 F.3d 1197, 1200 (9th Cir. 2000). However, in *U.S. v. Parga-Rosas,* 238 F.3d 1209, 1213–14 (9th Cir. 2001), the Ninth Circuit treated *Quintana-Torres* as a sufficiency of the evidence case and found that a person in the U.S. who was away from the border would have to demonstrate the speculative possibility that involuntary entry had taken place. *See also U.S. v. Rivera-Sillas,* 417 F.3d 1014, 1020–21 (9th Cir. 2005) [although §1326 is not a status or strict liability offense, involuntary presence in the U.S. is the rare exception not the rule, and an inference of voluntariness is raised where the person is found in the U.S. and has raised no evidence to the contrary].

10. *Miranda* Warnings—Where DHS gave confusing warning pursuant to *Miranda v. Arizona,* 384 U.S. 436 (1966), evidence was suppressed. *U.S. v. San Juan-Cruz,* 314 F.3d 384 (9th Cir. 2002) [where INS agent gave administrative warnings that said government does not provide counsel and then gave *Miranda* warnings saying government would, the confusion warrants reversal of conviction based upon person's statements]. When person was not deemed to be in custody at time he gave incriminating answers evidence would not be suppressed. *U.S. v. Hernandez-Hernandez,* 327 F.3d 703 (8th Cir. 2003) [where defendant detained as part of a *Terry* stop, his subsequent arrest after he admitted illegal entry to INS officer without prior *Miranda* warnings was lawful].

11. Arrest Improper as Defense—Person may not be detained under Fed. R. Crim. P. 5(a) for greater than 48 hours for a nonstatus crime without going before a magistrate. *Cf. U.S. v. Encarnacion,* 239 F.3d 395 (1st Cir. 2001). A person arrested pursuant to a potential charge under §1326 and not brought before a magistrate within 48 hours does not, absent collusion, violate Fed. R. Crim. Proc. 5(a), because §1326 is a status crime. *U.S. v. Tejada,* 255 F.3d 1, 3–5 (1st Cir. 2001); *U.S. v. Noel,* 231 F.3d 833, 837 (11th Cir. 2000).

12. Person Not Deported—If person not deported at immigration proceeding, government cannot sustain its burden that defendant was found in the U.S. after deportation. *U.S. v. Castillo-Basa,* 483 F.3d 896 (9th Cir. 2007) [although defendant need not be physically present at the time of his deportation order because an *in absentia* order will suffice, he could not be tried for perjury after being acquitted on the "found in" charge where he argued he was not present and the government was unable to prove he was deported].

13. Collateral Attack on Validity of First Deportation Order Permitted—*U.S. v. Mendoza-Lopez*, 481 U.S. 828 (1987) [collateral attack permitted where errors in first deportation hearing rendered hearing fundamentally unfair *and* respondent was denied effective judicial review of the validity of the deportation hearing because the IJ never advised respondent of his right to suspension and his waiver of appeal was therefore not intelligently and knowingly made]; *U.S. v. Charleswell,* 456 F.3d 347 (3d Cir. 2006) [collateral attack permitted on both reinstatement order under INA §241(a)(5) as well as underlying order]; *U.S. v. Lopez-Vasquez*, 227 F.3d 476, 483–85 (5th Cir. 2000) [summary removal proceeding is not fundamentally unfair and can be used as a basis for a prior removal order because the due process rights of an alien seeking admission are left to Congress]; *U.S. v. Gonzalez-Mendoza*, 985 F.2d 1014 (9th Cir. 1993) [no waiver of counsel where silent at deportation hearing]; *U.S. v. Lopez-Vasquez*, 1 F.3d 751 (9th Cir. 1993), *reh'g en banc denied* [mass silent waivers of appeal violated due process]; *U.S. v. Higareda-Ramirez,* 107 F.Supp.2d 1248 (D. Hawaii 2000) [failure to provide an interpreter or attorney at deportation hearing where respondent did not speak English and where no record of hearing exists to show fairness results in "fundamentally unfair" hearing]. Generally a party must show both prongs of *Mendoza-Lopez* (*i.e.*, hearing fundamentally unfair and no effective judicial review) to obtain relief. *U.S. v. Santos-Vanegas*, 878 F.2d 247 (8th Cir. 1989); *U.S. v. Palacios-Martinez*, 845 F.2d 89 (5th Cir.), *cert. denied*, 488 U.S. 844 (1988); *U.S. v. Zaleta-Sosa*, 854 F.2d 48, 51 (5th Cir. 1988); *U.S. v. Holland*, 876 F.2d 1533 (11th Cir. 1989). The passage of the REAL ID Act of 2005 may not bar the court's jurisdiction to hear a motion to dismiss the indictment under *Mendoza-Lopez. U.S. v. Villa-Melchor,* 389 F.Supp.2d 755, 758 (W.D. Tex. 2005) [court rejected both parties' view that case had to be transferred to circuit court under REAL ID Act].

13.a. General Criteria—Congress, in AEDPA, incorporated *Mendoza-Lopez* into statutory law under 8 U.S.C. §1326(d). The statute prevents a collateral attack to the validity of the deportation order unless the defendant (1) exhausted administrative remedies; (2) was deprived of judicial review; and (3) was ordered deported in a fundamentally unfair removal (or formerly a deportation/exclusion) hearing. 8 U.S.C. §1326(d). It applies to criminal proceedings initiated after Apr. 24, 1996. *U.S. v. Charleswell,* 456 F.3d 347, 354–63 (3d Cir. 2006) [upheld collateral attack on reinstatement order under INA §241(a)(5) because defendant was deprived of judicial review by not being informed of it and receiving a notice that mislead him as to his rights and because his hearing was fundamentally unfair]; *U.S. v. Zelaya,* 293 F.3d 1294 (11th Cir. 2002) [defendant failed to exhaust remedies when he failed to seek rescission of *in absentia* order]; *U.S. v. Gonzalez-Roque,* 301 F.3d 39, 46–49 (2d Cir. 2002) [defendant failed to comply with exhaustion requirement under §1326(d) when he failed to raise procedural due process issues and denial of continuance in his *pro se* appeal to the BIA]. A constitutional challenge against the exhaustion requirement under §1326(d)(1) has been rejected. *U.S. v. Johnson,* 391 F.3d 67, 73–74 (2d Cir. 2004) [failed to exhaust his administrative remedies and therefore ineligible to mount a collateral act on his deportation order]

13.b. Exhaustion of Administrative Remedies as Requisite for Relief Under §1326(d)(1)—The failure to exhaust administrative remedies has been used to deny a collateral challenge. *U.S. v. Deleon,* 444 F.3d 41, 48–51 (1st cir. 2006) [where respondent hid his true identity from the IJ he could not argue that he did not knowingly and intelligently give up his right to appeal because IJ failed to inform him of discretionary relief]; *U.S. v. Chavez-Alonso,* 431 F.3d 726 (10th Cir. 2005) [failure to exhaust is not excused by IJ's failure to inform defendant of his right to apply for INA §212(c) relief]; *U.S. v. Gonzalez,* 429 F.3d 1252 (9th Cir. 2005 [failure to appeal summary removal as an aggravated felon was a valid waiver as the bar to INA §212(h) relief under 8 U.S.C. §1228(b)(5), which barred all discretionary relief, could be retroactively applied]; *U.S. v. Rodriguez,* 410 F.3d 831, 834–35 (8th Cir. 2005) [IJ's failure to adequately inform respondent that drunk driving may not be an aggravated felony, did not make respondent's decision not to appeal to the BIA an involuntary or unknowing waiver]; *U.S. v. Roque-Espinoza,* 338 F.3d 724, 728–30 (7th Cir. 2003) [failure to appeal IJ denial of right to seek INA §212(c) relief to BIA on futility grounds was insufficient to overcome exhaust requirement under *Mendoza-Lopez* and §1326(d)]; *U.S. v. Gonzalez-Roque,* 301 F.3d 39, 46–49 (2d Cir. 2002) [defendant failed to comply with exhaustion requirement under §1326(d) when he failed to raise procedural due process issues and denial of continuance in his *pro se* appeal to the BIA]; *U.S. v. Hinojosa-Perez,* 208 F.3d 832 (9th Cir. 2000) [defendant failed to avail himself of a motion to reopen to challenge deportation order based upon defective notice and therefore failed to exhaust administrative remedies]; *U.S. v. Hernandez-Ochoa,* 346 F.Supp.2d 380, 382–83 (D.R.I. 2004) [EOIR transcript indicating defendant would file appeal and defendant's claim he did file appeal without more is insufficient to show exhaustion]. *But see U.S. v. Camacho-Lopez,* 450 F.3d 928 (9th Cir. 2006) [exhaustion not required where IJ erroneously advised defendant that he was ineligible for discretionary relief and he was not removable for aggravated felony as charged]; *U.S. v. Calderon,* 391 F.3d 370, 374–75 (2d Cir. 2004) [where IJ and respondent's counsel told him he was ineligible for §212(c) relief his waiver of appeal to BIA was not knowing and intelligently made]; *U.S. v. Sosa,* 387 F.3d 131, 136–37 (2d Cir. 2004) [failure to exhaust "must be excused" where it arises from an invalid waiver of the right to administrative appeal because it was not knowingly and intelligently made]; *U.S. v. Copeland,* 376 F.3d 61, 66–67 (2d Cir. 2004) [filing motion to reopen and appealing it to BIA satisfied exhaustion requirement]; *U.S. v. Pallares-Galan,* 359 F.3d 1088, 1096–98 (9th Cir. 2004) [defendant's failure to appeal his removal order was not "considered or intelligent" where IJ erroneously informed him that he was not eligible for relief from removal as an aggravated felon].

13.c. Denial of Judicial Review as a Requisite to Collateral Claim—In order to avail herself of relief under §1326(d) or *Mendoza-Lopez* a claimant must demonstrate that he was denied judicial review under §1326(d)(2). *U.S. v. Charleswell,* 456 F.3d 347, 354–63 (3d Cir. 2006) [where DHS provided a misleading notice to defendant in his reinstatement proceeding under INA §241(a)(5) that did not inform him of his right to a federal appeal, he was deprived of judicial review under §1326(d)(2)]; *U.S. v. Lopez,* 445 F.3d 90 (2d Cir. 2006) [followed *Copeland, Sosa and Calderon* and although the IJ/BIA had no obligation to inform the defendant of habeas relief, their statements that no relief was available deterred him from seeking judicial review]j; *U.S. v. Calderon,* 391 F.3d 370, 374–76 (2d Cir. 2004) [where IJ and respondent's counsel told him he was ineligible for §212(c) relief his waiver of appeal to BIA was not knowing and intelligently made and he was deprived of judicial review]; *U.S. v. Sosa,* 387 F.3d 131, 137–38 (2d Cir. 2004) [respondent did not have a realistic possibility of seeking judicial review through habeas because there was less than one month between entry of final order and physical deportation and he could not learn INA §212(c) relief *pro se* during that time given its complexity and he was not informed of it by IJ]; *U.S. v. Copeland,* 376 F.3d 61, 67–70 (2d Cir. 2004) [where defendant had no realistic opportunity for habeas review because he was physically deported quickly and because of the legal uncertainty as to the availability of habeas, he was denied judicial review for purposes of a collateral attack]. *But see U.S. v. Rodriguez,* 420 F.3d 831 (8th Cir. 2005)[where IJ, pre-*Leocal*, informed respondent that the BIA would most likely consider drunk driving an aggravated felony and respondent waived his appeal, the court rebuffed a challenge to the waiver because respondent's complaint is only that the IJ did not adequately inform him of a future change in the interpretation of the law]; *U.S. v. Rivera-Nevarez,* 418 F.3d 1104, 1107–11 (10th Cir. 2005) [although *Leocal* applied retroactively to render prior removal order invalid, defendant's failure to appeal removal order barred challenge]; *U.S. v. Mendez-Morales,* 384 F.3d 927, 929–30 (8th Cir. 2004) [statutory preclusion preventing judicial review of adjustment of status because respondent was an aggravated felon does not automatically bar an illegal re-entry prosecution where there is no due process deprivation by the agency and where habeas corpus jurisdiction was available]; *U.S. v. Vargas,* 479 F.Supp.2d 252, 254 (D. R.I. 2007) [where defendant claims lawyer improperly withdrew appeal of removal, it is insufficient to make a claim because nothing at removal hearing deprived him of opportunity for judicial review].

13.d. Fundamentally unfair proceeding where defendant was prejudiced—Generally a defendant under *Mendoza-Lopez* and §1326(d)(3) must show some that proceeding was fundamentally unfair *and* that respondent was prejudiced in the deportation/removal proceeding. *See e.g., U.S. v. Charleswell,* 456 F.3d 347, 354–63 (3d Cir. 2006) [where DHS provided a misleading notice to defendant in his reinstatement proceeding under INA §241(a)(5) that did not inform him of his right to a federal appeal, he was deprived of a fundamentally fair hearing and case was remanded to determine prejudice].

(1) The Standard for Prejudice—The circuits have varying standards to determine whether a person was prejudiced by errors committed during the removal proceedings. *Compare U.S. v. Charleswell,* 456 F.3d 347, 361–62 (3d Cir. 2006) [agreeing with majority of circuits that the standard for prejudice is a "reasonable likelihood that the result would have been different"]; *U.S. v. El Shami,* 434 F.3d 659, 664–66 (4th Cir. 2005) [applying a reasonable probability that respondent would have been granted INA §212(c) relief and not deported]; *U.S. v. Copeland,* 376 F.3d 61, 73–74 (2d Cir. 2004) [applying the "reasonable probability" standard as in ineffective assistance of counsel claims]; *U.S. v. Aguirre-Tello,* 353 F.3d 1199, 1207–08 (10th Cir. 2004) (*en banc*) [applying the "reasonable likelihood" standard to determine whether the defendant would have obtained relief or the outcome of the proceedings would have been different] *and U.S. v. Encarnacion-Galvez,* 964 F.2d 402, 407 (5th Cir. 1992) [defendant must show that "but for" the errors complained of he would not have been deported], *with U.S. v. Garcia-Martinez,* 228 F.3d 956, 963 (9th Cir. 2000) [must only show plausible grounds for relief to establish prejudice]. The prejudice inquiry may not extend beyond the fairness of the deportation/removal order itself and may not therefore encompass events subsequent to the order to find no prejudice *U.S. v. Scott,* 394 F.3d 111, 118–19 (2d Cir. 2005) [decision to deny dismissal of indictment was reversed where the district judge held there was no prejudice on theory that §212(c) relief would have been lost based upon a conviction subsequent to the deportation order]. At least one court has determined in the context of the denial of INA §212(c) relief, that the "reasonable probability" standard required that the applicant only show that s/he had a 20% chance of prevailing on the claim. *U.S. v. Copeland,* 369 F.Supp.2d 275, 285–88 (E.D.N.Y. 2005) [applying 20% rule but determining that defendant would not have been granted §212(c) relief and therefore there was no prejudice in denying him opportunity to apply]. Where the transcript of the removal proceeding is unavailable, the defendant still has the burden of overcoming the presumption that his deportation proceeding was conducted in a valid manner. *U.S. v. Arevalo-Tavares,* 210 F.3d 1198 (10th Cir. 2000). *U.S. v. Interian-Mata,* 363 F.Supp.2d 1246 (S.D. Cal. 2005) [where respondent who was deprived of INA §212(c) hearing would not have won his case on the merits, a motion to suppress was denied].

(2) Prejudice—*U.S. v. Camacho-Lopez,* 450 F.3d 928 (9th Cir. 2006) [exhaustion not required where IJ erroneously advised defendant that he was ineligible for discretionary relief and he was not removable for aggravated felony as charged]; *U.S. v. El Shami,* 434 F.3d 659, 664–66 (4th Cir. 2005) [the government's failure to provide notice of deportation proceeding prejudiced respondent because there was a reasonable probability that he would have been granted INA §212(c) relief and not deported]; *U.S. v. Ortiz-Lopez,* 385 F.3d 1202 (9th Cir. 2004) [conviction for illegal re-entry reversed where the IJ's failure to advise

defendant that he could get VD instead of deportation was prejudicial]; *U.S. v. Pallares-Galan,* 359 F.3d 1088 (9th Cir. 2004) [where IJ erroneously advised defendant in removal proceeding that he was not eligible for cancellation of removal because the IJ erroneously ruled that a conviction under a California statute for annoying or molesting a child under 18 was an aggravated felony, defendant was prejudiced and did not validly waive his right to appeal the IJ's order]; *U.S. v. Ubaldo-Figueroa,* 364 F.3d 1042 (9th Cir. 2004) [defendant prejudiced in immigration hearing, where his attorney said he would accept order as final but defendant did not intelligently or knowingly waive appeal; defendant was prejudiced because he had a plausible due process claim regarding the retroactivity of the aggravated felony definition and he had a right to apply for former INA §212(c) relief]; *U.S. v. Modica-Linos,* 399 F.Supp.2d 1114 (E.D. Wash. 2005) [IJ's statement that defendant was not eligible for §212(c) relief was erroneous, and defendant was therefore prejudiced in his removal proceeding].

(3) No Prejudice—*U.S. v. Luna,* 436 F.3d 312 (1st Cir. 2006) [where IJ failed to inform respondent about §212(c) relief, there was no prejudice because upon review of the facts respondent would not have obtained the relief]; *U.S. v. Jimenez-Borja,* 378 F.3d 853, 859 (9th Cir. 2004) [failure of IJ to advise respondent of his eligibility for INA §212(h) relief violated due process but he failed to show prejudice because he could not plausibly demonstrate the necessary extreme hardship to a qualifying relative]; *U.S. v. Mendoza-Mata,* 322 F.3d 829 (5th Cir. 2003) [where defendant had been deprived of his right to seek INA §212(c) relief he was not prejudiced because he could not show that there was a reasonable likelihood he would get the relief given his extensive criminal record]; *U.S. v. Gonzalez-Valerio,* 342 F.3d 1051, 1054–56 (9th Cir. 2003) [no prejudice in failing to inform respondent of his right to INA §212(c) relief where his second conviction was for an aggravated felony that arose subsequent to the passage of IIRIRA]; *U.S. v. Fernandez-Antonia,* 278 F.3d 150, 157–61 (2d Cir. 2002) [although IJ failed to instruct respondent on INA §212(h) relief, the respondent made no showing of prejudice]; *U.S. v. Medina,* 236 F.3d 1028 (9th Cir. 2001) [where there was a blank transcript of deportation hearing conviction was nevertheless upheld because unfairness of hearing is not an element of the offense, government must only prove prior deportation, and burden is on defendant to demonstrate prejudice]; *U.S. v. Muro-Inclan,* 249 F.3d 1180 (9th Cir. 2001) [although IJ never disclosed to defendant that he was eligible for 212(h) waiver, the facts did not demonstrate substantial prejudice]; *U.S. v. Perez-Ponce*, 62 F.3d 1120 (8th Cir. 1995) [reversed district court's vacation of conviction because, notwithstanding IJ's errors, there was no showing of prejudice]; *U.S. v. Espinoza-Farlo*, 34 F.3d 469 (7th Cir. 1994); *U.S. v. Meraz-Valeta*, 26 F.3d 992, 998 (10th Cir. 1994); *U.S. v. Fares*, 978 F.2d 52 (2d Cir. 1992); *U.S. v. Proa-Tovar*, 975 F.2d 592 (9th Cir. 1992) (*en banc*); *U.S. v. Encarnacion-Galvez*, 964 F.2d 402, 407 (5th Cir. 1992) [defendant must show that but for the errors complained of he would not have been deported].

13.e. Relief Granted—The courts have invalidated convictions or granted motions to dismiss pursuant to *Mendoza-Lopez* and §1326(d)

(1) **First Circuit**—*U.S. v. Diaz-Nin,* 221 F.Supp.2d 584 (D.V.I. 2002) [where person deprived of INA §212(c) relief and judicial review barred because government's position was that there was no review in habeas or on appeal *pre–St. Cyr* indictment dismissed];

(2) **Second Circuit**—*U.S. v. Scott,* 394 F.3d 111 (2d Cir. 2005) [following *U.S. v. Perez* and concluding that failure to seek §212(c) relief was a fundamental procedural error that was prejudicial]; *U.S. v. Calderon,* 391 F.3d 370 (2d Cir. 2004) [following *Sosa* and *Copeland* court, affirmed district court's dismissal of indictment where respondent was informed by both IJ and his own counsel that §212(c) relief was not available]; *U.S. v. Sosa,* 387 F.3d 131 (2d Cir. 2004) [reversed conviction where IJ failed to inform defendant of INA §212(c) relief, where defendant did not knowingly and intelligently waive administrative appeal rights, where there was no realistic opportunity for judicial review, where the procedural failure to inform demonstrated that case was fundamentally unfair and where the case was remanded for hearing on prejudice]; *U.S. v. Copeland,* 376 F.3d 61 (2d Cir. 2004) [failure to inform respondent in deportation hearing of INA §212(c) re-

lief was fundamentally unfair and case remanded on issue of prejudice]; *U.S. v. Velasco-Medina* distinguished]; *U.S. v. Perez,* 330 F.3d 97 (2d Cir. 2003) [indictment for illegal re-entry dismissed where lawyer failed to seek INA §212(c) relief and respondent only exhausted administrative remedies as to denial of motion to reopen]; *U.S. v. Duncan,* 396 F.Supp.2d 210 (D. Conn. 2005) [where respondent raised a derivative citizenship claim, he is entitled to evidentiary hearing before removal hearing can be used as basis for criminal proceeding]; *U.S. v. Garcia-Jurado,* 281 F.Supp.2d 498 (E.D.N.Y. 2003) [LPR deprived of fair hearing under §1326(d) where he was denied INA §212(c) hearing due to improper interpretation and then deported before BIA could rule on pending motion to reconsider]; *U.S. v. Frias-Gomez,* 262 F.Supp.2d 11 (E.D.N.Y. 2003) [where person improperly denied the opportunity to apply for INA §212(c) relief and he was deported before he could contest the decision indictment for illegal re-entry dismissed]; *U.S. v. Brown,* 148 F.Supp.2d 191 (E.D.N.Y. 2001) [where person was extradited to U.S., the failure to give him an opportunity to depart under the *Badalamenti* decision interpreting the former INA provision was fundamentally unfair].

(3) **Fourth Circuit**—*U.S. v. El Shami,* 434 F.3d 659, 664–66 (4th Cir. 2005) [the government's failure to provide notice of deportation proceeding prejudiced respondent because there was a reasonable probability that he would have been granted INA §212(c) relief and not deported].

(4) **Fifth Circuit**—*U.S. v. Campos-Asencio*, 822 F.2d 506 (5th Cir. 1987) [following *Mendoza-Lopez*, court reversed conviction where alien raised denial of counsel claim in his deportation hearing]; *U.S. v. Ojeda-Escobar,* 218 F.Supp.2d 839 (W.D. Tex. 2002) [motion granted where defendant was removed prior to *St. Cyr* and therefore denied application for INA §212(c) relief]; *U.S. v. Girosky-Garibay,* 176 F.Supp.2d 705 (W.D. Tex. 2001) [dismissed indictment where removal proceeding was fundamentally unfair because it was based on erroneous interpretation of law that felony DWI was an aggravated felony barring relief]; *U.S. v. Montano-Bentancourt*, 151 F.Supp.2d 794 (W.D. Tx. 2001) [where OSC was sent to wrong address and defendant deported in *in absentia* hearing was fundamentally unfair].

(5) **Eighth Circuit**—*U.S. v. Santos-Vanegas*, 878 F.2d 247 (8th Cir. 1989) [where deportation notice did not indicate respondent could appeal BIA's decision and where incorrect standard was used to evaluate asylum claim the conviction is reversed].

(6) **Ninth Circuit**—*U.S. v. Camacho-Lopez,* 450 F.3d 928 (9th Cir. 2006) [reversed district court where exhaustion was not required because IJ erroneously advised defendant that he was ineligible for discretionary relief and defendant was not removable for aggravated felony as charged]; *U.S. v. Ortega-Ascanio,* 376 F.3d 879 (9th Cir. 2004) [permitted withdrawal of plea before sentencing where defendant argued that intervening *St. Cyr* decision was basis to dismiss indictment for illegal re-entry because IJ, at removal hearing, failed to inform him of INA §212(c) relief even though he informed him of cancellation but only if he did not commit aggravated felony]; *U.S. v. Pallares-Galan,* 359 F.3d 1088 (9th Cir. 2004) [where IJ erroneously advised defendant in removal proceeding that he was not eligible for cancellation of removal because the IJ erroneously ruled that a conviction under a California statute for annoying or molesting a child under 18 was an aggravated felony, defendant was prejudiced and did not validly waive his right to appeal the IJ's order]; *U.S. v. Ubaldo-Figueroa,* 364 F.3d 1042 (9th Cir. 2004) [defendant prejudiced in immigration hearing where his attorney said he would accept order as final but defendant did not intelligently or knowingly waive appeal and defendant was prejudiced because he had a plausible due process claim regarding the retroactivity of the aggravated felony definition and he had a right to apply for former INA §212(c) relief]; *U.S. v. Leon Paz,* 340 F.3d 1003 (9th Cir. 2003) [where IJ erroneously told respondent he was ineligible for relief when in fact he was eligible for INA §212(c) relief his conviction was vacated; *U.S. v. Ahumada-Aguilar,* 295 F.3d 943 (9th Cir. 2002) [conviction reversed where IJ deprived person of his right to counsel in group hearing, where the waiver of right to appeal was not knowing and intelligent and where he was prejudiced by errors]; *U.S. v. Arrieta,* 224 F.3d 1076 (9th Cir. 2000) [defendant's mass deportation hearing where IJ failed to inform him of his apparent eligibility for an INA §212(h)

waiver resulted in prejudice]; *U.S. v. Calles-Pineda,* 627 F.2d 976 (9th Cir. 1980) [mass deportation hearing was denial of due process].

13.f. Relief Denied—More often than not in published cases, the courts have denied claims under *Mendoza-Lopez* and §1326(d).

(1) **First Circuit**—*U.S. v. Deleon,* 444 F.3d 41, 48–51 (1st cir. 2006) [where respondent hid his true identity from the IJ he could not argue that he did not knowingly and intelligently give up his right to appeal because IJ failed to inform him of discretionary relief]; *U.S. v. Vieira-Candelario*, 6 F.3d 12 (1st Cir. 1993) [where defendant was improperly denied right to seek INA §212(c) relief, filed appeal and later withdrew it, he was not denied judicial review];

(2) **Second Circuit**—*U.S. v. Gonzalez-Roque,* 301 F.3d 39 (2d Cir. 2002) [where IJ denied fourth continuance to permit respondent to file I-130 petition and respondent did not raise issue in *pro se* appeal to BIA he failed to comply with the exhaustion requirement under §1326(d)(1); due process was also not violated]; *U.S. v. Manragh,* 428 F.Supp.2d 130 (E.D.N.Y. 2006) [failure by appellate lawyer to file brief before the BIA did not substantially prejudice defendant because there was no reasonable probability that he would have avoided deportation]; *U.S. v. Cottone,* 244 F.Supp.2d 126 (E.D.N.Y. 2003) [IJ's erroneous claim to respondent that INA §212(c) relief was not available to him did not render proceeding fundamentally unfair]; *U.S. v. Bailey,* 56 F.Supp.2d 381 (S.D.N.Y. 1999) [motion to dismiss denied where immigration attorney told client not to appear and consequently his §212(c) application was deemed abandoned]; *U.S. v. Jimenez*, 921 F.Supp. 1054 (S.D.N.Y. 1995) [motion to dismiss indictment denied even where waiver of right to deportation hearing was coerced by threat of detention where no showing of prejudice because defendant would have been deported anyway];

(3) **Third Circuit**—*U.S. v. Torres,* 383 F.3d 92, 104–06 (3d Cir. 2004) [removal proceeding was not fundamentally unfair where IJ did not inform respondent of the right to seek §212(c) relief because grant of relief was speculative and a matter of "grace." Addressed *Greenholtz* finding it supported view that relief was speculative];

(4) **Fourth Circuit**—*U.S. v. Wilson,* 316 F.3d 506, 510–11 (4th Cir. 2003) [the proceeding was not fundamentally unfair where BIA denied INA §212(c) claim *pre–St. Cyr because* the failure of the BIA to consider a INA §212(c) claim is not a due process violation as there is no liberty or property interest in discretionary relief];

(5) **Fifth Circuit**—*U.S. v. Lopez-Ortiz,* 313 F.3d 225 (5th Cir. 2002), *cert. denied,* 537 U.S. 1135 (2003) [failure to inform defendant of eligibility for INA §212(c) relief does not rise to the level of fundamental unfairness and therefore does not affect the conviction because §212(c) relief is not a liberty or property interest warranting due process protection]; *U.S. v. Asibor*, 109 F.3d 1023, 1037–38 (5th Cir. 1997) [where attorney conducted case telephonically and defendant never notified of right to contact consulate, hearing was fundamentally fair]; *U.S. v. Saucedo-Velasquez*, 843 F.2d 832 (5th Cir. 1988) [conviction upheld where defendant was an unrepresented minor at his deportation hearing]; *U.S. v. Lubo,* 262 F.Supp.2d 727 734 (W.D. Tex. 2003) [no fundamental error because there was no prejudice where IJ entered reinstatement order denying withholding/CAT claim]; *U.S. v. Hernandez-Rodriguez,* 170 F.Supp.2d 700 (N.D. Tex. 2001) [motion to dismiss denied notwithstanding person's deportation because of incorrect retroactive application denying INA §212(c) relief pre–*St. Cyr*];

(6) **Sixth Circuit**—*U.S. v. Martinez-Rocha,* 337 F.3d 566 (6th Cir. 2003) [where respondent knowingly and intelligently waived his right to contest deportation he failed to exhaust his remedies and is barred under §1326(d)];

(7) **Seventh Circuit**—*U.S. v. De Horta Garcia,* 519 F.3d 658 (7th Cir. 2008) [defendant pled guilty after AEDPA and therefore barred from INA §212(c) relief]; *U.S. v. Santiago-Ochoa,* 447 F.3d 1015 (7th Cir. 2006) [where prior removal order was administrative under INA §238(b), defendant did not satisfy any requirements of 8 U.S.C. §1326(d)]; *U.S. v. Adame-Salgado,* 214 F.Supp.2d 853 (N.D. Ill. 2002) [failure to advise respondent

of INA §212(c) relief is insufficient to dismiss indictment because there was no showing that his right of judicial review or due process was violated];

(8) **Ninth Circuit**—*U.S. v. Rivera-Sillas,* 417 F.3d 1014, 1017–18 (9th Cir. 2005) [lack of counsel at deportation hearing does not violate Sixth Amendment]; *U.S. v. Corrales-Beltran,* 192 F.3d 1311, 1317–19 (9th Cir. 1999) [failure to advise person of right to appeal bond hearing where he gave up underlying administrative appeal on the merits was not in violation of *Mendoza-Lopez*]; *U.S. v. Arce-Hernandez,* 163 F.3d 559, 563–64 (9th Cir. 1998) [affirmed district court's determination that there was not sufficient prejudice where person married to USC with USC children and was not informed of right to apply for §212(h) waiver in violation of IJ's duty to do so]; *U.S. v. Contreras*, 63 F.3d 852, 856–57 (9th Cir. 1995) [refused to vacate even where there was telephonic mass hearing]; *U.S. v. Chavez-Huerto*, 972 F.2d 1087 (9th Cir. 1992) [affirmed conviction where defendant argued that he did not knowingly waive immigration appeal right where he was not told of the criminal bar to re-entry by IJ]; *U.S. v. Arroyo-Garcia*, 746 F.Supp. 1039 (D. Nev. 1990) [motion to dismiss indictment denied where defendant was not informed of his right to apply for registry, but the defect did not effectively foreclose judicial review or render the proceedings fundamentally unfair]: *U.S. v. Arroyo-Garcia*, 751 F.Supp. 172 (D. Nev. 1990) [same case].

(9) **Tenth Circuit**—*U.S. v. Aguirre-Tello,* 353 F.3d 1199, 1204–05 (10th Cir. 2004) (*en banc*) [rejected action to dismiss indictment in re-entry case because there is no constitutional right to be informed of discretionary relief that might be available such as INA §212 (c) and there was no prejudice]; *U.S. v. Meraz-Valeta*, 26 F.3d 992, 998 (10th Cir. 1994) [IJ's failure to consider improperly issued JRAD in drug case did not render deportation hearing fundamentally unfair]; *U.S. v. Valdez*, 917 F.2d 466 (10th Cir. 1990) [affirmed conviction where applicant claimed he was not given *Miranda* warnings before deportation hearing];

(10) **Eleventh Circuit**—*U.S. v. Holland*, 876 F.2d 1533 (11th Cir. 1989) [denial of judicial review alone insufficient; must show that specific error seriously prejudiced deportation hearing rendering the hearing fundamentally unfair].

13.g. Standard of Review—The collateral attack in these cases is a mixed question of law and fact and the courts will review them *de novo* when they involve constitutional rights. *U.S. v. Lopez-Vasquez*, 1 F.3d 751 (9th Cir. 1993), *rehearing en banc denied*; *U.S. v. Valdez*, 917 F.2d 466, 468 (10th Cir. 1990). The burden of proof is on the alien, not the government. *U.S. v. Martinez-Amaya*, 67 F.3d 678, 680–82 (8th Cir. 1995).

13.h. Defenses—Neither *Mendoza-Lopez* nor §1326 bars a defendant from asserting that s/he is not an alien notwithstanding the validity of the first deportation order. *U.S. v. Meza-Soria*, 935 F.2d 166 (9th Cir. 1991) [defendant could raise claim of USC without attacking previous order of deportation, because alienage is a separate element of 8 U.S.C. §1326]. Nor is a person collaterally estopped from asserting s/he is citizen. *U.S. v. Ortiz-Lopez*, 24 F.3d 53, 55–56 (9th Cir. 1994). However, the fact that a person legalized his or her status *after* the second entry is not a defense, in the view of at least one circuit. *U.S. v. Ramos-Quirarte*, 935 F.2d 162 (9th Cir. 1991) [rejected defense that defendant became a SAW after his return to U.S.].

13.i. Cannot Attack Underlying Conviction—The collateral attack doctrine may not extend to an attack on the conviction that formed the basis for the first deportation charge. *U.S. v. Arroyo-Garcia*, 751 F.Supp. 172 (D. Nev. 1990). However, the prior aggravated felony or other conviction may be challenged in a prosecution under 8 U.S.C. §1326 where it is used to enhance the penalties under §1326(b)(2) solely on the ground that defendant was denied counsel in the prior felony conviction. *U.S. v. Delacruz-Soto,* 414 F.3d 1158, 1164–67 (10th Cir. 2005). Congress has precluded a collateral attack of a summary exclusion order under INA §235(b)(1) and for purposes of the assessment of penalties (fines) because "no court shall have jurisdiction to hear claims collaterally attacking the validity of orders of exclusion, special (*i.e.*, summary) exclusion or deportation." INA §235(c), 8 U.S.C. §1225(c). The IIRIRA also prohibited collateral attacks of summary exclusion orders in criminal proceedings concerning unlawful entry (INA §275(c)) or unlawful re-entry (INA §276). INA §235(b)(1)(D). And at least one circuit has found that the lack of judicial review is not fundamentally unfair.

U.S. v. Lopez-Vasquez, 227 F.3d 476, 483–85 (5th Cir. 2000) [summary removal proceeding is not fundamentally unfair and can be used as a basis for a prior removal order because the due process rights of an alien seeking admission are left to Congress]. However, the general statutes prohibiting review of final orders of deportation under AEDPA of persons with convictions cannot be used to bar review of the validity of the initial deportation order. *U.S. v. Arce-Hernandez,* 163 F.3d 559, 561–63 (9th Cir. 1998) [court not barred by AEDPA §440(a) from deciding validity of deportation order in re-entry case].

13.j. Mootness—The government's appeal of a dismissal of the indictment is not moot where the respondent was removed from the U.S. after the indictment was dismissed. *U.S. v. Gonzalez-Roque,* 301 F.3d 39, 44–45 (2d Cir. 2002) [dismissal of indictment and defendant's subsequent removal by INS did not moot appeal because he would be subject to arrest and imprisonment if he sought re-entry].

13.k. Discovery—A defendant has a right to obtain a copy of his alien registration file in discovery to initiate collateral challenge. *U.S. v. Ponce-Covarrubias,* 227 F.Supp.2d 931 (W.D. Tenn. 2002) [defendant entitled to "A" file in discovery even if s/he failed to satisfy either the exhaustion of administrative remedies or the deprivation of judicial review as s/he is required to do under §1326(d) to obtain relief in collateral challenge]. «»

C. ***Convictions Under INA §274***—Includes: illegally bringing in [§274(a)(1)(A)(i)], transporting [§274(a)(1)(A)(ii)], harboring [§274(a)(1)(A)(iii)], and encouraging someone to come to, enter or reside in U.S. [§274(a)(1)(A)(iv)], conspiring or aiding and abetting these crimes [§274(a)(1)(A)(v)], or bringing someone to the U.S. [§274(a)(2)]. IRCA §112, PL 99-603, 100 Stat. 3359 (Nov. 6, 1986), amended INA §274(a), 8 U.S.C. §1324(a), to eliminate the ["Texas Proviso"] exception that employment is not harboring. However, INS regulatory comments, 52 Fed. Reg. 16217 (May 1, 1987), made it clear that this statute will not be applied to cases involving only employment. One court, ignoring the regulatory comments found that employment does constitute harboring. *U.S. v. Kim,* 193 F.3d 567, 572–74 (2d Cir. 1999). Another court found that it was not reversible error for a district judge to refuse to give a "mere employment" jury instruction to harboring and smuggling charges. *U.S. v. Khanani,* 502 F.3d 1281, 1285–89 (11th Cir. 2007) [failure to give mere employment jury instruction did not seriously impair the defendant's ability to conduct their defense because the instructions as given already required proof beyond mere employment]. *See also U.S. v. Tipton,* 518 F.3d 591 (8th Cir. 2008) [evidence was sufficient for harboring where persons were given employment, provided a place to live, given daily transportation, given money to purchase necessities, and maintained counterfeit immigration papers for the workers]; *U.S. v. Shum,* 496 F.3d 390 (5th Cir. 2007) [used defendant's employment of undocumented to establish that he facilitated their ability to remain in U.S. as an element necessary for a conviction for harboring, concealing or shielding undocumented]. Congress has exempt certain religious activities from the transporting, harboring or encouraging residence provisions where religious organizations enable persons to be volunteer ministers and provide them basic living expenses. INA §274(a)(1)(C). Congress in IIRIRA §203, in other contexts, made it a criminal penalty to knowingly hire for employment at least 10 individuals in a 12-month period with actual knowledge that the individuals are not authorized to work and have been brought to U.S. in violation of INA §274.

Violation of the "bringing in" provision or conspiring to do so is now punishable by up to 10 years. Violation of the transport, harboring and encouraging provision, if done for commercial advantage or financial gain, is also up to 10 years; otherwise it is up to 5 years. It is also up to 5 years for aiding and abetting and up to 5 years for knowingly hiring 10 persons, during any 12-month period, with knowledge that they are not authorized to be employed and have been brought to U.S. in violation of INA §274. Sentences may be increased by up to 10 years in the case of a person who has brought aliens into the U.S. if the offense was part of an ongoing commercial enterprise, the number of aliens transported were in groups of 10 or more and the aliens were transported in a manner that endangered their lives or the aliens presented a life-threatening risk to people in the U.S. INA §274(a)(4). If serious injury, penalties may be up to 20 years, and if death occurs the death sentence may be imposed. INA §274(a)(1)(B). *U.S. v. Matus-Leva,* 311 F.3d 1214, 1218–19 (9th Cir. 2002) [language requiring harsher sentence if smuggling "results in the death of any person" is not void for vagueness]. The statute now permits convictions for "reckless disregard." Prosecution generally must show willfulness. *U.S. v. Morales-Rosales*, 838 F.2d 1359 (5th Cir. 1988). Alienage and status are elements of the crime. *U.S. v. Alvarado-Machado*, 867 F.2d 209, 212 (5th Cir. 1989) [reversed conviction where no admissible evidence on alienage]. At least one court has found that the statutes apply extraterritorially. *U.S. v. Delgado-Garcia,* 374 F.3d 1337, 1343–51 (D.C.Cir. 2004) [§274(a) applies extraterritorially where Ecuadorian ship carrying potentially illegal persons was in international waters 170 nautical miles south of Guatemala and Mexico].

1. Bringing to the United States—"Bringing to" is under INA §274(a)(2), 8 U.S.C. §1324(a)(2), and has been broadly defined to include "leading," "escorting," or "causing [the alien] to come along" to the U.S. *U.S. v. Yoshida,* 303 F.3d 1145, 1151–52 (9th Cir. 2002) [where defendant guided undocumented persons to board aircraft, accompanied them on flight to U.S., and had their baggage claim receipts in phony names in her underwear, facts were sufficient for conviction]. "Bringing to" includes conduct where persons meet illegal aliens on U.S. side and transport them in U.S. *U.S. v. Aslam*, 936 F.2d 751 (2d Cir. 1991) [conduct covered not only under transporting provision, but also bringing in provision] as well as persons who fraudulently obtain officially issued visas for noncitizens. *U.S. v. Gasanova,* 332 F.3d 297 (5th Cir. 2003) [defendants who brought topless dancers into the U.S. on J-1 visas claiming they were conducting academic research could not argue that they had received official authorization]. *U.S. v. Calhelha,* 456 F.Supp.2d 350, 357–59 (D. Conn. 2006) [court upheld a count in the indictment over defendant's objection that persons brought to U.S. on visa waiver were facially legal even if defendant arranged their trips to work at his stores]. Includes aiding and abetting as well. *U.S. v. Angwin,* 263 F.3d 979, 997 (9th Cir. 2001), *reh'g denied* 271 F.3d 786, *cert. denied* 535 U.S. 966 (2002); *U.S. v. Nolasco-Rosas,* 286 F.3d 762 (5th Cir. 2002) [financial gain is not an element of an aiding and abetting charge]. But "bringing to" language does not include assisting someone to come to the U.S. where all fraudulent acts are committed by defendant abroad. *U.S. v. Assadi,* 223 F.Supp.2d 208 (D.D.C. 2002) [dismissed counts related to "bringing to" where person created false passports, bought them airline tickets to U.S., procured boarding passes, and took them to the airport, but never accompanied them to U.S.]. Or where the transporter completed all acts and dropped persons in the U.S. *before* defendant became involved. *U.S. v. Lopez,* 484 F.3d 1186 (9th Cir. 2007) [en banc[. *But see U.S. v. Villanueva,* 408 F.3d 193, 197–99 (5th Cir. 2005) [Congress intended statute prohibiting attempts to bring undocumented persons to the U.S. to apply to extraterritorial conduct]; *U.S. v. Calhelha,* 456 F.Supp.2d 350, 359–60 (D. Conn. 2006) [distinguished *Assadi* because defendant met future workers at the airport and transported them]. Commercial/financial gain must be proved to uphold conviction. *U.S. v. Munoz,* 412 F.3d 1043, 1046–48 (9th Cir. 2005) [where trial court gave jury instruction that relieved government of its burden to prove financial gain, conviction was reversed]; *U.S. v. Calhelha,* 456 F.Supp.2d 350, 360 (D. Conn. 2006) [commercial gain not only includes funds for transporting persons but also gain to defendant's business where persons were working]. The "bringing to" (as distinguished from bringing in) provision is a misdemeanor INA §274(a)(2)(A); however, penalties are substantially enhanced if the person was brought to U.S. to commit a crime or it was an offense done for commercial advantage or personal gain, or the alien was not immediately brought to the DHS inspection station. INA §274(a)(2)(B). The section was also amended to establish a violation for each alien. In order to obtain a conviction, the defendant must have had specific intent to violate U.S. immigration law. *U.S. v. Barajas-Montiel,* 185 F.3d 947, 951–52 (9th Cir. 1999). Attempt to commit a crime also requires specific intent. *U.S. v. Hernandez-Franco,* 189 F.3d 1151, 1158 (9th Cir. 1999). *But see U.S. v. Perez,* 443 F.3d 772, 780–81 (11th Cir. 2006) [upholding conviction on deliberate indifference standard].

2. Transporting—INA §274(a)(1)(A)(ii), 8 U.S.C. §1324(a)(1)(A)(ii)

   2.a. Government must prove: (1) defendant transported or moved an alien within the U.S.; (2) the alien was in the U.S. in violation of law; (3) the defendant knew or acted in reckless disregard of this fact; and (4) the defendant acted willfully in furtherance of the alien's violation of the law [illegal presence]. *U.S. v. Hernandez*, 913 F.2d 568 (8th Cir. 1990). Transporting "for gain" is no longer an element of the crime. *U.S. v. Romero-Cruz,* 201 F.3d 373, 378 (5th Cir. 2000). However, there is a separate aggravating circumstance for transporting for gain. 8 U.S.C. §1324(a)(1)(B)(i) that has been described as a separate offense. *U.S. v. Williams,* 449 F.3d 635, 646 (5th Cir. 2006). The government may prove a violation by circumstantial evidence. *U.S. v. Stonefish,* 402 F.3d 691, 695–97 (6th Cir. 2005) [upheld conviction without any direct evidence whether the illegal aliens in defendant's car paid anyone to get from China to the U.S.]. If a defendant is assisting a person to obtain lawful status, he is not acting "in furtherance of" the alien's illegal presence. *U.S. v. Merkt*, 764 F.2d 266 (5th Cir. 1985).

Conviction requires knowledge or reckless disregard of alien's illegal status. *U.S. v. Diaz*, 936 F.2d 786 (5th Cir. 1991); *U.S. v. Tapia*, 761 F.2d 1488 (11th Cir. 1985). Indictment need not allege willfulness if government alleges knowledge or reckless disregard. *U.S. v. Rivera*, 879 F.2d 1247 (5th Cir. 1989); *U.S. v. Mussaleen*, 35 F.3d 692, 698 (2d Cir. 1994) [reckless disregard standard upheld]. Defendant can have intent to further person's illegal presence in U.S. even if the defendant is engaged in a business to transport illegal aliens and is simply doing it to earn a living. *U.S. v. Hernandez-Guardado,* 228 F.3d 1017, 1022–24 (9th Cir. 2000).

2.b. Defense raising potential legality of alien's status unsuccessful. *U.S. v. Aguilar*, 883 F.2d 662, 676–80 (9th Cir. 1989) [assertion that Salvadorans are refugees under U.S. and international law not a defense]; *U.S. v. Alvarado-Machado*, 867 F.2d 209 (5th Cir. 1989) [alien informants with I-210s outside U.S. were not legally re-entering]; *U.S. v. Rivera*, 859 F.2d 1204, 1209 (4th Cir. 1988) [eligibility for amnesty not a defense where entry and transportation illegal]; *U.S. v. Rodriguez-Rodriguez*, 840 F.2d 697 (9th Cir. 1988) [where defendant picked up aliens and drove them from San Ysidio to L.A. it was not a defense that they were eligible for adjustment]; *U.S. v. Merkt*, 794 F.2d 950 (5th Cir. 1986) [assertion that transported aliens are refugees is not a defense]. *But see U.S. v. Medina-Garcia*, 918 F.2d 4 (1st Cir. 1990) [where informants given I-210s, they are not illegal aliens and no conviction for substantive offense possible, although conspiracy and attempt convictions upheld]; *U.S. v. Diaz*, 936 F.2d 786, 788 (5th Cir. 1991) [government must prove alien illegally in U.S., and cannot use his conviction for being undocumented in U.S. against defendant to prove element of crime]; *U.S. v. Darsan*, 811 F.Supp. 119 (W.D.N.Y. 1993) [rejected motion to dismiss based upon eligibility for waiver because nonimmigrants are presumed to be entering permanently and must prove their lack of intent]. A favorable subsequent official action is not a defense.

2.c. Religious beliefs or free speech rights may not be a defense. *U.S. v. Aguilar*, 883 F.2d 662, 687, 694–96 (9th Cir. 1989); *U.S. v. Merkt*, 764 F.2d 266, 270–71 (5th Cir. 1985) [defendant's religious convictions as a sanctuary worker not a defense]; *American Baptist Churches v. Meese*, 712 F.Supp. 756 (N.D. Cal. 1989).

2.d. *Mens rea* is an element of the statute, and the court must instruct the jury as to criminal intent. *U.S. v. Nguyen*, 73 F.3d 887 (9th Cir. 1995) [statute is not strict liability; must show criminal intent for conviction]. At least one circuit has distinguished between a charge of attempting to transport, which it regards as a specific intent crime because the government must prove conscious desire, and actual transporting, which is treated as a general intent crime because the government need only show knowledge or reckless disregard. *U.S. v. Ramirez-Martinez,* 273 F.3d 903, 913–15 (9th Cir. 2001).

2.e. Willful transportation of illegal aliens is not per se a violation of the statute, for the law prosecutes such conduct only when it furthers the alien's unlawful presence or entry. *U.S. v. Parmelee*, 42 F.3d 387, 391 (7th Cir. 1994) [defendant's guilty knowledge that transportation furthers an alien's illegal presence is an essential element of this crime]; *U.S. v. One 1982 Ford Pick-Up*, 873 F.2d 947 (6th Cir. 1989) [when defendant's intent was not to further illegal presence of Salvadorans being transported to find a job, no forfeiture]; *Merkt*, *supra* at 271; *U.S. v. Fierros*, 692 F.2d 1291, 1295 (9th Cir. 1982), *cert. denied*, 462 U.S. 1120 (1983) [transport of alien to and from work not violation of (a)(2)]; *U.S. v. Moreno*, 561 F.2d 1321, 1322 (9th Cir. 1977); *U.S. v. Moreno-Duque*, 718 F.Supp. 254 (D. Vt. 1989) [purpose of transportation must be to further violation of law]; *U.S. v. One 1984 Chevrolet Truck*, 701 F.Supp. 213 (N.D. Ga. 1988) [in forfeiture proceeding, government was not substantially justified where it sought forfeiture for bringing person to and from work]; *U.S. v. Bienvenido de la Rosa Basilio*, 682 F.Supp. 13 (D.P.R. 1988) [where alien was government informant and his transportation occurred while being informant, court granted motion to dismiss case at end of evidence because alien's illegal transportation was not in furtherance of illegal entry]; *U.S. v. One 1982 Toyota*, 642 F.Supp. 335 (N.D. Ill. 1986) [not all knowing transportation of alien is a violation of (a)(1)(B)]. *But see U.S. v. Hernandez-Garcia,* 284 F.3d 1138 (9th Cir. 2002) [a conviction for transporting undocumented persons within U.S. does not require the government to demonstrate an "entry" where the defendant knew that the persons who had "come to" the border were undocumented]; *U.S. v. Barajas-Chavez,* 162 F.3d 1285 (10th Cir. 1999) (*en banc*) [the "in furtherance language" is broad enough to encompass any person who transports someone, regardless of profit motive or close relationship, with knowledge or with reckless disregard of fact that the person transported is illegal and the transportation will help, advance, or promote the continued illegal presence]; *U.S. v. Velasquez-Cruz*, 929 F.2d 420 (8th Cir. 1991); *U.S. v. One 1982 Chevrolet Crew-Cab Truck*, 810 F.2d 178 (8th Cir. 1987).

Whether the alien made an entry into the U.S. is irrelevant in defending a smuggling charge. A conviction requires an entry under traditional standards. *U.S. v. Gonzalez-Torres*, 309 F.3d 594, 599–600 (9th Cir. 2002) [the concept of entry is not relevant to smuggling charges under §274(a)(2)(B)(iii) because Congress revised the smuggling provisions under PL 99-603, Title I, Part B, §112 (1986), and allowed for a conviction for "bringing to" the U.S., thereby deliberately overruling case law requiring that a smuggler "bring into" the U.S. an alien]; *U.S. v. Esparza*, 882 F.2d 143 (5th Cir. 1989) [transportation of Salvadorans out of Harlingen, Texas, who were released on their own recognizance but given written and verbal instructions to remain in area, is violation of statute].

3. Harboring/Concealing—INA §274(a)(1)(A)(iii), 8 U.S.C. §1324(a)(1)(A)(iii). Sheltering with knowledge of alien's illegal status may constitute harboring/concealing. *U.S. v. Shum,* 496 F.3d 390, 392 (5th Cir. 2007) [upholding the conviction of an employer who provided undocumented workers with false-identity documents and who failed to submit record-keeping paperwork to Social Security with respect to their employment]; *U.S. v. Zheng,* 306 F.3d 1080 (11th Cir. 2002) [provision of both housing and employment constitutes harboring]; *U.S. v. Kim,* 193 F.3d 567, 574–75 (2d Cir. 1999) [employment constitutes harboring where employer knew or recklessly disregarded person's illegal status and took steps to help her remain in employment undetected by INS]; *U.S. v. Sanchez*, 927 F.2d 376 (8th Cir. 1991); *U.S. v. Lopez*, 521 F.2d 437 (2d Cir.), *cert. denied*, 423 U.S. 995 (1975); *U.S. v. Rubio-Gonzalez,* 674 F.2d 1067, 1073 (5th Cir. 1982) [approving a jury charge defining harboring as "any conduct tending to substantially facilitate an alien's remaining in the United States illegally"]; *U.S. v. Cantu*, 557 F.2d 1173 (5th Cir. 1977) [where employer refused admittance to INS without warrant and aided aliens to leave work place, statute violated]; *U.S. v. Acosta de Evans,* 531 F.2d 428, 430 (9th Cir. 1976) *cert. denied* 429 U.S. 836 (1976) [holding that the word "harbor" means "to afford shelter to" and does not require the intent to avoid detection]; *U.S. v. Belevin-Ramales,* 458 F.Supp.2d 409 (E.D. Ky. 2006) [harboring does require proof that the defendant is seeking to assist the person in an attempt to evade and avoid detection]. *Cf. U.S. v. Khanani,* 502 F.3d 1281, 1285–89 (11th Cir. 2007) [although "mere employment" is a defense to harboring and smuggling charges, it was not reversible error for the district court to deny a jury instruction on mere employment because the instructions as given already required proof beyond mere employment]. Aiding and abetting harboring is also a crime that the government may prove by establishing that: (1) the alien entered or remained in the U.S. in violation of law; (2) the defendant concealed, harbored or sheltered the alien in the U.S.; (3) the defendant knew or recklessly disregarded that the alien entered or remained in the U.S. in violation of law; and (4) the defendant's conduct tended to substantially facilitate the alien remaining in the U.S. *U.S. v. De Jesus-Batres,* 410 F.3d 154, 160 (5th Cir. 2005) [upheld aiding and abetting conviction based upon circumstantial evidence and finding that financial gain is not an element of the crime]. Harboring also includes keeping persons in virtual slavery for personal benefit, *U.S. v. Bonetti,* 277 F.3d 441 (4th Cir. 2002) [upholding 78-month sentence and ordering restitution under Mandatory Victim Restitution Act for woman who was kept in virtually domestic slavery for years]. The government must show the defendant intended to violate the law. *U.S. v. You,* 382 F.3d 958, 965–66 (9th Cir. 2004).

4. Encouraging—INA §274(a)(1)(A)(iv), 8 U.S.C. §1324(a)(1)(A)(iv). This section applies to encouraging an alien to reside in the U.S. where such residence is or will be in violation of the law. Includes scheme to sell fraudulent work authorization and other documents to aliens in the U.S. even if they initially entered legally. *U.S. v. Oloyede*, 982 F.2d 133 (4th Cir. 1992) [lawyer's conviction for representing persons at INS who were sold false Social Security and employment documents by co-conspirator]. It also includes, in the view of one circuit, fraudulently obtaining a Social Security number for an undocumented person. *U.S. v. Ndiaye,* 434 F.3d 1270, 1296–98 (11th Cir. 2006) [where defendant obtained Social Security numbers with cards that were marked "valid for work only with INS authorization," the court still regarded it as encouraging an undocumented person to reside in the U.S.].

5. Conspiracy or aiding and abetting the commission of any of the acts in INA §274(a)(1)(A) is also a crime. INA §274(a)(1)(A)(v), 8 U.S.C. §1324(a)(1)(A)(v). However, a conviction for aiding and abetting cannot be sustained unless the jury unanimously agrees that the defendant was an aider and abettor.*U.S. v. Williams,* 449 F.3d 635, 647–48 (5th Cir. 2006) [where jury unanimously determined that defendant was culpable but was not unanimous on aiding and abetting, his conviction was reversed].

6. Bringing someone to the U.S. in reckless disregard of the fact that the alien has not received prior official authorization, even if the alien is brought to an inspection station, is a also crime under INA §274(a)(2)(B)(i),(ii), 8 U.S.C. §1324(a)(2)(B)(i),(ii). Under INA §274(a)(2)(B)(iii) a person may be convicted if s/he does not immediate bring and present the alien to an appropriate immigration officer at a designated port of entry. *United States v. Perez,* 443 F.3d 772, 782 (11th Cir. 2006) [a conviction will be sustained even if the defendant was stopped by police and therefore not given an opportunity to present the smuggled alien to an immigration officer at a port of entry].

7. Defenses

   7.a. *Government Misconduct—U.S. v. Valdovinos-Valdovinos*, 588 F.Supp. 551 (N.D. Cal.), *rev'd on other grounds*, 743 F.2d 1436 (9th Cir. 1984), *cert. denied*, 469 U.S. 1114 (1985) [INS agent passed as employer and lied to Mexican citizens about entering U.S. without papers to trap transporters]. *But see U.S. v. Alvarado-Machado*, 867 F.2d 209 (5th Cir. 1989) [use of alien informants not improper]; *U.S. v. Morales-Quinones*, 812 F.2d 604, 610–11 (10th Cir. 1987).

   7.b. *Mere Employment*—Although "mere employment" is a defense to harboring and smuggling charges, a least one court has found that it was not reversible error for the district court to deny a jury instruction on mere employment. *U.S. v. Khanani,* 502 F.3d 1281, 1285–89 (11th Cir. 2007) [failure to give mere employment jury instruction did not seriously impair the defendant's ability to conduct their defense because the instructions as given already required proof beyond mere employment].

   7.c. *Duress*—Duress offered as a legal excuse for committing the crime has no effect because a duress defense is only effective if it negates the specific intent element of attempted illegal entry. *U.S. v. Solorzano-Rivera,* 368 F.3d 1073, 1080–81 (9th Cir. 2004) [where defendant entered voluntarily but due to pressure from Mexican authorities chasing him, his defense went to a legal excuse but did not negate the specific-intent element of the crime]. The burden of proof remains on the defendant. *U.S. v. Leal-Cruz,* 431 F.3d 667 (9th Cir. 2005) [jury instruction placing the burden on the defendant to prove duress in this circumstance was correct]; *U.S. v. Hernandez-Franco,* 189 F.3d 1151, 1157–58 (9th Cir. 1999), *cert. denied,* 503 U.S. 1206 (2000) [proof must be by a preponderance of the evidence].

   7.d. *Public Authority Defense*—When a defendant engages in criminal conduct at the request of a government enforcement officer, with the reasonable belief that s/he is acting as an authorized government agent to assist law enforcement, s/he lacks the criminal intent to be convicted. *U.S. v. Burt,* 410 F.3d 1100 (9th Cir. 2005) [reversed conviction for trial judge's failure to give jury instruction on public authority defense].

   7.e. *Unconstitutionality of INA §274*—Attacks on the constitutionality of the enhancement provision of INA §274, 8 U.S.C. §1324, as violative of *Apprendi v. New Jersey,* 530 U.S. 466 (2000), on the theory that the statute permits increased penalties, or under the due process clause on the theory that §274(a)(1)(B)(iv) [smuggling resulting in the death of a person] is unconstitutionally vague, have been rejected prior to *Booker*. *U.S. v. Ramirez-Lopez,* 315 F.3d 1143, 1157–59 (9th Cir. 2003).

8. Forfeiture and Seizure

   8.a. *CBP Responsible for Processing Asset Forfeitures*—The general DHS forfeiture statute is INA §274(b), 8 U.S.C. §1324(b), predicated on a violation of §274(a). Judicial proceedings for forfeiture are *in rem* actions brought by the government pursuant to the Supplemental Rules for Certain Admiralty and Maritime Claims. As a result of the organizational changes in the legacy INS from the Homeland Security Act of 2002, the authority for forfeiture and seizure enforcement has primarily been transferred to CBP. 73 Fed. Reg. 9010–12 (Feb. 19,

2008). Under 8 C.F.R. §274.1 CBP and ICE officers may seize and forfeit that "has been or is being used in the commission of a violation of any statutory authority involving the unlawful introduction of aliens, contraband or proceeds of such introduction, pursuant to, but not limited to, section 274(a) of the Act (8 U.S.C. 1324(a)"). The processing of asset forfeitures, however, will be consolidated into CBP. Former regulations regarding forfeit and asset seizure under 8 C.F.R. §274 are *no longer* valid. The processing of all asset forfeiture will be done in accordance with the procedures in 19 C.F.R. §§162 and 171 and petitions for remission will be permitted in accordance with 19 U.S.C. §1618. Cases under legacy INS procedures included: *Garcia-Rubio v. INS*, 703 F.Supp. 859 (S.D. Cal. 1989) [failing to provide notice that owner can seek a waiver violated due process]; *Garcia v. Meza,* 235 F.3d 287, 292 (7th Cir. 2000) [notice by publication insufficient where individual's name and address are known or easily ascertainable]; *Small v. U.S.*, 136 F.3d 1334 (D.C. Cir. 1998); *U.S. v. Rogers,* 108 F.3d 1247, 1252–53 (10th Cir. 1997); *Matter of Sixty Seven Thousand Four Hundred Seventy Dollars ($67,470)*, 901 F.2d 1540 (11th Cir. 1990) [claimant who elects to rely on the remission or mitigation procedure may forfeit their right to seek judicial review]; *U.S. v. One Beechcraft King Air 300 Aircraft*, 107 F.3d 829 (11th Cir. 1997) [constitutionality of forfeiture based only upon a showing of probable cause was upheld. and cases cited therein]; *McCoy v. U.S.*, 758 F.Supp. 299 (E.D. Pa. 1991); *Gonzalez v. Rivkind*, 858 F.2d 657 (11th Cir. 1988) [vehicle owner was required to pay seizure related costs or sign indemnity agreement as a condition precedent to the return of the vehicles where there was no judicial determination that a violation of 8 U.S.C. §1324(a) had actually occurred].

Forfeiture can occur not only for transportation of aliens into the U.S. but "in" the U.S. as well. *U.S. v. One 1982 Chevrolet Crew-Cab Truck*, 810 F.2d 178 (8th Cir. 1987) [forfeiture upheld on summary judgment where owner put in no evidence that he took "reasonable precautions"]; *Tucson Ecumenical Council v. Ezell*, 704 F.Supp. 980 (D. Ariz. 1989) [forfeiture upheld where actions of owner were in furtherance of alien's illegal presence in this country]; *U.S. v. One 1985 Ford F-250 Pickup*, 702 F.Supp. 1308 (E.D. Mich. 1988) [8 U.S.C. §1324(a)(1)(B) covers transportation within U.S.]; *U.S. v. One 1984 Chevrolet Trans Star*, 623 F.Supp. 625 (D. Conn. 1985). Forfeiture may arise even if person has a valid visa but misrepresents herself as a USC to gain entry. *U.S. v. One 1989 Mercedes Benz*, 971 F.Supp. 124 (W.D.N.Y. 1997). But mere transportation of undocumented alien pursuant to employment is not a basis for forfeiture as a violation of 8 U.S.C. §1324(a)(2). *U.S. v. One 1984 Ford Van*, 826 F.2d 918 (9th Cir. 1987). Also government must demonstrate that the transportation was in furtherance of illegal entry. *See in this section* ¶ 2.e (p.241), *supra*. *But see U.S. v. One 1984 Ford Pickup Truck*, No. CA 3-88-2291-R (N.D. Tex. Aug. 30, 1989) [seizure based upon transportation to and from work], *reported in* 66 No. 36 *Interpreter Releases* 1033–34 (Sept. 18, 1989).

8.b. *Civil Asset Forfeiture Reform Act of 2000* (CAFRA)—Prior to the Civil Asset Forfeiture Reform Act of 2000 (CAFRA), the government needed only to establish probable cause for the institution of a forfeiture by making a *prima facie* showing. Many courts viewed this burden as more than mere suspicion, but less than probable cause. *U.S. v. One 1983 Homemade Vessel Named Barracuda*, 625 F.Supp. 893 (S.D. Fla. 1986). The statute defined certain proof, including government records, as establishing *prima facie* proof [INA §274(b)(3)]. The burden of proof, however, was strictly construed. *U.S. v. One 1982 Buick Regal*, 670 F.Supp. 808 (N.D. Ill. 1987). Once the government established its burden, the burden shifted to claimant to establish a defense to forfeiture. *U.S. v. One 1985 Ford F-250 Pickup*, *supra*; *U.S. v. One 1984 Chevrolet Truck*, 682 F.Supp. 1221, 1226 (N.D. Ga. 1988). Under CAFRA "a forfeiture proceeding commenced on or after [Aug. 23, 2000]" requires the government to prove forfeiture by "a preponderance of the evidence." The new burden of proof has generally not been found to apply retroactively to cases begun before, but pending on, Aug. 23, 2000. *U.S. v. One "Piper" Aztec "F" De Luxe Model 250 PA 23 Aircraft Bearing Serial, No. 27-7654057,* 321 F.3d 355 (3d Cir. 2003); *U.S. v. Miscellaneous Firearms, Explosives,* 399 F.Supp.2d 881 (C.D. Ill. 2005), *but see U.S. v. Real Property in Section 9,* 241 F.3d 796 (6th Cir. 2001). The government's procedures in administrative forfeitures have been found to violate the Fourth Amendment and the Fifth Amendment due process guarantees. *Gete v. INS*, 121 F.3d 1285 (9th Cir. 1997).

8.c. *Innocent Owner Defense*—The innocent owner defense, although eliminated in the statute, may not be eliminated as a constitutional matter. *Calero-Toledo v. Pearson Yacht Leasing Co.*, 416 U.S. 663 (1974). *See U.S. v. One 1983 Homemade Vessel Named Barracuda*, 858 F.2d 643 (11th Cir. 1988) [innocent owner requires proof that owner did everything he could to avoid unlawful use of property]; *U.S. v. Four Million, Two Hundred Fifty-Five Thousand Dollars in U.S. Currency*, 762 F.2d 895, 905–06 (11th Cir. 1985), *cert. denied*, 474 U.S. 1056 (1986) [defense turns on owner's actual, rather than constructive, knowledge]; *U.S. v. One 1985 Ford F-250 Pickup, supra* [innocent owner defense possible where vehicle is stolen or wrongfully possessed or owner did all that reasonably could be done to prevent illegal use]. Cannot rely on compliance with employer sanctions (verification) provisions as a basis to assert innocent owner defense. *U.S. v. One 1985 Ford F-250 Pickup, supra* at 1312. Lienholder's interest in automobile may not be sufficient to have standing to assert innocent owner defense. *U.S. v. One 1982 Oldsmobile Cutlass*, 709 F.Supp. 1542 (W.D. Okla. 1989). Although hearsay may be admissible in forfeiture proceedings, it is not admissible to rebut or establish the innocent owner defense. *U.S. v. All Monies ($477,048.62) in Acc't No. 90-3617-3, Israel Discount Bank*, 754 F.Supp. 1467, 1471 (D. Hawaii 1991).

8.d. *Unconstitutional Delay As a Defense*—Another defense to forfeiture may be the delay in the initiation of post-seizure forfeiture proceedings. Such delay may be unconstitutional as a violation of due process. *U.S. v. Eight Thousand Eight Hundred and Fifty Dollars in U.S. Currency*, 461 U.S. 555 (1983) [relying on criteria in *Barker v. Wingo*, 407 U.S. 514 (1972) to determine whether delay constitutional]; *Gonzalez v. Rivkind*, 858 F.2d 657 (11th Cir. 1988) [following *U.S. v. Eight Thousand Eight Hundred and Fifty Dollars* and *U.S. v. Von Neumann*, 474 U.S. 242 (1986) reversed lower court's requirement mandating a post-seizure hearing in all cases within 72 hours as too rigid because interested parties did have an opportunity to challenge government's seizure]. Delay in proceeding may also work against the claimant because if s/he failed to bring action timely, s/he may be barred by the doctrine of laches. *Little v. U.S.,* 35 F.Supp.2d 538 (E.D. Mich. 1999).

8.e. *Other Defenses*—Other defenses to forfeiture include: (1) duress, *U.S. v. One Lear Jet Aircraft*, 617 F.Supp. 769, 775–76 (S.D. Fla. 1985); (2) that the property was used as a common carrier; (3) that the property was taken in violation of the criminal laws by the perpetrator; (4) that the evidence used to form the basis for the forfeiture was in violation of the Fourth Amendment. *Vance v. U.S.*, 676 F.2d 183 (5th Cir. 1982); *U.S. v. $144,600 in U.S. Currency*, 757 F.Supp. 1342, 1345 (M.D. Fla. 1991); (5) no "substantial connection" between the property and the criminal activity in question. *U.S. v. One Hundred Thirty-Four Thousand, Seven Hundred and Fifty-Two Dollars ($134,752)*, 706 F.Supp. 1075 (S.D.N.Y. 1989); (6) the failure to inform a noncitizen who is interrogated during a seizure of her right to communicate with her embassy or consulate under Article 36 of the Vienna Convention on Consular Relations. *Jogi v. Voges,* 480 F.3d 822 (7th Cir. 2007) [allowed noncitizen convicted of aggravated battery and deported to bring civil rights claim for failure of state officials to notify him of the right to consular assistance under Article 36(1)(b)]. *But see Sanchez-Llamas v. Oregon,* 548 U.S. 331 (2006) [in criminal proceeding suppression is not an appropriate remedy for an Article 36 violation and regular state rules of procedural default apply to bar Article 36 claims]; *Medellin v. Texas,* 128 S.Ct. 1346 (2008) [the International Court of Justice *Avena* decision (*Case Concerning Avena and Other Mexican Nationals* (*Mex. v. U.S.*), 2004 I.C.J. 12 finding the U.S. had violated Article 36(1)(b) of the Convention was *not enforceable* in a state court to preempt state limitations on filing successive habeas petitions, notwithstanding the President's Memorandum directing enforcement, because the decision was not "self-executing" and the remedy under the Treaty is referral to the U.N. Security Council].

8.f. *Res Taken Out of Jurisdiction.* Jurisdiction over forfeiture does not cease where *res* taken out of jurisdiction while case on appeal. *Republic National Bank of Miami v. U.S.*, 506 U.S. 80 (1992). The government, however, may initially raise lack of jurisdiction on standing grounds to assert a claim either because claimant lacks an interest in the property, *U.S. v. One Parcel of Real Property*, 682 F.Supp. 694 (D.R.I. 1988).

8.g. *Fugitive Disentitlement Doctrine*—The fugitive from justice doctrine does not bar, *per se,* a party who is a fugitive from criminal proceedings from litigating a civil *in rem* forfeiture proceeding that is related to the criminal proceeding. *Degen v. U.S.,* 517 U.S. 820 (1996). Post-*Degen*, Congress under CAFRA, has now given the district judge authority to enforce the fugitive disentitlement doctrine under certain conditions. 28 U.S.C. §2466; *U.S. v. One 1988 Chevrolet Cheyenne Half-Ton Pickup Truck*, 357 F.Supp.2d 1321 (S.D. Ala. 2005) [where district court would not previously order DHS and DOS to allow claimant back into the U.S., the disentitlement doctrine applied where claimant was subsequently indicted]

8.h. Litigation may be initiated for the return of property under 28 U.S.C. §1331 and a claimant has a right to trial by jury where property seized on land. *U.S. v. One 1976 Mercedes Benz 280S*, 618 F.2d 453, 459 (7th Cir. 1980). A claimant also has a right to initiate a collateral due process attack on an administrative forfeiture where no notice was received. *U.S. v. Giraldo*, 45 F.3d 509 (1st Cir. 1995).

8.i. *Eight Amendment Applies For Excessive Fines*—Excessive nature of the forfeiture may be litigated. *Austin v. U.S.*, 509 U.S. 602 (1993). In *Austin*, the court determined that the Eighth Amendment's "excessive fine" language applied to civil forfeiture proceedings. *See also U.S. v. Bajakajian,* 524 U.S. 321 (1998) [forfeiture of full amount of money sought to be transported out of the country ($357,144) was excessive fine under Eight Amendment, where action was based on *in personam* jurisdiction arising from criminal statute]; *U.S. v. One Single Family Residence*, 13 F.3d 1493 (11th Cir. 1994).

8.j. *Attorney's Fees*—Attorney's fees are recoverable by the claimant "in any civil proceeding to forfeit property ... in which the claimant substantially prevails." 28 U.S.C. §2465 (b)(1). Fees are not limited to the statutory hourly cap set under EAJA. *U.S. v. $60,201.00 in U.S. Currency,* 291 F.Supp.2d 1126, 1129–30 (C.D. Cal. 2003) [granting prevailing market hourly rates of $300 and $225 per hour]. Prior to the Civil Asset Forfeiture Reform Act of 2000, which now provides for attorneys' fees, a claimant could recover fees under the Equal Access to Justice Act, where government's forfeiture was not substantially justified. *U.S. v. Marolf,* 277 F.3d 1156 (9th Cir. 2002) [administrative forfeiture without notice, argument that claimant's motion was barred by laches, and record as a whole demonstrated government lacked substantial justification]; *U.S. v. One 1984 Ford Van*, 873 F.2d 1281 (9th Cir. 1989) [government not substantially justified where they seized van even though the transportation of the alien was not in furtherance of illegal status]; *U.S. v. One 48 Foot White Colored Sailboat Named Libertine,* 59 F.Supp.2d 362, 365–66 (D.P.R. 1999) [government had no legal justification for forfeiture because persons presented themselves at port of entry]; *U.S. v. Eleven Vehicles*, 966 F.Supp. 361 (E.D. Pa. 1997) [even if government had probable cause to seize vehicle they were not substantially justified in defending forfeiture]; *U.S. v. One 1984 Chevrolet Truck*, 701 F.Supp. 213 (N.D. Ga. 1988); *Doe v. U.S.*, 16 Cl. Ct. 412 (Ct. Cl. 1989) [informer of immigration violations concerning Lear Jet granted fees under EAJA]; WSB ¶18,677a.16. *See also U.S. v. Certain Real Property at 2323 Charms Rd.*, 728 F.Supp. 1326 (E.D. Mich. 1990) [in drug related seizure magistrate's issuance of seizure warrant does not make government position substantially justified under EAJA]. *But see U.S. v. B&M Used Cars*, 860 F.2d 121 (4th Cir. 1988).

D. ***Aiding or Assisting Inadmissible Persons to Enter***—INA §277, 8 U.S.C. §1327. Any person is subject to a potential 10-year sentence for knowingly aiding or assisting a person to enter the U.S., if that person is inadmissible on criminal or security grounds. Knowing that the inadmissible person has a prior felony conviction is not an element of the crime that the U.S. must prove. *U.S. v. Flores-Garcia,* 198 F.3d 1119 (9th Cir. 2000) [the government need only prove that the defendant knew the person was inadmissible].

E. ***Marriage Fraud***—INA §275(c), 8 U.S.C. §1325(c). Imprisonment for up to 5 years and $250,000 fine. To convict a person under this statute the government generally must prove: (1) the person knowingly entered into a marriage; (2) the marriage was entered into for the purpose of evading a provision of the immigration laws; and (3) the person knew or had reason to know of the immigration laws. *U.S. v. Islam,* 418 F.3d 1125, 1128 (10th Cir. 2005) [upheld conviction on grounds a reasonable jury could have found that marriage was entered into to evade immigration laws and that defendant knew he was violating the immigration laws]; *U.S. v. Darif,* 446 F.3d 701, 709–11 (7th Cir. 2006) [government does not have to establish that parties did not intend to have a life together because defendant could have intended to establish a life together with the USC but still enter the marriage for purposes of evading the immigration laws]; *U.S. v. Vickerage*, 921 F.2d 143 (8th Cir. 1990) [upheld conviction where parties knew each other, had sex before and after marriage, but marriage was one of convenience]. *But see U.S. v. Orellana-Blanco,* 294 F.3d 1143, 1148–52 (9th Cir. 2002) [reversed conviction because admission of defendant's statement to INS was improper and the effect was prejudicial; in regard to conflicting evidence between husband and wife, the court found that: "An intent to obtain something other than or in addition to love and companionship from that life does not make a marriage a sham"]. However, it does not require that the government prove that the defendant knew of the specific immigration statute violated. *U.S. v. Chowdhury,* 169 F.3d 402, 406–07 (6th Cir. 1999) [relying on decision on willful conduct in *Bryan v. U.S.* 524 U.S. 184 (1998)]. Can also be charged with conspiracy to defraud the government by aiding and abetting others to enter into fraudulent marriages. *U.S. v. Anwar,* 428 F.3d 1102 (8th Cir. 2005) [defendant solicited female acquaintances to marry Pakistani men to allow the men to evade immigration laws].

F. *Fraudulent Documents for Entry/False Statements*—18 U.S.C. §1546(a)

1. Marriage Fraud—Marriage fraud charge possible where alien falsely stated (on I-485/I-130) that he and wife were living together. *U.S. v. Al-Kurna*, 808 F.2d 1072 (5th Cir. 1987); *U.S. v. Bartle*, 835 F.2d 646 (6th Cir.), *cert. denied*, 108 S.Ct. 1245 (1989); *U.S. v. Silien*, 825 F.2d 320 (11th Cir. 1987) [court rejected selective prosecution claim based on failure to prosecute USC spouses]. *But see U.S. v. Qaisi*, 779 F.2d 346 (6th Cir. 1985) [not material fact that parties not living together because separation not test]. To obtain conviction applicants have to make false statement under oath. *U.S. v. Chu*, 5 F.3d 1244 (9th Cir. 1993); the statement has to be made in an application, affidavit, or other documents required by immigration laws or regulations; and the defendant has to make the statement knowing it was false. And the statement must be a materially false statement *U.S. v. Kone,* 307 F.3d 430, 434–36 (6th Cir. 2002) [applying the *Kungys* materiality standard in arranged marriage cases]. There is some confusion among the circuit courts as to the significance of a marriage that is valid under state law even if it was entered into for a fraudulent purpose. *Compare U.S. v. Elzahabi,* 517 F.Supp.2d 1121 (D. Minn. 2007) [the formal validity of a marriage is not a defense to knowingly procuring a "green card" by means of any false claim or statement or otherwise procuring it by fraud] *with U.S. v. Diogo,* 320 F.2d 898 (2d Cir. 1963) [the technical validity of the marriage was a defense to both a charge under 18 U.S.C. §§1546 and §1001].

2. Fraudulent Documents Used for Entry—This section of the statute only applies to "documents whose primary *raison d'être* is the facilitation of entry into the country." *U.S. v. Campos-Serrano*, 404 U.S. 293, 299 (1971). A prior version of the statute did not permit a conviction for possession of a fraudulent passport from a nonexistent country. *U.S. v. Fox*, 766 F.Supp. 569 (N.D. Tex. 1991); *U.S. v. Vargas*, 380 F.Supp. 1162 (E.D.N.Y. 1974). The amended statute in 1986 provides for a conviction for someone found to possess a foreign counterfeit passport. *U.S. v. Rahman,* 189 F.3d 88, 118–19 (2d Cir. 1999) [distinguished *Vargas, Fox* and *Campos-Serrano* as pre-1986 Act cases and noted that the 1986 amendment to §1546 eliminated the language that a document must be "required" for entry and replaced it with language making it illegal to possess a fraudulent document that is "prescribed by statute or regulation" for entry] *U.S. v. Osiemi*, 980 F.2d 344 (5th Cir. 1993) [same in regard to fraudulent passport even where it did not contain a visa]. It may also include predicate documents such as labor certifications and I-140s. *U.S. v. Ryan-Webster,* 353 F.3d 353 (4th Cir. 2003) [upheld conviction for fraudulent drafting of ETA-750s and I-140s by lawyer]. Use of rubber stamp does not constitute "impression" for purpose of statute. *U.S. v. Naaman*, 813 F.2d 1577 (9th Cir. 1987). However, a person may not be convicted under paragraph one of §1546(a) unless the defendant not only procured a "green card" by fraud but that s/he possessed a fraudulent (forged, counterfeited, altered or falsely made) alien registration card. *U.S. v. Krstic,* 528 F.Supp.2d 1245 (D. Or. 2007) [court dismissed indictment for failure to alleged that alien card was fraudulent]. A person may be convicted under this statute for aiding and abetting even if the actual NIV or IV applicant lacked criminal intent. *U.S. v. West Indies Transport, Inc.*, 127 F.3d 299, 306–07 (3d Cir. 1997) [employer liable for aiding workers to obtain D-1s where they were working dry-dock and workers did not have criminal intent]. Because unlawful entry in a fraudulent document case is not an element of the crime, submission of evidence of unlawful entry may be excluded as prejudicial. *U.S. v. Amaya-Manzanares,* 377 F.3d 39, 45–46 (1st Cir. 2004) [reversed conviction in possession of fraudulent green card case where judge allowed relevant but prejudicial evidence by government that defendant made an unlawful entry].

2.a. Asylum Defense. Prosecuting a refugee for false documents may not be in violation of the UN Convention and Protocol Relating to the Status of Refugees. *U.S. v. Malenge,* 472 F.Supp.2d 269 (N.D.N.Y. 2007) [where defendant did not seek asylum at border and did not disclose that false passport was used to flee the Republic of the Congo, court declined to dismiss indictment as violation of the Refugee Convention]; *U.S. v. Barry,* 500 F.Supp.2d 125 (N.D.N.Y. 2007) [where defendant presented false passport at border and after being detained stated she was trying to get to U.S. to flee persecution, it did not violate the Convention and Protocol to prosecute her] .

3. False Statements on Application Submitted to DHS—The section requires that a defendant knowingly make a false material statement under oath in an application required by DHS statutes or regulations. *U.S. v. O'Connor,* 158 F.Supp.2d 697, 720–21 (E.D. Va. 2001) [fraud in applications for investors under the EB-5 program]. *See also U.S. v. Katkhordeh,* 477 F.3d 624 (8th Cir. 2007) [evidence of marriage in Iran sufficient to uphold conviction for fraud in visa application under second preference as unmarried son].

4. Materiality—At least one court has found that materiality must be judged based upon the entire immigration process and not one single document. *U.S. v. Wu,* 419 F.3d 142 (2d Cir. 2005) [where I-864 contained false statements that were not material, government can still convict by showing that I-864 was part of the larger process of falsely petitioning, though the use of an I-130 petition, for relatives].

5. Scope—Section 1546(a) covers not only false statements, but also the presentation of a document that "fails to contain any reasonable basis in law or fact." IIRIRA §214.

6. Includes All Fraudulent Immigration-Related Documents—Statute also includes knowingly accepting and receiving counterfeit immigration documents as evidence of employment authorization. *U.S. v. DeCruz*, 82 F.3d 856 (9th Cir. 1996). *See also U.S. v. Uvalle-Patricio,* 478 F.3d 699 (5th Cir. 2007) [statute includes the possession of blank I-551 permits even if they were fraudulent]. A person may be convicted under a deliberate indifference standard. *U.S. v. DeCruz*, 82 F.3d at 865–66. Willfulness is not required. *U.S. v. Polar*, 369 F.3d 1248, 1252–55 (11th Cir. 2004).

7. Penalties—The penalty for violation of §1546(a) is up to 25 years if committed to facilitate international terrorism; up to 20 years if committed to facilitate drug trafficking; up to 15 years if more than the second offense; and up to 10 years if first or second offense.

G. *Identification Document Fraud*—18 U.S.C. §1546(b). Whoever uses an identification document knowing that the document was not issued lawfully or is false or whoever submits a false attestation for purposes of satisfying the requirements for I-9/employer verification purposes is guilty of violating this subsection. A Social Security card in the view of one court is not an identification document for purposes of this section. *U.S. v. Tyson Foods, Inc.*, 258 F.Supp.2d 809, 812–19 (E.D. Tenn. 2003). At least one court has allowed the use of information from a spouse who battered the alien to obtain a conviction for a false I-9. *U.S. v. Maswai,* 419 F.3d 822 (8th Cir. 2005) [court rejected argument that 8 U.S.C. §1367, prohibiting the use of information about a battered spouse in removal proceedings applied to a criminal action under 18 U.S.C. §1546]. Penalties for violating §1546(b) include fine and imprisonment for not more than 5 years.

H. *Fraud and Related Activity in Connection with Identification Documents*—18 U.S.C. §1028. Includes knowingly and without lawful authority producing, transferring, possessing or possessing with intent to use an identification document or false identification document which appears to be issued by or under the authority of the U.S., a state, foreign government or international governmental or generic governmental organization. 18 U.S.C. §1028(b). Penalty may be up to 15 years or up to 20 if used to facilitate drug crime and up to 30 if used to facilitate terrorism. To obtain a conviction under the statute for possession there must be "a sufficient connection between the defendant and the contraband to support the inference that the defendant exercised dominion and control over the substance." *U.S. v. Barajas-Montiel,* 185 F.3d 947, 955–56 (9th Cir. 1999) [reversed conviction where documents found in vase in defendant's bedroom that was also used and occupied by other persons]. The statute also provides for possession of the identification of another during and in relation to a violation of 8 U.S.C. §1326 regarding entering or found in the U.S. 18 U.S.C. §1028A. *U.S. v. Crounsset,* 403 F.Supp.2d 475 (E.D. Va. 2005) [upheld conviction for using another person's alien registration number to illegally re-enter].

I. ***Knowing and Willful Use of a False Passport.*** 18 U.S.C. §1543. This section permits the prosecution of a person carrying a false passport from any country, not just the United States. *U.S. v. Dangdee,* 616 F.2d 1118, 1119 (9th Cir. 1980); *U.S. v. Simo,* 68 F.Supp.2d 706 (E.D. Va. 1999) [and cases cited therein]. Political asylum is not a duress defense unless defendant can show s/he had no legal alternative. *Simon, supra.*

J. ***Knowing and Willful False Statement to Obtain U.S. Passport***—18 U.S.C. §1542. Includes securing a passport through a false statement and making a false statement in an application for a passport. *U.S. v. Connors,* 441 F.3d 527, 531 (7th Cir. 2006) [upheld conviction where defendant's passport was confiscated at U.S.-Canadian border by customs officers and he applied for a new one stating his previous passport was "missing"]; *U.S. v. Suarez-Rosario,* 237 F.3d 1164 (9th Cir. 2001) [government did not have to prove real identity of defendant but only that he used a false statement to obtain a passport]. At least one court has found that the statute covers false statements made in accompanying documents. *U.S. v. Baum,* 380 F.Supp.2d 187, 204 (S.D.N.Y. 2005) [forgery of ex-husband's signature on accompanying letter for child's passport is part of passport application by virtue of 22 C.F.R. §51.20].

K. ***Destruction of Official Documents***—18 U.S.C. §2071(a). Willfully and unlawfully destroying or causing another person to destroy or attempt to destroy any record, paper document or other thing filed or deposited in a public office of with any public officer of the United States. *U.S. v. Salazar,* 455 F.3d 1022 (9th Cir. 2006) [upheld conviction of contract supervisor at California Service Center who directed others to shred thousands of documents that were scheduled to be interfiled in A files].

L. ***False Statements.*** 18 U.S.C. §1001. Any false or fraudulent misrepresentation regarding the actual purpose of a marriage in order to gain status may violate 18 U.S.C. §1001. *U.S. v. Zalman*, 870 F.2d 1047, 1055 (6th Cir. 1989). This includes an exculpatory denial during the course of questioning. *Brogan v. U.S.*, 522 U.S. 398 (1998) [rejected exculpatory no doctrine]. False ID at U.S. border is punishable under 18 U.S.C. §1001. *U.S. v. Popaw*, 821 F.2d 483 (8th Cir. 1987). Aiding and abetting in a false statement to a DHS officer that is material in the course of an investigation is a violation of §1001. *U.S. v. Mitchell,* 388 F.3d 1139 (8th Cir. 2004) [where person aided alien who was smuggled into U.S. for sex but who falsely said she was raped]. However, cannot convict where statement is not literally false. *U.S. v. Moses*, 94 F.3d 182, 188 (5th Cir. 1996).

M. ***Failure to Disclose Role as Document Preparer.*** It is a crime punishable by up to 5 years in prison to knowingly and willfully fail to disclose, conceal, or cover up the fact that a person has prepared or assisted in the preparation of a falsely made application for immigration benefits for a fee or other remuneration. INA §274C(e), 8 U.S.C. §1324c(e).

N. ***Aggravated Identity Theft in Conjunction with Immigration Crimes***—A person who uses the identification number of another person during the commission of various felonies including failure to depart, failure to register, false documents, or alien smuggling will receive an enhanced consecutive and mandatory penalty of 2 years, and, if related to terrorism, 5 years. 18 U.S.C. §1028A.

O. ***False Claim to U.S. Citizenship***—A person who "falsely and willfully represents himself to be a citizen of the United States" shall be fined or imprisoned. 18 U.S.C. §911. The 3 elements of the crime are a false claim, a willful misrepresentation, and a misrepresentation to someone with good reason to inquire into the defendant's citizenship. *U.S. v. Romero-Avila,* 210 F.3d 1017 (9th Cir. 2000) [rejecting the defense that the exact identity of the person lied to is an element of the offense]. To establish a willful violation the government must prove that the defendant acted with knowledge that his conduct was unlawful. *U.S. v. Ramirez,* 495 F.Supp.2d 92, 118–20 (D. Me. 2007) [quoting *Bryan v. United States* and finding that Cuban national willfully made a false claim to citizenship when purchasing a firearm]. But a person may not be convicted under §911 for a false claim to U.S. *nationality*. *U.S. v. Karaouni,* 379 F.3d 1139 (9th Cir. 2004) [where defendant checked off I-9 box that stated he was a citizen *or* national of the U.S., he could not be convicted under §911 that makes it a crime only to make a false claim to citizenship]. A knowingly false statement or claim that a person is or at any time has been a citizen or national of the U.S. with the intent to obtain for himself or another a federal or state benefit or the right to vote is also a crime. 18 U.S.C. §1015(e)–(f). Also, it is a crime to knowingly make any false statement under oath, in any case, proceeding, or matter relating to any law regarding naturalization, citizenship or registry of aliens. 8 U.S.C. §1015(a). This statute, in the view of one circuit, does not require materiality. *U.S. v. Abuagla,* 326 F.3d 277 (4th Cir. 2003). The Eleventh Circuit has held there is no "exculpatory no" defense in 18 U.S.C. §1001 cases to false claims of U.S.

citizenship. *U.S. v. Lopez-Iraeta*, 129 F.3d 1206 (11th Cir. 1997) [rejecting defense that person merely answering question during interrogation rather than affirmatively misrepresenting his citizenship]. *See also Brogan v. U.S.*, 522 U.S. 398 (1998) [rejecting exculpatory no doctrine in §1001 cases]. The statute has also withstood an over breadth attack under the First Amendment. *U.S. v. Esparza-Ponce,* 193 F.3d 1133, 1137–38 (9th Cir. 1999). In cases arising under 18 U.S.C. §1015(f) a defendant may not be charged if his or her: (1) parents were or are USCs; (2) the person permanently resided in the U.S. prior to 16; and (3) the person reasonably believed at the time of such violation that he or she was a USC. The exception is applied retroactively as if included in IIRIRA and applies to any person prosecuted on or after Sept. 30, 1996, as long as criminal proceedings were not concluded by Oct. 30, 2000.

P. ***Voting in Federal Election***—18 U.S.C. §611. It is unlawful for an alien to vote in a federal election. This section does not apply if the defendant's: (1) parents were or are USCs; (2) the person permanently resided in the U.S. prior to 16; and (3) the person reasonably believed at the time of voting that s/he was a USC. The exception is applied retroactively as if included in IIRIRA and applies to persons prosecuted on or after Sept. 30, 1996, unless criminal proceedings were concluded before Oct. 30, 2000. At least one circuit has found that the appropriate *mens rea* for conviction is "general intent" to engage in the prohibited conduct and not specific intent. *U.S. v. Knight,* 490 F.3d 1268 (11th Cir. 2007)

Q. ***Employer Sanctions***—INA §274A, 8 U.S.C. §1324a. IRCA makes it unlawful to "knowingly" hire, recruit, or refer for a fee an alien not authorized to be employed. Employees in employment before Nov. 7, 1986, are grandfathered. Civil penalties for first, second, and third offenses; criminal penalties for pattern or practice violations. There is also a criminal penalty for hiring 10 or more aliens in a 12-month period knowing they are not authorized to work *and* that they entered the U.S. in violation of INA §274; *U.S. v. Calhelha,* 456 F.Supp.2d 350, 363 (D. Conn. 2006) [facts sufficient to allege pattern and practice for person who arranged employees from Portugal to work at franchise stores]. Civil fines can be imposed for failure to complete and retain verification forms. *See* Ch. 12, ¶ VIII.A.3 (p.1261), *infra*.

R. ***Failure to Depart After Deportation Order***—INA §243, 8 U.S.C. §1253. Willful failure to depart U.S. within 90 days of final deportation order or to present oneself pursuant to bag and baggage letter is a felony punishable up to 4 years (or 10 years if person is deportable under the smuggling, criminal offense, security, or failure to register/falsification of documents ground) *U.S. v. Ayeni,* 66 F.Supp.2d 617 (M.D. Pa. 1999) [a collateral attack on the deportation order is permissible notwithstanding INA §242(a)(2)(C) in light of INA §242(b)(7), but counsel's failure to submit brief and to notify client of deportation order does not render deportation violative of due process]. The court may suspend the sentence based on criteria under the statute. One section includes conspiracy (with others, presumably an attorney) to take any action to prevent the person's departure. 8 U.S.C. §1253(a)(1)(C). If the validity of a removal order has not previously been decided, a person charged with a crime under §1253 may challenge the removal order by filing a motion before trial with the court. INA §242(b)(7)(A), 8 U.S.C. §1252(b)(7)(A). One court has recognized a necessity defense, where person denied asylum, but is afraid to return to his home country. *U.S. v. Kpomassie,* 323 F.Supp.2d 894 (W.D. Tenn. 2004) [person ordered deported who willfully resisted physical deportation may have a necessity defense that he fears return to his country despite his unsuccessful claim for asylum because the removal proceeding and the criminal proceeding are separate].

S. ***Willful Failure to Comply with Terms of Release Order***—INA §243(b), 8 U.S.C. §1253(b). When a person is released pursuant to INA §241(a)(3), 8 U.S.C. §1231(a)(3), and willfully fails to comply with regulations and requirements under the section, or knowingly gives false information in response to an inquiry under the section, s/he may be imprisoned not more than one year and fined not more than $1,000. *U.S. v. Nguyen,* 465 F.3d 1128, 1130–31 (9th Cir. 2006) [where supervised release order required respondent not "commit any crimes," his *nolo contendere* pleas were insufficient to establish guilt].

T. ***Amnesty and SAW Fraud***—Under INA §§210(b)(7)(A), 245A(c)(6), 8 U.S.C. §§1160(b)(7)(A), 1255a(c)(6), the filing of false applications or the creating of false documents for amnesty or SAW applicants is a criminal offense. *U.S. v. Sanchez*, 927 F.2d 376 (8th Cir. 1991).

U. ***Escape from Removal***—An escape from the custody of U.S. officers where there was a lawful arrest for removal proceedings is punishable by a $1,000 fine or one year imprisonment. 18 U.S.C. §751(a). The elements of the offense are that the defendant: (1) was confined in the detention facility at the direction of the AG; (2) for removal proceedings; and (3) escaped from confinement. *U.S. v. Rodriguez-Fernandez,* 234 F.3d 498 (11th Cir. 2000) [reversed conviction of person detained at Krome where there was no order, directive or document from the AG or her representative directing the detention, and the only evidence was testimony from an INS officer that, after review of the file, he determined detention]. The defense of fraud and duress has been successfully employed where the person established he would be persecuted if returned to his country. *U.S. v. Dagnachew*, 808 F.Supp. 1517 (D. Colo. 1992) [when Ethiopian who was denied asylum escaped from detention court acquitted him on grounds of duress, because he escaped INS detention to avoid persecution].

V. ***EWI / Attempt to Enter***—INA §275(a), 8 U.S.C. §1325(a)

1. Improper entry at time or place other than designated port of entry. Cannot collaterally attack validity of a summary exclusion order in this proceeding.
2. A conviction requires an entry under traditional standards. *U.S. v. Gonzalez-Torres*, 309 F.3d 594, 597–99 (9th Cir. 2002) [where defendant was under observation before crossing the Mexican border his conviction was reversed because he had not made an entry].
3. Civil penalty where apprehended for entering or attempting to enter ($50–$250).

W. ***High Speed Flight from Immigration Checkpoint***—18 U.S.C. §758. Fleeing or evading a checkpoint in a motor vehicle above speed limit.

X. ***Failure to Maintain a Green Card***—It is a criminal misdemeanor under 8 U.S.C. §1304(e) for an LPR to fail to keep his green card with him at all times.

Y. ***Aliens in Possession of a Firearm***—Under 18 U.S.C. §922(g)(5)(A), it is illegal for "an alien ... illegally or unlawfully in U.S." to possess a firearm. *U.S. v. Mendez,* 514 F.3d 1035, 1042–43 (10th Cir. 2008) [evidence was sufficient to find that defendant was illegal where he was born in Mexico, provided officers with a false Social Security number, and the government had no evidence of valid authorization to enter the country]. In order to prove a violation, the government must establish that the defendant was an "alien," that he was unlawfully in U.S., and that he knowingly possessed a firearm and ammunition in or affecting interstate commerce. *U.S. v. Diaz,* 519 F.3d 56, 66 (1st Cir. 2008) [knowing possession may be by either actual or constructive possession and alienage and unlawful status may be established by DHS records including warrants and orders of removal even if they may be established by a standard lower than beyond a reasonable doubt]. The type of ammunition or weapon possessed may be irrelevant. *See e.g., U.S. v. Guidry,* 406 F.3d 314, 322 (5th Cir. 2005) [type of weapon not an essential element of the crime]; *U.S. v. Levy,* 440 F.Supp.2d 162, 164 (E.D.N.Y. 2006) [type of ammunition not essential]. The law has been expanded to include nonimmigrants except in certain circumstances. 18 U.S.C. §922(g)(5)(B). NIV holders in certain circumstances are prohibited from possessing and/or transferring firearms and ammunition without a waiver under ATF regulations. 27 C.F.R. pt. 478. *U.S. v. Bazargan*, 992 F.2d 844 (8th Cir. 1993) [F-1 student who did not properly transfer schools under INS procedures convicted]; *But see U.S. v. Atandi,* 228 F.Supp.2d 1285 (D. Utah 2002) [although IJ made a finding of deportability regarding student who was out of status but did not enter final order of deportation because the student had relief in the form of AOS, the student was not illegally or unlawfully in the U.S. and district court dismissed indictment]. A person on bond during removal proceeding is still in illegal or unlawful status for purposes of §922(g)(5). *U.S. v. Bavo-Muzquiz.* 412 F.3d 1052 (9th Cir. 2005). And persons who are EWI without parole status are prohibited from possessing weapons under ATF regulations. 27 C.F.R. §478.11. So are applicants for TPS, *U.S. v. Flores,* 404 F.3d 320 (5th Cir. 2005) [a person who *applies* for TPS who entered the U.S. illegally may be charged criminally as an alien illegally or unlawfully in the U.S. in possession of a firearm in violation of 18 U.S.C. §922(g)(5)(A)] or adjustment applicants for LIFE, *U.S. v. Lucio,* 428 F.3d 519 (5th Cir. 2005) [adjustment of status applicant for LIFE with employment authorization convicted under 18 U.S.C. §922 (g)(5)(A)] on the theory that the status does not constitute lawful presence. However, a person *granted* TPS is not an illegal alien or unlawfully in U.S. for purposes of §922(g)(5)(A). *U.S. v. Orellana,* 405 F.3d 360 (5th Cir. 2005) [applying rule of lenity given the ambiguity of §922(g)(5)(A) and the questionable interpretation of the ATF regulation, Congress did not intend to criminalize the possession of firearms by persons granted TPS]. A defendant cannot be charged both under subsection (A) (illegally in US) and (B) (entered on NIV) because double jeopardy and the statute's construction prohibits double punishment for the same set of facts.*U.S. v. Elrawy,* 448 F.3d 309 (5th Cir. 2006).

Z. *Social Security Fraud*—42 U.S.C. §408(a)(7)(B). Imprisonment up to 5 years for the use of another person's Social Security number.

AA. *Withholding Documents to Further Trafficking in Persons*—18 U.S.C. §1592. Knowingly destroying, concealing, removing, confiscating, or possessing any actual or purported passport or other immigration document or government identification document to prevent or restrict a person's liberty, without lawful authority, in order to maintain the person's labor or services, when the person has been the victim of a severe form of trafficking (*e.g.,* the use of force, fraud, or coercion for sex trafficking and/or involuntary servitude, peonage, debt bondage, or slavery). The penalty for conviction is up to 5 years in prison.

BB. *International Marriage Brokers*—18 U.S.C. §1375a(d)(5)(B). Where international marriage broker discloses information about persons under 18, fails to collect information regarding U.S. client who may have predatory background or violent criminal history, fails to disclose U.S. client's background to prospective international client, and/or discloses information about international client to a third party, s/he is subject to criminal penalties up to 5 years in prison.

CC. *RICO Predicate Offenses*—AEDPA §433 and IIRIRA §202 have made certain immigration-related crimes predicate RICO offenses, even if they were not committed for financial gain. 18 U.S.C. §§1028, 1542, 1543, 1544 and 1546. However, in order for immigration-related offenses (INA §§274, 277, and 278; 8 U.S.C. §§1324, 1327 and 1328) to be RICO predicated offenses, the acts must have been committed for gain. *See Commercial Cleaning Services, L.L.C. v. Colin Service Systems, Inc.,* 271 F.3d 374 (2d Cir. 2001) [cleaning service's RICO action against competitor in civil case for hiring undocumented persons and therefore violating §1324 stated cause of action].

DD. *Other Criminal-Related Issues*

1. Agreements with U.S. Attorney as Part of Plea—A developing body of law provides that a U.S. Attorney in a plea bargain may bind the U.S. government, including the DHS, in regard to deportation of a person entering a plea. *Thomas v. INS*, 35 F.3d 1332 (9th Cir. 1994) [in plea agreement U.S. Attorney's agreement that "the Government will not oppose any motion by your counsel for ... relief from deportation to ... U.S. Immigration Service" binding on INS]; *Margalli-Olvera v. INS*, 43 F.3d 345 (8th Cir. 1994) [following *Thomas* enforced plea agreement]; *Ramallo v. Reno*, 931 F.Supp. 884 (D.D.C. 1996), *vacated on jurisdictional grounds*, 114 F.3d 1210 (D.C. Cir. 1997). *But see Morgan v. Gonzales,* 495 F.3d 1084, 1091 (9th Cir. 2007) [defendant did not allege that an explicit promise was made to him by the government]; *San Pedro v. U.S.*, 79 F.3d 1065 (11th Cir. 1996). The AG has sought to resolve the split in the circuits by promulgating a regulation that says INS shall not be bound by "plea agreements, cooperation agreements, or other agreements with or for the benefit of alien defendants, witnesses or informants, or other aliens cooperating with the United States Government, except by the authorization of the Commissioner of the Service or the Commissioner's delegate." 28 C.F.R. §0.197. The regulation, however, does not reach the unresolved constitutional argument of the enforceability of a plea or the court's authority to enforce a settlement.

2. Deportation and Fugitive Status—Deported alien charged with crime who does not ask U.S. consulate for permission to re-enter U.S. is considered fugitive. *U.S. v. Forty-Five Thousand Nine Hundred and Forty Dollars ($45,940)*, 739 F.2d 792 (2d Cir. 1984). Persons in fugitive status generally are not given the right to pursue an appeal at the BIA or federal court. *Wittgenstein v. INS*, 124 F.3d 1244 (10th Cir. 1997); *Bar-Levy v. INS*, 990 F.2d 33 (2d Cir. 1993). *But see Degen v. U.S.*, 517 U.S. 820 (1996) ["Fugitive disentitlement doctrine" does not apply to forfeiture].

3. Departure of Witnesses

   3.a. Under *U.S. v. Valenzuela-Bernal*, 458 U.S. 858 (1982), the moving party must show that the eyewitness evidence that was lost by deportation of a witness "would be both material and favorable to the defense" (458 U.S. at 873), and must "affect the judgment of the trier of fact" (458 U.S. at 874). The government's facilitation of voluntary departure is equivalent to the deportation of the witness. *U.S. v. Morales-Quinones*, 812 F.2d 604 (10th Cir. 1987). Some courts have held that the moving party must show bad faith and prejudice from the government's misconduct. *U.S. v. Gastelum-Almeida,* 298 F.3d 1167, 1174 (9th Cir. 2002) [affirmed transporting and harboring case where the defendant could not show prejudice or government bad faith in removing witnesses]; *U.S. v. Chaparro-Alcantara,* 226 F.3d 616, 622–25 (7th Cir.

2000) [bad faith required particularly in light of *Arizona v. Youngblood,* 488 U.S. 51, 57–58 (1988) and language in *Valenzuela-Bernal*]; *U.S. v. Ramirez-Jimenez*, 967 F.2d 1321, 1325 (9th Cir. 1992). *But see U.S. v. Hernandez,* 347 F.Supp.2d 375, 380–81 (S.D. Tex. 2004) [where standard was unclear in Fifth Circuit and defendant demonstrated that government did not act in good faith, indictment for assaulting border patrol agent was dismissed, where material witness was removed without notifying defendant]. A party may also waive the right to protest the deportation of material witnesses. *U.S. v. Ramirez-Lopez,* 315 F.3d 1143, 1149–53 (9th Cir. 2003) [right was waived and defendant could not show prejudice to him or bad faith by the government].

3.b. The taking of material witnesses depositions in lieu of their live testimony at trial was held to violate the Sixth Amendment confrontation clause. *U.S. v. Guadian-Salazar*, 824 F.2d 344 (5th Cir. 1987). *But see U.S. v. Rivera*, 859 F.2d 1204 (4th Cir. 1988) [no Sixth Amendment violation where defense counsel had opportunity to argue against deposition testimony and then participated in depositions that were used at trial].

3.c. In alien smuggling cases under INA §274(d), 8 U.S.C. §1324(d), a videotape deposition of a witness is admissible even if the witness was deported or expelled, if the witness "was available for cross-examination" and the deposition otherwise complies with the Federal Rules of Evidence.

3.d. The government cannot routinely detain undocumented aliens who are material witnesses unless it can prove the necessity for such detention. Either party can take depositions as an alternative. *Aguilar-Ayala v. Ruiz*, 973 F.2d 411, 421; 18 U.S.C. §3144 (1980). A material witness has the right to appointed counsel. 18 U.S.C. §3006A (1986).

4. Juvenile Aliens—Federal Juvenile Delinquency Act's requirements of parental notification and prompt arraignment when juvenile charged with federal crime are applicable to alien who is a juvenile when charged with smuggling. *U.S. v. Doe*, 862 F.2d 776 (9th Cir. 1988).

5. Criminal Forfeitures—18 U.S.C. §982. Criminal forfeiture includes most statutes related to passport and visa fraud. These include 18 U.S.C. §§1028, 1425–27, 1541–44, 1546, and 8 U.S.C. §1324(a)(1) and (2). For example, where there is a conviction for visa fraud under §1546, then 18 U.S.C. §982(a)(6)(A) provides for forfeiture of: (1) any proceeds of visa fraud; (2) any property derived from or traceable to the proceeds of visa fraud, (3) any property used to facilitate the crime and (4) any conveyance used in the commission of the offense. The criminal forfeiture proceedings are governed by Section 413 of the Comprehensive Drug Abuse Prevention and Control Act of 1970 (21 U.S.C. §853) except sections (a) and (d). Any criminal forfeitures under 18 U.S.C. §982 are therefore governed by the procedures set forth in 21 U.S.C. §853. Included within these procedures is the right of the government to seek preindictment issuance of an exparte TRO to seize property upon a showing of probable cause. *Restraint of Bowman Gaskins Financial Group,* 345 F.Supp.2d 613 (E.D. Va. 2004) [preindictment seizure of money in lawyer's account and other accounts upheld]. It also includes post-conviction seizure of property, even if it was not derived from the proceeds of the fraud, where it meets the "but-for" test. *U.S. v. Ivanchukov,* 405 F.Supp.2d 708 (E.D. Va. 2005) [court ordered the post-conviction forfeiture of $100,000 where one co-conspirator provided another a $100,000 blank check, which was not determined to be proceeds of their illegal immigration scheme but would have not been given "but for" their joint involvement in the conspiracy that required hiring a lawyer].

6. Reporting Criminal Conduct—If an employee or member of the public suspects criminal conduct by a USCIS, ICE, or CBP employee, s/he may report it to the DHS Office of Inspector General by calling 1-800-323-8603 or e-mailing *dhsoighotline@dhs.gov.*

7. Sentencing—The Sentencing Reform Act of 1984, as amended, 18 U.S.C. §3551 *et seq.*, 28 U.S.C. §§991–98, made far-reaching changes in federal sentencing by restraining the broad discretion that judges traditionally had and replaced it with guidelines based on aggravating and mitigating factors. Although the Court did allow for departures of sentences in certain circumstances, *see Koon v. U.S.*, 518 U.S. 81 (1996) [recognizing that discretion remained even under mandatory guidelines where factors were not adequately taken into account under the Guidelines or where the situation was atypical], generally the Guidelines were treated as mandatory. However, the Supreme Court in *U.S. v. Booker,* 543 U.S. 220 (2005) found that its holdings in *Blakely v.*

Washington, 542 U.S. 296 (2004), and *Apprendi v. New Jersey,* 530 U.S. 466, 477 (2000), apply to the U.S. Sentencing Guidelines and that the Sixth Amendment is violated by the imposition of an enhanced sentence under the Guidelines where it is based upon a sentencing judge's determination of a fact (other than a prior conviction) that was not found by a jury or admitted by the defendant. The Court then determined that, as a remedial matter, the Guidelines could no longer be mandatory but instead advisory. The courts can now "consult" the Guidelines, "take them into account when sentencing," and utilize a "reasonableness" standard. *Booker,* 125 S.Ct. at 765–67. In determining a sentence, the courts will be guided by the statutory factors set out in 18 U.S.C. §3553(a) together with the now-advisory Guidelines. The statutory factors under 18 U.S.C. §3553(a) state that the court, in determining a sentence, shall consider: (1) the nature and circumstances of the offense and the history and characteristics of the defendant; (2) the need for the sentence imposed: (a) to reflect the seriousness of the offense, to promote respect for the law, and to provide just punishment for the offense; (b) to afford adequate deterrence; (c) to protect the public; and (d) to provide the defendant with needed educational or vocational training, medical care, or other correctional treatment in the most effective manner; (3) the kinds of sentences available; (4) the kinds of sentences and the sentencing range established under the Guidelines; (5) any pertinent policy statement issued by the Sentencing Commission; (6) the need to avoid unwarranted sentence disparities; and (7) the need to provide restitution to the victims. To determine whether a sentence is reasonable the courts will look to the record to see if the sentencing judge gave "meaningful consideration" to the factors in §3553(a) and whether the factors were "reasonably applied to the circumstances of the case." *U.S. v. Vargas,* 477 F.3d 94, 100–01 (3d Cir. 2007) [upheld 41 month sentence for illegal reentry]. *See also U.S. v. Sanchez-Ramirez,* 497 F.3d 531 (5th Cir. 2007) [where judge imposed 80-month sentence for conspiring and aiding and abetting the transportation of undocumented persons, which was above Guideline range, the circuit court found it reasonable given the judge's finding of heinous conduct toward smuggled aliens]; *U.S. v. Roche-Martinez,* 467 F.3d 591, 595 (7th Cir. 2007) [rejects defendant's claim that he should have received downward departure for his cultural assimilation]; *U.S. v. Maciel-Vasquez,* 458 F.3d 994, 995 (9th Cir. 2006) [upheld 36 month sentence for reentry post-*Booker* despite defendant's claim that court relied on guidelines and failed to state why it chose a particular sentence]; *U.S. v. Ortiz-Delgado,* 451 F.3d 752, 758 (11th Cir. 2006) [upholding on post-*Booker* reasonableness grounds a 60 month sentence for re-entry after commission of crime of violence where the range was 57 to 71 months and holding that *Booker* does not require the sentencing judge to state on the record that he considered each of the §3553(a) factors]; *U.S. v. Perez-Nunez,* 368 F.Supp.2d 1265 (D.N.M. 2005) [court reduced sentence for re-entry after the commission of the aggravated felony of Third Degree Assault under Colorado law from 57 months to 24 months after applying 18 U.S.C. §3553(a) to the determination under the guidelines]; *U.S. v. Huerta-Rodriguez,* 335 F.Supp.2d 1019, 1025 (D. Neb. 2005) [rejected the government's contention that a criminal sentence should fall within the Guidelines range absent highly unusual circumstances as an effort to reinstitute mandatory guidelines].

7.a. Sentencing Cases in the Supreme Court Defining *Post-Booker* Sentencing—Subsequent to *Booker* the Supreme Court addressed the relationship between both within- and without-Guideline sentences and the presumptive reasonableness of a sentence under the §3553(a) factors.

(1) *Within Guideline Range Post-Booker Under Rita*—In *Rita v. United States,* 127 S.Ct 2456 (2007) the Court affirmed an appellate presumption of substantive reasonableness for sentences that are properly calculated to be within the Guidelines. The Court determined that an appellate presumption of reasonableness for within-Guideline sentencing is permissible, although not required. *Rita,* 127 S.Ct. at 2462. The Court went on to discuss how extensive a statement of reasons should be provided by the district court in rendering a sentencing decision. The Court noted that a within-Guidelines sentence will not necessarily require a lengthy explanation but that there may be circumstances where the parties raise nonfrivolous reasons for imposing a different sentence and in those cases the judge needs to explain why he rejected the arguments. Finally, where the judge imposes a sentence outside of the Guidelines range he will have to explain why he did so. *Rita,* 127 S.Ct. at 2468.; *U.S. v. Angel-Guzman,* 506 F.3d 1007 (10th Cir. 2007) [explaining and adopting *Rita* but also finding that a circuit court has no jurisdiction to review a district court's discretionary decision to deny a motion for a downward departure]; *U.S. v. Perez-Perez,* 512 F.3d 514 (9th Cir. 2008) [post-*Rita* a 62 month and two-week sentence within

the Guidelines was reasonable and the district court's sufficiently considered defendant's arguments].

(2) *Below Guideline Range Post-Booker Under Gall* and *Kimbrough.*—In *Gall v. United States*, 128 S.Ct. 586 (2007) the Supreme Court addressed whether a judge granting a sentence below the Guidelines had provide extraordinary reasons for doing so. In *Gall* the Guideline range suggested 30 to 37 month prison sentence and the judge granted 36 months probation instead. The Court determined that whether a sentence is within or outside the Guidelines range, the standard remains abuse of discretion and therefore no "extraordinary" finding need be made, nor mathematical calculation be computed when deviating from the Guidelines. 128 S.Ct. at 594–96. The Court detailed a procedure for calculating an appropriate sentence. First, a sentencing court should use the Guidelines as "the starting point and the initial benchmark" 128 S.Ct. at 596. The court should then give both parties and opportunity to argue for whatever sentence they deem appropriate. The judge should then consider all of the §3553(a) factors, but it doing so "should not presume that the Guidelines range is reasonable." 128 S.Ct. at 596–97. She must them make a individualized assessment based upon the facts and if she decides an outside-Guidelines sentence is appropriate, she must consider "the extent of the deviation and ensure that the justification is sufficiently compelling to support the degree of variance." 128 S.Ct at 597. Finally, the Court found it "uncontroversial" that a major departure be supported by a more significant justification than a minor one" and that the judge must adequately explain the chosen sentence for purposes of appellate review and to promote the perception of a fair sentencing system. In reviewing a sentence the appellate court will review it for abuse of discretion which ensuring that no significant procedural errors have occurred such as failing to calculate the Guidelines properly, treating them as mandatory, failing to consider all of the §3553(a) factors, selecting a sentence based upon clearly erroneous facts, or failing to explain the basis for the sentence. If it is procedurally sound the appellate court should review if for substantive reasonableness taking into account the totality of the circumstances. If it is within the Guidelines range the appellate court "may, but is not required to, apply a presumption of reasonableness" and but if it is outside the Guidelines range, the court "may not apply a presumption of unreasonableness." 128 S.Ct. at 597.

(3) In *Kimbrough v. United States,* 128 S.Ct.558 (2007) the Court held that a sentencing judge could consider the disparity within the Guidelines between crack and powder cocaine offenses and could determine in a particular case that the within-Guidelines sentence is "greater than necessary" to sever the sentencing objectives under §3553(a).

(4) Sentencing following *Gall* and *Kimbrough—U.S. v. Gonzalez-Carballo,* 519 F.3d 1232, 1236 (10th Cir. 2008) [24 month sentence for illegal reentry was below Guideline range and judge acknowledged the range and the PSR suggestion that the range overstated the seriousness of respondent's criminal history].

7.b. Guideline Sentencing Generally—As a result of the Sentencing Commission's desire to "achieve more proportionate punishment by providing tiered sentencing enhancement based on the period of imprisonment the defendant actually served for the prior aggravated felony" 66 Fed. Reg. 7962, 8008–09 (Jan. 26, 2001), the Commission substantially altered §2L1.2 on Nov. 1, 2001, to distinguish among various offenses for purposes of sentencing enhancement. Under these guidelines a person is only subject to a 16-level upward adjustment if he was previously deported or unlawfully remained in the U.S. after: (A) a conviction for a felony that is (i) a drug trafficking offense for which the sentence imposed exceeded 13 months; (ii) a crime of violence; (iii) a firearms offense; (iv) a child pornography offense; (v) a national security or terrorism offense; (vi) a human trafficking offense; or (vii) an alien smuggling offense committed for profit.

(1) A "sentence imposed" refers only to the portion "that was not probated, suspended, deferred, or stayed." Commentary to §2L1.2 note 1(a)(iv);

(2) A "crime of violence" for purposes of the 16 level enhancement is defined as "an offense under federal, state, or local law that has as an element the use, attempted use, or threatened use of physical force against the person of another; and includes murder, man-

slaughter, kidnapping, aggravated assault, forcible sex offenses (including sexual abuse of a minor), robbery, arson, extortion, extortionate extension of credit, and burglary of a dwelling." Commentary to §2L1.2 note 1(B)(ii); *U.S. v. Ortiz-Delgado,* 451 F.3d 752, 753–57 (11th Cir. 2006) [lewd acts upon a child in violation of Cal. Penal Code §288 is a crime of violence warranting post-*Booker* consideration of a 16 level upward adjustment because sexual abuse of a minor is defined as a crime of violence under §2L1.2(b)(1)(A)(ii)];

(3) Transporting aliens within the U.S. constitutes an alien smuggling offense. *U.S. v. Solis-Campozano,* 312 F.3d 164 (5th Cir. 2002).

(4) A "drug trafficking offense" means an offense under federal, state, or local law that prohibits the manufacture, import, export, distribution, or dispensing of a controlled substance (or a counterfeit substance) or the possession of a controlled substance (or a counterfeit substance) with intent to manufacture, import, export, distribute, or dispense." Commentary to §2L1.2 note 1(B)(iii). If the sentence was 13 months or more it carries the additional penalty of a 16 level upward adjustment under USSG §211.2(b)(1)(A)(i). *U.S. v. Chavez-Diaz,* 444 F.3d 1223, 1225–27 (10th Cir. 2006) [where defendant post-*Booker* was previously sentenced in a Wyoming court to 4 to 6 years for drug trafficking crime, the fact that he was deported and never served the full sentence does not take him out of USSG §2L1.2(b)(1)(A)(i) which requires a 16 level upward adjustment where the sentence was 13 months or more]; Under the Sentencing Guidelines simple possession of a controlled substance cannot constitute a controlled substance offense under the Guidelines Manual §4B1.1(a). *Salinas v. U.S.,* 547 U.S. 188 (2006).

(5) A person is subject to a 12-level upward adjustment if he is convicted for a felony drug trafficking offense for which the sentence imposed was 13 months or less. §2L1.2(b)(1)(B).

(6) A person is subject to an 8-level upward adjustment if he is convicted for an aggravated felony. §2L1.2(b)(1)(C);

(7) An "aggravated felony" has the meaning given that term in INA §101(a)(43), without regard to the date of conviction of the aggravated felony. Commentary to §2L1.2 note 2

(8) A person is subject to a 4-level upward adjustment if he is convicted of a felony other than an aggravated felony. §2L1.2(b)(1)(D). A person is also subject to a 4-level upward adjustment if he is convicted of 3 or more misdemeanors that are COVs or drug trafficking offenses. §2L1.2(b)(1)(E).

(9) A misdemeanor means any federal, state, or local offense punishable by a term of imprisonment of one year or less. Commentary to §2L1.2 note 3(A); *U.S. v. Cordova-Arevalo,* 456 F.3d 1229 (10th Cir. 2006) [although Colorado third degree assault conviction is a misdemeanor under state law, it is a felony under the federal definition pursuant to 18 U.S.C. §3559(a) and therefore enhancement of sentence was appropriate].

7.c. Sentencing Guidelines Cases *Post-Booker*

(1) Sentencing for Transportation of Undocumented Persons—*U.S. v. Sanchez-Ramirez,* 497 F.3d 531 (5th Cir. 2007) [where judge imposed 80 month sentence which was above Guideline range, the court found it reasonable given the judge's finding of heinous conduct toward smuggled aliens]; *U.S. v. Hussein Al Nasser,* 479 F.3d 1166, 1170–72 (9th Cir. 2007) [sentence reasonable even where there was no direct evidence that defendant received funds because under 2003 guidelines it did not matter]; *U.S. v. Martinez-Vives,* 475 F.3d 48, 54–56 (1st Cir. 2007) [giving greater sentence for person who goes to trial is permissible].

(2) Sentencing for Trafficking in False Documents—Sentencing Cases for Violations of 18 U.S.C. §1546(a) [using or attempting to use forged, counterfeit or altered immigration documents]—*U.S. v. Zapete-Garcia,* 447 F.3d 57 (1st Cir. 2006) [reversed sentence where judge used previous deportation to substantially enhance sentence when Guidelines already included a two level upward adjustment for previous deportation and judge did not explain why that was insufficient]; *U.S. v. Rivera,* 516 F.3d 500 (6th Cir. 2008)

[defendant entered guilty plea under 18 U.S.C. §1028 for causing unauthorized production of Tenn. driver's licenses and successfully challenged the use of §2L2.1 because he did not traffic in immigration documents]

(3) Sentencing for Illegal Re-Entry Cases—The court looks to the reasonableness of the sentence. *U.S. v. Juarez-Duarte,* 513 F.3d 204 (5th Cir. 2007) [upheld 87 month enhanced sentence where person illegally reentered after conviction for cocaine trafficking and received sentence enhancement for obstruction of justice by requesting a translator at his sentencing when he did not need one]; *U.S. v. Perez-Perez,* 512 F.3d 514 (9th Cir. 2008) [post-*Rita* a 62 month and two-week sentence within the Guidelines was reasonable and the district court's sufficiently considered defendant's arguments]; *U.S. v. Antuna-Moran,* 488 F.3d 1048 (5th Cir. 2007) [circuit court upheld a 46 month sentence for illegal reentry where district court improperly determined that prior conviction was a crime of violence but in the alternative provided the 46 month sentence if his Guideline determination was incorrect]; *U.S. v. Gama-Gonzales,* 469 F.3d 1109 (7th Cir. 2006) [37 month sentence was modest in light of defendant's history of criminal activity and his immediate illegal return to U.S. for a third time]; *U.S. v. Valtierra-Rojas,* 468 F.3d 1235 (10th Cir. 2006) [sentence above Guideline range is not presumptively unreasonable although the greater the divergence the more compelling the reasons should be; a 60 month sentence was reasonable even though it was 30 months above Guideline range]; *U.S. v. Turbides-Leonardo,* 468 F.3d 34 (1st Cir. 2006) [48 month sentence was reasonable and was within Guidelines]; *U.S. v. Cadenas,* 445 F.3d 1091 (8th Cir. 2006) [court upheld sentence over claim that judge did not sufficiently consider political conditions in Colombia causing duress]; *U.S. v. Montes-Pineda,* 445 F.3d 375, 377–78 (4th Cir. 2006) [court upheld 46 month sentence for aggravated felon who reentered notwithstanding defendant's claims that he reentered to be with his family, his aggravated felony conviction occurred 14 years ago and he has never served a lengthy jail sentence]; *U.S. v. Trejo-Martinez,* 481 F.3d 409 (6th Cir. 2007) [forty-six month sentence and 2 years supervised release upheld on reasonableness grounds]; *U.S. v. Ortiz-Delgado,* 451 F.3d 752, 758 (11th Cir. 2006) [upholding on post-*Booker* reasonableness grounds a 60 month sentence for re-entry after commission of crime of violence where the range was 57 to 71 months and holding that *Booker* does not require the sentencing judge to state on the record that he considered each of the 18 U.S.C. §3553(a) factors]; *U.S. v. Chavez-Diaz,* 444 F.3d 1223, 1227–30 (10th Cir. 2006) [30 month sentence for illegal reentry was within guideline range and district court was correct in not granting downward departure based on bad immigration advice or ignorance of the law where defendant entered the country not at a port of entry];*U.S. v. Martinez,* 434 F.3d 1318 (11th Cir. 2006) [an 87-month sentence for re-entry found not unreasonable, where defendant has a violent criminal history, the maximum penalty is 20 years, and the sentence was within the guideline range]. The court need not state why it chose a particular sentence if it considers the appropriate factors under §3553(a). *U.S. v. Maciel-Vasquez,* 458 F.3d 994, 995 (9th Cir. 2006) [upheld 36 month sentence for reentry post-*Booker* despite defendant's claim that court relied on guidelines and failed to state why it chose a particular sentence]. A sentence within the guideline range may be supported by simply a "general statement" of the reasons for the sentence, but a sentence outside the guideline range should provide specific reasons that must be stated with specificity in a written order. *U.S. v. Ruiz-Terrazas,* 477 F.3d 1196, 1199–1203 (10th Cir. 2007). The decision in *Booker* does not prohibit a judge from sentencing a defendant beyond the guideline range. *U.S. v. Hernandez-Villanueva,* 473 F.3d 118 (4th Cir. 2007) [where defendant was sentenced to 18 months because he re-entered to continue his association with a violent gang—MS-13—the court could exceed the guideline range of 0-6months without violating *Booker*]. However, where the court seeks to enhance a sentence, it must properly apply the law. *U.S. v. Scott,* 447 F.3d 1365 (11th Cir. 2006) [court improperly applied enhancement because defendant was not "found in" the U.S. after he was under a sentence of imprisonment].

(4) Sentencing for Found-In the United States—*U.S. v. Gordon,* 513 F.3d 659, 666–67 (7th Cir. 2008) [a 96 month sentence, although 25 month above the high end of the advisory guidelines, was not unreasonable or an abuse of discretion under *Gall v. United States,*

552 U.S.___, 128 S.Ct. 586 (2007) where defendant used former "green card" to reenter, where judge believed he would again take advantage of the most vulnerable people in our society by preying on the elderly, and where the judge believed he would return again because he had nothing in Belize]. The sentencing guidelines that are applicable in "found in" cases are those at the time the person is found in the U.S. not at time of voluntary re-entry. *U.S. v. Estrada-Quijas,* 183 F.3d 758 (8th Cir. 1999) [the "found in" violation is a continuing one and a defendant is therefore subject to the definition of "aggravated felony" at the time he is discovered]; *U.S. v. Rodriguez*, 26 F.3d 4 (1st Cir. 1994) [person sentenced under "found in" provision that changed after person's re-entry but before he was found in U.S. does not violate Ex Post Facto Clause]. *U.S. v. Whitaker*, 999 F.2d 38 (2d Cir. 1993); *U.S. v. Rivera*, 942 F.Supp. 247 (E.D. Vt. 1996). *But see U.S. v. Hernandez-Gonzalez,* 495 F.3d 55 (3d Cir. 2007) [for purposes of §4A1.2(e)(2) of the Guidelines, counting the past ten years of prior sentences begins from the date defendant re-entered the U.S. and not the date he was "found in" the U.S.].

7.d. Definition of a Sentence—Under prior law, a deferred adjudication is considered a conviction pursuant to sentencing guideline §4A1.2(f) even if it would not be a conviction for immigration purposes. *U.S. v. Valdez-Valdez*, 143 F.3d 196 (5th Cir. 1998) [Texas deferred adjudication statute deemed to be a conviction for sentence enhancement purposes]; *U.S. v. Campbell,* 167 F.3d 94 (2d Cir. 1999) [same]. Indeterminate sentences are deemed to be for maximum sentence and thus meet the 5-year requirement for an aggravated felony where 5 years is required. *Matter of Jean,* 23 I&N Dec. 373, 386 n.14 (AG 2002) [indeterminate sentence deemed to be for maximum period]; *U.S. v. Galicia-Delgado*, 130 F.3d 518 (2d Cir. 1997) [30- to 90-month sentence for attempted robbery is aggravated felony even where defendant served less than five years]; *U.S. v. Quinonez-Terrazas*, 86 F.3d 382 (5th Cir. 1996) [indeterminate sentence between 4 to 6 years is aggravated felony where definition required 5-year sentencing]; *U.S. v. Deleon-Rodriguez*, 70 F.3d 764 (3d Cir. 1995) [same]. A suspended sentence is still considered a term of imprisonment in determining whether crime is an aggravated felony. *U.S. v. Tejeda-Perez,* 199 F.3d 981 (8th Cir. 1999) [finding that INA §101(a)(48)(B) regarding treating suspension of sentence as the same as the term of imprisonment is the controlling provision rather than USSG §4A1.2(b)]. But probation is not a sentence to imprisonment under the requirements of §2L1.2. *U.S. v. Lopez-Vasquez*, 227 F.3d 476, 481 n.8 (5th Cir. 2000). A sentence that is imposed and then probated, however, may be considered a sentence under §101(a)(48)(B). *U.S. v. Ayala-Gomez*, 255 F.3d 1314 (11th Cir. 2001) [sentence that was probated is considered suspended for purposes of statute and therefore full sentence must be considered].

7.e. Definition of Aggravated Felony. An aggravated felony should not be defined rigidly—*U.S. v. Ballesteros-Ruiz,* 319 F.3d 1101 (9th Cir. 2003) [second conviction for possession of marijuana is not a felony triggering aggravated felony enhancement]; *U.S. v. Arellano-Torres,* 303 F.3d 1173, 1178 (9th Cir. 2002) [same]; *U.S. v. Hinds*, 803 F.Supp. 675 (W.D.N.Y. 1992) [where 2 felony marijuana convictions would have been misdemeanors in another state, 16-level increase unwarranted]. If statute did not define act as aggravated felony at the time it was committed, it is a violation of the constitutional prohibition against *ex post facto* laws to apply the 16-level upward adjustment. *U.S. v. Avila-Ramirez,* 170 F.3d 277 (2d Cir. 1999) [no 16-level enhancement for aggravated felony where conviction for indecent assault and the crime of re-entry were completed prior to the IIRIRA amendments making abuse of a minor an aggravated felony].

The USSG definition of aggravated felony incorporates the INA definition for the 8-level enhancement under USSG §2L1.2(b)(1)(C), but not for: (1) the 16-level enhancement under USSG §2L1.2(b)(1)(A) for certain designated crimes; (2) the 12-level enhancement under USSG §2L1.2(b)(1)(B) for drug trafficking offense for which the sentence imposed was 13 months or less, or (3) the felony enhancement under USSG §2L1.2(b)(1)(D). USSG §2L1.2 note 2. There is a question in the circuits as to whether an aggravated felony, for purposes of the sentencing guidelines and for the INA, are identical or distinct. *Cazarez-Gutierrez v. Ashcroft,* 382 F.3d 905, 912–14 (9th Cir. 2004) [distinguishing analysis for immigration purposes concerning the treatment of a state conviction as an aggravated felony from sentencing guideline cases where the "states possess primary authority for defining and enforcing the criminal law"]; *U.S. v. Pornes-Garcia,* 171 F.3d 142 (2d Cir. 1999) [finding definition of aggravated felony under USSG §2L1.2(b)(1)(A) distinct from INS definition; *Aguirre* distinguished]; *U.S. v. Lazo-Ortiz*, 136 F.3d 1282 (11th Cir. 1998) [neither the definition of aggravated felon at INA §101(a)(43), nor the definition under INA §276, 8 U.S.C. §1326, apply to the guidelines thereby permitting retroactive application of definition of crime of violence]; *U.S. v. Reyna-Espinosa*, 117 F.3d 826 (5th Cir. 1997) [possession of a firearm under §922(g)(5) while defined as an aggravated felony for the INA, is not an aggravated felony under USSG §2L1.2(b) (note)]; *U.S. v. Rios-Favela*, No. 96-50128 (9th Cir. June 25, 1997); *U.S. v. Munoz-Cerna*, 47 F.3d 207, 212 (7th Cir. 1995); *but see Cedano-Viera v. Ashcroft,* 324 F.3d 1062, 1067 (9th Cir. 2003) [reading *Matter of Yanez-Garcia* to require IJs to follow sentencing guideline as well as immigration cases interpreting aggravated felonies]; *U.S. v. Fuentes-Barahona,* 111 F.3d 651 (9th Cir. 1997) [suggesting date limitation under agg. felony statute applied to sentencing guidelines]; *U.S. v. Maul-Valverde*, 10 F.3d 544 (8th Cir. 1993) [citing to other cases addressing aggravated felony issues]. One court has also determined that even if a conviction would not be an aggravated felony for purposes of sentencing under §1326(b)(2), it could still be an aggravated felony for purposes of sentencing enhancement under USSG §2L1.2(b)(2). *U.S. v. Westcott,* 159 F.3d 107, 114–17 (2d Cir. 1998). The BIA previously determined that "crimes of violence" are defined differently for Sentencing Guidelines under USSG §4B1.2(1)(ii) than under the aggravated felony removal provision because the former finds a crime of violence if there is a risk of physical injury whereas the aggravated felony statute requires a risk of physical force. *Matter of Sweetser*, 22 I&N Dec. 709 (BIA 1999). In drug cases, however, the BIA agreed with a number of circuit courts that refused to make a distinction between sentencing enhancement cases and immigration cases when interpreting whether state felonies should be treated as aggravated felonies. *Matter of Yanez-Garcia,* 23 I&N Dec. 390, 396 (BIA 2002) [reversed *Matter of K-V-D-,* 22 I&N Dec. 1163 (BIA 1999) and found that state felony drug convictions will be considered aggravated felonies under federal law, even if the crime is a misdemeanor under federal law]. *See also U.S. v. Hernandez-Avalos,* 251 F.3d 505, 508–10 (5th Cir. 2001) [rejected both *Matter of L-G-* and *Matter of K-V-D-,* found that there was no basis to distinguish between sentencing guideline and immigration cases, and determined that possession of heroin is an aggravated felony because it was punishable under §844(a) *and* it is a felony under state law]. But the Supreme Court in *Lopez v. Gonzales,* 549 U.S. ___, 127 S.Ct. 625 (2006) rejected *Matter of Yanez-Garcia* to the extent it held that a state felony can be treated as an aggravated felony under the Controlled Substances Act if it is not a felony under federal law.

The Sentencing Commission sought to clarify some of these issues by amending the definitions under §2L1.2 in 2001 and again in 2003. The 2003 Sentencing Guideline for illegal reentry offenses imposes a 16-level increase for certain crimes of violence without regard to whether they would be aggravated felonies under the immigration law definition of crime of violence. *Compare* USSG §2L1.2 comment 1(B)(iii) *with* USSG §2L1.2 comment 3. For example, burglary is a crime of violence regardless of the sentence imposed under the Guidelines, but requires a one-year sentence to fall under the aggravated felony definition. *See, e.g., U.S. v. Pimentel-Flores,* 339 F.3d 959 (9th Cir. 2003) [approving the lawfulness of a 16-level enhancement sought pursuant to INA §276(b)(1), 8 U.S.C. §1226(b)(1)]. The 2003 amendments also redefined crime of violence to include sexual abuse of a minor, other sexual offenses, and burglary of a dwelling. It also added human trafficking offenses as defined in 18 U.S.C. §§1581–91, child pornography offenses under 18 U.S.C. §§2251–52A, and offenses under state and local law consisting of conduct that would have been a federal offense under those statutes for purposes of establishing a 16-level upward adjustment.

In certain circumstances the sentencing guidelines may conflict with the aggravated felony statute. For example, it is not clear that an enhancement sought under INA §276(b)(2), 8 U.S.C. §1226(b)(2), would be lawful because such enhancements are available only if the defendant has a prior aggravated felony conviction. The Supreme Court has given the Sentencing Commission broad authority, but the Sentencing Commission cannot contravene an Act of Congress. *See Stinson v. U.S.,* 508 U.S. 36 (1993) [holding that USSG Manual is binding on federal courts unless it is contrary to the statute].

There is also an issue as to whether INA §101(a)(48)(B) or USSG §4A1.2(b) applies in defining "term of imprisonment" for purposes of the enhancement provision. *U.S. v. Tejeda-Perez,* 199 F.3d 981, 982 (8th Cir. 1999) [INA §101(a)(48)(B) defines "term of imprisonment" for purposes of an enhancement under the sentencing guidelines as an aggravated felon]; *U.S. v. Maldonado-Ramirez,* 216 F.3d 940 (11th Cir. 2000) [same]. The term of imprisonment under the 2003 amendments now includes any terms of imprisonment given upon revocation of probation, parole, or supervised release.

The Supreme Court resolved the issue of whether a felony conviction under state law but not a felony under federal law can be considered an aggravated felony. A person must be convicted of a crime that is a felony under *federal* law. *Lopez v. Gonzales,* 549 U.S. ___, 127 S.Ct. 625 (2006). In *Lopez* the Court rejected the approach articulated in *Matter of Yanez-Garcia*, 23 I&N Dec. 390 (BIA 2002) that a state felony conviction is sufficient to be an aggravated felony under 18 U.S.C. §924(c)(2) even if it is not a felony under federal law. *Lopez* determined that a South Dakota conviction for aiding and abetting another person's possession of cocaine, while a felony under state law, could not be an aggravated felony because under federal law the conviction is treated as a misdemeanor. The Court held that "a state offense constitutes a 'felony punishable under the Controlled Substances Act' only if it proscribes conduct punishable as a felony under that federal law." 549 U.S. ___, ____, 127 S.Ct. 625, 633 (2006

Conversely, there is an issue as to whether a state conviction that is a misdemeanor under state law can be an aggravated felony for sentence enhancement. *U.S. v. Corona-Sanchez,* 291 F.3d 1201, 1208–09 (9th Cir. 2002) (*en banc*). [following language in *Apprendi* that "recidivism does not relate to the commission of the offense," the court would not consider petty theft as an aggravated felony where the maximum sentence was 6 months, notwithstanding the 2-year sentence received by defendant due to an enhancement statute]; *U.S. v. Gomez-Ortiz,* 62 F.Supp.2d 508 (D.R.I. 1999) [Mass. statute that was misdemeanor for first offense possession with intent to distribute was not aggravated felony under sentencing guidelines]. *But see U.S. v. Marin-Navarette,* 244 F.3d 1284 (11th Cir. 2001) [although attempted child molestation in the third degree is a misdemeanor under Washington State law it is an aggravated felony for sentencing enhancement]; *U.S. v. Christopher,* 239 F.3d 1191 (11th Cir. 2001), *cert. denied,* 122 S.Ct. 178 (2001) [theft by shoplifting although a misdemeanor under state law was agg. felony where sentence imposed, although suspended, was one year]; *U.S. v. Pacheco,* 225 F.3d 148, 154 (2d Cir. 2000); *Wireko v. Reno,* 211 F.3d 833, 835 (4th Cir. 2000); *U.S. v. Graham,* 169 F.3d 787, 792 (3d Cir.), *cert. denied,* 528 U.S. 845 (1999).

Sixteen-Level Adjustment Warranted (primarily under former USSG §2L1.2))—*U.S. v. Galinda-Gallegos,* 244 F.3d 728, 733 (9th Cir. 2001) [transporting aliens in the U.S. is an agg. felony even though it was not a conviction for smuggling]; *U.S. v. Polanco*, 47 F.3d 516 (2d Cir. 1995) [reversed refusal of district judge to grant 16-level enhancement of sentence as aggravated felon because of practice of NY defense bar to plead clients to low-level drug offenses and because the gross unfairness of the guidelines might raise due process concerns]; *U.S. v. Mendoza-Iribe,* 198 F.3d 742 (9th Cir. 1999) [upward 16-level adjustment applicable even if act was not aggravated felony at the time person convicted]; *U.S. v. Cazares-Gonzalez,* 152 F.3d 889 (8th Cir. 1998) [same]; *U.S. v. Lazo-Ortiz,* 136 F.3d 1282 (11th Cir. 1998) [same]; *U.S. v. Munoz-Cerna*, 47 F.3d 207 (7th Cir. 1995) [same]; *U.S. v. Campbell*, 94 F.3d 125 (4th Cir. 1996) [same]; *U.S. v. Garcia-Rico*, 46 F.3d 8 (5th Cir.), *cert. denied*, 115 S.Ct. 2596 (1996) [same]; *U.S. v. Nwene,* 20 F.Supp.2d 716, 723–25 (D.N.J. 1998) [same]; *Carvajales-Cepeda v. Meissner*, 966 F.Supp. 207 (S.D.N.Y. 1997) [same]; *U.S. v. Arzate-Nunez*, 18 F.3d 730, 733–35 (9th Cir. 1994) [rejected *ex post facto* argument where aggravated felony committed before aggravated felony act passed]; *U.S. v. Cabrera-Sosa*, 81 F.3d 998 (10th Cir. 1996) [same]; *U.S. v. Crawford*, 18 F.3d 1173 (4th Cir. 1994); *U.S. v. Lozano*, 138 F.3d 915 (11th Cir. 1998) [general *ex post facto* challenge to sentence enhancement provision rejected]; *U.S. v. Forbes*, 16 F.3d 1294 (1st Cir. 1994) [rejected *ex post facto* claim]; *U.S. v. Valdez*, 103 F.3d 95 (10th Cir. 1996) [same]; *U.S. v. Frios-Trujillo*, 9 F.3d 875 (10th Cir. 1993) [allowed enhancement where person committed burglary and pled guilty only to re-entry after commission of a felony under 8 U.S.C. §1326(b)(1) and not after commission of aggravated felony]. *But see U.S. v. Gomez-Ortiz,* 62 F.Supp.2d 508 (D.R.I. 1999) [Mass. statute that was misdemeanor for first offense possession with intent to distribute was not agg. felony under sentencing guidelines and 16-level enhancement was unwarranted]; *U.S. v. Fuentes-Barahona*, 111 F.3d 651 (9th Cir. 1997) [COV committed prior to Nov. 29, 1990, cannot be agg. felony for sentence enhancement]; *U.S. v. Campos-Martinez*, 976 F.2d 589 (9th Cir. 1992) [unless element was proven cannot enhance sentence].

*Downward Departure Post-*Booker—*U.S. v. Trujillo-Terrazas,* 405 F.3d 814 (10th Cir. 2005) [where 41 month sentence for an innocuous prior third degree arson conviction (throwing a match in a car) would have resulted in a sentence that would be "plain error" under *Booker* court reversed].

*Downward Departure Pre-*Booker—The sentencing guidelines to §2L1.2(b)(1)(A) at note 5 provide for a downward departure of the 16-level enhancement. Note 5 provides for a downward departure where: (1) the defendant has previously been convicted of only one felony; (2) such offense was not a COV or firearms offense; and (3) the term of imprisonment imposed for such offense did not exceed one year. A downward departure may also be given for delay in indicting a person in an illegal re-entry case. *U.S. v. Martinez-Salazar,* 318 F.Supp.2d 127 (S.D.N.Y. 2004). Downward departures was also permissible, pre-*Booker*, under *Koon v. U.S.,* 518 U.S. 81 (1996) if the court found that there was a mitigating circumstance of a kind, or to a degree, not adequately taken into consideration by the Sentencing Commission in formulating the guidelines. *U.S. v. Jauregui,* 314 F.3d 961 (8th Cir. 2003) [waiver of removal hearing by LPR is sufficient to give a 4-level downward adjustment in a sentencing for sale of drugs]; *U.S. v. Rodriguez-Montelongo,* 263 F.3d 429 (5th Cir. 2001) [cultural assimilation is a valid ground for downward departure in illegal re-entry case]; *U.S. v. Sanchez-Rodriguez,* 161 F.3d 556 (9th Cir. 1998) (*en banc*) [in §1326 case where the predicate offense was a $20 heroin sale, the court held that the district court may depart in its discretion based on the nature and circumstances of the underlying aggravated felony]; *U.S. v. Sanchez-Valencia,* 148 F.3d 1273, 1274 (11th Cir. 1998) [permitting downward departure for cultural assimilation]; *U.S. v. Diaz-Diaz,*135 F.3d 572, 581 (8th Cir. 1998) [the court affirmed a downward departure in a sale of 8.3 grams of marijuana because the seriousness of the offense was drastically overstated]; *U.S. v. Lipman,* 133 F.3d 726, 729–31 (9th Cir. 1998)] [same]. *But see U.S. v. Palomino-Rivera,* 258 F.3d 656 (7th Cir. 2001) [rejecting arguments under Note 5 and *Koon*]; *Flores-Diaz v. U.S.,* 516 F.Supp.2d 818, 828 (S.D. Tex. 2007) [where defendant was a repeat offender he was not culturally assimilated]. The status of being a deportable alien and therefore serving a harsher prison sentence because of ineligibility for prison programs such as a halfway house, is not a basis in the view of some courts for a downward adjustment, *U.S. v. Veloza*, 83 F.3d 380 (11th Cir. 1996); *U.S. v. Maung,* 320 F.3d 1305 (11th Cir. 2003) [sentencing court may not depart downward to take a crime out of the definition of an aggravated felony to shield defendant from immigration consequences]; *U.S. v. Aleskerova,* 300 F.3d 286, 300 (2d Cir. 2002); *U.S. v. Ebolum*, 72 F.3d 35 (6th Cir. 1995); *U.S. v. Mendoza-Lopez*, 7 F.3d 1483, 1486 (10th Cir. 1993), *cert. denied,* 511 U.S. 1036 (1994); *U.S. v. Alvarez-Cardenas*, 902 F.2d 734 (9th Cir. 1990); *U.S. v. Restrepo*, 999 F.2d 640 (2d Cir. 1993) [suggesting that departure may be permissible if the effect of deportation is beyond the ordinary]. *U.S. v. Santos v. U.S.*, 940 F.Supp. 275 (D. Hawaii 1996) [rejected equal protection argument]. *But see U.S. v. Smith*, 27 F.3d 649 (D.C. Cir. 1994). It is impermissible to give downward adjustment because the reason for the re-entry was to visit family or because drug conviction was minor. *U.S. v. Abreu-Cabrera*, 64 F.3d 67, 74–76 (2d Cir. 1995). Departure from sentencing guidelines because deportable person would not serve probation is impermissible. *U.S. v. Chavez-Botello*, 905 F.2d 279, 281 (9th Cir. 1990). *See also U.S. v. Amaya-Benitez*, 69 F.3d 1243 (2d Cir. 1995) [court cannot look at underlying circumstances of the aggravated felony conviction to grant downward adjustment and conviction was not so old (9 years) as to raise any issue]; *U.S. v. Gonzalez*, 112 F.3d 1325 (7th Cir. 1997) [age of aggravated felony convictions irrelevant]; *U.S. v. Maul-Valverde*, 10 F.3d 544 (8th Cir. 1993) [reversed judge's departure from upward 16-level adjustment where person had committed burglary and sentenced as aggravated felon]. *But see U.S. v. Sanchez-Rodriguez,* 161 F.3d 556, 559–63 (9th Cir. 1998) [can consider the nature and circumstances of the underlying aggravated felony in departing downward]; *U.S. v. Ortega-Mendoza*, 981 F.Supp. 694 (D.D.C. 1997) [downward departure appropriate because aggravated felony not serious, because conditions of detention would be more severe as deportable person and coercion and duress influence his return]. Moreover, a decision to deny a downward adjustment may not be reviewable. *U.S. v.*

Melendez-Torres, 420 F.3d 45, 50–52 (1st Cir. 2005) [denial of downward adjustment because defendant was culturally assimilated in the U.S. was not reviewable]. Presentation of false ID and false name to INS officers does not warrant enhancement of sentence absent a showing that it hindered the investigation. *U.S. v. Solano-Godines*, 120 F.3d 957, 963 (9th Cir. 1997).

7.f. *Stipulation to Deportation as Basis for Downward Departure*—Pre–*Booker*, certain circuits prohibited a defendant from obtaining a downward departure of his or her sentence simply because s/he is willing to stipulate to deportation absent a proffer of a nonfrivolous defense to deportation. *U.S. v. Mignott,* 184 F.3d 1288, 1290–91 (11th Cir. 1999) [citing First, Second, Third, and Ninth Circuit cases supporting the same view]. *But see U.S. v. Hernandez-Reyes,* 114 F.3d 800, 802 (8th Cir. 1999) [permitting downward departure where the parties filed a joint motion requesting it irrespective of defense to deportation]. Post-*Booker*, departure from the sentencing guidelines was also not permitted. *U.S. v. Hernandez-Montealegre,* 445 F.Supp.2d 646, 653–58 (E.D. Va. 2006) [where defendant had only frivolous defenses to removal departure was not appropriate].

8. *Former Rule Against Judicial Deportation*—The court, as part of the person's sentence, could not traditionally order him or her deported. *U.S. v. Tinoso,* 327 F.3d 864 (9th Cir. 2003) [court could not order as a condition of supervised release under 18 U.S.C. §3583(d) that person be deported; Court could order only that s/he be surrendered to immigration authorities for proceedings]; *U.S. v. Quaye*, 57 F.3d 447 (5th Cir. 1995) [same]; *U.S. v. Kassar*, 47 F.3d 562, 568–69 (2d Cir. 1995); *U.S. v. Ramirez*, 948 F.2d 66, 67–68 (1st Cir. 1991). IIRIRA abolished the right of the federal court to order deportation as a condition of release. *U.S. v. Mignott,* 184 F.3d 1288, 1291–92 (11th Cir. 1999) [Congress eliminated the right of U.S. district court judges to enter orders of deportation because INA §239(a)(3), 8 U.S.C. §1229(a)(3), makes hearing before IJ the exclusive procedure for deportation]. A court may therefore not enter a sentence that precludes a person from raising defenses to removal. *U.S. v. Maldonado-Ramirez,* 216 F.3d 940, 944–45 (11th Cir. 2000). *See also U.S. v. Velasquez-Velasquez,* F.3d (11th Cir. Apr. 21, 2008) [district court was reversed where he sought to impose a more severe sentence than he would have otherwise based upon unfounded assumptions regarding the defendant's immigration status or because of the court's personal views regarding immigration policy]. Congress, however, in IIRIRA §374(b), amended the statute regarding probation to permit deportation as a condition of probation either by stipulation of the parties or where the district court judge or magistrate orders deportation after notice and a hearing. At the hearing the AG must demonstrate deportability by clear and convincing evidence. 18 U.S.C. §3563(b)(21).

9. *Current Statutes Allowing Judicial Deportation*—Notwithstanding prior law, Congress, under the Immigration and Nationality Technical Corrections Act of 1994, established judicial deportation in the federal system. A sentencing judge in federal court may now enter an order of deportation as part of the sentence but only after certain procedural safeguards. *See in this chapter* "Judicial Deportation," ¶ X.S.11 (p.404), *infra*.

9.a. Federal parole commission guidelines do not consider immigration status as a basis to alter or reduce person's sentence.

10. *Extradition of Persons Who Are Not Citizens, Nationals, or LPRs*—18 U.S.C. §3181(b) permits the surrender of persons who are not citizens, nationals, or LPRs, even without an extradition treaty, if there is evidence that the person had committed a crime of violence against U.S. nationals and the charge is not political. Removal proceedings may also be instituted as: "Extradition proceedings are separate and apart from any immigration proceeding [citations omitted]" *Matter of Ruiz-Massieu,* 22 I&N Dec. 833 (BIA 1999). However, the Convention Against Torture is applicable to extradition proceedings. 22 C.F.R. §95.2 and it prevents extradition of a person who would face torture unless there are diplomatic assurance to the contrary. But such assurances must be reviewed under due process standards. *Khouzam v. Hogan,* 529 F.Supp.2d 543 (M.D. Pa. 2008) [stayed removal and released respondent from custody despite diplomatic assurances that Egyptian granted deferral of removal under CAT would not be tortured where the assurances were not subject to due process scrutiny].

11. *Prisoner Transfer Treaties*—The President is permitted to negotiate bilateral prison transfer treaties providing for incarceration in the country of the individual's nationality for the duration of his

prison term. IIRIRA §330. *See, e.g.*, Convention on the Transfer of Sentenced Persons, Mar. 21, 1983, T.I.A.S. No. 10824, 22 I.L.M. 530 (entered into force July 1, 1985). The prisoner's consent is not required. IIRIRA §330(c). Treaty countries and information regarding the transfer process may be found at *www.travel.state.gov/travel/tips/emergencies/emergencies_1200.html*. There may not be a due process right to be transferred and the decision to transfer may not be subject to review. *Marshall v. Reno*, 915 F.Supp. 426 (D.D.C. 1996). *But see Wong v. Warden, FCI Raybrook,* 999 F.Supp. 287 (N.D.N.Y. 1998) [constitutional due process right against refusal to transfer based on race, although plaintiff did not prove case]. At least one court has found that when a U.S. citizen is transferred back to the U.S. under the terms of a foreign sentence pursuant to the terms of the treaty, the district court does not have jurisdiction to alter the sentence even if it is not in compliance with U.S. law. *Bishop v. Reno,* 210 F.3d 1295 (11th Cir. 2000).

12. *Speedy Trial*—The Speedy Trial Act, which requires bringing criminal charges within the 30-day period between arrest and indictment under 18 U.S.C. §3161(b), generally does not run from detention by DHS. *U.S. v. Noel,* 231 F.3d 833 (11th Cir. 2000) [Speedy Trial Act does not run from detention by INS unless the INS detention is merely a "ruse" because the Act begins to run only after an individual is accused either by an arrest and charge or by an indictment]; *U.S. v. Cepeda-Luna*, 989 F.2d 353 (9th Cir. 1993) [same]; *U.S. v. Encarnacion,* 56 F.Supp.2d 151 (D.P.R. 1999) [same]. Similarly, the requirement in Fed. R. Crim. P. 5(a) that a person be taken before a magistrate within 48 hours or his case may be dismissed is not applicable where the person is charged under §1326(a)(2) [found in the U.S.] because it is a status offense. *U.S. v. Tejada,* 255 F.3d 1 (1st Cir. 2001); *U.S. v. Noel,* 231 F.3d 833, 837 (11th Cir. 2000). *See also U.S. v. Perez-Perez,* 337 F.3d 990, 997 (8th Cir. 2003) [civil deportation proceedings do not trigger the criminal rules of procedure including Rule 5(a)]. However, where there is collusion between INS and another agency for the purpose of bringing criminal charges, the Speedy Trial Act, will apply. *U.S. v. Tejada,* 255 F.3d at 4; *Noel, supra* at 836; *U.S. v. Vasquez-Escobar,* 30 F.Supp.2d 1364, 1367–68 (M.D. Fla. 1998) [found Speedy Trial Act applicable where there was collusion]; *U.S. v. Okuda,* 675 F.Supp. 1552 (D. Haw. 1987) [same]; *But see U.S. v. Dyer,* 325 F.3d 464, 468–70 (3d Cir. 2003) [no collusion between INS and U.S. Attorney's office].

IX. FINES

A. *In General*—The Immigration and Nationality Act has numerous provisions relating to civil and criminal fines. INA §231(d), 8 U.S.C. §1221(d) [failure to deliver manifest]; INA §241(e), 8 U.S.C. §1231(e) [failure to provide for deportation]; INA §251(d), 8 U.S.C. §1281(d) [alien crewmen]; INA §254(a), 8 U.S.C. §1284(a) [failure to control crew]; INA §255, 8 U.S.C. §1285 [employment of certain crew]; INA §256, 8 U.S.C. §1286 [improper discharge of crew]; INA §257, 8 U.S.C. §1287 [assisting unlawful entry of crew]; INA §271(a), 8 U.S.C. §1321(a) [prevent unauthorized entries]; INA §272(a), 8 U.S.C. §1322(a) [bringing in certain aliens]; INA §273, 8 U.S.C. §1323 [unlawful bringing of aliens]; and INA §274C(d)(3), 8 U.S.C. §1324c(d)(3) [document fraud].

Under the Immigration Act of 1990, the amounts of the fines have substantially increased. IMMACT90 §542. Also as a result of the Federal Civil Monetary Penalties Inflation Adjustment Act of 1990, PL 101-410 and the Omnibus Consolidated Rescissions and Appropriations Act of 1996, PL 104-134, §31001(s)(1), the DOJ revises penalties to adjust for inflation. For example, the penalties under INA §273, 8 U.S.C. §1323, which is the most invoked provision against airlines and vessels for bringing aliens into the U.S. who are not authorized, went from $3,000 to $3,300 per unauthorized alien. The funds are to be used to enhance enforcement authority including the construction of structures at the border to deter illegal entry and expediting preparation of transcripts of EOIR hearings. IMMACT90 §542.

Under INA §241(c)(3), carriers are once again liable for custodial and financial responsibility for stowaways, except where they cannot be removed. Under prior law airlines sued successfully to recover expenses for detaining TWOVs seeking asylum, *Aerolineas Argentinas v. U.S.*, 77 F.3d 1564 (Fed. Cir. 1996), and for an injunction. *Air Transport Ass'n of America v. Reno*, 80 F.3d 477 (D.C. Cir. 1996).

The procedures for the imposition and collection of fines are found at 8 C.F.R. §280 *et seq.* *See in this part* section B (p.264), *infra*. The only exception to these procedures is for fines under §274C which are found at 8 C.F.R. §§270, 1270.

The Service established a procedure where carriers may have their fines reduced if they establish procedures approved by the Service for the proper screening of passengers. 8 C.F.R. §273.3, 63 Fed. Reg. 23643 (Apr. 30, 1998). In order to receive the benefit of a reduction, refund or waiver of fines that are imposed, a carrier may enter into a memorandum of understanding with the Service to meet passenger screening standards, to train employees in documentary requirements, and to pay fines and user fees promptly. 65 Fed. Reg. 46742–43 (July 30, 2000).

In addition to fines, the AG may suspend the entry of aliens transported to the U.S. aboard a commercial airline that does not comply with AG regulations regarding fraudulent documents used by passengers. INA §212(f).

B. *Procedures for All Fines Except INA §274*

1. Proceedings initiated by the Associate Commissioner for Examinations, the Director for the National Fines Office, or the District Director by the issuance of Form I-79, Notice of Intent to Fine (NIF). The initiation of the fine proceeding does not preclude DHS from instituting its own civil suit pursuant to INA §280, 8 U.S.C. §1330. 8 C.F.R. §§280.1, 1280.1. Upon the service of a NIF, DHS under certain circumstances may prohibit the aircraft or vessel from departing the U.S. without security. 8 C.F.R. §§280.2, 280.3, 1280.2, 1280.3. The NIF must be personally served, 8 C.F.R. §§280.11, 1280.11. and an answer must be filed within 30 days following the service of the Notice of Intent to Fine. 8 C.F.R. §§280.12, 1280.12. The 30-day period may be extended another 30 days for good cause shown. *Id.* An answer should contain a written defense (filed in duplicate) under oath setting forth the reasons why "a fine should not be imposed, or if imposed, why it should be mitigated or remitted ..." *Id.* In addition, a party answering may request a personal appearance before an Immigration officer (who is not an IJ or ALJ).

2. Mitigation or Remission of Fine—A party may file an application for mitigation or remission of a fine within 30 days of receipt of the NIF. *Remission* is a complete forgiveness of the entire penalty, while *mitigation* is the imposition of a reduced penalty. An application for mitigation or remission shall be filed in duplicate under oath and "shall include information, supported by documentary evidence, as to the basis of the claim to mitigation or remission." 8 C.F.R. §§280.51(b), 1280.51(b). A petition for mitigation can only be filed in those cases where a mitigation procedure is permitted by statute. For example, INA §273 provides for both remission [INA §273(c)] and mitigation [INA §273(e)]. Regulations that a carrier must follow if it seeks to reduce, obtain a refund, or waive a fine can be found at 8 C.F.R. pt. 273. However, a carrier is not precluded from seeking remission or mitigation under 8 C.F.R. §§280.51, 1280.51.

3. A fine imposed under INA §273 may now be mitigated where (i) the carrier demonstrates that it had screened all passengers in accordance with procedures set forth at 8 C.F.R. pt. 273, *or* (ii) circumstances exist that the AG determines would justify such reduction, refund or waiver. INA §273(e). The former requires the carrier to sign a Memorandum of Understanding (MOU) with the INS. 8 C.F.R. §273.6.

4. Defenses—Each statute involves different defenses. For example, INA §273(c) permits remission (forgiveness in full) "where it appears that prior to the alien's departure from the last port outside the U.S., the carrier did not know, and could not have ascertained by the exercise of reasonable diligence, that the individual transported was an alien and that a visa was required." *See Matter of Varig Brazilian Airlines, Flight No. 830*, 21 I&N Dec. 744 (BIA 1997) [reasonable diligence standard applies both to whether person is an alien and needs a visa *and* to adequacy of carrier's inspection procedures. BIA decision remains unaffected by the passage of INA §273(e) and BIA applies reasonable person standard]; *Matter of Plane N-6104-C*, 6 I&N Dec. 819 (BIA 1955); *Matter of SS Florida*, 3 I&N Dec. 111 (AG 1954). Traditionally, the burden of proof is on the Service and the record must contain affidavits from witnesses and not simply statements from agents who did not witness the events. *M/V Saru Meru,* 20 I&N Dec. 592 (BIA 1992) [lack of affidavits from crew members or other stowaways was fatal]. However, carriers can generally not use as a defense that its employee overseas lacks the proper knowledge of U.S. immigration laws and regulations. *Matter of M/V Guadalupe*, 13 I&N Dec. 67 (BIA 1968). *See also Matter of Scandinavian Airlines Flight #SK 911*, 20 I&N Dec. 306 (BIA 1991) [airline is an insurer even where person had passport and visa, although airline may seek remission]. In addition, it is not a defense to a fine proceeding under INA §273 that the alien was subsequently admitted, even if a returning LPR, where he did not have the proper documentation at the time of his arrival. *Matter of Eastern Airlines, Inc. Flight No. 798*, 20

I&N Dec. 57 (BIA 1989); *Matter of Air India, "Flight No. 101,"* 21 I&N Dec. 890 (BIA 1997) [liability where the regulation did not provide for blanket waiver of visa when person granted waiver for inadmissibility]; Or that the passenger was subsequently granted a waiver where the passenger had to meet NIV documentary requirements. *United Airlines, Inc. v. Jones,* 337 F.Supp.2d 406 (E.D.N.Y. 2004) [where TWOV with diplomatic passport was subsequently paroled into the U.S. and carrier argued that because TWOV could have been granted a waiver the airline was not liable, the court held that the airline was liable, that BIA cases to the contrary misread the statute, and that the Supreme Court in *Hamburg-American Line v. U.S.*, 291 U.S. 420 (1934), and the statute clearly provided that even if person could obtain waiver the airline's liability arose from bringing the person to the U.S.]; *Matter of Finnair Flight AY103,* 23 I&N Dec. 140 (BIA 2001). *But see Matter of Plane "CUT-604,"* 7 I&N Dec. 701 (BIA 1957) [no carrier liability where regulation provides in express terms that a visa is not required when a waiver is granted for returning LPR]; *Matter of Plane Cca Cut 532,* 6 I&N Dec. 262 (BIA 1954) [same]. If waiver granted under §212(d)(4)(A) airline not subject to fine. *Matter of "Flight SR-4,"* 10 I&N Dec. 197 (BIA 1963). However, if the person is paroled into the U.S. when not in possession of valid passport or visa when required to do so, the airline is subject to a fine. *Matter of United Airlines Flight UA802,* 22 I&N Dec. 777 (BIA 1999) *aff'd United Airlines, Inc. v. Jones,* 337 F.Supp.2d 406 (E.D.N.Y. 2004). Airlines fined if TWOV absconds. O.I. §238.1a; 8 U.S.C. §1321. Laches is not a defense to fine proceedings, *Matter of United Airlines Flight UA802, supra* at 782. A carrier may obtain a remand of proceedings where the INS decision is cursory and inadequate for review. *Matter of Air India Flight No. 101,* 21 I&N Dec. 890 (BIA 1997) [case remanded for development of an adequate appellate record].

5. Appeal—If the District Director, Associate Commissioner for Examinations or the Director for the National Fines Office enters an order adverse to the party s/he may appeal it to the BIA within 15 days after the mailing of the notification of the decision, with an additional 3 days if received by mail.

6. Judicial Review—If a party is not satisfied with the decision, he may bring an action under the APA in the U.S.D.C. challenging the decision.

C. *Civil Penalties for Document Fraud*—INA §274C, 8 U.S.C. §1324c; 8 C.F.R. §§270, 1270 *et seq.*; 57 Fed. Reg. 33862 (July 31, 1992), 64 Fed. Reg. 7066 (Feb. 12, 1999).

1. It is unlawful for any person or entity *knowingly*:

1.a. to forge, counterfeit, alter or falsely make any document for the purpose of satisfying a requirement of, or to obtain a benefit under, the INA;

1.b. to use, attempt to use, provide, attempt to provide, *possess*, obtain, *accept*, or *receive* any forged, counterfeit, altered, or falsely made document in order to satisfy *any* requirement of the INA or to obtain a benefit under the INA. This includes, in the view of one court, the presentation of false documents to an employer for an I-9. *Villegas-Valenzuela v. INS*, 103 F.3d 805, 809–11 (9th Cir. 1996);

1.c. to use someone else's lawfully issued document for the purpose of satisfying *a* requirement of the Act, *Remileh v. INS*, 101 F.3d 66 (8th Cir. 1996) [use of cousin's birth certificate to gain employment];

1.d. to accept, receive, or use someone else's lawfully issued document for the purpose of complying with I-9 requirements or obtaining a benefit under the INA;

1.e. to prepare, file, or assist another in preparing or filing any application for benefits under the Act, or any document in connection with such application or document with knowledge or a reckless disregard of the fact that such application or document was falsely made or, in whole or in part, does not relate to the person on whose behalf it was or is being submitted. The Service has taken the view that the term "prepare" should be construed broadly to include actually filling out the form, completing other documents in support of the form (with knowledge of falsity and that the document will be attached to the form), or instructing another about filling it out. Memo, Virtue, Acting Exec. Assoc. Comm., HQ IRT 50/5.12, 96 Act. 052 (Sept. 3, 1997), *published on* AILA InfoNet at Doc. No. 97090391.

1.f. to present to a common carrier a document to board and then fail to present it to an immigration officer on arrival. The legislative history of IIRIRA §212 provides that this section, as well as the section regarding preparing or assisting in the preparation of false documents, apply only to offenses committed on or after Sept. 30, 1996.

2. The statute defines falsely made to include reckless disregard or having no basis in law or fact. INA §274C(f), 8 U.S.C. §1324c(f). This definition applies to preparation of applications before, on or after Sept. 30, 1996. IIRIRA §212(f). However, its retroactive affect is only limited to the "preparation of applications" and therefore does not apply to possession or use of a falsely made Social Security card prior to Sept. 30, 1996. *U.S. v. Davila*, 7 OCAHO no. 936 (June 16, 1997).

3. The attestation to false information on an I-9 does not constitute falsely making a document under the statute. *U.S. v. Remileh*, 5 OCAHO no. 724 (Feb. 7, 1995) [distinguishing falsely making a document from providing false information]. But the presentation of false documents (*e.g.*, green card and Social Security card) to employer filling out I-9 does constitute a violation under INA §274C. *U.S. v. Morales-Vargas*, 5 OCAHO no. 732 (Mar. 13, 1995).

4. Investigation

4.a. Gives DHS and ALJs power to investigate but only grants to ALJs the power to subpoena. However, the ALJ must go to U.S. district court to enforce the subpoenas.

4.b. Procedures for investigation and institution of proceedings closely parallel employer sanctions. 8 C.F.R. §§270, 1270.

(1) Any person may initiate complaint and a complaint may be initiated on the basis of hearsay (*e.g.*, Form I-213), 57 Fed. Reg. 33862 (July 31, 1993);

(2) DHS may conduct investigation on its own initiation without prior complaint;

(3) DHS may issue subpoenas pursuant to INA §274C(d)(1)(C), 8 C.F.R. §§235, 287.4, 1235, 1287.4 in accordance with procedures under §287.4 for the attendance of witnesses and the production of documents;

(4) If it is determined that there is a violation, DHS may issue and serve a notice of intent to fine (NIF). 8 C.F.R. §§270.2(e), 1270.2(e). The notice is personally served pursuant to 8 C.F.R. §103.5a(a)(2). Legacy INS was enjoined from using their original NIF form because it failed to properly advise a respondent of the proceeding and the consequences of the proceeding regarding deportation. *Walters v. Reno*, 145 F.3d 1032 (9th Cir. 1998), *cert. denied,* 526 U.S. 1003 (1999).

(5) If DHS moves forward on the case they will issue a complaint. 28 C.F.R. §68.5. Service on the complaint on the attorney of the respondent is sufficient even where respondent's notice has been returned as undeliverable. *U.S. v. Galvez-Melgarejo*, 4 OCAHO no. 684 (Sept. 9, 1994). After the complaint is served the respondent has 30 days to file an answer. 28 C.F.R. §68.9(a). If the respondent fails to answer, a default may be entered against him. When respondent answers, s/he may file affirmative defenses. 28 C.F.R. §68.9(c)(2). Affirmative defenses include selective prosecution, *res judicata*, and collateral estoppel.

(6) DHS should not institute INA §274C proceedings where there is an I-485 on file and an I-601 waiver to waive fraud unless the applications are denied. Memo, Puleo, Acting Exec. Assoc. Comm. Operations (HQ 274C-C) (Mar. 25, 1993), *reprinted in* 12 *AILA Monthly Mailing* 922–23 (Dec. 1993); Memo, Rees, Gen. Counsel, INS (May 18, 1993). However, the BIA has held that an INA §212(i) waiver is unavailable to waive §212(a)(6)(F) arising from a final order under INA §274C. *Matter of Delia Lazarte-Valverde*, 21 I&N Dec. 214 (BIA 1996) [distinguishing INS memo providing that a waiver may be filed as an exercise of prosecutorial discretion not a statement of law].

5. Hearing—The person or entity subject to a penalty is entitled to a hearing upon request with at least 30 days' notice. INA §274C(d)(2), 8 U.S.C. §1324c(d)(2). The hearing procedure that is utilized is the same as the procedure for employer sanctions and unfair immigration employment practices under 28 C.F.R. §68. If no hearing is requested, the AG's order is final *and not appealable.*

5.a. If the NIF is issued, respondent must request hearing within 60 days. Request is deemed filed when *received* by DHS. 8 C.F.R. §§270.2(f), 1270.2(f). In requesting a hearing, the respondent may, but is not required to, respond to each allegation listed in the NIF. The failure to timely file a request for a hearing will result in entry of a final order. 8 C.F.R. §§270.2(g), 1270.2(g).

5.b. The NIF as well as any complaint issued in these proceedings are governed by broad notice pleading and the DHS NIF or complaint will not be dismissed when the respondent is put on sufficient notice of the charges. *U.S. v. Villatoro-Guzman*, 3 OCAHO no. 540 (July 9, 1993).

5.c. The hearing is governed by ALJ procedures under 28 C.F.R. §68.1, utilizing many aspects of the Federal Rules of Civil Procedure (see "Employer Sanctions" discussion in Ch. 12, part V (p.1257), *infra*). Final rules published in 57 Fed. Reg. 57669–73 (Dec. 7, 1992). The hearing shall be held before an ALJ at the nearest practicable place to where the person or entity resides or where the alleged violation occurred. The hearing shall be conducted in accordance with the requirements of the APA, 5 U.S.C. §554, and the ALJ shall apply a preponderance of the evidence test. ALJ shall make findings of fact and issue an order served on the person or entity. The respondent can assert the Fifth Amendment. *U.S. v. Davila*, 6 OCAHO no. 903 (Nov. 21, 1996).

5.d. Evidence at hearings governed generally by APA, 5 U.S.C. §556(d); *Velasquez-Tabir v. INS*, 127 F.3d 456 (5th Cir. 1997) [will not exclude evidence even if it was obtained in violation of the NLRA]. Discovery is permitted including use of depositions. 28 C.F.R. §§68.18, 68.22.

5.e. Summary decision (like summary judgment) may be sought. 28 C.F.R. §68.38(c). *U.S. v. Ortiz*, 6 OCAHO no. 889 (Aug. 30, 1996) [reviewed law on summary decisions and concluded government had not established the knowledge requirement even though it could be inferred when a party avoids or ignores evidence]; *U.S. v. Kumar*, 6 OCAHO no. 833 (Feb. 6, 1996) [ALJ used I-213 to grant summary decision to government]; *Villegas-Valenzuela v. INS*, 103 F.3d 805, 811–14 (9th Cir. 1996) [upholding summary decision where respondent was not given opportunity to conduct discovery or cross examine deponent where affidavit was the basis for summary decision].

6. Penalties—INA §274C(d)(3), 8 U.S.C. §1324c(d)(3), 8 C.F.R. §§270.3, 1270.3.

6.a. The ALJ's order must contain a "cease and desist" provision if s/he finds a violation.

6.b. In addition, s/he may impose a civil penalty in an amount of:

(1) Not less than $375 and not more than $3,200 for each document used, *accepted*, or created and each instance of use, *acceptance*, or creation under INA §§274C(a)(1)–(4). For violations of §§274C(a)(5)–(6) not less than $275 or more than $2,200.

(2) If second or more penalty, then fines are from $3,200 to $6,500 for each violation of §§274C(a)(1)–(4). For a second penalty for §§274C(a)(5)–(6) not more than $2,200 or less than $5,500

6.c. In applying the penalties, "in the case of a person or entity composed of distinct, physically separate subdivisions, each of which provides separately for hiring, recruiting or referring for employment without reference to the practices of, and not under the control of or common contract with, another subdivision, each such subdivision shall be considered a separate person or entity."

6.d. The AG may waive the penalties for someone who does not present documents at the border if s/he is granted asylum or withholding.

6.e. The ALJ may consider mitigating and aggravating factors when imposing a civil penalty in a document fraud case. *U.S. v. Dominguez,* 8 OCAHO no. 1000 (1998).

7. Defenses

7.a. Double Jeopardy—*U.S. v. Dominguez*, 6 OCAHO no. 876 (July 1, 1996) [striking affirmative defense of double jeopardy on grounds that a plea to conspiracy does not bar a civil proceeding on the substantive offense and that respondent waived double jeopardy in his plea agreement]; *Noriega-Perez v. U.S.,* 179 F.3d 1166, 1171 (9th Cir. 1999) [no double jeopardy where criminal conviction and civil action for different offenses]. The Service has taken the view, based upon *Hudson v. U.S.,* 118 S.Ct. 488 (1997), that double jeopardy does not attach to civil fine proceedings. Memo, Virtue, G.C. (HQCOU 90/10.6-P: 90/5/5-P), *reprinted in* 76 No. 32 *Interpreter Releases* 1259, 1279–83 (Aug. 23, 1999).

7.b. Did not waive right to hearing—*Walters v. Reno,* 145 F.3d 1032 (9th Cir. 1998), *cert. denied,* 526 U.S. 1003 (1999) [the notice and waiver forms used by INS to require respondents to waive their right to an ALJ hearing did not properly inform the respondents of their rights; Court entered injunction vacating INA §274C final orders and required new notice form where "waiver" based on inadequate notice]. For class members seeking relief under the *Walters v. Reno* settlement, *see* 66 Fed. Reg. 48480–82 (Sept. 20, 2001). Under the settlement, persons with final orders of deportation arising from INA §274C had until Aug. 21, 2003, to file a written request with the INS to reopen his or her case.

7.c. Lack of knowledge of falsity of documents.

7.d. Separation of Powers—*Noriega-Perez v. U.S.,* 179 F.3d 1166, 1171–78 (9th Cir. 1999) [no violation of separation of powers to allow ALJ instead of Article III judge to impose fine].

7.e. All affirmative defenses must be supported by a statement of facts. 28 C.F.R. §68.8(c)(2).

8. Administrative and Judicial Review

8.a. Interlocutory appeal—ALJ may, *sua sponte* or on motion of a party within 10 days of an order, seek an interlocutory appeal if there is "an important question of law" for which there is a substantial difference of opinion *and* where the appeal will result in the ultimate termination of the proceedings or where subsequent review will be inadequate. 28 C.F.R. §68.53(a)(2).

8.b. ALJ's decision is final 60 days after the date it is issued unless the CAHO modifies, vacates, or remands the order or the order is referred to the AG. 28 C.F.R. §68.52(g). A party may seek review of the ALJ's order with CAHO within 10 days of the date of the entry of the order. 28 C.F.R. §68.54(a)(1).

8.c. A person or entity adversely affected by a final order has 45 days after the *date the order is issued* to seek review in the appropriate U.S. court of appeal. There is some ambiguity as to whether this became 45 days from the ALJ's order or 45 days from the time the order is final. *Velasquez-Tabir v. INS*, 127 F.3d 456, 458 n.5 (5th Cir. 1997).

8.d. Enforcement of the ALJ/AG's decision shall be through a suit in U.S. district court seeking compliance of the order. The validity and appropriateness of the ALJ/AG's order is not subject to review in such a proceeding.

D. ***Civil Penalty for Failure to Depart***—INA §274D. Any alien who willfully fails or refuses to depart the U.S. after a final order of removal is subject to pay a civil penalty of not more than $500/day.

X. REMOVAL PROCEDURES

A. ***Effect of Deportation***—Deportation has historically been viewed as having harsh consequences. *Fong Haw Tan v. Phelan*, 333 U.S. 6 (1948) [the equivalent to banishment]; *Jordan v. DeGeorge*, 341 U.S. 223 (1951) ["A sentence to life in exile ... a penalty"]; *Bridges v. Wixon,* 326 U.S. 135, 164 (1945) ["The impact of deportation upon the life of an alien is often as great if not greater than the imposition of a criminal sentence. A deported alien may lost his family, his friends, and his livelihood forever. Return to his native land may result in poverty, persecution and even death."]; *Ng Fung Ho v. White*, 259 U.S. 276 (1922) ["Loss of property or life or all that makes life worth living"]; *Lehmann v. U.S.,* 353 U.S. 685, 691 (1957) (Black, J., concurring) ["To banish [an immigrant] from home, family and adopted country is punishment of the most drastic kind."]; *Chrzanoski v. Ashcroft,* 327 F.3d 188, 197 (2d Cir. 2003) [quoting *Fong Haw Tan*]; *Padilla-Agustin v. INS*, 21 F.3d 970, 978 (9th Cir. 1994) [when an alien faces the threat of deportation the stakes are high.... He may face deprivation, torture or even death when he is returned to his homeland]; *Gonzalez v. INS*, 996 F.2d 804, 811 n.7 (6th Cir. 1993) [a drastic measure and at times the equivalent of banishment or exile ... A penalty]; *Yepes-Prado v. INS,* 10 F.3d 1363, 1369 n.11 (9th Cir. 1993) [quoting *Gonzalez* that "Deportation is a drastic measure and at times the equivalent of banishment or exile"]; *Klonis v. Davis*, 13 F.2d 630 (2d Cir. 1926) ["Exile, a dreadful punishment"]; *Matter of Hou*, 20 I&N Dec. 513, 520 (BIA 1992) [potentially drastic consequences of deportation].

B. *Due Process*—Person in removal (formerly deportation) proceeding is entitled to full due process. "It is well established that the Fifth Amendment entitles aliens to due process of law in deportation proceedings." *Reno v. Flores*, 507 U.S. 292, 306 (1993); "[T]he Due Process Clause applies to all 'persons' within the United States, including aliens, whether their presence here is lawful, unlawful, temporary, or permanent." *Zadvydas v. Davis,* 533 U.S. 678, 693 (2001) [indefinite detention is unconstitutional for post-removal cases beyond 6 months of incarceration because "Freedom from imprisonment—from government custody, detention, or other forms of physical restraint—lies at the heart of the liberty that Clause protects"]; *Accardi v. Shaughnessy*, 347 U.S. 260 (1954); *Bridges v. Wixon*, 326 U.S. 135 (1945); *Plyler v. Doe*, 457 U.S. 202 (1982); *Wong Yang Sung v. McGrath*, 339 U.S. 33 (1950)

1. Due process violations found

Second Circuit—*Burger v. Gonzales,* 498 F.3d 131 (2d Cir. 2007) [following the Ninth and Tenth Circuits the failure to give an asylum applicant from the former Yugoslavia the opportunity to respond to administrative findings of changed conditions in Serbia-Montenegro *before* making those finding is a violation of due process and is not cured by a motion to reopen]; *Montilla v. INS*, 926 F.2d 162, 169 (2d Cir. 1991) ["Careless observance by an agency of its own administrative processes weakens its effectiveness in the eyes of the public because it exposes the possibility of favoritism and of inconsistent application of the law"]

Third Circuit—*Cham v. Att'y Gen. of the U.S.,* 445 F.3d 683 (3d Cir. 2006) [IJ's conduct violated due process and deprived Gambian asylum application of a fair hearing where IJ assumed application was invalid, nitpicked the application and testimony for inconsistencies and contradictions, prevented applicant from presenting evidence/witnesses, and engaged in conduct that was abusive toward the applicant including preventing him from presenting his testimony by continually interrupting him]; *Muhanna v. Gonzales,* 399 F.3d 582, 588–89 (3d Cir. 2005) [a finding of frivolousness by IJ in asylum hearing violated due process where it was based solely on a credibility determination and not on the application as a whole and where respondent was not permitted to present testimony on his claim]; *Hossain v. Ashcroft,* 381 F.3d 29 (1st Cir. 2004) [where transcript and briefing schedule mailed to incorrect address and brief never filed, basic fairness requires that BIA's denial of motion to reconsider be reversed]; *Ezeagwuna v. Ashcroft,* 325 F.3d 396, 405–08 (3d Cir. 2003) [reliance on double and triple hearsay letter of Director of Office of Country Reports and Asylum Affairs in DOS to undermine credibility of documentary evidence in asylum/withholding claim violated due process]

Fifth Circuit—*Chike v. INS*, 948 F.2d 961 (5th Cir. 1991) [due process requires notice of BIA briefing schedule]

Sixth Circuit—*Alexandrov v. Gonzales,* 442 F.3d 395, 404–07 (6th Cir. 2006) [in Bulgarian asylum claim, IJ violated due process by relying on 2 highly unreliable hearsay memoranda from the U.S. Embassy in Sofia to prove that respondent's documents were fraudulent and he therefore filed a frivolous asylum claim]; *Ahmed v. Gonzales,* 398 F.3d 722 (6th Cir. 2005) [where IJ misunderstood testimony and based on his misunderstanding made improper rulings as to credibility denying asylum, due process was violated, the IJ's order was reversed, and the court ordered that a new judge hear the matter]; *Castellano-Chacon v. INS,* 341 F.3d 533, 552–53 (6th Cir. 2003) [IJ erred in not allowing respondent's counsel to make opening and closing arguments but found the error to be harmless in this case]

Seventh Circuit—*Bosede v. Mukasey,* 512 F.3d 946, 950–51 (7th Cir. 2008) [IJ violated fundamental due process in not considering evidence, in stating that petitioner might not have problems because he could bribe his way out of jail, and in applying "whatever rationale he could muster to justify a predetermined outcome"]; *Floroiu v Gonzales,* 481 F.3d 970, 973–76 (7th Cir. 2007) [where IJ characterized asylum applicants as "religious zealots" who were "offensive to the majority" his comments evidenced sufficient bias to deprive applicants of due process]; *Rodriguez Galicia v. Gonzales,* 422 F.3d 529, 538–40 (7th Cir. 2005) [IJ violated due process under the totality of the circumstances when he frequently interrupted respondent's counsel, assumed the role of counsel for the government and precluded 2 experts from testifying regarding Guatemalan asylum claim]; *Kerciku v. INS,* 314 F.3d 913 (7th Cir. 2003) [due process was violated where IJ foreclosed virtually all testimony in asylum hearing after he determined from brief questioning that respondent was not credible]; *Singh v. Reno,* 182 F.3d 504 (7th Cir. 1999) [INS improperly delayed a deportation hearing in violation of due process causing persons with criminal background to be denied any possibility of relief]; *Xiong v. INS,* 173 F.3d 601, 607–08 (7th Cir. 1999) [violation of due process to sustain deportability in federal appeal based on a different aggravated felony ground than the one charged and decided upon by IJ]; *Nazarova v. INS,* 171 F.3d 478 (7th Cir. 1999) [violation of due process to deprive person of meaningful opportunity to be heard at deportation proceeding where INS refused to reopen *in absentia* order]; *Podio v. INS,* 153 F.3d 506 (7th Cir. 1998) [where respondent denied the right to have siblings testify to corroborate persecution in Ukraine and where IJ stifled counsel's ability to allow client to testify by taking over and shortcutting the questioning, due process was denied]; *Kossov v. INS*, 132 F.3d 405, 408 (7th Cir. 1998) [where persons ordered deported to Russia but evidence taken on fear of return to Latvia, there was a "fundamental failure of due process"]; *Ademi v. INS*, 31 F.3d 517, 521 n.8 (7th Cir. 1994) [to discourage the right to appeal is to place an unconstitutional burden on the alien's right to due process]

Eighth Circuit—*Tun v. Gonzales,* 485 F.3d 1014 (8th Cir. 2007) [respondent's due process rights were violated where experts' testimony was excluded and interpretation was seriously flawed]; *Al Khouri v. Ashcroft,* 362 F.3d 461, 464–67 (8th Cir. 2004) [due process was violated where IJ made adverse credibility findings denying *pro se* respondent's asylum after refusing to allow respondent the opportunity to fully develop his record and giving him only 10 minutes to review his 200-page asylum application]

Ninth Circuit—*Yeghiazaryan v. Gonzales,* 439 F.3d 994 (9th Cir. 2006) [BIA violated due process where respondent's counsel filed a protective motion to reopen within 90 days and stated she would file the supporting briefs, but the BIA improperly denied the motion to reopen within the 90-day period because counsel did not simultaneously file the briefs and supporting documentation]; *Zolotukhin v. Gonzales,* 417 F.3d 1073 (9th Cir. 2005) [refusing to hear corroborative testimony from family members and expert testimony and cutting short respondent's testimony deprived him of due process in religious persecution claim from Russia where the violation could have "potentially…affect[ed] the outcome of the proceedings"]; *Lopez-Umanzor v. Gonzales,* 405 F.3d 1049 (9th Cir. 2005) [violation of due process not to permit expert testimony regarding domestic violence where it could have affected IJ's view of respondent's credibility and therefore affected whether IJ should believe respondent over police office about drug trafficking]; *Kaur v. Ashcroft,* 388 F.3d 734 (9th Cir. 2004) [due process violated where IJ precluded respondent's son from testifying and at the same time faulted her for not offering corroborating evidence at her asylum hearing]; *Martinez-De Bojorquez v. Ashcroft,* 365 F.3d 800 (9th Cir. 2004) [BIA violated due process by applying 8 C.F.R. §1003.4 to terminate an appeal of a person who departed the U.S. (when she briefly crossed the Mexican border for medical treatment) without being notified by the IJ that departure would terminate her appeal]; *Salgado-Diaz v. Ashcroft,* 395 F.3d 1158, 1162–65 (9th Cir. 2005) [failure to give respondent a hearing on whether he was previously removed illegally while he had a deportation hearing pending violated his due process rights]; *Garcia-Cortez v. Ashcroft,* 366 F.3d 749 (9th Cir. 2004) [petitioner denied due process where BIA summarily dismissed appeal for failure to file a brief when petitioners' notice of appeal was sufficiently detailed and they filed brief late]; *Flores-Chavez v. Ashcroft,* 362 F.3d 1150 (9th Cir. 2004) [reversed *in absentia* order against 15-year-old who was served with OSC pursuant to 8 C.F.R. §103.5a, but no service was provided to adult custodian. Court found that reading the statute to permit service solely on minor violated DHS regulations, was not entitled to *Chevron* deference, and raised serious constitutional questions]:*Reyes-Melendez v. INS,* 342 F.3d 1001 (9th Cir. 2003) [where IJ took over questioning, did not act as a neutral fact finder, and engaged in a stream of nonjudicious and snide comments demonstrating her hostility to the applicant for suspension, due process was violated and final order was reversed]; *Singh v. INS,* 362 F.3d 1164 (9th Cir. 2004) [due process violated where BIA sent transcript and briefing schedule to wrong address and then refused to allow respondent the opportunity to file a brief beyond the scheduled time]; *Ramirez-Alejandre v. Ashcroft,* 320 F.3d 858 (9th Cir. 2003) (*en banc*) [due process was violated where the BIA had no procedures for treating evidence that arose during the appeal process in suspension cases that often continued for years]; *Cano-Merida v. INS,* 311 F.3d 960, 964–65 (9th Cir. 2002) [IJ's off the record discussion with *pro se* respondent that he had no basis for asylum claim before respondent had opportunity to present testimony or documents was a violation of the full and fair hearing and neutral judge requirements that due process demands where respondent withdrew claim]; *Agyeman v. INS,* 296 F.3d 871 (9th Cir. 2002) [due process violated in deportation proceeding where the IJ demanded that the only evidence he would accept of the bona fide nature of respondent's marriage was his wife's testimony who did not appear because she has bipolar disorder]; *Abovian v. INS,* 219 F.3d 972, 978 (9th Cir. 2000) [failure by the BIA to give asylum applicant an opportunity to rebut adverse credibility findings by raising them for the first time before BIA violates due process]; *Sanchez-Cruz v. INS,* 255 F.3d 775, 779–80 (9th Cir. 2001) [where IJ refused to allow petitioner to present evidence that contradicted some of his findings, where he called her a liar, and where he focused almost exclusively on the period she accepted public assistance in denying suspension, she presented a colorable due process claim]; *Jacinto v. INS,* 208 F.3d 725 (9th Cir. 2000) [due process violated where IJ inadequately explained hearing procedures, and failed to adequately advise respondent of her various roles including the right to be a witness and the right to affirmatively present testimony instead of merely being subject to examination. Analogized asylum hearing to procedures in Social Security cases]; *Perez-Lastor v. INS,* 208 F.3d 773, 777–78 (9th Cir. 2000) [due process is violated by incompetent translation]; *Colmenar v. INS,* 210 F.3d 967, 971 (9th Cir. 2000) [failure to provide full and fair hearing of claims and a reasonable opportunity to present evidence violates due process and warrants reversal of asylum denial]; *Campos-Sanchez v. INS,* 164 F.3d 448 (9th Cir. 1999) [violation of due process to deny asylum on credibility finding at BIA where person found credible before IJ and never given opportunity to rebut]; *but see Pal v. INS,* 204 F.3d 935, 938–39 (9th Cir. 2000) [narrowing *Campos-Sanchez* where BIA credibility findings include IJs]; *Gonzalez-Julio v. INS*, 34 F.3d 820 (9th Cir. 1994) [struck down 10-day appellate filing deadlines for persons residing in Hawaii as violation of due process]; *Castillo-Villagra v. INS*, 972 F.2d 1017, 1029 (9th Cir. 1992) [denial of due process to take administrative notice of adjudicative facts without giving asylum applicant opportunity to be heard]; *Morisath v. Smith,* 988 F.Supp. 1333, 1340–41 (W.D. Wash. 1997) [DD written decision on bond and failure to provide bond hearing is a denial of due process]

Eleventh Circuit—*Ibrahim v. INS*, 821 F.2d 1547, 1550 (11th Cir. 1987) [due process but must show substantial prejudice]

Board of Immigration Appeals—*Matter of Ching*, 12 I&N Dec. 710, 712 (BIA 1968) [if in U.S., due process attaches].

2. Finding No Due Process Violation

U.S. Supreme Court—*Demore v. Kim*, 538 U.S. 510 (2003) [mandatory detention of LPRs under INA §236(c) does not violate due process]

First Circuit—*Aguilar v. ICE,* 510 F.3d 1, 21–24 (1st Cir. 2007) [substantive due process of parents to make decisions regarding the care, custody and control of their children is not violated when they are arrested and transported to out-of-state locations by ICE]; *Pena-Muriel v. Gonzales,* 489 F.3d 438 (1st Cir. 2007) [due process was not violated where the BIA refused to allow respondent, who was outside the United States, to reopen his deportation proceeding after five years because his conviction was vacated]; *Alsamhouri v. Gonzales,* 484 F.3d 117, 122, 124 (1st Cir. 2007) [no due process violation in denying continuance for new counsel to file asylum application];*Chickwendu v. Gonzales,* 415 F.3d 142 (1st Cir. 2005) [IJ's reconstruction of two witnesses testimony after forgetting to tape record them was not a due process violation where counsel participated and did not object to the reconstruction, where there were affidavits from the witnesses in evidence and where there was no showing of prejudice]

Second Circuit—*Cervantes-Ascencio v. INS,* 326 F.3d 83, 86–87 (2d Cir. 2003) [the requirement that respondent waive appeal in order to obtain VD does not violate due process]

Third Circuit—*Mudric v. Att'y Gen. of the U.S.,* 469 F.3d 94, 98–99 (3d Cir. 2006) [delay in adjudicating asylum and adjustment applications is not a violation of due process because there is no constitutional right to asylum and no property interest invoked in failing to timely decide a discretionary benefit]; *Romanishyn v. Attorney General of the U.S.*, 455 F.3d 175, 185–86 (3d Cir. 2006) [IJ's refusal to allow respondent to call more than two witnesses was not a violation of due process because submitting their testimony by affidavit did not render the proceeding fundamentally unfair]; *Kamara v. Att'y Gen. of the U.S.*, 420 F.3d 202, 211–12, 216–18 (3d Cir. 2005) [rejected a procedural due process challenge to bare nature of BIA's decision in CAT claim and a substantive due process challenge based upon the state-created danger exception holding it has no place in our immigration jurisprudence]; *Paripovic v. Gonzales,* 418 F.3d 240, 246 n.5 (3d Cir. 2005) [due process not violated where IJ refused to grant continuance to allow expert to testify where respondent did not ask for continuance prior to hearing that was in its 8th year];

Bonhometre v. Ashcroft, 414 F.3d 442, 448–50 (3d Cir. 2005) [no due process violation because INA §212(c)/212(h) relief was not available to temporary resident who committed aggravated felony]; *Dia v. Ashcroft,* 353 F.3d 228, 234–45 (3d Cir. 2003) (*en banc*) [AWO procedure does not violate due process because there is no right to a particular type of BIA decision]; *Abdulrahman v. Ashcroft,* 330 F.3d 587, 595–97 (3d Cir. 2003) [where IJ in certain places during the asylum hearing "did go beyond the bounds of propriety" her actions based on the record as a whole did not demonstrate sufficient bias to be due process violation]

Fifth Circuit— *Ahmed v. Gonzales,* 447 F.3d 433, 440 (5th Cir. 2006) [finding no due process violation in denying a continuance to permit approval of a labor certification for INA §245(i) eligibility because adjustment is discretionary]; *Rosales v. ICE,* 426 F.3d 733, 736–38 (5th Cir. 2005) [where respondent was not informed of rights under the Vienna Convention there was no due process violation because there was no showing of prejudice]; *De Zavala v. Ashcroft,* 385 F.3d 879 (5th Cir. 2004) [due process was not violated where respondent was incorrectly charged as inadmissible at entry as a nonimmigrant when she was inadmissible as an immigrant because there was no prejudice]

Sixth Circuit—*Matovski v. Gonzales,* 492 F.3d 722, 737–39 (6th Cir. 2007) [due process not violated where ground of inadmissibility—§212(a)(6)(C)(i)—is raised in relief phase of case although not charged as the ground of deportability because the IJ may rule on any ground of inadmissibility that arises during the course of proceedings]; *Garza-Moreno v. Gonzales,* 489 F.3d 239, 241–42 (6th Cir. 2007) [although "due process demands a reasonable accurate and complete transcript to allow for meaningful appellate review" the BIA's decision was not reversed despite 67 "indiscernible" notations in the transcript because there was no showing of prejudice]; *Bangura v. Hansen,* 434 F.3d 487, 494–96 (6th Cir. 2006) [INA §204(c) does not violate substantive or procedural due process]; *Elia v. Gonzales,* 431 F.3d 268, 275–76 (6th Cir. 2005) [substantive and procedural due process not violated by failure to give incarcerated respondent a hearing within 5 years so he could apply for §212(c) relief]; *Gilaj v. Gonzales,* 408 F.3d 275, 290 (6th Cir. 2005) [recognizing due process right to opening statement and closing argument but finding harmless error where respondent failed to demonstrate prejudice]

Seventh Circuit—*Alimi v. Gonzales,* 489 F.3d 829 (7th Cir. 2007) [admission of respondent's statement taken by officer at airport without presenting officer for cross-examination did not violate due process]; *Mireles v. Gonzales,* 433 F.3d 965, 969 (7th Cir. 2006) [no constitutional right to have removal proceedings initiated against respondent]; *Hussain v. Gonzales,* 424 F.3d 622, 626–27 (7th Cir. 2005) [due process was not violated where IJ set 60 days for submission of documents for asylum hearing rather than the 10 days under the local rules and there was no evidence that the earlier deadline prejudiced the respondent]; *Hamid v. Gonzales,* 417 F.3d 642, 645–47 (7th Cir. 2005) [no specific right to present evidence through oral testimony and IJ's refusal to allow live telephonic expert testimony while not precluding an expert affidavit is not a *per se* due process violation and no prejudice demonstrated]; *Ramos v. Gonzales,* 414 F.3d 800, 804–06 (7th Cir. 2005) [no due process violation where lawyer with EOIR-28 waived client's presence at all hearings and there was no showing of prejudice despite respondent's claim that IJ should have determined that lawyer was authorized to do so]; *Zaidi v. Ashcroft,* 377 F.3d 678, 682 (7th Cir. 2004) [where asylum applicant given only 3 weeks to present claim no due process violation absent showing of prejudice]; *Kuschchak v. Ashcroft,* 366 F.3d 597 (7th Cir. 2004) [IJ did not violate procedural due process in refusing to grant continuance where lawyer asked for expedited hearing on lottery adjustment and IJ insisted that he also proceed on asylum claim]; *Ciorba v. Ashcroft,* 323 F.3d 539, 544–45 (7th Cir. 2003) [IJ announcing at beginning of asylum hearing that he reviewed documents and thought asylum case was deficient but that he had not made up his mind was not bias or due process violation]

Eighth Circuit—*Abdelwase v. Gonzales,* 496 F.3d 904 (8th Cir. 2007) [BIA's refusal to accept late-filed brief was not prejudicial because BIA entered AWO and court reviewed IJ's decision]; *Vonhm v. Gonzales,* 454 F.3d 825, 829–30 (8th Cir. 2006) [where *pro se* respondent was not advised of right to present evidence at final hearing but was told to bring affidavit and did so, no due process violation]; *Obleshchenko v. Ashcroft,* 392 F.3d 970, 971–72 (8th Cir. 2004) [no due process right regarding ineffective assistance of counsel in asylum claim, because there is no liberty or property interest where relief is subject to the unfettered discretion of a governmental authority]; *Tamenut v. Ashcroft,* 361 F.3d 1060 (8th Cir. 2004) [where fax from U.S. consular section in

Ethiopia was used to impeach applicant's claim that he was in jail during periods fax showed he was employed at the consulate, due process was not violated by its submission because he could have rebutted them through his own testimony]; *Nyama v. Ashcroft,* 357 F.3d 812, 816–17 (8th Cir. 2004) [when asylum applications from other applicants with the same story and same alleged parent as respondent were offered to impeach respondent and not for their truth, they were admissible and did not violate respondent's due process rights because he had ample time to rebut them]

Ninth Circuit—*Shin v. Mukasey,* 519 F.3d 901, 906 (9th Cir. 2008) [due process not violated where deposition of corrupt DHS official who sold "green cards" was taken in consolidated cases for judicial economy and used in respondent's removal proceeding]; *Morales-Izquierdo v. Gonzales,* 486 F.3d 484, 495–98 (9th Cir. 2007) (en banc) [AG regulation that assigns reinstatement to a DHS officer rather than an IJ does not violate procedural due process; *Marcello v. Bonds,* 349 U.S. 302 (1955) cited]; *Salviejo-Fernandez v. Gonzales,* 455 F.3d 1063, 1065–66 (9th Cir. 2006) [due process was not violated where ICE did not charge respondent with an aggravated felony in the NTA but used the conviction to find respondent ineligible for cancellation]; *Theagene v. Gonzales,* 411 F.3d 1107, 1112–13 (9th Cir. 2005) [application by the BIA of an intervening *en banc* decision upon the government's motion to reconsider CAT grant in light of *en banc* decision does not violate due process]; *Khan v. Ashcroft,* 374 F.3d 825 (9th Cir. 2004) [upheld denial of motion to reopen *in absentia* hearing to seek asylum, where respondent attended master calendar, did not show up for continued hearing, and claimed due process violation because master calendar hearing was not translated]; *Munoz v. Ashcroft,* 339 F.3d 950, 954 (9th Cir. 2003) [no substantive due process right to remain in U.S. where respondent entered as one-year-old, has no family abroad, and is subject to removal because his parent failed to protect him by filing for relief from removal when he was a minor]; *Rojas-Garcia v. Ashcroft,* 339 F.3d 814, 823–24 (9th Cir. 2003) [due process is not violated where inadmissibility determination for "reason to believe" that person is a drug trafficker was based upon hearsay evidence as long as evidence was probative and fundamentally fair and ineffective assistance of counsel did not result in prejudice]; *Melkonian v. Ashcroft,* 320 F.3d 1061, 1072 (9th Cir. 2003) [aggressive and sometimes harsh questioning by IJ during asylum hearing is not a violation of due process]; *U.S. v. Barraza-Leon,* 575 F.2d 218, 220 (9th Cir. 1978)

Tenth Circuit—*Desta v. Ashcroft,* 329 F.3d 1179, 1184–86 (10th Cir. 2003) [no due process violation where BIA designates country because IJ forgets and respondent not given prior notice and opportunity to respond]

Eleventh Circuit—*Frech v. U.S. Att'y Gen.,* 491 F.3d 1277, 1280–82 (11th Cir. 2007) [where respondent argued that IJ's refusal to change venue violated his right to due process including the right to counsel and the ability to present evidence in NACARA waiver case, court found no prejudice]; *Zafar v. U.S. Att'y Gen.,* 461 F.3d 1357, 1362–67 (11th Cir. 2006) *reh'g en banc denied* 473 F.3d 1350 (2007) [finding no due process violation in denying a continuance to permit approval of a labor certification for INA §245(i) eligibility where adjustment is discretionary]; *Garcia v. Att'y Gen. of the U.S.,* 329 F.3d 1217, 1223–24 (11th Cir. 2003) [following *Mejia Rodriguez* there is no ineffective assistance of counsel that rises to a due process violation where the deficient representation "merely prevents the alien from being eligible" for discretionary relief such as INA §212(h)]; *Balogun v. U.S. Att'y Gen.,* 304 F.3d 1303 (11th Cir. 2003) [no constitutionally protected right to discretionary relief or to be eligible for discretionary relief and no constitutional right to be advised of consequences of accepting advance parole]

D.C. Circuit—*Narenji v. Civiletti,* 617 F.2d 745 (D.C. Cir. 1979), *cert. denied,* 446 U.S. 957 (1980).

3. *Relief in removal proceedings or before DHS is a matter of grace or right*—In *Arevalo v. Ashcroft,* 344 F.3d 1, 14–15 (1st Cir. 2003), the court addressed the issue whether INA §241(a)(5) (reinstatement of deportation order) may be applied retroactively to bar an AOS application filed prior to IIRIRA's effective date. In finding that the statute could not be applied retroactively the court noted that applying for AOS was a vested right even if the relief itself was discretionary. Citing *Accardi v. Shaughnessy,* 347 U.S. 260 (1954), and other cases, the court stated that "an alien is not precluded from having a vested right in a form of relief merely because the relief itself is ultimately at the discretion of the Executive Branch." *See also INS v. St. Cyr,* 533 U.S. 289, 307–08 (2001) ["Traditionally, courts recognized a distinction between eligibility for discretionary relief, on the one hand, and the favorable exercise of discretion, on the other hand. Eligibility that was 'governed by specific statutory standards' provided 'a right to a ruling on an applicant's eligibil-

ity,' even though the actual granting of relief was 'not a matter of right under any circumstances, but rather is in all cases a matter of grace.'"]; *Alcaraz v. INS,* 384 F.3d 1150, 1162–63 (9th Cir. 2004) [internal policies under *Accardi* principle have binding effect on agency, although court remanded to BIA to determine whether various memoranda were sufficient to establish policy in regard to repapering]; *U.S. v. Copeland,* 376 F.3d 61, 72 (2d Cir. 2004) [there is a distinction between "a right to seek relief and the right to the relief itself" and "[t]he decisions holding that a failure to inform an alien about Section 212(c) relief cannot be a fundamental error collapse this distinction and incorrectly assume that, because the grant of Section 212(c) relief is itself discretionary, the denial of a Section 212(c) hearing cannot be a fundamental procedural error"];*Rabiu v. INS,* 41 F.3d 879, 883 (2d Cir. 1994); *Mayers v. Reno,* 175 F.3d 1289, 1301 n.15 (11th Cir. 1999); *Gutierrez v. Ashcroft,* 289 F.Supp.2d 555, 567–68 (D.N.J. 2003) [rejected claim that because respondent has no due process right to obtain former INA §212(c) relief he has no due process claim to seek relief]. *But see Dekoladenu v. Gonzales,* 459 F.3d 500, 502–08 (4th Cir. 2006) [there is no due process violation in refusing to toll the VD period during a timely filed motion to reopen because motions to reopen and requests for adjustment are purely discretionary and there is no property or liberty interest at stake]; *Hernandez v. Gonzales,* 437 F.3d 341, 345–46 & n.7 (3d Cir. 2006) [no due process right to seek repealed suspension because there is no liberty interest to obtain relief from deportation or to be found ineligible for it]; *Hamdan v. Gonzales,* 425 F.3d 1051, 1060–61 (7th Cir. 2005) [rejected due process argument regarding IJ's conduct in reviewing adjustment application because adjustment is discretionary]; *Nguyen v. District Director,* 400 F.3d 255, 259 (5th Cir. 2005) [no due process right to eligibility for INA §212(c) discretionary relief]; *Guerra-Soto v. Ashcroft,* 397 F.3d 637, 641 (8th Cir. 2005) [affirmed BIA denial of reopening on alternative ground that when ineffective assistance of counsel touches upon respondent's chance to seek discretionary relief there is no due process issue]; *Jupiter v. Ashcroft,* 396 F.3d 487, 492–93 (1st Cir. 2005) [rejected due process claim where motion to reopen for AOS was denied based upon remaining beyond VD deadline on grounds there is no property interest in VD or AOS because they are discretionary]; *Ali v. Ashcroft,* 395 F.3d 722, 732 (7th Cir. 2005) [no due process violation in applying *Pickering* to use vacated conviction for removal and to bar cancellation because there is no liberty or property interest in discretionary relief or its denial]; *Obleshchenko v. Ashcroft,* 392 F.3d 970, 971–72 (8th Cir. 2004) [no due process right regarding ineffective assistance of counsel in asylum claim because there is no liberty or property interest where relief is subject to the unfettered discretion of a governmental authority]; *U.S. v. Torres,* 383 F.3d 92, 104–06 (3d Cir. 2004) [removal proceeding was not fundamentally unfair where IJ did not inform respondent of the right to seek §212(c) relief because grant of relief was speculative and a matter of "grace." Addressed *Greenholtz* finding it supported view that relief was speculative]; *Assaad v. Ashcroft,* 378 F.3d 471, 475–76 (5th Cir. 2004) [no due process violation and therefore no circuit court jurisdiction where counsel's ineffective assistance involved the failure to receive a discretionary waiver of conditional residency]; *Dave v. Ashcroft,* 363 F.3d 649, 652–53 (7th Cir. 2004) [rejected constitutional challenge to streamlining and ineffective assistance of counsel as to cancellation claim because there is no liberty or property interest in discretionary relief]; *Mireles-Valdez v. Ashcroft,* 349 F.3d 213, 219 (5th Cir. 2003) [no due process violation in regard to voluntary departure because eligibility for discretionary relief is not a liberty or property interest]; *Nativi-Gomez v. Ashcroft,* 344 F.3d 805 (8th Cir. 2003) [statutorily created relief such as adjustment of status and INA §212(h) that are subject to the "unfettered discretion" of a governmental authority cannot provide the constitutionally protected liberty interest necessary to give rise to a procedural due process claim]; *Smith v. Ashcroft,* 295 F.3d 425, 429–31 (4th Cir. 2002) [no due process right to challenge reinstatement order arising out of denial of INA §212(c) under AEDPA and IIRIRA because there is no property or liberty interest in discretionary statute]; *Ashki v. INS,* 233 F.3d 913, 921 (6th Cir. 2000) [no constitutionally protected liberty interest in obtaining discretionary relief from deportation]; *Tefel v. Reno*, 180 F.3d 1286, 1298–1305 (11th Cir. 1999), *cert. denied,* 120 S.Ct. 2657 (2000) [rejected due process claim on grounds that suspension is a matter of grace and therefore no liberty interest following *Connecticut Bd. of Pardons v. Dumschat,* 452 U.S. 458, 464–67 (1981)]; *Appiah v. INS,* 202 F.3d 704 (4th Cir. 2000), *cert. denied,* 531 U.S. 857 (2000) [same].

4. Deportation is considered a civil, not criminal, proceeding.

4.a. Ex Post Facto Clause inapplicable because deportation not criminal. *Collins v. Youngblood,* 497 U.S. 37, 110 S.Ct. 2715 (1990); *Lehmann v. U.S.*, 353 U.S. 685, 690 (1957); *Marcello v.*

Bonds, 349 U.S. 302, 314 (1955); *Harisiades v. Shaughnessy*, 342 U.S. 580 (1952); *Guaylupo-Moya v. Gonzales,* 423 F.3d 121, 131–32 (2d Cir. 2005) [rejected *ex post facto* challenged to expanded definition of aggravated felony that bars INA §212(h) relief]; *Csekinek v. INS,* 391 F.3d 819, 823–24 (6th Cir. 2004) [court rejects assertion that retroactive application of IIRIRA violates Ex Post Facto Clause]; *Perez v. Elwood,* 294 F.3d 552, 557 (3d Cir. 2002) [challenge to retroactive application of provision abolishing INA §212(c) not available under Ex Post Facto Clause because immigration is civil in nature]; *Montenegro v. Ashcroft,* 355 F.3d 1035, 1037 (7th Cir. 2004) [Ex Post Facto Clause does not apply to retroactive application of IIRIRA regarding finality of convictions]; *Hamama v. INS*, 78 F.3d 233 (6th Cir. 1996); *U.S. v. Yacoubian*, 24 F.3d 1, 9–10 (9th Cir. 1994); *Kelly v. Farquharson,* 256 F.Supp.2d 93, 101 n.7 (D. Mass. 2003).

4.b. Bill of Attainder Clause inapplicable because deportation is not a punishment or penalty. *Linnas v. INS*, 790 F.2d 1024 (2d Cir. 1986) [amendment to INA §241(a) deporting Nazis].

4.c. Speedy Trial inapplicable. Immigration proceedings not considered criminal proceedings for purpose of the Speedy Trial Act, *Argiz v. INS*, 704 F.2d 384 (7th Cir. 1983),

4.d. Sixth Amendment right to counsel inapplicable. *Morales-Izquierdo v. Gonzales,* 486 F.3d 484, 497 (9th Cir. 2007) (en banc) [in challenge to administrative reinstatement no Sixth Amendment right to counsel]; *Stroe v. INS,* 256 F.3d 498 (7th Cir. 2001) [no Sixth Amendment right to counsel; *dicta* suggests no Fifth Amendment right]; *U.S. v. Torres-Sanchez*, 68 F.3d 227, 230 (8th Cir. 1995); *Lozada v. INS,* 857 F.2d 10, 13 (1st Cir. 1988); *Mantell v. INS*, 798 F.2d 124 (5th Cir. 1986); *Deutsch v. INS*, 943 F.Supp. 276, 279 (W.D.N.Y. 1996) [failure to provide INS inmate with speedy trial was not Sixth Amendment violation],

4.e. Double Jeopardy inapplicable. *Seale v. INS,* 323 F.3d 150, 159–60 (1st Cir. 2003) [rejected respondent's *ex post facto* and double jeopardy arguments that a conviction for assault with intent to murder that arose before 1988 was not an aggravated felony]; *De La Teja v. U.S.*, 321 F.3d 1357, 1364–65 (11th Cir. 2003) [double jeopardy does not apply to immigration because it is a purely civil action]; *U.S. v. Yacoubian*, 24 F.3d 1, 10 (9th Cir. 1994); *Urbina-Mauricio v. INS*, 989 F.2d 1085, 1089 n.7 (9th Cir. 1993); *U.S. v. Garay-Burgos*, 961 F.Supp. 1321 (D. Ariz. 1997) [no double jeopardy for rehearing after deportation hearing]; *Scheidemann v. INS*, 83 F.3d 1517, 1521 n.4 (3d Cir. 1996).

4.f. *Miranda* warnings not required. *Miranda v. Arizona,* 384 U.S. 436 (1966). *U.S. v. Kiam,* 432 F.3d 524, 528–31 (3d Cir. 2005) [*Miranda* warning are no necessary when officer is determining admissibility at the border]; *U.S. v. Solano-Godines*, 120 F.3d 957 (9th Cir. 1997).

4.g. Incompetents not constitutionally prohibited from standing trial. *Brue v. Gonzales,* 464 F.3d 1227, 1232–34 (10th Cir. 2006) [trial of mentally incompetents does not violate substantive due process as it does in the criminal context]. *See also Mohamed v. Gonzales,* 477 F.3d 522, 526–27 (8th Cir. 2006) [court rejected claim that respondent was incompetent without a separate hearing on competency by basing its decision on respondent's actions at the removal hearing].

4.h. Eight Amendment may not apply. *Zamora-Mallari v. Mukasey,* 514 F.3d 679, 695 (7th Cir. 2008) [stripping LPR of residency by not allowing a §212(c) claim due to *Matter of Blake* because there is no comparable ground of inadmissibility is not a "fine" under the Eight Amendment because removal is not punishment]; *Cadet v. Bulger,* 377 F.3d 1173, 1196–97 (11th Cir. 2004) [the Eight Amendment does not apply to civil deportation claim by Haitian that he would suffer cruel and unusual punishment by being deported to Haiti where he would be imprisoned]; *Builes v. Nye,* 239 F.Supp.2d 518, 523–24 (M.D. Pa. 2003) [Colombian drug informant who would be killed upon return to Colombia could not rely on Eighth Amendment in removal proceeding]. *But see generally Austin v. U.S.*, 509 U.S. 602 (1993) [Eighth Amendment applies to civil forfeitures]; *U.S. v. Halper*, 490 U.S. 435 (1989). *But see U.S. v. Ursery*, 116 S.Ct. 2135 (1996) [forfeiture].

5. Failure of agency to follow its own rules is violative of due process. No showing of prejudice or harmful error is required. *Accardi v. Shaughnessy*, 347 U.S. 260 (1954); *Bridges v. Wixon*, 326 U.S. 135 (1945); *Singh v. DOJ,* 461 F.3d 290, 295–97 (2d Cir. 2006) [failure of BIA to follow its regulation regarding acceptance of evidence concerning hardship that occurred after conditional

residency is terminated was an abuse of discretion]; *Montilla v. INS*, 926 F.2d 162, 169 (2d Cir. 1991) ["Careless observance by an agency of its own administrative processes weakens its effectiveness in the eyes of the public because it exposes the possibility of favoritism and of inconsistent application of the law"]. *But see Mema v. Gonzales,* 474 F.3d 412, 420–21 (7th Cir. 2007) [no due process violation for failing to inform respondent under §1240.11(a)(2) of his right to withdraw his application for admission where there is no showing of prejudice]; *Martinez-Camargo v. INS,* 282 F.3d 487 (7th Cir. 2002) [where the violation of a regulation, here 8 C.F.R. §287.3, does not affect a constitutional right, the proceedings will not be invalidated where there is no showing of prejudice]; *Waldron v. INS*, 17 F.3d 511 (2d Cir.), *cert. denied,* 513 U.S. 1014 (1994) [automatic reversal required only when the violation is a fundamental right derived from the Constitution or federal statute]; *Mullen-Cofee v. INS*, 976 F.2d 1375, 1380 n.12 (11th Cir. 1992), *amended on denial of rehearing*, 986 F.2d 1364 (11th Cir. 1993) [failure to notify respondent of right to counsel not a due process violation where no substantive prejudice shown]; *Arzanipour v. INS*, 866 F.2d 743, 746 (5th Cir. 1989) [no due process violation unless regulation is required by the statute]; *U.S. v. Calderon-Medina*, 591 F.2d 529 (9th Cir. 1979); *Millian-Zamora v. Ashcroft,* 228 F.Supp.2d 272, 277–80 (E.D.N.Y. 2002) [where IJ violated the law, INA §240(b)(4)(C), and regulation (8 C.F.R. §240.9) by not recording a witness's testimony, prejudice need not be shown]; *Matter of Nwokoma*, 20 I&N Dec. 899 (BIA 1994) [citing *Brock v. Pierce County*, 476 U.S. 253 (1986), in finding that language of statutes and regulations compelling adjudication of petition within 90 days does not bar subsequent INS action].

6. Distinctions drawn by agency that are irrational cannot be upheld. *Servin-Espinoza v. Ashcroft,* 309 F.3d 1193 (9th Cir. 2002) [finding equal protection violation post *Fuentes-Campos* because of differing treatment between inadmissible persons (who had INA §212(c) rights) and deportable persons who did not; *Estrada-Torres* distinguished]; *Dillingham v. INS*, 267 F.3d 996, 1005–011 (9th Cir. 2001) [an irrebuttable presumption that a foreign conviction that is the equivalent of the Federal First Offender Act cannot expunge simple criminal possession of marijuana violates equal protection under *Stanley v. Illinois*]; *Yeung v. INS*, 76 F.3d 337 (11th Cir. 1995) [extending INA §212(h) to deportation]; *Garberding v. INS*, 30 F.3d 1187 (9th Cir. 1994) [struck down BIA interpretation of eligibility for first offender statute]; *Legalization Assistance Project v. INS*, 976 F.2d 1198, 1211 (9th Cir. 1992); *Francis v. INS*, 532 F.2d 268 (2d Cir. 1976); *Bedoya-Valencia v. INS*, 6 F.3d 891 (2d Cir. 1993) [extending INA §212(c) to EWI under *Francis* rule]; *Roman v. Ashcroft,* 181 F.Supp.2d 808 (N.D. Ohio 2002) [distinction between LPRs who are denied the right to file for §212(h) relief and non-LPRs who may still apply for cancellation of removal failed rational basis test]; *Wallace v. Reno,* 24 F.Supp.2d 104, 105–09 (D. Mass. 1998), *aff'd on other grounds* 194 F.3d 279 (1st Cir. 1999) [finding that the application of AEDPA §440(d) to deportable persons violates the equal protection clause]. *But see Klementanovsky v. Gonzales,* 501 F.3d 788 (7th Cir. 2007) [equal protection is not violated under a facially legitimate and bona fide standard by denying the use of a 212(h) waiver to defeat deportation while permitting it use to challenge inadmissibility; *Yeung* rejected]; *Granados-Oseguera v. Gonzales,* 464 F.3d 993, 996–97(9th Cir. 2006) [equal protection is not violated where persons who do not seek VD have 90 days to reopen their case but those who obtain VD from the IJ have only 30 or 60 days]; *Malagon De Fuentes v. Gonzales,* 462 F.3d 498, 503–05 (5th Cir. 2006) [equal protection is not violated under rational basis review where Congress treated only certain LPRs as arriving aliens and not others]; *Masnauskas v. Gonzales,* 432 F.3d 1067 (9th Cir. 2005) [denied equal protection challenge by Lithuanian spouse to NACARA §202 that provides that only Nicaraguan or Cuban spouses may obtain derivative adjustment]; *Flores-Ledezma v. Gonzales,* 415 F.3d 375, 381–82 (5th Cir. 2005) [equal protection not violated under a rational basis standard by giving the AG the choice to institute summary removal under INA §238(b) or proceedings before an IJ for nonresidents where relief may be obtained]; *Elkins v. Comfort,* 392 F.3d 1159 (10th Cir. 2004) [equal protection not violated under rational basis standard by refusal to extend FFOA treatment to foreign expunged conviction]. *Resendez-Alcaraz v. U.S. Att'y Gen.,* 383 F.3d 1262, 1271–72 (11th Cir. 2004) [the court utilized a highly deferential rational basis test to reject an equal protection challenge against treating expungements under state law differently than expungements under FFOA]; *Chen v. Ashcroft,* 381 F.3d 221, 227–28 (3d Cir. 2004) [the fact that statute provides only for spouses and not fiancées to receive asylum benefits for abortion/forced sterilization of girlfriend is both under/over-inclusive but neither under/over-inclusive is enough to render a statute irrational]. Under *Chevron* deferred to agency interpretation in *Matter of C-Y-Z-* and denied asy-

lum and withholding to fiancée]. *Alvarez-Garcia v. Ashcroft,* 378 F.3d 1094 (9th Cir. 2004) [under the "entry doctrine" fiction, a person seeking admission does not have an equal protection right to the same procedures for adjustment of status before the IJ as a deportable person]; *Latu v. Ashcroft,* 375 F.3d 1012, 1019–21 (10th Cir. 2004) [the §212(h) prohibition against granting LPRs the waiver if they are aggravated felons but allowing non–LPRs to apply has a rational basis that survives an equal protection challenge]; *Armendariz-Montoya v. Sonchik,* 291 F.3d 1116, 1122–23 (9th Cir. 2002) [not irrational to allow persons in exclusion proceedings under AEDPA to obtain INA §212(c) relief but deny it to those in deportation]; *Brooks v. Ashcroft,* 283 F.3d 1268, 1274 (11th Cir. 2002) [rejected equal protection challenge to differing treatment between those who go to trial and those who pled guilty under *St. Cyr* language regarding INA §212(c) relief]; *Lukowski v. INS,* 279 F.3d 644 (8th Cir. 2002) [rejected equal protection claim on rational basis test denying 212(h) eligibility to certain LPRs while granting it to nonresidents]; *Moore v. Ashcroft,* 251 F.3d 919, 923–25 (11th Cir. 2001) [on rational basis test court rejected equal protection claim denying §212(h) eligibility to certain LPRs while granting it to nonresidents]; *De Leon-Reynoso v. Ashcroft,* 293 F.3d 633, 637–40 (3d Cir. 2002) [same]; *Jankowski-Burczyk v. INS,* 291 F.3d 172 (2d Cir. 2002) [same]; *Lara-Ruiz v. INS,* 241 F.3d 934, 946–48 (7th Cir. 2001) [same]; *Rodriguez-Silva v. INS,* 242 F.3d 243, 248 (5th Cir. 2001) [benefits given to certain nationalities under NACARA does not violate equal protection because the Fifth Amendment does not "in any way restrict Congress' authority to set admission and naturalization criteria that are place of origin or nationality-sensitive..."]; *Requena-Rodriguez v. Pasquarell,* 190 F.3d 299, 308–09 (5th Cir. 1999) [equal protection not violated and *Francis* distinguished] *DeSousa v. Reno,* 190 F.3d 175, 183–85 (3d Cir. 1999) [same]; *Jurado-Gutierrez v. Greene,* 190 F.3d 1135, 1152 (10th Cir. 1999) [no equal protection violation regarding denial of §212(c)]; *Ram v. INS,* 243 F.3d 510, 517 (9th Cir. 2001) [no equal protection violation regarding application of statute cutting off suspension to certain nationalities]; *Pinho v. INS,* 249 F.3d 183 (3d Cir. 2001) [same]; *Bartoszewska-Zajac v. INS,* 237 F.3d 710, 714–15 (6th Cir. 2001) [same]; *Tefel v. Reno,* 180 F.3d 1286, 1298–99 (11th Cir. 1999), *cert. denied* 120 S.Ct. 2657 (2000) [same]; *Appiah v. INS,* 202 F.3d 704 (4th Cir. 2000) [same]; *Carr v. INS*, 86 F.3d 949 (9th Cir. 1996); *Campos v. INS*, 961 F.2d 309, 315–17 (1st Cir. 1992).

C. ***REAL ID Act Standard for Relief***—The REAL ID Act has altered the landscape in removal proceedings by placing all burdens on the respondent seeking relief. 8 U.S.C. §240(c)(4). This provision places the burden of proof on the applicant for relief to establish that: (1) s/he satisfies the applicable eligibility requirements; and (2) s/he merits a favorable exercise of relief. It also alters the standards to be applied as to the need for corroborative evidence, §240(c)(4)(B), and now grants IJs wide latitude in their basis for making credibility decisions. §240(c)(4)(C).

D. ***De Facto Deportation of USC or LPR Children***—*De facto* deportation of a USC child has not been recognized as a basis to stay or prevent the deportation of their undocumented or otherwise ineligible parents. *Payne-Barahona v. Gonzales,* 474 F.3d 1, 2–4 & n.1 (and cases cited therein) (1st Cir. 2006) [court rejected Fifth Amendment and international law claims as a basis to stop parent's removal where child was USC]; *Acosta v. Gaffney*, 558 F.2d 1153 (3d Cir. 1977); *Matter of Anaya*, 14 I&N Dec. 488 (BIA 1973); *Matter of A-K-,* 24 I&N Dec. 275 (BIA 2007) [parent cannot derivatively apply for asylum through her child and cannot establish a ground for asylum solely on fear of FGM to child]; *But see Abay v. Ashcroft,* 368 F.3d 634, 640–42 (6th Cir. 2004), [mother's fear that 9-year daughter would be subject to FGM qualifies for asylum]; *Nwaokolo v. INS,* 314 F.3d 303, 307–11 (7th Cir. 2002) [stay granted on BIA denial of motion to reopen under CAT where *USC daughter* might suffer female genital mutilation]; *Memije v Gonzales,* 481 F.3d 1163, 1164 (9th Cir. 2007) (Pregerson, J. dissenting); *but see Niang v. Gonzales,* 492 F.3d 505, 510–14 (4th Cir. 2007) [affirmed asylum denial where mother asserted derivative claim because USC daughter would be subject to FGM if she accompanied her to Senegal and because mother would suffer psychological harm if daughter accompanies her]; *Olowo v. Ashcroft,* 368 F.3d 692, 700–04 (7th Cir. 2004) [affirming IJ denial of asylum to mother of LPR children where mother claimed children, who were not required to leave U.S., would be subject to FGM if they returned to Nigeria]; *Oforji v. Ashcroft,* 354 F.3d 609, 614–18 (7th Cir. 2003) [same under CAT and distinguishing *Nwaokolo*]; *Coleman v. U.S.,* 454 F.Supp.2d 757, 766–69 & n.11 (N.D. Ill. 2006) [USC son who brought action enjoining mom's removal failed to state a cause of action because he suffers no cognizable constitutional violation]; *Matter of A-K-,* 24 I&N Dec. 275 (BIA 2007) [parent cannot establish ground for asylum solely on fear of FGM to child]. *See also Be-*

harry v. Reno, 183 F.Supp.2d 584 (E.D.N.Y. 2002), *rev'd on jurisdictional grounds,* 329 F.3d 51 (2d Cir. 2003) [reversed on jurisdictional grounds the grant of INA §212(h) relief to LPRs who committed crimes prior to AEDPA/IIRIRA but were convicted after passage of the acts because it violates the International Covenant on Civil and Political Rights and customary international law in that it results in separation from USC children]. *But see Oliva v. DOJ,* 433 F.3d 229 (2d Cir. 2005) [denied claim preventing the removal of the father of a USC child under Articles 3(1) and 7(1) of the U.N. Convention on the Rights of the Child, because cancellation of removal as a specific statutory provision governing the criteria to remain in the U.S. trumps any claim based upon customary international law]; *Arellano-Garcia v. Gonzales,* 429 F.3d 1183, 1187–88 (8th Cir. 2005) [same in regard to preventing deportation due to harm to child]; *Cabrera-Alvarez v. Gonzales,* 423 F.3d 1006, 1009–13 (9th Cir. 2005) [denied claim that U.N. Convention on the Rights of the Child, even assuming it has attained the status of customary international law, is violated or inconsistent with the cancellation statute because Article 9(4) recognizes the potential for parents to be deported and cancellation weighs the hardship to the child]; *Guaylupo-Moya v. Gonzales,* 423 F.3d 121, 132–37 (2d Cir. 2005) [finding *Beharry's* international law analysis inappropriate because Congress clearly intended to bar LPRs with aggravated felonies from obtaining the benefit of INA §212(h) and *Beharry* relied on Congress' ambiguity]. At least one court has also determined that a guardian ad litem need not be appointed for a 15-year-old Nicaraguan boy in deportation proceedings. *Calero v. INS*, 957 F.2d 50 (2d Cir. 1992). One circuit has also determined that the forced separation of parents from their children by arresting the parents and transferring them to other states awaiting removal proceedings does not violate substantive due process. *Aguilar v. ICE,* 510 F.3d 1, 21–24 (1st Cir. 2007) [substantive due process of parents to make decisions regarding the care, custody and control of their children is not violated when they are arrested and transported to out-of-state locations by ICE].

E. *Suppression of Illegally Obtained Evidence*

1. The basic issues to review in suppression matters are: (a) Was there a seizure? [*U.S. v. Mendenhall*, 446 U.S. 544 (1980); *U.S. v. Martinez-Fuerte*, 428 U.S. 543 (1976)]; (b) If it was not a seizure, was there a constitutional violation because there was no reasonable suspicion for the stop? [*Terry v. Ohio*, 392 U.S. 1 (1968)]; (c) If a seizure, was there probable cause? [*Dunaway v. New York*, 442 U.S. 200 (1979)]; (d) Does the party asserting the constitutional right have standing? [*Rakas v. Illinois*, 439 U.S. 128 (1978)]; (e) Does the Fourth Amendment apply at all? [*U.S. v. Verdugo-Urquidez*, 494 U.S. 259 (1990)]; (f) Is *Miranda v. Arizona,* 384 U.S. 436 (1966) applicable? *Missouri v. Seibert,* 542 U.S. 600 (2004) [confession obtained without *Miranda* warnings still inadmissible even if repeated after warnings were given].

2. An alien with insignificant ties to the U.S. has no Fourth Amendment right to prevent the seizure of his property located *outside* the U.S., even where the person is in the U.S. and the seizure failed to comply with Fourth Amendment standards. *U.S. v. Verdugo-Urquidez*, 494 U.S. 259 (1990).

3. In removal proceedings respondent/applicant cannot generally suppress evidence asserted to be procured in violation of the Fourth Amendment. *INS v. Lopez-Mendoza*, 468 U.S. 1032 (1984) [Fourth Amendment–based exclusionary rule inapplicable to deportation proceeding.] *Matter of Sandoval*, 17 I&N Dec. 70 (BIA 1979). But if there was a policy or widespread abuse, or if there are egregious Fourth Amendment violations which transgress notions of fundamental fairness, the exclusionary rule might apply. *Lopez Mendoza, supra* at 1050–51 and n.5; *Matter of Cervantes*, 21 I&N Dec. 351, 353 (BIA 1996); *Matter of* ___ (In removal proceedings in Immigration Court, New York) (Weisel, IJ) [terminated removal proceeding after suppressing evidence from coercive practices arising out of NSEERS process], *reprinted in* 82 No. 36 *Interpreter Releases* 1505, 1526–39 (Sept. 19, 2005). Seizing person outside of his apartment and conducting a nonconsensual warrantless search based solely on his Nigerian-sounding name is an egregious violation warranting suppression. *Orhorhaghe v. INS*, 38 F.3d 488 (9th Cir. 1994) [an egregious Fourth Amendment violation does not require that the violation undermine the probative value of the evidence]. Stopping someone based solely on race constitutes an egregious violation and the evidence will be suppressed. *Gonzalez-Rivera v. INS*, 22 F.3d 1441 (9th Cir. 1994) [where Border Patrol stopped Hispanic and all other reasons had low probative value, evidence suppressed]. Also, an improper arrest under INA §287(a)(2), 8 U.S.C. §1357(a)(2), raises "difficult questions." *Westover v. Reno,* 202 F.3d 475, 479–80 (1st Cir. 2000) [no right to suppress removal proceedings but recognizing that whether evidence from an illegal arrest should be used is a more difficult question under the statute]. *But see Chuyon Yon Hong v. Mukdasey,*518 F.3d 1030, 1034–36 (9th

Cir. 2008) [where former corrupt INS official used respondent's nonpublic information to gain an advantage in plea bargaining, respondent claimed unsuccessfully that the use of the information violated 5 C.F.R. §2635.703(a)]; *Melnitsenko v. Mukasey,* 517 F.3d 42, 47–49 (2d Cir. 2008) [motion to suppress denied because 3 hour detention, without *Miranda* or other warnings, after 4 or 5 uniformed officers escorted petitioner who was interrogated, fingerprinted and photographed was not so egregious under *Lopez Mendoza* to warrant suppression]; *Kandamar v. Gonzales,* 464 F.3d 65, 70–74 (1st Cir. 2006) [denied respondent's motion to suppress statements taken at the NSEERS interview as well as the improper seizure of his passport and rejected due process and equal protection challenge to NSEERS program on intermediate scrutiny and rational basis grounds]; *Almeida-Amaral v. Gonzales,* 461 F.3d 231, 234–37 (2d Cir. 2006) [stop of 17 year old Brazilian child at gas station not near the border was a violation of the Fourth Amendment but lacked evidence that it was based solely upon race as in *Gonzalez-Rivera* and was therefore not egregious]; *Navarro-Chalan v. Ashcroft,* 359 F.3d 19, 21–24 (1st Cir. 2004) [where respondent answered questions including information for I-213 before arrest warrant was issued he could not suppress name, identity and other I-213 information—no egregious violation].

4. Suppression is still possible under the Fifth Amendment. *Matter of Garcia-Flores*, 17 I&N Dec. 325 (BIA 1980); *Matter of Toro*, 17 I&N Dec. 340 (BIA 1980). Coerced confession has been held to be suppressible. *Navia-Duran v. INS*, 568 F.2d 803 (1st Cir. 1977); *Bong Youn Choy v. Barber*, 279 F.2d 642 (9th Cir. 1960). Also, evidence may be suppressed that is derived from illegal electronic surveillance. 18 U.S.C. §3504(a); *Matter of Hemblen*, 14 I&N Dec. 739 (BIA 1974). Review of the decision to deny disclosure of electronic surveillance information is in the court of appeals in a review of a final order of deportation. *U.S. v. Hamide*, 914 F.2d 1147, 1152–53 (9th Cir. 1990). *But see Ali v. Gonzales,* 440 F.3d 678, 681–82 (5th Cir. 2006) [even if NSEERS violated equal protection, the exclusionary rule does not apply].

5. Suppression is also possible under the administrative exclusionary rule of the BIA *see Matter of Garcia-Flores,* 17 I&N Dec. 325 (BIA 1980) where DHS violates regulations promulgated for the noncitizen's benefit, and noncitizens suffers prejudice.

6. Suppression under the First Amendment has been rejected in the context of an employer engaging in unfair labor practices to obtain DHS's intervention in a labor dispute. *Montero v. INS*, 124 F.3d 381, 386 (2d Cir. 1997).

7. Suppression of statements in forfeiture or otherwise not granted even where there was a violation of the Vienna Convention on Consular Relations for failure to notify the noncitizen of his right to communicate with his embassy. *Sanchez-Llamas v. Oregon,* 548 U.S. 331 (2006) [in criminal proceeding suppression is not an appropriate remedy for an Article 36 violation and regular state rules of procedural default apply to bar Article 36 claims].

8. A person's statement may be suppressed if there was substantial delay between the time of arrest, the time the statement was taken, and the time s/he was taken before a magistrate to be charged. *U.S. v. Superville,* 40 F.Supp.2d 672, 680–90 (D.V.I. 1999) [where INS took person into administrative detention, questioned him a second time 8 days later, and did not bring him before a judicial officer until another week, the delay violated Fed. R. Crim. P. 5(a), the *McNabb-Mallory* rule, and 18 U.S.C. §3501(c) and the statement was suppressed].

9. Evidence that is the fruit of the unlawful action is also suppressible. *Wong Sun v. U.S.*, 371 U.S. 471, 484 (1963) ["The exclusionary prohibition extends as well to the indirect as the direct products of such invasions"]. The "exclusionary sanctions applies to any 'fruits' of a constitutional violation—whether such evidence be tangible, physical material actually seized in an illegal search, items observed or words overheard in the course of the unlawful activity, or confessions or statements of the accused obtained during an illegal arrest and detention." *U.S. v. Crews*, 445 U.S. 463, 470 (1980). *See also U.S. v. Juarez-Torres,* 441 F.Supp.2d 1108, 1121–23 (D.N.M. 2006) [where vehicle stop 250 miles from border was unconstitutional, the court suppressed the defendant's A-file, fingerprints, evidence of identity, and all statements and observations]; *U.S. v. Khan,* 324 F.Supp.2d 1177, 1186–87 (D. Colo. 2004) [where officers did have reason to believe that LPR was in U.S. in violation of law because he procured his residency by fraud but did not have reasonable grounds to believe he would flee, arrest was unlawful and his subsequent *Mirandized* statements were suppressed as fruit of an unlawful arrest]. The commonly addressed excep-

tions to the rule are that the evidence was obtained from an independent source, that evidence of identity is not suppressible, or there was inevitable discovery or that the events between the unlawful activity and the information sought to be used were sufficiently attenuated. A motion to suppress must be very specific. There must be live testimony or a statement. *Matter of Barcenas*, 19 I&N Dec. 609 (BIA 1988).

10. Improper Use of Administrative Warrant—Documents and statements may also be suppressed where there is a "deliberate use by the Government of an administrative warrant for the purpose of gathering evidence in a criminal case," *Abel v. U.S.,* 362 U.S. 217, 226–29 (1960) [although on the record in the case the Court found no violation, it did note that using the INS administrative process to gather evidence for a criminal proceeding "to circumvent the latter's legal restrictions" would be a violation of the Fourth and Fifth Amendment].

11. Suppression of the Alien File—An alien ("A") file need not be suppressed even if there was an illegal arrest because the person does not have a legitimate expectation of privacy in the file and therefore has no standing to challenge its introduction into evidence. *U.S. v. Herrera-Ochoa,* 245 F.3d 495, 498 (5th Cir. 2001).

12. Suppression and Admission—Even if evidence could be suppressed, the person's admission of alienage and the other elements of a removal charge at the IJ hearing nullifies any claim to suppression of evidence. *Miguel v. INS*, 359 F.3d 408 (6th Cir. 2004).

13. A motion to suppress must be very specific. There must be live testimony or a statement. *Matter of Barcenas,* 19 I&N Dec. 609 (BIA 1988). There is no right to a separate suppression hearing. *Matter of Benitez*, 19 I&N Dec. 173 (BIA 1984).

F. *Encounters/Interrogation*

1. To determine the validity of an interrogation, court must first determine if it was a stop or a seizure. Standard to be used to determine if action was a seizure is whether a "reasonable person would have believed he was free to leave." *U.S. v. Mendenhall*, 446 U.S. 544 (1980); *INS v. Delgado*, 466 U.S. 210 (1984); *U.S. v. Alarcon-Gonzalez*, 73 F.3d 289 (10th Cir. 1996) [police officer yelling freeze turns stop into seizure]; *U.S. v. Alvarez-Sanchez*, 774 F.2d 1036 (11th Cir. 1985); *Martinez v. Nygaard*, 820 F.2d 1024 (9th Cir. 1987), *superseded by* 831 F.2d 822 (9th Cir. 1987); *Pearl Meadows Mushroom Farm, Inc. v. Nelson*, 723 F.Supp. 432, 447–48 (N.D. Cal. 1989).This standard is reflected in DHS's regulations. 8 C.F.R. §287.8(b). *But see U.S. v. Harrell*, 894 F.2d 120 (5th Cir. 1990) [investigative questioning by INS agents for one hour at airport checkpoint behind glass wall not a custodial interrogation when information gained in first few minutes].

2. For a stop, an officer needs reasonable suspicion based on specific articulable facts; probable cause is not necessary. *Terry v. Ohio*, 392 U.S. 1 (1968). Neither the actual motivation of the officer nor a determination of whether a stop would have occurred under "normal circumstances" are relevant. *Whren v. U.S.*, 116 S.Ct. 1769, 1774–76 (1997); *cf. U.S. v. Lopez-Moreno,* 420 F.3d 420, 432 (5th Cir. 2005) [under *Terry* even if an officer's subjective motivation for initiating a traffic stop was wrong because the defendant did not violate the statute, the constitutionality of the stop would be upheld if defendant was objectively violating a different traffic offense]; Whether the stop was justified depends on the "totality of the circumstances" confronting the officer. *U.S. v. Arvizu,* 122 S.Ct. 744, 750–53 (2002) [reversed court of appeals when it sought to analyze each factor to determine whether there was an innocent explanation rather than looking at the totality of the circumstances]; *U.S. v. Brignoni-Ponce*, 422 U.S. 873, 884 (1975) [lists factors to establish articulable facts]; *U.S. v. Cortez*, 449 U.S. 411, 418 (1981). Immigration officers have the right to stop and question a person "*only* for the purpose of determining whether he or she has a right to be or remain in the U.S." *Lau v. INS*, 445 F.2d 217 (D.C. Cir.), *cert. denied*, 404 U.S. 864 (1971); INA §287(a), 8 U.S.C. §1357(a). However, even this "statutory provision is *limited* by the Fourth Amendment." *Murillo v. Musegades*, 809 F.Supp. 487, 498 (W.D. Tex. 1992). A routine traffic stop is a seizure under the Fourth Amendment. *U.S. v. Baron-Cabrera*, 119 F.3d 1454, 1458 (10th Cir. 1997) [although it is seizure it doesn't require probable cause; it is investigatory detention requiring only reasonable suspicion].

ICE must have reasonable suspicion based upon articulable facts that the individual questioned is an illegal alien unless consent is given by the person whom the officer seeks to question. *Matter of King and Yang*, 16 I&N Dec. 502 (BIA 1978) [Oriental appearance, plus past history of illegal employment at restaurant, plus anonymous tip deemed sufficient for nondetentive questioning]; *U.S. v. Rodriguez*, 976 F.2d 592 (9th Cir. 1992). Race or alienage alone is insufficient to establish the "specifically articulable facts together with rational inferences from those facts" that suggest an illegal alien is present, notwithstanding DHS's broad authority under 8 U.S.C. §1357(a)(1). However, where there is reasonable suspicion to stop someone (*e.g.*, the person was speeding) the mere questioning of the individual about his immigration status does not, in and of itself, create a separate event requiring probable cause and such questions do not therefore constitute a Fourth Amendment violation. *Muehler v. Mena,* 544 U.S. 93, 100–01, 125 S.Ct. 1465 (2005) [officer did not need independent reasonable suspicion to ask the respondent her name, date and place of birth and immigration status where such questions did not prolong an otherwise valid detention]; *U.S. v. Torres-Monje,* 433 F.Supp.2d 1028, 1032–34 (D.N.D. 2006) [where officer stopped vehicle due to traffic violation it was not a violation of the Fourth Amendment to ask about driver and passenger's immigration status]

2.a. No reasonable suspicion to stop found

U.S. v. Espinoza, 490 F.3d 41, 46–48 (1st Cir. 2007) [where ICE agent observed nothing unusual or unlawful about a van's operation during his surveillance and where Boston was not a place generally associated with the smuggling of aliens, his observation that the van had a Texas license plate, that it was registered in the name of someone in a previous investigation for smuggling and that there were two or three similar passenger vans used for smuggling in the past year were insufficient for reasonable suspicion]; *U.S. v. Manzo-Jurado,* 457 F.3d 928 (9th Cir. 2006) [reversed conviction for misuse of Social Security number where the information was obtained through an illegal seizure based upon the officer's observation that Hispanic-looking men, who appeared to be a work crew, calmly conversed in Spanish at a football game where they appeared out-of-place]; *U.S. v. Sigmond-Ballesteros,* 285 F.3d 1117 (9th Cir. 2002) [reversed district court's denial of motion to suppress where defendant pulled off the road, attempted to obscure his face from the officer's shining light, was driving on a route notorious for alien smuggling, was driving a vehicle (pick up truck) typically used for smuggling without a back seat, was driving at 4:20am when the route was normally used for commercial traffic and was on a route to the border but not near the border]; *U.S. v. Lopez-Valdez,* 178 F.3d 282 (5th Cir. 1999) [reversed district court denial of suppression motion notwithstanding vehicle's proximity to border, numerous passengers in the vehicle, and the road the vehicle was traveling on could be used to circumvent an immigration checkpoint]; *U.S. v. Rodriguez-Rivas,* 151 F.3d 377 (5th Cir. 1998) [reversed district court denial of suppression motion where vehicle stopped by Border Patrol because it had no front license plate]; *U.S. v. Jones,* 149 F.3d 364 (5th Cir. 1998) [reversed district court finding of reasonable cause and held that under totality of circumstances the stop of the vehicle was unconstitutional]; *Gonzalez-Rivera v. INS*, 22 F.3d 1441 (9th Cir. 1994); *Illinois Migrant Council v. Pilliod*, 540 F.2d 1062 (7th Cir. 1976), *modified*, 548 F.2d 715 (7th Cir. 1977); *U.S. v. McDaniel*, 463 F.2d 129 (5th Cir. 1972); *Nicacio v. INS*, 797 F.2d 700 (9th Cir. 1985) [Mexican or Latin appearance alone are insufficient. "Articulable facts" forming the basis of reasonable suspicion are "measured against an objective reasonable man standard, not by the subjective impressions of a particular officer"]; *U.S. v. Juarez-Torres,* 441 F.Supp.2d 1108 (D.N.M. 2006) [where vehicle was stopped 250 miles from border, there was not a sufficient factual basis for the border patrol to stop the vehicle under the totality of the circumstances test]; *U.S. v. Espinoza,* 433 F.Supp.2d 186 (D. Mass. 2006) [a stop based solely upon the van having a Texas license plate and designed similar to 2 or 3 other vans seized with undocumented persons is not sufficient for a seizure]; *U.S. v. Ross,* 400 F.Supp.2d 939, 945–47 (W.D. Tex. 2005) [no reasonable suspicion to stop Jeep although there was reasonable suspicion to stop another car that appeared to be with it]; *U.S. v. Olivares-Rangel,* 324 F.Supp.2d 1218 (D.N.M. 2004) [when agent blocked car seizure took place without probable cause or reasonable suspicion and immigration records as well as all statements and fingerprint records are suppressed]; *U.S. v. Mendoza-Carrillo,* 107 F.Supp.2d 1098 (D.S.D. 2000) [no probable cause to detain passenger in car where minor traffic stop]; *U.S. v. Lopez-Valdez,* 102 F.Supp.2d 728 (W.D. Tex. 2000) [an anonymous tip was insufficient basis for investigative stop; evidence suppressed]; *U.S. v. Alvarado-Ramirez*, 975 F.Supp. 906 (W.D. Tex. 1997) [no probable cause or reasonable suspicion on stop]; *U.S. v. Covarrubia*, 911 F.Supp. 1409 (D.N.M. 1994) [where officer listed a series of factors but could not demonstrate how they related to his and fellow officer's experience in fighting transportation of illegal aliens, reasonable suspicion was not established]; *Murillo v. Musegades*, 809 F.Supp. 487, 498–99 (W.D. Tex. 1992) [the failure to answer an INS officer's questions or the refusal to cooperate with the officer cannot be the basis to draw an inference for probable cause or reasonable suspicion]; *U.S. v. Ramos*, 753 F.Supp. 75 (W.D.N.Y. 1990) [Hispanic appearance alone insufficient]; *Ramirez v. Webb*, 719 F.Supp. 610 (W.D. Mich. 1989) [INS illegally detained and used excessive force against USCs based upon their Hispanic appearance]; *McElrath v. Goodwin*, 713 F.Supp. 299, 303 n.3 (E.D. Ark. 1988). The objective reasonableness standard is applied in the context of what inferences a trained DHS enforcement officer might reasonably draw, rather than the inferences that might be drawn by a lay person. *U.S. v. Cortez*, 449 U.S. 411 (1981); *U.S. v. Sokolow*, 490 U.S. 1 (1989). The standard is equally applicable to state officers seeking to enforce immigration. *Farm Labor Organizing Comm. v. Ohio Hwy. Patrol,* 991 F.Supp. 895 (N.D. Ohio 1997), *rev'd in part,* 308 F.3d 523 (6th Cir. 2002 [state police enjoined from questioning motorists about their immigration status without reasonable suspicion based on articulable facts].

2.b. Reasonable suspicion to stop found

U.S. v. Berber-Tinoco, 510 F.3d 1083 (9th Cir. 2007) [reasonable suspicion for stop where officers narrowed their suspicion through deduction as to the location of the pick up of undocumented aliens and made reasonable factual inferences based on their experience regarding smuggling activities in the area]; *U.S. v. Hernandez,* 477 F.3d 210 (5th Cir. 2007) [reasonable suspicion for stop where events were close to the border, it was a notorious alien smuggling route, and the anonymous tip was not bare]; *U.S. v. Doe*, 701 F.2d 819 (9th Cir. 1983) [vehicle found in an area normally used to avoid checkpoints; when car was driving south it was riding high, but it was heavily laden when returning. *See also U.S. v. Cheromiah,* 455 F.3d 1216 (10th Cir. 2006) [roving patrol had reasonable suspicion to stop vehicle under totality of the circumstances and acted with permissible scope of the stop when he opened the side door of van even after ascertaining that the 4 occupants were USCs]; *U.S. v. Singh,* 415 F.3d 288 (2d Cir. 2005) [based upon the totality of the circumstances the Border Patrol agent had reasonable suspicion to stop NYC driver who was near the northern border in a remote areas]; *U.S. v. Quintana-Garcia,* 343 F.3d 1266, 1271–74 (10th Cir. 2003) [relying on *Brignoni-Ponce* factors and totality of the circumstances to affirm denial of motion to suppress where border patrol agent stopped car and drugs were found in it]; *U.S. v. Neufeld-Neufeld,* 338 F.3d 374 (5th Cir. 2003) [relying on the *Brignoni-Ponce* factors, which must be analyzed collectively and the use of the totality of the circumstances approach, even individually innocent actions may collectively result in sufficient suspicion where as here the defendant: (1) was 35 miles from the border, (2) was within 2 miles of a previous drug cache, (3) was using a known drug smuggling route in an area known for drug smuggling, and (4) appeared stiff, stared straight ahead, failed to acknowledge Border Patrol officers and slowed down considerably. Denial of motion to suppress in drug case affirmed.] *U.S. v. Gandara-Salinas,* 327 F.3d 1127 (10th Cir. 2003) [reversed lower court's grant of a motion to suppress because officer reasonably relied on a number of factors including the size of respondent's spare tire]; *U.S. v. Vasquez,* 298 F.3d 354 (5th Cir. 2002) [affirmed denial of motion to suppress where Border Patrol agent stopped new pickup truck that drove through private ranch instead of highway without stopping and where driver continually checked rear-view mirror]; *U.S. v. Guerrero-Barajas,* 240 F.3d 428 (5th Cir. 2001) [common route for smuggling, lawful vehicles infrequently travel the area at night, vehicle riding low, and driver slowed and began to swerve once agents followed him are sufficient specific and articulable facts]; *U.S. v. Chavez-Chavez,* 205 F.3d 145 (5th Cir. 2000) [agents identified the characteristics of the area of the stop, including the proximity to a checkpoint, the rigid suspension of the vehicle, the type of vehicle, the dirty appearance of the passengers, and the time of day]; *U.S. v. Orozco,* 191 F.3d 578 (5th Cir. 1999) [under *Brignoni-Ponce* criteria treated vehicle stop 200 miles from border as roving patrol requiring only reasonable suspicion]; *U.S. v. Samaguey,* 180 F.3d 195 (5th Cir. 1999) [the totality of the circumstances, including the reason to believe he was coming from border, alone, in out-of-state car, registered to a female, at an unusual hour, on a road known for illegal activity was sufficient]; *U.S. v. Nichols,* 142 F.3d 857 (5th Cir.

1998) [totality of circumstances sufficient for stop where clean truck, with no logo, coming from border with other factors]; *U.S. v. Doyle*, 129 F.3d 1372 (10th Cir. 1997) [stop reasonable under the totality of the circumstances where sensor indicated border crossing and other factors]; *U.S. v. Cruz-Hernandez*, 62 F.3d 1353 (11th Cir. 1995) [reasonable suspicion to stop vehicle even though it was not coming from border where person dressed in clothes typical of undocumented worker where he averted his eyes, where he appeared Hispanic, vehicle had out of state license plates, and was a typical van for smuggling]; *U.S. v. Tehrani*, 49 F.3d 54, 59–60 (2d Cir. 1995) [reasonable suspicion to detain based in part on companion's illegality]; *U.S. v. Espinoza-Santill*, 976 F.Supp. 561 (W.D. Tex. 1997) [reasonable suspicion where it was very early in the morning when there was very little traffic, where van was one mile from the border, where it was type of vehicle that could be used to haul illegal aliens, where driver was Hispanic, where he failed to yield and tried to evade agent]; *U.S. v. Vendrell-Pena*, 700 F.Supp. 1174 (D.P.R. 1988) [reasonable suspicion under *Terry* to stop taxi where: (1) area known to be entry point for illegal aliens; (2) city taxi in remote rural location; (3) taxi there in early morning hours]; *U.S. v. Galindo-Hernandez*, 674 F.Supp. 979 (E.D.N.Y. 1987) [reasonable suspicion established for stop where (1) defendants flew from Miami which agents knew was a departure point for illegal aliens; (2) their Hispanic appearance; (3) their nervous mannerisms; (4) their lack of luggage; (5) one defendant's expensive but ill-fitting attire; (6) their efforts to create appearance they were traveling alone while actually traveling together]. But subjective factors such as "avoiding eye contact" or giving a "suspicious look" are insufficient. *Nicacio, supra*; *Martinez v. Nygaard*, 831 F.2d 822, 827 (9th Cir. 1987) [stopping USC without objectively reasonable suspicion is unlawful detention]; *Ramirez, supra*.

2.c. Good faith exception—Evidence may be admissible even if an officer errs where s/he maintains a good faith and objectively reasonable belief that s/he has an adequate foundation to make a stop. *U.S. v. De Leon-Reyna*, 930 F.2d 396 (5th Cir. 1991) (*en banc*); *U.S. v. Alvarado-Ramirez*, 975 F.Supp. 906, 920–21 (W.D. Tex. 1997) [rejected good faith exception].

3. Frisking—In order to frisk someone who has not been arrested the ICE agent must have a reasonable suspicion based on specific articulable facts that the individual is armed. *Murillo v. Musegades*, 809 F.Supp. 487, 498 (W.D. Tex. 1992).

4. Seizures—A stop may ripen into a lawful seizure only when there is probable cause. *Dunaway v. New York*, 442 U.S. 200, 214–15 (1979); *Murillo v. Musegades,* 809 F.Supp. 487, 499 (W.D. Tex. 1992) ["A search or seizure will *never* be considered reasonable if the officer stops the vehicle *solely because of the Mexican ancestry of the occupant*"]; *Vasquez v. McPherson,* 285 F.Supp.2d 334, 341 (S.D.N.Y. 2003) [where there was immigration warrant for person meeting plaintiff's description and plaintiff responded with hostility, police officer had qualified immunity to arrest]; *Vendrell-Pena*, 700 F.Supp. 1174, 1178 (D.P.R. 1988) [where officers had sufficient suspicion to stop taxi and where alien admitted that she was Dominican, was unable to provide documentation and was evasive there was sufficient probable cause for arrest]. The refusal to answer questions cannot be considered in determining whether there is probable cause to arrest. *Florida v. Royer*, 460 U.S. 491 (1983); *Ramirez v. Webb*, 719 F.Supp. 610, 616 (W.D. Mich. 1989). Requesting the driver of a stopped van to turn off his engine may constitute a seizure. *U.S. v. Espinoza,* 490 F.3d 41, 48–50 (1st Cir. 2007) [where agent identified himself as ICE officer, was wearing a holstered firearm, displayed his badge and began asking questions, and in a commanding tone and manner indicated he wanted the driver to shut off the van's engine, it was not clearly erroneous for district court to draw inference that there was a seizure without probable cause]. *But see U.S. v. Torres-Lona,* 491 F.3d 750, 756–57 (8th Cir. 2007) [admission that he was born in Mexico, did not have immigration documents, and found in apartment complex known to house undocumented persons where others had been arrested and false documents found was enough for probable cause].

5. Interrogation Procedure—8 C.F.R. §§287.3 and 287.5. Statements taken on Form I-213. Arresting officer should not take statement, §287.3(a) unless no other officer available or it would result in unnecessary delay. *Martinez-Camargo v. INS,* 282 F.3d 487 (7th Cir. 2002) [where INS officer violated §287.3 but respondent was not prejudiced evidence was not excluded and removal order was affirmed]; *Matter of Garcia-Flores,* 17 I&N Dec. 325 (BIA 1980). Alien has to sign Form I-214 waiver form. Advice of rights should contain all rights under 8 C.F.R. §287.3 [advice includes: (1) reason for arrest; (2) right to be represented by counsel of alien's own choice; (3) list

of available free legal services; (4) self-incrimination; (5) notice that a decision will be made within 24 hours or less; (6) whether alien will continue in custody or be released on bond]. Advice of rights per regulation are given after interrogation. 8 C.F.R. §287.3. The Fourth and Fifth Amendments may require otherwise. *Navia-Duran v. INS*, 568 F.2d 803 (1st Cir. 1977). Statement cannot be taken from unaccompanied minor under18 on Form I-213. 8 C.F.R. §1240.10(c).

In the aftermath of Sept. 11, 2001, the AG announced an "interview" program targeted at young males from Middle Eastern countries whereby FBI and other law enforcement "partners" would interview these persons about "international terrorism." Memo, Deputy AG, Guidelines for the Interviews Regarding International Terrorism (Nov. 9, 2001), *reprinted in* 78 No. 46 *Interpreter Releases* 1816, 1829–35 (Dec. 3, 2001).

Department of Defense Interrogation—The uniform standards for the interrogation of persons under the United States Army Field Manual on Intelligence Interrogation do not apply to persons in the custody or under the effective control of the DOD pursuant to the criminal or immigration law of the U.S. National Defense Authorization Act for Fiscal Year 2006, PL 109-163, 119 Stat. 3136 (Jan. 6, 2006), Title XIV, Sec. 1402.

6. Use of Force—DHS can only use reasonable force to effect a particular seizure. *Murillo v. Musegades*, 809 F.Supp. 487, 500 (W.D. Tex. 1992) [Fourth Amendment protects against physically intrusive behavior during an arrest]; *Ramirez v. Webb*, 719 F.Supp. 610, 616–18 (W.D. Mich. 1989). To determine whether force is excessive court must balance the "nature and quality of the intrusion on the individual's Fourth Amendment interests against the countervailing governmental interest at stake." *Graham v. Connor*, 109 S.Ct. 1865 (1989); *Tennessee v. Garner*, 471 U.S. 1 (1985). DHS guidelines set forth at 8 C.F.R. §287.8.

G. *Area Control Operation/Investigative Searches / Worksite Enforcement Operations*

1. Broad factory sweeps are constitutional—*INS v. Delgado*, 466 U.S. 210 (1984) [factory sweeps/surveys are not work force seizures where persons believe they are free to leave and do not constitute seizure of any individual worker under *Terry v. Ohio*]. But detention of entire workforce is not permissible. *Pearl Meadows Mushroom Farm, Inc. v. Nelson*, 723 F.Supp. 432, 445–49 (N.D. Cal. 1989).

Area control operations may under the Constitution be lawful seizures. *Illinois Migrant Council v. Pilliod*, 531 F.Supp. 1011 (N.D. Ill. 1982) [reasonable suspicion not probable cause is standard for a control operation]; *English v. Sava*, 571 F.Supp. 1029 (S.D.N.Y. 1983). *But see Gallegos v. Haggerty*, 689 F.Supp. 93 (N.D.N.Y. 1988) [distinguishing and rejecting *English* in context of farmhouse raid]. Routinely boarding buses at scheduled stops and asking passengers for permission to search luggage, following *Delgado*, is not a per se seizure. *Florida v. Bostick*, 111 S.Ct. 2382 (1991). *But see U.S. v. Ellis,* 330 F.3d 677 (5th Cir. 2003) [where border patrol agents completed an immigration search of a bus they may not continue to detain passengers to look for drugs absent individualized suspicion].

The standard to be applied for warrant to inspect is a "relaxed standard." *Blackie's House of Beef, Inc. v. Castillo*, 659 F.2d 1211 (D.C. Cir. 1981), *cert. denied*, 455 U.S. 940 (1982) [provided "relaxed standard" of probable cause in searches of businesses for INS purposes]. *Accord International Molders & Allied Workers Local 164 v. Nelson*, 799 F.2d 547 (9th Cir. 1986) [preliminary injunction denied in part to restrain use of "warrants of inspection" to enter private business premises to search for unidentified or unknown aliens. The court accepted the lower standard for probable cause articulated by the D.C. Circuit in *Blackie's House of Beef, supra*. Persons need not be named in warrant unless it is warrant to *seize* a person (instead of search premises). However, part of basis for standard is that there were no employer sanctions at the time]. *See also Abel v. U.S.*, 362 U.S. 217 (1960).

Identification of Humanitarian Concerns in Worksite Enforcement. ICE has set forth guidelines to be applied by officer when conducting a worksite enforcement action that targets more than150 people. Guidelines For Identifying Humanitarian Concerns In Worksite Enforcement Operations *published on* AILA InfoNet at Doc. No. 07111631 [ICE should identify sole care givers and other humanitarian cases including persons with serious medical conditions, pregnant women and nursing mothers and parents needed to support seriously ill spouses or children so that they may be released or obtain help from DIHS (Division of Immigrant Health Services of HHS) or local or state SSSA (social security agency)

2. Standing to contest search/warrant—Following *Rakas v. Illinois*, 439 U.S. 128, 133–34 (1978), the Court found USCs or LPRs seized in factory raid had no standing under Fourth Amendment to challenge warrant because no expectation of privacy existed where work space was open and shared by 75 people. *Martinez v. Nygaard*, 831 F.2d 822, 825–26 (9th Cir. 1987). *But see International Molders v. Nelson*, 674 F.Supp. 294, 296 n.1 (N.D. Cal. 1987) [aliens have standing to challenge warrant where it was directed at seizing individuals, not just searching workplace as in *Martinez*]; *Gallegos v. Haggerty*, 689 F.Supp. 93 (N.D.N.Y. 1988) [following *Rakas* standing based on legitimate expectation of privacy, not on property rights, and tenants at property where landlord's ownership of migrant farm dwelling was in question, still have reasonable expectation of privacy].

3. Challenging the warrant

    3.a. Test is whether warrant and supporting affidavit contain sufficient specificity and reliability to prevent exercise of unbridled discretion by law enforcement officers. *International Molders v. Nelson*, 674 F.Supp. 294, 296 (N.D. Cal. 1987) [relying on *Delaware v. Prouse*, 99 S.Ct. 1391, 1395–97 (1979)].

    3.b. Seizure of all of lawyer's files may be permitted if there is a determination that lawyer's practice was "permeated by fraud." Attorney-client privilege may not be a basis to prevent search where it would protect the commission of a crime and where information put on INS forms constituted a waiver of privilege. *U.S. v. Oloyede*, 982 F.2d 133, 140–41 (4th Cir. 1992).

    3.c. Must determine whether it is warrant of inspection or general, open-ended seizure warrant. A general warrant is not permissible. *Marshall v. Barlow's, Inc.*, 436 U.S. 307 (1978); *See v. City of Seattle*, 387 U.S. 541 (1967); *International Molders v. Nelson*, 674 F.Supp. 294, 297–300 (N.D. Cal. 1987). If there is a warrant of inspection issued to conduct area-wide inspections to determine compliance, a less-than-probable-cause standard (as in *Blackie's House of Beef, Inc. v. Castillo*, 659 F.2d 1211 (D.C. Cir. 1981)) may apply. *Camara v. Municipal Court of City and County of San Francisco*, 387 U.S. 523 (1967). However, if the agency has used a warrant of inspection, the warrant may be challenged under a 2-part test. *Matter of Trinity Industries*, 876 F.2d 1485 (11th Cir. 1989). First, the court must determine whether the plan pursuant to which the warrant was issued is based on specific, neutral criteria. Second, the court must determine whether the warrant application clearly and adequately establishes that the particular company was selected pursuant to the application of the plan's neutral criteria.

4. Warrantless Searches/Seizures

    4.a. Open-field raids are not unlawful seizures. *Oliver v. U.S.*, 466 U.S. 170 (1984) [even where there were no-trespass signs and locked gates, there was no seizure]. But ICE, by statute, must have consent of owner or warrant to enter "farm or other outdoor agricultural operation." INA §287(e), 8 U.S.C. §1357(e). However, ICE claims that entry onto private land within 25 miles of the border (except private dwellings) may be done without a warrant. 8 C.F.R. §287.5(b). But 8 C.F.R. §287.8(f)(2) provides that a DHS officer may not enter into the nonpublic areas of a business, a residence (including the cartilage), or a farm or other outdoor agricultural operation absent a warrant or consent.

    4.b. Night-vision goggles when used are not considered an unlawful. *U.S. v. Vela*, 486 F.Supp.2d 587, 589–90 (W.D. Tex. 2005) [use of night-vision goggles does not constitute a search; *Kyllo v. U.S. distinguished*].

    4.c. Cannot enter migrant farm *dwellings* without warrant. *LaDuke v. Nelson*, 762 F.2d 1318 (9th Cir. 1985).

    4.d. Stops of Hispanic-looking persons on highways in State of Washington held violative of Fourth Amendment. *Nicacio v. INS*, 797 F.2d 700 (9th Cir. 1985).

    4.e. Warrantless searches are presumptively unreasonable and absent consent or probable cause *and* exigent circumstances *DHS cannot enter home to search or arrest. U.S. v. Castellanos,* 518 F.3d 965, 971–72 (8th Cir. 2008) [DHS officers cannot rely on 8 U.S.C. §1357 to conduct warrantless searches of homes, because it pertains to persons seeking entry]; *U.S. v. Troop,* 514 F.3d 405 (5th Cir. 2008) [criminal prosecution for transporting an alien reversed because exigent circumstances did not exist to justify border patrol's warrantless entry of defendant's home]; *U.S. v. You,* 198 F.Supp.2d 393 (S.D.N.Y. 2002) [evidence suppressed where agents made unlawful entry into home, where they made unlawful arrest, and where consent to search under circumstances was no voluntary]; *Gallegos v. Haggerty*, 689 F.Supp. 93 (N.D.N.Y. 1988). Warrantless searches, absent warrant exceptions, also are not permitted on "commercial curtilage" because such curtilage may be protected by the Fourth Amendment where there is a reasonable expectation of privacy. *Pearl Meadows Mushroom Farm, Inc.*, 723 F.Supp. at 438–43.

4.f. DHS cannot simply rely on claims of state officers that they will obtain a warrant for search. *Guerra v. Sutton*, 783 F.2d 1371 (9th Cir. 1986).

4.g. Consent to Search—Whether consent was knowingly given and voluntary is based on totality of circumstances. *U.S. v. Watson*, 423 U.S. 411 (1976); *Schneckloth v. Bustamonte*, 412 U.S. 218 (1973); *U.S. v. Cruz-Mendez,* 467 F.3d 1260 (10th Cir. 2006) [in illegal reentry case the renter of the apartment gave consent for officer to come into her living room and then her bedroom]; *U.S. v. Esparza-Mendoza,* 386 F.3d 953 (10th Cir. 2004) [upheld re-entry after deportation conviction where central evidence concerning identification was obtained voluntarily and officer's statement that she "needed" identification from the defendant did not, under the totality of the circumstances, make his compliance nonvoluntary]; *La Duke v. Nelson*, 762 F.2d 1318, 1329 (9th Cir. 1985); *U.S. v. You,* 198 F.Supp.2d 393, 405 (S.D.N.Y. 2002) [under circumstances including the fact that an unlawful arrest occurred, that defendant tried to shut the door to his home and INS agents prevented it, and 6 agents were standing inside his apartment or in the hallway at the time, his consent was not voluntary]; *U.S. v. Ramos*, 753 F.Supp. 75, 80 (W.D.N.Y. 1990) [where INS never established that defendant knew she had the right to refuse, consent was not established]. Where search occurred after illegal stop, INS has higher burden to show consent was voluntary. *U.S. v. Alvarado-Ramirez*, 975 F.Supp. 906, 919–20 (W.D. Tex. 1997). Where agent secured consent to search defendant's apartment by falsely representing to her that he could get a search warrant, consent was *not* voluntary. *U.S. v. Cruz*, 701 F.Supp. 440 (S.D.N.Y. 1988); *see also Pearl Meadows Mushroom Farm, Inc.*, 723 F.Supp. at 443–45. [coercive or misleading statements used to obtain consent impermissible]. Where person consented to speak with border patrol agent who made no gestures which objectively would constitute detention there was no seizure of the person. *U.S. v. Tehrani*, 826 F.Supp. 789, 798–99 (D. Vt. 1993), *aff'd*, 49 F.3d 54 (2d Cir. 1995).

4.h. Wiretaps—Congress provided DHS with authority to wiretap persons engaged in criminal activity related to alien smuggling or document fraud. IIRIRA §434, 18 U.S.C. §2516(*l*).

4.i. Consensual Recording—Where there is a reasonable expectation of privacy the government has no right to record a person's statements and such statements will not be deemed voluntarily provided. *Katz v. U.S.*, 389 U.S. 347 (1967). However, if an informer is invited to participate and if a person voluntarily divulges information to the informer, then that person is not protected by the Fourth Amendment. *Hoffa v. U.S.*, 385 U.S. 293 (1966). The First Amendment's Free Exercise Clause is also not a defense to an informer's entry into a church and his recording of the conversations of parishioners. *U.S. v. Aguilar*, 871 F.2d 1436, 1470–73 (9th Cir. 1989). However, the Free Exercise Clause does require the government to use the "least restrictive means" in the intrusion into church activities and it does prevent "unfounded and inappropriate covert activity which has as its purpose or objective the abridgement of the First Amendment freedoms of those involved." *Presbyterian Church (USA) v. U.S.*, 752 F.Supp. 1505, 1513–16 (D. Ariz. 1990).

5. Border/Checkpoint Search and Seizure

5.a. Border Search—The right of government agents to stop and search travelers at international borders does not implicate the Fourth Amendment, *U.S. v. Montoya de Hernandez*, 473 U.S. 531, 537 (1985); *Carroll v. U.S.*, 267 U.S. 132, 153–54 (1925), and probable cause is not required to justify a stop or search. *U.S. v. Ramsey*, 431 U.S. 606, 616 (1977); *U.S. v. Moreno-Vargas,* 315 F.3d 489 (5th Cir. 2002) [where drug interdiction was secondary purpose of fixed immigration checkpoint the checkpoint was reasonable and constitutional]; *U.S. v. Stevenson,* 274 F.Supp.2d 819, 820 (S.D. Tx. 2002) [immigration border search where dog alerted to drugs is lawful]; *U.S. v. Waldron,* 178 F.Supp.2d 738 (W.D. Tex. 2002) [same]. However, the detention of a person at the border does implicate the Fourth Amendment and such detention must be based on reasonable cause. *Ramirez v. U.S.*, 81 F.Supp.2d 532, 536–37 (D.N.J. 2000). Such border searches apply to persons exiting as well as entering the U.S. *U.S. v. Oriakhi*, 57 F.3d 1290 (9th Cir. 1995). Although Congress gave DHS agents broad authority to conduct such searches within a "reasonable distance" from the border, INA §287(a)(3), 8 U.S.C. §1357(a)(3), which the agency has defined as 100 miles, 8 C.F.R. §287.1(a)(2), the statute and regulation are subordinate to the Constitution. Even roving patrols within 20 miles of the border were deemed not to be the "functional equivalent" of the border, *Almeida-Sanchez v. U.S.*, 413 U.S. 266, 273 (1973), and therefore the Service was required to have probable cause, not reasonable suspicion, for any stop of vehicles. *Accord U.S. v. Venzor-Castillo*, 991 F.2d 634 (10th Cir. 1993) [where stop at point that allows someone to pass through 13 New Mexico towns before checkpoint it was not within reasonable distance from border]. *See also U.S. v. Castellanos,* 518 F.3d 965, 971–72 (8th Cir. 2008) [DHS officers cannot rely on 8 U.S.C. §1357 to conduct warrantless searches of homes, because it pertains to persons seeking entry]. However, if the court determines that the stop is by a roving patrol at the functional equivalent of the border then reasonable suspicion, not probable cause, is sufficient. *U.S. v. Brignoni-Ponce*, 422 U.S. 873 (1975). The roving patrol at least according to one court could be as far as 200–300 miles from the border. *U.S. v. Orozco,* 191 F.3d 578 (5th Cir. 1999). But the reasonable suspicion standard is not toothless. *U.S. v. Jones,* 149 F.3d 364 (5th Cir. 1998) [car more than 80 miles from border in area near a national park cannot be considered to have come from the border]; *Murillo v. Musegades*, 809 F.Supp. 487, 499 (W.D. Tex. 1992); *U.S. v. Alvarado-Ramirez*, 975 F.Supp. 906 (W.D. Tex. 1997) [where INS agent had no authority to stop for speeding, where there was a question as to whether person was speeding, and where car with Mexican license plate had no obligation to stop there was no reasonable suspicion]. *But see U.S. v. Barron-Cabrera*, 119 F.3d 1454 (10th Cir. 1997) [where officer observed person for nine–elevenths of a second he had sufficient time to observe him].

5.b. Fixed Checkpoints that are Equivalent to the Border—Similarly, fixed checkpoint stops need not meet the probable cause standard if they are deemed to be at the functional equivalent of the border. *U.S. v. Martinez-Fuerte*, 428 U.S. 543 (1976); *U.S. v. Ventura,* 447 F.3d 375 (5th Cir. 2006) [evidence of marijuana would not be suppressed because border patrol agents at fixed checkpoint on Interstate 35 near Laredo, Texas were entitled to sweep the restrooms and exterior luggage compartments of commercial buses as long as their primary purpose was to interdict illegal immigrants and the check did not unreasonably prolong the stop]; *U.S. v. Pollard,* 326 F.3d 397 (3d Cir. 2003) [checkpoint in U.S. Virgin Islands does not violate the Fourth Amendment and does not violate equal protection under the Fifth Amendment]; *U.S. v. Barnett*, 935 F.2d 178 (9th Cir. 1991) [search in secondary inspection]. Additionally, an airport stop in Puerto Rico pursuant to INA §212(d)(7) and 8 C.F.R. §§235.5(a), 1235.5(a) held constitutional as border stop and as within Fourth Amendment, but struck down practice of taking tickets as inconsistent with *Florida v. Royer*, 460 U.S. 491 (1983) and Fourth Amendment. *Lopez-Lopez v. Aran*, 844 F.2d 898 (1st Cir. 1988). A border search may also be conducted even where person was not admitted to Canada and upon return to the U.S. was searched. *U.S. v. Romm,* 455 F.3d 990, 996–97 (9th Cir. 2006) [USC with laptop containing child pornography who was not admitted into Canada was properly subject to border search upon his return to the US].

However, highway checkpoints that are not deemed to be the equivalent of the border cannot only be justified "by some quantum of individualized suspicion." *City of Indianapolis v. Edmond,* 531 U.S. 32, 121 S.Ct. 447, 457 (2000) [highway checkpoint whose primary purpose was to interdict illegal narcotics was held invalid because the program's purpose is indistinguishable from fighting crime generally]; *U.S. v. Jaime,* 473 F.3d 178, 181–83 (5th Cir. 2006) [followed *Edmond* but determined that person on bus gave consent to open luggage that contained drugs].

5.c. Laptop Searches at the Border—A developing area of law concerns the standard to be applied by CBP at the border for searching a passenger's laptop. In *U.S. v. Arnold,* 454 F.Supp.2d 999 (C.D. Cal. 2006) the court determined that the Fourth Amendment *does apply* to a laptop search at the border and that the standard for such search is reasonable suspicion which was not met in that case. *See also U.S. v. Irving,* 432 F.3d 401, 213–15 (2d Cir. 2005) [for non-routine searches at the border such as looking through luggage for diskettes, reasonable suspicion was needed but in this case there was reasonable suspicion]; *But see U.S. v. Romm,* 455 F.3d 990, 996–98 (9th Cir. 2006) [routine border search of laptop did not require probable, cause, reasonable suspicion or a warrant and court would not address whether First Amendment was violated]; *U.S. v. Ickes, Jr.*, 393 F.3d 501, 505–07 (4th Cir. 2005) [rejecting First Amendment argument in regard to border search of laptop}

5.d. Search in International Waters—The extent of the Service's authority to investigate and search in international waters has been challenged in that the investigating authority is limited to territorial waters under INA §287(a)(3), 8 U.S.C. §1357(a)(3). However, the court in *U.S. v. Chen*, 2 F.3d 330 (9th Cir. 1993) *cert. denied*, 511 U.S. 1039 (1994), rejected this theory on the grounds that the AG's authority, as delegated under what is now INA §103(c), provides no such limitation. *But see* 8 C.F.R. §287.1(a)(1), specifically defining enforcement authority as 12 nautical miles out into territorial seas.

6. Seizure of driver's license and return to state motor vehicle bureau not unlawful seizure. *Lopez v. INS*, 758 F.2d 1390 (10th Cir. 1985). Various states, *e.g.*, Florida, in light of the terrorist attacks on Sept. 11, 2001, have now established separate procedures for noncitizens to obtain drivers' licenses. These procedures, whose constitutionality has yet to be tested, will be affected by the requirements of the REAL ID Act of 2005. *See* "Driver's Licenses & REAL ID Act," in Ch. 6, section XIII.L (p.865), *infra*.

7. Sting Operations—Legacy INS established guidelines for sting operations that do not permit Service officers to make misrepresentations to induce persons to go to INS (*e.g.*, "you will receive a work permit"), but nevertheless allows the Service to send a person a letter saying they wish to discuss your immigration status. Memo, Meissner, Comm. HQ 243-P (Dec. 17, 1993), *reprinted in* 71 No. 23 *Interpreter Releases* 777, 796–99 (June 13, 1994).

8. Schools, Churches, and Funerals—INS also established guidelines providing that, generally, no enforcement operations that are likely to involve apprehensions should take place at schools, places of worship, or funerals, unless advanced written approval is given by the DD or Chief Patrol Agent. Memo, Puleo, Acting Assoc. Comm. INS, HQ 807-P (May 17, 1993). The procedures also require supervisory personnel to consider: (1) availability of alternative measures; (2) the importance of the enforcement action; (3) implementing measures to minimize the impact of the operation; and (4) whether the action has been requested or approved by the management of the institution involved. Memo, Wallis, Acting Reg. Director, Central Region, INS COR 50/19.1.5 (June 14, 2001), *published on* AILA InfoNet at Doc. No. 08050774.

H. *Subpoenas*—The AG or any immigration officer has the power to subpoena attendance and testimony and the production of documents "concerning any matter which is material and relevant to the enforcement of this Act and the administration of the Service, and to that end may invoke the aid of any court of the United States." INA §235(d)(4). But INA §235(a) has been held not to give the Service authority to issue "John Doe" subpoenas where the targets of a general investigation are known. *Peters v. U.S.*, 853 F.2d 692 (9th Cir. 1988) [quashed subpoena issued pursuant to §235(a) which ordered manager of labor camp to appear before INS and provide records and testimony relating to persons residing at the camp].

I. *Retention of Documents*—ICE has set forth a policy on confiscation or return of original documents to a person placed in removal proceedings. Memo, Torres, Acting Director, ICE (July 14, 2006), *published on* AILA InfoNet at Doc. No. 07100536. If the respondent is not legally entitled to possess the document, the document should be returned to the government agency that issued it absent ICE operational need to retain it. If the respondent legally possess the document, it should be returned to him or her. If the respondent legally possess the document but ICE has an operational need for the document, ICE maintains the right to retrain it.

1. Undocumented and Non-LPRs. ICE has a clear need for law enforcement purposes to retain domestically issued documents such as driver's licenses, Social Security cards, and ID cards, when the person is undocumented or not an LPR.

2. Lawful Permanent Residents. LPRs are entitled to evidence of permanent status and must be provided a temporary I-551 if ICE confiscates the original. If the card expires during the proceedings, ICE "shall renew and/or re-extend the card." If a final order is entered ICE should confiscate the

card. If relief is granted the I-551 should be returned. If the LPR is not detained she is "legally entitled to basic forms of identification such as driver's licenses and Social Security cards until an administrative final order…" and unless there is a clear operation need to retain the document it should be returned.

3. Government may seize and retain passport for purposes of removal hearing. *Onwubiko v. U.S.*, 969 F.2d 1392, 1397–98 (2d Cir. 1992). The U.S. courts and ICE have set forth a procedure at the end of a criminal case of returning U.S. passports to the DOS and foreign passports to the appropriate local office of DRO (Detention and Removal Office) of ICE. Memo, Lee, Acting Director, ICE (June 22, 2005), *published on* AILA InfoNet at Doc. No. 06071863; Memo, Gregoire, Chief, Policy and Operations Division, Administrative Office of the United States Court (July 21, 2005), *published on* AILA InfoNet at Doc. No. 06071865.

4. Requests By Foreign Governments. If foreign and/or domestic officials submit written requests for the return of documents, ICE may surrender the documents and place copies in the A-file.

5. Fraudulent Documents. Foreign and domestic government documents that are counterfeit or were obtained fraudulently will be confiscated and retained by ICE officials in all instances. Only authentic documents will be considered for return.

J. *Arrest*—An immigration officer has power to arrest a person without a warrant if the officer has reason to believe the alien is in the U.S. in violation of law or regulation and is likely to escape before a warrant can be obtained. INA §287(a)(2), 8 U.S.C. §1357(a)(2); 8 C.F.R. §287.5(c)(1); *U.S. v. Khan,* 324 F.Supp.2d 1177, 1186–87 (D. Colo. 2004) [where officers did have reason to believe that LPR was in U.S. in violation of law because he procured his residency by fraud but did not have reasonable grounds to believe he would flee, warrantless arrest was unlawful and his subsequent *Mirandized* statements were suppressed]. The Speedy Trial rule may apply in certain limited circumstances, *see in this chapter* ¶ VIII.DD.12 (p.263), *supra*. DHS officers may also arrest if the person has committed a felony under any law concerning the admission, exclusion or expulsion of persons, or any offense against the U.S., and the officer has reason to believe the person is guilty and there is a likelihood of the person escaping. INA §287(a)(5), 8 U.S.C. §1357(a)(5), 8 C.F.R. §287.5(c)(2), (3). A DHS officer may arrest if s/he has reasonable grounds to believe that the person has committed or is committing any felony as long as other conditions are met and the officer has completed appropriate training. 8 C.F.R. §287.5(c)(4); *U.S. v. Laija-Garcia,* 347 F.Supp.2d 350, 357–59 (W.D. Tex. 2004) [Border Patrol had authority to arrest person for what turned out to be a drug smuggling case because the arrest met all the criteria of §287(a)(5)(B)]; *Habeeb v. Castloo,* 434 F.Supp.2d 899, 907 (D. Mont. 2006) [border patrol officer had probable cause to arrest refugee who provided officer with a copy of his I-94 because he did not have the original I-94 he was required to have in his personal possession pursuant to 8 U.S.C. §1304(e)]. The "reason to believe" language has been interpreted to mean probable cause under constitutional standards. *U.S. v. Cortez*, 449 U.S. 411 (1981); *Martinez v. Nygaard*, 831 F.2d 822, 828 (9th Cir. 1987) [where LPR is detained and arrested during factory raid, arrest was reasonable because person did not have green card on her person, and therefore violated INA §264(e)]. *See also U.S. v. Villegas,* 495 F.3d 761, 769–71 (7th Cir. 2007) [police officer had probable cause to arrest defendant because he received information from other Milwaukee police officer that there was an immigration apprehension request for defendant because he had reentered the U.S. illegally after deportation]; *Murillo v. Musegades*, 809 F.Supp. 487, 500 (W.D. Tex. 1992); *U.S. v. Arzate-Nunez*, 18 F.3d 730, 735–36 (9th Cir. 1994) [where agents recognized person as having been deported 8 or 9 months earlier, they had probable cause to arrest].

1. An arrest in violation of §287(a)(2), however, does not result in the dismissal of removal proceedings. *Westover v. Reno,* 202 F.3d 475, 479–80 (1st Cir. 2000) [no right to suppress removal proceedings, but recognizing that whether evidence from an illegal arrest should be used is a more difficult question under the statute]. If person fails to produce alien resident card after admitting s/he is a LPR, probable cause exists for an arrest. *U.S. v. Wright*, 706 F.Supp. 1268, 1274 (N.D. Tex. 1989). *But see Mountain High Knitting, Inc. v. Reno*, 51 F.3d 216, 217–19 (9th Cir. 1995) [where persons without green card arrested then released when status verified, their arrest is illegal and use of INA §264(e), 8 U.S.C. §1304(e) (not carrying green card), is pretextual].

2. An arrest warrant may be issued only by authorized persons. 8 C.F.R. §287.5(e)(2). If an alien is arrested, his or her case shall be presented promptly "and in any event within 48 hours" for a de-

termination of *prima facie* evidence of illegality, to issue or not to issue an NTA and warrant of arrest, and to determine whether s/he should be released on bond. Memo, Hutchinson, Undersecretary DHS (Mar. 30, 2004), "Guidance on ICE Implementation of Policy and Practice Changes Recommended by the Department of Justice Inspector General," *published on* AILA InfoNet at Doc. No. 04041461 [reaffirming requirement of determination within 48 hours to charge individual, but giving ICE 72 hours to serve the NTA]. However in the case of "emergency or other extraordinary circumstance," the determination shall be made "within an additional reasonable period of time." 8 C.F.R. §287.3(d). An "emergency or other extraordinary circumstance" has been construed to mean: (1) a significant infrastructure or logistical disruption because of terrorism, weather, natural catastrophe, power outage, serious transportation emergency or serious disturbance; (2) a compelling law enforcement need such as an immigration emergency resulting in the influx of large numbers of people being detained; or (3) individual facts or circumstances unique to the person arrested including medical care or a compelling law enforcement need. A noncitizen subject to the emergency exception must be served with the NTA "as soon as practicable." Memo, Hutchinson (Mar. 30, 2004), *supra.*

3. An arrest may not be made in violation of INA §239(e). If an officer arrests a person subject to abuse (VAWA case), trafficking (T visa) or substantial physical or mental abuse resulting in a crime (U visa), the officer must certify that s/he has not solely relied on information from an abuser, trafficker or perpetrator of a crime in making the arrest and has not disclosed information obtained to anyone (except law enforcement). In making the arrest she must independently verify the information to support the arrest and must place the certificate on the NTA. INA §239(e); 8 U.S.C. §1367; Memo, Torres, Director of DRO and Form, Investigations, ICE (Jan 22, 2007), *published on* AILA InfoNet at Doc. No. 07022210; *see in this part* ¶ S.4.q (p.322), *infra*.

4. *Detention Without Charge*—The USA PATRIOT Act of 2001 permits the DHS to detain an individual for 7 days without filing a charging document if the AG certifies that the individual is a terrorist. INA §236A(a)(3), (5) He shall also be promptly informed of his rights. *Id.* Under the settlement reached in *Lopez v. INS*, Case No. 78-1912-WMB (C.D. Cal. Aug. 20, 1992), a person arrested without a warrant who wishes to consult with counsel will be given a minimum 2-hour period to communicate with counsel, during which time INS will cease interrogation. INS implementation of the settlement is described in Memo, McNary, Comm., CO-242 (Sept. 4, 1992), *reprinted in* 70 No. 5 *Interpreter Releases* 151, 160–68 (Feb. 1, 1993). The Service also placed greater restrictions and tighter controls on arrests at schools, places of worship, funerals or other religious ceremonies. Memo, Puleo, Acting Assoc. Comm., HQ 807-P (May 17, 1993), *reprinted in* 70 No. 25 *Interpreter Releases* 870, 885–87 (July 2, 1993).

5. *DEA Authority to Arrest*—Cross designation to arrest. The agreement between DEA and legacy INS to grant Border Patrol agents under Title 21 has been challenged as *ultra vires* of Title 21 and the INA. *U.S. v. Perkins,* 166 F.Supp.2d 1116, 1124–30 (W.D. Tex. 2001) [AG did not have the authority to cross designate Border Patrol agents to make narcotics arrests but evidence will not be suppressed]. However, all CBP personnel will be cross-designated to perform customs and immigration inspections.

6. *State and Local Authority to Arrest*—State and local law enforcement officials may arrest and detain a person who is "illegally present in the U.S." and who has previously been convicted of a felony in the U.S. and deported or left the U.S. after the conviction. State and local officials may arrest or detain only if they receive appropriate confirmation regarding the status of the person from DHS and only until DHS can take custody. AEDPA §439, 8 U.S.C. §1252c. *U.S. v. Villa-Velazquez,* 282 F.3d 553 (8th Cir. 2002). The AG asserts that state and local police, although not compelled to do so, have the "inherent authority to arrest individuals whose names have been entered into the FBI's National Crime Information Center (NCIC) database because they have both: (1) violated civil provisions of the Federal immigration laws that render them deportable and (2) been determined by Federal authorities to pose special risks, either because they present national security concerns or because they are absconders who have not complied with a final order of removal or deportation." Letter, Brown, Acting Asst. A.G., Office of Legal Affairs, DOJ (May 7, 2003), *published on* AILA InfoNet at Doc. No. 03051340 (May 13, 2003). One court has concluded however that failure to comply with the requirements of §1252c "does not limit or displace the preexisting general authority of state or local police officers to investigate and make arrests for violations of federal law, including immigration laws," as long as such arrests are not precluded

by state law. *U.S. v. Vasquez-Alvarez,* 176 F.3d 1294 (10th Cir. 1999). *Accord, U.S. v. Santana-Garcia,* 264 F.3d 1188, 1192–94 (10th Cir. 2001). But state and local law enforcement officials may not detain or question motorists about their immigration status or seize immigration documents without reasonable suspicion based on articulable facts. *Farm Labor Organizing Comm. v. Ohio Hwy. Patrol*, 991 F.Supp. 895 (N.D. Ohio 1997), *rev'd in part,* 308 F.3d 523 (6th Cir. 2002. Pursuant to IIRIRA §642, local and state entities or officials are prohibited from restricting any government entity or official from sending to or receiving from DHS any information. *City of New York v. U.S.,* 179 F.3d 29 (2d Cir. 1999) [statute upheld against City's facial challenge].

6.a. The AG may also enter into a written agreement with a state or political subdivision of a state to permit an officer or employee of the state or subdivision to perform functions of an immigration officer related to the investigation, apprehension, or detention of aliens. INA §287(g)(1), 8 U.S.C. §1357(g)(1). The state or political subdivision shall be the party paying all expenses. The officers will not be considered federal employees, but such persons "shall be considered to be acting under color of Federal authority for purposes of determining the liability, and immunity from suit, ... in a civil action brought under Federal or State law." INA §§287(g)(4), (5), and (8). Pursuant to INA §287(g)(1), the AG has entered into an agreement with the State of Florida to train 35 state and local law enforcement officers in immigration enforcement. MOU, AG/Gov. of Florida, Pilot Project to Authorize Training of Florida State and Local Law Enforcement Officers (June 13, 2002), 79 No. 30 *Interpreter Releases* 1120, 138–51 (July 29, 2002). ICE has also entered into an MOU with the Arizona Department of Corrections (Sept. 2005), giving state officials the authority to interview and charge detained respondents with removable offenses, *reprinted in* 10 No. 20 *Bender's Immigration Bulletin* 1552, 1601–14 (Oct. 15, 2005).

6.b. The AG has also promulgated regulations that authorize state and local law enforcement officers to be deputized as immigration enforcement officers during a "mass influx of aliens." INA §103(a)(10); 28 C.F.R. §§65.83–.84.

6.c. The DOJ and the DOD have also entered into a cooperative arrangement allowing the National Guard to assist DHS with border patrol on the northern and southern borders. "National Guard to Assist with Border Patrol," *published on* AILA InfoNet Doc. No. 02030432 (Mar. 4, 2002).

7. *FBI Given Authority to Make Immigration Arrests*—FBI agents have been authorized by the AG to exercise the power of DHS agents to arrest noncitizens without a warrant under INA §287, 8 U.S.C. §1357 (reason to believe person in U.S. in violation of immigration laws) and to exercise the function of immigration officers for the purpose of: (1) investigating, determining, the location of and apprehending, any alien who is in the U.S. in violation of the INA or any law or regulation regarding immigration status, or (2) enforcing any requirements of the INA and regulations. Memo, GC, FBI, Delegation of Authority to the FBI to Exercise the Powers and Duties of Immigration Officers (Feb. 26, 2003), *published on* AILA InfoNet at Doc. No. 03100915.

K. *Detention*

1. In removal proceedings a person subject to removal is generally entitled to release on bond unless s/he is subject to mandatory detention on criminal or terrorist grounds, or is an "arriving alien." *See in this chapter* "Detention of Inadmissible Persons," section IV.J (p. 135), *supra.* However, bond may be denied in the discretion of DHS/AG. INA §236(a), 8 U.S.C. §1226(a); *Matter of Patel,* 15 I&N Dec. 666 (BIA 1976) [presumption of release absent specific national security, danger or risk of flight]; *Carlson v. Landon*, 342 U.S. 524 (1952) [upholding discretionary denial of bond where security grounds were raised]. The inquiry is generally whether a person is a risk of flight or national security risk. This inquiry must be factually based and not simply by virtue of the person's status. *Carlisle v. Landon*, 73 S.Ct. 1179 (1953) (Douglas, J.); *Yanish v. Barber*, 73 S.Ct. 1105 (1953) (Douglas, J.); *Podolski v. Baird*, 94 F.Supp. 294 (E.D. Mich. 1950). *But see Matter of D-J-,* 23 I&N Dec. 572 (A.G. 2003) [emphasizing that AG's discretion to detain is not limited to danger and flight risk and justifying detention of Haitian asylum seekers based on government's general asserted national security interest in deterring mass migration of Haitians by boat rather than by an individualized determination of danger or flight risk]; *see also* 8 C.F.R. §§236.1(c)(8), 1236.1(c)(8) [purporting to shift *Matter of Patel* presumption of release to pre-

sumption of detention]. DHS must decide within 48 hours of the arrest or, in the case of an emergency or other extraordinary circumstance (*e.g.,* the bombing of the World Trade Center), "within an additional reasonable period of time," whether the person will be continued in custody or released. 8 C.F.R. §287.3(d). Before the entry of a final order of deportation, a party generally may seek release on bond under DHS/AG regulations or in a federal court habeas action. *See in this chapter* section IV.J (p. 135), *supra*.

2. Mandatory Detention for Aggravated Felons, Other Persons with Convictions, and Terrorists—*See in this part* "Special Rules…," section Q (p.302), *infra*.

3. Location of Detention—The DHS may have broad discretion to choose the situs of detention. *Sasso v. Milhollan*, 735 F.Supp. 1045 (S.D. Fla. 1990) [former 8 U.S.C. §1252(c) (now INA §241(g), 8 U.S.C. §1231(g)) confers broad discretion on AG]; *Justiz-Cepero v. INS*, 882 F.Supp. 1582 (D. Kan. 1995). Similarly, the Bureau of Prisons has broad discretion to determine the situs of incarceration of persons subject to deportation, including local contract jails and prisons. *Lato v. Attorney General*, 773 F.Supp. 973 (W.D. Tex. 1991). State officials can now request that DHS pay for undocumented DHS detainees or take custody of them. INA §241(i). For a listing of ICE detention facilities, *see* **Appendix I**, *infra*.

4. Transfer of Detainees—ICE has established standards and procedures for transfer of persons in ICE custody. *See* ICE Transfer Standards (June 16, 2004), *published on* AILA InfoNet at Doc. No. 04092167. These standards require that respondent's counsel who has a G-28 on file be notified of the transfer of his client *after* the client is en route. ICE Transfer Standards at ¶III. Detainees are not notified of the transfer until immediately prior to leaving the facility. Indigent detainees are granted a single domestic phone call at the government's expense upon arrival at their final destination. Some challenges to transfer have been barred on jurisdictional grounds. *See e.g., Aguilar v. ICE,* 510 F.3d 1 (1st Cir. 2007) [challenge to transfer as violating transferees right to counsel held barred under INA §242(b)(9) since claims could be brought as part of a petition for review of a removal order].

5. Conditions of Detention—DHS has published a Detention Operations Manual available at *www.ice.gov/partners/dro/opsmanual*, which provides detailed standards to be applied in all ICE and contractor detention facilities including: access to legal materials, telephones and facility equipment, visitation, law libraries, free legal services, correspondence, mail, classification, grievance procedures, group presentation of legal rights, religious services, and educational opportunities. The manual also has a section on policies regarding requests to be married in prison. It is a violation of a person's fundamental right to marriage to prohibit him or her from marrying while in detention. *Turner v. Safley,* 482 U.S. 78 (1987); *Theck v. Warden, INS,* 22 F.Supp.2d 1117 (C.D. Cal. 1998). Conditions of immigration detention are generally judged by the standards applicable to pretrial detainees under *Bell v. Wolfish,* 441 U.S. 520, 539 (1979). Thus, the petitioner must show either that the government intended to punish him or her or that the government's actions are arbitrary or purposeless and not reasonably related to legitimate government objectives. *Al Najjar v. Ashcroft,* 186 F.Supp.2d 1235, 1242–44 (S.D. Fla. 2002). *See also Ortega v. Rowe,* 796 F.2d 765 (5th Cir. 1986). *But see Lynch v. Cannatella,* 810 F.2d 1363 (5th Cir. 1987). *See also Jones v. Blanas,* 393 F.3d 918 (9th Cir. 2004) [suggesting more protective standard for civil detainees than "deliberate indifference" standard that applies to convicted prisoners).

6. DNA testing of detainees—42 U.S.C. §14135a. A federal agency that arrests, detains, or supervises noncitizens facing charges may collect DNA samples from the person arrested.

L. ***Release of Identity and Information Relating to Detainees***—State, local, and private detention facilities may not release information, including names, of DHS detainees being held in their facilities. Such information "shall be under the control of the Service and shall be subject to public disclosure only pursuant to the provisions of applicable federal laws, regulations and executive orders." 8 C.F.R. §§236.6, 1236.6. *Center for National Security Studies v. DOJ,* 331 F.3d 918 (D.C. Cir. 2003), *cert. denied,* 124 S.Ct. 1041 (2004) [the names, the attorneys' names, the dates of arrest and release, locations of arrest and detention and reasons for detention of post 9/11 detainees, including immigration, criminal and material witness detainees, are all exempt from disclosure under Exemption 7(A) of the FOIA regarding law enforcement proceedings]; *CEI Washington Bureau v. DOJ,* 404 F.Supp.2d 172 (D.D.C. 2005) [organization's request for personal information, such as alien numbers, in an electronic database regarding the administration of the State Criminal Alien Assistance Program was exempt under section 6 (privacy) and 7(C) (law enforcement purposes) of the FOIA].

M. *Bonds*—INA §236(a), 8 U.S.C. §1226(a). The INA provides for the release on bond of all persons except those deemed subject to mandatory detention under INA §236(c) as criminals or terrorists, or "arriving aliens." *See in this chapter* "Detention of Inadmissible Persons," section IV.J (p.135), *supra*. The AG may grant a minimum bond of $1,500, or may grant conditional parole. The AG may at any time revoke a bond or parole and re-arrest the person. INA §236(b).

1. Maintenance of status and departure bond—Bond of nonimmigrants to insure their return to country of origin.

2. Delivery bond—Applies to person arrested and is conditioned on promise of person to appear at each hearing or when requested by DHS. Where alien appeared one day late because he was ill, bond was considered breached. *Matter of Arbelaez-Naranjo*, 18 I&N Dec. 403 (R.C. 1983).

3. Public charge bond—To ensure that an individual is not a public charge in the U.S.

4. Standards, criteria, and conditions of bond—8 C.F.R. §§103.6(a)(2)(i), 1003.19(a)–(c)

4.a. Bond should be granted unless there is a finding that the individual is a threat to national security, likely to abscond or a poor bail risk. *Matter of Patel*, 15 I&N Dec. 666 (BIA 1976); *Matter of Daryoush*, 18 I&N Dec. 352 (BIA 1982). *But see* 8 C.F.R. §§236.1(c)(8), 1236.1(c)(8) [purporting to shift *Matter of Patel* presumption of release to presumption of detention]; *Matter of D-J-*, 23 I&N Dec. 572 (A.G. 2003) [emphasizing that AG's discretion to detain is not limited to danger and flight risk and justifying detention of Haitian asylum seekers based on the government's general asserted national security interest in deterring mass migration of Haitians by boat rather than by an individualized determination of danger or flight risk].

4.b. Criteria that are considered generally for bond under *Matter of Patel* and other cases are (a) whether the applicant has a fixed address in the U.S.; (b) length of residence in U.S.; (c) local family ties and whether the ties may entitle the applicant to reside in the U.S.; (d) record of appearances in court; (e) employment history or lack of employment; (f) criminal record, including the extensiveness of criminal activity, the recent nature of such activity and the seriousness of the offenses; (g) pending criminal charges; (h) history of immigration violations; (i) attempts to flee prosecution or otherwise escape from authorities; (j) manner of entry; (k) membership in community organization; (*l*) immoral acts or participation in subversive activities; and (m) financial ability to post bond. *Matter of Guerra,* 23 I&N Dec. 37, 40 (BIA 2006); *Matter of Patel*, *supra*; *U.S. ex rel. Barbour v. District Director, INS*, 491 F.2d 573 (5th Cir.), *cert. denied*, 419 U.S. 873 (1974); *Matter of San Martin*, 15 I&N Dec. 167 (BIA 1974). The determination of the IJ as to custody status or bond "may be based upon any information that is available to the immigration judge or that is presented to him or her by the alien or the Service." 8 C.F.R. §1003.19(d). The IJ has broad discretion in deciding what factors to consider. *Matter of Guerra,* 23 I&N Dec. 37 (BIA 2006) [IJ properly considered pending criminal charges absent a conviction when determining if the respondent was a danger to others]. An IJ also cannot consider the ability of the AG to actually deport someone as a criteria to grant bond. *Matter of P-C-M-*, 20 I&N Dec. 432 (BIA 1991). A change in the respondent's circumstances such as losing his deportation case may warrant an increase in bond. *Matter of Sugay*, 17 I&N Dec. 637 (BIA 1981). And a person facing serious criminal charges in another country in a proceeding whose fairness he doubts, can, without more, be denied bond. *Matter of Khalifah*, 21 I&N Dec. 107 (BIA 1995) [person deemed to be terrorist]. In addition, where respondent has no relief available to him, and is, therefore, a risk of flight and has a serious criminal history rendering him a threat, the BIA has upheld denial of any bond whatsoever. *Matter of Ellis*, 20 I&N Dec. 641 (BIA 1993). The BIA under a prior statute viewed the bond hearing as a 2-step process. First the person had to establish that s/he was not a danger to the community. If s/he was successful in rebutting the presumption that s/he was a danger, then the likelihood that s/he would abscond, became relevant. *Matter of Drysdale*, 20 I&N Dec. 815 (BIA 1994). The BIA held in *Matter of Melo*, 21 I&N Dec. 883 (BIA 1997) that the standards set forth in *Matter of Drysdale, supra*, also applied to the Transition Period Custody Rules.

4.c. Conditions of Release in Addition to Bond—The courts have long restricted the AG's authority to place certain conditions on a person's release. *Barton v. Sentner*, 353 U.S. 963 (1957) [cannot condition release on penalizing detainee if she violated the Smith Act or if she associated with communists]; *U.S. v. Witkovich*, 353 U.S. 194 (1957) [cannot force person to give INS information or associations as a condition of release]. A no-work condition on bond, however, has been determined to be within the statutory authority of the AG, so long as it only prohibits unauthorized employment *INS v. National Center for Immigrants Rights, Inc.*, 502 U.S. 183 (1991) [under former INA §241(a)(1)]. Under IIRIRA a person released will not be given authorization to work unless they are an LPR or otherwise (without regard to removal proceedings) would be given work authorization. INA §236(a)(3), 8 U.S.C. §1226(a)(3). However, an IJ may not refuse to consider nonmonetary conditions of bond. *Cevallos v. Ashcroft,* Case No. 04-CIV-23210-SEITZ (S.D. Fla. 2005) [granting injunctive and habeas relief that ordered the IJ to give respondent a bond hearing where matters, besides a monetary bond, would be considered; IJ initially refused to consider evidence or testimony regarding nonmonetary aspects of bond, including the use of an electronic bracelet].

4.d. Regulations Governing Release—Persons who are not subject to mandatory detention, including persons with criminal convictions that do not subject them to mandatory detention, are entitled to release under 8 C.F.R. §§236.1(c)(8), 1236.1(c)(8) which provides for discretionary release of an individual who can demonstrate that "release would not pose a danger to property or persons, and that [he] is likely to appear for any future proceeding." *Matter of Adeniji,* 22 I&N Dec. 1102 at 1111–13 (BIA 1999) [a test similar to that in *Matter of Drysdale,* 20 I&N Dec. 815 (BIA 1994) is appropriate].

4.e. Under prior statutes, the BIA determined that a comparable narrow release provisions in former INA §242(a)(2) (requiring a presumption against release of an LPR with an aggravated felony conviction) required the LPR to sustain the burden of demonstrating that s/he is not a threat to society and that s/he is likely to appear at any scheduled hearing. *Matter of De La Cruz*, 20 I&N Dec. 346 (BIA 1991). However, the fact that the felon has committed a "particularly serious crime" could not be used to foreclose bond for an LPR, or former INA §242(a)(2) would have been rendered meaningless. *Id.*

5. Bond procedure

5.a. DD initially sets bond. 8 C.F.R. §§236.1(c), 1236.1(c). Must state reasons for decision. *Matter of Daryoush*, 18 I&N Dec. 352 (BIA 1982). No right to discovery. *Matter of Khalifah*, 21 I&N Dec. 107 (BIA 1995). After initial determination by ICE, application for redetermination may be made to IJ. 8 C.F.R. §§1003.19, 236.1(d), 1236.1(d). The IJ cannot make a bond determination *sua sponte*. *Matter of P-C-M-*, 20 I&N Dec. 432 (BIA 1991). However, *no charging document* is required to be filed with the immigration court to commence bond proceedings. 8 C.F.R. §1003.14(a). The bond hearing is to be "separate and apart from, and shall form no part of, any deportation or removal hearing." 8 C.F.R. §1003.19(d) ; *Matter of R-S-H-,* 23 I&N Dec. 629, 630 n.7 (BIA 2003) ["We note that bond and removal are distinctly separate proceedings"]. However, the same IJ can hear both the bond and merits hearing. *Flores-Leon v. INS,* 272 F.3d 433, 440 (7th Cir. 2001) [court rejected recusal motion where IJ, notwithstanding former 3.19(d), heard both the bond and merits hearing]. The IJ may give DHS additional time to conduct a security check before setting the bond hearing. 8 C.F.R. §1003.47(k). As long as the person is in DHS's physical custody and has not received a final administrative removal order from the BIA, a party may make successive applications for bond to the IJ without filing a motion to reopen. *Matter of Uluocha*, 20 I&N Dec. 133 (BIA 1989). *But see Judulang v. Chertoff,* 535 F.Supp.2d 1129, 1132-33 (S.D. Cal. 2008) [detention lasting over 2½ years is unreasonable and district court ordered bond hearing before IJ over DHS objection that IJ lost jurisdiction over bond matters under 8 C.F.R. §1003.19(a) when administrative order became final]. After an initial bond redetermination, however, a subsequent redetermination can only be made in writing *and* upon a showing that "circumstances have changed materially since the prior bond redetermination." 8 C.F.R. §1003.19(e). If a bond determination is on appeal, the IJ has jurisdiction to determine a subsequent bond redetermination. *Matter of Valles*, 21 I&N Dec. 769 (BIA 1997). If the respondent is in state or federal custody, the existence of a DHS detainer does not give the IJ jurisdiction to hold a bond hearing where DHS has not set bond even if deportation proceedings have been initiated by respondent filing the NTA. *Matter of Sanchez*, 20 I&N Dec. 223 (BIA 1990); *Cruz v. Molerio*, 840 F.Supp. 303, 305–06 (S.D.N.Y. 1994). Where IJ has jurisdiction to set bond, the application must be made first to IJ nearest the place of detention,

8 C.F.R. §1003.19(c)(1), and thereafter to IJ who has control over case, 8 C.F.R. §1003.19(c)(2). A bond hearing may be requested orally or in writing. 8 C.F.R. §1003.19(b). IJ may raise or lower bond in deportation. *Matter of Spiliopoulos*, 16 I&N Dec. 561 (BIA 1978). DHS/AG cannot deny bond or use bond punitively because person sought judicial review. *Matter of Au*, 13 I&N Dec. 133 (BIA 1968). If respondent is released from custody, application to the IJ for redetermination of bond must be made within seven days after the date of release. 8 C.F.R. §§236.1(d)(1), 1236.1(d)(1). Thereafter, application for modification of bond or release may only be made to the DD. 8 C.F.R. §§236.1(d)(2), 1236.1(d)(2); *Matter of Chew*, 18 I&N Dec. 262 (BIA 1982). Also, if there are changed circumstances, the DD may redetermine bond or revoke bond even when bond was earlier redetermined by IJ, *Matter of Sugay*, 17 I&N Dec. 637 (BIA 1981), or after there is a final administrative order on removal. 8 C.F.R. §236.1(c)(9), 1236.1(c)(9). However, the DD cannot deny bond completely where it would prevent alien from showing up at criminal trial. *U.S. v. INS*, ___ F.Supp. ___, Case No. 89-1813 (S.D.N.Y. 1989), WSB ¶13,136.37.

5.b. Certain persons, by regulation, may not obtain review before an IJ of a DD's decision regarding bond. An IJ, by regulation, at 8 C.F.R. §§1003.19(h)(2)(i)(A)–(E), 236.1(c)(11) & (d)(1), and 1236.1(c)(11) & (d)(1), may not redetermine conditions of custody or have jurisdiction over bond matters with respect to: (A) persons in exclusion proceedings; (B) persons, including LPRs, who are "arriving aliens," *Matter of Oseiwusu,* 22 I&N Dec. 19 (BIA 1998) [decided under Transition Period Custody Rules (TPCR)]; (C) persons who are described in INA §237(a)(4), which provides for removal on terrorist or political grounds under INA §237(a)(4); (D) persons subject to mandatory detention under INA §236(c)(1); (E) persons with final administrative orders of removal.

6. Asylum applicants—Under the visa waiver program, an applicant for asylum/withholding is entitled to a bond if DHS issues an NTA. *Matter of Gallardo*, 21 I&N Dec. 210 (BIA 1996). The DHS has sought to avoid the provision of a bond hearing by issuing an I-863 to the alien rather than an NTA (I-862).

   Persons granted asylum, withholding, or CAT before the IJ may be released pending DHS appeal. DHS has issued a memo providing that: "In general, it is ICE policy to favor release of aliens who have been granted protection relief by an immigration judge, absent exceptional concerns such as national security issues or danger to the community and absent any requirement under law to detain.... Arriving aliens should [also] be considered for parole." Memo, Garcia, Asst. Sec. DHS (Feb. 9, 2004), *published on* AILA InfoNet at Doc. No. 04022462. *But see* ICE Parole Directive for Arriving Aliens, No. 7-1.0 (Nov. 6, 2007), *published on* AILA InfoNet at Doc. No. 07111264 [expressly superseding prior policy as applied to arriving aliens].

7. Juveniles—If a juvenile is detained pending removal proceedings, regulations provide for release of the juvenile to any of a large class of adult family members, legal guardians or to nonfamily members in certain limited situations. 8 C.F.R. §§236.3, 1236.3. The limitation on release of juveniles to nonfamily members only for unusual and compelling circumstances has been upheld in a facial challenge to its validity. *Reno v. Flores*, 507 U.S. 292 (1993) [rejecting facial challenge on substantive and procedural due process, equal protection and statutory grounds]. The Service established more liberal guidelines for release of unaccompanied minors. Memo, McNary (Dec. 13, 1991), *reprinted in* 69 No. 6 *Interpreter Releases,* 189, 205 (Feb. 10, 1992). These guidelines provide that no unaccompanied minor may be held in a detention facility for more than 72 hours unless s/he is: (1) charged or convicted of a criminal offense other than EWI; (2) adjudicated a delinquent or subject of pending delinquency proceedings; (3) engaged in violent or extremely disruptive conduct; (4) escaped from another facility; (5) an unrepresented Salvadoran under *Orantes* provisions; or there are (6) other extraordinary or compelling reasons. ICE also detains minors in family detention centers. In early January, 2008, ICE issued family detention standards that it posted on its website (*www.ice.gov/pi/familyresidential*).

8. Appeals to BIA—An appeal to BIA of a bond decision must be made with *30 days*, 8 C.F.R. §§1003.38, 236.1(d)(3)(i), 1236.1(d)(3)(i), unless it is an appeal of a DD's decision, in which case, it must be made within *10 days.* 8 C.F.R. §236.1(d)(3)(ii), 1236.1(d)(3)(ii). If a bond determination is on appeal, the IJ has jurisdiction to determine a subsequent bond redetermination. *Matter of Valles*, 21 I&N Dec. 769 (BIA 1997). DHS may seek an emergency stay from the BIA

regarding any bond order, 8 C.F.R. §1003.19(i)(1). The DHS may also obtain an *automatic* stay of an IJ's bond order simply by filing an EOIR-43 where the DD denied bond or set bond at $10,000 or more and the IJ authorized release on bond. The EOIR-43 must be filed within one business day of the IJ's order. 8 C.F.R. §1003.19(i)(2). Thereafter, DHS must file a notice of appeal consistent with §1003.38 to the BIA within 10 days of the IJ's decision or the stay will lapse. The notice of appeal, to preserve the stay, must be accompanied by a certification from a senior legal official that certifies that s/he has approved the filing of the notice of appeal and is satisfied that the contentions justifying the continued detention have evidentiary support and that the legal arguments are warranted by existing law or by a nonfrivolous argument for extension of the law. 8 C.F.R. §1003.6(c)(1). Once the notice of appeal is filed the IJ has 5 days to issue a written bond decision but may, in exigent circumstances, obtain an additional 5 days. 8 C.F.R. §1003.6(c)(2). If the BIA has not acted on the custody appeal within 90 days the automatic stay "shall" lapse. However, if the BIA grants a motion by the detainee to enlarge the time for submitting his brief, the 90 days are tolled. 8 C.F.R. §1003.6(c)(4). In addition, if the stay will lapse, DHS may seek a discretionary stay. 8 C.F.R. §1003.6(c)(5). If the BIA ultimately rules against DHS in its bond appeal, the release order is automatically stayed for 5 days to allow DHS to seek AG review. 8 C.F.R. §1003.6(d). *See also* Memo [Interim OPPM 06-03], Neal, Chief IJ (Oct. 31, 2006), *published on* AILA InfoNet at Doc. No. 06110264. The automatic-stay provision has been found to be unconstitutional, although these cases were all decided prior to the regulation's revision in 2006 to include the 90-day lapse provision. *Uritsky v. Ridge,* 286 F.Supp.2d 842 (E.D. Mich. 2003); *Bezmen v. Ashcroft,* 245 F.Supp.2d 446 (D. Conn. 2003). *Accord Zavala v. Ridge,* 310 F.Supp.2d 1071 (N.D. Cal. 2004) [automatic-stay provision violates substantive and procedural due process for person who is not subject to mandatory detention and not a national security threat]; *Zabadi v. Chertoff,* 2005 WL 1514122 (N.D. Cal. June 17, 2005) and 2005 WL 3157377 (N.D. Cal. Nov. 22, 2005) [same]; *Ashley v. Ridge,* 288 F.Supp.2d 662 (D.N.J. 2003) [same]. *But see Pisciotta v. Ashcroft,* 311 F.Supp.2d 445, 453–56 (D.N.J. 2004) [the stay provision is not unconstitutional under *Demore*].

9. Federal Court Review of Detention Pending Proceedings

9.a. INA §236(e), 8 U.S.C. §1226(e) provides that: "The Attorney General's discretionary judgment regarding the application of this section shall not be subjected to review. No court may set aside any action or decision by the Attorney General under this section regarding the detention or release of any alien or the grant, revocation or denial of bond or parole." In *Demore v. Kim,* 538 U.S. 510, 516–17 (2003) the Supreme Court held that INA §236(e) does not bar habeas jurisdiction over a constitutional challenge to mandatory detention legislation in the absence of a specific provision barring such habeas review. Although *Demore* involved a constitutional challenge to the mandatory detention statute, both pre- and post-*Demore* courts have found that habeas jurisdiction remains for statutory as well as constitutional challenges to mandatory detention. *See Gonzalez v. O'Connell,* 355 F.3d 1010, 1014–15 (7th Cir. 2004) [finding habeas jurisdiction to challenge mandatory detention even where the predicate issue to the constitutional claim was a statutory claim]; *Waffi v. Loiselle,* 527 F.Supp.2d 480, 483–85 (E.D. Va. 2007) [INA §236(e) does not bar habeas jurisdiction to determine statutory question whether person released from criminal custody can be subject to mandatory detention]; *Campbell v. Chadbourne,* 505 F.Supp.2d 191, 195–97 (D. Mass. 2007) [INA §236(e) does not bar constitutional challenge to detention where refugee claims he was detained for refusing to apply for AOS]; *Aguilar v. Lewis,* 50 F.Supp.2d 539, 542–43 (E.D. Va. 1999) [INA §236(e) bars discretionary decisions not statutory interpretation]; *Velasquez v. Reno,* 37 F.Supp.2d 663, 667–70 (D.N.J. 1999) [INA §236(e) barring review of detention decisions does not foreclose habeas challenge to application of statute]. *But see Hatami v. Chertoff,* 467 F.Supp.2d 637 (E.D. Va. 2006) [respondent's challenge that IJ failed to provide meaningful bond hearing was precluded by INA §§236(e), 242(a)(2)(B)(ii) and 242(b)(9)]; *Pisciotta v. Ashcroft,* 311 F.Supp.2d 445, 453 (D.N.J. 2004) [the decision by ICE to re-detain petitioner without bond or revoke his previous status because his removal hearing was reopened, notwithstanding a previous $12,000 bond, is not reviewable].

9.b. Discretionary Decisions May Be Reviewed Where They Raise Constitutional Issues—Courts have found jurisdiction to review even discretionary detention decisions where the detention violates due process or exceeds statutory authority. *See U.S. v. Grand China, Inc.* 376

F.Supp.2d 1150 (D.N.M. 2005) [reviewing denial of bond by ICE but upholding denial]. *But see Pisciotta v. Ashcroft,* 311 F.Supp.2d 445, 453 (D.N.J. 2004) [the decision by ICE to re-detain petitioner without bond or revoke his previous status because his removal hearing was reopened, notwithstanding a previous $12,000 bond, is not reviewable]; *Loa-Herrera v. Trominski,* 231 F.3d 984, 990–91 (5th Cir. 2000) [pre-*Demore* decision finding that INA §236(e) barred district court from considering challenge to lack of parole hearing for LPR stopped at the border]; *Galvez v. Lewis,* 56 F.Supp.2d 637 (E.D. Va. 1999) [pre-*Demore* decision finding no jurisdiction to review IJ's decision to apply INA §236(c) and refuse bond hearing].

9.c. Other Preclusion Statutes Do Not Bar Review of Detention Decisions—INA §242(g) does not bar review of detention decisions; nor does INA §242(b)(9) or INA §242(a)(2)(B)(ii). *Zadvydas v. Davis,* 533 U.S. 678, 686–89, 121 S.Ct. 2491, 2497–98 (2001) [INA §§236(e), 242(a)(2)(B)(ii), 242(a)(2)(C), and 242(g) did not bar habeas jurisdiction for challenge to post-removal detention]; *Sillah v. Davis,* 252 F.Supp.2d 589, 593–97 (W.D. Tenn. 2003) [INA §242(a)(2)(B)(ii) does not preclude habeas jurisdiction to challenge revocation of parole]; *Zhislin v. Reno,* 195 F.3d 810 (6th Cir. 1999) [INA §242(g) as interpreted by *Reno v. American-Arab Anti-Discrimination Comm.*, 119 S.Ct. 936, 943 (1999) does not bar review of challenge to indefinite detention]; *Parra v. Perryman,* 172 F.3d 954 (7th Cir. 1999) [in light of *American-Arab,* INA §242(g) does not bar habeas to review detention issue]; *Bouayad v. Holmes,* 74 F.Supp.2d 471, 473–74 (E.D. Pa. 1999) [government conceded that habeas jurisdiction existed to challenge mandatory detention and the court determined that neither INA §236(e) nor INA §242(b)(9) preclude jurisdiction over detention]; *Kiareldeen v. Reno,* 71 F.Supp.2d 402, 405–07 (D.N.J. 1999) [neither INA §236(e), nor §242(g) bars habeas jurisdiction to review detention based upon secret evidence]; *Alikhani v. Fasano,* 70 F.Supp.2d 1124, 1126–30 (S.D. Cal. 1999) [INA §§242(g), 242(b)(9) and 236(e) do not bar challenge to statutory and constitutional challenge to mandatory detention]; *But see Hatami v. Chertoff,* 467 F.Supp.2d 637 (E.D. Va. 2006) [respondent's challenge that IJ failed to provide meaningful bond hearing was precluded by INA §§236(e), 242(a)(2)(B)(ii) and 242(b)(9)]; *Loa-Herrera v. Trominski,* 231 F.3d 984, 990–91 (5th Cir. 2000) [no jurisdiction by district court to require DD to permit parole hearing for LPR stopped at the border].

9.d. REAL ID Act of 2005 and Judicial Review of Detention—With the passage of the REAL ID Act of 2005, PL 109-13, 119 Stat. 231, Div. B, §106 (May 11, 2005), Congress sought to eliminate habeas, mandamus, and All Writs jurisdiction in the district courts in regard to "judicial review of an order of removal entered or issued under any provision of this Act." INA §242(a)(5). The legislative history of the REAL ID Act of 2005, however, makes clear that it "will not preclude habeas review over challenges to detention that are independent of challenges to removal orders. Instead, the bill would eliminate habeas review only over challenges to removal orders." Joint Explanatory Statement of the Committee of Conference, H.R. Cong. Rep. No 109-72 at 175, 151 Cong. Rec. H2836, 2873 (May 3, 2005). *See also Hernandez v. Gonzales,* 424 F.3d 42 (1st Cir. 2005) [remanding habeas detention challenge by Mariel Cuban back to district court because habeas may be brought post-REAL ID Act when it is a challenge to detention]; *Ali v. Gonzales,* 421 F.3d 795, 797 n.1 (9th Cir. 2005) [the REAL ID Act does not apply to matters outside of challenges to removal orders]; *Bonhometre v. Ashcroft,* 414 F.3d 442, 446 n.4 (3d Cir. 2005); *Moallin v. Cangemi,* 427 F.Supp.2d 908, 918–21 (D. Minn. 2006) [citing the REAL ID Act legislative history a Somalian detained subsequent to his removal order can challenge his custody as violative of the constitution]; *Abdulle v. Gonzales,* 422 F.Supp.2d 774, 776 (W.D. Tex. 2006) [REAL ID does not preclude habeas related to detention only]. *But see Deljevic v. Baker,* 463 F.Supp.2d 699 (E.D. Mich. 2006) [no habeas jurisdiction to review detention where there is final order of removal and detention is challenged on ground that final order was improper].

9.e. Bond Pending Review in Circuit Court— At least one circuit court has also determined it has the inherent authority to grant bond while a petition for review is pending in the circuit court where petitioner has presented a substantial claim and there are extraordinary circumstances that make the grant of bail necessary to make the petition for review remedy effective. *Elkimya v. DHS,* 484 F.3d 151 (2d Cir. 2007) [finding court has inherent authority to grant bail pending resolution of a petition for review of returning LPR who has been out of the U.S. for

4 years, but concluding there were no extraordinary circumstances permitting bail); *Mapp v. Reno,* 241 F.3d 221 (2d Cir. 2001) [district courts have inherent authority to grant bail while habeas petition is pending where to do so is "necessary to make the habeas remedy effective"]; *but see Bolante v. Keisler,* 506 F.3d 618 (7th Cir. 2007) [admitting a person to bail while challenging admission is contrary to the INA and the inherent authority to admit persons to bail does not extend to persons deemed inadmissible at the border]; *Hassain v. Mukasey,* 510 F.3d 739 (7th Cir. 2007) [extending *Bolante* to prohibit circuit court from ordering release in the context of a habeas challenge to detention merely because challenge to removal order was also pending in the circuit court]. *See also Judulang v. Chertoff,* 535 F.Supp.2d 1129, 1132-33 (S.D. Cal. 2008) [detention lasting over 2½ years is unreasonable and district court ordered bond hearing before IJ over DHS objection that IJ lost jurisdiction over bond matters under 8 C.F.R. §1003.19(a) when administrative order became final and while case was on a petition for review in circuit court].

9.f. Exhaustion of Administrative Remedies—There is no statutory requirement of exhaustion of administrative remedies where a habeas petition challenges detention as opposed to removal. In addition, most courts have found that constitutional challenges to detention fall with the "futility" exception to prudential exhaustion requirements because the BIA lacks authority to decide constitutional issues. Even when a challenge is to the interpretation of a detention statute and thus within the BIA's authority, courts have found that exhaustion is not required either because the Board has previously decided the issue (making an administrative appeal futile) or because the time required for an administrative appeal to the Board would result in "irreparable injury." *Gonzalez v. O'Connell,* 355 F.3d 1010, 1015–18 (7th Cir. 2004) [habeas petitioner did not have to exhaust constitutional challenge to mandatory detention even though the predicate for the challenge was a statutory interpretation since the BIA had spoken on the statutory issue and it would have been futile]; *Soberanes v. Comfort,* 388 F.3d 1305, 1310 (10th Cir. 2004); *Ashley v. Ridge,* 288 F.Supp.2d 662, 666–67 (D.N.J. 2003) [need not exhaust administrative remedies where constitutionality of automatic-stay provision under 8 C.F.R. §1003.19(i)(2) cannot be addressed administratively before BIA]; *Baidas v. Jennings,* 123 F.Supp.2d 1052, 1055–57 (E.D. Mich. 1999) [exhaustion not required where it is not mandatory, it is futile, and constitutional issues are at stake]; *Vo v. Greene,* 109 F.Supp.2d 1281 (D. Colo. 2000) [exhaustion not required where BIA review is futile, because Board had upheld mandatory detention]; *Welch v. Reno,* 101 F.Supp.2d 347, 351 (D. Md. 2000) [no statutory exhaustion for habeas challenging detention, only for review of final orders of removal]. *See also Montero v. Cobb*, 937 F.Supp. 88 (D. Mass. 1996) [exhaustion not required in bond cases]. *Alikhani v. Fasano,* 70 F.Supp.2d 1124, 1129–30 (S.D. Cal. 1999); *Galvez v. Lewis,* 56 F.Supp.2d 637, 644 (E.D. Va. 1999); *Aguilar v. Lewis,* 50 F.Supp.2d 539, 541 (E.D. Va. 1999) [no federal statute imposes an exhaustion requirement concerning bond]; *Rowe v. INS,* 45 F.Supp.2d 144, 145–46 (D. Mass. 1999) (and cases cited therein); *Cabreja-Rojas v. Reno,* 999 F.Supp. 493 (S.D.N.Y. 1998); *Pastor-Camarena v. Smith*, 977 F.Supp. 1415, 1417 (W.D. Wash. 1997) (and cases cited therein); *Montero v. Cobb*, 937 F.Supp. 88, 90–91 (D. Mass. 1996) and *Shirkhani v. Greene*, 790 F.Supp. 1065 (D. Colo. 1992). *But see Boz v. U.S.* 248 F.3d 1299 (11th Cir. 2001) [habeas corpus properly dismissed where petitioner did not exhaust INS procedure for review after 90-day period]; *Al-Siddiqi v. Nehls,* 521 F.Supp.2d 870 (E.D. Wis. 2007) [where ICE refused to accept bond and conditions changed because FBI raised national security issues and the BIA directed petitioner to seek a new bond hearing before the IJ, petitioner had to exhaust his administrative remedies as a discretionary matter before seeking review]; *Campbell v. Chadbourne,* 505 F.Supp.2d 191 (D. Mass. 2007) [constitutional challenge by refugee to detention because of his failure to apply for adjustment should as a discretionary matter be exhausted]; *Bui v. INS,* 80 F.Supp.2d 1123 (D. Or. 1999); *Massoumi-Demaghi v. Weiss*, 631 F.Supp. 1525 (D. Conn. 1986) [must exhaust BIA remedy].

9.g. Jurisdiction / Venue / Proper Custodian

(1) In *Rumsfeld v. Padilla,* 542 U.S. 426 (2004), the Supreme Court addressed the issue of who is the proper respondent in a habeas corpus petition. Distinguishing *Braden v. 30th Judicial Circuit Court*, 410 U.S. 484, 494–95 (1973) [habeas not limited to place of petitioner's confinement but only to court's jurisdiction over custodian] and *Strait v. Laird,*

406 U.S. 341, 345 (1972) [habeas jurisdiction is proper even if custodian is not physically present in the district as long as the custodian is within reach of the court's process under *International Shoe* standards] and recognizing exceptions to the rule (such as in *Ex Parte Endo,* 323 U.S. 283, 304 (1994)), a majority of the Court, nevertheless determined that a habeas corpus action must be brought against the "immediate custodian" of the person detained and must be filed in the district court whose territorial jurisdiction includes the place where the custodian is located. The Court found the "immediate custodian" rule applicable in cases that involved challenges to physical detention (which it described as "core" cases), but declined to decide whether the rule would apply to persons in immigration custody "pending deportation." *Rumsfeld,* 121 S.Ct. at 2718 n.8. The Court's decision also noted the split in the circuits on the immediate custodian rule in immigration matters. *Id. Compare Ali v. Ashcroft,* 346 F.3d 873, 887–88 (9th Cir. 2003); and *Nolasco v. U.S.*, 358 F.Supp.2d 224, 231–34 (S.D.N.Y. 2004) [post-*Padilla*, the court determined that the AG or Secy. of DHS was the proper respondent and that the government waived objection to personal jurisdiction]; *Somir v. U.S.,* 354 F.Supp.2d 215, 216–18 (E.D.N.Y. 2005 [post-*Padilla,* the AG remains the proper custodian]; *Mandarino v. Ashcroft,* 318 F.Supp.2d 13, 16–17 (D. Conn. 2003 [AG is proper custodian for habeas purposes] *with Kholyavskiy v. Achim,* 443 F.3d 946 (7th Cir. 2006) [post-*Padilla*, neither the AG, the DHS Secretary nor the ICE Field Director are the proper custodians and the habeas petition should be directed to the warden of the state jail where the person is detained]; *Robledo-Gonzales v. Ashcroft,* 342 F.3d 667, 672–76 (7th Cir. 2003) [where petitioner was in custody of Bureau of Prisons awaiting trial on illegal reentry charge, his failure to name prison officials in habeas petition resulted in dismissal of his immigration claims]; *Roman v. Ashcroft,* 340 F.3d 314 (6th Cir. 2003) [DD is the immediate custodian and immediate custodian rule applies absent extraordinary circumstances]; *Samirah v. O'Connell,* 335 F.3d 545 (7th Cir. 2003) [district court lacked jurisdiction to review revocation of advance parole because habeas jurisdiction is unavailable where petitioner cannot obtain personal service over a custodian because there is none]; *Vasquez v. Reno,* 233 F.3d 688 (1st Cir. 2000), *cert. denied,* 534 U.S. 816 (2001) [AG is not subject to nationwide habeas and immediate custodian is the head of the detention facility]; *Yi v. Maugans*, 24 F.3d 500, 507 (3d Cir. 1994) [limited habeas to persons the DD had actual custody over and declined to include those he had constructive custody over and therefore could release, but who were not physically in the district]; *Excellent v. Ashcroft,* 359 F.Supp.2d 333, 335–36 (S.D.N.Y. 2005) [reading *Padilla* strictly to require naming of immediate custodian where petitioner was in Louisiana at time he filed petition in S.D.N.Y.]; *Diallo v. Holmes,* 288 F.Supp.2d 442 (E.D.N.Y. 2003) [where respondent was in detention in Batavia, N.Y., as a result of the ICE district director's decision, his transfer to Western District is appropriate]; *Andrade v. Ashcroft,* 270 F.Supp.2d 344 (E.D.N.Y. 2003) [on review of denied adjustment application, venue is properly in Oakdale where petitioner is detained because although his family resides in New York, they have not entered into a lease for property in N.Y. and the fact that case is on appeal to BIA is not persuasive where BIA remand or reversal will place case before IJ in Louisiana]. *Valdivia v. INS,* 80 F.Supp.2d 326, 332–33 (D.N.J. 2000) [no personal jurisdiction where custodian not within jurisdiction; but court transferred case under 28 U.S.C. §1631 rather than dismiss action]; *Wang v. Reno*, 862 F.Supp. 801, 811–13 (E.D.N.Y. 1994) [no habeas unless there is personal service over custodian]; *Chukwurah v. U.S.,* 813 F.Supp. 161, 168 (E.D.N.Y. 1993); *Peon v. Thornburgh*, 765 F.Supp. 155 (S.D.N.Y. 1991). For a general discussion of the service of process in habeas against the AG *see Henderson v. INS,* 157 F.3d 106, 122–28 (2d Cir. 1998).

(2) Immediate Custodian Is DHS or Local Warden—Even if one assumed that the immediate custodian is not the Attorney General, a question remains post-*Padilla* whether the immediate custodian is a DHS or ICE official or the local warden of a county, state, or federal prison where the respondent is detained. *See e.g., Campbell v. Ganter,* 353 F.Supp.2d 332, 336–38 (E.D.N.Y. 2004) [following *Padilla* and finding that because jurisdiction in a habeas case is not limited in a territorial sense but is a matter of venue and personal jurisdiction, the Field Director of ICE whose office is in the Southern District of New York may nevertheless be sued in the Eastern District of New York]. *Somir v. U.S.,* 354

F.Supp.2d 215, 218–19 (E.D.N.Y. 2005 [post-*Padilla,* venue was proper in the E.D.N.Y despite petitioner's detention in New Jersey]. *But see Kholyavskiy v. Achim,* 443 F.3d 946 (7th Cir. 2006) [post-*Padilla*, neither the AG, the DHS Secretary nor the ICE Field Director are the proper custodians and the habeas petition should be directed to the warden of the state jail where the person is detained]; *Galaviz-Medina v. Wooten*, 27 F.3d 487, 493–94 (10th Cir. 1994), *cert. denied,* 513 U.S. 1086 (1995) [habeas jurisdiction found where the custodian is a federal warden and not the Service because the Supreme Court has recognized that a challenge to future confinement is actionable and a warden acts as a Service agent where there is a detainer *and* a final deportation order].

10. Breach of Bond—Must be substantial. 8 C.F.R. §§103.6(c)(3), (e). *Bahramizadeh v. INS*, 717 F.2d 1170 (7th Cir. 1983). Federal court has found no breach where alien departed before interview at DHS (after OSC issued) and submitted SA-044 form from consul (verifying departure) as proof that he could not return to U.S. *Guirola-Beeche v. DOJ*, 662 F.Supp. 1414 (S.D. Fla. 1987). BIA and courts have found a breach where respondent did not surrender and filed federal habeas petition, *Matter of Allied Fidelity*, 19 I&N Dec. 124 (Comm. 1984); or where alien did not timely appear at hearing, *Matter of Arbelaez-Naranjo*, 18 I&N Dec. 403 (R.C. 1983); or where alien did not appear pursuant to bag and baggage letter and instead filed motion to stay which was denied. *Ruiz-Rivera v. Moyer*, 70 F.3d 498 (7th Cir. 1995) [failure to appear after stay denied]; *International Fidelity v. INS*, 623 F.Supp. 45 (S.D.N.Y. 1985). A bond breach can be appealed to the AAU. Where unrebutted evidence demonstrated that notice of breach was not received district court reinstated 30-day appeal period to AAU. *Hrubec v. INS*, 828 F.Supp. 251 (S.D.N.Y. 1993). *But see McLean v. Slattery*, 839 F.Supp. 188 (E.D.N.Y. 1993) [summary judgment for government where person failed to exhaust administrative remedies].

N. *Conditional Parole*—INA §236(a), in addition to bond, permits ICE officers to conditionally parole a person into the community pending a determination in her case or her testimony as a material witness. INA §236(a)(2)(B). However, a parole under this provision is not the same as a parole under INA §212(d)(5)(A) and may not permit the person to adjust status before the IJ. *Ortega-Cervantes v. Gonzales,* 501 F.3d 1111 (9th Cir. 2007) [a person apprehended near the border who was EWI and who was conditionally paroled under INA §236(a)(2)(B) after being detained for several weeks because he was a material witness in a smuggling case could not AOS under INA §245 because he was not paroled into the country within the meaning of INA §245].

O. *Detainers*

1. The DHS often places a notice with federal or state prison officials, called a "detainer," requesting the Bureau of Prisons (BOP) or its state equivalent to notify DHS if they intend to release the detained alien or to hold the alien for DHS. 8 C.F.R. §§236.1, 287.7, 1236.1. Regulations purport to provide authority for state or federal officials to hold aliens for 48 hours solely based on a DHS detainer request. 8 C.F.R. §287.7(d). DHS can only place a detainer on a person who is amenable to removal. 8 C.F.R. §287.7(a). A detainer may also have harsh consequences for noncitizen inmates. *Perez v. Neubert*, 611 F.Supp. 830 (D.N.J. 1985) [a detainer may justify solitary confinement]. The BOP, for example, may have the right to change classifications of prisoners when a formal (as opposed to notice) detainer is placed by DHS. *Mohammed v. Sullivan*, 866 F.2d 258 (8th Cir. 1989). Habeas corpus jurisdiction against DHS may be available once DHS places a detainer with the federal or state bureau of prisons because the noncitizen may then be considered to be in DHS custody for habeas purposes. *Guti v. INS*, 908 F.2d 495 (9th Cir. 1990); *Vargas v. Swan*, 854 F.2d 1028 (7th Cir. 1988); *Galaviz-Medina v. Wooten*, 27 F.3d 487, 492–94 (10th Cir. 1994), *cert. denied,* 513 U.S. 1086 (1995) [where detainer *and* final deportation order there is habeas jurisdiction against federal warden and INS]; *Lemeshko v. Wrona,* 325 F.Supp.2d 778, 782–83 (E.D Mich. 2004) [habeas jurisdiction where DHS placed detainer and state detainee already has final order of deportation even if s/he were not in DHS physical custody]; However, most courts, including the BIA, have found that a detainer alone is insufficient to constitute DHS custody. *Matter of Sanchez*, 20 I&N Dec. 223 (BIA 1990) [the filing of a detainer does not place a person in technical INS custody so as to grant IJ jurisdiction over the person's bond]; *Zolicoffer v. DOJ,* 315 F.3d 538 (5th Cir. 2003) [agreeing with other federal circuits and finding no habeas jurisdiction because person is not in custody of immigration authorities]; *Garcia v. Taylor*, 40 F.3d 299 (9th Cir. 1994) [INS detainer letter not custody for habeas purposes]; *Santana v. Chandler*, 961 F.2d 514 (5th Cir. 1992) [no jurisdiction to compel initiation of INS proceedings because

alien was not yet in INS custody]; *Prieto v. Gluch*, 913 F.2d 1159, 1162–64 (6th Cir.), *cert. denied*, 111 S.Ct. 976 (1991) [same]; *Orozco v. INS*, 911 F.2d 539 (11th Cir. 1990) [same]; *Mohammed, supra*; *Campillo v. Sullivan*, 853 F.2d 593, 595–96 (8th Cir.), *cert. denied*, 490 U.S. 1082 (1989) [no habeas jurisdiction to challenge detainer because alien not in INS custody]; *O'Georgia v. DOJ,* 370 F.Supp.2d 657 (N.D. Ohio 2005) [no mandamus jurisdiction where petitioner failed to exhaust internal BOP remedies and where there is no constitutional violation or statutory violation under INA §241, 8 U.S.C. §1231, to be removed promptly]; *Bell v. INS,* 292 F.Supp.2d 370, 373–74 (D. Conn. 2003); *Henriquez v. Ashcroft,* 269 F.Supp.2d 106, 108–09 (E.D.N.Y. 2003) [reviewing district court cases and finding no jurisdiction in habeas to review denial of certificate of citizenship where INS simply placed a detainer on applicant and he remains in the custody of the Bureau of Prisons]; *Kendall v. INS,* 261 F.Supp.2d 296, 300–03 (S.D.N.Y. 2003) [court lacks habeas jurisdiction over INS where it only posted a notice detainer and petitioner is not in INS custody]; *Deutsch v. U.S.*, 943 F.Supp. 276 (W.D.N.Y. 1996) [same, even where INS issues warrant of arrest and OSC while person in BOP custody]; *Severino v. Thornburgh*, 778 F.Supp. 5 (S.D.N.Y. 1991) [in action to compel INS to make a bond determination, the issuance of an OSC and warrant of arrest while detainee remains in state custody does not place person in INS custody for purposes of obtaining habeas jurisdiction]; *Payo v. Heyes*, 754 F.Supp. 164 (N.D. Cal. 1991); *Garcia v. INS*, 733 F.Supp. 1554 (M.D. Pa. 1990); *Cabezas v. Scott*, 717 F.Supp. 696 (D. Ariz. 1989); *D'Ambrosio v. INS*, 710 F.Supp. 269 (N.D. Cal. 1989); *Fernandez-Collado v. INS*, 644 F.Supp. 741 (D. Conn. 1986) [habeas rejected in challenge to detainer which prevented LPR from early release from BOP]. Even if habeas corpus relief is unavailable, declaratory and injunctive relief is not precluded. *Cruz v. Molerio*, 840 F.Supp. 303, 304 (S.D.N.Y. 1994).

The filing of a DHS detainer against a state alien inmate does not deny that inmate equal protection based on alienage where the detainer prevents participation in a family reunification program. *Isaraphanich v. Coughlin*, 716 F.Supp. 119 (S.D.N.Y. 1989) [rational basis test applied]; *Deutsch v. INS*, 943 F.Supp. 276, 280 (W.D.N.Y. 1996) [no constitutional right implicated by BOP classification based on INS detainer]; *Marshall v. Reno*, 915 F.Supp. 426, 433–34 (D.D.C. 1996); *Franklin v. Barry*, 909 F.Supp. 21 (D.D.C. 1995) [rejected equal protection and due process challenge based on different classifications of persons due to INS detainer] or where it prevents the inmate's efforts to reduce his time in prison. *McLean v. Crabtree,* 173 F.3d 1176, 1184–86 (9th Cir. 1999). *See also Paulino v. Connery*, 766 F.Supp. 209 (S.D.N.Y. 1991) [notice detainer not a violation of due process notwithstanding former 8 C.F.R. §242.2(c)(2)]. However, the automatic *revocation* of work release or other benefits solely because a detainer was filed may be a due process violation. *Severino v. Negron*, 996 F.2d 1439 (2d Cir. 1993). BOP has made a policy decision not to permit persons with a pending immigration detainer to participate in unescorted community activities (*e.g.*, halfway house, furlough). Letter, Quinlan, Director of BOP (Oct. 6, 1989), *reprinted in* 66 No. 43 *Interpreter Releases* 1241, 1252–53 (Nov. 6, 1989) and therefore they are also not permitted to obtain sentence reductions based on participation in community-based treatment programs. 28 C.F.R. §550.58, 61 Fed. Reg. 25121. One possible solution to this problem is to request the sentencing judge to nullify the effect of the detainer by ordering that it have no effect on unescorted community activities. BOP has also exempted inmates with confirmed orders of deportation, exclusion or removal from participating in literacy programs, thereby affecting their good time credit. 28 C.F.R. §523.20; 70 Fed. Reg. 66752–54 (Nov. 3, 2005) [although persons with final orders "represent a small fraction of all" persons seeking to participate in literacy and GED programs (about 6%) they are exempt from participating in the programs because the programs have long waiting lists and "we must concentrate our resources on inmates who will be released into U.S. communities"].

2. Under INA §287(d), 8 U.S.C. §1357(d), federal, state, and local law enforcement agencies are required to cooperate with DHS by informing DHS of aliens taken into custody for drug violations so DHS may place detainers on them; a detained alien for this purpose must be one who is physically taken into custody and is "booked, charged or otherwise officially processed." or "provided an initial appearance before a judicial officer where the alien has been informed of the charges and the right to counsel." 8 C.F.R. §287.1(d).

3. Time for Taking Person into Custody—The AG is required to "effectively and expeditiously take custody of alien" where detainer is issued and alien not detained, and the DHS is required "to de-

termine promptly" whether it will issue detainer. S. 2479, Sec. 5, 134 Cong. Rec. H. 9841 (Oct. 6, 1988). DHS regulations define that time period as 48 hours. 8 C.F.R. §287.7(d) [where INS issues a detainer and the person is not otherwise detained by a criminal justice agency the agency "shall maintain custody of the alien for a period not to exceed 48 hours excluding Saturdays, Sundays, and holidays in order to permit assumption of custody by the Service."].

4. Court in Pretrial Proceeding Makes Custody Determination, Not DHS—A least one federal court has taken the view that its decision on release of a criminal defendant awaiting trial under 18 U.S.C. §§3141–42 supersedes the DHS authority to take a criminal defendant into custody. *U.S. v. Adomako,* 150 F.Supp.2d 1302 (M.D. Fla. 2001).

5. A detainer will not be issued for an incarcerated noncitizen unless DHS intends to issue a NTA. Cadman, Telex (Dec. 5, 1986), *reprinted in* 63 *Interpreter Releases* 1163 (Dec. 15, 1986). Cannot issue detainer unless the incarcerated noncitizen would be subject to removal. 8 C.F.R. §287.7(b). A detainer can be issued for SAW or legalization applicants who are subject to removal. 56 Fed. Reg. 33204 (July 19, 1991).

6. The Interstate Agreement on Detainers (IAD), 18 U.S.C. §2, sets a 120-day time limit in which a prisoner subject to a detainer is brought to trial. IAD Art. IV(c). At least one court has found the IAD inapplicable to DHS detainers because their proceedings are not criminal. *U.S. v. Gonzalez-Mendoza*, 985 F.2d 1014 (9th Cir. 1993).

P. ***Bail Reform Act***—The federal bail statute, 18 U.S.C. §3142(d), which applies to persons under prosecution for federal crimes, includes a specific provision for "temporary detention" for up to 10 days of a defendant who "is not a citizen of the United States or lawfully admitted for permanent residence" and who poses a flight risk or danger to the community. Within the 10-day period, the U.S. Attorney must notify DHS. *U.S. v. Becerra-Cobo*, 790 F.2d 427 (5th Cir. 1986). If DHS fails or declines to take the person into custody within the 10-day period, the person is subject to ordinary federal bail provisions. The subsequent determination to continue to incarcerate an alien as a bail risk under 18 U.S.C. §3142(f) is permissible even if it is not within the first 5 days of arrest so long as it is within the 10-day detention under §3142(d). *U.S. v. Moncada-Pelaez*, 810 F.2d 1008 (11th Cir. 1987). This pretrial incarceration provision, however, should be applied sparingly. *U.S. v. Mendez-Hernandez*, 747 F.Supp. 846 (D.P.R. 1990) [admonishing U.S. Attorney and magistrate for interpreting the provision to permit pretrial detention for a minor immigration crime where there was no showing of danger to the community]. At least one federal court has taken the view that its decision on release of a criminal defendant awaiting trial under 18 U.S.C. §§3141-42 supersedes DHS's authority to take a criminal defendant into custody. *U.S. v. Adomoko,* 150 F.Supp.2d 1302 (M.D. Fla. 2001).

Q. ***Special Rules for Detention of Aggravated Felons, Persons Convicted of Certain Crimes, and Terrorists***—INA §236(c), 8 U.S.C. §1226(c).

1. Detention Laws from 1988 to 1996—Congress has legislated extensively as to when and under what circumstances persons convicted of crimes must be incarcerated pending immigration removal proceedings and after a final removal order. As a result of legislation in 1988 persons who were aggravated felons, including LPRs, were for the first time subject to mandatory detention pending removal proceedings without the possibility of release on bond. This mandatory detention provision was successfully challenged in many district courts. *Kellman v. District Director,* 750 F.Supp. 625 (S.D.N.Y. 1990); *Probert v. INS,* 750 F.Supp. 252 (E.D. Mich. 1990), *aff'd on other grounds,* 954 F.2d 1253 (6th Cir. 1992) [involving an NIV holder and finding the limitation on habeas authority under INA §242(a)(1) also unconstitutional]; *Paxton v. INS*, 745 F.Supp. 1261 (E.D. Mich. 1990), *dismissed as moot*, 925 F.2d 1465 (6th Cir. 1991); *Agunobi v. Thornburgh,* 745 F.Supp. 533 (N.D. Ill. 1990); *Leader v. Blackman,* 744 F.Supp. 500 (S.D.N.Y. 1990); *Davis v. Weiss,* 749 F.Supp. 47 (D. Conn. 1990); *Morrobel v. Thornburgh,* 744 F.Supp. 725 (E.D. Wa. 1990). Thereafter, amendments in IMMACT90 and the 1991 MTINA restored bond hearings for those aggravated felons who had been lawfully admitted to the U.S., including LPRs. Those individuals were eligible for bond if they could affirmatively demonstrate that their release would pose neither a danger or flight risk. *See* former INA §242(a)(2)(B), 8 U.S.C. §1252(a)(2)(B) (1994). However, in 1996, Congress enacted new legislation which greatly expanded the reach of the mandatory detention statute while eliminating the release policy for "lawfully admitted" noncitizens. The first provision enacted, on Apr. 26, 1996, as part of AEDPA, barred aggravated felons and others who had committed criminal acts from release even if they were LPRs. These pro-

visions were struck down by many district courts on retroactivity and constitutional grounds. *Lopez-Tellez v. INS*, Case No 96-1432-BTM (CGA) (S.D. Cal. Sept. 26, 1996) (Moskowitz, J); *Grodzki v. Reno*, 950 F.Supp. 339 (N.D. Ga. 1996); *Montero v. Cobb*, 937 F.Supp. 88, 92 (D. Mass. 1996); *Morales-Villagomez v. Smith*, 1996 WL 622451, Case No. C96-1141C (W.D. Wash. July 21, 1996) (Coughneour, J.); *Matter of Reyes*, Case No. B-94–80 (S.D. Tex. May 31, 1996) (Vela, J.). *See also in this section* "Constitutional and Statutory Challenges to Mandatory Detention," ¶ 3 (p.305), *infra*. Thereafter, on Sept. 30, 1996, the President signed IIRIRA, which mandates detention, without release, for virtually all persons who have committed crimes (as well as persons removable on terrorism grounds). Under the IIRIRA amendments, codified at INA §236(c), 8 U.S.C. §1226(c), the only persons who are eligible for release if subject to mandatory detention are persons who are a part of the Witness Protection Program or whose release will protect other witnesses. IIRIRA, however, also provided for limited exceptions to mandatory detention over a 2-year period if the AG invoked the Transition Period Custody Rules (TPCR). IIRIRA §303(b). The TPCR was invoked for 2 years from Oct. 9, 1996, to Oct. 9, 1998. While the TPCR mandated detention of virtually all noncitizens will criminal convictions, it permitted release of "lawfully admitted" noncitizens. Application of the TPCR was successfully challenged. *Pastor-Camarena v. Smith*, 977 F.Supp. 1415 (W.D. Wash. 1997) [finding that the "when release" language in TPCR limited the provision's application to persons with criminal convictions who had not yet been released from criminal incarceration].

2. The IIRIRA Provisions—INA §236 provides that the AG shall detain and shall not release the following categories of persons who are subject to removal from the U.S.: (a) persons who are inadmissible by reason of having committed any offense covered under INA §212(a)(2), 8 U.S.C. §1182(a)(2); (b) persons who are deportable by reason of having committed 2 or more crimes of moral turpitude, an aggravated felony, a drug offense, a firearm offense, *or* a miscellaneous crime as defined in INA §237(a)(2)(D), including espionage, sabotage, or treason for which a term of imprisonment of 5 years or more may be imposed, threatening the President in violation of 18 U.S.C. §871, violating the Neutrality Act under 18 U.S.C. §960, violating the Selective Service Act or Trading with the Enemies Act, committing travel control crimes under 8 U.S.C. §1185, or importing a person for an immoral purpose under INA §278, 8 U.S.C. §1328, (c) persons who have committed a CIMT for which the sentence of imprisonment is at least one year; or (d) persons involved in terrorist activity. The AG shall take them into custody "when the alien is released on parole, supervised release, or probation, and without regard to whether the alien may be arrested or imprisoned again for the same offense." If the person is subject to mandatory detention, the AG may only release such person if s/he is involved in the Witness Protection Program or to protect another witness and the AG is satisfied that the person will not pose a danger to the safety of either persons or property. The BIA has held that a person need not be charged in the NTA with the crime that would subject him to mandatory detention. *Matter of Kotliar,* 24 I&N Dec. 124 (BIA 2007) [person apprehended at home while on probation who was not charged in NTA with crime is still subject to mandatory detention for the crime].

2.a. Applicability. Only persons who are "released after" Oct. 9, 1998, are subject to mandatory detention. *Matter of Adeniji,* 22 I&N Dec. 1102, 1107–11 (BIA 1999). Therefore, persons who were released from parole, supervised release, probation or other detention on or before Oct. 9, 1998 remain eligible for a bond. Memo, Pearson, Ex. Asst. Comm. Field Operations (HQOPS (DDP) 50/10) (July 12, 1999), *reprinted in* 76 No. 27 *Interpreter Releases* 1082, 1099–1102 (July 19, 1999). The Board has also determined that the "when released" language under INA §236(c)(1) requires that the person must be released from *physical* custody for mandatory detention to apply. *Matter of West,* 22 I&N Dec. 1405 (BIA 2000) [where person was sentenced to probation after the effective date of INA §236(c)(1) he was not subject to mandatory detention because he was not "released" from physical custody]. However, the BIA has also determined that the timing of his or her release is not relevant as long as it is after the effective date of INA §236(c)(1). *Matter of Rojas,* 23 I&N Dec. 117 (BIA 2001) [person convicted of an offense that subjects him to mandatory detention will be mandatorily detained even if INS does not immediately take him into custody when he is released from his criminal sentence as long as he was released after Oct. 9, 1998]. Moreover, the BIA has held that an arrest is enough to satisfy the physical custody requirement even if no sentence was ever served fro the crime. Thus, a person who is released from arrest after Oct. 9, 1998 is subject to mandatory detention even if he is not picked up until later at home while serving probation and was never in physical custody after his conviction. *Matter of Kotliar,* 24 I&N Dec. 124 (BIA 2007) [person who did not serve a jail term for his criminal conviction, who was apprehended at home while on probation instead of immediately after his release from arrest, and who was not charged in NTA with a crime, is still subject to mandatory detention]. *But see Waffi v. Loiselle,* 527 F.Supp.2d 480, 485–88 (E.D. Va. 2007) [mandatory detention provision of INA §236(c) does not apply to a person who was released from state custody and only taken into ICE custody after he had been released (in this case one month) from state custody. INA §236(c) applies only when the person is taken immediately into ICE custody upon completing his state/federal sentence]; *Zabadi v. Chertoff,* 2005 U.S. Dist. LEXIS 31914 (N.D. Cal. 2005) [mandatory detention statute does not apply to petitioner who was taken into immigration custody 2 years after completion of criminal sentence]; *Quezada-Bucio v. Ridge,* 317 F.Supp.2d 1221, 1227–31 (W.D. Wash. 2004) [mandatory detention statute does not apply to petitioner who was taken into immigration custody 3 years after completion of criminal sentence].

ICE has also taken the position that *any* post-Oct. 1998 release from criminal custody triggers mandatory detention even if not for a crime that is a ground for mandatory detention, as long as the noncitizen was previously convicted of such a crime. *But see Cavazos v. Moore,* Civil Action M-03-347 (S.D. Tex. Jan. 7, 2005) [finding this interpretation violated plain language of statute]; *Cox v. Monica,* __F.Supp.2d___(M.D. Pa 2007), 2007 WL 1804335 [rejecting this interpretation based on retroactivity principles].

2.b. Effective Date—The effective date of INA §236(c) was Apr. 1, 1997, unless the AG notified the Congress of the lack of detention space, thereby invoking the "Transition Period Custody rules" (TPCR) and delaying implementation of INA §236(c) for one year. On Oct. 9, 1996, the INS Commissioner so notified the House Committee on the Judiciary. Letter, Meissner, Commissioner, HQCOM 50/12.1.1 (Oct. 9, 1996), *published on* AILA InfoNet at Doc. No. 96101590. A second notification was sent on Oct. 9, 1997, delaying the implementation of INA §236(c) until Oct. 9, 1998, *reported in* 74 No. 39 *Interpreter Releases* 1,552–53 (Oct. 10, 1997). The extension under the TPCR expired Oct. 9, 1998.

2.c. Procedures Under Mandatory Detention

(1) *Joseph* Hearing—Although IJs do not have authority to release a person subject to mandatory detention, they retain jurisdiction to determine whether the person is "properly included" within the mandatory detention provision. 8 C.F.R. §1003.19(h)(2)(ii). This hearing is referred to as a "Joseph" hearing based upon the BIA's decision in *Matter of Joseph*, 22 I&N Dec. 799 (BIA 1999), setting out the standard for making this determination. Under *Joseph* a person is "properly included" with the mandatory detention statute unless DHS is "substantially unlikely to prevail" in its charges that the person is removable on one of the grounds designated in INA §236(c). *But see Tijani v. Willis,* 430 F.3d 1241 (9th Cir. 2005) (Tashima, J concurring) [rejecting *Matter of Joseph* standard as a violation of due process, and arguing that INA §236(c) can not constitutionally be applied to any person who has a "substantial" argument against removability].

(2) If the government has not charged the person with the crime that would result in mandatory detention in the NTA, it must give notice of the basis for mandatory detention and provide an opportunity to challenge the detention before the IJ in a *Joseph* hearing. *Matter of Kotliar,* 24 I&N Dec. 124 (BIA 2007) [person charged in NTA as overstay was entitled to basis for mandatory detention and opportunity to challenge it].

(3) Automatic Stay—If an IJ issues an order releasing the respondent on the grounds that he is not "properly included" within the mandatory detention provision, DHS may obtain an automatic stay of the order simply by filing a notice of intent to appeal the bond on an EOIR-43. 8 C.F.R. §1003.19(i)(2); *See in this part* "Appeals to BIA," ¶ M.8 (p.295), *supra.* *Matter of Joseph,* 22 I&N Dec. 660 (BIA 1999) [automatic stay of IJ release order granted notwithstanding IJ's finding that person in not an aggravated felon and not subject to mandatory detention under INA §236(c)(1)]. In 2006, the automatic-stay regulations were revised to include an automatic 90-day lapse provision. Prior to this change, a number of courts found the automatic-stay provision to be unconstitutional. *Uritsky v.*

Ridge, 286 F.Supp.2d 842 (E.D. Mich. 2003); *Bezmen v. Ashcroft,* 245 F.Supp.2d 446 (D. Conn. 2003). *Accord Zabadi v. Chertoff,* 2005 WL 1514122 (N.D. Cal. June 17, 2005) and 2005 WL 3157377 (N.D. Cal. Nov. 22, 2005); *Zavala v. Ridge,* 310 F.Supp.2d 1071 (N.D. Cal. 2004); *Ashley v. Ridge,* 288 F.Supp.2d 662 (D.N.J. 2003) [automatic-stay provision violates substantive and procedural due process for person who is not subject to mandatory detention and not a national security threat]. *But see Pisciotta v. Ashcroft,* 311 F.Supp.2d 445, 453–56 (D.N.J. 2004) [the stay provision is not unconstitutional under *Demore*].

(4) Application to Individuals Previously Released Under TPCR or Pre-*Demore*—The Service's guidelines previously provided that a person who had obtained a bond need not be re-detained when the TPCR expired and INA §236(c) took effect. Memo, Pearson, Executive Assoc. Comm., HQOPS (DDP) 50/10-C (Oct. 7. 1998), *published on* AILA InfoNet at Doc. No. 98100791. In contrast, however, an ICE memo published subsequent to *Demore v. Kim*, directed all field officers to send demand letters to all persons who were released on bond prior to the *Demore* decision, but who remained subject to INA §236(c). If a person is subject to INA §236(c) and was released by ICE or EOIR s/he "shall be immediately detained and served with a revocation of release status." Memo, Tangeman, Director, Office of Detention and Removal, ICE, HQDRO 50/10 (May 15, 2003), *published on* AILA InfoNet at Doc. No. 03052340 (May 23, 2003). Under the Tangeman memo, if a person was released pursuant to a court order, however, s/he should not be immediately re-detained but local district counsel should be directed to take action in federal court to seek a vacatur of the release order. *Id.*

2.d. Constitutionality—The Supreme Court has held that the IIRIRA mandatory detention provision including detention of an LPR under INA §236(c) did not violate due process when the petitioner conceded deportability as an aggravated felon and did not request a hearing as to whether he was properly subject to mandatory detention under the statute, and where the detention was for a relatively brief period of time. *Demore v. Kim,* 538 U.S. 510 (2003). *See in this chapter* ¶ IV.J.5 (p.138), *supra.*

3. Constitutional and Statutory Challenges to Mandatory Detention—The detention-without-release provisions have been challenged on various grounds. These grounds include the inapplicability of the statute because the person is not charged as deportable or inadmissible under one of the grounds that triggers mandatory detention under the statute. *Probert v. INS*, 954 F.2d 1253 (6th Cir. 1992) [holding that prior mandatory detention statute under former INA §242(a)(2) did not apply to person not charged as an aggravated felon in the OSC].

3.a. Statutory Challenges—The principle statutory challenge to mandatory detention under INA §236(c) has been a challenge to its retroactive application. This challenge was based both on the language of INA §236(c)(1) which states that the AG "shall detain" designated individuals "when...released" as well as the effective date language in IIRIRA which states that INA §236(c) will apply to persons "released after" the expiration of the Transition Period Custody Rules (TPCR). Notwithstanding this language, upon expiration of the TPCR in October 1998, the INS began applying INA §236(c) to individuals who had been released from incarceration years before, or who had never been incarcerated for the offense in the first place. Numerous successful challenges followed: *Grant v. Zemski,* 54 F.Supp.2d 437, 439–41 (E.D. Pa. 1999) [INA §236(c) cannot be applied retroactively to persons released from criminal incarceration prior to Oct. 9, 1998]; *Velasquez v. Reno,* 37 F.Supp.2d 663 (D.N.J. 1999) [statute by its language can not apply retroactively to persons released from custody prior to end of TPCR on Oct. 9, 1998]; *Saucedo-Tellez v. Perryman,* 55 F.Supp.2d 882 (N.D. Ill. 1999) [same]; *Aguilar v. Lewis,* 50 F.Supp.2d 539, 542–44 (E.D. Va. 1999) [same]; *Alwaday v. Beebe,* 43 F.Supp.2d 1130 (D. Or. 1999). As a result of these statutory challenges, the Service changed its policy of retroactively applying INA §236(c) to individuals who had finished serving their criminal sentences years before. Memo, Pearson, Ex. Asst. Comm. Field Operations (HQOPS (DDP) 50/10) (July 12, 1999), *reprinted in* 76 No. 27 *Interpreter Releases* 1082, 1099–1102 (July 19, 1999). [applying INA §236(c) only to persons released from criminal incarceration on or after Oct. 9, 1998]. The BIA also adopted this interpretation of the statute. *Matter of Adeniji,* 22 I&N Dec. 1102, 1107–11 (BIA 1999) [mandatory detention does not apply to persons who completed their criminal custody prior to Oct. 10, 1998 based upon the TPCR language that INA §236(c) only applies to persons "released after" the TPCR expired]. Prior to IIRIRA, numerous courts used similar reasoning to reject the retroactive application of the AEDPA mandatory detention provision §440(c). *See e.g., Lopez-Tellez v. INS*, Case No. 96-1432-BTM (CGA) (S.D. Cal. Sept. 26, 1996) (Moskowitz, J); *Grodzki v. Reno*, 950 F.Supp. 339 (N.D. Ga. 1996); *Montero v. Cobb*, 937 F.Supp. 88 (D. Mass. 1996); *Morales-Villagomez v. Smith*, 1996 WL 622451, Case No. C96-1141C (W.D. Wash. July 21, 1996) (Coughneour, J.); *Matter of Reyes*, Case No. B-94–80 (S.D. Tex. May 31, 1996) (Vela, J.).

Litigation has also focused on whether the "when released" language limits INA §236(c)'s applicability to individuals who are actually incarcerated for their criminal offenses and who are taken into ICE custody *immediately* upon release from such incarceration. The Board has held that the "when released" language requires that the person must be released from *physical* custody for mandatory detention to apply. *Matter of West,* 22 I&N Dec. 1405 (BIA 2000) [where person was sentenced to probation after the effective date of INA §236(c)(1) he was not subject to mandatory detention because he was not "released" from physical custody]. However, the BIA has also held that the timing of his or her release is not relevant as long as it is after the effective date of INA §236(c)(1). *Matter of Rojas,* 23 I&N Dec. 117 (BIA 2001) [person convicted of an offense that subjects him to mandatory detention will be mandatorily detained even if INS does not immediately take him into custody when he is released from his criminal sentence]. *But see Waffi v. Loiselle,* 527 F.Supp.2d 480, 485–88 (E.D. Va. 2007) [mandatory detention provision of INA §236(c) does not apply to a person who was released from state custody and only taken into ICE custody after he had been released (in this case one month) from state custody. INA §236(c) applies only when the person is taken immediately into ICE custody upon completing his state/federal sentence]; *Quezada-Bucio v. Ridge,* 317 F.Supp.2d 1221, 1227–31 (W.D. Wash. 2004) [rejecting BIA's interpretation and citing several prior IIRIRA cases with similar holdings]; *Zabadi v. Chertoff,* 2005 U.S. Dist. LEXIS 31914 (N.D. Cal. 2005); *Pastor-Camarena v. Smith*, 977 F.Supp. 1415 (W.D. Wash. 1997) [construing similar "when released" language in TPCR as limiting applicability of statute to individuals taken into INS custody immediately after release].

More recently, litigation has challenged ICE's position that *any* post-Oct. 1998 release from criminal custody triggers mandatory detention even if not for a crime that is a ground for mandatory detention, as long as the noncitizen was previously convicted of such a crime. *See Cavazos v. Moore,* Civil Action M-03-347 (S.D. Tex. Jan. 7, 2005) [finding this interpretation violated plain language of statute]; *Cox v. Monica,* __F.Supp.2d___(M.D. Pa 2007), 2007 WL 1804335 [rejecting this interpretation based on retroactivity principles].

3.b. Constitutional Challenges—The Supreme Court upheld the constitutionality of INA §236(c). *Demore v. Kim*, 538 U.S. 510 (2003) [mandatory detention, for a brief period of time, of an LPR who conceded deportability as an aggravated felon, and did not request a hearing to challenge whether he was properly subject to the mandatory detention statute, did not violate due process, notwithstanding the lack of any hearing to determine whether he was a flight risk or likely to abscond]. In his concurring opinion that created a majority in *Demore,* Justice Kennedy, however, recognized that a person subject to mandatory detention "could be entitled to an individualized determination as to his risk of flight and dangerousness if the continued detention became unreasonable or unjustified" *Demore,* 538 U.S. at 532. Moreover, the majority opinion in *Demore* itself emphasized that detention pending removal proceedings was relatively brief—generally less than 45 days for those who do not appeal their removal orders to the BIA, and an additional 4 months for those who pursue a BIA appeal. *Id.* Subsequent to *Demore,* several courts have recognized the limited nature of the Supreme Court's holding. *Tijani v. Willis,* 430 F.3d 1241 (9th Cir. 2005) [ordered bond hearing before IJ for LPR who had been imprisoned for 2 years and 8 months, finding that mandatory detention only applied to "expeditious" removal proceedings and "it is constitutionally doubtful that Congress may authorize imprisonment of this duration for lawfully admitted resident aliens who are subject to removal"]; *Gonzalez v. O'Connell,* 355 F.3d 1010, 1019–21 (7th Cir. 2004) [noting that *Demore* left open the question of whether INA §236(c) would be constitutional as applied to an individual who raised colorable challenges to deportability, but finding no colorable claim in petitioner's case]; *Ly v. Hansen,* 351 F.3d 263 (6th Cir. 2003) [construing INA §236(c) as authorizing detention only for a period of time reasonably necessary to conclude removal proceedings, and finding Vietnamese immigrant's 1½ year detention, waiting a final order of removal, was unreasonable, particularly when it was unlikely he could actually be physically removed]; *Judulang v. Chertoff,* 535 F.Supp.2d 1129, 1132–33 (S.D. Cal. 2008) [detention lasting over 2½ years is unreasonable and district court ordered bond hearing before IJ over DHS objection that IJ lost jurisdiction over bond matters under 8 C.F.R. §1003.19(a) when administrative order became final and that his detention became voluntary when he chose to petition to the circuit court]; *Madrane v. Hogan,* 520 F.Supp.2d 654 (M.D. Pa. 2007) [reading *Demore* narrowly and ordering non-LPR petitioner's release after more than three years in custody fighting his removal to Morocco]; *Martinez v. Gonzales,* 504 F.Supp.2d 887 (C.D. Cal. 2007) [5 year detention was excessive and unauthorized under INA §236 and his successful requests for stays of removal cannot be a basis to deny release]; *Moallin v. Cangemi,* 427 F.Supp.2d 908, 25–27 (D. Minn. 2006) [if detention is treated as pre-removal, then year detention violated due process]; *Uritsky v. Ridge,* 286 F.Supp.2d 842 (E.D. Mich. 2003) [court in *Demore* operated on assumption that detention pre-removal was for a short duration and would be less than 6 months as in *Zadvydas* and therefore person in detention for over 11 months should be released notwithstanding mandatory detention provision]. *See also Tijani v. Willis,* 430 F.3d 1241 (9th Cir. 2005) (Tashima, J concurring) [rejecting *Matter of Joseph* standard as a violation of due process, and arguing that INA §236(c) cannot constitutionally be applied to any person who has a "substantial" argument against removability]; *But see Hussain v. Mukasey,* 510 F.3d 739, 742–44 (7th Cir. 2007) [no jurisdiction to challenge pre-final order of detention because of INA §242(a)(2)(B)(ii) and court could not enter order releasing petitioner while merits appeal is pending but would have to remand release issue to district court; however, the court did not rule out a constitutional challenge for inordinate delay in certain circumstances]; *Soberanes v. Comfort,* 388 F.3d 1305, 1311 (10th Cir. 2004) [reading *Zadvydas* and *Demore* to permit detention while removal proceeding and review is on going but recognizing that subsequent delays may warrant remedial action]; *Ali v. Achim*, 342 F.Supp.2d 769 (N.D. Ill. 2004) [reading *Demore* broadly to uphold constitutionality of 28-month discretionary detention of non-LPR refugee during removal proceedings].

3.c. Other Challenges to Detention

(1) Prolonged Detention Pending Judicial Review and Stay of Removal—Courts are divided as to what statute governs detention pending judicial review when there has been a stay of removal. Most courts have found that INA §236 continues to apply because the grant of a stay delays the start of the removal period. *See e.g.Tijani v. Willis,* 430 F.3d 1241 (9th Cir. 2005) [implicitly finding that §236 continues to apply]; *Wang v. Ashcroft,* 350 F.3d 130 (2d Cir. 2003); *Alafyouny v. Chertoff,* No. 3:06 CV 0204 M (N.D. Tex. May 19, 2006), 2006 WL 1581959 (collecting cases). ICE, however, takes the position that INA §241 governs, that the act of seeking a stay of removal serves to suspend the 90-day removal period, but that no bond is available under INA §241. *Id. See in this chapter,* "Application of INA §236 or INA §241," ¶ U.9.e (p.420), *infra.* Regardless of which statute applies, numerous courts have found that prolonged detention pending a stay of removal is subject to due process constraints under the principles of *Zadvydas* and *Demore* and have either ordered release or a meaningful custody hearing on due process grounds or have construed the statute to so require. *See e.g. Alafyouny v. Chertoff,* Case No. 3:06 CV 0204 M (N.D. Tex. May 19, 2006), 2006 WL 1581959 [ordering in-person interview and individualized custody determination for individual detained two years pending judicial review of removal order that had been stayed]; *Ovediji v. Ashcroft,* 332 F.Supp.2d 747 (M.D. Pa. 2004) [applying *Zadvydas* principles in order to release individual who was detained pending federal court review]; *Lawson v. Gerlinski,* 332 F.Supp. 2d 735 (M.D. Pa. 2004) [long-term LPR who obtained stay of removal and remained in detention for 18 months was granted release pending evidentiary hearing on underlying substantive due process claim to remain in the U.S.]; *Haynes v. DHS,* (M.D. Pa. July 8, 2005), 2005 WL 1606321. *See also Tijani v. Willis*, 430 F.3d 1241 (9th Cir. 2005) [ordering bond hearing for individual detained more than two years and eight months, much of this pending court of appeal review]; *Martinez v. Gonzales,* 504 F.Supp.2d 887 (C.D. Cal. 2007) [ordering

bond hearing for individual detained 5 years pending removal proceedings and judicial review]; *Del Toro-Chacon v. Chertoff,* 431 F.Supp.2d 1135, 1140-43 (W.D. Wash. 2006) [violation of due process to deny bond hearing before neutral adjudicator, whether or not person detained under INA §236 or INA §241]. *See also Nadarajah v. Gonzales,* 443 F.3d 1069 (9th Cir. 2006) [construing detention statutes not authorizing detention based upon national security as authorizing brief detention]. *But see Soberanes v. Comfort,* 388 F.3d 1305, 1311 (10th Cir. 2004) [reading *Zadvydas* and *Demore* to permit detention while removal proceedings and review is ongoing, but recognizing that subsequent delays may warrant remedial action]; *Hussain v. Mukasey,* 510 F.3d 739, 742-44 (7th Cir. 2007) [agreeing that due process imposes limits on prolonged pre–final-order mandatory detention, but finding no jurisdiction to order release once removal order was pending review in the court of appeals].

(2) Post–Final Order Indefinite Detention—*Zadvydas v. Davis,* 533 U.S. 678, 691–702 (2001) [due process remains to challenge indefinite detention for persons with final orders who can not be removed to any country because "Freedom from imprisonment—from government custody, detention, or other forms of physical restraint—lies at the heart of the liberty that Clause protects."]; *Clark v. Martinez,* 543 U.S. 371 (2005) [applying *Zadvydas's* 6-month ruling to inadmissible persons stopped at the border; finding as a matter of statutory construction that INA §241(a)(6), 8 U.S.C. §1231(a)(6), authorizes post–final order detention of such persons only for the period of time reasonably necessary to effectuate removal, and thus requiring the release of such persons after six months]; *Morales-Fernandez v. INS,* 418 F.3d 1116, 1122–25 (10th Cir. 2005) [post-*Clark* decision finding it impermissible to hold Mariel Cuban parolee beyond 6-month period]; *Rosales-Garcia v. Holland,* 322 F.3d 386, 403–15 (6th Cir. 2003) (*en banc*) [pre-*Clark* decision finding indefinite detention of Mariel Cubans would violate both the statute (as construed by *Zadvydas*) and the due process clause of the Fifth Amendment]; *Bah v. Cangemi,* 489 F.Supp.2d 905, 915–24 (D. Minn. 207) [court developed an "unencumbered-time" approach in determining that despite periods of time that stopped the 6 months post-final order from running, applicant had more than 6 months that were "unencumbered" and therefore should be released]; *Caballero v. Caplinger,* 914 F.Supp. 1374 (E.D. La. 1996) [Cuban EWI subjected to indefinite mandatory detention under former 8 U.S.C. §1252(a)(2)(A) could not be denied right to bond hearing under the Due Process Clause and the Eighth Amendment].

(3) Review of Discretionary Bond Determinations—Discretionary decisions may be reviewed where they raise constitutional issues. Courts have found jurisdiction to review even discretionary detention decisions, where the detention violates due process or exceeds statutory authority. *See U.S. v. Grand China, Inc.* 376 F.Supp.2d 1150 (D.N.M. 2005) [reviewing denial of bond by ICE but upholding denial]. *But see Pisciotta v. Ashcroft,* 311 F.Supp.2d 445, 453 (D.N.J. 2004) [the decision by ICE to re-detain petitioner without bond or revoke his previous status because his removal hearing was reopened, notwithstanding a previous $12,000 bond, is not reviewable]; *Loa-Herrera v. Trominski,* 231 F.3d 984, 990–91 (5th Cir. 2000) [pre-*Demore* decision finding that INA §236(e) barred district court from considering challenge to lack of parole hearing for LPR stopped at the border]; *Galvez v. Lewis,* 56 F.Supp.2d 637 (E.D. Va. 1999) [pre-*Demore* decision finding no jurisdiction to review IJ's decision to apply INA §236(c) and refuse bond hearing].

(4) Other Detention Without a Hearing Before an Impartial Adjudicator—*Olatunji v. Ashcroft,* 387 F.3d 383 (4th Cir. 2004) [ordering bond hearing for returning LPR, based upon retroactivity issues, who, post-IIRIRA, was deemed an "arriving alien"]; *Del Toro-Chacon v. Chertoff,* 431 F.Supp.2d 1135, 1140–43 (W.D. Wash. 2006) [although it was unclear whether the person was detained under INA §236 or INA §241 the court determined it was a violation of due process to deny the person a bond hearing before a neutral adjudicator such as an immigration judge]; *Cabreja-Rojas v. Reno,* 999 F.Supp. 493 (S.D.N.Y. 1998) [unconstitutional under *Eldridge* to deny returning LPRs a hearing before an independent IJ,]; *St. John v. McElroy*, 917 F.Supp. 243 (S.D.N.Y. 1996) [finding mandatory detention of returning LPR under former INA §236(e) unconstitutional and

ordering custody hearing before impartial adjudicator]; *Thomas v. McElroy*, 1996 WL 487953, Case No. 96-CV-5065 (JSM) (S.D.N.Y. August 23, 1996) (Martin, J) [same]; *Cruz-Taveras v. McElroy,* 1996 WL 455012, Case No. 96-CV-5068 (S.D.N.Y. Aug. 12, 1996) [same]; *Ekekhor v. Aljets*, 979 F.Supp. 640 (N.D. Ill. 1997) [same with respect to mandatory detention of returning LPR under the TPCR]; *Caballero v. Caplinger*, 914 F.Supp. 1374 (E.D. La. 1996) [former INA §242(a)(2)(B) barring bail to EWI is unconstitutional]. *But see Tineo v. Ashcroft,* 350 F.3d 382 (3d Cir. 2003) [rejecting retroactivity argument and upholding denial of bond hearing to returning LPR without addressing due process issue].

(5) Medical Release—Some courts have entertained release where health related issues have been raised notwithstanding mandatory detention provisions. *Diaz v. McElroy,* 134 F.Supp.2d 315, 320 (S.D.N.Y. 2001) [denying release because there was no indication that seizures were left untreated or that respondent's medical condition was deteriorating].

(6) *Bivens* Action for Unlawful Detention—There may also be jurisdiction for a *Bivens* claim based upon discrimination. *Kwai Fun Wong v. U.S.,* 373 F.3d 952, 968–75 (9th Cir. 2004) [finding that a *Bivens* claim for discrimination regarding the revocation of parole and rejection of adjustment of status were actionable because the entry fiction applies to a narrow class of procedural rights and does not apply to all constitutional claims of nonadmitted persons, but granting qualified immunity]; *Martinez-Aguero v. Gonzales,* 459 F.3d 618 (5th Cir. 2006 [entry fiction did not bar *Bivens* claim for false imprisonment and excessive force at port of entry]; *Arar v. Ashcroft,* 414 F.Supp.2d 250, 266–87 (E.D.N.Y. 2006) [*Bivens* action against DHS officials not barred by INA §§242(b)(9), 242(g), 242(a)(2)(B)(ii) or FARRA §2242(d)]. *But see Sissoko v. Rocha,* 509 F.3d 947 (9th Cir. 2007 [*Bivens* claim under the Fourth Amendment for improper detention of temporary resident in summary removal is barred by INA §242(g) in the limited circumstance where the temporary resident could have challenged his detention in habeas under INA §242(e)(2)]; *Foster v. Townsley,* 243 F.3d 210 (5th Cir. 2001) [INA §242(g) bars jurisdiction over claims arising from decision to execute removal order]; *Humphries v. Various Federal U.S. INS Employees,* 164 F.3d 936 (5th Cir. 1999) [INA §242(g) bars jurisdiction over claim of retaliatory exclusion but not over claims of involuntary servitude and mistreatment in detention]; *Khorrami v. Rolince,* 493 F.Supp.2d 1061 (N.D. Ill. 2007) [finding jurisdiction lacking over some but not all claims]. *But see Medina v. U.S.,* 92 F.Supp.2d 545 (E.D. Va. 2000) [disagreeing with reasoning of Humphries]

R. ***Mandatory Detention of Suspected Terrorists***—INA §236A, 8 U.S.C. §1226a; USA PATRIOT Act, PL 107-56 §412. The AG/ICE is authorized to mandatorily detain any person who he/it has certified as having reasonable grounds to believe is a person described in INA §237(a)(4)(A)(i) [engage in espionage, sabotage, or export control], §237(a)(4)(A)(iii) [opposition by violence or overthrow of U.S. government], or §212(a)(4)(B) [terrorist activity]. The certification may only be made by the AG or the Deputy AG, and may not be delegated further. The AG may detain the person for up to 7 days *prior* to placing him in a removal proceeding or charging him criminally. INA §236A(a)(5). If the person is not placed in removal proceedings or criminally charged the AG "shall release the alien." If s/he is placed in removal proceedings the AG shall mandatorily detain even if the person is eligible for relief or obtains relief (such as a CAT claim) until the AG determines that he no longer has reason to believe that the person falls under one of the basis for certification. However, if the person is finally found not to be removable, detention shall terminate. The AG shall review his certification subjecting the person to mandatory detention every six months and the detainee may request such review every 6 months and may submit documents and other evidence in support of his or her request. If the detainee has been ordered removed, but removal is unlikely in the reasonably foreseeable future, s/he may be detained for additional six- month periods only if his or her release will threaten the national security or the safety of the community or any person.

A person may seek judicial review by habeas corpus only of the AG's certification or his decision to keep someone in detention who is unlikely to be removed in the foreseeable future. INA §236A(b). The habeas court must apply the law of the Supreme Court and the D.C. Circuit. All appeals must go to the D.C. Circuit.

ICE may also detain suspected terrorists pursuant to INA §236(c)(1)(D) if they are inadmissible or deportable on terrorist grounds. The regulations at 8 C.F.R. §1003.19(h)(1)(i)(C) also authorize mandatory detention for individuals "described in INA §237(a)(4)."

1. *Military Commissions Act of 2006*—PL 109-366. This law establishes a statutory framework for the trial and appellate review of "alien unlawful enemy combatants." The Act establishes military commissions to try such persons, 10 U.S.C. ch. 47A, prohibits the use of the Geneva Convention as a source of rights for such persons, 10 U.S.C. §948b(g), allows for the use of hearsay evidence and restricts the use of classified information, 10 U.S.C. §§949a, 949d, prohibits the invocation of the Geneva Convention in any habeas proceeding or other civil action, Sect. 5 of PL 109-366, allows the President, through Executive Order, to define what satisfies the Geneva Convention except for "grave breaches," and prohibits the use of foreign or international law to do so, Sect. 6(a) of PL 109-366, and prohibits any court from hearing or considering a writ of habeas corpus by an alien "who has been determined by the United States to have been properly detained as an enemy combatant or is awaiting such determination, 28 U.S.C. §2241(e)(1), nor shall any court have jurisdiction to hear any aspect of the detention, transfer, treatment, trial or conditions of confinement of an alien who is or was detained by the United States and has been determined by the United States to have been properly detained as an enemy combatant or is awaiting such determination. 28 U.S.C. §2241(e)(2).

2. There is a serious question as to the constitutionality and the legality under international law of the establishment of the military tribunal by the President despite Congress' grant of authority. *Hamdan v. Rumsfeld,* 126 S.Ct. 2749 (2006); *Ex Parte Milligan,* 71 U.S. 2 (1866); *Duncan v. Kahanamoku,* 327 U.S. 304 (1946).

3. The detention of such persons based upon prior Presidential directives both within and outside the U.S. has raised serious legal questions. In *Rasul v. Bush,* 542 U.S. 466 (2004), the Court determined that aliens detained in military custody at Guantanamo, Cuba not only had a right to bring a habeas corpus action challenging their detention, they also are not barred from bringing an action pursuant to 28 U.S.C. §§1331 and 1350. In *Hamdi v. Rumsfeld,* 542 U.S. 507 (2004), the Court determined that "due process demands that a citizen held in the United States as an enemy combatant be given a meaningful opportunity to contest the factual basis for that detention before a neutral decisionmaker." *Hamdi,* 124 S.Ct. at 2635. The Court also decided in *Rumsfeld v. Padilla,* 542 U.S. 426 (2004), that a habeas action brought by a U.S. citizen detained as an enemy combatant must be brought against the "immediate custodian" of the detainee (and not the Secretary or the AG) and must be brought in the judicial district where the person is detained. However, the decision recognized certain exceptions to the "immediate custodian" doctrine including where the petitioner was confined overseas and not within any district court's territory, under which circumstances the person could file a habeas petition against the AG or other appropriate official in the place where that official resides (typically Washington DC). *Padilla,* 124 S.Ct. at 2725 n.16; *Gherebi v. Bush,* 374 F.3d 727, 739 (9th Cir. 2004) [following *Padilla* in action regarding Guantanamo detainees brought in Central District of California, court transferred case to D.C. where Bush resides]; *Gherebi v. Bush,* 338 F.Supp.2d 91 (D.D.C. 2004) [after transfer, D.C. district court held it had jurisdiction]; *Abu Ali v. Ashcroft,* 350 F.Supp.2d 28, 39–57 (D.D.C. 2004) [denied motion to dismiss habeas petition brought by a U.S. citizen being held in Saudi Arabia at the direction of the U.S.]. It also allowed for an exception pursuant to *Ex parte Endo,* 323 U.S. 283, 65 S.Ct. 208 (1944) where the physical location of a detainee is moved *after* a habeas petition is filed in the district of the immediate custodian. 124 S.Ct. at 2721. The Court left for another day the question as to whether the AG may be the proper custodian in immigration cases irrespective of the immediate custodian rule. 124 S.Ct. at 2718 n.8.

4. Cause of Action for Torture, Degrading and Inhumane Treatment, and Religious Freedom—At least one court has found that there is no Alien Tort Claim, Geneva Convention, *Bivens* action, or action under the Religious Freedom Restoration Act. *Rasul v. Myers,* 512 F.3d 644 (D.C. Cir. 2008) [no ATC claim because defendants acted within the scope of their employment and claim should be under the FTCA but procedures were not met; no Geneva Convention claim because the Westfall Act precludes it; no *Bivens* action because nonresident aliens outside the U.S. have no constitutional rights; and no RFRA claim because they are non–resident aliens and therefore not persons].

S. *Removal Hearing*—In light of IIRIRA's distinction between pre- and post–Apr. 1, 1997, hearings, DOJ maintains two sets of regulations governing removal hearings, 8 C.F.R. §§1240.1–.29, and exclusion/deportation hearings, 8 C.F.R. §§1240.40–.57. Only the post–Apr. 1, 1997, procedures will be addressed here.

1. Initiation—The proceeding is initiated by filing a notice to appear (NTA) on Form I-862 (formerly Order to Show Cause or OSC, Form I-221), INA §239(a), 8 U.S.C. §1229(a), with the Office of the IJ. 8 C.F.R. §§1003.14, 239.1(a), 1239.1(a), 1240.30, 1240.55. *Arenas-Yeses v. Gonzales,* 421 F.3d 111, 116–17 (2d Cir. 2005) [for purposes of suspension of deportation pre-IIRIRA, proceedings were not commenced when respondent was served with OSC because it had to be filed with the immigration court]; *Dandan v. Ashcroft,* 339 F.3d 567, 576 (7th Cir. 2003) [issuing of OSC was ineffective to trigger government responsibility regarding a removal hearing because the document must be filed]; *Armendariz-Montoya v. Sonchik,* 291 F.3d 1116, 1118–21 (9th Cir. 2002) [proceeding commenced only when OSC was filed with court]; *Asad v. Reno,* 242 F.3d 702, 705 (6th Cir. 2001) [proceedings do not commence under former 8 C.F.R. §3.14(a) until NTA was filed with the court]; *Costa v. INS,* 233 F.3d 31 (1st Cir. 2000) [person served with OSC but subsequent NTA was only document filed with court cuts off right to suspension because filing, not service, commences proceeding]; *Morales-Ramirez v. Reno,* 209 F.3d 977 (7th Cir. 2000) [a person served with an exclusion notice but not put into removal proceedings until after IIRIRA is barred from §212(c) because proceeding only commenced under 8 C.F.R. former §§3.14 and 240.30 after INS filed the NTA with the court]. *See Matter of Sanchez,* 20 I&N Dec. 223 (BIA 1990) for interpretation under previous regulations. For the list of immigration judges and their offices, *see* **Appendix C**, *infra*. Venue lies where NTA filed. 8 C.F.R. §1003.20. NTA contains statement of nature of proceedings, legal authority under which proceedings are conducted, factual allegations and designation of provisions that are violated.

2. Prosecutorial Discretion

2.a. Prosecutorial discretion includes a broad spectrum of discretionary enforcement decisions including: whether to charge an individual; what charge to bring; to drop any charges in an ongoing case; and to settle a case by plea bargain. Memo, Cooper, General Counsel HQCOU 90/16-P, *reprinted in* 77 No. 27 *Interpreter Releases* 946, 961–72 (July 17, 2000). The initiation of an NTA is a matter of prosecutorial discretion, *Cervantes v. Perryman*, 954 F.Supp. 1257, 1265 (N.D. Ill. 1997), akin to a prosecutorial decision to initiate criminal charges. *See also Reno v. American-Arab Anti-Discrimination Comm,* 525 U.S. 471 (1999). The BIA has stated it has no authority to review this discretion. *Matter of Bahta,* 22 I&N Dec. 1381, 1391–92 (BIA 2000). *But see Bravo-Pedroza v. Gonzales,* 475 F.3d 1358 (9th Cir. 2007) [court rejected argument of prosecutorial discretion and held that DHS counsel was barred under the doctrine of *res judicata* from instituting new removal proceeding on charges that could have been brought in prior proceeding].

2.b. The Service has issued guidelines concerning prosecutorial discretion. Memo, Meissner, Comm., HQOPP 50/4 (Nov. 17, 2000), *published on* AILA InfoNet at Doc. No. 00112702. They were readopted more recently in Memo, Myers, Asst. Sec., ICE (Nov 7. 2007), *published on* AILA InfoNet at Doc. No. 07111263 [noting that the end of the "catch and release" policy does not mean that officers should not exercise discretion and providing the example of nursing mothers]. The guidelines provide that the Service may decline to prosecute where there is not a substantial federal immigration enforcement interest. Memo at 5. It notes that even where there is a substantial immigration enforcement interest it may be outweighed by other interests, such as foreign policy considerations. Prosecutorial discretion may be appropriate "even when an alien is removable based on his or her criminal history and when the alien—if served with an NTA—would be subject to mandatory detention." Memo, Myers, Asst. Sec., ICE (Nov 7. 2007) at 6, *published on* AILA InfoNet at Doc. No. 07111263. Factors that should be taken into account in deciding whether to exercise prosecutorial discretion include, but are not limited to, the following: (1) Immigration status (LPRs warrant greater consideration); (2) Length of residence; (3) Criminal history (including nature and severity of criminal conduct, time elapsed since the offense and evidence of rehabilitation); (4) Humanitarian concerns (including medical conditions affecting the alien or the alien's family, entry into U.S. at a young age, ties to home country, extreme youth or advanced age, home country conditions); (5) Immigration history (past violations of immigration laws); (6) Likelihood of ultimately removing the alien; (7) Likelihood of achieving enforcement goal by other means; (8) Eligible or likely to be eligible for relief; (9) Effect on future admissibility (time-limited or permanent bar); (10) Current or past cooperation with law enforcement authorities; (11) Military service with honorable discharge; (12) Community attention (expressions of opinion in favor of or in opposition to removal); and (13) Resources available to the Service. Any decision by the Service should be based upon "the totality of the circumstances." Memo, Myers, Asst. Sec., ICE (Nov 7. 2007) at 8, *published on* AILA InfoNet at Doc. No. 07111263.

2.c. The agency may not consider: (1) an individual's race, religion, sex, national origin or political association, activities or beliefs (although they may be relevant in assessing asylum or terrorism); (2) the officer's personal feelings regarding the individual; or (3) the possible effect of the decision on the officer's own professional or personal circumstances. If prosecutorial discretion is exercised, the notice/letter granting the discretion should provide that it "does not confer any immigration status, ability to travel to the United States (unless the alien applies for and receives advance parole), immunity from future removal proceedings, or any enforceable right or benefit." Memo, Myers, Asst. Sec., ICE (Nov 7. 2007) at 12, *published on* AILA InfoNet at Doc. No. 07111263. In cases involving TPS or DED, the agency "should agree to administratively close proceedings" where individuals are *prima facie* eligible for the relief. In the case of TPS this is generally accomplished by agreeing to a continuance to allow the person to file for TPS and upon proof of filing agreeing to administratively close proceeding. As DED does not require an application the Service may agree to administratively close if the person is *prima facie* eligible. However, the Service should agree to administrative closure only *after* pleadings have been taken and the issue of removability has been established. Memo, Carpenter, Deputy Gen. Co., HQCOU 120/12.2-P (Feb. 7, 2002), *reported in* 79 No. 15 *Interpreter Releases* 524, 530–38 (Apr. 8, 2002). Any agreement may not be conditioned upon the applicant giving up any other rights including the right to apply for asylum or withholding of removal. *Id.*

2.d. ICE Memo on Prosecutorial Discretion. Subsequent to the Homeland Security Act of 2002 and the establishment of prosecutorial functions in ICE, the Office of the Principal Legal Advisor to ICE issued its own memorandum on prosecutorial discretion, Memo, Howard, Principal Legal Advisor (Oct. 24, 2005) *posted at* AILA InfoNet at Doc. No. 06050511, and parsed the issue as follows:

(1) Prosecutorial Discretion Prior to or in Lieu of NTA Issuance where

(a) Others options are available such as administrative, crewman, or expedited removal or reinstatement

(b) Clear eligibility for an immigration benefit that can be obtained outside of immigration court such as a clearly approvable I-130/I-485

(c) Administrative VD or VD under safeguard if detained

(d) NSEERS violator who is otherwise in status, has no criminal record and has a reasonable excuse for failing to register including being unaware of the registration requirements.

(e) Deferred Action for sympathetic humanitarian reasons including where the respondent has a child with a serious medical condition or disability or where the respondent or a close family member is undergoing treatment for a potentially life threatening disease.

(2) Prosecutorial Discretion After the NTA Has Issued but Before the NTA Has Been Filed where;

(a) Same factors as above

(b) Reasonable and rational decision not to prosecute where relief has been sought such as filing an application for a U or T visa.

(3) Prosecutorial Discretion after NTA Issuance and Filing—The ICE attorney may seek to dismiss: (a) because NTA improvidently issued; (b) because there is a change in circumstances such that continuation of the case is no longer in the government's interest. In these cases because an ICE attorney does not have the right to issue or terminate NTAs she must move to dismiss the proceedings without prejudice.; (c) because relief is otherwise available where "relief in the form of adjustment of status appears clearly approvable based on an approvable I-130 or I-140..." It may also be appropriate for special rule cancellation under NACARA; (d) because of appealing humanitarian factors such as a citizen child with a serious medical condition or disability. ICE attorneys need to investigate alternative dispositions; (e) because federal, state or local law enforcement entities desire to have the respondent remain in the U.S. These may alternatively be addressed by administrative closure of the case or the issuance of a stay of deportation. The ICE attorney may also: (1) remand a case to allow the respondent to pursue naturalization if she demonstrates prima facie eligibility or (2) resolve a case without lengthy proceedings such as not opposing relief, waiving appeal, making agreements that narrow issues, or stipulating to admissibility of evidence.

(a) Motion to Dismiss For Adjustment. In a prior memo, ICE set forth the following guidelines for initiating or agreeing to join in a motion to dismiss without prejudice where respondent seeks adjustment under INA §209 (asylum or refugee), INA §249 (registry), INA §245 (family- or employment-based): or Cuban Adjustment: (1) EOIR has jurisdiction; (2) respondent is *prima facie* eligible; (3) the application is clearly approvable to warrant exercising discretion; (4) there is no asylum application pending; and (5) the removal proceeding does *not* involve threats to national security, human rights violators, criminal convictions or conduct necessitating a INA §212(h) waiver or immigration fraud necessitating a INA §212(i) waiver or detained respondents unless there are unique or special circumstances including but not limited to the extent/or seriousness of criminal conduct, recency and/or significance of immigration fraud, or national security interests. Memo, Howard, Principal Legal Advisor, ICE (Oct. 6, 2005), *published on* AILA InfoNet at Doc. No. 05101360.

(4) Post Hearing Actions

(a) Decision to appeal should be guided by the "interests of judicial economy and fairness."

(b) Remanding to IJ or withdrawing an appeal where the respondent's brief is persuasive

(c) Joining in untimely motions to reopen for AOS or cancellation where respondent has "substantial equities, no serious criminal or immigration violations, and he is legally eligible to be granted that relief" but for the 90 day limitation.

(d) Remanding federal case to BIA where "there are potential litigation pitfalls or unusually sympathetic fact circumstances and where the BIA has the authority to fashion a remedy."

(e) Remanding *in absentia* orders particularly where the respondent simply appeared late for court.

(5) Final Orders—Stays and Motions to Reopen/Reconsider

(a) Where ineffective assistance of counsel deprived respondent of an opportunity to pursue relief and there was compliance with *Matter of Lozada* "it would be appropriate to join in or not oppose motions to reconsider.

(b) Where law enforcement want a respondent to testify, ICE counsel may recommend that a stay of removal be granted.

2.e. Prosecutorial Discretion Regarding Persons with U.S. Military Service—In exercising prosecutorial discretion for those who served in the U.S. military the initial inquiry is whether the person is eligible for U.S. citizenship by virtue of INA §§328 and 329. If not eligible, ICE counsel needs to look at: (1) the person's overall criminal history including whether they involve aggravated felonies, drug trafficking, violent crimes and crimes against children; (2) evidence of rehabilitation; (3) family and financial ties to the U.S.; (4) employment history, health and community service; and (5) specifics of military service including duty status, assignment to a war zone, number of years of services, and decorations awarded. Neither active service, nor honorable discharge, nor adverse publicity that may arise due to removal, are a basis to decline to issue an NTA. Memo, Forman, Acting Dir., Office of Investigations, ICE (June 21, 2004), *published on* AILA InfoNet at Doc. No. 06051664.

2.f. Guidelines Regarding USCIS and Initiating Referrals for NTAs—On July 11, 2006 Michael Aytes as Assoc. Dir, Domestic Operations, USCIS issued guidelines concerning NTAs issued in various cases based upon an MOA between ICE and USCIS. Memo, Aytes, Assoc. Dir. Domestic Operations, 70/1-P (July 11, 2006), *published on* AILA InfoNet at Doc. No. 06090871. The policy memorandum listed 5 categories of cases in order of seriousness/urgency in regard to issuance of NTAs: (1) egregious public safety cases (persons charged or convicted as aggravated felons under INA §§101(a)(43)(A), (C), (E), (F), (H), (I), and (N); human rights violators, suspected street gang members, Interpol hits, re-entry subsequent to a conviction for a felony, additional cases based upon local criteria) (2) other criminal cases; (3) cases where the NTA is prescribed by regulation; (4) cases denied by USCIS based on fraud; and (5) all other cases.

2.g. Agreeing to Dismiss to Permit Adjustment—Prosecutorial discretion to dismiss proceedings before the IJ without prejudice to allow USCIS to adjudicate the AOS application is appropriate where: (1) IJ has jurisdiction; (2) the respondent can demonstrate prima facie eligibility based upon a properly filed application for AOS including having an approved visa petition or (based upon a long-term relative relationship) a petition that is likely to be approved and will be immediately available; (3) the application appears clearly approvable; and (4) there is no asylum application pending before the IJ.

ICE Office of Chief Counsel should *not* agree to dismissal where the case involves: (1) threats to national security; (2) human rights violators; (3) criminal convictions or conduct necessitating a 212(h) or 212(i) waiver; or (4) detained respondents. Memo, Howard, Principal Legal Advisor, ICE, "Exercising Prosecutorial Discretion to Dismiss Adjustment Cases," (Oct. 6, 2005), *published on* AILA InfoNet at Doc. No. 05101360.

2.h. Decision to Seek a Remand from the Federal Court to the BIA. The government also has substantial discretion to seek a remand from the circuit court to the BIA. *See* "Remands" in Ch. 10, Section VI.M (p.1198), *infra*.

3. Issuance of NTAs

3.a. DHS has also set forth criteria for the issuance of NTAs when a benefit application is denied. NTAs should be issued in accordance with the Meissner Memo [Memo, Meissner, Comm., HQOPP 50/4 (Nov. 17, 2000), *published on* AILA InfoNet at Doc. No. 00112702], and should focus on all cases: (1) where the applicant's violation of the INA or other federal, state or local law constitutes a threat to public safety or national security; (2) where instances of a fraud scheme were detected; and (3) where the denial or withdrawal of certain TPS applications constitutes a ground of deportability/inadmissibility thereby triggering 8 C.F.R. §§244.10(c)(1), 244.14(b)(3), 1244.10(c)(1), 1244.14(b)(3). Memo, Yates, Assoc. Dir. Of Operations (Sept. 12, 2003), *published on* AILA InfoNet at Doc. No. 03100240 (Oct. 2, 2003).

3.b. When DHS Should Not Issue an NTA.

(1) If alien is in deferred action program. Considerations under program include: (a) the likelihood of ultimately removing the alien; (b) the presence of sympathetic factors (*e.g.*, age, hardship, physical condition); (c) adverse publicity if an effort is made to remove alien; (d) the person's continued presence is desired by law enforcement for an ongoing investigation or review; and (e) whether individual is a member of a class given high enforcement priority.

(2) If immigrant visa petition is pending, provided that approval would permit adjustment of status or voluntary departure. *Benslimane v. Gonzales,* 430 F.3d 828 (7th Cir. 2005) [IJ made legal error in denying continuance where respondent had filed I-130 and I-485 as part of marriage based adjustment but had not filed adjustment with IJ]; *Bull v. INS,* 790 F.2d 869 (11th Cir. 1986).

(3) If conviction is vacated or is about to be vacated. *See e.g., Matter of Ozkok*, 19 I&N Dec. 546 (BIA 1988) [relating to expungement of conviction which in light of *Matter of Roldan* reaffirmed in *Matter of Salazar* may no longer be a basis to prevent removal].

(4) If alien is a member or former member of the Armed Forces unless prior approval for NTA obtained from DHS.

(5) If person granted asylum unless asylum first revoked. 8 C.F.R. §§208.22, 1208.22.

4. NTA challenged—After commencement of proceedings any party may move the court for dismissal and only the court, upon motion, may then terminate. Prior to commencement the DHS has exclusive authority and the IJ has no jurisdiction. *Matter of G-N-C-*, 22 I&N Dec. 281 (BIA 1998); 8 C.F.R. §§239.2(c), 1239.2(c). U.S. Dept. of Justice Immigration Judge Benchbook, at p. 3-2, ¶5. These reasons for termination include that the NTA was "improvidently issued," 8 C.F.R. §239.2(a)(6) which may encompass all the grounds in former O.I. §239. An NTA which is not sufficient on its face may be dismissed even where an order of deportation has been entered. *Macleod v. INS*, 327 F.2d 453 (9th Cir. 1964).

4.a. Where application for NTA [Form I-862] not based on *prima facie* case of deportability, O.I. §239, or is not accompanied by substantial supporting evidence. *Bilokumsky v. Tod*, 263 U.S. 149 (1923).

4.b. Where issuance of NTA constitutes selective prosecution. *Adame-Hernandez v. INS*, 769 F.2d 1387 (9th Cir. 1985); *Lennon v. U.S.*, 387 F.Supp. 561 (S.D.N.Y. 1975). *See generally Wayte v. U.S.*, 470 U.S. 598 (1985); *U.S. v. O'Brien*, 391 U.S. 367 (1968); *U.S. v. Al Jibori*, 90 F.3d 22 (2d Cir. 1996); *American Baptist Churches v. Meese*, 712 F.Supp. 756, 762–64 (N.D. Cal. 1989). *But see Reno v. American-Arab Anti-Discrimination Committee,* 525 U.S. 471, 119 S.Ct. 936 (1999) [reversing 9th Cir. and finding that "an alien unlawfully in this country has no constitutional right to assert selective enforcement as a defense against his deportation" except in a "rare case in which the alleged basis of discrimination is so outrageous"]; *Kandamar v. Gonzales,* 464 F.3d 65, 70–74 (1st Cir. 2006) [absent outrageous discrimination, a selective prosecution claim because of NSEERS is precluded by *American-Arab*]; *Latu v. Ashcroft,* 375 F.3d 1012, 1019 (10th Cir. 2004) [action challenging the decision to commence removal proceedings in one venue versus another is barred by INA §242(g)].

4.c. Where NTA issuance accompanied by duress or lack of due process. *Matter of Rios-Carrillo*, 10 I&N Dec. 291 (BIA 1963).

4.d. Where deportability stated in the alternative, so that there is no notice of charges. *Browne v. Zurbrick*, 45 F.2d 931 (6th Cir. 1930) [stated as committing an act or was convicted]. *But see De Zavala v. Ashcroft,* 385 F.3d 879 (5th Cir. 2004) [due process was not violated where respondent was incorrectly charged as inadmissible at entry as a nonimmigrant when she was inadmissible as an immigrant because there was no prejudice];*Consola v. Karnuth*, 108 F.2d 178 (2d Cir. 1939).

4.e. Where there is *res judicata*. *U.S. v. Utah Constr. & Mining Co.*, 384 U.S. 394, 422 (1966); *Bravo-Pedroza v. Gonzales,* 475 F.3d 1358 (9th Cir. 2007) [court rejected argument of prosecutorial discretion and held that DHS counsel was barred from instituting new removal proceeding on charges that could have been brought in prior proceeding]; *Guevara v. Gonzales,* 450 F.3d 173 (5th Cir. 2006) [where DHS sought to collaterally attack, through a motion to reconsider, the BIA's jurisdiction to reopen respondent's case, it was barred by the doctrine of res judicata]; *Medina v. INS*, 993 F.2d 499 (5th Cir.), *reh'g denied*, 1 F.3d 312 (1993) [admission in exclusion proceeding bars deportation proceeding for same issues based on exclusion at time of entry stating that "Few legal doctrines are more intrinsic or necessary to our system than res judicata"]; *Ramon-Sepulveda v. INS*, 824 F.2d 749 (9th Cir. 1987) [when circuit court previously ruled that INS could not reopen proceedings to admit birth certificate which was not newly discovered evidence, INS was barred by *res judicata* from bringing new OSC]; *Matter of Cordero*, A29 989 441 (BIA Aug. 10, 1995) (unpublished), *reported in* 72 No. 38 *Interpreter Releases* 1330–31 (Oct. 2, 1995); *Murray v. Ashcroft,* 321 F.Supp.2d 385 (D. Conn. 2004) [where government's charge that respondent was an aggravated felon was not sustained on appeal, the court reversed a subsequent removal order using the same convictions to establish deportability under a different ground]. *See generally Johnson v.*

Ashcroft, 378 F.3d 164, 172 n.10 (2d Cir. 2004) [discussion regarding efforts to bring removal proceedings based upon different criminal charges known to the government when the charge in removal proceeding was vacated]. A *res judicata* challenge cannot be brought in federal court until the IJ/BIA makes a decision because INA §242(g) bar habeas review based upon initiation of proceedings. *Somir v. U.S.,* 354 F.Supp.2d 215, 220 (E.D.N.Y. 2005). *But see Bilali v. Gonzales,* 502 F.3d 470 (6th Cir. 2007) [collateral estoppel did not apply to IJ's determination that respondent had a valid marriage in an AOS proceeding to bar litigation whether USCIS improperly denied removal of their CR status]; *Valencia-Alvarez v. Gonzales,* 469 F.3d 1319, 1323–24 (9th Cir. 2006) [where BIA decision was not final and case remanded back to IJ, respondent's *res judicata* argument failed as to ICE's amendment of the charges on the NTA]; *Andrade v. Gonzales,* 459 F.3d 538, 545 (5th Cir. 2006) [res judicata does not apply to a decision on adjustment of status and the government was free to bring removal proceedings based upon criminal convictions that were disclosed at AOS hearing before residency was approved]; *Duvall v. Att'y Gen. of the U.S.,* 436 F.3d 382, (3d Cir. 2006) [although collateral estoppel applies in immigration proceedings barring the relitigation of alienage, it is a flexible concept and does not apply where a clearly deportable person continues to commit criminal acts after initial proceedings are terminated]; *Hamdan v. Gonzales,* 425 F.3d 1051, 1058–60 & n.15 (7th Cir. 2005) [res judicata does not apply where party gets remand before BIA to pursue a form of relief without a final judgment on his claim for relief]; *Santana-Albarran v. Ashcroft,* 393 F.3d 699, 703–05 (6th Cir. 2005) [AG not collaterally estopped from arguing respondent did not prove he entered the U.S. in 1985 for purposes of cancellation despite IJ's finding on removal charge that he entered EWI in 1985 because that date was not necessary and essential to find removability].

4.f. Where Respondent Raises Procedural Due Process Challenge—*Salgado-Diaz v. Ashcroft,* 395 F.3d 1158 (9th Cir. 2005) [respondent's removal order was vacated and respondent was entitled to a hearing on whether NTA should be dismissed where respondent alleges that he was arrested in violation of the Fourth Amendment and was illegally removed by legacy INS while he had a previous deportation hearing pending].

4.g. Where Respondent Raises Substantive Due Process Challenge—*Wang v. Reno,* 81 F.3d 808, 818–19 (9th Cir. 1996) [where U.S. officials created a Hobson's choice of testifying truthfully and risking further torture in China or perjuring himself and going to jail, they could not return him to China to face torture when he testified truthfully]; *Lawson v. Gerlinski,* 332 F.Supp.2d 735, 742–43 (M.D. Pa. 2004) [long term LPR with no relief who cooperated with government, received reduction in sentence and feared harm if returned to his country, was entitled to a substantive due process hearing on theory that the state created his danger]; *Builes v. Nye,* 239 F.Supp.2d 518, 525–26 (M.D. Pa. 2003) [substantive due process is violated where government informant would be sent to Colombia to face certain death]. But the Pennsylvania cases have been overruled by the Third Circuit. *Kamara v. Att'y Gen. of the U.S.,* 420 F.3d 202, 216–18 (3d Cir. 2005) [rejecting substantive due process challenge based on the state-created danger exception holding it has no place in immigration jurisprudence]. *See also Morgan v. Gonzales,* 495 F.3d 1084, 1092–94 (9th Cir. 2007) [recognizing state-created danger exception under *Morgan* but finding on the facts that convicted drug dealer's fear of return to country did not amount to gross negligence and deliberate indifference on the part of U.S. officials]; *Enwonwu v. Gonzales,* 438 F.3d 22, 29–31 (1st Cir. 2006) [following *Kamara* and rejecting state-created danger theory for persons facing removal]; *Momennia v. Estrada,* 268 F.Supp.2d 679 (N.D. Tex. 2003) [rejecting claim that FBI, through deliberate indifference, gave rise to a state-created danger to Iranian deportee who had provided assistance to the FBI, and that the government had a duty not to remove him to Iran].

4.h. Where DHS estopped—*Cf. INS v. Hibi,* 414 U.S. 5 (1973) [affirmative misconduct standard]; *Salgado-Diaz v. Ashcroft,* 395 F.3d 1158, 1165–68 (9th Cir. 2005) [government would be estopped from asserting fraudulent re-entry by respondent as a basis for removing him if respondent can prove that the legacy INS improperly deported him while his deportation hearing was pending]; *Otarola v. INS,* 270 F.3d 1272 (9th Cir. 2001) [government estopped from applying the stop time rule where IJ granted suspension and INS took a frivolous appeal to permit the stop-time rule to be applied]; *Fano v. O'Neill,* 806 F.2d 1262 (5th Cir. 1987) [reversed summary judgment for government where alien alleged "willful, wanton and reckless" conduct by INS in delaying application]; *Akbarin v. INS*, 669 F.2d 839, 843 (1st Cir. 1982); *Tejeda v. INS*, 346 F.2d 389 (9th Cir. 1965); *Corniel-Rodriguez v. INS*, 532 F.2d 301 (2d Cir. 1976) [when second preference applicant did not receive oral or written notice that marriage would invalidate petition]; *Harriott v. Ashcroft,* 277 F.Supp.2d 538, 542–45 (E.D. Pa. 2003) [ordered immigration to approve petition for citizenship and pay attorney's fees under equitable estoppel theory where certificate of citizenship denied because child turned 18 during delay and delay was 14 times longer than the 60 days normally contemplated for certificate].

No Estoppel. *INS v. Pangilinan*, 486 U.S. 875, 884, 108 S.Ct. 2210 (1988), *reh'g denied* 487 U.S. 1264 (1988) [cannot have equitable relief of estoppel if it overrides "a public policy established by Congress."]; *INS v. Miranda*, 459 U.S. 14 (1982); *INS v. Hibi,* 414 U.S. 5 (1973); *Shin v. Mukasey,* 519 F.3d 901, 906–07 (9th Cir. 2008) [where respondent unknowingly obtained her "green card" through fraud by a DHS official estoppel is inapplicable because the government is not bound by unauthorized acts of its agents]; *Mustanich v. Mukasey,* 518 F.3d 1084, 1087–90 (9th Cir. 2008) [followed *Pangilinan*, distinguished non–citizenship estoppel cases, and found estoppel could not be used to prevent removal where legacy INS failed to accept or act on adults' requests to naturalize petitioner before his 18th birthday]; *Morgan v. Gonzales,* 495 F.3d 1084, 1091–92 (9th Cir. 2007) [convicted drug dealer who was allowed to remain in U.S. for many years while cooperating with the government was not entitled to estoppel due to extreme delay in removing him absent a duty by the government not to do so]; *Mudric v. Att'y Gen. of the U.S.,* 469 F.3d 94, 99–100 (3d Cir. 2006) [respondent cannot claim equitable estoppel because prejudicial delay in adjudicating asylum and adjustment applications is not affirmative misconduct]; *Andrade v. Gonzales,* 459 F.3d 538, 545 n.2(5th Cir. 2006) [absent affirmative misconduct the DHS is not equitably estopped from bringing removal proceedings based upon criminal convictions that were presented to USCIS before granting adjustment]; *Savoury v. U.S. Att'y Gen.,* 449 F.3d 1307, 1318–19 (11th Cir. 2006) [DHS is not estopped from denying LPR status to a person who adjusted status and was had his condition removed despite fully disclosing his ineligibility due to a drug conviction because there is no showing that the government engaged in affirmative misconduct]; *Elia v. Gonzales,* 431 F.3d 268, 276 (6th Cir. 2005) [no affirmative misconduct by government and no reliance by incarcerated respondent in failing to hold removal hearing within 5 years so he could apply for §212(c) relief]; *Tovar-Alvarez,* 427 F.3d 1350, 1353–54 (11th Cir. 2005) [two year delay in deciding naturalization petition after interview does not equitably estop government from seeking removal]; *Raffington v. Cangemi,* 399 F.3d 900, 902–03 (8th Cir. 2005) [rejecting *Otarola* and holding that even if the government had filed a frivolous, but ultimately successful appeal, it would not constitute affirmative misconduct to estop the government]; *Rios v. Ziglar*, 398 F.3d 1201, 1208–10 (10th Cir. 2005) [where deadline passed for NACARA application but government told applicant to resubmit application and then kept the fee, the government's actions, even if affirmative misconduct, would not warrant estoppel because application was beyond the time period]; *Varela v. Ashcroft,* 368 F.3d 864 (8th Cir. 2004) [no affirmative misconduct in denial of adjustment application and in placing respondent in removal proceedings]; *Socop-Gonzalez v. INS,* 272 F.3d 1176, 1183–85 (9th Cir. 2001) (en banc) [no affirmative misconduct warranting equitable estoppel where INS negligently provided misinformation to the respondent that he could dismiss his appeal of his deportation order before the BIA and file an adjustment application with INS]; *Kowalczyk v. INS,* 245 F.3d 1143, 1149–51 (10th Cir. 2001) [nine-year delay in deciding asylum claim where country conditions have changed does not warrant estoppel]; *Cortez-Felipe v. INS,* 245 F.3d 1054, 1057 (9th Cir. 2001) [no equitable estoppel where INS fails to file OSC with Court after service and later files NTA thereby preventing suspension claim]; *Costa v. INS,* 233 F.3d 31, 37–38 (1st Cir. 2000) [same]; *Rojas-Reyes v. INS,* 235 F.3d 115, 126 (2d Cir. 2000) [no estoppel for INS's delay in promulgating repapering regulations to permit cancellation]; *Sulit v. Schiltgen,* 213 F.3d 449, 454 (9th Cir. 2000) [no estoppel where petitioner has not lost any rights and where it is simply negligent provision of misinformation]; *Westover v. Reno,* 202 F.3d 475, 481 (1st Cir. 2000) [no affirmative misconduct when stopped person on re-entry after advising her that she could leave and apply for a new visa]; *Tefel v. Reno,* 180 F.3d 1286, 1302–304 (11th Cir. 1999), *cert. denied,* 120 S.Ct. 2657 (2000) [where INS continued to accept suspension applications where there was a *possibility* Congress would amend the statute to pretermit such applications there is no estoppel]; *Moosa v. INS,* 171 F.3d 994,

1003–06 (5th Cir. 1999) [improper dismissal of an appeal as untimely and not complying with circuit precedent does not permit estoppel against INS]; *Clavis v. Ashcroft,* 281 F.Supp.2d 490, 497 (E.D.N.Y. 2003) [an unexplained 13-year delay in completing removal proceedings that resulted in the deprivation of an INA §212(c) hearing did not constitute the necessary affirmative misconduct for estoppel]; *Diallo v. Reno,* 61 F.Supp.2d 1361, 1369–71 (N.D. Ga. 1999) [no affirmative misconduct in processing lottery adjustment]; *Omni Packaging v. INS*, 930 F.Supp. 28, 33–35 (D.P.R. 1996) [INS not estopped from denying 3d preference petition on grounds that applicant is not a manager or executive notwithstanding previous L-1 approvals]; *Eskite v. District Director*, 901 F.Supp. 530, 538 (E.D.N.Y. 1995) [no estoppel to deport Haitian who had been "screened-in" after spending 18 months at Guantanamo]; *Azizi v. Thornburgh*, 719 F.Supp. 86, 97–98 (D. Conn. 1989), *aff'd*, 908 F.2d 1130, 1136 (2d Cir. 1990) [no affirmative misconduct where IJ and INS misadvised respondent about the effect of Sec. 5 of the Marriage Fraud Amendments Act]; *Mukherjee v. INS*, 793 F.2d 1006 (9th Cir. 1986) [no estoppel where no facts existed that incorrect negligent statement about not being subject to 2-year foreign residency was a deliberate lie]; *Sachdev v. INS*, 788 F.2d 912 (2d Cir. 1986) [distinguished *Corniel-Rodriguez* in 2d preference where State Dept. form specified marriage would invalidate petition]; *Jaa v. INS*, 779 F.2d 569 (9th Cir. 1986) [no estoppel where 58-month delay between alien's submission of adjustment of status application and denial due to neglect]; *Gonzalez v. McNary*, 765 F.Supp. 721, 724 (S.D. Fla.), *aff'd on other grounds*, 980 F.2d 1418 (11th Cir. 1993) [no estoppel where 3-year delay adjudicating petition and spouse's death resulted in denial]; *Matter of Izummi,* 22 I&N Dec. 169, 195–96 (Assoc. Comm. 1998) [INS not estopped where it approved scores of investor petitions under same program previously and where it informed petitioner prior to adjudication that it would approve petition]. The BIA takes the view that it has no authority to grant equitable estoppel against the Service to preclude it from taking a lawful course of action that it is empowered to pursue by statute or regulation. The BIA's power is limited to authority conferred upon it by AG. *Matter of Hernandez-Puente*, 20 I&N Dec. 335 (BIA 1991) [could not grant adjustment *nunc pro tunc* where person ineligible at present time due to INS error]. *See also Matter of United Airlines Flight UA802,* 22 I&N Dec. 777, 783 (BIA 1999); *Matter of Tayabji*, 19 I&N Dec. 264 (BIA 1985); *Matter of Tuakoi*, 19 I&N Dec. 341 (BIA 1985). *But see Matter of Truong,* 22 I&N Dec. 1090 (BIA 1999) [finding INS did not engage in affirmative misconduct when it placed respondent erroneously in exclusion proceedings].

Judicial Estoppel—The doctrine of judicial estoppel is a judge-made doctrine that seeks to prevent a litigant from asserting a position inconsistent with one that she had previously asserted in the same or in a previous proceeding to gain an unfair advantage. *See Young Wong Park v. Attorney General of the U.S.*, 472 F.3d 66, 73 (3d Cir. 2007) [court rejected claim of judicial estoppel where DHS amended charge to include aggravated felony after remand on whether respondent was deportable for committing a CIMT].

4.i. Where respondent makes a claim to citizenship—8 C.F.R. §§239.2(a)(2), 1239.2(a)(2), or where the respondent is a national of the U.S. 8 C.F.R. §§239.2(a)(1), 1239.2(a)(1); *Matter of Cruz,* 15 I&N Dec. 236 (BIA 1974) [IJ may terminate proceedings but only if respondent is prima facie eligible and the Service or the Court acknowledge that person is eligible]. An IJ may terminate deportation proceedings to permit a respondent to proceed to a final hearing on a pending naturalization case. *But see* INA §318, 8 U.S.C. §1429 ["No application for naturalization shall be considered by the Attorney General if there is pending against the applicant a removal proceeding pursuant to a warrant of arrest."]. But the IJ still has authority to terminate removal proceedings and permit the respondent to proceed to a final hearing on a pending naturalization application where there is *prima facie* eligibility for naturalization and the matters involves "exceptionally appealing or humanitarian factors" 8 C.F.R. §1239.2(f), but (according to the BIA) only if the DHS affirmatively communicates that respondent is *prima facie* eligible, *Matter of Acosta Hidalgo,* 24 I&N Dec. 103 (BIA 2007) [DHS *denial* of naturalization cannot be taken as a communication that respondent is *prima facie* eligible]; *Hernandez de Anderson v. Gonzales,* 497 F.3d 927, 932–35 (9th Cir. 2007) [upheld BIA's interpretation of §1239.2(f) under *Acosta Hidalgo* and *Cruz*]. It is also unconstitutional, under any circumstances, to deport a USC. *Trop v. Dulles*, 356 U.S. 86 (1957) [violates Eighth Amendment]; *Ng Fung Ho v. White*, 259 U.S. 276 (1922); *Fierro v. INS,* 66 F.Supp.2d 229, 231 (D. Mass. 1999) ["The INS has no discretion to execute removal orders against United States citizens."]. If respondent claims citizenship, s/he bears the burden by a preponderance of the evidence that s/he possess derivative citizenship. *Leal Santos v. Mukasey,* 516 F.3d 1, 4 (1st Cir. 2008) [once DHS establishes that respondent was born abroad, burden then shifts to her to prove derivative citizenship]; *Matter of Tijerina-Villarreal,* 13 I&N Dec. 327, 330–31 (BIA 1969).

Where respondent claims to be a national of the U.S., INA §101(a)(22)(B) defines a national of the U.S. as a citizen or "a person who, though not a citizen of the United States, owes permanent allegiance to the United States." In can only be achieved by birth or full naturalization. *Fernandez v. Keisler,* 502 F.3d 337, 348–53 (4th Cir. 2007) [rejected its former decision in *Morin, infra* as a case that gave a permissible construction of the "nationality" provision under INA §101(a)(22) but failed to provide an analysis deferring to the BIA under *Chevron*]. An LPR cannot be a national: (1) simply by long residence in the U.S., *U.S. v. Sotelo,* 109 F.3d 1446, 1448 (9th Cir. 1997), *Carreon-Hernandez v. Levi,* 543 F.2d 637, 638 (8th Cir. 1976), *Oliver v. INS,* 517 F.2d 426 (2d Cir. 1975); (2) because they filed a naturalization application or signed the oath of allegiance on the form. *Abiodun v. Gonzales,* 461 F.3d 1210, 1215–16 (10th Cir. 2006) [signing an oath of allegiance at a naturalization interview without taking the oath at a public ceremony does not trigger nationality]; *Okafor v. Gonzales,* 456 F.3d 531 (5th Cir. 2006) [same]; *Perdomo-Padilla v. Ashcroft,* 333 F.3d 964 (9th Cir.) *cert. denied* 124 S.Ct. 1041 (2004) [rejected *Hughes v. Ashcroft* and found that a person may only be a national by birth in a U.S. territory (American Samoa and Swains Island). *See also Omolo v. Gonzales,* 452 F.3d 404 (5th Cir. 2006) [a person may become a U.S. national only by birth or naturalization]; *Abou-Haidar v. Gonzales,* 437 F.3d 206 (1st Cir. 2006) [a person is not a national where he was an LPR for a long period, where he registered for Selective Service, and/or where he filed an application for naturalization, had an interview and swore an oath of allegiance but did not complete the naturalization process by attending a naturalization ceremony]; *Tovar-Alvarez v. U.S. Att'y General,* 427 F.3d 1350, 1352–53 (11th Cir. 2005) [neither long residence in the U.S. nor signing the oath of allegiance to the U.S. without taking the oath at a public ceremony results in citizenship]; *Marquez-Almanzar v. INS,* 418 F.3d 210, 216–19 (2d Cir. 2005) [finding that the statute requires someone to have been a national and therefore does not allow an LPR to become a national by manifesting allegiance even where it involved service in U.S. Army, an existing application for naturalization, registration with selective service and complete immersion in American society]; *Theagene v. Gonzales,* 411 F.3d 1107, 1112 (9th Cir. 2005) [service in Armed Forces without more is not a basis for national status]; *Sebastian-Soler v. U.S. Att'y Gen.,* 409 F.3d 1280, 1285–87 (11th Cir. 2005) [a person may only be a national of the United States by birth under §1408 or by naturalization]; *Alwan v. Ashcroft,* 388 F.3d 507, 512–13 (5th Cir. 2004) [filing a naturalization application, registering with the Selective Service, and swearing to the oath are insufficient objective demonstrations of allegiance to confer national status]; *Reyes-Alcaraz v. Ashcroft,* 363 F.3d 937 (9th Cir. 2004) [rejecting nationality claim under *Perdomo-Padilla* for LPR who served in the Armed Forces and took the standard military oath]; *U.S. v. Jimenez-Alcala,* 353 F.3d 858, 861 (10th Cir. 2003) [followed *Perdomo-Padilla*]; *Salim v. Ashcroft,* 350 F.3d 307 (3d Cir. 2003) [rejecting the view that filing an application for naturalization is sufficient to prove permanent allegiance to the U.S.]; *In re U.S.,* 316 F.3d 1071 (9th Cir. 2003) [where naturalization application is withdrawn there is no nationality claim]; *Oliver v. INS,* 517 F.2d 426, 428 n.3 (2d Cir. 1975); *De La Rosa v. U.S.,* 229 F.3d 80, 86 n.12 (1st Cir. 2000); *Shittu v. Elwood,* 204 F.Supp.2d 876 (E.D. Pa. 2002); *Matter of Navas-Acosta,* 23 I&N Dec. 586, 586–87 (BIA 2003). *But see U.S. v. Morin,* 80 F.3d 124, 126 (4th Cir. 1996) [finding that native Mexican who had submitted naturalization application was national under 8 U.S.C. §1101(a)(22) for purposes of 18 U.S.C. §2332; but *Morin* overruled by *Fernandez*]; *Hughes v. Ashcroft,* 255 F.3d 752 (9th Cir. 2001) [overruled by *Perdomo-Padilla*]; *Asemani v. Islamic Republic of Iran,* 266 F.Supp.2d 24 (D.D.C. 2003) [in the Foreign Sovereign Immunities Act context a national of the U.S. included someone who has filed an application for naturalization], or (3) because they took an oath upon enlisting in the U.S. Army Reserve. *Dragenice v. Gonzales,* 470 F.3d 183 (4th Cir. 2006) [distinguished *U.S. v. Morin.*

Federal Review. An adverse decision by the BIA on a nationality claim may only be reviewed in the courts of appeals. INA §242(b)(5); *Rivera-Martinez v. Ashcroft,* 389 F.3d 207 (1st Cir. 2004) [dismissed habeas and declined to transfer citizenship claim to circuit court where habeas was filed beyond 30-day period for circuit court review]; *Taniguchi v. Schultz,* 303 F.3d 950, 955 (9th Cir. 2002); *U.S. v. Morin,* 80 F.3d 124 (4th Cir. 1996); *Geronimo v. Mukasey,* 535 F.Supp.2d 808 (W.D. Tex. 2008) [declaratory judgment action in district court was dismissed because the petitioner had a removal hearing and an independent action is barred, although court transferred the case to the Fifth Circuit]; *Jones v. DHS,* 325 F.Supp.2d 551 (E.D. Pa. 2004) [habeas raising nationality claim should be transferred to circuit court even where person has been deported]; *Lee v. Ashcroft,* 268 F.Supp.2d 150 (E.D.N.Y. 2003) [transferring habeas action to Court of Appeals because it lacked jurisdiction under INA §242(b)(5)]; *Alvarez-Garcia v. INS,* 234 F.Supp.2d 283, 289–90 (S.D.N.Y. 2002. Review under INA §242(b)(5) does not extend, however, to a claim that an application for naturalization was improperly denied as that must be brought in a proceeding in the district court. *Abiodun v. Gonzales,* 461 F.3d 1210, 1216–17 (10th Cir. 2006) [court distinguished between a review of a claim that one is a citizen which is reviewed under INA §242(b)(5) and an improper denial of a naturalization petition which must be reviewed under 8 U.S.C. §1421(c)]. In addition, a claim to U.S. citizenship or nationality may not be barred for failure to exhaust administrative remedies under 8 U.S.C. §1252(d)(1). *Theagene v. Gonzales,* 411 F.3d 1107, 1110–12 (9th Cir. 2005) [distinguished *Taniguchi* and found that a nationality claim in the circuit court under INA §242(b)(5) is not subject to the exhaustion requirement of INA §242(d)(1)]; *Rivera v. Ashcroft,* 394 F.3d 1129 (9th Cir. 2005) [a habeas action to establish a nonfrivolous claim of U.S. citizenship cannot be barred even if respondent failed to exhaust his remedies because the Fifth and Fourteenth amendments are implicated; *Taniguchi* distinguished as frivolous claim]; *Moussa v. INS,* 302 F.3d 823, 825 (8th Cir. 2002) [in challenge to BIA's reversal of IJ's determination that person was citizen through naturalization of his father, the court had jurisdiction to determine whether applicant was an alien in order to decide whether statutory exhaustion under §1252(d)(1) even applied]. *But see Boyd v. ICE,* 344 F.Supp.2d 869 (E.D.N.Y. 2004) [dismissed habeas challenging reinstatement order on grounds that respondent failed to exhaust his administrative remedies in regard to his citizenship claim where he did not present citizenship claim to IJ, did not appeal IJ's decision and did not seek review in circuit court];. *DeJesus Corona v. Derosa,* 325 F.Supp.2d 516, 523–25 (D.N.J. 2004) [where petitioner had several previous opportunities to raise claim of citizenship before IJ or federal judge in criminal re-entry case and failed to do so, habeas barred to review USC claim];.*Atem v. Ashcroft,* 312 F.Supp.2d 792, 796–99 (E.D. Va. 2004) [where citizenship challenge was filed in habeas in the district court, but petitioner failed to appeal nationality issue to BIA, the case could not be transferred to circuit court because of failure to exhaust administrative remedies]; *Giap v. INS,* 311 F.Supp.2d 438, 440 (S.D.N.Y. 2004). A nationality claim that might otherwise be barred under INA §242(a)(2)(C) because the person has committed a criminal offense will, nevertheless, be heard in the circuit court because INA §242(a)(2)(D) preserves jurisdiction for legal claims. *Brue v. Gonzales,* 464 F.3d 1227, 1231–32 (10th Cir. 2006) [reviewed claim that aggravated felon acquired citizenship through adoptive parents].

4.j. Where respondent was a citizen at the time he was convicted of charges forming the basis of his removal. *Costello v. INS,* 376 U.S. 120 (1964) [denaturalized USC cannot be deported for two crimes involving moral turpitude when he was convicted of the crimes while he was a citizen]. *But see U.S. ex rel. Eichenlaub v. Shaughnessy,* 338 U.S. 521 (1950); *Matter of Gonzalez-Muro,* 24 I&N Dec. 472 (BIA 2008) [reaffirmed *Matter of Rossi,* 11 I&N Dec. 514 (BIA 1966) and distinguished *Costello* and held that respondent could be removed for crimes he was convicted of while a citizen, because he *committed* the crimes while he was an LPR, had his citizenship revoked because he committed the crimes before naturalization, and obtained his citizenship by concealing his activity]; *Matter of Rossi,* 11 I&N Dec. 514 (BIA 1966).

4.k. Where notice of proceeding or charge is insufficient. *Matter of Lopez-Barrios*, 20 I&N Dec. 203 (BIA 1990); *Chowdhury v. INS,* 249 F.3d 970 (9th Cir. 2001) [where NTA only charged person as agg. felon for money laundering conviction, INS could not prevail on theory that conviction for conspiracy to commit wire fraud was an agg. felony under other subsections of the statute because Respondent was not given notice nor charged with other agg. felony sections in NTA]; *Xiong v. INS,* 173 F.3d 601, 607–08 (7th Cir. 1999) [violation of due process to base deportability on an aggravated felony which was never charged nor used as the basis for deportation]. *But see Chambers v. Mukasey,* 520 F.3d 445 (5th Cir. 2008) [where NTA defectively alleged charge but respondent pled to it he waived challenge]. However, for purposes of relief, DHS need not charge the person with offense that would bar relief. *Matovski v. Gonzales,* 492 F.3d 722, 737–39 (6th Cir. 2007) [due process not violated where ground of inadmissibility—§212(a)(6)(C)(i)—is raised in relief phase of case although not charged as the ground of deportability because the IJ may rule on any ground of inadmissibility that arises during the course of proceedings]; *Salviejo-Fernandez v. Gonzales,* 455 F.3d 1063, 1065–66 (9th Cir. 2006) [due process was not violated where ICE did not charge respondent with an aggravated felony in the NTA but used the conviction to find respondent ineligible for cancellation]; *Taylor v. U.S.,* 396 F.3d 1322, 1329–30 (11th Cir. 2005) [upheld district court decision to bar §212(c) relief where respondent was not charged in NTA as an aggravated felon but where "conduct actually constituted an aggravated felony"]. Also, the failure to put down the date and time of the hearing on NTA does not render NTA ineffective where subsequent notice of hearing was sent to respondent. *Dababneh v. Gonzales,* 471 F.3d 806 (7th Cir. 2006) [where DHS served NTA without date and time but Immigration Court subsequently sent date and time notice, the NTA was sufficient]; *Haider v. Gonzales,* 438 F.3d 902, 906–08 (8th Cir. 2006) [upheld *in absentia* order and challenge to NTA that did not contain date and time of hearing where subsequent notice of date and time was sent to respondent]. Similarly, an illegible signature and title on the NTA does not render the NTA invalid or deprive the IJ of jurisdiction. *Kohli v. Gonzales,* 473 F.3d 1061 (9th Cir. 2007).

4.l. Where respondent is temporary resident and DHS has not revoked his or her residency. *Matter of Medrano*, 20 I&N Dec. 216 (BIA 1990). *But see Matter of Juarez*, 20 I&N Dec. 340 (BIA 1991) [termination of SAW status unnecessary to commence proceeding].

4.m. Where respondent was improperly charged as deportable when he was inadmissible. *Matter of R-D-,* 24 I&N Dec. 221 (BIA 2007) [deportation charge dismissed when person returning from Canada should have been charged as inadmissible].

4.n. Where DHS agrees to terminate proceeding because NTA improvidently issued. *Matter of Vizcarra-Delgadillo*, 13 I&N Dec. 51 (BIA 1968). DHS is authorized to cancel proceedings where respondent: (1) is a national of the U.S.; (2) is not deportable or inadmissible; (3) is deceased; (4) is not in the U.S.; (5) failed to file timely petition under INA §216(c) but the failure was excused; (6) NTA was improvidently issued; or (7) circumstances in the case have changed. 8 C.F.R. §§239.2(a), 1239.2(a). However, once proceeding have commenced the DHS cannot unilaterally terminate them. The decision rests with the IJ. *Matter of G-N-C-,* 22 I&N Dec. 281 (BIA 1998).

4.o. Where DHS has charged respondent with an NSEERS violation but believes that there is insufficient evidence that the violation was willful. Memo, Cerda, Acting Principal Legal Advisor, ICE, (Jan. 8. 2004), *published on* AILA InfoNet at Doc. No. 06050512.

4.p. Where the DHS agrees to administratively close cases and recharge someone in removal proceedings so that s/he would get the benefit of cancellation of removal. The process, called "repapering" will be used where the person: (1) would have been eligible for suspension of deportation under the 7- or 10-year provisions but for the stop-time rule under INA §240A(d)(1) or eligible for INA §212(c) relief but for AEDPA; and (2) is eligible for cancellation of removal and is not otherwise barred by INA §240A(d)(1). The DHS will not agree to reopen a case on this basis but once reopened they are generally required to agree to administratively close the case absent unusual circumstances. Memo, Cooper, G.C. (HQCOU 90/16.1-P) (Dec. 7 1999), Memo, Virtue, G.C. (HQCOU 90/16.1-P) (Dec. 7, 1998), *reprinted in* 77 No. 2 *Interpreter Releases* 39, 55–58 (Jan. 10, 2000). The BIA also agreed to administratively close files where repapering was available. Memo, Scialabba, Vice Chair of the BIA (Mar. 14, 2000), available at *www.usdoj.gov/eoir/chip6.pdf* and Memo, Schmidt, Chairman of the BIA (Aug. 20, 2000) available at *www.usdoj.gov/eoir/vll/genifo/streamimplem.pdf. See Alcaraz v. INS,* 384 F.3d 1150 (9th Cir. 2004) [found jurisdiction to review denial of administrative closure to repaper case and remanded case to BIA to determine whether repapering policy had been violated]; *Rojas-Reyes v. INS,* 235 F.3d 115, 125–26 (2d Cir. 2000) [failure to promulgate repapering regulations to permit cancellation did not create due process, equal protection or estoppel claims];*Checknan v. McElroy,* 313 F.Supp.2d 270, 274–76 (S.D.N.Y. 2004) [cannot mandamus Service to repaper applicant].

4.q. Where NTA not issued by proper authorities. Under DHS regulations only certain DHS officers may issue NTAs, 8 C.F.R. §239.1(a), although the Secretary of DHS has reserved the authority under 8 C.F.R. §2.1 to delegate other persons, presumably without additional regulation. 8 C.F.R. §§239.1(a)(41), 1239.1. *Ali v. Gonzales,* 435 F.3d 544 (5th Cir. 2006) [because issuing an NTA and signing an NTA are different concepts, an officer not authorized to issue an NTA may sign it as long as he was authorized by the appropriate official and the official ultimately signed the document submitted to the immigration court]. *But see Dailide v. U.S. Att'y Gen.,* 387 F.3d 1335, 1341 (11th Cir. 2004) [the Director of the Office of Special Investigations had the authority to issue an NTA although not on the list of officers named in 239.1(a) because the AG established the Office of Special Investigations to deport Nazis].

4.r. Where DHS violated the certification requirements of INA §239(e). When DHS initiates an enforcement action by arresting the respondent in certain locations, it must include on the NTA a statement it has complied with 8 U.S.C. §1367 prohibiting it from disclosing information to anyone and prohibiting the use of certain information from certain sources in generating the NTA. Under INA §239(e)(2) those locations are a domestic violence shelter, rape crisis center, supervised visitation center, family justice center, a victim services or victim services provider, a community based organization or a courthouse if the respondent is appearing in connection with a protection order case, child custody case, or other civil or criminal case relating to domestic violence, sexual assault, trafficking or stalking in which the respondent has been battered or subject to extreme cruelty, Under 8 U.S.C. §1367, DHS may not make an adverse determination on admissibility or deportability by relying on information obtained from abusers in VAWA cases, perpetrators of crimes in U visa cases and traffickers in T visa cases. Memo, Torres, Director of DRO and Form, Investigations, ICE (Jan. 22, 2007), *published on* AILA InfoNet at Doc. No. 07022210.

4.s. Where statute under which DHS seeks deportation is no longer effective. *Matter of B*, 5 I&N Dec. 255 (BIA 1953). *But see Attul v. INS*, 42 F.3d 958 (5th Cir. 1995).

4.t. Where DHS arrest and detention arise out of unfair labor practice by person's employer. O.I. §287.3a. *But see Montero v. INS*, 124 F.3d 381 (2d Cir. 1997) [rejecting claim that labor policy precludes deportation].

4.u. Where respondent is deceased or is not in U.S. 8 C.F.R. §239.2(a)(3), (4).

4.v. Where international law bars removal. At least one court has held that the International Covenant on Civil and Political Rights (ICCPR), 999 U.N.T.S. 171, particularly Article 13, may bar removal of a person who has children residing in the U.S. even if in compliance with U.S. law because "no one shall be subjected to arbitrary or unlawful interference with his...family..." *Maria v. McElroy,* 68 F.Supp.2d 206, 232 (E.D.N.Y. 1999). *See also Beharry v. Reno,* 183 F.Supp.2d 584 (E.D.N.Y. 2002), *rev'd on jurisdictional grounds,* 329 F.3d 51 (2d Cir. 2003) [finding person eligible for INA §212(h) relief under international law where the crime predates the 1996 changes but the conviction came after IIRIRA]; *But see Ayanbadejo v. Chertoff,* 517 F.3d 273, 278 (5th Cir. 2008) [upheld denial of motion to amend complaint to add an ICCPR claim because *Sosa v. Alvarez-Machain,* 542 U.S. 692 (2004) has explicitly held that it does not create obligations enforceable in federal courts]; *Martinez-Lopez v. Gonzales,* 454 F.3d 500, 502–03 (5th Cir. 2005) [international law and treaties that are not self-executing do not bar removal of aggravated felon whose conviction was a misdemeanor under federal law but a felony under state law]; *Guaylupo-Moya v. Gonzales,* 423 F.3d 121, 132–37 (2d Cir. 2005) [finding *Beharry's* international law analysis inappropriate because Congress clearly intended to bar LPRs with aggravated felonies from obtaining the benefit of INA §212(h) and *Beharry's* use of nonbinding international law norms relied on Congress's ambiguity]; *Flores v. Southern Peru Copper Corp.,* 343 F.3d 140, 163–64 n.35 (2d Cir. 2003) [in Alien Tort Claim case court in finding that ICCPR was an insufficient source of customary international law noted that it was also not self-executing under U.S. law]; *Naoum v. A.G.,* 300 F.Supp.2d 521 (N.D. Ohio 2004) [deportation of noncitizen parent does not violate ICCPR]; *Beshli v. DHS,* 272 F.Supp.2d 514, 525–26 (E.D. Pa. 2003) [no relief from removal because Articles 1-27 of ICCPR are not self-executing and since Congress has not passed any implementing legislation there is no enforceable action]; *Taveras-Lopez v. Reno,* 127 F.Supp.2d 598, 608–10 (M.D. Pa. 2000) [rejected use of ICCPR, customary international law or *jus cogens* to require that a waiver exist for aggravated felons otherwise barred by cancellation or INA §212(h)]. *See also U.S. v. Duarte-Acero,* 296 F.3d 1277, 1283 (11th Cir. 2002) [in criminal case court found that ICCPR violations do not create any judicially-enforceable rights because ICCPR is not self-executing].

4.w. Where the respondent is *prima facie* eligible for TPS or Deferred Enforced Departure. Memo, Carpenter, Deputy Gen. Co., HQCOU 120/12.2-P (Feb. 7, 2002), *reported in* 79 No. 15 *Interpreter Releases* 524, 530–38 (Apr. 8, 2002) [establishing Service policy of agreeing to administrative closure where someone is *prima facie* eligible].

4.x. Where the respondent has refugee status and the status has not been revoked. There is an open question in some circuits as to whether a person who became an LPR after achieving refugee or asylum status may be removed prior to revoking his or her refugee/asylum status. *Smriko v. Ashcroft,* 387 F.3d 279, 283–88 (3d Cir. 2004) [reviewing arguments but remanding issue to BIA to decide under *Chevron* deference principles]. On remand, however, the BIA held that a refugee who adjusts status and becomes an LPR may be placed in removal proceedings without first terminating refugee status. *Matter of Smriko,* 23 I&N Dec. 836 (BIA 2005). *See also Maiwand v. Gonzales,* 501 F.3d 101 (2d Cir. 2007) [respondent's AOS although not terminating his refugee status did not prohibit removal proceedings]; *Kaganovich v. Gonzales,* 470 F.3d 894, 897–98 (9th Cir. 2006) [in refugee case, agreed with *Smriko* under *Chevron* deference and as a matter of the plain language of the statute]; *Gutnik v. Gonzales,* 469 F.3d 683, 688–92 (7th Cir. 2006) [agreed with streamlined decision of one BIA member that refugee status is lost without revoking it when LPR placed in removal proceedings];

4.y. Where DHS asked for termination because respondent was previously removed and is not entitled to a hearing before an IJ to determine the reinstatement of the prior order under INA §241(a)(5). *Matter of W-C-B-,* 24 I&N Dec. 118 (BIA 2007) [the IJ has not authority to reinstate a prior order of removal or deportation and proceedings were properly terminated on DHS's motion].

5. Procedural Rights Before Hearing—INA §239, 8 U.S.C. §1229, 8 C.F.R. parts 239, 1239, and 1240.

5.a. Under IIRIRA §304 (effective Apr. 1, 1997), the following provisions are applicable:

(1) Notice of Issuance and Content of NTA

(a) Requires that NTA be given in person, or if personal service is not practicable, by mail (certified return receipt *no longer required*) to the respondent *or* his counsel of record. INA §239(a)(1), 8 U.S.C. §1229(a)(1), 8 C.F.R. §1003.13. However, if respondent does not appear the NTA must be served by personal service on him, on a responsible adult at his home, on his counsel, or by mail at his last known address. *Matter of Peugnet*, 20 I&N Dec. 233 (BIA 1991); *Matter of Huete*, 20 I&N Dec. 250 (BIA 1991) [IJ under former statute was sustained in dismissing a proceeding where the respondent was served by mail and the certified return receipt was not signed by respondent, or a responsible person at respondent's household]. If the Respondent does not receive the NTA and the notice of hearing it contains and therefore was never notified of the initiation of removal proceedings or his or her address obligations under INA §239(a)(1), then the IJ may not enter an *in absentia* order. *Matter of G-Y-R-,* 23 I&N Dec. 181 (BIA 2001). However, where the NTA is sent to the Respondent's correct address (for which there is no dispute) and the NTA is sent by certified return receipt but is left unclaimed at the post office by the Respondent, proper service has been made and Respondent's failure to appear resulted in a properly issued *in absentia* order. *Matter of M-D-,* 23 I&N Dec. 540 (BIA 2002) [respondent's defense that certified return receipt was not required and that regular mail would have been more reliable was rejected where certified return receipt came back unclaimed from Respondent's uncontested address].

(b) The NTA shall contain the following information: (1) the nature of the proceedings; (2) the legal authority for the proceedings; (3) the acts or conduct alleged to be in violation of law; (4) the charges against the respondent and the statutory provisions alleged to have been violated; (5) that the respondent may be represented by counsel and will be provided a list of counsel and a period of at least 10 days to procure counsel; (6) that the respondent must *immediately* provide the AG with a written address and telephone number (if any) where s/he may be contacted; (7) that the respondent must *immediately* provide the AG with a written record of any change of address or telephone number; (8) that if the respondent fails to comply with the notice requirements and does not provide his or her address (or change of address) and telephone number, a notice in writing need not be sent; (9) the time and place of the proceedings; and (10) that an *in absentia* order would be entered for failure to appear unless there are exceptional circumstances. INA §239(a)(1), 8 U.S.C. §1229(a)(1). Notice of an address or change of address must be provided by the respondent "immediately" on Form EOIR-33. INA §239(a)(1)(F)(ii), 1229(a)(1)(F)(ii). *But see Beltran v. INS,* 332 F.3d 407 (6th Cir. 2003) [in striking down an *in absentia* order the court found the EOIR-33 requirement to be ultra vires of the statute and that a letter notifying EOIR of the change of address was sufficient]. The notice shall include the person's name, "A" number, old address and telephone, new address and telephone, and the effective date of change. 8 C.F.R. §1003.15. The DHS must provide the address of IJ's office where NTA is filed. If person is in DHS custody, DHS has responsibility to notify the Immigration Court. 8 C.F.R. §1003.19(g); Memo, Hamilton, Assoc. Gen. Counsel (HQCOU 50/10.2) (Apr. 13, 1998), *reprinted in* 75 No. 17 *Interpreter Releases* 627, 636 (May 4, 1998).

(c) The NTA is in English and need *not* be in Spanish (H.R. Conf. Rep. No. 828, 104th Cong., 2d Sess. at 211), and shall notify the respondent about: (1) the right to be represented by counsel; (2) the 10-day period given to obtain counsel; and (3) a current list of free legal services. The AG may proceed after 10 days. INA §239(b), 8 U.S.C. §1229(b). The notice does not require that it be in any specific language. *Lopes v. Gonzales,* 468 F.3d 81, 85 (2d Cir. 2006) [rejecting claim that notice was deficient because it was not in Portuguese]. However, DHS may be required to translate charging document so person understands the nature of the proceedings. *Louis v. Meissner,* 530 F.Supp. 924 (S.D. Fla. 1981).

(d) If a respondent receives oral notice of the consequences of an *in absentia* order, absent exceptional circumstances, s/he is precluded for 10 years from obtaining virtually all forms of relief, including INA §240A (cancellation of removal, *e.g.*, former suspension and §212(c)); §240B (voluntary departure), §245 (adjustment), §248 (change of status), and §249 (registry). INA §240(b)(7), 8 U.S.C. §1229a(b)(7).

(2) Notice of Change in Time or Place of Proceeding

(a) In the case of a change or postponement in the time *and* place of the proceeding, *written* notice shall be given *in person* or (if personal service is not practicable) written notice by mail shall be given to the respondent or his counsel. INA §239(a)(2)(A), 8 U.S.C. §1229(a)(2)(A). The AG is no longer required to provide notice by certified return receipt. The notice shall state the new time or place for the hearing and the consequences of failing to appear, including an *in absentia* order. INA §239(a)(2)(A)(ii).

(b) Notice is not required at all if person failed to provide change of address. INA §239(a)(2)(B). If person is in DHS custody, DHS has responsibility to notify the Immigration Court. 8 C.F.R. §1003.19(g); Memo, Hamilton, Assoc. Gen. Counsel (HQCOU 50/10.2) (Apr. 13, 1998), *reprinted in* 75 No. 17 *Interpreter Releases* 627, 636 (May 4, 1998).

(3) *Effective Date*—IIRIRA §309 proceedings and the new removal procedure take effect Apr. 1, 1997. Cases pending on that date apply the former deportation and exclusion procedures under former INA §§235, 236, 242, and 242B. The only exceptions are: (1) if an evidentiary hearing has not commenced the AG may elect to use the new procedures, IIRIRA §309(c)(2); or (2) if the AG elects to terminate proceedings and restart the deportation proceeding as a removal proceeding, IIRIRA §309(c)(3). Courts have rejected a retroactive "settled expectation" argument where respondent seeks to be placed in deportation rather than removal proceedings. *Vasquez-Zavala v. Ashcroft,* 324 F.3d 1105,

1106–08 (9th Cir. 2003) [where respondent filed for asylum before Apr. 1, 1997 he did not have settled expectations that he would be put in deportation rather than removal proceedings]; *Lopez-Urenda v. Ashcroft,* 345 F.3d 783 (9th Cir. 2003) [following *Vasquez-Zavala* the court dismissed retroactivity argument for person who filed his asylum application before IIRIRA's passage on Sept. 30, 1996]; *Uspango v. Ashcroft,* 289 F.3d 226 (2d Cir. 2002) [same].

5.b. Service of OSC (now NTA) under former law. If respondent signed various parts of I-221, there is a fingerprint, and DHS officer states he served document, it may be assumed OSC was served personally. *Matter of Munoz-Santos*, 20 I&N Dec. 205 (BIA 1990);

5.c. Respondent must be granted at least 10 days after service of NTA before hearing can commence so that respondent has the opportunity to secure counsel, INA §239(b), unless respondent requests in writing an earlier date. *But see Matter of Santos*, 19 I&N Dec. 105 (BIA 1984) [must be harmful error];

5.d. There is a right to seek a change of venue once proceedings are initiated but there is no right to have proceedings initiated in a particular place. *Latu v. Ashcroft,* 375 F.3d 1012, 1019 (10th Cir. 2004) [action challenging the decision to commence removal proceedings in one venue versus another is barred by INA §242(g)];

5.e. Change of Venue—There is a right to seek a change of venue. 8 C.F.R. §1003.20(b). Venue may only be changed "only after the other party has been given notice and an opportunity to respond to the motion to change venue." *Id.* The regulation is violated where DHS *sua sponte* transfers venue to Oakdale without notice to the other side. *Jian v. INS*, 28 F.3d 256, 258–59 (2d Cir. 1994) [court affirmed deportation order because there was no harm to respondent]. Counsel filing a change of venue must include: (1) the date and time of the next scheduled hearing; (2) an admission or denial of the allegations in the NTA; (3) a designation or refusal to designate a country of removal: (4) if requesting relief a copy of the application and description of the basis for eligibility; (5) the address and telephone of place respondent would reside if the motion was granted; (6) if respondent has moved, a completed EOIR 33/IC form; and (7) a detailed explanation of the reasons for the request. Immigration Court Practice Manual at 5.10(c). The BIA has determined that in deciding a change of venue the IJ may change venue only for good cause after balancing the factors relevant to the venue issue. *Matter of Rahman*, 20 I&N Dec. 480 (BIA 1992). The factors include administrative convenience, expeditious treatment of the case, location of witnesses, cost of transporting witnesses or evidence to a new location and pursuant to regulation the provision of the address where the applicant could be reached. Where appropriate the motion should specify the witnesses, the nature of their possible testimony and why counsel could not be obtained in the present location. *Rahman* at 482. Other factors to be considered in determining change of venue include: (1) nature of evidence and its importance to alien's claim; (2) whether request is due to unreasonable conduct on alien's part; (3) number of prior continuances granted. *Campos v. Nail*, 43 F.3d 1285 (9th Cir. 1994) [class-wide injunctive relief granted where IJ had personal policy of denying all change of venue motions to Salvadoran and Guatemalan asylum seekers]; *Monter v. Gonzales,* 430 F.3d 546, 558–60 (2d Cir. 2005) [denial of change of venue from Buffalo to New York City reversed where government agreed to change and respondent was deprived of his right to rebut a finding that he made a material misrepresentation on his I-751 and was therefore not qualified to remove the condition on his residency]; *Romero-Morales v. INS*, 25 F.3d 125 (2d Cir. 1994) [reversed *in absentia* order where IJ did not consider basis for nonappearance, although respondent had filed a change of venue motion]; *Baires v. INS*, 856 F.2d 89 (9th Cir. 1988) [reversed deportation order where change of venue denied because IJ found request too close to hearing date]; *Chlomos v. DOJ*, 516 F.2d 310 (3d Cir. 1975) [where alien resided in New Jersey and retained counsel there, case should have been changed from Florida venue]; *Garcia-Guzman v. Reno,* 65 F.Supp.2d 1077 (N.D. Cal. 1999) [IJ clearly abused her discretion when she refused to change venue to cure the obvious deprivation of counsel even in absence of any prejudice in outcome]; *Matter of Seren*, 15 I&N Dec. 590 (BIA 1976). *But see Selimi v. INS,* 312 F.3d 854, 860–61 (7th Cir. 2002) [finding that granting change of venue based upon concession of removal was not *per se* coercive]; *Lovell v. INS*, 52 F.3d 458 (2d Cir. 1995) [upheld denial of change of venue in absence of demonstration of prejudice at INA §212(c) hearing where IJ improperly refused to consider change of venue]; *Hernandez-Vivas v. INS*, 23 F.3d 1557 (9th Cir. 1994) [filing timely motion to change venue does not establish reasonable cause not to appear; also rejected due process argument]; *Wijeratne v. INS*, 961 F.2d 1344, 1347 (7th Cir. 1992) [same]; *Maldonado-Perez v. INS*, 865 F.2d 328 (D.C. Cir. 1989) [denied change of venue in political asylum context]; *La Franca v. INS*, 413 F.2d 686 (2d Cir. 1969); *Matter of Chow*, 20 I&N Dec. 647 (BIA 1993) at 652–53 [not unreasonable for IJ to deny change of venue where alien's deportability remains at issue]; *Matter of Rivera*, 19 I&N Dec. 688 (BIA 1988) [where respondent cannot show prejudice and where govt.'s only witness was in venue where hearing held, denial of change upheld]; *Matter of Victorino*, 18 I&N Dec. 259 (BIA 1982). An applicant for change of venue must have a fixed street address at a new location before a change can be granted. 8 C.F.R. §1003.20(c).

De Novo Review of Prior Orders Not Permitted—The Chief IJ takes the view that the law of the case doctrine applies when a change of venue is granted and absent exceptional circumstances the receiving judge of a change of venue is "not free to hear the case *de novo* and ignore any orders prior to the venue change." Memo [OPPM 01-02], Creppy, Chief IJ, EOIR (Oct. 9, 2001), *reprinted in* 79 No. 3 *Interpreter Releases* 66, 84–88 (Jan. 14, 2002). The exceptions to the law of the case include: (1) a supervening rule of law; (2) compelling or unusual circumstances; (3) new evidence available to the transferee judge; (4) clear error in the previous order resulting in manifest injustice. *See also Zhang v. Gonzales,* 434 F.3d 993, 996–98 (7th Cir. 2006) [absent exceptional circumstances, such as a change in the law, new evidence, or compelling circumstances, a new IJ assigned to a case on remand should not make inconsistent rulings to the prior IJ based merely on differing impressions of credibility].

Completing as Much of the Case as Possible—The Chief IJ also takes the view that the IJ, "consistent with procedural due process requirements" should complete as much of the case as possible and should obtain pleadings, resolve the issue of deportability, removability, or inadmissibility, determine what forms of relief will be sought and set a date certain by which the relief applications, if any must be filed with the sending court. OPPM 01-02 (Oct. 9. 2001), *supra.*

Judicial Review—At least one circuit asserts that a decision regarding change of venue is not reviewable in federal court due to INA §242(a)(2)(B)(ii) because it is a discretionary decision. *Ballesteros v. Ashcroft,* 452 F.3d 1153, 1159–60 (10th Cir. 2006) [no jurisdiction to review claim that venue should be changed because DHS reorganization placed his case outside of the Ninth Circuit].

5.f. **Continuances**—A respondent may be entitled to a continuance for good cause and for a reasonable time. 8 C.F.R. §§1003.29, 1240.6. *Matter of Sibrun*, 18 I&N Dec. 354 (BIA 1983). In determining continuances (and change of venue), "a myopic insistence upon expeditiousness in the face of a justifiable request for delay can render the alien's statutory rights merely an empty formality." *Baires*, 856 F.2d 89, 91 (9th Cir. 1988). Moreover, an IJ's denial of a continuance to allow new attorney to prepare because his crowded docket would put off the cases for years is impermissible because "an immigrant's right to counsel should not be sacrificed because of the shortcomings of the immigration system itself." *Mendoza-Mazariegos v. Mukasey,* 509 F.3d 1074 (9th Cir. 2007) [cancellation applicant denied statutory right to counsel where he sought brief continuance so new attorney could familiarize himself with the case]. *See also Badwan v. Gonzales,* 494 F.3d 566 (6th Cir. 2007) [IJ erred in denying an unopposed first continuance where respondent sought to obtain a translation of his divorce to qualify for adjustment]; *Ahmed v. Gonzales,* 465 F.3d 806 (7th Cir. 2006) [IJ erred in not granting continuance to §245(i) eligible respondent with approved fourth preference petition who sought continuance to file labor certification to speed up process]; *Benslimane v. Gonzales,* 430 F.3d 828 (7th Cir. 2005) [rejected preclusion of review pursuant to INA §242(a)(2)(B) and found that IJ made legal error in denying continuance where respondent had filed I-130 and I-485 as part of marriage based adjustment but had not filed adjustment with IJ]; *Biwot v. Gonzales,* 403 F.3d 1094, 1098–1101 (9th Cir. 2005) [where detained respondent given only 5 working days to find counsel and then denied continuance, his due process right to have counsel was violated]; *Subhan v. Ashcroft,* 383 F.3d 591 (7th Cir. 2004) [rejected preclusion statutes and ruled that IJ's denial of a continuance to finalize labor certification without a reason consistent with §245(i) violated that statute]; *Lin v. Ashcroft,* 377 F.3d 1014, 1032–34 (9th Cir. 2004) [IJ erred in allowing asylum case of minor to go forward where counsel was obviously unprepared]; *Herbert v. Ashcroft,* 325 F.3d 68 (1st Cir. 2003) [it was arbitrary and capricious to deny a continuance where counsel was required to be before a federal magistrate at the same time he was required to appear before the IJ]. Similarly, it "is not the quantity of continuances that have been granted, but the adequacy of the postponement afforded." *Jiang v. Houseman*, 904 F.Supp. 971, 979 (D. Minn. 1995) [reversed exclusion order where applicant given inadequate opportunity to find counsel]; *Yi v. INS,* 257 F.Supp.2d 791, 796–97 (E.D. Pa. 2003) [citing language in *Baird* the district court reversed the BIA for abuse of discretion and denial of due process where IJ denied motion to continue for more evidence on CAT claim despite the fact that the motion was unopposed by the government and generally stated the information sought to be obtained]; *Colindres-Aguilar v. INS,* 819 F.2d 259 (9th Cir. 1987); *Castro Nuno v. INS,* 577 F.2d 577 (9th Cir. 1978).

Continuance Denied—*Singh v. DHS,* 517 F.3d 638, 646–47 (2d Cir. 2008) [denial upheld where petitioner sought continuance to obtain prior entry records to prove 7 years of residency necessary for cancellation and 212(h) where petitioner admitted entering on fraudulent documents]; *Elbahja v. Keisler,* 505 F.3d 125 (2d Cir. 2007) [IJ did not abuse his discretion in denying continuance pending approval of labor certification]; *Lendo v. Gonzales,* 493 F.3d 439 (4th Cir. 2007) [respondent's rights were not violated when IJ refused to continue case pending wife's labor certification]; *Frech v. U.S. Att'y Gen.,* 491 F.3d 1277, 1280–82 (11th Cir. 2007) [where respondent argued that IJ's refusal to change venue violated his right to due process including the right to counsel and the ability to present evidence in NACARA waiver case, court found no prejudice]; *Feliz v. Gonzales,* 487 F.3d 71 (1st Cir. 2007) [substantial evidence supported IJ denial of continuance where respondent never requested continuance, the case had previously been continued and there was no indication that respondent's wife would appear at continued hearing]; *Alsamhouri v. Gonzales,* 484 F.3d 117, 122, 124 (1st Cir. 2007) [no due process violation or abuse of discretion in denying continuance for new counsel to file asylum application where respondent given several months warning by former counsel that application would have to be filed]; *Berri v. Gonzales,* 468 F.3d 390, 394–95 (6th Cir. 2006) [continuance properly denied where motion was filed late and respondent sought continuance for new counsel one week before the final hearing that had been rescheduled several times over 5 years]; *Zafar v. U.S. Att'y Gen.,* 461 F.3d 1357, 1362–67 (11th Cir. 2006) *reh'g en banc denied* 473 F.3d 1350 (2007) [finding no abuse of discretion or due process or equal protection violation in denying a continuance to permit approval of a labor certification for INA §245(i) eligibility because no visa was immediately available and because as a constitutional matter adjustment is discretionary]; *Khan v. Att'y Gen. of the U.S.,* 448 F.3d 226, 233–36 (3d Cir. 2006) [IJ did not abuse discretion by denying continuance where wife's labor certification was pending and therefore a visa was not immediately available]; *Ahmed v. Gonzales,* 447 F.3d 433, 439–40 (5th Cir. 2006) [followed *Zafar* and found no statutory, due process or equal protection violation in denying continuance where labor certification was filed but no visa immediately available]; *Sanusi v. Gonzales,* 445 F.3d 193, 199–200 (2d Cir. 2006) [IJ did not abuse his discretion when he refused to grant a third continuance because respondent sought medical records to support his CAT claim]; *Pede v. Gonzales,* 442 F.3d 570 (7th Cir. 2006) [distinguished *Subhan* and *Benslimane* because here IJ gave a reason for denying a continuance for the adjustment which was the ultimate hopelessness of the adjustment application]; *Ali v. Gonzales,* 440 F.3d 678, 680–81 (5th Cir. 2006) [IJ did not abuse his discretion when he denied eight continuance where respondent failed to provide proof that his LC was filed before Apr. 30, 2001 making him eligible for INA §245(i) relief]; *Abu-Khaliel v. Gonzales,* 436 F.3d 627, 634 (6th Cir. 2006)[IJ did not abuse her discretion in denying continuance given the length of the previous continuance and the fact that respondent had prior criminal violations]; *Jean v. Gonzales,* 435 F.3d 475, 483–84 (4th Cir. 2005) [not a violation of due process to deny *pro se* respondent a continuance to obtain a lawyer where she had already virtually completed the submission of her formal testimony and documentary evidence and had been given a one year continuance to show rehabilitation during which time her attorney withdrew]; *Ramchandani v. Gonzales,* 434 F.3d 337, 338–40 (5th Cir. 2005) [distinguished *Subhan* and upheld denial of continuance where respondent failed to provide documentation that a labor certification had been filed prior to Apr. 30, 2001];

Salkeld v. Gonzales, 420 F.3d 804, 809–10 (8th Cir. 2005) [where counsel asked for continuance to withdraw due to rift with client, it was not a violation to deny motion when it was not made in advance and the hearing had been scheduled for four hours a year in advance];*Hasanaj v. Ashcroft,* 385 F.3d 780, 784–85 (7th Cir. 2004) [IJ did not violate due process by denying request for continuance on asylum case that was scheduled six months in advance and where no hearing was available for an additional six months]; *Kuschchak v. Ashcroft,* 366 F.3d 597 (7th Cir. 2004) [IJ did not violate due process in refusing to grant continuance where lawyer asked for expedited hearing on lottery adjustment and IJ insisted that he also proceed on asylum claim]; *Al Khouri v. Ashcroft,* 362 F.3d 461, 464 (8th Cir. 2004) [IJ did not violate due process in denying continuance for new counsel where previous counsel gave respondent six month notice before withdrawing]; *Ponce-Leiva v. Ashcroft,* 331 F.3d 369, 374–77 (3d Cir. 2003) [IJ did not abuse his discretion in denying asylum seeker's lawyer a last minute request for continuance where hearing set 8 months in advance and counsel did not allege emergency]; *Ambati v. Reno,* 233 F.3d 1054, 1061–62 (7th Cir. 2000) [due process not violated to deny continuance where lawyer entered case 2 weeks before asylum hearing but where client was given 7 months continuance and did not show prejudice in result]; *Michel v. INS,* 206 F.3d 253, 258–59 (2d Cir. 2000) [not error for judge to deny continuance where hearing was going badly and respondent wanted to rethink decision not to have a lawyer]; *Tavares v. Ashcroft,* 371 F.Supp.2d 61, 66–68 (D. Puerto Rico 2005) [granting several continuances to prepare for §212(c) hearing did not violate due process]; *U.S. v. Meraz-Vargas,* 35 F.Supp.2d 1272 (D. Kansas 1998) [granting two continuances was reasonable]; *Molina v. INS*, 981 F.2d 14, 16 (1st Cir. 1992) [IJ has broad legal power to decide continuance]; *Matter of Rivera*, 19 I&N Dec. 688 (BIA 1988) [unless continuance or change of venue granted, respondent must appear at hearing. Deportation *in absentia* upheld]; *Castaneda-Suarez v. INS*, 993 F.2d 142 (7th Cir. 1993) [denial of continuance to file INA §212(c) application where deadline had originally been missed upheld];

(1) Where visa petition/adjustment application are filed, cannot deny continuance solely because petition has not been approved. *Haswanee v. U.S. Att'y Gen.,* 471 F.3d 1212 (11th Cir. 2006) [where LC was approved, I-140 filed, and visa immediately available, but no I-485 filed, it was an abuse of discretion to deny continuance but not a violation of equal protection or due process]; *Ahmed v. Gonzales,* 465 F.3d 806 (7th Cir. 2006) [IJ erred in not granting continuance to §245(i) eligible respondent with approved fourth preference petition who sought continuance to file labor certification to speed up process]; *Merchant v. U.S. Att'y Gen.,* 461 F.3d 1375 (11th Cir. 2006) [where LC was approved and respondent filed I-140 and I-485 with DHS pursuant to INA §245(i) it was an abuse of discretion by IJ to deny a continuance. *Bull* supported and *Zafar* distinguished]; *Benslimane v. Gonzales,* 430 F.3d 828 (7th Cir. 2005) [IJ made legal error in denying continuance where respondent had filed I-130 and I-485 as part of marriage based adjustment but had not filed adjustment with IJ]; *Subhan v. Ashcroft,* 383 F.3d 591 (7th Cir. 2004) [IJ's denial of a continuance to finalize labor certification without a reason consistent with §245(i) violated that statute]; *Bull v. INS*, 790 F.2d 869 (11th Cir. 1986); *Matter of Velarde-Pacheco,* 23 I&N Dec. 253 (BIA 2002) [*Matter of Arthur* and *H-A-* modified to allow for motions to reopen where the I-485/I-130 are filed within 90 days, is not numerically barred, is not barred by *Matter of Shaar* o r any other procedural grounds, presents clear and convincing evidence that the marriage is bona fide, and the Service either does not oppose the motion or bases its opposition solely on *Matter of Arthur*]; *Matter of Garcia*, 16 I&N Dec. 653, 656 (BIA 1978); *Ssali v. Gonzales,* 424 F.3d 556, 562–64 (7th Cir. 2005) [vacated BIA's denial on motion to reopen for marriage adjustment and criticized government's analysis of *Matter of Arthur*]; *Singh v. Gonzales,* 404 F.3d 1024, 1027–29 (7th Cir. 2005) [where I-130 had been approved the BIA's reliance on *Matter of Velarde-Pacheco* to deny motion to reconsider to allow adjustment was error because *Velarde* involved an unadjudicated I-130; however under facts of case error was harmless]; *Singh v. Quarantillo,* 92 F.Supp.2d 386 (D.N.J. 2000) [released applicant, tolled voluntary departure until INS approved I-130 petition that had been pending for 2 years and adopted dissent in *Matter of H-A-*]. *But see Ilic-Lee v. Mukasey,* 507 F.3d 1044, 1047–48 (6th Cir. 2007) [BIA did not abuse its discretion in upholding IJ's denial of a continuance to allow USCIS to decide motion to reopen I-130 that had been pending 14 months]; *El-*

bahja v. Keisler, 505 F.3d 125 (2d Cir. 2007) [IJ did not abuse his discretion in denying continuance pending approval of labor certification]; *Pedreros v. Keisler,* 503 F.3d 162 (2d Cir. 2007) [IJ did not err in denying continuance where I-130 had been denied and was on appeal to BIA and no argument or evidence was advanced addressing DD's error in denying the I-130]; *Vargas-Hernandez v. Gonzales,* 497 F.3d 919, 923 (9th Cir. 2007) [IJ did not abuse its discretion where respondent was married for 7 years and he waited until final hearing five years after wife became a USC to ask for continuance to file an 1-130 petition]; *Lendo v. Gonzales,* 493 F.3d 439 (4th Cir. 2007) [respondent's rights were not violated when IJ refused to continue case pending wife's labor certification]; *Zafar v. U.S. Att'y Gen.,* 461 F.3d 1357, 1362–67 (11th Cir. 2006) *reh'g en banc denied* 473 F.3d 1350 (2007) [finding no abuse of discretion or due process or equal protection violation in denying a continuance to permit approval of a labor certification for INA §245(i) eligibility because no visa was immediately available and because as a constitutional matter adjustment is discretionary]; *Khan v. Att'y Gen. of the U.S.,* 448 F.3d 226, 233–36 (3d Cir. 2006) [IJ did not abuse discretion by denying continuance where wife's labor certification was pending and therefore a visa was not immediately available]; *Ahmed v. Gonzales,* 447 F.3d 433, 439–40 (5th Cir. 2006) [followed *Zafar* and found no statutory, due process or equal protection violation in denying continuance where labor certification was filed but no visa immediately available]; *Morgan v. Gonzales,* 445 F.3d 549 (2d Cir. 2006) [IJ did not abuse his discretion or deny due process when he denied continuance to permit the adjudication of an I-130 stemming from a marriage that had previously been determined to lack *bona fides*]; *Pede v. Gonzales,* 442 F.3d 570 (7th Cir. 2006) [distinguished *Subhan* and *Benslimane* because here IJ gave a reason for denying a continuance for the adjustment which was the ultimate hopelessness of the adjustment application]; *Ali v. Gonzales,* 440 F.3d 678, 680–81 (5th Cir. 2006) [IJ did not abuse his discretion when he denied eighth continuance where respondent failed to provide proof that his LC was filed before Apr. 30, 2001 making him eligible for INA §245(i) relief]; *Abu-Khaliel v. Gonzales,* 436 F.3d 627, 634 (6th Cir. 2006) [IJ did not abuse her discretion in denying continuance where I-130 filed by second wife who married respondent 5 days before the hearing given the length of the previous continuance and the fact that respondent had prior criminal violations].

In addition, the limitation imposed by *Matter of Shaar* is no longer good law in some circuits. *Ugokwe v. U.S. Att'y Gen.,* 453 F.3d 1325 (11th Cir. 2006) [a timely filed motion to reopen post-IIRIRA tolls the VD period and prohibits the application of *Matter of Shaar* to bar consideration of the merits of the motion]; *Barroso v. Gonzales,* 429 F.3d 1195, 1202–08 (9th Cir. 2005) [filing a motion to reconsider within the VD period automatically tolls VD]; *Kanivets v. Gonzales,* 424 F.3d 330, 334–36 (3d Cir. 2005) [distinguished *Bhiski* and found that *post*-IIRIRA a timely filed motion to reopen for AOS tolls the period of VD and allows the BIA to consider the motion]; *Sidikhouya v. Gonzales,* 407 F.3d 950 (8th Cir. 2005) [where motion to reopen for AOS was filed prior to the expiration of the VD period granted by the BIA, it was an abuse of discretion *post*-IIRIRA for the BIA to deny reopening based upon *Matter of Shaar* when VD expired before BIA ruled]; *Barrios v. Att'y Gen. of the U.S.,* 399 F.3d 272 (3d Cir. 2005) [rejecting *Matter of Shaar* for *pre*-IIRIRA cases, and holding that a timely filed motion to reopen prevents the BIA/IJ from applying the bar to adjustment under the former INA §242B(e)(2)(A) because the failure of the BIA/IJ to adjudicate the motion within the voluntary departure period is an "exceptional circumstance"]; *Azarte v. Ashcroft,* 394 F.3d 1278 (9th Cir. 2005) [where a motion to reopen is filed during the voluntary departure period and a stay of removal or VD is requested, the VD period is tolled for post-IIRIRA cases while the BIA considers the motion]. *But see Chedad v. Gonzales,* 497 F.3d 57 (1st Cir. 2007) [a timely filed motion to reopen does not stay the running of the VD period and if the motion is granted after VD has expired the respondent is barred from seeking relief §1229c(d)(1)]; *Dekoladenu v. Gonzales,* 459 F.3d 500, 502–08 (4th Cir. 2006) [a timely filed motion to reopen does not toll the VD period]; *Banda-Ortiz v. Gonzales,* 445 F.3d 387, 391 (5th Cir. 2006) [holding that BIA's decision to reopen case does not cure respondent's failure to depart during the voluntary departure period]; *Bhiski v. Ashcroft,* 373 F.3d 363, 370–72 (3d Cir. 2004) [legacy INS opposition to motion to reopen proceedings not based upon *Matter of Arthur* was upheld where respondent failed to depart upon expiration of VD under *Matter of Shaar*].

Decisions Contrary to or Denied Pursuant to *Matter of Velarde-Pacheco*—*Matter of Kotte*, 16 I&N Dec. 449 (BIA 1978); *Matter of Arthur*, 20 I&N Dec. 475 (BIA 1992) [modifying Garcia and declining to grant motion to reopen for a/s where petition not yet approved and where marriage entered into after deportation proceedings commenced, thus falling within INA §§204(g) and 245(e)]; *Matter of H-A-*, 22 I&N Dec. 728 (BIA 1999) [reaffirming *Matter of Arthur* notwithstanding 90-day limit on motions to reopen under 8 C.F.R. §3.2(c)(2)]; *Rezai v. INS*, 62 F.3d 1286, 1289–92 (10th Cir. 1995) [followed *Arthur* in face of First Amendment challenge]; *Dielmann v. INS*, 34 F.3d 851 (9th Cir. 1994) [followed *Arthur* in face of due process challenge]; *Pritchett v. INS*, 993 F.2d 80 (5th Cir. 1993) [followed *Arthur*]; *Onyeme v. INS*, 146 F.3d 227 (4th Cir. 1998) [distinguishing *Garcia* and finding IJ did not abuse its discretion in denying continuance where second I-130 was not prima facie approvable and beneficiary was ineligible to adjust without INA §212(i) waiver]; *Valderrama v. INS*, 260 F.3d 1083, 1086 (9th Cir. 2001) [staying the mandate to allow motion to reopen under §3.2(c)(2) because of marriage to USC would be inappropriate]

Denied Under *Velarde*—*Ilic-Lee v. Mukasey,* 507 F.3d 1044, 1049–53 (6th Cir. 2007) [BIA was correct to deny motion to reopen proceedings for AOS under *Velarde* where there was some evidence of a legal marriage but the weight of the evidence was slight and the government opposed reopening]; *Sarr v. Gonzales,* 485 F.3d 354, 362–64 (6th Cir. 2007) [BIA denial of motion to remand under *Velarde* upheld where applicant had testified falsely at asylum hearing and never filed waiver with *Velarde* motion]; *Ramchandani v. Gonzales*, 434 F.3d 337, 340–41 (5th Cir. 2005) [upheld BIA denial of motion to reopen under *Velarde* where DHS opposed motion because applicant didn't submit affidavit of support].

Distinguish Continuance for LC Approval vs. Petition for Adjustment—***Compare*** *Elbahja v. Keisler,* 505 F.3d 125 (2d Cir. 2007) [IJ did not abuse his discretion in denying continuance pending approval of labor certification]; *Lendo v. Gonzales,* 493 F.3d 439 (4th Cir. 2007) [respondent's rights were not violated when IJ refused to continue case pending wife's labor certification]; *Zafar v. U.S. Att'y Gen.*, 461 F.3d 1357, 1362–67 (11th Cir. 2006) *reh'g en banc denied* 473 F.3d 1350 (2007) [finding no abuse of discretion or due process or equal protection violation in denying a continuance to permit approval of a labor certification for INA §245(i) eligibility because no visa was immediately available and because as a constitutional matter adjustment is discretionary]; *Khan v. Att'y Gen. of the U.S.,* 448 F.3d 226, 233–36 (3d Cir. 2006) [IJ did not abuse discretion by denying continuance where wife's labor certification was pending and therefore a visa was not immediately available]; *Ahmed v. Gonzales,* 447 F.3d 433, 439–40 (5th Cir. 2006) [followed *Zafar* and found no statutory, due process or equal protection violation in denying continuance where labor certification was filed but no visa immediately available]; *Ali v. Gonzales,* 440 F.3d 678, 680–81 (5th Cir. 2006) [IJ did not abuse his discretion when he denied eight continuance where respondent failed to provide proof that his LC was filed before Apr. 30, 2001 making him eligible for INA §245(i) relief]; *Ramchandani v. Gonzales*, 434 F.3d 337, 338–40 (5th Cir. 2005) [distinguished *Subhan* and upheld denial of continuance where respondent failed to provide documentation that a labor certification had been filed prior to Apr. 30, 2001]; ***with*** *Haswanee v. U.S. Att'y Gen.,* 471 F.3d 1212 (11th Cir. 2006) [where LC was approved, I-140 filed, and visa immediately available, but no I-485 filed, it was an abuse of discretion to deny continuance but not a violation of equal protection or due process]; *Ahmed v. Gonzales,* 465 F.3d 806 (7th Cir. 2006) [IJ erred in not granting continuance to §245(i) eligible respondent with approved fourth preference petition who sought continuance to file labor certification to speed up process]; *Merchant v. U.S. Att'y Gen.,* 461 F.3d 1375 (11th Cir. 2006) [where LC was approved and respondent filed I-140 and I-485 with DHS pursuant to INA §245(i) it was an abuse of discretion by IJ to deny a continuance. *Bull* supported and *Zafar* distinguished]; *Subhan v. Ashcroft*, 383 F.3d 591 (7th Cir. 2004) [IJ's denial of a continuance to finalize labor certification without a reason consistent with §245(i) violated that statute]; *Bull v. INS*, 790 F.2d 869 (11th Cir. 1986) [where approval of I-130 petition would make visa immediately available it was abuse of discretion not to grant continuance], and *Benslimane v. Gonzales*, 430 F.3d 828 (7th Cir. 2005) [IJ made legal error in denying continuance where respondent had filed I-130 and I-485 as part of marriage based adjustment but had not filed adjustment with IJ].

Deferral of Review of Continuance—At least one court has determined that it will defer a decision on whether a denial of a continuance was an abuse of discretion until it is certain respondent qualified for INA §245(i). *Butt v. Gonzales,* 500 F.3d 130 (2d Cir. 2007) [remanded to BIA to answer questions regarding respondent's eligibility for INA §245(i) before it decides whether IJ abused his discretion in denying continuance].

(2) Denial of continuance to obtain counsel violates due process or the INA. *Gjeci v. Gonzales,* 451 F.3d 416 (7th Cir. 2006) [IJ's refusal to grant one continuance after respondent's counsel withdrew, where it was clear that respondent did not understand the difficulties he was facing in regard to documents, including those in the possession of his former counsel, due process was violated]; *Biwot v. Gonzales,* 403 F.3d 1094, 1098–1101 (9th Cir. 2005) [where detained respondent given only 5 working days to find counsel and then denied continuance, his due process right to have counsel was violated]; *Reyes-Palacios v. INS,* 836 F.2d 1154 (9th Cir. 1988); *Rios-Berrios v. INS*, 776 F.2d 859 (9th Cir. 1985); *Castaneda-Delgado v. INS*, 525 F.2d 1295 (7th Cir. 1975) [a two-day continuance to obtain counsel is insufficient]; *Jiang v. Houseman*, 904 F.Supp. 971, 979 (D. Minn. 1995) [reversed exclusion order where applicant given inadequate opportunity to find counsel]. *But see Jean v. Gonzales,* 435 F.3d 475, 483–84 (4th Cir. 2005) [not a violation of due process to deny *pro se* respondent a continuance to obtain a lawyer where she had already virtually completed the submission of her formal testimony and documentary evidence and had been given a one year continuance to show rehabilitation during which time her attorney withdrew].

(3) Policy of the Service to defer deportation hearing until party can obtain expungement. *Matter of Ozkok*, 19 I&N Dec. 546 (BIA 1988); *Matter of Tinajero*, 17 I&N Dec. 424 (BIA 1980). *But see Matter of Gabryelsky*, 20 I&N Dec. 750 (BIA 1993) [pendency of collateral attack on conviction not basis to stay proceeding in deportation]. However, this policy is now restricted to expungements under federal law, because state expungements no longer have any effect. *Matter of Roldan,* 22 I&N Dec. 512 (BIA 1999). *Roldan* was subsequently vacated *sub nom* in *Lujan-Armendariz v. INS,* 222 F.3d 728 (9th Cir. 2000). However, the BIA reaffirmed *Roldan* for cases outside of the Ninth Circuit. *Matter of Salazar,* 23 I&N Dec. 223 (BIA 2002).

(4) A conditional resident by marriage should be granted a continuance to file an application for a waiver under INA §216(c)(4) if s/he is *prima facie* eligible. *Matter of Mendes*, 20 I&N Dec. 833 (BIA 1994).

(5) IJ not required to automatically grant continuance when §245(i) will allow AOS in the future and person's return would subject him to 10-year bar. Letter, Creppy, Chief IJ, EOIR (Sept. 24, 1999), *reprinted in* 76 No. 40 *Interpreter Releases* 152, 1533–35 (Oct. 18, 1999). However, it is Service policy not to give priority to deportation proceedings against a person who is a grandfathered beneficiary. Memo, Bach, Exec. Assoc. Comm. (Apr. 14, 1999), *reprinted in* 76 No. 16 *Interpreter Releases* 621, 652, 658 (Apr. 26, 1999). ***Compare*** *Lendo v. Gonzales,* 493 F.3d 439 (4th Cir. 2007) [respondent's rights were not violated when IJ refused to continue case pending wife's labor certification]; *Zafar v. U.S. Att'y Gen.*, 461 F.3d 1357, 1362–67 (11th Cir. 2006) *reh'g en banc denied* 473 F.3d 1350 (2007) [finding no abuse of discretion or due process or equal protection violation in denying a continuance to permit approval of a labor certification for INA §245(i) eligibility because no visa was immediately available and because as a constitutional matter adjustment is discretionary]; *Khan v. Att'y Gen. of the U.S.*, 448 F.3d 226, 233–36 (3d Cir. 2006) [IJ did not abuse discretion by denying continuance where wife's labor certification was pending and therefore a visa was not immediately available]; *Ahmed v. Gonzales,* 447 F.3d 433, 439–40 (5th Cir. 2006) [followed *Zafar* and found no statutory, due process or equal protection violation in denying continuance where labor certification was filed but no visa immediately available]; *Ramchandani v. Gonzales,* 434

F.3d 337, 338–40 (5th Cir. 2005) [distinguished *Subhan* and upheld denial of continuance where respondent failed to provide documentation that a labor certification had been filed prior to Apr. 30, 2001]; ***with*** *Haswanee v. U.S. Att'y Gen.,* 471 F.3d 1212 (11th Cir. 2006) [where LC was approved, I-140 filed, and visa immediately available, but no I-485 filed, it was an abuse of discretion to deny continuance but not a violation of equal protection or due process]; *Ahmed v. Gonzales,* 465 F.3d 806 (7th Cir. 2006) [IJ erred in not granting continuance to §245(i)-eligible respondent with approved fourth-preference petition who sought continuance to file labor certification to speed up process]; *Merchant v. U.S. Att'y Gen.,* 461 F.3d 1375 (11th Cir. 2006) [where LC was approved and respondent filed I-140 and I-485 with DHS pursuant to INA §245(i) it was an abuse of discretion by IJ to deny a continuance. *Bull* supported and *Zafar* distinguished]; *Subhan v. Ashcroft,* 383 F.3d 591 (7th Cir. 2004) [IJ's denial of a continuance to finalize labor certification without a reason consistent with §245(i) violated that statute];

(6) IJ cannot continue hearing to allow person more time to establish his rehabilitation for relief. *Matter of Silva-Rodriguez,* 20 I&N Dec. 448 (BIA 1992) [reversed IJ decision to grant one year extension to demonstrate rehabilitation for former INA §212(c) relief].

(7) A denial of a continuance where respondent had to assert Fifth Amendment because of parallel criminal proceeding was upheld by one court. *Witter v. INS,* 113 F.3d 549, 555–56 (5th Cir. 1997) [difficult litigation choices do not infringe on Fifth Amendment].

(8) Judicial Review. Some circuit courts have determined that they lack jurisdiction to review an IJ's decision to deny a continuance. *Wood v. Mukasey,* 516 F.3d 564 (7th Cir. 2008) [no jurisdiction following *Ali* to review IJ's denial of a continuance to await approval of I-130]; *Iqbal Ali v. Gonzales,* 502 F.3d 659, 660–65 (7th Cir. 2007) [INA §242(a)(2)(B)(i) & (ii) bar jurisdiction to review continuances because when the underlying matter is not reviewable anything leading up to it is not reviewable; rejected argument that continuances are regulatory and therefore not barred; *Subhan* distinguished]; *Yerkovich v. Ashcroft,* 381 F.3d 990 (10th Cir. 2004) [no jurisdiction under INA §242(a)(2)(B)(ii) because decision to deny continuance due to pending IV petition is a discretionary decision]; *Grass v. Gonzales,* 418 F.3d 876, 878–89 (8th Cir. 2005) [followed *Onyinkwa,* the court determined it lacked jurisdiction to hear a challenge to the denial of a continuance to wait approval of an I-130 petition and the REAL ID Act of 2005 did not alter that lack of jurisdiction because the decision to grant a continuance was discretionary and not a question of law]; *Onyinkwa v. Ashcroft,* 376 F.3d 797 (8th Cir. 2004) [no jurisdiction under INA §242(a)(2)(B)(ii) to review discretionary decision to deny continuance but in dicta found it was not an abuse because USCIS issued a notice of intent to deny second IV petition and marriage was questionable]. *But see Zafar v. U.S. Att'y Gen.,* 461 F.3d 1357, 1360–62 (11th Cir. 2006) *reh'g en banc denied* 473 F.3d 1350 (2007) [review of the denials of respondents' requests for continuance were not precluded by INA §242(a)(2)(B)(ii) because that section applies only to statutes and continuances are governed by regulation]; *Khan v. Att'y Gen. of the U.S.,* 448 F.3d 226, 229–33 (3d Cir. 2006) [same]; *Ahmed v. Gonzales,* 447 F.3d 433, 436–37 (5th Cir. 2006) [same]; *Sanusi v. Gonzales,* 445 F.3d 193, 198–99 (2d Cir. 2006) [continuances are not even mentioned in the subchapter referred to (subchapter II of Chapter 12) by 242(a)(2)(B)(ii)]; *Abu-Khaliel v. Gonzales,* 436 F.3d 627, 631–34 (6th Cir. 2006) [INA §242(a)(2)(B)(ii) does not bar jurisdiction over the IJ's denial of a continuance because that section refers to matters in the discretion of the Attorney General and continuances are part of the removal hearing which Congress has specified under INA §240(a)(1) are conducted by IJs]. In addition, where a constitutional claim is made regarding the denial of a continuance, a court can review the claim. *Salkeld v. Gonzales,* 420 F.3d 804, 809–10 (8th Cir. 2005) [although court is barred under INA §242(a)(2)(B)(ii), it may review a constitutional claim pursuant to the REAL ID Act regarding the denial of a continuance]. At least one court has determined that it will defer a decision on whether a denial of a continuance was an abuse of discretion until it is certain respondent qualified for INA §245(i). *Butt v. Gonzales,* 500 F.3d 130 (2d Cir. 2007) [remanded to BIA to answer questions regarding respondent's eligibility for INA §245(i) before it decides whether IJ abused his discretion in denying continuance]

5.g. Explanation of Rights/Apparent Eligibility—Under 8 C.F.R. §1240.10(a)(1), the IJ must not only inform the applicant of the right to counsel, but must ascertain on the record if s/he desires counsel. *Matter of Michel*, 21 I&N Dec. 1101 (BIA 1998) [reversed removal order where IJ never asked respondent if he wanted counsel]. Under 8 C.F.R. §1240.10(a), a respondent must be informed of his rights, including right to counsel, to free legal services, to present evidence, cross-examine witnesses, and to appeal. *Picca v. Mukasey,* 512 F.3d 75 (2d Cir. 2008) [IJ's failure to advise respondent of a right to free legal services and to provide him with a list of those services requires reversal even if respondent had a lawyer at preliminary hearings and even if DHS claims they provided a list to him because it is the IJ's responsibility to inform him and the record indicates he never received a list]; *Jacinto v. INS,* 208 F.3d 725 (9th Cir. 2000) [due process violated where IJ inadequately explained hearing procedures, and failed to adequately advise respondent of her various roles including the right to be a witness whether or not she had an attorney and the right to affirmatively present testimony instead of merely being subject to examination. Analogized asylum hearing to procedures in Social Security cases where applicant unrepresented].

Apparent Eligibility—Pursuant to 8 C.F.R. §1240.11(a) the IJ must also notify the respondent of "all benefits enumerated in this chapter," *Matter of Cordova,* 22 I&N Dec. 966, 970 n.4 (BIA 1999), including all relief available to him under the Act, particularly pursuant to cancellation, adjustment and registry, if the respondent has "apparent eligibility" for such relief. 8 C.F.R. §1240.11(a)(2). Unlike the previous regulation this requires advising the applicant of both forms of voluntary departure. *Cordova, supra.* "Apparent eligibility" means "that where the record fairly reviewed by an individual who is intimately familiar with the immigration laws—as IJs no doubt are—raises a reasonable possibility that the petitioner may be eligible for relief, the IJ must advise the alien of the possibility and give him the opportunity to develop the issue." *Asani v. INS,* 154 F.3d 719, 727–28 (7th Cir. 1998) [IJ failed to advise as to suspension]; *Moran-Enriquez v. INS*, 884 F.2d 420 (9th Cir. 1989) [reversed deportation order where respondent apparently eligible for §212(h) relief]; *Duran v. INS*, 756 F.2d 1338 (9th Cir. 1985) [test applied to former §243(h)]; *U.S. v. Arrieta,* 224 F.3d 1076 (9th Cir. 2000) [IJ's failure to advise of apparent eligibility for INA §212(h) resulted in reversal of guilty plea for re-entering]; *U.S. v. Ortega-Ascanio,* 376 F.3d 879 (9th Cir. 2004) [permitted withdrawal of plea before sentencing where defendant argued that intervening *St. Cyr* decision was basis to dismiss indictment for illegal re-entry because IJ, at removal hearing, failed to inform him of INA §212(c) relief even though he informed him of cancellation but only if he did not commit aggravated felony]; *U.S. v. Arce-Hernandez,* 163 F.3d 559, 563 (9th Cir. 1998) [government concedes that failure to inform person married to USC of 212(h) waiver "taints" hearing, although court ruled it was not prejudicial in the case]; *U.S. v. Andrade-Partida,* 110 F.Supp.2d 1260 (N.D. Cal. 2000) [respondent never advised of INA §212(c) relief]; *Matter of Cordova, supra* [reversed final order where IJ improperly told applicant he was ineligible for voluntary departure at master calendar hearing because he lacked good moral character]; *Matter of Ulloa,* 22 I&N Dec. 725 (BIA 1999) [person found to be inadmissible as public charge and therefore ineligible for adjustment at deportation hearing had the right to be informed by IJ of a waiver under §213 under apparent eligibility test]. *But see Matter of R-S-H-, et al.,* 23 I&N Dec. 629, 644 (BIA 2003) [where respondents filed asylum/withholding, the failure of the IJ to advise respondents as to prehearing voluntary departure was not prejudicial because the respondents provided no reason to believe they would have waived their rights to other relief]; *Mema v. Gonzales,* 474 F.3d 412, 420–21 (7th Cir. 2007) [no due process violation for failing to inform respondent under §1240.11(a)(2) of his right to withdraw his application for admission where there is no showing of prejudice]; *Bejko v. Gonzales,* 468 F.3d 482, 487–88 (7th Cir. 2007) [same]; *Bonhometre v. Ashcroft,* 414 F.3d 442, 448–50 (3d Cir. 2005) [no due process violation for failure to inform respondent of INA §§212(c), 212(h) and CAT because respondent was not eligible for §212(c)/212(h), and no evidence was presented regarding the CAT claim]; *U.S. v. Aguirre-Tello,* 353 F.3d 1199, 1204–05 (10th Cir. 2004) (en banc) [no constitutional right to be informed of discretionary relief that might be available such as INA §212(c)]; *U.S. v. Lopez-Ortiz,* 313 F.3d 225 (5th Cir. 2002), *cert. denied,* 537 U.S. 1135 (2003) [failure to inform defendant of eligibility for INA §212(c) relief does not rise to the level of fundamental unfairness and therefore does not affect the conviction because §212(c) relief is not a liberty or property interest warranting due process protection].

5.h. *Termination of proceedings*—DHS cannot cancel the NTA once proceedings commence under §1003.14; 8 C.F.R. §§239.2(a), 1239.2(a) but it can seek to terminate them because the NTA was improvidently issued. *Matter of Vizcarra-Delgadillo*, 13 I&N Dec. 51 (BIA 1968).

6. Discovery

6.a. FOIA—8 C.F.R. §103; 58 Fed. Reg. 31147–50 (June 1, 1993); 9 FAM 40.4 N.4.

(1) Procedures for Filing

(a) DHS—Utilize G-639 Form. In requesting documents from the various DHS branches—ICE, CBP, USCIS—it is necessary to review the agency's document maintenance procedure. In most cases, separate requests to each individual field office must be made in addition to a request to the agency's headquarters. *Moayedi v. U.S. Customs and Border Protection,* 310 F.Supp.2d 73, 79–81 (D.D.C. 2007) [CBP made an "adequate search" of its records under the FOIA by searching only the TECS II system without searching any of its field offices because the FOIA request was made solely to CBP headquarters in Washington DC]. DHS also publishes the method in which it maintains records through a verification information system, 73 Fed. Reg. 10793 (Feb. 28, 2008).

i) CBP—Address: U.S. Customs and Border Protection, 1300 Pennsylvania Ave., NW, Attn: Mint Annex Building, FOIA Division, Washington, DC 20229; tel. no. 202 572-0640.

ii) USCIS—Has a three track system

a) Track 1 is for less complex requests that can be processed in 20 days or less

b) Track 2 is for complex requests that may require more than 20 working days

c) Track 3—NTA Track—Accelerated access to A files for individuals served with charging documents. It does not include cases where IJs have issued final orders, where an appeal has been filed, or the hearing date has passed and the respondent failed to appear resulting in closure or an *in absentia* order. The A file can be requested by filing a Form G-639 and G-28 along with the NTA or OSC, notice of continued hearing or I-863 (notice of referral to IJ), and a request to expedite. 72 Fed. Reg. 9017–18 (Feb. 28, 2007).

(b) EOIR—Do *not* use G-639 Form. Request should be writing and should describe the records sought. The respondent A# should be used. If a person is requesting information about himself a notarized statement or statement under penalty of perjury or a DOJ-361 form may be used. Notice, EOIR *discussed in* 83 No. 11 *Interpreter Releases* 465, 477 (Mar. 13, 2006). *See also* Immigration Court Practice Manual at Chap. 12.

(c) Genealogy Program—DHS has established a fee-for-service program to perform genealogical research for historical records (applicant files a G-1041 form) and/or a request to copy specific historical record if known (applicant files a G-1041A). 8 C.F.R. §§103.7(b)(1), 103.38–.41, Historical files are naturalization certificates from Sept. 27, 1906, to Apr. 1, 1956; visa files from July 1, 1924, to Mar. 31, 1944; registry files from Mar. 2, 1929, to Mar. 31, 1944; and A-number files below 8 million (A8). 8 C.F.R §103.39.

(2) DHS Response Process—DHS offices are ordered to respond to requests on a first in, first out basis unless there are complex and routine cases together requiring a two-tier system. Memo, Martinez, Asst. Comm. Records Systems Division, CO 1491-P (Apr. 29, 1992), *reprinted in* 69 *Interpreter Releases* 916–18 (July 27, 1993). Under the settlement agreement reached in *Mayock v. INS*, ___ F.Supp. ___, Case No. C-85-5169-Cal (N.D. Cal. May 22, 1992), the Service established a national policy which also permits requesters who demonstrate "exceptional need or urgency" to have his or her request processed out of turn on an expedited basis. To obtain expedited treatment the requester must show

that an individual's life or personal safety would be jeopardized or that substantial due process rights of the requestor would be impaired by the failure to process immediately and the information sought is not otherwise available. *Ray v. DOJ*, 770 F.Supp. 1544 (S.D. Fla. 1990) [INS ordered to comply with 10-day time requirements set forth in 5 U.S.C. §552(a)(6)(A), (B), and (C) and required not to invoke 10-day extension more than one time per FOIA request]; *But see Long v. DHS,* 436 F.Supp.2d 38 (D.D.C. 2006) [where an organization sought documents regarding government factual claims made in a cert. petition to the S.Ct. but failed to establish that they or others were filing an amicus brief or identify an imminent action, the government's failure to establish an unusual circumstance for not producing the documents within the statutory period was not a sufficient basis to obtain expedited treatment]. Whatever the time period for the search, the government must demonstrate its search was adequate. *Moayedi v. U.S. Customs and Border Protection,* 310 F.Supp.2d 73, 79–81 (D.D.C. 2007) [CBP made an "adequate search" of its records under the FOIA by searching only the TECS II system without searching any of its field offices because the FOIA request was made solely to CBP headquarters in Washington DC]; *Abdelfattah v. DHS*, 488 F.3d 178, 182 (3d Cir. 2007) [finding USCIS record search adequate but finding FBI search, without any supporting affidavit, inadequate]. The venue for alien that makes FOIA claim may be place of his or her residence. *Arevalo-Franco v. INS*, 889 F.2d 589 (5th Cir. 1989).

(3) FOIA Exceptions to be Narrowly Construed—The exceptions under the FOIA preventing disclosure are to be narrowly construed. *Department of the Interior v. Klamath Water Users Protective Ass'n,* 121 S.Ct. 1060 (2001); *DOJ v. Tax Analysts,* 492 U.S. 136, 151 (1989). The structure of the FOIA reflects "a general philosophy of full agency disclosure unless information is exempted under clearly delineated statutory language." *Department of the Air Force v. Rose*, 425 U.S. 352, 360–61 (1976). The burden is on the agency to justify its actions. 5 U.S.C. §552(a)(4)(B); *News Press v. DHS,* 489 F.3d 1173 (11th Cir. 2007) [narrowly construing exemption 6 regarding "unwarranted invasion" of privacy and granting release of addresses because DHS can not establish that the privacy interest in nondisclosure is greater than the public interest in disclosure]; *Lawyers Committee for Human Rights v. INS*, 721 F.Supp. 552 (S.D.N.Y. 1989) [government bears burden of asserting FOIA exemption]. Therefore, the agency's assertion of nondisclosure must be supported by a detailed affidavit explaining why no portions of any document may be segregated and released. *Perry-Torres v. DOS,* 404 F.Supp.2d 140 (D.D.C. 2005) [court recognized exemption from disclosure under INA §222(f) but held that DOS had to provide a more detailed affidavit explaining why no portion of any document could be released]. The agency's policy that it will decline to search for documents produced after the date of a requester's letter is inconsistent with the FOIA. *Public Citizen v. DOS,* 276 F.3d 634, 642–44 (D.C. Cir. 2002).

(4) Segregable Portions of a Record— Pursuant to 5 U.S.C. §552(b) "[a]ny reasonably segregable portion of a record shall be provided to any person requesting such record after deletion of the portions which are exempt." *Abdelfattah v. DHS*, 488 F.3d 178, 186 (3d Cir. 2007) [where Vaughn index and USCIS's declaration provided no basis to make a segregable finding, the case was remanded to district court to make the appropriate finding].

(5) Denied Disclosure—The government has often succeeded in challenging FOIA requests. *National Archives and Records Administration v. Favish,* __U.S.___, 124 S.Ct. 1570, 1581 (2004) [in the matter concerning the death/suicide of Vincent Foster, where there are privacy interests protected by Exemption 7(C) and a party seeks documents (in this case photos of Foster) to uncover government misconduct, the requester must establish "more than a bare suspicion in order to obtain disclosure."]; *DOS v. Ray*, 112 S.Ct. 541 (1991) [upholding privacy exception to request for names of Haitians forcibly returned]; *Department of Justice v. Reporters Committee for Freedom of Press,* 489 U.S. 749, 776, 109 S.Ct. 1468 (1989) [general prohibition against the disclosure of "rap sheet" information based upon a categorical balancing of individual privacy and public interest in disclosure]; *Juarez v. DOJ,* 518 F.3d 54 (D.C. Cir. 2008) [lower court's decision to uphold DEA's assertion of various privileges without reviewing the documents *in camera* pursu-

ant to 5 U.S.C. §552(a)(4)(B), or seeking to segregate out portions of the documents, was upheld where petitioner sought documents after being denied the renewal of her visa on grounds of money laundering]; *Bassiouni v. CIA,* 392 F.3d 244 (7th Cir. 2004) [upheld government's refusal to provide a Vaughn index or list of documents (called a *Glomar* response) where to do so would compromise intelligence gathering mechanisms]; *Center for National Security Studies v. DOJ,* 331 F.3d 918 (D.C. Cir. 2003), *cert. denied,* 124 S.Ct. 1041 (2004) [the names, the attorneys' names, the dates of arrest and release, locations of arrest and detention and reasons for detention of post 9/11 detainees, including immigration, criminal and material witness detainees, are all exempt from disclosure under Exemption 7(A) regarding law enforcement proceedings]; *Students Against Genocide v. DOS,* 257 F.3d 828 (D.C. Cir. 2001) [where DOS had released certain reconnaissance photographs to UN Security Council regarding Bosnia, it was not required to release the remainder]; *Essential Information, Inc. v. USIA*, 134 F.3d 1165 (D.C. Cir. 1998) [Internet and programming materials of USIA are exempt from disclosure under Smith-Mundt Act]; *Mapother v. DOJ*, 3 F.3d 1533 (D.C. Cir. 1993) [FOIA requested material withheld in Waldheim Report on grounds that it falls within exemption 5 (deliberative process) and exemption 7A (enforcement proceeding) because court found that the possibility that someone excludable under INA §212(a)(3)(E)(i) such as Waldheim might bring a challenge to his listing on AVLOS/NAILS Lookout constitutes an enforcement proceeding under 7A]; *Maynard v. CIA*, 986 F.2d 547, 564 (1st Cir. 1993) [INS search not inadequate simply because it took 17 months to locate request]; *American-Arab Anti-Discrimination Committee v. DHS,* 516 F.Supp.2d 83, 88–90 (D.D.C. 2007) [upheld ICE decision to withhold the gender and nationality of persons arrested during NSEERS under Exemption 7(A) on law enforcement grounds despite affidavit of former CIA official indicating there is no national security issue]; *Moayedi v. U.S. Customs and Border Protection,* 310 F.Supp.2d 73, 79–85 (D.D.C. 2007) [CBP made an "adequate search" of its records under the FOIA by searching only the TECS II system and properly asserted Exemption 2 regarding personal rules and practices of the agency where plaintiff sought information why he had been stopped 20 times at different airports when entering the U.S.]; *Eastern Carpet House v. DHS,* 430 F.Supp.2d 672, 675–76 (S.D. Tex. 2006) [government's reliance on Cejka Affidavit was sufficient to demonstrate due diligence by government because it relied upon a first-come first-serve basis where plaintiff's application was in line at approximately 12,000 of 52,000 pending requests]; *CEI Washington Bureau v. DOJ,* 404 F.Supp.2d 172 (D.D.C. 2005) [organization's request for personal information, such as alien numbers, in an electronic database regarding the administration of the State Criminal Alien Assistance Program was exempt under FOIA §6 (privacy) and §7(C) (law enforcement purposes)]; *Phillips v. ICE,* 385 F.Supp.2d 296 (S.D.N.Y. 2005) [documents, including A files, General Counsel e-mails, asylum application and attachments, notes of asylum interview, and investigative files regarding two Salvadoran military officers granted status in U.S. were exempt under Exemption 5/deliberative process, Exemption 7/investigative files, Exemption 6/personal privacy and attorney-client privilege. However, report to Congress summarizing findings as to propriety of officers' admission into U.S. was not exempt under Exemption 7(C) regarding law enforcement]; *Florida Immigrant Advocacy Center v. National Security Agency,* 380 F.Supp.2d 1332 (S.D. Fla. 2005) [one document of NSA properly withheld under exemptions 1 (Executive Orders) & 3 (statutes barring disclosure) where request was in regard to the basis of the AG's statement in *Matter of D-J-* that Haiti was a staging ground for migration of third country nationals]; *Schiller v. INS,* 205 F.Supp.2d 648, 657–64 (W.D. Tex. 2002) [the names and birth dates of persons arrested in an INS operation are shielded from disclosure under the law enforcement privilege and the privacy interests of the individuals under exemptions 6 and 7(C) of FOIA]; *Badalamenti v. DOS*, 899 F.Supp. 542, 546 (D. Kan. 1995) [DOS properly withheld certain documents pertaining to plaintiff's extradition]; *Cudzich v. INS*, 886 F.Supp. 101, 106–08 (D.D.C. 1995) [withheld documents under investigation-by-other-agency theory of (b)(7)(A) and refusal to reveal C.I. (b)(7)(D)]; *Buffalo Evening News v. U.S. Border Patrol*, 791 F.Supp. 386 (W.D.N.Y. 1992) [upheld extensive redaction of I-213s on internal, investigatory and privacy grounds]; *Ray v. DOJ*, 778 F.Supp. 1212 (S.D. Fla. 1991) [upholding privacy and investigatory exception concerning request for information about investigations of INS employees]; *Medina-Hincapie v. DOS*, 700 F.2d 737 (D.C. Cir. 1983) [upholding exemption under INA §222(f) to disclosure of visa documents]; *DeLaurentiis v. Haig*, 686 F.2d 192 (3d Cir. 1982) [same]; *Jan-Xin Zang v. FBI*, 756 F.Supp. 705 (W.D.N.Y. 1991).

(6) Granting Disclosure—Immigration related documents have been disclosed despite government challenges. *Abdelfattah v. DHS*, 488 F.3d 178, 184–86 (3d Cir. 2007) [remanded case to district court to review section 7 claimed exemption where USCIS did not identify any connection between its law enforcement authority and the information withheld when asserting the law enforcement exemption]; *National Council of La Raza, et al. v. DOJ,* 411 F.3d 350 (2d Cir. 2005) [ordered release of OLC memorandum regarding authority of state and local police to enforce immigration laws despite it being protected by the deliberative process privilege where DOJ waived the privilege by publicly adopting the memo]; *Perlman v. DOJ,* 312 F.3d 100 (2d Cir.) *reaff'd on remand* 380 F.3d 110 (2d Cir. 2004) [finding that OIG's report on EB-5 program should be released notwithstanding privacy interest of former general counsel because public interest outweighs law enforcement and privacy privileges except as to information regarding third parties and witnesses]; *Public Citizen Inc. v. DOS,* 100 F.Supp.2d 10, 29–30 (D.D.C. 2000) *aff'd in part and rev'd in part on other grounds* 276 F.3d 634 (D.C. Cir. 2002) [memo from USTR counsel to the USTR chief of staff analyzing a recent case is not *per se* exempt under §5 and is subject to *in camera* review]; *Ray v. DOJ*, 852 F.Supp. 1558 (S.D. Fla. 1994) [rejecting privacy exemption in request for unredacted logs of Haitian interdictees]; *U.S. v. Colima-Monge*, 978 F.Supp. 941 (D. Or. 1997) [court ordered disclosure of certain documents in deported co-defendant's "A" file over INS's FOIA objection].

(7) Standard of Review—The courts will use the "clear error" standard when it is a factual question and "de novo" review when it is a legal determination because the facts are not in controversy. *News Press v. DHS,* 489 F.3d 1173, 1187–89 (11th Cir. 2007).

6.b. Subpoenas—INA §240(b)(1), 8 U.S.C. §1229a(b)(1), provides that the IJ has authority to issue subpoenas for attendance of witnesses and presentation of evidence. 8 C.F.R. §§1003.35(b), 287.4(a)(2), 1287.4(a)(2); EOIR's Immigration Court Practice Manual, Chapter 4; *Kaur v. INS,* 237 F.3d 1098 (9th Cir. 2001) [removal order reversed and IJ directed to issue subpoena to compel the INS to produce resource material cited in INS's referral of respondent's asylum application to the IJ]; *Matter of Duran*, 20 I&N Dec. 1 (BIA 1989). *But see Skorusa v. Gonzales,* 482 F.3d 939, 943 (7th Cir. 2007) [IJ not required to continue case to obtain surveillance videos where respondent subpoenaed DHS officer but videos were in the possession of the FBI not DHS].

6.c. Depositions or interrogatories—8 C.F.R. §§1003.35, 1240.7(c); *Matter of R-*, 5 I&N Dec. 612, 613–14 (BIA 1954); *Shin v. Mukasey,* 519 F.3d 901, 906 (9th Cir. 2008) [due process not violated where deposition of corrupt DHS official who sold "green cards" was taken in consolidated cases for judicial economy and used in respondent's removal proceeding].

6.d. FBI Records Request—Pursuant to 28 C.F.R. §16.32, the FBI has established a procedure to request what is commonly called a "rap sheet" but under FBI nomenclature is called an FBI identification record. To obtain the record a person must submit in writing a request accompanied by name, date and place of birth and a set of fingerprints. The request is sent to: FBI, CJIS Division, 1000 Custer Hollow Road, Clarksburg, West Virginia 26306. The fee (currently $18) is submitted as a cashier's check/money order made payable to the Treasury of the U.S. If a lawyer is requesting the information an affidavit from the client stating his authority should be submitted.

6.e. Jencks Act—*Matter of C-*, 8 I&N Dec. 696 (BIA 1960); *Matter of L*, 9 I&N Dec. 14, 28 (BIA 1960); *Carlisle v. Rogers*, 262 F.2d 19 (D.C. Cir. 1958); *Great Lakes Airlines v. C.A.B. of U.S.*, 291 F.2d 354, 364 (9th Cir. 1961).

6.f. Privacy Act—S. Rept. 93-1183, 93d Cong., 2d Sess. (1974), *reprinted in* 1974 U.S.C.C.A.N. 6916; alien's I-213 and I-263B statements, 8 C.F.R. §103.2(b)(16); and copy of record of proceedings, 8 C.F.R. §§292.4(b), 1292.4(b). Right to records concerning oneself, 8 C.F.R. §103.21(a); 8 U.S.C. §1361 [entitled to all nonconfidential information]. The Privacy Act may only apply to USC or LPR. 5 U.S.C. §552a(d)(1); *Cudzich v. INS*, 886 F.Supp. 101, 105 (D.D.C. 1995) [LPR who lost residence status ineligible to obtain records under Privacy Act]. The unauthorized release of information to a third party is actionable. 5 U.S.C. §552a(g); *Orekoya v. Mooney,* 330 F.3d 1, 5–7 (1st Cir. 2003) [unauthorized and nonexempt release of one agency's documents to the public by another agency is actionable].

6.g. Right to production of favorable evidence—*Ibarra-Flores v. Gonzales,* 439 F.3d 614, 620–21 (9th Cir. 2006) [on remand, the court ordered the IJ to require the government to produce "all forms referencing petitioner's departure from the United States" where petitioner was seeking cancellation of removal and claimed he did not voluntarily depart under an order of administrative VD]; *U.S. ex rel. Schlueter v. Watkins*, 67 F.Supp. 556, 561 (S.D.N.Y.), *aff'd*, 158 F.2d 853 (2d Cir. 1946); *Demjanjuk v. Petrovsky*, 10 F.3d 338, 353 (6th Cir. 1993) [the *Brady* rule covers denaturalization and extradition cases where the government seeks denaturalization based on proof of alleged criminal activities]. Federal Rules do not apply. *Matter of Benitez*, 19 I&N Dec. 173 (BIA 1984) [upheld denial of continuance until FOIA response completed]. Right to discovery in regard to in camera submission made by the Service. *Naji v. Nelson*, 113 FRD 548 (N.D. Ill. 1986) [requiring INS, in challenge to §245 denial, to produce a list of documents with brief description that were submitted in camera by INS]. *But see Munoz-Santana v. INS*, 742 F.2d 561 (9th Cir. 1984) [too burdensome to require government to produce records as to approvals and denials of I-212 applications where records had to be hand searched].

6.h. In removal proceedings where the DHS seeks to remove someone who claims he is lawfully present by virtue of a prior admission, the applicant "shall have access to [her] visa or other entry document, if any, and any other records and documents ... pertaining to the [person's] admission or presence in the U.S." that are not confidential. INA §240(c)(2), 8 U.S.C. §1229a(c)(2).

6.i. Prehearing Conference and pretrial stipulations may be required by the IJ, including the production of documents prior to the hearing. 8 C.F.R. §1003.21; Immigration Court Practice Manual, Chapter 4.

7. **Hearing**

7.a. Hearing is conducted before an IJ, 8 U.S.C. §1229a, which may include the Chief Immigration Judge. *Demjanjuk v. Mukasey,* 514 F.3d 616 (6th Cir. 2008) [Chief Immigration Judge was IJ within the meaning of the definition of immigration judge under 8 U.S.C. §1101(b)(4) and may try cases]; 8 C.F.R. §1003.9(b)(5). DHS may lodge additional charges. 8 C.F.R. §1003.30, 8 C.F.R. §1240.10(e) ["At any time during the proceeding, additional or substituted charges of inadmissibility and/or deportability may be lodged by the Service in writing"]. *See Young Wong Park v. Attorney General of the U.S.*, 472 F.3d 66, 73 (3d Cir. 2007) [court rejected claim of judicial estoppel where DHS amended charge to include aggravated felony after remand on whether respondent was deportable for committing a CIMT]. Respondent must have notice of all charges. 8 C.F.R. §1240.10(e). *Zamora-Morel v. INS*, 905 F.2d 833, 839 (5th Cir. 1990) [where INS withdrew former INA §241(a)(11) charge based on a drug conviction the BIA could not rely upon it as a basis to deny relief]; *Matter of Ching*, 12 I&N Dec. 710 (BIA 1968). Additional charges may be lodged by motion to reopen after initial charge terminated because convictions vacated. *DeFaria v. INS*, 13 F.3d 422 (1st Cir. 1993). ICE's request to amend charges after case remanded by BIA not barred by *res judicata. Valencia-Alvarez v. Gonzales,* 469 F.3d 1319, 1323–24 (9th Cir. 2006) [where BIA decision was not final and case remanded back to IJ, respondent's *res judicata* argument failed as to ICE's amendment of the charges on the NTA]. *But see Bravo-Pedroza v. Gonzales,* 475 F.3d 1358 (9th Cir. 2007) [court rejected argument of prosecutorial discretion and held that DHS counsel was barred from instituting new removal proceeding on charges that could have been brought in prior proceeding that was final].

7.b. Procedural Issues at the Hearing—The EOIR has issued a Practice Manual that will detail the procedures to be used in all immigration courts throughout the U.S. It will end local rules and replace them with unified court rules such as a 30-day (instead of a 10-day) filing requirement for documents and motions to be heard prior to trial. Memo, Neal, Chief Immigration Judge, EOIR (Apr. 23, 2008), *reported on* AILA InfoNet at Doc. No. 08042860.

7.c. Closed Hearing

(1) On Sept. 21, 2001 the Chief Immigration Judge, Michael Creppy, issued a directive to all IJs requiring that removal hearings be closed to the public and the press in so-called "special interest" cases. The directive has been successfully challenged on First Amendment grounds. *Detroit Free Press v. Ashcroft,* 303 F.3d 681 (6th Cir. 2002) [stating that "democracies die behind closed doors"]; *Haddad v. Ashcroft,* 221 F.Supp.2d 799 (E.D. Mich. 2002) [ordering the government to release the respondent from detention or hold a new detention hearing that is open to the public]; *But see North Jersey Media Group, Inc. v. Ashcroft,* 308 F.3d 198 (3d Cir. 2002), *cert. denied,* 123 S.Ct. 2215 (2003) [upholding the constitutionality of the directive and disagreeing with *Detroit Free Press*].

(2) In an IJ proceeding concerning an abused spouse or child under INA §216(c)(4), the hearing is closed unless the party requests that it be opened. 8 C.F.R. §1003.27(c).

7.d. Right to counsel—INA §§240(b)(4)(A), 292, 8 C.F.R. §§292, 1240.3, 1292. Respondent has a right to representation by competent counsel. *Olvera v. INS*, 504 F.2d 1372 (5th Cir. 1974). This right to obtain counsel at a person's own expense is "fundamental" and a "due process" right that "must be respected in substance as well as in name." *Orantes-Hernandez v. Thornburgh*, 919 F.2d 549, 554 (9th Cir. 1990) (*quoting Baires v. INS*). It is "an integral part of the procedural due process to which the alien is entitled." *Saakian v. INS,* 252 F.3d 21, 24 (1st Cir. 2001) [quoting the 7th Cir in *Batanic v. INS,* 12 F.3d 662, 667 (7th Cir. 1993)]. Respondents have "a constitutional right to counsel based on the Fifth Amendment's guarantee of due process of law." *Borges v. Gonzales,* 402 F.3d 398, 408 (3d Cir. 2005); *U.S. v. Campos-Asencio*, 822 F.2d 506 (5th Cir. 1987) [denial of right to counsel violates Fifth Amendment]. The right extends to inadmissible as well as removable aliens. *Dakane v. U.S. Att'y Gen.*, 399 F.3d 1269, 1272–75 (11th Cir. 2005) [respondent in removal proceedings as inadmissible persons followed *Lozada* but did not show that counsel's failure to file brief prejudiced her claim despite a rebuttable presumption because prejudice requires a showing that counsel's performance was so inadequate that it may have affected the outcome of the proceeding]. A person's due process right to obtain counsel also includes a right to competent representation from retained counsel and a person is denied due process when his attorney provides ineffective assistance. *Fadiga v. Attorney General USA,* 488 F.3d 142, 155 (3d Cir. 2007) [a claim of ineffective assistance of counsel in removal proceedings is cognizable under the Fifth Amendment as a violation of due process and court reversed denial of motion to reopen for ineffective assistance holding that it violated due process]; *Ray v. Gonzales,* 439 F.3d 582, 587 (9th Cir. 2006) [respondent denied due process when two attorneys failed to properly file motions to reopen]. The denial of a continuance to obtain counsel may violate statutory right to counsel, *Mendoza-Mazariegos v. Mukasey,* 509 F.3d 1074 (9th Cir. 2007) [cancellation applicant denied statutory right to counsel where he sought brief continuance so new attorney could familiarize himself with the case]; *Hernandez-Gil v. Gonzales,* 476 F.3d 803 (9th Cir. 2007) [where respondent requested that hearing be continued because lawyer was not present, although in the building, his right to counsel was violated] and due process rights. *Montes-Lopez v. Gonzales,* 486 F.3d 1163 (9th Cir. 2007) [where BIA issued an AWO and failed to address respondent's statutory and constitutional claim that he had been denied the right to counsel and forced to proceed *pro se* when IJ refused to continue case despite counsel's temporary suspension, court reversed]; *Gjeci v. Gonzales,* 451 F.3d 416 (7th Cir. 2006) [IJ's refusal to grant one continuance after respondent's counsel withdrew, where it was clear that respondent did not understand the difficulties he was facing in regard to documents, including those in the possession of his former counsel, due process was violated]; *Biwot v. Gonzales,* 403 F.3d 1094, 1098–1101 (9th Cir. 2005) [where detained respondent given only 5 working days to find counsel, his right to due process was violated]; *Lin v. Ashcroft,* 377 F.3d 1014, 1032–34 (9th Cir. 2004) [reversed denial of motion to reopen where minor's counsel was ineffective in contacting, preparing, failing to appear personally, advocating and appealing his client's case and where IJ failed to continue hearing so minor could obtain competent counsel]. *Rios-Berrios v. INS*, 776 F.2d 859 (9th Cir. 1985); *Castaneda-Delgado v. INS*, 525 F.2d 1295 (7th Cir. 1975). Denial of right inherently prejudicial. *Cheung v. INS*, 418 F.2d 460 (D.C. Cir. 1969); *Jiang v. Houseman*, 904 F.Supp. 971, 979–80 (D. Minn. 1995) [no showing of prejudice necessary]. *See also Garcia-Guzman v. Reno,* 65

F.Supp.2d 1077, 1090 [INS conduct amounted to a "shocking interference with petitioner's attorney client relationship" where IJ denied change of venue]; *Molaire v. Smith*, 743 F.Supp. 839 (S.D. Fla. 1990). *But see Aguilar v. ICE,* 510 F.3d 1 (1st Cir. 2007) [no substantive due process right was violated in regard to ICE's interference in parent's relationship with their children and no pattern and practice claim may be brought to challenge ICE raids that resulted in precluding counsel, transferring respondents out of state and away from counsel, and depriving them of bond because these claims must be brought individually as INA §242(b)(9) requires]; *Zheng v. Gonzales,* 464 F.3d 60, 62–63 (1st Cir. 2006) [no due process violation where IJ failed to remind respondent of right to retain counsel at subsequent proceedings where respondent had counsel at the first proceeding who withdrew]; *Obleshchenko v. Ashcroft,* 392 F.3d 970, 971–72 (8th Cir. 2004) [no due process right regarding ineffective assistance of counsel in asylum claim because there is no liberty or property interest where relief is subject to the unfettered discretion of a governmental authority]; *Pop v. INS,* 279 F.3d 457, 460 (7th Cir. 2002) [suggesting that claim that constitutional right to counsel in the circuit is "virtually foreclosed" based on *dicta* in *Stroe v. INS*, 256 F.3d 498, 501].

(1) Ineffective Assistance of Counsel Claim

(a) Analysis—The analysis of an ineffective assistance claim requires the BIA to engage in a two-part analysis: (1) Would competent counsel have acted otherwise?; and (2) Was counsel's performance so inadequate that it may have affected the outcome of proceedings (and not whether the person would have won or lost his claim)? *Maravilla Maravilla v. Ashcroft,* 381 F.3d 855, 858 (9th Cir. 2004) [reversed BIA denial of motion to reopen for ineffective assistance of counsel where they improperly analyzed the standard by holding the respondent had to show the case outcome would have been different instead of "affecting" the outcome]; *Fadiga v. Attorney General USA,* 488 F.3d 142, 157–63 (3d Cir. 2007) [where BIA applied a clear probability standard in denying motion to reopen asylum claim from Guinea instead of applying a "reasonable probability" standard regarding ineffective assistance of counsel (*i.e.*, but for counsel's ineffective assistance there was a reasonable probability that the outcome would have been different) the court reversed and ordered the case reopened].

(b) Harmless Error Rule; No Ineffective Assistance of Counsel—BIA applies "harmless error" rule and rejects "inherent prejudice." *Matter of Assaad*, 23 I&N Dec. 553, 561–62 (BIA 2003) *appeal dismissed for lack of jurisdiction Assaad v. Ashcroft,* 378 F.3d 471 (5th Cir. 2004) [failure to file timely notice of appeal without any showing of further prejudice is insufficient to warrant reversal for ineffective assistance of counsel]; *Matter of G-N-C-,* 22 I&N Dec. 281 (BIA 1998) [no prejudice where INS without authorization unilaterally terminated removal proceeding because "the violation of a regulatory requirement invalidates a proceeding only where the regulation or procedure provides a benefit to the alien and the violation prejudiced the interest of the alien which was to be protected by the regulation."]; *Matter of Santos*, 19 I&N Dec. 105 (BIA 1984). *See also Matter of B-B-,* 22 I&N Dec. 309 (BIA 1998) [counsel's insistence on corroborative evidence for asylum claim that discouraged application is not ineffective assistance of counsel]; *Zeru v Gonzales,* 503 F.3d 59, 72–73 (1st Cir. 2007) [the respondent failed to demonstrate that the result of a proper appeal would have been different and therefore could not show that there was a reasonable probability of prejudice]; *Guerrero-Santana v. Gonzales,* 499 F.3d 90 (1st Cir. 2007) [rejected ineffective counsel claim where second motion to reopen by other lawyer was filed 14 months after BIA's denial allegedly caused by respondent's two initial lawyers]; *Desna v. Gonzales,* 454 F.3d 896, 899 (8th Cir. 2006) [rejected due process claim based upon ineffective assistance where it was unrelated to adverse credibility finding in asylum]; *Sako v. Gonzales,* 434 F.3d 857 (6th Cir. 2006) [upheld BIA denial of motion to reopen where respondent sought reopening so that he could file a timely petition for review which he alleges his lawyers incompetently failed to do]; *Orehhova v. Gonzales,* 417 F.3d 48, 53 n.3 (1st Cir. 2005) [claim that counsel should have handled matters better, including offering a different theory of asylum, does not amount to ineffective assistance]; *De Zavala v. Ashcroft,*

385 F.3d 879 (5th Cir. 2004) [due process was not violated where respondent's counsel conceded charge after respondent was incorrectly charged as inadmissible at entry as a nonimmigrant when she was inadmissible as an immigrant because there was no prejudice]; *Lara-Torres v. Ashcroft,* 383 F.3d 968, 973–77 (9th Cir. 2004) [poor legal advice to client that NTA would not apply retroactively to bar cancellation was not ineffective assistance of counsel because it did not occur during the course of the removal proceeding. Placing client in proceeding is not a due process violation]; *Dakane v. U.S. Att'y Gen.,* 399 F.3d 1269, 1272–75 (11th Cir. 2005) [respondent followed *Lozada* but did not show that counsel's failure to file brief prejudiced her claim despite a rebuttable presumption because prejudice requires a showing that counsel's performance was so inadequate that it may have affected the outcome of the proceeding];*Denko v. INS,* 351 F.3d 717, 722–25 (6th Cir. 2003) [where counsel wrote to client suggesting he could file motion to waive client's appearance and client did not show up at hearing it was not ineffective assistance requiring the *in absentia* order to be reopened]; *Rojas-Garcia v. Ashcroft,* 339 F.3d 814, 824–28 (9th Cir. 2003) [where respondent was found inadmissible on reason to believe charge and denied voluntary departure, counsel's failure to file brief to BIA, while ineffective, did not result in prejudice]; *Ponce-Leiva v. Ashcroft,* 331 F.3d 369, 377–78 (3d Cir. 2003) [absence of counsel at hearing did not prejudice asylum seeker who was allowed to present his case which clearly indicated he was in the U.S. for economic reasons only]; *Garcia v. Att'y Gen. of the U.S.,* 329 F.3d 1217, 1223–24 (11th Cir. 2003) [following *Mejia Rodriguez* there is no ineffective assistance of counsel that rises to a due process violation where the deficient representation "merely prevents the alien from being eligible" for discretionary relief such as INA §212(h)]; *Pop v. INS,* 279 F.3d 457, 460–62 (7th Cir. 2002) [where political conditions substantially changed in Romania no prejudice shown by denial of asylum]; *Hernandez v. Reno,* 238 F.3d 50, 56 (1st Cir. 2001) [rejected due process ineffective assistance claim where INA §212(c) case handled questionably and held that respondent must show reasonable probability that but for counsel's unprofessional errors the result would have been different]; *Huicochea-Gomez v. INS,* 237 F.3d 696, 699–700 (6th Cir. 2001) [no ineffective assistance where lawyer placed client in removal but applicant ineligible for cancellation]; *Ambati v. Reno,* 233 F.3d 1054, 1061–62 (7th Cir. 2000) [no due process denial of counsel to deny continuance where lawyer entered case 2 weeks before asylum hearing but where client was given 7 months continuance and did not show prejudice in result]; *Miranda-Lores v. INS*, 17 F.3d 84 (5th Cir. 1994) [where counsel failed to file INA §212(c) application respondent must still show actual prejudice regarding entitlement to relief]; *Mullen-Cofee v. INS*, 976 F.2d 1375, 1380 n.12 (11th Cir. 1992) *amended on denial of rehearing* 986 F.2d 1364 (11th Cir. 1993) [respondent who was never advised of his right to counsel in violation of INS regulations was not denied due process because there was no substantive prejudice]; *Cobourne v. INS*, 779 F.2d 1564 (11th Cir. 1986) [same].

(c) No Right to Relief and Therefore Ineffective Assistance Not Relevant—*Serrano v. Gonzales,* 469 F.3d 1317 (9th Cir. 2006) [no ineffective assistance of counsel where respondent sought motion to reopen after VD had expired on grounds of "exceptional circumstances" because that exceptional circumstances provision was removed from the Act]; *Gutierrez-Morales v. Homan,* 461 F.3d 605, 609–10 (5th Cir. 2006) [no constitutional claim for ineffective assistance of counsel in cancellation application because there is no constitutional right to discretionary relief or to eligibility for discretionary relief]; *Jamieson v. Gonzales,* 424 F.3d 765, 768 (8th Cir. 2005) [claim of ineffective assistance of counsel fails because in seeking adjustment of status there is no constitutionally-protected liberty interest at stake]; *Guerra-Soto v. Ashcroft,* 397 F.3d 637, 641 (8th Cir. 2005) [affirmed BIA denial of reopening on alternative ground that when ineffective assistance of counsel touches upon respondent's chance to seek discretionary relief there is no due process issue]; *Obleshchenko v. Ashcroft,* 392 F.3d 970, 971–72 (8th Cir. 2004) [no due process right regarding ineffective assistance of counsel in asylum claim because there is no liberty or property interest where relief is subject to the unfettered discretion of a governmental authority]; *Assaad v. Ashcroft,* 378 F.3d 471, 475–76 (5th Cir. 2004) [no due process violation and therefore no circuit court jurisdiction where counsel's ineffective assistance involved the failure to receive a discretionary waiver of conditional residency]; *Dave v. Ashcroft,* 363 F.3d 649, 652–53 (7th Cir. 2004) [rejected constitutional challenge to streamlining and ineffective assistance of counsel as to cancellation claim because there is no liberty or property interest in discretionary relief]. But these cases often confuse the lack of due process to obtain relief and a due process right to seek relief that Congress has made statutorily available. *See e.g., Arevalo v. Ashcroft,* 344 F.3d 1, 14–15 (1st Cir. 2003) the Court addressed the issue whether INA §241(a)(5) (reinstatement of deportation order) may be applied retroactively to bar an adjustment of status application filed prior to IIRIRA's effective date. In finding that the statute could not be applied retroactively the Court noted that applying for adjustment of status was a vested right even if the relief itself was discretionary. Citing *Accardi v. Shaughnessy*, 347 U.S. 260 (1954), and other cases the Court stated that "an alien is not precluded from having a vested right in a form of relief merely because the relief itself is ultimately at the discretion of the Executive Branch." *See also INS v. St. Cyr,* 533 U.S. 289, 307–08 (2001) ["Traditionally, courts recognized a distinction between eligibility for discretionary relief, on the one hand, and the favorable exercise of discretion, on the other hand. Eligibility that was 'governed by specific statutory standards' provided 'a right to a ruling on an applicant's eligibility,' even though the actual granting of relief was 'not a matter of right under any circumstances, but rather is in all cases a matter of grace.'"]; *Succar v. Ashcroft,* 394 F.3d 8, 10 (1st Cir. 2005) [struck down regulation as *ultra vires* on nonconstitutional grounds but held: "The mere fact that a statute gives the Attorney General discretion as to whether to grant relief after application does not by itself give the Attorney General the discretion to define eligibility for such relief]; *Alcaraz v. INS,* 384 F.3d 1150, 1162–63 (9th Cir. 2004) [internal policies under *Accardi* principle have binding effect on agency, although court remanded to BIA to determine whether various memoranda were sufficient to establish policy in regard to repapering]; *U.S. v. Copeland,* 376 F.3d 61, 72 (2d Cir. 2004) [there is a distinction between "a right to seek relief and the right to the relief itself" and "[t]he decisions holding that a failure to inform an alien about Section 212(c) relief cannot be a fundamental error collapse this distinction and incorrectly assume that, because the grant of Section 212(c) relief is itself discretionary, the denial of a Section 212(c) hearing cannot be a fundamental procedural error"]; *Rabiu v. INS,* 41 F.3d 879, 883 (2d Cir. 1994); *Mayers v. Reno,* 175 F.3d 1289, 1301 n.15 (11th Cir. 1999); *Gutierrez v. Ashcroft,* 289 F.Supp.2d 555, 567–68 (D.N.J. 2003) [rejected claim that because respondent has no due process right to obtain former INA §212(c) relief he has no due process claim to seek relief].

(d) Harmful Error Analysis Not Necessary for Ineffective Assistance

i) Ninth Circuit—The Ninth Circuit does not require a showing that ineffective assistance would have definitively changed the outcome but that it "may" have affected the outcome of the proceeding. *Morales Apolinar v. Mukasey,* 514 F.3d 893, 898–99 (9th Cir. 2008) [where former counsel failed to obtain school records and elicit testimony regarding physical presence and failed to establish qualifying relatives for hardship his performance prevented client from reasonably presenting her case for cancellation and client needed to show only "plausible grounds for relief"]; *Mohammed v. Gonzales,* 400 F.3d 785, 793–94 (9th Cir. 2005) [first counsel's failure to present evidence of FGM may have affected the outcome of the proceedings]. *See also Ray v. Gonzales,* 439 F.3d 582, 587–88 (9th Cir. 2006) [respondent denied due process when two attorneys failed to properly file motions to reopen and their performances were thus so poor that there is a presumption of prejudice because they prevented respondent from reasonably presenting his case]; *Baltazar-Alcazar v. INS,* 386 F.3d 940, 947–49 (9th Cir. 2004) [requiring respondent to proceed alone to establish extreme hardship given the complex nature of the task was prejudicial]; *Singh v. Ashcroft,* 367 F.3d 1182, 1189–90 (9th Cir. 2004) [presumption of prejudice where there is ineffective assistance of counsel and the presumption is not rebutted where respondent could show that the BIA could plausibly have determined that s/he was eligible for asylum]; *Bui v. INS*, 76 F.3d 268 (9th Cir. 1996) [BIA cannot engage in harmless error analysis that is speculative]; *Agyeman v. INS,* 296 F.3d 871, 884–85 (9th Cir. 2002) [reversed BIA because of "potential" prejudice where IJ insisted that only respondent's wife's testimony in an adjustment hearing is relevant]. In certain circumstances, the Ninth Circuit also maintains a "presumption of prejudice" which the government may rebut. *Grigoryan v. Keisler,* 515 F.3d 999, 1003–05 (9th Cir. 2007. The presumption of prejudice "may arise from counsel's failure to file a timely notice of appeal or petition for review, his failure to file a brief to the BIA or this court, or his filing of a boilerplate brief." *Grigoryan*, 515 F.3d 999, 1006. A presumption of prejudice also arises where ineffective assistance of counsel resulted in an *in absentia* removal order. *Lo v. Ashcroft,* 341 F.3d 934, 939 n.6 (9th Cir. 2003); *Grigoryan,* 515 F.3d at 1003.

ii) Other Circuits—*Waldron v. INS*, 17 F.3d 511, 518 (2d Cir. 1994), *cert. denied,* 513 U.S. 1014 (1994) [no showing of prejudice necessary where fundamental rights derived from the constitution or federal statute are implicated such as the right to counsel]; *Montilla v. INS*, 926 F.2d 162 (2d Cir. 1991) [reversed denial of §212(c) relief where IJ failed to comply with former 8 C.F.R. §242.16(a) by not requiring respondent to state on record whether or not he wanted counsel]; *Sewak v. INS*, 900 F.2d 667, 670 n.7 (3d Cir. 1990) [rejecting rule because INS must still prove *Woodby* standard where alien tried incorrectly *in absentia*]; *Rios-Berrios*, 776 F.2d 859, 863 n.1 (9th Cir. 1985) [criticizing *Santos* regarding counsel issue]; *Garcia-Guzman v. Reno,* 65 F.Supp.2d 1077, 1088 (N.D. Cal. 1999) [interference in attorney-client relationship was so egregious as to be a *per se* violation not requiring a showing of harm in outcome]; *Jiang v. Houseman*, 904 F.Supp. 971, 979–80 (D. Minn. 1995) [rejecting *Santos* in exclusion proceeding]; *Molaire v. Smith*, 743 F.Supp. 839 (S.D. Fla. 1990) [rejecting harmless error claim where excludable person never informed of free legal services and never voluntarily waived counsel]. *See also Matter of Michel*, 21 I&N Dec. 1101 (BIA 1998) [reversed order of removal where IJ failed to comply with 8 C.F.R. §240.10(a)(1) by not ascertaining on the record whether respondent desired counsel]; *Matter of Grijalva*, 21 I&N Dec. 472 (BIA 1996) [need not show prejudice to obtain reopening of *in absentia* order. Reopening predicated on ineffective assistance of counsel]; *Arizona v. Fulminante*, 499 U.S. 279, 309 (1991) [where "structural defects" in the trial they are not harmless errors].

(e) Denial of right where ineffective assistance of counsel—*Aris v. Mukasey,* 517 F.3d 595 (2d Cir. 2008) [ineffective assistance of counsel even if it occurs through a paralegal's misrepresentation is an exceptional circumstance in *in absentia* orders and also tolls the 180 day period]; *Sanchez v. Keisler,* 505 F.3d 641 (7th Cir. 2007) [reversed BIA's determination that lawyer's decision to proceed with regular cancellation rather than the lower standard for VAWA cancellation was a "strategic" decision rather than ineffective assistance and the case was remanded to the BIA]; *Fadiga v. Attorney General USA,* 488 F.3d 142, 155–63 (3d Cir. 2007) [a claim of ineffective assistance of counsel in removal proceedings is cognizable under the Fifth Amendment as a violation of due process and court reversed denial of motion to reopen for ineffective assistance holding that it violated due process]; *Mai v. Gonzales,* 473 F.3d 162, 165–67 (5th Cir. 2007) [reversed BIA denial of motion to reopen for ineffective assistance despite BIA's claim that the lawyer made a strategic decision when he admitted two grounds of removal where one required a §212(c) waiver and the second a waiver under §240A because once §212(c) granted for the first ground §240A was unavailable for the second]; *N'Diom v. Gonzales,* 442 F.3d 494 (6th Cir. 2006) [reversed asylum denial of person of Fulani ethnicity from Islamic Republic of Mauritania, where there was a combination of incompetent counsel resulting in evidence not being placed in the record, a coup in Mauritania and uncertainty about present conditions there, and the questionable rejection of respondent's testimony that appears plausible and consistent]; *Siong v. INS,* 376 F.3d 1030, 1037 (9th Cir. 2004) ["Failure to file a timely notice of appeal is obvious ineffective assistance of counsel ... [and] [p]rejudice is ordinarily presumed in immigration proceedings when counsel's error 'deprives the alien of the appellate proceeding entirely" although the presumption may be rebutted if the appellant has no plausible grounds for relief]; *Roe v. Flores-Ortega,* 528 U.S. 470, 120 S.Ct. 1029, 1038 (2000) [Sixth Amend. right to counsel violated where defendant can show reasonable probability that he would have appealed case]; *Rodriguez-Lariz v. INS,* 282 F.3d 1218, 1226–27 (9th Cir. 2002) [respondent's due process right to counsel was violated where notary and lawyers working for them failed to timely file suspension application]; *Saakian v. INS,* 252 F.3d 21 (1st Cir. 2001) [reversed BIA's failure to consider *Lozada* claim where BIA refusal was based upon *pro se* respondent's failure to present all aspects of *Lozada* claim to IJ]. *Dearinger ex rel. Volkova v. Reno,* 232 F.3d 1042 (9th Cir. 2000) [applying *Flores-Ortega* to Fifth Amendment immigration context where counsel filed notice in Circuit Court of Appeals one day late]; *Castillo-Perez v. INS,* 212 F.3d 518, 526–27 (9th Cir. 2000) [ineffective assistance of counsel is a denial of due process and the remedy is to remand and apply law on suspension that existed at time error was made which was pre-IIRIRA]; *Rabiu v. INS*, 41 F.3d 879 (2d Cir. 1994) [counsel's failure to file INA §212(c) application constituted ineffective assistance warranting reversal of deportation order]; *Colindres-Aguilar v. INS*, 819 F.2d 259 (9th Cir. 1987) [prejudice not harmless where counsel could have marshaled facts better on asylum and sought voluntary departure]; *Gutierrez v. Ashcroft,* 289 F.Supp.2d 555 (D.N.J. 2003) [where counsel affirmatively misrepresented that he had filed a habeas petition challenging the denial of the right to seek former INA §212(c) before respondent was physically removed but had not filed petition, his actions violated due process and permitted the court to accept the habeas *nunc pro tunc* to the time before respondent was physically removed from the U.S.]; *Saba v. INS,* 52 F.Supp.2d 1117, 1125–26 (N.D. Cal. 1999) [ineffective assistance of counsel amounts to due process violation and where counsel continues to represent person, the court has an independent duty to raise the claim]. *But see Then v. INS,* 37 F.Supp.2d 346, 359–62 (D.N.J. 1998) [not ineffective assistance under *Lozada* where no indication that client asked for appeal and was not present at hearing].

(f) *Lozada Criteria*—The BIA has determined criteria for ineffective assistance of counsel in *Matter of Lozada,* 19 I&N Dec. 637 (BIA 1988) [where ineffective assistance of counsel claim raised must (1) have motion supported by affidavit setting forth agreement and representations by counsel; (2) inform counsel against whom the claim is made and give counsel opportunity to respond; (3) reflect in motion whether bar charge has been filed and if not, why not]. *Tai v. Gonzales,* 423 F.3d 1, 5–6 (1st Cir. 2005) [where respondent failed to follow any of the *Lozada* criteria and failed to file a motion to reopen, BIA correctly denied ineffective assistance claim]; *See also Matter of Rivera,* 21 I&N Dec. 599 (BIA 1996) [elaborating on criteria related to bar complaints]. The BIA has reaffirmed the validity of *Lozada* notwithstanding DHS challenge to its constitutional underpinnings. *Matter of Assaad,* 23 I&N Dec. 553 (BIA 2003), *appeal dismissed for lack of jurisdiction, Assaad v. Ashcroft,* 378 F.3d 471 (5th Cir. 2004) [reaffirming validity of *Lozada* despite INS claim that under *Coleman v. Thompson,* 501 U.S. 722, 752–54 (1991) and *Wainwright v. Torna,* 455 U.S. 586, 587–88 (1982) that there is no constitutional right to counsel]. In the view of most courts, there must be a showing of prejudice, even where *Lozada* is met. *See e.g., Piranej v. Mukasey,* 516 F.3d 137, 142 n.6 (2d Cir. 2008) [must be showing of prejudice but it is likely on record where ineffectiveness resulted in denying AOS based upon USC wife]; *Zheng v. Gonzales,* 422 F.3d 98, 106–08 (3d Cir. 2005) [*Lozada* requirements were met but there was no showing of prejudice due to lawyer's failure to file BIA brief]; *Dakane v. U.S. Att'y Gen.,* 399 F.3d 1269, 1272–75 (11th Cir. 2005) [respondent followed *Lozada* but did not show that counsel's failure to file brief prejudiced her claim despite a rebuttable presumption because prejudice requires a showing that counsel's performance was so inadequate that it may have affected the outcome of the proceeding]. *See also in this section* "Harmless Error Rule," ¶ (b) (p.340), *supra*, and "No Right to Relief...," ¶ (c) (p.341), *supra*.

Applying Lozada to Accredited Representatives—The *Lozada* criteria may in some form apply to accredited representatives. *Matter of Zmijewska,* 24 I&N Dec. 87, 94–95 (BIA 2007) [where accredited representatives did not properly notify respondent of voluntary departure date, respondent sought to reopen his case and adjust status by filing formal complaint against representative and giving him the opportunity to respond thereby taking steps to satisfy the concerns expressed in *Lozada*]

(g) *Lozada Met Without Filing Bar Charge*—Under the third prong of the *Lozada* requirements, a respondent need not file a bar charge if s/he can explain why s/he did not file one with appropriate disciplinary authorities. *Morales Apolinar v. Mukasey,* 514 F.3d 893, 895–98 (9th Cir. 2008) [where petitioner's attorney was suspended from the bar after failing to respond to prior charges of ineffective assistance, it would be futile for petitioner to inform counsel of the accusations or file a complaint]; *Fadiga v. Attorney General USA,* 488 F.3d 142, 155–57 (3d Cir. 2007) [respondent not required to file a bar charge where lawyer confessed error and submitted a detailed affidavit regarding his ineffective assistance]; *Zheng v. Gonzales,* 422 F.3d 98, 106–07 (3d Cir. 2005) [third prong of *Lozada* was met where present attorney explained that respondent did not file bar charge because he was uncertain about former counsel's claim that the reason he failed to file brief is that he did not receive brief schedule. But lawyer diligently filed FOIA to find out. Court denied claim for lack of prejudice]; *Lo v. Ashcroft,* 341 F.3d 934 (9th Cir. 2003) [noting that there must be "flexibility in applying the *Lozada* requirements" the Court held that respondent was not required to file a bar charge against his attorney where the lawyer acknowledged the error in an affidavit and it was clear the lawyer's error was inadvertent in that his secretary calendared and gave the clients the wrong date to appear at the hearing].

(h) Not all courts require strict adherence to *Lozada. See e.g., Piranej v. Mukasey,* 516 F.3d 137, 142–45 (2d Cir. 2008) [where petitioner did not explain in sufficient detail the agreement he had with counsel, the court remanded the case for an evidentiary hearing to determine whether there was a general retainer which would have required counsel to explain INA §245(i) or just a retainer to represent him in removal proceedings];*Yang v. Gonzales,* 478 F.3d 133, 142–43 (2d Cir. 2007) [where respondent did not follow *Lozada* and simply raised incompetency issue to BIA, the court found it was sufficient in light of attorney's disbarment prior to BIA decision]; *Granados-Oseguera v. Gonzales,* 464 F.3d 993, 998–99 (9th Cir. 2006) [where ineffective counsel represented respondent improperly by filing motion to reopen beyond VD (30 day) deadline and by not requesting an extension of VD, the errors were "clear and obvious" and meeting the *Lozada* requirements was not a prerequisite to a petition for review]; *Barry v. Gonzales,* 445 F.3d 741, 746–47 (4th Cir. 2006) [although strict adherence to *Lozada* is not required, the BIA's denial of a motion to reopen was affirmed where there was not substantial compliance with *Lozada* because respondent's affidavit did not detail discussions with counsel, prior counsel was not served with papers and with an opportunity to respond to the motion to reopen, and there was no evidence that a bar charge was filed]; *N'Diom v. Gonzales,* 442 F.3d 494 (6th Cir. 2006) [*Lozada* not addressed where court reversed asylum denial of person of Fulani ethnicity from Islamic Republic of Mauritania due to a combination of incompetent counsel resulting in evidence not being placed in the record, a coup in Mauritania and uncertainty about present conditions there, and the questionable rejection of respondent's testimony that appears plausible and consistent]; *Ray v. Gonzales,* 439 F.3d 582, 589 (9th Cir. 2006) [as part of the notice criteria under *Lozada* the submission of a bar charge provided notice to the attorneys of respondent's complaints against them]; *Lo v. Ashcroft,* 341 F.3d 934 (9th Cir. 2003) [noting that there must be "flexibility in applying the *Lozada* requirements" the Court held that respondent was not required to file a bar charge against his attorney where the lawyer acknowledged the error in an affidavit and it was clear the lawyer's error was inadvertent in that his secretary calendared and gave the clients the wrong date to appear at the hearing]; *Rojas-Garcia v. Ashcroft,* 339 F.3d 814, 824–28 (9th Cir. 2003) [where administrative record demonstrates the legitimacy of the ineffective assistance claim and there was substantial compliance with *Lozada* failure to submit affidavits is not fatal; however respondent failed to show actual prejudice from ineffective assistance]; *Rodriguez-Lariz v. INS,* 282 F.3d 1218, 1226–27 (9th Cir. 2002) [respondent "substantially" complied with *Lozada* in asserting violation of due process right to counsel where notary and lawyers failed to file for suspension]; *Escobar-Grijalva v. INS,* 206 F.3d 1331, 1334–35 (9th Cir. 2000) [*Lozada* requirements need not be followed where the record demonstrates the ineffective assistance]; *Castillo-Perez v. INS,* 212 F.3d 518, 524–28 (9th Cir. 2000) [same]; *Ontiveros-Lopez v. INS,* 213 F.3d 1121, 1124–25 (9th Cir. 2000) [abuse of discretion to strictly adhere to *Lozada*]; *Saakian v. INS,* 252 F.3d 21 (1st Cir. 2001) [reversed BIA's refusal to consider ineffective assistance claim where all aspects of *Lozada* were not presented to IJ but were presented to BIA]; *Esposito v. INS*, 987 F.2d 108, 110–11 (2d Cir. 1993) [post-*Lozada* case not requiring bar complaint to establish ineffective assistance]; *Figeroa v. INS*, 886 F.2d 76 (4th Cir. 1989) [same].

(i) Greater Adherence to *Lozada* Criteria—*Omar v. Mukasey,* 517 F.3d 647 (2d Cir. 2008) [court upheld BIA dismissal where petitioner did not address any of the criteria in *Lozada* and particularly his contractual arrangements with a nonlawyer immigration consultant]; *Pepaj v. Mukasey,* 509 F.3d 725, 727 (6th Cir. 2007) [failure to file bar charge fatal to appeal and the court rejected an equal protection challenge to the requirement]; *Patel v. Gonzales,* 496 F.3d 829 (7th Cir. 2007) [BIA did not abuse its discretion in denying motion to reopen where respondent attached bar complaint but did not, *prior to filing the motion to reopen,* provide notice to ineffective counsel with time for an opportunity to respond]; *Garcia-Martinez v. DHS,* 448 F.3d 511 (2d Cir. 2006) [no review of ineffective assistance claim where BIA dismissed appeal for failure to comply with *Lozada*]; *Zheng v. DOJ,* 409 F.3d 43 (2d Cir. 2005) [respondent who fails to comply substantially with the *Lozada* requirements in filing a motion to reopen before the BIA forfeits an ineffective assistance claim before the court]; *Asaba v. Ashcroft,* 377 F.3d 9, 12 (1st Cir. 2004) [requiring strict adherence to *Lozada* and upholding BIA denial of motion to reopen where the respondent *inter alia* did not give ineffective counsel sufficient time to respond to charges *before* filing motion to reopen]; *Wang v. Ashcroft,* 367 F.3d 25 (1st Cir. 2004), [affidavit pursuant to *Lozada* failed to explain the agreement between counsel and client or the prejudice that resulted from counsel's misdeeds]; *Azanor v. Ashcroft,* 364 F.3d 1013, 1023 (9th Cir. 2004) [where respondent's affidavit did not include the details of his agreement with ineffective counsel court rejected claim]; *Betouche v. Ashcroft,* 357 F.3d 147, 149–51 (1st Cir. 2004) [upheld BIA denial of motion to reopen where *Lozada* requirements of an affidavit and notification to counsel were not met]; *Reyes v. Ashcroft,* 358 F.3d 592 (9th Cir. 2004) [where malpractice was not evident from the record, respondent's failure to file affidavit and his failure to provide former counsel an opportunity to respond *before* filing the motion to reopen did not comport with *Lozada*]; *Hamid v. Ashcroft,* 336 F.3d 465, 468–69 (6th Cir. 2003) [affirmed removal order and rejected ineffective assistance claim where applicant failed to allege in his affidavit following *Lozada* a detailed statement of the agreement that was entered into with former counsel with respect to the actions to be taken and what counsel did or did not represent]; *Lu v. Ashcroft,* 259 F.3d 127, 132–33 (3d Cir. 2001) [found *Lozada* criteria a reasonable exercise of authority, denied motion to reopen where respondent in exclusion proceeding did not comply with *Lozada,* but expressed concerned about inherent danger in applying a strict formulaic interpretation not allowing explanations for failing to file bar complaints]; *Stroe v. INS,* 256 F.3d 498 (7th Cir. 2001) [requiring strict adherence to *Lozada* and finding failure to do so barred ineffective assistance claim against lawyer who failed to file brief timely resulting in dismissal]; *Lara v. Trominski,* 216 F.3d 487, 495–99 (5th Cir. 2000) [BIA did not abuse discretion in denying motion to reopen where bar complaint could have been filed]; *Ortiz v. INS,* 179 F.3d 1148, 1153–54 (9th Cir. 1999) [no ineffective counsel claim where there is a failure to produce or proffer the evidence that counsel failed to introduce]; *Stewart v. INS,* 181 F.3d 587, 596 (4th Cir. 1999) [ineffective assistance of counsel claim not entertained where party failed to follow *Lozada*].

(j) *Lozada* applied in the context of *in absentia* order—*Habchy v. Gonzales,* 471 F.3d 858, 863–64 (8th Cir. 2006) [IJ did not abuse discretion in refusing to reopen proceedings where respondent failed to file bar charge and comply with *Lozada*]; *Asaba v. Ashcroft,* 377 F.3d 9 (1st Cir. 2004) [affirmed BIA denial of motion to reopen where *Lozada* requirements not strictly adhered to by respondent]; *Lo v. Ashcroft,* 341 F.3d 934 (9th Cir. 2003) [noting that there must be "flexibility in applying the *Lozada* requirements" and that prejudice is not required for a motion to reopen an *in absentia* order, the Court held that the BIA was arbitrary in not reopening the *in absentia* order where a bar charge was not filed but the lawyer acknowledged his error and it was clear that the lawyer's error was inadvertent in that his secretary calendared and gave the clients the wrong date to appear at the hearing]; *Riley v. INS,* 310 F.3d 1253, 1257–58 (10th Cir. 2002) [time limitation for filing motion to reopen may be equitably tolled for ineffective assistance of counsel and case will be remanded to BIA to determine respondent's due diligence and compliance with *Lozada* criteria]; *Matter of Grijalva*, 21 I&N Dec. 472 (BIA 1996) [failure to appear due to former counsel informing him incorrectly that he did not have to appear]; *Matter of Rivera*, 21 I&N Dec. 599 (BIA 1996) [suggesting that bar charge must be filed to meet *Lozada* conditions where challenging an *in absentia* order]; *Matter of Lei,* 22 I&N Dec. 113 (BIA 1998) (Rosenberg, J dissenting).

(k) Remedy for Ineffective Assistance—In *Castillo-Perez v. INS,* 212 F.3d 518, 528 (9th Cir. 2000) the Court determined that the appropriate remedy for an ineffective assistance claim was to remand the case to the BIA with instructions that the agency apply the law in existence at the time the claim should have been made. In *Castillo-Perez*, the BIA denied the motion to reopen for suspension on the grounds that post-IIRIRA the applicant was ineligible.

(l) Equitable Tolling for Ineffective Assistance or Fraud—The numerical limitations and time periods for filing a motion to reopen will be tolled where the respondent was provided ineffective assistance of counsel and the tolling continues until the respondent "definitively learns" of counsel's incompetence or fraud. *Albillo-De Leon v. Gonzales,* 410 F.3d 1090, 1100 (9th Cir. 2005) [where respondent was defrauded by nonlawyer who posed as a lawyer, the time period for filing a motion to reopen under NACARA §203(c) and 8 C.F.R. §1003.43(e)(1) was tolled until date that current attorney found out that motion was not filed]; *Aris v. Mukasey,* 517 F.3d 595 (2d Cir. 2008) [ineffective assistance of counsel even if it occurs through a paralegal's misrepresentation is an exceptional circumstance for *in absentia* case and also tolls the 180 day period]; *Ghahremani v. Gonzales*, 498 F.3d 993, 999–1001 (9th Cir. 2007) [reversing BIA denial of motion to reopen for equitable tolling, where respondent used due diligence in hiring several lawyers]; *Zhao v. INS,* 452 F.3d 154 (2d Cir. 2006) [reversed denial of first motion to reopen regarding numerical and time limits where second counsel did not timely file motion to reopen but argued that first counsel was ineffective and respondent was diligent in hiring second and third counsel]; *Ray v. Gonzales,* 439 F.3d 582, 588–92 (9th Cir. 2006) [both the numerical and time limitations on motions to reopen should be tolled where two attorneys failed to properly file motions to reopen and their performances were so poor that there is a presumption of prejudice because they prevented respondent from reasonably presenting his case]; *Singh v. Gonzales,* 416 F.3d 1006, 1015 (9th Cir. 2005) [remanded to BIA where BIA time barred a motion based upon ineffective assistance and equitable tolling where lawyer failed to file brief or specify grounds for appeal on form]; *Pervaiz v. Gonzales,* 405 F.3d 488, 490 (7th Cir. 2005) [because the 180-day period to reopen an *in absentia* determination is not jurisdictional, but a statute of limitations, it may be tolled for ineffective assistance of counsel where counsel failed to distinguish between the adequacy of notice and his client's failure to receive notice of a change in the time of the hearing]; *Borges v. Gonzales,* 402 F.3d 398 (3d Cir. 2005) [if notary working with lawyer committed fraud then 180 period is tolled, then motion to reopen is timely filed, and ineffectiveness of counsel would thereafter constitute an exceptional circumstance to rescind order; *Bejar* distinguished]; *Singh v. Ashcroft,* 367 F.3d 1182, 1185–86 (9th Cir. 2004) [where respondent filed motion to reopen on 91st day, the time limit for filing was equitably tolled due to former counsel's ineffective assistance in not filing brief resulting in summary dismissal]; *Iturribarria v. INS,* 321 F.3d 889, 897–99 (9th Cir. 2003) [90-day period for motion to reopen was equitably tolled until respondent met with his new counsel and became aware of previous counsel ineffectiveness, but no showing of prejudice was found in failure to file timely suspension application]; *Riley v. INS,* 310 F.3d 1253, 1257–58 (10th Cir. 2002) [time limitation for filling motion to reopen may be equitably tolled for ineffective assistance of counsel and case will be remanded to BIA to determine respondent's due diligence and compliance with *Lozada* criteria]; *Rodriguez-Lariz v. INS,* 282 F.3d 1218, 1223–26 (9th Cir. 2002) [numerical limitation on motions to reopen where ineffective assistance of counsel in failure to file for suspension]; *Varela v. INS,* 204 F.3d 1237 (9th Cir. 2000) [numerical limitation on motions to reopen is equitably tolled where second motion was filed after person was defrauded by notary purporting to provide legal representation];

No Tolling Because No Due Diligence—Most circuit courts will engage in a two-step analysis to determine tolling for ineffective assistance of counsel. First, the court must determine whether and when the ineffective assistance was or should have been discovered by a reasonable person. Second, the court must determine whether the person exercised due diligence in filing the motion to reopen after discovering the ineffective representation. *Wang v. Board of Immigration Appeals,* 508 F.3d 710, 715 (2d Cir. 2007) [upheld denial of motion to reopen where petitioner waited 8 months after learning of ineffective assistance and 5 months after complying with *Lozada* to file motion]. *See also Yuan Gao v. Mukasey,* 519 F.3d 376 (7th Cir. 2008) [a 75-day wait to file motion to reopen was deemed to be lack of due diligence]; *Singh v. Gonzales,* 491 F.3d 1090, 1096–97 (9th Cir. 2007) [upheld lack of due diligence where respondent waited approximately six months to take any action with a new lawyer after he became suspicious]; *Tapia-Martinez v. Gonzales,* 482 F.3d 417, 423–24 (6th Cir. 2007) [equitable tolling not applied to numerical limitations where respondent failed to exercise due diligence and file motions regarding her former lawyers]; *Valeriano v. Gonzales,* 474 F.3d 669 (9th Cir. 2007) [no equitable tolling where respondent's new counsel waited approximately 7 months, after filing *Lozada* complaint, to try and get district counsel to agree to joint motion to reopen]; *Habchy v. Gonzales,* 471 F.3d 858, 864–66 (8th Cir. 2006) [no equitable tolling where respondent's argument is that he lost the opportunity to reopen his case because of his own *pro se* initial motion to reopen]; *Patel v. Gonzales,* 442 F.3d 1011 (7th Cir. 2006) [court upheld BIA decision not to allow equitable tolling where respondent family failed to exercise due diligence as they waited almost 2 years to file motion to reopen based upon ineffective assistance]; *Cekic v. INS,* 435 F.3d 167 (2d Cir. 2006) [court would not toll deadline for filing motion to reopen due to ineffective assistance of counsel where respondent failed to exercise due diligence by waiting two years beyond the time they should have known for filing motion]; *Galvez Pineda v. Gonzales,* 427 F.3d 833, 838–39 (10th Cir. 2005) [although equitable tolling was appropriate for ineffective assistance, the motion to reopen under *Lozada* was properly denied for lack of due diligence when it was not filed within 90 days of receipt of the administrative record]; *Mahmood v. Gonzales,* 427 F.3d 248 (3d Cir. 2005) [recognized equitable tolling for ineffective assistance but denied petition for lack of due diligence by respondent]; *Chen v. Gonzales,* 415 F.3d 151, 153–54 (1st Cir. 2005) [denial of equitable tolling affirmed in Chinese family planning case where BIA found that respondent's could have raised ineffective assistance in first motion to reopen and therefore failed to exercise due diligence for tolling]; *Hernandez-Moran v. Gonzales,* 408 F.3d 496 (8th Cir. 2005) [court declined to toll 90-day period for motion to reopen where respondent failed to comply with *Lozada* and there was no showing of extraordinary circumstances beyond his control]; *Kanyi v. Gonzales,* 406 F.3d 1087, 1090–91 (8th Cir. 2005) [court did not decide equitable tolling of 180-day period for *in absentia* reopening because respondent did not act with due diligence]; *Scorteanu v. INS,* 339 F.3d 407, 412–14 (6th Cir. 2003) [where respondent failed to file motion to reopen within 180 days after he learned of prior lawyer's misfeasance the doctrine of equitable tolling did not apply because of lack of due diligence]; *Iavorski v. INS,* 232 F.3d 124 (2d Cir. 2000) [finding that 90-day time limitation may be equitably tolled because it is not jurisdictional but denying tolling on facts where counsel never filed appeal because Respondent did not act with due diligence]; *Mejia-Rodriguez v. Reno,* 178 F.3d 1139 (11th Cir. 1999) [upholding 90-day time limitation as not raising a constitutional concern even if person suffered a constitutional violation].

No Tolling Because Filing Period is Jurisdictional—Only the Eleventh circuit has adhered to the view that there is no equitable tolling for ineffective assistance of counsel on the theory that the 90/180 day period is jurisdictional. *Abidi v. U.S. Att'y Gen.,* 430 F.3d 1148 (11th Cir. 2005) [followed *Anin* and found that 90-day period to reopen could not be equitably tolled for ineffective assistance of counsel and failure to file motion to reopen within 90 days was jurisdictional]; *Dakane v. U.S. Att'y Gen.,* 399 F.3d 1269, 1272–73 n.3 (11th Cir. 2005) [no equitable tolling for ineffective counsel's failure to file appeal timely as issue is jurisdictional]; *Anin v. Reno,* 188 F.3d 1273, 1278–79 (11th Cir. 1999) *affirming Matter of A-A-,* 22 I&N Dec. 140 (BIA 1998) [the exceptional circumstance claim based upon counsel's failure to inform client of deportation hearing may not be heard because it was not brought within the 180-day period and that period is jurisdictional]. *But see generally Huerta v. Gonzales,* 443 F.3d 753 (10th Cir. 2006) [following *Eberhart v. U.S.,* 546 U.S. 12 (2005), and discussing difference between jurisdictional rules and mandatory claim-processing rules including the 30 day appeal period to the BIA which the court did not regard as jurisdictional]. There may also be a weakening of the 11th Circuit position. *Pereira v. U.S. Att'y Gen.,* 258 Fed. Appx. 277, 279-80 (11th Cir. 2007) [in unpublished decision seeking to distinguish *Anin* and *Abidi* as *dicta*].

(m) Exhaustion Requirement—The courts may not consider an ineffective assistance of counsel claim unless it was raised before the BIA either directly or through a motion to reopen. *Singh v. Gonzales,* 499 F.3d 969, 974 (9th Cir. 2007) [claim that first lawyer was ineffective because he made unauthorized changes to asylum application could have been raised at removal hearing by second lawyer]; *Puga v. Chertoff,* 488 F.3d 812 (9th Cir. 2007) [court would not address ineffective assistance of counsel claim because respondent failed to raise it in a motion to reopen before the BIA]; *Galvez Pineda v. Gonzales,* 427 F.3d 833, 837–38 (10th Cir. 2005) [where respondent timely appealed BIA's summary dismissal for failure to file brief and argued ineffective assistance of counsel, the court found the issue was not exhausted and respondent had to file a timely motion to reopen pursuant to *Lozada* and allow the BIA to rule]; *Etchu-Njang v. Gonzales,* 403 F.3d 577, 581–85 (8th Cir. 2005) [appellant was required to exhaust administrative remedies before raising ineffective assistance and no due process claim where ineffective assistance arose out of failure to seek discretionary relief of cancellation]; *Goonsuwan v. Ashcroft,* 252 F.3d 383 (5th Cir. 2001) [habeas dismissed because ineffective assistance of counsel claim had to be raised by motion to reopen before BIA in transitional rule case governed by 106(c) exhaustion requirement]; *Bernal-Vallejo v. INS,* 195 F.3d 56, 63–65 (1st Cir. 1999) [failure to raise ineffective assistance of counsel by way of motion to reopen barred claim in Court of Appeals even where ineffective counsel was attorney at BIA as well as IJ]; *Akinwunmi v. INS,* 194 F.3d 1340 (10th Cir. 1999) [same]. However, the BIA has been reversed for inconsistently applying the motion to reopen rule to deny an ineffective assistance of counsel claim. *Osei v. INS,* 305 F.3d 1205 (10th Cir. 2002) [reversed BIA denial of motion to reopen where BIA interpreted 8 C.F.R. §3.2(c)(1) to require production of newly discovered evidence despite ineffective assistance of counsel claim].

(n) Motion to Reopen Standard—Where ineffective assistance of counsel has been raised, the BIA has not required the production of new evidence under 8 C.F.R. §1003.2(c)(1) to reopen the proceedings. *Matter of N-K- & V-S-,* 21 I&N Dec. 879, 880 (BIA 1977); *Matter of Lozada,* 19 I&N Dec. 637, 639 (BIA), *aff'd,* 857 F.2d 10 (1st Cir. 1988); *Osei v. INS,* 305 F.3d 1205 (10th Cir. 2002) [BIA reversed where it required the production of new evidence for a motion based upon ineffective assistance of counsel]. However, the movant must show prejudice and therefore must produce evidence regarding his claim. *Canaveral v. Ashcroft,* 385 F.3d 40, 46 (1st Cir. 2004) [movant's claim against nonlawyer who committed fraud even if deemed ineffective assistance of counsel was insufficient because there was no showing of prejudice regarding CAT claim]. In addition, failure of counsel to raise an asylum/CAT/withholding claim before the IJ or BIA when there was an opportunity to do so, may waive the right and prevent a motion to reopen from being granted even if ineffective assistance is raised. *Maindrond v. Ashcroft,* 385 F.3d 98, 100–01 (1st Cir. 2004) [denial of motion to reopen for CAT upheld where movant was represented by counsel before IJ and BIA]. But the applicant need not show that he would win his case to obtain a motion to reopen. *Fadiga v. Attorney General USA,* 488 F.3d 142, 157–63 (3d Cir. 2007) [where BIA applied a clear probability standard in denying motion to reopen asylum claim from Guinea instead of applying a "reasonable probability" standard regarding ineffective assistance of counsel (*i.e.*, but for counsel's ineffective assistance there was a reasonable probability that the outcome would have been different) the court reversed and ordered the case reopened]; *Maravilla Maravilla v. Ashcroft,* 381 F.3d 855, 858 (9th Cir. 2004) [reversed BIA denial of motion to reopen for ineffective assistance of counsel where they improperly analyzed the standard for ineffective assistance of counsel and required respondent to show that he would win his case rather than that his claim may have been affected by counsel's ineffective assistance]. And the Board's claim that lawyer's actions were merely a strategic decision is reviewable under an abuse of discretion standard. *Mai v. Gonzales,* 473 F.3d 162, 165–67 (5th Cir. 2007) [reversed BIA denial of motion to reopen for ineffective assistance despite BIA's claim that the lawyer made a strategic decision when he admitted two grounds of removal where one required a §212(c) waiver and the second a waiver under §240A because once §212(c) granted for the first ground §240A was unavailable for the second].

(o) No Sixth Amendment Right—Although ineffective assistance of counsel is often considered a violation of due process under the Fifth Amendment, there may not be a Sixth Amendment right to counsel as a result of *U.S. v. Gouveia*, 467 U.S. 180 (1984) [no Sixth Amendment right to appointment of counsel for indigent inmates subject to admin. confinement during investigation of prison crimes]. *Accord Mantell v. INS*, 798 F.2d 124 (5th Cir. 1986). *See also Prichard-Ciriza v. INS*, 978 F.2d 219 (5th Cir. 1992); *Trench v. INS*, 783 F.2d 181, 183 (10th Cir.), *cert. denied*, 479 U.S. 961 (1986).

(2) Waiver of Right to Counsel—Denial of right where no intelligent or knowing waiver is made. *Hernandez-Gil v. Gonzales,* 476 F.3d 803, 806 (9th Cir. 2007) [where respondent requested that hearing be continued because lawyer was not present, although in the building, the IJ's denial of a continuance was a violation of respondent's right to counsel as he did not voluntarily waive counsel's presence and IJ had responsibility to take reasonable steps to ensure right to counsel]; *Biwot v. Gonzales,* 403 F.3d 1094, 1097–98 (9th Cir. 2005) [where respondent denied counsel and because of it he labored under the impression that he had no choice but to waive appeal, court retained jurisdiction on the denial of counsel claim and reversed removal order]; *Baltazar-Alcazar v. INS,* 386 F.3d 940 (9th Cir. 2004) [where IJ barred lawyer from his courtroom without a hearing and then gave respondents the Hobson's choice of undoing the consolidation of their cases or proceeding *pro se* without the lawyer of their choice, their waiver of counsel was not knowing or voluntary]; *Tawadrus v. Ashcroft,* 364 F.3d 1099 (9th Cir. 2004) [respondent did not intelligently and knowingly waive right to counsel and his due process rights were violated where his lawyer withdrew at the hearing and respondent was required to go forward with asylum claim without counsel on two hours notice]; *Montilla v. INS*, 926

F.2d 162 (2d Cir. 1991) [IJ may not conduct deportation hearing absent a clear waiver because case is complex and respondent not informed of his rights]. In order for a waiver to be valid an IJ must: (1) Inquire specifically of respondent about whether s/he wishes to continue without a lawyer and (2) receive a knowing, intelligent and voluntary affirmative response. *See e.g., Tawadrus v. Ashcroft,* 364 F.3d at 1103; *U.S. v. Mendoza-Lopez*, 481 U.S. 828, 107 S.Ct. 2148 (1987) [no waiver of right to appeal where there was no considered judgment and where aliens not told of their eligibility for suspension]; *Reyes-Palacios v. INS*, 836 F.2d 1154 (9th Cir. 1988); *Partible v. INS*, 600 F.2d 1094 (5th Cir. 1979); *Castro-O'Ryan v. INS*, 847 F.2d 1307 (9th Cir. 1987); *Corado-Rodriguez v. INS*, 828 F.2d 622 (9th Cir.), *amended and superseded*, 841 F.2d 865 (9th Cir. 1987) [denial of effective assistance where nonlawyer representative discouraged applicant for asylum to apply]. *U.S. v. Gonzalez-Mendoza*, 985 F.2d 1014, 1017 (9th Cir. 1993) [government has burden to prove that person intentionally relinquished or abandoned a known right or privilege]; *U.S. v. Lopez-Vasquez*, 1 F.3d 751 (9th Cir. 1993) [courts indulge every reasonable presumption against waiver]; *Cf. Bhiski v. Ashcroft,* 373 F.3d 363, 369–70 (3d Cir. 2004) [where respondent did not answer IJ's questions as to whether he would proceed without counsel, the court found it was too flimsy a foundation to argue a due process violation].

(3) Appointed Counsel—There may be a right to appointed counsel under Criminal Justice Act. *Johnson v. Ashcroft,* 378 F.3d 164, 169 n.5 (2d Cir. 2004) [noting appointment of counsel under the CJA to do appeal in circuit court]; *Saldina v. Thornburgh*, 775 F.Supp. 507 (D. Conn. 1991) [granting CJA appointment]; *Roman v. Ashcroft*, 162 F.Supp.2d 755 (N.D. Ohio. 2001) [citing to 18 U.S.C. §3006A(a)(2)(B) and CJA PLA §IV(a)(2) the Court found the CJA applied where habeas petitioner challenging constitutionality of mandatory detention]. *But see Perez-Perez v. Hanberry*, 781 F.2d 1477 (11th Cir. 1986) [rejected use of CJA counsel for parole hearing concerning release]. No *per se* right to appointed counsel. *Aguilera-Enriquez v. INS*, 516 F.2d 565 (6th Cir.), *cert. denied*, 423 U.S. 1050 (1976). *But see* dissent by DeMascio, J. in *Aguilera-Enriquez, supra.* There may be a right to appointed counsel in federal proceedings for *in forma pauperis* proceedings. 28 U.S.C. §1915(d). *Santana v. Chandler*, 961 F.2d 514 (5th Cir. 1992). But no constitutional right to appointed counsel in habeas proceeding. *Lemeshko v. Wrona,* 325 F.Supp.2d 778, 787 (E.D Mich. 2004) [*Pro se* habeas petitioner had no constitutional right to counsel].

(4) Transfer of Client Away from Lawyer—No *per se* right to prevent transfer of respondent away from his counsel. *Aguilar v. ICE,* 510 F.3d 1 (1st Cir. 2007) [no substantive due process right was violated in regard to ICE's interference in parent's relationship with their children and no pattern and practice claim may be brought to challenge ICE raids that resulted in precluding counsel, transferring respondents out of state and away from counsel, and depriving them of bond because these claims must be brought individually as INA §242(b)(9) requires]; *Committee of Central American Refugees v. INS*, 795 F.2d 1434 (9th Cir. 1986), *modified*, 807 F.2d 769 (9th Cir. 1986) [rejects constitutional and statutory right to prevent transfer of aliens where no ongoing attorney-client relationship]; *Sasso v. Milhollan*, 735 F.Supp. 1045 (S.D. Fla. 1990). No right to be detained where respondent's ability to obtain representation is the greatest. *Gandarillas-Zambrana v. BIA*, 44 F.3d 1251, 1256 (4th Cir. 1995); *Avramenkov v. INS,* 99 F.Supp.2d 210, 213–15 (D. Conn. 2000) [jurisdiction to contest transfer barred by 242(a)(2)(B)(ii) and no due process violation on interference with counsel or hindering witness absent factual showing]. *But see Orantes-Hernandez v. Thornburgh*, 919 F.2d 549, 566–67 (9th Cir. 1990) [distinguishing *Committee of Central American Refugees*]; *Louis v. Meissner*, 530 F.Supp. 924 (S.D. Fla. 1981). Right to have counsel is part of legislative history. *Castro-O'Ryan v. INS*, 847 F.2d 1307 (9th Cir. 1987) (*en banc*) [legislative history of INA §292 confirms Congress' intent to give the alien the right to have counsel at his or her own expense]. ICE has established standards and procedures for transfer of persons in ICE custody. *See* ICE Transfer Standards (June 16, 2004), *published on* AILA InfoNet at Doc. No. 04092167. These standards require that respondent's counsel who has a G-28 on file be notified of the transfer of his client *after* the client is en route. ICE Transfer Standards at ¶ III.

(5) Limited Appearances—No limited appearance of counsel where objection raised as to attorney's authority. *Matter of Velasquez*, 19 I&N Dec. 377 (BIA 1986). However, EOIR now recognizes that an IJ may allow a limited appearance, and that an attorney may appear for a specific hearing "on behalf of" another counsel. Immigration Court Practice Manual at 2.3(d), (j). Withdrawal of representation must be accomplished by written or oral motion. 8 C.F.R. §1003.17(b). *Matter of Rosales*, 19 I&N Dec. 655 (BIA 1988). Some authority indicates that counsel does not need to submit G-28 (now EOIR-28) to represent applicant. *Martinez-Zelaya v. INS*, 841 F.2d 294, 296 (9th Cir. 1988), but EOIR disagrees. Immigration Court Practice Manual at 2.1(b). There is no longer a signature required by the respondent on the EOIR-28, because there is no longer a signature line on the form for the respondent. If counsel has been the subject of disciplinary actions or other restrictions on his or her practice in *any* state, s/he must disclose it on the G-28 and EOIR-27/28, *Matter of Sparrow*, 20 I&N Dec. 920 (BIA 1994). If counsel changes his address, EOIR requires him to file new EOIR-27s in each case. EOIR Responses to EOIR/AILA Liaison Questions of Meeting Held Mar. 22, 2001(Q. 4), *reprinted in* 20 *AILA Monthly Mailing* 397 (July/Aug. 2001), *published on* AILA InfoNet at Doc. No. 01050902 (May 9, 2001). Counsel is obligated to file a EOIR-28 with the IJ even if he has filed a G-28 with the Service. *Ghounem v. Ashcroft,* 378 F.3d 740, 742 n.2 (8th Cir. 2004).

(6) Monitoring Attorney-Client Communications—The AG has put in place regulations that permit the monitoring of attorney-client communications including mail where, based upon information from the head of a federal law enforcement or intelligence agency, the AG believes that "it has substantial reason to believe that a particular inmate may use communications with attorneys or their agents to further or facilitate acts of violence or terrorism." 28 C.F.R. §501.3(d); 66 Fed. Reg. 55062–66 (Oct. 31, 2001). Except in the case of court authorization, prior to monitoring an attorney's conversations/mail with his client the regulation provides that written notice be given to the inmate and his attorney the reason for the monitoring and that the conversations are not protected by the attorney-client privilege. §501.3(d)(2).

(7) Notice to Counsel—Notice to counsel representing alien may be deemed sufficient notice to alien. *Sewak v. INS,* 900 F.2d 667, 670 n.6 ; *Tobeth-Tangang v. Gonzales,* 440 F.3d 537 (1st Cir. 2006) [motion to reopen BIA proceedings was denied where BIA decision was sent to respondent's attorney who never received it because he changed his address and did not submit an EOIR-33 pursuant to 8 C.F.R. §1003.38(e)]; *Wijeratne v. INS*, 961 F.2d 1344, 1347 (7th Cir. 1992). However, where the respondent insisted that notice went to an attorney who did not represent him, the notice is insufficient and respondent's due process rights could be implicated. *Sewak, supra*. The Service has also been taken to task for failing to provide notice to counsel in regard to proceedings (naturalization) for client. *Reeves v. Morschorak*, Case No. CV 92-2937 (C.D. Cal. July 7, 1992), *reported in* 11 *AILA Monthly Mailing* 679 (Sept. 1992). INS guidelines provided that an INS agent should notify attorney if they intended to interview her client. But such guidelines are not statutory and may not bar evidence obtained from illegal questioning. *U.S. v. Soto-Ornelas*, 863 F.2d 1487 (10th Cir. 1988).

(8) Admission/Stipulation by Counsel—"Absent egregious circumstances, a distinct and formal admission made before, during or even after a proceeding by an attorney acting in his professional capacity binds his client as a judicial admission." *Matter of Velasquez*, 19 I&N Dec. 377, 382 (BIA 1986); *Karim v. Gonzales,* 424 F.3d 109 (1st Cir. 2005) [where lawyer concedes removability and new lawyer asks to amend response to NTA to withdraw concession without offering any reason, court upheld BIA's brief denial]; *De Zavala v. Ashcroft,* 385 F.3d 879 (5th Cir. 2004) [due process was not violated where respondent's counsel conceded charge after respondent was incorrectly charged as inadmissible at entry as a nonimmigrant when she was inadmissible as an immigrant because there was no prejudice]; *Selimi v. INS,* 312 F.3d 854, 860–61 (7th Cir. 2002) [admission as to excludability by counsel to obtain change of venue barred insufficiency of evidence claim]; *Rarogal v. INS*, 42 F.3d 570 (9th Cir. 1994) [IJ bound by INS concession in INA §212(c) case that respondent was rehabilitated and deserved relief]; *Gordon v. INS*,

36 F.3d 249 (2d Cir. 1994) [where INS stipulates to stay of deportation, respondent does not become a fugitive by failing to comply with bag and baggage letter]; *Ali v. Reno*, 829 F.Supp. 1415, 1424–25 (S.D.N.Y. 1993), *aff'd*, 22 F.3d 442 (2d Cir. 1994). This includes tactical actions by counsel in the absence of egregious circumstances. *Matter of Gawaran*, 20 I&N Dec. 938 (BIA 1995). *See also INS v. Doherty*, 502 U.S. 314, 327, 112 S.Ct. 719 (1992). However, legal determinations may not be the subject of an admission. *Garcia v. Att'y Gen. of the U.S.*, 462 F.3d 287, 290 n.6 (3d Cir. 2006) [an admission that a person committed an aggravated felony and that his attorney did not contest it, is not binding because "the legal classification of prior convictions is not a factual proposition susceptible of admission by a litigant. It is a legal proposition that must be determined by a court…"]. Also counsel's decision to withdraw an application for relief from removal is not considered an admission and he may seek to reinstate it where he did so under a mistaken belief in the facts and he establishes a prima facie case for the relief. *Mendez-Gutierrez v. Ashcroft,* 340 F.3d 865 (9th Cir. 2003) [where applicant's lawyer withdrew asylum claim in the mistaken belief his client was eligible for cancellation, the IJ/BIA erred in not allowing him to reinstate the asylum application after demonstrating a prima facie case]. And even where counsel accepts an IJ's decision as final, the client is not deemed to have made an intelligent and knowing waiver of appeal where the proceedings were not translated. *U.S. v. Ubaldo-Figueroa,* 364 F.3d 1042, 1048 (9th Cir. 2004). *See also U.S. v. Calderon,* 391 F.3d 370, 375 (2d Cir. 2004) [the existence of representation alone is not enough to conclude there was a knowing and intelligent waiver of appeal]. And government counsel's stipulation may be overridden by the AG. *Matter of A-H-,* 23 I&N Dec. 774, 790–91 (A.G. 2005) [the AG has authority to remand a case for additional fact finding as he deems necessary and appropriate including the authority to override a stipulation by the DHS that respondent's life or freedom would be threatened if returned to his home country Algeria].

(9) Waiving Client's Appearance—*Ramos v. Gonzales,* 414 F.3d 800, 804–06 (7th Cir. 2005) [no due process violation where lawyer with EOIR-28 waived client's presence at all hearings and there was no showing of prejudice, despite respondent's claim that IJ should have determined that lawyer was not authorized to do so].

(10) Withdrawal of Counsel—Although an IJ has wide discretion to allow a counsel to withdraw, she must take into consideration the need to protect the client. *Immigration Judge's Benchbook* I:8:I.D.5. A "lawyer's professional responsibility upon withdrawal includes the duty to take reasonable steps to avoid foreseeable prejudice to the rights of the client, including giving notice to the client, allowing time for the employment of other counsel, and delivering to the client all papers and property to which the client is entitled. Model Rules of Prof. Conduct R. 1.16(d)." *Gjeci v. Gonzales,* 451 F.3d 416, 421–23 (7th Cir. 2006) [where IJ failed to take steps to protect respondent's interests before permitting withdrawal of counsel and then denied respondent a continuance, due process was violated].

7.e. Government Counsel—The obligation of government counsel is to see that the law is observed, not in victory or defeat. *Reid v. INS*, 949 F.2d 287 (9th Cir. 1991) ["Counsel for the government has an interest only in the law being observed, not in victory or defeat in any particular litigation"]; *Freeport-McMoRan Oil & Gas Co. v. F.E.R.C.*, 962 F.2d 45, 48 (D.C. Cir. 1992) [citing the ABA Code of Professional Responsibility holding government lawyers to a higher standard than private lawyers and finding "it astonishing that an attorney for a federal administrative agency could so unblushingly deny that a government lawyer has obligations that might sometimes trump the desire to pound an applicant into submission"]. The DHS counsel also has an obligation to "uphold international refugee law, including the United States' obligation to extend refuge where such refuge is warranted.... [T]he government wins when justice is done. *Matter of S-M-J-,* 21 I&N Dec. 722, 727 (BIA 1997) [trial attorney job as stated in the Handbook for Trial Attorney §1.3 (1964) requires that "the respondent should be aided in obtaining any procedural rights or benefits required by the statute, regulation and controlling court decision."]. Government counsel's obligations also extend to the preparation of the immigration court's transcript where it is flawed or missing. *Ortiz-Salas v. INS*, 992 F.2d 105, 107 (7th Cir. 1993) [government counsel's failure to remedy inadequate transcript described as prosecutorial misconduct]. In denaturalization cases based on proof of criminal activities, government counsel must follow the *Brady* rule and disclose all exculpatory evidence. *Demjanjuk v. Petrovsky*, 10 F.3d 338, 353 (6th Cir. 1993). At least one court has chastised government counsel for making arguments in an asylum case that are either "disingenuous or embarrassingly naïve." *Lusingo v. Gonzales,* 420 F.3d 193, 201–02 (3d Cir. 2005) [court disturbed at a government argument in an asylum case that relied on statements from the Ambassador of that country that no harm would come to the asylum applicant].

7.f. Unauthorized Practice of Law—The unauthorized practice of law is a matter of state law. State bars have enjoined UPL. *Florida Bar v. Corpa Immigration*, 642 So.2d 548 (Fla. 1994); *Cincinnati Bar Assn. v. Massengale*, 568 N.E.2d 1222 (Ohio 1991); *Matter of Taton*, 456 N.W.2d 717 (Minn. 1990). DHS/DOJ regulations under 8 C.F.R. §§292, 1292 also bar "visa consultants or any other person who is not a licensed attorney or authorized representative pursuant to 8 C.F.R. §292" from engaging in representation. Legal Opinion, Rees, General Counsel, CO 292.2 (June 9, 1992), *reprinted in* 69 No. 25 *Interpreter Releases* 803, 823–28 (July 6, 1992). "Representation" and "practice" and "preparation" are specifically defined in the regulations. 8 C.F.R. §§1.1(i) & (k), 1001.1(i) & (k). *See also* Memo, Virtue, Acting Gen. Counsel (Aug. 6, 1993), *reprinted in* 70 No. 35 *Interpreter Releases* 1205, 1213–18 (Sept. 13, 1993) [INS cannot authorize or endorse activity of nonaccredited organizations]; Letter, Rees, General Counsel, CO 292.2 (May 20, 1993), *reprinted in* 72 No. 37 *Interpreter Releases* 1311, 1321–24 (Sept. 25, 1995) [selecting forms does constitute giving legal advice]. DOS regulations, however, do not bar visa consultants. Letter, Adams, Deputy Asst. Secy. of State for Visa Services (Dec. 28, 1992), *reprinted in* 70 No. 6 *Interpreter Releases* 181, 196–97 (Feb. 8, 1993). A nonprofit organization may be recognized by the Board to practice before IJs under certain circumstances including the charging of only nominal fees. *Matter of American Paralegal Academy, Inc.*, 19 I&N Dec. 386 (BIA 1986); 8 C.F.R. §§292.2(a), 1292.2(a). The BIA may also withdraw its recognition. *Matter of Baptist Educational Center*, 20 I&N Dec. 723 (BIA 1993). Where adverse evidence and adverse recommendation presented by DD to deny recognition, organization has burden to rebut. *Matter of Chaplain Services, Inc.*, 21 I&N Dec. 578 (BIA 1996).

Law students may represent persons before DHS/ EOIR if they are participating in a legal aid program or clinic conducted by a law school or nonprofit organization under the direct supervision of a faculty member, attorney, or accredited representative, and they are appearing without direct or indirect remuneration from the person they represent. 8 C.F.R. §§292.1(a)(2)(ii)–(iv), 1292.1(a)(2)(ii)–(iv). In contrast, a law graduate need not appear through a legal aid program or clinic as long as s/he is appearing under the supervision of a licensed attorney or accredited representative and is appearing without direct or indirect remuneration from the client. 8 C.F.R. §292.1(a)(2)(iii). The law student and law graduate may be paid as long as they are not paid by the client. The DHS/EOIR official must approve the appearance of the law student or law graduate.

A lawyer who is not a member of the bar in a particular state may nevertheless practice immigration law in that state to the degree he limits the practice exclusively to federal immigration matters. *See generally Sperry v. State of Florida ex rel. Florida Bar,* 373 U.S. 379 (1963) [prohibited Florida Bar from enjoining nonlawyer the right to practice exclusively Patent Law in Florida].

7.g. Attorney Sanctions

(1) Contempt—The IJ now has authority to sanction by civil money penalty any action or inaction that is in contempt of the IJ's "proper exercise of authority" under the INA. INA §240(b)(1), 8 U.S.C. §1229a(b)(1).

(2) Frivolous Behavior—INA §240(b)(6), 8 U.S.C. §1229a(b)(6). The AG is directed under IIRIRA to promulgate regulations that (1) define frivolous behavior for which attorneys may be sanctioned; (2) specify the circumstances under which an administrative appeal of a decision or ruling will be considered frivolous and will be summarily dismissed; and impose appropriate sanctions (which may include suspension and disbarment) in the case of frivolous behavior. The regulations shall not limit the authority of the BIA pursuant to 8 C.F.R. §§292.3, 1292.3 to take action with respect to inappropriate behavior.

(3) Grounds for Discipline—Regulations now provide for disciplinary sanctions against an attorney who: (1) charges "grossly excessive" fees; (2) bribes or attempts to bribe, coerces, or attempts to coerce by any means whatsoever any person in connection with a case; (3) makes a false statement of material fact or law; (4) solicits professional employment through in-person or live telephone contact or through the use of runners; (5) is subject to a final order of disbarment or suspension or has resigned with an admission of misconduct; *Matter of Truong,* 24 I&N Dec. 52 (BIA 2006) [seven year suspension upheld following New York state disbarment]; *Matter of Ramos,* 23 I&N Dec. 843 (BIA 2005) [followed rebuttable presumption in *Gadda* and disbarred attorney from practice before BIA, IJ and DHS]; *Matter of Gadda,* 23 I&N Dec. 645, 648 (BIA 2003) [where proceeding brought based on a final order of disbarment by the state, such an order creates a rebuttable presumption that disciplinary sanctions should follow. 8 C.F.R. §1003.103(b)(2). Such a presumption can be rebutted only upon a showing that the underlying disciplinary proceeding resulted in a deprivation of due process, that there was an infirmity of proof establishing the misconduct, or that discipline would result in injustice]; *Gadda v. Ashcroft,* 363 F.3d 861 (9th Cir. 2004) [state supreme court had jurisdiction to disbar attorney who exclusively practiced immigration law and such action was not preempted]; (6) makes a false or misleading communication about his or her qualifications and services; (7) engages in contumelious or otherwise obnoxious conduct which would constitute contempt of court in a judicial proceeding; (8) has been found guilty of, or pleaded guilty or *nolo contendere* to a serious crime; (9) Falsely certifies a copy of a document as being a true and complete copy of an original; (10) engages in frivolous behavior in a proceeding before an immigration court, the Board, or any other administrative appellate body; (11) engages in conduct that constitutes ineffective assistance of counsel; (12) repeatedly fails to appear for scheduled hearings in a timely manner without good cause; or (13) assists any person, other than a practitioner in the performance of activity that constitutes the unauthorized practice of law. 8 C.F.R. §1003.102(a)– (m).

In regard to "grossly excessive" fees, DOJ commentary on the regulations has recognized that: "Expert jurists in immigration law who command higher fees for their services than other immigration practitioners would not be in violation of the regulations based solely on their fee." 65 Fed. Reg. 39513, 39518 (June 27, 2000). The commentary also notes that contumelious or obnoxious conduct requires a "finding of contempt [as a] prerequisite to the imposition of disciplinary action pursuant to this subsection." 65 Fed. Reg. at 39518. A "serious crime" under this section includes any felony and also includes any lesser crime involving interference with the administration of justice, false swearing, misrepresentation, fraud, willful failure to file income tax returns, deceit, dishonesty, bribery, extortion, misappropriation, theft, or attempt, conspiracy or solicitation to commit a serious crime. 8 C.F.R. §1003.102(h). Summary disciplinary proceedings cannot be concluded until all direct appeals shall have been completed. 8 C.F.R. §1003.103(b). Frivolous behavior occurs when an attorney "knows or reasonably should have known that his or her actions lack an arguable basis in law or in fact, or are taken for an improper purpose, such as to cause unnecessary delay." 8 C.F.R. §1003.102(j)(1).

(4) Procedures—8 C.F.R. §§292.3, 1003.104–06, 1292.3. Complaints are investigated by DHS when it involves the Service. 65 Fed. Reg. at 39514. The General Counsel of ICE must issue the charge. After the filing of an answer, the case will then be heard by EOIR according to procedures in 8 C.F.R. §§1003.106(a), (b), and (c). When it involves EOIR, the BIA makes the ultimate decision and the G.C. for the EOIR initiates the charges. *Id.* The attorney or representative shall have 30 days to answer. In her answer, the attorney must specifically request a hearing or the hearing officer will simply issue a decision. 8 C.F.R. §1003.105(c)(3). The Chief Immigration Judge shall designate an IJ to hold a hearing and render a decision. 8 C.F.R. §1003.106. *Either* party may appeal the decision to the BIA on an EOIR-45 and the BIA must receive the appeal with the proper fee, as in any appeal, within 30 days of the decision, if oral, or 30 days after mailing if mailed. 8 C.F.R. §1003.106(c). The Board has found that laches is not an affirmative defense in disciplinary proceedings. *Matter of Sparrow*, 20 I&N Dec. 920 (BIA 1994). If a party is expelled from the bar, he may subsequently seek reinstatement. 8 C.F.R. §1003.107.

(5) Sanctions for Violating Protective Order—DOJ has established procedures before the IJ for the admission of documents/information under a protective order which, if disclosed would "harm the national security ... or law enforcement interests of the United States." 8 C.F.R. §1003.46; *Matter of R-S-H, et al.,* 23 I&N Dec. 629 (BIA 2003). National security is defined under INA §219(c)(2), 8 U.S.C. §1189(c)(2) to include "the national defense, foreign relations, or economic interests of the United States." Failure to comply with a protective order issued under this section may result in the suspension of the attorney or accredited representative from practice before the EOIR or Service. 8 C.F.R. §1003.46(i).

(6) Reinstatement—A lawyer may apply for reinstatement if, after the expiration of the suspension period, s/he meets the definition of a lawyer or representative and can show by "clear, unequivocal, and convincing evidence that he or she possesses the moral and professional qualifications…" 8 C.F.R. §1003.107(a)(1). *Matter of Krivonos,* 24 I&N Dec. 292 (BIA 2007) [BIA declined to reinstate a lawyer "at this time" who had been convicted of immigration related fraud despite his reinstatement to the N.Y. Bar]. A lawyer who continues to practice after suspension may face additional sanctions and will not be reinstated after his first suspension is completed. *Matter of Jean-Joseph,* 24 I&N Dec. 294 (BIA 2007) [reinstatement denied to lawyer who continued to make appearances in immigration court after his suspension; BIA ordered he be suspended for 120 days which was twice the original suspension].

(7) The Board has previously sanctioned attorneys—*Matter of Shah,* 24 I&N Dec. 282 (BIA 2007) [attorney who knowingly made false statement on LCA and then used LCA to apply for H-1B on I-129 is subject to discipline for violating 8 C.F.R. §§1003.102(c), 1292.3(b)]; *Matter of Gadda,* 23 I&N Dec. 645 (BIA 2003) [disbarment]; *Matter of Sparrow*, 20 I&N Dec. 920 (BIA 1994); *Matter of De Anda*, 17 I&N Dec. 54 (BIA 1979); *Matter of Solomon*, 16 I&N Dec. 388 (AG 1977); *Matter of Koden*, 15 I&N Dec. 739 (BIA 1976), *aff'd*, 564 F.2d 228 (7th Cir. 1977); *Matter of Bogart*, 15 I&N Dec. 552 (BIA 1976).

(8) Courts Referring Cases to the Bar—In *Stroe v. INS,* 256 F.3d 498, 504 (7th Cir. 2001) the Court denied respondent's ineffective assistance of counsel claim for failure to follow *Lozada* but referred the lawyer's malpractice to the Illinois Bar where the case before the BIA was dismissed for the failure of the first counsel to timely file a brief.

7.h. Criminal charges against counsel related to immigration proceedings—IIRIRA has amended 18 U.S.C. §1546 to potentially ensnare lawyers who assist clients. Under 18 U.S.C. §1546, a lawyer who submits an application, affidavit or other document which "fails to contain any reasonable basis in law or fact" is subject to 10 years in jail. Congress also enacted INA §243(a)(1)(C), 8 U.S.C. §1253(a)(1)(C), which provides that an alien who "conspired, or takes any other action, designed to prevent or hamper ... the alien's departure" within 90 days of a removal order or from the date of final court order or from the date required to appear for a bag-and-baggage letter, is subject to a 4-year sentence and a fine. However, it is not a violation of INA §243(a)(1), 8 U.S.C. §1253(a)(1) to take any proper steps to secure cancellation or exemption from the order of removal or the person's release from custody. INA §243(a)(2), 8 U.S.C. §1253(a)(2). Whether a lawyer could be charged on a conspiracy or abetting theory under this statute is an open question in light of the language of the statute which seeks to convict only "an alien."

7.i. Right to present evidence and cross-examine witnesses—INA §§240(b)(1), (b)(4)(B), 8 U.S.C. §§1229a(b)(1) and (b)(4)(B), 8 C.F.R. §§ 1240.1(c), 1240.10(a)(4). *Tadesse v. Gonzales,* 492 F.3d 905, 909–11 (7th Cir. 2007) [refusal to consider expert's affidavit or testimony to rebut government's document expert and discounting affidavit of applicant's torture counselor, after sending him home without permitting his testimony, violated applicant's rights under INA §240(b)(4)(B)]; *Pronsivakulchai v. Gonzales,* 461 F.3d 903 (7th Cir. 2006) [reversed IJ's finding that respondent was ineligible for asylum on the grounds that there was reason to believe she had committed a drug trafficking crime in Thailand when she was deprived of the right to present evidence rebutting the government's evidence]; *Boyanivskyy v. Gonzales,* 450 F.3d 286 (7th Cir. 2006) [where IJ continued a hearing to a date when he knew respondent's three witnesses could not appear and on that date denied a further continuance and declared the hearing at an end, respondent denied his statutory and regulatory right to present evidence in his asylum case]; *Cham v. Att'y Gen. of the U.S.*, 445 F.3d 683 (3d Cir. 2006) [IJ's conduct violated due process and deprived Gambian asylum application of a fair hearing where IJ assumed application was invalid, nitpicked the application and testimony for inconsistencies and contradictions, prevented applicant from presenting evidence/witnesses, and engaged in conduct that was abusive toward the applicant including preventing him from presenting his testimony by continually interrupting him]; *Sosnovskaia v. Gonzales,* 421 F.3d 589, 592–94 (7th Cir. 2005) [reversed IJ's denial of asylum where s/he ignored the applicant's evidence and failed to give her a final hearing on her claim regarding anti-Semitism in the Ukraine finding that "the procedure that the IJ employed…is an affront to [the applicant's] right to be heard"]; *Zolotukhin v. Gonzales,* 417 F.3d 1073 (9th Cir. 2005) [refusing to hear corroborative testimony from family members and expert testimony and cutting short respondent's testimony deprived him of due process and the right to present evidence in religious persecution claim from Russia]; *Vasha v. Gonzales,* 410 F.3d 863, 872–75 (6th Cir. 2005) [although upholding adverse credibility determination, the court found the IJ's reliance on discussion with law clerk and other information of a witness after evidence was closed was a violation of due process]; *Hernandez-Guadarrama v. Ashcroft,* 394 F.3d 674, 681–83 (9th Cir. 2005) [it was fundamentally unfair to permit hearsay statement to be used against respondent when the government had deported the declarant thereby making her unavailable for cross-examination]; *Kaur v. Ashcroft,* 388 F.3d 734 (9th Cir. 2004) [due process violated where IJ precluded respondent's son from testifying and at the same time faulted her for not offering corroborating evidence at her asylum hearing]; *Kerciku v. INS,* 314 F.3d 913 (7th Cir. 2003) [due process was violated where IJ foreclosed virtually all testimony in asylum hearing after he determined from brief questioning that respondent was not credible]; *Agyeman v. INS,* 296 F.3d 871 (9th Cir. 2002) [IJ violated due process to insist that only the wife's testimony was relevant to the bona fide nature of the marriage when the husband could have brought other documentary evidence]; *Ladha v. INS,* 215 F.3d 889, 903–05 (9th Cir. 2000) [the IJ must mark documents for identification even if he excludes them so there is a record on appeal]; *Podio v. INS,* 153 F.3d 506 (7th Cir. 1998) [where IJ refused to allow asylum applicant to call his siblings as witnesses and where the respondent's counsel was hampered in presenting client's case by IJ taking over questioning, due process was violated]; *Hernandez-Garza v. INS,* 882 F.2d 945, 947–48 (5th Cir. 1989) [where district court denied respondent's counsel the right to cross-examine INS agents that took alien witness' affidavit on his fluency in Spanish it was error]; *Yi v. INS,* 257 F.Supp.2d 791, 797–99 (E.D. Pa. 2003) [IJ's refusal to allow evidence on alternate CAT claim theory that was stated in I-589 violated due process]. *But see Alimi v. Gonzales,* 489 F.3d 829 (7th Cir. 2007) [admission of respondent's statement taken by officer at airport without presenting officer for cross-examination did not violate due process]; *Mapouya v. Gonzales,* 487 F.3d 396, 415–16 (6th Cir. 2007) [refusal to allow respondent to call witnesses in a certain order did not violate due process because respondent could not show that the outcome of the case would have been different]; *Chakir v. Gonzales,* 466 F.3d 563, 567–69 (7th Cir. 2006) [where IJ's conduct was improper and respondent claimed he was precluded from presenting evidence, court found no statutory violation where respondent made no offer of proof and therefore did not show prejudice]; *Vonhm v. Gonzales,* 454 F.3d 825, 829–30 (8th Cir. 2006) [where *pro se* respondent was not advised of right to present evidence at final hearing but was told to bring affidavit and did so, no due process violation]; *Romanishyn v. Attorney General of the U.S.*, 455 F.3d 175, 185–86 (3d Cir. 2006) [IJ's refusal to allow respondent to call more than two witnesses was not a violation of due process because submitting their testimony by affidavit did not render the proceeding fundamentally unfair]; *Roman v. INS,* 233 F.3d 1027, 1032–33 (7th Cir. 2000) [IJ's brusque attitude and curtailing questioning but not preventing it entirely did not violate due process].

The agency also cannot submit documents (*e.g.*, affidavits) that deprive person of cross-examination, notwithstanding admissibility of hearsay, where admission goes to the core of the agency's case. *Alexandrov v. Gonzales,* 442 F.3d 395, 404–07 (6th Cir. 2006) [in Bulgarian asylum claim, IJ violated due process by relying on two highly unreliable hearsay memoranda from the U.S. Embassy in Sofia to prove that respondent's documents were fraudulent]; *Ezeagwuna v. Ashcroft,* 325 F.3d 396, 405–08 (3d Cir. 2003) [reliance on double and triple hearsay letter of Director of Office of Country Reports and Asylum Affairs in DOS to undermine credibility of documentary evidence in asylum/withholding claim violated due process]; *Olabanji v. INS*, 973 F.2d 1232 (5th Cir. 1992); *Cunanan v. INS*, 856 F.2d 1373 (9th Cir. 1988); *Baliza v. INS*, 709 F.2d 1231 (9th Cir. 1983). *Accord Zhen Nan Lin v. DOJ,* 459 F.3d 255, 268–72 (2d Cir. 2006) [BIA's adverse credibility finding that was based upon a consular report that a document was a forgery was reversed where the hearsay report was inherently unreliable because it relied upon statements from Chinese officials and lacked other indicia of reliability]; *Corovic v. Mukasey,* 519 F.3d 90, 95-96 (2d Cir. 2008) [U.S. government's request to Macedonian government to verify documents violated confidentiality provision of 8 C.F.R. §208.6 (now §1208.6) and the court, following *Zhen Nan Lin* prohibited the use of the Macedonian government's report and remanded the case but left open the possibility that the IJ could make the same finding that the document was fraudulent based upon other evidence]. *But see Matter of Lemhammad*, 20 I&N Dec. 316 (BIA 1991); *Rehman v. Gonzales,* 441 F.3d 506 (7th Cir. 2006) [where respondent failed to proffer evidence that he was precluded from presenting when IJ limited examination to three hours, court found no prejudice]; *Doumbia v. Gonzales,* 472 F.3d 957, 962–63 (7th Cir. 2007) [admission of Embassy report without cross-examination in asylum hearing on validity of summonses in Côte d'Ivoire court was not prejudicial or fundamentally unfair under 8 U.S.C. §1229a(b)(4)]; *Ocasio v. Ashcroft,* 375 F.3d 105 (1st Cir. 2004) [court upheld IJ's admission of spouse's affidavit regarding a sham marriage]; *Tamenut v. Ashcroft,* 361 F.3d 1060 (8th Cir. 2004) [where fax from U.S. Consular Section in Ethiopia was used to impeach applicant's claim that he was in jail during periods fax showed he was employed at the consulate, due process was not violated by its submission because he could have rebutted them through his own testimony]; *Nyama v. Ashcroft,* 357 F.3d 812, 816–17 (8th Cir. 2004) [when asylum applications from other applicants with the same story and same alleged parent as respondent were offered to impeach respondent and not for their truth, they were admissible and did not violate respondent's due process rights because he had ample time to rebut them]; *Bustos-Torres v. INS*, 898 F.2d 1053 (5th Cir. 1990) [where hearsay unimpeached it may be admissible]. The right to present witnesses absent a detailed showing of necessity was not prejudiced by transfer of the hearing to Oakdale, Louisiana. *Gandarillas-Zambrana v. BIA*, 44 F.3d 1251, 1256 (4th Cir. 1995). The right to present evidence and cross-examine witnesses is limited where national security information is presented by the government in opposition to the person's admission or request for discretionary relief. INA §240(b)(4)(B). The right to present evidence is also limited by compliance to local rules of court. *Sulaiman v. Gonzales,* 429 F.3d 347, 351 (1st Cir. 2005) [IJ did not err in refusing to admit documents submitted one day late in asylum hearing]; *Galicia v. Ashcroft,* 396 F.3d 446, 448 (1st Cir. 2005) [IJ did not abuse discretion in refusing to admit documents submitted in violation of local rules of court including timing of submission and failure to pre-mark exhibits]. Counsel should not give up right to present evidence. Where IJ off-the-record informed counsel that he need not put on certain evidence because he was going to rule in his favor and the BIA reversed the IJ's decision, counsel was precluded from raising in federal court the inadequacy of the record because he never raised it before the IJ. *Baria v. Reno*, 94 F.3d 1335, 1340 (9th Cir. 1996).

Immigration Court Manual and Presentation of Evidence—EOIR has established a formal set of procedures for the timing, presentation and acceptance of evidence by the IJ. *See Immigration Court Practice Manual* (available at *www.usdoj.gov/eoir*). For example, counsel is required to submit a "criminal history chart" if respondent has more than one conviction [Manual at 3.3(f), 4.16(b)(iii)], and witness lists must now contain a summary, the estimated length, and the language of the testimony [Manual at 3.3(g), 4.16(b)(ii)]. There are also formal rules for the manner in which evidence must be presented, including cover sheets, binding, tabs, and font size [Manual at 3.3(a)].

(1) *Expert Testimony*—As part of the right to present evidence a respondent may present expert testimony. *Tadesse v. Gonzales,* 492 F.3d 905, 909–11 (7th Cir. 2007) [refusal to consider expert's affidavit or testimony to rebut government's document expert was a violation of asylum applicant's right under INA §240(b)(4)(B)]; *Tun v. Gonzales,* 485 F.3d 1014 (8th Cir. 2007) [respondent's due process rights were violated where two experts' testimony was excluded];*Rodriguez Galicia v. Gonzales,* 422 F.3d 529, 538–40 (7th Cir. 2005) [IJ violated due process when he precluded two experts from testifying

regarding Guatemalan asylum claim even though one expert had submitted an affidavit]; *Koval v. Gonzales,* 418 F.3d 798, 806–09 & n.3 (7th Cir. 2005) [reversing IJ's refusal to allow former KGB agent Shvets's expert testimony on persecution of Mormons in Ukraine in light of the IJ's over reliance on the DOS country report despite its questionable admissibility and trustworthiness]; *Lopez-Umanzor v. Gonzales,* 405 F.3d 1049, 1056–58 (9th Cir. 2005) [violation of due process not to permit expert testimony regarding domestic violence where IJ was told that the expert would orally cover matters not in his affidavit and where IJ's claim of insufficient time was belied by his previous decision to have a separate hearing for a government witness]; *McDonald v. Gonzales,* 400 F.3d 684, 687–88 (9th Cir. 2005) [criticizing IJ for failure to allow expert testimony from former state prosecutor as to whether respondent would have been prosecuted for unlawfully voting in Hawaiian election]. In general, expert testimony in federal proceedings is governed by the *Daubert-Kumho Tire Company* standards as expressed in two Supreme Court decisions. *Daubert v. Merrell Dow Pharmaceuticals, Inc.,* 509 U.S. 579 (1993) and *Kumho Tire Company, Ltd. v. Carmichael,* 526 U.S. 137 (1999). The *Daubert* standard, however, may be too strict for administrative (as opposed to federal court) proceedings, but if it is applicable: "There is no ironclad requirement that an academic, to be qualified as an expert witness, must publish academic books or articles in the precise subject matter of her testimony." *Niam v. Ashcroft,* 354 F.3d 652, 660 (7th Cir. 2004) [reversed IJ where he struck expert affidavit on Bulgaria without voir dire of expert on the grounds that expert's major field was Russian banking even though she taught a course on Eastern Europe]. *But see Pasha v. Gonzales,* 433 F.3d 530, 535–46 (7th Cir. 2005) [reversed IJ where government documentary expert was unqualified to provide an opinion on Albanian documents noting that "junk science has no more place in administrative proceedings than in judicial ones"]. The unchallenged testimony of an expert cannot be rejected outright. *Banks v. Gonzales,* 453 F.3d 449, 453–54 (7th Cir. 2006) [IJ erred when he summarized but ignored expert on Liberia who testified that applicant from Krahn tribe would be persecuted and instead relied on his own views without any government expert; court noted that State Department reports are too general and that government needs expert witnesses];*Dia v. Ashcroft,* 353 F.3d 228, 258–59 (3d Cir. 2003) (*en banc*) [where handwriting expert testified that the signatures on passport and visa were not respondent's the IJ could not dismiss the testimony by opining that handwriting analysis is too speculative]. However, there may be no *per se* right to oral testimony of an expert. *Jarbough v. Att'y Gen. of the U.S.,* 483 F.3d 184, 192 (3d Cir. 2007) [in Syrian Druze case, IJ's refusal to grant continuance to allow for expert testimony was not a violation of due process where one expert's article was submitted and where other expert's affidavit was submitted]; *Shmyhelskyy v. Gonzales,* 477 F.3d 474, 482–83 (7th Cir. 2007) [due process not violated where IJ prohibited expert witness regarding abuse and torture from testifying but accepted her affidavit which was not challenged by DHS]; *Djedovic v. Gonzales,* 441 F.3d 547, 550–52 (7th Cir. 2006) [where respondent's counsel sought expert's telephonic testimony 2 days before hearing, the IJ did not violate the INA or due process by refusing telephonic testimony but permitting written or live testimony]; *Paripovic v. Gonzales,* 418 F.3d 240, 246 n.5 (3d Cir. 2005) [due process not violated where IJ refused to grant continuance to allow expert to testify where respondent did not ask for continuance prior to hearing that was in its 8th year]; *Hamid v. Gonzales,* 417 F.3d 642, 645–47 (7th Cir. 2005) [no specific right to present evidence through oral testimony and IJ's refusal to allow live telephonic expert testimony while not precluding an expert affidavit is not a *per se* due process violation and no prejudice demonstrated]. It is within the discretion of the IJ to reject expert testimony. *Almaghzar v. Gonzales,* 457 F.3d 915, 922–23 (9th Cir. 2006) [upheld IJ's determination that expert psychologist lacked credibility when he was unaware of respondent's conviction for distributing drugs but testified he was incapable of functioning in a linear fashion]; *Akinfolarin v. Gonzales,* 423 F.3d 39, 43 (1st Cir. 2005) [it was not error for IJ to refuse to admit psychiatric affidavit where doctor was not present for hearing, where he had a one-time consultation with the respondent that was not a thorough exam, where the affidavit contained information that contradicted respondent's testimony and where the IJ stated she would not give it much credence].

(2) *Polygraph Testimony*—One form of testimony that may be very useful in removal proceedings is polygraph testimony. Such testimony has been admitted in various proceedings. *Lenea v. Lane,* 882 F.2d 1171, 1174 (7th Cir. 1989) [finding polygraph testimony admissible in prison disciplinary proceedings and citing supporting cases]; *U.S. v. Piccinonna,* 885 F.2d 1529, 1535 (11th Cir. 1989) [although affirming the decision not to admit the polygraph results the court found that polygraph evidence is not inadmissible *per se* and stated that "there is no question that in recent years polygraph testing has gained increasingly widespread acceptance as a useful and reliable scientific tool."]; *U.S. v. Gilliard,* 133 F.3d 809 (11th Cir. 1998) [applying *Daubert* standard to determine admissibility of polygraph and finding under the facts it was not an abuse of discretion to deny its admissibility]. A polygraph examination may assist the IJ to determine whether a person has a subjective fear of persecution, but could not be used to establish the objective basis for a well-founded fear. *Goel v. Gonzales,* 490 F.3d 735 (9th Cir. 2007) [motion to reopen to submit polygraph evidence was denied because evidence was not unavailable during prior hearing].

(3) *Telephonic Testimony of Expert and Other Witnesses*—Where IJ denied expert the right to testify telephonically the Court reversed finding the IJ's decision "one of the odder rulings in our experience." *Niam v. Ashcroft,* 354 F.3d 652, 659 (7th Cir. 2004) [IJ agreed to allow telephonic testimony of expert from Dartmouth when the hearing was in Chicago but disallowed the telephonic testimony when he learned she was at an academic conference in Prague]; *Zolotukhin v. Gonzales,* 417 F.3d 1073, 1076 (9th Cir. 2005) [refusing to hear expert's telephonic testimony from Russia where prior motion was filed but IJ did not rule until day of the hearing and then required expert to appear in person or respondent to produce a phone card at her own expense]; *Beltran-Tirado v. INS,* 213 F.3d 1179, 1185–86 (9th Cir. 2000) [telephonic testimony of key witness was "fair"]. However, there may be no *per se* right to oral testimony of an expert. *Djedovic v. Gonzales,* 441 F.3d 547, 550–52 (7th Cir. 2006) [where respondent's counsel sought expert's telephonic testimony 2 days before hearing, the IJ did not violate the INA or due process by refusing telephonic testimony but permitting written or live testimony]; *Hamid v. Gonzales,* 417 F.3d 642, 645–47 (7th Cir. 2005) [no specific right to present evidence through oral testimony and IJ's refusal to allow live telephonic expert testimony while not precluding an expert affidavit is not a *per se* due process violation and no prejudice demonstrated]. A claim that telephonic testimony by a third-party was contrary to 8 C.F.R. §1003.25 has been rejected on the ground that the regulations only bars respondent's telephonic testimony if s/he objects to process. *Akinwande v. Ashcroft,* 380 F.3d 517, 521–22 (1st Cir. 2004) [upheld IJ's decision to allow ex-wife to testify telephonically that respondent's marriage to her was a sham and rejected claim that telephonic testimony of third party witnesses is barred by 8 C.F.R. §1003.25 if the respondent objects].

(4) *Posttraumatic Stress Disorder*—Courts have recognized that Posttraumatic Stress Disorder can affect a person's testimony and where the IJ/BIA failed to recognize its effects on person's asylum testimony, they have reversed the agency. *Fiadjoe v. Att'y Gen. of the U.S.,* 411 F.3d 135, 149–60 (3d Cir. 2005) [reversed BIA denial of asylum to woman from Trokosi sect in Ghana who had been repeatedly physically and sexually abused by her father].

(5) *Failure to Call Witness*—It was impermissible for IJ to draw negative credibility inference where respondent failed to call witness who was available. *Tabaku v. Gonzales,* 425 F.3d 417, 421–22 (7th Cir. 2005) [adverse credibility determination reversed where *inter alia* IJ applied the missing witness rule to witness who was sitting outside of courtroom and could have been called by the IJ].

7.j. Right to Opening Statement and Closing Argument—Denial of opportunity to present opening statement and closing argument may constitute a due process violation. *Gilaj v. Gonzales,* 408 F.3d 275, 290 (6th Cir. 2005) [recognizing right but finding harmless error where respondent failed to demonstrate prejudice].

7.k. Right to request relief—8 C.F.R. §1240.11. Applicant for relief can make request at any time prior to a decision by the IJ and it was error to deny an applicant, after the close of evidence but before a decision, to petition for former INA §241(f)(2) relief as untimely. *Zamora-Morel v. INS*, 905 F.2d 833, 839 (5th Cir. 1990); *Louis-Martin v. Ridge,* 322 F.Supp.2d 556, 561–62 (M.D.Pa. 2004) [despite counsel's failure to file I-589, CAT claim would not be deemed abandoned]. However, if person illegally re-enters U.S. after removal order s/he is not eligible for most forms of relief, except withholding and possibly asylum. INA §241(a)(5), 8 U.S.C. §1231(a)(5). *Alvarenga-Villalobos v. Ashcroft,* 271 F.3d 1169, 1172–73 (9th Cir. 2001) [rejected claim that person subject to INA §241(a)(5) should be allowed to reopen his case in light of the *Magana-Pizano* decision as that decision occurred subsequent to first deportation order]; *Matter of W-C-B-,* 24 I&N Dec. 118, 123 (BIA 2007) [remand from BIA to IJ inappropriate where 8 C.F.R. §1241.8(e) establishes administrative procedure through DHS to apply for withholding]. *But see Leitao v. Reno,* 311 F.3d 453 (1st Cir. 2002) [where person's denial of habeas was appealed and he was deported during pendency of appeal his claim is not moot because he may be permanently barred].

7.1. Security Checks—After Apr. 1, 2005, all persons seeking asylum and various forms of relief from removal, except voluntary departure, must comply with security clearance procedures. 8 C.F.R. §1003.47. The IJ's procedure is set forth at Memo [Interim OPPM 05-03], Creppy, Chief IJ, EOIR, (Mar. 28, 2005), *published on* AILA InfoNet at Doc. No. 05041565 [permitting the IJ to dictate a draft approval outside the presence of the parties if he is awaiting security checks but allowing him to make a final decision if he is denying the case]. Failure to file necessary documentation and comply with the requirements to provide biometrics and other biographical information within the time allowed by the IJ's order constitutes "abandonment of the application and the immigration judge may enter an appropriate order dismissing the application unless the applicant demonstrates that such failure was the result of good cause." 8 C.F.R. §1003.47(c) & (d). An IJ may not grant an application for relief until DHS has reported to the IJ that the appropriate investigation or examination is completed and reported relevant results to the IJ. 8 C.F.R. §1003.47(g). However, failure to act within a reasonable time may subject DHS to injunctive action. *Al Jabari v. Chertoff,* 536 F.Supp.2d 1029 (D. Minn. 2008) [In action to compel DHS to complete the security check involving the grant by an IJ of a marriage hardship waiver to lift conditional residence under 8 U.S.C. §1186a(c)(4), the court determined that although mandamus was unavailable because the statute does not impose a nondiscretionary duty, the APA permitted injunctive relief]. In addition, if the FBI has not completed its name check within 180 days, the IJ may now consider proceeding in light of the new USCIS memo. USCIS takes the position that if the FBI does not complete the name check within 180 days and the application is otherwise approvable "the adjudicator shall approve the I-485, I-601(waiver), I-687(temporary resident under 245A) or I-698 (temporary to permanent resident under 245A) and proceed with card issuance." Memo, Aytes, Assoc. Dir. Domestic Operations, USCIS, HQ70/23 & 70/28.1 (Feb. 4, 2008), *published on* AILA InfoNet at Doc. No. 08020760. The IJ has discretion to determine whether to conduct an additional hearing to consider new evidence if the security checks affect respondent's eligibility, but when there is no new information the IJ may not use the security check procedure as an opportunity to relitigate any issues. The IJ should simply enter an order granting the relief. *Matter of Alcantara-Perez,* 23 I&N Dec. 882 (BIA 2006). However, if new evidence becomes available that would normally support a motion to reopen because the security check revealed new information or because new circumstances developed after a case was remanded from the BIA, such as a marriage to a USC, the IJ may consider the new evidence even if she is barred from reconsidering the BIA's decision. *Matter of M-D-,* 24 I&N Dec. 138 (BIA 2007) [where record was remanded to IJ for security checks pursuant to 8 C.F.R. §1003.47(h) after BIA granted withholding and respondent had married a USC, IJ is authorized to consider adjustment]. In the event the person is granted relief and permanent residency but the name checks subsequently reveal actionable information, "DHS may detain and initiate removal proceedings against the permanent resident." Memo, Aytes, Assoc. Dir. Domestic Operations, USCIS, HQ70/23 & 70/28.1 (Feb. 4, 2008), *published on* AILA InfoNet at Doc. No. 08020760. Prior to Apr. 1, 2005, persons granted relief by the IJ were required to wait for long periods of time without documentation of their status because security checks were only initiated after they obtained the relief and USCIS, post Sept. 11, 2001, would not issue documents indicating LPR status until the checks were completed. This led to litigation. *See e.g., Santillan v. Gonzales,* 388 F.Supp.2d 1065, 1079–82 (N.D. Cal. 2005) [finding government's refusal to provide temporary status documentation to LPRs in proceedings and permanent status documentation within a reasonable time to persons granted relief by IJ was arbitrary and was not permitted by 8 U.S.C. §1304(d)].

(1) Procedure for Security Checks for Persons Filing for Asylum or Other Relief—An applicant seeking relief will be required to forward a photocopy of the application to the Texas Service Center (TSC) or the Nebraska Service Center (NSC). Applications regarding asylum, withholding and CAT are filed with the NSC. Applications for other forms of relief (I-485, EOIR-40, 42A, 42B, and I-881) including former INA §212(c) relief must be filed with TSC. The asylum and other applications must be submitted without attached supporting documentation, with the appropriate fee and the biometric fee, an EOIR-28, and a copy of the instructions. The service centers input the data and notice the applicant to appear at an ASC for biometrics. Subsequent to a grant of relief the respondent will be instructed to make an appointment (via INFOPASS) at the local USCIS office to initiate the process of obtain ID documentation and employment authorization. Memo, Yates, Assoc. Dir. Operations, USCIS, "Executive Office for Immigration Review (EOIR) Processing," (Mar.31, 2005), *published on* AILA InfoNet at Doc. No. 05051164. For persons who filed for relief prior to Apr. 1, 2005, they will be required to appear at a local ASC for biometrics.

7.m. Motions to suppress

(1) If "fundamentally unfair" may still suppress after *Lopez-Mendoza. See in this part* section E (p.278), *supra*. Motion must be specific, detailed and contain affidavits about the events.

(2) No right to separate suppression hearing. *Matter of Benitez*, 19 I&N Dec. 173 (BIA 1984).

(3) Administrative exclusionary rule. Where a regulation exists to benefit respondent, the regulation is violated and the respondent is harmed, the evidence is inadmissible. *Matter of Garcia-Flores*, 17 I&N Dec. 325 (BIA 1980). Evidence may also be suppressed if it violates DHS procedures. *Pieniazek v. Gonzales,* 449 F.3d 792 (7th Cir. 2006) [case remanded to BIA where respondent claimed he was deprived of opportunity to seek suppression of evidence based upon the Attorney General's Guidelines for Undercover Operations].

(4) A motion to suppress, however, may not affect a removal proceeding where the respondent admits the allegations of the NTA before the IJ. *Miguel v. INS,* 359 F.3d 408 (6th Cir. 2004) [even if there was a basis for the motion to suppress the respondent nullified the motion by admitting the elements of the removal charge before the IJ].

7.n. Privilege against self-incrimination

(1) *Kastigar v. U.S.*, 406 U.S. 441, 444 (1972) [may invoke privilege "in any proceeding, civil or criminal, administrative or judicial, investigatory or adjudicatory"]; *Bigby v. INS*, 21 F.3d 1059 (11th Cir. 1994); *Tashnizi v. INS*, 585 F.2d 781 (5th Cir. 1978); *Matter of King and Yang*, 16 I&N Dec. 502 (BIA 1978); *U.S. v. Alderete-Deras*, 743 F.2d 645 (9th Cir. 1984). Can limit the areas in which person wishes to answer questions about. *U.S. v. Soliz*, 129 F.3d 499 (9th Cir. 1997) [it was impermissible for Border Patrol to ask about smuggling where person had to answer only as to his citizenship]. The right against self-incrimination, however, does not extend to fear of foreign prosecution. *U.S. v. Balsys*, 524 U.S. 666, 118 S.Ct. 2218 (1998). Court may draw negative inferences from refusal to testify. *Bilokumsky v. Tod*, 263 U.S. 149, 154 (1923); *U.S. v. Solano-Godines*, 120 F.3d 957, 962 (9th Cir. 1997) *but see Hernandez-Guadarrama v. Ashcroft,* 394 F.3d 674, 680 n.6 (9th Cir. 2005) [where there were differences between the criminal and immigration anti-smuggling statutes, respondent's refusal to testify does not necessarily warrant an adverse inference regarding deportability]. DHS failed to prove alien smuggling under *Woodby* standard where limited evidence was not subject to cross-examination and was insufficiently reliable]. However, where INS offers no other evidence except the respondent's silence it is insufficient to meet its burden by clear, unequivocal and convincing evidence and the burden does not shift to respondent under INA §291. *Matter of Guevara*, 20 I&N Dec. 238 (BIA 1991). Attorney may invoke privilege. *Bigby* [although privilege is generally personal and must be invoked by individual,

his or her lawyer may invoke it where there is no objection that lawyer invoked it and judge assumed it was invoked]; *Matter of Castro-Olmedo*, A43 570 146 (BIA Oct. 22, 1996) (unpublished) [when respondent asserts Fifth Amendment as to identity, IJ cannot proceed *in absentia*]. *But see Garcia-Quintero v. Gonzales,* 455 F.3d 1006, 1019–20 (9th Cir. 2006) [where IJ forbade lawyer from invoking the Fifth Amendment for his client and instead required respondent to assert it as to each question, the IJ's finding of removal based upon respondent's admissions was upheld because attorney could have objected or asked to consult with his client].

(2) Fifth Amendment can be asserted to avoid *inter alia* the following crimes: INA §252(c) [alien crewman overstay]; INA §266(a) [if overstay after 30 days and no fingerprints/registration]; INA §264(e) [18 or over not carrying INS documentation]; INA §266(b) [failing to comply with change of address w/in 10 days under INA §265(a)]; INA §274C(e) [failure to disclose role as document preparer]; INA §275 [EWI]; INA §276 [previously deported and re-entered]; *U.S. v. Pantoja de Garcia*, Case No. 84-391 (S.D. Cal. 1984); 18 U.S.C. §1546 [false statements/fraudulent documents]; 18 U.S.C. §1028(b) [false documents]; 18 U.S.C. §1001 [false statement]; 18 U.S.C. §§911, 1015 [false claim to USC].

7.o. *Miranda v. Arizona,* 384 U.S. 436 (1966) inapplicable—*U.S. v. Solano-Godines*, 120 F.3d 957 (9th Cir. 1997) [did not have to give respondent *Miranda* warnings during deportation hearing]; *U.S. v. Khan,* 324 F.Supp.2d 1177, 1190–91 (D. Colo. 2004 [same]; *U.S. v. Kadem,* 317 F.Supp.2d 239 (W.D.N.Y. 2004 [same]; *U.S. v. Montoya-Robles*, 935 F.Supp. 1196 (D. Utah 1996) [same]; *Bustos-Torres v. INS*, 898 F.2d 1053, 1057 (5th Cir. 1990); *Trias-Hernandez v. INS*, 528 F.2d 366, 368 (9th Cir. 1975); *Alderete-Deras*, *supra*; *Chavez-Raya v. INS*, 519 F.2d 397, 402 (7th Cir. 1975). But INS must follow 8 C.F.R. §287.3. *See also U.S. v. Kiam,* 432 F.3d 524, 528–31 (3d Cir. 2005) [*Miranda* warnings are not necessary when officer is determining admissibility at the border]; *U.S. v. Lopez-Chamu,* 373 F.Supp.2d 1014 (C.D. Cal. 2005) [where ICE officers interviewed defendant in state jail knowing he was previously deported, motion to suppress nationality and citizenship information granted]; *U.S. v. Kadem supra* [although *Miranda* warnings did not have to be given as to questions regarding pedigree (name, place and date of birth), they should have been given as to inquiry into method of entry into country and documentation where Service officer interviewed person while serving criminal sentence];

7.p. Rules of evidence

(1) Rules relaxed in immigration hearing. *Matter of Wadud*, 19 I&N Dec. 182 (BIA 1984) [permit sentencing memo]; 8 C.F.R. §1240.7(a) ["Any oral or written statement which is material and relevant to any issue in the case previously made by the respondent or any other person during any investigation, examination, hearing or trial"]. DHS may now use information on respondent's asylum application as evidence to establish burden of proof in deportation proceedings. 8 C.F.R. §§208.3(c), 1208.3(c). Some circuits have found that evidentiary matters "are not subject to the Federal Rules of Evidence and we review evidentiary rulings by IJs only to determine whether such rulings have resulted in a violation of due process." *Hassan v. Gonzales,* 403 F.3d 429, 435 (6th Cir. 2005) [exclusion of untimely letter of asylum applicant's parents regarding persecutors current actions in looking for applicant did not violate due process]. *Accord Doumbia v. Gonzales,* 472 F.3d 957, 962–63 (7th Cir. 2007) [the Federal Rules of Evidence do not apply and the sole test is whether under 8 U.S.C. §1229a(b)(4) the evidence is probative and fundamentally fair]; *Zerrei v Gonzales,* 471 F.3d 342, 346 (2d Cir. 2006) ["The Federal Rules of Evidence do not apply in removal proceedings" and where respondent's counsel did not object to admission of a copy of respondent's passport at trial, it alone was sufficient to establish deportability as an overstay]. *Cf Leal Santos v. Gonzales,* 495 F.Supp.2d 180, 185 (D. Mass. 2007) [finding the FRE applies in *federal court* in a proceeding for derivative citizenship].

(2) Hearsay admissible—*Alimi v. Gonzales,* 489 F.3d 829 (7th Cir. 2007) [admission of respondent's statement taken by officer at airport without presenting officer for cross-examination did not violate due process]; *Rojas-Garcia v. Ashcroft,* 339 F.3d 814, 823–

24 (9th Cir. 2003) [due process is not violated where inadmissibility determination for "reason to believe" that person is a drug trafficker was based upon hearsay evidence as long as evidence was probative and fundamentally fair]; *Guerrero-Perez v. INS,* 242 F.3d 727, 729 n.2, *rehear'g denied* 256 F.3d 546 (7th Cir. 2001) [I-213 admissible and sufficient to establish removability by clear, unequivocal and convincing evidence]; *Nasir v. INS*, 122 F.3d 484 (7th Cir. 1997) [IJ erred in not admitting asylum applicant's letters verifying memberships in religious sect where he was not given opportunity to present witnesses because of change of venue]; *Espinoza v. INS*, 45 F.3d 308 (9th Cir. 1995) [I-213 admissible even where IJ did not permit cross examination of preparer despite the existence of 2 different handwritings on document and no indication as to who filled it out or when]; *Felzcerek v. INS*, 75 F.3d 112, 116 (2d Cir. 1996) [I-213 and DMV application admissible and may even qualify under hearsay exception, Federal Rule of Evidence 803(8)]; *Rosendo-Ramirez v. INS*, 32 F.3d 1085, 1087–89 (7th Cir. 1994) [I-213 admitted even after court states it "was obviously carelessly drafted"]; *Bustos-Torres v. INS*, 898 F.2d 1053 (5th Cir. 1990) [I-213 admissible even without supporting testimony where officer not present for cross-examination]; *Bauge v. INS*, 7 F.3d 1540, 1543 (10th Cir. 1993) [I-213 admissible with driver's license and passport]; *Tashnizi v. INS*, 585 F.2d 781 (5th Cir. 1978); *Glaros v. INS*, 416 F.2d 441 (5th Cir. 1969) [hearsay admissible when corroborative evidence]; *Matter of Gomez-Gomez,* 23 I&N Dec. 522, 523–27 (BIA 2002) [I-213 admissible and sufficient to establish deportability in *in absentia* case of 8-year-old where person who was allegedly the 8-year-old's father gave the statement]; *Matter of Ponce-Hernandez,* 22 I&N Dec. 784 (BIA 1999) [I-213 admissible and sufficient to establish deportability in *in absentia* hearing involving minor]. *See also, U.S. v. Torres-Villalobos,* 487 F.3d 607, 612–13 (8th Cir. 2007) (and cases cited therein) [conviction upheld for unlawful reentry after deportation despite Crawford challenge to warrants of deportation on the ground that the warrant was testimonial in nature because it attests that someone was deported on a particular date]; *U.S. v. Cervantes-Flores,* 421 F.3d 825, 830–33 (9th Cir. 2005) [Certificate of Nonexistence of Record to prove the AG did not give permission to re-enter U.S. was admissible and did not violate Sixth Amendment Confrontation Clause in criminal case, notwithstanding *Crawford v. Washington,* 541 U.S. 36 (2004) because it was nontestimonial like a business record]. *U.S. v. Earle,* 488 F.3d 537, 541–46 (1st Cir. 2007) [finding that the admission of the CNR, whether or not testimonial, was not harmful].

However, hearsay is only admissible if it is probative and its admission would not be fundamentally unfair. *Corovic v. Mukasey,* 519 F.3d 90, 95-96 (2d Cir. 2008) [U.S. government's request to Macedonian government to verify documents violated confidentiality provision of 8 C.F.R. §208.6 (now §1208.6) and the court, following *Zhen Nan Lin* prohibited the use of the Macedonian government's report and remanded the case but left open the possibility that the IJ could make the same finding that the document was fraudulent based upon other evidence]; *Silva v. Gonzales,* 463 F.3d 68, 72–73 (1st Cir. 2006) [upheld IJ's determination that asylum applicant's reliance on triple hearsay was not probative or reliable when finding respondent lacked credibility]; *Bao v. Gonzales,* 460 F.3d 426, 431–32 (2d Cir. 2006) [reversed IJ's adverse credibility decision in Chinese nationals' coercive family planning claims where IJ would not accept husband's affidavit because he could not be cross-examined but accepted asylum officer's memo of husband's asylum claim although officer could not be cross-examined]; *Zhen Nan Lin v. DOJ,* 459 F.3d 255, 268–72 (2d Cir. 2006) [BIA's adverse credibility finding that was based upon a consular report that a document was a forgery was reversed where the hearsay report was inherently unreliable because it relied upon statements from Chinese officials and lacked other indicia of reliability]; *Gu v. Gonzales,* 454 F.3d 1014, 1021–22 (9th Cir. 2006) [upheld denial of asylum where applicant's testimony, although deemed credible, consisted of hearsay evidence by friend as to what would occur to Gu in China if he returned and the statement, because of its limited probative value, cannot compel asylum]; *Alexandrov v. Gonzales,* 442 F.3d 395, 404–07 (6th Cir. 2006) [in Bulgarian asylum claim, IJ violated due process by relying on 2 highly unreliable hearsay memoranda from the U.S. Embassy in Sofia to prove that respondent's documents were fraudulent and he therefore filed a frivolous asylum claim]; *Hernandez-Guadarrama v.*

Ashcroft, 394 F.3d 674, 680–81 (9th Cir. 2005) [it was fundamentally unfair to permit hearsay statement to be used against respondent when the government had deported the declarant thereby making her unavailable for cross-examination. In addition, where a material statement in an I-213 was based upon another statement not admitted into evidence, the I-213 was not probative, was of no independent value and was entitled to no evidentiary weight]; *Ezeagwuna v. Ashcroft,* 325 F.3d 396, 405–08 (3d Cir. 2003) [reliance on double and triple hearsay letter of Director of Office of Country Reports and Asylum Affairs in DOS to undermine credibility of documentary evidence in asylum/withholding claim violated due process]; *Saidane v. INS*, 129 F.3d 1063 (9th Cir. 1997) [INS use of wife's affidavit to demonstrate sham marriage while declining to call her, rendered hearsay fundamentally unfair and denial of due process where wife refused to honor respondent's subpoena]; *Murphy v. INS*, 54 F.3d 605 (9th Cir. 1995) [I-213 and statement of INS officer containing double hearsay should not have been accorded any weight, nor used to establish charge by clear, convincing and unequivocal evidence]; *Olabanji v. INS*, 973 F.2d 1232 (5th Cir. 1992) [where affidavits of spouse who claimed marriage was fraudulent and handwriting expert who claimed spouse's signature on petition was fraudulent were unavailable for cross-examination, deportation order reversed]; *Hernandez-Garza v. INS*, 882 F.2d 945 (5th Cir. 1989) [BIA erred in admitting witness affidavit in smuggling case under former 8 U.S.C. §1251(a)(13) where INS failed to conclusively demonstrate it sought witness' presence at the hearing]; *Cunanan v. INS*, 856 F.2d 1373 (9th Cir. 1988) [denial of VD reversed where BIA relied upon I-213 hearsay declaration from respondent's wife but denied respondent opportunity for cross-examination by not making declarant available or informing respondent in advance it was going to use wife's affidavit]; *Baliza v. INS*, 709 F.2d 1231 (9th Cir. 1983); *Kiareldeen v. Reno,* 71 F.Supp.2d 402, 405–08 (D.N.J. 1999) [use of unclassified evidence based on statements from a person who would not testify that deprives applicant of bond is violation of right to cross-examine and of due process]. *See also Crawford v. Washington,* 541 U.S. 36 (2004)[in *criminal* context, out-of-court statements by witnesses that are testimonial (even if the statements are otherwise reliable) are barred by the Confrontation Clause unless the witnesses are unavailable and defendant had an opportunity to cross-examine them]. *But see Doumbia v. Gonzales,* 472 F.3d 957, 962–63 (7th Cir. 2007) [admission of Embassy report on validity of summonses in Côte d'Ivoire court was not prejudicial or fundamentally unfair under 8 U.S.C. §1229a(b)(4)]; *Ocasio v. Ashcroft,* 375 F.3d 105 (1st Cir. 2004) [court upheld IJ's admission of affidavit of spouse regarding sham marriage where spouse failed to appear at hearing and respondent/beneficiary-wife waived issue because she did not raise the claim that DHS failed to make reasonable efforts to secure spouse's appearance]; *Renteria-Gonzalez v. INS,* 322 F.3d 804, 816–20 (5th Cir. 2002) [where INS officer's hearsay statements about smuggling were admitted and the IJ did not require that the INS produce from Mexico the aliens who were smuggled or allow cross-examination by an interpreter to measure the officer's Spanish fluency, deportation order upheld]; *Dallo v. INS*, 765 F.2d 581 (6th Cir. 1985).

I-213 Statement of Minors—Statement taken from unaccompanied minor under18 on Form I-213 is not admissible. 8 C.F.R. §1240.10(c). *But see Matter of Amaya*, 21 I&N Dec. 583 (BIA 1996) [distinguishing *Davila-Bardales*, and finding that IJ can accept admissions of fact from minors but only after conducting specific inquiry]; *Matter of Ponce-Hernandez,* 22 I&N Dec. 784 (BIA 1999) [reversed IJ in an *in absentia* case involving a minor where the IJ found that submission solely of I-213 taken when the minor was 15 was insufficient to establish deportability]; *Matter of Gomez-Gomez,* 23 I&N Dec. 522, 523–27 (BIA 2002) [IJ's decision to terminate proceeding and to discount I-213 was reversed in *in absentia* hearing where INS relied on I-213 taken from person who was alleged to be parent of 8-year-old].

Under BIA decisions, where evidence is challenged (*e.g.*, veracity of I-213), alien must come forward with a *prima facie* case based on testimony (not affidavits alone) before DHS is called upon to respond. *Matter of Barcenas*, 19 I&N Dec. 609 (BIA 1988). *But see Murphy v. INS*, 54 F.3d 605, 612 (9th Cir. 1995) [burden remains on INS to establish alienage by clear and convincing evidence]; *Matter of Mejia*, 16 I&N Dec. 6 (BIA 1976). A respondent cannot complain about aspects of a hearsay document that he sought to admit after submitting it. *Johnson v. INS*, 971 F.2d 340, 343–44 (9th Cir. 1992) [where affidavit submitted by respondent for change of venue respondent could not later complain about derogatory information contained in it].

(3) Time for Submission of Evidence—The Immigration Court Practice Manual, Chapter 3 establishes general national rules for the submission of evidence in immigration court proceedings. Documents and evidence must be submitted in nondetained cases 30 days before a merits hearing or 15 days before a master calendar, and must be in the appropriate form, including a cover sheet, binding, tabs, and font size designated in the Immigration Court Practice Manual at 3.1(b), 3.2, 3.3. Untimely filings authorize the IJ to deny relief or not consider exhibits as evidence. Manual, 3.1(d)(ii). However, the IJ may set his or her own time for the submission of documentary evidence. 8 C.F.R. §1003.31(c) [the IJ "may set and extend time limits for the filing of applications and related documents and responses thereto, if any"]; *Hussain v. Gonzales,* 424 F.3d 622, 626–27 (7th Cir. 2005) [due process was not violated where IJ set 60 days for submission of documents for asylum hearing rather than the 10 days under the local rules and there was no evidence that the earlier deadline prejudiced the respondent].

(4) Authentication—Courts have recognized applicability of Fed. R. Civ. P. 44 in deportation proceedings. *Chew v. Boyd*, 309 F.2d 857 (9th Cir. 1962); *McNeil v. Kennedy*, 298 F.2d 323 (D.C. Cir. 1962); *Matter of Nand*, 13 I&N Dec. 336 (BIA 1964); *Baliza v. INS*, 709 F.2d 1231 (9th Cir. 1983). *But see Yongo v. INS,* 355 F.3d 27, 30–32 (1st Cir. 2004) [Fed. R. Evid. 901–02 regarding authentication do not apply and a document may be authenticated where immigration officer attests to where he obtained the documents and that he is familiar with these kind of records]; *Matter of Mejia*, 16 I&N Dec. 6 (BIA 1976); *Matter of Lopez*, 15 I&N Dec. 183 (BIA 1975); *Matter of Barcenas*, 19 I&N Dec. 609 (BIA 1988) [I-213 admissible to prove alienage and deportability because it is inherently reliable absent a showing that the information is incorrect or was obtained by coercion or duress]; *U.S. v. Agustino-Hernandez*, 14 F.3d 42 (11th Cir. 1994) [characterizing documents in "A" file, such as I-194 and warrant of deportation, as routinely and mechanically kept, and therefore their admission does not violate Fed. R. Evid. 803(8)(B)]. Also 8 C.F.R. §§287.6, 1287.6 requires attestation of a copy by the official having legal custody of an official record and under §§287.6(b), 1287.6(b) a foreign document must be authenticated by a consular officer unless the country is a signatory to convention abolishing such requirements. *Qin Wen Zheng v. Gonzales,* 500 F.3d 143, 146–49 (2d Cir. 2007) [BIA did not abuse its discretion in denying motion to reopen for changed country conditions where document from Changle Province, China was not authenticated under §287.6 in light of prior adverse credibility finding given the doctrine of *falsus in uno, falsus in omnibus*]; *Ali v. U.S. Att'y Gen.,* 443 F.3d 804, 812–13 (11th Cir. 2006) [BIA did not abuse its discretion in rejecting a photocopy of pardon that did not comply with the regulation, where respondent offered no compelling reason for his failure to obtain a properly certified copy].

Authentication Not the Exclusive Method—Vatyan v. Mukasey, 508 F.3d 1179 (9th Cir. 2007) [a petitioner's own testimony is a proper method that may be used to authenticate foreign public documents and IJ reversed, in asylum context, where he insisted that applicant obtain a certified document]; *Gebreeyesus v. Gonzales,* 482 F.3d 952, 955 (7th Cir. 2007) [reversed BIA denial of motion to reopen by Amharan from Ethiopia where BIA claimed that family members' letters had to be authenticated despite the letters not being official records]; *Jiang v. Gonzales,* 474 F.3d 25, 28–29 (1st Cir. 2007) [affidavit from father and declaration from parish priest are not "official records" requiring authentication pursuant to 8 C.F.R. §§287.6 and 287.6 is not an exclusive method for authenticating records in asylum cases]; *Shtaro v. Gonzales,* 435 F.3d 711, 717 (7th Cir. 2006) [failure to authenticate documents pursuant to §287.6 does not amount to presumptive proof of falsity and IJ reversed on credibility finding]; *Sukwanputra v. Gonzales,* 434 F.3d 627, 636–37 (3d Cir. 2006) [reversed IJ who refused to give any weight to unauthenticated documentary evidence on the basis of §287.6 and failed to afford the applicant an opportunity to authenticate the documents through other means]; *Cao He Lin v. DOJ,* 428 F.3d 391, 404–05 (2d Cir. 2005) [IJ reversed where she declined to accept the notarial birth certificate of an asylum applicant's child because it was not authenticated pursuant to 8 C.F.R. §287.6]; *Zhang v. Gonzales,* 405 F.3d 150, 155–56 (3d Cir. 2005) [where it was unclear whether IJ did not admit foreign documents or admitted them but gave them no weight because they were not authenticated pursuant to §287.6, the court remanded the case to BIA and ruled that §287.6 is not the exclusive means to authenticate documents]; *Leia v. Ashcroft,* 393 F.3d 427, 433–35 (3d Cir. 2005) [following *Liu* the court reversed the BIA's decision denying asylum and withholding on credibility grounds because respondent failed to present authenticated government documents pursuant to 8 C.F.R. §287.6. Section 287.6 is not the exclusive means to authenticate documents and the respondent had the right to present evidence when authentication was not possible]; *Liu v. Ashcroft,* 372 F.3d 529 (3d Cir. 2004) [IJ reversed where he admitted document without certification but gave it no weight; DHS conceded that the regulation is not an absolute rule of exclusion, nor the exclusive means of authenticating records]; *Yongo v. INS,* 355 F.3d 27, 31 (1st Cir. 2004) [regulation is one method, but not the exclusive method of authenticating documents]; *Wang v. INS,* 352 F.3d 1250, 1254 (9th Cir. 2003) [reversed IJ's adverse credibility finding based upon failure to authenticate documents solely because forensic experts could not determine authenticity]; *Khan v. INS,* 237 F.3d 1143 (9th Cir. 2001) [rejecting IJ's refusal to admit documents not certified by consular officer and finding that documents may be authenticated through any recognized procedure, including the Federal Rules of Civil Procedure]. Even if document is authenticated, under circumstances where testimony is critical, where the government makes no serious effort to locate the witness providing the authenticated document, the deport order on fraudulent marriage reversed. *Baliza*, 709 F.2d 1231 (9th Cir. 1983).

(5) Admission of a Crime—In *Matter of K,* 7 I&N Dec. 594, 598 (BIA 1957) the BIA adopted a three-part test for the acceptance of an admission: (1) the admitted conduct must constitute the essential elements of the crime; (2) the applicant must have been provided with a definition and the essential elements of the offense prior to his admission; and (3) the admission must be voluntary. The applicant must also admit all facts constituting the crime. *Matter of E-N-,* 7 I&N Dec. 153 (1956). *See also* 22 C.F.R. §40.21(a)(1); *Matter of G,* 1 I&N Dec. 225 (BIA 1942) [admission must be voluntary]; *Pazcoguin v. Radcliffe,* 292 F.3d 1209 (9th Cir. 2002) [beneficiary's admission to medical doctor during medical examination for IV in Philippines that he smoked marijuana for a number of years was used as the basis to deny visa upon entry to U.S. and to thereafter exclude him].

(6) Criminal convictions under 8 C.F.R. §1003.41—Docket entries, abstracts of records of conviction, minutes of a court proceeding or any document prepared by the court in which the conviction was entered that indicates the existence of the conviction. Documents may be submitted by electronic means as long as staff official certifies documents. The commentary to the regulations specifically recognize that admissibility of these documents and establishing deportability under *Woodby* are different. 58 Fed. Reg. 38952–54 (July 21, 1993); In *Huerta-Guevara v. Ashcroft,* 321 F.3d 883, 888 (9th Cir. 2003) the Ninth circuit determined that the only documents that may be relied upon in determining whether a conviction is for an aggravated felony under a divisible statute are the charging document, a signed plea agreement, jury instructions, the guilty plea, a transcript of the plea and the judgment. *See also Conteh v. Gonzales,* 461 F.3d 45, 57–59 (1st Cir. 2006) [cannot rely on respondent's after-the-fact statements or the PSI report to establish the record of conviction]; *Hernandez-Martinez v. Ashcroft,* 343 F.3d 1075 (9th Cir. 2003) [affirming *Huerta Guevara* and determining that a Presentence Report cannot be used to establish that a divisible statute is an aggravated felony]; *Matter of Pichardo,* 21 I&N Dec. 330, 331 (BIA 1996). *But see Savchuck v. Mukasey,* 518 F.3d 119, 122-23 (2d Cir. 2008) [Submission of a print-out of respondent's rap sheet, a copy of a Certificate of Disposition of his petit larceny conviction, a copy of the Sentence and Order of Commitment for his grant larceny conviction accompanied by a Certification of Records by DHS along with respondent's testimony admitting convictions was sufficient]; *Singh v. DHS,* 517 F.3d 638, 643–46 (2d Cir. 2008) [court found that DHS had established by clear and convincing evidence that petitioner was convicted of assault under N.Y. Penal

Law §120.05(1) by upholding the admission of a Conditions of Probation document, a Certificate of Disposition, and a post-conviction rap sheet which individually would be insufficient but in combination proved the conviction]; *Adefemi v. Ashcroft,* 386 F.3d 1022, 1029 (11th Cir. 2004) (*en banc*) [affirming the use of a City Court of Atlanta document that contains several ambiguities to establish deportability for a firearms offense by clear and convincing evidence because the court under the substantial-evidence test "must affirm the agency's decision unless there is no reasonable basis for that decision"]

Under INA §240(c)(3)(B), 8 U.S.C. §1229a(c)(3)(B) any of the following documents constitute proof of a criminal conviction: (a) an official record of judgment and conviction; (b) an official record of plea, verdict, and sentence; (c) a docket entry from court records that indicates the existence of the conviction; (d) official minutes of a court proceeding or a transcript of a court hearing in which the court takes notice of the existence of the conviction; (e) an abstract of a record of conviction; (f) any document or record prepared by or under the direction of the court indicating the existence of the conviction; or (g) any document or record maintained by a penal institution attesting to the conviction. INA §240(c)(3)(B). Electronic records are also admissible if certified by state official and certified by DHS official as having been received electronically. INA §240(c)(3)(C); 8 C.F.R. §1003.41(c). *Sinotes-Cruz v. Gonzales,* 468 F.3d 1190, 1195–97 (9th Cir. 2006) [where electronic records of conviction were not certified by state officials but respondent did not object before the IJ , the court found the conviction records were nevertheless admissible because the statutory and regulatory requirements only set forth when documents *must* be admitted (a "safe harbor") and not when they *can* be admitted without meeting the statutory or regulatory requirements if they are otherwise authenticated under any procedure that comports with common law rules of evidence]. The list of documents is also not exclusive and the government may offer "any other evidence" to establish deportability. 8 C.F.R. §1003.41(d); *Rosales-Pineda v. Gonzales,* 452 F.3d 627 (7th Cir. 2006) [court distinguished *Francis,* relied on the broad language of 8 C.F.R. §1003.41(d) and found that an FBI rap sheet, as distinguished from a foreign rap sheet, could be used as evidence of a conviction where there was other supporting evidence and the issue was denial of discretionary relief and not whether person was removable]; *Francis v. Gonzales,* 442 F.3d 131, 141–45 (2d Cir. 2006) [documents other than those listed in 1003.41 may be submitted as evidence but the court found a "rap sheet"/police report from Jamaica did not support a finding of a conviction under the *Woodby* standard even with an ambiguous oral admission of conviction]; *Fequiere v. Ashcroft,* 279 F.3d 1325, 1327 (11th Cir. 2002) [respondent's admission of drug conviction under oath established conviction for immigration purposes notwithstanding the absence of any document enumerated in INA §240(c)(3)(B)].

(7) What Constitutes the Record of Conviction—The Supreme Court has defined the "record of conviction" in a nonimmigration case involving a guilty plea to include the "charging document, written plea agreement, transcript of plea colloquy, and any explicit factual finding by the trial judge to which the defendant assented." *Shepard v. U.S.,* 544 U.S. 13, 125 S.Ct. 1254, 1257 (2005) [sentencing court cannot look to police reports in deciding whether a crime is a "generic burglary" for purposes of the Armed Career Criminal Act]. The record of conviction (including indictment or information, plea, verdict or judgment and sentence) can be considered to determine whether conviction is deportable offense. *Vue v. INS,* 92 F.3d 696, 700 (8th Cir. 1996) [IJ properly relied upon the amended criminal complaint to establish firearms offense]; *Matter of Madrigal,* 21 I&N Dec. 323 (BIA 1996) [transcript of plea and sentence hearing is part of record]; *Martinez-Perez v. Ashcroft,* 417 F.3d 1028–29 (9th Cir. 2005) [the documents to be considered as part of the record of conviction under the modified categorical approach are those specified in *Shepard v. U.S.,* 544 U.S. 13, 125 S.Ct. 1254, 1257 (2005)]; *Murray v. Ashcroft,* 285 F.Supp.2d 664, 670 (E.D. Pa. 2003) [not a violation of due process to rely on record of stipulated trial under Pennsylvania law to establish aggravated felony]. Testimony, however, is not part of the record of conviction and may not be used to establish an element of the conviction. *Tokatly v. Ashcroft,* 371 F.3d 613, 619–24 (9th Cir. 2004) [impermissible for IJ to rely on testimony of respondent or the victim to establish that respondent

committed a crime of domestic violence as IJ may only look at record of conviction not actual facts of the crime]. The record of conviction is also somewhat different if there was a conviction after a jury trial. If a person is convicted after trial (not by a plea) and there is no verdict form or jury instructions to demonstrate a finding regarding an element of the offense, the submission of an indictment and a judgment alone will *not* be sufficient. *Li v. Ashcroft,* 389 F.3d 892 (9th Cir. 2004) [where amount of loss due to fraud was not an element of the crime but where indictment alleges that more than $10,000 was involved in the fraud, the government may not prove under the modified categorical approach that this was a fraud or attempted fraud in excess of $10,000 by simply putting into evidence the charging document and the judgment without a verdict form or jury instructions because the government was not required to prove and the jury was not required to find a loss in excess of $10,000 in order to convict]. Whatever records are used they must establish deportability under *Woodby* standard. *Conteh v. Gonzales,* 461 F.3d 45, 57–59 (1st Cir. 2006) [cannot rely on respondent's after-the-fact statements or the PSI report to establish the record of conviction];*Matter of Pichardo*, 21 I&N Dec. 330 (BIA 1996) [cannot rely on testimony of respondent to establish element of crime]; *Matter of Sanudo,* 23 I&N Dec. 968, 974–75 (BIA 2006) [where the factual narrative of the police report was not incorporated into the charging document or the plea, it could not be considered in determining whether respondent may be removed]; *Matter of Teixeira,* 21 I&N Dec. 316 (BIA 1996). This list, however, is not exclusive and the government may offer "any other evidence" to establish deportability. 8 C.F.R. §1003.41(d). *Francis v. Gonzales,* 442 F.3d 131, 141–45 (2d Cir. 2006) [documents other than those listed in §1003.41 may be submitted as evidence but the court found a "rap sheet"/police report from Jamaica did not support a finding of a conviction under the *Woodby* standard even with an ambiguous oral admission of conviction]; *Fequiere v. Ashcroft,* 279 F.3d 1325, 1327 (11th Cir. 2002) [respondent's admission of drug conviction under oath established conviction for immigration purposes notwithstanding the absence of any document enumerated in INA §240(c)(3)(B)]. The courts have also ignored or sought to distinguish the *Shepard* limitations. *James v. Gonzales,* 464 F.3d 505, 510–14 (5th Cir. 2006) [where respondent pled guilty to one count of bank fraud resulting in a loss of $9,500 but the restitution amount exceeded $10,000, the court relied, in part, on the PSR report to find it was an aggravated felony]; *Adefemi v. Ashcroft,* 386 F.3d 1022, 1030 n.11 (11th Cir. 2004) (*en banc*) [distinguishing *Pichardo* and finding that respondent's admission corroborating his conviction for a firearms offense was relevant evidence]; *Lara-Ruiz v. INS,* 241 F.3d 934, 941 (7th Cir. 2001) [not improper for BIA to look beyond conviction records to determine that sexual assault was committed against a 4-year-old where no evidentiary hearing was required]; *Matter of Babaisakov,* 24 I&N Dec. 306, 319–21 (BIA 2007) [in an aggravated felony case under INA §101(a)(43)(M) where the government must prove loss to the victim in excess of $10,000 the IJ may not only rely on restitution orders, presentence reports, and admissions during plea colloquies but may also use "any evidence, otherwise admissible in removal proceedings, including witness testimony" and "testimonial admissions of the respondent made during the removal hearing" to prove the loss]; *Matter of Gertsenshteyn,* 24 I&N Dec. 111 (BIA 2007) [in an aggravated felony case under INA §101(a)(43)(K)(ii) where the government must demonstrate the conviction of a crime "if committed for commercial advantage" the IJ may go beyond the record of conviction to establish "commercial advantage" and use the presentence report, the respondent's admissions, and any other relevant evidence]; *Matter of Vargas,* 23 I&N Dec. 651 (BIA 2004) *aff'd* 448 F.3d 159 (2d Cir. 2006) [where record of conviction did not indicate which part of the statute respondent was convicted for purposes of deportation, the BIA found him deportable because he was charged with a crime of violence]. *See also Suazo Perez v. Mukasey,* 512 F.3d 1222, 1226–27 (9th Cir. 2008) [police report could be utilized in modified categorical approach where defendant checked a box on his plea that stated he agreed that "the court may review the police reports and/or statement of probable cause supplied by the prosecution to establish a factual basis of the plea"].

(8) Pre-Sentence/Probation Report may be "insufficient evidence to establish that the defendant pled guilty to the elements of the generic definition of a crime when the statute of

conviction is broader than the generic definition." *U.S. v. Corona-Sanchez,* 291 F.3d 1201, 1212 (9th Cir. 2002) (*en banc*). *See also Conteh v. Gonzales,* 461 F.3d 45, 57–59 (1st Cir. 2006) [cannot rely on respondent's after-the-fact statements or the PSI report to establish the record of conviction]; *Penuliar v. Ashcroft,* 435 F.3d 961, 969 (9th Cir. 2006) [rejected IJ reliance on probation report to establish that respondent pled guilty to crime of violence]; *Dickson v. Ashcroft,* 346 F.3d 44, 53 (2d Cir. 2003) [even if PSR were part of record of conviction reliance on narrative statement of facts contained in PSR was impermissible to establish aggravated felony conviction]; *Lara-Chacon v. Ashcroft,* 345 F.3d 1148, 1151–54 (9th Cir. 2003) [under modified categorical approach could not use pre-sentence report to determine that conviction under Arizona money laundering statute was a drug trafficking crime]; *Chang v. INS,* 307 F.3d 1185, 1191–92 (9th Cir. 2002) [pre-sentence report may not be used to establish an aggravated felony where to do so would contradict the terms of the plea agreement]; *Hernandez-Martinez v. Ashcroft,* 343 F.3d 1075, 1076 (9th Cir. 2003) [followed *Corona-Sanchez*]. *But see Ali v. Mukasey,* 521 F.3d 737 (7th Cir. 2008) [following *Matter of Babaisakov* and reinterpreting its own precedent post–*Brand X Internet Services,* the circuit court concluded the BIA could rely on the presentence investigation report to establish whether crime is a CIMT because "when deciding how to classify convictions under criteria that go beyond the criminal charge–such as the amount of the victim's loss, or whether the crime is one of 'moral turpitude' the agency has discretion to consider evidence beyond the charging papers and judgment of conviction"]; *James v. Gonzales,* 464 F.3d 505, 510–14 (5th Cir. 2006) [where respondent pled guilty to one count of bank fraud resulting in a loss of $9,500 but the restitution amount exceeded $10,000, the court relied, in part, on the PSR report to find it was an aggravated felony]; *Matter of Babaisakov,* 24 I&N Dec. 306, 319–21 (BIA 2007) [in an aggravated felony case under INA §101(a)(43)(M) where the government must prove loss to the victim in excess of $10,000 the IJ may not only rely on restitution orders, presentence reports, and admissions during plea colloquies but may also use "any evidence, otherwise admissible in removal proceedings, including witness testimony" and "testimonial admissions of the respondent made during the removal hearing" to prove the loss].

(9) Notations regarding special sentencing reasons or factors, *Larin-Ulloa v. Gonzales,* 462 F.3d 456, 468–69 (5th Cir. 2006) [BIA erroneously referred to a special sentencing factor notation in the Kansas journal entry form to determine under the modified categorical approach that respondent's conviction for aggravated battery was a crime of violence].

(10) Vacated Convictions—The burden of proof that a vacated conviction was vacated for other than procedural or substantive reasons rests with the government by clear, unequivocal and convincing evidence and not the respondent. *Pickering v. Gonzales,* 465 F.3d 263, 269 n.4 (6th Cir. 2006) [notwithstanding the respondent's immigration motive as expressed in his moving papers to the Canadian court, the Canadian vacatur of his conviction without explanation but with citation to authority was sufficient to vacate the conviction for immigration purposes and DHS had burden to prove that vacatur was not for a substantive or procedural reason]. *See in this chapter* "Burden of Proof," ¶ VI.A.9.b (p.210), *supra*.

(11) Statements in a brief should be treated as not conclusive—*Huerta-Guevara v. Ashcroft,* 321 F.3d 883, 888 (9th Cir. 2003) [respondent found not removable as aggravated felon for possession of stolen vehicle under Ariz. Stat. §13-1802, where statute encompasses acts that do not require criminal intent and concessions in respondent's appellate brief were not necessarily elements she pled guilty to.]

(12) Police/Arrest Reports—May not be used as a basis to determine eligibility for relief. *Matter of Arreguin*, 21 I&N Dec. 38 (BIA 1995); *Billeke-Tolosa v. Ashcroft,* 385 F.3d 708 (6th Cir. 2004) [IJ cannot look behind the applicant's conviction to deny adjustment based upon a police report]. *But see Henry v. INS,* 74 F.3d 1, 5–7 (1st Cir. 1996); *Matter of N-A-M-,* 24 I&N Dec. 336, 343–45 (BIA 2007) [BIA considered the Statement in Support of Warrantless Arrest and determined it could be used with any other reliable information to determine whether someone had committed a particularly serious crime barring withholding of removal]; *Matter of Grijalva,* 19 I&N Dec. 713 (BIA 1988). Police re-

ports may also not be used as a basis to determine conviction. *Matter of Teixeira*, 21 I&N Dec. 316 (BIA 1996) [reversed decision finding deportability for firearms conviction based on police report, but suggested police report could be used for discretionary relief purposes]; *Matter of Sanudo,* 23 I&N Dec. 968, 974–75 (BIA 2006) [where the factual narrative of the police report was not incorporated into the charging document or the plea, it could not be considered in determining whether respondent may be removed]; *Wala v. Mukasey,* 511 F.3d 102, 107–10 and n.5 (2d Cir. 2007) [relying on *Shepard* and determining that the BIA may rely only on facts that the petitioner "necessarily pleaded" the court held that the government could not rely on petitioner's police report to establish that burglary with an intent to commit larceny was a CIMT]; *See also Shepard v. U.S.,* 544 U.S. 13, 125 S.Ct. 1254, 1257 (2005) [sentencing court cannot look to police reports in deciding whether a crime is a "generic burglary" for purposes of the Armed Career Criminal Act].

(13) Abstract of Judgment—*Sandoval-Lua v. Gonzales,* 499 F.3d 1121, 1130 & n.8 (9th Cir. 2007) [cannot use abstract of judgment to prove conviction for aggravated felony purposes under modified categorical approach].

(14) Rap Sheet—*Francis v. Gonzales,* 442 F.3d 131, 141–45 (2d Cir. 2006) [after citing the regulatory history at 58 Fed. Reg. 38952, 38953 (July 21, 1993) and the AG's Order No. 1764-93, the court found that a "rap sheet"/police report from Jamaica, while admissible, did not support a finding of a conviction under the *Woodby* standard even where there was some admission of guilt]. *But see Singh v. DHS,* 517 F.3d 638, 643–46 (2d Cir. 2008) [court found that DHS had established by clear and convincing evidence that petitioner was convicted of assault under N.Y. Penal Law §120.05(1) by upholding the admission of a Conditions of Probation document, a Certificate of Disposition, and a post-conviction rap sheet which individually would be insufficient but in combination proved the conviction]; *Rosales-Pineda v. Gonzales,* 452 F.3d 627 (7th Cir. 2006) [court distinguished *Francis,* relied on the broad language of 8 C.F.R. §1003.41(d) and found that an FBI rap sheet, as distinguished from a foreign rap sheet, could be used where there was other supporting evidence and the issue was denial of discretionary relief and not whether person was removable].

(15) Interview Statements Taken from Respondent or Any Other Person—IJ may receive in evidence all oral or written prior statements of the respondent or any other person during any investigation, examination, hearing or trial. 8 C.F.R. §1240.7(a). *Prawira v. Gonzales,* 405 F.3d 661, 663 (8th Cir. 2005) [IJ did not err in admitting asylum officer's written notes and a status report on a pending overseas investigation into the authenticity of respondent's documents]; *Krasnopivtsev v. Ashcroft,* 382 F.3d 832, 837–38 (8th Cir. 2005) [admitting referral assessment of asylum officer]; *Ramsameachire v. Ashcroft,* 357 F.3d 169, 179–83 (2d Cir. 2004) [where record of airport interview indicates its reliability it may be used to challenge credibility]. However, such statements are subject to challenge concerning the manner and circumstances under which they are taken and the language of the parties. *Singh v. Gonzales,* 403 F.3d 1081 (9th Cir. 2005) [court reversed IJ's denial of asylum, withholding and CAT based upon adverse credibility assessment where there were perceived inconsistencies between asylum officer's Assessment to Refer and applicant's testimony because assessment is unreliable in light of the fact that it is only a short, conclusory written summary and there is no transcript, no indication of the language used or whether an oath was administered, no record of all the questions and answers, no contemporaneous notes, and no testimony of the asylum officer or the applicant]; *Stoyanov v. INS,* 172 F.3d 731 (9th Cir. 1999) [inconsistency between in-court testimony and application that lessens degree of persecution does not support adverse credibility finding]; *Balasubramanrim v. INS,* 143 F.3d 157 (3d Cir. 1998) [reversed BIA determination that applicant not credible because his testimony differed from unreliable statement taken at airport upon applicant's arrival]; *Senathirajah v. INS,* 157 F.3d 210, 218–21 (3d Cir. 1998) [same]; *Mulanga v. Ashcroft,* 349 F.3d 123, 137 (3d Cir. 2003) [same]; *Zubeda v. Ashcroft*, 333 F.3d 463, 476–77 (3d Cir. 2003) [challenged finding of lack of credibility by IJ where it was based upon contradiction between testimony and unreliable airport interview]; *Singh v. INS,* 292 F.3d 1017, 1020–24 (9th Cir. 2002) [air-

port interview lacked sufficient indicia of reliability to draw adverse credibility finding]; [same]; *Dia v. Ashcroft,* 353 F.3d 228, 257–58 (3d Cir. 2003) (*en banc*) [same]. No significant weight given to interview statement taken in English at person's arrival where his or her English is limited. *Matter of H-*, 21 I&N Dec. 337, 341 n.3 (BIA 1996). There is also a question as to whether the admission of statements of "any other person" would be fundamentally unfair when they are not subject to cross-examination. *See in this section* "Hearsay admissible," ¶ (2) (p.363), *supra*. In the view of one court a four-part test should be adopted to determine reliability of interviews including: (1) whether the record of the interview is verbatim or merely summarizes or paraphrases the person's statements; (2) Whether the questions asked were designed to elicit details and whether the officer asked follow-up questions that would aid in developing the account; (3) Whether the applicant was reluctant to reveal information because of prior interrogation sessions or other coercive experiences in his or her home country; and (4) Whether answers to questions suggested applicant did not understand English or the translation was not reliable. *Ramsameachire,* 357 F.3d at 180.

The danger in an immigration court relying on airport interview transcripts as a basis to determine lack of credibility was highlighted in a recent congressionally mandated study. *See* Keller, Rasmussen, Reeves and Rosenfeld, *Evaluation of Credible Fear Referral in Expedited Removal At Ports of Entry in the United States,* Study on Asylum Seekers in Expedited Removal, As Authorized by Section 605 of the International Religious Freedom Act of 1998 (Feb. 2005) at p. 30 ["The lack of congruence between the observations of our research assistants and the official records prepared by the investigating officers (A-files) suggests that the asylum process itself may be compromised by the use of these documents as official transcripts....The safeguard against inaccurate A-file records, asking aliens to attest to the accuracy of their statements, also appears inadequate as currently implemented"].

An IJ's reliance on such statements may also be challenged where it finds the respondent credible but relies on an airport interview that contradicts the remainder of respondent's claim. *Wu v. Ashcroft,* 393 F.3d 418, 423–25 (3d Cir. 2005) [where IJ failed to explain why it relied on an airport interview to contradict respondent's asylum claim when it found respondent's testimony credible, the court remanded].

(16) Asylum Applications—Information on the application may be used as a basis to institute removal proceedings or as evidence in the proceeding if filed after Jan. 4, 1995. 8 C.F.R. §208.3(c)(1). Information on application may be used to satisfy the burden of proof of deportability if filed after Jan. 4, 1995.

(17) Foreign Law—The party relying on foreign law must plead and prove it. *Matter of Soleimani*, 20 I&N Dec. 99 (BIA 1989); *Matter of Kodwo,* 24 I&N Dec. 479, 482 (BIA 2008); *Menghesha v. Gonzales,* 450 F.3d 142, 147 n.2 (4th Cir. 2006) [where government asserts that asylum applicant will face prosecution not persecution, it needed to plead and prove foreign law in regard to prosecution]. *But see Sadeghi v. INS*, 40 F.3d 1139, 1143 (10th Cir. 1994). Also, any foreign language document must be translated. 8 C.F.R. §1003.33. *Ramaj v. Gonzales,* 466 F.3d 520, 530 (6th Cir. 2006) [where the translated documents did not contain a statement that the translator was competent in Albanian and English the documents were properly excluded]; *Krasnopivtsev v. Ashcroft,* 382 F.3d 832, 837–38 (8th Cir. 2005) [it was not error for IJ to deny admitting untranslated foreign passport without certification].

(18) Presumption of Regularity—The presumption of regularity presumes that public officers, in the absence of clear evidence to the contrary, have properly discharged their official duties including placing information on forms. *U.S. v. Armstrong,* 517 U.S. 456, 464, (1996); *U.S. v. Chemical Foundation*, 272 U.S. 1, 14–15, (1926). But where a party identifies sufficient discrepancies in the documents or process, the presumption is rebutted. *U.S. v. Nunez-Garcia,* 262 F.Supp.2d 1073, 1084 (C.D. Cal. 2003) [rejected the presumption of regularity regarding naturalization interview and denied SJ to Service where they claimed that naturalized citizen made a false oral statement at his interview]

(19) Offer of Proof—An IJ may accept an offer of proof particularly where the testimony was not crucial. *Drobny v. INS*, 947 F.2d 241, 245 (7th Cir. 1991) [mother's testimony at INA §212(c) proceeding].

(20) Classified Information—The applicant's rights to examine or present evidence or cross-examine witnesses does not entitle him "to examine such national security information the government may proffer in opposition to the alien's *admission* to the U.S. or to an application ... for discretionary relief." INA §240(b)(4)(B), 8 U.S.C. §1229a (b)(4)(B). IJ may rely on undisclosed classified information in rendering his decision on asylum or other discretionary relief. 8 C.F.R. §§208.11(d), 1208.11(d) [in asylum, materials classified under Executive Order, E.O. 12958]; 8 C.F.R. §1240.11(a)(3), (c)(3)(iv). However, the use of undisclosed, classified and confidential information may violate due process. *Kiareldeen v. Reno,* 71 F.Supp.2d 402, 407–19 (D.N.J. 1999) [applying *Mathews* analysis and finding respondent's due process rights were violated "even if the interest is deemed to be the unarguably weighty one of national security"]; *American-Arab Anti-Discrimination Comm. v. Reno*, 883 F.Supp. 1365, 1376–78 (C.D. Cal. 1995). Also, note that INA §240(b)(4)(B) only applies to challenges to admission and for discretionary relief thus leaving the question of the use of such information for deportation and nondiscretionary relief (*e.g.,* withholding of removal) open. Also, a reviewing court must be given access to "unexpurgated copies of the Immigration Judge's classified decision and all classified materials presented to the Immigration Judge" so that it can "perform its statutory duty to review petitions from decisions of the Board." *Singh v. INS,* 328 F.3d 1205 (9th Cir. 2003) [circuit court ordered INS to produce documents in accordance with DOJ procedures where IJ rested his decision in part on inferences from classified information and the BIA adopted the IJ's factual findings].

(21) Information Under Seal/Protective Order—DOJ has established procedures before the IJ for the submission of documents/information under seal with a protective order which, if disclosed would "harm the national security...or law enforcement interests of the United States." 8 C.F.R. §1003.46. National security is defined under INA §219(c)(2), 8 U.S.C. §1189(c)(2) to include "the national defense, foreign relations, or economic interests of the United States." The EOIR guidelines provide that only the government is authorized to file a protective order under the regulations and the respondent may only appeal a decision granting a protective order after a final decision on the merits. Memo [Interim OPPM 02-02], Creppy, Chief IJ, EOIR (July 16, 2002) at ¶¶IIA, IIIB, *published on* AILA InfoNet at Doc. No. 02071870. The issuance of a protective order, however, does not preclude the respondent from challenging the admissibility of the information subject to the protective order. 8 C.F.R. §1003.46(g). If a respondent or his attorney or accredited representative discloses the information in violation of the protective order s/he becomes ineligible for "all forms of discretionary relief, except bond, unless the respondent fully cooperates with the Service or other law enforcement agencies in any investigation relating to noncompliance...and establishes by clear and convincing evidence either that extraordinary and extremely unusual circumstances exist or that failure to comply...was beyond the control of the respondent and his or her attorney or accredited representative." 8 C.F.R. §1003.46(i); *Matter of R-S-H-, et al.,* 23 I&N Dec. 629 (BIA 2003) [denied asylum, withholding and voluntary departure because of breach of protective order where respondent and counsel cooperated in the investigation of the breach but did not show extraordinary circumstances or that failure to comply was beyond their control].

(22) Hearings Involving Minors or Incompetents—The immigration court has adopted separate guidelines for proceedings involving unaccompanied children. Memo [OPPM 07-01], Neal, Chief IJ, EOIR (May, 22, 2007), *published on* AILA InfoNet at Doc. No. 07052360 [*replacing* Memo [Interim OPPM 04-07], Creppy, Chief IJ, EOIR (Sept. 16, 2004), *published on* AILA InfoNet at Doc. No. 04100568]. For purposes of court guidelines, unaccompanied children are defined as under 18 consistent with the Homeland Security Act of 2002. The "best interest of the child" standard is appropriate to determine the hearing environment but cannot be used to negate statutory or regulatory standards for asylum or other relief. Neither the regulations nor the INA permit the court to appoint a guardian *ad litem*. Hearings should be scheduled if possible on a separate docket, tele-

phonic and video conferencing may be waived, the IJ can disrobe, and the IJ should employ child-sensitive questioning and make appropriate credibility assessments given the child's age. An IJ should "not assume that inconsistencies are proof of dishonesty" as a child's testimony "may be limited not only by his or her ability to understand what happened, but also by his or her skill in describing the event in a way that is intelligible to adults." Guidelines, *supra* at ¶V(F). Motions to change venue may be granted without a pleading or application for relief and motions to continue should be considered in light of the fact that unaccompanied minors' cases are not subject to case or aged case completion deadlines.

An IJ can not accept admissions of removability from an unrepresented incompetent or unrepresented minor under the age of 18 who is not accompanied by a guardian, friend or near relative. 8 C.F.R. §1240.10(c). *Davila-Bardales v. INS*, 27 F.3d 1 (1st Cir. 1994) [IJ cannot take admission or use I-213 where minor made admission to establish deportability where minor not represented and not accompanied]; *Matter of Mejina-Andino,* 23 I&N Dec. 533 (BIA 2002) [personal service on uncle of 7-year-old is not sufficient when I-213 reveals there are parents in the U.S.]. *But see Matter of Amaya*, 21 I&N Dec. 583 (BIA 1996) [distinguishing *Davila-Bardales*, and finding that IJ can accept admissions of fact from minors but only after conducting specific inquiry]; *Matter of Ponce-Hernandez,* 22 I&N Dec. 784 (BIA 1999) [reversed IJ in an *in absentia* case involving a minor where the IJ found that submission solely of I-213 taken when the minor was 15 was insufficient to establish deportability]; *Matter of Gomez-Gomez,* 23 I&N Dec. 522, 523–27 (BIA 2002) [IJ's decision to terminate proceeding and to discount I-213 was reversed in *in absentia* hearing where INS relied on I-213 taken from person who was alleged to be parent of 8-year-old]. Where counsel is obtained, s/he must be competent. *Lin v. Ashcroft,* 377 F.3d 1014, 1023–27 (9th Cir. 2004) [reversed denial of motion to reopen where minor's counsel was ineffective in contacting, preparing, failing to appear personally, advocating and appealing his client's case].

Notice Involving Minor—When a minor is placed in the custody of a responsible adult pursuant to 8 C.F.R. §242.24, notice must be served upon the adult as well as the minor even if the minor is over 14. *Flores-Chavez v. Ashcroft,* 362 F.3d 1150 (9th Cir. 2004) [reversed *in absentia* order against 15-year-old who was served with OSC pursuant to 8 C.F.R. §103.5a but no service was provided to adult custodian. Court found that reading the statute to permit service solely on minor violated DHS regulations, was not entitled to *Chevron* deference, and raised serious constitutional questions]. DHS must also provide consular notification which cannot be waived by a minor. *U.S. v. D.L.,* 453 F.3d 1115, 1123 and n.6 (9th Cir. 2006).

Mental Incompetency—If the respondent cannot be present at his hearing because of mental incompetency the AG shall prescribe safeguards to protect his rights and privileges. INA §240(b)(3). By regulation the AG has allowed an attorney, legal representative, legal guardian, near relative or friend to appear on behalf of the respondent who is not competent. 8 C.F.R. §1240.4. However, in *Nelson v. INS,* 232 F.3d 258, 261–62 (1st Cir. 2000), the First Circuit found that an asylum applicant who stated that her memory was bad and that she was not capable of defending herself did not rise to the level of mental incompetence contemplated by the regulation and the IJ did not violate the Judge's Benchbook by proceeding with the case. Similarly, it does not violate substantive due process to proceed in a removal hearing involving a mentally incompetent person as it would in a criminal trial. *Brue v. Gonzales,* 464 F.3d 1227, 1232–34 (10th Cir. 2006) [where incompetent was represented by counsel there was no substantive due process violation and respondent was accorded the procedural protections provided by statute and regulations]. *See also Mohamed v. Gonzales,* 477 F.3d 522, 526–28 (8th Cir. 2006) [court rejected claim that respondent was incompetent without a separate hearing on competency by basing its decision on respondent's actions at the removal hearing] *reversing Mohamed v. Tebrake,* 371 F.Supp.2d 1043 (D. Minn. 2005) [IJ must inquire as to competency of respondent or §1240.4 would be a nullity and it was an abuse of discretion not to inquire where person was in a mental hospital and hearing was held via circuit television].

(23) Battered Spouse—Information obtained from a person who has battered a spouse or child cannot be used to make an adverse determination of admissibility or deportability. IIRIRA §384; 8 U.S.C. §1367. At least one court has allowed the use of information from a spouse who battered the alien to obtain a conviction for a false I-9. *U.S. v. Maswai,* 419 F.3d 822 (8th Cir. 2005) [court rejected argument that 8 U.S.C. §1367 prohibiting the use of information about a battered spouse in removal proceedings applied to a criminal action under 18 U.S.C. §1546].

(24) Amnesty Application—DHS cannot use information furnished pursuant to an amnesty application at a removal hearing. 8 U.S.C. §1255a(c)(5)(A), (B). In *Perez v. INS*, 72 F.3d 256 (2d Cir. 1995), the court found that INS could use the notices of the termination of temporary residency because the information was not furnished by respondent.

(25) Sequestration of Witnesses—At least one court in *dicta* has ruled that the Federal Rules of Evidence do not bind the IJ in a removal proceeding and therefore he was not required to sequester witnesses and it was not an abuse of discretion to fail to do so. *Podoprigora v. INS,* 98 F.Supp.2d 75, 79–80 (D. Mass. 2000).

(26) Evidence May Not Be Submitted After Close of Hearing—Where IJ has closed the hearing, a party may not submit evidence except on a motion to reopen. 8 C.F.R. §1003.31(c) [if application or document is not filed within time set by IJ, it is waived]; *Chay-Velasquez v. Ashcroft,* 367 F.3d 751, 756 (8th Cir. 2004) [upheld IJ's denial of the admission of a supplemental filing to asylum application after record was closed]; *Matter of Shanu,* 23 I&N Dec. 754, 764–65 (BIA 2005) [upheld denial of cancellation as abandoned for failure to timely file application]; *Matter of A-K-,* 24 I&N Dec. 275, 281 (BIA 2007) [rejected remand to IJ to apply for asylum because respondent was given opportunity at hearing and he declined to do so thereby waiving the right to apply].

(27) Failure to Present Evidence Deemed Abandonment of Application—Where respondent declined to abandon his application for adjustment, but his counsel said he would not present any evidence, court deemed application abandoned and IJ did not commit error in failing to rule on application already abandoned. *Bropleh v. Gonzales,* 428 F.3d 772, 778–79 (8th Cir. 2005).

(28) Negative Inference from Failure to Produce Evidence—Where a party withholds evidence, the court may draw a negative inference that the evidence is adverse to him. *Singh v. Gonzales,* 491 F.3d 1019, 1023–27 (9th Cir. 2007) [although IJ could have drawn a negative inference as to asylum applicant's credibility when he failed to sign a waiver that would have produced his Canadian file, the IJ could not simply draw a negative inference that he was not entitled to asylum].

7.q. Burden of Proof—Traditionally, INS was required to prove by "clear, unequivocal and convincing evidence" the alien's deportability. *Woodby v. INS*, 385 U.S. 276 (1966); *Pickering v. Gonzales,* 465 F.3d 263, 269 n.4 (6th Cir. 2006) [BIA precedent reversed where DHS failed to meet its burden by clear, unequivocal and convincing evidence under *Woodby* that vacated conviction was not for a substantive or procedural reason]; *Jaggernauth v. U.S. Atty. General,* 432 F.3d 1346, 1352–56 (11th Cir. 2005) [reversed removal order where the government failed to prove that respondent was an aggravated felon under *Woody* standard because grand theft under Florida Statute 812.014(1) is a divisible statute which includes under subsection (b) a temporary appropriation of the use of the property and therefore not necessarily "theft" under the common law definition]; *Hernandez-Guadarrama v. Ashcroft,* 394 F.3d 674, 678–83 (9th Cir. 2005) [removal order reversed because DHS failed to prove alien smuggling under *Woodby* standard where limited evidence was not subject to cross-examination and was insufficiently reliable]; *Murphy v. INS,* 54 F.3d 605 (9th Cir. 1995) [reversed deportation order based on questionable hearsay]; *Gameros-Hernandez v. INS*, 883 F.2d 839 (9th Cir. 1989); 8 C.F.R. §1240.8(a). *But see* 8 U.S.C. §§1229a(c)(2)(B), (c)(3)(A); 8 C.F.R. §1240.8(c); H.R. Conf. Rep. No. 828, 104th Cong., 2d Sess. at 212 (1996) providing for a "clear and convincing" standard. *See also e.g., Singh v. DHS,* 517 F.3d 638, 643–46 (2d Cir. 2008) [court found that DHS had established by clear and convincing evidence that petitioner was convicted of assault under N.Y. Penal Law §120.05(1) by upholding the admission of a

Conditions of Probation document, a Certificate of Disposition, and a post-conviction rap sheet which individually would be insufficient but in combination proved the conviction]. The differences between the "clear, unequivocal and convincing" standard and the "clear and convincing" standard are unclear and the *Woodby* standard may be considered constitutionally mandated. In *Addington v. Texas,* 441 U.S. 418, 432, 99 S.Ct. 1804 (1979) the Court in a civil law context stated that: "The term 'unequivocal' taken by itself, means proof that admits of no doubt, a burden approximating, if not exceeding, that used in criminal cases." The *Woodby* standard has been applied to various elements of the deportability charge. *See, e.g., Matter of Pichardo*, 21 I&N Dec. 330 (BIA 1996) [where document offered to prove firearms conviction does not specify that weapon was firearm, INS failed to meet burden even where respondent testified he used a gun]; *Matter of Tiwari*, 19 I&N Dec. 875 (BIA 1989), *modified Matter of Tiwari*, 20 I&N Dec. 254 (BIA 1991) [under former INA §241(a)(13) had to prove "for gain" by *Woodby* standard]; *Bigler v. U.S. Att'y Gen.,* 451 F.3d 728, 732–33 (11th Cir. 2006) [in abandonment of residency context the government was required to prove that respondent abandoned his residency by clear and convincing evidence]; *Cruz-Garza v. Ashcroft,* 396 F.3d 1125, 1128–29 (10th Cir. 2005) [DHS did not prove by clear and convincing evidence that reduced felony conviction was an aggravated felony because the reduction of respondent's conviction to a misdemeanor did not meet the *Roldan/Salazar* standards in light of the vagaries of the evidentiary record and the existence of a Utah statute permitting reduction which could have occurred for other than rehabilitative purpose]; *Sandoval v. INS,* 240 F.3d 577, 581–82 (7th Cir. 2001) [reversed deportation order where the IJ improperly placed burden on respondent to prove vacatur was not proper]. Despite the *Woodby* standard, a respondent may be required to go forward with evidence to rebut the government's *prima facie* case in certain circumstances. *Matter of Vivas*, 16 I&N Dec. 68 (BIA 1977) [although burden of proof remains with the government, the burden of going forward falls on respondent when the facts are within his particular knowledge and control and the government has made a *prima facie* case]. However, DHS cannot establish its prima facie case solely through inference drawn by the respondent's Fifth Amendment assertion of silence. *Matter of Guevara*, 20 I&N Dec. 238 (BIA 1991). Nor can it establish deportability by admission of the respondent where the admission was not transcribed but merely noted several months after a master calendar hearing. *Cortez-Acosta v. INS,* 234 F.3d 476 (9th Cir. 2000) [where the IJ did not make a verbatim transcript of the master calendar where the respondent allegedly admitted alien smuggling, but simply noted it in the file five months after the hearing, his notation is evidence but not a finding of fact and it alone is insufficient to meet the *Woodby* standard]. If the respondent denies the allegations, the IJ "shall receive evidence as to any unresolved issue" and one may read these regulations as prohibiting the IJ from obtaining that evidence by simply putting the respondent on the witness stand. *See* 8 C.F.R §§1240.10(c) & (d). On issues concerning alienage the burden remains always on DHS because "it is jurisdictional matter ..." *Murphy v. INS*, 54 F.3d at 608–09 (9th Cir. 1995). However, admission of foreign birth proves alienage and shifts burden to alien to prove time, place and manner of entry. *Matter of Benitez*, 19 I&N Dec. 173 (BIA 1984).

In addition, where time, place and manner of entry are at issue a different standard for going forward also applies. After proof of alienage, respondent must by statute prove time, place, and manner of entry. INA §291. Presumption under INA §291, applicable to deportation charges only where time, place and manner at issue. *Matter of Benitez, supra*. [INA §241(a)(1) charge as stowaway under INA §212(a)(18)]. *But see Iran v. INS*, 656 F.2d 469 (9th Cir. 1981) [presumption inapplicable to overstay cases].

(1) *Burden of Proof Under IIRIRA For Persons Seeking Admission*—Under IIRIRA, the burden of proof is altered for persons who are charged with not being admitted or paroled (EWI). 8 C.F.R. §1240.8(c). If the person is not an applicant for admission, DHS must first establish alienage. But if the respondent is charged as an applicant for admission, unless s/he can establish by clear and convincing evidence that s/he is lawfully present in the U.S. pursuant to a prior lawful admission, s/he must prove that s/he is clearly and beyond a doubt, entitled to be admitted to the U.S., and is not inadmissible as charged. If the person meets that burden, the DHS then has the burden to establish by "clear and convincing evidence" that the person is deportable. INA §§240(c)(2)(B), (c)(3)(A), 8 U.S.C. §§1229a(c)(2)(B), (c)(3)(A); 8 C.F.R. §1240.8(c); H.R. Conf. Rep. No. 828, 104th

Cong., 2d Sess. at 212 (1996). For burden of proof in cases concerning admission, *see in this chapter* ¶ IV.L.4.c (p.153), *supra.*

Access to Visa Documents in Meeting Burden. In meeting the respondent's burden of proof s/he "shall have access to [her] visa or other entry document, if any, and any other records and documents not considered by the [AG] to be confidential pertaining to [her] admission or presence in the United States." INA §240(c)(2).

(2) *Citizenship Cases*—If respondent claims citizenship, s/he bears the burden by a preponderance of the evidence that s/he possess derivative citizenship. *Leal Santos v. Mukasey,* 516 F.3d 1, 4 (1st Cir. 2008) [once DHS establishes that respondent was born abroad, burden then shifts to her to prove derivative citizenship]; *Matter of Tijerina-Villarreal,* 13 I&N Dec. 327, 330–31 (BIA 1969).

(3) Cases Involving Criminal Conduct

(a) *Admission by Respondent Regarding Criminal Conduct*—An admission as to conduct by a respondent is not sufficient to establish deportability under *Woodby* because the IJ must limit his inquiry to the record of conviction. *Matter of Pichardo,* 21 I&N Dec. 330 (BIA 1996) [BIA rejected use of respondent's admission that he used a gun when he was convicted of a weapons charge to establish deportability under *Woodby,* where record of conviction did not specify weapon]. *But see Lara-Ruiz v. INS,* 241 F.3d 934, 941 (7th Cir. 2001) [not improper for BIA to look beyond conviction records to determine that sexual assault was committed against a 4-year-old where no evidentiary hearing was required].

(b) *Vacated Convictions*—*See in this chapter* "Vacated Conviction May Not be a Conviction," ¶ VI.A.9 (p.209) and "Burden of Proof," ¶ VI.A.9.b (p.210), *supra.*

(c) *Aggravated Felony Standard for Summary Removal*—An aggravated felon shall be *conclusively presumed* to be deportable, INA §238(c), and the *Woodby* standard is inapplicable in summary proceedings.

(4) *Cases Involving Conditional Residency*—In deportation proceedings where *conditional residence* terminated because AG made adverse determination on the petition, the alien may request a review of the determination at his deportation hearing. At the hearing, the AG has the burden of proof to establish by a *preponderance of the evidence* that the facts and information described in the petition are not true with respect to the marriage. INA §216(c)(3)(D), 8 U.S.C. §1186a(c)(3)(D).

(5) *Burden and Standard of Proof in Seeking Relief from Removal*—Sec. 101(d) of the REAL ID Act of 2005, PL 109-13 (May 11, 2005) amended INA §240(c) for applications for relief filed on or after May 11, 2005 to clarify that the applicant for relief or protection from removal has the burden to establish: (i) s/he satisfies the applicable eligibility requirements; and (ii) s/he merits a favorable exercise of discretion (where the exercise of discretion is relevant). INA §240(c)(4)(A). The applicant must comply with the applicable information or documentary requirements specified by law, regulation and application instructions. IJ must weigh the credible testimony along with other evidence and can require corroboration unless the applicant does not have the evidence and cannot reasonably obtain it. INA §240(c)(4)(B). Credibility determinations will be made under the same totality of the circumstances test as asylum under INA §208(b)(1)(B)(iii) as well as the same method of determining credibility under that section. INA §240(c)(4)(C). The burden of proof to establish eligibility *and* to establish the privilege of the relief is on the applicant even for applications filed before May 11, 2005. 8 C.F.R. §§240.8(d), 240.11(e), 1240.8(d), 1240.11(e). However, when the applicant is seeking relief, such as cancellation, the burden shifts to the applicant, by a preponderance of the evidence, that he has not committed an aggravated felony or some other disqualifying act once "the evidence indicates" (*i.e.*, once the government presents) such disqualifying evidence of a mandatory ground of denial. 8 C.F.R. §1240.8(d). Thereafter, the burden is met, for example when the disqualifying event is a criminal conviction, by establishing the crime does not fit under the categorical approach and it was *inconclusive* under the modified categorical approach. *Sandoval-Lua v. Gonzales,* 499 F.3d 1121, 1129–32 (9th Cir. 2007) [when re-

spondent produced an *inconclusive* record of conviction on drug trafficking, he has met his burden that under the modified categorical approach he was not convicted of an aggravated felony].

(6) *Rule of Lenity and Rule Granting Presumption to Alien*—Deportation statutes must be narrowly construed in favor of aliens. *Leocal v. Ashcroft,* 543 U.S. 1, 125 S.Ct. 377, 384 n.8 (2004) [applied the rule of lenity as an alternative basis in its interpretation of why negligent acts would not constitute a crime of violence and therefore not an aggravated felony under 18 U.S.C. §16]; *INS v. St. Cyr,* 121 S.Ct. 2271, 2290 (2001) [recognizing the rule of lenity and "the longstanding principle of construing any lingering ambiguities in deportation statutes in favor of the alien"]; *Fong Haw Tan v. Phelan*, 333 U.S. 6 (1948) [matters of doubt should be resolved in favor of the alien in deportation proceedings]; *INS v. Cardoza-Fonseca*, 480 U.S. 421, 449 (1987); *INS v. Errico*, 385 U.S. 214, 225 (1966) [applying rule to provisions relating to relief]; *Rosenberg v. Fleuti*, 374 U.S. 449, 459 (1963); *Bonetti v. Rogers*, 356 U.S. 691, 699 (1958); *Barber v. Gonzalez*, 347 U.S. 637, 642–43 (1954); *Martinez v. Mukasey,* 519 F.3d 532, 542-45 (5th Cir. 2008) [under the first prong of *Chevron* and under longstanding principles construing statutes in favor of persons facing removal, the court concluded that the term "admitted" as used in INA §212(h) does not bar LPRs who were convicted of aggravated felonies from obtaining relief if they obtained LPR status through adjustment because they were not "admitted"]; *Esponda v. U.S. Att'y Gen.,* 453 F.3d 1319, 1322 (11th Cir. 2006) [the "longstanding principle" that deportation laws should be construed in favor of the alien barred summary dismissal of BIA appeal for failure to file a brief where another regulation provided that notice of appeal might be sufficient]; *Azarte v. Ashcroft,* 394 F.3d 1278, 1289 (9th Cir. 2005) [finding *Matter of Shaar* no longer good law for post-IIRIRA cases and reasoning that the motion to reopen statute and the VD statute must be read to toll the VD period while the motion to reopen is pending because *inter alia* deportation statutes should be construed in favor of the alien]; *Hernandez v. Ashcroft,* 345 F.3d 824, 840 (9th Cir. 2003) [in context of interpreting VAWA, the court stated "the general rule of construction that when the legislature enacts an ameliorative rule designed to forestall harsh results, the rule will be interpreted and applied in an ameliorative fashion ... This is particularly so in the immigration context where doubts are to be resolved in favor of the alien"]; *Francis v. Reno,* 269 F.3d 162, 170–71 (3d Cir. 2001) [applying rule of lenity to narrow interpretation of aggravated felony]; *Lennon v. INS*, 527 F.2d 187, 193 (2d Cir. 1975); *Martin v. Gantner,* 443 F.Supp.2d 367, 373 (E.D.N.Y. 2006) [in naturalization application court resolved interpretation of conviction as not being an aggravated felon because doubts are resolved in favor of the alien]; *Pottinger v. Reno,* 51 F.Supp.2d 349, 363 (E.D.N.Y. 1999) *aff'd* 242 F.3d 367 (2d Cir. 2000) [applying rule of lenity in conjunction with *Landgraf* analysis]; *Homayun v. Cravener,* 39 F.Supp.2d 837, 850 (S.D. Tex. 1999); *Matter of Tiwari*, 19 I&N Dec. 875 (BIA 1989); *Matter of Hou*, 20 I&N Dec. 513, 520 (BIA 1992); *Matter of Chartier*, 16 I&N Dec. 284, 287 (BIA 1977); *Matter of G*, 9 I&N Dec. 159, 164 (AG 1961). Similarly, where the immigration statutes are ameliorative doubts should be resolved in favor of aliens. *U.S. v. Sanchez-Guzman*, 744 F.Supp. 997, 1002 (E.D. Wash. 1990). The courts have also repeatedly recognized the complexity of immigration laws as having an effect on persons in INS proceedings. *Montilla v. INS*, 926 F.2d 162 (2d Cir. 1991); *Castro-O'Ryan v. INS*, 847 F.2d 1307, 1312 (9th Cir. 1987); *Doug Sik Kwon v. INS*, 646 F.2d 909, 919 (5th Cir. 1981); *Lok v. INS*, 548 F.2d 37, 38 (2d Cir. 1977). But the Rule of Lenity does not apply where the plain meaning of the statute precludes petitioner's interpretation. *Puello v. USCIS,* 511 F.3d 324, 334 (2d Cir. 2007) [in defining conviction, the plain language of the statute requires that a judgment be entered and therefore Rule of Lenity was inapplicable]; *Ruiz-Almanzar v. Ridge,* 485 F.3d 193, 198–99 (2d Cir. 2007) [Rule of Lenity cannot be applied whenever there is an ambiguity in a statute or *Chevron* deference would be meaningless; it is only applied when other cannons of statutory construction are not capable of resolving the statute's meaning and the BIA has not offered a reasonable interpretation]; *Spina v. DHS,* 470 F.3d 116, 129–30 (2d Cir. 2006) [where traditional rules of statutory construction permit the court to conclude that the statute is not ambiguous, the rule does not apply]. *See* "Deportation Statutes" in Ch. 10, Section X.C (p.1206), *infra*.

(7) *Review of IJ's finding is under the "substantial evidence" test*—8 U.S.C. §1252(b)(4)(B). *Thiam v. Gonzales,* 496 F.3d 912 (8th Cir. 2007) [substantial evidence supported EWI charge where respondent's passport indicated she left the country while she insisted and provided some proof she did not]; *Dia v. Ashcroft,* 353 F.3d 228, 248–61 (3d Cir. 2003) (*en banc*) [finding that 242(b)(4)(B) codified *Elias-Zacarias* thereby maintaining the traditional substantial evidence standard and reversed the IJ's credibility finding on asylum]. *But see Castaneda-Castillo v. Gonzales,* 488 F.3d 17, 22–26 (1st Cir. 2007) (*en banc*) [reversed adverse credibility determination and the *en banc* court noted that the language in 8 U.S.C. §1252(b)(4)(B) regarding reversal only if evidence "compels" reversal reflects a "gloss by the Supreme Court" and does not "eliminate[] the conventional requirement that an administrative agency's explanation be rational"]

Judicial review of *Woodby* standard under the substantial-evidence test is in dispute. ***Compare*** *Adefemi v. Ashcroft,* 386 F.3d 1022, 1029 (11th Cir. 2004) (*en banc*) [relying on a highly deferential view of the substantial-evidence test, the court affirmed the use of a City Court of Atlanta document that contains several ambiguities to establish deportability for a firearms offense by clear and convincing evidence because the court under the substantial-evidence test "must affirm the agency's decision unless there is no reasonable basis for that decision"] ***with*** *Francis v. Gonzales,* 442 F.3d 131, 138–39 (2d Cir. 2006) [joining the Sixth and Ninth Circuits the court determined that the substantial-evidence test required reversal where the government did not establish deportability by clear and convincing evidence (*i.e.*, "any rational trier of fact would be compelled to conclude that the proof did not rise to the level of clear and convincing evidence") and not as the Eleventh Circuit found that reversible error occurs only where there is no reasonable basis for the decision]. *But see also Bigler v. U.S. Att'y Gen.,* 451 F.3d 728, 732–33 (11th Cir. 2006) [substantial-evidence test used to establish that the government presented clear and convincing evidence that respondent abandoned his LPR status].

7.r. Interpretation—8 C.F.R. §1240.5. A person who does not understand English who is in proceeding has an absolute right to a translation as part of the right to present evidence and cross-examine witnesses. *Ememe v. Ashcroft,* 358 F.3d 446 (7th Cir. 2004) [where IJ made adverse credibility findings based upon statements at credible fear interview conducted in Italian and person's native language was Amharic case remanded to determine whether she comprehended questions]; *Amadou v. INS,* 226 F.3d 724 (6th Cir. 2000) [applicant for asylum deprived of due process right to a full and fair hearing because of incompetent translation]; *Abovian v. INS,* 219 F.3d 972, 979, 980 (9th Cir. 2000) [adverse credibility determination that may have been based on faulty interpretation reversed]; *Drobny v. INS*, 947 F.2d 241, 244 (7th Cir. 1991) [INA §212(c) proceeding]; *Haitian Refugee Center, Inc. v. Nelson*, 872 F.2d 1555 (11th Cir. 1989), *aff'd*, 111 S.Ct. 888 (1991) [constitutional right to translation at SAW interviews]; *Marincas v. Lewis*, 92 F.3d 195, 204 (3d Cir. 1996) [stowaways who are asylum applicants must have right to translator]; *Montecino v. INS*, 915 F.2d 518, 521 (9th Cir. 1990); *Augustin v. Sava*, 735 F.2d 32 (2d Cir. 1984) [exclusion/asylum proceeding]; *Tejeda-Mata v. INS*, 626 F.2d 721, 726 (9th Cir. 1980), *cert. denied*, 456 U.S. 994 (1982); *Bajrami v. Greene*, __ F.Supp. __, Case No. 94-S-1783 (D. Colo. June 2, 1995) (Sparr, J.). *But see Teng v. Mukasey,* 516 F.3d 12, 17–18 (2d Cir. 2008) [no due process violation where petitioner failed to point to any specific part of his testimony that was mistranslated]; *Mohamed v. Gonzales,* 477 F.3d 522, 527 (8th Cir. 2007) [failure to translate the Somali word for schizophrenia but numerous references in record to respondent's mental illness does not support due process violation because there is no showing of prejudice]; *Gishta v. Gonzales,* 404 F.3d 972, 978–80 (6th Cir. 2005) [court denied due process challenge where there were only isolated examples of mistranslations, where improper interpretation was not raised before IJ, and where there was no showing of prejudice]; *Kuqo v. Ashcroft,* 391 F.3d 856 (7th Cir. 2004) [where respondent failed to demonstrate either that the translation was actually flawed or that he was prejudiced, a translation of respondent's testimony in a different Albanian dialect was not a due process violation]; *Khan v. Ashcroft,* 374 F.3d 825 (9th Cir. 2004) [upheld denial of motion to reopen *in absentia* hearing to seek asylum, where respondent attended master calendar, did not show up for continued hearing, and claimed due process violation because master calendar hearing was not translated]; *Abdullah v. INS,* 184 F.3d 158, 164–66 (2d Cir. 1999) [distinguished and disagreed with *HRC v. Nelson* and found no right under *Mathews* analysis where person seeking a benefit in SAW context]. Where statements are written in a language a witness cannot understand, they are not admissible absent corroboration. *Hernandez-Garza v. INS*, 882 F.2d 945, 948 (5th Cir. 1989). Moreover, there is an absolute right to competent translation. *Matter of Tomas*, 19 I&N Dec. 464 (BIA 1987). In evaluating incompetent translation claims there are three kinds: (1) Direct evidence of incorrectly translated words; (2) Unresponsive answers by the witness; or (3) Witness's expression of difficulty understanding what is said to him. *Perez-Lastor v. INS,* 208 F.3d 773, 778 (9th Cir. 2000) [finding due process violation for failure to properly translate from Quiche because "an incorrect or incomplete translation is the functional equivalent of no translation"]; *Tun v. Gonzales,* 485 F.3d 1014 (8th Cir. 2007) [respondent's due process rights were violated where interpretation was seriously flawed because there was evidence of mistranslated words, that the witness was unable to understand the translator, and that there were unresponsive answers from the witness]. In the view of some courts, the respondent must show that a better translation would have made a difference in the outcome of the hearing before a decision will be reversed. *Meas v. Ashcroft,* 363 F.3d 729, 730 (8th Cir. 2004) [respondent failed to demonstrate how alleged deficiencies of the translator prejudiced her case]; *Gutierrez-Chavez v. INS,* 298 F.3d 824, 830 (9th Cir. 2003) *amended on denial of rehearing* 337 F.3d 1023 (9th Cir. 2003) [for due process violation must demonstrate that a better translation likely would have made a difference in the outcome]; *Hadjimehdigholi v. INS*, 49 F.3d 642, 649–50 (10th Cir. 1995); *Perez-Lastor v. INS,* 208 F.3d 773, 780–81 & n.8 (9th Cir. 2000). And the burden is on the respondent to clearly raise the issue of faulty translation. *Singh v. Ashcroft,* 367 F.3d 1139, 1143–44 (9th Cir. 2004) [although sharing the dissent's concern regarding the poor translation, the court affirmed the denial of asylum for lack of credibility because the "dissatisfied party bears the burden of ensuring the translations and their transcription are correct"]. There is also no *per se* right to simultaneous interpretation of the entire proceedings. *Matter of Exilus*, 18 I&N Dec. 276 (BIA 1982); *El Rescate Legal Services, Inc. v. EOIR*, 959 F.2d 742 (9th Cir. 1992) (*on rehearing*) [neither the INA nor the constitution mandates complete translation and plaintiff's facial challenge was rejected]. Also, the failure to object and to raise additional evidence that was precluded as a result of poor translation prevented reversal of deportation order on those grounds. *Cheo v. INS,* 162 F.3d 1227, 1230 (9th Cir. 1998). The BIA has also concluded that the government's interpreter has no requirement to assist someone to fill out an asylum application. *Matter of C-*, 20 I&N Dec. 529 (BIA 1992). The form for the translation, as well as the requirement that all documents be translated, is now specified at 8 C.F.R. §1003.33. *Ramaj v. Gonzales,* 466 F.3d 520, 530 (6th Cir. 2006) [where the translated documents did not contain a statement that the translator was competent in Albanian and English the documents were properly excluded]; *Krasnopivtsev v. Ashcroft,* 382 F.3d 832, 837–38 (8th Cir. 2005) [it was not error for IJ to deny admitting untranslated foreign passport without certification]. At least one court has determined that a person who waives the right to an interpreter, "cannot now blame inconsistencies in his testimony on his lack of fluency" in the face of an IJ determination that he lacked credibility. *Tarrawally v. Ashcroft,* 338 F.3d 180, 186 (3d Cir. 2003).

7.s. Administrative Closure—A case may not be administratively closed if opposed by either party. *Matter of Gutierrez*, 21 I&N Dec. 479, 480 (BIA 1996) (and cases cited therein). DHS will agree to administrative close a file where the respondent is *prima facie* eligible for TPS or Deferred Enforced Departure. Memo, Carpenter, Deputy Gen. Co., HQCOU 120/12.2-P (Feb. 7, 2002), *reported in* 79 No. 15 *Interpreter Releases* 524, 530–38 (Apr. 8, 2002) [establishing Service policy of agreeing to administrative closure where someone is *prima facie* eligible]. The DHS can also agree to administratively close cases and recharge someone in removal proceedings so that s/he would get the benefit of cancellation of removal. The DHS will not agree to reopen a case on this basis but once reopened they are generally required to agree to administratively close the case absent unusual circumstances. Memo, Cooper, G.C. (HQCOU 90/16.1-P) (Dec. 7 1999), Memo, Virtue, G.C. (HQCOU 90/16.1-P) (Dec. 7, 1998), *reprinted in* 77 No. 2 *Interpreter Releases* 39, 55–58 (Jan. 10, 2000). The BIA also has agreed to administratively close files where "repapering" is available. Memo, Scialabba, BIA Vice Chair (Mar. 14, 2000), available at *www.usdoj.gov/eoir/chip6.pdf*, and Memo, Schmidt, BIA Chairman (Aug. 20, 2000), available at *www.usdoj.gov/eoir/vll/genifo/streamimplem.pdf*. Where reopening is sought on certain issues in a case administratively closed, the BIA can review *those* issues as long as the party appeals those issues. All other issues that were administratively closed will remain so and the party does not waive any rights obtained when the case was administratively closed. *Matter of Gutierrez, supra* [motion to reopen for adjustment does not waive *ABC* settlement rights]. The circuit courts have jurisdiction to review the denial of administrative closure. *Garza-Moreno v. Gonzales,* 489 F.3d 239, 242–43 (6th Cir. 2007) [court has jurisdiction to review denial of administrative closure but there was no error where DHS opposed closure]; *Alcaraz v. INS,* 384 F.3d 1150 (9th Cir. 2004) [found jurisdiction to review denial of administrative closure to repaper case and remanded case to BIA to determine whether repapering policy had been violated], *but see Lopez-Reyes v. Gonzales,* 496 F.3d 20 (1st Cir. 2007) [failed to raise administrative closure argument resulted in failure to exhaust administrative remedies].

7.t. Harmless Error Doctrine—Violation of DHS/DOJ procedural rule or regulation *under* BIA does not *per se* invalidate deportation proceeding. Must have harmful prejudicial effect. *Matter of Santos,* 19 I&N Dec. 105 (BIA 1984); *Matter of R-S-H- et al.,* 23 I&N Dec. 629, 644 (BIA 2003) [where respondent never informed of prehearing voluntary departure there was no showing prejudice; *Matter of Cordova* distinguished]; *Tariq v. Keisler,* 505 F.3d 650, 657–58 (7th Cir. 2007) [BIA's failure to address asylum applicant's motion to supplement the record on appeal was harmless because even if fully credited it would not have effected the denial of asylum]; *Gilaj v. Gonzales,* 408 F.3d 275, 290 (6th Cir. 2005) [recognizing due process right to opening statement and closing argument but finding harmless error where respondent failed to demonstrate prejudice]; *Hernandez-Luis v. INS,* 869 F.2d 496 (9th Cir. 1989) [must show violation prejudiced an interest protected by the regulation]. The BIA now uses a two-part test to determine whether or not a deportation hearing should be invalidated: (1) whether the agency regulation that was violated serves a purpose or benefit to a respondent; and (2) whether the violation prejudiced interests of the respondent which were protected. *Matter of Hernandez,* 21 I&N Dec. 224 (BIA 1996); *U.S. v. Calderon-Medina,* 591 F.2d 529 (9th Cir. 1979). *But see Accardi v. Shaughnessy,* 347 U.S. 260 (1954); *Bui v. INS,* 76 F.3d 268 (9th Cir. 1996) [the BIA cannot speculate as to the claimed harmless error]; *Waldron v. INS,* 17 F.3d 511 (2d Cir. 1994), *cert. denied,* 513 U.S. 1014 (1994) [rejecting harmless error doctrine only where fundamental right derived from constitution or federal statute, such as the right to counsel, at stake]; *Montilla v. INS,* 926 F.2d 162 (2d Cir. 1991); *Sewak v. INS,* 900 F.2d 667, 670 n.7 (3d Cir. 1990) [rejecting harmless error argument even in absence of respondent's affirmative defense to deportation where respondent did not receive notice of hearing and INS still has *Woodby* burden]; *Haitian Refugee Center v. Smith,* 676 F.2d 1023 (5th Cir. 1982); *Shahandeh-Pey v. INS,* 831 F.2d 1384 (7th Cir. 1987) [if violation of procedural protection "actually had the potential for effecting the outcome of the deportation hearing"]; *Millian-Zamora v. Ashcroft,* 228 F.Supp.2d 272, 277–80 (E.D.N.Y. 2002) [where IJ violated the law and regulation by not recording a witness' testimony prejudice need not be shown]; *Matter of Michel,* 21 I&N Dec. 1101 (BIA 1998) [reversed order of removal where IJ failed to comply with 8 C.F.R. §240.10(a)(1) by not ascertaining on the record whether respondent desired counsel]. *See also Arizona v. Fulminante,* 499 U.S. 279, 309 (1991) [harmless error rule not applicable in cases involving "structural defects"].

7.u. Immigration Court Record—The record of proceeding in an immigration court may only be created by an IJ. No other "photographic, video, electronic, or similar recording device will be permitted to record any part of the proceeding." 8 C.F.R. §1003.28. Parties and members of the press, however, may have laptop computers, wireless telephones, and electronic calendars provided they do not disrupt the proceedings. Memo [OPPM 04-01], Creppy, Chief IJ, EOIR (Feb. 3, 2004), *published on* AILA InfoNet at Doc. No. 04022375. If the IJ permits the respondent to file a brief, need not record all parts of hearing. 8 C.F.R. §1240.9. Where IJ refused to go on record with party's objections concerning the case, it was reversed and remanded. *Matter of Garcia-Reyes,* 19 I&N Dec. 830 (BIA 1988). *See also Okoroha v. INS,* 715 F.2d 380, 383–84 (8th Cir. 1983). But IJ not reversed for excluding parts of record in absence of prejudice. *Brice v. INS,* 806 F.2d 415 (2d Cir. 1986); *Avila-Murrieta v. INS,* 762 F.2d 733 (9th Cir. 1985). Failure to put evidence in record because IJ suggested off-the-record it was unnecessary, precluded argument in federal court that record was inadequate. *Baria v.*

Reno, 94 F.3d 1335, 1340 (9th Cir. 1996). However, the failure to record a witness' testimony is so fundamental that it would require further proceedings even in the absence of a showing of prejudice. *Millian-Zamora v. Ashcroft,* 228 F.Supp.2d 272, 277–80 (E.D.N.Y. 2002) [where IJ violated the law §1229a(b)(4)(C) and regulation §240.9 by not recording a witness' testimony prejudice need not be shown]. The EOIR has now limited the use of off-the-record activity by IJs. Off-the-record dialogue should only occur "on rare occasions" when it is necessary "to the fair, expeditious and proper conduct of the hearing." If the IJ initiates the process he must inform the parties that the discussion will be summarized on the record, make it clear that the tape recorder is being turned off, summarize the discussion on the record and ask the parties if the summary is accurate and "if they have anything to add to the summary." Memo [OPPM 03-06], Creppy, Chief IJ, EOIR (Oct. 10, 2003), *published on* AILA InfoNet at Doc. No. 03121714. Where IJ has closed the hearing, a party may not submit evidence except on a motion to reopen. 8 C.F.R. §1003.31(c) [if application or document is not filed within time set by IJ, it is waived]; *Chay-Velasquez v. Ashcroft,* 367 F.3d 751, 756 (8th Cir. 2004) [upheld IJ's denial of the admission of a supplemental filing to asylum application after record was closed].

7.v. Presence of Applicant/Respondent at Hearing—IIRIRA provides for four forms of proceedings: (1) in person; (2) in the absence of respondent by agent of parties; (3) through video conference; and (4) telephonic hearing.

(1) Telephonic Hearing—A telephonic hearing may only be with the consent of the respondent. INA §240(b)(2), 8 U.S.C. §1229a(b)(2). A telephonic hearing held over the objection of the respondent may violate his or her right to be physically present at the hearing. *Purba v. INS*, 884 F.2d 516 (9th Cir. 1989) [under pre-IIRIRA statute the court reversed deportation order where hearing held telephonically over respondent's objection]. *But see Beltran-Tirado v. INS,* 213 F.3d 1179, 1185–86 (9th Cir. 2000) [telephonic testimony of key witness was "fair"]; *Bigby v. INS*, 21 F.3d 1059, 1063–64 (11th Cir. 1994) [unless credibility determination at issue, telephonic hearing is permissible]; *Matter of Villalba*, 21 I&N Dec. 842 (BIA 1997) [telephonic hearing *in absentia* and therefore without respondent's consent is permissible].

(2) Respondent Not Present at Hearing—If respondent cannot be present due to mental incompetency the AG shall prescribe safeguards to protect his rights and privileges. INA §240(b)(3). By regulation the AG has allowed an attorney, legal representative, legal guardian, near relative or friend to represent and appear on behalf of the respondent. 8 C.F.R. §1240.8. *See Ramos v. Gonzales,* 414 F.3d 800, 804–06 (7th Cir. 2005) [no due process violation where lawyer with EOIR-28 waived client's presence at all hearings and there was no showing of prejudice despite respondent's claim that IJ should have determined that lawyer was authorized to waive his appearance].

(3) Video Hearing—A hearing involving a video conference may have inherent problems that interfere with the right of representation and the ability of the IJ to engage in appropriate fact finding. In asylum hearings credibility findings are central and video conferencing "may render it difficult for a factfinder ... to make credibility determinations and to gauge demeanor." And "Because video conferencing permits the petitioner to be in one location and an IJ in another, its use results in a 'Catch 22' situation for the petitioner's lawyer. ... The effectiveness of the lawyer is diminished." *Rusu v. INS,* 296 F.3d 316, 322–24 (4th Cir. 2002) [finding inherent problems with video conferencing but determining on the facts in the case the respondent was not denied a full and fair hearing]. *See also* Letter, Creppy, Chief IJ, EOIR, Response to Chicago Appleseed Fund for Justice report on video conferencing in the Chicago court (Aug. 31, 2005), *published on* AILA InfoNet at Doc. No. 05110965. However, EOIR has adopted video conferencing on a national level. *See e.g.,* Letter, Rooney, Director EOIR (June 17, 2004), *published on* AILA InfoNet at Doc. No. 04062916 [supporting establishment of the Headquarters Immigration Court in Falls Church, Va., to do video hearing throughout the United States]. In *Eke v. Mukasey,* 512 F.3d 372, 382–83 (7th Cir. 2008) the circuit court relied on a *Mathews v. Eldridge* analysis to determine that petitioner had no due process right to a hearing in the physical presence of the IJ and on the facts of the case the court found that video conferencing was consistent with due process.

(4) Location of the Hearing for Circuit Court Review—The EOIR has also required IJs to specifically state the location of the hearing, which is often different than where the IJ may be physically sitting. In part, this is necessary to establish venue for purposes of judicial review. For example, an IJ sitting in Chicago but conducting a hearing with a respondent in Kansas City, Mo., must state on the record that the location of the hearing is Kansas City, which would result in review in the 8th Circuit instead of the 7th Circuit (Chicago). Memo [OPPM 04-06], Creppy, Chief IJ, EOIR, (Aug. 18, 2004), *published on* AILA InfoNet at Doc. No. 04081891.

7.w. Hearing *In Absentia*

(1) Under IIRIRA—INA §240(b)(5), 8 U.S.C. §1229a(b)(5). A person who fails to appear at his removal hearing after proper notice shall be ordered removed "if the Service establishes by clear, unequivocal, and convincing evidence that the written notice was so provided and that the alien is removable." *Williams-Igwonobe v. Gonzales,* 437 F.3d 453 (5th Cir. 2006) [in pre-IIRIRA case, where IJ proceeded *in absentia* and simply entered a boilerplate order finding respondent abandoned his applications for INA §212(h) rather than holding a hearing on it, he violated the *in absentia* requirement of holding a hearing on the merits before entering an *in absentia* order]; *Wellington v. INS*, 108 F.3d 631, 636–37 (5th Cir. 1997) [pre-IIRIRA case finding that government did not meet burden in INA §242B *in absentia* case where deportation order was reopened and thereafter *in absentia* order without proof was entered]. Written notice, pursuant to INA §239, 8 U.S.C. §1229, must be given in person or if personal service is not practicable through service by mail to the respondent or his attorney. *The use of certified return receipt mail is no longer required.* The new provisions that went into effect Apr. 1, 1997 under IIRIRA also provide:

(a) A person who, without reasonable cause, fails or refuses to attend a removal proceeding is barred from seeking entry to the U.S. within 5 years of her subsequent departure or removal. INA §212(a)(6)(B). Under the former statute (INA §242B) this included any time that a respondent failed to appear for a deportation hearing after proper notice, (when his or her appearance was not excused by the IJ), even if counsel appeared for the respondent and the issue of deportability had already been determined. *Matter of W-F-*, 21 I&N Dec. 503 (BIA 1996) [INA §242B applies to failure to appear at any hearing including those concerning relief after deportability was established].

i) Departure Prior to Hearing. At least one court has determined that an IJ is compelled to enter an *in absentia* order of removal and may not terminate proceedings for a person who departs prior to her scheduled hearing. *Ahmed v. Gonzales,* 432 F.3d 709 (7th Cir. 2005) [relying on 8 C.F.R. §1003.26 and 8 U.S.C. §1229a(b)(5), the court found that in the case of an incompetent minor who departed the U.S. prior to his final removal hearing that the IJ had no discretion to terminate proceedings and was required to enter an *in absentia* order].

(b) A person who has a final order entered against her *in absentia* after receiving *oral notice* is barred from most forms of relief for 10 years including cancellation of removal under INA §240A, voluntary departure under INA §240B, adjustment of status under INA §245, and registry under INA §249. *See* INA §240(b)(7). The bar was formerly 5 years. The bar only applies where the failure to appear was not due to exceptional circumstances and where the person was provided oral notice in her own language or a language she understands regarding the time and place of the hearing and the consequences for the failure to appear. INA §240(b)(7). Under the predecessor statute containing substantially similar language (§242B(e)(1)), the BIA has determined that a person who did not receive oral notice need not move to rescind the *in absentia* order, but can simply move to reopen based on other factors, *e.g.*, marriage to a USC. *Matter of M-S-,* 22 I&N Dec. 349 (BIA 1998). [allowed motion to reopen where *in absentia* order without oral notice was entered in January, motion to reopen was filed in March, and visa petition based on marriage to USC was approved in May]; *Wu v. INS,* 436 F.3d 157, 162–64 (2d Cir. 2006) [where respondent was not given oral warnings and where he sought asylum which was not barred by the former 5-year provision, the BIA abused its discretion in not considering his motion to reopen based upon a change-of-law argument, even if the BIA was correct in not rescinding its *in absentia* order]. *But see Grigous v. Gonzales,* 460 F.3d 156, 161–63 (1st Cir. 2006) [*Matter of M-S-* did not automatically require reopening where the relief sought was asylum which is not barred under INA §240(b)(7) and respondent failed to make the required showing for reopening].

(c) The *in absentia* order may be rescinded only if: (i) a motion to reopen is filed within 180 days of the date of the order and the person demonstrates there were exceptional circumstances; or (ii) a motion to reopen is filed at any time and the person can demonstrate that failure to appear was due to a lack of proper notice in accordance with INA §239 or that s/he was in state or federal custody and the failure to appear was through no fault of his or her own. INA §240(b)(5)(C), 8 U.S.C. §1229a(b)(5)(C) and 8 C.F.R. §1003.23(b)(4)(ii). The motion, in the view of one circuit, can only be made to an IJ, not the BIA. *Singh v. Gonzales,* 436 F.3d 484 (5th Cir. 2006) [upheld BIA decision that motion to reopen to rescind *in absentia* order could only be filed with the IJ, not the BIA]

The 180-day period is subject to equitable tolling where there is ineffective assistance of counsel. *Aris v. Mukasey,* 517 F.3d 595 (2d Cir. 2008) [ineffective assistance of counsel even if it occurs through a paralegal's misrepresentation is an exceptional circumstance and also tolls the 180 day period];*Pervaiz v. Gonzales,* 405 F.3d 488, 490 (7th Cir. 2005) [because the 180-day period to reopen an *in absentia* determination is not jurisdictional, but a statute of limitations, it may be tolled for ineffective assistance of counsel where counsel failed to distinguish between the adequacy of notice and his client's failure to receive notice of a change in time of hearing]; *Borges v. Gonzales,* 402 F.3d 398 (3d Cir. 2005) [if notary working with lawyer committed fraud, then 180-day period is tolled, then motion to reopen is timely filed, and ineffectiveness of counsel would thereafter constitute an exceptional circumstance to rescind order; *Bejar* distinguished]; *Lopez v. INS,* 184 F.3d 1097 (9th Cir. 1999). [where respondent did not appear at hearing because of fraudulent misrepresentation of nonlawyer, the 180-day period for filing reopening under former INA §242B(c)(3)(A) was tolled]. The numerical limits are also not jurisdictional and therefore subject to tolling. *Joshi v. Ashcroft,* 389 F.3d 732, 734–35 (7th Cir. 2004) [deadlines that govern transitions from one court to another such as from the BIA to the circuit court are jurisdictional but other deadlines such as the number or time limitation on motions to reopen are not and court could review BIA's denial of fourth motion to reopen *in absentia order*]; *Varela v. INS,* 204 F.3d 1237 (9th Cir. 2000) [numerical limitation on motions to reopen is equitably tolled where second motion was filed after person was defrauded by notary purporting to provide legal representation]. Equitable tolling is also appropriate where the fraudulent actions are by persons who are immigration consultants and not attorneys. *Fajardo v. INS,* 300 F.3d 1018 (9th Cir. 2002) [180-day period equitably tolled where immigration consultants made misrepresentations that prevented respondent from attending hearing or appealing; court suggested in fn.8 that misrepresentation would constitute an exceptional circumstance]. The limitations period is tolled until the respondent "definitively learns" of counsel's ineffectiveness or fraud.*Albillo-De Leon v. Gonzales,* 410 F.3d 1090, 1100 (9th Cir. 2005) [where respondent was defrauded by nonlawyer who posed as a lawyer, the time period for filing a motion to reopen under NACARA §203(c) and 8 C.F.R. §1003.43(e)(1) was tolled until date that current attorney found out that motion was not filed].

However, where a party fails to exercise due diligence in pursuing her rights, equitable tolling is unavailable. *Yuan Gao v. Mukasey,* 519 F.3d 376 (7th Cir. 2008) [a 75-day wait to file motion to reopen was deemed to be lack of due diligence]; *Singh v. Gonzales,* 491 F.3d 1090, 1096–97 (9th Cir. 2007) [upheld lack of due diligence where respondent waited approximately six months to take any action with a new lawyer after he became suspicious]; *Wang v. Board of Immigration Appeals,* 508

F.3d 710, 715 (2d Cir. 2007) [upheld denial of motion to reopen where petitioner waited 8 months after learning of ineffective assistance and 5 months after complying with *Lozada* to file motion].*Singh v. Gonzales,* 491 F.3d 1090, 1096–97 (9th Cir. 2007) [upheld lack of due diligence where respondent waited approximately six months to take any action with a new lawyer after he became suspicious]; *Tapia-Martinez v. Gonzales,* 482 F.3d 417, 423–24 (6th Cir. 2007) [equitable tolling not applied to numerical limitations where respondent failed to exercise due diligence and file motions regarding her former lawyers]; *Habchy v. Gonzales,* 471 F.3d 858, 864–66 (8th Cir. 2006) [no equitable tolling where respondent's argument is that he lost the opportunity to reopen his case because of his own *pro se* initial motion to reopen]; *Patel v. Gonzales,* 442 F.3d 1011 (7th Cir. 2006) [court upheld BIA decision not to allow equitable tolling where respondent family failed to exercise due diligence as they waited almost 2 years to file motion to reopen based upon ineffective assistance]; *Mahmood v. Gonzales,* 427 F.3d 248 (3d Cir. 2005) [recognized equitable tolling for ineffective assistance in failing to notify client about prior order thereby missing the time for filing a motion to reopen, but denied petition for lack of due diligence by respondent]; *Kanyi v. Gonzales,* 406 F.3d 1087, 1090–91 (8th Cir. 2005) [court did not decide equitable tolling of 180-day period for *in absentia* reopening because respondent did not act with due diligence]; *Scorteanu v. INS,* 339 F.3d 407, 412–14 (6th Cir. 2003) [where respondent failed to file motion to reopen within 180 days after he learned of prior lawyer's misfeasance the doctrine of equitable tolling did not apply because of lack of due diligence]; *Jobe v. INS,* 238 F.3d 96 (1st Cir. 2001) (en banc) [failure by respondent to file motion to reopen for several months after he received notice that removal order had been entered *in absentia* 6 months before prevents equitable tolling].

One circuit has taken the view that it is jurisdictional and times periods may not be waived. *Anin v. Reno,* 188 F.3d 1273, 1278–79 (11th Cir. 1999), *affirming Matter of A-A-,* 22 I&N Dec. 140 (BIA 1998) [the exceptional circumstance claim based upon counsel's failure to inform client of deportation hearing may not be heard because it was not brought within the 180-day period and that period is jurisdictional]. *But see generally Huerta v. Gonzales,* 443 F.3d 753 (10th Cir. 2006) [following *Eberhart v. U.S.,* 546 U.S. 12 (2005), and discussing difference between jurisdictional rules and mandatory claim-processing rules including the 30 day appeal period to the BIA which the court did not regard as jurisdictional]. There may also be a weakening of the 11th Circuit position. *Pereira v. U.S. Attorney General,* 258 Fed. Appx. 277, 279-80 (11th Cir. 2007) [in unpublished decision seeking to distinguish *Anin* and *Abidi* as *dicta*].

Numerical Limitation on Motions to Reopen Not Applicable—The filing of a motion to reopen for *deportation* cases is *not* subject to the one motion rule in *in absentia* cases that is imposed in other cases. 8 C.F.R. §1003.23(b)(4)(iii)(D); *Saakian v. INS,* 252 F.3d 21, 25 (1st Cir. 2001). A party may therefore make as many motions to reopen as he wishes to reopen to challenge the *in absentia* order in deportation and exclusion (but not removal) proceedings. *Matter of Cruz-Garcia,* 22 I&N Dec. 1155 (BIA 1999) [under *existing* regulations there are no time or numerical limitations for pre-242B cases to challenge the *in absentia* order and the "reasonable cause" test not the "exceptional circumstances" test applies]. Contrast requirements for *in absentia* orders in deportation proceedings 8 C.F.R. §1003.23(b)(4)(iii)(A) & (D) with those in removal proceedings. 8 C.F.R. §1003.23(b)(4)(ii). *Luntungan v. Att'y Gen. of the U.S.,* 449 F.3d 551, 555–57 (3d Cir. 2006) [finding numerical limit does apply to *in absentia* orders in removal under 8 C.F.R. §1003.23(b)(4)(ii) as distinguished from *in absentia* deportation orders and holding that equitable tolling did not apply to third motion to reopen where second motion was not numerically barred or denied due to incompetence of second counsel]; *Joshi v. Ashcroft,* 389 F.3d 732, 734 (7th Cir. 2004) [discussing the distinction and pointing to BIA's error, but allowing tolling because one motion rule is not jurisdictional]. *But see Montano Cisneros v. U.S. Att'y Gen.,* 514 F.3d 1224 (11th Cir. 2008) [numerical bar does not apply in removal proceedings to the case as a whole, but to each removal order, and where first motion to reopen was granted, respondent is not numerically barred from filing a motion to reopen second removal order].

No Time Limit on Motion Based on Lack of Notice—Andia v. Ashcroft, 359 F.3d 1181 (9th Cir. 2004) [where respondent alleged lack of notice of *in absentia* hearing, the 180-day time limit to reopen was inapplicable; the IJ erred in applying it and the BIA erred in determining that reopening was a matter of discretion]. *But see Derezinski v. Mukasey,* 516 F.3d 619, 620–21 (7th Cir. 2008) [BIA upheld in denying motion filed after 11 years where petitioner disappeared after first motion to reopen was denied and nothing had changed in 11 years].

(d) The *filing* of a motion to reopen for exceptional circumstances or failure to obtain notice *stays* deportation until the IJ rules. INA §240(b)(5)(C). If an appeal is taken to the BIA of the IJ's decision, deportation will be automatically stayed until the BIA rules. *Matter of Rivera*, 21 I&N Dec. 232 (BIA 1996); *But see Galvez-Vergara v. Gonzales,* 484 F.3d 798, 803 n.7 (5th Cir. 2007) [stay is automatic only until IJ rules]; *Bejar v. Ashcroft,* 324 F.3d 127, 132–33 (3d Cir. 2003) [following 8 C.F.R. §1003.23(b)(4)(ii) the court held that it was lawful to remove the respondent during the 30-day period between IJ's denial of the motion to reopen *in absentia* and the appeal to the BIA because "neither the INA nor the regulations provide for an automatic stay of...removal during the 30-day period"].

(e) There is no direct appeal to the BIA from an order of deportation entered *in absentia.* INA §240(b)(5)(C). The party can only file a motion to reopen before the IJ and appeal that decision to the BIA. *Matter of Guzman,* 22 I&N Dec. 722 (BIA 1999) [post-IIRIRA applied to removal proceedings]; *Matter of Gonzalez-Lopez*, 20 I&N Dec. 644 (BIA 1993) [pre-IIRIRA applied to deportation proceedings]. A motion made before an IJ may be reconsidered by another IJ who received the transferred case. *Singh-Bhathal v. INS,* 170 F.3d 943 (9th Cir. 1999) [where first IJ granted motion to reopen and to transfer case, the Court upheld the reconsideration and subsequent denial of the motion to reopen by the second IJ].

(f) When does an *in absentia* order become final? In light of the procedure to require first a motion to reopen and then an appeal, at least one court has held that a motion to reopen an *in absentia* order does not become final for some purposes until the BIA rules on the motion to reopen. *Kay v. Ashcroft,* 387 F.3d 664, 670–73 (7th Cir. 2004) [finding that in an *in absentia* case an order from the BIA does not become final for purposes of a motion to reopen under §208.18(b)(2) until there is a final decision by the BIA on the *in absentia* claim].

(g) Judicial review of an *in absentia* order "shall ... be confined to (i) the validity of the notice provided to the alien; (ii) the reasons for the alien's not attending the preceding; and (iii) whether or not the alien is removable." INA §240(b)(5)(D). *Abu Hasirah v. DHS,* 478 F.3d 474, 477 n.1 (2d Cir. 2007) [reversed *in absentia* order because respondent's unintentional lateness by 15 minutes was not a failure to appear]; *Cabrera-Perez v. Gonzales,* 456 F.3d 109 (3d Cir. 2006) [respondent's tardiness by 15-20 minutes because of traffic and unfamiliarity of the area by the driver was not a failure to appear]. *See also Nazarova v. INS,* 171 F.3d 478, 482 (7th Cir. 1999) [analysis under former judicial review statute].

(2) Immigration Act of 1990 (former INA §242B, 8 U.S.C. §1252b)—Prior to IIRIRA, Congress had established similar consequences and similar procedures when an *in absentia* order was entered. One major distinction, however, was that notice had to be sent by certified return receipt mail. Another distinction was that the bars to relief only applied for 5 years not 10. *Former* INA §242B(e). The procedures under this statute govern *in absentia* deportation orders entered between June 13, 1992 (the effective date of prior INA §242B) and Apr. 1, 1997 (the effective date of INA §240(b)).

(3) *In Absentia* Proceedings Prior to INA §242B—Prior to June 13, 1992, IJs conducted *in absentia* hearing based on regulation and case authority. Unlike IIRIRA or prior INA §242B, a person in proceedings before June 13, 1992 could have taken a direct appeal to the BIA at that time. *Matter of Gonzalez-Lopez, supra.* The pre-INA §242B procedure

applies if the OSC was issued before June 13, 1992. *Lahmidi v. INS,* 149 F.3d 1011 (9th Cir. 1998). Many of the cases under that law turned on whether persons received proper notice or had a reasonable cause for failing to appear at the hearing. *Adeyemo v. Ashcroft,* 383 F.3d 558 (7th Cir. 2004) [illegible signature on return receipt is insufficient to meet government's burden of demonstrating actual notice and *in absentia* order is vacated]; *U.S. v. Estrada-Trochez*, 66 F.3d 733 (5th Cir. 1995) [upheld *in absentia* order entered 9 years after §212(c) application was filed where no notice of hearing was given to counsel and applicant received no actual notice on theory that applicant failed to submit a change of address]; *Thomas v. INS*, 976 F.2d 786 (1st Cir. 1992) [upheld *in absentia* order where client and attorney showed up 10 minutes after IJ entered order]; *Maldonado-Perez v. INS*, 865 F.2d 328 (D.C. Cir. 1989) [upheld *in absentia* procedure preventing hearing on asylum application where applicant had reasonable opportunity to be present and failed to provide reasonable cause for his absence]; *Wijeratne v. INS*, 961 F.2d 1344 (7th Cir. 1992) [same]; *Matter of Patel,* 19 I&N Dec. 260 (BIA 1985), *aff'd*, *Patel v. INS*, 803 F.2d 804 (5th Cir. 1986); *Shah v. INS*, 788 F.2d 970 (4th Cir. 1986) [failure to appear solely because respondent appealing denial of change of venue to BIA is insufficient. Decision *in absentia* affirmed]. Notice of hearing was proper where notice sent to last known address. *U.S. v. Perez-Valdera*, 899 F.Supp. 181 (S.D.N.Y. 1995) [notice sent by first class mail to address where respondent was residing is sufficient even if no actual notice]. The OSC had to be personally served or by certified return receipt mail for the first hearing if regular mail did not result in respondent's appearance. *Former* 8 C.F.R. §242.1(c); *Matter of Peugnet*, 20 I&N Dec. 233 (BIA 1991). Where notice was improper IJ had to terminate proceedings unless both parties agreed to administrative closure. *Matter of Lopez-Barrios,* 20 I&N Dec. 203 (BIA 1990). A respondent can move to reopen her hearing on a showing of reasonable cause for absence. *Matter of Haim*, 19 I&N Dec. 641 (BIA 1988). In order to reopen, the respondent need not demonstrate a prima facie case for relief nor exceptional circumstances for failure to appear. A showing of reasonable cause was sufficient. *Matter of Ruiz,* 20 I&N Dec. 91 (BIA 1989); *Matter of Haim, supra.* Also the respondent was not required to show prejudice in order to rescind an order of deportation entered *in absentia*. *Matter of Grijalva*, 21 I&N Dec. 472, 473 n.2 (BIA 1996).

(4) No Failure to Appear—An *in absentia* order may not be entered where the respondent did not fail to appear. In *Perez v. Mukasey,* 516 F.3d 770 (9th Cir. 2008) a petitioner arrived two hours late for his court appearance due to his car overheating but the IJ was still on the bench. The IJ refused to hear the matter and entered an order *in* absentia. The court determined "that a petitioner who arrives late for his immigration hearing, but while the IJ is still in the courtroom, has not failed to appear for the hearing" and accordingly is not required to demonstrate exceptional circumstances to reopen the proceeding. *Perez*, 516 F.3d at 774–75. In *Alarcon-Chavez v. Ashcroft,* 403 F.3d 343 (5th Cir. 2005) the petitioner arrived at court 20 minutes after his scheduled hearing due to getting off at the wrong exit. He had attended all previous hearings and arrived 5 minutes after IJ entered his *in absentia* order. The IJ refused to return to the bench and subsequently denied a motion to reopen on the grounds that there were no exceptional circumstances. The Court ruled that it was "beyond cavil that there was no *failure* to appear and that when: "(1) there is no failure but only slight tardiness, (2) the IJ is either still on the bench or recently retired and still close by, and (3) the time of the immigrant's delayed arrival is still during 'business hours,' it is an abuse of discretion—if not worse—to treat such slight tardiness as a non-appearance," *Id.* at 346. The court noted "the curse of the robe" reminding judges "that they are appointed not anointed." *Id. See also Abu Hasirah v. DHS,* 478 F.3d 474 (2d Cir. 2007) [unintentional lateness at removal hearing by 15 minutes did not constitute a failure to appear]; *Cabrera-Perez v. Gonzales,* 456 F.3d 109 (3d Cir. 2006) [arrival at removal hearing 15 to 20 minutes late because respondent was waiting for a critical witness is not a failure to appear, but only slight tardiness].

(5) Failure to Provide Notice as a Defense—Notice to be valid no longer requires that it be by personal service or return receipt mail but simply by regular mail to the person's last address. INA §239(a)(1), 8 U.S.C. §1229(a)(1). Notice is deemed sufficient if it is given

at the most recent address provided by the respondent. INA §240(b)(5)(A). The notice must be "an address and telephone number (if any) at which the alien may be contacted." This does not require the address where the person is living, but merely where they may be contacted. *Arrieta v. INS*, 117 F.3d 429, 431 (9th Cir. 1997). The notice does not require that it be in any specific language. *Lopes v. Gonzales,* 468 F.3d 81, 85 (2d Cir. 2006) [rejecting claim that notice was deficient because it was not in Portuguese]. If the respondent provides evidence that he submitted a change of address, then an *in absentia* order must be vacated where notice was sent to an old address. *Terezov v. Gonzales,* 480 F.3d 558 (7th Cir. 2007) [court reversed denial of motion to reopen *in absentia* order where the BIA gave no weight to return receipts in respondent's possession with his new address and communications he received from USCIS to new address concerning employment authorization]. However, if the respondent fails to provide an address pursuant to INA §239(a)(1)(F) requiring notice of change of address then "no written notice shall be required." INA §240(b)(5)(B). Change of address under the statutory scheme must be provided "immediately." INA §239(a)(1)(F)(ii). *Dominguez v. U.S. Att'y Gen.,* 284 F.3d 1258 (11th Cir. 2002) [adhering strictly to §239(a)(1)(F) and finding notice was adequate because respondent had failed in her duty to provide change of address]. *But see Matter of G-Y-R-,* 23 I&N Dec. 181 (BIA 2001) [where the Respondent failed to receive the NTA and the initial notice of hearing it contains and therefore was never notified of the initiation of removal proceedings or his or her change of address obligations under INA §239(a)(1), s/he may not have an *in absentia* order entered against her/him. Upheld IJ decision to terminate proceeding because proper notice under INA §239(a)(1)(F) that requires that respondent first be informed of the statutory obligations under the NTA proceeding was not given; Failure to comply with the registration provisions of INA §265 and consequences flowing from it are unrelated to notice under INA §239]. Where notice is sent to the last known address, a presumption of receipt exists. *Lopes v. Gonzales,* 468 F.3d 81, 84–85 (2d Cir. 2006) [presumption exists even by regular mail but it may be rebutted].

(a) Form of Notice of Change of Address—The notice of a new address need not be given in the view of one court in accordance with 8 C.F.R. §1003.15(d)(2) on Form EOIR-33 to be valid. *Beltran v. INS,* 332 F.3d 407 (6th Cir. 2003) [where respondent through a friend who was a law student but not an attorney submitted change of address on letterhead but not on the EOIR-33 form and EOIR sent notice to old address, the court found the EOIR-33 requirement at 8 C.F.R. §1003.15(d)(2) to be ultra vires of the statute and the *in absentia* order was reversed].

(6) Failure to Receive Notice as a Defense—Courts have drawn a distinction between the failure to properly send notice and the failure of the respondent to receive it. *Lopes v. Gonzales,* 468 F.3d 81, 84 (2d Cir. 2006) [the statutory scheme draws a distinction between sending notice which can be the basis for an *in absentia* order, 8 U.S.C. §1229a(b)(5)(A) and receiving notice which can be the basis for a motion to reopen, 8 U.S.C. §1229a(b)(5)(C)(i),(ii)). *Accord Peralta-Cabrera v. Gonzales,* 501 F.3d 837, 843–46 (7th Cir. 2007) [pre-IIRIRA where respondent provided his location and who he was staying with he did not thwart notice by failing to tell DHS that the notice should be sent "care of" the homeowner]; *Joshi v. Ashcroft,* 389 F.3d 732, 735–36 (7th Cir. 2004) [reversed denial of fourth motion to reopen *in absentia* proceedings where respondent submitted affidavit and other documentation indicating he failed to receive notice notwithstanding evidence that the government properly sent it]. *See also Alrefae v. Gonzales,* 471 F.3d 353, 358–60 (2d Cir. 2006) [IJ's refusal to rescind *in absentia* order reversed where IJ merely recounted that notice was sent properly without considering respondent's claim that he never received it]; *Sabir v. Gonzales,* 421 F.3d 456, 458 (7th Cir. 2005) [the court held that when the IJ was presented with evidence that respondent did not *receive* the notice of hearing because it was returned to the court marked "Attempted-Not Known," he should have reopened the *in absentia* order because INA §240(b)(5)(C)(ii), 8 U.S.C. §1229a(b)(5)(C)(ii) allows reopening "if the alien demonstrates that the alien did not receive notice in accordance with …section 239(a)"]; *Ko v. Gonzales,* 421 F.3d 453 (7th Cir. 2005) [same]. *But see Maghradze v. Gonzales,* 462 F.3d 150, 153–55 (2d Cir. 2006) [where respondent claimed he never sent change of address

because he did not understand directions, court upheld BIA reasoning that his failure to file change of address amounts to constructive notice barring rescinding order even if he never actually received notice]. At least one circuit has found that the presumption favoring notice may be overcome by circumstantial evidence. *Lopes v. Gonzales,* 468 F.3d 81 (2d Cir. 2006) [IJ's *in absentia* order was reversed because the presumption of receipt of a properly addressed and mailed notice of hearing was overcome by "circumstantial evidence"]. The courts will review an IJ's decision for abuse of discretion. *Maknojiya v. Gonzales,* 432 F.3d 588 (5th Cir. 2005) [reversed IJ for abuse of discretion where respondent and counsel submitted affidavits stating they never received notice of the hearing in a case where certified return receipt notice was no longer required. *Grijalva* distinguished]; *Murtuza v. Gonzales,* 427 F.3d 508 (7th Cir. 2005) [finding no abuse where facts were ambiguous].

(a) Notice While in DHS Custody—If the person is in DHS custody, DHS has responsibility to notify the Immigration Court. 8 C.F.R. §1003.19(g); Memo, Hamilton, Assoc. Gen. Counsel, (HQCOU 50/10.2) (Apr. 13, 1998), *reprinted in* 75 No. 17 *Interpreter Releases* 627, 636 (May 4, 1998).

(b) Notice Involving Minor—When a minor is placed in the custody of a responsible adult pursuant to 8 C.F.R. §242.24, notice must be served upon the adult as well as the minor even if the minor is over 14. *Flores-Chavez v. Ashcroft,* 362 F.3d 1150 (9th Cir. 2004) [reversed *in absentia* order against 15-year-old who was served with OSC pursuant to 8 C.F.R. §103.5a but no service was provided to adult custodian. Court found that reading the statute to permit service solely on minor violated DHS regulations, was not entitled to *Chevron* deference, and raised serious constitutional questions]. DHS must also provide consular notification which cannot be waived by a minor. *U.S. v. D.L.,* 453 F.3d 1115, 1123 and n.6 (9th Cir. 2006).

(c) Notice to Counsel—In the view of some courts, notice to counsel is deemed sufficient even if counsel does not convey information to the respondent. *Dominguez-Capistran v. Gonzales,* 438 F.3d 876 (8th Cir. 2006) [where counsel failed to inform client of hearing date it was not deemed an exceptional circumstance, although court gave respondent a stay for 90 days to file a motion to reopen with the BIA because ineffective assistance was not alleged before the BIA or the circuit court]; *Scorteanu v. INS,* 339 F.3d 407, 412 (6th Cir. 2003) [where lawyer who committed malpractice received notice there is no lack of notice defense even if respondent may have a claim under exceptional circumstances]. However, notice to a former attorney where a different attorney was representing the respondent may violate due process even if respondent received notice directly. *U.S. v. Dorsett,* 308 F.Supp.2d 537, 543 (D.V.I. 2003).

(d) Notice to Others in Household—Notice to an adult relative is also sufficient notice. *Matter of Gomez-Gomez,* 23 I&N Dec. 522, 528 (BIA 2002) [notice to person who claimed to be father of 8-year-old is sufficient notice].

(e) No Time Limit on Motion Based on Lack of Notice—*Andia v. Ashcroft,* 359 F.3d 1181 (9th Cir. 2004) [where respondent alleged lack of notice of *in absentia* hearing, the 180-day time limit to reopen was inapplicable; the IJ erred in applying it and the BIA erred in determining that reopening was a matter of discretion].

(f) Deportation Does *Not* Bar Motion—At least one circuit has determined that 8 C.F.R. §1003.23(b)(4)(ii) permits reopening removal proceedings for lack of notice even if the person was deported because the regulation allows reopening at "any time." *Contreras-Rodriguez v. U.S. Att'y Gen.,* 462 F.3d 1314 (11th Cir. 2006) [although respondent was physically removed after *in absentia* order, he is not barred from filing a motion to reopen for lack of notice because §1003.23(b)(4)(ii) allows motion regarding lack of notice to be filed at "any time." *Patel* distinguished].

(g) Notice Successfully Challenged—Notice to be valid must be properly addressed. *Busquets-Ivars v. Ashcroft,* 333 F.3d 1008 (9th Cir. 2003) [where NTA and notice of hearing were sent to address with wrong zip code the order of removal *in absentia* was reversed]; *Ying Fong v. Ashcroft,* 317 F.Supp.2d 398, 400–03 (S.D.N.Y. 2004). The notice must also state the date, time and place for the hearing. *Ying Fong v. Ashcroft,* 317 F.Supp.2d 398, 405–06 (S.D.N.Y. 2004) [failure to provide date, time and place of hearing is inadequate notice to sustain an *in absentia* order]. The Respondent's failure to receive notice that a hearing date was changed may also be a sufficient basis to reopen an *in absentia* order. *Matter of Mancera,* 22 I&N Dec. 79 (BIA 1998) [where record demonstrated notice of first hearing but no notice of changed hearing date, IJ reversed and case reopened]; *Pervaiz v. Gonzales,* 405 F.3d 488, 490–91 (7th Cir. 2005) [counsel committed ineffective assistance when he failed to distinguish between the adequacy of notice by the government where notice was adequate under the regulations and not actually receiving notice of the change of the time of his client's hearing, which is a defense]. The applicant's failure to receive notice under current regular mail procedure may be established through a lesser standard than when return receipt mail was required. *See e.g., Kozak v. Gonzales,* 502 F.3d 34, 36 (1st Cir. 2007) [reversed BIA's reliance on *Grijalva* where respondent submitted affidavit and stated: "[W]e find that the use of regular mail renders the standard in *Grijalva* unworkable…We leave it to the BIA to come up with a new standard to be applied to aliens who claim non-receipt of notices sent by regular mail."] *See also in this section* "Burden of Proof," ¶ (k) (p.391), *infra.*

(h) Adequacy of Notice by Government Upheld—Where the NTA is sent to the Respondent's correct address (for which there is no dispute) and the NTA is sent by certified return receipt but is left unclaimed at the post office by the Respondent, proper service has been made and Respondent's failure to appear resulted in a properly issued *in absentia* order. *Matter of M-D-,* 23 I&N Dec. 540 (BIA 2002) [respondent's defense that certified return receipt was not required and that regular mail would have been more reliable was rejected where certified return receipt came back unclaimed from Respondent's uncontested address]; *Aragon-Munoz v. Mukasey,* 520 F.3d 82 (1st Cir. 2008) [notice sent to Rhode Island address given on corrected asylum application was sufficient in absence of other proof that petitioner lived in Arizona]; *Derezinski v. Mukasey,* 516 F.3d 619, 621–23 (7th Cir. 2008) [unclaimed return receipt was sufficient to show notice in light of petitioner's bare, uncorroborated affidavit denying service]. Failure to notify DHS of change of address generally bars challenge. *Haider v. Gonzales,* 438 F.3d 902, 906–08 (8th Cir. 2006) [where NTA did not state time and place of hearing but subsequent notice was sent to respondent at his former address and respondent failed to put in change of address, *in absentia* order was upheld]; *Sousa v. Ashcroft,* 393 F.3d 271 (1st Cir. 2005) [no abuse of discretion to deny motion to reconsider *in absentia* order where Respondent never notified INS of change of address and where NTA was not returned as undeliverable and Respondent failed to prove under *Matter of G-Y-R-* that he did not receive notice]. *See also Bhanot v. Chertoff,* 474 F.3d 71 (2d Cir. 2007) [respondent failed to overcome presumption by circumstantial evidence where he claimed nonreceipt of subsequent hearing but did not attend originally noticed hearing, and had uncorroborated affidavit with a major misstatement of fact].

(i) Pre-IIRIRA Notice Challenges—Under pre-IIRIRA the OSC was required to be given by personal service and the courts have reopened proceedings where neither the respondent nor his counsel received notice. *Chaidez v. Gonzales,* 486 F.3d 1079 (9th Cir. 2007) [where respondent submitted affidavit stating he did not know the person who signed the certified return receipt and she was not a "responsible person" at his residence, the court reversed the IJ's *in absentia* order and held that service for an OSC is more demanding than service for a hearing]; *Adeyemo v. Ashcroft,* 383 F.3d 558 (7th Cir. 2004) [illegible signature on return receipt is insufficient to meet government's burden of demonstrating actual notice of an OSC and *Matter of Huete,* not *Matter of Grijalva*, which relates to post-OSC notices of hearing, is controlling];*Kamara v. INS,* 149 F.3d 904 (8th Cir. 1998) [where INS at time of bond was given change of address they had obligation under §545 of IMMACT90 to place change in system]; *Urbina-Osejo v. INS,* 124 F.3d 1314, 1317 (9th Cir. 1997) [concluding that there is reasonable cause for failure to appear when an applicant has not received notice of the time and place of the hearing due to a change of address and s/he was not informed of a requirement to advise the INS of any change of address]; *Arrieta v. INS*, 117 F.3d 429 (9th Cir. 1997) [even if there is a presumption of effective delivery of the notice under *Matter of Grijalva*, it can be overcome where mailing address remains unchanged, where no one refused service of mail and where there was nondelivery or improper delivery of mail]; *Sewak v. INS*, 900 F.2d 667, 671 n.9 (3d Cir. 1990) [where reopening is discretionary there could be no proper exercise of discretion to deny reopening if the evidence produced established that respondent was denied notice]. *See also U.S. v. Montano-Bentancourt,* 151 F.Supp.2d 794, 796 (W.D. Tx. 2001) [finding that failure to send notice to address provided by respondent renders deportation proceeding fundamentally unfair in the context of a challenge under *Mendoza-Lopez* to a criminal prosecution for re-entry]. *Anin v. Reno,* 188 F.3d 1273, 1276–78 (11th Cir. 1999) [notice to attorney sufficient to counter statutory and due process challenge even if attorney failed to inform client]; *Farhoud v. INS,* 122 F.3d 794 (9th Cir. 1997) [notice mailed to last address where receipt was acknowledged; rejected due process challenge]. Counsel misplacing the notice does not alone amount to reasonable cause. *Wellington v. INS*, 108 F.3d 631, 635 (5th Cir. 1997). The burden is on the respondent to demonstrate she did not receive notice. *Giday v. INS*, 113 F.3d 230, 233 (D.C. Cir. 1997); *But see Matter of Powell*, 21 I&N Dec. 81 (BIA 1995) [failure of counsel to notify client not an exceptional circumstance]; *Matter of Grijalva*, 21 I&N Dec. 27 (BIA 1995).

(j) Method of Notice as a Constitutional Issue—A question may arise as to what method of notice is adequate to trigger the *in absentia* procedure. In *Mullane v. Center Hanover Bank & Trust Co.,* 339 U.S. 306, 314, 319 (1950), the Supreme Court determined that where property interests were at stake the notice that must be given consistent with due process is notice that is "reasonably calculated, under all the circumstances, to apprise interested parties of the pendency of the action and afford them an opportunity to present their objections." The Court further held that the "means employed must be such as one desirous of actually informing the [party] might reasonably adopt to accomplish it." *Id.* at 315. The Board has adopted the approach in *Mullane* in *Matter of M-D-,* 23 I&N Dec. 540, 542 (BIA 2002) [following *Mullane* the Board said the focus of the inquiry is whether the nature of the notice required is "reasonably calculated, under all the circumstances, to apprize interested parties of the pendency of the action."]. Similarly, in *Jones v. Flowers,* 547 U.S. 220, 226–27 (2006) the Court determined that when a certified letter threatening a tax foreclosure is returned unclaimed, the state must take additional steps to notify the property owner. *But see Derezinski v. Mukasey,* 516 F.3d 619, 621 (7th Cir. 2008) [distinguished *Flowers* determining that a property owner is less likely to avoid a hearing than an illegal immigrant]. However, the Supreme Court in *Dusenberry v. U.S.,* 122 S.Ct. 694 (2002) determined that notice reasonably calculated to apprise an interested party of an action and actual notice are separate and under the forfeiture statute at issue the government did not have to insure that the claimant received actual notice. *Dusenberry, supra* [finding the government did not have to make "heroic" efforts to insure actual notice where they sent notice by certified mail to three different locations including the prison defendant was incarcerated at].

(k) Burden of Proof

i) *Standard Under Grijalva*—In *Matter of Grijalva,* 21 I&N Dec. 27 (1995) the BIA set forth the type of proof that would be necessary to overcome the "strong presumption of effective service" to demonstrate that notice was not received by the respondent where respondent was served by *certified mail.* The BIA stated that the respondent must present "substantial and probative evidence from the Postal Service, third party affidavits, or other similar evidence..." 21 I&N Dec. at 37; *Rodriguez-Cuate v. Gonzales,* 444 F.3d 1015, 1017–19 (8th Cir. 2006) [respondent failed to overcome presumption of service under *Grijalva*]. *See also Derezinski v. Mukasey,* 516 F.3d 619, 621–23 (7th Cir. 2008) [unclaimed return receipt was sufficient to show notice in light of petitioner's bare, uncorroborated affidavit denying service]; *Thongphilack v. Gonzales,* 506 F.3d 1207 (10th Cir. 2007) [failed to meet burden where respondent informed the IJ orally and submitted his own affidavit but not an affidavit from the unidentified person who mailed his change of address]; *Gurung v. Ashcroft,* 371 F.3d 718, 722 (10th Cir. 2004) [failure to provide statement in affidavit form or to provide more than conclusory statements is insufficient to carry burden of proof under current statute and fact that notice was stamped rather than signed is unavailing].

ii) *Post-Grijalva* Involving Regular Mail—*Matter of Grijalva* was based upon the prior statute (former 8 U.S.C. §1252b(c)(1)) under a notice of hearing where notice was required to be given by certified mail and there was a strong presumption that the mail was delivered. Because the current statute requires service by *regular mail* of an NTA the presumption of delivery is far weaker and the nature of the proof to rebut service would not be the same. Many circuits have now rejected *Grijalva* completely and called upon the BIA to develop a new standard in light of the regular mail service. *Kozak v. Gonzales,* 502 F.3d 34, 36 (1st Cir. 2007) [reversed BIA's reliance on *Grijalva* where respondent submitted affidavit and stated: "[W]e find that the use of regular mail renders the standard in *Grijalva* unworkable…We leave it to the BIA to come up with a new standard to be applied to aliens who claim non-receipt of notices sent by regular mail."]. The Ninth Circuit has developed its own standard finding that where a respondent "initiates a proceeding to obtain a benefit, appears at an earlier hearing, and has no motive to avoid the hearing, a sworn affidavit...that neither she nor a responsible party residing at her address received the notice should ordinarily be sufficient to rebut the presumption of delivery and entitle [the respondent] to an evidentiary hearing to consider the veracity of her allegations." *Salta v. INS,* 314 F.3d 1076, 1079 (9th Cir. 2003) [reversed *in absentia* order and remanded case back for a hearing before IJ]. *See also Silva-Carvalho Lopes v. Mukasey,* 517 F.3d 156, 159–61 (2d Cir. 2008) [adopting the standard in *Salta* and reversing the BIA's denial of petitioner's motion to reopen a second time because it again improperly applied the *Grijalva* burden of proof]; *Santana Gonzalez v. Att'y Gen. of the U.S.,* 506 F.3d 274 (3d Cir. 2007) [*Grijalva* presumption only applies when notice is sent by certified mail and an affidavit of nonreceipt with other circumstantial evidence that the respondent had no incentive to refuse to appear (here the respondent was eligible for Cuban Adjustment Act) may meet the weaker presumption of notice sent by regular mail]; *Sembiring v. Gonzales,* 499 F.3d 981 (9th Cir. 2007) [following *Salta*, the court reversed the IJ's refusal to reopen an *in absentia* order and found that respondent overcame the presumption of effective service, despite filing only a *pro se* letter rather than an affidavit, because the circumstances, including respondent's affirmative asylum application and appearance on the originally scheduled date, demonstrated she was not avoiding the process]; *Alrefae v. Gonzales,* 471 F.3d 353, 358–60 (2d Cir. 2006) [IJ's refusal to rescind *in absentia* order reversed where IJ merely recounted that notice was sent properly without considering respondent's claim that he never received it]; *Lopes v. Gonzales,* 468 F.3d 81 (2d Cir. 2006) [IJ's *in absentia* order was reversed because the presumption of receipt of a properly addressed and mailed notice of hearing was overcome by "circumstantial evidence" in the form of an affidavit and other indicia that respondent would not abscond]; *Nibagwire v. Gonzales,* 450 F.3d 153 (4th Cir. 2006) [BIA abused its discretion by applying the strong presumption of delivery for certified mail and the now out-of-date standard in *Grijalva* for rebutting the presumption of delivery by certified mail because under the current regime service is by regular mail which has a much weaker presumption]; *Maknojiya v. Gonzales,* 432 F.3d 588 (5th Cir. 2005) [reversed IJ for abuse of discretion where he relied on *Grijalva* presumption to deny reopening in a case where certified mail was no longer necessary]; *Ghounem v. Ashcroft,* 378 F.3d 740, 743–45 (8th Cir. 2004) [following *Salta*, reversing IJ's denial of motion to reopen *in absentia* order, and holding that statutory change from certified return receipt mail to service by regular mail lessens the presumption that the mail was delivered].

Where person departed the U.S. prior to the initiation of removal proceedings, the *in absentia* order was reversed because proper notification was not provided. *Singh v. Gonzales,* 412 F.3d 1117, 1121–22 (9th Cir. 2005) [person who departs the U.S. before removal proceedings is not required to provide a change of address].

(l) Constructive Notice—At least one circuit has upheld the BIA's interpretation that the respondent's failure to provide her correct address under the statute results in "constructive notice" even if she never receives notice. *Maghradze v. Gonzales,* 462 F.3d 150, 153–55 (2d Cir. 2006) [where respondent claimed he never sent change of address because he did not understand directions, court upheld BIA reasoning that his failure to file change of address amounts to constructive notice even if he never actually received notice].

(7) Exceptional Circumstances as a Defense—Under INA §240(e), 8 U.S.C. §1229a(e), exceptional circumstances are defined as circumstances "beyond the control of the alien" such as battery or extreme cruelty to the alien or any child or parent of the alien, serious illness to the alien or serious illness or death of the spouse, parent or child of the alien, "but not including less compelling circumstances." The BIA, under the previous statute INA §242B, has employed a "totality of the circumstances" test to determine exceptional circumstances. *Matter of W-F-*, 21 I&N Dec. 503, 509 (BIA 1996). This view is supported by the legislative history under the former provision. H.R. Conf. Rep. No. 955, 101st Cong., 2d Sess. at 132 (1990), *reprinted in* 1990 U.S.C.C.A.N. 6784, 6797 ["(T)he conferees expect that in determining whether an alien's failure to appear was justifiable the Attorney General will look at the totality of the circumstances to determine whether the alien could not reasonably have been expected to appear."]. One court has defined the totality of the circumstances as including the following: (1) supporting documentary evidence; (2) respondent's efforts in contacting the immigration court; (3) respondent's promptness in filing the motion to reopen; (4) strength of the respondent's underlying claim; (5) the harm respondent would suffer if motion is denied; and (6) the inconvenience to the government. *Kaweesa v. Gonzales,* 450 F.3d 62, 68–69 (1st Cir. 2006) [citing to *Matter of B-A-S-* and holding that these concerns are grounded in due process]. The BIA has held that a respondent cannot make bare allegations regarding an exceptional circumstance but must submit detailed statements and medical or other records, including proof of his absence from work where appropriate. *Matter of J-P-,* 22 I&N Dec. 33 (BIA 1998) [migraine headache]; *Matter of B-A-S-,* 22 I&N Dec. 57 (BIA 1998) [twisted foot injury] *rev'd Singh v. INS,* 213 F.3d 1050 (9th Cir. 2000) [remanded because BIA imposed new requirements without notice]. However, where a respondent does make allegations regarding exceptional circumstances, it is insufficient for the IJ simply to iterate that service was properly made. *Alrefae v. Gonzales,* 471 F.3d 353, 360–61 (2d Cir. 2006) [IJ's refusal to rescind *in absentia* order reversed where IJ merely recounted that notice was sent properly without considering respondent's claim of exceptional circumstances].

Finding Exceptional Circumstance—The courts and the BIA under the current and former statute (INA §242B) have found exceptional circumstances in the following cases:

First Circuit. *Kaweesa v. Gonzales,* 450 F.3d 62 (1st Cir. 2006) [where respondent confused dates court found it was exceptional circumstances and held IJ failed to consider any of the factors that go into the "totality of the circumstances" in deciding exceptional circumstances]; *Herbert v. Ashcroft,* 325 F.3d 68 (1st Cir. 2003) [respondent had valid exceptional circumstances where IJ improperly entered an order *in absentia* because he denied a continuance to respondent's counsel who was required to be before a federal magistrate at the same time he was required to appear before the IJ]; *Saakian v. INS,* 252 F.3d 21, 25 (1st Cir. 2001) [under present statute ineffective assistance of counsel is exceptional circumstance]. **Second Circuit**. *Aris v. Mukasey,* 517 F.3d 595 (2d Cir. 2008) [ineffective assistance of counsel even if it occurs through a paralegal's misrepresentation is an exceptional circumstance]; *Romero-Morales v. INS,* 25 F.3d 125 (2d Cir.

1994) [suggesting a broader reading of exceptional circumstances]. **Third Circuit.** *Borges v. Gonzales,* 402 F.3d 398 (3d Cir. 2005) [ineffectiveness of counsel would constitute an exceptional circumstance to rescind order, if 180 period had already been tolled due to fraud; *Bejar* distinguished]. **Fifth Circuit.** *Galvez-Vergara v. Gonzales,* 484 F.3d 798 (5th Cir. 2007) [reversed BIA for failure to follow *Matter of Grijalva* where respondent argued exceptional circumstances due to ineffective assistance of counsel]; **Sixth Circuit.** *Scorteanu v. INS,* 339 F.3d 407, 413–14 (6th Cir. 2003) [counsel's misfeasance and fraud in not informing client of hearing date and his subsequent disbarment is an "exceptional circumstance" but 180-day period was not tolled where respondent did not exercise due diligence in filing motion to reopen]. **Seventh Circuit.** *Nazarova v. INS,* 171 F.3d 478 (7th Cir. 1999) [where respondent was two hours late for court after waiting for a translator that she reasonably thought was necessary it was an exceptional circumstance]. **Ninth Circuit.** *Chete Juarez v. Ashcroft,* 376 F.3d 944 (9th Cir. 2004) [in a pre-IIRIRA case, the court viewed the totality of the circumstances and respondent's eligibility for relief in determining that the "circumstances surrounding" his case render it exceptional]; *Lo v. Ashcroft,* 341 F.3d 934 (9th Cir. 2003) [the BIA was arbitrary in not reopening an *in absentia* order even in the absence of showing prejudice where there was ineffective assistance of counsel and therefore an exceptional circumstance but a bar charge under *Lozada* was not filed because the lawyer acknowledged his error in an affidavit and the lawyer's error was inadvertent in that his secretary calendared and gave the clients the wrong date to appear at the hearing]; *Monjaraz-Munoz v. INS,* 327 F.3d 892 (9th Cir. 2003) [where attorney's agent gave negligent advice to travel to Tijuana the day before the deportation hearing resulting in respondent's failure to appear there were exceptional circumstances]; *Jerezano v. INS,* 169 F.3d 613 (9th Cir. 1999) [where person arrived to court tardy and IJ was still on the bench "it seems both harsh and unrealistic" to enter *in absentia* order]; *Romani v. INS,* 146 F.3d 737 (9th Cir. 1998) [in *absentia* order reversed because misadvice by legal assistant not to go into courtroom did not require finding of exceptional circumstance as respondent did appear at courthouse pursuant to notice]. **Eleventh Circuit.** *Montano Cisneros v. U.S. Att'y Gen.,* 514 F.3d 1224 (11th Cir. 2008) [BIA abused its discretion in denying motion to reopen where the Board ignored its own precedent– *Matter of Grijalva–* in circumstance where person impersonated a lawyer and told client he did not have to appear]; **Board of Immigration Appeals.** *Matter of Grijalva,* 21 I&N Dec. 472 (BIA 1996) [where ineffective assistance of counsel resulted in advice by counsel that respondent did not have to appear at hearing because it was "continued," the respondent demonstrated exceptional circumstances].

Exceptional Circumstances Not Found

First Circuit. *Asaba v. Ashcroft,* 377 F.3d 9 (1st Cir. 2004) [although recognizing that ineffective assistance of counsel may be an exceptional circumstance, the court, nevertheless, affirmed the BIA's denial of a motion to reopen where *Lozada* requirements not strictly adhered to by respondent]; *Georcely v. Ashcroft,* 375 F.3d 45, 49–51 (1st Cir. 2004) [where respondent knew his hearing was set, his failure to appear simply because his lawyer filed a motion to change venue that the lawyer believed would be granted was not an exceptional circumstance]; *Rojas-Reynoso v. INS,* 235 F.3d 26, 30 n.3 (1st Cir. 2000) [the filing of a request for extension of voluntary departure or a motion to reopen is not an exceptional circumstance]. **Second Circuit**. *Webb v. Weiss,* 69 F.Supp.2d 335, 338 (D. Conn. 1999) [failure of lawyer to appear and instruction to client not to appear is not an exceptional circumstance where respondent failed to raise ineffective assistance of counsel]. **Third Circuit**. *Bejar v. Ashcroft,* 324 F.3d 127, 131–32 (3d Cir. 2003) [failure of counsel to inform client of hearing date and time is not an exceptional circumstance].**Fifth Circuit.** *Magdeleno de Morales v. INS,* 116 F.3d 145 (5th Cir. 1997) [mechanical breakdown of auto on the way to the court coupled with other factors was not an exceptional circumstance]. **Sixth Circuit.** *Denko v. INS,* 351 F.3d 717, 722–25 (6th Cir. 2003) [where counsel wrote to client suggesting he could file motion to waive client's appearance and client did not show up at hearing it was not ineffective assistance requiring the *in absentia* order to be reopened]. **Seventh Circuit**. *Uriostegui v. Gonzales,* 415 F.3d 660, 663–64 (7th Cir. 2005) [mishearing correct month for hearing is not per se an exceptional circumstance]; *Kay v. Ashcroft,* 387 F.3d 664, 671 (7th Cir. 2004) [suffering from PTSD, being *pro se,* understanding little English and notifying the court of a change of address are not exceptional circumstances]; *Ursachi v. INS,* 296 F.3d 592 (7th Cir. 2002) [conclusory allegations in the form of general affidavit of illness by respondent and general note by physician was insufficient to establish exceptional circumstances due to illness]. **Eighth Circuit**. *Dominguez-Capistran v. Gonzales,* 438 F.3d 876 (8th Cir. 2006) [where counsel failed to inform client of hearing date it was not deemed an exceptional circumstance although court gave respondent a stay for 90 days to file a motion to reopen with the BIA because ineffective assistance was not alleged before the BIA or the circuit court]. **Ninth Circuit**. *Valencia-Fragoso v. INS,* 321 F.3d 1204 (9th Cir. 2003) [appearing 4½ hours late for hearing because respondent mistakenly believed hearing was later without any showing of relief is not an "exceptional circumstance"]; *Celis-Castellano v. Ashcroft,* 298 F.3d 888 (9th Cir. 2002) [upheld BIA determination that there was insufficient showing of exceptional circumstances where respondent failed to present evidence of severity of asthma attack]; *Singh-Bhathal v. INS,* 170 F.3d 943 (9th Cir. 1999) [erroneous advice of an immigration consultant did not constitute exceptional circumstances]; *Sharma v. INS,* 89 F.3d 545 (9th Cir. 1996) [traffic congestion not exceptional circumstance and does not raise due process concern]. **Tenth Circuit**. *Tang v. Ashcroft,* 354 F.3d 1192 (10th Cir. 2003) [failure to show up at hearing after making two motions to change venue that were not ruled upon is not an exceptional circumstance and respondent could not assert ineffective assistance of counsel where he failed to comply with *Lozada*]. **Eleventh Circuit**. *Lonyem v. U.S. Att'y Gen.,* 352 F.3d 1338 (11th Cir. 2003) [where respondent submitted sworn affidavits attesting to contracting malaria the day before the hearing, the court affirmed the denial of a motion to reopen giving deference to the IJ's conclusion while questioning respondent's failure to notify the court]. **Board of Immigration Appeals.** *Matter of S-M-,* 22 I&N Dec. 49 (BIA 1998) [respondent's questionable claims that the date on the notice of hearing was illegible and that he did not speak English were not exceptional circumstances]; *Matter of J-P-,* 22 I&N Dec. 33 (BIA 1998) [serious headache resulting in person being bedridden is not an exceptional circumstance in absence of documented proof]; *Matter of Powell,* 21 I&N Dec. 81 (BIA 1995) [failure of counsel to inform client of notice is not an exceptional circumstance]; *Matter of W-F-*, 21 I&N Dec. 503 (BIA 1996) [failure to appear because of employment on a fishing vessel is not an exceptional circumstance]; *Matter of Rivera*, 21 I&N Dec. 599 (BIA 1996) [failure to file bar charge under *Matter of Lozada* regarding ineffective assistance of counsel where respondent claimed her counsel refused to speak with her and inform her of hearing was insufficient to establish exceptional circumstance based on ineffective assistance of counsel]; *Matter of Lei,* 22 I&N Dec. 113 (BIA 1998) [ineffective assistance of counsel claim as an "exceptional circumstance" must be filed within 180-day period]; *Matter of Shaar*, 21 I&N Dec. 541 (BIA 1996), *aff'd, Shaar v. INS,* 141 F.3d 953 (9th Cir. 1998) [neither the filing of a motion to reopen to apply for suspension of deportation during the pendency of a period of VD, nor the IJ's failure to adjudicate the motion prior to the expiration of VD constitutes an "exceptional circumstance" that would prevent the harsh consequences of denial of relief]; *but see Ugokwe v. U.S. Att'y Gen.,* 453 F.3d 1325 (11th Cir. 2006) [a timely filed motion to reopen post-IIRIRA tolls the VD period and prohibits the application of *Matter of Shaar* to bar consideration of the merits of the motion]; *Barroso v. Gonzales,* 429 F.3d 1195, 1202–08 (9th Cir. 2005) [filing a motion to reconsider within the VD period automatically tolls VD]; *Kanivets v. Gonzales,* 424 F.3d 330, 334–36 (3d Cir. 2005) [distinguished *Bhiski* and found that *post*-IIRIRA a timely filed motion to reopen for AOS tolls the period of VD and allows the BIA to consider the motion]; *Sidikhouya v. Gonzales,* 407 F.3d 950 (8th Cir. 2005) [where motion to reopen for AOS was filed prior to the expiration of the VD period granted by the BIA, it was an abuse of discretion *post*-IIRIRA for the BIA to deny reopening based upon *Matter of Shaar* when VD expired before BIA ruled]; *Barrios v. Att'y Gen. of the U.S.,* 399 F.3d 272 (3d Cir. 2005) [rejecting *Matter of Shaar* for *pre*-IIRIRA cases, and holding that a timely filed motion to reopen prevents the BIA/IJ from applying the bar to adjustment under the former INA §242B(e)(2)(A) because the failure of the BIA/IJ to adjudicate the motion within the voluntary departure period is an "exceptional circumstance"]; *Azarte v. Ashcroft,* 394 F.3d 1278 (9th Cir.

2005) [disavowing *Shaar* for post-IIRIRA cases and holding that when a motion to reopen is filed within the VD period in a removal proceeding and a stay of removal or stay of VD is requested, the VD period is tolled while the BIA is considering the motion to reopen].

Judicial Review—One court has found that there is no habeas review of the denial of a motion to reopen for exceptional circumstances. *Lopez v. Ashcroft,* 267 F.Supp.2d 150 (D. Mass. 2003).

(8) Other Defenses—The respondent was barred from entering the courthouse. *Twum v. INS,* 411 F.3d 54 (2d Cir. 2005) [where IJ misconstrued *in absentia* motion in exclusion as an ineffective assistance of counsel claim under *Lozada* rather than a claim that security guards barred his entry to the court, the circuit court reversed and remanded]. The respondent was tardy but the IJ was still on the bench. *Jerezano v. INS,* 169 F.3d 613 (9th Cir. 1999) [in *absentia* order reversed as too "harsh and unrealistic."]. The respondent appeared at courthouse but was told, improperly, by his counsel's staff not to enter courtroom. *Romani v. INS,* 146 F.3d 737 (9th Cir. 1998) [in *absentia* order reversed because respondent appeared at courthouse and therefore exceptional circumstance did not have to be established]. The respondent reasonably believed she needed a translator after first appearance and she waited for translator arriving at deportation hearing two hours late. *Nazarova v. INS,* 171 F.3d 478 (7th Cir. 1999) [violation of due process by depriving person of meaningful hearing and noting "with disfavor their (BIA) refusal to distinguish between a failure to appear at all and failure to appear at exactly the appointed hour."]. The denial to reopen leads to the unconscionable result of deporting an individual "eligible for relief from deportation." *Singh v. INS,* 295 F.3d 1037 (9th Cir. 2002) [where respondent appeared at 1 pm for an 11 am hearing the case was reopened because respondent diligently appeared for all previous hearings, had no reason to delay the hearing, easily confused the time based upon previous hearings and relief was available because of his marriage to a USC].

(9) The Right Against Self-Incrimination and *In Absentia* Hearings—The assertion of a Fifth Amendment right at a removal hearing cannot be used as a basis to proceed *in absentia* on the theory that the person is not present. *Matter of Castro*, A43 570 146 (BIA Oct. 22, 1996) (unpublished decision).

(10) *In Absentia* Proceedings Involving Minors—*Matter of Ponce-Hernandez,* 22 I&N Dec. 784 (BIA 1999) [reversed IJ in an *in absentia* case involving a minor where the IJ found that submission solely of I-213 taken when the minor was 15 was insufficient to establish deportability]; *Matter of Gomez-Gomez,* 23 I&N Dec. 522, 523–27 (BIA 2002) [IJ's decision to terminate proceeding and to discount I-213 was reversed in *in absentia* hearing where INS relied on I-213 taken from person who was alleged to be parent of 8-year-old]. When a minor is placed in the custody of a responsible adult pursuant to 8 C.F.R. §242.24, notice must be served upon the adult as well as the minor even if the minor is over 14. *Flores-Chavez v. Ashcroft,* 362 F.3d 1150 (9th Cir. 2004) [reversed *in absentia* order against 15-year-old who was served with OSC pursuant to 8 C.F.R. §103.5a but no service was provided to adult custodian. Court found that reading the statute to permit service solely on minor violated DHS regulations, was not entitled to *Chevron* deference, and raised serious constitutional questions].

7.x. Summary Decision—Where deportability is determined on the pleadings and the respondent did not make an application for relief under 8 C.F.R. §1240.11, is statutorily ineligible for relief, or has been granted VD by the IJ, the IJ may enter a summary decision. 8 C.F.R. §1240.12(b). A summary decision may not be entered where further fact-finding or analysis is necessary to resolve an issue that remains after the respondent has admitted to the factual allegations and charges of removability. *Matter of A-P-,* 22 I&N Dec. 468 (BIA 1999) [where further fact finding was required to determine whether an asylum application should be pretermitted under INA §241(b)(3)]. *But see Matter of Rodriguez-Carrillo,* 22 I&N Dec. 1031 (BIA 1999) [distinguishing *Matter of A-P-* and finding additional proceedings were unnecessary even where respondent did not concede removability].

7.y. Self-Deportation—A person can only "self-deport" if s/he leaves the U.S. *after* an order of deportation has been entered. 8 C.F.R. §§241.7, 1241.7; 8 U.S.C. §1101(g). *Mrvica v. Esperdy*, 376 U.S. 560, 563 (1964). However, an *in absentia* order may be entered where person served with OSC and then fails to appear and court may thereafter decline to review the order. *Joo v. INS*, 813 F.2d 211 (9th Cir. 1987). The BIA has also held that someone who lawfully entered the U.S. but wishes to leave may be held for removal proceedings. *Matter of Ruiz-Massieu,* 22 I&N Dec. 833 (BIA 1999) [person seeking to leave U.S. within 24 hours of lawful entry held for removal proceeding for four years on grounds that Secy. of State determined his presence would have serious foreign policy consequences].

7.z. Deportation by Stipulation—Parties can now stipulate to deportation "which shall constitute a conclusive determination" of removability. INA §240(d), 8 U.S.C. §1229a(d).

7.aa. Collateral Estoppel—Applies in deportation proceeding where citizen's denaturalization proceeding in federal court raised same issues as to misrepresentation on a visa, *Kairys v. INS*, 981 F.2d 937 (7th Cir. 1992); *Schellong v. INS*, 805 F.2d 655 (7th Cir. 1986) or the same factual matters *Szehinskyj v. Att'y Gen. of the U.S.*, 432 F.3d 253 (3d Cir. 2005) [former concentration camp guard and SS member who was denaturalized for illegal procurement was collaterally estopped from asserting he did assist in the persecution of others]; *Dailide v. U.S. Att'y Gen.,* 387 F.3d 1335, 1342–43 (11th Cir. 2004) [where Lithuanian was denaturalized for illegally procuring his citizenship because he did not qualify as a displaced person due to his persecution of Jews, the record of the denaturalization proceeding was admitted in immigration court and used to determine removal by collateral estoppel]; *Hammer v. INS,* 195 F.3d 836, 840–42 (6th Cir. 1999). *But see Palciauskas v. INS*, 939 F.2d 963 (11th Cir. 1991) [reversed deportation order finding denaturalization proceeding did not collaterally estop respondent in deportation]. The doctrine has also been applied to bar relitigation in deportation proceedings where issue of entry was raised and decided in district court case involving respondent's adjustment. *Ramsay v. INS*, 14 F.3d 206 (4th Cir. 1994). The doctrine has also been applied in a deportation proceeding to the question of alienage where the respondent had a prior criminal conviction and a finding of alienage was essential to that conviction. *Howard v. INS*, 930 F.2d 432 (5th Cir. 1991); *but see Duvall v. Att'y Gen. of the U.S.,* 436 F.3d 382, (3d Cir. 2006) [although collateral estoppel applies in immigration proceedings barring the relitigation of alienage, it is a flexible concept and does not apply where a clearly deportable person continues to commit criminal acts after initial proceedings are terminated]. However, a finding of alienage in a deportation proceeding cannot be used to collaterally estop a defendant in a criminal proceeding where alienage is an element of the crime. *U.S. v. Meza-Soria*, 935 F.2d 166, 169 (9th Cir. 1991) [prior deportation order does not collaterally estop defendant in 8 U.S.C. §1326 prosecution from arguing he is a USC]. The doctrine of collateral estoppel can only apply where: (1) the issue at stake is identical to the one involved in the prior litigation; (2) the issue was actually litigated in the prior litigation; and (3) the determination of the issue in the prior litigation was a critical and necessary part of the judgment in that earlier action. *Palciauskas v. INS*, 939 F.2d 963 (11th Cir. 1991). Where issue was not "necessary and essential" to prior action, it cannot be used to collaterally estop a party. *Santana-Albarran v. Ashcroft,* 393 F.3d 699, 703–05 (6th Cir. 2005) [AG not collaterally estopped from arguing respondent did not prove he entered the U.S. in 1985 for purposes of cancellation despite IJ's finding on removal charge that he entered EWI in 1985 because that date was not necessary and essential to find removability].

7.bb. Filing Documents—Where applicant fails to timely file applications or documents (*e.g.*, I-191/I-589 applications) as required by IJ, application deemed waived or abandoned. 8 C.F.R. §1003.31; *Green v. INS*, 46 F.3d 313 (3d Cir. 1995) [an INA §212(c) application deemed abandoned when counsel failed to file it timely]; *Matter of Villarreal-Zuniga,* 23 I&N Dec. 886, 892 (BIA 2006) [adjustment application deemed abandoned when not filed on time]; *Matter of Shanu,* 23 I&N Dec. 754, 764–65 (BIA 2005) [upheld denial of cancellation as abandoned for failure to timely file application]. *But see Louis-Martin v. Ridge,* 322 F.Supp.2d 556, 561–62 (M.D.Pa. 2004) [despite counsel's failure to file I-589, CAT claim would not be deemed abandoned]. Any request for relief is deemed filed when document actually received by the Office of the IJ. 8 C.F.R. §1003.13. All documents or applications requiring a fee must be paid to *DHS* and fee receipt must be thereafter filed with Office of IJ. 8 C.F.R. §§103.7(a), 1003.31, 1103.7(a). Where respondent declined to abandon his application for adjustment but his counsel said he would not present any evidence, court deemed application abandoned and IJ did not commit error in failing to rule on application already abandoned. *Bropleh v. Gonzales,* 428 F.3d 772, 778–79 (8th Cir. 2005).

7.cc. Paying Application Fees—Procedure. When a respondent is applying for relief from removal the fee must be paid to DHS and not to the immigration court. 8 C.F.R. §1103.7(a)(3). Upon payment to DHS, the respondent shall receive a receipt from DHS and any documents relating to the proceeding. The fee receipt and the application or motion shall then be submitted to the EOIR. Appeals, however, are filed with the fee directly to the BIA. 8 C.F.R. §§1003.8, 1103.7(a)(2), (b). When a motion is filed with the BIA that includes an application for relief that has a separate fee (*e.g.,* I-485), the fee for the motion is sent to the BIA and if the BIA grants the motion, the movant will then pay the fee for the application for relief to DHS when the case is remanded to the IJ. 8 C.F.R. §1003.8(b).

7.dd. Recusal and Misconduct of IJ—Under *Matter of Exame*, 18 I&N Dec. 303 (BIA 1982), the BIA recognized three distinct grounds for recusal: (1) "[T]he constitutional due process requirement that the hearing be before a fair and impartial arbiter"; (2) the immigration judge had a personal, rather than judicial bias stemming from an "extrajudicial" source; or (3) the IJ engaged in "such pervasive bias and prejudice" as shown by his judicial conduct. These grounds are consistent with the recusal provisions of 28 U.S.C. §§144, 455. Recusal under 28 U.S.C. §144 requires that affidavits be filed supporting the claim. Sec. 455 does not have such a requirement but instead placed the duty upon the IJ to disqualify himself. This is consistent with 8 C.F.R. §1240.1(b). An IJ's recusal decision prior to a hearing should always be rendered in writing, provide a well-reasoned opinion for the grant or denial and be served upon the parties. It must be issued in every case as simple form or blanket orders will not suffice unless the IJ had a role in the case as a DHS or private attorney. If the grounds do not become apparent until the hearing the IJ may do it orally on the record. Memo [OPPM 05-02], Creppy, Chief IJ, EOIR, (Mar. 21, 2005), at section IV, *published on* AILA InfoNet at Doc. No. 05032369.

The standards for disqualification are to be liberally applied. *Liljeberg v. Health Services Acquisition Corp.*, 108 S.Ct. 2194 (1988); *Hall v. SBA*, 695 F.2d 175 (5th Cir. 1983). *See also Nicodemus v. Chrysler Corp.*, 596 F.2d 152 (6th Cir. 1979); *U.S. v. Kelly,* 888 F.2d 732, 744 (11th Cir. 1989) [holding that 28 U.S.C. §455 eliminated the doctrine that a judge had a "duty to sit" in a case]; *Matter of Osterloh*, 34 F.2d 223 (S.D. Tex. 1929). Moreover, when a legally sufficient motion is present, it is inappropriate for the IJ to pass upon the truthfulness of the facts. It should be given to another IJ to decide. *Berger v. U.S.*, 255 U.S. 22 (1921). Further, there is no doubt that the Code of Judicial Conduct is applicable to IJs, as it is to all administrative judges. *See Three Mile Island Alert, Inc. v. N.R.C.*, 771 F.2d 720 (3d Cir. 1985); *Faulkner Radio, Inc. v. FCC*, 557 F.2d 866 (D.C. Cir. 1977); *Amos Treat & Co. v. FCC*, 306 F.2d 260 (D.C. Cir. 1962); *Matter of Chocallo*, 2 MSPB 23 (1978), *aff'd*, 2 MSPB 20 (1980).

The court's conduct toward counsel may also be the basis for recusal. *U.S. v. Kelley*, 712 F.2d 884, 890 (1st Cir. 1983); *Bell v. Chandler*, 569 F.2d 556 (10th Cir. 1978); *U.S. v. Ritter*, 540 F.2d 459 (10th Cir. 1976), *cert. denied*, 429 U.S. 951 (1976); *U.S. v. Panzardi-Alvarez*, 678 F.Supp. 353 (D.P.R. 1988). As judicial officers, IJs have a "responsibility to function as neutral and impartial arbiters" and "must assiduously refrain from becoming advocates for either party" *Aguilar-Solis v. INS,* 168 F.3d 565, 569 (1st Cir. 1999). *See also Schweiker v. McClure,* 456 U.S. 188, 195 (1982) [due process demands impartiality on the part of those who function in judicial or quasi-judicial capacities]; *Zhang v. Gonzales,* 405 F.3d 150, 157–61 (3d Cir. 2005) (McKee, J concurring) [where IJ appears to have decided case before hearing all the testimony because respondent used the word "persecution" in her testimony, case should be remanded to BIA and new judge assigned]; *Reyes-Melendez v. INS,* 342 F.3d 1001 (9th Cir. 2003) [where IJ took over questioning, did not act as a neutral fact finder, and engaged in a stream of nonjudicious and snide comments demonstrating her hostility to the applicant for suspension, due process was violated and final order was reversed]; *Marincas v. Lewis,* 92 F.3d 195, 204 (3d Cir. 1996). *But see Vargas-Hernandez v. Gonzales,* 497 F.3d 919, 925–27 (9th Cir. 2007) [upheld denial of recusal motion despite IJ's invitation to file the motion where there was no evidence of prejudgment and applicant was given a full and fair opportunity to present his case]. A judge should not necessarily recuse himself, according to EOIR, because a party sues or threatens to sue him. Memo [OPPM 05-02], Creppy, Chief IJ, EOIR, (Mar. 21, 2005) at ¶III(A), *published on* AILA InfoNet at Doc. No. 05032369. Nor would events that were remote in time or an IJ's cutting or hostile comments to an attorney regarding his skill mandate recusal according to EOIR. *Id.*

But whether recusal is appropriate, the IJ's testiness, inappropriate comments, and overly abrupt or intimidating manner may raise a due process claim or at least removal from the case. The A.G. issued a directive to improve the manner that IJ's conducted themselves on the bench in light of substantial concerns raised by the press and the public. Memo, Rooney, Director, EOIR (undated, c. Apr. 2007), *published on* AILA InfoNet at Doc. No. 07041165 (Apr. 11, 2007). *See also Floroiu v Gonzales,* 481 F.3d 970, 973–76 (7th Cir. 2007) [where IJ characterized asylum applicants as "religious zealots" who were "offensive to the majority" his comments evidenced sufficient bias to deprive applicants of due process]; *Islam v. Gonzales,* 469 F.3d 53 (2d Cir. 2006) [where IJ repeatedly addressed the respondent in "an argumentative, sarcastic, impolite, and overly hostile manner that went beyond fact-finding and questioning" the court reversed also stating that: "Even when, as here, the IJ firmly believes a petitioner is not truthful, repetitive verbally abusive comments and questions taint the proceedings, erode the appearance of fairness and call into question the result of the proceeding."]; *Huang v. Gonzales,* 453 F.3d 142, 148–51 (2d Cir. 2006) [where negative credibility assessment was reversed in forced abortion case, the IJ's apparent bias against the applicant required reassignment on remand to a different IJ]. In *Cham v. Att'y Gen. of the U.S.,* 445 F.3d 683 (3d Cir. 2006) the court determined that that IJ's conduct violated due process and deprived Gambian asylum applicant of a fair hearing where IJ assumed application was invalid, nitpicked the application and testimony for inconsistencies and contradictions, prevented applicant from presenting evidence/witnesses, and engaged in conduct that was abusive toward the applicant including preventing him from presenting his testimony by continually interrupting him. The court reversed the IJ and quoted *Iliev v. INS,* 127 F.3d 638, 643 (7th Cir. 1997) stating: "It is a hallmark of the American system of justice that anyone who appears as a litigant in an American courtroom is treated with dignity and respect. That expectation must be met regardless of the citizenship of the parties or the nature of the litigation. In a country built on the dreams and accomplishments of an immigrant population, a particularly severe wound is inflicted on the principle when an immigration matter is not conducted in accord with the best of our tradition of courtesy and fairness." *Cham,* 445 F.3d at 685. *See also Sukwanputra v. Gonzales,* 434 F.3d 627, 637–38 (3d Cir. 2006) [without reaching the due process issue, the court determined that the IJ's comments were so intemperate, it suggested a different IJ on remand because "justice must satisfy the appearance of justice" and there is a need to ensure fairness and satisfy the appearance of impartiality]; *Giday v. Gonzales,* 434 F.3d 543, 547–50 (7th Cir. 2006) [although resolving the case on other issues, the court applied the totality of the circumstances test to the IJ's conduct and noted both that the IJ asked far more questions than the assistant district counsel and that "when the questioning becomes so aggressive that it frazzles applicants and nit-picks inconsistencies" any benefit to the development of the record is lost]; *Wang v. Att'y Gen. of the U.S.,* 423 F.3d 260, 267–71 (3d Cir. 2005) [where the "tone, the tenor, the disparagement, and the sarcasm of the IJ seem[ed] more appropriate to a court television show than a federal court proceeding, the court reversed the adverse credibility finding on asylum, remanded to the BIA and suggested a new IJ be assigned to the case]; *Rodriguez Galicia v. Gonzales,* 422 F.3d 529, 538–40 (7th Cir. 2005) [IJ violated due process under the totality of the circumstances when he frequently interrupted respondent's counsel, assumed the role of counsel for the government and precluded two experts from testifying regarding Guatemalan asylum claim]; *Ahmed v. Gonzales,* 398 F.3d 722 (6th Cir. 2005) [where IJ misunderstood testimony and based on his misunderstanding made improper rulings as to credibility denying asylum, due process was violated, the IJ's order was reversed, and the court ordered that a new judge hear the matter]. *But see Yosd v. Mukasey,* 514 F.3d 74, 77–79 (1st Cir. 2008) [court rejected claim that, as an institutional matter, an IJ should always be recused where a case was remanded to her after she made an adverse credibility finding]; *Jarbough v. Att'y Gen. of the U.S.,* 483 F.3d 184, 192–93 (3d Cir. 2007) [it was not improper for IJ to rebuke attorney for asking leading questions]; *Apouviepseakoda v. Gonzales,* 475 F.3d 881, 884–89 (7th Cir. 2007) [although IJ's conduct "was hardly a model of patience and decorum," it did not impede Togo asylum applicant's "reasonable opportunity" to be heard]; *Boci v. Gonzales,* 473 F.3d 762, 768–69 (7th Cir. 2007) [although IJ cut off line of inquiry, insisted on moving things along, and asked many questions, a less than desirable demeanor, in and of itself, does not violate due process]; *Ishak v. Gonzales,* 422 F.3d 22, 31 (1st Cir. 2005) [IJ's brusque and impatient manner in questioning respondent was not so obviously bias or unfair that hearing was a violation of due process]; *Hassan v. Gonzales,* 403 F.3d 429, 436–37 (6th Cir. 2005) [IJs brusque and sarcastic manner is insufficient to raise prejudgment]; *Shoaira v. Ashcroft,* 377 F.3d 837, 842–43 (8th Cir. 2004) [IJ's inappropriate comments scattered through the asylum transcript did not work any prejudice against respondent and therefore did not violate due process]; *Abdulrahman v. Ashcroft,* 330 F.3d 587, 595–97 (3d Cir. 2003) [where IJ in certain places during the asylum hearing "did go beyond the bounds of propriety" her denial was not reversed because of the deferential standard of review of the record]; *Kuciemba v. INS,* 92 F.3d 496, 501–02 (7th Cir. 1996); *Ivezaj v. INS,* 84 F.3d 215, 220 (6th Cir. 1996). Nor does the IJ's statement at the beginning of the hearing concerning his views of the case amount to a due process violation. *Ciorba v. Ashcroft,* 323 F.3d 539, 544–45 (7th Cir. 2003) [IJ announcing at beginning of asylum hearing that he reviewed documents and thought asylum case was deficient but that he had not made up his mind was not bias or due process violation]. Moreover, a judge's vigorous questioning of an applicant does not violate due process. *Melkonian v. Ashcroft,* 320 F.3d 1061, 1072 (9th Cir. 2003) [aggressive and sometimes harsh questioning by IJ during asylum hearing is not a violation of due process]. Nor does the IJ's efforts to shorten the hearing or acting stern or short-tempered amount to a due process violation. *Laurent v. Ashcroft,* 359 F.3d 59 62–63 (1st Cir. 2004) [cutting off cumulative or redundant testimony does not violate due process and the fact that an IJ forms a preliminary opinion about the facts does not render the proceeding fundamentally unfair]; *Albathani v. INS,* 318 F.3d 365, 374–75 (1st Cir. 2003) [finding that if the asylum applicant was an admitted person with due process rights, the IJ's efforts to expedite the hearing and her acting in a stern and short-tempered manner were insufficient to establish due process violation].

Several circuit courts, however, have on occasion remanded cases back to BIA with the request or order that a different IJ be assigned. *Mapouya v. Gonzales,* 487 F.3d 396, 416 (6th Cir. 2007) [urged the BIA on remand to assign a different IJ where IJ made numerous errors in asylum and withholding hearing of applicant from Brazzaville, Congo, but there was no evidence discussing IJ misconduct]; *Shahinaj v. Gonzales,* 481 F.3d 1027, 1029 (8th Cir. 2007) [where IJ's adverse credibility finding in Albanian's homosexual persecution claim was based in part on belief that respondent was not credible because he did not speak, dress or act like a homosexual, the decision was reversed and the court recommended reassignment of the case to a different IJ]; *Shah v. Attorney General of the U.S.* 446 F.3d 429, 437–38 (3d Cir. 2006) [where court reversed adverse credibility finding in Pakistani asylum case, with a suggestion that IJ was looking for ways to deny case, it requested that BIA on remand select a new IJ to hear the case]; *Pavlova v. INS,* 441 F.3d 82, 92 (2d Cir. 2006) [vacated IJ's credibility findings on asylum case and strongly suggested case be assigned to a different judge on remand]; *Wang v. Att'y Gen. of the U.S.,* 423 F.3d 260, 271 (3d Cir. 2005) [where court found that the IJ made intemperate and humiliating remarks that failed the basic requirement of being a neutral and impartial arbiter the "parties would be far better served by the assignment of these proceedings to a different IJ"]; *Zhang v. Gonzales,* 405 F.3d 150, 157–61 (3d Cir. 2005) (McKee, J concurring) [where IJ appears to have decided case before hearing all the testimony because respondent used the word "persecution" in her testimony, case should be remanded to BIA and new judge assigned]; *Nuru v. Gonzales,* 404 F.3d 1207, 1229 (9th Cir. 2005) [where IJ's comments against asylum applicant during hearing were caustic and without substance and where IJ denied counsel's request for closing argument and suggested without basis that counsel coached his witness, court ordered that case be assigned to a new IJ on remand]; *Huang v. Gonzales,* 403 F.3d 945, 948–51 (7th Cir. 2005) [where IJ exceeded his proper role in questioning the asylum applicant and his conduct tainted the credibility findings, decision reversed and court encouraged the BIA to assign a new judge]; .*Korytnyuk v. Ashcroft,* 396 F.3d 272, 287 n.20 (3d Cir. 2005) [IJ's exchanges with respondent were so troubling that on remand the parties would be better served by assignment of proceedings to a different judge]; *Yi-Tu Lian v. Ashcroft,* 379 F.3d 457, 462 (7th Cir. 2004) ["The inadequate performance of the immigration judge leads us to recommend that the case be reassigned to another immigration judge"]; *Guchshenkov v. Ashcroft,* 366 F.3d 554 (7th Cir. 2004) [criticizing and removing IJs from asylum cases where they did not present a reasoned decision]; *Muhur v. Ashcroft,* 355 F.3d 958, 961 (7th Cir. 2004) [in view of IJ's "mishandling" of asylum claim by applying an incorrect standard, BIA urged to remand to a different IJ]; *Bace v. Ashcroft,* 352 F.3d 1133, 1141 (7th Cir. 2003) [suggested new hearing officer where circuit court thought IJ made numerous errors]; *Paramasamy v. Ashcroft,* 295 F.3d 1047, 1055 n.4 (9th Cir. 2002) [suggesting that after remand if IJ is necessary another be assigned].

Transfer of case to a new IJ does not mean that all matters should be relitigated. *Zhang v. Gonzales,* 434 F.3d 993, 996–98 (7th Cir. 2006) [absent exceptional circumstances, such as a change in the law, new evidence, or compelling circumstances, a new IJ assigned to a case on remand should not make inconsistent rulings to the prior IJ based merely on differing impressions of credibility]; *Ko v. Gonzales,* 421 F.3d 453 (7th Cir. 2005) [where first IJ reopened *in absentia* order and transferred case and second IJ reversed the first IJ, the court determined that the second IJ abused his discretion because there was evidence in the record of lack of notice and litigants have " a right to expect that a change in judges will not mean going back to square one"]. The Chief IJ also takes the view that the law of the case doctrine applies when a change of venue is granted and absent exceptional circumstances the receiving judge of a change of venue is "not free to hear the case *de novo* and ignore any orders prior to the venue change." Memo [OPPM 01-02], Creppy, Chief IJ, EOIR (Oct. 9, 2001), *reprinted in* 79 No. 3 *Interpreter Releases* 66, 84–88 (Jan. 14, 2002). The exceptions to the law of the case include: (1) a supervening rule of law; (2) compelling or unusual circumstances; (3) new evidence available to the transferee judge; (4) clear error in the previous order resulting in manifest injustice.

As a constitutional matter, we have "long recognized that combining the roles of prosecutor and adjudicator in a single entity is a recipe for fundamentally unfair and erroneous decision making. *See, e.g., Schweiker v. McClure*, 456 U.S. 188, 195 (1982) ...." *Flores by Galvez-Maldonado v. Meese*, 942 F.2d 1352, 1368 (9th Cir. 1991) (*en banc*) (Tang, J. concurring), *rev'd on other grounds, Reno v. Flores*, 507 U.S. 292 (1993). The court in *Flores-Leon v. INS,* 272 F.3d 433, 440 (7th Cir. 2001), however, had no difficulty in rejecting a recusal motion based upon a claim that an IJ may not hear both the bond and merits hearing because 8 C.F.R. §1003.19(d) requires that they be "separate and apart."

7.ee. Right to Notify Embassy—8 C.F.R. §§236.1(e), 1236.1(e). Detained alien must be notified that he may communicate with the consul or diplomatic officer of the country of his nationality where country is on treaty list. 8 C.F.R. §§236.1(e), 1236.1(e) [list includes Canada, UK and many European and South American countries]. The right applies even if person is in federal custody as long as a deportation proceeding is held. *Waldron v. INS*, 17 F.3d 511, 515–16 (2d Cir.), *cert. denied,* 513 U.S. 1014 (1994). Under Ninth Circuit law the failure to notify alien of his right to contact his country's consulate or embassy may result in reversal of a deportation order where he produces evidence that: (1) he did not know of right; (2) he would have availed himself of the right had he known of it; and (3) there was a likelihood that the contact would have resulted in assistance to him in resisting deportation. *U.S. v. Rangel-Gonzalez*, 617 F.2d 529, 533 (9th Cir. 1980) [in challenge to underlying deportation order in illegal reentry context]. The defendant would also have to demonstrate that the violation of the regulation "prejudiced [his] interests." *U.S. v. Cerda-Pena,* 799 F.2d 1374, 1377 (9th Cir. 1986) [same]. *See also U.S. ex rel. Madej v. Schomig,* 223 F.Supp.2d 968, 977–80 (N.D. Ill. 2002) [applying Convention and the International Court of Justice ruling in *LaGrand Case (Germany v. U.S.),* 2001 I.C.J. 104 (June 27) to vacate death penalty because notification to consul could have made a difference at death penalty phase]. Under State Department Guidelines a person should be notified under the Convention at time of booking. *Consular Notification and Access* (1998), U.S. Department of State. *But see Torres De La Cruz v. Maurer,* 483 F.3d 1013, 1023–24 (10th Cir. 2007) [the default rules specified in *Sanchez-Llamas* barred claim that Article 36 was violated as to LPR in removal proceeding because the LPR did not raise the issue with the IJ and the BIA determined that it was waived]; *Rosales v. ICE,* 426 F.3d 733, 736–38 (5th Cir. 2005) [where respondent was not informed of rights under the Vienna Convention there was no due process violation because there was no showing of prejudice].

Notification to Minors—DHS must also provide consular notification to a minor which cannot be waived by the minor. *U.S. v. D.L.*, 453 F.3d 1115, 1123 and n.6 (9th Cir. 2006).

Violation of Article 36—The violation of Article 36 (as distinguished from violation of the DHS regulation on consular notification, 8 C.F.R. §§236.1, 1236.1) does not create an enforceable right. *Sanchez-Llamas v. Oregon,* 548 U.S. 331 (2006) [in criminal proceeding suppression of evidence is not an appropriate remedy for an Article 36 violation and regular state rules of procedural default apply to bar Article 36 claims]; *Medellin v. Texas,* 128 S.Ct. 1346 (2008) [the International Court of Justice *Avena* decision (*Case Concerning Avena and Other Mexican Nationals* (*Mex. v. U.S.*), 2004 I.C.J. 12 finding the U.S. had violated Article 36(1)(b) of the Convention was not enforceable in a state court to preempt state limitations on filing successive habeas petitions, notwithstanding the President's Memorandum directing enforcement, because the decision was not "self-executing" and the remedy under the Treaty is referral to the U.N. Security Council]; *U.S. v. De La Pava,* 268 F.3d 157, 163–66 (2d Cir. 2001) *and cases cited therein* [no fundamental right implicated by failure to give consular notification and indictment should not be dismissed]; *Matter of Rivera-Valencia,* 24 I&N Dec. 484, 491–92 (BIA 2008) [court-martial is a conviction under INA §101(a)(48)(A) and Art. 36 of the Vienna Convention cannot be a basis to collaterally attack the conviction].

The failure to notify an individual of his right to consular assistance may result in an action for civil damages and injunctive relief. *Jogi v. Voges,* 480 F.3d 822 (7th Cir. 2007) [allowed noncitizen convicted of aggravated battery and deported to bring civil rights claim under §1983 for failure of state officials to notify him of the right to consular assistance under Article 36 ¶1(b)]; *Standt v. City of New York,* 153 F.Supp.2d 417 (S.D.N.Y. 2001) [private right permissible]. *But see Cornejo v. County of San Diego,* 504 F.3d 853 (9th Cir. 2007) [Article 36 does not create an independent enforceable right under §1983 for Mexican nationals who were not advised on their consular rights]; *Bieregu v. Ashcroft,* 259 F.Supp.2d 342, 352–54 (D.N.J. 2003) [no ATCA claim for violation of Article 36 because there is no tort].

7.ff. Relation Back Doctrine—The BIA recognizes that a declaration of an invalid marriage could relate back to the date of the marriage for immigration purposes absent fraud, misrepresentation or manipulation. *Matter of Astorga*, 17 I&N Dec. 1, 4 (BIA 1979). However, the doctrine is only applied "where to do so would bring about a just result," *Matter of Magana*, 17 I&N Dec. 111, 114 (BIA 1979) [relation back doctrine rejected where respondent believed to have committed fraud], and may therefore not cure a misrepresentation when made to obtain a visa. *Garcia v. INS*, 31 F.3d 441 (7th Cir. 1994) [where IJ determined that respondent in deportation proceeding for misrepresentation in obtaining second preference approval intended to misrepresent marital status, the decision by foreign court determining marriage was void ab initio not sufficient to cure misrepresentation]; *Hendrix v. INS*, 583 F.2d 1102 (9th Cir. 1978).

8. **Summary Removal for Nonresident Aggravated Felons**—INA §238(b), 8 U.S.C. §1228(b), 8 C.F.R. §§238.1, 1238.1 *et seq.*

8.a. Establishes a nonjudicial summary proceeding for nonresidents who the DHS seeks to deport as aggravated felons. ICE will conduct these proceedings through trial attorneys, except that the person initiating the charges shall not enter the final order. Respondent is served with an I-851 and has 10 days to respond. 8 C.F.R. §§238.1(c), 1238.1(c).

8.b. Applies to persons who are not LPRs. It also applies to conditional residents. Some courts have found that the statute also applies to parolees notwithstanding the statutory language making the statute applicable to aggravated felons and thus only to persons who commit aggravated felonies "after admission." *Bamba v. Riley, Jr.*, 366 F.3d 195 (3d Cir. 2004); *Bazan-Reyes v. INS,* 256 F.3d 600, 604–05 (7th Cir. 2001).

8.c. Person must be given reasonable notice of the charges and an opportunity to inspect the evidence and rebut the charges. 8 C.F.R. §§238.1(b)(2) and (c), 1238.1(b)(2) and (c). The proceedings need not be conducted in a language the person understands. An order can be entered without a finding of clear, convincing and unequivocal evidence. An order of summary deportation may not be executed until 14 days after its issuance, unless waived by the respondent.

8.d. Conclusive presumption of deportability. INA §238(c).

8.e. No relief available because the AG is barred from granting any relief. INA §238(b)(5), *U.S. v. Gonzalez,* 429 F.3d 1252 (9th Cir. 2005 [the bar to INA §212(h) relief under 8 U.S.C. §1228(b)(5), which barred all discretionary relief for a person subject to expedited removal who was a non-LPR aggravated felon, could be retroactively applied]; *but see Matter of Michel,* 21 I&N Dec. 1101 (BIA 1998) [INA §212(h) availability]; *U.S. v. Arrieta,* 224 F.3d 1076, 1080–81 (9th Cir. 2000) [rejected argument that §1228(b)(5) bars all relief for aggravated felons including those who are not in expedited removal]. However, the person may seek protection under the Convention Against Torture. 8 C.F.R. §§208.31, 1208.31.

8.f. Judicial review by habeas was abolished for persons convicted of most crimes, INA §§242(a)(2)(C), (a)(5). However, review remains in the court of appeals solely to review constitutional questions and questions of law. INA §242(a)(2)(D), 8 U.S.C. §1252 (a)(2)(D). *Flores-Ledezma v. Gonzales,* 415 F.3d 375, 379–81 (5th Cir. 2005) [the REAL ID Act of 2005 enacting INA §242(a)(2)(D) preserved constitutional review and the review of questions of law for summary removal proceedings under INA §238(b) notwithstanding 242(a)(2)(C) or 242(g)].

8.g. Constitutionality and retroactivity of the summary removal procedure upheld. *Graham v. Mukasey,* 519 F.3d 549 (6th Cir. 2008) [expedited-removal procedure does not violate due process, because there was no prejudice, and does not violate equal protection, because there is a rational basis]; *U.S. v. Calderon-Segura,* 512 F.3d 1104, 1107–08 (9th Cir. 2008) [expedited removal proceedings under 8 U.S.C. §1228(b) did not violate equal protection under rational basis test on claim that persons similarly situated may or may not be placed in expedited removal]; *Gonzalez v. Chertoff,* 454 F.3d 813, 816–18 (8th Cir. 2006) [followed *Fernandez-Vargas* and found that application of 238(b) to a 1988 conviction was not impermissibly retroactive and there was no equal protection claim]; *Flores-Ledezma v. Gonzales,* 415 F.3d 375, 381–82 (5th Cir. 2005) [rational basis for giving the AG the choice to institute summary removal under INA §238(b) or proceedings before an IJ for nonresidents where relief may be obtained]; *U.S. v. Rangel De Aguilar,* 308 F.3d 1134 (10th Cir. 2002) [constitutionality of procedure for taking a waiver of hearing under §1228(b)(4) was upheld where defendant challenged the lack of a neutral magistrate to take the waiver and the lack of an audible record]; *U.S. v. Benitez-Villafuerte,* 186 F.3d 651 (5th Cir. 1999) [statute meets minimum due process notice requirements and the commingling of prosecutorial and adjudicative functions is permissible]; *Ogundipe v. DHS,* 295 F.Supp.2d 513, 517 (E.D. Pa. 2003) [expedited process does not violate due process]; *Bamba v. Elwood,* 252 F.Supp.2d 195, 203–06 (E.D. Pa. 2003) [no due process violation regarding opportunity to be heard, adequate time to respond, or inability to return].

9. **Expedited Removal Proceedings for Persons Serving Prison Sentences**—INA §238(a), 8 U.S.C. §1228(a).

9.a. Provides for removal proceedings for persons detained in federal, state and local prisons. INA §238(a)(1), 8 U.S.C. §1228(a)(1). Includes any person convicted of criminal offenses: aggravated felons, drugs, firearms, 2 CIMTs committed within 5 years of entry and miscellaneous crimes under 237(a)(2)(D). INA §238(a)(1).

9.b. Proceedings under INA §238.

9.c. Requires that hearing be conducted in a manner which eliminates the need for additional detention at any DHS processing center and that assures expeditious deportation where warranted following the end of the alien's sentence. Also requires AG to provide for the availability of special deportation proceedings at prisons so that the initiation and, if possible, the completion of deportation proceedings can occur before end of prison sentence. Conducting a deportation and INA §212(c) hearing in a prison was not found to violate *per se* due process. *Burgos-Abril v. INS*, 58 F.3d 475 (9th Cir. 1995).

9.d. Aliens shall be detained to the maximum extent possible at facilities where other such aliens are detained and the AG shall make reasonable efforts to ensure the alien's access to counsel and right to counsel under INA §292 are not impaired. Aliens must be detained consistent with section 236(c). INA §238(a)(2).

9.e. The AG shall have 30 days to effect person's departure who has been convicted of one of the crimes recited above. The AG may waive it if the person is cooperating with law enforcement authorities or for national security reasons.

9.f. An alien convicted of an aggravated felony shall be *conclusively presumed* to be deportable from the U.S. INA §238(c), 8 U.S.C. §1228(c). The DHS still has the burden of proving alienage. In the case of aggravated felons, the AG is mandated to initiate and complete removal proceedings when the person is incarcerated for the aggravated felony.

9.g. The passage of INA §238(a) does not limit the discretion of prison officials to change security classifications. *Mohammed v. Sullivan*, 866 F.2d 258, 260 (8th Cir. 1989) [under former version of statute at 8 U.S.C. §1252(a)]. Nor does INA §238(a) create a private right of action by a detained alien to an expedited deportation hearing. INA §238(a)(1) ["Nothing in this section shall be construed to create any substantive or procedural right or benefit that is legally enforceable by any party against the United States or its agencies or officers or any other person"]. Immigration and Nationality Technical Corrections Act of 1994 §225 ["No amendment made by this Act and nothing under INA §242(i) shall be construed to create a substantive or procedural right"]; *Campos v. INS*, 62 F.3d 311 (9th Cir. 1995); *Hernandez-Avalos v. INS*, 50 F.3d 842 (10th Cir. 1995); *Channer v. Hall*, 112 F.3d 214 (5th Cir. 1997); *Matter of Sanchez*, 20 I&N Dec. 223 (BIA 1990), or a right of an excludable alien to expedited treatment. *Lopez-Mejia v. INS*, 798 F.Supp. 625 (C.D. Cal. 1992) [section inapplicable to person in exclusion]. Moreover, a party may be entitled to an expedited hearing only when s/he is in DHS custody. *Paulino v. Connery*, 766 F.Supp. 209, 211–12 (S.D.N.Y. 1991) [expedited proceeding only applicable after person is in INS custody]. In any event, INA §238(a) does not compel a person's physical deportation prior to completion of sentence. *Perez v. INS*, 979 F.2d 299 (3d Cir. 1992).

(1) Government's conduct under this program severely criticized. *Fadare v. Reno*, 819 F.Supp. 1196 (E.D.N.Y. 1993) [INS required to show cause for failure to initiate deportation proceeding before completion of sentence]; *Iheme v. Reno*, 819 F.Supp. 1192 (E.D.N.Y. 1992) [chastising government for delay in deportation proceedings]; *Nwankwo v. Reno*, 819 F.Supp. 1186 (E.D.N.Y. 1993) [mandatory detention provision does not give AG right to ignore speedy disposition requirement under INA §242(c)].

9.h. Relief Unavailable—Many forms of relief including asylum, cancellation of removal, and voluntary departure, are not available to aggravated felons. *See, e.g.*, INA §§208(b)(2)(A), 240A(a)(3), 240B(a)(1). Withholding of removal may also be unavailable if the person has been convicted of an aggravated felony. INA §241(b)(3). Aggravated felons are automatically considered persons convicted of particularly serious crimes under INA §241(b)(3)(B)(ii). However, if a person was not sentenced to 5 years the AG may determine that the person has not been convicted of a particularly serious crime. *See* "Particularly Serious Crime, Danger to the Community," in. Ch. 4, ¶ IV.D.3 (p.479), *infra*.

10. **Stipulated Judicial Order of Deportation**—Pursuant to Fed. R. Crim. P. 11, a person subject to removal may waive his or her right to a hearing and stipulate to a judicial order of deportation as a condition of the plea agreement. INA §238(c)(5), 8 U.S.C. §1228(c)(5). If s/he stipulates a judge or magistrate may order deportation as a condition of probation. 18 U.S.C. §3563(b)(21).

11. **Judicial Deportation**—INA §238(c), 8 U.S.C. §1228(c).

11.a. A district court may enter an order of removal or grant relief to a criminal defendant—The district court judge has authority to enter the order "at the time of sentencing."

11.b. Procedure—The U.S. Attorney initiates the process by filing with the U.S. district court prior to commencement of the trial or entry of a guilty plea, a notice of intent to request judicial deportation, which shall be served upon the defendant and the DHS. INA §238(c)(2)(A). At least 30 days prior to the date set for sentencing, the U.S. Attorney with the concurrence of the Commissioner shall file removal charges with the court regarding the alienage of the defendant and identifying the crimes which make him or her deportable. INA §238(c)(2)(B). A defendant cannot initiate the process. *U.S. v. Flores-Uribe*, 106 F.3d 1485, 1487 (9th Cir. 1997). And in the view of one court, the government's failure to comply with the procedural rights established in §238(b)(2) will not reverse a deportation order absent proof that the government's lapse affected the defendant's "substantial rights." *U.S. v. Nguyen,* 255 F.3d 1335,

1345–47 (11th Cir. 2001) [where government failed to raise alienage in papers it submitted, the lack of notice and violation of §238(b)(2) would not alter the order of deportation absent a showing that the defendant's "substantial rights" were affected]. If the defendant has presented substantial evidence to establish a prima facie case for eligibility for relief, the Commissioner shall provide the court with a recommendation and report. The court shall either grant or deny the relief sought. The defendant shall have an opportunity to review and cross examine the witnesses and the evidence and present witnesses on his own behalf. However, the court shall only consider evidence admissible in INA §240 proceedings. If the U.S. district judge denies the request to remove, the AG may initiate deportation proceedings under INA §240. The Service has issued initial guidance on these cases. Memo, Meissner, Comm. INS, CO 766.9 (Feb. 22, 1995), *reprinted in* 72 No. 13 *Interpreter Releases* 449, 462 (Mar. 31, 1995).

11.c. Appeal—To circuit court, consistent with INA §242.

12. **Terrorist Removal Courts**—The Congress established special provisions for the removal of persons suspected of being terrorists in AEDPA §401(a) *et seq.* (as amended under IIRIRA §354), INA §501 *et seq.*, 8 U.S.C. §1531 *et seq.*

(1) Establishes a special court of 5 U.S. district court judges designated by the Chief Justice who will hear terrorist alien cases initiated by the AG through application to the court for someone who the AG believes meets the definition of terrorist under INA §237(a)(4)(B), 8 U.S.C. §1227(a)(4)(B). The situs of the court will be the U.S. Courthouse in the District of Columbia. A single judge may grant the request/application for the hearing.

(2) The hearing is expedited but open to the public. INA §504(a). There is a right to appointed counsel if the person is "financially unable to obtain counsel." The burden of proof on the government is only by a preponderance of the evidence and the Federal Rules of Evidence do not apply. Although the respondent may introduce evidence, cross-examine witnesses and subpoena persons nationwide, the government may introduce classified information that the respondent has no right to review nor suppress, even if unlawfully obtained. INA §504(e)(1), (3). Request for Subpoenas under Rule 12 of the Court Rules must be made to the court at least 10 days prior to the removal hearing. The government is to provide the respondent a summary of the classified information unless the judge determines that the person's continued presence would cause serious and irreparable harm to national security *and* death or serious injury to any person. If the judge makes this determination and if respondent is an LPR, the other special procedures apply, including the fact that a special attorney is appointed to review the confidential material and if he discloses it to his client it is a criminal offense. INA §504(e)(3)(F).

(3) The respondent has no right to seek the following forms of relief before the judge: asylum, withholding, cancellation, removal, voluntary departure, adjustment or registry. INA §504(k). However, a removal order may not be executed that would violate the Convention Against Torture after the Secy. of State and the AG confer. 28 C.F.R. §200.1.

(4) Expedited appeal. Must file notice within 20 days in U.S. Court of Appeals for D.C. Circuit and court must render a decision within 60 days. INA §505(a)(1), (c)(4)(B).

(5) Detention and removal. Only an LPR may seek release pending a removal determination if the AG decides to detain. INA §506(a)(2)(A). The judge's decision is not subject to review except if AG wishes to appeal. If judge decides person should be removed, they are detained pending removal even if previously released. If AG cannot remove, she must give respondent a report every 6 months on success in obtaining removal. INA §507(b)(2)(C).

(6) There is no judicial review of the continued detention except in the U.S. Court of Appeals for D.C. Circuit and then only to challenge the constitutionality of detention. INA §505(e)(2).

(7) Respondent can designate the country of deportation but AG need not agree if deportation to that country would impair a treaty obligation or adversely effect U.S. foreign policy. INA §507(b)(2)(B).

13. **Reinstatement of Removal Order**—INA §241(a)(5), 8 U.S.C. §1231(a)(5), 8 C.F.R. §§241.8, 1241.8. Where AG finds that a person removed or given VD under an order of removal re-enters the U.S. illegally, DHS can reinstate the prior order of removal and the person may not seek to reopen the original order, review the reinstated order, or seek relief from removal. The statute encompasses exclusion, deportation, removal, as well as summary removal orders. *Warner v. Ashcroft,* 381 F.3d 534, 537–38 (6th Cir. 2004); *Delgado v. Mukasey,* 516 F.3d 65 (2d Cir. 2008) [INA §241(a)(5) applicable to reentry after summary removal order]. There is no right to a hearing before an IJ. 8 C.F.R. §§241.8(a), 1241.8(a). *Lorenzo v. Mukasey,* 508 F.3d 1278, 1283–84 (10th Cir. 2007) [regulation does not violate due process by limiting hearing to DHS officer]; *Morales-Izquierdo v. Gonzales,* 486 F.3d 484 (9th Cir. 2007) (en banc) [DHS regulation regarding the procedure for reinstatement of removal cases that permits removal without a hearing before the IJ is not inconsistent with INA §241(a)(5) under *Chevron* and removal before a DHS officer does not violate due process or the right to counsel]; *De Sandoval v. U.S. Att'y Gen.,* 440 F.3d 1276, 1279–83 (11th Cir. 2006) [the AG's decision under 8 C.F.R. §241.8 to allow immigration officers to carry out the ministerial task of reinstating existing removal orders constitutes a permissible interpretation of both §§1229a(a) and 1231(a)(5)]; *Ochoa-Carrillo v. Gonzales,* 437 F.3d 842, 845 (8th Cir. 2006) [finding that 8 C.F.R. §241.8 permitting reinstatement through a DHS officer is a valid interpretation of the reinstatement statute]; *Lattab v. Ashcroft,* 384 F.3d 8, 17–20 (1st Cir. 2004) [under *Chevron* deference regulations permitting reinstituting removal without a hearing before IJ are not inconsistent with 241(a)(5)]; *Matter of W-C-B-,* 24 I&N Dec. 118 (BIA 2007) [the IJ has not authority to reinstate a prior order of removal or deportation and proceedings were properly terminated on DHS's motion].

A person subject to reinstatement still retains the right to seek withholding of removal and a claim based upon the Convention Against Torture. 8 C.F.R. §§208.31, 241.8(d), 1208.31, 1241.8(d). S/he may also initiate a constitutional or statutory challenge to the original removal proceeding. *Debeato v. Att'y Gen. of the U.S.,* 505 F.3d 231 (3d Cir. 2007) [post-REAL ID Act, there is jurisdiction under INA §242(a)(2)(D) to review a legal challenge to a reinstated removal order notwithstanding preclusion provision of INA §241(a)(5), although court found no gross miscarriage of justice warranting collateral attack on original removal order]; *Ramirez-Molina v. Ziglar,* 436 F.3d 508, 513–14 (5th Cir. 2006) [same]; *Chacon-Corral v. Weber,* 259 F.Supp.2d 1151 (D. Colo. 2003) [*Pre*-REAL ID Act, finding habeas jurisdiction to challenge the constitutional infirmity of the original removal proceeding]. *But see Morales-Izquierdo v. Gonzales,* 486 F.3d 484, 497 (9th Cir. 2007) (en banc) [reinstatement of a prior order—regardless of the process afforded—does not offend due process; *Arreola-Arreola v. Ashcroft,* 383 F.3d 956 (9th Cir. 2004) reversed].

Application of Deportation Orders Entered Before IIRIRA—In *Fernandez-Vargas v. Gonzales,* 126 S.Ct. 2422 (2006), the Court resolved a split in the circuits and determined that the application of INA §241(a)(5) to persons who reentered the U.S. after deportation but before Apr. 1, 1997 was not impermissibly retroactive even if the person applied for relief from removal, such as adjustment of status, after Apr. 1, 1997.

Reinstatement May Not Retroactively Eliminate Substantive Defenses—The Court in *Fernandez-Vargas v. Gonzales,* 126 S.Ct. 2422 (2006) also determined that applications for relief filed *after* Apr. 1, 1997 were barred by INA §241(a)(5) and INA §241(a)(5) was *not* impermissibility retroactive as to that relief. *Delgado v. Mukasey,* 516 F.3d 65 (2d Cir. 2008) [same, agreeing with *Torres-Garcia* and *Gonzales*]; *Gonzales v. DHS,* 508 F.3d 1227, 1234–42 (9th Cir. 2007) [reversed its prior decision in *Perez-Gonzales v. Ashcroft,* 379 F.3d 783 (9th Cir. 2004) and upheld on *Chevron* deference under *National Cable & Telecommunications Ass'n v. Brand X,* 545 U.S. 967 (2005) the BIA's decision in *Matter of Torres-Garcia*]; *Labojewski v. Gonzales,* 407 F.3d 814 (7th Cir. 2005) [reinstatement not impermissibly retroactive for person who re-entered the U.S. before IIRIRA but applied for AOS after; *Faiz-Mohammad* distinguished]; *Lattab v. Ashcroft,* 384 F.3d 8, 17–20 (1st Cir. 2004) [same]; *Matter of Torres-Garcia,* 23 I&N Dec. 866 (BIA 2006) [an I-212 waiver cannot retroactively waive inadmissibility under INA §212(a)(9)(C)(i)(II) because the applicant cannot seek admission under that section for 10 years after the date of his last departure from the U.S.]. *See also De Sandoval v. U.S. Att'y Gen.,* 440 F.3d 1276, 1284–85 (11th Cir. 2006) [INA §245(i) is not in conflict with the reinstatement provision that bars most forms of relief because §245(i) applies to persons who had never before been removed]. The Court in *Fernandez-Vargas,* 126 S.Ct. 2422, 1432–33 (2006) however, left open the question of whether someone who filed his application for relief prior to Apr. 1, 1997, could be barred by INA §241(a)(5). In *Valdez-Sanchez v. Gonzales,* 485 F.3d 1084 (10th Cir. 2007) the Tenth Circuit addressed the issue left open in *Fernandez-Vargas* and found that where a person married and adjusted status to that of a conditional resident before IIRIRA, the application of INA §241(a)(5) to respondent was impermissibly retroactive. In *Silva Rosa v. Gonzales,* 490 F.3d 403 (5th Cir. 2007), however, the court found that INA §241(a)(5) was not impermissibly retroactive where person married LPR before IIRIRA and had approved I-130 before that date, but a visa number was not available and respondent did not file AOS until *after* IIRIRA's effective date.

Prior to *Fernandez*-Vargas, courts found that while DHS may retroactively apply the statute to prior deportation orders, INA §241(a)(5) may not retroactively eliminate substantive defenses to removal where the relief was filed or sought prior to the effective date of IIRIRA (Apr. 1, 1997). *Faiz-Mohammad v. Ashcroft,* 395 F.3d 799, 809–10 (7th Cir. 2005) [pre-*Fernandez-Vargas* finding that INA §241(a)(5) may not retroactively bar relief where person entered and applied for relief/AOS before Apr. 1, 1997]; *Lopez-Flores v. DHS,* 387 F.3d 773 (8th Cir. 2004) [pre-*Fernandez-Vargas,* the court found it was impermissible to invoke INA §241(a)(5) retroactively where respondent had potential relief of AOS if I-212 waiver granted and initial labor certification application was filed prior to IIRIRA's effective date]; *Arevalo v. Ashcroft,* 344 F.3d 1 (1st Cir. 2003) [pre-*Fernandez-Vargas* an adjustment of status application based upon father's second preference petition that was filed prior Apr. 1, 1997 is not barred by INA §241(a)(5)].

Constitutional challenges to reinstatement order procedures have been rejected by most courts. Although it was possible to challenge the unconstitutionality/due process violations regarding the original removal order, most courts determined that current reinstatement of removal procedures under 8 C.F.R. §241.8 withstand constitutional scrutiny. *Lorenzo v. Mukasey,* 508 F.3d 1278, 1283–84 (10th Cir. 2007) [regulation at 8 C.F.R. §241.8 does not facially violate due process and there was no showing of prejudice]; *De Sandoval v. U.S. Att'y Gen.,* 440 F.3d 1276, 1285 (11th Cir. 2006) [procedural due process claim rejected where petitioner could demonstrate no prejudice]; *Ochoa-Carrillo v. Gonzales,* 437 F.3d 842, 846–48 (8th Cir. 2006) [procedure does not violate due process noting that under 8 C.F.R. §103.2(b)(16)(i) and 103.10 respondent's counsel can get access to respondent's file before submitting a written response]; *Morales-Izquierdo v. Gonzales,* 486 F.3d 484, 496 (9th Cir. 2007) (*en banc*) [we agree with the Attorney General that a reinstatement order implemented under 8 C.F.R. §241.8 is not facially unconstitutional; *Arreola-Arreola v. Ashcroft,* 383 F.3d 956, 962 (9th Cir. 2004) *overruled*]; *Warner v. Ashcroft,* 381 F.3d 534, 538–39 (6th Cir. 2004) [no due process violation because respondent failed to show prejudice when reinstating exclusion order]; *Duran-Hernandez v. Ashcroft,* 348 F.3d 1158, 1162–63 (10th Cir. 2003) [rejected claim that additional procedural safeguards were necessary or that denying adjustment and then instituting removal violates due process]; *Padilla v. Ashcroft,* 334 F.3d 921 (9th Cir. 2003) [did not reach constitutional issue as there is no prejudice to respondent because her pending INA §245(i) application does not trump the reinstatement provision that bars relief]; *Avila-Macias v. Ashcroft,* 328 F.3d 108, 114–15 (3d Cir. 2003) [statute does not violate due process because there is no prejudice]; *Ojeda-Terrazas v. Ashcroft,* 290 F.3d 292, 302 (5th Cir. 2002) [same]; *Gomez-Chavez v. Perryman,* 308 F.3d 796, 800–02 (7th Cir. 2002) [procedure does not violate due process where decision to reinstate is made by an administrative rather than a judicial officer]; *Alvarenga-Villalobos v. Ashcroft,* 271 F.3d 1169, 1173 (9th Cir. 2001) [no due process violation where 241(a)(5) bars respondent from collaterally attacking prior deportation order]; *Briones-Sanchez v. Heinauer,* 319 F.3d 324 (8th Cir. 2003) [same]; *U.S. v. Martinez-Vitela,* 193 F.3d 1047, 1052–53 (9th Cir. 1999) [reinstatement proceedings comply with due process under *Mathews* analysis].

Constitutional challenge to underlying removal order—A respondent may have no right to challenge the constitutionality of the underlying removal order that triggers INA §241(a)(5). *Martinez-Merino v. Keisler,* 504 F.3d 1068 (9th Cir. 2007) [following *Morales-Izquierdo* the court held that respondent could not challenge the constitutional validity of the underlying original order of removal]. *But see* INA §242(a)(2)(D) allowing for constitutional and legal challenges. An applicant, however, may not be able to challenge an underlying order if it is a *summary* removal order, notwithstanding INA §242(a)(2)(D). *Lorenzo v. Mukasey,* 508 F.3d 1278, 1281 (10th Cir. 2007) [petitioner could not challenge her underlying summary removal order in INA §241(a)(5) proceedings, notwithstanding INA §242(a)(2)(D) which allows for legal and constitutional challenges to removal orders, because INA §235(b)(1) precludes legal challenges to summary removal orders].

Procedures—Pursuant to 8 C.F.R. §241.8 ICE may not enter a removal order until the officer determines that: (1) the person has been subject to a prior order; (2) the person identified is the same person as the one with the prior order and if disputed identity shall be established through fingerprint identification; and (3) the person unlawfully re-entered the United States. If the officer determines that the person is subject to removal he shall provide the respondent a written notice and advise her that she may make a written or oral statement contesting the determination. If a statement is made the officer shall consider whether the statement warrants reconsideration of the determination. Notwithstanding reinstatement of removal a person may apply for withholding of removal and HRIFA or NACARA benefits. An applicant seeking to challenge the reinstatement order must make an administrative record. *Ochoa-Carrillo v. Gonzales,* 437 F.3d 842, 845–46 (8th Cir. 2006) [respondent failed to make an administrative record contesting identity].

Administrative Review—The BIA has held that it has no jurisdiction to consider a challenge to a reinstated deportation/exclusion/removal order. *Matter of G-N-C-,* 22 I&N Dec. 281 (BIA 1998). Even where INS violated its regulations and terminated removal proceedings to institute a proceedings under INA §241(a)(5) instead of seeking termination from the Court, there was no prejudice. *Matter of G-N-C-, supra.*

Judicial Review—Prior to the REAL ID Act and INA §242(a)(2)(D), 8 U.S.C. §1252(a)(2)(D) the review of the underlying removal/deportation order in reinstated removal cases was precluded in the circuit court under INA §241(a)(5) because such order "is not subject to being reopened or reviewed." *Garcia-Marrufo v. Ashcroft,* 376 F.3d 1061, 1063–64 (10th Cir. 2004) [rejected challenge under *Mendoza-Lopez* and found that there was no jurisdiction to review underlying deportation order even where the criminal conviction that was the basis for the order had been vacated]; *Avila-Macias v. Ashcroft,* 328 F.3d 108, 115 (3d Cir. 2003) [review of underlying deportation order precluded in court of appeals]. However, INA §242(a)(2)(D) now provides for the right to initiate legal and constitutional challenges in the circuits courts notwithstanding any preclusion statute. *Ramirez-Molina v. Ziglar,* 436 F.3d 508, 513–14 (5th Cir. 2006) [jurisdiction under INA §242(a)(2)(D) to review legal challenge to reinstated removal order notwithstanding preclusion provision of INA §241(a)(5), although court found no miscarriage of justice warranting collateral attack on removal order]. Even prior to INA §242(a)(2)(D), a reinstatement order could be challenged by petition for review on the grounds that the respondent is a USC. *Batista v. Ashcroft,* 270 F.3d 8 (1st Cir. 2001). And the circuit courts always had jurisdiction to review the lawfulness of the application of INA §241(a)(5). *Duran-Hernandez v. Ashcroft,* 348 F.3d 1158 (10th Cir. 2003) [habeas case transferred to circuit court because jurisdiction only in circuit court]; *Arevalo v. Ashcroft,* 344 F.3d 1, 9 (1st Cir. 2003) [recognizing that it may not revisit the validity of the original deportation order but having the authority "to determine the appropriateness of its resurrection"]; *Ojeda-Terrazas v. Ashcroft,* 290 F.3d 292, 295 (5th Cir. 2002); *Velasquez-Gabriel v. Crocetti,* 263 F.3d 102, 105 (4th Cir. 2001) [same] *Bejjani v. INS,* 271 F.3d 670, 674 (6th Cir. 2001) [same] *Castro-Cortez v. INS,* 239 F.3d 1037, 1043–45 (9th Cir. 2001) [same]. The petition for review to the circuit court must be filed within 30 days of the date of the reinstatement order. *Ponta-Garca v. Ashcroft,* 386 F.3d 341 (1st Cir. 2004) [petition for review was dismissed because the 30-day period also applies to orders of reinstatement entered pursuant to INA §241(a)(5) and the petitioner's response to DHS of the order does not toll the 30 days].

Res Judicata/Collateral Estoppel—Criminal conviction to illegal re-entry does not necessarily bar habeas action to challenge unconstitutionality of original removal order. *Nolasco v. U.S.,* 358 F.Supp.2d 224, 237–38 (S.D.N.Y. 2004) [res judicata was inapplicable to *St. Cyr* challenge to original deportation order where eligibility for INA §212(c) relief was never litigated in the criminal proceeding].

FTCA action—One person improperly deported under INA §241(a)(5) has successfully brought a federal tort claim for money damages against the federal government. *Araujo v. U.S.,* 301 F.Supp.2d 1095 (N.D. Cal. 2004) [summary judgment on liability granted to plaintiff on collateral estoppel grounds following *Castro-Cortez*].

T. *Cancellation of Visa*—DHS officers are not authorized to cancel NIVs upon commencement of deportation hearing. DHS can only cancel visas in deportation if DHS permits person to depart voluntarily prior to final hearing or if persons is ordered deported or excluded. 22 C.F.R. §41.122(h)(2), and (4).

U. *Physical Removal*—INA §241(b)(2), 8 U.S.C. §1231(b)(2)

1. *There is a 4-step process in physical removal*—First, a person will be removed to the country s/he designates. INA §241(b)(2)(A). A person may not designate a contiguous territory, adjacent island, or island adjacent to contiguous territory unless s/he is a native, citizen, subject, national or resident of that territory or island. Second, the IJ may disregard the designation by the person subject to removal if: (i) s/he fails to designate a country promptly; (ii) the government of the designated country does not inform the Secretary of DHS within 30 days that it will accept her; (iii) the government designated is not willing to accept her; or (iv) the Secretary of DHS decides that removal to the designated country is prejudicial to the U.S. INA §241(b)(2)(C). Third, if the person cannot be removed to a designated country, then the IJ can remove her to a country where she is a subject, national or citizen unless: (i) the country does not inform the Secretary of DHS within 30 days or another reasonable time the Secretary of DHS decides that it will accept her; or (ii) the country decides it will not accept her. INA §241(b)(2)(D). Fourth, if none of the above alternatives can be utilized then the Secretary of DHS shall remove the person to any of the following countries: (1) the country from which the person was admitted; (ii) the country from the foreign port which person left for the U.S. or a foreign territory contiguous to U.S.; (iii) the country of person's residence before entry to U.S.; (iv) the country of person's birth; (v) the country that had sovereignty over person's birthplace when they were born; (vi) the country in which person's birthplace is located at time of removal order; (vii) another country that will accept the person. INA §241(b)(2)(E). Under INA §242(b)(2)(E)(i)–(vi) ICE need not demonstrate that the country is willing to accept her. *Jama v. ICE,* 543 U.S. 335, ____, 125 S.Ct. 694, 698–706 (2005) [the designations of potential countries of removal under 8 U.S.C. §1231(b)(2)(E)(i)–(vi) do not require the receiving countries' consent, unlike subsection (vii) of §1231(b)(2)(E), which specifically requires consent]; *Jama v. Gonzales,* 431 F.3d 230 (5th Cir. 2005) [followed Supreme Court decision in *Jama* and allowed removal to Somalia even if country has not accepted them]. If respondent does not designate a country then IJ can send her to a country that she is a citizen, subject or national. *Pavlovich v. Gonzales,* 476 F.3d 613, 61–16 (8th Cir. 2007) [where respondent who was born in Russian and raised in Latvia declined to designated a country of removal, the IJ can designate a country and DHS can send the person to any country consistent with §1231(b)(2)(E)(i)-(vi) without the country's consent]; *but see Hadera v. Gonzales,* 494 F.3d 1154 (9th Cir. 2007) [IJ's determination that respondent was *not* a citizen of Ethiopia did not permit the IJ to order him removed there after he failed to designate a country because he was not a citizen, subject or national]. However, if he is not a citizen, subject or national of any country or they will not accept him than INA §241(b)(2)(E) applies. *Bejet-Viali Al-Jojo v. Gonzales,* 424 F.3d 823, 828 (8th Cir. 2005) [followed *Jama* and allowed designation of countries over objection of respondent that Great Britain, a place he resided for four years, or Sierra Leone, his country of birth, would not accept him]; 8 C.F.R. §§241.15, 1240.10, 1241.15; 70 Fed. Reg. 661–75 (Jan. 5, 2005) [amending the regulations to clarify that consent of the receiving country is unnecessary for removals by DHS or the IJ under §1231(b)(2)(E)(i)–(vi), that the receiving country does not require a functioning government, and that acceptance from the receiving country is not necessary prior to DHS making travel arrangements or transporting the person]. Under INA §241(b)(2)(E)(vii) the Secretary of DHS may only designate the country if he can show that the country *will* accept the respondent. *Wangchuck v. DHS,* 448 F.3d 524, 530–32 (2d Cir. 2006) [where Tibetan living in India did not fall under first six categories of 8 U.S.C. §1231(b)(2) and there was no indication that China would accept him, the BIA's alternate order of removal to China was erroneous]; *Himri v. Ashcroft,* 378 F.3d 932, 938–40 (9th Cir. 2004) [Jordan was improperly designated as a country for Palestinian asylum seeker where there was no showing by the government before the designation that Jordan would take the respondent]. *But see Zahren v. Gonzales,* 487 F.3d 1039 (7th Cir. 2007) [where Palestinian designates Jordan, has a temporary Jordanian passport and did not contest he was a citizen of Jordan in the NTA, the IJ did not err in designating Jordan as the country of removal despite his obvious Palestinian birth and despite asylum claim from the Palestinian territory due to conversion to Christianity].

2. *Respondent in removal proceeding has right to designate country of deportation*—INA §241(b)(2), 8 U.S.C. §1231(b)(2), 8 C.F.R. §1240.10(f). *Bui v. INS*, 76 F.3d 268 (9th Cir. 1996) [IJ failure to permit respondent to designate country of deportation is reversible error]. If person does not designate country, IJ given broad authority to do so. *Al Najjar v. Ashcroft,* 257 F.3d 1262, 1295–96

(11th Cir. 2001) [IJ decision to designate Saudi Arabia when Palestinian refused to designate country is not error]. The statute also provides for alternate places of deportation. However, the respondent cannot designate a contiguous territory to U.S. unless he is a native, citizen, subject or national of that territory. *Matter of A-A-*, 20 I&N Dec. 492, 505 (BIA 1992). It is a fundamental failure of due process to deport someone to a country while hearing asylum claim only from another country without opportunity to present evidence regarding country of deportation. *Kossov v. INS*, 132 F.3d 405 (7th Cir. 1998) [evidence of persecution in Latvia, but deportation to Russia]. *Accord Kuhai v. INS,* 199 F.3d 909 (7th Cir. 1999) [evidence of a well-founded fear regarding Uzbekistan, but BIA ordered removal to Ukraine]; *Andriasian v. INS,* 180 F.3d 1033, 1041 (9th Cir. 1999) [a last minute switch by the IJ of the country of deportation violates due process because it fails to give proper notice]; *Palavra v. INS,* 287 F.3d 690 (8th Cir. 2002) [reversed BIA removal order to Croatia on substantial evidence standard where respondent claimed citizenship in Bosnia and sought asylum from there]; *But see Al Najjar, supra* [no error where IJ gave petitioner ample time to contest designation].

3. *Due Process Challenges to Designation and Removal—Zadvydas v. Davis,* 533 U.S. 678, 121 S.Ct. 2491 (2001) [the continued detention of a person beyond the time that his removal is "reasonably foreseeable" is unconstitutional as a violation of due process and the INS may not hold a person six months after a removal order absent evidence that his or her removal is reasonably foreseeable]; *Clark v.Martinez,* 543 U.S. 371 (2005) [following *Zadvydas* and finding that as a matter of statutory construction of 8 U.S.C. §1231(a)(6) inadmissible persons must be released after 6 months unless their removal is reasonably foreseeable]; *Kholyavskiy v. Schlecht,* 479 F.Supp.2d 897, 908–09 (E.D. Wis. 2007) [In EAJA context, ICE position in reading *Zadvydas* to permit 6 months detention even if person's removal is not reasonably foreseeable was not substantially justified];*Wong v. Warden, FCI Raybrook,* 999 F.Supp. 287, 289–90 (N.D.N.Y. 1998) [person who is non–USC/LPR serving criminal sentence has a 5th Amend. due process right against discriminatory denial of transfer to his home country based on race, although he was unable to prove claim in the case]; *Matter of Linnas*, 19 I&N Dec. 302 (BIA 1985) [rejecting constitutional due process challenge to IJ's designation of the U.S.S.R. as country of deportation where alien Nazi established he was tried in sham proceeding in U.S.S.R. and sentenced to death].

4. The Secretary of DHS has authority ("may") disregard designation to a country respondent chooses where it is prejudicial to U.S., where the person fails to designate a country promptly, where the receiving government is not willing to accept the person or does not inform U.S. within time requested by U.S. INA §241(b)(2)(C), 8 U.S.C. §1231(b)(2)(C). The BIA may designate the country under one of these conditions if the IJ fails to do so. *Desta v. Ashcroft,* 329 F.3d 1179, 1184–86 (10th Cir. 2003) [no due process violation where BIA designates country because IJ forgets and respondent not given prior notice and opportunity to respond]. The decision of the AG to designate a country, absent fraud, lack of jurisdiction or unconstitutionality, may not be reviewable. *Doherty v. Meese*, 808 F.2d 938 (2d Cir. 1986); *Doherty v. DOJ,* 908 F.2d 1108, 1113–14 (2d Cir. 1990), *rev'd on other grounds*, *INS v. Doherty*, 502 U.S. 314, 112 S.Ct. 719 (1992). INA §242(g).

If the Secretary of DHS does not or cannot deport person to place person designates, Secretary of DHS may deport him to country from which he was admitted, born, or resident or any other country willing to accept him. INA §241(b)(2)(E), 8 U.S.C. §1231(a)(2)(E). The Secretary of DHS also has authority to remove someone even to a country that the U.S. does not recognize. *Osmani v. INS*, 14 F.3d 13, 15 (7th Cir. 1994). In addition the BIA has the authority to change the country of designation where original country ceased to exist. *Ademi v. INS*, 31 F.3d 517, 520–21 (7th Cir. 1994). The Supreme Court has determined that the Secretary of DHS may deport a respondent under sections 8 U.S.C. §1231(b)(2)(E)(iv) to his country of birth (Somalia) even if the Secretary has not established that the country will accept him. *Jama v. ICE,* 543 U.S. 335, ____, 125 S.Ct. 694, 698–706 (2005) [the designations of potential countries of removal under 8 U.S.C. §1231(b)(2)(E)(i)-(vi) do not require the receiving countries' consent, unlike subsection (vii) of §1231(b)(2)(E), which specifically requires consent]; *Jama v. Gonzales,* 431 F.3d 230 (5th Cir. 2005) [followed Supreme Court decision in *Jama* and allowed removal to Somalia even if country has not accepted them]; *Bejet-Viali Al-Jojo v. Gonzales,* 424 F.3d 823, 828 (8th Cir. 2005) [followed *Jama* and allowed designation of countries over objection of respondent that Great Britain, a place he resided for four years, or Sierra Leone, his country of birth, would not accept him]; 8 C.F.R. §§241.15, 1240.10, 1241.15; 70 Fed. Reg. 661–75 (Jan. 5, 2005) [amending the regulations to clarify that consent of the receiving country is unnecessary for removals by DHS or the IJ under §1231(b)(2)(E)(i)–(vi), that the receiving country does not require a functioning government, and that acceptance from the receiving country is not necessary prior to DHS making travel arrangements or transporting the person]. *Cf. Himri v. Ashcroft,* 378 F.3d 932, 938–40 (9th Cir. 2004) [under subsection (E)(vii) Jordan was improperly designated as a country for Palestinian asylum seeker where there was no showing by the government before the designation that Jordan would take the respondent].

Lack of Administrative Review—Although the IJ designates the country of removal, 8 C.F.R. §1240.12, the inability to remove the person to that country does not prevent DHS from removing him to another country under 8 C.F.R. §241.15 and his decision may not be reviewable by the IJ or the BIA. 8 C.F.R. §1241.15.

5. An alien sentenced to imprisonment shall not be deported until such imprisonment has been terminated by the release of the alien from confinement. Parole, supervised release, probation, or possibility of arrest or further imprisonment, shall not be a ground to defer deportation. INA §241(a)(4)(A), 8 U.S.C. §1231(a)(4)(A). *Walford v. INS*, 48 F.3d 477 (10th Cir. 1995) [cannot mandamus court to order deportation before completion of sentence in light of former INA §242(h)]; *U.S. v. Abreu*, 940 F.Supp. 443 (D.R.I. 1996).

6. *Notification of Deportation*—Counsel has a right to notification of client's imminent physical deportation. *Zepeda-Melendez v. INS*, 741 F.2d 285 (9th Cir. 1984); Regulations for deportation (8 C.F.R. §241.33(b)) and for exclusion (8 C.F.R. §241.22) provide for 72 hours notice before removal. *Arreaza-Cruz v. INS*, 39 F.3d 909 (9th Cir. 1994).This prior notice provision was eliminated for removal proceedings. However, the removal of a respondent prior to a 72 hour period is unconstitutional in the view of one district court. *Ying Fong v. Ashcroft,* 317 F.Supp.2d 398, 400–03 (S.D.N.Y. 2004) [removal in less than 72 hours was a violation of due process and court required that respondent be returned to the U.S.].

7. *Sedation of Deportee*—At least one court has found that use of sedatives that are not antipsychotic drugs is permissible to sedate deportee. *U.S. v. Bechara*, 935 F.Supp. 892 (S.D. Tex. 1996). In the light of negative publicity and litigation, ICE no longer will sedate an employee to execute a removal order unless it obtains an order from a federal district court. Memo, Torres, Director, ICE (Jan. 9, 2008), *published on* AILA InfoNet at Doc. No. 08011661.

8. *Mandatory Detention During Removal Period*—INA §241(a)(2), 8 U.S.C. §1231(a)(2). DHS shall detain the person during the removal period and "under no circumstance" shall they release a person who has been found inadmissible or removable under criminal or terrorism grounds. *Khotesouvan v. Morones,* 386 F.3d 1298 (9th Cir. 2004) [a person detained under the mandatory detention provision may not contest detention during the 90-day period even if his removal is not reasonably foreseeable]; The application of the provision has been contested. *Quezada-Bucio v. Ridge,* 317 F.Supp.2d 1221, 1223–24 (W.D. Wash. 2004) [where a stay pending appeal is granted, the mandatory detention section does not apply because the 90-day removal period is not in effect and therefore the person's detention is subject to INA §236 and not INA §241(a)(2)]; *Del Toro-Chacon v. Chertoff,* 431 F.Supp.2d 1135, 1140–43 (W.D. Wash. 2006) [although it was unclear whether the person was detained under INA §236 or INA §241 the court determined it was a violation of due process to deny the person a bond hearing before a neutral adjudicator such as an immigration judge].

9. **Time Limitation on Removal**

Where a final order of removal is made the DHS shall have only 90 days to effect the alien's removal. The 90 days run from the date the removal order becomes administratively final, *or* the date of a federal court's final order if judicial review is sought *or* the date the person is released from federal or state confinement if serving a criminal sentence. INA §241(a)(1)(A) & (B), 8 U.S.C. §1231(a)(1)(A) & (B). DHS takes the legal position that it is not required to act with "reasonable dispatch" *within* the 90-day period established by INA §241(a)(1)(A). Legal Memo, Philbin, Deputy Asst. A.G., Limitation on the Detention Authority of the INS, (Feb. 20, 2003), *published on* AILA InfoNet at Doc. No. 04021965. The 90-day period, in the view of one court, is triggered by the end of the appeal period after entry of a final order (BIA decision +30 days) and not by DHS's decision to take the person into custody. *Ulysse v. DHS,* 291 F.Supp.2d 1318, 1324–

26 (M.D. Fla. 2003) [rejected DHS interpretation of the initiation of the 90-day period and ordered the release of the petitioner]. If the DHS does not remove the detainee within that time or if the detainee does not leave within that time, s/he "shall be subject to supervision under regulations" prescribed by DHS. INA §241(a)(3), 8 U.S.C. §1231(a)(3). Release under supervision may be conditioned by statute on certain requirements including periodic reporting, bond, and restrictions on activity and conduct. INA §241(a)(3). *But see U.S. v. Witkovich,* 353 U.S. 194 (1957) [construing scope of authority conveyed by similar statutory language as limited to assuring appearance at removal].

Beyond 90-Day Detention—The Secretary of DHS, as a statutory matter, may detain beyond the removal period any person ordered removed who is inadmissible under INA §212 or removable because s/he (1) has violated his or her NIV status or condition of entry [INA §237(a)(1)(C)]; (2) has committed a crime covered under the Act [INA §237(a)(2)]; (3) has been engaged in security-related terrorist or foreign policy matters [INA §237(a)(4)]; or (4) the AG has determined that the person is a risk to the community or unlikely to comply with the order of removal. INA §241(a)(6), 8 U.S.C. §1231(a)(6); 8 C.F.R. §§241.4(a). Under regulations, if the person can demonstrate by clear and convincing evidence that the release would not pose a danger to the community or significant risk of flight, the DD may release him. 8 C.F.R. §§241.4(d)(1); 8 C.F.R. §1241.14. *Matter of Saelee,* 22 I&N Dec. 1258 (BIA 2000) [relying on detainee's clear and convincing burden to uphold detention]. However, once removal is not longer reasonably foreseeable, detention may not be continued under the statute, INA §241(a)(6). *Clark v. Martinez,* 543 U.S. 371 (2005); *Tran v. Mukasey,* 515 F.3d 478 (5th Cir. 2008).

Constitutional Challenge to Continue Detention—Under the statute (8 U.S.C. §1231(a)(6)), the continued detention of a person beyond the time that his removal is "reasonably foreseeable," however, would raise serious constitutional problems, and thus the statute has been construed as not authorizing such indeterminate detention. *Zadvydas v. Davis,* 533 U.S. 678, 121 S.Ct. 2491 (2001) [designating 6 months as a presumptively reasonable period of time to effect removal]; *Clark v. Martinez,* 543 U.S. 371 (2005) [following *Zadvydas* and finding that as a matter of statutory construction of 8 U.S.C. §1231(a)(6) inadmissible persons whose removal is not reasonably foreseeable must be released after 6 months]. Under the *Zadvydas* analysis the person seeking release may have the initial burden to demonstrate that there is a "good reason to believe that there is no significant likelihood of removal in the reasonably foreseeable future." *Hajbeh v. Loiselle,* 490 F.Supp.2d 669 (E.D. Va. 2007) [quoting *Zadvydas* and finding that the government did not rebut the initial burden]. Following *Zadvydas* the Ninth Circuit held that it was not reasonably foreseeable to believe that the petitioner in that case would be returned to Cambodia in light of the lack of a repatriation agreement and other factors. *Ma v. Ashcroft,* 208 F.3d 815 (9th Cir.), *aff'd,* 121 S.Ct. 2491 (2001), *on remand,* 257 F.3d 1095 (9th Cir. 2001). Similarly, the Fifth Circuit in *Zadvydas* held on remand that immigration authorities did not rebut applicant's showing that his removal was not reasonably foreseeable. *Zadvydas v. Davis,* 533 U.S. 678, 121 S.Ct. 2491 (2001), *on remand,* 285 F.3d 398 (5th Cir. 2002). *See also Morales-Fernandez v. INS,* 418 F.3d 1116, 1122–25 (10th Cir. 2005) [post-*Clark* finding it impermissible to hold Cuban beyond 6-month period]; *Ali v. Cangemi,* 384 F.3d 989 (8th Cir. 2004) [Somali in detention for 18 months who could not be deported as member of class in action precluding deportation to Somalia was ordered released]; *Hashi v. Chertoff,* 535 F.Supp.2d 1125 (S.D. Cal. 2008) [Somali kept in detention 9 months after final order is beyond the presumptively reasonable period]; *Andreasyan v. Gonzales,* 446 F.Supp.2d 1186, 1189–92 (W.D. Wash. 2006) [where ICE asked for a few more weeks to deport LPR ordered removed to Uzbekistan and ICE had not removed him eight months later, they failed to rebut LPR's claim that his removal was not reasonably foreseeable]; *Moallin v. Cangemi,* 427 F.Supp.2d 908, 925–28 (D. Minn. 2006) [government could rebut applicant's initial showing that his removal to Somalia was not reasonably foreseeable]; *Abdel-Muhti v. Ashcroft,* 314 F.Supp.2d 418, 424–26 (M.D.Pa. 2004) [Palestinian detained for over 2 years subsequent to final removal order was granted release where Honduras and Jordan would not accept him and there was no concrete evidence that Palestinian authorities would accept him];*Rajigah v. Conway,* 268 F.Supp.2d 159, 166–67 (E.D.N.Y. 2003) [the fact that foreign government regularly issues travel documents does not make removal reasonably foreseeable]; *Habtegaber v. Jenifer,* 256 F.Supp.2d 692, 697 (E.D. Mich. 2003) [ordered petitioner released because no country would take him and the 6-month period began to run from the date of the removal order and not from the date BIA appeal was withdrawn, *see* 8 C.F.R. §1003.4]; *Seretse-Khama v. Ashcroft,* 215 F.Supp.2d 37, 49

(D.D.C. 2002) [where Service did not carry its burden under 8 C.F.R. §241.13(f) of reasonable foreseeable removal by stating they had removed others to Liberia and where respondent's noncooperation consisted solely of telling the consulate he did not want to return to Liberia, the court ordered his release]. *But see Andrade v. Gonzales,* 459 F.3d 538, 543–44 (5th Cir. 2006) [*Zadvydas* created "no specific limit on detention" and the government could detain after the 6 month period where respondent failed to meet his burden that there is not a significant likelihood of removal]; *Khotesouvan v. Morones,* 384 F.3d 1046, 1048–49 (9th Cir. 2004) [an action may not be brought for release within the 90-day period even if the government concedes that removability is not reasonably foreseeable because INA §241(a)(2) mandates detention for that period and *Zadvydas* construed INA §241(a)(6), not §241(a)(2)]; *Wang v. Ashcroft,* 320 F.3d 130, 145–47 (2d Cir. 2003) [due process not violated where court entered final order and removal is not only reasonably foreseeable but imminent]; *Akinwale v. Ashcroft,* 287 F.3d 1050 (11th Cir. 2002) [placing the burden on the respondent to show both "post-removal order detention in excess of six months" and also to provide evidence of a good reason to believe that there is no significant likelihood of removal in the "reasonable foreseeable future"]; *NMA v. Ridge,* 286 F.Supp.2d 469 (E.D. Pa. 2003) [habeas petition denied after 9 months of detention where Liberian consulate stated it would issue travel document after interim government is installed, and thus it was reasonably foreseeable that respondent would be deported]; *Khan v. Fasano,* 194 F.Supp.2d 1134 (S.D. Cal. 2001) [person failed to meet burden of showing that his removal was not reasonably likely to Pakistan]; *Fahim v. Ashcroft,* 227 F.Supp.2d 1359 (N.D. Ga. 2002) [the 6-month period must accrue before habeas petition is filed and not during pendency of petition and petitioner failed to demonstrate that there was no significant likelihood in being sent back to Egypt because we have diplomatic relations and treaty that permits return]. *But see Olajide v. ICE,* 402 F.Supp.2d 688, 691–93 (E.D. Va. 2005) [habeas seeking release from detention post-removal order was ripe because petitioner had been in detention for more than six months at the time the court was adjudicating the matter even though the petition had been filed prior to six months].

Subsequent to *Zadvydas* the government promulgated regulations purporting to authorize continued detention of persons whose removal was not reasonably foreseeable in "special circumstances." 8 C.F.R. §§241.14, 1241.14. *See in this section* ¶ 9.b(4) (p.418), *infra.* The regulations have been successfully challenged as *ultra vires* because under *Zadvydas* the statute only authorizes detention insofar as removal is reasonably foreseeable. *Tran v. Mukasey,* 515 F.3d 478 (5th Cir. 2008); *Tuan Thai v. Ashcroft,* 366 F.3d 790 *reh'g and reh'g en banc denied* 389 F.3d 967 (9th Cir. 2004) [neither INA §241(a)(6), nor DHS regulations authorize continued detention beyond the 6-month *Zadvydas* period because of mental illness or potential criminal conduct or danger to the community; regulations cannot authorize what statute does not].

The Supreme Court has determined that *Zadvydas'* analysis of 8 U.S.C. §1231(a)(6) applies to inadmissible persons. *Clark v. Martinez,* 543 U.S. 371 (2005) [following *Zadvydas* and finding that as a matter of statutory construction of 8 U.S.C. §1231(a)(6) inadmissible persons whose removal is not reasonably foreseeable must be released after 6 months]; *Morales-Fernandez v. INS,* 418 F.3d 1116, 1122–25 (10th Cir. 2005) [post-*Clark* finding it impermissible to hold Cuban beyond 6-month period]. *See also Rosales-Garcia v. Holland,* 322 F.3d 386 (6th Cir. 2003) [pre-*Clark* decision finding that *Zadvydas's* 6-month release requirement applied to inadmissible Mariel Cubans both as a matter of statutory construction and due process]. Prior to *Clark,* at least one court held that a person who entered EWI, although "inadmissible" was nevertheless entitled to due process protection and therefore covered by *Zadvydas. Heng Meng Lin v. Ashcroft,* 247 F.Supp.2d 679, 683–85 (E.D. Pa. 2003) [for purposes of due process right of release under *Zadvydas* and application of Service regulation 8 C.F.R. §241.13, person who entered EWI has entered and is entitled to due process notwithstanding treatment in removal proceeding as an inadmissible person]. *But see Wilson v. Zeithern,* 265 F.Supp.2d 628 (E.D.Va. 2003) [liberty interest of EWI attenuated in relation to an LPR under *Zadvydas,* although it does not strip the EWI of all protection under the Due Process Clause].

Timing the 90 Day Period—The 90-day removal period runs from the later of:

(1) the final administrative order of removal, INA §241(a)(1)(B)(i), *Habtegaber v. Jenifer,* 256 F.Supp.2d 692, 697 (E.D. Mich. 2003) [final administrative order begins to run from the IJ order where the BIA appeal was withdrawn prior to entry of BIA order under 8 C.F.R. §3.4 (now §1003.4)]; *Dalis v. Brady,* 766 F.Supp. 901, 905–07 (D. Colo. 1991) [a removal order is measured

from the time a party failed to file a timely appeal and not from the BIA's dismissal for untimeliness]. *But see Fahim v. Ashcroft,* 227 F.Supp.2d 1359 (N.D. Ga. 2002) [the 6-month period did not begin to run until court of appeals rejected underlying appeal].

(2) the date of the reviewing court's final order if the removal order was judicially stayed pending federal review, INA §241(a)(1)(B)(ii) *Akinwale v. Ashcroft,* 287 F.3d 1050, 1052 n.4 (11th Cir. 2002) [suggesting that seeking a stay of removal constitutes an act to prevent removal and therefore tolls the 90-day removal period]; *Dennis v. ICE,* 426 F.Supp.2d 252, 254–55 (M.D. Pa. 2006) [respondent's detention for more than 2 years did not yet trigger procedures for post-removal orders because a stay remained in effect until court of appeals ruled on merits]; *Kothandaraghipathy v. DHS,* 396 F.Supp.2d 1104, 1106–07 (D. Ariz. 2005) [district court could not review habeas detention based upon 90-day limit when petitioner had an appeal pending and stay from circuit court and petitioner was therefore detained under INA §236 not §241]; *but see Bah v. Cangemi,* 489 F.Supp.2d 905, 915–24 (D. Minn. 2007) [where stay was denied but circuit court ultimately granted petition, the court counted the six month period between the denial of the stay and the reversal of the removal order on appeal]; *Moallin v. Cangemi,* 427 F.Supp.2d 908, 921–24 (D. Minn. 2006) [the *Ali* injunction granting a stay of physical removal to Somalia was not a stay of removal within the statute which contemplated a stay pending review of a removal order]; *Abdulle v. Gonzales,* 422 F.Supp.2d 774 (W.D. Tex. 2006) [same]; *Oyedeji v. Ashcroft,* 332 F.Supp.2d 747 (M.D. Pa. 2004) [government could not argue that 90-day period had not yet run by virtue of voluntary stay under 2nd Circuit procedure that respondent had received after appealing his case to circuit court because no formal stay order was issued. In addition, respondent's almost 5 years of detention was unjustified because the paper review of his detention was inadequate and the court found that: "While a stay of removal may suspend the running of the removal period, it does not toll the clock of the life of a person held in prison awaiting adjudication of the merits of his challenge to the validity of a removal order"];*Arevalo v. Ashcroft,* 260 F.Supp.2d 347 (D. Mass. 2003) [seeking a stay of removal cannot be construed as a person acting to prevent her removal]. Whether or not the court may determine that the 90 day period has been stayed does not prevent a court from entering an order providing for bond where the length of non–final order removal is unreasonably long. *Judulang v. Chertoff,* 535 F.Supp.2d 1129, 1132-33 (S.D. Cal. 2008) [detention lasting over 2½ years is unreasonable and district court ordered bond hearing before IJ over DHS objection that IJ lost jurisdiction over bond matters under 8 C.F.R. §1003.19(a) when administrative order became final].

(3) the date the person is released from non-DHS detention. INA §241(a)(1)(B)(iii); *Duamutef v. INS,* 386 F.3d 172, 179–80 (2d Cir. 2004) [a conditional parole for deportation only (CPDO) by the N.Y. State Parole Board is not a release from state custody triggering the 90-day period]; *Rodney v. INS*, 462 F.Supp.2d 285, 287–89 (D. Conn. 2006) [neither mandamus nor habeas provide jurisdictional basis because there is no clear right to deportation prior to the expiration of term of incarceration, statute prohibits removal until sentence is served and INS has no obligation to remove respondent prior to release from state custody, *see* 8 U.S.C. §§ 1228(a)(3)(B), 1231(a)(1)(B)(iii), 1231(1)(4)(A)];

Tolling of 90-Day Period Due to Detainee's Conduct—Where the detainee refuses to cooperate in his/her removal, the 90-day removal period is tolled. INA §241(a)(1)(C), 8 U.S.C. §1231(a)(1)(C). This arises where the person has demonstrated some sort of bad faith failure to cooperate in his removal. *Lema v. INS,* 341 F.3d 853 (9th Cir. 2003) [where person told Ethiopian officials he was Eritrean the Court affirmed the denial of his habeas petition because "when an alien refuses to cooperate fully and honestly with officials to secure travel documents from a foreign government, the alien cannot meet his or her burden to show there is no significant likelihood of removal in the reasonably foreseeable future"]; *Pelich v. INS,* 329 F.3d 1057 (9th Cir. 2003) [where person subject to removal order refused to fill out passport application and gave conflicting information regarding his and parents' background there was no due process violation under *Zadvydas*]; *Balogun v. INS*, 9 F.3d 347 (5th Cir. 1993) [under former statute six months tolled if detainee's conduct prevented deportation]; *Dor v. District Director, INS,* 891 F.2d 997 (2d Cir. 1989) [finding5-year detention permissible under pre-IIRIRA statute where client obstructed removal]; *Agbanyo v. Cabral,* 518 F.Supp.2d 326 (D. Mass. 2007) [detainee told Liberian consulate that he was a USC]; *Davis v. Gonzales,* 482 F.Supp.2d 796 (W.D. Tex. 2007) [where Nigerian did not take any overt steps to thwart removal, but did not exhaust readily available resources in making a good faith effort toward removal, habeas was denied]; *Olajide v. ICE,* 402 F.Supp.2d 688,

693–95 (E.D. Va. 2005) [petitioner delayed removal by insisting on an operation from an unqualified doctor when he was provided a qualified doctor]; *Riley v. Greene,* 149 F.Supp.2d 1256, 1262 (D. Colo. 2001) [refusal to complete travel documents]; *Sango-Dema v. District Director INS,* 122 F.Supp.2d 213, 221 (D. Mass. 2000) [detainee cannot trigger due process right to be released where he refused to cooperate with INS in obtaining travel documents]. *But see Martinez v. Gonzales,* 504 F.Supp.2d 887, 897–98 (C.D. Cal. 2007) [nothing in INA §241(a)(1)(C) suggests that a petitioner exercising his right to appeal or obtaining a stay stops the 90 days from running]; *Bah v. Cangemi,* 489 F.Supp.2d 905, 922 (D. Minn. 2007) [a foreign government's refusal to issue travel documents while the applicant is seeking legal relief from his removal does not constitute an action by respondent frustrating his removal under INA §241(a)(1)(C) and the court developed an "unencumbered-time" approach to determine how to count the 90 days where a person was successful on appeal to the federal court]; *Khan v. Gonzales,* 481 F.Supp.2d 638 (W.D. Tex. 2006) [rejected government argument that cooperation included original acts of destroying passport before removal proceedings to Bangladesh began and the court ordered respondent's release after 9 months of custody post-removal]; *Singh v. Gonzales,* 448 F.Supp.2d 1214, 1218–20 (W.D. Wash. 2006) [where ICE fails to comply with 8 C.F.R. §§241.4(g)(1)(ii) and (5)(ii) and fails to provide respondent a Notice of Failure to Comply *before* the expiration of the removal period, the court ordered respondent's release under *Zadvydas*]; *Abdel-Muhti v. Ashcroft,* 314 F.Supp.2d 418, 426–30 (M.D.Pa. 2004) [Palestinian detained for over 2 years subsequent to order was granted release where his misrepresentations about his identity occurred years before and he has since cooperated]; *Rajigah v. Conway,* 268 F.Supp.2d 159, 164–67 (E.D.N.Y. 2003) [there was no bad faith preventing release where detainee's counsel truthfully advised Guyanese Ambassador that he intended to file a court action and the policy of the Guyanese government was to decline to issue travel documents to its national while action was pending]; *Seretse-Khama v. Ashcroft,* 215 F.Supp.2d 37, 49 (D.D.C. 2002) [where respondent's noncooperation consisted solely of telling consulate he did not want to return to Liberia, it did not constitute noncooperation and court ordered his release].

DHS Procedures—In determining the appropriate procedures and standards to apply following *Zadvydas*, DHS now distinguishes between detainees who are subject to final orders of removal that can presumably be effectuated and detainees who are subject to final removal orders but whose removal is not "significantly likely." The former are governed by 8 C.F.R. §§241.4. The latter by §§241.13 & 241.14, 1241.14; 66 Fed. Reg. 56967–82, 56969–70 (Sept. 14, 2001). If the DHS determines that there are changed circumstances so that a person who was not significantly likely to be removed is now likely to be so, his case will be governed by §241.4, 66 Fed. Reg. at 56969; 8 C.F.R. §§241.4(b)(4). Section 241.13, however, does not apply to arriving aliens (*e.g.,* Mariel Cubans) even if their removal is not significantly likely. *Id.* Mariel Cubans will continue to be governed by §212.12. Other arriving aliens with final orders will be governed by §241.4. Section 241.13, however, will apply to inadmissible persons who are EWI as they are not considered to be arriving aliens. *Id.* In any event, pursuant to *Clark*, all detainees must be released when removal is not reasonably foreseeable.

In order to enhance its legal position as to the tolling of the 90-day period for noncooperation immigration authorities now place the detainee on notice, by form letter, that s/he is required to produce documentation necessary to facilitate her removal before immigration will consider her request for release including: (1) copies of passports, birth certificates and other nationality documents; (2) copies of correspondence indicating all good faith efforts to obtain a passport from the country of nationality or the country indicated on the order of removal; (3) copies of receipts and responses from embassies regarding travel documents; and (4) any other evidence showing removal is not reasonably foreseeable. Letter to Detainee, INS HQPDU, *reprinted in* 79 No. 18 *Interpreter Releases* 621, 637 (Apr. 29, 2002). However, the regulations require that DHS shall provide Notice of Failure to Comply to the detainee. 8 C.F.R. §241.4(g)(5)(i)-(ii). *Singh v. Gonzales,* 448 F.Supp.2d 1214, 1218-20 (W.D. Wash. 2006) [where ICE fails to comply with 8 C.F.R. §§241.4(g)(1)(ii) and (5)(ii) and fails to provide respondent a Notice of Failure to Comply *before* the expiration of the removal period, the court ordered respondent's release under *Zadvydas*].

9.a. Detainees Subject to Final Orders of Removal Within the 90-Day Removal Period, 8 C.F.R. §§241.4

Under 8 C.F.R. §§241.4(e), the Field Officer Director has mandatory and discretionary factors he must consider prior to release. Before making any decision to release, the Field

Officer Director must conclude that: (1) No travel documents are available for the detainee or removal is not otherwise practical or in the public interest; (2) The detainee is presently a nonviolent person; (3) The detainee is likely to remain nonviolent if released; (4) The detainee is not likely to pose a threat to the community following release; (5) The detainee is not likely to violate the conditions of release; and (6) S/he does not pose a significant risk of flight if released. 8 C.F.R. §§241.4(e). If the person is not a threat to public safety or a flight risk, the Field Officer Director "should release the alien on an order of supervision." Memo, Hutchinson, Undersecretary DHS (Mar. 30, 2004), "Guidance on ICE Implementation of Policy and Practice Changes Recommended by the Department of Justice Inspector General," *published on* AILA InfoNet at Doc. No. 04041461. The Field Officer Director should also consider the following factors: (1) Disciplinary problems while incarcerated; (2) The nature and seriousness of the alien's criminal convictions including time actually served, probation history and evidence of recidivism; (3) Psychiatric and psychological reports regarding detainee's mental health; (4) Evidence of Rehabilitation; (5) Favorable factors such as ties to the U.S. including number of close relatives; (6) Prior immigration violations and history; (7) The likelihood that s/he is a significant flight risk; and (8) Any other information that is probative of whether alien is likely (i) to adjust to life in the community; (ii) engage in future acts of violence; (iii) engage in future criminal acts; (iv) pose a danger to himself, others or property; (v) violate the conditions of release. 8 C.F.R. §241.4(f). Review will be denied if the detainee refuses to cooperate in the process of obtaining travel documents. 8 C.F.R. §241.4(g)(4). The detainee's past failure to cooperate in obtaining a travel document shall be considered an adverse factor but the existence of a criminal history does not create a presumption in favor of continued detention. Memo, Pearson, Exec. Assoc. Comm. (HQOPS 50/14.6-C) (Aug. 6, 1999), *reprinted in* 76 No. 33 *Interpreter Releases* 1285, 1300–03 (Aug. 30, 1999). Failure or refusal to make timely application in good faith for travel documents is a basis, without more, to deny release. 8 C.F.R. §241.4(g)(5)(i). DHS shall provide the detainee a notice of failure to comply in seeking removal. §241.4(g)(5)(ii).

(1) Procedure for Review—8 C.F.R. §§241.4(h)–(k).

   (a) First Review—The Field Officer Director is required to review every case on the administrative record before the 90-day removal period expires. The Field Officer Director must provide the detainee with 30 days notice to submit any additional information. The Field Officer Director may grant an interview at his or her discretion. The Field Officer Director may hold the case an additional 90 days to make a further determination as to release or detention.

   (b) Second Review by Panel—If the Field Officer Director decides to continue the detention the Executive Associate Commissioner shall have a review panel recommend whether the person should be released or kept in detention. The detainee has a right to a personal interview before the Panel and may be accompanied by a person of his or her choice. 8 C.F.R. §241.4(i)(3). The Executive Associate Commissioner is not bound by the panel's determination. The review by the panel would normally take place after six months, although the decision in *Zadvydas v. Davis,* 533 U.S. 678, 121 S.Ct. 2491 (2001) casts serious doubt that a person can be continued in detention for more than six months from the final order, except in extraordinary circumstances.

(2) Extension of the 90-day period—DHS regulations provide that the 90-day period for removal is extended pursuant to INA §241(a)(1)(C) where the detainee "fails or refuses to make timely application in good faith for travel or other documents necessary" to depart the U.S. 8 C.F.R. §241.4(g)(1)(ii). DHS shall provide Notice of Failure to Comply to the detainee and the notice shall have the effect of extending the removal period. §241.4(g)(5)(i)–(ii). *Singh v. Gonzales,* 448 F.Supp.2d 1214, 1218–20 (W.D. Wash. 2006) [where ICE fails to comply with 8 C.F.R. §§241.4(g)(1)(ii) and (5)(ii) and fails to provide respondent a Notice of Failure to Comply *before* the expiration of the removal period, the court ordered respondent's release under *Zadvydas*].

9.b. Detainees Subject to a Final Order of Removal Where There Is No Significant Likelihood of Removal in the Reasonably Foreseeable Future, 8 C.F.R. §§241.13–14, 1241.14.

(1) Presenting Claim—A detainee may seek release under this provision "at any time after the removal order becomes final" even if it is within the 90-day period if s/he can demonstrate that "there is no significant likelihood of removal in the reasonably foreseeable future." 66 Fed. Reg. at 56970; 8 C.F.R. §241.4(i)(7). However, the regulations state that DHS Headquarters Post-order Detention Unit (HQPDU) "has no obligation to release an alien under this section until HQPDU has had the opportunity during a six-month period, dating from the beginning of the removal period...to make its determination as to whether there is a significant likelihood of removal in the reasonably foreseeable future." 8 C.F.R. §241.13(b)(2)(ii). The criteria to determine if removal is reasonably foreseeable are at 8 C.F.R. §241.13(f).

(2) Provision Does Not Apply to Certain Detainees—Section 241.13, does not apply to: (a) arriving aliens including those denied entry, those paroled into the U.S. and Mariel Cubans; (b) detainees with final orders of removal who are within the removal period (90 days) including persons whose removal period was extended because of their lack of cooperation; (c) detainees who are ordered removed by the Alien Terrorist Removal Court pursuant to Title 5 of the INA. 8 C.F.R. §241.13(b)(3)(i)–(iii). However, post–*Clark v. Martinez*, these regulations are *ultra vires* as applied to arriving aliens, including Mariel Cubans, all of whom are entitled to the foreseeability reviews and release procedures provided under the regulations. *See e.g., Morales-Fernandez v. INS,* 418 F.3d 1116, 1122–25 (10th Cir. 2005) [post-*Clark* finding it impermissible to hold Cuban beyond presumptively reasonable 6-month period].

(3) Procedure for Release—8 C.F.R. §241.13(d).

(a) Must make written request to HQPDU demonstrating that there is no significant likelihood that in the reasonably foreseeable future. The written request "shall" include information regarding the detainee's cooperation in obtaining travel documents. §241.13(d)(2).

(b) Within 10 days of receipt HQPDU will respond in writing to the detainee, with a copy to counsel, explaining the procedures that will be used to evaluate the request. §241.13(e). IF HQPDU determines that the detainee has not cooperated in obtaining travel documents, it shall notify her of that fact and no further action will be taken until the detainee complies. If HQPDU determines there are further grounds to review the request, it may forward a copy of the request to the DOS for information and assistance.

i) HQPDU in evaluating the request shall consider all the factors including but not limited to: (1) the history of the detainee's efforts to comply with the order of removal; (2) the history of the DHS's efforts to remove persons to the country in question or to third countries including (a) the ongoing nature of the DHS's efforts to remove the detainee, (b) the detainee's assistance with those efforts, (c) the reasonably foreseeable results of those efforts, (d) the view of the DOS regarding the prospects for removal, and (e) the receiving country's willingness to accept the detainee into its territory. §241.13(f).

ii) Thereafter, the DHS shall permit the detainee an opportunity to respond to the evidence on which the DHS shall rely including the DOS's information. §241.13(e)(4). HQPDU may grant the detainee an interview by telephone or in person.

(c) HQPDU Decision—The HQPDU may decide the following: (1) There is no significant likelihood of removal and, absent special circumstances pursuant to 8 C.F.R. §241.14, the DHS "shall promptly make arrangements for [his] release." §241.13(g)(1); (2) Deny Release by informing the detainee that there is a significant likelihood that he will be removed in the reasonably foreseeable future. There is no appeal of the decision. §241.13(g)(2).

i) HQPDU may set conditions for release under an order of supervision that include requiring the detainee to make efforts to obtain travel documents and attendance at rehabilitative/sponsorship programs. §241.13(h). The DHS may also grant employment authorization. §241.13(h)(2).

ii) The DHS may also withdraw or revoke release if removal is reasonably foreseeable or detainee has violated the conditions of release. §§241.13(h)(4) & (i), 1241.14(h)(4) & (i). DHS must notify the person released of the reasons for revocation. §241.13(i)(3). *See* 8 U.S.C. §1253(b) [providing for criminal prosecution for willful violation of conditions of release].

(4) Special Circumstances Requiring Continued Detention Even if Return is Not Reasonably Foreseeable. 8 C.F.R. §§241.14, 1241.14.

(a) Under these regulations, promulgated subsequent to *Zadvydas* and prior to *Clark,* DHS is purportedly authorized to continue detention of persons whose removal is not reasonably foreseeable where: (a) Detainee has highly contagious disease that is a threat to public safety; (b) Detainee is a person described in INA §212(a)(3)(C) or 237(a)(4)(C), whose release would have serious adverse foreign policy consequences, and no condition of release can be expected to avoid those consequences; (c) Detainee is a person described in INA §§212(a)(3)(A) or (B) or §237(a)(4)(A) or (B), his release presents a significant threat to the national security or a significant risk of terrorism and no condition of release can reasonably be expected to avoid the threat; (d) Detainee determined to be specially dangerous because he has committed one or more crimes of violence, he is likely to engage in acts of violence in the future due to his mental condition or personality disorder and behavior associated with that condition or disorder and no conditions of his release can reasonably be expected to ensure the safety of the public. 8 C.F.R. §§241.14(b)–(f), 1241.14(f). Even prior to *Clark* there were strong arguments that these provisions were *ultra vires* in light of *Zadvydas'* holding that INA §241(a)(6) only authorizes detention insofar as removal is reasonably foreseeable. *Tuan Thai v. Ashcroft,* 366 F.3d 790, *reh'g and reh'g en banc denied,* 389 F.3d 967 (9th Cir. 2004) [finding regulation purporting to authorize continued detention of detainees who are mentally ill and dangerous *ultra vires* in that the regulation cannot authorize what statute does not]. Subsequent to *Clark,* these arguments were even more persuasive. *Tran v. Mukasey,* 515 F.3d 478, 484–85 (5th Cir 2008) ["The Supreme Court has twice held that §1231(a)(6) does not authorize indefinite detention for any class of aliens covered by the statute" and "based on the clear language of *Clark*, this Court must conclude that the presumptive six-month period established in *Zadvydas* is applicable to all categories of aliens covered by the statute"].

i) Detention Due to Highly Contagious Disease—DHS shall not invoke this provision except upon the express recommendation of the Pubic Health Service. If detainee can be treated at an appropriate medical facility s/he may be released. 8 C.F.R. §§241.14(b)(1) and (2).

ii) Detention Due to Foreign Policy Consequences—This section can only be invoked if the AG or Deputy AG, after consultation of the DOS and recommendation of the Secy. of State, certifies that the detainee should not be released because of the foreign policy consequences. The certification is subject to on going review. 8 C.F.R. §241.14(c)(2).

iii) Detention Due to Security or Terrorism—The Commissioner must certify this ground of detention to the AG. Before certification the detainee must be notified of the factual basis for the decision and be given an opportunity to respond. If the detainee was not ordered deported on security/terrorism grounds, INS must first conduct an interview and take a sworn statement from the detainee who has the right to have counsel present. Before making the certification to the AG, the party making the certification shall take into account: (1) the recommendations of INS enforcement officials and the FBI or other law enforcement and national security agencies; (2) the detainee's statements; (3) the detainee's previous conduct and (4) other special circumstances. The Commissioner's recommendation to the AG shall be in writing and the AG shall certify the detention based on the record developed by the INS and upon the recommendation of the FBI and INS Commissioner. 8 C.F.R. §§241.14(d)(2)–(5). This regulation in addition to being *ultra vires* is arguably superfluous in light of the USA PATRIOT Act §412(a), 115 Stat. 350 (enacted Oct. 25, 2001) (codified at 8 U.S.C. §1226a(a)(6)), which provides that a person whose removal is not reasonably foreseeable and who has been certified by the AG as presenting a national security threat or as having been involved in terrorist activities may be detained beyond the removal period in 6-month increments. *Clark v. Martinez,* 543 U.S. 371, 387 (O'Connor J. concurring) [citing 8 U.S.C. §1226a(a)(6) [INA §236A] as support for the Court's holding that INA §241(a)(6) does not authorize indefinite detention because "The Government has other statutory means [apart from §241(a)(6)] for detaining aliens whose removal is not foreseeable and whose presence poses security risks"].

iv) Detention Due to Special Danger to Public—The INS Commissioner shall request a report from the PHS on the medical and psychiatric condition of the detainee. The report should address whether, given the detainee's condition, he is likely to engage in acts of violence in the future. If the INS Commissioner makes the determination that the detainee poses a special danger and orders his continued detention, he shall refer the matter to an IJ for a hearing. The IJ shall first determine whether there is reasonable cause for the INS's position and the hearing shall commence within 10 business days of the INS filing an I-863. Only the INS may appeal a decision at this stage. If the IJ determines that there is reasonable cause s/he will hold a merits hearing. Either party may appeal that decision. 8 C.F.R. §§241.14(f), 1241.14(f). The Immigration Court has set forth procedures for IJs in regard to reasonable cause and merit hearings. Memo [OPPM 01-03], Creppy, Chief IJ, EOIR, (Nov. 19, 2001), *reprinted in* 79 No. 3 *Interpreter Releases* 66, 74–83 (Jan 14, 2002). The regulations have been successfully challenged in light of *Zadvydas. Tuan Thai v. Ashcroft,* 366 F.3d 790 *rehearing and rehearing en banc denied* 389 F.3d 967 (9th Cir. 2004 [absent a national security threat neither §1231(a)(6), nor DHS regulations permit continued detention beyond *Zadvydas* period because of mental illness or potential criminal conduct danger]; *Tran v. Mukasey,* 515 F.3d 478 (5th Cir. 2008) [under *Zadvydas* and *Clark*, the government may not detain a person indefinitely pursuant to §241.14(f) on the grounds the person is a threat to the public due to his mental illness].

9.c. Supervised Release and the ISAP Program—If a person is not deported and is released s/he will be subject to supervision of ICE. INA §241(a)(3), 8 U.S.C. §1231(a)(3).

(1) ISAP Program—ICE, through private contract, now maintains an Intensive Supervision Assistance Program (ISAP) that utilizes electronic "bracelets" and other intense supervision and reporting devices and procedures to insure close and frequent contact with an individual granted supervised release. The ISAP program is used for three categories of respondents: (1) those in removal proceedings who have not been issued final orders of removal and may be a flight risk; (2) those who have been issued final orders and are considered potentially dangerous but cannot legally be held in custody any longer; and (3) those with final orders who have been released but who have violated their orders of supervision by committing crimes or otherwise failing to comply with release conditions. There are three phases of the program: intense, intermediate and regular. For a detailed description of the program *see Nguyen v. B.I. Inc.* 435 F.Supp.2d 1109 (D. Or. 2006) [finding no substantive or procedural due process violation for post-removal noncitizens place in ISAP; nor does ISAP violate the APA notice and comment requirements].

(2) Bond Conditions for Supervised Release—The DHS may place reasonable conditions if it chooses to release someone. *Doan v. INS*, 311 F.3d 1160 (9th Cir. 2002) [a $10,000 bond is a reasonable condition of release after the 90-day period]; *CAO v. INS,* 189 F.Supp.2d 1082 (S.D. Cal. 2001) [upheld bond regulation at 8 C.F.R. §241.5(b)]. *Cf.*

Hmaidan v. Ashcroft, 258 F.Supp.2d 832, 838–40 (E.D. Ill. 2003) [it is inconsistent with *Zadvydas* to permit the Service to set a bond that a detainee is unable to post].

(3) Criminal Proceedings and Supervised Release—Failure to comply with an order of supervised release can result in the initiation of criminal proceedings under 8 U.S.C. §1253(b). *See in this chapter* "Willful Failure to Comply with Terms of Release Order," section VIII.S (p.250), *supra.*

9.d. Federal Jurisdiction over Detention during Removal Process—A writ of habeas corpus may be brought to challenge indefinite detention notwithstanding various preclusion statutes. *Zadvydas v. Davis,* 533 U.S. 678, 687–88 (2001) [INA §§236(e), 242(a)(2)(B)(ii), 242(a)(2)(C), 242(g) did not bar habeas jurisdiction for challenge to post-removal order indefinite detention]; *Fahim v. Ashcroft,* 227 F.Supp.2d 1359, 1365–68 (N.D. Ga. 2002).

(1) Effect of the REAL ID Act—With the passage of the REAL ID Act of 2005, PL 109-13, 119 Stat. 231, Division B §106 (May 11, 2005), Congress sought to eliminate habeas, mandamus and All Writs jurisdiction in the district courts in regard to "judicial review of an order of removal entered or issued under any provision of this Act." INA §242(a)(5). Habeas was also eliminated for matters covered under INA §§242(b)(9), (g). The REAL ID Act of 2005, however, no longer bars the court of appeals from considering constitutional claims or questions of law in a petition for review even where other sections (*e.g.,* criminal aliens, discretionary decision, §242(g)) would bar or limit review. The legislative history of the REAL ID Act of 2005 also makes clear that it "will not preclude habeas review over challenges to detention that are independent of challenges to removal orders. Instead, the bill would eliminate habeas review only over challenges to removal orders." Joint Explanatory Statement of the Committee of Conference, H.R. Cong. Rep. No 109-72 at 173–75, 151 Cong. Rec. H2836, 2873 (May 3, 2005). *See also Hernandez v. Gonzales,* 424 F.3d 42 (1st Cir. 2005) [remanding habeas detention challenge by Mariel Cuban back to district court because habeas may be brought post-REAL ID Act when it is a challenge to detention]; *Ali v. Gonzales,* 421 F.3d 795, 797 n.1 (9th Cir. 2005) [the REAL ID Act does not apply to matters outside of challenges to removal orders and the court declined to transfer a habeas case to the circuit court where petitioners challenged solely their physical removal]; *Bonhometre v. Ashcroft,* 414 F.3d 442, 446 n.4 (3d Cir. 2005); *Moallin v. Cangemi,* 427 F.Supp.2d 908, 918–21 (D. Minn. 2006) [citing the REAL ID Act legislative history a Somalian detained subsequent to his removal order can challenge his custody as violative of the constitution]; *Abdulle v. Gonzales,* 422 F.Supp.2d 774, 776 (W.D. Tex. 2006) [REAL ID does not preclude habeas related to detention only]. *But see Deljevic v. Baker,* 463 F.Supp.2d 699 (E.D. Mich. 2006) [no habeas jurisdiction to review detention where there is final order of removal and detention is challenged on ground that final order was improper].

(2) Exhaustion and Ripeness—Generally, a detainee must exhaust his administrative remedies and his claim must be ripe for review. *Boz v. U.S.* 248 F.3d 1299 (11th Cir. 2001) [habeas corpus properly dismissed where petitioner did not exhaust INS procedure for review after 90-day period]; *Ali v. Barlow,* 446 F.Supp.2d 604, 609–10 (E.D. Va. 2006) [where respondent was not in custody for six months subsequent to the final order, his *Zadvydas* claim for release is not yet ripe]; *Smith v. DOJ,* 218 F.Supp.2d 357, 363–64 (W.D.N.Y. 2002) [must exhaust administrative remedies, including BIA, before asking the court for release under INA §241]; *Bui v. INS,* 80 F.Supp.2d 1123 (D. Or. 1999) [same]. *But see Welch v. Reno,* 101 F.Supp.2d 347, 351 (D. Md. 2000) [finding no exhaustion requirement in habeas action challenging pre-removal detention under mandatory detention statute; statutory exhaustion only for review of final orders of removal]; *Alikhani v. Fasano,* 70 F.Supp.2d 1124, 1129–30 (S.D. Cal. 1999) [same]; *Aguilar v. Lewis,* 50 F.Supp.2d 539, 541 (E.D. Va. 1999) [same]; *Rowe v. INS,* 45 F.Supp.2d 144, 145–46 (D. Mass. 1999) (Same, and cases cited therein); *Pastor-Camarena v. Smith*, 977 F.Supp. 1415, 1417 (W.D. Wash. 1997) (Same and cases cited therein); *Montero v. Cobb*, 937 F.Supp. 88, 90–91 (D. Mass. 1996).

9.e. Application of INA §236 or INA §241—When a detainee seeks federal court review of a removal order and the government detains the respondent, the government will assert that INA

§241 applies and therefore the Court may not order the respondent's release from custody. *See* INA §241(a)(2) [during the removal period the AG shall detain the respondent and under no circumstances shall he be released if he is being detained under 237(a)(2) regarding criminal grounds]. *See e.g., Andrade v. Gonzales,* 459 F.3d 538, 542–43 (5th Cir. 2006) [government deflected a challenge to prolonged mandatory detention by successfully arguing that once respondent had a final order his detention was governed by INA §241 and not INA §236(c)]. However, INA §241 may not be applicable until the federal court issues a final order. INA §241(a)(1) [the 90-day removal period runs from the date of the reviewing court's final order]. *See Al-Siddiqi v. Nehls,* 521 F.Supp.2d 870, 874–75 (E.D. Wis. 2007) [bond proceeding in district court is governed by INA §236 and not INA §241 because there is no final order of removal where petitioner filed for review in circuit court and obtained stay of removal]; *Martinez v. Gonzales,* 504 F.Supp.2d 887, 892–94 (C.D. Cal. 2007) [petitioner was held for 5 years under INA §236 and not §241 because his removal order was on appeal and he had obtained a stay from the circuit court]; *Chalas-Zapata v. Ashcroft,* 305 F.Supp.2d 333, 336–37 (S.D.N.Y. 2004) for discussion regarding the distinction between INA §§236 and 241. The determination as to what periods of time will be counted as pre-final order under *Demore*, as staying a final order as a result of respondent's actions so the 90 day/6 months period does not run, or as post-final order so that *Zadvydas* applies is not always clear. *Bah v. Cangemi,* 489 F.Supp.2d 905, 915–24 (D. Minn. 207) [court ordered habeas applicant's release based upon *Zadvydas* by utilizing an "unencumbered-time" approach in determining which periods of time were stopped for the 90 day/6 month time period due to respondent's conduct and which were considered post-order removal because no stay had been granted by the circuit court]. However, there may be jurisdiction to release even where the government asserts that 90 days of detention have not been reached because of a stay of removal. *Oyedeji v. Ashcroft,* 332 F.Supp.2d 747 (M.D. Pa. 2004) [government could not argue that 90-day period had not yet run by virtue of voluntary stay under 2nd Circuit procedure that respondent had received after appealing his case to circuit court where no formal stay order was entered. In addition, respondent's almost 5 years of detention was unjustified because the paper review of his detention was inadequate and the court found that: "While a stay of removal may suspend the running of the removal period, it does not toll the clock of the life of a person held in prison awaiting adjudication of the merits of his challenge to the validity of a removal order"].

10. Exception to *Zadvydas* and *Clark*—The USA PATRIOT Act §412(a), 115 Stat. 350 (enacted Oct. 25, 2001) (codified at 8 U.S.C. §1226a(a)(6) provides that a person whose removal is not reasonably foreseeable and who has been certified by the AG as presenting a national security threat or as having been involved in terrorist activities may be detained beyond the 6-month period in six month increments. Congress's express authorization of prolonged detention for this purpose was cited by both the Supreme Court and the Ninth Circuit as support for their finding that the general detention provisions in the INA do not authorize indefinite detention. *Clark v. Martinez,* 543 U.S. at 379 n.4 [explaining the *Zadvydas* did not create an exception to its statutory construction of §1231(a)(6) for alien terrorists "for the simple reason that sustained detention of alien terrorists is a 'special arrangement' authorized by a different statutory provision"]; *Nadarajah v. Gonzales,* 443 F.3d 1069 (9th Cir. 2006) ["The Supreme Court has held that the existence of statutes authorizing the detention of suspected terrorists specifically precludes the use of general detention statutes to authorize the unlimited detention of terrorists"].

11. Withholding or Deferral of Removal—DHS has authority to release a person who has a final order of removal and who has been granted withholding or deferral of removal before the 90-day removal period has expired if it is not actively pursuing the person's removal. Memo, Cooper, INS General Counsel, HQCOU 50/1.1 (Apr. 21, 2000), *reprinted in* 77 No. 39 *Interpreter Releases* 1445, 1460 (Oct. 9, 2000).

12. Self-Removal—8 C.F.R. §§241.7, 1241.7. Field Officer Director may permit an alien ordered removed to depart at his or her own expense to a destination of his or her choice.

13. Employment Authorization—A person ordered removed is ineligible for EA unless person cannot be removed because receiving country would not take him or his removal is impractical or contrary to public interest. INA §241(a)(7), 8 U.S.C. §1231(a)(7).

14. Absconders—The Service initiated an Absconder Apprehension Initiative. The purpose of this program is to identify persons who have final orders of deportation/ removal and to ascertain: (1) whether they pose a terrorist threat; (2) whether they will be criminally charged under 8 U.S.C. §1253 for the federal crime of Failure to Depart after a final order of removal has been issued; or (3) whether they will be taken into custody and physically deported promptly. The Service guidelines require that when an "absconder" is apprehended and interviewed that s/he be given warnings under *Miranda v. Arizona,* 384 U.S. 436 (1966) and be informed that consular officials of her or his country may be notified of her detention under the Vienna Convention on Consular Relations. Thompson, Memo, Deputy AG, (Jan. 25, 2002), *published on* AILA InfoNet at Doc. No. 03100648.

V. ***Stays of Deportation***—Respondent may petition the DD (8 C.F.R. §§241.6, 1241.6), the IJ (8 C.F.R. §1003.23(b)(1)(v)) and the BIA (8 C.F.R. §1003.6) to stay his removal. The filing of a federal petition "shall not delay execution of the Warrant of Removal except upon an affirmative order of the court." 8 C.F.R. §241.3(c). There is no requirement that the petitioner seek a stay from *both* the BIA *and* the DD. *Naragan v. Ilchert*, 799 F.Supp. 1047, 1049 (N.D. Cal. 1992). Where a stay is sought to permit respondent to seek judicial review of a claim that is nonfrivolous and that has not been decided by a circuit court or the Supreme Court, the stay should be granted. *Biancada v. Turnage*, 883 F.2d 836 (9th Cir. 1989). Similarly, where stay is sought to reopen BIA proceedings, BIA abused its discretion in denying request, *Anderson v. McElroy*, 953 F.2d 803 (2d Cir. 1992), particularly where the decision was "merely conclusory." *Butros v. INS*, 804 F.Supp. 1336 (D. Or. 1991).

Jurisdictional Question—The DHS takes the view that INA §242(g), 8 U.S.C. §1252(g) as interpreted by *Reno v. American-Arab Anti-Discrimination Comm.*, 525 U.S. 471, 119 S.Ct. 936 (1999) bars any action in federal court to stay the deportation/removal of a noncitizen. *Moussa v. Jenifer,* 389 F.3d 550, 554–55 (6th Cir. 2004) [although habeas petitioner raised statutory and constitutional claims regarding the denial of motion to stay before ICE they were nothing more than an effort to review the nonreviewable discretionary decision of the DD to execute an order of removal barred by INA §242(g)]; *Fedorca v. Perryman,* 197 F.3d 236 (7th Cir. 1999); *Botezatu v. INS,* 195 F.3d 311 (7th Cir. 1999); However, where the court has habeas jurisdiction to review deportability, its ancillary jurisdiction to stay deportation pending that review is not barred by INA §242(g) or *American-Arab. Wallace v. Reno,* 194 F.3d 279, 285 (1st Cir. 1999). *See also Hope v. Immigration Service (ICE)*, 349 F.Supp.2d 490, 495 (E.D.N.Y. 2004) [stay of removal granted pending motion to reopen before the BIA]; INA §242(g). The REAL ID Act, however, has dramatically changed the landscape and generally prohibits district court action. *Tejada v. Cabral,* 424 F.Supp.2d 296 (D. Mass. 2006) [although the district court has jurisdiction to review the validity of noncitizen's state court conviction, it does not have jurisdiction *post*-REAL ID Act to review noncitizen's removal proceeding and therefore has no jurisdiction to seek a stay of removal].

Stay Order and Contempt—Failure to stay removal when court has ordered stay may result in contempt against the government. *Dimitrov v. Ashcroft,* 368 F.3d 960 (7th Cir. 2004) [issued order to show cause but declined to issue contempt in light of government procedural changes and fact that person was not physically removed]. But if the government has no actual or constructive notice of the court's order a person would not be considered to be deported in violation of the order. *U.S. v. Garcia-Echaverria,* 374 F.3d 440, 449–50 (6th Cir. 2004) [government unaware of stay order issued by the Southern District of New York before it deported respondent whose habeas case had been transferred to the Western District of Louisiana].

W. ***Early Removal of Nonviolent Offenders***—INA §241(a)(4)(B), 8 U.S.C. §1231(a)(4)(B).

1. The AG may allow the removal of a person prior to completion of his criminal sentence where he is determined to be a nonviolent offender. If he is in federal custody he may obtain early removal if the AG determines it is in the best interest of the U.S. and he is not confined for alien smuggling and certain aggravated felonies as defined in 8 U.S.C. §1101(a)(43)(B), (C), (E), (I) and (L) [drug trafficking, arms trafficking, certain firearms offenses, child pornography, violating national defense]. If he is in state custody he may obtain early removal if he submits a written request to the AG, the AG determines it is in the best interest of the state to remove him and he has not been convicted of arms trafficking [8 U.S.C. §1101(a)(43)(C)] or certain firearms offenses [8 U.S.C. §1101(a)(43)(E)].

2. There is no private right of action under the statute. INA §241(a)(4)(D), 8 U.S.C. §1231(a)(4)(D); *Duamutef v. INS,* 386 F.3d 172, 182 (2d Cir. 2004) [the district court lacked habeas jurisdiction to compel ICE to take custody over state prisoner and to execute order of removal because prisoner had no standing]; *U.S. v. Aispuro*, 127 F.3d 1133 (9th Cir. 1997) [finding no private right under similar statute enacted under AEDPA]; *Thye v. U.S.*, 109 F.3d 127 (2d Cir. 1997) [same]; *Lemeshko v. Wrona,* 325 F.Supp.2d 778, 784–85 (E.D Mich. 2004) [no due process right to be deported prior to completion of criminal sentence]; *Cepeda v. INS,* 273 F.Supp.2d 222 (E.D.N.Y. 2003) [no private right of action or due process right to be released from prison before completion of criminal sentence]; *U.S. v. Abreu*, 940 F.Supp. 443, 446–48 (D.R.I. 1996) [mandamus does not lie because AG's discretion is broad]; *U.S. v. Lopez*, 940 F.Supp. 920 (E.D. Va. 1996) [same]; *Chacon-Castellanos v. Reno*, 943 F.Supp. 26 (D.D.C. 1996) [decision to deport is within sole and unfettered discretion of the AG; no private right; no writ of mandamus]; *Sjogreen v. Reno*, 943 F.Supp. 29 (D.D.C. 1996) [same].
3. There is also no right to compel the AG to deport someone. *Koos v. Holm,* 204 F.Supp.2d 1099, 1108–09 (W.D. Tenn. 2002) (and cases cited therein).

CHAPTER 4
FLEEING PERSECUTION: REFUGEES, ASYLEES, AND OTHERS

CHAPTER 4
FLEEING PERSECUTION: REFUGEES, ASYLEES, AND OTHERS

I. CATEGORIES OF PROTECTION FOR PERSONS FLEEING PERSECUTION

A. ***Introduction***—In the past decade, there has been no area of immigration law that has generated more controversy, resulted in more litigation, and caused more confusion than the law relating to persons coming to the U.S. after fleeing persecution in their homeland. The law is no longer limited, as it once was, to persons fleeing Communism or to persons paroled into the U.S., as were tens of thousands of Hungarians, Cubans, and Vietnamese during the 1950s to 1970s. It now involves international as well as domestic law—and the application of numerous complex statutes and regulations concerning not only asylees and refugees, but parolees, persons seeking withholding of removal, persons making claims under the Convention Against Torture, and temporary protected status. This chapter explains each of these terms, the rights of people who seek freedom from persecution on our shores, and the procedures that apply to them.

B. ***Sources of Law***—The two major sources of law affecting persons fleeing persecution are international agreements and instruments and U.S. domestic law.

1. *International Law*

1.a. *United Nations Convention & Protocol*—The principal international agreement governing U.S. obligations toward refugees is the 1967 United Nations Protocol Relating to the Status of Refugees, to which the U.S. acceded in 1968. Opened for signature Jan. 31, 1967, 19 U.S.T. 6223, T.I.A.S. No. 6577, 606 U.N.T.S. 267 (1967). The Protocol adopted Articles 2–34 of the U.N. Convention Relating to the Status of Refugees, which has been in force since 1951. Opened for signature July 28, 1951, 19 U.S.T. 6577, 189 U.N.T.S. 137, 150, 152 (1951). The Protocol is important because it governs the treatment of asylees and persons fleeing persecution, and because it contains provisions that have been incorporated into domestic law, such as the definition of "refugee," [compare Art. I, §2 of the Protocol and Art. I of the Convention with INA §101(a)(42), 8 U.S.C. §1101(a)(42)], and the prohibition under Art. 33 of the return of a person whose life or freedom would be threatened in the country s/he fled. Although the Protocol is important as an independent source of law, one U.S. court has found that Article 33 is not self-executing and therefore not binding on U.S. courts, *Haitian Refugee Center, Inc. v. Baker*, 949 F.2d 1109 (11th Cir. 1991), and the Supreme Court has found that it does not apply outside the physical territory of the U.S. *Sale v. Haitian Centers Council, Inc.*, 509 U.S. 155 (1993). The customary international law of safe haven and nonreturn has also been rejected as a separate basis for jurisdiction before the immigration court. *Galo-Garcia v. INS*, 86 F.3d 916 (9th Cir. 1996) [because Congress enacted an extensive legislative scheme for the admission of refugees, customary international law cannot confer jurisdiction].

1.b. *UNHCR Handbook*—Perhaps the greatest importance of the Convention and Protocol is that it can be a source of interpretation and authority for U.S. refugee and asylum law. The BIA and the federal courts have looked to *The Handbook on Procedures and Criteria for Determining Refugee Status Under the 1951 Convention and the 1967 Protocol Relating to the Status of Refugees* (Geneva 1979) ("Handbook"), published by the Office of the U.N. High Commissioner for Refugees (UNHCR), as an important source for interpreting the meaning of terms and procedural matters under our own domestic law. *See Cardoza-Fonseca v. INS*, 480 U.S. 421, 437–39 and 439 n.2 (1987) [Handbook "provides significant guidance" in construing the Protocol]; *Poradisova v. Gonzales,* 420 F.3d 70, 79–81 (2d Cir. 2005) [IJ ignored Handbook requirement that events of persecution be viewed cumulatively instead of in isolation; isolated events may be taken "out of context" and can be "misleading"]; *Chang v. INS*, 119 F.3d 1055, 1061–62 (3d Cir. 1997) [regarding prosecution as persecution]; *Rodriguez-Roman v. INS*, 98 F.3d 416, 425–26 (9th Cir. 1996); *Singh v. Ilchert*, 63 F.3d 1501, 1511 (9th Cir. 1995); *Ramos-Vasquez v. INS*, 57 F.3d 857, 863 (9th Cir. 1995); *Canas-Segovia v. INS*, 902 F.2d 717 (9th Cir. 1990), *aff'd on alternate grounds after remand*, 970 F.2d 599 (9th Cir. 1992); *Zavala-Bonilla v. INS*, 730 F.2d 562, 567 n.7 (9th Cir. 1984); *Yang v. Carroll*, 852 F.Supp. 460, 470 n.22 (E.D. Va. 1994); *Matter of S-M-J-*, 21 I&N Dec. 722, 724–25, 729 (BIA 1997); *Matter of Acosta*, 19 I&N Dec. 211, 221 (BIA 1985) ["[w]hile we do not consider the ... Handbook to be controlling, the Handbook nevertheless is a useful tool"]; *Matter of Frentescu*, 18 I&N Dec. 244, 246–47 (BIA 1982); *Matter of Rodriguez-Palma*, 17 I&N Dec. 465, 468–69 (BIA 1980). The Supreme Court, however, has also recognized that the "U.N. Handbook may be a useful interpretative aid, but it is not binding on the Attorney General, the BIA, or United States courts." *INS v. Aguirre-Aguirre,* 526 U.S. 415, 427 (1999); *Abdulai v. Ashcroft,* 239 F.3d 542, 552–53 (3d Cir. 2001) [following *Aguirre-Aguirre*].

1.c. *Other International Agreements*—In addition to the U.N. Convention and Protocol, there are other international agreements that are relevant to the treatment of applicants for asylum or refugee status, even if they are not legally binding on U.S. courts. *See, e.g.,* Universal Declaration of Human Rights; International Covenant on Economic, Social and Cultural Rights. Virtually all of the important international agreements affecting persons fleeing persecution can be found in one volume in the *Collection of International Instruments Concerning Refugees* (Geneva 1979), published by UNHCR. The BIA has also determined that the Geneva Convention Relative to the Protection of Civilian Persons in Time of War does not create a remedy from deportation. *Matter of Medina*, 19 I&N Dec. 734 (BIA 1988); *Bradvica v. INS*, 128 F.3d 1009, 1014 (7th Cir. 1997)

1.d. *U.N. Convention Against Torture (CAT)*—The most significant recent development in the use of international instruments for the protection of persons facing persecution is the U.N. Convention Against Torture and Other Cruel, Inhuman or Degrading Treatment or Punishment, opened for signature Feb. 4, 1985, G.A. Res. 39/46, 39 U.N. GAOR Supp. No. 51 at 197, U.N. Doc. A/Res/39/708 (1984), *reprinted in* 23 I.L.M. 1027 (1984), *modified* in 24 I.L.M. 535 (1985). The CAT was enacted into U.S. law on Oct. 21, 1998. FY1999 Omnibus Consolidated and Emergency Supplemental Appropriations Act, PL 105-277, div. G, sub. B, tit. XXI Foreign Affairs Reform and Restructuring Act of 1998, §2242, 112 Stat. 2681–822, 105th Cong. 2d Sess. (1998), 136 Cong. Rec. S17486, 36198 (1990); *Committee on Foreign Relations, Convention Against Torture and other Cruel, Inhuman or Degrading Treatment or Punishment,* S. Exec. Rep. 101-30 (1990). Although the treaty is not self-executing, *Pierre v. Gonzales,* 502 F.3d 109, 119–20 (2d Cir. 2007) [because CAT is not self-executing an applicant cannot rely on international law and international treatment under the treaty to establish a judicially enforceable right]; *Renkel v. U.S.,* 456 F.3d 640 (6th Cir. 2006) [treaty does not permit a private cause of action against the U.S. arising out of conditions of confinement in the U.S.] it should be construed consistent with the Convention. Article 3(1) states, "[n]o State Party shall expel, return ('refouler') or extradite a person to another State where there are substantial grounds for believing that he would be in danger of being subjected to torture." In making this determination the U.S. "shall take into account all relevant considerations including, where applicable, the existence in the State concerned of a consistent pattern of gross, flagrant, or mass violations of human rights." Art. 3(2). Congress has stated, "[i]t shall be the policy of the United States not to expel, extradite, or otherwise effect the involuntary return of any person to a country in which there are substantial grounds for believing the person would be in danger of being subjected to torture, regardless of whether the person is physically present in the United States." PL 105-277, §2242(a), *supra.* DOJ has published regulations to effectuate the Convention at 8 C.F.R. §§208.16–.18, 1208.16–.18, which have been upheld as they relate to the definition of torture and the burden of proof. *Reyes-Sanchez v. Ashcroft,* 261 F.Supp.2d 276, 290–92 (S.D.N.Y. 2003) [finding that 8 C.F.R. §§208.16(c)(2) and 208.18(a)(2)&(5) were lawful and that CAT was not "self-executing"]. Congress has also authorized the establishment of centers within and outside the U.S. to treat victims of torture. Torture Victims Relief Reauthorization Act of 2003. PL 108-179, 117 Stat. 2643 (Dec. 15, 2003); H.R. Report No. 108-261 (II). *See also in this chapter*, "Convention Against Torture / Deferral of Removal," part V (p. 484), *infra*.

1.e. *Customary International Law*—The BIA has determined that customary international law does not create a remedy from deportation that can be sought by individuals beyond that provided by the INA. *Matter of Medina*, 19 I&N Dec. 734 (BIA 1988). *Accord Bradvica v. INS*, 128 F.3d 1009, 1014 (7th Cir. 1997); *Echeverria-Hernandez v. INS*, 923 F.2d 688 (9th Cir. 1991) [there are no international norms establishing a right to temporary asylum and it is preempted by legislative and executive action]; *American Baptist Churches v. Meese*, 712 F.Supp. 756 (N.D. Cal. 1989) [Refugee Act of 1980 rejects norm of temporary refuge]. *But see Filartiga v. Pena-Irala*, 630 F.2d 876 (2d Cir. 1980); *Rodriguez-Fernandez v. Wilkinson*, 505 F.Supp. 787 (D. Kan. 1980), *aff'd on other grounds*, 654 F.2d 1382 (10th Cir. 1981).

2. *Domestic Law*

2.a. *Refugee Act of 1980*—U.S. domestic law, as it affects persons fleeing persecution, is found principally in the Refugee Act of 1980, PL 96-212, 94 Stat. 102 (1980). The principal sections concerning persons fleeing persecution are found at INA §§101(a)(42), 207–09, 212(d)(5), 241(b)(3) [formerly 243(h)], and 244; 8 U.S.C. §§1101(a)(42), 1157–59, 1182(d)(5), 1231(b)(3) [formerly 1253(h)], and 1254a. In addition to the INA, regulations were promulgated by DOJ, which are principally found at 8 C.F.R. §§207–09, 212.5, 235.3, 1207.3, 1208–09, 1235.3, 1240.11(c), 1240.33, and 1240.49(c).

2.b. *Administrative Interpretation*—Interpretation of the statutes and regulations is generally made by DOJ, and principally by the BIA, although its decisions may be reviewed by the Attorney General (AG), who is vested with the ultimate authority for all decisions under the INA. *See, e.g., Matter of Y-L-, A-G-, R-S-R-*, 23 I&N Dec. 270 (AG 2002); *Matter of Leon-Orosco and Rodriguez-Colas*, 19 I&N Dec. 136 (AG 1984). DHS (and its various components, including USCIS, ICE, CBP) and DOS also make administrative determinations relevant to persons fleeing persecution.

2.c. *Judicial Interpretation*—Since neither DHS nor DOJ may entertain constitutional or other challenges to the validity of their own regulations or statutes, such challenges can only be brought in the federal courts. Since 1980, federal courts have been active in addressing both constitutional and nonconstitutional challenges to the federal government's treatment of persons seeking protection from persecution. Such challenges have generally arisen through direct litigation in the federal courts under the APA or the INA, *see, e.g., Gonzalez v. Reno,* 212 F.3d 1338 (11th Cir. 2000); *Haitian Refugee Center v. Civiletti,* 503 F.Supp. 442 (S.D. Fla. 1980), *modified sub nom. Haitian Refugee Center v. Smith*, 676 F.2d 1023 (5th Cir. 1982); *Jean v. Nelson*, 472 U.S. 846 (1985); *American Baptist Churches v. Meese*, 712 F.Supp. 756 (N.D. Cal. 1989); *but see Sale v. Haitian Centers Council, Inc.*, 509 U.S. 155 (1993); *Haitian Refugee Center, Inc. v. Baker*, 953 F.2d 1498, 1505–09 (11th Cir. 1992), or through the statutorily prescribed review process (INA §242), providing direct appellate review of BIA decisions. *Augustin v. Sava*, 735 F.2d 32 (2d Cir. 1984); *Chavarria v. DOJ*, 722 F.2d 666, 668 (11th Cir. 1984).

C. *Persons Protected Under U.S. Law*—U.S. immigration laws permit persons fleeing persecution to seek protection under several different categories:

1. Normal flow refugees under INA §207(a);
2. Emergency flow refugees (refugees of special humanitarian concern) under INA §207(b);
3. Asylum seekers under INA §208;
4. Persons seeking withholding of removal under INA §241(b)(3) (or before Apr. 1, 1997, withholding of exclusion and deportation under INA §243(h)) whose life or freedom would be threatened;
5. Persons seeking protection under CAT; 8 C.F.R. §§208.16–.18, 1208.16–.18.
6. Parolees under INA §212(d)(5);
7. Persons granted extended voluntary departure (EVD) or deferred enforced departure (DED); and
8. Persons granted temporary protected status (TPS).

II. OVERSEAS REFUGEES

A. *Definition of Refugee*—A refugee is defined as any person outside his or her country of nationality, or in the case of a person having no nationality, his or her last habitual residence, who is unable or unwilling to return to, and is unable or unwilling to avail himself or herself of the protection of that country because of persecution or a "well-founded fear of persecution on account of race, religion, nationality, membership in a particular social group or political opinion." INA §101(a)(42)(A), 8 U.S.C. §1101(a)(42)(A). The refugee definition also includes persons with a well-founded fear of persecution who are still within the country of persecution under such special circumstances as the President may specify after consultation with Congress. INA §101(a)(42)(B), 8 U.S.C. §1101(a)(42)(B). The definition incorporates the refugee standard of the U.N. Convention and Protocol Relating to the Status of Refugees, *supra,* and specifically excludes persons who participated in the persecution of others. The definition also includes forced abortion, involuntary sterilization or other coercive population control programs as constituting persecution on account of political opinion. The present law's ideologically neutral definition substitutes the former statute's "would be subject to persecution" language, which was applied solely to persons fleeing certain countries.

B. *Persecution of Others as Bar to Status*—The definition bars asylee and refugee status to "any person who ordered, incited, assisted, or otherwise participated in the persecution of any person on account of race, religion, nationality, membership in a particular social group, or political opinion." INA §101(a)(42)(B); 8 U.S.C. §1101(a)(42)(B). *See also* INA §§208(b)(2)(A)(i), §241(b)(3)(B)(i); 8 U.S.C. §§1158(b)(2)(A)(i), 1231(b)(3)(B)(i). Under 8 C.F.R. §§208.13(c), 1208.13(c), the applicant has the burden of proving by a preponderance of the evidence that he did not commit such an act if evidence indicated s/he did. *Matter of A-H-,* 23 I&N Dec. 774, 783–85 (AG 2005) [remanding to BIA under AG's broader standard for assisting in persecution of others]. The BIA has determined that "assisted" may include involuntary or compelled assistance and that it is necessary to look at the "objective effect" of the persecution and not the persecutor's state of mind. *See Matter of Laipenieks*, 18 I&N Dec. 433, 464–65 (BIA 1983), *rev'd on other grounds*, *Laipenieks v. INS*, 750 F.2d 1427, 1435 (9th Cir. 1985) [former Nazi collaborator stripped of citizenship was also denied asylum on ground that he had assisted in the persecution of others]; *Matter of McMullen*, 19 I&N Dec. 90 (BIA 1984); *Fedorenko v. U.S.*, 449 U.S. 490, 512 & n.34 (1981) [no basis for an involuntary assistance exception regarding persecution of others]. Some courts have found that there must be both a particularlized showing of personal involvement and a demonstration that the assistance was material. *Doe v Gonzales,* 484 F.3d 445 (7th Cir. 2007) [remanding to BIA where applicant, who was present when Salvadoran military executed Jesuits, but did not discourage escape attempts, help to maintain order or otherwise contribute to persecution; raising issues as to whether "assist" and "participate" are the same and whether an un-planned cover-up subsequent to events constitutes persecution]; *Miranda Alvarado v. Gonzales,* 449 F.3d 915, 925–33 (9th Cir. 2006) [interpreter for torturers of persons suspected of assisting Sendero Luminoso in Peru was found to have assisted in the persecution of others because his conduct was a necessary part of the violative interrogation]. *See also Chen v. U.S. Att'y Gen.,* 513 F.3d 1255 (11th Cir. 2008) [finding that person who guarded women detained for forced abortions in Chinese province participated in persecution of others, and holding that the determination of whether one should be denied as assisting in persecution "is a particularized, fact-specific inquiry into whether the applicant's personal conduct was merely indirect, peripheral and inconsequential association or was active, direct and integral to the underlying persecution"]; *U.S. v. Hansl,* 439 F.3d 850 (8th Cir. 2006) [upholding denaturalization of member of Death's Head Battalion who guarded concentration camp as "personally assisting" in the persecution of others within the meaning of the Refugee Relief Act, whether involuntary or not]; *Higuit v. Gonzales,* 433 F.3d 417, 420–21 (4th Cir. 2006) [military intelligence officer for Marcos government in Philippines who acknowledged that people he provided information about were imprisoned or killed, assisted, or otherwise participated in the persecution of others even if he was not directly involved in their physical harm or torture]; *Xie v. INS,* 434 F.3d 136 (2d Cir. 2006) [transporting captive women to undergo forced abortions in China was assistance in persecution even if it was not voluntary]; *Singh v. Gonzales,* 417 F.3d 736, 739–41 (7th Cir. 2005) [respondent assisted or otherwise participated in persecution where, as police officer, he brought Sikhs into custody whom he knew were being physically abused]; *Bah v. Ashcroft,* 341 F.3d 348 (5th Cir. 2003) [member of RUF in Sierra Leone who executed a prisoner and mutilated civilians]; *U.S. v. Friedrich,* 402 F.3d 842 (8th Cir. 2005) [position of guard at Nazi concentration camp was sufficient, without more, to establish assisting in persecution for purposes of denaturalization]; *Ofosu v. McElroy*, 933 F.Supp. 237 (S.D.N.Y. 1995) [member of CDR in Ghana who arrested political activists who were later tortured]. *But see Hernandez v. Reno,* 258 F.3d 806 (8th Cir. 2001) [reversing denial of asylum for Guatemalan member of ORPA on grounds BIA did not follow *Fedorenko*]. There must also be an act of persecution that the individual participated in. *Xu Sheng Gao v. U.S. Att'y Gen.,* 500 F.3d 93, 100–02 (2d Cir. 2007) [as the Chief Officer of the Quingdao City Cultural Management Bureau applicant's responsibility to inspect bookstores to determine if they were selling prohibited material was not assisting persecution where there was no evidence that either his job duties required, or in actual practice, that anyone was arrested, detained, charged, prosecuted or imprisoned for selling prohibited material that included pornography as well as political materials]. Self-defense does not constitute persecution of others. *Vukmirovic v. Ashcroft,* 362 F.3d 1247, 1252–53 (9th Cir. 2004) [reversing asylum denial on grounds that Bosnian-Serb acted in self-defense]. Activity directly related to a civil war, including forced recruitment, destruction of property, military attacks, or mere membership in an organization that involves such activities is not persecution. *Matter of Rodriguez-Majano*, 19 I&N Dec. 811 (BIA 1988). Persecution of others cannot be imputed from membership in a particular group. *Vukmirovic*, 362 F.3d at 1252 [imputed actions of other Bosnian-Serbs cannot be basis to deny asylum as persecutor]. In the view of one circuit, a person had to have prior or contemporaneous knowledge about the persecution for the bar to apply even where the objective effect of his actions was to assist in persecution. The court distinguished between involuntariness, which raises issues of duress and obeying orders, and the scienter requirement of prior or contemporaneous knowledge, which is not in conflict with stating that even involuntary actions bar relief. *Castaneda-Castillo v. Gonzales,* 488 F.3d 17 (1st Cir. 2007) (*en banc*) [remanded to apply scienter requirement to determine whether Peruvian army officer had prior or contemporaneous knowledge of massacre and therefore assisted in persecution; court noted that once government established applicant's association with persecution the burden shifted to the applicant to establish lack of scienter]. *See also Xu Sheng Gao v. U.S. Att'y Gen.,* 500 F.3d 93, 102–03 (2d Cir. 2007) [the persecutor bar, following the First Circuit, "requires some level of culpable knowledge that the consequences of one's actions assist in acts of persecution].

C. ***Normal Flow Refugees***—INA §207(a), 8 U.S.C. §1157(a) provides for the admission of refugees who apply for admission from outside the U.S. or its borders. Such "normal flow refugees" are designated on an annual basis by the President, in consultation with Congress, based on humanitarian or national interest concerns. INA §207(a)(1), 8 U.S.C. §1157(a)(1).

D. ***Emergency Flow Refugees***—Refugees of special humanitarian concern (emergency flow refugees) are refugees for whom the President determines, after appropriate consultation with Congress, that an unforeseen emergency exists such that their admission is justified by "grave humanitarian concerns or is otherwise in the national interest" and could not be accomplished through the normal flow of refugee admissions determined for each fiscal year. INA §207(b), 8 U.S.C. §1157(b). The President, under special circumstances and after consultation with Congress, may also designate "any person who is within the country of such person's nationality" as a refugee who otherwise meets the definition. INA §101(a)(42)(B), 8 U.S.C. §1101(a)(42)(B). For example, in 1980, 3,500 Cubans in the Peruvian Embassy in Havana were designated as refugees by the President.

E. ***Designation of Certain Groups for Refugee Protection***—Throughout the years, Congress has designated different groups of persons who may receive refugee protection by asserting a well-founded fear and demonstrating a lower standard of proof that requires only a "credible basis for concern about the possibility of persecution." Foreign Operations, Export Financing, and Related Programs Appropriations Act, 1990, PL 101-167, 103 Stat. 1195 (Nov. 21, 1989) at tit. V, §599D; Consolidated Appropriations Act, 2004, PL 108-199, 118 Stat. 3 (Jan. 23, 2004) at div. E, tit. II, §213. The groups currently include nationals and residents of: (1) the former Soviet Union who share common characteristics; (2) Vietnam, Laos, and Cambodia who share common characteristics or are recognized by the AG as members of certain categories of individuals; (3) the former Soviet Union who are Jews or Evangelical Christians; (4) the former Soviet Union who are members of the Ukrainian Catholic Church or the Ukrainian Orthodox Church; and (5) the Islamic Republic of Iran who are members of a religious minority.

F. ***Iraqis Employed by the U.S. Government in Iraq***—The FY 08 National Defense Appropriations Act designates as refugees of special humanitarian concern eligible for Priority 2 processing (which is a group, rather than an individual, referral program to process refugees by the DOS in consultation with USCIS): (1) Iraqis who were or are employed by the U.S. government in Iraq; (2) Iraqis who establish to the Secy. of State that they are or were employed in Iraq by: (i) a media or NGO headquartered in the U.S. *or* (ii) an organization or entity closely associated with the U.S. mission in Iraq that received funding from the U.S.; (3) spouses, children, and parents of the Iraqis designated above whether or not accompanying or following to join as well as sons, daughters and siblings; and (4) Iraqis who are members of a religious or minority community that have been identified by the Secy. of State as a persecuted group and who have immediate relatives or family-preference relatives in the U.S. All groups are subject to the annual refugee admission quotas. PL 110-181, tit. XII, subtit. C, §1243.

G. ***North Korean Human Rights Act***—A national of the Democratic People's Republic of Korea (North Korea) shall not be considered a national of the Republic of Korea (South Korea) so that refugee/asylum status will not be barred on the theory that he could be returned to the Republic of Korea. North Korean Human Rights Act of 2004, PL 108-333, 118 Stat. 1287; 22 U.S.C. §7842. However, if a North Korean avails himself of South Korean citizenship he may be ineligible for asylum due to firm resettlement. *Matter of K-R-Y- and K-C-S-,* 24 I&N Dec. 133 (BIA 2007).

H. ***"Bring Them Home Alive Act"***—Congress has offered refugee status to persons from certain countries (Vietnam, Laos, Cambodia, China, N. Korea, countries of former Soviet Republic) who personally deliver into U.S. custody, any living American missing or held prisoner from the Vietnam or Korean wars. PL 106-484, 114 Stat. 2195, 146 Cong. Rec. H10703-04 (Nov. 9, 2000). The law also grants refugee status to the parents, spouse and children of the designated refugee. In 2002 the law was expanded to include any national of Iraq or "nation of the Greater Middle East Region." PL 107-258, 116 Stat. 1738 (Oct. 29, 2002).

I. ***Removal of Refugees***—Admission as a refugee does not preclude subsequent proceedings to remove the person if s/he was not a refugee at the time of admission, 8 C.F.R. §207.9, or if s/he has engaged in activities making him or her inadmissible *and* where there is a "compelling reason of national security or public order" warranting removal. 8 C.F.R. §§240.35(c), 1240.35(c); *Shamoun v. District Director*, 967 F.Supp. 1051 (N.D. Ill. 1997). Refugees are conditionally admitted into the U.S., not paroled or permanently admitted. *Matter of Jean,* 23 I&N Dec. 373, 374 n.4 (AG 2002) [refugee admitted under INA §207 is conditionally admitted which has the "effect of deferring her admissibility, inspection and examination"]. A person seeking refugee status may waive certain grounds of inadmissibility. 8 C.F.R. §§207.3, 1207.3. However, a person denied refugee status may not sue to waive inadmissibility. *Reznik v. DOJ, INS*, 901 F.Supp. 188 (E.D. Pa. 1995).

J. ***Spouses and Children of Refugees***—Spouses and children of refugees are admitted as refugees even if they would not qualify as such on their own. INA §207(c)(2), 8 U.S.C. §1157(c)(2). DHS policy permits admission of a spouse and children as long as the relationship existed prior to the principal refugee's admission to the U.S. and continues to exist at the time of admission. 8 C.F.R. §207.7(c). This includes a child who was *in utero* at the time of admission. 8 C.F.R. §207.7(c); Memo, Aytes, Asst. Comm. for Benefits Division, INS, HQ COU 120/11.30-P (Aug. 27, 1996), *reprinted in* 73 No. 40 *Interpreter Releases* 1462, 1486–87 (Oct. 21, 1996). Even if a child "ages-out" and becomes 21 during the process of admission or thereafter, s/he will be considered a child if s/he is unmarried and was under 21 at the time his or her parent applied for refugee status. INA §207(c)(2)(B), 8 U.S.C. §1157(c)(2)(B). The application is filed on Form I-730 within 2 years of the principal refugee's admission unless the period is extended for "humanitarian reasons." 8 C.F.R. §207.7(d). Other relatives of the refugee (*e.g.,* a grandparent or brother) may not enter the U.S. as an accompanying relative under INA §207(c)(2). However, if they reside in the same household, they may be given a refugee interview to qualify for refugee status in their own right. 63 Fed. Reg. 43957 (Aug. 17, 1998).

III. ASYLUM

A. ***Definition of Asylee***—An asylee is a person who meets the definition of refugee under INA §101(a)(42) [*see in this chapter* sections II.A & B (p.432), *supra*], but who is either physically present in the U.S. or is at a land border or port of entry of the U.S. at the time he seeks refuge. INA §208(a), 8 U.S.C. §1158(a).

1. *Interdiction on the High Seas*—The right to seek asylum may not extend to persons interdicted on the high seas or detained outside the physical territory of the U.S. *Sale v. Haitian Centers Council, Inc.*, 509 U.S. 155 (1993) [former INA §243(h) and U.N. Convention does not apply to bar interdiction program on high seas]; *In re Li,* 71 F.Supp.2d 1052 (D. Hawaii 1999) [no right to asylum interview or hearing because Midway Island is not part of the U.S. as defined in INA §101(a)(38)]. *See also* Legal Opinion, Virtue, G.C. to Meissner, Comm. (HQCOU 90/15) (Sept. 1,

1998), *reprinted in* 76 No. 13 *Interpreter Releases* 529, 536–45 (Apr. 2, 1999) [INS had no authority to operate Guantanamo as a screening and detention camp for Haitians because it was outside U.S.]. Under INA §§212(f) and 215(a)(1), the President delegated authority to the AG to maintain custody of persons interdicted on the high seas and to conduct asylum interviews and to take "any other appropriate actions" with respect to such persons. Memo, Clinton, President of the U.S. (Sept. 24, 1999), 64 Fed. Reg. 55809 (Oct 15, 1999), *reprinted in* 76 No. 38 *Interpreter Releases* 1457 (Sept. 30, 1999) and 76 No. 39 *Interpreter Releases* 1490 (Oct. 11, 1999). A subsequent Executive Order was issued by President George W. Bush directing the AG to provide a screening process for persons interdicted or intercepted in the Caribbean region, directing the Secy. of State to provide for the custody, transportation and other needs for persons needing protection including finding third countries for them, and requiring the Secy. of Defense to make Guantanamo available if it does not interfere with the operation and security of the base. Executive Order 13276, George W. Bush (Nov. 15, 2002), *reprinted in* 79 No. 46 *Interpreter Releases* 1747, 1774 (Nov. 25, 2002). The government has also adhered to a "wet foot/dry foot" policy that allows for interdiction and return of any person after screening on a coast guard vessel as long as they do not set foot on dry land. *See* Office of Legal Counsel, Department of Justice, "Immigration Consequences of Undocumented Aliens Arrival in United States Territorial Waters" (1993); *Movimiento Democracia, Inc. v. Chertoff,* 417 F.Supp. 2d 1343 (S.D. Fla. 2006) [Cuban migrants who landed on Seven Mile Bridge in Florida Keys were on U.S. land within meaning of "dry foot" policy].

2. *Nationality and Statelessness*—Before deciding an asylum/refugee claim, the applicant's nationality must first be addressed. *Dhoumo v. BIA,* 416 F.3d 172 (2d Cir. 2005) [reversing denial of asylum/withholding where IJ made no specific finding as to nationality]; *Wangchuck v. DHS,* 448 F.3d 524, 528–29 (2d Cir. 2006) [same]. *But see Fedosseeva v. Gonzales,* 492 F.3d 840, 845–46 (7th Cir. 2007) [questions about whether the designated country will accept the alien are to be dealt with by the AG after, and independent of, the asylum case; citing to *Pavlovich*]. Inability to establish nationality cannot be a basis to deny refugee or asylum status. *Dulane v. INS*, 46 F.3d 988, 996–99 (10th Cir. 1995) [reversing BIA's denial of asylum based on failure to establish nationality]. For stateless persons, the IJ/BIA must determine where the applicant "last habitually resided." *Paripovic v. Gonzales,* 418 F.3d 240, 243–45 (3d Cir. 2005) [upholding IJ's finding under *Chevron* deference, that applicant's 2½ year stay in Serbia established that he habitually resided there]. A stateless Palestinian can establish eligibility for asylum if: (1) his expulsion, denial of reentry or the uncompensated confiscation of his property constituted a violation of his basic human rights so serious as to constitute persecution; and (2) he suffered these violations on account of one of the enumerated grounds in the refugee definition. Legal Opinion, Martin, General Counsel, CO-208 (Oct. 27, 1995), *reprinted in* 72 No. 44 *Interpreter Releases* 1553, 1557–63 (Nov. 13, 1995). *But see Fedosseeva v. Gonzales,* 492 F.3d 840, 845 (7th Cir. 2007) [statelessness alone is not a ground of asylum and refugee definition is explicit that person must show persecution]; *Sharari v. Gonzales,* 407 F.3d 467, 474–75 (1st Cir. 2005) [discrimination against stateless Palestinian in Lebanon not sufficient for withholding]; *Ahmed v. Ashcroft,* 341 F.3d 214 (3d Cir. 2003) [discrimination against stateless Palestinian in Saudi Arabia did not amount to persecution and statelessness alone does not warrant asylum]; *Al Najjar v. Ashcroft,* 257 F.3d 1262, 1293–94 (11th Cir. 2001) [statelessness alone does not warrant asylum; country of "last habitual residence" was not Israel]. Similarly, an applicant need not prove that the country from which he seeks asylum would otherwise accept him if deported. *Ouda v. INS,* 324 F.3d 445, 452–53 (6th Cir. 2003) [rejecting INS argument that asylum could not be granted to Palestinian from Kuwait because Kuwait would not take her back].

3. *Persecution*—Defined as "a threat to the life or freedom of, or the infliction of suffering or harm upon, those who differ in a way regarded as offensive." *Acosta*, 19 I&N Dec. at 222; *Li v. Att'y Gen. of the U.S.,* 400 F.3d 157, 164–68 (3d Cir. 2005) [discussing legislative history of persecution]; *Sanchez Jimenez v. U.S. Att'y Gen.,* 492 F.3d 1223, 1232–33 (11th Cir. 2007) [being shot at constitutes past persecution where there was evidence that FARC sought to kill, albeit unsuccessfully, Colombian businessman]; *Gomes v. Gonzales,* 473 F.3d 746, 753–54 (7th Cir. 2007) [Christians in Bangladesh suffered more than harassment at hands of Muslim fundamentalists when they were physically abused and terrorized in their home with a knife to their throat]; *Narayan v. Ashcroft,* 384 F.3d 1065, 1067–68 (9th Cir. 2004) [Indo-Fijian who was physically harmed on

several occasions and repeatedly robbed]; *Montoya-Ulloa v. INS*, 79 F.3d 930 (9th Cir. 1996) [beatings by Sandinista youths sufficient]; *Matter of L-K-*, 23 I&N Dec. 677, 682–83 (BIA 2004) [home invasions resulting in serious injury]. *But see Sahi v. Gonzales*, 416 F.3d 587 (7th Cir. 2005) [remanding to the BIA for failure to define persecution in context of member of Ahmadi faith in Pakistan]. Persecution need not be physical, *Borca v. INS*, 77 F.3d 210, 215–17 (7th Cir. 1996) [recognizing substantial economic deprivation as persecution], but must be more than harassment. *Mikhailevitch v. INS*, 146 F.3d 384, 390 (6th Cir. 1998); *Balazoski v. INS*, 932 F.2d 638, 642 (7th Cir. 1991). Persecution has also been defined as: "the infliction of suffering or harm, under government sanction, upon persons who differ in a way regarded as offensive (*e.g.*, race, religion, political opinion, etc.), in a manner condemned by civilized governments. The harm or suffering need not be physical, but may take other forms, such as the deliberate imposition of severe economic disadvantage or the deprivation of liberty, food, housing, employment or other essentials of life." *Abdel-Masieh v. INS*, 73 F.3d 579, 583 (5th Cir. 1996), *quoting Matter of Laipenieks*, 18 I&N Dec. 433, 456–57 (BIA 1983), *rev'd on other grounds*, 750 F.2d 1427 (9th Cir. 1985). INS Supplementary Refugee/Asylum Adjudications Guidelines, *reprinted in* 67 No. 4 *Interpreter Releases* 85,101–02 (Jan. 22, 1990) [relegation to substandard dwellings, exclusion from institutions of higher learning, enforced social and civil inactivity, passport denial, constant surveillance and pressure to become an informer may all constitute persecution]. Persecution includes a forced medical examination where a woman is fighting population control policies. *Li v. Ashcroft*, 356 F.3d 1153, 1158–59 (9th Cir. 2004) (en banc) and where she faces severe economic sanctions if she refused abortion. *Matter of T-Z-*, 24 I&N Dec. 163 (BIA 2007) [case remanded to determine whether wife of applicant did face severe economic sanctions if she refused abortion].

3.a. *Permanent or Serious Injury Not Required*—Persecution does not require that an applicant establish permanent or serious injuries. *Matter of O-Z- & I-Z-*, 22 I&N Dec. 23, 25–26 (BIA 1998) [persecution "encompasses a variety of forms of adverse treatment, including non–life threatening violence and physical abuse or non-physical forms of harm"]; *De Santamaria v. U.S. Att'y Gen.*, ___ F.3d ___ (11th Cir. Apr. 22, 2008) [IJ reversed where cumulative persecution of Colombian by FARC amounted to past persecution and minor physical injuries did not effect finding because "we have not required serious physical injury where the petitioner demonstrates repeated threats combined with other forms of severe mistreatment"]; *Delgado v. Mukasey*, 508 F.3d 702, 707–08 (2d Cir. 2007) [reversed BIA's denial of asylum where the BIA misread its own decision in *Matter of V-T-S-* and improperly suggested that kidnapping was not persecution]; *Mejia v. U.S. Att'y Gen.*, 498 F.3d 1253 (11th Cir. 2007) [IJ reversed where Colombian who was member of Liberal Party was threatened over 18 month period, had large rock thrown at him, was hit with butt of rifle breaking his nose by FARC members, and was sent written death threat *cumulatively* faced past persecution]; *Sanchez Jimenez v. U.S. Att'y Gen.*, 492 F.3d 1223, 1232–33 (11th Cir. 2007) [where Colombian applicant received numerous threats from FARC, was shot at while in his car but not hit, and FARC unsuccessfully sought to kidnap his daughter, the facts amounted to persecution and court stated that being shot at alone constitutes past persecution]; *Sholla v. Gonzales*, 492 F.3d 946 (8th Cir. 2007) [Albanian who spent 2 years in a hard-labor camp with his wife and toddler daughter and who thereafter was threatened with death and brutally beaten with rubber batons on several occasions suffered past persecution]; *Ruiz v. Gonzales*, 479 F.3d 762, 766 (11th Cir. 2007) [beatings, threatening telephone calls, and kidnapping cumulatively amounted to persecution]; *Beskovic v. Gonzales*, 467 F.3d 223, 226–27 (2d Cir. 2006) [reversing IJ denial where Muslim from Montenegro was detained, interrogated and beaten by Serbian police on 2 separate occasions]; *Edimo-Doualla v. Gonzales*, 464 F.3d 276, 282–83 (2d Cir. 2006) [reversing BIA denial of asylum for Cameroonian where IJ required applicant to show permanent or serious injuries despite numerous beatings and arrests]; *Kantoni v. Gonzales*, 461 F.3d 894, 897–98 (7th Cir. 2006) [reversing asylum denial of Togo woman who was detained briefly, and threatened but not beaten because a "credible threat that causes a person to abandon lawful political or religious association or beliefs is persecution"]; *Tamara-Gomez v. Gonzales*, 447 F.3d 343, 348–49 n.8 (9th Cir. 2006) [finding persecution without physical violence against Colombian petitioner who helped police against the FARC, but denying asylum and withholding for lack of nexus]; *Canales-Vargas v. Gonzales*, 441 F.3d 739, 744–46 (9th Cir. 2006) [anonymous death threats are sufficient to establish well-founded fear of future persecution given the "low standard"]; *Quan v. Gonzales*, 428 F.3d 883, 888 (9th Cir.

2005) [electrocution with a rod even if applicant did not seek medical attention or sustain injuries is persecution]; *Smolniakova v. Gonzales,* 422 F.3d 1037, 1048–49 (9th Cir. 2005) [assault and death threats sufficient to establish past persecution of Russian Jew]; *Nakibuka v. Gonzales,* 421 F.3d 473, 476–77 (7th Cir. 2005) [where soldiers' invaded the home, slapped, kicked and bound the applicant, pointed a gun to her head and threatened to kill and rape her, persecution was established because one incident of detention if severe enough is sufficient]; *Un v. Gonzales,* 415 F.3d 205, 210 (1st Cir. 2005) [credible verbal death threats may fall within the meaning of persecution]; *Marcos v. Gonzales,* 410 F.3d 1112, 1118–21 (9th Cir. 2005) [reversing IJ finding of no well-founded fear because persecutors had not yet carried out threats]; *Thomas v. Ashcroft,* 409 F.3d 1177, 1187–89 (9th Cir. 2005) (en banc), *vacated on other grounds*, 126 S.Ct. 1613 (2006) [escalating scheme of intimidation and real threat of physical violence are enough to establish persecution]; *Gilaj v. Gonzales,* 408 F.3d 275, 283–88 (6th Cir. 2005) [Albanian woman who was beaten during first search of home, was threatened by police with death, was beaten and bruised and deprive of food during two-day detention and had police attempt to sexually molest her during second search suffered persecution]; *Mihalev v. Ashcroft,* 388 F.3d 722, 728–30 (9th Cir. 2004) [where Gypsy from Bulgaria was jailed for 10 days and beaten every day with bags of sand, but suffered no significant injury, he suffered past persecution]; *Faruk v. Ashcroft,* 378 F.3d 940, 943 (9th Cir. 2004) [no permanent injuries where mixed marriage led to persecution but husband was beaten and abducted, wife was physically attacked twice in her home and both were consistently verbally assaulted and assailed with rocks]; *Lopez v. Ashcroft,* 366 F.3d 799, 803 (9th Cir. 2004) [where guerrillas attempted to murder applicant by placing him in building and setting it on fire, the fact that his burns were not severe did not undermine his claim of persecution]; *Begzatowski v. INS,* 278 F.3d 665, 670 (7th Cir. 2002) [reversing denial of asylum where BIA focused on whether applicant had permanent injuries as an ethnic Albanian in the Yugoslavian army; distinguishing its own opinion in *Meghani*]. *But see Rodriguez-Ramirez v. Ashcroft,* 398 F.3d 120, 124–25 (1st Cir. 2005) [6-year-old child who witnessed his father being beaten by guerillas and later witnessed others being executed was not persecution].

3.b. *Custodial Interrogation*—Custodial interrogation can be persecution where it is abusive. *Voci v. Gonzales,* 409 F.3d 607, 614–16 (3d Cir. 2005) [Albanian who suffered multiple beating from police including one instance which broke his knee and resulted in extended hospitalization is persecution]; *Phommasoukha v. Gonzales,* 408 F.3d 1011 (8th Cir. 2005) [Laotian soldier's imprisonment for 4 to 6 years in a Pathet Lao concentration camp for re-education was persecution even if there was lack of physical harm]; *Vladimirova v. Ashcroft,* 377 F.3d 690, 696–97 (7th Cir. 2004) [where several detentions were abusive and the last encounter involved being hit in the abdomen resulting in a miscarriage, applicant suffered past persecution]; *Singh v. Ilchert*, 69 F.3d 375 (9th Cir. 1995) [Sikh beaten and shot during interrogation].

3.c. *Rape or Sexual Assault*—Persecution may also be in the form of rape or sexual assault. *Boer-Sedano v. Gonzales,* 418 F.3d 1082, 1088 (9th Cir. 2005) [Mexican homosexual forced to perform oral sex nine times on police officer suffered past persecution]; *Ali v. Ashcroft,* 394 F.3d 780, 784–87 (9th Cir. 2005) [United Somali Congress militia's gang-rape of applicant was at least in part motivated by her political opinion and membership in Midgan clan]; *Garcia-Martinez v. Ashcroft,* 371 F.3d 1066, 1072–74 (9th Cir. 2004) [rape of villager by Guatemalan soldiers]; *Shoafera v. INS,* 228 F.3d 1070 (9th Cir. 2000) [Ethiopian citizen of Amharic ethnicity raped in part because of ethnicity]; *Hernandez-Montiel v. INS,* 225 F.3d 1084, 1097 (9th Cir. 2000) [gay man with female sexual identity was raped and assaulted]; *Matter of D-V-*, 21 I&N Dec. 77 (BIA 1993) [Haitian woman who was Aristide supporter gang-raped during coup]. *But see Menendez-Donis v. Ashcroft,* 360 F.3d 915 (8th Cir. 2004) [rape, absent evidence of identity or motive of attackers, which occurred four years after death of husband and before death of son, was not past persecution]; *Ochave v. INS,* 254 F.3d 859 (9th Cir. 2001) [no substantial evidence to support the nexus between rape and a protected ground]; *Molina-Morales v. INS,* 237 F.3d 1048 (9th Cir. 2001) [rape and murder of aunt was personal dispute with no evidence of political motive]. *See also in this chapter*, "Evidence of Gender-Based Persecution," ¶ XII.B.2.h(10) (p.580), *infra*.

3.d. *Forced Medical Examination*—Persecution includes a forced medical examination where a woman is fighting population control policies. *Li v. Ashcroft*, 356 F.3d 1153, 1158–59 (9th Cir. 2004) (en banc).

3.e. *Physical Harm or Detention Not Amounting to Persecution*—In some cases, physical harm or detention may not amount to persecution. *Bejko v. Gonzales,* 468 F.3d 482, 485–86 (7th Cir. 2006) [Albanian subject to 2-week detention in harsh conditions and subsequent questioning not persecution]; *Zhu v. Gonzales,* 465 F.3d 316, 318–20 (7th Cir. 2006) [boyfriend of woman forced to have an abortion did not suffer past persecution when he was kicked and struck with fists and hit over the head with a brick requiring stitches but not detained in a single act of violence by government officials]; *Zheng v. U.S. Att'y Gen.,* 451 F.3d 1287 (11th Cir. 2006) [follower of Falun Gong who was detained for 5 days and required to watch reeducation videos, lost his job, and was subject to periodic searches did not suffer persecution]; *Samedov v. Gonzales,* 422 F.3d 704, 707 (8th Cir. 2005) [4-day detention without physical injury of Azerbaijani applicant of Lezghin ethnicity is not past persecution]; *Topalli v. Gonzales,* 417 F.3d 128 (1st Cir. 2005) [no persecution for Albanian arrested 7 times and beaten each time by police but did not require medical attention]; *Bocova v. Gonzales,* 412 F.3d 257, 263–64 (1st Cir. 2005) [Albanian who was arrested and beaten twice by police for his support of the Albanian Democratic Party did not suffer past persecution]; *Prela v. Ashcroft,* 394 F.3d 515, 518 (7th Cir. 2005) [Albanian from Kosovo who was interrogated at various times by Serbian police, detained for 24 hours, harassed for money and beaten causing injury, while suffering harassment and intimidation was not persecution]; *Liu v. Ashcroft,* 380 F.3d 307, 313–14 (7th Cir. 2004) [no persecution where Chinese minor was detained for 2 days, her hair was pulled and she was twice pushed to the ground because of belief she followed Falun Gong, where she was expelled from school, and officials came to her home and overturned furniture]; *Shoaira v. Ashcroft,* 377 F.3d 837, 843–45 (8th Cir. 2004) [psychological harm arising from rough treatment by Egyptian authorities and from witnessing father's arrest does not constitute persecution]; *Dinu v. Ashcroft,* 372 F.3d 1041 (9th Cir. 2004) [former soldier beaten by police and threatened with death while being interrogated is not persecution even though no charges were brought because police investigation was legitimate]; *Tawm v. Ashcroft,* 363 F.3d 740, 743 (8th Cir. 2004) [member of Lebanese Forces who was detained twice, four years apart, for a few hours each, without serious injury is not persecution]; *Dandan v. Ashcroft,* 339 F.3d 567, 572–74 (7th Cir. 2003) [3-day interrogation, where respondent was deprived of food and beaten resulting in a swollen face does not "compel" a finding of past persecution]; *Guzman v. INS,* 327 F.3d 11, 15–16 (1st Cir. 2003) [army officer kidnapped and beaten by persons who may have been guerrillas insufficient to establish past persecution]; *Fisher v. INS*, 79 F.3d 955 (9th Cir. 1996) (en banc); *Zalega v. INS*, 916 F.2d 1257 (7th Cir. 1990) [detention for brief periods without mistreatment, and harassment concerning work not persecution].

3.f. *Persecution Arising from Emotional Trauma*—Persecution may be emotional or psychological as well as physical. *Mashiri v. Ashcroft,* 383 F.3d 1112, 1120–21 (9th Cir. 2004) [where Afghan woman in Germany watched neighbor's store firebombed, had her home vandalized, was chased by a mob, had her son beaten-up by neo-Nazis, read about German man who shot over the heads of two Afghan school children on the same route to school as her son, and knew of violent attacks against her husband, these events cumulatively established past persecution]; *Abay v. Ashcroft,* 368 F.3d 634, 640–42 (6th Cir. 2004), [mother's fear that 9-year daughter would be subject to FGM qualifies for asylum]; *Kovac v. INS*, 407 F.2d 102, 106–07 (9th Cir. 1969) [finding that persecution encompasses both physical and mental suffering and that, by deleting the qualifier "physical" from the statute's definition of persecution in 1969, Congress intended to include mental suffering]; *but see Niang v. Gonzales,* 492 F.3d 505, 510–14 (4th Cir. 2007) [affirmed withholding denial where mother asserted derivative claim because USC daughter would be subject to FGM if she accompanied her to Senegal and because mother would suffer psychological harm if daughter accompanies her but noted mom may qualify for humanitarian asylum because of "Sophie's choice"].

3.g. *Harassment*—Persecution does not include harassment without more. *Tobon-Marin v. Mukasey,* 512 F.3d 28, 31–32 (1st Cir. 2008) [attempted coercive conscription by FARC where there was no physical harm and no persistent effort was not persecution]; *Ferdinandus v. Gonzales,* 504 F.3d 61 (1st Cir. 2007) [harassment by rioters against Indonesian Christian who was never incarcerated or beaten is not persecution]; *Setiadi v. Gonzales,* 437 F.3d 710, 713 (8th Cir. 2006) [where Indonesian Catholic married Muslim woman, past persecution does not include unfulfilled threats of physical injury]; *Firmansjah v. Gonzales,* 424 F.3d 598, 604–07 (7th Cir. 2005) [Catholic Indonesian woman of Chinese descent who was forced to change her name to avoid harassment did not suffer persecution]; *Hernandez-Baena v. Gonzales,* 417 F.3d 720, 723 (7th Cir. 2005) [unfulfilled death threat by guerillas without extraordinary threats of an immediate and menacing nature is not persecution]; *Zheng v. Gonzales,* 416 F.3d 97 (1st Cir. 2005) [storming of the village church by unarmed officials where respondent was member was not persecution]; *Sepulveda v. U.S. Att'y Gen.,* 401 F.3d 1226, 1230–31 (11th Cir. 2005) [menacing telephone calls and threats to brother amounts to harassment, not persecution because "persecution is an extreme concept requiring more than a few isolated incidents of verbal harassment or intimidation"]; *Hasanaj v. Ashcroft,* 385 F.3d 780, 782 (7th Cir. 2004) [where Albanian was threatened at gunpoint and car was set on fire but he was not physically harmed, no persecution]; *Krasnopivtsev v. Ashcroft,* 382 F.3d 832, 839 (8th Cir. 2005) [no persecution were applicant was simply harassed by police in Georgia because of his Russian ethnicity]; *Khalil v. Ashcroft,* 337 F.3d 50, 55–56 (1st Cir. 2003) [harassment of Coptic Christian in Egypt including denial of building permits and civil suits regarding his property are not sufficient to show persecution]; *Ciorba v. Ashcroft,* 323 F.3d 539, 545–46 (7th Cir. 2003) [harassment in the form of regular questioning and searches by police did not rise to level of persecution]; *Mousa v. INS,* 223 F.3d 425, 430 (7th Cir. 2000) [where DOS advisory opinion notes that the Palestinian applicant is listed in the Jordanian police database as a potential spy and threat, the resulting harassment did not constitute persecution]; *Khourassany v. INS,* 208 F.3d 1096, 1100–01 (9th Cir. 2000) [denying asylum where shop owner was repeatedly brought to office of the secret police but was not physically harmed in any manner]. *But see Ouda v. INS,* 324 F.3d 445, 454 (6th Cir. 2003) [requiring Palestinians to leave Kuwait because they were perceived enemies is sufficient alone to establish past persecution].

3.h. *Discrimination*—Persecution does not include discrimination, except in extraordinary cases. *Zehatye v. Gonzales,* 453 F.3d 1182, 1185–90 (9th Cir. 2006) [social ostracism and economic hardship for Jehovah's Witness from Eritrea was insufficient]; *Sharari v. Gonzales,* 407 F.3d 467, 474–75 (1st Cir. 2005) [discrimination against stateless Palestinian in Lebanon is not sufficient for withholding]; *Berte v. Ashcroft,* 396 F.3d 993, 996–97 (8th Cir. 2005) [refusal to provide citizenship documents to citizens in northern part of Ivory Coast is discrimination not persecution]; *Mansour v. Ashcroft,* 390 F.3d 667 (9th Cir. 2004) [discrimination of Coptic Christians in Egypt]; *Gormley v. Ashcroft,* 364 F.3d 1172, 1177–80 (9th Cir. 2004) [white South African's loss of work and economic opportunities due to Employment Equity Act 55 of 1998 does not amount to persecution]; *Vatulev v. Ashcroft,* 354 F.3d 1207, 1210 (10th Cir. 2003) [Moldovan of Russian descent suffered discrimination not persecution]; *Ahmed v. Ashcroft,* 341 F.3d 214 (3d Cir. 2003) [discrimination against stateless Palestinian in Saudi Arabia did not amount to persecution]; *Nagoulko v. INS,* 333 F.3d 1012, 1016–18 (9th Cir. 2003) [job discrimination and harassment due to religious beliefs as a Pentecostal Christian in the Ukraine during Communist rule does not amount to persecution]; *Fisher v. INS,* 291 F.3d 491 (8th Cir. 2002) [harassment and slurs due to Lutheran faith in Ukraine does not amount to persecution]; *Barreto-Claro v. U.S. Att'y Gen.,* 275 F.3d 1334, 1340 (11th Cir. 2001) [employment discrimination in Cuba when person fell out of favor with Communist Party that stops short of depriving an individual of a means of earning a living does not constitute persecution]; *Bucur v. INS*, 109 F.3d 399, 402–03 (7th Cir. 1997) [discrimination against Hungarian minority in Romania is not persecution]; *Faddoul v. INS*, 37 F.3d 185 (5th Cir. 1994) [Palestinian in Saudi Arabia]; *Ghaly v. INS*, 58 F.3d 1425, 1431 (9th Cir. 1995); *V-F-D-,* 23 I&N Dec. 859, 863–64 (BIA 2006) [discrimination in school, neighborhood and employment against non-Muslim in Egypt does not amount to past persecution]; *Matter of A-M-,* 23 I&N Dec. 737, 739–40 (BIA 2005) [discrimination and harassment based on Chinese ethnicity and Christian religion for Indonesian citizen insufficient]; *Matter of Salama,* 11 I&N Dec. 536 (BIA 1966). *But see Ouda v. INS,* 324 F.3d 445, 453–56 (6th Cir. 2003) [reversing BIA finding that conduct amounted to discrimination, not persecution, where Palestinians in Kuwait were deprived of food, water, a livelihood and the ability to leave the house as well as threatened and beaten up and ultimately expelled without full pension]; *Duarte de Guinac v. INS,*

179 F.3d 1156 (9th Cir. 1999) [reversing BIA finding of discrimination where Quiche Indians were physically abused in Guatemalan army]; *Korablina v. INS,* 158 F.3d 1038 (9th Cir. 1998) [reversing IJ finding of discrimination where repeated attacks against Jewish woman and her family in the Ukraine amounted to persecution]; *Singh v. INS*, 94 F.3d 1353, 1359 (9th Cir. 1996) [proof that persecutor discriminated against a group to which applicant belongs is *always* relevant to asylum]; *Matter of Salama*, 11 I&N Dec. 536 (BIA 1966) [Jewish professionals denied licenses to practice in their field due to government campaign of discrimination were persecuted].

3.i. *Economic Deprivation*—In *Matter of Acosta,* 19 I&N Dec. 211, 222 (BIA 1985), the BIA recognized that economic deprivation can be persecution if the deprivation is "so severe that [it] constitute[s] a threat to an individual's life or freedom." In *Matter of T-Z-,* 24 I&N Dec. 163, 170–72 (BIA 2007), the BIA reiterated and clarified its standard for persecution based upon economic deprivation. The BIA determined it requires "severe" deprivation as specified in H.R. Rep. No. 95-1452 at 5, as *reprinted in* 1978 U.S.C.C.A.N. 4700, 4704, 1978 WL 8575 and as stated in *Matter of Laipenieks* 18 I&N Dec. 433, 457 (BIA 1983) [the "deliberate imposition of severe economic disadvantage or the deprivation of liberty, food, housing, employment or other essentials of life"]. The Board also held the "economic difficulties must be above and beyond those generally shared by others in the country" but an applicant "need not demonstrate a total deprivation of livelihood or a total withdrawal of all economic opportunity in order to demonstrate harm amounting to persecution ... [because] ... [g]overnment sanctions that reduce an applicant to an impoverished existence may amount to persecution even if the victim retains the ability to afford the bare essentials of life" and thus a "particularly onerous fine, a large-scale confiscation of property, or a sweeping limitation of opportunities to continue to work in an established profession or business may amount to persecution." *Matter of T-Z-,* 24 I&N Dec. 163, 173–74 (BIA 2007) [reversed persecution finding and remanded for a new hearing to determine whether, for example, the applicant's spouse who was forced to abort due to claimed economic persecution had other sources of income if she lost her job as threatened]; *Mirzoyan v. Gonzales,* 457 F.3d 217 (2d Cir. 2006) [where ethnic Armenian in the Republic of Georgia suffered economic hardship, the case was remanded to the BIA prior to *Matter of T-Z-* to establish a consistent standard of economic persecution]; *Koval v. Gonzales,* 418 F.3d 798, 805–06 (7th Cir. 2005) [Ukrainian citizens of Mormon faith who demonstrated a "probability of deliberate imposition of substantial economic disadvantage" established past persecution due to economic hardship]; *Krotova v. Gonzales,* 416 F.3d 1080, 1084–85 (9th Cir. 2005) [sustained economic pressure because of anti-Semitism coupled with physical violence and restrictions on the practice of Judaism constituted persecution]; *Zhang v. Gonzales,* 408 F.3d 1239, 1247–50 (9th Cir. 2005) [cumulative effect of economic deprivation, denial of education and violence directed to applicant's father in her presence may amount to persecution]; *Li v. Att'y Gen. of the U.S.,* 400 F.3d 157, 164–70 (3d Cir. 2005) ["deliberate imposition of severe economic disadvantage which threatens a petitioner's life or freedom may constitute persecution"]; *Ghebremedhin v. Ashcroft,* 385 F.3d 1116, 1119, *modified*, 392 F.3d 214 (7th Cir. 2004) [reversing denial of asylum to Jehovah's Witness who fled Eritrea given the country's documented harsh treatment toward that group including preventing respondent from obtaining employment]; *Baballah v. Ashcroft,* 367 F.3d 1067 (9th Cir. 2004) [threats and attacks coupled with economic persecution that made it virtually impossible to earn a living constituted persecution]; *Ouda v. INS,* 324 F.3d 445, 453–56 (6th Cir. 2003) [Palestinians in Kuwait who were deprived of food, water, a livelihood and the ability to leave the house and were threatened and beaten up were persecuted]; *Borca v. INS*, 77 F.3d 210, 215–17 (7th Cir. 1996) [rejecting requirement that persecution must be total withdrawal of all economic opportunities instead of substantial deprivation]; *Surita v. INS*, 95 F.3d 814 (9th Cir. 1996) [Indo-Fijian subject to multiple robberies, home invasions, threats of rape and murder]; *Gonzalez v. INS*, 82 F.3d 903, 910 (9th Cir. 1996) [death threats, marking house, taking ration cards and property amounts to persecution]; *Kovac v. INS*, 407 F.2d 102 (9th Cir. 1969); *Dunat v. Hurney*, 297 F.2d 744 (3d Cir. 1961); *Matter of Salama*, 11 I&N Dec. 536 (BIA 1966); *Matter of Eusaph*, 10 I&N Dec. 453 (BIA 1964).

Economic Deprivation Insufficient—*Yun Jian Zhang v. Gonzales,* 495 F.3d 773, 776–78 (7th Cir. 2007) [damage to Chinese applicant's home due to his opposition to population control was not severe enough to constitute persecution]; *Makatengkeng v. Gonzales,* 495 F.3d 876,

882–84 (8th Cir. 2007) [Indonesian albino under any theory of economic persecution suffered only harassment]; *Musabelliu v. Gonzales,* 442 F.3d 991, 994–95 (7th Cir. 2006) [where general in Albanian military was dismissed because he sought to expose corruption, "losing a job is not persecution"]; *Ahmed v. Ashcroft,* 396 F.3d 1011, 1013–14 (8th Cir. 2005) [lack of employment because of membership in the Mohajir and Bihari ethnic groups in Pakistan is not persecution]; *Lie v. Ashcroft,* 396 F.3d 530, 536 (3d Cir. 2005) [robberies motivated by Chinese ethnicity in Indonesia without more is not persecution]; *Damko v. INS,* 430 F.3d 626 (2d Cir. 2005) [following *Acosta* and determining that Albanian's economic deprivation did not threaten his life or freedom under substantial evidence review]; *Gormley v. Ashcroft,* 364 F.3d 1172, 1177–80 (9th Cir. 2004), [white South African's loss of work and economic opportunities due to Employment Equity Act 55 of 1998 does not amount to persecution]; *Capric v. Ashcroft,* 355 F.3d 1075, 1092–95 (7th Cir. 2004) [loss of job, economic hardships and harassment do not amount to past or future persecution]; *Medhin v. Ashcroft,* 350 F.3d 685, 689 (7th Cir. 2003) [loss of one job due to Eritrean ethnicity is insufficient to show past persecution]; *Barreto-Claro v. U.S. Att'y Gen.,* 275 F.3d 1334, 1340 (11th Cir. 2001) [employment discrimination in Cuba when person fell out of favor with Communist Party that stops short of depriving an individual of a means of earning a living is not persecution]; *Sofinet v. INS,* 196 F.3d 742, 746–47 (7th Cir. 1999) [unhappiness with employment as police officer because of religious discrimination is not persecution]. *Matter of H-M-*, 20 I&N Dec. 683 (BIA 1993) [loss of ration card and deprivation of employment do not constitute persecution].

3.j. *Stripping Citizenship*—A government's decision to strip persons of their citizenship may be a form of persecution. *Haile v. Gonzales,* 421 F.3d 493, 495–96 (7th Cir. 2005) [decision to strip Eritreans of their Ethiopian citizenship based on ethnicity may be persecution and IJ was reversed for rejecting the claim]; *Giday v. Gonzales,* 434 F.3d 543, 553–54 (7th Cir. 2006) [same].

3.k. *Conscription by Guerilla Organizations is Not Per Se Persecution—INS v. Elias-Zacarias,* 502 U.S. 478 (1992); *Rodriguez Morales v. U.S. Att'y Gen.,* 488 F.3d 884 (11th Cir. 2007) [evidence did not compel a finding other than FARC persecuted applicant who was a dentist because they wanted his medical services]; *Sanchez v. U.S. Att'y Gen.,* 392 F.3d 434 (11th Cir. 2004) [Colombian fearing conscription by FARC denied asylum where no evidence of actual or imputed political opinion and no nexus between political opinion and alleged FARC persecution]; *Habtemicael v. Ashcroft,* 370 F.3d 774, 780 (8th Cir. 2004) [no persecution or well-founded fear for Ethiopian who successfully escaped conscription by EPLF]; *Velasquez-Valencia v. INS,* 244 F.3d 48 (1st Cir. 2001); *Tecun-Florian v. INS,* 207 F.3d 1107 (9th Cir. 2000) [no showing that torture by Guatemalan guerillas was on account of religion/politics]; *Pedro-Mateo v. INS,* 224 F.3d 1147 (9th Cir. 2000) [indigenous Indians not social group and therefore no evidence that conscription was on account of any characteristic]; *Sebastian-Sebastian v. INS,* 195 F.3d 504, 509 (9th Cir. 1999); *Matter of R-O-*, 20 I&N Dec. 455 (BIA 1992); *Matter of Vigil*, 19 I&N Dec. 572 (BIA 1988). *But see Rivas-Martinez v. INS*, 997 F.2d 1143 (5th Cir. 1993) [criticizing BIA's reasoning and application of *Elias-Zacarias* in forced conscription case]; *Maldonado-Cruz v. INS*, 883 F.2d 788 (9th Cir. 1989). Forcible recruitment or other harm resulting from generalized strife is not persecution. *Matter of Rodriguez-Majano*, 19 I&N Dec. 811 (BIA 1988).

3.l. *Civil War, General Conditions*—Harsh conditions shared by many, or general civil strife or anarchy are generally not considered persecution by the BIA and the courts. *Sela v. Mukasey,* 520 F.3d 44 (1st Cir. 2008) [rioting against Christians in Indonesia was reflective of civil unrest and do not rise to the level of persecution]; *Maryam v. Gonzales,* 421 F.3d 60, 63 (1st Cir. 2005) [denying Indonesian asylum case of moderate Muslim and noting that "evidence of widespread violence and human rights violations affecting all citizens is insufficient to establish persecution"]; *Al-Fara v. Gonzales,* 404 F.3d 733, 740 (3d Cir. 2005) [notwithstanding harsh conditions in Gaza, the denial of asylum to Palestinian involving 38-year-old incident was supported by substantial evidence]; *Awad v. Ashcroft,* 328 F.3d 336, 342 (7th Cir. 2003) [general evidence of mistreatment of women in Lebanon does not provide a basis for asylum]; *Gonzalez v. Reno,* 212 F.3d 1338, 1355 (11th Cir. 2000) [political conditions which affect the populace as a whole, such as re-education and indoctrination, are not synonymous with persecution]; *Matter of Sanchez and Escobar*, 19 I&N Dec. 276 (BIA 1985) [tragic and widespread violence affecting all Salvadorans as a result of civil strife and anarchy is not persecution]; *Rejaie v. INS*, 691 F.2d 139 (3d Cir. 1982); *Matter of T-*, 20 I&N Dec. 571 (BIA 1992) [violence in Sri Lanka in regard to Tamil Tigers is not ethnic or political persecution against Tamils generally]; *Matter of Janus and Janek*, 12 I&N Dec. 866, 876 (BIA 1968). But fear based on a specific ground is not negated simply because of general violence and disorder. *Konan v. Att'y Gen. of the U.S.*, 432 F.3d 497, 503–06 (3d Cir. 2005) [where gendarme in Côte d'Ivoire was killed by rebel forces, gendarme's son had imputed claim for asylum because attack was in part to kill government supporters, not simply police officers and general civil unrest does not negate claim]; *Vente v. Gonzales,* 415 F.3d 296, 301–02 (3d Cir. 2005) [IJ reversed where he mischaracterized claim as one regarding general conditions of violence in Colombia notwithstanding specific evidence of persecution]; *Ndom v. Ashcroft,* 384 F.3d 743, 752–56 (9th Cir. 2004) [person subject to past persecution where there is widespread civil strife need not show s/he has been "singled out" because to show s/he was appreciably different than the general population under strife would have the perverse effect of protecting governments that engage in widespread abuse]; *Eduard v. Ashcroft,* 379 F.3d 182, 190 (5th Cir. 2004) [IJ's denial of asylum and withholding for Indonesia Christian was reversed because it was not based solely upon general civil violence and disorder]. Moreover, the BIA has acknowledged "that persecution can and often does take place in the context of civil war. *Matter of Villalta*, 20 I&N Dec. 142 (BIA 1990)." *Matter of H-*, 21 I&N Dec. 337, 343 (BIA 1996) [interclan violence in Somalia]. Torture in the interrogation of a perceived dissident is grounds for asylum even if government had right to investigate. *Senathirajah v. INS,* 157 F.3d 210, 221–22 (3d Cir. 1998) [Sri Lankan tortured for information regarding Tamil Tigers].

3.m. *Laws of General Application*—Persecution may arise from laws of general application. *Beskovic v. Gonzales,* 467 F.3d 223, 226–27 (2d Cir. 2006) [reversing IJ denial where Muslim from Montenegro was detained, interrogated and beaten by Serbian police on two occasions ostensibly for violating general laws]; *Guchshenkov v. Ashcroft,* 366 F.3d 554, 559 (7th Cir. 2004) [reversing IJ for lack of a reasoned decision where he misunderstood concept that persecution can arise out of formally approved laws as in Nazi Germany].

3.n. *Prosecution*—Persecution does not generally include prosecution. *Tesfamichael v. Gonzales,* 469 F.3d 109, 117–18 (5th Cir. 2006) [Ethiopia's prosecution against smuggler during time of war was not persecution]; *Scheerer v. U.S. Att'y Gen.,* 445 F.3d 1311, 1315–17 (11th Cir. 2006) [chemist charged under Germany's racial hatred law and sentenced to 14 months for arguing there were no gas chambers at Auschwitz had no claim for persecution]; *Li v. Gonzales,* 420 F.3d 500, 507–11 (5th Cir. 2005) [applicant who was punished in China because of his religious belief, not entitled to withholding because his prosecution was pursuant to a law of general applicability regarding unregistered churches]; *Movsisian v. Ashcroft,* 395 F.3d 1095, 1097 (9th Cir. 2005) [Pentecostal Christian's fear of prosecution for refusing to perform military service without proof that he was targeted for conscription because of his religion is not persecution]; *Shardar v. Ashcroft,* 382 F.3d 318, 323–24 (3d Cir. 2004) [Bangladesh citizen who would be prosecuted for participating in violent demonstration did not establish persecution]; *Chanco v. INS,* 82 F.3d 298 (9th Cir. 1996) [fear of prosecution for involvement in military coup is not persecution]; *Castaneda v. INS,* 23 F.3d 1576, 1577–78 (10th Cir. 1994) [fear of mistaken prosecution not persecution]; *Behzadpour v. U.S.*, 946 F.2d 1351 (8th Cir. 1991) [fear of criminal charges for passport fraud]; *Mabugat v. INS*, 937 F.2d 426 (9th Cir. 1991) [criminal charges for fraud not persecution]; *Yang v. Carroll*, 852 F.Supp. 460, 466–68 (E.D. Va. 1994) [prosecution for assault when wife in PRC subject to forced sterilization is not persecution]; *Matter of H-M-,* 20 I&N Dec. 683 (BIA 1993) [punishment for black market sales and currency speculation is not persecution]. However, if prosecution is motivated by political opinion or another enumerated factor and the punishment is sufficiently serious, prosecution under a law of general applicability can be persecution. *Edimo-Doualla v. Gonzales,* 464 F.3d 276, 286–87 (2d Cir. 2006) [recognizing that there may be a political purpose to prosecution and that that the government would not "summon a political dissident with forms that indicate an intent to persecute"]; *Toure v. Att'y Gen. of the U.S.,* 443 F.3d 310, 321–22 (3d Cir. 2006) [former military officer who fled country because his family was in grave danger of being harmed by government officials could not have asylum denied on theory that his prosecution for desertion upon return would not be persecution because breaking a law to escape persecution cannot be considered prosecution upon return]; *Hoque v.*

Ashcroft, 367 F.3d 1190, 1197 (9th Cir. 2004) [IJ's determination that applicant's arrest for demonstration was prosecution was not supported by substantial evidence where applicant stated he was wrongly accused and government arresting opponents took power]; *Lin v. INS,* 238 F.3d 239, 244 (3d Cir. 2001) [reversing BIA denial of withholding and asylum to Chinese student who demonstrated during Tiananmen Square era despite being sought through lawful subpoena for arrest]. Persecution does not necessarily include:

(1) *Prosecution for Evading Military Service—Abdel-Rahman v. Gonzales,* 493 F.3d 444 (4th Cir. 2007) [applicant's potential punishment for desertion from military is not persecution]; *Rodriguez v. Gonzales,* 441 F.3d 593 (8th Cir. 2006) [no evidence that applicant was physically harmed or threatened on account of his refusal to join Guatemalan military or that he would be persecuted for evading service]; *Djedovic v. Gonzales,* 441 F.3d 547, 548–49 (7th Cir. 2006) [substantial evidence supported IJ's determination that Moslem Serbian would not suffer persecution for refusing conscription and facing imprisonment for military desertion]; *Pelinkovic v. Ashcroft,* 366 F.3d 532, 537–39 (7th Cir. 2004) [upholding BIA denial of motion to reopen by Montenegrins where evidence indicated only lukewarm, sporadic attempts to punish for avoiding Serbian military service]; *Mekhoukh v. Ashcroft,* 358 F.3d 118, 125–28 (1st Cir. 2004) [applicant failed to meet burden of proof on punishment for conscientious objection where he never requested alternative service]; *Foroglou v. INS,* 170 F.3d 68 (1st Cir.) [fear of prosecution for objection to military service not sufficient]; *Mojsilovic v. INS,* 156 F.3d 743 (7th Cir. 1998) [refusal to serve in Serbian army not enough for asylum without showing punishment for refusal]; *Alonzo v. INS*, 915 F.2d 546 (9th Cir. 1990); *Zepeda-Melendez v. INS*, 741 F.2d 285 (9th Cir. 1984); *Matter of A-G-*, 19 I&N Dec. 502 (BIA 1987), *aff'd sub nom. M.A. v. INS*, 899 F.2d 304 (4th Cir. 1990) (en banc) [refusal to serve in military not persecution unless disproportionately severe punishment]; *Matter of Vigil*, 19 I&N Dec. 572 (BIA 1988) [same, citing to Handbook ¶40]; *Matter of Canas*, 19 I&N Dec. 697 (BIA 1988) [religious objection to military service does not *per se* establish eligibility for asylum even if persecuted], *rev'd*, *Canas-Segovia v. INS*, 902 F.2d 717 (9th Cir. 1990), *aff'd on alternate grounds after remand*, 970 F.2d 599 (9th Cir. 1992) [affirmed on imputed political motive]; *Sadeghi v. INS*, 40 F.3d 1139 (10th Cir. 1994). *See also Harutyunyan v. Gonzales,* 421 F.3d 64, 69–70 (1st Cir. 2005) [no well-founded fear of persecution for ethnic Azeri's compulsory service in Armenian army]. *But see Toure v. Att'y Gen. of the U.S.,* 443 F.3d 310, 321–22 (3d Cir. 2006) [former military officer who fled country because his family was in grave danger of being harmed by government officials could not have asylum denied on theory that his prosecution for desertion upon return would not be persecution because breaking a law to escape persecution cannot be considered prosecution upon return]; *Ilchuk v. Att'y Gen. of the U.S.,* 434 F.3d 618, 624–26 (3d Cir. 2006) [reversing BIA denial of withholding for Pentecostal who refused service in Ukraine military; if certain religions are given alternative service while others are sent to jail, that would constitute religious persecution]; *Nuru v. Gonzales,* 404 F.3d 1207, 1227–29 (9th Cir. 2005) [tortured member of Eritrean military who spoke against war with Sudan and would face charges for desertion had well-founded fear]; *Ghebremedhin v. Ashcroft,* 385 F.3d 1116, 1120 *amended* 392 F.3d 214 (7th Cir. 2004) [reversing denial of asylum for Jehovah's Witness who would have suffered harsher treatment than others for his refusal to serve in the Eritrean military]; *Lukwago v. Ashcroft,* 329 F.3d 157 167–70 (3d Cir. 2003) [distinguishing *Elias-Zacarias* and finding that forced conscription by guerrillas engaged in attacks on the government is different than evading country's military laws].

Evasion of military service can be grounds for fear of future persecution where person would "suffer disproportionately severe punishment for the military offense" on account of one of the specified grounds, Handbook ¶169; *Matter of R-R*, 20 I&N Dec. 547 (BIA 1992), or "where the type of military action ... is condemned by the international community as contrary to basic rules of human conduct." Handbook ¶170-71; *Barraza-Rivera v. INS*, 913 F.2d 1443 (9th Cir. 1990) [where applicant forcibly recruited into military and given a choice to assassinate 2 men or be killed, his refusal was tantamount to conscientious objection]; *Tagaga v. INS,* 228 F.3d 1030 (9th Cir. 2000) [officer who went AWOL because he would face trial for treason in Fiji as a result of his refusal to disassociate with Indo-Fijians entitled to asylum and withholding]; *Ramos-Vasquez v. INS*, 57 F.3d 857 (9th Cir. 1995). *See also Miljkovic v. Ashcroft,* 376 F.3d 754 (7th Cir. 2004) [Croatian who was drafted solely for hazardous duty because of his opposition to Milosevic regime and place of birth has well-founded fear]; *Vujisic v. INS,* 224 F.3d 578 (7th Cir. 2000) [Slovenian who was drafted into Serbian military and fled after beatings and accusation that he was a spy based on ethnicity]; *Islami v. Gonzales,* 412 F.3d 391, 396–97 (2d Cir. 2005) [forcing a Muslim/ethnic Albanian soldier to serve in Yugoslavian army whose military campaigns were "condemned by the international community as contrary to the basic rules of human conduct" and were "directed at members of the [soldier's] own race, religion, nationality or social or political group" is sufficient to establish persecution, although the government rebutted the claim because of changed circumstances].

(2) *Prosecution for Evading Exit Visa Laws—Matter of Sibrun,* 18 I&N Dec. 354 (BIA 1983); *Lin v. DOJ,* 432 F.3d 156 (2d Cir. 2005) [CAT claim based solely on fact that applicant is part of the large class of persons who illegally departed China and who may be subject to administrative detention where some people have been tortured is insufficient to establish claim absent particularized evidence]; *Barreto-Claro v. U.S. Att'y Gen.,* 275 F.3d 1334, 1340 (11th Cir. 2001) [prosecution for violating Cuba's travel laws is not persecution]; *Si v. Slattery*, 864 F.Supp. 397, 406 (S.D.N.Y. 1994); *Henry v. INS*, 552 F.2d 130 (5th Cir. 1977); *Yang v. Carroll*, 852 F.Supp. 460, 468 (E.D. Va. 1994); *Edmond v. Nelson*, 575 F.Supp. 532 (E.D. La. 1983); *Matter of Leon-Orosco and Rodriguez-Colas,* 19 I&N Dec. 136 (AG 1984) [Cubans leaving from Mariel does not constitute a social group]. *But see Yi-Tu Lian v. Ashcroft,* 379 F.3d 457 (7th Cir. 2004) [possible CAT claim for person smuggled to U.S. where it is illegal for Chinese citizen to emigrate without government permission and government was likely to discover he had returned]; *Al-Harbi v. INS,* 242 F.3d 882, 893–94 (9th Cir. 2001) [illegal departure from Iraq by U.S. evacuation designed to save Iraqi dissidents does not bar claim of future persecution]; *Rodriguez-Roman v. INS*, 98 F.3d 416, 431 (9th Cir. 1996) [three-year sentence would be severe punishment triggering persecution]; *Chang v. INS*, 119 F.3d 1055 (3d Cir. 1997) [prosecution under China's state security law may be persecution]; *Coriolan v. INS*, 559 F.2d 993, 1000 (5th Cir. 1977); *Sovich v. Esperdy,* 319 F.2d 21, 29 (2d Cir. 1963) [imprisonment for violating exit visa laws may constitute persecution]; *Matter of Janus and Janek*, 12 I&N Dec. 866 (BIA 1968).

(3) *Expulsion as Noncitizen During Wartime*—Memo, Miller, Acting Asst. Comm., HQ 1453-C (June 18, 1993), *reprinted in* 70 No. 31 *Interpreter Releases* 1068, 1088–89 (Aug. 16, 1993) [Palestinians from Saudi Arabia].

(4) *Enforcement of Dress and Conduct Rules Concerning Women in Moslem Countries—Fisher v. INS*, 79 F.3d 955, 961–62 (9th Cir. 1996) (en banc); *Sharif v. INS*, 87 F.3d 932 (7th Cir. 1996) [same].

3.o. *Intent to Harm Distinct from Persecution*—An applicant is not required to prove that the persecutor engaged in persecution with the malignant or punitive intent to harm. It is not the persecutor's subjective intent that is relevant, but rather the objective persecution, whatever his reason. *Pitcherskaia v. INS*, 118 F.3d 641 (9th Cir. 1997) [applicant institutionalized to "cure" her of homosexuality was persecuted]; *Matter of Kasinga*, 21 I&N Dec. 357, 365–67 (BIA 1996) [subjective, punitive, or malignant intent to harm is not required].

3.p. *Breach of Confidentiality of Asylum*—Persecution may arise from violation of the confidentiality provision. *Zhen Nan Lin v. DOJ,* 459 F.3d 255, 260–68 (2d Cir. 2006) [where consulate violated the confidentiality provision of 8 C.F.R. §208.6 (now §1208.6) by asking the Chinese government to verify certain documents, it created a "new risk of persecution … independent of [the applicant's] original claim" and the court remanded the case for a new hearing finding that the government's interpretation of the regulation as only pertaining to "sensitive" information is inconsistent with the plain language of the regulation and its own prior interpretations]. *See also Corovic v. Mukasey,* 519 F.3d 90, 95-96 (2d Cir. 2008) [U.S. government's request to Macedonian government to verify documents violated confidentiality provision of 8 C.F.R. §208.6 (now §1208.6) and the court, following *Zhen Nan Lin* prohibited the use of the Macedonian government's report and remanded the case but left open the possibility that the IJ could make the same finding that the document was fraudulent based upon other evidence]. *See generally* Memo, Cooper, G.C., "Confidentiality of Asylum Applications and Overseas Verification of Documents and Application Information" (June 21, 2001), *http://judiciary.house.gov/legacy/82238.pdf, but see Averianova v. Mukasey,* 509 F.3d 890, 897–900 (8th Cir. 2007) [under Bo Cooper memo disclosures would have to give rise to a reasonable inference that the person has applied for asylum and in this case the request to the Uzbek government for copies of applicants' birth certificates did not]; *Abdel-Rahman v. Gonzales,* 493 F.3d 444, 453–54 (4th Cir. 2007) [where DHS did disclose existence of asylum application to Egyptian Embassy, court dismissed argument that it was a separate basis for asylum because his fears of government retaliation were already outlined and there was no need for a remand].

Exceptions to Confidentiality—There are exceptions, including the use of information in defense of a legal action or a U.S. criminal or civil investigation. 8 C.F.R. §§208.6(c), 1208.6(c); Memo, Langlois, Director, Asylum Division, USCIS, HQASM 120/12.8 (June 15, 2005), *published on* AILA InfoNet at Doc. No. 05062440 (May 24, 2005) [ICE and CBP may have access to information as they are not considered third parties under the regulations; information contained in RAPS and APSS system should not be disclosed to third parties except in the limited circumstances stated under §208.6(c)]. An officer may not disclose information to unauthorized third parties even if the applicant makes it public because the applicant must provide written consent. *Id.* The U.S. has also entered into an agreement with Canada through a *Statement of Mutual Understanding on Information Sharing* that permits exchanging information and records on a case-by-case basis which may include asylum applications and information. Memo, Aguirre, Acting Director, USCIS, HQIAO 120/12.8 (July 28, 2003), *published on* AILA InfoNet at Doc. No. 03102790].

3.q. *Single Incident Sufficient*—A single incident can be sufficient to find persecution. *Corado v. Ashcroft,* 384 F.3d 945 (8th Cir. 2004) [reversing IJ who denied asylum because the single incident at respondent's home did not constitute a pattern and practice of mistreatment]; *But see Chen v. Ashcroft,* 381 F.3d 221, 234–35 (3d Cir. 2004) [isolated incidents that do not result serious injury not persecution]; *Dandan v. Ashcroft,* 339 F.3d 567, 573–74 (7th Cir. 2003) [same].

3.r. *Periodic Persecution*—Arrests need not be imminent at the time applicant leaves his country. He may even return to his home country for a short period of time or leave his country without difficulty. INS Supplementary Refugee/Asylum Adjudications Guidelines, *reprinted in* 67 No. 4 *Interpreter Releases* 85, 101–02 (Jan. 22, 1990)

3.s. *Persecution Should be Treated Cumulatively*—The severity of each incident should not be addressed in isolation without considering the cumulative effect of events. *De Santamaria v. U.S. Att'y Gen.,* ___ F.3d ___ (11th Cir. Apr. 22, 2008) [IJ denial of past persecution reversed where Colombian suffered cumulative persecution by FARC where they repeatedly threatened her, twice physically attacked her including dragging her out of her vehicle by her hair, tortured and murdered a family friend who refused to give information on her whereabouts, and finally kidnapped and beat her, although she eventually escaped]; *Niftaliev v. U.S. Att'y Gen.,* 504 F.3d 1211, 1217 (11th Cir. 2007) [cumulative effects of discrimination in Ukraine due to mixed ethnicity, beatings, arrests, searches and interrogations for speaking out in Ukraine, 15 day detention where he was deprived of food, beaten, and threatened at gunpoint, and beatings and threats after he left country by Ukrainian officials in Argentina warranted past persecution]; *Mejia v. Att'y Gen. of the U.S.,* 498 F.3d 1253 (11th Cir. 2007) [IJ reversed where Colombian who was member of Liberal Party was threatened over 18-month period, had large rock thrown at him, was hit by FARC members with butt of rifle, breaking his nose, and was sent written death threat *cumulatively* faced past persecution]; *Manzur v. DHS,* 494 F.3d 281, 289–90 (2d Cir. 2007) [IJ reversed where he made numerous legal errors and he maintained a practice of dividing the patterns of harm against the wife of a former executed general in Bangladesh instead of explaining their cumulative effect]; *Tchemkou v. Gonzales,* 493 F.3d 785, 790–92 (7th Cir. 2007) [where Cameroonian woman endured serious bodily harm on 2 occasions, was threatened with additional retaliation, and had her freedom curtailed the cumulative *Delgado v. U.S. Att'y Gen.,* 487 F.3d 855, 861 (11th Cir. 2007) [Venezuelan who had gun pointed at him and his son, suffered numerous threats, son beaten, and car vandalized twice had established past persecution]; *Jiang v. Gonzales,* 485 F.3d 992, 997 (7th Cir. 2007) [where IJ in Chinese Christian case focused solely on beating without looking at the entire sequence of events, the denial of past persecution was reversed]; *Gjolaj v. USCIS,* 468 F.3d 140, 142–43 (2d Cir. 2006) [reversing IJ where he did not treat arrests of Albanian cumulatively]; *Ruiz v. Gonzales,* 479 F.3d 762, 767 (11th Cir. 2007) [reversing IJ/BIA where applicant established that cumulative actions constituted past persecution and ICE failed to establish by preponderance of the evidence that applicant could reasonably relocate within Colombia]; *Edimo-Doualla v. Gonzales,* 464 F.3d 276, 283–84 (2d Cir. 2006) [reversing BIA denial of asylum in Cameroonian case where IJ considered incidents of persecution separately instead of cumulatively]; *Cecaj v. Gonzales,* 440 F.3d 897 (7th Cir. 2007) [IJ reversed on denial of past persecution where he failed to consider cumulative evidence concerning member of Democratic Party of Albania]; *Poradisova v. Gonzales,* 420 F.3d 70, 79–81 (2d Cir. 2005) [reversing BIA denial of asylum where it ignored the Handbook requirements that events be viewed cumulatively instead of in isolation]; *Krotova v. Gonzales,* 416 F.3d 1080, 1084–85 (9th Cir. 2005) [cumulative effect of mistreatment due to anti-Semitism in Russia amounted to persecution]. This also means that events should be treated correlatively, and not as merely coincidental. *Beskovic v. Gonzales,* 467 F.3d 223, 226–27 (2d Cir. 2006) [reversing IJ denial where Muslim from Montenegro was detained, interrogated and beaten by Serbian police on two occasions and IJ failed to consider the context of the actions].

4. *Government Unable or Unwilling to Control Persecutors*—The applicant must be unable or unwilling to avail him- or herself of the protection of the country of persecution. Therefore, it must be shown that the persecution is inflicted either by the government or by persons or organizations the government is unable or unwilling to control. *Nabulwala v. Gonzales,* 481 F.3d 1115 (8th Cir. 2007) [reversing denial of asylum to lesbian from Uganda where IJ made no findings as to whether the government was unable or unwilling to control others]. The applicant is not required to demonstrate that the government/police refused to protect him or that the refusal was on account of one of the enumerated grounds. *Valdiviezo-Galdamez v. Att'y Gen.,* 502 F.3d 285, 288–29 (3d Cir. 2007) [IJ erred when he held that Honduran claiming persecution from gang members was required to prove that the government "refused" to protect him and that the refusal was on account of his particular social group or opinion]. The applicant is also not required to report third-party persecution to government authorities as a condition for seeking withholding based upon such persecution where it would be futile or result in further abuse. *Lopez v. U.S. Att'y Gen.,* 504 F.3d 1341, 1345 (11th Cir. 2007) [remanding case to BIA because applicant's failure to report to police does not automatically bar relief where applicant can demonstrate under *Matter of S-A-* that the authorities would have been unable or unwilling to protect her and for that reason she could not rely on them]; *Ornelas-Chavez v. Gonzales,* 458 F.3d 1052, 1057 (9th Cir. 2006) [failure to report an incident of persecution by private parties is not required if doing so would be futile or subject the applicant to further abuse]. However, where the applicant does report persecution to the government and the government provides a prompt response, it may be telling evidence of the government's willingness to protect him. *Ortiz-Araniba v. Keisler,* 505 F.3d 39, 42 (1st Cir. 2007) [where woman from El Salvador claiming persecution by member of Mara Salvatrucha gang reported him to police and he was promptly arrested, substantial evidence supported denial of future persecution claim because government was willing to protect her].

Cases Reversing Denial of Relief: *Pavlova v. INS,* 441 F.3d 82, 91–92 (2d Cir. 2006) [reversing IJ who required applicant to show persecution by the government despite claim that the Russian government was unwilling to control the RNU's persecution of Baptists]; *Fiadjoe v. Att'y Gen. of the U.S.,* 411 F.3d 135, 160–63 (3d Cir. 2005) [reversing BIA denial of asylum of woman who was sexually and emotionally abused by her father who was priest in Trokosi sect in Ghana where DOS country report indicated that it would have been futile for her to go to police]; *Deloso v. Ashcroft,* 393 F.3d 907, 858, 866 n.5 (9th Cir. 2005) [government unwilling or unable to stop persecution in rural Philippines where applicant had to travel two hours to the nearest police station and persecution escalated after he reported incidents to police]; *Faruk v. Ashcroft,* 378 F.3d 940, 944 (9th Cir. 2004) [police provided no assistance in investigating or protecting an inter-religious Fijian couple from harm]; *Avetova-Elisseva v. INS,* 213 F.3d 1192 (9th Cir. 2000) [Armenian in

Russia had well-founded fear based on ethnicity, in light of the "pattern and practice" of persecution that Russian authorities were unable or unwilling to stop]; *Mgoian v. INS,* 184 F.3d 1029, 1036 (9th Cir. 1999) [Armenian government is unable or unwilling to stop persecution of Kurdish-Moslem families]; *Singh v. INS*, 94 F.3d 1353, 1360 (9th Cir. 1996) [Indo-Fijian reported assaults to police who took no action]; *Gomez-Saballos v. INS*, 79 F.3d 912 (9th Cir. 1996) [reversing denial where former prison director would be subject to persecution by former National Guardsmen and documentary evidence supported claim that government is unable to control them]; *Sotelo-Aquije v. Slattery*, 17 F.3d 33, 37 (2d Cir. 1994) [reversing denial of asylum for persecution by Sendero Luminoso]; *McMullen v. INS*, 658 F.2d 1312, 1315 (9th Cir. 1981); *Matter of S-A-*, 22 I&N Dec. 1328, 1333, 1335 (BIA 2000) [Moroccan government would have been unable or unwilling to control orthodox Muslim father from abusing his daughter]; *Matter of Tan*, 12 I&N Dec. 564 (BIA 1967)

Cases Upholding Denial: *Sidabutar v. Gonzales,* 503 F.3d 1116, 1124 (10th Cir. 2007) [applicant could not demonstrate that the government was unable or unwilling to protect Christian in Indonesian from persecution]; *Garcia v. Gonzales,* 500 F.3d 615 (7th Cir. 2007) [Colombian applicant was unable to demonstrate that government was unwilling to provide protection from the FARC]; *Lolong v. Gonzales,* 484 F.3d 1173, 1178–81 (9th Cir. 2007) (en banc) [relying on fears common to Chinese Christian women in Indonesia was insufficient to establish asylum where no claim that individual was targeted and no showing that the government was unable or unwilling to stop persecution based on DOS reports]; *Nikijuluw v. Gonzales,* 427 F.3d 115, 120–22 (1st Cir. 2005) [no evidence that government sponsored, supported or condoned sporadic instances of discrimination and violence against Christian Indonesians by Muslims]; *Harutyunyan v. Gonzales,* 421 F.3d 64, 68–69 (1st Cir. 2005) [where police investigated and made arrests in incidents involving physical violence and arson by Armenian locals against applicant because of his Azeri ethnicity, no showing that government was involved in the persecution]; *Menjivar v. Gonzales,* 416 F.3d 918, 920–21 (8th Cir. 2005) [failure of police to respond promptly to attack by Salvadoran gang member does not mean the government is unable or unwilling to stop persecution; applicant must show the government has condoned it or is completely helpless to protect against it]; *Castro-Perez v. Gonzales*, 409 F.3d 1069, 1072 (9th Cir. 2005) [respondent who was raped twice by head of local gang in Honduras failed to demonstrate that government was unable or unwilling to stop rape even if it was assumed to be persecution against member of a social group]; *Adebisi v. INS*, 952 F.2d 910, 914 (5th Cir. 1992) [government unwillingness to protect applicant not found where applicant was afraid to approach the government for protection for personal reasons].

5. *On Account of Race, Religion, National Origin, Political Opinion, or Membership in a Particular Social Group*—The applicant must demonstrate that the persecution is "on account of" one of the five enumerated grounds. *See INS v. Elias-Zacarias*, 502 U.S. 478 (1992) [fear of forced recruitment by guerillas must be "on account of" or because of applicant's political opinion]. An applicant is not required to prove that the persecutor acted with the malignant or punitive intent to harm. *Matter of Kasinga*, 21 I&N Dec. 357, 365 (BIA 1996). It is not the persecutor's subjective intent that is relevant, but rather the objective persecution, whatever his reason. *Pitcherskaia v. INS*, 118 F.3d 641 (9th Cir. 1997) [applicant subject to institutionalization to "cure" her of being gay was persecution; rejecting *Matter of Mogharrabi* definition to the extent it confuses punishment and persecution]. The fact that a persecutor's threat has an entirely rational and strategic purpose behind it does not diminish the persecution. *Montecino v. INS*, 915 F.2d 518, 520 (9th Cir. 1990).

5.a. *Persecutor's Views as an Element*— A determination of persecution requires more than an inquiry into whether the applicant's persecution arises out of race, religion, national origin, political opinion or membership in a particular social group. It requires an examination of the persecutor's views of the applicant's actions or lack of action. *INS v. Elias-Zacarias*, 502 U.S. 478 (1992); *Muhur v. Ashcroft,* 355 F.3d 958 (7th Cir. 2004) [reversing IJ's determination that Jehovah's Witness was not entitled to asylum because she could escape notice by hiding her religion without looking at persecutor's motives in suppressing religion]; *Avetova-Elisseva v. INS,* 213 F.3d 1192 (9th Cir. 2000) [Armenian in Russia who could not establish past persecution could establish a well-founded fear in light of the "pattern and practice" of persecution which Russian authorities were unable or unwilling to stop]. However, the victim's political opinion (or one of the other enumerated categories) is the relevant criterion, not the persecutor's for determining whether a person has been persecuted "on account of" an enumerated ground. *Elias-Zacarias, supra. See also in this section*, "Imputed Political Opinion," ¶ 5.b(2) (p.449), *infra.*

5.b. *Political Opinion*—According to the BIA, political opinion requires an active specific opinion or belief. However, one need not use the word "political" in order to express a political view. *Bu v. Gonzales,* 490 F.3d 424 (6th Cir. 2007) [demonstrating against government corruption in China resulting in persecution]; *Fedunyak v. Gonzales,* 477 F.3d 1126, 1129–30 (9th Cir. 2007) [political opinion expressed through whistleblowing where Ukrainian involved in the automobile business complained to higher government officials about local officials and police extortion and corruption]; *Sagaydak v. Gonzales*, 405 F.3d 1035, 1041–45 (9th Cir. 2005) [retaliation against government auditor for exposing corruption in a private company in the context of political reforms rooting out corruption in the Ukraine met both the imputed political opinion and the "on account of" criteria for asylum]; *Mamouzian v. Ashcroft*, 390 F.3d 1129, 1134–35 (9th Cir. 2004) [reversing IJ's determination that Armenian, who was persecuted because she wrote about public corruption, cannot state a basis for asylum]; *Hasan v. Ashcroft*, 380 F.3d 1114, 1120–21 (9th Cir. 2004) [exposing government corruption by publishing article constituted a political statement]; *Grava v. INS*, 205 F.3d 1177, 1181–82 (9th Cir. 2000) [whistleblowing may be a political opinion]; *Reyes-Guerrero v. INS*, 192 F.3d 1241 (9th Cir. 1999) [Colombian prosecutor forced into exile by repeated threats after prosecuting members of another political party]; *Chang v. INS*, 119 F.3d 1055, 1062 n.4 (3d Cir. 1997) [explanation for failure to report persons to Chinese authorities is political opinion]. *But see Li v. Gonzales*, 416 F.3d 681, 685 (7th Cir. 2005) [upholding denial where Chinese woman was harassed due to her desire to cohabitate with her boyfriend]. In addition, one circuit has raised the issue that in light of the Supreme Court's decision in *Garcetti v. Ceballos,* 543 U.S. 1186 (2005) that characterized the speech of government employees pursuant to their official duties as not free speech protected by the First Amendment, it would be anomalous to grant asylum to prosecutors because they speak out against corruption. *Pavlyk v. Gonzales,* 469 F.3d 1082, 1089 (7th Cir. 2006). Political opinion also encompasses more than electoral political and formal political ideology or action. *Ahmed v. Keisler,* 504 F.3d 1183, 1193–98 (9th Cir. 2007) [reversed BIA determination that Bihari living in Bangladesh was not persecuted on account of his political opinion where he voiced his opposition through a hunger strike and demonstrations to the treatment of Biharis];

(1) *Neutrality as Political Opinion*—The BIA has rejected the concept that neutrality constitutes political opinion. *Matter of Acosta*, 19 I&N Dec. 211 (BIA 1985) [member of taxi co-op who was threatened by guerrillas for failure to participate in work stoppage had a position of neutrality not a "political opinion"]; *Matter of Maldonado-Cruz*, 19 I&N Dec. 509 (BIA 1988) [denying asylum to Salvadoran who feared persecution from government and guerrillas after being kidnapped by guerrillas because he remained neutral], *rev'd*, *Maldonado-Cruz v. INS*, 883 F.2d 788 (9th Cir. 1989); *Matter of Vigil*, 19 I&N Dec. 572 (BIA 1988). The BIA has even asserted that torture to obtain information about a militant Sikh organization is not a basis for asylum because "the purpose of the mistreatment was to extract information ... rather than to persecute the applicant because of his political opinion." *Matter of R-*, 20 I&N Dec. 621 (BIA 1992), *remanded sub nom. Rana v. Moschorak*, 37 F.3d 1506 (9th Cir. 1994). The courts, however, have taken a different view. *See Sangha v. INS,* 103 F.3d 1482, 1488 (9th Cir. 1997) [recognizing the doctrine of "hazardous neutrality" where showing neutrality in an environment in which political neutrality is fraught with hazard may constitute political opinion]; *Canas-Segovia v. INS*, 970 F.2d 599, 601 (9th Cir. 1992) [reading *Elias-Zacarias* as permitting imputed motive]; *Ramirez-Rivas v. INS*, 899 F.2d 864 (9th Cir.), *vacated on other grounds*, 502 U.S. 1025 (1992); *Novoa-Umania v. INS*, 896 F.2d 1, 3 (1st Cir. 1990) [establishing tripartite test for neutrality]; *Maldonado-Cruz v. INS*, 883 F.2d 788 (9th Cir. 1989); *Argueta v. INS*, 759 F.2d 1395 (9th Cir. 1985); *Bolanos-Hernandez v. INS*, 767 F.2d 1277 (9th Cir. 1984) [position of neutrality during civil war can constitute political opinion]; *Coriolan v. INS*, 559 F.2d 993, 1000–02 (5th Cir. 1977). The neutrality must be the result of an affirmative decision to remain neutral rather than mere apathy. *Lopez v. INS*, 775 F.2d 1015 (9th Cir. 1985).

(2) *Imputed Political Opinion*—The courts, the BIA and INS General Counsel have recognized that imputed political opinion can exist no matter what the asylum seeker's actual political opinion may be. *INS v. Elias-Zacarias*, 502 U.S. 478 (1992). An asylum applicant claiming imputed political opinion is not required to have any knowledge about the political belief that is being imputed to him. *Singh v. Gonzales,* 406 F.3d 191, 196–97 (3d Cir. 2005) [reversing IJ's denial of asylum in Sikh mixed-motive case]. *See also Delgado v. Mukasey,* 508 F.3d 702, 706–07 (2d Cir. 2007) [reversed BIA's denial of asylum where kidnapping was due to petitioner's expertise in computers, but her refusal to provide assistance could be imputed political opinion and viewed as political betrayal]; *Ahmed v. Keisler,* 504 F.3d 1183, 1194–95 (9th Cir. 2007) [where applicant was beaten when captured with his uncle suggests the army imputed uncle's political onion to him]; *Vumi v. Gonzales,* 502 F.3d 150, 155–59 (2d Cir. 2007) [remanded to determine if persecution of the wife of the bodyguard of Kabila at time he was assassinated in the DRC could be on account of imputed political opinion relying on criteria in *Matter of S-P-*]; *Koudriachova v. Gonzales,* 490 F.3d 255, 263–64 (2d Cir. 2007) [reversed BIA denial of asylum to defected KGB agent where BIA confused applicant's imputed political claim regarding future persecution with a requirement to demonstrate past persecution]; *Uwais v. U.S. Att'y Gen.,* 478 F.3d 513, 517–18 (2d Cir. 2007) [where police arrested, beat and sexually assaulted applicant because *they* believed she was affiliated with the Tamil Tigers, BIA denial was reversed on grounds of imputed political opinion]; *Tun v. INS,* 445 F.3d 554, 570–71 (2d Cir. 2006) [political activities that give rise to persecution do not require applicant to be motivated by political beliefs and IJ's claim that Burmese citizen's engagement in pro-democracy movement in the U.S. was self-serving was insufficient to support denial]; *Zhou v. Gonzales,* 437 F.3d 860, 868–69 (9th Cir. 2006) [Chinese government perceived applicant as supporter of Falun Gong and anti-government because she brought articles into country critical of government's treatment of Falun Gong]; *Kumar v. Gonzales,* 444 F.3d 1043, 1053–54 (9th Cir. 2006) [the fact that Indian police imputed to applicant a political opinion associated with a Muslim separatist group in Jammu and Kashmir was a sufficient nexus for asylum]; *Konan v. Att'y Gen. of the U.S.,* 432 F.3d 497, 503–06 (3d Cir. 2005) [where gendarme in Côte d'Ivoire was killed by rebel forces in attack, gendarme's son had imputed claim for asylum because attack was in part to kill government supporters not simply police officers; distinguishing *Matter of Fuentes*]; *Gao v. Gonzales,* 424 F.3d 122, 129 (2d Cir. 2005) [reversing IJ denial of asylum where court focused on whether applicant was a follower of Falun Gong instead of whether authorities would have perceived him as such]; *Nakibuka v. Gonzales,* 421 F.3d 473, 478–79 (7th Cir. 2005) [soldiers imputed political opinion to housekeeper of prominent political opponent of Ugandan regime]; *Zhang v. Gonzales,* 408 F.3d 1239, 1246–47 (9th Cir. 2005) [parents' refusal and resistance to forced abortion is imputed political opinion to child]; *De Brenner v. Ashcroft,* 388 F.3d 629, 635–39 (8th Cir. 2004) [where Shining Path mistakenly imputed political involvement to wealthy Peruvian, BIA's decision that persecution was based on wealth and not due to a protected ground was reversed]; *Jahed v. INS,* 356 F.3d 991 997–1001 (9th Cir. 2004) [where Iranian soldier extorted respondent on threat to expose him to the government as a former member of the Mujahedin, respondent had well-founded fear on account of political reasons]; *Ndom v. Ashcroft,* 384 F.3d 743, 752–56 (9th Cir. 2004) [where membership in an organization was imputed to applicant by Senegalese authorities resulting in his persecution, IJ's denial of asylum was reversed]; *Garcia-Martinez v. Ashcroft,* 371 F.3d 1066, 1074–78 (9th Cir. 2004) [rape of applicant was persecution on account of imputed political opinion because Guatemalan soldiers mistakenly believed villagers were aiding guerillas]; *Mejia v. Ashcroft,* 298 F.3d 873, 877–80 (9th Cir. 2002) [confidential informant had imputed political opinion]; *Rios v. Ashcroft,* 287 F.3d 895, 900–01 (9th Cir. 2002) [family of murdered Guatemalan army officer who were kidnapped and threatened established persecution because imputed political opinion]; *Ventura v. INS,* 264 F.3d 1150 (9th Cir. 2001), *rev'd on other grounds,* 537 U.S. 12, (2002) [where applicant's family was closely associated with military and were targeted because of military affiliation, and where applicant was readily associated with pro-military and anti-guerrillas views and received death threats, persecution was on account of imputed political opinion, notwith-

standing his lack of knowledge of guerrillas]; *Al-Harbi v. INS,* 242 F.3d 882 (9th Cir. 2001) [finding well-founded fear of future persecution for person opposed to Hussein, who was airlifted out of Iraq by U.S. because the Iraqi government would treat him as a traitor]; *Agbuya v. INS,* 241 F.3d 1224, 1229- 31 (9th Cir. 2001) [Communist guerillas in Philippines imputed political motive to former employee of mining company who was perceived to be against workers]; *Lim v. INS,* 224 F.3d 929, 934 (9th Cir. 2000) [Philippine intelligence officer threatened with death by Communist group he infiltrated]; *Navas v. INS,* 217 F.3d 646, 658–62 (9th Cir. 2000) [soldiers' action against respondent was based in part on his family's political association and resulting imputed political opinion]; *Chanchavac v. INS,* 207 F.3d 584, 591–92 (9th Cir. 2000) [Guatemalan military imputed guerrilla sympathy to applicant]; *Yazitchian v. INS,* 207 F.3d 1164 (9th Cir. 2000) [in case involving extortion and imputed political opinion, court reversed BIA denial and found that *Elias-Zacarias* did not overrule *Desir*]; *Briones v. INS,* 175 F.3d 727 (9th Cir. 1999) (en banc) [informant in ideological struggle had imputed political opinion]; *Cf. Vasquez v. INS,* 177 F.3d 62 (1st Cir. 1999) [where applicant witnessed political assassination and forced to tell police no imputed political opinion]; *Ratnam v. INS,* 154 F.3d 990 (9th Cir. 1999) [rejecting claim that torture was legitimate intelligence gathering]; *Vera-Valera v. INS,* 147 F.3d 1036 (9th Cir. 1998) [president of street vendors had imputed political opinion]; *Meza-Manay v. INS*, 139 F.3d 759, 764 (9th Cir. 1998) [imputed political motive by Shining Path sufficient for asylum]; *Gomez-Saballos v. INS*, 79 F.3d 912 (9th Cir. 1996) [Nicaraguan prison director threatened by former inmate who was member of Somoza national guard had well-founded fear based on political opinion]; *Singh v. Ilchert*, 63 F.3d 1501 (9th Cir. 1995); *Osorio v. INS*, 18 F.3d 1017, 1029–31 (2d Cir. 1994) [union activity posed a political threat]; *Shirazi-Parsa v. INS*, 14 F.3d 1424, 1430 (9th Cir. 1994) *overruled on other grounds by Fisher v. INS,* 79 F.3d 955 (9th Cir. 1996) (en banc); *Carranza-Hernandez v. INS*, 12 F.3d 4 (2d Cir. 1993) [persecutor's motive was related to union activity]; *Canas-Segovia v. INS*, 970 F.2d 599 (9th Cir. 1992); *Desir v. Ilchert*, 840 F.2d 723 (9th Cir. 1988); *Maldonado-Cruz v. INS*, 883 F.2d 788 (9th Cir. 1989); *Lazo-Majano v. INS*, 813 F.2d 1432, 1435 (9th Cir. 1987); *Hernandez-Ortiz v. INS*, 777 F.2d 509, 517 (9th Cir. 1985); *Sovich v. Esperdy*, 319 F.2d 21 (2d Cir. 1963); *Yiu Sing Chun v. Sava*, 708 F.2d 869 (2d Cir. 1983); *Ratnam v. Lewis*, 892 F.Supp. 619, 638 (D.N.J. 1995); *Rajaratnam v. Moyer*, 832 F.Supp. 1219 (N.D. Ill. 1993); *Matter of S-P-*, 21 I&N Dec. 486, 489–90 (BIA 1996); *Matter of Izatula*, 20 I&N Dec. 149 (BIA 1990); *Matter of A-G-*, 19 I&N Dec. 502, 506 (BIA 1987); Legal Opinion, Rees, Gen. Counsel (Jan. 13, 1993) and addendum (Mar. 4, 1993), *reprinted in* 70 No. 14 *Interpreter Releases* 485, 498–512 (Apr. 12, 1993).

(3) *Imputed Religious Views—Mezvrishvili v. U.S. Att'y Gen.*, 467 F.3d 1292, 1296 (11th Cir. 2006) [reversing IJ/BIA in case involving Jehovah's Witness from Rep. of Georgia, recognizing that persecutor may impute religious views].

(4) *No Imputed Opinion—Chikkeur v. Mukasey,* 514 F.3d 1381 (1st Cir. 2008) [no imputed political opinion because of extortion by radical Islamists against shop keeper]; *Pascal v. Mukasey,* 514 F.3d 483, 486–88 (6th Cir. 2007) [Guatemalan Mayan caught between army and guerrillas could not establish imputed political opinion because both groups were simply pursuing their own political objectives and not designed to persecute the applicant]; *Rivera v. U.S. Att'y Gen.,* 487 F.3d 815, 820–23 (11th Cir. 2007) [persecution by FARC in Colombia due to failure to pay "war tax" is not imputed political opinion]; *Ochoa v. Gonzales,* 406 F.3d 1166, 1171–72 (9th Cir. 2005) [no imputed political opinion where Colombian businessman fears narcotics traffickers because he owes them a large sum of money]; *Makhoul v. Ashcroft,* 387 F.3d 75. 82 (1st Cir. 2004) [political speech limited to Internet chat rooms is too insubstantial under the facts of the case]. *Molina-Morales v. INS,* 237 F.3d 1048 (9th Cir. 2001) [rape and murder of applicant's aunt was personal dispute]. *Al Najjar v. Ashcroft,* 257 F.3d 1262, 1289 (11th Cir. 2001) [recognizing imputed political opinion but denying it for failure to show that persecution would be because of it]; *Lwin v. INS,* 144 F.3d 505, 509 (7th Cir. 1998) [recognizing imputed political opinion but finding no proof in Burmese citizen's case].

5.c. *Membership in a Particular Social Group*—As defined by the BIA, refers to persons who hold a "common, immutable characteristic" which may be "an innate one such as sex, color, kinship ties, or in some circumstances…a shared past experience such as former military leadership or land ownership." *Matter of Acosta*, 19 I&N Dec. 211, 233–34 (BIA 1985). The BIA requires the characteristic to be one "that the group either cannot change, or should not be required to change because it is fundamental to their individual identities or consciences." *Id.* In *Acosta*, the BIA found that membership in a taxi collective that was being persecuted did not constitute "membership in a particular social group" because the applicant was free to quit the group. *Id.* Although the Board does not require an element of cohesiveness or homogeneity among group members, it has held that "social visibility is a "relevant factor" such that members of a society perceive those with the characteristic in question as members of a social group. *Matter of C-A-*, 23 I&N Dec. 951, 959–61 (BIA 2006) *affirmed Castillo-Arias v. U.S. Att'y Gen.*, 446 F.3d 1190, 1197–99 (11th Cir. 2006) [noncriminal drug informants in Colombia are not part of a social group because *inter alia* their social visibility is different in kind from groups afforded protection under the INA]; *Matter of A-T-*, 24 I&N Dec. 296, 302–04 (BIA 2007) [following *Matter of C-A-*, BIA expressed doubt that "young female members of the Bambara tribe who oppose arranged marriage" have the kind of social visibility that would make them readily identifiable to those who would be inclined to persecute them]; *Matter of A-M-E & J-G-U-*, 24 I&N Dec. 69, 73–76 (BIA 2007), *aff'd, Ucelo-Gomez v. Mukasey,* 509 F.3d 70 (2d Cir. 2007) [following *Matter of C-A-* and finding that "affluent Guatemalans" did not constitute a social group]. The BIA has also declined to recognize as a social group persons engaged in past criminal conduct or shared criminal enterprise, because such actions are not immutable characteristics and recognition would have negative public policy implications. *Arteaga v. Mukasey,* 511 F.3d 940 (9th Cir. 2007) [former member of gang in El Salvador does not qualify for social group status both because it would undermine the humanitarian purpose of the INA to give protection to violent, drug dealing gangs and disassociating from a gang is not a social group]; *Elien v. Ashcroft,* 364 F.3d 392, 396–98 (1st Cir. 2004) [declining to recognize as a social group, Haitians who commit crimes in the U.S. and are deported to dangerous conditions]; *Toussaint v. Att'y Gen. of the U.S.,* 455 F.3d 409, 417–18 (3d Cir. 2006) [same]. It is up to the BIA in the first instance, and not the federal courts, to decide what constitutes a cognizable social group. *Gonzales v. Thomas,* 547 U.S. 183 (2006) [vacating 9th Cir. *en banc* decision that defined a social group before giving the BIA the opportunity to determine whether "the members of a family can and do constitute a 'particular social group' within the meaning of the Act]; *Gonzales v. Tchoukhrova,* 127 S.Ct. 57 (2006) [vacating social group finding of disabled children in light of *Thomas*]; *Koudriachova v. Gonzales,* 490 F.3d 255, 262–63 (2d Cir. 2007) [remanding back to BIA to determine in first instance, following *Thomas*, whether defected KGB agents constitute a social group].

(1) *U.N. Guidelines*—The U.N. Handbook defines social group as persons with similar backgrounds, habits or social status. *See* Handbook at ¶77. The High Commissioner's Office has also published guidelines that take into consideration external factors as well as internal/immutable characteristics. *Guidelines on International Protection: "Membership of a particular social group" within the context of Article 1A(s) of the 1951 Convention and/or its 1967 Protocol relating to the Status of Refugees,* U.N. Refugee Agency, U.N. Doc. HCR/GIP/02/02 (May 7, 2002). "A group of persons who share a common characteristic other than their risk of being persecuted, *or who are perceived as a group by society.* The characteristic *will often* be one which is innate, unchangeable, or which is otherwise fundamental to identity, conscience or the exercise of one's human rights." *Guidelines* at ¶11.

(2) *Past vs. Future Persecution Social Group Claims*—In *Lukwago v. Ashcroft,* 329 F.3d 157, 172 (3d Cir. 2003), the Third Circuit distinguished social group definitions for past and future persecution claims, finding that a social group for past persecution claims must "exist independently of the persecution" and "have existed before the persecution began." The court found that "children from Northern Uganda who are abducted and enslaved" by a guerilla organization are not part of a particular social group for past persecution, but that "children who have escaped from involuntary servitude after being ab-

ducted and enslaved" by the same organization in Uganda have a social group claim for future persecution.

(3) *Imputed Social Group—Amanfi v. Ashcroft,* 328 F.3d 719, 727–30 (3d Cir. 2003) [recognizing imputed social group claim for Ghanian mistakenly believed to be homosexual].

(4) *Membership in Group*—To present a "membership" claim, the applicant must establish that she is a member of the particular social group. *Eke v. Mukasey,* 512 F.3d 372, 382 (7th Cir. 2008) [where IJ doubted Nigerian petitioner's claim that he was a homosexual, petitioner had the burden of demonstrating that he was part of that social group].

(5) *Ninth Circuit*—The Ninth Circuit has defined a particular social group as one in which the members are united by a voluntary association *or* by an innate characteristic that is so fundamental to the identities or consciences of its members, that members either cannot or should not be required to change it. *Hernandez-Montiel v. INS,* 225 F.3d 1084 (9th Cir. 2000). In *Sanchez-Trujillo*, 801 F.2d 1571, 1574–75 (9th Cir. 1986), the court recognized four criteria for establishing social group persecution: (a) Is the group cognizable? (b) Does the alien qualify as member? (c) Has the group been targeted because of characteristics as a group? (d) Are "special circumstances" present that permit *per se* finding and that do not require findings of individual persecution of members of group?

(6) *First Circuit—Silva v. Ashcroft,* 394 F.3d 1, 4–6 (1st Cir. 2005) [adhering to immutability whether innate or experiential as a requirement but recognizing that refugees' situations "vary widely" in whistleblower case and accepting "that current or former employment status can, at least theoretically, form the linchpin for assembling a protected social group"]. *See also Ang v. Gonzales,* 430 F.3d 50, 55–56 (1st Cir. 2005) [employment at the U.S. Embassy or support for Americans can constitute social group because membership stems from an "innate characteristic or shared experience"]; *Alvarez-Flores v. INS,* 909 F.2d 1, 7 (1st Cir. 1990).

(7) *Second Circuit*—Previously adopted the "voluntary associational relationship" standard and noted that the members of a social group must be externally distinguishable. *Gomez v. INS,* 947 F.2d 660, 664 (2d Cir. 1991); *Saleh v. DOJ,* 962 F.2d 234, 240 (2d Cir. 1992). *See also Gao v. Gonzales,* 440 F.3d 62, 66–70 (2d Cir. 2006) [broadly interpreting *Acosta*, distinguishing *Gomez,* and finding that women subject to forced marriage in China is a social group]. More recently, it has adopted the standard in *Matter of Acosta* and drawing on *Matter of C-A-* it has also found that shared past experience may constitute an immutable characteristic for purposes of a social group, if the fear of persecution derives "primarily" from that status and not some other reason. *Koudriachova v. Gonzales,* 490 F.3d 255, 260–62 (2d Cir. 2007) [upholding on *Chevron* grounds the *Acosta/C-A-* definition and finding that BIA applied an improper test to defected KGB agents because there is no requirement that defected KGB agents maintain an associational relationship and the BIA failed to address why shared past experience was not sufficient for social group purposes]. The Second Circuit has also affirmed the BIA's "social visibility" and "well defined boundaries" theories in determining social group. *Matter of A-M-E- & J-G-U-,* 24 I&N Dec. 69, 73–76 (BIA 2007) *aff'd, Ucelo-Gomez v. Mukasey,* 509 F.3d 70 (2d Cir. 2007) [following *Matter of C-A-* and finding that "affluent Guatemalans" did not constitute a social group].

(8) *Third Circuit*—Has adopted the *Acosta* definition. *Lukwago v. Ashcroft,* 329 F.3d 157, 170–73 (3d Cir. 2003).

(9) *Sixth Circuit*—Has adopted the BIA's immutable characteristic approach but has recognized that the BIA itself in cases such as *Matter of R-A-,* 22 I&N Dec. 906 (BIA 1999) (remanding to the BIA in light of future regulations, 23 I&N Dec. 694 (AG 2005)) may be moving toward recognizing external perception of a group as a factor. "[S]ociety's reaction to a 'group' may provide evidence in a specific case that a particular group exists, as long as the reaction by persecutors to members of a particular social group is not the touchstone defining the group." *Castellano-Chacon v. INS,* 341 F.3d 533, 548 (6th Cir. 2003). A social group must share a "narrowing characteristic other than their risk of be-

ing persecuted." *Rreshpja v. Gonzales,* 420 F.3d 551, 556 (6th Cir. 2005) [young Albanian women who are forced into prostitution is not a social group].

(10) *Seventh Circuit*—In *Lwin v. INS,* 144 F.3d 505, 510 (7th Cir. 1998) the court adopted the first two criteria above and maintained as a third that the person establish that his well-founded fear is based on his membership in the group. *But see Ahmed v. Ashcroft,* 348 F.3d 611, 6116–18 (7th Cir. 2003) ["immutability, while important, has never been the last or only word on the definition of a social group"].

(11) *Eighth Circuit*—Has recognized that a social group may arise from voluntary associations not just immutable characteristics. *Safaie v. INS*, 25 F.3d 636, 640 (8th Cir. 1994) [while all Iranian women could not be a social group, Iranian women who advocate women's rights could be].

(12) *Tenth Circuit*—Has adopted the *Acosta* definition. *Niang v. Gonzales,* 422 F.3d 1187, 1198–2001 (10th Cir. 2005) [female member of the Tukulor Fulani tribe in Senegal that practices FGM is subject to social group persecution because gender and tribal membership are immutable characteristics].

(13) *Eleventh Circuit*—*Castillo-Arias v. U.S. Att'y Gen.,* 446 F.3d 1190, 1195–99 (11th Cir. 2006) [rejecting a noncriminal informant who provided information to the police against a Colombian drug cartel as part of a social group, and stating, "we do not doubt the reasonableness of the BIA's requirement of a 'common, immutable characteristic'"].

(14) *Cases Finding Social Group*—*Ahmed v. Keisler,* 504 F.3d 1183, 1198–99 (9th Cir. 2007) [a Bihari living in Bangladesh is part of a particular social group]; *Vumi v. Gonzales,* 502 F.3d 150, 154–55 (2d Cir. 2007) [recognizing that membership in a nuclear family may support a social group and remanding back to BIA to make the determination in regard to woman from DRC who was persecuted because government sought her husband in connection with Kabila's assassination]; *Sepulveda v. Gonzales,* 464 F.3d 770 (7th Cir. 2006) [former employees of the AG's office in Colombia]; *Gao v. Gonzales,* 440 F.3d 62, 66–70 (2d Cir. 2006) [women who have been sold into marriage and who live in a part of China where forced marriages are considered valid and enforceable]; *Konan v. Att'y Gen. of the U.S.,* 432 F.3d 497, 501–02 (3d Cir. 2005) [remanding where IJ failed to consider whether status as an immediate family member of a gendarme in Côte d'Ivoire was a social group]; *Ang v. Gonzales,* 430 F.3d 50, 55–56 (1st Cir. 2005) [employment at the U.S. Embassy or support for Americans can constitute social group membership but denying asylum because IJ fairly considered and denied claim]; *Bhasin v. Gonzales,* 423 F.3d 977, 983–85 (9th Cir. 2005) [Indian mother was part of family constituting a social group where sons and daughters were missing in retaliation by Islamic militants for capture of their leader]; *Tapiero De Orejuela v. Gonzales,* 423 F.3d 666, 672–73 (7th Cir. 2005) [educated, landowning class of cattle farmers targeted by FARC in Colombia was social group]; *Boer-Sedano v. Gonzales,* 418 F.3d 1082, 1087–88 (9th Cir. 2005) [Mexican homosexual is part of a social group]; *Karouni v. Gonzales,* 399 F.3d 1163, 1171–72 (9th Cir. 2005) [*all* alien homosexuals are members of a particular social group]; *Mihalev v. Ashcroft,* 388 F.3d 722, 726 (9th Cir. 2004) [Gypsies are an identifiable ethnic group]; *Lukwago v. Ashcroft,* 329 F.3d 157, 170–73 (3d Cir. 2003) [finding that "children from Northern Uganda who are abducted and enslaved" by a guerilla organization are not part of a social group for past persecution, but that "children who have escaped from involuntary servitude after being abducted and enslaved" by the same organization in Uganda have a social group claim for future persecution]; *Yadegar-Sargis v. INS,* 297 F.3d 596, 603 (7th Cir. 2002) [Christian women in Iran who did not adhere to the Islamic female dress code is a social group]; *Hernandez-Montiel v. INS,* 225 F.3d 1084 (9th Cir. 2000) [gay men with female sexual identities are social group]; *Lwin v. INS,* 144 F.3d 505, 512 (7th Cir. 1998) [parents of Burmese student dissidents are a social group]; *Fatin v. INS,* 12 F.3d 1233 (3d Cir. 1993) [could have social group based on women who refused to conform to gender specific laws in Iran]; *Gebremichael v. INS,* 10 F.3d 28, 36 (1st Cir. 1993) ["[t]here can, in fact, be no plainer example of a social group based on common, identifiable and immutable characteristics than that of the nuclear family"]; *Aguilera-Cota v. INS,* 914 F.2d 1375, 1380 n.3 (9th Cir. 1990) [employment by government may

constitute social group membership]; *Sanchez-Trujillo v. INS,* 801 F.2d 1572 (9th Cir. 1986) [family is a social group]; *Ananeh-Firempong v. INS,* 766 F.2d 621, 626 (1st Cir. 1985) [broad definition of social group]; *Matter of Toboso-Alfonso,* 20 I&N Dec. 819 (AG 1994) [homosexual is a member of a social group]. Legacy INS also recognized that "in certain circumstances ... persons with HIV or AIDS may constitute a particular social group under refugee law." Memo, Martin, General Counsel (Feb. 16, 1996) *reported in* 73 *Interpreter Releases* 909 (July 8, 1996).

(a) *Cases Finding Clan as Social Group*— Clan membership is also a social group. *Mohammed v. Gonzales,* 400 F.3d 785, 796–98 (9th Cir. 2005) [in cases involving FGM, membership in a particular social group may be defined by clan or as all Somali females given the widespread practice]; *Ali v. Ashcroft,* 394 F.3d 780, 784–87 (9th Cir. 2005) [gang-rape of applicant was at least in part motivated by her membership in Midgan clan in Somalia]; *Matter of H-,* 21 I&N Dec. 337 (BIA 1996) [Somali clan is a social group citing DOJ Basic Law Manual at p.48]; *Matter of Kasinga,* 21 I&N Dec. 357, 365–66 (BIA 1996) [young women of particular African tribe subject to, but opposed to, female genital mutilation is a social group]; *But see Matter of A-T-,* 24 I&N Dec. 296, 302–04 (BIA 2007) [following *Matter of C-A-,* BIA rejected claim by Mali female who suffered FGM in past and is now subject to an arranged marriage that "young female members of the Bambara tribe who oppose arranged marriage" constitute a particular social group].

(b) *HIV/AIDS Victims as Social Group*—Legacy INS also recognized that "in certain circumstances ... persons with HIV or AIDS may constitute a particular social group under refugee law." Memo, Martin, General Counsel (Feb. 16, 1996) *reported in* 73 *Interpreter Releases* 909 (July 8, 1996).

(15) *Cases Rejecting Social Group*—*Matter of A-T-,* 24 I&N Dec. 296, 303–04 (BIA 2007) [following *Matter of C-A-,* BIA rejected claim by Mali female who suffered FGM in past and is now subject to an arranged marriage that "young female members of the Bambara tribe who oppose arranged marriage" constitute a particular social group]; *Matter of A-M-E- & J-G-U-,* 24 I&N Dec. 69, 73–76 (BIA 2007) *aff'd, Ucelo-Gomez v. Mukasey,* 509 F.3d 79 (2d Cir. 2007) ["affluent Guatemalans" did not constitute a particular social group under social visibility theory]; *Matter of C-A-,* 23 I&N Dec. 951 (BIA 2006) *affirmed Castillo-Arias v. U.S. Att'y Gen.,* 446 F.3d 1190, 1195–99 (11th Cir. 2006) [noncriminal drug informants are potentially too numerous and too inchoate to be a social group]; *Arteaga v. Mukasey,* 511 F.3d 940 (9th Cir. 2007) [former member of gang in El Salvador does not qualify for social group status both because it would undermine the humanitarian purpose of the INA to give protection to violent, drug dealing gangs and disassociating from a gang is not a social group]; *Pavlyk v. Gonzales,* 469 F.3d 1082, 1087–89 (7th Cir. 2006) ["Ukrainian prosecutors" or "uncorrupt prosecutors" is not a social group because the characteristic is not immutable particularly where applicant did not demonstrate that he possessed particular knowledge that would make him vulnerable]; *Mwembie v. Gonzales,* 443 F.3d 405, 414–15 (5th Cir. 2006) [government employee in national palace in Democratic Republic of Congo the day President Kabila was killed, who sought asylum based upon being an employee at the national palace was not a member of a particular social group]; *Ruzi v. Gonzales,* 441 F.3d 611, 614–16 (8th Cir. 2006) [Albanian could not demonstrate that persecution was at least partially on account of his political opinion]; *Rreshpja v. Gonzales,* 420 F.3d 551, 554–57 (6th Cir. 2005) [young Albanian women forced into prostitution are not a social group]; *Escobar v. Gonzales,* 417 F.3d 363 (3d Cir. 2005) [Honduran street children do not constitute a social group]; *Cruz-Funez v. Gonzales,* 406 F.3d 1187, 1190–91 (10th Cir. 2005) [small businessmen ruined by Hurricane Mitch and are indebted to unscrupulous private creditors connected to the corrupt Honduran business and political system are not a social group]; *Ochoa v. Gonzales,* 406 F.3d 1166, 1170–71 (9th Cir. 2005) [business owners in Colombia who rejected demands by narcotics traffickers to participate in illegal activities are not a social group]; *Elien v. Ashcroft,* 364 F.3d 392, 396–98 (1st Cir. 2004) [declining, as a matter of public policy, to recognize as a social group Haitians who commit crimes in the U.S. and are deported to dangerous conditions]; *Castellano-Chacon v. INS,* 341 F.3d

533, 545–51 (6th Cir. 2003) [tattooed youths facing return to Honduras is not a social group]; *Raffington v. INS,* 340 F.3d 720, 721–23 (8th Cir. 2003) [mentally ill female Jamaicans are not a social group because they are not "a collection of people closely affiliated with each other, who are actuated by some common impulse or interest"]; *Cruz-Navarro v. INS,* 232 F.3d 1024, 1028–29 (9th Cir. 2000) [current police or military are not social group although former police/military may be; distinguishing *Matter of Fuentes,* 19 I&N Dec. 658 (BIA 1988)]; *Pedro-Mateo v. INS,* 224 F.3d 1147 (9th Cir. 2000) [Kanjobal Indians from Guatemala described as indigenous Indians are not social group]; *Najafi v. INS*, 104 F.3d 943, 947–48 (7th Cir. 1997) [Iranians who left Iran, studied in U.S., and declined to fight in revolutionary army are not a social group]; *Gomez v. INS*, 947 F.2d 660, 663–64 (2d Cir. 1991) [women battered and raped in El Salvador are not a social group]; *Arriaga-Barrientos v. INS*, 937 F.2d 411, 414 (9th Cir. 1991) [military is not a social group]; *Yang v. Carroll*, 852 F.Supp. 460, 469–71 (E.D. Va. 1994) [PRC families having more than one child not social group]; *Matter of Sanchez and Escobar*, 19 I&N Dec. 276 (BIA 1985), *aff'd*, *Sanchez-Trujillo v. INS*, 801 F.2d 1571 (9th Cir. 1986) [a purely statistical showing that many of those killed in El Salvador are young, working class, urban males of military age is insufficient when those in armed conflict are usually in that group anyway].

5.d. *Mixed-Motive Cases*—In mixed-motive cases (*i.e.*, interrogation because of imputed political views or because the interrogator wanted intelligence information), an applicant is required to establish that race, religion, nationality, membership in a particular social group, or political opinion "was or will be at least one *central* reason for persecuting the applicant." INA §208(b)(1)(B)(i). This standard was enacted as part of the REAL ID Act and applies to all cases filed on or after May 11, 2005. The purpose of the legislation fixing the "central reason" standard was to clarify the law and to discontinue reliance on cases, principally from the Ninth Circuit, that benefited potential terrorists by establishing a presumption in favor of the applicant where the government used force against the applicant and there was no legitimate basis for prosecution. H.R. Cong. Rep. No 109-72 at 173–75, 151 Cong. Rec. H2831, H2869-70 (May 3, 2005).

(1) *BIA on Mixed Motive*—Prior to the legislation, the BIA recognized that in mixed-motive cases, decisions should be made by keeping in mind "the fundamental humanitarian concerns of asylum law." *Matter of S-P-*, 21 I&N Dec. 486 (BIA 1996). In *Matter of S-P-*, the BIA suggested 5 criteria to determine whether the motive for abuse was directed toward punishing or modifying a perceived political view or punishing a criminal act: (1) indications the abuse was directed toward modifying or punishing a person rather than conduct (*e.g.*, statements by perpetrators or abuse out of proportion to nonpolitical ends); (2) treatment of others in similar circumstances; (3) conformity to procedures for criminal prosecutions or military law; (4) the extent to which anti-terrorism laws are defined and apply to suppress political opinion as well as illegal conduct; and (5) the extent to which suspected political opponents are subjected to arbitrary arrest, detention, and abuse. *Matter of S-P-*, 21 I&N Dec. at 494. In presenting evidence on these issues the applicant does not bear an "unreasonable burden" of establishing the exact motivation. Subsequent to *Matter of S-P-*, the BIA in *Matter of T-M-B-*, 21 I&N Dec. 775, 777–78 (BIA 1997), *rev'd sub nom., Borja v. INS,* 175 F.3d 732 (9th Cir. 1999) (en banc), and *Matter of V-T-S-*, 21 I&N Dec. 792, 798 (BIA 1997), narrowly construed the mixed motive concept by rejecting extortion in the former and kidnapping in the latter as having anything other than a pecuniary motive. More recently, in a decision interpreting the REAL ID Act changes to the law, the BIA reaffirmed its decision in *Matter of S-P-* and found that mixed motive can be established by testimonial evidence, by "direct or circumstantial evidence," and that the protected ground cannot be "incidental, tangential, superficial or subordinate to another reason for harm." *Matter of J-B-N- & S-M-*, 24 I&N Dec. 208, 214 (BIA 2007).

(2) *Appellate Court Decisions*—The circuit courts have also interpreted mixed motives in asylum cases. *Delgado v. Mukasey,* 508 F.3d 702, 706–07 (2d Cir. 2007) [reversed BIA's denial of asylum where kidnapping was due to petitioner's expertise in computers, but her refusal to provide assistance could be imputed political opinion and viewed as politi-

cal betrayal]; *Vumi v. Gonzales,* 502 F.3d 150, 155–59 (2d Cir. 2007) [remanded to determine if persecution of the wife of the bodyguard of Kabila at time he was assassinated in the DRC was based upon a mixed motive, including imputed political opinion]; *Sanchez Jimenez v. U.S. Att'y Gen.,* 492 F.3d 1223, 1235–36 (11th Cir. 2007) [where Colombian businessman was persecuted by FARC for money and his political participation in Conservative Party, IJ's decision reversed]; *Menghesha v. Gonzales,* 450 F.3d 142, 147–49 (4th Cir. 2006) [where IJ determined that Ethiopian was subject to prosecution for obstructing justice while serving as a government security officer, his failure to inquire into other motives besides prosecution was reversible error]; *Gjerzai v. Gonzales,* 435 F.3d 800, 811–13 (7th Cir. 2006) [kidnapping of Albanian applicant's 2-year-old son and an invasion of his home, even if economically motivated in part does not exclude the possibility of a mixed motive; reversing IJ denial]; *Mohideen v. Gonzales,* 416 F.3d 567, 570–71 (7th Cir. 2005) [recognizing mixed motive and reversing BIA denial of asylum to Sri Lankan Moslems for its failure to evaluate the evidence]; *Singh v. Gonzales,* 406 F.3d 191, 197–99 (3d Cir. 2005) [in Sikh mixed-motive case the court reversed the IJ's denial of asylum where persecution was in part motivated by political beliefs]; *Nuru v. Gonzales,* 404 F.3d 1207, 1227–29 (9th Cir. 2005) [where tortured member of Eritrean military who spoke against war with Sudan would also face charges for desertion his fear of persecution was well founded]; *Ali v. Ashcroft,* 394 F.3d 780, 784–87 (9th Cir. 2005) [United Somali Congress militia's gang-rape of applicant was at least in part motivated by her political opinion and membership in Midgan clan]; *Deloso v. Ashcroft,* 393 F.3d 858, 864–66 (9th Cir. 2005) [where attacks could have been for vengeance or political motivation by Communist enforcer/gangster, IJ reversed]; *Mamouzian v. Ashcroft,* 390 F.3d 1129, 1134–35 (9th Cir. 2004) [reversing BIA because persecution against Armenian was motivated in part because of her participation in rallies and writing articles opposing corruption]; *De Brenner v. Ashcroft,* 388 F.3d 629, 635–39 (8th Cir. 2004) [where Shining Path mistakenly imputed political opinion to wealthy Peruvian, BIA's decision that it was based on wealth and not due to a protected ground was reversed]; *Garcia-Martinez v. Ashcroft,* 371 F.3d 1066, 1074–78 (9th Cir. 2004) [although soldiers who raped villager said they wanted to be with a woman, their treatment of applicant also arose out of their mistaken belief that the villagers were aiding the guerillas]; *Hoque v. Ashcroft,* 367 F.3d 1190, 1198 (9th Cir. 2004) [where political opponents were jealous of applicant's organizing ability but applicant also established politically-based persecution, the IJ erred in ignoring the mixed motive]; *Jahed v. INS,* 356 F.3d 991 997–1001 (9th Cir. 2004) [where Iranian soldier extorted respondent on threat to expose him to the government as a former member of the Mujahedin, respondent had well-founded fear on account of political reasons]; *Tarubac v. INS,* 182 F.3d 1114, 1118–19 (9th Cir. 1999) ["A finding that the persecution was motivated by nonpolitical factors is largely irrelevant to an applicant's eligibility for asylum, unless the BIA finds substantial evidence that the *only* motivation for the persecution was nonpolitical"]; *Gafoor v. INS,* 231 F.3d 645, 650–54 (9th Cir. 2000) [reversing BIA using mixed motive analysis and finding that were motivated in part by Indian background and purported opposition to the army and not because he witnessed a rape by an army officer]. *But see Rivera v. U.S. Att'y Gen.,* 487 F.3d 815, 820–23 (11th Cir. 2007) [recognizing mixed motive as a valid basis generally but finding in the case that persecution by FARC in Colombia due to failure to pay "war tax" is not imputed political opinion even if family refused payment for political reasons]; *Girma v. INS,* 283 F.3d 664 (5th Cir. 2002) [recognizing mixed motive analysis but finding under *Elias-Zacarias* standard that BIA did not err in determining that applicant did not in part suffer persecution on account of her membership in a particular social group].

5.e. *Cases Finding "On Account of" Nexus for Asylum/Withholding—De Santamaria v. U.S. Att'y Gen.,* ___ F.3d ___ (11th Cir. Apr. 22, 2008) [where FARC threatened and used physical violence against Colombian woman because of her support for the Colombian government and her work with democratic organizations, it was on account of her political opinion]; *Ahmed v. Keisler,* 504 F.3d 1183, 1193–1200 (9th Cir. 2007) [reversed BIA determination that Bihari living in Bangladesh was not persecuted on account of his political opinion or membership in a particular social group]; *Boctor v. Gonzales,* 474 F.3d 488 (7th Cir. 2007) [Coptic Christian who was threatened by Muslim extremists for reporting threats against fellow Christian who married Muslim woman that converted to Christianity was persecuted on account of his religion]; *Edimo-Doualla v. Gonzales,* 464 F.3d 276, 282–83 (2d Cir. 2006) [reversing IJ finding in Cameroonian asylum case that persecution was not on account of political views where applicant was arrested numerous times after political activity]; *Zhou v. Gonzales,* 437 F.3d 860, 868–69 (9th Cir. 2006) [reversing IJ where Chinese government perceived applicant as supporter of Falun Gong because she brought articles into country critical of government's treatment of Falun Gong]; *Smolniakova v. Gonzales,* 422 F.3d 1037, 1049–50 (9th Cir. 2005) [reversing IJ for lack of substantial evidence regarding Jewish religious persecution in Russia where testimony demonstrated that assault and threats were based on religion]; *Sagaydak v. Gonzales,* 405 F.3d 1035, 1041–45 (9th Cir. 2005) [retaliation against government auditor for exposing corruption in a private company in the context of political reforms rooting out corruption in the Ukraine, met both the imputed political opinion and the "on account of" criteria for asylum]; *Nuru v. Gonzales,* 404 F.3d 1207, 1225–27 (9th Cir. 2005) [finding IJ's determination that Eritrean soldier who spoke against war with Sudan did so because he was a coward and therefore did not express a political opinion, purely speculative]; *Mihalev v. Ashcroft,* 388 F.3d 722, 727–28 (9th Cir. 2004) [nexus established where police officers beat partygoers, stated that Gypsies don't deserve to live and arrested the applicant as the instigator who was organizing Gypsy gatherings]; *De Brenner v. Ashcroft,* 388 F.3d 629, 635–39 (8th Cir. 2004) [where Shining Path mistakenly imputed political involvement to wealthy Peruvian, BIA's decision that persecution was based upon wealth and not due to a protected ground was reversed]; *Garcia-Martinez v. Ashcroft,* 371 F.3d 1066, 1074–78 (9th Cir. 2004) [although applicant had not articulated a political position, her rape constituted persecution on account of imputed political opinion because Guatemalan soldiers mistakenly believed villagers were aiding guerillas]; *Lopez v. Ashcroft,* 366 F.3d 799, 804 (9th Cir. 2004) [refusal to cooperate with guerrillas by person perceived as a political opponent may constitute political opinion]; *Popova v. INS,* 273 F.3d 1251, 1257–59 (9th Cir. 2001) [BIA determination that applicant was not persecuted "on account of" her religious and political affiliations because she received education and employment from the government is not supported by substantial evidence]; *Ventura v. INS,* 264 F.3d 1150 (9th Cir. 2001) *rev'd on other grounds,* 537 U.S. 12 (2002) [where applicant's family members were closely associated with military, were targeted because of military affiliation, and where applicant is readily associated with pro-military and anti-guerrillas views and has received death threats, persecution is on account of imputed political opinion notwithstanding his lack of knowledge of guerrillas]; *Del Carmen Molina v. INS,* 170 F.3d 1247, 1249 (9th Cir. 1999) [guerrillas' threats motivated in part by an interest in recruiting her did not negate claim where there was fear that FMLN would kill her because she did not agree with them and where they had killed family members]; *Vera-Valera v. INS,* 147 F.3d 1036 (9th Cir. 1998) [president of street vendors did have imputed political asylum claim]; *Rodriguez-Roman v. INS*, 98 F.3d 416, 429–30 (9th Cir. 1996) [illegal departure statute meets *Elias-Zacarias* test because it imputes to those prosecuted, a political opinion (disloyalty) warranting severe punishment]. Persecution "on account of" does not mean "solely on account of" and if persecutor was motivated only in part by victim's political opinion, membership, race or religion, that would be sufficient. *Borja v. INS,* 175 F.3d 732 (9th Cir. 1999) (en banc) [where Philippine communist guerillas extorted money after applicant articulated her political opposition, persecution was at least in part on account of her political opinion]; *Chang v. INS*, 119 F.3d 1055, 1065 (3d Cir. 1997); *Osorio v. INS*, 18 F.3d 1017, 1028 (2d Cir. 1994); *Matter of H-*, 21 I&N Dec. 337, 343–46 (BIA 1996); *Matter of Kasinga*, 21 I&N Dec. 357, 366–67 (BIA 1996) [because female genital mutilation is practiced at least "in some significant part" to overcome sexual characteristics, it is "on account of"]; *Ratnam v. Lewis*, 892 F.Supp. 619, 638 (D.N.J. 1995) [opinion can be erroneously attributed to applicant].

5.f. *Cases Denying Asylum/Withholding for Lack of "On Account of" Nexus—Tobon-Marin v. Mukasey,* 512 F.3d 28, 31–32 (1st Cir. 2008) [coercive conscription alone by FARC is insufficient]; *Lopez de Hincapie v. Gonzales,* 494 F.3d 213 (1st Cir. 2007) [Colombian could not demonstrate that the threats that she received was on account of her political opinion or family membership]; *Babani v. Gonzales,* 492 F.3d 20 (1st Cir. 2007) [Albanian who was not directly involved in politics failed to demonstrate that mistreatment of her and husband were on account of her political opinion]; *Rodriguez Morales v. U.S. Att'y Gen.,* 488 F.3d 884 (11th Cir. 2007) [evidence did not compel a finding other than FARC persecuted applicant who was a dentist because they wanted his medical services]; *Rivera v. U.S. Att'y Gen.,* 487 F.3d 815, 820–23 (11th Cir. 2007) [finding persecution by FARC in Colombia due to failure to pay "war tax" was not "on account of" political opinion];*Mouawad v. Gonzales,* 485 F.3d 405, 412 (8th Cir. 2007) [no withholding based on imputed political opinion where applicant refused to give military secrets to Hezbollah]; *Lengkong v. Gonzales,* 478 F.3d 859, 862–63 (8th Cir. 2007) [Indonesian whose home was attacked, was attacked on a bus and whose car was vandalized did not establish that incidents were more than criminal conduct or general unrest]; *Silva v. U.S. Att'y Gen.,* 448 F.3d 1229, 1238 (11th Cir. 2006) [where Colombian applicant received death threats signed by the FARC while working on a political campaign and thereafter received threatening phone calls, was shot at while driving in her car, followed by more daily telephonic threats until she left the country, the evidence regarding the shooting did not compel a reversal of the IJ decision that it was not on account of political opinion]; *Tamara-Gomez v. Gonzales,* 447 F.3d 343, 349–51 (9th Cir. 2006) [finding persecution against Colombian petitioner who helped police against the FARC, but denying asylum and withholding for lack of nexus to any political view held by petitioner]; *Jun Ying Wang v. Gonzales,* 445 F.3d 993 (7th Cir. 2006) [fearing retaliation for testifying against others in a criminal proceeding is not "on account of" any protected ground]; *Gandziami-Mickhou v. Gonzales,* 445 F.3d 351, 358–59 (4th Cir. 2006) [applicant beaten and raped in jail and suffering PTSD properly denied asylum because she could not show it was on account of her political opinion]; *Mwembie v. Gonzales,* 443 F.3d 405 (5th Cir. 2006) [government employee in national palace in Democratic Republic of Congo the day President Kabila was killed, who was beaten and rape while in prison in connection with investigation, was persecuted, but not on account of an enumerated ground]; *Ruzi v. Gonzales,* 441 F.3d 611, 614–16 (8th Cir. 2006) [Albanian could not demonstrate that persecution was at least partially on account of his political opinion]; *Topalli v. Gonzales,* 417 F.3d 128, 133 (1st Cir. 2005) [where respondent was beaten to prevent his sister from being sold into prostitution and where the Albanian government is unwilling or unable to stop such acts, asylum was still denied because the harm was not on account of any enumerated ground]; *Turay v. Ashcroft,* 405 F.3d 663, 668 (8th Cir. 2005) [burning of respondent's home to force him to serve guerillas in Sierra Leone did not merit asylum because respondent did not demonstrate political opinion or nexus to conscription]; *Mohamed v. Ashcroft,* 396 F.3d 999, 1004–05 (8th Cir. 2005) [Somali woman could not demonstrate that she was attacked and son killed on account of her membership in the Benadir clan]; *Sanchez v. U.S. Att'y Gen.,* 392 F.3d 434 (11th Cir. 2004) [it is not enough to show that applicant would be tortured or persecuted for refusal to cooperate with FARC; must show that it is on account of actual or imputed political opinion]; *Silva v. Ashcroft,* 394 F.3d 1, 6–8 (1st Cir. 2005) [former employee / whistleblower could not show connection between persecution and group membership in what was essentially a personal dispute]; *Lopez-Soto v. Ashcroft,* 383 F.3d 228, 235–39 (4th Cir. 2004) [where notorious gang executed applicant's brother, there was no persecution on account of one of the enumerated grounds]; *Ustyan v. Ashcroft,* 367 F.3d 1215 (10th Cir. 2004) [refusal by ethnic Armenian and Georgian citizen from Abkhazia who resisted recruitment from Georgian and Abkhazian separatists during armed conflict did not have imputed political opinion]; *Samayoa Cabrera v. Ashcroft,* 367 F.3d 10 (1st Cir. 2004) [Guatemalan who received numerous threats did not provide any evidence of persecutors' motives]; *Dominguez v. Ashcroft,* 336 F.3d 678 (8th Cir. 2003) [Guatemalan's fears of forced recruitment does not amount to persecution on account of political opinion]; *Kharkhan v. Ashcroft,* 336 F.3d 601, 605 (7th Cir. 2003) [concerns that removal to Ukraine would limit employment and expose applicant to criminal element is not sufficient]; *Velasquez-Valencia v. INS,* 244 F.3d 48 (1st Cir. 2001) [Guatemalan guerillas' recruitment of applicant without more is insufficient to establish asylum]; *Cruz-Navarro v. INS,* 232 F.3d 1024 (9th Cir. 2000) [police officer could not show persecution on account of his status or political opinion]; *Pedro-Mateo v. INS,* 224 F.3d 1147 (9th Cir. 2000) [indigenous Indians not a social group and therefore no evidence that conscription was on account of any characteristic]; *Kozulin v. INS,* 218 F.3d 1112, 1115–17 (9th Cir. 2000) [Russian merchant sailor who was beaten could not establish it was on account of political reasons instead of his disclosing corruption by his captain]; *Fisher v. INS*, 79 F.3d 955, 962 (9th Cir. 1996) (*en banc*) [punishment for dress and conduct rules concerning women does not amount to persecution absent showing that it is on account of woman's religious or political views]; *Adhiyappa v. INS*, 58 F.3d 261, 267–68 (6th Cir. 1995) [informer for Sri Lankan government who feared retaliation was not being persecuted on account of his political opinion but rather as informer]; *Bartesaghi-Lay v. INS*, 9 F.3d 819 (10th Cir. 1993) [Peruvian who refused to assist guerrilla group in drug dealing would not be persecuted "on account of" any political opinion]; *Adebisi v. INS*, 952 F.2d 910 (5th Cir. 1992) [applicant failed to show that his fear of persecution was on account of his membership in his tribe as opposed to a personal dispute among tribe members]; *Matter of R-A-*, 22 I&N Dec. 906 (AG 2001), *remanded by AG,* 23 I&N Dec. 694 (AG 2005) (remanding to BIA for reconsideration under the final rule published as a proposed rule at 65 Fed. Reg. 76588 (Dec. 7, 2000)) [rejecting claim of battered wife brutalized by husband in Guatemala because there was no showing that brutality was on account of her beliefs, opinion or membership in a particular social group]; *Matter of T-M-B-*, 21 I&N Dec. 775 (BIA 1997), *rev'd Borja v. INS,* 175 F.3d 732 (9th Cir. 1999) (en banc) [where group in Philippines extorted applicant to pay "revolutionary tax," she did not qualify for asylum on account of enumerated grounds]; *Matter of C-A-L-*, 21 I&N Dec. 754 (BIA 1997) [former Guatemalan soldier wanted by guerrillas after they obtained his personnel file because of his artillery experience has not established persecution on account of enumerated grounds]; *Matter of R-*, 20 I&N Dec. 621 (BIA 1992), *remanded sub nom. Rana v. Moschorak*, 37 F.3d 1506 (9th Cir. 1994) [finding that torture of Sikh was to extract information and was not on account of political opinion]; *Matter of K-S-*, 20 I&N Dec. 715 (BIA 1993) [reaffirming *Matter of R-*, notwithstanding district court remand of that case].

B. *Past Persecution Claim*—If the applicant establishes past persecution, there is a presumption that s/he has a well-founded fear of future persecution. This presumption may be overcome only if DHS can establish by a preponderance of the evidence that there are changed country conditions. 8 C.F.R. §§208.13(b)(1)(i), 1208.13(b)(1)(i). If DHS meets this burden, the applicant may still be granted asylum if there are "compelling reasons" for being unwilling to return, 8 C.F.R. §§208.13(b)(1)(iii)(A), 1208.13(b)(1)(iii)(A), or if there is "a reasonable possibility that he or she may suffer other serious harm upon removal to that country." 8 C.F.R. §§208.13(b)(1)(iii)(B), 1208.13(b)(1)(iii)(B).

1. *IJ Required to Make a Finding on Past Persecution*—If a past persecution claim is presented, an IJ is required to make a finding regarding the claim. *Un v. Gonzales,* 415 F.3d 205, 208–10 (1st Cir. 2005) [remanding case where IJ failed to make finding regarding past persecution when evidence was presented]; *Antipova v. U.S. Att'y Gen.*, 392 F.3d 1259 (11th Cir. 2004) [reversing IJ for failure to follow the regulatory requirement under §208.16(b) to make a finding whether Jewish Russian national suffered past persecution for purposes of withholding]; *Hernandez-Barrera v. Ashcroft,* 373 F.3d 9, 20–26 (1st Cir. 2004) [reversing BIA where it failed to determine past persecution and, if so, whether the Service rebutted the claim and established changed circumstances]; *But see Ambartsoumian v. Ashcroft,* 388 F.3d 85, 90 n.3 (3d Cir. 2004) [where IJ failed to state whether applicant suffered past persecution that was rebutted, or had not suffered past persecution, substantial evidence supported either conclusion].

2. *Pattern or Practice in Past Persecution Claim*— Past persecution claims do not necessarily require proof of particularized persecution where the applicant proves a pattern or practice of persecution of a group of persons similarly situated to the applicant. 8 C.F.R. §§208.13(b)(2)(iii); 1208.13(b)(2)(iii); *Banks v. Gonzales,* 453 F.3d 449, 452–53 (7th Cir. 2006) [IJ erred in requiring Liberian of Krahn tribe to present evidence that she was singled out for persecution because all parties conceded the Krahn tribe was persecuted and the applicant's lawyer does not have the burden of asserting §1208.13(b)(2)(iii)]; *Sukwanputra v. Gonzales,* 434 F.3d 627, 637 (3d Cir. 2006) [reversing IJ for failure to consider whether Indonesian of Chinese ethnicity is subject to pattern or practice of persecution]; *Himri v. Ashcroft,* 378 F.3d 932, 936–38 (9th Cir. 2004) [Palestinians who lived in Kuwait were persecuted minority]; *Knezevic v. Ashcroft,* 367 F.3d 1206, 1211–12 (9th Cir. 2004) [reversing denial of asylum of Serb despite lack of evidence of particularized persecution where Serb fled hometown of Brvar in Bosnia-Herzegovina which was bombed and invaded by Croats bent on ethnic cleansing].

3. *Presumption of Well-Founded Fear*—A person who has suffered past persecution is presumed to have a well-founded fear of future persecution and it is the government's burden to rebut that pre-

sumption. 8 C.F.R. §§208.13(b)(1)(ii), 1208.13(b)(1)(ii). *Balliu v. Gonzales,* 467 F.3d 609 (7th Cir. 2006) [IJ erred in placing burden on Kosovo native who had established past persecution to prove he would be persecuted in the future]; *Youkhana v. Gonzales,* 460 F.3d 927, 931–33 (7th Cir. 2006) [where past persecution established, the IJ erred in finding changed country conditions for Assyrian Christian in Iraq simply because the Ba'ath Party was no longer in power, without looking further]; *Bushira v. Gonzales,* 442 F.3d 626 (8th Cir. 2006) [reversing IJ who placed burden on Ethiopian applicant to demonstrate a well-founded fear without making a determination of past persecution]; *Phommasoukha v. Gonzales,* 408 F.3d 1011 (8th Cir. 2005) [where IJ mistakenly failed to recognize that imprisonment of Laotian soldier in a Pathet Lao concentration camp for re-education was past persecution, the court remanded to determine whether conditions have sufficiently changed to overcome presumption]; *Bace v. Ashcroft,* 352 F.3d 1133, 1140–42 (7th Cir. 2003) [Albanian who established past persecution did not have burden on internal relocation or continuing dangerous conditions]; *Ruano v. Ashcroft,* 301 F.3d 1155, 1159–62 (9th Cir. 2002) [Guatemalan UCN party member who received multiple death threats at home and business, who was followed and narrowly escaped an assassination attempt and who had been targeted because of his UCN membership established past persecution]; *Krastev v. INS,* 292 F.3d 1268, 1275–79 (10th Cir. 2002) [where BIA relied on 1995 Profile from Bulgaria that did not rebut past persecution, the court reversed and remanded]; *Yang v. McElroy,* 277 F.3d 158 (2d Cir. 2002) [remanding for more current country condition reports in case involving 4-year delay between the BIA decision and the IJ decision which relied on a 5-year-old DOS Country report]; *Chouchkov v. INS,* 220 F.3d 1077 (9th Cir. 2000) [where Jewish engineer who opposed technology sale to Iran received threatening telephone calls, had a car accident and his father had a car accident, court reversed denial of past persecution]; *Garrovillas v. INS,* 156 F.3d 1010, 1016–17 (9th Cir. 1998) [informant for Philippine military received 3 death threat letters]; *Korablina v. INS,* 158 F.3d 1038 (9th Cir. 1998) [BIA determination of discrimination and not persecution reversed where Jewish woman was threatened and her family and boss beaten in Ukraine]; *Kossov v. INS*, 132 F.3d 405, 409 (7th Cir. 1998) (Rovner concurring) [where woman was taunted and beaten until she miscarried because of her religious beliefs, was threatened by police and lost her property, past persecution from Latvia was established]; *Lopez-Galarza v. INS*, 99 F.3d 954, 960–63 (9th Cir. 1996) [where person suffered atrocious persecution through rape and beatings, past persecution was severe enough]; *Surita v. INS*, 95 F.3d 814 (9th Cir. 1996) [Indo-Fijian subject to multiple robberies, home invasions and threats of rape and murder by ethnic Fijians after coup]; *Gebremichael v. INS*, 10 F.3d 28 (1st Cir. 1993); *Desir v. Ilchert*, 840 F.2d 723, 729 (9th Cir. 1988); *Matter of S-A-*, 22 I&N Dec. 1328, 1333, 1335 (BIA 2000) [daughter was persecuted by Muslim orthodox father through physical assault, imposed isolation, and deprivation of education]; *Matter of O-Z- & I-Z-* , 22 I&N Dec. 23 (BIA 1998) [harm to Jews in Ukraine]; *Matter of H-*, 21 I&N Dec. 337 (BIA 1996) [member of Somali clan]; *Matter of D-V-*, 21 I&N Dec. 77 (BIA 1993) [harm to Aristide supporter in Haiti]; *Matter of B-*, 21 I&N Dec. 66 (BIA 1995) [Afghani citizen in prison for 14 months]; *Singh v. Ilchert*, 69 F.3d 375 (9th Cir. 1995); *Shukoor v. Rogers*, 954 F.Supp. 1415 (C.D. Cal. 1997). A past persecution claim therefore need not rest on a past "atrocious form" of persecution to meet the requirements of 8 C.F.R. §§208.13(b)(1)(i), 1208.13(b)(1)(i). *Matter of C-Y-Z-*, 21 I&N Dec. 915, 919 (BIA 1997). *See also Smolniakova v. Gonzales,* 422 F.3d 1037, 1048–49 (9th Cir. 2005) [past persecution based on an assault and death threats was sufficient to establish past persecution regarding Jewish religious persecution in Russia]; *Asani v. INS,* 154 F.3d 719, 722–25 (7th Cir. 1998) [past persecution requires no greater punishment than future persecution]. Past persecution does not require physical violence. *Leiva-Montalvo v. INS,* 173 F.3d 749 (9th Cir. 1999) [threats against Salvadoran who did not want to join new guerilla organization subsequent to the 1992 Peace Accords suffered past persecution].

4. *Past Persecution and Withholding*—A finding of past persecution gives rise to a presumption that the applicant's life or freedom would be threatened for purposes of withholding of removal under INA §241(b)(3). 8 C.F.R. §§208.16(b)(1)(i), 1208.16(b)(1)(i); *Makadji v. Gonzales,* 470 F.3d 450, 458–59 (2d Cir. 2006) [IJ reversed where citizen of Mauritania established past persecution and burden was not shifted to the government]; *Ali v. Ashcroft,* 394 F.3d 780, 791 (9th Cir. 2005) [where Somali clan member was gang raped by another clan, a finding of past persecution gave rise to a presumption of withholding of removal]; *Ndom v. Ashcroft,* 384 F.3d 743, 756 (9th Cir. 2004) [presumption of withholding for person from Casamance region of Senegal who suffered past persecution]; *Rios v. Ashcroft,* 287 F.3d 895, 900–02 (9th Cir. 2002) [family of murdered

Guatemalan army officer who were kidnapped and threatened established past persecution for withholding]; *Duarte de Guinac v. INS,* 179 F.3d 1156, 1164 (9th Cir. 1999); *Korablina v. INS,* 158 F.3d 1038, 1046 (9th Cir. 1998); *Fergiste v. INS,* 138 F.3d 14, 20 (1st Cir. 1998). *But see Kobugabe v. Gonzales,* 440 F.3d 900 (7th Cir. 2006) [recognizing but ignoring shifting burden in Ugandan withholding case where there was past persecution and finding that there was no showing by applicant of future harm].

5. *Rebuttal of Well-Founded Fear Presumption*—Where the applicant establishes past persecution, the applicant is presumed to have a well-founded fear of future persecution and the burden shifts to DHS to establish by a preponderance of the evidence a "fundamental change in circumstances" (generally changed country conditions) or that relocation, where it would be reasonable to do so under all the circumstances, would avoid the persecution. 8 C.F.R. §§1208.13(b)(1)(i)(A),(B), (ii). If DHS rebuts the presumption, the applicant will be denied unless s/he demonstrates " 'compelling reasons for being unwilling or unable to return' to his or her country of nationality, or 'a reasonable possibility that he or she may suffer other serious harm upon removal to that country.' 8 C.F.R. 1208.13(b)(1)(iii)(A),(B)." *Matter of D-I-M-,* 24 I&N Dec. 448, 450 (BIA 2008) [reversed IJ denial in Kenyan asylum case where past persecution was found but the IJ did not explicitly provide the presumption of future persecution and failed to shift the burden to DHS]. An AO shall refer, and an IJ shall deny, in the exercise of discretion, an asylum application based on past persecution if (A) there has been a fundamental change in circumstances such that the applicant no longer has a well-founded fear of persecution in his or her country of nationality or last habitual residence, or (B) the applicant could avoid future persecution by relocating to another part of his or her country of nationality or last habitual residence. 8 C.F.R. §§208.13(b)(1)(i), 1208.13(b)(1)(i). Where an applicant has established past persecution, the government bears the burden of establishing these requirements by a preponderance of the evidence. 8 C.F.R. §§208.13(b)(1)(ii), 1208.13(b)(1)(ii).

   a. *Standard for Rebuttal*—At least one court has recognized that "a State Department report on country conditions, standing alone, is not sufficient to rebut the presumption of future persecution when a petitioner has established past persecution." *Molina-Estrada v. INS,* 293 F.3d 1089, 1096 (9th Cir. 2002). *See also Ali v. Ashcroft,* 394 F.3d 780, 788 (9th Cir. 2005). *See also Niang v. Mukasey,* 511 F.3d 138, 148–49 (2d Cir. 2007) [BIA's one-sentence determination that applicant was ineligible for withholding because conditions in Mauritania have "improved dramatically" without any support in the record is error or indisputable historical fact]; *De Brenner v. Ashcroft,* 388 F.3d 629, 638–39 (8th Cir. 2004) [where BIA did not make a finding as to past persecution, it erred in making an alternative finding that changed country conditions did not warrant asylum and placing the burden on the applicant to rebut country conditions]; *Awale v. Ashcroft,* 384 F.3d 527, 531–32 (8th Cir. 2004) [administrative record, including the DOS report, did not contain substantial evidence rebutting past persecution]; *Berishaj v. Ashcroft,* 378 F.3d 314, 326–28 (3d Cir. 2004) [the use of generalized information is not permissible where no explanation was given as to how or why the DOS report rebutted the claim]. *But see Sillah v. Mukasey,* 519 F.3d 1042, 1044-45 (9th Cir. 2008) [respondent could return to Sierra Leone because, although evidence indicated that the Revolutionary United Front was still committing abuses, there was not compelling evidence that they would target respondent]; *Chreng v. Gonzales,* 471 F.3d 14, 20–24 (1st Cir. 2006) [DHS rebutted past persecution from Cambodia based upon membership in San Rainsy political party by detailed reference to DOS report]; *Hoxhallari v. Gonzales,* 468 F.3d 179, 187–88 (2d Cir. 2006) [IJ was not required to make a "specific finding premised on record evidence" regarding changed country conditions in Albanian asylum case]; *Waweru v. Gonzales,* 417 F.3d 199, 203–05 (1st Cir. 2006) [affirming IJ's determination that past persecution from Kenya under the Moi regime was rebutted]; *Islami v. Gonzales,* 412 F.3d 391, 396–97 (2d Cir. 2005) [where persecution of Muslim/Albanian arose out of his participation as a soldier in the Serb controlled Yugoslav army, but his future fear is related to sporadic events of continued Serb persecution, but without their control over Kosovo or its army, the government met its lesser burden of rebutting the past persecution claim]; *Brucaj v. Ashcroft,* 381 F.3d 602, 605–08 (7th Cir. 2004) [government rebutted ethnic Albanian claim of persecution by presenting country reports and demonstrating regime change in the former Yugoslavia]; *Gonzalez-Hernandez v. Ashcroft,*

336 F.3d 995, 999–1000 (9th Cir. 2003) [relying on *INS v. Ventura* and giving deference to the manner in which the BIA construed the country report in Guatemalan asylum case].

b. *Changed Conditions*—Under the regulation the government has the burden to demonstrate a "fundamental change in circumstances" such that the applicant no longer has a well-founded fear. Generally, the change applies to changed political conditions in the country, but it may apply to personal changes that affect the applicant's well-founded fear. *Ixtlilco-Morales v. Keisler,* 507 F.3d 651 (8th Cir. 2007) [BIA could rely on applicant's status as an adult as a changed circumstance concerning future persecution because his claim was based upon his mistreatment as a homosexual child]. *See also* 65 Fed. Reg. 76121, 76127 (Dec. 6, 2000) [noting that a fundamental change in personal circumstances is contemplated in the regulatory change]. In terms of changed country conditions, a change in regime does not necessarily rebut past persecution because it does not "necessarily eliminate the objective basis for an applicant's fear of persecution at the hands of his former oppressors." *Mihaylov v. Ashcroft,* 379 F.3d 15, 23 (1st Cir. 2004) [reversing IJ denial of asylum from Bulgaria based on lack of credibility and rebuttal of past persecution through changed country conditions]. *See also Gabuniya v. Att'y Gen. of the U.S.,* 463 F.3d 316, 324–25 (3d Cir. 2006) [IJ's reliance solely on the resignation of the President of Georgia as basis to establish changed conditions was insufficient]. Nor does the simple passage of time constitute sufficient rebuttal of past persecution. *Matter of Y-T-L-,* 23 I&N Dec. 601 (BIA 2003) [in coercive family planning case, reversing the IJ and finding that "the passage of time since the forced sterilization…coupled with the lack of enforcement of coercive family planning measures during that period" did not constitute a fundamental change in circumstances sufficient for rebuttal because forced sterilization is a "permanent and continuing act of persecution"]. However, the BIA has suggested that changed conditions (*i.e.*, changed government) alone is sufficient to shift the burden back to the applicant. *Matter of N-M-A-,* 22 I&N Dec. 312 (BIA 1998) [once changed conditions are established, the burden shifts back to the applicant to demonstrate the reasonableness of his fear from any potential new source of harm]. They have also held that where the persecution will not reoccur because it is a one-time event, such as FGM, past persecution has been rebutted. *Matter of A-T-,* 24 I&N Dec. 296 (BIA 2007) [Mali female subject to FGM in past denied withholding because despite past persecution it is not continuing persecution and therefore future harm not established; distinguished sterilization].

c. *Safe Relocation—Ruiz v. Gonzales,* 479 F.3d 762, 767 (11th Cir. 2007) [ICE failed to establish by preponderance of the evidence that applicant could reasonably relocate within Colombia]; *Singh v. Ilchert*, 69 F.3d 375, 379–81 (9th Cir. 1995); *Matter of H-*, 21 I&N Dec. 337, 349 n.7 (BIA 1996) [noting that where government claims that the applicant would not face persecution in a protected area, it should clarify how it will accomplish the deportation of the individual to the protected area]. Where the government fails to demonstrate that the applicant can be relocated or that relocation is reasonable under the circumstances, the IJ's decision denying asylum must be reversed. *Ruiz v. Gonzales, supra; Essohou v. Gonzales,* 471 F.3d 518, 522–23 (4th Cir. 2006) [member of Congolese Movement for Democracy and Integral Development could not safely relocate in the Congo]; *Boer-Sedano v. Gonzales,* 418 F.3d 1082, 1090–91 (9th Cir. 2005) [government did not overcome past persecution where homosexual man from Mexico would face social and cultural constraints if returned and where his AIDS condition would likely result in serious harm, including his inability to obtain medication]; *Gambashidze v. Ashcroft,* 381 F.3d 187, 192–94 (3d Cir. 2004) [government must prove that relocation would be successful and reasonable]; *Eduard v. Ashcroft,* 379 F.3d 182, 193–94 (5th Cir. 2004) [IJ erred in confusing whether a person could relocate within their country "if necessary" with whether it was reasonable to do so]; *Knezevic v. Ashcroft,* 367 F.3d 12061214–16 (9th Cir. 2004) [relocation to Serb held areas of Bosnia-Herzegovina is not reasonable where asylum applicants are elderly, have no home, no business, no possessions and the quality of life is abysmal].

d. *Safe Relocation vs. Changed Conditions*—Arguments regarding "safe relocation" and "changed conditions" are analytically distinct and failure to address those issues separately could result in dismissal of an appeal. *Steevenez v. Gonzales,* 476 F.3d 114 (2d Cir. 2007) [respondent failed to exhaust administrative remedies by failing to address the "safe relocation" issue on the theory that it was addressed in his argument that the government failed to establish changed country conditions].

e. *Cases Failing to Rebut Past Persecution—Ruiz v. Gonzales,* 479 F.3d 762, 767 (11th Cir. 2007) [ICE failed to establish by preponderance of the evidence that applicant could reasonably relocate within Colombia]; *Youkhana v. Gonzales,* 460 F.3d 927, 931–33 (7th Cir. 2006) [IJ erred in finding changed country conditions for Assyrian Christian in Iraq simply because the Ba'ath Party was not longer in power]; *Naizgi v. Gonzales,* 455 F.3d 484, 488–89 (4th Cir. 2006) [having established past-persecution, the IJ/BIA decision denying asylum was reversed because there was no finding in Eritrean case that DHS rebutted finding by establishing changed circumstances]; *Banks v. Gonzales,* 453 F.3d 449, 453–54 (7th Cir. 2006) [IJ erred when he ignored expert on Liberia who testified that applicant from Krahn tribe would be persecuted and instead relied on his own views; court noted that DOS reports are too general and that government needs expert witnesses]; *Berishaj v. Ashcroft,* 378 F.3d 314, 326–28 (3d Cir. 2004) [use of generalized information was not permissible where no explanation was given as to how or why the DOS report rebutted the claim]; *Lopez v. Ashcroft,* 366 F.3d 799, 804–07 (9th Cir. 2004) [information about general changes in Guatemala was insufficient to meet government's burden to rebut past persecution]; *Krastev v. INS,* 292 F.3d 1268, 1275–79 (10th Cir. 2002) [reliance on 1995 Profile of Bulgaria was insufficient to overcome past persecution]; *Rios v. Ashcroft,* 287 F.3d 895, 900–02 (9th Cir. 2002) [family of murdered Guatemalan army officer who were kidnapped and threatened established past persecution which was not rebutted by general statement concerning peace accord in 1998 country report]; *Salazar-Paucar v. INS,* 281 F.3d 1069, 1076–77 (9th Cir. 2002) [neither the passage of time because the case was pending at the BIA for 6 years, nor a 1993 Amnesty Report was sufficient to demonstrate changed circumstances in Peru]; *Lal v. INS,* 255 F.3d 998, 1010–11 (9th Cir. 2001), *amended on reh'g,* 268 F.3d 1148 (9th Cir. 2001) [BIA failed to undertake the required individual analysis to establish changed conditions]; *Manzoor v. DOJ,* 254 F.3d 342 (1st Cir. 2001) [BIA impermissibly relied solely on DOS report about lack of countrywide persecution in the face of applicant's contrary testimony and impermissibly put burden of proof to establish countrywide persecution on applicant who had established past persecution]; *Agbuya v. INS,* 241 F.3d 1224, 1231 (9th Cir. 2001) [INS failed to overcome presumption where country conditions indicated that kidnapping continued to exist by Philippine communists]; *Kataria v. INS,* 232 F.3d 1107, 1115–16 (9th Cir. 2000) [INS did not overcome presumption where country conditions report indicated that extrajudicial killings still exist]; *Vujisic v. INS,* 224 F.3d 578, 582 (7th Cir. 2000) [where BIA merely asserts, without evidence in the record, that country conditions have changed, it is insufficient for rebuttal]; *Galina v. INS,* 213 F.3d 955, 958–59 (7th Cir. 2000) [BIA misapplied the principle of administrative notice by relying on opinions in the Country Reports and treating them as uncontested facts]; *Borja v. INS,* 175 F.3d 732, 737–38 (9th Cir. 1999) (*en banc*) [where Philippine communist guerillas extorted money and physically harmed applicant, DOS profile stating that "*generally* [it is] possible to seek internal resettlement" was insufficient to meet burden]; *Tarubac v. INS,* 182 F.3d 1114, 1119–20 (9th Cir. 1999) [same]; *Leiva-Montalvo v. INS,* 173 F.3d 749, 751–52 (9th Cir. 1999) [INS introduction of DOS report describing improvements in human rights situation insufficient to overcome presumption]; *Del Carmen Molina v. INS,* 170 F.3d 1247, 1250 (9th Cir. 1999) [must show how changed country conditions "will affect the specific petitioner's situation...[i]nformation about general changes...is not sufficient"]; *Duarte de Guinac v. INS,* 179 F.3d 1156, 1163–64 (9th Cir. 1999) [Guatemalan Profile failed to rebut specific facts]; *Meza-Manay v. INS,* 139 F.3d 759, 765–66 (9th Cir. 1998) [BIA did not address INS's failure to rebut presumption in case involving Shining Path]; *Fergiste v. INS,* 138 F.3d 14, 17–19 (1st Cir. 1998) [rejecting simple administrative notice and citation to *Matter of E-P-,* 21 I&N Dec. 860 (BIA 1997) as a basis to rebut past persecution where applicant presented evidence of continuing problems in Haiti]; *Vallechilo-Castillo v. INS,* 121 F.3d 1237 (9th Cir. 1997) [government does not overcome presumption by simply asking for administrative notice of changed conditions in Nicaragua where applicant provided direct evidence of current conditions]; *Osorio v. INS,* 99 F.3d 928, 932 (9th Cir. 1996); *Surita v. INS,* 95 F.3d 814, 821 (9th Cir. 1996); *Prasad v. INS,* 101 F.3d 614 (9th Cir. 1996); *Gebremichael v. INS,* 10 F.3d 28, 37 n.23 (1st Cir. 1993); *Matter of D-I-M-,* 24 I&N Dec. 448, 450 (BIA 2008) [reversed IJ denial in Kenyan asylum case where past persecution was found but the IJ did not explicitly provide the presumption of future persecution and failed to shift the burden to DHS]; *Matter of C-Y-Z-,* 21 I&N Dec. 915 (BIA 1997).

f. *Cases Supporting Rebuttal of Past Persecution—Pascual v. Mukasey,* 514 F.3d 483, 488–89 (6th Cir. 2007) [DOS reports indicating the end of the civil war and the disbanding of civil patrols undercut Guatemalan Mayan's claim that he was subject to persecution as a result of the civil war and the civil patrols] *Chreng v. Gonzales,* 471 F.3d 14, 20–24 (1st Cir. 2006) [DHS rebutted past persecution claim from Cambodia based on membership in San Rainsy party by detailed reference to DOS report regarding changed conditions]; *Hoxhallari v. Gonzales,* 468 F.3d 179, 187–88 (2d Cir. 2006) [upholding IJ's decision that conditions had changed sufficiently in Albania, noting that the IJ is not required to make a "specific finding premised on record evidence" when considering changed country conditions]; *Bollanos v. Gonzales,* 461 F.3d 82 (1st Cir. 2006) [Albanian asylum claim rebutted by 2003 DOS Country Report and 2004 Asylum Profile]; *Tota v. Gonzales,* 457 F.3d 161, 166–69 (1st Cir. 2006) [evidence from DOS report that "since 1998" treatment of DP members in Albania improved provided substantial evidence to rebut presumptive well-founded fear regarding events in 2000 absent applicant's rebuttal]; *Shehu v. Gonzales,* 443 F.3d 435, 438–40 (5th Cir. 2006) [DOS reports *post*-Milosevic demonstrated changed country conditions in Kosovo for Muslim]; *Palma-Mazariegos v. Gonzales,* 428 F.3d 30, 34–36 (1st Cir. 2005) [DOS Country Report on Guatemala alone directly rebutted applicant's particular fear that he would be persecuted by the guerillas]; *Shardar v. Ashcroft,* 382 F.3d 318, 324 (3d Cir. 2004) [relying on one statement in a 1997 DOS Profile to rebut past persecution claim]; *Meas v. Ashcroft,* 363 F.3d 729 (8th Cir. 2004) [relying on DOS reports to rebut presumption of future persecution and fact that there was no reported persecution of repatriated Cambodian refugees]; *Gonzalez-Hernandez v. Ashcroft,* 336 F.3d 995, 999–1000 (9th Cir. 2003) [relying on *INS v. Ventura* and giving deference to the manner in which the BIA construed the country report in Guatemalan asylum case]; *Quevedo v. Ashcroft,* 336 F.3d 39, 44–45 (1st Cir. 2003) [DOS report on Guatemala rebutted past persecution and applicant failed to overcome government's rebuttal through expert affidavit or other reports]; *Koliada v. INS,* 259 F.3d 482 (6th Cir. 2001) [relying on a highly deferential standard, the court found that the INS overcame the presumption in light of changes in the Ukraine]; *Yatskin v. INS,* 255 F.3d 5 (1st Cir. 2001) [where applicant does not contradict DOS report, it may be used to overcome past persecution]; *Gonahasa v. INS,* 181 F.3d 538, 542 (4th Cir. 1999) [DOS profile is "highly probative" and in "most cases" will provide substantial evidence to overcome presumption]; *Vaduva v. INS,* 131 F.3d 689 (7th Cir. 1997) [finding INS overcame presumption based on DOS report and rejecting Amnesty International report even where applicant was beaten up in Romania after the first democratic election]; *Dhine v. Slattery,* 3 F.3d 613 (2d Cir. 1993) [where persecuting government fell and new government in place, the preponderance of evidence is established absent countervailing evidence]; *Matter of A-T-,* 24 I&N Dec. 296 (BIA 2007) [Mali female subject to FGM in past denied withholding because despite past persecution it is not continuing persecution and therefore future harm not established]; *Matter of H-M,* 20 I&N Dec. 683 (BIA 1993) [in past persecution case, administrative notice of changed conditions meets rebuttable presumption test].

g. *Humanitarian Asylum for Severe Past Persecution*—Where the presumption of future persecution has been rebutted, an applicant may still obtain asylum if s/he can demonstrate a compelling reason s/he is unable or unwilling to return because of severe past persecution, *i.e.,* "humanitarian" asylum. 8 C.F.R. §§208.13(b)(1)(iii)(A), 1208.13(b)(1)(iii)(A); *Matter of Chen,* 20 I&N Dec. 16, 21 (BIA 1989); *Matter of S-A-K- and H-A-H-,* 24 I&N Dec. 464 (BIA 2008) [mother and daughter from Somalia who suffered FGM and continue to suffer side effects from it are entitled to asylum on humanitarian grounds]; *Matter of B-,* 21 I&N Dec. 66 (BIA 1995); *Matter of H-,* 21 I&N Dec. 337, 347–48 (BIA 1996) [compelling factors include "age, health, and family" factors]; *Mohammed v. Gonzales,* 400 F.3d 785, 801 (9th Cir. 2005) [suggesting that person subject to FGM may be eligible for humanitarian asylum given the severity of the past persecution]; *Brucaj v. Ashcroft,* 381 F.3d 602, 608–11 (7th Cir. 2004) [remanding because BIA's decision was unclear in dismissing humanitarian claim]; *Lal v. INS,* 255 F.3d 998, 1002–10 (9th Cir. 2001), *amended on reh'g,* 268 F.3d 1148 (9th Cir. 2001) [BIA denial of asylum and withholding reversed where the BIA, contrary to *Chen,* regulations, and BIA and 9th Cir. case law, added a requirement that "ongoing disability" should be considered as a factor for persons subject to severe past persecution]; *Vongsakdy v. INS,* 171 F.3d 1203, 1206–07 (9th Cir. 1999) [Laotian in labor camp suffered "atrocious forms of persecution" that do not require any further inquiry regarding future persecution]; *Rodriguez-Matamoros v. INS*, 86 F.3d 158, 160–61 (9th Cir. 1996) [past persecution and remand to determine discretionary exercise]; *see also Niang v. Gonzales,* 492 F.3d 505, 514 n.13 (4th Cir. 2007) [humanitarian asylum may be an option for woman facing "Sophie's choice" of taking USC child with her who will suffer from FGM in Senegal or leaving her here alone], *but see Jalloh v. Gonzales,* 498 F.3d 148 (2d Cir. 2007) [applicant from Sierra Leone did not provide evidence that his persecution had long-lasting physical or mental effects]; *Naizgi v. Gonzales,* 455 F.3d 484, 487–88 (4th Cir. 2006) [affirmed BIA reversal of humanitarian asylum grant for Eritrean because status reserved only for atrocious forms of persecution]; *Shehu v. Gonzales,* 443 F.3d 435, 440–41 (5th Cir. 2006) [where some facts related to relatives of Kosovo Muslim and not to her, where others, such as forced exile, were not more severe than others who faced persecution, humanitarian asylum was denied];*Reyes-Morales v. Gonzales,* 435 F.3d 937, 942 (8th Cir. 2006) [despite applicant being beaten unconscious by members of Salvadoran military which left him physically deformed and where friends were also killed during the incident, it was not arbitrary and capricious for BIA to deny relief]; *Ang v. Gonzales,* 430 F.3d 50, 57–58 (1st Cir. 2005) [suggesting that humanitarian asylum for people who assist the U.S. in other countries "would rip a mammoth hole in the fabric of the immigration laws"]; *Ngarurih v. Ashcroft,* 371 F.3d 182, 189–91 (4th Cir. 2004) [torture of applicant while in prison was not one of the "rare" case warranting humanitarian asylum]; *Quevedo v. Ashcroft,* 336 F.3d 39, 45 (1st Cir. 2003) [a single incident of persecution of short duration where there were no subsequent acts of recrimination not severe enough]; *Woldemeskel v. INS*, 257 F.3d 1185, 1187–90 (10th Cir. 2001) [past persecution not severe where Ethiopian of Amhara background was tortured and kept in prison, but since release has married, has two children and lived in Ethiopia for many years]; *Dobrota v. INS,* 195 F.3d 970, 974 (7th Cir. 1999) [only in rare cases is past persecution so severe that it would be inhumane to return the alien to his native country even in the absence of future persecution]; *Gonahasa v. INS,* 181 F.3d 538, 544 (4th Cir. 1999) [eligibility based on severity alone is reserved for the "most atrocious abuse"]; *Bachkova v. INS*, 109 F.3d 376 (7th Cir. 1997) [no asylum for applicant who was interrogated, incarcerated, forced to act against her political will and beaten by former communist authorities]; *Acewicz v. INS*, 984 F.2d 1056, 1062 (9th Cir. 1993) [persecution must be atrocious]; *Tokarska v. INS*, 978 F.2d 1, 2 (1st Cir. 1992); *Rivera-Cruz v. INS*, 948 F.2d 962, 969 (5th Cir. 1991) [asylum denied where level of past persecution did not indicate that repatriation was inhumane]; *Kapcia v. INS*, 944 F.2d 702, 708 (10th Cir. 1991) [where past persecution not severe and there is little likelihood of future persecution, asylum denied]. *Skalak v. INS*, 944 F.2d 364 (7th Cir. 1991) [past persecution is rebuttable presumption]; *Matter of N-M-A-,* 22 I&N Dec 312 (BIA 1998) [denying asylum notwithstanding torture where "the degree of harm suffered by the applicant, the length of time over which the harm was inflicted, and the lack of evidence of severe psychological trauma stemming from the harm" did not rise to the level of "compelling circumstances"].

h. *Other Serious Harm*—Where the government has successfully rebutted the past persecution claim by demonstrating that the applicant is not likely to suffer future persecution, s/he may still be able to obtain asylum if there is "a reasonable possibility that he or she may suffer other serious harm upon removal to that country." 8 C.F.R. §§208.13(b)(1)(iii)(B), 1208.13(b)(1)(iii)(B); 63 Fed. Reg. 31945, 31947 (June 11, 1998); *Liti v. Gonzales,* 411 F.3d 631, 641–42 (6th Cir. 2005) [staying removal to allow BIA to *sua sponte* consider humanitarian claim]; *Belishta v. Ashcroft,* 378 F.3d 1078 (9th Cir. 2004) [upholding denial of asylum on the record but staying order to permit BIA to reopen case under this regulation which the circuit court interprets not to require serious harm as a result of any particular animus].

6. *Corroboration*—Past persecution, like other asylum claims, does not require corroborative evidence but may be established through the applicant's own credible testimony. 8 C.F.R. §208.13(a); *Garrovillas v. INS,* 156 F.3d 1010, 1016–17 (9th Cir. 1998); *Bace v. Ashcroft,* 352 F.3d 1133, 1140–41 (7th Cir. 2003) [where asylum claim based upon specific events corroborative evidence of general conditions not needed]. *See in this chapter* "REAL ID Act of 2005 and Corroboration," ¶ XII.B.2.f(5) (p.531) & XII.B.2.g(3) (p.545), *infra*.

C. *Well-Founded Fear Claim*— A person need not have actually suffered persecution in the past to qualify for asylum. A person may also qualify for asylum if s/he has a well-founded fear of future persecution. INA §101(a)(42), 8 U.S.C. §1101(a)(42). To prevail on a well-founded fear claim, the applicant must show that a "reasonable person in his circumstances would fear persecution." *Matter of Mogharrabi*, 19 I&N Dec. 439, 445 (BIA 1987); *Matter of Barrera*, 19 I&N Dec. 837, 845 (BIA 1989). The quantum of proof is a reasonable possibility which may be as little as a 10% chance of future persecution occurring. *See INS v. Cardoza-Fonseca*, 480 U.S. 421 (1987); 8 C.F.R. §208.13(b)(2)(i)(B); §1208.13(b)(2)(i)(B) [must show reasonable possibility of persecution]; *Kaiser v. Ashcroft,* 390 F.3d 653, 658–59 (9th Cir. 2004) [BIA reversed where it held that former Pakistani military officer had not met burden of proof because threatened harm against him by MQM was not carried out]. *See also in this chapter "Standard of Persuasion—Asylum,"* ¶ XII.B.2.c (p.524), *infra*. The well-founded fear test involves both a *subjective* component (fear) *and* an *objective* component (reasonable possibility of persecution). *See e.g., Jorgji v. Mukasey,* 514 F.3d 53, 58 (1st Cir. 2008) [Albanian applicant who saw people being executed as a child may have a subjective fear but she did not have an objective basis for fear regarding events of religious and other persecution that occurred 15 to 35 years ago during a Stalinist government that no longer exists]. The persecutor's knowledge of the applicant's activities or that he would become aware of the applicant is a consideration. *Myat Thu v. Attorney General of the USA,* 510 F.3d 405, 413–15 (3d Cir. 2007) [political activities in Japan with BDA and in Burma with the NLD may establish basis for asylum if the Burmese military is aware of the applicant and case was remanded in light of DOS reports and letters indicating that the Burmese military would be aware of applicants activities]. Must show that "the alien possesses a characteristic a persecutor seeks to overcome by punishing the individuals who possess it, that a persecutor is aware or could become aware the alien possesses this characteristic, that a persecutor has the capability of punishing the alien, and that a persecutor has the inclination to punish the alien." *Matter of Mogharrabi, supra* at 446. Compare with Handbook ¶¶42 and 45, which provide that a well-founded fear exists if the applicant finds his return "intolerable" or otherwise wishes to avoid return because it entails some risk. "Fear" is defined as "a genuine apprehension or awareness of danger in another country." *Matter of Acosta*, 19 I&N Dec. 211, 221 (BIA 1985). Where IJ, in analyzing subjective fear component, failed to distinguish fortitude in the face of danger from the absence of fear, denial of asylum was reversed. *Singh v. Moschorak*, 53 F.3d 1031, 1034 (9th Cir. 1995) [Sikh who continued demonstration in the face of repeated arrests improperly denied asylum]. *See also De Santamaria v. U.S. Att'y Gen.,* ___ F.3d __ (11th Cir. Apr. 22, 2008) [Colombian applicant's return trips home in the face of FARC persecution did not negate her subjective fear]. *But see Aruta v. INS*, 80 F.3d 1389 (9th Cir. 1996) [no reasonable fear of return to Philippines]. *Del Valle v. INS*, 776 F.2d 1407, 1412 (9th Cir. 1985); *Platero-Cortez v. INS*, 804 F.2d 1127 (9th Cir. 1986).

1. *Persecutor Need Not be Presently Aware of Offending Act*—It is not relevant that the persecutor be aware of the offending act, but rather, whether he will become aware of it. *Eduard v. Ashcroft,* 379 F.3d 182, 192–93 (5th Cir. 2004) [IJ erred in requiring Indonesian Christians to prove that persecutor was aware of their religion and race rather than that persecutor could become aware of it]; *Najafi v. INS*, 104 F.3d 943, 949 (7th Cir. 1997) [Iranian who converted to Christianity need not show that Iranian authorities knew about it]. *cf. Myat Thu v. Attorney General of the USA,* 510 F.3d 405, 413–15 (3d Cir. 2007) [political activities in Japan with BDA and in Burma with the NLD may establish basis for asylum if the Burmese military is aware of the applicant and case was remanded in light of DOS reports and letters indicating that the Burmese military would be aware of applicants activities]. Similarly, an applicant is also not required to prove that he fled his country due to persecution if he has a valid claim now. *Wiransane v. Ashcroft,* 366 F.3d 889, 899 (10th Cir. 2004); *Melkonian v. Ashcroft,* 320 F.3d 1061, 1068 (9th Cir. 2003) [fear of persecution need not be the only motivation for leaving and the fact that someone seeks asylum based on future persecution means that the reasons for leaving while probative are not the ultimate issues].

2. *Disclosure of Asylum Application As Independent Basis*—Under 8 C.F.R. §1208.6(a) DHS officers are precluded from disclosing that a respondent has sought asylum. If a DHS officer does disclose the information through inadvertence or neglect to officials from the applicant's country, it may be a separate basis for asylum. *See in this part* "Breach of Confidentiality of Asylum," ¶ A.3.p (p.444), *supra*.

3. *Burden of Proof in Pattern and Practice Cases*—In well-founded fear cases, the applicant need not establish that s/he would be "singled out individually for persecution" if there is a "pattern or

practice" of persecution of people "similarly situated to the applicant." 8 C.F.R. §§208.13(b)(2)(iii)(A)–(B), 1208.13(b)(2)(iii)(A)–(B); *Mufied v. Mukasey,* 508 F.3d 88 (2d Cir. 2007) [remanded case to BIA whether Christians in Indonesia of ethnicities other than Chinese are subject to a pattern and practice of persecution; *Matter of A-M-* distinguished]; *Ghebrehiwot v. Att'y Gen. of the U.S.,* 467 F.3d 344, 353–55 (3d Cir. 2006) [where IJ failed to consider DOS report and 30 other document submitted by Eritrean Pentecostal Christian and focused only on past persecution, the court remanded to consider whether there is a pattern and practice of future persecution]; *Banks v. Gonzales,* 453 F.3d 449, 452–53 (7th Cir. 2006) [IJ erred in requiring Liberian of Krahn tribe to present evidence that she was singled out for persecution because all parties conceded the Krahn tribe was persecuted and the applicant does not have the burden of asserting §1208.13(b)(2)(iii)]; *Tun v. INS,* 445 F.3d 554, 569–71 (2d Cir. 2006) [Burmese citizen who engaged in pro-democracy political demonstrations in the U.S. against Burmese government was eligible for well-founded fear claim based upon Burmese government's pattern and practice of punishing exiles who are politically active and IJ was reversed where he believed applicant had to show individualized claim or even that the Burmese government was aware of him as an individual]; *Sukwanputra v. Gonzales,* 434 F.3d 627, 637 (3d Cir. 2006) [reversing IJ for failing to consider whether Indonesian of Chinese ethnicity is subject to pattern or practice of persecution]; *Himri v. Ashcroft,* 378 F.3d 932, 936–38 (9th Cir. 2004) [Palestinians who lived in Kuwait were persecuted minority]; *Eduard v. Ashcroft,* 379 F.3d 182, 192 (5th Cir. 2004) [IJ erred in requiring Indonesian Christians to prove they were singled out for persecution when evidence indicated a pattern and practice of persecution of Christians]. To establish a pattern or practice of persecution an applicant must present evidence of systematic persecution of a group and that persecutors target the group specifically on account of one of the five statutory grounds. *Kho v. Keisler,* 505 F.3d 50, 54–55 (1st Cir. 2007) [no ongoing pattern or practice of persecution against ethnic Chinese or Christians in Indonesia]. *See also Matter of A-M-,* 23 I&N Dec. 737, 740–41 (BIA 2005) [record did not show pattern or practice of persecution in Indonesia against Chinese Christians]; *Kaharudin v. Gonzales,* 500 F.3d 619, 623–25 & n.4 (7th Cir. 2007) [Chinese Christians in Indonesia are not subject to a pattern and practice of persecution and cases cited therein];*Gomes v. Gonzales,* 429 F.3d 1264, 1267 (9th Cir. 2005) [denying pattern and practice claim of Christian in Bangladesh where country report stated government did not countenance attacks]; *Avetova-Elisseva v. INS,* 213 F.3d 1192 (9th Cir. 2000) [Armenian in Russia who could not establish past persecution could nevertheless establish a well-founded fear of future persecution based upon her ethnicity in light of the "pattern or practice" of persecution which Russian authorities were unable or unwilling to stop]; *Chen v. INS,* 195 F.3d 198, 203 (4th Cir. 1999) ["[t]he 'well founded fear' standard ... does not require an asylum petitioner to show that he will be individually targeted or 'singled out' for persecution"]; *Hamzehi v. INS*, 64 F.3d 1240, 1250 (8th Cir. 1995) (Godbold, dissenting). *See also Singh v. INS*, 94 F.3d 1353 (9th Cir. 1996) [rejecting BIA concept that because all Indo-Fijians may be persecuted asylum is unavailable to them]; *Makonnen v. INS*, 44 F.3d 1378, 1382–84 (8th Cir. 1995) [reversing BIA where it ignored regulation and sought to require all members of the group to show persecution]; *Kotasz v. INS*, 31 F.3d 847 (9th Cir. 1994) [reversing BIA denial where person was member of anticommunist subgroup]. However, at least one circuit has taken the position that the identifiable group must "suffer systematic or pervasive persecution." *Woldemeskel v. INS,* 257 F.3d 1185, 1191 (10th Cir. 2001) [discrimination against Amhara ethnicity in Ethiopia is not sufficient to show systematic and pervasive persecution]. *See also Sela v. Mukasey,* 520 F.3d 44, 46 (1st Cir. 2008) [sporadic violence toward Christians in Indonesia is insufficient]; *Woldemichael v. Ashcroft,* 448 F.3d 1000, 1003–05 (8th Cir. 2006) [a 54-year old Jehovah's Witness could not demonstrate pattern and practice persecution in Eritrea because State Department's. documentation focused on persecution only against those who refused to vote for independence or refused to obey the requirement of national service and neither was applicable to the applicant].

4. *Burden of Proof, Disfavored Group*—Even if there is no pattern or practice, applicants may still obtain asylum if they are a member of a "disfavored group." *Sael v. Ashcroft,* 386 F.3d 922, 925–30 (9th Cir. 2004) [ethnic Chinese minority is a disfavored group in Indonesia and the applicant submitted evidence establishing the required "comparatively low" level of individualized risk for a member of a disfavored group (*i.e.,* various incidents of discrimination, harassment and threats) to prove a well-founded fear of future persecution]; *Hoxha v. Ashcroft*, 319 F.3d 1179, 1183–84 (9th Cir. 2003) [in regard to Albanians persecuted in Serbia, to the degree that the record reveals a

particular group is targeted, even if there is no "pattern or practice" of persecution under §208.13(b)(2), the individual's burden of proof is lessened]. *Cf. Lolong v. Gonzales,* 484 F.3d 1173, 1178–81 (9th Cir. 2007) (*en banc*) [relying on fears common to Chinese Christian women from Indonesia was insufficient where there was no argument of being targeted individually and no showing that the government was unable or unwilling to stop persecution in light of DOS reports]. *But see Kho v. Keisler,* 505 F.3d 50, 55 (1st Cir. 2007) [rejected "disfavored group" rule established by the Ninth Circuit as beyond the regulatory and statutory scheme].

5. *No Well-Founded Fear if Relocation is Reasonable*—In a case based upon a well-founded fear of future persecution, the applicant has the burden of demonstrating that it would not be reasonable to internally relocate unless the government is the persecutor. To be "unable or unwilling to return" to his or her home country, the applicant must demonstrate that s/he has a well-founded fear of returning to any place in the country, not just that s/he is unable to return to a particular place, city or abode within that country. 8 C.F.R. §§208.13(b)(2)(ii), 1208.13(b)(2)(ii) ["[a]n applicant does not have a well-founded fear of persecution if the applicant could avoid persecution by relocating to another part of the applicant's country of nationality...if under all the circumstances it would be reasonable...."]; 8 C.F.R. §208.16(b)(1)(i)(B), 1208.16(b)(1)(i)(B) [applicant could avoid a future threat to his or her life or freedom by relocating to another part of the country of removal and it would be reasonable to do so]; *Matter of Acosta*, 19 I&N Dec. 211 (BIA 1985). Criteria for reasonableness of internal relocation include, but are not limited to, whether person would face other serious harm in place of relocation; any ongoing civil strife within the country; administrative, economic, or judicial infrastructure; geographical limitations; and social and cultural constraints such as age, gender, health and social and familial ties. 8 C.F.R. §208.13(b)(3); *Hagi-Salad v. Ashcroft,* 359 F.3d 1044 (8th Cir. 2004) [where BIA failed to follow the criteria in §208.13(b)(3) and instead found that the applicant could not "reasonably fear harm" if relocated, the court reversed the denial of asylum]. Where the applicant has not established past persecution, or that the persecution is by the government or is government sponsored, he bears the burden of establishing that relocation is unreasonable. 8 C.F.R. §§208.13(b)(3)(i), 1208.13(b)(3)(i); *Mohamed v. Ashcroft,* 396 F.3d 999, 1006–07 (8th Cir. 2005) [IJ did not have to make reasonableness determination in returning applicant to any part of Somalia because applicant did not suffer past persecution and the burden therefore was on the applicant]; *Lopez-Gomez v. Ashcroft,* 263 F.3d 442 (5th Cir. 2001) [applicant has burden to demonstrate that persecution is not geographically limited when claim is not based on the government as persecutor]. Where the persecutor is the government, persecution is government sponsored, or the applicant has established past persecution, it is presumed that internal relocation is unreasonable unless the Service establishes by a preponderance of the evidence that relocation is reasonable. 8 C.F.R. §208.13(b)(3)(ii); *Yang v. Gonzales,* 427 F.3d 1117, 1122 (8th Cir. 2005) [where IJ speculated that applicant could avoid persecution in China under coercive population policy by relocating, court reversed because the Service has the burden]; *Melkonian v. Ashcroft,* 320 F.3d 1061, 1069–71 (9th Cir. 2003) [Armenian Christian escaping Muslim held Abkhazia had rebuttable presumption that threat existed nationwide and government had the burden to show that he could reasonably relocate]; *Manzoor v. DOJ,* 254 F.3d 342 (1st Cir. 2001) [reversing denial of asylum where BIA impermissibly relied solely on DOS report in finding lack of countrywide persecution despite applicant's contrary testimony and where BIA improperly put burden on applicant who had established past government sponsored persecution]; *Abdel-Masieh v. INS,* 73 F.3d 579, 586–87 (5th Cir. 1996); *Singh v. Moschorak*, 53 F.3d 1031, 1034 (9th Cir. 1995); *Singh v. Ilchert*, 69 F.3d 375, 379–81 (9th Cir. 1995); *Matter of H-*, 21 I&N Dec. 337, 349 n.7 (BIA 1996).

5.a. *Cases Finding Relocation Unreasonable/Countrywide Persecution—Ruiz v. Gonzales,* 479 F.3d 762, 767 (11th Cir. 2007) [ICE failed to establish by preponderance of the evidence that applicant could reasonably relocate within Colombia]; *Mema v. Gonzales,* 474 F.3d 412, 419 (7th Cir. 2007) [reversed IJ's finding that asylum applicant was not sought by police while in hiding where adverse credibility determination was not supported by the record];*Arboleda v. U.S. Att'y Gen.,* 434 F.3d 1220 (11th Cir. 2006) [where government conceded past persecution, its submission of a 1997 Asylum Profile and 1999 and 2000 DOS reports on Colombia did not establish that respondent could relocate to avoid the FARC which the court stated "operates country-wide in Colombia"]; *Gao v. Gonzales,* 440 F.3d 62, 71–72 (2d Cir. 2006) [reversing IJ finding that women who had been sold into marriage could relocate within China]; *Tapiero De Orejuela v. Gonzales,* 423 F.3d 666, 674 (7th Cir. 2005) [educated, landowning class of cattle farmers targeted by FARC would face nationwide persecution given FARC's presence throughout Colombia]; *Kaiser v. Ashcroft,* 390 F.3d 653, 659–60 (9th Cir. 2004) [former Pakistani military officer would be persecuted nationwide by MQM]; *Eduard v. Ashcroft,* 379 F.3d 182, 193–94 (5th Cir. 2004) [IJ erred in confusing whether a person could relocate within their country "if necessary" with whether it was reasonable to do so]; *Knezevic v. Ashcroft,* 367 F.3d 12061214–16 (9th Cir. 2004) [relocation to Serb held areas of Bosnia-Herzegovina is not reasonable where applicants were elderly, had no home, no business, no possessions, no place to go and the quality of life was abysmal]; *Cardenas v. INS,* 294 F.3d 1062 (9th Cir. 2002) [reversing BIA determination that Peruvian suffering persecution from the Shining Path had not demonstrated fear that was countrywide]; *Hengan v. INS,* 79 F.3d 60, 62–63 (7th Cir. 1996) [Romanian government unable or unwilling to stop persecution of Hungarian minority]; *Matter of Kasinga*, 21 I&N Dec. 357, 367 (BIA 1996) [where country small and there is evidence police would not protect women, countrywide persecution was established]. Moreover, courts have held that where a persecutor shows no intent to limit his persecution to any one area and the alien can be readily identified, he is at risk countrywide. *Damaize-Job v. INS*, 787 F.2d 1332 (9th Cir. 1986) [Miskito Indian in Nicaragua].

5.b. *Cases Finding Relocation Reasonable/No Countrywide Persecution—Guillaume v. Gonzales,* 504 F.3d 68, 73 (1st Cir. 2007) [applicant could not demonstrate that if he moved to Gonaives from Port-au-Prince he would continue to face persecution]; *Tendean v. Gonzales,* 503 F.3d 8, 10–11 (1st Cir. 2007) [Indonesian from small village where he claims father's opponents persecute him could relocate to another village in the country because there was no showing that political opponents had any capacity or inclination to pursue him]; *Singh v. BIA,* 435 F.3d 216, 219 (2d Cir. 2006) [Sikh could relocate in India without facing religious persecution]; *Galicia v. Ashcroft,* 396 F.3d 446, 448 (1st Cir. 2005) [Guatemalan gay man failed to rebut claim that he could return to other places in country without persecution]; *Mazariegos v. INS,* 241 F.3d 1320 (11th Cir. 2001) [denying asylum to low level Guatemalan soldier who failed to establish countrywide nongovernmental persecution]; *Etugh v. INS*, 921 F.2d 36, 39 (3d Cir. 1990) [Nigerian denied asylum where he feared tribal conflict in one area of country]; *Abdel-Masieh v. INS*, 73 F.3d 579, 585–86 n.5 (5th Cir. 1996) [Sudanese CDPHC did not have to return to rebel area]; *Matter of C-A-L-*, 21 I&N Dec. 754, 757–58 (BIA 1997) [where problem confined to applicant's hometown, he failed to establish countrywide persecution]; *Matter of R-*, 20 I&N Dec. 621 (BIA 1992), *remanded to the district court sub nom. Rana v. Moschorak*, 37 F.3d 1506 (9th Cir. 1994) [Sikh may not be persecuted in other parts of India].

5.c. *No Deportation to Third Country Without Considering Well-Founded Fear*—The BIA cannot order deportation to a different country on appeal where no evidence was taken on whether the person has a well-founded fear of persecution in that country. *Kossov v. INS*, 132 F.3d 405 (7th Cir. 1998) [evidence of persecution in Latvia, but deportation to Russia]. *Accord Kuhai v. INS,* 199 F.3d 909 (7th Cir. 1999) [evidence of well-founded fear regarding Uzbekistan, but removal to Ukraine]; *Andriasian v. INS,* 180 F.3d 1033, 1041 (9th Cir. 1999) [IJ's last-minute switch of country of deportation violates due process for lack of proper notice].

D. *Mandatory Denial of Asylum*—Congress has mandated by statute numerous exceptions and exclusions to the grant of asylum. INA §208(a)(2) and (b)(2), 8 U.S.C. §1158(a)(2) and (b)(2). An Asylum Officer (AO) or IJ may not grant an asylum application filed after Apr. 1, 1997 [8 C.F.R. §§208.13(c)(1), 1208.13(c)(1)] if:

1. *Persecution of Others*—The applicant ordered, incited, assisted or otherwise participated in the persecution of others; *see in this chapter* section II.B (p.432), *supra.*

2. *Particularly Serious Crime*—The applicant, having been convicted by a final judgment of a particularly serious crime in the U.S., constitutes a danger to the community;

3. *Serious Nonpolitical Crime*—There are serious reasons for believing that the applicant has committed a serious, nonpolitical crime outside the U.S. prior to arrival [the aggravated felony bar was not made applicable to this section by statute]; *Khouzam v. Ashcroft,* 361 F.3d 161, 165–66 (2d Cir. 2004) [serious reasons under this statute is equivalent to probable cause]; *Pronsivakulchai v. Gonzales,* 461 F.3d 903 (7th Cir. 2006) [reversing IJ's finding that there was reason to believe the

applicant had committed a drug trafficking crime in Thailand when she was deprived of the right to present rebuttal evidence];

4. *Danger to U.S. Security*—There are reasonable grounds for regarding the alien as a danger to the security of the U.S.;

5. *Terrorism*—The applicant is described as a terrorist under INA §212(a)(3)(B)(i)(I)–(IV) or (VI), or §237(a)(4)(B). This provision applies to asylum applications filed on or after May 11, 2005. *See* REAL ID Act of 2005 §101(b), PL 109-13 (May 11, 2005). For applications filed before May 11, 2005, the bar to asylum applies only to persons found inadmissible or deportable as a terrorist. The burden is on the applicant to demonstrate otherwise by clear and convincing evidence. *Matter of S-K-* 23 I&N Dec. 936, 942 n.5 (BIA 2006) [finding respondent barred from withholding and asylum because the Chin National Front in Burma is a terrorist organization and a contribution of $685 over an 11-month period was sufficient to establish "material" support]. *Cf. Matter of S-K-,* 24 I&N Dec. 289 (AG 2007) [maintaining precedential value of BIA decision but remanding case to BIA in light of DHS decision to grant a waiver under INA §212(d)(3)(B)(i) and not to apply the "material support" bar on asylum to certain persons providing support to the CNF]. INA §212(a)(3)(B)(i)(IV) does not apply if the AG determines that there are not reasonable grounds for regarding the applicant as a danger to U.S. security. Subsequent to the A.G.'s decision, the Secretary of DHS and the Secretary of State were given broader powers to waive the provision under the Consolidated Appropriations Act, 2008, PL 110-161, Div. J, §691(a), 121 Stat. 1844, 2364–65 and the Act itself exempted certain groups, including the CNF, that was the subject of the AG's decision in *Matter of S-K-*. The Secretary of DHS also exercised his authority to waive the "material support" provision for persons who provided support under "duress" to terrorist organizations (*e.g.*, asylees who were required to pay ransom or extortion money). Memo, Chertoff, Secy. of DHS, Exercise of Authority Under Sec. 212(d)(3)(B)(i) (Apr. 27, 2007), *published on* AILA InfoNet at Doc. No. 07050168. For a detailed discussion of criteria to grant waiver, *see* Ch. 3, ¶ III.H.2.d(6)(b) (p.105), *supra.*

   In light of Congress' Act DHS granted the respondent asylum and the BIA vacated its grant of deferral of removal and found no need to address withholding. *Matter of S-K-,* 24 I&N Dec. 475 (BIA 2008). *See generally McAllister v. Att'y Gen. of the U.S.,* 444 F.3d 178, 188–89 (3d Cir. 2006) [upheld ineligibility for asylum or withholding where respondent found deportable under INA §237(a)(4)(B)]; *Bellout v. Ashcroft,* 363 F.3d 975 (9th Cir. 2004) [upholding bar to asylum because there was substantial evidence that person was engaged in terrorist activity; distinguishing *Cheema* as a case under prior law]; *Matter of U-H-,* 23 I&N Dec. 355, 356 (BIA 2002) [finding that §412 of the USA PATRIOT Act did not alter the "reasonable grounds to believe" standard]; *Cheema v. Ashcroft,* 383 F.3d 848, 857–59 (9th Cir. 2004) [reversing BIA finding that persons who supported terrorist activity in India are ineligible for asylum and rejecting BIA's analysis as collapsing a finding of terrorism and a danger to security into one]; *Perinpanathan v. INS,* 310 F.3d 594, 598–99 (8th Cir. 2002) [where applicant voluntarily participated in activities of the Tamil Tigers, asylum was barred].

6. *Firm Resettlement*—The applicant has been firmly resettled in another country prior to arriving in the U.S. 8 C.F.R. §§208.13(c)(2)(i)(B), 208.15. The applicant will be deemed firmly resettled if, prior to arriving in the U.S., he or she entered another country with, or while in that country received, an offer of permanent resident status, citizenship or some other type of permanent resettlement, unless s/he establishes (a) that her entry into the country was a necessary consequence of her flight from persecution, she remained in that country only as long as necessary to make further travel arrangements, and she did not establish significant ties to that country; or (b) that the conditions of her residence were so "substantially and consciously restricted" by the authority of the country that she was not in fact resettled. 8 C.F.R. §§208.15, 1208.15. The offer must be for permanent, not temporary, residence in a third country where the applicant lived peacefully and without restriction. *Maharaj v. Gonzales,* 450 F.3d 961, 969 (9th Cir. 2006) (*en banc*). Where firm resettlement is found, the bar applies even if the country where the person was resettled will no longer accept her because of expired travel documents. *Sultani v. Gonzales,* 455 F.3d 878, 883–84 (8th Cir. 2006) [Afghan's claim that Australian refugee status expired is not a basis for an exception to the bar and there was no evidence regarding possible persecution from Australia]; *Firmansjah v. Gonzales,* 424 F.3d 598, 601–04 (7th Cir. 2005) [Catholic Indonesian woman of Chinese descent whose resident status in Singapore may have lapsed due to her prolonged stay was

still barred because "firm resettlement" relates to the time "prior to" the applicant's arrival in the U.S.]; *Vang v. INS,* 146 F.3d 1114, 1117 (9th Cir. 1998). *See also Abdalla v. INS,* 43 F.3d 1397, 1400 (10th Cir. 1994); *Salazar v. Ashcroft,* 359 F.3d 45 (1st Cir. 2004) [Peruvian given residency in Venezuela was firmly resettled]. In determining whether a person's life was so restrictive that s/he was not resettled, the AO and IJ shall consider the living conditions of other residents, the type and extent of housing and employment opportunities, the right of the applicant to obtain property, and the right to enjoy other privileges and rights of the country including travel, education, re-entry, public relief and naturalization. 8 C.F.R. §§208.15(b), 1208.15(b). Length of stay alone in a country is not determinative of firm resettlement. *Camposeco-Montejo v. Ashcroft,* 384 F.3d 814, 818–21 (9th Cir. 2004) [Guatemalan who lived 16 years in Mexico but with no official permanent status]; *Elizour v. Ashcroft,* 378 F.3d 1143, 1151–52 (10th Cir. 2004) [stay in Canada for four years where government denied permanent status, refused asylum, and ordered deportation is not firm resettlement].

6.a. *Totality of the Circumstances*—At least three circuits have strictly adhered to the language of 8 C.F.R. §208.15 and rejected a "totality of the circumstances approach" in determining firm resettlement. *Maharaj v. Gonzales,* 450 F.3d 961, 971–76 (9th Cir. 2006) (*en banc*) [court adopted an "offer-based approach" where the government has the burden to demonstrate that a formal offer of official status has been made to the applicant permitting her to remain indefinitely in the country before the burden shifts to the applicant]; *Diallo v. Ashcroft,* 381 F.3d 687 (7th Cir. 2004) [reversing IJ's finding of firm resettlement of Mauritanian citizen in Senegal and noting that the IJ could not consider factors such as respondent's length of stay until determining that the applicant had been given a permanent offer]; *Abdille v. Ashcroft,* 242 F.3d 477 (3d Cir. 2001) [where person granted asylum for 2 years in South Africa, court reversed firm resettlement finding and remanded case for further evidentiary proceedings to determine whether as a matter of law or policy applicant was firmly resettled]. *See also Matter of Soleimani,* 20 I&N Dec. 99 (BIA 1989) [notwithstanding Israel's law of return permitting Jews to resettle in Israel, an Iranian Jew who stayed in Israel on a tourist visa and then sought more permanent status was *not* firmly resettled. The BIA used additional criteria to determine firm resettlement such as: (1) time between flight and asylum application; (2) family ties; (3) intent; and (4) business and property connections]. *But see Sall v. Gonzales,* 437 F.3d 229, 232–34 (2d Cir. 2006) [applying the "totality of the circumstances" approach, noting other circuits adopting the same, and finding that a citizen of Mauritania was not firmly resettled in Senegal].

6.b. *Burden of Proof*—The government has the burden of proving that the applicant is firmly resettled. The applicant may rebut firm resettlement by demonstrating an exception in 8 C.F.R. §208.15(a), (b). *See also Mussie v. INS*, 172 F.3d 329 (4th Cir. 1999) [where person granted asylum in Germany, issued travel documents and lived in Germany for 6 years, INS had introduced "some evidence" and petitioner failed to overcome it]; *Cheo v. INS*, 162 F.3d 1227, 1229–30 (9th Cir. 1998) [where Cambodians lived in Malaysia for three years they failed to rebut inference of firm resettlement]; *Abdalla v. INS*, 43 F.3d 1397 (10th Cir. 1994) [Sudanese citizen living in the UAE for 20 years]. *But see Maharaj v. Gonzales,* 450 F.3d 961, 977–78 (9th Cir. 2006) (*en banc*) [where applicant left Canada before being granted permanent residency, the government had the burden of demonstrating the significance of that process and whether it was an offer of permanent residency at the stage the applicant left so that the burden shifts to the applicant]; *Makadji v. Gonzales,* 470 F.3d 450, 454–58 (2d Cir. 2006)[reversing IJ's finding of firm resettlement based simply on length of residence because government did not meet initial burden]; *Wangchuck v. DHS,* 448 F.3d 524, 529 (2d Cir. 2006) [applicant raised in India from Tibetan parents improperly put burden on applicant to establish he was not firmly resettled in India]; *Sall v. Gonzales,* 437 F.3d 229, 232–34 (2d Cir. 2006) [reversing IJ who placed burden of proof on applicant because government has initial burden to establish firm resettlement, but a peaceful stay in a third country may create a presumption that the applicant must rebut]; *Diallo v. Ashcroft,* 381 F.3d 687, 693 (7th Cir. 2004) [government has the initial burden of demonstrating that applicant was firmly resettled and only then does burden shift to the applicant to rebut the presumption]; *Firmansjah v. Gonzales,* 424 F.3d 598, 601–04 (7th Cir. 2005) [Indonesian woman who is Catholic and of Chinese decent testified to her residence status in Singapore]

6.c. *Fear in Third Country*—Firm resettlement is not applicable to a person who settled in a third country, but has a well-founded fear of remaining in that country. *Siong v. INS,* 376 F.3d 1030, 1040 (9th Cir. 2004) [Laotian of Hmong ethnicity who became a citizen of France but who is being targeted by Laotian communists for his previous CIA work is not firmly resettled in France if he is seeking asylum from France].

6.d. *Parent Status Imputed to Child*—For purposes of determining resettlement, the parent's status is determinative of a minor child's status even if the child is now over 21 and petitioning separately. *Vang v. INS,* 146 F.3d 1114 (9th Cir. 1998) [22-year-old denied asylum because his parents were firmly resettled while he was a minor].

6.e. *Cases Finding No Resettlement*—*Makadji v. Gonzales,* 470 F.3d 450, 454–58 (2d Cir. 2006)[IJ reversed in finding firm resettlement simply because Mauritanian lived in Mali for 10 years, because government did not meet initial burden]; *Haile v. Gonzales,* 421 F.3d 493, 497 (7th Cir. 2005) [possession of Eritrean passport without ever being in Eritrea is insufficient to demonstrate firm resettlement]; *Ali v. Ashcroft,* 394 F.3d 780, 789–91 (9th Cir. 2005) [although applicant lived in Ethiopia for five years after fleeing Somalia, she was not offered permanent residence or its equivalent and therefore was not firmly resettled]; *Elizour v. Ashcroft,* 378 F.3d 1143, 1151–52 (10th Cir. 2004) [stay in Canada for four years where government denied permanent status, refused asylum and ordered deportation is not firm resettlement]; *Cheo v. INS,* 162 F.3d 1227, 1230 (9th Cir. 1998) [temporary stay in a third country is not firm resettlement]. *See generally Rosenberg v. Woo,* 402 U.S. 49 (1971).

6.f. *Cases Finding Resettlement*—*Sultani v. Gonzales,* 455 F.3d 878 (8th Cir. 2006) [Afghan was firmly resettled in Australia]; *Firmansjah v. Gonzales,* 424 F.3d 598, 601–04 (7th Cir. 2005) [Catholic Indonesian woman of Chinese descent was firmly resettled in Singapore]; *Nahrvani v. Gonzales,* 399 F.3d 1148, 1151–52 (9th Cir. 2005) [where Iranian resided in Germany for 10 years, worked and traveled freely throughout the country, and married a German citizen, he was firmly resettled]; *Rife v. Ashcroft,* 374 F.3d 606, 610–12 (8th Cir. 2004) [where family granted Israeli citizenship under law of return, lived and worked in Israel for 3 years, and received some government benefits, they were firmly resettled]; *Desta v. Ashcroft,* 329 F.3d 1179, 1186–87 (10th Cir. 2003) [Ethiopian firmly resettled in Canada]; *Ali v. Reno,* 237 F.3d 591, 593–96 (6th Cir. 2001) [where Iraqi citizen was granted refugee status by the Danish government before entering that country and upon arrival was given a Danish passport and residence permit, she was firmly resettled]; *Matter of K-R-Y- and K-C-S-,* 24 I&N Dec. 133 (BIA 2007) [although the North Korean Human Rights Act of 2004 does not bar a North Korean from receiving asylum in the U.S. even if he could get South Korean citizenship, the firm resettlement doctrine still applies and North Koreans who became South Korean citizens, have their children living in South Korea, and were employed and could freely move about the country and make speeches were firmly resettled].

7. *Safe Third Country: Canadian-U.S. Agreement*—The applicant may also be removed, pursuant to a bilateral or multilateral agreement, to a safe third country in which the person's life or freedom would not be threatened and where s/he would have access to a full and fair procedure for determining asylum, unless the AG finds it is in the public interest to grant asylum, INA §208(a)(2)(A). The U.S. entered into a "Safe Third Country Agreement" with Canada effective Dec. 29, 2004. *See* 8 C.F.R. §§208.4(a)(6), 208.30(e)(6), 212.5(e)(2), 1003.42(h), 1208.4(a)(6), 1240.11; 69 Fed. Reg. 69480–97 (Nov. 29, 2004); 69 Fed. Reg. 10620–27 (Mar. 8, 2004).

7.a. *Procedure*—The Canadian-U.S. Agreement bars persons arriving from Canada or in transit during removal from Canada from applying for asylum, withholding or CAT and requires them to return to Canada for consideration of these claims. In effect, the agreement requires persons seeking refugee protection to make a claim in the first country they arrive in (U.S. or Canada) unless they qualify for an exception to the agreement. The agreement does not apply to citizens of the U.S. or Canada and does not apply to stateless persons who are habitual residents of Canada or the U.S. 8 C.F.R. §208.30(e)(6)(iii)(A). The agreement applies only to persons seeking admission at land border ports of entry as defined in 8 C.F.R. §100.4(c)(2) and 19 C.F.R. §101.3(b)(1), on the U.S./Canadian border and to certain persons deported from Canada who are in transit through the U.S. A determination as to the applicability of the agreement, as well as any exceptions to it, will be made by an AO, not by CBP. Memo,

Ahern, Asst. Comm. Field Operations, CBP, "Safe Third Country Agreement Implementation," (Dec. 22, 2004), *published on* AILA InfoNet at Doc. No. 05033110; 8 C.F.R. §208.30(e)(6). If a deported person from Canada is transiting through the U.S. and seeks asylum, he will be returned to Canada to seek asylum there or, if brought to CBP's attention at any airport within the U.S., will have his parole status revoked and will be treated as an arriving alien for purposes of expedited removal/credible fear processing. If a person seeking refugee status in Canada has been illegally in the U.S., he will be returned to the U.S. and put in removal proceedings as a deportable person. Memo, Ahern (Dec. 22, 2004); 69 Fed. Reg. at 69484 [unless the person is a parolee in the U.S., individuals returned from Canada "will not be subject to expedited removal because they will not meet the definition of 'arriving alien'"]. *But see Matter of R-D-,* 24 I&N Dec. 221 (BIA 2007) [deportation charge dismissed where person should have been charged as an arriving alien where he was returned to the U.S. pursuant to the Reciprocal Agreement of July 13, 2000 between the U.S. and Canada].

7.b. *Exceptions to Enforcement of the Agreement*—8 C.F.R. §208.30(e)(6)(i)-(iii). If the applicant establishes by a "preponderance of the evidence" that one of the following exceptions applies, he will be given the normal credible fear interview:

(1) S/he is a citizen of Canada or stateless and habitually residing in Canada;

(2) S/he has a USC spouse, son, daughter, parent, legal guardian, sibling, grandparent, grandchild, aunt, uncle, niece, or nephew who has been granted asylum, refugee, or other lawful status in the U.S. except B visa or VWP status;

(3) S/he has one of the qualifying relatives above who is at least 18 and has an asylum application pending before USCIS, EOIR or the federal courts;

(4) S/he is a minor with no parent or legal guardian in the U.S. or Canada;

(5) S/he arrived in the U.S. with a valid visa or admission document or, being required to hold a visa to enter Canada, was not required to obtain a U.S. visa;

(6) USCIS determines in its "unreviewable discretion" that it is in the public interest to allow the applicant to pursue his claim in the U.S.

7.c. *Moratorium on Removal*—Notwithstanding the agreement, Canada has placed a moratorium on removal of persons from certain countries who therefore may first make a claim in the U.S. and then seek protection in Canada. Those countries currently are: Afghanistan, Burundi, Democratic Republic of the Congo, Haiti, Iraq, Liberia, Rwanda and Zimbabwe.

7.d. *IJ Jurisdiction*—If a person is being returned to Canada pursuant to a decision by DHS under the Agreement, the IJ does not have jurisdiction to review the decision that the person should be returned to Canada. 8 C.F.R. §§1003.42(h). But the IJ does have jurisdiction to review, in the first instance, a claim by DHS that a respondent is barred from asylum because of the Agreement under INA §208(a)(2)(A). 8 C.F.R. §§1208.4(a)(6), 1240.11(g). The IJ has the authority to determine whether, by a preponderance of the evidence, the Agreement or any of the exceptions apply to the applicant. 8 C.F.R. §1240.11(g)(2). Even if the Agreement applies and no exception is available, the applicant may still apply for any other available relief. 8 C.F.R. §1240.11(g)(4); Memo [Interim OPPM 04-09], Creppy, Chief IJ, EOIR (Dec. 28, 2004), *published on* AILA InfoNet at Doc. No. 05012472 (Jan. 24, 2005). The AG however, by regulation, has determined that withholding and CAT relief, in addition to asylum, are not available. 8 C.F.R. §1240.11(g)(4).

8. *Previous Asylum Application*—The applicant previously applied for and was denied asylum, unless the applicant demonstrates the existence of changed circumstances which materially affect the applicant's eligibility for asylum. INA §208(a)(2)(C), (D); 8 U.S.C. §1158(a)(2)(C), (D). The applicant may file a successive application for asylum prior to a final order of removal if he can demonstrate changed circumstances. However, if there is a final order, the applicant may only file a successive application through a motion to reopen and only under the "changed country condition" standards of §1229a(c)(7)(C)(ii). *Zheng v. Mukasey,* 509 F.3d 869 (8th Cir. 2007) [there is no conflict between §1158(a)(2)(D), which allows for changed circumstances when filing successive applications for asylum, and §1229a(c)(7)(C)(ii), which permits successive applications in a motion to reopen only for changed country conditions when there is a final order of removal];

Matter of C-W-L-, 24 I&N Dec. 346 (BIA 2007) [denied untimely motion to reopen where only "changed personal circumstances" and not changed country conditions were alleged]. *See in this section,* "Changed Circumstances," ¶ 9.a (p.474), *infra.*

9. *Time Limit*—The applicant did not file his asylum claim within 1 year after his arrival in the U.S. unless the applicant demonstrates the existence of changed circumstances which materially affect the applicant's eligibility for asylum or extraordinary circumstances relating to the delay in filing the application. INA §208(a)(2)(B), (D); 8 U.S.C. §1158(a)(2)(B), (D). The one-year deadline begins to run from the person's *last* arrival in the U.S. or Apr. 1, 1997, whichever is later. 8 C.F.R. §§208.4(a)(2)(ii), 1208.4(a)(2)(ii); *Joaquin-Porras v. Gonzales,* 435 F.3d 172, 178–80 (2d Cir. 2006) [applicant who had been in the U.S. for a number of years but had traveled several times on advance parole was precluded from seeking asylum despite last entering the U.S. on the advance parole within one year]. However, at least one court has found that the one year time period for a person who has asylum revoked runs for the date of revocation and not the date of last entry. *Diallo v. Gonzales,* 447 F.3d 1274, 1282 (10th Cir. 2006) If the year falls on a weekend or holiday, the one year runs until the next weekday. 8 C.F.R. §§208.4(a)(2)(ii), 1208.4(a)(2)(ii). In making the one-year determination the application is considered filed upon receipt by USCIS or EOIR. If USCIS has not received the application within one year of the applicant's arrival, the mailing date may be considered the filing date if the applicant has "clear and convincing evidence of mailing the application within the 1-year period." 8 C.F.R. §§208.4(a)(2)(ii), 1208.4(a)(2)(ii). *Nakimbugwe v. Gonzales,* 475 F.3d 281 (5th Cir. 2007) [regulations applies and application is timely filed where it was put in the mail before the one year but received after]. The one year deadline may apply to minors. *Compare Bernal-Rendon v. Gonzales,* 419 F.3d 877, 880–81 (8th Cir. 2005) [one-year filing deadline applies to minor daughter from Colombia] *with El Himri v. Ashcroft,* 378 F.3d 932 (9th Cir. 2004) [one-year filing requirement does not apply to minors]. The provision has withstood constitutional challenges. *Ticoalu v. Gonzales,* 472 F.3d 8, 11 (1st Cir. 2006) [no due process right because asylum is discretionary]; *Sukwanputra v. Gonzales,* 434 F.3d 627, 631–32 (3d Cir. 2006) [rejecting Supremacy Clause and Due Process challenges to one year filing deadline].

9.a. *Changed Circumstances*—The term "changed circumstances" refers to circumstances that "materially affect[] the applicant's eligibility for asylum." 8 C.F.R. §§208.4(a)(4), 1208.4(a)(4). These include: (1) changes in conditions in the country of nationality; *Matter of A-M-*, 23 I&N Dec. 737, 738–39 (BIA 2005) [terrorist bombing in Bali was an insufficient changed circumstance for claim based on Chinese ethnicity and Christian faith]; (2) changes in the applicant's circumstances that materially affect eligibility for asylum including changes in applicable U.S. law and activities the applicant becomes involved in outside the country of persecution that place the applicant at risk; *Guan v. BIA,* 345 F.3d 47, 49 (2d Cir. 2003) ["changed circumstances" encompasses changed personal circumstances arising in the U.S.]; or (3) aged-out or divorced/widowed dependent who must now file his or her own application. 8 C.F.R. §§208.4(a)(4), 1208.4(a)(4). The applicant must file an asylum application within "a reasonable period" given the "changed circumstances" *Id. But see Chen v. Gonzales,* 498 F.3d 758 (7th Cir. 2007) [notwithstanding §208(a)(2)(D), an applicant's subsequent marriage and birth of two children cannot be a basis to reopen proceedings for fear of sterilization in China because the changed contemplated under INA §240(c)(7)(C)(ii) relates to changed country conditions not personal circumstances].

9.b. *Extraordinary Circumstances*—The term "extraordinary circumstances" refers to events or factors directly related to the failure to meet the 1-year deadline. The one-year deadline may be excused as long as the person filed within a reasonable period given those extraordinary circumstances. The burden is on the applicant to demonstrate: (1) that the circumstances were not intentionally created through action or inaction; (2) that the circumstances were directly related to the person's failure to file within 1-year; and (3) the delay was reasonable under the circumstances. Extraordinary circumstances may include: (1) serious illness or mental or physical disability including effects of persecution; (2) legal disability (*e.g.*, minor or mental impairment); (3) ineffective assistance of counsel relying on *Lozada* criteria; (4) maintaining TPS status, maintaining lawful immigrant or nonimmigrant status or given parole until a reasonable period before filing the asylum application; (5) filing within one year but having USCIS reject the application as incomplete and thereafter re-filing in a reasonable time, or (6) the death or serious illness or incapacity of the applicant's legal representative or a member of the applicant's immediate family. 8 C.F.R. §§208.4(a)(5), 1208.4(a)(5). "[T]he list is not all-inclusive, and it is recognized that there are many other circumstances that might apply if the applicant is able to show that but for such circumstances the application would have been filed ..." 62 Fed. Reg. 10312, 10316 (Mar. 6, 1997). However, in addition to the existence of the regulatory extraordinary circumstance, the applicant must also demonstrate that the circumstance was directly related to the failure to file within the one-year period and that the delay was reasonable under the circumstances. *Matter of Y-C-*, 23 I&N Dec. 286 (BIA 2002) [extraordinary circumstances existed where minor was in INS custody for more than one year after his arrival and after release to his uncle's custody, sought to file an application 5½ months later while still a minor]. *See also Al-Mousa v. Mukasey,* 518 F.3d 738 (9th Cir. 2008) [remanding case to BIA to determine the definition of minor for purposes exempting the applicant from the one-year filing deadline, where he was under 21 but over 18].

9.c. *Final Order of Removal*—There is a question as to what standard to apply in seeking to file an application for asylum after the one year deadline if a final order of removal has been entered. Prior to a final order, an applicant may seeking to file an asylum application if he can show changed or extraordinary circumstances as discussed *supra*. However, if there is a final order, the applicant may only file a successive application through a motion to reopen and only under the "changed country condition" standards of §1229a(c)(7)(C)(ii). *Zheng v. Mukasey,* 509 F.3d 869 (8th Cir. 2007) [there is no conflict between §1158(a)(2)(D), which allows for changed circumstances when filing successive applications for asylum, and §1229a(c)(7)(C)(ii), which permits successive applications in a motion to reopen only for changed country conditions when there is a final order of removal]; *Chen v. Gonzales,* 498 F.3d 758 (7th Cir. 2007) [notwithstanding §208(a)(2)(D), an applicant's subsequent marriage and birth of two children cannot be a basis to reopen proceedings for fear of sterilization in China because the changed contemplated under INA §240(c)(7)(C)(ii) relates to changed country conditions not personal circumstances]; *Matter of C-W-L-*, 24 I&N Dec. 346 (BIA 2007) [denied untimely motion to reopen where only "changed personal circumstances" and not changed country conditions were alleged].

10. *Applications Filed Before April 1, 1997*—Applicants who filed *before* Apr. 1, 1997 are not barred by the Canadian-U.S. Agreement or the one-year filing deadline, but are still barred by the other grounds. *Compare* 8 C.F.R. §§208.13(c)(1) and (2), 1208.13(c)(1) and (2). *See also Kankamalage v. INS,* 335 F.3d 858 (9th Cir. 2003) [although 8 C.F.R. §208.13(c)(2), which bars persons who commit particularly serious crimes, applies to asylum applications filed before Apr. 1, 1997, the court, following *St. Cyr,* held it may not be applied retroactively to a person whose conviction arose before that date].

11. *Burden of Proof Regarding Disqualification*—The applicant has the burden of proving by clear and convincing evidence that he filed the application within one year. 8 C.F.R. §§208.4(a)(2), 1208.4(a)(2). The applicant has the burden of disproving by a preponderance of the evidence, a disqualifying act under the mandatory grounds of asylum, if the evidence indicates a ground applies. 8 C.F.R. §§208.13(c)(2)(ii), 1208.13(c)(2)(ii); *Chay-Velasquez v. Ashcroft,* 367 F.3d 751, 755 (8th Cir. 2004) [asylum applicant failed to meet burden of proof to establish that he did not commit a serious nonpolitical crime]. Although the regulations provide for mandatory denial of asylum, such action may be violative of our international treaty obligations and *ultra vires* of INA §208. *But see Yang v. INS*, 79 F.3d 932 (9th Cir. 1996) [rejecting challenge to firm resettlement bar, citing *Reno v. Flores*, 507 U.S. 292 (1993), regarding blanket procedures and *Chevron*]; *Ahmetovic v. INS*, 62 F.3d 48 (2d Cir. 1995) [rejecting argument that mandatory denial for crime that was not an aggravated felony is contrary to the statute or to international law].

12. *Judicial Review*—There is no judicial review of a decision to bar an asylum application because of a safe third country, because the applicant was previously denied asylum, because the applicant did not file the application within one year of entry, because the AG determines there are no changed circumstances warranting an exception to the one-year deadline or because the applicant is deemed to be a terrorist. INA §208(a)(3) and (b)(2)(D). However, there may be certain exceptions. *See in this chapter*, "Judicial Review," ¶ XII.C.4 (p.593), *infra*. *See also* "Asylum Review" in Ch. 10, ¶ IV.A.16 (p.1128), *infra*.

E. *Criminal Bars to Asylum*—The criminal bars to asylum are now statutory. INA §208(b)(2)(A)(ii) [applicant having been convicted by a final judgment of a particularly serious crime constitutes a danger to the community of the U.S.] and INA §208(b)(2)(A)(iii) [serious reasons for believing that the applicant has committed a serious nonpolitical crime outside the U.S. prior to arrival]; *Chay-Velasquez v. Ashcroft,* 367 F.3d 751, 755–56 (8th Cir. 2004) [denying asylum and withholding because applicant committed nonpolitical crimes in burning buses which served the civilian population, breaking windows, and fighting with police]; *Efe v. Ashcroft,* 293 F.3d 899, 905–06 (5th Cir. 2002) [affirming BIA decision that applicant was barred from asylum because he stabbed and killed a police officer during a demonstration]. Conviction of an aggravated felony is considered a conviction of a particularly serious crime. INA §208(b)(2)(B), 8 U.S.C. §1158(b)(2)(B).

1. *Mandatory Denial*—The regulations do not allow for balancing the crime against the severity of the persecution as these are mandatory grounds for denial. *Matter of B-,* 20 I&N Dec. 427 (BIA 1991) [aggravated battery with a firearm is a particularly serious crime]; *Ahmetovic v. INS*, 62 F.3d 48, 51–53 (2d Cir. 1995) [no separate finding that person is a danger to the community is necessary to bar asylum where the crime is particularly serious]; *Martins v. INS*, 972 F.2d 657 (5th Cir. 1992) [finding that the statute applies retroactively to convictions prior to the enactment of the 1988 aggravated felony statute and that no finding of danger to the community is necessary]. The constitutionality of the preclusive effect on aggravated felons has been challenged unsuccessfully. *Martins*, 972 F.2d at 661–62 [no violation of due process to deny aggravated felons the right to apply for asylum or withholding].

2. *Discretionary Denial for Other Crimes*—Where a crime does not require mandatory denial, a well-founded fear "should generally outweigh all but the most egregious of adverse factors," in deciding whether to grant discretionary asylum. *Matter of Pula*, 19 I&N Dec. 467 (BIA 1987). *But see Kouljinski v. Keisler,* 505 F.3d 534 (6th Cir. 2007) [denied asylum on discretionary grounds because refugee had three DUI convictions]; *Alsagladi v. Gonzales,* 450 F.3d 700 (7th Cir. 2006) [upheld denial of asylum on discretionary grounds where applicant from Yemen committed fraud by entering the U.S. as a tourist when his intent was to remain]; *Dhine v. Slattery*, 3 F.3d 613 (2d Cir. 1993) [numerous misdemeanors on balance sufficient to deny asylum]. The AG, however, has stated that even if an applicant is not statutorily barred, he would be "highly disinclined to exercise [his] discretion" to grant asylum where there is a dangerous or violent felon, unless there are "extraordinary circumstances, such as those involving national security or foreign policy considerations" or the denial would result in "exceptional and extremely unusual hardship." *Matter of Jean,* 23 I&N Dec. 373, 384–85 (AG 2002) *affirmed Jean v. Gonzales,* 452 F.3d 392, 396–98 (5th Cir. 2006) [declining to exercise discretion to grant asylum where Haitian woman was convicted of second degree manslaughter in the death of an infant; on appeal court rejected argument that AG's standard was *ultra vires*]; *Ali v. Achim,* 468 F.3d 462, 465–67 (7th Cir. 2006) *cert. dismissed* 128 S.Ct. 828 (2007) [AG did not exceed his authority when he articulated the heightened waiver standard in *Matter of Jean*]. The IJ however, must first make a finding that the crime is violent or dangerous before determining the need to demonstrate exceptional and extremely unusual hardship. *Rivas-Gomez v. Gonzales,* 441 F.3d 1072, 1074–79 (9th Cir. 2006).

3. *Pre-Apr. 1, 1997 Applications*—If the application was filed prior to Apr. 1, 1997, 8 C.F.R. §§208.13(c)(2), 1208.13(c)(2) govern and aggravated felonies and certain other crimes bar asylum. *Matter of C-*, 20 I&N Dec. 529 (BIA 1992); *Matter of U-M-,* 20 I&N Dec. 327 (BIA 1991). *See also Komarenko v. INS,* 35 F.3d 432, 435–36 (9th Cir. 1994) [upholding challenge to pre-1997 regulations]. Prior to the statutory bar, a person applying after Nov. 29, 1990 but before Apr. 1, 1997, who was convicted of an aggravated felony, was ineligible to *apply for* or be granted asylum under former INA §208(d), whether the conviction occurred before, on, or after the enactment date. *Matter of A-A-*, 20 I&N Dec. 492 (BIA 1992); *Feroz v. INS*, 22 F.3d 225 (9th Cir. 1994); *Buitrago-Cuesta v. INS*, 7 F.3d 291, 295 (2d Cir. 1993); *Martins v. INS*, 972 F.2d 657, 660 (5th Cir. 1992); *Eskite v. District Director*, 901 F.Supp. 530, 534–35 (E.D.N.Y. 1995). Under IIRIRA §321(b) the aggravated felony definition is retroactive so convictions occurring before, on, or after Apr. 1, 1997 would be covered. *But see Kankamalage v. INS,* 335 F.3d 858 (9th Cir. 2003) [although 8 C.F.R. §208.13(c)(2) applies to applications filed before Apr. 1, 1997, following *St. Cyr,* it may not be applied retroactively to a person whose conviction arose before that date]; *see also Batanic v. INS*, 12 F.3d 662 (7th Cir. 1993) [a person subject to the former regulations could still be eligible for asylum notwithstanding a conviction if due to a procedural error he was unable to apply].

F. *Discretionary Grounds for Denial*—An IJ may deny asylum as a matter of discretion even if a person is statutorily eligible. INA §208(a), 8 U.S.C. §1158(a) ["the alien may be granted asylum in the discretion of the Attorney General..."]; INA §208(b)(1), 8 U.S.C. §1158(b)(1) ["[t]he Attorney General may grant asylum to an alien..."]; 8 C.F.R. §1208.14(a); *Matter of A-H-,* 23 I&N Dec. 774, 780–83 (A.G. 2005) [AG denied asylum in the exercise of discretion to applicant connected to the FIS in Algeria because of his links to armed Islamic groups that committed human rights violations and because of his tax evasion in the U.S., notwithstanding other equities]. *See Huang v. INS,* 436 F.3d 89, 96–102 (2d Cir. 2006) [IJ acted contrary to law under INA §242(b)(4)(D) in denying asylum as a matter of discretion, where he failed to examine the totality of the circumstances and focused solely on the embellishment of peripheral testimony and the applicant's payment to a smuggler]; *Kalubi v. Ashcroft,* 364 F.3d 1134 (9th Cir. 2004) [BIA should weigh all positive and negative factors in deciding to grant asylum as a matter of discretion]. However, when exercising discretion, an IJ should not consider a temporary stay in a third country and should give little weight to a true refugee's use of false documents or false statements to immigration officers to escape persecution. *Dong v. Gonzales,* 421 F.3d 573, 578–79 (7th Cir. 2005) [rejecting the use of false documents to enter as a basis to determine lack of credibility because it has no bearing on applicant's forced abortion claim]; *Mamouzian v. Ashcroft,* 390 F.3d 1129, 1138 (9th Cir. 2004) [reversing IJ's denial of asylum and cautioning the IJ in the exercise of his discretion]. *But see Ibrahim v. Gonzales,* 434 F.3d 1074, 1079 (8th Cir. 2006) [where IJ denied asylum in the exercise of discretion, the court upheld denial and noted that a history of submitting falsehoods to immigration and law enforcement officers is a valid consideration in the AG discretion]. Prior INS regulations provided for the discretionary denial of asylum if the applicant could be removed to a third country which offered resettlement and in which the alien would not face harm or persecution. The courts were reluctant to permit this form of discretionary denial. *Andriasian v. INS,* 180 F.3d 1033, 1043–47 (9th Cir. 1999) [reversing BIA's determination that asylum can be denied as a matter of discretion where a person could be sent to a third country despite the lack of an offer of resettlement]; *Melkonian v. Ashcroft,* 320 F.3d 1061, 1071 (9th Cir. 2003) [rejecting IJ's conclusion that asylum could be denied because person decided to come to the U.S. rather than stay in Russia for economic reasons after fleeing Abkhazia]. *But note* INA §208(a)(2)(A), 8 U.S.C. §1158(a)(2)(A) now makes removal to a safe third country pursuant to a bilateral or multilateral agreement mandatory.

G. *Reconsideration of Asylum Denial*—Where asylum is denied on discretionary grounds, but withholding granted, the IJ should reconsider the denial when a spouse and children are involved. 8 C.F.R. §§208.16(e), 1208.16(e). The IJ must consider the impact of the asylum denial on the applicant's ability "to be reunited with his spouse and minor child." *Matter of T-Z-,* 24 I&N Dec. 163, 176 (BIA 2007) [remanding to IJ to consider asylum if withholding is sustained and to also consider reunification with family in a third country]. The asylum applicant may not be required to file a formal motion to reopen or reconsider the asylum denial. *Huang v. INS,* 436 F.3d 89, 92–94 (2d Cir. 2006) [applicant denied asylum as a matter of discretion but granted withholding exhausted his claim for reconsideration by filing an appeal challenging the denial of asylum and a separate motion was not necessary to invoke §1208.16(e)].

IV. WITHHOLDING OF REMOVAL

INA §241(b)(3) [formerly INA §243(h)], 8 U.S.C. §1231(b)(3). While the Refugee Act applies the "well-founded fear" standard for persons who are refugees and asylees, it adopts a different standard for withholding of removal to one's home country based on a probability of harm. *Compare INS v. Cardoza-Fonseca*, 480 U.S. 421 (1987) [asylum standard], *with INS v. Stevic*, 467 U.S. 407 (1984) [former §243(h) standard]. INA §241(b)(3) is based on Article 33 of the Protocol, which places a mandatory prohibition against the return of someone to a country where his or her "life or freedom would be threatened." However, at least one court has found that Article 33 is not enforceable under U.S. law because it is not "self-executing," *Haitian Refugee Center, Inc. v. Baker*, 949 F.2d 1109, 1110 (11th Cir. 1991), and the Supreme Court has held that former INA §243(h) is inapplicable to persons interdicted on the high seas or detained outside of the physical territory of the U.S. *Sale v. Haitian Centers Council, Inc.*, 509 U.S. 155 (1993). *See also* Legal Opinion, Virtue, G.C. to Meissner, Comm. (HQCOU 90/15) (Sept. 1, 1998), *reprinted in* 76 No. 13 *Interpreter Releases* 529, 536–45 (Apr. 2, 1999) [INS had no authority to operate Guantanamo because it was outside U.S.]. In the REAL ID Act of 2005, Congress established new standards for corroboration and credibility determinations in the asylum, withholding of removal and CAT context. The new standards apply to all cases filed on or after May 11, 2005. *See* INA §§208(b)(1)(B), 240(c)(4), 241(b)(3)(C), 8 U.S.C. §§1158(b)(1)(B), 1230(c)(4), 1231(b)(3)(C). *See also in this chapter*, "REAL ID Act of 2005 and Corroboration" and "REAL ID Act of 2005 and Credibility Determinations," ¶¶ XII.B.2.f(5) (p.531) and XII.B.2.g(3) & (4) (p.545), *infra*.

A. *Mandatory Prohibition Against Removal*—In contrast to the discretionary authority of the AG under the asylum provisions, INA §241(b)(3) provides for a mandatory prohibition against removal of a person found who establishes that his "life or freedom would be threatened on account of race, religion, nationality, membership in a particular social group or political opinion." *Popova v. INS,* 273 F.3d 1251 (9th Cir. 2001) [Bulgarian doctor threatened repeatedly by police and anonymous callers because of religious and political views was entitled to withholding]; *Leiva-Montalvo v. INS,* 173 F.3d 749 (9th Cir. 1999) [Salvadoran who was threatened, detained and shot at by new guerilla organization subsequent to the 1992 Peace Accords entitled to withholding]. The standard does not include withholding *per se* for persons who are war refugees. *Matter of Medina*, 19 I&N Dec. 734 (BIA 1988).

B. *Past Persecution and Withholding*—A finding of past persecution gives rise to a presumption of withholding of removal. 8 C.F.R. §§208.16(b)(1)(i), 1208.16(b)(1)(i) ["[i]f the applicant is determined to have suffered past persecution...it shall be presumed that the applicant's life or freedom would be threatened in the future..."]; *Ali v. Ashcroft,* 394 F.3d 780, 791 (9th Cir. 2005) [in case where Somali clan member was gang raped by another clan, a finding of past persecution gave rise to a presumption of withholding]; *Antipova v. U.S. Att'y Gen.,* 392 F.3d 1259, 1264–65 (11th who were kidnapped and threatened established past persecution for withholding of removal which was not rebutted by general statement concerning peace accord in 1998 country report]; *Duarte* Cir. 2004) [reversing IJ for failure to follow the regulatory requirement to make a finding whether Jewish Russian national suffered past persecution]; *Rios v. Ashcroft,* 287 F.3d 895, 900–02 (9th Cir. 2002) [family of murdered Guatemalan army officer *de Guinac v. INS,* 179 F.3d 1156, 1164 (9th Cir. 1999); *Korablina v. INS,* 158 F.3d 1038, 1046 (9th Cir. 1998); *Fergiste v. INS,* 138 F.3d 14, 20 (1st Cir. 1998). If a person has not established past persecution, s/he must demonstrate that it is more likely than not that s/he would be persecuted on one of the five protected grounds if returned to her country. 8 C.F.R. §208.16(b)(2). *See in this chapter* "On Account of Race, Religion, National Origin, Political Opinion, or Membership in a Particular Social Group," ¶ III.A.5 (p.447), *supra*.

C. *AO Cannot Decide Withholding*—An AO cannot decide withholding of removal requests. 8 C.F.R. §§208.16(a), 1208.16(a). An IJ in removal proceedings, of course, may decide it.

D. *Grounds of Disqualification for Withholding*—INA §241(b)(3)(B), 8 U.S.C. §1231(b)(3)(B) sets forth grounds for disqualification of certain categories of persons who might otherwise have a valid withholding claim. These exclusions have been codified in the regulations and are to be applied by AOs and IJs. 8 C.F.R. §§208.16(d)(2), 1208.16(d)(2). Under INA §241(b)(3)(B), deportation of an alien whose life or freedom would be threatened will not be withheld, if:

1. *Nazism or Genocide*—The applicant was a Nazi or engaged in genocide under INA §237(a)(4)(D), or:

2. *Persecution of Others*—The applicant ordered, incited, assisted or otherwise participated in the persecution of any person on account of race, religion, nationality, membership in a particular social group or political opinion, INA §241(b)(3)(B)(i), 8 U.S.C. §1231(b)(3)(B)(i); *Matter of A-H-*, 23 I&N Dec. 774, 783–85 (AG 2005) [remanding to BIA under AG's broader standard]. In *Matter of A-H-*, the AG established a broad standard for determining whether an applicant for withholding participated in the persecution of others. The AG held that assistance does not require "direct personal involvement in the acts of persecution" and that "in certain circumstances statements of encouragement alone can suffice." 23 I&N Dec. at 784–85. The AG cited as examples of evidence that could support a finding of inciting, assisting, or participating in persecution: (1) that the leader was instrumental in creating and sustaining the ties between the political movement and the armed group and was aware of the atrocities committed by the armed group; (2) that he used his profile and position of influence to make public statements that encouraged those atrocities; (3) that he made statements that appear to have condoned the persecution without publicly and specifically disassociating himself and his movement from the acts of persecution, particularly if his statements appear to have resulted in an increase in the persecution. *See also in this chapter* section II.B (p.432), *supra*.

3. *Particularly Serious Crime, Danger to the Community*—The applicant, having been convicted by a final judgment of a particularly serious crime, constitutes a danger to the U.S. community. INA §241(b)(3)(B)(ii), 8 U.S.C. §1231(b)(3)(B)(ii);

3.a. *Particularly Serious Crimes*—The BIA historically relied on the criteria established in *Matter of Frentescu,* 18 I&N Dec. 244, 247 (BIA 1982) in determining whether someone has been convicted of a particularly serious crime. The criteria included: (1) the nature of the conviction; (2) the circumstances and underlying facts of the conviction; (3) the type of sentence imposed; and (4) whether the type and circumstances of the crime indicate that the respondent is a danger to the community. More recently, however, the BIA in *Matter of N-A-M-,* 24 I&N Dec. 336, 342–43 (BIA 2007) noted that its view of whether a conviction is a particularly serious crime has "evolved" since the issuance of *Frentescu* and the Board no longer engages in a separate determination to address whether the respondent is a danger to the community but under *Matter of Carballe,* 19 I&N Dec. 357 (BIA 1986) focuses on the "nature of the crime and not the likelihood of future serious misconduct" *Matter of N-A-M-* at 342. It also noted that it no longer focuses on the sentence imposed because it "is not the most accurate or salient factor to consider in determining the seriousness of an offense." *Id.* At 343. The Board also rejected the idea that a conviction must be an aggravated felony to be a particularly serious crime. *Matter of N-A-M-,* 24 I&N Dec. 336 (BIA 2007) [finding that felony menacing under Colorado Revised Statutes 18-3-206(1), although not an aggravated felony, is a particularly serious crime]. *But see Alaka v. Attorney General,* 456 F.3d 88, 104–05 (3d Cir. 2006) [only aggravated felonies can be particularly serious crimes]. The Board has further determined that once it finds that the crime by its nature, irrespective of the facts, bring it within the "range" of a particularly serious crime, either party may bring in any otherwise reliable evidence to determine whether it should be treated so. *Matter of N-A-M-,* 24 I&N Dec. 336, 343–45 (BIA 2007) [BIA considered the Statement in Support of Warrantless Arrest and determined it would not be limited to the record of conviction or sentencing information]. *Accord Ali v. Achim,* 468 F.3d 462, 467–71 (7th Cir. 2006) *cert. dismissed* 128 S.Ct. 828 (2007) [particularly serious crimes are not limited to aggravated felonies and court upheld BIA's case-by-case approach]. *But see Morales v. Gonzales,* 478 F.3d 972, 981–83 (9th Cir.2007) [relying on prior BIA precedent *Matter of L-S-,* 22 I&N Dec. 645 (BIA 1999) the court determined the IJ erred in relying on facts in an appellate court's decision for crimes respondent was not convicted of instead of limiting the inquiry to the record of conviction and sentencing evidence]. The inquiry, however, does not involve "an examination of the respondent's family or community ties, the risk of persecution in the alien's native country" or going "behind the record of conviction to redetermine the alien's innocence or guilt." *Matter of L-S-,* 22 I&N Dec. 645, 650–51 (BIA 1999). The "rebuttable presumption" approach favoring a finding that an aggravated felony is always a "particularly serious crime" in *Matter of Q-T-M-T-,* 21 I&N Dec. 639 (BIA 1996) has been rejected for removal cases. *Matter of S-S-,* 22 I&N Dec. 458 (BIA 1999). But in *Matter of Y-L-,* 23 I&N Dec. 270 (AG 2002) the AG reversed *Matter of S-S-* as it relates to aggravated felony for unlawful trafficking which is now presumptively a particularly serious crime and ground for denial even if the sentence is less than 5 years.

The BIA in conducting its analysis must determine whether the person has committed a particularly serious crime by reviewing each case separately. *Afridi v. Gonzales,* 442 F.3d 1212, 1217–21 (9th Cir. 2006) [BIA erred in failing to apply each of the factors in *Frentescu*]; *Yousefi v. INS,* 260 F.3d 318, 327–30 (4th Cir. 2001) [reversing BIA and IJ as abuse of discretion where neither applied the *Frentescu* factors to the case]; *Steinhouse v. Ashcroft,* 247 F.Supp.2d 201 (D. Conn. 2003) [following *Yousefi* and distinguishing *Ahmetovic,* the district court determined that the BIA improperly failed to consider the fourth factor in *Frentescu*]. *But see Solis v. Mukasey,* 515 F.3d 832 (8th Cir. 2008) [IJ did not violate due process in relying on a police report that contradicted petitioner's testimony regarding his conviction for delivery of a controlled substance]; *Chong v. District Director, INS,* 264 F.3d 378, 386–87 (3d Cir. 2001) [BIA did not have to remand case to IJ for individualized determination under *Matter of S-S-* where the information was already in the record on appeal because agency is only required to make individualized determination not give individualized hearing before an IJ]; *Tunis v. Gonzales,* 447 F.3d 547, 548–50 (7th Cir. 2006) [noting that of the six criteria to overcome the presumption that a drug crime is particularly serious under *Matter of Y-L-,* the IJ incorrectly applied criteria four by finding that all drug crimes are violent. However, the court upheld the denial of asylum because the applicant must satisfy all six criteria and as the applicant was the person who sold the drugs she could not have had merely peripheral involvement under the third criteria]; *Perez v. Loy,* 356 F.Supp.2d 172, 176–77 (D. Conn. 2005) [following *Matter of Y-L-,* and finding that the AG's opinion is not subject to retroactivity analysis]; *Ali v. Ashcroft,* 395 F.3d 722, 729–30 (7th Cir. 2005) [affirmed denial of withholding where applicant did not present evidence to rebut presumption of *Matter of Y-L-*]; *Chinchilla-Jimenez v. INS*, 226 F.Supp.2d 680, 684–85 (E.D. Pa. 2002).

Not Particularly Serious Crimes—The BIA has found that burglary with intent to commit theft is not a particularly serious crime under former INA §243(h)(2)(B), *Matter of Frentescu*, 18 I&N Dec. 244, 247 (BIA 1982), nor are single misdemeanor offenses. *Matter of Juarez*, 19 I&N Dec. 664 (BIA 1988) [assault with a deadly weapon]. The validity of these cases, however, may be in question in light of subsequent statutory changes making aggravated felonies where the persons has been sentenced to five years in prison particularly serious crimes *per se.* INA §241(b)(3)(B). *See, e.g., Matter of C-,* 20 I&N Dec. 529 (BIA 1992) [analysis in *Matter of Frentescu* has been superseded by statutory changes]. But the crime must be an aggravated felony. *Alaka v. Att'y Gen. of the U.S.*, 456 F.3d 88, 105–09 (3d Cir. 2006) [finding that conviction for bank fraud under 18 U.S.C. §1344 was not a particularly serious crime because it was not an aggravated felony as the amount of loss was less than $10,000].

Particularly Serious Crimes—The BIA has found the following crimes to be particularly serious: felony menacing under Colorado Revised Statutes 18-3-206(1), *Matter of N-A-M-,* 24 I&N Dec. 336 (BIA 2007); substantial battery with a dangerous weapon, *Ali v. Achim,* 468 F.3d 462, 467–71 (7th Cir. 2006) *cert. dismissed* 128 S.Ct. 828 (2007); burglary of a dwelling which included aggravating circumstances, *Matter of Garcia-Garrocho*, 19 I&N Dec. 423 (BIA 1986); shooting with intent to kill, *Nguyen v. INS*, 991 F.2d 621, 626 (10th Cir. 1993); and robbery, *Matter of Carballe*, 19 I&N Dec. 357 (BIA 1986); *Cepero v. BIA*, 882 F.Supp. 1575, 1580 (D. Kan. 1995). The courts have held that possession of cocaine for sale and possession of heroin with intent to distribute are particularly serious crimes. *Crespo-Gomez v. Richard*, 780 F.2d 932 (11th Cir. 1986) [cocaine]; *Mahini v. INS,* 779 F.2d 1419, 1421 (9th Cir. 1986) [heroin], but simple possession of cocaine is not, *Matter of Toboso-Alfonso*, 20 I&N Dec. 819 (AG 1994). The BIA takes the view that any drug trafficking crime as defined under federal law, no matter how small, is a particularly serious crime. *Matter of U-M-*, 20 I&N Dec. 327 (BIA 1991). *But see Beltran-Zavala v. INS*, 912 F.2d 1027 (9th Cir. 1990) [rejecting view that all drug crimes are *per se* "particularly serious" and requiring that BIA view them on a case-by-case basis]. Handbook ¶¶152-156.

3.b. *Aggravated Felony Conviction*—A person convicted of an aggravated felony for which s/he was sentenced to an aggregate term of imprisonment of 5 years is considered to have committed a particularly serious crime. INA §241(b)(3)(B). However, if a person was not sentenced to 5 years, the AG may determine that the person has not been convicted of a particularly serious crime. *Matter of L-S-,* 22 I&N Dec. 645 (BIA 1999) ["bringing in" an alien to the U.S. under §1324(a)(2)(B)(ii) is not a particularly serious crime]; *Matter of S-S-,* 22 I&N Dec. 458 (BIA 1999). In making that determination, the BIA must look to the factors in *Frentescu* as now modified by *Matter of N-A-M-,* 24 I&N Dec. 336 (BIA 2007. *Brue v. Gonzales,* 464 F.3d 1227, 1234–35 (10th Cir. 2006) [upholding BIA determination that respondent's conviction for second degree sexual assault of a minor under Colorado law was a particularly serious crime that barred withholding under *Frentescu* factors]; *Afridi v. Gonzales,* 442 F.3d 1212, 1217–21 (9th Cir. 2006) [BIA erred in failing to apply each of the factors in *Frentescu* to determine whether respondent was convicted of a particularly serious crime, where his sentence for an aggravated felony was under 5 years].

The AG, however, has determined that an aggravated felony involving unlawful trafficking in a controlled substance *presumptively* constitutes a particularly serious crime and is therefore always a bar to withholding absent "extraordinary and compelling circumstances." *Matter of Y-L-,* 23 I&N Dec. 270 (AG 2002) [reversing *Matter of S-S-* as it relates to aggravated felony for unlawful trafficking]; *Miguel-Miguel v. Gonzales,* 500 F.3d 941, 945–52 (9th Cir. 2007) [AG did not exceed his authority by creating the presumption in *Matter of Y-L-*, the presumption is constitutional, but it may not be applied retroactively]; *Perez v. Loy,* 356 F.Supp.2d 172, 176–77 (D. Conn. 2005) [following *Matter of Y-L-* and finding that the AG's opinion is not subject to retroactivity analysis]; *Ali v. Ashcroft,* 395 F.3d 722, 729–30 (7th Cir. 2005) [affirming denial of withholding where applicant did not present evidence to rebut presumption of *Matter of Y-L-*]; *Reyes-Sanchez v. Ashcroft,* 261 F.Supp.2d 276, 285–88 (S.D.N.Y. 2003) [AG's decision to create blanket rule in *Matter of Y-L-* upheld on *Chevron* grounds]; *Chinchilla-Jimenez v. INS*, 226 F.Supp.2d 680, 684–85 (E.D. Pa. 2002). The bar is not absolute as the AG may depart from it "only under the most extenuating circumstances that are both extraordinary and compelling." *Matter of Y-L-,* 23 I&N Dec. at 274. The AG suggested six criteria that would be necessary at a "minimum" to constitute extraordinary and compelling circumstances: (1) a very small quantity of controlled substance; (2) a very modest amount of money paid for the drugs in the offending transaction; (3) merely peripheral involvement by the alien in the criminal activity, transaction or conspiracy; (4) the absence of any violence or threat of violence, implicit or otherwise, associated with the offense; (5) the absence of any organized crime or terrorist organization involvement, direct or indirect, in relation to the offending activity; and (6) the absence of any adverse or harmful effect of the activity or transaction on juveniles. *Id.* at 277. All the criteria would have to be present. *Id.* Where the IJ/BIA does not conduct an individualized review to determine whether these criteria have been met, the decision will be reversed. *Bosede v. Mukasey,* 512 F.3d 946, 950–51 (7th Cir. 2008) [IJ violated fundamental due process in failing to consider evidence rebutting the AG's presumption and the court therefore had jurisdiction under INA §242(a)(2)(D) notwithstanding INA §242(a)(2)(C)]; *Ford v. ICE,* 294 F.Supp.2d 655, 659–63 (M.D. Pa. 2003) [following *Chong v. District Director, INS,* 264 F.3d 378, the BIA's generalized statement that respondent did not comply with the criteria in *Matter of Y-L-* violated due process because it failed to discuss individual factors]. *See also Lavira v. Att'y Gen. of the U.S.,* 478 F.3d 158, 164–66 (3d Cir. 2007) [IJ failed to consider factual basis of drug trafficking conviction which was a $10 sale to an undercover police officer and therefore failed to follow *Matter of Y-L-*); *Tunis v. Gonzales,* 447 F.3d 547, 548–50 (7th Cir. 2006) [noting that of the six criteria to overcome the presumption that a drug crime is a particularly serious crime under *Matter of Y-L-* the IJ misapplied the fourth criterion by holding that all drug crimes are violent. However, the court upheld the denial of asylum by the IJ because all six criteria must be satisfied and as the applicant was the person who sold the drugs, she could not have had merely peripheral involvement as required by the third criterion]. Under IIRIRA §321(b) the term aggravated felony applies regardless of whether the conviction was before, on, or after date of enactment (Sept. 30, 1996). *Matter of L-S-J-*, 21 I&N Dec. 973 (BIA 1997) [finding robbery with a handgun a particularly serious crime barring withholding even though sentence was only 2½ years]. For purposes of determining an "aggregate term of imprisonment under INA §241(b)(3)(B), concurrent sentences should not be added together but instead should be equal in length to the longest concurrent sentence. *Matter of Aldabesheh,* 22 I&N Dec. 983, 988–89 (BIA 1999).

3.c. *Danger to the Community*—Under 8 C.F.R. §§208.16(d)(2), 1208.16(d)(2), a person who has been convicted of a particularly serious crime shall be considered a danger to the community. *See Matter of Q-T-M-T-*, 21 I&N Dec. 639, 655–56 (BIA 1996); *Matter of C*, 20 I&N Dec. 529 (BIA 1992); *Matter of U-M-*, 20 I&N Dec. 327 (BIA 1991) [finding all aggravated felonies and drug trafficking crimes particularly serious and not requiring a further finding of danger to the community]; *Ahmetovic v. INS*, 62 F.3d 48, 53 (2d Cir. 1995) (and cases cited therein); *Kofa v. INS*, 60 F.3d 1084 (4th Cir. 1995) (en banc) [finding plain language, legislative history and Protocol supports BIA view]; *Al-Salehi v. INS*, 47 F.3d 390 (10th Cir. 1995); *Mansoori v. INS*, 32 F.3d 1020 (7th Cir. 1994); *Feroz, supra* at 227; *Garcia v. INS*, 7 F.3d 1320 (7th Cir. 1993) [a separate finding that person constitutes danger to the community is unnecessary]; *Mosquera-Perez v. INS*, 3 F.3d 553 (1st Cir. 1993) [same]; *Martins v. INS*, 972 F.2d 657 (5th Cir. 1992) [separate finding of danger to the community is not necessary where drug crime is defined as "particularly serious"]; *Crespo-Gomez v. Richard*, 780 F.2d 932 (11th Cir. 1986); *Matter of Carballe*, 19 I&N Dec. 357 (BIA 1986); *Ramirez-Ramos v. INS*, 814 F.2d 1394 (9th Cir. 1987). However, there is no legislative finding that such persons *per se* constitute a danger to the community, thereby leaving open the possibility that a particularly serious conviction does not automatically invoke this bar to relief.

4. *Serious Nonpolitical Crime*—There are serious reasons for considering that the alien has committed a serious, nonpolitical crime before arrival in the U.S., INA §241(b)(3)(B)(iii), 8 U.S.C. §1231(b)(3)(B)(iii); *Khouzam v. Ashcroft,* 361 F.3d 161, 165–66 (2d Cir. 2004) [serious reasons under this statute is equivalent to probable cause]; *Pronsivakulchai v. Gonzales,* 461 F.3d 903 (7th Cir. 2006) [reversing IJ's finding that respondent was ineligible for asylum and withholding on the grounds that there was reason to believe she had committed a drug trafficking crime in Thailand when she was deprived of the right to present rebuttal evidence]. To determine whether a crime is "nonpolitical" under INA §241(b)(3)(B)(iii), the standard is that set forth by the BIA under the prior statute in *Matter of McMullen,* 19 I&N Dec. 90 (BIA 1984), which was upheld by the Supreme Court in *INS v. Aguirre-Aguirre,* 526 U.S. 415 (1999). Under *McMullen*, the BIA found that whether a crime is political in nature turns on whether "the political aspects of the offense outweigh its common-law character." *McMullen* at 97–98. The balance need not be struck if "the crime is grossly out of proportion to the political objective or if it involves acts of an atrocious nature." *Id.* The BIA is not required to balance the "criminal acts against the risk of persecution he would face if returned..." *INS v. Aguirre-Aguirre,* 526 U.S. 415 (1999). The BIA is also not required to consider the "atrocious nature" of the offense if it has determined that the common-law (*i.e.,* criminal) aspects of the offense outweigh the political nature of the crime. *Id* at 429–31. And where it has determined that the acts were not political based on the lack of proportion with the objectives, the BIA need not engage in a detailed analysis of the "political necessity and success" of the applicant's methods. *Id.* at 431–32. A person was ineligible under former INA §243(h)(2)(C) where he facilitated or assisted terrorists in committing a serious nonpolitical crime, even if he had not "pulled the trigger." *McMullen v. INS*, 788 F.2d 591 (9th Cir. 1986). *Accord Chay-Velasquez v. Ashcroft,* 367 F.3d 751, 755–56 (8th Cir. 2004) [denying asylum and withholding because applicant committed nonpolitical crimes in burning buses which served the civilian population, breaking windows, and fighting with police]. Participation in a *coup d'état*, however, may be political, and therefore not a bar to withholding, where there is no opportunity for citizens to freely and peacefully change their laws, officials or form of government. *Dwomoh v. Sava*, 696 F.Supp. 970 (S.D.N.Y. 1988). *But see Matter of S-K-* 23 I&N Dec. 936, 942 n.5 (BIA 2006) [barring withholding to an applicant who contributed money to the Chin National Front that fights against repression by the illegitimate Burmese military government as providing "material" support to a terrorist organization]; *cf.* . *Matter of S-K-,* 24 I&N Dec. 289 (AG 2007) [maintaining precedential value of BIA decision but remanding case to BIA in light of DHS decision to grant a waiver under INA §212(d)(3)(B)(i) and not to apply the "material support" bar on asylum to certain persons providing support to the CNF]; or

5. *Danger to U.S. Security*—There are reasonable grounds to believe the alien is a danger to the security of the U.S. INA §241(b)(3)(B)(iv), 8 U.S.C. §1231(b)(3)(B)(iv). Any person described in INA §237(a)(4)(B) [terrorist] shall be considered such a person and shall be denied withholding. In *Matter of A-H-,* 23 I&N Dec. 774, 787–90 (AG 2005) the AG addressing former §243(h)(2)(D), which contained similar language ("reasonable grounds for regarding"), interpreted the statute to provide: (1) that the level of danger need not be serious, significant or grave and therefore any nontrivial level of danger to the nation's defense, foreign relations or economic interests is sufficient to trigger the provision; (2) that reasonable grounds means a standard "substantially less stringent than preponderance of the evidence" and is more akin to probable cause which would be satisfied "if there is information that would permit a reasonable person to believe that the alien may pose a danger to national security;" and (3) the information relied on to support a reasonable grounds determination "need not meet standards for admissibility of evidence in court proceedings." *Yusupov v. Att'y Gen. of the U.S.,* 518 F.3d 185 (3d Cir. 2008) [affirming on *Chevron* grounds the AG's reading of the statute except the part stating that the government need only show that the respondent "may" be a danger rather than "is" a danger to the U.S.]. *See also Matter of U-H-,* 23 I&N Dec. 355, 356 (BIA 2002) [finding that the USA PATRIOT Act §412 did not alter the "reasonable grounds to believe" standard]. Post–REAL ID, a person may also be barred from withholding under the CAT or nondeferral CAT, if the person knew or should have known they were providing material support to a terrorist organization. *Matter of S-K-* 23 I&N Dec. 936, 942 n.5 (BIA 2006) [finding that the Chin National Front is a terrorist organization, that contributions need not have been for terrorist purposes, and that a contribution of $685 over an 11 month period was sufficient to establish "material" support]; *cf. Matter of S-K-,* 24 I&N Dec. 289 (AG 2007) [maintaining precedential value of BIA decision but remanding case to BIA in light of DHS

decision to grant a waiver under INA §212(d)(3)(B)(i) and not to apply the "material support" bar on asylum to certain persons providing support to the CNF]. Subsequent to the AG's decision, the Secretary of DHS and the Secretary of State were given broader powers to waive the material support provision under the Consolidated Appropriations Act, 2008, PL 110-161, Div. J, §691(a), 121 Stat. 1844, 2364–65 and the Act itself exempted certain groups, including the CNF, that was the subject of the AG's decision in *Matter of S-K-*. In light of Congress' Act DHS granted the respondent asylum and the BIA vacated its grant of deferral of removal and found no need to address withholding. *Matter of S-K-,* 24 I&N Dec. 475 (BIA 2008). For Pre-REAL ID *see Cheema v. INS,* 383 F.3d 848, 857–59 (9th Cir. 2004) [pre–REAL ID, the court reversed the BIA's finding that persons who support terrorist activity in India are ineligible for withholding and rejected the BIA's analysis as collapsing a finding of terrorism and a danger to security into one]. The Secretary of DHS also exercised his authority to waive the "material support" provision for persons who provided support under "duress" to terrorist organizations (*e.g.,* asylees who were required to pay ransom or extortion money). Memo, Chertoff, Secy. of DHS, Exercise of Authority Under Sec. 212(d)(3)(B)(i) (Apr. 27, 2007), *published on* AILA InfoNet at Doc. No. 07050168. For a detailed discussion of criteria to grant waiver, *see* "Waiver Provision" in Ch. 3, ¶ III.H.2.d(6)(b) (p.105), *supra.*

6. *Burden of Proof*—If the evidence indicates that one or more grounds of denial apply, the burden shifts to the applicant to prove by a preponderance of the evidence that the grounds are inapplicable. 8 C.F.R. §§208.16(d)(2), 1208.16(d)(2); The BIA is also to be given broad deference under *Chevron* in the construction of the statute. *INS v. Aguirre-Aguirre,* 526 U.S. 415 (1999).

7. *Standard of Proof*—The government need not prove any of these exclusion categories by "clear and convincing evidence." *McMullen,* 788 F.2d at 598 n.2. It need only find probable cause to establish "serious reasons" for considering the crime to be nonpolitical. *Id.* at 599; *Khouzam v. Ashcroft,* 361 F.3d 161, 165–66 (2d Cir. 2004) [serious reasons under the statute is equivalent to probable cause]. Similarly, the government may prove that there are "reasonable grounds for regarding" an alien as a danger to the national security where there is information that would permit a reasonable person to believe that the alien may pose such a danger. *Matter of A-H-,* 23 I&N Dec. 774, 786–87 (AG 2005); *Yusupov v. Att'y Gen. of the U.S.,* 518 F.3d 185 (3d Cir. 2008) [affirming on *Chevron* grounds the AG's reading of the statute regarding standard of proof]. However, the applicant has a right to present evidence. *Pronsivakulchai v. Gonzales,* 461 F.3d 903 (7th Cir. 2006) [reversing IJ's finding that respondent was ineligible for asylum on the grounds that there was reason to believe she had committed a drug trafficking crime in Thailand when she was deprived of the right to present rebuttal evidence]. If the evidence indicates that one or more grounds of exclusion apply, the burden shifts to the applicant to prove by a preponderance of the evidence that the grounds are inapplicable. 8 C.F.R. §§208.16(d)(2), 1208.16(d)(2). The BIA is also given broad deference under *Chevron* in the construction of the statute. *INS v. Aguirre-Aguirre,* 526 U.S. 415 (1999).

8. *Mandatory Denial*—The prohibitions of INA §241(b)(3)(B)(ii) and (iii) [formerly INA §§243(h)(2)(B) and (C)] are mandatory, 8 C.F.R. §208.16(d)(2)and the nature of a person's criminal conduct or activity may not be balanced against the severity of the persecution when denying withholding. *INS v. Aguirre-Aguirre,* 526 U.S. 415 (1999); *Crespo-Gomez v. Richard*, 780 F.2d 932 (11th Cir. 1986); *Matter of Rodriguez-Coto*, 19 I&N Dec. 208 (BIA 1985). *But see* Handbook ¶156. INA §241(b)(3) [formerly 243(h)] relief has been denied on the grounds that assault with a firearm with intent to murder, *Gjonaj v. INS*, 47 F.3d 824 (6th Cir. 1995), armed robbery, *Matter of Rodriguez-Coto, supra*; *Hernandez-Gonzalez v. Moyer*, 907 F.Supp. 1224, 1227 (N.D. Ill. 1995), robbery, *Matter of Rodriguez-Palma*, *supra*, burglary, *Matter of Ballesteros-Garcia*, *supra*, and embezzlement, *Matter of Castellon*, 17 I&N Dec. 616 (BIA 1981), constitute "serious nonpolitical crimes" under former INA §243(h)(2)(C).

E. *Judicial Review of Discretionary Denial*—There may be judicial review to determine whether a conviction is a particularly serious crime barring withholding. *Alaka v. Att'y Gen. of the U.S.,* 456 F.3d 88, 95–102 (3d Cir. 2006) [following reasoning in *Spencer* and determining that discretionary bar does not apply to determination of particularly serious crime exception to withholding of removal]; *Afridi v. Gonzales,* 442 F.3d 1212, 1217–19 (9th Cir. 2006) [distinguishing its own precedent in *Unuakhaulu v. Gonzales,* 416 F.3d 931 (9th Cir. 2005), and holding that INA §242(a)(2)(B)(ii) did not bar review of the BIA's determination that respondent committed a particularly serious crime because respondent challenged the failure to apply the proper legal standard under *Frentescu*]; *Steinhouse v. Ashcroft,* 247 F.Supp.2d 201, 205–06 (D. Conn. 2003) [finding habeas jurisdiction to review the standard applied by BIA to determine a particular serious crime]. *But see Ali v. Achim,* 468 F.3d 462, 465–66, 470 (7th Cir. 2006) *cert. dismissed* 128 S.Ct. 828 (2007) [jurisdiction to review whether proper standard was applied to determine a particularly serious crime but there was no jurisdiction to review BIA's exercise of discretion under the proper legal standard including whether it misapplied its own precedent]; *Matsuk v. INS,* 247 F.3d 999, 1002 (9th Cir. 2001) [no jurisdiction to review decision to deny withholding based on the determination that a crime is particularly serious because INA §242(a)(2)(B)(ii) bars review of all discretionary decisions].

F. ***Effective Dates***—For deportation and exclusion cases (*i.e.,* cases arising before Apr. 1, 1997) AEDPA §413(f) provided discretionary authority to the AG to override the bars to relief under former §243(h)(2) if she determined that it was "necessary to ensure compliance with the 1967 United Nations Protocol Relating to the Status of Refugees." Former INA §243(h)(2), 8 U.S.C. §1253(h)(2). The Board interpreted this provision to mean that a person who had been convicted of an aggravated felony and sentenced to at least 5 years in prison was conclusively barred from withholding, but that a sentence of less than 5 years was subject to a "rebuttable presumption" that could overcome the particularly serious crime bar. *Matter of Q-T-M-T-,* 21 I&N Dec. 639 (BIA 1996). *See Choeum v. INS,* 129 F.3d 29, 40–43 (1st Cir. 1997) [upholding INS/BIA interpretation that a separate finding is unnecessary if conviction more than 5 years]. Former INA §243(h)(3) was eliminated by IIRIRA §305(a).

V. CONVENTION AGAINST TORTURE / DEFERRAL OF REMOVAL

A. ***Generally***—8 C.F.R. §§208.16–.18, 1208.16–.18. Under international and domestic law, a person may not be returned to a country where s/he will be tortured. United Nations Convention Against Torture and Other Cruel, Inhuman or Degrading Treatment or Punishment, opened for signature Feb. 4, 1985, G.A. Res. 39/46, 39 U.N. GAOR Supp. No. 51 at 197, U.N. Doc. A/Res/39/708 (1984), *reprinted in* 23 I.L.M. 1027 (1984), *modified* in 24 I.L.M. 535 (1985). The CAT was enacted into U.S. law on Oct. 21, 1998 by Fiscal Year 1999 Omnibus Consolidated and Emergency Supplemental Appropriations Act, PL 105-277, Div. G, Sub. B, Tit. XXI §2242 of the Foreign Affairs Reform and Restructuring Act of 1998, 112 Stat. 2681–822, 105th Cong. 2d Sess. (1998) [FARRA]; 144 Cong. Rec. H11044-03; 136 Cong. Rec. S17486, 36198 (1990); *Committee on Foreign Relations, Convention Against Torture and other Cruel, Inhuman or Degrading Treatment or Punishment,* S. Ex. Rept. 101-30, 101st Cong. 2d Sess. (Aug. 30, 1990). *See also* 136 Cong. Rec. S17486, S17491-92 (Daily ed. 1990). *See also* Burgers & Danelius, *The United Nations Convention Against Torture: A Handbook on the Convention Against Torture and Other Cruel, Inhuman or Degrading Treatment or Punishment* (1988).

Article 3(1) of the Convention states, "[n]o State Party shall expel, return ('refouler') or extradite a person to another state where there are substantial grounds for believing that he would be in danger of being subjected to torture." In making this determination, the U.S. "shall take into account all relevant considerations including, where applicable, the existence in the State concerned of a consistent pattern of gross, flagrant, or mass violations of human rights." Article 3 (2). Congress has stated that: "[i]t shall be the policy of the United States not to expel, extradite, or otherwise effect the involuntary return of any person to a country in which there are substantial grounds for believing the person would be in danger of being subjected to torture, regardless of whether the person is physically present in the United States." Section 2242 ¶1, *supra.*

Congress in FARRA barred challenges to the regulations adopted to implement CAT. FARRA §2242(d) ["[n]otwithstanding any other provision of law…no court shall have jurisdiction to review the regulations adopted to implement [CAT] or any other determination made with respect to the application of the policy [regarding expelling, extraditing or otherwise involuntarily returning someone] except as part of the review of a final order of removal pursuant to [INA §242]"]. *See also* 8 C.F.R. §§208.18(e), 1208.18(e). Based on this language, some courts have found that CAT is not self-executing and therefore does not provide a source of independent enforceable rights. *Pierre v. Gonzales,* 502 F.3d 109, 119–20 (2d Cir. 2007) [because CAT is not self-executing an applicant cannot rely on international law and international treatment under the treaty to establish a judicially enforceable right]; *Renkel v. U.S.,* 456 F.3d 640 (6th Cir. 2006) [CAT does not permit a private cause of action for improper and degrading treatment against the U.S. arising out of conditions of confinement in the U.S.]; *Wang v. Ashcroft,* 320 F.3d 130,

140 (2d Cir. 2003) [CAT is not self-executing and does not provide independent enforceable rights but regulations may be enforced]; *Reyes-Sanchez v. Ashcroft,* 261 F.Supp.2d 276, 290–92 (S.D.N.Y. 2003); *Calderon v. Reno,* 39 F.Supp.2d 943, 956–57 (N.D. Ill. 1999). However, even if CAT is not "self-executing," FARRA regulations are enforceable in federal court proceedings, including (pre-REAL ID) habeas. *Auguste v. Ridge,* 395 F.3d 123, 137–38 (3d Cir. 2005) [following *Ogbudimkpa* but also noting that scope of review is "limited to constitutional issues and errors of law, including both statutory interpretation and application of law to undisputed facts or adjudicated facts, but does not include review of administrative fact findings or the exercise of discretion"]; *Habtemicael v. Ashcroft,* 360 F.3d 820, 825–28 (8th Cir. 2004) [reversing IJ denial of CAT claim for failure to engage in sufficient fact finding to determine whether there is a violation]; *Cadet v. Bulger,* 377 F.3d 1173, 1181–83 (11th Cir. 2004) [recognizing that *Richardson v. Reno* was overruled by *St. Cyr* and holding that federal courts retain jurisdiction under 28 U.S.C. §2241 to challenge removal orders under CAT]; *Singh v. Ashcroft,* 351 F.3d 435, 440–42 (9th Cir. 2003) [following *Cornejo-Barreto* the court found that FARRA does not preclude a habeas action challenging a decision on a CAT claim even if the habeas claim does not raise a "purely legal question"]; *Ogbudimkpa v. Ashcroft,* 342 F.3d 207, 212–22 (3d Cir. 2003) [district courts have habeas jurisdiction to review violations of CAT or FARRA because as a practical matter they are the same]; *Wang, supra; Saint Fort v. Ashcroft,* 329 F.3d 191, 200–04 (1st Cir. 2003) [applicant's claim does not rest on whether CAT is self-executing because Congress passed enabling legislation under FARRA and the agency issued regulations].

B. *CAT Regulations*—DOJ published regulations to effectuate CAT. *See* 8 C.F.R. §208.16 to 208.18, 64 Fed. Reg. 8478 (Feb. 19, 1999), *reprinted in* 76 No. 7 *Interpreter Releases* 275, 288–305 (Feb. 22, 1999). In §2242 of the FARRA, *supra,* Congress also determined that regulations limiting time to reopen a removal/deportation case to apply for CAT benefits was lawful. *Huang v. Ashcroft,* 390 F.3d 1118, 1120–23 (9th Cir. 2004) [deadline for filing motion to reopen by Mar. 22, 1999 applied to CAT claim seeking deferral as well as withholding]; *Foroglou v. Reno,* 241 F.3d 111, 113 (1st Cir. 2001) [upholding BIA's refusal to consider CAT claim not filed within time proscribed by §208.18(b)(2)]; *but see Guo v. DOJ,* 422 F.3d 61 (2d Cir. 2005) [where applicant did not have final order before Mar. 22, 1999, he did not have to file motion to reopen to have CAT claim heard]. Regulations relating to the definition of torture and to the burden of proof have been upheld. *Reyes-Sanchez v. Ashcroft,* 261 F.Supp.2d 276, 290–92 (S.D.N.Y. 2003) [8 C.F.R. §§208.16(c)(2), 208.18(a)(5) are lawful].

C. *Extradition Proceedings*—To comply with CAT as it applies to extradition proceedings, DOS has issued corresponding regulations. 22 C.F.R. §95, 64 Fed. Reg. 9435–37 (Feb. 26, 1999), *reprinted in* 76 *Interpreter Releases* No. 9, 372, 381–83 (Mar. 8, 1999). These regulations utilize a "more likely than not" standard that the person would be tortured. 22 C.F.R. §§95.1(c), 95.2(b). The regulations suggest that a presentation under CAT is made after a judicial officer has found the person extraditable and before s/he is extradited. 22 C.F.R. §95.3(a). A fear of torture or even the grant of asylum, in the view of some courts, may not be considered in the extradition proceeding. *Hoxha v. Levi,* 465 F.3d 554, 563 (3d Cir. 2006) [noninquiry principle does not permit the court in an extradition proceeding to inquire into humanitarian considerations such as torture or death upon return as that is a function of the Executive branch]; *Mironescu v. Costner,* 345 F.Supp.2d 538 (M.D.N.C. 2004) [no review of CAT claim in extradition but Secy. of State must consider evidence if magistrate orders extradition and must notify defendant of Secretary's decision with enough time to seek habeas review]; *In re Extradition of Mironescu,* 296 F.Supp.2d 632 (M.D.N.C. 2003) [consideration under CAT is left to the Secy. of State and cannot be considered in extradition]. The Secy. of State may surrender the fugitive to the requesting State, deny surrender of the fugitive, or surrender the fugitive subject to conditions. There is no judicial review. 22 C.F.R. §95.4. The Ninth Circuit has held that 22 C.F.R. §95.4 only applies to judicial review of the regulations themselves and does not preclude a challenge to the statute's implementation under the APA. *Cornejo-Barreto v. Seifert,* 218 F.3d 1004 (9th Cir. 2000) [fugitive fearing torture may petition for review of the Secretary's decision to surrender him and such review is subject to an abuse of discretion standard under 5 U.S.C. §706(2)(a) of the APA]. *Accord Singh v. Ashcroft,* 351 F.3d 435, 440–42 (9th Cir. 2003). Judicial review, consistent with due process, must also be provided where a person *granted* deferral of removal has had the status revoked on the grounds of diplomatic assurances that he would not be tortured if returned to his country. *Khouzam v. Hogan,* 529 F.Supp.2d 543 (M.D. Pa. 2008) [stayed removal and released respondent from custody despite diplomatic assurances that Egyptian granted deferral of removal under CAT would not be tortured where the assurances were not subject to due process scrutiny].

D. ***Definition of Torture***—8 C.F.R. §§208.18, 1208.18. Torture is defined as "any act by which severe pain or suffering, whether physical or mental, is intentionally inflicted on a person for such purposes as obtaining from him or her or a third person information or a confession, punishing him or her for an act he or she or a third person has committed or is suspected of having committed, or intimidating or coercing him or her or a third person, or for any reason based on discrimination of any kind...." 8 C.F.R. §§208.18(a)(1), 1208.18(a)(1). In order for acts which constitute mental pain or suffering to be considered torture, they must be caused by or result from: (i) intentional or threatened infliction of severe physical pain or suffering; (ii) administration or threat of mind altering substances or other procedures to disrupt profoundly senses or personality; (iii) threat of imminent death; or (iv) threat that another will be subject to (ii) or (iii) above. 8 C.F.R. §§208.18(a)(4), 1208.18(a)(4). *Ni v. BIA,* 439 F.3d 177, 179–80 (2d Cir. 2006) [whether forced sterilization constitutes torture is an open question, but IJ's failure to consider CAT claim in context of China's "one child policy" was reversible error]; *Al-Saher v. INS,* 268 F.3d 1143 (9th Cir. 2001) [reversing BIA's denial of CAT protection and finding that Iraqi subject to repeated beating and cigarette burns was tortured within the meaning of INS regulations]. Rape can constitute torture. *Zubeda v. Ashcroft,* 333 F.3d 463, 472–73 (3d Cir. 2003) (and cases cited therein) [citizen of the Republic of Congo could claim CAT benefits because of fear of detention that would result in rape]. Murder can constitute torture. *Comollari v. Ashcroft,* 378 F.3d 694, 697 (7th Cir. 2004) [rejecting government's argument that torture does not include assassination because a person can have a painless death]. FGM may constitute torture. *Tunis v. Gonzales,* 447 F.3d 547, 550 (7th Cir. 2006) [reaffirming its view that FGM can be torture because "involuntary excision, even if unaccompanied by infibulation, is torture"]; *Mohammed v. Gonzales,* 400 F.3d 785, 802 (9th Cir. 2005) [FGM may be considered torture under DHS regulations].

1. *BIA Definition of Torture*—The BIA has defined torture as: (1) an act causing severe physical or mental pain or suffering that must be "an extreme form of cruel and inhuman treatment" and not lesser forms; (2) the act must be "specifically intended" to inflict severe physical or mental pain or suffering and an act that results in unanticipated or unintended severity of pain or suffering does not constitute torture; (3) the act must have an "illicit purpose" such as "obtaining information or a confession, punishment for a victim's or another's act, intimidating or coercing a victim or another or any discriminatory purpose;" (4) the act must be an intentional government act directed against a person in the offender's custody or control and "negligent acts or acts by private individuals not acting on behalf of the government" are not covered; and (5) the act "does not include pain or suffering arising only from, inherent in or incidental to lawful sanctions" such as a judicially imposed death penalty. *Matter of J-E-,* 23 I&N Dec. 291, 297–99 (BIA 2002) [indefinite detention of criminal deportees by Haitian authorities in substandard prisons does not constitute torture because there is no intention to inflict pain or suffering]. *Accord Pierre v. Gonzales,* 502 F.3d 109 (2d Cir. 2007) [agreeing with *Matter of J-E-* in Haitian detention case and determining that there must be "specific intent" to torture by the government or a private actor the government acquiesces in]; *Toussaint v. Att'y Gen. of the U.S.,* 455 F.3d 409 (3d Cir. 2006) [agreeing with *Matter of J-E-* in Haitian detention case and finding that BIA's reversal of IJ in short opinion was sufficient]; *Francois v. Gonzales,* 448 F.3d 645, 652 n.6 (3d Cir. 2006) [following *Auguste* but declining to suggest that conditions of confinement "could never satisfy the burden…for relief under the CAT"]; *Auguste v. Ridge,* 395 F.3d 123 (3d Cir. 2005) [following *Matter of J-E-* and determining that applicant must prove "specific intent" to establish torture]; *Cadet v. Bulger,* 377 F.3d 1173, 1181, 1186–96 (11th Cir. 2004) [following *Matter of J-E-* and 5-part test for torture claim finding that cruel, degrading and inhumane treatment in Haitian prisons and/or by Haitian police officers does not amount to torture under CAT]; *Settenda v. Ashcroft,* 377 F.3d 89, 95–96 (1st Cir. 2004) [applying analysis in *Elien* and *Matter of J-E-* to person facing detention in Uganda]; *Elien v. Ashcroft,* 364 F.3d 392, 398–99 (1st Cir. 2004) [following *Matter of J-E-* and holding that because there was no evidence that Haiti used torture pervasively or as a matter of policy on detainees, the IJ did not err in denying CAT claim]; *Thelemaque v. Ashcroft,* 363 F.Supp.2d 198 (D. Conn. 2005) [following *Matter of J-E-* regarding Haitian detention conditions]. *See also Zhang v. Gonzales,* 432 F.3d 339, 345 (5th Cir. 2005) [fear that Falun Gong member will be sanctioned for not reporting to the police after his arrest and for violating Chinese immigration laws is not torture but lawful sanction]. *But see Jean-Pierre v. U.S. Att'y Gen.,* 500 F.3d 1315, 1322–27 (11th Cir. 2007) [the BIA failed to give reasoned consideration to the claim of a Haitian petitioner who is mentally ill with AIDS that he will face torture if returned to Haiti because he will be imprisoned which will result in his being singled out for crawl-space confinement, beatings with metal rods,

and "kalot marassa" (severe boxing of the ears leading to deafness)]; *Lavira v. Att'y Gen. of the U.S.,* 478 F.3d 158, 166–72 (3d Cir. 2007) [distinguishing *Auguste* because Lavira suffers from HIV and is an above-the-knee amputee].

Noncompliance with applicable legal procedural standards does not *per se* constitute torture. 8 C.F.R. §§208.18(a)(8), 1208.18(a)(8). Although the Convention and the BIA recognize that "lawful sanctions" cannot be torture, a government cannot exempt itself from the proscriptions of the Convention simply by defining torture as lawful punishment. The exclusion of pain and suffering arising from lawful sanctions under 8 C.F.R. §§208.18(a)(3), 1208.18(a)(3) does *not* permit a state to engage in torture by authorizing permissible forms of punishment under its domestic law. *Ghebrehiwot v. Att'y Gen. of the U.S.,* 467 F.3d 344, 358–59 (3d Cir. 2006) [simply because the respondent was punished as a deserter does not necessarily mean that he cannot also establish that he suffered torture under CAT]; *Nuru v. Gonzales,* 404 F.3d 1207, 1218–23 (9th Cir. 2005) [where Eritrean soldier who questioned purpose of war with Sudan was subjected to almost daily beatings, deprived of adequate food and water for 25 days, and thereafter severely beaten, IJ's determination that this was simply lawful punishment was reversed].

2. *DOJ Analysis of Torture Definition*—DOJ has issued its own analysis of the definition of torture under CAT for purposes of analyzing the appropriate criminal statutes under 18 U.S.C. §§2340–40A. Legal Memorandum, Levin Acting Asst. A.G., Office of Legal Counsel, DOJ (Dec. 30, 2004), *published on* AILA InfoNet at Doc. No. 05010462 [defining the terms "severe," "severe physical pain or suffering," "severe mental pain or suffering," and "specifically intended" and recognizing that there is no "good motive" or good reason exception to the use of torture].

3. *Torture Does Not Include*—(i) lesser forms of cruel and inhumane treatment; (ii) acts that result in unintended severity of pain and suffering; or (iii) lawful sanctions judicially imposed including the death penalty. 8 C.F.R. §§208.18(a) (2), (3), & (5), 1208.18(a) (2), (3), & (5); *Mohamed v. Gonzales,* 477 F.3d 522, 527–28 (8th Cir. 2006) [general ostracism and abuse at the hands of other Somalis because of mental illness does not constitute torture]; *Jo v. Gonzales,* 458 F.3d 104 (2d Cir. 2006) [destruction, theft, expropriation or other deprivations of property do not constitute torture because mental pain must have its origin in actual or threatened infliction of harm to the person]; *Raffington v. Cangemi,* 399 F.3d 900, 904 (8th Cir. 2005) [denial of access to public or private mental health care is not torture]; *Auguste v. Ridge,* 395 F.3d 123, 138–47 (3d Cir. 2005) [applicant must prove "specific intent" to establish torture and horrible prison conditions are not enough to establish that Haitian officials had specific intent to commit torture]; *Prela v. Ashcroft,* 394 F.3d 515, 519 (7th Cir. 2005) [ethnic Albanian in Kosovo was not tortured where he was detained for 24 hours, harassed for bribes, interrogated, threatened and sustained an unspecified injury to his hands]; *Cadet v. Bulger,* 377 F.3d 1173, 1186–96 (11th Cir. 2004) [inhumane treatment of Haitian deportees subject to indefinite detention and mistreatment by prison officials does not amount to torture under CAT]; *Gui v. INS,* 280 F.3d 1217, 1230 (9th Cir. 2002) [harassment, tapping telephones, trying to run respondent off the road do not represent torture]. *But see Jean-Pierre v. U.S. Att'y Gen.,* 500 F.3d 1315, 1322–27 (11th Cir. 2007) [the BIA failed to give reasoned consideration to the claim of a Haitian petitioner who is mentally ill with AIDS that he will face torture if returned to Haiti because he will be imprisoned which will result in his being singled out for crawl-space confinement, beatings with metal rods, and "kalot marassa" (severe boxing of the ears leading to deafness)]; *Lavira v. Att'y Gen. of the U.S.,* 478 F.3d 158, 166–72 (3d Cir. 2007) [distinguishing *Auguste* because Lavira suffers from HIV and is an above-the-knee amputee].

4. *Reason for Torture Need Not be Political*—Neither the genuineness of the applicant's political beliefs, nor the basis of the government's torture are relevant to a claim under CAT. *Tun v. INS,* 445 F.3d 554, 571–72 (2d Cir. 2006) [IJ reversed where she denied CAT relief because torture would be in retaliation for alleged criminal activity for not paying taxes and jumping ship as a crewman and because IJ did not believe that Burmese citizen's actions demonstrating against his government while in the U.S. were genuinely motivated instead of self-serving].

E. ***Acquiescence by Government Officials***—The act must be done "by or at the instigation of or with the consent or acquiescence of a public official or other person acting in an official capacity." 8 C.F.R. §§208.18(a)(1), 1208.18(a)(1). *Mouawad v. Gonzales,* 485 F.3d 405, 413–14 (8th Cir. 2007) [failure of the IJ to address acquiescence of Lebanese government to violence by Hezbollah did not permit review; CAT denial reversed]; *Morales v. Gonzales,* 478 F.3d 972, 983–84 (9thCir. 2007) [IJ erred where he sought and addressed only direct government involvement in determining CAT claim while ignoring willful blindness or outright acceptance by the police of respondent's repeated sexual abuse]; *Habtemicael v. Ashcroft,* 370 F.3d 774, 780–83 (8th Cir. 2004) [reversing denial of CAT claim where IJ failed to make findings about the status of the EPLF in Ethiopia at the time respondent fled]. Acquiescence must include awareness of the torture and failure to intervene in breach of a legal responsibility to do so. 8 C.F.R. §§208.18(a)(7), 1208.18(a)(7). In *Matter of S-V-,* 22 I&N Dec. 1306 (BIA 2000), the BIA set the standard for "acquiescence" and determined that an applicant's burden of proof must include either actual knowledge or proof that government officials "are willfully accepting" of the nongovernmental torture. But many courts have rejected this view and have accepted a lower threshold for government acquiescence that would include a "willful blindness" standard. *Delgado v. Mukasey,* 508 F.3d 702, 708–09 (2d Cir. 2007) [reversing BIA's denial of CAT where it implied a standard different than "willful blindness" and ignored testimony and human rights reports suggesting acquiescence by the government]; *Silva-Rengifo v. Att'y Gen. of the U.S.,* 473 F.3d 58, 65–71 (3d Cir. 2007) [rejected standard in *Matter of S-V-* requiring actual knowledge of torture and finding instead that standard includes willful blindness]; *Rafiq v. Gonzales,* 468 F.3d 165 (2d Cir. 2006) [reversing IJ for failing to apply "willful blindness" standard as required by *Khouzam*]; *Amir v. Gonzales,* 467 F.3d 921, 926–27 (6th Cir. 2006) [accepted willful blindness standard and rejected *Matter of S-V*]; *Ornelas-Chavez v. Gonzales,* 458 F.3d 1052, 1060 (9th Cir. 2006) [reversing denial of CAT where BIA found that torture was not "sanctioned" because the court determined that "sanction" and "acquiescence" were different standards]; *Rafix v. Gonzales,* 458 F.3d 36 (2d Cir. 2006) [denial of CAT claim of Muslim who converted to Christianity was reversed where IJ failed to use "willfully blind" test and ignored substantial evidence]; *Lopez-Soto v. Ashcroft,* 383 F.3d 228, 239–41 (4th Cir. 2004) [adopting willful blindness standard but finding no evidence to support CAT claim where father reported son's death to police and no one was arrested]; *Khouzam v. Ashcroft,* 361 F.3d 161, 168–71 (2d Cir. 2004) [disapproving of *Matter of Y-L-, A-G-, R-S-R* in that a CAT applicant does not have to prove that the state consented or approved of torture, but only that "government officials know of or remain willfully blind" to the torture]; *Zheng v. Ashcroft,* 332 F.3d 1186 (9th Cir. 2003) [disapproving of *Matter of S-V-* and finding that congressional intent only requires "awareness" by government officials and not "willful acceptance" of torture which suggests actual knowledge and not just "willful blindness"]; *Perez v. Loy,* 356 F.Supp.2d 172, 177–79 (D. Conn. 2005) [following *Khouzam* and *Zheng* and reversing BIA for applying the incorrect "willfully accepting" standard]. *See also* S. Exec. Rep. 101-30 at 9 (1990).

1. *Physical Custody/Control Not Required*—The Convention does not require that the person face torture while under a public official's custody or physical control. *Reyes-Reyes v. Ashcroft,* 384 F.3d 782 (9th Cir. 2004) [reversing IJ denial of CAT claim for homosexual male with female identity from El Salvador where IJ erroneously determined that applicant had to be tortured by someone in the government or acting for the government without addressing acquiescence]; *Azanor v. Ashcroft,* 364 F.3d 1013, 1019–20 (9th Cir. 2004) [reversing BIA determination suggesting that applicant was required to be in the physical control or custody of a government official and rejected language in *Matter of J-E-* that BIA relied upon]; *Valdiviezo-Galdamez v. Attorney General,* 502 F.3d 285, 292–93 (3d Cir. 2007) [where police ignored five reports filed by applicant regarding violence and threats by gang members, their failure to act "could arguably constitute government 'acquiescence' to torture"].

2. *Reporting of Torture to the Government Not Required.* There is no requirement that an applicant for CAT report his alleged torture to public officials to qualify for relief. *Ornelas-Chavez v. Gonzales,* 458 F.3d 1052, 1059–61 (9th Cir. 2006) [failure to report an incident of persecution by private parties is not required for CAT because there is no requirement that the public official have actual knowledge of the torture; it is enough that the public official could have inferred the alleged torture was taking place, remained willfully blind to it or simply stood by because of inability or unwillingness].

3. *Cases Finding No Acquiescence—Arteaga v. Mukasey,* 511 F.3d 940, 948–49 (9th Cir. 2007) [rejected claim that ex-gang members in El Salvador would face torture at hands of the government because they would not be protected in prison]; *Purwantono v. Gonzales,* 498 F.3d 822, 855–26 (8th Cir. 2007) [Muslim Indonesian who opposed being recruited by Laskar Jihad denied CAT because, *inter alia,* he could not demonstrate that the Indonesian government would acquiesce in his torture as it had taken action against Laskar Jihad]; *Tolego v. Gonzales,* 452 F.3d 763, 767 (8th

Cir. 2006) [ethnic Chinese from Indonesia who complained about acts of violence could not demonstrate that they were committed by, at the direction of, or with the acquiescence of public officials]; *Tamara-Gomez v. Gonzales,* 447 F.3d 343, 351 (9th Cir. 2006) [where Colombian applicant cooperated with the police against the FARC, petitioner could not sustain claim of government acquiescence where the government merely failed to apprehend the persons threatening petitioner or lacked the financial resources to eradicate the threat of torture]; *Rreshpja v. Gonzales,* 420 F.3d 551, 557 (6th Cir. 2005) [where local police did not ignore complaint of young Albanian woman's attempted kidnapping for prostitution but were unable to solve crime, there was no acquiescence]; *D-Muhumed v. U.S. Att'y Gen.,* 388 F.3d 814, 819–20 (11th Cir. 2004) [where Somalia has no central government and the clans controlling various sections of the country do not do so through official power, there is no government sanctioned torture or acquiescence]; *Reyes-Sanchez v. U.S. Att'y Gen.,* 369 F.3d 1239 (11th Cir. 2004) [based on the regulatory language, the police investigation of the terrorists' acts against respondent and the DOS country reports, the government would not acquiesce in torture]; *Guzman v. INS,* 327 F.3d 11, 16–17 (1st Cir. 2003) [BIA properly denied motion to reopen where there was no evidence that government official consented or acquiesced]; *Cano-Merida v. INS,* 311 F.3d 960, 965–66 (9th Cir. 2002) [same]; *Lukwago v. Ashcroft,* 329 F.3d 157, 182–83 (3d Cir. 2003) [child enslaved and conscripted by guerrilla organization in Northern Uganda did not have CAT claim because Ugandan government did not initiate, condone or acquiesce in torture but in fact opposed guerrillas]; *Ontunez-Tursios v. Ashcroft,* 303 F.3d 341, 354–55 (5th Cir. 2002) [stating that "willful blindness" suffices to prove acquiescence but finding that evidence did not prove that Honduran officials would turn a blind eye to torture]; *Ali v. Reno,* 237 F.3d 591, 596–98 (6th Cir. 2001) [in domestic violence case, finding that acquiescence includes "willful blindness," but determining that the Danish police intervened to stop the violence even if they were unable to do so and therefore they did not acquiesce to torture]; *Builes v. Nye,* 239 F.Supp.2d 518, 524–25 (M.D. Pa. 2003) [evidence of widespread bribery, corruption and intimidation of government officials in Colombia, and intimidation and powerlessness to stop torture does not equal acquiescence]; *Chinchilla-Jimenez v. INS,* 226 F.Supp.2d 680, 685 (E.D. Pa. 2002) [where report on Honduras only indicated that certain officials may undertake corrupt activity, applicant did not meet burden of showing government acquiescence]. The applicant must establish that "current government officials acting in an official capacity would be responsible for such abuse." *Matter of Y-L, A-G-, R-S-R,* 23 I&N Dec. 270, 280 (AG 2002).

F. *Burden of Proof: More Likely Than Not*—The standard to be applied is the same as withholding of removal under INA §241(b)(3), which requires the respondent to prove that s/he is "more likely than not" to be subject to torture upon removal and allows proof of a claim by the applicant's own testimony, if credible, without corroboration. 8 C.F.R. §§208.16(c)(2), 1208.16(c)(2). "To prevail, the respondent must show that 'he is more likely than not to suffer intentionally-inflicted cruel and inhuman treatment that either (1) is not lawfully sanctioned by that country or (2) is lawfully sanctioned by that country, but defeats the object and purpose of CAT....' The government need not prove the opposite..." *Matter of J-F-F-,* 23 I&N Dec. 912, 917 (AG 2006) [reversing the IJ/BIA grant of CAT relief to a *pro se* respondent with a severe mental disorder from the Dominican Republic where the IJ "strung together a series of suppositions" by speculating what would happen to the respondent if he did not take his medication and was arrested and tortured by the police and by "flip[ping] the burden [of proof] on its head" by finding facts based on the absence of evidence]. *But see Tran v. Gonzales,* 447 F.3d 937, 941–44 (6th Cir. 2006) [where applicant from Vietnam argued that BIA disaggregated his claims thereby requiring 51% on each claim and where BIA's decision lacked any discussion of a standard of review, court reversed and remanded for a determination under the correct standard of review and burden of proof]; *Kamara v. Att'y Gen. of the U.S.,* 420 F.3d 202, 213–15 (3d Cir. 2005) [finding that the BIA applied the wrong quantum of proof required for a CAT claim when it treated the likelihood of torture from different entities in Sierra Leone as noncumulative claims instead of aggregating them statistically to reach 51%]. The standard of review is substantial evidence and under 8 U.S.C. §1252(b)(4)(B) "administrative findings of fact are conclusive unless any reasonable adjudicator would be compelled to conclude to the contrary." *Lin v. DOJ,* 432 F.3d 156 (2d Cir. 2005) [upholding BIA's determination under the "compelled" standard where CAT claim based solely on fact that applicant is part of the large class of persons who illegally departed China and who may be subject to detention where some people have been tortured was insufficient to establish claim absent particularized evidence]. The burden of proof, however, does not necessarily require the applicant to attach a document that is easily available to the BIA. *Abassi v. INS,* 305 F.3d 1028, 1031 (9th Cir. 2002) [*pro se* litigant was not required to produce country reports that were readily available to the BIA].

1. *Objective Nature of Standard*—The standard of proof is more objective and the subjective elements of asylum and withholding are not applicable. *Hosseini v. Gonzales,* 471 F.3d 953, 959–61 (9th Cir. 2006) [although BIA made adverse credibility finding in regard to whether applicant would be tortured upon return, the objective evidence from two DOS reports indicated he was likely to be tortured and therefore deferral of removal should be granted even if person engaged in terrorist activities]; *Singh v. Ashcroft,* 398 F.3d 396, 404–06 (6th Cir. 2005) [IJ reversed for failure to separately analyze credibility issues for CAT after making a generalized negative credibility finding]; *Camara v. Ashcroft,* 378 F.3d 361, 371–72 (4th Cir. 2004) [following *Ramsameachire* and other circuits and finding that credibility determinations as to asylum/withholding claims are not dispositive of a CAT claim because the latter is objective while the former applies to applicant's subjective state of mind]; *Ramsameachire v. Ashcroft,* 357 F.3d 169, 184–86 (2d Cir. 2004) [same]. *But see Guo v. Gonzales,* 463 F.3d 109, 113–14 (2d Cir. 2006) [*Ramsameachire* and other cases do not apply where the adverse credibility finding on asylum/withholding eliminates all of the factual basis for CAT]; *Gandziami-Mickhou v. Gonzales,* 445 F.3d 351 (4th Cir. 2006) [where IJ based her decision on totality of the circumstances her failure to individually address specific pieces of evidence did not negate the denial; *Camara* distinguished]; *Ibrahim v. Gonzales,* 434 F.3d 1074, 1079–80 (8th Cir. 2006) [where respondent relied on same evidence to prove torture as to prove likelihood of persecution, the IJ did not err in failing to separately analyze the credibility issues under CAT]. However, general evidence that there are instances of torture in a country are not sufficient to meet the burden under CAT in the absence of specific evidence that respondent will be targeted. *Rashiah v. Ashcroft,* 388 F.3d 1126, 1133 (7th Cir. 2004).

2. *Evidence*—In assessing whether a person is more likely than not to be tortured in the future, all evidence shall be considered including: (1) evidence of past torture; (2) evidence that the applicant could relocate to another part of the country where s/he would not likely be tortured; (3) evidence of gross, flagrant, or mass violations of human rights within the country; and (4) other relevant information regarding country conditions. 8 C.F.R. §§208.16(c)(3), 1208.16(c)(3); *Matter of J-E-,* at 303. Country conditions are relevant in assessing withholding, *Matter of G-A-,* 23 I&N Dec. 366, 368–72 (BIA 2002), even if they are insufficient, standing alone, to obtain withholding. *Yi-Tu Lian v. Ashcroft,* 379 F.3d 457 (7th Cir. 2004) [reversing IJ because applicant may have viable CAT claim for being smuggled to U.S. where IJ ignored evidence that it is illegal for Chinese citizens to emigrate without permission of the Chinese government and that government is likely to find out applicant was deported]; *Mapouya v. Gonzales,* 487 F.3d 396, 414–15 (6th Cir. 2007) [IJ's denial of CAT from Brazzaville, Congo reversed and remanded where IJ failed to analyze claim under the factors enumerated in the regulations and in *Ali v. Reno,* 237 F.3d 591, 596–97 (6th Cir. 2007)]; *Mostafa v. Ashcroft,* 395 F.3d 622 (6th Cir. 2005) [BIA's failure to address country condition reports regarding Iran in CAT claim as in *Matter of G-A-* is reversible error]; *Zubeda v. Ashcroft,* 333 F.3d 463, 477–78 (3d Cir. 2003) [the BIA did not sufficiently consider the evidence in country reports and human rights reports]. The Board should also consider evidence the applicant could relocate to a part of the country of removal where he or she is not likely to be tortured. 8 C.F.R. §208.16(c)(3)(ii); *Yakovenko v. Gonzales,* 477 F.3d 631, 637 (8th Cir. 2007) [applicant did not establish that harm inflicted by certain criminals was sufficient to establish that it would be unsafe or unreasonable to relocate within Ukraine].

3. *Cases Where Burden of Proof Was Met*—*Matter of G-A-,* 23 I&N Dec. 366 (BIA 2002) [burden met where due to a combination of factors including Christian religion, Armenian ethnicity, long duration in the U.S., drug related conviction, and extreme conditions in Iranian prisons, it was more likely than not that he would be tortured if returned to Iran]; *Tchemkou v. Gonzales,* 495 F.3d 785, 794–95 (7th Cir. 2007) [reversed BIA and found evidence compelled finding that Cameroonian woman would face torture if returned given her past treatment]; *Muradin v. Gonzales,* 494 F.3d 1208, 1210–11 (9th Cir. 2007) [where IJ found Armenian applicant who was tortured while in the military credible, and the BIA made no country finding in reversing the CAT grant, the court reversed and cited to DOS report on Armenia]; *Ali v. Achim,* 468 F.3d 462, 471–72 (7th Cir. 2006) *cert. dismissed* 128 S.Ct. 828 (2007) [BIA reversed in Somalian CAT claim where the BIA ignored key evidence, overlooked expert testimony and focused narrowly are general conditions]; *Zewdie v. Ashcroft,* 381 F.3d 804, 808–10 (8th Cir. 2004) [where IJ/BIA found Ethiopian

respondent not credible because she failed to produce medical evidence that her scars were from beatings, the court held that no reasonable fact finder under the *Elias-Zacarias* standard could fail to find respondent eligible for CAT]; *Khup v. Ashcroft,* 376 F.3d 898, 904–06 (9th Cir. 2004) [applicant established that there was at least a 51% chance of being tortured given the torture of a fellow preacher by the military and DOS country reports and AI press release on torture in Burma]; *Sackie v. Ashcroft,* 270 F.Supp.2d 596, 601–03 (E.D. Pa. 2003) [where child soldier in Liberia was threatened with death on numerous occasions, frequently given mind altering substances and suffered cuts to his back and arms, he met burden that he was tortured].

4. *Cases Where Burden of Proof Was Not Met—Lin v. DOJ,* 432 F.3d 156 (2d Cir. 2005) [claim based solely on illegal departure from China]; *Auguste v. Ridge,* 395 F.3d 123, 148–49 (3d Cir. 2005) [Haitian prison conditions case]; *Cadet v. Bulger,* 377 F.3d 1173, 1180 (11th Cir. 2004) [same]; *Settenda v. Ashcroft,* 377 F.3d 89, 95–96 (1st Cir. 2004) [applied analysis in *Elien* and *Matter of J-E-* to person facing detention in Uganda]; *Elien v. Ashcroft,* 364 F.3d 392, 398–99 (1st Cir. 2004) [no evidence that Haiti used torture pervasively or as a matter of policy on detainees; applicant failed to meet his burden of proof]; *Wang v. Ashcroft,* 320 F.3d 130, 143–45 (2d Cir. 2003) [military deserter from PRC failed to meet burden of proof to demonstrate he would be tortured as opposed to simply placed in prison]; *Thelemaque v. Ashcroft,* 363 F.Supp.2d 198 (D. Conn. 2005) [failure to provide meet burden of proof that he would be tortured in Haitian detention]; *Ford v. ICE,* 294 F.Supp.2d 655, 663–66 (M.D. Pa. 2003) [under the "some evidence" standard, court upheld BIA's judgment that respondent could not demonstrate it was "more likely than not" that he would suffer torture]; *Matter of M-B-A-,* 23 I&N Dec. 474 (BIA 2002) [Nigerian woman convicted of drug offense in the U.S. did not meet burden of proof to establish deferral claim based on the enforcement against her of Decree No. 33 of the Nigerian National Drug Law Enforcement Agency that would result in her incarceration and torture]; *Matter of J-E-,* 23 I&N Dec. 291, 302 (BIA 2002) [where there were isolated instances of torture of indefinite detainees in Haiti, it was insufficient to establish that it is more likely than not that respondent would be tortured if returned to Haiti]; *Antoine v. U.S.*, 204 F.Supp.2d 119 (D. Mass 2002) [no evidence that applicant would be tortured by Haitian government].

5. *Burden of Proof and Asylum/Withholding*—Where the burden of proof was met on CAT and the court determined that the applicant's persecution stemmed from a political opinion, it was unnecessary to remand under *INS v. Ventura,* 537 U.S. 12 (2002) because in light of the higher burden for CAT, the applicant would obtain asylum and withholding based upon future persecution. *Fedunyak v. Gonzales,* 477 F.3d 1126, 1130–31 (9th Cir. 2007).

G. *Difference Between Asylum/Withholding and Deferral of Removal Under CAT*—*See in this chapter* ¶ XI.B.8.e (p.512), *infra*.

H. *Termination of Deferral of Removal*—At any time deferral of removal is in effect counsel for the government may file a motion with the IJ to terminate removal if the motion "is accompanied by evidence that is relevant to the possibility that the alien would be tortured … and that was not presented at the previous hearing." 8 C.F.R. §208.17(d)(1). The person granted deferral is given the right to respond to the government's information, a hearing is held before the IJ where the burden is on the alien and the eligibility standards are those set forth under the original proceeding at 8 C.F.R. §208.16(c). The IJ can decide to retain deferral or order the person removed. Any appeal shall be to the BIA. 8 C.F.R. §§208.17(d)(3), (4).

I. *Termination through Diplomatic Assurances Against Torture*—Unlike asylum or withholding, the Secy. of State may obtain assurances from the foreign government that the applicant will not be tortured if removed to that country. If the AG in consultation with the Secy. of State believes the assurances are sufficiently reliable, the CAT claim shall not be further considered by the IJ, BIA or AO and if the CAT claim has been granted the person may be removed. The AG may delegate this authority to the Deputy AG or the INS Comm. 8 C.F.R. §§208.18(c), 1208.18(c). A challenge to petitioner's claim that DHS failed to follow its regulations in revoking CAT relief is subject to judicial review. *Khouzam v. Hogan,* 497 F.Supp.2d 615 (M.D. Pa. 2007) [denied DHS motion to dismiss habeas where petitioner challenged DHS revocation of deferral of removal under CAT on grounds that DHS failed to comply with its own regulations, violated procedural and substantive due process, and violated CAT as implemented by FARRA]. Moreover, the decision to rely on diplomatic assurances and thereby revoke deferral and remove the grantee is subject to a due process review. *Khouzam v. Hogan,* 529 F.Supp.2d

543 (M.D. Pa. 2008) [stayed removal and released respondent from custody despite diplomatic assurances that Egyptian granted deferral of removal under CAT would not be tortured where the assurances were not subject to due process scrutiny].

J. ***CAT Claims in Streamlined or Expedited Removal Proceedings***—A CAT claim may be made if the applicant is: (i) ordered removed under INA §235(c), 8 C.F.R. §§208.18(d), 1208.18(d); (ii) subject to expedited removal, 8 C.F.R. §§208.30, 1208.30; or (iii) subject to expedited removal as an aggravated felon under INA §238(b) or due to reinstatement under INA §241(a)(5). 8 C.F.R. §§208.31, 1208.31. Applications are made before an AO and only in the case of expedited removal, expedited removal of an aggravated felon and reinstatement may an IJ entertain an application after a finding of reasonable fear of torture.

K. ***Application***—There is no formal application to submit a CAT claim. However, "[b]ecause there is no separate and distinct procedure for seeking CAT relief, then Petitioners' [I-589] application responses, which clearly evinced their fear of torture, constitute claims for relief under the CAT." *Eduard v. Ashcroft,* 379 F.3d 195–96 (5th Cir. 2004) [remanding to IJ to consider CAT where answers on I-589 indicated a fear of torture]. Failure to timely file I-589 is not an abandonment of CAT claim. *Louis-Martin v. Ridge,* 322 F.Supp.2d 556, 561–62 (M.D. Pa. 2004).

L. ***Judicial Review of CAT Claims***—Prior to the REAL ID Act of 2005, §242(a)(2)(C) barred judicial review in the circuit courts where an applicant for CAT relief has been convicted of certain crimes. *Balogun v. Ashcroft,* 270 F.3d 274 (5th Cir. 2001) [once threshold issues were determined that INA §242(a)(2)(C) applied, that section barred review of CAT claim]. Former §106(a)(10) as amended by AEDPA §440 and IIRIRA §309(c)(4)(G) barred judicial review of a CAT claim. *Diakite v. INS,* 179 F.3d 553 (7th Cir. 1999). Other circuit courts have refused to address a CAT claim unless it was first raised before the IJ/BIA. *Oliva-Muralles v. Ashcroft,* 328 F.3d 25, 26 (1st Cir. 2003); *Ortiz v. INS,* 179 F.3d 1148 (9th Cir. 1999); *Khourassany v. INS,* 208 F.3d 1096 (9th Cir. 2000) [denying motion to remand but agreeing to stay mandate for 90 days to allow application to BIA to reopen]. Prior to the REAL ID Act, applicants for CAT who were barred from circuit court review could file their claims in the district court through a habeas petition, as long as they exhausted their administrative remedies including motions to reopen for claims filed prior to Mar. 22, 1999. *Huang v. Ashcroft,* 390 F.3d 1118 (9th Cir. 2004); *Singh v. Ashcroft,* 351 F.3d 435, 440–42 (9th Cir. 2003) [following *Cornejo-Barreto*, finding that FARRA does not preclude a habeas action challenging a CAT decision even if the claim does not raise a "purely legal question"]; *Ogbudimkpa v. Ashcroft,* 342 F.3d 207, 212–22 (3d Cir. 2003) [district courts have habeas jurisdiction to review violations of CAT or FARRA because as a practical matter they are the same]; *Saint Fort v. Ashcroft,* 329 F.3d 191, 200–04 (1st Cir. 2003) [FARRA does not expressly repeal 28 U.S.C. §2241]; *Wang v. Ashcroft,* 320 F.3d 130, 140–45 (2d Cir. 2003) [habeas was not expressly barred by FARRA for review of CAT claims]; *Cornejo-Barreto v. Seifert,* 218 F.3d 1004, 1016 n.13 (9th Cir. 2000); *Builes v. Nye,* 239 F.Supp.2d 518, 525 (M.D. Pa. 2003) [habeas jurisdiction exists to challenge misinterpretation of a statute or regulation under CAT]; *Julmiste v. Ashcroft,* 212 F.Supp.2d 341, 344–45 (D.N.J. 2002) [habeas jurisdiction exists to review CAT claim notwithstanding the bar under INA §242(a)(2)(C) for criminal conduct]. But under the REAL ID Act of 2005, habeas, mandamus, and the All Writs Act were eliminated as a source of jurisdiction to review CAT claims and the courts of appeal "shall be the sole and exclusive means for judicial review of any cause or claim" under CAT. INA §242(a)(4). In the courts of appeal an applicant may raise constitutional questions or questions of law. INA §242(a)(2)(D). *But see Khouzam v. Hogan,* 497 F.Supp.2d 615 (M.D. Pa. 2007) [denied DHS motion to dismiss habeas under REAL ID Act, INA §242(g) and political question doctrine where petitioner challenged DHS revocation of deferral of removal under CAT on grounds that DHS failed to comply with its own regulations, violated procedural and substantive due process, and violated CAT as implemented by FARRA];. In the final decision in *Khouzam v. Hogan,* 529 F.Supp.2d 543 (M.D. Pa. 2008) the court determined that the decision to rely on diplomatic assurances and thereby revoke deferral of removal was subject to a review under Due Process and the court vacated the decision to revoke petitioner's removal and ordered him released.

VI. PAROLEES

A. ***Generally***—Prior to the Refugee Act of 1980, the AG was permitted to parole persons into the U.S. without formal admission for emergency reasons or reasons deemed strictly in the public interest. Former INA §212(d)(5)(A), 8 U.S.C. §1182(d)(5)(A). Under the Refugee Act, the AG's parole authority was limited to individual parole determinations based on "compelling reasons in the public interest with respect to that particular alien." INA §212(d)(5)(B), 8 U.S.C. §1152(d)(5)(B). IIRIRA further amended the parole authority by eliminating the former language under INA §212(d)(5)(A) and providing that the AG may parole "only on a case-by-case basis for urgent humanitarian reasons or significant public benefit." INA §212(d)(5)(A), 8 U.S.C. §1182(d)(5)(A). This represents a significant change from previous practice when the AG's parole authority was used broadly to parole tens of thousands of refugees at a time. For example, between 1959 and 1961, INA §212(d)(5) was used to parole 20,000 Cuban refugees at a time when no Cuban Refugee Act existed. By enacting this new limitation on the AG's authority, Congress clearly expressed its desire to channel people through the refugee or asylum process designated under the Act, rather than permitting the broad discretionary authority of the AG to be utilized to parole persons fleeing persecution. Parole is not deemed "an admission," INA §212(d)(5)(A), and exclusion proceedings have been initiated against parolees, such as Nicaraguans, Iranians and Haitians, even when they have sought political asylum. Under IIRIRA §603 parolees will be counted against the worldwide family quota. INA §201(c)(4), 8 U.S.C. §1151(c)(4).

B. ***The Lautenberg Amendment***—This amendment to the Foreign Operations Appropriations Act (PL 101-167) established a "public interest parole" procedure which was offered "on an exceptional basis only for an unspecified but limited period of time." Memo, McNary, Comm., 207-P (Jan. 8, 1990), *reprinted in* 67 No. 4 *Interpreter Releases* 85, 99 (Jan. 22, 1990). Certain groups (*e.g.*, Soviet Jews, Laotians, Cambodians) paroled under this category but denied refugee status between Aug. 15, 1988 and Sept. 30, 1994 are eligible for adjustment of status. *Id.*; 8 C.F.R. §§245.7, 1245.7. The Lautenberg provisions relating to refugees and adjustment were extended until the end of September 1999. The Lautenberg Amendment standard of credible fear for refugees coming from certain countries does *not* apply to asylum adjudications in the view of INS. Legal Opinion, Martin, General Counsel (Oct. 6, 1995), *reprinted in* 72 No. 45 *Interpreter Releases* 1575, 1594–96 (Nov. 20, 1995). *Accord Halaim v. INS,* 358 F.3d 1128, 1132–36 (9th Cir. 2004) [Lautenberg Amendment did not give Pentecostal Christian from former Soviet Union any greater rights to asylum or any lower standard of proof in asylum proceedings than those contained in the social group provisions of 8 C.F.R. §208.13(b)(2)].

VII. EXTENDED VOLUNTARY DEPARTURE (EVD); DEFERRED ENFORCED DEPARTURE (DED)

A. ***Extended Voluntary Departure***—Extended Voluntary Departure (EVD) is a term of art for programs that permit the AG in his discretion to temporarily enjoin the removal of persons from particular countries who fear return because of sudden political changes in their countries of origin or other reasons. For example, an EVD program was established for Polish citizens who entered the U.S. before July 21, 1984, during the Polish government's efforts to destroy the Solidarity movement. Prior programs existed for citizens of Cuba (1960 to Nov.2, 1966), Dominican Republic (Sept. 18, 1966 to Apr. 26, 1978), Czechoslovakia (Aug. 21, 1968 to Dec. 30 1977), Chile (Apr. 1971 to Dec. 1977), Cambodia (1975 to Oct. 28, 1977), Vietnam (Apr. 4, 1975 to Oct. 28, 1977), Lebanon (Feb. 12, 1976-withdrawn), Hungary (Dec. 30, 1977-Apr. 29, 1981), Romania (Dec. 30, 1977 to Apr. 29, 1981), Uganda (June 8, 1978 to Sept. 30, 1986), Iran (Apr. 1979 to Nov. 13, 1979), Nicaragua (July 3, 1979 to Sept. 28, 1980); Afghanistan (arrival before July 31, 1984); Ethiopia (arrival before July 31, 1984); and China (arrival before Apr. 11, 1990). As EVD is discretionary, at least one court has found that the AG's failure to grant EVD to Salvadorans is not reviewable where it is a facially legitimate exercise of discretion. *Hotel & Restaurant Employees Union v. Smith*, 594 F.Supp. 502 (D.D.C. 1984), *aff'd by divided court on other grounds*, 846 F.2d 1499 (D.C. Cir. 1988). *But see American Baptist Churches v. Thornburgh*, Case No. C-85-3255-RFP (N.D. Cal. Sept. 11, 1989), *reported in* 66 *Interpreter Releases* 1061–63 (Sept. 25, 1989). There is no formal application process for EVD or DED, but a person may be the beneficiary of a program.

Chinese Student Protection Act—Although the government no longer takes applications of principals under the Act, regulations allow late arriving dependents to adjust based on spouse's priority date. 8 C.F.R. §§245.9(m), 1245.9(m). The BIA does not permit adjustment under the Act for persons who entered EWI, notwithstanding INA §245(i). *Matter of Wang,* 23 I&N Dec. 924 (BIA 2006); *Ri Kai Lin v. Bureau of Citizenship and Immigration Services,* 514 F.3d 251, 254–55 (2d Cir. 2008) [upheld *Wang* as a reasonable interpretation of the statutes].

B. ***Deferred Enforced Departure***—A variant of EVD is DED. It was previously used by President Bush to assist Chinese students in the U.S. after the incident in Tiananmen Square. Executive Order 12711 (Apr. 11, 1990). It was also used during the Persian Gulf War and for Salvadorans. On Dec. 23, 1997, President Clinton announced a Haitian DED program pending the passage of legislation for Haitians. The DED program covered Haitians who were paroled into the U.S. or who applied for asylum prior to Dec. 31, 1995, and had been continuously present since that date. The program covered spouses, parents or children included in the asylum application. Memo, Cronin, Acting Exec. Assoc. Comm., INS, HQ 120/12.1 (Mar. 3, 1998), *reprinted in* 75 No. 9 *Interpreter Releases* 326, 350–53 (Mar. 9, 1998). The Haitian Refugee Immigration Fairness Act of 1998, PL 105-277, 112 Stat. 2681-538 was enacted, which allowed certain Haitians paroled into the U.S. before Dec. 31, 1995 or who applied for asylum before that date to apply for lawful permanent residency before Apr. 1, 2000. DED has also been granted to Liberians. Memo, Attorney General (Sept. 27, 1999), *reprinted in* 76 No. 38 *Interpreter Releases* 1456, 1471 (Sept. 30, 1999); Memo, Pearson, Exec. Assoc. Comm. HQISD 120/12.1 (Sept. 29, 1999), *reprinted in* 76 No. 42 *Interpreter Releases* 1579, 1594–1601 (Nov. 1, 1999). DED was extended several times but expired on Sept. 29, 2002 when TPS was initiated for a one-year period. 67 Fed. Reg. 61665–66 (Oct. 1, 2002).

Administrative Closure of Removal Case for Persons Eligible for DED—The Service "should agree to administratively close proceedings," where individuals are *prima facie* eligible for DED. However, the Service should agree to administrative closure only *after* pleadings have been taken and the issue of removability has been established. Memo, Carpenter, Deputy Gen. Co., HQCOU 120/12.2-P (Feb. 7, 2002), *reported in* 79 No. 15 *Interpreter Releases* 524, 530–38 (Apr. 8, 2002). Any agreement to administratively close the file may not be conditioned upon the applicant giving up any other rights including the right to apply for asylum or withholding of removal. *Id.*

VIII. TEMPORARY PROTECTED STATUS (TPS)

A. ***Generally***—INA §244, 8 U.S.C. §1254a.; 8 C.F.R. §§244, 1244; 56 Fed. Reg. 23491 (May 22, 1991). Establishes a temporary safe haven in the U.S. for nationals of a foreign state (or if stateless if person habitually resided in the foreign state) if the AG, after consultation with appropriate government agencies, determines with respect to that foreign state that:

1. There is an ongoing armed conflict within the state (or a part of the state) posing a serious threat to the personal safety of the country's nationals if returned there. INA §244(b)(1)(A), 8 U.S.C. §1254a(b)(1)(A); *or*
2. There has been an earthquake, flood, drought, epidemic or other environmental disaster resulting in a substantial but temporary disruption of living conditions in the area affected; the foreign state is unable temporarily to handle the return of its nationals and the foreign state has affirmatively requested designation, INA §244(b)(1)(B), 8 U.S.C. §1254a(b)(1)(B); *or*
3. There exists extraordinary and temporary conditions in the foreign state that prevent aliens who are nationals from returning safely. However, if AG determines that it is contrary to national interest to allow nationals to remain temporarily, s/he may decline ...." INA §244(b)(1)(C), 8 U.S.C. §1254a(b)(1)(C).

B. ***A Person Granted TPS***—

1. Is granted such status for 6 to 18 months, which may be extended.
2. Shall not be deported during TPS period. INA §244(a)(1)(A), 8 U.S.C. §1254a(a)(1)(A). Moreover, if the applicant is in proceedings, the AG shall notify him "in a form and language" he understands, of the availability of TPS. INA §244(a)(3), 8 U.S.C. §1254a(a)(3).
3. Shall be granted employment authorization during the initial TPS period or one year, whichever is shorter, and thereafter for any extensions of TPS. INA §§244(a)(1)(B) and (2), 8 U.S.C. §§1254a(a)(1)(B) and (2); 8 C.F.R. §§244.12(a), 1244.12(a).
4. Shall not be detained on the basis of his or her status. INA §244(d)(4), 8 U.S.C. §1254a(d)(4).
5. May travel abroad with permission. INA §244(f)(3), 8 U.S.C. §1254a(f)(3). Must apply for and receive permission (I-131) before traveling. 8 C.F.R. §§244.15, 1244.15. If person received advance parole and returns timely, he is admitted in same status and is not considered to have failed

to maintain continuous physical presence. MTINA of 1991, PL 102-232, 105 Stat. 1733, §304(c). However, a person with TPS who travels may still be subject to the 3/10 year bars under INA §§212(a)(9)(B)(i)(I) & (II).

6. May adjust or change status and is considered in status for those purposes. INA §244(f)(4), 8 U.S.C. §1254a(f)(4). However, if a person was out of status (because of unlawful employment or overstay) before getting TPS, he is ineligible to adjust. Letter, Miller, Acting Asst. Comm. Adjudications (Mar. 30, 1993), *reprinted in* 70 No. 22 *Interpreter Releases* 753, 770–71 (June 7, 1993). Similarly, EWIs cannot adjust even if they obtained advance parole and reentered the U.S. (unless s/he is IR or special immigrant under INA §101(a)(27)(H)). Legal Opinion, Virtue, Acting G.C. (Mar. 4, 1991), *reprinted in* 68 No. 15 *Interpreter Releases* 461, 483–86 (Apr. 22, 1991). Thus, the bar is only applicable when a person's stay would have expired but for TPS. *But see Matter of Escobar-Turcios*, Case No. A24 848 532 (IJ Oct. 21, 1992), *reported in* 69 No. 42 *Interpreter Releases* 1400 (Nov. 2, 1992) [clear language of INA §244(f)(4) permits persons to adjust even if they were EWI].

7. May not be granted Social Security benefits because SSA has determined that persons granted TPS are not permanently residing in the U.S. under color of law. (PRUCOL) 58 Fed. Reg. 41181–82 (Aug. 3, 1993).

8. May apply for asylum since TPS is designed to supplement, not eviscerate, asylum. By establishing TPS, Congress did not intend to allow asylum applicants to use that status as an element of proof. *Gomez v. INS*, 947 F.2d 660 (2d Cir. 1991).

9. May apply for cancellation of removal once TPS expires. Time in TPS does not cause a break in time period for cancellation of removal. However, time period does not count toward cancellation of removal unless AG determines that extreme hardship exists. INA §244(e), 8 U.S.C. §1254a(e).

10. An applicant for TPS is not necessarily considered in a lawful status if TPS has not yet been granted. *U.S. v. Flores,* 404 F.3d 320 (5th Cir. 2005) [TPS applicant who entered the U.S. illegally may be charged as an alien illegally or unlawfully in the U.S. in possession of a firearm in violation of 18 U.S.C. §922(g)(5)(A)]. However, a person *granted* TPS has generally been considered to be in a lawful status. *U.S. v. Orellana,* 405 F.3d 360, 364–65 n.21 (5th Cir. 2005) [courts that have considered whether TPS is a lawful status have found that it is and the court applying rule of lenity given the ambiguity of §922(g)(5)(A) and the questionable interpretation of the ATF regulation, found that Congress did not intend to criminalize the possession of firearms by persons granted TPS].

C. *Eligibility for TPS*—INA §244(c), 8 U.S.C. §1254a(c); 8 C.F.R. §§244.2, 1244.2

1. Must establish identity and nationality of TPS country, or if stateless, habitually resided in TPS country, and proof of continuous residence in the U.S. for required period. 8 C.F.R. §§244.9, 1244.9.

    1.a. Evidence of nationality in descending preference includes: passport; birth certificate accompanied by photo ID; national identity document bearing photo or fingerprint; or affidavit as to inability to obtain documents with any other proof.

    1.b. Evidence of residence may consist of employment records, rent receipts, school records, hospital or medical records, attestation by churches, unions or other organizations and other documents including passport entries, children's U.S. birth certificates, bank books, tax receipts or any other relevant documents.

2. Must be physically present and continuously residing in U.S. since date of designation. INA §244(c)(1), 8 U.S.C. §1254a(c)(1)—Allowing brief, casual and innocent absence without disrupting physical presence or residence requirement and temporary trip abroad due to emergency or extenuating circumstances outside control of applicant does not disturb residence requirement. INA §244(c)(4), 8 U.S.C. §1254a(c)(4); 8 C.F.R. §§244.1, 1244.1.

3. Must be otherwise admissible, 8 C.F.R. §§244.3, 1244.3—Certain noncriminal and nonsecurity grounds [§§212(a)(4), (5)(A), (B), 7(a)(i)] automatically waived. Other noncriminal and nonsecurity grounds may be waived "for humanitarian purposes, to assure family unity or where it is oth-

erwise in the public interest." INA §244(c)(2)(A), 8 U.S.C. §1254a(c)(2)(A); 8 C.F.R. §§244.3(b), 1244.3(b).

4. Must not be ineligible because of 8 C.F.R. §§244.4, 1244.4—Conviction of a felony or *two* or more misdemeanors or because applicant is a person described in INA §241(b)(3)(B).

   4.a. Felony is a crime committed in U.S. punishable by imprisonment of more than one year, irrespective of actual confinement. A felony does not include an offense defined by the state as a misdemeanor where the sentence actually imposed is one year or less. 8 C.F.R. §§244.1, 1244.1.

   4.b. Misdemeanor is defined as any crime punishable by one year or less, irrespective of actual time served. However, any crime punishable by a maximum of five days or less shall not be considered a misdemeanor. 8 C.F.R. §§244.1, 1244.1.

5. Register for TPS within the period provided by AG. A person who did not initially register, but was a nonimmigrant, granted VD, had a change of status, adjustment of status, VD, asylum or other relief application pending before the immigration court or subject to further review or appeal, or was a parolee, or is the spouse or child of a person currently eligible for TPS, may submit a TPS application within 60 days immediately following the expiration or termination of the status above. 8 C.F.R. §§244.2(f)(2) and (g), 1244.2(f)(2) and (g).

D. ***Spouse and Children***—The spouse or child of a person granted TPS may registered after the initial registration period during subsequent extensions of TPS as long as the relationship existed at the time of the spouse's or parent's initial registration. 8 C.F.R. §244.2(f)(iv).

E. ***Termination/Withdrawal of Status***—INA §244(c)(3), 8 U.S.C. §1254a(c)(3); 8 C.F.R. §§244.14, 1244.14.

1. If AG finds person was not eligible. *See e.g., Bah v. Cangemi,* 489 F.Supp.2d 905, 912–14 (D. Minn. 207) [court had no jurisdiction to review AAO decision to withdraw Liberian's TPS on the grounds that his vacated conviction for second-degree criminal sexual conduct under *Matter of Pickering* was still a conviction and therefore he was ineligible for TPS]

2. Person fails to maintain continuous physical presence. *See* INA §244(c)(4), 8 U.S.C. §1254a(c)(4) for treatment of brief, casual, and innocent departures and other absences.

3. Person fails, without good cause, to register *annually* with AG. INA §244(c)(3)(C), 8 U.S.C. §1254a(c)(3)(C). Legislative Wire #67, IMMACT90, McNary, Comm. (Aug. 13, 1991), *reported in* 68 No. 32 *Interpreter Releases* 1069, 1083 (Aug. 26, 1991).

4. AG terminated program. INA §244(b)(3)(B), 8 U.S.C. §1254a(b)(3)(B)—Must publish in Federal Register and give 60 days notice of termination. If program terminated, person's designation and EAD remain valid until expiration. INA §244(d)(3), 8 U.S.C. §1254a(d)(3).

F. ***Temporary Treatment for Eligible Applicant***—INA §244(a)(4), 8 U.S.C. §1254a(a)(4); 8 C.F.R. §§244.5, 244.10(e), 1244.5, 1244.10(e)—If applicant establishes *prima facie* case, can get benefits (stay of deportation and employment authorization) before registration period begins and after it begins until application decided if s/he applies within first 30 days of TPS program. No fee is required for temporary benefits but persons must apply with fee (or waiver) within first 30 days of program. 8 C.F.R. §244.5.

G. ***Application Procedure***—8 C.F.R. §§244.6, 244.9, 1244.6, 1244.9.

1. Must submit I-821, I-765, 2 photos, evidence of nationality and identity and proof of residency in accordance with 8 C.F.R. §244.9. If I-765 is not needed because applicant has or does not need employment authorization, it must be completed anyway for biographic purposes without fee. Fingerprints are required.

2. Application filed during registration period and with fee established by program. 8 C.F.R. §§103.7(b)(1), 244.7, 1103.7(b)(1), 1244.7. Fee may be waived. 8 C.F.R. §§244.20, 1244.20; IMMACT90 Wire #50, McNary, Comm., CO I588-C (Apr. 4, 1991), *reprinted in* 68 No. 14 *Interpreter Releases* 431, 456 (Apr. 15, 1991). If applicant has pending removal proceeding before the IJ or BIA s/he shall be given written notice of TPS program and an opportunity to apply. 8 C.F.R. §§244.7(d), 1244.7(d).

3. *Late Filing*—8 C.F.R. §§244.2(f)(2) and (g), 1244.2(f)(2) and (g). A person who failed to apply during the initial registration period may apply during any subsequent extension if at the time of the initial registration period, the applicant was a nonimmigrant, had been granted voluntary departure, had a change of status, adjustment of status, VD, asylum or other application for relief pending before the immigration court or subject to further review or appeal, or was a parolee, or is the spouse or child of a person currently eligible for TPS. An application for late registration must be filed within 60 days immediately following the expiration or termination of the status described.

4. Applicant may be required to appear in person, but has right to counsel. 8 C.F.R. §§244.8, 1244.8.

5. Must register annually within 30 days prior to anniversary of the grant, which includes submitting I-821 (without fee) and I-765 (with fee) if employment desired. 8 C.F.R. §§244.17, 1244.17.

H. ***Administrative Closure for Person in Removal Proceedings***—The Service "should agree to administratively close proceedings," where individuals are *prima facie* eligible for TPS. However, the Service should agree to administrative closure only *after* pleadings have been taken and the issue of removability has been established. Memo, Carpenter, Deputy Gen. Co., HQCOU 120/12.2-P (Feb. 7, 2002), *reported in* 79 No. 15 *Interpreter Releases* 524, 530–38 (Apr. 8, 2002). Any agreement may not be conditioned upon the applicant giving up any other rights including the right to apply for asylum or withholding of removal. *Id.*

I. ***Judicial Review***

1. No judicial review of any determination with respect to designation, termination or extension of TPS with respect to a foreign state. INA §244(b)(5)(A), 8 U.S.C. §1254a(b)(5)(A). One court has also found that there is no judicial review of the denial of TPS in an individual case. *Rodas v. Chertoff,* 399 F.Supp.2d 697, 704–06 (E.D. Va. 2005) [INA §242(a)(2)(B)(ii) bars review of the denial of an individual's application for TPS]. Another has found there is no jurisdiction to review a withdrawal of TPS. *Bah v. Cangemi,* 489 F.Supp.2d 905, 912–14 (D. Minn. 207) [court had no jurisdiction to review AAO decision to withdraw Liberian's TPS on the grounds that his vacated conviction for second-degree criminal sexual conduct under *Matter of Pickering* was still a conviction and therefore he was ineligible for TPS].

2. AAO may review the denial of an application for TPS. 8 C.F.R. §§244.10, 1244.10. The notice is filed with the DD. Review shall not preclude the applicant from raising TPS eligibility in removal proceedings or before the BIA. INA §244(b)(5)(B), 8 U.S.C. §1254a(b)(5)(B), 8 C.F.R. §§244.11, 1244.11; *Matter of Barrientos,* 24 I&N Dec. 100 (BIA 2007) [IJ may review TPS eligibility *de novo* even if AAO denied claim].

3. Employment authorization is granted during AAO appeal or while in removal proceedings. 8 C.F.R. §§244.12(d), 1244.12(d).

J. ***Confidentiality***—AG shall establish procedure to ensure information is confidential. INA §244(c)(6), 8 U.S.C. §1254a(c)(6). However, information may be used for purposes of enforcing the INA or in any criminal proceedings. 8 C.F.R. §§244.16, 1244.16.

K. ***Special Adjustment Program***—Senate required to have super-majority (3/5 of Senate) approval before a program may be established to grant group adjustment to TPS beneficiaries. INA §244(h), 8 U.S.C. §1254a(h).

L. ***Salvadorans and Guatemalans***

1. *TPS for Salvadorans*—66 Fed. Reg. 14214–16 (Mar. 9, 2001). Nationals of El Salvador who have been continuously physically present in the U.S. since Mar. 9, 2001 and have continuously resided in the U.S. since Feb. 13, 2001 are eligible for TPS if they registered between Mar. 9, 2001 and Sept. 9, 2002 or late registered under 8 C.F.R. §244.2(f)(2). Applying for other benefits does not bar a TPS application. The program has most recently been extended until Mar. 9, 2009 [72 Fed. Reg. 46649 (Aug. 21, 2007)].

2. *Salvadoran and Guatemalan Program*—Pursuant to the settlement agreement entered in *American Baptist Churches v. Thornburgh*, 760 F.Supp. 796 (N.D. Cal. 1991) ("ABC") all Salvadorans in the U.S. as of Sept. 19, 1990 and all Guatemalans in the U.S. as of Oct. 1, 1990 can obtain a *de novo* asylum interview under the Oct. 1, 1990, asylum regulations if the Salvadoran applied for TPS or in-

dicated to INS in writing before Oct. 31, 1991, his or her desire for a *de novo* asylum interview or if the Guatemalan files a written request for a *de novo* asylum application or and intent to receive the benefits of ABC in writing between July 1, 1991 and Dec. 31, 1991. *Chaly-Garcia v. U.S.,* 508 F.3d 1201 (9th Cir. 2007) [Guatemalan who filed an asylum application after October 1, 1990 is considered to have expressed in writing a desire to receive ABC benefits and is therefore a covered class member]. These provisions do not apply to persons who had asylum interviews between Oct. 1, 1990 and Nov. 23, 1990, who are aggravated felons, or who were apprehended at the time of entering after Dec. 19, 1990. The agreement contains provisions staying deportation and deportation proceedings of class members until the class member can effectuate his or her rights under the agreement. *Melendez v. DOJ*, 926 F.2d 211 (2d Cir. 1991) [remanded to agency in light of *ABC* rather than deciding Salvadoran asylum claim]; *Matter of Morales*, 21 I&N Dec. 130 (BIA 1996) [setting forth criteria to stay deportation/exclusion]. Salvadorans who register for TPS are deemed to have automatically registered for *ABC*. USCIS has established change of address procedures for *ABC* class members. 70 Fed. Reg. 45410–12 (Aug. 8, 2005).

3. *Special Rule Cancellation for Salvadorans and Guatemalans*—Section 203 of the Nicaraguan Adjustment and Central American Relief Act, PL 105-100, 111 Stat. 2160, Tit. II, Div. A (Nov. 19, 1997), as amended by PL 105-139, 111 Stat. 2644 (Dec. 2, 1997). *See* Ch. 8, ¶ IV.C.12 (p.995), *infra*.

M. *TPS for Nationals of Somalia*—Somalis who have been continuously physically present and continuously residing in the U.S. since Sept. 16, 1991, are eligible if they apply within 12-months from Sept. 16, 1991 to Sept. 16, 1992. [56 Fed. Reg. 46804 (Sept. 16, 1991)]. The program has most recently been extended until Sept. 17, 2009 [73 Fed. Reg. 13245 (Mar. 10, 2008)].

N. *TPS for Nationals of Burundi and Sudan*

1. *Burundi*—Nationals of Burundi must have been continuously physically present and continuously resided in U.S. since Nov. 4, 1997, and registered by Nov. 3, 1998. The program is terminating effective May 2, 2009. [72 Fed. Reg. 61172 (Oct. 29, 2007)].

2. *Sudan*—Nationals of Sudan must have been continuously physically present and continuously resided in the U.S. since Nov. 4, 1997. The program was extended until Nov. 2, 2005 [69 Fed. Reg. 60168–70 (Oct. 7, 2004)]. DHS redesignated Sudan, thereby allowing Sudanese who have been physically present and continuously residing in the U.S. since Oct. 7, 2004 to register for the first time by Apr. 5, 2005. *Id.* The program was most recently extended until Nov. 2, 2008 [72 Fed. Reg. 10541 (Mar. 8, 2007)].

O. *TPS for Hondurans and Nicaraguans*—Nationals of Honduras and Nicaragua must have continuously resided in the U.S. since Dec. 30, 1998 and have been physically present since Jan. 5, 1999. 64 Fed. Reg. 524–28 (Jan. 5, 1999); 65 Fed. Reg. 30440–42 (May 11, 2000). Any national of Honduras or Nicaragua who had applied for, or planned to apply for asylum, but whose asylum application had not yet been approved, may also apply for TPS. The application period ran from Jan. 5, 1999 to Aug. 20, 1999. The program was most recently extended until Jan. 5, 2009 [72 Fed. Reg. 29534 (May 29, 2007) for Nicaragua; 72 Fed. Reg. 29529 (May 29, 2007 for Honduras]. For Nicaraguans, TPS status or an application for TPS has no effect on a NACARA application.

IX. EXTRADITION OF PERSONS FEARING PERSECUTION OR TORTURE

The relationship between extradition and asylum has become a topic of concern in light of the CAT. *See, e.g., Cornejo-Barreto v. Seifert,* 218 F.3d 1004 (9th Cir. 2000). Extradition proceedings are governed by 18 U.S.C. §3184 (2000). If the magistrate or district judge determines that there is sufficient probable cause that an extraditable offense has been committed and there is no bar to extradition, s/he must issue a warrant for the extradition. The decision to extradite may be subject to collateral review in habeas proceedings, although review is quite limited. *Kastnerova v. U.S.,* 365 F.3d 980, 984 (11th Cir. 2004). Once a person is found extraditable and habeas corpus has concluded, the Secy. of State may determine, as a matter of discretion, whether the person should be surrendered for extradition. The Sec. must address whether the person would be subject to torture upon extradition. *See* United Nations Convention Against Torture and Other Cruel, Inhuman or Degrading Treatment or Punishment, Art. 3; Foreign Affairs Reform and Restructuring Act, PL 105-277, §2277, *and* 22 C.F.R. §95.2.

Extradition procedures have traditionally been regarded as separate and independent from removal procedures under the INA. *Barapind v. Reno,* 225 F.3d 1100 (9th Cir. 2000); *Cornejo-Barreto, supra,* at 1009–11; *McMullen v. INS,* 788 F.2d 591, 596 (9th Cir. 1986); Restatement (Third) of Foreign Relations §478 n.6 (1986). However, a number of extradition treaties contain a political offense exception. *Quinn v. Robinson,* 783 F.2d 776 (9th Cir. 1986) [declining extradition of Irish-American who conspired with PIRA]; *Ramos v. Diaz,* 179 F.Supp. 459, 463 (S.D. Fla. 1959) [denying extradition of Cuban convicted of murder during Cuban revolution]; *In re Ezeta,* 62 F. 972 (N.D. Cal. 1894) [Salvadorans accused of murder while unsuccessfully thwarting revolution]; *Ornelas v. Ruiz,* 161 U.S. 502 (1896) [providing criteria for political offenses but permitting extradition]; *Eain v. Wilkes,* 641 F.2d 504 (7th Cir. 1981) [permitting extradition of PLO member to Israel]; *Sandhu v. Bransom,* 932 F.Supp. 822, 826 (N.D. Tex. 1996); *Matter of Extradition of Sandhu,* 886 F.Supp. 318, 323–24 (S.D.N.Y. 1993). Documents that are certified for extradition are reviewed under 7 FAM 1633.

At least one court has found that the BIA may stay consideration of an asylum case until extradition is completed. *Barapind v. Reno,* 225 F.3d 1100 (9th Cir. 2000). Another panel of the same circuit found jurisdiction to review the Secretary's decision to extradite after denying CAT relief. *Cornejo-Barreto v. Seifert,* 218 F.3d 1004 (9th Cir. 2000). Other courts have determined that the Convention does not obligate the extradition judge to consider human rights conditions in the country of extradition. *Hoxha v. Levi,* 465 F.3d 554, 563 (3d Cir. 2006) [noninquiry principle does not permit the court to inquire into humanitarian considerations such as torture or death upon extradition as that is a function of the Executive branch]; *Mironescu v. Costner,* 345 F.Supp.2d 538 (M.D.N.C. 2004) [no review to consider evidence of CAT claim in extradition but Secy. of State must consider evidence if magistrate orders extradition and must notify defendant of Secretary's decision with enough time to permit habeas review]; *In re Extradition of Mironescu,* 296 F.Supp.2d 632 (M.D.N.C. 2003) [CAT consideration must be left to the Secy. of State and cannot be considered in extradition].

X. SUBSTANTIVE DUE PROCESS

Under certain circumstances, a person may claim that it would violate substantive due process to remove him to a country where he may face certain death. *Wang v. Reno,* 81 F.3d 808, 818–19 (9th Cir. 1996) [where U.S. officials created a Hobson's choice of testifying truthfully and risking further torture in China or perjuring himself and going to jail, they could not return him to China to face torture when he testified truthfully]; *Lawson v. Gerlinski,* 332 F.Supp.2d 735, 742–43 (M.D. Pa. 2004) [long term LPR with no relief who cooperated with government, received reduction in sentence and feared harm if returned to his country, was entitled to a substantive due process hearing on theory that the state created his danger]; *Builes v. Nye,* 239 F.Supp.2d 518, 525–26 (M.D. Pa. 2003) [substantive due process is violated where government informant would be sent to Colombia to face certain death]. But the Pennsylvania cases have been overruled by the Third Circuit. *Kamara v. Att'y Gen. of the U.S.,* 420 F.3d 202, 216–18 (3d Cir. 2005) [rejecting substantive due process challenge based on the state-created danger exception holding it has no place in immigration jurisprudence]. *See also Morgan v. Gonzales,* 495 F.3d 1084, 1092–94 (9th Cir. 2007) [recognizing state-created danger exception under *Morgan* but finding on the facts that convicted drug dealer's fear of return to country did not amount to gross negligence and deliberate indifference on the part of U.S. officials]; *Enwonwu v. Gonzales,* 438 F.3d 22, 29–31 (1st Cir. 2006) [following *Kamara* and rejecting state-created danger theory for persons facing removal]; *Momennia v. Estrada,* 268 F.Supp.2d 679 (N.D. Tex. 2003) [rejecting claim that FBI, through deliberate indifference, gave rise to a state-created danger to Iranian deportee who had provided assistance to the FBI, and that the government had a duty not to remove him to Iran].

XI. THE APPLICATION PROCESS

A. *Processing of Refugees*

1. *Annual Refugee Quotas*—Each year the President, after consultation with Congress, designates certain countries and areas of the world as places from which the U.S. will fill the annual refugee quota. For fiscal year 2008 the designations were as follows:

Africa	16,000	Latin America/Caribbean	3,000
East Asia	20,000	Near East/South Asia	28,000
Europe and Central Asia	3,000	Unallocated Reserve	10,000

If a person seeks refugee status from an area/country that was not designated under the fiscal year allocation, the consular officer cannot accept the application. *See* Refugee Processing Guidelines, Department of State. The officer must refer the person to UNHCR. Persons within their own countries who may be considered refugees, if they otherwise qualify, for FY 2008 are applicants from Vietnam, Cuba, the former Soviet Union, and in exceptional circumstances persons identified by a U.S. Embassy in any location.

2. *Refugee Requirements for Approval*—A person outside the U.S. seeking admission to this country as a refugee must file a Refugee Application (I-590) and, if 14 years old or older, a Biographical Form (G-325A) and fingerprints with an overseas DHS officer or, if in an area too far from a DHS office, at a designated consular office. 8 C.F.R. §§207.1(a), 207.2(a). An applicant must also submit to the standard medical examination. 8 C.F.R. §207.2(c). Refugee status will not be authorized until the refugee is sponsored by a responsible person or organization that can provide assurances of both employment and housing on entry and of transportation from the applicant's present residence to his final destination in the U.S. 8 C.F.R. §207.2(d). This usually is accomplished through an umbrella organization called the American Council for Voluntary Agencies.

3. *Categories of Inadmissibility*—Even if an applicant meets all the requirements for refugee status, s/he may still be denied admission if s/he falls within certain categories of inadmissibility under INA §212(a).

   3.a. *Inadmissibility Automatically Waived*—INA §207(c)(3), 8 U.S.C. §1157(c)(3). The categories that are waived automatically, and do not require a waiver application are INA §212(a)(5) [persons coming to work, unless they have labor certification]; (a)(4) [persons likely to become a public charge]; §212(a)(7)(A) [immigrant without valid documentation on entry]; §212(a)(5)(B) [certain medical graduates who have not passed the U.S. medical examinations].

   3.b. *No Waiver Available*—Categories of inadmissibility that cannot be waived under any circumstances notwithstanding refugee eligibility are INA §212(a)(2)(C) [drug trafficking]; §212(a)(3) [except subparagraph (D)] [relating to security, terrorism, foreign policy and Nazi grounds].

   3.c. *Waiver Available*—All other categories of inadmissibility under INA §212(a) may be waived by the AG for humanitarian purposes, to assure family unity or when otherwise in the public interest. INA §207(c)(3); 8 C.F.R. §§207.3(b), 1207.3(b). Guidelines have been established for waivers of inadmissibility due to HIV status. Memo, Cummings, Deputy Dir. OIA (June 16, 1999), *reprinted in* 76 No. 41 *Interpreter Releases* 1551, 1563–64 (Oct. 25, 1999) [allowing refugees to rely on their eligibility for certain public funds when considering that there would be no cost to U.S. government].

   3.d. *Form 1-602*—A refugee must submit the application to the officer in charge at the consulate accepting applications. The refugee has the burden of proof and the denial of the waiver is not administratively appealable. 8 C.F.R. §§207.3(b), 1207.3(b). One court found there was no judicial review of a DHS officer's decision to deny a refugee waiver, determining that the officer is the functional equivalent of a consular officer and therefore not subject to judicial review. *Doan v. INS,* 160 F.3d 508 (8th Cir. 1998).

4. *Ineligibility Due to Firm Resettlement*—The AG may only admit a refugee "who is not firmly resettled in any foreign country." INA §207(c)(1). Under 8 C.F.R. §207.1(b), any offer of residency, citizenship or some other type of permanent resettlement by another nation will be considered to fall within the definition of "firmly resettled." An applicant who claims not to be firmly resettled, must establish that his or her condition of residence in the third country has been substantially and consciously restricted by the authorities of that country so as to effectively deny resettlement. 8 C.F.R. §207.1(c). *But see Matter of Moy*, 12 I&N Dec. 121 (Comm. 1967); *Matter of Hung*, 12 I&N Dec. 178 (Comm. 1967). The regulations look to criteria such as housing, employment, permission to hold property, and enjoyment of other rights and privileges of residents of that country, to determine whether the refugee is living under conditions that may be considered restrictive. 8 C.F.R. §207.1(c). Absent from these considerations is the extent to which a third country can protect the refugee against physical harm from agents of the country of origin. A parent's status in regard to firm resettlement will be conclusive on a child even if the child is now a

separately petitioning adult. *Vang v. INS,* 146 F.3d 1114 (9th Cir. 1998). *See in this chapter*, "Firm Resettlement," ¶ III.D.6 (p.470), *supra*.

5. *Admission to the U.S.*—The refugee has four months from the approval of the application to be admitted into the U.S. 8 C.F.R. §207.4. The failure to do so presumably will result in the invalidation of the application.

6. *Admission of Refugees by AG*—The AG is given broad latitude to admit refugees on a basis other than by priority date from the date of filing the application. The AG may select from a list of approved applicants in a manner that will "best support the policies and interests of the U.S." The AG is authorized to set up criteria for the selection and assignment of processing priorities in each refugee group based on such considerations as: "reuniting families, close associations with the U.S., compelling humanitarian concerns and public interest factors." 8 C.F.R. §207.5. A refugee who could otherwise enter the U.S. within the preference system will not be processed as a refugee unless to do so would be in the public interest. If the refugee has a visa currently available to him, he will be advised, but not required, to seek the classification.

7. *Termination of Refugee Status*—The AG may terminate the status of a refugee if he determines s/he was not, in fact, a refugee within the meaning of INA §101(a)(42). INA §207(c)(4); 8 C.F.R. §207.9; *Matter of Garcia-Alzugaray*, 19 I&N Dec. 407 (BIA 1986) [Cuban admitted as refugee under INA §207 could not have status terminated for committing crime after admission]. The refugee may not be placed in *removal* proceedings unless his refugee status is terminated under 8 C.F.R. §207.9.

8. *Spouse and Children of Refugees*—The Act specifically provides for the admission of spouses and children of refugees, even if they are not refugees themselves, when they are accompanying or "following to join" the refugee and are not otherwise inadmissible under INA §212(a). INA §207(c)(2), 8 U.S.C. §1157(c)(2). To initiate the process for the family, a refugee must file an I-730 with DHS. 8 C.F.R. §207.7(d). The application must be filed within two years of the refugee's admission to the U.S. unless DHS extends the filing period for "humanitarian reasons." *Id.* The admission of spouses and children will be charged against the numerical limitation for refugee entries of the refugee's country. *Refugee Processing Guidelines*, Department of State at. 27. For example, the British-born wife of an Ethiopian refugee will be charged against the Ethiopian refugee allocation. There is no provision, however, for the granting of refugee status to a spouse or child acquired after the principal refugee's admission into the U.S., except for a child *in utero* at the time of admission. 8 C.F.R. §207.7(c). They must qualify on their own as refugees. O.I. §207.8.

B. ***Applying for Asylum, Withholding of Removal, and Protection Under CAT***

1. *Establishment of Procedures*—The Refugee Act of 1980 directed the AG to establish procedures for people physically present in the U.S. or at land borders or ports of entry to apply for asylum if they fall within the definition of refugee. INA §208(a), 8 U.S.C. §1158(a). *Matter of Gharadaghi*, 19 I&N Dec. 311 (BIA 1985) [IJ erred in refusing to hear asylum claim because applicant was outside the U.S. in Canada]. DOJ promulgated Interim Regulations on June 2, 1980. INS published final rules on July 27, 1990 (55 Fed. Reg. 30674), that became effective Oct. 1, 1990 and additional rules on Dec. 5, 1994 (59 Fed. Reg. 62284) that became effective Jan. 4, 1995. Following IIRIRA, a new set of asylum rules was published on Mar. 6, 1997 (62 Fed. Reg. 10336). In 1998 Congress enacted into law the Convention Against Torture. FY 1999 Omnibus Consolidated and Emergency Supplemental Appropriations Act, PL 105-277, Div. G, Sub. B, Tit. XXI Foreign Affairs Reform and Restructuring Act of 1998, §2242, 112 Stat. 2681-822, 105th Cong. 2d Sess. (1998), 144 Cong. Rec. H11044-03; 136 Cong. Rec. S. 17486, 36198 (1990). This Act and the subsequent regulations, 64 Fed. Reg. 8478–96, *reprinted in* 76 No. 7 *Interpreter Releases* 275, 288–305 (Feb. 22, 1999), govern procedures under CAT. In addition, new asylum rules on past persecution and country-wide persecution, and the one-year filing deadline were published on Dec. 6, 2000 (65 Fed. Reg. 76121–76138).

2. *Effective Dates*—Asylum and withholding applications filed *prior to* Apr. 1, 1997 will be considered under current regulations, except where regulations expressly provide otherwise. 8 C.F.R. §§208.1(a), 1208.1(a) . The CAT rules apply as of Mar. 22, 1999. 8 C.F.R. §§208.18(b)(1), 1208.18(b)(1).

3. *Asylum at the Border*—INA §235(b), 8 U.S.C. §1225(b); 8 C.F.R. §208.30. Under IIRIRA §302, Congress established an expedited removal procedure for anyone seeking asylum in the U.S. who is inadmissible under 8 U.S.C. §§1182(a)(6)(C) (false statements) or 1182(a)(7) (no documents). Unless the person who is inadmissible indicates an intention to apply for asylum or a fear of persecution, s/he is summarily removed. If the person does indicate an intention for one or the other, s/he is referred to an asylum officer. If the AO determines the applicant has a credible fear of persecution s/he is referred to an IJ to present an asylum claim. Persons other than AOs can conduct credible fear interviews but several requirements, including supervision by an AO, must be met under INA §235(b)(1) before permission is granted. "Credible fear" of persecution means that there is a significant possibility, taking into account the credibility of the statements and other factors, that the person could establish eligibility for asylum. 8 C.F.R. §208.30(e)(2). The "significant possibility" standard also applies to a determination that there is credible fear of torture. 8 C.F.R. §208.30(e)(3). If the officer determines there is no credible fear, the applicant has a right to an expedited appeal to an IJ that must occur within 7 days. Judicial review is limited. *See* "Expedited Removal" in Ch. 3, section IV.C (p.131), *supra*.

4. *Asylum, Withholding and CAT Relief Before the Asylum Officer.*

   4.a. *Processing the Asylum Application*—The regulations provide for a corps of asylum officers (AO) to hear and decide asylum applications filed or pending after Oct. 1, 1990. The AOs receive special training in international relations and international law, 8 C.F.R. §§208.1(b), 1208.1(b), are under the jurisdiction of the DHS Director of International Affairs, 8 C.F.R. §§208.2(a), 1208.2(a), and "shall maintain a documentation center with information on human rights conditions." 8 C.F.R. §§208.1(b), 1208.1(b). The application includes an I-589 application in triplicate, plus an additional copy for each dependent family member in the U.S. (*see* 8 C.F.R. §§208.3(a), 1208.3(a), copies of all passports or other travel documents, photographs of the applicant and each dependent, proof of family relationships for dependents and all documents supporting the asylum claim. The application must be thorough, detailed, complete, must be signed, must contain a response to *each* question on the I-589 and must be accompanied by all required materials. Incomplete applications will be returned and will toll the 150-day period for employment authorization. 8 C.F.R. §§208.3(c)(3), 1208.3(c)(3). If the I-589 is received by USCIS before a dependent child turns 21, s/he will continue to be treated as a child, as long as s/he is unmarried, under the Child Status Protection Act (CSPA). Memo, Langlois, Asylum Office, HQIAO 120/12.9 (Aug. 7, 2002), *published on* AILA InfoNet at Doc. No 02090531 (Sept. 5, 2002). An application for asylum is automatically deemed an application for withholding of deportation or removal as well. 8 C.F.R. §§208.3(b), 1208.3(b). The AG is authorized to charge a fee for asylum applications. INA §208(d)(3), 8 U.S.C. §1158(d)(3). The applicant must file the application within 1 year of arrival in the U.S. unless there were changed circumstances or extraordinary circumstances as defined in 8 C.F.R. §§208.4(a)(5), 1208.4(a)(5). INA §208(a)(2)(B), 8 C.F.R. §§208.4(a)(2), 1208.4(a)(2). An applicant is also barred if s/he previously filed an asylum application that was denied unless there were changed circumstances. INA §208(a)(2)(C). The bars *do not* apply to applications for withholding of removal. 8 C.F.R. §§208.4(a), 1208.4(a). The application is filed by mail directly with the regional Service Center with jurisdiction over the applicant's residence unless the Director of Asylum or the director of the local asylum office directs the applicant to file with the asylum office or unless the person is an "aged-out" derivative in which case s/he should file her own application with the local asylum office with an explanation. 8 C.F.R. §§208.4(b)(1), (2), 1208.4(b)(1), (2). The AO is required to notify the applicant of the right to counsel, the consequences of a frivolous application, and to provide the applicant with a list of pro bono services. INA §208(d)(4), 8 U.S.C. §1158(d)(4).

   4.b. *Consequences of Filing Asylum Application*—The filing of an asylum application has substantial consequences. 8 C.F.R. §§208.3(c), 1208.3(c):

      (1) Information on the application may be used as a basis to institute removal proceedings or as evidence in the proceeding if filed after Jan. 4, 1995. 8 C.F.R. §§208.3(c)(1), 1208.3(c)(1).

      (2) Information may be used to satisfy the burden of proof of deportability if filed after Jan. 4, 1995.

(3) Mailing to the address provided by the applicant on the asylum application shall constitute adequate service except for service of I-122/I-221.

(4) Applications are signed under penalty of perjury, and the applicant's signature establishes a presumption that s/he is aware of the contents. 8 C.F.R. §§208.3(c)(2), 1208.3(c)(2); *Pang v. USCIS,* 448 F.3d 102, 107–08 (2d Cir. 2006) [where applicant signed first signature line under penalty of perjury, the presumption was effective even if the preparer did not sign on the second signature line and the applicant did not sign and swear to the application in front of an immigration official on the third signature line as required. However, the court failed to make findings as to the accuracy of the application in light of the applicant's explanation of its inadequacy]. Moreover, the knowing placement of false information may subject the person to criminal and civil penalties under §274C. 8 C.F.R. §§208.3(c)(4), 1208.3(c)(4).

(5) *Frivolous Applications*—An applicant who knowingly makes a frivolous application "shall be permanently ineligible for any benefits" under the Act if s/he was given notice of the consequences of filing a frivolous application. INA §208(d)(6), 8 U.S.C. §1158(d)(6), 8 C.F.R. §§208.3(c)(5), 208.20, 1208.3(c)(5), 1208.20. The IJ or AO must notify the applicant of such consequences at the time s/he files the application. INA §208(d)(4)(A), 8 U.S.C. §1158(d)(4)(A). The IJ must find that material aspects of the application were false and that such fabrications were knowingly and deliberately made. 8 C.F.R. §§208.20, 1208.20. Therefore, an application is frivolous "if any of its material elements is deliberately fabricated." 8 C.F.R. §§208.20, 1208.20; *Luciana v. Att'y Gen. of the U.S.,* 502 F.3d 273, 280 (3d Cir. 2007) [Applying the standard in *Kungys v. U.S.* the court determined that the applicant's misrepresentation was not material because the IJ had declined to allow the application as untimely]. *Cf. Kalilu v. Mukasey,* 516 F.3d 777, 779 n.2 (9th Cir. 2008) [where petitioner's falsehood went to the question of whether his application was time barred, it was material]. A frivolous finding can only be made by the IJ or BIA in a final order if, during the course of proceedings, the IJ or BIA is satisfied that the applicant had sufficient opportunity to account for discrepancies. 8 C.F.R. §§208.20, 1208.20; *Alexandrov v. Gonzales,* 442 F.3d 395, 404–07 (6th Cir. 2006) [IJ's frivolous finding based on two highly unreliable hearsay memoranda from the U.S. Embassy in Sofia was a violation of due process]; *Farah v. Ashcroft,* 348 F.3d 1153, 1156–58 (9th Cir. 2003) [where asylum applicant was not given an adequate opportunity to explain the discrepancies that led to the IJ's frivolous ruling, the decision was reversed as inconsistent with the regulation]. But what if the applicant withdraws the application? In *Mei Juan Zheng v. Mukasey,* 514 F.3d 176, 181–82 (2d Cir. 2008) the court remanded the case to determine whether the statutory language allows a frivolous finding when the application is withdrawn. *But see Lazar v. Gonzales,* 500 F.3d 469, 479 (6th Cir. 2007) [the IJ's frivolous finding was not mooted by the withdrawal of petitioner's asylum application].The court in *Mei Juan Zheng*, 514 F.3d at182-84 also remanded the case to determine whether the IJ had the discretion to decline to make a finding of frivolousness based upon the statutory language.

i) *Standard*—In *Matter of Y-L-,* 24 I&N Dec. 151, 155 (BIA 2007) *on remand Liu v. DOJ,* 455 F.3d 106 (2d Cir. 2006), the BIA clarified the standard an IJ must follow in making a frivolous finding. 8 C.F.R. §§208.20, 1208.20 sets forth a "comprehensive framework" that requires the IJ to meet the following requirements: "(1) notice to the alien of the consequences of filing a frivolous application; (2) a specific finding by the Immigration Judge or the Board that the alien knowingly filed a frivolous application; (3) sufficient evidence in the record to support the finding that a material element of the asylum application was deliberately fabricated; and (4) an indication that the alien has been afforded sufficient opportunity to account for any discrepancies or implausible aspects of the claim." *Matter of Y-L-,* 24 I&N Dec. at 155. *See also* 65 Fed. Reg. 76121, 76128 (Dec. 6, 2000). The BIA indicated that "fraudulent may be more appropriate than frivolous" in light of the deliberate fabrication requirement, *Id.* at 155 n.1, and that a deliberate fabrication involves a "knowing and intentional misrepresentation of the truth." *Id.* at 156. The IJ should bring his concerns to the attention of the applicant "prior to the conclusion of the proceedings."

Id.; *Kalilu v. Mukasey,* 516 F.3d 777, 779 (9th Cir. 2008) [reversed frivolous finding for determination under new standard in *Matter of Y-L-*]. In *Biao Yang v. Gonzales,* 496 F.3d 268 (2d Cir. 2007) the court vacated the BIA's frivolous finding and remanded the case to the Board to clarify its decision in *Matter of Y-L-* because the decision was unclear on the need for a frivolous finding separate from an adverse credibility finding as well as several other issues.

ii) *Burden of Proof*—The IJ's finding must be supported by "cogent and convincing reasons" and the government has the burden of proof. *Id.* at 158. The respondent's concession that statements on his first asylum application were erroneous "is not enough in and of itself to indicate that he knowingly filed an application containing a deliberate fabrication" even if signing the document establishes a presumption that he was aware of its content pursuant to 8 C.F.R. §§208.3(c)(2), 1208.3(c)(2). *Id.* at 161 & n.4.

iii) *Effect of Adverse Credibility Finding*—A frivolous finding cannot be based solely on an adverse credibility determination. *Mingkid v. U.S. Att'y Gen.,* 468 F.3d 763, 768–69 (11th Cir. 2006) [IJ's determination that Indonesian brothers' asylum claim was frivolous was reversed where IJ failed to make findings based on 8 C.F.R. §208.20 regarding deliberate fabrication and failed to permit applicants to explain discrepancies]; *Scheerer v. U.S. Att'y Gen.,* 445 F.3d 1311, 1317–18 (11th Cir. 2006) [where IJ found that person charged under Germany's racial hatred law and sentenced to 14 months for arguing there were no gas chambers at Auschwitz was not deemed credible, a lack of credibility does not alone equate to a frivolous finding]; *Muhanna v. Gonzales,* 399 F.3d 582, 588–89 (3d Cir. 2005) [a finding of frivolousness violated due process where it was based solely on a credibility determination and not on the application as a whole and where respondent was not permitted to present testimony on his claim].

iv) *No Mitigation*—In the view of at least one circuit, a frivolous finding is not mitigated by any subsequent recantation. *Barreto-Claro v. U.S. Att'y Gen.,* 275 F.3d 1334, 1337–39 & n.8 (11th Cir. 2001) [where Cuban applicant, after warning, had materially misrepresented his status in a third country, his subsequent recantation did not alleviate the IJ/BIA finding of frivolousness]. However, a finding that an applicant filed a frivolous asylum application does not preclude seeking withholding of removal. *Id.*

v) *Motion to Reopen*—An applicant may file a motion to reopen to challenge the frivolous finding. *Verano-Velasco v. U.S. Att'y Gen.,* 456 F.3d 1372, 1377 (11th Cir. 2006) [motion to reopen was granted reversing a frivolous finding on Colombian asylum claim where evidence surfaced that government's witness had committed fraud in custody proceedings regarding the asylum applicant]. However, an applicant who files a motion to reopen for other relief, such as AOS, without previously challenging the frivolous finding (or even raising it in the motion to reopen) cannot obtain review of the frivolous finding and will therefore be barred from the additional relief. *Tchuinga v. Gonzales,* 454 F.3d 54, 60–61 (1st Cir. 2006)

vi) *Frivolous Finding Upheld*—*Ceraj v. Mukasey,* 511 F.3d 583, 588–91 (6th Cir. 2007) [where incident regarding punishment by Albanian authorities appeared fro the first time in testimony and was not in his 1991 refugee application or 1997 asylum application, the frivolous finding was upheld]; *Lazar v. Gonzales,* 500 F.3d 469 (6th Cir. 2007) [where respondent had multiple opportunities to retract his two fraudulent asylum applications and only did so during cross-examination, he could not rely on his first counsel's malfeasance in urging him to lie as a defense to a frivolous finding]; *Aziz v. Gonzales,* 478 F.3d 854, 857–58 (8th Cir. 2007) [upholding IJ's finding that Iraqi woman who submitted asylum claim under false name and claimed her husband compelled her to do it, filed frivolous application]; *Kifleyesus v. Gonzales,* 462 F.3d 937, 944–45 (8th Cir. 2006) [upholding IJ finding that Ethiopian asylum claim was frivolous where applicant filed a false application, failed to modify it when given a chance, swore to the truth of it, lied in response to IJ's questions and subsequently admitted the falsity of testimony and her application]; *Sterkaj v. Gonzales,*

439 F.3d 273, 278–79 (6th Cir. 2006) [submission of fraudulent "summons" and questionable "wanted" document that went to heart of Albanian asylum seeker's claim was sufficient for IJ to find application frivolous]; *Ignatova v. Gonzales,* 430 F.3d 1209, 1214–15 (8th Cir. 2005) [upholding post–REAL ID Act, frivolous finding based on fraudulent documents]; *Fongwo v. Gonzales,* 430 F.3d 944, 947–49 (8th Cir. 2005) [denying applicant's motion to reconsider frivolous finding by IJ under abuse of discretion standard where IJ's finding was based on entry documents that applicant said presented a false identity but IJ believed to be true]; *Selami v. Gonzales,* 423 F.3d 621, 624–26 (6th Cir. 2005) [submission of a fraudulent newspaper article that supported a key element of Albanian's asylum claim was sufficient to support frivolous finding where court gave the applicant failed to explain fraudulent document]; *Efe v. Ashcroft,* 293 F.3d 899, 908 (5th Cir. 2002) [upholding frivolous finding where applicant misrepresented his case several times and never clarified discrepancies]; *Barreto-Claro v. U.S. Att'y Gen.,* 275 F.3d 1334, 1337–39 & n.8 (11th Cir. 2001) [where Cuban applicant materially misrepresented his status in a third country, his subsequent recantation did not alleviate the IJ/BIA finding of frivolousness].

vii) *De Novo Review*—The frivolous determination is reviewed *de novo. Mingkid v. U.S. Att'y Gen.,* 468 F.3d 763, 769 (11th Cir. 2006) [reversing IJ's frivolous finding].

(6) *Unlawful Presence*—The filing of a meritorious asylum application stops the accrual of unlawful presence *if* the applicant does not engage in unauthorized employment while the application is pending. *See* Ch. 3, ¶ III.E.3.d(2) (p.93), *supra.*

4.c. *Consequences of Making False Statement in Asylum Interview*—A false oral statement under oath during an asylum interview is a bar to good moral character under INA §101(f)(6), 8 U.S.C. §1101(f)(6). *Medina v. Gonzales,* 404 F.3d 628, 633–37 (2d Cir. 2005) [applicant statutorily ineligible for suspension because she lacked good moral character as a result of false statement to the asylum officer]; *Ramos v. INS,* 246 F.3d 1264, 1265–66 (9th Cir. 2001); *Matter of R-S-J-,* 22 I&N Dec. 863 (BIA 1999) [false oral statement under oath to asylum officer].

4.d. *Confidentiality*—Information contained in or pertaining to an asylum application, or any records pertaining to a credible fear or reasonable fear determination, "shall not be disclosed without the written consent of the applicant." 8 C.F.R. §§208.6(a), 1208.6(a). The disclosure may be an independent ground for asylum. There are exceptions to the confidentiality requirements. *See in this chapter* "Breach of Confidentiality of Asylum," ¶ III.A.3.p (p.444), *supra.*

4.e. *Nonimmigrant Status and Asylum Application*—If an asylum applicant was maintaining a valid NIV status at the time of filing the application, and asylum is denied before the NIV status expires or the applicant obtains an extension of NIV status while the asylum application is pending, the applicant is restored to NIV status and proceedings are not commenced. 8 C.F.R. §§208.23, 1208.23. Legal Opinion, Cook, General Counsel, CO 1453-P, 241.9-P, 208-P (Apr. 4, 1990), *reprinted in* 67 No. 19 *Interpreter Releases* 561, 568 (May 14, 1990); Letter, Bednarz, Chief NIV Branch, Adjudications, CO 893-C (Oct. 21, 1993), *reprinted in* 12 *AILA Monthly Mailing* 931 (Dec. 1993). The filing of an asylum application does not by itself extend the NIV status of an applicant. Letter, LaFleur, Chief NIV Branch, Adjudications, HQ 214-C, 248-C, 208-C (Nov. 14, 1995), *reprinted in* 72 No. 48 *Interpreter Releases* 1700, 1708 (Dec. 18, 1995). However, even if NIV status lapses during the pendency of the asylum claim, it may be a "technical" violation through "no fault of his own," to allow the person to adjust status as long as the application is still pending and has not been referred to the immigration court. *Matter of L-K-,* 23 I&N Dec. 677, 680–81 (BIA 2004) [DV lottery winner cannot adjust where case was referred to immigration court; but recognizing that if application was still pending with DHS it would be considered a technical reason under 8 C.F.R. §1245.1(d)(2)(ii)]. Under current interpretation a person may be unlawfully present for purposes of the 3/10 year bar if she worked one-day without employment authorization while her claim for asylum was pending.

4.f. *Asylum Offices*—DHS now has asylum offices in eight major metropolitan areas. These areas are: Arlington, Va., Chicago, Houston, Los Angeles, Miami, New York City, Newark, N.J., and San Francisco. *See* **Appendix E,** *infra* for address and jurisdiction of each office. AOs will circuit ride to cities within a 300 mile radius. *See* Appendix E, *infra* for circuit areas. The AO must forward a copy of each application it receives to DOS. 8 C.F.R. §§208.11(a), 1208.11(a).

4.g. *Asylum Interview*—The AO shall conduct an asylum interview "in a nonadversarial manner and, at the request of the applicant, separate and apart from the public." 8 C.F.R. §§208.9(b), 1208.9(b). The applicant may have counsel or a representative present and may submit affidavits of witnesses, 8 C.F.R. §§208.9(b), 1208.9(b), and any documentary or other corroborating evidence. *Haitian Refugee Center v. Civiletti*, 503 F.Supp. 442 (S.D. Fla. 1980), *modified sub nom. Haitian Refugee Center v. Smith*, 676 F.2d 1023 (5th Cir. 1982). The AO may administer oaths, question the applicant and witnesses. The applicant must bring an interpreter if s/he cannot proceed in English but the interpreter must be at least 18 and cannot be a witness or the applicant's attorney or representative. Counsel may bring a member of his or her staff to interpret as long as the person is not a witness. Memo, Cummings, Acting Asst. Comm. (Aug. 17, 1992), *reported in* 11 *AILA Monthly Mailing* 751 (Oct. 1992). Failure without good cause to comply with this provision may be deemed an abandonment of the application. 8 C.F.R. §§208.9(g), 1208.9(g). If the applicant fails to appear, the application may be dismissed or other sanctions imposed. INA §208(d)(5)(A)(v). Failure to appear will be excused if the notice of interview was not mailed to the applicant's current address as provided to USCIS prior to the interview or if the applicant demonstrates the failure to appear was the result of exceptional circumstances. 8 C.F.R. §§208.10, 1208.10. *See also* 8 C.F.R. §§103.2(b)(9), (13); AFM at 15.1(b)(2) & (d). A motion to reopen may be filed, 8 C.F.R. §103.2(b)(15), but the applicant must demonstrate that a request to reschedule for good cause was postmarked, faxed, or received telephonically, or a notification of a change of address was received prior to the interview. AFM at 15.1(d)(3)(B).

(1) *Timing of Interview and Adjudication*—Absent exceptional circumstances, the asylum interview "shall commence not later than 45 days after the date an application is filed." The application shall be adjudicated within 180 days. Any administrative appeal shall be filed within 30 days of the decision. INA §208(d)(5)(A)(ii)–(iv). At least one court has rejected a claim that the failure to timely adjudicate an asylum application resulted in a denial of due process due to changed circumstances. *Tamas-Mercea v. Reno,* 222 F.3d 417, 427 (7th Cir. 2000) [application submitted in 1991 but not decided until 1997]. Upon completion of the interview, the applicant or his representative shall have an opportunity to make a statement or comment on the evidence which may be limited in the AO's discretion. 8 C.F.R. §§208.9(d), 1208.9(d). The applicant may also be given a brief extension of time to supplement the record. 8 C.F.R. §§208.9(e), 1208.9(e).

(2) *Application at Land Border*—The land border provisions require a person seeking asylum to return to the contiguous territory to await a decision. *Matter of Gharadaghi*, 19 I&N Dec. 311 (BIA 1985).

(3) *DOS and Other Government Materials*—The AO may rely on DOS or other government materials or "other credible sources such as international organizations, private voluntary agencies, news organizations, or academic institutions." 8 C.F.R. §§208.12(a), 1208.12(a). Regulations preclude discovery however. 8 C.F.R. §§208.12(b), 1208.12(b). At its option, DOS may provide detailed information on country conditions relevant to the application. 8 C.F.R. §§208.11(b), 1208.11(b). DOS may also provide: (1) an assessment of the accuracy of the application; (2) information about whether persons similarly situated are suffering persecution; or (3) other relevant information. 8 C.F.R. §§208.11(b), 1208.11(b). AOs and IJs may request specific comments. 8 C.F.R. §§208.11(c), 1208.11(c). At least one court has found that the failure to provide complete or detailed information is not a basis to reverse the IJ's decision because the applicant has the right to respond. *Ghaly v. INS*, 58 F.3d 1425, 1429 (9th Cir. 1995). Unless classified, DOS comments are made part of the record. 8 C.F.R. §§208.11(d), 1208.11(d). The failure of the BIA to consider the factual assertions contained in the DOS opinion is error. Moreover, the right to rebut its determination is particularly important because it often lacks objectivity. *See in this chapter* "Country Reports and Profiles," ¶ XII.B.2.f(16)(b) (p.539), *infra*.

(4) *Retention of the Applicant's Documents*. USCIS retains the right to hold a document provided to it during the affirmative asylum process to determine its validity. If the AO takes the document it must provide a receipt on Form I-72 to the applicant. If the AO determines the document is authentic it must be "promptly return[ed]" to the applicant. If the AO determines that the document is fraudulent or fraudulently obtained s/he has the right to retain the document in the A-file. Memo, Melmed, Chief Counsel, USCIS (Nov. 30, 2007), *published on* AILA InfoNet at 07122065.

(5) *Background Checks*—The identity of the applicant must be checked against all appropriate records and databases maintained by the AG and the Secy. of State, including CLASS, to determine the applicant's inadmissibility, deportability or ineligibility for asylum. INA §208(d)(5)(A)(i), 8 U.S.C. §1158(d)(5)(A)(i). Failure to appear without good cause for fingerprinting/biometrics will stop the "clock" for employment authorization purposes and can be a basis to deny an affirmative application for asylum if it occurs more than one time and it was without good cause. Memo, Langlois, Chief, Asylum Division, USCIS HQRAIO 120/9.3a (Sept. 12, 2006), *published on* AILA InfoNet at Doc. No. 06091360. *See also in this chapter* "Security Procedures in Asylum Applications," ¶ XII.A.11 (p.522), *infra*.

(6) *Direct Review of Denial by BIA*—Where the applicant presents his or her case to the AO, and seeks review directly with the BIA (and not the IJ), any credibility decisions must be based upon a full transcription of the interview with the applicant, *Matter of S-S-*, 21 I&N Dec. 121 (BIA 1995), or other documentary evidence in the record. *Matter of M-S-*, 21 I&N Dec. 125 (BIA 1995).

4.h. *Jurisdiction and Referral to IJ by AO.*

(1) *The AO's Decision*—The AO's decision may grant, deny or refer an applicant to a removal hearing. The decision must be in writing and if denied must contain a credibility assessment unless the denial is due to statutory or regulatory ineligibility (*e.g.*, aggravated felony). 8 C.F.R. §§208.19, 1208.19. If the applicant appears to be inadmissible or deportable, the AO will refer him to the IJ. 8 C.F.R. §§208.14(c)(1), 1208.14(c)(1). The AO is empowered to issue an NTA. 8 C.F.R. §§239.1(a)(20), 1239.1(a). If a person is in valid immigrant, nonimmigrant, TPS status or parole status, the AO will deny the asylum application and *not* refer the case to the IJ. 8 C.F.R. §§208.14(c)(2), (3), 1208.14(c)(2), (3). An AO shall not decide withholding of removal. 8 C.F.R. §§208.16(a), 1208.16(a). Notices of intent to deny are eliminated except for asylum applicants in lawful status, *ABC* class members, and class members of the *Mendez* Settlement Agreement in Los Angeles. Asylum Officer Training Manual, "Decision Writing Part I" (Feb. 1998).

(2) *Effect of Denial on Family Members*—The denial of a principal results in denial of family members only if they are included on the application. 8 C.F.R. §§208.14(f), 1208.14(f).

(3) *Limited Hearing Before the IJ*—Stowaways, crewmen, visa waiver applicants, visa waiver overstays, S applicants, persons ordered removed under INA §235(c) may be referred to an IJ for a limited hearing solely on asylum or withholding. The hearing may not be used to challenge removability or to seek any other forms of relief. Prior to referral, a stowaway is given a credible fear determination. 8 C.F.R. §§208.5(b)(1)(i), 1208.5(b)(1)(i). A crew member is given 10 days to submit an asylum application to DHS who then serves the applicant with an I-863 and forwards the case to an IJ. §§208.5(b)(1)(ii), 1208.5(b)(1)(ii). Similarly, persons subject to reinstatement of removal under INA §241(a)(5) or expedited removal under INA §238 may be referred by the AO to an IJ, but the hearing may only address withholding. An appeal of the IJ's decision may be made to the BIA. Courts of appeal have jurisdiction under INA §242(a)(1) to review the IJ/BIA decision on asylum/withholding even if there is no jurisdiction to review the order of removal. *Kanacevic v. INS,* 448 F.3d 129, 133–36 (2d Cir. 2006) [no jurisdiction to review asylum only hearing for VWP applicant]; *Nreka v. U.S. Att'y Gen.,* 408 F.3d 1361, 1366–68 (11th Cir. 2005) [same]. The IJ is not permitted to review other matters in an asylum only hearing such as adjustment of status. *Ferry v. Gonzales,* 457 F.3d

1117, 1126–28 (10th Cir. 2006) [statutory provision allowing VWPs to apply for AOS before DHS does not give the IJ authority to review it in removal proceedings]; *Zine v. Mukasey,* 517 F.3d 535, 541–44 (8th Cir. 2008) [same]. *But see Freeman v. Gonzales,* 444 F.3d 1031, 1034–37 (9th Cir. 2006) [a VWP who is an immediate relative of a USC has the right to adjust status in the U.S. INA §245(c)(4), 8 U.S.C. §1255(c)(4) and where husband died she remained a spouse under INA and had the right to contest denial of AOS in same manner as other AOS applicants].

4.i. *Withholding of Removal and CAT Applications before AO*—The AO will not decide a withholding application unless the applicant alleges resistance to coercive population procedures and no quota number is available. 8 C.F.R. §§208.16(a), 1208.16(a). The AO will decide CAT claims in the context of persons ordered removed under INA §238(b) or reinstatement of removal under INA §241(a)(5). 8 C.F.R. §§208.31, 1208.31. The AO will also consider CAT claims of stowaways. 8 C.F.R. §§208.2(c)(1)(ii), 1208.2(c)(1)(ii).

5. *AO's Criteria for Deciding Asylum Claims*—The AO may, in the exercise of discretion, grant asylum if the applicant meets the refugee definition under INA §101(a)(42), 8 U.S.C. §1101(a)(42). The AO must carefully consider the claim under the Convention and Protocol standards. *INS v. Cardoza-Fonseca*, 480 U.S. 421 (1987); *Carvajal-Munoz v. INS*, 743 F.2d 562 (7th Cir. 1984). The AO cannot prejudge any asylum claim. *Haitian Refugee Center v. Smith*, 676 F.2d 1023 (5th Cir. 1982).

5.a. *Mandatory Denial of Asylum*—INA §208(a)(2) and (b)(2), 8 U.S.C. §1158(a)(2) and (b)(2), 8 C.F.R. §§208.13(c), 1208.13(c). Asylum will be denied where the person can be removed to a third country pursuant to a bilateral or multilateral agreement, where her life would not be threatened and where she could have access to a full and fair asylum process. INA §208(a)(2)(A).

5.b. *Discretionary Factors*—The IJ may also deny asylum solely on discretionary grounds even if the applicant qualifies. *Alsagladi v. Gonzales,* 450 F.3d 700 (7th Cir. 2006) [upheld denial of asylum on discretionary grounds where applicant from Yemen committed fraud by entering the U.S. as a tourist when his intent was to remain]; *Matter of Pula*, 19 I&N Dec. 467 (BIA 1987) [BIA adopted a "totality of the circumstances" test to determine a discretionary denial]. Discretionary denials may occur for several reasons:

(1) *Safe Third Country*—Prior INS regulations provided for the discretionary denial of asylum if the applicant could be removed to a third country which offered resettlement and in which the alien would not face harm or persecution, *Matter of Pula*, 19 I&N Dec. 467 (BIA 1987), although courts were reluctant to uphold such a finding. *Andriasian v. INS,* 180 F.3d 1033, 1043–47 (9th Cir. 1999) [reversing BIA's determination that asylum could be denied as a matter of discretion where a person could be sent to a third country despite the lack of an offer of resettlement]; *Melkonian v. Ashcroft,* 320 F.3d 1061, 1071 (9th C ir. 2003) [rejecting IJ's conclusion that asylum could be denied because person decided to come to the U.S. rather than stay in Russia for economic reasons after fleeing Abkhazia]; *Damaize-Job v. INS*, 787 F.2d 1332 (9th Cir. 1986); *Garcia-Ramos v. INS,* 775 F.2d 1370, 1374–75 (9th Cir. 1985). The prior regulation expired on Jan. 5, 2001 and any decision denying asylum based on a discretionary decision regarding "safe haven" is impermissible on or after that date. *Tandia v. Gonzales,* 437 F.3d 245, 248–49 (2d Cir. 2006) [where IJ issued decision regarding safe haven on Jan. 8, 2001, three days after the repeal of the regulation, the court reversed the finding and determined case could only be judged under firm resettlement standards which it did not meet]. *But note* INA §208(a)(2)(A), 8 U.S.C. §1158(a)(2)(A) now makes removal to a safe third country pursuant to a bilateral or multilateral agreement mandatory.

(2) *Circumventing Refugee Procedures*—Previously, asylum could also be denied as a matter of discretion where the applicant sought to circumvent the procedures for obtaining refugee status abroad and instead entered the U.S. with fraudulent documents. *See Matter of Shirdel*, 19 I&N Dec. 33 (BIA 1984); *Matter of Salim,* 18 I&N Dec. 311 (BIA 1982). However, following *Salim*, the BIA found that this ground for denial should be narrowly construed because "the danger of persecution should outweigh all but the most extreme adverse factors." *Matter of Pula*, 19 I&N Dec. 467 (BIA 1987) [withdrawing from *Salim*

"insofar as it suggests that circumvention of orderly refugee procedures alone is sufficient to require the most unusual showing of countervailing equities"]. In *Pula*, the BIA adopted a "totality of the circumstances" test and stated that among the factors to be considered in exercising discretion are: (1) whether the applicant passed through any other (third) country or arrived in the U.S. directly from his home country; (2) whether orderly refugee procedures were available in the third country; (3) the length of time the applicant remained in the third country; (4) the applicant's living conditions, safety and potential for long-term residency in the third country; (5) whether the applicant has relatives legally in the U.S. or has other personal ties in the U.S. motivating his desire to seek asylum here; (6) the applicant's ties to any other country where he does not fear persecution; (7) the seriousness of the applicant's fraud if he engaged in fraud to circumvent refugee procedures (the use of fraudulent documents to escape the country of persecution itself is *not* a significant adverse factor, although fraudulent entry as USC would be); (8) general humanitarian considerations such as the alien's tender age or poor health; and (9) whether discretionary factors should be weighed in light of the unusual harsh consequences of deportation where the applicant has met his burden for asylum, but not for INA §243(h). *Accord Matter of Soleimani*, 20 I&N Dec. 99 (BIA 1989); *Matter of Gharadaghi*, 19 I&N Dec. 311 (BIA 1985); *Gulla v. Gonzales,* 498 F.3d 911 (9th Cir. 2007) [IJ abused his discretion under the "totality of the circumstances" in *Matter of Pula* in denying, on discretionary grounds, asylum to a Chaldean Christian from Iraq where the applicant went through three countries before coming to the U.S., where he had U.S. family, and where he presented himself at the border to apply for asylum].

Moreover, false statements made at the airport should not be a basis for any adverse credibility determination. *Uanreroro v. Gonzales,* 443 F.3d 1197, 1210–11 (10th Cir. 2006) [false statements made at the airport alone should not be basis for adverse credibility finding because IJ must look at totality of the circumstances and "[i]t is readily apparent that lying to gain entry to the United States may be entirely consistent with fleeing persecution"]; *Paramasamy v. Ashcroft,* 295 F.3d 1047, 1054 (9th Cir. 2002) [the use of false documents for travel is not a proper basis for an adverse credibility determination]; *Akinmade v. INS,* 196 F.3d 951, 955–56 (9th Cir. 1999) [presentation of fraudulent documents on entry does not affect credibility of asylum claim]. *But see Alsagladi v. Gonzales,* 450 F.3d 700 (7th Cir. 2006) [upheld denial of asylum on discretionary grounds where applicant from Yemen committed fraud by entering the U.S. as a tourist when his intent was to remain].

5.c. *Revocation of Asylum/Withholding*—The AO is also permitted under limited circumstances to revoke asylum and withholding. 8 C.F.R. §§208.24(a), (b), 1208.24(a), (b). For asylum, these include: (1) a showing of fraud; (2) application was filed after Apr. 1, 1997 and any of the conditions in INA §208(c)(2) exist; or (3) application was filed before Apr. 1, 1997 and the applicant no longer fears persecution based on changed circumstances in the home country, or the applicant committed a disqualifying act under 8 C.F.R. §§208.13(c)(2), 1208.13(c)(2). Withholding of removal may also be terminated where: (1) there are changed conditions in the home country; (2) there is fraud; (3) the applicant has committed disqualifying acts under INA §241(b)(3)(B); or (4) the applicant filed before Apr. 1, 1997 and committed disqualifying acts under former INA §243(h)(2).

5.d. *Issuance of AO's Decision*—The applicant must appear in person to receive the AO's decision (unless the AO allows the applicant to waive his appearance in writing), or the clock will stop for employment authorization. 8 C.F.R. §§208.9(d), 208.19, 1208.9(d), 1208.19. The decision of the AO to grant an application or refer it to removal proceedings is not appealable. However, it may be renewed in removal proceedings as discussed below. 8 C.F.R. §§208.14(b), (c), 1208.14(b), (c). An applicant may separately challenge the AO's denial of asylum in federal court. *Fleurinor v. INS*, 585 F.2d 129, 135 (5th Cir. 1978), especially where a procedural or "pattern and practice" claim is raised. *See Jean v. Nelson*, 727 F.2d 957, 979 (11th Cir. 1984) (*en banc*); *Haitian Refugee Center v. Smith*, 676 F.2d 1023 (5th Cir. 1982). *But see Kashani v. Nelson*, 793 F.2d 818 (7th Cir. 1986); *Yim Tong Chung v. Smith*, 640 F.Supp. 1065 (S.D.N.Y. 1986). IIRIRA removed jurisdiction to challenge the mandatory denial of asylum. INA §208(a)(3), (b)(2)(D).

6. *AO and Credible Fear Determinations*—INA §235(b), 8 C.F.R. §§1003.42, 208.30, 1208.30.

6.a. *Generally*—Stowaways, crewmen and persons subject to expedited removal who seek asylum, withholding or protection under CAT will be given a credible fear interview by an AO or someone who receives AO training consistent with INA §235(b)(1)(E). 8 C.F.R. §§208.5(b)(1), 208.30, 1208.5(b)(1), 1208.30. Credible fear defined as "a significant possibility ... that the alien could establish eligibility for asylum under 208." INA §235(b)(1)(B)(v). Methods have been suggested to streamline the credible fear process including the use of telephone interviews and ending the requirement that notes and answers be typed. Memo, Langlois, Acting Dir. Asylum Division, HQASM 120/10.19 (Dec. 8, 2000), *reprinted in* 78 No. 6 *Interpreter Releases* 337, 357–59 (Feb. 5, 2001).

6.b. *Credible Fear Procedures*—The interview to determine credible fear may be reasonably limited by the AO. The applicant is entitled to consult with counsel or another person of his or her choosing, at no expense to the government, and such person may be present at the interview and in the AO's discretion may present a statement at the end of the interview. 8 C.F.R. §§208.30(d), 1208.30(d). The applicant has the right to correct errors in a summary decision by AO. If credible fear is established: (1) the stowaway/crewman is referred to the IJ by I-863 for a hearing under 8 C.F.R. §§208.2(c)(1), 1208.2(c)(1); and (2) all other applicants are referred to the IJ by I-862 for immigration court hearing. 8 C.F.R. §§208.30(f), 1208.30(f). If no credible fear: (1) stowaway is referred to DHS for removal under INA §235(a)(2); and (2) all other cases are referred to IJ if person so wishes. 8 C.F.R. §§208.30(g), 1208.30(g).

6.c. *IJ Review of Credible Fear Determination*—8 C.F.R. §§1003.42, 208.30(f), (g), 1208.30(f), (g). The IJ creates a separate record of proceeding from any later §240 proceeding. The IJ takes a statement under oath from the applicant. The applicant "may consult with a person [attorney] ... prior to review." 8 C.F.R. §1003.42(c). The IJ must conclude the review within 24 hours and no later than 7 days. 8 C.F.R. §1003.42(e). The IJ's review is *de novo* to determine whether there is a "significant possibility" that an asylum, withholding or CAT claim could be established. The IJ has no authority to review custody status in the course of the credible fear review. 8 C.F.R. §1003.42(g). If the IJ determines that the applicant has a credible fear, the applicant will be able to apply for asylum before the IJ. 8 C.F.R. §§208.30(f), 1208.30(f). If the IJ determines that no credible fear exists, she is returned to ICE for removal.

6.d. *Re-interview After Denial/Before Departure*—An applicant may seek to be re-interviewed prior to removal even if his application has been denied by the AO and the IJ if the Office of International Affairs determines that the applicant "has made a reasonable claim that compelling new information concerning the case exists and should be considered." Memo, Benson, Exec. Assoc. Comm. for Field Operations, INS (Dec. 30, 1997), *published on* AILA InfoNet at Doc. No. 98021090.

7. *AO and Reasonable Fear Determination for Withholding of Removal*—8 C.F.R. §§208.31, 1208.31.

7.a. *Generally*—A person subject to expedited removal under INA §238(b) or reinstatement of removal under INA §241(a)(5) who expresses a fear of returning to his country of removal will be given a "reasonable fear" interview by an AO. The interview will be conducted in a nonadversarial manner and the applicant may be represented by counsel. The AO shall create a summary of the interview and shall review it with the applicant to allow him to correct any errors. 8 C.F.R. §§208.31(c), 1208.31(c). The AO, without reference to any bars to eligibility, shall determine whether there is "a reasonable possibility that [the person] would be persecuted on account of his or her race, religion, nationality, membership in a particular social group or political opinion, or a reasonable possibility that he or she would be tortured in the country of removal." *Id.*

7.b. *Reasonable Fear Found*—If the applicant is determined to have a reasonable fear s/he will be referred to an IJ for consideration of withholding of removal in accordance with §208.16. 8 C.F.R. §§208.31(e), 1208.31(e).

7.c. *No Reasonable Fear Found*—An applicant may seek IJ review of an AO's decision of no reasonable fear. 8 C.F.R. §§208.31(f), (g), 1208.31(f), (g). If the IJ concurs with the AO, the case is returned to ICE for the applicant's removal. There is no appeal of the IJ's decision. 8 C.F.R. §§208.31(g)(1), 1208.31(g)(1). If the IJ determines the applicant does have a reasonable fear, the applicant can file an I-589 for consideration by the IJ. 8 C.F.R. §§208.31(g)(2), 1208.31(g)(2).

8. *Asylum, Withholding [*INA §241(b)(3)], *and CAT Claim Before the IJ*

8.a. *Generally*—Aliens served with an NTA (I-862) can file an application for asylum only before the IJ and not with the AO. 8 C.F.R. §1003.14(b); 8 C.F.R. §§208.2(b), 1208.2(b); *Gerrero v. Moyer*, 738 F.Supp. 1164 (N.D. Ill. 1990) [cannot mandamus DD to decide asylum application when case is before the IJ]. Once the NTA is served, the IJ has jurisdiction over the respondent and cannot terminate proceedings because an asylum application is pending with the AO. *Matter of P-L-P-*, 21 I&N Dec. 887 (BIA 1997). The I-589, as well as the other forms and documents listed above must be filed in triplicate with the court. 8 C.F.R. §§208.3, 208.4(c), 1208.3, 1208.4(c), 1240.11(c)(2). An I-589 will also be considered a request for withholding of removal under INA §241(b)(3), and a request for protection under CAT. 8 C.F.R. §§208.3(b), 1208.3(b) and §§208.16 & .17, 1208.16 & .17. *Chavarria v. DOJ*, 722 F.2d 666 (11th Cir. 1984); *Matter of Castellon*, 17 I&N Dec. 616 (BIA 1981). A copy of the application (without supporting documentation) with a biometric fee and application fee (if any) and an EOIR-28 must also be filed with the Nebraska Service Center. 8 C.F.R. §1003.47, Memo, Yates, Assoc. Dir. Operations, USCIS, "Executive Office for Immigration Review (EOIR) Processing," (Mar. 31, 2005), *published on* AILA InfoNet at Doc. No. 05051164 (May 11, 2005). An application that is not filed within the time frame set by the IJ will be deemed waived. 8 C.F.R. §1003.31(c); *Matter of R-R-*, 20 I&N Dec. 547 (BIA 1992) [waived when attorney mistakenly filed with DD instead of court]. If an applicant withdraws his asylum claim before the IJ, s/he may seek to reinstate it if s/he is prima facie eligible. *Mendez-Gutierrez v. Ashcroft,* 340 F.3d 865 (9th Cir. 2003) [where applicant withdrew asylum claim in the mistaken belief he was eligible for cancellation, the IJ/BIA erred in not allowing him to reinstate the application after demonstrating a prima facie case].

8.b. *Asylum Only Proceeding*—8 C.F.R. §208.2(c)(1). Crewmen and stowaways who have a credible fear of persecution, along with persons in the visa waiver program, persons ordered removed under INA §235(c), and persons admitted under the S visa may now have asylum claims heard by an IJ. 8 C.F.R. §§208.2(c)(1), 1208.2(c)(1). *But see* §§208.18(d), 1208.18(d), not permitting IJ hearings for persons under §235(c) for CAT claims. Case law also requires hearings before IJs: (1) for stowaways who seek asylum. *See Selgeka v. Carroll,* 184 F.3d 337 (4th Cir. 1999); *Marincas v. Lewis*, 92 F.3d 195 (3d Cir. 1996); *Yiu Sing Chun v. Sava*, 708 F.2d 869 (2d Cir. 1983); *Garcia v. Smith*, 674 F.2d 838 (11th Cir. 1982); *Cheng v. Ilchert*, 698 F.Supp. 825 (N.D. Cal. 1988); *Fang-Sui Yau v. Gustafson*, 623 F.Supp. 1515 (C.D. Cal. 1985). *But see Matter of Waldei*, 19 I&N Dec. 189 (BIA 1984); (2) for persons in the visa waiver program who seek asylum even if subject to summary removal. *Matter of Kanagasundram,* 22 I&N Dec. 963 (BIA 1999) [not subject to summary removal even if inadmissible under §§212(a)(6)(C) or (7)]; *Matter of L-*, 20 I&N Dec. 553 (BIA 1992); *Matter of H-*, 20 I&N Dec. 611 (BIA 1992); and (3) for persons subject to INA §235(c) who seek asylum. *Rafeedie v. INS*, 880 F.2d 506 (D.C. Cir. 1989). The IJ may only consider asylum/withholding claims as "all parties are prohibited from raising or considering any other issues including...eligibility for waivers...and any [other] form of relief...." 8 C.F.R. §§208.2(c)(3)(i), 1208.2(c)(3)(i). The application is initially filed with DHS who forwards it to the court. 8 C.F.R. §§208.4(b)(5), 1208.4(b)(5). The IJ's decision may be appealed to the BIA. Courts of appeal have jurisdiction under INA §242(a)(1) to review the IJ/BIA decision on asylum/withholding even if there is no jurisdiction to review the order of removal. *Kanacevic v. INS,* 448 F.3d 129, 133–36 (2d Cir. 2006) [finding jurisdiction to review asylum only hearing for VWP applicant]; *Nreka v. U.S. Att'y Gen.,* 408 F.3d 1361, 1366–68 (11th Cir. 2005) [same].

8.c. *IJ Advisement Regarding Frivolous Applications*—The IJ is required to advise the asylum applicant of the right to counsel and the consequences of filing a frivolous application. INA

§208(d)(4)(A), 8 U.S.C. §1158(d)(4)(A). If the IJ determines that the applicant knowingly made a frivolous application after notice, the applicant "shall be permanently ineligible for any benefits under the Act." INA §208(d)(6), 8 U.S.C. §1158(d)(6), 8 C.F.R. §§208.20, 1208.20, 1240.11(c)(1)(iii). *Ignatova v. Gonzales,* 430 F.3d 1209, 1214–15 (8th Cir. 2005) [post-REAL ID, upholding frivolous finding based on fraudulent documents]; *Barreto-Claro v. U.S. Att'y Gen.,* 275 F.3d 1334, 1337–39 & n.8 (11th Cir. 2001) [where Cuban applicant materially misrepresented his status in a third country, his subsequent recantation did not alleviate the IJ/BIA finding of frivolousness].

8.d. *Differences Between Asylum and Withholding*—Although asylum requests are considered with requests to withhold removal, 8 C.F.R. §§208.3, 1208.3, the BIA has noted significant differences between the two. *See Matter of Lam*, 18 I&N Dec. 15 (BIA 1981). For example, a denial of asylum for lack of credibility is not fatal to a withholding claim. *Paul v. Gonzales,* 444 F.3d 148, 156–57 (2d Cir. 2006) [adverse credibility finding for asylum from Pakistan does not bar motion to reopen on different grounds as a Christian for withholding or CAT because a withholding claim premised on objective evidence may be sustained even if IJ has found asylum testimony regarding past persecution as not credible]. Also, a request for withholding is country specific as it seeks to withhold removal from *a particular country* where the applicant's "life or freedom would be threatened." In addition, the doctrine of "firm resettlement" in a third country while potentially invalidating a request for asylum has no effect on withholding because it is country specific. In contrast, asylum is not country specific. Moreover, an asylee becomes eligible for LPR status after one year. *See* INA §209(b), 8 U.S.C. §1159(b). A grant of withholding, however, will not result in permanent residence. The IJ has no discretion to deny a valid application for withholding, but does have discretion to deny a valid asylum claim. *Matter of Lam, supra*; *Matter of Pula*, 19 I&N Dec. 467 (BIA 1987); *Osorio v. INS*, 18 F.3d 1017, 1021–22 (2d Cir. 1994) [burden of proof different]. An applicant for withholding is not subject to the prohibitions against filing for asylum more than one year after admission or after a previous asylum denial. INA §208(a)(2)(B), (C), 8 C.F.R. §§208.4(a), 1208.4(a). In cases filed on or after May 11, 2005, a trier of fact is required to apply the same corroboration and credibility criteria for asylum and withholding. INA §208(b)(1)(B)(ii),(iii) and §241(b)(3)(C). Some courts have now held that withholding, unlike asylum, does not grant derivative benefits to family members so that a grant of withholding to a husband or parent does not give derivative benefits to the spouse or child. *Arif v. Mukasey,* 509 F.3d 677, 680–82 (5th Cir. 2007) [wife of withholding applicant does not obtain a derivative status and 8 C.F.R. §1208.16(e) supports that reading of the statute]; *Delgado v. U.S. Att'y Gen.,* 487 F.3d 855, 862 (11th Cir. 2007) [where Venezuelan father and son were granted withholding, mother could not obtain withholding because the statute does not provide for derivative benefits as does asylum].

8.e. *Difference Between Asylum, Withholding, and Deferral Under CAT*—8 C.F.R. §§208.16 & .17, 1208.16 & .17; 64 Fed. Reg. 8478–79 (Feb. 19, 1999), *reprinted in* 76 No. 7 *Interpreter Releases* 275, 288–89 (Feb. 22, 1999).

(1) *Application Procedure*—Unlike asylum/withholding there is no formal application for CAT. However, "[b]ecause there is no separate and distinct procedure for seeking CAT relief, then Petitioners' [I-589] application responses, which clearly evinced their fear of torture, constitute claims for relief under the CAT." *Eduard v. Ashcroft,* 379 F.3d 195–96 (5th Cir. 2004). Failure to timely file an I-589 may not be deemed an abandonment of a CAT claim. *Louis-Martin v. Ridge,* 322 F.Supp.2d 556, 561–62 (M.D. Pa. 2004).

(2) *Mandatory Bars to Withholding Not Applicable to Deferral Under CAT*—Withholding under CAT is analytically distinct from deferral under CAT. *Compare* 8 C.F.R. §§208.16, 1208.16 *with* 8 C.F.R. §§208.17, 1208.17. Withholding under CAT permits withholding in a manner similar to INA §241(b)(3), and includes mandatory grounds of denial (§§208.16(d)(2), 1208.16(d)(2)). Conversely, deferral does *not* consider any of the bars to withholding under INA §241(b)(3)(B). CAT relief may be granted even if the applicant was involved in the persecution of others, *Vukmirovic v. Ashcroft,* 362 F.3d 1247, 1253 (9th Cir. 2004) [reversing IJ denial of motion to reopen for CAT relief for Bosnian-Serb where IJ found he was ineligible for the persecution of others], or is a terrorist or supported terrorist activity. *Hosseini v. Gonzales,* 471 F.3d 953, 957–61 (9th Cir. 2006) [upholding denial of withholding under CAT because person was a terrorist, but granting

deferral because terrorist activities were not relevant]. *See also Matter of Jean,* 23 I&N Dec. 373, 376 n.7 (AG 2002) [applicant's criminal history is "irrelevant in examining his or her entitlement to *deferral* of removal under the Convention"].

(3) *Burden in CAT*—In determining eligibility for withholding under CAT: (1) the burden is on the applicant; (2) the burden is the "more likely than not" standard articulated in *Stevic;* and (3) the applicant's own testimony, if credible, may be sufficient. 8 C.F.R. §§208.16(c)(2), 1208.16(c)(2); *Matter of J-E-,* 23 I&N Dec. 291, 302 (BIA 2002). In addition, unlike asylum or withholding where past persecution shifts the burden to the government to prove relocation to avoid persecution, a CAT applicant always maintains the burden of demonstrating that s/he will be tortured irrespective of where she relocates in the country. *Hasan v. Ashcroft,* 380 F.3d 1114, 1122–23 (9th Cir. 2004) [denial of asylum reversed but denial of CAT upheld on grounds that included the failure to meet the burden that internal relocation is not a possibility].

(4) *Must Consider All Evidence of Torture*—In assessing whether a person is more likely than not to be tortured all evidence of future torture shall be considered including: (1) evidence of past torture; (2) evidence that the applicant could relocate to another part of the country where s/he would not likely be tortured; (3) evidence of gross, flagrant, or mass human rights violations within the country; and (4) other relevant country conditions. 8 C.F.R. §§208.16(c)(3), 1208.16(c)(3); *Matter of J-E,* 23 I&N Dec. 291, 303 (BIA 2002); *Matter of G-A-,* 23 I&N Dec. 366 (BIA 2002) [burden met where due to a combination of factors including the applicant's Christianity, Armenian ethnicity, long duration in the U.S., drug related conviction, and extremely harsh conditions in Iranian prisons, it is more likely than not that he would be tortured upon his removal to Iran]. While relevant, country conditions are insufficient, standing alone, to obtain withholding. "Specific grounds must exist that indicate the individual would be personally at risk." *Id.; Sevoian v. Ashcroft,* 290 F.3d 166 (3d Cir. 2002) [affirming BIA's denial of reopening on failure to establish *prima facie* case under §208.16(c)(3)]; *Sulaiman v. Att'y Gen.,* 212 F.Supp.2d 413, 417 (E.D. Pa. 2002) [although respondent presented substantial evidence, the BIA did not violate §208.16(c)(3) in finding otherwise]; *Julmiste v. Ashcroft,* 212 F.Supp.2d 341, 346–49 (D.N.J. 2002) [rejecting CAT claim based on general political and prison conditions in Haiti].

(5) *Government Acquiescence*—For relief under CAT, the torture must be by or with the acquiescence of a public official but need not be on account of one of the five grounds for asylum or withholding. *See* 8 C.F.R. §§208.18, 1208.18; *Matter of J-E-, supra,* at 297–99; *Cano-Merida v. INS,* 311 F.3d 960, 965–66 (9th Cir. 2002) [BIA properly denied motion to reopen where there was no evidence that government official consented or acquiesced].

(6) *Different Analysis for CAT and Asylum/Withholding Claims*—The determination that there is no basis for withholding/asylum does not necessarily mean the person is ineligible for CAT relief. *Li Fang Lin v. Mukasey,* 517 F.3d 685, 696–97 (4th Cir. 2008) [reversed and remanded CAT denial where BIA erroneously failed to engage in a separate analysis of petitioner's CAT claim from China based upon facts separate from her "resistance to population control" asylum claim]; *Paul v. Gonzales,* 444 F.3d 148, 156–57 (2d Cir. 2006) [adverse credibility finding for asylum from Pakistan does not bar motion to reopen on different grounds as a Christian for withholding or CAT because a withholding claim premised on objective evidence may be sustained even if IJ has found asylum testimony regarding past persecution as not credible]; *Singh v. Ashcroft,* 398 F.3d 396, 404–06 (6th Cir. 2005) [reversing IJ for failure to separately analyze credibility issues for CAT after making a generalized negative credibility finding]; *Hamoui v. Ashcroft,* 389 F.3d 821, 827–28 (9th Cir. 2004) [BIA abused its discretion in applying asylum standard for CAT, relying on asylum testimony to deny motion to reopen for CAT and where counsel was ineffective]; *Taha v. Ashcroft,* 389 F.3d 800, 802 (9th Cir. 2004) [reversing where IJ and BIA used adverse credibility finding on asylum to deny CAT]; *Mihalev v. Ashcroft,* 388 F.3d 722, 731 (9th Cir. 2004) [remanding IJ's decision because he failed to address respondent's CAT claim; standards for asylum and CAT are different]; *Camara v. Ashcroft,* 378 F.3d 361, 371–72 (4th Cir. 2004) [following *Ramsameachire* and other circuits and reversing IJ's denial of CAT because credibility determinations as

to asylum/withholding claims are not dispositive of a CAT claim]; *Settenda v. Ashcroft,* 377 F.3d 89, 94–95 (1st Cir. 2004) [a *per se* rule that an adverse credibility determination on an asylum claim automatically defeats a CAT claim would be erroneous because it may doom some but not others]; *Kamalthas v. INS,* 251 F.3d 1279 (9th Cir. 2001) [reversing BIA's refusal to consider CAT claim because it had previously determined that applicant's claim for asylum was not credible]; *Sivakaran v. Ashcroft,* 368 F.3d 1028, 1029 (8th Cir. 2004) [reversing denial of CAT claim because adverse credibility determination and adverse decision on asylum and withholding are not determinative of CAT]; *Ramsameachire v. Ashcroft,* 357 F.3d 169, 184–86 (2d Cir. 2004) [credibility finding used to deny asylum/withholding cannot be basis for CAT denial]; *Zubeda v. Ashcroft,* 333 F.3d 463, 476 (3d Cir. 2003) ["[a]llowing the taint of the earlier adverse credibility determination [on asylum] to bleed through to the BIA's consideration of her claim under [CAT] without further explanation is [] error."]; *Kamalthas v. INS,* 251 F.3d 1279 (9th Cir. 2001) [reversing BIA refusal to hear CAT claim because it had previously determined that applicant's claim for asylum was not credible]; *Mansour v. INS,* 230 F.3d 902 (7th Cir. 2000). *But see Lin-Jian v. Gonzales,* 489 F.3d 182, 192–93 (4th Cir. 2007) [under *Camara* there must be additional evidence to support CAT claim or IJ can use credibility finding from withholding/asylum]; *Kebede v. Gonzales,* 481 F.3d 562, 565 (8th Cir. 2007) [separate analysis of CAT is only required where there is evidence that applicant might be tortured for reasons unrelated to her asylum/withholding claim]; *Guo v. Gonzales,* 463 F.3d 109, 113–14 (2d Cir. 2006) [*Ramsameachire* and other cases do not apply where the adverse credibility finding on asylum/withholding eliminates all factual bases for CAT]; *Ibrahim v. Gonzales,* 434 F.3d 1074, 1079–80 (8th Cir. 2006) [where respondent relied on same evidence to prove torture as to prove likelihood of persecution, the IJ did not err in failing to separately analyze the credibility issues under CAT]; *Yang v. DOJ,* 426 F.3d 520, 522–23 (2d Cir. 2005) [distinguishing *Ramsameachire* and *Zubeda* because the factual finding that determined lack of credibility was the respondent's claim of forced sterilization which was not analytically distinct from the withholding claim]; *Aden v. Ashcroft,* 396 F.3d 966, 969 (8th Cir. 2005) [where adverse credibility finding could be used for asylum and CAT and no additional evidence was offered, a separate analysis was not necessary]; *Efe v. Ashcroft,* 293 F.3d 899, 907–08 (5th Cir. 2002) [distinguishing *Mansour* and *Kamalthas*]. One court has determined "while deferral is a separate *form* of protection, it is not an independent *basis* upon which entitlement exists" and "deferral may be granted only after the alien has shown that he is entitled to protection under §200.16(c)." *Huang v. Ashcroft,* 390 F.3d 1118, 1120–23 (9th Cir. 2004) [rejecting respondent's habeas claim that he is not subject to Mar. 22, 1999 motion to reopen deadline because that pertains to withholding for CAT and not deferral].

(7) *Detention*—The granting of deferral will not necessarily result in release of a detained applicant. *See* 8 C.F.R. §§208.17(b)(1)(ii) & (c), 1208.17(b)(1)(ii) & (c). However, where DHS is not actively pursuing removal, it has authority to release a person with a final order who has been granted withholding or deferral of removal before the 90-day removal period has expired. Memo, Cooper, INS Gen. Counsel, HQCOU 50/1.1 (Apr. 21, 2000), *reprinted in* 77 No. 39 *Interpreter Releases* 1445, 1460 (Oct. 9, 2000).

(8) *Application of REAL ID*—For cases filed on or after May 11, 2005, the standards for corroboration of evidence for asylum and withholding do not necessarily apply to CAT claims, *see* INA §208(b)(1)(B)(ii) and §243(b)(1)(B), although the credibility standards may apply to all three forms of relief. *Compare* INA §208(b)(1)(B)(iii) and §241(b)(3)(C) *with* INA §240(c)(4)(C).

(9) *Termination of Deferral*—8 C.F.R. §§208.17(d), 1208.17(d). The regulations provide a more streamlined method of terminating deferral of removal than withholding or asylum. DHS need not file a motion to reopen to terminate, but may instead simply set the matter for an IJ hearing.

(10) *No CAT Claim in §235 Proceedings*—Unlike asylum an IJ may not hear a CAT claim for a person in a proceedings under INA §235(c). 8 C.F.R. §§208.18(d), 1208.18(d). For a detailed discussion of the IJ role in CAT claims *see* Memo [OPPM 99-5], Creppy, Chief IJ, EOIR (May 14, 1999), *reprinted in* 76 No. 24 *Interpreter Releases* 971, 986–98 (June 28, 1999)

8.f. *Role of the Department of State*—The IJ must forward a copy of the asylum application to the DOS Office of Asylum Affairs in the Bureau of Democracy, Human Rights and Labor, and to calendar the hearing. 8 C.F.R. §§1240.11(c)(2), 1240.49(c)(3) [pre–Apr. 1, 1997]; *Matter of Saban*, 18 I&N Dec. 70 (BIA 1981). The IJ in his discretion may ask for a new DOS opinion if s/he believes that conditions have substantially changed since the original opinion was obtained. *Doe v. INS*, 867 F.2d 285 (6th Cir. 1989) [IJ abused his discretion when he failed to request second opinion]. Any removal hearing presumably would be held in abeyance until the opinion is received. If the court has not previously determined deportability, it will do so first at the resumed hearing. If deportability is established, the court will then consider the asylum or withholding application and will permit the applicant to present documentary, expert and other testimonial evidence. If the IJ determines that the mandatory grounds for denial of asylum/withholding exist, no further hearing is necessary. 8 C.F.R. §§1240.11(c) (3), 1240.49(c)(4) [pre–Apr. 1, 1997]. In CAT claims, DOS may obtain diplomatic assurances that the country will not torture the applicant upon return. If the AG, Deputy AG, or INS Comm. concur, the applications "shall not be considered further by an immigration judge, the Board of Immigration Appeals, or an asylum officer." 8 C.F.R. §§208.18(c), 1208.18(c).

8.g. *Hearings and Procedural Issues on Asylum and Other Claims*— IJ procedures are generally set forth in Memo [Revised OPPM 00-01], Creppy, Chief IJ, EOIR (Aug. 4, 2000), *published on* AILA InfoNet at 00080490. For detailed local operating procedures in immigration court, *see www.usdoj.gov/eoir/efoia/ocij/locopproc.htm.*

(1) *Hearing*—An asylum/withholding hearing is open to the public unless the applicant requests otherwise. 8 C.F.R. §§1240.11(c)(3)(i), 1240.49(c)(4)(i) [pre–Apr. 1, 1997]. An IJ must have an initial hearing on an asylum application within 45 days and complete the hearing within 180 days absent exceptional circumstances. An IJ cannot enter an order granting withholding of removal without first entering a removal order where asylum has not been granted. *Matter of I-S- & C-S-*, 24 I&N Dec. 432 (BIA 2008). [in the absence of a grant of asylum, withholding of removal may not be granted, without first entering a removal order].

(2) *Employment Authorization*—For a discussion of work authorization and the EAD clock, *see in this chapter* ¶ XII.A.9 (p.521), *infra.*

(3) *Failure to Appear*—If the applicant fails to appear for the hearing, the application "shall be denied" unless he did not receive notice, was in federal or state custody or his failure to appear was due to exceptional circumstances as defined under INA §240(e)(1). 8 C.F.R. §§208.2(c)(3)(ii), 1208.2(c)(3)(ii). Only one motion to reopen may be filed within 90 days if failure to appear is based on exceptional circumstances. The filing of the motion does not stay deportation unless the IJ separately grants a stay. 8 C.F.R. §§208.2(c)(3)(iii), 1208.2(c)(3)(iii). However, if the motion to reopen is to rescind an *in absentia* order and if it is filed within the appropriate time period, the applicant receives an automatic stay. INA §240(b)(5), 8 U.S.C. §1229a(b)(5).

(4) *Evidence and Testimony*—The IJ must place an asylum applicant under oath and testimony must be taken. 8 C.F.R. §§1240.11(c)(3)(iii), 1240.49(c)(3)(iii) [pre–Apr. 1, 1997]; *Matter of Fefe*, 20 I&N Dec. 116 (BIA 1989) [cannot rely exclusively on I-589]. However, at least one circuit has concluded that this does not mean that the applicant must do more than swear to the truthfulness of the application. *Grava v. INS,* 205 F.3d 1177, 1180–81 (9th Cir. 2000) [BIA not warranted in requiring stipulation by parties that oral testimony would be the same as written application before accepting written application where applicant's only testimony was to acknowledge under oath that application was valid]. The IJ may hear evidence on asylum and withholding at one hearing; however, in adjudicating the applications, the court's findings should be clearly delineated between the standard of proof for withholding under *INS v. Stevic*, 467 U.S. 407 (1984), and the standard of proof for asylum under *INS v. Cardoza-Fonseca*, 480 U.S. 421 (1987). *Matter of Mogharrabi*, 19 I&N Dec. 439, 446 (BIA 1987). The IJ should adjudicate asylum applications first because of the lower standard of proof. *Id.*

(5) *Frivolous Application*—If the applicant is deemed to have knowingly made a frivolous application after being notified of the consequences, s/he "shall be permanently ineligible for any benefits under this Act." INA §208(d)(5), (6), 8 U.S.C. §1158(d)(5), (6). *Ignatova v. Gonzales,* 430 F.3d 1209, 1214–15 (8th Cir. 2005) [*post*-REAL ID, upholding frivolous finding based on fraudulent documents].

(6) *Mandatory Denial Asylum/Withholding*—The grounds for mandatory denial of asylum apply to renewed applications before the IJ, even if the original application was filed with the AO or DD prior to Oct. 1, 1990. *Matter of B-*, 20 I&N Dec. 427 (BIA 1991); *Silwany-Rodriguez v. INS*, 975 F.2d 1157 (5th Cir. 1992); *Cepero v. BIA*, 882 F.Supp. 1575, 1580–81 (D. Kan. 1995). The IJ may hold an evidentiary hearing limited to issues regarding a mandatory ground for denial of asylum/withholding. 8 C.F.R. §1240.11(c)(3). If the IJ determines that a mandatory ground for denial of asylum/withholding exists, no further hearing is necessary. 8 C.F.R. §§1240.11(c) (3), 1240.49(c)(4) [pre–Apr. 1, 1997].

(7) *Discretionary Denial of Asylum/Withholding Grant*—Where the IJ denies asylum on discretionary grounds, but grants withholding, the IJ should reconsider the asylum denial if a child and/or a spouse is involved. 8 C.F.R. §§208.16(e), 1208.16(e). *Huang v. INS,* 436 F.3d 89, 96–102 (2d Cir. 2006) [IJ acted contrary to law under INA §242(b)(4)(D) in denying asylum as a matter of discretion where he failed to examine the totality of the circumstances and focused solely on the embellishment of peripheral testimony and the applicant's payment to a smuggler].

(8) *Asylum Grant*—The IJ may grant asylum for an indefinite period. 8 C.F.R. §§208.14(e), 1208.14(e), subject to termination under §§208.24, 1208.24.

8.h. *Equal Treatment in Adjudication of Asylum Claims*—Courts have expressed concern about the inconsistent treatment of asylum applicants. *Zhang v. Gonzales,* 452 F.3d 167, 172–74 (2d Cir. 2006) [where husband was granted asylum for fear of future sterilization but wife denied on the same grounds, the court reversed noting that "[a] rational system of law would seem to require consistent treatment of such identical claims or, at the very least, an explanation from the BIA for their seemingly inconsistent treatment"]; *Njuguna v. Ashcroft,* 374 F.3d 765, 771 n.4 (9th Cir. 2004) [finding it "disturbing" that three Kenyans were granted asylum but a fourth was not involving the same incident because "it is a foundation of the rule of law that similarly situated individuals be treated similarly"]; *Wang v. Ashcroft,* 341 F.3d 1015, 1019 n.2 (9th Cir. 2003) [husband granted asylum based on his wife being subject to coercive population control, but wife denied asylum].

9. *Special Limited Hearings On Asylum and Withholding*—Stowaways, crewmen, visa waiver applicants, visa waiver overstays, S visa applicants, persons ordered removed under INA §§235(c), 238(b), or 241(a)(5) are given special limited IJ hearings if the AO denies or does not decide their asylum claims. 8 C.F.R. §§208.2(c)(1), (2), 1208.2(c)(1), (2). Persons who are stowaways, crewmen, visa waiver applicants, visa waiver overstays, and S visa applicants, as well as a person ordered removed under INA §235(c) may be referred to an IJ solely to conduct a hearing on asylum and withholding. This hearing may not be used, for example, to challenge removability or seek other waivers. 8 C.F.R. §§208.2(c)(3)(i), 1208.2(c)(3)(i). Similarly, an AO may refer a person to an IJ who is subject to reinstatement of removal under INA §241(a)(5) or expedited removal under INA §238, but the hearing may only address withholding of removal or deferral. In either case, the AO initiates the removal process by issuing an I-863 referring the matter to the IJ. The IJ's decision in this asylum only proceeding may be appealed to the BIA. The circuit courts of appeal have jurisdiction under INA §242(a)(1) to review the IJ/BIA decision on asylum/withholding even if there is no jurisdiction to review the order of removal. *Kanacevic v. INS,* 448 F.3d 129, 133–36 (2d Cir. 2006) [finding jurisdiction to review asylum only hearing for VWP applicant]; *Nreka v. U.S. Att'y Gen.,* 408 F.3d 1361, 1366–68 (11th Cir. 2005) [same].

10. *Children Applying for Asylum*—A child has an independent right to seek asylum in the U.S. Memo, Guidelines for Children's Asylum Claims, Weiss, Acting Director, Office of International Affairs (120/11.26) (Dec. 10, 1998), *reprinted in* 76 No. 1 *Interpreter Releases* 1, 5–34 (Jan. 4, 1999). *See also* 75 No. 21 *Interpreter Releases* 757 (June 1, 1998); Memo [OPPM 07-01], Neal, Chief IJ, EOIR, "Guidelines for Immigration Court Cases Involving Unaccompanied Alien Children," (May 22, 2007), *published on* AILA InfoNet at Doc. No. 07052360; UNHCR, *Guidelines*

on Policies and Procedures in dealing with Unaccompanied Minors Seeking Asylum (Feb. 1997). Under the *Guidelines*, testimony of a child under 16 should be given a liberal "benefit of the doubt" treatment. *Hernandez-Ortiz v. Gonzales,* 496 F.3d 1042 (9th Cir. 2007) [reversed IJ for not thoroughly considering the impact of events on the petitioner when he was a small child as a result of the actions of the Guatemalan army, and the court affirmed the legal rule that "injuries to a family must be considered in an asylum case where the events that form the basis of the past persecution claim were perceived when the petitioner was a child"]; *Liu v. Ashcroft,* 380 F.3d 307, 314 (7th Cir. 2004) [citing Guidelines and recognizing that the harm a child fears may be relatively less than an adult and still qualify for asylum, but finding that a 16-year-old might only get a "slight calibration," which in this case was insufficient to alter the outcome]; *Abay v. Ashcroft,* 368 F.3d 634, 639–40 (6th Cir. 2004) [reversing IJ's denial of asylum to 9-year-old child facing FGM]; *Jorge-Tzoc v. Gonzales,* 435 F.3d 146 (2d Cir. 2006) [failure to consider effect of respondent's status as a small child when the events occurred required reversal and remand to determine past persecution]; *Matter of Chen*, 20 I&N Dec. 16 (BIA 1989). *But see Jiang v. Gonzales,* 500 F.3d 137 (2d Cir. 2007) [following *Shi Liang Lin* the court held that a claim by a child of persecution based *solely* on forced abortion of his mother is insufficient and rejected his economic past persecution claim because unlike in *Jorge-Tzoc* did not share the characteristic that motivated the persecution and therefore there was no nexus to a protected ground]; *Gonzalez v. Reno,* 212 F.3d 1338 (11th Cir. 2000) [INS's rejection of unadmitted 6-year-old's application for asylum did not violate 8 U.S.C. §1158]. There are many successful theories regarding asylum for children. *See* Nugent and Schulman, *Giving Voice to the Vulnerable: On Representing Detained Immigrant and Refugee Children,* 78 No. 39 *Interpreter Releases* 1569–91 (Oct. 8, 2001).

The one-year filing deadline for asylum does not apply to minors. 8 C.F.R. §§ 208.4(a)(5)(ii), 1208.4(a)(5)(ii). *Matter of Y-C-,* 23 I&N Dec. 286 (BIA 2002) [extraordinary circumstances existed where minor was in INS custody for more than one year after his arrival and, after release to his uncle's custody, sought to file an application 5½ months later while still a minor]. *See also Al-Mousa v. Mukasey,* 518 F.3d 738 (9th Cir. 2008) [remanding case to BIA to determine the definition of minor for purposes exempting the applicant from the one-year filing deadline where he was under 21 but over 18].

11. *Parents Cannot Apply Derivatively Through Their Child*—Although children may individually apply or derivatively apply through their parents, a child's parents cannot derivatively apply through their child. *Matter of A-K-,* 24 I&N Dec. 275 (BIA 2007) [parent cannot establish ground for asylum solely on fear of FGM to child]; *Niang v. Gonzales,* 492 F.3d 505, 510–14 (4th Cir. 2007) [affirmed asylum denial where mother asserted derivative claim because USC daughter would be subject to FGM if she accompanied her to Senegal and because mother would suffer psychological harm if daughter accompanies her]; *Olowo v. Ashcroft,* 368 F.3d 692, 700–04 (7th Cir. 2004) [affirming IJ denial of asylum to mother of LPR children where mother claimed children, who were not required to leave U.S., would be subject to FGM if they returned to Nigeria]; *Oforji v. Ashcroft,* 354 F.3d 609, 614–18 (7th Cir. 2003) [same under CAT and distinguishing *Nwaokolo*]. However, where a child is with his or her parents and the child is the direct victim, it would be devastating to require parents to make the choice of abandoning their child or taking the child back to the country of persecution. *Abay v. Ashcroft,* 368 F.3d 634, 640–42 (6th Cir. 2004) [mother's fear that 9-year old daughter would be subject to FGM qualifies for asylum]; *Nwaokolo v. INS,* 314 F.3d 303, 307–11 (7th Cir. 2002) [stay granted on BIA denial of motion to reopen under CAT where *USC daughter* might suffer FGM]; *see also Hassan v. Gonzales,* 484 F.3d 513, 519 (8th Cir. 2007) [acknowledging that mother may have asylum claim for fear of FGM against children].

12. *Derivative Benefits Under Withholding*—Some circuit courts have now held that withholding, unlike asylum, does not grant derivative benefits to family members so that a grant of withholding to a husband or parent does not give derivative benefits to the spouse or child. *Arif v. Mukasey,* 509 F.3d 677, 680–82 (5th Cir. 2007) [wife of withholding applicant does not obtain a derivative status and 8 C.F.R. §1208.16(e) supports that reading of the statute]; *Delgado v. U.S. Att'y Gen.,* 487 F.3d 855, 862 (11th Cir. 2007) [where Venezuelan father and son were granted withholding, mother could not obtain withholding because the statute does not provide for derivative benefits as does asylum].

XII. REPRESENTING THE ASYLUM, CAT, AND §241(b)(3) APPLICANT

A. *Pre-Hearing and Pre-Merits Representation*

1. *Generally*—Several major problems confronting counsel representing an applicant for asylum or withholding prior to a hearing are: (1) access to the applicant in detention; (2) the release of the applicant from detention; (3) if released, the applicant's right to work pending a determination of his claim; and (4) the right to travel.

2. *Access to the Client*—In 1981 the INS dramatically altered its policy with respect to the release of inadmissible aliens seeking asylum in the U.S. *See Louis v. Nelson*, 544 F.Supp. 973, 979–81 (S.D. Fla. 1982), *aff'd on other grounds*, 472 U.S. 846 (1985). Since 1981, inadmissible aliens in many instances have been detained until a final determination is made in their cases. 8 C.F.R. §§235.3, 1235.3. This change, in some cases, has also been accompanied by the transfer of inadmissible aliens from one detention center to another, often thousands of miles apart. *See, e.g., Ledesma-Valdes v. Sava*, 604 F.Supp. 675 (S.D.N.Y. 1985); *Louis v. Meissner*, 530 F.Supp. 924 (S.D. Fla. 1981); *Matter of Alphonse*, 18 I&N Dec. 178 (BIA 1981). At the same time, DHS has systematically increased the minimum bond for deportable aliens, and the BIA has sustained the increased bonds, thus ensuring the long-term detention of deportable aliens. Moreover, post-IIRIRA, detention is more likely the norm for asylum seekers arrested prior to proceedings. Persons stopped at the border who are subject to expedited removal and credible fear determinations are usually detained until a determination is made. AG Ashcroft announced that all Haitians and others arriving by sea, except Cubans, who are subject to expedited removal will be detained, with minor humanitarian exceptions, throughout the entire credible fear *and* asylum process. Others who enter the country EWI may be detained because they were not lawfully admitted. Still others who have been convicted of certain crimes will be detained under the mandatory detention provisions of INA §236. Finally, DHS regulations preclude IJ's from considering bond if the person is an arriving alien. 8 C.F.R. §§236.1(c)(11), 1003.19(h)(2)(i)(B), 1236.1(c)(11). UNHCR has raised serious concerns regarding the detention policies of asylum seekers in the U.S. Letter, Guebre-Christos, Regional Representative UNHCR (Apr. 15, 2002), *reprinted in* 79 No. 18 *Interpreter Releases* 620, 630–36 (Apr. 29, 2002).

3. *Right to Counsel*—Under INA §292, 5 U.S.C. §555(b), and 8 C.F.R. §§1240.3, 292, an alien has the right to be represented by counsel. *Partible v. INS*, 600 F.2d 1094 (5th Cir. 1979); *Cheung v. INS*, 418 F.2d 460 (D.C. Cir. 1969); *Rose v. Woolwine*, 344 F.2d 993 (4th Cir. 1965). This right has been characterized as "fundamental" and a "due process" right in the asylum context. *Orantes-Hernandez v. Thornburgh*, 919 F.2d 549, 554 (9th Cir. 1990). Similarly, counsel has a First Amendment right to speak with his client, at least when the attorney is not receiving any remuneration for his services. *Jean v. Nelson*, 727 F.2d 957, 983–84 (11th Cir. 1984) (*en banc*), *aff'd on other grounds*, 472 U.S. 846 (1985); *Haitian Centers Council, Inc. v. Sale*, 823 F.Supp. 1028, 1040–43 (E.D.N.Y. 1993); *Orantes-Hernandez v. Meese*, 685 F.Supp. 1488, 1511 (C.D. Cal. 1988), *aff'd*, 919 F.2d 549 (9th Cir. 1990). *But see Cuban American Bar Ass'n, Inc. v. Christopher*, 43 F.3d 1412, 1429–30 (11th Cir. 1995) [First Amendment access does not extend to persons in INS custody held outside the physical territory of the U.S.]; *Haitian Refugee Center, Inc. v. Baker*, 953 F.2d 1498, 1511–15 (11th Cir.) [same]. In addition to the right of access to counsel, the detained alien has a right to access legal materials. *Perez-Funez v. District Director*, 619 F.Supp. 656 (C.D. Cal. 1985) [including updated lists of free legal services]; *Orantes-Hernandez v. Smith*, 541 F.Supp. 351 (C.D. Cal. 1982) [INS cannot ban written materials, particularly those regarding legal rights of aliens]. To obtain access to a detained client, counsel must file Form G-28 (Notice of Appearance as Counsel) with ICE. 8 C.F.R. §§292.4(a), 1292.4(a). If the applicant does not have counsel, he is to be informed of the right to counsel after his arrest when a decision is made to initiate removal proceedings. 8 C.F.R. §287.3. The applicant must also be informed at that time, and again before the IJ, of the availability of free legal services. 8 C.F.R. §§287.3, 236.2(a), 1240.10(a)(2); *Molaire v. Smith*, 743 F.Supp. 839 (S.D. Fla. 1990). The IJ must ascertain on the record whether counsel is desired. 8 C.F.R. §1240.10(a)(1); *Matter of Michel*, 21 I&N Dec. 1101 (BIA 1998), and advise the applicant of the consequences of filing a frivolous application. INA §208(d)(4), 8 U.S.C. §1158(d)(4). Once the applicant obtains counsel, the IJ may only communicate with counsel concerning the applicant's immigration proceedings. 8 C.F.R. §292.5(a). But there may not be a constitutional right to require the government to inform a detained asylum

seeker of offers of assistance. *Ukrainian-American Bar Ass'n v. Baker*, 893 F.2d 1374, 1380–82 (D.C. Cir. 1990) [INS cannot be ordered to provide Eastern Block and Soviet asylum seekers information regarding Bar Ass'n offer of assistance]. The right to counsel extends to asylum seekers deemed inadmissible. *Jean v. Nelson*, 727 F.2d at 983–84. However, at least one circuit has recognized that there is no due process violation arising out of ineffective assistance of counsel in an asylum claim. *Obleshchenko v. Ashcroft,* 392 F.3d 970, 971–72 (8th Cir. 2004) [no due process right regarding IAC in asylum claim because there is no liberty or property interest where relief is subject to the unfettered discretion of a governmental authority].

4. *Transfer of Detainee*—The transfer of the applicant from one detention center to another can result in a denial of access to counsel, particularly where the alien was previously represented. *Orantes-Hernandez v. Meese*, 685 F.Supp. 1488 (C.D. Cal. 1988), *aff'd*, 919 F.2d 549, 566 (9th Cir. 1990) [transfer of represented detainee interferes with the attorney-client relationship; unrepresented detainees cannot be transferred for seven days to give them an opportunity to obtain counsel]; *Louis v. Meissner*, 530 F.Supp. 924 (S.D. Fla. 1981). *But see Committee of Central American Refugees v. INS*, 795 F.2d 1434 (9th Cir. 1986); *Ledesma-Valdes v. Sava*, 604 F.Supp. 675 (S.D.N.Y. 1985).

5. *Duty to Asylum Seekers in Custody*—DHS recognizes a special duty toward aliens in custody seeking asylum or withholding. 8 C.F.R. §§208.5, 1208.5. Where a person in custody requests asylum, or withholding, or expresses fear of persecution or harm upon return to his country, DHS shall make the appropriate application forms available and shall provide a list of persons or private agencies that can Asst. 8 C.F.R. §§208.5(a), 1208.5(a). Where possible, expedited consideration shall be given to applications of detained aliens. 8 C.F.R. §§208.5(a), 1208.5(a).

6. *Change of Venue*—The IJ has jurisdiction to change the venue of cases involving inadmissibility, 8 C.F.R. §1003.20(b); *Matter of Dobere*, 20 I&N Dec. 188 (BIA 1990) [overruling *Matter of Alphonse*, 18 I&N Dec. 178 (BIA 1981)], and in deportation proceedings. *Matter of Rahman*, 20 I&N Dec. 480 (BIA 1992) [factors for IJ to consider in changing venue]; *Matter of Wadas*, 17 I&N Dec. 346 (BIA 1980) [exclusion]; *Baires v. INS*, 856 F.2d 89 (9th Cir. 1988) [deportation]; *Chlomos v. DOJ and INS*, 516 F.2d 310 (3d Cir. 1975); *Matter of Victorino*, 18 I&N Dec. 259 (BIA 1982); *Campos v. Nail*, 43 F.3d 1285 (9th Cir. 1994) [class-wide injunctive relief where IJ as a matter of personal policy routinely denied change of venue to Guatemalans and Salvadorans seeking asylum and entered *in absentia* orders]. *But see Maldonado-Perez v. INS*, 865 F.2d 328 (D.C. Cir. 1989).

7. *Right to Apply for Asylum*—Every alien has a protected interest, whether statutory or constitutional, to apply for asylum or withholding. *Maldonado-Perez v. INS*, 865 F.2d 328, 332 (D.C. Cir. 1989); *Jean v. Nelson*, 727 F.2d 957, 976, 981–83 (11th Cir. 1984) (en banc); *Yiu Sing Chun v. Sava*, 708 F.2d 869, 877 (2d Cir. 1983) ["[r]efugee who has a well founded fear of persecution in his homeland has a protectable interest recognized by both treaty and statute"]; *Haitian Refugee Center v. Smith*, 676 F.2d 1023, 1038 (5th Cir. 1982) ["[i]n this case we conclude that Congress and the Executive have created, at a minimum, a constitutionally protected right to petition our government for political asylum"]. *See* INA §208, 8 U.S.C. §1158; 8 C.F.R. §§1240.11(c)(1), 1240.33(a), 1240.49(c)(2). *But see Gonzalez v. Reno,* 212 F.3d 1338 (11th Cir. 2000) [upholding rejection by INS of unadmitted 6-year-old's application for asylum]. The protected interest in applying for relief is stronger with respect to withholding, which is mandatory, than asylum, which is discretionary. *Jean v. Nelson, supra,* at 981 n.33. However, Congress has restricted that right by barring applications for asylum that are filed more than one year after arrival in the U.S., unless there are changed or extraordinary circumstances. Absent such circumstances, a person is also barred if his or her asylum application was previously denied. INA §208(a)(2)(B), (C).

7.a. *Right to Notice*—At least some courts have found that INS does not have to provide *per se* notice of the right to apply for asylum, even where the alien is detained. *Jean v. Nelson, supra* at 981–83. *See also Beer v. INS*, 68 F.3d 216 (8th Cir. 1995) [where respondent did not indicate fear of return, IJ did not have notice obligation]; *Ramirez-Osorio v. INS*, 745 F.2d 937 (5th Cir. 1984). Other courts, however, have recognized the right to notice. *See, e.g., Orantes-Hernandez v. Smith*, 541 F.Supp. 351, 374–78 (C.D. Cal. 1982) and 685 F.Supp. 1488 (C.D. Cal. 1988), *aff'd*, 919 F.2d 549, 556–57 (9th Cir. 1990) [failure to advise Salvadorans of right to apply for asylum and obtaining coerced VD agreements invalidates waiver under due process clause of the Fifth Amendment]. The Fifth and Eleventh Circuits have recognized the right to notice under certain circumstances. *Villegas v. INS*, 745 F.2d 950 (5th Cir. 1984) [notice required when alien notified of right to counsel and expressed fear of return]; *Jean v. Nelson, supra* at 983 n.35 ["if INS officials were refusing to inform aliens of their right to seek asylum even if they did indicate that they feared persecution if returned to their home countries, our conclusion [that no notice is required] would be different"]. Regulations now require that notice be given where a person expresses fear of returning to his or her home country. 8 C.F.R. §§208.5, 235.3(b)(4), 1240.11(c)(1), 1208.5, 1235.3(b)(4). The right to notice of withholding exists by regulation. 8 C.F.R. §1240.11(a)(2). *But see Ramirez-Gonzalez v. INS*, 695 F.2d 1208 (9th Cir. 1983), and *Minwalla v. INS*, 706 F.2d 831 (8th Cir. 1983), adopting the "apparent eligibility" test that notice need not be given if the alien designates the country of deportation and the claim for withholding is not apparent.

7.b. *No Right to Asylum*—Although there is a right to apply for asylum, there is no right to asylum itself. *Mudric v. Att'y Gen. of the U.S.*, 469 F.3d 94, 98–99 (3d Cir. 2006) [delay in adjudicating asylum and adjustment applications is not a violation of due process because there is no constitutional right to asylum and no property interest invoked in failing to timely decide a discretionary benefit]; *Haitian Refugee Center v. Smith, supra* at 1039. The BIA has also suggested that there is no right to government assistance in completing an application for asylum notwithstanding a serious language barrier. *Matter of C-*, 20 I&N Dec. 529, 531 (BIA 1992) [court interpreter is not required to assist person in filling out asylum application].

8. *Right to Release from Detention*—A removable alien who is detained has the right to a bond hearing unless he is being removed for security reasons, is subject to mandatory detention because of the commission of certain crimes, or is an arriving alien, which may include returning LPRs. INA §§101(a)(13), 236, 8 C.F.R. §§236.1(c)(5), (d), 1236.1(c)(5), (d). The alien should not be detained or required to post bond unless there is a finding that he is a threat to national security or is a poor bail risk. *U.S. ex rel. Barbour v. Dist. Dir., INS*, 491 F.2d 573 (5th Cir. 1974); *Matter of Daryoush*, 18 I&N Dec. 352 n.3 (BIA 1982); *Matter of Patel*, 15 I&N Dec. 666 (BIA 1976). A person with a criminal conviction is not eligible for release except under limited circumstances. INA §236(c)(1), 8 C.F.R. §§236.1(c), 1236.1(c). An asylum or withholding applicant is also detained if s/he falls within the expedited removal provisions and cannot get bond until credible fear is established and are detained pending IJ's review. 8 C.F.R. §§208.30(f), 1208.30(f). ICE has established criteria for granting parole to a person who has been determined to have a credible fear of persecution. *See* ICE Directive 7-1.0, Myers, Asst. Secy. (Nov. 6, 2007), *published on* AILA InfoNet at Doc. No. 07111264. *See also* Ch. 3, ¶ IV.J.11 (p.141), *supra.* If a person claims fear of persecution at a land border port of entry and the fear is unrelated to Canada or Mexico, the person may be required to wait in Canada or Mexico. If the fear of persecution is related to Canada or Mexico, the person must be detained pending the IJ's review. Memo, Meissner, Comm., 96 Act. 049, HQ CO-90/20, 50/1, 50/10 (July 14, 1997), *published on* AILA InfoNet at Doc. No. 97071490. Similarly, if a person is not deemed to have been lawfully admitted, s/he is denied bond. DOJ regulations also appear to preclude all persons seeking admission from obtaining bond before an IJ. 8 C.F.R. §§236.1(c)(5), 1236.1(c)(5). For a discussion on parole for inadmissible persons, *see* Ch. 3, section IV.H (p.134), *supra.* Under the VWP, an applicant for asylum/withholding is entitled to bond if DHS issues an NTA. *Matter of Gallardo,* 21 I&N Dec. 210 (BIA 1996). DHS has sought to avoid the provision of a bond hearing by issuing an I-863 to the alien rather than an NTA (I-862).

8.a. *Mandatory Detention*—The constitutionality of mandatory detention has been upheld. *Demore v. Kim,* 538 U.S. 510 (2003). *But see Tijani v. Willis,* 430 F.3d 1241 (9th Cir. 2005) [ordering bond hearing for LPR who has been imprisoned for two years and eight months, finding that "it is constitutionally doubtful that Congress may authorize imprisonment of this duration for lawfully admitted resident aliens who are subject to removal"]; *Ly v. Hansen,* 351 F.3d 263 (6th Cir. 2003) [post-*Demore* it is a violation of substantive due process to detain a person subject to deportation for 1 ½ years, particularly when it is unlikely he can be physically removed]; *Judulang v. Chertoff,* 535 F.Supp.2d 1129, 1132–33 (S.D. Cal. 2008) [detention lasting over 2½ years is unreasonable; district court ordered bond hearing before IJ over DHS objection that IJ lost jurisdiction over bond matters under 8 C.F.R. §1003.19(a), when administrative order became final, and that his detention became voluntary when he chose to petition to the circuit court]; *Madrane v. Hogan,* 520 F.Supp.2d 654 (M.D. Pa. 2007) [reading *Demore* narrowly and ordering non-LPR petitioner's release after more than three years in custody fighting his removal to Morocco]; *Lawson v. Gerlinski,* 332 F.Supp.2d 735, 744–46 (M.D. Pa. 2004) [long term LPR who obtained stay of removal and remained in detention for 18 months was granted release pending evidentiary hearing on underlying substantive due process claim to remain in U.S.]. For a detailed discussion of bond for deportable persons subject to removal, *see* Ch. 3, sections X.M (p.293) and X.Q (p.302), *supra.*

8.b. *Release Pending Appeal*—Persons granted asylum, withholding or CAT by the IJ may be released pending DHS appeal. Although under DHS regulations, persons *granted* deferral of removal under CAT may remain in detention, 8 C.F.R. §§208.17(b)(1)(ii), 1208.17(b)(ii), DHS has stated, "[i]n general, it is ICE policy to favor release of aliens who have been granted protection relief by an [IJ], absent exceptional concerns such as national security issues or danger to the community and absent any requirement under law to detain....Arriving aliens should [also] be considered for parole." Memo, Garcia, Asst. Sec. DHS (Feb. 9, 2004), *published on* AILA InfoNet at Doc. No. 04022462.

8.c. DHS also has authority to release a person for whom it is not actively seeking removal, who has a final order of removal and who has been granted withholding or deferral of removal before the 90-day removal period has expired. Memo, Cooper, INS General Counsel, HQCOU 50/1.1 (Apr. 21, 2000), *reprinted in* 77 No. 39 *Interpreter Releases* 1445, 1460 (Oct. 9, 2000).

9. *The Right to Work*—Pursuant to the U.S. Enhanced Border Security and Visa Entry Reform Act, PL 107-173, 116 Stat. 543 (May 14, 2002) §309, an alien *granted* asylum or withholding is automatically granted employment authorization. *See also* INA §208(c)(1)(B) and 8 C.F.R. §§208.7, 274a.12(a)(5), (10), 1208.7, 1274a.12(a)(5), (10). Similarly, where an asylum applicant is recommended for a grant and has not yet received it, s/he can obtain employment authorization. DHS has issued a notice stating that the I-94 may serve as evidence of employment authorization. 67 Fed. Reg. 64911–12 (Oct. 22, 2002). Like LPRs, asylees and refugees are authorized to work incident to their status and need not apply for an EAD to work. Moreover, the dates on an EAD are not relevant to the person's continuing authorization to work incident to their status. Memo, Yates, Acting Assoc. Director, Operations USCIS, HQADJ 70/21.1.13 (Mar. 10, 2003), *published on* AILA InfoNet at Doc. No. 03040140; Legal Memo, Carpenter, Deputy GC, HQCOU 90/15 (June 17, 2002), *reprinted in* 80 No. 14 *Interpreter Releases* 511–14, 523–31 (Apr. 7, 2003). Letter, Friedman, Special Policy Counsel, Civil Rights Division, DOJ (Oct. 18, 2002), *reprinted in* 79 No. 43 *Interpreter Releases* 1640–41, 1653–54 (Nov. 4, 2002). However, under INA §208(d)(2), 8 U.S.C. §1158(d)(2), "an applicant for asylum is not entitled to employment authorization except as may be provided by regulation in the discretion of the Attorney General."

9.a. *The EAD Clock*—For asylum applications filed after Jan. 4, 1995, employment authorization will not be granted at the time of filing. 8 C.F.R. §§208.7(a)(1), 274a.12(c)(8), 274a.13(a), 1208.7(a)(1), 1274a.12(c)(8), 1274a.13(a). An applicant for asylum may not *receive* work authorization for 180 days after the submission of an asylum application. INA §208(d)(2). An EAD application may not be filed prior to 150 days after the date on which a complete asylum application, as defined in 8 C.F.R. §§208.3(c)(3), 1208.3(c)(3), has been received by DHS or the IJ under 8 C.F.R. §208.4. 8 C.F.R. §§208.7(a)(1), 274a.12(c)(8), 1208.7(a)(1), 1274a.12(c)(8). After 150 days, if no decision on the asylum application is made, the applicant may apply for an EAD on Form I-765 and DHS shall have 30 days to either grant or deny it. If the asylum application is denied within the 150 days, the person is not eligible for work authorization. 8 C.F.R. §§208.7(a)(1), 1208.7(a)(1). If the asylum application is not adjudicated within the 30 days that the EAD application is pending, the applicant is eligible for an interim EAD. If asylum is denied within the 30 days, the EAD request shall be denied. Where the AO refers the case to the IJ, the 150-day period includes the referral and the final decision of the IJ. It is only when the IJ denies asylum before 180 days have lapsed that a person will be completely denied work authorization. Otherwise s/he will be eligible for an interim EAD, 8 C.F.R. §§208.7(a)(1), 1208.7(a)(1), which will continue for the period of time necessary to decide the asylum application and "for completion of any administrative or judicial review." 8 C.F.R. §§208.7(b), 1208.7(b). The applicant must provide proof of appeal. 8 C.F.R. §§208.7(c), 1208.7(c).

9.b. *Tolling of the EAD Clock*—If an asylum application is returned as incomplete, the 150 days does not start to run until a complete application is resubmitted. 8 C.F.R. §§208.7(a)(2), 1208.7(a)(2). Continuances at the request of the applicant also stop the EAD clock. *See* Memo, [OPPM 05-07], Creppy, Chief IJ, "Definitions and Use of Adjournment, Call-Up and Case Identification Codes" (June 16, 2005), *published on* AILA InfoNet at Doc. No. 05070660, which sets forth the 27 codes that will stop the clock and the few that will let the clock continue to run. *See also* **Appendix D**, *infra* (180-Day Asylum Clock Matrix). Failure to appear for fingerprinting/biometrics will stop the "clock," if the failure was without good cause. Memo, Langlois, Chief, Asylum Division, USCIS HQRAIO 120/9.3a (Sept. 12, 2006), *published on* AILA InfoNet at Doc. No. 06091360.

9.c. *Aggravated Felons*—Persons convicted of an aggravated felony shall not be granted work authorization and shall have work authorization terminated if previously granted, when asylum or withholding is denied because of the conviction. 8 C.F.R. §§208.7(a)(1), 1208.7(a)(1).

9.d. *Failure to Appear*—An applicant who fails to appear without good cause for the AO interview or IJ hearing shall not be granted employment authorization. 8 C.F.R. §§208.7(a)(4), 1208.7(a)(4).

9.e. *Renewal/Termination of EAD*—Requests for renewals of work authorization should be filed 90 days before expiration. 8 C.F.R. §§208.7(d), 1208.7(d). However, if asylum is denied by an AO, employment authorization terminates on the date of the EAD or 60 days after the denial whichever is longer. 8 C.F.R. §§208.7(b)(1), 1208.7(b)(1). If asylum is denied by the IJ, BIA or federal court, work authorization terminates upon the expiration of the EAD, unless the applicant filed for administrative or judicial review. 8 C.F.R. §§208.7(b)(2), 1208.7(b)(2).

9.f. In NYC and LA, INS was enjoined from denying EADs to asylum applicants where they could not locate the I-589. *Merida-Turcios v. Reno*, No. CV 94-5220 (C.D. Cal. July 1, 1996) and *Najera-Boria v. McElroy*, 1995 WL 151775 (E.D.N.Y. June 14, 1996). *See* National Guidelines for Forms I-765 Filed at Service Centers, etc., *reprinted in* 74 No. 10 *Interpreter Releases*, 465, 479–82 (Mar. 17, 1997).

9.g. *Pre-Jan. 4, 1995 Applications*—For asylum applications filed before Jan. 4, 1995 the prior regulation applies. Under former 8 C.F.R. §§208.7(a), "the asylum officer to whom an initial application for employment authorization accompanying an application for asylum or withholding of deportation is referred *shall* authorize employment for a period not to exceed one year to aliens who are not in detention and whose applications for asylum or withholding of deportation the asylum officer determined are not frivolous." "Frivolous" was defined as "manifestly unfounded or abusive." *See also* former 8 C.F.R. §§274a.12(c)(8), 274a.13(a). The INS instructed its officers to apply the test broadly so that an application will not be deemed frivolous if there was at least one fact that supported the fear that was related to one of the five grounds for asylum and there was no clear mandatory bar. Memo, Inzunza, Deputy Comm., CO 208.8.5-P (June 2, 1992), *reprinted in* 69 No. 23 *Interpreter Releases* 744, 756–61 (June 22, 1992).

10. *The Right to Travel*—Regulations permit but restrict the right of an asylum/withholding *applicant* to travel. Although an applicant may receive advance parole permitting her to travel pursuant to 8 C.F.R. §§212.5(f), IFM at 16.3(a), her return to the country of claimed persecution will be deemed an abandonment of the application, unless the applicant can establish compelling reasons for having assumed the risk of persecution in returning. 8 C.F.R. §§208.8, 1208.8.

11. *Security Procedures in Asylum Applications*—Post–Apr. 1, 2005, all persons seeking asylum and various other forms of relief, except VD, must comply with security clearance procedures. 8 C.F.R. §1003.47. The applicant is required to forward a photocopy of the asylum application to the NSC, without supporting documentation, with the appropriate fees, an EOIR-28, and a copy of the instructions. The NSC inputs the data and notifies the applicant to appear at an ASC for biometrics. Subsequent to a grant of relief the respondent will be instructed to make an appointment (via INFOPASS) at the local USCIS office to initiate the process of obtaining ID documentation and employment authorization. Memo, Yates, Assoc. Dir. Operations, USCIS, "Executive Office for Immigration Review (EOIR) Processing," (Mar.31, 2005), *published on* AILA InfoNet at Doc. No. 05051164. Persons who filed prior to Apr. 1, 2005, will be required to appear at a local ASC

for biometrics. Failure to file necessary documentation and comply with the requirements to provide biometrics and other biographical information within the time allowed by the IJ's order constitutes "abandonment of the application and the immigration judge may enter an appropriate order dismissing the application unless the applicant demonstrates that such failure was the result of good cause." 8 C.F.R. §1003.47(c) & (d). The IJ's procedures are set forth in Memo [Interim OPPM 05-03], Creppy, Chief IJ, EOIR, (Mar. 28, 2005), *published on* AILA InfoNet at Doc. No. 05041565 [permitting the IJ to dictate a draft approval outside the presence of the parties if he is awaiting security checks but allowing him to make a final decision if he is denying the case]. An IJ may not grant an application for relief until DHS has completed the appropriate investigation and reported the results to the IJ. 8 C.F.R. §1003.47(g). The IJ has the discretion to conduct an additional hearing to consider new evidence if the security checks affect respondent's eligibility, but when there is no new information, the IJ may not use the security check procedure as an opportunity to relitigate the issues, and should simply enter an order granting the relief. *Matter of Alcantara-Perez,* 23 I&N Dec. 882 (BIA 2006). Although a person may not be granted asylum until her identity has been checked against all appropriate records or databases maintained by the AG and the Secy. of State, including AVLOS, to determine inadmissibility, deportability or ineligibility. INA §208(d)(5)(A)(i), 8 U.S.C. §1158(d)(5)(A)(i), this provision may not be used to alter the burden of proof and deny asylum by presuming the person is of unknown identity and requiring them to prove their identity. *Kalouma v. Gonzales,* 512 F.3d 1073 (9th Cir. 2008) [reversed IJ who relied on INA §208(d)(5)(A)(i) to deny asylum unless the "unknown" person before him proved his identity]. In the event the person is granted relief and permanent residency but the name checks subsequently reveal actionable information, "DHS may detain and initiate removal proceedings against the permanent resident." Memo, Aytes, Assoc. Dir. Domestic Operations, USCIS, HQ70/23 & 70/28.1 (Feb. 4, 2008), *published on* AILA InfoNet at Doc. No. 08020760. *See also* "Security Checks" in Ch. 3, ¶ X.S.7.1 (p.361), *supra.*

12. *Disclosure of Application to Third Parties*—DOJ regulations specifically preclude the disclosure of an application for asylum or withholding to third parties except as permitted by the DHS Sec. in his discretion or as narrowly prescribed in the regulations. 8 C.F.R. §§208.6, 1208.6. *See in this chapter* "Breach of Confidentiality of Asylum," ¶ III.A.3.p (p.444), *supra.*

B. *The Hearing Process*

1. *Generally*—In representing an asylum or withholding applicant before the immigration court, counsel must be apprised of the prehearing procedures, the rights of the applicant at trial, and the burden, standard and nature of proof needed to prove a claim. Asylum seekers have a fundamental right of access to the courts. *Orantes-Hernandez v. Meese*, 685 F.Supp. 1488, 1510 (C.D. Cal. 1988), *aff'd*, 919 F.2d 549 (9th Cir. 1990). They also have a right to competent interpretation, *Ememe v. Ashcroft,* 358 F.3d 446 (7th Cir. 2004) [remanding where IJ made adverse credibility findings based on statements at credible fear interview conducted in Italian and person's native language was Amharic]; *Matter of Tomas*, 19 I&N Dec. 464 (BIA 1987), although EOIR is not required to provide simultaneous interpretation. *El Rescate Legal Services, Inc. v. EOIR*, 959 F.2d 742 (9th Cir. 1992); *Matter of Exilus*, 18 I&N Dec. 276 (BIA 1982). "Justice requires that an applicant for asylum or withholding of deportation be afforded a meaningful opportunity to establish his or her claim." *Senathirajah v. INS,* 157 F.3d 210, 221 (3d Cir. 1998). An IJ cannot enter an order granting withholding of removal without first entering a removal order where asylum has not been granted. *Matter of I-S- & C-S-,* 24 I&N Dec. 432 (BIA 2008). [in the absence of a grant of asylum, withholding of removal may not be granted, without first entering a removal order].

2. *Proving the Asylum, Withholding, or CAT Claim*

   2.a. *Burden of Proof*—The ultimate burden of proof is placed upon the applicant for asylum, withholding, or CAT relief. 8 C.F.R. §§208.13(a), 208.16(b), 208.16(c) 1208.13(a), 1208.16(b), 1208.16(c), 1240.11(c)(3)(iii), 1240.33(c)(3), 1240.49(c)(4)(iii). *See e.g., Matter of J-F-F-,* 23 I&N Dec. 912 (AG 2006) [reversing the IJ/BIA grant of CAT relief to a *pro se* respondent with a severe mental disorder from the Dominican Republic, where the respondent failed to meet his burden of proof because the IJ speculated what would happen to the respondent and "flipped the burden [of proof] on its head" by finding facts in the absence of evidence]. However, there are shifting burdens in the process. Where the applicant establishes past persecution, the applicant is presumed to have a well-founded fear of future persecution and the burden shifts to DHS to establish by a preponderance of the evidence a fundamental change in circumstances (usually changed country conditions) or that relocation, where it would be reasonable to do so under all the circumstances, would avoid the persecution. 8 C.F.R. §§1208.13(b)(1)(i)(A),(B), (ii). If DHS rebuts the presumption, the applicant will be denied unless s/he demonstrates " 'compelling reasons for being unwilling or unable to return' to his or her country of nationality, or 'a reasonable possibility that he or she may suffer other serious harm upon removal to that country.' 8 C.F.R. 1208.13(b)(1)(iii)(A),(B)." *Matter of D-I-M-,* 24 I&N Dec. 448, 450 (BIA 2008) [reversed IJ denial in Kenyan asylum case where past persecution was found but the IJ did not explicitly provide the presumption of future persecution and failed to shift the burden to DHS]. An applicant may also meet the burden of proof by demonstrating a well-founded fear of future persecution separate from past persecution. The applicant has the burden in that case of demonstrating that it would not be reasonable to internally relocate unless the government is the persecutor.

In a revocation proceeding, the burden is on the government to prove the ground of revocation by a preponderance of the evidence. *Ntangsi v. Gonzales,* 475 F.3d 1007 (8th Cir. 2007) [reversing IJ's revocation of asylum where he impermissibly placed burden on asylee to demonstrate she had not committed fraud].

2.b. *Standard of Persuasion for Withholding*—In *INS v. Stevic*, 467 U.S. 407 (1984), the Court found that the applicant must prove his claim for withholding by showing a "clear probability" of persecution. The Court interpreted "clear probability" to mean that persecution was "more likely than not," a "preponderance of the evidence" standard. Legacy INS adopted the *Stevic* standard for withholding claims under CAT. 64 Fed. Reg. 8478–8501 at 8480 (Feb. 19, 1999); 8 C.F.R. §§208.16(c)(2), 1208.16(c)(2); *Matter of G-A-,* 23 I&N Dec. 366 (BIA 2002) [burden met where due to a combination of factors, it is more likely than not that applicant would be tortured upon his removal to Iran]; *Kamara v. Att'y Gen. of the U.S.,* 420 F.3d 202, 213–15 (3d Cir. 2005) [BIA applied the wrong quantum of proof for CAT claim when it treated the likelihood of torture from different entities in Sierra Leone as noncumulative claims instead of aggregating them to reach 51%]; *Khup v. Ashcroft,* 376 F.3d 898, 906–07 (9th Cir. 2004) [finding at least a 51% chance of torture in Burma given torture of applicant's fellow preacher by the military, DOS country reports and AI press release]. *But see Settenda v. Ashcroft,* 377 F.3d 89, 95–96 (1st Cir. 2004) [applying analysis in *Elien* and *Matter of J-E-* to person facing detention in Uganda]; *Elien v. Ashcroft,* 364 F.3d 392, 398–99 (1st Cir. 2004) [following *Matter of J-E-* and finding no evidence that Haiti used torture pervasively or as a matter of policy on detainees and that IJ did not err in denying CAT]; *Wang v. Ashcroft,* 320 F.3d 130, 143–45 (2d Cir. 2003) [military deserter from PRC failed to demonstrate he would be tortured as opposed to simply placed in prison]; *Matter of J-F-F-,* 23 I&N Dec. 912, 917 (AG 2006) [AG applied the "more likely than not standard" and reversed the IJ's grant and the BIA's affirmance of CAT relief where the IJ speculated what would happen to the respondent and "flipped the burden [of proof] on its head" by finding facts based on the absence of evidence]; *Matter of M-B-A-,* 23 I&N Dec. 474 (BIA 2002) [Nigerian woman convicted of drug offense in the U.S. did not establish that Decree No. 33 of the Nigerian National Drug Law Enforcement Agency would be enforced against her and would result in her incarceration and torture]; *Matter of J-E-,* 23 I&N Dec. 291, 303 (BIA 2002).

2.c. *Standard of Persuasion for Asylum*—In *INS v. Cardoza-Fonseca*, 480 U.S. 421 (1987), the Court held that the "well-founded fear" standard for asylum is more generous than withholding and therefore, can be satisfied by a lesser standard of persuasion and by different evidence. [discussing a "10% chance" *Id.* at 440 and stating that, "[o]ne can certainly have a well-founded fear of an event happening when there is less than a 50% chance of the occurrence taking place." *Id.* at 431]; *see Sanchez Jimenez v. U.S. Att'y Gen.,* 492 F.3d 1223, 1234 (11th Cir. 2007) [recognizing the 10% standard in *Cardoza-Fonseca* and finding that if there is a 10% chance of being shot at to obtain future persecution, then actually being shot at constitutes past persecution]; *Sun Wen Chen v. Att'y Gen. of the U.S.,* 491 F.3d 100, 105–09 (3d Cir. 2007) [BIA applied wrong standard in expecting spouse to prove more than a 10% chance of future persecution in forced sterilization case where BIA held that applicant did not meet burden of proof because it found that forced sterilization policy is not "uniformly applied" or is "uncertain"]; *Haoua v. Gonzales,* 472 F.3d 227 (4th Cir. 2007) [IJ erred in determining that Niger applicant for asylum had only a 10% chance of being subject to FGM]; *Canales-Vargas v. Gonzales,* 441 F.3d 739, 744–46 (9th Cir. 2006) [substantial evidence did not support IJ's denial of asylum because anonymous death threats were sufficient under the "low standard" requiring a 10% chance to establish a well-founded fear of future persecution]; *Abebe v. Gonzales,* 432 F.3d 1037, 1041–43 (9th Cir. 2005) (*en banc*) [substantial evidence did not support IJ's determination that there was less than a 10% chance that USC child of Ethiopian parents would be subject to FGM]; *Quan v. Gonzales,* 428 F.3d 883, 889 (9th Cir. 2005) [IJ reversed where he required applicant to show that all practicing Christians in China are persecuted as a pattern and practice rather than applying the 10% rule]; *Marcos v. Gonzales,* 410 F.3d 1112, 1118–21 (9th Cir. 2005) [reversing IJ determination that respondent did not have well-founded fear where persecutors had not yet carried out threats because "even a one-tenth possibility of persecution might effect a well-founded fear"]; *Bellido v. Ashcroft,* 367 F.3d 840, 845 n.7 (8th Cir. 2004) [reversing IJ's denial of asylum to Bolivian union leader and noting that burden is less than 50% chance]; *Hoxha v. Ashcroft,* 319 F.3d 1179, 1184 (9th Cir. 2003) [well-founded fear does not require certainty or even a probability of persecution]; *Lim v. INS,* 224 F.3d 929, 934 (9th Cir. 2000) [10% risk sufficient following *Cardoza-Fonseca*]; *Bajwa v. Cobb*, 727 F.Supp. 53, 58 (D. Mass. 1989); *Perez-Alvarez v. INS*, 857 F.2d 23, 25 (1st Cir. 1988) [if one out of 10 persons in applicant's country is in danger, there is a well-founded fear]; *Mendoza-Perez v. INS*, 902 F.2d 760 (9th Cir. 1990) [claim that person employed by land reform organization received death threat by letter was sufficient even in absence of letter]. Following *Cardoza-Fonseca*, the BIA determined that asylum may be granted where "a reasonable person in his circumstances would fear persecution." *Matter of Mogharrabi*, 19 I&N Dec. 439 (BIA 1987). The Seventh Cir. has interpreted this to mean "good reason" to fear persecution. *Kubon v. INS*, 913 F.2d 386 (7th Cir. 1990). *See also Wangchuck v. DHS,* 448 F.3d 524, 530 (2d Cir. 2006) [IJ reversed where he mixed withholding standard regarding "more likely than not" that Tibetan applicant "would be persecuted" instead of applying the "well-founded fear" standard]; *Mikhael v. INS*, 115 F.3d 299 (5th Cir. 1997) [reversing BIA for applying higher standard than well-founded fear]; *Karaj v. Gonzales,* 462 F.3d 113, 117–19 (2d Cir. 2006) [reversing IJ denial where IJ required respondent to establish that he "would be persecuted" upon return to Albania]. The applicant must establish that there is a "reasonable possibility" of persecution, which can be satisfied by less than a preponderance of the evidence so long as there is a subjective fear and an objective basis for the fear. *Cardoza-Fonseca, supra,* at 440. The Board takes the view that the applicant must show that the fear of persecution is both subjectively genuine and objectively reasonable. *Matter of R-O-*, 20 I&N Dec. 455 (BIA 1992); *Sayaxing v. INS,* 179 F.3d 515, 520 (7th Cir. 1999) [objective fear requires applicant to present specific, detailed facts]. The objective component requires a showing by credible, direct and specific evidence, facts supporting a reasonable fear. Therefore an applicant must show that: (1) s/he possesses a belief or characteristic a persecutor seeks to overcome in others by means of punishment of some sort; (2) the persecutor is aware or could become aware that the applicant possesses this belief or characteristic; (3) the persecutor has the capability of punishing the applicant; and (4) the persecutor has the inclination to punish the applicant. *Matter of Mogharrabi, supra.*

2.d. *Relationship Between Standards for Withholding and Asylum*—The BIA has also found that where an applicant satisfies "the higher burden of proof required for withholding of removal, it follows that she has satisfied the lesser 'well-founded fear' standard of proof required for asylum." *Matter of Soleimani*, 20 I&N Dec. 99 (BIA 1989); *Ramirez-Rivas v. INS*, 899 F.2d 864, 866 (9th Cir.), *vacated on other grounds*, 502 U.S. 1025 (1992). However, if the applicant does not meet the asylum standard, she *a fortiori* cannot meet the standard for withholding. *Alvarez-Flores v. INS*, 909 F.2d 1, 4 (1st Cir. 1990). Moreover, meeting the asylum standard does not mean that the applicant will meet the withholding standard. *Lim v. INS,* 224 F.3d 929, 937–39 (9th Cir. 2000) [BIA findings were insufficient in regard to denial of asylum but not for denial of withholding].

Standard for Juveniles—The same standards apply to juveniles in the view of one court. *Cruz-Diaz v. INS*, 86 F.3d 330, 331 (4th Cir. 1996).

2.e. *Nature of Proof*

(1) *Generally*—As a result of the differing standards of persuasion for withholding and asylum, the evidence presented may differ under each standard. Courts may require more objective and corroborative evidence to sustain a withholding claim than for asylum. *Compare Chavarria v. DOJ*, 722 F.2d 666 (11th Cir. 1984) *with Bolanos-Hernandez v. INS*, 767 F.2d 1277 (9th Cir. 1984).

(2) *Specific and Detailed Claim*—Whatever standard is applied, the applicant's claim must be specific and detailed. *INS v. Elias-Zacarias*, 502 U.S. 478 (1992). Counsel must emphasize the special circumstances of the applicant's situation and both documentary and testimonial evidence should be submitted when possible. Expert testimony is also permitted and should be utilized. *See, e.g., Banks v. Gonzales,* 453 F.3d 449, 453–54 (7th Cir. 2006) [noting that DOS reports are too general and that government needs expert witnesses]; *Dia v. Ashcroft,* 353 F.3d 228, 258–59 (3d Cir. 2003) (*en banc*) [where handwriting expert testified in asylum case that the signatures on the passport and visa were not respondent's the IJ erred in dismissing the testimony as too speculative]. When individuals are unavailable to testify, affidavits attesting to the veracity of an applicant's claim should be utilized to corroborate the claim.

(3) *Pattern and Practice*—DHS regulations recognize that an applicant is not required to provide evidence that s/he would be "singled out individually" for persecution if s/he established "that there is a pattern and practice" in the country of persecution of groups of persons similarly situated to the applicant on account of one of the five enumerated grounds *and* that the applicant establishes his own inclusion within the group. 8 C.F.R. §§208.13(b)(2)(iii), 208.16(b)(2)(i), (ii), 1208.13(b)(2)(iii), 1208.16(b)(2)(i), (ii). *Ghebrehiwot v. Att'y Gen. of the U.S.,* 467 F.3d 344, 353–55 (3d Cir. 2006) [where IJ failed to consider DOS reports and other documents submitted by Eritrean Pentecostal Christian and focused solely on past persecution, the court remanded to consider a pattern and practice of future persecution]; *Banks v. Gonzales,* 453 F.3d 449, 452–53 (7th Cir. 2006) [IJ erred in requiring Liberian of Krahn tribe to present evidence that she was singled out for persecution because all parties conceded the Krahn tribe was persecuted and the applicant's lawyer does not have the burden of asserting §1208.13(b)(2)(iii)]; *Tun v. INS,* 445 F.3d 554, 569–71 (2d Cir. 2006) [Burmese citizen who engaged in pro-democracy political demonstrations in the U.S. against Burmese government was eligible for well-founded fear claim based upon Burmese government's pattern and practice of punishing exiles who are politically active and IJ was reversed where he believed applicant had to show individualized claim or even that the Burmese government was aware of him as an individual]; *Sukwanputra v. Gonzales,* 434 F.3d 627, 637 (3d Cir. 2006) [reversing IJ for failure to consider whether Indonesian of Chinese ethnicity is subject to pattern and practice persecution]; *Zhao v. Gonzales,* 404 F.3d 295, 308 (5th Cir. 2005) [reversing denial of asylum and concluding that Falun Gong member did not have to "prove that he had been personally targeted" in establishing future persecution]; *Himri v. Ashcroft,* 378 F.3d 932, 936–38 (9th Cir. 2004) [Palestinians who lived in Kuwait were persecuted minority]; *Eduard v. Ashcroft,* 379 F.3d 182, 192 (5th Cir. 2004) [IJ erred in requiring Indonesian Christians to prove they were singled out for persecution when evidence indicated a pattern and practice of persecution of Christians]; *Avetova-Elisseva v. INS,* 213 F.3d 1192 (9th Cir. 2000) [Armenian in Russia who could not establish past persecution could establish a well-founded fear in light of the "pattern and practice" of persecution of Armenians which Russian authorities were unable or unwilling to stop]; *Chen v. INS,* 195 F.3d 198, 203 (4th Cir. 1999). *See also Najafi v. INS*, 104 F.3d 943, 949 (7th Cir. 1997) [Iranian who converted to Christianity need not show that Iranian authorities are aware of the conversion]. *Osaghae v. INS*, 942 F.2d 1160 (7th Cir. 1991) ["asylum is not limited to the notorious"]. *But see Matter of A-M-,* 23 I&N Dec. 737, 740–41 (BIA 2005) [BIA did not find pattern and practice of persecution in Indonesia against Chinese Christians]; *Wijono v. Gonzales,* 439 F.3d 868, 873–74 (8th Cir. 2006) [Chinese Christian withholding applicant did not establish that persecution was "systemic, pervasive, or organized" to constitute a pattern or practice in Indonesia]; *Sepulveda v. U.S. Att'y Gen.,* 401 F.3d 1226, 1231 (11th Cir. 2005) [to establish causal connection between political opinion and

feared persecution, the applicant must show s/he would be "singled out" for persecution]. Group persecution of this nature is prevalent in most asylum applications. *Singh v. INS*, 94 F.3d 1353, 1358–60 (9th Cir. 1996) [reversing BIA denial, and "reject[ing] the notion that an applicant is ineligible for asylum merely because all members of a persecuted group might be eligible for asylum"]; *Makonnen v. INS*, 44 F.3d 1378, 1382–84 (8th Cir. 1995) [reversing BIA where it ignored regulation and sought to require all members of the group to show persecution]; *Kotasz v. INS*, 31 F.3d 847 (9th Cir. 1994) [reversing BIA denial for member of anticommunist subgroup].

(4) *Current Political Context*—When evaluating an asylum claim, changed country conditions, as properly established in the record, may be a significant factor in concluding that an applicant has not established a well-founded fear of persecution. *Matter of E-P-*, 21 I&N Dec. 860 (BIA 1997) [changed conditions in Haiti post-Aristide]. The applicant's claim can only be understood in the context of the current political climate and where conditions change, courts may remand cases to determine the validity of the claim in light of new conditions. *Yang v. McElroy,* 277 F.3d 158 (2d Cir. 2002) [where there was a four-year delay between the BIA decision and the IJ decision which relied on a five-year-old DOS report, the court remanded for current reports]; *Osaghae v. INS*, 942 F.2d 1160 (7th Cir. 1991) [remanding where Nigerian claimed he had newly discovered evidence while case was pending in court of appeals]; *Desir v. Ilchert*, 840 F.2d 723, 730 (9th Cir. 1988) [validity of Haitian's claim after Duvalier's departure]; *Gonzalez v. INS*, 82 F.3d 903, 910–12 (9th Cir. 1996); *Castillo-Villagra v. INS*, 972 F.2d 1017 (9th Cir. 1992). Alternatively, if there is new evidence of changed conditions, the applicant should file a motion to reopen with the BIA. *Al-Fara v. Gonzales,* 404 F.3d 733, 743–44 (3d Cir. 2005) [court would not consider new evidence outside the record as respondent should file motion to reopen with BIA]; *Asani v. INS,* 154 F.3d 719, 725–26 (7th Cir. 1998) [where conditions changed subsequent to BIA denial, the case was remanded to permit the applicant to file a motion to reopen]. *See also Cordero-Trejo v. INS*, 40 F.3d 482, 490–91 (1st Cir. 1994) [reversing BIA denial where testimony and evidence not considered "in light of general conditions" in country as required by 8 C.F.R. §208.13(a)]. The existence of general conditions of violence cannot be used as a basis to hold that a person did not suffer persecution. *Ndom v. Ashcroft,* 384 F.3d 743, 752–56 (9th Cir. 2004) [person subject to past persecution need not show s/he has been "singled out" because to require a showing s/he is appreciably different than the general population under strife would have the perverse effect of protecting governments that engaged in widespread abuse]; *Baballah v. Ashcroft,* 335 F.3d 981, 990 (9th Cir. 2003) *amended* 367 F.3d 1067 (9th Cir. 2004) [rejecting IJ opinion that applicant who suffered persecution was no different than rest of society]. The BIA has suggested that general background information about a country must be included in the record as a foundation for the applicant's claim. *See Matter of S-M-J-*, 21 I&N Dec. 722, 724–25 (BIA 1997). *See also Gramatikov v. INS*, 128 F.3d 619, 620 (7th Cir. 1997) [criticizing uncorroborated claims about country conditions].

(5) *Administrative Notice of Conditions*—The BIA may take administrative notice of "commonly known facts such as current events or the contents of official documents." 8 C.F.R. §1003.1(d)(3)(iv). Official documents include "country condition reports prepared by the Department of State, including its foreign policy expertise, analysis and opinion." 67 Fed. Reg. 54878, 54892 (Aug. 26, 2002). The AG has concluded that he has the authority *sua sponte* to remand a case for additional fact-finding. *Matter of A-H-,* 23 I&N Dec. 774, 790–91 (AG 2005) [AG has authority to remand a case for additional fact finding, including the authority to override a DHS stipulation that respondent's life or freedom would be threatened if returned to his home country]. The BIA may take administrative notice of changed country conditions as long as it does not blindly apply a noticed fact and engages in an individualized review of the case. *Useinovic v. INS,* 313 F.3d 1025, 1030–31 (7th Cir. 2002) [affirming BIA denial where Yugoslavian government that was the basis for fear no longer is in power]. Other courts have determined that administrative notice is only appropriate where there are uncontroverted facts concerning asylum. *Galina v. INS,* 213 F.3d 955, 958–59 (7th Cir. 2000) [BIA misapplied the princi-

ple of administrative notice by relying on opinions in DOS Reports and treating them as uncontested facts]; *Fergiste v. INS,* 138 F.3d 14, 17–19 (1st Cir. 1998) [rejecting simple administrative notice as a basis to rebut past persecution where applicant presented evidence of continuing problems in Haiti]; *Kowalczyk v. INS,* 245 F.3d 1143 (10th Cir. 2001) [abuse of discretion to take administrative notice of changed political conditions in Poland 9 years after brief submitted]. Courts have also taken notice of events that are "troubling" and "well publicized," *Gafoor v. INS,* 231 F.3d 645, 654–57 (9th Cir. 2000) [taking judicial notice of more recent coup in Fiji that was not reflected in the record], or where the BIA's adverse credibility finding was based upon a failure to recognize a fact that is beyond dispute. *Singh v. Ashcroft,* 393 F.3d 903 (9th Cir. 2004) [where BIA made adverse credibility finding because applicant did not prove the existence of the Indian intelligence service (RAW), the court reversed, citing Fed. R. Evid. 201, and rejected the government's argument that the court could not take notice of such an obvious fact as "nonsense"]. *But see INS v. Ventura,* 537 U.S. 12 (2002) [reversing 9th Cir. finding on changed circumstances where BIA had not reached the issue because the appropriate procedure required a remand to the agency]; *Gonzales v. Thomas,* 547 U.S. 183 (2006) [vacating 9th Cir. *en banc* decision that defined a particular social group before giving the BIA the opportunity to determine whether "the members of a family can and do constitute a 'particular social group' within the meaning of the Act"]. *See also Ezeagwuna v. Ashcroft,* 325 F.3d 396, 398 & 411 (3d Cir. 2003) [on rehearing, vacating previous grant of asylum/withholding after determining court misapplied credibility issues and remanding case to IJ to make those decisions].

(6) *Right to Respond to Administrative Notice*—The failure to provide an applicant the right to respond to administrative notice is a violation of due process. *Burger v. Gonzales,* 498 F.3d 131 (2d Cir. 2007) [following the Ninth and Tenth Circuits the failure to give an asylum applicant from the former Yugoslavia the opportunity to respond to administrative findings of changed conditions in Serbia-Montenegro *before* making those finding is a violation of due process and is not cured by a motion to reopen]; *Chhetry v. DOJ,* 490 F.3d 196 (2d Cir. 2007) [although BIA could take administrative notice of new developments, it violated due process when it denied motion to reopen based on changed conditions in Nepal by citing to recent sources that indicated positive developments in Nepal after motion was filed without giving applicant an opportunity to respond]; *Circu v. Gonzales,* 450 F.3d 990 (9th Cir. 2006) (*en banc*) [failure to give asylum applicant the right to rebut DOS report violated due process]; *Getachew v. INS*, 25 F.3d 841 (9th Cir. 1994); *De La Llana-Castellon v. INS*, 16 F.3d 1093 (10th Cir. 1994); *Castillo-Villagra v. INS*, 972 F.2d 1017 (9th Cir. 1992) [reversing where BIA took administrative notice of adjudicative facts and not merely legislative facts without providing opportunity to rebut]. *But see Acewicz v. INS*, 984 F.2d 1056, 1059–61 (9th Cir. 1993) [distinguishing *Castillo-Villagra* where person had opportunity to raise issue before IJ]; *Matter of H-M-*, 20 I&N Dec. 683 (BIA 1993). In the view of some circuits, the applicant must challenge administrative notice through a motion to reopen. *Toptchev v. INS,* 295 F.3d 714, 723–24 (7th Cir. 2002) [applicants could not have been surprised by BIA's use of DOS reports in light of their frequent use and could have filed a motion to reopen]; *Gutierrez-Roque v. INS*, 954 F.2d 769, 772–73 (D.C. Cir. 1992); *Wojcik v. INS*, 951 F.2d 172, 173 (8th Cir. 1991); *Rivera-Cruz v. INS*, 948 F.2d 962 (5th Cir. 1991); *Janusiak v. INS*, 947 F.2d 46, 48 n.1 (3d Cir. 1991); *Kaczmarczyk v. INS*, 933 F.2d 588, 593–97 (7th Cir. 1991). The AG takes the view that administrative notice may be challenged in a motion to reopen which will be liberally construed so that the "not available" and "could not have been discovered" requirements of 8 C.F.R. §1003.2(c) "should not stand in the way of such a review and determination on the merits of the motion." 67 Fed. Reg. 54878, 54893 (Aug. 26, 2002). The denial of a stay when a motion to reopen is pending would raise significant due process concerns. *Gutierrez-Roque*, 954 F.2d at 773. *Accord Kaczmarczyk*, 933 F.2d at 597 n.9.

(7) *Difficulty in Establishing Claim*—"[A]n alien seeking asylum is often limited in the evidence he can obtain to show proof of potential persecution." *Artiga-Turcios v. INS*, 829 F.2d 720, 723 (9th Cir. 1987). "Persecutors are hardly likely to provide their victims with affidavits attesting to their acts of persecution." *Bolanos-Hernandez v. INS*, 767 F.2d

1277, 1285 (9th Cir. 1984). The failure of the persecutor to place his identity and motivations in writing does not undercut the applicant's credibility and cannot be the basis for denial because it does not rest on the "legitimate nexus required in credibility findings." *Secaida-Rosales v. INS,* 331 F.3d 297, 311 (2d Cir. 2003) [BIA reversed where IJ made unwarranted credibility determinations based on lack of documents and nonessential omissions]. Moreover, an applicant fleeing persecution should not be expected to bring documentary evidence to prove her asylum claim. *Niftaliev v. U.S. Att'y Gen.,* 504 F.3d 1211, 1217 (11th Cir. 2007) [in reversing IJ's denial of past persecution from the Ukraine, the court found that testimony alone was sufficient and noted that it was "troubled by the notion of condemning the petitioner for failing to obtain some sort of documentation from the same government that persecuted and imprisoned him, concerning incidents that occurred approximately ten years ago"]; *Gjerzai v. Gonzales,* 435 F.3d 800, 809 (7th Cir. 2006) ["it seems illogical to require a family fleeing a country to take precious time to search for and collect documents in order to corroborate an asylum claim"]; *Abovian v. INS,* 219 F.3d 972, 978 (9th Cir. 2000) [documentary evidence not required to support asylum claim]. Some evidentiary burdens are "too great for an alien who has fled his native country and cannot obtain information through official governmental sources." *Gomez-Saballos v. INS*, 79 F.3d 912, 916 (9th Cir. 1996) [need not obtain testimony about treatment of subsequent prison directors]. "Evidence of proof of intent and motive would be particularly hard to provide because both involve proof of a persecutor's state of mind." *Canas-Segovia v. INS*, 902 F.2d 717, 727 (9th Cir.), *aff'd on alternate grounds after remand*, 970 F.2d 599 (9th Cir. 1992). However, where corroborative evidence is available, the general rule is that such evidence should be presented. *Matter of S-M-J-*, 21 I&N Dec. 722 (BIA 1997); *Matter of M-D-*, 21 I&N Dec. 1180 (BIA 1998), *rev'd, Diallo v. INS,* 232 F.3d 279 (2d Cir. 2000) [corroborating evidence should be presented where available, but reversing the denial where it was not reasonable to expect it]; *Matter of Dass*, 20 I&N Dec. 120 (BIA 1989); *Dorosh v. Ashcroft*, 398 F.3d 379, 381–83 (6th Cir. 2004) [approving BIA's corroboration rule in *Matter of S-M-J-* and affirming IJ's denial of asylum for lack of corroboration]; *El-Sheikh v. Ashcroft,* 388 F.3d 643, 647 (8th Cir. 2004) [adopting *Matter of S-M-J* as well as the standard in the 2d and 3d Circuits in *Diallo* and *Abdulai* that before asylum can be denied for lack of corroboration the IJ must make a credibility determination, provide an explanation for the need for corroboration, and assess why it was not reasonable to produce corroborative evidence it if it could not be produced]; *Qui v. Ashcroft,* 329 F.3d 140, 153–54 (2d Cir. 2003) [reversing BIA under *Diallo* and *Alvarado-Carillo* because the BIA did not point to the specific pieces of missing information that the applicant should have produced and did not demonstrate that the corroborative documentation was reasonably available to the applicant]. *But see Guo v. Ashcroft,* 361 F.3d 1194, 1201 (9th Cir. 2004) [when applicant's credibility is in question, corroborative evidence should be produced where it is "easily available" and it is inappropriate to make an adverse credibility finding for failure to produce affidavits from relatives or acquaintances living outside the U.S.]; *Uwase v. Ashcroft,* 349 F.3d 1039, 1044–45 (7th Cir. 2003) [failure of sister to testify to corroborate claim cannot be basis to deny claim where sister's testimony was of little value]; *Ladha v. INS,* 215 F.3d 889, 901 (9th Cir. 2000) [disapproving of *Matter of S-M-J-* and *Matter of M-D-* and reversing finding of need for corroborative evidence where testimony was specific and credible]. Under the BIA's standard, the weaker the applicant's testimony, the greater the need for corroborative evidence. *Matter of Y-B-*, 21 I&N Dec. 1136 (BIA 1998). *But see Kataria v. INS,* 232 F.3d 1107 (9th Cir. 2000) [rejecting the standard and finding that absent a determination that the person is not credible, his testimony alone is sufficient]. Moreover, where an applicant submits corroborative identity documents that are fraudulent, it indicates an overall lack of credibility regarding his claim absent an explanation or rebuttal. *Matter of O-D-*, 21 I&N Dec. 1079 (BIA 1998). *But see Hanaj v. Gonzales,* 446 F.3d 694 (7th Cir. 2006) [following *Kourski* the court reversed the IJ for ignoring evidence by the Albanian applicant and his witnesses regarding his credibility and determining, instead, lack of credibility based solely on a fraudulent birth certificate without any findings that applicant knew or suspected the document was fraudulent]; *Yeimane-Berhe v. Ashcroft,* 393 F.3d 907, 911–13 (9th Cir. 2005) [where applicant presented testimony that was detailed and consistent, the submission of a fraudulent medical certificate to corroborate persecution where there was no evidence that she knew it to be fraudulent could not be the sole basis to deny relief]; *Kourski v. Ashcroft,* 355 F.3d 1038 (7th Cir. 2004) [where fraudulent birth certificate was submitted to show Jewish religion, IJ improperly inferred that person was not credible without any showing that person knew document was fraudulent].

2.f. *Documentary Evidence*

(1) *General Political Conditions*—The BIA and the courts have accepted the view that evidence of general political conditions in a country is admissible at a withholding, asylum and CAT claim hearing. *Mostafa v. Ashcroft,* 395 F.3d 622 (6th Cir. 2005) [BIA's failure to address country condition reports regarding Iran in CAT claim is reversible error]; *Zubeda v. Ashcroft,* 333 F.3d 463, 477–78 (3d Cir. 2003) [quoting extensively from Amnesty International, Human Rights Watch and DOS reports and finding the BIA did not sufficiently consider such evidence in denying CAT]; *Melendez v. DOJ*, 926 F.2d 211, 219 (2d Cir. 1991) ["[w]e and other courts have expressly held that objective evidence of violent conditions in the subject country is especially probative of a well founded fear"]; *Sanon v. INS*, 52 F.3d 648, 652–53 (7th Cir. 1995) [criticizing INS for lack of current country condition information]; *Bolanos-Hernandez v. INS*, 767 F.2d 1277, 1285 (9th Cir. 1984) ["[t]he significance of a specific threat to an individual's life or freedom is not lessened by the fact that the individual resides in a country where the lives and freedom of large numbers of people are threatened"]; *McMullen v. INS*, 658 F.2d 1312 (9th Cir. 1981); *Coriolan v. INS*, 559 F.2d 993 (5th Cir. 1977); *Haitian Refugee Center v. Civiletti*, 503 F.Supp. 442 (S.D. Fla. 1980), *aff'd sub nom. Haitian Refugee Center v. Smith*, 676 F.2d 1023 (5th Cir. 1982); *U.S. v. Shaughnessy*, 234 F.2d 715 (2d Cir. 1955); *Matter of Exame*, 18 I&NDec. 303 (BIA 1982). Evidence of general conditions compiled by other sources may not only come from DOS reports but also "other credible sources, such as international organizations, private voluntary agencies, news organizations, or academic institutions." 8 C.F.R. §§208.12(a), 1208.12(a).

(2) *Availability of Corroborating Evidence*—At the same time courts have recognized that it is unlikely that persecutors will provide "their victims with affidavits attesting to their acts of persecution." *Ramos-Vasquez v. INS,* 57 F.3d 857, 862–63 (9th Cir. 1995) (quoting *Bolanos-Hernandez v. INS,* 767 F.2d 1277, 1285 (9th Cir. 1984)); *Diallo v. Gonzales,* 439 F.3d 764, 766 (7th Cir. 2006) [unreasonable for IJ to expect Guinean asylum applicant to provide documents from opposition political party and from newspapers about a demonstration they might not have covered]; *Dawoud v. Gonzales,* 424 F.3d 608, 612–13 (7th Cir. 2005) ["[t]o expect [asylum applicants] to stop and collect dossiers of paperwork before fleeing is both unrealistic and strikingly insensitive to the harrowing conditions they face"]. Therefore, "the purpose of country conditions evidence...is not to corroborate specific acts of persecution (which can rarely be corroborated through documentation), but to provide information about the context in which the alleged persecution took place, in order that the factfinder may intelligently evaluate the petitioner's credibility." *Zahedi v. INS,* 222 F.3d 1157 (9th Cir. 2000).

(3) *Credible Testimony Sufficient*—Under 8 C.F.R. §208.13(a), the testimony of the applicant, if credible, may be sufficient to sustain the burden of proof without corroboration. *Niftaliev v. U.S. Att'y Gen.,* 504 F.3d 1211, 1217 (11th Cir. 2007) [where IJ did not make adverse credibility determination and applicant relied on testimony alone, the appeal does not concern corroboration issues under 8 U.S.C. §1252(b)(4) and the evidence was sufficient to establish past persecution from Ukraine]; *Karouni v. Gonzales,* 399 F.3d 1163, 1173–74 (9th Cir. 2005) [reversing IJ who required corroborative evidence because "[o]nce an applicant's testimony is deemed credible...no further corroboration is required to establish the facts to which the applicant testified"]; *Zewdie v. Ashcroft,* 381 F.3d 804, 808–09 (8th Cir. 2004) [reversing denial of CAT relief where IJ/BIA requirement that applicant produce medical evidence that scars were from beatings was unreasonable]; *Secaida-Rosales v. INS,* 331 F.3d 297, 311 (2d Cir. 2003) [failure to produce medical records of injuries or letters that detail persecutors' names and motivations does not undercut applicant's credibility, and is not essential to claim]; *Georgis v. Ashcroft,* 328 F.3d

962, 969 (7th Cir. 2003) [asylum applicant need not submit corroborating evidence in order to sustain her burden of proof]; *Chen v. Slattery*, 842 F.Supp. 814, 824 (E.D.N.Y. 1994) [reversing IJ's denial of asylum based in part on applicant's refusal to provide documentary evidence]. However, the BIA has held that corroborating evidence should be produced where it is reasonable to expect it, or an explanation should be provided as to why it was not presented. *Matter of S-M-J-*, 21 I&N Dec. 722, 725–26 (BIA 1997) [evidence includes place of birth, media accounts, evidence of publicly held office, documentation of medical treatment].

(4) *Lack of Corroboration*—The absence of corroborating evidence when required, can lead to a finding that an applicant failed to meet his burden of proof. INA §§208(b)(1)(B), 240(c)(4), 241(b)(3)(C); *Matter of S-M-J-, supra* at 725–26.; *Matter of M-D-*, 21 I&N Dec. 1180 (BIA 1998), *rev'd, Diallo v. INS,* 232 F.3d 279 (2d Cir. 2000) [upholding BIA finding that corroborating evidence should be presented where available, but reversing the denial where it was not reasonable to expect corroborative evidence]; *Tun v. INS,* 445 F.3d 554, 567–69 (2d Cir. 2006) [failure to produce parents who were LPRs to corroborate political activity in the former Burma was basis to deny past persecution claim]; *Liti v. Gonzales,* 411 F.3d 631, 640 (6th Cir. 2005) [upholding IJ's finding that corroboration of murder of Albanian political activist was reasonably available and respondent failed to provide an explanation for the lack of corroboration]; *Madjakpor v. Gonzales,* 406 F.3d 1040, 1044–45 (8th Cir. 2005) [upholding denial of withholding for lack of corroboration where respondent testified he was unable to obtain documents because he was detained]; *Dorosh v. Ashcroft*, 398 F.3d 379, 381–83 (6th Cir. 2004) [approving corroboration rule in *Matter of S-M-J-* and affirming IJ's denial of asylum for lack of corroboration]; *El-Sheikh v. Ashcroft,* 388 F.3d 643, 647 (8th Cir. 2004) [adopting *Matter of S-M-J* as well as the standard in the 2d and 3d Circuits in *Diallo* and *Abdulai* that before asylum can be denied for lack of corroboration, the IJ must make a credibility determination, must explain the need for corroboration, and must assess why it was not reasonable to produce it if it could not be produced]; *Balogun v. Ashcroft,* 374 F.3d 492, 501–02 (7th Cir. 2004) [failure to present evidence that is "reasonably available" casts a cloud on the applicant's testimony or when the applicant's testimony "while not mendacious, cannot be accepted at face value"]; *Lin v. Ashcroft,* 371 F.3d 18, 22 (1st Cir. 2004) [where undisputed country reports state that documents from certain provinces in China are subject to widespread fabrication and fraud, it was reasonable for IJ to require authentication of document]; *Nyama v. Ashcroft,* 357 F.3d 812, 817 (8th Cir. 2004) [where Cameroon applicant was deemed not credible, IJ's demand for corroborative evidence was not error].

(5) *REAL ID Act of 2005 and Corroboration*—Congress has legislated on corroboration issues for all cases filed on or after May 11, 2005. *See* INA §§208(b)(1)(B), 240(c)(4), 241(b)(3)(C), 8 U.S.C. §§1158(b)(1)(B), 1230(c)(4), 1231(b)(3)(C); *Matter of S-B-,* 24 I&N Dec. 42 (BIA 2006) [new standards only apply where application was filed first with asylum office or IJ on or after May 11, 2005; where application was filed with asylum office before May 11th but with IJ after, the new standards do not apply]. Although corroboration is unnecessary where the trier of fact is satisfied that the "applicant's testimony is credible, is persuasive, and refers to specific facts sufficient to demonstrate that the applicant is a refugee," the trier of fact can require the applicant to corroborate otherwise credible testimony "unless the applicant does not have the evidence and cannot reasonably obtain the evidence." In determining whether the applicant has met her burden, the trier of fact may weigh the credible testimony along with other record evidence. INA §§208(b)(1)(B)(ii), 240(c)(4)(B), 241(b)(3)(C).

(6) *Cases Reversing IJ/BIA Under S-M-J/Diallo Corroboration Standard*—*Lin v. Gonzales,* 445 F.3d 127, 135 (2d Cir. 2006) [following *Diallo* IJ reversed where the IJ failed to explain why it was reasonable to expect applicant to have documents or why applicant's explanation was insufficient]; *Poradisova v. Gonzales,* 420 F.3d 70, 79–81 (2d Cir. 2005) [reversing BIA under *Diallo* standard for requiring corroboration without discussing materiality or reasonableness to obtain]; *El-Sheikh v. Ashcroft,* 388 F.3d 643, 647 (8th Cir. 2004) [reversing denial of asylum and remanded to agency to engage in three-part analysis articulated in *Diallo* and *Abdulai*]; *Miah v. Ashcroft,* 346 F.3d 434 (3d Cir. 2003) [up-

holding *Matter of S-M-J-* following *Abdulai*, but reversing BIA where it failed to conduct an independent analysis of whether corroboration was necessary]; *Abdulai v. Ashcroft,* 239 F.3d 542, 550–55 (3d Cir. 2001) [upholding validity of BIA's requirement for corroboration but reversing the decision because the BIA did not explain its reasons for the denial]; *Alvarado-Carillo v. INS,* 251 F.3d 44, 53–55 (2d Cir. 2001) [reversing BIA denial where general information provided support for claim and where the BIA failed to identify any particular document or type of document it believed was missing].

(7) *Prior Notice Required Before Finding Deficiency*—An IJ's concern for more specific information does not constitute a valid ground for denying asylum where the applicant was not given notice that the information submitted was insufficient. *Qui v. Ashcroft,* 329 F.3d 140, 153–54 (2d Cir. 2003) [reversing BIA under *Diallo* and *Alvarado-Carillo* because the BIA did not point to specific pieces of missing information that the applicant should have produced and did not demonstrate that the documentation was reasonably available]. *Paramasamy v. Ashcroft,* 295 F.3d 1047, 1054 (9th Cir. 2002) [failure to provide letter from mother corroborating applicants account of sexual abuse was impermissible because IJ never questioned applicant about the perceived deficiency]; *Akinmade v. INS,* 196 F.3d 951, 957 (9th Cir. 1999).

(8) Circuit Courts on Corroboration

(a) *Third Circuit*—The three-part corroboration inquiry as stated in the 3d Cir. is: (1) an identification of facts for which it is reasonable to expect corroboration; (2) an inquiry as to whether the applicant has provided information corroborating those facts; and, if he or she has not, (3) an analysis of whether an applicant has adequately explained why s/he was unable to do so. *See, e.g., Toure v. Att'y Gen. of the U.S.,* 443 F.3d 310, 323–25 & n.8 (3d Cir. 2006) [reversed the IJ's finding of the need for corroboration because she failed to follow the 3-part test set forth in *Abdulai v. Ashcroft,* 239 F.3d 542, 551–52 (3d Cir. 2001)] *Voci v. Gonzales,* 409 F.3d 607, 616–17 (3d Cir. 2005) [where BIA did not engage in three-part analysis or even explain if there was a need for corroboration, asylum denial reversed]; *Berishaj v. Ashcroft,* 378 F.3d 314, 326 (3d Cir. 2004) [recognizing three part test but reversing IJ in ethnic Albanian case on grounds that it was unreasonable for the IJ to require corroboration because, "[w]artime persecution is surely among those matters—exigency, strife, and destruction all conspire to destroy what records there might once have been"]; *Mulanga v. Ashcroft,* 349 F.3d 123, 134 (3d Cir. 2003) [reversing IJ where findings on lack of corroboration were not supported by substantial evidence where applicant was unable to obtain proof of husband's membership in a political organization from the Republic of the Congo]. The 3d Cir. has adhered to its view post-REAL ID and has determined that REAL ID does not alter its corroboration requirements. *Chukwu v. Att'y Gen. of the U.S.,* 484 F.3d 185, 191–93 (3d Cir. 2007) [reversing IJ's lack of corroboration finding as to medical, police and court documents in Nigerian asylum claim].

(b) *Seventh Circuit*—Before denying asylum for lack of corroboration the 7th Cir. requires the IJ to: (1) make an explicit credibility finding; (2) explain why additional corroboration is reasonable; and (3) explain why the alien's explanation for not producing the requested corroboration is inadequate. *Tandia v. Gonzales,* 487 F.3d 1048, 1054–56 (7th Cir. 2007) [where IJ never addressed citizen of Mauritania's explanation for lack of documents adverse credibility finding reversed]; *Dong v. Gonzales,* 421 F.3d 573, 579 (7th cir. 2005) [where IJ never explained why corroboration was reasonable and why respondent never provided documentation, the lack of corroboration finding could not support the decision]; *Soumahoro v. Gonzales,* 415 F.3d 732 (7th Cir. 2005) [granting petition for review where IJ failed to make a credibility finding and failed to explain why respondent's unsuccessful efforts to obtain corroborating evidence was unreasonable]; *Ayi v. Gonzales,* 460 F.3d 876, 880–81 (7th Cir. 2006) [reversing IJ's adverse credibility determination in case of Togo native where IJ *inter alia* expected respondent to corroborate persecutors' knowledge of his political activity]; *Ikama-Obambi v. Gonzales,* 470 F.3d 720, 725–26 (7th Cir. 2006) [reversing IJ decision requiring corroboration where IJ failed to first make explicit credibility finding].

(c) *Eighth Circuit*—The 8th Cir. agrees with the 2d and 3d Circuit's analysis. *El-Sheikh v. Ashcroft,* 388 F.3d 643, 647 (8th Cir. 2004) [adopting *Matter of S-M-J* as well as the standard in the 2d and 3d Circuits in *Diallo* and *Abdulai* that before asylum can be denied for lack of corroboration, the IJ must make a credibility determination, offer an explanation for the need for corroboration, and assess why it was not reasonable to produce it if it could not be produced].

(d) *Ninth Circuit*—The 9th Cir. rejected *Matter of S-M-J-. Ladha v. INS,* 215 F.3d 889, 901 (9th Cir. 2000) ["[w]e reaffirm that an alien's testimony, if un-refuted and credible, direct and specific, is sufficient to establish the facts testified without the need for any corroboration"]. *See also Smolniakova v. Gonzales,* 422 F.3d 1037, 1047 (9th Cir. 2005) [reversing adverse credibility finding in part, where it was unreasonable for IJ to expect a corroborating letter from a stranger who witnessed an attack against respondent]; *Shire v. Ashcroft,* 388 F.3d 1288, 1298–99 (9th Cir. 2004) [failure to obtain flight records through NIIS, medical records from abroad, and UN statement acknowledging presence in a refugee camp was very difficult to obtain; reversing IJ for demanding corroborative evidence]; *Kaur v. Ashcroft,* 379 F.3d 876, 889–90 (9th Cir. 2004) [affidavits of relatives and acquaintances living outside U.S. are almost never easily available and therefore could not be required]; *Guo v. Ashcroft,* 361 F.3d 1194, 1201 (9th Cir. 2004) [when applicant's credibility is in question, corroborative evidence should be produced but only where it is "easily available"]. *But see Unuakhaulu v. Gonzales,* 416 F.3d 931, 937–39 (9th Cir. 2005) [upholding denial of Nigerian asylum claim where applicant failed to present evidence that was readily available such as membership in his tribe]. The 9th Circuit's position may no longer be valid for post-May 11, 2005 cases, in light of INA §208(b)(1)(B)(ii).

(9) *Standard of Review for Corroboration*—The REAL ID Act established a new standard of review of the IJ/BIA's decision to require corroboration. The decision to require corroboration in asylum or other relief-from-removal cases may only be reversed if "a reasonable trier of fact is compelled to conclude that such corroborating evidence is unavailable." INA §242(b)(4), 8 U.S.C. §1252(b)(4). (REAL ID Act §101(e)). Although the corroboration requirements are effective only for cases filed on or after May 11, 2005, the federal review provision under INA §242(b)(4)(D) applies to all final orders concerning asylum, withholding, and other forms of relief issued before, on or after May 11, 2005. REAL ID Act §101(h)(3), 119 Stat. at 305–06. However, there is an issue whether the REAL ID Act changes the standard of review. In *Toure v. Att'y Gen. of the U.S.,* 443 F.3d 310, 323–25 & n.8 (3d Cir. 2006) the Third Circuit, in a *post*-REAL ID Act case, reversed the IJ's finding of the need for corroboration because she failed to follow the standard set forth in *Abdulai v. Ashcroft,* 239 F.3d 542, 551–52 (3d Cir. 2001) and questioned whether the REAL ID Act provision under 8 U.S.C. §1252(b)(4)(D) was applicable, while noting that the Act did not alter the rules requiring the IJ to develop and applicant's testimony and to adequately explain the basis for its decision. *See also Ikama-Obambi v. Gonzales,* 470 F.3d 720, 725–26 (7th Cir. 2006) [reversing *Post*-REAL ID IJ decision requiring corroboration where IJ first failed to make explicit credibility finding]; *Edimo-Doualla v. Gonzales,* 464 F.3d 276, 284–86 (2d Cir. 2006) [reversing IJ finding that corroboration was necessary in Cameroonian asylum case where IJ speculated that medical records were necessary regarding beating where applicant never said he had permanent injuries and said he received no medial treatment]; *Hor v. Gonzales,* 421 F.3d 497, 500–01 (7th Cir. 2005) [reversing IJ's corroboration findings post-REAL ID; although the IJ's findings are entitled to deference, the IJ must first explain, unless it is obvious, why he thinks corroborating evidence would have been available]. *Accord. Zhang v. Gonzales,* 434 F.3d 993, 998–99 (7th Cir. 2006) [quoting *Hor* and reversing IJ's demand for corroboration]. *But see Chen v. Gonzales,* 434 F.3d 212, 217–20 (3d Cir. 2005) [*post*-Real ID, upholding IJ's denial of asylum even where the IJ did not make a valid credibility assessment because even a credible applicant may be required to produce corroborative

evidence and respondent failed to do so]; *Zheng v. Gonzales,* 417 F.3d 379, 383 n.2 (3d Cir. 2005) [finding that the IJ's requirement to corroborate what may be speculative records is subject to the "compelling" review standard which is "effective immediately" including cases begun before May 11, 2005]. However, the standard may not apply to motions to reopen before the BIA because it applies only to review of a decision by the "trier of fact" (which is the IJ not the BIA) and does not, by its terms, apply to the provision on motions to reopen at INA §240(c)(7), 8 U.S.C. §1229a(c)(7), *Fessehaye v. Gonzales,* 414 F.3d 746, 752–53 (7th Cir. 2005).

(10) *Corroboration Not Required—Niftaliev v. U.S. Att'y Gen.,* 504 F.3d 1211, 1217 (11th Cir. 2007) [where IJ did not make adverse credibility determination and applicant relied on testimony alone, the appeal does not concern 8 U.S.C. §1252(b)(4) and the court was also "troubled by the notion of condemning the petitioner for failing to obtain some sort of documentation from the same government that persecuted and imprisoned him, concerning incidents that occurred approximately ten years ago"]; *Edimo-Doualla v. Gonzales,* 464 F.3d 276, 284–86 (2d Cir. 2006) [reversing IJ finding that corroboration was necessary in Cameroonian asylum case where IJ speculated that medical records were necessary regarding beating where applicant never said he had permanent injuries and received no medial treatment]; *Ayi v. Gonzales,* 460 F.3d 876, 880–81 (7th Cir. 2006) [reversing IJ's adverse credibility determination in case of Togo native where IJ *inter alia* expected respondent to corroborate persecutors' knowledge of his political activity]; *San Kai Kwok v. Gonzales,* 455 F.3d 766, 771 (7th Cir. 2006) [IJ reversed in pre-REAL ID Act case, where he required documentary evidence that was irrelevant to forced abortion claim including an abortion certificate that the court has recognized "probably does not exist"]; *Li Zu Guan v. INS,* 453 F.3d 129, 140–41 (2d Cir. 2006) [reversed IJ's lack of credibility finding where he requested applicant to produce children's birth certificates when it was not reasonable to expect to have contemporaneous documentation given the fact that the parents took great pains to conceal birth in the PRC because the IJ's request "must be calibrated to the norms and practices of the aliens' home countries and the circumstances of the aliens' departure"];*Diallo v. Gonzales,* 439 F.3d 764, 766 (7th Cir. 2006) [vacating denial of asylum where IJ did not make an adverse credibility finding and did not adequately explain his reasons for requiring corroboration]; *Cao He Lin v. DOJ,* 428 F.3d 391, 404–05 (2d Cir. 2005) [demands for corroboration without a reasoned explanation for the need is error requiring reversal]; *Dawoud v. Gonzales,* 424 F.3d 608, 612–14 (7th Cir. 2005) [rejecting BIA's insistence on corroboration where story was credible and supported by DOS report.]; *Rodriguez Galicia v. Gonzales,* 422 F.3d 529, 536–38 (7th Cir. 2005) [reversing adverse credibility assessment based in part on IJ's requested corroboration of a car registration that was irrelevant to the applicant's claim]; *Fessehaye v. Gonzales,* 414 F.3d 746, 755–57 (7th Cir. 2005) [in motion to reopen by Jehovah Witness in Ethiopia, applicant's own affidavit was sufficient and no corroboration was necessary for *prima facie* case]; *Vasha v. Gonzales,* 410 F.3d 863, 871 n.3 (6th Cir. 2005) [upholding an adverse credibility determination, but finding that the IJ's insistence on requiring Albanian respondent to produce police and medical records more than 9 years old when country was under communist rule and where country now has generalized lawlessness and corruption was not reasonable]; *Huang v. Gonzales,* 403 F.3d 945, 951 (7th Cir. 2005) [reversing IJ's credibility determination based upon lack of corroboration where documents were irrelevant because they were based upon IJ's speculation or unreasonable to obtain]; *Guo v. Ashcroft,* 361 F.3d 1194, 1201 (9th Cir. 2004) [when applicant's credibility is in question, corroborative evidence should be produced but only where it is easily available; it is inappropriate to make an adverse credibility finding for failure to produce affidavits from relatives or acquaintances living outside the U.S.]; *Uwase v. Ashcroft,* 349 F.3d 1039, 1044–45 (7th Cir. 2003) [failure of sister to testify to corroborate claim cannot be basis for denial where sister's testimony was of little value]; *Kataria v. INS,* 232 F.3d 1107 (9th Cir. 2000) [absent a determination that the person is not credible his testimony alone is sufficient]; *Ladha v. INS,* 215 F.3d 889, 901 (9th Cir. 2000) [disapproving of *Matter of S-M-J-* and *Matter of M-D-* and reversing finding of need for corroborative evidence where testimony was specific and credible]; *Mukamusoni v. Ashcroft,* 390 F.3d 110, 123–25 (1st Cir. 2004) [reversing IJ for overstat-

ing the role of missing corroborative evidence while ignoring the bulk of evidence including country condition reports]; *Lin v. Ashcroft,* 385 F.3d 748, 756–57 (7th Cir. 2004) [in forced abortion case, corroboration is not necessary when the applicant's testimony is otherwise credible]; *Gontcharova v. Ashcroft,* 384 F.3d 873 (7th Cir. 2004) [reversing IJ and recommending that case be sent to a different judge where IJ offered no reason for requesting certain documents and failed to discuss why it was reasonable to expect the documentation in light of respondent's explanation and country conditions].

(11) *General Corroborating Evidence and Evidence of Country Conditions Shall Be Produced—Matter of R-S-H-*, 23 I&N Dec. 629, 643 (BIA 2003) [emphasizing that IJs and BIA frequently rely on DOS reports]; *Matter of S-M-J-*, supra at 725–26; *Matter of Dass*, 20 I&N Dec. 120 (BIA 1989) [evidence of background conditions not merely optional because application cannot be properly evaluated without it]. *See also Matter of V-T-S-*, 21 I&N Dec. 792, 797 (BIA 1997). Where IJ ignores corroborative evidence of country conditions, denial of asylum may be reversed. *Mukamusoni v. Ashcroft*, 390 F.3d 110, 123–25 (1st Cir. 2004) [reversing IJ for overstating the role of missing corroborative evidence while ignoring the bulk of evidence including country reports].

(12) *Credibility and Documentary Evidence*

(a) *Fraudulent Documents Affect Credibility*—Where an applicant submits an ID document that is found or suspected to be counterfeit, it effects the credibility of her entire claim in the absence of an explanation or rebuttal. *Matter of O-D-*, 21 I&N Dec. 1079 (BIA 1998). *Accord Averianova v. Mukasey,* 509 F.3d 890, 895–97 (8th Cir. 2007) [fraudulent birth certificates that contradicted nationality claims and Jewish identity affected credibility where IJ made explicit findings and explanation for discrepancies by applicants were not believed]; *Selami v. Gonzales*, 423 F.3d 621, 624–26 (6th Cir. 2005) [submission of a fraudulent newspaper article that supported a key element of Albanian's asylum claim is sufficient to support an adverse credibility finding]; *Eta-Ndu v. Gonzales*, 411 F.3d 977, 984–86 (8th Cir. 2005) [where forensic document analyst testified that two documents were typed on same typewriter when they allegedly came from two different branches of an organization, and the court was unsatisfied with respondent's explanation, asylum could be denied for lack of corroboration]; *Hysi v. Gonzales*, 411 F.3d 847 (7th Cir. 2005) [where legacy INS Forensic Document Lab determined that applicant's name as author of newspaper articles had been inserted and where applicant's claim rested on retaliation for articles, IJ's adverse credibility determination and denial of asylum upheld]; *Yongo v. INS*, 355 F.3d 27, 32–35 (1st Cir. 2004) [upholding IJ decision where there was enough evidence for judge to conclude that Zairian asylum applicant lied about previous application in Germany and was therefore not credible]. The Second Circuit upheld an adverse credibility determination, recognizing that a false document may signify that the entire claim is false (*falsus in uno, falsus in omnibus*) but noted five exceptions where false documents would not necessarily signify a lack of credibility: (1) evidence is independently corroborated; (2) false document used to escape persecution; (3) false documents are ancillary to the claim; (4) false statements made at an airport interview; and (5) applicant does not know or have reason to know document is false. *Siewe v. Gonzales,* 480 F.3d 160, 170–71 (2d Cir. 2007).

(b) *Fraudulent Documents Not Fatal—Corovic v. Mukasey,* 519 F.3d 90, 97–98 (2d Cir. 2008) [reversed adverse credibility determination where court believed 2 documents were fraudulent but there was no indication that respondent knew or had reason to know they were fraudulent]; *Chen v. BIA,* 461 F.3d 153 (2d Cir. 2006) [IJ's conclusion that only fraud by respondent, instead of government error, explained discrepancy in documents was speculative and did not support adverse credibility determination]; *Hanaj v. Gonzales,* 446 F.3d 694 (7th Cir. 2006) [following *Kourski* the court reversed the IJ for ignoring evidence by the Albanian applicant and his witnesses regarding his credibility and determining, instead, lack of credibility based solely on a fraudulent birth certificate without any findings that applicant knew or suspected the document was fraudulent]; *Lin v. Gonzales,* 445 F.3d 127, 132–34 (2d

Cir. 2006) [IJ erred in mistaken belief that applicant's presentation of a false sterilization certificate to Chinese authorities to escape persecution called into question the authenticity of all her documentary evidence; the assumption that *falsus in uno, falsus in omnibus* (false in one thing, false in everything) has its limits]; *Kumar v. Gonzales,* 444 F.3d 1043, 1050 (9th Cir. 2006) [IJ erred in making an adverse credibility assessment based on his uninformed conclusion that a document was fraudulent without submitting the document to a handwriting expert or forensic laboratory]; *Gjerzai v. Gonzales,* 435 F.3d 800, 810–11 (7th Cir. 2006) [where IJ refused to send documents to Forensic Document Lab and where there was no proof that the applicant knew or had reason to know that the documents submitted were fraudulent, it was error for the IJ, despite specific, detailed and consistent testimony, to exclude the documents and determine that the lack of corroboration resulted in a failure of the applicant to meet his burden of proof]; *Yeimane-Berhe v. Ashcroft,* 393 F.3d 907, 911–13 (9th Cir. 2005) [where testimony was detailed and consistent, the submission of a fraudulent medical certificate where there was no evidence that she knew it to be fraudulent could not be the sole basis to deny relief]; *Kourski v. Ashcroft,* 355 F.3d 1038 (7th Cir. 2004) [where fraudulent birth certificate was submitted to show Jewish religion court improperly inferred that person was not credible without any showing that person knew document was fraudulent]. *See also Hoque v. Ashcroft,* 367 F.3d 1190, 1195–97 (9th Cir. 2004) [alteration of the date on a letter does not support lack of credibility finding by IJ where respondent was never asked to explain the marking, to provide the history of its submission, and did not aid asylum claim]; *Shtaro v. Gonzales,* 435 F.3d 711, 717 (7th Cir. 2006) [applicant may not be found incredible simply because she used a false passport to enter the U.S.]; *Nreka v. U.S. Att'y Gen.,* 408 F.3d 13611368 (11th Cir. 2005) [although upholding IJ's denial of asylum and adverse credibility determination, the court observed that "documents to facilitate travel or gain entry into the United States cannot in and of themselves be used as a basis to deny asylum" or to draw an adverse credibility determination]; *Kaur v. Ashcroft,* 379 F.3d 876, 889 (9th Cir. 2004) [lies and misstatements to border officials and presentation of a false passport do not reflect on credibility and were "entirely consistent with her asylum claim"].

(c) *Standard for Credibility of Documents*—The standard for credibility of documents should be the same as credibility of testimony and therefore, any adverse decision must be "based on specific, cogent reasons that bear a legitimate nexus to the finding." *Zahedi v. INS,* 222 F.3d 1157, 1165 (9th Cir. 2000) [reversing IJ's decision that documents lacked credibility based on ambiguous decision from Forensic Document Laboratory]. The IJ cannot rely on speculation regarding her view of what a document should look like. *Niang v. Mukasey*, 511 F.3d 138, 147 (2d Cir. 2007) [in Mauritanian asylum case, the tenuousness of the IJ's suspicions regarding applicant's documents, where the suspicions were based upon error or speculation, cannot support an adverse credibility determination where the applicant was otherwise credible]; *Chen v. BIA,* 461 F.3d 153 (2d Cir. 2006) [IJ's conclusion that only fraud by respondent, instead of government error, explained discrepancy in personal identification number on documents was speculative]; *Li Zu Guan v. INS,* 453 F.3d 129, 138–40 (2d Cir. 2006) [reversed IJ where his analysis of documents was flawed and other evidence contradicted his assertions in Chinese family planning case]; *Lin v. Gonzales,* 434 F.3d 1158, 1162–63 (9th Cir. 2006) [reversing IJ's adverse credibility finding based on her view that corroborating documents were suspicious because of her speculation as to perceived deficiencies in the documents and what she believed they should look like]; *Chen v. DOJ,* 426 F.3d 104, 114–15 (2d Cir. 2005) [on coercive population control claim, IJ's determination that birth control certificates appeared to be fabricated because they were not sequential was speculation]; *Hoque v. Ashcroft,* 367 F.3d 1190, 1195–97 (9th Cir. 2004) [alteration of the date on a letter does not support lack of credibility finding by IJ where respondent was never asked to explain the marking, to provide the history of its submission, and did not aid asylum claim]; *Uwase v. Ashcroft,* 349 F.3d 1039, 1042 (7th Cir. 2003) [determination that a person lacked credibility because of IJ's speculation about the meaning of a stamp on a document is impermissible]. *But see Onsongo v. Gonzales,* 457 F.3d 849, 854–55 (8th Cir. 2006) [in Kenyan asylum claim upheld IJ's determination that documents bore hallmarks of fraud because forensic evidence of fraud is not necessary where the documents bore readily identifiable indications of fraud]. The mere failure to authenticate a document does not constitute a sufficient foundation for an adverse credibility finding in the absence of evidence undermining the reliability of the document. *Zhou v. Gonzales,* 437 F.3d 860, 868–69 (9th Cir. 2006) [IJ's adverse credibility determination was reversed where he determined he would give "diminished weight" to documents because the asylum applicant could not obtain live testimony from persons living abroad to corroborate the documents despite the fact that there was no evidence that the documents were forged or unreliable]; *Wang v. INS,* 352 F.3d 1250, 1254 (9th Cir. 2003) [reversing IJ's adverse credibility finding based on failure to authenticate documents solely because forensic experts could not determine authenticity]. Minor discrepancies between documents is insufficient to make an adverse credibility determination. *Wang v. INS, supra.*

(d) In addition, hearsay documents even if admissible can not be the basis for an adverse credibility finding where they lack reliability. *Zhen Nan Lin v. DOJ,* 459 F.3d 255, 268–72 (2d Cir. 2006) [BIA's adverse credibility finding that was based on a consular report that a document was a forgery was reversed where the hearsay report was inherently unreliable]; *Corovic v. Mukasey,* 519 F.3d 90, 95–96 (2d Cir. 2008) [same following *Zhen Nan Lin*]; *Alexandrov v. Gonzales,* 442 F.3d 395, 404–07 (6th Cir. 2006) [in Bulgarian asylum claim, IJ violated due process by relying on two highly unreliable hearsay memoranda from the U.S. Embassy in Sofia to prove that respondent's documents were fraudulent]; *Ezeagwuna v. Ashcroft,* 325 F.3d 396, 405–08 (3d Cir. 2003) [reliance on double and triple hearsay DOS letter to undermine credibility of documentary evidence violated due process].

(e) *Government Criteria for Document Credibility*—The government has set forth criteria for determining when its own investigative documents and reports are reliable and they must at a minimum identify: (1) the investigator and his or her qualifications; (2) the objective and extent of the investigation; and (3) the methods used to verify the information discovered. *See* Memo, Cooper, G.C., "Confidentiality of Asylum Applications and Overseas Verification of Documents and Application Information" (June 21, 2001), *http://judiciary.house.gov/legacy/82238.pdf.* Failure to comply with these standards has resulted in reversal. *See Corovic v. Mukasey,* 519 F.3d 90, 95–96 (2d Cir. 2008) [U.S. government's request to Macedonian government to verify documents violated confidentiality provision of 8 C.F.R. §208.6 (now §1208.6) and the court, following *Zhen Nan Lin* prohibited the use of the Macedonian government's report as unreliable and remanded the case but left open the possibility that the IJ could make the same finding that the document was fraudulent based upon other evidence]; *Zhen Nan Lin v. DOJ,* 459 F.3d 255, 270–72 (2d Cir. 2006) [Same regarding Chinese Embassy].

(13) *Documentary Evidence Must Be Evaluated*—Where documentary corroborating evidence is produced by an asylum applicant, the IJ and BIA must evaluate the evidence. *Mukamusoni v. Ashcroft,* 390 F.3d 110, 120–22 (1st Cir. 2004 [reversing IJ where he discounted applicant's detailed affidavit as well as country report and expert's report because 8 C.F.R. §1208.3(c)(1) requires that all information should be considered in meeting burden of proof]; *Gailius v. INS,* 147 F.3d 34 (1st Cir. 1998) [reversing IJ/BIA where there was no evaluation of the credibility, authenticity or effect of the corroborative documentary evidence].

(14) *Authentication Requirements for Documents*—Documentary evidence, when it is in the form of official records, generally needs to comply with authentication requirements in 8 C.F.R. §§287.6, 1287.6 including proper certification by a consular officer if the documents are from abroad. §§287.6(b), 1287.6(b). The authentication requirement is not always strictly adhered to by the federal courts. *Vatyan v. Mukasey,* 508 F.3d 1179 (9th Cir. 2007) [a petitioner's own testimony is a proper method that may be used to authenti-

cate foreign public documents and IJ reversed, in asylum context, where he insisted that applicant obtain a certified document]; *Gebreeyesus v. Gonzales,* 482 F.3d 952, 955 (7th Cir. 2007) [reversing BIA denial of motion to reopen by Amharan from Ethiopia where BIA claimed that family members' letters had to be authenticated despite the letters not being official records]; *Xue Deng Jiang v. Gonzales,* 474 F.3d 25, 28–29 (1st Cir. 2007) [affidavit from father and declaration from parish priest are not "official records" requiring authentication pursuant to 8 C.F.R. §287.6 and §287.6 is not an exclusive method for authenticating records in asylum cases]; *Shtaro v. Gonzales,* 435 F.3d 711, 717 (7th Cir. 2006) [failure to authenticate documents pursuant to §287.6 does not amount to presumptive proof of falsity and IJ reversed on credibility finding]; *Sukwanputra v. Gonzales,* 434 F.3d 627, 636–37 (3d Cir. 2006) [reversing IJ who refused to give any weight to unauthenticated documentary evidence on the basis of §287.6 and failed to afford the applicant an opportunity to authenticate the documents through other means]; *Cao He Lin v. DOJ,* 428 F.3d 391, 404–05 (2d Cir. 2005) [IJ reversed where she declined to accept notarial birth certificate of applicant's child because it was not authenticated pursuant to 8 C.F.R. §287.6]; *Zhang v. Gonzales,* 405 F.3d 150, 155–56 (3d Cir. 2005) [where it was unclear whether IJ did not admit foreign documents or admitted them but gave them no weight because they were not authenticated pursuant to §287.6, the court remanded the case to BIA and ruled that §287.6 is not the exclusive means to authenticate documents]; *Leia v. Ashcroft,* 393 F.3d 427, 433–35 (3d Cir. 2005) [following *Liu*, reversing BIA's decision denying relief on credibility grounds because respondent failed to present authenticated government documents pursuant to 8 C.F.R. §287.6 because §287.6 is not the only means of authenticating documents]; *Liu v. Ashcroft,* 372 F.3d 529 (3d Cir. 2004) [reversing IJ where he admitted document without certification but gave it no weight; DHS conceded that the regulation is not the exclusive means of authenticating]; *Yongo v. INS,* 355 F.3d 27, 31 (1st Cir. 2004) [regulation is not the exclusive method of authenticating documents]; *Wang v. INS,* 352 F.3d 1250, 1254 (9th Cir. 2003) [reversing IJ's adverse credibility finding based on failure to authenticate documents solely because forensic experts could not determine authenticity]; *Khan v. INS,* 237 F.3d 1143 (9th Cir. 2001) [rejecting IJ's refusal to admit documents not certified by consular officer and finding that documents may be authenticated through any recognized procedure, including the Federal Rules of Civil Procedure]. However, the BIA does not abuse its discretion when it requires authentication if there has been an adverse credibility finding. *Qin Wen Zheng v. Gonzales,* 500 F.3d 143, 146–49 (2d Cir. 2007) [BIA did not abuse its discretion in denying motion to reopen for changed country conditions where document from Changle Province, China was not authenticated under §287.6 in light of prior adverse credibility finding given the doctrine of *falsus in uno, falsus in omnibus*].

(15) *Excluding Documentary Evidence*—Corroborating documentary evidence may not be excluded where the IJ finds that the lack of the document is a basis for an adverse credibility determination and denial of asylum. *Sall v. Gonzales,* 437 F.3d 229, 235–36 (2d Cir. 2006); *Gjerzai v. Gonzales,* 435 F.3d 800, 810–11 (7th Cir. 2006) [where IJ refused to send documents to Forensic Document Lab and where there was no proof that the applicant knew or had reason to know that the documents were fraudulent, it was error for the IJ, despite specific, detailed and consistent testimony, to exclude the documents and determine that the applicant to meet his burden of proof]; *Georgis v. Ashcroft,* 328 F.3d 962, 969 (7th Cir. 2003) [error to exclude police letter from Ethiopia and to determine applicant lacked credibility because she lacked corroboration]; *Khan v. INS,* 237 F.3d 1143, 1144 (9th Cir. 2001) [IJ erred in excluding police certificate for lack of authentication when the lack of corroboration was cited as a reason for denial of asylum]. This principle extends to refusing to consider rebuttal evidence. *Tadesse v. Gonzales,* 492 F.3d 905, 909–11 (7th Cir. 2007) [refusal to consider expert's affidavit or testimony to rebut government's document expert and discounting affidavit of applicant's torture counselor, after sending him home without permitting his testimony, violated applicant's right under INA §240(b)(4)(B)];

(16) *Types of Documentary Evidence*—Evidence of persecution may be presented "through affidavits, journalistic accounts [although no] particular amount or kind of evidence to demonstrate that his fear is well founded" is necessary. *Carcamo-Flores v. INS*, 805 F.2d

60, 64 (2d Cir. 1986). *Accord. Mukamusoni v. Ashcroft,* 390 F.3d 110, 120–22 (1st Cir. 2004 [IJ reversed where he discounted asylum applicant's detailed affidavit and didn't consider other corroborative evidence including an expert report and country conditions report]; *Castaneda-Hernandez v. INS*, 826 F.2d 1526 (6th Cir. 1987). For the evidence to be useful, however, it must be related in some manner to the individual's claim. *Zavala-Bonilla v. INS*, 730 F.2d 562 (9th Cir. 1984) [letters concerning government harassment of unions relevant in claim by union member]. Even evidence that is 10 years old is admissible unless there is some basis to exclude it. *Perez-Alvarez v. INS*, 857 F.2d 23 (1st Cir. 1988) [IJ reversed where he excluded evidence of union membership that was 10 years old based on his unsubstantiated belief that information was stale]. In *Matter of S-M-J-*, 21 I&N Dec. 722, 726–28 (BIA 1997), the BIA clarified that it expected the INS as well as the IJ to provide evidence of country conditions and other available evidence through the Resource Information Center, or otherwise that would shed light on the applicant's claim.

(a) *Background Material*—To obtain background country information and materials, the applicant should consult human rights and educational organizations that may provide specific and reliable information on various countries. *See* **Appendix H**, *infra,* for a list of such organizations. The applicant may also consult the Resource Information Center which was created by INS to assist AOs in adjudicating asylum claims, as well as the DOS reports.

(b) *Country Reports and Profiles*—The BIA has relied on the DOS Profile of Asylum Claims and Country Conditions, which are prepared pursuant to 8 C.F.R. §§208.11(a), 1208.11(a) and the government's view of country conditions in specific countries. *Matter of R-S-H-*, 23 I&N Dec. 629, 643 (BIA 2003) [emphasizing that IJs and the BIA frequently rely on DOS Country Reports]; *Matter of A-E-M-,* 21 I&N Dec. 1157 (BIA 1998) [profile on Peru that stated that Sendero Luminoso have reduced ability to act and operate in only a few areas of Peru used to deny asylum]; *Matter of V-T-S-*, 21 I&N Dec. 792, 798–99 (BIA 1997) ["[c]ountry condition profiles described by the State Department have been found to be 'the most appropriate and perhaps the best resource for information on conditions in foreign nations'"].

i) Circuit Court Cases

First Circuit—*Tota v. Gonzales,* 457 F.3d 161, 166–69 (1st Cir. 2006) [evidence from DOS report that "since 1998" treatment of DP members in Albania improved provided substantial evidence to rebut presumptive well-founded fear regarding events in 2000 absent applicant's rebuttal]; *Palma-Mazariegos v. Gonzales,* 428 F.3d 30, 34–36 (1st Cir. 2005) [DOS report on Guatemala alone directly rebutted applicant's particular fear that he would be persecuted]; *Negeya v. Gonzales,* 417 F.3d 78, 84 (1st Cir. 2005) [upholding denial of asylum from Ethiopian based on recent DOS report and noting that, "[g]enerally, State Department reports are a highly probative source of evidence in cases that turn on the objective reasonableness of an asserted fear of future persecution"]; *Lin v. Ashcroft,* 371 F.3d 18, 22 (1st Cir. 2004) [where undisputed country reports provide that documents from certain provinces in China are subject to widespread fabrication and fraud, it was reasonable for IJ to require authentication of document].

Second Circuit—*Serafimovich v. Ashcroft,* 456 F.3d 81 (2d Cir. 2006) [where IJ/BIA ignored information in country reports that conditions worsened in Belarus the decision denying withholding was reversed]; *Chen v. Gonzales,* 417 F.3d 268, 272–75 (2d Cir. 2005) [reversing IJ's denial of asylum where IJ ignored DOS report supporting PRC respondent's claim of religious persecution]; *Melgar de Torres v.Reno,* 191 F.3d 307, 314 (2d Cir. 1999) [relying on Profile of El Salvador for positive view of country].

Third Circuit—*Myat Thu v. Attorney General of the USA,* 510 F.3d 405, 413–15 (3d Cir. 2007) [political activities in Japan with BDA and in Burma with the NLD may establish basis for asylum and case is remanded in light of DOS reports and letters indicating that the Burmese military may be aware of applicants activities]; *Ghebrehiwot v. Att'y Gen. of the U.S.,* 467 F.3d 344, 353–55 (3d Cir. 2006) [where IJ failed to consider DOS reports and other documents submitted by Eritrean Pentecostal Christian, court remanded case to consider whether there is a pattern and practice of persecution]; *Ambartsoumian v. Ashcroft,* 388 F.3d 85, 93 (3d Cir. 2004) [relying on DOS reports considered by IJ as "objective evidence" to find no past persecution from Georgia]; *Xie v. Ashcroft,* 359 F.3d 239, 243–44 (3d Cir. 2004) [describing Country Reports as "the most appropriate and perhaps the best resource for information on political situations in foreign nations" and denying relief due to lack of credibility including claim of forced sterilization of wife in 1979 when China's policy according to Report did not take affect until early 1980s]; *Kayembe v. Ashcroft,* 334 F.3d 231, 235–37 (3d Cir. 2003) [where DOS Country Report stated that the government of the Congo no longer persecutes Tutsis, substantial evidence supported denial].

Fifth Circuit—*Zhao v. Gonzales,* 404 F.3d 295, 304–06 (5th Cir. 2005) [BIA abused its discretion in refusing to grant a motion to reopen to admit the DOS Reports which supported respondent's contention that Falun Gong members were persecuted].

Sixth Circuit—*Shkulaku-Purballori v. Mukasey,* 514 F.3d 499, 503 (6th Cir. 2007) [where the IJ relied on DOS reports to show that democratic changes occurred in Albania, the applicant's response that the reports did not reflect every incident and that the country has a long history of instability were insufficient to rebut the reports].

Seventh Circuit—*Gebreeyesus v. Gonzales,* 482 F.3d 952, 955 (7th Cir. 2007) [reversing BIA denial of motion to reopen by Amharan from Ethiopia based on changed country conditions where BIA offered no reasoned explanation for its decision in light of DOS report regarding government repression]; *Huang v. Gonzales,* 453 F.3d 942 (7th Cir. 2006) [IJ's adverse credibility determination upheld despite errors where PRC respondent presented certificate of forced abortion and IJ relied on DOS report stating certificates are only given for voluntary abortions]; *Dawoud v. Gonzales,* 424 F.3d 608, 612–14 (7th Cir. 2005) [rejecting the BIA's insistence on corroboration where story was credible and supported by DOS report and reversing BIA denial of motion to reconsider because BIA misread DOS report]; *Toptchev v. INS,* 295 F.3d 714, 722 (7th Cir. 2002) [BIA entitled to consider reports and may reasonably rely on DOS's assessment of current country conditions, given the Department's expertise in international affairs].

Eighth Circuit—*Diallo v. Mukasey,* 508 F.3d 451, 455–56 (8th Cir. 2007) [many aspects of country reports supported the determination that conditions have improved in Sierra Leone and precluded a finding of future persecution]; *Gebrehiwot v. Ashcroft,* 374 F.3d 723, 725–26 (8th Cir. 2004) [IJ may reasonably rely on DOS's assessment of current country conditions given their expertise in international affairs]; *Meas v. Ashcroft,* 363 F.3d 729 (8th Cir. 2004) [relying on DOS report that there was no reported persecution of repatriated Cambodian refugees to rebut future persecution]; *Navarijo-Barrios v. Ashcroft,* 322 F.3d 561, 564 (8th Cir. 2003) [given DOS's expertise in international affairs, BIA may reasonably rely on the Department's assessment of current country conditions as they related to the likelihood of future persecution].

Ninth Circuit—*Lanza v. Ashcroft,* 389 F.3d 917, 934–35 & n.13 (9th Cir. 2004) [relying on absence of evidence in DOS report and noting that the reports are "the most appropriate and perhaps the best resource for information on the political situations in foreign nations"]; *Duarte de Guinac v. INS,* 179 F.3d 1156, 1162 (9th Cir. 1999) [purpose of DOS reports is to "provide information about the context in which the alleged persecution took place, in order that the fact finder may intelligently evaluate the petitioner's credibility"];

Tenth Circuit—*Yuk v. Ashcroft,* 355 F.3d 1222, 1236 (10th Cir. 2004) [DOS report on Cambodia can constitute substantial evidence supporting an IJ's decision].

Eleventh Circuit—*Reyes-Sanchez v. U.S. Att'y Gen.,* 369 F.3d 1239, 1243 (11th Cir. 2004) [BIA entitled to "heavily rely" on DOS reports in determining that Peru does not acquiesce in torture].

ii) *Negative View of Reports*—One court has noted that DOS reports are more like litigation documents than accurate analysis. *See Koliada,* 259 F.3d 482, 487–88 (6th Cir. 2001) [although upholding the denial of asylum, the court, in referring to the DOS reports, found that, "[i]t stands to reason that a report produced by one executive department to aid the litigation of another executive department would often support the second department's point of view"]. Another court has severely criticized the over-reliance on DOS reports and even questioned their admissibility. *Koval v. Gonzales,* 418 F.3d 798, 806–09 & n.3 (7th Cir. 2005) [reversing IJ's denial of asylum to Mormon from Ukraine, in light of IJ's over-reliance on DOS country report despite its questionable admissibility, anonymity, generality, lack of trustworthiness and respondent's inability to verify its truth through cross-examination]. Other courts have recognized that the observations in the reports do not automatically discredit contrary evidence. *Banks v. Gonzales,* 453 F.3d 449, 453–54 (7th Cir. 2006) [DOS reports are too general and the IJ erred in ignoring expert testimony supporting persecution claim of Liberian from Krahn tribe]; *Cao He Lin v. DOJ,* 428 F.3d 391, 403–04 (2d Cir. 2005) [where IJ did not heed court's admonition "not to place excessive reliance" on DOS reports, its decision that the China profile provided substantial evidence without giving an explanation why it credited the report over the applicant's testimony was error]; *Mece v. Gonzales,* 415 F.3d 562, 573 (6th Cir. 2005) [differing descriptions between the DOS report and respondent regarding the political coloration of the socialist government in Albania do not reflect on respondent's credibility]; *Sosnovskaia v. Gonzales,* 421 F.3d 589, 593–94 (7th Cir. 2005) [criticizing IJ's reliance on DOS Report on Ukraine to deny asylum claim in light of court's admonition regarding the potential for bias in the reports and "the inability of asylum-seekers to question the conclusions contained therein"]; *Zheng v. Gonzales,* 409 F.3d 804, 810–11 (7th Cir. 2005) [DOS Country Reports "cannot substitute for an individualized determination of an asylum or withholding claim"]; *Zhang v. Gonzales,* 405 F.3d 150, 157 (3d Cir. 2005) [counseling wariness in the wholesale reliance on DOS reports particularly where the data the report relied on was old and there is only a single paragraph in the DOS report that addresses the issue]; *Tian-Yong Chen v. INS,* 359 F.3d 121, 130–32 (2d Cir. 2004) [court should not place "excessive reliance" on DOS reports which "are sometimes skewed toward the governing administration's foreign-policy goals and concerns" including "half-truths about human rights abuses in friendly countries"]. Another court has recognized that while the reports are trustworthy, "the factual summaries and assessments...are sometimes colored by diplomatic relations and are at best generalizations of the human rights situations in foreign countries." *Kanivets v. Riley,* 286 F.Supp.2d 460, 466 (E.D. Pa. 2003) [for purposes of likelihood of success on a stay petition, individual specific descriptions of persecution cannot be refuted by general Country Reports]. *Accord. Kanivets v. Riley,* 320 F.Supp.2d 297, 300 (E.D. Pa. 2004) [legal error for IJ to rely on DOS report to rebut testimony IJ found credible]. Reports may have little relevance where the applicant has already endured actual persecution. *Bellido v. Ashcroft,* 367 F.3d 840, 845 n.6 (8th Cir. 2004) [observations in report cannot outweigh actual persecution of Bolivian union official]. Nor can such evidence of background conditions alone establish that specific acts of persecution did or did not occur. *Ornelas-Chavez v. Gonzales,* 458 F.3d 1052, 1057 (9th Cir. 2006) [reversing lack of credibility finding where the BIA improperly relied *inter alia* on DOS report to establish lack of credibility].

iii) *Inaccuracies and Hearsay*—Statements and reports may be challenged for factual inaccuracies or because they represent highly unreliable hearsay. *Corovic v. Mukasey,* 519 F.3d 90, 95-96 (2d Cir. 2008) [U.S. government's request to Macedonian government to verify documents violated confidentiality provision of 8 C.F.R. §208.6 (now §1208.6) and the court, following *Zhen Nan Lin* prohibited the use of the Macedonian government's report and remanded the case but left open the possibility that the IJ could make the same finding that the document was fraudulent based upon other evidence]; *Zhen Nan Lin v. DOJ,* 459 F.3d 255, 268–72 (2d Cir. 2006) [BIA's adverse credibility finding that was based on a consular report that a document was a forgery was reversed where the hearsay report was inherently unreliable]; *Alexandrov v. Gonzales,* 442 F.3d 395, 404–07 (6th Cir. 2006) [in Bulgarian asylum claim, IJ violated due process by relying on two highly unreliable hearsay memoranda from the U.S. Embassy in Sofia to prove that respondent's documents were fraudulent]; *He Chun Chen v. Ashcroft,* 376 F.3d 215, 225–26 (3d Cir. 2004) [criticizing IJ and BIA for finding a lack of credibility of abortion certificates from PRC by relying on "nothing more" than the DOS Country Report that stated that abortion certificates are only issued to women who voluntarily seek abortions because such Reports are not the "Holy Writ" and the BIA "cannot hide behind the State Department's letterhead"]; *Ezeagwuna v. Ashcroft,* 325 F.3d 396, 405–08 (3d Cir. 2003) [reliance on double and triple hearsay letter of Director of Office of Country Reports and Asylum Affairs in DOS to undermine credibility of documentary evidence violated due process; criticizing efforts "to use the prestige of the State Department letterhead to make its case and give credibility to the letter's contents"]; *Galina v. INS,* 213 F.3d 955, 958–99 (7th Cir. 2000) [statements in Country Reports are not only not incontestable, they "are not even facts"; "the Board should treat it with a healthy skepticism, rather than, as is its tendency, as Holy Writ"]; *Gramatikov v. INS*, 128 F.3d 619, 620 (7th Cir. 1997) ["[t]here is perennial concern that the Department soft pedals human rights violations by countries that the United States wants to have good relations with"]; *Gailius v. INS,* 147 F.3d 34, 46 (1st Cir. 1998) [quoting *Gramatikov* regarding DOS reports]; *Vaduva v. INS*, 131 F.3d 689, 691 (7th Cir. 1997) ["[i]f it is reasonable to suspect the State Department has a tendency to soft pedal human rights violations...it may be just as reasonable to suspect that Amnesty International exaggerates them so they will not go without notice"]; *Okoroha v. INS*, 715 F.2d 380, 383 (8th Cir. 1983); *Zamora v. INS*, 534 F.2d 1055, 1061 (9th Cir. 1976); *Paul v. INS*, 521 F.2d 194, 200 (5th Cir. 1975); *Ratnam v. Lewis*, 892 F.Supp. 619, 625–26 (D.N.J. 1995) [criticizes BHRHA's analysis of Sri Lanka]; *Dhine v. District Director*, 818 F.Supp. 671, 677 (S.D.N.Y.), *rev'd on other grounds*, 3 F.3d 613 (2d Cir. 1993) [criticizing DOS Country Report on Ethiopia as factually inaccurate]; *Molina-Estrada v. INS,* 293 F.3d 1089, 1096 (9th Cir. 2002) ["a State Department report on country conditions, standing alone, is not sufficient to rebut the presumption of future persecution when a petitioner has established past persecution"].

iv) *Generalized Information to Rebut or Support Claim is Impermissible*—The use of generalized information in the reports to rebut a specific claim is impermissible. *Mapouya v. Gonzales,* 487 F.3d 396, 411–13 (6th Cir. 2007) [even if the government could prove that country conditions have changed in Brazzaville, Congo, it must show by a preponderance of the evidence that the changed conditions negate the applicant's *individualized* fear and where documents rebutted the country report, they had to be weighed against the report]; *Gomes v. Gonzales,* 473 F.3d 746 (7th Cir. 2007) [in case involving Christians from Bangladesh who were attacked by Muslims, court reversed IJ's finding that there was no likelihood of future persecution where the IJ overrelied on DOS reports while ignoring specific contradictory testimony]; *Ornelas-Chavez v. Gonzales,* 458 F.3d 1052, 1057 (9th Cir. 2006) [background evidence alone can not be used to establish whether or not persecution occurred; reversing adverse credibility finding where the BIA improperly relied *inter alia* on the DOS report]; *Sunthara-*

linkam v. Gonzales, 458 F.3d 1034, 1047–48 (9th Cir. 2006) [government expert's general testimony about trends and conditions in Sri Lanka not based upon individualized facts concerning the respondent cannot be the basis for an adverse credibility finding]; *Tambadou v. Gonzales,* 446 F.3d 298, 300–04 (2d Cir. 2006) [BIA reversed on changed country conditions findings where it used an outdated DOS report, ignored the complexities of the reported information, did not make an individualized assessment, and failed to consider evidence by Mauritanian applicant which contradicted the changed conditions described in the report]; *Kllokoqi v. Gonzales,* 439 F.3d 336, 343 (7th Cir. 2006) [a general statement in a Country Report regarding Kosovo was insufficient to rebut the applicant's detailed, specific testimony, establishing his place of origin]; *Hoque v. Ashcroft,* 367 F.3d 1190, 1197–98 (9th Cir. 2004) [BIA's reliance on country report's claim of widespread violence in Bangladesh to support claim that respondent was involved in violence is impermissible]. *Accord Berishaj v. Ashcroft,* 378 F.3d 314, 326–28 (3d Cir. 2004) [use of generalized information to rebut claim was not permissible where no explanation was given as to how or why the DOS report rebutted the claim]. The IJ "may not discredit a petitioner's testimony based on a statement in a DOS report that is itself based on speculation or conjecture. *See Shah v. INS,* 220 F.3d 1062, 1069 (9th Cir. 2000). *Zheng v. Ashcroft,* 397 F.3d 1139, 1144 (9th Cir. 2005) [statements in the country report were not inconsistent with applicant's testimony when local variances, as recognized by the report, regarding sterilization policy and fines, are taken into account]. The same is true for supporting claims by generalized information. *Chen v. Gonzales,* 470 F.3d 1131 (5th Cir. 2006) [upholding denial of religious persecution claim of Chinese Protestant despite DOS Country Reports and Religious Freedom Report because the statements that religious adherents experienced persecution were vague and the specific examples of persecution pointed to other religions].

v) *Inferences from DOS Reports Must be Rational*—Any inference that the IJ/BIA draws from a country report must be rational. *Dawoud v. Gonzales,* 424 F.3d 608, 612–14 (7th Cir. 2005) [where BIA misread DOS report as not supporting Egyptian Coptic's persecution claim, court reversed denial of motion to reconsider]; *Zarouite v. Gonzales,* 424 F.3d 60 (1st Cir. 2005) [where BIA asserted that country report for Morocco rebutted past persecution claim, the court reversed finding that the inference drawn by the BIA was not rationally related to the report]. However, the failure of a report to mention a specific fact or group should not be used to infer that fact or group did not exist. *Vladimirova v. Ashcroft,* 377 F.3d 690, 697 (7th Cir. 2004) [IJ reversed where it drew adverse inference from DOS failure to name religious group in its annual report because failure to name a specific religious organization does not imply that the group does not exist or was not persecuted]; *Nagi El Moraghy v. Ashcroft,* 331 F.3d 195, 203–04 (1st Cir. 2003) [IJ erred in employing the country condition reports as a test of direct corroboration]. *But see Lanza v. Ashcroft,* 389 F.3d 917, 934–35 (9th Cir. 2004) [relying on fact that DOS report did not mention persecution of members of UCR in Argentina].

vi) *Overcoming DOS Reports with Expert Testimony*—*Mapouya v. Gonzales,* 487 F.3d 396, 411–13 (6th Cir. 2007) [even if the government could prove that country conditions have changed in Brazzaville, Congo, it must show by a preponderance of the evidence that the changed conditions negate the applicant's *individualized* fear and where documents rebutted the country report, they had to be weighed against the report]; *Banks v. Gonzales,* 453 F.3d 449, 453–54 (7th Cir. 2006) [DOS reports are too general and the IJ erred in ignoring expert testimony supporting persecution claim of Liberian from Krahn tribe]; *Yang v. Gonzales,* 427 F.3d 1117, 1121–22 (8th Cir. 2005) [following *Zheng* and finding that expert affidavit was "sufficient to dispute the information in the State Department reports"]; *Zheng v. Gonzales,* 415 F.3d 955, 960–63 (8th Cir. 2005) [specific and expert testimony overcame DOS Report that Fujian province was lax in enforcement policy and that children born abroad are not considered as violative of one–child policy]; *Guo v. Ashcroft,* 386 F.3d 556, 563–66 (3d Cir. 2004) [BIA erred in denying motion to reopen because expert affidavit rebutted the DOS Profile and provided sufficient evidence to meet *prima facie* case]. *But see Matter of C-C-,* 23 I&N Dec. 899, 901–02 (BIA 2006) [denying motion to reopen based in part on expert affidavit refuting DOS position regarding forced sterilization in China because it found that affidavit was not based on personal knowledge and referred to events prior to the DOS report it challenged]; *Wang v. BIA,* 437 F.3d 270, 274–76 (2d Cir. 2006) [expert affidavit that was not prepared specifically for petitioner and was not particularized as to his circumstances was limited in relevance].

(c) *Other Sources of Information*—DHS regulations now provide that AOs may not only rely on DOS and country conditions reports but "other credible sources, such as international organizations, private voluntary agencies, news organizations, or academic institutions." 8 C.F.R. §§208.12(a), 1208.12(a). *See also Tobon-Marin v. Mukasey,* 512 F.3d 28, 3e (1st Cir. 2008) [discussing UNICEF report that Colombia's civil unrest affects about 17.5% of its child population but finding that "affects" does not necessarily connote that the children suffer persecution]; *Jorge-Tzoc v. Gonzales,* 435 F.3d 146, 149 (2d Cir. 2006) [quoting from CEH report on war in Guatemala and reversed IJ denial of asylum for Mayan from Guatemala where IJ failed to consider report]; *Zubeda v. Ashcroft,* 333 F.3d 463, 467–69, 477–78 (3d Cir. 2003) [quoting extensively from Human Rights Watch report on Republic of Congo and challenging BIA's failure to give sufficient weight and meaning to such reports]; *Navas v. INS,* 217 F.3d 646, 653–54 (9th Cir. 2000) [quoting extensively from Americas Watch reports on El Salvador]; *Chanchavac v. INS,* 207 F.3d 584, 590 (9th Cir. 2000) (discussing Amnesty International finding regarding Guatemalan military]; *Feleke v. INS*, 118 F.3d 594, 599 (8th Cir. 1997) [relying in part on Amnesty International Report on Ethiopia]; *Chang v. INS*, 119 F.3d 1055, 1064–65 (3d Cir. 1997) [referring to Human Rights Watch/Asia]; *Hengan v. INS*, 79 F.3d 60, 62–63 (7th Cir. 1996) [recognition that Helsinki Watch and other human rights reports may have greater weight than DOS]; *Orantes-Hernandez v. Gonzales,* 504 F.Supp.2d 825, 838–43 (C.D. Cal. 2007) [in the context of vacating a part of the original *Orantes* injunction the court discusses the current political conditions in El Salvador]; *Matter of G-A-,* 23 I&N Dec. 366, 369–70 (BIA 2002) [relying extensively on a report prepared by Iranian Christians International, Inc. in granting CAT claim]; *Matter of T-*, 20 I&N Dec. 571, 576–77 (BIA 1992) [BIA relies extensively on Amnesty International reports]. *But see Matter of A-G-*, 19 I&N Dec. 502 (BIA 1987), *aff'd sub nom. M.A. v. INS*, 899 F.2d 304, 312–14 (4th Cir. 1990) (*en banc*) ["statements of opinion of private unofficial bodies (referring to Americas Watch), do not constitute evidence of condemnation by recognized international government bodies, which would be necessary at a minimum for U.S. to accept [the claim that the Salvadoran army violates international law"]; *Agada v. Ashcroft,* 368 F.3d 867, 870 (8th Cir. 2004) [where lesser known source reports were tangentially relevant to asylum claim in comparison to DOS Country Report, court upheld IJ's decision to deny asylum].

2.g. *Testimonial Evidence*

(1) *Generally*—The applicant's testimony cannot be rejected solely because it may be viewed as self-serving. *Matter of Acosta*, 19 I&N Dec. 211 (BIA 1985). Uncorroborated but credible testimony by the applicant may be sufficient to sustain the burden of proof. 8 C.F.R. §§208.13(a), 208.16(b), 1208.13(a), 1208.16(b). *Dawoud v. Gonzales,* 424 F.3d 608, 612–14 (7th Cir. 2005) [rejecting the BIA's insistence on corroboration where applicant's story was credible and supported by DOS report. "To expect [asylum seekers] to stop and collect dossiers of paperwork before fleeing is both unrealistic and strikingly insensitive to the harrowing conditions they face"]; *Yang v. U.S. Att'y Gen.*, 418 F.3d 1198, 1201 (11th Cir. 2005) [noting that: "[u]ncorroborated but credible testimony may be sufficient to sustain the burden of proof for demonstrating eligibility for asylum," but finding that the evidence did not establish persecution]; *Karouni v. Gonzales,* 399 F.3d

1163, 1173–74 (9th Cir. 2005) [reversing IJ's requiring corroborative documentary evidence because: "[o]nce an applicant's testimony is deemed credible...no further corroboration is required to establish the facts to which the applicant testified"]; *Njuguna v. Ashcroft,* 374 F.3d 765 (9th Cir. 2004) [where respondent's testimony is credible and there was no contradictory evidence, the BIA's decision to deny relief on the grounds that the testimony was "unsupported and implausible speculation" was not based upon substantial evidence]. Virtually all courts have found that uncorroborated testimony is sufficient to establish a claim for asylum so long as it is credible, persuasive and specific. *See Matter of Mogharrabi*, 19 I&N Dec. 439 (BIA 1987); *Ahmadshah v. Ashcroft,* 396 F.3d 917, 920–21 (8th Cir. 2005) [reversing denial of asylum and noting documentary evidence was not necessary where applicant's claim was clear and consistent]; *Bellido v. Ashcroft,* 367 F.3d 840, 844 (8th Cir. 2004) [lack of corroboration of Bolivian union leader's claim is not basis to deny asylum]; *Georgis v. Ashcroft,* 328 F.3d 962, 969 (7th Cir. 2003) [not necessary for an asylum applicant to submit corroborating evidence in order to sustain burden of proof]; *Secaida-Rosales v. INS,* 331 F.3d 297, 311 (2d Cir. 2003) [testimony alone is sufficient; reversing BIA where it relied on IJ's credibility findings based, in part, on failure to produce documents]; *Ladha v. INS,* 215 F.3d 889, 901 (9th Cir. 2000) ["[w]e reaffirm that an alien's testimony, if unrefuted and credible, direct and specific, is sufficient to establish the facts testified without the need for any corroboration"]; *Senathirajah v. INS,* 157 F.3d 210, 216 (3d Cir. 1998) ["[c]ommon sense establishes that it is escape and flight, not litigation and corroboration, that is foremost in the mind of an alien who comes to these shores fleeing detention, torture and persecution. Accordingly, corroboration is not required to establish credibility"]; *Sotelo-Aquije v. Slattery*, 17 F.3d 33, 36 n.2 (2d Cir. 1994); *Mendoza-Perez v. INS*, 902 F.2d 760 (9th Cir. 1990); *Damaize-Job v. INS,* 787 F.2d 1332 (9th Cir. 1986) ["[m]inor discrepancies in dates that are attributable to the applicant's language problems or typographical errors cannot be viewed as attempts by the applicant to enhance his claim of persecution [and] have no bearing on credibility."]; *Canjura-Flores v. INS*, 784 F.2d 885 (9th Cir. 1985) [when IJ/BIA are silent on credibility of the alien's testimony, court will presume credibility]; *Bolanos-Hernandez v. INS*, 767 F.2d 1277 (9th Cir. 1984); *Aguilera-Cota v. INS*, 914 F.2d 1375, 1380–81 (9th Cir. 1990) [IJ cannot draw adverse inference from fact that threatening note left for the applicant was not signed and that applicant did not retain it]; *Carvajal-Munoz v. INS*, 743 F.2d 562 (7th Cir. 1984). *But see Gu v. Gonzales,* 454 F.3d 1014, 1021–22 (9th Cir. 2006) [upheld denial of asylum where applicant's testimony, although deemed credible, consisted of hearsay evidence by friend as to what would occur to Gu in China if he returned and the statement, because of its limited probative value, cannot compel asylum]; *Huaman-Cornelio v. BIA*, 979 F.2d 995, 1000 (4th Cir. 1992) ["[p]etitioner offers nothing beyond his own barebones statement...."].

(2) *Credibility Analysis and Failure of Proof*—A credibility determination must be independent of an analysis of the sufficiency of the applicant's evidence. *Abdulai v. Ashcroft,* 239 F.3d 542, 551 n.6 (3d Cir. 2001) ["[a] failure of proof is not a proper ground per se for an adverse credibility determination. The latter finding is more appropriately based upon inconsistent statements, contradictory evidence, and inherently improbable testimony"]. *But see Chen v. Gonzales,* 434 F.3d 212, 220–22 (3d Cir. 2005) [*post*-REAL ID, upholding denial of asylum even where IJ did not make a valid credibility assessment because even a credible applicant may be required to produce corroborative evidence].

(3) *REAL ID Act of 2005 and Corroboration*—For cases filed on or after May 11, 2005. Corroboration may be unnecessary where the trier of fact is satisfied that the "applicant's testimony is credible, is persuasive, and refers to specific facts sufficient to demonstrate that the applicant is a refugee." However, the trier of fact can require the applicant to corroborate otherwise credible testimony "unless the applicant does not have the evidence and cannot reasonably obtain the evidence." In determining whether the applicant has met her burden the trier of fact may weigh the credible testimony along with other record evidence. INA §208(b)(1)(B)(ii).

(4) *REAL ID Act of 2005 and Credibility Determinations*—For cases filed on or after May 11, 2005. *Matter of S-B-,* 24 I&N Dec. 42 (BIA 2006) [new standards only apply where

application was filed first with asylum office or IJ on or after May 11, 2005; where application was first filed with asylum office before May 11th but with IJ after, the new standards do not apply]. Credibility is now determined by the "totality of the circumstances and all relevant factors." The trier of fact may base credibility on "demeanor, candor, or responsiveness of the applicant or witness, the inherent plausibility of the applicant's or witness's account, the consistency between the applicant's or witness's written and oral statements (whenever made and whether or not under oath, and considering the circumstances under which the statements were made), the internal consistency of each such statement, the consistency of such statements with other evidence of record (including the reports of the Department of State on country conditions) and any inaccuracies or falsehoods in such statements, without regard to whether an inconsistency, inaccuracy, or falsehood goes to the heart of the applicant's claim, or any other relevant factor." INA §208(b)(1)(iii), 8 U.S.C. §1158(b)(1)(B)(iii); *Matter of J-Y-C-,* 24 I&N Dec. 260, 263–66 (BIA 2007) [upheld IJ's finding of lack of credibility under the REAL ID Act for Chinese asylum claim where IJ relied upon the totality of the circumstances, including some inconsistencies that did not go to the heart of the claim, some inconsistencies between respondent's testimony and his airport statements, his demeanor and his lack of corroboration]; *Chen v. U.S. Att'y Gen.,* 463 F.3d 1228, 1230–32 (11th Cir. 2006) [rejecting the argument that an adverse credibility determination could not be based on "trivial" issues or ones "irrelevant to the dispositive issues" under the REAL ID Act]. *But see Kadia v. Gonzales,* 501 F.3d 817, 821–22 (7th Cir. 2007) [although the case was pre-REAL ID the court determined that under the REAL ID Act, IJ may consider inaccuracies or falsehoods that do not go to the heart of the asylum application but can do so only as part of his consideration of the "totality of the circumstances, and all relevant factors" and the court reversed IJ where he failed to distinguish between material lies and innocent mistakes, trivial inconsistencies and harmless exaggerations and adhered to the discredited doctrine of *falsus in uno, falsus in omnibus* (false in one thing, false in all things)].

(5) *Presumption of Credibility*—Post-REAL ID Act of 2005, there is no longer a presumption of credibility. However, the applicant has a rebuttable presumption on appeal if no adverse credibility determination is explicitly made. INA §§208(b)(1)(B)(iii), 240(c)(4)(C), 241(b)(3)(C), 8 U.S.C. §§ 158(b)(1)(B)(iii), 1229a(c)(4)(C), 1231(b)(3)(C). Prior to REAL ID, where an IJ did not make a credibility finding, the court presumed credibility. *Li Fang Lin v. Mukasey,* 517 F.3d 685, 687–88 (4th Cir. 2008) [in pre-REAL ID Act case the court followed the other circuits and determined that where the BIA expressly declined to address the IJ's determination of lack of credibility, the court would presume credibility]; *Niftaliev v. U.S. Att'y Gen.,* 504 F.3d 1211, 1216–17 (11th Cir. 2007) [where IJ did not make adverse credibility determination and applicant relied on testimony alone, credibility assumed and IJ's denial of past persecution from Ukraine was reversed]; *Kayembe v. Ashcroft,* 334 F.3d 231, 237–39 (3d Cir. 2003) [reversing where BIA noted IJ's negative credibility finding but made no credibility finding of its own and did not point to anything in the record to refute the claim]; *See also Li v. Att'y Gen. of the U.S.,* 400 F.3d 157, 163–64 (3d Cir. 2005) [where BIA found no past persecution "assuming" credibility after IJ had found adverse credibility, the court treated his testimony as credible]; *Artiga-Turcios v. INS,* 829 F.2d 720, 723 (9th Cir. 1987). Also pre-REAL ID, "absent an explicit finding that a specific statement by the petitioner is not credible we are required to accept her testimony as true." *Lukwago v. Ashcroft,* 329 F.3d 157, 164 (3d Cir. 2003) [quoting *Hartooni v. INS,* 21 F.3d 336, 342 (9th Cir. 1994) in context of a case involving a former child soldier as a particular social group in Uganda]. Under pre-REAL ID decisions, where an IJ did not expressly make an adverse credibility determination, the BIA may not imply such a finding without violating the applicant's due process right to notice. *Mendoza Manimbao v. Ashcroft,* 329 F.3d 655 (9th Cir. 2003) [BIA must remand to IJ for new determination on credibility, give applicant notice and an opportunity to respond to the BIA's concern, or accept the testimony as credible]. *But see Zaman v. Mukasey,* 514 F.3d 233, 237–38 (2d Cir. 2008) [although court's decision in *Diallo v. INS,* 232 F.3d 279, 287 requires an explicit credibility determination be made, the IJ's analysis in the case was sufficient to qualify as an explicit adverse credibility determination]; *Kho v. Keisler,* 505 F.3d 50, 56 (1st Cir. 2007) [rejected the propo-

sition that applicants are entitled to a presumption of credibility on review if there is no express credibility determination made by an IJ]. Where the IJ made a favorable credibility determination and the BIA reversed without providing applicant the right to respond to the BIA's claims, it also violated due process if the adverse finding formed the basis for the denial. *Stoyanov v. INS,* 172 F.3d 731, 735 (9th Cir. 1999); *Akinmade v. INS,* 196 F.3d 951, 957 (9th Cir. 1999); *Campos-Sanchez v. INS,* 164 F.3d 448 (9th Cir. 1999). *But see Pal v. INS,* 204 F.3d 935, 938–39 (9th Cir. 2000) [narrowing *Campos-Sanchez* where BIA credibility findings include IJs]. Also, when the BIA was reversed in a case where it expressly abstained from ruling on credibility, the case was remanded to the Board for a credibility finding. *Krastev v. INS,* 292 F.3d 1268, 1279 (10th Cir. 2002) (and cases cited therein); *Briones v. INS,* 175 F.3d 727, 730 (9th Cir. 1999) (*en banc*). [where IJ made adverse credibility finding but BIA expressly decline to rule on that issue and instead denied asylum on another basis, the court reversed on the legal issue and remanded for credibility finding].

(6) *Pre-REAL ID Credibility Determinations*—Prior to REAL ID, IJ credibility determinations were ordinarily given great weight and the BIA applied a clearly erroneous standard of review. 8 C.F.R. §1003.1(d)(3)(i); *Matter of A-H-,* 23 I&N Dec. 774, 786–87 (AG 2005) [when IJ's adverse credibility determination was based on the applicant's demeanor and sincerity as well as omissions and discrepancies, BIA erred in reversing]; *Matter of R-S-H-,* 23 I&N Dec. 629, 637 & 641 (BIA 2003) [applying the clearly erroneous standard to the adverse credibility determination by the IJ]; *Matter of A-S-*, 21 I&N Dec. 1106, 1109–11 (BIA 1998); *Matter of Pula*, 19 I&N Dec. 467 (BIA 1987); *Feto v. Gonzales,* 433 F.3d 902, 911 (7th Cir. 2005) [credibility determinations are findings of fact and should only be overturned under extraordinary circumstances]; *Gao v. U.S. Att'y Gen.,* 400 F.3d 963, 964 (2d Cir. 2005) [finding review of IJ's credibility findings "highly deferential" and "conclusive" unless reasonable adjudicator would be compelled to find otherwise]; *Loulou v. Ashcroft,* 354 F.3d 706, 709–10 (8th Cir. 2003) [upholding adverse credibility finding where respondent did not have mother testify who was major witness and where father's arrest was inconsistent with prior statements]; *Krouchevski v. Ashcroft,* 344 F.3d 670 (7th Cir. 2003) [ethnic Macedonian from Bulgaria could not overcome adverse credibility finding by explaining discrepancies or presenting documentary evidence]; *Chen v. INS,* 344 F.3d 272 (2d Cir. 2003) [*ex post* justifications for discrepancies were insufficient to overcome BIA's lack of credibility finding]; *Kalitani v. Ashcroft,* 340 F.3d 1 (1st Cir. 2003) [upholding IJ adverse credibility finding under *Elias-Zacarias* standard where testimony was inherently incredible, applicant's Ugandan identity documents raised doubts as to her identity, and her demeanor demonstrated she was evasive, less than candid and unresponsive]; *Pop v. INS,* 270 F.3d 527 (7th Cir. 2001) [affirming IJ's adverse credibility determination]. The IJ "must make "clean determinations of credibility" or the court will assume credibility. *Yang v. U.S. Att'y Gen.,* 418 F.3d 1198, 1201 (11th Cir. 2005) [upholding IJ's denial but noting that referring to the applicant's claims as "ridiculous fabrication" or stating that her testimony was "extremely inconsistent and made absolutely no sense whatsoever" did not amount to a specific finding that her testimony lacked credibility]. *Siewe v. Gonzales,* 480 F.3d 160, 167–71 (2d Cir. 2007) [quoting *Lavender v. Kurn,* 327 U.S. 645, 653 (1946) and distinguished between fair inference, which the court believed occurred here, and bald speculation where there is a complete absence of probative facts and gave deference to the IJ as it would a district judge].

(7) *BIA Standard*—The BIA will not uphold a credibility determination by an IJ if it is not supported by the record. *Matter of S-A-*, 22 I&N Dec. 1328 (BIA 2000) [reversing IJ's negative credibility finding of young Moroccan woman abused by her father]; *Matter of B-*, 21 I&N Dec. 66 (BIA 1995) [where applicant's testimony was plausible, detailed, internally consistent, consistent with the asylum application and embellished during probing cross-examination, IJ's adverse credibility finding was reversed]. The BIA will only defer to an adverse credibility determination based on inconsistencies and omissions regarding events central to the claim where a review of the record reveals that (1) the discrepancies and omissions described by the IJ are actually present in the record; (2) such

discrepancies and omissions provide specific and cogent reasons to conclude that the alien provided incredible testimony; and (3) the alien has failed to provide a convincing explanation for the discrepancies and omissions. *Matter of S-A-,* 22 I&N Dec. 1328 (BIA 2000) [quoting *Matter of A-S-,* 21 I&N Dec. 1106, 1109 (BIA 1998) and reversing IJ's adverse credibility determination].

(8) *Demeanor*—Credibility determinations based on demeanor are often given great deference. *Singh-Kaur v. INS,* 183 F.3d 1147, 1149–51 (9th Cir. 1999); *Matter of A-H-,* 23 I&N Dec. 774, 786–87 (AG 2005) [when IJ's adverse credibility determination was based on the applicant's demeanor and sincerity as well as omissions and discrepancies, BIA erred in reversing]. But where the IJ's findings on demeanor rest on the respondent's testimony which is ascertainable but unsupported by the record, they will not be credited. *Arulampalam v. Ashcroft,* 353 F.3d 679, 685–87 (9th Cir. 2003) [where demeanor finding does not adequately address the factors such as countenance, how the person sits, whether they are nervous, her/his coloration of events, modulation or pace of speech and other nonverbal factors, court will not credit finding]. Adverse credibility findings based on boilerplate demeanor determinations must be reversed. *Paramasamy v. Ashcroft,* 295 F.3d 1047, 1048 (9th Cir. 2002) [where IJ made adverse credibility determinations in three asylum cases based on identical demeanor findings and BIA cited the boilerplate language as evidence of individualized determinations, the court reversed, stating that "[t]he integrity of the adjudicative process…is called into question when boilerplate findings masquerade as individualized credibility determinations']. *See also Castaneda-Castillo v. Gonzales,* 488 F.3d 17, 22–26 (1st Cir. 2007) (*en banc*) [adverse credibility based in part on IJ's determination that the respondent was "blinking his eyes in an unusually rapid rate" was error in light of other erroneous credibility findings]. Also, adverse credibility findings based upon erroneous facts cannot be sustained. *Li Zu Guan v. INS,* 453 F.3d 129, 139–40 (2d Cir. 2006) [where IJ found that applicant for asylum based upon the PRCs family planning policy lacked credibility due to his demeanor because he *inter alia* took two or three water breaks to formulate answers when in fact he took only one break, the IJ's analysis of the applicant's demeanor was compromised by factual error and is a flawed basis for denial].

(9) *Critical of IJ's Credibility Assessments*—Courts will not defer to the IJ's credibility findings when they are unsupported by the record; the IJ's conclusions must be supported by substantial evidence. *Niang v. Mukasey*, 511 F.3d 138, 145–47 (2d Cir. 2007) [in Mauritanian asylum case, the tenuousness of the IJ's suspicions regarding applicant's documents, where the suspicions were based upon error or speculation, cannot support an adverse credibility determination where the applicant was otherwise credible]; *Zahedi v. INS,* 222 F.3d 1157, 1165 (9th Cir. 2000) [credibility determination must be "based on specific, cogent reasons that bear a legitimate nexus to the finding"]; *Tewabe v. Gonzales,* 446 F.3d 533, 538–40 (4th Cir. 2006) [IJ reversed in Ethiopian asylum claim where he stated that testimony was "implausible" without providing specific or cogent reasons why speaking out at a meeting, making airplane reservations quickly, or applying for asylum upon arrival were implausible]. The IJ "must have a legitimate articulable basis to question the petitioner's credibility, and must offer a specific, cogent reason for any stated disbelief." *Wiransane v. Ashcroft,* 366 F.3d 889, 898 (10th Cir. 2004), [IJ's finding that person was not ethnic Chinese was based upon speculation]; *Gui v. INS,* 280 F.3d 1217, 1225 (9th Cir. 2002) [quoting from *Hartooni v. INS,* 21 F.3d 336, 342 and reversing adverse credibility findings]. Adverse credibility determinations that are based on general and conclusory statements will not be sustained. *Butt v. Gonzales,* 429 F.3d 430, 436–37 (3d Cir. 2005) [IJ's claim that respondent's testimony was "thin" or "extremely vague" and his documents were "equally flimsy" is not enough to support an adverse credibility finding]. An IJ's interjection of personal views and his reliance on personal experience and beliefs to make credibility findings that are unsupported by specific and cogent reasons in the record will not be upheld. *Huang v. Gonzales,* 403 F.3d 945, 948–51 (7th Cir. 2005) [IJ's personal views about Catholicism was an inappropriate basis to make a credibility finding]. "Inconsistencies due to an unscrupulous preparer without other evidence of dishonesty (such as evasiveness in answering questions) do not provide a specific and cogent basis for an adverse credibility finding." *Alvarez-Santos v. INS,* 332

F.3d 1245, 1254 (9th Cir. 2003) [recognizing that asylum applications are frequently filled out by "poor, illiterate people who do not speak English" or by "preparers, whether lawyers or non-lawyers [who] are not always scrupulous" but finding independent reasons to discredit testimony]. Moreover, "credibility findings resting on analysis of testimony rather than on demeanor may deserve less than usual deference." *Secaida-Rosales v. INS,* 331 F.3d 297, 307 (2d Cir. 2003) [quoting *Aguilero-Cota v. INS,* 914 F.3d 1375, 1381 (9th Cir. 1990) in reversing IJ's credibility finding]. The IJ must allow the applicant to create a record before he makes an adverse credibility finding. *Muhanna v. Gonzales,* 399 F.3d 582, 589–90 (3d Cir. 2005) [where IJ concluded that asylum application was frivolous based on adverse credibility and abruptly ended the hearing, respondent was precluded from presenting a full record and IJ's denial was reversed for lack of substantial evidence]. An IJ's determination on credibility in one aspect of the case does not automatically carry over to another aspect. *Lin-Jian v. Gonzales,* 489 F.3d 182, 191–93 (4th Cir. 2007) [where court upheld IJ's adverse credibility finding as to future persecution, the IJ's failure to make a credibility determination as to past persecution requires the assumption that the testimony was credible and the denial was not supported by substantial evidence].

(10) *Confrontation of Inconsistency Prior to Making Credibility Assessment*—The IJ must give the asylum applicant an opportunity to explain a nonobvious inconsistency before relying on it to make an adverse credibility finding. *Suntharalinkam v. Gonzales,* 458 F.3d 1034, 1045–46 (9th Cir. 2006) [failure to give Sri Lankan an opportunity to explain discrepancy regarding medical records or manner of arrest was reversible error]; *Pang v. USCIS,* 448 F.3d 102, 109–11 (2d Cir. 2006) [in forced abortion case, "[w]hen putative inconsistencies or implausibilities are not dramatic and the need to clarify is not obvious, an IJ has an obligation to inform the petitioner that his testimony is being viewed as potentially flawed, and the IJ must give the petitioner a chance to explain"]; *Xue v. BIA,* 439 F.3d 111 (2d Cir. 2006) [IJ may not rest an adverse credibility finding on nondramatic putative contradictions or incongruities in an applicant's testimony without first giving the applicant a chance to explain]; *Damaize-Job v. INS,* 787 F.2d 1332 (9th Cir. 1986).

(11) *Credibility and the Doctrine of Falsus in Uno, Falsus in Omnibus*—The doctrine of *falsus in uno, falsus in omnibus* (false in one thing, false in all things) has been given substantial weight in the Second Circuit. *Siewe v. Gonzales,* 480 F.3d 160, 170–71 (2d Cir. 2007) ["*Falsus in uno* is a natural and instinctive tool of the factfinder, like a carpenter's hammer or plumber's wrench" and "a single false document or a single instance of false testimony may (if attributable to the petitioner) infect the balance of the alien's uncorroborated or unauthenticated evidence"]; *Qin Wen Zheng v. Gonzales,* 500 F.3d 143, 146–49 (2d Cir. 2007) [BIA did not abuse its discretion in denying motion to reopen for changed country conditions where document from Changle Province, China was not authenticated under §287.6 in light of prior adverse credibility finding given the doctrine of *falsus in uno, falsus in omnibus*]; *Niang v. Mukasey,* 511 F.3d 138, 146 (2d Cir. 2007) [quote *falsus in uno* language in *Siewe* but held that IJ's adverse credibility determination based upon his belief that documents were not authentic was error]. *But see Kadia v. Gonzales,* 501 F.3d 817, 821–24 (7th Cir. 2007) [post-REAL ID, IJ failed to distinguish between material lies and innocent mistakes, trivial inconsistencies and harmless exaggerations and adhered to the discredited doctrine of *falsus in uno, falsus in omnibus* while engaging in defective "gotcha" questioning of applicant]; *Lin v. Gonzales,* 445 F.3d 127, 132–34 (2d Cir. 2006) [IJ erred in mistaken belief that applicant's presentation of a false sterilization certificate to Chinese authorities to escape persecution called into question the authenticity of all her documentary evidence; the assumption that *falsus in uno, falsus in omnibus* (false in one thing, false in everything) has its limits]. *See also in this section* "Fraudulent Documents Not Fatal," ¶ 2.f(12)(b) (p.535), *supra.*

(12) *Failure to Seek Asylum In Third Country and Credibility*—Credibility does not turn on an applicant's failure to seek asylum in a third country he may have passed through on his journey to the U.S.

(13) *False Travel Documents and Credibility*—Credibility does not turn on whether someone presented a fraudulent document at the border because he was fleeing persecution. *Edimo-Doualla v. Gonzales,* 464 F.3d 276, 288–89 (2d Cir. 2006) [reversing IJ finding that applicant lacked credibility in Cameroonian asylum case because the use of fraudulent documents on entry cannot alone form the basis for an adverse credibility determination where the person is in immediate danger or imminent persecution]; *Zhang v. Gonzales,* 434 F.3d 993, 997 (7th Cir. 2006) [quoting *Dong v. Gonzales,* 421 F.3d 573, 577 (7th Cir. 2005) *and Matter of O-D-,* 21 I&N Dec. 1079, 1081 (BIA 1998): "[t]he use of false documents to facilitate travel or gain entry does not serve to impute a lack of credibility to the petitioner"]; *Kaur v. Ashcroft,* 379 F.3d 876, 889 (9th Cir. 2004) [false passport and misrepresentations to border officials to get into U.S. are consistent with asylum claim and do not reflect on credibility]; *Paramasamy v. Ashcroft,* 295 F.3d 1047, 1054 (9th Cir. 2002) [the use of false documents for travel is not a proper basis for an adverse credibility determination]; *Akinmade v. INS,* 196 F.3d 951, 955–56 (9th Cir. 1999) [distinguishing for purposes of credibility, false statements made to establish an asylum claim which do affect credibility, and false statements made to evade INS officials (such as a false passport or material misrepresentation at inspection) which do not affect credibility]. *But see Fongwo v. Gonzales,* 430 F.3d 944, 947–49 (8th Cir. 2005) [no abuse of discretion in denying motion to reconsider IJ's frivolous finding, where IJ's finding was based on entry documents that applicant said presented a false identity but IJ believed to be true].

(14) *Alcohol or Drug Use and Credibility*—Credibility does not turn on the IJ's concern about the applicant's use of alcohol. *Mihaylov v. Ashcroft,* 379 F.3d 15, 22–23 (1st Cir. 2004) [no evidence that respondent was an alcoholic and IJ did not explain what bearing respondent's alcohol use had on asylum claim].

(15) *Failure to Call Witnesses or Produce Evidence and Credibility*—It was impermissible for the IJ to make an adverse credibility finding where respondent failed to call a witness who was available. *Tabaku v. Gonzales,* 425 F.3d 417, 421–22 (7th Cir. 2005) [reversing adverse credibility determination where IJ drew the conclusion that a witness who was sitting outside of courtroom was afraid to testify because she could not withstand cross-examination even though IJ could have called her into courtroom to testify]. *But see Singh v. Gonzales,* 491 F.3d 1019, 1023–27 (9th Cir. 2007) [where a party withholds evidence, the court may draw a negative inference that the evidence is adverse to him. Although IJ could have drawn a negative inference as to asylum applicant's credibility when he failed to sign a waiver that would have produced his Canadian file, the IJ could not simply draw a negative inference that he was not entitled to asylum].

(16) *Credibility and Hearsay*—*Gu v. Gonzales,* 454 F.3d 1014, 1021–22 (9th Cir. 2006) [upheld denial of asylum where applicant's testimony, although deemed credible, consisted of hearsay evidence by friend as to what would occur to Gu in China if he returned and the statement, because of its limited probative value, cannot compel asylum].

(17) *Credibility and Forum Shopping*—At least one court has relied upon the applicant's lack of credibility in stating where they lived in the U.S. as a basis for denying, in part, their asylum claim. *Singh v. Gonzales,* 495 F.3d 553 (8th Cir. 2007) [adverse credibility sustained in part because applicants lied about where they were living in the U.S. by stating they were living in California instead of Missouri so they could gain a "forum shopping" advantage].

(18) *Credibility and IJ's Conduct*—*Wang v. Att'y Gen. of the U.S.,* 423 F.3d 260, 267–71 (3d Cir. 2005) [in Chinese forced sterilization case, the court remanded to the BIA and suggested a new IJ be assigned where the "tone, the tenor, the disparagement, and the sarcasm of the IJ seem[ed] more appropriate to a court television show than a federal court proceeding" and therefore "so tainted the proceedings below" that the court was not confident that the applicant was able to present his claim]. *See also Elias v. Gonzales,* 490 F.3d 444 (6th Cir. 2007) [remanded case where the behavior of the IJ, who was since removed from the bench, affected the adverse credibility ruling]; *Floroiu v Gonzales,* 481 F.3d 970, 973–76 (7th Cir. 2007) [where IJ characterized asylum applicants as "religious

zealots" who were "offensive to the majority" his comments evidenced sufficient bias to deprive applicants of due process]; *Huang v. Gonzales,* 453 F.3d 142, 148–51 (2d Cir. 2006) [where negative credibility assessment was reversed in forced abortion case, the IJ's apparent bias against the applicant required reassignment on remand to a different IJ]; *Cham v. Att'y Gen. of the U.S.,* 445 F.3d 683 (3d Cir. 2006) [IJ's conduct violated due process and deprived Gambian asylum application of a fair hearing where he assumed his application was invalid, nitpicked the application and testimony for inconsistencies and contradictions, prevented applicant from presenting evidence/witnesses, and engaged in conduct that was abusive toward the applicant including preventing him from presenting his testimony by continually interrupting him]. *But see Sunoto v. Gonzales,* 4504 F.3d 56, 59–61 (1st Cir. 2007) [rejected claim of prejudgment by the IJ in Indonesian asylum case where there was evidence to support lack of credibility other than the IJ's initial erroneous assessment].

(19) *Lack of Knowledge Regarding Geography*—Failure to know the geography of a particular area is not a basis alone to support an adverse credibility finding. *Suntharalinkam v. Gonzales,* 458 F.3d 1034, 1040–41 (9th Cir. 2006) [IJ's adverse credibility determination because respondent from Sri Lanka was unaware of the geography of North America was based upon speculation given the fact that studies show that more than ten percent of 18- to 24-year-old USCs cannot locate the U.S. on the map].

(20) *Credibility and Inconsistent Asylum Applications*—Failure to file an application that is not as complete as petitioner's testimony does not mean testimony is not credible. *Suntharalinkam v. Gonzales,* 458 F.3d 1034, 1042–44 (9th Cir. 2006) [IJs adverse credibility determination regarding Sri Lankan suspected of terrorism was reversed because testimony that is more detailed than an asylum application cannot be the basis for the determination]; *Smolniakova v. Gonzales,* 422 F.3d 1037, 1044–45 (9th Cir. 2005) [reversing adverse credibility finding regarding Jewish persecution in Russia, noting that "an applicant's testimony is not per se lacking in credibility simply because it includes details that are not set forth in the asylum application"]; *Liti v. Gonzales,* 411 F.3d 631, 637–39 (6th Cir. 2005) [finding past persecution rebutted in light of changed country conditions in Albania, but reversing the BIA's adverse credibility finding because of omissions on the asylum application stating, "we reject, the BIA's underlying rationale that the [applicants] are required to provide an exhaustive, detailed list of their...activities in their asylum application"]; *Vasha v. Gonzales,* 410 F.3d 863, 871 n.4 (6th Cir. 2005) [upholding adverse credibility determination, but noting that "an asylum applicant is not required to provide an exhaustive, detailed list of all incidents of persecution in his asylum application"]; *Taha v. Ashcroft,* 389 F.3d 800, 801 (9th Cir. 2004) [reversing denial of asylum where person offered considerably more detail in his testimony than his application]; *Chanchavac v. INS,* 207 F.3d 584, 588 n.2 (9th Cir. 2000) [differing focus at trial from asylum application does not mean the two are contradictory]; *Aguilera-Cota v. INS*, 914 F.2d 1375, 1382 (9th Cir. 1990) [reversing adverse credibility finding because the application did not refer to incidents given in testimony, noting that applications "are frequently filled out by poor illiterate people who do not speak English and are unable to retain counsel"].

Similarly, failure to file a complete application, even if lacking in corroborating affidavits is not a basis to make an adverse credibility determination absent a "legitimate nexus" between the omission or inconsistency and credibility. *Secaida-Rosales v. INS*, 331 F.3d 297, 306–13 (2d Cir. 2003) [failure to place all details on application and failure to produce certain corroborative evidence was not a basis for an adverse credibility determination]; *Stoyanov v. INS,* 172 F.3d 731 (9th Cir. 1999) [inconsistency between in-court testimony and application that lessens degree of persecution does not support adverse credibility finding]; *Lopez-Reyes v. INS*, 79 F.3d 908 (9th Cir. 1996); *Osorio v. INS*, 99 F.3d 928, 932 (9th Cir. 1996) [inconsistencies between poorly filled out application and statements].

The fact that an event is omitted on the application, but testified to at the hearing does not warrant an adverse credibility finding. *Heng v. Gonzales,* 493 F.3d 46, 49 (1st Cir. 2007) [adverse credibility determination of Cambodian reversed where failure to include incident of husband's arrest in asylum application was not a major part of her claim]; *Ssali v. Gonzales,* 424 F.3d 556, 562–64 (7th Cir. 2005) [BIA's adverse credibility determination based on failure to disclose on an asylum application an event in Uganda that respondent testified to in greater detail at trial is not inconsistent and in fact "supports an applicant's credibility"]. Particularly where it was not legally relevant previously. *Kim v. Gonzales,* 458 F.3d 40, 46–48 (2d Cir. 2006) [applicant's failure to initially testify in 1992 that wife was sterilized when it was not legally relevant because it was before Congress addressed forced abortion/sterilization cannot be the basis for an adverse credibility finding. *Cheng Tong Wang v. Gonzales,* 449 F.3d 451 (2d Cir. 2006) distinguished]. *But see Ismaiel v. Mukasey,* 516 F.3d 1198, 1205–06 (10th Cir. 2008) [omission of torture in application and supplemental letters by Syrian where counsel assisted is a basis to draw adverse credibility finding].

Mistranslation and Inconsistent Application—Where the inconsistency between the I-589 and the testimony of the applicant from Brazzaville, Congo is due to translation errors and the applicant neither spoke nor read English, the IJ's finding that he lacked credibility was reversed. *Mapouya v. Gonzales,* 487 F.3d 396, 406–11 (6th Cir. 2007) [the perceived inconsistencies resulting from mistranslations were not material to applicant's claim].

Incompetent Counsel—Where inconsistencies between the application and the presentation of evidence at trial may be due to incompetency of counsel, court properly reversed adverse credibility finding and remanded case to BIA. *Yang v. Gonzales,* 478 F.3d 133, 142–44 (2d Cir. 2007) [where IJ's lack of credibility determination rested in large measure on the belief that counsel was competent, the lawyer's disbarment for incompetency should have resulted in BIA's remand]. *But see Lazar v. Gonzales,* 500 F.3d 469 (6th Cir. 2007) [where respondent had multiple opportunities to retract his two fraudulent asylum applications and only did so during cross-examination, he could not rely on his first counsel's malfeasance in urging him to lie as a defense to a frivolous finding].

Upholding adverse credibility where application inconsistent—Rivera v. Mukasey, 508 F.3d 1271, 1274–76 (9th Cir. 2007) [inconsistencies between application and testimony were sufficient for adverse credibility determination of asylum claimant from the Philippines based upon opposition to the NPA]; *Tarraf v. Gonzales,* 495 F.3d 525, 532–34 (7th Cir. 2007) [Lebanese withholding claim denied where applicant sought to embellish his claim by testifying about physical violence and torture that was not in his asylum application]; *Shmyhelskyy v. Gonzales,* 477 F.3d 474, 480–81 (7th Cir. 2007) [Ukrainian asylum claim properly denied where respondent failed to explain why he did not list most severe beating in his asylum application, although he listed arrest]; *Amir v. Gonzales,* 467 F.3d 921, 925–26 (6th Cir. 2006) [inconsistencies regarding arrests, incidents, and basis for detention between application and testimony regarding Muslim's claim of conversion to Christianity]; *Desna v. Gonzales,* 454 F.3d 896 (8th Cir. 2006) [person claiming persecution as Jew from Ukraine did not mention issue in application, check off ethnic persecution, or provide hospital records of assault]; *Cheng Tong Wang v. Gonzales,* 449 F.3d 451 (2d Cir. 2006) [failure to mention wife's forced sterilization in asylum application based upon opposition to China's family planning program was grounds for adverse credibility assessment]; *Ye v. DHS,* 446 F.3d 289 (2d Cir. 2006) [where Chinese applicant failed to mention in I-589 that he had been detained for 3 days and beaten for speaking out against abortion, the court upheld the IJ's adverse credibility finding]; *Majidi v. Gonzales,* 430 F.3d 77, 80–81 (2d Cir. 2005) [upholding denial asylum for Bangladesh applicant due to inconsistencies between testimony and application; IJ was not required to bring inconsistencies to applicant's attention]; *Sharari v. Gonzales,* 407 F.3d 467, 474–75 (1st Cir. 2005) [where respondent omitted incidents of harm from his asylum application, two affidavits, and his asylum interview, adverse credibility determination upheld]; *Falaja v. Gonzales,* 418 F.3d 889, 894–97 (8th Cir. 2005) [where major events of persecution in Nigeria were not recounted in application or interview, and where testimony was inconsistent, court upheld adverse credibility finding]; *Dong v. Ashcroft,* 406 F.3d 110 (2d Cir. 2005) [Chinese citizen's failure to mention in three applications that he was forced to undergo forced sterilization without an anesthetic is legitimate basis to make an adverse credibility finding]; *Esaka v. Ashcroft,* 397 F.3d 1105, 1109–10 (8th

Cir. 2005) [distinguishing *Zewdie* and finding that where person spoke English the failure to mention beating during asylum interview was a basis for adverse credibility]; *Ali v. Gonzales,* 401 F.3d 11, 15 (1st Cir. 2005) [upholding adverse credibility finding of Ethiopian woman where she failed to mention her rape to female AO at interview]; *Prokopenko v. Ashcroft,* 372 F.3d 941, 945 (8th Cir. 2004) [failure to mention beatings in applicant's original affidavit gave rise to IJ's adverse credibility determination that deserved deference]; *Bellido v. Ashcroft,* 367 F.3d 840, 843 (8th Cir. 2004) [reversing IJ credibility finding for Bolivian union leader where original asylum application omitted certain details of claim]; *Xie v. Ashcroft,* 359 F.3d 239, 243–46 (3d Cir. 2004) [failure to mention wife's sterilization in application and inconsistencies concerning applicant's detention reflected on credibility notwithstanding his claim that a travel agent filled out the application improperly]; *Navarijo-Barrios v. Ashcroft,* 322 F.3d 561 (8th Cir. 2003) [affirming denial of Guatemalan asylum claim based on inconsistencies between testimony and I-589]; *Pop v. INS,* 270 F.3d 527 (7th Cir. 2001) [failure to mention beating in interview or on application raises credibility issue].

Regulatory Presumption Regarding Credibility—A presumption of negative credibility under 8 C.F.R. §§208.3(c)(2), 1208.3(c)(2) that arises from statements on an I-589 inconsistent with testimony, may be overcome by the applicant. *Pang v. USCIS,* 448 F.3d 102, 107–08 (2d Cir. 2006) [reversing adverse credibility decision where the applicant challenged the accuracy of the I-589 and the IJ failed to evaluate his explanation and determine whether he rebutted the presumption under 208.3(c)(2)]; *Liu v. Ashcroft,* 372 F.3d 529, 534 (3d Cir. 2004) [IJ erred in basing adverse credibility on inconsistency in I-589 because presumption that respondent was aware of I-589 content had been successfully rebutted given his lack of knowledge of English]. *See also Chen v. Gonzales,* 420 F.3d 707, 710–11 (7th Cir. 2005) [where the heart of PRC national's asylum claim was not in his application, the IJ's conclusion that respondent was involved in the narrative of the application and therefore now lacks credibility was not supported by substantial evidence]. *But see Kasnecovic v. Gonzales,* 400 F.3d 812, 814–15 (9th Cir. 2005) [discrepancies regarding nationality and residence went to the heart of the claim of person born in Montenegro claiming withholding from Kosovo, where she first listed Kosovo as her place of birth on TPS and asylum applications].

Sibling's Application—Inconsistencies between a sibling's I-589 application and the applicant's I-589 may be used to establish lack of credibility. *Obale v. Att'y Gen. of the U.S.,* 453 F.3d 151, 163–64 (3d Cir. 2006) [failure in sibling's application to make any reference to applicant's past persecution was used as a basis to deny asylum].

(21) *Similarities in Different Asylum Applications as a Basis for Lack of Credibility*—An immigration judge may draw an adverse credibility finding where there are inter-proceeding similarities, including similarities between affidavits submitted by two different asylum applicants, if there are sufficient evidentiary safeguards imposed by the immigration judge. *Mei Chai Ye v. DOJ,* 489 F.3d 517, 524–27 (2d Cir. 2007) [where IJ meticulously pointed out 23 striking similarities between affidavits in respondent's and another person's asylum case, gave the respondent and his counsel substantial time to explain the similarities as not being "canned" affidavits, and considered plausible explanations for the similarities before making an adverse credibility determination, the finding was upheld].

(22) *Inconsistencies and Omissions at Airport and Other Interviews*—Cannot necessarily be basis to make lack of credibility finding. *Moab v. Gonzales,* 500 F.3d 656 (7th Cir. 2007) [reversed BIA's reliance on airport interview given its unreliability and held that BIA erred in its determination that adding an additional harm to Liberian applicant's claim not mentioned in the airport interview–persecution on account of sexual orientation–demonstrated lack of credibility]; *Ucelo-Gomez v. Gonzales,* 464 F.3d 163, 167 (2d Cir. 2006) [case remanded where IJ cited inconsistencies between airport statements and testimony but did not address respondent's explanation for it]; *Bao v. Gonzales,* 460 F.3d 426 (2d Cir. 2006) [reversing IJ's adverse credibility determination due to inconsistencies between wife's testimony and husband's asylum application and interview, where IJ disregarded husband's affidavit because he could not be cross-examined but accepted

AO's memo of husband's claim although officer could not be cross-examined]; *Latifi v. Gonzales,* 430 F.3d 103, 105 (2d Cir. 2005) [where credible fear interview was only inconsistent with testimony in trivial matters and where applicant offered an explanation for why he was not forthcoming in his airport interview, court reversed adverse credibility finding]; *Rodriguez Galicia v. Gonzales,* 422 F.3d 529, 536–38 (7th Cir. 2005) [reversing adverse credibility assessment based on irrelevant inconsistencies between credible fear interview and testimony at trial and recognizing that false statements to an immigration officer where person fears deportation to a persecuting country "can be entirely *consistent* with a fear of persecution"]; *Dong v. Gonzales,* 421 F.3d 573, 579 (7th Cir. 2005) [where Chinese forced abortion applicant told immigration officials she came to U.S. "for fun" court discounted it because "[a]irport interviews…are not always reliable indicators of credibility" and the interview as a whole supported applicant's claim]; *Fiadjoe v. Att'y Gen. of the U.S.,* 411 F.3d 135, 159 (3d Cir. 2005) [reversing BIA's adverse credibility finding of woman from Trokosi sect in Ghana, analogizing asylum interview conducted in prison 17 days after arrival to an airport interview and stating that "inconsistencies between an airport statement and an asylum seeker's testimony before an IJ is not sufficient, standing alone, to support a BIA finding that the petitioner was not credible"]; *Singh v. Gonzales,* 403 F.3d 1081 (9th Cir. 2005) [reversing IJ's denial of relief based on adverse credibility where there were perceived inconsistencies between AO's Assessment to Refer and applicant's testimony because Assessment is only a short, conclusory written summary and there is no transcript, no indication of the language used or whether an oath was administered, no record of all the questions and answers, no contemporaneous notes, and no testimony of the AO or the applicant]; *Huang v. Gonzales,* 403 F.3d 945, 950 (7th Cir. 2005) [IJ should not have relied on airport interview to make adverse credibility determination where applicant was never asked whether she feared returning home or wanted to seek asylum]; *Wu v. Ashcroft,* 393 F.3d 418, 423–25 (3d Cir. 2005) [remanding where IJ failed to explain why he relied on an airport interview to contradict respondent's asylum claim when it found respondent's testimony credible]; *Jamal-Daoud v. Gonzales,* 403 F.3d 918, 922–23 (7th Cir. 2005) [relying on four-part test in *Balogun v. Ashcroft,* 374 F.3d 492, 505 (7th Cir. 2004) court determined that airport interview was reliable]; *Kebede v. Ashcroft,* 366 F.3d 808, 811 (9th Cir. 2004) [reversing IJ's credibility finding based on failure to disclose rape in asylum interview or application because such failure is not a bellwether of truth]; *Balasubramanrim v. INS,* 143 F.3d 157 (3d Cir. 1998) [reversing BIA determination that applicant was not credible because his testimony differed from an unreliable airport statement]; *Senathirajah v. INS,* 157 F.3d 210, 218–21 (3d Cir. 1998) [same]; *Mulanga v. Ashcroft,* 349 F.3d 123, 137 (3d Cir. 2003) [same]; *Dia v. Ashcroft,* 353 F.3d 228, 257–58 (3d Cir. 2003) (*en banc*) [same]; *Chen v. Slattery*, 842 F.Supp. 814, 824 (E.D.N.Y. 1994) [minor inconsistencies between statements at entry and at hearing are insufficient]; *But see Kanacevic v. INS,* 448 F.3d 129, 136–38 (2d Cir. 2006) [airport statement was substantially inconsistent with asylum claim of Montenegro national of Albanian ethnicity]; *Diallo v. Gonzales,* 445 F.3d 624, 631–33 (2d Cir. 2006) [adverse credibility claim of applicant upheld where court determined that the asylum interview, unlike an airport interview, was reliable notwithstanding the officer's failure to provide a verbatim transcript or to record any questions asked]; *Guan v. Gonzales,* 432 F.3d 391 (2d Cir. 2005) [where airport statement is "materially different" than application and the airport interview was reliable, the "entirely different" claims regarding persecution in China can be the basis for an adverse credibility finding]; *Jalloh v. Gonzales,* 423 F.3d 894, 898–99 (4th Cir. 2005) [applicant from Sierra Leone lacked credibility where there were significant discrepancies between airport statement and his asylum application and testimony]; *Aden v. Ashcroft,* 396 F.3d 966 (8th Cir. 2005) [upholding adverse credibility finding where there were inconsistencies between the I-589 and respondent's testimony regarding rape of Somali woman due to clan membership]; *Li v. Ashcroft,* 378 F.3d 959 (9th Cir. 2004) [inconsistencies between airport interview and testimony at asylum hearing were basis to deny Chinese forced sterilization asylum claim]; *He Chun Chen v. Ashcroft,* 376 F.3d 215, 224 (3d Cir. 2004) [discrepancies between airport interview and testimony that go to the heart of the claim support an adverse credibility determination]; *Balogun v. Ashcroft,* 374 F.3d 492, 504–05

(7th Cir. 2004) [following *Ramsameachire* criteria to determine whether airport interview was fair and accurate and concluding it was]; *Ramsameachire v. Ashcroft,* 357 F.3d 169, 179–83 (2d Cir. 2004) [where record of airport interview indicates its reliability it may be used to challenge credibility]; *Disu v. Ashcroft,* 338 F.3d 13, 17–18 (1st Cir. 2003) [adverse credibility upheld where the core of applicant's claim regarding arrests, interrogations, and physical abuse was absent in his asylum application and unmentioned in his initial interview]; *Bojorques-Villanueva v. INS,* 194 F.3d 14 (1st Cir. 1999) [where there are multiple inconsistencies going to the central facts deferral to the BIA is warranted].

The danger of an immigration court relying on airport interview transcripts as a basis to determine credibility was highlighted in a recent congressionally mandated study. *See* Keller, Rasmussen, Reeves and Rosenfeld, *Evaluation of Credible Fear Referral in Expedited Removal At Ports of Entry in the United States,* Study on Asylum Seekers in Expedited Removal, As Authorized by Section 605 of the International Religious Freedom Act of 1998 (Feb. 2005) at p. 30 ["The lack of congruence between the observations of our research assistants and the official records prepared by the investigating officers (A-files) suggests that the asylum process itself may be compromised by the use of these documents as official transcripts....The safeguard against inaccurate A-file records, asking aliens to attest to the accuracy of their statements, also appears inadequate as currently implemented"].

(23) *Post-traumatic Stress Disorder and Credibility*—Courts have recognized that PTSD can affect a person's testimony and where the IJ/BIA failed to recognize its effects on an applicant's testimony, they have reversed. *Fiadjoe v. Att'y Gen. of the U.S.,* 411 F.3d 135, 149–60 (3d Cir. 2005) [reversing BIA's adverse credibility finding and denial of asylum to woman from Trokosi sect in Ghana who had been repeatedly physically and sexually abused by her father. Court referred to USCIS guidelines for Considerations for Asylum Officers Adjudicating Asylum Claims from Women].

(24) *False Statements and Credibility*—False statements are not determinative of credibility, but must be viewed under the particular circumstances. *Rodriguez Galicia v. Gonzales,* 422 F.3d 529, 536–38 (7th Cir. 2005) [reversing adverse credibility based on irrelevant inconsistencies between credible fear interview and testimony at trial and recognizing that false statements to an immigration officer where person fears deportation to a persecuting country "can be entirely *consistent* with a fear of persecution"]; *Marcos v. Gonzales,* 410 F.3d 1112, 1116–18 (9th Cir. 2005) [reversing IJ determination that lying to obtain immigrant visa demonstrates lack of credibility on asylum claim because visa fraud was not an effort to enhance his asylum claim]; *Kaur v. Ashcroft,* 379 F.3d 876, 889 (9th Cir. 2004) [lies and misstatements to border officials and presentation of a false passport do not reflect on credibility and "are entirely consistent with her asylum claim"]; *Turcios v. INS*, 821 F.2d 1396, 1400–01 (9th Cir. 1987) [lying to INS about nationality not inconsistent with asylum claim]. *But see Toure v. Ashcroft,* 400 F.3d 44, 47–49 (1st Cir. 2005) [providing false testimony at husband's asylum hearing was relevant to IJ's determination of credibility in her own case]. Conversely, an IJ does not have to determine that an applicant's statements are "clearly false" to make an adverse credibility determination as long as the determination is supported by specific, cogent, reasons. *Onsongo v. Gonzales,* 457 F.3d 849, 854 (8th Cir. 2007) [adverse credibility determination regarding Kenyan asylum claim was supported by substantial evidence].

(25) *Minor Inconsistencies and Credibility*—"Minor inconsistencies in the record that do not relate to the basis of an applicant's alleged fear of persecution, go to the heart of the asylum claim, or reveal anything about an asylum applicant's fear for his safety are insufficient to support an adverse credibility finding." *Mendoza Manimbao v. Ashcroft,* 329 F.3d 655, 660 (9th Cir. 2003) [reversing BIA adverse credibility finding without prior notice and opportunity for applicant to respond where IJ failed to make an express adverse credibility ruling]. "[A]dverse credibility determinations based on minor discrepancies, inconsistencies, or omissions that do not go to the heart of the applicant's asylum claim cannot constitute substantial evidence." *Chen v. INS,* 266 F.3d 1094, 1098 (9th Cir. 2001) *vacated by INS v. Chen* 123 S.Ct. 549 (2002) *but reinstated as to credibility issue*

326 F.3d 1316, 1317 (9th Cir. 2003). *See also Tadesse v. Gonzales,* 492 F.3d 905, 910–11 (7th Cir. 2007) [minor inconsistencies such as when Eritrean applicant left hairdressing school in Italy cannot be the basis for adverse credibility finding]; *Adekpe v. Gonzales,* 480 F.3d 525, 530–33 (7th Cir. 2007) [IJ's failure to consider documentary evidence that bolstered claim from Togo was error even if the IJ believed the applicant's claim lacked credibility]; *Zhong v. DOJ,* 480 F.3d 104, 125–38 (2d Cir. 2007) [minor inconsistencies at the periphery of the applicant's claim are an impermissible basis to find lack of credibility]; *Sarr v. Gonzales,* 474 F.3d 783, 789–93 (10th Cir. 2007) [where inconsistencies regarding applicant's birth certificate and mother's death either did not exist or were minor and corrected, denial of asylum from Mauritania was reversed]; *Suntharalinkam v. Gonzales,* 458 F.3d 1034 (9th Cir. 2006) [IJ's adverse credibility determination regarding asylum claim of Sri Lankan suspected of terrorism was reversed where the discrepancies were related to the date of the father's death or where other minor discrepancies may have been the result of poor translation or an inadequate transcript]; *Kim v. Gonzales,* 458 F.3d 40, 44–45 (2d Cir. 2006) [a five day error on third child's birth date (April 15th vs April 10) is minor and cannot be the basis of an adverse credibility finding]; *Kumar v. Gonzales,* 444 F.3d 1043, 1051–52 (9th Cir. 2006) [where a discrepancy may be attributable to a clerical error, it may not form the basis of an adverse credibility finding unless the IJ or BIA specifically explain its significance or point to respondent's evasiveness about it]; *Giday v. Gonzales,* 434 F.3d 543, 550–53 (7th Cir. 2006) [reversing IJ credibility finding that was based on minor and irrelevant discrepancies]; *Butt v. Gonzales,* 429 F.3d 430, 437 n.10 (3d Cir. 2005) [Pakistani asylum case quoting *Gao* that "generally, minor inconsistencies and minor admissions that reveal nothing about an asylum applicant's fear for his safety are not an adequate basis for an adverse credibility finding"]; *Quan v. Gonzales,* 428 F.3d 883, 886–88 (9th Cir. 2005) [minor inconsistencies and unclear testimony where applicant not given an opportunity to clarify cannot be the basis for an adverse credibility finding]; *Pergega v. Gonzales,* 417 F.3d 623, 628–29 (6th Cir. 2005) [where there was a discrepancy over whether the applicant filed a police report was an irrelevant inconsistency because whether he reported the incident is less relevant than whether it actually occurred]; *Singh v. Gonzales,* 403 F.3d 1081, 1090–92 (9th Cir. 2005) [poor date recollection cannot be a basis to find lack of credibility where IJ focused on minutely disparate dates]; *Chen v. Ashcroft,* 362 F.3d 611, 620 (9th Cir. 2004) [reversing adverse credibility finding where person subjected to forced abortion was denied relief because of inconsistencies in minor matters]; *Sylla v. INS,* 388 F.3d 924, 926–27 (6th Cir. 2004) [reversing adverse credibility where there were minor inconsistencies as to the amount applicant paid for his political party membership card and whether he was properly listed as a student on his card]; *Liu v. Ashcroft,* 372 F.3d 529, 534 (3d Cir. 2004) [in coerced abortion case applicant's testimony that she was either 4 or 5 months pregnant is trivial and it was error to base a lack of credibility on that testimony]; *Uwase v. Ashcroft,* 349 F.3d 10391042–43 (7th Cir. 2003) [conflicting testimony regarding applicant's source of support in the U.S. is a minor inconsistency with various explanations that does not affect her asylum claim]; *Singh v. INS,* 362 F.3d 1164, 1169–72 (9th Cir. 2004) [minor inconsistencies in Sikh's claim were insufficient to support adverse credibility]; *Georgis v. Ashcroft,* 328 F.3d 962, 967–70 (7th Cir. 2003) [where minor inconsistencies concerning dates and actions are easily resolved by other facts in evidence and explained by improperly excluded evidence, BIA reversed]; *Singh v. Ashcroft,* 301 F.3d 1109 (9th Cir. 2002) [an omission of a detail in a corroborative medical letter does not create inconsistency, nor does a minor discrepancy or unidentified unresponsiveness make the asylee's account not credible]; *Akinmade v. INS,* 196 F.3d 951, 954 (9th Cir. 1999); INS Supplementary Refugee/Asylum Adjudication Guidelines, *reprinted in* 67 No. 4 *Interpreter Releases* 85, 101–03 (Jan. 22, 1990) ["Minor inconsistencies, misrepresentations, or concealment in a claim should not lead to a finding of incredibility where the inconsistency, misrepresentation or concealment is not material to the claim"]. *But see* REAL ID Act of 2005, INA §208(b)(1)(B)(iii) finding that inconsistency does not necessarily have to go to the "heart of the applicant's asylum claim" for all post-May 11, 2005 cases. *See also Pan v. Gonzales,* 489 F.3d 80, 86–87 (1st Cir. 2007) [cumulative effect of minor inconsistencies between trial and before asylum officer were sufficient to uphold adverse credibility find-

ing]; *Chen v. U.S. Att'y Gen.,* 463 F.3d 1228, 1230–32 (11th Cir. 2006) [post-REAL ID, rejecting the applicant's argument that an adverse credibility determination could not be based upon "trivial" issues or ones "irrelevant to the dispositive issues"].

(26) *Materiality of Inconsistent Statements*—To affect an asylum or withholding claim, an inconsistency must be material. *Wang v. Ashcroft,* 341 F.3d 1015, 1021–22 (9th Cir. 2003) [inconsistencies were not material to forced abortion claim]. *But see Kaur v. Gonzales,* 418 F.3d 1061 (9th Cir. 2005) [where inconsistencies that weaken a claim for asylum are accompanied by other indications of dishonesty, and where respondent admitted she lied but argued that her true story should be believed because it was less powerful, the IJ's adverse credibility determination was supported by substantial evidence]; *Barreto-Claro v. U.S. Att'y Gen.,* 275 F.3d 1334, 1337–39 & n.8 (11th Cir. 2001) [where Cuban applicant, after warning, materially misrepresented his status in a third country on an asylum application, his subsequent recantation did not alleviate the IJ/BIA finding of frivolousness]; *Matter of A-H-,* 23 I&N Dec. 774, 786–87 (AG 2005) [where IJ's adverse credibility determination was based on the applicant's demeanor and sincerity as well as omissions and discrepancies, BIA erred in reversing]. *See also* INA §208(b)(1)(B)(iii) for post-May 11, 2005 cases.

(27) *Credibility and Fraudulent Documents*—Credibility will not necessarily turn on the presentation of fraudulent documents. *Kumar v. Gonzales,* 444 F.3d 1043, 1050–51 (9th Cir. 2006) [IJ erred in making an adverse credibility assessment based on his uninformed conclusion that a document was fraudulent without submitting it to a handwriting expert or forensic laboratory]; *Gjerzai v. Gonzales,* 435 F.3d 800, 810–11 (7th Cir. 2006) [where IJ refused to send documents to Forensic Document Lab and where there was no proof that the applicant knew or had reason to know that the documents were fraudulent, it was error for the IJ, despite specific, detailed and consistent testimony, to exclude the documents and determine that the lack of corroboration resulted in a failure of the applicant to meet his burden of proof]; *Yeimane-Berhe v. Ashcroft,* 393 F.3d 907, 911–13 (9th Cir. 2005) [where testimony was detailed, internally consistent and consistent with other testimony and documents, the submission of a fraudulent medical certificate where there was no evidence that she knew it to be fraudulent could not be the sole basis to deny relief]; *Kourski v. Ashcroft,* 355 F.3d 1038 (7th Cir. 2004) [where fraudulent birth certificate was submitted to show Jewish religion it was improper to infer adverse credibility without showing that person knew document was fraudulent]; *Hoque v. Ashcroft,* 367 F.3d 1190, 1195–97 (9th Cir. 2004) [alteration of date on a letter does not support adverse credibility finding by IJ where respondent was never asked to explain the marking, to provide the history of its submission, and it did not aid asylum claim].

(28) *Adverse Credibility Cannot be Based on Speculation and Conjecture*—The IJ cannot resort to "speculation and conjecture" in concluding that an applicant is not credible.

(a) *Second Circuit—Huang v. Gonzales,* 453 F.3d 142, 147–49 (2d Cir. 2006) [IJ's statement that uneducated villager in China would not confront local authorities about human rights, or that family would give up first child because she was a girl, and IJ's unsupported medical opinion regarding sterilization were all speculative and could not sustain adverse credibility finding]; *Tandia v. Gonzales,* 437 F.3d 245, 249–51 (2d Cir. 2006) [IJ impermissibly drew inference that applicant's failure to remember specific matters in his un-transcribed and un-recorded conversation with the AO signified that those matters were true]; *Secaida-Rosales v. INS,* 331 F.3d 297, 307 (2d Cir. 2003) [reversing IJ's adverse credibility finding against Guatemalan where IJ relied on inappropriate standards for testimony and corroboration and speculation and conjecture in assessing the evidence]; *Alvarado-Carillo v. INS,* 251 F.3d 44, 51–52 (2d Cir. 2001) [reversing where there was a discrepancy of 4 months in testimony over one of several matters].

(b) *Third Circuit—Dia v. Ashcroft,* 353 F.3d 228, 247–60 (3d Cir. 2003) (*en banc*) [IJ's credibility determinations rested on conjecture and were "more puzzling than plausible, more curious than commonsense"]; *Zubeda v. Ashcroft,* 333 F.3d 463, 476–77 (3d Cir. 2003) [challenging adverse credibility finding by IJ based on contradiction between testimony and unreliable airport interview]; *Gao v. Ashcroft,* 299 F.3d 266, 278 (3d Cir. 2002) [reversing denial of asylum based on adverse credibility determination which included the IJ's "unsupported opinion as to how an authoritarian government operates"].

(c) *Fourth Circuit—Camara v. Ashcroft,* 378 F.3d 361, 368–69 (4th Cir. 2004) [reversing some of IJ's credibility findings based on speculation or minor inconsistencies but affirming lack of credibility on others].

(d) *Fifth Circuit—Mwembie v. Gonzales,* 443 F.3d 405, 409–14 (5th Cir. 2006) [although court upheld denial on lack of nexus to an enumerated ground, it severely criticized the IJ's credibility findings that rested on "incorrect and irrational assumptions about human behavior and especially the behavior of people from foreign cultures" and her "lack of familiarity with the record and her ability to comprehend it"];

(e) *Sixth Circuit—Alexandrov v. Gonzales,* 442 F.3d 395, 407–09 (6th Cir. 2006) [in Bulgarian asylum claim, IJ's adverse credibility assessment was reversed where it was based on IJ's personal beliefs about how long beatings and detention should last].

(f) *Seventh Circuit—Tadesse v. Gonzales,* 492 F.3d 905, 910–11 (7th Cir. 2007) [adverse credibility finding against Eritrean reversed where testimony was not implausible and claimed inconsistencies were not inconsistent]; *Mema v. Gonzales,* 474 F.3d 412, 419 (7th Cir. 2007) [reversed IJ's finding that asylum applicant was not sought by police while in hiding where adverse credibility determination was not supported by the record]; *San Kai Kwok v. Gonzales,* 455 F.3d 766, 769–71 (7th Cir. 2006) [IJ reversed in pre-REAL ID Act case concerning forced abortion, despite existence of a serious inconsistency about the manner and location of applicant's custody, where other adverse credibility findings were based upon speculation or minor discrepancies]; *Pramatarov v. Gonzales,* 454 F.3d 764 (7th Cir. 2006) [IJ reversed in Bulgarian Roma case because adverse credibility was based on "factual error, bootless speculation, and errors of logic"]; *Kllokoqi v. Gonzales,* 439 F.3d 336, 344 (7th Cir. 2006) [reversing IJ's speculative finding that injury of ethnic Albanian in Kosovo was due to bicycle accident when both the applicant's testimony and medical testimony confirmed his injury was due to severe beatings]; *Huang v. Gonzales,* 403 F.3d 945, 948–51 (7th Cir. 2005) [IJ's personal views about Catholicism were an inappropriate basis for credibility findings]; *Grupee v. Gonzales,* 400 F.3d 1026, 1027 (7th Cir. 2005) [IJ's "unexplained incredulity" over Liberian's return to work for two days after release from prison and before departure despite applicant's explanation is not a basis to challenge credibility]; *Uwase v. Ashcroft,* 349 F.3d 1039 (7th Cir. 2003) [IJ credibility finding based on speculation regarding the significance of certain evidence or conjecture regarding the failure of a family member to testify was reversed]; *Ememe v. Ashcroft,* 358 F.3d 446 (7th Cir. 2004) [remanding case where IJ's adverse credibility finding was based on statements at credible fear interview conducted in Italian where applicant's native language was Amharic].

(g) *Eighth Circuit—Shahinaj v. Gonzales,* 481 F.3d 1027 (8th Cir. 2007) [reversing IJ's adverse credibility finding regarding Albanian homosexual because of IJ's statements that respondent did not speak, dress or act like a homosexual].

(h) *Ninth Circuit— Suntharalinkam v. Gonzales,* 458 F.3d 1034 (9th Cir. 2006) [IJ's adverse credibility determination regarding asylum claim of Sri Lankan suspected of terrorism was reversed where IJ speculated about respondent's knowledge of geography, his physical description of torture, and the manner in which hospital records were kept in Sri Lanka and relied upon a government report that was also speculative]; *Kumar v. Gonzales,* 444 F.3d 1043, 1050–51 (9th Cir. 2006) [IJ erred in making adverse credibility assessment based on his uninformed conclusion that the document was fraudulent without submitting the document to a handwriting expert or forensic laboratory]; *Lin v. Gonzales,* 434 F.3d 1158, 1162–63 (9th Cir. 2006) [reversing IJ's adverse credibility finding based on her view that documents were suspicious because of her conjecture and speculation as to perceived deficiencies in the documents and what she believed they should look like]; *Jibril v. Gonzales,* 423 F.3d 1129, 1135–39 (9th Cir. 2005) [reversing IJ's credibility determination where court speculated that respondent could not have 'played dead" when Somalian militia kicked him, but court stated it would have reached a different result if REAL ID credibility determinations applied]; *Smolniakova v. Gonzales,* 422 F.3d 1037, 1044–53 (9th Cir. 2005) [reversing adverse credibility finding based on misconstruction of the record, insufficient evidence and improper speculation regarding asylum claim]; *Shire v. Ashcroft,* 388 F.3d 1288, 1295–99 (9th Cir. 2004) [speculation regarding the impossibility of respondent's fraudulent entry into the U.S., the lack of a careful immigration inspection, and the failure to recall minor details unrelated to his claim, were an impermissible basis to make an adverse credibility finding]; *Ding v. Ashcroft,* 387 F.3d 1131, 1136 (9th Cir. 2004) [reversing IJ's credibility finding in Chinese forced abortion case because it was based on speculation, conjecture and an inappropriate legal standard]; *Kaur v. Ashcroft,* 379 F.3d 876, 886–87 (9th Cir. 2004) [IJ's determination that applicant's claim that the Indian government misspelled her name in her passport was implausible, was based on IJ's own personal conjecture about the manner in which Indian passport officials carry out their duty]; *Ge v. Ashcroft,* 367 F.3d 1121 (9th Cir. 2004) [reversing denial of asylum based on forced abortion because IJ's adverse credibility determination rested on speculation]; *Guo v. Ashcroft,* 361 F.3d 1194, 1200–02 (9th Cir. 2004) [adverse credibility determination based on speculation, conjecture, and lack of difficult-to-obtain corroborative documents was not supported by substantial evidence]; *Paramasamy v. Ashcroft,* 295 F.3d 1047, 1052–54 (9th Cir. 2002) [remanding Sri Lankan asylum case for new hearing where IJ, among other things, perceived inconsistencies not based on the evidence including that the failure to disclose sexual assault to male Service officers at the airport indicated later testimony was not credible]; *He v. Ashcroft,* 328 F.3d 593 (9th Cir. 2003) [reversing adverse credibility determination in forced sterilization case on grounds it was not supported by substantial evidence]; *Bandari v. INS,* 227 F.3d 1160, 1165–68 (9th Cir. 2000) [personal beliefs of IJ about events or causation cannot substitute for evidence]; *Shah v. INS,* 220 F.3d 1062 (9th Cir. 2000) [reversing adverse credibility determinations based on applicant's failure to produce sufficient corroborating evidence and DOS general assertions contradicting the applicant]; *Abovian v. INS,* 219 F.3d 972, 978–80 (9th Cir. 2000) [where there were no misrepresentation and no specific and direct evidence that contradicted applicant's testimony there was no basis to determine that petitioner lacked credibility]; *Akinmade v. INS,* 196 F.3d 951 (9th Cir. 1999) [record did not support denial of asylum on credibility grounds of Nigerian student]; *Garrovillas v. INS,* 156 F.3d 1010–16 (9th Cir. 1998) [where IJ demonstrated hostility and predisposition to discredit applicant and where inconsistency was a discrepancy between a statement in the asylum application and in-court testimony but the discrepancies "lessen the degree of persecution he experienced, rather than to increase it," BIA's denial reversed]; *Martinez-Sanchez v. INS*, 794 F.2d 1396, 1400 (9th Cir. 1986) [reversing denial of asylum where IJ's claim that applicant lacked credibility not supported by the record]; *Aguilera-Cota v. INS*, 914 F.2d 1375, 1381 (9th Cir. 1990) [reversing denial because IJ's reasons must be based on "a rational and supportable connection between the reasons cited and the conclusion that the petitioner is not credible"]; *Mosa v. Rogers*, 89 F.3d 601, 604–05 (9th Cir. 1996) [same]; *Vilorio-Lopez v. INS*, 852 F.2d 1137, 1142 (9th Cir. 1988) [minor inconsistencies in the record such as discrepancies in dates which reveal nothing about an asylum applicant's fear for his safety are not an adequate basis for adverse credibility finding]; *Turcios v. INS*, 821 F.2d 1396 (9th Cir. 1987) [reversing IJ finding that former INA §243(h) applicant not credible where finding not supported by record. IJ must "offer a specific cogent reason for his disbelief"]; *Hartooni v. INS*, 21 F.3d 336, 343 (9th Cir. 1994) [BIA's credibility determination not supported by record]; *Ramos-Vasquez v. INS*, 57 F.3d 857 (9th Cir. 1995) [same].

(i) *Tenth Circuit—Chaib v. Ashcroft,* 397 F.3d 1273, 1278–80 (10th Cir. 2005) [reversing IJ's negative credibility finding based on speculation regarding Algerian government's treatment of suspected terrorist supporters that was contrary to country reports and speculation regarding Algerian bank's computer system]; *Elizour v. Ashcroft,* 378 F.3d 1143, 1152–54 (10th Cir. 2004) [IJ may not rest credibility determinations on his own unsupported opinion].

(j) *BIA—Matter of Kasinga*, 21 I&N Dec. 357, 364–65 (BIA 1996); *Matter of Lok*, 18 I&N Dec. 101, 106 (BIA 1981); *Matter of Becerra-Miranda*, 12 I&N Dec. 358, 368 (BIA 1967). *See also Matter of Lugo-Guadiana*, 12 I&N Dec. 726, 729 (BIA 1968); *Matter of Yaldo*, 12 I&N Dec. 830, 838 (BIA 1968).

(29) *Lack of Credibility Not Always Fatal— Lin-Jian v. Gonzales,* 489 F.3d 182, 191–93 (4th Cir. 2007) [where court upheld IJ's adverse credibility finding as to future persecution, the IJ's failure to make a credibility determination as to past persecution requires the assumption that the testimony was credible and the denial was not supported by substantial evidence]; *Gebreeyesus v. Gonzales,* 482 F.3d 952, 955 (7th Cir. 2007) [reversing BIA denial of motion to reopen by Amharan from Ethiopia based on changed country conditions where BIA ignored analytical distinction between future and past persecution claims and focused on IJ's adverse credibility assessment of past persecution]; *Adekpe v. Gonzales,* 480 F.3d 525, 530–33 (7th Cir. 2007) [IJ's failure to consider documentary evidence that bolstered claim from Togo was error even if the IJ believed the applicant's claim to lack credibility]; *Paul v. Gonzales,* 444 F.3d 148, 153–55 (2d Cir. 2006) [Christian from Pakistan was granted motion to reopen based upon changed circumstances, despite IJ's prior adverse credibility finding, because he may prevail on a theory of future persecution as long as the factual predicate for the claim is independent of the testimony the IJ found not credible]; *Niang v. Gonzales,* 422 F.3d 1187, 1198–2001 (10th Cir. 2005) [notwithstanding adverse credibility determination a female member of the Tukulor Fulani tribe in Senegal that practices FGM can be subject to persecution on account of membership in a particular social group; remanding for a determination as to whether she had suffered persecution because she was subject to FGM]; *Forgue v. U.S. Att'y Gen.,* 401 F.3d 1282, 1287 (11th Cir. 2005) [upholding denial of asylum under substantial evidence rule, but noting that "an adverse credibility determination does not alleviate the IJ's duty to consider other evidence produced by an asylum applicant"]; *Guo v. Ashcroft,* 386 F.3d 556, 562–64 (3d Cir. 2004) [BIA could not rely on IJ's prior, unrelated adverse credibility determination concerning religious persecution in China to deny a motion to reopen for asylum based on China's family planning policy]; *Camara v. Ashcroft,* 378 F.3d 361, 369–71 (4th Cir. 2004) [upholding adverse credibility finding but reversing denial of relief where IJ overlooked documentary evidence that provided a strong basis to support claim]; *Kamalthas v. INS,* 251 F.3d 1279, 1284 (9th Cir. 2001) [negative-credibility determination in an asylum claim can not "wash over" the CAT claim]; *Al-Harbi v. INS,* 242 F.3d 882 (9th Cir. 2001) [upholding denial of Iraqi applicant's past persecution claim because his testimony was found to lack credibility, but determining that notwithstanding lack of credibility there was sufficient evidence to support future persecution claim]; *Mansour v. INS,* 230 F.3d 902, 905–06 (7th Cir. 2000) [upholding IJ's determination that Iraqi was not credible because of inconsistency between testimony at trial and asylum application but reversing on CAT claim because CAT is based on other standards].

(30) *Substantial Evidence Standard of Review*—Credibility determinations are subject to the substantial evidence standard of review. *Dia v. Ashcroft,* 353 F.3d 228, 248–61 (3d Cir. 2003) (*en banc*) [finding that §242(b)(4)(B) codified *Elias-Zacarias* thereby maintaining the traditional substantial evidence standard and reversing the IJs credibility finding]. A credibility analysis "assesses the applicant's claim only for internal consistency, detail and plausibility in light of the applicant's testimony and the background evidence." *Balogun v. Ashcroft,* 374 F.3d 492, 499 (7th Cir. 2004) [upholding adverse credibility under highly deferential *Elias-Zacarias* standard].

(31) *IJ Error in Credibility Assessment May Not Result in Reversal*—Even if an IJ erred in her credibility assessment, the court may still uphold the denial if there is sufficient alternative evidence or an alternative ground. *Chen v. DOJ,* 471 F.3d 315, 332–42 (2d Cir. 2006) [although IJ engaged in improper speculation and his decision contained errors, the

court upheld the decision where substantial evidence supported it and it was clear the same decision would be made on remand]. In *Chen,* the 2d Cir. articulated a standard first announced in *Cao He Lin v. DOJ,* 428 F.3d 391 (2d Cir. 2005): an IJ decision may be upheld even if there were errors where: (1) the IJ explicitly relies on a valid alternative ground for denying relief that is not tainted by error; (2) the error is so "tangential" to the ultimate ruling that there is no realistic possibility of a different result on remand; *or* (3) the untainted evidence in support of the IJ's conclusion is so "overwhelming" that there is no realistic possibility of a different result on remand. 471 F.3d at 338–39. *See also Tu Lin v. Gonzales,* 446 F.3d 395 (2d Cir. 2006) [where IJ erred in forced abortion case in identifying certain discrepancies and in relying on country profile report to discredit testimony, there was sufficient evidence for an adverse credibility finding based upon facts the applicant should have revealed]; *Hoxhallari v. Gonzales,* 468 F.3d 179 (2d Cir. 2006) [where IJ may have erred in credibility assessment regarding past persecution, his finding that the government met its burden of showing changed country conditions was sufficient even where the IJ did not make a "specific finding premised on record evidence" regarding changed country conditions in Albanian]; *Qyteza v. Gonzales,* 437 F.3d 224 (2d Cir. 2006) [notwithstanding IJ's erroneous credibility determination, there was substantial evidence in the record to "confidently predict" that the IJ would render the same decision in the absence of error]; *Chen v. Gonzales,* 434 F.3d 212, 220–22 (3d Cir. 2005) [*post*-Real ID, the court upheld the denial of asylum even where the IJ did not make a valid credibility assessment because even a credible applicant may be required to produce corroborative evidence]; *Djouma v. Gonzales,* 429 F.3d 685, 688 (7th Cir. 2005) [although IJ erred in credibility determination, applicant failed to prove he had been persecuted or was likely to be persecuted in the future]. *But see Li Zu Guan v. INS,* 453 F.3d 129 (2d Cir. 2006) [the standards in *Cao* and *Chen* did not prevent the reversal and remand of the IJ's credibility findings where there were numerous errors and a paucity of valid findings by the IJ]; *Lin Li Hua v. DOJ,* 453 F.3d 99, 105–12 (2d Cir. 2006) [the standard in *Cao* did not prevent the court from reversing the IJ's decision to deny withholding despite numerous important inconsistencies where the respondent testified to her pain in being forcibly sterilized and the IJ relied upon pure speculation to find her claim incredible despite saying it was the most critical issue in the case].

(32) *Adverse Credibility Determination Not Supported by Substantial Evidence*

(a) *First Circuit—Heng v. Gonzales,* 493 F.3d 46 (1st Cir. 2007) [adverse credibility determination of Cambodian reversed where inconsistencies were explained by poor translation, where failure to include husband's arrest in asylum application was not a major part of her claim, and where there were translation problems throughout case]; *Castaneda-Castillo v. Gonzales,* 488 F.3d 17, 22–26 (1st Cir. 2007) (*en banc*) [adverse credibility based in part on IJ's determination that the respondent was blinking his eyes in an unusually rapid rate and four other erroneous credibility findings reversed and the *en banc* court noted that the language in 8 U.S.C. §1252(b)(4)(B) regarding reversal only if evidence "compels" reversal reflects a "gloss by the Supreme Court" and does not "eliminate[] the conventional requirement that an administrative agency's explanation be rational"]; *Mihaylov v. Ashcroft,* 379 F.3d 15 (1st Cir. 2004) [Bulgarian case where IJ based adverse credibility on belief that respondent was alcoholic and confused evidence regarding persecutor's motives as credibility matters]; *Cordero-Trejo v. INS*, 40 F.3d 482 (1st Cir. 1994).

(b) *Second Circuit—Corovic v. Mukasey,* 519 F.3d 90, 97-98 (2d Cir. 2008) [reversed adverse credibility determination where court believed 2 documents were fraudulent but there was no indication that respondent knew or had reason to know they were fraudulent]; *Gao v. BIA,* 482 F.3d 122 (2d Cir. 2007) [reversing denial of Chinese sterilization case based on IJ's erroneous factual determinations]; *Zhong v. DOJ,* 480 F.3d 104, 125–38 (2d Cir. 2007) [minor inconsistencies at the periphery of applicant's claim based on coercive population control program is an impermissible basis to find lack of credibility]; *Yang v. Gonzales,* 478 F.3d 133, 142–44 (2d Cir. 2007) [where IJ's adverse credibility determination rested in large measure on the belief that counsel was competent, the lawyer's disbarment for incompetency should have resulted in BIA's remand]; *Ucelo-Gomez v. Gonzales,* 464 F.3d 163, 167 (2d Cir. 2006) [remanding where IJ did not address respondent's explanation for inconsistencies or how his claim that affluent Guatemalans were a social group would affect the credibility determinations]; *Chen v. BIA,* 461 F.3d 153 (2d Cir. 2006) [IJ's conclusion that fraud by respondent, instead of government error, explained discrepancy in personal identification number on documents was speculative and did not support adverse credibility assessment]; *Bao v. Gonzales,* 460 F.3d 426 (2d Cir. 2006) [reversing IJ's decision that coercive family planning claims were not credible due to inconsistencies between wife's testimony and husband's asylum application and interview]; *Zhen Nan Lin v. DOJ,* 459 F.3d 255, 268–72 (2d Cir. 2006) [reversing BIA's adverse credibility finding that was based on a consular report that a document was forged where the report was inherently unreliable]; *Kim v. Gonzales,* 458 F.3d 40, 44–48 (2d Cir. 2006) [where inconsistency about the date of applicant's third child's birth was minor, where the IJ based another discrepancy on speculation, and where applicant from China failed to mention his wife's sterilization before it was a legal basis for asylum, the IJ's adverse credibility determination was not supported by the record]; *Li Zu Guan v. INS,* 453 F.3d 129, 138–42 (2d Cir. 2006) [IJ reversed in family planning case where he based lack of credibility upon speculation as to authenticity of documents, incorrect facts relating to demeanor, and requests for documents that were unreasonable]; *Lin Li Hua v. DOJ,* 453 F.3d 99, 105–12 (2d Cir. 2006) [in Chinese forced sterilization case, IJ reversed despite numerous important inconsistencies where the respondent testified to her pain in being forcibly sterilized and the IJ relied upon pure speculation to find her claim incredible despite saying it was the most critical issue in the case]; *Pang v. USCIS,* 448 F.3d 102 (2d Cir. 2006) [IJ did not evaluate the applicant's claim rebutting the signed I-589 and did not inform the applicant that it would rely on nonobvious matters to view testimony as flawed]; *Lin v. Gonzales,* 445 F.3d 127, 132 (2d Cir. 2006) [IJ's credibility determination was based upon a mischaracterization of the testimony because he confused applicant's claim of forced sterilization in China with whether Chinese authorities would allow applicant to have two children]; *Rizal v. Gonzales,* 442 F.3d 84, 90–94 (2d Cir. 2006) [where IJ denied case without considering affidavit and background evidence because she believed the applicant was not a follower of Christianity given his low level of doctrinal knowledge, the IJ's opinion was not supported by substantial evidence]; *Pavlova v. INS,* 441 F.3d 82, 85–91 (2d Cir. 2006) [reversing IJ's adverse credibility findings for Russian Baptist facing persecution by the RNU]; *Zheng v. Gonzales,* 440 F.3d 76 (2d Cir. 2006) [reversing IJ's adverse credibility findings in PRC forced sterilization case, where she misrepresented the record and where the inconsistencies were minor and isolated]; *Yang v. Gonzales,* 440 F.3d 72 (2d Cir. 2006) [IJ's adverse credibility findings in Chinese Christian case were not supported by substantial evidence, where he failed to provide cogent and specific reasons for his disbelief, where inconsistencies did not exist, and where he misconstrued testimony]; *Latifi v. Gonzales,* 430 F.3d 103, 105 (2d Cir. 2005) [where Albanian's credible fear interview was only inconsistent with testimony in trivial matters and when he offered an explanation why he was not forthcoming in his airport interview, court reversed adverse credibility finding]; *Gao v. Gonzales,* 424 F.3d 122, 130–32 (2d Cir. 2005) [reversing IJ's adverse credibility determination in Falun Gong case].

(c) *Third Circuit—Chukwu v. Att'y Gen. of the U.S.,* 484 F.3d 185, 188–91 (3d Cir. 2007) [in Nigerian MASSOB case, IJ's adverse credibility finding was reversed where alleged inconsistencies were explained by record testimony]; *Gabuniya v. Att'y Gen. of the U.S.,* 463 F.3d 316 (3d Cir. 2006) [reversing IJ's adverse credibility finding in Georgian case where finding was based on speculation and minor inconsistencies]; *Shah v. Attorney General of the U.S.* 446 F.3d 429, 437–38 (3d Cir. 2006) [reversed IJ in Pakistani asylum case where many inconsistencies were minor or nonexistent and the alleged major inconsistency regarding the father's death was explained by a witness, was evident in newspaper articles, and was verified by the death certificate]; *Sukwanputra v. Gonzales,* 434 F.3d 627, 636–37 (3d Cir. 2006) [reversing IJ's adverse credibility finding in Chinese Indonesian's case where determination was based on speculation, conjecture and improper treatment of documents not authenticated under 8 C.F.R. §287.6]; *Butt v. Gonzales,* 429 F.3d 430 (3d Cir. 2005) [asylum claim of Pakistani member of the PPP was improperly denied on credibility grounds where the IJ misunderstood the plain language of a doctor's note and gave general and conclusory reasons for denial]; *Wang v. Att'y Gen. of the U.S.,* 423 F.3d 260, 267–71 (3d Cir. 2005) [in forced sterilization case, remanding to the BIA and suggesting a new IJ be assigned to the case where the "tone, the tenor, the disparagement, and the sarcasm of the IJ seem[ed] more appropriate to a court television show than a federal court proceeding" and therefore "so tainted the proceedings below" that the court was not confident that the applicant was able to present his claim]; *Fiadjoe v. Att'y Gen. of the U.S.,* 411 F.3d 135, 152–60 (3d Cir. 2005) [reversing BIA adverse credibility finding of woman from Trokosi sect in Ghana suffering PTSD, who was repeatedly emotionally and sexually abused by her father, where inconsistencies existed between asylum interview, which was conducted in prison 17 days after arrival, and statements before IJ]; *Cao v. Att'y Gen. of the U.S.,* 407 F.3d 146 (3d Cir. 2005) [where applicant was persecuted because she spoke out against Chinese policy of infanticide, IJ's adverse credibility finding was not supported by substantial evidence because it was based *inter alia* on IJ's failure to credit applicant's actions arising out of a moral distinction between abortion and infanticide]; *Liu v. Ashcroft,* 372 F.3d 529, 534 (3d Cir. 2004) [IJ erred in basing adverse credibility on inconsistency in I-589 because presumption that respondent was aware of contents of I-589 had been successfully rebutted given his lack of knowledge of English]; *Guo v. Ashcroft,* 386 F.3d 556, 562–64 (3d Cir. 2004) [BIA could not rely on the IJ's prior, unrelated adverse credibility finding in religious persecution claim to deny a motion to reopen for asylum based on entirely separate coercive family planning claim because "one adverse credibility finding (does not) beget another"]; *Berishaj v. Ashcroft,* 378 F.3d 314, 323–26 (3d Cir. 2004) [reversing IJ's credibility determination that was based on speculation regarding ethnic Albanian from Montenegro's persecution by Serbs as both a civilian and in the military]; *Kayembe v. Ashcroft,* 334 F.3d 231, 235–37 (3d Cir. 2003) [where DOS Country Report finds that the government of the Congo no longer persecutes Tutsis, substantial evidence supported denial of claim].

(d) *Fourth Circuit— Lin-Jian v. Gonzales,* 489 F.3d 182, 191–93 (4th Cir. 2007) [where court upheld IJ's adverse credibility finding as to future persecution, the IJ's failure to make a credibility determination as to past persecution requires the assumption that the testimony was credible and the denial was not supported by substantial evidence]; *Tewabe v. Gonzales,* 446 F.3d 533, 538–40 (4th Cir. 2006) [IJ reversed in Ethiopian asylum claim where he stated that testimony was "implausible" without providing specific or cogent reasons why speaking out at a meeting, making airplane reservations quickly, or applying for asylum upon arrival were implausible].

(e) *Sixth Circuit—Mapouya v. Gonzales,* 487 F.3d 396, 406–11 (6th Cir. 2007) [applicant from Brazzaville, Congo had statements that appeared to be inconsistent due to mistranslation but were in fact discrepancies that were explained and were not material]; *Chen v. Gonzales,* 447 F.3d 468 (6th Cir. 2006) [forced sterilization case where adverse credibility determinations were based upon error or speculation]; *Alexandrov v. Gonzales,* 442 F.3d 395, 407–09 (6th Cir. 2006) [reversing IJ's adverse credibility finding in Bulgarian case where it was based on IJ's personal beliefs about how long beatings and detention should last, reversing IJ's denial of asylum as frivolous where it was based on two unreliable reports from U.S. Embassy in Sofia regarding alleged fraudulent documents]; *Mece v. Gonzales,* 415 F.3d 562 (6th Cir. 2005) [providing detailed analysis demonstrating that IJ's examples of adverse credibility were either trivial, not consistent with the evidence, or a misconstruction of the evidence]; *Pergega v. Gonzales,* 417 F.3d 623, 627–31 (6th Cir. 2005) [reversing BIA where inconsistencies were either irrelevant or nonexistent]; *Singh v. Ashcroft,* 398 F.3d 396, 404–06 (6th Cir. 2005) [IJ reversed for failure to separately analyze credibility issues for CAT after making a generalized negative credibility finding]; *Sylla v. INS,* 388

F.3d 924 (6th Cir. 2004) [reversing BIA adverse credibility finding where inconsistencies were minor, where findings were contrary to the evidence, and where speculation about the similarity of respondent's testimony to another were not supported by the record].

(f) *Seventh Circuit—Kadia v. Gonzales,* 501 F.3d 817, 821–24 (7th Cir. 2007) [post-REAL ID, IJ failed to distinguish between material lies and innocent mistakes, trivial inconsistencies and harmless exaggerations, and adhered to the discredited doctrine of *falsus in uno, falsus in omnibus* (false in one thing, false in all things) while engaging in defective "gotcha" questioning of applicant]; *Tandia v. Gonzales,* 487 F.3d 1048 (7th Cir. 2007) [adverse credibility finding regarding citizen of Mauritania involved in political opposition to the government was reversed because inconsistencies were insignificant, IJ speculated about ability to obtain passport and leave the country, and testimony was not vague as the IJ suggested]; *Jiang v. Gonzales,* 485 F.3d 992 (7th Cir. 2007) [adverse credibility finding of Chinese Christian reversed where IJ relied on doctrinal knowledge of Christianity and made findings unsupported by the record]; *Adekpe v. Gonzales,* 480 F.3d 525, 530–33 (7th Cir. 2007) [reversing IJ's negative credibility finding in Togo case where it was based on unimportant discrepancies and IJ failed to consider supportive documentary evidence]; *Mema v. Gonzales,* 474 F.3d 412, 419 (7th Cir. 2007) [reversed IJ's finding that asylum applicant was not sought by police while in hiding where adverse credibility determination was not supported by the record]; *Ayi v. Gonzales,* 460 F.3d 876 (7th Cir. 2006) [reversing IJ's adverse credibility determination in Togo case where IJ engaged in speculation, expected respondent to corroborate persecutors' knowledge, and assumed lack of credibility because respondent avoided persecution for extended period of time]; *San Kai Kwok v. Gonzales,* 455 F.3d 766, 769–71 (7th Cir. 2006) [IJ reversed in pre-REAL ID Act case concerning forced abortion, despite existence of a serious inconsistency about the manner and location of applicant's custody, where all other adverse credibility findings were based upon speculation or minor discrepancies]; *Pramatarov v. Gonzales,* 454 F.3d 764 (7th Cir. 2006) [IJ reversed in Bulgarian Roma case because adverse credibility was based on "factual error, bootless speculation, and errors of logic"]; *Hanaj v. Gonzales,* 446 F.3d 694 (7th Cir. 2006) [following *Kourski* the court reversed the IJ for ignoring evidence by the Albanian applicant and his witnesses regarding his credibility and determining, instead, lack of credibility based solely on a fraudulent birth certificate without any findings that applicant knew or suspected the document was fraudulent]; *Kllokoqi v. Gonzales,* 439 F.3d 336, 344 (7th Cir. 2006) [reversing IJ's adverse credibility finding in case involving ethnic Albanian from Kosovo because the IJ engaged in speculation, the inconsistencies were minor, and general statements in a Country Report cannot rebut specific testimony]; *Durgac v. Gonzales,* 430 F.3d 849, 852–54 (7th Cir. 2006) [reversing IJ's adverse credibility assessment of Kurdish student in Turkey]; *Zhang v. Gonzales,* 434 F.3d 993, 997–1001 (7th Cir. 2006) [reversing IJ's credibility assessment in forced abortion case where second IJ unnecessarily made new credibility findings, relied on the use of a false passport, improperly requested corroborating documents, he ignored country conditions evidence and improperly found that testimony contradicted DOS report]; *Gjerzai v. Gonzales,* 435 F.3d 800, 810–11 (7th Cir. 2006) [reversing IJ's adverse credibility assessment which was, in part, based on his own view of the validity of documents which he refused to send to a forensic document lab and where there was no proof that the applicant knew or had reason to know that the documents were fraudulent]; *Shtaro v. Gonzales,* 435 F.3d 711 (7th Cir. 2006) [adverse credibility finding reversed where IJ relied on speculation, mistakenly found inconsistencies between applicant's testimony and the DOS report, failed to explain why he doubted authenticity of documents, and rejected document because it was not authenticated pursuant to 8 C.F.R. §287.6]; *Giday v. Gonzales,* 434 F.3d 543, 550–53 (7th Cir. 2006) [reversing IJ credibility finding that was based on minor and irrelevant discrepancies where Eritrean was forcibly deported to Ethiopia]; *Lhanzom v. Gonzales,* 430 F.3d 833 (7th Cir. 2005) [reversing IJ where Tibetan's testimony was not inconsistent with her written statement and her father's testimony]; *Djouma v. Gonzales,* 429 F.3d 685, 688 (7th Cir. 2005) [although IJ erred in credibility determination, asylum denied on alternative ground that applicant failed to prove past persecution or likelihood of future persecution]; *Tabaku v. Gonzales,* 425 F.3d 417, 421–22 (7th Cir. 2005) [adverse credibility determination reversed where it was based on the missing witness rule where witness was sitting outside of courtroom and could have been called by the IJ]; *Ssali v. Gonzales,* 424 F.3d 556, 562–64 (7th Cir. 2005) [reversing adverse credibility finding where the BIA's "very significant mistake (regarding what part of Uganda respondent came from) suggests that the Board was not even aware of the most basic facts" of the case]; *Rodriguez Galicia v. Gonzales,* 422 F.3d 529, 536–38 (7th Cir. 2005) [reversing adverse credibility assessment and recognizing that false statements to an immigration officer where person fears deportation to a persecuting country "can be entirely *consistent* with a fear of persecution"]; *Dong v. Gonzales,* 421 F.3d 573 (7th Cir. 2005) [in forced abortion case, adverse credibility reversed because findings were either not supported by the record or not central to the claim]; *Chen v. Gonzales,* 420 F.3d 707 (7th Cir. 2005) [IJ's denial of asylum to PRC national whose claim was based on religious persecution was reversed because substantial evidence did not support the adverse credibility finding]; *Huang v. Gonzales,* 403 F.3d 945, 948–51 (7th Cir. 2005) [reversing IJ where IJ interjected his personal views about Catholicism in making inappropriate credibility findings]; *Jishiashvili v. Att'y Gen. of the U.S.,* 402 F.3d 386 (3d Cir. 2005) [where Georgian applicant presented testimony that was detailed, internally consistent, and materially in accord with his application and there is corroborative evidence, the IJ's adverse credibility was not supported where it was based on a few equivocal aspects of the claim not logically compelled by the record]; *Grupee v. Gonzales,* 400 F.3d 1026, 1027 (7th Cir. 2005) [IJ's "unexplained incredulity" over Liberian's return to work for two days after release from prison and before departure despite applicant's explanation is not a basis to challenge credibility]; *Lin v. Ashcroft,* 385 F.3d 748, 756–57 (7th Cir. 2004) [in forced abortion case, adverse credibility determination was not supported by substantial evidence]; *Tolosa v. Ashcroft,* 384 F.3d 906 (7th Cir. 2004) [reversing IJ's adverse credibility determination regarding Ethiopian of Oromo ethnicity]; *Ememe v. Ashcroft,* 358 F.3d 446 (7th Cir. 2004) [where IJ's adverse credibility findings were based on statements at credible fear interview conducted in Italian and applicant's native language was Amharic, case remanded to determine whether she comprehended questions]; *Uwase v. Ashcroft,* 349 F.3d 1039 (7th Cir. 2003) [reversing case involving mixed Hutu-Tutsi where IJ decision was not based on substantial evidence and where undue weight was given to lack of corroborating testimony]; *Georgis v. Ashcroft,* 328 F.3d 962, 967–70 (7th Cir. 2003) [where minor inconsistencies concerning dates and actions were resolved by other facts in evidence and explained by improperly excluded evidence, BIA's decision not supported by substantial evidence under *Elias-Zacarias*].

(g) *Eighth Circuit—Shahinaj v. Gonzales,* 481 F.3d 1027 (8th Cir. 2007) [reversing IJ's adverse credibility finding regarding Albanian homosexual because of IJ's statements that respondent did not speak, dress or act like a homosexual]; *Zewdie v. Ashcroft,* 381 F.3d 804, 808–09 (8th Cir. 2004) [where IJ/BIA found Ethiopian respondent not credible because she failed to produce medical evidence that her scars were from beatings, the court found it unreasonable under *Elias-Zacarias* to meet this extraordinary level of corroboration and reversed CAT denial]; *Bellido v. Ashcroft,* 367 F.3d 840 (8th Cir. 2004) [reversing IJ credibility finding for Bolivian union leader where application omitted certain details]; *but see Onsongo v. Gonzales,* 457 F.3d 849, 853 (8th Cir. 2007) [adverse credibility determination regarding Kenyan asylum claim could be based upon implausibility of testimony which does not make it speculative].

(h) *Ninth Circuit—Suntharalinkam v. Gonzales,* 458 F.3d 1034 (9th Cir. 2006) [IJs adverse credibility determination regarding asylum claim of Sri Lankan suspected of terrorism was reversed where IJ did not give respondent an opportunity to explain inconsistencies or where they were based upon speculation, minor or nonexistent discrepancies between asylum application and testimony or generalized expert testimony]; *Singh v. Gonzales,* 439 F.3d 1100 (9th Cir. 2006) [adverse credibility determination reversed where IJ relied on minor inconsistencies and speculation and ignored Sikh's explanation]; *Zhou v. Gonzales,* 437 F.3d 860, 865–66 (9th Cir. 2006) [reversing IJ's adverse credibility findings in Falun Gong case where determination was based on speculation, unexplained alleged discrepancies, and a demand for corroboration of documents from people living outside the U.S. when there was no indication that the documents were fraudulent or unreliable]; *Kumar v. Gonzales,* 444 F.3d 1043 (9th Cir. 2006) [reversing IJ's adverse credibility findings based on speculation about documents, minor and purported inconsistencies]; *Lin v. Gonzales,* 434 F.3d 1158, 1162–63 (9th Cir. 2006) [reversing IJ's adverse credibility finding where her view that documents were suspicious was based on conjecture and speculation as to perceived deficiencies and what she believed they should look like]; *Quan v. Gonzales,* 428 F.3d 883, 886–88 (9th Cir. 2005) [minor inconsistencies and unclear testimony where applicant not given an opportunity to clarify cannot be the basis for an adverse credibility finding]; *Quan v. Gonzales,* 423 F.3d 997, 999–1002 (9th Cir. 2005) [in PRC religious persecution claim, court reversed adverse credibility determination based upon minor inconsistencies, speculation and unclear testimony]; *Smolniakova v. Gonzales,* 422 F.3d 1037, 1044–53 (9th Cir. 2005) [reversing adverse credibility finding based on misconstruction of the record, insufficient evidence and improper speculation in case involving Jewish persecution in Russia]; *Marcos v. Gonzales,* 410 F.3d 1112, 1116–18 (9th Cir. 2005) [reversing IJ determination that lying to obtain immigrant visa demonstrates lack of credibility on asylum claim because his visa fraud was not an effort to enhance his asylum claim]; *Yeimane-Berhe v. Ashcroft,* 393 F.3d 907, 911–13 (9th Cir. 2005) [where Ethiopian of Amhara ethnicity presented testimony that was detailed and consistent, the submission of a fraudulent medical certificate where there was no evidence that she knew it to be fraudulent could not be the sole basis to make an adverse credibility finding]; *Kaur v. Ashcroft,* 379 F.3d 876 (9th Cir. 2004) [reversing IJ's five credibility findings in Sikh case that did not go to the heart of the claim, were based on speculation and conjecture, and where IJ did not provide specific and cogent reasons supporting his findings]; *Ge v. Ashcroft,* 367 F.3d 1121 (9th Cir. 2004) [reversing adverse credibility finding in forced abortion case where it rested upon speculation and was not supported by substantial evidence]; *Chen v. Ashcroft,* 362 F.3d 611, 620 (9th Cir. 2004) [reversing adverse credibility finding based on inconsistencies in minor matters]; *Arulampalam v. Ashcroft,* 353 F.3d 679, 687–89 (9th Cir. 2003) [where airport interview was as consistent and coherent as later testimony but not as detailed, adverse credibility was not supported by substantial evidence]; *Wang v. Ashcroft,* 341 F.3d 1015, 1021–22 (9th Cir. 2003) [substantial evidence did not support adverse credibility finding where inconsistencies were not material].

(i) *Tenth Circuit—Solomon v. Gonzales,* 454 F.3d 1160 (10th Cir. 2006) [IJ's adverse credibility determination that applicant was not truthful about her Ethiopian citizenship and was in fact Eritrean was reversed because the applicant explained why she didn't have corroborating evidence, the passport's missing pages did not compel a finding of deceit and sister's affidavit was sufficient]; *Uanreroro v. Gonzales,* 443 F.3d 1197, 1205–11 (10th Cir. 2006) [adverse credibility reversed regarding FGM case from Nigeria where it was based upon a misreading of the DOS reports, erroneous view of alleged inconsistent statements due to mother's poor English, and applicant's false statements at the airport]; *Chaib v. Ashcroft,* 397 F.3d 1273, 1278–80 (10th Cir. 2005) [reversing IJ's negative credibility findings that were based on speculation regarding Algeria's treatment of suspected terrorist supporters that was contrary to country reports and speculation regarding Algerian bank's computer system]; *Elizour v. Ashcroft,* 378 F.3d 1143, 1152–54 (10th Cir. 2004) [IJ's adverse credibility finding in Syrian case was based on unsupported opinion and unsubstantiated skepticism without record support].

(j) *Eleventh Circuit—Mezvrishvili v. U.S. Att'y Gen.*, 467 F.3d 1292, 1296 (11th Cir. 2006) [reversing IJ/BIA in case involving Jehovah's Witness from Georgia for *inter alia* not making a "clean" adverse credibility finding where IJ found applicant credible but then denied case because IJ determined applicant did not know enough about his religion].

(33) *Adverse Credibility Determination Was Supported by Substantial Evidence*

(a) *First Circuit—Teng v. Mukasey,* 516 F.3d 12, 16–17 (1st Cir. 2008) [in Cambodian withholding case the IJ premised her adverse credibility determination in part on Teng's demeanor, in part on inconsistencies and implausibilities regarding his behavior and in part on minor inconsistencies in his testimony]; *Chanthou Hemv. Mukasey,* 514 F.3d 67, 71–73 (1st Cir. 2008) [Cambodian couple who did not support the Cambodian Peoples Party lacked credibility on major issues that go to the heart of their claim] *Segran v. Mukasey,* 511 F.3d 1 (1st Cir. 2007) [major inconsistencies in Liberian case between testimony and recitals to asylum officer during credible fear interview]; *Tun v. Gonzales,* 503 F.3d 159 (1st Cir. 2007) [Cambodian with inconsistencies between her application and testimony]; *Lin v. Gonzales,* 503 F.3d 4 (1st Cir. 2007) [coercive birth control case from China]; *Yu v. Gonzales,* 502 F.3d 17 (1st Cir. 2007) [forced IUD claim where inconsistencies in testimony and documents]; *Melhem v. Gonzales,* 500 F.3d 78 (1st Cir. 2007) [Lebanese claiming Syrian agents were seeking to persecute him where testimony was inconsistent with application and affidavit]; *Pan v. Gonzales,* 489 F.3d 80, 86–87 (1st Cir. 2007) [cumulative effect of minor inconsistencies between trial and before asylum officer of person claiming religious persecution in the PRC were sufficient to uphold adverse credibility finding]; *Mewengkank v. Gonzales,* 486 F.3d 737 (1st Cir. 2007) [no credible in claim by Christian claiming persecution if returned to Indonesia *Gao v. Gonzales,* 467 F.3d 33 (1st Cir. 2006) [applicant's testimony that his wife was involuntarily sterilized and that he suffered religious persecution was not credible]; *Zheng v. Gonzales,* 464 F.3d 60, 63–65 (1st Cir. 2006) [adverse credibility upheld in case involving Catholic from PRC, where court employed three part test: (1) the discrepancies and omissions described by the IJ must actually be present in the record; (2) the discrepancies and omissions must provide specific and cogent reasons to conclude that the alien provided incredible testimony; and (3) a convincing explanation for the discrepancies or omissions must not have been supplied by the alien]. *See also Dine v. Gonzales,* 464 F.3d 89 (1st Cir. 2006) [Albanian political persecution claim denied where testimony was inconsistent with documentary evidence and evasive]; *Jean v. Gonzales,* 461 F.3d 87 (1st Cir. 2006) [Haitian's persecution by Aristide supporters based on family and political opinion not credible]; *Stroni v. Gonzales,* 454 F.3d 82, 88–89 (1st Cir. 2006) [activist on behalf of the Democratic Party in Albania found not credible]; *Estrada-Henao v. Gonzales,* 453 F.3d 38 (1st Cir. 2006) [numerous inconsistencies between testimony and application including failure to mention threats by FARC in application]; *Hoxha v. Gonzales,* 446 F.3d 210 (1st Cir. 2006) [rejecting Albanian's claim that there was no nexus between the discrepancies and the IJ's adverse credibility finding and that there were other measures establishing credibility]; *Lumaj v. Gonzales,* 446 F.3d 194 (1st Cir. 2006) [upholding IJ's adverse credibility finding where there were several discrepancies in Albanian's claim]; *Simo v. Gonzales,* 445 F.3 7 (1st Cir. 2006) [where Albanian applicant gave inconsistent account of how he procured his false passport, failed to mention any persecution at the airport interview, and gave unconvincing answers to inconsistencies, IJ upheld]; *Huang v. Gonzales,* 438 F.3d 65 (1st Cir. 2006) [Chinese applicant claiming persecution for violation of one-child policy who gave inconsistent answers and neglected to discuss wife's forced sterilization until 10 years after application filed]; *Tai v. Gonzales,* 423 F.3d 1, 4–5 (1st Cir. 2005) [Chinese forced abortion case where applicant did not mention contraception or abortion in his initial interview]; *Long v. Gonzales,* 422 F.3d 37 (1st Cir. 2005) [discrepancies between Cambodian's statements in his application, to the AO and to the IJ]; *Chen v. Gonzales,* 418 F.3d 110 (1st Cir. 2005) [IJ's adverse credibility determination regarding PRC national was amply supported by the record where there were numerous inconsistencies, gaps and contradictions]; *Dhima v. Gonzales,* 416 F.3d 92 (1st Cir. 2005) [where IJ identified numerous inconsistencies in Albanian asylum claim, credibility finding was unassailable]; *Kasneci v. Gonzales,* 415 F.3d 202 (1st Cir. 2005) [after IJ presented cogent reasons for making adverse credibility finding in Albanian asylum case, court was not compelled to conclude otherwise]; *Singh v. Gonzales,* 413 F.3d 156, 159–60 (1st Cir. 2005) [where testimony was inconsistent and implausible and applicant had trouble answering questions, adverse credibility upheld]; *Olujoke v. Gonzales,* 411 F.3d 16, 21–23 (1st Cir. 2005) [upholding IJ's adverse credibility finding in case involving religious persecution]; *Toure v. Ashcroft,* 400 F.3d 44, 47–49 (1st Cir. 2005) [providing false testimony at husband's asylum hearing was relevant to IJ's credibility determination in her own case]; *Qin v. Ashcroft,* 360 F.3d 302 (1st Cir. 2004) [record supported IJ's finding that forced abortion claim was fabricated]; *Albathani v. INS,* 318 F.3d 365, 373–74 (1st Cir. 2003) [upholding IJ's adverse credibility findings in claim by member of Lebanese Forces because under *Elias-Zacarias* and 8 U.S.C. §1252(b)(4)(B) the evidence did not "compel" reversal]; *Aguilar-Solis v. INS,* 168 F.3d 565, 570–71 (1st Cir. 1999) [applicant's purchase of fraudulent documents, factual variances between applications, and improbable claims that he did not know documents he possessed were bogus properly cast doubt on his credibility].

(b) *Second Circuit—Shu Wen Sun v. Board of Immigration Appeals,* 510 F.3d 377 (2d Cir. 2007) [substantial evidence supported IJ's decision that husband, making withholding claim primarily on wife's forced sterilization, was not credible given his evasive and nonresponsive answers and his conflicting testimony]; *Yan v. Mukasey,* 509 F.3d 63 (2d Cir.2007) [substantial evidence in the record supported IJ's decision that Chinese forced sterilization claim was inherently implausible]; *Mei Chai Ye v. DOJ,* 489 F.3d 517, 524–27 (2d Cir. 2007) [where IJ meticulously pointed out 23 striking similarities between affidavits in respondent's and another person's asylum case, gave the respondent and his counsel substantial time to explain the similarities as not being "canned" affidavits, and considered plausible explanations for the similarities before making an adverse credibility determination, the finding was upheld]; *Iouri v. Ashcroft,* 487 F.3d 76, 81–82 (2d Cir. 2007) [upholding adverse credibility finding in case involving persecution of member of the Ukraine Orthodox Church because of discrepancies between asylum application, addendum and testimony]; *Siewe v. Gonzales,* 480 F.3d 160, 167–71 (2d Cir. 2007) [in Cameroon case, quoting *Lavender v. Kurn,* 327 U.S. 645, 653 (1946) and distinguishing between fair inference, which the court believed occurred here, and bald speculation where there is a complete absence of probative facts]; *Chen v. DOJ,* 471 F.3d 315, 332–42 (2d Cir. 2006) [where the IJ engaged in improper speculation and his decision contained errors, the decision will be upheld if substantial evidence supports it and it is clear the same decision would be made on remand]; *Jian Hui Shao v. BIA,* 465 F.3d 497, 500–01 (2d Cir. 2006) [upholding IJ's adverse credibility finding in PRC family planning case]; *Guo v. Gonzales,* 463 F.3d 109, 113–14 (2d Cir. 2006) [where an adverse credibility finding on asylum/withholding eliminates all of the factual basis for CAT, it may be used in the CAT claim]; *Liu v. DOJ,* 455 F.3d 106, 110–12 (2d Cir. 2006) [adverse credibility finding regarding Chinese applicant's opposition to forced abortion of wife upheld where there were glaring discrepancies between first I-589 based upon Falun Gong and second/testimony]; *Chen v. U.S. Att'y Gen.,* 454 F.3d 103 (2d Cir. 2006) [in forced abortion case, the IJ could look at the cumulative impact of inconsistencies and not consider the effect of each individual discrepancy or omission]; *Cheng Tong Wang v. Gonzales,* 449 F.3d 451 (2d Cir. 2006) [failure to mention wife's forced sterilization in asylum application based upon opposition to China's family planning program]; *Kanacevic v. INS,* 448 F.3d 129, 136–38 (2d Cir. 2006) [airport statement was substantially inconsistent with asylum claim of Montenegro national of Albanian ethnicity]; *Singh v. BIA,* 438 F.3d 145 (2d Cir. 2006) [upholding IJ's findings that Sikh's claim lacked credibility because of inconsistencies and vagueness, notwithstanding court's determination that IJ was incorrect on 2 of the 8 grounds he relied upon]; *Borovikova v. DOJ,* 435 F.3d 151 (2d Cir. 2006) [in case of anti-Semitic persecution from the Ukraine, the court upheld the IJ's adverse credibility finding where the applicant's birth certificate was likely fraudulent, her application and supplemental application presented contradictory stories, and testimony was inconsistent]; *Chen v. BIA,* 435 F.3d 141, 146 (2d Cir. 2006) [upholding adverse credibility finding where IJ did not believe claim that Chinese respondent escaped detention because her jailors were not paying attention and that she could be found in a city of one million persons simply by looking in a neighborhood where young people live]; *Guan v. Gonzales,* 432 F.3d 391 (2d Cir. 2005) [where airport statement was "materially different" than application and the airport interview was reliable, adverse credibility finding upheld]; *Yang v. Gonzales,* 431 F.3d 84 (2d Cir. 2005) [Chinese woman claiming forced birth control had inconsistencies and discrepancies in her case]; *Majidi v. Gonzales,* 430 F.3d 77, 80–81 (2d Cir. 2005) [upholding denial in Bangladesh asylum case due to inconsistencies between testimony and application; IJ was not required to bring inconsistencies to applicant's attention]; *Ni v. DOJ,* 424 F.3d 172 (2d Cir. 2005) [coercive population control case from China]; *Lin v. DOJ,* 413 F.3d 188, 190–93 (2d Cir. 2005) [applicant's submission of documents showing sterilization without proof that it was forced could not overcome adverse credibility finding where applicant could also not recall when she was married and where there were many inconsistencies]; *Zhang v. INS,* 386 F.3d 66 (2d Cir. 2004) [two inconsistent statements as to the date applicant's wife was sterilized and the date he learned of it, were a sufficient basis to uphold IJ's adverse credibility determination]; *Shi v. BIA,* 374 F.3d 64 (2d Cir. 2004) [adverse credibility upheld where applicant's withdrawn claim that wife had abortion in 1992 was followed by new claim that wife was sterilized in 1998]; *Ramsameachire v. Ashcroft,* 357 F.3d 169, 179–83 (2d Cir. 2004) [where record of airport interview indicates its reliability, its use to challenge credibility provided substantial evidence]; *Chen v. INS,* 344 F.3d 272 (2d Cir. 2003) [*ex post* justifications for discrepancies were insufficient to overcome substantial evidence standard supporting BIA's adverse credibility finding].

(c) *Third Circuit—Zheng v. Gonzales,* 417 F.3d 379 (3d Cir. 2005) [adverse credibility upheld in forced sterilization case despite IJ errors regarding minor inconsistencies and speculation]; *He Chun Chen v. Ashcroft,* 376 F.3d 215, 223–26 (3d Cir. 2004) [despite reservations about a number of the IJ/BIA credibility findings in husband's case based on wife's forced abortion, the court upheld credibility finding given the "extraordinary deferential standard"]; *Reynoso-Lopez v. Ashcroft,* 369 F.3d 275, 277–79 (3d Cir. 2004) [record supported adverse credibility in Guatemalan case].

(d) *Fourth Circuit—Dankam v. Gonzales,* 495 f.3d 113, 121–23 (4th Cir. 2007) [citizen of Cameroon provided documents that were inconsistent with her testimony]; *Camara v. Ashcroft,* 378 F.3d 361, 369–71 (4th Cir. 2004) [upholding adverse credibility on some of IJ's findings under highly deferential standard but reversing denial of relief where IJ overlooked documentary evidence that supported claim].

(e) *Sixth Circuit—Sarr v. Gonzales,* 485 F.3d 354, 359–62 (6th Cir. 2007) [although the IJ misinterpreted some evidence, the failure to include certain events in a later filed application and in testimony coupled with a lack of documentation was sufficient to uphold denial]; *Hamida v. Gonzales,* 478 F.3d 734, 736–38 (6th Cir. 2007) [Tunisian who claimed persecution but was permitted by government to complete college and graduate school paid by the government]; *Ramaj v. Gonzales,* 466 F.3d 520, 527–28 (6th Cir. 2006) [Albanian seeking asylum based on Catholic faith and political activities had inconsistent asylum applications and contradictory testimony as to why he fled]; *Bah v. Gonzales,* 462 F.3d 637 (6th Cir. 2006) [Guinean woman claiming fear of persecution because of involvement in RPG and because daughters would be subject FGM was found not credible]; *Sterkaj v. Gonzales,* 439 F.3d 273, 278–79 (6th Cir. 2006) [submission of fraudulent "summons" and questionable "wanted" document that went to the heart of Albanian claim along with testimony that conflicted with DOS Reports and implausible claims were sufficient reasons to uphold adverse credibility determination]; *Shkabari v. Gonzales,* 427 F.3d 324 (6th Cir. 2005) [inconsistencies in IJ's analysis were not sufficient to diminish the substantial evidence in the record supporting adverse credibility finding]; *Selami v. Gonzales,* 423 F.3d 621, 624–26 (6th Cir. 2005) [submission of a fraudulent newspaper article that supported a key element in Albanian claim was sufficient to support adverse credibility finding]; *Hassan v. Gonzales,* 403 F.3d 429, 434–35 (6th Cir. 2005) [asylum denied to Palestinian on grounds that there were inconsistencies between testimony, application, and documents]; *Pilica v. Ashcroft,* 388 F.3d 941, 950–55 (6th Cir. 2004) [inconsistencies between applicant's and brother's testimony and failure to corroborate testimony was sufficient to uphold adverse credibility ruling in Albanian case]; *Yu v. Ashcroft,* 364 F.3d 700, 703–04 (6th Cir. 2004) [inconsistencies regarding applicant's connection to Falun Gong between his airport interview, application, credible fear interview and testimony were sufficient to uphold adverse credibility finding].

(f) *Seventh Circuit—Song Wang v. Keisler,* 505 F.3d 615, 620–22 (7th Cir. 2007) [adverse credibility determination regarding forced abortion claim by husband and wife was upheld based upon inconsistencies in husband's account and their failure to go into hiding]; *Ye Mon Aung v. Gonzales,* 495 F.3d 742 (7th Cir. 2007) [Burmese citizen who opposed military government where his stated reasons for fearing persecution fell apart upon cross-examination and revealed they were based upon rumor and speculation]; *Singh v. Gonzales,* 487 F.3d 1056 (7th Cir. 2007) [Indian Sikh claiming persecution had inconsistencies between application and testimony]; *Sina v. Gonzales,* 476 F.3d 459 (7th Cir. 2007) [Albanian not credible because he submitted false documents and numerous inconsistencies]; *Apouviepseakoda v. Gonzales,* 475 F.3d 881, 889–93 (7th Cir. 2007) [evidence did not compel a contrary result in denial of Togo woman's asylum claim]; *Doumbia v. Gonzales,* 472 F.3d 957, 963–64 (7th Cir. 2007) [admission of Embassy report on validity of summonses in Côte d'Ivoire court demonstrating invalidity of documents and other inconsistencies provided sufficient evidence of adverse credibility finding]; *Huang v. Gonzales,* 453 F.3d 942 (7th Cir. 2006) [IJ's adverse credibility determination upheld despite errors where PRC respondent presented certificate of forced abortion and IJ relied on DOS report stating certificates are only given for voluntary abortions]; *Hussain v. Gonzales,* 424 F.3d 622, 627–30 (7th Cir. 2005) [Pakistani who claimed membership in TJP lacked credibility]; *Nigussie v. Ashcroft,* 383 F.3d 531, 535–38 (7th Cir. 2004) [where testimony was self-serving, inconsistent, and lacked credibility and corroboration, the IJ's denial of relief was supported by substantial evidence]; *Balogun v. Ashcroft,* 374 F.3d 492, 498 (7th Cir. 2004) [IJ's adverse credibility determination in FGM case upheld under highly deferential *Elias-Zacarias* standard]; *Korniejew v. Ashcroft,* 371 F.3d 377 (7th Cir. 2004) [finding that one of the three discrepancies relied on by the IJ was incorrect and cautioning IJs against perceived inconsistencies, but upholding adverse credibility determination while noting that changed country conditions would be fatal to the applicant's claim of persecution in Poland due to her Jewish background]; *Malek v. INS,* 198 F.3d 1016 (7th Cir. 2000) [Lebanese Christian's claim not credible where BIA offered cogent reasons for its adverse determination]; *Bhatt v. Reno,* 172 F.3d 978 (7th Cir. 1999) [Hindu alleging religious persecution for his support of Muslims provided no corroboration of his claim that he was beaten]; *Ahmad v. INS,* 163 F.3d 457, 461–63 (7th Cir. 1999) [IJ's reasons did bear a reasonable nexus to the adverse credibility finding].

(g) *Eighth Circuit—Zine v. Mukasey,* 517 F.3d 535, 541–42 (8th Cir. 2008) [Algerian had inconsistent and uncorroborated testimony]; *Chen v. Mukasey,* 510 F.3d 797 (8th Cir. 2007) [claim of persecution related to mother's membership in Falun Gong was implausible]; *Singh v. Gonzales,* 495 F.3d 553 (8th Cir. 2007) [adverse credibility sustained in part because applicants lied about where they were living in the U.S. by stating they were living in California instead of Missouri so they could gain a "forum shopping" advantage]; *Gebresadik v. Gonzales,* 491 F.3d 846 (8th Cir. 2007) [upheld IJ's adverse credibility determination of Ethiopian who claimed persecution due to membership in the AAPO]; *Yakovenko v. Gonzales,* 477 F.3d 631 (8th Cir. 2007) [Ukrainian woman alleging anti-Semitism found not credible because she told an unbelievable story regarding the timing of how she obtained a visa to Mexico and entered the US]; *Jallow v. Gonzales,* 472 F.3d 569 (8th Cir. 2007) [Gambian seeking CAT relief did not present credible documents which undermined his credibility]; *Zhuang v. Gonzales,* 471 F.3d 884, 889–90 (8th Cir. 2006) [Chinese applicant lacked credibility where there were cumulative inconsistencies, omissions in testimony, and statement contradicted country conditions evidence]; *Celaj v. Gonzales,* 468 F.3d 1094 (8th Cir. 2006) [upheld IJ's adverse credibility determination regarding Albanian where DOS reports and respondent's written submissions, including Human Rights Watch report and other DOS reports, and other corroborating evidence contradicted his testimony or was unreliable]; *Onsongo v. Gonzales,* 457 F.3d 849, 852–57 (8th Cir. 2007) [adverse credibility determination regarding Kenyan asylum claim was supported by substantial evidence where IJ found testimony was implausible and documents had hallmark of fraud]; *Fofanah v. Gonzales,* 447 F.3d 1037 (8th Cir. 2006) [Sierra Leone citizen claimed persecution by Revolutionary United Front was denied due to contradictions in evidence regarding the RUF and death of his father]; *Desna v. Gonzales,* 454 F.3d 896 (8th Cir. 2006) [person claiming persecution as Jew from Ukraine did not discuss issue in application, check off ethnic persecution, or provide hospital records of assault]; *Ibrahim v. Gonzales,* 434 F.3d 1074, 1078–79 (8th Cir. 2006) [member of Midgan clan from Somalia not credible when he presented a fabricated story on his initial asylum application]; *Mamana v. Gonzales,* 436 F.3d 966, 968–69 (8th Cir. 2006) [Togo applicant's testimony was not plausible]; *Hoxha v. Gonzales,* 432 F.3d 919 (8th Cir. 2005) [Albanian's testimony not corroborated and IJ provided specific, cogent reasons for adverse credibility findings]; *Sheikh v. Gonzales,* 427 F.3d 1077, 1080–82 (8th Cir. 2005) [Somali's testimony conflicted with other family members and asylum application]; *Jalloh v. Gonzales,* 423 F.3d 894, 898–99 (4th Cir. 2005) [applicant from Sierra Leone lacked credibility where there were significant discrepancies between airport statement, application and testimony]; *Ombongi v. Gonzales,* 417 F.3d 823 (8th Cir. 2005) [Kenyan asylum claim lacked detail and corroboration and his explanations for bigamy and inability to contact family were not credible]; *Falaja v. Gonzales,* 418 F.3d 889, 894–97 (8th Cir. 2005) [where major events were not recounted in application or interview regarding religious persecution in Nigeria, and where there were inconsistencies in testimony, court upheld adverse credibility finding]; *Ambroise v. Gonzales,* 411 F.3d 932 (8th Cir. 2005) [IJ's adverse credibility determination upheld where respondent presented fraudulent documents relating to a core issue, failed to provide a satisfactory explanation for having done so, and failed to present other credible documentary evidence]; *Ismail v. Ashcroft,* 396 F.3d 970 (8th Cir. 2005) [upholding adverse credibility determination in Somalian claim]; *Mohamed v. Ashcroft,* 395 F.3d 835 (8th Cir. 2005) [same]; *Begna v. Ashcroft,* 392 F.3d 301, 304 (8th Cir. 2004) [uncorroborated testimony of Ethiopian of Eritrean descent was implausible]; *Amin v. Ashcroft,* 388 F.3d 648 (8th Cir. 2004) [person of Beharis ethnicity was properly denied asylum where kidnapping not mentioned in first asylum application and there were other discrepancies in his story]; *Gemechu v. Ashcroft,* 387 F.3d 944, 947–48 (8th Cir. 2004) [failure of Ethiopian to present evidence corroborating his claim and inconsistencies with country conditions reports]; *Kondakova v. Ashcroft,* 383 F.3d 792, 796–99 (8th Cir. 2004) [Seventh Day Adventist from Ukraine denied asylum where omissions, inconsistencies and failure to provide corroborating evidence provided specific and cogent reasons to support adverse credibility determination]; *Hassanein v. Ashcroft,* 380 F.3d 324, 327–28 (8th Cir. 2004) [inconsistent answers between adjustment and asylum applications regarding organizational membership and family background sufficient to demonstrate lack of credibility].

(h) *Ninth Circuit—Don v. Gonzales,* 476 F.3d 738 (9th Cir. 2007) [Sri Lankan claiming persecution by LTTE not credible because of inconsistency on important date and because IJ found he had a propensity for not telling the truth]; *Almaghzar v. Gonzales,* 457 F.3d 915, 922–23 (9th Cir. 2006) [upholding IJ's finding that expert psychologist lacked credibility when he was unaware of respondent's drug conviction but testified he was incapable of functioning in a linear fashion]; *Kaur v. Gonzales,* 418 F.3d 1061 (9th Cir. 2005) [where inconsistencies that weaken a claim are accompanied by other indications of dishonesty, the IJ's adverse credibility finding was supported by substantial evidence]; *Kasnecovic v. Gonzales,* 400 F.3d 812, 814–15 (9th Cir. 2005) [discrepancies regarding nationality and residence went to the heart of the claim of person born in Montenegro claiming withholding from Kosovo]; *Li v. Ashcroft,* 378 F.3d 959 (9th Cir. 2004) [inconsistencies between former asylum claims, airport interview and testimony were basis to deny Chinese forced sterilization claim]; *Singh v. Ashcroft,* 367 F.3d 1139 (9th Cir. 2004) [upholding adverse credibility finding in Sikh claim].

(i) *Eleventh Circuit—Chen v. U.S. Att'y Gen.,* 463 F.3d 1228, 1230–32 (11th Cir. 2006) [in Falun Gong case, the court found that under REAL ID, an adverse credibility determination need not be based on the heart of the claim]; *Alim v. Gonzales,* 446 F.3d 1239, 1254–57 (11th Cir. 2006) [IJ's credibility determinations were specific, cogent and supported by substantial evidence where Christian respondent from Syria committed multiple acts of fraud]; *Ruiz v. U.S. Att'y Gen.,* 440 F.3d 1247, 1254–56 (11th Cir. 2006) [upholding adverse credibility determination of Colombian claiming persecution by the FARC where, *inter alia*, respondent's family remained in Colombia unharmed and he testified that FARC members only told him to leave the region, not the country]; *Forgue v. U.S. Att'y Gen.,* 401 F.3d 1282 (11th Cir. 2005) [upholding denial where Haitian applicant claiming persecution by *Fanmi Lavalas* never mentioned the details of his claim prior to his hearing and never provided corroborative evidence]; *D-Muhumed v. U.S. Att'y Gen.,* 388 F.3d 814 (11th Cir. 2004) [upholding adverse credibility findings where there were numerous inconsistencies between application, testimony and documentary evidence].

(34) *Right to Present Evidence and Credibility*—The IJ cannot deny the applicant the right to present evidence because he does not believe he is credible. *Kaur v. Ashcroft,* 388 F.3d 734 (9th Cir. 2004) [due process violated where IJ precluded respondent's son from testifying and at the same time faulted her for not offering corroborating evidence]; *Kerciku v. INS,* 314 F.3d 913 (7th Cir. 2003) [due process was violated where IJ foreclosed virtually all testimony after he determined from brief questioning that respondent was not credible].

(35) *Brief Testimony and Credibility*—The Applicant's testimony cannot be considered vague simply because it is brief. *Alvarado-Carillo v. INS,* 251 F.3d 45, 52 (2d Cir. 2001) [where applicant gave brief but detailed testimony regarding events that occurred more than 10 years before, BIA's denial was reversed].

(36) *Nontransfer of Credibility Finding*—An adverse credibility finding for one claim does not necessarily affect the ability to obtain other relief. *Lin-Jian v. Gonzales,* 489 F.3d 182, 191–93 (4th Cir. 2007) [where court upheld IJ's adverse credibility finding as to future persecution, the IJ's failure to make a credibility determination as to past persecution requires the assumption that the testimony was credible and the denial was not supported by substantial evidence]; *Singh v. Ashcroft,* 398 F.3d 396, 404–06 (6th Cir. 2005) [IJ reversed for failure to separately analyze credibility issues for CAT after making a generalized negative credibility finding]; *Camara v. Ashcroft,* 378 F.3d 361, 371–72 (4th Cir. 2004) [reversing IJ's denial of CAT because credibility determinations as to asylum/withholding claims are not dispositive of a CAT claim]; *Sivakaran v. Ashcroft,* 368 F.3d 1028, 1029 (8th Cir. 2004) [reversing denial of CAT claim because adverse credibility determination and adverse decision on asylum/withholding are not determinative of CAT claim]; *Ramsameachire v. Ashcroft,* 357 F.3d 169, 184–86 (2d Cir. 2004) [credibility finding used to deny asylum/withholding cannot be basis for CAT denial]; *Zubeda v. Ashcroft,* 333 F.3d 463, 476 (3d Cir. 2003) ["[a]llowing the taint of the earlier adverse credibility determination [on asylum] to bleed through to the BIA's consideration of her claim under [CAT] without further explanation is [] error."]. *But see Lin-Jian v. Gonzales,* 489 F.3d 182, 192–93 (4th Cir. 2007) [under *Camara* there must be additional evidence to support CAT claim or IJ can use credibility finding from withholding/asylum]; *Guo v. Gonzales,* 463 F.3d 109, 113–14 (2d Cir. 2006) [*Ramsameachire* does not apply where adverse credibility finding on asylum/withholding eliminates all of the factual basis for CAT]; *Ibrahim v. Gonzales,* 434 F.3d 1074, 1079–80 (8th Cir. 2006)

[where respondent relied on same evidence to prove torture as to prove likelihood of persecution, IJ did not err in failing to separately analyze the credibility issues under CAT]; *Yang v. DOJ,* 426 F.3d 520, 522–23 (2d Cir. 2005) [distinguishing *Ramsameachire* and *Zubeda* because the factual finding that determined adverse credibility was the claim of forced sterilization which was not analytically distinct from the asylum claim]; *Aden v. Ashcroft,* 396 F.3d 966, 969 (8th Cir. 2005) [where adverse credibility could be used for asylum and CAT and no additional evidence was offered, a separate analysis was not necessary]; *Efe v. Ashcroft,* 293 F.3d 899, 907–08 (5th Cir. 2002).

(37) *Testimony Providing Alternate Theory*—Where applicant stated alternate reasons for CAT claim that were included in I-589, the IJ erred in refusing to hear the claim. *Yi v. INS,* 257 F.Supp.2d 791, 797–99 (E.D. Pa. 2003) [violation of right to present evidence under 8 U.S.C. §1229a(b)(4)(B)].

2.h. *Type of Evidence*

(1) *Evidence of Persecution of Family Members Sufficient*—Evidence concerning the treatment of a person's family is probative of a threat against the applicant and may be basis for relief. *Ahmed v. Keisler,* 504 F.3d 1183, 1194–95 (9th Cir. 2007) [where applicant was beaten when captured with his uncle suggests the army imputed uncle's political onion to him]; *Binrashed v. Gonzales,* 502 F.3d 666 (7th Cir. 2007) [reversed IJ's denial of future persecution of Yemen man who claimed he would be persecuted in retaliation against his father's actions]; *Vumi v. Gonzales,* 502 F.3d 150, 154–59 (2d Cir. 2007) [where wife of bodyguard of Kabila who was assassinated in DRC was sought by authorities, court remanded case to BIA to determine if bodyguard's wife was persecuted on account of her social group (nuclear family) or imputed political opinion]; *Hernandez-Ortiz v. Gonzales,* 496 F.3d 1042 (9th Cir. 2007) [reversed IJ for not thoroughly considering the impact of events on the petitioner when he was a small child as a result of the actions of the Guatemalan army, and the court affirmed the legal rule that "injuries to a family must be considered in an asylum case where the events that form the basis of the past persecution claim were perceived when the petitioner was a child"]; *Ticoalu v. Gonzales,* 472 F.3d 8, 11–12 (1st Cir. 2006) [BIA erred in Indonesian asylum case in not addressing brother's grant of asylum in its decision]; *Jorge-Tzoc v. Gonzales,* 435 F.3d 146 (2d Cir. 2006) [failure to consider effect of respondent's status as a small child when the events occurred required reversal and remand to determine past persecution];*Konan v. Att'y Gen. of the U.S.,* 432 F.3d 497, 501–02 (3d Cir. 2005) [remanding to BIA where IJ failed to consider whether status as an immediate family member of a gendarme in Côte d'Ivoire was a particular social group]; *Bhasin v. Gonzales,* 423 F.3d 977, 983–85 (9th Cir. 2005) [Indian mother was part of family membership constituting a particular social group where sons and daughters were missing as retaliation by Islamic militants for capture of their leader]; *Bernal-Rendon v. Gonzales,* 419 F.3d 877, 881 (8th Cir. 2005) [recognizing that a nuclear family can constitute a social group, but denying case on merits]; *Lopez-Soto v. Ashcroft,* 383 F.3d 228, 235–39 (4th Cir. 2004) [family constitutes a particular social group but upholding denial of asylum on grounds that claim not based on family persecution]; *Abay v. Ashcroft,* 368 F.3d 634, 640–42 (6th Cir. 2004), [mother who fears that 9 year daughter would be subject to FGM qualifies for asylum]; *Rios v. Ashcroft,* 287 F.3d 895, 900–01 (9th Cir. 2002) [family of murdered Guatemalan army officer who were kidnapped and threatened established persecution because political opinion was imputed to them by guerrillas]; *Ventura v. INS,* 264 F.3d 1150, 1154–55 (9th Cir. 2001) *rev'd on other grounds* 537 U.S. 12 (2002) ["[p]ast political persecution of family members provides evidence of imputed political opinion of an asylum applicant"]; *Mgoian v. INS,* 184 F.3d 1029, 1035–36 (9th Cir. 1999) [murder of uncle and persecution of other family members who were also Kurdish-Muslims in Armenia]; *Lwin v. INS,* 144 F.3d 505, 512 (7th Cir. 1998) [parents of Burmese student dissidents are a social group]; *Meza-Manay v. INS,* 139 F.3d 759 (9th Cir. 1998) [where ex-husband was a target of the Shining Path, wife would still be granted asylum notwithstanding divorce]; *Gebremichael v. INS,* 10 F.3d 28 (1st Cir. 1993) [persecution because of family membership is social group persecution]; *Draganova v. INS,* 82 F.3d 716, 721–22 (7th Cir. 1996); *Abudu v. INS,* 802 F.2d 1096, 1102 (9th Cir. 1986), *rev'd on other grounds,* 485

U.S. 94 (1988); *Ananeh-Firempong v. INS*, 766 F.2d 621 (1st Cir. 1985); *Chavarria v. DOJ*, 722 F.2d 666, 668 (11th Cir. 1984); *Sanchez v. INS*, 707 F.2d 1523, 1527–28 (D.C. Cir. 1983); *Fleurinor v. INS*, 585 F.2d 129, 134 (5th Cir. 1978); *Chavez v. INS*, 723 F.2d 1431, 1434 (9th Cir. 1984); *Shoaee v. INS*, 704 F.2d 1079, 1084 (9th Cir. 1983); *Rasool v. INS*, 758 F.Supp. 188 (S.D.N.Y. 1991); *Matter of Villalta*, 20 I&N Dec. 142 (BIA 1990) [Salvadoran whose family was killed]; *Matter of Chen*, 20 I&N Dec. 16 (BIA 1989); Handbook ¶43.

(a) *Evidence of Family Persecution Insufficient—Mabasa v. Gonzales,* 455 F.3d 740, 745–47 (7th Cir. 2006) [where applicant's family members in Zimbabwe were harmed because they were high ranking members of the Movement for Democratic Change, but applicant was simply a member, he cannot obtain withholding through derivative persecution and must establish evidence of his own future harm]; *Caushi v. Att'y Gen. of the U.S.,* 436 F.3d 220, 231–32 (3d Cir. 2006) [BIA did not abuse its discretion in failing to reopen where counsel simply submitted his own affidavit, without supporting documentation, stating that case should be reopened because applicant's sister obtained asylum]; *Jalloh v. Gonzales,* 418 F.3d 920 (8th Cir. 2005) [execution of parents and sister by rebel army was not sufficient to establish past persecution where it was an isolated event]; *Eta-Ndu v. Gonzales,* 411 F.3d 977, 983 (8th Cir. 2005) [where uncle was murdered and father's business burned down because of their political views, no claim based on family membership]; *Roy v. Ashcroft,* 389 F.3d 132, 138–39 (5th Cir. 2004) [although father was given asylum due to his evangelical preaching, son, who was not present at any incidents where father was persecuted, lived in a different district with his mother, and demonstrated no serious involvement in Christianity was not entitled to relief]; *Shoaira v. Ashcroft,* 377 F.3d 837, 843–45 (8th Cir. 2004) [psychological harm arising from rough treatment by Egyptian authorities and from witnessing her father's arrest does not constitute persecution]; *Francois v. INS,* 283 F.3d 926, 931–32 (8th Cir. 2002) [although brothers were granted asylum, respondent's claim was rejected because information regarding brothers was outdated]; *Pop v. INS,* 279 F.3d 457, 462–63 (7th Cir. 2002) [ex-wife's grant of asylum did not require same treatment for applicant because claims were "materially different" and they were not based on the same persecution or same facts]; *Matter of A-K-,* 24 I&N Dec. 275, 277–79 (BIA 2007) [a derivative claim for withholding or CAT based upon future harm (FGM) to an applicant's child is not sufficient because it is not directed against the respondent]; *Matter of Jean,* 23 I&N Dec. 373, 387–88 (AG 2002) [denying withholding to Haitian woman where husband was targeted and attacked but no evidence presented for imputed theory or to link her to husband's affiliations].

(b) *Failure to Persecute Family Members Not Relevant*—However, the fact that family members are *not* persecuted is not relevant to a claim. *Uwais v. U.S. Att'y Gen.,* 478 F.3d 513, 519 (2d Cir. 2007) [where applicant's daughter went to Sri Lanka and her mother returned to Sri Lanka after visiting the U.S., the BIA erred in drawing inference that applicant did not have a well-founded fear]; *Edimo-Doualla v. Gonzales,* 464 F.3d 276, 286–87 (2d Cir. 2006) [reversing IJ's finding that the fact that applicant's mother and wife were not persecuted undercut his claim where applicant testified that mother and wife were not politically active]; *Kumar v. Gonzales,* 444 F.3d 1043, 1055 (9th Cir. 2006) [the fact that parents of Indian applicant from Jammu and Kashmir region have remained unharmed was not relevant because there was no evidence that police suspected them of associating with the same Muslim separatist faction]; *Toure v. Att'y Gen. of the U.S.,* 443 F.3d 310, 318–19 (3d Cir. 2006) [claim of past persecution is not undercut by wife's continued presence in Cot d'Ivoire both because she is in hiding and her presence goes to future persecution, not past persecution]; *Vente v. Gonzales,* 415 F.3d 296, 302 (3d Cir. 2005) [it was irrelevant that family members remained in Colombia unharmed]; *Bellido v. Ashcroft,* 367 F.3d 840, 844 (8th Cir. 2004) [reversing IJ denial for Bolivian union leader where family was not persecuted]; *Lim v. INS,* 224 F.3d 929, 935 (9th Cir. 2000) [unharmed family member was not relevant where they were not subject to similar risk]; *Hartooni v. INS*, 21 F.3d 336, 342 (9th Cir. 1994). *But see De Oliveira v. Mukasey,* 520 F.3d 78,

80 (1st Cir. 2008) [Brazilian asylum claim undercut by fact that wife and children continued to live in Brazil particularly when the threats against the respondent contemplated harm to his children]; *Sou v. Gonzales,* 450 F.3d 1, 8 (1st Cir. 2006) [where children continue to live peacefully in Cambodia undercuts parents' future persecution claim]; *Krasnopivtsev v. Ashcroft,* 382 F.3d 832, 839 (8th Cir. 2005) [the reasonableness of a fear of persecution is diminished when family members remain in the native country unharmed and the applicant himself has not been singled out for abuse]; *Toptchev v. INS,* 295 F.3d 714, 725 (7th Cir. 2002) [the fact that petitioner's family members continue to live unharmed in Bulgaria supports lack of well-founded fear]; *Hakeem v. INS,* 273 F.3d 812, 816 (9th Cir. 2001) ["[a]n applicant's claim of persecution upon return is weakened, even undercut, when similarly-situated family members continue to live in the country without incident"]; *Sofinet v. INS,* 196 F.3d 742, 747 (7th Cir. 1999) [absence of evidence of harm to family undermines petitioner's claim].

(c) *No derivative benefit for family member seeking withholding of removal*— Some circuits have now held that withholding, unlike asylum, does not grant derivative benefits to family members so that a grant of withholding to a husband or parent does not give derivative benefits to the spouse or child. *Arif v. Mukasey,* 509 F.3d 677, 680–82 (5th Cir. 2007) [wife of withholding applicant does not obtain a derivative status and 8 C.F.R. §1208.16(e) supports that reading of the statute]; *Delgado v. U.S. Att'y Gen.,* 487 F.3d 855, 862 (11th Cir. 2007) [where Venezuelan father and son were granted withholding, mother could not obtain withholding because the statute does not provide for derivative benefits as does asylum].

(d) *Evidence of Intra-Family Persecution*—Family member's persecution by other family members is a basis for relief where the government is unable or unwilling to take any action. *Faruk v. Ashcroft,* 378 F.3d 940, 943 (9th Cir. 2004) [attack by family members due to inter-faith marriage of Christian and Muslim Fijians supports claim]; *Matter of S-A-,* 22 I&N Dec. 1328 (BIA 2000) [past persecution in Morocco at the hands of respondent's father].

(e) *Persecution of Non-Family Household Members*—A person who is part of household may also suffer persecution by implication. *Nakibuka v. Gonzales,* 421 F.3d 473 (7th Cir. 2005) [housekeeper of high-ranking political opponent of Ugandan government subjected to persecution by the military].

(2) *Evidence of Religious Persecution*—Evidence of treatment of certain religious groups is probative of a threat against an applicant claiming religious persecution. *Boctor v. Gonzales,* 474 F.3d 488 (7th Cir. 2007) [Coptic Christian who was threatened by Muslim extremists for reporting threats against fellow Christian who married Muslim woman that converted to Christianity was persecuted on account of his religion]; *Gomes v. Gonzales,* 473 F.3d 746 (7th Cir. 2007) [court reversed BIA where Christians from Bangladesh were attacked by Muslims and IJ did not appear to consider cumulative persecution and overrelied on DOS reports while ignoring specific contradictory testimony]; *Mezvrishvili v. U.S. Att'y Gen.,* 467 F.3d 1292, 1296 (11th Cir. 2006) [reversing IJ/BIA in case involving Jehovah's Witness from Rep. of Georgia, recognizing that persecutor may impute religious view to person]; *Youkhana v. Gonzales,* 460 F.3d 927, 931–33 (7th Cir. 2006) [IJ erred in finding changed country conditions for Assyrian Christian in Iraq simply because the Ba'ath Party was not longer in power]; *Rafix v. Gonzales,* 458 F.3d 36 (2d Cir. 2006) [denial of CAT claim of Muslim who converted to Christianity was reversed where IJ failed to use "willfully blind" test and ignored substantial evidence]; *Smolniakova v. Gonzales,* 422 F.3d 1037, 1048–49 (9th Cir. 2005) [past persecution based on an assault and death threats was sufficient to establish past persecution regarding Jewish persecution in Russia]; *Ivanishvili v. DOJ,* 433 F.3d 332, 339–43 (2d Cir. 2006) [remanding where IJ failed to evaluate Jehovah's Witness testimony about religious persecution in Georgia]; *Koval v. Gonzales,* 418 F.3d 798 (7th Cir. 2005) [remanding case regarding persecution of Mormons in the Ukraine]; *Poradisova v. Gonzales,* 420 F.3d 70, 81–82 (2d Cir. 2005)[where Jewish applicants from Belarus submitted reports

from DOS and international organizations demonstrating that hostility to Jews had worsened since IJ/BIA decision, the BIA abused its discretion in not reopening]; *Fessehaye v. Gonzales,* 414 F.3d 746, 755 and n.9 (7th Cir. 2005) [persecution of Jehovah's Witness in Ethiopia]; *Chen v. Gonzales,* 417 F.3d 268, 272–75 (2d Cir. 2005) [reversing IJ's denial of asylum where IJ ignored DOS report supporting claim of religious persecution in China]; *Krotova v. Gonzales,* 416 F.3d 1080 (9th Cir. 2005) [cumulative effects of mistreatment due to anti-Semitism in Russia]; *Zhang v. Ashcroft,* 388 F.3d 713, 719–21 (9th Cir. 2004) [China has prohibited the practice of Falun Gong and members would be unable to practice it without harm]; *Ghebremedhin v. Ashcroft,* 385 F.3d 1116 *amended* 392 F.3d 214 (7th Cir. 2004) [reversing denial to Jehovah's Witness who fled Eritrea given the country's documented harsh treatment toward that group and his refusal to serve in Eritrean military on religious grounds]; *Mamedov v. Ashcroft,* 387 F.3d 918 (7th Cir. 2004) [reversing denial of asylum where person denied employment and beaten by the police because he practiced Judaism]; *Eduard v. Ashcroft,* 379 F.3d 182, 192 (5th Cir. 2004) [IJ erred in requiring Indonesian Christians to prove they were singled out for persecution when evidence indicated a pattern and practice of persecution of Christians]; *Vladimirova v. Ashcroft,* 377 F.3d 690, 697 (7th Cir. 2004) [failure of DOS to name religious group in its annual report does not imply that religious group does not exist or was not persecuted]; *Khup v. Ashcroft,* 376 F.3d 898 (9th Cir. 2004) [Seventh Day Adventist in Burma granted relief where a fellow preacher was arrested, tortured and killed and applicant went into hiding]; *Guo v. Ashcroft,* 361 F.3d 1194, 1202–04 (9th Cir. 2004) [citizen of PPC who was beaten and detained by police for 15 days for resisting efforts of police in removing cross from a tomb during a funeral established past persecution]; *Muhur v. Ashcroft,* 355 F.3d 958 (7th Cir. 2004) [reversing IJ's determination that Jehovah's Witness not entitled to asylum because she could escape notice by hiding her religion]; *Baballah v. Ashcroft,* 335 F.3d 981, 990–91 (9th Cir. 2003) *amended* 367 F.3d 1067 (9th Cir. 2004) [Muslim Israeli established that threats and attacks coupled with economic persecution were sufficient to reverse IJ denial]; *Bandari v. INS,* 227 F.3d 1160 (9th Cir. 2000) [BIA reversed where Christian in Iran persecuted for interfaith dating and not for violating general law against public display of affection]; *Ladha v. INS,* 215 F.3d 889 (9th Cir. 2000) [reversing BIA denial regarding persecution of Khoja sect of Islam in Pakistan]; *Maini v. INS,* 212 F.3d 1167 (9th Cir. 2000) [reversing BIA denial of claim arising from intermarriage between Hindu and Sikh]; *Korablina v. INS,* 158 F.3d 1038 (9th Cir. 1998) [Jewish woman in Ukraine suffered persecution]; *Najafi v. INS*, 104 F.3d 943, 948–50 (7th Cir. 1997) [Iranian conversion to Christianity is apostasy punishable by death in Iran]; *Matter of O-Z- & I-Z-,* 22 I&N Dec. 23 (BIA 1998) [anti-Semitism in the Ukraine]; *Matter of Salama,* 11 I&N Dec. 536 (BIA 1966); *Dolores v. INS*, 772 F.2d 223, 226 (6th Cir. 1985); *Kanivets v. Riley,* 320 F.Supp.2d 297, 299 (E.D. Pa. 2004) [in Jewish persecution claim, IJ made legal errors including relying on DOS report to repute evidence IJ deemed credible]; *Bajwa v. Cobb*, 727 F.Supp. 53 (D. Mass. 1989) [Sikh religion]; *Matter of L-K-,* 23 I&N Dec. 677, 682–83 (BIA 2004) [evangelical Christian living in the Ukraine who was seriously injured during a series of home invasions was persecuted on account of her religious beliefs]; *Matter of G-A-,* 23 I&N Dec. 366 (BIA 2002) [burden met in CAT claim where due to a combination of factors including applicant's Christian religion, it is more likely than not that he would be tortured upon his removal to Iran]. The BIA has also found that abuse suffered by a woman in a Muslim country due to her father's orthodoxy amounts to religious persecution. *Matter of S-A-,* 22 I&N Dec. 1328 (BIA 2000).

(a) *Evidence of Religious Conversion After Leaving Home Country*—Where an applicant converted to another religion after leaving his home country, it is also probative. *Rafix v. Gonzales,* 458 F.3d 36 (2d Cir. 2006) [denial of CAT claim of Muslim who converted to Christianity was reversed where IJ failed to use "willfully blind" test and ignored substantial evidence]; *Bastanipour v. INS*, 980 F.2d 1129 (7th Cir. 1992) [Iranian's conversion to Christianity may result in religious persecution]; *Doe v. INS*, 867 F.2d 285 (6th Cir. 1989) [Chinese student converted to Christianity after arrival in U.S. and spoke out against anti-religious atmosphere in China]; *Shirazi-Parsa v. INS*, 14 F.3d 1424 (9th Cir. 1994) [Mormon in Iran] *overruled on other grounds by*

Fisher v. INS, 79 F.3d 955 (9th Cir. 1996) (*en banc*); *But see Chakir v. Gonzales,* 466 F.3d 563, 569–70 (7th Cir. 2006) [Christian convert from Morocco could not establish that Moroccan government would not protect him as Moroccan law is not based on Sharia law].

(b) *Lack of Doctrinal Knowledge*—Denying relief because IJ believes that a certain level of doctrinal knowledge of the religion is necessary is reversible error. *Jiang v. Gonzales,* 485 F.3d 992, 995 (7th Cir. 2007) [IJ reversed where he discredited Chinese Christian's asylum claim based on applicant's lack of doctrinal knowledge of Christianity]; *Mezvrishvili v. U.S. Att'y Gen.,* 467 F.3d 1292, 1295–97 (11th Cir. 2006) [reversing IJ/BIA in case involving Georgian Jehovah's Witness where applicant's credibility was not challenged but agency found he did not know enough about his religion]; *Rizal v. Gonzales,* 442 F.3d 84, 90–94 (2d Cir. 2006) [where IJ denied case because she believed the applicant was not a follower of Christianity given his low level of doctrinal knowledge, the court "expressly reject[ed] this approach"]; *Iao v. Gonzales,* 400 F.3d 530 (7th Cir. 2005) [reversing denial to Falun Gong follower noting *inter alia*, the IJ's lack of familiarity with relevant foreign culture and his exaggerated notion of how much religious people know about their religion]; *Ahmadshah v. Ashcroft,* 396 F.3d 917, 920–21 and n.2 (8th Cir. 2005) [reversing denial of asylum for Christian convert from Afghanistan, rejecting assertion that applicant must have a clear understanding of Christian doctrine before he could claim he had a commitment to Christianity].

(c) *Relief Based on Religious Persecution Denied*—*Sipayung v. Gonzales,* 491 F.3d 18 (1st Cir. 2007) [Christian in Indonesia did not suffer past persecution and could not show pattern and practice of persecution]; *Quomsieh v. Gonzales,* 479 F.3d 602 (8th Cir. 2007) [Christian Palestinians could not establish persecution by Muslims]; *Chen v. Gonzales,* 470 F.3d 1131 (5th Cir. 2006) [upholding denial of religious persecution claim of Chinese Protestant despite delving into doctrinal knowledge of individual and DOS Reports because the statements of persecution were vague and the specific examples of persecution pointed to other religions]; *Chakir v. Gonzales,* 466 F.3d 563, 569–70 (7th Cir. 2006) [Christian convert from Morocco could not establish that Moroccan government would not protect him as Moroccan law is not based upon Sharia law]; *Zehatye v. Gonzales,* 453 F.3d 1182, 1185–90 (9th Cir. 2006) [Jehovah's Witness from Eritrea who suffered social ostracism and economic hardship denied relief]; *Zheng v. U.S. Att'y Gen.,* 451 F.3d 1287 (11th Cir. 2006) [follower of Falun Gong who was detained for 5 days and required to watch reeducation videos, lost his job, and was subject to periodic searches denied relief]; *Woldemichael v. Ashcroft,* 448 F.3d 1000, 1003–05 (8th Cir. 2006) [a 54-year old Jehovah's Witness could not demonstrate pattern and practice persecution in Eritrea because State Department's. documentation focused on persecution only against those who refused to vote for independence or refused to obey the requirement of national service and neither was applicable to the applicant]; *Alim v. Gonzales,* 446 F.3d 1239, 1256–57 (11th Cir. 2006) [Syrian Christian could only demonstrate harassment not persecution]; *Gomes v. Gonzales,* 429 F.3d 1264, 1267 (9th Cir. 2005) [Christian in Bangladesh denied pattern and practice claim where country report stated government did not countenance attacks]; *Li v. Gonzales,* 420 F.3d 500, 507–11 (5th Cir. 2005) [Chinese applicant who was punished because of his religious beliefs, not entitled to withholding because his prosecution was pursuant to a law of general applicability regarding unregistered churches]; *Zaidi v. Ashcroft*, 377 F.3d 678, 681–82 (7th Cir. 2004) [upholding BIA denial where only one incident of beating by anti-Shia group, and no details or other documentary evidence was presented]; *Prokopenko v. Ashcroft,* 372 F.3d 941, 946 (8th Cir. 2004) [IJ denial upheld where despite evidence that police/security forces harass and beat religious minorities, the applicant was not an "actively practicing Baptist"]; *Khalil v. Ashcroft,* 337 F.3d 50, 55–56 (1st Cir. 2003) [harassment of Coptic Christian in Egypt not sufficient to show persecution]; *Nagoulko v. INS,* 333 F.3d 1012, 1016–18 (9th Cir. 2003) [job discrimination and harassment due to religious beliefs as a Pentecostal Christian in the Ukraine does not amount to persecution]; *Tesfu v. Ashcroft,* 322 F.3d 477 (7th Cir. 2003) [discrimination and poor treatment of Jehovah's Witnesses in Eritrea does not amount to persecution]; *Ambati v. Reno,* 233 F.3d 1054 (7th Cir. 2000) [Indian of Christian faith suffering mild harassment by Hindus insufficient]; *Karapetian v. INS,* 162 F.3d 933 (7th Cir. 1998) [applying highly deferential standard even where other family members granted relief because of persecution]; *Mejia-Paiz v. INS*, 111 F.3d 720 (9th Cir. 1997); *Refahiyat v. DOJ*, 29 F.3d 553 (10th Cir. 1994); *Elnager v. INS*, 930 F.2d 784, 788–89 (9th Cir. 1991).

(3) *Evidence of Union or Other Organizational Membership*—Evidence of persecution against certain types of organizations, such as unions, is probative of a threat against the applicant. *Bellido v. Ashcroft,* 367 F.3d 840 (8th Cir. 2004) [reversing IJ credibility finding and lack of substantial evidence for Bolivian union leader]; *Agbuya v. INS,* 241 F.3d 1224 (9th Cir. 2001) [former employee of mining company that was targeted by guerillas]; *Vera-Valera v. INS,* 147 F.3d 1036 (9th Cir. 1998) [president of street vendors had imputed political opinion]; *Osorio v. INS*, 18 F.3d 1017 (2d Cir. 1994) [reversing BIA denial of asylum to union leader]; *Carranza-Hernandez v. INS*, 12 F.3d 4 (2d Cir. 1993) [reversing BIA denial of asylum to union organizer]; *Mendoza-Perez v. INS*, 902 F.2d 760 (9th Cir. 1990) [land reform organization]; *Perez-Alvarez v. INS*, 857 F.2d 23 (1st Cir. 1988); *Zavala-Bonilla v. INS*, 730 F.2d 562 (9th Cir. 1984); *Haitian Refugee Center v. Civiletti*, 503 F.Supp. 442 (S.D. Fla. 1980). *See also* 8 C.F.R. §§208.13(b)(2)(i), 1208.13(b)(2)(i); *Makonnen v. INS*, 44 F.3d 1378, 1382–84 (8th Cir. 1995) [regulation covers organized, systematic or pervasive persecution]. But a person need not be a "card-carrying member of a political party to be considered persecuted on account of political opinion." *Toure v. Att'y Gen. of the U.S.*, 443 F.3d 310, 319–20 (3d Cir. 2006) [applicant from Côte d'Ivoire did not have to be member of RDR to have a political opinion or to suffer due to imputed political opinion].

(4) *Evidence of Return Trip to Home Country—De Santamaria v. U.S. Att'y Gen.*, ___ F.3d ___ (11th Cir. Apr. 22, 2008) [Colombian applicant's return trips home in the face of FARC persecution did not negate her subjective fear]; *Smolniakova v. Gonzales,* 422 F.3d 1037, 1049–50 (9th Cir. 2005) [reversing IJ's determination that respondent would not face future persecution because she traveled back to Russia on three occasions to tend to her dying mother]; *Boer-Sedano v. Gonzales,* 418 F.3d 1082, 1091 (9th Cir. 2005) [return trips alone cannot rebut a presumption of past persecution]; *Karouni v. Gonzales,* 399 F.3d 1163, 1175–76 (9th Cir. 2005) [returning to Lebanon for two months and one month respectively because parents were dying does not constitute substantial evidence that his fear of persecution was not well-founded]. *But see Toloza-Jimenez v. Gonzales,* 457 F.3d 155, 161 (1st Cir. 2006) [Colombian failed to satisfy the subjective prong of the well-founded fear test by returning home to Colombia after traveling twice to the US]; *Madjakpor v. Gonzales,* 406 F.3d 1040, 1045 (8th Cir. 2005) [where applicant returned to Togo two times, he failed to demonstrate an objectively reasonable fear of arrest]; *Diab v. Ashcroft,* 397 F.3d 35, 42 (1st Cir. 2005) [Coptic Christian's return to Egypt three times for short visits supported IJ's adverse credibility finding regarding subjective fear]; *Carcamo-Recinos v. Ashcroft,* 389 F.3d 253, 258–59 (1st Cir. 2004) [willing return to Guatemala on several occasions during time respondent was threatened, remaining in Guatemala for more than two years after alleged persecution peaked, and no persecution of family members during entire time is substantial evidence supporting denial].

(5) *Evidence of Valid Visa or Passport—Tandia v. Gonzales,* 487 F.3d 1048, 1053–54 (7th Cir. 2007) [where political activist from Mauritania obtained passport to leave the country through a bribe, the IJ's claim that he had official approval to leave and therefore was not credible was reversed]; *Mema v. Gonzales,* 474 F.3d 412, 419 (7th Cir. 2007) [ability to obtain passport by Albanian is not probative of fear of future persecution because "governments are often all too happy to see undesirables and dissidents depart"]; *Durgac v. Gonzales,* 430 F.3d 849, 852 (7th Cir. 2006) [that Kurdish national of Turkey was given a passport after 18-day detention cannot be a basis for adverse credibility assessment because governments are often happy to see "undesirable" ethnic groups leave]; *Nakibuka v. Gonzales,* 421 F.3d 473, 480 (7th Cir. 2005) [obtaining a visa from Ugandan

government does not show lack of persecution because "oppressive governments that want to eliminate their political opponents may find that allowing them to leave the country is easier than having them jailed or killed"]; *Grupee v. Gonzales,* 400 F.3d 1026, 1027 (7th Cir. 2005) [reversing adverse credibility finding based in part on fact that Liberian could obtain a passport]; *Khup v. Ashcroft,* 376 F.3d 898, 905 (9th Cir. 2004) [reversing IJ's determination that applicant did not have a well-founded fear because he was able to obtain a passport and renew it twice where respondent paid a large sum of money to obtain passport]; *Hoxha v. Ashcroft,* 319 F.3d 1179, 1184 (9th Cir. 2003) [rejecting government's argument that fear of persecution of Albanian in Serbia was belied by ease of applicant in obtaining a passport because Serbs wanted Albanians to leave]; *Perkovic v. INS*, 33 F.3d 615, 623 n.7 (6th Cir. 1994) [persecution is not inconsistent with legally obtaining a passport]; *Cordero-Trejo v. INS*, 40 F.3d 482, 490 (1st Cir. 1994) [evidence of passport does not bar refugee status, citing Handbook]; *But see Toptchev v. INS,* 295 F.3d 714, 725 (7th Cir. 2002) [that petitioners were able to obtain passports and permission to leave and fact that their property in Bulgaria was not confiscated undermines claim]; *Alvarez-Flores v. INS*, 909 F.2d 1, 5 (1st Cir. 1990).

(6) *Remaining In Country Unharmed—Sanchez Jimenez v. U.S. Att'y Gen.,* 492 F.3d 1223 (11th Cir. 2007) [Colombian's return to country for two years to take care of dying mother before finding return to the U.S. and seeking asylum did not effect court's determination that he suffered past persecution when FARC shot at his car attempting to kill him]; *Ayi v. Gonzales,* 460 F.3d 876, 881 (7th Cir. 2006) [in case involving Togo native, reversing IJ's adverse credibility finding that was based in part on his avoiding persecution for an extended period of time]; *Dong v. Gonzales,* 421 F.3d 573, 578 (7th Cir. 2005) [that Chinese woman remained in her country for four years after abortion and avoided persecution is irrelevant]; *Awale v. Ashcroft,* 384 F.3d 527, 531–32 (8th Cir. 2004) [Somali woman from Galglae clan who remained in country for four years established past persecution; no substantial evidence to rebut claim based on changed country conditions or ability to relocate]; *Ramirez-Rivas v. INS*, 899 F.2d 864, 871 (9th Cir. 1990), *vacated on other grounds*, 502 U.S. 1025 (1992) [remaining in El Salvador 6 months]; *Damaize-Job v. INS*, 787 F.2d 1332, 1336 (9th Cir. 1986) [remaining 2 years in Nicaragua]; *Turcios v. INS*, 821 F.2d 1396, 1402 (9th Cir. 1987); *Garcia-Ramos v. INS*, 775 F.2d 1370, 1374 n.7 (9th Cir. 1985); Handbook ¶48. *But see Yuk v. Ashcroft,* 355 F.3d 1222, 1234 (10th Cir. 2004) [where Cambodian stayed in country 12 years after his son's detention, torture and death indicated that father did not suffer persecution]; *Matter of A-M-,* 23 I&N Dec. 737, 740 (BIA 2005) [that Chinese Christian remained in Indonesia for 2 years after his store was looted with no additional incidents was "significant" as was his spouse and children's continued residence in Indonesia].

(7) *Commission of Crimes Cannot Disestablish Fear of Persecution—Karouni v. Gonzales,* 399 F.3d 1163, 1177–78 (9th Cir. 2005) [objective fear of persecution cannot be disestablished by his commission of crimes].

(8) *Evidence of Military Action Directed at Applicant*—Evidence that the government asserted its military strength against an individual, absent evidence of criminal conduct, creates a presumption that such action is politically motivated. *Platero-Cortez v. INS*, 804 F.2d 1127 (9th Cir. 1986); *Rajaratnam v. Moyer*, 832 F.Supp. 1219, 1222 (N.D. Ill. 1993) [beating and torture of detainee cannot be viewed as legitimate right to arrest and interrogate]; *Singh v. Ilchert*, 801 F.Supp. 313 (N.D. Cal. 1992), *aff'd*, 69 F.3d 375 (9th Cir. 1995) [Sikh's beating and shooting by police cannot be treated as legitimate custodial interrogation]; *Shukoor v. Rogers*, 954 F.Supp. 1415 (C.D. Cal. 1997). *But see Perlera-Escobar v. EOIR*, 894 F.2d 1292, 1299 (11th Cir. 1990) [government's desire to punish guerrilla is not persecution based on political opinion but rather prosecution of a traitor]; *Matter of R-*, 20 I&N Dec. 621 (BIA 1992) [torture by police not political persecution].

(9) *Evidence of Inconsistent Treatment by Government*— Inconsistent treatment by government officials provides an insufficient basis to deny asylum where person has suffered persecution. *Matter of Pula*, 19 I&N Dec. 467 (BIA 1987) [applicant persecuted by

Yugoslavian officials not denied relief where Yugoslav government also gave him citizenship]; *Popova v. INS,* 273 F.3d 1251, 1258–59 (9th Cir. 2001) [the fact that applicant was allowed to work for government as a physician and travel does not mean she was not persecuted]. Evidence that someone was persecuted and released cannot be used to infer that the person does not have a well-founded fear of persecution. *Lopez-Galarza v. INS*, 99 F.3d 954 (9th Cir. 1996) [release after rape and abuse in prison]; *Shirazi-Parsa v. INS*, 14 F.3d 1424 (9th Cir. 1994) [Iranian interrogated but released had well-founded fear when he received summons to appear] *overruled on other grounds by Fisher v. INS,* 79 F.3d 955 (9th Cir. 1996) (*en banc*); *Del Valle v. INS*, 776 F.2d 1407, 1413 (9th Cir. 1985). INS Supplementary Refugee/Asylum Adjudications Guidelines, *reprinted in* 67 *Interpreter Releases* 101–03 (Jan. 22, 1990).

(10) *Evidence of Gender-Based Persecution*— INS developed guidelines for the treatment of gender-based persecution claims. Memo, Coven, Office of International Affairs (May 26, 1995), *reprinted in* 72 No. 22 *Interpreter Releases* 771, 781–90 (June 5, 1995). The BIA regards the Guidelines as "instructive" but not binding. *Matter of R-A-,* 22 I&N Dec. 906, 913 (BIA 1999) *vacated and remanded for reconsideration under future final regulations,* 23 I&N Dec. 694 (AG 2005). UNHCR has also developed guidelines for gender-related persecution. *See* UNHCR, Guidelines On International Protection: Gender-Related Persecution Within the Context of Article 1A(2) of the 1951 Convention and/or Its 1967 Protocol Relating to the Status of Refugees, HCR/GIP/02/01 (May 7, 2002), *reprinted in* 81 No. 17 *Interpreter Releases* 545, 561–75 (Apr. 26, 2004).

(11) *Evidence of Rape and Physical Abuse—Kantoni v. Gonzales,* 461 F.3d 894 (7th Cir. 2006) [reversing asylum denial for Togo woman who was raped by country's President in reprisal for father's opposition]; *Boer-Sedano v. Gonzales,* 418 F.3d 1082, 1088 (9th Cir. 2005) [Mexican homosexual forced to perform oral sex nine times on police officer suffered past persecution]; *Ali v. Ashcroft,* 394 F.3d 780, 784–87 (9th Cir. 2005) [United Somali Congress militia's gang-rape of applicant was motivated in part by her political opinion and membership in Midgan clan]; *Lazo-Majano v. INS*, 813 F.2d 1432 (9th Cir. 1987) *overruled on other grounds by Fisher v. INS,* 79 F.3d 955 (9th Cir. 1996) (*en banc*) [political opinion must relate "the political opinion of the victim as seen by their persecutors"]; *Paramasamy v. Ashcroft,* 295 F.3d 1047, 1052–54 (9th Cir. 2002) [remanding Sri Lankan woman's asylum claim based on sexual assault by Army members where IJ determined that her failure to disclose assault to male officers at the airport upon entry demonstrated lack of credibility]; *Shoafera v. INS,* 228 F.3d 1070 (9th Cir. 2000) [rape of Ethiopian citizen of Amharic ethnicity]; *Angoucheva v. INS*, 106 F.3d 781 (7th Cir. 1997) [reversing to determine whether sexual assault was politically motivated]; *Lopez-Galarza v. INS*, 99 F.3d 954 (9th Cir. 1996) [reversing BIA on past persecution claim where applicant was raped and abused in prison]; *Matter of D-V-*, 21 I&N Dec. 77 (BIA 1993) [Haitian woman who was Aristide supporter gang-raped during coup]. *But see Joaquin-Porras v. Gonzales,* 435 F.3d 172, 180–82 (2d Cir. 2006) [isolated instance of rape by police officer and subsequent brief detention because of sexual orientation was insufficient to warrant withholding or CAT]; *Thuri v. Ashcroft,* 380 F.3d 788 (5th Cir. 2004) [rape arising out of rogue police officer's retaliation because of applicant's father's actions is not political]; *Menendez-Donis v. Ashcroft,* 360 F.3d 915 (8th Cir. 2004) [politically motivated death threats to applicant and her family, followed by the murder of three family members and her own gang rape did not establish persecution under the substantial evidence standard]; *Ochave v. INS,* 254 F.3d 859 (9th Cir. 2001) [asylum denied where there was no substantial evidence to support the nexus between the rape and a protected ground]; *Molina-Morales v. INS,* 237 F.3d 1048 (9th Cir. 2001) [rape and murder of aunt was personal dispute with no evidence of applicant's opposing political view]; *Klawitter v. INS*, 970 F.2d 149 (6th Cir. 1992); *Gomez v. INS*, 947 F.2d 660 (2d Cir. 1991); *Guevara-Flores v. INS*, 786 F.2d 1242 (5th Cir. 1986); *Matter of R-A-,* 22 I&N Dec. 906 (BIA 1999) *vacated and remanded for reconsideration under future final regulations,* 23 I&N Dec. 694 (AG 2005) [woman subject to repeated sexual and emotional abuse by her husband was not considered part of a social group; rejecting social group of "Guatemalan women who have been involved intimately with Guatemalan male companions, who believe that women are to live under male domination"]. Rape can also

constitute torture for purposes of CAT claim. *Zubeda v. Ashcroft,* 333 F.3d 463, 472–73 (3d Cir. 2003) (and cases cited therein) [finding that Republic of Congo citizen could claim CAT benefits because of fear of detention upon return that would result in rape].

Failure to Disclose Rape—In rape or sexual assault cases, failure to report the event at a first interview is not a "bellwether of truth." *Kebede v. Ashcroft,* 366 F.3d 808, 811 (9th Cir. 2004) [quoting *Paramasamy v. Ashcroft,* 295 F.3d 1047, 1053 (9th Cir. 2002), reversing IJ's adverse credibility finding based on failure to disclose rape in asylum interview or application].

(12) *Evidence of Generalized Persecution of Women*—*Gao v. Gonzales,* 440 F.3d 62, 66–70 (2d Cir. 2006) [women who have been sold into marriage and who live in a part of China where forced marriages are considered valid and enforceable constitutes a particular social group]; *Safaie v. INS*, 25 F.3d 636, 640 (8th Cir. 1994) [Iranian woman advocating women's rights]; *Fatin v. INS*, 12 F.3d 1233 (3d Cir. 1993) [Iranian women supportive of Shah's government]; U.N. Guidelines on the Protection of Refugee Women (Geneva 1991).

(13) *Evidence of Sexual Orientation*—*Boer-Sedano v. Gonzales,* 418 F.3d 1082, 1087–88 (9th Cir. 2005) [Mexican homosexual was part of a particular social group]; *Karouni v. Gonzales,* 399 F.3d 1163, 1171–72 (9th Cir. 2005) [*all* alien homosexuals are members of a particular social group; finding no difference between being persecuted for being homosexual and engaging in homosexual acts]; *Amanfi v. Ashcroft,* 328 F.3d 719, 727–30 (3d Cir. 2003) [persecution claim is viable for Ghanaian citizen alleging imputed social group claim as homosexual]; *Hernandez-Montiel v. INS,* 225 F.3d 1084 (9th Cir. 2000) [gay men with female sexual identities]; *Matter of Toboso-Alfonso*, 20 I&N Dec. 819 (AG 1994) [homosexuals as social group]; *Pitcherskaia v. INS*, 118 F.3d 641 (9th Cir. 1997) [institutionalization for being gay to "cure" person is persecution]. *But see Kimumwe v. Gonzales,* 431 F.3d 319, 321–24 (8th Cir. 2005) [the record supported IJ's characterization of applicant's expulsion from school and arrest as arising from sexual misconduct and not homosexuality]. Failure to mention persecution because of sexual orientation at airport interview may not be fatal. *Moab v. Gonzales,* 500 F.3d 656 (7th Cir. 2007) [reversed BIA's reliance on airport interview given its unreliability and held that BIA erred in its determination that adding an additional harm to Liberian applicant's claim not mentioned in the airport interview–persecution on account of sexual orientation–demonstrated lack of credibility].

(14) *Evidence of Female Genital Mutilation*—FGM may serve as a basis for asylum or CAT relief. *Matter of Kasinga*, 21 I&N Dec. 357 (BIA 1996). The Board, however, has determined that once a person suffers FGM she may not have a well-founded fear of future persecution because it has already occurred. *Matter of A-T-,* 24 I&N Dec. 296 (BIA 2007) [Mali female subject to FGM in past denied withholding because despite past persecution it is not continuing persecution and therefore future harm not established]. *But see Hassan v. Gonzales,* 484 F.3d 513, 517–18 (8th Cir. 2007) [joining the growing number of circuits that have concluded that FGM rises to the level of persecution and rejecting the argument that future harm is rebutted because applicant already subject to FGM]; *Mohammed v. Gonzales,* 400 F.3d 785, 796–801 (9th Cir. 2005) [a person subject to FGM can claim past persecution or well-founded fear because FGM like forced sterilization is a continuing harm, and social group may be defined by clan or as "all Somalian females," given the widespread practice]. Notwithstanding *Matter of A-T-*, the Board has recognized that FGM is so traumatic a person may obtain asylum on humanitarian grounds and future persecution need not be demonstrated. *Matter of S-A-K- and H-A-H-,* 24 I&N Dec. 464 (BIA 2008) [mother and daughter from Somalia who suffered FGM and continue to suffer side effects from it are entitled to asylum on humanitarian grounds]. *See also Agbor v. Gonzales,* 487 F.3d 499 (7th Cir. 2007) [BIA's decision to deny future persecution claim based upon FGM from Cameroon was not supported by substantial evidence where BIA disregarded key evidence, relied on DOS report that does not specifically contradict respondent, and then faulted applicant for not responding]; *Haoua v. Gonzales,* 472 F.3d 227 (4th Cir. 2007) [IJ erred in determining that Niger ap-

plicant for asylum had only a 10% chance of being subject to FGM]; *Tunis v. Gonzales,* 447 F.3d 347, 350–52 (7th Cir. 2006) [reversing IJ's denial of CAT relief where IJ misunderstood the distinction between clitoridectomy and infibulation and failed to recognize the possibility of further excision in Sierra Leone, where procedures are common and condoned by the government]; *Barry v. Gonzales,* 445 F.3d 741, 745 (4th Cir. 2006) [although denying a motion to reopen asylum, the court recognized that FGM constituted persecution within the meaning of the INA]; *Abebe v. Gonzales,* 432 F.3d 1037, 1041–43 (9th Cir. 2005) (*en banc*) [substantial evidence did not support IJ's determination that there was a less than 10% chance that USC child of Ethiopian parents would be subject to FGM]; *Niang v. Gonzales,* 422 F.3d 1187, 1198–2001 (10th Cir. 2005) [notwithstanding adverse credibility determination, a female member of the Tukulor Fulani tribe in Senegal that practices FGM can be subject to persecution on account of membership in a particular social group]; Whether a parent can obtain asylum based upon the fear of his/her child's FGM is in controversy. *Abay v. Ashcroft,* 368 F.3d 634, 640–42 (6th Cir. 2004) [mother who fears that 9 year daughter would be subject to FGM qualifies for asylum]; *Nwaokolo v. INS,* 314 F.3d 303, 307–11 (7th Cir. 2002) [stay granted on BIA denial of motion to reopen under CAT where *USC daughter* might suffer FGM]; *Abankwah v. INS,* 185 F.3d 18 (2d Cir. 1999). *But see Matter of A-K-,* 24 I&N Dec. 275 (BIA 2007) [parent cannot establish ground for asylum solely on fear of FGM to child]; *Olowo v. Ashcroft,* 368 F.3d 692, 700–04 (7th Cir. 2004) [affirming IJ denial of asylum to mother of LPR children where mother claimed children, who were not required to leave U.S., would be subject to FGM if they returned to Nigeria]; *Oforji v. Ashcroft,* 354 F.3d 609, 614–18 (7th Cir. 2003) [same]. DHS and DOS are now required to make available to NIV and IV holders, information on the severe harm to physical and psychological health caused by FGM. IIRIRA §644. Cable, DOS 01-State-88175 (May 18, 2001), *reprinted in* 78 No. 22 *Interpreter Releases* 935–37 (June 4, 2001). It is now a crime to engage in FGM in the U.S. 18 U.S.C. §116.

(15) *Marriage as Basis for Persecution*—Persecution "for marrying between races, religions, nationalities, social group memberships, or...political opinion is...persecution on account of a protected ground." *Faruk v. Ashcroft,* 378 F.3d 940, 943 (9th Cir. 2004) (quoting from *Baballah v. Ashcroft,* 367 F.3d 1067, 1077 (9th Cir. 2004) which quoted *Maini v. INS,* 212 F.3d 1167, 1175 (9th Cir. 2000)) [persecution arising out of marriage between Christian and Muslim Fijians]. *But see Matter of A-T-,* 24 I&N Dec. 296, 302–04 (BIA 2007) [Mali woman from Bambara tribe who is subject to an arranged marriage after suffering FGM is not part of a social group and despite arranged marriage to first cousin that could result in birth defects to future children she was denied withholding because the BIA did "not see how the reluctant acceptance of family tradition over person preference can form the basis of a withholding of removal claim].

(16) *Evidence of Extortion by Government*—Evidence of extortion by government or quasi-government officials directed against one person is persecution. *Jahed v. INS,* 356 F.3d 991, 997–1001 (9th Cir. 2004) [where Iranian soldier threatened to expose applicant to the government as a former member of the Mujahedin, he had well-founded fear on account of political reasons]; *Yazitchian v. INS,* 207 F.3d 1164 (9th Cir. 2000) [in case involving extortion and imputed political opinion, court reversed BIA denial and found that *Elias-Zacarias* did not overrule *Desir*]; *Desir v. Ilchert*, 840 F.2d 723 (9th Cir. 1988) [extortion by Tonton Macoutes]; *Borja v. INS,* 175 F.3d 732 (9th Cir. 1999) (*en banc*) [where Philippine communist guerillas extorted money after applicant articulated her political opposition, circumstances indicated that persecution was at least in part on account of political opinion]. Evidence that government agents are searching for applicant may be sufficient. *Rasool v. INS*, 758 F.Supp. 188 (S.D.N.Y. 1991).

(17) *Anti-Government Actions in the U.S.*—Evidence of anti-government actions while in the U.S. is sufficient to establish well-founded fear. *Matter of Mogharrabi*, 19 I&N Dec. 439 (BIA 1987) [Iranian student who participated in anti-Khomeini demonstrations in U.S. and got into dispute at Iranian Interest Section granted asylum]; *Myat Thu v. Attorney General of the USA,* 510 F.3d 405, 413–15 (3d Cir. 2007) [political activities in Japan with BDA and in Burma with the NLD may establish basis for asylum and case is re-

manded in light of DOS reports and letters indicating that the Burmese military may be aware of applicants activities]; *Tun v. INS,* 445 F.3d 554, 570–71 (2d Cir. 2006) [Burmese citizen who engaged in pro-democracy political demonstrations in the U.S. against Burmese government was eligible for asylum and IJ's claim that such actions were self-serving is not sufficient to support decision because political activities that give rise to persecution do not require applicant to be motivated by political beliefs]. *See also Ghadessi v. INS,* 797 F.2d 804, 807–08 (9th Cir. 1986).

(18) *Evidence of Specific Threats by Guerrillas*—Specific threats by guerillas, even where applicant was never actually seized is sufficient. *Salazar-Paucar v. INS,* 281 F.3d 1069, 1074–76 (9th Cir. 2002) [where respondent only received death threats but Shining Path harmed members of his family and murdered his political counterparts, past persecution was proven]; *Lim v. INS,* 224 F.3d 929, 934–37 (9th Cir. 2000) [where former police officer received threats it was sufficient to establish asylum, but not withholding]; *Sotelo-Aquije v. Slattery*, 17 F.3d 33, 37 (2d Cir. 1994) [that applicant had not yet been physically harmed or had a face-to-face confrontation with persecutor is not determinative of well-founded fear]; *Arteaga v. INS*, 836 F.2d 1227, 1232 (9th Cir. 1988). *See also Maldonado-Cruz v. INS*, 883 F.2d 788 (9th Cir. 1989) [actual seizure by guerrillas]. *But see INS v. Elias-Zacarias*, 502 U.S. 478 (1992) [rejecting forced conscription by guerillas as a basis for asylum where there was no showing that persecution arose from his political opinion]; *Perlera-Escobar, supra* [adopting BIA view that guerrillas efforts to discipline deserters is not a political opinion]; *Matter of R-O-*, 20 I&N Dec. 455 (BIA 1992).

(19) *Circumstantial Evidence*—Circumstantial evidence and inference may be persuasive particularly in establishing the persecutor's motive. *Karouni v. Gonzales,* 399 F.3d 1163, 1173–74 (9th Cir. 2005) [circumstantial evidence and reasonable inference where there is no other logical explanation for the persecution may be used to show persecutor's motives]; *Popova v. INS,* 273 F.3d 1251, 1258–59 (9th Cir. 2001) [cumulative circumstantial evidence should not be treated as coincidence]; *Ramirez-Rivas v. INS*, 899 F.2d 864, 869 (9th Cir. 1990), *vacated on other grounds*, 502 U.S. 1025 (1992).

(20) *Treatment Toward Prisoners*—General evidence of treatment toward prisoners is probative of persecution claim. *Matter of Izatula*, 20 I&N Dec. 149 (BIA 1990).

(21) *Evidence of Forced Abortion or Involuntary Sterilization or Resistance to Coercive Population Control Programs*—Is now defined as persecution on account of political opinion. INA §101(a)(42), 8 U.S.C. §1101(a)(42). *Chao Qun Jiang v. USCIS,* 520 F.3d 132, 135-36 (2d Cir. 2008) [remanded to determine whether forced insertion of IUD constitutes persecution]; *Li Fang Lin v. Mukasey,* 517 F.3d 685, 692–97 (4th Cir. 2008) [remanded case to determine whether forced insertion *and* mandatory continued usage of an IUD can be persecution for resistance to coercive population control program]; *Zheng v. Gonzales,* 497 F.3d 201 (2d Cir. 2007) [remanded case to BIA to obtain clear determination whether force insertion of IUD constitutes persecution]; *Zi Zhi Tang v. Gonzales,* 489 F.3d 987, 992 (9th Cir. 2007) [forced abortion and forced sterilization share unusual characteristics and there is no way to distinguish them for withholding eligibility]; *Dong v. Gonzales,* 421 F.3d 573, 578 (7th Cir. 2005) [one forced abortion is sufficient to show persecution and IJ impermissibly denied asylum because person remained in country for four years after abortion]; *Zheng v. Gonzales*, 409 F.3d 804, 809–11 (7th Cir. 2005) [where BIA held that repeated involuntary IUD insertion constitutes persecution but denied withholding, the court reversed]; *Cao v. DOJ*, 421 F.3d 149, 155–56 (2d. Cir. 2005) [in granting motion to remand, the court found that once a person is subjected to forced abortion under the standards in *Matter of C-Y-Z-,* there is "an irrebuttable presumption of a well founded fear" under *Matter of Y-T-L-*]; *Cao v. Att'y Gen. of the U.S.,* 407 F.3d 146 (3d Cir. 2005) [addressing but not deciding whether doctor who spoke out against infanticide was eligible but reversing IJ's negative credibility finding and remanding]; *Wang v. Ashcroft*, 341 F.3d 1015, 1019–21 (9th Cir. 2003) [reversing denial of asylum based on forced abortion claim where evidence established persecution under INA §101(a)(42) and government failed to rebut]. IIRIRA §601, which amended the definition of refugee at INA §101(a)(42) sought to reverse the courts that held that it was not a political opin-

ion to oppose government population control programs. *See Matter of X-P-T-,* 21 I&N Dec. 634 (BIA 1996) [superseding *Matter of Chang*, 20 I&N Dec. 38 (BIA 1989) in light of changes due to IIRIRA §601]. For pre-IIRIRA §601 cases see *Matter of G-*, 20 I&N Dec. 764 (BIA 1993); *Chen v. INS*, 95 F.3d 801 (9th Cir. 1996); *Zhang v. Slattery,* 55 F.3d 732 (2d Cir. 1995); *Chai v. Carroll,* 48 F.3d 1331 (4th Cir. 1995). INA §101(a)(42), when coupled with the presumption under 8 C.F.R. §§208.16(b)(2), 1208.16(b)(2) will result in withholding. *Matter of X-P-T-,* 21 I&N Dec at 637–38.

(a) *Relief Not Automatic*—However, neither asylum nor withholding are automatic under the new provision. *Matter of J-H-S-,* 24 I&N Dec. 196 (BIA 2007) [a husband may not automatically receive asylum based upon future persecution simply because he has more than one child born in China]; *Matter of C-C-,* 23 I&N Dec. 899 (BIA 2006) [denying motion to reopen finding insufficient evidence to establish prima facie eligibility that respondent would be persecuted in China because of birth of children in U.S.; distinguishing *Guo v. Ashcroft,* 386 F.3d 556 (3d Cir. 2004)]; *Zheng v. Gonzales,* 475 F.3d 30 (1st Cir. 2007) [mere opposition to China's family planning policies by single woman does not *compel* finding of future well-founded fear]; *Huang v. Gonzales,* 453 F.3d 942 (7th Cir. 2006) [IJ's adverse credibility determination upheld where respondent presented certificate of forced abortion and IJ relied on DOS report stating certificates are only given for voluntary abortions]; *Yang v. Gonzales,* 427 F.3d 1117, 1121–22 (8th Cir. 2005) [following *Zheng* and finding that expert affidavit of John Aird was "sufficient to dispute the information in the State Department reports"]; *Huang v. INS,* 421 F.3d 125 (2d Cir. 2005) [where first child was a daughter and second child born in U.S., no showing that foreign born child would violate one-child policy]; *Zheng v. Gonzales,* 415 F.3d 955, 960–63 (8th Cir. 2005) [overcoming DOS Report that Fujian province was lax in enforcement policy and that children born abroad are not considered violating one–child policy by providing specific and expert testimony]; *Li v. Gonzales,* 405 F.3d 171 (4th Cir. 2005) [neither a fine nor the routine medical insertion of an IUD without forced resistance is persecution]; *Zhang v. INS,* 386 F.3d 66 (2d Cir. 2004) [inconsistent statements by applicant as to the date his wife was sterilized and the date he learned of it, were a sufficient basis to uphold IJ's adverse credibility determination]; *S-Cheng v. Ashcroft,* 380 F.3d 320, 322–24 (8th Cir. 2004) [denying asylum and withholding where claim was based on speculative facts and IJ found respondent lacked credibility]; *Xie v. Ashcroft,* 359 F.3d 239 (3d Cir. 2004) [denying relief due to lack of credibility where applicant claimed wife was forcibly sterilization in 1979 and DOS report indicated that China's policy did not take effect until early 1980s]; *Liao v. DOJ,* 293 F.3d 61 (2d Cir. 2002) [denying forced sterilization claim on merits]; *Chen v. INS,* 195 F.3d 198 (4th Cir. 1999) [asylum denied where person failed to show that he had been individually targeted or that he belonged to a group, such as those in a particular province or region that is subject to the enforcement of the 'one child' program].

(b) *Rebutting Past Persecution.* Forced abortion and forced sterilization constitute past persecution and raise a presumption of future persecution. DHS may rebut and overcome the presumption of past persecution. 8 C.F.R. §§208.13(b)(1)(i), 1208.13(b)(1)(i). However, the BIA has found that the passage of time cannot cure forced sterilization because it is a "permanent and continuing act of persecution." *Matter of Y-T-L-,* 23 I&N Dec. 601 (BIA 2003) ["the passage of time since the forced sterilization of the respondent's wife, coupled with the lack of enforcement of coercive family planning measures during that period" did not constitute a fundamental change in circumstances sufficient for rebutting past persecution]. The regulatory presumption of future persecution also applies in forced abortion cases. *Zhu v. Gonzales,* 493 F.3d 588, 599–602 (5th Cir. 2007); *See also Ge v. Ashcroft*, 367 F.3d 1121 (9th Cir. 2004) [reversing denial of asylum because IJ's adverse credibility determination rested upon speculation and was not supported by substantial evidence].

(c) *Children Born Abroad—Matter of S-Y-G-,* 24 I&N Dec. 247 (BIA 2007) [on remand from the Second Circuit, the BIA denied applicant's motion to reopen because she could not overcome heavy burden to show changed country conditions that would result in her persecution because of second child born in U.S.]; *Matter of J-W-S-*, 24 I&N Dec. 185, 192 (BIA 2007) [on remand from the Second Circuit, the BIA reviewed numerous documents including the Aird affidavit and concluded that the record evidence "does not demonstrate that the Chinese Government has a national policy of requiring forced sterilization of parents who return with a second child born outside of China"]; *Matter of C-C-*, 23 I&N Dec. 899 (BIA 2006) [denying motion to reopen finding there was insufficient evidence to establish *prima facie* eligibility that respondent had a well-founded fear of persecution in China because of birth of children in U.S.]; *Yu v. Att'y Gen. of the U.S.*, 513 F.3d 346 (3d Cir. 2008) [in light of *Matter of C-C-* court determined that petitioner's claim of forced sterilization due to birth of child in U.S. could not be sustained]; *Chen v. Gonzales*, 498 F.3d 758 (7th Cir. 2007) [notwithstanding §208(a)(2)(D), an applicant's subsequent marriage and birth of two children cannot be a basis to reopen proceedings for fear of sterilization in China because the changed contemplated under INA §240(c)(7)(C)(ii) relates to changed country conditions not personal circumstances]; *Huang v. INS*, 421 F.3d 125 (2d Cir. 2005) [where first child was a daughter and second child born in U.S., there was no showing that foreign-born child would violate one-child policy]. *But see Gao v. Mukasey*, 508 F.3d 86 (2d Cir. 2007) [remanded case post-*S-Y-G-* where child born in U.S. because documentary evidence is different]; *Li v. U.S. Att'y Gen.*, 488 F.3d 1371, 1375–76 (11th Cir. 2007) [BIA erred in not granting motion to reopen and basing denial in part on the fact that Li's children were born in the U.S. and that Chinese policy distinguishes between children born abroad and in China]; *Lin v. DOJ*, 473 F.3d 48 (2d Cir. 2006) [in light of documents presented in *Guo*, court remanded case to consider new evidence of forced sterilization in Fujian province, although recognizing that it could not remand for new evidence at petitioner's suggestion]; *Guo v. Gonzales*, 463 F.3d 109, 114–15 (2d Cir. 2006) [BIA erred in refusing to reopen where evidence was submitted after close of proceedings that local authorities in Changle City did consider a child born abroad to be in violation of one-child policy]; *Yang v. Gonzales*, 427 F.3d 1117, 1121–22 (8th Cir. 2005) [following *Zheng* and finding that expert affidavit of John Aird was "sufficient to dispute the information in the State Department reports"]; *Zheng v. Gonzales*, 415 F.3d 955, 960–63 (8th Cir. 2005) [overcoming DOS Report that Fujian province was lax in enforcement policy and that children born abroad are not considered violating one–child policy]; *Guo v. Ashcroft*, 386 F.3d 556, 563–66 (3d Cir. 2004) [BIA should not have denied motion to reopen based on fear of future persecution due to children born in the U.S. because Aird affidavit provided sufficient evidence to meet *prima facie* case].

(d) *Child's Right to Asylum/Withholding*—The children of persons subject to forced abortion or sterilization are not automatically entitled to asylum under §101(a)(42)(B). *Jiang v. Gonzales*, 500 F.3d 137 (2d Cir. 2007) [following *Shi Liang Lin* the court held that a claim by a child of persecution based *solely* on forced abortion of his mother is insufficient and rejected his economic past persecution claim because unlike in *Jorge-Tzoc* he did not share the characteristic that motivated the persecution and therefore lacked a nexus to a protected ground]; *Chen v. DOJ*, 417 F.3d 303 (2d Cir. 2005) [IIRIRA §601(a) was not intended to extend to children of parent subject to forced abortion or sterilization]; *Zhang v. Gonzales*, 408 F.3d 1239, 1244–46 (9th Cir. 2005) [BIA's refusal to extend automatic asylum eligibility to children must be accorded deference under *Chevron*]; *Wang v. Gonzales*, 405 F.3d 134, 142–43 (3d Cir. 2005) [child is not a spouse and if an unmarried parent cannot obtain relief under *Matter of C-Y-Z* then *a fortiori* a potential sibling cannot]. However, the fact that a child may not have automatic eligibility does not foreclose an asylum claim. *Zhang v. Gonzales*, 408 F.3d 1239, 1246–50 (9th Cir. 2005) [parents' resistance to forced abortion is imputed political opinion to child and economic deprivation, denial of access to education and violence directed to her father in her presence amounted to persecution].

(e) *Spouse's Right to Asylum/Withholding*—The husband of a woman forced to undergo an abortion, or the spouse of person forced to undergo sterilization, may independently claim asylum, but there is no *per se* right to asylum based on the relationship. *Matter of J-S-*, 24 I&N Dec. 520, 536 (AG 2008) [overruling in part (regarding *per se* persecution) *Matter of C-Y-Z-,* 21 I&N Dec. 915 (BIA 1997) and *Matter of S-L-L-,* 24 I&N Dec. 1 (BIA 2006)]; *Shi Liang Lin v. DOJ,* 494 F.3d 296 (2d Cir. 2007) (*en banc*) [rejecting *Matter of C-Y-Z-* and finding that the unambiguous language of IIRIRA §601(a) does *not* extend *automatic* refugee status to spouses, unmarried partners, or fiancées of persons protected under the statute]. *But see Sun Wen Chen v. Att'y Gen. of the U.S.,* 491 F.3d 100, 105–09 (3d Cir. 2007) [upholding BIA analysis that spouse qualifies for asylum under *Chevron* but reversing denial of asylum because BIA applied wrong standard in expecting spouse to prove more than a 10% chance of future persecution]. Similarly, nonspouses must also independently establish persecution arising out of their own forced abortion, involuntary sterilization, other resistance to coercive population control, or a well-founded fear that they will be forced to undergo such a procedure or be subjected to persecution for such failure, refusal, or resistance. *Matter of S-L-L-,* 24 I&N Dec. 1, 8–10 (BIA 2006) [boyfriends, fiancés and other unmarried persons do not qualify as a spouse would, but may demonstrate persecution based on "other resistance" to coercive population control programs]; *Yang v. U.S. Att'y Gen.,* 494 F.3d 1311, 1316–18 (11th Cir. 2007) [traditional Chinese marriage is not recognized as legal marriage and therefore cannot be basis for forced abortion claim]; *Chen v. Gonzales,* 457 F.3d 670, 674 (7th Cir. 2006) [boyfriend of woman forced to abort a pregnancy is not covered under statute]; *Wang v. USCIS,* 437 F.3d 276 (2d Cir. 2006) [where applicant not married to woman forced to undergo abortion, he cannot assert her abortion as a basis for his claim]; *Yang v. U.S. Att'y Gen.,* 418 F.3d 1198, 1204 n.6 (11th Cir. 2005) [noting *Matter of C-Y-Z-* requirement that a person must be a spouse to qualify]; *Zhang v. Ashcroft,* 395 F.3d 531 (5th Cir. 2004) [boyfriend who impregnated girlfriend could not qualify]; *Chen v. Ashcroft,* 381 F.3d 221 (3d Cir. 2004) [deferring to agency interpretation in *Matter of C-Y-Z-* and denying asylum and withholding to fiancée]; *Cf. Chen v. Ashcroft,* 376 F.3d 215, 223 n.2 (3d Cir. 2004) [criticizing rule as contributing to the "destruction of a family union"]. *But see Pan v. U.S. Att'y Gen.,* 449 F.3d 408 (2d Cir. 2006) [following *Lin* and requiring BIA to clarify *Matter of C-Y-Z-* whether girlfriend's forced abortion is covered under statute]; *Zhang v. Gonzales,* 434 F.3d 993, 1001–02 (7th Cir. 2006) [where husband was spouse at time of forced abortion but wife has now divorced and remarried, husband's claim to past persecution is still valid]; *Lin v. DOJ,* 416 F.3d 184 (2d Cir. 2005) [where BIA in *Matter of C-Y-Z-* failed to explain its rationale for *spousal* eligibility, its decision is not accorded *Chevron* deference and the fiancée or boyfriend of persons subjected to Chinese population control may qualify for asylum]. A spouse whose marriage would be legally recognized but for China's coercive family planning policies is considered a spouse in certain circuits for asylum purposes. *Zhang v. Gonzales,* 434 F.3d 993, 998–99 (7th Cir. 2006) [where couple had marriage ceremony but because of age restrictions the government would not recognize it, marriage was still valid]; *Ma v. Ashcroft,* 361 F.3d 553 (9th Cir. 2004) [where China would not legally register a traditional marriage because husband was under 22, he was nevertheless considered a husband under asylum law]; *see also Zheng v. Ashcroft,* 397 F.3d 1139, 1148 (9th Cir. 2005) [agreeing with *Ma* regarding validity of relationship for purposes of asylum and finding in the alternative that respondent would be eligible for relief because of the forced abortion of his child]. *But see Chen,* 381 F.3d 221 at 231–34. At least one circuit has found that the spouse is also entitled to withholding without any additional showing beyond the criteria necessary to demonstrate persecution for asylum. *Qili Qu v. Gonzales,* 399 F.3d 1195 (9th Cir. 2005) [where wife sterilized, husband is entitled to withholding by that fact alone and the government may not rebut it by establishing there is no cause for fear of future persecution]; *Zi Zhi Tang v. Gonzales,* 489 F.3d 987, 992 (9th Cir. 2007) [withholding also available to husband for forced abortion of spouse]. However, a husband may not automatically receive asylum based upon future persecution simply because he has more than one child born in China. *Matter of J-H-S-,* 24 I&N Dec. 196 (BIA 2007).

(f) *Other Relatives Right To Asylum*—The parents and in-laws of people persecuted by coercive family planning policies are not *per se* refugees within the meaning of INA §101(a)(42)(B). *Shi Liang Lin v. DOJ,* 494 F.3d 296 (2d Cir. 2007) (*en banc*).

(g) *Force Defined*—The term "forced" under the statute does not require physical restraint, but is a much broader concept including "compelling, obliging or constraining by mental, moral, or circumstantial means." *Ding v. Ashcroft,* 387 F.3d 1131, 1138–39 (9th Cir. 2004) [reversing denial of asylum because credibility determinations were based on speculation and the force used to compel abortion did not require physical restraint]; *Zi Zhi Tang v. Gonzales,* 489 F.3d 987, 990–92 (9th Cir. 2007) [followed *Ding* and reversed IJ who relied on incorrect standard for "force" including imputing a "hiding" and "summons" requirement to show abortion was forced]. The BIA, however, has defined "forced" to undergo abortion or sterilization to mean "subjected to harm of sufficient severity that it amounts to persecution" if the applicant declines to abort or sterilize. *Matter of T-Z-,* 24 I&N Dec. 163, 168–69 (BIA 2007) [persecution is not limited to physical harm or threats of physical harm and may include threats of economic harm but the definition of "forced" in the statute is not *less* than persecution]; *see Xiu Fen Xia v. Mukasey,* 510 F.3d 162 (2d Cir. 2007) [not forced abortion where no government official was aware of the pregnancy because applicant arranged to have abortion to avoid what she speculated would be government punishment in the form of abortion, sterilization, fines or other sanctions]; *see also* Memo, Martin, General Counsel, INS (Oct. 21, 1996), *reprinted in* 73 No. 43 *Interpreter Releases* 1597, 1600 (Nov. 11, 1996); *But see Sui v. Ashcroft,* 395 F.3d 863, 871 (8th Cir. 2005) [denying asylum in forced abortion case and reading the phrase "forced to abort" to mean "some sort of physical force or undue pressure with the intent" to cause and did cause an abortion]. Where a person has an abortion under circumstances where she would face negative legal, social and economic ramifications of the pregnancy, including the possibility of sterilization or physically compelled abortion later if she did not abort, her decision to abort is still forced and cannot reasonably be considered a "choice." *Zhu v. Gonzales,* 493 F.3d 588, 597–99 (5th Cir. 2007) [analyzed case under *Matter of T-Z-* , reversed denial of past persecution, and rejected DHS claim that because Chinese authorities were not aware of pregnancy until she got abortion and because boyfriend wanted her to have abortion that abortion was not forced]; *Xiu Ling Chen v. Gonzales,* 489 F.3d 861 (7th Cir. 2007) [case remanded prior to *Matter of T-Z-* for BIA to determine what level of economic sanction constitutes force and what is the PRC's policy toward those who do not pay the sanction].

(h) *Other Resistance to Population Control*—The statute also encompasses "other resistance" to population control policies. *Lin v. Gonzales,* 472 F.3d 1131, 1134–35 (9th Cir. 2007) [brother's attempted interference with officials who were destroying his brother's property for violating birth control policies constituted "other resistance" under INA §101(a)(42)(B)]; *Yang v. U.S. Att'y Gen.,* 418 F.3d 1198, 1203–05 (11th Cir. 2005) [although applicant could not prove forced sterilization, her opposition to an "atrocious injection procedure" for birth control and two forced IUD procedures could be considered "other resistance"]; *Li v. Ashcroft,* 356 F.3d 1153 (9th Cir. 2004) (en banc) [young couple resisted minimum marriage age requirement and also fought the limitation on family size]. *But see Huang v. U.S. Att'y Gen.,* 429 F.3d 1002, 1009–11 (11th Cir. 2005) [a painful gynecological exam and a 20-day detention for failure to attend the next examination did not constitute "other resistance" to population control warranting asylum; *Yang* and *Li* distinguished].

(i) *Cap Abolished*—The REAL ID Act of 2005, §101(g) abolished the 1,000 per year cap on granting asylum or refugee status for resisting coercive population control programs.

(22) *Former Police, Army Personnel, Court Personnel, and Security Personnel*—May be eligible for asylum or withholding. *Konan v. Att'y Gen. of the U.S.,* 432 F.3d 497, 503–06 (3d Cir. 2005) [where gendarme in Côte d'Ivoire was killed by rebel forces in attack on

camp, gendarme's son had imputed claim for asylum because attack was in part to kill government supporters not simply police officers; *Matter of Fuentes* distinguished]; *Reyes-Guerrero v. INS,* 192 F.3d 1241 (9th Cir. 1999) [Colombian prosecutor who investigated and convicted persons from opposing political party and who received death threats was entitled to withholding]; *Velarde v. INS,* 140 F.3d 1305 (9th Cir. 1998) [distinguishing *Matter of Fuentes* and finding a former member of the Peruvian President's personal security team established claim for asylum]. *But see Matter of Fuentes,* 19 I&N Dec. 658 (BIA 1988) [police officer receiving threats because of his duties did not suffer persecution]; *Tamara-Gomez v. Gonzales,* 447 F.3d 343, 349–51 (9th Cir. 2006) [finding persecution where Colombian petitioner helped police against the FARC, but denying relief for lack of nexus because assistance to the police is insufficient to establish a political view]; *Estrada-Escobar v. Ashcroft,* 376 F.3d 1042 (10th Cir. 2004) [major in Peruvian National Police who provided security to terrorist judges did not suffer persecution because threats were due to his employment not political opinion]; *Cruz-Navarro v. INS,* 232 F.3d 1024, 1028–29 (9th Cir. 2000) [distinguishing between former and current police and army personnel and finding that the latter do not constitute a social group].

(23) *Drug and Other Informants*—An informant in a fiercely ideological struggle is eligible for asylum. *Mejia v. Ashcroft,* 298 F.3d 873, 877–80 (9th Cir. 2002) [confidential informant in Philippines had imputed political opinion]; *Briones v. INS,* 175 F.3d 727 (9th Cir. 1999) (en banc). *See also Garrovillas v. INS,* 156 F.3d 1010, 1016–17 (9th Cir. 1998) [informant for Philippine military received 3 death threat letters]. *But see Carmenatte-Lopez v. Mukasey,*518 F.3d 540, 542 (8th Cir. 2008) [witness or informant of political crime not eligible]. A drug informant may also be eligible on a "state-created danger" theory. *Lawson v. Gerlinski,* 332 F.Supp.2d 735, 742–43 (M.D. Pa. 2004) [long term LPR with no relief who cooperated with government, received reduction in sentence and feared harm if returned to his country, was entitled to a substantive due process hearing on theory that the state created his danger]; *Builes v. Nye,* 239 F.Supp.2d 518, 525–26 (M.D. Pa. 2003) [substantive due process is violated where government informant would be sent to Colombia to face certain death]. But this Pennsylvania line of cases has now been overruled in the 3d Cir. *Kamara v. Att'y Gen. of the U.S.,* 420 F.3d 202, 216–18 (3d Cir. 2005) [rejecting substantive due process challenge based on the state-created danger exception as having no place in immigration jurisprudence]. *See also Matter of C-A-,* 23 I&N Dec. 951 (BIA 2006), *aff'd by Castillo-Arias v. U.S. Att'y Gen.,* 446 F.3d 1190, 1195–99 (11th Cir. 2006) [noncriminal informant who provided information to the police against drug cartel in Cali, Colombia was not part of a particular social group]; *Enwonwu v. Gonzales,* 438 F.3d 22, 29–31 (1st Cir. 2006) [following *Kamara* and rejecting state-created danger theory for persons who cooperated with DEA and are now facing removal]; *Saldarriaga v. Gonzales,* 402 F.3d 461, 466–68 (4th Cir. 2005) [where association with DEA drug informant may result in harm if returned to Colombia, asylum denied because applicant neither articulated a political opinion nor demonstrated how persecution would be on account of his political opinion].

(24) *Whistleblowing and Exposing Corruption*—Where applicant was a whistleblower, exposed government corruption as a journalist or otherwise opposed government corruption beyond refusal to be extorted, her actions may be considered a political opinion. *Haxhiu v. Mukasey,* 519 F.3d 685, 690-92 (7th Cir. 2008) [petitioner's anticorruption activities in the Albanian military which persisted beyond his employment constituted political opinion]; *Bu v. Gonzales,* 490 F.3d 424 (6th Cir. 2007) [demonstrating against government corruption in China resulting in persecution]; *Fedunyak v. Gonzales,* 477 F.3d 1126, 1129–30 (9th Cir. 2007) [political opinion expressed through whistleblowing where Ukrainian involved in the automobile business complained to higher government officials about local officials and police extortion and corruption]; *Zhang v. Gonzales,* 426 F.3d 540, 544–48 (2d Cir. 2005) [reversing IJ denial because "opposition to endemic corruption or extortion, no less than opposition to other government practices or policies, may have a political dimension when it transcends mere self-protection and represents a challenge to the legitimacy or authority of the ruling regime"]; *Sagaydak v. Gonzales,* 405 F.3d 1035, 1041–45 (9th Cir. 2005) [retaliation against government auditor for exposing corruption in a private company met both the imputed political opinion and the

"on account of" criteria for asylum]; *Mamouzian v. Ashcroft,* 390 F.3d 1129, 1134–35 (9th Cir. 2004) [reversing IJ's denial of asylum for Armenian who wrote about public corruption stating "we have repeatedly held that retaliation against an individual who opposes government corruption can constitute persecution on account of political opinion"]; *Hasan v. Ashcroft,* 380 F.3d 1114, 1120–21 (9th Cir. 2004) [exposing government corruption by publishing an article constituted a political statement]; *Li Wu Lin v. INS,* 238 F.3d 239, 244 (3d Cir. 2001); *Grava v. INS,* 205 F.3d 1177, 1181–82 (9th Cir. 2000) [whistleblowing may be a political opinion]; *Reyes-Guerrero v. INS,* 192 F.3d 1241 (9th Cir. 1999) [Colombian prosecutor who investigated and convicted persons from opposing political party and who received death threats was entitled to withholding]; *Gonahasa v. INS,* 181 F.3d 538, 543 (4th Cir. 1999); *Desir v. Ilchert,* 840 F.2d 723, 727 (9th Cir. 1988). *See Silva v. Ashcroft,* 394 F.3d 1, 4–6 (1st Cir. 2005) [although ruling against whistleblower, the court recognized "that current or former employment status can, at least theoretically, form the linchpin for assembling a protected social group"]. *But see Marku v. Ashcroft,* 380 F.3d 982 (6th Cir. 2004) [refusing to engage in government corruption without any evidence that action was ideologically motivated or that persecutor perceived them to be is insufficient].

(25) *Bribery of Government Officials to Avoid Persecution.* The Seventh Circuit has expressly held in a number of cases that suggesting that someone could use bribery to escape persecution is "an irrational and altogether improper consideration in deciding a claim for asylum or other relief." *Bosede v. Mukasey,* 512 F.3d 946, 951 (7th Cir. 2008) [court was "appalled that the IJ would rest his decision on the absurd proposition that Bosede could evade imprisonment, mistreatment, and possibly death by approaching his jailers and trying to buy his way out"]

(26) *Economic Status*—The fact that the applicant had two homes and a car and was a surgeon educated by the government did not mean that he was not persecuted. *Gui v. INS,* 280 F.3d 1217, 1227–28 (9th Cir. 2002) ["[i]f his life was so comfortable in Romania—a car, multiple homes, a sizable income—why would he be so eager to leave?"].

(27) *Identifying Assailants*—Failure to identify attackers is "not critical" to a claim for past persecution. *Bace v. Ashcroft,* 352 F.3d 1133, 1138 (7th Cir. 2003).

(28) *Treatment toward others similarly situated is not required. Sanchez Jimenez v. U.S. Att'y Gen.,* 492 F.3d 1223, 1235 (11th Cir. 2007) [where FARC tried to kill Colombian businessman for assisting in Conservative Party campaign, but there was no evidence that actual political candidate was threatened, the lack of evidence was not relevant; nor was applicant's minor role in Party];

(29) *Classified Information*—USCIS may rely on its own classified information or that from other agencies in deciding the asylum or withholding case. 8 C.F.R. §§208.11(d), 1208.11(d); *Ali v. Reno*, 829 F.Supp. 1415, 1434–36 (S.D.N.Y. 1993), *aff'd*, 22 F.3d 442 (2d Cir. 1994). While the IJ may rely on classified information, DHS must provide the applicant with a summary detailed enough to permit a response. 8 C.F.R. §1240.11(a)(3).

(30) *Information Under Seal/Protective Order*—DOJ has established procedures before the IJ for the submission of documents and information under seal with a protective order which, if disclosed would "harm the national security...or law enforcement interests of the United States." 8 C.F.R. §1003.46. National security is defined under INA §219(c)(2), 8 U.S.C. §1189(c)(2) to include "the national defense, foreign relations, or economic interests of the United States." The issuance of a protective order does not preclude the respondent from challenging the admissibility of the information. 8 C.F.R. §1003.46(g). If a respondent or his/her attorney or accredited representative discloses the information in violation of the protective order, s/he becomes ineligible for "all forms of discretionary relief, except bond, unless the respondent fully cooperates with the Service or other law enforcement agencies in any investigation relating to noncompliance...and establishes by clear and convincing evidence either that extraordinary and extremely unusual circumstances exist or that failure to comply...was beyond the control of the respondent and his or her attorney or accredited representative." 8 C.F.R. §1003.46(i);

Matter of R-S-H-, 23 I&N Dec. 629 (BIA 2003) [denying asylum, withholding and VD because of breach of protective order where respondent and counsel cooperated in the investigation but did not show extraordinary circumstances or that failure to comply was beyond their control].

C. *Post-Trial Relief*

1. *Motion to Reopen*—A person previously found deportable may move to reopen his or her case to apply for asylum before the IJ if the motion is filed within 90 days of the final order. 8 C.F.R. §§1003.2(c)(2), 208.4(b)(3)(ii), 1208.4(b)(3)(ii). Only one motion to reopen may be filed. 8 C.F.R. §1003.2(c)(2). Regulations limiting the time to reopen to apply for CAT relief have been deemed lawful. *Foroglou v. Reno,* 241 F.3d 111, 113 (1st Cir. 2001) [upholding BIA's refusal to consider CAT claim not filed within time proscribed by §208.18(b)(2)]. However, the BIA's interpretation of when an order is final for purposes of filing a motion to reopen for CAT relief has been challenged. *Kay v. Ashcroft,* 387 F.3d 664, 670–73 (7th Cir. 2004) [in an *in absentia* case, an order from the BIA does not become final for purposes of a motion to reopen under §208.18(b)(2) until there is a final decision on the *in absentia* claim]. The BIA has also established regulations governing the content of a motion to reopen that is filed during a judicial proceeding. 8 C.F.R. §1003.2(e). For an in-depth discussion of motions to reopen and reconsider, *see* "Motion to Reopen or Reconsider before EOIR" in Ch. 9, part XIII (p.1046), *infra*.

1.a. *Exceptions to the Time and Numerical Limitations on Motions to Reopen*—There are five exceptions to the 90-day/1-motion rule:

(1) where order was entered *in absentia* and there are exceptional circumstances or no notice 8 C.F.R. §1003.2(c)(3)(i);

(2) the BIA may reopen a proceeding *sua sponte*, 8 C.F.R. §1003.2(a); *Matter of G-D-,* 22 I&N Dec. 1132 (BIA 1999) [declining *sua sponte* reconsideration because the change in law under *Matter of O-Z- & I-Z-* was not sufficiently compelling to warrant extraordinary intervention]; *Matter of X-G-W-,* 22 I&N Dec. 71 (BIA 1998) [change in law was significant and its impact unambiguous thereby warranting extraordinary relief]; *But see Matter of G-C-L-,* 23 I&N Dec. 359 (BIA 2002) [overruling *Matter of X-G-W-* regarding reopening in coercive population control cases on grounds that "the interest of finality in immigration proceedings now takes precedence" over asylum claims]; *But see Cyrus v. Keisler,* 505 F.3d 197, 203 (2d Cir. 2007) [no jurisdiction to review *sua sponte* denial by BIA of a motion to reopen].

(3) the parties agree to reopening, 8 C.F.R. §1003.2(c)(3)(iii);

(4) DHS asks for reopening where there was fraud in the original proceeding or a crime supports termination of asylum, 8 C.F.R. §1003.2(c)(3)(iv); *Hailemichael v. Gonzales,* 454 F.3d 878 (8th Cir. 2006) [reversed reopening for asylum fraud where no showing by DHS that evidence was new and previously unavailable because this section only excepts the time and numerical limitations and not other requirements for reopening]; *Efe v. Ashcroft,* 293 F.3d 899, 904 (5th Cir. 2002) [affirming BIA's decision to reopen because of new laboratory evidence]; and

(5) in asylum, withholding and CAT cases, there may be reopening due to changed circumstances in the country of deportation that could not have been discovered or presented in the previous proceeding. INA §240(c)(7)(C)(ii); 8 C.F.R. §§1003.2(c)(3)(ii), 1003.23(b)(4)(i). The provision applies to *in absentia* orders as well even in the absence of reasonable cause for failing to appear. *Matter of A-N- & R-M-N-,* 22 I&N Dec. 953 (BIA 1999) [Afghan citizen did not have reasonable cause for failing to appear but could reopen *in absentia* order based on changed circumstances]. For a detailed exposition of the case law, *see* "Motions to Reopen" in Ch. 9, section XIII.C (p.1048), *infra*.

1.b. *Motions Must Comply With Regulations*—All motions to reopen must be consistent with 8 C.F.R. §§208.4(b)(3)(ii), 1003.2, 1208.4(b)(3)(ii). *INS v. Abudu,* 485 U.S. 94 (1988); *Matter of R-R-*, 20 I&N Dec. 547 (BIA 1992) [for motion to reopen, traditional criteria including showing that evidence was not previously available are applied; *Matter of Jean* reversed]. *See Goel v. Gonzales,* 490 F.3d 735 (9th Cir. 2007) [motion to reopen asylum case to submit polygraph evidence regarding applicant's torture was denied because evidence was not unavailable during prior hearing]; *Ivanov v. Gonzales,* 487 F.3d 635 (8th Cir. 2007) [where DHS sought to reopen proceedings because birth certificate in asylum case was allegedly fraudulent, the IJ/BIA grant of the motion to reopen was reversed because DHS failed to show that the document was unavailable and undiscoverable at the time of the prior hearing; however, DHS could bring new proceeding to revoke asylum based upon fraud]; *Hailemichael v. Gonzales,* 454 F.3d 878 (8th Cir. 2006) [court challenged reopening where there was no showing that evidence of asylum fraud was previously unavailable and court rejected DHS claim that they were exempt from requirement of unavailability].

1.c. *Grounds for Denial of Motion to Reopen*—There are at least three additional independent grounds for the denial of a motion to reopen: (1) where the applicant has failed to establish a *prima facie* case for the underlying substantive relief; (2) for asylum, the movant has not reasonably explained the failure to apply for asylum initially; and (3) where the ultimate relief is discretionary, such as asylum, "the BIA may leap ahead...over the two threshold concerns...and simply determine that even if they were met, the movant would not be entitled to the discretionary grant of relief." *INS v. Abudu*, 485 U.S. 94 (1988). *Accord INS v. Doherty*, 502 U.S. 314 (1992) [discretion applies equally to motions to reopen claims of asylum and withholding]; *Fesseha v. Ashcroft,* 333 F.3d 13, 20–21 (1st Cir. 2003) [applying *Abudu* standards and finding no abuse of discretion in denial of motion to reopen for Ethiopian who failed establish a prima facie case]; *Al Najjar v. Ashcroft,* 257 F.3d 1262, 1302 (11th Cir. 2001) [upholding BIA denial of motion to reopen for CAT on ground that *Abudu* places "heavy burden" on applicant]. Denials for failure to reasonably explain why an application was not previously made, as well as denials where relief is discretionary, are subject to an abuse of discretion standard. *Zhao v. DOJ,* 265 F.3d 83, 95–97 (2d Cir. 2001) [reversing denial of reopening in forced sterilization claim where BIA relied on cursory and speculative statements that appeared to acknowledge that sterilization had occurred but refused to allow reopening to present proof]; *Doherty v. DOJ*, 908 F.2d 1108, 1115–16 (2d Cir. 1990) [AG abused his discretion in relying on a "foreseeability" standard to determine that applicant failed to apply previously]; *Mickeviciute v. INS,* 327 F.3d 1159 (10th Cir. 2003) [reversing BIA where it failed to articulate which of the three *Abudu* grounds it relied on in denying motion to reopen]. The Supreme Court specifically declined in *INS v. Abudu* to articulate the standards or criteria for review of a *prima facie* case.

1.d. *Motions to Reopen for Withholding*—A motion to reopen for withholding is governed by 8 C.F.R. §1003.23(b)(3), (4), which in addition to the criteria stated above, also prohibits the granting of such a motion where the IJ advised the applicant pursuant to 8 C.F.R. §§1240.11(c), 1240.49(c) [pre–April 1] of the right to seek withholding of removal. 8 C.F.R. §1003.2(c)(1).

1.e. *No Prima Facie Case*—Courts have denied motions to reopen for failure to establish a *prima facie* case for asylum, CAT, or withholding. *Allabani v. Gonzales,* 402 F.3d 668, 675–78 (6th Cir. 2005) [upholding BIA denial of motion to reopen for CAT to native of northern Yemen even where counsel was ineffective because applicant failed to establish prima facie case]; *Selimi v. Ashcroft,* 360 F.3d 736 (7th Cir. 2004) [no abuse of discretion where BIA determined that Macedonian failed to establish a prima facie case of asylum]; *Fesseha v. Ashcroft,* 333 F.3d 13, 20–21 (1st Cir. 2003) [applying *Abudu* in Ethiopian context]; *M.A. v. INS*, 899 F.2d 304, 310 (4th Cir. 1990) (*en banc*) [ambiguities should not necessarily be resolved in alien's favor thereby rejecting summary judgment procedures as model]; *Haftlang v. INS*, 790 F.2d 140 (D.C. Cir. 1986) [conclusory evidence even if believable is insufficient]; *Chavarria v. DOJ*, 722 F.2d 666 (11th Cir. 1984); *Minwalla v. INS*, 706 F.2d 831 (8th Cir. 1983); *Rejaie v. INS*, 691 F.2d 139, 142 (3d Cir. 1982); *Matter of Leon-Orosco and Rodriguez-Colas*, 19 I&N Dec. 136 (AG 1984) [where claim showed little likelihood of success on the merits, reopening denied], *aff'd Garcia-Mir v. Smith,* 766 F.2d 1478 (11th Cir. 1985).

1.f. *Prima Facie Case*—If a *prima facie* case is established, reopening must be granted unless discretionary reasons under *INS v. Rios-Pineda*, 471 U.S. 444 (1985) and *INS v. Abudu, supra*, warrant denial. *Kay v. Ashcroft,* 387 F.3d 664, 673–75 (7th Cir. 2004) [where evidence established a *prima facie* case and BIA's denial was made without rational explanation, court reversed]; *Mengistu v. Ashcroft,* 355 F.3d 1044 (7th Cir. 2004) [reversing BIA denial of Eritrean motion to reopen despite continuing evidence of persecution]; *Zhao v. DOJ,* 265 F.3d 83, 95–97 (2d Cir. 2001) [reversing denial of reopening where BIA relied on cursory and speculative statements where IJ appeared to acknowledge that sterilization had occurred, but refused to allow reopening to present proof regarding it]; *Aviles-Torres v. INS*, 790 F.2d 1433 (9th Cir. 1986). To obtain reopening, the applicant need only file an asylum application with an affidavit that is not "inherently unbelievable" and which, if true, would establish a claim. No corroboration is necessary. *Haftlang v. INS*, 790 F.2d 140 (D.C. Cir. 1986); *Hernandez-Ortiz v. INS*, 777 F.2d 509 (9th Cir. 1985). *But see Maghradze v. Gonzales,* 462 F.3d 150, 155–56 (2d Cir. 2006) [IJ/BIA may deny reopening for CAT where evidence was not previously unavailable even if respondent establishes prima facie case]; *Caushi v. Att'y Gen. of the U.S.,* 436 F.3d 220, 231–32 (3d Cir. 2006) [BIA did not abuse its discretion in refusing to reopen where counsel simply submitted his own affidavit, without supporting documentation, stating that case should be reopened because applicant's sister obtained asylum]. The BIA should not make credibility determinations on motions to reopen. *Ghadessi v. INS*, 797 F.2d 804 (9th Cir. 1986). The prima facie standard does not require a showing of clear probability. *Fadiga v. Attorney General USA,* 488 F.3d 142, 157–63 (3d Cir. 2007) [where BIA applied a clear probability or more-likely-than-not standard in denying motion to remand/reopen asylum claim from Guinea, instead of applying a "reasonable likelihood" (*i.e.*, a realistic chance that the petitioner can at a later time establish that asylum should be granted), the court reversed and ordered the case reopened].

1.g. *No Automatic Stay of Removal*—A motion to reopen accompanied by an asylum application *does not* automatically stay exclusion, deportation or removal. 8 C.F.R. §§208.5(c), 1208.5(c).

1.h. *Post-Departure Motions*—A motion to reopen or reconsider shall not be made after the applicant's physical removal from the U.S. Also, any departure from the U.S. while the motion is pending shall be considered a withdrawal. 8 C.F.R. §1003.2(d). *Pena-Muriel v. Gonzales,* 489 F.3d 438 (1st Cir. 2007), *reh'g denied*, 510 F.3d 350 (1st Cir. 2007) [due process was not violated where the BIA refused to allow respondent, who was outside the United States, to reopen his deportation proceeding because his conviction was vacated]; *But see William v. Gonzales,* 499 F.3d 329 (4th Cir. 2007) [striking down 8 C.F.R. §1003.2(d) where person files motion outside of the U.S. as contrary to INA §240(c)(7)(A), 8 U.S.C. §1229a(c)(7)(A)]. However, this section bars only persons who depart *after* removal proceedings begin. *Singh v. Gonzales,* 412 F.3d 1117, 1120–21 (9th Cir. 2005) [person who departs before removal proceedings are initiated and seeks to reopen to vacate *in absentia* order is not barred by §1003.2(d)]. The Ninth Circuit also excepts a person whose conviction is vacated when the conviction was a key part of the removal proceeding. *Cardoso-Tlaseca v. Gonzales,* 460 F.3d 1102 (9th Cir. 2006) [where respondent's conviction is vacated after physical removal, court reversed BIA for denying motion to reopen because conviction was a "key part" of removal proceeding]. *See also Contreras-Rodriguez v. U.S. Att'y Gen.,* 462 F.3d 1314 (11th Cir. 2006) [although respondent was physically removed after *in absentia* order, he is not barred from filing a motion to reopen for lack of notice because §1003.23(b)(4)(ii) allows motion regarding lack of notice to be filed at "any time"].

1.i. *Scope of Review of Reopened Case*—If the BIA reopens and remands, the IJ is not limited to the reopened grounds unless the BIA expressly states the limitation. The BIA's decision to retain jurisdiction or to narrow the issues that the IJ may consider must be expressly stated and cannot be inferred. *Johnson v. Ashcroft,* 286 F.3d 696 (3d Cir. 2002) [following *Matter of Patel,* 16 I&N Dec. 600, 601 (BIA 1978), reversing BIA's decision that IJ did not have discretion to consider asylum claim after BIA reopened case for CAT claim].

1.j. *Pro se Litigant and Motions to Reopen*—At least one circuit has found that when a *pro se* litigant refers to Country Reports in his motion, the BIA is obligated to evaluate the motion in the context of the most *recent* DOS profiles. *Abassi v. INS,* 305 F.3d 1028, 1030–32 (9th Cir. 2002).

2. *Appeal to BIA*—The review of an IJ's decision on asylum/withholding/CAT claims will be subject to *de novo* review on nonfactual issues and the clearly erroneous standard regarding factual issues,

including credibility. 8 C.F.R. §1003.1(d)(3); *Matter of S-H-,* 23 I&N Dec. 462 (BIA 2002) [clearly erroneous rule requires IJs to make detailed findings of facts]. *De novo* review will apply to the application of legal standards such as whether the facts establish past persecution or a well-founded fear of future persecution. Thus, while the IJ's "determination of 'what happened' to the individual is a factual determination that will be reviewed under the clearly erroneous standard, the IJ's determination of whether those facts demonstrate harm that rises to the level of 'persecution' and whether the harm inflicted was 'on account of' a protected ground will not be limited by the 'clearly erroneous' standard. 67 Fed. Reg. 54878–01, 54890 (Aug. 26, 2002). *Matter of R-S-H-*, 23 I&N Dec. 629, 637 & 641 (BIA 2003) [applying the clearly erroneous standard to the adverse credibility determination by the IJ]. An applicant may also file a motion to reopen to request asylum if his case is on appeal before the BIA where asylum was not requested. The motion must explain the reason for not applying to the IJ initially. 8 C.F.R. §§208.4(b)(4), 1208.4(b)(4). However, failure to raise an asylum/CAT/withholding claim before the IJ/BIA when there was an opportunity to do so on appeal, may waive the right and prevent a motion to reopen from being granted. *Maindrond v. Ashcroft,* 385 F.3d 98, 100–01 (1st Cir. 2004) [denial of motion to reopen for CAT upheld where movant was represented by counsel before IJ and BIA].

3. *Motion to Remand*—A motion to remand is discretionary and the BIA need not remand a case unless it "would likely change the result in the case." *Berte v. Ashcroft,* 396 F.3d 993, 997 (8th Cir. 2005) [upholding the BIA's denial of remand to provide additional country reports and other documentary evidence in Ivory Coast asylum case]. *But see Fadiga v. Attorney General USA,* 488 F.3d 142, 157–63 (3d Cir. 2007) [where BIA applied a clear probability or more-likely-than-not standard in denying motion to remand/reopen asylum claim from Guinea, instead of applying a "reasonable likelihood" (*i.e.*, a realistic chance that the petitioner can at a later time establish that asylum should be granted), the court reversed and ordered the case reopened]. The standard of review is abuse of discretion. *Ticoalu v. Gonzales,* 472 F.3d 8, 11–13 (1st Cir. 2006) [BIA abused its discretion when it failed to remand Indonesian asylum case where proof was presented that new violence had occurred near applicant's city and where BIA failed to address brother's grant of asylum]. The AG, however, has concluded that he has the authority *sua sponte* to remand a case for additional fact-finding. *Matter of A-H-,* 23 I&N Dec. 774, 790–91 (AG 2005) [the AG has authority to remand a case for additional fact-finding as he deems necessary and appropriate including the authority to override a DHS stipulation that respondent's life or freedom would be threatened if returned to Algeria].

4. *Judicial Review*—If an applicant's claim for asylum or withholding or motion to reopen is denied by the BIA and the applicant is in removal proceedings, he may seek review of those decisions in the U.S. Court of Appeals. INA §242(a)(1), 8 U.S.C. §1252(a)(1); *Perkovic v. INS*, 33 F.3d 615, 618–20 (6th Cir. 1994) [rejecting INS claim that BIA's reversal of asylum grant is not a final order for circuit court review]. Courts may review legal questions, for abuse of discretion and whether there was substantial evidence on the record as a whole *unless* there is some other preclusion statute barring review. *See e.g., Matsuk v. INS,* 247 F.3d 999, 1002 (9th Cir. 2001) [review of the decision to deny withholding based on determination that crime is particularly serious was barred by INA §242(a)(2)(B)(ii), which bars review of discretionary decisions]. An applicant in an asylum only proceeding under 8 C.F.R. §208.2(c)(1), may also seek judicial review. *Kanacevic v. INS,* 448 F.3d 129, 133–36 (2d Cir. 2006) [court has jurisdiction to review asylum only hearing for VWP entrant]; *Nreka v. U.S. Att'y Gen.,* 408 F.3d 1361, 1366–68 (11th Cir. 2005) [same]. In general, the discretionary decision of the AG to grant or deny relief "shall be conclusive unless manifestly contrary to law and an abuse of discretion." INA §242(b)(4)(D); *Huang v. INS,* 436 F.3d 89, 96–102 (2d Cir. 2006) [IJ acted manifestly contrary to law in denying asylum as a matter of discretion where he failed to examine the totality of the circumstances and focused solely on the embellishment of peripheral testimony and the applicant's payment to a smuggler]. Under the REAL ID Act, all transition rule (deportation or exclusion) cases are now reviewed under INA §242 (instead of former INA §106) and habeas, mandamus, and the All Writs Act are eliminated as a source of jurisdiction regarding "an order of removal entered or issued under any provision of this Act." REAL ID preserved appellate court review of constitutional claims and questions of law in a petition for review notwithstanding other preclusion provisions such as INA §§242(a)(2)(C) or 242(g). *See* INA §§242(a)(2)(D), (a)(5). *Berhe v. Gonzales,* 464 F.3d 74, 86–87 (1st Cir. 2006) [the adequacy of the BIA's reasoning is a legal question and therefore not barred under INA

§242(a)(2)(C) for an applicant with a conviction]; *Ramos v. Gonzales,* 414 F.3d 800, 802–04 (7th Cir. 2005) [Congress added §242(a)(2)(D) to consider all constitutional and statutory claims in review of a final order]; *Papageorgiou v. Gonzales,* 413 F.3d 356, 357–58 (3d Cir. 2005) [section 242(a)(2)(D) restores jurisdiction to the circuit court for persons who previously were barred from such review under §242(a)(2)(C) because of criminal convictions and makes the restoration retroactive by applying it to any order issued before, on or after May 11, 2005]; *Fernandez-Ruiz v. Gonzales,* 468 F.3d 1159, 1163 (9th Cir. 2006) [same]. However, review of constitutional and statutory claims under INA §242(a)(2)(D) may not extend to the review of factual issues where Congress has barred that review. *Conteh v. Gonzales,* 461 F.3d 45, 62–63 (1st Cir. 2006) [post-REAL ID Act, the court had no authority to engage in substantial evidence review of a withholding of removal claim for an applicant who was convicted of an aggravated felony because such review is otherwise barred under INA §242(a)(2)(C) and no constitutional or legal question was presented]; *Hamid v. Gonzales,* 417 F.3d 642, 647 (7th Cir. 2005) [declining to consider whether the IJ's factual conclusions are supported by substantial evidence in aggravated felon case for failure to raise a constitutional or statutory claim under INA §242(a)(2)(D)]. The bar to habeas, mandamus and All Writs review also includes review of CAT claims and the courts of appeals "shall be the sole and exclusive means for judicial review of any cause or claim under" CAT. INA §242(a)(4).

4.a. *No Judicial Review of Certain Claims*—There is no judicial review to challenge the decision to deny an applicant the right to seek asylum because the applicant: (1) can go to a safe third country; (2) was previously denied asylum; (3) did not file the application within 1 year of entry; (4) is deemed to be a terrorist or (5) did not demonstrate to the AG/DHS changed circumstances warranting an exception to the one-year or previously denied asylum claim or no extraordinary circumstances relating to the one-year filing deadline. INA §§208(a)(3) and (b)(2)(D), 8 U.S.C. §§1158(a)(3) and (b)(2)(D); *Zine v. Mukasey,* 517 F.3d 535, 539 (8th Cir. 2008) [no review of timeliness or extraordinary circumstances issue]; *Pepaj v. Mukasey,* 509 F.3d 725, 727–28 (6th Cir. 2007) [followed *Almuhtaseb* and held no review for abuse of discretion regarding solely factual questions in denying motion to reopen for changed country conditions]; *Zhu v. Gonzales,* 493 F.3d 588, 594–96 (5th Cir. 2007) [where applicant filed asylum six months after B-2 stay expired, the definition of whether that was a reasonable time was fact intensive and therefore not a question of law reviewable under INA §242(a)(2)(D)]; *Mouawad v. Gonzales,* 485 F.3d 405, 410–11 (8th Cir. 2007) [INA §242(a)(2)(d) did not alter the bar to the review of the one-year filing deadline]; *Chen v. DOJ,* 471 F.3d 315, 323–32 (2d Cir. 2006) [although broadly reading the "questions of law" language in INA §242(a)(2)(D), the assertion that the IJ failed to apply the law was insufficient to overcome the bar to review of extraordinary or changed circumstances]; *Almuhtaseb v. Gonzales,* 453 F.3d 743, 746–49 (6th Cir. 2006) [INA §242(a)(2)(D) does not alter bar to review of changed circumstances to the degree it is a factual question]; *Tan v. U.S. Att'y Gen.,* 446 F.3d 1369, 1374 (11th Cir. 2006) [no jurisdiction to review whether IJ erroneously concluded that the applicant failed to establish extraordinary circumstances]; *Sukwanputra v. Gonzales,* 434 F.3d 627, 633–35 (3d Cir. 2006) [changed circumstances affecting one-year deadline is not reviewable]; *Ignatova v. Gonzales,* 430 F.3d 1209, 1213–14 (8th Cir. 2005) [no jurisdiction to review determinations concerning exceptions to the one-year filing deadline for asylum]; *Mehilli v. Gonzales,* 433 F.3d 86, 92–94 (1st Cir. 2005) [following *Vasile* and other circuits, *post*-REAL ID, and determining that issues regarding timeliness in filing an asylum claim were factual and discretionary and could not be reviewed under INA §242(a)(2)(D)]; *Chacon-Botero v. U.S. Att'y Gen.,* 427 F.3d 954, 957 (11th Cir. 2005) [following *Vasile* and finding that the issue of timely filing an asylum claim was not reviewable because it was not a constitutional claim or question of law under INA §242(a)(2)(D)]; *Vasile v. Gonzales,* 417 F.3d 766, 768 (7th Cir. 2005) [INA §242(a)(2)(D) allowing review of constitutional and legal questions does not allow review of the failure to file within one year or that there were no extraordinary circumstances excusing the delay because these are factual and discretionary issues]; *Sharari v. Gonzales,* 407 F.3d 467, 473 (1st Cir. 2005) [no jurisdiction to review whether asylum application was filed within one year and if not, whether exceptional circumstances excused delay]; *Vladimirova v. Ashcroft,* 377 F.3d 690, 695–96 (7th Cir. 2004) [following *Zaidi* and finding no jurisdiction over whether "extraordinary circumstances" overcame one-year filing deadline]; *Zaidi v. Ashcroft*, 377 F.3d 678, 680–81 (7th Cir. 2004) [joining other circuits in finding no jurisdiction to review IJ decision that asylum application was untimely]; *Castellano-Chacon v. INS,* 341 F.3d 533, 541–44 (6th Cir. 2003) [no jurisdiction to review changed circumstances to excuse untimely asylum]; *Tarrawally v. Ashcroft,* 338 F.3d 180, 184–86 (3d Cir. 2003) [no jurisdiction to review compliance with one-year filing requirement for asylum *or* whether extraordinary circumstances excuse untimely filing]; *Mendoza v. U.S. Att'y Gen.,* 327 F.3d 1283, 1286–87 (11th Cir. 2003) [same]; *Tsevegmid v. Ashcroft,* 336 F.3d 1231, 1234–35 (10th Cir. 2003) [same]; *Fahim v. U.S. Att'y Gen.,* 278 F.3d 1216 (11th Cir. 2002) [same]; *Hakeem v. INS,* 273 F.3d 812, 815–16 (9th Cir. 2001) [no jurisdiction to review IJ denial of asylum for failure to file within year although separate habeas action may not be precluded]; *Izmailov v. Reno,* 263 F.3d 851 (8th Cir. 2001) [no jurisdiction to review denial of asylum for failing to file within one year]. The bar to judicial review regarding the one-year filing deadline was not unconstitutional under the due process clause. *Hana v. Gonzales,* 503 F.3d 39, 43–44 (1st Cir. 2007) [applicant who had nervous breakdown when he entered U.S. that prevented his filing for asylum unsuccessfully challenged the constitutionality of the preclusion statute].

4.b. *Judicial Review Notwithstanding Bar*—Although there is no review of the one-year bar, there may be review regarding the interpretation of the regulation governing the bar, *Nakimbugwe v. Gonzales,* 475 F.3d 281 (5th Cir. 2007) [court found there was jurisdiction to reverse IJ's determination that bar applied where person mailed application within the one year but EOIR did not received it until after the year]; *Diallo v. Gonzales,* 447 F.3d 1274, 1281–82 (10th Cir. 2006) [in the case of an asylee whose status was revoked there was jurisdiction to interpret that the one year period to apply for asylum should run from the time of revocation and not last entry]. There is also jurisdiction to review a due process claim regarding submission of evidence of exceptional or changed circumstances, *Somakoko v. Gonzales,* 399 F.3d 882 (8th Cir. 2005) [entertaining but rejecting due process challenge to IJ's refusal to hear evidence regarding exceptional circumstances]; *Kanivets v. Riley,* 320 F.Supp.2d 297, 300 (E.D. Pa. 2004) and 286 F.Supp.2d 460, 468 (E.D. Pa. 2003) [habeas jurisdiction to review whether changed circumstances warranted extension of one-year time bar], or a claim that the application of the law required a reasoned decision. *Gjyzi v. Ashcroft,* 386 F.3d 710, 713–14 (6th Cir. 2004) [where BIA reversed IJ's adverse credibility finding that was the basis for concluding that the application was filed beyond one year, but still upheld the IJ's decision, a due process issue was raised for lack of a reasoned decision and the court vacated the order]. One circuit has also determined that there is jurisdiction to review the IJ/BIA failure to address a properly raised extraordinary circumstances claim to the one-year bar. *Sagaydak v. Gonzales,* 405 F.3d 1035, 1039–41 (9th Cir. 2005) [where petitioner alleges failure to file in one year was due to extraordinary circumstances and both the IJ and the BIA failed to address whether the exception applies, the court has jurisdiction to review the failure to make the determination]. *See also Ramadan v. Gonzales,* 479 F.3d 646, 648–54 (9th Cir. 2007), *reh'g en banc denied,* 504 F.3d 973 (2007) [court can review the issue of whether changed circumstances excuse the failure to file for asylum within one year as a mixed question of law and fact under INA §242(a)(2)(D)].

4.c. *Stays of Removal During Judicial Review*—An applicant post-IIRIRA must apply for a stay of removal from the court as stays are no longer automatic and habeas corpus actions in the district court seeking review of removal orders are not permitted. For further discussion regarding stays of removal, *see* Ch. 10, section VI.B (p.1191), *infra*.

4.d. *Old or Stale Administrative Record*—The review of an asylum/withholding/CAT claim must be based on the administrative record, but such records are often out-of-date. *Ambartsoumian v. Ashcroft,* 388 F.3d 85, 87–88, 94–96 (3d Cir. 2004) [noting the problem with stale administrative records and reproducing, in the appendix to the opinion, OIL's policy regarding remanding cases within old/stale records]; *Berishaj v. Ashcroft,* 378 F.3d 314, 317 (3d Cir. 2004) [noting that administrative records in asylum cases are "grossly out-of-date" and calling upon Congress and the Executive Branch to restructure the process]. *See Kamara v. Att'y Gen. of the U.S.,* 420 F.3d 202, 218–19 (3d Cir. 2005) [reminding the AG that the internal remand procedure outlined in *Ambartsoumian* is appropriate not only for cases where country conditions have deteriorated but where conditions have so improved that withholding or CAT relief can no longer be justified]. The AG has concluded that he has *sua sponte* authority to remand a case for additional fact-finding where the record may be stale. *Matter of A-H-*, 23 I&N Dec. 774, 790–91 (A.G. 2005) [AG has authority to remand a case for additional fact-finding as he deems necessary and appropriate].

4.e. *Standard of Review for Motions To Reopen*—The denial of a motion to reopen or reconsider for asylum or withholding is generally reviewed under the traditional abuse of discretion standard. *INS v. Abudu*, 485 U.S. 94 (1988) [broad discretion given to INS]; *Li v. U.S. Att'y Gen.*, 488 F.3d 1371, 1374–76 (11th Cir. 2007) [BIA abused its discretion in not granting motion to reopen where Chinese applicant demonstrated that local government officials have intensified their punishment against those who violate the one child policy]; *Kebe v. Gonzales,* 473 F.3d 855 (7th Cir. 2007) [BIA abused its discretion in not granting motion to reopen due to changed country conditions where Ethiopian citizen and member of the Oromo Liberation Front (OLF) provided evidence that before the 2005 elections conditions worsened]; *Paul v. Gonzales,* 444 F.3d 148, 153–55 (2d Cir. 2006) [BIA abused its discretion in not reopening case of Christian from Pakistan based upon changed circumstances, despite IJ's prior adverse credibility finding, because applicant may prevail on a theory of future persecution as long as the factual predicate for the claim is independent of the testimony the IJ found not credible]; *Dawoud v. Gonzales,* 424 F.3d 608, 611–12 (7th Cir. 2005) [BIA abused its discretion in refusing to reopen case of Coptic from Egypt who was persecuted by security forces where BIA misread DOS report that supported respondent's claim]; *Poradisova v. Gonzales,* 420 F.3d 70, 81–82 (2d Cir. 2005) [where Jewish applicants from Belarus submitted reports from DOS and international organizations that showed that hostility to Jews had worsened, the BIA abused its discretion in not reopening]; *Fessehaye v. Gonzales,* 414 F.3d 746, 754–56 (7th Cir. 2005) [BIA abused its discretion in failing to articulate why evidence was insufficient to warrant reopening where applicant relied on her own affidavit of religious persecution as a Jehovah's Witness in Ethiopia]; *Ven v. Ashcroft,* 386 F.3d 357, 360–61 (1st Cir. 2004) [no abuse of discretion in denying Cambodian's motion to reconsider the denial of a motion to reopen based on changed country conditions because there was no legal error]; *Mickeviciute v. INS,* 327 F.3d 1159 (10th Cir. 2003) [reversing BIA where it failed to articulate which of the three *Abudu* grounds it relied on in denying respondent's motion to reopen]; *Zhao v. DOJ,* 265 F.3d 83, 95–97 (2d Cir. 2001) [reversing denial of reopening in forced sterilization asylum case where BIA relied on cursory and speculative statements where IJ appeared to acknowledge that sterilization had occurred]. *But see Fesseha v. Ashcroft,* 333 F.3d 13, 20–21 (1st Cir. 2003) [applying *Abudu* standards and finding no abuse of discretion in denying Ethiopian motion to reopen]. The abuse of discretion standard has not been lessened by the codification of motions to reopen by IIRIRA. *Fessehaye v. Gonzales, supra* [rejecting argument that the statutory recognition of motions to reopen under IIRIRA lessened the degree of deference owed the BIA]. The question of whether a person factually establishes a *prima facie* case for reopening may be subject to the less deferential substantial-evidence test. *Al Najjar v. Ashcroft,* 257 F.3d 1262, 1304 (11th Cir. 2001) [denial of motion to reopen for CAT supported by substantial evidence]; *Kamalthas v. INS,* 251 F.3d 1279 (9th Cir. 2001) [reviewing factual finding of denial for failure to establish prima facie case under substantial evidence and decision to deny under abuse of discretion]; *Sevoian v. Ashcroft,* 290 F.3d 166 (3d Cir. 2002) [same]; *But see M.A. v. INS*, 899 F.2d 304, 307–10 (4th Cir. 1990) (*en banc*) [subjecting *prima facie* claim to abuse of discretion].

4.f. *Standard of Review of Withholding vs. Asylum*—The denial of a claim for withholding is subject to the less stringent substantial-evidence test because withholding is mandatory if the applicant proves his claim. *Melendez v. DOJ*, 926 F.2d 211, 216–19 (2d Cir. 1991); *Chavarria v. DOJ*, 722 F.2d 666, 669–70 (11th Cir. 1984); *Rajaratnam v. Moyer*, 832 F.Supp. 1219 (N.D. Ill. 1993); *Rasool v. INS*, 758 F.Supp. 188 (S.D.N.Y. 1991). The standard of review for asylum claims is more complicated. Although the ultimate grant of asylum is discretionary, the factual determination of whether an applicant has a "well-founded fear" is not. In light of this distinction, courts have developed a bifurcated system of review.

4.g. *Review of Factual Determinations under Substantial-Evidence Test*—The factual determination concerning the applicant's well-founded fear is reviewed under the substantial-evidence test. INA §242(b)(4)(B). *See INS v. Elias-Zacarias*, 502 U.S. 478 (1992) [Court will reverse the Board only if the evidence presented was so compelling that no reasonable fact finder could fail to find the requisite fear of persecution]. But one circuit has described the review as a "highly deferential version of the substantial evidence test." *Dobrota v. INS,* 195 F.3d 970, 973 (7th Cir. 1999). Another circuit has found that DOS Country Reports supply the substantial evidence necessary to uphold a BIA decision denying asylum. *Kayembe v. Ashcroft,* 334 F.3d 231, 235–37 (3d Cir. 2003) [where DOS Country Report states that the Congo no longer persecutes Tutsis, it provided substantial evidence needed to deny the claim based on ethnic persecution]. One circuit has suggested that factual determinations by IJs may not be reversed even if clearly erroneous. *Eusebio v. Ashcroft,* 361 F.3d 1088, 1091 (8th Cir. 2004) [upholding denial of asylum where person subject to arrest and physical abuse].

4.h. *Cases Reversing IJ or BIA's Denial of Asylum/Withholding/CAT under Elias-Zacarias Standard*

(1) *Second Circuit—Edimo-Doualla v. Gonzales*, 464 F.3d 276, 282–88 (2d Cir. 2006) [reversing IJ's findings that arrests and beatings did not amount to persecution, that actions were not on account of political opinion, that the applicant lacked credibility, and that applicant failed to corroborate claim in Cameroonian asylum case]; *Tun v. INS,* 445 F.3d 554, 570–71 (2d Cir. 2006) [reversing IJ's denial of asylum where Burmese citizen engaged in pro-democracy political demonstrations in the U.S. against Burmese government]; *Jorge-Tzoc v. Gonzales*, 435 F.3d 146 (2d Cir. 2006) [failure to consider evidence in Guatemalan Mayan Indian case and failure to consider effect of respondent's status as a small child when the events occurred required reversal and remand to determine past persecution]; *Ivanishvili v. DOJ*, 433 F.3d 332, 339–43 (2d Cir. 2006) [remanding to IJ where he failed to evaluate Jehovah's Witness testimony about religious persecution in Georgia]; *Qui v. Ashcroft*, 329 F.3d 140 (2d Cir. 2003) [denial of asylum reversed where BIA confused vague testimony with testimony that lacked detail, failed to support its findings by substantial evidence and failed to consider key elements in the record]; *Alvarado-Carillo v. INS*, 251 F.3d 44, 49 (2d Cir. 2001) [reversing BIA denial where it made impermissible credibility and corroboration findings and where it failed to address all events in asylum claim]; *Abankwah v. INS*, 185 F.3d 18, 22–23 (2d Cir. 1999) [reversing BIA notwithstanding *Elias-Zacarias* where BIA misinterpreted facts]; *Carranza-Hernandez v. INS*, 12 F.3d 4 (2d Cir. 1993).

(2) *Third Circuit—Chavarria v. Gonzales,* 446 F.3d 508, 520–22 (3d Cir. 2007) [reversing BIA denial of future persecution because it failed to recognize that subsequent incident was related to applicant witnessing abuse by paramilitaries in Guatemala]; *Toure v. Att'y Gen. of the U.S.,* 443 F.3d 310 (3d Cir. 2006) [reversing IJ on past and future persecution, credibility, and corroboration issues]; *Caushi v. Att'y Gen. of the U.S.,* 436 F.3d 220, 226–31 (3d Cir. 2006) [reversing IJ in Albanian claim of past persecution where IJ ignored testimony and incorrectly found sister's testimony not credible]; *Konan v. Att'y Gen. of the U.S.*, 432 F.3d 497, 503–06 (3d Cir. 2005) [where gendarme in Côte d'Ivoire was killed by rebel forces in attack on camp, gendarme's son had imputed claim for asylum because attack was in part to kill government supporters not simply police officers; reversing IJ] *Awolesi v. Ashcroft,* 341 F.3d 227 (3d Cir. 2003) [where IJ granted asylum to Nigerian businessman and BIA reversed by stating only that "the evidence was insufficient" and that the arguments made by the INS on appeal were "persuasive," the court was unable to tell the basis for the decision and reversed]; *Lukwago v. Ashcroft,* 329 F.3d 157, 180 (3d Cir. 2003) [reversing BIA determination that there was no factual basis for future persecution claim of child soldier who escaped guerrillas in Uganda because he is in no greater danger than general population]; *Senathirajah v. INS,* 157 F.3d 210 (3d Cir. 1998) [reversing denial of asylum based on erroneous assessment of applicant's credibility]; *Balasubramanrim v. INS,* 143 F.3d 157 (3d Cir. 1998) [same].

(3) *Fourth Circuit—Lin-Jian v. Gonzales,* 489 F.3d 182, 191–93 (4th Cir. 2007) [where court upheld IJ's adverse credibility finding as to future persecution, the IJ's failure to make a credibility determination as to past persecution requires the assumption that the testimony was credible and the denial was not supported by substantial evidence]; *Haoua v. Gonzales,* 472 F.3d 227 (4th Cir. 2007) [IJ erred in determining that Niger applicant for asylum had only a 10% chance of being subject to FGM]; *Essohou v. Gonzales,* 471 F.3d 518, 522–23 (4th Cir. 2006) [substantial evidence did not support BIA's claim that a

member of Congolese Movement for Democracy and Integral Development could safely relocate in the Congo because she was in hiding for many months].

(4) *Fifth Circuit—Zhao v. Gonzales,* 404 F.3d 295, 30610 (5th Cir. 2005) [Falun Gong member had a well-founded fear of future persecution and the BIA was reversed]; *Abdel-Masieh v. INS*, 73 F.3d 579, 585 (5th Cir. 1996) [reversing BIA notwithstanding *Elias-Zacarias* where BIA did not address relevant considerations].

(5) *Sixth Circuit—N'Diom v. Gonzales,* 442 F.3d 494 (6th Cir. 2006) [reversing asylum denial of person of Fulani ethnicity from Mauritania where there was a combination of incompetent counsel resulting in evidence not being placed in the record, a coup in Mauritania, uncertainty about present conditions there, and the questionable rejection of respondent's testimony that appeared plausible and consistent]; *Alexandrov v. Gonzales,* 442 F.3d 395, 407–09 (6th Cir. 2006) [in Bulgarian claim, reversing IJ's lack of credibility where it was based on IJ's personal beliefs about how long beatings and detention should last, and reversing IJ's denial of asylum as frivolous where it was based on highly unreliable reports from the U.S. Embassy in Sofia regarding alleged fraudulent documents]; *Gjyzi v. Ashcroft,* 386 F.3d 710, 715–16 (6th Cir. 2004) [in Albanian case, where BIA failed to address past persecution but reversed IJ on an adverse credibility assessment, the court reversed the BIA's denial of withholding and remanded the case for a new determination].

(6) *Seventh Circuit—Binrashed v. Gonzales,* 502 F.3d 666 (7th Cir. 2007) [reversing IJ's denial of future persecution of Yemen man who claimed he would be persecuted in retaliation against his father's actions]; *Oyekunle v. Gonzales,* 498 F.3d 715 (7th Cir. 2007) [BIA erred in relying on a country report about FGM in Lagos when events occurred in Nigeria and other factors to demonstrate that there was no objective basis for well-founded fear]; *Tchemkou v. Gonzales,* 495 F.3d 785, 794–95 (7th Cir. 2007) [reversing BIA and holding evidence compelled finding that Cameroonian woman would face torture if returned given her past treatment]; *Agbor v. Gonzales,* 487 F.3d 499 (7th Cir. 2007) [BIA's decision to deny future persecution claim based upon FGM from Cameroon was not supported by substantial evidence where BIA disregarded key evidence, relied on DOS report that does not specifically contradict respondent, and then faulted applicant for not responding]; *Boctor v. Gonzales,* 474 F.3d 488 (7th Cir. 2007) [Coptic Christian who was threatened by Muslim extremists for reporting threats against fellow Christian who married Muslim woman that converted to Christianity compelled conclusion of past persecution]; *Ali v. Achim,* 468 F.3d 462, 471–72 (7th Cir. 2006) *cert. dismissed* 128 S.Ct. 828 (2007) [reversing BIA in Somalian CAT claim where the BIA ignored key evidence, overlooked expert testimony and focused narrowly are general conditions]; *Cecaj v. Gonzales,* 440 F.3d 897 (7th Cir. 2007) [reversing IJ's denial of past persecution where he failed to consider cumulative evidence concerning member of Democratic Party of Albania]; *Hor v. Gonzales,* 421 F.3d 497 (7th Cir. 2005) [reversing IJ's denial for lack of corroboration because his decision was based on "unsubstantiated conjectures" and the deferential standard of review under REAL ID does not alter the lack of basis for the IJ's decision]; *Sosnovskaia v. Gonzales,* 421 F.3d 589, 592–94 (7th Cir. 2005) [reversing IJ's denial of asylum where s/he ignored the applicant's evidence and failed to give her a final hearing on her claim regarding anti-Semitism in the Ukraine]; *Georgis v. Ashcroft,* 328 F.3d 962, 967–70 (7th Cir. 2003) [denial of asylum reversed under *Elias-Zacarias* standard where minor inconsistencies concerning dates and actions were easily resolved by other facts in evidence and explained by improperly excluded evidence]; *Sanon v. INS*, 52 F.3d 648 (7th Cir. 1995) [reversing BIA denial of asylum under *Elias-Zacarias*].

(7) *Eighth Circuit—Brima Bah v. Gonzales,* 448 F.3d 1019 (8th Cir. 2006) [reversing IJ's denial of past persecution by Liberian who was persecuted by Charles Taylor due to membership in a tribal group and imputed political opinion]; *Bushira v. Gonzales,* 442 F.3d 626 (8th Cir. 2006) [reversing IJ where he placed burden on Ethiopian applicant to demonstrate a well-founded fear of future persecution without making a determination of past persecution]; *Zewdie v. Ashcroft,* 381 F.3d 804, 808–10 (8th Cir. 2004) [where IJ/BIA found respondent not credible because she failed to produce medical evidence

that her scars were from beatings, the court reversed, holding that no reasonable fact finder could fail to find respondent eligible for CAT]; *Bellido v. Ashcroft,* 367 F.3d 840 (8th Cir. 2004) [reversing IJ credibility finding and lack of substantial evidence for Bolivian union leader].

(8) *Ninth Circuit—Ahmed v. Keisler,* 504 F.3d 1183, 1193–1200 (9th Cir. 2007) [reversing BIA determination that Bihari in Bangladesh did not suffer persecution on account of his political opinion or social group]; *Zhang v. Ashcroft,* 388 F.3d 713, 718–21 (9th Cir. 2004) [reversing IJ's determination that Falun Gong member would not face persecution on return to China in light of family members arrests, his identification by authorities, and country condition reports]; *Mihalev v. Ashcroft,* 388 F.3d 722, 727–30 (9th Cir. 2004) [in case involving Gypsy from Bulgaria, substantial evidence did not support IJ's conclusion that the applicant failed to establish past persecution]; *He v. Ashcroft,* 328 F.3d 593 (9th Cir. 2003) [reversing adverse credibility determination by BIA on grounds it was not supported by substantial evidence]; *Melkonian v. Ashcroft,* 320 F.3d 1061, 1069 (9th Cir. 2003) [reversing BIA denial of asylum to Armenian Christian who fled Muslim controlled Abkhazia]; *Popova v. INS,* 273 F.3d 1251, 1257–59 (9th Cir. 2001) [reversing BIA denial of asylum where there were cumulative circumstantial events of persecution that lead to the conclusion that their occurrence was not coincidental; BIA claim that applicant was not entitled to asylum because she was educated and allowed to work and travel abroad were "non-evidence based assumptions regarding conduct in another culture"]; *Tagaga v. INS,* 228 F.3d 1030, 1033–34 (9th Cir. 2000) [reversing BIA denial of relief under *Elias-Zacarias* standard for Fijian officer who would face treason for refusing to disassociate with Indo-Fijians]; *Cordon-Garcia v. INS,* 204 F.3d 985 (9th Cir. 2000) [reversing BIA denial of asylum under *Elias-Zacarias* standard]; *Mgoian v. INS,* 184 F.3d 1029, 1034 (9th Cir. 1999) [reversing BIA where its findings were not supported by substantial evidence]; *Hartooni v. INS,* 21 F.3d 336 (9th Cir. 1994) [reversing denial where BIA made findings not based on the record].

(9) *Tenth Circuit—Yan v. Gonzales,* 438 F.3d 1249 (10th Cir. 2006) [where Chinese Christian testified that authorities broke up his home church, confiscated his Bible and threw him in jail where he was beaten, the IJ's decision to deny relief, based on a DOS report that indicated that persons with small home churches were ordinarily not attacked and based on a minor inconsistency in the applicant's story, was not supported by substantial evidence].

(10) *Eleventh Circuit—Niftaliev v. U.S. Att'y Gen.,* 504 F.3d 1211, 1217 (11th Cir. 2007) [where IJ did not make adverse credibility determination and applicant relied on testimony alone, the cumulative effects of treatment by Ukrainian authorities were sufficient to establish past persecution and the court was also "troubled by the notion of condemning the petitioner for failing to obtain some sort of documentation from the same government that persecuted and imprisoned him, concerning incidents that occurred approximately ten years ago"]; *Mejia v. U.S. Att'y Gen.,* 498 F.3d 1253 (11th Cir. 2007) [reversing IJ where Colombian, who was member of Liberal Party, was threatened over 18 month period, had large rock thrown at him, was hit with butt of rifle breaking his nose by FARC members, and was sent written death threat *cumulatively* faced past persecution]; *Sanchez Jimenez v. U.S. Att'y Gen.,* 492 F.3d 1223, 1232–33 (11th Cir. 2007) [reversing IJ's denial of past persecution because being shot at constitutes past persecution where there was evidence that FARC sought to kill, albeit unsuccessfully, Colombian businessman]; *Delgado v. U.S. Att'y Gen.,* 487 F.3d 855, 861 (11th Cir. 2007) [reversing IJ where Venezuelan who had gun pointed at him and his son, suffered numerous threats, son beaten, and car vandalized twice had established past persecution through cumulative evidence notwithstanding identification of assailants]; *Ruiz v. Gonzales,* 479 F.3d 762, 767 (11th Cir. 2007) [reversing IJ/BIA where applicant established that cumulative actions constituted past persecution and ICE failed to establish by preponderance of the evidence that applicant could reasonably relocate within Colombia]; *Mezvrishvili v. U.S. Att'y Gen.,* 467 F.3d 1292 (11th Cir. 2006) [reversing IJ/BIA in case involving Jehovah's Witness from Georgia because they failed to render a reasoned decision]; *Tan v. U.S. Att'y Gen.,* 446 F.3d 1369, 1375–77 (11th Cir. 2006) [in case involving Chinese

Indonesian woman, the IJ did not give reasoned consideration to withholding claim because he misstated the contents of the record, failed to consider all the evidence, failed to explain why sexual assault was not based on the applicant's race after accepting applicant as credible, and failed to support his finding by record facts].

4.i. Cases Upholding Denial of Asylum/Withholding/CAT under Elias-Zacarias Standard

(1) *First Circuit—Chikkeur v. Mukasey,* 514 F.3d 1381 (1st Cir. 2008) [no imputed political opinion because of extortion by radical Islamists against Algerian shop keeper]; *Jorgji v. Mukasey,* 514 F.3d 53, 58 (1st Cir. 2008) [Albanian applicant did not have an objective basis for fear regarding events of religious and other persecution that occurred 15 to 35 years ago during Stalinist government]; *Lumanauw v. Mukasey,,* 510 F.3d 5 (1st Cir. 2007) [substantial evidence supports denial of asylum/withholding regarding threats by ex-fiancée and police because of applicant's Christian beliefs]; *Journal v. Keisler,* 507 F.3d 9 (1st Cir. 2007) [anti-Lavalas activist did not suffer past persecution or have a well-founded fear of future persecution in Haiti]; *Butt v. Keisler,* 506 F.3d 86 (1st Cir. 2007) [Shi'a in Pakistan waived past persecution claim and could not demonstrate future persecution]; *Ouk v. Keisler,* 505 F.3d 63 (1st Cir. 2007) [pharmacist at Cambodian Ministry of Health did not suffer past persecution or have a well-founded fear of future persecution]; *Boukhtouchen v. Gonzales,* 498 F.3d 78 (1st Cir. 2007) [member of Berber minority denied asylum from Algeria]; *Wang v. Mukasey,* 508 F.3d 80 (1st Cir. 2007) [fears forced abortion if returned to China because she has one child in the U.S. and wants more]; *Tendean v. Gonzales,* 503 F.3d 8 (1st Cir. 2007) [substantial evidence demonstrated Indonesian would not likely suffer torture]; *Sipayung v. Gonzales,* 491 F.3d 18 (1st Cir. 2007) [Christian in Indonesia did not suffer past persecution and could not show pattern and practice of persecution]; *Jiang v. Gonzales,* 474 F.3d 25, 29–32 (1st Cir. 2007) [Chinese future religious persecution claim based upon one isolated incident five years before did not compel asylum]; *Alibeaj v. Gonzales,* 469 F.3d 188 (1st Cir. 2006) [Albanian woman's claim properly denied where events happened in the distant past or were too tenuous to establish political motivation for the harm]; *Orelien v. Gonzales,* 467 F.3d 67 (1st Cir. 2006) [no evidence other than harassment to support claim by Haitian opponent of Lavalas]; *Ouk v. Gonzales*, 464 F.3d 108 (1st Cir. 2006) [Cambodian who only suffered minor injuries from crowd movement in 1997 and some emotional harm did not establish a well-founded fear]; *Awad v. Gonzales*, 463 F.3d 73 (1st Cir. 2006) [Coptic Christian from Egypt denied withholding]; *Sou v. Gonzales,* 450 F.3d 1 (1st Cir. 2006) [substantial evidence supported denial of asylum where parents' involvement in political organizations in Cambodia were at a low-level or nonexistent, where they left country freely, where children continue to live peacefully in Cambodia and where government authorities took 17 months to question applicant after release from arrest]; *Chahid Hayek v. Gonzales*, 445 F.3d 501 (1st Cir. 2006) [denial of withholding and CAT to a Maronite Christian and former member of Lebanese Forces upheld]; *Pan v. Gonzales,* 445 F.3d 60 (1st Cir. 2006) [upheld BIA denial where applicant failed to demonstrate that she was persecuted as a young unmarried woman from rural China who resisted forced marriage]; *Susanto v. Gonzales*, 439 F.3d 57 (1st Cir. 2006) [substantial evidence supported IJ's determination that ethnic Chinese applicant from Indonesia did not suffer past persecution and failed to establish a well-founded fear of future persecution]; *Sulaiman v. Gonzales*, 429 F.3d 347 (1st Cir. 2005) [denial of Syrian asylum/CAT claim upheld where he suffered only harassment]; *Harutyunyan v. Gonzales*, 421 F.3d 64, 68–69 (1st Cir. 2005) [where Armenian locals used physical violence and arson against applicant because of his Azeri ethnicity but police investigated incidents and made arrests, there was no showing of government acquiescence and the applicant's fear of future persecution due to conscription in the army was not supported by substantial evidence]; *Negeya v. Gonzales*, 417 F.3d 78, 83–85 (1st Cir. 2005) [where Ethiopian's future persecution claim was based on events in the 1990s and the government offered a 2002 DOS report, substantial evidence supported IJ's decision]; *Ziu v. Gonzales*, 412 F.3d 202 (1st Cir. 2005) [Albanian denial of asylum/withholding upheld under *Elias-Zacarias* standard where respondent's children were harassed, there were two episodes of physical abuse not requiring hospitalization, a police search and various threats]; *Njenga v. Ashcroft*, 386 F.3d 335, 339–40 (1st Cir. 2004) [substantial evidence supported denial of withholding

and CAT to Kenyan claim of FGM]; *Romilus v. Ashcroft*, 385 F.3d 1, 5–8 (1st Cir. 2004) [Haitian applicant could not establish nexus between harm and one of five grounds for asylum]; *Pieterson v. Ashcroft*, 364 F.3d 38, 44 (1st Cir. 2004) [Sierra Leone applicant could not establish that general violence was directed toward her in light of DOS Reports and no specific evidence]; *Mabikas v. INS*, 358 F.3d 145, 149–50 (1st Cir. 2004) [substantial evidence did not support applicant's fear of persecution from the Republic of the Congo]; *Khem v. Ashcroft*, 342 F.3d 51 (1st Cir. 2003) [low-level member of opposition party during coup where husband died guarding weapons warehouse did not "compel" asylum]; *Keo v. Ashcroft*, 341 F.3d 57 (1st Cir. 2003) [substantial evidence supported denial of Cambodian citizen's claim]; *Gebremichael v. INS*, 10 F.3d 28, 34 n.17 (1st Cir. 1993); *Debab v. INS*, 163 F.3d 21 (1st Cir. 1998) [Algerian applicant failed to prove threats came from armed Islamist insurgents]; *Tokarska v. INS*, 978 F.2d 1 (1st Cir. 1992).

(2) *Second Circuit—Lin v. Att'y Gen. of the U.S.*, 441 F.3d 193 (2d Cir. 2006) [upholding IJ determination that Chinese national did not have a well-founded fear]; *Joaquin-Porras v. Gonzales*, 435 F.3d 172, 180–82 (2d Cir. 2006) [isolated instance of rape by police officer and subsequent brief detention because of applicant's sexual orientation was insufficient to warrant withholding or CAT and IJ's decision upheld under substantial evidence standard].

(3) *Third Circuit—Shehu v. Gonzales*, 482 F.3d 652 (3d Cir. 2007) [Albanian who was attacked by criminal gang]; *Kibinda v. Att'y Gen. of the U.S.*, 477 F.3d 113 (3d Cir. 2007) [military officer from Cabinda in Angolan army who deserted]; *Celaj v. Att'y Gen. of U.S.*, 471 F.3d 483 (3d Cir. 2006) [anonymous death threats were not sufficient to establish persecution, nor did applicant prove events in Albania were on account of his political opinion]; *Chen v. Gonzales*, 434 F.3d 212, 217–20 (3d Cir. 2005) [post–REAL ID, the court upheld the denial of asylum even where the IJ did not make a valid credibility assessment because even a credible applicant may be required to produce corroborative evidence and respondent failed to do so]; *Al-Fara v. Gonzales*, 404 F.3d 733 (3d Cir. 2005) [denial of asylum to Palestinian involving 38-year-old incident was supported by substantial evidence]; *Abdulrahman v. Ashcroft*, 330 F.3d 587, 595–99 (3d Cir. 2003) [upholding denial of asylum despite the fact that IJ's conduct fell "well below" appropriate standards of impartiality and she went "beyond the bounds of propriety"].

(4) *Fourth Circuit—Ngarurih v. Ashcroft*, 371 F.3d 182, 184–89 (4th Cir. 2004) [substantial evidence supported denial where applicant had returned to country of persecution for several months to fight his brother's incarceration]; *Huaman-Cornelio v. BIA*, 979 F.2d 995, 999 (4th Cir. 1992).

(5) *Fifth Circuit—Hongyok v Gonzales*, 492 F.3d 547 (5th Cir. 2007) [substantial evidence supported BIA denial of withholding and CAT to victim of sex trafficking from Thailand]; *Chen v. Gonzales*, 470 F.3d 1131 (5th Cir. 2006) [denial of asylum for Chinese Protestant upheld despite DOS Reports because the statements that religious adherents experienced persecution were vague and the specific examples of persecution pointed to other religions]; *Majd v. Gonzales*, 446 F.3d 590 (5th Cir. 2006) [IJ did not err in denying asylum, withholding and CAT to Libyan holding Palestinian Authority passport despite two detentions by Israeli forces, search of his home, and detention of family members]; *Zamora-Morel v. INS*, 905 F.2d 833, 837–38 (5th Cir. 1990).

(6) *Sixth Circuit—Shkulaku-Purballori v. Mukasey*, 514 F.3d 499 (6th Cir. 2007) [the evidence did not "compel" granting withholding or CAT to Albanian who was arrested, beaten and shot at]; *Kouljinski v. Keisler*, 505 F.3d 534, 544–45 (6th Cir. 2007) [rejected withholding and CAT claim of Russian Jew claiming anti-Semitism in Russia]; *Mohammed v. Keisler*, 507 F.3d 369 (6th Cir. 2007) [Shia's beating by mob in Pakistan without government reaction and a single incident of detention were insufficient to establish claim]; *Berri v. Gonzales*, 468 F.3d 390 (6th Cir. 2006) [upheld IJ denial where claim by Lebanese citizens was based upon intermarriage and imputed political opinion]; *Lumaj v. Gonzales*, 462 F.3d 574 (6th Cir. 2006) [where Albanian woman was beaten and suffered bodily injury, court upheld IJ denial of asylum because persecution requires greater se-

verity and the respondent could not show the attempted kidnapping was political]; *Klawitter v. INS*, 970 F.2d 149, 152 (6th Cir. 1992).

(7) *Seventh Circuit—Tariq v. Keisler,* 505 F.3d 650 (7th Cir. 2007) [Pakistani fearing persecution due to Western upbringing]; *Garcia v. Gonzales,* 500 F.3d 615 (7th Cir. 2007) [Colombian government was willing to assist applicant claiming persecution from FARC]; *Tarraf v. Gonzales,* 495 F.3d 525, 534–35 (7th Cir. 2007) [Lebanese applicant failed to provide details of his alleged detention and torture]; *Fedosseeva v. Gonzales,* 492 F.3d 840, 847–48 (7th Cir. 2007) [ethnic Russian's fear of return to Latvia was not objective and not supported by substantial evidence]; *Boci v. Gonzales,* 473 F.3d 762 (7th Cir. 2007) [Albanian who claimed he and family were targeted because of membership in Democratic Party could not demonstrate physical harm or abuse]; *Ahmed v. Gonzales,* 467 F.3d 669 (7th Cir. 2006) [Somalian applicant failed to demonstrate persecution as member of the Midgan clan]; *Chakir v. Gonzales,* 466 F.3d 563, 569–70 (7th Cir. 2006) [Christian convert from Morocco could not establish that Moroccan government would not protect him as Moroccan law is not based upon Sharia law]; *Firmansjah v. Gonzales,* 424 F.3d 598, 604–07 (7th Cir. 2005) [upholding denial of withholding for Catholic Indonesian woman of Chinese decent, who studied in U.S.]; *Mitreva v. Gonzales,* 417 F.3d 761 (7th Cir. 2005) [upholding denial of asylum to Roma from Bulgaria]; *Ahmed v. Ashcroft,* 348 F.3d 611 (7th Cir. 2003) [former member of Algerian military and police force could not provide substantial evidence that he had suffered or will suffer persecution]; *Sivaainkaran v. INS*, 972 F.2d 161, 163 (7th Cir. 1992).

(8) *Eighth Circuit—Miah v. Mukasey,* 519 F.3d 784 (8th Cir. 2008) [evidence did not compel reversal of IJ's denial of asylum, withholding, and CAT from applicant from Bangladesh]; *Zacarias-Velasquez v. Mukasey,* 509 F.3d 429 (8th Cir. 2007) [Guatemalan who served in civil patrol and was detained and threatened by guerrillas]; *Bartolo-Diego v. Gonzales,* 490 F.3d 1024 (8th Cir. 2007) [Guatemalan who fled guerillas did not establish imputed political opinion for asylum and did not compel withholding or CAT]; *Kebede v. Gonzales,* 481 F.3d 562 (8th Cir. 2007) [Ethiopian who supported AAPO party and was put in jail for two days could not establish past or future persecution]; *Quomsieh v. Gonzales,* 479 F.3d 602 (8th Cir. 2007) [Christian Palestinians could not establish persecution by Muslims]; *Pavlovich v. Gonzales,* 476 F.3d 613 (8th Cir. 2007) [Russian Jew in Latvia denied past persecution, well-founded fear of future persecution, withholding and CAT]; *Flores-Calderon v. Gonzales,* 472 F.3d 1040, 1043–44 (8th Cir. 2007) [substantial evidence did not support asylum for former member of Peruvian Navy who was attacked by persons he speculated were guerrillas and therefore could not demonstrate that claim was related to a protected ground]; *Vonhm v. Gonzales,* 454 F.3d 825 (8th Cir. 2006) [Liberian who feared harm based upon opposition to Charles Taylor could not establish past persecution or well-founded fear of future persecution]; *Suprun v. Gonzales,* 442 F.3d 1078 (8th Cir. 2006) [substantial evidence supported BIA finding that Russian did not suffer past persecution due to his Jewish faith]; *Cao v. Gonzales,* 442 F.3d 657 (8th Cir. 2006) [IJ's denial of Chinese husband's claim for asylum, based on forced abortion and sterilization of wife was supported by substantial evidence]; *Abrha v. Gonzales,* 433 F.3d 1072 (8th Cir. 2006) [Ethiopian failed to establish past or future persecution]; *Gomez v. Gonzales,* 425 F.3d 543 (8th Cir. 2005) [record did not *compel* finding that Guatemalan was beaten by soldiers because of imputed political opinion]; *Salkeld v. Gonzales,* 420 F.3d 804, 808–09 (8th Cir. 2005 [although record contained evidence of fear of persecution based on homosexuality, court could not say it was "so compelling" that the IJ could not have reasonably denied asylum]; *Lorenzo-Gonzales v. Gonzales,* 419 F.3d 754 (8th Cir. 2005) [Guatemalan member of Civil Patrol failed to show past persecution based on one threat to his wife by unidentified armed men and future persecution in light of the DOS reports noting peace accords]; *Yang v. Gonzales,* 413 F.3d 757 (8th Cir. 2005) [vague claims of detention and interrogation for one month upon return to Laos and current political conditions did not support past or future persecution claim]; *Eta-Ndu v. Gonzales,* 411 F.3d 977, 982–86 (8th Cir. 2005) [highly deferential review upholding denial of claim from Cameroon]; *Mompongo v. Gonzales,* 406 F.3d 512 (8th Cir. 2005) [substantial evidence supported IJ's finding that applicant from the Democratic Republic of the Congo would not face persecution notwithstanding his credible testimony]; *Alemu v. Gonzales,* 403 F.3d 572,

575–76 (8th Cir. 2005) [where DOS reports undercut applicant's claim that she faced future persecution because of her Oromos ethnicity and membership in the OLF in Ethiopia, where she remained in the country for years, and where her family remained and live there unharmed, IJ's denial upheld]; *Hassan v. Ashcroft,* 388 F.3d 661, 666–69 (8th Cir. 2004) [substantial evidence supported IJ's denial of relief based on his determination that applicant was not a member of Midgan clan in Somalia and was not persecuted because of his membership if he was a member]; *Mwangi v. Ashcroft,* 388 F.3d 623, 627–28 (8th Cir. 2004) [where applicant offered no proof of her participation in demonstrations in Kenya where she applied for F-1 visa, never mentioned political fears and returned home on three occasions, court upheld denial]; *Molathwa v. Ashcroft,* 390 F.3d 551 (8th Cir. 2004) [Botswanan homosexual who was harassed by police did not prove withholding]; *Zakirov v. Ashcroft,* 384 F.3d 541 (8th Cir. 2004) [person of Tartar nationality returning to Russian Federation]; *Gemechu v. Ashcroft,* 387 F.3d 944, 947–48 (8th Cir. 2004) [failure of Ethiopian to present evidence corroborating his claim and inconsistencies with country conditions reports]; *Ngure v. Ashcroft,* 367 F.3d 975, 989–93 (8th Cir. 2004) [IJ not compelled to find that respondent's prior arrests established persecution]; *Wondmneh v. Ashcroft,* 361 F.3d 1096 (8th Cir. 2004) [Ethiopian who resisted recruitment into Mengistu militia failed to show past persecution or a well-founded fear]; *Menendez-Donis v. Ashcroft,* 360 F.3d 915 (8th Cir. 2004) [politically motivated death threats to the petitioner and her family, followed by the murder of three of her family members and her own gang rape did not establish persecution under the substantial evidence standard]; *Alsheweikh v. INS*, 990 F.2d 1025 (8th Cir. 1993).

(9) *Ninth Circuit—Lolong v. Gonzales,* 484 F.3d 1173, 1178–81 (9th Cir. 2007) (*en banc*) [relying on fears common to Chinese Christian women from Indonesia was insufficient to establish asylum where there was no argument of being targeted individually, and no showing that the government was unable or unwilling to stop persecution in light of DOS reports demonstrating government's commitment to freedom of religion]; *Gu v. Gonzales,* 454 F.3d 1014, 1021–22 (9th Cir. 2006) [upheld denial of asylum where applicant's testimony, although deemed credible, consisted of hearsay evidence by friend as to what would occur to Gu in China if he returned and the statement, because of its limited probative value, cannot compel asylum]; *Zehatye v. Gonzales,* 453 F.3d 1182, 1185–90 (9th Cir. 2006) [substantial evidence supported denial of asylum/withholding for Jehovah's Witness from Eritrea who suffered social ostracism and economic hardship]; *Zhang v. Ashcroft,* 388 F.3d 713, 721–22 (9th Cir. 2004) [although evidence of record compelled reversal on withholding for future persecution of Falun Gong member, the likelihood of future harm amounting to torture was not compelled]; *Marcu v. INS,* 147 F.3d 1078 (9th Cir. 1998); *Abedini v. INS*, 971 F.2d 188, 191 (9th Cir. 1992).

(10) *Tenth Circuit—Tulengkey v. Gonzales,* 425 F.3d 1277 (10th Cir. 2005) [Christians of Chinese descent in Indonesia]; *Kapcia v. INS*, 944 F.2d 702, 707 (10th Cir. 1991);

(11) *Eleventh Circuit—Djonda v. U.S. Att'y Gen.,* 514 F.3d 1168 (11th Cir. 2008) [where applicant from Togo was beaten in prison and received threats from other students, the record did not compel past persecution; nor did record compel future persecution where brother disappeared and students made accurate threats]; *Rodriguez Morales v. U.S. Att'y Gen.,* 488 F.3d 884 (11th Cir. 2007) [evidence did not compel a finding other than FARC persecuted applicant who was a dentist because they wanted his medical services]; *Rivera v. U.S. Att'y Gen.,* 487 F.3d 815, 820–23 (11th Cir. 2007) [finding persecution by FARC in Colombia due to failure to pay "war tax" was not "on account of" political opinion]; *Zheng v. U.S. Att'y Gen.,* 451 F.3d 1287 (11th Cir. 2006) [follower of Falun Gong who was detained for 5 days and required to watch reeducation videos, lost his job, and was subject to periodic searches did not suffer past persecution or establish a well-founded fear of future persecution]; *Silva v. U.S. Att'y Gen.,* 448 F.3d 1229 (11th Cir. 2006) [where Colombian applicant received death threats signed by the FARC while working on a political campaign, received threatening phone calls and was shot at while driving in her car, the evidence did not compel a reversal of the IJ]; *Sepulveda v. U.S. Att'y Gen.,* 401 F.3d 1226, 1231–33 (11th Cir. 2005) [evidence did not compel reversal of IJ's denial in case involving Colombian student opposed to ELN]; *Fahim v. U.S. Att'y*

Gen., 278 F.3d 1216, 1218 (11th Cir. 2002) [affirming BIA denial of withholding and CAT following *Elias-Zacarias* and INA §§242(b)(4)(A)–(B)]; *Mazariegos v. INS,* 241 F.3d 1320, 1323–24 (11th Cir. 2001); *Lorisme v. INS*, 129 F.3d 1441 (11th Cir. 1997); *Perlera-Escobar v. EOIR*, 894 F.2d 1292, 1296 (11th Cir. 1990); *Rasool v. INS*, 758 F.Supp. 188 (S.D.N.Y. 1991).

4.j. Not Applying Elias-Zacarias in Reversing IJ/BIA

(1) *First Circuit—Berhe v. Gonzales,* 464 F.3d 74, 86–87 (1st Cir. 2006) [reversing BIA where the IJ offered two reasons for granting withholding and the BIA addressed only one in reversing the decision]; *Gailius v. INS,* 147 F.3d 34, 44 (1st Cir. 1998); *Cordero-Trejo v. INS*, 40 F.3d 482, 487 (1st Cir. 1994).

(2) *Second Circuit—Gjolaj v. USCIS,* 468 F.3d 140, 143 (2d Cir. 2006) [IJ's finding that there was a lack of connection between applicant's political activities and mistreatment by Albanian police was not supported by substantial evidence]; *Lin v. Gonzales,* 445 F.3d 127, 135–36 (2d Cir. 2006) [IJ's decision that mother of two who fled China to avoid sterilization would not face persecution because there was no evidence that she would get pregnant again was based upon speculation]; *Tian-Yong Chen v. INS,* 359 F.3d 121, 123–30 (2d Cir. 2004) [where IJ overlooked critical evidence of respondent's beating and BIA mistakenly recounted that respondent was not beaten, the decision was vacated and remanded].

(3) *Third Circuit—Sun Wen Chen v. Att'y Gen. of the U.S.*, 491 F.3d 100, 105–09 (3d Cir. 2007) [upholding BIA analysis that spouse qualifies for asylum under *Chevron* but reversing denial of asylum because BIA applied wrong standard in expecting spouse to prove more than a 10% chance of future persecution]; *Cham v. Att'y Gen. of the U.S.,* 445 F.3d 683 (3d Cir. 2006) [IJ's conduct violated due process and deprived Gambian asylum application of a fair hearing where he assumed his application was invalid, nitpicked the application and testimony for inconsistencies and contradictions, prevented applicant from presenting evidence/witnesses, and engaged in conduct that was abusive toward the applicant including preventing him from presenting his testimony by continually interrupting him]; *Lusingo v. Gonzales,* 420 F.3d 193, 199–201 (3d Cir. 2005) [BIA erred in denying asylum to teenager from Tanzania whose disappearance in U.S. became an embarrassment to Tanzanian government]; *Wu v. Ashcroft,* 393 F.3d 418 (3d Cir. 2005) [where IJ failed to explain why it relied on an airport interview to contradict respondent's asylum claim when it found his testimony credible, the court remanded pointing out that conclusion was not "compelled"].

(4) *Seventh Circuit—Gomes v. Gonzales,* 473 F.3d 746 (7th Cir. 2007) [in case involving Christians from Bangladesh who were attacked by Muslims, court reversed IJ's finding that respondents were harassed where evidence clearly demonstrated severe physical abuse and the IJ's overreliance on DOS reports while ignoring specific contradictory testimony]; *Kantoni v. Gonzales,* 461 F.3d 894 (7th Cir. 2006) [reversing asylum denial of Togo woman where IJ erred by considering each alleged incident of persecution in isolation rather than as a pattern]; *Banks v. Gonzales,* 453 F.3d 449, 453–54 (7th Cir. 2006) [IJ erred in ignoring expert testimony supporting persecution claim of Liberian from Krahn tribe by relying on the DOS report and supplying his own expertise]; *Iao v. Gonzales,* 400 F.3d 530 (7th Cir. 2005) [reversing denial of asylum to Falun Gong follower noting the IJ's lack of familiarity with relevant foreign culture, his exaggerated notion of how much people know about their religion, his exaggerated notion of the availability, especially in poor nations, of documentary evidence of religious membership, his insensitivity to translation difficulties, his failure to make clean credibility determinations, and affirmances by the BIA with no opinion or a short, unhelpful, boilerplate opinion]; *Guchshenkov v. Ashcroft,* 366 F.3d 554 (7th Cir. 2004) [reversing IJs in two separate cases where they did not provide reasoned decisions for denying asylum seekers]; *Niam v. Ashcroft,* 354 F.3d 652 (7th Cir. 2004) [reversing IJ without addressing *Elias-Zacarias* on denial of asylum claims where IJ's analysis "was so inadequate as to raise questions of adjudicative competence"]; *Uwase v. Ashcroft,* 349 F.3d 1039 (7th Cir. 2003) [reversing IJ denial of mixed Hutu-Tutsi claim where undue weight was given to lack of corroborating

testimony]; *Begzatowski v. INS,* 278 F.3d 665, 668–69 (7th Cir. 2002) [reversing BIA denial without reference to *Elias-Zacarias* standard].

(5) *Eighth Circuit—Yang v. Gonzales,* 427 F.3d 1117, 1121–22 (8th Cir. 2005) [following *Zheng* and finding that expert affidavit of John Aird was "sufficient to dispute the information in the State Department reports"]; *Zheng v. Gonzales,* 415 F.3d 955, 960–63 (8th Cir. 2005) [overcoming DOS Report that Fujian province was lax in enforcement policy and that children born abroad are not considered violating one-child policy by providing specific and expert testimony].

(6) *Ninth Circuit—Muradin v. Gonzales,* 494 F.3d 1208, 1210 (9th Cir. 2007) [where IJ and BIA failed to address social group claim that applicant was a member of Armenian military, court reversed]; *Ding v. Ashcroft,* 387 F.3d 1131, 1136 (9th Cir. 2004) [IJ reversed in Chinese forced abortion case because credibility finding was based on speculation, conjecture and an inappropriate legal standard]; *Njuguna v. Ashcroft,* 374 F.3d 765 (9th Cir. 2004) [where respondent's testimony was credible and there was no contradictory evidence, the BIA's decision to deny relief on the grounds that testimony was "unsupported and implausible speculation" was not based on substantial evidence]; *Chen v. Ashcroft,* 362 F.3d 611, 620 (9th Cir. 2004) [applying substantial evidence standard, reversing adverse credibility finding based on inconsistencies in minor matters]; *Ghebllawi v. INS*, 28 F.3d 83 (9th Cir. 1994) [*Elias-Zacarias* did not reverse traditional substantial evidence standard and extreme deference should not be accorded BIA/IJ in these cases]; *Stoyanov v. INS,* 149 F.3d 1226 (9th Cir. 1998) [where BIA relied on clear factual error, its decision will be reversed]; *Gailius, supra.* [where IJ/BIA failed to evaluate corroborative documentary evidence, its decision was reversed].

4.k. *Credibility Assessments under Substantial-Evidence Standard*—The IJ's determination as to the applicant's credibility will also be judged under a substantial-evidence test. *See in this part* "Testimonial Evidence," ¶ B.2.g (p. 544), *supra.* Where the IJ makes a negative credibility determination and it is affirmed, the case may still be reversed where there was substantial corroborative evidence supporting the applicant's claim that the IJ failed to consider. *See in this part* "Lack of Credibility Not Always Fatal," ¶ B.2.g(29) (p.560), *supra.* Also an applicant may raise due process issues where, for example, he was not given an opportunity to rebut an adverse credibility determination because an IJ made a positive credibility determination but denied asylum on other grounds and the BIA affirmed based solely on lack of credibility. *Campos-Sanchez v. INS,* 164 F.3d 448 (9th Cir. 1999). However, where the IJ erred in its credibility assessment, the court may still uphold the denial if there is sufficient alternative evidence or an alternate ground for denial. *Chen v. DOJ,* 471 F.3d 315, 332–42 (2d Cir. 2006) [although IJ engaged in improper speculation and his decision contained errors, the court will uphold the decision if there is substantial evidence to support it and the same decision would be made on remand]; *Djouma v. Gonzales,* 429 F.3d 685, 688 (7th Cir. 2005) [although the IJ erred in its credibility determination, there was an alternative ground for denying asylum where applicant failed to prove past or future persecution].

4.l. *Manifestly Contrary to Law Standard*—The ultimate decision to grant asylum to a person who has a well-founded fear is reviewed under the manifestly contrary to law standard. INA §242(b)(4)(D) [the AG's discretionary judgment "whether to grant relief" shall be conclusive "unless manifestly contrary to the law and an abuse of discretion"]; *Huang v. INS,* 436 F.3d 89, 96–102 (2d Cir. 2006) [IJ acted manifestly contrary to law in denying asylum as a matter of discretion where he failed to examine the totality of the circumstances and focused solely on the embellishment of peripheral testimony and the applicant's payment to a smuggler]; *Kalubi v. Ashcroft,* 364 F.3d 1134 (9th Cir. 2004) [BIA should weigh all positive and negative factors in deciding to grant asylum in its discretion but may not make an adverse credibility finding for purposes of discretion when it did not do so when assessing relief]. An IJ should not consider a temporary stay in a third country and should give little weight to a true refugee's use of false documents or false statements to immigration officers when escaping persecution. *Dong v. Gonzales,* 421 F.3d 573, 578–79 (7th Cir. 2005) [quoting *Matter of O-D* and rejecting the use of false documents to enter as a basis to determine lack of credibility because it had no bearing on applicant's forced abortion claim]; *Mamouzian v. Ashcroft,* 390

F.3d 1129, 1138 (9th Cir. 2004) [reversing IJ's denial of asylum and cautioned the IJ in the exercise of his discretion].

4.m. *Application of Incorrect Standard*—If the BIA applies an incorrect legal standard or fails to address the IJ's application of an incorrect standard, the decision will be reversed. *Berhe v. Gonzales,* 464 F.3d 74, 86–87 (1st Cir. 2006) [IJ offered two reasons for granting withholding and the BIA addressed only one in reversing the decision]; *Kamara v. Att'y Gen. of the U.S.,* 420 F.3d 202, 213–15 (3d Cir. 2005) [post-REAL ID, reversing the BIA denial of CAT claim where BIA applied the wrong quantum of proof required for the claim]; *Poradisova v. Gonzales,* 420 F.3d 70, 79–81 (2d Cir. 2005)[IJ applied incorrect legal standards to the treatment of evidence including when corroboration was necessary, when adverse weight should be given to the failure to produce documents, the failure to give weight to persecution claims of friends, and the refusal to treat incidents of persecution cumulatively]; *Stankovic v. INS*, 94 F.3d 1117 (7th Cir. 1996) [decision of BIA was irrational because it had no application to the facts]; *Draganova v. INS*, 82 F.3d 716, 720–21 (7th Cir. 1996) [IJ's statement that applicant must "conclusively" prove a claim is erroneous]; *Hengan v. INS*, 79 F.3d 60, 63–64 (7th Cir. 1996) [where IJ relied on several inappropriate or irrelevant considerations, decision reversed]; *Perkovic v. INS*, 33 F.3d 615, 621 (6th Cir. 1994) [BIA misconstrued statutory definition of refugee in denying ethnic Albanian from Yugoslavia]; *Tarvand v. INS*, 937 F.2d 973, 976–77 (4th Cir. 1991) [when IJ applied wrong asylum standard and BIA failed to correct it, decision reversed]; *Michael v. Slattery*, 852 F.Supp. 211, 217 (S.D.N.Y. 1994) [BIA's incorrect application of clear probability instead of reasonable possibility standard reversed]. However, even if the BIA articulates the correct standard, a case will be remanded if the BIA did not in fact apply it. *Rodriguez v. INS*, 841 F.2d 865 (9th Cir. 1987) [rejecting use by BIA of boiler-plate language]; *Castaneda-Hernandez v. INS*, 826 F.2d 1526, 1530 (6th Cir. 1987). *See also Corado-Rodriguez v. INS*, 828 F.2d 622 (9th Cir. 1987) [in post-*Acosta* decision BIA must clearly delineate findings on each claim]. Finally, court review requires a separate review of withholding requiring "objective evidence" and asylum claim proving fear is "both subjectively genuine and objectively reasonable." *Blanco-Comarribas v. INS*, 830 F.2d 1039 (9th Cir. 1987) [affirming denial of withholding and reversing denial of asylum].

4.n. *Legal Questions Reviewed De Novo*—Review of INS's interpretation of the INA are reviewed *de novo. INS v. Cardoza-Fonseca,* 480 U.S. 421, 446–48 (1987). However, the BIA interpretation is given deference. *INS v. Aguirre-Aguirre,* 526 U.S. 415, 424 (1999); *Al Najjar v. Ashcroft,* 257 F.3d 1262, 1284 (11th Cir. 2001).

4.o. *Pattern and Practice Cases*—The decision of the AO on asylum may also be directly reviewable in federal court but only if it is part of a pattern and practice to deny rights to aliens. *Compare McNary v. HRC, Inc.*, 498 U.S. 479 (1991); *Jean v. Nelson*, 727 F.2d 957, 979 (11th Cir. 1984); *Haitian Refugee Center v. Smith*, 676 F.2d 1023 (5th Cir. 1982), *with Kashani v. Nelson*, 793 F.2d 818 (7th Cir. 1986) *and Chung v. Smith*, 640 F.Supp. 1065 (S.D.N.Y. 1986).

4.p. *Rule under INS v. Ventura*—Federal court review of asylum, withholding or other related claims cannot result in the grant of those claims if the agency previously denied them. "Well established principles of administrative law" require the courts to remand cases to the agency for fact-finding rather than make those determinations at the appellate level. *INS v. Ventura,* 537 U.S. 12, 16 (2002) [reversing the 9th Cir. for addressing changed circumstances in an asylum case where the BIA had not reached the issue]. The Court also determined that it is up to the BIA in the first instance, and not the federal courts, to decide what might constitute a cognizable social group. *Gonzales v. Thomas,* 547 U.S. 183 (2006) [vacating 9th Cir. *en banc* decision that defined a particular social group before giving the BIA the opportunity to determine whether "the members of a family can and do constitute a 'particular social group' within the meaning of the Act"]; *Gonzales v. Tchoukhrova,* 127 S.Ct. 57 (2006) [vacating social group finding of disabled children in light of *Thomas*]. For a detailed discussion regarding remands, *see* Ch. 10, section VI.M (p.1198), *infra*.

4.q. *Judicial Review of CAT Claims*—The review of CAT claims will vary depending upon whether it is for withholding of removal or deferral as the latter involves a criminal conviction which implicates the bar under INA §242(a)(2)(C). Thus, while withholding under CAT may be reviewed under the substantial evidence standard, deferral may only be reviewed for constitutional questions or questions of law. For a detailed discussion, *see* Ch. 10, ¶ IV.A.17 (p.1130), *infra*. *See also in this chapter*, "Convention Against Torture / Deferral of Removal," Part V (p.484), *supra*.

4.r. *Judicial Review of Decisions Regarding Corroboration*—The AG's decision to require corroboration in asylum or other relief from removal may only be reversed if "a reasonable trier of fact is compelled to conclude that such corroborating evidence is unavailable." INA §242(b)(4), 8 U.S.C. §1252(b)(4) (REAL ID Act §101(e)). Although the IJ's corroboration standards set forth in the REAL ID Act are effective only for cases filed on or after May 11, 2005, the federal review provision under INA §242(b)(4) is effective for all final orders concerning asylum, withholding, and other forms of relief or protection from removal issued before, on or after May 11, 2005. REAL ID Act §101(h)(3), 119 Stat. at 305–06; *Hor v. Gonzales,* 421 F.3d 497, 500–01 (7th Cir. 2005) [reversing IJ's corroboration findings because "[a]ll that this (new provision) means is that an immigration judge's determination…is entitled to reasonable deference (but that) the precondition to deference is that the immigration judge explain (unless it is obvious) why he thinks corroborating evidence, if it existed, would have been available to the alien"]; *Accord, Zhang v. Gonzales,* 434 F.3d 993, 998–99 (7th Cir. 2006) [quoting *Hor* and reversing IJ's demand for corroboration]. *But see Chen v. Gonzales,* 434 F.3d 212, 217–20 (3d Cir. 2005) [*post*-REAL ID, upholding the denial of asylum even where the IJ did not make a valid credibility assessment because even a credible applicant may be required to produce corroborative evidence and respondent failed to do so]; *Zheng v. Gonzales,* 417 F.3d 379, 383 n.2 (3d Cir. 2005) [finding that the IJ's requirement to corroborate what may be speculative records is subject to the "compelling" review standard which is "effective immediately" including cases begun before May 11, 2005]. However, the standard may not apply to motions to reopen before the BIA because it applies only to review of a decision by the "trier of fact" (which is the IJ not the BIA) and does not, by its terms, apply to the provision on motions to reopen at INA §240(c)(7), 8 U.S.C. §1229a(c)(7). *Fessehaye v. Gonzales,* 414 F.3d 746, 752–53 (7th Cir. 2005).

XIII. ASYLUM GRANTS AND REVOCATION

A. *Asylum Grant*—When asylum is granted, it is granted for an indefinite period, 8 C.F.R. §208.14(e), 1208.14(e), but it does not convey a right to remain permanently. INA §208(c)(2), 8 U.S.C. §1158(c)(2). The grant of asylum, however, means that as long as asylum is granted, the person cannot be returned to any country. *Andriasian v. INS,* 180 F.3d 1033, 1042 n.14 (9th Cir. 1999) [if a petitioner is granted asylum, then the persecution that he would face is no longer relevant–because he may not be deported to that country or any other]. Under INA §208(c)(2) and the regulations, a person granted asylum may have his asylum or withholding of removal revoked under certain circumstances by the AO, 8 C.F.R. §§208.24(a) & (b), 1208.24(a) & (b), or the IJ. 8 C.F.R. §§208.24(f), 1208.24(f).

1. *Spouse and Children of Asylee*—The spouse or children of the principal asylee may also be granted asylum if accompanying or following to join the principal. INA §208(b)(3), 8 U.S.C. §1158(b)(3), 8 C.F.R. §§208.21(a), (d) 1208.21(a), (d). The relationship must have existed at the time the principal's asylum was approved, except for children born or adopted after approval. 8 C.F.R. §§208.21(b), 1208.21(b). If an asylee wishes to bring his spouse and children to the U.S. he may do so by filing an I-730 application with the Nebraska Service Center within 2 years of the asylum grant. The agency can extend the 2-year period for humanitarian reasons. 8 C.F.R. §208.21(c). If approved, USCIS will forward the approved I-730 to the Embassy in the jurisdiction where the family is located. 8 C.F.R. §§208.21(d), 1208.21(d). If the spouse or child is in U.S. but not included in principal's application, the principal must file I-730 with the NSC within 2 years. 8 C.F.R. §§208.21(c), 1208.21(c). A child who turns 21 during the course of the I-730 application period or after s/he has arrived in the U.S. will continue to be classified as a child if s/he is unmarried and was under 21 *at the time the principal parent filed the I-589.* INA §208(b)(3)(B), 8 U.S.C. §1158(b)(3)(B); Memo, Langlois, Asylum Office, HQIAO 120/12.9 (Aug. 7, 2002), *published on* AILA InfoNet at Doc. No 02090531 (Sept. 5, 2002). The after-acquired spouse and children of the principal are not eligible to accompany or follow to join. Because the review of a denial of an I-730 is not part of a final order of removal, any action seeking review must be brought in the district court. *Nnadika v. Att'y Gen. of the U.S.,* 484 F.3d 626 (3d Cir. 2007) [remanding a

claim for injunctive and declaratory relief seeking review of a denied I-730 to the district court]. DOJ regulations require that a person denied asylum as a matter of discretion but granted withholding should have his application reconsidered because it precludes spouses and children from joining him. Factors to consider are the reasons for the denial and reasonable alternatives available to the applicant such as reunification with his family in a third country. 8 C.F.R. §§208.16(e), 1208.16(e). *Huang v. INS*, 436 F.3d 89, 96–102 (2d Cir. 2006) [IJ acted manifestly contrary to law under INA §242(b)(4)(D) in denying asylum as a matter of discretion where he failed to examine the totality of the circumstances and focused solely on the embellishment of peripheral testimony and the applicant's payment to a smuggler].

2. *Withholding Does Not Result In Derivative Benefits*— Some courts have now held that withholding, unlike asylum, does not grant derivative benefits to family members so that a grant of withholding to a husband or parent does not give derivative benefits to the spouse or child. *Arif v. Mukasey,* 509 F.3d 677, 680–82 (5th Cir. 2007) [wife of withholding applicant does not obtain a derivative status and 8 C.F.R. §1208.16(e) supports that reading of the statute]; *Delgado v. U.S. Att'y Gen.,* 487 F.3d 855, 862 (11th Cir. 2007) [where Venezuelan father and son were granted withholding, mother could not obtain withholding because the statute does not provide for derivative benefits as does asylum].

3. *Immediate Employment*—A person granted asylum is immediately authorized for employment. INA §208(c)(1)(B), 8 C.F.R. §§208.7, 1208.7; *Ngwanyia v. Ashcroft*, 302 F.Supp.2d 1076, 1084–89 (D. Minn. 2004) [ordering DHS to comply with Border Security Act, PL 107-173, 116 Stat. 543 (May 14, 2002), requiring immediate grant of employment authorization upon grant of asylum]. An asylee no longer needs to wait until s/he gets an EAD card to obtain a Social Security card and persons granted asylum or refugee status can now receive unrestricted Social Security cards. Memo, Clay-Thompson, Acting Director ORR, HHS, State Letter #01-09 (Apr. 5, 2001), reprinted in 78 No. 19 *Interpreter Releases* 812, 819–23 (May 14, 2001); Memo, Limon, Director ORR, HHS, State Letter #00-14 (July 12, 2000), reprinted in 78 No. 19 *Interpreter Releases* 812, 824–25 (May 14, 2001).

4. *Refugee Travel Document*—A person granted refugee status under INA §207 or asylum under INA §208 may obtain a refugee travel document for one year's duration by filing an I-131 application. INA §208(c)(1)(C), 8 U.S.C. §1158(c)(1)(C), 8 C.F.R. §223.2. A returning asylee with an expired refugee travel document is inadmissible and may not resume her status unless she applies for and is granted a refugee travel document under 8 C.F.R. §223.2(b)(2)(ii) at a U.S. Consulate or port of entry, granted parole under INA §212(d)(5) or granted refugee status upon a new application at the border. Memo, Cooper, G.C., HXCOU90/15-P (c. Sept. 2000), *reprinted in* 77 No. 37 *Interpreter Releases* 1384, 1391–98 (Sept. 25, 2000). If inadmissible, INS may terminate asylum and initiate removal proceedings. 8 C.F.R. §§208.24(f), 1208.24(f). However, the "alien's lack of an advance parole document or his inadmissibility to the United States created by the lack of a valid refugee travel document should be viewed in light of the compelling circumstances that led to the alien's status as a refugee or asylee. Accordingly, it is often appropriate for INS to facilitate the return of refugees and asylees to the United States when they are stranded overseas due to the absence or expiration of a refugee travel document." Memo, Cooper (HXCOU90/15-P), *supra.* In determining parole, the DD should consider factors including: (1) compelling circumstances that led to the original refugee/asylum approval; (2) the circumstances surrounding the expiration or failure to obtain the refugee travel document; (3) whether the person returned to his or her country and why; (4) family reunification; and (5) the person's current circumstances. *Id.* A person's return to his country of origin after obtaining asylum/refugee status may endanger his continued status because he may be considered to have "voluntarily re-availed himself of the protection of his country of nationality." 1951 Convention Relating to the Status of Refugees, Article 1(C)(1). A return to the country of origin is not, however, a *per se* ground to revoke asylum/refugee status. Rather "a fact-specific investigation is necessary." Memo, Cooper (HXCOU90/15-P), *supra.*

B. *Revocation of Asylum*—An asylee may lose his or her status if: (1) there is fraud in the application; (2) the application is filed after Apr. 1, 1997 and the person meets one of the categories of ineligibility specified in INA §208(c)(2), or (3) the application was filed before Apr. 1, 1997 and the applicant no longer has a well-founded fear because there are changed conditions in the country of origin. 8 C.F.R. §§208.24, 1208.24. Under USCIS guidelines AOs may seek to terminate affirmative grants of asylum where: (1) the asylee no longer meets the definition of refugee due to changed circumstances; (2) the grounds traditionally for denial, such as being a persecutor or firmly resettled, are now in existence; (3) the asylee acquires a new nationality; or (4) the asylee travels back to the country of persecution and avails himself of the country's protection including the possibility of obtaining residency. *Affirmative Asylum Procedures Manual* (Nov. 2007), *www.uscis.gov/files/nativedocuments/AffrmAsyManFNL.pdf*; "Traveling Outside the United States as an Asylum Applicant, an Asylee or a Lawful Permanent Resident Who Obtained Such Status Based on Asylum Status," USCIS (Jan. 4, 2007) *found at www.uscis.gov/files/pressrelease/AsylumTravel122706FS.pdf*; *Diallo v. Gonzales,* 447 F.3d 1274, 1279–80 (10th Cir. 2006) [where asylee failed to disclose on asylum application other name he used to previously apply for asylum, there was sufficient basis to revoke asylum status]. In a revocation proceeding, the burden is on the government by a preponderance of the evidence to prove the ground of revocation. *Ntangsi v. Gonzales,* 475 F.3d 1007 (8th Cir. 2007) [IJ reversed where he revoked Cameroonian's asylum status by impermissibly placing burden on asylee to demonstrate she had not committed fraud]; *Hailemichael v. Gonzales,* 454 F.3d 878, 884–86 (8th Cir. 2006) [where DHS submitted documents in motion to reopen that contradicted asylee's testimony regarding her husband's incarceration but no evidence was produced to show she knew that fact or otherwise concealed material facts with knowledge of their falsity, court reversed termination of asylum].

C. *Revocation of Withholding*—A person granted withholding may also have her status revoked if: (1) s/he no longer fears persecution because conditions have changed in his or her country; (2) there is fraud in the application; or (3) s/he falls under a ground that would have initially barred withholding (*e.g.*, serious nonpolitical crime). If such action is taken by the AO, the applicant's spouse and children also have their status terminated, although they may be able to reassert it before the IJ. 8 C.F.R. §§208.24(d), 1208.24(d). If the principal is terminated, employment authorization is also terminated. 8 C.F.R. §208.24(c).

XIV. ADJUSTMENT OF STATUS AND SPECIAL LEGISLATION

A. *Generally*—A person granted refugee status or asylum may apply for permanent residence in the U.S. after one year. The one year begins from the time the person is admitted as a refugee, the date the person receives a final grant of asylum, or, if in the U.S., the date the I-730 was approved. Memo, Yates, Deputy Ex. Assoc. Comm. Office of Field Operations, HQ 70/20.11, 70/6.1.5., 70/6.1.6, 70/34.2 (May 15, 2000), *reprinted in* 77 No. 24 *Interpreter Releases* 832, 837–48 (June 26, 2000). Refugees and asylees adjust under INA §209, not §245, and they do not need to leave the U.S. to adjust even if they initially entered without inspection. Derivative family members may adjust even where principal refugee has not or will not. Memo Gibson, Acting Assoc. Comm., Examinations, CO 209-P (Oct. 4, 1985), *reprinted in* 62 *Interpreter Releases* 1030–31 (Oct. 25, 1985). Congress has separately addressed the problem of children who "age-out" during the adjustment process. Under the Child Status Protection Act (CSPA), as long as the child is unmarried, was under 21 at the time the principal parent "applied for asylum," and was listed as a child, s/he "shall continue to be classified as a child for purposes" of asylum/refugee processing, I-730 and adjustment. INA §208(b)(3)(B), 8 U.S.C. §1158(b)(3)(B). "Applied for asylum" means that USCIS received the I-589 before the child turned 21. Memo, Yates, Assoc. Dir. Operations, USCIS, HQOPRD 70/6.1 (Aug. 17, 2004), *published on* AILA InfoNet at Doc. No. 04091561; Memo, Langlois, Asylum Office, HQIAO 120/12.9 (Aug. 7, 2002), *published on* AILA InfoNet at Doc. No 02090531 (Sept. 5, 2002). However, a child who later marries is ineligible for CSPA benefits. *Akhtar v. Gonzales,* 406 F.3d 399, 406–08 (6th Cir. 2005) [rejecting equal protection and due process challenges where child was married because his mother was granted asylum before the effective date of CSPA]. A refugee placed in removal proceedings may apply for AOS under INA §209 and may apply for a waiver of inadmissibility under INA §209(c). *Matter of H-N-,* 22 I&N Dec. 1039 (BIA 1999); 8 C.F.R. §§209.2, 1209.2. INA §212(e) is not a bar to obtaining residency. Memo, Yates (Aug. 17, 2004), *supra.*

1. *Parolee Adjustment*—Under special legislation, certain persons who were paroled into the U.S. may also seek residence after one year. *See* Indochinese Refugee Adjustment Act, PL 95-145, Title 1; the Hungarian Refugee Act, PL 85-559, 72 Stat. 419; the Cuban Refugee Adjustment Act of 1966, PL 89-732; the Cuban-Haitian Adjustment Act, PL 99-603, 100 Stat. 3359; and the Nicaraguan Adjustment and Central American Relief Act, PL 105-100, 111 Stat. 2160, Tit. II, Div. A (Nov. 19, 1997) as amended by PL 105-139, 111 Stat. 2644 (Dec. 2, 1997).

2. *Cuban Refugee Adjustment*—Only the Cuban Refugee Adjustment Act is open-ended and provides no cutoff date for applicants. Under the Act, any native or citizen of Cuba or the immediate relative of any Cuban native or citizen (including after-acquired spouses and children) can apply for permanent residence in the U.S. one year after he or she has been inspected, admitted or paroled into the country. A temporary absence outside the U.S. during the one-year period does not interrupt the time period as long as the person had no intention of abandoning his or her residence and is readmitted or paroled upon return. 8 C.F.R. §245.2(a)(4)(iii). The spouse or child of the Cuban need not be a native or citizen of Cuba as long as s/he resides with the Cuban. *Gonzalez v. McNary*, 980 F.2d 1418 (11th Cir. 1993) [where Cuban native died during pendency of application, spouse and child had no right to residency, because they were not residing with him]. A battered spouse/child or one subject to extreme cruelty need not reside with the Cuban spouse/parent to petition. Also a battered spouse may self-petition for 2 years after the termination of the marriage if there is a demonstrated connection between the termination of the marriage and the battering or extreme cruelty by the Cuban spouse. PL 109-162, 119 Stat. 2960 (Jan. 5, 2006) §823(a) of the Violence Against Women and Department of Justice Reauthorization Act. Even in the absence of any claim of abuse, the Cuban Adjustment Act *permits a self-petition for two years after the Cuban spouse dies* as long as the non-Cuban resided with the Cuban spouse. *Id.* However, a spouse is not eligible for Cuban Adjustment if his or her Cuban spouse was not paroled, or inspected and admitted as a nonimmigrant. *Matter of* ____ (AAO Feb. 18, 2005), 2005 WL 2101359 [Cuban husband who entered U.S. as refugee and was therefore not paroled, or inspected and admitted as an NIV, could not transmit Cuban adjustment benefits to non-Cuban spouse]. The spouse is also not eligible if his or her Cuban spouse is now a USC.

There is no bar for Cubans to obtain the benefit of the Act even if they have no fear of returning to Cuba and would not qualify for asylum. For example, a Cuban native or citizen who enters the U.S. from Venezuela on a B-2 (tourist) visa can become an LPR, without proving fear of persecution, if he simply can remain in the U.S. for one year because he was inspected and admitted as an NIV. A Cuban native or citizen may even adjust after entering under the VWP. *In re* A76 940 152 (AAO Aug 10, 2000), *reported in* 77 No. 34 *Interpreter Releases* 1291, 1292 (Sept. 1, 2000). A Cuban born in, or native to, Cuba may also adjust even if s/he entered the U.S. as a citizen of another country. *Matter of* ___ (AAO Dec. 16, 2002), *reported in* 80 No. 5 *Interpreter Releases* 156 (Feb. 3, 2003) [Cuban national who entered on Venezuelan passport as Venezuelan citizen is eligible for AOS]. The applicant, however, must provide proof of Cuban citizenship but USCIS will now recognize a Cuban birth certificate or a Cuban consulate certificate of birth abroad as meeting the necessary burden of proof of Cuban citizenship. *Matter of Vazquez,* (AAO July 31, 2007) [overruled *Matter of Buschini* (AAO June 30, 2006) and the Library of Congress' determination that Cuban citizenship has a residency requirement and finding that "a Cuban consular certificate indicating that a person was born abroad to parents at least one of whom was a Cuban citizen at the time of the person's birth" meets the burden of establishing Cuban residency]. INS Guidelines have also clarified that a Cuban who enters EWI may still qualify for adjustment by obtaining a parole. Memo, Meissner, Comm. "Eligibility for Permanent Residence Under the Cuban Adjustment Act Despite Having Arrived at a Place Other than a Designated Port of Entry" HQCOU 120/17-P (Apr. 19, 1999), *reprinted in* 76 No. 17 *Interpreter Releases* 676, 684–90 (May 3, 1999) [EWI eligible if he surrenders to the Service and the Service paroles him pending a final determination or an IJ releases him under §236]. *See also* Memo, Renaud, Chief, Field Operations, USCIS (Mar. 4, 2008), *published on* AILA InfoNet at Doc. No. 08040132. In addition, an applicant for adjustment may apply to the IJ for adjustment even if he is an arriving alien. *Matter of Artigas,* 23 I&N Dec. 99 (BIA 2001). The effective date of the acquisition of LPR status is 30 months prior to the grant of residency. This roll back is for the principal applicant and his or her immediate family members who also adjust. For purposes of former INA §212(c) LPR status was measured from the beginning of the 30-month period. *Matter of Rivera-Rioseco*, 19 I&N Dec. 833 (BIA 1988). Presumably, the same would apply for cancellation of removal. The Cuban Refugee Adjustment Act has been conditionally repealed upon the determination by the President under §203(c)(3) of PL 104-114 (Cuban Liberty and Democratic Solidarity Act) that a democratically elected government in Cuba is in power. IIRIRA §606. But it shall not apply to those whose applications for adjustment are pending on the date of repeal. The Nicaraguan Adjustment and Central American Relief Act, PL 105-100, 111 Stat. 2160, Tit. II, Div. A (Nov. 19, 1997) as amended by PL 105-139, 111 Stat. 2644 (Dec. 2, 1997) provides for AOS for Cubans, their spouses, children, *and* sons and daughters who were continuously physically present in U.S. since Dec. 1, 1995. The Act also provides for AOS for Nicaraguans who were continuously physically present since Dec. 1, 1995.

In addition to the Cuban Adjustment Act, there is also a special lottery program for Cuba, and Cubans who are beneficiaries of approved family-based petitions who are not immediate relatives may now be paroled into the U.S. while awaiting their priority dates. Cuban Family Reunification Parole Program, 72 Fed. Reg. 65588 (Nov. 21, 2007); *See also* CIS Fact Sheets and FAQs at 12 No. 24 *Bender's Immigration Bulletin* 1815, 1857–64 (Dec. 15, 2007).

B. *Adjustment of Status*

1. *Refugees*—A refugee who is admitted into the U.S. can adjust his or her status to LPR after one year of continuous physical presence. INA §209(a)(1), 8 U.S.C. §1159(a)(1), 8 C.F.R. §§209.1, 1209.1. Spouses and children may be admitted and adjusted even if not refugees themselves. INA §207(c)(2), 8 U.S.C. §1157(c)(2).

1.a. *Inadmissibility*—Certain grounds of inadmissibility are automatically waived for refugees and asylees: INA §212(a)(4) [public charge]; §212(a)(5) [labor certification]; and §212(a)(7)(A) [immigrant documentation requirement]. Certain grounds cannot be waived: INA §212(a)(2)(C) [drug trafficking]; and §§212(a)(3)(A)–(C) and (E) [security, terrorist, foreign policy and Nazi persecutor grounds]. All other grounds of inadmissibility, including criminal grounds, may be waived under INA §209(c). However, a waiver for serious ("violent or dangerous") crimes will almost never be granted absent extraordinary circumstances such as those involving national security or foreign policy considerations or where the denial would result in exceptional and extremely unusual hardship. *Matter of Jean,* 23 I&N Dec. 373, 381–84 (AG 2002), *aff'd, Jean v. Gonzales,* 452 F.3d 392, 396–98 (5th Cir. 2006) [denying adjustment to person convicted of second degree manslaughter in the death of a baby and reversing BIA where the focus was on the family's hardship without considering the nature of the criminal offense; on appeal court rejected argument that AG's standard was *ultra vires*]; *Ali v. Achim,* 468 F.3d 462, 465–67 (7th Cir. 2006) *cert. dismissed* 128 S.Ct. 828 (2007) [AG did not exceed his authority when he articulated the heightened waiver standard in *Matter of Jean*]. *But see Rivas-Gomez v. Gonzales,* 441 F.3d 1072, 1074–79 (9th Cir. 2006) [reversing IJ for denying §209(c) waiver where respondent was convicted of an aggravated felony (statutory rape) and IJ determined there was insufficient hardship without first determining that the crime was a violent or dangerous felony].

1.b. *Waiver Application*—An application for a waiver is typically filed on Form I-602. USCIS policy provides that except for §212(a)(1) [health related grounds] with its own unique waiver under §212(g), an adjudicator may grant a waiver *without* an I-602 "provided that USCIS records and other information available to the adjudicator contain sufficient information to assess eligibility for the waiver and there is no evidence to suggest that negative factors would adversely impact the exercise of discretion to grant a waiver." Memo, Aytes, Acting Dir. Operations, USCIS, HQPRD 70/23.10 (Oct. 31, 2005), *published on* AILA InfoNet at Doc. No. 05110962; AFM at 41.6.

2. *Asylees*—There is no longer a cap on adjustment for persons who are asylees or refugees. PL 109-13, 119 Stat. 231 (May 11, 2005), Div. B, "REAL ID Act of 2005," §101(g). For an asylee to adjust his status he must: (1) apply for adjustment; (2) be physically present in the U.S. for at least one year after being granted asylum; (3) continue to be a refugee within the meaning of INA §101(a)(42); (4) not be firmly resettled in another country; and (5) be admissible to the U.S. as an immigrant under the Act upon examination for adjustment. The grounds of inadmissibility, the waivers, and the procedures for a waiver are the same as stated for refugees, above. *See also* 8 C.F.R. §§209.2(b), 1209.2(b); AFM at 41.6.

2.a. *Spouse and Children*—If the asylee's spouse or children (under 21) are not included in the principal's asylum application, they can still be accorded derivative asylum status. Although USCIS maintains that the spousal or child relationship had to pre-date the grant of asylum or refugee status, the regulation provides no such limitation. 8 C.F.R. §209.2(a)(1)(iii); *but see* Memo, Carmichael, Assoc. Comm., Examinations, "Asylum Procedures and Adjustment of Status," CO 208-P (May 18, 1984), *reprinted in* 61 *Interpreter Releases* 522–28 (June 29,

1984). They may also adjust independent of the principal as long as the principal continues to meet the refugee definition and the spouses remain married. Memo, Gibson, Acting Assoc. Comm. Examination, INS CO-209-P (Oct. 4, 1985), *reprinted in* 62 *Interpreter* Releases 1030-31 (Oct. 25, 1985).

2.b. *Divorce and Continuing Right to Adjustment*—If the parties are divorced or the principal dies before final adjustment, the spouse is ineligible to adjust status through the principal. Legal Opinion, Virtue, CO 209(b) (July 27, 1989). However, s/he does not lose her asylum status. In order not to remain in limbo s/he may seek to adjust by filing her own I-589, have it approved *nunc pro tunc* to the date her original derivative asylum was granted (or their I-730 was approved) and then file her own adjustment application. *Affirmative Asylum Procedures Manual*, Office of International Affairs, Asylum Division, Affirmative Asylum Process at pp. 71-74 (Feb. 2003). If the spouse is from the same country as the principal, the USCIS will normally grant the asylum application. *Id.* The same is true for children who have aged-out and do not qualify for the Child Status Protection Act or where the parent dies.

2.c. *Aged-Out Children and CSPA*—INA §208(b)(3)(B), 8 U.S.C. §1158(b)(3)(B). A child who is under 21 *and listed* on their parents' asylum (I-589) or refugee (I-590) applications on the date the asylum application is received by USCIS or the refugee application is filed with USCIS (*i.e.*, interviewed by USCIS) will continue to be classified as a child for purposes of the asylum/refugee determination, the I-730 petition and the AOS application under INA §209. Memo, Yates, Assoc. Dir. Operations, USCIS, HQOPRD 70/6.1 (Aug. 17, 2004), *published on* AILA InfoNet at Doc. No. 04091561.

3. *Procedures*— An application for adjustment by a refugee or an asylee is filed on I-485 at the service center designated by the DHS. 8 C.F.R. §§209.1(b), 209.2(c), 1209.1(b), 1209.2(c). If political conditions change during the pendency of the adjustment application, so that the person no longer fears persecution, adjustment may be denied. The denial of an application for adjustment is not appealable. The applicant does have the right, however, to renew the application in removal proceedings. 8 C.F.R. §§209.2(c), 1209.2(c). A person granted asylum may submit a written request to have his family members join him. In his discretion, the AG may waive for asylees and refugees all grounds of inadmissibility under INA §212(a) except §212(a)(2)(C) or (3)(A), (B), (C), or (E) if it is for humanitarian purposes, to ensure family unity, or in the public's interest. INA §209. Waivers are filed on Form I-602.

4. *Travel*—During the pendency of an application under INA §209 an asylee may travel abroad. Letter, Combs, Asst. Comm. CORAP (Dec. 20, 1988), *reprinted in* 66 *Interpreter Releases* 100, 116–17 (Jan. 23, 1989). If s/he travels abroad and is inadmissible because the refugee travel document expired or one was not obtained, s/he may still adjust her status if paroled into the U.S. INA §209(b); Memo, Cooper, Gen. Counsel, HXCOU90/15-P, *reprinted in* 77 No. 37 *Interpreter Releases* 1384, 1391–98 (Sept. 25, 2000). Departure without advance parole of an asylee/refugee while their adjustment application is pending is *not* an abandonment of the application because adjustment is governed by 8 C.F.R. §§209.1(a)(1) & (2), 1209.1(a)(1) & (2) and not by §§245.2(a)(4)(ii), 1245.2(a)(4)(ii). Memo, Cooper (Sept. 25, 2000), *supra.*

5. *Effect of Grant*—UNHCR advises that the grant of LPR status to a refugee or asylee does not end the individual's status as a refugee or asylee. Letter, Painter, Senior Protection Officer, UNHCR (Feb. 28, 2003), *reprinted in* 80 No. 11 *Interpreter Releases* 413–14, 423–29 (Mar. 17, 2003).

6. *Removal of LPRs Who Held Asylum or Refugee Status*—The BIA has held that a refugee who adjusts status and becomes an LPR may be placed in removal proceedings without first terminating refugee status. *Matter of Smriko,* 23 I&N Dec. 836 (BIA 2005). *See also Vong Xiong v. Gonzales,* 484 F.3d 530, 533–34 (8th Cir. 2007) [followed BIA and 9th Cir.]; *Gutnik v Gonzales,* 469 F.3d 683, 688–92 (7th Cir. 2006) [agreed with streamlined decision of one BIA member that refugee status is lost without revoking it when LPR placed in removal proceedings]; *Kaganovich v. Gonzales,* 470 F.3d 894, 897–98 (9th Cir. 2006) [in refugee case, agreeing with the BIA in *Smriko* under *Chevron* deference and as a matter of the plain language of the statute]; *Romanishyn v. Attorney General of the U.S.*, 455 F.3d 175 (3d Cir. 2006) [followed *Smriko* under *Chevron* deference] The Board has further held that once a person who is admitted as a refugee under INA §207 adjusts status and becomes an LPR, s/he can not reapply for adjustment as a refugee/asylee in a subsequent removal hearing or apply for a waiver under INA §209(c). *Matter of S-I-K-,* 24 I&N Dec.

324, 330 (BIA 2007); *Saintha v. Mukasey,* 516 F.3d 243, 251–53 (4th Cir. 2008) [upheld BIA view under *Chevron* deference that refugee could not readjust in IJ proceedings as a refugee/asylee because of INA §209(a)(1)(C)]. Even when a refugee/asylee can adjust, a waiver for serious ("violent or dangerous") crimes will almost never be granted absent extraordinary circumstances such as those involving national security or foreign policy considerations or where the denial would result in exceptional and extremely unusual hardship. *Matter of Jean,* 23 I&N Dec. 373, 381–84 (AG 2002) *affirmed Jean v. Gonzales,* 452 F.3d 392, 396–98 (5th Cir. 2006) [denying adjustment to person convicted of second degree manslaughter in the death of a baby and reversing BIA where the focus was on the family's hardship without considering the nature of the criminal offense; on appeal court rejected argument that AG's standard was *ultra vires*]; *Ali v. Achim,* 468 F.3d 462, 465–67 (7th Cir. 2006) *cert. dismissed* 128 S.Ct. 828 (2007) [AG did not exceed his authority when he articulated the heightened waiver standard in *Matter of Jean*]. *But see Rivas-Gomez v. Gonzales,* 441 F.3d 1072, 1074–79 (9th Cir. 2006) [reversing IJ for denying §209(c) waiver where respondent was convicted of an aggravated felony (statutory rape) and IJ determined there was insufficient hardship without first determining that the crime was a violent or dangerous felony].

XV. REFERENCE MATERIAL AND LEGISLATIVE HISTORY:

Office of the United Nations High Commissioner for Refugees, *Handbook on Procedures and Criteria for Determining Refugee Status* (Geneva 1979)

Office of the United Nations High Commissioner for Refugees, *Collection of International Instruments Concerning Refugees* (Geneva 1979)

Hearings on H.R. Rep. No. 2816, The Refugee Act of 1979, before the Subcommittee on Immigration, Refugees, and International Law of the House of Representatives Committee of the Judiciary, 96th Congress, 1st Session, 26 (1979)

S. Rep. No. 96-256, 96th Congress, 1st Session (1979), Report on the Refugee Act of 1979

H.R. Rep. No. 96-608, 96th Congress, 1st Session (1979), House Report with Additional, Separate and Minority Views of The Refugee Act of 1979

H.R. Conf. Rep. No. 104-828, 104th Cong. 2d Sess. (Sept. 24, 1996), Report on Illegal Immigration Reform and Immigrant Responsibility Act of 1996

Congressional Research Service, Performed at Request of Senate Committee of the Judiciary, 96th Congress, 2d Session, Review of U.S. Refugee Resettlement Programs and Policies (Comm. Print 1980).

INS Master Exhibits on Country Conditions, 58 Fed. Reg. 26165 (Apr. 30, 1993).

CHAPTER 5
NONIMMIGRANT VISAS

CHAPTER 5
NONIMMIGRANT VISAS

I. DISTINGUISHING IMMIGRANTS FROM NONIMMIGRANTS

A. ***In General***—Nonimmigrants, unlike immigrants, enter the U.S. for a temporary period of time and are restricted to the activity consistent with their visas. Unlike immigrants, however, they are less subject to numerical restrictions and more likely to obtain waivers of inadmissibility.

B. ***Nonimmigrants: General Characteristics***

1. Generally nonimmigrants must represent that their stay in the U.S. is temporary

   1.a. Intending Immigrant Problem—A consular officer must determine whether the nonimmigrant actually seeks to enter the U.S. permanently. Under INA §214(b), 8 U.S.C. §1184(b), there is a legal presumption that all persons seeking entry are immigrants. The section explicitly applies to B, E, F, J, M, O-2, P, Q, and TN applicants. Cable, DOS, 04-State-274068 (Dec. 28, 2004), *published on* AILA InfoNet at Doc. No. 05032279. The Immigration Act of 1990, however, exempted H-1 and L categories from INA §214(b); 22 C.F.R. §41.11. Congress has also exempted V visas from the statutory presumption. Cable, 04-State-274068, *supra.* A DOS cable has confirmed the H and L exemption by determining that "even if the [H-1B, H-4, L-1 or L-2] alien has a clearly articulated intention of acquiring permanent residence, the application may not be denied for that reason." Cable, DOS, 91-State-171115, ¶8 (May 24, 1991), *reprinted in* 68 No. 21 *Interpreter Releases* 681–84 (June 3, 1991). Moreover, DHS regulations recognize that the filing of an application for or approval of a labor cert or IV petition or the filing of an AOS application "shall not" be a basis for denying H-1 or L-1 petitions, extensions or C/S to an H-1 or L-1 classification or for the dependent family members. 8 C.F.R. §§214.2(h)(16), (*l*)(16).

   A decision under INA §214(b) is different than a decision of inadmissibility under INA §212(a). A person may be denied a visa under 214(b), even if not inadmissible, if he fails to meet "any one of the specific requirements of the applicable NIV category..." Cable, DOS, 04-State-274068 (Dec. 28, 2004), *published on* AILA InfoNet at Doc. No. 05032279. The applicant must prove to the satisfaction of the consular officer that his "intended activities are consistent with the claimed non-immigrant status." *Id.* Thus, DOS has broadly construed 214(b) not simply as a measure of immigrant intent, but whether the applicant meets the objective criteria to obtain a specific visa.

   In general, an NIV applicant's desire to remain must be distinguished from his or her intent to remain. *Lauvik v. INS*, 910 F.2d 658, 660–61 (9th Cir. 1990) [reversed denial of E-2 where applicant expressed desire to immigrate but did not intend to immigrate if not permitted]. In determining whether a person is likely to return to their home country, consuls are to consider the "long term view" and they are not to consider present short-term emergencies (*e.g.,* conditions in Lebanon, Liberia) in deciding to issue visas from those countries. Minutes, AILA-DOS Liaison Meeting (Oct. 3, 1989), *reprinted in* 9 *AILA Monthly Mailing* 42 (Jan. 1990).

   1.b. Dual Intent Doctrine—Even though a nonimmigrant must demonstrate genuinely that his or her intent is to remain in the U.S. temporarily, s/he may have both a short term intent to leave and a long term intent to remain permanently. This is known as the doctrine of dual intent. *Matter of H-R-*, 7 I&N Dec. 651, 654 (R.C. 1958). In the General Counsel's view, the "mere desire ... to obtain permanent residence in the future does not, by itself, automatically disqualify an alien from admission as a nonimmigrant. *Matter of Hosseinpour,* 15 I&N Dec. 191, 192 (BIA 1975)"; Legal Opinion, Martin, 97-9 (June 25, 1997), *reprinted in* 75 No. 16 *Interpreter Releases* 596, 598–99 (Apr. 27, 1998).

The doctrine of dual intent is recognized by USCIS for H/L and O/P visa categories. 8 C.F.R. §§214.2(h)(16), (*l*)(16), (o)(13), (p)(15). *See also Int'l Auto Exchange, Inc. v. Attorney General*, 643 F.Supp. 616, 618 (D.D.C. 1986) [upholding restrictive interpretation of temporary employment on L-1 but recognizing dual intent doctrine]; *Matter of Hosseinpour*, 15 I&N Dec. 191 (BIA 1975). DOS has determined that if the H-1/L-1 obtained a change of status, the fact that s/he "is the beneficiary of an application for a preference status filed under section 204 or has otherwise sought permanent residence in the United States shall not constitute evidence of an intention to abandon a foreign residence for purposes of obtaining a visa as a nonimmigrant described in subparagraphs (H)(1) or (L) of section 101(a)(15)." Cable, DOS, 91-State-171115, ¶5 (May 24, 1991), *reprinted in* 68 No. 21 *Interpreter Releases* 681–84 (June 3, 1991).

The doctrine of dual intent is also recognized for persons in E status. Letter, Bednarz, HQ 214e-C, 245-C (Oct. 1, 1993), *reprinted in* 70 No. 42 *Interpreter Releases* 1444, 1456–58 (Nov. 1, 1993).

Because dual intent exists for persons in H-1 and L status, and because there is regulatory authority to permit them to do so, persons in any of these categories can file for an extension even *after* she files an application for AOS. 8 C.F.R. §§214.2(h)(16)(i), (*l*)(16)(ii).

Similarly, DOS recognized the doctrine in regard to family members waiting under the family-sponsored second preference. In a letter to Congress, DOS stated that with respect to issuing a NIV to an alien registered on an immigration visa waiting list, whether as the spouse or child of a permanent resident or any other basis, the Department has long recognized the concept of "dual intent." Cable, DOS, 92-State-193038 (June 17, 1992), *reprinted in* 69 No. 27 *Interpreter Releases* 872–73 (July 20, 1992).

The DOS however takes a narrower view with respect to extensions of J-1 status. Although the mere filing of an INA §212(e) waiver application will not disqualify a J-1 physician from extending the period of J-1 status, the adjudication of the waiver by DOS will result in the ineligibility of the J-1 to extend status. Letter, Jin, USIA G.C. (Dec. 18, 1995), *reprinted in* 73 No. 2 *Interpreter Releases* 47, 51 (Jan. 10, 1996)

The dual intent doctrine has also been rejected in the TN context, 8 C.F.R. §214.6(b) [Definition of Temporary Entry]; 63 Fed. Reg. 1331, 1333 (Jan. 9, 1998).

2. Domicile in U.S. by NIVs—A person in B or F status lacks the legal capacity to establish domicile in the U.S. because the status requires that the person have the intent not to abandon a foreign residence. *Toll v. Moreno,* 458 U.S. 1, 14 & n.20, 102 S.Ct. 2977 (1982); *Elkins v. Moreno,* 435 U.S. 647, 665, 98 S.Ct. 1338 (1978); *Gaudin v. Remis,* 379 F.3d 631, 637 (9th Cir. 2004) [parent who entered the U.S. on B-2 status could not relocate to U.S. and therefore her claim under the International Child Abduction Remedies Act is not moot]; *DeQuervain v. Desguin,* 927 So.2d 232 (2d DCA Fla. 2006) [absent LPR status person is nonresident for homestead tax exemption].

3. No Numerical Limitations on Most NIVs—There are no numerical limitations on the number of nonimmigrant visas (NIVs) that may be issued or the number of people with NIVs that may enter the U.S. except as to E-3, H-1B, H-1C, H-2B, Q-2, S, T and U visas. All grounds of exclusion under INA §212(a), 8 U.S.C. §1182(a) (quality restrictions) apply in determining the issuance of a NIV and the entrance of a nonimmigrant. The Secy. of State shall also direct consular officers to discontinue granting NIVs (and IVs) in countries that refuse to accept their deported citizens. INA §243(d), 8 U.S.C. §1253(d).

4. Waivers of Grounds of Inadmissibility—All grounds of inadmissibility under INA [except INA §§212(a)(3)(A)(i)(I), (3)(A)(ii), (3)(A)(iii), (3)(C) and (3)(E)(i),(ii)] can be waived for NIVs under INA §212(d)(3), 8 U.S.C. §1182(d)(3); 22 C.F.R. §40.301(a).

5. State Sponsors of Terrorism—Restrictions on NIVs for persons from countries designated as state sponsors of terrorism. 8 U.S.C. §1735(a). The Secretary of State may not issue a NIV from any country the Secretary of State has determined to be a state sponsor of terrorism under one of several laws (22 U.S.C. §§2371(a), 2780(d)) until he consults with the AG and the heads of other appropriate agencies and determines that such person does not pose a threat to the safety or national security of the U.S.

6. Valid Passport Requirement—NIV applicants need a passport valid for 6 months beyond the time of anticipated stay and a valid nonimmigrant visa or border crossing card. INA §212(a)(7)(B)(i), (ii), 8 U.S.C. §1182(a)(7)(B)(i), (ii); 22 C.F.R. §41.104. This provision can be waived by Secy. of State and AG acting jointly. INA §212(d)(4), 8 U.S.C. §1182(d)(4). The entry and visa requirements for each country are found at DOS, Bureau of Consular Affairs, *Publication 10432,* Mar. 1997, *reprinted in* 75 No. 13 *Interpreter Releases* 472, 490 (Apr. 6, 1998). The U.S., by agreement with certain countries, will allow persons to enter the U.S. even if their passports are not valid for 6 months because those countries have agreed to extend automatically passport validity six months beyond the expiration date of the passports. For a list of the countries which include Argentina, Canada, Colombia, Mexico, the UK, Venezuela and many others *see* 64 Fed. Reg. 14300–01 (Mar. 24, 1999), *reprinted in* 76 No. 12 *Interpreter Releases* 504 (Mar. 29, 1999). An applicant for admission may also have his or her visa in an invalid passport if it is a multiple entry indefinite visa and s/he is in possession of a valid passport. 22 C.F.R. §41.112(b)(3).

7. Barred After Overstay—An NIV holder will not be readmitted into the U.S. if s/he overstays the time authorized in the U.S. on his or her last entry unless s/he obtained a new visa at the consular office in the country of his or her nationality or another consular office if no consular office exists in her country of nationality, or the Secy. of State finds extraordinary circumstances. INA §222(g)(2), 8 U.S.C. §1202(g)(2). This provision applies to persons who first overstayed after Sept. 30, 1996. Memo, Crocetti, Assoc. Comm., Examinations (1997), *reprinted in* 16 *AILA Monthly Mailing* 347 (May 1997). It does not include persons who are out of status or status violators for reasons other than an overstay (*e.g.,* worked without authorization). *Id.* A person whose visa is automatically canceled may apply for an INA §212(d)(4) waiver at the border. IFM at 15.15(a), (k), *reprinted in* 76 No. 6 *Interpreter Releases* 243, 252–56 (Feb. 8, 1999). The section does not apply to: (1) persons on Visa Waiver Program; (2) Canadians without I-94s; (3) persons in parole status; (4) persons who are EWI; and (5) Persons from Mexico who enter without I-94s. Cable, DOS (99-State-105097) (June 7, 1999), *reprinted in* 76 No. 24 *Interpreter Releases* 977–80 (June 28, 1999); Letter, Hrinyak, (HQINS 70/12.1) (Apr. 1, 1999), *published on* AILA InfoNet at Doc. No. 99040191.

8. Only One NIV Status at a Time—A person cannot hold more than one nonimmigrant status at a time. Letter, Weinig, Deputy Asst. Comm., Adjudications, CO 214h-C, 214e-C (Nov. 28, 1989), *reprinted in* 67 No. 2 *Interpreter Releases* 39, 53 (Jan. 8, 1990).

9. Visa validity and change in employment—A visa remains valid in H, L, O, or P classifications during its validity period regardless of a change in the beneficiary's employer. As long as the beneficiary remains in the same NIV classification, the visa is considered valid. Memo, Aytes, Assoc. Comm. (July 8, 1997), *reprinted in* 74 No. 36 *Interpreter Releases* 1459 (Sept. 22, 1997). Although this does not mean the employee is authorized to work for another employer, it does mean if he changes employment and then reconsiders and returns to original employer the visa would still be valid.

II. PROCEDURES

A. *Consular and Immigration Inspection*

1. Consular Review—There are two levels of scrutiny for persons seeking to enter the U.S. as nonimmigrants. First, the applicant must seek and obtain a visa at a U.S. embassy or consulate unless s/he is visa exempt. The applicant must submit an electronic DS-160 form unless directed by a consular officer to submit the written DS-156. 22 C.F.R. §41.103(a). All males between the ages of 16 and 45, except those applying as A, G and NATO applicants, are required to fill out a DS-157 post-Sept 11, 2001. Cable, DOS, 02-State-6020 (Jan. 11, 2002), *reprinted in* 79 No. 4 *Interpreter Releases* 118–19 (Jan. 21, 2002). [Note: Some posts require the DS-157 for female applicants as well]. Male applicants in A-3, G-5 and NATO-7 categories are not exempt and must also fill out a DS-157 form. Cable, DOS, 02-State-7129 (Jan. 12, 2002), *published on* AILA InfoNet at Doc. No. 02011531 (Jan 12, 2002).

   1.a. BIOVISA Program—Photos and fingerprints are now required for each visa applicant under what the DOS calls the BIOVISA (Biometric Visa) Program. This program is a "partner program" of US-VISIT. 69 Fed. Reg. 78515 (Dec. 30, 2004).Under the program there is strict compliance with the requirement that all visa applicants must have their fingerprints taken unless they are physically unable to appear at the post for medical reasons or are physically unable to have their prints taken. There are no other exceptions. Cable, DOS, 05-State-00191641 (Oct. 17, 2005), *published on* AILA InfoNet at Doc. No. 06011870. If a visa is issued, the Secretary of State must establish an electronic version of the visa file so that it will be available to DHS officers at the ports of entry. INA §221(a)(2), 8 U.S.C. §1201(a)(2).

1.b. Personal Appearance—Generally, an applicant is required to go to the consular office having jurisdiction over her place of residence. 22 C.F.R. §41.101. Although a person is generally required to seek the visa in his country of residence, there may be circumstances where NIV-posts are closed and DOS will direct applicants to other posts. Memo, DOS (Apr. 2002), *reprinted in* 79 No. 17 *Interpreter Releases* 596–98 (Apr. 22, 2002). In addition, all consular posts can issue NIVs. 9 FAM 41.101 N.2. If an NIV holder overstays, s/he *must* return to the consular office in the country of her nationality unless extraordinary circumstances are found to exist by the Secy. of State. If no consular office exists in the country of nationality, the Secy. of State shall designate a consular post. INA §222(g)(2). An applicant who decides to get his visa at a post in another country and needs a duplicate approval sent to that post must submit an I-824 to USCIS. 8 C.F.R. §103.5b. INA §222(h) now requires everyone between 14 and 79 to submit to an in person interview before a consular officer when requesting an NIV. The provision may be waived by the consular officer for: (1) persons under 14; (2) persons over 79; (3) A, G and NATO visa holders; (4) a person who is granted a diplomatic or official visa on a diplomatic or official passport; or (5) a person who is seeking a new biometric visa not more than 12 months after her prior visa expired in the same visa classification and is seeking it from the consular post in the country of her residence unless there is an indication of visa ineligibility or noncompliance with U.S. immigration laws or regulations. 22 C.F.R. §§41.102(b)(1)–(5). The statute also provides a waiver for C-3s not contained in the regulation. Alternatively, the consular officer can waive the requirement if it is in the national interest or there are unusual or emergent circumstances. 22 C.F.R. §41.102(b)(6). However, neither a consular officer nor the Deputy Assistant Secretary of State may waive the requirement of an in-person interview unless it is for an A, G, NATO, or diplomatic or official visa if the person: (1) is not a national or resident of the country where the consulate is located; (2) was previously refused a visa, is listed in CLASS, or otherwise requires a Security Advisory Opinion unless the refusal was subsequently overcome or inadmissibility was waived; *or* (3) is a national of a country officially designated as a state sponsor of terrorism; (4) is identified as a member of a group or sector the Secy. of State determines possess a substantial risk of submitting inaccurate information to obtain the visa, has a higher rate of visa denials than average or poses a security threat to the United States. 22 C.F.R. §41.102(d).

1.c. DHS Involvement In Consular Processing—In light of the establishment of the Department of Homeland Security (DHS) changes have been made in consular processing. Under §428 of the Homeland Security Act of 2002, PL 107-296, 116 Stat. 2135 (Nov. 25, 2002), 6 U.S.C. §236, DHS has now been given final responsibility for regulatory visa guidance in most areas of NIVs as well as IVs. Under a MOU between DOS and DHS, the Department of Homeland Security: will now be responsible for all visa guidance regarding (1) waivers except INA §§212(d)(4)(B) and 212(*l*) waivers; (2) NIVs except A, C (transits to the UN), E (determining qualifying treaties and substantiality question), G, I, J (designated qualifying programs) visas; and (3) inadmissibility except certain grounds relating to Presidential proclamations under INA §212(f) and certain terrorist and religious freedom violator grounds and (4) evidentiary criteria to establish eligibility for a visa, for admissibility and for classification of IVs and NIVs. Memorandum of Understanding Between the Secretaries of State and Homeland Security Concerning Implementation of Section 428 of the Homeland Security Act of 2002 (Sept. 30, 2003), *published on* AILA InfoNet at Doc. No. 03101641 and Doc. No. 03092913 at ¶3. An officer of DHS may now also be on-site at a consular post and may review any visa application. In Saudi Arabia, on site DHS personnel "shall" review all visa applications prior to adjudication. If a visa is denied by a consular officer, a second officer may review the denial but only after s/he has: (1) reviewed the information in the data system; (2) indicated that the information has been reviewed on the visa application form; and (3) states the reason s/he is issuing the visa (or waiver) in spite of the information in the data system. Homeland Security Act of 2002, §429. Under the Homeland Security Act of 2002 §428(e), the DHS may also assign employees to consular and diplomatic posts to: (1) provide expert advice and training regarding specific security threats relating to individual or classes of visa applicants; (2) review any visa application; and (3) conduct investigations with respect to consular matters. In Saudi Arabia, on-site personnel of DHS "shall" review all visa applications prior to adjudication. HSA §428(i).

1.d. Consideration of Visa Application—Consular officers are permitted to consider all available information, 22 C.F.R. §§41.102(b), 41.103(b) and 41.105(a), and in the view of one court, may consider hearsay evidence to establish a reasonable belief to deny a visa. *Adams v. Baker*, 909 F.2d 643, 649 (1st Cir. 1990). Consular officers are also required to act on visa applications before them. 22 C.F.R. §42.81; *Patel v. Reno*, 134 F.3d 929 (9th Cir. 1997) [mandamus jurisdiction is available to compel decision on case]. Where the consular officer finds a DHS-generated basis for inadmissibility when checking the Consular Lookout and Support System (CLASS), s/he "must assume that the finding was correct" and, except in cases involving nonpermanent ineligibilities, "should not look behind a definitive DHS finding or re-adjudicate the alien's eligibility with respect to the provision..." Cable, DOS, 05-State-066722 (Apr. 12, 2005) at ¶¶7–8, *published on* AILA InfoNet at Doc. No. 05052060; 9 FAM 40.6 N.3.2. If the applicant insists that the information is incorrect, the consular officer can direct or assist the applicant to contact DHS.

1.e. Reciprocal Procedures—The U.S. government has a policy of reciprocity in its treatment of applicants for visas from all counties. Reciprocal procedures of nationals from other countries includes treatment regarding (1) fingerprinting (only if they do); (2) validity of the period of the visa, INA §221(c), 8 U.S.C. §1201(c); and (3) fees for visa processing, INA §281, 8 U.S.C. §1351. Reciprocity is not only extended to citizens of that country but to residents or refugees residing in the foreign country who are from a third country. 22 C.F.R. §41.112(b).

1.f. Stateside Third-Country Nationals—Appointments for visas for stateside third-country nationals (TCNs) at border posts in Canada and Mexico are now made by telephone or online. The numbers for Canada are 1-888-840-0032 and 1-900-443-3131; for Mexico, call 1-900-476-1212 or 1-800-919-1754. (The 1-900 numbers have a per-minute charge; the 1-800/888 numbers will take credit-card payments.) For online appointments, see *www.nvars.com* (Canada) or *www.usvisa-mexico.com* (Mexico). Persons who are from one of the countries that is designated a state sponsor of terrorism (Cuba, Iran, Syria, Sudan, or North Korea) may not apply stateside for a visa.

B. *Visa Processing of NIVs*

1. Denials. If a consular officer denies a visa s/he "shall provide the applicant a timely written notice" that states the basis for the determination and lists the specific provisions of the law. INA §212(b), 8 U.S.C. §1182(b); 22 C.F.R. §41.121(b). Any refusal of an NIV must now be reviewed by a consular supervisor or a designated alternate "to ensure compliance with applicable laws and procedures." 22 C.F.R. §41.121(c). The refusal must be reviewed without delay which the regulation requires to be "on the day of refusal or as soon as is administratively possible." If the reviewing officer has a consular title or commission he can take control over the case and if not he must consult with the Visa Office or the officer to resolve the conflict. §41.121(c). If the applicant has indicated an intention to overcome the denial through the submission of additional evidence, a review of the refusal "must be deferred for not more than 120 days." 22 C.F.R. §41.121(c). A similar law applies to the review of the issuance of visas. 22 C.F.R. §113(i).

The Secy. of State may waive the written denial provision in regard to any individual or class of inadmissible persons and the provision does not apply to removal orders under INA §212(a)(2) or (a)(3). DOS continues to require posts to explain the reasons for a denial to an applicant. Cable, DOS, 97-State-114760 (1997), *reprinted in* 74 No. 25 *Interpreter Releases* 1037–38 (July 7, 1997); 9 FAM 41.121, 42.81. Before denying a visa: (1) a consular officer should give the applicant an opportunity to be interviewed in person with "every reasonable opportunity to establish their eligibility to receive a visa"; (2) they should inform the applicant of the section of the law under which the visa was refused, *"as well as the underlying factual basis for the refusal* unless the facts are classified or secret but unclassified"; and (3) they should explain the refusal in person. Cable, 01-State-102813 (June 12, 2001), *reprinted in* 78 No. 26 *Interpreter Releases* 1145–47 (July 9, 2001). Also, a consular officer cannot deny a visa for discriminatory reasons based exclusively on a profile. *Olsen v. Albright*, 990 F.Supp.31 (D.D.C. 1997) [in the review of the legality of the discharge of a consular officer, the court found the consulate's practices discriminating]. However, a visa must be denied without prejudice if the application is delayed more than 60 days due to an agency's investigation of inadmissibility for security grounds under INA §212(a)(3). Consolidated Appropriations Act, 2004, PL 108-199, 118 Stat. 3 (Jan. 23, 2004), Sec. 406. In granting a visa, consular officers should grant them for the full period of validity under reciprocity schedules and should not grant limited visa validity because they have doubts about the applicant's immigrant intent. Cable, DOS, 01-State-45943 (Mar. 15, 2001), *reprinted in* 78 No. 14 *Interpreter Releases* 644–45 (Apr. 9, 2001).

2. Advisory Opinions—The factual assertions of consular officers are not subject to review by the Secy. of State, INA §104(a)(1), 8 U.S.C. §1104(a)(1), although a party may seek an advisory opinion from DOS on any legal issue. If the advisory opinion involves a legal question, then the applicant's attorney may ask for an advisory review through *Legalnet@state.gov*. At least one court has found, however, that when the Deputy Assistant Secy. of State for Visa Services revokes a visa under 8 U.S.C. §1201(i), it is committed to agency discretion and is not reviewable. *Mansur v. Albright,* 130 F.Supp.2d 59 (D.D.C. 2001). Under the MOU between DOS and DHS any advisory opinion that seeks to change DOS guidance to consular officers must first be reviewed by DHS. Memorandum of Understanding Between the Secretaries of State and Homeland Security Concerning Implementation of Section 428 of the Homeland Security Act of 2002 (Sept. 30, 2003), *published on* AILA InfoNet at Doc. Nos. 03092913 & 03101641, at ¶4a.

3. Judicial Review—Where a consular post denies a visa there are several courts that have taken the view that the denial is not subject to judicial review, *Saavedra Bruno v. Albright,* 197 F.3d 1153 (D.C. Cir. 1999) [distinguished *Abourezk* and finding no review of decision to grant or to revoke a visa; noting that traditionally these were matters for diplomatic protest]; *Centeno v. Shultz*, 817 F.2d 1212 (5th Cir. 1987), *cert. denied*, 484 U.S. 1005 (1988); *Li Hing of Hong Kong v. Levin*, 800 F.2d 970 (9th Cir. 1986); *Burrafato v. DOS*, 523 F.2d 554 (2d Cir. 1975), *cert. denied*, 424 U.S. 910 (1976) [no review even where DOS fails to follow own regulations]; *El-Hadad v. U.S.*, 377 F.Supp.2d 42 (D.D.C. 2005) [no habeas or other jurisdiction to review denial of B-1/B-2 visa or advance parole to return to pursue litigation]; *Chun v. Powell,* 223 F.Supp.2d 204, 206–07 (D.D.C. 2002) [no jurisdiction to review by declaratory judgment whether consular officer has weighed all factors in denying on §214(b) grounds a B-2 visa to plaintiff's sister]; *Romero v. Consulate of U.S., Barranquilla, Colombia*, 860 F.Supp. 319 (E.D. Va. 1994) [no jurisdiction on denial of NIVs in Colombian "reason to believe" cases]; *Garcia v. Baker*, 765 F.Supp. 426 (N.D. Ill. 1990). *But see Patel v. Reno*, 134 F.3d 929 n.1 (9th Cir. 1997) [mandamus action compelling consular officer to decide IV case]; *Abourezk v. Reagan*, 785 F.2d 1043 (D.C. Cir. 1986), *aff'd per curiam by an equally divided court*, 108 S.Ct. 252 (1987); *Legal Assistance for Vietnamese Asylum Seekers v. DOS*, 45 F.3d 469 (D.C. Cir. 1995), *remanded on other grounds*, 117 S.Ct. 378 (1996) [Standing and jurisdiction to challenge DOS change of policy]; *Academy of Religion v. Chertoff,* 463 F.Supp.2d 400, 416–19 (S.D.N.Y. 2006) [First Amendment challenge by academic organizations to refusal/revocation of visa to Islamic scholar is subject to review because it involves a constitutional issue and the DHS and other agencies involved in security advisory opinions (SAO) are involved in the decision-making process]. *See also U.S. v. Kumpf,* 438 F.3d 785, 788 (7th Cir. 2006) [rejected claim that consular nonreviewability precluded review of visa issuance in denaturalization case, where government claimed visa was issued unlawfully under Refugee Relief Act]; *Raduga USA Corp. v. DOS,* 440 F.Supp.2d 1140, 1149–52 (S.D. Cal. 2006) [allowed plaintiff to amend mandamus complaint to encompass review of consulate's bad faith denial of employee's IV after court ordered mandamus]. Moreover, even if a court has jurisdiction to review a denial, it cannot order the consulate to issue the visa, but only to apply the appropriate standard in determining issuance. *City of New York v. Baker*, 878 F.2d 507 (D.C. Cir. 1989). In addition, the Homeland Security Act of 2002 §428(f) specifically states that it does not create a private right of action to challenge the decision of a consular officer or other U.S. official or employee to grant or deny a visa. The Supreme Court's decision in *Rasul v. Bush,* 542 U.S. 466 (2004), however, may have dramatically altered these doctrines. In *Rasul,* the Court found that there was habeas jurisdiction to review the physical custody of aliens being held at the military base in Guantanamo, Cuba. The Court distinguished *Johnson v. Eisentrager*, found that habeas applies extraterritorially to aliens, that aliens like U.S. citizens can invoke federal court authority, and that the presence of the detainee in the territorial jurisdiction of a federal court is not a juris-

dictional requirement for habeas as long as there is jurisdiction over the custodian. The Court also found that jurisdiction existed under 28 U.S.C. §1331 (General Federal Question jurisdiction) and §1350 (Alien Tort Claims Act) for aliens outside the U.S. and noted that: "The courts of the United States have traditionally been open to nonresident aliens." *Rasul,* 124 S.Ct. at 2698–99. *See also Abu Ali v. Ashcroft,* 350 F.Supp.2d 28, 39–57 (D.D.C. 2004) [denied motion to dismiss habeas petition brought by a U.S. citizen being held in Saudi Arabia at the direction of the U.S.].

4. Hs, Ls, Ks, Os, Ps, and Qs need prior approval at USCIS service center of I-129 petitions (H, L, O, P, and Q visas) or I-129F (K visas) petitions before applying at a consular post. INA §214(c), 8 U.S.C. §1184(c). To determine where the I-129 work-related petitions are filed review the petition instructions and check USCIS websites. If the I-129 is approved, the approved I-129 petition is routed to the Kentucky Consular Center (KCC) rather then sending them to the consular post overseas. The KCC then scans the information and consular posts now access it through a system called Petition Information Management Service (PIMS). Cable, 07-State-155679 (Nov. 13, 2007), *published on* AILA InfoNet at Doc. No. 08040331. I-129Fs (for fiancées and K-3s), however, are still sent through the National Visa Center. Cable, DOS, 04-State-150760 (July 10, 2004), *published on* AILA InfoNet at 04071264 (July 12, 2004). When an approval notice is lost or when there is a desire to notify a new U.S. Consulate about an approval, a duplicate approval notice is requested on an I-824. 8 C.F.R. §103.5b. Fs, Ms, and Js need certification from school/program sponsor. Burden of proof is on petitioner for all petitions. *Matter of Brantigan,* 11 I&N Dec. 493 (BIA 1966).

5. Security Issues—For general background clearance information the DOS relies on the Consular Lookout and Support System (CLASS) name check system. For procedures under CLASS when there is a match *see* Cable, DOS, 05-State-066722 (Apr. 12, 2005), *published on* AILA InfoNet at Doc. No. 05052060 (May 20, 2005). Where the use of the CLASS system leads to a "hit" on security, INA §212(f), Section 306 of the Enhanced Border Security and Visa Entry Reform Act (alien from country that sponsors terrorism), or VGTOF (violent gang or terrorist organization file), the consular officer is instructed to submit a Visa Donkey request. Cable, 05-State-066722, *supra.* In addition, the DOS has developed several computerized systems to collect and transmit data on terrorists and other malefactors. DOS has developed the Visas Viper terrorist reporting program which is designed to collect data on suspected terrorists worldwide who are not currently visa applicants for the purpose of watch listing them. Appropriate information is then placed in the CLASS and IBIS lookout systems. Cable, DOS, 01-State-182167 (Oct. 18, 2001), *reprinted in* 78 No. 47 *Interpreter Releases* 1865–71 (Dec. 10, 2001). Organized crime suspects from the former Soviet Union and Baltic Republics are placed in the Visas Shark and Visa EEL program. *Id,* 9 FAM 40.31 N.4. DOS also maintains a Technology Alert List (TAL) to deny admission to persons who may engage in technology transfer. The TAL consists of a Critical Field List that designates major fields of controlled goods and technologies that raise technological transfer concerns and the DOS list of state sponsors of terrorism. 9 FAM 40.31 N5.1-2 to N5.1-5 & Ex. 1; Cable, DOS, 02-State-147566 (Aug. 2, 2001), *published on* AILA InfoNet at Doc. No. 03030449. DOS has developed a procedure to help consular officers find reason to believe that certain persons (including visiting students and scholars) might be ineligible under §212(a)(3)(A)(i)(II). Cable, DOS, (98-State-015652) (Jan. 28, 1998), *reprinted in* 75 No. 27 *Interpreter Releases* 980–84 (July 17, 1998); 9 FAM 40.31 N.5. If a visa applicant has not been cleared within 45 days, s/he may request the status of her case by inquiring at *SAOInquiries@state.gov* with a caption stating "overdue SAO." Where the consular officer finds a DHS-generated basis for inadmissibility, s/he "must assume that the finding was correct" and except in cases involving nonpermanent ineligibilities "should not look behind a definitive DHS finding or re-adjudicate the alien's eligibility with respect to the provision…" Cable, DOS, 05-State-066722 (Apr. 12, 2005), *published on* AILA InfoNet at Doc. No. 05052060 (May 20, 2005); 9 FAM 40.6 N.3.2. Denials based upon security advisory opinions may be reviewable because they are not necessarily made by consular officers. *Academy of Religion v. Chertoff,* 463 F.Supp.2d 400, 416–19 (S.D.N.Y. 2006) [First Amendment challenge by academic organizations to refusal/revocation of visa to Islamic scholar is subject to review because it involves a constitutional issue and the DHS and other agencies involved in security advisory opinions (SAO) are involved in the decision-making process].

   Removing Information from CLASS—An LPR or USC seeking to remove their names from CLASS should write to Chief, Systems Liaison and Procedures Division, Visa Office, U.S. Department of State, Washington, D.C. 20522-0113. If the person is not a USC or LPR, s/he must go back to the consular post that placed the information into the system and ask for a correction or deletion. If the consular post was not responsible for the information, the concerned person must write to the agency that placed the information in the database. 9 FAM Appendix D, 203.4

DHS Traveler Redress Inquiry Program (DHS TRIP). If applicant for admission or entry has been denied or delayed entry or placed in secondary continuously, s/he may lodge a complaint with DHS's Trip on line. Complainant needs to go to *www.dhs.gov/trip* to file the complaint.

Security Advisory Opinions—DOS has established special processing requirements for certain nationalities regarding security issues. Cable, DOS, 01-State-109933 (June 23, 2001), *reprinted in* 78 No. 38 *Interpreter Releases* 1536, 1549–67 (Oct. 1, 2001); Cable, DOS (99-State-025434), *reprinted in* 76 *Interpreter Releases* 634–48 (Apr. 26, 1999); 9 FAM Appendix G, 501 *et seq.* They include relying on a Visa Mantis cable process to verify the applicant's background. Cable, DOS (99-State-158241) (Aug. 24, 1999), *reprinted in* 76 No. 47 *Interpreter Releases* 1768–73 (Dec. 13, 1999). For a description of the Visa Mantis process see 79 No. 18 *Interpreter Releases* 623–28 (Apr. 29, 2002); 80 No. 26 *Interpreter Releases* 904–05 (July 7, 2003). The DOS now requires Security Advisory Opinions (SAOs) for: (1) nationals from certain countries, 9 FAM Appendix G 502.2; (2) persons the consular officer knows or has reason to believe are ineligible to enter the U.S. because of espionage, terrorism, foreign policy reasons or Nazi affiliation, 9 FAM Appendix G 502.3; (3) persons seeking a waiver for membership in the Communist Party, 9 FAM Appendix G 502.4; (4) persons falling under certain entries in the CLASS system ("00" class), 9 FAM Appendix G 502.5, 9 FAM 40.31 N.3; (5) applicants who the consular officer knows or has reason to believe are on the Economic Defense List, 9 FAM Appendix G 502.6; (6) nationals of Communist or Communist controlled countries who are being sponsored by USG employee, 9 FAM Appendix G 502.7; and (7) persons who are subject to the Technology Alert List (TAL), 9 FAM 40.31 N.5.1-5. DHS is authorized to make the final determination of whether to grant, refuse or revoke a visa after a DOS determination on the Security Advisory Opinion. Memorandum of Understanding Between the Secretaries of State and Homeland Security Concerning Implementation of Section 428 of the Homeland Security Act of 2002 (Sept. 30, 2003), *published on* AILA InfoNet at Doc. Nos. 03092913 & 03101641, at ¶4b. Consular Officers may also obtain information from the National Crime Information Center's Interstate Identification Index (NCIC-III) in the form of abstract and summaries. 22 C.F.R. §40.5. If needed, they may also seek full files. USA PATRIOT Act of 2001, §403(b). If the database indicates that an NIV may have a criminal background the consular officer must request fingerprints and submit them to the FBI for a criminal records check. 22 C.F.R. §41.105(b)(2). The NCIC system has been exempt from the Privacy Act requirement that it maintain records "with such accuracy, relevance, timeliness and completeness as is reasonably necessary to assure fairness." Letter, Brown, Acting Asst. AG (May 13, 2003) Ans. 33, *reprinted in* 80 No. 21 *Interpreter Releases* 743–44, 756–57 (May 23, 2003).

In sum, consular officers generally engage in several types of security checks: (1) Visa Condor checks that arise from information disclosed on Form DS-157 or because a person is from one the designated terrorist countries (Cuba, Iran, Syria, Sudan, or North Korea) or the broader list of countries found at 9 FAM Appendix G 502.2; (2) Visa Mantis checks arising from the TAL list relating to a person who because of his actions or background may be involved in the transfer of sensitive technology, 9 FAM 40.31 N.5; (3) Visa Donkey requests where there are hits for security, INA §212(f), Section 306 of the Enhanced Border Security and Visa Entry Reform Act (alien from country that sponsors terrorism), or VGTOF (violent gang or terrorist organization file) issues, Cable, DOS, 05-State-066722 (Apr. 12, 2005), *published on* AILA InfoNet at Doc. No. 05052060 (May 20, 2005); and (4) Criminal background checks which arise from a "hit" in the NCIC database or from other sources, 9 FAM 40.31 N.5.3.

If a visa applicant has not been cleared within 45 days and s/he may request the status of her case by inquiring at *SAOInquiries@state.gov.* If the SAO involves a legal question then the applicant may ask for an advisory review through *Legalnet@state.gov.*

6. Immigration Admission—After obtaining the visa (or in some cases entering without a visa under the VWP or other statutory or regulatory exemptions), the applicant must apply for admission into the U.S. at the border or pre-flight inspection station by a CBP officer. A CBP inspector conducts an interview at the airport, seaport, or land border to determine if the applicant is admissible; this is called a primary inspection. If an issue is raised as to admissibility, the officer may direct the

person to a "secondary inspection" on site. At times the CBP officer may decide to grant the person a deferred inspection at another time in another place. In any of these scenarios, the inspector may utilize translators when necessary under restricted criteria. IFM at 17.18. If admitted, s/he will be given an I-94 card. This card will govern the terms of his or her stay in the U.S. If entry is denied, the nonimmigrant may be summarily removed or put in a removal proceeding before an IJ to remove her from the U.S. If a consular post has issued a visa, however, it is prima facie evidence of admissibility sufficient to shift the burden of producing evidence to the DHS at a removal hearing where admissibility is questioned. *Matter of Walsh & Pollard*, 20 I&N Dec. 60 (BIA 1988). Where an I-94 was issued by USCIS or an asylum office *after* entry, but contains erroneous information, USCIS district offices are authorized to correct any error. If the error arose at admission/port-of-entry due to a mistake by CBP, the person should be directed to CBP. Memo, Yates, Assoc. Dir. For Operations, USCIS, "I-94 Errors Issued by U.S. Citizenship and Immigration Services," HQOPRD 70/42.10 (Mar. 30, 2004), *published on* AILA InfoNet at Doc. No. 04042769.

C. *INA §221(g), 8 U.S.C. §1201(g) Denial Procedures*—No visa issued if:

1. "It appears" to consular officer ... "from statements in the application, or in the papers submitted therewith, that such alien is ineligible to receive a visa ..." INA §221(g)(1), 8 U.S.C. §1201(g)(1), 22 C.F.R. §41.121; 9 FAM 41.121.
2. Application does not comply with INA or regulations. When a case is refused under 221(g) consular officers "should explain clearly to the applicant and attorney of record what documents or other evidence is needed, or what procedural step needs to be completed (*e.g.,* case being submitted to the Department for advisory opinion ...)" Cable, DOS, 97-State-12958 (June 18, 1997), *reprinted in* 16 *AILA Monthly Mailing* 585 (July/Aug. 1997).
3. Consular officer "knows or has reason to believe that alien is ineligible ... " (*e.g.,* drugs). "Reason to believe" is a determination "based upon facts or circumstances which would lead a reasonable person to conclude ... ineligibility ...." 22 C.F.R. §40.6. It may include hearsay. *Adams v. Baker*, 909 F.2d 643, 649 (1st Cir. 1990).
4. Processing delayed by any agency more than 60 days due to a determination regarding inadmissibility on security and related grounds (212(a)(3), including terrorism. Denial is without prejudice. Consolidated Appropriations Act, 2004, PL 108-199, 118 Stat. 3 (Jan. 23, 2004), Sec. 406.

D. *Validity of Issued Visa*

1. The time granted by U.S. on visa depends on:
   - 1.a. Nature of the visa;
   - 1.b. Reciprocity with foreign nations setting maximum periods of validity. 22 C.F.R. §41.112(b).
2. Period of validity of the visa is generally unrelated to the length of stay in the U.S. given by USCIS. 9 FAM 41.112 N.2.11. It is only related to the time when an application for entry must be made. However, if an NIV holder stays beyond the period granted his or her visa is void. INA §222(g)(1), 8 U.S.C. §1202(g)(1).
3. Visa Symbols. The DOS maintains a detailed list of symbols it uses for each immigrant and nonimmigrant category in the visa issuance process. *See* **Appendix N,** *infra.*

E. *INA §222(g) / Overstays*

1. Generally—If an NIV overstays the period authorized by AG, or if USCIS or IJ formally find that a status violation has occurred for person in D/S or another status (*e.g.,* works without authorization), his or her visa is void under §222(g). DOS will use the INS definition of the "period of stay authorized by the AG" Cable, DOS 98-State-051296 (Mar. 23, 1998), *published on* AILA InfoNet at Doc. No. 98032392; 9 FAM 40.68 [DOS procedures regarding §222(g)]. Section 222(g) applies to visas issued before, on, or after Sept. 30, 1996. IIRIRA §631(b). However, the person must have first overstayed after Sept. 30, 1996 and the provision does *not* include persons who are out of status for any other reason, such as working without authorization Memo, Crocetti, Assoc. Comm., Examinations (1997), *reprinted in* 16 *AILA Monthly Mailing* 347 (May 1997) unless there is a formal finding of status violation. Cable, DOS, 98-State-051296, *supra.* The visa holder who

overstays cannot be readmitted to the U.S. until s/he returns to the consular office in the country of his or her nationality to obtain a new visa. However, a person whose visa is automatically canceled may apply for an INA §212(d)(4) waiver at the border. Inspector's Field Manual at 15.15 (k); Memo, Pearson, Exec. Assoc. Comm., Field Operations, (HQADN 70/12-P, IN 00-14) (Mar. 3, 2000), *reprinted in* 77 No. 10 *Interpreter Releases* 300, 322–27 (Mar. 13, 2000); Memo, Williams, Ex. Assoc. Comm. Field Operations, HQINS 70/12.2.1 (Sept. 30, 2002), *published on* AILA InfoNet at Doc. No. 02111340. The DHS may also cancel any other visa in a person's passport if it was not issued in the country of the person's nationality. *Id* at sect. 15.15(f).

2. Extraordinary Circumstances—If the Secy. of State finds that extraordinary circumstances permit presentation at another consular office or there is no consular office in the country of nationality s/he may obtain the visa elsewhere. INA §222(g)(2), 8 U.S.C. §1202(g)(2). If there is no consulate in country of nationality the person may apply in her last country of permanent residence or at a consular post designated under 9 FAM Part IV, Appendix C. *See also* 9 FAM 42.61 N1-4. If the person is a dual national, then s/he may go to either country. If stateless, the person shall be considered a national of the country that issued her travel documents. 22 C.F.R. §41.101(c), (d).
3. Physicians—Extraordinary circumstances also apply to a physician who is working in a medically underserved area when applying for an H-1B visa in state/federal waiver program where prior to J status expiring, the physician applied for a waiver and an employer filed an I-129 petition which were subsequently granted. He may therefore apply at any consulate where he is physically present. 22 C.F.R. §41.101(c)(i).
4. Asylum, TPS, and §222(g)—The submission of an asylum application is not considered to be a time of authorized stay in U.S. Cable, DOS, 96-State-232251 (Nov. 8, 1996), *reprinted in* 73 No. 44 *Interpreter Releases* 1614 (Nov. 18, 1996). Thus, an applicant for asylum should apply for E/S to keep NIV current. *Id.* However, persons who were granted TPS *before* their NIV status expired are not subject to §222(g). IFM at 15.15(d), *reprinted in* 76 No. 6 *Interpreter Releases* 243, 252–56 (Feb. 8, 1999); Cable, DOS, (99-State-105097) (June 7, 1999), *reprinted in* 76 No. 24 *Interpreter Releases* 977–80 (June 28, 1999).
5. Voluntary Departure and §222(g)—The Service and the DOS have adopted the view that a person who is given VD after overstaying or found to have violated his status is subject to §222(g). IFM §15.15(h); Memo, Pearson, Exec. Assoc. Comm., Field Operations, (HQADN 70/12-P, IN 00-14) (Mar. 3, 2000), *published on* AILA InfoNet at Doc. No. 00030773; Cable, DOS, 98-State-051296 (Mar. 23, 1998), *published on* AILA InfoNet at Doc. No. 98032392.
6. Extensions of Stay or Change of Status and §222(g)—A person who timely files a nonfrivolous application for a C/S or E/S and who has not worked without authorization, will not be considered to be in unlawful status during the pendency of the application. Any unlawful presence that would otherwise accrue during the time the c/s or e/s is pending will be tolled until a decision is reached. Unlawful presence will accrue only from the time of the denial. A person with an NIV to a specific date who departs the U.S. before a C/S or E/S is decided will not be subject to 222(g) if he can establish that his application was timely and nonfrivolous and that he did not engage in unauthorized employment. IFM §15.15(g); Memo, Pearson, Exec. Assoc. Comm., Field Operations, (HQADN 70/12-P, IN 00-14) (Mar. 3, 2000), *published on* AILA InfoNet at Doc. No. 00030773; Cable, DOS, No. 00-State-102274 (May 30, 2000), *reprinted in* 77 No. 22 *Interpreter Releases* 727–29 (June 5, 2000). NIVs who are D/S and file E/S or C/S and depart the U.S. will not be subject to 222(g) even if the application is subsequently denied unless it was for a status violation that would have resulted in the termination of the period of authorized stay. IFM §15.15(g)(2).
7. H-1B Cap—For a discussion concerning the cap, change of status, and the "cap-gap," *see in this chapter* ¶ VII.C.1.h(4) (p.678). *infra*.
8. A and G Visas and 222(g)—The provisions of 222(g) will not be applied to A-1, A-2, G-1, G-2, G-3 and G-4 visa holders. Cable, DOS No. 225321, Christopher, Secy. of State, 96-State-208799/212382 (1996), *reprinted in* 73 No. 42 *Interpreter Releases* 1544–46 (Nov. 4, 1996). C-2, C-3 and NATO-1 through NATO-6 visa holders are also exempt. Cable, Albright, Secy. of State, 96-State-208799/225321/232219 (Jan. 23, 1997), *reprinted in* 74 No. 4 *Interpreter Releases* 183–85 (Jan. 27, 1997). The only exception may be if USCIS or an IJ find a status violation has occurred. Cable, DOS, 98-State-051296 (Mar. 23, 1998), *published on* AILA InfoNet at Doc. No. 98032392.

9. VWP, EWI, Parole, and §222(g)—Persons on VWP who overstay, or persons who enter EWI or are granted parole are not subject to 222(g). Cable, DOS, 98-State-051296 (Mar. 23, 1998) *supra*; IFM at 15.15(c), *reprinted in* 76 No. 6 *Interpreter Releases* 243, 252–56 (Feb. 8, 1999); Cable, DOS (99-State-105097) (June 7, 1999), *reprinted in* 76 No. 24 *Interpreter Releases* 977–80 (June 28, 1999).

10. F, I, and J Visas, and Others with D/S and §222(g)—Persons with D/S will not be subject to 222(g) unless USCIS finds a status violation while adjudicating a request for an immigration benefit or an IJ finds a status violation in proceedings against the person. Cable, DOS, 98-State-051296 (Mar. 23, 1998), *published on* AILA InfoNet at Doc. No. 98032392.

11. Canadians/Mexicans and §222(g)—Persons admitted from Canada or Mexico with an I-68 (for Canadian boaters) or DSP-150 border crossing card (BCC) are not subject to INA §222(g). Nor are Canadians or Mexicans who enter on a visa but are not issued an I-94 unless they are formally found to be out of status. Letter, Hrinyak, (HQINS 70/12.1) (Apr. 1, 1999), *published on* AILA InfoNet at Doc. No. 99040191.

12. Impossibility—A person will not be deemed an overstay, if due to circumstances it is impossible to depart the U.S. *Matter of C-C-*, 3 I&N Dec. 221, 222 (BIA 1948) [a person held in custody pending trial for a criminal charge past the time of his authorized stay was not deportable under the principle that the law does not compel the impossible].

F. *Revocation of Visas*—22 C.F.R. §41.122, 9 FAM 41.122. Revocation by a consular officer can occur where there is:

1. Ineligibility under INA §212(a);
2. Nonentitlement to visa classification;
3. An immigrant visa issued; or
4. A physical removal of the visa from the passport.

INA §221(i), 8 U.S.C. §1201(i); 22 C.F.R. §41.122(a). Revocations of visas are often initiated by the Terrorist Screening Center, which then informs the Visa Office and DHS so the information is placed in the CLASS and IBIS systems. Once there is a formal revocation the information is sent to consular post by cable and e-mailed to ICE and the National Terrorist Center. Letter, Hary, Asst. Secy. of State, DOS to Hutchinson, Under Sec. DHS (Aug. 2. 2004) *reported in* 81 No. 33 *Interpreter Releases* 1138–39 (Aug. 23, 2004). DOS guidelines provide notice of intent to revoke with an opportunity to respond before the visa is revoked. Cable, DOS, 00-State-245040, *reprinted in* 77 No. 8 *Interpreter Releases* 241–43 (Feb. 28, 2000), §41.122(b); *Wong v. DOS and INS*, 789 F.2d 1380 (9th Cir. 1986) [Secy. of State cannot revoke when visa improperly issued solely because L-2 spouse and children not physically present at embassy where they were not otherwise inadmissible under INA §212(a) or ineligible for L-2]. *But see Noh v. INS,* 248 F.3d 938 (9th Cir. 2001) [Asst. Secy. of State is not required to comply with regulations regarding revocation of visa because he did not revoke visa in his capacity as a consular officer but rather as the Secy. of State's delegate. *Wong* distinguished on those grounds. His decision is, however, subject to the facially legitimate and bona fide standard]; *Mansur v. Albright,* 130 F.Supp.2d 59 (D.D.C. 2001) [when the Deputy Assistant Secy. of State for Visa Services revokes a visa under 8 U.S.C. §1201(i), it is committed to agency discretion and is not reviewable]; *Knoetze v. DOS*, 634 F.2d 207 (5th Cir. 1981) [can revoke without notice where applicant committed crime of moral turpitude prior to entry]; *Ruston v. DOS,* 29 F.Supp.2d 518, 523 (E.D. Ark. 1998) [no jurisdiction to review revocation of visa by consular officer because notice of intent to revoke is not mandatory].

DHS may also revoke a visa under 9 FAM 41.122 PN 16 if: (1) the visa holder obtains an IV or AOS; (2) the visa holder is ordered removed as inadmissible or deportable; (3) the visa holder is notified by a CBP officer during an inspection that s/he is inadmissible and she withdraws her application for admission; (4) the visa holder is granted voluntary departure; (5) an INA §212(d)(3)(A) waiver used to obtain the visa is now revoked; (6) the visa holder presents a fraudulent visa; (7) the visa has been physically removed from the passport. But, an unexpired visa in an expired passport remains valid. 22 C.F.R. §41.112(b)(3).

Limited Judicial Review—Habeas corpus, mandamus and All Writs Act jurisdiction are eliminated under INA §221(i) regarding the revocation of an immigrant visa or NIV, except in the context of a removal proceeding and only then if the revocation provides the sole ground for removal under INA

§237(a)(1)(B). *Bolante v. Achim,* 457 F.Supp.2d 896 (E.D. Wis. 2006) [no habeas jurisdiction to review claim that revocation was improper under 22 C.F.R. §41.122(a)].

G. ***Disclosure of Records***—DOS has a statutory exemption from disclosure of documents pertaining to the issuance or refusal of visas or permits to enter the U.S. INA §222(f), 8 U.S.C. §1202(f). In order to accommodate DHS's need to disclose information to rejected applicants where application is revoked or not approved, 8 C.F.R. §§103.2(b)(16) and 205.2(b), DOS and the Service agreed to permit the Service disclosure. Cable, DOS, 89-State-028963 (Jan.31, 1989), *reprinted in* 66 No. 6 *Interpreter Releases* 159 (Feb. 6, 1989). DOS may also successfully raise privacy exemptions under FOIA to prevent disclosure of a person's name. *DOS v. Ray*, 502 U.S. 164, 112 S.Ct. 541 (1991) [upheld refusal to release names of Haitians who were deported]. *But see Ray v. DOJ*, 852 F.Supp. 1558 (S.D. Fla. 1994) [unredacted logs of Haitian interdictees ordered released].

H. ***Revalidation/Reissuance of Visas***—22 C.F.R. §41.111(b), 69 Fed. Reg. 35121 (June 23, 2004). A person already holding an A-1, A-2, G-1 to G-4, NATO-1 to NATO-6 visa may apply directly to the Department of State in Washington, D.C., to reissue or revalidate his visa. For revalidation, the requirements are: (1) the person's nationality must be the same as it was when the previous visa was issued; (2) the previous visa must be the same classification as the visa which the applicant is now seeking; (3) the previous visa must not have a remaining validity of more than 60 days; and (4) if the previous visa has expired the application for revalidation must be submitted within one year of the expiration. Visa Office Responses to AILA/VO Liaison Questions, 20 *AILA Monthly Mailing* 64 (Jan./Feb. 2001). Must submit original I-94, I-797 approval notice, completed electronic DS-160, PP valid for six months, and supporting documentation for the visa including a comprehensive letter from the employer. If the applicant's previous visa was annotated "Visas Mantis" s/he must have an interview abroad. AILA-VO Liaison (Oct. 15, 2003) at question 71. The DOS discontinued visa revalidation for C, E, H, I, L, O, and P visas. 69 Fed. Reg. 35121 (June 23, 2004), *reprinted in* 81 No. 25 *Interpreter Releases* 825, 826, 842 (June 28, 2004).

DOS may also issue initial visas to persons in the U.S. in the status of A, C-2, C-3 or G.

I. ***Returning Petitions to USCIS***—On occasion a consular officer, rather than deny a visa under INA §221(g), 8 U.S.C. §1201 will return the petition to USCIS to request reconsideration and revocation. DOS's position is that returning petitions to USCIS should be used judiciously since the process is lengthy and the evidentiary standard to revoke the petition is high. "Posts should not use the revocation request process as a means of disposing of problematic cases in which fraud, misrepresentation or ineligibility for status is only suspected but cannot be clearly established." Cable, DOS, 01-State-121801 (July 13, 2001), *reprinted in* 78 No. 30 *Interpreter Releases* 1276–78 (Aug. 6, 2001). Consular officers should consider three principles in seeking to revoke a petition: (1) there should be substantial evidence supporting return not previously considered by DHS because revocation is not merely to readjudicate a petition; (2) the memo supporting the petition return must clearly show the factual and concrete reasons for recommending revocation; and (3) the applicant must be provided in writing as full an explanation as possible of the legal and factual basis for visa denial and petition return. Cable, DOS, 04-State-41682 (Feb. 25, 2004) at ¶¶6-10, *published on* AILA InfoNet at Doc. No. 04030364. *See also Matter of Arias,* 19 I&N Dec. 568 (BIA 1988) [reversed revocation where it was based on consul's memorandum which was conclusory, speculative, equivocal and irrelevant]. The return of a petition is accomplished on an Form DS-3096. 9 FAM 42.43 N.3, PN1.Consular officers should return K-1 and K-3 visas to the National Visa Center and *not* to DHS when recommending revocation. Cable, DOS, 04-State-41682 (Feb. 25, 2004) ¶2, *published on* AILA InfoNet at Doc. No. 04030364.

J. ***Electronic Filing (E-Filing)***—68 Fed. Reg. 23010–12 (Apr. 29, 2003). USCIS has established a procedure that permits applicants to file petitions electronically. Applicants may file I-90, I-129 (except L-1, H-1B, H-2B), I-129S, I-131, I-140, I-539, I-765, I-821, and I-907 petitions electronically. *See www.uscis.gov/e-filing*. Signatures on the forms are completed electronically. 8 C.F.R. §103.2(a)(2). Confirmation is received upon completion of the document and applicants will receive notice in the mail for a USCIS-scheduled appointment for capturing biometrics and photographs at an application support center. Supporting documentation (usually photocopies rather than originals), along with a print-out of the confirmation receipt (*not* a copy of the e-filed application) and the original LC (if applicable), needs to be promptly submitted afterwards, in accordance with the form's instructions (*see, e.g.,* I-140 instructions, requiring that the necessary initial evidence be *received* by the Service Center within 7 business days (*not* 30 days) after the e-filing). Failure to submit the required documentation in the requisite time period can be a basis for denying the application.

USCIS has also proposed a variety of forms to allow employers to establish customer accounts and to allow the employers or their agents and attorneys to file applications electronically. 70 Fed. Reg. 77171–74 (Dec. 29, 2005).

III. ADMISSION TO U.S.

A. ***Issuance of visa does not guarantee admission to the U.S.***—It only permits boarding of transportation to U.S. INA §221(h), 8 U.S.C. §1201(h).

B. ***Must Present to CBP an Unexpired Visa and Passport Valid for 6 Months***—8 C.F.R. §212.1. *Exceptions*: (a) Canadians and Mexicans are visa-exempt (b) Reciprocity with certain countries, 9 FAM 41.104 N.2.1, even when passport not valid for 6 months. The U.S., by agreement with most countries, will allow persons to enter even if their passports are not valid for 6 months; those countries have agreed to extend automatically passport validity 6 months beyond their expiration date. For a complete list, *see* 9 FAM 41.104 Exh. 1. See also "Documents Required for Travelers Departing from or Arriving in the United States at Sea and Land Ports-of-Entry from Within the Western Hemisphere, 73 Fed. Reg. 18383 (Apr. 3, 2008).

C. ***US-VISIT***—U.S. Visitor & Immigrant Status Indicator Technology Program (US-VISIT), 69 Fed. Reg. 468–83 (Jan 5, 2004), 8 C.F.R. §214.1(a)(3), 215.8(a)(1), 235.1(d)(1) and (f)(1); 8 U.S.C. §1365a. DHS has been mandated by Congress to establish an automated entry and exit control system to track records of entries and departures and to identify overstays and persons posing a national security threat. IIRIRA §110 [directed AG to develop an automated entry and exit control system to collect records of arrivals and departure from every foreign visitor entering and leaving the U.S.]; Immigration and Naturalization Service Data Management Improvement Act (DMIA) of 2000, PL 106-215, 114 Stat. 337, 8 U.S.C. §1365a [amended and replaced IIRIRA §110 and directed the integration of existing DOJ/DOS electronic foreign visitor arrival and departure data systems]; USA PATRIOT Act of 2001 §414 [requiring that AG and Secy. of State focus on biometric and tamper resistant technologies]; Enhanced Border Security and Visa Entry Reform Act [mandated the electronic arrival/departure manifest requirement, the use of biometrics, and the integration of an exit/entry control system with other enforcement and intelligence systems].

1. The law required that an automated entry/exit program be implemented at air and seaports by Dec. 31, 2003; the 50 most highly trafficked land ports of entry (POEs) by Dec. 31, 2004; and all ports of entry by Dec. 31, 2005. For a more realistic timetable and technical analysis of the program *see* US-VISIT Program: Privacy Impact Assessment Update (July 1, 2005), DHS, 70 Fed. Reg. 39300–23 (July 7, 2005).
2. Entry—The program covers only nonimmigrant visitors including persons entering under the VWP. CBP personnel in addition to the initial inspection will take biometric information. 8 C.F.R. §235.1(f)(1)(ii). The biometric information initially included only one digital photograph and two electronic (index fingers) fingerprints. DHS Secretary Michael Chertoff announced in mid-July, 2005 that DHS will strengthen the US-VISIT program by requiring 10 finger scans for all first time visitors to the U.S. Subsequent entries and exits by air, sea, and land border posts will require two finger scans for verification. Any passports issued by visa waiver passport countries on or after Oct. 26, 2005, must include digital photographs on each of the new passports and data pages and must be machine-readable. Unexpired passports issued before Oct. 26, 2005 will still be valid for travel under the VWP, provided they are machine-readable. The machine-readable passports issued after Oct. 26, 2005, must incorporate biometric identifiers that comply with standards established by the International Civil Aviation Organization (ICAO) which at present are facial recognition biometrics. 8 U.S.C. §1732(c)(1). In addition all consular posts must require applicants to comply with the biometric information requirements under US-VISIT before they can issue visas. All visa applicants, except those exempt, are required to make personal appearances at consulates so their fingerprints and digital photo may be taken.

   The biometric identification requirements do not apply to: (1) persons younger than 14 and older than 79; (2) A-1, A-2, C-3(except for attendants, servants or personal employees of accredited officials), G-1 through G-4, NATO 1 through NATO-6. The Secretary of State and Secretary of DHS may jointly determine, however, to require the inclusion of any of these classes or may exempt others. An individual may not be subject if DHS, DOS or CIA director determines to grant waiver. 8 C.F.R. §235.1(f)(1)(iv)(D). Most Canadians are not subject to US-VISIT. But NSEERS initial fingerprinting/identification requirements may still be in effect for Canadians born in certain countries. Failure of an individual to provide the biometric identification required may result in a finding that the person is inadmissible under INA §212(a)(7), 8 U.S.C. §1182(a)(7); 8 C.F.R. §§214.1(a) & 235.1(f)(1)(ii).

3. Exit—Require NIVs with visas to use a self-service check out system located within secure areas of major international airports or seaports. The same persons who are exempt on entry are exempt from the exit requirements. 8 C.F.R. §215.8(a)(2). The process may require the departing individual to also provide fingerprints, photographs or other specified biometric identifiers. 8 C.F.R. §215.8(a)(1). This exit process began during 2004. DHS takes the position that failure to provide biometric and other information upon departure may lead to a determination that the individual failed to maintain the terms of his or her immigration status.8 C.F.R. §§214.1(a)(3)(ii), 215.8(b). It may also lead to a determination that the person is ineligible to receive a future visa or other immigration benefit or be admitted to the U.S. *Id.*; 69 Fed. Reg. 468, 474 (Jan. 5, 2004). In making a determination of lost benefits the officer will consider "the totality of the circumstances, including, but not limited to, all positive and negative factors related to the alien's ability to comply with the departure procedures." 8 C.F.R. §215.8(b). DHS, however, has abandoned the use of kiosks at airports where international passengers would register and is instead seeking to integrate the exit visa system into the normal departure process. DHS Announcement that International Visitors Are No Longer Required To USE US-VISIT Kiosks When Leaving the Country (May 4, 2007) *reported in* 84 No. 20 *Interpreter Releases* 1069, 1087–88 (May 14, 2007).
4. Traveling in the U.S.—TSA officials are now checking driver's licenses and other documentation when individuals are bordering aircraft *within* the U.S.
5. Challenging Information in US-VISIT—Challenging US-VISIT Records. Need to send the following information by mail or fax (202 298-5201) to US-VISIT Privacy Officer, US-VISIT Program, Border and Transportation Security, U.S. Department of Homeland Security, Washington, D.C. 20528: name, address, contact numbers, date and place of birth, date of arrival in and/or departure from the U.S., port of arrival and/or departure in U.S., name of airline or sea vessel and flight number or cruise line ticket number, passport number and country of issuance, and U.S. visa number. The requestor must sign the request *and the signature must be notarized or submitted under penalty of perjury* under 28 U.S.C. §1746. Privacy officer may also be called 202-298-5200. 69 Fed. Reg. 2615 (Jan. 16, 2004).

D. ***Advanced Passenger Information System (APIS)***—CBP also maintains the Advanced Passenger Information System (APIS) which allows it to obtain information from carriers on persons entering and leaving the U.S. before the passengers enter or depart. 70 Fed. Reg. 17820 (Apr. 7, 2005) *reported in* 82 No. 16 *Interpreter Releases* 657, 664–65 (Apr. 18, 2005). Airlines and cruise ships must now send to DHS electronically in advance of arrival in or departure from the U.S. biographical and other passenger information on all passengers in carriers arriving or departing the U.S. CBP has adopted final rules requiring various forms of notification of passenger and crew lists at least 30 minutes before flight departs. 72 Fed. Reg. 48320 (Aug. 23, 2007).

E. ***Arrival/Departure Information System (ADIS)***—The arrival and departure records obtained through US-VISIT and APIS will be stored in ADIS and will be used to verify overstays and to notify schools through the Student and Exchange Visitor Information System (SEVIS) that a student should be enrolling within 30 days of entry. The biometric identification information will be entered into an automated identification system (IDENT). The information obtained through ADIS or IDENT can be checked against DOS consular records to determine biometric matches. The DOS information can be accessed through Interagency Border Inspection System (IBIS) at a port of entry. For Privacy Act compliance issues and challenges to ADIS or ENFORCE/IDENT system, *see* Ch. 3, ¶¶ IV.A.4 to .7 (p.129), *supra*.

F. ***Cannot Have Preconceived Intent to Enter for Purpose Different from that Permitted Under Visa***—(*e.g.*, B-2 really immigrant; B-2 really H-1), with very limited exceptions. However, at least one court has found that an adjustment of status bars a later deportation for initial entry with preconceived intent to remain. *Choe v. INS*, 11 F.3d 925 (9th Cir. 1993).

G. ***If Admitted at Border***—Applicant is given an I-94 (document authorizing stay), recording arrival/departure and stamped with port of entry/date.

H. ***Time of Initial Admission Provided at 8 C.F.R. §214.2***—H and L visa holders can be admitted only during validity of petition. All visa holders, including H/L, can be admitted to the U.S. for a period extending beyond the date of the visa. 22 C.F.R. §41.112(a); 9 FAM 41.112 N. 2.11. Where an error is made in the time given for admission that is not consistent with granting a person until the validity period of his petition plus 10 days, *e.g.,* 8 C.F.R. §214.2(h)(13)(i)(A), it may be corrected by bringing the I-94 to the local inspections unit to be corrected or sending it to the supervisor at the port of entry. IFM at 15.12(c). *Evangelical Lutheran Church in America v. INS,* 288 F.Supp.2d 32, 48–49 n.11 (D.D.C. 2003), *appeal dismissed,* 2004 WL 434067 (D.C. Cir. Mar. 3, 2004)

I. ***Grace Period to Depart the U.S.***—Certain periods of stay also include a "grace period" before someone must depart the United States. For example, by regulation, a student in F-1 status is given 60 days after completion of study to depart. 8 C.F.R. §214.2(f)(5)(iv). An H-1B is given 10 days after expiration of the validity period." Letter, Hernandez, Director, Business and Trade Services Branch, INS (Mar. 21, 2001), *reprinted in* 78 No. 13 *Interpreter Releases* 608, 615 (Apr. 2, 2001). An H-1B is also not employment authorized during the 10-day grace period. ***Unpaid Leave.*** At least one court has recognized that placing an employee on unpaid leave until his immigration status is resolved is consistent with IRCA and not in violation of law. *Incalza v. Fendi North America, Inc.,* 479 F.3d 1005 (9th Cir. 2006) [where E-1 Italian national was fired after company changed from Italian to French ownership, employee's award of damages for wrongful termination under California law was upheld because company could have requested H-1B status or placed him on temporary unpaid leave until he married a USC instead of terminating him].

J. ***Criminal Activity in U.S.***—A conviction of an NIV in the U.S. for a crime of violence for which a sentence of more than one year imprisonment *may* be imposed (regardless of whether such sentence is in fact imposed) constitutes a failure to maintain status under INA §237(a)(1)(C)(i). 8 C.F.R. §214.1(g).

K. ***Extension of Stay***—8 C.F.R. §214.1(c); USCIS SOPs on Extension of Status (Mar. 2003), *published on* AILA InfoNet at Doc. No. 07090760.

1. All NIVs are eligible for extension except: (a) Visa Waiver entrants; (b) C-1, C-2, C-3; (c) D-1, D-2; (d) K-1, K-2; and (e) Person admitted as D/S except F-1 students not completing full course of study (8 C.F.R. §214.2(f)(7)); (f) S beyond 3 years; (g) Q-2 beyond 3 years. 8 C.F.R. §214.1(c)(3).

2. Procedure—8 C.F.R. §214.1(c)(2):

   2.a. Apply on Form I-539—All nonimmigrants except:

   (1) Exchange visitors (J)—SEVIS DS-2019.

   (2) NIV temporary workers (E, H, L, O, P, Q, R, TN)—Form I-129 with appropriate supplement. Dependents holding derivative status may be included on I-129. 8 C.F.R. §214.1(c)(1).

   2.b. Applications filed before the expiration of the applicant's current status are timely. The failure to file timely may be excused. 8 C.F.R. §214.1(c)(4).

   2.c. Give reasons requesting stay; attach I-94; provide documentation. Person must agree to maintain passport validity during extension period.

   2.d. USCIS service center decides.

   2.e. No appeal. 8 C.F.R. §§214.1(c)(5) and 214.2(p)(9). May file motion to reconsider with USCIS. Does not stay decision and therefore ICE may seek deportation in absence of stay.

   2.f. If extension is denied there is a question post-IIRIRA whether there is federal jurisdiction to review the denial. *Compare CDI Information Services, Inc. v. Reno,* 278 F.3d 616 (6th Cir. 2002) [no jurisdiction under INA §242(a)(2)(B)(ii) to review a denial of an H-1B extension] *with Evangelical Lutheran Church in America v. INS,* 288 F.Supp.2d 32, 40–45 (D.D.C. 2003) *appeal dismissed* 2004 WL 434067 (D.C. Cir. Mar. 3, 2004) [rejected the discretionary decision bar, INA §242(g) bar, and committed to agency discretion bar in reviewing the denial of an untimely filed H-1B extension and reversed former INS decision]. Jurisdiction clearly existed pre-IIRIRA. *Chung v. INS*, 662 F.Supp. 474 (W.D. Wash 1987) [review of denial of E-2 extension].

2.g. Out-of-Time Request—Where a request for extension is filed out-of-time, USCIS may grant the extension *nunc pro tunc* where the failure to timely file was due to "extraordinary circumstances" beyond the applicant's control and the delay was "commensurate with the circumstances," the applicant is a bona fide NIV not in removal proceedings and has not otherwise violated his or her NIV status. 8 C.F.R. §214.1(c)(4).

2.h. Travel While Extension Is Pending—A person in the H, L, O, P category who travels for personal or business reasons during the pendency of the extension may request USCIS to send a cable to the U.S. consulate so the applicant can obtain a new visa. 8 C.F.R. §§214.2(h)(15)(i), (*l*)(15)(i), (o)(12)(i), (p)(14)(i).

L. *Change of Status*—INA §248, 8 U.S.C. §1258; 8 C.F.R. §248; USCIS SOPs on Change of Status (Mar. 2003), *published on* AILA InfoNet at Doc. No. 07090760.

1. Can change from one nonimmigrant status to another pursuant to INA §248, 8 U.S.C. §1258 (*e.g.,* B-2 can change to F-1) on Form I-539. All NIV temporary workers (except family members who continue to use I-539s) must use I-129. To change status an applicant must be in lawful status, absent extraordinary circumstances. 8 C.F.R. §248.1(b). The agency interprets lawful status to include not only up to the time of filing but up to the time the new status becomes operative. *L.A. Closeout, Inc. v. DHS,* 513 F.3d 940 (9th Cir. 2007) [rejected claim that person had to be in lawful status on a B-2 only until the time the c/s was filed under 8 C.F.R. §248.1 and not until the H-1B status became available (because of the cap) months after the B-2 stay expired].

1.a. Students

(1) A B-1/B-2 cannot begin to attend school until his or her change of status to F-1/M-1 has been approved. 8 C.F.R. §248.1(c)(3). When a Service officer is adjudicating a C/S he must ensure that applicant did not begin and will not begin a course of study before C/S is granted. Memo, Williams, Ex. Assoc. Comm. Field Operations, HQISD 70/6.2.2 P (Apr. 12, 2002), *reprinted in* 79 No. 17 *Interpreter Releases* 595, 605–07 (Apr. 22, 2002).

(2) A student in F-1 status is given D/S + 60-day grace period to depart the U.S. after completion of F-1 status, including optional practical training. A person may C/S to H-1B (or another status) during the 60-day departure period (including after completion of OPT). Memo, Pearson, Exec. Assoc. Comm. Field Operations, HQ 70.23.1 RS-P (Aug. 19, 1998), *reprinted in* 75 No. 32 *Interpreter Releases* 1147, 1167 (Aug. 24, 1998).

1.b. Certain categories cannot change—8 C.F.R. §§248.1(c)(1), 248.2.

(1) Persons who are inadmissible including under INA §212(a)(9)(B)(i) because they stayed 6 months or a year or more longer than they were given or were otherwise unlawfully present in the U.S. for that period of time, unless AG granted a waiver of the inadmissibility.

(2) C (transit); D (crewman); K (fiancée) TWOV, J (exchange visitor/student if subject to two-year foreign residency requirement), S (informant), Visa waiver program entrant, M-1 to F-1, and M-1 to H-1 if H-1 based on training received as an M-1.

(3) J can change if he obtains waiver of 2-year foreign residency requirement or is not subject to requirement. Js who are foreign medical graduates can also now change status to H-1B if they meet INA §212(e) requirements and meet all commitments concerning their contract with health facility including 3-year commitment. INA §214(*l*)(2), 8 U.S.C. §1184(*l*)(2); 8 C.F.R. §212.7(c)(9).

(4) Exception. Restrictions on changing status do not apply to those seeking U or T status. INA §248(b).

1.c. Intent Problem—B-2 to F-l. If a request for a change from B to F-1 occurs within 60 days of entry, the Service views the change as improper on the grounds that the applicant's admission as a B-2 was improper because he had the "preconceived intent" to enter as a student (F-1). If person obtained school certificate before entry as B-2, it is evidence of preconceived intent to be a student. Where request for change of status occurred within four months of entry and the SEVIS I-20 A/B was requested from the school within 45 days of entry, INS's denial of change of status was upheld. *Tsui v. Attorney General*, 445 F.Supp. 832 (D.D.C. 1978).

1.d. Departure during pendency of application for C/S has traditionally constituted an abandonment. Memo, Cook, Acting Asst. Comm. Program, HQ 70/6.2.9 (June 18, 2001), *reprinted in* 78 No. 33 *Interpreter Releases* 1378, 1395 (Aug. 27, 2001); Letter, Bednarz, Chief, NIV Branch, Adjudications, CO 248-C (Oct. 29, 1993), *reprinted in* 70 No. 46 *Interpreter Releases* 1604, 1626 (Dec. 6, 1993). It also results in a problem regarding cancellation of the person's current visa under INA §222(g) if he is o/s when he departs. However, departure during the course of a nonfrivolous C/S or E/S is considered an extraordinary circumstance for purposes of 222(g) and the person need not return to his home country to obtain a new visa. The person may also be eligible for a INA §212(d)(4) waiver at the border. *See in this chapter* "INA §222(g)/Overstays," section II.E, (p.625), *supra.*

1.e. Departure After C/S Granted—A change of status takes effect automatically on the effective date noted on the I-797 and any intervening departure or admission should not negate the effective date. Letter, Hernandez, Chief, Business and Trade Services Branch, Adjudications, USCIS, HQOPRD 70/6.2 (Aug. 18, 2004) exchange of letters, *published on* AILA InfoNet at Doc. No. 05042565 [where F-1 obtains C/S to H-1B but start-up date for H-1B is months away and person departs after approval and returns on valid F-1 status before H-1B status takes effect, she is eligible to begin H-1B status on its effective date noting that C/S approval of H-1B is on a tear-off I-94].

1.f. May also C/S even if out of status if it is due to "extraordinary circumstances beyond the control of the applicant or petitioner" and the applicant "has not otherwise violated his or her nonimmigrant status." 8 C.F.R. §248.1(b)(1), (2). *Eyoum v. INS*, 125 F.3d 889, 892 (5th Cir. 1997) [rejected argument because applicant had also worked without authorization].

1.g. H and L visas—If the maximum period has been reached for the H or the L an applicant cannot C/S to the other category because a petition may not be approved once the maximum period (6 years for H and 5/7 years for an L) has been reached. The 6-year limit applies to spouses and dependents in H-4 status. 8 C.F.R. §214.2(h)(9)(iv). Time spent in L-1 status counts toward the 6-year period for H. 8 C.F.R. §214.2(*l*)(12)(i); Letter, Bednarz, Chief, NIV Branch, Adjudications, CO 214L-C (Feb. 14, 1994), *reprinted in* 71 No. 10 *Interpreter Releases* 351, 373–74 (Mar. 14, 1994) LOS-N-83573 (WRSC May 19, 1988), EAC 88-053 0121 (NYC June 21, 1988), *reported in* 7 *AILA Monthly Mailing* 497 (Oct. 1988). However, a person in H-4 or L-2 status is free to change his status to an H-1B or L-1 because the time spent in H-4 or L-2 status is not counted toward the six year maximum on H-1Bs or 5/7 years on L-1s. Memo, Aytes, Assoc. Dir., Domestic Operations, USCIS, HQPRD 70/6.2.8, 70/6.2.12, AD 06-29 (Dec. 5, 2006), *published on* AILA InfoNet at Doc. No. 06122063 [recognizing that H-1B and H-4 after 6 years can switch positions with each obtaining a new 6 years]; AFM §31.2(d)(2). There is also an issue as to whether the "time spent" waiting for the approval of the grant of a c/s from the DHS can be deducted from the 5-, 6-, or 7-year limitation. The c/s bar does not effect a c/s to categories other than H or L, and a person who has reached the maximum period may still c/s, for example, to an O or E visa.

1.h. H-1B Cap—If person applies for C/S and the cap has been reached they will be treated as out of status if they fall out of status before the beginning of the next fiscal year on Oct 1st. For a detailed discussion, *see in this chapter* "Change of Status and H-1B Cap ('Cap-Gap') Problem," ¶ VII.C.1.h(4) (p.678), *infra*.

2. I-129 Petition—For all NIVs who are temporary workers (E, H, L, O, P, Q, R, TN) when simultaneously filing request for another NIV status. Dependents holding derivative status may be included in the petition if the form version specifically provides for their inclusion. In all other cases family members/dependents of the worker should submit Form I-539. All applications are filed with VSC/CSC having jurisdiction over the person's place of employment in the U.S.

   Not needed where change is (1) from B-2 to B-l or B-l to B-2, or (2) from A, G, E, F, H, I, J, L or M of accompanying family member to F-1.

3. A and G changing status must also file an I-566 with the I-539.

4. No appeal on denial of change of status, 8 C.F.R. §214.2(p)(9)—However, applicant can make a motion to reconsider before the regional service center director.

M. *Maintenance of Present Status*—8 C.F.R. §248.1(b)

1. To maintain status applicant must:

   1.a. File Change of Status or Extension of Status Timely—Failure to submit change or extension of status before authorized stay expires results in a violation of status unless the DD is satisfied it was excusable. If tardiness is less than one week, strong consideration given to excusing it. However, if a person is determined to be an overstay his visa is void and he must return to his country of nationality to obtain a new visa. INA §222(g)(1), (2), 8 U.S.C. §1202(g)(1), (2).

   1.b. Not Violate Status—Unauthorized employment is a per se failure to maintain status. 8 C.F.R. §214.1(e) (F-l who worked without authorization). Leave under the Family and Medical Leave Act does not terminate the employer-employee relationship (in H-1B context) and the person is therefore in status. Letter, Hernandez, Acting Director, Business and Trade Service (HQ 70/6.2.8) (Feb. 2, 2000), *reprinted in* 77 No. 8 *Interpreter Releases* 243, 252 (Feb. 28, 2000). An unpaid leave in order to address status may also be consistent with the law. *Incalza v. Fendi North America, Inc.,* 479 F.3d 1005 (9th Cir. 2006) [where E-1 Italian national was fired after company changed from Italian to French ownership, employee's award of damages for wrongful termination under California law was upheld because company could have requested H-1B status or placed him on temporary unpaid leave until he married a USC instead of terminating him].

   1.c. Not Be In Deportation Proceedings.

2. An applicant's adjustment of status to LPR is barred if he does not maintain his status, unless INA §§245(i) and 245(k) is applicable.

N. *Adjudication of Petitions*

1. Premium Processing of Certain Applications—PL 106-553, 114 Stat. 2762 (Dec. 21, 2000), INA §286(u), 8 U.S.C. §1356(u); 8 C.F.R. §§103.2(f), 103.7(b)(1), (c)(1); 66 Fed. Reg. 29682–86 (June 1, 2001). The Service established a procedure that guarantees that it will process certain employment-based petitions and applications within 15 calendar days if the petitioner pays a premium processing fee. The current fee is $1,000 in addition to the regular I-129 Fee. An I-907 Form must be filed with the I-129 Petition currently designated for premium processing. Petitioners in the following categories are eligible for premium processing: E-1/E-2, H-1B, H-2B, H-3, L-1, O-1/O-2, P-1/P-2/P-3, Q-1, TN NAFTA. Within the 15-day period USCIS will issue an approval notice, notice of intent to deny, request for evidence or notice of an investigation for fraud or misrepresentation. 66 Fed. Reg. at 29682. If USCIS does not issue a response within 15 days it will refund the fee and still expedite the case. 8 C.F.R. §103.2(f)(1).The 15-day period begins when USCIS receives the application or petition. 8 C.F.R. §103.2(f)(1). The use of premium processing for applications may change over time and USCIS will post on its website (*www.uscis.gov/premiumprocessing*) which application and petitions can use premium processing. 8 C.F.R. §103.2(f)(2)

2. Expedited Processing of Cases—USCIS service centers will accept requests to expedite cases separate and apart from Premium Processing. They will accept expedite requests based on the following criteria: (1) Severe financial loss to the company or individual; (2) Extreme emergent situation; (3) Humanitarian situation; (4) Nonprofit status of requesting organization in furtherance of the cultural and social interests of the U.S.;(5) DOD or National Interest Situation (Note: Request must come from U.S. government entity and explain why delay would be detrimental); (6) USCIS error; or (7) Compelling interest of the Service. Memo, Ohata, Assoc. Comm. Service Center Operations, HQ 70/1 (Nov. 30, 2001), *reprinted in* 79 No. 5 *Interpreter Releases* 146, 159–62 (Jan. 28, 2002); Memo, Ohata, Assoc. Comm. Service Center Operations, HQ70/1 (Apr. 20, 2001), *reprinted in* 78 No. 25 *Interpreter Releases* 1072, 1118 (July 2, 2001) [provides telephone and fax numbers to make requests at service centers]. There is also a general number for information at all service centers. 1-800-375-5283.

3. Questioning Prior Determinations—USCIS has the authority to question prior determinations on petitions and applications and adjudicators are not bound to approve subsequent I-129 or other petitions or applications for benefits simply because of a prior erroneous approval. Where the same parties are seeking an extension on the same underlying facts a prior determination should be given deference. However, a prior approval need not be followed where there was: (1) a material error; or

there is (2) a substantial change in circumstances; or (3) new material information adversely effecting eligibility. Memo, Yates, Assoc. Dir. Of Operations, USCIS, HQOPRD 72/11.3 (Apr. 23, 2004), *published on* AILA InfoNet at Doc. No. 04050510 (May 5, 2004) [defining material error, substantial change and new material information and recognizing that material error does not include subjective determinations such as the prior adjudicator's evaluation of a degree equivalency]. *Accord Royal Siam Corp. v. Chertoff,* 484 F.3d 139, 148 (1st Cir. 2007) [H-1B petitioner for restaurant manager has no automatic entitlement to second approval where first approval was in error; no estoppel].

4. Request for Evidence (RFE) & Notice of Intent to Deny (NOID)—8 C.F.R. §103.2(b); AFM at §§10.1(c), 11.1(m), 25.2(d)(3), 38.1(e). The regulations do not require adjudicators to issue RFEs or NOIDs *before denying* an application. 8 C.F.R. §103.2(b)(8). USCIS, however, intends to exercise this authority only where cases "are filed with little more than a signature and proper fee, and therefore are substantially incomplete or where the applicant or petitioner has failed to demonstrate a basis for eligibility for the benefit sought" (for example an AOS as an IR where no evidence of the relationship is provided). 72 Fed. Reg. 19100, 19103 (Apr. 17, 2007). Conversely, an RFE/NOID should also not be issued where all statutory or regulatory evidence required has been submitted (*i.e.,* the record is complete) and the applicant or petitioner demonstrated eligibility by a preponderance of the evidence. The applicant/petitioner does *not* have to establish eligibility beyond a reasonable doubt. Memo, Yates, Assoc. Dir. Operations, USCIS, HQOPRD 70/2 (Feb. 16, 2005), *published on* AILA InfoNet at Doc. No. 05021810 (rescinding May 4, 2004 memo) ["Adjudicators too often issue a RFE for additional types of evidence that could tend to eliminate all doubt and all possibility for fraud"]. "RFEs should, if possible, be avoided." AFM at 10.5(a). An RFE should only be issued where a specific piece of information is missing and the request should not be a "broad brush" request. It is not normally appropriate for officers to "dump" the entire RFE template and send it to the applicant. Memo, Yates (Feb. 18, 2005), *supra.* A NOID is more appropriate than a RFE when the initial evidence is predominantly present but: (1) the filing does not appear to establish eligibility by the preponderance of the evidence; (2) the case appears to be ineligible for approval but not necessarily incurable; (3) the adjudicator intends to rely for denial on evidence not submitted by the petitioner/applicant; or (4) a statute or regulation requires a NOID. Memo, Yates (Feb. 18, 2005), *supra.* A NOID is required for VAWA petitions (8 C.F.R. §§204.2(c)(3)(ii) and (e)(3)(ii), AOS involving certain physicians (8 C.F.R. §245.18(i)) and certain legalization applications (8 C.F.R. §245a.20(a)(2)). By regulation, USCIS has also instituted a procedure where the time period to respond to an RFE is "flexible" depending upon the subject matter and can be less, but never more, than 12 weeks. 8 C.F.R. §103.2(b)(8)(iv). A NOID always only allows 30 days to respond. *Id.* An RFE/NOID may also direct an applicant to appear for a "biometrics capture." If the applicant fails to appear for a biometrics capture or other required in-person process, the application or petition "shall be considered abandoned and denied" unless by the appointment date USCIS had received a change of address or rescheduling request that the agency concludes warrants the failure to appear. 8 C.F.R. §103.2(b)(13)(ii).

5. Copies vs. Originals—Petitioner must submit originals of the application or petition and the documents issued to support them such as a labor certification, Form DS-2019, medical examinations, affidavits, formal consultations, letters of current employment and all other documents needed to support the benefit sought unless it is an document issued by USCIS or the legacy INS. 8 C.F.R. §§103.2(b)(4). The agency may request that other originals be submitted as well and failure to submit them by the deadline may result in denial or revocation. 8 C.F.R. §103.2(b)(5). If a petitioner or applicant submits unrequested originals they will not be returned unless a written request is made for them. AFM at 11.1(m)(3); 8 C.F.R. §§103.2(b)(4),(5). Documentary requirements for petitioner's lawful status are found at 8 C.F.R. §103.2(b)(17).

6. Considering government error or delay and compelling circumstances. USCIS has recognized that there may be circumstances where due to "government error or delay and compelling humanitarian factors," the officer may exercise his judgment to render an "extraordinary favorable" decision to the applicant Memo, Divine, Acting Deputy Director, USCIS (May 3, 2006), *published on* AILA InfoNet at Doc. No. 06051562.

O. *Employment of Nonimmigrants*—8 C.F.R. §§214.1(e), 274a.12–.14

1. Unauthorized work can result in deportation for failure to maintain status—INA §237(a)(1)(C), 8 U.S.C. §1227(a)(1)(C). Unauthorized employment is not a bar to adjustment of status if the applicant is eligible for INA §245(i), 8 U.S.C. §1255(i) or is an immediate relative.

2. Work Authorization Procedures

   2.a. Regulations under 8 C.F.R. §274a.12–14.

   2.b. If person lawfully employed under A-3, E-1, E-2, E-3, G-5, H-1B, H-2A/B, H-3, I, J-1, L-1, O-1/O-2, P-1/P-2/P-3 or R status, or NIV under §214(e) (NAFTA) and files timely application for extension consistent with 8 C.F.R. §214.1, is automatically given 240 days from date of expiration. 8 C.F.R. §274a.12(b)(20). This extension does not apply if person is seeking a change of status. During 240 days, there is no INA §245(c) bar to adjustment of status.

   2.c. If nonimmigrant changes employers, s/he must file new petition and cannot work for new employer until approval of new petition. Letter, Weinig, Deputy Asst. Comm. Adjudications (June 2, 1988), *reprinted in* 65 No. 28 *Interpreter Releases* 735, 751–52 (July 25, 1988). The exception to this rule is for H-1Bs who are allowed "portability" and can begin working for a new H-1B employer at the time the new H-1B petition is filed if certain conditions are met.

3. Revocation—8 C.F.R. §274a.14(b).

   3.a. DD can revoke work authorization if:

      (1) Good cause shown;

      (2) Conditions that favored granting permission no longer exist;

      (3) Information in application was not true.

   3.b. DD must provide notice of revocation and a 15-day period for applicant to respond. 8 C.F.R. §274a.14(b)(2).

4. Procedure—For a discussion regarding which NIVs are authorized to work incident to status and which require an EAD and submission I-765, *see* "Employment Authorization" in Ch. 12, part X (p.1265), *infra*.

IV. VISA-EXEMPT PERSONS

A. *Canadians*—Canadians do not need visas to enter the U.S., unless they seek entry on an E, K, S or V visa. 8 C.F.R. §212.1(a); 22 C.F.R. §41.2(m). But they now need passports. A Canadian citizen will need a passport to enter the U.S. unless s/he is: (1) a participant in NEXUS, FAST, or SENTRI programs; (2) a Canadian Indian; or (3) a child under 16 or, if in a group, under 19. 8 C.F.R. §212.1(a). CBP officers are now prohibited from accepting oral declarations of Canadian citizenship at land borders and a Canadian must provide documentary evidence of citizenship. 72 Fed. Reg. 72744–45 (Dec. 21, 2007). Residents but not citizens of Canada must present a visa as well as a passport. Admission is for 6 months maximum as B-l/B-2. If a different visa is desired, applicant needs to show approved petition (*e.g.,* 1-797 for H-1B), or certificate (*e.g.,* SEVIS I-20 A/B for F/M) or apply at the border (TN, L-1). Must show proof of Canadian citizenship at border. The form for Canadians border crossing cards has been eliminated although Canadians who need to obtain waivers can enter with a I-194. Canadian pleasure boaters (including landed immigrants from a visa waiver country) may now also get an I-68 which permits them to avoid inspection each time they boat into U.S. waters. 8 C.F.R. §§235.1(g)(1), (4) and (5). Persons admitted without visa from Canada at the border are not subject to INA §222(g). Nor are Canadians who enter on a visa but are not issued an I-94 unless there are formally found to be out of status. Letter, Hrinyak, Acting Assoc. Comm. INS (HQINS 70/12.1) (Apr. 1, 1999), *published on* AILA InfoNet at Doc. No. 99040191. Also, Canadians inspected at the border but not given a visa or I-94 are treated as duration of status similar to F/J for purposes of the 3/10 year bar according to a DOS cable interpreting INS's position. Cable, DOS, 97-State-23545, *reprinted in* 76 No. 41 *Interpreter Releases* 1552–53 (Oct. 25, 1999). However, the Service has not provided a written opinion on this subject. Canadians subject to INA §212(e) can satisfy the 2-year foreign residency requirement by living in Canada and working in the U.S. Minutes, Liaison Meeting Between USIA/AILA ¶19, *reprinted in* 18 *AILA Monthly Mailing* 52 (Jan. 1999). Most Canadians are not subject to US-VISIT. But NSEERS initial fingerprinting/identification requirements may still be in effect for Canadians born in certain countries. The U.S. and Canada have developed a system called NEXUS that allows low risk, pre-approved users simplified entry into Canada and the U.S.

Canadian citizens seeking to enter the U.S. to perform as musicians and athletes may enter the U.S. on H-2Bs that are precertified if they are going to perform within 50 miles of the U.S. border. They do not need an H-2B visa, for example. Procedures for Temporary Labor Certification in the Entertainment Industry under the H-2B Visa Program, TEGL 31-05, DeRocco, Asst. Sec. ETA, DOL (May 31, 2006) at ¶4C, *reprinted in* 12 No. 1 *Bender's Immigration Bulletin* 1, 42–54 (Jan. 1, 2007).

Previously, persons who had a common nationality with Canadians or British subjects in Bermuda, including citizens of all commonwealth countries and Ireland (*e.g.,* India, Namibia, New Zealand, Pakistan), who resided in Canada or Bermuda had both passport and visa requirements waived. Former 9 FAM 41.2 N.1.1; 22 C.F.R. §41.2(b); 8 C.F.R. §212.1(a); O.I. 212.1(b). Residence for this purpose was found to include refugee status in Canada. *Matter of Thumbimuthu,* Case No. A70 521 400 (IJ Mar. 29, 1993), *reported in* 12 *AILA Monthly Mailing* 461 (June 1993). This waiver has been eliminated. Cable, Powell, Secy. of State, 03-State-029504 (Feb. 1, 2003), *published on* AILA InfoNet at Doc. No. 03030446. Citizens from Bermuda do not need a visa but do need a passport if arriving by air. 22 C.F.R. §41.2(b).

B. ***Mexicans***—No visa/passport required if: (1) Have DSP-150, B-1/B-2 Visa and Border Crossing Card, containing a machine readable biometric identifier, (2) Coming from contiguous territory by land or sea; and applying for B-l/B-2 entry. In every other situation a Mexican national is required to have a passport. 8 C.F.R. §212.1(c); 22 C.F.R. §41.2(g). Also, to obtain a Border Crossing Card and B-1/B-2 visa, the Mexican citizen must present a Mexican passport at the consulate. 22 C.F.R. §41.32(a)(2)(iii). CBP officers are now prohibited from accepting oral declarations of Mexican citizenship at land borders and Mexican citizens must provide documentary evidence of citizenship. 72 Fed. Reg. 72744–45 (Dec. 21, 2007). Mexicans are issued I-94s like other entrants. Mexican Border Visitor's Permits have been eliminated. Border crossing cards are valid until cancelled. 22 C.F.R. §41.32(c). Persons admitted from Mexico with BCCs may remain in U.S. up to 30 days without needing an I-94 and may travel not more than 25 miles from the border, unless it is in Arizona where they may travel up to 75 miles from the border. 8 C.F.R. §235.1(h)(1)(v). Persons admitted from Mexico with a DSP-150 border crossing card (BCC) are not subject to INA §222(g). Nor are Mexicans who enter on a visa but are not issued an I-94 unless there are formally found to be out of status. Letter, Hrinyak, (HQINS 70/12.1) (Apr. 1, 1999), *published on* AILA InfoNet at Doc. No. 99040191.

C. ***North American Free Trade Agreement (NAFTA)***—58 Fed. Reg. 69205–19 (Dec. 30, 1993); 58 Fed. Reg. 69226–28 (Dec. 30, 1993); 58 Fed. Reg. 68526–28 (Dec. 28, 1993); 8 C.F.R. §§214.2(b)(4), 214.6; 9 FAM 41.59. NAFTA was signed Dec. 8, 1993. Chapter 16 of the Agreement related to immigration issues. To comply with the Agreement, INA §214(e), 8 U.S.C. §1184(e), has been added to provide for the admission to the U.S. of Mexican and Canadian citizens who are coming to engage in professional activities as defined by the NAFTA.

1. Visitors for Business—8 C.F.R. §214.2(b)(4) provides for an expanded class of persons who can enter the U.S. as business visitors so long as they receive no salary or other remuneration from a U.S. source other than expense allowances; they provide proof of Canadian or Mexican citizenship; they provide a description of the purpose of entry and evidence that they will engage in one of the occupations or professions set forth in Appendix 1603.A.1 to Annex 1603 of NAFTA, 8 C.F.R. §214.2(b)(4)(i)(A)–(G), and that they are otherwise eligible under existing law. A citizen of Canada is not required to present an NIV. A Mexican must present a passport and either an NIV or border crossing card. Cable, INS, HQ 1815-P (Dec. 30, 1993). These occupations/professions include:
    - research and design;
    - growth, manufacture and production;
    - marketing (including trade fair and promotional personnel attending a convention);
    - sales (for representatives and agents taking orders or negotiating contracts for goods or services, but not delivering goods or providing services);
    - distribution (including transportation operators and customs brokers, except Mexico has exempt this activity);
    - after-sales services, including installation, repair and maintenance personnel;
    - general service, including management and supervisory personnel engaged in commercial transactions, financial service personnel, public relations personnel, tourism personnel, tour bus operators, translators and other professionals set out in Appendix 1603.D.1 (TN) to Annex 1603 of NAFTA.
2. L Petitions—Requirements are the same as other Ls but the procedure is different for Canadians. A Canadian beneficiary of an L petition can present the petition at a Class A port of entry or pre-

clearance/preflight station. 8 C.F.R. §214.2(*l*)(17). The Canadian spouse and Canadian children of an L-1 are entitled to an L-2. Non-Canadian spouse or children must apply for the L-2 visa at the U.S. Embassy or Consulate. Mexican citizens must submit an I-129 and L Supplement as any other L applicant.

3. Professionals—TNs

3.a. TN status is for Canadian and Mexican persons engaged in activities at a professional level. 8 C.F.R. §214.6. This category is designated "TN," is similar to H-1B except there is no statutory limitation on stay such as exists for Hs and Ls, and it generally covers a broader range of job categories. However, TNs unlike H-1Bs are subject to INA §214(b) and must prove their intent not to immigrate. 9 FAM 41.59 N5. "Activities at a Professional Level" under NAFTA is defined as requiring "at least a baccalaureate degree or appropriate credentials demonstrating status as a professional." A baccalaureate degree under the former U.S. Canada Free Trade Agreement did not require the completion of a 4-year program where the Canadian university grants a degree in 3 years. Letter, Puleo, Asst. Comm., Adjudications, CO 1773-C (Dec. 22, 1989), *reprinted in* 67 No. 22 *Interpreter Releases* 639, 655 (June 4, 1990). The regulations specify various categories of professions that are covered by Appendix 1603.D.1 to Annex 1603. 8 C.F.R. §214.6(c). These include: accountant (BA, CPA, CA, CGA, or CMA); actuary (included within term mathematician and therefore requires a BA and recognition by a professional actuarial association or society); architect (BA or state/provincial license); computer systems analyst (BA or post-secondary diploma and 3 years experience); disaster relief claims adjuster (BA or 3 years experience in field); economist (BA); engineer (BA or state/ provincial license); forester (BA or state/provincial license); graphic designer (BA or post-secondary diploma + 3 years experience); hotel manager (BA in hotel/ rest. management or post-secondary diploma in hotel/rest. management and 3 years experience in field); industrial designers (BA or post-secondary diploma + 3 years experience); interior designer (BA or post-secondary diploma + 3 years experience); land surveyor (BA or state/provincial/federal license); landscape architect (BA); lawyer (member of bar in state or province or LLB, JD, LLL, or BCL); librarian (MLS or BLS); management consultant (BA or 5 years experience in management consulting or a related field); mathematician (BA); medical/allied professionals [including dentists, dietitians, medical technologists, nutritionists, occupational therapists, Pharmacists, physicians (teaching or research only), physio/physical therapist, psychologist, recreational therapist, and RN (state/ provincial license)]; veterinarian (DVM, DMV or state/provincial license); range manager (BA); research assistant; scientific technician/technologist; scientist (Agriculturist including Agronomist, Animal Breeder, Animal Scientist, Apiculturist, Astronomer, Biochemist, Biologist, Chemist, Dairy Scientist, Entomologist, Epidemiologist, Geneticist, Geochemist, Geologist, Geophysicist, Horticulturist, Meteorologist, Pharmacologist, Plant Paleontologist, Physicist including Oceanographer in Canada, Plan Breeder, Poultry, Soil Scientist and Zoologist—all of whom require either a BA or Licenciatura Degree); social worker (BA); sylviculturist (BA); teacher (college, seminary or university); technical publications writer (BA or post-secondary diploma + 3 years experience); urban planner (BA); and vocational counselor (BA).

3.b. The Service narrowed the grounds for the entry of a person as a management consultant under the former U.S. Canada Free Trade Agreement. The INS Guidelines provided that: "A management consultant should generally not be a regular, full-time employee, of the entity requiring service ... In cases [of full-time employment] the management consultant should not be assuming an existing position, replacing someone in an existing position, or filling a newly created permanent position. In short, the management consultant should either be an independent consultant or the employee of a consulting firm under contract to a U.S. entity or the consultant, if salaried, should be in a supernumerary temporary position." Memo, Puleo, Asst. Comm., Adjudications CO 1773-C (Oct. 4, 1989), *reprinted in* 9 *AILA Monthly Mailing* 253-54 (Apr., 1990).

3.c. Self-Employment Prohibited—8 C.F.R. §214.6(b) [defines "Engage in Business Activities"]. A TN may not be self-employed in U.S. However, a TN who is entering the U.S. to perform work for a U.S. company where s/he owns an interest (even a controlling interest) in the *Canadian* company contracted to perform the management consultancy may be granted TN status. Letter, LaFleur, Chief Business and Trade Branch, Adjudications, HQ 1815-C (Feb. 5, 1996), *reprinted in* 73 No. 8 *Interpreter Releases* 235, 249–50 (Feb. 26, 1996); 63 Fed. Reg. 1331–35, 1333 (Jan. 9, 1998).

3.d. Engineers—The Service determined that "software engineers" are included within NAFTA as engineering is not limited to any field. Memo, Cronin, Acting Ex. Assoc. Comm., Office of Programs, HQINS 70/6.2.23, *reprinted in* 77 No. 42 *Interpreter Releases* 1550, 1556–57 (Oct. 30, 2000). The engineer would still be required to demonstrate a B.A. or B.S. degree in engineering. *Id.*

3.e. Scientific Technician/Technologist (ST/T)—Appendix 1603.D.1 codified at 8 C.F.R. §214.6(c) requires a technologist to possess: (1) theoretical knowledge of any of the following disciplines: agricultural sciences, astronomy, biology, chemistry, engineering, forestry, geology, geophysics, meteorology, or physics; and (b) the ability to solve practical problems in any of these disciplines, or the ability to apply principles of any of those disciplines to basic or applied research. No degree or post-secondary diploma is required. Memo, Cronin, Acting Ex. Assoc. Comm., Office of Programs, HQINS 70/ 6.2.23, *reprinted in* 77 No. 42 *Interpreter Releases* 1550, 1556–57 (Oct. 30, 2000). Scientific Technician/Technologist position must involve the use of principles of science, research and development and/or scientific observations and calculations. The position must be in direct support of a professional in one of the sciences and primarily include activity consistent with the support of a science professional. The technician who assists the engineer in the lab to design and develop new technology may qualify, but the mechanic who repairs and maintains the same technology after it is built is not. DOS, Guidance on Qualification as a Scientific Technician/Technologist under NAFTA (Jan. 4, 2008), *published on* AILA InfoNet at Doc. No. 08022774. In evaluating whether a person qualifies under this category the following principles should be considered: (a) the ST/T must be providing support to a person who is a professional in one of the named fields; (b) the offer of employment must specifically demonstrate that the work of the ST/T will be inter-related with that of the supervisory professional and that it will therefore be managed, coordinated and reviewed by a professional; (c) the ST/T's theoretical knowledge has been acquired through the successful completion of a least two years of training in a relevant educational program. The training may be documented by presentation of a diploma, a certificate, or a transcript accompanied by evidence of relevant work experience; (d) the Occupational Outlook Handbook will be relied upon to determine whether the job functions are consistent with those of an ST/T; (e) Persons normally doing work in the construction trades even if in a specialized industry such as aircraft or power distribution will not be admitted. IFM at 15.5(f)(2)(A); Memo, Williams, Ex. Assoc. Comm. Field Operations, HQINS 70/6.2.2 (Nov. 7, 2002), *published on* AILA InfoNet at Doc. No. 02121331.

4. Procedures — 8 C.F.R. §§214.6(d), (e). Documentation must include proof of citizenship, a letter from the prospective employer describing in detail the activities to be performed to show they are in a professional capacity, diplomas, degrees, certificates or professional memberships and must affirm (a) professional activity to be engaged in; (b) purpose of entry; (c) anticipated length of stay; (d) beneficiary's educational qualifications; (e) beneficiary's compliance with applicable state law; and (f) arrangements for remuneration. Must have evaluations of Canadian or Mexican degree where required. Education requirements need to be demonstrated. 9 FAM 41.59 N1.2(3). Degrees outside of the U.S., Canada or Mexico should be accompanied by an evaluation. Evidence of licensure at the time of application for admission or a visa is *no longer required.* Memo, Hrinyak, Acting Ex. Dir. Immigration Policy and Programs, CBP, "Additional TN Occupations" (Oct. 26, 2004), *published on* AILA InfoNet at Doc. No. 05033173. Licensure to practice a given profession is a post-entry requirement subject to enforcement by the appropriate state agency and is *not* a prerequisite to obtain entry as a TN. 9 FAM 41.59 N1.4. Documentation for Canadians may be presented at a Class A port of entry or at a preclearance station. No prior petition, labor certification or approval required for Canadians. Nor is an LCA required. 8 C.F.R. §214.6(e), (h). I-94 given for one year as a multiple entry with designation TN. Can be used for all re-admissions while valid. Part-time employment under TN is permissible. 9 FAM 41.59 N1.5. To apply for an extension or change of status or change of U.S. employer the applicant must apply through the appropriate Service Center designated on the application or USCIS websites. An extension or change of status must be filed on an I-129. 83 No. 15 *Interpreter Releases* 643, 676–77 (Apr. 10, 2006). However, a new application is unnecessary where a TN's jobsite is changed by the same employer. 8 C.F.R. §214.6(i)(3).

Mexicans desiring TN status are no longer required to obtain approved petitions or LCAs. 8 C.F.R. §214.6(d), but they are still required to obtain a visa. 9 FAM 41.59 N2.3; IFM at 15.5. However, if a Mexican (or Canadian) is requesting an extension of status or change of status in the U.S. s/he must file an I-129. 83 No. 15 *Interpreter Releases* 643, 676–77 (Apr. 10, 2006). If it is not pursuant to an e/s or c/s, the TN applicant need only submit the request at the consulate with a passport and a visa application form, with a letter of employment in the U.S. that indicates the position in question and why the position requires a professional consistent with NAFTA Chapter 16, Annex 1603, Appendix 1603.D.1. The applicant must also present evidence that s/he is a professional. A list of professions is found at 9 FAM 41.59, Exhibit II. A license to practice certain professions, while required by a state (*e.g.,* law license/Bar admission), is *not* required to issue the TN visa. However, where a bachelor's degree is specifically required experience cannot be used in lieu of the degree. Cable, DOS, 04-State-3646 (Jan. 7, 2004), *published on* AILA InfoNet at Doc. No. 04022562. Approvals for Mexicans are no longer subject to a numerical cap. 69 Fed. Reg. 11287–90 (Mar. 10, 2004)

Denials—The Service will permit a Canadian citizen who applies for the TN at the border but cannot demonstrate that s/he is admissible to ask for a hearing before an IJ or withdraw her application for admission. If s/he declines to and she is inadmissible under INA §212(a)(6)(C) or (7)(A), the officer may initiate expedited removal procedures. IFM at 15.5(f)(10).

5. Spouses and unmarried minor children accompanying or following to join TN will get a TD visa. They shall not accept employment unless they are otherwise authorized. 8 C.F.R. §214.6(j). The are permitted to attend school on a full time basis. 9 FAM 41.59 N5.1
6. Domestic Servants—A domestic servant of a TN who meets the requirements for domestic servants entering the U.S. under 9 FAM 41.31 N9.3-3 may be issued a B-1 visa. 9 FAM 41.59 N5.2.
7. In-State Tuition—A TD/TN visa holder cannot possess the legal capacity to be a resident for in-state tuition purposes in California. *Carlson v. Reed,* 249 F.3d 876 (9th Cir. 2001) [person with TN/TD lacks intent under *Toll v. Moreno and Elkins v. Moreno* to establish permanent residency in the U.S. and scheme does not violate due process or equal protection.]
8. Doctrine of Dual Intent Inapplicable to TN—INA §214(b) is fully applicable, although there is no limitation on the number of years TN status may be granted. The doctrine of dual intent is not applicable to persons in TN status. 63 Fed. Reg. 1331 at 1333 (Jan. 9, 1998). 8 C.F.R. §214.6(b) [Definition of Temporary Entry]; 22 C.F.R. §41.59(c). Thus, a TN with an approved I-140 petition may be denied admission at the border as an intending immigrant. Letter, LaFleur, Business and Trade Services, Benefits Branch, INS, HQ 1815-C (June 18, 1996), *reprinted in* 73 No. 28 *Interpreter Releases* 970, 979–80 (July 22, 1996).
9. E Visas—NAFTA provides for E1/E2 status for Canadians and Mexicans. This status includes E1/E2 status in the U.S. Virgin Islands. Minutes of AILA and DOS Meeting (Oct. 3, 1989), *reprinted in* 9 *AILA Monthly Mailing* 42 (Jan. 1990).

D. *Groups Exempt By Statute, Treaty and Compact*—22 C.F.R. §41.1

1. U.S. Armed Forces, American Indians born in Canada, Aliens entering from Guam, Puerto Rico or U.S. Virgin Islands; foreign officials. TWOV may enter only if s/he has a valid visa to a third country.
2. Bahamian nationals or British subjects living in Bahamas, Cayman or Turks and Caicos can be exempted from visa (not passport) requirement if they satisfy the officer that they are "clearly and beyond doubt entitled to admission in all other respects." 22 C.F.R. §41.2(c), (d). Need certificate showing no criminal record.
3. British, French and Netherlands nationals having residence in respective territories in Caribbean (*e.g.,* French in Martinique).
4. Nationals and residents of the British Virgin Islands if: they have a passport; are proceedings by aircraft from St. Thomas, VI; are traveling to some other U.S. port solely for B visa purposes; and they have a current Certificate of Good Conduct issued by the Royal VI Police Dept. 22 C.F.R. §41.2(f); 8 C.F.R. §212.1(b)(2).
5. Persons from the Freely Associated States (Citizens of Federated States of Micronesia, the Republic of the Marshall Islands and the Republic of Palau). *See* Employer Information Bulletin 106,

Office of Business Liaison, DHS (Dec. 8, 2004), *reprinted in* 82 No. 7 *Interpreter Releases* 322, 341–42 (Feb. 14, 2005) [need only have a passport or in the case of Palau a travel document or birth certificate and will then be issued an I-94 with D/S allowing them to work in U.S.]. *See also* Fact Sheet, USCIS *discussed in* 82 No. 8 *Interpreter Releases* 353, 367–68 (Feb. 21, 2005).

6. Where unforeseen emergency and approval of DD. 22 C.F.R. §41.2(j).

E. ***Automatic Revalidation/Extension of Validity of Visa***—22 C.F.R. §41.112(d). An alien can re-enter the U.S. with an expired visa in her passport:

1. If the alien had maintained her status in the U.S., has a valid passport, and is in possession of an I-94 which has not yet expired; and

2. If the alien is applying for readmission from contiguous territory (without need of a waiver) after absence not exceeding 30 days. Fs and Js (and their accompanying spouse and children) can also go to adjacent islands on a current SEVIS I-20 or SEVIS DS-2019 whichever is appropriate.

3. This provision is inapplicable to: (1) persons who have applied for a new visa while abroad; and (2) persons who come from countries that are designated as state sponsors of terrorism 22 C.F.R. §§41.112(d)(2)(vii) & (3); 9 FAM 41.112 N.4.2 & 4.3; 9 FAM 41.121 PN1.2-15; Cable, DOS, 02-State-50158 (Mar. 14, 2002), *published on* AILA InfoNet at Doc. No. 02040432; IFM at 15.3(b). When a person is denied a visa abroad, the consular officer no longer needs to annotate the last page of the passport because the denial will appear electronically but should cancel the expired NIV and retrieve the I-94. Cable, DOS, 07-State-004819 (Jan.13, 2007), *published on* AILA InfoNet at Doc. No. 07050461; Cable, DOS, 02-State-50181 (June 2002), *published on* AILA InfoNet at Doc. No. 02061947, Memo, Williams, Ex. Assoc. Comm. Field Operations HQINS 70/11.1 (Mar. 29, 2002), *published on* AILA InfoNet at Doc. No. 02060434.

4. This provision may also not apply where the person simply changed status in the U.S. and never had a visa or the visa has now expired. Letter, Hernandez, HQ 70/6.2.5 (Nov. 2, 2001), *reprinted in* 79 No. 2 *Interpreter Releases* 38, 54–56 (Jan. 7, 2002) [a Canadian who had expired E visa and left with valid I-94 for less than 30 days could return; however, if he had obtained a c/s to an E in the U.S. instead of obtaining the visa he could not return on the I-94].

F. ***Visa Waiver Program (VWP)***—INA §217, 8 U.S.C. §1187; 8 C.F.R. §217.1-217.6; 22 C.F.R. §41.2.

1. Waiver for persons from certain countries applying as B-1/B-2 for a period not in excess of 90 days with nonrefundable ticket (at present Andorra, Australia, Austria, Belgium, Brunei, Denmark, Finland, France, Germany, Iceland, Ireland, Italy, Japan, Liechtenstein, Luxembourg, Monaco, Netherlands, New Zealand, Norway, Portugal, San Marino, Singapore, Slovenia, Spain, Sweden, Switzerland, and the U.K. It does not apply to British overseas citizens, British dependent territories' citizens, or citizens of British Commonwealth countries). 8 C.F.R. §§212.1(i), 217.2.

   1.a. The Immigration Act of 1990 expanded the program to all countries that are designated provided the country has machine-readable passports and the AG determines the country's inclusion will not compromise law enforcement. Under IIRIRA §635, Congress modified the grounds for disqualifying a country from the program. If a country has a 2%, but less than 3.5%, disqualification rate they are placed on probation. If within two fiscal years the country has failed to develop a machine-readable passport or has a disqualification rate of 2% or more they are terminated. If a country has a disqualification rate over 3.5% they are disqualified.

   Upon entry a person coming for a B-1/B-2 purpose receives a WB status. A person can also be admitted under the WB category if coming for H-3 training (*i.e.,* B-1 in lieu of H-3). Letter, Weinig, Acting Assoc. Comm., Examinations, HQ 217-C (Jan. 4, 1994), *reprinted in* 71 No. 6 *Interpreter Releases* 221, 236 (Feb. 7, 1994). An applicant may enter at a land border as well as at air or seaports. 8 C.F.R. §§217.2(b), (c). An applicant may also use the status to transit the U.S. 8 C.F.R. §217.2(d). Applicants are given an I-94W form. 8 C.F.R. §217.2(b). Can re-enter with same I-94W after temporary absence to adjacent island. Cable, DOS, 89-State-169930 (May 22, 1989), *reprinted in* 66 No. 25 *Interpreter Releases* 722 (July 3, 1989); 8 C.F.R. §217.3(b). For example, U.K. citizen enters on program, given 90 days and transits to Bahamas for 20 days, may re-enter on I-94W. To be eligible for the program if arriving by air or sea: (1) need to present a passport from the designated country; (2) need to be in possession of a round trip ticket unless waived, INA §217(a)(8), 8 U.S.C. §1187(a)(8), which ticket must be nontransferable and valid for a period of not less than one year and must transport the person to a destination that is not an adjacent island or contiguous territory. 8 C.F.R. §217.2(c)(1); and (3) need to arrive on a carrier that has an agreement with the DHS even if it is not the carrier that issued the ticket. INA §217(a)(5), 8 U.S.C. §1187(a)(5); 8 C.F.R. §217.2(c).

1.b. An applicant arriving by land, in addition to providing a machine-readable passport and desiring to come solely as a B visitor for a period not in excess of 90 days, must provide evidence of financial solvency and a domicile abroad to which s/he intends to return. 8 C.F.R. §217.2(c)(2). If the person is a visitor for business (B-1) he will be designated WB; if tourist for pleasure (B-2) he will be designated WT. Each person, including infants, must have there own machine-readable passport. Cable, DOS, 04-State-205166 (Sept. 23, 2004) ¶9, *published on* AILA InfoNet at Doc. No. 05030164.

1.c. US-VISIT Program / Machine Readable Passports—Visa waiver countries are subject to US-VISIT. [*See in this chapter* section III.C (p.629), *supra*.] In addition, visa waiver countries must certify by Oct. 26, 2005 that they have programs to issue their nationals both machine-readable passports (MRP) and MRPs that incorporate biometric identifiers that comply with standards established by the International Civil Aviation Organization (ICAO) which at present are facial recognition biometrics. 8 U.S.C. §1732(c)(1). If they are unable to comply and the date for compliance is not changed individuals from those countries will need to obtain visas to enter the U.S. If they enter without a visa and without a MRP *after* Oct. 26, 2005, they will be granted a one-time parole and will not be treated *the first time* to have violated the terms of the VWP under INA §217(g). If they return the next time with a MRP they will be considered admissible. Memo, Hrinyak, Acting Ex. Dir. Immigration Policy and Programs, CBP, (IPP:BZ) (Oct. 21, 2004), *published on* AILA InfoNet at Doc. No. 05033175. No formal parole application is required and no fee is taken to get the "first-time" parole for entry without a MRP. Memo, Ahern, Asst. Comm. Field Operations, CBP, (OFO:IPP:JBK) (Oct. 22, 2004), *published on* AILA InfoNet at Doc. No. 05033174. The machine-readable requirement does not apply to other programs or groups that are visa-waived or visa-exempt such as Canadian citizens or certain persons from the Caribbean. Cable, DOS, 04-State-16751 (Jan. 26, 2004), *reprinted in* 81 No. 9 *Interpreter Releases* 280 (Mar. 1, 2004). Most countries have complied and provide a digital photo passport.

1.d. Not Eligible for C/S, E/S or AOS—If admitted under this program, not eligible for change of status, extension of status, or adjustment of status unless it is on the basis of an immediate-relative petition 8 C.F.R. §245.1, or INA §245(i). However, a VWP placed in a removal (asylum only) proceeding may be ineligible to AOS even if an immediate relative. 8 C.F.R. §1208.2(c)(3)(i). *See e.g., Zine v. Mukasey,* 517 F.3d 535, 541–44 (8th Cir. 2008) [VWP who is married to a USC and who was placed in asylum only proceeding could not AOS]. If an emergency prevents departure the DD is authorized to grant up to 30 days satisfactory departure. 8 C.F.R. §217.3(a). A DD is also authorized to give up to 120 days pre-hearing VD under INA §240B(a)(2)(A) but may now give an even longer period to permit a person to continue to receive medical treatment. INA §240B(a)(2)(B). If otherwise inadmissible, cannot use program even if person has INA §212(d)(3) waiver. If person is denied admission or is otherwise inadmissible s/he must obtain a visa to enter. 8 C.F.R. §217.4(a); 22 C.F.R. §41.2(*l*)(2).

1.e. Waiver of Rights—If inadmissible, or if deportable after admission, person waives right to and will be removed from the U.S. without a removal hearing, except for an asylum-only hearing if requested. 8 C.F.R. §§217.4(b), (c), 208.2(c)(1)(iii), 1208.2(c)(1). The waiver of rights under the visa waiver program includes all nonasylum forms of relief. *Schmitt v. Maurer,* 451 F.3d 1092 (10th Cir. 2006) [ineligible to apply for AOS as abused spouse under VAWA]; *Nose v. Attorney General*, 993 F.2d 75, 80 (5th Cir. 1993); *American-Arab Anti-Discrimination Comm. v. Ashcroft,* 241 F.Supp.2d 1111 (C.D. Cal. 2003) [although VWP applicant had adjustment of status pending based upon IR, he was subject to removal under VWP when picked up during course of special registration program]. However, a VWP who is an immediate relative of a USC has the right to adjust status in the U.S. INA §245(c)(4), 8 U.S.C. §1255(c)(4). *Freeman v. Gonzales,* 444 F.3d 1031, 1034–37 (9th Cir. 2006) [AOS spouse whose husband died remained a spouse under INA and had the right to contest denial of AOS in same manner as other AOS applicants]. *But see Zine v. Mukasey,* 517 F.3d 535, 541–44 (8th Cir. 2008) [ineligible to AOS after petitioner placed in asylum-only proceeding but the court declined to resolve the issue of the effect of INA §245(c)(4) for a person who seeks AOS *before* being placed in an asylum-only proceeding or a different proceeding].

The visa waiver applicant also waives the right to appear before an IJ. *Handa v. Clark,* 401 F.3d 1129, 1133–35 (9th Cir. 2005) [deference given to DHS regulation denying access to an IJ where statute, 8 U.S.C. §1187(b), seems to bar IJ hearing], unless she is in an "asylum-only" proceeding. 8 U.S.C. §1187(b)(2). If she seeks asylum she will be issued an I-863 (instead of an NTA) and will be referred to an IJ for an "asylum-only" hearing where she is ineligible to seek any other form of relief. 8 C.F.R. §1208.2(c)(1)(iv), (c)(3)(iii). *Zine v. Mukasey,* 517 F.3d 535, 541–44 (8th Cir. 2008) [ineligible to AOS because Algerian petitioner fraudulently entered under VWP and is bound by its terms]; *Lacey v. Gonzales,* 499 F.3d 514 (6th Cir. 2007); *Ferry v. Gonzales,* 457 F.3d 1117, 1126–28 (10th Cir. 2006) [the statutory provision allowing VWPs to apply for AOS before DHS does not give the IJ authority to review it in removal proceedings]; *Schmitt v. Maurer,* 451 F.3d 1092 (10th Cir. 2006) [ineligible to apply for AOS as abused spouse under VAWA]; *Handa v. Clark,* 401 F.3d 1129, 1133 (9th Cir. 2005) [in visa waiver removal case, all nonasylum forms of relief were waived but respondent had the right to contest whether the visa waiver program applied at all or whether respondent had right to appear before IJ]; *Wigglesworth v. INS,* 319 F.3d 951 (7th Cir. 2003) [VWP entrant mistakenly placed in removal proceeding was not entitled to apply for suspension of deportation because she waived her right to a hearing and because INA §242(g) precludes review seeking recommencement of deportation proceedings]; *Itaeva v. INS,* 314 F.3d 1238, 1241–43 (10th Cir. 2003) [finding that INA §217(b)(2) does not bar jurisdiction and on the merits finding that a VWP applicant may not apply for suspension in a removal hearing where asylum is addressed]; However, at least one circuit has determined that a VWP entrant who files for AOS as an immediate relative pursuant to INA §245(c)(4) is entitled to the procedural guarantees of adjustment applicants under 8 C.F.R. §245.2 and is no longer subject to the "no-contest clause" of the VWP. *Freeman v. Gonzales,* 444 F.3d 1031, 1034–37 (9th Cir. 2006) [AOS spouse whose husband died remained a spouse under INA and had the right to contest denial of AOS in same manner as other AOS applicants]. A visa waiver entrant also must be provided an asylum-only hearing, if requested, even if she would otherwise be subject to summary removal for fraud or lack of documentation under INA §§212(a)(6)(C) or (7). *Matter of Kanagasundram,* 22 I&N Dec. 963 (BIA 1999) [person with fraudulent passport entering on visa waiver program entitled to asylum hearing before IJ under 8 C.F.R. §§208.2(b) & 217.4(a)(1)]; *Matter of L,* 20 I&N Dec. 553 (BIA 1992) [in former deportation proceedings]; *Matter of H,* 20 I&N Dec. 611 (BIA 1992) [in former exclusion proceedings]. But she may not be able to use the fraudulent entry as a basis to argue she is not subject to the VWP restrictions because she does not come from a VWP country. *Zine v. Mukasey,* 517 F.3d 535, 542–43 (8th Cir. 2008) [Algerian who fraudulently entered under the VWP as a French citizen is not relieved of the VWP restrictions]. Once an applicant is put in proceedings s/he is also entitled to a bond hearing. *Matter of Gallardo,* 21 I&N Dec. 210 (BIA 1996). DHS has sought to avoid the provision of a bond hearing by issuing an I-863 rather than an NTA (I-862) to a VWP asylum applicant. An asylum only hearing before the IJ may be appealed to the BIA. The circuit courts of appeal have jurisdiction under INA §242(a)(1) to review the IJ/BIA decision on asylum/withholding even if there is no jurisdiction to review the order of removal of a visa waiver applicant. *Kanacevic v. INS,* 448 F.3d 129, 133–36 (2d Cir. 2006) [court of appeals does have jurisdiction to review asylum only hearing for VWP applicant]; *Nreka v. U.S. Att'y Gen.,* 408 F.3d 1361, 1366–68 (11th Cir. 2005) [court has jurisdiction to review BIA decision regarding an asylum only proceeding]. However, at least one court has determined that there is no jurisdiction to review a denial of AOS by a VWP applicant who stayed beyond the 90 day period because there is no review of the denial in a removal hearing. *Lacey v. Gonzales,* 499 F.3d 514 (6th Cir. 2007).

1.f. The constitutionality of the provision has been upheld in the face of a due process and equal protection challenges. *McGuire v. INS District Director*, 804 F.Supp. 1229 (N.D. Cal. 1992) [person sought to challenge prior deportation order under VWPP because IJ denied VD in the second case on the grounds that he had been deported previously]. Similarly, the DHS determination that a person under the program is not entitled to a hearing before an IJ has been upheld. *Prasil v. Meissner*, 941 F.Supp. 91, 93 (N.D. Ill. 1996). An applicant may assert that s/he did not knowingly waive his or her rights. *Nose v. Attorney General*, 993 F.2d 75, 78–79 (5th Cir. 1993); *Polizio v. Jenifer,* 217 F.Supp.2d 811, 814–16 (E.D. Mich. 2002) [a 17-year-old waived right to hearing; due process challenge to lack of hearing and detention in VWP was denied; but court urged waiver of 10-year bar at consulate]; *But see Auguste v. Reno,* 152 F.3d 1325, 1329 (11th Cir. 1998) *reh'g denied* 162 F.3d 1179 (11th Cir. 1998) [pre-*American-Arab* no jurisdiction under INA §242(g) to review whether waiver was knowingly and intelligently made]; *Tsukamoto v. Radcliffe,* 29 F.Supp.2d 660 (D. Hawaii 1998) [same].

1.g. If person inadmissible, carrier will also be fined for bringing person to U.S. without a visa. INA §217(e)(1)(C), 8 U.S.C. §1187(e)(1)(C), INA §273(a)(1), 8 U.S.C. §1323(a)(1).

V. VISAS FOR TEMPORARY VISITORS (B-1/B-2)—INA §101(a)(15)(B); 8 U.S.C. §1101(a)(15)(B); 22 C.F.R. §41.31; 9 FAM 41.31

A. *Criteria*

1. Alien (other than student, one performing skilled or unskilled labor, law enforcement, or representative of foreign information media). The B classification is not meant to be "a catch-all classification available to all who wish to come to the United States temporarily for whatever purpose." *Matter of Healy and Goodchild*, 17 I&N Dec. 22 (BIA 1979) [cannot use B to enter as student].
2. Has a residence in a foreign country (need not have his own home), 9 FAM 41.31 N.2, but must be "actual dwelling place in fact." INA §101(a)(33), 8 U.S.C. §1101(a)(33).
3. Has no intention of abandoning foreign residence.
4. Visiting temporarily for business or pleasure.
5. Initial Admission—1-year maximum with 6-month extensions, 8 C.F.R. §214.2(b). B-2s are automatically admitted for 6 months in most circumstances.

B. *Must demonstrate pursuant to 22 C.F.R. §41.31(a)*

1. Intention to depart at expiration of requested stay.

   1.a. Must show employment, family, social ties to residence abroad. 9 FAM 41.31 N.3.4.

   1.b. May require posting of bond with DD at port of entry INA §221(g), 8 U.S.C. §1201(g), 8 C.F.R. §221.1.

2. Permission to enter foreign country at end of stay.
3. Adequate financial arrangements to carry out purpose of visit (*e.g.,* for travel in the U.S. need money). 9 FAM 41.31 N.4.2—Does individual have money or proof of support from friends and relatives in U.S. or abroad. Are ties sufficient between "sponsor" and applicant to insure support?
4. Documentation showing all the above.

C. *Time Limitation*—Admittance for up to 1 year with extension of 6 months. 8 C.F.R. §214.2(b)(1). B-2 previously given automatic 6 months. 8 C.F.R. §214.2(b)(2) but proposed rule seeks to eliminate the 6-month rule and replace it with a 30-day period. The fact that someone may be staying in the U.S. for an extended period of time is not a bar to B-2 classification as long as the consular officer is satisfied that there is a time limitation and the stay is not indefinite in nature. 9 FAM 41.31 N.3.1. Also once admission is determined to be "fair and reasonable" the six month admission period should be granted. O.I. §214.2(b). But DHS is concerned about the "revolving door problem." An applicant for admission cannot use a temporary visa as a means to create permanent residency by leaving and returning every six months. *Mwongera v. INS,* 187 F.3d 323, 328 (3d Cir. 1999) [upholding BIA determination that person's stay was not temporary and that he had violated his B-1 status because he "set no definite goals and made no plans to accomplish those goals"]; *Matter of Lawrence,* 15 I&N Dec. 418, 420 (BIA 1975).

D. *B-1 / B-2 Engaging in Student Studies*—8 C.F.R. §§214.2(b)(7), 248.1(c)(3). A person entering the U.S. as a B-1/B-2 can no longer begin to attend school as an F-1/M-1 without first obtaining a change of status in the U.S. or an F-1/M-1 visa abroad. If a student with a B-1/B-2 begins to attend school without an F-1/M-1 or a c/s he will be denied a change of status to an F-1/M-1. Memo, Williams, Ex. Assoc. Comm. Field Operations, HQISD 70/ 6.2.2 P (Apr. 12, 2002), *reprinted in* 79 No. 17 *Interpreter Releases* 595, 605–07 (Apr. 22, 2002).

E. *B-1 Visitors for Business*

1. Admissible if: [9 FAM 41.31 N.4-N.8 or O.I. §214.2(b)]:

1.a. Engaging in commercial transactions not involving gainful employment, *e.g.*, negotiating contracts, litigation, consulting with clients or business associates. It is *not* gainful employment if business visitor is "making phone calls, giving employees instructions or taking clients to their cars." *Garavito v. INS*, 901 F.2d 173, 175 (1st Cir. 1990) [reversed INS's denial of C/S from B-1 to E-2 on grounds that B-1 was unlawfully employed]. However, where business activity almost exclusively involved full-time management of a U.S. enterprise B-1 not valid. *Matter of Lawrence*, 15 I&N Dec. 418, 420 (BIA 1975). May also study, if it is part of work or recreational activities. Letter, Weinig, Deputy Asst. Comm., Examination (Jan. 4, 1988), *reprinted* in 65 No. 4 *Interpreter Releases* 86, 96 (Jan. 25, 1988).

1.b. Participating in scientific, educational, professional, religious or business conventions. A person may receive an honorarium and incidental expenses for "usual academic activity" from an academic institution as long as it does not last more than 9 days at a single academic institution and as long as the foreign national has not accepted more than five such honoraria in a six-month period. INA §212(q), 8 U.S.C. §1182(q).

1.c. B-1 in Lieu of H-1—Traditionally, an alien who would otherwise be H-1 (other than entertainment professionals) but receives no salary or remuneration other than an expense allowance or other reimbursement incidental to temporary stay could enter as B-1. A controversy arose over the extent to which a B-1 can be used in lieu of an H-1.

(1) DHS and DOS have determined that foreign workers hired under a contract labor arrangement between a foreign software company and a U.S. telecommunications company were not eligible for B-1 visitor visas. Cable, DOS, 93-State-011402 (Jan. 13, 1993), *reprinted in* 70 No. 5 *Interpreter Releases* 147, 152–54 (Feb. 1, 1993).

(2) Sculptor/painter who wanted to come to U.S. for less than six months a year and have shows and receive commissions is not deemed a B-1 because he is simply extending his business to the U.S. with the U.S. becoming a profit center, without any international trade. Letter, Weinig, Deputy Asst. Comm., Adjudications (1988), *reprinted in* 65 No. 15 *Interpreter Releases* 415, 481–82 (Apr. 18, 1988).

(3) Family members. A B-2 is the appropriate visa for a family member of someone entering the U.S. as a B-1 in lieu of H-1B (or H-3). As derivatives the children would be able to attend school. 9 FAM 41.11, Note 5.2; Notes from VO-AILA Liaison (Mar. 30, 2000), *published on* AILA InfoNet at Doc. No. 00050905 (May 9, 2000).

1.d. B-1 in Lieu of J-1—Certain visitors to the U.S. may have their travel funded by the U.S. government but do not fall within the J-1 category. For example, an employee of an embassy or consulate (Foreign Service National Employee) may travel to the U.S. at U.S. government expense to participate in a wide variety of programs (*e.g.*, CIA/DIA training) that are not authorized exchange visitor programs. These travelers need not be issued J-1 visas and can be issued another appropriate visa such as a B-1. Cable, DOS, 04-State-13720 (Jan. 21, 2004), *published on* AILA InfoNet at Doc. No. 04022564; Memo, Ahern, Asst. Comm., Field Operations, CBP, "B-1 in Lieu of J-1 Visa for U.S. Government Funded Travel," (Feb. 10, 2004), *published on* AILA InfoNet at Doc. No. 05040471.

1.e. H-3 who will receive salary abroad and only expense allowance or other reimbursement.

1.f. Religious workers coming temporarily to do missionary work if such work does not involve the selling of articles or solicitation and acceptance of donations, and receives no salary/remuneration except expenses. Persons who do not qualify for R visas may nevertheless qualify for B-1. 9 FAM 41.31 N 9.1; Cable, DOS, 01-State-135944 (Aug. 7, 2001), *reprinted in* 78 No. 31 *Interpreter Releases* 1315–16 (Aug. 13, 2001).

1.g. Minister who will exchange pulpits but will be reimbursed by his own church abroad.

1.h. Minister on evangelical tour supported by contributions at evangelical meeting.

1.i. Personal/Domestic servants who accompany returning USCs who are temporarily assigned to U.S. or who permanently reside in a foreign country.

1.j. Personal/Domestic servant of a B, E, F, H, I, J, L, O, P, Q or R, provided employee can show under 8 C.F.R. §274a.12(c)(17) and 9 FAM 41.31:

(1) Not abandoning residence abroad;

(2) Has worked for employer for 1 year or has had on-going employment relations with him and employee has at least 1 year prior experience as servant. But LPRs cannot bring servants because it indicates the servant's permanency.

(3) Must be paid by contract the prevailing wage as a domestic. Cable, DOS, 05-State-00141634 (Aug. 8, 2005), *published on* AILA InfoNet at Doc. No. 06011867 [address prevailing wage and issues of involuntary servitude regarding trafficking in persons]; Cable, DOS, 04-State-67428 (Mar 26, 2004), *published on* AILA InfoNet at Doc. No. 04040861; 9 FAM 41.21 N. 6.2; 9 FAM 41.31 N. 9.3.

1.k. Professional athletes such as golfers and race drivers who receive no salary, only tournament money.

1.l. An airline employee who would otherwise be an E except no treaty between U.S. and airline's country or alien is not national of treaty country (*e.g.,* Swede working for Colombia airline).

1.m. A foreign medical student seeking to take "elective clerkship" without remuneration.

1.n. An alien who is the member of the Board of Directors of U.S. corporation and who is coming to U.S. for board meeting.

1.o. Foreign corporate personnel to set up U.S. subsidiary, as well as persons exploring E-2 investment. 9 FAM 41.31 N.9.7.

1.p. Alien installing equipment pursuant to contract of sale—IFM §15.4(b)(1)(B)(3). Subsequent to *International Union of Bricklayers v. Meese*, 616 F.Supp. 1387 (N.D. Cal. 1985) [declaring former OI 214.2(b)(5) invalid], a regulation was issued that modified the OI so as not to include building or construction work (other than supervisory or training not involving any "hands on" work). 8 C.F.R. §214.2(b)(5). DOS guidelines also provide that building or construction work, whether on-site or in-plant, is considered local employment or labor for hire and is not permissible on a B-1 even if it involves an after sales contract. 9 FAM 41.31 N.10.1; Cable, DOS, 01-State-92023 (May 24, 2001), *reprinted in* 78 No. 22 *Interpreter Releases* 937–38 (June 4, 2001). However, persons engaged in supervision or training of others in building or construction work may enter as B-1s. *Id.*

1.q. Commercial Truck Drivers engaged only in international hauling—IFM 15.5(c)(1)(E). Notwithstanding NAFTA a commercial truck driver, consistent with B-1status, may only be transporting goods across international borders. They may not engage in cabotage (*i.e.,* carrying goods picked up at one point in the U.S. and dropped of at another point in the U.S.). To be consistent with B-1 status certain general principles must be applied to international trucking: (1) the goods must be leaving or entering and remain in the stream of international commerce; (2) once the goods have come to rest in the U.S. they assume a domestic character; (3) a driver bringing goods from Canada or Mexico may not load, haul or deliver a cargo that has its origin and its final destination within the U.S.; (4) a driver may pick up goods in Canada or Mexico, regardless of whether they are foreign or U.S. made, and deliver them to a U.S. location; (5) the entry of the driver must be for the purpose of the international movement of goods; (6) drivers may not engage in any activity that qualifies as local labor for hire; and (7) the burden of proof remains on the driver.

(1) DHS recognized the following permissible activities under these guidelines: (1) deadheading trailers; (2) driving an empty tractor; (3) back-up and relay drivers; (4) tractor replacements; (5) yard moves; (6) trailer switches; and activities that are a necessary incident to international commerce.

(2) Activities that are not permissible include: (1) transporting goods from one U.S. location to another; (2) repositioning empty trailers between two points in the U.S. when the driver did not enter with or depart with the trailer; (3) topping up an international ship-

ment with a U.S. domestic shipment; (4) traveling through Canada or Mexico while delivering goods from one U.S. point to another; and (5) directly soliciting shipments for deliveries while in the U.S.

(3) CBP also requires that truck carriers transporting Border Release Advanced Screening and Selectivity (BRASS) merchandise may only use drivers registered under the Free and Secure Trade (FAST) program and carrying a FAST Driver Card. CBP announcement *reported in* 81 No. 45 *Interpreter Releases* 1653, 1661–62 (Nov. 22, 2004).

1.r. Tour Bus Operators. 8 C.F.R. §§214.2(b)(4)(i)(E)(1) and (G)(6). A tour bus operator may also not engage in cabotage and therefore cannot take passengers to different destinations in the U.S. Memo, Pearson, Ex. Assoc. Comm., Office of Field Operations, HQ 70/6.2.2-C/HQ70/13.1/HQ70/21.11 (Jul. 2, 1998), *published on* AILA InfoNet at Doc. No. 06081766. Passengers may be dropped off in the U.S. but the bus must then go back empty or reload and take the passengers out of the U.S.

1.s. Participating in voluntary service program if religious only. Includes any service (*e.g.*, carpenter). O.I. §214.2(b)(7); IFM §15.4(b)(1)(B)(24).

1.t. Attending an executive seminar.

1.u. Race track personnel including jockeys, sulky drivers, trainers or grooms who are accompanying a foreign based employer. They need not be of the same nationality as the foreign employer. Cable, DOS, 05-State-178837 (Sept. 27, 2005), *published on* AILA InfoNet at Doc. No. 06011869; 9 FAM 41.31 N. 9.8.

1.v. Observing the conduct of business or other professional or vocational activity that does not involve hands-on business activity.

2. Basic Eligibility Test—22 C.F.R. §41.31(b), *Matter of B- & K-*, 6 I&N Dec. 827 (BIA 1955).

2.a. Business Defined—22 C.F.R. §41.31(b).

(1) Legitimate commercial or professional activity; or

(2) Not local employment or labor for hire.

2.b. Criteria

(1) Clear intent to continue foreign residence.

(2) Principal place of business and actual accrual of profits predominantly in foreign country.

(3) Various U.S. entries of plainly temporary nature. *Matter of B- & K-*, 6 I&N Dec. 827 (BIA 1955) [Canadian farmers periodic trips to U.S. to sell produce are B-1]; *Matter of W.*, 6 I&N Dec. 832 (BIA 1955) [Canadian bought fish in Canada, transported to U.S., paid to transport by U.S. company in Canadian money valid B-1]; *Matter of Hira*, 11 I&N Dec. 824 (BIA 1966), *aff'd* (AG 1966) [Hong Kong tailor who entered U.S. to measure customers—valid B-1]; *but cf. Matter of Minei*, 11 I&N Dec. 430 (R.C. 1965) [when alien painter sold work in U.S. B-1 denied].

(4) Further international commerce or business. *Karnuth v. U.S. ex rel. Arbro*, 279 U.S. 231 (1929); *Mwongera v. INS,* 187 F.3d 323, 329 (3d Cir. 1999) [upheld removal based upon BIA's findings that B-1s time in U.S. was central to the company's extension into the U.S. and therefore was not simply delivering goods internationally]; *Matter of Neill*, 15 I&N Dec. 331 (BIA 1975) [engineer coming to U.S. to consult with clients and expand work here—invalid B-1]; *cf. Matter of Opferkuch*, 17 I&N Dec. 158 (BIA 1979) [nonprincipal of business granted B-1; suggests that *Neill* means principal cannot get visa]; *Matter of Duckett*, 19 I&N Dec. 493 (BIA 1987) [Canadian railroad clerk who spends 2/3 hours in U.S. and rest in Canada every day to check on RR cars is eligible for B-1].

(5) Foreign employer who directs the employment; profits must go to employer; profits must accrue abroad; services in U.S. must be incidental to international trade and commerce (*e.g.*, exchange of merchandise). *Matter of Sriniasan*, Case No. A23 192 575 (C.O. 1982), *reprinted in* 70 No. 35 *Interpreter Releases* 1189 (Sept. 13, 1993) [consultant employed and paid by Tata Burroughs, Ltd. which is 50% owned by Burroughs in United States. Consult-

ant under direction of U.S. Corp. while in United States. U.S. Burroughs is dependent on having Tata Burroughs employees as consultants to sell equipment in U.S.—proper B-1].

(6) Payment to B-1 should generally be abroad. However, salary remuneration, so long as the source is outside the U.S., may be arranged through U.S. banking or other financial institution. Arrangements between the foreign employer and the business visitor regarding expenses and per diem have no bearing on eligibility for B-1. Moreover, the purchase of property or the establishment of a bank account are not *per se* prohibited. Letter, Miller, Deputy Asst. Comm., Adjudications, CO 214b-C (Nov. 5, 1992), *reprinted in* 70 No. 7 *Interpreter Releases* 221, 239–40 (Feb. 22, 1993).

(7) Services being performed are not ones which a U.S. worker would have to be hired for, are not inherently part of the U.S. labor market, and are not primarily benefiting the U.S. entity as local work. Memo, Williams, Regional Director Western Region, WRINS 70/20 (undated, c. 2000), *published on* AILA InfoNet at Doc. No. 03040190.

(8) INA does not extend to outer continental shelf and foreign workers are not required to obtain visas (B-1, H-2B or otherwise) to work. *United Ass'n of Journeymen AFL-CIO v. Reno*, 73 F.3d 1134 (D.C. Cir. 1996).

3. Employment Authorization—Domestic servants and employees of airlines of nontreaty countries may obtain employment authorization to work in U.S. in these fields. 8 C.F.R. §§274a.12(c)(17), 1274a.12(c)(17).

F. *B-2 Visitors for Pleasure*

1. Admissible if— [9 FAM 41.31 N.13-14]:
   - Tourists.
   - Social visits to friends/relatives.
   - Health purposes.
   - Participants in conventions of social organizations.
   - Participants in amateur musical, sports or similar events with no remuneration.
   - Dependants of U.S. Armed Forces personnel.
   - Accompanying D or B-1 aliens.
   - If coming to U.S. to marry USC but will depart. 9 FAM 41.31 N.14.1-1.
   - If coming to U.S. to marry nonimmigrant. Must thereafter get spouse's derivative status.
   - If eligible for H-4 but inconvenient or impossible to obtain it, the spouse or child can enter on B-2. 9 FAM 41.53 N.18.4
   - Nonspouse partner (regardless of gender) that accompanies a principal E, H or L for duration of stay. However, the B-2 must show entitlement to B-2 status in his/her own right (*i.e.,* no §214(b) problem), but the primary purpose of the travel must be to accompany his or her significant other. The fact that the cohabitating partner may be living in the U.S. for an extended period is not a bar to B-2 classification. 9 FAM 41.31 N 14.1; Cable, 01-State-118790 (July 9, 2001), *published on* AILA InfoNet at Doc. No. 01071131; Letter, Miller, Deputy Asst. Comm., Adjudications, CO 893-C (Jan. 12, 1993), *reprinted in* 70 No. 12 *Interpreter Releases* 440–41 (Mar. 29, 1993); Letter, Weinig, Deputy Asst. Comm., Examinations (Dec. 3, 1987), *reprinted in* 64 No. 47 *Interpreter Releases* 1373, 1385–87 (Dec. 14, 1987). *See also* 9 FAM 41.31 N14.4 [DOS uses this section by analogy to apply to significant others who do not qualify for derivative visas]
   - Parent seeking to remain with F-1 child is not in and of itself a basis to deny B-2. Letter, LaFleur, Chief, Business and Trade Branch, Benefits Division, INS, HQ 70/6.2.2 (June 6, 1996), *reprinted in* 73 No. 28 *Interpreter Releases* 970, 976–77 (July 22, 1996).
   - Language students in course of short duration when the course of study is under 18 hours per week. Cable, DOS, 93-State-202275 (July 2, 1993), *reprinted in* 70 No. 28 *Interpreter Releases* 978 (July 26, 1993).

2. Pleasure defined. "Legitimate activities of a recreational character, including tourism, amusement, visits with friends or relatives, rest, medical treatment and activities of a fraternal, social or service

nature." 22 C.F.R. §41.31(b)(2). Employment not permitted even where only remuneration is room, board and pocket change. *Matter of Hall*, 18 I&N Dec. 203 (BIA 1982).

G. ***Out of Status***—Incarceration of a nonimmigrant visitor for conviction is deemed a breach of status (because status cannot be pursued in jail). *Matter of A*, 6 I&N Dec. 762 (BIA 1955). *See also Matter of Halabi*, 15 I&N Dec. 105 (BIA 1974); *Matter of Siffre*, 14 I&N Dec. 444 (BIA 1973); *Matter of Neely & Whylie*, 11 I&N Dec. 864 (BIA 1966).

VI. VISAS FOR STUDENTS AND TRAINEES (F, M, J, H-3)

A. *Academic Students (F Visa)*

1. Criteria—Statutes/Regulations—INA §101(a)(15)(F), 8 U.S.C. §1101(a)(15)(F); 8 C.F.R. §214.2(f), 9 FAM 41.61; 67 Fed. Reg. 76256 (Dec. 11, 2002); 68 Fed. Reg. 28129 (May 23, 2003) [interim SEVIS rule]; 70 Fed. Reg. 7853 (Feb. 16, 2005) [final SEVIS rule]

1.a. Applicant has foreign residence with no intention of abandoning it.

(1) In determining a student's immigrant intent "[t]he fact that the alien plans on studying a subject for which there is no or little employment opportunity in his country of residence is not a basis for denying the visa … nor … is the fact that the country of residence can provide for equivalent quality courses in the same subject matter. Cable, DOS, 05-State-180015 (Sept. 28, 2005) ¶5, *published on* AILA InfoNet at Doc. No. 05110115. Conversely, the fact that an education program, such as ESL, may be available in the student's own country is not itself a ground to refuse the applicant. 9 FAM 41.61 N6.4; Cable, 08-State-024930 (Mar. 11, 2008) ¶4, *published on* AILA InfoNet at Doc. No. 08040255. Nor should the consular officer accord different schools different weight in determining the validity of the student's request and consular officers "should not go behind the I-20 to adjudicate the alien's qualifications as a student." Cable, 05-State-180015, *supra* at ¶7. Although consular officers may consider the usefulness of a degree from a community or lesser-known college, attendance at such a college or university "is not, in itself, a ground of ineligibility and applicants cannot be refused a visa for that reason." 9 FAM 41.61 N2.3. The consular officer should focus on the student applicant's immediate intent instead of focusing primarily on his ties or long term goals. *Id.* at ¶4; 9 FAM 41.61 N. 5.1-5.4.

1.b. Applicant is a *bona fide* student qualified to pursue a full course of study.

1.c. Applicant seeks to enter the U.S. as a student "temporarily and solely for the purpose of pursuing such a course of study at an established institution of learning or other recognized place of study in the United States."

1.d. Applicant will study only at an institution particularly designated by him and approved by ICE in compliance with the SEVIS program. 8 C.F.R. §214.2(f)(1)(i)(A). To maintain their status as an approved school, the school must meet certain reporting and other requirements.

1.e. Will not attend a public elementary school or publicly funded adult education program and will not attend a public secondary school unless s/he attends the secondary school for a period *not* in excess of 12 months *and* demonstrates s/he has reimbursed the school board the full, unsubsidized per capita cost of the education. INA §214(m)(1), 8 U.S.C. §1184(m)(1). Publicly funded adult education programs means education, training, ESL or other intensive English program operated by, through or for a local public school district regardless of whether the program charges fees or tuition. The bar does not apply to post-secondary schools such as public community or junior colleges which receive public funds, but charge full nonresident tuition to foreign students. Memo, Crocetti, Assoc. Comm., HQ 50/5.12, 96 Act.011 (Jan. 27, 1997), *reprinted in* 74 No. 5 *Interpreter Releases* 226, 227–29 (Feb. 3, 1997). This provision also does not apply to persons in J-1, F-2, L-2, or H-4 status who may be attending school, or even a person who enters EWI or on B status and attends school. Cable, DOS (2000-State-051174) (Mar. 17, 2000), *reprinted in* 77 No. 16 *Interpreter Releases* 547–49 (Apr. 21, 2000). It applies solely to foreign students presenting SEVIS I-20s from public schools in the U.S. *Id.* If the foreign student violates this provision, INA §212(a)(6)(G) bars his or her entry for 5 years. *Id.*

1.f. Family members, on F-2s, may not attend school without c/s to F-1, except that a child may attend elementary through 12th grade. 8 C.F.R. §214.2(f)(15). F-2s may not attend school while the c/s is pending.

2. Criteria—In practice, an applicant must:

2.a. Meet all the above requirements;

2.b. Present a SEVIS Form I-20 issued in her name by a school approved by the Service 8 C.F.R. §214.2(f)(1)(i)(A) and paid the SEVIS Fee (I-901). 8 C.F.R. §§214.2(f)(19), 214.13. The fee may be paid by credit card via the Internet at *www.fmjfee.com* or by mailing a U.S. dollar check or international money order to a lockbox address in the U.S. Cable, DOS, 04-State-162300 (Aug. 31, 2004), *published on* AILA InfoNet at Doc. No. 04092160. If record of fee payment has not been entered at time of admission, CBP will admit the student for 30 days and issue a I-515A but only if his record reflects his being in active or initial status as a student. Memo, Hrinyak, Acting Ex. Dir. Immigration Policy and Programs, CBP, (OFO:IPP:CB) (Dec. 1, 2004), *published on* AILA InfoNet at Doc. No. 05033166; IFM at 15.16(f).

2.c. Have sufficient financial support, 22 C.F.R. §41.61(b)(1)(ii), *e.g.,* I-134. 9 FAM 41.61 N.6.1-1 ["Sufficient funds to cover expenses" means "the applicant is required to establish the unlikelihood of becoming a public charge ... and of resorting to unauthorized U.S. employment to maintain solvency"]. Must show availability of funds, not possession of them. Officer can consider currency restrictions in home country. 9 FAM 41.61 N. 6.2. Also look to whether person giving I-134 has resources and legal obligation. *Matter of Buckland*, 10 I&N Dec. 706 (R.C. 1964); *Matter of Haddad*, 10 I&N Dec. 785 (R.C. 1964).

2.d. Be proficient in English or will receive training to make her proficient. The school may explain, where appropriate, why English proficiency is not required. 9 FAM 41.61 N.5.

2.e. Intend to depart the U.S.

2.f. Have sufficient academic credentials to attend particular institution. 9 FAM 41.61 N.7.

2.g. Maintain a full course of study which is defined as: [8 C.F.R. §214.2(f)(6)]

(1) Postgraduate study certified by DSO as full course.

(2) Undergraduate college or university—12 semester/ quarter hours if all undergraduates are enrolled for 12 hours and are charged full tuition or considered full-time for other administrative purposes.

(3) Post-secondary nonvocational (*e.g.,* junior college, fine arts school)—12 hours; credits must be accepted by at least 3 schools.

(4) Study in any other language, liberal arts or fine arts nonvocational program—18 hours in classroom or 22 hours if mostly lab.

(5) Elementary, middle school, or academic high school.

(6) Online Classes. An F-1 student may only take one class or three credits online or through distance education per term and no online language study program. 8 C.F.R. §214.2(f)(6)(i)(G).

(7) Reduced Course Load. A student may not reduce her course load below a full course of study as outlined above without first obtaining permission from the DSO and then may only reduce it, at a minimum, to 6 semester/ quarter hours or half the clock hours of a full course of study. 8 C.F.R. §214.2(f)(6)(iii). S/he may only reduce her course load one time unless it is for medical reasons and then only for a maximum of 12 months. 8 C.F.R. §§214.2(f)(6)(iii)(A), (B). A student may also have a reduced course load his final term to complete her studies. 8 C.F.R. §§214.2(f)(6)(i)(B), (iii)(C).

3. Commuter students from Canada and Mexico may attend school part time or full time in the U.S. as F-3 visa holders as long as they are not residing in the U.S. INA §101(a)(15)(F)(iii); 22 C.F.R. §41.61(b)(1)(iii). As border commuter students they will be given a date certain on their I-94, instead of D/S. 8 C.F.R. §214.2(f)(18). Border commuter students are subject to SEVIS but may not obtain F-2 status for their dependents. 68 Fed. Reg. 28129, 28130 (May 23, 2003).

4. Consular Procedure—Consul issues F-1 visa. Consular officers must verify the SEVIS I-20 and the data in the SEVIS system before issuing a visa. Consular officers are directed to deny F-1/F-2 visas under INA §221(g) where a person presents the appropriate form from the school but there is no SEVIS record in the computerized system, Cable, DOS, 03-State-40362 (Feb. 12, 2003) at ¶10, *published on* AILA InfoNet at Doc. No. 03030443 (Mar. 4, 2003) or where the person fails to pay the SEVIS (I-901) fee. Cable, DOS, 04-State-162300 ¶5 (Aug. 31, 2004), *published on* AILA InfoNet at Doc. No. 04092160. If a visa is issued they must enter the information in the SEVIS database. 22 C.F.R. §41.61(d). DHS will no longer allow a person in B-1/B-2 status to begin school until s/he has changed status to F-1 or obtained an F-1 visa abroad and re-entered. 8 C.F.R. §§214.2(b)(7). And a c/s to F-1 will be denied if B-1/B-2 enrolled in course of study prior to obtaining the c/s. 8 C.F.R. §248.1(c)(3). The prohibition against studying prior to obtaining Service approval of a change of NIV status is limited to B-1/B-2s. Memo, Williams, Ex. Assoc. Comm. Field Operations, HQISD 70/6.2.2-P (Apr. 12, 2002), *published on* AILA InfoNet at Doc. No. 02041532. Students may not enter the U.S. in F status more than 30 days in advance of their program start date but may enter after the start date so long as they are enrolled for the next academic period. Cable, DOS, 04-State-70079 (June 22, 2004), *published on* AILA InfoNet at Doc. No. 04080964. Consular officers may not physically issue initial-entry student visas more than 120 days before the program start date, but must warn students they cannot enter the U.S. more than 45 days before the start date. 9 FAM 41.61 Note 14.2. If they wish to enter before, they may be given a B visa, in addition to the F-1, but they may then have difficulty c/s to F-1 and may be required to depart the U.S. and re-enter on their F-1. The 120- and 45-day rules do not apply to returning students who may be issued an F visa at any time and return to school at any time as long as they are maintaining student status and their SEVIS records are current. Cable, DOS, 06-State-021872 (Feb. 9, 2006), *published on* AILA InfoNet at Doc. No. 06031360.

   Students renewing visas during the course of their study should generally have the visas renewed in the normal course of business, unless circumstances have changed significantly from the time of the previous issuance. Cable, DOS, 05-State-180015 (Sept. 28, 2005) ¶6, *published on* AILA InfoNet at Doc. No. 05110115 ["If students feel that they will encounter difficulties in seeking a new student visa or that a visa will not be issued to them so they can continue their studies, they may be less inclined to leave the United States during their studies and hence may distance themselves culturally from their homeland. Posts should facilitate the reissuance of student visas so that these students can travel freely back and forth between the homeland and the United States."].

5. Duration of status—All students will be admitted a maximum of 30 days before program start date. 8 C.F.R. §214.2(f)(5)(i); Cable, DOS, 03-State-74670 (Mar. 21, 2003) ¶¶6-8, *reprinted in* 80 No. 13 *Interpreter Releases* 476–78 (Mar. 31, 2003) [suggesting a possibility of extension to 90 days]. If changing status s/he will be given duration of status for period needed to complete one educational program including progression to higher levels if accomplished in accordance with DHS transfer procedures (thus no extension of stay needed). D/S = completion of educational program (including practical training) + 60 days. 8 C.F.R. §214.2(f)(5)(iv). The 60 days can be used to prepare for departure or transfer to another school in accordance with §214.2(f)(8). A person may C/S to H-1B (or another status) during the 60-day departure period. Memo, Pearson, Exec. Assoc. Comm. Field Operations, HQ 70.23.1 RS-P (Aug. 19, 1998), *reprinted in* 75 No. 32 *Interpreter Releases* 1147, 1167 (Aug. 24, 1998). In cases where F-1 timely files a C/S to H-1B and the H-1B cap has been reached, the regulations now *automatically extend* the student's F-1 stay (whether or not in OPT) and employment authorization (if in OPT) until Oct 1 of the following fiscal year, so that there is no "gap" between the time her F-1 stay would have expired and the Oct. 1 start-up date for the H-1B. 8 C.F.R. §214.2(f)(5)(vi)(A). It also applies to F-2s. The Commissioner may extend duration of status beyond the 60-day period until the next fiscal year. 8 C.F.R. §214.2(f)(5)(vi). The Commissioner exercised that authority during FY 2000 and determined that an F-1 waiting to C/S can accept a signing bonus from the prospective employer. 65 Fed. Reg. 15178–80 (Mar. 21, 2000).

6. SEVIS Identification—Students are issued SEVIS I-20 identification. 8 C.F.R. §214.2(f)(1)(i)(A) [I-94 still required as well]. Spouse and children issued separate SEVIS I-20s. 8 C.F.R. §214.2(f)(3).

   6.a. SEVIS I-20 not surrendered if temporarily departing.

   6.b. SEVIS I-20. endorsed with duration of status.

7. Transfers—8 C.F.R. §214.2(f)(8).

   7.a. Transfer Requirements—Can transfer if:

   (1) *Bona fide* student;

   (2) Has been pursuing full course of study;

   (3) Intends to pursue full course;

   (4) Has financial ability to attend transferred school; and

   (5) Begins classes at transferred school within 5 months of transferring out of current school or within 5 months of the program completion date whichever is earlier. 8 C.F.R. §214.2(f)(8)(i). The student must request from the school s/he attends, no later than 60 days after completion of the program, the release of the SEVIS record to the new school. Failure to do this means the student is out-of-status and forced to apply for reinstatement to student status. Where the student is engaged in OPT s/he must be able to resume classes within 5 months of transferring out of the school that recommended OPT or the date OPT ends whichever is earlier.

   7.b. Transfer Procedures—8 C.F.R. §214.2(f)(8)(ii).

   (1) Student must first notify the current school and then obtain a properly completed SEVIS I-20 A/B from school he intends to transfer to.

   (2) The student must notify the DSO at the school he has transferred to within 15 days of the start date listed on the SEVIS Form I-20. The transfer is effected when the transfer school notifies SEVIS that the student has enrolled in classes within 30 days as required by 8 C.F.R. §214.3(g)(3)(iii).

   (3) Cannot transfer schools if student not pursuing a full course of study or is engaged in unauthorized employment unless reinstated to student status. 8 C.F.R. §214.2(f)(8)(i).

   (4) Failure to comply with transfer procedure renders student out of status. *U.S. v. Bazargan*, 992 F.2d 844, 877 (8th Cir. 1993).

   (5) May not transfer to public elementary or publicly funded adult education program. May not transfer to public secondary school unless student pays for secondary school and only attends a maximum of 12 months. INA §214(m)(2), 8 U.S.C. §1184(m)(2). In order to obtain an F-1 the student must reimburse the public secondary school the "full, unsubsidized per capita cost of education" covering the period and must do it *before* the visa or F-1 status is issued. Cable, DOS, 97-State-032114 (1997), *reprinted in* 74 No. 20 *Interpreter Releases* 860–61 (May 23, 1997). If the student enters, attends a private school and then jumps to a public school without meeting the conditions of INA §214(m), his or her visa is cancelled and s/he is inadmissible into the U.S. for 5 years. INA §§214(m)(2), 212(a)(6)(G).

8. Withdrawing from Educational Institution—An F-1 authorized to withdraw from school is given 15 days to depart. However, if the F-1 fails to obtain permission to withdraw, s/he is not afforded the 15-day grace period to depart. 8 C.F.R. §214.2(f)(5)(iv); 67 Fed. Reg. 76256, 76262 (Dec. 11, 2002). When the student is ready to resume study, the school must issue a new I-20 with a new SEVIS number and the student must pay the SEVIS I-901 fee. Cable, DOS, 05-State-00232385 (Dec. 28, 2005) ¶7, *published on* AILA InfoNet at Doc. No. 06011873.

9. Employment

   9.a. No employment 1st academic year (*i.e.*, 9 months) except for on-campus work which can begin as soon as the student is admitted in F-1 status. 8 C.F.R. §214.2(f)(9)(ii). Students who transfer after being given work authorization need new authorization to work. After 1st year a student in good standing may obtain employment off campus as determined by the DSO if:

   (1) Severe Economic Hardship—A student may obtain work authorization where there is severe economic hardship caused by unforeseen circumstances beyond the student's control. 8 C.F.R. §214.2(f)(9)(ii)(C). To work off-campus the student must be in good academic standing and carrying a full course of study. Supporting documentation as to eco-

nomic hardship is needed. May only work 20 hours per week when school is in session. A student granted permission may work full time during holidays or school vacations.

(2) Internship with International Organization—A bona fide student offered employment by a recognized international organization must apply for employment at the service center on Form I-765 with fee. Must obtain written certification from employer that work is within scope of the organization sponsorship, and must submit SEVIS I-20 I.D. endorsed by DSO within last 30 days with completed I-765.

9.b. On-Campus Employment

(1) First-year prohibition is inapplicable. 8 C.F.R. §214.2(f)(9)(i).

(2) Includes work performed on school premises (including on location commercial firms which provide services for students such as the student bookstore) *or* at an off-campus location which is educationally affiliated with the school. The educational affiliation must be associated with school's established curriculum or related to contractually funded research projects if post graduate level and it must be an integral part of the student's educational program. 8 C.F.R. §214.2(f)(9)(i). While school is in session, F-1s can only work 20 hours/week. Permitted to work only when it will not displace U.S. workers. When school is not in session permitted to work full-time. 8 C.F.R. §214.2(f)(9)(i). On campus employment not permitted if course of study completed unless it is practical training. *Id.*

9.c. Off-Campus Employment

(1) Employment Due to Emergent Circumstances—The Secretary of DHS may suspend all or some of the requirements of on- and off-campus employment by notice in the Federal Register. The suspension may permit the students to work full time and to reduce their course load during the period of the notice's effect. 8 C.F.R. §§214.2(f)(5)(v), (6)(i)(F), (9)(i).

The INS designated students from Indonesia, South Korea, Malaysia, Thailand, and the Philippines, and suspended the 20-hour limit on and off campus as well as the requirement of a full course of study. In the case of on-campus employment the DSO must note it on the SEVIS I-20 after receiving evidence that it was necessary to avoid severe economic hardship. 63 Fed. Reg. 31872 (June 10, 1998).

9.d. Practical Training

(1) Training available when:

(a) Full-time student for at least one academic year which is normally 8-9 consecutive months (unless a graduate student in a special program);

(b) It is related to a course of study;

(c) It is employment for the purpose of practical training; and

(d) It is not for English language training.

(2) Procedure—8 C.F.R. §214.2(f)(10). There are two types of practical training:

(a) Curricular Practical Training, 8 C.F.R. §214.2(f)(10)(i):

i) This type of training is defined to be alternate work/study, internship, cooperative education or any other type of required internship or practicum.

ii) If student obtained one year or more of full-time curriculum practical training, then post-completion training is not available. Curricular practical training may be granted on a "part-time" basis (no more than 20 hours/week) or a "full-time" basis. Part-time training is defined as 20 hours or fewer per week and full-time training is defined as more than 20 hours. A student working 20 hours or less for 2 years or a student working more than 20 hours for one year is not eligible for post-completion practical training Letter, Hernandez, Director, Business and Trade Branch, HQADN 70/6.2.6 (Nov. 22, 2002), *reprinted in* 80 No. 6 *Interpreter Releases* 210–11, 220–21 (Feb. 10, 2003). Part-time curricular practical training does not impact optional practical training (pre- or post-completion of studies).

iii) Cannot accept any practical training unless student for one academic year or if in language program prior to completion of studies.

iv) A job offer is required to apply for curricular practical training.

v) Must submit to DSO request for CPT. Students must follow internal procedures established by DSO.

(b) Optional Practical Training. 8 C.F.R. §214.2(f)(10)(ii); 73 Fed. Reg. 18944–56 (Apr. 8, 2008)

i) Optional practical training may be exercised in one of four circumstances:

a) during student's annual vacation and at other times when school not in session;

b) while school is in session as long as it does not exceed 20 hours per week;

c) after completion of all course requirements (excluding thesis or equivalent) for bachelor's, master's or doctoral degree program; and

d) after completion of the course of study.

ii) Limited to 12 months for non-STEM students and must complete training within 14 months of graduation. The 12 and 14 month limitations do *not* apply to STEM (science, technology, engineering or mathematics) students who can obtain one additional 17 month period (29 months in total) of OPT if the employer is enrolled in the E-verify program and agrees to report the student's departure within 48 hours. 8 C.F.R. §214.2(f)(10)(ii)(C). The STEM student also has reporting requirements in 6 month increments to the DSO. 8 C.F.R. §214.2(f)(12). The STEM Designated Degree Program List is found at **Appendix M**, *infra,* and updates can be found at *www.ice.gov/sevis*. F-1 must request OPT before the completion of his program and no earlier than 90 days before the end of one full academic year. 8 C.F.R. §214.2(f)(10)(ii)(A). All students can qualify for a new 12 months of OPT based upon a higher degree level program.

iii) Automatic extension of OPT for F-1 students who timely filed for a C/S to H-1B and are the beneficiaries of H-1B petitions where there is a "gap" between the end of the OPT and the start-up date for the H-1B due to the H-1B cap. 8 C.F.R. §214.2(f)(5)(vi)(A).

iv) Obtaining OPT. 8 C.F.R. §214.2(f)(11). To obtain practical training the DSO must make a recommendation for OPT under SEVIS. The DSO must indicate whether it will be part-time or full-time training and note the start and end dates. The F-1 will then be given the SEVIS Form I-20 and s/he must file the employment page of the SEVIS Form I-20 with an I-765 to obtain an Employment Authorization Document (EAD). It is advisable to include photocopies of the previous I-20, I-94 and biographic photo page of the passport. Form I-538 and signature card are no longer required. The student *cannot* get employment authorization without filing an I-765 and cannot begin employment until s/he is issued an EAD. The F-1 students may apply for the I-765 up to 90 days prior to the program end-date but not later than 60 days after the end-date. A STEM student may apply for an extension prior to the expiration of the first 12 month OPT and his employment authorization is extended automatically for 180 days. 8 C.F.R. §274a.12(b)(6)((iv). A student cannot begin employment until the start day on the employment authorization but cannot request a start date later than 60 days after completion of the program. No job offer is required to apply for optional practical training.

(c) Unused practical training. Unused portion of practical training cannot be used at a later time, O.I. §214.2(f)(10)(viii), unless "reserved" in accordance with OIs.

(d) Termination of practical training is automatic when student transfers to another school.

(e) Unemployment During OPT. Student cannot accrue more than 90 days of unemployment during OPT. If STEM student granted extension s/he cannot accrue more than 120 days unemployment for the 29 months. 8 C.F.R. §214.2(f)(10)(ii)(E).

(f) Duration of Status. 60 days after the OPT employment authorization expires.

(g) Cap-Gap. If F-1 student in OPT is the beneficiary of an H-1B petition and timely filed a C/S her F-1/OPT stay is automatically extended until Oct 1st of the following fiscal year so that there is no "gap" between the time her OPT would have expired and the Oct. 1 start-up date for the H-1B. 8 C.F.R. §214.2(f)(5)(vi)(A). It also applies to F-2s.

(h) Other C/S. A person may also C/S to H-1B (or another status) during the authorized 60-day departure period after the completion of optional practical training. Memo, Pearson, Exec. Assoc. Comm. Field Operations, HQ 70.23.1 RS-P (Aug. 19, 1998), *reprinted in* 75 No. 32 *Interpreter Releases* 1147, 1167 (Aug. 24, 1998).

9.e. Temporary Absence Abroad with Work Authorization

(1) If re-entering on SEVIS I-20 I.D. with EAD it is valid only if the student is admitted to attend the same school.

(2) If student has unexpired EAD for post-completion practical training s/he may resume employment as long as the EAD is accompanied by SEVIS I-20 signed within last 6 months by DSO. The student is also advised to obtain a job offer letter or letter of employment in order to re-enter the U.S. after completion of studies.

(3) Student must present the EAD at the port of entry upon return. 8 C.F.R. §214.2(f)(13)(ii).

(4) If student has completed studies and is on optional practical training, s/he must present a valid F-1 visa when returning from an absence abroad

9.f. Obtaining a Social Security Card—The SSA has established procedures for students to apply for SSN or replacement card. Policy Instruction, SSA, EM-02093 (Aug. 8, 2002), *reprinted in* 79 No. 34 *Interpreter Releases* 1280, 1335–37 (Aug. 26, 2002). The student must submit evidence of age and identify, a I-20, a current I-94 and evidence of authorization to work and full-time attendance at school which may include an original letter from the DSO providing that the student is authorized to work on campus and currently enrolled in a full course of study. *Id.*

10. Out-of-Status Problem—8 C.F.R. §§214.2(f)(5), (f)(6). If student is employed without authorization, or not pursuing full course of study, or transfers schools without permission or fails to complete a full course of study in time and is ineligible for a program extension, s/he is out of status and subject to deportation. *Matter of Yazdani*, 17 I&N Dec. 626 (BIA 1981). A student who drops below a full course of study without prior approval of the DSO is considered out of status. 8 C.F.R. §214.2(f)(6)(iii). A student who is out of the country for more than five months should be terminated from the SEVIS. 8 C.F.R. §§214.2(f)(4), (f)(8)(i). The student is also required to obtain a new visa as the visa is invalid if he has been out of the country for more than five months. 22 C.F.R. §41.122(h)(3). If the student wishes to re-enter, a new SEVIS I-20 must be issued for the "initial attendance," and a new visa issued. Where the student is out for a temporary absence for five months or less he may be readmitted for study upon presentation of a valid I-20. Cable, DOS, 05-State-00232385 (Dec. 28, 2005), *published on* AILA InfoNet at Doc. No. 06011873; 8 C.F.R. 214.2(f)(4). Prior regulations were not applied to bar status to student who had minor disruptions in his full course of study. *Mashi v. INS*, 585 F.2d 1309 (5th Cir. 1978) [student arrested for misdemeanor and who temporarily dropped below 12 credits maintained status]. Conviction of a student that does not interrupt studies is not necessarily a violation. *Matter of C*, 9 I&N Dec. 100 (BIA 1960). *But see* 8 C.F.R. §214.1(g), [making certain convictions violations of any nonimmigrant status]. Students considered to be in status even if not engaged in full course where:

10.a. They remain for summer or annual vacation, so long as they are eligible and intend to register for the next term. 8 C.F.R. §214.2(f)(5)(iii).

10.b. They are compelled by illness or other medical condition to interrupt studies or reduce course load below full course as long as the total time does not exceed 12 months. 8 C.F.R. §214.2(f)(6)(iii)(B).

10.c. They take less than a full course of study for valid academic reasons on advice of DSO. However, the need for a reduced course load must arise out of the student's "initial difficulty with the English language or reading requirements, unfamiliarity with U.S. teaching methods, or improper course level placement. The student must resume a full course of study at the next available term..." And a student who drops below a full course is not eligible for a second authorization to take less than a full course of study by the DSO due to academic reasons. 8 C.F.R. §214.2(f)(6)(iii)(A).

10.d. They take fewer than a full course to complete their program in the final term. 8 C.F.R. §214.2(f)(6)(iii)(C).

10.e. They enroll in more than one DHS approved school where joint credits total full time. 8 C.F.R. §214.2(f)(6)(iv).

11. Change of Status from B-1/B-2—8 C.F.R. §§214.2(b)(7), 248.1(c)(3). A person entering the U.S. as a B-1/B-2 can no longer begin to attend school as an F-1/M-1 without first obtaining a change of status in the U.S. or an F-1/M-1 visa abroad. If a student with a B-1/B-2 begins to attend school without an F-1/M-1 or a C/S he will be denied a change of status to an F-1/M-1. Memo, Williams, Ex. Assoc. Comm. Field Operations, HQISD 70/6.2.2 P (Apr. 12, 2002), *reprinted in* 79 No. 17 *Interpreter Releases* 595, 605–07 (Apr. 22, 2002). This prohibition only applies to study prior to approval for B-1/B-2s. *Id.*

12. Change of Status During 60 Day Grace Period—A person may C/S to H-1B (or another status) during the authorized 60-day departure period, including the 60 days after completion of optional practical training. Memo, Pearson, Exec. Assoc. Comm. Field Operations, HQ 70.23.1 RS-P (Aug. 19, 1998), 75 No. 32 *Interpreter Releases* 1147, 1167 (Aug. 24, 1998).

13. Overstays—F-1s are not considered an overstay for purposes of INA §222(g) unless a USCIS officer or IJ has made a determination that a status violation has occurred. Cable, DOS, 98-State-051296 (Mar. 23, 1998), *published on* AILA InfoNet at Doc. No. 98032392. Thus, where USCIS or IJ have made the determination, the F-1 visa holder can no longer simply leave the country and re-enter with his SEVIS I-20. He must return home and obtain new visa. An F-1 who stays beyond the 60-day grace period has overstayed for purposes of E/S or C/S.

14. Reinstatement—Students may be reinstated by filing an I-539 accompanied by a properly completed SEVIS Form I-20 indicating the DSO's recommendation for reinstatement and demonstrating that: (1) S/he has not been out of status for more than 5 months or that there were exceptional circumstances and that the request was filed as promptly as possible; (2) S/he does not have a record of repeated or willful violations of Service regulations; (3) S/he is currently pursuing or intending to pursue a full course of study; (4) S/he has not engaged in unauthorized employment; (5) S/he is not deportable on any ground other than being out-of-status; and (6) S/he establishes to the satisfaction of the Service either that the violation resulted from circumstances beyond her control such as serious injury or illness, closure of the institution, a natural disaster or inadvertence, oversight or neglect by the DSO *or* the violation relates to reduction in the student's course level that the DSO could have authorized and that failure to reinstate will result in extreme hardship to the student. 8 C.F.R. §214.2(f)(16). If a student's status is reinstated his F-1 visa remains valid; but if reinstatement is denied the visa is lost because denial of status would result in invalidation of the visa under INA §222(g). Cable, DOS, 05-State-00232385 (Dec. 12, 2005), *published on* AILA InfoNet at Doc. No. 06011873. A student denied reinstatement is not barred from seeking another visa but consular officer should review the circumstances surrounding why the student ceased full-time study and lost status in the first place, including any actual status violation. *Id.* Reinstatement is generally a discretionary matter. *Matter of Yazdani*, *supra*; *DeSousa v. Demore,* 169 F.Supp.2d 1169 (N.D. Cal. 2001) [denied request to reinstate former student who was out of status while applying for adjustment based on marriage that was eventually denied].

15. Extension of Stay.

15.a. A student is not required to apply for E/S as long as s/he is maintaining status and making normal progress toward completing the educational objective. 8 C.F.R. §214.2(f)(7).

15.b. Extension of status must be requested where studies not completed timely (*e.g.,* if supposed to be completed in 2 years on SEVIS I-20 but student needs additional 6 months). The DSO may grant program extension if he certifies that the delays are caused by compelling medical or academic reasons such as changes of major or research topics, unexpected research problems, or documented illness. 8 C.F.R. §214.2(f)(7)(iii). Delays caused by academic probation or suspension are not acceptable reasons for program extensions.

15.c. The student must apply for the extension before the end-date on his program and his failure to do so would make the student o/s but subject to application for reinstatement. 8 C.F.R. §214.2(f)(7)(iii). If student is unable to complete program within period and is ineligible for a program extension s/he is out of status and must apply for reinstatement. *Id.*

16. Family may follow to join F-1 if the F-1 student is or will be within 30 days enrolled in a full course of study or is engaged in approved practical training. Each family member must be separately issued a SEVIS I-20. 8 C.F.R. §214.2(f)(3). Family members may not be employed and may not attend school except that a child may attend elementary through twelfth grade. 8 C.F.R. §214.2(f)(15). Also where a minor child is attending school, a parent is not *per se* barred from entering on B-2 and seeking extension of B-2 if the parent can show lack of intent to remain permanently. Letter, LaFleur, Chief, Business and Trade Branch, Benefits Division, HQ 70/6.2.2 (June 6, 1996), *reprinted in* 73 No. 28 *Interpreter Releases* 970, 976–77 (July 22, 1996).

17. Strikes and Lockouts—Students EAD is automatically suspended during a strike or lockout. 8 C.F.R. §214.2(f)(14).

18. Name and Address Registration—8 C.F.R. §214.2(f)(17). The change of address requirement under INA §265 is satisfied by SEVIS notification within 10 days even though the school is not required to update SEVIS data until 21 days after the change. Any student who has gone through special registration and moves must file a change of address on form AR 11.

19. SEVIS/Data Collection—Under IIRIRA §641, Congress now requires approved institutions for F programs to keep computerized data on students and exchange visitors as well as accompanying family members that includes their current address and status at the institution. The students are required to pay a fee to operate the program. The program called SEVIS (Student and Exchange Visitor Information System) is now mandatory for all schools issuing SEVIS I-20s. 8 C.F.R. §214.2(f)(1)(iii). DHS will no longer recognize I-20s that are not issued under the SEVIS program. *Id.* The schools have been provided an Internet site to access SEVIS at *www.ice.gov/sevis/schools.* 8 C.F.R. §214.12(b)(1). Under SEVIS the school must report if the student commences a full course of study, drops below a full course of study, transfers schools, extends her stay, is reinstated to student status, or engages in off-campus employment, curricular practical training or optional practical training. The school is also required to notify DHS of any student who reports or fails to report within 30 days of the institution's registration deadline. 8 C.F.R. §214.3(g)(3)(iii)(A); Memo, Williams, Ex. Assoc. Comm., Field Operations, HQINS 70/6.2.6 (Aug. 20, 2002) at 3, *reprinted in* 79 No. 45 *Interpreter Releases* 1706–07, 1715–18 (Nov. 18, 2002). The 30-day reporting requirement is based upon the "program start date" for new students and "next session start date" for continuing students. The school needs to report whether "the student reported to the academic institution as expected" even if the course enrollment process has not been fully determined because that can be reported at a later date. Memo, Garcia, Acting Asst. Sec. DHS, SEVIS Reporting Requirements At the Start of Each Term or Session (Oct. 17, 2003), *reprinted in* 81 No. 1 *Interpreter Releases* 5, 29–30 (Jan. 5, 2004).

Consular officers must also verify the SEVIS I-20 and the data in the SEVIS system before issuing a visa. Consular officers are directed to deny F-1/F-2 visas under INA §221(g) where a person presents the appropriate form from the school but there is no SEVIS record in the computerized system. Cable, DOS, 03-State-40362 (Feb. 12, 2003) at ¶10, *published on* AILA InfoNet at Doc. No. 03030443. If a visa is issued they must enter the information in the SEVIS database. 22 C.F.R. §41.61(d).

20. School Certification—The application for School Certification (I-17) must now be submitted to the Student and Exchange Visitor Program (SEVP) of ICE, instead of to USCIS. Memo, Drury, Director SEVP, DHS, HQSEV 20 (Oct. 31, 2003), *reprinted in* 80 No. 47 *Interpreter Releases* 1684-85, 1693–94 (Dec. 15, 2003).

21. In-State Tuition and Undocumented Status—Certain states, by statute, permit undocumented students to gain resident tuition status: California, Illinois, New York, Oklahoma, Texas, Utah and Washington. Certain states, by statute, prohibit undocumented students from obtaining in-state tuition: Alaska, Mississippi. *See also* Suthers, Opinion of Colorado Attorney General, 07-03 (Aug. 14, 2007), *reprinted in* 12 No. 18 *Bender's Immigration Bulletin* 1255, 1339- 44 (Sept. 15, 2007). *But see Toll v. Moreno,* 458 U.S. 1, 14 & n.20, 102 S.Ct. 2977 (1982); *Elkins v. Moreno,* 435 U.S.

647, 665, 98 S.Ct. 1338 (1978); Forehand, Opinion of the Virginia Attorney General (Domicile Matter) (Mar. 6, 2008), *reprinted in* 13 No. 8 *Bender's Immigration Bulletin* 504 (Apr. 15, 2008) [undocumented persons may never be domicile in Virginia but USC children of undocumented may be].

B. ***Vocational Students (M Visa)***—INA §101(a)(15)(M), 8 U.S.C. §1101(a)(15)(M); 8 C.F.R. 214.2(m), 67 Fed. Reg. 76256–80 (Dec. 11, 2002); 68 Fed. Reg. 28129 (May 23, 2003) [interim SEVIS rule]; 70 Fed. Reg. 7853 (Feb. 16, 2005) [final SEVIS rule]. Similar to F-1 except at a vocational/nonacademic institution.

1. Full Course Defined—8 C.F.R. §214.2(m)(9).

   1.a. Study in community/junior college for 12 semester/quarter hours leading to a specific educational and/or vocational objective.

   1.b. Study at a post-secondary vocational/business school (other than language training program) which confers a degree or has its credits accepted by 3 accredited academic institutions. Twelve hours of instruction/week or its equivalent are required.

   1.c. Study in vocational or other nonacademic curriculum (including a language training program taken at the school to further vocational training); 18 hours/week if predominantly classroom or 22 hours if predominantly shop/lab. Flight schools, cooking schools and other vocational schools would be included. Under section 113 of the Aviation and Transportation Security Act of 2001 flight school trainers are now required to provide to the AG a noncitizen's identification who wishes to be trained on an aircraft with a maximum certified takeoff weight of 12,500 pounds or more before so that the AG can assess the security risk prior to the training. 28 C.F.R. §105.10–.14

   1.d. Study in vocational or other nonacademic high school curriculum for not less than minimum number of hours for normal progress toward degree.

   1.e. No Online Courses—Distance education or online courses cannot count toward an M-1 student's full course of study unless the course requires the student's physical presence. 8 C.F.R. §214.2(m)(9)(v).

   1.f. Reduced Course Load—M-1 can take a reduced course load but only for a maximum aggregate of 5 months and only because of medical reasons. 8 C.F.R. §214.2(m)(9)(vi).

2. Commuter students from Canada and Mexico may attend school part time or full time in the U.S. as M-3 visa holders as long as they are not residing in the U.S. INA §101(a)(15)(M)(iii); 22 C.F.R. §41.61(b)(1)(iii). As border commuter students they will be given a date certain on their I-94, instead of D/S. 8 C.F.R. §214.2(m)(19). Border commuter students are subject to SEVIS but may not obtain F-2 status for their dependents. 68 Fed. Reg. 28129, 28130 (May 23, 2003).

3. In order to obtain M must present SEVIS Form I-20 to consular officer, 22 C.F.R. §41.61(b)(1), pay the SEVIS (I-901) fee, and meet the same general criteria for an F-1 student, *supra.* Initial student can not enter U.S. more than 45 days before school and consul can issue initial visa up to 120 days before. Cable, DOS, 06-State-021872 (Feb. 9, 2006), *published on* AILA InfoNet at Doc. No. 06031360.

4. The SEVIS fee may be paid by credit card via the Internet at *www.fmjfee.com* or by mailing a U.S. dollar check or international money order to a lockbox address in the U.S. Cable, DOS, 04-State-162300 (Aug. 31, 2004), *published on* AILA InfoNet at Doc. No. 04092160. 8 C.F.R. §§214.2(m)(20), 214.13.

5. Admitted for time necessary to complete course + 30 days, or for one year, whichever is less. 8 C.F.R. 214.2(m)(5). An M student may now be subject to INA §222(g) as well as the 3/10 year bar because he will be given an "end date" stamped on his SEVIS form that will be 30 days beyond the program end date. Information Sheet, U.S. ICE (Jan. 15, 2004), *reprinted in* 81 No. 6 *Interpreter Releases* 188, 205 (Feb. 9, 2004). However, it is unclear what will be stamped on the M student's I-94.

6. Extension of Stay—Can cumulatively obtain extensions up to 3 years (+30 days) from the original start date to complete program. 8 C.F.R. §214.2(m)(10).

7. Cannot begin vocational studies until student enters the U.S. with the M-1 visa or c/s to M-1. 8 C.F.R. §214.2(b)(7) [cannot begin program on B-1/B-2]. And a c/s to M-1 will be denied if B-1/B-2 enrolled in course of study prior to obtaining the c/s. 8 C.F.R. §248.1(c)(3). This prohibition only applies to study prior to approval for B-1/ B-2s. Memo, Williams, Ex. Assoc. Comm. Field Operations, HQISD 70/6.2.2 P (Apr. 12, 2002), *reprinted in* 79 No. 17 *Interpreter Releases* 595, 605–07 (Apr. 22, 2002).

8. SEVIS/Data Collection—Under IIRIRA §641, Congress now requires approved institutions for M programs to keep computerized data on students and exchange visitors and their accompanying family members that includes their current address and status at the institution. The students are required to pay a fee to operate the program. The program called SEVIS (Student and Exchange Visitor Information System) is now mandatory for all schools issuing SEVIS I-20s. 8 C.F.R. §214.2(m)(1)(iii). DHS will no longer recognize I-20s that are not issued under the SEVIS program. *Id.* The schools have been provided an Internet site to access SEVIS, at *www.ice.gov/sevis/schools.* 8 C.F.R. §214.12(b)(1). Under SEVIS the school must report if the student commences a full course of study, drops below a full course of study, transfers schools, extends her stay, is reinstated to student status, or engages in practical training. The school is also required to notify DHS of any student who reports or fails to report within 30 days of the institution's registration deadline. 8 C.F.R. §214.3(g)(3)(iii)(A); Memo, Williams, Ex. Assoc. Comm., Field Operations, HQINS 70/6.2.6 (Aug. 20, 2002) at 3, *reprinted in* 79 No. 45 *Interpreter Releases* 1706–07, 1715–18 (Nov. 18, 2002). The 30-day reporting requirement is based upon the "program start date" for new students and "next session start date" for continuing students. The school needs to report whether "the student reported to the academic institution as expected" even if the course enrollment process has not been fully determined because that can be reported at a later date. Memo, Garcia, Acting Asst. Sec. DHS, SEVIS Reporting Requirements at the Start of Each Term or Session (Oct. 17, 2003), *reprinted in* 81 No. 1 *Interpreter Releases* 5, 29–30 (Jan. 5, 2004).

   Consular officers must verify the SEVIS I-20 and the data in the SEVIS system before issuing a visa. Consular officers are directed to deny M-1/M-2 visas under INA §221(g) where a person presents the appropriate form from the school but there is no SEVIS record in the computerized system, Cable, DOS, 03-State-40362 (Feb. 12, 2003) at ¶10, *published on* AILA InfoNet at Doc. No. 03030443 or where the student fails to pay the SEVIS (I-901) fee. Cable, DOS, 04-State-162300 ¶5 (Aug. 31, 2004), *published on* AILA InfoNet at Doc. No. 04092160. If a visa is issued they must enter the information in the SEVIS database. 22 C.F.R. §41.61(d). Consulate may issue visa 120 days in advance but must inform the student that he may not enter the U.S. more than 30 days in advance. 9 FAM 41.61 Note 14.2. The 120- and 30-day rules do not apply to continuing students who are maintaining status.

9. Family Members—Must individually obtain SEVIS Form I-20s. 8 C.F.R. §214.2(m)(3). Cannot obtain employment. Cannot engage in full time study unless it is a child attending primary or secondary school. 8 C.F.R. §214.2(m)(17). Can only obtain an extension of stay if M-1 obtains extension. 8 C.F.R. §214.2(m)(10)(iii).

10. Reinstatement—A student may ask for reinstatement on I-539 to the Service. It may be considered only if the student: (1) was not out of status for more than 5 months at the time of filing the request; (2) does not have a record of repeated or willful violations of Service regulations; (3) is currently pursuing or intends to pursue a full course of study; (4) has not engaged in unlawful employment; (5) is not deportable other than being out-of-status; and (6) establishes that the violation of status resulted form circumstances beyond his control such as illness, injury, natural disaster, closure of the institution or negligence by the DSO *or* the violation relates to a reduction in the student's course load that would have been within a DSO's power to authorize. 8 C.F.R. 214.2(m)(16). If a student's status is reinstated his M-1 visa remains valid; but if reinstatement is denied the visa is lost because denial of status would result in invalidation of the visa under INA §222(g). Cable, DOS, 05-State-00232385 (Dec. 12, 2005), *published on* AILA InfoNet at Doc. No. 06011873. A student denied reinstatement is not barred from seeking another visa but consular officer should review the circumstances surrounding why the student ceased full-time study and lost status in the first place, including any actual status violation. *Id.* Reinstatement is generally a discretionary matter. *Matter of Yazdani, supra*; *DeSousa v. Demore,* 169 F.Supp.2d 1169 (N.D. Cal. 2001) [denied request to reinstate former student who was out of status while applying for adjustment based on marriage that was eventually denied].

11. Differences from F-1

11.a. Can only be authorized to reduce course load for medical reasons and only for a maximum aggregate period of five months.

11.b. No online courses or distance courses permissible unless person is required to be physically present for class.

11.c. Can only attend school with extensions for a maximum of 3 years.

11.d. Can transfer schools only in first 6 months unless reason for not being able to remain at present school was "due to circumstances beyond the student's control." And must get DHS permission prior to transfer on I-539. 8 C.F.R. §214.2(m)(11).

11.e. Cannot change educational objectives. 8 C.F.R. §214.2(m)(12).

11.f. Cannot accept employment, 8 C.F.R. §214.2(m)(13), except practical training. But practical training may only be obtained after completion of study. 8 C.F.R. §214.2(m)(14). Must have job in field of study; can only be given one period of practical training for period of time "equal to 1 month of each 4 months" student pursued full course of study. Not exceeding 6 months, §214.2(m)(14)(iii). Application must be submitted on I-765 before expiration of authorized stay and not more than 60 days before to 30 days after completion of course of study. 8 C.F.R. §214.2(m)(14)(ii).

11.g. Cannot change to H status if basis of H was training or education received as M-1 student. 8 C.F.R. §248.1(d). Nor can student's request to change nonimmigrant status be granted to M if student is doing it to ultimately qualify for H. 8 C.F.R. §248.1(c). M also cannot change to F. 8 C.F.R. §248.1(c). However, none of these regulations apply to M-2s.

C. *Exchange Visitor (J Visa)*—INA §101(a)(15)(J), 8 U.S.C. §§1101(a)(15)(J), 1182(e); Legislative history at H. Rept. 721, 87th Cong. 1st Sess. 121 (1961); S. Rept. 372, 87th Cong. 1st Sess. 19 (1961); H. Conf. Rept. 87-1197 (Sept. 15, 1961), H. Conf. Rept. 87-1088 (Aug. 30, 1961); H. Rept. 87-1094 (Aug. 31, 1961); 1961 U.S.C.C.A.N. 2775 *et seq.*; 58 Fed. Reg. 15180–15220 (Mar. 19, 1993); 67 Fed. Reg. 76256–80, 76307–16 (Dec. 11, 2002); 68 Fed. Reg. 28129 (May 23, 2003) [interim SEVIS rule]; 70 Fed. Reg. 7853 (Feb. 16, 2005) [final SEVIS rule]. IIRIRA §621, H. Conf. Rep. 208 and 863, 104th Cong., 2d Sess. at 246–47 (1996);

1. Criteria set forth in 9 FAM 41.62 N. 1, 22 C.F.R. pt. 62. Program is for a nonimmigrant visitor who has no intention of abandoning foreign residence and who:

1.a. Is a professor or research scholar [22 C.F.R. §62.20], short-term scholar [§62.21], *bona fide* trainee or intern [§62.22], college or university student [§62.23], teacher [§62.24], secondary school student [§62.25], nonacademic specialist [§62.26], foreign physician [§62.27], international visitor [22 C.F.R. §62.28], government visitor [22 C.F.R. §62.29], camp counselor [22 C.F.R. §62.30], au pair [22 C.F.R. §62.31], or summer student in a travel/work program [22 C.F.R. §62.32].

1.b. Has sufficient funds and fluency in English. 22 C.F.R. §§41.62(a)(2) and (a)(3);

1.c. Maintains sufficient medical insurance for accident and illness for participant and J family members in a minimum amount of $50,000 per accident or illness. 22 C.F.R. §62.14;

2. Consulates may issue the visa at any time as long as the DS-2019 is valid. The DS-2019 replaced the IAP-66. An exchange visitor may not enter the U.S. more than 30 days before the program start date on the DS-2019 to participate in an exchange visitor program. 9 FAM 41.62 N. 9.3; 8 C.F.R. §214.2(j)(1)(ii).

3. On issue in J-1 cases: Is the training in a field which can be utilized in the foreign country? 9 FAM 41.62 N5.2;

4. Trainee and Internship Programs—DOS substantially revised the trainee program for private host companies and replaced it with a more rigorous trainee program and internship program, 22 C.F.R. §62.22; 72 Fed. Reg. 33669 (June 19, 2007).

4.a. Internship Program Criteria—Foreign national who is either currently enrolled in and pursuing studies at a degree-or certificate-granting post-secondary institution outside the U.S. *or* graduated from such an institution no more than 12 months prior the start date of the exchange program. Must also have verifiable English language skills sufficient to function on a day-to-day basis. §62.22(a),(d).

4.b. Trainee Program Criteria—Foreign national who either has a degree or professional certificate from a foreign post-secondary academic institution *and* a least one year of prior related work experience in their occupation field outside the U.S. *or* five years of work experience outside the U.S. in their occupational field. §62.22(d)(2)

4.c. Time Limitation—The trainee program is generally for 18 months, except in the case of agriculture and hotel and tourism which are limited to 12 months with certain exceptions, *see infra.* 22 C.F.R. §62.22(k). Interns are limited to 12 months.

(1) Additional Training—To get additional training the program must address the development of more advanced skills or a different field of expertise. Interns may participate in an additional program as long as they maintain student status or begin a new internship program within 12 months of graduation. Trainees must be out of U.S. for a 2 year period before they can get additional training. Similarly, interns who no longer qualify for an internship program must be out of the U.S. for 2 years before starting a trainee program. 22 C.F.R. §62.22(n).

4.d. Occupational categories limited to— (i) Agriculture, forestry and fishing; (ii) arts and culture; (iii) aviation; (iv) construction and building trades; (v) education, social sciences, library science, counseling and social services; (vi) health related occupations; (vii) hospitality and tourism; (viii) information media and communications; (ix) management, business, commerce and finance; (x) public administration and law; and (xi) the sciences, engineering, architecture, mathematics, and industrial occupation. 22 C.F.R. §62.22(c)(2).

(1) Exclusions—Under 22 C.F.R. §62.22(j) a sponsor cannot: (1) place the person in an unskilled or casual labor position; (2) place them in a position, occupation or business that would bring the program into notoriety or disrepute; (3) contract with a staffing/employment agency to recruit, screen, evaluate or trainee interns or trainees; (4) have training involve more than 20 % clerical work; (5) have a hospitality or tourism program of greater than six months duration that does not have at least three departmental or functional rotations; and (6) have interns in the field of aviation (trainees in aviation are permitted but only consistent with the restrictions noted by DOS in its 2006 Statement of Policy, 71 Fed. Reg. 3913 (Jan.24, 2006)).

5. Au Pair Program—22 C.F.R. §62.31. The program permits youths from abroad to be placed with American host families seeking child care. Although the program was previously limited to European youths, the DOS has expanded it to include all nations except those lacking diplomatic relations with the U.S. 61 Fed. Reg. 8215 (Mar. 4, 1996). DOS has also issued rules requiring greater oversight of the program. 64 Fed. Reg. 53930 (Oct. 5, 1999); 62 Fed. Reg. 34632–34 (June 27, 1997). DOS has now developed a second au pair program called EduCare that provides for less child care work and a greater academic component. Under EduCare an au pair will provide child care services only for 30 hours (instead of 45 hours) per week and will take no less than 12 (instead of 6) semester hours of academic credit or its equivalent per year. 22 C.F.R. §§62.31(a), (c), (k). 66 Fed. Reg. 43087–08 (Aug. 17, 2001). Although the program is for a 12 month period, DOS, in its sole discretion, may approve extensions of the au pair program for a one-time extension of six, nine or 12 months but the au pair must demonstrate she has complied with certain educational requirements and must file it at least 30 days prior to her current expiration. 22 C.F.R. §§62.31(k), (o).

6. B-1 in Lieu of J-1—Certain visitors to the U.S. may have their travel funded by the U.S. government but do not fall within the J-1 category. For example, an employee of an Embassy or Consulate (Foreign Service National Employee) may travel to the U.S. at U.S. government expense to participate in a wide variety of programs (*e.g.*, CIA/ DIA training) that are not authorized exchange visitor programs. These travelers need not be issued J-1 visas and can be issued another appropriate visa such as a B-1. Cable, DOS, 04-State-13720 (Jan. 21, 2004), *published on* AILA InfoNet at Doc. No. 04022564; Memo, Ahern, Asst. Comm., Field Operations, CBP, "B-1 in Lieu of J-1 Visa for U.S. Government Funded Travel," (Feb. 10, 2004), *published on* AILA InfoNet at Doc. No. 05040471.

7. Two-Year Foreign Residence Requirement

7.a. Certain J visa holders are subject to a requirement that they must return to their home country or country of last residence upon completion of their training in the U.S. before they are eligible to adjust status, apply for an immigrant visa, or apply for an H or L visa, or change status inside the U.S. (except for change to A or G, or except for change to H-1B for physicians receiving waivers on the basis of a three-year waiver job). INA §§212(e), 214(*l*), and 248, 8 U.S.C. §§1182(e), 1184(*l*), and 1258; 22 C.F.R. §41.63. Those J visa holders subject to this 2-year foreign residence requirement are persons:

(1) Whose participation "was financed in whole or in part, directly or indirectly, by an agency of the government of the U.S. or by the government of his nationality or last residence";

(2) Who at the time of admission or acquisition of status was engaged in a field which was on the DOS Skills List. The most recent "Skills List" governing programs beginning on or after Mar. 17, 1997 is found at 62 Fed. Reg. 2447–2516 (Jan. 16, 1997), *reprinted in* 74 No. 15 *Interpreter Releases* 644, 670–704 (Apr. 21, 1997), and should also be in 9 FAM 41.62, Exhibit II; *http://exchanges.state.gov/education/jexchanges/participation/skills_list.pdf* *See also http://exchanges.state.gov/education/jexchanges/participation/waivers.htm*. The previous Skills List was issued on July 12, 1984 and governs all persons who entered on or after July 12, 1984 to Mar. 17, 1997.

(3) Who came to the U.S. or acquired J status after Jan. 10, 1977 to receive graduate medical education or training. INA §212(e), 8 U.S.C. §1182(e).

7.b. A person subject to the 2-year foreign residence requirement is ineligible to apply for an immigrant visa/adjustment of status, change of status (except as to A and G categories or to H-1B for a physician taking a three-year J-1 waiver job), or to apply for an H or L visa unless he returns home and physically resides in his country for 2 years following departure from the U.S. or obtains a waiver. 8 U.S.C. §1182(e); 8 C.F.R. §§248.2(c), (d); 22 C.F.R. §41.63(a)(1); *Friedberger v. Schultz*, 616 F.Supp. 1315 (D.C. Pa. 1985). A foreign physician is not precluded from applying for an O visa, although he would still remain subject to the 2-year foreign residence requirement. Letter, Bednarz, Chief, NIV Branch, Adjudications, HQ 214.42-C (Aug. 30, 1994), *reprinted in* 71 No. 39 *Interpreter Releases* 1360, 1376 (Oct. 7, 1994).

7.c. A person is subject to the 2-year foreign residence requirement even if he obtained the J visa by fraud. *Espejo v. INS,* 311 F.3d 976 (9th Cir. 2002); *Matter of Park,* 15 I&N Dec. 436 (1975).

8. Waiver of 2-year requirement. 8 C.F.R. §§212.7(c), 1212.7(c); 22 C.F.R. §41.63(a)(2)–(g).

8.a. Procedure—USCIS can grant waiver only after DOS makes favorable recommendation to USCIS. *Dina v. Attorney General*, 793 F.2d 473 (2d Cir. 1986); *Silverman v. Rogers*, 437 F.2d 102 (1st Cir. 1970), *cert. denied*, 402 U.S. 983 (1971) [DOS can veto hardship waiver by INS]; *Matter of Tayabji*, 19 I&N Dec. 264 (BIA 1985) [upholding rescission of adjustment of status where DD granted waiver after DOS recommended denial of waiver].

(1) DOS procedure to obtain waiver is now a four-part process: (1) Applicant must first submit a Data Sheet to Department of State/Waiver Review Division with two stamped self-addressed envelopes and a fee (presently $215). Data Sheet and fees now sent to St. Louis, MO site. (2) DOS sends case number and instruction sheet for waiver application to applicant. The instruction sheet will depend upon the nature of waiver indicated on the Data Sheet. (3) Under INA §212(e) there are four kinds of J-1 waivers. All commence with filing of the Data Sheet, as noted above. For two categories (persecution and hardship), the next step is filing Form I-612 with the USCIS Service Center having jurisdiction over the applicant's place of residence. The other two categories (Interested Government Agency and No Objection) do not require a filing with USCIS. For those, the next step is an application to the agency or to the foreign government, as described below. (4) DOS reviews the application and forwards the recommendation to USCIS with a copy to the applicant and J-1 sponsor. To check on status of case, call (202) 663-1600 or see *http://travel.state.gov/visa/temp/info/info_1296.html.*

(2) In hardship and persecution cases, a waiver application is made to USCIS on Form I-612 after DOS issues a DOS waiver file number. 8 C.F.R. §212.7(c)(5). The USCIS Form I-612 is only used for two of the four kinds of J waivers (hardship and persecution). The

other two waivers (interested government agency and no objection) do not start with a filing to the USCIS, and they do not involve the Form 1-612 at any point. If DHS grants the persecution or hardship waiver it then transmits the information to the Waiver Review Division of DOS which shall make a recommendation after reviewing the "program, policy, and foreign relations aspects of the case" §41.63(b)(2) and transmit its decision to DHS.

(3) If request denied by USCIS prior to the referral to DOS, an appeal can be made to the AAO, 8 C.F.R. §212.7(c)(11), If a waiver is denied due to a negative DOS recommendation, there is no appeal, but it may be possible to pursue a *de* non application.

8.b. Basis for waiver:

(1) Possible Persecution—"Would be subject to persecution on account of race, religion or political opinion." Under this section, DOS has the authority to deny a waiver on "program and policy" grounds even if USCIS finds that the exchange visitor would be subject to persecution. J-1 persecution waivers are very rare and they take a long time to process because there are several internal reviews at DOS. An exchange visitor granted asylum under INA §207 may adjust status under INA §209, even if subject to the J-1 foreign residence requirement which would prevent him from adjusting under INA §245(a). 8 C.F.R. §209.2(b); 22 C.F.R. §41.63(a)(2).

(2) Exceptional Hardship—Departure from U.S. would impose exceptional hardship on USC/LPR spouse or child. *Keh Tong Chen v. AG,* 546 F.Supp. 1060 (D.D.C. 1982); H.R. Rep. No. 721, 87th Cong., 1st Sess. 121 (1961); 22 C.F.R. §41.63(a)(2).

(a) Exceptional Not Extreme Hardship—Decision reversed where director relied on suspension cases where the standard was "extreme hardship" instead of the appropriate exceptional hardship standard. *Matter of* ___,(AAO Feb. 6, 2007) *reported in* 84 No. 22 *Interpreter Releases* 1189, 1217 (June 4, 2007) [USC wife suffered from hypothyroidism, depression and had malignant basal cell carcinomas would suffer exception hardship if accompanied husband to Syria and that wife's depression would affect her ability to work as athletic trainer if husband returned to Syria without her].

(b) In determining a hardship waiver: (1) applicant must show hardship if spouse/child accompanying him abroad for two years; and (2) hardship if spouse/child remain in U.S. *Matter of* ___, A77 851 910 (AAO Oct. 3, 2000) [waiver granted where spouse's ongoing medical problems if she stayed in U.S. would be exacerbated by spouse's absence and return to Colombia would create hardship given unstable political situation, coupled with financial hardship] *reported in* 77 No. 44 *Interpreter Releases* 1611–12 (Nov. 13, 2000); *Accord Matter of* ___, A74 944 520 (AAO Feb. 7, 2001) *reported in* 78 No. 12 *Interpreter Releases* 564–65 (Mar. 26, 2001).

(c) Self-imposed separation, not grounds. *Matter of Mansour*, 11 I&N Dec. 306 (DD 1965).

(d) Factors to consider: economic, physical and emotional hardship; loss of employment, educational and health opportunities.

(e) Hardship to nonqualifying relatives will be given weight if there also exists hardship to a qualifying relative. *Matter of Kawasaki*, 12 I&N Dec. 864 (DAC 1968) [mother-in-law's depression if separated from wife of applicant].

(f) More "liberal attitude" taken where:

i) Alien imparted some benefit to U.S. *Matter of Coffman*, 13 I&N Dec. 206 (DAC 1969) [taught German to USC/LPR].

ii) Alien participated in program at own expense.

iii) Program of short duration. *Matter of Coffman, supra,* [90 days].

iv) Some time spent overseas fulfilling requirement of residency.

(g) Hardship to Spouse:

i) Educational/career hardship. Where spouse would have to disrupt her education/career. *Matter of Chong*, 12 I&N Dec. 793 (DD 1968).

ii) Allegation that they could not financially maintain 2 households.

iii) Give up medical practice to accompany spouse. *Matter of Savetamal*, 13 I&N Dec. 249 (R.C. 1969).

iv) Psychological and other hardship:

a) Where USC husband would suffer economic and cultural hardship if accompanied wife to Korea and when husband had history of psychological problems the refusal by INS to grant hardship waiver was reversed. *Huck v. Attorney General*, 676 F.Supp. 10 (D.D.C. 1987).

b) Wife is Christian and husband may not be able to leave Egypt after 2 years because of exit laws. *Matter of Mansour*, 11 I&N Dec. 306 (DD 1965).

c) Alcoholism and psychiatric problems of husband as well as harm to USC child if accompanying physician wife to Colombia and husband's inability to care for family if remained here was sufficient for hardship waiver. In *Matter of*___ A77 851 910 (AAO Oct. 3, 2000), *reported in* 77 No. 44 *Interpreter Releases* 1611 (Nov. 13, 2000).

d) USC spouse psychologically disabled with a history of clinical depression resulting in financial dependence on the applicant. *Matter of* ___ (AAO Feb. 14, 2000), 2000 WL 33538895 (Jan. 1, 2002).

(h) Child Hardship—where applicant unable to support family and child needs surgery unavailable in home country. *Matter of Santillano*, 11 I&N Dec. 146 (DD 1965) [Philippine doctor returned home unable to support family with child needing corrective surgery]; where USC child of 3 has atrophic dermatitis which would make it dangerous to require smallpox vaccine and child required to get vaccine if returned to India with J parents—waiver granted, *Matter of Ambe*, 13 I&N Dec. 3 (DD 1968); where USC child got sick in India returning there would result in hardship. *Matter of Gupta*, 13 I&N Dec. 477 (DAC 1970). But: (1) where parents would take salary cut affecting ability to support USC child and child would not have same educational opportunities—waiver denied, *Matter of Lai*, 13 I&N Dec. 188 (R.C. 1969); and (2) when children would be subject to more infections, diseases—no waiver. *Matter of Amin*, 13 I&N Dec. 209 (R.C. 1969).

(3) No objection waiver. 22 C.F.R. §41.63(a)(3)

(a) If J country issues a no objection statement regarding J's decision not to return home.

(b) Not available to foreign medical graduates except if they came to U.S. as J to observe, consult, teach, or do research. 22 C.F.R. §41.63(a)(3); §62.27(g)(2);

(c) A no objection statement from the home country is generally held insufficient if U.S. government provided direct or indirect funding for the purpose of participating in an educational or cultural program. *See generally* 22 C.F.R. §62.2. The amount of money received from the U.S. government, whether the funds have been earmarked for exchange purposes, and the exchange visitor's contributions to the U.S., however, are relevant.

(d) Procedure—Apply through country's embassy in U.S. unless J has returned home, then through foreign office.

(4) Request by U.S. Federal Executive Agency. 22 C.F.R. §41.63(c)

(a) Initiated by U.S. agency (generally other than DOS) that has interest in case. Any feral agency can do this, whether or not it has an established J waiver program. Must show granting of waiver is: (i) in public interest; and (ii) compliance with 2-year return would be "clearly detrimental" to a program/activity of official interest to agency (*e.g.*, NASA, NIH).

(b) Procedure—The individual or office of the agency recognized by DOS to submit waiver applications must transmit the waiver application to DOS.

Dept. of Education regulations previously found at 34 C.F.R. §50 *et seq.* but Dept. has withdrawn from program; HUD has withdrawn program. Memo, Cisneros (Dec. 13, 1996), *reprinted in* 74 No. 5 *Interpreter Releases* 236, 241 (Feb. 3, 1997). USDA also announced it will no longer serve as an interested government agency. USDA, Release No. FSJ-1 visa.02, *reprinted in* 79 No. 11 *Interpreter Releases* 376, 392 (Mar. 11, 2002). HHS, which historically supported waivers principally for researchers, has broadened its program to include waivers for primary care physicians and general psychiatrists in medically undeserved areas, 45 C.F.R. §50.1 *et seq.* Under HHS guidelines: (1) Physicians limited to primary care doctors and general psychiatrists who have completed their training program and are willing to work in a HPSA or MUA/P or Mental Health HPSA. Defines primary care physicians as internal medicine, pediatrics, family practice or obstetrics/gynecology; (2) Petitioning health care facility must document good faith but unsuccessful effort to recruit qualified U.S. physician; (3) Head of petitioning facility must execute a statement that facility is located in specific HPSA or MUA/P area and that it provides medical care to Medicaid and Medicare eligible patients and the uninsured indigent; (4) Physician must execute statement that s/he does not have pending and will not submit another IGA waiver request while HHS one is pending; and (5) Need employment contract that states specific primary care medical field, that is for a minimum of three years and 40 hours per week in a HPSA or MUA/P area, that does not contain a noncompete clause limiting practice in a medically underserved area, that is terminable for good cause and not by mutual consent, and that may be assigned to another employer with HHS approval. 68 Fed. Reg. 35226 (June 12, 2003). HHS has narrowed the possible positions by requiring that waivers will only be available for locations with a HPSA score of 14 or higher which are: (a) Health centers as defined under Section 330 of the Public Health Service Act; (2) Rural health clinics as defined under Sections 1102 and 1871 of the Social Security Act; or (3) Native American/Alaskan Native tribal medical facilities as defined by the Self-Determination and Education Assistance Act (PL 93-638). HHS, Application for Waiver *reproduced in* 81 No. 3 *Interpreter Releases* 82–83, 91–100 (Jan. 19, 2004).

(5) International Medical Graduate—INA §214(*l*), 22 C.F.R. §41.63(a)(3); 8 C.F.R. §212.7(c)(9); Memo, Pearson, Exec. Assoc. Comm. (HQADN70/21.1)(Oct. 4 1999), *reprinted in* 76 No. 39 *Interpreter Releases* 1504–08 (Oct. 11, 1999). A FMG may obtain a waiver through a recommendation issued by an interested state or federal agency interested in facilitating the physician's employment in a designated medically underserved area.

(a) State Agency—22 C.F.R. §41.63(e) The Immigration and Nationality Technical Corrections Act of 1994 at §220 provided for a special ("Conrad 20" now called "Conrad 30") program to waive the 2-year foreign residence requirement for foreign physicians who acquire J status or enter as Js and work in a state medically underserved area. The program has been extended (IIRIRA §622(a), PL 103-416, and PL 109-477) until June 1, 2008. Memo, Aytes, Assoc. Dir. Domestic Operations, USCIS HQ 70/6.2.10 (Jan. 29, 2007), *published on* AILA InfoNet at Doc. No. 07030668. The program provides that an "interested" state department of public health or its equivalent may recommend up to 30 waivers per year if the applicant: (1) obtains a no objection letter (if the medical education or training was funded by the home country); (2) agrees to accept *bona fide* full time employment at health facility or health care organization within 90 days of receiving the waiver; (3) practices primary care or specialty medicine for a total of 3 years in a shortage area unless the DHS determines that extenuating circumstances, such as the closure of the facility or hardship to the alien, would justify a lesser period, in which case the applicant must demonstrate another *bona fide* offer of employment in a shortage area for the remainder of the 3-year period; *Matter of Southeastern Pediatric and Adolescent Medicine,* LIN-02-111-54784 (AAO Feb. 10, 2003) [failure to pay promised salary as represented on LCA and employment contract was extenuating circumstance] *reported in* 80 No. 15 *Interpreter Releases* 555 (Apr. 14, 2003); (4) does not practice medicine in an area not designated as a shortage area; and (5) fulfills all the terms of the contract with the state health care facility.

i) The state agency may use up to 5 of its 30 visas to locate FMGs in a facility that serves patients in a medically underserved area even if the facility itself is not within the area. INA §214(*l*)(1)(D)(ii).

ii) In the case of specialty medicine, a waiver may be granted if the agency can demonstrate, based upon criteria it establishes, that there is a shortage of health care professionals able to provide services in the appropriate medical specialty to the patients who will be served by the FMG. 60 Fed. Reg. 16785, 16786 (Apr. 3, 1995).

(b) Procedures for state waivers, 22 C.F.R. §41.63, 60 Fed. Reg. 53122–26 (Oct. 12, 1995); 8 C.F.R. §212.7(c)(9). For updated list of state programs *see* 5 *Bender's Immigration Bulletin* 151-59 (Feb. 1, 2000):

i) Each state must designate to DOS the agency within the state responsible for the waivers.

ii) A completed application to DOS must contain:

a) data sheet for DOS, DS-3035

b) letter from director of state agency which identifies the FMG by name, country, and date of birth and states it is in the public interest to grant the waiver;

c) three-year contract between FMG and health care facility that demonstrates that faculty is in shortage area as designated by HHS and that FMG will abide by all the terms of INA §214(*l*);

d) proof that facility is within a shortage area as designated by HHS;

e) copies of all IAP-66/DS-2019;

f) FMG's curriculum vitae;

g) no objection letter (if required owing to funding from a governmental source); and

h) each application for state is numbered sequentially so that they will not exceed 30.

(c) Federal Agency Criteria—To obtain a waiver of the 2-year foreign residence requirement the FMG must: (1) obtain a no-objection letter from the country the FMG must return to (only if government funding was received); (2) agrees to accept *bona fide* full time employment at health facility or health care organization within 90 days of receiving the waiver; (3) practices primary care or specialty medicine for a total of 3 years in a shortage area unless DHS determines that extenuating circumstances, such as the closure of the facility or hardship to the alien, would justify a lesser period, in which case the applicant must demonstrate another *bona fide* offer of employment in a shortage area for the remainder of the 3-year period.

i) In the case of a request by the Dept. of Veterans Affairs, or a physician performing teaching or training services, the FMG shall not be required to practice medicine in a shortage area;

ii) In the case of specialty medicine, a waiver may be granted if the agency can demonstrate, based upon criteria it establishes, that there is a shortage of health care professionals able to provide services in the appropriate medical specialty to the patients who will be served by the FMG.

(d) Federal agency—Procedures for interested U.S. Government Agency, 22 C.F.R. §41.63(c).

i) U.S. gov't agency must explain in writing why waiver "would be in the public interest and the detrimental effect that would result to the program or activity ..." if J-1 could not continue.

ii) Request must include:

a) All SEVIS DS-2019 forms and J-1's current address and nationality;

b) Copy of employment contract between the FMG and facility. Contract must be for 3 years and require the FMG to perform no less than 40 hours/week of primary or specialty care medicine in a Health Professional Shortage Area (HPSA) or Medically Underserved Area or Population (MUA/ P) or psychiatric care in a Mental Health Professional Shortage Area (MHPSA). If FMG employed by Veterans Administration, need not work in HPSA/MUA area. Agreement *cannot* include noncompete clause;

c) Statement by head of facility that facility is located in a MUA/ P, HPSA or MHPSA and provides medical care to Medicaid or Medicare eligible patients and indigent uninsured patients. The statement must include I.D. number of the designated area and "FIPS" (Federal Information Processing Standards) county code and census track or 9-digit zip code where the facility is located;

d) Statement by FMG under penalty of perjury that s/he is not applying with any other U.S./state agency for waiver;

e) Evidence of efforts to recruit U.S. doctors were insufficient.

(e) The provisions concerning the 3-year commitment also apply to medical graduates seeking a waiver through an interested federal agency unless person is being employed full-time in medical research or training.

(f) If a medical graduate obtained a C/S to H-1B and fails to fulfill the terms of the contract s/he is ineligible to apply for IV, LPR status or C/S without meeting the 2-year foreign residence requirement. Under certain "extenuating circumstances" which include closure of the health care facility or hardship to the physician. 8 C.F.R. §212.7(c)(9)(iv).

(g) Health profession shortage areas are defined by HHS as Health Professional Shortage Areas (HPSAs), Mental Health Professional Shortage Areas (MHPSA) and Medically Underserved Areas or Population (MUA/P). The HPSA listing was last published at 65 Fed. Reg. 56028–56186 (Sept. 15, 2000). The current MUA/P can be obtained from *www.hpsafind.hrsa.gov*.

(h) Overstays who are FMGs on J-1s—The overstay provisions of INA §222(g) regarding cancellation of visas automatically do not apply to FMG's working in medically underserved areas who had an I-140 filed and a 212(e) waiver application filed prior to the expiration of the J where the petition and waiver was subsequently granted. Cable No. 208799/212382, Christopher, Secy. of State, 96-State-225321 (1996), *reprinted in* 73 No. 42 *Interpreter Releases* 1544–46 (Nov. 4, 1996).

8.c. Administrative Review—Regulations provide for secondary review of waiver applications within DOS by the Waiver Review Board which is referred cases at the discretion of the Chief, Waiver Review Division. 22 C.F.R. §41.63(g).

8.d. Judicial Challenge—Although AG's determination may be subject to judicial review under an abuse of discretion standard, *Al-Khayyal v. INS*, 818 F.2d 827 (11th Cir. 1987), *Chang v. Reno*, 986 F.Supp. 19 (D.D.C. 1997) [extreme hardship denial] the DOS's determination (*e.g.*, refusal to agree to INA §212(e) waiver) is committed to agency discretion. *Korvah v. Brown*, 66 F.3d 809 (6th Cir. 1995); *Singh v. Moyer*, 867 F.2d 1035 (7th Cir. 1989); *Abdelhamid v. Ilchert*, 774 F.2d 1447 (9th Cir. 1985); *Slyper v. Attorney General*, 827 F.2d 821 (D.C. Cir. 1987), *cert. denied,* 485 U.S. 941 (1988); *El-Omrani v. Director, USIA*, 638 F.Supp. 430 (W.D. Pa. 1986); *Dina v. Attorney General*, 793 F.2d 473 (2d Cir. 1986). *But see Chong v. Director, USIA*, 821 F.2d 171 (3d Cir. 1987) [disagreeing with *Abdelhamid*].

9. Clarification of Other Issues Relating to the Waiver

9.a. Third-Country Residency—Cannot meet 2-year requirement by residence in third country. Must return to country that J is a national and resident of, or if not a national, a legal permanent resident. 22 C.F.R. 41.62(c)(3). DOS looks at the country of residence listed on Form IAP-66/DS-2019 to determine where the 2-year residence requirement must be satisfied. In FMG cases, DOS looks to the country that issued the "Statement of Need" for purposes of ECFMG (Education Commission for Foreign Medical Graduates) Certification.

9.b. Repayment of Funds—Repayment to U.S. or foreign country will not satisfy waiver requirement.

9.c. Impossibility of Performance/Loss of Citizenship—There are certain circumstances where a person subject to the 2-year foreign residence requirement cannot comply with it because the home country no longer exists or the home country has denied an NIV to the person who desires to return. DOS in those circumstances will act as the interested government agency. This theory will not work in situations where a person subject to the residence requirement has acquired citizenship in Canada or some other third country and claims to have lost home country citizenship. DOS has rejected the position that a person would be entitled to a waiver because his home country has revoked, by operation, of law, their citizenship due to the acquisition of citizenship or legal permanent residence in another country. *See* 63 Fed. Reg. 42233 (Aug. 7, 1998).

9.d. EU Countries—Cannot fulfill the 2-year foreign residence requirement if J-1 is from one EU country by living in another EU country for the 2-year period. Questions and Answers for AILA Liaison Meeting With the Visa Office on Oct. 26, 2001, *published on* AILA InfoNet at Doc No. 01103032 (Oct. 30, 2001).

9.e. Temporary absence or second program:

(1) If J who is not subject to 2-year residence requirement leaves U.S. temporarily and needs new J visa to return, he returns in same J status.

(2) If J is subject to 2-year requirement but then switches to J program that is not subject to J requirement—must still meet 2-year requirement but may re-enter on new J before satisfying the 2-year requirement.

9.f. Error in Annotation Regarding Foreign Residence Requirement on J Documentation—DHS inspector/examiner or DOS consular officer is not bound by an incorrect notation on the IAP-66/DS-2019, on the J visa, or on other documents such as the I-94, suggesting that a person in J status is or is not subject to the two-year foreign residence requirement. Such annotations may be wrong and an incorrect annotation is not legally binding on DHS or DOS. The lawyer must make an independent determination pursuant to INA §212(e) including reviewing the applicable skills list to determine whether the client is or is not subject to the two-year requirement. When in doubt request advisory opinion from DOS.

(1) An advisory opinion may be requested by sending a letter (there is no form or fee) to: Waiver Review Division CA/VO/L/W, Visa Services, U.S. Department of State, 2401 E. Street, N.W. (SA-1), Washington, DC 20522-0106. An opinion letter is typically issued within 4 months. While technically not binding on DHS, in practice, DHS will defer to a DOS advisory opinion.

9.g. Which "skills list" applies? If person is re-entering U.S. to continue program that began prior to Mar. 17, 1997, s/he will be governed by the 1984 skills list. This is also true even if person returns to consulate to renew a visa if the renewal is for a program that began prior to Mar. 17, 1997. Only entry on a new program that began after Mar. 17, 1997 will be governed by the Mar. 17th skills list. 74 No. 19 *Interpreter Releases* 832–33 (May 19, 1997). If a country is removed from the skills list, exchange visitors from that country are no longer subject to 212(e) based upon the skills list for that country, regardless of when they entered. 62 Fed. Reg. 67431 (Dec. 24, 1997) ["in the case of all governments which have requested removal from the skills list, their citizens are retroactively no longer required, on the basis of the skills list, to comply with the two-year home residence requirement of 212(e)"]. The latest version of the skills list is electronic, *see http://exchanges.state.gov/education/jexchanges/participation/skills_list.pdf.*

9.h. Canadians subject to INA §212(e) can satisfy the 2-year foreign residence requirement even if they work in the U.S. as long as they live in Canada. Minutes, Liaison Meeting between USIA & AILA ¶19, *reprinted in* 18 *AILA Monthly Mailing* 52 (Jan. 1999).

9.i. Waiver Hotline—Can call DOS through 24-hour line regarding J waivers. The number is (202) 663-1600. Case status inquiries can also be e- mailed to *legalnet@state.gov.*

10. General Procedures for Js

10.a. SEVIS/Data Collection—Under IIRIRA §641, Congress now requires approved institutions for J programs to keep computerized data on students and exchange visitors and their accompanying family members that includes their current address and status at the institution. The exchange visitor is required to pay a SEVIS fee to obtain J status. 8 C.F.R. §§214.2(j)(5), 214.13. The SEVIS (I-901) fee may be paid by credit card via the Internet at *www.fmjfee.com* or by mailing a U.S. dollar check or international money order to a lockbox address in the U.S. Cable, DOS, 04-State-162300 (Aug. 31, 2004), *published on* AILA InfoNet at Doc. No. 04092160. SEVIS (Student and Exchange Visitor Information System) is now mandatory for all exchange programs. 22 C.F.R. §62.70(a). DOS is phasing out the IAP-66 and has replaced it with a SEVIS DS-2019. 22 C.F.R. §62.70(a)(6); Cable, DOS, 02-State-113328 (June 12, 2002) at ¶9, *published on* AILA InfoNet at Doc. No. 02062444. The exchange programs have been provided an Internet site to access SEVIS at *www.ice.gov/sevis/schools*. 8 C.F.R. §214.12(b)(1). Under SEVIS the responsible officer (RO) must report if the exchange visitor commences academic training, transfers schools, extends her stay, is reinstated to the exchange program, or engages in employment. The school is also required to notify DHS of any student who reports or fails to report within 30 days of the institution's registration deadline. 8 C.F.R. §214.3(g)(3)(iii)(A); Memo, Williams, Ex. Assoc. Comm., Field Operations, HQINS 70/6.2.6 (Aug. 20, 2002) at 3, *reprinted in* 79 No. 45 *Interpreter Releases* 1706–07, 1715–18 (Nov. 18, 2002). The 30-day reporting requirement is based upon the "program start date" for new students and "next session start date" for continuing students. The school needs to report whether "the student reported to the academic institution as expected" even if the course enrollment process has not been fully determined because that can be reported at a later date. Memo, Garcia, Acting Asst. Sec. DHS, SEVIS Reporting Requirements At the Start of Each Term or Session (Oct. 17, 2003), *reprinted in* 81 No. 1 *Interpreter Releases* 5, 29–30 (Jan. 5, 2004).

Consular officers may issue a J visa at any time but must warn the first time J recipient that s/he may not enter the U.S. for the first time until thirty (30) days before the program start date. Cable, DOS, 04-State-144850 (July 15, 2004), *published on* AILA InfoNet at Doc. No. 04080965. Consular officers must also verify the SEVIS I-20 and the data in the SEVIS system before issuing a visa. Consular officers are directed to deny J-1/J-2 visas under INA §221(g) where a person presents the appropriate form from the school but there is no SEVIS record in the computerized system, Cable, DOS, 03-State-40362 (Feb. 12, 2003) at ¶10, *published on* AILA InfoNet at Doc. No. 03030443 or where the SEVIS (I-901) fee was not paid. Cable, DOS, 04-State-162300 ¶5 (Aug. 31, 2004), *published on* AILA InfoNet at Doc. No. 04092160. If a visa is issued they must enter the information in the SEVIS database. 22 C.F.R. §41.61(d).

10.b. Transfer or change of category to other J programs

(1) Transfers are no longer done through USCIS with I-539. DOS will assume responsibility through responsible school officials on SEVIS DS-2019. 22 C.F.R. §§62.42, 62.76. The regulations specify the procedure between SEVIS programs and between SEVIS and non-SEVIS programs. §62.76. The current sponsor and the transfer sponsor "shall communicate appropriately to ensure an uninterrupted transfer, continuous status of the exchange visitor and proper change of address reporting…" 22 C.F.R. §62.76(b).

(2) Change of program category will be denied unless transfer "is clearly consistent and closely related to the participant's original exchange objective." 22 C.F.R. §62.41(a) [may grant change from research scholar to student, 22 C.F.R. §62.41(b)].

10.c. Period of stay

(1) Different times specified for different fields.

(a) Post-Secondary Student—time needed to complete degree + 18 months practical (academic) training. 22 C.F.R. §62.23(f)(4). Can also get *summer* work and travel if in final year during the summer vacation. Cable, DOS, 07-State-03175 ¶8-11 (Mar. 13, 2007), *published on* AILA InfoNet at Doc. No. 07042460.

(b) Post Doctoral Degree—degree plus up to 36 months academic training, granted in increments of up to 18 months at a time. 22 C.F.R. §62.23(f)(4).

(c) Business/Industrial trainees—18 months unless it is in hospitality and tourism or in agriculture then it is 12 months, 22 C.F.R.. §62.22(k). However, two exceptions apply. An agriculture trainee can be granted 18 months if the additional six months consists of classroom participation and studies. §62.22(k). In addition both agriculture and hospitality and tourism may have management programs (*e.g.,* hotel or restaurant management, turf grass management) and management programs may be for an 18 month duration. 72 Fed. Reg. 33669, 33671 (June 19, 2007)

(d) Internships—maximum duration is 12 months. 22 C.F.R. §62.22(k).

(e) Professor and Scholars—limit of 5 years, prohibited under certain circumstances if in the U.S. on another J for more than 6 of the 12 months immediately preceding the start of the program, Cable, 07-State-03175, *supra;* 22 C.F.R. §62.20(d)(2), and at end of 5 year program cannot participate in new professor/scholar program for 2 years. 22 C.F.R. §62..20(i)(2); 9 FAM 41.62 N4.6, n4.7 and N11.4. An extension for a maximum of an additional 5 years may be given where the J-1 is engaged in a research project under the direct sponsorship of a Federally Funded National Research and Development Center or U.S. Federal laboratory, the J-1's continued involvement is beneficial to the successful conclusion of the project as determined after peer review, and DHS has agreed to the extension. 22 C.F.R. 62.20(i)(3).

(f) Short Term Scholars—6 months; exempt from bar that exists for professors and scholars if they previously had J for 6 of 12 months immediately preceding this J. 9 FAM 41.62 N4.6, N4.7.

(g) Flight School Trainees—24 months.

(h) Summer Work/Travel—4 months

(2) Admission and Extension of Stay.

(a) Admission for D/S on I-94—Duration of status is defined as the completion of the J program + 30 days. 8 C.F.R. §214.2(j)(1)(ii). However, if the J-1 has applied for C/S to H-1B and the H-1B cap has been reached, the Commissioner may extend her D/S until the next fiscal year when H-1B status can commence. 8 C.F.R. §214.2(j)(1)(vi). The Commissioner exercised that authority during FY 2000 determined that a J-1 waiting to C/S could accept a signing bonus from the prospective employer. 65 Fed. Reg. 15178–80 (Mar. 21, 2000). A J-1 who has obtained a waiver pursuant to the State 30 program is not subject to the H-1B cap. Memo, Cronin, Acting Ex. Assoc. Comm. Program, HQPGM 70/6.2.8 (June 19, 2001) at ¶II B, *reprinted in* 78 No. 25 *Interpreter Releases* 1069, 1108–17 (July 2, 2001).

(b) Extension of stay are achieved in one of two ways

i) For periods up to the maximum period of authorized stay for the particular J-1 category, the Responsible Officer of the J-1 program is authorized to grant the stay without coming to the DOS for approval. Thus, if program is authorized for 18 months but J-1 entered to participate for 12 months, the sponsor need not report to DOS if s/he determines that trainee needs an additional 6 months for additional or advanced training in the same area. E-Mail, DOS Exchange Visitor Program, Second J-1 Training Programs Not Permitted, *published on* AILA InfoNet at Doc. No. 03100640.

ii) For extensions beyond the maximum period authorized for the program up to 18 months, the, RO/ARO Officer must file with DOS a request for an "Extension Beyond the Maximum Duration of Program Participation" through SEVIS. The RO/ARO must provide evidence to establish the request is due to exceptional or unusual circumstances. This situation would apply to a person who has enrolled in a 12-month program but the sponsor believes that there should be an extension beyond 12 months up to 18 months. E-Mail, DOS Exchange Visitor Program, Second J-1 Training Programs Not Permitted, *published on* AILA InfoNet at Doc. No. 03100640.

(c) No Second J-1 Training Program—A sponsor is prohibited from issuing a Form DS-2019 to a foreign national to participate in a second J-1 training program. E-Mail, DOS Exchange Visitor Program, Second J-1 Training Programs Not Permitted, *published on* AILA InfoNet at Doc. No. 03100640.

(d) Timing for Request—A request for an extension must be filed at least 60 days prior to expiration of the current SEVIS DS-2019. 61 Fed. Reg. 29285–87 (June 10, 1996). RO may issue new SEVIS DS-2019 even when 212(e) waiver is pending provided extension does not extend beyond the regulatory cap for the category. Prior to 1995, an extension was not likely to be granted if the applicant had applied for a waiver of the two-year foreign residence requirement. Letter, Colvin, G.C., USIA (Nov. 3, 1993), *reprinted in* 71 No. 4 *Interpreter Releases* 170 (Jan. 24 1994). Since 1995, however, the mere application for a waiver has not blocked the ability to get an extension. However, once a waiver is granted, the exchange visitor can complete the duration of the program, but s/he cannot get an extension. Letter, Jin, General Counsel, USIA (Dec. 18, 1995), *reprinted in* 73 No. 2 *Interpreter Releases* 47, 51–52 (Jan. 10, 1996).

(e) Overstay—A J-1 (except certain FMGs who have applied for §212(e) waiver) are subject to the requirements of INA §222(g) that result in canceling visas of persons who overstay but only if USCIS or IJ have made a status violation determination or their J-1 requires them to leave on a date certain (as opposed to D/S). Cable, DOS, 98-State-051296 (Mar. 23, 1998), *published on* AILA InfoNet at Doc. No. 98032392. A J-1 overstays for other purposes if s/he stays beyond the 30-day grace period for J-1s.

10.d. Full course of study for Js at colleges and universities:

(1) Full course defined by "the accredited educational institutions in which the student is registered." 22 C.F.R. §62.2.

(2) The DOS allows numerous exceptions to the full course of study rule ranging from medical problems to a *bona fide* academic reason presented to the responsible officer. 22 C.F.R. §62.23(e).

10.e. Employment:

(1) Method of Obtaining Employment. Employment must be authorized in writing by the RO/ARO prior to commencement of employment either by listing the source of funding on the SEVIS DS-2019 or by writing a separate letter authorizing the specific employment for periods of up to one year at a time.

(2) Students—22 C.F.R. §62.23(g).

(a) Employment limited to on campus if pursuant to scholarship, fellowship or assistantship or off-campus if it is a summer work/travel exchange program or if it is necessary because of serious, urgent and unforeseen economic circumstances that have arisen since acquiring exchange visitor status.

i) Participation in summer work/travel (SWT) exchange program is only available to students pursuing a degree or full-time course of study at an accredited post-secondary institution. Students can participate if they are transferring from one school to another, if they have finished an academic program and are going on to another academic program, or if they are continuing on to graduate school. There is no prohibition against a student participating in an SWT program for more than one year. Cable, DOS, 04-State-13720 (Jan. 21, 2004), *published on* AILA InfoNet at Doc. No. 04022567. SWT participants are not required to have a job offer before their program starts and have a 30-day grace period after the program ends. Cable, 08-State-024930 (Mar. 11, 2008) ¶¶7-9, *published on* AILA InfoNet at Doc. No. 08040255.

(b) Employment is only available to students in good academic standing, who continue in a full course of study, and who have been approved by school officer. Employment may not exceed 20 hours per week except during official school breaks and annual vacation.

(c) DOS has suspended certain requirements governing program status and on-campus and off-campus employment for J-1 students whose means of financial support is from Indonesia, South Korea, Malaysia, Thailand and the Philippines. 63 Fed. Reg. 34276–77, *reprinted in* 75 No. 24 *Interpreter Releases* 877, 896 (June 29, 1998).

(3) Academic (practical) training.

(a) Employment for academic training must commence within 30 days of completion of studies. 22 C.F.R. §62.23(f)(2)(ii). This requires job offer within that period, not actual commencement of work. Letter, Hitt, Director Exchange Visitor Program Service, USIA (May 6, 1993), *reprinted in* 70 No. 21 *Interpreter Releases* 710, 722–23 (May 27, 1993).

(4) Employment of Spouse or Child. Only if it is not for support of principal J-1, 8 C.F.R. §214.2(j)(1)(v), and spouse is not also a J-1. Employment request is filed on I-765 and employment is authorized for the length of J-1's stay or 4 years, whichever is shorter.

10.f. Reinstatement Into J-1 Status. 22 C.F.R. 62.45

(1) Technical Violations. These violations include: (i) failure to extend the IAP-66 in a timely manner due to inadvertence or neglect; (ii) failure to conclude a transfer of program prior to the expiration on the IAP-66 due to delay, oversight, inadvertence or neglect; (iii) failure to receive prior approval for customary honorarium. The Responsible School official may correct these *status quo ante* by issuing a SEVIS DS-2019 to correct the record, provided the following apply: no more than 120 calendar days have passed since the expiration of the current SEVIS DS-2019 and the exchange visitor has maintained program objectives, has maintained the required insurance coverage, has not worked without authorization, has maintained a full course of study (or received RO permission in advance), has paid the SEVIS fee, and has not been suspended or terminated from the program. The RO notifies DOS by sending a copy of the SEVIS DS-2019. Alternatively, this can be accomplished by letter to DOS as well. 22 C.F.R. §62.45(c)(4).

(2) Substantive Violations. These violations include: (i) failure to maintain valid program status for more than 120 days beyond the end date of the SEVIS DS-2019; (ii) failure to maintain a full course of study under 22 C.F.R. §62.2 without prior consultation with school. To remedy these violations the applicant and Responsible Officer must apply to DOS and demonstrate that the violation resulted from circumstances beyond the control of the applicant or from administrative delays or oversight, inadvertence or neglect *or* that failure to receive reinstatement will result in "unusual hardship." DOS in the preamble defined unusual hardship to include a situation where an exchange visitor had one more semester of a seven-year program to fulfill his requirements. 64 Fed. Reg. 44123 (Aug. 13, 1999). DOS states that if the person is in violation over 120 days (but less than 270 days), he needs to show both inadvertence or neglect *and* unusual hardship. DOS will react to reinstatement request within 45 days of delivery. Reinstatement, if approved is approved as of the date of receipt by DOS and will be approved *nunc pro tunc*. To make request, RO sends the filing fee, sends the DS-2019 indicating it is for reinstatement while leaving the beginning date blank but requesting an end date, and submits a written statement.

(3) Violations Precluding Reinstatement. 22 C.F.R. §62.45(f). These violations include: (i) knowingly or willful failure to obtain or maintain required health insurance while in U.S.; (ii) engaged in unauthorized employment; (iii) suspension or termination from the most recent exchange program; (iv) Failed to maintain status for more than 270 days; (v) received a §212(e) waiver; and (vi) failed to maintain CIPRIS fees.

10.g. Estoppel—If person issued J visa due to INS misinformation when they could have obtained another visa without 2-year requirement—estoppel granted. *Hetzer v. INS*, 420 F.2d 357 (9th Cir. 1970).

10.h. Ineligible for suspension even if obtained INA §212(e) waiver if doctor. 8 U.S.C. §1254(f); *Matter of Mangaser*, 19 I&N Dec. 28 (BIA 1983).

11. Spouses and Children (J-2)—Also subject to foreign-residence requirement. 8 C.F.R. §212.7(c)(4). *Matter of Tabcum*, 14 I&N Dec. 113 (R.C. 1972). May be subject to requirement even if they enter U.S. after spouse completes program with 2-year foreign residence requirement if they obtained visa as spouse and children of applicant. *Sheku-Kamara v. Karn*, 581 F.Supp. 582 (E.D. Pa. 1984). However, if J-1 spouse has fulfilled the 2-year foreign residence requirement the J-2 spouse and children may not be subject to it. Letter, Weinig, Deputy Asst. Comm., Adjudications, CO 212e-C (Sept. 27,

1989), *reprinted in* 66 No. 42 *Interpreter Releases* 1207, 1223–24 (Oct. 30, 1989). *But see* Notes from VO-AILA Liaison, Mar. 30, 2000, *published on* AILA InfoNet at Doc. No. 00050905 (May 9, 2000) ["VO has concluded that individuals who come to the United States in J-2 status are subject to the same requirement as the J-1, and are obligated to satisfy the two-year foreign residence requirement even when the principal J-1 has already fulfilled the obligation."] and *see* Legal Opinion 90-17, Cook, Gen. Counsel, CO 212.43-C/214j-C (Apr. 4, 1990) [the J-2 dependent remains subject to the foreign residence requirement even if the former J-1 has satisfied the requirement]. Where waiver granted to J-1, J-2 spouse and children may automatically get waiver. Letter, Miller, Deputy Asst. Comm., Adjudications, CO 214j-C (Nov. 27, 1988), *reprinted in* 66 No. 48 *Interpreter Releases* 1415, 1433 (Dec. 18, 1989). *But see* Legal Opinion 90-17, *supra.* [J-2 dependent only gets waiver where J-1 obtained waiver *and* specifically included J-2 in the waiver application consistent with 8 C.F.R. §212.7(c)(5)].

11.a. DOS itself will act as an IGA to recommend a waiver for a J-2 in certain circumstances. In cases of death or divorce from the J-1,or when a J-2 child teaches age 21, the Waiver Review Division may entertain requests for waivers on behalf of the J-2. The Division will need a completed data sheet, DS-2019/IAP-66 forms of the J-1, divorce decree or death certificate, whichever is applicable, and, for a dependent son or daughter turning 21, a copy of his or her birth certificate.

12. Exchange Visitor Program Designation, Suspension, and Revocation Board—Procedures for reprimanding, probating, revoking or suspending J program for violations even if they are not willful or *negligent. See* 72 Fed. Reg. 72245 (Dec. 20, 2007), *amending* 22 C.F.R. §§62.50–.62. The regulations provide for graduated sanctions and procedural hearings. 22 C.F.R. §§62.50–.62. In *National Collegiate Recreation Services v. Powell,* Case No. 9:02cv02676 (D.S.C. Nov. 26, 2002) *reported in* 80 No. 7 *Interpreter Releases* 244–46 (Feb. 19, 2003), the district court determined that the revocation of American Hospitality Academy's J-1 program designation was arbitrary and capricious because the DOS imposed the harshest penalty without basis and its fact finding was deficient.

D. *H-3 Visa*—INA §101(a)(15)(H)(iii), 8 U.S.C. §1101(a)(15)(H)(iii); 8 C.F.R. §214.2(h)(7).

1. Definition—Temporary worker invited by an individual or organization for purposes of receiving instruction and training other than to receive graduate medical education or training. The training program must be one "that is not designed primarily to provide productive employment."

1.a. Must have foreign residence to which s/he must return.

1.b. Regulatory criteria for H-3 are: 8 C.F.R. §214.2(h)(7)(ii)(A):

(1) Proposed training not available in alien's home country;

(2) Beneficiary will not be placed in a position in which citizen and resident workers are regularly employed;

(3) No productive employment unless it is incidental and necessary to the training and pursuing a career outside the U.S.

(4) The training will benefit the beneficiary in pursuing a career outside the U.S.

2. However, if the program has any of the following flaws, it is unacceptable:

2.a. Deals in generalities with no fixed schedule, objectives, or means of evaluation;

2.b. Is incompatible with the nature of the petitioner's business or enterprise;

2.c. Is on behalf of a beneficiary who already possesses substantial training and expertise in the proposed field of training;

2.d. Is in a field in which it is unlikely that the knowledge or skill will be used outside the U.S.;

2.e. Will result in productive employment beyond that which is incidental and necessary to the training;

2.f. Is designed to recruit and train aliens for the ultimate staffing of domestic operations in the U.S.;

2.g. Does not establish that the petitioner has the physical plant and sufficiently trained manpower to provide the training specified; or

2.h. Is designed to extend the total allowable period of practical training previously authorized a nonimmigrant student.

8 C.F.R. §214.2(h)(7)(iii), 55 Fed. Reg. 2628–29.

3. The training program by regulation [8 C.F.R. §214.2(h)(7)(ii)(B)] and by case law [*Matter of Frigon*, 18 I&N Dec. 164 (Comm. 1981)], should include:

   3.a. Kind of training, supervision to be given, and structure of the training program.

   3.b. The proportion of time that will be devoted to productive employment. Productive employment should be minimal because applicant should be receiving training and not performing productive work that displaces USCs/LPRs. *See Matter of St. Pierre*, 18 I&N Dec. 308 (Reg.Comm. 1982).

   3.c. Number of classroom instruction hours. This should be as high as possible to show that petition is not really to work, but to train.

   3.d. Number of hours of on-the-job training both supervised and unsupervised. Unsupervised work should be minimal. Supervised work should always be oriented toward training.

   3.e. The position and duties for which the training will prepare the applicant. Must be preparing someone for the type of work that is not available or is new in country where they will work, *e.g.,* IBM develops new software which is unknown in another country, but which they will market there. IBM can petition to train people to use that software so that they can use it when the software is sold in their home country.

   3.f. The reason why the applicant *cannot* obtain the training in the country of origin and why the training must be given here. Must show that this type of program does not exist in alien's country of origin, that it is unique to the degree that it does exist in the U.S. and that it is not readily available in *any* other country.

   3.g. The reason why a training program is a benefit to the petitioning company willing to hire the trainee.

   3.h. The source of remuneration received by the trainee.

4. Externs and Nurses—Extern may qualify for H-3 if attending residency or internship at AMA or AOA hospital and will engage in externship during school vacation. 9 FAM 41.53 N.20. Nurses may also obtain H-3 if have unrestricted license in country where they received medical education, or if education in Canada/U.S., and the petition provides statement that nurse is qualified under state law to receive the training. 8 C.F.R. §214.2(h)(7)(i)(B). *But see Matter of* ___ EAC 03 085 52660 (AAO Oct. 30, 2003) (Vermont Service Center) [affirmed denial where insufficient information on teaching staff, where proposed trainees' experience and background from Philippines were unclear, where the petitioner had not established sufficiently that trainees would not be doing normal nursing care, and where training might be incompatible with petitioner's business as recruiter of highly trained nurses].

5. Distinguishing B-l and J-l from H-3—A person otherwise eligible for an H-3 may obtain a B-1 if s/he receives salary abroad or a J-1 if s/he is in a J program.

6. Admission and Extension

   6.a. Admitted for length of training program, but in no event longer than 2 years. 8 C.F.R. §214.2(h)(9)(iii)(C)(1). No extension, change of status or readmission to H or L status granted after the 2 years unless alien resided and is physically present out of the U.S. for 6 months. 8 C.F.R. §214.2(h)(13)(iv). If training is seasonal, intermittent, or 6 months or less, this rule does not apply. 8 C.F.R. §214.2(h)(13)(v).

   6.b. The approval of a permanent labor certification or the filing of a preference petition by the same employer for the same or a different job is grounds to deny extension of training program. 8 C.F.R. §214.2(h)(16)(ii).

   6.c. Must file application by employer on I-129. Can have multiple beneficiaries. 8 C.F.R. §214.2(h)(2)(ii).

7. Special Education Exchange Program—IMMACT90 §223; 55 Fed. Reg. 2606, 2628 (Jan. 26, 1990); 8 C.F.R. §214.2(h)(7)(iv).

7.a. Extends exchange status to participants in a special education program which provides for practical training and experience in the education of children with physical, mental or emotional disabilities.

7.b. Limited to 18-month stay and limited to 50 visas/status per year.

7.c. Procedure:

(1) Processed under H-3 category.

(2) Petition must be filed by facility that has professional, trained staff and a structured program for children that provides training and hands-on experience. Must have description of the training program.

(3) Need evidence that participant is nearing completion of a BA or higher degree or has extensive prior training or experience.

(4) If in U.S. for 18 months under H/L status may not seek C/S, E/S or readmission under H/L categories unless s/he has resided and been physically present outside U.S. for immediate prior 6 months. 8 C.F.R. §214.2(h)(13)(iv).

VII. VISAS FOR BUSINESS PERSONNEL (H, L, E, I, O, P, Q, AND R VISAS)

A. *Characteristics*

- Permits employment in U.S.
- Longer duration than B.
- Facilitates residency (L, E).
- Duration of stay—For tax implications, *see* Ch. 6, section XIII.H (p.861), *infra.*

B. *H Visas*—INA §101(a)(15)(H), 8 U.S.C. §1101(a)(15)(H)

1. Seven Categories of H Visas:

   - H-1B: Specialty occupation.
   - H-1B1: Fast Track H-1Bs
   - H-1C: Professional Nurses Working in Health Professional Shortage Areas (HPSAs).
   - H-2A: Temporary agricultural workers.
   - H-2B: Skilled/unskilled workers provided USCs/LPRs unavailable.
   - H-3: Trainees.
   - H-4: Accompanying family members (spouse/children)

2. General Criteria

2.a. USCIS must first approve petition of employer. INA §214(c), 8 U.S.C. §1184(c); 8 C.F.R. §214.2(h)(1).

C. *H-1B Visas*—INA §101(a)(15)(H)(i)(b), 8 U.S.C. §1101(a)(15)(H)(i)(b). Legislative History, H.R. Rep. No. 851, 91st Cong. 2d Sess., 1970 U.S.C.C.A.N. 2750-55 (1970). *See also* Immigration Act of 1990, H.R. Conf. Rep. No. 955, 101st Cong. 2d Sess. 125 (1990); Miscellaneous and Technical Immigration and Naturalization Amendments of 1991, PL 102-232 (Dec. 12, 1991); 59 Fed. Reg. 41818–42 (Aug. 15, 1994); Omnibus Appropriations Act (OAA) for FY 2005, PL 108-447, 118 Stat. 2809, Div. J, Tit. IV, Subtit. B—H-1B Visa Reform, Section 426, PL 108-447 (Dec. 8, 2004).

1. Criteria—INA §101(a)(15)(H)(i)(b), 8 U.S.C. §1101(a)(15)(H)(i)(b); 8 C.F.R. §214.2(h); 22 C.F.R. §41.53:

1.a. Person in a specialty occupation, fashion model of distinguished merit and ability, or person providing service related to Department of Defense (DOD) cooperative research and development project or co-production project.

1.b. Coming temporarily to U.S. *Matter of Ord*, 18 I&N Dec. 285 (R.C. 1982).

1.c. Approval of labor certification or the filing of immigrant visa petition does not preclude granting an H-1B petition or extension. INA §214(h), 8 U.S.C. §1184(h). Alien may legitimately have "dual intent." Memo, Gibson, Acting Assoc. Comm., CO 214h-P, 214L-P (Sept. 23, 1985), *reprinted in* 62 *Interpreter Releases* 965–67 (Oct. 4, 1985); 8 C.F.R. §214.2(h)(16)(i).

1.d. Does not require maintenance of a foreign residence. IMMACT90 §205(e); IFM §15.4; 9 FAM 41.53 N3.1. In light of the elimination of the foreign residence requirement, DOS's position is that "the intent of the H-1 applicant in regard to nonimmigrant or immigrant status is totally irrelevant. Thus, not only shall the consular officers not refuse an H-1 visa on this basis, facts relating to foreign residence and nonimmigrant intent shall not be considered by the officer when adjudicating the H-1 visa application." Cable, DOS, 91-State-171115, ¶6 (May 24, 1991), *reprinted in* 68 No. 21 *Interpreter Releases* 681–84 (June 3, 1991).

1.e. Self-Petitioning/Owner as Petitioner—Although an owner of a petitioning employer *may* be barred from obtaining a labor certification, nonprecedent AAO decisions support the right of a corporation to petition for its owner for an H-1B if the owner is H-1B qualified. *Matter of X, ___,* SRC 98 101 50785 (AAO Aug. 9, 1999), 21 *Immigr. Rep.* B2-6 [following *Matter of Aphrodite Investments, Ltd.,* a sole owner and sole employee of the petitioning company is not precluded from receiving an H-1B]. *Matter of X* (AAO Feb. 23, 2006), *published on* AILA InfoNet at Doc. No. 08041470. *But see Administrator, Wage and Hour Division v. Avenue Dental Care,* 6-LCA-29 (ALJ June 28, 2007) at 20–21 [suggesting that more than a 50% ownership interest may defeat the employee-employer relationship but deciding that 50% does not].

1.f. Labor Condition Application (LCA) Requirement—INA §212(n)(1), 8 U.S.C. §1182(n)(1). Applies to all H-1Bs including fashion models, 8 C.F.R. §214.2(h)(1)(ii)(B)(3), and physicians. The petitioner is required to obtain a certification from DOL that it has filed an LCA in the occupational specialty. 8 C.F.R. §214.2(h)(4)(i)(B)(1). Memo, Weinig, Asst. Comm., Adjudications, CO 214h-P (Mar. 5, 1992), *reprinted in* 69 No. 12 *Interpreter Releases* 378, 390 (Mar. 30, 1992). There are special attestation requirements for employers who previously committed willful violations of the law or for employers who are deemed to be H-1B dependent. 20 C.F.R. §§655.736–.739. DOD category does not require an LCA. However, LCAs are required for H-1B, H-1B1, and E-3 employees. H-2Bs required a labor certification.

1.g. Payment of Fees By Employer

(1) Fees to the DHS—The employer must pay three sets of fees to the government. First, they must pay the standard petition fees for the I-129 petition and if the employee is abroad the additional fees at the consulate. Second, the employer must pay a fee of $1,500 unless she is an employer with not more than 25 full-time equivalent employees and then she must only pay one-half the required fee which is now $750. INA §214(c)(9). Third, the employer is now required to pay to the government a $500 fraud prevention and detection fee. INA §214(c)(12). All fees are paid to the Department of Homeland Security. The fraud prevention fee must be paid in a separate check but other fees can be bundled. The petitioner pays the $1,500 fee *one* time to initially grant the H-1B, to extend the stay of an H-1B (if not paid at a prior extension) *or* to change status to an H-1B. A primary or secondary education institution, an institution of higher education, as defined in section 20 U.S.C. §1001(a), a nonprofit entity related to or affiliated with any such institution, a nonprofit entity which engages in established curriculum-related clinical training of students registered at any such institution, a nonprofit research organization or a governmental research organization are exempt from the fee. INA §214(c)(9)(A); 8 C.F.R. §214.2(h)(19)(iii)-(iv). The fraud fee must be paid one time but is limited to initial applications or to invoke portability to switch employers. Nonprofits are *not* exempt. INA §214(c)(12)(A). Neither fee applies to spouses or dependent children.

(2) Payment of Salary and Costs to Employee

(a) Payment of Salary. Employer must begin paying petition-stated wage within 30 days of employee's entry or 60 days from employee's C/S application if in the U.S. INA §212(n)(2)(C)(vii)(III). The wage must now be 100% of the prevailing wage. INA §§212(p)(3) & (n)(1)(A)(i)(II). Nor may the employer "bench" a full time or part time H-1B due to lack of work. INA §212(n)(2)(C)(vii)(I)(II). An employer may give a prospective employee monetary or nonmonetary (stock option) signing bonus. Letter, Hernandez, Acting Branch Chief, Business and Trade Services HQ 70/6.2.8 (May 3, 2000). Employee entitled to leave under the Family Medical Leave Act to the same extent as other employees without being out-of-status *See* AILA InfoNet at Doc. No. 00091503 [report of teleconference call with Immigration Service Division of INS].

(b) Payment of Transportation Costs Home. If employer dismisses employee it is liable for reasonable costs of transportation home. INA §214(c)(5)(A), 8 U.S.C. §1184(c)(5)(A); 8 C.F.R. §214.2(h)(4)(iii)(E). The enforcement of this provision is regarded as a private contractual matter. Letter, Simmons, Branch Chief, Business and Trade Service (HQ 70/6.2.8) (May 20, 1999), *reprinted in* 76 No. 28 *Interpreter Releases* 1125, 1140 (July 26, 1999). An employer may not impose a penalty on an H-1B employee for leaving his employment. INA §212(n)(2)(C)(vi)(I); 20 C.F.R. §655.731(c)(10)(i)(C). However, an employer may require an employee to sign a liquidated damages clause as long as such clause is valid under state law.

1.h. Cap of 65,000 H-1B Visas Per Year—The H-1B visas per year are capped at 65,000 per fiscal year *less* the Free Trade Visas for Chile and Singapore resulting in 58,200 H-1B Visas. INA §§214(g)(1)(A), 214(g)(8)(B)(iv), 8 U.S.C. §§1184(g)(1)(A), 1184(g)(8)(B)(iv); PL 108-77 and 108-78. The cap does *not* include an additional 20,000 visas per year for persons who have earned a master's or higher degree *from a United States institution of higher education* (as defined in 20 U.S.C. §1001(a)). INA §214(g)(5)(C), AFM at 31.3(g)(10). Also, medical doctors who obtain an INA §212(e) waiver upon the request of an interested Federal or State agency are cap exempt. INA §214(*l*)(2)(A). Only "new employment" is covered under the cap. USCIS can no longer count against the cap any person who has already been counted within the past six years unless the H-1B applicant would be eligible for a new full six years of authorized H-1B admission at the time the new petition is filed. INA §214(g)(7). An H-1B could be eligible for a full 6 years if s/he was out of the country for a year or if the work s/he was performing in the U.S. was seasonal, intermittent or less than 6 months per year.

(1) Categories that cannot be counted in the 65,000 cap include

(a) J-1 physicians who have obtained a waiver pursuant to the State 30 program or federal programs. Memo, Cronin, Acting Ex. Assoc. Comm. Program, HQPGM 70/6.2.8 (June 19, 2001) at ¶II B, *reprinted in* 78 No. 25 *Interpreter Releases* 1069, 1108–17 (July 2, 2001); INA §214(*l*)(2)(A).

(b) Beneficiaries of employment offers at institutions of higher education (as defined in 20 U.S.C. §1001(a) or related or affiliated nonprofit entities, or nonprofit research organizations, or governmental research organizations; INA §214(g)(5)(A)&(B).

i) Private employers may petition under this provision if their employees are working "at" the institution of higher education. In order to do so, the employer must demonstrate both that the employee is physically working at the institution of higher education or related or affiliated nonprofit *and* that there is "nexus" between the work performed and the normal purpose of the nonprofit. AFM at 31.3(g)(13)(A) Examples 1-4; Memo, Aytes, Assoc. Dir. Domestic Operations, USCIS, HQPRD 70/23.12 (June 6, 2006), *published on* AILA InfoNet at Doc. No. 06060861; Memo, Cronin, Acting Ex. Assoc. Comm. Programs, HQPGM 70/6.2.8 (June 19, 2001), *published on* AILA InfoNet at Doc. No. 01062031, 8 C.F.R. §214.2(h)(19)(iii)(C); 20 C.F.R. §656.40(e)(1)(iii) & (e)(2);

ii) Nonprofit research organization is one primarily engaged in basic research and/or applied research. Government research organization is defined as a U.S. government entity. 8 C.F.R. §§214.2(h)(19)(iii)(C) and (iv); AFM at 31.3(g)(13)(C);

iii) Texas school district petitioner may *not* be subject to the CAP if the proffered position is part of a collaboration between the school and an institute of higher education that is exempt under the cap. *Matter of ___*, EAC 06 216 52028 (AAO Sept. 8, 2006) (VSC) *reported in* 12 No. 2 *Bender's Immigration Bulletin* 57, 88 (Jan. 15, 2007) [Texas high school affiliated with Texas institute of higher education where position was a collaboration between the two].

(c) Persons (up to 20,000) who possess a U.S. earned master's or higher degree. INA §214(g)(5)(C); AFM at 31.3(g)(10), 70 Fed. Reg. 23775 (May 5. 2005).

(d) A person who has already be counted against the cap within the past six years and applies for another H-1B with another employer (including under portability provisions) is *not* considered to be applying for new employment and is not subject to the cap. 65 Fed. Reg. 15178–80 (Mar. 21, 2000)

(e) Spouse and children of H-1B

(f) Extensions of H-1B status

(g) Fraudulent Petitions—Approved petitions later found to be issued by fraud or a material misrepresentation are restored to the numerical cap irrespective of the fiscal year the fraud was discovered. INA §214(g)(3). However, if a petition is subsequently revoked for any reason other than a material misrepresentation/fraud it will only be restored if it was revoked in the year it was approved. 69 Fed. Reg. 8675–76 (Feb. 25, 2004).

(2) Fast Track and the Cap—The U.S. has entered into Fast Track Trade legislation with Chile and Singapore. At present, Chile receives a maximum of 1,400 H-1B1s and Singapore a maximum of 5,400 H-1B1s. To the degree these are used they are reduced from the overall H-1B cap, thus reducing the overall cap for all others to 58,200. If they are not used, they are made available between Oct 1st and Nov. 15th of the next fiscal year. 69 Fed. Reg. 8675–76 (Feb. 25, 2004); Memo, Yates, Assoc. Dir. Operations, USCIS (Jan. 8, 2004), *published on* AILA InfoNet at Doc. No. 04030361. The numerical cap is filled in the order that petitions are filed. Persons with U.S. based master's or higher degrees will not be counted as part of the cap until 20,000 visas are reached and will be counted thereafter. 70 Fed. Reg. 23775, 23777 (May 5, 2005). Once the cap is reached the following issues may arise:

(3) Persons awaiting visa availability—DOS has agreed to allow foreign medical graduates who require an extension beyond the period of actual training or education to take their exams to be given an extension of their J-1 status until the cap has been lifted. This only pertains to persons who have received a §212(e) waiver, who are not unlawfully employed and who are sitting for specialty Boards. The extension is limited until the end of the month in which the Board examination is given but not to exceed 6 months. 64 Fed. Reg. 34982–83 (June 30, 1999), *reprinted in* 76 No 26 *Interpreter Releases* 1053, 1074 (July 12, 1999).

(4) Change of Status and H-1B Cap ("Cap-Gap") Problem—If person applies for C/S and the H-1B cap has been reached s/he will be treated as O/S if s/he falls O/S before the beginning of the next fiscal year on Oct 1st. For example, a person who is in valid B-2 status until June 1 applies for C/S in April. The H-1B cap is reached on April 1 for an Oct. 1 employment start-up date. The applicant will be considered out-of-status beginning June 1 even if the application is approved for an Oct. 1 start date. The H-1B petition will be approved but due to the "gap" between June 1 and Oct 1, the C/S will be denied. Memo, Pearson, Ex. Assoc. Comm. (HQ 70/23.1RS-P) (Aug. 19, 1998), *reprinted in* 75 No. 32 *Interpreter Releases* 1146, 1165 (Aug. 24, 1998); *L.A. Closeout, Inc. v. DHS,* 513 F.3d 940 (9th Cir. 2007) [Pearson memo upheld under *Auer* deference where the court rejected the claim that the person had to be in lawful status on a B-2 only until the time the c/s was filed under 8 C.F.R. §248.1 and not until Oct. 1st]. The H-1B petition that is not adjudicated before the cap is reached will be adjudicated and given a starting date no earlier than Oct. 1 of the following fiscal year, regardless of the date requested on the petition. 8 C.F.R. §214.2(h)(8)(ii)(E). A petition filed after the cap is reached will not be accepted because petitions are currently accepted at the beginning of April for the start of the next fiscal year (Oct. 1), and a sufficient number of petitions are filed in the first days of April of each year to meet the H-1B visa allocations for the next fiscal year.

For F-1 and J-1 beneficiaries (and their dependents) seeking C/S, their D/S (which is normally 60 (F-1) and 30 (J-1) days respectively beyond the completion of studies) can be used to file the c/s and if the Oct. 1 day is reached during those periods they are within status. In addition, an F-1 student (whether or not in OPT) who is the beneficiary of an H-1B petition and who has timely filed a C/S will now have her status and work authorization (if in OPT) *automatically extended* until Oct 1st of the following fiscal year so that there is no "gap" between the time her F-1 stay would have expired, and the Oct. 1 start-up date for the H-1B. 8 C.F.R. §214.2(f)(5)(vi)(A). It also applies to F-2s. The Commissioner of USCIS may also by announcement in the Federal Register extend the time necessary to complete the adjudication of the H-1B, usually until the next fiscal year, so that a J-1 does not become O/S. 8 C.F.R. §§214.2(j)(1)(vi). The Commissioner exercised that authority during FY 2000 and determined that a J-1 waiting to C/S can accept a signing bonus from the prospective employer. 65 Fed. Reg. 15178–80 (Mar. 21, 2000).

Portability and Cap-Exempt to Cap-Subject Status. An H-1B may port from a cap-exempt employer to a cap-subject employer during a period when there are no H-1B numbers as long as the cap-subject H-1B application is eventually approved and the LCA covers the entire period of employment. Letter, Hernandez III, Chief, Business and Trade Services, USCIS (May 23, 2007), *published on* AILA InfoNet at Doc. No. 07052563

(5) INA §222(g)—Where person applies for C/S to H-1B but the C/S is denied because the cap is reached before change can be granted, it could be considered an extraordinary circumstance under INA §222(g) thus permitting the person to go to a third country as long as s/he did not work without authorization. Cable, DOS (99-State-105097) (June 7, 1999), *reprinted in* 76 No. 24 *Interpreter Releases* 977–80 (June 28, 1999).

(6) Procedure to Select H-1B Petitions—An employer may not file more than one H-1B petition for each prospective employee during the fiscal year so that each prospective employee who qualifies for the "master's cap" of 20,000 can not file two petitions to encompass the "regular" H-1B and the master's H-1B. Only one petition will be permitted. 8 C.F.R. §214.2(h)(2)(i)(G); 72 Fed. Reg. 15389, 15391–92 (Mar. 24, 2008). The one petition limitation also applies to preclude an employer from filing multiple petitions for different jobs for the same employee. 72 Fed. Reg. at 15392. However, the rule does not preclude related employers (*e.g.*, parent and subsidiary companies or affiliates) from filing petitions on behalf of the same beneficiary. *Id.* But the burden rests of the employer to demonstrate it has a legitimate business need to do so and if it fails to meet that burden all petitions on behalf of that beneficiary will be denied or revoked. 8 C.F.R. §214.2(h)(2)(i)(G). USCIS will accept all applications during the first five (5) business days before conducting a random selection process so that applicants need not file the application exactly on April 1st of the year. 8 C.F.R. §214.2(h)(8)(ii)(B).

1.i. Must be permanent position (unlike H-2), which must be temporarily filled.

1.j. Petitioner must be U.S. employer—8 C.F.R. §214.2(h)(4)(ii). Employer defined as: (1) engages a person to work within the U.S.; (2) has employer-employee relationship in that it may hire, pay, fire, supervise or otherwise control work; *and* (3) has an Internal Revenue Service Tax ID Number. Includes partnership or sole proprietor. Letter, Bednarz, Chief, INS, NIV Branch, Adjudications, CO 214h-C (July 29, 1993), *reprinted in* 13 *AILA Monthly Mailing* 22 (Jan. 1994). U.S. employer must have control of the H-1B but does not necessarily need to be the entity paying her salary. Letter, LaFleur, Chief, Business and Trade Branch, Benefits Division, INS, HQ 70/6.2.8 (July 22, 1996), *reprinted in* 73 No. 30 *Interpreter Releases* 1045, 1062–63 (Aug. 5, 1996) [acknowledged that foreign former employer could continue to pay salary]. At least one court has found that where an employment agency is involved, USCIS may treat the employer as the entity where the person will ultimately work. *Defensor v. Meissner,* 201 F.3d 384 (5th Cir. 2000) [affirmed INS's denial of H-1Bs to nurses with bachelor degrees because the hospitals where they would work did not require B.N.S. degrees even if the employment agency that hired them did]. Where employer hires a professional employer organization (PEO) to handle its administrative matters in regard to its employees such as payroll and health insurance but the employer still retains control over the day-to-day activities of the H-1B, the employer can petition (and would be responsible) for the H-1B because it would still be considered the U.S. employer as defined under 8 C.F.R. §214.2(h)(4)(ii). Letter, Hernandez, Director, Business and Trade Services, INS, HQ 70/6.2.8 (Dec. 20, 2000), *reprinted in* 78 No. 27 *Interpreter Releases* 1171, 1191–94 (July 16, 2001). A PEO could file for an H-1B if it met the definition of a U.S. employer under the regulations and was not simply a record keeper or accountant. *Id.*

1.k. Portability—New employment upon *filing* petition. A person in H-1B status may accept new employment upon the *filing* of a new petition by the prospective employer if: (1) s/he was lawfully admitted; (2) the new petition is "nonfrivolous"; (3) the new petition was filed before the date of expiration of the period of stay authorized by the AG; and (4) subsequent to such lawful admission the H-1B beneficiary has not been employed without authorization before the filing of such petition. INA §§214(n)(1) and (n)(2)(A)–(C). Filing is defined at 8 C.F.R. §103.2(a)(7)(i) as physically received by USCIS. The Service has determined that a "nonfrivolous" petition is one that "is not without basis in law or fact." Memo, Pearson, Ex. Assoc. Comm. HQOPS 70/20 (Jan 29, 2001), *reprinted in* 78 No. 7 *Interpreter Releases* 365, 381–83 (Feb. 12, 2001). A "period of stay authorized by the AG" allows a person to port even if their last approved petition has expired in some cases including where the current employer may have filed an extension of stay that is still pending beyond the current petition validity. Memo, Yates, Assoc. Dir. Operations, USCIS, HQOPRD 70/6.2.8-P (May 12, 2005) at p. 11, *published on* AILA InfoNet at Doc. No. 05051810 (May 18, 2005). There may also be successive H-1B portability petitions filed while a previous portability petition has been filed as long as the beneficiary remains in a status authorized by the AG. *Id.* at 11–12.

Portability and Cap-Exempt to Cap-Subject Status—An H-1B may port from a cap-exempt employer to a cap-subject employer during a period when there are no H-1B numbers as long as the cap-subject H-1B application is eventually approved and the LCA covers the entire period of employment. Letter, Hernandez III, Chief, Business and Trade Services, USCIS (May 23, 2007), *published on* AILA InfoNet at Doc. No. 07052563.

In order to be admitted at the border under the portability provisions an applicant must meet the following requirements: (1) S/he must otherwise be admissible; (2) S/he must be in possession of a valid unexpired passport and visa, unless exempt under 8 C.F.R. §§212.1, 1212.1; (3) S/he must establish that she was previously admitted in H-1B status by presenting the I-94 or I-797; and (4) S/he must present the filing receipt Form I-797 for the new H-1B or other evidence of timely filing prior to expiration of previous H-1B. If the H-1B is not in possession of I-797 and a CLAIMS inquiry shows no evidence of the new petition being filed or if the original petition has expired and there is no evidence of the approval of a new one, the person may not be admitted in H-1B status. Memo, Pearson, Ex. Assoc. Comm. HQOPS 70/20 (Jan. 29, 2001), *supra.* Under DOS guidelines a person may also be readmitted under the H-1B visa obtained through the original employer as long as it has not expired and the other above conditions are met. Cable, DOS 01-State-27960 (Feb. 14, 2001), *reprinted in* 78 No. 11 *Interpreter Releases* 529 (Mar. 19, 2001). *See also* Memo, Cronin, Acting Ex. Assoc. Comm. Program, HQPGM 70/6.2.8 (June 19, 2001) at ¶II D, *reprinted in* 78 No. 25 *Interpreter Releases* 1069, 1108–17 (July 2, 2001). An H-1B employee may also return to the original employer after switching to another employer (through the portability provision or otherwise) if his original petition is still valid because H-1B "petitions remain valid until they either expire or are revoked..." Letter, Hernandez, Director, Business and Trade Services, HQ 70/6.2.8 (Apr. 24, 2002), *reprinted in* 79 No. 32 *Interpreter Releases* 1198–99, 1220–23 (Aug. 12, 2002).

1.l. Lawful Status and Termination—An H-1B who is terminated from his position or is unemployed is not considered to be maintaining lawful status. Letter, Hernandez, Director, Business and Trade Services, HQ 70/6.2.8 (Apr. 24, 2002), *reprinted in* 79 No. 32 *Interpreter Releases* 1198–99, 1220–23 (Aug. 12, 2002).

2. Analyses/Definitions

2.a. Specialty Occupation is defined under INA §214(i)(1), 8 U.S.C. §1184(i)(1), 8 C.F.R. §214.2(h)(4)(ii) and 20 C.F.R. §655.715 ("Specialty Occupation" for H-1B defined in subsection (1)) as requiring:

(1) Theoretical and practical application of a body of highly specialized knowledge *and*

(2) Attainment of a bachelor's or higher degree in the specific specialty (*or its equivalent*) as a minimum for entry into the occupation in the U.S.

2.b. Standards to Determine Specialty Occupation, 8 C.F.R. §214.2(h)(4)(iii)(A) require that the position must meet one of the following criteria:

(1) A baccalaureate or higher degree *or equivalent* is normally the minimum requirement for entry into the particular position; *The Button Depot, Inc. v. DHS,* 386 F.Supp.2d 1140 (C.D. Cal. 2005) [reversed denial of H-1B petition for accountant where DHS abused its discretion by failing to apply the relevant standards regarding an equivalent foreign degree in business administration as meeting the industry standard, by failing to consider evidence, and by relying on unrelated factors]; *Unical Aviation, Inc. v. INS,* 248 F.Supp.2d 931 (C.D. Cal. 2002) [reversed AAO because position of senior market analyst was indistinguishable from a marketing research analyst which INS acknowledged was a specialty occupation and company demonstrated in normally requires a baccalaureate degree]; *Tapis Intern v. INS,* 94 F.Supp.2d 172 (D. Mass. 2000) [reversed AAO because it denied H-1B on grounds that job did not require bachelor's degree while ignoring that regulation permit equivalency]. *But see Fred 26 Importers, Inc. v. DHS,* 445 F.Supp.2d 1174, 1179–80 (C.D. Cal. 2006)[upheld AAO requirement that degree must directly relate to the proffered position where human resource manager position did not require a degree solely in human resource management; however, court reversed AAO on grounds that nature of duties was specialized and complex].

(2) Degree requirement is common in industry in parallel positions among similar organizations or alternatively that the particular position is so complex or unique that a degree is required;

(3) Employer normally requires a degree or equivalent; *or*

(4) Nature of specific duties so specialized and complex that knowledge required to perform the duties is usually associated with attainment of degree. *Fred 26 Importers, Inc. v. DHS,* 445 F.Supp.2d 1174, 1180–81 (C.D. Cal. 2006)[court reversed AAO where it failed to address expert and other evidence that a human resource manager position in a small export/import company required duties which were specialized and complex and, instead, simply asserted that small company did not require specialized and complex duties].

2.c. Criteria In Evaluating the Position Include Under *Matter of Michael Hertz Assoc.*, 19 I&N Dec. 558 (Comm. 1988):

(1) Focus on tasks, demands, duties and actual requirements of position as specified both by petitioner and industry documents;

(2) Position requires knowledge, both theoretical and applied, which is almost exclusively obtained through studies and institution of higher learning;

(3) Position requires a precise and specific course of study which relates directly and closely to the position;

(4) Obtaining a college degree in business or liberal arts, without further specification, does not establish eligibility. Requirement of college degree for sake of general education or to obtain higher caliber employee insufficient;

(5) Other factors considered: Form, method, extent of compensation (*e.g.,* if percent of net income suggests a permanent job); Form of agreement/contract (must have termination date).

2.d. Cases referring to Members of the Professions Relevant to Definition of Specialty Occupation—*Matter of Essex Cryogenics Industries, Inc.*, 14 I&N Dec. 196 (Comm. 1972); *Matter of General Atomic Co.*, 17 I&N Dec. 532 (Comm. 1980); INA §101(a)(32), 8 U.S.C. §1101(a)(32).

2.e. Specialty occupation encompasses the definition of professional. A "professional" has been previously defined to include:

Accountant, *Matter of Arjani*, 12 I&N Dec. 649 (R.C. 1967); *Matter of Doultsinos*, 12 I&N Dec. 153 (DD 1957); *The Button Depot, Inc. v. DHS,* 386 F.Supp.2d 1140 (C.D. Cal. 2005) [reversed denial of H-1B petition for accountant where DHS abused its discretion by failing to apply the relevant standards regarding an equivalent foreign degree in business administration as meeting the industry standard]. *But see E.G. Enterprises, Inc. v. DHS,* 467 F.Supp.2d 728 (E.D. Mich. 2006) [although position was titled accountant, USCIS concluded that it was not a specialty occupation because the job offered was a bookkeeper's position]. **Acupuncturist**, *Cutler v. Ilchert*, ___ F.Supp. ___ (N.D. Cal. 1985) [without degree]. *But see Matter of* ___, WAC 94-064-50122 (AAU Sept. 9, 1994), *published on* AILA InfoNet at Doc. No. 95020190. **Chef**, *Matter of* __,EAC 03 143 51185 (AAO Jan. 28, 2005) [sous chef of pastry operations where restaurant employed 140 people at 3 different locations and had an annual income of $8million and the facility of employment was a world-renowned patisserie] *reported in* 11 No. 24 *Bender's Immigration Bulletin* 1367, 1396–97 (Dec. 15, 2006); *Matter of* ___, WAC 02-136-52595 (AAO Dec. 13, 2002) [executive pastry chef where job required a BA degree and level of complexity and supervisory responsibility was more than food service manager as described in OOH]. **Chiropractor**, *Matter of McGowan*, 11 I&N Dec. 898 (DD 1966). **Computer Programmer**, *Matter of Precision Programming, Inc.*, EAC 9220251006 (AAU Apr. 22, 1993) [programmer for business may be specialty occupation], *reported in* 70 No. 21 *Interpreter Releases* 702–04 (May 27, 1993). Memo, Way, NSC Director, NSC 70/44.4 (Dec. 22, 2000), *reprinted in* 78 No. 16 *Interpreter Releases* 714, 725–26 (Apr. 23, 2001) [regarding position of programmer as generally considered a specialty occupation especially if the position "involves providing clients with programming analysis, custom designs, modifications, and/or problem solving of software."]. **Database Administrator (Document Quality Specialist)**, *Matter of* ____, (AAO Aug. 12, 2004) [where database systems were so specialized and complex for company developing new technology in endovascular temperature therapy, H-1B for database administrator was justified as requiring a BA or higher] *reported in* 10 No. 18 *Bender's Immigration Bulletin* 1401, 1426 (Sept. 15, 2005). **Dietician**, *Matter of DeVera*, 13 I&N Dec. 340 (DD 1966); *Matter of Roldan*, 11 I&N Dec. 869 (DD 1966). **Electronics specialist**, *Matter of Sea, Inc.*, 19 I&N Dec. 817 (Comm. 1988). **Fashion designer**, *Mindseye v. Ilchert*, 1985 U.S. Dist. LEXIS 17986, No. C-84-6199-FJW (N.D. Cal. July 11, 1987); 65 No. 3 *Interpreter Releases* 58, 60 (Jan. 15, 1988). **Film and Video Director,** *Matter of* ____, WAC 04 172 53199 (AAO Aug. 15, 2006). **General Manager,** (but only where business is complex). *Arctic Catering, Inc. v. Thornburgh*, 769 F.Supp. 1167 (D. Colo. 1991). *But see Shanti, Inc. v. Reno,* 36 F.Supp.2d 1151, 1164–66 (D. Minn. 1999) [general manager and restaurant manager positions not specialty occupations per se]. **Graphic Designer**, *Young China Daily v. Chappell*, 742 F.Supp. 552 (N.D. Cal. 1989). **Hotel management**, *Matter of Sun*, 12 I&N Dec. 535 (DD 1966). **Human Resource Manager,** *Fred 26 Importers, Inc. v. DHS,* 445 F.Supp.2d 1174 (C.D. Cal. 2006); **Industrial designer (with B.A.)**, *Matter of Michael Hertz Assoc.*, 19 I&N Dec. 558 (BIA 1988) [reversed *Matter of Huckenbeck*, 13 I&N Dec. 118 (R.C. 1969)]. **Interior designer (commercial)**, *Matter of* ___, WAC89 (AAU Nov. 30, 1989), *reported in* 67 No. 3 *Interpreter Releases* 61–62 (Jan. 12, 1990). **Investment Analyst**, *Matter of Tight Knot, Inc.,* LIN 99 089 51751 (AAO June 20, 2000) *reported in* 77 No. 34 *Interpreter Releases* 1291, 1292–93 (Sept.1, 2000). **Journalist**, *Matter of Perez*, 12 I&N Dec. 701 (DD 1968). **Librarian**, *Matter of Yaakov*, 13 I&N Dec. 203 (R.C. 1969). **Marketing Research Analyst/Senior Market Analyst**, *Unical Aviation, Inc. v. INS,* 248 F.Supp.2d 931 (C.D. Cal. 2002). **Medical records librarian**, *Matter of Villanueva*, 13 I&N Dec. 733 (DAC 1977). **Medical Technologist**, *Matter of Panganiban*, 13 I&N Dec. 581 (DAC 1970). **Minister**, *Matter of Wu*, 11 I&N Dec. 697 (DD 1966). **Orthopedist**, *Children's Medical Center of Dallas v. INS,* Case No. 3-87-2330-T (N.D. Tex. 1988). **Painting Restorer,** *Matter of* ___,EAC 04 086 52877 (AAO Aug. 3, 2005) *reported in* 11 No. 13 *Bender's Immigration Bulletin* 675, 712–13 (July 1, 2006). **Pharmacist**, *Matter of Rabbani*, 12 I&N Dec. 15 (DD 1966). **Rehabilitation Coordinator,** *Matter of* ___, WAC 02 198 51280 (AAO Apr. 25, 2005) [position required a bachelor's degree and was a combination of medical and health services manager and physical and occupation therapist] *reported in* 11 No. 23 *Bender's Immigration Bulletin* 1323, 1339–40 (Dec. 1, 2006). **Showroom Manager**, *Tapis Intern v. INS,* 94 F.Supp.2d 172 (D. Mass. 2000) [reversed AAO because it denied H-1B on grounds that job did not require bachelor's degree while ignoring that regulation permitted equivalency]. **Social Worker**, *Matter of Reyes*, 13 I&N Dec. 406 (R.C. 1969). **Software Design Engineer**, *Matter of Shanmukam/Matter of Aditi Corp.,* LIN 99 243 50365 (AAO May 23, 2000), *reported in* 77 No. 25 *Interpreter Releases* 861–63 (June 30, 2000). **Soil Conservationist,** *Matter of* ___, LIN 04 088 51403 (AAO Aug. 24, 2005) *reported in* 11 No. 13 *Bender's Immigration Bulletin* 675, 712–13 (July 1, 2006). **Teacher (public primary and secondary),** *Matter of Garland I.S.D.*, EAC 06 216 52028 (AAO Sept. 8, 2006) [teaching position in public primary or secondary schools where teacher is only required to have a probationary certification and a degree in any academic major with the completion of specialized courses and teacher training]; **Technical Publications Writer**, *Matter of Desai*, 17 I&N Dec. 569 (R.C. 1980). **Vocational Counselor**, *Matter of Wu*, 12 I&N Dec. 459 (DD 1967). **Webographer**, *Matter of Image Plant___*, EAC 00 247 50368 (AAO Feb. 15, 2002) *reprinted in* 79 No. 12 *Interpreter Releases* 406, 415–18 (Mar. 18, 2002) [treated webographer as graphic designer]

2.f. A position will be considered professional position if listed in INA §101(a)(32); 8 U.S.C. §1101(a)(32). *Turbomotive, Inc. v. Weiss*, Case No. H-88-563 (JAC) (D. Conn. July 27, 1989); 66 No. 30 *Interpreter Releases* 879 (Aug. 7, 1989) [mechanical engineer position not requiring a B.S. or B.A. still professional position because engineer is listed in the statute as a professional position]. In addition, the DOL has provided a list of professional occupations for recruitment purposes for labor certifications that require a person to customarily hold a bachelors or higher degree. *See* 69 Fed. Reg. 77325, 77377–84 (Dec. 27, 2004), *published on* AILA InfoNet at Doc. No. 04122312. Although DOL has explicitly stated that the list is not intended to be used to qualify a person for eligibility under the H-1B or H-1B1 category, 69 Fed. Reg. at 77346 (Dec. 27, 2004), it may serve as some guidance. *See* **Appendix A**, *infra.*

2.g. The Service views a position as professional where it meets one of four criteria established in 8 C.F.R. §214.2(h)(4)(ii). *Royal Siam Corp. v. Chertoff,* 484 F.3d 139 (1st Cir. 2007) [upheld denial by USCIS of previously approved restaurant manager position where USCIS relied on Occupational Handbook and asserted that generalized business administration degree was insufficient to support specialized knowledge claim]; *E.G. Enterprises, Inc. v. DHS,* 467 F.Supp.2d 728 (E.D. Mich. 2006) [although position was titled accountant, USCIS concluded that it was not a specialty occupation because the job offered was a bookkeeper's position]; *Fred 26 Importers, Inc. v. DHS,* 445 F.Supp.2d 1174, 1179–80 (C.D. Cal. 2006)[upheld AAO requirement that degree must directly relate to the proffered position where human resource manager position did not require a degree solely in human resource management; however, court reversed AAO on grounds that it failed to explain why the nature of the duties was not sufficiently specialized and complex];*Blacher v. Ridge,* 436 F.Supp.2d 602, 604–05 (S.D.N.Y. 2006) [professional travel manager position not a professional position; case dismissed on jurisdictional grounds]; *Shanti, Inc. v. Reno,* 36 F.Supp.2d 1151, 1164–66 (D. Minn. 1999) [restaurant manager position not specialty occupation]; *All Aboard Worldwide Couriers v. Attorney General,* 8 F.Supp.2d 379 (S.D.N.Y. 1998) [upheld denial of public affairs consultant position in shipping industry because applicant failed to prove degree requirement in this specific industry even if public affairs consultants are professionals in other industries]; *Matter of Caron International Inc.*, 19 I&N Dec. 791 (Comm. 1988) [general manager occupations such as vice-president or first line supervisor not necessarily a professional position]; *Matter of Ling*, 13 I&N Dec. 35 (R.C. 1968); *Matter of___,* WAC 03 066 50015 (AAO June 9, 2004) [Montessori teacher was not a professional position]. The position, under INS's view, qualifies as a specialty occupation if it always or nearly always requires a B.A. degree or higher rather than "usually" requires a degree. *Louisiana Philharmonic Orchestra v. INS,* 2000 W.L. 282785 (E.D. La. Mar. 15, 2000). Generally, look to industry standards. *Matter of Michael Hertz Assoc., Inc.*, 19 I&N Dec. 558 (Comm. 1988). *But see Safer, Inc. v. INS,* CA 3-87-2761-R (N.D. Tex. 1989); 66 No. 11 *Interpreter Releases* 328–29 (Mar. 20, 1989). But it is also a professional position where the employer or the job require a degree or its *equivalent* and thus some combination of education and experience may be sufficient. *Tapis Intern v. INS,* 94 F.Supp.2d 172 (D. Mass. 2000) [reversed AAO because it denied H-1B on grounds that job did not require bachelor's degree while ignoring that the regulation also permitted equivalency]. An exception to the "industry standard" requirement would permit a finding that a *position* is professional where it is a "transitional occupation." *Hird/Blaker Corp. v. Sava*, 764 F.Supp. 872 (S.D.N.Y. 1991). One court has looked to the definition of professional contained in the FLSA. 29 C.F.R. §541. *Full Gospel Portland Church v. Thornburgh*, 730 F.Supp. 441, 446–47 (D.D.C. 1988). "[T]he vocations included in the term 'professional' in our modern highly industrialized society are constantly expanding." *Matter of Shin*, 11 I&N Dec. 686 (DD 1966). Whether position is professional is unrelated to size of company, salary or prior company history of maintaining position. *Fred*

26 Importers, Inc. v. DHS, 445 F.Supp.2d 1174, 1180–81 (C.D. Cal. 2006)[reversed AAO where it failed to address expert affidavits and other evidence that human resource manager position was sufficiently complex and rejected H-1B because it was a small company]; *Young China Daily v. Chappell,* 742 F.Supp. 552 (N.D. Cal. 1989); [graphics designer position is professional job]. Position can be considered professional based on "the complexity of the duties alone." *American Bictech, Inc. v. INS*, No. Civ-2-88-262 (E.D. Tenn. Mar. 27, 1989), *reported in* 66 No. 23 *Interpreter Releases* 653–55 (June 19, 1989) [president of injection molded plastic company is professional position]; *Arctic Catering, Inc. v. Thornburgh*, 769 F.Supp. 1167 (D. Colo. 1991) [general manager of business catering to needs of workers at geophysical drilling and mining camps in remote regions of the world]. *But see E.G. Enterprises, Inc. v. DHS,* 467 F.Supp.2d 728, 737 (E.D. Mich. 2006) [upheld denial of H-1B for accountant position where USCIS determined that the duties of the proffered position, *combined* with the position title and business size demonstrated it was a bookkeeping position]. Moreover, INS should give deference to the employer's view, should consider fully the employer's evidence and should not rely simply on "standardized government classification systems, [Occupational Outlook Handbook]." *Unico American Corp. v. Watson*, Case No. CV 89-6958 (C.D. Cal. Mar. 19, 1991), *reported in* 68 No. 34 *Interpreter Releases* 1161 (Sept. 9, 1991).

2.h. Where position is considered specialty occupation does person have credentials? 8 C.F.R. §214.2(h)(4)(iii)(C).

(1) Employee requirements needed for specialty occupation under INA §214(i)(2), 8 U.S.C. §1184(i)(2) are:

(a) Full state licensure to practice in the occupation, if such licensure is required to practice in the occupation; Where the state or local authority requires proof of lawful employment *before* granting the license and the license is required to practice the profession, USCIS will grant a one-year H-1B approval to allow the beneficiary to obtain the license. In order to issue the "one-year H-1B" the adjudicator must determine: (1) the beneficiary has filed an application in accordance with state or local rules and procedures; (2) the beneficiary is fully qualified to receive the state or local license but for the lawful employment requirement; and (3) the beneficiary is otherwise qualified to receive the H-1B. Approval of the H-1B does not mean that the beneficiary has approval to engage in employment without the appropriate license. A request for an extension of the one year will be denied where the beneficiary cannot establish she has obtained the license. Memo, Neufeld, Deputy Assoc. Dir. Domestic Operations, USCIS, HQ 70/6.2.8 (Mar. 21, 2008), *published on* AILA InfoNet at Doc. No. 08032432; AFM at 31.3(d)(3)

(b) Completion of the degree required for the occupation; *or*

(c) *Experience* in the specialty equivalent to the completion of such degree; and

(d) Recognition of expertise in the specialty through progressively responsible positions relating to the specialty.

Degree or its equivalent is sufficient if it is a requirement for the job. 8 C.F.R. §214.2(h)(4)(iii)(C)(2); *Matter of Shin*, 11 I&N Dec. 686 (DD 1966).

Where employee has mixture of education and experience, it may be sufficient where applicant has at least some formal college level training and the training and education are the equivalent of the degree. 8 C.F.R. §214.2(h)(4)(iii)(C)(4); *Matter of Sea, Inc.*, 19 I&N Dec. 817 (Comm. 1988); *Matter of Yaakov*, 13 I&N Dec. 203 (R.C. 1969).

But a general degree, such as a B.A. in business administration or its equivalent, absent specialized experience may be insufficient because there must be a showing of a degree in a specialized field. *Shanti, Inc. v. Reno,* 36 F.Supp.2d 1151, 1162–66 (D. Minn. 1999) [distinguished *Matter of Sun* because applicant only had equivalent general degree in business and not hotel management degree]. *But see The Button Depot, Inc. v. DHS,* 386 F.Supp.2d 1140 (C.D. Cal. 2005) [reversed denial of H-1B petition for accountant where DHS abused its discretion by failing to apply the relevant standards regarding an equivalent foreign degree in business administration, by failing to consider evidence, and by relying on unrelated factors].

(2) Experience Alone May Be Sufficient—8 C.F.R. §214.2(h)(4)(iii)(C)(4) ("education, specialized training, *and/or* progressively responsible experience that is equivalent to BA"). *See Matter of Minnesota Mining and Mfg. Co. (3M)*, Case No. A27 228 517 (AAU Oct. 24, 1989), *reported in* 66 No. 48 *Interpreter Releases* 1411–12 (Dec. 18, 1989) [22 years experience in document systems manager position]. *But see Matter of Portugues Do Atlantico Information Bureau, Inc.*, 19 I&N Dec. 194 (Comm. 1984) [decided before regulatory change permitting experience as sole basis for qualifications]. Where experience is substituted for education it *must* include the theoretical and practical application of specialized knowledge required at the professional level. Not any on-the-job training is sufficient. *Matter of Sea, Inc.,* 19 I&N Dec. 817 (Comm. 1988).The courts have found experience alone sufficient. *Turbomotive, Inc. v. Weiss,* ___ F.Supp. ___, Case No. H-88-563 (JAC) (D. Conn. July 27, 1989), *reported in* 66 No. 30 *Interpreter Releases* 879 (Aug. 7, 1989) [twenty-four years in engineering and $48,000 salary qualifies person as professional]; *Hong Kong TV Video Program, Inc. v. Ilchert*, 685 F.Supp. 712 (N.D. Cal. 1988) [company president, 20 years of experience without degree]; *Globenet, Inc. v. Attorney General,* ___ F.Supp. ___ No. 88-1261 (D.D.C. Jan. 10, 1989) [twenty-three years experience in data processing for position of electrical and electronics engineer], *reported in* 66 No. 3 *Interpreter Releases* 59 (Jan. 13, 1989).

(3) Evaluations—An evaluation of work experience can be accomplished by: (1) an evaluation from an official who has authority to grant college level credit; (2) a recognized college level equivalency exam; (3) an evaluation by a reliable evaluation credential service as to *education* only; (4) evidence of certification or registration from a nationally recognized professional association; or (5) a determination by the DHS that the equivalent of college level training has been reached through a formula counting three years of experience as one year of college and that the alien has professional recognition. *Shanti, Inc. v. Reno,* 36 F.Supp.2d 1151, 1161–66 (D. Minn. 1999) [upheld denial because notwithstanding evaluation applicant could not show that combined education and experience constituted equivalent in specialized area]. To demonstrate expertise must have recognition by two authorities in the field, membership in an association, publications by or about the applicant, licensure or achievements which a recognized authority has determined to be significant. 8 C.F.R. §214.2(h)(4)(iii)(D)(5). For an equivalence to an MA must have BA plus five years of experience. 8 C.F.R. §214.2(h)(4)(iii)(D)(5). For PhD applicant must hold the degree. The Service should not challenge the credential evaluation if it is from a reputable company unless the evaluation contains obvious errors. Memo, Examinations (Nov. 13, 1995), *reprinted in* 73 No. 12 *Interpreter Releases* 364 (Mar. 25, 1996). However, a credential evaluating service can only evaluate *education*, not experience or training, according to USCIS by virtue of 8 C.F.R. §214.2(h)(4)(iii)(D)(3). *See e.g., Matter of* ___,WAC 02 273 55874 (AAO Apr. 25, 2005) (Cal. S.C.) and *Matter of* ___ , LIN 04 065 52086 (AAO 25, 2005) (Neb. S.C.) *reported in* 12 No. 1 *Bender's Immigration Bulletin* 1, 33 (Jan 1, 2007) [academic credential evaluator could address education evaluation but cannot address training or work experience under 8 C.F.R. §214.2(h)(4)(iii)(D)(1)]. Education and training can be evaluated by an independent evaluator but it must be "from an official who has authority to grant college-level credit for training and/or experience in the specialty at an accredited college or university which has a program for granting such credit based on an individual's training and/or work experience." 8 C.F.R. §214.2(h)(4)(iii)(D)(1). *Compare* section (D)(1) *with* (D)(3).

2.i. Judicial Review—The denial of an I-129 petition for an H-1B may not be subject to judicial review because INA §242(a)(2)(B)(ii) bars judicial review of discretionary decisions of DHS. *Blacher v. Ridge,* 436 F.Supp.2d 602 (S.D.N.Y. 2006) [notwithstanding employer's claim that USCIS violated its due process rights by erroneously interpreting the definition of specialty occupation under the H-1B category when it determined that a professional travel manager was not a professional position, the court held that 8 U.S.C. §1184(a)(1) regarding the admission of nonimmigrants leaves the decision to USCIS's discretion and therefore bars review under INA §242(a)(2)(B)(ii); the court also found that venue was not proper because neither defendants nor plaintiffs resided in the Southern District and the decision was made in Vermont]. A petitioner must also generally exhaust its administrative remedies by appealing to the AAO. *But see E.G. Enterprises, Inc. v. DHS,* 467 F.Supp.2d 728, 732–33 (E.D. Mich. 2006) [where H-1B petitioner missed deadline to file AAO court held there was still jurisdiction to review denial.

3. Attestation Requirements for H-1B—INA §212(n)(1), 8 U.S.C. §1182(n)(1); 137 Cong. Rec. S 18242, 18245, 18506–11 (Nov. 25, 1991), 137 Cong. Rec. H 11485 (Nov. 25, 1991); 59 Fed. Reg. 65646–79 (Dec. 20, 1994). Before an H-1B application can be submitted an employer must obtain certification of a labor condition application. 20 C.F.R. §655.700(a)(3). Companies deemed to be "dependent employers" or "willful violators" have special attestation requirements including that they have made good faith efforts to recruit U.S. workers. INA §§212(n)(1)–(3); 20 C.F.R. §§655.736–39; 65 Fed. Reg. 80110–80254 (Dec. 20, 2000).

3.a. The labor condition application or attestation for H-1B and H-1B1 purposes must be filed *electronically* on ETA 9035E unless a "physical disability or lack of access to the Internet prevents an employer from using the electronic filing system." 20 C.F.R. §655.720(a). 70 Fed. Reg. 72556–64 (Dec. 5, 2005) [requiring electronic filings except in narrow circumstances]. The electronic form is submitted to the Chicago NPC. 73 Fed. Reg. 11954–56 (Mar. 5, 2008); 20 C.F.R. §655.720(b). If an employer meets the criteria to send the form by mail he must first get approval from DOL to send LCAs by mail, 20 C.F.R. §655.720(c) and then file the request by mail on form ETA 9035. 20 C.F.R. §655.720(d). The faxback system is no longer used.

(1) Required Wage Defined—The employer must pay the H-1B employee the "required wage," which is defined as: the greater of the actual wage level paid by the employer to all other individuals with similar experience and qualifications for the specific employment at the place of employment *or* the prevailing wage for the occupation in the area of employment based on the best information available. In regard to the former standard, the wage is in relation to employees working in "substantially the same duties and responsibilities" with "substantially similar experience and qualifications." 20 C.F.R. §655.731(a)(1).

(2) Prevailing Wage—The prevailing wage must be determined at the time of filing the LCA. The prevailing wage determination is determined by the collective bargaining agreement (CBA) if one exists that pertains to the occupation. 20 C.F.R. §655.731(a)(2)(i). If there is no CBA the state employment security agency (SESA) now known as State Workforce Agency (SWA) shall establish a prevailing wage based upon the "best information available" that is "the arithmetic mean of the wages of workers similarly employed in the area of intended employment." §655.731(a)(2)(ii)(A). The Bureau of Labor Statistics Occupational Employment Statistics (OES) shall be used to determine the arithmetic mean. Alternatively, an employer may provide a prevailing wage based upon the Davis Bacon Act or the McNamara-O'Hara Service Contract Act, 20 C.F.R. §655.731(b)(3)(i) *or* a survey that is based upon the "median wage of workers similarly employed in the area of intended employment" conducted by an independent authoritative source. §655.731(b)(3)(iii)(B) or another legitimate source. §655.731(b)(3)(iii)(C). An independent authoritative source "shall mean a survey of wages published in a book, newspaper, periodical, loose-leaf service, newsletter, or other similar medium." *Id.* It must be the last published survey of the source and conducted within the past 24 months. *Id.* If another legitimate source is used employer will have to demonstrate the legitimacy of the wage if an investigation is conducted. 20 C.F.R. §655.731(a)(2)(ii)(C). If SESA/SWA is relied upon the LCA must be filed within the validity period of the SWA determination (from 90 days to one year) or it is not valid. 20 C.F.R. §655.731(a)(2)(ii)(A)(1). The determination of the prevailing wage is based upon persons "similarly employed" throughout the area of intended employment, *i.e.,* "having substantially comparable jobs in the occupational classification in the area of intended employment." 20 C.F.R. §655.731(a)(2)(iii). If this definition of "similarly employed" cannot yield a representative sample of workers, then "similarly employed" may be defined as: (1) having jobs requiring a substantially similar level of skill or (2) having substantially comparable jobs with employers outside of the area of intended employment. An employer, however, may never pay a wage lower than that required under any applicable Federal, state or local law. 20 C.F.R §655.731(a)(2)(iv). If the employer cannot wait for a SWA determination of the prevailing wage and relies on its own independent source, it can file the LCA but

if the information relied upon subsequently is below the prevailing wage determined by SWA, it must pay the H-1B employee the difference within 30 days to avoid a wage violation. 20 C.F.R. §655.731(a)(2)(ii)(A)(2). DOL provided guidance on prevailing wage standards in its publication of the PERM regulations, 69 Fed. Reg. 77325, 77365–72 (Dec. 27, 2004), *published on* AILA InfoNet at Doc. No. 04122312; and in its field memoranda, Memo, DeRocco, Asst. Sec., ETA, "Prevailing Wage Guidance" (May 17, 2005), *published on* AILA InfoNet at Doc No. 05052066 (May 20, 2005); New FAQs on Prevailing Wage (Aug. 1, 2005), *published on* AILA InfoNet at Doc. No. 05081067. *See formerly* GAL No. 1-00, Jacobs-Simmons, Deputy Asst. Sec., ETA (May 16, 2000), *reprinted in* 77 No. 21 *Interpreter Releases* 701, 706–15 (May 26, 2000) [addresses employer surveys and discusses access to OES data which is now broken down into ALC data for most industries and EDU data for nonprofits/educational institutions]; GAL No. 2-98, McConnell, Acting Admin. of Regional Management (Oct. 31, 1997), *reprinted in* 74 No. 43 *Interpreter Releases* 1712, 1716–27 (Nov. 7, 1997) [providing criteria to be used if employer wishes private wage survey]; GAL No. 4-95, Farmer, Admin. for Regional Management (May 18, 1995), *reprinted in* 72 No. 24 *Interpreter Releases* 838, 848–55 (June 26, 1995). "Wages paid" is any compensation treated as earnings for income tax and FICA purposes. 20 C.F.R. §655.731(c)(2). "Wage rate" is remuneration exclusive of fringe benefits. 20 C.F.R. §655.715. Certain deductions such as the cost of attorneys fees for the H-1B/LCA if paid by the applicant, under certain circumstances, may be deducted from the wages paid to him to determine whether the applicant has received the appropriate prevailing wage rate. 20 C.F.R. §§655.731(c)(9)(iii)(C) and (c)(11).

(a) 100% of Prevailing Wage—An employer can no longer pay 95% of the prevailing wage but must pay 100% of the determined prevailing wage. INA §212(p) and §§212(a)(5)(A), (n)(a)(A)(i)(II), (t)(1)(A)(i)(II).

(b) Prevailing Wage for Employees of Institutions of Higher Education and Nonprofits—INA §212(p), 8 U.S.C. §1182(p), 20 C.F.R. §§655.731(a)(2)(vii), 656.40(e). Special provision that bases the prevailing wage only by comparison with the same type of institution or organization in the area of employment.

(c) Calculation of Prevailing Wage by Hour or Year on LCA—For purposes of filing an LCA, an employer may convert a prevailing wage from an hourly salary to a yearly salary by multiplying the hourly wage by 2080. Conversely, where the employer obtains a prevailing wage that is expressed in a yearly salary it may divide the salary by 2080 to convert it to an hourly wage. 20 C.F.R. §655.731(a)(2)(vi).

(d) Calculation of Prevailing Wage Where There is a Range of Wages. Where a range of wages is paid in an occupational classification or among individuals with similar experience and qualifications, a range is considered to meet the prevailing wage as long as the bottom of the wage range is at least the prevailing wage. 20 C.F.R. §655.731(a)(2)(v).

(e) Safe Harbor—Under the INA an employer has the option of: (1) requesting a prevailing wage determination (PWD) from the SWA; (2) using a survey conducted by an independent authoritative source; or (3) using another legitimate source. However, by obtaining a PWD from the SWA the employer is given "safe-harbor status" protecting him from any Wage and Hour Division investigation challenging the validity of the PWD as long as it was applied properly. New FAQs on Prevailing Wage ("Question 2") (Aug. 1, 2005), *published on* AILA InfoNet at Doc. No. 05081067.

(3) To provide working conditions for H-1Bs that will not adversely affect other workers similarly employed. Working conditions commonly refer to matters "including hours, shifts, vacation periods, and fringe benefits." 20 C.F.R. §655.732(b).

(4) To attest that there is no strike or lockout in occupational classification at the place of employment. Employers are prohibited from placing H-1Bs in a place where there is a strike or lockout or work stoppage in that occupation. 20 C.F.R. §655.733(a)(1).

(5) To provide notice to the bargaining representative if any, or to *post* notice that a labor condition application has been filed. *See in this section* "Posting Notice," ¶ 3.c(10)(a) (p.689), *infra.*

3.b. Employer—To file attestation employer must be within the U.S., must have an employer/employee relationship with applicant, and must have an IRS tax I.D. number. 20 C.F.R. §655.715. Job contractors and employers with multiple employees may petition and the regulations do not preclude foreign employers from petitioning as long as they meet the above qualifications. The entity that files the LCA will be deemed to be the employer. *Administrator, Wage and Hour Division v. Avenue Dental Care,* 6-LCA-29 (ALJ June 28, 2007) at 18–19 [where employer used assumed business name in filing LCAs, it could not claim that aggrieved employee should have been listed under a different corporate name and therefore the employer was the corporate entity]. The DOL may also pierce the corporate veil and use an alter ego theory for liability purposes. *Id* at p. 19 n.2.

3.c. Procedure

(1) Attestation shall contain the number of workers sought, the occupational classification for each, the prevailing wage and method for determining it, and the wage rate and working conditions. Employer must make attestation available for public inspection within one day of filing with DOL.

(2) The labor condition application or attestation for H-1B and H-1B1 purposes must be filed electronically on ETA 9035E unless a "physical disability or lack of access to the Internet prevents an employer from using the electronic filing system." 20 C.F.R. §655.720(a). The electronic form is submitted through DOL's website at *www.lca.doleta.gov.* 20 C.F.R. §655.720(b). If an employer meets the criteria to send the form by mail he must first get approval from DOL to send LCAs by mail, 20 C.F.R. §655.720(c) and then file the request by mail on Form ETA 9035. 20 C.F.R. §655.720(d). The faxback system is no longer used. Under the electronic filing system, the ETA 9035E must be printed and signed by the employer immediately after ETA provides the electronic certification. The signed form must be maintained in the employer's file, a copy of the signed form must be maintained in the public access file, and another copy submitted with the I-129. §655.730(c)(3). To track the status of the LCA, DOL e-mail is *lcstatus06@doleta.gov.*

(3) Providing Copy of LCA to Employee. The employer shall provide a signed copy of the certified ETA 9035 or 9035E to the H-1B employee no later than the date s/he reports to work. 20 C.F.R. §655.734(a)(3).

(4) Each LCA must be limited to a single occupation but can list multiple locations where the H-1B employee will be working. 20 C.F.R. §655.730(c)(5).

(5) The position covered by LCA may be either full-time or part-time employment. Full-time and part-time positions cannot be combined on a single LCA. 20 C.F.R. §655.730(c)(6).

(6) The LCA is valid for the period of employment on the ETA 9035 and for no greater than a period of 3 years. A new prevailing wage does not have to be obtained every year but the SWA prevailing wage is valid for a period of not less than 90 days and not more than one year. 20 C.F.R. §655.731(a)(2)(iii)(A). The period of validity of an LCA may not exceed 3 years. 20 C.F.R. §655.750(a). Thus, if subsequent employees are hired in the same occupational classification in the same area of intended employment beyond the validity period of the prevailing wage determination by the SWA, a new determination must be obtained because the prevailing wage does not "relate back" for purposes of the new LCA. 20 C.F.R. §655.731(a)(2)(viii).

(7) The Public Access File. An employer must maintain a public access file which is accessible to interested and aggrieved parties. The public access file must be available at either the employer's principal place of business in the U.S. or at the worksite. 20 C.F.R. §655.760(a). An interested party is not necessarily adversely affected by the LCA but simply one that has "notified the DOL of his or her/its interest or concern in the administrator's determination." The employer must retain and make available for public inspection a "public access file" within one day after the LCA is filed with all documentation supporting the LCA, including:

(a) A copy of the completed LCA

(b) Documentation which provides the wage rate to be paid H-1B nonimmigrants;

(c) A full, clear explanation of the system that the employer used to set the "actual wage" paid in the position, *e.g.*, memorandum to the file summarizing the system or a copy of the employer's pay system (payroll records are not required for public display although they *must* be retained for 3 years from date of creation for enforcement purposes);

(d) A copy of the documentation used to establish the prevailing wage which may be solely a general description of the source and methodology (Davis-Bacon, SESA, etc.), although wage data must be kept for enforcement purposes;

(e) Copy of the notice given to the union/ employees. If to employees directly need hard copy posted notice or electronic notice;

(f) A summary of the benefits offered to U.S. workers in the same occupational classification, a statement as to how any differentiation in benefits is made (without divulging proprietary information) where there are differences, *see* 20 C.F.R. 655.731(c)(3);

(g) Where the employer undergoes a change in corporate structure (*e.g.*, a successor corporation or "spin off") a sworn statement by a responsible official of the new employing entity that it accepts all obligations, liabilities and undertakings under the LCAs filed by the predecessor employing entity, together with a list of each affected LCA and its date of certification, and a description of the actual wage system and the EIN of the new employing entity *see* 20 C.F.R. §655.730(e)(1); The sworn statement should be completed *before* the H-1B is employed. Letter, Hernandez, Director, Business and Trade Services, HQ 70/6.2.8 (June 7, 2001), *published on* AILA InfoNet at Doc. No. 01062832.

(h) Where the employer utilizes the definition of "single employer" in the Internal Revenue Code, a list of any entities included as part of the single employer in making H-1B determinations, *see* 20 C.F.R. §655.736(d)(7);

(i) Where the employer is H-1B dependent or a willful violator and it indicates an employee is exempt under 20 C.F.R. §655.737, a list of such exempt H-1B employees;

(j) Where the employer is H-1B dependent or a willful violator a summary of recruitment methods used and the time frames of recruitment of U.S. workers, *see* 20 C.F.R. §655.739(i)(4).

(8) Approval of application is required by the statute to occur within 7 days of filing unless application is incomplete or obviously inaccurate. 20 C.F.R. §§655.740(a)(1), (2). The Secy. of Labor reviews it only for completeness and obvious inaccuracies. INA §212(n)(1)(D).

(9) Retention of records. All records must be retained one year beyond LCA period or, if complaint is filed, until the complaint is determined. Payroll records must also be retained for these periods but in any event, no less than the 3-year period mentioned above.

(10) Certain posting and per diem payments to employees are also required. Although a number of these were successfully challenged in *National Ass'n of Manufacturers v. DOL*, 1996 WL 420868 (D.D.C. July 22, 1996) [striking some requirements on APA notice and comment grounds], *reported in* 73 No. 29 *Interpreter Releases* 999–1,002 (July 29, 1996), DOL regulations were republished, *see, e.g.*, 20 C.F.R. §655.734 [regarding posting notices].

(a) Posting Notice. The notice must be posted, or where there is a union it must be given to the union *before* filing LCA, 20 C.F.R. §§655.730(d)(4), 655.734(a)(1). The notice may be the LCA or may be a document of sufficient size and visibility that indicates: (1) that H-1Bs are sought; (2) the number of H-1Bs; (3) the occupational classification; (4) the wages offered; (5) the period of employment; (6) the location(s) at which the H-1Bs will be employed; and (7) that the LCA is available for public inspection. The notices shall contain a provision stating where complaints for misrepresentations may be filed. The posting notice includes posting "in a least two conspicuous locations at each place of employment where any H-1B nonimmigrant will be employed" and the notices "shall be posted on or within 30 days before the date the labor condition application is filed and shall remain posted for a total of 10 days." §655.734(a)(1)(ii)(A)(1)–(3). Hard copy notices may be posted in such areas as those including areas where wage and hour and Occupational Safety and Health notices are posted. 20 C.F.R. §655.734(a)(1)(ii)(A)(2). Alternatively an employer may provide electronic notice to employees in the "occupational classification" for which H-1Bs are sought. The employer may accomplish this through any means it normally communicates with employees including a "home page," "electronic bulletin board" or "e-mail." If accomplished through e-mail it need only be sent once; other electronic forms (*e.g.,* home page) should be "posted" for 10 days. §655.734(a)(1)(ii)(B). Notices must be posted at each worksite including ones not originally contemplated at the time of filing but which are within the area of intended employment listed on the LCA. §655.734(a)(2). The H-1B employee must be provided with a copy of the certified LCA when he begins employment. §655.734(a)(3).

(b) Benching/Per Diem/Payment Requirements. An employer must continue to pay H-1B employee who is not performing work if it is due to a nonproductive status at the direction of the employer (*e.g.,* benching an H-1B because of lack of assigned work, lack of a permit or license). 20 C.F.R. §655.731(c)(7)(i). It does not include circumstances where there is a nonproductive status unrelated to employment (*e.g.,* caring for an ill relative) §655.731(c)(7)(ii).

(11) Amending LCA—No provisions to amend LCAs. If change is material must file new LCA. Where employee promoted to a more advanced level need not file new LCA but must develop and maintain documentation explaining the changes and showing that the required wage has been met. Letter, Norris, Chief, Division of Foreign Labor Certifications, DOL (Nov. 4, 1996), *reprinted in* 73 No. 44 *Interpreter Releases* 1,634-36 (Nov. 18, 1996). Any change in occupational classification or permanent relocation to a place not reflected on LCA would require a new LCA. *Id.* Where an employer corporation changes its corporate structure as the result of an acquisition, merger, "spin-off" or other such action, the new employing entity is not required to file a new LCA and H-1B petition with respect to transferred employees even if there is a change in the FEIN. 20 C.F.R. §655.730(e). The "new" employer prior to employing the H-1B should maintain a sworn statement assuming all obligations, liabilities, and undertakings in all existing LCAs. 20 C.F.R. §655.730(e)(1); the sworn statement must be completed *before* the H-1B is employed. Letter, Hernandez, Director, Business and Trade Services, HQ 70/6.2.8 (June 7, 2001), *published on* AILA InfoNet at Doc. No. 01062832. A name change also does not require a new LCA. Letter, Norris, Chief, Division of Foreign Labor Certifications, DOL (Mar. 4, 1997), *reprinted in* 74 No. 26 *Interpreter Releases* 1083, 1094–95 (July 14, 1997). The "new" employer, however, must file new LCAs if it subsequently hires new employees or when it seeks extensions for the transferred employees, 20 C.F.R. §655.730(e)(iv)(C)(2). Moving within the same MSA does not require a new LCA. Letter, Richardson, Chief, Div. of Foreign Labor Certification, DOL (July 16, 1996), *reprinted in* 15 *AILA Monthly Mailing* 510 (Sept. 1996).

3.d. DOL has established a procedure to process complaints by an aggrieved person or organization or through its own initiated investigation relating to the failure of the employer to meet the above conditions or because of misrepresentation of those conditions. INA §212(n)(2), 8 U.S.C. §1182(n)(2); 20 C.F.R. §655.800 *et seq.* The DOL has 60 days to investigate, 120 days to bring a complaint after it determines there is a violation and 120 days to make a finding after the hearing. INA §(n)(2)(G)(viii). The former 30- and 60-day provisions for investigation and resolution of complaints under INA §212(n)(2)(B), 8 U.S.C. §1182(n)(2)(B) are not jurisdictional and do not bar the DOL Secretary from proceeding in a case against a defaulting employer. *Administrator, Wage and Hour Division v. Synergy Systems, Inc.* 04-LCA76 (June 30, 2006) [rejected the defendant's claim that the Administrator and the OALJ's failure to comply with the statutory deadlines was jurisdictional]; *Employment Standards Administration v. Synergy Systems, Inc.,* 04-LCA-22 (OALJ Mar. 5, 2004). However, absent a decision by the Administrator that an investigation on a complaint is warranted, no hearing may be brought. 29 C.F.R. §655.806(b); *Goel v. Bion Healthcare Staffing LLC,* 07-LCA-21 (ALJ July 18, 2007) [complaint dismissed where DOL did not conduct investigation and respondent asked to withdraw to pursue other action]. At least one court has also found that there is no private right of action on behalf of an employee allegedly terminated in favor of an H-1B even if that status was obtained through a fraudulent application. *Watson v. Bank of America,* 196 Fed. Appx. 306 (5th Cir. 2006) [affirmed dismissal of suit by USC against DOL, DHS DOS and employers for conspiracy to grant H-1B to detriment of U.S. workers]; *Watson v. U.S.,* __F. 3d ___(Fed. Cir. June 6, 2007) [no action for damages due to DOL "taking" USC's job under Tucker Act for failure to investigate and adjudicate his claim because there was no property right in his job with the private employer].

3.e. Penalties/Sanctions

(a) General Penalties—Failure to comply with all LCA requirements may result in a fine ($1,000 to $35,000 per violation) and a debarment from all future approvals of any NIVs, IVs, or LCs for at least one year. 20 C.F.R. §655.810; *Administrator, Wage and Hour Division v. Avenue Dental Care,* 6-LCA-29 (ALJ June 28, 2007) [willful failure to pay wages resulted in 2 year debarment]; *Cleveland v. QuikCAT.com Inc.,* 03-LCA-19 (ALJ June 9, 2005) [debarment for 2 years was upheld, along with back wages and penalties, where employer willfully failed to pay the appropriate wage, then stopped paying H-1Bs completely, and failed to provide notice of the filing of its LCA] *reported in* 10 No. 24 *Bender's Immigration Bulletin* 1843, 1871 (Dec. 15, 2005). However, for most matters it must be a "substantial failure" to comply. INA §212(n)(2)(C). And there is a "good faith" exception so that an employer is considered to have complied with the LCA requirements "notwithstanding a technical or procedural failure to meet such requirements, if there was a good faith attempt to comply..." INA §212(n)(2)(H)(i). There are exceptions to the "good faith" defense. INA §212(n)(2)(H)(ii). The violation must also be a willful failure which requires knowledge or reckless disregard. 20 C.F.R. §655.810(b); *Guy Santiglia v. Sun Microsystems, Inc.* Case No. 03-076 (ARB July 29, 2005) [where there was no substantial or willful violation of posting and public access requirements company's violations did not subject it to civil money penalties]. In determining penalty, DOL looks at: (1) previous history of violations; (2) the number of workers affected by the violations; (3) the gravity of the violation; (4) the violator's good faith compliance efforts; (5) the violator's explanation; (6) the violator's commitment to future compliance; and (7) the extent of financial gain by the violation or the extent of others' loss. 20 C.F.R. §655.810(c).

(b) Reinstatement—*Talukdar v. U.S. Dep't of Veterans Affairs,* 04-LCA-100 (Jan. 31, 2007) [where doctor was discriminated against because of his union activity regarding the differential pay between H-1B doctors and others, the employer was ordered to reinstate him and to pay backpay].

(c) Back Pay and Front Pay—If the employer has not paid the "required wage," (*i.e.*, the greater of the actual wage level paid by the employer to all other individuals with similar experience and qualifications for the specific employment at the place of employment *or* the prevailing wage for the occupation in the area of employment based on the best information available) it can be ordered to pay backpay or make up the deficiency. 20 C.F.R. §§655.810(a), 655.805(a)(2). To determine what "wages" were paid to the employee and whether those wages met the "required wage," the regulations define actual wages at 20 C.F.R. §655.731(c)(2). The DOL, in determining what wage was actually paid, looks to the LCA or the actual wage rather than giving effect to any private oral agreement. *Srikanth Dola v. Infoamerica,* 06-LCA-11 (ALJ Apr. 6, 2007) at 21–22 [ALJ declined to give effect to an oral agreement in determining what was the employee's wages]. Similarly, it will not count any sums, including per diem payments or advances that were not reported to the IRS in computing the "wages" the employee received. *Id.* At 23-27; 20 C.F.R. §§655.731(c)(2)(ii) and (iv). Payments made as a share of profits are *not* considered part of the wage owed and are also not a proper deduction from wages within the meaning of the regulations. *Administrator, Wage and Hour Division v. Avenue Dental Care,* 6-LCA-29 (ALJ June 28, 2007) at 19–20. Any deduction from wages that are paid an employee will not be considered, such as a deduction for a previous loan to the employee, unless the employee voluntarily agreed to it and provided written authorization. 20 C.F.R. §655.731(c)(9)(iii)(A); . *Srikanth Dola v. Infoamerica,* 06-LCA-11 (ALJ Apr. 6, 2007) at 26–28. In certain cases where reinstatement is not possible the employer may also be required to pay frontpay *Matter of Rung,* 2004-LCA-006 (AAO Sept. 26, 2006) [where termination was not *bona fide* and irreparable animosity between the parties makes return to work not possible ALJ ordered frontpay for the remainder of the term of the LCA]. Also, an employee may not be considered properly terminated for purposes of cutting off backpay and frontpay unless the employer follows 20 C.F.R. §655.731(c)(7)(iii) and notifies USCIS that the employment relationship has been terminated so that the I-129 petition is canceled *and* provides the employee with payment for transportation home. *Matter of Rung, supra.; Amtel Group of Florida, Inc. v. Yongmahapakorn,* 04-LCA-87 (OALJ Sept. 29, 2006), 2006 WL 2821406 [where employer notified employee but never notified USCIS of termination of H-1B it remained valid until the end of the LCA period and the former employee was able to collect back pay and interest]. *See, e.g., Administrator, Wage and Hour Division v. Mohan Kutty, M.D. et al.,* 01-LCA-00010 to 00025 (OALJ Oct. 9, 2002) [backpay award of over $980,000 including attorney's fees for J-1 waiver and H-1B petitions]; *Administrator, Wage and Hour Division v. Ken Technologies, Inc.,* 03-LCA-00015 (OALJ July 18, 2003) [failure to notify DHS of termination kept clock running for back pay even where employee misrepresented his credentials] 8 No. 22 *Bender's Immigration Bulletin* 1770-71 (Nov. 15, 2003); *Matter of Rajan,* 02-LCA-00012 (OALJ Apr. 30, 2003) [employer required to pay back wages from date employee reported to date INS revoked H-1B notwithstanding lack of actual work during the entire period; employer also required to reimburse for H-1B fees] *reported in* 8 No. 21 *Bender's Immigration Bulletin* 1716 (OALJ Nov. 1, 2003); *Matter of Miller,* 02-LCA-00004 (Feb. 7, 2003) [employer not required to pay wages from date of H-1B filing under portability provision where employer sent INS a letter stating employment would not begin until after petition approved] *reported in* 8 No. 18 *Bender's Immigration Bulletin* 1529-30 (OALJ Sept. 15, 2003). However, even where the employer does notify USCIS that employee is terminated but then continues to take steps to keep her employed, the employment relationship is continuing. *Innawalli v. American Information Technology Corp.* 05-LCA-165 (Sept. 29, 2006) In the portability context, damages begin to accrue after the portability application is filed and the person enters into employment (*i.e.*, when the employee first makes herself available). *Chellaurai v. Infinite Solutions, Inc.,* 03-LCA-72 (April 26, 2006). [damages accrued from time employee first made herself available even if there was no work].

3.f. Employers will be penalized for intimidating or threatening "whistleblowers"—INA §212(n)(2)(C)(iv). An employer will also be fined $1,000 for requiring an H-1B to pay a penalty for leaving the employer, but it shall not include lawful liquidated damages. INA §212(n)(2)(C)(vi).

3.g. Attorney Sanctions—Lawyer who submitted false LCA to USCIS to obtain H-1B visa was disciplined by BIA. *Matter of Shah,* 24 I&N Dec. 282 (BIA 2007)

3.h. Hearing—20 C.F.R. §655.820. The employer is entitled to an APA hearing before an ALJ. Must request hearing within 15 days of administrator's decision. 20 C.F.R. §655.820(d). Apply to Administrative Review Board. Failure to timely file, absent equitable tolling, results in dismissal of claim. *Administrator, Wage & Hour Division v. Gurukrupa LLC,* 07-LCA-19 (ALJ July 5, 2007) [dismissed case and found there was not equitable tolling absent extraordinary circumstances because respondent's actions did not amount to anything more than excusable neglect]; *Seyanabou Ndiaye v. CVS Store No. 6081,* 05-LCA-24 (May 9, 2007) and Nov. 29, 2006) [filing with state unemployment agency and EEO both of which dismissed her claims did not equitably toll the time for filing]; *Wakileh v. Western Kentucky University,* 03-LCA-23 (ALJ Oct. 6, 2003) [dismissed case where complainant's failure to file request due to moving did not equitably toll the time for filing] *reported in* 80 No. 42 *Interpreter Releases*

1523–24 (Nov. 3, 2003); For a survey of LCA cases 73 No. 20 *Interpreter Releases* 673–78 (May 20, 1996), 80 No. 25 *Interpreter Releases* 868–72 (June 30, 2003). *But see Ravikumar Gupta v. Jain Software Consulting, Inc.*, 05-LCA-08 (Mar. 30, 2007) [complaint for benching was timely filed because it is a continuing violation and the time period is measured from the end of the time period specified on the LCA].

(1) Settlement—The parties may settle the case and absent fraud or that the agreement was not entered into knowingly or voluntarily, the settlement will not be rescinded. *Administrator, Wage and Hour Division v. API Accounting and Computer Consulting,* 07-LCA-81 (Jan. 25, 2008) [settlement binding on the employer who belatedly sought to back out]. Parties may enter into consent decrees to resolve cases. *See e.g., Administrator, Wage and Hour Division v. Piminco, Inc.* 06-LCA-17 (ALJ Oct. 26, 2006).

3.i. Review of ALJ determination and federal court action—If a party is dissatisfied with the decision of an ALJ s/he may appeal the decision to the Secretary of Labor. 20 C.F.R. §655.840, 655.845. If a party is dissatisfied with the Secretary's decision s/he may seek review in the U.S. District Court. 20 C.F.R. §655.850. At least one court has rejected a direct action in federal court for violations of the labor condition application statute, 8 U.S.C. §1182(n) without first exhausting the administrative process set forth above. *Shah v. Wilco Systems, Inc.*, 126 F.Supp.2d 641, 646–48 (S.D.N.Y. 2000). [no private right of action to enforce 1182(n) violations or violations under unfair immigration employment practices §1324b].

3.j. Dependent Employers and Employers Who Willfully Violate Attestation Provisions—INA §212(n)(1)–(3); 8 U.S.C. §1182(n)(1)–(3); 20 C.F.R. §§655.700–.760, 655.800–.855; 65 Fed. Reg. 80110–54 (Dec. 20, 2000); 144 Cong. Rec. S 10877-01 at S10878 (Sept. 24, 1998), S12741-04 at S12750 (Oct 21, 1998) [statements of Senator Abraham]; 144 Cong. Rec. H8584 (Sept. 24, 1998), E2323-01 at E2324 (Nov 14, 1998) [statements of Rep. Smith].

Companies, who after Oct. 21, 1998, had been found to have willfully violated the attestation provisions in the past five years *or* employers who were considered "dependent employers" because they had a certain percentage of H-1B employees are required to file new attestation provisions with the DOL after Jan 19, 2001. A dependent employer is defined as an employer: (a) with 25 or fewer full time equivalent employees who employs more than 7 H-1Bs; (b) with at least 26 and not more than 50 full time equivalent employees and employs more than 12 H-1Bs; or (c) with at least 51 full time equivalent employees and employs a number of H-1Bs that is equal to at least 15% of the full time equivalent employees. 20 C.F.R. §655.736(a). If the employer is petitioning for a person who holds a master's degree or higher (or its equivalent) in a specialty related to the intended employment or the employee will receive wages (including cash bonuses and similar compensation but not benefits) at an annual rate of at least $60,000, its applications are exempt from the attestation requirements. 20 C.F.R. §655.737. In determining the "equivalency" for a master's degree, the employer cannot utilize work experience. 65 Fed. Reg. 80110 at 80137–38. In determining whether it is a "specialty related to the intended employment" DOL suggests the employer look to the Occupational Outlook Handbook and O*NET. 65 Fed. Reg. 80110 at 80138–39. The dependent employer must attest that the placement of the H-1B, either directly with the employer or indirectly with a contractor, did not and will not displace a U.S. worker in an essentially equivalent job between 90 days before until 90 days after the date of filing the visa petition. This includes U.S. employees of the employer as well as displacement of U.S. employees of another employer if the H-1B is placed at another employer's worksite. For this "secondary placement" of workers, displacement cannot occur within 90 days before and until 90 days after the placement of the workers at the secondary placement. INA §212(n)(2)(E). *Cyberworld Enterprise Technologies, Inc. d/b/a Tekstrom, Inc. v. Administrator, Wage and Hour Division,* 04-LCA-49 (May 24, 2006) [company violated §1182(n)(1)(F) by failing to make secondary displacement inquiries prior to placement]. The employer must also attest that he has taken good faith steps to recruit U.S. workers at a compensation level and under procedures consistent with industry wide standards and that he has offered the job to any U.S. worker who is qualified. 20 C.F.R. §655.739. The recruitment attestation is not required for H-1B nonimmigrants who qualify under the employment-based first preference. INA §212(n)(1)(G)(i). The employer's obligations arise whenever it seeks new H-1Bs or extensions of H-1Bs. 20 C.F.R. §655.736(g). The burden is upon the employer to determine whether it is H-1B dependent. The employer who believes they may be "borderline" dependent should generally follow a short-hand test, called a "snap-shot" test to determine whether or not it is dependent. 20 C.F.R. §655.736(c)(2). The AG will establish an arbitration procedure to review an employer's failure to offer a job to a qualified U.S. worker. An aggrieved job applicant may file a complaint. INA §212(n)(5).

(1) Defining An Employer for Dependent Status. INA §212(n)(3)(C)(ii). A "single employer" for purposes of determining dependent employer status is defined with reference to the Internal Revenue Code, 26 U.S.C. §414(b), (c), (m) and (o). 20 C.F.R. §§655.736(b). Where there is a change in corporate structure such as an acquisition, merger, "spin-off" or other such action, the new employing entity is not required to file new LCAs or H-1B petitions with respect to H-1Bs transferred to the new employer even where the Employer Identification Number (EIN) is changed. 20 C.F.R. §655.730(e).

(2) Defining Full Time Equivalent Employees (FTE). 20 C.F.R. §655.736(a)(2). FTE does not include bona fide consultants and independent contractors. 20 C.F.R. §655.736(a)(2)(i). An FTE is one who works 40 hours/week unless 35 hours would be considered bona fide full time. Part-time employees are aggregated to FTEs under a formula specified in the regulations. §655.736(a)(2)(ii)–(iv).

(3) Defining Essentially Equivalent Job. 20 C.F.R. §655.738(b)(2). To determine essential equivalency between the job of the laid off U.S. worker and the H-1B nonimmigrant DOL compares the following: (1) whether the job responsibilities were the same; (2) whether the qualifications and experience of the workers for the job were the same; and (3) whether the jobs were in the same area of employment. The "area of employment" is defined as "the area within normal commuting location where the work of the H-1B nonimmigrant is, or will be, performed. If such worksite or location is within a Metropolitan Statistical Area, any place within such area is deemed to be within the area of employment." §655.738(b)(2)(iii). DOL has suggested the EPA standards provide a useful source of standards for assessing the essential equivalence of jobs. 65 Fed. Reg. 80110–01 at 80145–46 (Dec. 20, 2000).

(4) Defining Employed by the Employer. The common law standard applies in determining whether a U.S. worker is employed by a dependent employer or employed at another employer's worksite where the H-1B worker is placed. DOL suggests that it will look to EEOC guidance to determine an individual's employment status while rejecting IRS criteria as a model. 65 Fed. Reg. 80141–42 (Dec. 20, 2000).

(5) Defining Displacement of U.S. Workers. The displacement of U.S. workers only arises where there is a layoff of a U.S. worker and not: (1) a valid termination for cause, (2) retirement, (3) voluntary departure from employment, or (4) expiration of a contract of employment of the U.S. worker. 20 C.F.R. §655.738(b)(1). Displacement also does not occur if the U.S. worker was first offered but refused a similar employment opportunity with the same employer. INA §212(n)(4)(D)(i)(II), 20 C.F.R. §655.738(b)(1)(iv).

(a) Documents Required Regarding Nondisplacement—20 C.F.R. §655.738(e). Employer is required to retain the following documents to meet the displacement requirements:

i) Direct displacement: (1) All employer records regarding circumstances that U.S. worker left; (2) employee's name, last-known mailing address, occupational title and job description; (3) documentation concerning the employee's experience and qualifications and principal assignments; (4) documents concerning the employee's departure such as notification of termination by employer and the employee's responses; (5) employee evaluations; and (6) terms of any offers by employer to employee of similar employment.

ii) Secondary displacement: (1) documentation showing the manner in which the employer satisfied its obligation to make inquiries as to the displacement of U.S. workers by the secondary employer;

(6) Defining Acceptable Recruitment Methods for U.S. Workers 20 C.F.R. §655.739(e). The employer's recruiting methods "shall be at a level and through methods and media which

are normal, common or prevailing in the industry, including those strategies that have been shown to be successfully used by employers in the industry to recruit U.S. workers." Can use active (direct communication) or passive (advertising) solicitation and external or internal company solicitation. §655.739(d).

3.k. Mexican TN Applicants—Mexicans desiring TN status are no longer required to obtain approved petitions or LCAs. 8 C.F.R. §214.6(d). And there is no longer a numerical cap of Mexican TNs. 69 Fed. Reg. 11287–90 (Mar. 10, 2004).

4. Payment of Transportation by Employer

4.a. If H-1B is dismissed before the end of the period for admission the employer is liable for "the reasonable costs of return transportation of the alien abroad." INA §214(c)(5)(A), 8 U.S.C. §1184(c)(5)(A), 8 C.F.R. §214.2(h)(4)(iii)(E). The enforcement of this provision is regarded as a private contractual matter. Letter, Simmons, Branch Chief, Business & Trade Service (HQ 70/6.2.8) (May 20, 1999), *reprinted in* 76 No. 28 *Interpreter Releases* 1125, 1140 (July 26, 1999). However, failure to comply with 20 C.F.R. §655.731(c)(7)(ii) which includes notifying USCIS of the termination *and* paying the employee's transportation home could result in the continued accrual of front and back pay because there is no *bona fide* termination until these steps are taken. *Matter of Rung,* 2004-LCA-006 (AAO Sept. 26, 2006) [where employer failed to notify USCIS of termination and failed to pay former employee's transportation costs home, the employment relationship did not result in a *bona fide* termination and the employer was required to pay front pay].

5. Procedure for H-1Bs: 8 C.F.R. §214.2(h)(2)

5.a. Employer or agent files petition on Form I-129. Agent must have contract and itinerary where appropriate. 8 C.F.R. §214.2(h)(2)(i)(F).

5.b. Fees to the DHS—The employer must pay three sets of fees to the government. First, they must pay the standard petition fees for the I-129 petition and if the employee is abroad the additional fees at the consulate. Second, the employer must pay a fee of $1,500 unless she is an employer with not more than 25 full-time equivalent employees and then she must only pay one-half the required fee which is now $750. INA §214(c)(9). Third, the employer is now required to pay to the government a $500 fraud prevention and detection fee. INA §214(c)(12). All fees are paid to the Department of Homeland Security. The fraud prevention fee must be paid in a separate check but other fees can be bundled. The $1,500 fee is paid *one* time to initially grant the H-1B, to extend the stay of an H-1B (if not paid at a prior extension) *or* to change status to an H-1B. A primary or secondary education institution, an institution of higher education, as defined in section 20 U.S.C. §1001(a), a nonprofit entity related to or affiliated with any such institution, a nonprofit entity which engages in established curriculum-related clinical training of students registered at any such institution, a nonprofit research organization or a governmental research organization are exempt from the fee. INA §214(c)(9)(A); 8 C.F.R. §214.2(h)(19)(iii)-(iv). The fraud fee must be paid one time but is limited to initial applications or to invoke portability to switch employers. Nonprofits are *not* exempt. INA §214(c)(12)(A). Neither fee applies to spouses or dependent children.

5.c. Petitions Filed with VSC/CSC—Depending on the geographic location where the H-1B services will be performed, the H-1B petition is filed with VSC or CSC. *See* Instructions on Form I-129. For certain H-1B petitioners claiming an exemption from the cap, the petitions are filed with the CSC. *See* USCIS Update (Jan. 30, 2008), *posted on* AILA InfoNet at Doc. No. 08021272. Those petitioners claiming exemption because they are institutions of higher education, or related or affiliated nonprofit entities, nonprofit research organizations, or governmental research organizations file with CSC. Petitions for individuals who are cap-exempt, *e.g.*, certain physicians serving in shortage areas and petitions for those already counted are filed according to normal filing rules. *Id.*

5.d. If new employer, must file new petition (I-129). Requests for extensions or change of status are included directly on I-129 and separate application is not filed. But I-539 must be filed for accompanying family members.

5.e. Proof that LCA has been certified must be submitted. *See, e.g.*, SOPs on I-129/H-1B, *published on* AILA InfoNet at Doc. No. 07072668.

5.f. Petition validity will be recorded as of date of work not date of approval if submitted before work begins. Memo, Norton (Mar. 2, 1988), *reprinted in* 7 *AILA Monthly Mailing* 153 (Apr., 1988). Petition may be submitted up to 6 months before work begins. 8 C.F.R. §214.2(h)(9)(i)(B).

5.g. Documentation—8 C.F.R. §214.2(h)(4)(iv).

(1) Degrees; evidence of experience; written contracts. Sometimes need educational evaluation of person whose credentials were obtained abroad or evaluation of experience and education; affidavits of experts; translations.

(2) Evaluations. *See in this section* ¶ 2.h(3) (p.685), *supra.*

(3) License, temporary license, or without any license where person authorized to fully perform work under state law. Memo, Puleo, Asst. Comm., Adjudications, CO 214h-P (Dec. 3, 1987), *reprinted in* 64 No. 46 *Interpreter Releases* 1338 (Dec. 7, 1987). 8 C.F.R. §214.2(h)(4)(v). Can only receive approval for the period of temporary licensure. 8 C.F.R. §214.2(h)(4)(v)(E). Where lack of license is solely due to inability to obtain Social Security card which H-1B may not obtain because s/he is not in employment authorized, an H-1B petition may be approved if s/he provides evidence from state licensing board that the lack of an SS card is the only obstacle to licensure. Memo, Cook, Act. Asst. Comm. Adjudications, HX 70/6.2.8 (Nov. 20, 2001), *reprinted in* 78 No. 46 *Interpreter Releases* 1825, 1839–40 (Dec 3, 2001). Where the state or local authority requires proof of lawful employment *before* granting the license and the license is required to practice the profession, USCIS will grant a one-year H-1B approval to allow the beneficiary to obtain the license. In order to issue the "one-year H-1B" the adjudicator must determine: (1) the beneficiary has filed an application in accordance with state or local rules and procedures; (2) the beneficiary is fully qualified to receive the state or local license but for proof of lawful employment; and (3) the beneficiary is otherwise qualified to receive the H-1B. Approval of the H-1B does not mean that the beneficiary has approval to engage in employment without the appropriate license. A request for an extension of the one year will be denied where the beneficiary cannot establish she has obtained the license. Memo, Neufeld, Deputy Assoc. Dir. Domestic Operations, USCIS, HQ 70/6.2.8 (Mar. 21, 2008), *published on* AILA InfoNet at Doc. No. 08032432; AFM at 31.3(d)(3).

(4) Photocopies may be submitted. 8 C.F.R. §214.2(h)(2)(i)(A).

(5) H-1B (unlike I-140) need not provide proof of ability to pay salary. Memo, Examinations (Nov. 13, 1995), *supra.*

5.h. Changes in employment—INA §214(c)(10); 8 C.F.R. §214.2(h)(2)(i)(D); 20 C.F.R. §655.730(e)

(1) Successor Companies, No New Petition—An amended H-1B petition shall not be required where the petitioning employer is involved in a corporate restructuring, including but not limited to a merger, acquisition, or consolidation, where a new corporate entity succeeds to the interests and obligations of the original petitioning employer and where the terms and conditions of employment remain the same but for the identity of the petitioner. INA §214(c)(10), 8 U.S.C. §1184(c)(10). Where an employer corporation changes its corporate structure as the result of an acquisition, merger, "spin-off" or other such action, the new employing entity is not required to file a new LCA and H-1B petition with respect to transferred employees even if there is a change in the EIN provided the new employing entity assumes all LCA and immigration related obligations and liabilities and maintains certain documentation in its public access file. 20 C.F.R. §655.730(e). Where successor corporation assumes petitioning company's posture, it is not required to file new petition (although with L-1 it would). Letter, Hernandez, Acting Director, Business and Trade Services, HQ 70/6/2/8 (Feb. 4, 2000), *reprinted in* 77 No. 11 *Interpreter Releases* 585, 590–91 (May 1, 2000); Letter, Weinig, Deputy Asst. Comm., Adjudications (June 2, 1988), *reprinted in* 65 No. 28 *Interpreter Releases* 735, 751–52 (July 25, 1988). New H-1Bs also do not have to be filed where one company purchases several others and consolidates them under one of the purchased companies, where there would be no material change in working conditions. Letter, Brown,

Acting Chief, Business and Trade Services Branch, Benefits Division, INS, HQ 70/6.2.8 (Dec. 17, 1996), *reprinted in* 74 No. 4 *Interpreter Releases* 188, 205–07 (Jan. 27, 1997). Even if the new employer does not comply with the LCA requirements of maintaining a sworn statement assuming liability for the existing LCA employees and therefore violates §655.730(e)(1), DHS does not require a new H-1B petition if it is simply a corporate merger or reorganization that does not affect employment. Letter, Hernandez, Director, Business and Trade Services, HQ 70/6.2.8 (June 7, 2001), *published on* AILA InfoNet at Doc. No. 01062832. However, a new LCA must be filed if the new entity hires new employees or when it seeks extensions for the transferred employees, 20 C.F.R. §655.730(e)(iv)(C)(2).

(a) Returning at Port of Entry—When there is a successor employer and H-1B returning at port of entry, s/he should present a letter stating that the new corporate entity has succeeded the previous employer and that the terms and conditions of employment remain the same. Memo, Cronin, Acting Ex. Assoc. Comm. Program, HQPGM 70/6.2.8 (June 19, 2001) at ¶III B 1, *reprinted in* 78 No. 25 *Interpreter Releases* 1069, 1108–17 (July 2, 2001).

(2) Minor Changes, No New Petition—A new or amended petition is *also not* needed when: (1) employer changes its name; or (2) employer changes ownership/ a successor-in-interest, unless a new LCA must be filed. Letter, Hernandez, Acting Director, Business and Trade Services, HQ 70/6/2/8 (Feb. 4, 2000), *reprinted in* 77 No. 17 *Interpreter Releases* 585, 590–91 (May 1, 2000); Memo, Aleinikoff, Exec. Assoc. Comm., HQ 70/6.2.8-P (Aug. 22, 1996), *reprinted in* 73 No. 35 *Interpreter Releases* 1222, 1231–32 (Sept. 16, 1996); Memo, Hogan, Exec. Assoc. Comm., Operations, CO 214h-C (Oct. 22, 1992), *reprinted in* 69 No. 43 *Interpreter Releases* 1439, 1448–49 (Nov. 9, 1992); or (3) the employee's place of employment is changed and a new LCA is filed. A new or amended petition is *not* required simply on the basis of an employee's geographic move "[a]s long as the LCA has been filed and certified for the new employment location, the appropriate worksite posting has taken place, and other wage and hour obligations are met..." Letter, Hernandez, Director, Business and Trade Branch, USCIS (Oct. 23, 2003), *published on* AILA InfoNet at Doc. No. 03112118. Minor changes in job duties or salary increase do not require a new petition, only material changes do. If an amended petition is filed it must be accompanied by an LCA. A promotion to a higher position within the same occupation would not normally require filing an amended petition provided applicant utilizes same academic training. Letter, LaFleur, Chief, NIV Branch, Adjudications, HQ 214h-C (Oct. 12, 1995), *reprinted in* 72 No. 45 *Interpreter Releases* 1578, 1599–1601 (Nov. 20, 1995).

(3) Substantial Changes, New Petition Required—A new or amended petition, however, must be filed where: (1) the location of employment is changed and is outside the area of employment specified on the LCA, but no new LCA has been filed (2) there is a change in the person's duties from one specialty occupation to another; (3) there is a material change in the terms and conditions of employment; or (4) a new LCA must be filed pursuant to DOL regulations. By regulation, DHS requires a petitioner to "immediately notify the Service of any changes in the terms and conditions of employment of a beneficiary which may affect eligibility" under the H category. 8 C.F.R. §214.2(h)(11)(i)(A).

(4) Termination of Employment—Leave under the Family and Medical Leave Act does not terminate the H-1B relationship with the employer. Letter, Hernandez, Acting Director, Business and Trade Service (HQ 70/6.2.8) (Feb. 2, 2000), *reprinted in* 77 No. 8 *Interpreter Releases* 243, 252 (Feb.28, 2000). Unpaid leave may also be permitted. *Incalza v. Fendi North America, Inc.*, 479 F.3d 1005 (9th Cir. 2006) [where E-1 Italian national was fired after company changed from Italian to French ownership, employee's award of damages for wrongful termination under California law was upheld because company could have requested H-1B status or placed him on temporary unpaid leave until he married a USC instead of terminating him]. If the petitioner no longer employs the beneficiary, the petitioner "shall" send a letter explaining the change to the director who approved the petition. 8 C.F.R. §214.2(h)(11)(i)(A). Failure to comply with this requirement and the requirement to pay the former employee's transportation costs home means that the employment relationship has not been terminated and the employer will still be

liable for back and front pay. *See Matter of Rung,* 2004-LCA-006 (AAO Sept. 26, 2006); 20 C.F.R. §655.731(c)(7)(ii).

(5) Portability—Employment upon *filing* petition. A person in H-1B status may commence new employment upon the *filing* of a new petition by the prospective employer if: (1) s/he was lawfully admitted; (2) the new petition is "nonfrivolous"; (3) the new petition was filed before the date of expiration of the period of stay authorized by the AG of the H-1B beneficiary; and (4) subsequent to such lawful admission the H-1B beneficiary has not been employed without authorization before the filing of such petition. INA §§214(n)(1), (2)(A)–(C). Filing is defined at 8 C.F.R. §103.2(a)(7)(i) as physically received by USCIS. The Service has determined that a "nonfrivolous" petition is one that "is not without basis in law or fact." Memo, Pearson, Ex. Assoc. Comm. HQOPS 70/20 (Jan 29, 2001), *reprinted in* 78 No. 7 *Interpreter Releases* 365, 381–83 (Feb. 12, 2001). In order to be admitted at the border under the portability provisions an applicant must meet the following requirements: (1) S/he must otherwise be admissible; (2) S/he must be in possession of a valid unexpired passport and visa, unless exempt under 8 C.F.R. §212.1; (3) S/he must establish that she was previously admitted in H-1B status by presenting the I-94 or I-797; and (4) S/he must present the filing receipt Form I-797 for the new H-1B or other evidence of timely filing prior to expiration of previous H-1B. If the H-1B is not in possession of I-797 and a CLAIMS inquiry shows no evidence of the new petition being filed or if the original petition has expired and there is no evidence of the approval of a new one, the person may not be admitted in H-1B status. Memo, Pearson, supra; Memo, Cronin, Acting Ex. Assoc. Comm. Program, HQPGM 70/6.2.8 (June 19, 2001) at ¶II D, *reprinted in* 78 No. 25 *Interpreter Releases* 1069, 1108–17 (July 2, 2001).

(6) Where beneficiary switches employers and obtains a longer date on the petition and extension of stay filed by the second employer, his stay will be governed by the longer date. This is true if the employee was admitted into the U.S. under the first petition while the extension of stay was still pending. Letter, Simmons, Branch Chief, Business and Trade Services (HQ 70/6.2.8) (Oct. 20, 1999), *reprinted in* 76 No. 46 *Interpreter Releases* 1723, 1745 (Dec. 3, 1999).

(7) If an amended petition is filed it must be accompanied by a new LCA. However, where an LCA exists at another worksite, transfer to that worksite does not require an amended petition. Letter, Russell, Acting Branch Chief of Business and Trade Services Branch, Benefits Division, INS, HQ 70/6.2.8 (Mar. 12, 1997), *reprinted in* 74 No. 22 *Interpreter Releases* 934, 950–52 (June 9, 1997). Letter, Simmons, Branch Chief, Benefits & Trades Section (HQ 70/6.2.8) (Nov. 12, 1998), *reprinted in* 75 No. 48 *Interpreter Releases* 1740, 1750–51 (Dec. 21, 1998) [if H-1B approved for site A and person is then transferred to site B and there are LCAs for both sites an amended H-1B petition is not necessary. However, if the person never worked at site A then a *new* (not simply amended) petition must be filed to work at site B]. "As long as the LCA has been filed and certified for the new employment location, the appropriate worksite posting has taken place, and other wage and hour obligations are met, no amended petition would be required regardless of when the LCA was filed and certified, as long as the certification took place before the employee was moved." Letter, Hernandez, Director, Business and Trade Branch, USCIS (Oct. 23, 2003), *published on* AILA InfoNet at Doc. No. 03112118.

(8) Short Term Placement—20 C.F.R. §655.735(c). An H-1B in the U.S. under an LCA may be sent to a new worksite which is not covered by an LCA in the occupation but only up to a maximum of 30 days each year and up to 60 days each year if the H-1B spends substantial time at a permanent worksite, if s/he continues to maintain an office or work station at the permanent worksite and if her U.S. residence or place of abode is located in the area of the permanent worksite.

(9) Multiple Employers. H-1B can work (part-time or full-time) for more than one employer, but each must file a petition. Letter, Bednarz, Chief, NIV Adjudications, CO 214h-C (June 29, 1994), *reprinted in* 71 No. 27 *Interpreter Releases* 936, 952 (July 18, 1994); Letter, Gorsky, Acting Chief Advisory Opinions Division, DOS (Apr. 13, 1998), *reprinted in* 75 No. 17 *Interpreter Releases* 631, 648 (May 4, 1998). When H-1B switches to a second

company for several months and returns to initial company, the second company needs to file an H-1B but the first company need not file a petition upon the H-1B's return as the first petition remains valid. Letter, LaFleur, Chief, Business and Trade Branch, Benefits Division, INS, HQ 70/6.2.8 (Apr. 29, 1996), *reprinted in* 73 No. 22 *Interpreter Releases* 764, 774–75 (June 3, 1996); Letter, Hernandez, Director, Business and Trade Services, INS (Apr. 24, 2002), *published on* AILA InfoNet at Doc. No. 02051432. There is no set number of hours that beneficiary must work for each employer. Letter, Brown, Acting Chief, Business and Trade Services, Benefits Division, INS, HQ 70/ 6.2.8 (July 18, 1997), *reprinted in* 74 No. 30 *Interpreter Releases* 1219, 1232–33 (Aug. 11, 1997).

(10) Extension of stay to work for same employer, if timely filed, continues employment for 240 days beyond expiration of the I-94 while decision pending. 8 C.F.R. §274a.12(b)(20).

(11) Reduction in Force (RIF) as termination. If company has RIF policy but gives H-1B employee several months severance after RIF, the H-1B ceases status from the day he stops employment not the day his severance ends. Letter, Simmons, Branch Chief, Business and Trade Branch (HQ 70/6.2.8, HQ 70/6.2.12), *reprinted in* 76 No. 9 *Interpreter Releases* 378, 385–87 (Mar. 8, 1999).

(12) Employer Where Person Referred

(a) Who is the employer when an agency hires the employee and refers her to the ultimate employer? At least one court has found that the employer for purposes of determining H-1B status is the ultimate employer not the agency. *Defensor v. Meissner,* 201 F.3d 384 (5th Cir. 2000) [affirmed INS's denial of H-1Bs to nurses with bachelor degrees because the hospitals where they would work did not require B.N.S. degrees even if the employment agency that hired them did].

(b) Professional Employer Organizations (PEO). Where employer hires a PEO to handle its administrative matters in regard to its employees such as payroll and health insurance but the employer still retains control over the day-to-day activities of the H-1B, the employer can petition (and would be responsible) for the H-1B because it would still be considered the U.S. employer as defined under 8 C.F.R. §214.2(h)(4)(ii). Letter, Hernandez, Director, Business and Trade Services, INS, HQ 70/ 6.2.8 (Dec. 20, 2000), *reprinted in* 78 No. 27 *Interpreter Releases* 1172, 1191–94 (July 16, 2001). A PEO could file for an H-1B if it met the definition of a U.S. employer under the regulations and was not simply a record keeper or accountant. *Id.*

(13) Revocation—8 C.F.R. §214.2(h)(11)—Automatic if petitioner dies, goes out of business or withdraws petition.

5.i. By notice—May revoke if: (a) beneficiary is no longer employed in same capacity; (b) petitioner violated the terms of the approved petition, and (c) where statements in original petition incorrect. Petitioner may rebut evidence presented by Director.

5.j. Appeal

(1) No appeal from automatic revocation.

(2) Appeal from Notice of Denial to Associate Commissioner.

6. Admission and Extension for H-1B—8 C.F.R. §§214.2(h)(9), (13), (15).

6.a. Petition approval for up to 3 years on I-797. However, in a specialty occupation it may not exceed the period of validity of the LCA, 8 C.F.R. §214.2(h)(9)(iii)(A)(1), and in a DOD project it may be up to 5 years. USCIS officers should not be arbitrarily limiting approvals to time period left on professional license when such license, *e.g.,* teaching, is renewable. Letter, Brown, Acting Chief, NIV Branch, Adjudications, CO 214h-C (July 14, 1995), *reprinted in* 72 No. 31 *Interpreter Releases* 1093, 1109–10 (Aug. 14, 1995).

6.b. Admission is for maximum (including extensions) of 6 years—8 C.F.R. §214.2(h)(13)(iii). *Nair v. Coultice,* 162 F.Supp.2d 1209 (S.D. Cal. 2001) [reversed INS's recent interpretation and found that time abroad was not part of the 6 years]. The 6-year limit applies to spouses and dependents in H-4 status. 8 C.F.R. §214.2(h)(9)(iv). However, a person in H-4 or L-2 status is free to change his status to an H-1B or L-1 because the time spent in H-4 or L-2 status is not counted toward the six year maximum on H-1Bs or 5/7 years on L-1s. Memo, Aytes, Assoc. Dir., Domestic Operations, USCIS, HQPRD 70/6.2.8, 70/6.2.12, AD 06-29 (Dec. 5, 2006), *published on* AILA InfoNet at Doc. No. 06122063 (Dec. 20, 2006) [recognizing that H-1B and H-4 after 6 years can switch positions with each obtaining a new 6 years]; AFM §31.2(d)(2).The 6-year limitation does not apply to an alien who resides less than 6 mos./yr in U.S., or who is a seasonal or intermittent employee. 8 C.F.R. §214.2(h)(13)(v). Periods where alien unemployed in U.S. or failed to maintain status would be counted toward the 6-year limitation. Memo, Puleo, Asst. Comm. (Apr. 17, 1989), *reprinted in* 66 No. 16 *Interpreter Releases* 455, 471–72 (Apr. 24, 1989). All time spent out of the U.S. is subtracted and does not count toward the six year period and therefore time out of the U.S. may be added back/recaptured to the six year period. *Matter of IT Ascent*, EAC 04 047 53189 (AAO Sept. 2, 2005) [time working abroad is not counted] *published on* AILA InfoNet at Doc. No. 05102760; *Nair v. Coultice supra*, [finding that all time out of U.S. is not considered]; Memo, Aytes, Acting Assoc. Dir. Operations, HQPRD 70/6.2.8, 70/6.2.12, AD 05-21 (Oct. 21, 2005), *published on* AILA InfoNet at Doc. No. 05110363 [finding that any days spent outside U.S. will not be counted toward maximum period provided beneficiary is able to submit independent documentary evidence]; AFM at 31.3(g)(9) [evidentiary standards to recapture time]. Cannot generally exceed 6 years by changing from H to L (although a 7th year from H to L-1A is possible). Cannot exceed 6 years by changing from L to H and cannot extend 6-year rule by changing employers at end of the 5th year. *Id.*; *Matter of Safetran*, 20 I&N Dec. 49 (Comm. 1989). Time spent in L status counted toward the 6-year period for H. LOS-N-83573 (WRSC May 19, 1988), EAC 88-053 0121 (NYC June 21, 1988), *reported in* 7 *AILA Monthly Mailing* 497 (Oct. 1988). There is an issue, however, as to whether the "time spent" waiting for the approval of the grant of a c/s from the DHS from L-1 to H-1B status can be deducted from the 6-year limitation.

If a person remains outside of the U.S. for one year, s/he may begin the 6 year period anew. However, the new six year period would be subject to the numerical cap on H-1Bs. Thus, a person, for example, who has an H-1B for 5 years and then departs for one year may not wish to begin a new six year period. Rather, s/he may wish to recapture the final year of the first six years thereby avoiding the numerical cap on H-1Bs. USCIS now explicitly permits this alternative. Memo, Aytes, Assoc. Dir., Domestic Operations, USCIS, HQPRD 70/6.2.8, 70/6.2.12, AD 06-29 (Dec. 5, 2006) at pp. 4-5, *published on* AILA InfoNet at Doc. No. 06122063 (Dec. 20, 2006) [recognizing that person seeking readmission as H-1B who has been outside of the U.S. for one year may choose to use the "remainder" of her six years and avoid a new numerical cap]; AFM §31.1(g)(14).

Admission will be for the validity period of the petition, plus a period of up to 10 days before the period runs and 10 days after expiration. 8 C.F.R. §214.2(h)(13)(i)(A). The 10-day period however does not apply to an H-1B who is terminated. There is no "grace period" for a terminated employee. Letter, Hernandez, Director, Business and Trade Services Branch, Off. of Adjudications (Mar. 27, 2001), *reprinted in* 78 No. 13 *Interpreter Releases* 608, 616–18 (Apr. 2, 2001). It is also DHS policy that an H-1B should not enter the U.S. more than 10 days prior to the start of his authorized employment and therefore visas should not be issued more than 10 days before the beginning of employment unless the issuance is from a high volume post in anticipation of the fiscal year (Oct 1st) rush. Cable, DOS, 04-State-74313 (Apr. 2, 2004), *published on* AILA InfoNet at Doc. No. 04040862.

6.c. Extensions Beyond 6 Years

(1) Section 106(a) Extension—An H-1B may extend his or her status beyond the 6-year limitation if a labor certification, an I-140 or employment-based adjustment application has been filed at least 365 days prior to the expiration of his current period of H-1B status. H-1B status shall be extended in one-year increments. *See* AC21, PL 106-313 §106(a); AFM at 31.1(b), 31.2(d) and 31.3; Memo, Cronin, Acting Ex. Assoc. Comm. Program, HQPGM 70/6.2.8 (June 19, 2001) at ¶II E, *reprinted in* 78 No. 25 *Interpreter Releases* 1069, 1108–17 (July 2, 2001); 21st Century Department of Justice Appropriations Authorization Act, PL 107-273, §11030A (Nov. 2, 2002); Memo, Yates, Acting Assoc. Dir. Operations,

USCIS (Apr. 24, 2003), *published on* AILA InfoNet at Doc. No. 03050145 (May 1, 2003). The H-1B extension in one-year increments also applies to the filing of an I-360 religious worker petition that is pending more than 365 days. Letter, Hernandez, Director, Business and Trade Branch, BUSCIS, HQADN 70/21 (June 6, 2003), *reprinted in* 80 No 26 *Interpreter Releases* 902, 927–28 (July 7, 2003). An extension may be given for more than one year only when there is time remaining on the first 6-year period. AFM at 31.3(g)(8) Note.

(2) The LC and I-140 may be from prior employer, Letter, Hernandez, Dir., Business & Trade Servs., HQ70/9.1 (Apr. 24, 2002), *published on* AILA InfoNet at Doc. No. 02050231 (May 2, 2002), as there is no requirement that they must be from the same employer to obtain the extension. Memo, Yates, Assoc. Dir. Operations, USCIS, HQOPRD 70/6.2.8-P (May 12, 2005) at p. 9, *published on* AILA InfoNet at Doc. No. 05051810 (May 18, 2005). USCIS will also not deny an extension where the LC was filed more than 365 days, has now been approved, but the I-140/I-485 has not been filed. Memo, Yates (May 12, 2005) at p.9. An extension may be granted even if the I-140 petition has been denied if the denial is on appeal. *Id.* Similarly, an extension may be granted if an LC is denied if the LC is within the 30 days for appeal to BALCA or on appeal to BALCA. AFM at 33.3(g)(8) [the LC will still be considered "pending" while the denial of such certification may be appealed or while the appeal is actually pending]. Where an LC is re-filed under PERM, the filing date of the original ETA-750 will be used: (1) where the DOL allows the original filing date to be maintained by noting it in Section "O" of the ETA 9089 or (2) where DOL does not permit the original filing date to be used but the petitioner can demonstrate that the elements relating to the job opportunity and the alien beneficiary on the new LC are not "materially different" from those specified on the ETA-750. AFM at 33.3(g)(8). The request for extension may be filed before the 365 days are reached as long as the 365 days will be reached prior to the H-1B's requested start date. If there is a gap, however, the extension of stay cannot be granted. Memo, Yates, Assoc. Dir. Operations, USCIS, HQOPRD 70/6.2.8-P (May 12, 2005) at p. 8, *published on* AILA InfoNet at Doc. No. 05051810; Cable, 01-State-102000 (June 11, 2001), *reprinted in* 78 No. 24 *Interpreter Releases* 1042–43 (June 18, 2001).

(3) Section 104(c) Extension—An H-1B may also be extended beyond the 6-year period for any person who is the beneficiary of a first, second, or third employment-based petition but due to per country limitations is unable to file for or obtain his or her immigrant visa. AC21 §104(c). However, the person must have an *approved* I-140 petition to qualify. An extension may be granted more than one time for periods of up to three years at a time. Memo, Yates, Assoc. Dir. Operations, USCIS, HQOPRD 70/6.2.8-P (May 12, 2005) at pp. 10-11, *published on* AILA InfoNet at Doc. No. 05051810.

(4) Extensions for Spouse/Children—H-1B extensions beyond 6 years are also given to H-4 family members and a person who is an H-1B for the maximum period may c/s to H-4 and remain in the U.S. based on the principal's status. Memo, Yates, Acting Assoc. Director, USCIS, HQBCIA 70/6.2.8-P (Apr. 24, 2003) at B, *published on* AILA InfoNet at Doc. No. 03050145 (May 1, 2003); Memo, Yates, Assoc. Dir. Operations, USCIS, HQOPRD 70/6.2.8-P (May 12, 2005) at p. 10, *published on* AILA InfoNet at Doc. No. 05051810. However, a person in H-4 or L-2 status is free to change his status to an H-1B or L-1 because the time spent in H-4 or L-2 status is not counted toward the six year maximum on H-1Bs or 5/7 years on L-1s. Memo, Aytes, Assoc. Dir., Domestic Operations, USCIS, HQPRD 70/6.2.8, 70/6.2.12, AD 06-29 (Dec. 5, 2006), *published on* AILA InfoNet at Doc. No. 06122063 (Dec. 20, 2006) [recognizing that H-1B and H-4 after 6 years can switch positions with each obtaining a new 6 years]; AFM §31.2(d)(2).

The H-1B may obtain extensions in one-year increments until: (1) the LC is finally denied or if LC is approved until the EB petition is denied; (2) the EB immigrant petition is denied where no LC was filed; or (3) the grant or denial of the IV or AOS. Memo, Yates, Acting Assoc. Director, BUSCIS, HQBCIA 70/6.2.8-P (Apr. 23, 2003) at B, *published on* AILA InfoNet at Doc. No. 03050145 (May 1, 2003); Memo, Cronin, Acting Ex. Assoc. Comm. Program, HQPGM 70/6.2.8 (June 19, 2001) at ¶II C 1, *published on* AILA InfoNet at Doc. No. 01062031. The extension may be filed by the H-1B's current employer or a new employer.

Memo, Yates, Acting Assoc. Director, BUSCIS, HQBCIA 70/6.2.8-P (Apr. 23, 2003) at D, *published on* AILA InfoNet at Doc. No. 03050145.

To qualify for the extension the person "need not be in H-1B status in order to benefit from sections 106 and 104(c) of AC21. The alien may obtain such additional periods of H-1B admission through a petition to change status from another nonimmigrant classification, or through H-1B visa issuance at a U.S. consulate (unless visa exempt) and admission from abroad." Memo, Aytes, Assoc. Dir., Domestic Operations, USCIS, HQPRD 70/6.2.8, 70/6.2.12, AD 06-29 (Dec. 5, 2006) at pp. 3-4, *published on* AILA InfoNet at Doc. No. 06122063 (Dec. 20, 2006) [recognizing that H-1B and H-4 after 6 years can switch positions with each obtaining a new 6 years]; AFM §31.2(d)(5).

6.d. Extensions of visa petition *and extension of stay* all filed on an I-129. 8 C.F.R. §§214.2(h)(14), (15). A request for a petition extension cannot be filed if stay expired. The request for an extension must be accompanied by the new LCA. A person must be in the U.S. when an extension is filed, but may travel abroad while an extension is pending. Approval via cable will be sent to the appropriate consular post upon petitioner's request. 8 C.F.R. §214.2(h)(15)(i). Extensions are given up to a total period of 6 years unless one of the circumstances mentioned above applies. Extensions are authorized for a period of up to 3 years at any one time. If extensions are permitted beyond the 6-year period they are given in one-year increments, except that AC 21 §104(c) extensions are given in 3-year increments. Extensions are not counted in the numerical cap on H-1Bs. A denial of an extension may not be subject to judicial review. *CDI Information Services, Inc. v. Reno,* 278 F.3d 616 (6th Cir. 2002) [no jurisdiction under INA §242(a)(2)(B)(ii) to review a denial of an H-1B extension]; *But see Evangelical Lutheran Church in America v. INS,* 288 F.Supp.2d 32, 40–45 (D.D.C. 2003) *appeal dismissed* 2004 WL 434067 (D.C. Cir. Mar. 3, 2004) [rejected the discretionary decision bar, INA §242(g) bar, and committed to agency discretion bar in reviewing the denial of an untimely filed H-1B extension and reversed former INS decision].

6.e. Filing During Pendency of LPR Applications—An H–1B may apply for an extension of status (including dependents), a new H-1B petition, or a change of status to another L category even if s/he has filed an application for or received an approval of a LC, an IV petition or filed an AOS application. 8 C.F.R. §214.2(h)(16)(i). But cannot change to another H category if LC is approved or I-140 has been filed. 8 C.F.R. §214.2(h)(16)(ii). In addition, if H-1B with pending AOS applies for an EAD based on the AOS and then works for another employer, her H-1B status is violated. AFM at 30.1, App. 23.4, 31–2a. AC21 changes that for those H-1Bs whose AOS applications are pending more than 180 days, assuming they follow the requirements of INA §204(j).

6.f. Attending Classes—There is nothing in the INA or the regulations that prohibits an H-1B from attending classes as long as the studies are incidental to H-1B status. Letter, Bednarz, Chief, NIV Branch, Adjudications, CO 214h-C (Jan. 5, 1995), *reprinted in* 72 No. 6 *Interpreter Releases* 211, 227 (Feb. 6, 1995).

7. Family Members—Immediate family (spouse and children) accompanying H-1B (or H-2A & -2B or H-3) will be granted an H-4 visa. The 6-year limit on admission and extensions for an H-1 applies to spouses and dependents in H-4 status. 8 C.F.R. §214.2(h)(9)(iv), but H-4s will get the benefit of any extension the H-1B can obtain beyond the six years where an LC, I-140 or I-360 was filed at least 365 days before the end of the 6th year. AC21 §106 permits extensions till AOS or IV applications are approved. However, a person in H-4 or L-2 status is free to change his status to an H-1B or L-1 because the time spent in H-4 or L-2 status is not counted toward the six year maximum on H-1Bs or 5/7 years on L-1s. Memo, Aytes, Assoc. Dir., Domestic Operations, USCIS, HQPRD 70/6.2.8, 70/6.2.12, AD 06-29 (Dec. 5, 2006), *published on* AILA InfoNet at Doc. No. 06122063 (Dec. 20, 2006) [recognizing that H-1B and H-4 after 6 years can switch positions with each obtaining a new 6 years]; AFM §31.2(d)(2). An H-4 is not necessary and a child or spouse can accompany or follow to join the beneficiary with a B-2 if it is inconvenient or impossible to apply for H-4. 9 FAM 41.53 N. 18.4. An H-4 in status need not file an extension when the principal H-1B changes employment. Letter, LaFleur, HQ 70/6.2.8-C (Dec. 28, 1995), *reprinted in* 73 No. 3 *Interpreter Releases* 78, 95 (Jan. 16, 1996). Servants accompanying family may enter on B-1s. 9 FAM 41.53 N.16. Spouses battered or subjected to extreme cruelty are eligible for work authorization, INA §106, to be filed with the Vermont Service Center unit that adjudicates VAWA self-petitions, U and T visas.

8. Travel and Employment Authorization, While Adjustment Application is Pending—If an H-1 is not under exclusion, deportation, and removal proceedings and is in valid H-1 status, s/he may travel while her AOS application is pending without an advance parole if she: (1) is coming to resume employment with the same employer her H-1 is authorized for and (2) is in possession of a valid H visa. The former requirement that she also have in her possession the AOS receipt has been removed. 72 Fed. Reg. 61791 (Nov. 1, 2007). Dependent family members in lawful H-4 status may also travel during the AOS if the same conditions for the H-1 principal exist. 8 C.F.R. §§245.2(a)(4)(ii)(C), 1245.2(a)(4)(ii)(C). However, if s/he travels and re-enters on an advance parole and she has a valid and approved H-1B petition, she may apply for an extension of her status and DHS will terminate her parole and admit her as an H-1B. *Adjudicator's Field Manual,* Appendix 23-4, Memo, Cronin, Acting Assoc. Comm., Office of Programs HQADJ 70/2.8.6, 2.8.12, 10.18 (May 16, 2000), *Published on* AILA InfoNet at Doc. No. 00051801. The employer may also apply for a new H-1B or the employee with a valid H-1B visa may depart and re-enter as an H-1B. AFM, Appendix 23-4. Even if the employee re-enters on an advance parole and continues her H-1B employment she will not be considered to engage in unauthorized employment. *Id.*

D. *Fashion Models*—8 C.F.R. §214.2(h)(4)(ii)

1. Standard—Fashion models are retained under the H-1B category if they can demonstrate they are of distinguished merit and ability. The applicable standard requires the model to show that s/he is prominent in his or her field and that the position requires prominence. Prominence means a "high level of achievement as evidenced by a degree of skill and recognition substantially above that ordinarily encountered ... The person must be renowned, leading or well known." *See Matter of Shaw*, 11 I&N Dec. 277 (DD 1965). This category does not include support occupations such as hair stylists and make-up artists who may apply through O-1 or H-2B categories. 59 Fed. Reg. 41818 (Aug. 15, 1994).

2. Criteria—8 C.F.R. §214.2(h)(4)(vii):

   2.a. Petitioner's Requirements:

   (1) Copies of written contract or summary of the terms of the oral agreement;

   (2) Services are to be performed for a distinguished event or production or for an organization that has a distinguished reputation or record of employing prominent persons.

   2.b. Beneficiary's Requirements—Documentation of any *two* of the following

   (1) Achieved national or international recognition evidenced by critical reviews, articles, news stories;

   (2) Performing for employers that have a distinguished reputation;

   (3) Experts' or critics' recognition;

   (4) Commands high salary in relation to others.

3. Fashion Models Under O-1 Category—Fashion models may also qualify under O-1 as extraordinary persons in business but not in the arts. *Matter of Ford Models, Inc.*, EAC 9217150797 (AAU Oct. 16, 1992), *discussed in* 70 No. 6 *Interpreter Releases* 180–81 (Feb. 8, 1993).

E. *Defense Department Visas for Cooperative Research, Development, and Co-production*—IMMACT90 §222. NIV coming to U.S. on basis of reciprocity to perform services of an exceptional nature requiring exceptional merit and ability in a research, development, and/or co-production project provided under a government-to-government agreement administered by the Secretary of Defense.

   1.a. Procedures—Visa is for maximum of 10 years. Extensions will be granted in 2-year increments.

   (1) Only 100 such visas/status permitted at any one time.

   (2) Persons will be processed under the H-1B category. Petitions/extensions should be accompanied by letter from DOD Project Manager. Letter must describe the applicant's duties but details about the project are not required. Must also show person has a baccalaureate or higher degree, or its equivalent. 8 C.F.R. §214.2(h)(4)(vi).

   1.b. Must have foreign residence that applicant does not intend to abandon.

   1.c. Spouse and children can accompany or follow to join.

F. *Nurses*—INA §101(a)(15)(H)(i)(c), 8 U.S.C. §1101(a)(15)(H) (i)(c); INA §212(m), 8 U.S.C. §1182(m); 66 Fed. Reg. 31107–14 (June 11, 2001); The Nursing Relief for Disadvantaged Areas Act of 1999, PL 106-95, 113 Stat. 1312 (Nov. 12, 1999), 145 Cong. Rec. D1307 (Nov. 16, 1999).

1. H-1A—Prior to 1998, Congress established the H-1A category generally for nurses. The provisions of the Immigration Nursing Relief Act of 1989 ended on Sept. 1, 1995, thereby ending the H-1A category that had been established for professional nurses. Congress extended the H-1A program until Sept. 30, 1997. PL 104-302 (Oct. 11, 1996). INA §§101 (a)(15)(H)(i)(c), 212(m), 8 U.S.C. §§1101(a)(15)(H)(i)(c), 1182(m); 8 C.F.R. §214.2(h)(3); 59 Fed. Reg. 875–903 (Jan. 6, 1994) [final labor attestation regulations]; *Beverly Enterprises Inc., v. Herman,* 119 F.Supp.2d 1 (D.D.C. 2000) [regulation requiring the employer to pay the greater of the facility or prevailing wage rate, 20 C.F.R. §§655.310(e)(1) & (f), instead of simply the facility wage rate was struck down as inconsistent with congressional intent]. INS established guidance regarding pending adjustment applications of H-1A nurses, including the need to submit I-129 extension applications in certain circumstances. Memo, Redman, Deputy Asst. Comm., HQ 70/6.2.8 (Aug. 21, 1997), *reprinted in* 74 No. 35 *Interpreter Releases* 1394, 1420–22 (Sept. 15, 1997). H-1A was officially repealed by PL 106-95 §2. The DOS, through consular officers sending telegrams to DOL to investigate INRA violations, constituted an "aggrieved party or organization" under 8 U.S.C. §1182(m)(2)(E)(ii) and therefore had authority to make a proper complaint. *Alden Management Services, Inc. v. Chao,* 529 F.Supp.2d 882, 888–90 (N.D. Ill. 2007).
2. H-1C—Permits foreign trained nurses to work temporarily at hospitals in Health Professional Shortage Areas (HPSAs). The classification applies to: (1) a person who is coming temporarily to perform services as a registered nurse; (2) who meets the requirements of INA §212(m)(1); and (3) who is seeking admission to perform services at a facility described in INA §212(m)(6) for which there was an unexpired attestation on file. 8 C.F.R. §214.2(h)(1)(ii)(A). The program was reauthorized by PL 109-423 (Dec. 20, 2006) and currently expires on December 20, 2009. Memo, Aytes, Assoc. Dir. Domestic Operations, USCIS, HQ 70/6.2.8 (Dec. 26, 2006), *published on* AILA InfoNet at Doc. No. 07010866.
3. H-1B—A professional nurse may qualify under H-1B if s/he can establish that the position is a specialty occupation and that s/he has a degree or its equivalent pursuant to H-1B regulations. Passing the foreign nurses exam (NCLEX-RN) and state licensure are still required to obtain H-1B status. However, if the only barrier to obtaining a state license is the lack of a Social Security number, USCIS will approve the H-1B petition. Memo, Hernandez, Director, Business and Trade Branch, HQ 70/6.2.8 (Feb. 27, 2003), *published on* AILA InfoNet at Doc. No. 03031142. Also where the state or local authority requires proof of lawful employment *before* granting the license and the license is required to practice the profession, USCIS will grant a one-year H-1B approval to allow the beneficiary to obtain the license. In order to issue the "one-year H-1B" the adjudicator must determine: (1) the beneficiary has filed an application in accordance with state or local rules and procedures; (2) the beneficiary is fully qualified to receive the state or local license but for proof of lawful employment; and (3) the beneficiary is otherwise qualified to receive the H-1B. Approval of the H-1B does not mean that the beneficiary has approval to engage in employment without the appropriate license. A request for an extension of the one year will be denied where the beneficiary cannot establish she has obtained the license. Memo, Neufeld, Deputy Assoc. Dir. Domestic Operations, USCIS, HQ 70/6.2.8 (Mar. 21, 2008), *published on* AILA InfoNet at Doc. No. 08032432. AFM at 31.3(d)(3).

   The Service has maintained that nurses would qualify for H-1B only where the position was filled in the past by degreed nurses or in states whose licensing requirements mandate a B.A. Memo, Aytes, Acting Asst. Comm., Adjudications, HQ 214h-C (Nov. 17, 1995), *published on* AILA InfoNet at Doc. No. 95121290. More recently, the Service has recognized that a nurse's position would be considered H-1B qualified where: (a) a bachelor's or higher degree (or its equivalent) is normally a minimum requirement; (b) the degree requirement is common to the industry for parallel nursing positions; (c) the employer normally requires a degree or its equivalent; or (d) the nature of the position's duties is so specialized and complex that the knowledge required to perform the duties is usually associated with the attainment of a bachelor's or higher degree or its equivalent. Employer Information Bulletin 19, USCIS, Office of Business Liaison (Dec. 7, 2004) at 3, *reprinted in* 81 No. 47 *Interpreter Releases* 1733, 1742–43, 1749–56 (Dec. 13, 2004). The Service has also recognized that nurses who are certified as advanced practice registered nurses (APRN) where the employer requires such certification would qualify for H-1B status. APRNs include Clinical Nurse Specialists (acute care, adult, critical care, gerontological, family, hospice and palliative care, neonatal, pediatric, psychiatric and mental health, neonatal, women's health), Nurse Practitioner (acute care, adult, family, gerontological, pediatric, psychiatric and mental health, neonatal, women's health), Certified Registered Nurse Anesthetist, Certified Nurse-Midwife. Also nurses in administrative positions such as upper level nurse managers where the nurses hold bachelor's degrees may qualify. Memo, Williams, Executive Assoc. Comm., Office of Field Operations, HQISD 70/ 6.2.8-P (Nov. 27, 2002), *published on* AILA InfoNet at Doc. No. 02121746. Nurses in certain administrative positions such as an upper-level "nurse manager" in a hospital may also be H-1B eligible. Employer Information Bulletin 19, USCIS, Office of Business Liaison (Dec. 7, 2004) at 3, *supra*. However, if the hospital does not require a bachelor's degree USCIS will not grant H-1B status simply because the agency that hired and referred the nurse required a bachelor's degree. *Defensor v. Meissner,* 201 F.3d 384 (5th Cir. 2000) [affirmed INS's denial of H-1Bs to nurses with bachelor degrees because the hospitals where they would work did not require B.N.S. degrees even if the employment agency that hired them did]. And USCIS recently cautioned that: "H-1B status generally is not available to most RNs because every State and the District of Columbia permits a person who does not hold a bachelor's degree in nursing, but who meets the education and testing requirements set by law, to obtain an RN license." Employer Information Bulletin 19, USCIS, Office of Business Liaison (Dec. 7, 2004) at 2, *supra*. Having a BSN is not, by itself, sufficient to make the nursing position an H-1B position as the critical factor is whether the degree is required. *Id.* at 3.

4. H-2B Nurses—USCIS does not view H-2B nurses favorably and will only "rarely" approve them because "most U.S. nursing positions constitute permanent employment." Employer Information Bulletin 19, USCIS, Office of Business Liaison (Dec. 7, 2004) at 2, *reprinted in* 81 No. 47 *Interpreter Releases* 1733, 1742–43, 1749–56 (Dec. 13, 2004).

5. TN-1 Nurses—Under NAFTA, Canadian *and Mexican citizens* can enter the U.S. as nurses under the TN category without being subject to the H-1B time (6 years) limitation. Mexican national professionals are also no longer required to obtain approval of an I-129 petition and a corresponding labor condition application before obtaining a visa. Nor do they need an LCA when filing an extension on an I-129 in the U.S. 69 Fed. Reg. 11287 (Mar. 10, 2004).

6. Nurses may also enter as H-3—8 C.F.R. §214.2(h)(7)(i)(B). *But see Matter of* ___ EAC 03 085 52660 (AAO Oct. 30, 2003) (Vermont Service Center) [affirmed denial where insufficient information on teaching staff, where proposed trainees' experience and background from Philippines were unclear, where the petitioner had not established sufficiently that trainees would not be doing normal nursing care and where training might be incompatible with petitioner's business as recruiter of highly trained nurses].

7. Visa Screen/Inadmissibility—Nurses are also subject to both temporary and permanent inadmissibility as foreign health care workers if they have not been certified ("visa screen") by the CGFNS (or an equivalent certified independent credentialing agency), INA §§212(a)(5)(C), 212(r), 22 C.F.R. §40.53(a). The ground of inadmissibility applies even to a person who did their training in the U.S. 8 C.F.R. §212.15(c); 68 Fed. Reg. 43901, 43904–05 (July 25, 2003). The legislative history suggests that this section applies to persons seeking entry through NAFTA or any other treaty, H.R. Conf. Rep. 828, 104th Cong., 2d Sess. at 227 (1996); 68 Fed. Reg. 43901, 43904 (July 25, 2003) and USCIS now requires TN nurses from Canada and Mexico to obtain the visa screen. 69 Fed. Reg. 43729 (July 22, 2004). It includes licensed practical nurses, licensed vocational nurses, and registered nurses. 8 C.F.R. §§212.15(c)(1), 1212.15(c)(1). It also includes persons indirectly involved in health care work such as a supervisory nurse even if she does not engage in clinical work. 63 Fed. Reg. 55007 at 55009 (Oct. 14, 1998). DHS has interpreted the statute to apply at the present time only to those professions listed in the legislative history. 8 C.F.R. §212.15(c), 1212.15(c). However, the Conference Report did allow DHS to designate other categories and DHS will consult extensively with HHS regarding any future additions. 68 Fed. Reg. 43901, 43905–06 (July 25, 2003). The DOS has agreed and suggested the DOT as guidance for defining the professions. Cable, DOS, (98-State-079570), *reprinted in* 75 No. 19 *Interpreter Releases* 697 (May 18, 1998).

7.a. The ground of inadmissibility under INA §212(a)(5)(C) does not apply to: (1) nurses performing nonclinical health care such as teachers, researchers, and managers of health care facilities; (2) persons receiving training under F, J or H-3; (3) spouse and dependent children of an immigrant or NIV holder; and (4) persons obtaining AOS or IV under family-based petitions, employment-based petitions not involving direct medical care, refugee adjustment, registry, cancellation or legalization. 8 C.F.R. §§212.15(b), 1212.15(b), 68 Fed. Reg. 43901, 43904 (July 25, 2003). In order to avoid inadmissibility, the nurse must obtain a certified statement pursuant to the criteria established under INA §212(r) or a certification under INA §212(a)(5)(C).

7.b. Procedure for Certification Under INA §212(a)(5)(C)—A person seeking to enter as a nurse is inadmissible unless s/he presents a certificate from the appropriate accrediting agency verifying that: (1) The person's education, training, license and experience are comparable with that required for an American health care worker of the same type; (2) The education, training, license and experience are authentic and in the case of a license, unencumbered; (3) The education, training license and experience meet all applicable statutory and regulatory requirements for admission into the U.S. although the verification is not binding on the DHS; (4) The applicant has passed a predictor licensing or occupation examination recognized by a majority of states licensing the occupation or has passed the actual occupation licensing or certification examination; and (5) The applicant meets certain English language requirements by either graduating from a school in one of several English-speaking countries or by passing an English language test administered by ETS, TOEIC or IELTS. 8 C.F.R. §§212.15(f), (g), 1212.15(f), (g). The English language examination is administered through either the Educational Testing Service (ETS) (which includes the TOEFL), the Test of English for International Communication Service International (TOEIC) or the International English Language Testing System (IELTS). 8 C.F.R. §§212.15(g)(3), 1212.15(g)(3). The organization affiliated with the Michigan English Language Assessment Battery (MELAB) has decided not to be designated any longer. 68 Fed. Reg. 43901, 43914 (July 25, 2003). Persons are exempt from the English language requirement if they attended college, university or a professional training school in Australia, Canada (except Quebec), Ireland, New Zealand, U.K., or the U.S. 8 C.F.R. §§212.15(g)(2), 1212.15(g)(2). Nurses may also be exempt from an English language proficiency test (as well as a comparability review) if they meet the streamline certification process in their occupation. 8 C.F.R. §212.15(i). A nurse may meet the requirements by taking a predictor examination as specified in 8 C.F.R. §§212.15(f)(1)(iv) instead of the National Council Licensure Examination for Nurses ("NCLEX-RN"). 68 Fed. Reg. 43901, 43914 (July 25, 2003). In addition, a nurse who has graduated from an entry level program accredited by the National League for Nursing Accreditation Commission (NLNAC) or the Commission on Collegiate Nursing Education (CCNE) is exempt from the educational comparability review and English language proficiency testing. If the nurse is not exempt from the English language exam either because of graduation from one of the accredited program under NLNAC or CCNE or because of graduation from a program in an English-speaking country, 8 C.F.R. §§212.15(g) & (i), 1212.15(g), s/he must attain a certain score on the ETS (TOEFL), TOEIC, or IELTS exam. 8 C.F.R. §§212.15(g)(4)(ii), 1212.15(g)(4)(ii).

7.c. Under INA §212(r), 8 U.S.C. §1182(r) and 8 C.F.R. §§212.15(h) a nurse may obtained a certified statement necessary to meet the requirements of INA §212(a)(5)(C) instead of a certification as outlined above. Under the Nursing Relief for Disadvantaged Areas Act of 1999, PL 106-95 §4, CGFNS (or an equivalent approved independent credentialing organization) may issue a certified statement (instead of a certificate) if: (1) the individual has a valid unrestricted license as a nurse in a state where the individual is to be employed and the state has verified that any foreign licenses are authentic and unencumbered; (2) the nurse has passed the NCLEX-RN; and (3) the nurse is a graduate of an English-language nursing program; (4) the nursing program was located in Australia, Canada, Ireland, New Zealand, South Africa, the United Kingdom, or the U.S. or in any other country designated by unanimous agreement of CGFNS (or another equivalent credentialing service) approved for certification of nurses and (5) the nursing program was in operation on or before Nov. 12, 1999 or has been approved by unanimous agreement by CGFNS or another equivalent credentialing service. CGFNS has designated nursing programs. 8 C.F.R. §§212.15(h)(2). If a certified statement is issued, the nurse need not comply with the certificate requirements or the English language requirements for certification in the regulations.

G. *Athletes and Entertainers*—Athletes and entertainers have been removed from the H-1B category and placed in new categories as O and P nonimmigrants.

H. *Physicians*—8 C.F.R. §214.2(h)(4)(viii)

1. Effective Dec. 12, 1991 by virtue of the Miscellaneous and Technical Immigration and Naturalization Amendments of 1991, PL 102-282, §303(a)(5), a foreign physician may now enter the U.S. under certain conditions to practice medicine with an H-1B. This provision amends INA §§212(j)(2) and 101(a)(15)(H)(i)(b) to permit a graduate of a medical school who is coming to the U.S. to perform services as a member of the medical profession, if:

   1.a. S/he is coming pursuant to an invitation from a public or nonprofit private educational or research institution or agency in the U.S. to teach or conduct research, or both, at or for such institution or agency (physician may do incidental patient care); *or* has complied with each of the following

      (1) Has passed the Federation licensing examination (administered by the Federation of State Medical Boards of the U.S.) or an equivalent recognized test credential examination as determined by the Secretary of Health and Human Services. Parts 1 & 2 of FLEX (Federation Licensing Examination), and Steps 1, 2, and 3 of the NBME (National Board of Medical Examiners) have been replaced by Steps 1, 2, and 3 of the USMLE (U.S. Medical Licensing Examination). The Service will not accept a combination of these examinations for establishing eligibility for H-1B status. Letter, Bednarz, INS Acting Asst. Comm. Adjudications, HQ 214h-C,(July 29, 1994), *reprinted in* 71 No. 43 *Interpreter Releases* 1482, 1493 (Nov. 7, 1994); *and*

      (2) Has competency in oral and written English, as demonstrated by passage of the English language proficiency test given by ECFMG (Educational Commission for Foreign Medical Graduates), or is a graduate of a school of medicine which is accredited by a body or bodies approved for the purpose by the Secretary of Education (regardless whether the school of medicine is in the U.S.).

         (a) ECFMG certification is required for all foreign physicians as a prerequisite for entering medical training programs in the U.S. Applicants must pass three examinations for ECFMG certification: USMLE Steps 1, 2CK (clinical knowledge) and 2CS (clinical skills). The English language examination has now been folded into USMLE-Step 2, although previous passage of TOEFL (Test of English as a Foreign Language) will still be recognized. For more information go to *www.ecfmg.org/usmle*.

   1.b. Foreign physicians seeking H-1B status must also

      (1) Have a license to practice medicine from a foreign state, or have graduated from a medical school in the U.S. or in a foreign state, and

      (2) If s/he will provide direct patient care, must also have a medical license *or other authorization* to practice medicine required by the state of intended employment. Where the state or local authority requires proof of lawful employment *before* granting the license and the license is required to practice the profession, USCIS will grant a one-year H-1B approval to allow the beneficiary to obtain the license. In order to issue the "one-year H-1B" the adjudicator must determine: (1) the beneficiary has filed an application in accordance with state or local rules and procedures; (2) the beneficiary is fully qualified to receive the state or local license but for proof of lawful employment; and (3) the beneficiary is otherwise qualified to receive the H-1B. Approval of the H-1B does not mean that the beneficiary has approval to engage in employment without the appropriate license. A request for an extension of the one year will be denied where the beneficiary cannot establish she has obtained the license. Memo, Neufeld, Deputy Assoc. Dir. Domestic Operations, USCIS, HQ 70/6.2.8 (Mar. 21, 2008), *published on* AILA InfoNet at Doc. No. 08032432. AFM at 31.3(d)(3)

   1.c. A person in a residency program may also be approved for an H-1B. 60 Fed. Reg. 62021–22 (Dec. 4, 1995) [withdrawing bar to H-1B for residents in final rule].

2. As in the case of all H-1Bs, the employer must submit with the petition certification from the DOL that it has filed an LCA, as well as all necessary documentation to establish the above licenses and examinations.

3. Foreign physicians may also enter without the certifying examinations where

   3.a. Physician is of national or international renown. Under INA §101(a)(41), 8 U.S.C. §1101(a)(41), doctors of national or international renown are not within the definition of foreign medical graduates and are therefore exempt from the restriction.

   3.b. Physician not "coming to perform services as members of the medical profession" under INA §101(a)(15)(H)(i)(b), 8 U.S.C. §1101(a)(15)(H)(i)(b) (*e.g.*, administrator of drug company). *Matter of Sheikh*, 17 I&N Dec. 634 (R.C. 1980). Physicians who are seeking to enter as physician's assistant or medical researchers not eligible for H-1 if they are involved "in any manner whatsoever in direct patient care." Cable, DOS, 95-State-06254 (Mar. 2, 1995), *reprinted in* 72 No. 14 *Interpreter Releases* 504–06 (Apr. 10, 1995).

   3.c. Graduated from a U.S. medical school. 8 C.F.R. §214.2(h)(4)(viii)(B)(2).

4. C/S for foreign medical graduates with INA §212(e) problem—May now C/S to H-1B if s/he otherwise meets requirements for C/S and 212(e) waiver issued under INA §214(*l*) . However, if s/he does C/S s/he is ineligible for IV or AOS or any other NIV if s/he fails to fulfill the terms of the contract with the health facility in shortage area which now requires a 3-year commitment. INA §214(*l*)(2)(A); 8 C.F.R. §§212.7(c)(9), 1212.7(c)(9); Memo, Pearson, Exec. Assoc. Comm. (HQADN70/ 21.1) (Oct. 4 1999), *reprinted in* 76 *Interpreter Releases* 1504–08 (Oct. 11, 1999). In addition INA §222(g) does not apply to J-1 foreign physicians in D/S unless USCIS or an IJ has determined a status violation. Cable, DOS, 98-State-051296 (Mar. 23, 1998), *published on* AILA InfoNet at Doc. No. 98032392. For criteria and procedures regarding waivers of the 2-year foreign residence requirements for doctors, *see in this chapter* ¶ VI.C.8.b(5) (p.665), *supra.*

5. Overstays—DOS has recognized that foreign physicians who are meeting the requirements of §214(*l*) are going to work in a medically underserved area, and have timely applied for the waiver or petition but have overstayed while waiting for an approval will be treated under the extraordinary circumstances provision of the overstay provisions of INA §222(g) if the waiver and petition were subsequently approved. Cable, DOS, 96-State-225321, Christopher, Secy. of State (1996), *reprinted in* 73 No. 42 *Interpreter Releases* 1544–46 (Nov. 4, 1996).

6. Extensions / H-1B Cap—DOS will allow J-1 alien physicians to extend their status beyond the period of actual training to take their specialty Board examinations. The maximum duration of any such extension is six months. The extension is limited until the end of the month in which the Board examination is given but not to exceed 6 months. 64 Fed. Reg. 34982–83 (June 30, 1999). The mere filing of a INA §212(e) waiver application will not disqualify a J-1 physician from extending the period of J-1 status; rather, it is only upon adjudication of the waiver by DOS which results in an ineligibility to extend status. Letter, Jin, USIA G.C. (Dec. 18, 1995), *reprinted in* 73 No. 2 *Interpreter Releases* 47, 51 (Jan. 10, 1996). A J-1 who has obtained a waiver pursuant to the request by an interested Federal or State agency is not subject to the 65,000 cap. INA §214(*l*)(2)(A). In addition, a physician holding an M.D. from a U.S. university will qualify for the 20,000 visa supplement for foreign nationals who have earned a master's or higher degree from a U.S. institution of higher education (as defined in 20 U.S.C. §1101(a)). INA §214(g)(5)(C).

7. Foreign physician not statutorily eligible for H-2B, H-3 or TN—9 FAM 41.53 N.4.2-7. However, medical students may qualify for H-3s if the student will engage in employment as an extern during his or her medical school vacation. 9 FAM 41.53 N.20. Also foreign physicians may enter under TN category but only to teach or do research (with incidental patient care). They may not enter to practice medicine under TN even if they graduated from a U.S. medical school (although they were permitted to do so under the former TC category). Letter, Bednarz, Chief, NIV Branch, Adjudications, HQ 1815-C (Mar. 13, 1995), *reprinted in* 72 No. 14 *Interpreter Releases* 508, 518 (Apr. 10, 1995).

8. Physician eligible for O visa—Although a J-1 physician subject to the 2-year foreign residence requirement under INA §212(e) cannot C/S to an O because INA §248 prohibits it, s/he may still obtain an O visa by going abroad. Letter, Hernandez, Director, Business and Trade Services, HQ 70/6.2.8 (Oct. 19, 2001), *reprinted in* 79 No. 2 *Interpreter Releases* 38, 52–54 (Jan. 7, 2002). However, at completion of O s/he is still subject to the 2-year foreign residence requirement. Letter, Bednarz, Chief, NIV Branch, Adjudications HQ 214.42-C (Aug. 30, 1994), *reprinted in* 71 No. 39 *Interpreter Releases* 1376 (Oct. 7, 1994).

9. Physicians as Investors—A foreign physician may invest in a medical practice and obtain an E-2 visa if s/he is from a treaty country and is not involved in patient care. Letter, Schlosser, U.S. Consul Toronto (Jan. 25, 1994), *published on* AILA InfoNet at Doc. No. 94080490.

10. Foreign Medical Student.

 10.a. May obtain H-1B for residency program.

 10.b. May obtain B-1 (in lieu of H-3) if coming to take an "elective clerkship." But if person has already graduated (FMG) the B-1 (and F-1) is unavailable. Letter, LaFleur, Chief, Business and Trade Services Branch, Benefits Division, INS, HQ 70/6.2.2-C (1996), *reprinted in* 73 No. 22 *Interpreter Releases* 764, 776–77 (June 3, 1996).

I. *Fast-Track H-1B1 Visas*—INA §101(a)(15)(H)(i)(b)(1), 8 U.S.C. §1101(a)(15)(H)(i)(b)(1); INA §212(g)(8)(A), 8 U.S.C. §1101(g)(8)(A); H.R. 2738, PL 108-77, 117 Stat. 909, H.R. 1739, PL 108-78, 117 Stat. 947; H.R. Rep. No. 108-224, pt. 2 at 6–11, 15–20, 36–46 (2003); H.R. Rep. No. 108-225, pt. 2. at 5–11, 15–16 (2003); 9 FAM 41.53 N27–28

1. The U.S.-Chile Free Trade Agreement and the U.S.-Singapore Free Trade Agreement provide for E-1 (Treaty Trader) and E-2 (Treaty Investor) visas as well as a new category of H-1B1 visas.

2. H-1B1 Visas:

 2.a. For persons in a "specialty occupation" that requires: (i) theoretical and practical application of a body of specialized knowledge and (ii) attainment of a bachelor's degree or higher in the specific specialty (or its equivalent) as a minimum for entry into the occupation in the U.S. According to the legislative history of this provision: "The requirement is to be interpreted identically to the requirement to qualify as a professional under the H-1B category (except as regarding four professions listed in appendix 14.3(D)(2) of the U.S.-Chile Free Trade Agreement)." H.R. Rep. No. 108-224, pt. 2 at 17 (2003). Four categories are added to those covered under H-1B1: Agricultural Manager and Physical Therapist (for persons from Chile) and Management Consultants and Disaster Relief Claims Adjusters (for persons from Chile or Singapore). 20 C.F.R. §655.715 ("Specialty Occupation" for H-1B1 defined in subsection (2)) For these categories alternative credentials are accepted. 9 FAM 41.53 N28.4(B).

 2.b. No DHS petition required—Applicant gets visa directly at U.S. consulate. 9 FAM 41.53 N.28.2 & 28.8. Submits proof of filing LCA and written offer of employment. However, if he wishes to c/s, obtain an initial extension of status, or change from one H-1B1 employer to another, he must file the I-129 with the attendant applications (LCA, H-1B Data Collection Supplement), the filing fee for an H-1B petition, plus the $1,500 fee (unless there are less than 26 employees and then it is $750). The fraud prevention and detection fee of $500 does *not* have to be paid by an H-1B1. USCIS announcement on H-1B1 fees (June 21, 2005) *reported in* 82 No. 26 *Interpreter Releases* 1061, 1062–63 (July 1, 2005).

 2.c. No licensure requirement as a prerequisite to admission on H-1B1—Applicant expected to comply with licensure requirement following their admission where profession requires state license. Memo, Yates, Assoc. Dir. Operations, USCIS (Jan. 8, 2004), *published on* AILA InfoNet at Doc. No. 04030361; 9 FAM 41.53 N28.6.

 2.d. Labor condition attestation on Form 9035 or 9035E must be filed with DOL and annotated as H-1B1—Chile or H-1B1—Singapore. 20 C.F.R. §655.700(d)(3); 9 FAM 41.53 N28.3 & 28.8(B). Therefore, a prevailing wage determination is also needed; *see in this part* "Attestation Requirements for H-1B," ¶ C.3 (p.686), *supra*.

 2.e. Admission is for one year—Extensions granted in one year increments. Extensions are *not* limited to six years. However, every third extension will require a new 2-year LCA because, after the second extension, the next extension may only be granted if the Secy. of Labor certifies to DHS and DOS that the intending employer has filed a new 2-year LCA. E/S and C/S granted through the Vermont Service Center. Spouses and dependent children given H-4s. Memo, Ahern, Asst. Comm. Field Operations, CBP, OFO:IPP:JBK (Apr. 19, 2004), *published on* AILA InfoNet at Doc. No. 05040166.

 2.f. Subject to INA §214(b) and proof H-1B1 applicant has no intention of abandoning his residency abroad and becoming an LPR. 9 FAM 41.53 N28.5

2.g. Change of Status—A I-129 application should be accompanied by: (1) Letter from U.S. employer stating activity to be engaged in, anticipated length of stay and arrangements for remuneration; (2) Evidence that education requirements are met; and (3) Labor attestation. Memo, Yates, Assoc. Dir. Operations, USCIS (Jan. 8, 2004), *published on* AILA InfoNet at Doc. No. 04030361.

2.h. Numerical Limit of Visa Reduces H-1B cap to Extent used—Chile: 1,400; Singapore: 5,4000

J. *E-3 Visa-Australian Special Occupation Visa*—The REAL ID Act of 2005 established a new category, E-3 which allows persons to enter the U.S. "solely to perform services in a specialty occupation in the United States if the alien is a national of the Commonwealth of Australia" and files a labor attestation under INA §212(t). It is limited to 10,500 per fiscal year. Although the E-3 has characteristics that are the same as H-1Bs or Fast Track H-1B1s, it is a separate visa with separate benefits and requirements. For example, E-3 spouses may work and E-3 applicants are not required to pay the special fees required of H-1Bs. Aytes, Acting Assoc. Dir., Domestic Operations, USCIS, "Processing Guidelines for E-3 Australian Specialty Occupation Workers and Employment Authorization for E-3 Dependent Spouses," *published in* 83 No. 3 *Interpreter Releases* 121, 123–24, 140–45 (Jan. 17, 2006). However, like H-1Bs and H-1B1s, E-3s are required to provide an LCA and prevailing wage determination. *See in this part* ¶ C.3.a (p.686), *supra*, and ¶ Q.2.c (p.742), *infra*. Spouses battered or subjected to extreme cruelty by the E-3 are eligible for work authorization, INA §106, 8 U.S.C. §1105a(a), to be filed with the Vermont Service Center unit that adjudicates VAWA self-petitions, U and T visas.

K. *H-2A, H-2B Visas*—INA §101(a)(15)(H)(ii)(a)–(b), 8 U.S.C. §1101(a)(15)(H)(ii)(a)–(b); 8 C.F.R. §214.2(h)(5)–(6); 9 FAM 41.53 N. 4-5

1. Definition

1.a. H-2 category is divided between temporary workers performing "agricultural labor or services ... of a temporary or seasonal nature," INA §101(a)(15)(H)(ii)(a), and temporary workers performing "other temporary service or labor." INA §101(a)(15)(H)(ii)(b).

1.b. To qualify for H-2:

(1) Applicant must be coming temporarily to U.S.

(2) Applicant must be performing temporary services/labor.

(3) Employer must demonstrate that no U.S. workers capable of performing such service/labor are available in U.S. Under the H-2A program there is a 50% rule, which requires employers to hire qualified U.S. farmworkers who apply for the job until 50% of the contract period has been completed. 55 Fed. Reg. 29356 (July 19, 1990). Employer must engage in serious recruitment, including use of electronic data banks via SWAs. Memo No. 17-97, Farmer, Admin. for Regional Management (Jan. 6, 1997), *reprinted in* 74 No. 19 *Interpreter Releases* 828, 835–37 (May 19, 1997).

2. Requirements for H-2A—INA §101(a)(15)(H)(ii)(a); INA §218; 20 C.F.R. §§651.10, 653 (Subparts B & F), 654 (Subpart E), 655 (Subpart B), 658 (Subpart F)); Memo to Field 16-10; TEGL No. 31-01; GAL No. 1-02; DeRocco, Asst. Sec., ETA, TEGL No. 11-07 (Nov. 6, 2007), *published on* AILA InfoNet at Doc. No. 07110736; DeRocco, Asst. Sec. ETA, TEGL No. 11-07, Change 1 (Nov. 14, 2007), *published on* AILA InfoNet at Doc. No. 07111560; Round 1, TEGL 11-07, Change 1, DOL (Feb. 5, 2008), *reprinted in* 85 No. 7 *Interpreter Releases* 417, 465–75 (Feb. 11, 2008); Round 2, TEGL 11-07, Change 1, DOL (Mar. 6, 2008), *reprinted in* 85 No. 11 *Interpreter Releases* 757, 826–29 (Mar. 10, 2008; TEGL 11-07, Change 1, Questions from SWA Training Webinars—Round 3, *published on* AILA InfoNet at Doc. No. 08050163; Memo, Jacob, Solicitor of Labor, DOL (Mar. 14, 2008), *reprinted in* 85 No. 16 *Interpreter Releases* 1247 (Apr. 14, 2008) The visa/status is for foreign workers to enter the U.S. to perform agricultural labor or services of a temporary or seasonal nature.

2.a. Procedures through SWA and NPC—DeRocco, Asst. Sec., ETA, TEGL No. 11-07 (Nov. 6, 2007), *supra*. An employer must demonstrate that there are insufficient workers who are able, willing, qualified and available to perform the agricultural work at the time and place where the H-2A worker is to perform the work *and* his or her employment will not adversely affect the wages and working conditions of similarly employed U.S. workers. The procedures generally are as follows:

(1) Filing—File with the SWA in location where work will be performed and if performed in more than one location or state where the work will begin. TEGL No. 11-07, *supra* at ¶4(A)(ii).

(2) Timing—The Secy. of DOL is required to make an LC determination at least 30 calendar days before the start date and therefore the SWA must conduct a housing inspection, the employer must provide a recruitment report to the NPC and the employer must provide proof of worker's comp. insurance to the NPC before the 30 calendar days before the start date. INA §218(c)(3)(A).

(3) Recruitment—Employer must follow recruitment procedures in 20 C.F.R. §655.103(d)(2)(ii) including placing ads that direct potential employees to apply or send resumes to the nearest SWA office. If potential employees appear at the employer's place of business he must interview them and if not present respond to messages within 24 hours. TEGL No. 11-07, *supra* at ¶4(B).

(4) Verification of Employment and Housing—The SWA is required to verify the applicant's authorization to work and the employer's housing. TEGL No. 11-07, *supra* at ¶4(B)(ii) and (C); Memo, Jacob, Solicitor of Labor, DOL (Mar. 14, 2008), *published on* AILA InfoNet at Doc. No. 08040762; Round 1, H-2As TEGL 11-07, Change 1, DOL FAQs (Feb. 5, 2008), *reprinted in* 85 No. 7 *Interpreter Releases* 417, 465–75 (Feb. 11, 2008). The employer must comply with either OSHA housing standards for temporary labor camps at 29 C.F.R. §1910.142 or ETA standards at 20 C.F.R. §654.404-654.417; *See also* DeRocco, Asst. Sec. ETA, TEGL 15-06 (Feb. 9, 2007). This means it must complete and retain I-9 forms for persons who appear at their offices and use the E-Verify system. TEGL 11-07, Change 1, Questions from SWA Training Webinars—Round 3 ¶14–16, *published on* AILA InfoNet at Doc. No. 08050163.

3. **Requirements for H-2B**—8 C.F.R. §214.2(h)(6); DeRocco, Asst. Sec., ETA, TEGL No. 21-06 Attachment A (Apr. 4, 2007), *published on* AILA InfoNet at Doc. No. 07040960; DeRocco, Asst. Sec., ETA, TEGL No. 21-06, Change 1 Attachment A (June 25, 2007), *published on* AILA InfoNet at Doc. No. 07062530; Round 1 H-2B FAQs, DOL, *published on* AILA InfoNet at Doc. No. 07071871; Special requirements for Tree Planting and Related Reforestation Occupations. DeRocco, Asst. Sec. ETA, TEGL No. 27-06 (June 12, 2007), *posted in* AILA InfoNet at Doc. No. 07061361; GAL No. 1-95 (Nov. 10, 1994), *reprinted in* 72 No. 3 *Interpreter Releases* 100, 106 (Jan. 13, 1995), *published on* AILA InfoNet at Doc. No. 94020790; 72 Fed. Reg. 19961 (Apr. 20, 2007); 72 Fed. Reg. 36504 (July 3, 2007); 72 Fed. Reg. 38621 (July 13, 2007).

3.a. Must get temporary labor certification, 20 C.F.R. §655, demonstrating that: (1) No USC/LPR workers are available for position; (2) Employment of aliens will not adversely affect wage rate and working conditions of similarly employed workers in the U.S. 8 C.F.R. §§214.2(h)(6)(i), (6)(iv)(A)(1). Application for LC submitted to Chicago NPC. 73 Fed. Reg. 11954–56 (Mar. 5, 2008).

3.b. Must demonstrate that the request for labor is a one-time occurrence, a seasonal need, a peakload need, or an intermittent need. Period of employment must be a year or less unless there are extraordinary circumstances. 8 C.F.R. §214.2(h)(6)(ii). If more than a year a new LC is needed. Seasonal or peakload need of longer than 10 months, which is of a recurring nature, will not be accepted. TEGL No. 21-06 at II(C).

(1) One-Time Occurrence. Must demonstrate that either: (1) it has not employed people in the past *and* will not need them in the future; or (2) it has permanent employment situation but a temporary event of short duration has created the need for a temporary worker.

(2) Seasonal Need. The labor is traditionally tied to a season of the year by an event or pattern *and* is of a recurring nature. Must specify the times that the labor will *not* be needed and these times cannot be unpredictable, subject to change, or vacation.

(3) Peakload Need. The labor is needed to supplement the permanent staff *and* the temporary additions to staff will not become permanent.

(4) Intermittent Need. Need labor occasionally or intermittently for short period of time and has not employed permanent or full time workers for the position.

3.c. Multiple beneficiaries may be requested if they will do the same type of work on the same terms and conditions in the same occupation and area of employment. But cannot request more beneficiaries than job openings.

3.d. If work done in more than one location, application must include the itinerary of locations and dates of work in each location. Must file application with SWA where employment will begin.

3.e. Must demonstrate that there is no labor dispute at the workplace.

3.f. Not available to doctors. Also, not available to Virgin Islands employers except entertainers and athletes for periods not to exceed 45 days. 8 C.F.R. §214.2(h)(6)(iv)(B).

3.g. Position is temporary

(1) To determine whether job is temporary the Service does not look to the nature of the duties, but rather, to the nature of the employer's need. 8 C.F.R. §214.2(h)(6)(ii)(B); *Matter of Artee Corp.*, 18 I&N Dec. 366 (Comm. 1982) [employment agency that provided temporary help on continuous basis because of chronic shortage denied H-2 because continuous temporary need is equal to a permanent need]. *Accord Seven Star, Inc. v. U.S.*, 873 F.2d 225 (9th Cir.), *cert. denied* 110 S.Ct. 242 (1989) [adopts *Artee* and rejects equal protection argument finding that agency may make "different decisions in different cases in different years"]; *Sussex Engineering, Ltd. v. Montgomery*, 825 F.2d 1084 (6th Cir. 1987), *cert. denied*, 108 S.Ct. 1473 (1988); *Volt Technical Servs. Corp. v. INS*, 648 F.Supp. 578 (S.D.N.Y. 1986); *Blumenfeld v. Attorney General*, 762 F.Supp. 24 (D. Conn. 1991) [rejected child monitor as temporary]; *But see Wilson v. Smith*, 587 F.Supp. 470 (D.D.C. 1984). DOL has adopted *Artee* to determine temporary labor certifications. *See* GAL No. 1-95 (Nov. 10, 1994), *supra*. *See also* Legal Opinion, Kmick, Deputy Asst. AG, Office of Legal Counsel (Apr. 23, 1987), *reprinted in* 67 No. 7 *Interpreter Releases* 178, 193–98, 202 (Feb. 26, 1990).

3.h. *Procedure*—DOL procedure set forth in TEGL and published in the Federal Register, *supra* as follows:

(1) DOL Procedure

(a) File ETA Form 750 Part A with SWA in area where employment will begin. The application cannot be filed earlier than 120 days before employment or later than 60 days. An association or other organization of employers cannot file and a job contractor cannot file if the job contractor's need for the workers is permanent.

(b) Application must include: (i) Two ETA 750, Part A forms and the Part B forms are not needed; (ii) Documentation of efforts to advertise and recruit prior to filing, if any, but if not state on Item 21 of ETA that will comply with supervised recruitment; (iii) A *detailed temporary need* statement on the employer's letterhead explaining the job opportunity and number of workers being requested and how the job meets the temporary standard. A labor shortage in the area does *not* meet the temporary standard; and (iv) supporting evidence.

i) Supporting Evidence. The documentary list is not exhaustive and the employer is not required to produce every item on the list. Round 1 H-2B FAQs, DOL, *published on* AILA InfoNet at Doc. No. 07071871. The following are recommended:

a) Signed work contracts, letters of intent from clients, and/or monthly invoices from previous calendar years clearly showing that work will be performed for each month during the requested period as proof that the work is tied to a season and will reoccur;

b) Annualized and/or multi-year work contracts supplemented with signed work contracts specifying start and end dates during each year;

c) Summarized monthly payroll reports for previous year that identifies for each month, permanent and temporary workers separately in the occupation.

d) Insufficient documentation includes work contracts with no termination date or solely with temporary workers; staffing charts, graphs or other documentation that do not correspond to the period of need; and applications that only include weather charts, event calendars, hotel occupancy rates or annual/quarterly tax reports (IRS 941s)

(c) Can request multiple workers on ETA Form 750, Part A at Item 18a, assuming it is the same work, area of employment (MSA), and conditions. To determine the MSA (Metropolitan Statistical Area), contact the U.S. Census Bureau (1-866-758-1060) or see *www.census.gov/population/www/estimates/metroarea.html.* If the employment is all in one MSA but there are different prevailing wage rates, the highest rate must be used. Round 1 H-2B FAQs, DOL, *published on* AILA InfoNet at Doc. No. 07071871.

(d) Employer must sign authorizing an agent or attorney if there is one and a G-28 must be filed by attorney. There are currently *no prohibitions* on passing on administrative or legal costs of applying for the H-2B to the H-2B worker. Round II, H-2B FAQs, DOL, *published on* AILA InfoNet at Doc. No. 07121661. *But see Rivera v. Brickman Group Ltd.,* ___ F.Supp.2d ___(E.D. Pa. Jan. 7, 2008) 2008 WL 81570 [H-2B landscapers entitled to receive transportation, visa, and payments to recruiters as costs under the FLSA] *Castellanos-Contreras v. Decatur Hotels, L.L.C.,* 488 F.Supp.2d 565, 572 n.5 (E.D. La. 2007) [finding that the FLSA applies to H-2B workers and suggesting that hotel workers may have a claim for reimbursement for travel, visa, recruitment and other expenses incurred in migrating to the U.S.].

(e) If multiple locations must include the names and physical addresses of each location.

(f) Must pay the prevailing wage in accordance with ETA and cannot have must meet typical requirements for LCs such as the job cannot have unduly restrictive job requirements or a combination of duties.

(g) SWA will place job in its job bank for 10 calendar days.

(h) During 10 day posting by SWA, the employer shall place ad for 3 consecutive calendar days in local newspaper unless SWA determines the ad should be in a professional, trade or ethnic publication. The ad does not have to be placed on a Sunday. Round 1 H-2B FAQs, DOL, *published on* AILA InfoNet at Doc. No. 07071871.

  i) The ad must describe the job opportunity including hours, rate of pay, duration of employment and all locations of employment; state the minimum requirements; identify the employer; direct applicants to report or send resumes to SWA; and state the number of job openings. The employer must provide the SWA with tear sheets or other proof of publication

  ii) Employer must document use of union (if they exist for the occupation) and other recruitment sources.

  iii) Recruitment Report—The report shall identify each recruitment source by name; the name, address, telephone number and resume of each U.S. worker who applied; and explain lawful job-related reasons for not hiring. In determining qualified workers, the CO may take into consideration not only workers in the area but also workers who "are willing to move from elsewhere to take the job at their own expense or at the employer's expense, if the prevailing practice…" TEGL No. 21-06 at Attachment A part V(2)

(i) SWA forwards application to NPC Chicago. The CO at the NPC may issue may issue one Request for Information (RFI) to the employer giving the employer seven days to correct a deficiency. The CO's decision is advisory to USCIS and there is no provision for reconsideration or appeal of the decision. TEGL No. 21-06, Change 1 and Attachment A, *supra.*

(2) Obtain labor certification approval—20 C.F.R. §§655.1–.4 [nonagriculture]; 20 C.F.R. §655.101 *et seq.* [agriculture]. 60- to 120-day notice for H-2Bs, 45-day notice for H-2As; For procedures *see* TEGL No. 21-06, Attachment A (Apr. 4, 2007), *supra*; 70 Fed. Reg. 41430–37 (July 19, 2005).

(3) Submit approval with I-129 to USCIS—In "emergent situations" where all the beneficiaries are not known, multiple petitions may be filed for beneficiaries subsequent to the initial filing. 8 C.F.R. §214.2(h)(2)(iii). Allowing petitions with unnamed beneficiaries is "the exception, not the norm" and the Service should not grant the exception without evidence from the employer clearly describing the business reasons why beneficiaries are unnamed. Memo, Cook, Acting Asst. Comm. Programs, HQ 70/6.2.9 (July 5, 2001), *reprinted in* 79 No. 8 *Interpreter Releases* 272, 289–90 (Feb. 18, 2002). There is now a $150 fraud prevention fee which must be filed with the DHS application.

(a) DOL's approval or denial given great weight by USCIS, O.I. §214.2(h)(5)(iv)(A), but USCIS not bound by Dept. of Labor's decision. *Matter of Golden Dragon Chinese Restaurant*, 19 I&N Dec. 238 (Comm. 1984). If DOL denies application for a temporary labor certification, the employer may file I-129 petition with USCIS along with countervailing evidence. 8 C.F.R. §214.2(h)(6)(iv)(D)–(E). If temporary LC is lost only USCIS can request a duplicate LC from DOL. Round II, H-2B FAQs, DOL, *published on* AILA InfoNet at Doc. No. 07121661.

(4) Substitution of Beneficiaries—8 C.F.R. §214.2(h)(2)(iv). USCIS may substitute H-2B beneficiaries where (a) petition was approved for unnamed beneficiaries; (b) the approval is for a group; or (c) the job does not require education, teaching or experience. This may be done by letter with a copy of the approval notice and the beneficiaries' credentials. A consular officer may substitute beneficiaries on approved H-2B group petitions without obtaining the Service's approval if the qualifications of individual beneficiaries on the group petition will not be or were not considered in according the H classification. Cable, DOS, No. 90-State-096324 (Mar. 26, 1990), *reported in* 67 No. 16 *Interpreter Releases* 475 (Apr. 23, 1990). However, now an H-2B petition must include the worker's full name, if he is a returning worker a certification to that effect, and a fraud prevention fee of $150 per application.

(5) Transportation home—If H-2B is dismissed before the end of the period for admission the employer must pay "the reasonable costs of return transportation of the alien abroad." INA §214(c)(5)(A), 8 U.S.C. §1184(c)(5)(A); 8 C.F.R. §214.2(h)(6)(vi)(E).

3.i. *H-2Bs in the Entertainment Industry*—There are special procedures for employers seeking to hire persons for limited appearances in the entertainment industry. Procedures for Temporary Labor Certification in the Entertainment Industry under the H-2B Visa Program, TEGL 31-05, DeRocco, Asst. Sec. ETA, DOL at ¶4C (May 31, 2006), *reprinted in* 12 No. 1 *Bender's Immigration Bulletin* 1, 42–54 (Jan. 1, 2007). The H-2B includes performers and "all technical and support personnel involved with a performance." *Id.* At ¶4E. To complete an application the employer must submit: (1) ETA-750; (2) itinerary of locations and duration of work in each location if more than one worksite; (3) documentation if any to recruit U.S. workers. The wage must meet or exceed the prevailing wage. The employer may advertise the job opportunity before or after filing the ETA-750 in a national publication that is likely to bring responses. The employer must provide the agency (which will be a SWA specializing in entertainment called an OSE) a copy of the ad. The OSE will then write to the appropriate national union. If a recruitment sources asserts qualified U.S. workers it must provide specific information. The OSE can require additional recruitment. In making the determination, the CO must consider circumstances unique to the entertainment industry. A denial of certification can be appealed to DHS. If employment is certified in can not exceed 12 months/364 days.

3.j. Admission and Extension

(1) Admitted for time on LC but no more than 1 year. 8 C.F.R. §214.2(h)(9)(iii)(B); §214.2(h)(6).

(2) Extension not more than 12 months and maximum of 3 years, given only in extraordinary circumstances. 8 C.F.R. §214.2(h)(15)(ii)(C); GAL 1-95, *supra.* Must have new labor cert. or notice that certification cannot be made. Cannot obtain C/S, E/S or readmission as an H/L if H-2B was previously in U.S. for 3 years in H/L category unless s/he has resided and been physically present outside U.S. for 6 months immediately prior to application. 8 C.F.R. §§214.2(h)(13)(iv);

(3) *H-2B Cap*—H-2B is limited to 66,000 visas a year. Extensions of stay and change of employer applications are not counted in the cap. The H-2B petitions subject to the cap are issued in order of filing and the limitation is not applicable to spouse and children. From May 2005 until Sept. 30, 2007 (when the returning H-2B provisions of the Save Our Small and Seasonal Business Act sunset), returning workers were not counted in the cap if the worker was counted in one of the last 3 years prior to the approved start date. INA §214(g)(9). The numerical cap is allocated so that no more than 33,000 visas may be used for the first six months. This avoids the differential advantage that winter employees (who file first) had over summer employees. INA §214(g). Prior to the new legislation, a due process challenge to the numerical procedure which placed no cap on winter temporary employees and therefore allowed them the use of the full 66,000 was denied. *Daylily Farms, Inc. v. Chao,* 357 F.Supp.2d 356 (D. Mass. 2005) [DOL procedures in allowing filing for H-2Bs only 120 days before employment was rational despite its impact on employers who need summer workers and who may have no visas because the cap is reached through winter workers]. The DOL will not amend previously certified LCs so that they may be used in the second half of the fiscal year. Round 2 H-2B FAQs, DOL, *published on* AILA InfoNet at Doc. No. 07121661 [a temporary LC is only valid for the period of time specified].

(a) Fish roe processors, fish roe technicians and supervisors of fish roe processing are exempt from the H-2B cap. Department of Defense Appropriations Act, 2005, PL 108-287, 118 Stat. 951 (Aug. 6, 2004), Title X, Ch. IV, §14006.

(4) Can submit multiple beneficiaries on one petition if they will be performing the same service, for the same period of time in the same location. 8 C.F.R. §214.2(h)(2)(ii).

(5) Visa Issuance for H-2B/H-2R— Need an approved I-129 petition. Prior to Sept. 30, 2007 (when the H-2R program ended), an employer could attest to the fact that the H-2B is a returning H-2 and therefore should be treated as an H-2R. Can have multiple workers on a petition. A consular officer may issue the visa after obtaining verification from KCC that a previous H-2B visa was issued, if returning H-2R or by otherwise verifying it. 9 FAM 41.53 N.4–5. If an applicant is not entitled to an H-2R visa because s/he cannot establish that she was previously issued an H-2B visa, the consul may process the applicant under the H-2B category if she is otherwise available and the annual limit on visas has not been reached. Cable, DOS, 05-State-00126721 (July 7, 2005), *published on* AILA InfoNet at Doc. No. 05120166.

3.k. *Employer's Obligations*—The employer on an H-2A or H-2B who terminates the employees services must provide him transportation back to his country. 8 C.F.R. §214.2(h)(6)(vi)(E). In addition, if the employer terminates the employee or changes any terms and conditions of employment of the employee, the employer must notify USCIS *immediately.* 8 C.F.R. §214.2(h)(11)(i)(A).

3.l. H-2 to Employment-Based Preference

(1) Where same employer need to show position is different.

(2) If present labor certification is approved or preference petition is filed DHS regulation provides no H-2 extension will be granted. 8 C.F.R. §214.2(h)(16)(ii). *But see North American Industries v. Feldman*, 722 F.2d 893 (1st Cir. 1983) [struck down INS O.I. finding INS wrong in focusing on duties rather than *employer's* need].

3.m. *Administrative Penalties*—If there is a substantial failure to meet any of the conditions of the H-2B petition or a willful misrepresentation of a material fact, DHS may impose, in addition to all other penalties and only after a hearing, civil monetary penalties of $10,000 per violation and refusal to grant petitions for a period of 1 to 5 years. INA §214(c)(14)(A). Substantial failure is defined as "willful failure to comply with the requirements of this section that constitutes a significant deviation from the terms and conditions of the petition." The highest penalties are reserved for willful failures.

3.n. *Judicial Review*—A USC denied job advertised for H-2B position has no standing to sue under INA or False Claims Act, but may have claim under 42 U.S.C. §1981(a) [Civil Rights Act]. *U.S. v. Richard Dattner Architects*, 972 F.Supp. 738 (S.D.N.Y. 1997). A challenge to

GAL Nos. 10-84 and 1-95 as contrary to H-2B regulations and statute was rejected in *Martinez v. Reich*, 934 F.Supp. 232 (S.D. Tex. 1996).

L. *O Visas*—INA §101(a)(15)(O), 8 U.S.C. §1101(a)(15)(O); 137 Cong. Rec. part 2 S18242-01 at 18247 (Nov. 26, 1991), 8 C.F.R. §214.2(o)(1); 22 C.F.R. §41.55; 59 Fed. Reg. 41818–42 (Aug. 15, 1994): 72 Fed. Reg. 18856 (Apr. 16, 2007)

1. O-1—8 C.F.R. §214.2(o)(1)(i):

 1.a. O-1A—Person who "has extraordinary ability in the sciences, arts, education, business or athletics which has been demonstrated by sustained national or international acclaim." 8 C.F.R. §214.2(o)(1)(ii)(A)(1).

 1.b. O-1B—If in motion picture or TV production, the person must have "a demonstrated record of extraordinary achievement." Person needs to demonstrate that his or her achievements have been recognized in the field "through extensive documentation." 8 C.F.R. §214.2(o)(1)(ii)(A)(2).

 1.c. The Service interprets the statute to encompass "any field of endeavor" including craftsmen and lecturers. Memo, Weinig, Acting Asst. Comm., CO 214O.1-C, 214P.1-C (June 25, 1992), *reprinted in* 69 No. 33 *Interpreter Releases* 1070, 1084–86 (Aug. 31, 1992). For an extensive list of examples of what might include "any field of creative activity or endeavor," *see* 137 Cong. Rec. Part 2 S18247 (Nov. 26, 1991). The term art also includes not only the principal creators and performers, but also other essential personnel such as directors, set designers, choreographers, orchestrates, coaches, arrangers, costume designers, make-up artists, stage technicians and animal trainers. 8 C.F.R. §214.2(o)(3)(ii). It also includes the culinary arts. *Id.*

 1.d. Must seek to enter for the purpose of continuing the type of work, but there is no requirement that the person is coming to the U.S. to perform services requiring a person of O-1 caliber. 59 Fed. Reg. 41818 at 41820 (Aug. 15, 1994); *Matter of ___*, LIN 02 184 53385 (AAO Sept. 17, 2002), *reprinted in* 26 Immig. Rptr. B2-92 [following comments in Federal Register and rejecting Service Center's position that the position must require someone of extraordinary ability].

 1.e. Dual intent recognized, as there is no foreign residence requirement but there is a requirement that there be a temporary intent to remain. 8 C.F.R. §214.2(o)(13); *Matter ___*, WAC 01-250-52367, CSC (AAO 4. 2002) [reversed denial by regional director because a culinary chef opening a new restaurant as part of a series of restaurants around the world can be considered to have a temporary intent to remain], *reported in* 8 No. 8 *Bender's Immigration Bulletin* 688-89 (Apr. 15, 2003). Dual intent is permissible for O-1s. Office of Business Liaison, USCIS, Employer Information Bulletin 15 (Dec. 8, 2004) at 4, *reprinted in* 82 No. 3 *Interpreter Releases* 149, 160, 180–84 (Jan. 17, 2005).

2. O-2—8 C.F.R. §214.2(o)(1)(ii)(B):

 2.a. Only for person accompanying and assisting an O-1 artist or athlete in the artistic or athletic performance for a specific event or events so long as:

  (1) S/he is an integral part of such actual performance.

  (2) S/he has critical skills and experience with the O-1 that are not of a general nature and which cannot be performed by other individuals.

   (a) For motion picture or TV productions, person has skills and experience which are not general, which are critical and which are based on a pre-existing long-standing working relationship. In the case of a specific production a long-standing relationship is unnecessary where there is significant pre or post production work that will take place inside and outside U.S. and the person's presence needed for successful completion.

  (3) S/he has foreign residence which s/he has no intention of abandoning.

3. O-3—8 C.F.R. §214.2(o)(6)(iv): Includes spouse and children accompanying and following to join as O-3s.

4. Extraordinary Ability/Extraordinary Achievement Defined—8 C.F.R. §214.2(o)(3)(ii):

 4.a. Extraordinary ability in science, education, business or athletics is "a level of expertise indicating that the person is one of the small percentage who have arisen to the very top of the field of endeavor." *See, e.g., Matter of* ___ SRC 02-245-52561, TSC (AAO Nov. 1, 2002) [discoverer of master gene Cbfal and one of 20 of America's Most Promising Biomedical Researchers met criteria for O-1], *reported in* 8 No. 2 *Bender's Immigration Bulletin* 150-52 (Jan. 15, 2003).

4.b. Extraordinary ability in the arts means "distinction," "a high level of achievement in the field of arts evidenced by a degree of skill and recognition substantially above that ordinarily encountered ..." This category requires the petitioner to establish only that the artist is "prominent in his or her field of endeavor." 59 Fed. Reg. 41818 at 41820 (Aug. 15, 1994); *Matter of* ___, WAC 02-196-50736 CSC (AAO Sept. 16, 2002) [recognizing that the standard for extraordinary ability in the arts, while high, is less that in science, business or athletics and granting O-1 to juggler who had toured with Ringling Brothers Circus and won an international competition] *reported in* 8 No. 4 *Bender's Immigration Bulletin* 294-95 (Feb. 15, 2003); *Matter* ___, WAC 01-250-52367, CSC (AAO 4. 2002) [reversed denial by regional director of Executive Chef position] *reported in* 8 No. 8 *Bender's Immigration Bulletin* 688-89 (Apr. 15, 2003).

4.c. Extraordinary achievement means a "very high level of accomplishment in the motion picture or TV industry evidenced by a degree of skill and recognition significantly above that ordinarily encountered ..." The person must be "outstanding or notable." 59 Fed. Reg. 41818 at 41821 (Aug. 15, 1994).

4.d. Proving extraordinary ability in science, education, business or athletics—8 C.F.R. §214.2(o)(3)(iii)—Beneficiary may prove sustained national or international acclaim by receipt of a major internationally recognized award such as the Nobel Prize, or documenting at least 3 of the suggested criteria: (a) receipt of nationally or internationally recognized awards; (b) membership in organization that requires outstanding achievement; (c) published materials about the applicant in professional or major trade publications; (d) judgment of the work of others; (e) original scientific or scholarly work of major significance in his or her field; (f) evidence of authorship of scholarly work; (g) evidence that s/he has been employed in a critical or essential capacity at an organization with a distinguished reputation; (h) has commanded or will command a high salary in relation to others in the field.

4.e. Proving distinction in the arts—8 C.F.R. §214.2(o)(3)(iv)—Beneficiary must prove s/he is prominent in his or her field by being nominated for or the recipient of a significant international or national award or prize, such as an Academy Award, Emmy, Grammy or Director's Guild Award, or by documenting at least 3 of the following suggested criteria:

(1) lead in production having a distinguished reputation;

(2) critical reviews in major newspapers or trade journals;

(3) lead for organization that has a distinguished reputation;

(4) record of major commercial or critically acclaimed successes;

(5) significant recognition from organizations, critics, government agencies or other recognized experts in the field;

(6) has commanded or will command a high salary.

4.f. Proving extraordinary achievement in motion picture or TV industry—8 C.F.R. §214.2(o)(3)(v)—The Service relies on the same criteria used to prove distinction in the arts, except that it will weigh the evidence differently by requiring a person of extraordinary achievement "to meet a higher standard." 59 Fed. Reg. 41818 at 41821 (Aug. 15, 1994).

4.g. Comparable Evidence—To prove extraordinary ability in the arts or science, education, business or athletics (but not in the motion picture or TV industry), the petitioner may submit comparable evidence if the above does not readily apply to his or her occupation. 8 C.F.R. §§214.2(o)(3)(iii)(C), (iv)(C). O-1 petitioners are not required to demonstrate that the work requires someone of O-1 caliber. 59 Fed. Reg. 41818, 41820 (Aug. 15, 1994).

4.h. Proving the O-2 standard—8 C.F.R. §214.2(o)(4). Evidence needs to establish current essentiality, critical skills and experience with the O-1 not possessed by U.S. worker. For motion picture and TV, critical skills/experience with O-1 based on longstanding work relationship *or* for a specific production (including pre- and post-production work) has taken and will take place in and out of the U.S. and the beneficiary's participation is essential to complete production.

4.i. General documentary requirements for all O categories—8 C.F.R. §§214.2(o)(2)(ii), (iii). Can use affidavits by employers and experts, contracts, awards, and similar documentation. Need explanation of nature, time frame and itinerary of events. Need advisory opinion from consultative organization.

5. Consultations—8 C.F.R. §214.2(o)(5)—O-1/O-2:

5.a. Motion picture/TV O-1 petitions *must* include written advisory opinions from appropriate union *and* management group, describing beneficiary's achievements in motion picture/TV field. Motion picture/TV O-2 petitions *must* include written advisory opinions from appropriate union *and* a management group, describing beneficiary's skills/experience with O-1 and whether longstanding relationship exists or, for continuity purposes, whether O-2's continuing participation in production is essential because significant production will take/has taken place in and out of the U.S.

5.b. All other O-1 petitions *must* contain written advisory opinion from appropriate union, if one exists, describing beneficiary's ability/achievements in field and duties to be performed. Petition *may* contain nonunion opinions from any expert source. All other O-2 petitions *must* have written advisory opinion from appropriate union, if one exists, describing alien's essentiality to and working relationship with the O-1. Memo, Weinig, Acting Asst. Comm., CO 214O.1C, 214P.1C (June 25, 1992), *reprinted in* 69 No. 33 *Interpreter Releases* 1070, 1084–86 (Aug. 31, 1992). If the consultation does not contain all the elements necessary, the Service should approve the petition if it is otherwise approvable. Memo, Weinig (June 25, 1992), *supra.*

5.c. O-2 petitions must contain consultations from each union with appropriate expertise over activities of the O-2 beneficiaries. Memo, Weinig (June 25, 1992), *supra.*

5.d. Negative advisory opinions *must* contain specific statement of facts supporting the conclusion reached. Positive opinions may take the form of a letter stating "no objection." All opinions are advisory only, not binding on USCIS.

5.e. Waiver of Consultation—Consultation requirement waived if petitioner demonstrates no appropriate union exists. 8 C.F.R. §214.2(o)(5)(i)(G). Consultation waived for O-1s of extraordinary ability in arts who are re-entering the U.S. to perform similar services within 2 years of obtaining consultation. 8 C.F.R. §214.2(o)(5)(ii)(B). New consultations not required for extensions of stay. Letter, Bednarz, Chief, NIV Branch, Adjudications, CO 214h-C (Sept. 29, 1992), *reprinted in* 69 No. 44 *Interpreter Releases* 1460, 1471–72 (Nov. 16, 1992).

5.f. Expedited Treatment—The regulations make a theoretical provision for the Service to obtain consultation in expedited cases and routine ones where petition includes nonlabor consultation. 8 C.F.R. §214.2(o)(5)(i)(E) and (F).

6. Petition Process—8 C.F.R. §214.2(o)(2).

6.a. I-129 application—O-1 cannot petition for himself. Letter, Weinig, Acting Asst. Comm., Adjudications, CO 214o.1C (July 24, 1992), *reprinted in* 69 No. 33 *Interpreter Releases* 1071, 1087 (Aug. 31, 1992). Must use U.S. agent to file in cases involving persons traditionally self-employed or where there is a foreign employer. 8 C.F.R. §214.2(o)(2)(i). Cannot file petition more than *one year* before person's work. O-2 petition must be filed separately from O-1. Adjudication at service center even in emergency. Photocopies may be submitted. Approval on I-797.

6.b. Work at multiple locations—Include itinerary. File I-129.

6.c. Work for multiple employers—Each employer must file at Service Center. One employer/agent can petition for entire itinerary.

6.d. Change employer—New employer must file with Service Center and request E/S. O-2 *cannot* change unless O-1 does.

6.e. Amended petition—Need only file if change is material. Promotion is not a material change. Letter, Brown, Acting Branch Chief, Business and Trade Services Branch, Benefits Division, INS, HQ 70/6.2.18 (Oct. 14, 1997), *reprinted in* 75 No. 4 *Interpreter Releases* 130, 155 (Jan. 26, 1998).

6.f. Notice to USCIS—If there are any changes in the terms and conditions of employment which may affect eligibility, the petitioner "shall immediately notify the Service." And if the petitioner no longer employs the beneficiary, s/he "shall send a letter explaining the change to the Director who approved the petition." 8 C.F.R. §214.2(o)(8)(i)(A).

6.g. Agents—Can file I-129 involving multiple employers as the representative of the employers and beneficiary if s/he includes itinerary and contract.

6.h. Multiple beneficiaries—May include multiple O-2s on one petition where they are assisting O-1 in same performance for same time.

6.i. The approval of a labor certification or filing of a preference petition shall not be a basis to deny an O petition or an extension of an O or admission to the U.S. 8 C.F.R. §214.2(o)(13).

6.j. All extensions filed on I-129 at VSC. Granted in increments of one year for the same event. Office of Business Liaison, USCIS, Employer Information Bulletin 15 (Dec. 8, 2004) at 3, *reprinted in* 82 No. 3 *Interpreter Releases* 149, 160, 180–84 (Jan. 17, 2005). No documentation needed for extension of petition. For an extension of stay need only provide a statement explaining reason for stay request. No new consultation required. 8 C.F.R. §214.2(o)(12). *See* Letter, Bednarz, (Sept. 29, 1992), *supra*; If the beneficiary leaves the U.S. for business or personal reasons while the extension request is pending, s/he may request that USCIS send cable notification of approval to consular office abroad. 8 C.F.R. §214.2(o)(12)(i). An O is not precluded from traveling while an extension of stay is pending. Memo, Cook, Acting Asst. Comm., INS HQ 70/6.2.9 (June 18, 2001), *posted on* AILA InfoNet at Doc. No. 01081635. An O petition and extension of status by a new employer or for a new position by the same employer is a new "event" under 8 C.F.R. §214.2(o)(3) and may be approved for 3 years. Summary of Oct. 3, 2002 ISD Teleconference, *published on* AILA InfoNet at Doc. No. 02110470.

6.k. Professional Athletes—When traded from one team to another, employment authorization (EA) will continue with new team for 30 days during which time I-129 must be filed. If filed, EA extended until petition is adjudicated. 8 C.F.R. §214.2(o)(2)(iv)(G).

7. Admission—Period of authorized stay for O category is for such time as the AG may specify to provide for the event(s), but no more than 3 years. INA §214(a)(2)(A), 8 U.S.C. §1184(a)(2)(A); 8 C.F.R. §214.2(o)(6)(iii)(A). The beneficiary may be admitted 10 days before and stay until 10 days after validity period, 8 C.F.R. §214.2(o)(10), but cannot work during this time. There is no overall time limit on O-1s similar to the overall time limits on H-1Bs and L-1s.

8. Return Transportation Costs—The petitioner and employer are jointly and severally liable for reasonable transportation costs of beneficiary's return home if s/he is terminated. INA §214(c)(5)(B), 8 U.S.C. §1184(c)(5)(B), 8 C.F.R. §214.2(o)(16).

9. Denial—8 C.F.R. §214.2(o)(7)—If based on derogatory information that the petitioner was unaware of, s/he gets 30 days to respond. Otherwise final order entered and person can appeal to AAU.

10. Revocation—8 C.F.R. §214.2(o)(8)—The service center automatically revokes petition if petitioner, or in the case of an agent the underlying employer, goes out of business, files a written withdrawal or notifies USCIS that the beneficiary is no longer employed. All other circumstances require notice prior to revocation.

M. P Visas—INA §101(a)(15)(P), 8 U.S.C. §1101(a)(15)(P); 8 C.F.R. §214.2(p); 22 C.F.R. §41.56; 59 Fed. Reg. 41818–42 (Aug. 15, 1994): 72 Fed. Reg. 18856 (Apr. 16, 2007); Creating Opportunities for Minor League Professionals, Entertainers, and Teams Through Legal Entry Act of 2006 (COMPETE Act of 2006)—PL 109-463, 120 Stat. 3477 (Dec. 22, 2006).

1. P-1 Athletes and Group Entertainers

1.a. Person who performs as an athlete, individually or as part of a group or team that is "internationally recognized"(P-1A) *or* a person who performs with or is an integral or essential part of an entertainment group that has been recognized internationally as being outstanding in the discipline for a sustained and substantial period of time (P-1B), and in the case of the performer has had a sustained and substantial relationship with the group over a period of at least one year. P-1As have now been expanded to include minor league professional/entertainers under certain circumstances to include: (1) an athlete, whether or not professional, who performs at an internationally recognized level of performance; (2) an amateur athlete or coach of sports teams in the U.S. that are members of a foreign league or association if (i) the foreign league or association is the highest level of amateur performance of that sport in that country; (ii) participation renders the athlete ineligible for U.S. scholarships under NCAA rules; and (iii) a significant number of the players in the league are drafted into major league teams or minor teams affiliated with them; *or* (3) professional or amateur ice skater who performs individually or as part of a group theatrical production.

(1) Internationally recognized means "a high level of achievement...evidenced by a degree of skill and recognition substantially above that ordinarily encountered, to the extent such achievement is renowned, leading or well-known in more than one country." 8 C.F.R. §214.2(p)(3);

(2) An entertainment group or athletic team may be as few as 2 persons. The manner in which the act is billed is not a determinative factor. If solo artist or entertainer traditionally performs with back up singers or musician the act can be classified as a group so long as 75% of them have been together for one year or more. If they do not meet the 75% rule then the solo artist must qualify as O-1 and the musicians as O-2s. Memo, Weinig (June 25, 1992), *supra*.

(3) Both the international recognition and one year prior relationship may be waived for performers and entertainers in some cases. INA §214(c)(4)(B)(ii) & (iii), 8 U.S.C. §§1184(c)(4)(B)(ii) & (iii). A group that is nationally recognized for a sustained and substantial period of time may obtain a waiver if there are special circumstances. The one year prior relationship does not apply to 25% of performers or entertainers in any group and the AG may waive this requirement for any performer or entertainer who replaces an essential member of the group because of that member's illness or other exigent circumstances or because the performer or entertainer augments the group by performing a critical role.

(4) Circus personnel performing as part of a circus or circus group are exempt from international recognition and one-year requirements provided they are part of, or are joining, a circus with sustained national recognition. 8 C.F.R. §214.2(p)(4)(iii)(C)(1); Memo, Weinig (June 25, 1992), *supra*.

1.b. Seeks to enter temporarily and solely for purpose of performing in a "competition, event or performance." This includes short vacations, promotional appearances and incidental stopovers, and can include an entire season, itinerary and contract. 8 C.F.R. §214.2(p)(3).

1.c. Individual entertainers are omitted if performing separate and apart from group. Must get O-1

1.d. Visas cannot be issued to a national of a country that is a state sponsor of international terrorism unless the Secretary of State in consultation with the Secretary of Homeland Security and the heads of other appropriate U.S. agencies grants a waiver.

2. P-2 Reciprocal Exchange Program. 8 C.F.R. §214.2(p)(5)

2.a. Performs as artist or entertainer individually or as part of a group, or is an integral part of the performance.

2.b. Seeks to enter temporarily and solely for performing and

2.c. Is under a reciprocal exchange program between an organization or organizations in the U.S. and one or more foreign organizations and which provides for the temporary exchange of artists, entertainers or groups.

3. P-3. 8 C.F.R. §214.2(p)(6)

3.a. Performs as an artist, entertainer, individual or as part of a group or is an integral part of the performance *and*

3.b. Enters temporarily and solely to perform, teach or coach in a culturally unique program. There is no requirement that group exist before tour.

3.c. May be commercial or noncommercial program. 8 C.F.R. §214.2(p)(6)(i)(B). It need not be sponsored by educational, cultural or government agency. 59 Fed. Reg. 41818, 41825 (Aug. 15, 1994).

4. Essential Support Personnel—8 C.F.R. §214.2(p)(3). Person who is an integral part of the performance of a P-1, P-2 or P-3 "because he or she performs support services which cannot be readily performed by a United States worker and which are essential to the successful performance of services." The person must have the appropriate qualifications to perform the services, critical knowledge of the specific services and experience in providing such support. Multiple support personnel may be on one petition if it involves the same period of time and the same services. Instructions to Form I-129, *revised* July 30, 2007. For example, the P-1 classification includes support personnel for athletes such as coaches, scouts, trainers and other team officials. It may also include referees, linesmen or officials to conduct the games if they are traditionally employed in the sport. Memo, Weinig (June 25, 1992), *supra*. However, coaches or other officials of teams which are comprised totally of USCs do not qualify. *Id.* Need to apply separately for O-1. To obtain a P status the support personnel must submit a consultation with a labor organization, a statement regarding person's prior essentiality, critical skills and experience with principal petitioner and a copy of the contract or summary of oral contract. 8 C.F.R. §214.2(p)(4)(iv).

5. P-4—Spouses and Children—Can enter as accompanying or following to join as P-4s. No employment unless authorized. Granted same term of admission as spouse. 8 C.F.R. §214.2(p)(8)(iii)(D).

6. Foreign Residence Abroad Requirement—All "P" applicants must have a foreign residence that they do not intend to abandon, but regulations permit dual intent. 8 C.F.R. §214.2(p)(15).

7. Petition Process—8 C.F.R. §214.2(p)(2), (4), (5), (6).

   7.a. Filing—8 C.F.R. §214.2(p)(2).

      (1) I-129 petition must be filed within the *one year* period prior to services at the Appropriate Service Center designated on the petition and USCIS website. Photocopies can be submitted. P petitions may be filed by U.S. employer, U.S. sponsor, established U.S. agent or foreign employer through U.S. agent. P-2 petitions may also be filed by U.S. union involved in the exchange program. Separate petition for essential support personnel. Amended petitions must be filed if there are material changes.

      (2) Multiple employers/multiple work/agents. If multiple work area must submit itinerary. Petition filed at Service Center. If multiple employers, each may file I-129 at Service Center *or* one petitioner can petition for entire itinerary. If change in employers, the new employer must file a petition and request to extend stay. If agent is the petitioner, s/he must have itinerary and contract. 8 C.F.R. §214.2(p) (2)(iv)(E). Must have U.S. agent as petitioner where P is self-employed or there is a foreign employer. 8 C.F.R. §214.2(p)(2)(iv)(E). Multiple beneficiaries may be included on petition if they are members of a group seeking classification based on the reputation of the group or if they provide essential support.

      (3) Substitution of beneficiaries—8 C.F.R. §214.2(p)(2)(iv)(H). Can substitute all P categories. Employer must submit letter at consular post or port of entry requesting substitution along with copy of petitioner's approval notice.

   7.b. Evidence for all P petitions—8 C.F.R. §§214.2(p)(2)(ii), (iii). Copies of written contracts or summaries of oral contract. Affidavits, awards, or similar documentation regarding achievements, expert opinions.

   7.c. P-1 Athletes—8 C.F.R. §214.2(p)(4)(ii). Need documentation showing that: (1) athlete or team internationally recognized; (2) athletic competition must have a distinguished reputation; and (3) competition must require participation of athlete or team with international reputation

      (1) Petition must include tendered contract with major U.S. sports league or team or one commensurate with international recognition; *and*

      (2) Any 2 of the following:

         (a) significant participation in a prior season in majors;

         (b) international competition with national team;

(c) significant participation in a prior season for U.S. college or university or intercollegiate competition;

(d) written statement from U.S. official in sport about person or team's international recognition;

(e) written statement from expert or sport's media as to international recognition;

(f) team or individual ranking; or

(g) significant honor or award in sport. *or*

(3) Perform as a professional athlete employed by either a professional sports team in association with 6 or more teams that have combined revenues in excess of $10,000,000 or a minor league team affiliated with such association

7.d. P-1 Entertainment Groups—8 C.F.R. §214.2(p)(4)(iii). Need documentation showing that: (1) group internationally recognized for sustained and substantial period of time; (2) 75% of members of the group have had sustained and substantial relationship with group for one year.

(1) Petition must include evidence that:

(a) group has been performing for at least one year;

(b) list of members and dates employed;

(c) group has been nominated or has received significant international awards *or* any three of the following documentation regarding international recognition:

i) star or lead in performance that has distinguished reputation;

ii) reviews in major publication;

iii) star or lead in performance for organization that has distinguished reputation;

iv) major commercial or critically acclaimed success;

v) testimonials regarding group's significant recognition; or

vi) group will command or has commanded high salary.

(2) Certain Groups Exempt—8 C.F.R. §214.2(p)(4)(iii)(C).

(a) Circuses do not have to meet one-year group membership requirement or international recognition. Need only show they have been recognized nationally as outstanding for sustained period.

(b) Director may waive international recognition for group recognized nationally for sustained period where there are special circumstances.

(c) One-year relationship may also be waived in exigent circumstances.

7.e. P-1 Minor League or Amateur Athletes—Must demonstrate that the coach or athletes are: (1) part of an international league or association of 14 or more amateur sports teams: (2) that the foreign league is operating at the highest level of amateur performance in the foreign country; (3) that participation in the foreign league renders the players ineligible for scholarship or amateur athletics under the NCAA; and (4) that a significant number of players who play in the foreign leagues are drafted by major league or minor league affiliates in the U.S. Memo, Aytes, Assoc. Dir. of Domestic Operations, USCIS, HQ 70/6.2.19 (Dec. 28, 2006), *published on* AILA InfoNet at Doc. No. 07010865.

7.f. P-2 Reciprocal Exchange—8 C.F.R. §214.2(p)(5). Need documentation showing that: (1) persons performing under reciprocal exchange program; (2) exchange is between a U.S. organization and foreign organization; (3) provision is for temporary exchange; and (4) the exchange is between similar caliber performers employed under similar conditions.

Documents needed:

(1) formal reciprocal exchange agreement;

(2) statement from sponsoring organization regarding exchange;

(3) evidence that appropriate labor organization in U.S. was involved in negotiating or concurs in reciprocal program; *and*

(4) evidence that all exchange artists or entertainers are artists with comparable skills and that the terms and conditions of employment are similar.

7.g. P-3 Culturally Unique Program—8 C.F.R. §214.2(p)(6). Need documentation showing that: (1) Artists or entertainers, individually or as a group, coming to the U.S. for the purpose of developing, interpreting, representing, coaching, or teaching a unique or traditional ethnic, folk, cultural, musical, theatrical or artistic performance or presentation; and that the (2) Artist or entertainer must be coming to the U.S. to participate in a *commercial* or noncommercial cultural event which will further understanding or development of his or her art form.

Documentation needed:

(1) Affidavits, testimonials, or letters from recognized experts with the basis of their knowledge attesting to the applicant's skills in performing, presenting, coaching or teaching the unique or traditional art form;

(2) Documentation that performance is culturally unique, as evidenced by published materials and

(3) Evidence that all performances will be culturally unique events.

8. Consultations—8 C.F.R. §214.2(p)(7).

8.a. Consultation with an appropriate union regarding the nature of the work to be done and the person's qualification is mandatory before any P visa petition is approved. Advisory opinion, however, is not binding on USCIS.

8.b. Petitioner must submit a written advisory opinion from union with I-129 petition. The union may submit a specific opinion or letter of no objection.

8.c. Two exceptions

(1) Where USCIS handles case expeditiously and obtains opinion telephonically; or

(2) No appropriate labor organization exists.

8.d. If a detailed opinion is written for P-1s, it must evaluate person's or group's ability, comment on their international recognition and state whether services being performed are appropriate for an internationally recognized athlete or entertainment group. P-2 advisory opinions must comment on the *bona fides* of the reciprocal program and whether it meets appropriate regulatory standards. P-3 opinions must evaluate the cultural uniqueness of the person's skills, state whether the events are mostly cultural in nature, and state whether the event or activity is appropriate for P-3 classification. For essential support personnel, the advisory opinion must evaluate the person's essentiality to and working relationship with the artist or entertainer and state whether U.S. workers are available. Consultations not needed for an extension. Letter, Bednarz, Chief, NIV Branch, Adjudications, CO 214p-C (Sept. 29, 1992), *reprinted in* 69 No. 44 *Interpreter Releases* 1460, 1471–72 (Nov. 16, 1992). Negative consultations *must* contain specific statement of facts supporting conclusions. Alternatively, a union may simply submit a no objection letter. 8 C.F.R. §214.2(p)(7)(ii).

9. Admission/Extension—8 C.F.R. §214.2(p)(8)(iii), (13), (14)(ii).

9.a. P-1 athletes may be admitted for a period of up to 5 years with one extension up to 5 years. INA §214(a)(2)(B), 8 U.S.C. §1184(a)(2)(B). A petition for a P-1 athletic team may not exceed one year. A petition for a P-1 entertainment group may not exceed one year.

9.b. P-2/P-3 and essential support personnel granted admission for time necessary to complete event up to one year and extensions for a similar period. A petition for a P-2 or P-3 artist or entertainer, therefore, may not exceed one year.

9.c. Spouse and Dependents—A spouse and dependents may only be admitted for the same period as the principal. 8 C.F.R. §214.2(p)(8)(iii)(D).

9.d. For extension of visa petition no supporting documents are required unless requested and no consultation is required. For extension of stay for the same event or activity petitioner needs only a statement or letter explaining need for extension unless additional requests are made by USCIS. Beneficiary must be in the U.S. at the time request for an extension is filed. All requests are on Form I-129. Approval on I-797. 8 C.F.R. §214.2(p)(13) and (14); *See* Letter, Bednarz (Sept. 29, 1992), *supra*. If the beneficiary leaves the U.S. for business or personal reasons while the extension request is pending, s/he may request that USCIS send cable notification of approval to consular office abroad. 8 C.F.R. §214.2(p)(14)(i). A person is not precluded from traveling while an extension of stay is pending. Memo, Cook, Acting Comm. INS, HQ 70/6.2.9 (June 18, 2001), *published on* AILA InfoNet at Doc. No. 01081635.

9.e. The approval of LC or filing of a preference petition shall not be a basis to deny a P petition or extension. 8 C.F.R. §214.2(p)(15).

9.f. Transportation costs—The petitioner and employer are jointly and severally liable for reasonable costs of the beneficiary's trip home if s/he is terminated. INA §214(c)(5)(B); 8 C.F.R. §214.2(p)(18).

9.g. Traded Athletes—Employment authorization remains for 30 days with new team during which time a new I-129 must be filed. If filed, EA continues until petition decided. 8 C.F.R. §214.2(p)(2)(iv)(C)(2).

10. Denial—8 C.F.R. §214.2(p)(9). Petitioner has right to appeal from the denial of the petition. However, there is no appeal from the denial of an extension of stay or change of status.

11. Revocation—8 C.F.R. §214.2(p)(10). May occur automatically if petitioner or employer if there is an agent goes out of business, files a written withdrawal or notifies the DHS that the beneficiary is no longer employed. Otherwise, revocation must be by notice.

12. Consular Processing—Consular officers "do not have the authority to question the approval of P petitions without specific evidence, unavailable to DHS at the time of petition approval, that the beneficiary may not be entitled to status." Cable, DOS, 05-State-133398 (July 19, 2005) ¶5, *published on* AILA InfoNet at Doc. No. 05072661. Consular officer also should not, as a routine matter, require applicants to perform without an indication that the performer is not a bona fide member of the group. *Id* at ¶6. Group members are not required to apply together for the visa and the consulate is urged to utilize expediting procedures where the group's schedule may be disrupted by unforeseen events. *Id* at ¶¶2-3.

N. *L Visas*—INA §101(a)(15)(L), 8 U.S.C. §1101(a)(15)(L), 8 C.F.R. §214.2(*l*); 22 C.F.R. §41.54. Legislative history, H.R. Rep. No. 851, 91st Cong. 2d Sess.; 1970 U.S.C.C.A.N. 2750, 116 Cong. Rec. 5730 (1970). *See also* Immigration Act of 1990, H.R. Conf. Rep. No. 955, 101st Cong., 2d Sess. 126 (1990); 1990 U.S.C.C.A.N. 6784; Omnibus Appropriations Act (OAA) for FY 2005, PL 108-447, 118 Stat. 2809, Div. J, Tit. IV, "L-1 Visa Reform Act of 2004" (Dec. 8, 2004).

1. Definition—8 C.F.R. §214.2(*l*)(1)(ii):

1.a. Alien must be employed continuously abroad for 1 of the past 3 years by parent, branch, affiliate or subsidiary of U.S. company preceding his application for admission. The Immigration Act of 1990 eliminated the "immediately preceding" requirement, so that a person may now be transferred into the U.S. if s/he worked for the entity abroad continuously for one year at any time within the preceding *three years*. In the case of a person being transferred where the importing employer has filed a blanket L, the transferee must also have worked for the company abroad for at least 12 months. INA §214(c)(2)(A); AFM at 32.5.

1.b. Employment by a firm, corporation or other legal entity or its parent, branch, affiliate or subsidiary. Includes profit, nonprofit, religious, charitable organizations. 9 FAM 41.54 N.7.3; *Matter of Church of Scientology International*, 19 I&N Dec. 593 (Comm. 1988); Form of entity not relevant. *Id.*; *Johnson-Laird, Inc. v. INS*, 537 F.Supp. 52 (D. Or. 1981). Also includes accounting or management consulting firms with an internationally recognized presence notwithstanding their status as partnerships. IMMACT90 §206(a). Even if international management consulting firm separates from an international accounting firm and is no longer connected to it, but continues to maintain the qualifying worldwide organizational structure, they may obtain L-1s. PL 106-95 §6 (Nov. 12, 1999); AFM at 32.2(a)(2) and 22.5(b); Memo, Yates, Deputy Ex. Assoc. Comm., Immigration Service Division, Office of Field Operations,

HQADN 70/ 6.2.12, AD 00-17 (Aug. 10, 2000), *reprinted in* 77 *Interpreter Releases* 1211–13 (Aug. 21, 2000).

1.c. Alien seeks to enter U.S. temporarily to continue to work for same employer or its affiliate or subsidiary. The employee is not required to perform full-time services in the U.S. but must dedicate a significant portion of his or her time on a regular and systematic basis. O.I. §214.2(*l*)(5)(ii)(B). The DOS takes the view that while full time employment is anticipated the beneficiary does not have be in the U.S. on a full-time basis. Cable, DOS (98-State-095200) (May 28, 1998), *reprinted in* 75 No. 22 *Interpreter Releases* 813, 814 (June 8, 1998) and *published on* AILA InfoNet at Doc. No. 98060591 (June 5, 1998); 9 FAM 41.54 N.8.5. The person's principal purpose in the U.S., however, must be consistent with L status. DOS Cable, 98-State-102426, *supra.*

1.d. Must continue to work in capacity that is managerial or executive (L-1A) or involves specialized knowledge (L-1B). IMMACT90 §206(a).

1.e. The INA §214(b) presumption of immigrant intent is no longer applicable to Ls. Thus, a petition for an immigrant visa may be pending while person maintains L-1 status.

2. One-Year Employment Requirement

2.a. One-year cannot be met by working part of year for affiliate or branch in U.S. *Karmali v. INS*, 707 F.2d 408 (9th Cir. 1983). But time spent in U.S. will not interrupt one year. 8 C.F.R. §214.2(*l*)(1)(ii)(A); O.I. §248.4. 9 FAM 41.54 N.11.3. Prior authority distinguished. *See Matter of Continental Grain Co.*, 14 I&N Dec. 140 (DD 1972). [five months training in U.S. and then seven months abroad with corp. is sufficient]. Also, time spent in U.S. in another status (*e.g.,* H-1B) in excess of 3 years does not interrupt the one-out-of-three year requirement if the companies have qualifying (*e.g.,* parent-subsidiary) relationship. Letter, Bednarz, Chief, NIV Branch, Adjudications, CO 214L-C (Feb. 14, 1994), *reprinted in* 71 No. 10 *Interpreter Releases* 351, 373–74 (Mar. 14, 1994; 8 C.F.R. §214.2(*l*)(1)(ii)(A) [periods not interruptive of the one year but such period not counted toward fulfillment of the one year]. Where applicant never physically worked abroad 1 year not met. *Matter of Kloeti*, 18 I&N Dec. 295 (R.C. 1981) [B-1 employed by foreign company but never physically present abroad working for them, L denied]. Working in American Samoa or another outlying possession is sufficient to meet the one-year abroad requirement. Letter, Ohata, Asst. Comm. Service Center Operations, 70/100 (Feb. 13, 2003), *published on* AILA InfoNet at Doc. No. 03030345.

2.b. Part-time employment—Can use combination of part-time employment to meet one-year continuous requirement if part-time work is for affiliated companies (*i.e.,* parent, subsidiary, branch); 9 FAM 41.54 N. 11.1.

2.c. Blanket Ls—As a result of the L-1 Visa Reform Act, PL 108-447, Div. J, Title IV (Dec. 8, 2004) amending INA §214(c)(2)(A) blanket L employees are required once again to show that they worked for the company abroad for one year. Previously 6 months of past employment was sufficient

2.d. One year preceding admission vs. one year preceding filing petition for L. The statute and regulations appear to be in conflict in regard to whether the one-year requirement abroad must be met prior to seeking admission into the U.S. or prior to filing the I-129 petition for the L visa. *Compare* INA §101(a)(15)(L) ["an alien who, within 3 years preceding the time of his application for admission into the United States, has been employed continuously for one year..."] and 8 C.F.R. §214.2(*l*)(1)(ii)(A) ["an alien who, within three years preceding the time of his or her application for admission into the United States, has been employed abroad continuously for one year..."] and Letter, Bednarz, Chief, NIV Branch Adjudications, CO 214L-C (Mar. 25, 1994), *reprinted in* 71 No. 27 *Interpreter Releases* 936, 955 (July 18, 1994) ["Based on the statutory definition, it is clear that it was the intent of Congress to require that the alien's qualifying L-1 employment must have occurred within the three-year period immediately *preceding the alien's application for admission* to the United States"] *with* 8 C.F.R. §214.2(*l*)(3)(iii) [evidence of one-year employment "within the three years preceding the filing of the petition"] and 8 C.F.R. §214.2(*l*)(3)(v)(B) ["The beneficiary has been employed for one continuous year in the three-year period preceding the filing of the petition"]. Thus, a person who attends post-graduate school in the U.S. for 1 year in 2004 on an F-1 and worked for the company 2 years before in 2001 would qualify if the date of "admission" was used but would not qualify if the date of filing the petition was used if s/he did not file the petition until after she completed her studies in 2005.

3. "Employee"

3.a. If majority or substantial stockholder of U.S./foreign corp.—Can also be L-1 employee. *Matter of Aphrodite Investments Ltd.*, 17 I&N Dec. 530 (Comm. 1980). *See also Matter of Allan Gee, Inc.*, 17 I&N Dec. 296 (R.C. 1979); *Matter of Tessel, Inc.*, 17 I&N Dec. 631 (AAC 1981) [alien owned 93% of foreign corp., 60% of U.S. corp.].

3.b. If sole stockholder. *Matter of M*, 8 I&N Dec. 24 (AG 1958); *Edwards Fish Enterprises, Inc. v. INS*, ___ F.Supp. ___ (W.D. Wash. 1986) [beneficiary sole owner of U.S. company petitioner]; 9 FAM 41.54 N.7.6

3.c. If sole proprietor. *Johnson-Laird, Inc. v. INS*, 537 F.Supp. 52 (D. Or. 1981).

3.d. Where beneficiary is owner or major stockholder special requirements for eligibility. 8 C.F.R. §214.2(*l*)(3)(vii).

3.e. Compensation

(1) Employment does not necessarily depend upon amount or existence of a salary. *Johnson-Laird, Inc. v. INS*, 537 F.Supp. 52 (D. Or. 1981); *Matter of Tessel, Inc.*, 17 I&N Dec. 631 (AAC 1981) [nonsalaried chairman can qualify as L-1]; *Matter of Pozzoli*, 14 I&N Dec. 569 (RC 1974) [power of control over employee's activity rather than salary is essential element].

(2) Payment by foreign or U.S. company is not material. *Matter of Pozzoli*, 14 I&N Dec. 569 (R.C. 1974); 9 FAM 41.54 N.9.1

(3) There is no prevailing wage requirement, and therefore consular officers should only determine whether person would be public charge. Cable, DOS, 96-State-75033 (1996), *reprinted in* 73 No. 28 *Interpreter Releases* 963–64 (July 22, 1996).

(4) Beneficiary employed in U.S. directly by a foreign company, who is *not* controlled in any way by the foreign company's office in the U.S. will *not* qualify for L status. 9 FAM 41.54 N.9.2.

3.f. Outsourced or Agency Employment—As a result of the L-1 Visa Reform Act, PL 108-447, Div. J, Tit. IV (Dec. 8, 2004) enacting INA §214(c)(2)(F), there are now only limited circumstances where an employee who is in L-1B (specialized knowledge) status may be outsourced to another company. *See in this section* "Job Shop/Offsite Work," ¶ 10 (p.730), *infra*; AFM at 32.3(c). *See also* DOS Cable: "The essential element in determining the existence of an 'employer-employee' relationship is the right of control, that is, the right of the employer to order and control the employee in the performance of his or her work. This, rather than the source of the salary, is the controlling factor in determining the existence of an employer/employee relationship." Cable, DOS, 04-State-33493 (Feb. 14, 2004) at ¶6, *published on* AILA InfoNet at Doc. No. 04022410; 9 FAM 41.54 N.9, 9.1–9.2. USCIS requires the L-1B employer to retain ultimate authority over the worker. Press Release, USCIS Implements L-1 Visa Report Act of 2004 (June 23, 2005), *reprinted in* 82 No. 26 *Interpreter Releases* 1061, 1062, 1083–84 (July 1, 2005).

4. Temporariness

4.a. Whether the L-1 transferee is coming to the U.S. solely for a temporary period of time is no longer an issue of substantial concern to USCIS or DOS. *See* INA §214(h), 8 U.S.C. §1184(h) [L visa holder applying for permanent residency shall not constitute evidence of intention to abandon foreign residence for purpose of continuing to obtain L visas] and INA §214(b) [eliminating L category as persons presumed to be immigrants]. Thus both USCIS and DOS no longer focus on the question of temporariness. AFM at 32.3(b) Note [Section 214(h) eliminates the need to adjudicate the issue of whether an L is actually being transferred on a temporary basis]; 9 FAM 41.54 N.4 [indicating that the consular officer's evaluation of the applicant's eligibility for an L visa shall *not* focus on temporariness]. Prior to §214(h) and the amendments to 214(b) temporariness was a substantial concern in adjudicating L petitions. *See Matter of Isovic*, 18 I&N Dec. 361 (Comm. 1982) [although corp. fiction maintained, L denied where no showing that transfer is temporary];

International Auto Exc., Inc. v. Attorney General, 643 F.Supp. 616 (D.D.C. 1986) [upholding INS strict interpretation of temporariness]; *Edwards Fish Enterprises, Inc. v. INS*, ___ F.Supp. ___ (W.D. Wash. 1986) [beneficiary's statement that she would return home in 36 months must be accepted absent contrary facts demonstrating that statement is unbelievable]. Factors in prior determinations concerning temporariness included whether: (1) U.S. operation was limited; (2) Beneficiary's commercial interests require his departure?; (3) Specific showing that beneficiary's services have temporary limits; and (4) U.S. company's operation after departure of beneficiary. Note however that when the beneficiary is the owner, operator or major stockholder the I-129 petition must include evidence of temporariness. 8 C.F.R. §214.2(*l*)(3)(vii). And the burden of proof always remains with the petitioner. *Matter of Brantigan*, 11 I&N Dec. 493 (BIA 1966).

5. Qualifying Organization

5.a. A majority stock ownership in both companies sufficient. *Matter of Tessel, Inc.*, *supra* [but watch employee/ temporary problem].

5.b. Joint Ventures—Less than majority ownership, but control, may be sufficient to qualify relationship as subsidiary/affiliate. *Matter of Hughes*, 18 I&N Dec. 289 (Comm. 1982) [joint venture where U. S. company owned 50% but had control over management and policy]; 9 FAM 41.54 N.7.1-4b. Where 2 parent companies own 50% (joint venture) of a company, the company (joint venture) is a *subsidiary* of *both* parent companies. *Matter of Siemens Medical Systems, Inc.*, 19 I&N Dec. 362 (Comm. 1986); Even less than 50% ownership would be sufficient for subsidiary if the parent/owners can show control. 8 C.F.R. §214.2(*l*)(1)(ii)(K) and (L). USCIS, however, makes a distinction between equity joint-ventures (financially contributing company owns 50% and exercises control) and nonequity joint ventures (contractual arrangement where one or more of the contributing companies provides noncapital resources such as patents, trademarks, manufacturing process, managerial know-how) which does *not* establish a qualifying L-1 relationship. AFM at 32.3(d) Note ("Joint Ventures"). *See also* 9 FAM 41.54 N.7.1-4b provides that a contractual joint venture does not qualify as a subsidiary.

5.c. Contractual relationship (*e.g.*, licensing/franchising) is generally *not* sufficient to establish necessary relationship. DOL Technical Assistance Guide, No. 656 (TAG) at 1(A)(1)(d). [Schedule A Group IV does not include license/franchise relationships]; *Matter of Schick*, 13 I&N Dec. 647 (R.C. 1970). *But see Matter of Budget Rent-A-Car*, Case No. MIA-N-12807 (R.C. 1981) [when franchise agreement controls policies and advertisement it is sufficient]. Both the *Foreign Affairs Manual* and the *Adjudicator's Field Manual* no longer seem to support the approach in *Budget Rent-A-Car.* 9 FAM 41.54 N.7.1-4b provides that a contractual joint venture does not qualify as a subsidiary; *See also* AFM at 32.3(d) Note ("Joint Ventures").

5.d. Proprietorships—In cases where the business is not a separate legal entity from the owner(s), the petitioner's statement of ownership and control must be accompanied by evidence, such as a license to do business, record of registration as an employer with IRS, business tax returns or other evidence which identifies the owners of the business. AFM at 32.3(d) Note (Proprietorships).

5.e. Ownership by common group (*e.g.*, where U.S. affiliate owned one-third by family corp. one-third by person who owns foreign corp. and one-third by family of person) or same individuals. To establish affiliate each individual in the group must own approximately the same share or proportion of each entity. A more restrictive interpretation requiring identical ownership has been struck down as too restrictive. *Sun Moon Star Advanced Power, Inc. v. Chappell*, 773 F.Supp. 1373 (N.D. Cal. 1990) [where family owned U.S. company in part through holding company which the family controlled, but which owned no interest in foreign company, affiliation was recognized]. Also, the AAO has recognized that where persons own different amounts of shares in parent and affiliate but vote in majority block by agreement, the parent/affiliate relationship would be approved because there is no danger of one group controlling the foreign entity and another the U.S. one. *Matter of ___*, WAC 93-128-50463 (AAU Sept. 3, 1993). Control as well as ownership are the defining characteristics. In fact, as the BIA noted in *Matter of Hughes*, 18 I&N Dec. 289, 293 (Comm. 1982): "Ownership need not be majority if control exists."

5.f. Church organizations may qualify as parent/subsidiary or affiliates under certain circumstances. *Matter of Church of Scientology International*, 19 I&N Dec. 593 (Comm. 1988) [Catholic Church, but not Scientologists, meet parent/subsidiary model].

5.g. Factors

- Common name.
- Regular sharing and exchange of personnel.
- Cross directorship.
- Sharing of technical, financial and research skills.
- Size and general recognition of organization.

5.h. Partnerships that market accounting or marketing services under internationally recognized name and under an agreement with a worldwide coordinating organization that is owned and controlled by the member firms, are affiliates. 8 C.F.R. §214.2(*l*)(1)(ii)(L)(3).

5.i. A branch is an operating division or office of the same organization in a different location. The office or operating division is *not* a separate business entity. 9 FAM 41.54 N.7.1-3; 8 C.F.R. §214.2(*l*)(1)(ii)(J).

6. Rendering services to same employer.

6.a. Must have employment relationship with U.S. company. Cannot transfer someone to work here without U.S. business entity having control/salary. *Matter of Penner*, 18 I&N Dec. 49 (Comm. 1982) [where oil well rigger "transferred" to work on project which is directed from abroad and salary paid abroad, no L]. For example, if a foreign construction company mans a project in the U.S. with a workforce it sends to the U.S. from a foreign country, the workers are not eligible for L visas. *See* 9 FAM 41.54 N.9.2

6.b. If U.S. company is less than one year old, it must show proof of physical premises (lease/deed). 8 C.F.R. §214.2(*l*)(3)(v)(A).

6.c. *Both* U.S. and *foreign* company must be active. 8 C.F.R. §214.2(*l*)(1)(ii)(G), overruled, *Matter of Thompson*, 18 I&N Dec. 169 (Comm. 1981), and explained, *Matter of Chartier*, 16 I&N Dec. 284 (BIA 1977).

(1) Doing business requires activity not just registration of business or office or presence of an agent. 8 C.F.R. §214.2(*l*)(1)(ii)(H); 9 FAM 41.54 N.10.2

6.d. L classification is not created for self-employment. 9 FAM 41.54 N.10.4.

7. Must Work in Managerial, Executive or Specialized Skill

7.a. Must be manager, executive or worked in specialized skill abroad; may be any of these three in U.S. The transferee "does not have to be transferred to the United States in the same capacity in which he or she was employed abroad." AFM at 32.3(b); *Matter of Vaillancourt*, 13 I&N Dec. 654 (R.C. 1970) [specialized knowledge abroad, manager in U.S.]. Managers and Executives fall under the L-1A category. Persons with specialized knowledge fall under the L-1B category. If an L-1A subsequently seeks LPR status he may apply through EB-1 without the need for a labor certification. A person of specialized knowledge however will need a labor certification to obtain LPR status.

7.b. Managerial capacity is defined under INA §101(a)(44)(A), 8 U.S.C. §1101(a)(44)(A); 8 C.F.R. §214.2(*l*)(1)(ii)(B)—Managerial capacity means an assignment with an organization in which the employee *primarily*:

(1) manages the organization, department, subdivision, function or component;

(2) supervises and controls the work of other supervisory, professional or managerial employees, *or manages an essential function within the organization* or department or subdivision of the organization;

(3) has authority to hire and fire or recommend personnel actions (if other employees directly supervised), or if no direct supervision, functions at a senior level within hierarchy or as to function managed *and*

(4) exercises discretion over day-to-day operations of the activity or function;

First-line supervisors are not considered managers unless the employees they supervise are professionals. Statute was not intended to limit managers or executives to persons who supervise a large number of persons or large enterprise. *National Hand Tool Corp. v. Pasquarell*, 889 F.2d 1472, n.5 (5th Cir. 1989); *Mars Jewelers, Inc. v. INS*, 702 F.Supp. 1570, 1573 (N.D. Ga. 1988). Supervision includes supervising independent contractors as well as employees. 9 FAM 41.54 N.8.2-1a. A person may be a manager or executive under new regulations, even if he is the sole employee of the company where he utilizes outside independent contractors or where business is complex. He may be a "functional manager." *Matter of Irish Dairy Board, Ltd.*, Case No. A28 845 421 (AAU Nov. 16, 1989) [Schedule A, Group IV case], *reported in* 66 No. 46 *Interpreter Releases* 1329–30 (Dec. 4, 1989); *IKEA U.S., Inc. v. DOJ, INS*, 48 F.Supp.2d 22 (D.D.C. 1999) [applied essential function analysis but found that petitioner in I-140 case failed to present sufficient documentation that employee worked "primarily" as manager]; 9 FAM 41.54 N. 8.2-1c. Validity of more restrictive managerial definition under previous and current regulations has been upheld for L-1 petition. *Republic of Transkei v. INS*, 923 F.2d 175 (D.C. Cir. 1991), and in Schedule A, Group IV case. *Family Inc v. USCIS*, 469 F.3d 1313 (9th Cir. 2006) [substantial evidence supported denial of I-140 petition and the court determined that size of the company could be one factor that the agency considers where applicant was president, wife was the manager, there were only four other employees, the company had one shareholder in Korea, and the business was small]; *Omni Packaging, Inc. v. INS*, 930 F.Supp. 28, 32–33 (D.P.R. 1996) [technical support specialist not manager or executive for Schedule A, Group IV purposes]; *National Hand Tool Corp., supra*; *Fedin Bros. Co., Ltd. v. Sava*, 724 F.Supp. 1103 (E.D.N.Y. 1989) [affirm denial of 6th preference petition where petition repeated language of regulation but did not provide detailed description of job duties].

7.c. Executive capacity defined under INA §101(a)(44)(B), 8 U.S.C. §1101(a)(44)(B), 8 C.F.R. §214.2(*l*)(1)(ii)(C), means an assignment in an organization in which the employee primarily:

(1) Directs the management of the organization or a major component or function;

(2) Establishes goals and policies;

(3) Exercises wide latitude in discretionary decision making *and*

(4) Receives only general supervision or direction from higher level executives, board of directors or stockholders. In determining whether an individual is acting in a *managerial or executive capacity*, AG shall take into account the reasonable needs of the organization, component or function in light of the overall purpose and stage of development of the organization, component or function. *The number of employees supervised is not determinative.* 9 FAM 41.54 N.8.2.

(5) Validity of previous regulations upheld in *Fedin Bros. Co., Ltd., supra.*

8. Specialized knowledge is defined to include a person who has special knowledge of the company product, service, research, equipment, techniques, management or other interests and its application in international markets or has an advanced level of knowledge of processes and procedures of the company. 8 C.F.R. §214.2(*l*)(1)(ii)(D). It includes a type of specialized or advanced knowledge that is different from that generally found in a particular industry but need not be proprietary or unique. Memo, Ohata, HQSCOPS 70/6.1 (Dec. 20, 2002), *published on* AILA InfoNet at Doc. No. 03020548. Where the specialized knowledge is of a company product, the knowledge must be "noteworthy or uncommon." Memo, Ohata (Dec. 20, 2002), *supra.* Where it involves the company's processes and procedures it must be "advanced." *Id.* The advanced knowledge need not be narrowly held throughout the company. *Id.* Specialized knowledge includes knowledge which is advanced and generally not known of a process or product which would be difficult to impart to another without significant economic inconvenience to the U.S. or foreign firm. *Id.* In addition, 9 FAM 41.54 N.8.2-2 further defines specialized knowledge as:

(1) Not simply a skilled worker. *Matter of Penner*, 18 I&N Dec. 49 (Comm. 1982). Rather someone whose advanced level of expertise and proprietary knowledge of the employer organization's product, service, research, equipment, techniques, management or other activity is not readily available in the U.S. labor market. The term "proprietary" however, is no longer in the regulations.

(2) Characteristics include: [Memo, Norton, Assoc. Comm., Examinations (Oct. 27, 1988), *reprinted in* 65 No. 43 *Interpreter Releases* 1170, 1194 (Nov. 7, 1988)].

(a) Possesses knowledge that is valuable to the employer's competitiveness in the market place;

(b) Is uniquely qualified to contribute to the U.S. employer's knowledge of foreign operating conditions;

(c) Has been utilized as a key employee abroad and has been given significant assignments which have enhanced the employer's productivity, competitiveness, image or financial position; and

(d) Possesses knowledge that can be gained only through extensive prior experience with that employer.

(3) Knowledge contributes to the uninterrupted operation of the specific business for which the applicant's services are sought and the knowledge is not the type of knowledge generally found in the particular industry. Knowledge must also be of a certain complexity. Memo, Ohata, Dir. Service Center Operations, USCIS (Sept. 4, 2004), *published on* AILA InfoNet at Doc. No. 04091666 [finding Chefs and Specialty Cooks are generally not considered to have specialized knowledge].

This definition substantially modifies the narrow criteria expressed in *Matter of Sandoz Crop Protection Corp.*, 19 I&N Dec. 666 (Comm. 1988). *See also* Cable, DOS, 96-State-222894 (1995), *reprinted in* 72 No. 39 *Interpreter Releases* 1378–80 (Oct. 6, 1995). Refer to 9 FAM 41.54, Exhibit 1, for the specialized-knowledge questionnaire.

9. Cases addressing specialized knowledge—Oil well rigger not "specialized knowledge [*Matter of Penner*]; Marketing manager of company with specialized patented herbicide not "specialized knowledge." *Matter of Sandoz Crop Protection Corp.*, 19 I&N Dec. 666 (Comm. 1988). Specialty chefs not "specialized knowledge." *1756, Inc. v. Attorney General*, 745 F.Supp. 9 (D.D.C. 1990) [upheld INS regulation concerning specialized knowledge]; *See also* Ohata (2004) memo re: Chefs and Specialty Cooks. But executive secretary, aerial computer photographers and interior designers have been designated as persons with specialized knowledge. *Matter of Raulin*, 13 I&N Dec. 618 (R.C. 1970); *Matter of Colley*, 18 I&N Dec. 117 (Comm. 1981); *IKEA, Inc. v. DOJ*, ___ F.Supp. ___, No. 87-2025 (D.D.C. Dec. 23, 1987) [where 100 employees possessed the knowledge of interior designers still specialized knowledge in company of 10,000. Court did not understand why phrase "held by a few" was a proper requirement for L-1] *reported in* 65 No. 7 *Interpreter Releases* 163 (Feb. 22, 1988)

10. Job Shops/Offsite Work—INA §214(c)(2)(F), 8 U.S.C. §1184(c)(2)(F). An L-1 is ineligible for classification as a specialized knowledge worker (L-1B) if s/he will be "stationed primarily" at the worksite of an employer other than the petitioner or an affiliate, subsidiary, or parent and the beneficiary will be "principally" under the "control and supervision" of the unaffiliated employer *or* the placement in the nonaffiliated worksite is "essentially an arrangement to provide labor for hire for the unaffiliated employer." USCIS interprets the "control and supervision" provision as requiring the L-1B employer to retain ultimate authority over the worker. Press Release, USCIS Implements L-1 Visa Report Act of 2004 (June 23, 2005), *reprinted in* 82 No. 26 *Interpreter Releases* 1061, 1062, 1083–84 (July 1, 2005). USCIS interprets the "control and supervision" provision as requiring the L-1B employer to retain ultimate authority over the worker. Press Release, USCIS Implements L-1 Visa Report Act of 2004 (June 23, 2005), *reprinted in* 82 No. 26 *Interpreter Releases* 1061, 1062, 1083–84 (July 1, 2005).This provision applies to all initial petitions, amendments to petitions or extensions of L-1B petitions filed on or after June 6, 2005. AFM at 32.3(c).

11. Specialized knowledge professional—8 C.F.R. §214.2(*l*)(1)(ii)(E)—Person with specialized knowledge who is a member of the professions under INA §101(a)(32), 8 U.S.C. §1101(a)(32). This provision is used in connection with blanket petitions. 8 C.F.R. §214.2(*l*)(4)(i)(D). These persons typically have a professional degree.

12. Nature/Size of Company

12.a. Parent and subsidiary companies do not have to be in same business.

12.b. No size limitation of company. 9 FAM 41.54 N.7.5 But depending upon the size of the company, different types of evidence may be required. AFM at 32.3(d) .

12.c. No country limitation as with Es. *Matter of Barsai*, 18 I&N Dec. 13 (R.C. 1981) [subsidiary of Hungarian governmental agency].

12.d. Can be transferred from one U.S. affiliate to another but must file new I-129.

13. New Office—USCIS regulations detail special provisions when a new parent, subsidiary, branch or affiliate office is opened in the U.S. and wishes to employ a manager or executive but typically does not have proof of extensive business activity in the U.S. because it was recently opened. 8 C.F.R. §§214.2(*l*)(1)(ii)(F) and (H), (3)(v), (7)(i)(A)(3). A new office is defined as "an organization which has been doing business in the United States through a parent, branch, affiliate, or subsidiary for less than one year." As the definition requires the new office to be "doing business" the "mere presence of an agent or office" is not enough to satisfy even the new office requirement for an L-1. 8 C.F.R. §214.2(*l*)(1)(ii)(H). In order to qualify for an L-1 where a new office is involved the petitioner must submit evidence that: (1) sufficient physical premises for the office have been secured (usually by providing a lease); (2) the beneficiary meets the one-year continuous employment requirements; and (3) the intended U.S. operation within one year "will support an executive or managerial position." 8 C.F.R. §214.2(*l*)(3)(v). In order to meet this last requirement the petitioner must provide information regarding: (1) the proposed nature of the office describing the scope of the entity, its organizational structure, and its financial goals; (2) the size of the U.S. investment and the financial ability of the foreign entity to remunerate the beneficiary and to commence doing business; *and* (3) the organization structure of the foreign entity. 8 C.F.R §214.2(*l*)(3)(v)(C)(1)–(3). A "new office" petition may only be approved for one year. Thereafter it may be extended upon presentation of evidence that the business is active and operating. 8 C.F.R. §214.2(*l*)(7)(i)(A)(3).

14. Procedural Aspects

14.a. I-129 filed by employer (petitioner) at appropriate service center (except for Canadians under NAFTA or emergency expedited applications with the DD) where beneficiary will perform the services. 8 C.F.R. §214.2(*l*)(2). Photocopies of documents may be submitted.

14.b. Special Fraud Fee—A fraud prevention and detection fee of $500 is for a new petition and will be collected only one time for a petition involving a beneficiary and an employer. Once the fee is collected there will be no fraud detection fee for a subsequent petition involving the same beneficiary and employer. CBP will collect the fee for L-1s presented at the Canadian border under NAFTA. Memo, Hrinyak, Acting Ex. Dir., Immigration Policy and Programs, CBP, "Implementation of Fraud Prevention and Detection Fee ($500)," (Mar. 18, 2005), *published on* AILA InfoNet at Doc. No. 05041262.

14.c. Petition Approved for 3 Years—8 C.F.R. §214.2(*l*)(7)(i)(A)(2). If new office, USCIS can only approve for *one* year, 8 C.F.R. §214.2(*l*)(7)(i)(A)(3), and thereafter petitioner must show compliance with managerial/ executive standards. To obtain first year approval need to show that sufficient physical premises have been secured and that within one year business will support an executive or managerial position. 8 C.F.R. §214.2(*l*)(3)(v). A business plan projecting staff levels by the end of the first year can be submitted. To determine extension after first year, USCIS looks to "number of employees, significant growth in cash flow, presence of significant customers and clientele, or similar elements ..." 65 No. 7 *Interpreter Releases* 157 (Feb. 22, 1988). There is a 7-year maximum for managers and executives and a 5-year maximum for specialized knowledge, INA §214(c)(2)(D)(i)–(ii), 8 U.S.C. §1184(c)(2)(D)(i)–(ii), 8 C.F.R. §214.2(*l*)(12), unless in U.S. for seasonal or intermittent work or for less than 6 months per year. 8 C.F.R. §214.2(*l*)(12)(ii). The maximum limitation periods for Ls has been upheld. *Fibermaster, Ltd. v. INS*, ___ F.Supp. ___, Case No. 88-2001 (D.D.C. July 3, 1990), *reported in* 67 No. 29 *Interpreter Releases* 864–66 (Aug. 6, 1990). All time spent out of the U.S. is subtracted and does not count toward the maximum 5/7 year period and therefore time out of the U.S. may be added back/recaptured to the maximum period. *Matter of IT Ascent*, EAC 04 047 53189 (AAO Sept. 2, 2005), *published on* AILA InfoNet at Doc. No. 05102760; *Nair v. Coultice, supra*, [finding that all time out of U.S. in H status is not considered]; Memo, Aytes, Acting Assoc. Dir. Operations, HQPRD 70/6.2.8, 70/6.2.12, AD 05-21 (Oct. 21, 2005), *published on* AILA InfoNet at Doc. No. 05110363 [finding that any days spent outside U.S. will not be counted toward maximum period for H or L status provided beneficiary is able to submit independent documentary evidence]; AFM at 32.6(g) [evidentiary standards to recapture time]. The 5/7 year limitation applies to spouses and dependents as well. 8 C.F.R. 214.2(*l*)(7)(ii). The 5-year specialized knowledge limitation may be overcome where employee becomes a manager or executive at least 6 months before 5 years expires and USCIS approves the change. S/he may thereafter get the benefit of the full 7 years. 8 C.F.R. §214.2(*l*)(15)(ii). The 5/7 year limit does not apply to E status so a person could change status to E after 5/7 years as L or H. However, time in H status will count toward 5/7 years and a person cannot change status to an H after reaching the 5/7 year maximum. 8 C.F.R. §214.2(*l*)(12)(i); Letter, Bednarz, Chief, NIV Branch, Adjudications, CO 214L-C (Feb. 14, 1994), *reprinted in* 71 No. 10 *Interpreter Releases* 351, 373–74 (Mar. 14, 1994). Extensions granted upon filing I-129 (and L supplement) with approval notice (I-797) and letter from employer. 8 C.F.R. §§214.2(*l*)(14), (15). Approval via cable will be sent to appropriate consular post if the person travels abroad for business or personal reasons while the extension is pending. 8 C.F.R. §214.2(*l*)(15)(i). It is possible to travel abroad and re-enter the U.S., if the person's visa and I-94 are still valid. Extensions of stay given in 2-year increments.

14.d. Admission—8 C.F.R. §214.2(*l*)(11). The beneficiary of an individual petition may only be admitted for a period of three years or the validity period of the petition whichever is shorter. This applies whether or not the person enters on an individual petition or a I-129S petition pursuant to a blanket petition. However, the beneficiary of a blanket petition may be admitted for three years even though the initial validity period of the company's blanket petition may have expired before that time.

14.e. Expedited treatment under IMMACT90 requires USCIS to render a decision on an L-1 petition within 30 days after "a completed petition has been filed." INA §214(c)(2)(C), 8 U.S.C. §1184(c)(2)(C). However, absent premium processing, the normal processing times of the Service Centers indicate that the 30-day deadline is not being followed.

14.f. Part-Time Employment—Transferees can work part-time for more than one subsidiary of the same international corporation. But to work at second company need to file new petition to establish qualifying relationship. Do not need to file new petition for first company because the change in hours not significant enough. Letter, Weinig, Deputy Asst. Comm. (Dec. 18, 1987), *reprinted in* 65 No. 19 *Interpreter Releases* 509, 518–19 (May 16, 1988). Part-time employment has also been recognized in the context of maternity leave under the Family and Medical Leave Act of 1993 and for medical reasons or vacation. Letter, Hernandez, Chief Business and Trade Services Branch, Office of Program and Regulations Development, HQOPRD 70/6.2.8 (Mar. 9, 2004), *published on* AILA InfoNet at Doc. No. 04031165.

14.g. Amendments to Petition: Must file amended petition with USCIS where there are changes in the approved relationships, additional qualifying organizations and any information which would affect the beneficiary's employment. 8 C.F.R. §214.2(*l*)(7)(i)(C).

(1) Changes requiring amended petition include (1) a significant change in beneficiary's duties (*e.g.,* specialized knowledge to managerial/executive); and (2) transfer from one company to another in same organization where beneficiary becomes employee of new company. Memo, Hogan, Exec. Assoc. Comm., Operations, CO 214l-C (Oct. 22, 1992), *reprinted in* 69 No. 43 *Interpreter Releases* 1439, 1449–50 (Nov. 9, 1992).

(2) Different rules apply for amendments to blanket petitions; *see in this section* ¶ 14.n(2)(e) (p.734), *infra*.

14.h. RFEs, NOIDs, and Readjudication of Petition—Petitioner must comply with all reasonable documentary requests by USCIS or suffer denial. *Calexico Warehouse, Inc. v. Neufeld,* 259 F.Supp.2d 1067, 1075–80 (S.D. Cal. 2002) [failure to provide the Service with the company's stock ledger, organizational chart, and further evidence of managerial/executive duties was sufficient under the abuse of discretion standard to affirm revocation of the petition]. For additional discussion on RFEs and NOIDs, *see in this chapter* ¶ III.N.4 (p.635), *supra*.

14.i. Administrative and Judicial Review. An appeal of a denial of an L-1 petition by the regional service center is filed with the Administrative Appeals Office. A review of the AAO's decision may be filed in federal court but will generally be based on the agency's record. *Balaton, Inc. v. Reno,* 93 F.Supp.2d 61 (D.D.C. 2000) [court declined to allow petitioner to supplement record based on claim that AAO continuously pursued an unlawful policy to deny L-1 visa extensions to small business petitioners]. A federal district court may be jurisdictionally barred under INA §242(a)(2)(B)(ii) from the review of a denial of an L-1 by the USCIS. *Eastern Carpet House, Inc. v. DHS,* 430 F.Supp.2d 672, 674–75 (S.D. Tex. 2006) [no review of AAO denial of L-1 extension because 8 U.S.C. §1184 provides that the admission of a nonimmigrant is discretionary and 8 U.S.C. §1252(a)(2)(B)(ii) bars review of discretionary decisions]; *Global Export/Import Link v. U.S. Bureau of Citizenship and Immigration Services,* 423 F.Supp.2d 703 (E.D. Mich. 2006) [where USCIS denied an I-129 petition for L-1A classification in its authority under 8 U.S.C. §1184(c), the decision is not reviewable because it is a discretionary decision barred from review under INA §242(a)(2)(B)(ii)].

14.j. Revocation: It is automatic when petitioner withdraws petition or when petitioner fails to request indefinite validity of a blanket petition. Notice of an intent to revoke is sent when one or more entities no longer qualifies. 8 C.F.R. §214.2(*l*)(9). An abuse of discretion standard applies to review revocation. *Calexico Warehouse, Inc. v. Neufeld,* 259 F.Supp.2d 1067, 1075–80 (S.D. Cal. 2002) [failure to provide the Service with the company's stock ledger, organizational chart, and further evidence of managerial/executive duties was sufficient under the abuse of discretion standard to affirm revocation of the petition].

14.k. Filing During Pendency of LPR Applications—An L-1 may apply for an extension of status (including dependents), a new L-1 petition, or a change of status to another L or H category even if s/he has filed an application for or received an approval of a LC or an IV petition or filed an AOS application. 8 C.F.R. §214.2(*l*)(16)(i). However, if L-1 with pending AOS applies for an EAD based on the AOS application and works for another employer, his L-1 status is violated. AFM §30.1 and Appendix 23.4, 31.2a.

14.l. Travel and Employment Authorization While Adjustment Application is Pending—If an L-1 is not under exclusion, deportation, or removal proceedings and is in valid L-1 status, s/he may travel while her AOS application is pending without an advance parole if she: (1) is coming to resume employment with the same employer her L-1 is authorized for and (2) is in possession of a valid L visa (if required). The former requirement that she also have in her possession the AOS receipt has been removed. 72 Fed. Reg. 61791 (Nov. 1, 2007). Dependent family members in lawful L-2 status may also travel during the AOS if the same conditions for the L-1 principal exist. 8 C.F.R. §245.2(a)(4)(ii)(C). However, if s/he travels and re-enters on an advance parole and s/he has a valid and approved L-1 petition, s/he may apply for an extension of her status and USCIS will terminate her parole and admit her as an L-1. *Adjudicator's Field Manual,* Appendix 23-4, Memo, Cronin, Acting Assoc. Comm., Office of Programs HQADJ 70/2.8.6, 2.8.12, 10.18 (May 16, 2000), *reprinted in* 77 No. 20 *Interpreter Releases* 672, 677–80 (May 22, 2000). The employer may also apply for a new L-1 or if the person retains a valid L-1, s/he may depart and re-enter on the L-1. AFM at Appendix 23-4. Even if the employee re-enters on an advance parole and continues her L-1 employment she will not be considered to engage in unauthorized employment. *Id.*

14.m. Spouse/Children—Receive L-2 visas. Regarding adjustment of L-2s refer to 8 C.F.R. §245.2(a)(4).

(1) Admission and Extensions. The 5/7 year limitation on admission and extensions for L-1s applies to spouses and dependents as well. 8 C.F.R. §214.2(*l*)(7)(ii). If the limitation is not reached, however, an L-2 may remain in the U.S. and change status even if the L-1 departs. Letter, LaFleur, Chief, Business and Trade Branch, Benefits Division, HQ 70/6.2.8 (July 16, 1996), *reprinted in* 73 No. 29 *Interpreter Releases* 1010, 1024 (July 29, 1996). In addition, a person in L-2 (or H-4) status is free to change his status to an L-1A or L-1B (or H-1B) because the time spent in L-2 (or H-4) status is not counted toward the 5/7 year maximum on L-1s (or the six year maximum on H-1Bs). Memo, Aytes, Assoc. Dir., Domestic Operations, USCIS, HQPRD 70/6.2.8, 70/6.2.12, AD 06-29 (Dec. 5, 2006), *published on* AILA InfoNet at Doc. No. 06122063 (Dec. 20, 2006) [recognizing that L-2 and L-1A/B after 7/5 years can switch positions with each obtaining a new 7/5 year period]; AFM §32.6(h).

(2) Employment Authorization for Spouse. Spouse is now eligible for employment authorization. INA §214(c)(2)(E); Cable, DOS, 02-State-17328 (Jan. 29, 2002), *published on* AILA InfoNet at Doc. No. 02013032. Employment authorization filed on I-765 at the Service Center with jurisdiction over spouse's place of residence. Must provide: (i) proof of principal's current status including the petition approval notice if available; and (ii) I-94s of principal and spouse to verify marital relationship. Employment will be granted for period of admission and/or status not to exceed 2 years. In the event spouse does not receive a Form I-766 (proof of employment authorization) within 90 days, s/he is eligible to receive employment authorization for 240 days. Memo, Yates, Deputy Ex. Assoc. Comm., Field Operations, HQ 70/6.2.5, 6.2.12 (Feb. 22, 2002), *published on* AILA InfoNet at Doc. No 02022832 (Feb. 28, 2002).

14.n. Blanket Procedure—8 C.F.R. §214.2(*l*)(4); Memo, Cook, Acting Asst. Comm. for Adjudications, HQ 70/6.2.8 (Feb. 13, 2001), *reprinted in* 78 No. 11 *Interpreter Releases* 526, 546–49 (Mar. 19, 2001).

(1) Requirements

(a) Petitioner has office and has been doing business in U.S. for one year.

(b) Petitioner has 3 or more domestic and foreign branches, subsidiaries or affiliates. Petitioner and entities are engaged in commercial trade or services.

(c) Combined U.S. annual sales of $25 million, U.S. workforce of 1,000 *or* received approval of at least 10 L petitions in last 12 months.

(d) Nonprofit organizations cannot file blanket petitions. 9 FAM 41.54 N.14.2b.

(e) Employee must work abroad for parent, affiliate or subsidiary for 12 months. INA §214(c)(2)(A). AFM at 32.4 Note.

(f) Anti-Job Shop Provision of INA §214(c)(2)(F) applies. *See in this section* ¶ 10 (p.730), *supra*; AFM at 32.5.

(2) Procedure

(a) Obtain approval of blanket from the service center. All extensions, change of status must be filed with service centers. 8 C.F.R. §214.2(*l*)(7)(i).

(b) Petition initially approved for 3 years; must then apply for extension. 8 C.F.R. §214.2(*l*)(7)(i)(B).

(c) Fill out Form I-129S, attach I-171C demonstrating "blanket approval," and submit to consular officer to obtain visa (unless visa exempt). No longer required to file individual petitions for blanket L-1s. However, must continue to establish beneficiary's managerial, executive, or specialized knowledge professional qualifications in each case. 8 C.F.R. §214.2(*l*)(5)(ii).

(d) Blanket L procedures may not be used for specialized knowledge positions that are not "professional" in nature. 8 C.F.R. §214.2(*l*)(5)(ii)(D)

(e) A new Certificate of Eligibility (I-129S) *is* required where beneficiary is reassigned to an organization listed in the approved petition *and* will be performing different job duties. 8 C.F.R. §214.2(*l*)(5)(ii)(G). A new Certificate is not needed for transfers to any organization listed on a blanket petition if the job duties are virtually the same.

O. *E Visas*—INA §101(a)(15)(E), 8 U.S.C. §1101(a)(15)(E); 8 C.F.R. §214.2(e); 22 C.F.R. §41.51; 62 Fed. Reg. 48138 at 48146–55 (Sept. 12, 1997); Immigration Acts of 1924; July 6, 1932; and 1952.

1. Definition:

1.a. Person is entering U.S. (for indefinite time).

1.b. Based upon treaty of friendship, commerce and navigation or Bilateral Investment Treaty or other arrangements (NAFTA-Canada and Mexico) between U.S. and country of which s/he is a national. Some countries may have only E-1 treaties or E-2 treaties. Some have both. 9 FAM 41.51, Exh. 1; *See* **Appendix L**, *infra*, for list.

1.c. Person is entering

(1) Solely to carry on substantial trade which is international in scope principally between U.S. and the foreign state of which s/he is a national (E-1 treaty trader), or

(2) Solely to develop and direct the operations of an enterprise in which the alien has invested, or is actively in the process of investing a substantial amount of capital in a *bona fide* enterprise (E-2 treaty investor), or

(3) As a key employee from treaty country of either E-1 or E-2, including executives and supervisors or persons whose services are "essential to the efficient operation of the enterprise." 8 C.F.R. §214.2(e)(3), or

(4) As a principal employer who is: (a) a person with nationality of treaty country whether in or outside U.S.; or (b) an enterprise or organization that is 50% or more owned by treaty nationals, or

(5) A dependent of one of the above referenced persons.

2. General considerations

2.a. Need not show proceeding to U.S. for a specific period of time, so long as there is an ultimate intention to depart the U.S. and not permanently remain. 8 C.F.R. §214.2(e)(1)(ii), (2)(iii), (5); 9 FAM 41.51 N.1.1, N.1.2, N.15; *Lauvik v. INS*, 910 F.2d 658, 660–61 (9th Cir. 1990) [reversed DD denial of E-2 extension where DD failed to distinguish between applicant's desire not to depart from his intent to do so].

2.b. Except as described above, no temporariness or intent to return to foreign residence is required. Nor is proof of foreign residence required. An application should not be denied solely on the basis of an approved labor certification or for a filed or approved immigrant visa petition. However, the applicant must have an intent to depart and DOS requires a visa applicant to establish that s/he will not seek adjustment of status within the United States. 8 C.F.R. §214.2(e)(5); 9 FAM 41.51 N.15.

2.c. Each treaty may contain specific provisions that create subtle but important differences in the treatment of treaty nationals. For example, the treaty with the United Kingdom requires a UK citizen to be domiciled in the UK to obtain the benefits of the treaty. This is not true for any other E treaty with any other country.

2.d. INS and DOS issued final regulations, which are identical in most important respects. 62 Fed. Reg. 48138–55 (Sept. 12, 1997). INS traditionally followed DOS regulations and FAM. O.I. §214.2(e); *Kim v. District Director*, 586 F.2d 713, 716 (9th Cir. 1978); *Matter of Walsh & Pollard*, 20 I&N Dec. 60 (BIA 1988); *Matter of Csonka*, 17 I&N Dec. 254 (R.C. 1978); *Matter of Tamura*, 10 I&N Dec. 717 (R.C. 1964), *overruled on other grounds in Matter of Udagawa,* 14 I&N Dec. 578 (BIA 1974).

3. Time of Admission—2-year admission and extensions of stay up to 2 years at a time. 8 C.F.R. §214.2(e)(19), (20). Admission will be for 2 years even if the visa is valid for less than 30 days at the time of entry. Cable, Brooks, Asst. Comm., Inspections (Oct. 10, 1989), *reprinted in* 8 *AILA Monthly Mailing* 761 (Dec. 1989); 22 C.F.R. §41.112(a).

4. E-l—INA §101(a)(15)(E)(i), 8 U.S.C. §1101(a)(15)(E)(i).

4.a. Substantial trade:

(1) Trade. Under 8 C.F.R. §214.2(e)(9), 22 C.F.R. §41.51(a)(7) and (8), 9 FAM 41.51 N.4, trade is defined as "the existing *international* exchange of items of trade for consideration between the U.S. and the treaty country." Domestic trade is not international trade and is therefore not counted when considering what is substantial trade. According to DOS, Items of trade "include but are not limited to goods, services, international banking, insurance monies, transportation, communications, data processing, advertising, accounting, design and engineering, management consulting, tourism, technology and its transfer, and some news-gathering activities." The USCIS definition also includes "data processing, advertising, accounting, design and engineering, and management consulting." Goods are "tangible commodities or merchandise having extrinsic value." Services

are "legitimate economic activities which provide other than tangible goods." Service is interpreted "in an expansive fashion." 62 Fed. Reg. 48138 at 48141 (Sept. 12, 1997). Union official sent to U.S. for organizing, eligible for E. Includes export or import. For example, if equipment purchase involves transfer of component parts for assembly in U.S. it is trade. IMMACT90 defined trade to include trade in services and technology.

(2) "Principal" trade. 8 C.F.R. §214.2(e)(11), 9 FAM 41.51 N.7

(a) Trade must be principally between U.S. and treaty country.

(b) More than 50% of total volume of *international* trade between U.S. and treaty country.

(c) Domestic trade not counted in calculation of "more than 50%."

(d) If business does more than 50%, each E-l owner does not need more than 50% trade.

(e) If it is only a U.S. branch office, then the foreign company has to have more than 50% of its trade with the U.S. since it is not considered a separate legal entity. However, a U.S. subsidiary is considered independently from its foreign company owner.

(3) "Substantial." 8 C.F.R. §214.2(e)(10), 22 C.F.R. §41.51(a)(9), 9 FAM 41.51 N.6

(a) "An amount of trade sufficient to insure a continuous flow of international trade between the U.S. and the treaty country."

(b) Cannot be based on a single transaction, regardless of how protracted or monetarily valuable.

(c) Trade can be binding contracts which call for the immediate exchange of items of trade.

(d) *Volume* of exchanges is given more weight than the value of the exchanges. No minimum requirement for either.

(e) Smaller businesses. Income derived from the value of numerous transactions which is sufficient to support trader and her family constitutes a favorable factor in assessing existence of substantial trade.

(f) Sources of proof include, but are not limited to, bills of lading, customer receipts, letters of credit, insurance papers documenting commodities imported, purchase orders, carrier inventories, trade brochures, insurance papers documenting commodities imported, purchase orders, courier inventories and sales contracts. 62 Fed. Reg. 48138 at 48141 (Sept. 12, 1997).

4.b. Nationality of Corporation. 8 C.F.R. §214.2(e)(7), 62 Fed. Reg. 48138 at 48140 (Sept. 12, 1997); 22 C.F.R. §41.51(a)(6); 9 FAM 41.51 N.2, N.3.2

(1) At least 50% of stock owned by nationals of treaty country. Permits joint venture. 9 FAM 41.51 N.3.1; 51 Fed. Reg. 6911–7001 (Feb. 27, 1986). Where foreign corporation is owner of the U.S. entity the nationality of the foreign corporation is determined by its owners, not by its place of incorporation or the location of the company's business activity. *Matter of* ___, EAC 90-123-50664 (AAU May 14, 1993). However, if it is a publicly traded company, the firm's nationality is presumed to be that of the country in which the firm's stock is physically listed and traded on the stock exchange. 9 FAM 41.51 N.3.2.

(2) LPRs from the treaty country who own stock in the U.S. company can not have their stock counted in the determination of the nationality of the company. E or non-E nationals of the treaty country who are not LPRs, can count their stock when determining the nationality of the company. 9 FAM 41.51 N.14.1.

(3) In order to employ persons from the treaty country, at least 50% of the corporation must be owned by persons having the nationality of the treaty country who are maintaining E status if residing in the U.S. or, if not residing in the U.S., who would be classifiable as E nonimmigrants. 9 FAM 41.51 N.14.1, 22 C.F.R. §41.51(a)(2). *Cf Incalza v. Fendi North America, Inc.*, 479 F.3d 1005 (9th Cir. 2006) [where Italian national was fired after company changed to French ownership, employee's award of damages was upheld because company could have requested H-1B status or given him unpaid leave until he resolved his immigration status].

4.c. Employee's Work—Unlike L-1, employee can be a new hire and need not have worked for the company previously. 9 FAM 41.51 N.14.3–4. For a discussion of the nature of the employees' position with the company, *see in this section* ¶ 6 (p.739), *infra*.

4.d. Special problems with E-1 related to embargoes—Where the U.S. places an economic embargo or sanctions on a country, the country's E-1 privileges are often rendered inoperable. For example, U.S. sanctions against Yugoslavia resulted in the suspension of the issuance of E-1 visas. 12 *AILA Monthly Mailing* 140-43 (Feb. 1993). Also, embargo against Iran prohibits E-1 for Iranians. Executive Order 12959 (May 6, 1995), 60 Fed. Reg. 24757 (May 9, 1995). But an E-2 may be permissible. *See, e.g.,* Cable, DOS (98-State-128375) (July 8, 1999), *reprinted in* 76 No. 28 *Interpreter Releases* 1124–25 (July 26, 1999) [permitting E-2s for Iranians providing that person is not coming to U.S. to work as an agent, employee or contractor of Iran government or for a business entity or other organization in Iran].

5. E-2—INA §101(a)(15)(E)(ii), 8 U.S.C. §1101(a)(15)(E)(ii); 22 C.F.R. §41.51.

5.a. Nationality of Investment Enterprise—Same as E-l; 50% is sufficient (joint venture). 22 C.F.R. §41.51(b)(6), 9 FAM 41.51 N.3.1.

5.b. Investment—Has invested or is actively in the process of investing. 22 C.F.R. §41.51(b)(1).

(1) Funds in employer's possession/control.

(a) Funds must be "at risk." 9 FAM 41.51 N.8.1-2 (*e.g.,* must be unsecured loan or collateral for loan must be from personal assets). The capital must be subjected to partial or total loss if investment fortunes reverse. It must be "the investor's unsecured personal business capital or capital secured by personal assets." 8 C.F.R. §214.2(e)(12); 22 C.F.R. §41.51(b)(7). Mortgage debt or commercial loan secured by enterprise assets is not sufficient. 9 FAM 41.51 N.8.1-2, 62 Fed. Reg. 41138 at 48142 (Sept. 12, 1997). A second mortgage on a home, unsecured or unencumbered loans or assets and loans on the person's personal signature are acceptable. 62 Fed. Reg. 41138 at 48142 (Sept. 12, 1997). Inheritance of a business is not an investment. 9 FAM 41.51 N.8.1-1, although applicant may use inherited funds for an investment. *See also* Letter, Weinig, Deputy Asst. Comm., Adjudications, CO 214e-C (Jan. 17, 1992), *reprinted in* 69 No. 13 *Interpreter Releases* 438 (Apr. 6, 1992). The statute does not require that the source of the funds be outside the U.S. *Id.* 9 FAM 41.51 N8.1-1.

(b) Intent or prospective plans insufficient. *Matter of Chung*, 15 I&N Dec. 681 (R.C. 1976). Uncommitted funds in a bank account insufficient. 9 FAM 41.51 N.8.1-3; *Matter of Heitland*, 14 I&N Dec. 563 (BIA 1974). However, a reasonable amount of case held in a business bank account, to be used for routine operations, may be counted as investment funds. 9 FAM 41.51 N. 8.1-3. Funds must be irrevocably committed to enterprise and applicant has burden of showing irrevocable commitment. 8 C.F.R. §214.2(e)(12); 22 C.F.R. §41.51(b)(7); 9 FAM 41.51 N.8.1-3.

(c) Escrowed Funds. Placing funds in escrow pending approval of E classification with legal mechanism that irrevocably commits funds but also protects investor if application is denied is permissible. 8 C.F.R. §214.2(e)(12); 22 C.F.R. §41.51(b)(7).

(2) Funds cannot be obtained directly or indirectly through criminal activity. 8 C.F.R. §214.2(e)(12). Criminal activity includes matters illegal under U.S. law and does *not* include activity which would be lawful under U.S. law. Thus, the violation of foreign laws restricting the exit of capital from the country would not be considered using funds that came from a criminal activity. 62 Fed. Reg. 48138 at 48142. (Sept. 12, 1997).

(3) Valuation of investment. 9 FAM 41.51 N.8.2-1, N.8.2-2.

(a) Rent paid on equipment or property is investment, but limited to funds devoted to item in any *month* (unless rent paid in advance). *Matter of Shaw*, 15 I&N Dec. 794 (BIA 1976). Purchase of equipment/inventory counted. *Matter of Khan*, 16 I&N Dec. 138 (BIA 1977). 9 FAM 41.51 N.8.2-1.

(b) Transfer of goods and machinery so long as it is demonstrated they will be or are being put to use in the enterprise. 9 FAM 41.51 N.8.2-2.

(c) Must establish that funds are the investor's. *Nice v. Turnage*, 752 F.2d 431 (9th Cir. 1985) [must demonstrate that it is alien's funds and that s/ he is not simply investing a third party's (*e.g.*, parent/in-law) money].

(d) Inherited business does not qualify as investment. 9 FAM 41.51 N.8.1-1. *But see* Letter, Weinig, Deputy Asst. Comm., Adjudications, CO 214e-C (Jan. 17, 1992), *reprinted in* 69 No. 13 *Interpreter Releases* 425, 438 (Apr. 6, 1992). Inherited funds, however, can be used to make a qualified investment. 9 FAM 41.51 N.8.1-1.

5.c. Commercial Enterprise:

(1) Not passive investment (*e.g.*, stocks, undeveloped land). 9 FAM 41.51 N.9.

(2) Entrepreneurial. Land development as opposed to land investment. *Matter of Heitland, supra*.

(3) Nonprofit institutions (schools, associations) are *not* considered commercial enterprises and therefore investing in a nonprofit will not result in eligibility for E-2. 62 Fed. Reg. 48138 at 48142 (Sept. 12, 1997); 22 C.F.R. §41.51(b)(8); 9 FAM 41.51 N.9.

5.d. Substantiality of investment—Department of State by statute is charged with the responsibility for defining "substantial." INA §101(a)(45), 8 U.S.C. §1101(a)(45). Currently, DOS uses relative/proportionality test.

(1) Test is: (i) the amount of qualifying funds invested weighed against the total cost of purchasing or creating the enterprise; (ii) the amount normally considered sufficient to ensure the investor's financial commitment to the successful operation of the enterprise; and (iii) a magnitude of investment to support the likelihood that the investor will successfully develop and direct the enterprise. 8 C.F.R. §214.2(e)(14); 9 FAM 41.51 N.10; 22 C.F.R. §41.51(b)(9).

(2) Small and medium size businesses. The lower the cost of the enterprise, the higher, proportionally, the investment must be to be considered a substantial amount. 8 C.F.R. §214.2(e)(14)(iii); 9 FAM 41.51 N.10.4 [suggesting that if total investment is $100,000 or less E-2 investor should provide 100% of the investment]. The 50%+ rule formerly required by INS has been abandoned. 62 Fed. Reg. 48138 at 48142 (Sept. 12, 1997).

(3) DOS recognizes that the value (cost) of the business is dependent upon the nature of the enterprise and the cost of the business *per se* is not independently relevant or determinative of qualification for E-2 status, as long as all other requirements are met. 9 FAM 41.51 N.10.3. For example, the cost to establish a service business may be relatively low and the DOS will look at the "amount necessary to establish a viable enterprise." Supports decision reached in *Matter of Walsh & Pollard*, 20 I&N Dec. 60 (BIA 1988) [British company set up U.S. subsidiary to fulfill its contractual obligations with GM by sending engineers. Investment was less than $50,000]. Airgram, DOS (Apr. 3, 1989), *reprinted in* 66 No. 13 *Interpreter Releases* 381, 387–92 (Apr. 3, 1989); 9 FAM 41.51 N.13.

5.e. Cannot Be Marginal—9 FAM 41.51 N.11; 8 C.F.R. §214.2(e)(15); 22 C.F.R. 41.51(b)(10).

(1) Enterprise marginal if it does not have the present or *future* capacity to generate more than minimal living for investor and family. If future capacity at issue you need to demonstrate what will occur within a 5-year period; therefore the applicant should provide a *5-year plan*. 22 C.F.R. §41.51(b)(10); 8 C.F.R. §214.2(e)(15).

(2) Investment cannot be solely to earn a living for the investor and his family. *Lauvik v. INS*, 910 F.2d 658, 661–62 (9th Cir. 1990); *Kim v. District Director*, 586 F.2d 713 (9th Cir. 1978). Investor's employment as skilled or unskilled labor in business is unrelated to the marginality issue. 62 Fed. Reg. 48138 at 48143 (Sept. 12, 1997)

(3) Factors [Memo, Assoc. Comm., Adjudications, CO 214e-C (June 14, 1985)]:

(a) Investment will expand job opportunities;

(b) Generate other sources of income;

(c) Investment will generate income substantially above what would be considered a living;

(d) Investor will not work simply as a skilled or unskilled worker.

(4) Where INS did not consider record evidence of other income, court reversed finding that investment was marginal. *Chung v. INS*, 662 F.Supp. 474 (W.D. Wash. 1987). However, current language of the FAM strongly suggests that evidence of other income is no longer a factor. 9 FAM 41.51 N. 11.

5.f. Develop and Direct, 9 FAM 41.51 N.12.1:

(1) Must manage business and not compete directly in the market as skilled laborer. *Lauvik v. INS*, 910 F.2d 658, 661–62 (9th Cir. 1990) [reversed DD denial of E-2 extension where applicant performed "some menial tasks"]. "Hands-on" management that is purely incidental to developing business is permissible. 62 Fed. Reg. 48138 at 48144 (Sept. 12, 1997).

(2) Has controlling interest in business. *Matter of Lee*, 15 I&N Dec. 187 (R.C. 1975). Control may be by negative veto and therefore 50% ownership may be sufficient to establish the "develop and direct" criteria so long as s/he is not contractually precluded from taking action. 9 FAM 41.51 N.12. Under regulations, control may be established by: (1) 50% ownership; (2) operational control through managerial position; or (3) other means. 8 C.F.R. §214.2(e)(16), 22 C.F.R. §41.51(b)(11). What constitutes control may vary depending on factors such as the structure of the enterprise involved. 9 FAM 41.51 N. 11.

(3) Develop and direct only applies to principal investor, not to employees. 62 Fed. Reg. 48138 at 48150; *Matter of Walsh and Pollard, supra*. Visa Office response to Interrogatory 17, *digested in* 66 No. __ *Interpreter Releases* 369 (Apr. 3, 1989).

(4) In small corporation, stock ownership is generally indicia of control. However, majority ownership of stock is not enough where majority owner cedes managerial control over the enterprise. *U.S. v. Matsumaru,* 244 F.3d 1092, 1100–01 (9th Cir. 2001). [upheld conviction of immigration lawyer who took control of business enterprise].

(5) In large corporation look to corporate/stock structure and corporate practice. 9 FAM 41.51 N.12. Negative control of joint-venture qualifies. *Id.*

5.g. Intent to depart, 8 C.F.R. §214.2(e)(1)(ii), (2)(iii), (5); 22 C.F.R. 41.51(b)(3); 9 FAM 41.51 N.1.2(9).

(1) Investor's statement sufficient. *Lauvik v. INS*, 910 F.2d 658, 660–61 (9th Cir. 1990) [distinguished E-2 desire from intent to depart]

(2) Do not need objective criteria (*i.e.,* existing home abroad). *Id.*

(3) May not be denied solely on basis of an approved LC or IV petition. However, DOS requires the visa applicant to establish that he or she will not seek adjustment of status within the U.S. 8 C.F.R. §214.2(e)(5); 9 FAM 41.51 N.15.

6. Employees of E-1/E-2 must have same nationality as treaty employer *and* must be either:

6.a. Executives and Supervisors—8 C.F.R. §214.2(e)(17); 9 FAM 41.51 N.14; 22 C.F.R. §§41.51(a)(11) and (b)(12).

(1) Position must be principally and primarily, as opposed to incidentally or collaterally, executive or supervisory.

(2) Duties must provide the employee ultimate control and responsibility for the enterprise's overall operation or a major component of it.

(a) To determine the requirements control and responsibility, DHS/DOS shall consider: (i) whether the executive position provides great authority to determine policy and direction; (ii) whether the supervisory position provides supervision for a significant portion of the operation and does not generally involve supervision over low-level employees; (iii) whether the applicant possesses executive/supervisory skills and experience; (iv) whether salary and position title are commensurate with executive/supervisory position; (v) the relationship of the position to the organizational structure; (vi) the responsibility of the applicant for making discretionary decisions, setting policies, directing and managing business operations, and/or supervising other professional and supervisory personnel; and (vii) if the position requires performance of routine staff work or if it is only of an incidental nature;

6.b. Nonsupervisory person with special qualifications who is an essential employee—8 C.F.R. §214.2(e)(18), 9 FAM 41.51 N.14.3; 22 C.F.R. §§41.51(a)(12) and (b)(13). *See also Matter of Walsh & Pollard, supra.*

(1) In determining if essential employee, the factors to consider are as follows:

(a) the employee's degree or proven expertise in area of operations;

(b) the uniqueness of the specific skills;

(c) the function of the job to which the applicant is destined;

(d) the salary such special expertise can command. 9 FAM 41.51 N.14.3-2(b); and

(e) the availability of U.S. workers. 9 FAM 41.51 N.14.3-2(c). In determining uniqueness/specialization for purposes of essential employee status (E-2) can also look at whether U.S. workers are available. *Matter of Nago*, 16 I&N Dec. 446, 447 (BIA 1978); *Matter of Udagawa*, 14 I&N Dec. 578, 582 (BIA 1974); 8 C.F.R. §214.2(e)(18)(ii).

(2) Knowledge of a foreign language and culture, knowledge of country conditions, or previous employment do not by themselves meet the special qualifications requirement. Need to analyze their essentiality in relationship to the enterprise. 8 C.F.R. §214.2(e)(18)(i).

(3) An essential employee's skills do not have to be "unique" or "one of a kind," but rather, "indispensable to the success of the enterprise." 62 Fed. Reg. 48138 at 48144 (Sept. 12, 1997).

(4) Whether essential skills are needed or available will vary over the time of an enterprise (after start-up need employee's skills) when the provision of the service is not generally available in the U.S. 8 C.F.R. §214.2(e)(18)(ii); 22 C.F.R. §§41.51(a)(12) and (b)(13); 9 FAM 41.51 N.14.3-1.

6.c. For E-1/E-2 employee to qualify, the employer must hold treaty status if in U.S. *or be so classifiable.* 62 Fed. Reg. 48138 at 48150 (Sept. 12, 1997); 22 C.F.R. §§41.51(a)(2) and (b)(2).

7. Procedures. 8 C.F.R. §214.2(e)(19), (20), and (21)

7.a. Application for E status filed on Form I-129 if seeking change of status in U.S. If filing application at consular post, most posts use the DS-156E supplemental form in addition to the Form DS-156 visa application. Applicant must provide supporting evidence of the investment. The burden of proof is on the applicant. *Matter of Khan, supra; Matter of Shaw, supra.*

7.b. Visa Reciprocity—To determine the length of time of the visa must look to country of nationality to determine the maximum time they grant to USCs. The time period is published in the DOS reciprocity schedule. The maximum time is usually 5 years. Continuously renewable depending upon compliance with the requirements.

7.c. Admission is for 2 years. 8 C.F.R. §214.2(e)(19)(i). If E entrant does not leave the U.S. during that time, s/he must file I-129 before the expiration of the time period. 8 C.F.R. §214.2(e)(20).

7.d. Special qualification/essential employee's responsible for start-up operations, generally only given 2 years absent special circumstances. 8 C.F.R. §214.2(e)(20)(ii).

7.e. Substantive and nonsubstantive changes in employer, 8 C.F.R. §214.2(e)(8)(iii) and (iv).

(1) A substantive change requires filing a new I-129 with employer supplement. A change is substantive if there has been a fundamental change in the employer's basic characteristics such as merger, acquisition or sale where the applicant is employed.

(2) Nonsubstantive change—No I-129 or prior approval necessary if there is no substantive or fundamental change in the national's employment which would affect eligibility for E classification. No prior approval necessary if corporate changes occur which do not affect the previously approved employment relationship. 8 C.F.R. §214.2(e)(8)(iv). Nonsubstantive changes include mere change in name of treaty company, where one treaty national owner is replaced by another, or in some merger and acquisition where there is no effect on the [person's] employment or relationship to the approved treaty activity. 62 Fed. Reg. 48138 at 48141 (Sept. 12, 1997).

(3) If employer is unsure about the effect of change, s/he may seek USCIS advice by filing with fee completed I-129 and seeking USCIS's advice. 8 C.F.R. §214.2(e)(8)(v).

(4) If there is a substantive change, a new *visa* may also be required.

7.f. Subsidiary Employment—8 C.F.R. §214.2(e)(8)(ii). May perform work for parent or subsidiary of employer enterprise without it being deemed substantive change of E status if: (a) subsidiary independently qualifies as a treaty organization at the time the E treaty status was determined; (b) the work requires an executive, supervisor or essential skill person; *and* (c) work is consistent with E status.

7.g. Multiple Employees—A person is not precluded from hiring multiple employees in E-2 status, Letter, Lorr, Acting Chief, Business and Trade Branch, Benefits Division, INS, HQ 70/6.2.5-6 (1996), *reprinted in* 73 No. 37 *Interpreter Releases* 1290, 1308–10 (Sept. 30, 1996) [need to file I-129 with supplement E if in U.S.], but employment cannot be inconsistent with terms and conditions of E. 8 C.F.R. §214.2(e)(8). An unauthorized change of employment to a new employer is a failure to maintain status. 8 C.F.R. §214.2(e)(8)(vii).

7.h. E-1/E-2 in Lieu of H-1B—Notwithstanding *Matter of Walsh & Pollard*, the Service will not grant E-2 (essential employee) status to persons who are paid by job-shop to work at another company (that is U.S. owned). Letter, Lorr, Acting Chief, Benefits Division, INS, HQ 70/6.2.5-6 (Aug. 28, 1996), *reprinted in* 73 No. 37 *Interpreter Releases* 1290, 1311–14 (Sept. 30, 1996). *See* 9 FAM 41.51 N.13.1.

7.i. An E-1 applicant generally must demonstrate that trade is already in existence at the time of the application. *Matter of Seto*, 11 I&N Dec. 290 (R.C. 1965). An exception is a showing of binding contracts calling for immediate trade. 9 FAM 41.51 N.4.4. An E-2 may have a start up business.

7.j. No E visas for Mexico/Canada if there is a labor dispute. 8 C.F.R. §214.2(e)(22); 22 C.F.R §41.51(a)(13). A similar restriction also applies to nationals of Chile and Singapore, although the DOS and USCIS regulations have not yet been amended to reflect this fact. INA §214(j)(2).

8. Family of Es

8.a. Spouse and children accompanying or following to join principal E—Nationality not important. 8 C.F.R. §214.2(e)(4); 22 C.F.R. §§41.51(a)(3) and (b)(3).

8.b. Employment Authorization Issues

(1) Spouse of E visa holder who enters U.S. as E spouse can now obtain employment authorization. INA §214(e)(6); Cable, DOS, 02-State-17328 (Jan. 29, 2002), *published on* AILA InfoNet at Doc. No. 02013032. Employment authorization filed on I-765 at the Service Center set forth in the application instructions and on USCIS websites. For employment authorization the spouse must provide: (i) proof of principal's current status including the petition approval notice if available; and (ii) I-94s of principal and spouse to verify marital relationship. Employment will be granted for period of admission and/or status not to exceed 2 years. In the event spouse does not receive a Form I-765 (proof of employment authorization) within 90 days, s/he can go to local district office and obtain employment for 240 days. Memo, Yates, Deputy Ex. Assoc. Comm., Field Operations, HQ 70/6.2.5, 6.2.12 (Feb. 22, 2002), *published on* AILA InfoNet at Doc. No 02022832 (Feb. 28, 2002).

(2) Children are still not employment authorized but they can attend school without changing status. Inspector's Field Manual §§15.4(e), 15.5(d).

9. Employment discrimination and wrongful termination issues—Under traditional "E" treaties relating to friendship, commerce and navigation, hiring only foreign nationals for employment may be contrary to Title VII. *Sumitomo Shoji America, Inc. v. Avagliano*, 457 U.S. 176 (1982); *Weeks v. Samsung Heavy Industries Co., Inc.*, 126 F.3d 926 (7th Cir. 1997); *Wallace v. SMC Pneumatics Inc.*, 103 F.3d 1394 (7th Cir. 1997); *Papaila v. Uniden America Corp.*, 51 F.3d 54 (5th Cir. 1995), *cert. denied*, 116 S.Ct. 187 (1995); *Fortino v. Quasar Co.*, 950 F.2d 389 (7th Cir. 1991); *McNamara v. Korean Air Lines*, 863 F.2d 1135 (3d Cir. 1988), *cert. denied*, 493 U.S. 944 (1989); *Spiess v. C. Itoh & Co.*, 643 F.2d 353 (5th Cir. 1981), *vacated on other grounds*, 457 U.S. 1128 (1982); *Wickes v. Olympic Airways*, 745 F.2d 363 (6th Cir. 1984). In addition, an E employee may have a cause of ac-

tion for wrongful termination. *Incalza v. Fendi North America, Inc.,* 479 F.3d 1005 (9th Cir. 2006) [where E-1 Italian national was fired after company changed from Italian to French ownership, employee's award of damages was upheld because company could have requested H-1B status for him or given him unpaid leave to resolve his immigration status]. The FCN treaty may also not preempt state employment claims. *Ventress v. Japan Airlines,* 486 F.3d 1111, 1114–18 (9th Cir. 2007) [Japan-US FCN does not preempt California whistleblower claim.

P. ***Bilateral Investment Treaties***—Traditionally, most E-1/E-2 treaty rights arose out of Treaties of Friendship, Commerce and Navigation (FCNs) which governed both trade and investment. More recently, the U.S. has signed treaties directed solely to investment called Bilateral Investment Treaties (BIT) and to Free Trade Agreements (NAFTA/Fast Track) which contain both E-1 and E-2 components. BITs allow for E-2 status only; however, they are more expansive than the traditional FCNs because they apply to foreign nationals who establish, administer or advise an enterprise and not simply develop or direct it. 66 No. 2 *Interpreter Releases* 32, 59 (Jan. 9, 1989). *See* **Appendix L**, *infra,* for list.

Q. ***E-3 Visa (Australian Special Occupation)***—INA §101(a)(15)(E)(iii), 8 U.S.C. §1101(a)(15)(E)(iii); PL 109-13, 119 Stat. 231, Div. B, Tit. V, §501 (May 11, 2005); 22 C.F.R. §41.51(c); AFM at 34.6.

1. Establishes a new category, E-3 which allows persons to enter the U.S. "solely to perform services in a specialty occupation in the United States if the alien is a national of the Commonwealth of Australia" and files a labor attestation under INA §212(t). It is limited to 10,500 per fiscal year. Although the E-3 has characteristics that are the same as H-1Bs or Fast Track H-1B1s, it is a separate visa with separate benefits and requirements. For example, E-3 spouses may work and E-3 applicants are not required to pay the special fees required of H-1Bs. Aytes, Acting Assoc. Dir., Domestic Operations, USCIS, "Processing Guidelines for E-3 Australian Specialty Occupation Workers and Employment Authorization for E-3 Dependent Spouses," *published in* 83 No. 3 *Interpreter Releases* 121, 123–24, 140–45 (Jan. 17, 2006). However, like H-1Bs and H-1B1s, E-3s are required to provide an LCA and prevailing wage determination.

2. To qualify for an E-3 visa, the applicant must (22 C.F.R. §41.51(c)(1) / AFM 34.6(a)):

   2.a. Possess the nationality of the designated country. To date, the only country is Australia.

   2.b. Demonstrate that he satisfies the "specialty occupation" requirements under INA §214(i)(1) and DHS regulations;

      (1) Requirements include the submission of a certified copy of any license or permission to practice if required before practice in the area of employment or evidence that s/he will meet the licensure requirements if it is not required immediately to practice. AFM at 34.6(a)(2); 9 FAM 41.51 N.16.7.

      (2) Does not include fashion models of distinguished merit and ability.

   2.c. Present an LCA in accordance with INA §212(t)(1);

      (1) Cannot submit LCA used in conjunction with a previous H-1B application. The E-3 LCA is the same as that for H-1B and H-1B1 applicants. 20 C.F.R. §655t.730; 73 Fed. Reg. 19944–50 (April 11, 2008). The applicant must file the standard LCA on Form ETA-9035.

   2.d. Present to proof of his academic or other credentials demonstrating he qualifies for the position under INA §214(i)(1);

   2.e. Present a job offer letter or other documentation from the employer establishing that he will be engaged in a specialty occupation and that he will be paid the higher of the actual or prevailing wage pursuant to INA §212(t)(1);

   2.f. Have a visa number available under INA §214(g)(11)(B); and

   2.g. Intends to depart the U.S. upon termination of his E-3 status.

3. Application Process—AFM 34.6(b)

   3.a. Apply directly at consulate for E-3 visa or apply for C/S or E/S on an I-129 petition at the VSC with the information required for eligibility, described above (¶ 2, *supra*).

4. Admission and Extension of Stay

4.a. Admitted initially for period not to exceed the validity of LCA. The term of admission normally granted is two years—the same as E-1s and E-2s. Memo, Hrinyak, Acting Ex. Dir. Immigration Policy and Planning, CPB, OFC:IPP:BZ (Sept. 19, 2005), *published on* AILA InfoNet at Doc. No. 06040712. Extensions of stay may be granted *indefinitely* in increments not to exceed the LCA. AFM 34.6(a)(3).

4.b. CAP of 10,500 Visas. Does not apply to extensions of E-3s provided applicant remains with the same employer named in the original visa application abroad or in the C/S. Dependents do not count against the cap. AFM 34.6(a)(3) Note 3.

5. Spouse and Dependent Children—Receive the same E-3 classification. They need not have the same nationality as the principal and they are not subject to the numerical limitations. 22 C.F.R. §41.51(c)(2); AFM 34.6(a)(3) Note 1. Spouses are eligible for employment authorization. INA §214(e)(6). They are processed in a similar manner to applications by E-1/E-2 spouses except that they must be filed at the VSC. If the principal E-3 has not extended his or her E-3 status, then dependents should file I-539 based upon their place of residence. AFM 34.6(a)(3) Note 2. In addition, spouses battered or subjected to extreme cruelty by the principal E-3 are independently eligible for work authorization, INA §106, 8 U.S.C. §1105a(a), to be filed with the Vermont Service Center unit that adjudicates VAWA self-petitions, U and T visas.

R. *Q Nonimmigrants*—INA §101(a)(15)(Q), 8 U.S.C. §1101(a)(15)(Q); 8 C.F.R. §214.2(q); 57 Fed. Reg. 55056 (Nov. 24, 1992); 22 C.F.R. §41.57.

1. NIV for a participant in an international cultural exchange program designated by the AG for the purpose of providing practical training, employment *and* the sharing of the history, culture and traditions of the country of the person's nationality. The program applies to an employer who has employees not simply an agent or office and who provides on a regular, continuous, systematic basis goods and/or services (including lectures, seminars and other types of cultural programs). 8 C.F.R. §214.2(q)(1).

2. Conditions of Visa:

2.a. Cannot exceed 15 months.

2.b. Beneficiary must have foreign residence.

2.c. Beneficiary must be employed under the same wages and working conditions as U.S. workers.

2.d. Limitation on admission—If beneficiary has spent 15 months in U.S. under a visa cannot be readmitted under the same status until physically outside of the U.S. for 1 year. Brief trips to U.S. under B-1/B-2 do not break the continuity of the one-year foreign residence requirement. 8 C.F.R. §214.2(q)(2)(ii).

3. Application process—I-129 used for both employer program approval and employee petition. Petition can be filed at service center where employer's headquarters located or where beneficiary will do work. 8 C.F.R. §214.2(q)(5). Petition only approved for duration of program (not to exceed 15 months) plus 30 days. A new petition must be filed each time qualified employer wants to bring additional cultural exchange visitors. However, the employer may replace or substitute a participant named in a previously approved petition. 8 C.F.R. §§214.2(q)(3), (q)(6). If beneficiary will work in more than one location need an itinerary. Petition must be accompanied by documentary evidence supporting application, including: (1) a certification that the wages and working conditions are comparable to those accorded local workers; (2) proof that employer is actually doing business in U.S. and has the financial ability to pay participants; and (3) designation of a particular company official to represent company before USCIS and to administer the program. In addition, petition must provide the date of birth, nationality, education, title and job description for each visitor and a certification that s/he can perform the work. All of the above supporting documentation needs to be produced with I-129 unless the employer files multiple petitions in the same year. 8 C.F.R. §§214.2(q)(4), (11)(ii). Petitioner may be employer or designated agent working in an executive or managerial capacity. 8 C.F.R. §214.2(q)(1).

4. Requirements for Program Approval—8 C.F.R. §214.2(q)(3)(iii). All the following must be met:

   4.a. Interaction with American Public—Program must take place in school, museum, business or other establishment where the American public or a segment of the public sharing a common cultural interest, is exposed to aspects of a foreign culture as part of a structured program. Private homes or isolated business settings do not qualify.

   4.b. Cultural component which must be designed on the whole "to exhibit or explain the attitude, customs, history, heritage, philosophy or traditions" of the person's country. Standard instructional activities such as courses or lectures are acceptable.

   4.c. Work Component—The work must serve as the vehicle to achieve the cultural objective and cannot be separate from it.

5. Requirements for Participants—8 C.F.R. §214.2(q)(3)(iv).

   5.a. Must be 18 at time petition filed;

   5.b. Must be qualified to perform work;

   5.c. Must have ability to communicate cultural attributes of country;

   5.d. Must have resided and been physically present outside the U.S. for the immediate prior year if previously admitted as Q.

6. Extension of Stay—Extension only granted up to a total of 15 months. A new petition must be filed for each extension. 8 C.F.R. §214.2(q)(10).

7. Revocation of Petition—8 C.F.R. §214.2(q)(9). Automatic revocation if employer goes out of business, files a withdrawal of the petition or terminates the program. Petition for other reasons may be revoked by notice. An appeal may be taken to the AAO.

8. Judicial Review. At least one court has held that denial of a petition for a Q-1 organization is reviewable. *National Collegiate Recreation Services v. Chertoff,* 447 F.Supp.2d 527 (D. S.C. 2006) [followed *Spencer Enterprises Inc*. and held that INA §242(a)(2)(B)(ii) did not bar judicial review of denial of Q-1 because neither the statute nor the regulations specifically state that the decision is in the discretion of DHS].

S. *Q-2 Nonimmigrants from Northern Ireland*—INA §101(a)(15)(Q)(ii), 8 U.S.C. §1101(a)(15)(Q)(ii). P.L.105-319 (Oct. 30, 1998); 22 C.F.R. §§41.57(b), 101(f), 139; 8 C.F.R. §§214.1(a)(1)(vii), (b)(4), 214.2(q), 248.3(d); 65 Fed. Reg. 14764–80 (Mar. 17, 2000).

Visa is for a person 35 years or younger who resides in Northern Ireland or the counties of Louth, Monaghan, Cavan, Leitrim, Sligo, or Donegal within the Republic of Ireland and seeks to temporarily enter the U.S. for a period not longer than 36 months to participate in a cultural and training program for the purpose of providing practical training, employment, and the experience of coexistence and conflict resolution in a diverse society.

Only 4,000 visas per year. The program must be approved by the Secy. of State and the AG. It will be administered by a designated Program Administrator under the regulations and will include programs in hospitality and tourism, customer service, information and communications technology, pharmaceuticals, engineering, sales, marketing and promotion, agriculture/horticulture diversification, food processing and furniture. 22 C.F.R. §139.8. The current Program Administrator is Northrop Grumman IT at *www.walshvisa.net.* Employer Information Bulletin 17, Office of Business Liaison, Q-1 and Q-2 Programs (Jan. 28, 2004), *reprinted in* 81 No. 5 *Interpreter Releases* 157, 167–69 (Feb. 2, 2004). In order for the trainee to qualify s/he must: (1) be between 18 and 35; (2) have been physically resident in Northern Ireland or one of the border counties for 3 months prior to applying; (3) meet U.S. immigration/visa requirements; (4) be unemployed for a least 3 months or have completed or currently be enrolled in a training program in Ireland (FAS) or Northern Ireland (T&EA) or be a currently employed person whose employer has nominated him. 22 C.F.R. §139.5, 8 C.F.R. §214.2(q)(15) (includes requirement that applicant not intend to come to U.S. for more than 36 months). The Program Administrator must prepare a certification letter sent to the consular officer that details the applicants background and qualifications for the program. 22 C.F.R. §41.57(b)(1)(ii). An applicant may change programs but must do so through the Program Administrator 8 C.F.R. §214.2(q)(15)(viii) and the applicant cannot hold two jobs. §214.2(q)(15)(ix). The visa expires in FY 2006. Allows spouse and minor children to enter.

T. *R Nonimmigrants*—INA §101(a)(15)(R), 8 U.S.C. §1101(a)(15)(R); 22 C.F.R. §41.58; 8 C.F.R. §214.2(r); 60 Fed. Reg. 42034–37 (Aug. 15, 1995).

1. NIV for:

   1.a. A minister:

      (1) Deacons, practitioners of Christian Science and officers of the Salvation Army may be deemed ministers. 9 FAM 41.58 N.9.2; 9.3, and 9.4. *or*

   1.b. A person working in a professional capacity in a religious vocation or occupation;

      (1) Professional capacity is occupation defined at INA §101(a)(32) or B.A. as minimal requirement. 22 C.F.R. §41.58. However, USCIS defines it only as B.A. degree or foreign equivalent degree. 8 C.F.R. §214.2(r)(2).

      (2) Religious occupation is activity which relates to traditional religious function, *e.g.*, cantors, liturgical workers, translators, religious broadcasters, workers in religious hospitals, but not if they are performing lay work (*e.g.*, nurses not eligible). Does not include clerks, fundraisers or maintenance workers. 8 C.F.R. §214.2(r)(2).

      (3) Religious vocation relates to traditional religious function, *e.g.*, nun, monk. If person practices religious vocation it does not matter what job s/he performs (*e.g.*, could include janitor). 9 FAM 41.58 N.10.2-1; *or*

   1.c. A person working for a religious organization (or its IRC §501(c)(3) affiliate) in a religious vocation or occupation; *and*

   1.d. Who for 2 years immediately preceding the application has been a *member* of the religious denomination having a *bona fide* nonprofit religious organization in the U.S. Does *not* require prior employment with the organization as in special immigrant category. If person is merely member of denomination that is sufficient. 22 C.F.R. §41.58(a)(2). USCIS cannot require proof that someone has been practicing in a profession prior to entering on an R-1. *Ten Acre Foundation v. INS*, 892 F.Supp. 289 (D.C. Cir. 1995), *aff'd*, 78 F.3d 693 (D.C. Cir. 1996) [rejecting INS requirement that person seeking to enter program as nurse for Christian Scientists must be fully qualified for position and show previous experience in occupation].

      (1) Factors to consider to determine *bona fide* religious denomination are the presence of some form of ecclesiastical government, a recognized creed and form of worship, a formal code of doctrine and disciplines; religious services and ceremonies, established places of religious worship, and religious congregations. 22 C.F.R. §41.58(b).

      (2) Membership established by letter from appropriate official.

2. Entry limited to 5 years—Not subject to INA §214(b). 9 FAM 41.58 N.2-N.3

3. Spouse and children may accompany or follow to join (R-2).

4. No prior USCIS petition or approval needed if filed at consulate. 8 C.F.R. §214.2(r)(3).

5. Evidence, Procedures and Admission—8 C.F.R. §214.2(r)(4)–(7).

   5.a. Must apply at consular post or if in U.S. on I-129 for C/S. Applicant does *not* need an approved I-129 to obtain visa at the consular post. 8 C.F.R. §214.2(r)(3). Canadians may apply at the border for the R-1.

   5.b. Initial admission is for 3 years with E/S on I-129 for a period up to 2 years. Total period of stay is 5 years. After 5 years must reside and be physically present outside U.S. for one year, except for brief visits, to be eligible again. R visa holders are to be admitted for a period of three years, regardless of the expiration date of the NIV. Memo, Hrinyak, Acting Ex. Dir. Immigration Policy and Programs, CBP, "Guidance on Period of Admission for Religious Workers (R-1) (Oct. 14, 2004), *published on* AILA InfoNet at Doc. No. 05040469.

   5.c. Spouse and children granted R-2 status. May not accept employment. Office of Business Liaison, USCIS, Employer Information Bulletin 18 (Dec. 8, 2004) at 2, *reprinted in* 82 No. 3 *Interpreter Releases* 149, 161, 185–87 (Jan. 17, 2005)

   5.d. If change employer must file new I-129. New employer must be same denomination.

5.e. Evidence—8 C.F.R. §214.2(r)(3):

(1) Tax exemption of U.S. organization or documentation required to obtain IRC §501(c)(3).

(2) Letter from authorized official employing person. The letter must establish that person has the required 2-year membership. If the membership was maintained in whole or part outside the U.S., the letter must establish that the foreign and U.S. religious organization belong to the same religious denomination. The letter must also establish the person's qualifications, remuneration and the name and location of the U.S. organization.

5.f. Premium Process Suspended. In light of concerns regarding fraud USCIS has suspended premium processing. USCIS Extends Suspension, *published on* AILA InfoNet at Doc. No. 08010469

U. *I Visas (Representatives of Media)*—INA §101(a)(15)(I), 8 U.S.C. §1101(a)(15)(I).

1. Criteria:

1.a. *Bona fide* representative.

1.b. Of foreign press, radio, film or other foreign information media.

(1) Includes not only primary employees of foreign information media engaged in filming news events or documentaries, but also employees of independent production companies if the employees either: (1) hold a credential issued by a professional journalistic association; or (2) if no such credential is available because the sending country has no credentialing authority or the authority does not offer credentialing to the class of media representatives to which the employees belong. 9 FAM 41.52 N2.2

(2) Does not include film production/distribution unless film is informational or educational. 9 FAM 41.52 N.2.

(3) Television included. O.I. §214.2(i). Private production crews where film will be distributed for information or news not commercial entertainment are also included. O.I. §214.2(i).

(4) If producing for commercial entertainment/advertising purpose, camera crew and other workers obtain O-1 and O-2 visas even if no U.S. remuneration and film solely for foreign distribution. Under O.I. §214.2(i) they formerly sought H or B-1 visas.

(5) Foreign press includes a foreign press owned by U.S. shareholders if staffed in large part by non-Americans to collect information for foreign audience. Letter, Odom, Deputy Chief, Visa Services, V-101(a)(15)(i) (Jan. 9, 1986). I visa holder may be employed by a U.S. branch office or U.S. subsidiary of the foreign company provided his or her activities are being conducted principally for the benefit of the foreign-based media. Letter, Odom, Chief, Advisory Opinions Division, DOS (Nov. 27, 1995), *reprinted in* 72 No. 47 *Interpreter Releases* 1654, 1675 (Dec. 11, 1995).

1.c. Entering *solely* to engage in vocation.

1.d. Only if "home office" is in foreign country (foreign correspondent for *N.Y. Times* needs L/H visa).

1.e. Overstay—Not subject to INA §222(g) until there is finding of unauthorized stay by IJ or USCIS because I visa holders are given D/S upon entry. Cable, DOS (99-State-105097) (June 7, 1999), *reprinted in* 76 No. 24 *Interpreter Releases* 977–80 (June 28, 1999).

2. Conditions of entry—reciprocity between U.S. and *home country*. 22 C.F.R. §41.52(a); O.I. §214.2(i). Cannot enter on a B visa or on visa waiver to perform I functions. Cable, DOS, 03-State-155061 (June 6, 2003), *published on* AILA InfoNet at Doc. No. 03070111.

3. Procedure

3.a. Admission for duration of status; extensions for 1 year. 8 C.F.R. §214.2(i).

3.b. No limitation on extensions. May remain indefinitely. No requirement of residence abroad.

3.c. No restrictions on adjustment.

3.d. Employment of spouse/children—Dependents must be employment authorized to work. 8 C.F.R. §§274a.12(b)(10), 1274a.12(b)(10) [employer subject to sanctions].

VIII. DIPLOMATIC & INTERNATIONAL ORGANIZATION ALIENS (A, G, C-2/C-3)

A. *Diplomatic/Official Visas Distinguished*

1. Diplomatic visa eligibility—22 C.F.R. §41.26. Heads of state; royal family; governor generals; cabinet members; justices of highest court; presiding members of legislatures; ambassadors; military at or above rank of brigadier general; military attaché; G-4 visa holders if Sec. General of U.N. or other high U.N. official or officer on diplomatic missions; and all immediate family members of those persons.

2. Official visas—22 C.F.R. §41.27. Persons eligible to receive diplomatic visa but not in possession of diplomatic passport; A visas; C visas within INA §212(d)(8), 8 U.S.C. §1182(d)(8) [reciprocal continuous transit], and all other G visas, except G-3, unless from government recognized by U.S.; members of legislatures and justices of lower courts; clerical and custodial employees attached to foreign government delegations or international organization; members of the family; or servants and personal employees of diplomatic visa holders.

3. Purpose of diplomatic designation—expedited processing at border. Stamped on visa. (*e.g.*, F-1 with diplomatic designation)

4. Section 13 of the Immigration and Nationality Act of 1957, PL 85-316, 71 Stat. 642, *as modified*, PL 97-116, 95 Stat. 1611 (Dec. 29, 1981), permits adjustment of status for A or G visa holders, without any other basis for adjustment, if they have failed to maintain status and can demonstrate compelling reasons why s/he cannot return to home country. The applicant must also demonstrate it is in the U.S. national interest and not contrary to national welfare, safety and security to grant LPR status. Only 50 Section 13 visas are available each year.

5. If person is LPR, must go from LPR to A (or G or E), if occupation would grant him the status, unless s/he obtains a waiver. 8 U.S.C. §1257; 8 C.F.R. §247. If diplomat wishes to retain his or her LPR status, s/he may file an I-508 waiver (of diplomatic immunities) within 10 days of the DD notifying him or her of USCIS's intention to adjust him or her to A, G or E status. If the LPR does not respond to the DD, the diplomat will automatically be changed to NIV status. 8 C.F.R. §§247.11, 247.12.

B. ***A Visas***—INA §101(a)(15)(A), 8 U.S.C. §1101(a)(15)(A). Diplomats, officials and employees of foreign governments recognized by the U.S. coming on official business.

1. Three categories

   1.a. A-1—22 C.F.R. §41.22(b). Ambassadors, public ministers or career diplomats/ officers and their immediate families. Also "career couriers." 22 C.F.R. §41.22(h)(1); 9 FAM 41.22 N.1-N.1.5.

   1.b. A-2—Other accredited officials and employees of foreign governments and their immediate families.

   1.c. A-3—Attendants, servants, personal employees of A-1 or A-2 and members of *their* immediate families.

2. Credentials

   2.a. A-1—accepted by President or Secy. of State. Holding diplomatic passport or government employment without approval of credentials by U.S. is insufficient to obtain visa. A-2—Secy. of State. A-2 and A-3—Only on basis of reciprocity—8 U.S.C. §1101(a)(15)(A). The possession of the visa, standing alone, also does not prove diplomatic status. *U.S. v. Al-Hamdi,* 356 F.3d 564, 573 (4th Cir. 2004) [upheld interpretation of Vienna Convention on Consular Relations that did not provide continuing A-1 status for son or daughter that turned 21]; *U.S. v. Kostadinov,* 734 F.3d 905, 912 (2d Cir. 1984) [issuance of A-1 visa does not confer diplomatic immunity because such status is recognized by identification on official lists and by issuance of diplomatic immunity card].

   2.b. If foreign official/employee not coming on official business—not an A-l/A-2. Should be given B or other NIV visa.

   2.c. If no *de jure* recognition by U.S. only given B, C or G-3 visa. *De jure* does not equal formal diplomatic relations. May have *de jure* status even without diplomatic relations (*e.g.*, Cuba).

3. Inadmissibility

3.a. A-l—Limited only to certain security grounds, INA §212(a)(3)(A)–(C), 9 FAM 41.21 PN4; A-2—Same as A-1 limitation; A-3—Subject to all grounds of inadmissibility, except that if a bona fide A-3 employee s/he cannot be subject to being an intending immigrant under INA §214(b). 9 FAM 41.22 N.4.4(c).

3.b. Visa not issued to persona non grata. 22 C.F.R. §41.21(d)(1).

4. Procedure

4.a. Issuance of A is *prima facie* eligibility under INA §101(a)(15)(A), 8 U.S.C. §1101(a)(15)(A), but it is subject to Secy. of State accepting credentials. 8 C.F.R. §214.2(a)(1).

4.b. Admitted for duration of status. 8 C.F.R. §214.2(a)(1).

5. A-3

5.a. Different procedures. A-3 is for personal employee of A-1/A-2. The employer must be in valid A-1/A-2 status for applicant to receive A-3. 9 FAM 41.22 N.4.

5.b. Subject fully to all grounds of inadmissibility except intending immigrant. 9 FAM 41.22 N.4.4(c).

5.c. Must prove admissibility. If consular officer believes person is seeking A-3 but intends to work someone else or in a position other than as a personal employee of the A-1/A-2 he may deny the visa on INA §214(b) or INA §212(a)(6)(C) grounds. 9 FAM 41.22 N.4.2 and N. 4.4(c).

5.d. No prior domestic experience needed. 9 FAM 41.21 N.6.1.

5.e. Admission for 3 years plus 2-year periods. 8 C.F.R. §214.2(a).

5.f. Family members of A-3—No employment, 8 C.F.R. §214.2(a)(2), except spouses battered or subjected to extreme cruelty are eligible for work authorization, INA §106, to be filed with the Vermont Service Center unit that adjudicates VAWA self-petitions, U and T visas.

6. Families A-l/A-2

6.a. Defined, 8 C.F.R. §214.2(a)(2)(i)-(v). Includes, spouse, unmarried children, *and* unmarried sons and daughters under certain limited circumstances. For example, an unmarried son or daughter under the age of 23 who is in full-time attendance as a student at a post-secondary educational institution is considered a dependent and may obtain employment. 8 C.F.R. §214.2(a)(2)(iii).

6.b. Employment (spouse and unmarried dependent children, sons and daughters):

(1) Must seek permission. 8 C.F.R. §§274a.12(c)(1), 1274a.12(c)(1), 8 C.F.R. §214.2(a)(2), (5), (6). Employment permitted upon recommendation of DOS only if there is a formal bilateral employment agreement or informal de facto reciprocal agreement. 8 C.F.R. §214.2(a)(5). An applicant cannot work in a Schedule B position, 8 C.F.R. §214.2(a)(5)(ii)(D), or if his or her employment is contrary to the interest of the U.S. which includes prior unauthorized employment or failure to pay income tax on money previously earned. 8 C.F.R. §214.2(a)(5)(ii)(E). The applicant must submit an I-566 form to the DOS for approval. If endorsed, then s/he may make an application for employment for dependents to be filed at the Nebraska Service Center. 63 Fed. Reg. 50584 at 50585 (Sept. 22, 1998). In addition, spouses battered or subjected to extreme cruelty are eligible for work authorization, INA §106, to be filed with the Vermont Service Center unit that adjudicates VAWA self-petitions, U and T visas.

(2) Subject to deportation for employment without permission under INA §237(a)(1)(C)(i). *See* 8 C.F.R. §214.2(a)(10).

Former O.I. §214.2(a)(10). USCIS will only notify DOS of visa status. Will not deport as long as DOS accepts credentials of diplomat. Will not even notify DOS if job involves "educational, nursing and cultural pursuits."

6.c. Procedure

(1) Where work authorization is sought pursuant to a formal agreement or an informal *de facto* reciprocal arrangement, the dependent under 8 C.F.R. §214.2(a)(6) needs to:

(a) File I-566 with Office of Protocol at DOS.

(b) DOS makes recommendation and if positive dependent applies to USCIS.

(c) For approval need to demonstrate: (i) alien will be here more than 6 months; (ii) has qualification for position under 214.2(a)(2); (iii) not Schedule B work (*i.e.,* oversupply), except if full time student working 20 hrs; (iv) reciprocity of work in foreign country; (v) alien must not have criminal record, violated DHS laws, including unauthorized employment, or failed to pay taxes;

(2) No appeal from denial.

(3) Approval in 2-year increments.

6.d. Overstays—The provisions of INA §222(g) concerning overstays returning to their country of origin to obtain a new visa are inapplicable to A-1 and A-2 visa holders. Cable No. 225321, Christopher, Secy. of State, State No. 208799/212382 (1996), *reprinted in* 73 No. 42 *Interpreter Releases* 1,544-50 (Nov. 4, 1996) other than a determination by a USCIS officer or IJ that he has committed a status violation. Cable, DOS, 98-State-051296 (Mar. 23, 1998), *published on* AILA InfoNet at Doc. No. 98032392. A-3s are subject to INA §222(g). 9 FAM 41.22 N.4.4(c).

6.e. LPR status—Children of diplomats born in the U.S. are considered to be LPRs. 8 C.F.R. §§101.3, 1101.3; *Matter of Chu*, 14 I&N Dec. 241 (R.C. 1972); *Matter of Huang*, 11 I&N Dec. 190 (R.C. 1965), unless they abandon their residency by returning to their home country with their parents. *Nikoi v. Attorney General*, 939 F.2d 1065 (D.C. Cir. 1991).

C. *G Visas*—INA §101(a)(15)(G), 8 U.S.C. §1101(a)(15)(G), 9 FAM 41.24

1. Authority: International Organizations Immunities Act, 22 U.S.C. §288.

2. Five categories

2.a. G-1

(1) Principal resident representative, family and staff (of any rank, including clerical and custodial employees, so long as they are assigned on "resident basis"). G-1s are for members of a permanent mission of a recognized government. 9 FAM 41.24 N.1

(2) Foreign government has U.S. *de jure* recognition.

(3) International organization listed (*e.g.,* IMF, U.N., OAS, OAU).

(4) If G-1 to G-4 seek entry to go to UN or any other international organization they are only subject to certain security grounds of inadmissibility INA §212(a)(3)(A)–(C). If they are inadmissible on these grounds they may seek an advisory opinion to permit admission. 9 FAM 41.24 N. 2.3

(5) G-l—G-4—Duration of status so long as DOS recognizes credentials. 8 C.F.R. §214.2(g)(1).

2.b. G-2

(1) Representatives of a recognized government and their immediate family. Military officers assisting the UN with peacekeeping matters. Attendees of course at IMF and World Bank. Other accredited representatives and immediate family.

(2) Interpretation at 9 FAM 41.24 N.1(2)

(a) Personnel of any rank including clerical/custodial and immediate family;

(b) *Temporary* delegation (*e.g.,* includes working groups of international organization);

(c) Inadmissible under certain security grounds; *see in this section* ¶ 2.a(4) (p.749), *supra.*

2.c. G-3

(1) G-1/G-2 from government without *de jure* recognition from U.S.; or

(2) Nonmember country of international organization.

2.d. G-4

(1) Officers and employees of international organization and immediate family. Includes "personnel of any rank." 9 FAM 41.24 N.1(4).

(2) Special expeditious treatment to U.N. reps. because U.S. host country. 9 FAM 41.24 N.3.1.

(3) Inadmissible only under certain security grounds, INA §102, 8 U.S.C. §1102.

(4) Sons and daughters, widows and retirees in G-4 status can apply for permanent residence as "special immigrants." INA §101(a)(27)(I), 8 U.S.C. §1101(a)(27)(I).

(5) G-4s include officers and employees of INTELSAT who worked for the company prior to its privatization as long as they either held G-4 status and were employed by INTELSAT for at least 6 months prior to privatization on July 17, 2001 *or* held G-4 status and were employed by a successor or separated entity of INTELSAT after 6 months of employment. Immediate family members are also covered but attendants, servants and person employees of officers and employees are not. 22 C.F.R. §41.24(a)(2) and (c).

2.e. G-5

(1) Attendants, servants and personal employees of G-1 to G-4.

(2) Subject to exclusion on all grounds.

(3) May be admitted for 3 years, plus renewals in increments of 2 years, but extensions must be accompanied by a letter from employer describing G-5's work. 8 C.F.R. §214.2(g)(1).

2.f. General criteria

(1) If person is eligible for both A and G (*i.e.,* foreign diplomat conducting business for government and also attending organization) will be given an A visa. 22 C.F.R. §41.24(b)(3).

(2) If person is G and has other nonimmigrant visa will be given G.

(3) Admission on G subject to DOS credential approval.

(4) Visa usually issued upon international organization's request.

(5) Not required to have domicile abroad as with other nonimmigrant visas. Can establish intent to reside in the U.S. *Elkins v. Moreno*, 435 U.S. 647 (1978).

(6) If consular officer issues incorrect visa and DHS grants c/s to correct visa the U.S. Mission at the U.N. can reissue the correct A or G visa. 9 FAM 41.24 N.16.

3. Employment—No provision for authorizing employment of family in G-2 status, except that spouses of any G visa holder who are battered or subjected to extreme cruelty are eligible for work authorization, INA §106, to be filed with the Vermont Service Center unit that adjudicates VAWA self-petitions, U and T visas. In addition, the spouse and unmarried dependent children, sons or daughters of G-1, G-3 or G-4s may also seek employment authorization. 8 C.F.R. §§274a.12(c)(4), 214.2(g)(2), (5), (6), 1274a.12(c)(4). For G-1 and G-3, dependents' employment can only be pursuant to a formal bilateral employment agreement or an informal *de facto* reciprocal agreement if they are a national of that country. Dependents must first apply to DOS on Form I-566. If approved, the dependent must apply to USCIS. The same criteria generally apply to G-1, G-3, and G-4 that apply to A-1 (*see in this part* ¶ B.6.b (p.748), *supra.*) The application for employment for dependents must be filed at the Nebraska Service Center. 63 Fed. Reg. 50584–01 at 50585 (Sept. 22, 1998), *reprinted in* 75 No. 37 *Interpreter Releases* 1337, 1356 (Sept. 28, 1998).

3.a. It is a violation of status for dependents to work without authorization *and* for principal alien when s/he works outside scope of his or her official position. 8 C.F.R. §214.2(g)(10).

3.b. G-1 through G-5 authorized to work pursuant to their status for international organization. 8 C.F.R. §§274a.12(b)(7)–(8), 1274a.12(b)(7)–(8).

3.c. Adjustment—INA §§245, 247, 8 U.S.C. §§1255, 1257—Same as A visa.

4. Overstays—The provisions of INA §222(g) are not currently applied to A-1, A-2, G-1, G-2, G-3 and G-4 visa holders. Cable No. 225321, Christopher, Secy. of State, State No. 208799/212382 (1996), *reprinted in* 73 No. 42 *Interpreter Releases* 1544–46 (Nov. 4, 1996) unless USCIS or IJ make a determination that a status violation has occurred. Cable, DOS, 98-State-051296 (Mar. 23, 1998), *published on* AILA InfoNet at Doc. No. 98032392. It is applied to A-3 visa holders. 9 FAM 41.22 N.4.4(c).

5. LPR Status—Children of diplomats born in the U.S. are LPRs. *See in this part* ¶ B.6.e (p.749), *supra*.

D. *NATO*—8 C.F.R. §214.2(s)

1. Special visas for certain employees of NATO; Countries that are parties to NATO listed at 9 FAM 41.25 N1.1.

2. 22 C.F.R. §§41.21, 41.25;

3. Exempt from overstay requirements of INA §222(g) unless USCIS or IJ make a status determination.

4. Employment authorization for NATO principal is incident to status. 8 C.F.R. §274a.12(b)(17), (18). Dependents may also be given employment authorization if there is a written bilateral dependent employment agreement or a de facto agreement. 8 C.F.R. §214.2(s)(3)-(5). The application for employment for dependents must be filed at the Nebraska Service Center. 63 Fed. Reg. 50584–85 (Sept. 22, 1998), *reprinted in* 75 No. 37 *Interpreter Releases* 1337, 1356 (Sept. 28, 1998).

5. Civilian employees of NATO as well as their spouse and children may obtain special immigrant status under INA §101(a)(27)(L) in the same manner as G-4 employees.

E. *UN Transits (C-2 Visa)*

1. Definition

1.a. Representative (from non–*de jure* and nonmember country, *e.g.,* Hamas official Abu Marzouk), or expert that U.N. needs.

1.b. Under U.N. "Headquarters Agreement" (61 Stat. 758)—No impediment to travel for representatives or those requested by U.N. (*e.g.,* expert on refugee matters).

1.c. Inadmissible only under INA §§212(a)(3)(A), (3)(B), (3)(C) and (7)(B) if seeking entry pursuant to UN Headquarters Agreement. 9 FAM 41.71 N5.1. C-2 can obtain INA §212(d)(3)(A) waiver for these grounds. Criteria may be less stringent in C-2 "Headquarters" cases. 9 FAM 41.71 N.5.3.

1.d. Given 29 days. Extensions difficult. 8 C.F.R. §214.2(c)(3). Must stay within NYC area and proceed directly to U.N. When leaving U.N. business must leave U.S. 8 C.F.R. §214.2(c)(2).

1.e. Exempt from overstay requirements of INA §222(g) unless IJ or USCIS make status determination.

F. *Foreign Government Transits (C-3 Visa)*—INA §212(d)(8), 8 U.S.C. §1182(d)(8)

1. Definition:

1.a. Accredited official of foreign government.

1.b. Passing in transit through U.S.

1.c. U.S. has reciprocal right in foreign country.

1.d. Must be on official business.

2. Inadmissible only as to INA §212(a)(3)(A)–(C) and (7)(B).

IX. FAMILY-RELATED VISAS FOR FIANCÉES, SPOUSES, AND CHILDREN OF U.S. CITIZENS OR LPRs

A. *K-1 Visa*—INA §101(a)(15)(K)(i), 8 U.S.C. §1101(a)(15)(K)(i); 9 FAM 41.81

1. Criteria:

   1.a. A fiancé(e) of USC.

   1.b. Seeks to enter U.S. *solely* to conclude a valid marriage with petitioner.

   1.c. Marry within 90 days after entry.

   1.d. Minor children of fiancés can accompany them (K-2).

2. Procedure:

   Requires petition approval by USCIS. INA §214(d), 8 U.S.C. §1184(d).

   2.a. USC must file I-129F petition with USCIS, not at consulate. INA §214(d); 9 FAM 41.81 N.2; O.I. §214.2(k).

   2.b. Must be filed where petitioner is residing. 8 C.F.R. §214.2(k).

   2.c. Must provide proof that:

   (1) There is a *bona fide* intention to marry within 90 days of fiancé's entry

   (2) No legal impediments to marriage;

   (3) Have previously met in person within two years of filing petition. USCIS may waive in person requirement, where extreme hardship or long established custom. 8 C.F.R. §214.2(k)(2); *Matter of* ___ (AAO Feb. 28, 2003) [not extreme hardship where USC refused to meet personally with fiancé during Afghanistan war because they could have met in a third country] *reported in* 80 No. 21 *Interpreter Releases* 750–51 (May 23, 2003).

   (4) Must provide the criminal record, if any, of the *petitioner*. INA §214(d)(1)

   (a) USCIS has limited the reporting to domestic violence, sexual assault, child abuse and neglect, dating violence, elder abuse, stalking, certain violent crimes, and crimes related to a controlled substance or alcohol where the petitioner has been convicted on at least three occasions not arising out of a single act. Memo, Aytes, Assoc. Dir. Domestic Operations, USCIS, HQOPRD 70/6.2.11 (July 21, 2006), *published on* AILA InfoNet at Doc. No. 06080164. Certified copies of all court and police records showing dispositions are required. *Id.*

   2.d. Petition valid for 4 months. Can be revalidated for 4-month periods. No extensions of stay. 8 C.F.R. §214.1(c)(3).

   2.e. Petition automatically terminated where petitioner dies or withdraws petition.

   2.f. Approved petition goes to consul. Consul must determine that fiancé would be eligible to receive *immigrant* visa before approving K. 22 C.F.R. §41.81(d). However, consular officer cannot require K-1 applicant as a condition of entry to get all vaccinations under vaccine-preventable diseases as required by INA §212(a)(1)(A)(ii). Memo, Virtue, Acting Exec. Assoc., Comm. (Sept. 29, 1997), *published on* AILA InfoNet at Doc. No. 97101090.

   2.g. Can obtain K petition approval even if fiancé in deportation proceeding where s/ he has been granted voluntary departure. Letter, Weinig, Deputy Asst. Comm., Adjudication (Sept. 16, 1988), *reprinted in* 7 *AILA Monthly Mailing* 540 (Nov. 1988).

   2.h. Disclosure of Petitioner's Criminal History to Beneficiary—USCIS may disclose to a beneficiary or her legal guardian, a petitioner's criminal history involving violence or sex offenses. The disclosure must be consistent with the requirements of 5 U.S.C. §552a(b)(8) that disclosure is "pursuant to a showing of compelling circumstances affecting the health and safety of an individual…" The fact of disclosure must also be provided in writing to the petitioner. Memo, Divine, Acting Deputy Director, HQOPRD 70/6.1.1 (May 3, 2006), *published on* AILA InfoNet at Doc. No. 06051563. DOS will disclose the information to the beneficiary at the consular interview. Memo, Virtue, Acting Exec. Assoc., Comm. (Sept. 29, 1997) at 2, *published on* AILA InfoNet at Doc. No. 97101090

2.i. Visa not issued:

(1) If marriage would not be legal. *Matter of Manjoukis*, 13 I&N Dec. 705 (DD 1971) [fourteen-year-old women cannot legally marry]; *Matter of Souza*, 14 I&N Dec. 1 (R.C. 1972) [existing prior marriage. Where divorce filed although likely to be finalized within 90 days, was not yet finalized].

(2) Where beneficiary is inadmissible under INA §212(a). Can get INA §212(d)(3)(A) waiver. But only granted where, if married, the exclusion ground is waivable under INA §212(g), (h), (i), or where I-212 would be approved for waiver of INA §212(a)(9)(A)(i) [prior removal for inadmissibility] and INA §212(a)(9)(A)(ii) [prior deportation].

(3) Denial Due to Prior Petitions—Where petitioner previously filed petitions for two or more fiancées if the previously approved petition was filed within 2 years. In addition, once a petitioner has had two fiancée or spousal petitions approved, if a subsequent petition is filed in less than 10 years after the date the first petition was filed DHS shall notify both the petitioner and the beneficiary of any subsequent petition about the number of previously approved fiancée or spousal petitions. INA §214(r)((4)(B)(i). Consul is required to disclose the criminal record of the *petitioner* to the applicant. 8 U.S.C. §1375a(b)(1)(A).

(4) Denial Due to Petitioner's Criminal Conviction—Where petitioner was convicted of a specified offense against a minor unless granted a waiver. INA §§101(a)(15)(K), 204(a)(1)(A)(viii)(I). A USC who has been convicted of a specified offense against a minor as defined in sec. 111(7) of the Adam Walsh Child Protection and Safety Act of 2007, PL 109-248, 120 STAT. 587 (July 27, 2006) is prohibited from petitioning for his or her fiancé(e), unless the Secretary of Homeland Security, in the Secretary's "unreviewable discretion" determines that the USC or LPR poses no risk to the beneficiary of the petition. Section 111(7) defines a "specified offense against a minor" as an offense against a minor that *involves* any of the following: (A) an offense (unless committed by a parent or guardian) involving kidnapping; (B) an offense (unless committed by a parent or guardian) involving false imprisonment; (C) solicitation to engage in sexual conduct; (D) use in a sexual performance; (E) solicitation to practice prostitution; (F) video voyeurism as described in 18 U.S.C. §1801; (G) possession, production or distribution of child pornography; (H) criminal sexual conduct involving a minor, or the use of the Internet to facilitate or attempt such conduct; or (I) any conduct that by its nature is a sex offense against a minor. USCIS views this list as "stated in relatively broad terms" that "takes into account that these offenses may be named differently in a wide variety of federal, state, and foreign criminal statutes. Memo, Aytes, Assoc. Dir., Domestic Operations, USCIS, HQDOMO 70/1-P at ¶3 C (Feb. 8, 2007), *published on* AILA InfoNet at Doc. No. 07030669.

(5) Waivers of time and numerical limitations with or without a criminal history. DHS may waive the time and numerical bars in its discretion but a waiver shall not be granted if the petitioner has a record of violent criminal offenses against a person unless s/he can establish s/he has been battered or subjected to extreme cruelty and was not the primary perpetrator of the violence. INA §214(d)(2). The petitioner may submit the request for a waiver in writing. Factors to consider regarding a waiver are: (1) whether there are unusual circumstances such as the death or incapacity of a previous beneficiary; (2) whether the petitioner has a history of domestic violence; (3) whether the petitioner has a pattern of filing multiple petitions for different beneficiaries at the same time, of filing and withdrawing petitions, or obtaining approvals every few years. Memo, Aytes, Assoc. Dir. Domestic Operations, USCIS, HQOPRD 70/6.2.11 (July 21, 2006) at 2–3, *published on* AILA InfoNet at Doc. No. 06080164. If the petitioner has a history of violent offenses "the adjudicator may not waive the filing limitations unless extraordinary circumstances exist..." Aytes, *supra*. Evidence of rehabilitation with other compelling factors may be considered extraordinary circumstances.

(a) Mandatory Waiver. If convicted petitioner was battered or subject to extreme cruelty at the time he committed the offense and was not the primary perpetrator of violence, was acting in self-defense, violated a protective order aimed at protecting him *or* conviction was for crime that did not result in serious bodily injury and there was a connection between the crime and the battery or extreme cruelty.

(6) Waiver of the Criminal Bar under the Adam Walsh Act—The waiver under this provision is in the "sole and unreviewable discretion" of the DHS upon a determination that the "petitioner poses no risk to the beneficiary." Memo, Aytes, Assoc. Dir. Domestic Operations, 70/1-P (July 28, 2006), *published on* AILA InfoNet at Doc. No. 06080264. In determining the waiver, USCIS must take into consideration that the purpose of section 402 of Adam Walsh Act is "to ensure that an intended alien beneficiary is not placed at risk of harm" from the petitioner. Memo, Aytes, Assoc. Dir., Domestic Operations, USCIS, HQDOMO 70/1-P at ¶3D (Feb. 8, 2007), *published on* AILA InfoNet at Doc. No. 07030669. "USCIS interprets the "poses no risk to the beneficiary" provision to mean that the petitioner must pose no risk to the safety or well-being of the beneficiary, which includes the principal beneficiary and any alien derivative beneficiary." Memo, Aytes (Feb. 8, 2007), *supra*, at ¶3D.

(a) Petitioner's Evidence to Support Waiver—USCIS believes the petitioner must submit evidence of rehabilitation and any other relevant evidence that demonstrates, beyond a reasonable doubt, that s/he poses no risk to the safety and well-being of the beneficiaries. USCIS will presume risk if the beneficiary is a child "irrespective of the nature and severity of the petitioner's specified offense and other past criminal acts and irrespective of whether the petitioner and beneficiary will be residing either in the same household or within close proximity to one another. The burden is upon the petitioner to rebut and overcome the presumption of risk…" Memo, Aytes (Feb. 8, 2007) *supra,* at D 2. Proof may include: (1) certified records indicating successful completion of counseling or rehabilitation programs; (2) certified psychological evaluations attesting to rehabilitation or behavior modification; (3) evidence of service to the community; (4) certified copies of police and court records relating to the offense; and (5) news accounts and transcripts describing the nature and circumstances of the offense. Memo, Aytes (Feb. 8, 2007), *supra,* at D 1.

(b) USCIS Decision Criteria—USCIS shall consider all known factors that are relevant to determine whether the petitioner poses any risk including: (1) the nature and severity of the offense; (2) petitioner's criminal history; (3) the nature, severity, and mitigating circumstances of prior violent or criminal behavior that may pose a risk; (4) the relationship between the petitioner and the beneficiary and derivative beneficiaries; (5) the age and gender of the beneficiary; (6) whether petitioner and beneficiary will be residing in the same house; (7) the degree that rehabilitation or behavior modification alleviate the risk. Memo, Aytes (Feb. 8, 2007), *supra,* at D 2. Unless the adjudicator can conclude, based upon the evidence, that the petitioner poses no risk to the beneficiary, s/he must deny the petition. Any approval must be cleared through USCIS headquarters.

2.j. Work Authorization—K-1 and K-2 are authorized. 8 C.F.R. §§274a.12(a)(6), 1274a.12(a)(6).

3. Procedure for adjustment of status/residency:

3.a. Adjustment procedure under INA §214(d) eliminated under Immigration Marriage Fraud Amendments Act (IMFA).

3.b. Now must obtain conditional resident status for two years and obtain LPR status through lifting conditions.

3.c. With K-1 visa cannot change status, INA §248, 8 U.S.C. §1158, or adjust status based on grounds other than marriage to person who filed K-1 petition. INA §245(d), 8 U.S.C. §1255(d). And under K-1 provision, if the marriage to the K-1 petitioner does not occur "within three months after the admission....[the K-1 and minor children]..shall be required to depart from the United States and upon failure to do so shall be removed in accordance with section 1229a and 1231..." 8 U.S.C. §1184(d); *Markovski v. Gonzales,* 486 F.3d 108 (4th Cir. 2007) [notwithstanding §245(i), respondent could not adjust based upon approved I-140 petition because §245(d) bars adjustment except based upon K-1 petition]; *Kalal v. Gonzales,* 402 F.3d 948, 950–51 (9th Cir. 2005) [upheld rescission of CR status to person who did not marry K-1 petitioner within 90 days and instead married a different USC]. However, 8 U.S.C. §1255(d) may be read to permit adjustment even if the marriage does not take place within 90 days if it is to the "citizen who filed the petition to accord" the K-1 status. *See also Matter of Zampetis,* 14 I&N Dec. 125 (BIA 1972)

3.d. K-2 can adjust status even if s/he is over 18 at the time her parent marries the USC spouse because she is not entering as a step-child but rather as the child (under 21) of the K-1. 8 C.F.R. §214.2(k)(6)(ii); Memo, Aytes, Assoc. Dir. Domestic Operations, HQOPRD AD07-04 (Mar. 15, 2007), *published on* AILA InfoNet at Doc. No. 07040618. However, if she is under 18 at the time her parent married the USC and needs the benefit of the CSPA, the USC step-parent may file an I-130 petition for her. AFM at 21.2(e)(2)(ii)

4. Administrative and Judicial Review. One court has found that there is no jurisdiction to compel DHS to approve an I-129F petition or even to adjudicate it. *Sharif v. Chertoff,* 497 F.Supp.2d 928 (N.D. Ill. 2007) [requiring the approval of the 129F petition or seeking to compel an adjudication is barred by INA §242(a)(2)(B)(ii)]. Another dismissed an FTCA and Bivens claim for failure to adjudicate and other actions by DOS and DHS. *Chiang v. Skeirik,* 529 F.Supp.2d 166 (D. Mass. 2007).

B. *K-3 Visa (Spouse of USC)*—INA §101(a)(15)(K)(ii), 8 U.S.C. §1101(a)(15)(K)(ii); 22 C.F.R. §41.81; 9 FAM 41.81; 8 C.F.R. §214.2(k); 66 Fed. Reg. 42587–95 (Aug. 14, 2001).

1. Established a K-3 visa for a person who has a valid marriage to a USC, the USC has filed an I-130 petition on his or her behalf, and s/he seeks to enter the U.S. to await the approval. Includes minor children of beneficiary. If the I-130, IV or AOS is denied, the authorized admission under the K-3 terminates 30 days after the denial

2. Children of K-3—An unmarried child of a K-3 applicant need only establish that s/he is the child of a K-3 to receive a K-4 visa. S/he does not need a separate petition by USC. Cable, DOS 00-State-242292 at ¶11 (Jan. 30, 2001), *reprinted in* 78 No. 6 *Interpreter Releases* 339–42 (Feb. 5, 2001). Even if K-4 child is inadvertently left off the I-129F form, the consular officer should process his or her visa. Cable, DOS, 01-State-167548, *supra* at ¶34. Note that a child of the USC petitioner, if s/he is also not the child of the K-3, may *not* receive a K-4. Most K-4s are likely to be the step-children of the USC petitioner. *Id* at ¶33. K-4 children are not given the benefit of the Child Status Protection Act if they "age-out." But a K-4 step-child may utilize the CSPA when adjusting status in the U.S. if the USC step-parent filed an I-130 for her. AFM at 21.2(e)(2)(i). If the K-4 is not a step-child, however (because USC marriage to person's parent was after the child's 18th birthday), the child can still come to the U.S. on a K-4 until his 21st birthday.

3. Inadmissibility Waived—The applicant is exempt from INA §212(a)(1) [vaccination requirements] and §212(a)(5) [labor certification].

4. Effective date—The K-3 status became effective Dec. 21, 2000 and applies to all petitions filed before, on, or after that date.

5. Procedures

5.a. Issuing Post—If the potential K-3 applicant was married abroad, s/he must apply for the visa in the country in which the marriage took place or if there is no consular post in that country at a post designated by the Deputy Asst. Secy. of State for Visa Services. 22 C.F.R. §41.81(b)(2); Section 1103(b)(2) of the LIFE Act.

5.b. File I-129F—The USC petitioner files an I-129F petition with USCIS through the Missouri Service Center (MSC). The petition should include proof that an I-130 petition has been filed. All stand-alone I-130s must be filed with the Chicago Lockbox. USCIS Update, USCIS Revises Filing Instructions for Petition for Alien Relative (Mar. 21, 2008), *published on* AILA InfoNet at Doc. No. 08032130. In addition, must include the criminal record, if any, of the *petitioner.* INA §214(r)(1). Once approved, the MSC forwards the file to the NVC where an NCIC check will be performed. If the person clears the NCIC check the I-129F is electronically forwarded to the post. Once the consular post receives the I-129F they send the beneficiary a letter/Packet 3 outlining the documentary requirements necessary for the issuance of the visa including the location for the medical exam. Documentary requirements are similar to the K-1 and require completing an electronic DS-160 form. Neither an I-134, nor an I-864 is required and posts should not routinely require I-134s except where it is needed to overcome a public charge consideration from the documents presented. Cable, DOS 02-State-79357 (Apr. 26, 2002) at ¶23, *reprinted in* 79 No. 19 *Interpreter Releases* 665–69 (May 6, 2002). The 129-F approval is only valid for 4 months but may be revalidated by the consul. 9 FAM 48.81 N 5.2, 6.1 & 6.2, Cable, DOS 02-State-79357, *supra* at ¶20. Visas will be multiple entry/2-year validity visas. All grounds of ineligibility apply (unlike V visa) so K-3/K-4 may be subject to 3/10 year bar. Cable, DOS, 01-State-167548 (Sept. 27, 2001), *reprinted in* 78 No. 40 *Interpreter Releases* 1621–25 (Oct. 15, 2001).

5.c. Documentary Requirements for Consulate—Similar to K-1 fiancé visas. Includes IV medical examination, NCIC check, local police certificates, public charge documentation. An I-864 is not required but an I-134 may be required. Cable, DOS 00-State-242292, *supra* at ¶13-14, Consul must receive an approved notice pursuant to INA §214(r)(1) before issuing the visa. 22 C.F.R. §41.81(b)(1). Consul is required to disclose the criminal record of the *petitioner* to the applicant. 8 U.S.C. §1375a(b)(1)(A).

5.d. Notification of Multiple Filings by Petitioner—Once a petitioner has had two fiancée or spousal petitions approved, if a subsequent petition is filed in less than 10 years after the date the first petition was filed DHS shall notify both the petitioner and the beneficiary of any subsequent petition about the number of previously approved fiancée or spousal petitions. INA §214(r)((4)(B)(i).

5.e. Denial Due to Petitioner's Criminal Conviction—Where petitioner was convicted of a specified offense against a minor unless granted a waiver. INA §§101(a)(15)(K), 204(a)(1)(A)(viii)(I). A USC who has been convicted of a specified offense against a minor as defined in sec. 111 (7) of the Adam Walsh Child Protection and Safety Act of 2007, PL 109-248, 120 STAT. 587 (July 27, 2006) is prohibited from petitioning for his or her spouse under the K-3 category, unless the Secretary of DHS, in her "unreviewable discretion" determines that the USC or LPR poses no risk to the beneficiary of the petition. Section 111(7) defines a "specified offense against a minor" as an offense against a minor that involves any of the following: (A) an offense (unless committed by a parent or guardian) involving kidnapping; (B) an offense (unless committed by a parent or guardian) involving false imprisonment; (C) solicitation to engage in sexual conduct; (D) use in a sexual performance; (E) solicitation to practice prostitution; (F) video voyeurism as described in 18 U.S.C. §1801; (G) possession, production or distribution of child pornography; (H) criminal sexual conduct involving a minor, or the use of the Internet to facilitate or attempt such conduct; or (I) any conduct that by its nature is a sex offense against a minor.

(1) Waiver of the Criminal Bar Under the Adam Walsh Act. The waiver under this provision is in the "sole and unreviewable discretion" of the DHS upon a determination that the "petitioner poses no risk to the beneficiary." Memo, Aytes, Assoc. Dir. Domestic Operations, 70/1-P (July 28, 2006), *published on* AILA InfoNet at 06080264

5.f. Disclosure of Petitioner's Criminal History to Beneficiary—USCIS may disclose to a beneficiary or her legal guardian, a petitioner's criminal history involving violence or sex offenses. The disclosure must be consistent with the requirements of 5 U.S.C. §552a(b)(8) that disclosure is "pursuant to a showing of compelling circumstances affecting the health and safety of an individual..." The fact of disclosure must also be provided in writing to the petitioner. Memo, Divine, Acting Deputy Director, HQOPRD 70/6.1.1 (May 3, 2006), *published on* AILA InfoNet at Doc. No. 06051563

5.g. Approved I-130 Problem: If the K-3's I-130 petition has been approved *and* received at the consular post, a K-3 visa will *not* be issued. 66 Fed. Reg. 19390, 19392 (Apr. 16, 2001) because the post will simply go forward and adjudicate the IV. If the K-3 began the IV process at the post by returning the DS-2001 thereby notifying the post they are ready to be interviewed, s/he may opt to continue the K-3 processing even if the approved I-130 has arrived at the post. Cable, DOS, 01-State-167548, *supra* at ¶30, *published on* AILA InfoNet at Doc. No. 01092702.

5.h. Admission and Extensions—K-3/K-4 are admitted to the U.S. for a 2-year period. 8 C.F.R. §214.2(k)(8). An extension of stay will be granted for additional 2-year intervals but only if the USC spouse has filed and has not yet received an approval of an I-130 petition or the K-3 has filed for an IV or AOS and has not yet received an approval. If the I-130 has been approved then the K-3 in order to obtain an extension must file the IV or AOS or show "good cause" why s/he has not done so. Good cause "may include an illness, a job loss, or some other catastrophic event that has prevented the filing of an adjustment of status application by the K-3/K-4." 8 C.F.R. §214.2(k)(10). Extensions for K-4s must be filed concurrently with the parent's K-3 extension. In addition the citizen parent of a K-4 should file an I-130 on the K-4s behalf if a qualifying step-child relationship exists. *Id.* If USCIS proposes to deny an extension, it will provide the K-2/K-4 with a notice of intent to deny and give the applicant 30 days to respond.

5.i. Termination of K-3/K-4 status—Termination of status will occur 30 days following: (1) the denial or revocation of the I-130; (2) the denial or revocation of the IV or AOS; (3) the K-3's divorce of the USC; or (4) the K-4's marriage. The denial of the K-3 also results in the termination of the K-4. 8 C.F.R. §214.2(k)(11).

5.j. Change of Status—K-3/K-4 cannot change their status in the U.S., nor can an NIV change to a K-3/K-4 status. 8 C.F.R. §248.1(a).

5.k. Adjustment of Status—K-3 cannot adjust status except on the basis of the marriage to the same USC who petitioned for the K-3 status. 8 C.F.R. §§245.1(c)(6)(i), 1245.1(c)(6)(i).

(1) Medical Examinations. A K-3/K-4 adjustment applicant need not take another medical exam if s/he was medically examined prior to the K-3/K-4 issuance and the exam is not more than a year old at the time of filing the AOS application. 8 C.F.R. §§245.5, 1245.5.

(2) Child (K-4) Adjustment. A separate I-130 petition should be filed by the step-parent for the K-4 seeking AOS if a step-parent relationship exists. 8 C.F.R. 245.1(i). The CSPA applies in this circumstance. AFM at 21.2(e)(2)(i).

5.l. Employment Authorization—A K-3/K-4 has employment incident to status but must nevertheless apply for EA on I-765. Renewal of EA will not be granted unless the K-3/K-4 makes the showing in regard to obtaining an extension of stay (*i.e.,* filing of I-485 or I-130). 8 C.F.R. §214.2(k)(9).

5.m. Travel—K-3/K-4 may travel outside the U.S. without obtaining an advance parole as long as they are in valid K-3/K-4 status and they are returning on a valid K-3/K-4 visa. 8 C.F.R. §§245.2(a)(4)(ii)(C), 1245.2(a)(4)(ii)(C).

C. *V Visa (Spouse/Child of LPR)*—INA §101(a)(15)(V), 8 U.S.C. §1101(a)(15)(V), INA §214(q), 8 U.S.C. §1184(q); PL 106-553, 114 Stat. 2762 (Dec. 21, 2000); 22 C.F.R. §41.86; 8 C.F.R. §214.15; 66 Fed. Reg. 46697–46705 (Sept. 7, 2001).

1. Visa for spouses (V-1) and children (V-2) of LPRs or dependent children of the spouses (V-3)—(1) if the LPR filed an I-130 petition for the spouse or child prior to Dec. 21, 2000 and (2) if the petition is pending for 3 or more years or if the petition has been approved but 3 or more years have elapsed and a visa number is not immediately available or a visa number is available but the IV/adjustment application remains pending. V eligible persons may apply for NIV status in the U.S. 8 C.F.R. §214.15(c).

2. Pending Defined—Under DOS regulations an IV is deemed to "remain pending" at the consulate if the applicant has applied for an IV in accordance with 22 C.F.R. §40.1(*l*)(2) and the visa has not been issued or denied. 22 C.F.R. §41.86(a). This means that the IV applicant "has personally appeared before a consular officer and verified ....the statements contained on the Form OF-230 and in all supporting documents, has previously submitted all forms and documents required in advance of the appearance and paid the visa application processing fee, but no decision has been made...." 66 Fed. Reg. 19390, 19391 (Apr. 16, 2001). An I-130 petition is deemed pending if it has not been adjudicated after being properly filed. If the petition is returned for an RFE then it must be timely returned. If it is denied but the denial is on appeal it will be deemed to be pending while on appeal. However, a petition which was rejected by USCIS as not properly filed is not considered to be pending. 8 C.F.R. §214.15(d).

3. V-3 Unmarried Children—Must demonstrate that s/he is the child of a principal entitled to V-1 classification. Issuance of visa may precede V-1 issuance as child is not relegated to accompanying or following to join. Cable, DOS, 00-State-242292 at ¶4 (Jan. 30, 2001), *reprinted in* 78 No. 6 *Interpreter Releases* 325, 339–42 (Feb. 5, 2001).

4. Aging Out Cases—If child of LPR ages-out while waiting the 3-year period, s/he is not eligible for the V visa 66 Fed. Reg. at 19391, and s/he is deemed to be in unlawful status subject to removal and accruing unlawful presence. Cable, DOS, 01-State-151917 at ¶18-19 (Sept. 1, 2001), *reprinted in* 78

No. 35 *Interpreter Releases* 1440–44 (Sept. 10, 2001). At a consular post the maximum validity of the visa is only until the day before the child's 21st birthday. Cable, DOS 02-State-79357 (Apr. 26, 2002) at ¶18, *reprinted in* 79 No. 19 *Interpreter Releases* 665–69 (May 6, 2002). Child Status Protection Act does not apply. *Alvidrez v. Ridge,* 311 F.Supp.2d 1163, 1165 (D. Kan. 2004) [CSPA does not cover V visa holders and therefore person who aged-out under V-3 visa and brought constitutional claim for employment authorization could not use the CSPA to establish standing]. However, a V-2 or V-3 child is eligible for an extension beyond his 20th birthday as a result of a Ninth Circuit decision in *Akhtar v. Burzynski,* 384 F.3d 1193 (9th Cir. 2004) [struck down 8 C.F.R. §214.15(g) that prevented extension of V-2/V-3 status beyond child's 20th birthday] which has been adopted nationally by USCIS. Memo, O'Reilly, Director, Field Operations, USCIS "Adjudication of Form I-539 for V-2 or V-3 Extension," (Jan. 10, 2005), *published on* AILA InfoNet at Doc. No. 05020460; Memo, Aytes, Assoc. Dir. Domestic Operations, USCIS, HQPRD 70/23.12 (June 14, 2006), *published on* AILA InfoNet at Doc. No. 06062870; AFM at 37.4.

5. Inadmissible Grounds Exempt—A V visa applicant is exempt from INA §212(a)(6)(A) [presence without admission or parole], §212(a)(7)(A) [no valid PP or visa] and §212(a)(9)(B) [unlawful presence].

   5.a. Unlawful Presence—The 3/10 year bar does not affect obtaining V status. 8 C.F.R. §214.15(i)(3)(i) [no 3/10 year bar even if person has accrued more than 180 days unlawful status in U.S.]. However, the 3/10 year bar is applicable when the person seeks permanent residence and absent a waiver or an exception s/he is barred from residency. 8 C.F.R. §214.15(i)(3)(ii).

6. Employment—Provides for a grant of employment authorization for a period equal to the V's authorized admission as an NIV. 8 C.F.R. §214.15(h). However, a V-3 cannot obtain employment authorization where he has reached 21 and aged-out. *Alvidrez v. Ridge,* 311 F.Supp.2d 1163, 1165 (D. Kan. 2004) [V-3 visa holder had no standing to seek employment authorization because he had not, and could not, file an extension of his V-3 status or application for visa].

7. Travel—Cannot travel abroad on I-797. If person has V status but no visa, they must obtain the visa at the consulate before re-entering the U.S. 8 C.F.R. §214.15(i)(1). However, if the person has a V visa they do not need an advance parole to travel while their AOS application is pending. §214.15(i)(2). And travel outside the U.S. by AOS applicant in valid V status shall not be deemed an abandonment of the application if s/ he is admissible as a V upon returning to the U.S. 8 C.F.R. §§245.2(a)(4)(ii)(D), 1245.2(a)(4)(ii)(D).

8. Termination of Status—The V status is automatically terminated 30 days following:

   8.a. The denial, withdrawal or revocation of the I-130, the IV, or the AOS

   8.b. The V-1 spouse's divorce from the LPR becomes final

   8.c. The marriage of a V-2 or V-3;

   8.d. The naturalization of the petitioning LPR in which case the V status will terminate only for immediate relatives (*children* and spouses) but not for sons and daughters after the current period of admission ends; 8 C.F.R. §214.15(k). AFM at 37.4(k)(1)

   8.e. When a principal V's status is terminated the V-3 dependent is also terminated.

   8.f. If termination is appealed, status terminated 30 days after the administrative appeal is dismissed.

9. Procedure:

   9.a. At the Consular Post:

      (1) Documentary Requirements. Similar to K-1 fiancé visas. Includes IV medical examination, NCIC check, local police certificates, public charge documentation. An I-864 is not required but an I-134 may be required. Cable, DOS 00-State-242292, *supra* at ¶13-14; 66 Fed. Reg. 19390 at 19391–92. However, the I-134 should only be requested in exceptional cases. Cable, DOS 02-State-79357 (Apr. 26, 2002) at ¶12, *reprinted in* 79 No. 19 *Interpreter Releases* 665–69 (May 6, 2002). In addition to the electronic DS-160 form an applicant is required to complete a DS-3052 and DS-157.

(2) Issuing Post. A V visa may only be issued at the post processing the underlying IV. 22 C.F.R. §41.86(d); 66 Fed. Reg. 19390 at 19391.

(3) Validity of Visa. Consular officers are instructed to issue visa for full validity period of 10 years subject to shorter period for person who will age-out, for security concerns, or ineligibility for waivers. 66 Fed. Reg. 19390 at 19391.

9.b. Before DHS:

(1) At the border. A V visa applicant applying at a port of entry must have a visa. 8 C.F.R. §214.15(e)(2).

(2) Change of Status in the U.S. must file:

(a) I-539; fingerprints; medical exam; proof of qualifying for benefit including LPR's petition or I-797 receipt, marriage license, birth certificates. 8 C.F.R. §§214.15(f)(1) and (2).

(b) Not required to have maintained status to change status. 8 C.F.R. §248.1(b). Admission and Extension of Status. Period of admission is 2 years. For a child the period of admission is 2 years or the day before the child becomes 21, whichever is earlier. 8 C.F.R. §214.15(g)(1) and (2). Extensions of stay will be granted on the same basis. §214.15(g)(3). However, if the applicant has a current priority date but has not filed an AOS or requested an IV, the DHS will only grant a one-time 6-month extension. §214.15(g)(4).

9.c. Before IJ/BIA:

(1) If in proceedings, the V applicant can request the IJ to administratively close the file to permit her to apply for V status. Or if a motion to reopen was previously filed before the BIA to request it be indefinitely continued in order to allow the applicant to pursue the V visa with USCIS. 8 C.F.R. §214.15(*l*).

X. TRANSIT, CREWMEN, AND NATO/G-4 FAMILY (C, D, N)

A. *C Visas (Transits) and TWOV*—INA §101(a)(15)(C), 8 U.S.C. §1101(a)(15)(C).

1. Categories:

1.a. If alien in "immediate and continuous transit through U.S."—C-l (*e.g.,* Crewmen joining ship. Businessmen traveling from Belize to Jamaica through U.S.).

1.b. Includes U.N. transits (*e.g.,* non *de jure* and nonmember reps., *e.g.,* Chairman Arafat or U.N. experts) as C-2s.

1.c. Foreign representative passing through U.S.—C-3.

2. Requirements of C-1—22 C.F.R. §41.71:

2.a. Passing in immediate and continuous transit through U.S.

(1) Immediate defined as reasonably expeditious departure in normal course of travel as elements permit and prearranged itinerary assumes. No unreasonable layover privileges. If want to visit friends, etc. need other visa. 22 C.F.R. §41.71, 9 FAM 41.71 N.1.

(2) If C-1 is for a crewmen joining a ship, s/he needs a letter from shipping company agreeing to pay cost of removal if necessary. 9 FAM 41.41 N.3.1.

2.b. In possession of ticket or other assurance of transportation to destination.

2.c. Sufficient funds for transit.

2.d. Has permission to enter third country.

2.e. Period of stay cannot exceed 29 days. 8 C.F.R. §214.2(c)(3).

3. Other issues

3.a. Cannot change status. INA §248, 8 U.S.C. §1258.

3.b. Can adjust under INA §245, 8 U.S.C. §1255.

(1) But preconceived intent problem.

(2) Cannot adjust if C-1 crewman.

(3) Ineligible for extension of stay, 8 C.F.R. §214.1(c)(3), or employment, 8 C.F.R. §214.1(e).

4. Transit Without Visa (TWOV)—INA §212(d)(4)(C), 8 U.S.C. §1182(d)(4)(C); 8 C.F.R. §§212.1(f); 68 Fed. Reg. 46926–28, 46948–49 (Aug. 7, 2003) [suspending program].

4.a. The TWOV program as well as the International-to-International (ITI) program (which allowed passengers to transit only from one airport by not leaving the international transit lounge) have been suspended by DHS for security reasons. All person who previously transited through the U.S. under TWOV or ITI are now required to obtain a visa. 68 Fed. Reg. 46926–28, 46948–49 (Aug. 7, 2003) [suspending program for 60 days]. Foreign government officials may continue to transit the U.S. *Id.*; 8 C.F.R. §212.1(f)(3).

4.b. For Persons Formerly Eligible for TWOV or International-to-International the Following Rules and Procedures Applied:

(1) Waiver of visa under INA §212(d)(4)(C), 8 U.S.C. §1182(d)(4)(C), of persons proceeding in immediate and continuous transit through U.S. on authorized carrier.

(2) Requirements—8 C.F.R. §214.2(c)(1); 22 C.F.R. §41.2(i). At port of entry TWOV must establish:

(a) Otherwise admissible.

(b) Confirmed onward reservation to next country.

(c) Continue journey on same or connecting line within 8 hrs. or next available transport. Cannot change carrier more than 2 times.

(d) The carrier transporting the person has signed an agreement with the DHS pursuant to INA §233(c);

(e) The applicant is in route to a specified foreign country; and

(f) The applicant possesses documentation establishing identity, nationality, and the ability to enter a country other than the U.S.;

(3) Other factors:

(a) Ineligible for: *extensions of stay*, *employment*, 8 C.F.R. §214.1(c)(3), (e), and *adjustment*, 8 C.F.R. §§245.1(b)(1), 1245.1(b)(1) except under INA §245(i).

(b) Formerly TWOV was unavailable to citizens and residents of certain countries. 8 C.F.R. §§212.1(f)(2), 1212.1(f)(2), 22 C.F.R. §41.2(i)(1) [*e.g.*, Afghanistan, Angola, Bangladesh, Belarus, Bosnia-Herzegovina, Burma, Burundi, Central African Republic, People's Republic of China, Colombia, Congo (Brazzaville), Cuba, India, Iran, Iraq, Libya, Nigeria, North Korea, Pakistan, Serbia, Sierra Leone, Somalia, Sri Lanka, and Sudan].

(c) May permit entry on parole under 212(d)(5) or waiver for unforeseen emergency. 8 C.F.R. §§212.1(g), 1212.1(g). *Matter of United Airlines Flight UA802,* 22 I&N Dec. 777 (BIA 1999).

(d) If waiver granted under §212(d)(4)(A) airline not subject to fine. *Matter of "Flight SR-4,"* 10 I&N Dec. 197 (BIA 1963). However, if the person is paroled into the U.S. when not in possession of valid passport or visa, the airline is subject to a fine. *Matter of United Airlines Flight UA802,* 22 I&N Dec. 777 (BIA 1999). Airlines fined if TWOV absconds. O.I. §238.1a; 8 U.S.C. §1321.

B. *D Visas (Crewmen)*—INA §101(a)(15)(D), 8 U.S.C. §1101(a)(15)(D); 8 C.F.R. §214.2(d).

1. Description—Crewman (person serving in good faith in any capacity required for normal operating and service on board a vessel).

   1.a. Includes people employed by owners or concessionaire (*e.g.,* beautician).

   1.b. Includes trainees.

   1.c. Does *not* include persons on U.S. based fishing vessels, except for those landing temporarily on Guam. 9 FAM 41.41 N.6.

   1.d. Does *not* include persons not needed for normal operation or where numbers are in excess. 22 C.F.R. §41.41(b).

   1.e. Does not include persons performing longshoreman's work unless it is prevailing practice (established by a collective bargaining agreement or employer attestation if no agreement), there is reciprocity for crewman aboard U.S. vessels, or it is being done by automated equipment. INA §258, 8 U.S.C. §1288; 8 C.F.R. §258, 22 C.F.R. §89 (containing reciprocity list).

   1.f. At least one court has relied upon 3 factors to determine alien crewman status:

      (1) the nature of the employee's duties;

      (2) when those duties are performed;

      (3) whether any employee has a permanent connection with the ship, and whether their presence facilitates the operation of the vessel. *ILWU v. Meese*, 891 F.2d 1374 (9th Cir. 1989) [finding that on-board crane operators not *bona fide* alien crewmen].

2. Two types of visas—Traditionally there were two methods of obtaining D visas: Individual D visas (22 C.F.R. §41.41(a)) or crew list visa (all members of crew listed on manifest 22 C.F.R. §41.42). Crew list visas have been eliminated for security reasons. 69 Fed. Reg. 12797–99 (Mar. 18, 2004); 69 Fed. Reg. 43515–16 (July 21, 2004). D-1 visas for crew on all types of vessels except U.S. based fishing vessels and D-2 visas for U.S. based fishing vessels temporarily visiting Guam.

3. Procedure

   3.a. Can get D even if not employed at time of application. 9 FAM 41.41 N.2.2. Cannot use visa unless employed. Under D status not authorized to work in U.S. even if incident to status. 55 Fed. Reg. 25928 at 25930 (June 25, 1990).

   3.b. 29 days maximum period of admission. 9 FAM 41.41 N.4.

   3.c. *No extensions* of stay. 8 C.F.R. §252.1(f). *No change of status* under INA §248. *No adjustment* except INA §245(i). *No suspension* under INA §244(a), (f). Equal protection claim rejected as to suspension, *Guinto v. INS*, 774 F.2d 991 (9th Cir. 1985). Can get EVD. *Matter of King & Yang*, 16 I&N Dec. 502 (BIA 1978).

   3.d. Not eligible for D if:

      (1) Family member (B-2).

      (2) Entering U.S. to join ship (C-1).

      (3) Coasting officer (B-1)—officer hired by carrier to replace officer of foreign vessel on crew leave.

      (4) A strike or lockout is in progress unless person had been employed by the company for at least a year. INA §214(f), 8 U.S.C. §1184(f).

   3.e. Inspection and admission of crew—8 C.F.R. §§251, 252:

      (1) Crew detained in ship until CBP inspection. 8 C.F.R. §252.1:

         (a) CBP inspectors have right to waive visa requirement, O.I. §251.1b; INA §212(d)(4), 8 U.S.C. §1182(d)(4), and passport requirements, O.I. §252.1c.

(2) D-l/D-2 visas:

(a) No inspection if no departure: Alien on ship that goes into international waters and then returns without stopping at any foreign ports (sea escape) has not made a departure, is not inspected on return and *cannot* qualify for crewman's visa.

(b) If inspected: (i) CBP satisfied D intends to depart on same aircraft/vessel (D-1 or D-2); or (ii) satisfied intends to depart on different aircraft/ vessel within time given (D-1); and (iii) crew cannot be paid off or discharged from arriving vessel until CBP assured D-1/D-2 made other departure arrangements. 8 C.F.R. §252.1(d).

(c) Under INA §101(a)(13)(B) a crewman permitted to land is not deemed admitted.

(3) D must demonstrate under 8 C.F.R. §252.1(c):

(a) Not inadmissible;

(b) Clearly and beyond doubt entitled to land.

4. D issued Form I-95 Conditional Landing Permit—Can switch from D-1 to D-2 if s/he gets paid off ship.

5. No Hearing Before IJ—INA §252(b), 8 U.S.C. §1282(b)—Summary procedure:

5.a. DHS given authority to revoke conditional permit, take into custody and deport, but revocation must be within 29-day period of D-1. If jump ship and apprehended after D-l/D-2 permit expires then entitled to regular removal hearing.

5.b. Summary procedure also on initial determination to issue I-95. No appeal. 8 C.F.R. §252.2.

C. *N Visas*—INA §101(a)(15)(N), 8 U.S.C. §1101(a)(15)(N), 8 C.F.R. §214.2(n). Parents and children of G-4s and NATO employees accorded special immigrant status under INA §101(a)(27)(I) or (L) if child given visa during the time s/he is under 21.

XI. LAW ENFORCEMENT VISAS (S, T, U)

A. *S Visas*—INA §101(a)(15)(S), 8 U.S.C. §1101(a)(15)(S), 8 C.F.R. §§212.4(i), 212.1, 214.2, 245.11, 248.3(h), 1212.1, 1212.4(i), 1245.1; 60 Fed. Reg. 44258, 44260 (Aug. 25, 1995); 22 C.F.R. §41.83.

1. S-1 Visa—Person in possession of critical reliable information concerning a criminal organization or enterprise who is willing to supply or has supplied such information to federal or state law enforcement authorities or court *and* whose presence in the U.S. the AG determines is essential to the success of an authorized criminal investigation or prosecution.

2. S-2 Visa—Persons who both the Secy. of State and AG jointly determine:

2.a. Is in possession of critical reliable information concerning a terrorist organization, enterprise or operation;

2.b. Is willing or has supplied such information to federal law enforcement authorities or federal court;

2.c. Will be or has been placed in danger as a result of providing such information; *and*

2.d. Is eligible to receive an award under 22 U.S.C. §2708(a).

3. Number of Visas/Length of Stay

3.a. 200 visas for S-1 per year; 50 for S-2. The DHS code numbers for S-1 and S-2 will be S-5 and S-6 because of prior use of the S codes. Family members are designated S-7. 60 Fed. Reg. 44258 at 44260 (Aug. 25, 1995).

3.b. Maximum admission is 3 years. AG not permitted to grant extension.

3.c. No C/S from S visa. However, can C/S to S. 8 C.F.R. §248.3(h).

3.d. Reporting provisions tied to visa.

3.e. AG can waive grounds of inadmissibility under INA §212(d)(1), except Nazis.

3.f. Must waive right to contest removal, except for withholding.

4. Spouse, married or unmarried sons and daughters, and parents may accompany or follow to join if AG (S-1) or Secy. of State and AG (S-2) deem it appropriate.

5. Adjustment of Status—S-1 or S-2 and family (spouse, children, son or daughter, parents) if admitted as S may adjust if they are not inadmissible as a Nazi *and* the provision of information has substantially contributed to the success of the investigation, and in the case of S-2s, has also resulted in receiving a DOS reward. Must submit approved I-854 with I-485. INA §245(j), 8 C.F.R. §§245.11, 1245.11.

6. Removal—DOJ regulations provide special removal provisions through DD for persons in S status. 8 C.F.R. §§236.4, 1236.4.

7. Procedure to apply for S visa. 8 C.F.R. §214.2(t)(4)

   7.a. Application made on I-854. Application shall include evidence of: (i) applicant's cooperation; (ii) the need for her presence; (iii) grounds of inadmissibility; (iv) factors warranting favorable exercise of discretion. 8 C.F.R. §214.2(t)(4)(i)(C).

   7.b. Can only be filed by federal or state law enforcement agency (LEA).

   7.c. Filed with the Asst. AG, Criminal Division, who will then certify and forward it to ICE Commissioner.

   7.d. U.S. Attorney with jurisdiction over the investigation or prosecution, as well as the highest level of state or federal LEA, must also endorse the I-854.If approved S visa holder, must report quarterly to LEA. Must also report change of telephone number, address and travel plans.

   7.e. Can lose S status if: (i) terms of status not met; (ii) conviction of a criminal offense punishable by one year or more; (iii) it is in the public interest. 8 C.F.R. §214.2(t)(11).

8. Parole—DHS may also parole a person into the U.S. where state or federal LEA is prepared to apply for S visa. 8 C.F.R. §§212.14, 1212.14.

9. Judicial Intervention—At least one court declined to direct the then INS to issue an S visa because the government's obligation under the plea agreement is to bring defendant's cooperation to the government and not issue an S visa. *Hernandez v. U.S.,* 280 F.Supp.2d 118, 126 (S.D.N.Y. 2003)

B. *T Visas*—INA §§101(a)(15)(T), 212(d)(13), 214(o), 245(*l*), 8 U.S.C. §§1101(a)(15)(T), 1182(d)(13), 1184(o), 1255(*l*); Trafficking Victims Protection Act of 2000, Div. A of PL 106-386, 114 Stat. 1464 (Oct. 28, 2000), Victims of Trafficking and Violence Protection Act; H.R. Conf. Report No. 106-939; 8 C.F.R. §214.11; 67 Fed. Reg. 4784 (Jan. 31, 2002); Torture Victims Protection Reauthorization Act of 2003, PL 108-193, 117 Stat. 2875 (Dec. 19, 2003), H.R. 2620; Violence Against Women and Department of Justice Reauthorization Act of 2005, PL 109-162, 119 Stat. 2960 (Jan. 5. 2006), Title VIII, Sec. 802 H.R. Rep. 109-233

1. Provides 5000 visas per year for persons: (i) who have been subject to "severe trafficking" as defined in 22 U.S.C. §7102 (the use of force, fraud, or coercion for sex trafficking and/or involuntary servitude, peonage, debt bondage, or slavery); (ii) who are physically present in the U.S. (iii) who the AG and Secy. of DHS agree have complied with a reasonable request by Federal, State or Local law enforcement authorities to assist in the investigation or prosecution of such trafficking or in the investigation of crimes where acts of trafficking are at least one central reason for the crime; and (iv) who would "suffer extreme hardship involving unusual and severe harm upon removal." INA §101(a)(15)(T)(i); 8 C.F.R. §214.11(b). If under 18 years of age s/he is not required to assist law enforcement agencies to obtain the visa. If under 21 the principal may include her spouse, parents, unmarried siblings under 18 at time of principal's filing, and children who may accompany or follow to join. INA §101(a)(15)(T)(ii). If 21 or over, she may include only her spouse and children. The annual limitation does not apply to T derivatives. INA §214(o)(3), 8 U.S.C. §1184(o)(3). The U.S. has now signed and ratified the U.N. Convention Against Transnational Organized Crime (TOC) and the Protocols on human trafficking (Protocol to Prevent, Suppress and Punish Trafficking in Persons, Especially Women and Children) and smuggling (Protocol Against the Smuggling of Migrants by Land, Sea and Air) (Dec. 3, 2005).

   1.a. Severe Forms of Trafficking in Persons Defined, 8 C.F.R. §214.11(a). It means "sex trafficking in which a commercial sex act is induced by force, fraud, or coercion, in which the person induced to perform such act has not attained 18 years of age." It also includes the "recruitment, harboring, transportation, provision, or obtaining of a person for labor or services through the use of force, fraud, or coercion for the purpose of subjection to involuntary servitude, peonage, debt bondage, or slavery."

1.b. Reasonable Request for Assistance means a reasonable request made by a law enforcement officer or prosecutor to a victim to assist in the investigation or prosecution of the acts of trafficking in persons. Reasonableness depends upon the "totality of the circumstances taking into account general law enforcement and prosecutorial practices, the nature of the victimization, and the specific circumstances of the victim, including fear, severe traumatization (both mental and physical) and the age and maturity of young victims." 8 C.F.R. §214.11(a). Children under 18 are not required to comply with a request, even if reasonable, to provide assistance to law enforcement personnel as a result of amendments to the law in 2003. Memo, Yates, Assoc. Dir. Operations, USCIS, HQOPRD 70/6.2 (Apr. 15, 2004), *published on* AILA InfoNet at Doc. No. 04060110. Secondary evidence regarding the age of the applicant pursuant to 8 C.F.R. §103.2(b)(2)(i) is acceptable. Memo, Yates, Assoc. Dir. Operations, USCIS, HQOPRD 70/6.2 (Apr. 15, 2004), *published on* AILA InfoNet at Doc. No. 04060110. If an applicant is unable to cooperate with a request for assistance due to psychological or physical trauma, the request is deemed to be unreasonable. INA §101(a)(T)(iii).

1.c. Law Enforcement Agency includes State or local law enforcement agency and Federal agencies that have the responsibility and authority for the detection, investigation, or prosecution of severe forms of trafficking in persons. INA §101(a)(15)(T)(iii)

1.d. Application Process—8 C.F.R. §214.11(d)(2). Form I-914 is the application for T status and must be filed with the Vermont Service Center only. In addition the applicant must submit: (i) The fee; (ii) 3 current photos; (iii) Fingerprint fee; (iv) Evidence that applicant is a victim of severe form of trafficking; (v) Evidence that applicant is physically present in the U.S. on account of the trafficking; (vi) Evidence of compliance with a reasonable request for assistance in the investigation or prosecution or evidence that applicant is younger than 18; and (vi) Evidence that the applicant would suffer extreme hardship involving unusual and severe harm if removed from the U.S. There are fingerprint and may be interview requirements and failure to appear may result in the denial of the application. §214.11(d)(7). If waiver is necessary under INA §212(d)(13) [waiving medical grounds and all other grounds except security, international child abduction and renouncing citizenship] or INA §212(d)(3)(B) [waiving most other grounds], the T applicant files it on Form I-192 which accompanies Form I-914. 8 C.F.R. §214.11(j). Applicants are exempt from the public charge ground. INA §212(d)(13)(A), 8 U.S.C. §1182(d)(13)(A).

1.e. Evidentiary Standard—Any "credible evidence." §214.11(d)(3). To prove that an applicant is a victim of a severe form of trafficking in persons s/he can submit secondary evidence describing the nature and scope of any force, fraud, or coercion used against her/him (unless the victim was under 18). The application must also contain a statement by the applicant describing the acts of her or his victimization. 8 C.F.R. §214.11(f) and (f)(3). Some types of secondary evidence are: trial transcripts, court documents, police reports, news articles and affidavits of witnesses. *Id.* Alternative to this proof an applicant may submit a Law Enforcement Agency (LEA) endorsement on Supplement B to I-914. 8 C.F.R. §214.11(f)(1). This endorsement will be deemed sufficient. In establishing physical presence, applicant must submit a statement addressing the date, manner, purpose and place of his or her entry and any other secondary proof. 8 C.F.R. §214.11(g)(1). Must also provide proof that the applicant did not "have a clear chance to leave" the U.S. if she escaped the traffickers before law enforcement became involved. §214.11(g)(2). To establish the requirement that the applicant complied with a reasonable request for assistance by an LEA the LEA endorsement on Supplement B would be sufficient. §214.11(h)(1). May also submit secondary evidence in the form of affidavits and other documents. Applicant must submit an original statement that indicates the reason the LEA endorsement does not exist or is unavailable and the good faith efforts to obtain it. §214.11(h)(2). In presenting evidence of "extreme hardship involving unusual and severe harm," factors that may be considered include but are not limited to: (i) Age and personal circumstances of the applicant; (ii) serious physical or mental illness of the applicant; (iii) the nature and extent of the physical and psychological consequences of severe forms of trafficking on persons; (iv) the impact of the loss of U.S. courts to address applicant's claim; (v) the punishment applicant will receive upon his return to his country because of being a victim; (vi) the likelihood of re-victimization; (vii) the likelihood that the traffickers would retaliate; and (viii) the likelihood that the applicant's individual safety would be seriously threatened civil by the existence of civil war and armed conflict as demonstrated by TPS designation. 8 C.F.R. §214.11(i)(1).

1.f. Filing Deadlines—If victimization occurred prior to Oct. 28, 2000 (effective date of the Act), then applicant must file within one year of Jan. 31, 2002, or, if under 21 at the time, then one year from his 21st birthday or Jan. 31, 2002, whichever is later.

1.g. In proceedings—Applicant may seek T status and request a joint motion with ICE counsel to administratively close the case if before the IJ/BIA or to defer indefinitely a motion to reopen/reconsider if one is before the IJ/BIA. 8 C.F.R. §214.11(d)(8). If there is a final order, the DHS may grant T status and cancel the final order. 8 C.F.R. §214.11(d)(9). ICE may not rely solely on information obtained from traffickers to initiate removal proceedings but must independently verify any information it receives, 8 U.S.C. §1367(a)(1)(F), and must place a certificate on the NTA indicating that it has neither disclosed information to any person nor relied solely on such information. INA §239(e). *See* Ch. 3, ¶ X.S.4.r (p.322), *supra*.

1.h. Age Out Provision—Siblings and children who are under 21 do not age-out if application is filed before they are 21 and principal who is under 21 will continue to be treated as under 21 for purposes of being accompanied by family. Memo, Yates, Assoc. Dir. Operations, USCIS, HQOPRD 70/6.2 (Apr. 15, 2004), *published on* AILA InfoNet at Doc. No. 04060110.

1.i. Ground of Inadmissibility under INA §212(d)(13)—NIV applicants are exempt from the public-charge ground, and all inadmissibility grounds may be waived except for INA §212(a)(3) [security, terrorism, and related grounds], INA §212(a)(10)(C) [international child abductors], and INA §212(a)(10)(E) [former USCs who renounced to avoid taxes] if it is in the national interest and the activities triggering inadmissibility were caused by or incident to the victimization. Those ineligible under the health ground, INA §212(a)(1) need only show it is in the national interest to grant the waiver. A person is ineligible for the visa if there is reason to believe that s/he has committed an act of a severe form of trafficking in persons. INA §214(o)(1), 8 U.S.C. §1184(o)(1). 8 C.F.R. §214.11(c).

2. Employment Authorization and other benefits—A person granted a T visa may also obtain employment authorization. The employment authorization is incident to their status. INA §101(i)(2), 8 U.S.C. §1101(i)(2); 8 C.F.R. §214.11(*l*)(4). In addition, persons granted T status may receive benefits "to the same extent" as persons admitted as refugees. 67 Fed. Reg. 4784, 4789, *supra.*

3. Removal After Grant of T Status—Nothing shall prevent the AG from initiating removal proceeding for conduct committed after the person's admission or for conduct or a condition that was not disclosed prior to admission on a T visa. 8 C.F.R. §214.11(t).

4. 5000 Cap—The Act provides for a cap of 5,000 principal T-status (T-1) persons in any fiscal year. Once the cap is reached USCIS will continue to review applications but will not issue any additional T-1 status. The applicant, instead, is put on a waiting list and receives notice of that fact. 8 C.F.R. §214.11(m). During subsequent fiscal years when new T-1s become available they will be issued in priority order. While on the waiting list, USCIS may provide some "status" to the applicant in the form of deferred action, parole or stay of removal. 8 C.F.R. §214.11(m). Derivatives are exempt from the annual 5,000 cap. INA §214(o)(3).

5. Family Members—If accompanying or following to join the principal T-1, a spouse, sibling under 18, parent or child could obtain a T-2 through T-5 if the principal is under 21. If the principal is over 21 then s/he can bring her spouse and children only. INA §101(a)(15)(T)(ii); 22 C.F.R. §41.84(a). Applicants need to submit evidence of family relationship. The family relationship must exist at the time the T-1 application was filed. The extreme hardship requirement for family members was eliminated by the Violence Against Women and Department of Justice Reauthorization Act of 2005, PL 109-162, 119 Stat. 2960 (Jan. 5, 2006).

6. Duration of T status—A T-1 is given for a maximum period of 4 years. It is not renewable except that the status may be extended if law enforcement officials certify that her presence is necessary to assist in the investigation or prosecution of trafficking activity. INA §212(o)(7). DHS shall notify the T-1 that s/he can apply for AOS within the 90-day period before the 3-year anniversary of

the grant of the T-1. If the T-1 does not apply her/his status is terminated. If the T-1 does apply, her T-1 status continues. DHS may also revoke the T-1 status if the applicant violated the terms of her status; T-1 was issued in error; and/or the LEA notifies DHS that the T-1 has unreasonably refused to cooperate with the investigation or prosecutor. The T-1 is given notice and an opportunity to respond. §214.11(p). A T-2 spouse's visa may be revoked when a divorce from the T-1 becomes final.

7. Change of Status—Notwithstanding the prohibitions under INA §248 regarding a change of status, those bars do not apply to a change of status to T classification. INA §248(b)

8. Adjustment—May adjust up to 5,000 principal T visa holders per year: (1) if physically present in U.S. for three years in T status or physically present in the U.S. during investigation and prosecution of trafficking case and the AG opines the investigation or prosecution is complete, whichever time period is less; (2) if s/he has maintained good moral character throughout her status; and (3) has complied with any reasonable request for assistance in the investigation or prosecution of acts of trafficking or would suffer extreme hardship involving unusual and severe harm if removed. The AG may also adjust the status of any spouse, sibling, parent, or child admitted under the T visa and "spouses, sons and daughters or parents" are not included in the 5,000 cap. A departure from the U.S. for any period in excess of 90 days or an aggregate of 180 days breaks the physical presence requirement. A person may not adjust if he is otherwise inadmissible unless the AG determines that it is in the national interest to do so in which case he may waive INA §§212(a)(1) [health grounds] and INA §212(a)(4) [public charge], and waive any other provisions (except §§212(a)(3), (10)(C), and (10)(E)) if the activities rendering the person inadmissible were caused by, or were incident to, the severe trafficking. INA §245(*l*), 8 U.S.C. §1255(*l*).

9. Prohibition Against Petitioning for Abusers—A VAWA self-petitioner or a person who had T or U status cannot file a nonimmigrant or immigrant visa petition on behalf of the person who abused her or her child. INA §204(a)(1)(L).

10. DHS Assistance to Other Agencies—Under 28 C.F.R. §1100.35 DHS is authorized to determine the appropriate status to give a person who DHS or another law enforcement agency encounters who it believes is a noncitizen victim of severe forms of trafficking who is a potential witness. DHS is empowered to use a "variety of statutory and administrative mechanisms" to ensure the person's presence in the U.S. including parole, VD, stay of final order, and applicable NIVs.

C. *U Visas*—INA §§101(a)(15)(U), 212(d)(14), 214(p), 245(m), 8 U.S.C. §§1101(a)(15)(U), 1182(d)(14), 1184(p), 1255(m); Trafficking Victims Protection Act of 2000, Div. A of PL 106-386 §1513(a)(2), 114 Stat. 1464, 1533–34 (Oct. 28, 2000), Victims of Trafficking and Violence Protection Act; H.R. Conf. Report No. 106-939; 8 C.F.R. §214.11; 67 Fed. Reg. 4784 (Jan. 31, 2002); Torture Victims Protection Reauthorization Act of 2003, PL 108-193, 117 Stat. 2875 (Dec. 19, 2003), H.R. 2620; Violence Against Women and DOJ Reauthorization Act of 2005, PL 109-162 §862, 119 Stat. 2960, 3066 (Jan. 5. 2006), Title VIII, Sec. 802 H.R. Rep. 109-233 *amended by* Violence Against Women and DOJ Reauthorization Act—Technical Corrections, PL 109-271, 120 Stat. 750 (2006); 8 C.F.R. §§212.17, 214.14; 72 Fed. Reg. 53014 (Sept. 17, 2007); AFM at Chap. 39.

1. *Eligibility*—Provides 10,000 visas per year. An applicant must show she: (a) has suffered substantial physical or mental abuse as a result of having been a victim of "qualifying criminal activity;" (b) possesses credible and reliable information establishing that he or she has knowledge of the details concerning the qualifying criminal activity upon which his or her petition is based; (c) has been helpful, is being helpful, or is likely to be helpful to a certifying agency in the investigation or prosecution of the qualifying criminal activity; *and* (d) the qualifying criminal activity occurred in the U.S. (including Indian country and U.S. military installations), in U.S. territories or possessions, or violated a U.S. federal law that provides for extraterritorial jurisdiction. INA §101(a)(15)(U), 8 C.F.R. §214.14(b).

1.a. Qualifying Criminal Activity is defined as including one or more of the following *or any similar activities* in violation of federal, state, or local criminal laws: abduction; blackmail; domestic violence; extortion; false imprisonment; felonious assault; female genital mutilation; hostage (being held as a); incest; involuntary servitude; kidnapping; manslaughter; murder; obstruction of justice; peonage; perjury; prostitution; rape; sexual assault; sexual contact (abusive); sexual exploitation; slave trade; torture; trafficking; unlawful criminal restraint;

witness tampering; or attempt, conspiracy, or solicitation to commit any of these crimes. INA §101(a)(15)(U)(iii); 8 C.F.R. §214.14(a)(9).

1.b. Victim of Qualifying Criminal Activity means: (i) a person who has suffered direct and proximate harm as a result of the commission of one of the criminal acts named in the statute; (ii) family members where the direct victim is deceased due to murder or manslaughter or is incompetent or incapacitated and where the family is the spouse and children under 21 and if the direct victim was under 21 his or her siblings under 18 and parents as well as spouse and children; or (iii) where the person is the victim of witness tampering, obstruction of justice or perjury, including attempt, solicitation or conspiracy to commit one or more of those offenses *if* s/he has been directly and proximately harmed by the perpetrator of those crimes and the perpetrator committed them as a means to avoid or frustrate efforts to investigate, arrest, prosecute or otherwise bring to justice the perpetrator for other criminal activity *or* to further the perpetrator's abuse or exploitation of or undue control over the petitioner. 8 C.F.R. §214.14(a)(14)). *See also* 72 Fed. Reg. 53014, 53017 (Sept. 17, 2007) for a further discussion regarding direct and indirect victims. A person is not a victim if he or she is culpable for the criminal activity. 8 C.F.R. §212.14(a)(14)(iii); 72 Fed. Reg. at 53017–18

1.c. Substantial Physical or Mental Abuse Defined—Physical or mental abuse means injury or harm to the victim's physical person, or harm to or impairment of the emotional or psychological soundness of the victim. 8 C.F.R. §214.14(a)(8); 72 Fed. Reg. at 53018. Factors considered include but are not limited to the nature of the injury; the severity of the perpetrator's conduct; the severity of the harm suffered; the duration of the infliction of harm; any permanent or serious harm to appearance, health and physical or mental soundness, and any aggravation of a victim's pre-existing conditions. No single factor is required and a series of acts may suffice, even where no single act meets the standard. 8 C.F.R. §214.14(b)(1).

2. *Procedure/Application Process*—8 C.F.R. §214.14(c).

2.a. What Petition is Filed?—A petitioner must file Form I-918 with the USCIS.

2.b. When May the Petition Be Filed?—An petitioner may file a I-918 if s/he is in pending immigration proceedings, has a final order of removal, deportation or exclusion, or seeks NIV status outside of any proceeding. If in proceedings or has a final order, ICE may agree to a joint motion to terminate or reopen as appropriate, but if the petitioner is in detention pending execution of the order of removal the filing of a U-1 petition has no effect on removal and the person must file a request for a stay of removal. 8 C.F.R. §214.14(c)(1)(ii). USCIS and not the IJ has "sole jurisdiction over all petitions for U nonimmigrant status." 8 C.F.R. §214.14(c)(1). *See also Fonseca-Sanchez v. Gonzales,* 484 F.3d 439, 442 n.5 (7th Cir. 2007) [dismissing petition for review of U visa denial because there was no jurisdiction as denial was not part of a final order of removal].

2.c. What Is Included in the Petition?—The I-918 must contain: (1) a signed statement by the petitioner describing the facts of the victimization that supports eligibility for the U status; (2) any additional evidence demonstrating victimization including proof of physical or mental abuse; (3) a I-192 waiver pursuant to INA §212(d)(14) and 8 C.F.R. §212.17 if the petitioner is inadmissible *and* (4) a Supplement B that is signed by a certifying official within 6 months of filing the petition. The Supplement B must contain the following information: (1) how the person qualifies to be a certifying official; (2) that the petitioner has been a victim of qualifying criminal activity that the certifying official's agency is investigating or prosecuting; (3) that the petitioner possesses information concerning the activity; (4) that the petitioner has been, is being, or is likely to be helpful; and (5) that the criminal activity violated U.S. law or occurred in the U.S. or its possessions and territories including but not limited to Indian country or on a military installation. A petitioner who previously received interim relief may simply submit the Form I-918 without supporting evidence. 8 C.F.R. §214.14(c)(1), but USCIS is not bound by its previous determination. 8 C.F.R. §214.14(c)(4). The burden is on the petitioner to demonstrate eligibility. 8 C.F.R. §214.14(c)(2). USCIS shall consider any credible evidence submitted to support the claim. INA §214(p)(4); 8 C.F.R. §214.14(c)(2).

(1) A certifying official is defined as: (a) the head of a certifying agency (*i.e.*, a Federal, State, or local law enforcement agency or prosecutor, judge, or other authority involved in the investi-

gation or prosecution of the criminal activity); (b) supervisor who has been designed by the head of the agency to issue U status certifications; or (c) a Federal, State, or local judge.

3. *Cap on U-1 Status*—10,000 visas/status may be issued annually and the limit only applies to principal aliens. If the 10,000 has been reached persons granted U-1 status will be put on a waiting list and grantees and their family will be given deferred action or parole. AFM at 39(d). During the time of deferred action or parole, the grantee awaiting a visa/status will not be considered to be accruing unlawful presence for purposes of INA §212(a)(9)(B). INA §214(p)(2); 8 C.F.R. §214.14(d).

4. *Approval of the Petition*—If approved any outstanding order of removal, deportation or exclusion, "will be deemed cancelled by operation of law as of the date of USCIS's approval…" The order may be cancelled by filing with the IJ or the BIA a motion to reopen and terminate removal proceeding which ICE "may agree, as a matter of discretion" to overcome time and numerical bars. 8 C.F.R. §214.14(c)(5)(i).

5. *Employment Authorization*—Employment is authorized incident to status and therefore USCIS will automatically issue an EAD. However, to extend or replace an EAD must file an I-765. INA §214(p)(3)(B); 8 C.F.R. §214.14(c)(17).

6. *Admission and Duration of Status*—Approved for a period of 4 years. Status may be revoked but notice is required unless the U visa holder notifies the USCIS that she will not seek admission to the U.S. 8 C.F.R. §214.14(h). The four years may be extended if the certifying official attests that the U-1s presence in the U.S. is necessary to assist in the investigation or prosecution of qualifying criminal activity. INA §214(p)(6); 8 C.F.R. §214.14(g).

7. *Family Members*—Family members are the spouse and children (under 21) of the U-1 where the U-1 is 21 or over. Where the U-1 is under 21 then family members include, spouse, children, parents and unmarried siblings (under 18). Family members are eligible for U-2 (spouse), U-3(child), U-4 (parent) and U-5 (unmarried sibling). INA §101(a)(15)(U)(ii); 8 C.F.R. §214.14(a)(10), (f). The Form I-918, Supplement A is filed to petition for family members. Evidence of the relationship and a waiver if necessary must accompany the petition. Parents and unmarried siblings will qualify as long as the U-1 was under 21 at the time the I-918 and the Supplement A was filed. 8 C.F.R. §214.14(f)(2). For those granted interim relief, USCIS has determined that the "family member's age on the date of the U interim relief filing shall be controlling for the age eligibility requirement…" Memo, Aytes, Assoc. Dir. Domestic Operations, USCIS (Mar. 27, 2008), *published on* AILA InfoNet at Doc. No. 08040256. Visas issued to family members do not count toward the annual 10,000 cap. INA §214(p)(2)(B).

8. *Nondisclosure and Prohibited Use*—DHS, DOJ and DOS officers may not use or disclose (other than legitimate law enforcement purposes) any information relating to the beneficiary of a pending or approved U petition. 8 U.S.C. §1367(a)(1)(E); 8 C.F.R. §214.14(e).

9. *Grounds of Inadmissibility*—All grounds of inadmissibility except for INA §212(a)(3)(E) are waivable by DHS if in the "public or national interest." INA §212(d)(14). Inadmissibility is not waived for Nazis, participants in genocide, or persons who committed, ordered, incited, assisted or otherwise participated in torture or extrajudicial killings under INA §212(a)(3)(E). If the applicant is inadmissible on criminal or related grounds, USCIS will consider the number and severity of the offenses. In cases involving violent or dangerous crimes or inadmissibility based on security or related grounds under INA §212(a)(3) USCIS will only exercise discretion in "extraordinary circumstances." 8 C.F.R. §212.17(b)(2). No appeal from the denial of the waiver. 72 Fed. Reg. 53014, 53021–22 (Sept. 17, 2007) [discussing waivers for violent crimes in the context of *Matter of Jean*]. INA §212(d)(14); 8 C.F.R. §212.17.

10. *Removal Proceedings*—ICE may not rely solely on information obtained from the perpetrators of the crime against the respondent to initiate removal proceedings but must independently verify any information it receives and must place a certificate on the NTA indicating that it has neither disclosed information to anyone nor relied on such information if it arrested respondent at certain locations. INA §239(e), 8 C.F.R. §214.14(e)(3). *See* Ch. 3, ¶ X.S.4.r (p.322), *supra*. In addition, a person who may be *prima facie* eligible for a U visa can seek a joint motion with DHS to continue, stay, or terminate proceedings, to allow for the adjudication of U status. 8 C.F.R. §214.14(c)(1); 72 Fed. Reg. 53022 at n.10 (Sept. 17, 2007); *Ramirez Sanchez v. Mukasey,* 508 F.3d 1254 (9th Cir. 2007) [remanded case to BIA to consider petitioner's request for a continu-

ance or motion to stay or terminate proceedings to permit the adjudication of the U status request]. If petitioner is subject to a final order of removal, s/he may also request a stay of removal pending a determination of U status. 8 C.F.R. §214.14(c)(ii).

11. *Change of Status*—Notwithstanding the prohibitions under INA §248 regarding a change of status, those bars do not apply to a change of status to U classification. INA §248(b).

12. *Adjustment of Status*—Unless the Secy. of DHS determines based on affirmative evidence that the U visa holder unreasonably refused to provide assistance in a criminal investigation or prosecution, s/he may adjust the status of such person if: (1) s/he has been physically present in the U.S. for a continuous period of 3 years; and (2) in the opinion of the Secretary her continued presence in the U.S. is justified on humanitarian grounds to ensure family unity or is otherwise in the public interest. Physical presence is broken if the person is outside the U.S. in excess of 90 days or an aggregate of 180 days unless the absence is to assist in an investigation or prosecution or a person involved in the investigation certifies that the absence was otherwise justified. The Secretary may adjust the spouse and children of the U visa holder. In the case of a U visa holder who is a child, the AG may adjust the parent if s/he considers the grant necessary to avoid extreme hardship. INA §245(m).

13. *Prohibition Against Petitioning for Abusers*—A VAWA self-petitioner or a person who had T or U status cannot file a nonimmigrant or immigrant visa petition on behalf of the person who abused her or her child. INA §204(a)(1)(L).

CHAPTER 6
PERMANENT RESIDENT STATUS

XII. DIFFERENCES BETWEEN VISA PROCESSING & ADJUSTMENT OF STATUS

XIII. OTHER MATTERS CONCERNING LPRs

CHAPTER 6
PERMANENT RESIDENT STATUS

I. GENERAL

A. ***Definition***—INA §101(a)(20), 8 U.S.C. §1101(a)(20). Status of being lawfully accorded the privilege of permanently residing in the U.S. as an immigrant. *See e.g., Savoury v. U.S. Att'y Gen.,* 449 F.3d 1307, 1313–17 (11th Cir. 2006) [where DHS granted adjustment of status and had respondent's condition removed despite his fully disclosing his ineligibility due to a drug conviction, the BIA was correct in asserting that he was not an LPR for purposes of INA §212(c) relief because LPR status acquired by fraud *or* mistake nullifies the status].

B. ***Intent to Keep U.S. Permanent Residence***—If there is an absence of intent coupled with objective circumstances, a lawful permanent resident (LPR) can lose his or her status even if s/he visits the U.S. often. Although person may have multiple residences, U.S. residence must be permanent one. *See also in this chapter,* "Abandonment of Residency," section XIII.E (p.859)

C. ***What Lawful Permanent Residence Does Not Give***

1. Citizenship
2. Permanence in the sense that the status cannot be lost
   - 2.a. LPRs can be deported if they are subject to a ground of deportation. For example, LPRs can be deported for the commission of a drug offense. INA §237(a)(2)(B), 8 U.S.C. §1227(a)(2)(B).
   - 2.b. LPR status may be lost if status is deemed abandoned. *Matter of Huang*, 19 I&N Dec. 749 (BIA 1988). *See in this chapter* section XIII.E (p.859), *infra*. This may be true even if the person does not renounce his residency by signing an I-407 or have a formal removal hearing to determine abandonment. *U.S. v. Yakou,* 428 F.3d 241, 247–51 (D.C.Cir. 2005) [person deemed to have lost his LPR status without filing an I-407 or have a removal hearing where he intentionally abandoned his status].
   - 2.c. However, LPRs are accorded full constitutional due process rights as to their admission, *Landon v. Plasencia*, 459 U.S. 21 (1982); *Kwong Hai Chew v. Colding*, 344 U.S. 590 (1953); *Rafeedie v. INS*, 880 F.2d 506 (D.C. Cir. 1989), the determination of their right to remain, *Bridges v. Wixon*, 326 U.S. 135 (1945), and their right to an evidentiary hearing on parole upon seeking re-entry. *Hamaya v. McElroy*, 797 F.Supp. 186 (E.D.N.Y. 1992). They also retain other constitutional rights such as First Amendment rights. *Rafeedie v. INS*, 795 F.Supp. 13, 21–23 (D.D.C. 1992).
3. Automatic entry to U.S.—LPR must demonstrate s/he is admissible each time s/he seeks entry under certain circumstances. INA §101(a)(13)(C), 8 U.S.C. §1101(a)(13)(C).

D. ***Green Card***—I-151 or I-551. Status, not card, is determinative. Person becomes LPR upon first admission to U.S. with immigrant visa or upon adjustment of status in U.S. Card is merely evidence of such status.

E. ***Process for Obtaining Lawful Permanent Residency***

1. Immigration selection system—INA §§201–09, 8 U.S.C. §§1151–59. Consists of:
   - 1.a. Family-sponsored immigrants.
   - 1.b. Employment-based immigrants.

1.c. Diversity immigrants.

1.d. Refugees and asylees.

1.e. Persons not subject to limitations.

2. Persons not subject to limitations

2.a. Registry—INA §249; 8 U.S.C. §1259

(1) Entry before Jan. 1, 1972, and maintained continuous residence—Residence defined in INA §101(a)(33), 8 U.S.C. §1101(a)(33) as actual place of abode, regardless of intent. *Matter of Jalil*, 19 I&N Dec. 679 (BIA 1988) [holding that financial connections, home, financial interests and personal property in U.S. were insufficient to show residence where actual dwelling place outside U.S. for several year period]; *Manzo-Fontes v. INS*, 53 F.3d 280 (9th Cir. 1995) [13-month absence where employed and paid taxes in Mexico indicates residence abroad].

(2) Petitioner needs to show that s/he is a person of good moral character, is not ineligible for citizenship, is not deportable as a terrorist or Nazi, and is not inadmissible under §212(a) insofar as it relates to criminals, procurers and other immoral persons, subversives, violators of the narcotics laws and smugglers of aliens. Criteria for good moral character discussed in *Matter of Sanchez-Linn*, 20 I&N Dec. 362 (BIA 1991); *Matter of P*, 8 I&N Dec. 167 (BIA 1958) and *Matter of Locicero*, 11 I&N Dec. 805 (BIA 1966). Unlike cancellation of removal and voluntary departure awarded by the EOIR at the end of a removal hearing, there is no requisite time period for good moral character for registry. Applicant must show only that s/he is currently a person of good moral character. However, past deeds will reflect current character. *Matter of Sanchez-Linn, supra*. The Service has also determined that, because of inadmissibility under INA §212(a)(5)(B), being a foreign medical graduate is a negative factor, and that INA §212(e) is a bar to registry. Memo, Norton, Asst. Comm., Examinations (May 19, 1987), *reprinted in* 64 No. 20 *Interpreter Releases* 622, 636–37 (May 26, 1987); *But see Matter of Mulenga,* A22 199 560 (Chicago, Ill.) (Fujimoto, J. Sept. 2, 1994) [finding INA §212(e) not applicable to registry after Congress advanced date to 1972]. Medical exam is *not* required.

(3) Person ineligible for registry if they had or have a record of lawful entry into the U.S. as LPR. *Angulo-Dominguez v. Ashcroft,* 290 F.3d 1147, 1149–51 (9th Cir. 2003) [finding that a person who entered EWI but later became a lawful permanent resident could not apply for registry because the purpose of the statute is to "create a legal record of entry for those who have none" and denying an equal protection challenge to the statute]; *Matter of M-P-*, 9 I&N Dec. 747 (BIA 1968) [LPR in deportation proceeding could not apply for registry because registry is only available where there was no record of lawful admission].

(4) Person may apply for registry even if s/he was in former exclusion proceedings. *Hernandez v. Chandler*, ___ F.Supp. ___, Case No. CA 3-88-0224-R (N.D. Tex. June 23, 1989); 66 No. 30 *Interpreter Releases* 885–87 (Aug. 7, 1989).

2.b. Suspension and Cancellation of Removal—Former INA §§244(c), (d), 8 U.S.C. §§1254a(c), (d), and INA §240A(b)(3), 8 U.S.C. §1229b(b)(3). *See* "Cancellation of Removal," Ch. 8, part IV (p.972), *infra*. Maximum of 4,000 per year, INA §240A(e)(1).

2.c. Special immigrants—INA §101(a)(27), 8 U.S.C. §1101(a)(27), only as it relates to subsections (A) (returning LPRs), 22 C.F.R. §42.22, and (B) (certain former USCs), 22 C.F.R. §42.23.

2.d. Children of Diplomats—Children of foreign diplomats born in the U.S. are not USCs but may be considered LPRs. 8 C.F.R. §§101.3(a), (c), (d); *Matter of Chu*, 14 I&N Dec. 241 (R.C. 1972); *Matter of Huang*, 11 I&N Dec. 190 (R.C. 1965). However, such children may lose their residency if they have abandoned it by returning to the home country with their diplomatic parents. *Nikoi v. Attorney General*, 939 F.2d 1065 (D.C. Cir. 1991).

2.e. Persons receiving LPR status through legalization and SAW programs.

II. IMMEDIATE RELATIVES

A. ***Part of Overall Cap***—Under the Immigration Act of 1990, immediate relatives (IRs) are now part of the overall cap on immigration.

1. IRs, however, are not subject to a numerical limit. They are deducted from the overall cap of 480,000.
2. IRs not exempt from grounds of inadmissibility where applicable under INA §212(a). However, waivers may be available based upon family relationships. Procedures to obtain waivers are addressed in an AILA-CBP Liaison Committee Practice Guide, *published on* AILA InfoNet at Doc. No. 07060774. *See also* Index, waivers.

B. *Restricted to:* [INA §§101(b)(1) & 201(b)(2)(A)(i), 8 U.S.C. §§1101(b)(1) & 1151(b)(2)(A)(i)]

1. "Children, spouses and parents" of a USC.
2. If applying for a parent, the USC must be a son or daughter (*i.e.,* at least 21).
3. If applying for a child, the child must be under 21 and unmarried at time of filing petition. INA §201(f), 8 U.S.C. §1151(f).
4. Widow(er) of a USC if married for at least 2 years, petitions within 2 years of spouse's death, not remarried, and was not legally separated from spouse at time of his or her death. 8 C.F.R. §204.2(b)(1). Includes as IRs children of the widow(er). INA §§201(b)(2)(A)(i), 204(a)(1)(A)(ii), 8 U.S.C. §§1151(b)(2)(A)(i), 1154(a)(1)(A)(ii). The children are derivative beneficiaries and need not (and cannot) file a separate petition. *Matter of Minkova,* 22 I&N Dec. 1161 (BIA 1999). It does not extend to the unmarried or married sons or daughters of widow(er)s. *See Id.;* 8 C.F.R. §204.2(b)(4). 60 Fed. Reg. 38947–48 (July 31, 1995), *reprinted in* 72 No. 30 *Interpreter Releases* 1052, 1066–67 (Aug. 7, 1995). DOS has also decided that the deceased need not have been a USC for 2 years as long as he was a USC at time of death. Cable, DOS, 92-State-052354 (Feb. 20, 1992), *reprinted in* 69 No. 9 *Interpreter Releases* 301 (Mar. 9, 1992). The Service agrees. 8 C.F.R. §204.2(b)(1)(i). The widow/widower application is submitted on I-360 form. If the petition was filed as an I-130 and the petitioner dies, it is automatically converted into an I-360 petition if the widow(er) otherwise qualifies for an I-360 because she was married to the USC for 2 years and petitioned within 2 years of his death. 8 C.F.R. §204.2(i)(1)(iv) and §205.1(a)(3)(i)(C)(1).

   The Ninth Circuit has gone further and has now determined that INA §204(b)(2)(A)(i) cannot be read to bar a widow who has been married *less than* 2 years and who has already applied for AOS at the time of her spouse's death from being considered a spouse eligible for AOS. *Freeman v. Gonzales,* 444 F.3d 1031, 1037–43 (9th Cir. 2006) [the text, structure, and context of 8 U.S.C. §1151(b)(2)(A)(i), as well as DHS's willingness to adjust spouses regardless of the marriage's duration, demonstrate that USCIS's interpretation barring widows who have already applied for adjustment to adjust because they are no longer "spouses" is unwarranted]. The court in *Freeman* determined that the two year marriage requirement does not apply if the spouse has a pending AOS because it only applies to widows who wish to file a new petition. *See also Lockhart v. Chertoff,* Case No. 1:07CV823 (N.D. Ohio Jan. 7, 2008), 2008 WL 80225 [agreeing with analysis in *Freeman* and *Taing* and rejecting approach in *Turek*]; *Taing v. Chertoff,* 526 F.Supp.2d 177 (D. Mass. 2007) [BIA's decision in *Matter of Varela,* 13 I&N Dec. 453, 454 (BIA 1970) stating that the marriage had to be in effect for two years could not be given any deference because the BIA, in a subsequent decision, determined it had no jurisdiction in *Varela* because it was a review of a petition from a beneficiary]. *But see Turek v. DHS,* 450 F.Supp.2d 736 (E.D. Mich. 2006) [disagrees with *Freeman* and finds no equal protection violation because the Ninth Circuit law may differ]. USCIS maintains the view that *Freeman* is only binding in the Ninth Circuit, that the Ninth Circuit's analysis is in error and that *Matter of Sano,* 19 I&N Dec. 299 (BIA 1985) and *Matter of Varela,* 13 I&N Dec. 453 (BIA 1970) continue to apply in other circuits, and that even in the Ninth Circuit after the petition is approved pursuant to *Freeman* it is automatically revoked (because it is not automatically converted to an I-360 petition) and the spouse (now widow) must seek humanitarian reinstatement and file an I-864. AFM at 21.2(a)(4)(A) and (B)(2).
5. Battered Spouse, Child, or Parent—Violence Against Women Act of 1994, PL 103-322, 108 Stat. 1902-55, 8 U.S.C. §§1151, 1154, 1186a, 1186a note, 1254, 2245 (1994); Victims of Trafficking and Violence Protection Act (VTVPA), Tit. V (Battered Immigrant Women Protection Act) PL 106-386, 114 Stat. 1464 (Oct. 28, 2000); 2000 H.R. 3244; Violence Against Women and DOJ Reauthorization

Act of 2005, PL 109-162, 119 Stat. 2960 (Jan. 5, 2006), Cong. Rec. S13753 *et seq.* (Dec. 16, 2005) (Summary); Violence Against Women Reauthorization Act—Technical Corrections, PL 109-271, 120 Stat. 750 (2006).

5.a. Eligibility—The spouse, child or parent who is subject to extreme cruelty or battered may file a self-petition independently of the abusive USC/LPR spouse or parent. INA §§204(a)(1)(A)(iii)–(vii) & (B)(ii)–(iii); 8 U.S.C. §§1154(a)(1)(A)(iii)–(vii) & (B)(ii)–(iii); 8 C.F.R. §204.2(c), (e). A derivative child of a battered spouse is also included without a separate petition. 8 C.F.R. §204.2(c)(4). In battered spouse or child cases the spouse or child must demonstrate that s/he resided with USC/LPR spouse/parent; was battered or subject to extreme cruelty (or, in the case of a spouse self-petitioner, the child was battered or subjected to extreme cruelty) during the marriage with USC/LPR, the marriage was entered into in good faith, s/he is otherwise eligible for IR or preference status, and has good moral character. Any credible evidence of battery or extreme cruelty may be considered. INA §204(a)(1)(J); 8 C.F.R. §204.2(c)(2), (e)(2). The spouse no longer must be married to the LPR or USC abuser at the time the petition is properly filed with USCIS because a battered spouse now includes: (1) someone who in good faith believed they were married but was subject to bigamy, (2) someone who was married but the abusing spouse who was a USC died within the 2 years immediately preceding the filing of the self-petition; (3) the abusing spouse renounced his U.S. citizenship/LPR status or lost his status within the 2 years immediately preceding the filing of the self-petition, and the loss was related to or due to an incident of domestic violence; or (4) the abused spouse can demonstrate a connection between the legal termination of the marriage within the past 2 years and the battering/extreme cruelty by the USC/LPR spouse. AFM at 21.14(q). A self-petitioner who had a bigamous marriage needs to demonstrate that: (1) she married a USC/LPR whom s/he believed was free to enter into the marriage; (2) the marriage ceremony was actually performed; and (3) the requirements for the establishment of a bona fide marriage were otherwise met. Memo, Williams, Ex. Assoc. Comm., Field Operations HQADN/70/8 (Aug. 21, 2002), *published on* AILA InfoNet at Doc. No. 02091042. In demonstrating the connection between the legal termination of the marriage and the battering/extreme cruelty "the evidence submitted to meet the core eligibility requirements may be sufficient to demonstrate a connection..." Memo, Pearson, Ex. Assoc. Comm. Field Operations, HQADN/70/8 (Jan. 2, 2002), *published on* AILA InfoNet at Doc. No. 03101649. These provisions also cover abused spouses and children living abroad if their abusers are USC/LPR members of the U.S. military or are U.S. government employees or if some of the abuse perpetrated by the USC/LPR spouse/parent took place in the U.S. They also permit persons to be divorced after the petition is filed without the need to demonstrate a connection between battering/extreme cruelty and the divorce. INA §204(a)(1)(B)(v)(I). A battered spouse may even remarry after, *but not before,* the self-petition is approved without the self-petition being invalidated. INA §204(h). However, if remarriage occurs *prior* to the petition's approval, USCIS's position that it is not approvable has been upheld. *Delmas v. Gonzales,* 422 F.Supp.2d 1299 (S.D. Fla. 2005). If the self-petitioner is a stepchild, the parent-child relationship must exist for the child to self-petition and the step-child can file even if the abusing parent is no longer a USC/LPR where the abusing spouse renounced his U.S. citizenship/LPR status or lost his status within the 2 years immediately preceding the filing of the self-petition, and the loss was related to or due to an incident of domestic violence. A self-petitioning child/parent may adjust even if the abusing parent/spouse loses his or her LPR status after the filing of the petition. INA §204(a)(1)(B)(v)(I). All I-360 petitions for self-petitioning battered spouses and children are filed with the Vermont Service Center. Memo, Virtue, Acting Exec. Assoc. Comm., INS (May 6, 1997), *reprinted in* 74 No. 23 *Interpreter Releases* 962, 971–77 (June 16, 1997). USCIS will also send notices that the petitioner has established a prima facie case so that s/he may qualify for means-tested benefits. 8 C.F.R. §204.2(c)(6).

5.b. Aged-Out Children—An abused child of a U.S. citizen may petition until the age of 25 if he can demonstrate that the "abuse was at least one central reason for the filing delay." INA §204(a)(1)(D)(v). Otherwise, a self-petitioning child must be unmarried and under 21 years old when the I-360 is filed but will not "age-out" even if the petition is not approved until after 21 years of age. INA §204(a)(1)(D)(i)(1). Nor do derivative children age-out. Instead they automatically are transferred to the relevant preference category as approved self-petitioners. INA §204(a)(1)(D)(i)(III). They maintain their original priority date (or, in the case of derivatives, the principal's priority date) and receive the protection of the Child Status Protection Act even if they lost their status due to the death of, or termination of parental relationship by, the abusive parent. INA §§201(f)(4), 203(h)(4), 204(a)(1)(D).

5.c. Self Petitioning for Abused Parent—A parent may self-petition under VAWA if s/he is the parent of a current U.S.C (who subjected them to battery or extreme cruelty) or the parent of an abusive USC who, within the past two years, lost or renounced U.S. citizenship related to an incident of domestic violence, or died. The parent can apply if the parent is a person of good moral character, is eligible to be classified as an IR, resides or has resided with the USC daughter or son, and demonstrates that she has been battered or subject to extreme cruelty by the USC daughter or son. INA §204(a)(1)(A)(vii).

5.d. Good Moral Character—If the person lacks good moral character, the petition will be denied. *Matter of ______*, A76 093 795 EAC 99 034 52692 (AAO Aug. 11, 1999), *reported in* 77 No. 5 *Interpreter Releases* 155, 168 (Feb. 1, 2000) [petitioner's convictions barred a finding of good moral character]. However, an act or conviction that otherwise would statutorily bar good moral character under INA §101(f) may be excused if it is "waivable" and if the act or conviction was connected to the spouse/child having been battered or subject to extreme cruelty. INA §204(a)(1)(C). The adjudicator does not have to find that the waiver would be granted "only that one would be available for filing at the time of adjustment of status." To establish that the conviction was connected to the battering or extreme cruelty the evidence must establish that the battering or extreme cruelty "compelled or coerced" the applicant to commit the crime or act so that "the self-petitioner would not have committed the act or crime in the absence of the battering or extreme cruelty." The evidence submitted must demonstrate: (1) the circumstances surrounding the act or conviction and the abuser's role in it; (2) the requisite causal relationship between the crime or act and the battering or extreme cruelty; and (3) that the battering or extreme cruelty must have been perpetrated by the self-petitioner's qualifying relative but the crime or act need not have occurred during the marriage. Memo, Yates, Assoc. Dir. Operations, USCIS, HQOPRD 70/8.1/8.2 (Jan. 19, 2005), *published on* AILA InfoNet at Doc. No. 05012561.

5.e. Employment Authorization/Deferred Action—Upon approval of the I-360, a VAWA self-petitioner is eligible for employment authorization, INA §204(a)(1)(K). Memo, Cronin, Acting Assoc. Comm., Office of Programs (HQ 204-P) (Dec. 22, 1998). Requests for deferred action are filed with the Vermont Service Center. Memo, Cronin, Acting Ex. Assoc. Comm., Office of Programs, HQ/AND/70/6.1P (Sept. 8, 2000), *reprinted in* 77 No. 38 *Interpreter Releases* 1413, 1432–33 (Oct. 2, 2000). The battered spouse of a NIV in the A, E-3, G, and H status is eligible for employment authorization. INA §106.

5.f. Prohibition on Petitioning for an Abuser—A VAWA self-petitioner or a person who had T or U status cannot file a nonimmigrant or immigrant visa petition on behalf of the person who abused her or her child. INA §204(a)(1)(L)

5.g. Evidence in VAWA Cases—USCIS shall consider any credible evidence in adjudicating a VAWA case. INA §204(a)(1)(J).

(1) Proving a VAWA Case—Evidence of battery/extreme cruelty includes, but is not limited to, reports and affidavits from police, judges and other court officials, medical personnel, school officials, clergy, social workers, and other social service agency personnel. Other evidence may include an order of protection against the abuser or other legal or practical steps to end and/or document the abuse, such as seeking refuge in a battered women's shelter or similar place, consulting with a psychologist or other mental health professional, maintaining photographs showing visible injuries, consulting a lawyer specializing in family law, or even documenting "nonqualifying abuses" to show a pattern of abuse and violence. 8 C.F.R. §§204.2(c)(2)(iv) and (e)(2)(iv). Acts that may not initially appear violent may be considered acts of violence if they are part of an overall pattern of violence. 8 C.F.R. §204.2(c)(1)(vi) and 8 C.F.R. §204.2(e)(1)(vi).

For resources specializing in relief for immigrant victims of domestic violence and other crimes, *see www.asistaonline.org* (ASISTA Immigration Technical Assistance); *www.NationalImmigrationProject.org* (National Immigration Project of the National Lawyer's Guild); www.ilrc.org (Immigrant Legal Resource Center).

5.h. Confidentiality of Information Provided—Section 384 of IIRIRA, 8 U.S.C. §1367(a)(2) made it illegal to release any information concerning an applicant for a battered spouse or battered child provision. Section 1367(a)(1) prohibits officials or employees of DOJ, DHS, or DOS from making an adverse determination of admissibility or deportability using information provided solely by the abusive spouse or parent or another member of the household. If a government agent receives such information s/he cannot act on it unless it is independently corroborated by an unrelated person. Violation of the prohibition can result in disciplinary action or civil penalties up to $5,000. 8 U.S.C. §1367(c). DHS has set up a reporting procedure for violations through its Office for Civil Rights and Civil Liberties; an e-mail should be sent to *civil.liberties@dhs.gov*. Exceptions are provided for: (i) disclosure of census information as may be described by the Secy. of Commerce under 13 U.S.C. §8; (ii) disclosure to law enforcement officers for legitimate law enforcement purposes; (iii) judicial review; (iv) battered individuals, if they are adults, have waived the statute's restrictions; (v) benefit-eligibility determinations pursuant to 8 U.S.C. §1641(c); (vi) disclosure to Congress; and (vii) certain communications with nonprofit victims' rights organizations. 8 U.S.C. §1367(b). Memo, Virtue, Acting Exec. Assoc. Comm. (May 5, 1997), *reprinted in* 74 No. 18 *Interpreter Releases* 783, 795–97 (May 12, 1997). At least one court has allowed the use of information from a spouse who battered the alien to obtain a conviction for a false I-9. *U.S. v. Maswai,* 419 F.3d 822 (8th Cir. 2005) [court rejected argument that 8 U.S.C. §1367 prohibiting the use of information about a battered spouse in removal proceedings applied to a criminal action under 18 U.S.C. §1546]. The petitioner must provide evidence of the abuser's status, but if she is unable to do so USCIS will attempt to electronically verify the citizenship or immigration status of the abuser. 8 C.F.R. §103.2(b)(17)(ii).

5.i. Three- and Ten-Year Bar—If battered spouse has been unlawfully present after Apr. 1, 1997, s/he may be inadmissible for 3/10 years under INA §212(a)(9)(B), 8 U.S.C. §1182 (a)(9)(B). *See* "Persons Unlawfully Present" in Ch. 3, ¶ III.E.3 (p.89), *supra*. There is an exception to the 3/10 year bar if the applicant can show a substantial connection between the domestic violence and the unlawful presence or the applicant "first arrived" before Apr. 1, 1997. INA §212(a)(9)(B)(iii)(IV).

5.j. Others Grounds of Inadmissibility and Waivers—Special exceptions/waivers for VAWA petitioners are found at INA §§212(g)–(i) and (s), (a)(9)(B) and (C), and for cancellation of removal.

5.k. AOS and EWI—All approved self-petitioners who applied for adjustment on or after Jan. 14, 1998 or whose adjustment applications were pending on that date are eligible to adjust under INA §245(a) even if they entered without inspection or parole. Memo, Aytes, Assoc. Director, Domestic Operations, USCIS, HQDOMO 70/23.1 (Apr. 11, 2008), *published on* AILA InfoNet at Doc. No. 08042161; AFM at 23.5(k) [no requirement to show relationship between battery and EWI]. They are also exempt from all bars to adjustment under INA §245(c) But no grounds of inadmissibility, other than EWI, is automatically waived. Memo, Aytes, Assoc. Dir., Domestic Operations, USCIS, HQDOMO 70/23.1 (Apr. 11, 2008), AFM at 23.5(k).

5.l. VWP and VAWA—At least one circuit has held that a VAWA petition is subject to the bar on AOS for visa waiver entrants. *Schmitt v. Maurer,* 451 F.3d 1092 (10th Cir. 2006) [ineligible to apply for AOS as abused spouse under VAWA];

5.m. Initiating Removal Proceedings—DHS may not rely solely on information obtained from abusers to initiate removal proceedings but must independently verify any information it receives and must place a certificate on the NTA indicating that it has neither disclosed information nor relied on such information if it arrests respondent in certain sensitive locations. INA §239(e). *See* Ch. 3, ¶ X.S.4.r (p.322), *supra*.

5.n. Motions to Reopen Removal/Deportation Proceedings for Battered Spouse, Parent, or Child—A battered spouse, parent or child seeking to reopen removal proceedings as a self-petitioner or to seek cancellation of removal may file the application within one year of the entry of a final order as long as the applicant is physically present in the U.S. The AG in his or her discretion may waive the one-year requirement if the applicant demonstrates extraordinary circumstances or extreme hardship to his or her child. INA §240(c)(7)(C)(iv), 8 U.S.C. §1229a(c)(6)(C)(iv). The one-motion rule also does not apply to battered spouse, parent or child cases. INA §240(c)(7)(A). If the motion to reopen is to seek suspension or adjustment as a self-petitioner and the person is in deportation (as distinguished from removal) proceedings, there is no time limit for the filing of the motion and one motion may be filed notwithstanding the numerical limitation. Sec. 825(b) of PL 109-162, 119 Stat. 2960, Violence Against Women and DOJ Reauthorization Act of 2005.

5.o. Naturalization and VAWA—A spouse or child of a USC who obtained LPR status because of battering or extreme cruelty may also apply for citizenship within a 3-year period under INA §319(a), 8 U.S.C. §1430(a). The requirement that the spouse live with and remain married to his or her USC spouse for the 3-year period is waived. The requirement that a child be defined as a child under the INA at the time s/he became an LPR is also waived, although the requirement that the child be at least 18 to petition is not waived. Memo, Yates, Deputy Ex. Assoc. Comm., Field Operations, HQISD 70/33 (Oct. 15, 2002), *published on* AILA InfoNet at Doc. No. 02103143. In addition, a CR who obtained LPR status through an approved waiver of the joint filing requirement due to abuse under INA §216(c)(4)(C) is eligible to apply for naturalization after 3 years under INA §319(a). Memo, Yates, Assoc. Dir. Operations, HQOPRD 70/33.1 (Jan. 27, 2005), *published on* AILA InfoNet at Doc. No. 05020760.

5.p. "VAWA Self-Petitioner"—Defined at INA §101(a)(51) to include conditional residents, battered spouses and children of Cuban Adjustment, HRIFA and NACARA beneficiaries, as well as abused spouses, children, and parents described herein.

6. Spouse, Parent, or Child of Member of Armed Forces Who Died in Combat. PL 108-136, §1703

6.a. Allows self-petitioning for the spouse, parent or child of a USC who served honorably in the Armed Forces and died as a result of injury or disease incurred in or aggravated by combat as long as s/he petitions within 2 years of the USC's death. The spouse may apply as long as she was not legally separated from her spouse at the time of his death and does not remarry during the petitioning process. A child may apply even if s/he becomes 21 or marries after the USC's death. INA §201(b)(2)(A)(i). A parent of the deceased USC may also file an immediate-relative petition even if the deceased USC child was under 21 years of age. Public charge is waived as a ground of inadmissibility. The application is made on an I-360 and an I-485 may be filed *concurrently* with it. AFM at 21.11(d)(1).

6.b. A spouse, parent, or child of an LPR who honorably served, died as a result of injury or disease incurred in or aggravated by combat, and who posthumously became a USC, can self-petition as an immediate relative if filed within 2 years of LPR's death. The spouse, parent, or child is also eligible for deferred action, advance parole and work authorization. Public charge is waived as a ground of inadmissibility.

6.c. A spouse, parent, or child of a USC who served honorably in active duty status, who died as a result of injury or disease incurred in or aggravated by combat, and who was granted posthumous citizenship under INA §329A) may adjust his or her status to permanent residency if the adjustment was filed prior to the USC's death.

6.d. Definitions: USCIS has defined "died as a result of injury or disease incurred in or aggravated by combat" to mean: (i) the death is attributable to an injury or disease for which the member was awarded the Purple Heart *or* (ii) the death resulted from an injury or disease that was incurred or aggravated: (A) as a direct result of armed conflict; (B) while engaged in hazardous service; (C) in the performance of duty under conditions simulating war; *or* (D) through an instrumentality of war. Memo, Aytes, Acting Dir. Domestic Operations, USCIS, HQPRM 70/6.1.1P (Apr. 3, 2006), *reprinted in* 83 No. 19 *Interpreter Releases* 869, 897–910 (May 8, 2006)

(1) Armed conflict includes instances when the service member was a prisoner of war or while escaping or attempting to escape. AFM at 21.11(b)(2)(A)

(2) Hazardous service includes aerial flight, parachute duty, demolition duty, experimental stress duty, and diving duty. AFM at 21.11(b)(2)(B)

(3) Conditions simulating war includes military training, such as war games, practice alerts, tactical exercises, airborne operations, leadership reaction course, grenade and live fire weapons practice, bayonet training, hand-to-hand combat training, repelling, and negotiation of combat confidence and obstacle courses. AFM at 21.11(b)(2)(C)

(4) Instrumentality of war includes a vehicle, vessel, or device designated primarily for Military Service and intended for use in military service but may also include instrumentalities not designated primarily for military service if its use subjects the service member to hazard or risk peculiar to military service. It may therefore include wounds caused by a military weapon, accidents involving a military combat vehicle, or injury or sickness caused by fumes, gases, or explosion of military ordinance, vehicles or material. AFM at 21.11(b)(2)(D).

C. *Child defined*

1. Definition of a child under INA is a critical definition as it also provides the basis for the definition of:

1.a. Parent—INA §101(b)(2), 8 U.S.C. §1101(b)(2).

1.b. Sibling—INA §203(a)(4), 8 U.S.C. §1153(a)(4).

1.c. Son or daughter—INA §§203(a)(1), (3), 8 U.S.C. §§1153(a)(1), (3).

2. INA §101(b)(1), 8 U.S.C. §1101(b)(1) defines child as an unmarried person under 21 years of age who is a:

2.a. Child born in wedlock (formerly called legitimate child).

2.b. Step-child, whether legitimate or not, as long as child was under 18 at time step-relationship was created.

2.c. Child legally legitimated before 18 if in custody of father at time of legitimation.

2.d. Child born out-of-wedlock (formerly called illegitimate child) where relationship is either with the mother or with the father if, in the case of the father, a *bona fide* parent-child relationship exists.

2.e. Children adopted before 16, and having 2 years legal custody and residence with adopting parents. However, if the family has already adopted a sibling the second brother or sister who is adopted may be under 18 at time of adoption. *See in this section* ¶ 6 (p.782), *infra.*

2.f. Certain orphans. *See in this section* ¶ 7 (p.784), *infra.*

3. Step-child—INA §101(b)(1)(B), 8 U.S.C. §1101(b)(1)(B):

3.a. Old standard—Child, whether legitimate or illegitimate lived with and was cared for as the child of step-parent or the step-parent evinced an active parental interest in the support and welfare of the child. *Matter of Moreira*, 17 I&N Dec. 41 (BIA 1979).

3.b. Present standard more liberal—Literal reading of statute requires only that step-parent relationship be formed before child reaches 18, *Medina-Morales v. Ashcroft,* 371 F.3d 520, 531–32 (9th Cir. 2004) [reversed BIA denial of motion to reopen where IJ contrary to precedent relied on the strength of a step-parent relationship, rather than simply the fact of the relationship, to determine whether to grant motion to reopen for adjustment]; *Palmer v. Reddy*, 622 F.2d 463 (9th Cir. 1980); *Matter of McMillan*, 17 I&N Dec. 605 (BIA 1981), and that parents have real marriage. *Matter of Awwal*, 19 I&N Dec. 617 (BIA 1988).

3.c. Significance—Where natural mother and/or father is LPR but step-parent is USC, child can avoid family 2d preference backlog by step-parent's petition.

3.d. Problem areas:

(1) Adulterine child born after step-parent relationship could qualify as step-child. *Matter of Stultz*, 15 I&N Dec. 362 (AG 1975).

(2) Effect of step-parent divorce—If step-relationship continues, petition is valid, notwithstanding divorce. *Matter of Pagnerre*, 13 I&N Dec. 688 (BIA 1971); *Matter of Mowrer*, 17 I&N Dec. 613 (BIA 1981). The same is true for step-siblings. *Matter of Mourillon*, 18 I&N Dec. 122 (BIA 1981).

(3) USC may petition for natural parent and step-parent. *Matter of Fong*, 17 I&N Dec. 212 (BIA 1980).

4. Children born in- or out-of-wedlock—INA §§101(b)(1)(A), (D), 8 U.S.C. §§1101(b)(1)(A), (D):

4.a. Born out-of-wedlock—Children born out-of-wedlock previously could only obtain benefits through mother. *Fiallo v. Bell*, 430 U.S. 787 (1977). Child can now obtain benefits through natural father if father has or had *bona fide* parent-child relationship when child was under 21 and not married. INA §101(b)(1)(D), 8 U.S.C. §1101(b)(1)(D); 8 C.F.R. §§204.2(d)(2)(iii), (f)(2)(iii). Applies even if child is 21 or over on date of the Act's passage, as long as relationship was previously formed. *Matter of Vizcaino*, 19 I&N Dec. 644 (BIA 1988).

BIA has provided general characteristics for determining when there is or was a "bona-fide parent-child relationship," noting that this language should be generously interpreted. *Matter of Vizcaino, supra* ["Some evidence of emotional and/or financial ties should be shown ... some attempt to help support the child and/or some showing of communication with or about the child."]. A *bona fide* relationship exists "where the father demonstrates or has demonstrated an active concern for the child's support, instruction and general welfare." 8 C.F.R. §204.2(d)(2)(iii). The evidence relevant to establish a parent-child relationship is "varied and widespread ... It may include money order receipts or cancelled checks showing the petitioner's financial support of the beneficiary at any point in her life ... medical or insurance records, school records on the beneficiary ... correspondence between the parties ... notarized affidavits of friends, neighbors, school officials or other knowledgeable associates attesting to the existence of the parent-child relationship." *Matter of Pineda*, 20 I&N Dec. 70 (BIA 1989).

4.b. Born in wedlock—INA §101(b)(1)(A), 8 U.S.C. §1101(b)(1)(A)—If born in wedlock, parent need only prove relationship.

5. Legitimated children—INA §101(b)(1)(C), 8 U.S.C. §1101(b)(1)(C):

5.a. Legitimation is defined as "the act of putting a child born out-of-wedlock in the same legal position as a child born in wedlock." *Matter of Cabrera*, 21 I&N Dec. 589 (BIA 1996) [where law in Dominican Republic was changed so that there is no distinction between children born in wedlock or out-of-wedlock if parent recognizes child, the petition of the father should be granted. (Overruling *Matter of Reyes*, 17 I&N Dec. 512 (BIA 1980))].

5.b. Four requirements:

(1) Action to legitimate child under the law of child's residence or domicile, or under the law of the father's residence or domicile. *Kaliski v. District Director*, 620 F.2d 214 (9th Cir. 1980) [relied on California law because it was domicile of father, even though father domiciled in state after child was 18, where legitimating act occurred before 18]. *But see* 8 C.F.R. §204.2(d)(2)(ii) [for legitimation based on laws of father's residence or domicile, father must have resided—while child was under 18—in country or state under whose laws the child was legitimated].

(2) Child under 18 at time of legitimation.

(3) Legal custody with father at time of legitimation.

(4) Natural child of father. *Matter of Bueno*, 21 I&N Dec. 1029 (BIA 1997). Paternity may be established by primary evidence (birth certificate) or secondary evidence (historical documents, *e.g.,* medical or school records, or blood test). USCIS must inform applicant that they may use a blood test if no other secondary evidence is available. *Matter of Pagan,* 22 I&N Dec. 547 (BIA 1999).

5.c. Methods of legitimating:

(1) Laws of country (or state) of child or father's domicile or residence that eliminate all legal distinctions;

(2) Subsequent marriage of natural parents; *Matter of Rowe,* 23 I&N Dec. 962 (BIA 2006) [Guyana]

(3) Judicial decree;

(4) Formal recognition of paternity;

(5) Open/notorious acknowledgment of paternity.

5.d. Legal custody:

(1) Actual custody by natural right or court decree.

(2) Presumption:

(a) Old standard provided for presumption of maternal custody unless proof to the contrary. *Matter of De La Rosa*, 14 I&N Dec. 728 (BIA 1974).

(b) Present standard permits a presumption that father has not been divested of custody where child legitimated. *Matter of Rivers*, 17 I&N Dec. 419 (BIA 1980).

5.e. Age at legitimation (before 18):

Retroactivity to birth?

(1) Despite country's law BIA does not give retroactive effect. *Matter of Obando*, 16 I&N Dec. 278 (BIA 1977). Must establish requisite degree of proof of parent-child relationship, and child must be under 18 at time of law's passage. *Matter of Martinez-Gonzalez,* 21 I&N Dec. 1035.

(2) When country's law changes it is as of date of change. *Matter of Clahar*, 18 I&N Dec. 1 (BIA 1981). Legitimate status counted from the time the distinction was abolished. *Matter of Martinez-Gonzalez, supra*; *Matter of Torres,* 22 I&N Dec. 28 (BIA 1998) [Peruvian law abolished distinctions on Nov. 14, 1984].

5.f. Legitimation also occurs where the laws of the country make no distinction between child born in wedlock or out-of-wedlock. *Matter of Martinez-Gonzalez*, 21 I&N Dec. 1035 at n.3 (BIA 1997) [Dominican Republic]

Countries where law has eliminated distinction between children born in or out-of-wedlock. *Matter of Moraga,* 23 I&N Dec. 195 (BIA 2001) [El Salvador]; *Matter of Torres,* 22 I&N Dec. 28 (BIA 1998) [Peru]; *Matter of Martinez-Gonzalez*, 21 I&N Dec. 1035 (BIA 1997) [Dominican Republic]; *Matter of Patrick*, 19 I&N Dec. 726 (BIA 1988) [Trinidad and Tobago]; *Matter of Campuzano*, 18 I&N Dec. 390 (BIA 1983) [Ecuador]; *Matter of Martinez,* 18 I&N Dec. 399 (BIA 1983) [Cuba]; *Matter of Richard*, 18 I&N Dec. 208 (BIA 1982) [Haiti]; *Matter of Pavlovic*, 17 I&N Dec. 407 (BIA 1980) [Yugoslavia]; *Matter of Espinoza*, 17 I&N Dec. 522 (BIA 1980) [Bolivia]; *Matter of Sanchez*, 16 I&N Dec. 671 (BIA 1979) [Honduras]; *Matter of Hernandez*, 17 I&N Dec. 7 (BIA 1979) [Guatemala].

(1) Look for equality of final rights. Must be complete equality or the distinction is not considered eliminated. *Matter of Breninzon*, 19 I&N Dec. 40 (BIA 1984); *Matter of Reyes,* 17 I&N Dec. 512, 514 (BIA 1980); *De Los Santos v. INS*, 690 F.2d 56 (2d Cir. 1982).

6. Adopted children—INA §101(b)(1)(E), 8 U.S.C. §1101(b)(1)(E):

6.a. Adopted under 16, and with 2 years of legal custody, and residing with parents for 2 years. *Matter of Repuyan*, 19 I&N Dec. 119 (BIA 1984) [addressing issue of residency for adoption].

(1) Two years residency with child may occur before or after adoption. 8 C.F.R. §204.2(d)(2)(vii)(C); *Matter of M*, 8 I&N Dec. 118 (BIA 1958). Can occur at any time, but must be full 2 years. *Matter of Lee*, 11 I&N Dec. 911 (BIA 1966). However, must have legal custody of child during those 2 years even if the child is not yet adopted. Under Consular Efficiency Bill, PL 99-653, §2, custody or residency requirement can be fulfilled simultaneously.

(2) Satisfied if custody and residence with the adopting parent or parents. 8 C.F.R. §204.2(d)(2)(vii). Evidence must be submitted to show that beneficiary resided with the *petitioner*. 8 C.F.R. §204.2(d)(2)(vii)(B). There is some ambiguity in regard to the statute and regulations because it appears that the 2-year legal custody requirement can be met by either parent, INA §101(b)(1)(E)(i), and therefore the requirement in the regulation that the *petitioning* parent must have had the 2 years of legal custody may not be a valid requirement. *See* general discussion in *Bustamante-Barrera v. Gonzales,* 447 F.3d 388, 396–98 (5th Cir. 2006) [distinguishing former derivative naturalization statute, which required that child be in the sole custody of one parent, from the adoption statute, which

defines an adopted child as one in "the legal custody of and has resided with the adopting parent or parents"].

(3) Legal custody for 2 years requires either final adoption decree or official document in the form of a custody award by the court or recognized governmental entity. Informal documents, such as sworn affidavits, are insufficient. Memo, Puleo, Asst. Comm., Adjudications (Feb. 17, 1989), *reprinted in* 66 No. 9 *Interpreter Releases* 260 (Mar. 6, 1989); 8 C.F.R. §204.2(d)(2)(vii)(A).

(4) Battered Children. If a child "has been battered or subject to extreme cruelty by the adopting parent or by a family member of the adopting parent residing in the same household," the legal-custody and 2-year residency requirements are waived. INA §101(b)(1)(E)(i).

(5) Adoption must be *before* child is 16. Adoption *nunc pro tunc* after 16 will not be given retroactive effect. *Matter of Cariaga*, 15 I&N Dec. 716, 717 (BIA 1976). *See also generally Bustamante-Barrera v. Gonzales,* 447 F.3d 388, 399–401 (5th Cir. 206) [in citizenship context, state court order amending custody *nunc pro tunc* to provide mother with sole custody does not bind USCIS as a matter of federal law]; *But see Messina v. USCIS,* __F.Supp.2d __, 2006 WL 374564 (E.D. Mich. Feb. 16, 2006) [rejected *Cariaga* and held that a lawful *nunc pro tunc* adoption had to be recognized by USCIS]; *Allen v. Brown*, 953 F.Supp. 199 (N.D. Ohio 1997). If it is an adoption of a sibling the sibling can be under 18. INA §101(b)(1)(E)(ii).

(6) USCIS will inquire into *bona fides* of adoption, particularly where adoptive parents are relatives of natural parents. *Matter of Marquez*, 20 I&N Dec. 160 (BIA 1990). Where adopted child continues to reside with natural parent(s) and adoptive parents, the burden is on the adoptive parents to establish that they exercised primary parental control. *Matter of Cuello*, 20 I&N Dec. 94 (BIA 1989). 8 C.F.R. §204.2(d)(2)(vii)(B).

(7) Adoption of Sibling by Same Family. PL 106-139, 113 Stat. 1696 (Dec. 7, 1999); 1999 HR 2886; 145 Cong. Rec. H10136-02; 145 Cong. Rec. S12931-04(1999). A family who adopts a child who is under 16 may also adopt his or her sibling even if the sibling is over 16, as long as s/he is under 18 at the time of adoption. INA §101(b)(1)(E)(ii). Legacy INS has taken the position that the under-16-year-old must be adopted first or at the same time as the under-18-year-old. Memo, Cronin, Acting Assoc. Comm. Office of Programs (HQADN 70/1) (Dec. 28, 1999), *reprinted in* 77 No. 14 *Interpreter Releases* 476, 484–85 (Apr. 10, 2000) [noting PL 106-139 applicable to both LPR status and naturalization under INA §322(a)(4)]. However, the BIA has held that the over-16-year-old sibling may be adopted first and that the statute does not mandate any order of adoption. *Matter of Anifowoshe,* 24 I&N Dec. 442 (BIA 2008). The Service defines "natural sibling" for purposes of this act to include children "sharing one or both biological parents." Memo, Pearson, Exe. Assoc. Comm. HQADN 70/8.3 (Nov. 13, 2000), *reprinted in* 78 No 6 *Interpreter Releases* 336, 353–56 (Feb. 5, 2001).

6.b. Natural parents of adopted child cannot obtain immigration benefits through natural child if child was adopted in accordance with INA §101(b)(1)(E) and an immigration benefit has resulted. *Matter of Li*, 20 I&N Dec. 700 (BIA 1993). This is different than step-children, who can petition for natural parent. If the child did not and now cannot acquire any immigration benefits through the adoptive parents, the natural parents may possibly be able to petition for the child. *Matter of Li*, 21 I&N Dec. 13 (BIA 1995). A natural parent relationship can be re-established even if there was an adoption under INA §101(b)(1)(E) where: (1) petitioner did not receive any benefit as a result of the adoptive relationship; (2) petitioner can demonstrate that a natural parent-child relationship meeting the requirement of §101(b) once existed; (3) the subsequent adoption that satisfied §101(b)(1)(E) has been lawfully terminated; and (4) the natural parent's relationship has been re-established. *Matter of Li*, 21 I&N Dec. 13, 17–18 (BIA 1995).

6.c. Adopted child *cannot* petition for natural siblings if the child was adopted in accordance with INA §101(b)(1)(E), even if the child obtained *no* immigration benefit from adopted parents. *Matter of Li*, 20 I&N Dec. 700 (BIA 1993) [overruling *Matter of Lum*, 11 I&N Dec. 55 (BIA

1964) and disregarding *Matter of Fujii*, 12 I&N Dec. 495 (DD 1967) as not binding on BIA]; *Kosak v. Aguirre,* 519 F.3d 210 (3d Cir. 2008) [upholding *Matter of Li* on *Chevron* deference grounds]; *Young v. Reno*, 114 F.3d 879 (9th Cir. 1997) [upholding *Matter of Li* when it was applied to petition pending for many years before the decision in *Li*]; *Kosak v. Devine,* 439 F.Supp.2d 410 (E.D. Pa. 2006) [upheld *Matter of Li* under *Chevron* deference]. *Li* suggests that if child was adopted after 16 [if not in accordance with INA §101(b)(1)(E)], then he could apply for siblings and perhaps natural parents. *Matter of Li, supra,* at 703 (BIA 1993)

6.d. Must conform to country's/place's law of adoption. *Matter of Garcia-Rodriguez*, 16 I&N Dec. 438 (BIA 1978). In Islamic countries, adoption is virtually nonexistent. *See www.travel.state.gov/family/adoption/intercountry/intercountry_3132.html.*

6.e. Customary adoptions:

(1) Heavy burden.

(2) Rarely approved. *Matter of Yue*, 12 I&N Dec. 747 (BIA 1968) [Hong Kong pursuant to Chinese traditional law]. *But see Matter of Palelei*, 16 I&N Dec. 716 (BIA 1979) [customary adoption unacceptable because Tongan law does not recognize it], *disapproved by Kaho v. Ilchert*, 765 F.2d 877 (9th Cir. 1985).

6.f. Procedural issues regarding adoptions

(1) Priority Date. Child can obtain priority date of parents even if legal custody requirement is not completed, as long as child was adopted and was a member of the principal's household prior to adoptive parents' admission into U.S. Child can then enter as a derivative following to join the principal once s/he has 2 years of legal custody and residence. Letter, Odom, Chief, Advisory Opinion Division (May 19, 1993), *reprinted in* 70 No. 19 *Interpreter Releases* 1014, 1022–23 (Aug. 2, 1993).

(2) LPR parent cannot rely on 8 C.F.R. §211.1(b)(1). Under USCIS regulations an LPR giving birth abroad can bring her child into the U.S. as an LPR on her first trip back to the U.S. 8 C.F.R. §211.1(b)(1). DOS has determined this provision does *not* apply to adopted children. Cable, DOS, 96-State-118649 (June 8, 1996), *reprinted in* 73 No. 25 *Interpreter Releases* 869–70 (July 1, 1996).

(3) Federal Courts Reluctant to Interfere in Immigration Process. *Guadarrama-Garcia v. Acosta,* 217 F.Supp.2d 802 (S.D. Tex. 2002) [court declined injunction to prevent removal of child who was being adopted by U.S. citizens despite state court order on adoption].

6.g. Hague Convention. For procedural aspects and how it changes the law of adoption *see in this section* ¶ 8 (p.786), *infra*.

7. Orphans—INA §101(b)(1)(F), 8 U.S.C. §1101(b)(1)(F). Distinguish orphans and adopted children:

7.a. Orphans do not have 2-year legal custody/residence requirement. Also do not contemplate pre-existing family relationship.

7.b. For orphan, need establish that s/he is adopted *abroad*. 8 C.F.R. §204.3(k)(2). The adoption process must conform to the Hague Convention if both countries are state parties to the Convention.

(1) If already here, then not an orphan, but, rather, an adoption. *Matter of Handley*, 17 I&N Dec. 269 (BIA 1978).

(2) Benefits available to orphan in U.S. in parole status who is not adopted in the U.S.; but an orphan illegally in U.S. or on nonimmigrant visa is ineligible to receive the benefits of an orphan petition and to adjust. 8 C.F.R. §204.3(k)(3). However, under the Hague Convention the child can be in the U.S. as an NIV, parolee, or even EWI, but cannot adjust unless otherwise eligible and the Central Authority of the other country approves adoption. Otherwise, petition can be approved provisionally but the child must return for an IV. 8 C.F.R. §309(b)(4).

7.c. Criteria. *Matter of Greenwood*, 18 I&N Dec. 417 (BIA 1983).

(1) Adoption while child under 16.

(2) Orphan by reason of death or disappearance, abandonment and/or desertion, separation, or loss of both parents.

(a) Abandonment requires parents forsake all parental rights. INA §101(b)(1)(F), 8 U.S.C. §1101(b)(1)(F). "Abandonment by both parents means that the parents have willfully forsaken all parental rights, obligations, and claims to the child, as well as all control over and possession of the child, without intending to transfer, or without transferring, these rights to any specific person(s)" 8 C.F.R. §204.3(b). It includes not only the intention to abandon but also the actual act of surrendering all rights, obligations, claims, control, and possession. *Id.* A relinquishment or release by the parents to the prospective adoptive parents or for a specific adoption *does not constitute* an abandonment. *Rogan v. Reno,* 75 F.Supp.2d 63, 65–68 (E.D.N.Y. 1999) [where birth parents did not abandon the child and where biological mother was capable of proving support for the child and proper care, the BIA's decision denying the petition was affirmed]; 8 C.F.R. §204.3(b).

(b) If one parent—only requirement is that s/he must be incapable of providing proper care and irrevocably in writing release child. 8 C.F.R. §204.3(d)(1)(iii)(C);

(c) If child born out-of-wedlock—previously treated as if one parent. *Matter of Rodriguez*, 18 I&N Dec. 9 (BIA 1980). But as a result of recognition of fathers under INA §101(b)(1)(D), abandonment by one parent no longer permits release of child for adoption where father of child born out-of-wedlock has relationship with the child. Memo, Puleo, Asst. Comm., Adjudications (Nov. 2, 1987), *reprinted in* 64 No. 44 *Interpreter Releases* 1293, 1294 (Nov. 16, 1987); 65 No. 3 *Interpreter Releases* 54, 55–55 (Jan. 15, 1988); 65 No. 25 *Interpreter Releases* 661, 675, 683 (July 1, 1988). However, if natural father has disappeared or abandoned or deserted the child or if the father has in writing irrevocably released the child for emigration and adoption, he is not considered a parent for purposes of this section, INA §101(b)(2), and the mother is considered a sole parent. 8 C.F.R. §204.3(b) [definition of "sole parent"]. In these circumstances the mother is considered the sole parent even if the country makes no distinction between legitimate children and illegitimate children, since Congress replaced these terms with child born in and out-of-wedlock. *See* Cable, INS (Dec. 26, 1995), *reprinted in* 73 No. 1 *Interpreter Releases* 13 (Jan. 2, 1996).

(d) Adoption must be by husband and wife or by a single parent at least 25 years old. 8 C.F.R. §204.3(b) [definition of prospective adoptive parents].

(3) If there are step-parents, family treated as if there are 2 parents for INA §101(b)(1)(F).

(4) No limitations on number of orphans person can adopt.

(5) USCIS must be satisfied that there will be proper care for the child. Home study required [8 C.F.R. §204.3(e)], includes analysis of parents capabilities and living conditions. Also includes history of any substance abuse, sexual or child abuse or domestic violence even if there was no arrest or conviction. Letter, Chang, Director Residence and Status Branch, Adjudications, HQ70/ 8.3, *reprinted in* 77 No. 31 *Interpreter Releases* 1166, 1183 (Aug. 14, 2000).

(6) Adoption by homosexual approved. *Matter of Gressin*, Case No. A72 457 702 (AAU Sept. 13, 1993), *reported in* 70 No. 46 *Interpreter Releases* 1603–64 (Dec. 6, 1993).

7.d. As with adoptions, natural parents precluded from immigration benefits.

7.e. Procedures for Non-Convention Countries—For review of procedures including the filing of application for advanced processing (I-600A) that permits adopting parent(s) to file application *prior* to identifying child, *see* 8 C.F.R. §204.3; 9 FAM 42.21 N.12 and 13; Memo, Puleo, Exec. Assoc. Comm., INS, HQ 204.26-C (Sept. 30, 1994), *reprinted in* 71 No. 41 *Interpreter Releases* 1418, 1433–37 (Oct. 24, 1994). An orphan petition (I-600) may be filed concurrently with advanced processing application, while advanced processing application is pending or after it has been approved. 8 C.F.R. §204.3(d). The approval of the I-600A is valid for 18 months unless extended due to SARS outbreak in adopting country. 8 C.F.R. §204.3(h)(3). In addition to the I-600A process, USCIS has adopted an "Adjudicate Orphan Status First" pilot program in Haiti, Honduras, Philippines, Poland, and Sierra Leone that allows USCIS to determine whether the child is truly an orphan within the meaning of the INA *prior to* the final adjudication of the I-600 (orphan status petition). Memo, Yates, Acting Assoc. Director, Operations BUSCIS, HQOPS 70/8.3 (June 4, 2003), *published on* AILA InfoNet at Doc. No. 03070115. For adoption procedure pursuant to the Hague Convention, *see in this section* ¶ 8 (p.786), *infra*.

(1) DOS has also established procedure to accredit and oversee adoption agencies and individuals involved in the adoption process. 22 C.F.R. §96; 68 Fed. Reg. 54064 (Sept. 15, 2003). 71 Fed. Reg. 8161–64 (Feb. 16, 2006)

8. Procedures for Adoption in Hague Convention Countries for Orphans and Nonorphan Adoptions—INA §101(b)(1)(G), 8 U.S.C. §1101(b)(1)(G); 8 C.F.R. §§204.3(a)(2), 204.301–.310; 22 C.F.R. §42.24; 72 Fed. Reg. 56831–67 (Oct. 4, 2007). 72 Fed. Reg. 61301 (Oct. 20, 2007). U.S. is now a signatory to the Hague Convention on the Protection of Children and Co-operation in Respect of Intercountry Adoption, 29 May 1993, *entered into force* April 1, 2008. Congress, pursuant to implementing the Hague Convention, has authorized DOS to be the central authority for the U.S. to monitor requests for overseas adoptions to prevent fraud. PL 106-279; H.R. Report No. 106-691(I) (2000). Hague Convention adoptions apply when both countries are signatories to the Convention and have entered the Convention into force in their respective countries. By the beginning of 2008 there were 94 signatory countries.

8.a. Definition of Who May Adopt is Different Under the Hague Convention. INA §101(b)(1)(G).

(1) *Only* a married USC whose spouse also adopts the child *or* an unmarried USC who is 25 or older may adopt. Thus, for nonorphan adoptions, LPRs *may not apply*.

(2) The visa *petition* must be filed *before* the child's 16th birthday.

(3) The 2-year legal-custody and joint-residence requirements do not apply as in nonorphan cases.

(4) The child must be adopted *abroad*.

(5) The adopting parents must be habitually residing in the U.S. and the child must be an habitual resident of the Convention country. INA §204(d)(2). A USC who is living abroad but is returning to establish a domicile in the U.S. on or before the child's admission with an IV will be considered to be habitually residing in the U.S., 8 C.F.R. §204.303(a)(2). Similarly a USC who will be bringing the child back to the U.S. after the adoption and before the child's 18th birthday so the child may be naturalized under INA §322 will be considered an habitual resident and subject to the Convention. USCs serving in the Armed Forces or working with the U.S. government are considered habitually residing in the U.S. 8 C.F.R. §204.313(b)(2). However, U.S. citizens who are living abroad and adopt the child abroad and are not returning are *not* subject to the Convention but can bring the child into the U.S. under INA §101(b)(1)(E). 72 Fed. Reg. 56831, 56835 (Oct. 4, 2007). If the child is in the U.S. as an NIV, parolee, or EWI, s/he will be treated as an habitual resident of the Convention country and an adoption can proceed under the Convention. 8 C.F.R. §204.309(b)(4). However, if the child is otherwise ineligible to adjust or if the Central Authority in the other country requires the child's return to approve the adoption, then the petition may be provisionally approved but the child must return to the country and obtain an immigrant visa. 8 C.F.R. §204.309(b)(4).

(6) No provision for older siblings adopted by the same parents.

(7) Child does *not* have to be an orphan as defined under INA §101(b)(1)(F) to utilize Convention procedures

(8) The child's birth parents (or parent in the case of a child who has one sole or surviving parent because of the death or disappearance of, or the child's abandonment or desertion by, the other parent), or other persons or institutions that retain legal custody of the child:

(a) Must have freely given their written irrevocable consent to the termination of their legal relationship with the child and to the child's emigration and adoption *and*

(b) In the case of a child placed for adoption by both living birth parents, both parents are incapable of providing proper care for the child.

(9) Procedures Under the Convention, 8 C.F.R. §§204.3(a)(2), 204.301–.310; 22 C.F.R. §42.24. The procedures under the Hague Convention require that USCIS must *first* determine that the USCs are suitable adoptive parents *before* authorities in other countries place the child with the USCs for adoption and the other country must agree that the adoption is in the best interests of the child. The U.S. must then decide before the adoption that it will meet the requirements of the Convention and U.S. immigration law. Thus, a Convention adoption will only occur if both governments agree and the child will be able to enter the U.S.

(10) Applications for adoption under the Convention are on different forms. The Convention form is the I-800 (Petition) and I-800A (Application for determination of suitability to adopt). The I-800A *must be approved before* approval of the I-800. The I-800 may then be approved but only *provisionally* until the foreign state determines that the child will be authorized to immigrate. If a Convention adoption began through the filing of an I-601 or I-601A before April 1, 2008 (the day the Convention went into force in the U.S.) then the adoption can proceed under non-Convention procedures.

(11) No funds to birth parents. The new regulations prohibit the exchange of any funds to the birth parents for the adoption. However, payment of certain expenses related to the birth of the child, care of the child, or care of the birth mother while pregnant are permissible. 8 C.F.R. §§204.304(a)–(b).

9. No adjustment—A child in the U.S. either illegally or as a nonimmigrant is ineligible for the benefits of an orphan petition. However, a child who has been paroled *and* who has not been adopted in the U.S. is eligible for the benefits of an orphan petition and may therefore be eligible to adjust. 8 C.F.R. §204.3(k)(3).

10. Citizenship Immediately Available—The Child Citizenship Act of 2000 (PL 106-395) provides that orphans who were *adopted abroad prior* to issuance of the IV (IR-3 classification) are now immediately eligible for citizenship. Cable, DOS, 01-State-105804 (June 16, 2001), *reprinted in* 78 No. 25 *Interpreter Releases* 1077–78 (July 2, 2001). Because they are immediately eligible for citizenship, the I-864 affidavit of support is no longer required in their cases. Cable, DOS 01-State-105806 (June 16, 2001*), published on* AILA InfoNet at Doc. No. 01061691; 8 C.F.R. §320, 66 Fed. Reg. 32138–66 (June 13, 2001), and the sponsor need only file an I-864W to demonstrate exemption from the affidavit of support requirement.

D. *Parents*—INA §101(b)(2), 8 U.S.C. §1101(b)(2)

1. Parent, father or mother established by reason of child definition.

2. Child can only petition for parent when child is 21 or older (*i.e.,* a son or daughter under INA). INA §201(b)(2)(A)(i), 8 U.S.C. §1151(b)(2)(A)(i).

3. Once criteria of child-parent is met, advanced age of child is irrelevant in petitioning for parent. *Matter of Citino*, 12 I&N Dec. 427 (BIA 1967) [where relationship formed prior to 18th birthday, the step-daughter could petition for step-mother even though step-daughter was older than 18 at time of petition]. *See Young v. Reno*, 114 F.3d 879 (9th Cir. 1997). 8 C.F.R. §204.2(f).

E. *Brothers and sisters*—Siblings can petition for one another only if they meet the definition of a child from one or both parents. *Matter of Garner*, 15 I&N Dec. 215 (BIA 1975). Half-siblings may petition for one another. *Matter of Mahal*, 12 I&N Dec. 409 (BIA 1967). Sibling adopted by another family is not considered a brother or sister for immigration purposes if adoption was in accordance with INA §101(b)(1)(E). *Matter of Li*, 20 I&N Dec. 700 (BIA 1993) [revoked sibling petition]; *Kosak v. Aguirre,* 519 F.3d 210 (3d Cir. 2008) [upholding *Matter of Li* on *Chevron* deference grounds];

Young v. Reno, 114 F.3d 879 (9th Cir. 1997) [upholding *Matter of Li* when it was applied to petition pending for many years before the decision in *Li*]; *Kosak v. Devine,* 439 F.Supp.2d 410 (E.D. Pa. 2006) [upheld *Matter of Li* under *Chevron* deference].

F. *Spouses and sham marriages*

1. Immigration Marriage Fraud Amendments Act of 1986 (IMFA), PL 99-639 §5(b), 100 Stat. 3537, 3543 (Nov. 10, 1986), Legislative History at H.R. Rep. No. 906, 99th Cong. 2d Sess. (on H.R. 3737), *reprinted in part in* 1986 U.S.C.C.A.N. 5978-86; Sen. Rep. No. 99-491 (Sept. 26, 1986) (on S. 2270); *Castillo Ison v. INS,* 308 F.3d 1036 (9th Cir. 2002) [Act's requirements only apply to marriages entered into on or after Nov. 10, 1986].

1.a. Marriage now results in conditional residence status unless it is more than 2 years old at time of granting the immigrant status. INA §216, 8 U.S.C. §1186a. Two-year period is measured from the time residency is granted. Thus, if a person obtained an immigrant visa packet at a U.S. embassy indicating that he is a conditional resident, but he entered the U.S. after his marriage was more than 2 years old, he would enter as an LPR not a conditional resident. 8 C.F.R. §§235.11(b), 1235.11(b).

1.b. Conditional residence terminated if, before second anniversary of the grant of conditional residence, USCIS determines that:

(1) Marriage judicially annulled or terminated other than through death of spouse;

(2) Marriage entered into for purpose of procuring noncitizen's entry for a fee, or other consideration was given for filing a petition (except fee to attorney); or

(3) Noncitizen and spouse fail to petition USCIS within 90-day period before second anniversary of conditional residence, or noncitizen and spouse fail to jointly appear at USCIS interview (unless good cause is shown), unless the noncitizen has filed Form I-751 seeking a waiver of the joint filing requirement.

1.c. Procedures:

(1) Must file joint petition (Form I-751) within 90 days of second anniversary of grant of conditional residence and before the end of the 2-year period. 8 C.F.R. §§216.4(a)(1), 1216.4(a)(1). Conditional residence becomes permanent after second anniversary of status if it is not terminated. However, the Service takes the position that if it does not adjudicate the petition within the 90-day period, it is not barred from denying the petition, Legal Opinion, Cook, General Counsel, CO 216-P (June 21, 1990), *reprinted in* 67 No. 33 *Interpreter Releases* 979, 991–97 (Aug. 31, 1990), and the BIA has held that failure to adjudicate a petition within 90 days of the interview under INA §216(c)(3)(A) does not result either in the INS's loss of jurisdiction over the joint petition or the automatic removal of the conditional basis. *Matter of Nwokoma*, 20 I&N Dec. 899 (BIA 1994); *Robertson v. Attorney General*, 957 F.Supp. 1035 (N.D. Ill. 1997) [90-day not mandatory to extent permitting mandamus]. Submission of I-751 petition must be accompanied by evidence of valid marriage such as: (1) joint ownership of property; (2) lease showing joint tenancy; (3) commingling of finances; (4) birth certificates of children; (5) affidavits of third parties; and (6) other documentation. 8 C.F.R. §§216.4(a)(5), 1216.4(a)(5).

(a) Dependent Children Filing I-751. A child who received his or her conditional residence on the same date as or within 90 days thereafter of his or her parent need *not* file a separate I-751 petition. However, if the child received his conditional residence status more than 90 days after his or her parent (*e.g.*, because the parent adjusted and the children were abroad), each child must file a separate I-751. 8 C.F.R. §216.4(a)(2).

(b) There are special procedures for persons in the military in regard to completing I-751 interviews. Memo, Pearson, Ex. Assoc. Comm. Field Operations, HQADN 70/23.12 (Jan. 7, 2002), *published on* AILA InfoNet at Doc. No. 02030632.

(2) If parties cannot file jointly (Form I-751) noncitizen may file waiver on Form I-751. 8 C.F.R. §§216.5, 1216.5. Previously there were two separate forms (I-751/I-752). They are now combined into two parts of the same (I-751) form. For example, where spouse dies, waiver part should be filed because a joint petition cannot be filed. Letter, Miller,

Dep. Asst. Comm. (Aug. 7, 1989), *reprinted in* 66 No. 33 *Interpreter Releases* 970, 982 (Aug. 28, 1989). Similarly, an I-751 waiver may be filed if the parties are divorced. But a party may not apply for the waiver on an I-751 until they are divorced. Memo, Yates, Acting Assoc. Director Operations, BUSCIS (Apr. 10, 2003), *published on* AILA InfoNet at Doc. No. 03050643 (May 6, 2003) [cannot apply for waiver until final divorce]. If waiver cannot be timely filed because divorce is not final, the applicant may be placed in removal proceedings, where s/he can ask the IJ for a continuance until divorce is final. Memo, Yates (Apr. 10, 2003), *supra*. I-751 waiver may be filed before, during, or after the 90-day filing window that applies to jointly filed I-751 petitions. *Matter of Stowers,* 22 I&N Dec. 605 (BIA 1999); 8 C.F.R. §216.5 [does not contain 90-day requirement]. An applicant may also seek to reopen proceedings based upon the finality of the divorce and the ability to now file an I-751. *Alrefae v. Gonzales,* 471 F.3d 353, 361–63 (2d Cir. 2006) [reversed IJ for failure to consider reopening proceedings where respondent was now divorced and could file I-751 but offered no view on whether it was now untimely]. The filing of joint petition or waiver automatically extends the alien's status until the I-751 is adjudicated. Memo, Yates, Acting Assoc. Dir. Operations, BUSCIS, HQADN 70/23.12 (Dec. 2, 2003), *published on* AILA InfoNet at Doc. No. 03120940. A CR is entitled to receive an I-551 stamp in his passport or if no passport on an I-94 for a period of one year while awaiting a decision. *Id.* If petition was not timely filed but was accepted for filing by USCIS, it should be treated as timely. *Flores-Salgado v. Caplinger*, 872 F.Supp. 1521 (E.D. La. 1995).

(3) Waivers may be granted under INA §216(c)(4), 8 U.S.C. §1186a(c)(4), 8 C.F.R. §§216.5, 1216.5 even if the marriage is terminated or there is another disqualifying reason where:

(a) Extreme hardship if alien deported; and extreme hardship occurred only during period of conditional residency. *But see* 8 C.F.R. §216.5(e)(1) [take into account only those factors that arose *subsequent* to entry as a conditional resident]; *but see Singh v. DOJ,* 461 F.3d 290, 296–98 (2d Cir. 2006) [finding jurisdiction to review denial of reopening for extreme hardship, determining that the statute and regulation are in conflict; that the regulation permits consideration of extreme hardship that arose subsequent to the termination of conditional residency and finding the BIA erred in not considering extreme hardship that arose after the IJ's hearing]. On remand, *Matter of Singh,* 24 I&N Dec. 331 (BIA 2007), the Board claimed there was no conflict between the regulation and the statute as stated by the Second Circuit but, in any event, would have denied the application as a matter of discretion and because respondent failed to adhere to the procedures regarding motions to reopen when he raised the extreme-hardship issue. One circuit has held that a person may seek an extreme-hardship waiver even if his marriage was not in good faith. *Waggoner v. Gonzales,* 488 F.3d 632, 634–38 (5th Cir. 2007) [the language of the extreme-hardship waiver statute is clear and does not require a good-faith marriage to qualify for the waiver]. *But see Velazquez v. INS*, 876 F.Supp. 1071, 1075–78 (D. Minn. 1995) [cannot use provision to waive sham marriage]; or

(b) Qualifying marriage entered into in good faith by alien and terminated other than through death of spouse. *Oropeza-Wong v. Gonzales,* 406 F.3d 1135, 1141–49 (9th Cir. 2005) [Section 1252(a)(2)(B)(ii) did not bar the court's jurisdiction to review whether a conditional resident in removal proceedings qualified for good-faith-marriage waiver under §1186a(c)(4)(B), but IJ's denial of waiver was upheld on the merits]; *Cho v. Gonzales,* 404 F.3d 96, 98–102 (1st Cir. 2005) [court had jurisdiction notwithstanding §1252(a)(2)(B)(ii) to review whether CR in removal proceedings qualified for good-faith-marriage waiver under §1186a(c)(4)(B), and court reversed BIA for lack of substantial evidence, where parties had long courtship, USC husband terminated relationship, there was substantial documentary evidence, and alien wife's filling out applications and submitting them promptly and lack of knowledge of husband's extramarital affair were irrelevant]; *Damon v. Ashcroft,* 360 F.3d 1084 (9th Cir. 2004) [reversing denial of removal of conditional residence for lack of substantial evidence where IJ erred by imposing her own views about a "real" marriage. It was impermissible for her to make a finding of marriage invalidity on the basis that the wife rushed into the marriage, did not share a common language or culture with husband, did not take his last name and had a nonreligious wedding]. The requirement that the divorce be for good cause and the requirement that the alien must petition for the divorce were eliminated by the Immigration Act of 1990 (PL 101-649).

i) INA §204(c) Distinguished. An IJ's determination that the qualifying marriage was not entered into in good faith is different than a finding under INA §204(c) that the marriage was entered into for the purpose of evading the immigration laws. *Singh v. DOJ,* 461 F.3d 290, 294–95, n.3 (2d Cir. 2006) [where government did not argue §204(c) and where IJ found first wife's testimony equivocal, the court found that respondent's failure to prove a good-faith marriage is not enough to establish a sham marriage to evade the immigration laws]; or

(c) Qualifying marriage entered in good faith and that during the marriage the beneficiary spouse or child was "battered by or was the subject of extreme cruelty perpetrated by his or her spouse and the beneficiary was not at fault in failing to meet the petitioning requirements." This waiver does not require that the parties be divorced. USCIS has defined this exception as including, but not limited to, "being the victim of any act or threatened act of violence, including any forceful detention which results or threatens to result in physical or mental injury. Psychological or sexual abuse or exploitation ... shall be considered acts of violence." 8 C.F.R. §§216.5(e)(3)(i), 1216.5(e)(3)(i). A waiver based upon extreme mental cruelty may be supported by any credible evidence. INA §216(c)(4), 8 U.S.C. §1186a(c)(4). USCIS will maintain the confidentiality of the information. 8 C.F.R. §§216.5(e)(3)(viii), 1216.5(e)(3)(viii).

(d) These waivers are separate and independent and multiple grounds should be asserted where applicable. *Matter of Balsillie*, 20 I&N Dec. 486 (BIA 1992); *Matter of Anderson*, 20 I&N Dec. 888 (BIA 1994) [IJ has no authority to review request for waiver where respondent asserted a different basis for the waiver before INS].

(4) Immigration Marriage Fraud Amendments Act covers spouses, children of spouses, and K fiancé(e)s. Does not cover derivatives (*e.g.,* spouse of 3d preference). It also does not include children where parent did not obtain residency through marriage. Legal Opinion, Cook, General Counsel (Jan. 12, 1990), *reprinted in* 67 No. 6 *Interpreter Releases* 159, 166–68 (Feb. 5, 1990) [child is not conditional permanent resident where parent did not obtain residency through qualifying marriage under INA §216].

(5) USCIS required to notify alien of filing procedures at time of residency and 90 days before alien must reapply, but failure to notify does not relieve parties of responsibility. 8 C.F.R. §§216.2(a)–(c), 1216.2(a)–(c).

(6) Noncitizen need not be physically present in U.S. to file petition so long as s/he returns for the USCIS interview. 8 C.F.R. §§216.4(a)(4), 1216.4(a)(4). If conditional resident, may return within one year of the date of expiration of the conditional residence card if alien is in possession of a receipt showing that he or she filed an I-751 form within previous 6 months. 8 C.F.R. §211.1(a)(5). *But see* 8 C.F.R. §§235.11(c), 1235.11(c), which suggests person may be put in removal proceedings if petition has not been approved. The CR, however, has a right to a temporary I-551 while s/he obtains review of the termination. Memo, Redman, Acting Asst. Comm., Adjudications, DOS, HQ 70/23.13-C (Oct. 9, 1997), *reprinted in* 74 No. 43 *Interpreter Releases* 1714, 1731 (Nov. 7, 1997).

(7) Procedures for waiver. 8 C.F.R. §§216.5, 1216.5.

(a) If waiver is based on marriage entered in good faith, document requirements include records showing combined assets, length of time parties cohabitated and grounds for which marriage was terminated (including divorce decree). If waiver based on other reasons, *see* 8 C.F.R. §§216.5(e)(1), 1216.5(e)(1) (for hardship) and §§216.5(e)(1), 1216.5(e)(1) (for battered or abused).

(b) Where USCIS has terminated conditional residence status, the former conditional resident may file a waiver before or after the 90-day period. *Matter of Stowers,* 22 I&N Dec. 605 [where INS terminated CR status and placed person in removal proceeding, the former CR could file waiver with INS and IJ must grant continuance until application is adjudicated]. Regulations that specifically allow waivers based on cruelty to be filed at any time under 8 C.F.R. §§216.5(e)(3)(ii), 1216.5(e)(3)(ii) are now, by BIA decision in *Stowers*, extended to all waivers. *See also Mersereau v. Ingham*, 875 F.Supp. 148, 154 (W.D.N.Y. 1995) [finding 8 C.F.R. §235.11(c) contemplated filing outside U.S.].

(c) USCIS may grant I-751 waiver before or subsequent to 90-day period. Legal Opinion, Cook, General Counsel (Jan. 9, 1990), *reprinted in* 67 No. 6 *Interpreter Releases* 159, 168–70 (Feb. 5, 1990). IJ must grant continuance to allow USCIS to adjudicate the waiver. *Matter of Stowers, supra*; *Matter of Mendes,* 20 I&N Dec. 833 (BIA 1994).

(8) Denial of Adjustment. In accordance with INA §245(d), a person who entered as a conditional resident under INA cannot adjust status under INA §245. However, this does not prevent person from adjusting under a different section of the INA (*e.g.,* §§209, 240A). IMFA Questions at 1990 AILA National Conference Q.7, *reprinted in* 68 No. 35 *Interpreter Releases* 1197, 1209, 1211 (Sept. 16, 1991). In addition, if conditional resident status is terminated, person may adjust if there is a legal basis to do so. *Matter of Stockwell*, 20 I&N Dec. 309 (BIA 1991) [marriage to new USC]. Also, if person was previously a conditional resident and makes a new entry as a nonimmigrant, s/he may adjust. IMFA Questions, *supra*, Q.8.

(9) Termination of Conditional Residence

(a) Can occur in three ways:

i) USCIS can affirmatively terminate prior to 2-year expiration. INA §216(b)(1).

ii) USCIS can adjudicate petition and find it not valid. INA §216(c)(3)(C).

iii) CR fails to timely file petition or appear for interview. INA §216(c)(2)(A).

(b) A withdrawal of support of the joint petition by the spouse results in treating the petition as not filed for purposes of this section. *Matter of Mendes*, 20 I&N Dec. 833 (BIA 1994).

(c) If USCIS terminates CR status it must still provide a temporary I-551 or an I-94 while the CR obtains review of the termination. Memo, Redman, Acting Asst. Comm., Adjudications, DOS, HQ 70/23.13-C (Oct. 9, 1997), *reprinted in* 74 No. 43 *Interpreter Releases* 1714, 1731 (Nov. 7, 1997).

(10) Removal Proceeding for Terminated Conditional Residents.

(a) No appeal from denial of petition except in removal proceedings. 8 C.F.R. §§216.4(d), 1216.4(d). If petition denied, applicant put in removal proceedings. INA §237(a)(1)(D), 8 U.S.C. §1227(a)(1)(D); 8 C.F.R. §§216.4(d)(2), 1216.4(d)(2). If applicant does not petition USCIS, applicant cannot petition IJ in first instance. Legal Opinion, Cook, General Counsel (Jan. 9, 1990), *reprinted in* 67 No. 6 *Interpreter Releases* 159, 170 (Feb. 5, 1990). Similarly, an IJ can only review the denial of a waiver by USCIS. If a waiver is filed where USCIS has terminated the CR status, the IJ shall continue the matter until USCIS rules on the waiver. *Matter of Stowers,* 22 I&N Dec. 605 (BIA 1999) [continuance should be granted even where waiver is filed outside or before 90-day period]. If applicant does not file a joint petition or waiver (I-751) with USCIS in the first instance, applicant cannot file before IJ, *Matter of Lemhammad*, 20 I&N Dec. 316 (BIA 1991); 8 C.F.R. §§216.5(f), 1216.5(f), but he may still obtain review before the IJ. *Matter of Mendes*, 20 I&N Dec. 833 (BIA 1994). However, where USCIS has denied the waiver on the grounds requested by the respondent, the respondent may not seek consideration before the IJ of an alternate waiver under INA §216(c)(4). *Matter of Anderson*, 20 I&N Dec. 888 (BIA 1994) [where INS denies extreme hardship waiver under INA §216(c)(4)(A), the IJ had no authority to determine waiver on the alternate grounds of good faith under INA §216(c)(4)(B)]. Similarly, the IJ has no authority to review the validity of the denial of a joint petition where the parties are subsequently divorced because the party becomes statutorily ineligible for approval under INA §216(c)(1). *Matter of Tee*, 20 I&N Dec. 949 (BIA 1995). Also, once the applicant loses his conditional residence status, he may be unable to file a motion to reopen before the IJ to obtain an approved I-751. *Molina de Massenet v. Gonzales,* 485 F.3d 661 (1st Cir. 2007). Collateral estoppel may not apply to the IJ's review regarding conditional residency. *Bilali v. Gonzales,* 502 F.3d 470 (6th Cir. 2007) [collateral estoppel did not apply to IJ's determination that respondent had a valid marriage in an AOS proceeding to bar litigation whether USCIS improperly denied removal of their CR status].

(b) Burden of Proof. USCIS must establish basis for termination under INA §216(b)(1) by a preponderance of the evidence. INA §216(b)(2). *Matter of Lemhammad,* 20 I&N Dec. 316 (BIA 1991). 8 C.F.R. §§216.4(d)(2), 1216.4(d)(2); *Smolniakova v. Gonzales,* 422 F.3d 1037, 1053–54 (9th Cir. 2005) [reversed IJ who placed burden incorrectly on respondent to prove validity of marriage]; IJ reviews waivers *de novo*, but the Service believes applicant has burden of proof on waiver. Legal Opinion, Rees, Gen. Counsel, CO 216-C (Dec. 3, 1991). The applicant has the burden of proof in cases terminated for failure to file or to appear under INA §216(c)(2)(A); 8 C.F.R. §§216.4(a)(6), 1216.4(a)(6).

(c) Closed Hearing. In an IJ proceeding concerning an abused spouse or child under INA §216(c)(4), the hearing is closed unless the party requests that it be opened. 8 C.F.R. §1003.27(c).

(d) Respondent should be given reasonable opportunity to file waiver under INA §216(c)(4) where s/he is *prima facie* eligible, *Matter of Mendes*, 20 I&N Dec. 833 (BIA 1994).

(11) Administrative and Judicial Review. The denial of the I-751 petition to remove conditional residence by the IJ may be appealed to the BIA. If the respondent is not successful before the BIA s/he may seek review in the court of appeals. In the court of appeals the DHS is likely to raise the issue that review of discretionary matters is precluded in federal court under INA §242(a)(2)(B)(ii). *Ebrahim v. Gonzales,* 471 F.3d 880, 883–84 (8th Cir. 2006) [no jurisdiction to review good-faith-marriage exception under INA §216(c)(4)(B), 8 U.S.C. §1186a(c)(4)(B)]; *Atsilov v. Gonzales,* 468 F.3d 112, 116 (2d Cir. 2006) [INA §242(a)(2)(B)(ii) bars review of the AG's decision to deny a waiver under 8 U.S.C. §1186a(c)(4) as a matter of discretion]; *Suvorov v. Gonzales,* 441 F.3d 618, 621–22 (8th Cir. 2006) [same]; *Ignatova v. Gonzales,* 430 F.3d 1209, 1212–13 (8th Cir. 2005) [post–REAL ID Act, the court found no jurisdiction following *Urena-Tavarez* to review hardship waiver under §1186a(c)(4)(A) for extreme hardship]; *Urena-Tavarez v. Ashcroft,* 367 F.3d 154, 157–61 (3d Cir. 2004) [no jurisdiction to review IJ's denial of a waiver of conditional residency under 8 U.S.C. §1186a(c)(4) because it is a discretionary decision barred from review under INA §242(a)(2)(B)(ii)]; *Assaad v. Ashcroft,* 378 F.3d 471, 475 (5th Cir. 2004) [following *Urena-Tavarez* and finding no jurisdiction to review good-faith-marriage waiver under 8 U.S.C. §1186a(c)(4)(B) even in context of motion to reopen]. *But see Singh v. DOJ,* 461 F.3d 290, 293–94 & n.2 (2d Cir. 2006) [finding jurisdiction to review BIA's refusal to remand a case to consider a hardship waiver. The case does not involve the review of the substance of the hardship waiver, which would be precluded, but rather whether the BIA erred in not remanding it for consideration]; *Monter v. Gonzales,* 430 F.3d 546 (2d Cir. 2005) [the Second Circuit adopted the 4-part test in *Kungys* and found that respondent's failure to list a separate address for his wife on the I-751 was material, but that the IJ's refusal to change venue deprived respondent of the opportunity to rebut the presumption that he procured his permanent residency by a material misrepresentation, and to show he was nevertheless qualified to receive his permanent residency]; *Oropeza-Wong v. Gonzales,* 406 F.3d 1135, 1141–49 (9th Cir. 2005) [Section 1252(a)(2)(B)(ii) did not bar the court's jurisdiction to review whether a CR in removal proceedings qualified for good-faith-marriage waiver under §1186a(c)(4)(B), but IJ's denial of waiver was upheld on the merits]; *Cho v. Gonzales,* 404 F.3d 96, 98–102 (1st Cir. 2005) [court had jurisdiction notwithstanding §1252(a)(2)(B)(ii) to review whether CR in removal proceedings qualified for good-faith-marriage waiver under §1186a(c)(4)(B), and court reversed BIA for lack of substantial evidence]; *Mendes v. INS,* 197 F.3d 6, 12–13 (1st Cir. 1999) [finding jurisdiction but applying the highly def-

erential *Elias-Zacarias* standard]; *Al Jabari v. Chertoff,* 536 F.Supp.2d 1029 (D. Minn. 2008) [In action to compel DHS to complete the security check involving a grant by an IJ of a marriage hardship waiver to lift conditional residence under 8 U.S.C. §1186a(c)(4), the court determined that, although mandamus was unavailable because the statute does not impose a nondiscretionary duty, the APA permitted injunctive relief].

1.d. Marriage in removal proceeding—IMFA §5, INA §§204(g), 245(e), 8 U.S.C. §§1154(g), 1255(e).

(1) *Procedure and Clear and Convincing Standard*—May not adjust status to permanent resident or have visa petition for permanent status as spouse approved if marriage entered into while administrative or judicial proceedings are pending, unless the parties establish by "clear and convincing evidence ... that the marriage was entered into in good faith." INA §§245(e)(2) and (3), 204(g); 8 U.S.C. §§1255(e)(2) and (3), 1154(g); 8 C.F.R. §§204.2(a)(1)(iii), 245.1(c)(8)(iii)(F), 1245.1(c)(8)(iii)(F); *Matter of Fuentes*, 20 I&N Dec. 227 (BIA 1991). The addition of the "good faith" exception is applicable to all marriages entered into before, on or after Nov. 29, 1990, the date of the Immigration Act of 1990. No waiver application is required. However, the applicant must request the waiver *in writing* when submitting the I-130 petition. 8 C.F.R. §§204.2(a)(1)(iii)(A). Applicant must submit evidence with application that meets the clear and convincing standard. *See* 8 C.F.R. §§245.1(c)(8)(iii)(F), 1245.1(c)(8)(iii)(F), initial paragraph of 8 C.F.R. §204.2(a)(1)(iii), and 8 C.F.R. §204.2(a)(1)(iii)(B)(1)–(6). All stand-alone I-130s must be filed with the Chicago Lockbox. USCIS Update, USCIS Revises Filing Instructions for Petition for Alien Relative (Mar. 21, 2008), *published on* AILA InfoNet at Doc. No. 08032130. If the petition is approved, it is considered primary evidence of eligibility for the *bona fide*–marriage exemption. 8 C.F.R. §§245.1(c)(8)(v), 1245.1(c)(8)(v). If the petition is approved, it would be an abuse of discretion for the BIA to request additional evidence beyond the approval. *Patel v. Ashcroft,* 375 F.3d 693 (8th Cir. 2004) [BIA abused its discretion in denying a remand for an AOS application based upon a marriage and requiring the production of additional evidence of a bona fide marriage where the beneficiary in proceedings submitted an approved petition]. If the petition is denied for failing to meet the *bona fide*–marriage exemption it is appealable to the BIA. 8 C.F.R. §204.2(a)(1)(iii)(E). If application for adjustment is denied for failure to establish the *bona fide*–marriage exception, the appeal is to the AAU. 8 C.F.R. §§103.3(a)(1)(ii), 1103.3(a)(1)(ii).

Procedure under *Matter of Velarde-Pacheco.* Under earlier BIA decisions, an application for adjustment of status couldn't be filed, where the marriage was entered into during removal proceeding, until the I-130 is approved. *Matter of H-A-,* 22 I&N Dec. 728 (BIA 1999) [following *Matter of Arthur*, 20 I&N Dec. 475 (BIA 1992) a person may not file adjustment application until I-130 is approved even if the adjustment application would subsequently be time-barred because of the 90-day reopening period under 8 C.F.R. §1003.2(c)]. *But see Matter of Velarde-Pacheco,* 23 I&N Dec. 253 (BIA 2002) [*Matter of Arthur* and *H-A-* modified to allow for motions to reopen, where the I-485/I-130 are filed within 90 days, are not numerically barred, are not barred by *Matter of Shaar*, 21 I&N Dec. 541 (BIA 1996), or any other procedural grounds, presents clear and convincing evidence that the marriage is *bona fide*, and the Service either does not oppose the motion or bases its opposition solely on *Matter of Arthur*]; *Melnitsenko v. Mukasey,* 517 F.3d 42, 48–52 (2d Cir. 2008) [BIA cannot deny a motion under *Velarde-Pacheco* where petitioner meets all five criteria solely on the fact of DHS's opposition]; *Ssali v. Gonzales,* 424 F.3d 556, 562–64 (7th Cir. 2005) [vacated BIA's denial on motion to reopen for marriage adjustment and criticized government's analysis of *Matter of Arthur*]; *Singh v. Gonzales,* 404 F.3d 1024, 1027–29 (7th Cir. 2005) [where I-130 had been approved, the BIA's reliance on *Matter of Velarde-Pacheco* to deny motion to reconsider to allow adjustment was error, because *Velarde* involved an unadjudicated I-130; however, under facts of case error was harmless].

The limitation to adjustment imposed by *Matter of Shaar*, after respondent failed to depart within time allowed by VD order, is no longer valid in some circuits. *Ugokwe v. U.S. Att'y Gen.,* 453 F.3d 1325 (11th Cir. 2006) [a timely filed motion to reopen post-

IIRIRA tolls the VD period and prohibits the application of *Matter of Shaar* to bar consideration of the merits of the motion]; *Barroso v. Gonzales,* 429 F.3d 1195, 1202–08 (9th Cir. 2005) [filing a motion to reconsider within the VD period automatically tolls VD]; *Kanivets v. Gonzales,* 424 F.3d 330, 334–36 (3d Cir. 2005) [distinguished *Bhiski* and found that *post*-IIRIRA, a timely filed motion to reopen for AOS tolls the period of VD and allows the BIA to consider the motion]; *Sidikhouya v. Gonzales,* 407 F.3d 950 (8th Cir. 2005) [where motion to reopen for AOS was filed prior to the expiration of the VD period granted by the BIA, it was an abuse of discretion post-IIRIRA for the BIA to deny reopening based upon *Matter of Shaar*, when VD expired before BIA ruled]; *Barrios v. Att'y Gen. of the U.S.,* 399 F.3d 272 (3d Cir. 2005) [rejecting *Matter of Shaar* for *pre*-IIRIRA cases, and holding that a timely filed motion to reopen prevents the BIA/IJ from applying the bar to adjustment under the former INA §242B(e)(2)(A), because the failure of the BIA/IJ to adjudicate the motion within the voluntary departure period is an "exceptional circumstance"]; *Azarte v. Ashcroft,* 394 F.3d 1278 (9th Cir. 2005) [where a motion to reopen is filed in a removal proceeding post-IIRIRA during the voluntary departure period and a stay of removal or VD is requested, the VD period is tolled while the BIA considers the motion]; *Singh v. Quarantillo,* 92 F.Supp.2d 386 (D.N.J. 2000) [the district court adopted the dissent in *Matter of H-A-,* found that the majority opinion "produced manifest injustice [and] flouted Congressional intent," ordered applicant released, and tolled VD until INS approved I-130 petition that had been pending for 2 years]. *But see Chedad v. Gonzales,* 497 F.3d 57 (1st Cir. 2007) [a timely filed motion to reopen does not stay the running of the VD period and if the motion is granted after VD has expired the respondent is barred from seeking relief under INA §240B(d)(1), 8 C.F.R. §1229c(d)(1)]; *Hadayat v. Gonzales,* 458 F.3d 659, 663–64 (7th Cir. 2006) [where respondent filed motion to reopen before VD expired but then stayed after motion was denied without seeking stay from circuit court, he was ineligible for relief whether or not *Matter of Shaar* remains good law]; *Dekoladenu v. Gonzales,* 459 F.3d 500, 502–08 (4th Cir. 2006) [a timely filed motion to reopen does not toll the VD period]; *Banda-Ortiz v. Gonzales,* 445 F.3d 387, 391 (5th Cir. 2006) [holding that BIA's decision to reopen case does not cure respondent's failure to depart during the voluntary departure period].

In addition, the bar to AOS may apply even if a person is successful in reopening proceedings. *Chedad v. Gonzales,* 497 F.3d 57 (1st Cir. 2007) [a timely filed motion to reopen does not stay the running of the VD period and if the motion is granted after VD has expired the respondent is barred from seeking relief under INA §240B(d)(1), 8 C.F.R. §1229c(d)(1)]; *Singh v. Gonzales,* 468 F.3d 135 (2d Cir. 2006) [IJ's granting of MTR does *not* vacate the effect of prior noncompliance with a VD order that now bars respondent's adjustment of status]; *Dacosta v. Gonzales,* 449 F.3d 45 (1st Cir. 2006) [BIA properly denied adjustment after granting motion to reopen, because granting a motion to reopen where applicant had previously remained beyond the VD period without a stay did not expunge the previous violation for purposes of barring adjustment]. *Compare Banda-Ortiz v. Gonzales,* 445 F.3d 387, 391 (5th Cir. 2006) [BIA's decision to reopen does not cure respondent's failure to depart during VD period and respondent is therefore ineligible for cancellation]. *But see Orichitch v. Gonzales,* 421 F.3d 595 (7th Cir. 2005) [in granting petitioner's joint MTR for AOS, the BIA permanently "disposed of" the VD order and thus eliminated the §240B(d) issue].

Review of motions to remand for adjustment during removal proceedings is governed by abuse of discretion standard. *Ilic-Lee v. Mukasey,* 507 F.3d 1044, 1049–53 (6th Cir. 2007) [BIA was correct to deny motion to reopen proceedings for AOS under *Velarde* where there was some evidence of a legal marriage but the weight of the evidence was slight and the government opposed reopening]; *Sarr v. Gonzales,* 485 F.3d 354, 362–64 (6th Cir. 2007) [BIA denial of motion to remand under *Velarde* upheld where applicant had testified falsely at asylum hearing and never filed waiver with *Velarde* motion]; *Conteh v. Gonzales,* 461 F.3d 45, 64–65 (1st Cir. 2006) [*Velarde* standard did not apply where there was not a visa immediately available because spouse was only an LPR]; *Malhi v. INS*, 336 F.3d 989, 999–1000 (9th Cir. 2003) [following "clear and convincing" evidence requirement in *Matter of Velarde-Pacheco* and 8 C.F.R. §204.2(a)(1)(iii)(B) evidentiary requirements but upholding denial by BIA of motion to remand under abuse of discretion standard]; *Ramchandani v. Gonzales,* 434 F.3d 337, 340–41 (5th Cir. 2005) [upheld BIA denial of motion to reopen under *Velarde* where DHS opposed motion because applicant didn't submit affidavit of support]. *See also Castillo Ison v. INS,* 308 F.3d 1036 (9th Cir. 2002) [Act's requirements as interpreted in *Matter of Arthur* only apply to marriages entered into on or after Nov. 10, 1986]; *Matter of McKee,* 17 I&N Dec. 332 (BIA 1980).

Marriage Need Only be Viable at Inception to be Valid—An adjustment of status application may not be denied solely because the marriage is no longer viable and the parties are not living together if it was not fraudulent or a sham marriage at its inception and the parties are not legally separated or divorced. *Matter of Boromand,* 17 I&N Dec. 450 (BIA 1980); *Hernandez v. Ashcroft,* 345 F.3d 824, 845–49 (9th Cir. 2003) [the nonviability of a marriage cannot alone be the basis to deny adjustment even if immigration characterizes its decision to deny adjustment as discretionary].

BIA Discretion to Deny—The BIA is given broad discretion to deny a motion to reopen where it believes the applicant has not met the "clear and convincing standard" or where it believes there was a history of recurrent marriage fraud. *Miah v. Mukasey,* 519 F.3d 784, 789–90 (8th Cir. 2008) [denied motion to reopen under *Velarde* on insufficiency of the evidence and distinguished *Velarde* because motion was filed after BIA ruled]; *Ilic-Lee v. Mukasey,* 507 F.3d 1044, 1049–53 (6th Cir. 2007) [BIA was correct to deny motion to reopen proceedings for AOS under *Velarde* where there was some evidence of a legal marriage but the weight of the evidence was slight and the government opposed reopening]; *Mahmoud v. Gonzales,* 485 F.3d 175 (1st Cir. 2007) [discretionary denial of adjustment due to eleventh-hour marriage with few equities upheld]; *Falae v. Gonzales,* 411 F.3d 11, 14–15 (1st Cir. 2005) [although respondent in motion to remand made a prima facie showing of eligibility for adjustment of status based upon his marriage, and the BIA made no finding of a "sham marriage," the BIA did not abuse its discretion in refusing to reopen where respondent persistently used fraudulent documents, had a checkered previous marital history that indicated fraud, and lacked credibility]; *Krazoun v. Ashcroft,* 350 F.3d 208 (1st Cir. 2003) [where respondent had 2 previous marriages that BIA deemed fraudulent, it was within discretion to deny reopening]. However, it may not refuse consideration of an adjustment application for lack of evidence where the I-130 petition has been approved. *Patel v. Ashcroft,* 375 F.3d 693 (8th Cir. 2004) [BIA abused its discretion in denying a remand for an AOS application based upon a marriage and requiring the production of additional evidence of a *bona fide* marriage, where the beneficiary in proceedings submitted an approved petition].

(a) Administrative proceedings begin with the issuance of an I-122 or the issuance of the OSC if before June 20, 1991, or the filing of the OSC with the IJ if after June 20, 1991, or the filing with the IJ of the NTA if after Apr. 1, 1997. 8 C.F.R. §§ 245.1(c)(8)(i) 1003.14(a), 1245.1(c)(8)(i); *Matter of Casillas,* 22 I&N Dec. 154 (BIA 1998). A person who only has a detainer placed on him is not in proceeding. INS Response to AILA Questions Regarding IMFA, 67 No. 11 *Interpreter Releases* 314, 345 (Feb. 26, 1990).

(b) Administrative proceedings are "pending" until order of deportation or voluntary departure is carried out and person physically departs U.S. or if proceedings are cancelled or respondent prevails. 8 C.F.R. §204.2(a)(1)(iii); *Blackwell v. Thornburgh,* 745 F.Supp. 1529, 1533–37 (C.D. Cal. 1989); *Minatsis v. Brown,* 713 F.Supp. 1056 (S.D. Ohio 1989); *Matter of Enriquez,* 19 I&N Dec. 554 (BIA 1988). Under INS view, a case is also deemed pending even if it is administratively closed. Legal Opinion, Cook, General Counsel, CO 204.21-P (Oct. 17, 1990), *reprinted in* 68 No. 3 *Interpreter Releases* 83, 89 (Jan. 18, 1991).

(2) Must remain outside U.S. for 2 years before residency visa granted. INA §204(g), 8 U.S.C. §1154(g), unless petitioner establishes by clear and convincing evidence that the marriage was entered into in good faith, INA §245(e)(3)

(a) Two years need not be continuous, as long as aggregate is 2 years. 53 Fed. Reg. 30011 at 30012–13 [comments on Final Regulation].

(b) If person marries while in removal proceedings the 2-year ban not applicable if they get voluntary departure, get divorced, remarry outside U.S. and then submit petition. Memo, Puleo, Asst. Comm., Adjudications (July 13, 1988), 1988 *AILA Monthly Mailing* 541. However, INS general counsel said IMFA §5 would apply if it was a sham divorce. Memo, G.C., CO 204.21C (Jan. 31, 1989), *reprinted in* 66 No. 22 *Interpreter Releases* 627, 637–41 (June 6, 1989). The Service takes the same view where marriage is annulled in contemplation of remarriage outside U.S. Memo, General Counsel Office, 204.21-P (Nov. 10, 1989), *reprinted in* 66 No. 48 *Interpreter Releases* 1413, 1424–27 (Dec. 18, 1989).

(3) Due process and equal protection challenges to pre-1990 Immigration Act permitting 2-year ban. *Azizi v. Thornburgh*, 908 F.2d 1130 (2d Cir. 1990) [rejected procedural due process challenge finding IMFA §5 a substantive, not procedural, rule]; *Anetekhai v. INS*, 876 F.2d 1218 (5th Cir. 1989) [rejected due process, equal protection, and 9th and Tenth Amendment arguments as interference with divorce laws]; *Almario v. INS*, 872 F.2d 147 (6th Cir. 1989); *Gomez-Arauz v. McNary*, 746 F.Supp. 1071 (W.D. Okl. 1990); *Blackwell v. Thornburgh*, 745 F.Supp. 1529, 1537–39 (C.D. Cal. 1989); *Minatsis v. Brown*, 713 F.Supp. 1056 (S.D. Ohio 1989); *Smith v. INS*, 684 F.Supp. 1113 (D. Mass. 1988); *But see Manwani v. DOJ*, 736 F.Supp. 1367 (W.D.N.C. 1990).

1.e. Petition for subsequent marriage

(1) No 2d preference spouse petition can be approved for 5 years from the date petitioner obtained permanent residence if that LPR obtained his or her status through marriage. INA §204(a)(2)(A)(i), 8 U.S.C. §1154(a)(2)(A)(i); 8 C.F.R. §204.2(a)(1)(i)(A).

(2) Exception if LPR can establish by "clear and convincing evidence" that prior marriage not entered into for purpose of evading immigration law or terminated by death of spouse. 8 C.F.R. §204.2(a)(1)(i)(A); *Matter of Patel*, 19 I&N Dec. 774 (BIA 1988) [BIA applied statute retroactively, relying on standard in *Bradley v. School Bd. of City of Richmond*, 416 U.S. 696 (1974)]. If 5 years have elapsed USCIS cannot use this test to deny new petition. *Matter of Pazandeh*, 19 I&N Dec. 884 (BIA 1989) [approval of 2d preference petition appropriate even if 5 years had not elapsed, when petition was filed but had elapsed while on appeal]. If USCIS believes there was fraud in first marriage, then its remedy is to take action other than applying the clear and convincing standard where 5 years have elapsed. *Id.* Documentation needed to prove clear and convincing standard found at 8 C.F.R. §204.2(a)(1)(i)(C).

1.f. Naturalization and other benefits

(1) Period of conditional residence counts toward naturalization. A CR may even file for naturalization, if s/he qualifies, while her I-751 (to remove conditional residency) is pending. Letter, Novak, Director, VSC (Dec. 18, 2001), *reprinted in* 79 No. 3 *Interpreter Releases* 66, 89–90 (Jan. 14, 2002). INA §216(e), 8 U.S.C. §1186a(e); 8 C.F.R. §§216.1, 1216.1.

(2) Conditional resident has same benefits and responsibilities accorded all other residents (*e.g.*, employment authorization, petition for children). 8 C.F.R. §216.1.

2. *The validity of the marriage*—AFM at 21.3 (revised Mar. 20, 2003*), published on* AILA InfoNet at Doc. No. 03072915.

2.a. If the marriage was valid at inception, it is valid for immigration purposes even if partners are separated and the marriage is no longer viable. *Matter of Boromand,* 17 I&N Dec. 450, 454 (BIA 1980) ["in the absence of evidence to support a finding of a fraudulent or sham marriage or evidence showing the legal dissolution of the marriage at the time of the adjustment, the denial of an adjustment of status application or the subsequent rescission of such grant cannot be based solely on the nonviability of the marriage at the time of the adjustment application."]; *Matter of McKee,* 17 I&N Dec. 332 (BIA 1980) [visa petition could not be denied solely because the parties to the marriage were no longer living together]; *Hernandez v. Ashcroft,* 345 F.3d 824, 845–49 (9th Cir. 2003) [the nonviability of a marriage cannot alone be the basis to deny adjustment even if immigration characterizes its decision to deny adjustment as discretionary]; *Dabaghian v. Civiletti*, 607 F.2d 868 (9th Cir. 1979) [visa petition could not be denied solely because people not living together]. If marriage was entered into in good faith, a petition remains approvable even if the parties are no longer in love with one another. *Agyeman v. INS,* 296 F.3d 871, 883 (9th Cir. 2002) [where IJ told respondent that he was ineligible to adjust if his wife was no longer in love, court of appeals reversed]. The key is whether the parties intended "to establish a life together at the time of their marriage." *Bark v. INS,* 511 F.2d 1200, 1202 (9th Cir. 1975). *Accord Damon v. Ashcroft,* 360 F.3d 1084 (9th Cir. 2004) [reversing denial of removal of conditional residence for lack of substantial evidence, where IJ erred by imposing her own views about a "real" marriage. It was impermissible to make a finding of marriage invalidity on the basis that the wife rushed into the marriage, did not share a common language or culture with husband, did not take his last name, and had a nonreligious wedding]. One court recognized that "marriages for green cards [may be] genuine. An intent to obtain something other than or in addition to love and companionship from that life does not make a marriage a sham. Rather, the sham arises from the intent not 'to establish a life together." *U.S. v. Orellana-Blanco,* 294 F.3d 1143, 1151 (9th Cir. 2002).

2.b. Law of place of marriage governs

(1) The relevant analysis involves determining first whether the marriage is valid under a state's or a country's law, and then whether the marriage qualifies under the INA. *Matter of Lovo*, 23 I&N Dec. 746, 748 (BIA 2005) [marriage of postoperative transsexual that is valid under North Carolina law is valid for immigration purposes, because the Defense of Marriage Act, PL 104-199, 110 Stat. 2419 (1996), does not preclude a marriage involving a postoperative transsexual]. But note USCIS position regarding transsexuals in Memo, Yates, Assoc. Dir. Of Operations, USCIS, HQOPRD 70/6 (Apr. 16, 2004), *published on* AILA InfoNet at Doc. No. 04080367. [USCIS does not recognize transsexual marriage for any purpose].

(2) Marriages that are merely voidable, but not void, will be recognized for USCIS purpose. *Matter of G.*, 9 I&N Dec. 89 (BIA 1960) [marriage between minors].

(3) Common law marriage. Where state recognizes common law marriage, the marriage would be valid for immigration purposes. *U.S. v. Gomez-Orozco,* 28 F.Supp.2d 1092, 1095–98 (C.D. Ill. 1998), *rev'd on other grounds,* 188 F.3d 422 (7th Cir. 1999). *But see Ma v. Ashcroft,* 361 F.3d 553 (9th Cir. 2004) [where China, due to its population-control policies, would not legally register a traditional marriage because husband was under 22, he was nevertheless considered a husband under asylum law].

(4) Religious Marriage. A religious marriage is considered a valid marriage for immigration purposes if it is recognized by the sovereign in that country or state as a valid marriage. *Matter of Ceballos,* 16 I&N Dec. 765 (BIA 1979) [religious marriage in Colombia has the same validity as a civil marriage]; *Matter of Alvarez-Quintana,* 14 I&N Dec. 255 (BIA 1973) [religious marriage is not valid under Mexican law because civil authorities have exclusive jurisdiction]; *Matter of Coletti,* 11 I&N Dec. 551 (BIA 1965) [under Italian law a religious marriage to be effective must be recorded, but once recorded it is retroactive to date of religious ceremony]

2.c. Marriage cannot be contrary to public policy. *Matter of H.*, 9 I&N Dec. 640 (BIA 1962) [polygamy though valid under foreign law is against U.S. public policy and will not be recognized]. Public policy issue is also dependent on state laws, *e.g.,* if uncle-niece marriage is permitted under state law, it is recognized for immigration purposes. *Matter of E.*, 4 I&N Dec. 239 (BIA 1951).

2.d. For marriage to be valid, prior divorce must be valid. *Chan v. Bell*, 464 F.Supp. 125 (D.D.C. 1978). The divorce must be valid under the laws of the jurisdiction granting the divorce.

Matter of Hann, 18 I&N Dec. 196 (BIA 1982); *Matter of Darwish,* 14 I&N Dec. 307 (BIA 1973); *Matter of Miraldo,* 14 I&N Dec. 704 (BIA 1974) and if so would be recognized unless it would violate our public policy to recognize the divorce. *Jahed v. Acri,* 468 F.3d 230 (4th Cir. 2006) [where parents were both physically present in Pakistan for the divorce and both consented, the divorce was not valid for immigration purposes under *Matter of Ma* because they were never citizens of Pakistan and were never domiciled there]; *Matter of Luna,* 18 I&N Dec. 385, 386 (BIA 1983) [accepting Dominican Republic divorce pronouncement that was not irregular on its face]; *Matter of Ma,* 15 I&N Dec. 70, 71 (BIA 1974) [establishing a test for validity of a foreign divorce, and finding that although the divorce was valid in Korea even if both parties were not domiciled there, it was invalid under U.S. law].

(1) The validity of the remarriage, however, will be determined by reference to the place of remarriage. *Matter of P-,* 4 I&N Dec. 610, 614 (A.G. 1952); Legal Opinion, Martin, General Counsel, 97-9 (June 25, 1997), *reprinted in* 75 *Interpreter Releases* 596 (Apr. 27, 1998). Thus, depending on state law, a second marriage, where divorce is not final, may only be voidable not void. *Matter of Arenas*, 15 I&N Dec. 174 (BIA 1975).

(2) If divorce is initiated in the U.S., whether an undocumented alien can get a divorce is a matter of state law. *Nicolas v. Nicolas*, 444 So.2d 1118 (Fla. 3d DCA 1984); *Das v. Das*, 603 A.2d 139 (N.J. Super. 1992). If it is a foreign divorce, it must be recognized under state law. *Matter of Hosseinian*, 19 I&N Dec. 453 (BIA 1987).

(3) The prior divorce must be final, and not simply a separation. *Matter of Miraldo*, 14 I&N Dec. 704 (BIA 1974).

(4) In the absence of fraud or misrepresentation, a decree obtained *ab initio* to annul first marriage is legal and will relate back to cure defects of petition. *Matter of Astorga*, 17 I&N Dec. 1, 4 (BIA 1979). *But see Garcia v. INS*, 31 F.3d 441 (7th Cir. 1994) (and cases cited therein).

(5) Tribal Divorce—Proof of customary divorce includes: (1) the tribe to which person belongs; (2) the current customary divorce law of that tribe; (3) the fact that the pertinent ceremonial procedures were followed; (4) evidence of the customary procedure derived from reported cases, legal treaties, and commentaries, and depositions of legal scholars; (5) advisory opinions as to the procedure from organizations traditionally recognized by the government as possessing knowledge of customary law; and (6) evidence that the divorce was properly perfected, including affidavits that include the full names and birth dates of the parties, the date of the customary marriage, the date of, and grounds for, the dissolution of the marriage, the names, birth dates of and custody agreement for any children born of the marriage, and a description of tribal formalities that were observed, including the names of the tribal leaders, the name of the tribe, the place, the type of divorce, and any other relevant information. *Matter of Kodwo,* 24 I&N Dec. 479 (BIA 2008) [reversed USCIS denial of customary divorce because under current Ghanian law affidavits may be sufficient to establish a divorce for immigration purposes]. *Cf. Iyamba v. INS,* 244 F.3d 606 (8th Cir. 2001) [rejected customary divorce, where beneficiary failed to demonstrate by substantial evidence that all ceremonial procedures were followed]

(6) Religious Divorce—*Matter of M*, 7 I&N Dec. 556 (BIA 1957) [divorce under Jordanian-Moslem law by resident of Connecticut not recognized], *quoting Matter of H*, 6 I&N Dec. 470 (BIA 1954) ["a Jewish rabbinical divorce obtained in [NY] has been held invalid … Similarly, a church divorce of the Mormon church was not regarded as valid when it was not secured through judicial proceedings and failed to conform with the statutory requirements for divorce in the State of Utah"].

2.e. Proxy Marriages—If parties not in each other's presence at marriage ceremony there must be proof of consummation. INA §101(a)(35), 8 U.S.C. §1101(a)(35); *Matter of B-,* 5 I&N Dec. 698, 699 (BIA 1954) [person is not spouse under INA unless proxy marriage was consummated]; *Moussa v. INS,* 302 F.3d 823, 826–27 (8th Cir. 2002) [in derivative naturalization case parents who were remarried by proxy but had not consummated their remarriage were not in a marital relationship that would have barred naturalization to their child].

2.f. Proof Necessary to Establish *Bona Fide* Marriage—*Matter of Laureano*, 19 I&N Dec. 1 (BIA 1983) [look to evidence including "proof that the beneficiary has been listed as the petitioner's spouse on insurance policies, property leases, income tax forms, or bank accounts, and testimony or other evidence regarding courtship wedding ceremony, shared residence, and experiences"]; *See also Matter of Phillis,* 15 I&N Dec. 385 (BIA 1975).

3. *Presumption of Validity of Marriage*—If a marriage petition is approved, it would be an abuse of discretion for the BIA to request additional evidence beyond the approval. *Patel v. Ashcroft,* 375 F.3d 693 (8th Cir. 2004) [BIA abused its discretion in denying a remand for an AOS application based upon a marriage and requiring the production of additional evidence of a *bona fide* marriage where the beneficiary in proceedings submitted an approved petition]; 8 C.F.R. §§245.1(c)(8)(v), 1245.1(c)(8)(v).

4. *Presumption of Fraud*—INA §237(a)(1)(G)(i), 8 U.S.C. §1227(a)(1)(G)(i) [INA §241(c) eliminated by IMMACT90]

4.a. Marriage presumed to be fraudulent and alien subject to deportation under this section if: married within 2 years prior to obtaining LPR and marriage judicially annulled or terminated within 2 years subsequent to LPR entry. This rule has a *de minimis* effect in light of conditional residency under INA §216.

4.b. Burden on alien to rebut presumption after USCIS establishes that marriage took place less than 2 years prior to entry and was terminated less than 2 afterwards. *Rodriguez v. INS,* 204 F.3d 25 (1st Cir. 2000) [state-court judgment ending marriage that was specifically based upon a finding of fraudulent intent to evade the immigration laws was a "presumption plus" that was not sufficiently rebutted]. *Matter of Neto-Domingos*, 15 I&N Dec. 310 (BIA 1975); *Vasquez-Mondragon v. INS*, 560 F.2d 1225 (5th Cir. 1977). Burden may be easily rebutted. *See Matter of Boromand*, 17 I&N Dec. 450 (BIA 1980).

5. *Sham Marriage*—INA §237(a)(1)(G)(ii); 8 U.S.C. §1227(a)(1)(G)(ii)

5.a. Removal also under INA §212(a)(6)(C) and INA §§237(a)(1) and (2):

(1) If USCIS is satisfied that the alien has failed or refused to fulfill marital agreement, which marriage was made to procure LPR status (*e.g.*, gigolo marriage; unwary USC).

(2) If alien refuses to consummate marriage, §212(a)(6)(C) applies. But if USC fails to fulfill marriage, §212(a)(6)(C) may not apply. *Matter of M*, 7 I&N Dec. 601 (BIA 1957).

5.b. Test for fraudulent-at-inception:

(1) Did bride and groom intend to establish life together? *Lutwak v. U.S.*, 344 U.S. 604 (1954); *Agyeman v. INS,* 296 F.3d 871, 883 (9th Cir. 2002); *Bark v. INS*, 511 F.2d 1200 (9th Cir. 1975); *Matter of McKee*, 17 I&N Dec. 332 (BIA 1980); *Matter of Laureano*, 19 I&N Dec. 1 (BIA 1983).

(2) Look to subjective state of mind. Objective facts only to shed light on state of mind.

(a) Conduct of parties before and after marriage relevant. Petitioner must present evidence that may include insurance policies, property, leases, income tax, bank accounts. *Matter of Soriano*, 19 I&N Dec. 764 (BIA 1988).

(b) Government investigation must be reasonable. *Stokes v. INS*, 393 F.Supp. 24 (S.D.N.Y. 1975); *Ali v. INS*, 661 F.Supp. 1234 (D. Mass. 1986).

(c) Inconsistency in statements made by couple may be the basis for denial. *Nikrodhanondha v. Reno,* 202 F.3d 922 (7th Cir. 2000) [although couple had 2 children, court upheld BIA denial where couple gave different years for when they first met, different reasons for the initial breakup, and different periods of time when wife in Thailand for wedding, coupled with false information as to when they were living together].

(d) Recantation of affidavit may not overcome fraud finding. *Rodriguez Del Carmen v. Gonzales,* 441 F.3d 41(1st Cir. 2006) [where spouse recanted affidavit stating marriage was fraudulent and mother testified that she was coerced into signing affidavit, IJ's decision that it was a fraudulent marriage, nevertheless, was upheld].

(3) BIA will not uphold denial of marriage petition by DD where specific basis for denial and evidence underlying denial are absent. *Matter of Pradieu*, 19 I&N Dec. 419 (BIA 1986).

(4) Cohabitation and consummation not absolute prerequisites:

(a) Elderly couple separate bedrooms. *Matter of Peterson*, 12 I&N Dec. 663 (BIA 1968).

(b) Same-sex spouse not recognized. *Adams v. Howerton*, 673 F.2d 1036 (9th Cir. 1982); *See also* Defense of Marriage Act, PL 104-199, 110 Stat. 2419 (1996) at §7 defining marriage as a union between one man and one woman, and spouse as referring only to a person of the opposite sex; Memo, Yates, Assoc. Dir. Of Operations, USCIS, HQOPRD 70/6 ¶III (Apr. 16, 2004), *published on* AILA InfoNet at Doc. No. 04080367 [USCIS agrees "that no legal authority permits recognition of homosexual relationships as 'marriages' for purposes of immigration and nationality laws, regardless of whether the relationship may be recognized as a 'marriage' under the law where the relationship came into existence"]

(c) Postoperative Transsexual Marriage is Recognized. *Matter of Lovo*, 23 I&N Dec. 746, 748 (BIA 2005) [marriage of postoperative transsexual that is valid under North Carolina law is valid for immigration purposes, because the Defense of Marriage Act, PL 104-199, 110 Stat. 2419 (1996) does not preclude a marriage involving a postoperative transsexual]. *But see,* USCIS does not recognize validity of transsexual marriages for any purpose. Memo, Yates, Assoc. Dir. Of Operations, USCIS, HQOPRD 70/6 (Apr. 16, 2004) ¶2, *published on* AILA InfoNet at Doc. No. 04080367.

(5) Where prior withdrawal of application, to obtain approval and to overcome previous withdrawal:

(a) Need explanation for withdrawal.

(b) Evidence supporting *bona fides* of marriage. *Matter of Laureano*, 19 I&N Dec. 1 (BIA 1983) [look to evidence including "proof that the beneficiary has been listed as the petitioner's spouse on insurance policies, property leases, income tax forms, or bank accounts, and testimony or other evidence regarding courtship wedding ceremony, shared residence, and experiences"]

(6) Judicial Review. *Nakamoto v. Ashcroft,* 363 F.3d 874, 878–81 (9th Cir. 2004) [court's jurisdiction was not precluded by INA §242(a)(2)(B)(ii) to review AG's decision to deport for marriage fraud under INA §237(a)(1)(G)(ii), but there was substantial evidence to support AG's decision where marriage was annulled on fraud grounds].

6. *Relief from Fraudulent Marriages*—INA §237(a)(1)(H), 8 U.S.C. §1227(a)(1)(H)

If misrepresentation/fraud made in procuring visa/entry and beneficiary is spouse, parent, son or daughter of USC or LPR, USCIS, in its discretion, can waive it if the person was in possession of an immigrant visa or equivalent document and was otherwise admissible to the U.S. except for §§212(a)(5)(A) & (a)(7)(A). A VAWA self-petitioner is also covered. But cannot use fraudulent marriage to form necessary family relationship to obtain relief. *Matter of Matti*, 19 I&N Dec. 43 (BIA 1984) [cannot use fraudulent marriage to obtain waiver]. The section is inapplicable to persons who are removable as Nazis under INA §237(a)(4)(D). Waiver may not be reviewable in federal court. *Singh v. Gonzales,* 451 F.3d 400, 410–11 [no jurisdiction to review the discretionary aspects of the denial of an INA §237(a)(1)(H) waiver]; *San Pedro v. Ashcroft,* 395 F.3d 1156 (9th Cir. 2005) [same].

7. INA §204(c), 8 U.S.C. §1154(c)

7.a. Bar to approval of subsequent immigrant visa petition (immediate or preference) where:

(1) Alien previously granted a non quota or preference status as spouse of USC/LPR *Matter of La Grotta*, 14 I&N Dec. 110 (BIA 1972); *Matter of Calilao*, 16 I&N Dec. 104 (BIA 1977), or attempted to obtain LPR status, and

(2) USCIS determined that marriage was entered into to evade immigration laws.

(a) INA §204(c) now punishes an applicant for attempt or conspiracy to enter into a marriage for the purpose of evading the immigration laws. DHS need only show that beneficiary attempted or conspired to enter into a fraudulent marriage. INA §204(c)(2). Thus, prior decisions such as *Matter of Anselmo*, 16 I&N Dec. 152 (BIA 1977) and *Matter of Concepcion*, 16 I&N Dec. 10 (BIA 1976) that denied the applicability of INA §204(c) because there was no first marriage in fact, or *Matter of Rubino*, 15 I&N Dec. 194 (BIA 1975) that denied INA §204(c) applicability because the adjustment of status had not been completed, may have little applicability because the attempt itself is sufficient to invoke INA §204(c).

(b) Evidentiary basis for INA §204(c). Conviction or prosecution unnecessary if evidence of fraudulent marriage or attempt documented in alien's file. 8 C.F.R. §204.2(a)(1)(ii). *Salas-Velazquez v. INS*, 34 F.3d 705, 708 (8th Cir. 1995) [statute includes attempt]; *Syed v. Ashcroft,* 389 F.3d 248 (1st Cir. 2004) [court upheld INA §204(c) finding where documents submitted were fraudulent, where respondent's testimony was inconsistent and not credible and where photographs with first wife appeared to be staged]. However, DD ordinarily should not give conclusive effect to determination made in a prior administrative proceeding but rather should reach his own independent conclusion based on the evidence before him. *Matter of Tawfik*, 20 I&N Dec. 166 (BIA 1990); *Matter of Samsen*, 15 I&N Dec. 28 (BIA 1974). Such evidence must be substantial and probative. *Tawfik*, *supra*; *Matter of Kahy*, 19 I&N Dec. 803 (BIA 1988); *Matter of Rahmati*, 16 I&N Dec. 538 (BIA 1978). At least one court applied the arbitrary and capricious standard to review a revocation of an approved petition based on INA §204(c). *Oddo v. Reno,* 17 F.Supp.2d 529 (E.D. Va. 1998).

(3) Where evidence in record that beneficiary was active participant in fraudulent marriage, burden shifts to second petitioner to establish that beneficiary did not seek to obtain status based on prior fraudulent marriage. *Matter of Kahy*, 19 I&N Dec. 803 (BIA 1988); *Ghaly v. INS*, 58 F.3d 1425 (9th Cir. 1995).

7.b. INA §204(c) is inapplicable to second marital visa petition filed by the same spouse on behalf of the same original beneficiary. *Matter of Isber*, 20 I&N Dec. 676 (BIA 1993).

7.c. An applicant who commits marriage fraud and is placed in removal proceedings because he was inadmissible as an LPR due to the fraudulent marriage may obtain a INA §237(a)(1)(H) waiver, notwithstanding INA §204(c), if he is otherwise admissible. *Virk v. INS,* 295 F.3d 1055 (9th Cir. 2002); *Matter of Manchisi,* 12 I&N Dec. 132 (BIA 1967) *overruled in Matter of Diniz,* 15 I&N Dec. 447 (1975) *but reinstated in Matter of Da Lomba,* 16 I&N Dec. 616 (BIA 1978).

7.d. The bar applies to all petitions filed after Nov. 10, 1986, but may be based on fraud occurring before that date. *Ramilo v. DOJ,* 13 F.Supp.2d 1055, 1058 (D. Hawaii 1998). Includes employment-based petition as well as family-based ones. *Oddo v. Reno,* 17 F.Supp.2d 529 (E.D. Va. 1998) [upheld revocation of I-140 petition].

7.e. Government cooperation does not mitigate bar. *Matter of ____,* (AAO Apr. 23, 2004) [beneficiary's cooperation with the Service to go after the corrupt attorney who promoted the fraudulent marriage did not mitigate bar to approval of subsequent employment-based petition], *reported in* 81 No. 43 *Interpreter Releases* 1573, 1582–83 (Nov. 8, 2004).

7.f. INA §204(c) has withstood a constitutional challenge based upon substantive and procedural due process, *Bangura v. Hansen,* 434 F.3d 487, 494–96 (6th Cir. 2006) and cruel and unusual punishment. *Barmo v. Reno*, 899 F.Supp. 1375, 1380–85 (E.D. Pa. 1995).

7.g. INA §212(a)(6)(C)(i) in lieu of INA §204(c)—Court upheld BIA's denial of employment-based AOS where it found that respondent's previous marriage constituted a fraudulent scheme to obtain an immigration benefit under INA §212(a)(6)(C)(i) without addressing INA §204(c). *Coelho v Gonzales,* 452 F.3d 104 (1st Cir. 2006)

7.h. Judicial Review—*Ikenokwalu-White v. Gonzales,* 495 F.3d 919, 924–26 (8th Cir. 2007) [review of revocation of I-130 despite it potentially affecting mother's removal was not part of a removal order and the case had to be pursued in the district, not circuit, court]; *But see Cedeno v. Ridge,* 336 F.Supp.2d 147, 150–52 (D.P.R. 2004) [jurisdiction over adjustment to review INA §204(c) determination because it is nondiscretionary, but review is in circuit court not district court]. *See also Bangura v. Hansen,* 434 F.3d 487 (6th Cir. 2006) [permitting district court review of constitutional, APA and INA challenges to INA §204(c) procedure and denial of I-130 petition]; *Hanif v. DHS,* 472 F.Supp.2d 914, 920–22 (E.D. Mich. 2007) [court has jurisdiction to review denial of I-130 petition under the APA but there is no final agency action by the BIA so the petition must be dismissed]. *But see Ginters v. Cangemi,* 419 F.Supp.2d 1124, 1128–31 (D. Mass. 2006) [no habeas jurisdiction to review denial of I-130 because the requirement under 8 C.F.R. §204.2(a)(1)(ii) regarding the USCIS director's determination of whether there is "substantial and probative evidence" of immigration fraud in previous marriage is a discretionary decision].

8. *Potential criminal violations*

8.a. Visa fraud. 18 U.S.C. §1546. *U.S. v. Al-Kurna*, 808 F.2d 1072 (5th Cir. 1987) [false statement on I-485 or I-130 regarding residence of parties is material]. *But see U.S. v. Qaisi*, 779 F.2d 346 (6th Cir. 1985). There is some confusion among the circuit courts as to the significance of a marriage that is valid under state law even if it was entered into for a fraudulent purpose. *Compare U.S. v. Elzahabi,* 517 F.Supp.2d 1121 (D. Minn. 2007) [the formal validity of a marriage is not a defense to knowingly procuring a "green card" by means of any false claim or statement or otherwise procuring it by fraud] *with U.S. v. Diogo,* 320 F.2d 898 (2d Cir. 1963) [the technical validity of the marriage was a defense to both a charge under 18 U.S.C. §1546 and §1001].

8.b. False statement. 18 U.S.C. §1001; *U.S. v. Zalman*, 870 F.2d 1047, 1055 (6th Cir. 1989).

8.c. Conspiracy. 18 U.S.C. §371.

8.d. Marriage fraud—INA §275(c); 8 U.S.C. §1325(c). Imprisonment for up to 5 years and $250,000 fine. To convict a person under this statute the government generally must prove: (1) the person knowingly entered into a marriage; (2) the marriage was entered into for the purpose of evading a provision of the immigration laws; and (3) the person knew or had reason to know of the immigration laws. *U.S. v. Islam,* 418 F.3d 1125, 1128 (10th Cir. 2005) [upheld conviction on grounds a reasonable jury could have found that marriage was entered into to evade immigration laws and that defendant knew he was violating the immigration laws]; *U.S. v. Vickerage*, 921 F.2d 143 (8th Cir. 1990) [upheld conviction where parties knew each other, had sex before and after marriage, but marriage was one of convenience]. *But see U.S. v. Orellana-Blanco,* 294 F.3d 1143, 1148–52 (9th Cir. 2002) [reversed conviction because admission of defendant's statement to INS was improper and the effect was prejudicial; in regard to conflicting evidence between husband and wife the court found that: "An intent to obtain something other than or in addition to love and companionship from that life does not make a marriage a sham"]. However, it does not require that the government prove that the defendant knew of the specific immigration statute violated. *U.S. v. Chowdhury,* 169 F.3d 402, 406–07 (6th Cir. 1999) [relying on S.Ct. decision on willful conduct in *Bryan v. U.S.* 524 U.S. 184, 118 S.Ct. 1939 (1998)]. Can also be charged with conspiracy to defraud the government by aiding and abetting others to enter into fraudulent marriages. *U.S. v. Anwar,* 428 F.3d 1102 (8th Cir. 2005) [defendant solicited female acquaintances to marry Pakistani men to allow the men to evade immigration laws].

9. *Civil Action*

9.a. Mail-order bride brought suit in federal court against marriage bureau, operator, and former husband for fraud, negligence, and other causes of action as a result of husband's abuse. *Fox v. Encounters International,* 318 F.Supp.2d 279 (D. Md. 2002).

10. *Viability of marriage*

10.a. If no legal separation or dissolution at time of petition, USCIS cannot deny petition because parties not living together or solely because marriage is not viable. *Matter of McKee*, 17 I&N Dec. 332 (BIA 1980); *Matter of Pierce*, 17 I&N Dec. 456 (BIA 1980); *Matter of Mowrer,*

17 I&N Dec. 613 (BIA 1981); *Hernandez v. Ashcroft,* 345 F.3d 824, 845–49 (9th Cir. 2003) [the nonviability of a marriage cannot alone be the basis to deny AOS even if government characterizes its decision to deny adjustment as discretionary]; *Chan v. Bell*, 464 F.Supp. 125 (D.D.C. 1978); *Dabaghian v. Civiletti*, 607 F.2d 868 (9th Cir. 1979); *U.S. v. Qaisi*, 779 F.2d 346 (6th Cir. 1985).

10.b. Non–legal separation only relevant for determining whether marriage was fraudulent at inception. *Matter of McKee*, 17 I&N Dec. 332 (BIA 1980).

10.c. Subsequent conduct after marriage, no matter how unconventional, does not prove lack of marital intent. *Bark v. INS*, 511 F.2d 1200 (9th Cir. 1975).

10.d. Death of spouse does not automatically result in termination of USCIS petition if USCIS finds that for humanitarian reasons revocation would be improper. 8 C.F.R. §205.1(a)(3)(i)(C)(2), 1205.1(a)(3)(i)(C)(2). DOS criteria in evaluating a request for humanitarian reinstatement include whether there is: (1) disruption of an established family unit; (2) hardship to USCs or LPRs; (3) a beneficiary who is elderly or in poor health; (4) a beneficiary who has had lengthy residence in the U.S.; (5) a beneficiary who has no home to go to; (6) undue delay by INS or consular officers in processing the petition and the visa; and (7) a beneficiary who has strong family ties in the U.S. 9 FAM 42.42 PN2. However, even if the petition is not revoked, the person may not be able to obtain his or her residency because s/he cannot meet the affidavit of support requirement because the petitioner (now deceased) is the only person who can file the affidavit of support. Letter, Cook, Acting Asst. Comm. Adjudications, (HQ 70/9) (Nov. 8, 1999), *reprinted in* 76 No. 46 *Interpreter Releases* 1722, 1742–43 (Dec. 3, 1999). Congress created an exception to address this problem in the Family Sponsor Immigration Act of 2002, PL 107-150 (Mar. 13, 2002). This Act permits the substitution of certain relatives to meet the affidavit of support requirements under INA §213A(f)(5), when the petitioning relative has died and the AG, on humanitarian grounds, decides to reinstate the I-130 petition that has been automatically revoked upon petitioner's death. Under the Act, a spouse, parent, mother-in-law, father-in-law, sibling, child (if at least 18 years of age), son, daughter, son-in-law, daughter-in-law, sister-in-law, brother-in-law, grandparent, grandchild, or legal guardian of the beneficiary qualify to substitute for the deceased petitioner. The beneficiary of the I-130 must ask the AG to reinstate the petition *and* must demonstrate that s/he has a substitute sponsor under the Act. If a beneficiary does not have another qualifying relative, s/he may seek to make an estoppel argument. *Pierno v. INS*, 397 F.2d 949 (2d Cir. 1968). *But see INS v. Miranda*, 459 U.S. 14 (1982) [18-month delay not basis for estoppel].

The death of a spouse also does not automatically revoke the I-130 petition where a widow or widower qualifies for an I-360 self-petition. If the widow(er) qualifies because s/he was married to the petitioner for 2 years at the time of his death and has not remarried, the I-130 petition is adjudicated as an I-360. 8 C.F.R. §§204.2(i)(1)(iv), 205.1(a)(3)(i)(C)(1), 1205.1(a)(3)(i)(C)(1). In addition, one circuit has now determined that INA §204(b)(2)(A)(i) cannot be read to bar a widow married less than 2 years, who has already applied for AOS at the time of her spouse's death, from receiving her residency. *Freeman v. Gonzales,* 444 F.3d 1031, 1037–43 (9th Cir. 2006). For a more detailed discussion, *see in this part* ¶ B.4 (p.775), *supra.*

10.e. Battered Spouse—A spouse/child who is battered or subject to extreme cruelty may file a petition independently of USC/LPR spouse or parent. INA §§204(a)(1)(A)(iii)–(iv) & (B)(ii)–(iii); 8 C.F.R. §204.2(c), (e). For a detailed discussion, *see in this part* ¶ B.5, (p.775), *supra.*

11. *Marriage Abroad*

11.a. Petition Can be Filed at Consulate if Petitioner's Residence is Abroad—*See in this chapter* "Venue for Petition," section XI.I (p.827), *infra.*

11.b. NIV Only from Country of Marriage—INA §214(r)(2) (pertaining to K-3 visas) and Section 1103(b) of the LIFE Act, PL 106-553, 114 Stat. 2762 (Dec. 21, 2000) provide that the spouse of a USC who marries the USC abroad is inadmissible into the U.S. with an NIV unless the NIV was issued by a consular officer in the foreign state in which she was married.

12. *Sham Divorces. Matter of Aldecoaotalora*, 18 I&N Dec. 430 (BIA 1983) [BIA will not recognize sham divorce to obtain an immigration benefit, *e.g.*, family 2d preference].

13. *Marriage in Detention*—ICE has published a Detention Operations Manual, available at *www.ice.gov/partners/dro/opsmanual*, which provides detailed standards to be applied in all ICE and contractor detention facilities. Included in the manual is a section on Marriage Requests. The request to be married in the detention facility "will be granted" unless: (1) Detainee is not legally eligible to be married; (2) Detainee is not mentally competent; (3) The intended spouse has not affirmed in writing, his or her intent to marry; (4) The marriage would present a threat to the security or orderly operation of the facility; (5) Compelling government interests exist for denying the request, *e.g.,* if there is a final order and performance of the marriage ceremony would require postponement of the detainee's physical removal from the U.S. or if the detainee is an arriving alien having limited constitutional rights. However, compelling interests cannot include administrative inconvenience, or because a detainee may pursue relief from removal. The request must be in writing and must be accompanied by a writing from the intended spouse containing an affirmation of intention to marry. Notwithstanding ICE limitations, a detainee has a constitutional right to marry. *Turner v. Safley,* 482 U.S. 78 (1987); *Theck v. Warden, INS,* 22 F.Supp.2d 1117 (C.D. Cal. 1998). *But see Williams v. Wisconsin,* 336 F.3d 576 (7th Cir. 2003) [upholding Wisconsin's right to prevent person on probation from leaving country to marry a person abroad].

III. NUMERICAL LIMITATION (PREFERENCE) IMMIGRANT

A. *Maximum Divided into Categories*—The maximum number of visas issued per fiscal year (Oct. 1 to Sept. 31) is divided into family-sponsored immigration, employment-based immigration, and diversity immigration. For numerical statistics, *see* Policy Directorate, DHS Office of Immigration Statistics, Annual Flow Report (March 2008), *published on* AILA InfoNet at Doc. No. 08042362.

1. *Family-Sponsored*

   1.a. 480,000 visas less immediate relatives plus unused employment-based visas.

   1.b. Floor for family-based immigration at 226,000 visas—The law maintains a floor on family visas for persons who are not IRs so that the increase in the numbers of IRs will not affect at least 226,000 visas for persons who are not IRs. INA §201(c)(1)(B)(ii).

   1.c. Long-term parolees are now counted against the worldwide quota for family-sponsored immigration. INA §201(c)(1)(A)(ii) and (c)(4). The Service interprets long term parolees to include persons who do not depart within one year of parole. It also includes long-term parolees who adjust under special legislation. Memo, Virtue, Acting Exec. Assoc. Comm., HQ IRT 50/5.12, 96 Act.039 (Aug. 7, 1997), *reprinted in* 74 No. 31 *Interpreter Releases* 1248, 1260–64 (Aug. 18, 1997).

2. *Employment-Based*—140,000 visas, plus left over family visas. INA §201(d)(1)

3. *Diversity Immigrants*—50,000 per year [55,000, per INA §201(e), less up to 5,000, per NACARA §203(d)]. *See in this chapter* part IV (p.812), *infra.*

4. *Per-Country Levels*

   4.a. No state favored over another.

   4.b. 7% of total for independent countries (26,120 in 2007). INA §202(a)(2).

   4.c. 2% of total for dependent areas ["colony or other component … overseas from the governing foreign state," 22 C.F.R. §401(f)] (7,463 in 2007). INA §202(a)(2).

   4.d. A separate 7% per country cap will apply to diversity immigrants. INA §203(c)(1)(E)(v).

B. *Preference System*—Preference system is divided between family preferences, INA §203(a), 8 U.S.C. §1153(a), and employment-based preferences, INA §203(b), 8 U.S.C. §1153(b).

1. Preference System for Family-Sponsored Immigrants—INA §203(a).

   1.a. First Preference—Unmarried sons and daughters of USC—23,400 plus unused Fourth Preference, INA §203(a)(1), 8 U.S.C. §1153(a)(1);

1.b. Second Preference—Spouses and unmarried children and sons and daughters of LPR, INA §203(a)(2)(A) and (B), 8 U.S.C. §1153(a)(2)(A) and (B).

(1) Divides them between 2A and 2B—114,200 plus excess over 226,000 plus unused First Preference.

(2) 2A—spouses and unmarried children of LPR. 77% of visas to the 2A category and 75% of the 77% is not subject to per country limitations (2A exempt).

(3) 2B—unmarried sons and daughters of LPRs are given 23% of the visas.

1.c. Third Preference (former Fourth Preference) married sons and daughters of USCs. 23,400 plus unused 1st and 2d Preference, INA §203(a)(3), 8 U.S.C. §1153(a)(3).

1.d. Fourth Preference (former Fifth Preference) brothers and sisters of USCs. 65,000 plus any unused in preference categories 1-3, INA §203(a)(4), 8 U.S.C. §1153(a)(4).

2. Employment-Based Immigration—INA §203(b), 8 U.S.C. §1153(b).

2.a. First Preference—Priority Workers, INA §203(b)(1), 8 U.S.C. §1153(b)(1). 28.6% of worldwide visas plus unused investor and special immigrant visas.

(a) Persons of extraordinary ability, INA §203(b)(1)(A), 8 U.S.C. §1153(b)(1)(A);

(b) Outstanding professors and researchers, INA §203(b)(1)(B), 8 U.S.C. §1153(b)(1)(B);

(c) Multinational executives and managers, INA §203(b)(1)(C), 8 U.S.C. §1153(b)(1)(C);

2.b. Second Preference—Members of the Professions Holding Advanced Degrees or Aliens of Exceptional Ability, INA §203(b)(2), 8 U.S.C. §1153(b)(2)—28.6% or worldwide visas plus unused priority workers.

2.c. Third Preference—Skilled Workers, Professionals and Other Workers, INA §203(b)(3), 8 U.S.C. §1153(b)(3)—28.6% of worldwide visas plus unused visas in the priority worker and professional categories.

2.d. Fourth Preference—Special Immigrants, INA §203(b)(4), 8 U.S.C. §1153(b)(4)—7.1% of worldwide visas per year with a 5,000 limitation on religious workers other than ministers. Does not include returning LPRs or former citizens seeking reacquisition of citizenship as they are considered outside of the quota.

2.e. Fifth Preference—Employment Creation (investors), INA §203(b)(5), 8 U.S.C. §1153(b)(5)—7.1% of visas per year of which 3,000 are set aside for targeted employment areas.

3. Nonpreference has been closed since 1978.

4. Derivative Status—Visas given to spouse and children who accompany or follow to join the principal beneficiary. INA §203(d), 8 U.S.C. §1153(d). *These visas are charged to principal beneficiary's preference category.*

C. *Foreign State Chargeability*—INA §202(b), 8 U.S.C. §1152(b); 22 C.F.R. §42.12

1. The determination as to which country's quota an applicant/ beneficiary gets charged to is important where countries are oversubscribed (*e.g.*, Mexico).

2. General rule—Chargeable to country of birth. Country of citizenship/nationality does not control.

3. Four exceptions (cross-chargeability):

3.a. Alien child may be charged to foreign state of either parent (where accompanying or following to join parent). 22 C.F.R. §42.12(b); 9 FAM 42.12 N5

3.b. Spouse may be charged to state of accompanying spouse. 22 C.F.R. §42.12(c).

3.c. USC who lost citizenship charged to country of current citizenship or, if citizenship is nonexistent, to country of last residence. 22 C.F.R. §42.12(d).

3.d. Alien born in location where neither parent was born or had their residence may be charged to foreign state of either parent. (No accompanying requirement). This provision could be used where parents are refugees (*e.g.*, from China to Hong Kong). 22 C.F.R. §42.12(e). *But see Matter of Ascher*, 14 I&N Dec. 271 (BIA 1973). *See* 9 FAM 42.12 Notes

3.e. In DV cases, the nonapplicant spouse's country of birth may be charged to the applicant spouse to allow the applicant spouse to qualify for DV as long as the parties were married prior to submitting the entry in the lottery. E-Mail Correspondence, Beirne, Deputy Chief, Advisory Opinions Division, DOS *reported in* 82 No. 24 *Interpreter Releases* 985, 990–91 (June 13, 2005). *See* 72 Fed. Reg. 57089 (Oct. 5, 2007)

4. Cross-chargeability does not rest on principal beneficiary—9 FAM 40.1 N.8. *Example* (4th family preference): Brother (principal beneficiary) is from Mexico—visa is unavailable. His wife is from Sweden. Consul can charge beneficiary to wife's Swedish quota, but only if spouse and principal beneficiary simultaneously apply for immigrant visa and admission.

4.a. "Accompanying"—Enter U.S. as LPR with principal beneficiary or within 6 months of principal beneficiary's entry or appearance at consulate for chargeability request. 22 C.F.R. §40.1(a)(1). An accompanying or following-to-join derivative beneficiary may adjust status even if they preceded the alien to the U.S., as long as they did not precede the principal person to the U.S. as an immigrant. *Matter of Naulu*, 19 I&N Dec. 351 (BIA 1986). An accompanying spouse or child will be given the same preference category as their spouse or parent. INA §§203(d), 216(g), 8 U.S.C. §§1153(d), 1186a(g). Thus, a spouse of a 3rd-preference beneficiary does not become a conditional resident but rather an LPR, even if married less than 2 years. Spouse or child acquired after admission cannot accompany or follow to join—a separate petition is required. Congress, through the Child Status Protection Act, PL 107-208, 116 Stat. 927 (Aug. 6, 2002), H.R. 1209 established rules for children for purposes of accompanying or following to join that permit a person to be considered a child who would otherwise age-out. Whether a child has "aged-out" will be determined by taking the child's age at the time an immigrant visa number became available to the parent and deducting the number of days/years the petition has been pending. For example, a child who is 21 years old and 9 months at the time the immigrant visa number became available to his parents, but the immigrant visa petition (*e.g.*, I-140) has been pending for 11 months will be treated as a child under the INA and may accompany or follow to join his parents. A child must seek to acquire LPR status within one year of the time the priority date is current to benefit from the CSPA. For following-to-join cases, the date that will meet the one-year filing requirement is the date that the parent files Form I-824 (which form can be filed with the I-485). Cable, DOS, 03-State-15049 (Jan. 17, 2003) at ¶22, *published on* AILA InfoNet at Doc. No. 03020550; 8 C.F.R. §103.5b.

4.b. "Following to join"—After 6 months, the relative is not "accompanying" the person, but, rather, "following to join" him or her. 22 C.F.R. §40.1(a)(1). The criteria for following to join are: (1) that person seeking entry is the spouse or child of principal beneficiary before the beneficiary's entry into the U.S. *Matter of G*, 7 I&N Dec. 731 (BIA 1958); (2) that the spouse or child not precede the principal beneficiary to U.S. *Matter of Kahn*, 14 I&N Dec. 122 (BIA 1972); *Santiago v. INS,* 526 F.2d 488, 490 (9th Cir. 1975); and (3) that the time period of child or spouse's entry is more than 4 months and without time limit so long as child or spouse maintain their respective status. A following-to-join spouse or child will be given the same preference category as his or her spouse or parent. 8 U.S.C. §§1153(d); 1186a(g). Thus, a spouse of a 3rd-preference beneficiary does not become a conditional resident but rather an LPR even if married less than 2 years. The child or spouse will still be given a derivative status without filing separate preference petitions, and will obtain cross chargeability if a child.

D. *Priority date*

1. Determines order of availability of visas.

2. For relative petitions (1st, 2nd, 3rd, and 4th preferences), the priority date is the date the preference petition (I-130) was filed, 22 C.F.R. §42.53(a), 9 FAM 42.53 N.1, which under DHS regulations requires receipt of the filing fee and a signed petition. 8 C.F.R. §204.1(d). It is not the date petition approved. However, where petition denied because of ineligibility and later resubmitted when eligible, the priority date is the time of the resubmission. *Matter of Carbajal*, 20 I&N Dec. 461 (BIA 1992).

2.a. Conversion of Family-Based Petitions and Retention of Priority Dates—Certain petitions automatically convert to others but retain, if relevant, their original priority date. 8 C.F.R. §204.2(i). For example:

(1) 1st to 3rd preference upon marriage of son or daughter;

(2) child of USC marries and goes from immediate relative to 3rd preference;

(3) divorce of child or son or daughter goes from 3rd preference to immediate relative or 1st preference (whether beneficiary is treated as a child or a son or daughter is based on his or her age on the date of the termination of the marriage);

(4) child beneficiary of immediate relative on reaching 21 goes to 1st preference, unless he was under 21 on the date that the IR petition was filed, INA §201(f)(1);

(5) naturalization of petitioner changes 2nd-preference child or son or daughter to immediate relative or 1st preference [To determine whether beneficiary will be treated as a child or son or daughter, his or her age on the date of naturalization is controlling, INA §201(f)(2); if the child is the child of 2nd-preference spouse beneficiary, USC petitioner must now file separate IR application. A son or daughter in preference 2B may elect not to accept the automatic transfer to first preference but instead remain in preference 2B. If s/he wishes to do so, s/he must file a request with USCIS that the conversion not occur and s/he will retain the original priority date under the 2B preference, as long as the original petition was properly filed, even if not approved at time of naturalization, INA §204(k)];

(6) a child accorded 2A status derivatively loses entitlement to such status upon reaching 21 and petitioner must file new petition for 2B preference (accorded initial priority date);

(7) a son or daughter who marries *after* parent naturalizes has the 2B petition converted to §203(a)(3) petition because it first automatically converts to §203(a)(1) upon the naturalization of the parent [*see* 8 C.F.R. §204.2(i)(3)] and then the §203(a)(1) petition automatically converts to a §203(a)(3) petition, 8 C.F.R. §204.2(i)(1)(i).

3. Battered spouses and children may transfer priority dates from petitions filed by their abusers to their new self-petitions "without regard to the current validity" of the previous petition. 8 C.F.R. §204.2(h)(2); Memo, Aleinikoff, Exec. Assoc. Comm., Programs HQ 204-P (Apr. 16, 1996).

4. Employment-Based Priority Dates

4.a. For employment-based immigration the priority date is either

(1) The date the labor certification filed (preference 2 and 3 require LC); or

(2) The date that the preference petition is filed with USCIS under the 1st pref. or any category (4th/5th preference) not needing a LC.

4.b. Subsequent Petitions—An EB 1st, 2nd, or 3rd preference is entitled to earliest priority date where subsequent 1st, 2nd, or 3rd preference submitted, unless the prior petition is revoked due to fraud, not simply employer's withdrawal. 11 *AILA Monthly Mailing* 823 (Nov. 1992). Priority dates under the first 3 employment-based categories are transferable. 9 FAM 42.53 N. 3.6. But the priority date is not transferable to 4th/5th preference or family-sponsored petitions. In addition, under certain circumstances a new 1st, 2nd, or 3rd preference employment-based petition does not have to be filed when the employee changes employment. An adjustment of status application based upon an approved 1st preference (outstanding researchers/professors or multinational transferees) or a 2nd or 3rd preference employment-based petition that is pending more than 180 days "shall remain valid with respect to a new job if the individual changes jobs or employers if the new job is in the same or a similar occupational classification as the job for which the petition was filed." INA §§204(j) (referring to INA §204(a)(1)(F)), §212(a)(5)(A)(iv). *See Krishnamoorthy v. Ridge,* 2003 U.S. Dist. LEXIS 8381 (N.D. Ill. May 19, 2003) [ordering the Service to adjudicate plaintiff's petition in accordance with INA §204(j)]. If the employee is in a removal proceeding, the BIA has stated, however, that the IJ has no jurisdiction over the visa petition pursuant to INA §204(j), and therefore cannot decide to adjust the respondent. *Matter of Perez Vargas,* 23 I&N Dec. 829 (BIA 2005). But the decision was *vacated* in *Perez-Vargas v. Gonzales,* 478 F.3d 191 (4th Cir. 2007) [the BIA's decision that the IJ has no jurisdiction to decide the continuing validity of an employment-based petition under INA §204(j) was reversed because 8 C.F.R. §1245.2(a)(1) provides IJs with exclusive jurisdiction to adjust applicants in removal proceedings and a determination under INA §204(j) is simply an act of fact finding incidental to AOS]. *See also*

Sung v. Keisler, 505 F.3d 372 (5th Cir. 2007) [adopted reasoning of *Perez-Vargas v. Gonzales* and found that IJ does have jurisdiction over portability determination because it is incidental to AOS]; *Matovski v. Gonzales,* 492 F.3d 722 (6th Cir. 2007) [court reversed IJ's refusal to consider AOS for person who "ported," because 8 C.F.R. §245.2(a)(5)(ii) made the portability issue irrelevant as the IJ had authority to adjust a person if he was eligible to adjust at the time he filed with the USCIS director, and because there was no regulation that barred the IJ from considering portability].

5. Derivative Beneficiaries—Spouse/children get same priority date as beneficiary—22 C.F.R. §42.53(a).

5.a. Date available as long as marriage still exists, child under 21 pursuant to Child Status Protection Act, and family "accompanying" or "following to join."

5.b. Children of immediate relatives are not derivative beneficiaries—If it is the child of the beneficiary of an immediate-relative petition, s/he is not a derivative and the petitioner or beneficiary must file a separate petition, and there is a separate priority date. For example, the child of a person who marries a USC must be the beneficiary of a separate petition by the parent beneficiary or, where applicable, the petitioning USC step-parent. The child does not ride on the USC step-parent's petition for the child's parent.

(1) *Exception*—Children of persons applying as abused spouses are derivatives, however. 8 C.F.R. §204.2(c)(4); *see also* Preamble to Interim Regulations, 61 Fed. Reg. 13061 at 13068–69 (Mar. 26, 1996) ["A qualified derivative child of a self-petitioning spouse of an abusive citizen of the United States is also considered to be an immediate relative"].

5.c. "Aged-Out" Children. Child Status Protection Act (CSPA), PL 107-208, 116 Stat. 927 (Aug. 6, 2002), H.R. 1209; INA §201(f), 8 U.S.C. §1151(f); AFM at 21.2(e). The CSPA does not apply retroactively. If a child aged-out before Aug. 6, 2002, s/he is not eligible for the benefits described below except if the family or employment-based petition that s/he is the direct or derivative beneficiary under was filed before Aug. 6, 2002, and was pending on that date, or was approved and the IV or AOS was not denied before that date. Although legacy INS required that the IV or AOS application also had to be filed on or *before* Aug. 6, 2002, Memo, Williams, Ex. Assoc. Comm. Office of Field Operations, INS, HQADN 70/6.1.1 (Feb. 14, 2003) at p.2, *published on* AILA InfoNet at Doc. No. 03031040, that position has been rejected by the BIA. *Matter of Avila-Perez,* 24 I&N Dec. 78 (BIA 2007) [where respondent filed and received an approval of his family petition prior to August 6, 2002, but did not file his AOS application until after that date, he retained his status as a child and was eligible to adjust] and has now been rejected by USCIS. Memo, Neufeld, Acting Assoc. Director, Domestic Operations, USCIS, HQ DOMO 70/6.1 (May 6, 2008), *published on* AILA InfoNet at Doc. No. 08050669 [CSPA is extended to persons who had approved visa petitions prior to Aug. 6, 2002 even if they did not have a pending AOS or IV application filed on or before that date]; AFM at Chapter 21.2(e)(2)(iii) & (iv). USCIS will now entertain motions to reopen without fee for persons who qualify and who were previously denied solely because they did not have an AOS or IV pending on Aug. 6, 2002. Memo, Neufeld (May 6, 2008) *Id.* The DOS view is that CSPA will not apply to a petition approved before Aug. 6, 2002, unless the child aged out on or after that date *or* the child aged out before Aug. 6, 2002, and prior to aging out had applied for and been denied an IV under INA §221(g). Cable, DOS, 03-State-15049 (Jan. 17, 2003) at ¶8, *published on* AILA InfoNet at Doc. No. 03020550; Cable, DOS, 02-State-163054 (Aug. 26, 2002) at ¶17, *published on* AILA InfoNet at Doc. No. 02090940. DOS's position is also that a refusal during the one year prior to Aug. 6, 2002 will not be considered a final determination and therefore CSPA applies. If the refusal occurred prior to one year (prior to Aug. 6, 2001) it will also not be considered final if it was denied on the basis of §221(g) and the case was not terminated under §203(g) or if the applicant applied for a waiver that was still pending on Aug. 6, 2002. Cable, DOS, 03-State-131625 (May 17, 2003), *published on* AILA InfoNet at Doc. No. 03060243. *See also Padash v. INS,* 358 F.3d 1161, 1167–74 (9th Cir. 2004) [final determination under section 8 does not mean final determination by the agency (DHS/DOS) but final determination of the matter which includes a final decision by a court and therefore denied adjustment application pending judicial review on Aug. 6, 2002 is covered by the CSPA].

"Pending" for purposes of this section includes "agency action on the petition, including an appeal or motion to reopen" filed with the AAO or BIA if such appeal or motion "was filed and/or pending on Aug. 6, 2002." Memo, Williams, (Feb. 14, 2003), *supra.* A motion to reopen filed after Aug. 6, 2002 based solely on the grounds that a person would now be eligible for CSPA benefits could not be granted. Memo, Williams (Feb. 14, 2003), *supra.* at ¶4.

"Final determination" for purposes of the AOS means "agency approval or denial issued by the Service or Executive Office for Immigration Review." Memo, Williams (Feb. 14, 2003), *supra.* at ¶4. *But see Padash v. INS,* 358 F.3d 1161, 1167–74 (9th Cir. 2004) [final determination under CSPA §8 does not mean final determination by the agency (DHS/DOS), but final determination of the matter that includes a final decision by a court; therefore denied adjustment application pending judicial review on Aug. 6, 2002, is covered by the CSPA].

USA PATRIOT Act and CSPA—The 45-day extension provided in the USA PATRIOT Act applies and can be used to benefit persons who are eligible and who would have turned 21 before Aug. 6, 2002. Memo, Williams (Feb. 14, 2003), *supra* at n.1.

The CSPA provisions do not apply to NIVs such as V or K visas, to NACARA, HRIFA, Family Unity, and Special Immigrant Juveniles. Memo, Williams (Feb. 14, 2003), *supra* p.2; Cable, DOS, 03-State-15049 (Jan. 17, 2003) at ¶31, *published on* AILA InfoNet at Doc. No. 03020550; *Alvidrez v. Ridge,* 311 F.Supp.2d 1163, 1165 (D. Kan. 2004) [CSPA does not cover V visa holders, and therefore person who aged-out under V-3 visa and brought constitutional claim for employment authorization could not use the CSPA to establish standing]. However, a K-4 seeking adjustment could utilize the CSPA. Memo, Williams (Feb. 14, 2003), *supra.* at ¶5; and a K-2 could also utilize the CSPA, but only if a separate I-130 petition (which is not normally required) is filed by the USC step-parent. AFM at 21.2(e)(2)(i)–(ii).

(1) Immediate-Relative Children. The appropriate date to determine whether a person remains an immediate-relative child is the child's age on the date the immediate-relative petition was filed. Thus, an unmarried child who becomes 21 while the petition is pending would not be placed in the 1st-preference category, but would remain an immediate relative as long as the child does not marry. INA §201(f)(1), 8 U.S.C. §1151(f)(1); Cable, DOS, 02-State-163054 (Aug. 26, 2002) at ¶7, *published on* AILA InfoNet at Doc. No. 02090940. However, the DOS would allow a child to be processed as a 1st preference instead of an immediate relative if his priority date is current. Cable, DOS, 03-State-15049 (Jan. 17, 2003) at ¶30, *published on* AILA InfoNet at Doc. No. 03020550.

(2) Married Sons and Daughters. If a petition is filed under the family-based 3rd preference and the son or daughter divorces, the relevant date for treating the son or daughter as a child for immediate-relative status or 2B preference is the date of divorce, as long as s/he remains unmarried. INA §201(f)(3), 8 U.S.C. §1151(f)(3); Cable, DOS, 02-State-163054, *supra* at ¶9. For example, if a married son or daughter gets divorced during the pendency of a 3rd-preference petition and on the date of the termination of the marriage the son or daughter is 20 years old, s/he will be considered an immediate relative child. If s/he is over 21 then she would be eligible for 1st-preference status. AFM at 21.2(e)(1)(i)(C)

(3) Naturalization of Parent

   (a) If LPR files 2nd preference for child and subsequently naturalizes, the child's age on the date of naturalization is controlling. Thus, a child who is 19 at the time the second preference petition for the child is filed and the petitioning parent naturalizes when the child is 20 years and 10 months, the child will be considered an immediate relative. INA §201(f)(2).

   (b) If LPR files 2nd preference for son or daughter under section 2B and then naturalizes, the petition is automatically converted to a 1st preference petition. However, a son or daughter may elect not to accept ("opt-out") the automatic transfer to first preference but instead remain in preference 2B. If s/he wishes to do so she must file a request with USCIS that the conversion not occur and she will retain the original priority date under the section 2B preference filing as long as the original petition was properly filed even if not approved at time of naturalization. INA §204(k), 8 U.S.C. §1154(k). Cable, DOS, 02-State-163054 (Aug. 26, 2002) at ¶19, *published on* AILA InfoNet at Doc. No. 02090940. If the petition is converted she will also retain the original priority date. The reasons for not accepting the automatic conversion is due to the availability of visas. For example, a son or daughter from the Philippines may not wish to be transferred to first preference because first preference for Philippines may be further backlogged than the second preference. This provision also applies to unmarried children who are under F2A, reach 21 and whose parent naturalizes. Thus if LPR filed an I-130 for his child, the child then became 21 and the parent thereafter naturalized, the child (now a son or daughter) can utilize this provision to decide to opt-out of the first preference and retain section 2B status. Memo, Aytes, Assoc. Dir. Domestic Operations, USCIS HQ 70/6.1.3 (June 14, 2006), *published on* AILA InfoNet at Doc. No. 06062870 [reversing previous policy of denying F2A the right to opt-out]; AFM at 21.2(e)(4)(C).

(4) Family, Employment and Diversity Petitions For Derivative Children. Congress under the Child Status Protection Act, PL 107-208, 116 Stat. 927 (Aug. 6, 2002), H.R. 1209 mitigated the harshness of previous provisions by providing for the protection of children who are beneficiaries under the preference categories (such as family-based 2A preference) or who are derivative beneficiaries of their parents' priority date in family, employment (including EB-5 investors) or diversity-based categories. INA §203(h)(3).

How to Calculate the Age. The formula for determining whether a child has "aged-out" for purposes of family, employment or diversity-based petitions is determined as follows: (1) Calculate the age of the child on the date when an immigrant visa number becomes available or the approval date, whichever is later; and (2) Reduce that number by the days the I-130, I-140, I-360, I-526 or diversity visa petition has been *pending*. The "child," however, *must* file for LPR status (adjustment/immigrant visa) *within one year of the approval of the petition or the availability of the visa, whichever is later,* to obtain the benefits of the CSPA. Memo, Williams (Feb. 14, 2003), *supra.* at ¶ 6. *Martinez v. DHS,* 502 F.Supp.2d 631, 636–37 (E.D. Mich. 2007) [where "child" applied for AOS more than one year after the availability of his mother's visa he did not receive the protection of the CSPA].

(a) The definition of the petition "pending" is the period of time from the receipt (not the priority) date of a properly filed petition to the date an approval is issued. *Id.* AFM at 21.2(e)(1)(ii)(B). For DV cases the period used to determine when a petition is pending is the first day of the DV mail-in period to the date of the letter notifying the principal alien that his or her application has been selected. *Id* at 4; Cable, DOS, 02-State-163054 (Aug. 26, 2002) at ¶15, *published on* AILA InfoNet at Doc. No. 02090940. [Note: However, a DV visa cannot be issued after the end of the fiscal year for that lottery "regardless of whether a derivative might benefit from age-out protection under the CSPA." Cable, DOS, 03-State-15049 (Jan. 17, 2003) at ¶12, *published on* AILA InfoNet at Doc. No. 03020550]. At least one circuit rejected the argument that "pending" is measured from the time the petition is filed until a visa number is available rather than until the petition is approved. *Ochoa-Amaya v. Gonzales,* 479 F.3d 989 (9th Cir. 2007) [motion to reopen properly denied because applicant did not qualify under CSPA for adjustment].

(b) The definition date for when an immigrant visa number becomes *available* for purposes of the calculation and the one year filing deadline "is the first day of the month of the Department of State (DOS) Visa Bulletin, which indicates availability of a visa for that preference category." Memo, Williams, Ex. Assoc. Comm. Office of Field Operations, INS, HQADN 70/6.1.1 (Feb. 14, 2003) p.2-3, *published on* AILA InfoNet at Doc. No. 03031040. Where the priority date regresses the date the I-485 was filed (if filed before regression) is considered the visa availability date. *Id.* p. 3. If the I-485 is not filed until after regression is over and a visa is available, the subsequent date should be used.

(c) The definition of "filing" for purposes of the one year filing date for an IV is the date the beneficiary child (not his parent) submits the completed DS-230, Part I form and it is recorded in the IV system. Cable, DOS, 03-State-15049 (Jan. 17, 2003) at ¶¶17–20, *published on* AILA InfoNet at Doc. No. 03020550. For "following to join" cases it will be the date the parent files Form I-824 (which form can be filed with the I-485) or takes a "concrete step" towards seeking to acquire LPR status. *Id* at ¶¶22, 23. *See also* 8 C.F.R. §103.5b.

Examples. A son who is 22 years and 2 months old on the date his visa number becomes available (which may or may not be the date of approval of the petition) whose parents' petition has been pending for 2 years and 2 months would remain eligible as a child to obtain LPR status as long as s/he pursued the residency within the year. Conversely, if an I-130 was filed in 1998 when the derivative beneficiary was 20 and approved one year later, but the priority date was not reached until 2003, the child would not be eligible for benefits because s/he would have been 25 in 2003 and would be considered 24 for purposes of the CSPA because her age would be 25 less the one year the petition was pending. Similarly, a derivative beneficiary would be ineligible where an I-140 was filed in 1998 when the derivative beneficiary was 20, and the parents' I-140 petition was approved in 2000 (and the visa number was current on approval), but s/he waited until the year 2002 to apply for adjustment. S/he is ineligible because s/he failed to file within one year of the availability of the visa. Similarly, a person on whose behalf an I-140 was filed and approved a year and a half ago thereafter files a I-485, s/he is ineligible for CSPA (because s/he didn't file within the year) and if under 21 must ask to expedite the file. An I-130 was filed in 1998 when the child was 20. The priority date became available the next year. However, the I-130 was not adjudicated until 5 years later. An I-485 was filed within the year. The person would be considered a child. Memo, Williams, Ex. Assoc. Comm. Office of Field Operations, INS, HQADN 70/6.1.1 (Feb. 14, 2003) pp. 4–5 & n.4, *published on* AILA InfoNet at Doc. No. 03031040.

(5) Other Avenues for Age-Outs. If the child does not qualify under the Child Status Protection Act s/he may still receive some benefit. First, if s/he is approaching 21, USCIS may still expedite the approval. *Id.* Also a child who is a derivative beneficiary under the second preference can still receive the priority date accorded the parents under their petition. 8 C.F.R. §204.2(a)(4). Also, derivatives of approved battered spouse or child petitioners are transformed into petitioners in the relevant preference category when they age-out. INA §204(a)(1)(D)(i)(III).

(6) Prior efforts to sue INS to obtain adjudication prior to child reaching 21 have generally been unsuccessful. *Maldonado-Coronel v. McElroy*, 943 F.Supp. 376 (S.D.N.Y. 1996); *Zheng v. INS*, 933 F.Supp. 338 (S.D.N.Y. 1996). *But see Fano v. O'Neill*, 806 F.2d 1262 (5th Cir. 1987). *See also Afsharzadehyadzi v. Perryman,* 214 F.Supp.2d 884 (N.D. Ill. 2002) [no jurisdiction under mandamus due to INA §242(a)(2)(B)(i) and failure to exhaust before IJ to consider AOS application that had already been denied for "aged-out" child].

(7) Battered Spouses and Children. Aging out derivatives of battered spouses and children are automatically placed in the relevant son or daughter preference category without losing the priority date based upon the original self-petition. INA §204(a)(1)(D). Provides Child Status Protection Act protection and preserves original priority date of self-petitioning LPR or derivative subject to domestic violence (including child who may have lost his LPR status because abusive parent dies or terminates the parent child relationship) and who has now aged-out. INA §§201(f)(4), 203(h)(4), 204(a)(1)(D). Also allows children of U.S. citizens subject to abuse to petition until the age of 25 if they can demonstrate that the "abuse was at least one central reason for the filing delay." INA §204(a)(1)(D)(v).

(8) A spouse or child acquired before principal's admission or adjustment gets the principal's priority date as accompanying or following to join. In addition, if the child is born of a marriage which existed prior to the principal's admission, s/he gets the principal's priority date as accompanying or following to join, even if born *after* principal's admission. 22 C.F.R. §42.53(c), 9 FAM 42.53 N.6.2. Similarly, if spouse or child acquired af-

ter visa issuance but before admission they are entitled to derivative status and priority date. 9 FAM 42.53 N.6.4.

(9) No derivative priority date for offspring of derivative children. 9 FAM 42.53 N.6.6. However, in legalization beneficiary cases the child of a beneficiary is not required to file a new visa petition and can enter under 2nd preference based on the priority date of parent beneficiary. Letter, Odom, Chief Advisory Opinions, DOS (Apr. 20, 1992), *reprinted in* 69 No. 28 *Interpreter Releases* 906, 923 (July 27, 1992).

(10) Priority date for adopted children. Adopted child who has been adopted and is a member of the principal's household obtains parents' priority date even if the two-year legal custody requirement is not completed and child can enter as derivative after two years of legal custody and residence. Letter, Odom, Chief, Advisory Opinion Division (May 19, 1993), *reprinted in* 70 No. 29 *Interpreter Releases* 1014, 1022–23 (Aug. 2, 1993).

6. Loss of Priority—INA §203(e)(1), 8 U.S.C. §1153(e)(1), establishes a priority system for family and employment-based immigrants. INA §203(g), 8 U.S.C. §1153(g), provides that Secy. of State shall terminate the registration of any person who fails to apply for an IV within one year of notification of availability. But the Sec. can, within 2 years following notification, reinstate registration if the person can establish that the failure was due to circumstances beyond his control.

E. *Presumption Against Admissibility*—INA §203(f), 8 U.S.C. §1153(f), establishes a burden of proof on the applicant (presumption against admissibility) under the family-preference (including widows), employment-based, and special immigrant categories.

F. *If Country Oversubscribed*—INA §202(e), 8 U.S.C. §1152(e)

1. If country has reached its maximum allowance (*see in this part* "Per-Country Levels," ¶ A.4 (p.804), *supra*), its allocated visas must be divided between family-based and employment-based preference categories in proportion to each of their preferences. Ensures visa availability in each category for the country.
2. For a country to be oversubscribed, DOS must actually grant the full number of visas in one fiscal year. *Olivares v. INS*, 685 F.2d 1174 (9th Cir. 1982).
3. INA §202(a)(5) provides that any unused employment-based visas for the fiscal year may be made available without regard to the per-country limit.

IV. DIVERSITY IMMIGRANTS—INA §203(c), 8 U.S.C. §1153(c), 22 C.F.R. §42.33, 66 Fed. Reg. 39435–37 (July 31, 2001)

A. *Number Available*. DHS/DOS determine by a complex formula based on number of persons from each foreign state who were provided LPR status during the most recent 5-year period for which data is available. INA §203(c)(1). The number of diversity visas available is 55,000 each year [§201(e)], reduced by up to 5,000 by the number of grants of special cancellation under NACARA §203(d).

B. *Regions*

1. AG shall identify high admission and low admission regions and states. The regions are (1) Africa; (2) Asia; (3) Europe; (4) North America (other than Mexico); (5) Oceania; and (6) South America, Mexico, Central America and the Caribbean.
2. For purposes of this program, Northern Ireland and Hong Kong SAR are considered separate foreign states and each colony, component or dependent of a foreign state is treated as part of that state.
3. A high admission region is defined as a region where the states have greater than 1/6 of all visas issued. All other regions are defined as low-admission. High admission state is a state which has had greater than 50,000 admissions in the 5-year FY period. All others are defined as low admission.
4. No visas will be issued to high admission states.
5. Visas will be divided between low admission states and high admission regions, with priority given to those in low admission regions.
6. No state can get more than 7% (3,850) of the total diversity visas available in any one fiscal year.

C. *Eligibility*—22 C.F.R. §42.33:

1. Applicant not eligible unless s/he:

   1.a. Is a native of a low admission state designated under diversity program. 22 C.F.R. §42.33(a)(1). But note, cross-chargeability is permissible because the nonapplicant spouse's country of birth may be charged to the applicant spouse to allow the applicant spouse to qualify for DV as long as the parties were married prior to submitting the entry in the lottery. 72 Fed. Reg. 57089 (Oct. 5, 2007); E-Mail Correspondence, Beirne, Deputy Chief, Advisory Opinions Division, DOS, *reported in* 82 No. 24 *Interpreter Releases* 985, 990–91 (June 13, 2005); 9 FAM 42.33 N. 4.2(3);

   1.b. Has either:

      (1) a high school diploma or its equivalent as defined under 22 C.F.R. §42.33(a)(2) [a GED degree is *not* equivalent. Memo, Puleo, Exec. Assoc. Comm., CO 245-P (Nov. 2, 1994), *reprinted in* 71 No. 44 *Interpreter Releases* 1505, 1524, 1527 (Nov. 14, 1994)]. To meet the high-school equivalency in another country "a foreign course of study must provide the alien with the minimum academic records required for admission to study in U.S. universities or colleges as determined in the most recent edition of the publication entitled 'Foreign Credentials Required for Consideration of Admission to Universities and Colleges in the United States." 22 C.F.R. §42.33(a)(2); or

      (2) within 5 years of applying, at least 2 years of work experience in an occupation requiring at least 2 years' training or experience. The occupation must require an SVP of 7. Memo, Puleo (Nov. 2. 1994), *supra*; Cable, DOS (98-State-199837) (Oct. 28, 1998) at ¶7, *reprinted in* 75 No. 46 *Interpreter Releases* 1662, 1664 (Dec. 7, 1998). The DOS relies on the DOL's O*NET Online to determine qualifying work experience. 22 C.F.R. §42.33(a)(3). *See* 80 No. 34 *Interpreter Releases* 1237–38, 1259–67 (Sept. 8, 2003) [listing all O*NET occupations requiring 2 years training or experience]; and

   1.c. Has obtained visa within the fiscal year s/he applied. "Under no circumstances may a consular officer issue a visa...after the end of the fiscal year." 22 C.F.R. §42.33(a)(1).

2. Family Members Are Eligible—Spouse and children are eligible including spouses and children acquired subsequent to the DV entry submission. Cable, DOS (98-State-099723) (June 3, 1998*), reprinted in* 75 No. 22 *Interpreter Releases* 815 (June 8, 1998) as long as the marriage took place prior to the principal's admission into the U.S. under the DV program. E-Mail Correspondence, Beirne, Deputy Chief, Advisory Opinions Division, DOS *reported in* 82 No. 24 *Interpreter Releases* 985, 990–91 (June 13, 2005); 9 FAM 42.33 N. 6.8. For children covered under the Child Status Protection Act, the period used to determine when a petition is pending is the first day of the DV mail-in period to the date of the letter notifying the principal alien that his or her application has been selected. *Id* at 4; Cable, DOS, 02-State-163054 (Aug. 26, 2002) at ¶15, *published on* AILA InfoNet at Doc. No. 02090940. However, a DV visa cannot be issued after the end of the fiscal year for that lottery "regardless of whether a derivative might benefit from age-out protection under the CSPA." Cable, DOS, 03-State-15049 (Jan. 17, 2003) at ¶12, *published on* AILA InfoNet at Doc. No. 03020550.

D. *Procedure*

1. DOS has ended the mail-in system for the diversity visa lottery. It is now replaced it with an electronic filing system. The electronic diversity visa entry form can be accessed by going to *http://dvlottery.state.gov*. An electronic confirmation notice will be sent upon receipt of a completed EDV Entry Form. Recent photographs of the applicant and his or her spouse and each child under 21 years of age (unless a USC or LPR) must be submitted electronically with the EDV Entry Form. A separate digital photo for each person must meet the following specifications: (1) JPEG (Joint Photographic Experts Group) Format; (2) Color or grayscale (monochrome images will not be accepted); (3) Resolution of 320 pixels wide by 240 pixels high and a color depth of either 24-bit color, 8-bit color or 8-bit grayscale; If scanned the print must be 2x2inches square and must be scanned at a resolution of 150 dots per inch and with a color depth of either 24-bit color, 8-bit color or 8-bit grayscale; (4) Maximum image size of 62,500 bytes; (5) Directly facing the camera with no tilt up, down or to the side and the face should cover about 50% of the area of

the photo; (6) Background for photo should be neutral and light-colored; (7) No sunglasses or other paraphernalia in picture is acceptable; nor is out-of-focus picture; and (8) Hats and head coverings not acceptable except if for religious beliefs and only then if no portion of the person's face is obscured; Tribal or other headgear that is not religious is not acceptable nor are military, airline or other personnel wearing hats. Signatures are no longer required on applications. Applicants will be selected by random generation through the computer and person who are not selected will not be notified. No fee is charged to enter. 22 C.F.R. §42.33(b).

2. The selection process is random selection (lottery) in each fiscal year. The Secy. of State will designate the time and place for filing. An applicant may only file *one* petition. If more than one petition is submitted all petitions submitted by the applicant for that period are void. Often a problem arises because USCIS or a consular post fail to grant AOS or an IV before the fiscal year ends. The Service has said they will accept adjustment applications 90 days in advance of the actual date when a visa is available. Memo, Yates, Deputy Ex. Assoc. Comm. (HQ 70/23.1, HQ 70/33) (July 22, 1999), *reprinted in* 76 No. 13 *Interpreter Releases* 1116, 1135–37 (July 26, 1999); Letter, Podolny, Assoc. Gen. Counsel (Dec. 16, 2002), 80 No. 3 *Interpreter Releases* 88–89, 109–11 (Jan. 20, 2003). Actions filed or pending beyond the fiscal year that the visa had to be granted have generally been unsuccessful. *Mohamed v. Gonzales,* 436 F.3d 79 (3d Cir. 2006) [court is without authority to hear claim that is now moot because the Service lacks the statutory authority to issue a DV visa beyond the fiscal year]; *Coraggioso v. Ashcroft,* 355 F.3d 730 (3d Cir. 2004) [affirmed order of removal because legacy INS did not adjudicate adjustment within one year period]; *Carrillo-Gonzalez v. INS,* 353 F.3d 1077 (9th Cir. 2003) [equitable tolling not applicable to one year period]; *Ahmed v. DHS,* 328 F.3d 383 (7th Cir. 2003) [following *Iddir* the Court held that mandamus should be denied not on jurisdictional grounds but on the grounds that no relief could be granted]; *Nyaga v. Ashcroft,* 323 F.3d 906 (11th Cir. 2003) [mandamus action dismissed as moot where claim was filed after the end of the fiscal year because court cannot compel issuance of visas after fiscal year ended]; *Iddir v. INS,* 301 F.3d 492, 499–501 (7th Cir. 2002) [denying mandamus relief because INS does not have a clear duty to adjudicate petitions and in fact lacks the statutory authority to award diversity visas beyond the fiscal year]; *Gebre v. Rice,* 462 F.Supp.2d 186 (D. Mass. 2006) [same]; *Kracun v. U.S.,* 392 F.Supp.2d 594 (S.D.N.Y. 2005) [although failure to issue lottery visa was due to dilatory and confused conduct of government agencies, court could not grant relief beyond the fiscal year]; *Basova v. Ashcroft,* 373 F.Supp.2d 192, 199–200 (E.D.N.Y. 2005) [petitioners who as part of amended complaint filed subsequent to fiscal year could not relate their claims back to those who filed before the end of the fiscal year]; *Ticheva v. Ashcroft,* 241 F.Supp.2d 1115 (D. Nev. 2002) [as INS is without power to grant visa beyond the fiscal year, injunctive action is dismissed as moot]; *Zapata v. INS,* 93 F.Supp.2d 355 (S.D.N.Y. 2000) [court declined to issue order preserving right to obtain visa where visa lottery had ended for the year]; *Rahman v. McElroy,* 884 F.Supp. 782 (S.D.N.Y. 1995) [no liberty or property interest in obtaining LPR status if picked and person selected cannot compel INS to schedule adjustment interviews]. *But see Przhebelskaya v. U.S. Bureau of Citizenship and Immigration Services,* 338 F.Supp.2d 399 (E.D.N.Y. 2004) [where action to compel INS to adjust lottery applicant before the end of the fiscal year and INS fails to do so the court had continuing jurisdiction to compel grant]; *Paunescu v. INS,* 76 F.Supp.2d 896 (N.D. Ill 1999) [same]. In one case the court dismissed as moot a claim brought prior to the end of the fiscal year where the government demonstrated that all visas had been used. *Basova v. Ashcroft,* 383 F.Supp.2d 390 (E.D.N.Y. 2005) [where government provided statistics demonstrating that all visa numbers had been used for the diversity lottery, court reversed former opinion and entered order dismissing case as moot against applicants who brought their claims prior to the end of the fiscal year].

V. POLISH AND HUNGARIAN PAROLEES—8 C.F.R. §245.12

The Congress in IIRIRA §646 established a special adjustment of status program for persons who (1) are nationals of Hungary and Poland; (2) were inspected and granted parole into the U.S. during the period Nov. 1, 1989 to Dec. 31, 1991 after being denied refugee status; (3) have been physically present in the U.S. for at least one year and physically present on the date the AOS application is made; and (4) are admissible into the U.S. without regard to INA §212(a)(4), (5), (7)(A). The AG may also waive all other provisions of INA §212(a) except §212(a)(2)(C) and §212(a)(3)(A)–(C) and (E) for humanitarian purposes, to assure family unity, or when it is otherwise in the public interest. Application submitted on I-485. No cut off date for applying. If depart need to obtain advance parole as law does not cover person outside U.S. Family members do *not* join on the application. They must separately qualify or await a second preference petition. Memo, Crocetti, Assoc. Comm. (Dec. 23, 1996), *reprinted in* 74 No. 14 *Interpreter Releases* 608, 618–24 (Apr. 14, 1997); 8 C.F.R. §§245.12, 1245.12.

VI. NICARAGUAN AND CUBAN ADJUSTMENT—Nicaraguan Adjustment and Central American Relief Act (NACARA), PL 105-100, 111 Stat. 2160, 2193 (Nov. 19, 1997); 8 C.F.R. §§245.13, 1245.13

A. *Generally*—Provides under §202 for AOS for Nicaraguans or Cubans physically present in the U.S. since Dec. 1, 1995 if s/he applies for AOS before Apr. 1, 2000.

Person can adjust even if ordered excluded, deported, removed or failed to depart voluntarily after VD order. *But see Sherifi v. INS,* 260 F.3d 737 (7th Cir. 2001) [persons may not apply for NACARA benefits if they were in exclusion proceedings as suspension historically has been denied persons seeking exclusion]. No separate motion to reopen is required, but an application for a stay of removal must be filed on Form I-246 with the application. 8 C.F.R. §§245.13(d)(5), 1245.13(d)(5).

B. *INA Provisions Waived*—INA §212(a)(4) [public charge]; INA §212(a)(5) [labor certification], §212(a)(6)(A) [EWI], §212(a)(7)(A) [no documents], and §212(a)(9)(B) [3/10 year bar] are waived. USCIS may also waive INA §212(a)(9)(A) [persons previously removed] and §212(a)(9)(C) [persons unlawfully present after EWI]. The criteria for waiver under §§212(a)(9)(A) & (C) are the same as those used when making a determination on a person's application for consent to reapply. Memo, Pearson, Ex. Assoc. Comm. HQADN 70/23.1-P, 70/6.1.3-P (Feb. 14, 2001), *published on* AILA InfoNet at Doc. No. 01022007. Thus it is a benefit to EWI Cubans ineligible for AOS under the Cuban Refugee Act. In addition, INA §241(a)(5) [reinstatement of removal/deportation order] is not applicable. 8 C.F.R. §§241.8(d), 1241.8(d).

C. *Motion to Reopen before DHS/EOIR re LIFE Act*—A person may file a motion to reopen before USCIS or the IJ/BIA if s/he has been made eligible for AOS as a result of the LIFE Act and Amendments potentially waiving §§212(a)(9)(A) & (C) and disregarding INA §241(a)(5). A motion may be made before USCIS even if the NACARA application was previously denied as long as the person has not been issued an NTA or other charging document and he pays the filing fee for the motion. Memo, Pearson, Ex. Assoc. Comm. HQADN 70/23.1-P, 70/6.1.3-P (Feb. 14, 2001), *published on* AILA InfoNet at Doc. No. 01022007. It may also be filed before the IJ/BIA if there is a final order. Memo, Pearson, Ex. Assoc. Comm. HQADN 50/14.1-P, 70/23.1-P (Feb. 14, 2001), *published on* AILA InfoNet at Doc. No. 00122040. A motion to reopen may also be filed before USCIS or IJ/ BIA (depending upon the status of the case) even if the applicant never previously requested NACARA benefits if s/he is now eligible for NACARA because of the changes regarding INA §§212(a)(9)(A) or (C) or 241(a)(5). 8 C.F.R. §§245.13(d)(4)(ii), 1245.13. The waiver of INA §§212(a)(9)(A) or (C) is filed on I-601 and the motion to reopen must be filed on or before June 19, 2001. 8 C.F.R. §§245.13(c)(2), (d)(4)(ii), 1245.13(c)(2), 1245.13(d)(4)(ii).

D. *Physical Presence*—Allowed 180 days absence (in aggregate) without breaking physical presence requirement. Proof of presence prior to Dec. 1, 1995, includes asylum application, issuance of OSC or placement in exclusion proceedings, AOS application under INA §245, application for EA, Social Security records, any other benefit under the INA, income tax records, or other documents specified in 8 C.F.R. §§245.13(e), 1245.13(e).

E. *Employment Authorization*—EA granted upon filing AOS application if USCIS has proof in its file that person is eligible for benefit. Otherwise applicant must wait 180 days. 8 C.F.R. §§245.13(j) 1245.13(j).

F. *Parole*—Person may receive advance parole to travel. A person may also be paroled into the U.S. if they qualify for NACARA. 8 C.F.R. §245.13(k). Memo, Yates, Deputy Exec. Assoc. Comm. (HQPGM 70/19) (Oct. 15, 1999), *reprinted in* 76 No. 44 *Interpreter Releases* 1661, 1665–66 (Nov. 15, 1999).

G. *Motions to Reopen before IJ/BIA*—Allows NACARA applicants from Cuba and Nicaragua with final orders of removal, deportation or exclusion to file one motion to reopen but it must be filed by June 19, 2001. The time period to file the motion may be equitably tolled. *See e.g., Albillo-De Leon v. Gonzales,* 410 F.3d 1090 (9th Cir. 2005) [where respondent was defrauded by nonlawyer who posed as a lawyer, the time period for filing a motion to reopen under NACARA §203(c) and 8 C.F.R. §1003.43(e)(1) was tolled until date that current attorney found out that motion was not filed].

H. ***Spouses and Children***—Spouse, children and unmarried sons and daughters eligible to AOS if:

1. They are Nicaraguan or Cuban.
2. They apply for AOS before Apr. 1, 2000.
3. Only sons and daughters need to show they have been in U.S. since Dec. 1, 1995.
4. The same sections under INA §212 are waived.
5. Spouse/children who were battered or subject to extreme cruelty are also eligible. A battered spouse or child may apply even if the *abuser never applied* for NACARA benefits as long as the petition is filed within 18 months of Jan. 5, 2006. Sec. 815 of the Violence Against Women and Department of Justice Reauthorization Act, PL 109-162, 119 Stat. 2960 (Jan. 5, 2006).

I. ***Administrative and Judicial Review***

1. Administrative review the same as all other AOS applicants before IJ except where person previously ordered deported the hearing is limited to NACARA eligibility. 8 C.F.R. §§245.13(m)–(n), 1245.13(m)–(n).
2. No judicial review of the AG's decision "as to whether the status of any alien should be adjusted." NACARA §202(f); *Centeno v. U.S. Att'y Gen.,* 441 F.3d 904 (11th Cir. 2006) [no jurisdiction to review denial of NACARA for failure to present evidence of presence]; *Cifuentes Ruiz v. Gonzales,* 455 F.3d 661 (6th Cir. 2006) [no jurisdiction to challenge determination that applicant timely filed for benefit]; *Ortega v. U.S. Att'y Gen.,* 416 F.3d 1348 (11th Cir. 2005) [no jurisdiction to review denial of NACARA adjustment by BIA]. *See also Chapinski v. Ziglar,* 278 F.3d 718 (7th Cir. 2002) [mandamus, declaratory and injunctive relief to compel INS to place person in removal proceedings to obtain benefit as NACARA spouse is barred by INA §242(g)]. However, at least one circuit has determined that it will stay a person's deportation to give the person an opportunity to file for the benefits of NACARA. *Aguilar-Escobar v. INS,* 136 F.3d 1240, 1241 (9th Cir. 1998). Moreover, §202(f) does not bar constitutional claims. *Frech v. U.S. Att'y Gen.,* 491 F.3d 1277, 1280–81 (11th Cir. 2007) [court had jurisdiction to review claim in NACARA case that the IJ's refusal to change venue violated respondent's right to due process including the right to counsel and the ability to present evidence].

VII. HAITIAN REFUGEE IMMIGRATION FAIRNESS ACT OF 1998 (HRIFA)—Div. A, Tit. IX, Sec. 902 of PL 105-277, 112 Stat. 2681-538 (Oct. 21, 1998); 8 C.F.R. §§245.15, 1245.15

A. ***Generally***—Provides for equal treatment for Haitian refugees with Nicaraguans receiving benefits under the Nicaraguan Adjustment and Central American Relief Act. Applications must have been filed at any time between June 11, 1999 and Mar. 31, 2000.

Provides for AOS for Haitians who: (1) filed for asylum before Dec. 31, 1995; (2) were paroled into the U.S. prior to Dec. 31, 1995, after having been identified as having a credible fear of persecution, or paroled for emergent reasons or reasons deemed strictly in the public interest; *or* (3) were children as defined in the INA at the time of their arrival in the U.S. before Dec. 31, 1995 and (i) arrived without parents and remained without parents; (ii) became orphaned subsequent to arrival; or (iii) were abandoned by parents or guardians prior to Apr. 1, 1998 and have remained abandoned. For those who remained without parents in the U.S., the issue is "who has or has had parental control over the child since his or her arrival into the United States." 65 Fed. Reg. 15835 at 15839 (Mar. 24, 2000); 8 C.F.R. §§245.15(b)(1)(iii)(A), 1245.15(b)(1)(iii)(A). The term "orphan" includes children where one parent was lost and presumed dead by the Haitian government and the other is unable to provide proper care and provides a written release to the child. Similarly, a child will be considered an orphan if both parents died after the child reached 21. 65 Fed. Reg. 15835 at 15839–40; 8 C.F.R. §§245.15(a), 1245.15(a).

Applications are filed at the Nebraska Service Center, PO Box 87245, Lincoln, NE 68501-7245

B. ***Physical Presence***—Requires the person to be physically present in the U.S. since Dec. 31, 1995, but permits up to 180 days absence in the aggregate during that period without losing physical presence. The principal applicant and his or her unmarried son or daughter must prove that they were in the U.S. on Dec. 31, 1995, and were continuously physically present since that date. The spouse need not prove that s/he was here on Dec. 31, 1995 or continuously physically present. S/he need only show that s/he is physically present at the time the application is filed. 8 C.F.R. §§245.15(c), (d)(1), (d)(5), 1245.15(c), (d)(1), (d)(5). A person who is otherwise eligible to receive benefits under the act but is outside the U.S. may seek parole to enter by filing an application with the Nebraska Service Center. 8 C.F.R. §§245.15(t)(2), (u)(2), 1245.15(t)(2), (u)(2). USCIS will continue to parole qualifying Haitian dependents after Mar. 31, 2000 because dependents are eligible for the benefits of HRIFA if they file after Mar. 31, 2000 as long as the principal family member filed by that date. 65 Fed. Reg. 15924–25 (Mar. 24, 2000). Children who "age-out" before they adjust are not eligible and the Child Status Protection Act does not protect them. The documentary requirements are detailed at 8 C.F.R. §§245.15(j) & (k), 1245.15(j) & (k).

C. ***Persons Ordered Removed or in Proceedings***—Can adjust even if in proceedings or ordered excluded, deported, removed, or failed to depart voluntarily. If a person has a final order of deportation or exclusion s/he must file his or her application at: USCIS, Nebraska Service Center, PO Box 87245, Lincoln, NE 68501-7245. 8 C.F.R. §§245.15(g)(1), 1245.15(g)(1). The applicant must also file a request for a stay consistent with 8 C.F.R. §§241.6, 1241.6 on Form I-246. Absent evidence of statutory ineligibility or significant negative discretionary factors, the stay shall be approved. 8 C.F.R. §§245.15(g)(3)(ii), 1245.15(g)(3)(ii). If the person is in deportation or exclusion proceedings, or has a pending motion to reopen or reconsider those proceedings before June 11, 1999, then the request must be filed with the immigration court. 8 C.F.R. §§245.15(g)(2) and (p), 1245.15(g)(2) and (p). Similarly, if a person's case is pending at the BIA on appeal or the person filed a motion to reopen or reconsider at the BIA before June 11, 1999 s/he can file her request with the BIA. 8 C.F.R. §§245.15(g)(2) and (p), 1245.15(g)(2) and (p). If there is jurisdiction before the IJ, the applicant may request the IJ adjudicate the application or administratively close it. 8 C.F.R. §§245.15(p)(4), 1245.15(p)(4). Closure requires the Service's concurrence. 8 C.F.R. §§245.15(p)(4)(i), 1245.15(p)(4)(i). HRIFA applicants with final orders of removal, deportation or exclusion may file one motion to reopen but it must be filed by June 19, 2001. As a result of the LIFE Act and Amendments, INA §241(a)(5) is no longer applicable to HRIFA applicants. Under DHS regulations an immigration officer may not reinstate the prior order unless and until a final decision to deny the application for adjustment has been made. 8 C.F.R. §§241.8(d), 1241.8(d).

D. ***INA Provisions Waived***—Waives INA §212(a)(4) [public charge]; INA §212(a)(5) [labor certification]; INA §212(a)(6)(A) [EWI]; INA §212(a)(7)(A) [no documents] and INA §212(a)(9)(B). USCIS may also waive INA §212(a)(9)(A) [persons previously removed] and §212(a)(9)(C) [persons unlawfully present after EWI]. The criteria for waiver under §§212(a)(9)(A) & (C) are the same as those used when making a determination on an person's application for consent to reapply. Memo, Pearson, Ex. Assoc. Comm. HQADN 70/23.1-P, 70/6.1.3-P (Feb. 14, 2001), *published on* AILA InfoNet at Doc. No. 01022007. May apply for other waivers if eligible. 8 C.F.R. §§245.15(e)(2), 1245.15(e)(2).

E. ***Motion to Reopen before DHS/EOIR re LIFE Act Changes***—A person may file a motion to reopen before USCIS or the IJ/BIA if s/he has been made eligible for AOS as a result of the LIFE Act and Amendments potentially waiving §§212(a)(9)(A) & (C) and disregarding INA §241(a)(5). A motion to reopen the originally denied HRIFA application may be made before USCIS as long as the applicant has not been issued an NTA or other charging document and s/he pays the filing fee for the motion. S/he may also file a motion to reopen before the IJ/BIA if s/he has a final order. Memo, Pearson, Ex. Assoc. Comm. HQADN 50/14.1-P, 70/23.1-P (Feb. 14, 2001), *reprinted in* 78 No. 8 *Interpreter Releases* 407, 425–27 (Feb. 26, 2001). A motion to reopen may also be filed before USCIS or IJ/BIA (depending upon the status of the case) even if the applicant never previously requested HRIFA benefits if s/he is now eligible for HRIFA because of the changes regarding INA §§212(a)(9)(A) or (C) or 241(a)(5). 8 C.F.R. §§245.15(g)(3)(ii), 1245.15(g)(3)(iii). The waiver of INA §§212(a)(9)(A) or (C) is filed on I-601 and the motion to reopen must have been filed on or before June 19, 2001. 8 C.F.R. §§245.15 (e)(3), (g)(3)(ii), (r)(4), 1245.15(e)(3), (g)(3)(iii), (r)(4).

F. ***Employment Authorization and Travel***—Authorizes employment upon filing the application. However, under the interim regulations employment authorization will not be issued during the first 180 days. 8 C.F.R. §§245.15(n), 1245.15(n). A person may not travel outside of the U.S. without obtaining advance parole. 8 C.F.R. §§245.15(t)(1), 1245.15(t)(1). The time period out of the country on advance parole does not count toward the 180-day absence. 8 C.F.R. §§245.15(c)(4)(ii), 1245.15(c)(4)(ii). However, if a person has a final order of exclusion, deportation, or removal their departure from the U.S. (even with an I-512 parole document) will execute the order and thus bar reentry. 8 C.F.R. §§245.15(t)(3), 1245.15(t)(3).

G. *Spouses and Children*—Allows for AOS of spouse, child, or unmarried son or daughter if they are Haitian nationals, they are otherwise admissible except for the sections waived (*see in this part* section D (p.818), *supra*), they are physically present in the U.S. on the date of the application; and in the case of an unmarried son or daughter they have continuously been physically present in the U.S. since Dec. 31, 1995. The unmarried son or daughter get the benefit of the physical presence definition which permits 180 days absence in the aggregate. The documentary requirements, which include for principal beneficiaries and unmarried sons and daughters' proof of presence in the U.S. on Dec. 31, 1995, are extensive and are listed at 8 C.F.R. §§245.15(i)–(k), 1245.15(i)–(k). Dependents may file applications subsequent to Mar. 31, 2000 provided the principal filed by that date. Thus, USCIS will continue to grant advance paroles to dependents to enter the U.S. subsequent to Mar. 31, 2000. 65 Fed. Reg. 15924–25 (Mar. 24, 2000). Spouses/children who were battered or subject to extreme cruelty are also covered. And battered spouses and children are eligible even if the principal HRIFA applicant *never applied for benefits* under HRIFA. Violence Against Women and DOJ Reauthorization Act, PL 109-162 (Jan. 5, 2006), §824.

H. *Denial of HRIFA Application*—If USCIS denies the application and the applicant is out-of-status, his case may be referred to the IJ if he is not already subject to a final order of exclusion, deportation, or removal. If DHS initiates removal proceedings, the applicant may renew his application for HRIFA before the IJ. 8 C.F.R. §245.15(r)(2). If the applicant already has a final order, his case should be referred to the IJ under 8 C.F.R. §245.15(r)(3) and DHS shall notify the court by Notice of Certification (I-290C) to deny the HRIFA application.

I. *Judicial Review*—HRIFA §902(f) precludes judicial review of the denial of an application for adjustment. *Alexis v. U.S. Att'y Gen.*, 431 F.3d 1291 (11th Cir. 2005) [no jurisdiction to review denial of adjustment absent a substantial constitutional claim].

VIII. SYRIAN ADJUSTMENT ACT—PL 106-378, 114 Stat. 1442 (HR 4681) (Oct. 27, 2000); 8 C.F.R. §§245.20, 1245.20

A. *Generally*—Allows for the adjustment of status of Syrian Jews: (1) who arrived in the U.S. after Dec. 31, 1991 after being allowed to depart Syria by the Syrian government; and (2) who are physically present in the U.S. at the time of filing the AOS application. The application must have been filed no later than Oct. 26, 2001. The applicant must have been physically present in the U.S. for one year after being granted asylum; must not be firmly resettled in any foreign country; and must be otherwise admissible. A spouse, child, or unmarried son or daughter of the principal applicant may also apply. The total number of persons who may be adjusted is 2,000.

1. Inadmissibility Waived—Grounds of inadmissibility relating to INA §212(a)(4) [public charge] and §212(a)(7)(A) [documentation] are waived. Applicant may apply for INA §§212(h), (i) & (k) waivers if necessary. 8 C.F.R. §§245.20(c), 1245.20(c).

2. Filing Applications—All applications are filed with the Nebraska Service Center and the must be received by Oct. 26, 2001. 8 C.F.R. §§245.20(d), 1245.20(d). If AOS application is already filed on other grounds, may request a change in the basis for the AOS. Must request change before Oct. 27, 2001.

    2.a. Evidence, 8 C.F.R. §§245.20(e), 1245.20(e). Must submit: (1) Passport; (2) I-94 or other evidence of inspection and admission or parole after Dec. 21, 1991; (3) Documents evidencing physical presence for one year after asylum grant; (4) Spouse's marriage certificate and/or child's birth certificate.

    2.b. Can get EA and advance parole. 8 C.F.R. §§245.20(f), (g), 1245.20(f), (g).

3. Date of Adjustment—The law grants the date of adjustment as one year prior to the date of approval of AOS on the I-181. Memo, Cronin, Acting Ex. Assoc. Comm. Programs, HQADN 70/23 (May 24, 2001), *reprinted in* 78 *Interpreter Releases* 1010–14 (June 11, 2001).

IX. VIETNAM, CAMBODIA AND LAOS ADJUSTMENT ACT—PL 106-429 §586 (Nov. 1, 2000); H.R. Rep. No. 106-997; 8 C.F.R. §§245.21, 1245.21

A. *Generally*—Allows for the adjustment of status of Vietnamese, Cambodian and Laotian nationals who were paroled into the U.S. before Oct 1, 1997 and who were physically present on the date and eligible for adjustment. An applicant had to be a parolee from: (a) Vietnam under the auspices of the

Orderly Departure Program; (b) From a refugee camp in East Asia; *or* (c) from a displaced person's camp administered by the U.N. High Commissioner for Refugees in Thailand. The 5,000 cap and the 3 year filing deadline originally placed in the law were eliminated by PL 108-447 §534. Although the regulation has not been updated at 8 C.F.R. §245.21, USCIS issued a press release announcing the changes. USCIS Announces New Guidance Regarding Indochinese Parolee Adjustments (March 30, 2005). The adjustment date will be the date of parole into the U.S.

B. *Criteria*—To be eligible a person must demonstrate that s/he: (1) Is a citizen or native of Vietnam, Cambodia, or Laos; (2) Was inspected and paroled into the U.S. before Oct. 1, 1997; (3) Was physically present in the U.S. prior to and on Oct. 1, 1997; (4) Was paroled from Vietnam under the Orderly Departure Program, from a refugee camp in East Asia or from a displaced persons camp administered by the UNHCR in Thailand; (5) Applied for adjustment between Jan. 27, 2003 and Jan. 25, 2006 and paid all appropriate fees; and (6) Is otherwise eligible to receive an IV and otherwise admissible except that inadmissibility due to public charge (212(a)(4)), labor certification (212(a)(5)), lack of possession of documents for residency upon entry (212(a)(7)(A)), or prior removal or 3/10 year bar (212(a)(9)) is waived. 8 C.F.R. §§245.21(a), (e), 1245.21(a), (e).

C. *Procedure*

1. Filing Application—AOS application must be submitted in all circumstances to the Service. Neither the IJ nor the BIA have jurisdiction to AOS. If in removal proceedings, the applicant, after filing an application with the Service, must request the consent of the Service to file a joint motion to administratively close the case. Unless the Service consents, neither the IJ nor the BIA may defer proceedings. 8 C.F.R. §§245.21(b), (c). If the applicant has a final order of removal he must request a stay and the Service will generally not grant a stay if the person is inadmissible on a ground for which a waiver is necessary. 8 C.F.R. §245.21(d).

   1.a. Satisfactory Documentation—The regulations provide what documents will be satisfactory to demonstrate physical presence, 8 C.F.R. §241.22 and other requirements. 8 C.F.R. §245.21(g).

2. Waivers—Inadmissibility under INA §212(a)(1) [health related grounds], §212(a)(6)(B) [failure to appear at removal hearing], §212(a)(6)(C) [material misrepresentation], §212(a)(6)(F) [final civil penalty], §212(a)(8)(A) [ineligibility for citizenship], §212(a)(10)(B) [guardian required to accompany helpless person], and §212(a)(10)(D) [unlawful voting] may be waived upon a showing of extreme hardship to the applicant or his spouse, parent, or son or daughter who is a USC/LPR. Applications are filed on I-601 waivers. Certain criminal grounds may be waived under INA §212(h) where appropriate. 8 C.F.R. §§245.21(f).

3. Travel and Employment—An applicant may seek employment by filing an I-765 and may obtain permission to travel. 8 C.F.R. §§245.21(h), (i).

X. USA PATRIOT ACT—Uniting and Strengthening America by Providing Appropriate Tools Required to Intercept and Obstruct Terrorism Act of 2001, PL 107-56, 115 Stat. 272 (Oct. 26, 2001), Title IV, Subtitle C §§421–28; 22 C.F.R. §42.32(d)(9).

A. *Generally*—Provides for special benefits for family members of persons who were victims of the Sept. 11, 2001, attacks by allowing them to become special immigrants or to self-petition. It allows for the extension of certain deadlines for children who have become 21, for persons granted voluntary departure or for persons who missed the diversity lottery deadline as a result of the events of Sept. 11.

B. *Special Immigrant Status under §421*—Section 421 of the Act provides special immigrant status to: (1) persons whose family/employment-based petitions, fiancé(e) petitions, or LC were revoked/terminated or rendered null by the death, disability or loss of employment of the petitioner, applicant or beneficiary as a result of the events of Sept 11; (2) Spouse and children of such persons who were accompanying or following to join the principal no later than Sept 11, 2003; (3) Grandparents of child of USC/LPR parents who died in attack. The public charge ground of inadmissibility does not apply and therefore an affidavit of support (I-864) is not required. Memo, Anderson, Ex. Assoc. Comm., Office of Policy and Planning, HQADN 70/23.1 (Jan. 31, 2002), *published on* AILA InfoNet at Doc. No. 02032533. The grandparent to qualify must demonstrate that they will assume legal custody of the orphaned child before s/he becomes 21. The spouse or child of the grandparent may accompany or follow to join. Cable, DOS, 01-State-79359 (Apr. 26, 2002) ¶20, *published on* AILA InfoNet at Doc. No. 02042690; 9 FAM 42.32(d)(9), N.1-4. Special immigrant status is recognized at 22 C.F.R. §42.32(d)(9) and public charge is waived as a ground of inadmissibility. 22 C.F.R. §42.32(d)(9)(i)(B)(ii).

1. Procedures—The applicant applies for special immigrant status on I-360 in the service center with jurisdiction over the applicant's place of residence. Need to indicate on the form the specific basis for eligibility and note in Part II, Box K that s/he is applying for benefits under the USA PATRIOT Act. An applicant should include with the I-360 the following: (a) evidence that demonstrates the requisite death, disability, or loss of employment; (b) a statement describing, or evidence of, the petition or application that was revoked, terminated, or rendered null by the events of Sept. 11, 2001. Evidence may include a receipt issued by the INS. For grandparent who is petitioning s/he must demonstrated that s/he is coming to U.S. to assume legal custody of the orphaned grandchild before the child turns 21 or the child was under the age of 18 at the time the petition was filed and is not older than 21. Memo, Anderson (Jan. 31, 2002), *supra*, at 3. Once the I-360 is approved, the applicant may file for AOS on I-485. *Id.*

C. *Protection for NIVs*—Section 422 of the Act provides protection for NIVs who were disabled as a direct result of 9/11. They may remain in the U.S. the latter of the date their status terminates or one year after the onset of the disability. Also, NIVs who were unable to depart due to 9/11 will be considered to have timely departed if the departure occurred before Nov. 11, 2001, and will not be considered to have accrued unlawful presence until that time. This section also gives DV 2001 lottery winners until Apr. 1, 2002, to adjust status if, as a direct result of the terrorist attacks, they were prevented from using the diversity visa before the (Sept. 30) end of the DV 2001 year. If the principal lottery winner died as a result of 9/11 and obtained his DV status, his spouse and children would still be eligible. If the principal obtained DV status before his or her death and the family members were following to join, they must have sought that status before June 30, 2002, under the provisions of section 422(c)(3). Family members must provide death certificate or other evidence of principal's death due to terrorist attack. Cable, DOS, 02-State-032257 (Feb. 20, 2002), *published on* AILA InfoNet at Doc. No. 02022131. Section 422 also extended grants of parole for 90 days so that a person returning to the U.S. with an expired I-512 with an expiration date on or after Sept. 11, 2001, will be admitted as if the I-512 was not expired for a 90-day period after expiration if s/he can establish that s/he was prevented from returning to the U.S. by a specified terrorist activity. Section 422 also extended VD for a period of 30 days if VD expired between Sept. 11, 2001, and Oct. 11, 2001. There is no requirement that the person who received VD shows that the delay in departure was due to terrorism. Memo, Anderson, Ex. Assoc. Comm., Office of Policy and Planning, HQADN 70/23.1 (Jan. 31, 2002) at 7, *published on* AILA InfoNet at Doc. No. 02032533. For those provisions requiring such a showing of delay, the circumstances that would be considered include: office closures, airline flight cessations or delays and other closures, cessations, or delays affecting case processing or travel necessary to satisfy legal requirements. *Id* at 8.

D. *Self-Petitions for LPR Status*—Section 423 provides that the alien spouse or children of U.S. citizens who died in the terrorist attacks may self-petition for LPR status. 22 C.F.R. §42.21(b), (c). It does not include a fiancé(e) where USC did not petition. Cable, DOS, 01-State-79359 (Apr. 26, 2002) ¶10, *reprinted in* 79 No. 21 *Interpreter Releases* 782–86 (May 20, 2002) Need not wait two years as widow/widower. In order to qualify the spouse and children would have to petition within two years and the spouse could not have been legally separated from the deceased USC or remarried. The petitioning children will be considered to remain immediate relatives for 2 years regardless of age or marriage. Memo, Anderson, Ex. Assoc. Comm., Office of Policy and Planning, HQADN 70/23.1 (Jan. 31, 2002) at 9, *published on* AILA InfoNet at Doc. No. 02032533. The section also provides that where an LPR died in the terrorist attacks and his spouse, child or unmarried adult son/daughter had been the beneficiary of an I-130 petition, the petition is still valid and they remain eligible for LPR status. The spouse, child, or son or daughter of an LPR who died on Sept 11, 2001, as a result of the terrorist attack may also self-petition if they were present in the U.S. on Sept. 11, 2001. *See also* Cable, DOS, 01-State-190946 (Nov. 2, 2001), *reprinted in* 78 No. 47 *Interpreter Releases* 1871, 1872–74 (Dec. 10, 2001) [reviewing general and most immediate provisions of USA PATRIOT Act]. Section 423(c) also provides for the admissibility of a spouse or child of an employment-based LPR or person who had an employment-based I-485 pending; the survivor may continue to have his or her I-485 adjudicated, provided the I-485 was filed on or before Sept. 11, 2002, and s/he was in the U.S. before Sept. 11, 2001. Memo, Anderson (Jan. 31, 2002), *supra*, at 10; Cable, DOS, 01-State-79359, *supra* at ¶25.

1. Procedures—If the person was the spouse or child of a USC, s/he must file an I-130 within 2 years of the death of the USC. The petitioner should write in box A of the I-130, "USA PATRIOT Act, Section 423(a)." Memo, Anderson (Jan. 31, 2002), *supra*, at 9. If the person was the spouse or child of an LPR, s/he may apply for employment authorization and may request deferred action. No petition is required for the retention of the priority date where an I-130 was already filed. If an I-130 was not filed the spouse or child or the LPR may self-petition by filing the petition at the service center having jurisdiction over the petitioner's place of residence. During the time, the self-petitioner awaits a visa s/he may request deferred action and employment authorization. When the priority date becomes current s/he may apply for AOS. *Id.* For the person seeking AOS through a person who was an LPR through an employment-based petition or who had filed an I-485, no new application or petition was required. For any of the petitions filed under Section 423, the public-charge ground of inadmissibility is waived, and a person need not file an affidavit of support. *Id.* at 11.

E. *Aged-Out Children*—Section 424 provides for an automatic 45-day extension for any child beneficiary of a petition, asylum, or refugee application, an E/S, C/S, or AOS application filed on or before Sept. 11, 2001, for a child under the age of 21. USCIS shall consider the child to remain in that status for an additional period of 45 days after his or her 21st birthday. (Extension was 90 days if the child's 21st birthday occurred in the month of Sept. 2001.) DOS agrees. Cable, DOS, 02-State-123775 (June 26, 2002), *published on* AILA InfoNet at Doc. No. 02070941. If the I-485 was filed on or prior to Sept. 11, 2001, or is based upon a visa petition filed on or before Sept. 11, and the applicant's 21st birthday occurred after Sept. 2001, the application may be approved for an additional 45 days from the date of his or her 21st birthday. This section does not require any link to the events of Sept. 11. *Id.* The 45-day period provided here may also works in conjunction with the Child Status Protection Act (CSPA), PL 107-208, to determine whether a child aged-out before Aug. 6, 2002, the effective date of the Act. Memo, Williams, Ex. Assoc. Comm., Office of Field Operations, INS, HQADN 70/6.1.1 (Feb. 14, 2003), *published on* AILA InfoNet at Doc. No. 03031040. DOS has taken the position that they will consular process immediate relatives even if the child is over 21, and they will issue visas "regardless of age or marital status." Cable, DOS, 01-State-79359 (Apr. 26, 2002) ¶9, *published on* AILA InfoNet at Doc. No. 02042690.

F. *Administrative Relief*—Section 425 authorizes the AG to grant administrative relief to any person lawfully present in the U.S. on Sept. 10, 2001 who was the spouse, parent, or child of a person who died or was disabled as a direct result of a specified terrorist activity. The AG may grant the person deferred action and employment authorization. *Id* at 11–12.

G. *Evidence/Documentation of Death, Disability, or Loss of Employment* [Section 426]

1. Documentation evidencing death that may be used to qualify: (a) an official death certificate; (b) an interim death certificate; (c) flight records; (d) public records listing the deceased as a victim; and (e) other official or nonofficial documentation.

2. Disability is defined as "A physical or mental impairment that substantially limits one or more of the major life activities of such individual." A licensed psychiatrist or medical doctor must provide documentation that the physical or mental impairment meets this definition and is a direct result of the specified terrorist activity. Memo, Anderson (Jan. 31, 2002), *supra*, at 13–14.

3. Documentation of loss of employment—The following documentation may be used to demonstrate loss of employment due to physical damage: (a) a letter from the employer; (b) official records indicating that the business was completely destroyed; or (c) other documentation showing the complete destruction of the business. If the person can continue to be employed but at a different location, s/he will not be considered to have lost employment. Cable, DOS, 01-State-79359 (Apr. 26, 2002) ¶31-35, *reprinted in* 79 No. 21 *Interpreter Releases* 782–86 (May 20, 2002).

H. *Exception for Perpetrators*—Section 427 provides that no benefits under the above provisions will be provided to family members of persons culpable for the terrorist attacks on Sept. 11.

I. *Definition of Terrorist Activity*—Section 428 defines "specified terrorist activity" as "any terrorist activity conducted against the Government or people of the United States on September 11, 2001." It includes the attacks on the World Trade Center and the Pentagon as well as the crash of Flight 93. It does not include the subsequent anthrax attacks or threats or other previous or subsequent terrorist activities.

XI. PETITION PROCESS

A. ***Immediate Relatives; 1st to 4th Family Preferences***—For immediate-relative or family-related preferences (1st, 2nd, 3rd, 4th preference), the petitioner is the USC/LPR who is applying for his or her alien-beneficiary relative. The petitioner files the application on an I-130 petition. In the case of a widow(er) and widow(er)'s children, a battered spouse, a spouse whose children were battered by the USC/LPR spouse (even if they are not the children of the USC/LPR), or the battered child of USC/LPR (or where there is extreme cruelty by USC/LPR), the government provides for a self-petition. Self-petitions are filed on I-360 petitions. However, in the case of widow(er)s, if the petition was filed as an I-130, the couple had been married for 2 years, and the petitioner dies, the spouse's petition is automatically converted into an I-360 petition if the widow(er) otherwise qualifies for an I-360. 8 C.F.R. §204.2(i)(1)(iv).

B. ***Battered Spouses or Children***—The spouse or child who is subject to extreme cruelty or battered may file a self-petition independently of USC/LPR abusive spouse or parent. INA §§204(a)(1)(A)(iii)–(iv); 8 U.S.C. §§1154(a)(1)(A)(iii)–(iv), (a)(1)(B)(ii)–(iii); 8 C.F.R. §204.2(c), (e). For a detailed discussion, *see in this chapter* ¶ II.B.5, (p.775), *supra.*

C. ***Widow(er)s***—In the case of widow(er)s and their children their applications are filed on an I-360. However, if the petition was filed as an I-130 and then the petitioner dies after two years of marriage, it is automatically converted into an I-360 petition if the widow(er) otherwise qualifies for an I-360. 8 C.F.R. §204.2(i)(1)(iv). For a more lengthy discussion, *see in this chapter* ¶ II.B.4 (p.775), *supra.*

D. ***Spouse, Parent, or Child of Member of Armed Forces Killed in Combat***—Allows self-petitioning for the spouse, parent, or child of a USC who served honorably in the Armed Forces and died as a result of injury or disease incurred in or aggravated by combat, as long as s/he petitions within 2 years of the USC's death. The spouse may apply as long as she is not legally separated from her spouse at the time of his death and does not remarry during the petitioning process. A child may apply even if s/he becomes 21 or marries after the USC's death. INA §201(b)(2)(A)(i). The parent's petition will be treated as an immediate-relative petition even if the USC child was under 21 years of age. Also allows a spouse, parent, or child of an LPR (who honorably served, died as a result of injury or disease incurred in or aggravated by combat, and who posthumously became a USC) to self-petition as an immediate relative if filed within 2 years of LPR's death. The spouse, parent, or child is also eligible for deferred action, advance parole, and work authorization. Public charge is waived as a ground of inadmissibility. A spouse, parent, or child (of a USC who served honorably in active duty status, who died as a result of injury or disease incurred in or aggravated by combat and who was granted posthumous citizenship under INA §329A) may also adjust his or her status to permanent residency if the adjustment was filed prior to the USC's death.

E. ***Procedures***

1. DD or service center may withhold adjudication of a petition or application (including I-130s, I-140s, I-360s, and I-485s) when an investigation is pending and disclosure of evidence would prejudice the investigation. 8 C.F.R. §103.2(b)(18). However, this process is not indefinite and requires procedurally that the director, the regional commissioner, and, finally the associate commissioners for enforcement and adjudications certify the need for the delay in 6-month increments. *Dong v. Chertoff,* 513 F.Supp.2d 1158, 1166–68 (N.D. Cal. 2007) [8 C.F.R. §103.2(b)(18) limits the discretion of USCIS to continue/withhold the adjudication of a petition/application and therefore *is subject* to judicial review and is not precluded by INA §242(a)(2)(B)(ii)]; *But see Qui v. Chertoff,* 486 F.Supp.2d 412, 418–19 (D.N.J. 2007) [reading the regulation for the opposite position]. If USCIS requires additional documents or requests clarification, petitioner has 12 weeks to supply missing information or to rebut USCIS findings. 8 C.F.R. §103.2(b)(8). During this period the priority date may be unaffected, but no interim benefits (*e.g.,* employment authorization) will be granted. 8 C.F.R. §103.2(b)(10).
2. Issuance of Request for Evidence (RFE) or Notice of Intent to Deny (NOID)—When an application/petition is neither immediately denied for being clearly ineligible, nor approved because the record is complete and the applicant/petitioner met the appropriate evidentiary standard, USCIS may issue either an RFE or NOID. For a discussion of each, *see* Ch. 5, ¶ III.N.4 (p.635), *supra.*

3. Beneficiary Must be Eligible at Time Petition is Filed—*Matter of Drigo*, 18 I&N Dec. 223 (BIA 1982). The Service interprets this to mean that "the standard for amending a petition is ... whether the petition was approvable on the date it was filed. Any amendment based on facts...that come into existence after the filing date, must be made in a new petition with a new filing and priority date." Letter, Dixon, Deputy Gen. Counsel, (HQCOU 70/11.1-C) (Sept. 10, 1998) at p.6, *reprinted in* 75 No. 37 *Interpreter Releases* 13351344-55 (Sept. 28, 1998); *Matter of Izumii,* 22 I&N Dec. 169, 175 (1998); *Matter of Katigbak,* 14 I&N Dec. 45 (Reg. Com. 1971). Beneficiary must also be eligible at the time he is receiving his immigrant visa or adjustment of status. *Pazcoguin v. Radcliffe,* 292 F.3d 1209 (9th Cir. 2002) [beneficiary's admission to medical doctor during medical examination for IV in Philippines that he smoked marijuana for a number of years was used as the basis to deny visa upon entry to U.S. and to thereafter exclude him]; *Shaikhs v. INS,* 181 F.3d 823 (7th Cir. 1999) [where respondent divorced one month before he entered U.S. as LPR his status was invalid]. Where petitioner is LPR *and* living in the U.S., his or her status cannot be attacked by the Service in visa petition proceedings. *Matter of Umale*, 16 I&N Dec. 682 (BIA 1979).

4. Approved Petition—When an approved petition is already used to obtain residency, it cannot be used a second time. *Matter of Villarreal-Zuniga,* 23 I&N Dec. 886 (BIA 2006) [cannot adjust status based upon an approved I-130 petition that was previously used to obtain residency]; 8 C.F.R. §204.2(h)(2).

5. Burden of Proof is on the Petitioner—*Matter of Brantigan*, 11 I&N Dec. 493 (BIA 1966); *Egan v. Weiss*, 119 F.3d 106 (2d Cir. 1997) [BIA did not abuse discretion in denying petition by refusing to accept order of Nigerian court where there was substantial fraud]. Where petitioner filed a relative petition for a beneficiary but never disclosed on previously filed petition (*e.g.,* I-485/N-400) that petitioner had the relative s/he is now petitioning for, s/he must establish family relationship by "clear and convincing" evidence. *Matter of Ma*, 20 I&N Dec. 394 (BIA 1991). But the burden of proof is not insurmountable and the Service will abuse its discretion when it relies on information that is demonstrably false. *Camarena v. Meissner,* 78 F.Supp.2d 1044 (N.D.Cal. 1999) [INS abused its discretion in denying extension of family unity benefits by relying on information that was rebutted and shown to be demonstrably false].

6. Considering Government Error or Delay and Compelling Circumstances—USCIS has recognized that there may be circumstances where due to "government error or delay and compelling humanitarian factors," the officer may exercise his judgment to render an "extraordinary favorable" decision to the applicant. Memo, Divine, Acting Deputy Director, USCIS (May 3, 2006), *published on* AILA InfoNet at Doc. No. 06051562

7. Inadmissibility and Petition Approval—Under INA §204(b) a petition may not be denied based upon the conclusion that the beneficiary is inadmissible. *Matter of O-,* 8 I&N Dec. 295 (BIA 1959); Memo, Divine, GC, USCIS, HQOCC 70/6.22/04 (Oct. 14, 2004), *published on* AILA InfoNet at Doc. No. 04111566 [a willful and unexcused failure to comply with NSEERS cannot support the denial of a visa petition].

8. Copies vs. Originals—Petitioner must submit originals of the application or petition and the documents issued to support them such as a labor certification, Form DS-2019, medical examinations, affidavits, formal consultations, letters of current employment and all other documents needed to support the benefit sought unless it is an document issued by USCIS or the legacy INS. 8 C.F.R. §§103.2(b)(4). The agency may request that other originals be submitted as well and failure to submit them by the deadline may result in denial or revocation. 8 C.F.R. §103.2(b)(5). Documentary requirements for petitioner's lawful status are found at 8 C.F.R. §103.2(b)(17). An applicant or petitioner may sign for him- or herself even if s/he is a minor. 8 C.F.R. §103.2(a)(2).

9. Unavailability of records—Where record does not exist, applicant or petitioner must obtain letter on original government letterhead unless the FAM indicates the document does not exist, in which case the letter requirement is waived. 8 C.F.R. §103.2(b)(2)(ii). *Cf. Hernandez v. Ashcroft,* 345 F.3d 824, 842–44 (9th Cir. 2003) [reversed DHS denial of adjustment based upon failure to produce approved visa petition where applicant provided a letter from the Transitional Immigrant Visa Processing Center including her priority date].

10. Birth Certificates—If a birth certificate is required and a petitioner fails to produce it, s/he may submit secondary evidence. However, the Service takes the view that "the unavailability of a birth

certificate creates a presumption of ineligibility for the benefit, and any alternative evidence submitted must be evaluated for its authenticity and credibility.8 C.F.R. §103.2(b)(2)(i) and 204.2(d)(2)(v)." Memo, Cronin, Acting Ex. Assoc. Comm. Office of Programs, HQADN 70/11 (July 14, 2000), *reprinted in* 77 No. 29 *Interpreter Releases* 1096, 1104–12, 1105 (July 31, 2000). Delayed birth certificates, even when unrebutted by contradictory evidence may be deemed insufficient to prove paternity. *Matter of Bueno*, 21 I&N Dec. 1029, 1032–34 (BIA 1997) [finding delayed birth certificate and affidavit from mother insufficient to establish father's paternity]; *Matter of Pagan,* 22 I&N Dec. 547 (BIA 1999) [reaffirming *Bueno* but allowing proof by blood test alone under 8 C.F.R. §204.2(d)(2)(vi)]. If documents are not produced, the Service may suggest HLA or DNA testing, but they may only be done through labs accredited by the AABB (formerly American Association of Blood Banks). Memo, Aytes, Assoc. Dir. Domestic Operations, USCIS (Mar. 19, 2008), *published on* AILA InfoNet at Doc. No. 08032430 [to find accredited testers applicant can go to *www.aabb.org*]. However, DOS has informed consular officers that they "should use other methods, such as conducting a thorough interview, to determine whether the necessary relationship exists, leaving the applicant the option of providing DNA evidence if other available evidence is insufficient." Cable, DOS 01-State-22995 (Feb. 8, 2001*), reprinted in* 78 No. 11 *Interpreter Releases* 532–33 (Mar. 19, 2001). DNA testing may be offered as an alternative to the beneficiary where the consular officer has developed sufficient evidence to return the petition to USCIS. *Id.* Only the polymerase chain reaction-short tandem repeats (PCR-STR) and the restriction fragment length polymorphism (RFLP) methods of DNA testing are acceptable and they must be done by a lab accredited by the American Association of Blood Banks (AABB). *Id.* Similarly, USCIS officers should only ask for DNA testing where "credible evidence is insufficient to prove the claimed biological relationship" and the officer can never "require" DNA testing. Memo, Aytes, Assoc. Dir. Domestic Operations, USCIS (Mar. 19, 2008), *published on* AILA InfoNet at Doc. No. 08032430.

10.a. Proof of U.S. Citizenship. An applicant may prove U.S. citizenship through: (i) a birth certificate that was issued by a civil authority; (ii) a certificate of naturalization; (iii) an unexpired U.S. passport issued for the full validity to the petitioner as a citizen (and not as a noncitizen national); (iv) Form FS-240 Report of Birth Abroad; and (v) secondary evidence (but a petition with such evidence would be considered "not clearly approvable" and forwarded to USCIS office). Cable, 07-State-081258 (June 12, 2007), *published on* AILA InfoNet at Doc. No. 08031930; 8 C.F.R. §204.1(g)(1)(i); 9 FAM Appendix 200, §201.2.

11. Disclosure of Petitioner's Criminal History to Beneficiary—USCIS may disclose to a beneficiary or her legal guardian, a petitioner's criminal history involving violence or sex offenses. The disclosure must be consistent with the requirements of 5 U.S.C. §552a(b)(8) that disclosure is "pursuant to a showing of compelling circumstances affecting the health and safety of an individual..." The fact of disclosure must also be provided in writing to the petitioner. Memo, Divine, Acting Deputy Director, HQOPRD 70/6.1.1 (May 3, 2006), *published on* AILA InfoNet at Doc. No. 06051563.

12. Confidential evidence—Government may rely on confidential evidence in deciding both discretionary and nondiscretionary applications. 8 C.F.R. §103.2(b)(16)(iv). However, due process is offended when such information is used to deny a nondiscretionary grant such as legalization. *Compare American-Arab Anti-Discrimination Comm. v. Reno*, 70 F.3d 1045, 1066–71 (9th Cir. 1995), enjoining the Service from using undisclosed classified information in legalization process, *with Jay v. Boyd*, 351 U.S. 345, 358–60 (1956) relying on classified information to deny discretionary relief.

13. Evidence in Cases Involving Battery and Extreme Cruelty to Spouses and Children—A special "any credible evidence" standard applies to all elements of petitions by spouses and children subject to battery or extreme cruelty. INA §204(a)(1)(J). USCIS recognizes that evidence normally available to family-based petitioners may not be accessible because of the dynamics of domestic violence. 8 C.F.R. §204.2(c)(2)(i).

14. Expedited Processing of Cases—USCIS Service Centers do accept requests to expedite cases separate and apart from Premium Processing. They will accept expedite requests based on the following criteria: (1) Severe financial loss to the company or individual; (2) Extreme emergent situation; (3) Humanitarian situation; (4) DOD or National Interest Situation (Note: Request must

come from U.S. government entity and explain why delay would be detrimental); and (5) USCIS error. Memo, Ohata, 70/1 (Apr. 20, 2001), *reprinted in* 78 No. 25 *Interpreter Releases* 1072, 1118 (July 2, 2001) [provides telephone and fax numbers to make requests at Service Centers]. In addition, the Vermont Service Center has a dedicated unit that addresses all battered spouse and child petitions nationwide and a special telephone number for attorneys to call to request expedited consideration of such cases.

15. Fee Schedule—The fee for each petition is listed at 8 C.F.R. §§103.7(b), 1103.7(b). Fees may be waived by USCIS where there is an inability to pay. INS has provided general guidance as to the grant of such a waiver. In determining whether someone can demonstrate "inability to pay" under the regulation INS officers should consider: (1) whether person qualified for and received federal means-tested public benefits; (2) whether her household income is below the poverty guidelines; (3) whether the person is elderly (65 or over); (4) whether a person is disabled as determined by a federal agency; (5) the age and number of dependents in the person's household who are seeking derivative status or concurrent benefits; (6) humanitarian or compassionate reasons (*e.g.,* temporary destitution or in a nursing home). INS should also take into consideration whether person is a self-petitioning abused spouse or child. Memo, Pearson, Exec. Assoc. Comm. for Field Operations, (HQ 70/5.5) (Oct. 9, 1998), *reprinted in* 75 No. 41 *Interpreter Releases* 1478, 1497–1503 (Oct. 26, 1998); 8 C.F.R. §§103.7(c), 1103.7(c). Fact Sheet, USCIS Fee Waiver Guidance (Mar. 29, 2004), *published on* AILA InfoNet at Doc. No. 04033164 [addressing documentation necessary to establish basis for waiver].

F. *What does approval mean?*

1. Certifies alien eligible for LPR status.

2. Does Not Grant Lawful Permanent Residence—Beneficiary of petition must still obtain adjustment of status or visa approval. Beneficiary must be eligible at the time he is receiving his immigrant visa or adjustment of status. *Shaikhs v. INS,* 181 F.3d 823 (7th Cir. 1999) [where respondent divorced one month before he entered U.S. as LPR his status was invalid]. Both qualitative restrictions (*e.g.,* spouse of LPR obtains approval of petition; however, the spouse is ineligible for residency because drug conviction bars residency under INA §212(a)(2)(A)(i)(II)), and quantitative (quota) restrictions apply (*e.g.,* under 2nd preference backlog for spouses is approximately 6 years). Beneficiary of petition needs to meet both sets of restrictions before s/he can obtain residency based on the approved I-130 petition.

3. Approval of Petition Does Not Necessarily Stay Deportation or Removal Proceeding—*Morgan v. Gonzales,* 445 F.3d 549 (2d Cir. 2006) [IJ did not abuse his discretion or deny due process when he denied continuance to permit the adjudication of an I-130 stemming from a marriage that had previously been determined to lack *bona fides*]; *Ngongo v. Ashcroft,* 397 F.3d 821 (9th Cir. 2005) [affirmed AWO decision to deport on grounds first I-130 was fraudulent even though a three judge panel reversed the DD's denial of a second I-130 filed by the same spouse]; *Matter of H-A-,* 22 I&N Dec. 728 (BIA 1999) [following *Matter of Arthur* the Board ruled that where I-130 petition was approved more than 90 days after final order reopening is barred by former 8 C.F.R. §3.2(c)]; *Matter of Arthur*, 20 I&N Dec. 475 (BIA 1992) [modifying *Garcia* and declining to grant motions to reopen for AOS where unapproved petition is based on marriage entered into after deportation proceedings commenced, thus falling within INA §§204(g) and 245(e)]; *Dielmann v. INS*, 34 F.3d 851 (9th Cir. 1994) [same]; *Rezai v. INS*, 62 F.3d 1286, 1289–92 (10th Cir. 1995) [followed *Arthur*]; *Pritchett v. INS*, 993 F.2d 80 (5th Cir.), *cert. denied*, 114 S.Ct. 345 (1993) [same]. *But see Haswanee v. U.S. Att'y Gen.,* 471 F.3d 1212 (11th Cir. 2006) [where LC was approved, I-140 filed, and visa immediately available, but no I-485 filed, it was an abuse of discretion to deny continuance but not a violation of equal protection or due process]; *Merchant v. U.S. Att'y Gen.,* 461 F.3d 1375 (11th Cir. 2006) [where LC was approved and respondent filed I-140 and I-485 with DHS pursuant to INA §245(i) it was an abuse of discretion by IJ to deny a continuance. *Bull* supported and *Zafar* distinguished]; *Benslimane v. Gonzales,* 430 F.3d 828 (7th Cir. 2005) [IJ made legal error in denying continuance where respondent had filed I-130 and I-485 as part of marriage based adjustment but had not filed adjustment with IJ]; *Bull v. INS*, 790 F.2d 869 (11th Cir. 1986); *Matter of Velarde-Pacheco,* 23 I&N Dec. 253 (BIA 2002) [*Matter of Arthur* and *H-A-* modified to allow for motions to reopen where the motion for I-485/ I-130 are filed within 90 days, is not numerically barred, is not barred by *Matter of Shaar* or any other procedural

grounds, presents clear and convincing evidence that the marriage is bona fide, and the Service either does not oppose the motion or bases its opposition solely on *Matter of Arthur*]; *Singh v. Gonzales,* 404 F.3d 1024, 1027–29 (7th Cir. 2005) [where I-130 had been approved the BIA's reliance on *Matter of Velarde-Pacheco* to deny motion to reconsider to allow adjustment was error because *Velarde* involved an unadjudicated I-130; however under facts of case error was harmless].

4. Filing or Approval of I-130 Petition Alone Does Not Grant Prehearing VD—Can no longer obtain work authorization with prehearing voluntary departure even if visa available within 60 days, 8 C.F.R. §240.25. Can obtain up to 120 days of prehearing VD. 8 C.F.R. §240.25. A denial may not be subject to judicial review because it is committed to agency discretion. *Lalani v. Perryman*, 105 F.3d 334, 337–38 (7th Cir. 1997); *Perales v. Casillas*, 903 F.2d 1043 (5th Cir. 1990) [prehearing voluntary departure and employment authorization decision is committed to agency discretion].

G. *Persons Precluded from Petitioning*

1. Sex Offenders Against Minors—INA §§204(a)(1)(A)(viii), 204(a)(1)(B)(i)(II). A USC or LPR who has been convicted of a specified offense against a minor as defined in Sec. 111(7) of the Adam Walsh Child Protection and Safety Act of 2007, PL 109-248, 120 Stat. 587 (July 27, 2006), is prohibited from petitioning for family members, unless the Secretary of DHS, in her "unreviewable discretion" determines that the USC or LPR poses no risk to the beneficiary of the petition. Section 111(7) defines a "specified offense against a minor" as an offense against a minor that involves any of the following: (A) an offense (unless committed by a parent or guardian) involving kidnapping; (B) an offense (unless committed by a parent or guardian) involving false imprisonment; (C) solicitation to engage in sexual conduct; (D) use in a sexual performance; (E) solicitation to practice prostitution; (F) video voyeurism as described in 18 U.S.C. §1801; (G) possession, production or distribution of child pornography; (H) criminal sexual conduct involving a minor, or the use of the Internet to facilitate or attempt such conduct; or (I) any conduct that by its nature is a sex offense against a minor.

   1.a. Waiver of Criminal Bars under Adam Walsh Act—The waiver under this provision is in the "sole and unreviewable discretion" of the DHS upon a determination that the "petitioner poses no risk to the beneficiary." Memo, Aytes, Assoc. Dir. Domestic Operations, 70/1-P (July 28, 2006), *published on* AILA InfoNet at 06080264. For a more detailed discussion of the evidentiary issues and the criminal bar, see Ch. 5, ¶ IX.A.2.i(6) (p.754), *supra*.

H. *Denials of Petitions*

1. Applicant entitled to obtain adverse evidence where denial is based on adverse or derogatory information and must be given an opportunity to rebut it. 8 C.F.R. §103.2(b)(16). Evidence must be part of record. *Matter of Pradieu*, 19 I&N Dec. 419 (BIA 1986) [reversed denial where specific basis for denial and evidence underlying denial were absent from record]. Where petitioner is not given the opportunity to rebut adverse evidence and he proffers rebuttal evidence on appeal, the denial will be reversed and the case remanded. *Matter of Cuello*, 20 I&N Dec. 94 (BIA 1989); *Matter of Soriano*, 19 I&N Dec. 764 (BIA 1988). *But see Ghaly v. INS*, 58 F.3d 1425, 1431 (9th Cir. 1995) [INS can produce derogatory evidence in summary form].

2. Applicant must be given a reasonable opportunity to rebut evidence. *Matter of Obaigbena*, 19 I&N Dec. 533 (BIA 1988). Criteria to determine whether a request for extension to respond should be granted, include:

   2.a. limited time requested, preferably no more than a few weeks;

   2.b. unavailability of certain persons for affidavits and reasons for unavailability;

   2.c. need to obtain sworn statements from a significant number of persons; and

   2.d. need to obtain documents from distant sources. *Id.* DD does not need to give extension to produce documents that should have been produced originally.

3. Motion to Reopen or Reconsider—The procedure for motions to reopen or reconsider before USCIS are governed by 8 C.F.R. §103.5. Each Service Center maintains its own detailed procedures on how to treat appeals and motions to reopen and reconsider. *See e.g.*, Way, Director, Ne-

braska Service Center, NSC Motions and Appeals Processes for other than Special Agricultural Worker and Legalization Cases, NSC 70/41.1.1 (Feb. 10, 2004), *published on* AILA InfoNet at Doc. No. 04021763.

4. Administrative and Judicial Review. A denial of an I-130 petition may be reviewed by the BIA. 8 C.F.R. §1003.1(b). The petitioner may seek judicial review of the denial. *Bangura v. Hansen,* 434 F.3d 487 (6th Cir. 2006) [permitting district court review of constitutional, APA and INA challenges to INA §204(c) procedure and denial of I-130 petition]; *Hanif v. DHS,* 472 F.Supp.2d 914, 920–22 (E.D. Mich. 2007) [court has jurisdiction to review denial of I-130 petition under the APA but there is no final agency action by the BIA so the petition must be dismissed]; *Cedeno v. Ridge,* 336 F.Supp.2d 147, 150–52 (D.P.R. 2004) [jurisdiction over adjustment to review INA §204(c) determination because it is nondiscretionary, but review is in circuit court not district court].

I. *Venue for Petitions*

1. If filing a visa petition:

   1.a. Must file I-130 or I-360 with service center at place of petitioner's residence. The residence of the beneficiary is not relevant or controlling. 8 C.F.R. §204.1(e). In battered spouse/children cases all petitions are filed with the Vermont Service Center.

   1.b. If petitioner's residence is in U.S. but temporarily visiting in foreign country, must file I-130 in U.S. 8 C.F.R. §204.1(e)(1). If the petitioner resides abroad in a country where there is a DHS office, s/he must file application there. 8 C.F.R. §204.1(e)(2). If petitioner resides in another country, the consular officer may accept the application. 8 C.F.R. §204.1(e)(3). Petitioner must demonstrate that s/he has permission to reside in the country and has been residing there for six months. U.S. military personnel may also file abroad if residing in the consular district. Even if petitioner does *not* reside in consular district, he may accept the petition in "emergent or humanitarian cases and cases in the national interest." 8 C.F.R. §204.1(e)(3).; USCIS Update, Consular Offices Abroad Resume Accepting I-130 Petitions (Mar. 26, 2007), *published on* AILA InfoNet at Doc. No. 07032762. Special humanitarian reasons may arise where: (1) The qualifying marriage took place abroad; or (2)The beneficiary is very young or very old in need of care by petitioner. Comments to Regulations, 54 Fed. Reg. 34141–42, *reprinted in* 66 No. 33 *Interpreter Releases* 963, 974–75 (Aug. 28, 1989). Family emergencies that would warrant filing in the district include minor children unexpectedly left without a caretaker. National interest includes facilitating the travel of U.S. military and other U.S. government direct-hire employees assigned overseas who are pending transfer. *See* 84 No. 13 *Interpreter Releases* 725, 739 (Mar. 26, 2007).

2. If filing in conjunction with an application for adjustment of status:

   Applications filed at the place of residence of beneficiary when filing petition and adjustment application together. 8 C.F.R. §204.1(e).

J. *Revocation of approved petitions*

1. Forms of revocation—USCIS may revoke petition for "good and sufficient cause" with notice. INA §205, 8 U.S.C. §1155.

   1.a. Revoked on grounds other than those specified as "automatic" grounds. 8 C.F.R. §205.2.

   1.b. Revocation cannot be based on unsupported statements, unstated presumptions or where the petitioner is unaware and has not been advised of derogatory information. *Matter of Estime,* 19 I&N Dec. 450 (BIA 1987) [review by BIA of revocations where notice is required]; *Matter of Arias*, 19 I&N Dec. 568 (BIA 1988) [reversed revocation where it was based on consul's memorandum which was conclusory, speculative, equivocal and irrelevant]. *But see Ghaly v. INS*, 58 F.3d 1425, 1434 (9th Cir. 1995) [derogatory information may be in summary form; regulation does not mandate full document].

   1.c. A petition may be revoked whether or not the beneficiary is in the U.S. *Matter of Vilos,* 12 I&N Dec. 61 (BIA 1967), *But see Firstland International, Inc. v. INS,* 377 F.3d 127 (2d Cir. 2004) [under plain language of 8 U.S.C. §1155 legacy INS had no authority to revoke petition for someone who is out of the country]. The notice requirement and the penalty for failure to properly notify under INA §205, however, have been eliminated and the elimination was made retroactive for any revocation made before, on, or after Dec. 17, 2004. Intelligence Reform and Terrorism Prevention Act of 2004, PL 108-458, 118 Stat. 3638 §5304(d). *See also Estrada-Canales v. Gonzales,* 437 F.3d 208, 218–19 (1st Cir. 2006) [failure to provide notice before revocation of IV does not bar CBP from challenging admission in a removal proceeding and following *Matter of Alarcon,* 17 I&N Dec. 574 (BIA 1980) does not bar a finding of inadmissibility].

1.d. Burden of proof in revocation proceedings to establish eligibility for the benefit sought is on the petitioner. *Matter of Estime, supra* at 2. *But see Full Gospel Portland Church v. Thornburgh*, 730 F.Supp. 441, 445 (D.D.C. 1988), *rev'd in part on other grounds* 927 F.2d 628 (D.C. Cir. 1991).

2. Automatic Revocation by DHS [8 C.F.R. §205.1(a)]

2.a. Beneficiary's registration at the consulate is terminated, then DHS automatically terminates the petition. Thus, where a brother failed to register at the consulate for the immigrant visa under the fourth preference, the underlying I-130 petition was revoked and he could not AOS based upon the petition. *Park v. Gonzales,* 450 F.Supp.2d 1153 (D. Or. 2006) [upheld validity of the automatic revocation of the I-130 petition under 8 C.F.R. §205.1(a)(1) as well as DOS's authority to terminate the immigrant visa process under 8 U.S.C. §1153(g) for failure of the beneficiary to apply].

2.b. Withdrawal by petitioner in writing or death of beneficiary.

2.c. Death of petitioner unless USCIS decides that for humanitarian reasons petition should not be revoked and there is a substitute sponsor under the Family Sponsor Immigration Act of 2002, PL 107-150, 116 Stat. 74 (Mar. 13, 2002). 8 C.F.R. §§205.1(a)(3)(i)(C), 1205.1(a)(3)(i)(C). The beneficiary of the I-130 must ask the AG to reinstate the petition *and* must demonstrate that s/he has a substitute sponsor under the Act. 8 C.F.R. §§205.1(a)(3)(i)(C), 1205.1(a)(3)(i)(C). Memo, Williams, Ex. Assoc. Comm., Field Operations, HQADJ/70/21.1.13 (June 15, 2002), *reprinted in* 79 No. 31 *Interpreter Releases* 1169, 1187 (Aug. 5, 2002). Under the Family Sponsor Immigration Act a spouse, parent, mother-in-law, father-in-law, sibling, child (if at least 18 years of age), son, daughter, son-in-law, daughter-in-law, sister-in-law, brother-in-law, grandparent, grandchild or legal guardian of the beneficiary qualifies as a substitute for the deceased petitioner in regard to the affidavit of support. DOS criteria in evaluating a request for humanitarian reinstatement include whether there is: (1) disruption of an established family unit; (2) hardship to USCs or LPRs; (3) a beneficiary who is elderly or in poor health; (4) a beneficiary who has had lengthy residence in the U.S.; (5) a beneficiary who has no home to go to; (6) undue delay by INS or consular officers in processing the petition and the visa; and (7) a beneficiary who has strong family ties in the U.S. 9 FAM 42.42 PN2.

However, a petition may not be reinstated on humanitarian grounds if the petitioner dies *before* the petition is approved. *Abboud v. INS*, 140 F.3d 843, 849 (9th Cir. 1998); *Dodig v. INS,* 9 F.3d 1418 (9th Cir. 1993). Similarly, death of a principal beneficiary invalidates the petition for derivative beneficiaries. 9 FAM 42.53 N.7.2.

An I-130 petition filed by a spouse who dies is not automatically revoked where the surviving spouse qualifies as a widow(er) under the INA. If the beneficiary is the spouse of a USC and they were married for 2 years and the surviving spouse is not remarried, the I-130 petition is automatically converted into an I-360 self-petition and no affidavit of support is required. 8 C.F.R. §§204.2(i)(1)(iv), 205.1(a)(3)(i)(C)(1), 1205.1(a)(3)(i)(C)(1). At least one circuit, however, has now determined that INA §204(b)(2)(A)(i) cannot be read to bar a widow, who has been married less than two years and who has already applied for AOS at the time of her spouse's death, from receiving an approved I-130. *Freeman v. Gonzales,* 444 F.3d 1031, 1037–43 (9th Cir. 2006). For a more detailed discussion, *see in this chapter* ¶ II.B.4 (p.775), *supra.*

At least one court has also found that it was improper to automatically revoke a petition without considering a humanitarian exception where petitioner died before the application was approved but INS approved it. *Estate of Tow v. INS*, 1990 WL 608204 (N.D. Cal. Nov.

16, 1990). *See also Sanchez-Trujillo v. INS*, 620 F.Supp. 1361 (W.D.N.C. 1985); *Pierno v. INS*, 397 F.2d 949, 950 (2d Cir. 1968).

2.d. Marriage of 2d preference son or daughter. *See Corniel-Rodriguez v. INS*, 532 F.2d 301 (2d Cir. 1976) [no revocation where child not given written or oral notice that marriage would invalidate 2d preference petition]. *But see Sachdev v. INS*, 788 F.2d 912 (2d Cir. 1986).

2.e. Legal termination of husband-wife relationship, except in cases of battered spouses or children. INA §204(h), 8 U.S.C. §1154(h).

2.f. Upon the remarriage of the spouse of an abusive USC or LPR unless self-petition has already been approved. INA §204(h).

3. Revocation, but petition and priority date remain valid where:

3.a. Child (immediate relative) reached age of 21. Becomes 1st preference application.

3.b. Child (immediate relative) marries—becomes 3d preference petition.

3.c. Child (1st preference) marries—becomes 3d preference petition.

4. Automatic revocation retroactive to date of approval—Automatic revocation cannot be reviewed by IJ/BIA. *Matter of Zaidan*, 19 I&N Dec. 297 (BIA 1985); *Matter of Aurelio*, 19 I&N Dec. 458 (BIA 1987). Under regulations, except in case of death of petitioner, AG has no discretion to reinstate petition. 57 Fed. Reg. 41053 (Sept. 9, 1992).

K. *Registration, Termination, and Revocation by Department of State*

1. Revocation by Secy. of State—INA §203(g), 8 U.S.C. §1153(g); 22 C.F.R. §42.83; 52 Fed. Reg. 49678 (Oct. 1, 1991); *Park v. Gonzales,* 450 F.Supp. 2d1153 (D. Or. 2006) [upheld revocation and termination by DOS and revocation of I-130 by DHS barring adjustment]. The notice of revocation is now from the NVC and not the consulate under §42.83

1.a. Alien's eligibility/registration for visa at consulate terminates where "alien ... fails to apply for an immigrant visa within one year following notification to [him] of availability of such visa."

1.b. Reinstatement possible if within 2 years of notification of availability applicant can show failure "due to circumstances beyond the alien's control."

2. Return of Petition by Consular Officer to USCIS—On occasion a consular officer, rather than deny a visa under INA §221(g) will return the petition to DHS to request reconsideration and revocation. DOS's position is that returning petitions to DHS should be used judiciously since the process is lengthy and the evidentiary standard to revoke the petition is high. "Posts should not use the revocation request process as a means of disposing of problematic cases in which fraud, misrepresentation or ineligibility for status is only suspected but cannot be clearly established." Cable, DOS, 01-State-121801 (July 13, 2001), *reprinted in* 78 No. 30 *Interpreter Releases* 1276–77 (Aug. 6, 2001); 9 FAM 42.43. Consular officers should consider three principles in seeking to revoke a petition: (1) There should be substantial evidence supporting return not previously considered by DHS because revocation is not merely to readjudicate a petition; (2) the memo supporting the petition return must clearly show the factual and concrete reasons for recommending revocation; and (3) the applicant must be provided in writing as full an explanation as possible the legal and factual basis for visa denial and petition return. Cable, DOS, 04-State-41682 (Feb. 25, 2004) at ¶¶6-10, *published on* AILA InfoNet at Doc. No. 04030364. *See also Matter of Arias,* 19 I&N Dec. 568 (BIA 1988) [reversed revocation where it was based on consul's memorandum which was conclusory, speculative, equivocal and irrelevant]. Consular officers should return K-1 and K-3 visas to the National Visa Center and *not* to DHS when recommending revocation. Cable, DOS, 04-State-41682 (Feb. 25, 2004) at ¶2, *published on* AILA InfoNet at Doc. No. 04030364.

3. Revocation of Immigrant Visa—INA §221(i) governs the revocation of immigrant and nonimmigrant visas. Review of the revocation may only be challenged under INA §242 in the review of a removal proceeding if the revocation was the sole reason for the removal under INA §237(a)(1)(B). The REAL ID Act removed the right to challenge revocation by habeas, mandamus or the All Writs Act in district court. INA §221(i). *Bolante v. Achim,* 457 F.Supp.2d 896 (E.D. Wis. 2006) [no habeas jurisdiction to review claim that revocation was improper under 22 C.F.R. §41.122(a)].

L. *Judicial Review of Petition/IV Revocation*—Some courts have adopted the view that revocation of a petition is not subject to judicial review under INA §242(a)(2)(B)(ii), 8 U.S.C. §1252(a)(2)(B)(ii). *Holy Virgin Protection Cathedral v. Chertoff,* 499 F.3d 658 (7th Cir. 2007) [no jurisdiction to review revocation of religious worker petition]; *Hamilton v. Gonzales,* 485 F.3d 564 (10th Cir. 2007) [revocation of I-130/adoption petition that was affirmed by BIA is not reviewable in circuit court because it is not part of a final order, the APA is not an independent jurisdictional ground, and it is precluded by INA §242(a)(2)(B)]; *Ghanem v. Upchurch,* 481 F.3d 222 (5th Cir. 2007) [revocation of I-130 petition is not reviewable]; *Jilin Pharmaceutical USA, Inc. v. Chertoff,* 447 F.3d 196 (3d Cir. 2006) [distinguished *Soltane* regarding denial of visa petitions and found that there was no jurisdiction to review a revocation of an I-140 petition because it was a discretionary decision barred by INA §242(a)(2)(B)(ii)]; .*El-Khader v. Monica,* 366 F.3d 562 (7th Cir. 2004) [no jurisdiction to review revocation of employment-based visa petition under 8 U.S.C. §1155 because of previous marriage fraud. Citing *Samirah v. O'Connell* the court rejected the claims that the discretionary decision bar is limited to removal, deportation and exclusion proceedings and that marriage fraud is not discretionary]; *Hanif v. DHS,* 472 F.Supp.2d 914 (E.D. Mich. 2007) [no jurisdiction to review revocation of I-130 petition]. *But see Ayanbadejo v. Chertoff,* 517 F.3d 273, 276–78 (5th Cir. 2008) [jurisdiction exists to review denial of I-130 petition and regulatory language that may suggest it is a discretionary decision cannot bind the court because Congress precluded review only of decisions described as discretionary under the *statute*]; *Ikenokwalu-White v. Gonzales,* 495 F.3d 919, 924–26 (8th Cir. 2007) [review of revocation of I-130 should have been brought in district, not circuit, court because it was not part of a removal order despite its potential effect on the mother's removal]; *Ana International Inc. v. Way,* 393 F.3d 886, 893–95 (9th Cir. 2005) [following *Spencer* and holding that INA §242(a)(2)(B)(ii) does not bar judicial review of an I-140 visa revocation of an EB-1 decision under 8 U.S.C. §1155 because the "good and sufficient cause" language of the statute provides a legal standard, as does the "managerial capacity" criteria of EB-1]; *Firstland International Inc. v. INS,* 377 F.3d 127, 130–31 (2d Cir. 2004) [no bar to review of AG's nondiscretionary decision to revoke I-140 petition where person is in U.S., because it raises a pure legal question of whether §1155 permits revocation where beneficiary is in the US]. In regard to the revocation of an immigrant visa or NIV, habeas corpus, mandamus and All Writs Act jurisdiction are eliminated under INA §221(i) except in the context of a removal proceeding and only then if the revocation provides the sole ground for removal under INA §237(a)(1)(B). *Bolante v. Achim,* 457 F.Supp.2d 896 (E.D. Wis. 2006) [no habeas jurisdiction to review claim that revocation was improper under 22 C.F.R. §41.122(a)].

XII. DIFFERENCES BETWEEN VISA PROCESSING & ADJUSTMENT OF STATUS

A. *Generally*

1. Visa processing through National Visa Center and consular post. INA §§221–22, 8 U.S.C. §§1201–02. The Secy. of State has authority to determine both the procedures for the processing of Immigrant Visas (IVs) and the location where they will be processed. INA §202(a)(1)(B), 8 U.S.C. §1152(a)(1)(B). This broad discretionary authority may not be reviewable even if it involves discrimination. *Legal Assistance for Vietnamese Asylum Seekers v. DOS*, 104 F.3d 1349, 1352–53 (D.C. Cir. 1997).

2. Adjustment of status through USCIS. INA §245, 8 U.S.C. §1255. *See in this part* section C (p.834), *infra*.

B. *At Consular Post*

1. When outside U.S. or ineligible to adjust status or when person prefers processing at consulate for strategic or convenience reasons.

2. Approved I-130/I-140 petition forwarded to National Visa Center (NVC) which performs all preinterview functions. 8 C.F.R. §204.2(c)(3)(i), (g)(3), (h)(2), (n). The DOS has eliminated the old numbered package system. The new system requires the applicant to pay fees up-front by sending a Immigrant Visa Fee Bill and Affidavit of Support Fee Bill. After payment, the applicant receives the Instruction Package which now asks the applicant to complete, gather, and forward: (1) the applicant's document processing information/documentation (all of applicant's *original or certified copies* of civil documents such as police reports, marriage licenses, etc) and (2) an I-864 (affidavit of support). Thereafter, an applicant will receive an "appointment letter" for the date to ap-

pear at the consulate and instructions on the medical exam. The immigrant visa form currently in use is the DS-230, Parts 1 & 2. The NVC will forward petitions and accompanying documents to the consular post after all documentation is complete and the appointment letter generally signifies that documents and forms are complete and have been forwarded. NVC will send a Form DS-3032 at the time it sends the I-864 to the beneficiary to allow her to designate a representative (like Form G-28) if no attorney has been representing the applicant. The address of NVC is 32 Rochester Avenue, Portsmouth, New Hampshire 03801-2909, (603) 334-0700, fax (603) 334-0759/0791.

2.a. Usually place of last residence abroad, not country of nationality is designated place. 9 FAM 42.61 N.l.1, 1.2, 2.1

(1) Residence—"principal actual dwelling place"—INA §101(a)(33), 8 U.S.C. §1101(a)(33).

2.b. Exception to residence rule—Discretionary acceptance. 22 C.F.R. §42.61(a):

(1) Hardship—9 FAM 42.61 N.2.2-1, 2.2-2, 2.2-3

(a) U.S. consulate in another country may take case if: (1) Alien is in U.S., (2) will experience hardship if required to return to residence; (3) additional workload at consulate is acceptable. When hardship is clearly demonstrated consulates "encouraged" to accept case, 9 FAM 42.61 N.2.2-2. Hardship includes the "presence of war, wide spread civil disturbance, revolution or other similar phenomena" in the person's country or an inability to travel long distances "because of physical infirmity or advanced age." 9 FAM 42.61 N2.2-3.

(b) Travel expense, military service or inconvenience are not bases for acceptance by consul on hardship grounds.

(2) Homeless visa cases. DOS defines homeless visa cases as ones "in which the beneficiary is a national and resident of, or if in the United States, is a national of and has had his or her last foreign residence in, a country which is not within the consular jurisdiction of any U.S. immigrant visa issuing post." Cable, DOS, 92-State-197870 (June 20, 1992), *reprinted in* No. 28 69 *Interpreter Releases* 901–03 (July 27, 1992); 9 FAM 42.61 N.3.2-1. DOS is using Ciudad Juarez to process IVs for persons in the U.S. Other homeless cases and the posts that will take them are as follows:

- Afghanis: Islamabad
- Bosnians: Zagreb
- Cubans: Ciudad Juarez
- Iranians: Abu Dhabi, Ankara, Vienna, Naples, Frankfurt (family-based only)
- Iraqis: Amman, Casablanca
- Libyans: Tunis
- Somalis: Nairobi, Dar es Salaam, Djibouti
- Sudan: Cairo

9 FAM 42.61 Exhibit I

3. Application at consular post

3.a. In general, if applicant has been unlawfully in U.S. for more than 180 days or one year after Apr. 1, 1997, s/he will be barred from the U.S. for 3 or 10 years respectively. INA §212(a)(9)(B). Limited waivers are available. *See* "Waivers of Inadmissibility," Ch. 3, section III.I (p.113), *supra*, and "Consular Decision on Waiver," Ch. 3, section III.K (p.128), *supra*.

3.b. Applicant still has burden to prove s/he is eligible notwithstanding approved petition. 22 C.F.R. §42.41. The applicant must demonstrate that s/he is "documentarily qualified." 9 FAM 42.55 PN1.2, 42.63 N.1.2

3.c. Must prove that s/he is not inadmissible on any INA §212(a) grounds.

3.d. Must enter U.S. within 6 months of issuance of IV. 22 C.F.R. §§42.72, 42.64(b).

3.e. Consul's Return of Petition to USCIS

(1) Consular officer is to review not re-adjudicate petition. 9 FAM 42.43 N1(b).

(2) DOS's view is that unless a petition was clearly approved in error it shall not be returned to USCIS unless consul has knowledge of evidence that was not available to USCIS, and that USCIS would not have approved the petition if it had knowledge of such evidence. DOS's position is that returning petitions to USCIS should be used judiciously since the process is lengthy and the evidentiary standard to revoke the petition is high. "Posts should not use the revocation request process as a means of disposing of problematic cases in which fraud, misrepresentation or ineligibility for status is only suspected but cannot be clearly established." Cable, DOS, 01-State-121801 (July 13, 2001), *reprinted in* 78 No. 30 *Interpreter Releases* 1276–77 (Aug. 6, 2001).

(3) Petitions that are being returned to USCIS for revocation must now be sent first to National Visa Center by the consular post.

(4) The consul must process the case when USCIS reaffirms its approval and the consul has no additional facts to submit to support belief. 9 FAM 42.43 N.4.

(5) In the rare case where the consular officer disagrees with the USCIS decision to uphold the validity of the petition, it should be sent to DOS for review. 9 FAM 42.43 N.4.1. "Such referrals shall be rare, however, since the burden of proof still rests with the INS and protracted delay without sufficient reason is *not* equitable." Cable, DOS, 95-State-079723 (Apr. 1, 1995), *reprinted in* 72 No. 14 *Interpreter Releases* 507 (Apr. 10, 1995).

3.f. Police certificates are no longer required for the time applicant resided in U.S., country of nationality or residence if it was less than 6 months or for all other residences if they were less than 1 year. 22 C.F.R. §42.65(c)(1). DOS has also abandoned the requirement for police and military records altogether in those countries where records have been determined to be of no value in deciding eligibility. Cable, No. 90-State-385673, DOS (Nov. 14, 1990), *reprinted in* 68 No. 8 *Interpreter Releases* 251 (Mar. 4, 1991). Applicants should check with the consular post. The FBI fingerprint checks are generally not used, Cable, DOS, 91-State-093410 (Mar. 23, 1991), *reprinted in* 68 No. 14 *Interpreter Releases* 440–41 (Apr. 15, 1991), but fingerprint checks have been re-instituted in a pilot project for persons over the age of 16 in certain posts: Port-au-Prince; Toronto; Montreal; Vancouver; Manila; Warsaw; Dublin; Santo Domingo; New Delhi; Bombay; Madras; Ciudad Juarez; San Salvador and Guangzhou.

3.g. Affidavit of support (I-864) with more binding, detailed and stringent requirements is now mandatory for family-based and, in some limited cases, employment-based, applications. INA §213A, 8 U.S.C. §1183a, 8 C.F.R. §213a.2. The petitioner must be the sponsor and must be domiciled in U.S. under USCIS regulations, thereby precluding USCs living abroad from petitioning for their relatives. The sponsor or joint sponsor must demonstrate that her income is 125% above poverty guidelines. For a detailed discussion about the I-864 requirements, *see* Ch. 3, ¶ III.B.1.a (p.60), *supra.*

3.h. Must include copies of tax returns filed with IRS over the previous 3 years if employed in the U.S.

3.i. Medical Exam—Must be performed by doctor overseas; cannot do examination in U.S. 9 FAM 42.66 PN 7. Facts learned by doctor (*e.g.,* admission of marijuana use) can be used to deny admission. *Pazcoguin v. Radcliffe,* 292 F.3d 1209 (9th Cir. 2002) [beneficiary's admission to medical doctor during medical examination for IV in Philippines that he smoked marijuana for a number of years was used as the basis to deny visa upon entry to U.S. and to thereafter exclude him].

3.j. Name Check procedure—Congress has mandated that person's names be checked for any criminal activity before IVs are issued. DOS has instituted a program to check applicant's names through the National Crime Information Center's Interstate Identification Index (NCIC-III). Cable, DOS 94-State-327494, Letter, Dillard, Deputy Asst. Sec. for Visa Services DOS (Feb. 15, 1995), *reprinted in* 4 *AILA Monthly Mailing* 275, 292 (Apr. 1995). Under the USA PATRIOT Act of 2001, DHS and consular officers will be given extracts/summaries of information contained in NCIC-III and may be given full files. 22 C.F.R. §40.5. If the check reveals that an IV applicant may have a criminal background then the consular officer may request fingerprints. 22 C.F.R. §42.67(c)(2). Consular officers utilize the Consular Lookout and Support System (CLASS) for name checks. For procedures under CLASS *see* Cable, DOS, 05-State-066722 (Apr. 12, 2005), *published on* AILA InfoNet at Doc. No. 05052060 (May 20, 2005). A name-check is valid for 15 months. Memo, Aytes, Assoc. Dir. Domestic Operations, USCIS (Dec. 21, 2006), *published on* AILA InfoNet at Doc. No. 07022660.

3.k. Homeland Security Act Procedures—Under HSA §428(e), the DHS may assign employees to consular and diplomatic posts to: (1) provide expert advice and training regarding specific security threats relating to individual or classes of visa applicants; (2) review any visa application; and (3) conduct investigations with respect to consular matters. In light of the establishment of the Department of Homeland Security (DHS) changes have been made in consular processing. Under section 428 of the Homeland Security Act of 2002, PL 107-296, 116 Stat. 2135 (Nov. 25, 2002), 6 U.S.C. §236, DHS has now been given final responsibility for regulatory visa guidance in most areas of IVs. Under a Memorandum of Understanding (MOU) between DOS and DHS, the Department of Homeland Security will now be responsible for all visa guidance regarding (1) waivers except INA §§212(d)(4)(B) and 212(*l*) waivers; (2) NIVs except A, C (transits to the UN), E (determining qualifying treaties and substantiality question), G, I, J (designate qualifying programs) visas; (3) inadmissibility except certain grounds relating to Presidential proclamations under INA §212(f) and certain terrorist, religious freedom violators, and Nazi grounds; and (4) evidentiary criteria to establish eligibility for a visa, for admissibility and for classification of IVs and NIVs. Memorandum of Understanding Between the Secretaries of State and Homeland Security Concerning Implementation of Section 428 of the Homeland Security Act of 2002 (Sept. 30, 2003) at ¶3, *published on* AILA InfoNet at Doc. No. 03101641. An officer of DHS may now also be on-site at a consular post and may review any visa application. In Saudi Arabia, on site DHS personnel "shall" review all visa applications prior to adjudication. HSA §428(i).

4. Denials at Consular Posts

4.a. No judicial review—*But see* APA §702; *Kleindienst v. Mandel*, 408 U.S. 753 (1972); *Abourezk v. Reagan*, 785 F.2d 1043 (D.C. Cir. 1986), *aff'd per curiam by an equally divided court*, 108 S.Ct. 252 (1987); *American Academy of Religion v. Chertoff,* 463 F.Supp.2d 400, 416–19 (S.D.N.Y. 2006) [First Amendment challenge by academic organizations to refusal/revocation of visa to Islamic scholar is not subject to consular nonreviewability because it involves a constitutional issue and the DHS and other agencies involved in security advisory opinions are involved in the decision-making process]; *Rogan v. Reno,* 75 F.Supp.2d 63, 65–66 (E.D. N.Y. 1999) [INA §242(g) does not bar review of denial of individual family/orphan petition]. Person entitled to know legal basis for decision, 22 C.F.R. §42.81(b), and s/he must be given a written explanation detailing grounds of ineligibility. Applicant usually given opportunity to overcome ineligibility, 22 C.F.R. §42.81(b) and (c); if applicant who is within one year of refusal "adduces further evidence tending to overcome the ground of ineligibility," the case shall be reconsidered. 22 C.F.R. §42.81(e). *Patel v. Reno*, 134 F.3d 929 (9th Cir. 1997). See discussion in Ch. 10, ¶ IV.C.2 (p.1147), *infra.*

4.b. Applicant may seek advisory opinion from Visa Office Advisory Opinions Division to obtain the review of a legal (not factual) issue. 22 C.F.R. §41.121(d), 9 FAM 41.121(d) and 9 FAM 40.6 N.1.

5. Waivers may be available—INA §§212(i) and 212(h) waivers can no longer be pre-processed. Can only apply for waivers once applicant has been refused. Consul does not make a recommendation on the waiver request "but merely forwards the case to DHS for a decision." Cable, DOS, 05-State-066722 ¶2 (Apr. 12, 2005), *published on* AILA InfoNet at Doc. No. 05052060 (May 20, 2005); 9 FAM Appendix N, 400. Applications for waivers are adjudicated at the USCIS overseas office nearest to the consulate. In Ciudad Juarez the consulate has established an expedited procedure to address I-601 waivers. Appointment Waiver Enhancements (I-601) U.S. Consulate Ciudad Juarez Waiver Pilot Program, *published on* AILA InfoNet at Doc. No. 07122060 and Doc. No. 08010364.

6. Third country processing—USCIS may grant advance parole (I-512) pursuant to 8 C.F.R. §§212.5(f) to pursue visa in third country. IFM at 16.1.

7. Issuance of Replacement Visas—Where IV is not used within 6 months of issuance, a consular officer may issue a replacement visa if: (1) the immigrant is unable to use the visa during the period of its validity for reasons beyond her control; (2) the visa is issued during the same fiscal year or in the following year if an IR and the visa number was recaptured; (3) the number has not been returned to DOS as recaptured in the case of a preference or diversity immigrant;(4) the immigrant pays all fees; *and* (5) the consular officer ascertains whether the original issuing office knows of any reason why a new visa should not be issued. 22 C.F.R. §42.74.

C. *Adjustment of Status Under §245*—INA §245, 8 U.S.C. §1255; Leg. Hist. at S. Rep. No. 1651, 86th Cong. 2d Sess. (1960); 1960 U.S.C.C.A.N. 3124, 3147; PL 103-317, Title V §506(b), 108 Stat. 1724, 1765 (Adjustment for EWI and others); 1994 U.S.C.C.A.N. p.1801 (regarding S visa); H.R. Rep. No. 104-828 at p.230 (IIRIRA §375); 8 C.F.R. §245.1 *et seq.*

1. Requirements Under Regular Adjustment Procedures

1.a. Inspected and admitted or paroled (EWIs, stowaways, and TWOVs cannot adjust).

A person is inspected and admitted when he presents himself for inspection and makes no knowing false claim to U.S. citizenship. *Matter of Areguillin*, 17 I&N Dec. 308 (BIA 1980) [Mexican citizen not questioned at border while riding in a car that was stopped was "inspected and admitted" even though she had no lawful basis to enter]; *But see* 8 C.F.R. §101.2 and INA §101(a)(13)(A) [defining admission as *lawful* entry]; *Orozco v. Mukasey,* 521 F.3d 1068 (9th Cir. 2008) [a person who is inspected and admitted at the border through the use of fraudulent documents is ineligible to adjust status because admission under §101(a)(13)(A) now requires *lawful entry*. The court found that *Matter of Areguillin* is not longer good law in light of the passage of §101(a)(13)(A)]. Also, a person who claims to be a USC and fraudulently obtains entry in that manner is considered EWI, *Reid v. INS,* 420 U.S. 619, 624, 95 S.Ct. 1164, 1167–68 (1975) (and cases cited therein) [a person who makes an entry into the country by falsely representing himself as a citizen is not only excludable under former 212(a)(19) for fraud but is deportable as one who has "entered the United States without inspection"], *Ramsay v. INS*, 14 F.3d 206, 211 n.6 (4th Cir. 1994), and may therefore be ineligible to adjust status. However, the BIA has held that any misrepresentation may be waived despite the ability to bring an EWI charge. *Matter of Y,* 8 I&N Dec. 143 (BIA 1958) [recognizing that a waiver for any misrepresentation is available even if respondent fraudulently claimed he was a USC at the border and could be charged for that reason as having made an EWI].

1.b. Parolee. A person paroled under INA §212(d)(5)(A) can AOS. However, a person granted conditional parole under INA §236(a)(2)(B) is not the same as a parolee under INA §212(d)(5)(A) and at least one circuit has determined that she may not adjust status. *Ortega-Cervantes v. Gonzales,* 501 F.3d 1111 (9th Cir. 2007) [a person apprehended near the border who was EWI and who was conditionally paroled under INA §236(a)(2)(B) after being detained for several weeks because he was a material witness in a smuggling case could not AOS under INA §245 before the IJ because he was not paroled into the country within the meaning of INA §245].

1.c. Must be lawfully here, except for immediate relatives, battered spouses and children, and special immigrant under INA §101(a)(27)(H) [certain FMGs], §101(a)(27)(I) [certain spouse and children of G's], §101(a)(27)(J) [juvenile dependents], and §101(a)(27)(K) [certain veterans]. Thus, INA §§245(c)(2), (c)(7) and (c)(8) do not bar AOS for IRs and these special immigrants.

1.d. A visa number must be immediately available at time of filing. 8 C.F.R. §§245.2(a)(5)(ii), 1245.2(a)(5)(ii). If visa numbers regress after filing, except for immediate relatives, so that no visa can actually be issued, the case is held in abeyance until a visa is available. *Hernandez v. Ashcroft,* 345 F.3d 824, 843–45 (9th Cir. 2003) [availability of a visa does not mean that the individual must actually possess an allocated visa number to be eligible to adjust]. If the applicant files an I-130 and then a visa number becomes available because the priority date is reached or because circumstances change (*e.g.*, petitioner becomes USC and petition goes from 2nd preference to IR), the adjustment applicant can file the I-485 with proof that the petitioner filed the I-130 and it will be treated in the same manner as if the I-130 had been filed with the I-485. Memo, Yates, Assoc. Dir. Operations, USCIS, "Petitions for Alien Relative (Form I-130) Pending at Service Centers," (Apr. 22, 2004), *published on* AILA InfoNet at Doc. No. 04052161 (May 21, 2004).

1.e. Applicant must make adjustment application—8 C.F.R. §§245.2, 1245.2

1.f. Applicant must pass medical and security clearances. To find a doctor to conduct the medical exam, see *www.uscis.gov/civilsurgeons* or call the USCIS main number, 1-800-375-5283 or online at. Because of long delays in AOS applications the reports of medical examinations are valid until the time of adjudication if no Class A or Class B medical condition is certified by the physician. Memo, Aytes, Assoc. Dir. Operations, HQ 70/21.1.1-P (Jan. 7, 2008) [extending policy until Jan. 1, 2009], *published on* AILA InfoNet at Doc. No. 08041566.

1.g. Applicant must be eligible and otherwise admissible—Ineligible under INA §§245(c), (d), 8 U.S.C. §§1255(c), (d), or otherwise if:

(1) Alien crewmen, including those with "B" and "C," as well as "D" visas.

(2) Worked without authorization. *Matter of Hall*, 18 I&N Dec. 203 (BIA 1982) [Unification Church member receiving both necessary and nonessential expenses is employed in absence of fixed salary]; 8 C.F.R. §§245.1(b)(4), 1245.1(b)(4). IIRIRA §375 amended §245(c) to include *any* alien who was employed while being an unauthorized alien as defined in INA §245(c)(8), 8 U.S.C. §1255(c)(8). *See* INA §274A(h)(3), 8 U.S.C. §1324a(h)(3). Bar applies if applicant *ever* worked without authorization. Memo, Aytes, Assoc. Dir. Domestic Operations, USCIS HQDOMO 70/23.1 (Jan. 12, 2007) ¶B, *published on* AILA InfoNet at Doc. No. 07030661 [bar applies even if person paroled into U.S. but on any previous trip was employed without authorization].This section does *not* bar immediate relatives or special immigrants under §101(a)(27)(H), (I), (J), or (K) [medical doctors, "G" relatives, veterans, or juvenile court dependents] to adjust status. *See also Salehpour v. INS*, 761 F.2d 1442 (9th Cir. 1985). INA §245(c) is not bar to adjustment where F-1 timely filed change of status to H-1 but began work before approval. However, *Salehpour* may not be good law after 8 C.F.R. §§274a.12, 1274a.12.

(a) No bar where beneficiary of employment-based petition (former 3d pref. petition) works without authorization if he is also immediate relative. 65 No. 6 *Interpreter Releases* 138, 149–50 (Feb. 28, 1988). *But see* Legal Opinion, Cook, General Counsel, CO 245-C (May 18, 1990) [suggesting that IR status must be tested by obtaining an approved petition before beneficiary can rely on relationship for adjustment on other grounds].

(b) Immediate Relative for purposes of avoiding the INA §245(c) bar includes spouses even where the marriage may no longer be valid. *Matter of Adalatkhah*, 17 I&N Dec. 404 (BIA 1980).

(c) Asylee or exchange student granted waiver under INA §212(e) because of persecution is barred from adjustment of status if s/he worked without permission or was out-of-status before asylum granted. 65 No. 14 *Interpreter Releases* 380–81, 400–02 (Apr. 11, 1988) (applies where adjustment sought under provisions other than INA §209).

(d) Unauthorized employment as a bar to adjustment applies to persons who engaged in unauthorized employment *after* adjustment application is filed. 8 C.F.R. §§274a.12(c)(9), 1274a.12(c)(9); 62 Fed. Reg. 39417 at 39421.

(e) Bar does not apply to employment-based petitions where person worked no more than an aggregate period exceeding 180 days without permission since his last entry into the U.S. INA §245(k).

(3) Person not in "lawful immigration status" (other than immediate relative) on date of filing application or who has failed to maintain continuously a legal status except if it was through no fault of his own *or* for technical reasons. 8 C.F.R. §1245.1(d)(2). DHS regulations do not permit adjustment if applicant was *ever* out of status during any prior entries.

8 C.F.R. §§245.1(b)(5), (6) and (c)(1), 1245.1(b)(5), (6) and (c)(1); Letter, Miller, Deputy Asst. Comm., Adjudications, CO 245-C (Jan. 8, 1990), *reprinted in* 67 No. 5 *Interpreter Releases* 120, 151 (Jan. 29, 1990); Memo, Aytes, Assoc. Dir. Domestic Operations, USCIS HQDOMO 70/23.1 (Jan. 12, 2007) ¶B, *published on* AILA InfoNet at Doc. No. 07030661 [bar applies even if person paroled into U.S. but on any previous trip failed to maintain lawful status]. A person in lawful status who files for asylum and then falls out of status is not eligible to adjust if DHS takes action on the asylum request by denying, referring or dismissing it. However, an asylee may be able to adjust if the application is pending. *Matter of L-K-*, 23 I&N Dec. 677, 680–81 (BIA 2004) [falling out of status during asylum process is not for a "technical reason" and therefore lottery winner cannot adjust where case was referred to immigration court; but the BIA recognized that if application was still pending with DHS it would be considered a technical reason under 8 C.F.R. §1245.1(d)(2)(ii)]. However, persons granted TPS who entered lawfully even if out of status subsequent to obtaining TPS may adjust their status. INA §244(f)(4), 8 U.S.C. §1254a(f)(4). Also, a person who is in status at time of filing adjustment may pursue application even if he falls out of status after adjustment application is filed provided s/he does not work without permission. AFM at 20.1(e); *Matter of Ho*, 15 I&N Dec. 692 (BIA 1976). Under INA §245(c)(7), a person may not adjust who is seeking employment-based residency if s/he is not in lawful NIV status. Any alien who was employed without authorization or has violated the terms of his or her NIV may not adjust under 245a. INA §245(c)(8). Violating the terms of status does not include: (1) violation that was not the applicant's fault or occurred through technical reasons as described in 8 C.F.R. §§245.1(d)(2), 1245.1(d)(2); (2) grant of extension of status (E/S) or change of status (C/S) which was not approved until after stay expired; or (3) reinstatement to student status on the basis of circumstances beyond the student's control. Memo, Crocetti, Assoc. Comm., INS, HQ 50/5.12, 96 Act.034 (May 1, 1997), *reprinted in* 74 No. 18 *Interpreter Releases* 777, 791–94, 793 (May 12, 1997). Unauthorized employment for purposes of §245(c)(8) includes working without authorization after an AOS application is filed or *ever* engaging in unauthorized employment. 8 C.F.R. §§245.1(b)(9), (10), 1245.1(b)(9), (10). However, an employment-based applicant can adjust even if she worked unlawfully or was otherwise out of status as long as the unauthorized employment or out of status did not exceed 180 days. INA §245(k).

(4) Paroled person barred from adjusting under employment-based petition under INA §203(b) because a parolee is not in a "lawful nonimmigrant status" within INA §245(c)(7). Memo, Aytes, Assoc. Dir. Domestic Operations, USCIS HQDOMO 70/23.1 (Jan. 12, 2007) ¶B, *published on* AILA InfoNet at Doc. No. 07030661 [arriving alien or any other person paroled into U.S. may not adjust if the adjustment is based upon an employment petition].

(5) Alien is TWOV—8 C.F.R. §§245.1(b)(1), 1245.1(b)(1).

(6) "A," "G," or "E" unless alien waives privileges and immunities on Form I-508. 8 C.F.R. §§245.1(c)(3), 1245.1(c)(3).

(7) "A" or "G" without other typical basis for adjustment, unless "compelling reason" and failed to maintain status. Show compelling reasons that A-1, A- 2/G-1, G-2 unable to return to their country. 8 U.S.C. §1255 n.9 or 8 U.S.C. §1255b(b). Must also demonstrate that it is in U.S. national interest and not contrary to national welfare, safety and security to grant adjustment. Section 13 of Act of 1957, *as modified* by PL 97-116, 95 Stat. 1611 (Dec. 29, 1981). In order to qualify, person must have failed to maintain "A" or "G" status. Only 50 persons annually can adjust.

(8) J not meeting 2-year foreign residence requirement or obtaining waiver. 8 C.F.R. §§245.1(c)(2), 1245.1(c)(2). However, if applicant has approval from USIA for waiver, J can submit AOS even if the Service has not yet approved waiver. Memo, Virtue, Exec. Assoc. Comm., INS, HQ 70/23.1-P, 70/12.2 (Feb. 17, 1998), *reprinted in* 75 No. 9 *Interpreter Releases* 327, 354–55 (Mar. 9, 1998).

(9) Alien seeking to adjust by virtue of a marriage entered into while administrative or judicial proceedings are pending concerning person's status. *Matter of Egbunine*, 19 I&N

Dec. 478 (BIA 1987) [proceeding begins with filing of OSC]; *Matter of Enriquez*, 19 I&N Dec. 554 (BIA 1988) [proceeding ends when person departs]; 8 C.F.R. §§245.1(c)(9), 1245.1(c)(8). However, a waiver is available upon showing of clear and convincing evidence. 8 C.F.R. §§245.1(c)(8)(iii)(F), 1245.1(c)(8)(iii)(F); *Malhi v. INS*, 336 F.3d 989, 999–1000 (9th Cir. 2003) [following "clear and convincing" evidence requirement in *Matter of Velarde-Pacheco* and 8 C.F.R. §204.2(a)(1)(iii)(B) evidentiary requirements but upholding denial by BIA of motion to remand under abuse of discretion standard]. *Accord. Sarr v. Gonzales,* 485 F.3d 354, 362–64 (6th Cir. 2007) [BIA denial of motion to remand under *Velarde* upheld where applicant had testified falsely at asylum hearing and never filed waiver with *Velarde* motion]; *Falae v. Gonzales,* 411 F.3d 11, 14–15 (1st Cir. 2005) [although respondent in motion to remand made a prima facie showing of eligibility for adjustment of status based upon his marriage, and the BIA made no finding of a "sham marriage," the BIA did not abuse its discretion in refusing to reopen where respondent persistently used fraudulent documents, had a checkered previous marital history that indicated fraud, and lacked credibility]. *But see Melnitsenko v. Mukasey,* 517 F.3d 42, 48–52 (2d Cir. 2008) [BIA cannot deny a motion under *Velarde-Pacheco* where petitioner meets all five criteria solely on the fact of DHS's opposition].

Under prior BIA decisions, a person who marries during deportation proceedings may not file an adjustment application until his or her I-130 petition is approved. *Matter of Arthur,* 20 I&N Dec. 475 (BIA 1992); *Matter of H-A-*, 22 I&N Dec. 728 (BIA 1999) [following *Arthur* even where person barred from filing adjustment because it was not within the 90-day reopening period under former 8 C.F.R. §3.2(c)]. *But see Matter of Velarde-Pacheco,* 23 I&N Dec. 253 (BIA 2002) [*Matter of Arthur* and *H-A-* modified to allow for motions to reopen where the I-485/I-130 are filed within 90 days, is not numerically barred, is not barred by *Matter of Shaar* or any other procedural grounds, presents clear and convincing evidence that the marriage is bona fide, and the Service either does not oppose the motion or bases its opposition solely on *Matter of Arthur*]; *Melnitsenko v. Mukasey,* 517 F.3d 42, 48–52 (2d Cir. 2008) [BIA cannot deny a motion under *Velarde-Pacheco* where petitioner meets all five criteria solely on the fact of DHS's opposition]; *Benslimane v. Gonzales,* 430 F.3d 828 (7th Cir. 2005) [IJ made legal error in denying continuance where respondent had filed I-130 and I-485 as part of marriage based adjustment with USCIS but had not filed adjustment with IJ]; *Singh v. Gonzales,* 404 F.3d 1024, 1027–29 (7th Cir. 2005) [where I-130 had been approved the BIA's reliance on *Matter of Velarde-Pacheco* to deny motion to reconsider to allow adjustment was error because *Velarde* involved an unadjudicated I-130; however under facts of case error was harmless]; *Bull v. INS*, 790 F.2d 869 (11th Cir. 1986); *Matter of Garcia*, 16 I&N Dec. 653, 656 (BIA 1978). *Cf. Miah v. Mukasey,* 519 F.3d 784, 789–90 (8th Cir. 2008) [denied motion to reopen under *Velarde* on insufficiency of the evidence, and distinguished *Velarde* because motion was filed after BIA ruled]; *Ilic-Lee v. Mukasey,* 507 F.3d 1044, 1049–53 (6th Cir. 2007) [BIA was correct to deny motion to reopen proceedings for AOS under *Velarde* where there was some evidence of a legal marriage but the weight of the evidence was slight and the government opposed reopening]; *Ramchandani v. Gonzales,* 434 F.3d 337, 340–41 (5th Cir. 2005) [upheld BIA denial of motion to reopen under *Velarde* where DHS opposed motion because applicant didn't submit affidavit of support].

Note that the limitation imposed by *Matter of Shaar* is no longer valid in some circuits. *Ugokwe v. U.S. Att'y Gen.,* 453 F.3d 1325 (11th Cir. 2006) [a timely filed motion to reopen post-IIRIRA tolls the VD period and prohibits the application of *Matter of Shaar* to bar consideration of the merits of the motion]; *Barroso v. Gonzales,* 429 F.3d 1195, 1202–08 (9th Cir. 2005) [filing a motion to reconsider within the VD period automatically tolls VD]; *Kanivets v. Gonzales,* 424 F.3d 330, 334–36 (3d Cir. 2005) [distinguished *Bhiski* and found that *post*-IIRIRA a timely filed motion to reopen for AOS tolls the period of VD and allows the BIA to consider the motion]; *Sidikhouya v. Gonzales,* 407 F.3d 950 (8th Cir. 2005) [where motion to reopen for AOS was filed prior to the expiration of the VD period granted by the BIA, it was an abuse of discretion *post*-IIRIRA for the BIA to deny reopening based upon *Matter of Shaar* when VD expired before BIA ruled]; *Barrios v. Att'y Gen. of the U.S.,* 399 F.3d 272 (3d Cir. 2005) [rejecting *Matter of Shaar* for *pre*-IIRIRA cases, and holding that a timely filed motion to reopen prevents the

BIA/IJ from applying the bar to adjustment under the former INA §242B(e)(2)(A) because the failure of the BIA/IJ to adjudicate the motion within the voluntary departure period is an "exceptional circumstance"]; *Azarte v. Ashcroft,* 394 F.3d 1278 (9th Cir. 2005) [where a motion to reopen is filed during the voluntary departure period in a post-IIRIRA removal proceeding and a stay of removal or VD is requested, the VD period is tolled while the BIA considers the motion]. *But see Chedad v. Gonzales,* 497 F.3d 57 (1st Cir. 2007) [a timely filed motion to reopen does not stay the running of the VD period and if the motion is granted after VD has expired the respondent is barred from seeking relief §1229c(d)(1)].

Nevertheless, the bar to adjustment of status may apply even if a person is successful in reopening proceedings. *Chedad v. Gonzales,* 497 F.3d 57 (1st Cir. 2007) [a timely filed motion to reopen does not stay the running of the VD period and if the motion is granted after VD has expired the respondent is barred from seeking relief §1229c(d)(1)]; *Singh v. Gonzales,* 468 F.3d 135 (2d Cir. 2006) [IJ's granting of MTR does *not* vacate the effect of prior noncompliance with a VD order that now bars respondent's adjustment of status]; *Dacosta v. Gonzales,* 449 F.3d 45 (1st Cir. 2006) [BIA properly denied adjustment after granting motion to reopen because granting a motion to reopen where applicant had previously remained beyond the voluntary departure period without a stay did not expunge the previous violation for purposes of barring adjustment]; *Banda-Ortiz v. Gonzales,* 445 F.3d 387, 391 (5th Cir. 2006) [BIA's decision to reopen does not cure respondent's failure to depart during VD period and respondent is therefore ineligible for cancellation]. *But see Orichitch v. Gonzales,* 421 F.3d 595 (7th Cir. 2005) [in granting petitioner's joint MTR for AOS, the BIA permanently "disposed of" the VD order and thus eliminated the §240B(d) issue].

(10) Respondent in Removal Proceedings Who Fails To Take Certain Action. IIRIRA withdraws the right to seek adjustment of status for a period of 10 years after entry of the order of removal for persons who: (a) fail to appear at a removal hearing after receiving oral notice unless there are exceptional circumstances, INA §240(b)(7), 8 U.S.C. §1229a (b)(7); (b) fails to depart after a grant of voluntary departure (no exceptional circumstances written into statute), INA §240B(d), 8 U.S.C. §1229c(d); or (c) re-enters U.S. illegally after being removed, INA §241(a)(5), 8 U.S.C. §1231(a)(5) [applying to *all* forms of relief]. *See e.g., Chedad v. Gonzales,* 497 F.3d 57 (1st Cir. 2007) [a timely filed motion to reopen does not stay the running of the VD period and if the motion is granted after VD has expired the respondent is barred from seeking relief §1229c(d)(1)]; *Naeem v. Gonzales,* 469 F.3d 33 (1st Cir. 2006) [where LPR wife became USC and her I-130 petition was approved for her husband during the VD period, but husband's motion to reopen, although filed within 90 days of the BIA's decision, was filed after the end of the VD period, BIA was correct in finding husband statutorily ineligible for AOS]; *De Martinez v. Ashcroft,* 363 F.3d 1022 *amended on r'hearing* 374 F.3d 759 (9th Cir. 2004) [where motion to reopen for adjustment of status was filed within the 90-day time limit but after VD expired, the movant was ineligible to adjust notwithstanding *Matter of Velarde-Pacheco*]. *But see Orichitch v. Gonzales,* 421 F.3d 595 (7th Cir. 2005) [where BIA granted motion to reopen after IJ denied motion to reopen to adjust because respondent was barred by INA §240B(d) for failure to timely voluntarily depart, case was reopened for all purposes and respondent was eligible to adjust].

The same provision denying relief existed under pre-IIRIRA law. INA §242B(e), although it barred the relief for 5 years. *Matter of Powell,* 21 I&N Dec. 81 (BIA 1995) [notice given by IJ bars relief even if there was appeal to BIA and BIA did not provide additional notice]; *Matter of Ali,* 21 I&N Dec. 1058 (BIA 1997) [neither minor longstanding illness existing prior to grant of VD nor allegations of serious illness to others, including family members, is an exceptional circumstance for stopping the effects of §242B(e) when person does not depart within VD period]; *Rojas-Reynoso v. INS,* 235 F.3d 26, 29–30 & n.3 (1st Cir. 2000) [filing a motion to extend voluntary departure and waiting beyond VD period for response is not an exceptional circumstance; nor is filing a motion to reopen];*Mardones v. McElroy,* 197 F.3d 619 (2d Cir. 1999) [finding that the passage of §245(i) or the INS's failure to respond to a request for extension of VD are not exceptional circumstances and adjustment was properly denied]. *But see Velezmoro v. Ashcroft,* 362 F.3d 1231 (9th Cir. 2004) [where person remained in the U.S. more than five years beyond the expiration of her voluntary departure period s/he may now be eligible to adjust because five years had elapsed]; *Ordonez v. INS,* 345 F.3d 777, 783–84 (9th Cir. 2003) [under former INA §242B(e) the IJ was required to give oral and written notice of loss of relief for failing to depart and where IJ did not specifically list the forms of relief that would be lost the denial of the right to suspension was reversed].

(11) Adjustment of status must be withdrawn if a person violates a protective order when a document is submitted under seal. DOJ has established procedures before the IJ for the submission of documents/information under seal with a protective order which, if disclosed would "harm the national security...or law enforcement interests of the United States." 8 C.F.R. §1003.46. National security is defined under INA §219(c)(2), 8 U.S.C. §1189(c)(2) to include "the national defense, foreign relations, or economic interests of the United States." If a respondent or his attorney or accredited representative discloses the information in violation of the protective order s/he becomes ineligible for "all forms of discretionary relief, except bond, unless the respondent fully cooperates with the Service or other law enforcement agencies in any investigation relating to noncompliance...and establishes by clear and convincing evidence either that extraordinary and extremely unusual circumstances exist or that failure to comply...was beyond the control of the respondent and his or her attorney or accredited representative." 8 C.F.R. §1003.46(i); *Matter of R-S-H-, et al.,* 23 I&N Dec. 629 (BIA 2003) [denied asylum, withholding and voluntary departure because of breach of protective order where respondent and counsel cooperated in the investigation of the breach but did not show extraordinary circumstances or that failure to comply was beyond their control].

(12) Person who obtained conditional LPR status under INA §216, 8 U.S.C. §1186a; 8 C.F.R. §§245.1(c)(5), 1245.1(c)(5) or INA §216A, 8 U.S.C. §1186b, and seeks adjustment on another basis. However, if INA §216 status terminated person may thereafter adjust if s/he has legal basis to do so. *Matter of Stockwell*, 20 I&N Dec. 309 (BIA 1991).

(13) Inadmissible under INA §212(a), 8 U.S.C. §1182(a), *Matter of Vindman*, 16 I&N Dec. 131 (R.C. 1977), except in the case of S visa adjustment unless the visa holder is inadmissible under INA §212(a)(3)(E). *See also Rodriguez v. Gonzales,* 451 F.3d 60, 65 (2d Cir. 2006) [where respondent was convicted under 18 U.S.C. §1542 for making a false statement on a passport where he obtained passport by representing himself as a USC, his adjustment of status application was barred because he was inadmissible for making a false claim to U.S. citizenship]; *Falaja v. Gonzales,* 418 F.3d 889, 897–99 (8th Cir. 2005) [where IJ/BIA found that inconsistencies in asylum application were the basis for an adverse credibility finding and were willfully made, court upheld denial of AOS based upon an employment-based petition because the applicant was ineligible under 212(a)(6)(C)(i)]; *Billeke-Tolosa v. Ashcroft,* 385 F.3d 708 (6th Cir. 2004) [IJ cannot look behind the applicant's conviction to deny adjustment based upon a police report]. Can file waivers concurrently with adjustment application. 8 C.F.R. §§245.1(f), 1245.1(f). This includes an I-212 waiver for prior removal. 8 C.F.R. §212.2(e) [waiver filed with DD who has jurisdiction over applicant's residence]; *Lopez-Flores v. DHS,* 376 F.3d 793, 795 n.2 (8th Cir. 2004) [AOS applicant may ask for *nunc pro tunc* permission to reapply even if in removal proceedings]. If health care worker, must also obtain a certificate before s/he is admissible. INA §212(a)(5)(C). 8 C.F.R. §§245.14, 1245.14.

(14) Entered under visa waiver program, unless an immediate relative. 8 C.F.R. §§217.3(a), 245.1(b)(8), 1245.1(b)(8) or grandfathered under former INA §245(i). At least one circuit has determined that a VWP entrant who files for AOS as an immediate relative pursuant to INA §245(c)(4) while in lawful status is entitled to the procedural guarantees of adjustment applicants under 8 C.F.R. §245.2 and is no longer subject to the "no-contest clause" of the VWP. *Freeman v. Gonzales,* 444 F.3d 1031, 1034–37 (9th Cir. 2006) [AOS spouse whose husband died remained a spouse under INA and had the right to contest denial of AOS in same manner as other AOS applicants]. *But see Lacey v. Gonzales,* 499 F.3d 514 (6th Cir. 2007) [no jurisdiction to review a denial of AOS by a VWP appli-

cant who stayed beyond the 90 day period because there is no review of the denial in a removal hearing];*Schmitt v. Maurer,* 451 F.3d 1092 (10th Cir. 2006) [ineligible to apply for AOS as abused spouse under VAWA]; *Ferry v. Gonzales,* 457 F.3d 1117, 1127–28 (10th Cir. 2006). *See also Zine v. Mukasey,* 517 F.3d 535, 543–44 (8th Cir. 2008) [once VWP placed in asylum-only proceedings cannot seek AOS based upon USC marriage].

(15) K visa holder except if s/he is married within 90 days pursuant to K status and K petitioner is the petitioner in the I-130. 8 U.S.C. §1255(d), INA §245(d); 8 C.F.R. §§245.1(c)(6), 1245.1(c)(6). Under K-1 provision, if the marriage to the K-1 petitioner does not occur "within three months after the admission....[the K-1 and minor children]..shall be required to depart from the United States and upon failure to do so shall be removed in accordance with section 1229a and 1231..." 8 U.S.C. §1184(d); *Markovski v. Gonzales,* 486 F.3d 108 (4th Cir. 2007) [notwithstanding §245(i), respondent could not adjust based upon approved I-140 petition because §245(d) bars adjustment except based upon K-1 petition]; *Kalal v. Gonzales,* 402 F.3d 948, 950–51 (9th Cir. 2005) [upheld rescission of CR status to person who did not marry K-1 petitioner within 90 days and instead married a different USC]. However, 8 U.S.C. §1255(d) may be read to permit adjustment even if the marriage does not take place within 90 days if it is to the "citizen who filed the petition to accord" the K-1 status. *See also Matter of Zampetis,* 14 I&N Dec. 125 (BIA 1972) *But see* 8 C.F.R. §245.1(c)(6). Also, INA §245(i) may not be used to waive the requirements of §245(d). *Kalal v. Gonzales,* 402 F.3d 948, 951–52 (9th Cir. 2005) [INA §245(i) waives §§245(a) and (c) and not §245(d)].

(16) S visa holders except as provided under the special provisions for S adjustment. C.F.R. §§245.11, 1245.11. *See* "S Visa" in Ch. 5, section XI.A (p.762), *supra.*

(17) A person deportable as an alien terrorist. 8 C.F.R. §§245.10(g), 1245.10(g).

(18) Orphans. A child in the U.S. either illegally or as a nonimmigrant is ineligible for the benefits of an orphan petition and may therefore not adjust. However, a child who has been paroled *and* who has not been adopted in the United States is eligible for the benefits of an orphan petition and may therefore be eligible to adjust. 8 C.F.R. §204.3(k)(3).

1.h. Deportability Generally Does Not Bar Adjustment—Persons deportable but not inadmissible under INA §212(a) may adjust status. *Matter of Rainford,* 20 I&N Dec. 598 (BIA 1992) [person subject to deportation on a gun charge is nevertheless eligible to adjust]; *Matter of Azurin,* 23 I&N Dec. 695 (BIA 2005) [for convictions prior to AEDPA, the Board reaffirmed *Rainford* and *Gabryelsky* and determined a §212(c) waiver was available in conjunction with an application for adjustment even if the ground of deportation (gun charge) could not be waived because it did not have an equivalent ground of inadmissibility].

1.i. Security Check/Name Check All applicants for adjustment of status must be subject to an IBIS and FBI security/name check. AFM at 10.3; Memo, Yates, Assoc. Dir., Operations, USCIS, IBIS Record Check Requirements (Jan. 20. 2004), *published on* AILA InfoNet at Doc. No. 04063071. In the event the security check/name check is not completed within 180 days by the FBI and the application is otherwise approvable, "the adjudicator shall approve the I-485, I-601(waiver), I-687 (temporary resident under §245A) or I-698 (temporary to permanent resident under §245A) and proceed with card issuance." Memo, Aytes, Assoc. Dir. Domestic Operations, USCIS, HQ70/23 & 70/28.1 (Feb. 4, 2008), *published on* AILA InfoNet at Doc. No. 08020760. *See also* Ch. 3, ¶ X.S.7.1 (p.361), *supra.*

1.j. Battered Spouse and Children. Approved VAWA self-petitioners are exempt from the INA §245(c) bar. *See also in this chapter* ¶ II.B.5 (p.775), *supra.*

1.k. Immigrant visa must be immediately available. 8 C.F.R. §§245.1(g), 1245.1(g).

(1) An approved I-130/I-140/I-360 is a precondition. The I-130/I-140 petitions may be filed simultaneously with adjustment of status (I-485) application if the priority date is current. As a practical matter this means that I-130 petitions and the I-485 application can be simultaneously filed only where it is for an immediate relative because there is a backlog in every other category requiring that the petition be approved first. Where categories for employment-based residency are current, the I-140 may be filed at the same time as the I-485. The former rule requiring an approved I-140 petition *before* filing the adjustment

of status application has been withdrawn 8 C.F.R. §245.2(a)(2)(i) except that the I-485 may not be filed where there is a backlog or regression in a particular category or country. Memo, Yates, Assoc. Dir. Operations, USCIS, HQOPRD 70/11.1 (Dec. 29, 2004), *published on* AILA InfoNet at Doc. No. 04122862 [regarding concurrent filing and withdrawals of I-485 due to regression of employment-based, third preference, visa numbers]. I-360 petitions must be filed and approved first, except in the case of a Special Immigrant Juvenile, where the I-360 and I-485 may be filed simultaneously.

(2) Priority date must be reached or immediate relative/special immigrant.

(3) Can ask for visa number on expedited basis if available. AFM at 10.11

(4) Aged-out cases. *See in this chapter* ¶ III.D.5.c (p.808), *supra*.

1.l. USCIS has discretion to deny adjustment.

(1) In absence of adverse factors, it is usually granted. *Matter of Arai*, 13 I&N Dec. 494 (BIA 1970); *Matter of Lam*, 16 I&N Dec. 432 (BIA 1978). However, the Service cannot grant adjustment *nunc pro tunc* to person no longer eligible for adjustment. *Matter of Hernandez-Puente*, 20 I&N Dec. 335 (BIA 1991) [derivative under former 5th preference could not be granted adjustment retroactively after he became 21 due to INS error]. *But see Przhebelskaya v. U.S. Bureau of Citizenship and Immigration Services,* 338 F.Supp.2d 399 (E.D.N.Y. 2004) [where action to compel INS to adjust lottery applicant before the end of the fiscal year and INS fails to do so the court had continuing jurisdiction to compel grant];*Paunescu v. INS,* 76 F.Supp.2d 896 (N.D. Ill. 1999) [same]. *See also Billeke-Tolosa v. Ashcroft,* 385 F.3d 708 (6th Cir. 2004) [in the exercise of discretion IJ may not look behind the applicant's conviction to deny adjustment based upon a police report].

(2) Factors considered in exercise of discretion:

(a) Existence of family ties in U.S.

(b) Hardship in traveling abroad.

(c) Length of residence in U.S.

(d) Preconceived intent:

i) Preconceived intent to immigrate at the time of entering as a nonimmigrant can be a basis to deny an adjustment application. *Jain v. INS*, 612 F.2d 683 (2d Cir.), *cert. denied*, 446 U.S. 937 (1980); *Ameeriar v. INS*, 438 F.2d 1028 (3d Cir.), *cert. denied*, 404 U.S. 801 (1971); *But see* INA §245(i);

ii) When an immediate-relative petition is at issue, preconceived intent alone is not enough. *Matter of Cavazos*, 17 I&N Dec. 215 (BIA 1980). But where it concerns a former 5th preference petition, it is sufficient. *Matter of Ibrahim*, 18 I&N Dec. 55 (BIA 1981).

(e) Existence of repeated violations of immigration law. *Mamoka v. INS*, 43 F.3d 184 (5th Cir. 1995).

(3) Where AOS is pending but applicant requests I-824 for IV processing, USCIS will treat the request as a request to withdraw the AOS application and after notice will withdraw it. Similarly, if the applicant files a "duplicate" I-130 requesting visa processing, it will do the same. Memo, Cronin, Acting Ex. Assoc. Comm., Office of Programs, HQ 70/23.1P (Aug. 8, 2000), *reprinted in* 77 No. 42 *Interpreter Releases* 1551, 1558 (Oct. 30, 2000). *See also* 8 C.F.R. §103.5b.

1.m. Rescheduling Adjustment Interview and Denial for Abandonment—USCIS may deem any application abandoned where the individual fails to appear for a scheduled interview and USCIS does not receive the request by the applicant or his attorney for rescheduling by the date of the interview (which request was required to be filed *prior to* the date and time of the interview), does not file notification of a change of address, or the application has not been withdrawn. 8 C.F.R. §§103.2(b)(9) & (13); AFM at 15.1(b)(2) & (d). A motion to reopen may be filed, 8 C.F.R. §103.2(b)(15) but the applicant must demonstrate that a request providing good cause to reschedule was postmarked, faxed, or received telephonically before the date and time of the scheduled interview or a notification of a change of address was received prior to adjudication of the petition. AFM at 15.1(d)(3)(B).

1.n. Transferring Adjustment to New or Subsequent Family- or Employment-Based Immigrant Visa Petitions—AFM at 23.2(k); Memo, Pearson, Ex. Assoc. Comm., Office of Field Operations HQ 70/23.1-P, 6.1.3-P (May 9, 2000), *reprinted in* 77 No. 21 *Interpreter Releases* 695, 716–7 (May 26, 2000). A person can transfer a second approved I-130 or I-140 petition to an existing I-485 adjustment application as long as the priority date for the petition is current.

1.o. Status at time of filing—Some courts in the criminal context pursuant to 18 U.S.C. §922(g)(5)(A) have found that a person cannot be convicted of being illegally present with a firearm if they have filed for adjustment of status. *U.S. v. Bruno-Muzquiz,* 412 F.3d 1052, 1054 (9th Cir. 2005); *U.S. v. Hernandez,* 913 F.2d 1506, 1513–14 (10th Cir. 1990). *But see U.S. v. Latu,* 479 F.3d 1153 (9th Cir. 2007) and cases cited therein.

1.p. AOS Is Not An Entry. The BIA has found that a person seeking adjustment of status is *not* making an entry into the U.S., although he may be assimilated to the person making entry for purposes of deciding whether he meets the requirements of INA §245(a), including the grounds of inadmissibility under INA §212(a). *Matter of Rainford*, 20 I&N Dec. 598 (BIA 1992) [person deportable for gun violation may nevertheless AOS because a gun charge does not make him inadmissible and he is not subject to deportation after he AOS]; *Matter of Connelly*, 19 I&N Dec. 156, 159 (BIA 1984) [former INA §241(f) inapplicable to waive fraud committed after entry at an adjustment interview]; *Matter of Mendez-Moralez,* 21 I&N Dec. 296, 299 (BIA 1996); *Jankowski-Burczyk v. INS,* 291 F.3d 172, 175 & n.2 (2d Cir. 2002). Under current law "admission" is *not* defined as including AOS but rather the prior "lawful entry of the alien into the United States after inspection and authorization by an immigration officer." INA §101(a)(13)(A) *Zhang v. Mukasey,* 509 F.3d 313 (6th Cir. 2007) [5 years is not measured from AOS for purposes of a CIMT committed within 5 years of admission, because AOS does not constitute an admission for purposes of calculating the time period]; *Shivaraman v. Ashcroft,* 360 F.3d 1142 (9th Cir. 2004) [rejecting interpretation of INA §237(a)(2)(A)(i) that would permit counting the 5 years from AOS instead of admission under INA §101(a)(13)(A)]. *Accord Martinez v. Mukasey,* 519 F.3d 532, 542–45 (5th Cir. 2008) [under the first prong of *Chevron* and under longstanding principles construing statutes in favor of persons facing removal, the court rejected *Matter of Rosas* in interpreting the exclusion provision of INA §212(h) and concluded that the term "admitted" as used in INA §212(h) does not bar LPRs who were convicted of aggravated felonies from obtaining relief if they were adjusted]; *Abdelqadar v. Gonzales,* 413 F.3d 668, 672–74 (7th Cir. 2005) [questioning and rejecting *Matter of Rosas* in the context of a commission of a CIMT under §237(a)(2)(A)(i) within 5 years of admission where person entered more than 5 years but adjusted status within 5 years]; *Aremu v. DHS,* 450 F.3d 578 (4th Cir. 2006) [same; reversing *Matter of Shanu* and finding §101(a)(13)(A) is clear and that admission applies to lawful entry and not to AOS]. *But see Matter of Shanu,* 23 I&N Dec. 754, 756–59 (BIA 2005) *reversed Aremu v. DHS,* 450 F.3d 578 (4th Cir. 2006) [the term "date of admission" in 237(a)(2)(A)(i) includes the date of AOS and applies to *any* admission]; *Matter of Rosas,* 22 I&N Dec. 616 (BIA 1999). In *American-Arab Anti-Discrimination Comm. v. Reno*, 70 F.3d 1045, 1067–68 (9th Cir. 1995), the Ninth Circuit held that due process applied to legalization adjustment proceedings and applicants were not assimilated to persons seeking entry. Also persons in valid H-1/L-1 status and their dependents may continue their status including applying for extensions of stay as H/L during the AOS period. 8 C.F.R. §214.2(h)(16)(i), (*l*)(16).

1.q. Adjustment before the IJ— If DHS denies AOS, the application may be renewed in a removal proceeding under certain circumstances. *Compare* 8 C.F.R. §245.2(a)(5)(ii) *with* 8 C.F.R. §1245.2(a)(1). At the time of the renewal of the application for AOS before the IJ, "an applicant does not need to meet the statutory requirement of section 245(c) of the Act [*e.g.*, not working without authorization] or §245.1(g) [immediate availability of an immigrant visa], if, in fact, those requirements were met at the time the renewed application was initially filed with the director." 8 C.F.R. §245.2(a)(5)(ii). *Accord, Matovski v. Gonzales,* 492 F.3d 722 (6th Cir. 2007) [court reversed IJ's refusal to consider adjustment of status for person who "ported" because 8 C.F.R. §245.2(a)(5)(ii) made the portability issue irrelevant as the IJ had authority to adjust a person if he was eligible to adjust at the time he filed with the USCIS director and because there was no regulation that barred the IJ from considering portability]. In removal proceedings, the applicant for AOS has the burden to establish both statutory eligibility and that s/he merits a favorable exercise of discretion. *Matovski, supra.*

As a result of regulatory changes arising from nationwide litigation, *see e.g., Bona v. Gonzales,* 425 F.3d 663 (9th Cir. 2005) [agreeing with *Succar v. Ashcroft,* 394 F.3d 8 (1st Cir. 2005) and disagreeing with *Mouelle v. Gonzales,* 416 F.3d 923 (8th Cir. 2005) *vacated* 126 S.Ct. 2964 (2006) and finding that an arriving alien in removal proceeding may adjust status] "arriving aliens" are no longer barred from AOS before USCIS. They may only seek to adjust status before the IJ if they are returning on an advance parole, USCIS has denied their AOS, they are placed in removal proceedings, and they are renewing a previously filed AOS application. 8 C.F.R. §§245.2(a)(1)(ii), 245.2(a)(5)(ii), 1240.11(a)(1), 1245.2(a)(1), 1245.2(a)(5)(ii); 71 Fed. Reg. 27585–92 (May 12, 2006) [withdrawing 8 C.F.R. §§245.1(c)(8) and 1245.1(c)(8) that barred arriving aliens from adjusting status]; AFM at 23.2(b) [discussing jurisdiction of USCIS and IJ regarding arriving aliens seeks to adjust]; Memo, Aytes, Assoc. Dir. Domestic Operations, USCIS HQDOMO 70/23.1 (Jan. 12, 2007), *published on* AILA InfoNet at Doc. No. 07030661. *But see Chambers v. Mukasey,* 520 F.3d 445, 450–51 (5th Cir. 2008) [IJ had no jurisdiction to address an AOS application that was filed 3 years after advance parole and was not the original denied AOS application, because the regulation only permits IJ review of a previously filed application]. The regulation limiting adjustment to USCIS for arriving aliens has been upheld. *Scheerer v. U.S. Att'y Gen.,* 513 F.3d 1244 (11th Cir. 2008) [8 C.F.R. §1245.2(a)(1), limiting arriving aliens' adjustment in most cases solely to USCIS was valid under *Chevron* because it did not eliminate adjustment but merely limited the forum for it]; *Vakker v. Att'y Gen. of the U.S.,* 519 F.3d 143, 148-50 (3d Cir. 2008) [upholding denial of remand of AOS to IJ for arriving alien under new regulations that require application is filed with USCIS and not IJ]. *See also Matter of Artigas,* 23 I&N Dec. 99 (BIA 2001) [a Cuban adjustment applicant who is an arriving alien may adjust before the IJ, because his application is under section 1 of the Cuban Adjustment Act and not under §245]. Some courts have held that it is an abuse of discretion for an IJ/BIA to deny a motion to reopen or motion to continue to allow the filing and processing of an adjustment application before USCIS. *Kalilu v. Mukasey,* 516 F.3d 777, 779–81 (9th Cir. 2008) [BIA abused its discretion by denying motion to reopen contrary to *Matter of Velarde-Pacheco* and on the grounds that only USCIS had jurisdiction because motion should have been granted to give USCIS the time to adjudicate the AOS]; *See also Shen Gao Ni v. BIA,* 520 F.3d 125 (2d Cir. 2008) [the BIA's recital in denying the motion to reopen because the IJ had no jurisdiction to adjust arriving aliens under the new regulation, "even if technically accurate" does not adequately discharge the BIA's duty to consider the record facts and offer an explanation, where respondents sought to reopen to terminate proceedings and go before USCIS]. *But see Jiang v. Gonzales,* 425 F.3d 649, 652–53 (9th Cir. 2005) [applicant who first entered U.S. under TWOV was arriving alien even though he subsequently obtained an advance parole and therefore was ineligible to adjust before the IJ under the Chinese Student Protection Act]. Under pre-IIRIRA law a paroled alien could adjust before DD but not in an exclusion proceeding. *Alvarez-Garcia v. Ashcroft,* 378 F.3d 1094 (9th Cir. 2004) [upholding limitation on adjustment before DD for excludable persons who were paroled into the U.S. because under the "entry doctrine" fiction, a person seeking admission does not have an equal protection right to the same procedures for AOS before the IJ as a deportable person]

The BIA has stated that an IJ also has no jurisdiction to determine the continuing validity of an employment-based visa petition pursuant to INA §204(j). Therefore, an IJ may not adjust the status of a person in removal proceedings pursuant to INA §204(j), who has an approved employment-based petition and an adjustment application pending where the employee has changed jobs and the adjustment application is pending more than 180 days. *Matter of Perez Vargas,* 23 I&N Dec. 829 (BIA 2005). But *Matter of Vargas* was *vacated Perez-Vargas v. Gonzales,* 478 F.3d 191 (4th Cir. 2007) [the BIA's decision that the IJ has no jurisdiction to decide the continuing validity of a employment-based petition under INA §204(j) was reversed because 8 C.F.R. §1245.2(a)(1) provides IJs with exclusive jurisdiction to adjust applicants in removal proceedings and a determination under INA §204(j) is simply an act of fact finding incidental to AOS]. *See also Sung v. Keisler,* 505 F.3d 372 (5th Cir. 2007) [adopted reasoning of *Perez-Vargas v. Gonzales* and found that IJ does have jurisdiction over portability determination because it is incidental to AOS]; *Matovski v. Gonzales,* 492 F.3d 722 (6th Cir. 2007) [court reversed IJ's refusal to consider adjustment of status for person who "ported" because 8 C.F.R. §245.2(a)(5)(ii) made the portability issue irrelevant as the IJ had authority to adjust a person if he was eligible to adjust at the time he filed with the USCIS director and because there was no regulation that barred the IJ from considering portability].

Refugee seeking to readjust status—A refugee who became an LPR and was then placed in removal proceedings who seeks to readjust as a refugee/asylee may be barred because INA §209(a)(1)(C). *Saintha v. Mukasey,* 516 F.3d 243, 251–53 (4th Cir. 2008) [upheld BIA view under *Chevron* deference that refugee could not readjust in IJ proceedings].

Prosecutorial Discretion to Dismiss Proceeding and Allow USCIS to Adjudicate—The Office of Chief Counsel for ICE has set forth guidelines for agreeing to dismiss proceedings *without prejudice* to permit an adjustment application to proceed before USCIS. *See* Chapter 3, X (P) (Prosecutorial Misconduct).

When an approved petition is already used to obtain residency, it cannot be used a second time to adjust status. *Matter of Villarreal-Zuniga,* 23 I&N Dec. 886 (BIA 2006) [cannot adjust status based upon an approved I-130 petition that was previously used to obtain residency]; 8 C.F.R. §204.2(h)(2).

2. Special Adjustment Provision—INA §245(i), 8 U.S.C. §1255(i), PL 103-317 Title V §506(b), 108 Stat. 1724 (Aug. 26, 1994), PL 106-554, Title XV 114 Stat. 2763 (Dec. 21, 2000); 2000 U.S.C.C.A.N. 2705; 8 C.F.R. §§245.10, 1245.10; 146 Cong. Rec. S11263-01 (daily ed. Oct. 27, 2000); 146 Cong. Rec. S11850-52 (daily ed. Dec. 15, 2000).

2.a. Section 245(i) allows a person to apply to adjust status notwithstanding the fact that s/he entered without inspection, overstayed, or worked without authorization. Thus a person who is EWI, notwithstanding INA §245(a), or is within one of the classes of INA §245(c) can adjust status if s/he paid the special fee required (currently $1,000). 8 C.F.R. §§103.7(b)(1), 1103.7(b)(1), as long as s/he (including her spouse and children) is the beneficiary of any labor certification or petition under section 204 (including I-140, I-130, I-360, I-526) that was filed on or before Apr. 30, 2001. The law had previously sunset on Jan. 14, 1998 but was revived under the LIFE Act amendments to include any application filed before Apr. 30, 2001. The LIFE Act amendment applies to a person who filed after Jan. 14, 1998 and before Apr. 30, 2001 *if the person was physically present in the U.S. on Dec. 21, 2000.* Memo, Cronin, Acting Executive Assoc. Comm. (HQ 70/23.1-P) (Jan. 26, 2001), *reprinted in* 78 No. 6 *Interpreter Releases* 325, 346–52 (Feb. 5, 2001) and *reprinted as amended* 78 No. 10 *Interpreter Releases* 473, 501–04 (Mar. 12, 2001). Persons who filed *before* Jan. 14, 1998 do not have to prove physical presence. The fee of $1,000 may not be waived by an IJ. *Matter of Fesale,* 21 I&N Dec. 114 (BIA 1995). Persons who are eligible include stowaways, crewmen, visa waiver entrants and TWOVs.

Section 245(i), however, does not waive any ground of inadmissibility, so INA §212(a) fully applies. 8 C.F.R. §§245.1(a), 1245.1(a). *Singh v. Gonzales,* 413 F.3d 156, 161 (1st Cir. 2005) [found person ineligible for INA §245(i) relief because of several intentional misrepresentations]. Thus, there was a facial conflict between this section and INA §212(a)(6)(A) which makes EWIs inadmissible (except if you are the spouse or child or an LPR or USC). The conflict was resolved by the GC who determined that §245(i) was applicable to persons who entered EWI and, therefore, they were able to adjust, notwithstanding §212(a)(6)(A). Legal Opinion, Martin, General Counsel, INS, CO 245(i), CO 212(a)(6)(A) (Feb. 19, 1997), *reprinted in* 74 No. 11 *Interpreter Releases* 499, 516–22 (Mar. 24, 1997). Other grounds of inadmissibility have not been waived and INA §245(i) does not waive INA §212(a)(9)(C)(i)(I), notwithstanding the fact that it involves EWI. *Matter of Briones,* 24 I&N Dec. 355 (BIA 2007) [INA §245(i) adjustment is unavailable to someone who is subject to INA §212(a)(9)(C)(i)(I)]; *Matter of Torres-Garcia,* 23 I&N Dec. 866 (BIA 2006) [an I-212 waiver cannot retroactively waive inadmissibility under INA §212(a)(9)(C)(i)(II) because the applicant cannot seek admission under that section for 10 years after the date of his last departure from the U.S.]; *Ramirez-Canales v. Mukasey,* 517 F.3d 904, 907–10 (6th Cir. 2008 [followed *Briones* under *Chevron* but remanded for potential *nunc pro tunc* relief]; *Delgado v. Mukasey,* 516 F.3d 65 (2d Cir. 2008) [same, agreeing with *Torres-Garcia* and *Gonzales*];

Gonzales v. DHS, 508 F.3d 1227, 1234–42 (9th Cir. 2007) [reversed its prior decision in *Perez-Gonzales v. Ashcroft,* 379 F.3d 783 (9th Cir. 2004) and upheld on *Chevron* deference under *National Cable & Telecommunications Ass'n v. Brand X,* 545 U.S. 967 (2005) the BIA's decision in *Matter of Torres-Garcia*];*Mortera-Cruz v. Gonzales,* 409 F.3d 246 (5th Cir. 2005) [*Chevron* deference granted to BIA's determination that a person inadmissible under INA §212(a)(9)(C)(i) may not adjust under INA §245(i)]; *Berrum-Garcia v. Comfort,* 390 F.3d 1158, 1166–68 (10th Cir. 2004) [applicant for §245(i) adjustment who re-enters after removal/deportation is *not* eligible to waive INA §212(a)(9)(C)(i)(II) with an I-212 without returning to his home country for 10 years]; *But see Acosta v. Gonzales,* 439 F.3d 550, 552–56 (9th Cir. 2006) [following *Perez-Gonzales*, the court held that INA §245(i) also applies to persons inadmissible under INA §212(a)(9)(C)(i)(I) but that the waiver under INA §212(a)(9)(B)(v) for unlawful presence is not available]; *Padilla-Caldera v. Gonzales,* 453 F.3d 1237 (10th Cir. 2006) [applicant for INA §245(i) adjustment who is subject to inadmissibility under INA §212(a)(9)(C)(i)(I) because s/he has been unlawfully present in the U.S. for an aggregate period of more than one year and re-entered the country illegally may adjust status. *Berrum-Garcia* distinguished and Crocetti INS memo not given *Chevron* deference]; *Perez-Gonzalez v. Ashcroft,* 379 F.3d 783, 790–91 (9th Cir. 2004) *motion to r'consd denied* 403 F.3d 1116 (2005) [DHS decision to deny §245(i) adjustment on grounds that it was barred by §212(a)(6)(A) reversed; however, the remainder of the opinion regarding the application of waivers after unlawful reentry is, as a practical matter, vacated under *Gonzales v. DHS,* 508 F.3d 1227 (9th Cir. 2007)]. However, adjustment under INA §245(i) is also unavailable to a person who is inadmissible under INA §212(a)(9)(B)(i)(II) [ten-year bar]. *Matter of Lemus,* 24 I&N Dec. 373 (BIA 2007).

INA §241(a)(5) bars illegal reentrants from seeking AOS under INA §245(i). *See e.g., Lino v. Gonzales,* 467 F.3d 1077, 1079 (7th Cir. 2006) [mother from Mexico who is married to USC with three USC children, two of whom have severe developmental disabilities could not adjust; citing to other circuits]; *De Sandoval v. U.S. Att'y Gen.,* 440 F.3d 1276, 1284–85 (11th Cir. 2006) [INA §245(i) is not in conflict with the reinstatement provision that bars most forms of relief because §245(i) applies only to persons who had never before been removed]. However, a person subject to §241(a)(5) may be able to adjust status under §245(i) if the application was filed prior to the effective date of IIRIRA (Apr. 1, 1997). *Faiz-Mohammad v. Ashcroft,* 395 F.3d 799, 809–10 (7th Cir. 2005) [pre-*Fernandez-Vargas* finding that INA §241(a)(5) may not retroactively bar relief where person entered and applied for relief/AOS before Apr. 1, 1997]; *Lopez-Flores v. DHS,* 387 F.3d 773 (8th Cir. 2004) [pre-*Fernandez-Vargas,* the court found it was impermissible to invoke INA §241(a)(5) retroactively where respondent had potential relief of AOS if I-212 waiver granted and initial labor certification application was filed prior to IIRIRA's effective date]; *Arevalo v. Ashcroft,* 344 F.3d 1 (1st Cir. 2003) [pre-*Fernandez-Vargas* an adjustment of status application based upon father's second preference petition that was filed prior Apr. 1, 1997 is not barred by INA §241(a)(5)]. The Court in *Fernandez-Vargas,* 548 U.S. 30 (2006) barred AOS for persons subject to INA §241(a)(5) who filed for relief after April 1, 1997 (the effective date of IIRIRA) but left open the question of whether someone who filed his application for relief prior to Apr. 1, 1997 is eligible for relief. In *Valdez-Sanchez v. Gonzales,* 485 F.3d 1084 (10th Cir. 2007) the Tenth Circuit addressed the issue left open in *Fernandez-Vargas* and found that where a person married and adjusted status to that of a conditional resident before IIRIRA, the application of INA §241(a)(5) to respondent was impermissibly retroactive. In *Silva Rosa v. Gonzales,* 490 F.3d 403 (5th Cir. 2007), however, the court found that INA §241(a)(5) was not impermissibly retroactive where person married LPR before IIRIRA and had approved I-130 before that date, but a visa number was not available and respondent did not file AOS until *after* IIRIRA's effective date.

Other sections require waivers before use of §245(i). A J visa holder subject to the 2-year foreign residency requirement must file an INA §212(e) waiver, and an A, E, or G visa holder is required to file an I-508 or I-566 waiver.

Other sections prohibit the use of §245(i). Because §245(i) waives §§245(a) & (c) but not §245(d), other persons who are ineligible to adjust or get the benefit of §245(i) include K-1 visa holders, persons who are conditional residents, S visa holders, and persons seeking adjustment based on marriage entered into while in exclusion, deportation, or related judicial proceedings, unless there is clear and convincing evidence that marriage is *bona fide*. INA §245(d), 8 U.S.C. §1255(d); 8 C.F.R. §§245.1(c), 1245.1(c); *Markovski v. Gonzales,* 486 F.3d 108 (4th Cir. 2007) [notwithstanding §245(i), respondent could not adjust based upon approved I-140 petition because §245(d) bars adjustment except based upon K-1 petition]; *Kalal v. Gonzales,* 402 F.3d 948, 951–52 (9th Cir. 2005) [in case where K-1 visa holder did not marry within 90 days and did not marry K-1 petitioner, the court upheld the rescission of her improperly granted CR status and upheld her removal because *inter alia* INA §245(i) does not waive the requirements of §245(d)]. *But see Matter of Stockwell,* 20 I&N Dec. 309 (BIA 1991) [a person whose status was terminated under INA §216 may thereafter adjust if s/he has legal basis to do so]. It is also not available to persons seeking adjustment under the Chinese Student Protection Act of 1992, *Matter of Wang,* 23 I&N Dec. 924 (BIA 2006) *Chan v. Reno*, 113 F.3d 1068 (9th Cir. 1997). Diversity visas also do not qualify under §245(i) since they were not petitions filed with the AG. However, a post–Jan. 14, 1998 diversity visa applicant may use a grandfathered petition as a basis to apply for diversity.

2.b. Proving Physical Presence on Dec. 21, 2000. 8 C.F.R. §§245.10(n), 1245.10(n); 66 Fed. Reg. 16383–90 (Mar. 26, 2001). Only the principal applicant and not his or her dependent family members must prove physical presence. 8 C.F.R. §§245.10(a)(1)(ii), 1245.10(n)(1); 66 Fed. Reg. 16383 at 16387. If documents are unavailable to prove physical presence on Dec. 21, 2000, an applicant can rely on documents proving s/he was present prior to and after that date. §§245.10(n)(1), 1245.10(n)(1). An applicant can rely on INS documentation such as I-94, NTA, OSC, I-122 for exclusion hearing, or photocopy of any application or petition showing relevant dates. §§245.10(n)(2), 1245.10(n)(2). An applicant can rely on other government documents such as a state driver's license or identification card, county or municipal hospital records, public college or public school transcripts, income tax records, benefit records for local, state, or federal government. §§245.10(n)(3), 1245.10(n)(3). An applicant can also rely on nongovernment records such as school records, rental or other dated receipts, utility bills, personal checks, employment records, credit card statement, or family records. The Service will not accept a personal affidavit attesting to physical presence without requiring an interview or additional evidence to validate the affidavit. §§245.10(n)(5), 1245.10(n)(5).

2.c. Grandfathered Petition—The Service has taken the view that it is the individual beneficiary (and his spouse and children) who are grandfathered by filing on or before Apr. 30, 2001 and not the petition, so that a beneficiary can adjust status based on a petition submitted and approved after Apr. 30, 2001 or a diversity visa application submitted after that date as long as there was an application/petition filed on or before Apr. 30, 2001 that was "approvable when filed." Therefore, once an applicant meets the requirements for grandfathering under 8 C.F.R. §245.10, s/he continues to be grandfathered until AOS. She is not limited to seeking AOS based upon the original petition and may seek AOS on any other basis. Moreover, there is *no* limit to the number of applications a grandfathered applicant may file. Memo, Yates, Assoc. Dir. Operations, USCIS, HQOPRD 70/23.1 (Mar. 9, 2005) ¶3(E), *published on* AILA InfoNet at Doc. No. 05031468. Even if the applicant "has been denied adjustment of status, has withdrawn or abandoned the application for adjustment of status, or has otherwise not adjusted under section 245(i), [she] remains grandfathered." Memo, Yates (Mar. 9, 2005), *supra* at ¶3.

(1) Approvable When Filed. 8 C.F.R. §§245.10(a)(3), 1245.10(a)(3). To be grandfathered an immigrant visa petition or labor certification application on or before Apr. 30, 2001 had to be: (1) properly filed and (b) approvable when filed. 8 C.F.R. §§245.10(a)(2), 1245.10(a)(2). Properly filed means that the petition was physically received by the Service on or before Apr. 30, 2001 or if mailed that it was postmarked on or before that date. Applications received without a postmark or with an illegible postmark "shall be considered timely filed if physically received by the Service by the close of business May 3, 2001." Memo, Yates, Deputy Ex. Assoc. Comm. Field Operations (Apr. 26, 2001), *reprinted in* 78 No. 18 *Interpreter Releases* 774, 790–93 (May 7, 2001). The same rule applies for private mail service delivered without a legible date and metered mail. *Id.* With respect to LC, it means that it was properly filed and accepted pursuant to 20 C.F.R. §656.21 by the State Employment Security Agency (SESA).

"Approvable When Filed" means that as of the date of filing, the petition or LC was: (1) properly filed; (2) meritorious in fact; and (3) nonfrivolous (frivolous being defined as patently without substance). §§245.10(a)(3), 1245.10(a)(3). This determination is made based on the circumstances that existed at the time the petition was filed and not whether it "was later withdrawn, denied, or revoked due to circumstances that have arisen after the time of filing." *Id;* §§245.10(i), 1245.10(i). *But see Lasprilla v. Ashcroft,* 365 F.3d 98 (1st Cir. 2004), [upheld decision on motion to reopen to deny grandfathering to spouse on I-130 petition where petition was denied]. Such changed circumstances include but are not limited to "a child who has reached age 21 before the principal alien could adjust status, an employer going out of business, or a valid, bona fide marriage ending in divorce before the alien could adjust status." 66 Fed. Reg. at 16385; §§245.10(a)(4), 1245.10(a)(4).

(a) Labor Certifications. For purposes of an LC the DOL/DHS take the view that "approvable when filed" means that the ETA 750 was properly filed. Thus, the Labor Department "considers every properly filed application for permanent labor certification to be approvable when filed for section 245(i) grandfathering purposes. The 'approvable when filed' standard can be met merely by properly filing the application on Form ETA 750. The Form ETA 750, as a statement from the employer, will meet the burden of establishing that the employment is nonfrivolous and meritorious in fact." Letter, Chang, Director, Residence and Status Branch, INS, HQADN 70/23.1 (May 15, 2001), *reprinted in* 78 No. 22 *Interpreter Releases* 931, 980–82 (June 4, 2001).

(b) Marriage Petitions. If the grandfathering is based upon a marriage petition filed before April 30, 2001, then the beneficiary has the burden to demonstrate that the marriage was bona fide. *Matter of Jara Riero and Jara Espinol,* 24 I&N Dec. 267 (BIA 2007) [upheld denial of AOS under §245(i) where beneficiary failed to prove that first marriage was bona fide because he failed to overcome contradictions cited in denial of first I-130]. The BIA encourages the IJ to take testimony on the issue and the beneficiary should present evidence of the bona fides of the first marriage consistent with *Matter of Laureano,* 19 I&N Dec. 1, 3 (BIA 1983) [proof through insurance policies, property leases, income tax forms, bank accounts and testimony or other evidence regarding courtship, wedding ceremony, shared residence and experiences]. The denial of the first marriage petition is not conclusive as to the question of the bona fide nature of the marriage. *Matter of Jara Riero and Jara Espinol, supra* at 269. *But see Echevarria v. Keisler,* 505 F.3d 16, 20 (1st Cir. 2007) [IJ/BIA are not required to revisit an original visa determination to establish whether the petition was "approvable when filed" if it was made on the merits, did not depend on changed circumstances, and could have been effectively reviewed at the time, although the IJ or BIA may choose to review it as a matter of grace].

(2) Asylum and Diversity Visa Applications. Filing an asylum application, diversity visa lottery application, or receipt of a winning diversity letter does *not* serve as a basis to grandfather a subsequent application. However, a diversity winner may use a valid grandfathered petition (*e.g.*, I-130/I-140/L.C.) to file for adjustment. 8 C.F.R. §1245.10(h). *See also Matter of L-K-,* 23 I&N Dec. 677, 678–79 (BIA 2004)

(3) Aged-Out Children, Divorced Spouses and After Acquired Family. The spouse or child of a grandfathered applicant is also grandfathered for §245(i) purposes even if she does not adjust with the principal. A spouse or child is also grandfathered "even after losing the status of spouse or child, such as by divorce or by becoming 21 years of age" as long as the relationship existed with the principal applicant at the time a qualifying petition or application was properly filed on or before Apr. 30, 2001. Memo, Yates, Assoc. Dir. Operations, USCIS, HQOPRD 70/23.1 (Mar. 9, 2005) at ¶3(D), *published on* AILA InfoNet at Doc. No. 05031468; Memo, Bach, Ex. Asst. Comm., Policy and Programs (HQ 70/23.1-P, HQ 70/8-P) (Jun. 10, 1999), *reprinted in* 76 No. 25 *Interpreter Releases* 1017, 1028–32 (July 2, 1999). Thus, aged-out children and divorced spouses are grandfathered and can file any petition or application they wish independently of the principal and need

not AOS or follow to join or accompany the principal. In addition, after-acquired children and spouse are allowed to adjust as a dependent under §245(i) with the principal. However, they are not grandfathered and therefore do not get the benefit of the principal's §245(i) and may not adjust if the principal has already adjusted. Thus, a person who becomes the spouse or child of a grandfathered person after the person acquired LPR status cannot accompany or follow to join the principal and cannot AOS under §245(i) unless he has an independent basis for grandfathering. Memo, Yates (Mar. 9, 2005) at ¶3(D).

(4) Substitution of Beneficiaries on LC. Cannot substitute a different beneficiary on the LC for purposes of grandfathering because grandfathering only applies to the original beneficiary. 66 Fed. Reg. 16383 at 16385; §245.10(j).

(5) Unlawful Presence. Grandfathering is unrelated to unlawful presence and a person may accrue unlawful presence even if s/he is grandfathered. §§245.10(m), 1245.10(m).

2.d. The excess fee is not required for children under 17, nor for spouses or children of legalized persons if they meet the family unity test. 8 C.F.R. §§103.7(b)(1), 1103.7(b)(1).

2.e. IJ may hear adjustment application under INA §245(i). *Matter of Grinberg*, 20 I&N Dec. 911 (BIA 1994). And may hear it in conjunction with a waiver as long as the petition was filed before Apr. 30, 2001. *Matter of Michel*, 21 I&N Dec. 1101 (BIA 1998) [application with §212(h) waiver]. INA §245(i) does not preclude the IJ from denying AOS as a discretionary matter based on applicant's transgressions. *Westover v. Reno,* 202 F.3d 475, 480 (1st Cir. 2000). An IJ may deny a §245(i) application for discretionary reasons. *Usmani v. Att'y Gen. of the U.S.,* 483 F.3d 1147 (11th Cir. 2007) [court rejected argument that §245(i) was mandatory if person qualified]. However, failure to grant a continuance to finalize a labor certification based §245(i) adjustment may be a violation of the statute and is reviewable in the circuit court. *Ahmed v. Gonzales,* 465 F.3d 806 (7th Cir. 2006) [IJ erred in not granting continuance to §245(i) eligible respondent with approved fourth preference petition who sought continuance to file labor certification to speed up process]; *Subhan v. Ashcroft,* 383 F.3d 591 (7th Cir. 2004) [rejected preclusion statutes and ruled that IJ's denial of a continuance to finalize labor certification without a reason consistent with §245(i) violated that statute] *but see Hadayat v. Gonzales infra. See also Haswanee v. U.S. Att'y Gen.,* 471 F.3d 1212 (11th Cir. 2006) [where LC was approved, I-140 filed, and visa immediately available, but no I-485 filed, it was an abuse of discretion to deny continuance but not a violation of equal protection or due process]; *Merchant v. U.S. Att'y Gen.,* 461 F.3d 1375 (11th Cir. 2006) [where LC was approved and respondent filed I-140 and I-485 with DHS pursuant to INA §245(i) it was an abuse of discretion by IJ to deny a continuance. *Bull* supported and *Zafar* distinguished]. *But see Lendo v. Gonzales,* 493 F.3d 439 (4th Cir. 2007) [respondent's rights were not violated when IJ refused to continue case pending wife's labor certification so they could adjust under INA §245(i)]; *Zafar v. U.S. Att'y Gen.,* 461 F.3d 1357 (11th Cir. 2006) *reh'g en banc denied* 473 F.3d 1350 (2007) [review of the denials of respondents' requests for continuance were not precluded by INA §242(a)(2)(B)(ii) because that section applies only to statutes and continuances are governed by regulation; nevertheless it was not an abuse of discretion to deny a continuance where the labor certification was not approved and adjustment was not immediately available; nor was it a violation of due process because adjustment is discretionary]; *Hadayat v. Gonzales,* 458 F.3d 659, 662–63 (7th Cir. 2006) [where adjustment date under approved fourth preference family petition was not current and where respondent failed to comply with voluntary departure, BIA did not err in denying motion to reconsider and court distinguished *Subhan* as granting reversal only due to court's failure to provide a reason for denial]; *Khan v. Att'y Gen. of the U.S.,* 448 F.3d 226, 233–36 (3d Cir. 2006) [IJ did not abuse discretion by denying continuance where wife's labor certification was pending and therefore a visa was not immediately available]; *Ahmed v. Gonzales,* 447 F.3d 433, 439–40 (5th Cir. 2006) [followed *Zafar* and found no statutory, due process or equal protection violation in denying continuance where labor certification was filed but no visa immediately available]; *Ali v. Gonzales,* 440 F.3d 678, 680–81 (5th Cir. 2006) [IJ did not abuse his discretion when he denied eighth continuance where respondent failed to provide proof that his LC was filed before Apr. 30, 2001 making him eligible for INA §245(i) relief]; *Ramchandani v. Gonzales,* 434 F.3d 337, 338–40 (5th Cir. 2005) [distinguished *Subhan* and upheld denial of continuance where respondent failed to provide documentation that a labor certification had been filed prior to Apr. 30, 2001]; *Grass v. Gonzales,* 418 F.3d 876, 877–89 (8th Cir. 2005) [no jurisdiction to stay proceedings or grant continuance to allow for approval of I-130 or I-140 for §245(i) protection and the REAL ID Act of 2005 did not alter that lack of jurisdiction because the decision to grant a continuance was discretionary and not a question of law]. Motions to reopen must be filed in accordance with the existing one motion/90-day rules or by consent of the Service. 66 Fed. Reg. 16383 at 16386; 8 C.F.R. §§245.10(f), 1245.10(f). *But see Padilla v. Ashcroft,* 334 F.3d 921 (9th Cir. 2003) [respondent's pending INA §245(i) application does not trump the reinstatement provision that bars relief].

2.f. Enforcement Issues—Legacy INS Headquarters provided guidance to field officers that they: "shall not initiate removal proceedings against an alien who is eligible for adjustment under section 245(i), if such action is based solely on the filing of an immigrant petition, labor certification application, or application for adjustment of status filed by, or on behalf of, that alien on or after the date of this memorandum seeking to legalize the alien's status under section 245(i)." Memo, Pearson, Executive Assoc. Comm. Office of Field Operations, INS, HQOPS 50/12.2 (Apr. 27. 2001), *reprinted in* 78 No. 19 *Interpreter Releases* 809, 817–18 (May 14, 2001). If a person in undocumented status is encountered in the course of routine enforcement, s/he may be processed under routine procedures. However, the memo notes that the Service may also exercise its prosecutorial discretion not to place the person in proceedings. *Id.*

2.g. Reinstatement of Removal—INA §§241(a)(5) and 245(i). The Court in *Fernandez-Vargas v. Gonzales,* 126 S.Ct. 2422 (2006) determined that applications for relief filed after Apr. 1, 1997 were barred by INA §241(a)(5). *Delgado v. Mukasey,* 516 F.3d 65 (2d Cir. 2008) [same, agreeing with *Torres-Garcia* and *Gonzales*]; *Gonzales v. DHS,* 508 F.3d 1227, 1234–42 (9th Cir. 2007) [reversed its prior decision in *Perez-Gonzales v. Ashcroft,* 379 F.3d 783 (9th Cir. 2004) and upheld on *Chevron* deference under *National Cable & Telecommunications Ass'n v. Brand X,* 545 U.S. 967 (2005) the BIA's decision in *Matter of Torres-Garcia*]; *Lino v. Gonzales,* 467 F.3d 1077, 1079 (7th Cir. 2006) [mother from Mexico who is married to USC with three USC children, two of whom have severe developmental disabilities, could not adjust, notwithstanding §245(i); citing to other circuits];*De Sandoval v. U.S. Att'y Gen.,* 440 F.3d 1276, 1284–85 (11th Cir. 2006) [INA §245(i) is not in conflict with the reinstatement provision that bars most forms of relief because §245(i) applies to persons who had never before been removed]; *Labojewski v. Gonzales,* 407 F.3d 814 (7th Cir. 2005) [reinstatement not impermissibly retroactive for person who re-entered the U.S. before IIRIRA but applied for AOS after; *Faiz-Mohammad* distinguished]; *Lattab v. Ashcroft,* 384 F.3d 8, 17–20 (1st Cir. 2004) [same]; *Warner v. Ashcroft,* 381 F.3d 534, 539–40 (6th Cir. 2004) [found that INA §245(i) "has no effect upon §241(a)(5)'s preclusion of relief"]; *Flores v. Ashcroft,* 354 F.3d 727, 730–31 (8th Cir. 2003) [reinstatement provision bars adjustment except in limited circumstances for persons seeking relief under NACARA or HRIFA]; *Padilla v. Ashcroft,* 334 F.3d 921 (9th Cir. 2003) [pending INA §245(i) application does not trump the reinstatement provision that bars relief]; *Matter of Torres-Garcia,* 23 I&N Dec. 866 (BIA 2006). The Court in *Fernandez-Vargas,* 126 S.Ct. 2422, 2432–33 (2006) however, left open the question of whether someone who filed his application for relief prior to Apr. 1, 1997, could be barred by INA §241(a)(5). In *Valdez-Sanchez v. Gonzales,* 485 F.3d 1084 (10th Cir. 2007) the Tenth Circuit addressed the issue left open in *Fernandez-Vargas* and found that where a person married and adjusted status to that of a conditional resident before IIRIRA, the application of INA §241(a)(5) to respondent was impermissibly retroactive. In *Silva Rosa v. Gonzales,* 490 F.3d 403 (5th Cir. 2007), however, the court found that INA §241(a)(5) was not impermissibly retroactive where person married LPR before IIRIRA and had approved I-130 before that date, but a visa number was not available and respondent did not file AOS until *after* IIRIRA's effective date. *See also Faiz-Mohammad v. Ashcroft,* 395 F.3d 799, 809–10 (7th Cir. 2005) [pre-*Fernandez-Vargas* finding that INA §241(a)(5) may not retroactively bar relief where person entered and applied for relief/AOS before Apr. 1, 1997]; *Lopez-Flores v. DHS,* 387 F.3d 773 (8th Cir. 2004) [pre-*Fernandez-Vargas,* the court found it was impermissible to invoke INA §241(a)(5) retroactively where respondent had potential relief of AOS if I-212 waiver granted and initial labor certification application was filed prior to IIRIRA's effective date]; *Arevalo v. Ashcroft,* 344 F.3d 1 (1st Cir. 2003) [pre-*Fernandez-Vargas* an adjustment of status application based upon father's second preference petition that was filed prior Apr. 1, 1997 is not barred by INA §241(a)(5)].

3. Special Exemption for Employment-based Petitioners Seeking Adjustment—INA §245(k), 8 U.S.C. §1255(k), PL 105-119, 111 Stat. 2440, §111(c) (Nov. 26, 1997).

3.a. Persons who are beneficiaries of employment-based petitions approved under §203(b)(1), (2) or (3), or §203(b)(4) in the case of religious workers described in 101(a)(27)(C), are exempt from ineligibility on grounds of §245(c)(2), (7) or (8) [unauthorized employment or out-of-status] if they were lawfully admitted and had not violated the terms of their status [by working unlawfully, overstaying, or otherwise violating the terms and conditions] for more than an aggregate period exceeding 180 days.

(1) USCIS maintains the position that the 180 days may occur *after* the filing of adjustment under §245(k). For example, if a person has 160 days of unlawful status, then files an AOS under §245(k) but proceeds to work for another 21 days without an authorization, he would be barred in the Service's view. AILA/USCIS Liaison Minutes at q. 3 (Oct. 28, 2004), *published on* AILA InfoNet at Doc. No. 05012163.

(2) The 180 days are measured only from the employee's last entry. AILA/TSC Liaison Minutes (Apr. 7, 2003) at q. 11, *published on* AILA InfoNet at Doc. No. 03051242 (May 12, 2003).

3.b. They must be otherwise eligible to adjust.

3.c. No additional fee for adjustment like §245(i).

4. Jurisdiction

4.a. Family-Based—Beginning Dec. 2004, family-based AOS applications from most states and territories are required to be filed at the "Chicago Lockbox." The fees are accepted and the interview schedules, and the file is then sent to the local district office where the interview will take place. For states that are not required to file at the Chicago Lockbox, applications are still filed directly with the USCIS district office where the adjustment applicant resides, even if petitioner on the I-130 is in another venue.

4.b. Employment-Based—The first three categories of employment-based applications (including persons of extraordinary ability) are filed on an I-140. Application for special immigrants are filed on Form I-360. Investor applications are filed on Form I-526. 8 C.F.R. §§204.5(a), 204.6(a). All applications were formerly filed with the service center having jurisdiction over the intended place of employment. 8 C.F.R. §§204.5(b), 204.6(b), although some employers were granted permission to consolidate all petitions at one Service Center. Now petitions are filed as follows: I-140—Nebraska Service Center (which may forward applications to the Texas Service Center); I-360—Service Center for residence; I-526—California Service Center. Fact Sheet, USCIS, Notifies Employers of Filing Changes (Mar. 24, 2006), *reprinted in* 83 No. 13 *Interpreter Releases* 548, 567–71 (Mar. 24, 2006).

4.c. If it is filed subsequent to issuance of NTA, the adjustment application can only be filed with IJ. 8 C.F.R. §§245.2(a)(1), 1245.2(a)(1). The DHS may thereafter agree with the respondent to remand the case back to USCIS for adjustment (Form I-471C). However, where DHS does not agree to a remand, the IJ has no authority to remand the adjustment application to USCIS. *Matter of Roussis*, 18 I&N Dec. 256 (BIA 1982). The IJ must determine the application. 8 C.F.R. §1240.11(a)(1). Concurrent applications to overcome inadmissibility under §§212(g), 212(h), 212(i), or 212(k) may be filed with the adjustment application pursuant to INA §245. 8 C.F.R. §§245.1(f), 1245.1(f). The IJ has no jurisdiction over I-130, I-140 or I-360 petitions. These must be filed with and approved by USCIS prior to the IJ considering the adjustment application (I-485).

4.d. If applicant has moved to another district, the DD in the district where the application was filed has discretion to retain application or transfer it. Letter, Puleo, Asst. Comm. Adjudications, CO 245-C (Dec. 6, 1989), *reprinted in* 67 No. 3 *Interpreter Releases* 66, 80 (Jan. 12, 1990). To extend employment authorization, the applicant must apply in district of residence. *Id.*

4.e. No jurisdiction to AOS in former exclusion proceeding unless person travels outside U.S. on advance parole after previously filing AOS application. *Matter of Castro*, 21 I&N Dec. 379

(BIA 1996). *See Chambers v. Mukasey,* 520 F.3d 445, 450–51 (5th Cir. 2008) [IJ had no jurisdiction to address an AOS application that was filed 3 years after advance parole and was not the original denied AOS application, because the regulation only permits IJ review of a previously filed application]. DHS still maintains this distinction by excluding "arriving aliens" from filing AOS applications in removal proceedings before the IJ. However, the application may be filed with USCIS. 8 C.F.R. §§245.2(a)(1), 1245.2(a)(1). The regulation limiting adjustment to USCIS for arriving aliens has been upheld. *Scheerer v. U.S. Att'y Gen.,* 513 F.3d 1244 (11th Cir. 2008) [8 C.F.R. §1245.2(a)(1), limiting arriving aliens' adjustment in most cases solely to USCIS was valid under *Chevron* because it did not eliminate adjustment but merely limited the forum for it]. *See in this section* "Arriving Aliens and Adjustment," ¶ 5.g (p.853), *infra.*

4.f. No jurisdiction to AOS if there is a final order of removal/deportation unless the IJ grants a motion to reopen. If the time for filing a motion to reopen has passed because it is more than 90 days from the decision of the IJ/BIA, a motion may still be granted if DHS consents. 8 C.F.R. §1003.2(c)(3)(iii); *Bolshakov v. INS*, 133 F.3d 1279, 1281–82 (9th Cir. 1998) [not required to exhaust because agreement of parties to reopening is not a remedy]. The Service's General Counsel has stated that consent should be given "only under exceptional and compelling circumstances." Memo, Martin, General Counsel, INS, HQ COU 90/16.11-P (Dec. 23, 1997), *reprinted in* 75 No. 7 *Interpreter Releases* 259, 275–77 (Feb. 23, 1998). However, this position was modified for persons seeking a motion to reopen to obtain residency through adjustment of status. The INS Gen. Counsel has decided that INS may join in a motion to reopen for consideration of AOS under INA §245 "if such adjustment of status was not available to the respondent at the former hearing, the alien is statutorily eligible...and the respondent merits a favorable exercise of discretion." Memo, Cooper, Gen. Counsel, HQCOU 90/ 16.22.1 (May 17, 2001), *reprinted in* 78 No. 27 *Interpreter Releases* 1166, 1181–84 (July 16, 2001).

5. Advance parole [8 C.F.R. §§212.5(f)]

5.a. Departure from U.S. without advance permission to leave during pendency of adjustment application is considered abandonment. 8 C.F.R. §§245.2(a)(4)(ii), 1245.2(a)(4)(ii); IFM at 16.1(b); *Le v. Waters*, 863 F.Supp. 1104 (N.D. Cal. 1994). However, there is now an exception for persons in valid H and L status and their dependents and for K-3 and K-4 visa holders.

(1) If an L-1 or H-1B is not under exclusion, deportation, and removal proceedings and is in valid L-1 or H-1B status, s/he may travel while her AOS application is pending without an advance parole if she: is coming back to the U.S. to resume employment with the same employer for which her H-1B/L-1 is authorized and (2) is in possession of a valid L or H visa (if required). The former requirement that she also have in her possession the AOS receipt has been removed. 72 Fed. Reg. 61791 (Nov. 1, 2007). Dependent family members in lawful H-4/L-2 status may also travel during the AOS if the same conditions for the H-1B/L-1 principal exist. 8 C.F.R. §§245.2(a)(4)(ii)(C), 1245.2(a)(4)(ii)(C). However, if s/he travels and re-enters on an advance parole and s/he has a valid and approved H-1B/L-1 petition, s/he may apply for an extension of her status and DHS will terminate her parole and admit her as an H-1B/L-1. *Adjudicator's Field Manual,* Appendix 23-4, 31–2a, Memo, Cronin, Acting Assoc. Comm., Office of Programs HQADJ 70/2.8.6, 2.8.12, 10.18 (May 16, 2000), *reprinted in* 77 No. 20 *Interpreter Releases* 672, 677–80 (May 22, 2000). The employer may also apply for a new H-1B/L-1 or if the person retains a valid H-1B/L-1, s/he may depart and re-enter on the H-1B/L-1. Adjudicator's Field Manual, Appendix §23-4. Even if the employee re-enters on an advance parole and continues her H-1B/ L-1 employment she will not be considered to engage in unauthorized employment. *Id.*

(2) The departure of someone who is in lawful K-3 or K-4 status and is not under exclusion, deportation or removal proceedings is not deemed an abandonment of the application for adjustment, if, upon returning to the U.S. s/he is in possession of a valid K-3/K-4 visa and remains eligible for the status. 8 C.F.R. §245.2(a)(4)(ii)(C). The same is true for a person in valid V status. 8 C.F.R. §245.2(a)(4)(ii)(D).

(3) The departure of someone in the U.S. for more than a year on an advance parole may prohibit him from seeking asylum. *Joaquin-Porras v. Gonzales,* 435 F.3d 172, 178–80 (2d Cir. 2006) [return on DHS authorized parole does not constitute a new arrival for purposes of 8 C.F.R. §208.4(a)(2)(ii) and an applicant who had been in the U.S. for a number of years but had traveled several times on an advance parole was precluded from seeking asylum despite last entering the U.S. on the advance parole within one year].

5.b. The District Directors have jurisdiction to grant advance parole (I-131/I-512) under INA §212(d)(5)(A), 8 U.S.C. §1182(d)(5)(A). AILA Midwest Regional Conference NBC Panel Questions and Answers, Apr. 7, 2006, *published on* AILA InfoNet at Doc. No. 06042664; 8 C.F.R. §212.5; IFM at 16.1. Advance parole can be granted to a person whose adjustment application is pending and who must leave the U.S. "for *bona fide* business or personal reason." This does *not* require a showing of emergent or extreme need to travel. Rather it includes "travel for any reason which is not contrary to law or public policy." Memo, Puleo, Assoc. Comm., Adjudications, CO 212.28-C (July 6, 1992), *reprinted in* 69 No. 26 *Interpreter Releases* 846, 851–52 (July 13, 1992). For persons seeking adjustment, advance parole will be granted for multiple entries and for the time period required to complete adjustment of status, not to exceed one year. Memo, Puleo, Exec. Assoc. Commissioner (Apr. 20, 1995); Memo, Virtue, Acting Exec. Assoc. Comm., HQ 120/17.2 (Aug. 15, 1997), both memos *reprinted in* 74 No. 32 *Interpreter Releases* 1292, 1303–05 (Aug. 25, 1997). If the person applying for advance parole is in removal proceedings his or her request must be adjudicated by the Office of International Affairs (formerly Office of Refugees, Asylum and Parole) at Headquarters, and not the DD. Letter, Cummings, Acting Director Refugee, Asylum and Parole, CO 212.5, (Oct. 8, 1993), *reprinted in* 71 No. 1 *Interpreter Releases* 18, 46–47 (Jan. 3, 1994).

5.c. Advance parole can also be granted to: LPR who has applied to USCIS for a duplicate I-551 or visa waiver under INA §211(b), but who must depart for emergent reasons prior to approval of application, IFM at 16.1(b); or a person (except a J subject to foreign residency requirement, a beneficiary of a private bill or a person in deportation proceedings) who the DD authorizes for emergent or humanitarian reasons, IFM at 16.1(c), (h), or a person whose parole, prior to embarkation abroad, has been authorized by the DD.

5.d. Advance Parole for Person out of U.S.—An advance parole cannot be granted to a person outside of the U.S. *El-Hadad v. U.S.,* 377 F.Supp.2d 42, 48–49 & n.6 (D.D.C. 2005) [person is not eligible for advance parole who is outside of the U.S. and there is no judicial or habeas review of his denial where he sought parole solely to pursue litigation in US].

5.e. Advance Parole and NSEERS—If applicant who had previously registered travels on advance parole, he does not have to register upon his return at the port of entry, because he "would be a parolee and not a non-immigrant applicant." Memo, Williams, Ex. Assoc. Comm. Field Operations, "Standard Operating Procedures for Alien Registration—IFM Update IN02-34, HQINS 70/28 (Sept. 5, 2002) at 1–2, 18, *published on* AILA InfoNet at Doc. No. 03043048.

5.f. Status Upon Return. If a party is granted advance parole but his or her admissibility is challenged on return, s/he will be placed in removal proceedings challenging her admissibility, even if s/he was in a deportable status before leaving. *Balogun v. U.S. Att'y Gen.,* 304 F.3d 1303 (11th Cir. 2002) [no constitutionally protected right to discretionary relief or to be eligible for discretionary relief upon return from advance parole and no constitutional right to be advised of consequences of accepting advance parole]; *Barney v. Rogers*, 83 F.3d 318 (9th Cir. 1996) [overstay who obtained advance parole was placed in exclusion proceedings after adjustment application was denied upon return]; *Brito-Deleon v. Ashcroft,* 188 F.Supp.2d 340, 345 n.3 (S.D.N.Y. 2002) [in *dicta* the court found that there was nothing to prevent INS from initiating removal proceedings against an applicant for adjustment with drug conviction who was given a re-entry permit]; *Matter of G-A-C-,* 22 I&N Dec. 83 (BIA 1998) [person in advance parole properly placed in exclusion proceeding; followed *Barney* distinguished *Navarro-Aispura*]; *Matter of S-O-S-,* 22 I&N Dec. 107 (BIA 1998) [regarding advance parole in Ninth Circuit]; *But see Navarro-Aispura v. INS*, 53 F.3d 233 (9th Cir. 1995) [registry adjustment applicant improperly placed in exclusion on his return]. S/he will not be subject to summary removal proceedings however. 8 C.F.R. §§1.1(q), 1001.1(q).

5.g. Arriving Aliens and Adjustment. As a result of regulatory changes arising from nationwide litigation, *see e.g., Bona v. Gonzales,* 425 F.3d 663 (9th Cir. 2005) [agreeing with *Succar v. Ashcroft,* 394 F.3d 8 (1st Cir. 2005), and disagreeing with *Mouelle v. Gonzales,* 416 F.3d 923 (8th Cir. 2005) *vacated* 126 S.Ct. 2964 (2006), and finding that an arriving alien in removal proceeding may adjust status] "arriving aliens" are no longer barred from AOS before USCIS. They may seek to adjust status before the IJ only if they are returning on an advance parole, USCIS has denied their AOS, they are placed in removal proceedings, and they seek review of a previously filed AOS application. 8 C.F.R. §§245.2(a)(1), 245.2(a)(5)(ii), 1240.11(a)(1), 1245.2(a)(1), 1245.2(a)(5)(ii); 71 Fed. Reg. 27585–92 (May 12, 2006) [withdrawing 8 C.F.R. §§245.1(c)(8) and 1245.1(c)(8), which barred arriving aliens from adjusting status]; AFM at 23.2(b) [discussing jurisdiction of USCIS and IJ regarding arriving aliens who seek to adjust]; Memo, Aytes, Assoc. Dir. Domestic Operations, USCIS HQDOMO 70/23.1 (Jan. 12, 2007), *published on* AILA InfoNet at Doc. No. 07030661. *Cf. Chambers v. Mukasey,* 520 F.3d 445, 450–51 (5th Cir. 2008) [IJ had no jurisdiction to address an AOS application that was filed 3 years after advance parole and was not the original denied AOS application, because the regulation only permits IJ review of a previously filed application]. The regulation limiting adjustment to USCIS for arriving aliens has been upheld. *Scheerer v. U.S. Att'y Gen.,* 513 F.3d 1244 (11th Cir. 2008) [8 C.F.R. §1245.2(a)(1), limiting arriving aliens' adjustment in most cases solely to USCIS was valid under *Chevron* because it did not eliminate adjustment but merely limited the forum for it]; *Vakker v. Att'y Gen. of the U.S.,* 519 F.3d 143, 148–50 (3d Cir. 2008) [upholding denial of remand of AOS to IJ for arriving alien under new regulations that require that the application be filed with USCIS and not IJ]. *See also Matter of Artigas,* 23 I&N Dec. 99 (BIA 2001) [a Cuban adjustment applicant who is an arriving alien may adjust before the IJ, because his application is under section 1 of the Cuban Adjustment Act and not under §245]. Some courts have held that it is an abuse of discretion for an IJ/BIA to deny a motion to reopen or motion to continue to allow the filing and processing of an adjustment application before USCIS. *Kalilu v. Mukasey,* 516 F.3d 777, 779–81 (9th Cir. 2008) [BIA abused its discretion by denying motion to reopen contrary to *Matter of Velarde-Pacheco* and on the grounds that only USCIS had jurisdiction because motion should have been granted to give USCIS the time to adjudicate the AOS]; *See also Shen Gao Ni v. BIA,* 520 F.3d 125 (2d Cir. 2008) [the BIA's recital in denying the motion to reopen because the IJ had no jurisdiction to adjust arriving aliens under the new regulation, "even if technically accurate" does not adequately discharge the BIA's duty to consider the record facts and offer an explanation where respondents sought to reopen to terminate proceedings and go before USCIS]. *But see Jiang v. Gonzales,* 425 F.3d 649, 652–53 (9th Cir. 2005) [applicant who first entered U.S. under TWOV was arriving alien even though he subsequently obtained an advance parole and therefore was ineligible to adjust before the IJ under the Chinese Student Protection Act]. Under pre-IIRIRA law a paroled alien could adjust before DD but not in an exclusion proceeding. *Alvarez-Garcia v. Ashcroft,* 378 F.3d 1094 (9th Cir. 2004) [upholding limitation on adjustment before DD for excludable persons who were paroled into the U.S. because under the "entry doctrine" fiction, a person seeking admission does not have an equal protection right to the same procedures for AOS before the IJ as a deportable person]. However, where adjustment is denied, the person who was paroled into the country on the advance parole *does not* revert to his original status, *e.g.*, an admitted person who overstayed, but is treated as an arriving alien under 8 C.F.R. §1.1(q) and subject to removal as an inadmissible alien. *Ibragimov v. Gonzales,* 476 F.3d 125, 132–38 (2d Cir. 2007) [an adjustment applicant reentering on an advance parole is an arriving alien under 8 C.F.R. §1.1(q) and if his adjustment application is denied he remains a parolee and does not revert to a person admitted as an overstay].

5.h. Advance Parole and Three/Ten Year Bar. A person granted advance parole who was unlawfully present in the U.S. for 180 days/1 year prior to filing an AOS application will be subject to the 3/10 year bar upon return. The grant and use of the advance parole does not mean the applicant is in the U.S. in a *bona fide* capacity. USCIS should *not* issue advance parole if USCIS knows the person would be subject to removal upon his return unless it appears likely that a waiver would be granted. Memo, Virtue, Acting Exec. Comm., HQ IRT 50/5.12, 96 Act.068 (Nov. 26, 1997), *reprinted in* 74 No. 46 *Interpreter Releases* 1842, 1864–68 (Dec. 8, 1997).

5.i. Advance Parole and Suspension or Cancellation of Removal. In the view of one circuit, the advance parole regulation, 8 C.F.R. §245.2(a)(4)(ii) which treats returning adjustment applicants as seeking admission if their AOS is denied is not *ultra vires* of the suspension statute. *Geach v. Chertoff,* 444 F.3d 940, 943–44 (8th Cir. 2006) [advance parole is not *ultra vires* of the suspension statute because suspension is discretionary and respondent's equal protection and due process rights were not violated]

5.j. Effect on Family's Status—Where person in valid NIV status applies for AOS and departs on advance parole, he loses NIV status on return and therefore family loses NIV status when it is based on principal's (*e.g.,* L-2). Letter, Skerrett, Chief IV Branch, Adjudications, HQ 245-C (Sept. 15, 1995), *reprinted in* 72 No. 38 *Interpreter Releases* 1343, 1362 (Oct. 2, 1995).

5.k. Revocation of Advance Parole—Where DD revoked advance parole at the time someone was out of the U.S., at least one court has determined that there was no jurisdiction to review the decision. *Samirah v. O'Connell,* 335 F.3d 545 (7th Cir. 2003) [district court lacked jurisdiction to review revocation because INA §242(a)(2)(B)(ii) precludes review of discretionary decisions and because habeas jurisdiction was unavailable to someone outside the U.S. who is not in custody and is unable to have personal service over a custodian].

6. Employment authorization

6.a. Eligible when application submitted. 8 C.F.R. §§274a.12(c)(9), 1274a.12(c)(9). Filed on I-765. In the view of at least one court the grant of work authorization is mandatory, not a matter of the Service's discretion. *Gomez-Arauz v. McNary*, 779 F.Supp. 1308 (W.D. Okl. 1991). If a second application for employment authorization is filed because adjustment not adjudicated, USCIS must resolve it within 90 days or the persons work authorization is automatically extended for 240 days pursuant to 8 C.F.R. §§274a.13(d), 1274a.13(d).

6.b. Applicant in valid NIV work status (*e.g.,* H-1B) would maintain that status and need not apply for E.A. If status expired during pendency of adjustment process s/he could apply for extension of NIV status or for E.A. Letter, Weinig, Deputy Asst. Comm., Adjudications, CO-214h-C (Feb. 7, 1992), *reprinted in* 69 No. 13 *Interpreter Releases* 425, 432 (Apr. 6, 1992). Person in E-1 or E-2 status could seek extension of his stay *after* filing adjustment application in light of the doctrine of dual intent. Memo, Virtue, Acting Exec. Assoc. Comm. (Aug. 5, 1997).

6.c. H-1B and L-1 status holders may now apply for E/S, C/S to H or L, or seek new H-1B/L-1 petition while AOS is pending. 8 C.F.R. §§214.2(h)(16)(i), 214.2(*l*)(16)(i); AFM at 30.1 and Appendix §23-4, 31.2a.

7. Denial of adjustment/Administrative and Judicial Review

7.a. No appeal on denial. 8 C.F.R. §§245.2(a)(5)(ii), 1245.2(a)(5)(ii).

7.b. May make motion to reopen or reconsider. 8 C.F.R. §103.5.

(1) If denial is final, can renew adjustment application in deportation proceedings. 8 C.F.R. §§245.2(a)(1), 1245.2(a)(1).

7.c. Judicial Review. For issues concerning the judicial review of adjustment of status *see* Ch. 10, ¶ IV.A.3.g (p.1121), *infra. See also* "Mandamus" in Ch. 10, section III.D (p.1103), *infra.*

8. Rescission of adjustment—INA §246(a), 8 U.S.C. §1256(a); 8 C.F.R. §§246, 1246

8.a. Seek rescission within 5 years if person was ineligible for adjustment or suspension.

(1) Not applicable where IV was obtained at the consulate abroad. In that circumstance DHS must seek to remove under INA §237(a)(1), 8 U.S.C. §1227(a)(1).

(2) Alien does not have same safeguards as in deportation proceeding when DHS exercises rescission. Alien may have affirmative defenses to rescission (*e.g.,* was eligible to adjust under another provision of law).

(3) May be brought when returning resident placed in deferred inspection, in the view of one court. *Ali v. Reno*, 829 F.Supp. 1415, 1426–31 (S.D.N.Y. 1993), *aff'd*, 22 F.3d 442 (2d Cir. 1994).

(4) If respondent answers in writing and requests hearing before IJ within 30 days of DD's notice that he intends to rescind residency, respondent is entitled to a hearing before the IJ. 8 C.F.R. §§246.1, 246.3, 1246.1, 1246.3. In the view of one court, the rescission hearing before the IJ may be combined with a removal hearing. *Kalal v. Gonzales,* 402 F.3d 948 (9th Cir. 2005) [upheld rescission of CR status and procedure combining it with removal hearing of person who did not marry K-1 petitioner within 90 days and instead married a different USC]. If s/he fails to do so within 30 days, no hearing is required. *Ali v. Reno*, 22 F.3d 442 (2d Cir. 1994) [where applicant requests continuance to respond and asked for documents, response not deemed to be answer or request for a hearing]. If DD decides issue, IJ does not have jurisdiction to review a decision rescinding residency entered by the DD, *Matter of Rodriguez-Esteban*, 20 I&N Dec. 88 (BIA 1989), but IJ should terminate proceedings pending a motion to reopen before the DD. *Rodriguez-Esteban, supra.*

8.b. If there is rescission, person placed in nonimmigrant status as overstay.

8.c. All family members who derived status from person rescinded also lose status.

8.d. Traditionally, rescission did not prevent INS from bringing deportation proceeding after 5 years if they found cause (*e.g.,* INA §212(a)(6)(C) fraud). *Monet v. INS*, 791 F.2d 752 (9th Cir. 1986); *Oloteo v. INS*, 643 F.2d 679 (9th Cir. 1981); *Asika v. Ashcroft,* 362 F.3d 264 (4th Cir. 2004) [under *Chevron* deference the 5-year statutory limit on rescission does not prohibit removal proceedings where LPR status was obtained in error]; *Matter of Belenzo,* 17 I&N Dec. 374, 380 (AG 1981). *But see Bamidele v. INS*, 99 F.3d 557 (3d Cir. 1996) [the running of the limitation period under INA §246(a) prohibits INS from initiating deportation proceedings based on fraud in AOS]. IIRIRA §378 amended the rescission proceedings to permit the AG to initiate removal proceedings instead of rescission at any time. Thus, DHS no longer needs to initiate rescission proceedings, but can simply institute removal proceedings. INA §246(a), 8 U.S.C. §1256(a). Also DHS may not be required to bring rescission where persons were ineligible for adjustment because they were already subject to final orders of removal. *Sulit v. Schiltgen,* 213 F.3d 449 (9th Cir. 2000).

8.e. In rescission, the DHS must only prove ineligibility on grounds originally asserted for adjustment. It need not address any other grounds on which applicant could have sought adjustment. *Shoo Hwan Kim v. Meese*, 810 F.2d 1494 (9th Cir. 1987).

8.f. Procedure. 8 C.F.R. §246

(1) DD sends notice of intent to rescind.

(2) If LPR contests within 30 days, there is hearing before IJ.

(3) Rules of evidence not binding.

(4) Standard is "clear, convincing and unequivocal." *Yaldo v. INS*, 424 F.2d 501 (6th Cir. 1970).

(5) Can appeal adverse decision of IJ on rescission to BIA. 8 C.F.R. §§3.1(b)(8), 246.7, 1246.7.

9. Judicial Review

9.a. District court review of BIA rescission order was permissible, *Baria v. Reno*, 94 F.3d 1335, 1337–40 (9th Cir. 1996) [review permissible in district court of BIA's rescission order under former §1329 while deportation proceedings are pending and before final order of deportation entered] if deportation proceedings are not completed. District court also retained review power when party does not seek review of final order. *Gottesman v. INS*, 922 F.Supp. 605, 610 (N.D. Ga. 1996).

9.b. Circuits split over whether there is review of DD decision in circuit court as part of final order of deportation. *Compare Gottesman v. INS*, 33 F.3d 383 (4th Cir. 1994) [no jurisdiction] with *Bachelier v. INS*, 625 F.2d 902, 904 (9th Cir. 1980) [jurisdiction].

9.c. Post-IIRIRA, DHS is likely to raise as a jurisdictional bar to the review of rescission in the district or circuit courts, INA §242(a)(2)(B)(ii), 8 U.S.C. §1252(a)(2)(B)(ii), on the theory that rescission is a "discretionary" decision by DHS. *But see Spencer Enterprises, Inc. v. U.S.,* 345 F.3d 683, 689 (9th Cir. 2003) for a narrow reading of the discretionary decision bar.

10. Removal Proceedings After Adjustment or While Adjustment is Pending—Notwithstanding adjustment of status, DHS can initiate removal proceedings for any ground under INA §237 including inadmissibility on original entry. INA §246(a), 8 U.S.C. §1256(a). *But see Matter of Rainford*, 20 I&N Dec. 598 (BIA 1992). However, one court has held that AOS bars later deportation for initial entry with preconceived intent to remain. *Choe v. INS*, 11 F.3d 925 (9th Cir. 1993). At least one court has determined that the filing of an adjustment application does not stay removal proceedings and DHS may proceed with removal proceedings notwithstanding pending I-485. *Roudnahal v. Ridge,* 310 F.Supp.2d 884, 892–94 (N.D. Ohio 2003), [pending adjustment application does not prevent the initiation of removal proceedings]. ICE however may, as a matter of prosecutorial discretion, join or initiate a motion to dismiss without prejudice to allow AOS before USCIS if removal is pending. *See* "Prosecutorial Discretion" in Ch. 3, ¶ X.S.2 (p.311), *supra.*

XIII. OTHER MATTERS CONCERNING LPRs

A. *Travel and Re-entry Document*

1. LPR must present admission document upon entry to U.S. or s/he is inadmissible. INA §212(a)(7)(A), 8 U.S.C. §1182(a)(7)(A).

   Must present special immigrant visa, green card (I-551), or re-entry permit. But USCIS may waive requirement. 8 C.F.R. §211.1(b).

2. If LPR is considered seeking admission into the U.S., *see Rosenberg v. Fleuti*, 374 U.S. 449 (1963), s/he is subject to all inadmissibility grounds. IIRIRA eliminated the definition of "entry" and replaced it with "admission." Returning LPRs are not applicants for admission except under certain circumstances listed in INA §101(a)(13). Mere fact of possession of an entry document (*e.g.,* green card) is not *per se* protection.

3. Special immigrant ("returning resident") visa

   3.a. Obtained at consulate abroad.

   3.b. File DS-117 with evidence of: LPR status (*e.g.,* I-551); intent to return; ties to the U.S.; and proof that the protracted stay was for reasons beyond the applicant's control.

4. Re-entry permits—INA §223, 8 U.S.C. §1203

   4.a. May be issued to LPRs or CRs. 8 C.F.R. §223.2(b).

   4.b. Apply in U.S. before departure and must remain in U.S. until biometrics are taken. Departure before the decision but after the biometrics are taken does *not* effect the validity of the document and it may be picked up at consulate or overseas DHS offices. May be issued document during deportation or exclusion proceedings with no effect on the proceedings. 8 C.F.R. §223.2(f).

      (1) File I-131 together with copy of I-551 or other evidence of status (endorsed I-94), photos, tax returns, and fee at Nebraska Service Center.

      (2) Valid for 2 years and not renewable, but may return to U.S. and get new one after 2 years. 8 C.F.R. §§223.2, 223.3. May have up to almost 6 years absence from the U.S. 8 C.F.R. §223.2(c)(2).

      If outside U.S. longer than period of permit need special immigrant ("returning resident") visa.

   4.c. Generally sought when going to be out of U.S. more than one year, or when need travel document (*e.g.,* Cuban w/out valid passport).

   4.d. Possession of re-entry permit does not prevent DHS from inquiring as to whether holder abandoned his residency. It simply prevents the DHS from relying *solely* on the duration of the holder's absence as a basis to determine abandonment. 8 C.F.R. §223.3(d)(1). Letter, Weinig, Field Manual Project Director, INS (Aug. 17, 1997), *reprinted in* 74 No. 31 *Interpreter Releases* 1256, 1274–76 (Aug. 18, 1997); *Moin v. Ashcroft,* 335 F.3d 415, 419 (5th Cir. 2003) [upheld abandonment under substantial evidence standard and noted that a re-entry permit merely serves as evidence of intent to return which the government may refute]; *But see Matter of V-*, 4 I&N Dec. 143 (BIA 1950). Further, the grant of a re-entry permit does not

cp ➡ sp: divided by equitable distribution
sp ➡ cp: quasi community property [treated like cp]

n to the permit holder at the border and placing inadmissibility. *See generally Brito-Deleon v.* .Y. 2002) [in *dicta* the court found that there was val proceedings against an applicant for adjust-e-entry permit].

sent in the U.S. at the time of filing. A applicant biometrics associated with the re-entry permit. If ics, the permit may be denied as abandoned.

g—Former O.I. §235.1(k)(4) gave DD discretion during removal proceedings. Legacy INS's inter-appeal to the BIA. Letter, Cronin, Asst. Comm., 497–99 (July/Aug. 1991). *See generally,* IFM at r refugee to travel during deportation/ exclusion entry permit or refugee travel document to a per-t affect those proceedings"].

nquished, lawful permanent residence (2) after R. §211.1(a).

a few days or even very often does not "auto-ctually resides abroad. DHS can independently

year of the date of expiration of the conditional eipt showing that he or she filed an I-751 form (5). *But see* 8 C.F.R. §§235.11(c), 1235.11(c), proceedings if petition has not been approved. -551 while s/he obtains review of the termina-Adjudications, DOS, HQ 70/23.13-C (Oct. 9, *ses* 1714, 1731 (Nov. 9, 1997). The spouses or children of military personnel or civilian employees of the U.S. government may return on expired conditional I-551 if they were overseas with spouse. 8 C.F.R. §211.1(a)(6).

2. Replacement I-551

2.a. Need to file an I-90 with photographs to replace I-551. Permanent resident card ("green cards"), but not LPR status, now expires every 10 years and a replacement must be sought. If applicant filed for naturalization six months or more prior to expiration of card, s/he need not apply for a new card. However, within six months s/he must apply for it. Memo, Pearson, Exec. Assoc. Comm. (HQ 70/5.9) (Sept. 29, 1999), *reprinted in* 76 No. 39 *Interpreter Releases* 1479, 1495–02 (Oct. 11, 1999). If CBP encounters a person with an expired 10-year card at the border, s/he will furnish him with I-90 and take no further action. Carriers have been notified that they should permit boarding of any bona fide LPR with an expired I-551. Memo, Pearson (Sept. 29, 1999), *supra.* CBP officers cannot cut, clip, or otherwise mutilate an expired card. Memo, Hrinyak, Acting Ex. Dir. Immigration Policy and Programs, CBP, OFO:IPP:CB (July 26, 2004), *published on* AILA InfoNet at Doc. No. 05040167. Photos for I-551 cards are now full-front instead of ¾ side view. Memo, Hrinyak, Acting Ex. Dir. Immigration Policy and Programs, CBP, OFO:IPP:CB (Aug. 4, 2004), *published on* AILA InfoNet at Doc. No. 05040470. USCIS may waive the photograph requirement or make arrangements for a home visit for a person who cannot provide a photograph because of confinement due to "advanced age or physical infirmity." Memo, Williams, Ex. Assoc. Comm., Field Operations, HQEXM 70/28 (Feb. 14, 2003), *published on* AILA InfoNet at Doc. No. 03032020.

2.b. While I-90 is pending, DHS must promptly provide an unambiguous temporary substitute or replacement. *Etuk v. Blackman*, 748 F.Supp. 990 (E.D.N.Y. 1990), *aff'd sub nom. Etuk v. Slattery*, 936 F.2d 1433 (2d Cir. 1991). If providing a receipt the document must unambiguously state it is a receipt of an I-90. *Etuk v. Slattery*, 803 F.Supp. 644 (E.D.N.Y. 1992). Immigration regulations now provide for the issuance of a properly endorsed I-94 if the LPR has not received his I-551 card prior to departure from the U.S. 8 C.F.R. §264.1(h). Immigration must also provide a person in removal proceedings a temporary I-551 or evidence of permanent residence status until the proceedings are complete. 8 C.F.R. §264.5(g). Policy of confiscating green cards of deportable residents and not promptly providing an adequate temporary substitute is in violation of the INA employer sanctions and unfair immigration employment practice provisions of the INA. *Etuk, supra.* An I-94 with a temporary I-551 stamp is an adequate temporary substitution. *Etuk v. Slattery*, 973 F.2d 60 (2d Cir. 1992). The court of appeals, however, would allow the DHS to deny temporary proof if the DHS has reason to believe that the person is not an LPR or that the card was not lost or stolen. *Etuk v. Slattery*, 936 F.2d 1433, 1447–48 (2d Cir. 1991). *But see Loa-Herrera v. Trominski,* 231 F.3d 984 (5th Cir. 2000) [reversed order relying on INS Memorandum governing issuance of temporary proof to persons whose green cards were confiscated and noted that process is governed by 8 C.F.R. §264.5(g)].

2.c. Security Checks. Post–Apr. 1, 2005 all persons seeking various forms of relief from removal must comply with security clearance procedures including providing biometrics both before and after a grant. 70 Fed. Reg. 4743, 4753 (Jan. 31, 2005), 8 C.F.R. §1003.47; Memo, Yates, Assoc. Dir. Operations, USCIS, "Executive Office for Immigration Review (EOIR) Processing," (Mar. 31, 2005), *published on* AILA InfoNet at Doc. No. 05051164 (May 11, 2005). If USCIS receives a national security concern or its check reveals a criminal record, officers are instructed to cease processing the I-90 and immediately refer the matter to ICE or in less egregious cases seek the criminal records and court dispositions through an RFE. Memo, Aytes, Assoc. Dir. Domestic Operations, USCIS, 70/28 (Jan. 4, 2008), *published on* AILA InfoNet at Doc. No. 08010762. If the applicant for a benefit fails to appear for a biometrics capture or other required in-person process, the application or petition "shall be considered abandoned and denied" unless by the appointment date USCIS had received a change of address or rescheduling request that the agency concludes warrants the failure to appear. 8 C.F.R. §103.2(b)(13)(ii). Prior to Apr. 1, 2005, persons granted relief by the IJ were required to wait for long periods of time without documentation of their status because security checks were only initiated after they obtained the relief and USCIS, post Sept. 11, 2001, would not issue documents indicating LPR status until the checks were completed. This led to litigation. *See e.g., Santillan v. Gonzales,* 388 F.Supp.2d 1065, 1079–82 (N.D. Cal. 2005) [finding government's refusal to provide temporary status documentation to LPRs in proceedings and permanent status documentation within a reasonable time to persons granted relief by IJ was arbitrary and was not permitted by 8 U.S.C. §1304(d)]. *See also* Ch. 3, ¶ X.S.7.1 (p.361), *supra*.

C. *Verifying Residency*

1. LPR status is verified by reference to official records, including service files, arrival manifests, arrival records, service index cards, immigrant identification cards, certificates of registry, declaration of intention issued after July 1, 1929, alien registration receipt cards/permanent resident cards (Forms AR-3, AR-103, I-151, I-551), passports and re-entry permits. 8 C.F.R. §103.2(b)(17). Also, if applicant or petitioner needs further action on approved residency, s/he would file I-824. If family members are following to join principal who is adjusting status, then I-824 should be filed at the same time as the I-485 is filed. 8 C.F.R. §103.5b.

2. Although temporary I-551 stamps in a passport, like the "green card," are merely evidence of residency, INS action in repeatedly placing such stamps in person's passport over a number of years resulted in injunctive relief granting residency. *Reid v. INS*, 1994 WL 132397 (S.D.N.Y. Apr. 8, 1994), *reported in* 71 No. 26 *Interpreter Releases* 890–90 (July 11, 1994). *But see Nelson v. Reno,* 204 F.Supp.2d 1355 (S.D. Fla. 2002), *aff'd without opinion,* 61 Fed. Appx. 670 (Table) [INS officer's placement of I-551 stamp in passport where officer failed to stamp the I-130/I-485/I-181 did not result in granting applicant LPR status]; *Bassey v. INS,* 2002 WL 31298854 (N.D. Cal. Oct. 10, 2002) [relying on *Nelson* and finding that stamping the applicant's passport and sending a notice of approval had no legal effect where I-130 was not approved]. *See also Dar-Salameh v. Gonzales,* 468 F.3d 47 (1st Cir. 2006) [respondent with not deprived of due process when he was ordered deported despite his claim that his status was adjusted because he had an I-94 stamp in his passport].

D. *Obtain Second Residency*—DOS in correspondence has acknowledged that a person is eligible to receive an IV even if he is already an LPR. Letter, Odom, Chief, Advisory Opinions Division (Nov. 27, 1991/Jan. 3, 1992), *reprinted in* 69 No. 11 *Interpreter Releases* 354, 365–66 (Mar. 23, 1992) [Iranian who obtained asylum and did not want asylum code on her I-551 could obtain LPR another way and a person who did not want to bring wife in as 2nd preference could reapply for IV under EB-1 category and bring wife in as accompanying spouse]. However, the Service's position is that an LPR cannot AOS on a different basis. Letter, Skerrett, Chief Immigrant Branch Adjudications HQ 245-C (July 19, 1993), *reprinted in* 70 No. 34 *Interpreter Releases* 1172, 1186–87 (Sept. 3, 1993). LPR must go overseas and relinquish LPR status by filing I-407 at consulate and then seek to re-immigrate. Similarly, DOL's position is that an LPR cannot apply for an LC. Letter, Richardson, Chief, Div. of Foreign Labor Certification DOL (Nov. 7, 1994), *reprinted in* 71 No. 45 *Interpreter Releases* 1553, 1565 (Nov. 18, 1994). Also, cannot adjust status based upon an approved I-130 petition that was previously used to obtain residency *Matter of Villarreal-Zuniga,* 23 I&N Dec. 886 (BIA 2006); 8 C.F.R. §204.2(h)(2).

E. *Abandonment of Residency*—INA §§101(a)(20), (27)(A), 8 U.S.C. §§1101(a)(20), (27)(A); 22 C.F.R. §42.22; 9 FAM 42.22; 8 C.F.R. §211.1(a)(2); 8 C.F.R. §316.5(c)(1)(i) [regarding citizenship]; *Matter of Huang*, 19 I&N Dec. 749 (BIA 1988); *Matter of Zamora*, 17 I&N Dec. 395 (BIA 1980); *Matter of Muller*, 16 I&N Dec. 637 (BIA 1978); *Matter of Umale*, 16 I&N Dec. 682 (BIA 1979); *Matter of Quijencio*, 15 I&N Dec. 95 (BIA 1974); *Matter of Kane*, 15 I&N Dec. 258 (BIA 1975); *Hana v. Gonzales,* 400 F.3d 472, 475–77 (6th Cir. 2005) [where LPR had permanent job, real property and immediate family in Iraq and never worked, paid taxes, or procured a bank account or driver's license in the U.S. and was absent for the vast majority of four years, the court determined that her trip was, nevertheless, temporary in nature because her failure to put down roots was due to her desire to help her family safely flee Iraq and to take care of her terminally ill mother-in-law and her return was fixed by an early event—the safe emigration of her family from Iraq to the U.S.]; *Khodagholian v. Ashcroft,* 335 F.3d 1003 (9th Cir. 2003) [LPR who made three trips out of U.S. and the last trip exceeded one year did not abandon his residency]. *But see Bigler v. U.S. Att'y Gen.,* 451 F.3d 728, 732–33 (11th Cir. 2006) [test is not one of desire but whether respondent's intent is supported by actions and where respondent's "absence is not relatively short in duration [he] must show a continuous uninterrupted intention to return to the United States during the entirety of his visit." Upheld abandonment under clear and convincing evidence standard where respondent was outside of U.S. for more than a year, signed a document at consulate abandoning his residency, and only after his divorce from his Colombian wife sought the return of his residency]; *Katebi v. Ashcroft,* 396 F.3d 463 (1st Cir. 2005) [where LPR remained in Canada for three years and became Canadian citizen after brief stay in U.S. upon receipt of LPR status abandonment upheld under substantial evidence standard]; *Moin v. Ashcroft,* 335 F.3d 415 (5th Cir. 2003) [abandonment upheld on substantial evidence standard where LPR made several trips into U.S. with a stay of approximately 6 months in total of the last 54 months including entries with a re-entry permit]; *Ahmed v. Ashcroft,* 286 F.3d 611 (2d Cir. 2002) [abandonment upheld where person outside U.S. for 9 years despite one re-entry permit, BIA statement that he "probably never formed the subjective intent of abandoning" LPR status, and conduct for 11 years subsequent to returning to US]; *Aleem v. Perryman*, 114 F.3d 672 (7th Cir. 1997) [abandonment found even where person paid U.S. taxes, had association memberships and child who was USC]; *Singh v. Reno*, 113 F.3d 1512 (9th Cir. 1997); *Diosa-Ortiz v. Ashcroft,* 334 F.Supp.2d 27 (D. Mass. 2004) [LPR who mistakenly thought that a "notice to deliver alien" after case was administratively closed was a final order of deportation and therefore left the U.S., abandoned his residency under all the circumstances when he did not return for more than a year];

1. If LPR out of U.S. continuously for more than one year, DHS takes the position that residency has been abandoned. 8 C.F.R. §211.1(a)(2). However, residency may be abandoned even if less than one year where person lives and works abroad. *Singh, supra* [lived abroad to be with wife and child while awaiting priority date, but returned to U.S. and worked during summers]; *Alvarez v. District Director*, 539 F.2d 1220 (9th Cir. 1976). *But see Saxbe v. Bustos,* 419 U.S. 65, 95 S.Ct. 272 (1974) [LPR does have the privilege of living abroad]; *Khodagholian v. Ashcroft,* 335 F.3d 1003, 1006–07 (9th Cir. 2003) [the test is whether LPR intended to be temporarily abroad and not whether the s/he exceeded one year].

2. In the view of one court a person may lose her LPR status even if she does not renounce her residency by signing an I-407 or have a formal removal hearing to determine abandonment. *U.S. v. Yakou,* 428 F.3d 241, 247–51 (D.C. Cir. 2005) [in prosecution for violation of the Arms Control

Export Act and the International Traffic in Arms Regulations, a person who abandoned his U.S. residency but did not sign an I-407 or have a removal proceeding brought against him was nevertheless no longer an LPR and therefore not a U.S. person within the meaning of the law even though he re-entered the U.S. 10 times after abandonment and used his "green card" to enter on a number of occasions].

3. If temporary absence abroad, residency is not deemed abandoned. *Matter of Guiot*, 14 I&N Dec. 393 (DD 1973); *Matter of Vielma-Ortiz*, 11 I&N Dec. 414 (BIA 1965) [loss of U.S. citizenship does not result in automatic loss of LPR]; *Hana v. Gonzales,* 400 F.3d 472, 475–77 (6th Cir. 2005) [no abandonment where petitioner spent majority of time in Iraq ensuring the safety of her family while awaiting their visas and attending to terminally ill mother-in-law].

   Temporary visit abroad under INA §101(a)(27)(A), 8 U.S.C. §1101(a)(27)(A) occurs only when (a) the visit abroad is for a period relatively short, fixed by some early event or (b) the visit will terminate upon the occurrence of an event having reasonable possibility of occurring within a relatively short period of time (*e.g.,* taking care of an ill relative). If the event does not occur within a relatively short period of time, the visit will be considered a temporary visit abroad only if the alien has a continuous uninterrupted intention to return to the U.S. during the entirety of his or her visit. Criteria to determine continuous uninterrupted intention include family ties, property holdings, and business affiliations in the U.S. and foreign country. *Khodagholian v. Ashcroft,* 335 F.3d 1003, 1007 (9th Cir. 2003) [citing *Chavez-Ramirez* criteria and finding LPR did not abandon residency]; *Chavez-Ramirez v. INS*, 792 F.2d 932 (9th Cir. 1986); *Gamero v. INS*, 367 F.2d 123 (9th Cir. 1966); *Angeles v. District Director*, 729 F.Supp. 479 (D. Md. 1990). *But see Ahmed, supra* [focusing solely on length of time abroad].

4. BIA/DOS criteria (*Kane/Huang/*9 FAM 42.22 N.1.1, 1.2, 1.4)

   4.a. Purpose of departure.

   4.b. Existence of fixed termination date for visit abroad.

   4.c. Objective intention to return to U.S. as place of permanent employment or actual home. Look at family ties, job, income tax returns, club memberships, mortgages.

5. Notwithstanding INA §101(a)(33), 8 U.S.C. §1101(a)(33), lack of fixed dwelling place in U.S. not dispositive because 8 C.F.R. §211.1(a) requires only "unrelinquished lawful permanent residence." *Matter of Huang, supra*; *Saxbe v. Bustos*, 419 U.S. 65 (1974).

6. Burden of Proof—DHS has burden by clear, unequivocal and convincing evidence to prove that LPR's status has changed. *Hana v. Gonzales,* 400 F.3d 472, 475 (6th Cir. 2005); *Singh v. Reno,* 113 F.3d 1512, 1514 (9th Cir. 1997). Once a colorable claim to LPR status made, the burden is on DHS by *Woodby* standard ["clear, unequivocal and convincing evidence"] to show abandonment. *Matter of Huang, supra*; *Angeles v. District Director*, 729 F.Supp. 479, 482 (D. Md. 1990).

7. "An extended period of absence from U.S., in appropriate circumstances, can be viewed as a temporary visit abroad if the end of the period of absence can be fixed by some early event." *Matter of Huang, supra. See also Hana v. Gonzales,* 400 F.3d 472, 475–77 (6th Cir. 2005) [where LPR had permanent job, real property and immediate family in Iraq and never worked, paid taxes, or procured a bank account or driver's license in the U.S. and was absent for the vast majority of four years, the court determined that her trip was, nevertheless, temporary in nature because her failure to put down roots was due to her desire to help her family safely flee Iraq and to take care of her terminally ill mother-in-law and her return was fixed by an early event—the safe emigration of her family from Iraq to the U.S.].

8. LPR returning on a visitor's visa from abroad does not necessarily indicate relinquishment. 9 FAM 41.31 N.15 42.22 N.10.

9. Abandonment by a parent is imputed to his or her accompanying child. *Matter of Zamora*, 17 I&N Dec. 395 (BIA 1980).

10. Surrender of green card and signing statement abandoning residency does not necessarily preclude maintenance of LPR status. *Matter of Wood*, Case No. A24 653 925 (BIA Jan. 13, 1992), *reported in* 69 No. 16 *Interpreter Releases* 512–14 (Apr. 27, 1992) [notwithstanding surrender of card and statement respondent did not intend to abandon LPR status].

11. Filing Tax Return as Nonresident—Filing income tax return as a nonresident alien raises rebuttable presumption that person has abandoned Lawful Permanent Resident status. Memo, Martin, General Counsel, INS, HQ 70/11-P, 70/33-P (May 7, 1996), *reprinted in* 73 No. 27 *Interpreter Releases* 929, 948–50 (July 15, 1996); 8 C.F.R. §316.5(c)(2).

12. Liquidation of assets abroad is a valid basis for proceeding abroad for a prolonged period of time. *Matter of Souqi*, 14 I&N Dec. 390 (R.C. 1973).

13. *Rosenberg v. Fleuti*, 374 U.S. 449 (1963); [avoids a problem with inadmissibility by finding that no new entry was made]; IFM at 13.4, 13.5, 17.17. *But see* INA §101(a)(13)(C), 8 U.S.C. §1101(a)(13)(C); *Matter of Collado-Munoz*, 21 I&N Dec. 1061 (BIA 1997) [finding in detention context *Fleuti* no longer requires the admission of an LPR whose trip was brief, casual and innocent but who had a conviction that would bar him under INA §212(a)(2)]; *Tineo v. Ashcroft,* 350 F.3d 382 (3d Cir. 2003) [determining that Congress did abolish the *Fleuti* doctrine in the passage of INA §101(a)(13)(C) for certain returning LPRs and upholding *Matter of Collado-Munoz* on *Chevron* deference grounds].

F. *Termination of Residency*—An LPR, once placed in removal proceedings, doesn't lose his or her status until a final administrative order of removal is issued. 8 C.F.R. §§1.1(p), 1001.1(p); *Perez-Rodriguez v. INS*, 3 F.3d 1074, 1077–79 (7th Cir. 1993); *Matter of Gunaydin*, 18 I&N Dec. 326 (BIA 1982), *aff'd*, 742 F.2d 776 (3d Cir. 1984); *Etuk v. Slattery*, 936 F.2d 1433, 1447 (2d Cir. 1991). However, in the view of one court a person may lose her LPR status even if she does not renounce her residency by signing an I-407 or have a formal removal hearing to determine abandonment. *U.S. v. Yakou,* 428 F.3d 241, 247–51 (D.C. Cir. 2005) [in prosecution for violation of the Arms Control Export Act and the International Traffic in Arms Regulations, a person who abandoned his U.S. residency but did not sign an I-407 or have a removal proceeding brought against him was nevertheless no longer an LPR and therefore not a U.S. person within the meaning of the law even though he re-entered the U.S. 10 times after abandonment and used his "green card" to enter on a number of occasions].

G. *Children of LPRs Born Abroad are LPRs if:* [8 C.F.R. §211.1(b)(1)]

1. Child born subsequent to issuance of parents' visa and within time of validity of visa.

2. If child is under 2, is accompanied by parent upon 1st return of parent who is applying to re-enter as LPR, and parent admissible. Child should be issued I-181 upon first entry. IFM at 14.5 (Admission of Certain Immigrant Children Without Immigrant Visas).

H. *Tax Information*

1. Applicant for LPR status must provide information with respect to whether or not s/he was required to file income tax return for the "most recent 3 taxable years." 26 U.S.C. §6039E(b)(3). However, IRS form 9003 is no longer required as part of the IV/AS process. Cable, DOS, 02-State-094440 (May 16, 2002), *published on* AILA InfoNet at Doc. No. 02052043 (May 20, 2002). IRS exempts F, H-3, H-4 and J visa holders from the requirement anyway if they receive no gross income from U.S. sources other than allowances and expenses and/or payments for services furnished incident to status or with employment authorization applicable to status. 56 Fed. Reg. 3034 (Jan. 28, 1991). INS and IRS entered into an agreement to share information to ensure compliance with 26 U.S.C. §6039E. Memorandum of Understanding Between IRS and INS, 11 *AILA Monthly Mailing* 489-90 (June 1992).

   1.a. Alien may be taxed as resident alien or nonresident alien. If resident alien s/he is taxed on worldwide income like USC. If nonresident alien s/he is taxed only on income from sources within the United States. U.S. Tax Guide for Aliens, IRS Publication 519 (2007). *See www.irs.gov/publications/p519.*

   1.b. A person is considered a resident for tax purposes if s/he meets the "green card test" (*i.e.,* is an LPR) or "the substantial presence test." A person who is not a USC or LPR may be taxed as one if s/he meets either of the substantial presence tests. If a person is here 183 days during the year s/he meets the substantial presence test and will be considered a resident for U.S. tax purposes. Alternatively, s/ he may meet the test if s/he is physically present in U.S. for 31 days of the tax year and a total of 183 days during a 3-year period by counting all days of current year, 1/3 of the days of previous year and 1/6 of the days of the second previous year. If alien does not meet 183 days under this formula s/he is considered a nonresident. In determining the number of days, some days may be exempt because under tax law and IRS regulations certain individuals are exempt for a limited number of calendar years (F, J, M, and Q) or unlimited period of calendar years (A or G); Others may be physically unable to leave (Form 8843 required), are in transit between two points outside the U.S., or commute to employment in the U.S. from a residence in Canada or Mexico. Moreover, even if s/he meets the substantial presence test, if s/he is not physically present in the U.S. for 183 days during the tax year s/he will be treated as a nonresident if s/he can show a tax home in a foreign country and a closer connection to that country than the U.S. (Form 8840 required).

1.c. Abandonment of residence for tax purposes for LPR may be achieved by sending a letter or I-407 to DHS or a consular officer stating the decision to abandon residency and by enclosing the green card. 57 Fed. Reg. 15237–54 (Apr. 27, 1992). A long-term resident whose LPR status ended after June 3, 2004, will not be relieved of his or her obligation to file U.S. tax returns and report his or her worldwide income as a resident alien until he or she has also submitted Form 8854 to the IRS reporting his or her termination of LPR status, as required by 26 U.S.C. §7701(n). A former LPR is a long-term resident if he or she was an LPR for at least 8 of 15 consecutive tax years ending with the tax year that LPR status ended. Certain former long-term residents must submit Form 8854 annually to comply with 26 U.S.C. §6039G information-reporting requirements.

1.d. The tax liability of an individual may also depend upon whether the U.S. has a tax treaty with the person's country of citizenship. A dual resident (a resident of both the U.S. and treaty country) may be able to support U.S. nonresidency and treaty country residency under the tie-breaker rule of the treaty article on residency. **Appendix G**, *infra,* contains a chart concerning those countries that maintain tax treaties with the U.S. The treaties with Greece and Pakistan lack a tie-breaker rule.

2. Estate Tax—Estate taxation varies depending on whether the decedent was a nonresident alien or resident alien on his or her date of death in the U.S. For U.S. estate, gift, and generation-skipping transfer tax purposes, a nonresident alien is an individual who is neither a citizen nor resident of the U.S., 26 U.S.C. §2101(a) and §2501(a). Resident status is not the same as for income tax purposes but rather is determined based on domicile. Nonresidents are subject to transfer tax on assets situated in the U.S., such as U.S. real estate and U.S. stocks and bonds, using the same rates as for citizens, but with an exemption equivalent of only $60,000. Special rules require worldwide debt to be allocated *pro rata* to U.S. situs and non-U.S. situs assets. Residents (*i.e.*, domiciliaries) are subject to estate, gift, and generation-skipping taxes in the same manner as citizens. Residents can use the exemption-equivalent amount, which increases as a result of the Economic Growth and Tax Relief Reconciliation Act (H.R. 1836), 26 U.S.C. §2010(c), but is scheduled to revert to prior law levels in 2011. *See* Jones, *The Effect of EGTRA '01 on LPR Estate Tax Issues,* 20 *AILA Monthly Mailing* 491–92 (Oct. 2001). An unlimited marital deduction is allowed for transfer to a USC spouse, but is not allowed for transfers to a non-USC spouse unless the property passes to the non-USC spouse through a qualified domestic trust (QDOT), 26 U.S.C. §2056(d). A marital deduction or other benefits may be available under an estate tax treaty, or, in the case of Canada, the income tax treaty. *See* **Appendix G**, *infra.*

I. *Social Security Payments*

1. A person who is not a USC is prohibited from receiving Social Security payments if s/he has been outside U.S. for more than 6 months unless the person's country has a Social Security or pension system that reciprocates for USCs (Totalization Agreements). Social Security Act §202(t)(1), 42 U.S.C. §402(t). 71 No. 4 *Interpreter Releases* 171–72 (Jan. 24, 1994); *Taylor v. Barnhart,* 399 F.3d 891, 894–95 (8th Cir. 2005) [totalization agreement with UK that could be construed to provide disability benefits to illegal person in U.S. is trumped by subsequently enacted statutes requiring lawful presence to receive benefits]; *Dragan v. Heckler*, 1985 U.S. Dist. LEXIS 18961 (D.D.C.) [rejected effort to totalize pension payments from a nonagreement country]. Countries that have totalization agreements and thus allow payments abroad are: Austria, Australia, Belgium, Canada, Chile, France, Finland, Germany, Greece, Ireland, Italy, Japan, Luxembourg, Netherlands, Norway, Portugal, South Korea, Spain, Sweden, Switzerland, and United Kingdom.

In addition to these countries we also have reciprocal agreements with Albania, Bosnia, Czech Republic, Hungary, Macedonia, Slovak Republic and Uruguay.

2. SSA publishes a guide discussing whether and how individuals can receive payments when they are outside the U.S. *See www.ssa.gov/pubs/10137.html#countries*. With a few exceptions, Social Security restrictions prohibit sending payments to individuals in Cambodia, Vietnam, or areas that were in the former Soviet Union (other than Armenia, Estonia, Latvia, Lithuania, and Russia).

3. Aliens who are deported under INA §241(a), removed as inadmissible for EWI, or removed under 237(a) (except for failure to maintain status, and smuggling) lose their Social Security benefits after notice to Secy. of HHS by the AG unless the persons are subsequently readmitted as LPRs. Social Security Act §202(n), 42 U.S.C. §402(n). The SSA had to receive notice that the person was deported or removed under certain exceptions (*i.e.,* failure to maintain status or smuggling) *before* Mar. 3, 2004 to retain benefits. 20 C.F.R. §404.464(a). *Flemming v. Nestor*, 363 U.S. 603 (1960); *Smart v. Shalala*, 9 F.3d 921 (11th Cir. 1993) [rejected PRUCOL status as basis for benefits]; 65 No. 43 *Interpreter Releases* 1167, 1169 (Nov. 7, 1988); 68 No. 22 *Interpreter Releases* 718 (June 17, 1991).

4. NIVs May Be Excluded from Social Security Coverage—A student (F, M, J and Q) enrolled and regularly attending classes in a school, college, or university is exempt from Social Security and Medicare taxes. 26 U.S.C. §3121(b)(10). Nonresident aliens in F, J, M and Q status are exempt from Social Security and Medicare taxes on services performed to carry out the purpose of their status. These exemptions do not apply to residents or aliens in derivative status. 26 U.S.C. §3121(b)(19). Social Security exclusion from coverage provided by 20 C.F.R. §404.1036 is overridden by the tax law defining nonresidents. 26 U.S.C. §7701(b).

5. Eligibility of Children—Even if a person is ineligible himself to receive Social Security benefits, his or her children may be eligible if they are USCs (*e.g.*, in the case of someone who is deported but has earned benefits, the USC children may be able to get those benefits if they are still living in the U.S.).

J. *Social Security Cards*—The Social Security Administration (SSA) has set forth regulations guiding when noncitizens may obtain Social Security cards. 20 C.F.R. pt. 422. 62 Fed. Reg. 63681 (Dec. 2, 1997), 63 Fed. Reg. 56552 at 56553 (Oct. 22, 1998); 68 Fed. Reg. 55304 (Sept. 25, 2003). The SSA will issue a Social Security card to the following persons: USCs, LPRs or persons authorized to work as determined by SSA under 20 C.F.R. §422.105. SSA will also issue Social Security cards to persons for nonwork purposes where they need a number to satisfy a federal statute or regulation to receive a federally funded benefit (*e.g.,* TANF) and they reside in or out of the U.S. *or* to satisfy a state or local law that requires a Social Security number to receive public assistance benefits and they are legally in the U.S. 20 C.F.R. §422.104(a)(3). A Social Security card will not be given for the nonwork purpose of obtaining a driver's license or because a person has difficulty in obtaining "cell phones, credit cards, mortgages, bank accounts, marriage and professional licenses, various forms of insurance, admission to academic institutions and financial aid for student loans." 68 Fed. Reg. 55304 at 55306–07 (Sept. 23, 2003). A Social Security card issued for nonwork purposes will be annotated with the legend Not Valid for Employment. 20 C.F.R. §422.104(b). Generally a noncitizen must fill out an SS-5 form when requesting a Social Security card, unless SSA has entered into an agreement with DHS/DOS to share information in which case they will receive it electronically. 20 C.F.R. §§422.103(b)(3), (c)(3). If s/he seeks a change in the name or other personal identifying information on the card, s/he must file a new Form SS-5. 20 C.F.R. §422.110(a). If an applicant comes to the SSA with an I-94 that reflects a classification permitting work, s/he is presumed to have permission to engage in employment. 20 C.F.R. §422.105. However, all applicants 12 or older are required to be personally interviewed and all applicants, regardless of age (including those under 7) must provide evidence of age, U.S. citizenship or alien status and true identity. 20 C.F.R. §422.107(a). F-1 students are required to present additional evidence if they do not have an EA from DHS and their SEVIS I-20 is not endorsed for curricular practical training. 20 C.F.R. §422.107(e)(2) [documentation includes letter from DSO regarding authorized employment and letter from employer]. All requests for a Social Security card are now checked against the SAVE system instituted by legacy INS. If the SAVE system cannot provide positive verification, the SSA will then send a G-845 form. If the information cannot be verified the application will be noted as fraudulent and sent to the Inspector General's office. Policy Instruction, SSA, EM-02086, EM-02091 (July 12, 2002, Aug. 2, 2002), *reprinted in* 79 No. 34 *Interpreter Releases* 1278–80, 1312–37 (Aug. 26, 2002). If earnings are reported on a Social Security card that is not valid for employment, the SSA will inform DHS of the reported earnings. 20 C.F.R. §422.104(b). A person may only obtain a replacement Social Security card 3 times in a year and 10 Social Security cards per lifetime. 20 C.F.R. §422.103(e).

An Individual Taxpayer Identification Number (ITIN) may be requested on form W-7, for the purposes of filing a tax return. ITINs are usually now issued at the same time as a tax return is filed. The W-7 form and the required documents demonstrating a need for ITIN are filed with the U.S. tax return. 26 C.F.R. §301.6109-1(d)(3). Need to submit evidence such as passport, birth certificate or other documentation showing alien status. IRS requires persons to use ITINs when filing individual returns.

A person who is an LPR who does not have a Social Security number must apply for a number on form SS-5 or furnish to the employer a signed and dated statement containing his or her name, address, place and date of birth, sex, father's name and mother's maiden name. The employer must advise the person to apply for a card and must submit a copy of the person's statement with the W-2 form or a copy of the person's receipt if s/he has applied. 26 C.F.R. §31.6011(b)–(2). DHS may now require any noncitizen to put her Social Security number on any record designated by the AG. INA §264(f).

No-Match and Mismatched Social Security Numbers—When the SSA receives a W-2 with a nonexistent or mismatched Social Security number, they will send the employer a letter indicating the mismatch. *See* "No-Match Social Security Numbers" in Ch. 12, ¶ I.D.2.c(1) (p.1251), *infra*.

Social Security Fraud—42 U.S.C. §408(a)(7)(B). Imprisonment up to 5 years for the use of another person's Social Security number.

K. *Public Benefits*—As a result of the Personal Responsibility and Work Opportunity Reconciliation Act of 1996, PL 104-193, 110 Stat. 2105 (Aug. 22, 1996), Congress dramatically altered the rights of LPRs and others to obtain benefits. 8 U.S.C. §1601-45. *See* **Appendix F**, *infra*. In so doing, it preempted state statutes or initiatives, such as California's Proposition 187, designed to accomplish a similar purpose. *LULAC v. Wilson*, 997 F.Supp. 1244 (C.D. Cal. 1997). Persons who are not "qualified" aliens under the law are not eligible for most federal benefits while states are not barred from providing benefits if they chose to do so. Qualified alien is defined in 8 U.S.C. §1641(b) and (c) and includes: LPR; asylee; refugee; parolee under INA §212(d)(5) for at least one year; conditional entrant; person granted withholding; and Cuban/Haitian entrants. *Joubert v. Barnhart,* 396 F.Supp.2d 1320 (S.D. Fla. 2005) [Haitian who adjusted under Special Immigrant Juvenile provision is eligible for SSI based upon the definition of Cuban-Haitian Entrant]; *Nodarse v. Barnhart,* 319 F.Supp.2d 1333 (S.D. Fla. 2004) [Cuban who adjusted under NACARA is eligible for SSI based upon definition of Cuban-Haitian Entrant]. It also includes a battered spouse or child, parent of a battered child, and child of a battered parent, where there is a relationship between the battery or cruelty and the need for the benefits. Battered immigrants need to have an approved visa petition filed by a spouse/parent, a pending self-petition which sets forth a prima facie case under VAWA or an application for suspension of deportation/cancellation of removal under VAWA. Victims of trafficking and their derivative beneficiaries, although not included among the "qualified" immigrants, are also eligible for federal public benefits to the same extent as refugees. Qualified immigrants who physically entered the U.S. on or after Aug. 22, 1996 are barred from obtaining federal means-tested public benefits programs for five years, unless they meet an exception to the bar. Federal means-tested public benefits have been defined to include only: nonemergency Medicaid, the State Children's Health Insurance Program (SCHIP), Temporary Assistance for Needy Families (TANF), Food Stamps, and Supplemental Security Income (SSI). There are more extensive immigrant restrictions in the SSI program. Qualified immigrant children and certain additional groups of immigrants are exempt from the 5-year bar on Food Stamps. Those who enter subject to the new legally enforceable affidavits of support (I-864) may be financially ineligible after the 5-year bar is over, due to sponsor-to-applicant deeming of income. There are exceptions to these deeming rules. 8 U.S.C. §1631. The statutory restrictions on federal benefits in this scheme has withstood a constitutional challenge. *See e.g., Rodriguez v. U.S.*, 983 F.Supp. 1445 (S.D. Fla. 1997); *but see Aliessa v. Novello,* 96 N.Y.2d 418 (2001) [NY law denying state-funded medical services to a sub-group of immigrants violates the Equal Protection Clause of the U.S. and NY State Constitutions]. Termination of SSI benefits because refugee, asylee or LPR status are not being granted due to prolonged security checks in violation of the 120-day provision is not actionable. *Kaplan v. Chertoff,* 481 F.Supp. 2d 370, 377–98 (E.D. Pa. 2007) However, the *Kaplan* class-action was settled permitting class members who received SSI benefits and who have AOS or naturalization petitions pending 6 months or more to request expedited treatment of their naturalization or AOS applications. *Kaplan v. Chertoff,* No. 06-5304 (E.D. Pa. Mar. 5, 2008), *published on* AILA InfoNet at Doc.

No. 08050533. Certain types of benefits and programs are generally exempt from these provisions, *e.g.,* emergency Medicaid, immunizations and testing for communicable disease symptoms (outside of Medicaid), school breakfast and school lunch, short-term noncash disaster assistance, and WIC (at state option). In addition, in-kind services that are not conditioned on an individual's income or resources and are necessary to protect life or safety are available without immigration status restrictions. Such services include police, domestic violence and child abuse prevention, short-term shelter or housing assistance, soup kitchens, substance abuse and mental health services, public health services, programs to protect the life or safety of workers, youth, community residents, fire, transportation, crisis counseling. *See e.g.,* Final Order of the Attorney General, 66 Fed. Reg. 3613 at 3615 (Jan. 16, 2001). To establish citizenship for Medicaid benefits, HHS has published rules at 72 Fed. Reg. 38662–97 (July 16, 2007). These citizenship-verification rules apply only to citizens, and do not affect immigrants' eligibility for Medicaid or the procedures for verifying immigration status in that program.

L. *Driver's Licenses & REAL ID Act*

1. Driver's Licenses/Identification Documents—REAL ID Act of 2005, PL 109-13, 119 Stat. 231 (May 11, 2005), Title II, §201

   1.a. Sets standards for new driver's licenses and identification documents issued by states. Includes minimum information requirements such as digital photo, signature, physical security features, and a common machine-readable technology. Before issuing a driver's license or identification card the applicant must show proof of lawful status and other documents. Requires compliance by May 11, 2008. DHS has now promulgated final regulations to standardize driver's licenses. 6 C.F.R. §37; 73 Fed. Reg. 5272–5340 (Jan. 29, 2008).

   1.b. Criminalized the use of a false driver's license at an airport and amended 18 U.S.C. §1028(a)(8) to include actual authentication features on documents.

2. State Prohibitions—Some states refuse to grant driver's licenses to undocumented persons on the grounds that they could not be lawful residents of the State. Cox, Opinion of the Attorney General of Michigan (Dec. 27, 2007), *reprinted in* 13 No. 2 *Bender's Immigration Bulletin* 85-89 (Jan. 15, 2008) [a person who is not an LPR cannot be a resident of the State of Michigan for purposes of obtaining a driver's license].

CHAPTER 7
EMPLOYMENT BASED IMMIGRATION AND LABOR CERTIFICATION

CHAPTER 7
EMPLOYMENT-BASED IMMIGRATION AND LABOR CERTIFICATION

I. EMPLOYMENT BASED IMMIGRATION—INTRODUCTION—INA §203(b), 8 U.S.C. §1153(b)

The Immigration Act of 1990 (IMMACT90) altered traditional employment-based immigration to the U.S. Effective Oct. 1, 1991, the former Third and Sixth Preferences were eliminated and replaced by five categories. The First Preference is for priority workers including persons of extraordinary ability, outstanding professors and researchers, and multinational organization executives and managers. The Second Preference is for members of the professions holding advanced degrees or persons of exceptional ability. The Third Preference is for professionals, skilled and other workers. The Fourth Preference provides for special immigrants including religious workers, court dependents, returning residents and others. The Fifth Preference is an investor provision, which grants residency to persons who invest significant funds in the U.S. and create (or maintain in certain circumstances) 10 jobs for U.S. workers.

II. FIRST PREFERENCE—PRIORITY WORKERS (EB-1 Category)—INA §203(b)(1), 8 U.S.C. §1153(b)(1)

A. ***Generally***—28.6% of worldwide visas plus unused investors and special immigrant visas. Not subject to labor certification.

B. ***Persons of Extraordinary Ability***—INA §203(b)(1)(A), 8 U.S.C. §1153(b)(1)(A).

1. Alien with extraordinary ability in sciences, arts, education, business or athletics which has been demonstrated by sustained national or international acclaim and whose achievements have been recognized in the field through extensive documentation; *and*
2. Alien seeks entry to continue work in the area of extraordinary ability; *and*
3. Entry will substantially benefit prospectively the U.S. While the regulations do not require any evidence on the prospective benefit and the Service Centers may not require a submission regarding the benefit, Letter, Skerrett, Chief, Immigration Branch, Adjudications, HQ 204-23-C (Mar. 8, 1995), *reprinted in* 72 No. 12 *Interpreter Releases* 443, 445 (Mar. 27, 1995), it is wise to do so. Often, the substantial benefit criteria is met through the other two criteria, but there may be very rare instances where the person's admission may be damaging or detrimental to the interests of the U.S. *Id.*
4. No Employer Needed—INA §204(a)(1)(E), 8 U.S.C. §1154(a)(1)(E); 8 C.F.R. §204.5(h)(1). Person does need proof that s/he intends to pursue in U.S. work in area of expertise. 8 C.F.R. §204.5(h)(5), although no specific offer of employment is required. If applicant had approved petition filed by prospective employer, but intends to pursue other vocational pursuits, petition would still be valid even if s/he did not work for employer as long as s/he demonstrated how s/he plans to continue her work. Letter, Skerrett, Chief Immigrant Branch, Adjudications (Jan. 23, 1993), *published on* AILA InfoNet at Doc. No. 93031040. However, the beneficiary must intend to continue in the area of his or her expertise. 8 C.F.R. §204.5(h)(5); AFM at 22.2(i)(1)(C).
5. The legislative history indicates among other things that this category is intended to be "for the small percentage of individuals who have risen to the very top of their field of endeavor." H.R. Rep. No. 101-723 (I), 101st Cong., 2d Sess. 59 (1990); 1990 U.S.C.C.A.N. 6710 at 6739; 56 Fed. Reg. 60897–99 (1991); 8 C.F.R. §204.5(h)(2).

6. Evidence. 8 C.F.R. §204.5(h)(3); AFM at 22.2(i).

6.a. Applicant must demonstrate "sustained or international acclaim" and that his or her achievements have been recognized in his or her field of expertise. Evidence shall include evidence of a one-time achievement—a major international recognized award (*e.g.*, Nobel Prize). If the applicant is not the recipient of such an award then documentation of any *three* of the following is required:

(1) Receipt of lesser nationally or internationally recognized prizes or awards (academic awards to students are generally ignored).

(a) Nomination for an award does not carry as much weight as winning and one must prove sustained acclaim. *Matter of* ____ (AAO June 1, 2004) *reported in* 81 No. 42 *Interpreter Releases* 1533, 1546–47 (Nov. 1, 2004) [denial upheld for member of Filipino music group Prettier Than Pink, but fact that a nomination or award goes to the group instead of the individual applicant is not relevant].

(2) Membership in association in the field for which classification is sought, which requires outstanding achievement of their members, as judged by recognized national or international experts.

(3) Published material about the person in professional or major trade publications or other major media.

(4) Participation as a judge of the work of others.

(5) Evidence of original scientific, scholastic, artistic, athletic or business-related contributions of major significance.

(6) Authorship of scholarly articles in the field.

(7) Artistic exhibitions or showcases.

(8) Performance in a leading or cultural role for organizations or establishments that have a distinguished reputation.

(9) High salary or remuneration in relation to others in the field.

(10) Commercial success in the performing arts.

6.b. The submission of evidence of 3 of the 10 categories may not be dispositive. It establishes the initial evidence, but such threshold evidence may fall short of proving extraordinary ability and USCIS may require additional evidence. Letter, Skerrett, Chief, Immigrant Branch, Adjudications, HQ 204.23-C (May 20, 1993), *reprinted in* 70 No. 22 *Interpreter Releases* 750, 764–65 (June 7, 1993). However, if an applicant does demonstrate extraordinary ability in three categories, USCIS cannot deny the petition simply because it believes documents in other categories should be available if the person were extraordinary. AFM at 22.2(i)(1)(C). An applicant may also submit "comparable evidence" (8 C.F.R. §204.5(h)(4)) if the above standards do not readily apply. Comparable evidence may include expert opinion letters attesting to the applicant's abilities. AFM at 22.2(i)(1)(F). A person who is an athlete, particularly one new to major league competition, may not otherwise qualify. 56 Fed. Reg. 60897, 60899 (Nov. 29, 1991). For an excellent discussion of the evidence needed to prove extraordinary ability, *see* Lawler, *Professionals: A Matter of Degree* (AILA June 2003) at Chapter 2.

6.c. INS has been reversed for incorrectly applying its regulations, *Buletini v. INS*, 860 F.Supp. 1222 (E.D. Mich. 1994), and abusing its discretion. *Muni v. INS*, 891 F.Supp. 440 (N.D. Ill. 1995) [INS misapplied definition in denying professional hockey player on grounds he was an all-star or one of League's highest paid players]; *Grimson v. INS*, 934 F.Supp. 965 (N.D. Ill. 1996) [reversed INS where he was found to be one of best hockey "enforcers"]; *Matter of Price*, 20 I&N Dec. 953 (AAU 1994) [although not all "major league" athletes qualify, golfer ranked 10th best in professional tour qualifies]; *Matter of* ___, VSC, EAC 02-099-53226 (AAO Mar. 24, 2003) [reversed denial of Taekwondo instructor because the standard is "sustained national acclaim" and not being at the "top of their field"] *reported in* 8 No. 18 *Bender's Immigration Bulletin* 1529 (Sept. 15, 2003).

(1) Sciences. Biophysicist. *Matter of* ___, CSC, WAC 02-070-52665 (AAO Feb. 27, 2003) [leading expert in synchrotron radiation] *reported in* 8 No. 19 *Bender's Immigration Bulletin* 1574 (Oct. 1, 2003); Market Research. *Matter of* ___, NSC (AAO Aug. 29, 2002) [user researcher specializing in the emotional needs and reactions of product users] *reported in* 8 No. 5 *Bender's Immigration Bulletin* 605 (Apr. 1, 2003); Plant Biologist. *Matter of* ___, (AAO May 27, 2004) [emphasized peer review and reversed DD denial] *reported in* 81 No. 42 *Interpreter Releases* 1533, 1547–48 (Nov. 1, 2004);

(2) Arts. *Matter of* ___, WAC 01-245-53659, CSC (AAO Oct. 1, 2002) [acrobat and member of Cirque de Soleil] *reported in* 8 No. 6 *Bender's Immigration Bulletin* 480 (Mar. 15, 2003); *Matter of* ___ (AAO Oct. 8, 2002) [Chinese artist was required to meet only three and not all of the criteria set forth in 8 C.F.R. §204.5(h)] *reported in* 80 No. 6 *Interpreter Releases* 216–17 (Feb. 10, 2003);

(3) Education;

(4) Business. Journalism. *Matter of* ___, CSC, WAC 01-283-53346 (AAO Mar. 11, 2003) [Editor-In-Chief/Journalist of Chinese newspaper] *reported in* 8 No. 19 *Bender's Immigration Bulletin* 1574 (Oct. 1, 2003);

(5) Athletics/Coaching. USCIS recognizes that among the most problematic cases are those of internationally acclaimed athletes who wish to enter the U.S. to coach. If the person has been a coach for a prolonged period of time the application must place heavier emphasis on his coaching. However, where the athlete has received recent acclaim as an athlete the adjudicator should take into account the totality of the circumstances of the athletics and coaching. AFM at 22.2(i)(1)(C). *Matter of* ___ (AAO Sept 16, 2003) (Nebraska Service Center) [professional hockey player met 3 out of the 10 criteria] *reported in* 81 No. 7 *Interpreter Releases* 222–23 (Feb. 16, 2004); *Matter of* ___, VSC, EAC 02-099-53226 (AAO Mar. 24, 2003) [Taekwondo instructor] *reported in* 8 No. 18 *Bender's Immigration Bulletin* 1529 (Sept. 15, 2003); *Matter of* ___ (AAO Dec. 10, 2002) [marathon runner granted status upon showing that he would work in U.S. as marathon runner] *reported in* 80 No. 8 *Interpreter Releases* 276 (Feb. 24, 2003); *Matter of* ___ A76 093 176 (AAO Aug. 19, 1999) [swimming coach for disabled students] *reported in* 77 No. 18 *Interpreter Releases* 611 (May 8, 2000); *Matter of Sapunar*, Case No. A73 400 252 (NSC) (AAU Apr. 1, 1996), *reported in* 73 No. 29 *Interpreter Releases* 1005 (July 29, 1996) [judo coach]. *But see Lee v. Ziglar,* 237 F.Supp.2d 914, 918 n.3 (N.D. Ill. 2002) [extraordinary baseball player from Korea did not qualify as extraordinary baseball coach].

6.d. INS G.C. has taken the view that lawyers are not considered within the term "sciences" or "arts" for extraordinary ability EB-1 purposes. Legal Opinion, Aleinikoff, General Counsel, INS, CO 203-P (Jan. 20, 1995), *reprinted in* 72 No. 5 *Interpreter Releases* 175, 184 (Jan. 30, 1995).

6.e. O-1 vs. EB-1—The AAO's position is that the approval of an O-1 petition does not compel USCIS to approve an EB-1 classification and that the standard is higher for EB-1. *Matter of* ___, WAC 02-254-54529 (AAO Sept. 29, 2003) *reported in* 81 No. 3 *Interpreter Releases* 83–86 (Jan. 19, 2004). AFM at 22.2(i)(1)(G) [approval of O-1 may be a "relevant" consideration].

C. *Outstanding Professors and Researchers*—INA §203(b)(1)(B), 8 U.S.C. §1153(b)(1)(B).

1. Recognized internationally as outstanding in a specific academic area;

2. Has 3 years experience in teaching or research in the academic area;

2.a. Experience in teaching or research counted while working on advanced degree if degree is acquired, person had full responsibility for the class taught, or the research has been recognized as outstanding in the academic field. 8 C.F.R. §204.5(i)(3)(ii).

3. Seeks entry:

3.a. For a tenure (or tenure track) teaching position;

3.b. Comparable position at university or institute of higher education to conduct research; *or*

3.c. Comparable position to conduct research with private employer if it employs at least 3 persons full-time in research activities and the departmental, division or institution has achieved documented accomplishments in an academic field. Research will not include engineering or product design because such activity is the "technological application of existing research." *Matter of* ___, WAC 99-016-52605 (AAO Feb. 6, 2001) *reported in* 7 No. 18 *Bender's Immigration Bulletin* 1095-1104 (Sept. 15, 2002).

3.d. If it is a research position it may be tenured, tenure track *or* a permanent offer, that is, an offer of indefinite or unlimited duration in which the researcher will have an expectation of continued permanent employment unless there is good cause for termination. 8 C.F.R. §204.5(i)(2). In recognition that modern business practices often have "at will" contracts that do not include "good cause" provision and that are year-to-year, USCIS does not require the contract to have a "good cause" provision to prove permanent employment but will accept other evidence from the employer that the researcher will continued to be employed that demonstrates "the intent to continue to seek funding and a reasonable expectation that funding will continue (such as demonstrated prior renewals for extended long-term research projects)..." AFM at 22.2(i)(2)(C); Memo, Aytes, Acting Dir. Domestic Operations, USCIS, (June 6, 2006), *published on* AILA InfoNet at Doc. No. 06060860. If the position is tenure or tenured track there is no requirement to demonstrate permanency. *Id.*

4. Evidence that the professor or researcher is recognized internationally as outstanding in the academic field must include at least *two* of the following:
   - Receipt of major prizes or awards for outstanding achievement.
   - Membership in an association which requires outstanding achievement.
   - Published material in professional publications written by others about the applicant's work.
   - Evidence of the person's participation as a judge of the work of others.
   - Evidence of original scientific research.
   - Authorship of scholarly books or articles in the field.

5. Submission of evidence in two categories is the minimum required. USCIS must evaluate the evidence presented. A book by the applicant published by a "vanity" press, a footnoted reference to the applicant's work without evaluation, an unevaluated listing of the applicant's work in a subject matter index, or a negative or neutral review of the applicant's work would be of little or no value. Letter, Weinig, Acting Asst. Comm., Examinations, CO 204.23-C (July 30, 1992), *reprinted in* 69 No. 32 *Interpreter Releases* 1037, 1052 (Aug. 24, 1992). On the other hand, peer review presentations at symposia or in articles about the applicant's work, testimony from scholars regarding the applicant's contributions, a good number of entries in a citation index that cites the person's work as authoritative, and a PhD thesis, adviser or reviewer of peer-review journal, are all examples of solid evidence. *Id.* A recent nonprecedent AAO decision, however, provides that peer review is common and will not be considered a significant factor unless the applicant has reviewed an unusually large number of articles, has reviewed for numerous journals or is on the journal's editorial board. *Matter of* ____, Case No. LIN 03-165-52241 (AAO Apr. 5, 2005).

6. No labor certification is required although an offer of employment is required in the form of a letter from the sponsoring employer. 8 C.F.R. §204.5(i)(3)(iii). *Matter of* ___, LIN 03 122 52049 (AAO Jan. 3, 2005), 2005 WL 2160025 (Nebraska Service Center) [letters from personnel at the university indicating their desire to provide permanent employment to the applicant were insufficient in the absence of a written employment officer from the employer to the beneficiary, setting out the title, terms and conditions of employment].

7. Cases Supporting Outstanding Professors and Researchers. *Matter of* ___, WAC 99-051-51587, CSC (AAO, Oct. 2, 2001) *reported in* 7 No. 10 *Bender's Immigration Bulletin* 604 (May 15, 2002) [designer of hearing aids for petitioning company where two criteria were met];

D. *Multinational Executives and Managers*—INA §203(b)(1)(C), 8 U.S.C. §1153(b)(1)(C)

1. Employed abroad for one year (*in last 3 years*) by "firm or corporation or other legal entity or an affiliate or subsidiary thereof."

1.a. Affiliates include entities owned and controlled by the same group of individuals, in approximately the same share or proportion of each entity. 8 C.F.R. §204.5(j)(2). Includes accounting firms that have "internationally recognized name(s)" as affiliates, notwithstanding the fact that they are actually separate partnerships. IMMACT90 §206(a). Firms will be considered affiliates if they market accounting services under the same internationally recognized name and the same agreement. 8 C.F.R. §204.5(j)(2). Under PL 106-95, 113 Stat. 1312 (Nov. 12, 1999) §6, affiliate now also includes management consulting firms that work with accounting firms as long as they market under an internationally recognized name or work with a successor worldwide coordinating organization even if it is not collectively owned or controlled. International management consulting firms that separate from an international accounting firm, yet continue to maintain the qualifying worldwide organizational structure may continue to use the EB-1 category even if it is no longer connected to an accounting firm. AFM at 32.2(a)(2) and 22.5(b); Memo, Yates, Deputy Ex. Assoc. Comm., Immigration Service Division, Office of Field Operations, HQADN 70/ 6.2.12, AD 00-17 (Aug. 10, 2000), *reprinted in* 77 No. 32 *Interpreter Releases* 1203, 1211–13 (Aug. 21, 2000).

1.b. Subsidiary can be joint venture if there is equal control and veto power; or can be less than one-half ownership if there is control in fact. Memo, Yates (Aug. 10, 2000), *supra.* An LLC may also be a subsidiary. AFM at 22.2(i)(3)(B)(4).

1.c. The "one of three year requirement" may be met even if person is in U.S. for more than 3 years if s/he is working for same employer, affiliate, or subsidiary in U.S. and was employed for at least 1 of last 3 by company abroad before entering in valid nonimmigrant status. 8 C.F.R. §204.5(j)(3)(i)(B).

2. Seeks to enter U.S. in order to continue to render services to the same employer or to a subsidiary or affiliate thereof in a capacity that is managerial or executive. Unlike the L-1 applicant, cannot be a specialized knowledge worker abroad. 8 C.F.R. §204.5(j)(3)(i)(A).

3. No labor certification, but a job offer by the U.S. organization, is required.

4. Managerial and executive capacity defined under INA §101(a)(44), 8 U.S.C. §1101(a)(44); 8 C.F.R. §204.5(j)(2).

4.a. Managerial capacity means an assignment with the organization in which the employee *personally*:

(1) manages the organization, department, subdivision, function or component;

(2) supervises and controls the work of other supervisory, professional or managerial employees, or manages an essential function within the organization or department or subdivision of the organization;

(3) has authority to hire and fire or recommend personnel actions (if another directly supervises employees), or if no direct supervision, functions at a senior level; *and*

(4) exercises discretion over day-to-day operations of the activity or function.

(5) First line supervisors are not considered managers unless the employees they supervise are professional. 8 C.F.R. §204.5(j)(4). Even if the employees are professionals, the position must be *primarily* managerial. *Q Data Consulting, Inc. v. INS,* 293 F.Supp.2d 25 (D.D.C. 2003) [where former position as Senior Software Consultant was only 60 to 65% managerial and where prospective position as Team Manager over 5 to 14 employees was not primarily managerial, INS did not abuse its discretion in denying petition even if it subsequently granted an L-1a petition for the same position.

(6) The definition of manager includes a "functional manager" who is managing a function of the organization. AFM at 22.2(i)(3)(E)(1). Functional manager need not oversee any employees but must manage "an essential function" or operation within the organization 8 C.F.R. §204.5(j)(2).

4.b. Executive capacity means an assignment in an organization in which the employee primarily:

(1) directs the management of the organization or a component or function;

(2) establishes goals and policies;

(3) exercises wide latitude in discretionary decision making; *and*

(4) receives only general supervision or direction from higher level executives, board of directors or stockholders.

4.c. Professional may be a manager or an executive. *Immediate Business Systems, Inc. v. Richards*, 645 F.Supp. 355 (N.D. Ga. 1986); *but see Matter of Cantec Representatives, Inc.*, 19 I&N Dec. 241 (Comm. 1984). A technical support specialist was determined not to be an executive or a manager under former Schedule A, Group IV. *Omni Packaging, Inc. v. INS*, 930 F.Supp. 28, 32–33 (D.P.R. 1996). *See also Q Data Consulting, Inc. v. INS*, 293 F.Supp.2d 25 (D.D.C. 2003). In determining whether an individual is acting in a managerial or executive capacity, USCIS shall take into account the reasonable needs of the organization, component or function in light of the overall purpose and stage of development of the organization, component or function. *The number of employees supervised is not determinative.* 8 C.F.R. §204.5(j)(2).

5. Evidence—8 C.F.R. §204.5(j)(3).

5.a. Generally need statement from U.S. employer concerning person's employment with company in one of the past three years and that U.S. employer has been doing business (*i.e.,* holding goods and/or services out for sale) for one year.

5.b. Managerial/Executive Evidence—8 C.F.R. §204.5(j)(4), (5). Where staffing levels are used as a factor, employer must show the reasonable needs of the organization in light of the overall purpose and stage of development. Employer must provide a job offer in the form of a statement describing the duties of the position and the capacity in which the person will be employed. If petitioner is seeking to assert that person is a manager of an essential function, it must still provide sufficient evidence that the beneficiary is working "primarily" as a manager. *Family Inc v. USCIS,* 469 F.3d 1313 (9th Cir. 2006) [substantial evidence supported denial of I-140 petition and the court determined that size of the company could be one factor that the agency considers where applicant was president, wife was the manager, there were only four other employees, the company had one shareholder in Korea, and the business was small]; *Q Data Consulting, Inc. v. INS,* 293 F.Supp.2d 25 (D.D.C. 2003) [where former position as Senior Software Consultant was only 60 to 65% managerial and where prospective position as Team Manager over 5 to 14 employees was not primarily managerial, INS did not abuse its discretion in denying petition even if it subsequently granted L-1A petitions]; *IKEA U.S., Inc v. DOJ,INS,* 48 F.Supp.2d 22 (D.D.C. 1999) [applied essential function analysis but found that petitioner in I-140 case failed to present sufficient documentation that employee worked "primarily" as manager].

5.c. Need to show company is operating abroad. If foreign entity stops operating prior to visa appointment the person is ineligible for status. Letter, Odom, Chief Advisory Opinions Division (Nov. 17, 1992), *reprinted in* 70 No. 6 *Interpreter Releases* 182, 198–99 (Feb. 8, 1993). However, INS takes the view that absent revocation of the I-140, it is *not* a grounds to deny AOS "solely because the overseas subsidiary or affiliates ceased operations after the I-140 was approved but prior to the 245 interview." Letter, LaFleur, Chief, Business and Trade Services Branch, INS (July 15, 1996), *reprinted in* 15 *AILA Monthly Mailing* 511 (Sept. 1996).

5.d. Need to show that company is not merely shelf corporation but is active, conducting substantial business, and truly needs an executive or manager. *Systronics Corp. v. INS*, 153 F.Supp.2d 7 (D.D.C. 2001) [revocation upheld in *dicta* on grounds that there were 2 employees, that the company seemed to be operating out of two locations with a small sublease, and that the deputy manager who would be running the company in the beneficiary's absence only had six months experience].

6. Judicial Review—The discretionary decision bar pursuant to the REAL ID Act, PL 109-13, 119 Stat. 231 (May 11, 2005), Div. B §101(f), applies to nonremoval decisions as well as removal cases because it made INA §242(a)(2)(B) applicable in all matters "regardless of whether the judgment, decision, or action is made in removal proceedings." INA §242(a)(2)(B), 8 U.S.C. §1252(a)(2)(B). Although all discretionary matters are now covered as a result of the REAL ID Act of 2005, courts differ on the scope of INA §242(a)(2)(B). *Compare Jilin Pharmaceutical USA, Inc. v. Chertoff,* 447 F.3d 196 (3d Cir. 2006) [distinguished *Soltane* regarding denial of visa petitions and found that there was no jurisdiction to review a revocation of an I-140 petition because it was a discretionary decision barred by INA §242(a)(2)(B)(ii)]; and *El-Khader v. Monica,* 366 F.3d 562, 565–67 (7th Cir. 2004) [quoting *Samirah v. O'Connell* and finding that the discretionary decision bar under INA §242(a)(2)(B)(ii) is *not* limited solely to matters arising in re-

moval, deportation, or exclusion proceeding thereby barring judicial review of the revocation of a visa petition]; *Systronics Corp. v. INS*, 153 F.Supp.2d 7 (D.D.C. 2001) [no jurisdiction, but even if there was jurisdiction the standard of review is highly deferential] *with Ana International Inc. v. Way,* 393 F.3d 886, 893–95 (9th Cir. 2005) [following *Spencer* and holding that INA §242(a)(2)(B)(ii) does not bar judicial review of an I-140 visa revocation decision of an EB-1 under 8 U.S.C. §1155 because the "good and sufficient cause" language of the statute provides a legal standard, as does the "managerial capacity" criteria of EB-1]; *Spencer Enterprises, Inc v. U.S.,* 345 F.3d 683, 689 (9th Cir. 2003) [finding there was review of the denial of an EB-5 investor petition and narrowly construing the section to include only "acts the *authority* for which is *specified* under the INA to be discretionary" and not simply any discretionary decision. The court found that the section includes only acts that are matters of "pure discretion" and not "discretion guided by legal standards." *Id* at 690]; *Soltane v. DOJ,* 381 F.3d 143, 146–48 (3d Cir. 2004) [followed *Spencer* in regard to special immigrant/religious worker case]. *See generally* Chapter 10, section on INA §242(a)(2)(B)(ii).

III. SECOND PREFERENCE—MEMBERS OF PROFESSIONS HOLDING ADVANCED DEGREES OR ALIENS OF EXCEPTIONAL ABILITY (EB-2 Category)—INA §203(b)(2), 8 U.S.C. §1153(b)(2); 8 C.F.R. §204.5(k)

A. *Generally*—28.6% of worldwide visas plus unused first preference. Today, with no visa backlog under the second (except China and India) and substantial backlog of the third employment-based preferences, there is an advantage to EB-2 over EB-3 classification. Only EB-2 applicants may waive the labor certification requirement if granted a national interest waiver (*see also* section C (p.875), *infra,* regarding Schedule A). EB-2 qualified applicants are eligible to file an EB-3 professional or skilled worker petition as well, although given the current backlog in EB-3 there would be little interest in doing so.

B. *Eligibility*—Members of the professions holding advanced degrees or their equivalent, or who because of their exceptional ability in the sciences, arts or business will substantially benefit prospectively the national economy, cultural or educational interests, or welfare of the U.S. and whose services are sought by an employer in the U.S. The position must require a member of the professions holding an advanced degree *and* the person must possess an advanced degree as shown by a master's degree or its equivalent in education and work experience. Memo, Cronin, Acting Assoc. Comm. Office of Program and Yates, Deputy Exec. Assoc. Comm., Field Operations (HQ 70/6.2) (Mar. 20, 2000), *published on* AILA InfoNet at Doc. No. 00032703; AFM, Appendix 22-1. A foreign master's degree is sufficient if through evaluation it can be demonstrated that it is equivalent to a U.S. master's degree. *Matter of* ___, LIN 06 164 51652 (AAO Dec. 5, 2007) *reprinted in* 13 No. 7 *Bender's Immigration Bulletin* 371, 405–09 (Apr. 1, 2008).

C. *Labor Certification, National Interest Waiver, or Schedule A*—Applicant must have a job offer and labor certification. However, USCIS may waive requirement if it is in the national interest to do so. INA §203(b)(2)(B), 8 U.S.C. §1153(b)(2)(B). A national interest waiver is not available in the EB-1 category. *Matter of* ___ (AAO Apr. 14, 2004) [dismissed appeal because beneficiary cannot obtain a national interest waiver as an outstanding professor or researcher under EB-1], *reported in* 81 No. 43 *Interpreter Releases* 1573, 1583–84 (Nov. 8, 2004). In addition certain persons may fall under Schedule A of the LC process. If a person's profession falls within Schedule A, s/he does not have to test the labor market but must submit an ETA 9089 when filing the I-140 and satisfy other criteria. *See in this chapter,* ¶ VIII.D.6 (p.948), *infra.*

D. *Definition of Advanced Degree*—8 C.F.R. §204.5(k)(2)

1. BA/BS or foreign academic equivalent plus 5 years of progressive experience in the specialty is equivalent to MA. 8 C.F.R. §204.5(k)(3)(i)(B). The Conference Committee Report provides that a person with a bachelor's degree plus at least 5 years of professional work experience in the profession has the equivalent of an advanced degree. H.R. Rep. No. 955, 101st Cong. 2d Sess. 121 (1990). USCIS policy is that the bachelor's degree cannot be demonstrated by a combination of experience and education. However, it can be demonstrated by a combination of degrees/education. Letter, Hernandez, Director, Business and Trade Services, USCIS, HQ 70/6.2.8 (Jan. 7, 2003), *published on* AILA InfoNet at Doc. No. 03041544. *But see Snapnames.com v. Chertoff,* 2006 WL 3491005 (D. Or. 2006) [upholding

USCIS position that bachelors or "foreign degree equivalent" for purposes of defining a professional or a person with advance degree means *one foreign degree* equivalent and *not* a combination of degrees]. An applicant can satisfy the advanced degree requirement, therefore, by the following: (1) a U.S. master's degree or higher or a foreign degree evaluated to be the equivalent of a U.S. master's degree or higher; or (2) a U.S. bachelor's degree or foreign degree equivalent plus five years of progressive, post-degree work experience. However, the applicant must possess *at least* a bachelor's degree or foreign degree equivalent. AFM at 22.2(j)(1)(B). If the applicant relies on work experience to attain the 5 years of experience post-BA, it must be *progressively more responsible* experience and USCIS may require an affidavit or statement under penalty of perjury that such progressive experience is necessary. USCIS defines progressive experience as "employment experience that reveals progress, moves forward, and advances toward increasingly complex or responsible duties. In short, progressive experience is demonstrated by advancing levels of responsibility and knowledge in the specialty." Memo, Cronin, Acting Assoc. Comm. Office of Program and Yates, Deputy Exec. Assoc. Comm., Field Operations (HQ 70/6.2) (Mar. 20, 2000), *published on* AILA InfoNet at Doc. No. 00032703; AFM, Appendix 22-1.

1.a. There is currently a conflict between the SVP under DOL and the use of a college degree plus 5 years experience. If a position carries an SVP of 7 then a master's degree would be within the range, but a bachelor's degree plus 5 years experience would exceed the SVP. Thus, a labor certification that listed an MA or BA plus 5 years may be rejected by the DOL. Letter, Richardson (Apr. 30, 1993), *reprinted in* 70 No. 26 *Interpreter Releases* 905, 922–24 (July 12, 1993). Conversely, DHS has determined that DOL's acceptance of a bachelor's degree plus 3 years experience as the equivalent of a master's degree does not satisfy the EB-2 requirement. Employer Information Bulletin 14, Office of Business Liaison, USCIS, "Employment-Based Permanent Residence." 80 No. 45 *Interpreter Releases* 1607, 1614 at 1618 (Nov. 24, 2003).

1.b. Treatment of 5 years of work experience—Under current USCIS regulations 5 years of progressive experience are necessary to establish a master's degree equivalent for a person who has a bachelor's degree or its equivalent. 8 C.F.R. §204.5(k)(3)(i)(B) ["To show that the alien is a professional holding an advanced degree, the petition must be accompanied by ... [a] ... baccalaureate degree or a foreign degree equivalent ... and evidence showing ... at least five years of progressive post-baccalaureate experience in the specialty"]; *See also* 8 C.F.R. §214.2(h)(4)(iii)(D)(5) [in H-1B context]. However, INS in memoranda has taken the position that unless the L.C. or the I-140 indicates otherwise, the 5 years of experience may be used both to establish the equivalency for a masters *and* any experience required for the position apart from the master's degree. Thus, an L.C. that requires a master's degree or equivalent and 3 years experience can be fulfilled by a person with a bachelor's degree and 5 years progressive experience because the 5 years will be counted toward establishing the master's degree and toward the 3-year experience requirement. A petitioner can include a person's "5 year post-baccalaureate progressive experience *both* to make the [person's] baccalaureate the equivalent of a Master's degree *and* to meet the ... experience that someone who actually does have a Master's degree must have." Memo, Cronin and Yates, *supra*; AFM, Appendix 22-1. See also *Chintakuntla v. INS*, Case No. C 99-5211 MMC (N.D. Cal. May 4, 2000) *reported in* 77 No. 19 *Interpreter Releases* 627, 642–48 (May 15, 2000) [issuing a permanent injunction to protect persons with 5 years of experience and BS/BA degree as having the equivalent of a MA degree under the statute and regulations and found that since the Cronin & Yates memo was not a regulation and did not have the force of law an injunction was necessary]. Subsequent to the court's injunction in *Chintakuntla*, INS issued a notice incorporating the Mar. 20, 2000 Cronin & Yates memo and specifying that persons previously denied had the right to file untimely motions to reconsider beyond the 30-day period. 65 Fed. Reg. 41093, 41097 (June 30, 2000), *reprinted in* 77 No. 26 *Interpreter Releases* 903, 927–31 (July 10, 2000).

2. If PhD required cannot use equivalent work experience. Must have PhD or foreign academic equivalent.

E. *Definition of Exceptional Ability*

1. A degree of expertise significantly above that ordinarily encountered. May include more than former H-1 "distinguished merit and ability." *Matter of Kim*, 12 I&N Dec. 758 (A.C. 1968) [H-1 confined to ability within limited area of field; former third preference was preeminence in field as a whole];

Matter of Tagawa, 13 I&N Dec. 13 (DD 1967) [defining art]. "Rare or unusual talent, or unique or extraordinary ability." *Matter of Frank*, 11 I&N Dec. 657 (DD 1966). *See also Matter of Medical University of South Carolina*, 17 I&N Dec. 266 (R.C. 1978); AFM at 22.2(j)(2)

2. Proof of exceptional ability—8 C.F.R. §204.5(k)(3)(ii).

   2.a. Any *three* of the following:

   - Degree relating to area of exceptional ability;
   - Letter from current or former employer showing at least 10 years experience;
   - License to practice profession;
   - Person has commanded a salary or remuneration demonstrating exceptional ability;
   - Membership in professional association;
   - Recognition for achievements and significant contributions to the industry or field by peers, governmental entities, or professional or business organization.

   2.b. Comparable evidence may be submitted if above categories are inapplicable. This evidence may include expert opinion letters. 8 C.F.R. §204.5(k)(3)(iii).

3. What is science, art? Art includes athletes and entertainers. AFM at 22.2(j)(3); *Matter of Masters*, 13 I&N Dec. 125 (DD 1969); Legal Opinion, Aleinikoff, General Counsel, INS CO-203P (Jan. 20, 1995), *reprinted in* 72 No. 5 *Interpreter Releases* 175, 184 (Jan. 30, 1995).

F. *National Interest Waiver*—INA §203(b)(2)(B), 8 U.S.C. §1153(b)(2)(B); AFM at 22.2(j)(4)

1. Employer or Applicant Can Sign Petition—To qualify for a national interest exemption a ETA-9089 form must be submitted with statement supporting national interest claim. 8 C.F.R. §204.5(k)(4)(ii). Employer *or* applicant can sign the petition.

2. Waiver Available Only to EB-2s—A national interest waiver is not available in the EB-1 category. *Matter of* ___ (AAO Apr. 14, 2004) [dismissed appeal because beneficiary cannot obtain a national interest waiver as an outstanding professor or researcher under EB-1] *reported in* 81 No. 43 *Interpreter Releases* 1573, 1583–84 (Nov. 8, 2004).

3. Evidentiary Criteria—The "national interest" exemption must be significantly higher than that required to establish prospective national benefit required for all persons seeking "exceptional" status. In *Matter of New York State Department of Transportation,* 22 I&N Dec. 215 (Acting Assoc. Comm. 1998) ["*NYSDOT*"], the legacy INS has given guidance regarding the threshold for a waiver including the following criteria: (1) the person seeks employment in an area of substantial intrinsic merit; (2) the benefit will be national in scope; and (3) the national interest would be adversely affected if a labor certification were required. Having exceptional ability is not by itself sufficient to grant the waiver. Nor would work such as local pro bono lawyering, teaching in a single school, or providing nutritional information in a localized setting be sufficient to meet the national criteria. A national interest waiver is not warranted solely to ameliorate a local labor shortage. The petitioner must prove that the benefit his unique skills would provide substantially outweighs the inherent national interest in protecting U.S. workers through the labor certification process.

4. Other Evidentiary Factors Pre-*NYSDOT*—The AAU suggested seven factors to be considered in determining the grant or denial of a national interest waiver pre-*NYSDOT:* (1) improving the U.S. economy; (2) improving wages and working conditions for U.S. workers; (3) improving education and programs for U.S. children and underqualified workers; (4) improving health care; (5) providing more affordable housing; (6) improving the U.S. environment and making more productive use of natural resources; and (7) interested government agency request. *Matter of* ___, Case No. EAC 92 091 50126 (AAU July 21, 1992) [Mississippi Phosphate], *reported in* 69 No. 41 *Interpreter Releases* 1364–65 (Oct. 26, 1992); 70 No. 23 *Interpreter Releases* 773–83 (June 14, 1993).

5. Denied Cases Post-*NYSDOT*—Following *NYSDOT*, many cases have been denied including: (1) a bilingual counselor at a university; (2) a China-U.S. attorney/ trade specialist; (3) director of a day camp for the elderly; (4) special education teacher; (5) physicians working in HPSAs; *but see* PL 106-95 §5 permitting NIW for physicians in shortage areas, 8 C.F.R. §204.12; (6) media safety directors; (7) computer systems analysts. The INS, however has stated that petitions approved prior

to *NYSDOT* will not be revisited during the §245 adjustment. Memo, Cronin, Acting Assoc. Comm., Program (Apr. 7, 1999), *reprinted in* 18 *AILA Monthly Mailing* 439 (May, 1999).

6. Approved Cases Post-*NYSDOT*—AAO decisions include::

6.a. Coaching, Sculling—*Matter of* ___, NSC 76-863-824 (AAO Sept 16, 1998), 1998 WL 34022277.

6.b. Computer Work—*Matter of* ___, WAC 03-216-54354 (AAO Mar. 7, 2005)[information management systems—date mining] *reported in* 11 No. 2 *Bender's Immigration Bulletin* 49, 81–82 (Jan. 15, 2006); *Matter of* ___, EAC 03-031051783 AAO Jan. 31, 2005) [software developer of stock option valuation] *reported in* 11 No. 4 *Bender's Immigration Bulletin* 153, 184 (Feb. 15, 2006); *Matter of* ___, NSC (AAO Apr. 11, 2002) [modeling sheet metal parts] *reported in* 7 No. 16 *Bender's Immigration Bulletin* (Aug. 15, 2002).

6.c. Corporate president/business owner—*Matter of* ___, VSC, EAC 01-010-50438 (AAO Feb. 4, 2003) [managing director for nonprofit organization that creates jobs in the inner cities] *reported in* 8 No. 15 *Bender's Immigration Bulletin* 1283 (Aug. 1, 2003), *Matter of* ___, EAC 98-076-51659 (AAO June 21, 1999) [owner not eligible for LC and business employed 210 to 270 persons and reduces trade deficit]; *Matter of* ___, EAC 99-144-51371, VSC (AAO Aug. 22, 2002) [Nigerian businessman served national interest by improving U.S.-Nigerian business relations in the oil business].

6.d. Engineer, Mechanical Engineer—*Matter of* ___, WAC 03-083-53964 (AAO Mar, 7, 2005) [computational mechanics engineer including the development of the AGILE software]; *Matter of Kaiser Aerospace and Electronics Corp,* A75 653 615, CSC (AAO Mar. 28, 2003) [where it was a nonresearch, narrow field most letters of support were from colleagues. Applicant was a specialist in gear machinery who designed system in aircraft to reduce failure]

6.e. Investment Analyst—*Matter of* ___ (AAO Sept. 12, 2000) *reported in* 6 *Bender's Immigration Bulleting* 674-75 (July 1, 2001).

6.f. Music. *Matter of* ___ (AAO Aug. 18, 2002) [accordion (Bayan) musician] *reported in* 80 No. 15 *Interpreter Releases* 553–54 (Apr. 14, 2003).

6.g. Research—Medical. AIDS: *Matter of* ___, LIN-98-230-53484 (AAO Jan. 12, 1999); Avian Flu, *Matter of* ___, LIN 02-218-51584 (AA) Jan. 18, 2005) [molecular biologist and researcher focusing on avian flu] *reported in* 10 No. 24 *Bender's Immigration Bulletin* 1843, 1870–71 (Dec. 15, 2005); Biochemistry. *Matter of* ___ (AAO Oct. 18, 2001) [basis of mood stabilizers]; *Matter of* ___, NSC (AAO Oct. 15, 2002) [research on two anticancer drugs, one of which can be used to treat Alzheimer's] *reported in* 8 No. 11 *Bender's Immigration Bulletin* 975 (June 1, 2003); *Matter of* ___, WAC 97-191-51059 (AAO Sept. 24, 2002) *reported in* 80 No. 15 *Interpreter Releases* 552–53 (Apr. 14, 2003); Biology. *Matter of* ___, CSC, WAC 02-207-53549 (AAO Sept. 30, 2003) [therapeutic antibodies for prion diseases] *reported in* 9 No. 5 *Bender's Immigration Bulletin* 242 (Mar. 1, 2004); Cancer. *Matter of* __, EAC 98-070-50006 (AAO June 21, 1999) [suppression of cancer cells]; *Matter of* ___, EAC 98-070-50114 (AAO June 21, 1999) [prostate/breast cancer]; Diabetes *Matter of* ___, EAC 99 14950456, VSC (AAO Dec. 11, 2001) *reported in* 7 No. 10 *Bender's Immigration Bulletin* 605 (May 15, 2002); Genetics Research. *Matter of* ___, EAC 99 077 51640 (AAO Oct. 2, 2001) [neurodegenerative and infectious diseases]; *Matter of* ___, EAC 99-092-52192 (AAO, Apr. 27, 2001) [genetic disorders]; Hemoglobinopathies *Matter of* ___ (AAO Aug 3, 2002) *reported in* 80 No. 15 *Interpreter Releases* 552, 554–55 (Apr. 14, 2003); Leprosy and arthritis research, *Matter of* ___ (AAO Mar. 17, 2001); Microbiologist. *Matter of* ___ (AAO Mar. 16, 2001) [development of salmonella vaccines]; Multiple sclerosis: *Matter of* ___ EAC 99-019-53051; Obesity, *Matter of* ___, EAC 99-012-51220, VSC (AAO Apr. 29, 2002) *reported in* 7 No. 19 *Bender's Immigration Bulletin* 1159-60 (Oct. 1, 2002); Pathology. *Matter of* ___, EAC 98 216 50785 (AAO Mar. 16, 2001) [research at Armed Forces Institute of Pathology]; Pharmaceutical, *Matter of* ___, EAC 98-120-50192 (AAO June 29, 1999); Radiology: *Matter of* ___, WAC 98-131-50087 (AAO Apr. 6, 1999).

6.h. Research—Nonmedical. Acoustic Technology (buried land mines), *Matter of* ___, TSC (AAO Aug. 18, 2002) *reported in* 8 No. 8 *Bender's Immigration Bulletin* 691 (Apr. 15, 2003); Animal pregnancy. *Matter of* ___, NSC (AAO Apr. 10, 2002) *reported in* 7 No. 16 *Bender's*

Immigration Bulletin 1028 (Aug. 15, 2002); Atmospheric research, *Matter of Shi,* LIN 98 197 51825 (AAO) (Apr. 27, 2000); Bioremediation, *Matter of* ___, NSC (AAO Nov. 2, 2001) *reported in* 7 No. 10 *Bender's Immigration Bulletin* 604-05 (May 15, 2002); Chemistry, *Matter of* ___, LIN 02-108-51863(AAO June 16, 2003) [nuclear magnetic resonance spectroscopy to examine chemical composition of drugs] *reported in* 9 No. 7 *Bender's Immigration Bulletin* 383, 416 (Apr. 1, 2004); *Matter of* ___, NSC (AAO May 23, 2002) [analytical chemistry including capillary electrochromatography] *reported in* 8 No. 6 *Bender's Immigration Bulletin* 480 (Mar. 15, 2003); *Matter of* ___, A76-447-742 (AAO Nov. 9, 1998), 1998 WL 34622379; *Matter of* ___, WAC 99-132-51823 (AAO Oct. 18, 2001) [chemical synthesis of nanowires]; Dairy Nutrition, *Matter of* ___ (Aug. 29, 2002) [lactating dairy cow feeding methods] *reported in* 8 No. 13 *Bender's Immigration Bulletin* 1128 (July 1, 2003); Entomology, *Matter of* ___, WAC 03-042-54861 (AAO Feb. 24, 2004) [research improved environmental ways of controlling insect populations] *reported in* 9 No. 20 *Bender's Immigration Bulletin* 1213, 1243 (Oct. 15, 2004); Geochemical Research. *Matter of* ___, NSC LIN 02-248-50383 (AAO July 8, 2003) [investigate mineral/fluid reactions using spectroscopy] *reported in* 8 No. 5 *Bender's Immigration Bulletin* 282 (Mar. 1, 2004); Genome and Signaling Pathways, *Matter of* ___, WAC 02-089-52983 (AAO June 3, 2003) *reported in* 9 No. 7 *Bender's Immigration Bulletin* 383, 416 (Apr. 1, 2004); Nanotechnology, *Matter of X–, W*AC 03-095-51671 (AAO Jan 31, 2005) [integration of nanostructured germanium with current silicon technology], *reported in* 11 No. 4 *Bender's Immigration Bulletin* 153, 184 (Feb. 15, 2006); Nuclear Reactor Safety, *Matter of* ___, VSC 00-059-54055 (AAO Oct. 2, 2002), *reported in* 8 No. 11 *Bender's Immigration Bulletin* 974-75 (June 1, 2003); Pollution (Hydrologic Modeling for pollution and groundwater contamination), *Matter of* ___NSC (AAO, Mar. 11, 2002), *reported in* 7 No. 16 *Bender's Immigration Bulletin* 1027-28 (Aug. 15, 2002); Physics, *Matter of* ___, EAC 99178-51980, VSC (AAO Dec. 17, 2001), *reported in* 7 No. 10 *Bender's Immigration Bulletin* 605-06 (May 15, 2002); Semiconductors and Rock and Fluid Physics, *Matter of* ___, EAC 98-126-53308 (AAO, July 19, 1999); Plant Physiology, *Matter of* ___, NSC (AAO Dec. 21, 2001), *reported in* 7 No. 10 *Bender's Immigration Bulletin* 606 (May, 15, 2002), *Matter of* ___, EAC 00-032-51205 VSC (AAO May 13, 2002), *reported in* 8 No. 5 *Bender's Immigration Bulletin* 398-99 (Mar. 1, 2003); Telecommunications /Aircraft: *Matter of* ___, EAC 98-101-54452 (AAO June 21, 1999) [advanced atmospheric turbulence modeling, high performance computing methods and data-parallel techniques].

6.i. TV Reporter. *Matter of* ___, WAC 02-196-53090 (AAO Dec. 16, 2003) [reporter serving Asian community could show his reporting had national, not just local impact in Bay Area] *reported in* 9 No. 8 *Bender's Immigration Bulletin* 477, 517 (Apr. 15, 2004).

7. Change in Employer—Where national interest waiver was based on applicant's work with a particular employer, a petition filed by the employer would no longer be valid if employer was out of business or no longer wished to hire applicant. However, where waiver was based on applicant's contribution to an industry which could be utilized by another employer, it is still valid. Letter, Skerrett, Chief, Immigr. Branch, Adjudications, HQ 204.24-C (Aug. 10, 1995), *reprinted in* 72 No. 36 *Interpreter Releases* 1274, 1281–82 (Sept. 18, 1995), *published on* AILA InfoNet at Doc. No. 95083091.

8. Judicial Review—One court has held that national interest waiver decisions are discretionary and judicial review is therefore barred under INA §242(a)(2)(B)(ii). *Zhu v. Gonzales,* 411 F.3d 292 (D.C. Cir. 2005) [rejecting analysis relied upon in *Spencer* and holding that review of national interest waivers is barred under 8 U.S.C. §1252(a)(2)(B)(ii)].

G. *Foreign Medical Graduates*—Special Problems:

1. Precluded from entering U.S. as an immigrant principally to perform services as members of the medical profession. INA §212(a)(5)(B), 8 U.S.C. §1182(a)(5)(B).

2. Ground of inadmissibility does not apply if:

2.a. Possesses a certificate from the Educational Commission on Foreign Medical Graduates (ECFMG) on the basis of passage of parts I and II of the National Board of Medical Examiners Examination (or equivalent) which is now steps 1-2 of the United States Medical Licensing Examination (USMLE), is competent in oral and written English (which is now the Test of English as a Foreign Language or the TOEFL exam), and the Clinical Skills Assessment (CSA) examination. 8 C.F.R. §214.2(h)(4)(viii)(B).

(1) In order to take the CSA examination an applicant need only pass Step 1 of the USMLE and the TOEFL exam. Cable, DOS, 02-State-032247 (Feb. 20, 2002), *reprinted in* 79 No. 10 *Interpreter Releases* 342 (Mar. 4, 2002).

2.b. Doctor of national or international renown;

2.c. Graduate of accredited medical school in U.S. (including Puerto Rico and Canada); or

2.d. Not entering U.S. to perform medical services.

(1) Person filling position does not need to be M.D. For example, M.D. enters as professor of environmental epidemiology. *Matter of Sheikh*, 17 I&N Dec. 634 (R.C. 1980); *Matter of Washington University School of Medicine*, Case No. A23 643 743 (Comm. AAU Feb. 5, 1992), *reported in* 69 No. 27 *Interpreter Releases* 864–66 (July 20, 1992) [research Asst. professor of rheumatology requiring MD degree or equivalent]; or

(2) Where M.D. enters as immediate relative or as relative under preference system.

(3) Where the M.D. enters as a refugee or asylee, under the diversity lottery program, or any other provision of the Act in which the basis for immigration is other than employment as a physician (such as a software engineer developing medical software).

2.e. NIW for Physicians In Medically Underserved Areas—INA §203(b)(2)(B)(ii); 8 C.F.R. §§204.12(a)-(c), 245.18(e); AFM at 22.2(j)(6), 23.5; 65 Fed. Reg. 53889. If immigration is based on an employment offer as a physician, must also obtain labor certification unless exempted from that requirement. Physicians working in medically underserved areas qualify for national interest waivers (once again) pursuant to PL 106-95 §5. INA §203(b)(2)(B)(ii). To obtain the benefit of this law: (1) the physician must agree to work full-time in a health shortage area or for the VA; (2) a federal agency or state public health department has to determine that the work is in the public interest; and (3) the physician must work full-time for an aggregate of 5 years (not including time on J-1) before s/he is eligible for AOS or IV. 8 C.F.R. §§204.12(a)–(c). The prior requirement that the FMG's service had to be completed within six (6) years (8 C.F.R. §204.12(b)(1)) as well as a requirement that the five years can only begin to run after the petition and national interest waiver are approved (8 C.F.R. §245.18(e) were struck down as *ultra vires* of the statute. *Schneider v. Chertoff,* 450 F.3d 944 (9th Cir. 2006); USCIS applied *Schneider* nationwide and also agreed to accept national interest waivers on behalf of physicians who provide specialty care rather than solely primary-care medicine in any federally designated underserved area, including Physician Scarcity Areas. But USCIS emphasized that the physician must be pursuing the type of medical service that is the basis for the NIW. Memo, Aytes, Assoc, Dir. Domestic Operations, USCIS HQ 70/6.2, AD06-46 (Jan. 23, 2007), *published on* AILA InfoNet at 07021262. Petitions and AOS applications can be filed prior to the date the 5-year service is completed provided that an immigrant visa number is available. 8 C.F.R. §204.12(e). Waivers approved prior to Nov. 12, 1999 are unaffected and waivers filed before Nov. 1, 1998 are approved if physician has worked full-time for 3 years in shortage area. INA §203(b)(2)(B)(ii); 8 C.F.R. §§204.12, 245.18, 1245.18. To support a national interest waiver a physician must present with the I-140: (1) contract of employment or if self-employed an attestation; (2) evidence of employment in a HPSA or VA and in a designated specialty by HHS for the HPSA; (3) a letter dated within 6 months of filing the petition from a federal agency or from the department of public health of the State attesting that the physician's work is in the public interest; (4) evidence that the physician meets the admissibility requirements of INA §212(a)(5)(B) regarding USMLE; and (5) evidence of §212(e) waiver if applicable. 8 C.F.R. §204.12(c). Although comments to the regulations limit the waivers to physicians practicing in "family or general medicine, pediatrics, general internal medicine, obstetrics/gynecology, and psychiatry." 65 Fed. Reg. 53889, 53890 (Sept. 6, 2000), this suggested limitation has been eliminated by USCIS memorandum and NIW eligibility is now expanded to specialty care physicians. Memo, Aytes (Jan. 23, 2007), *supra.*

2.f. USCIS Acceptance of Adjustment Application. USCIS has determined that a physician who is the beneficiary of an approved I-140 with a national interest waiver may file (and USCIS must accept) his or her adjustment of status application even if s/he has not completed his or her 3- or 5-year medical-service requirement in H-1B status, pursuant to INA §214(*l*). However, USCIS may not approve the AOS until the physician has fulfilled the 3- or 5-year requirement. AFM at 23.5(e)(3)(A); Memo, Yates, Deputy Ex. Assoc. Comm. Field Operations, HQ 70/6.1.3-P (Oct 1, 2001), *reprinted in* 78 No. 41 *Interpreter Releases* 1649, 1658–60 (Oct. 22, 2001). Portability provisions do *not* apply to NIW physicians. AFM at 23.5(e)(3)(F).

2.g. Labor Certifications for Physicians. When an NIW is not possible, a physician may seek residency through the labor certification process. To obtain labor certification physician must have state license in state where labor certification is filed *at the time* it is filed or must be able to obtain license within a proximate time of the person's entry through the completion of a ministerial process. *Matter of Perla-Tate*, 90-INA-175 (BALCA Dec. 4, 1992) (*en banc*), 1992 WL 382136 [where physicians had to go through residency program they were barred under former 20 C.F.R. §656.20(c)(4)]; *Matter of Glendale Family Medical Center*, 95-INA-40 (BALCA Oct. 3, 1996), 1996 WL 566414 [CO can require employer to obtain opinion from state licensing board whether or not license is needed or whether any other requirements have been met].

H. *Nurses*—EB-2 Issues. Registered nurses may often face a problem if the seek EB-2, instead of EB-3 status. Although many nurses have advanced degrees, USCIS often takes the position that the job they are filling does not require a nurse with an advanced degree. AFM at 22.2(j)(1)(D) ["the DOL's *Occupational Outlook Handbook* indicates that, in the nursing profession, only managerial jobs (director of nursing or assistant director of nursing) or advanced level jobs (clinical nurse specialist, nurse practitioner, etc) generally require advanced degrees. A registered nurse job, by contrast, usually does not require an advanced degree holder"].

I. *Soviet Scientists*—Soviet Scientists Immigration Act of 1992 (SSIA), PL 102-509, 106 Stat. 3316; Foreign Relations Authorization Act, Fiscal Year 2003, PL 107-228, 116 Stat. 1350 (Sept. 30, 2002).

1. Allows certain scientists/engineers from the independent states of the former Soviet Union (Armenia, Azerbaijan, Belarus, Georgia, Kazakhstan, Kyrgyzstan, Moldova, Russia, Tajikistan, Turkmenistan, Ukraine and Uzbekistan) or Baltic states (Latvia, Lithuania and Estonia) to apply for LPR status under the Second Preference, without obtaining an L.C. or National Interest Waiver, if they are scientists or engineers "who have expertise in nuclear, chemical, biological, or other high-technology field which is clearly applicable to the design, development or production of ballistic missiles, nuclear, biological, chemical or other high technology weapons of mass destruction" or working on defense projects in the same area. 8 C.F.R. §204.10(b) (Definition)
2. Procedure—File I-140 by applicant or anyone on his behalf. No offer of employment is required. A letter from the Bureau of Nonproliferation of DOS regarding applicant's background with evidence of nationality is sufficient. 8 C.F.R. §204.10(c). Must file before Sept. 30, 2006. Allows for 950 IVs/adjustments per year, but bars any scientist previously admitted as an LPR from benefits under the Act.

IV. THIRD PREFERENCE—PROFESSIONALS, SKILLED AND OTHER WORKERS (EB-3 Category)—INA §203(b)(3), 8 U.S.C. §1153(b)(3)

A. *Generally*—28.6% of worldwide visas plus unused first and second preference.

B. *Eligibility*

1. Professionals—Baccalaureate degree (or foreign university equivalent) and person who is a member of the professions.
2. Skilled Workers—Full-time permanent job requiring *at least 2 years* training *or* work experience. Relevant post-secondary education may be considered as training. 8 C.F.R. §204.5(*l*)(2).
3. Other Workers—Includes foreign nationals with less than two years of training and work experience.
4. A labor certification is needed for all third preference categories. A national interest waiver is not available for EB-3. However, a person may fall under Schedule A of the DOL regulations in

which case s/he does not have to test the labor market but must submit an ETA 9089 and meet other requirements when filing the I-140. *See in this chapter* ¶ VIII.D.6 (p.948), *infra*.

C. *Professional/Skilled Workers*

1. One relevant concern under EB-3 is between professionals and skilled workers versus other workers because historically there has been a substantial backlog of visa numbers for "other workers." Backlogs have become appreciably worse as a result of INA §245(i) and a 50% reduction in visa numbers in the other worker category because of NACARA which reduced the other worker category by 5,000 visas per year. These categories are distinguished by the job requirements on the labor certification and the years of training or experience for each. Training and experience under DOL standards are useful to show the professional character of the job. DOL standards found in:

1.a. O*NET—This is a computerized system that contains a lists by category of all positions of employment in the U.S. and the requirements, by education, training and experience, necessary to perform the work (*see www.onetcenter.org*). O*NET is the successor to and the modified computerized version of the Dictionary of Occupational Titles (DOT), which is generally no longer relied upon by the DOL. 69 Fed. Reg. 77325, 77332 (Dec. 27, 2004), *published on* AILA InfoNet at Doc. No. 04122312. O*NET operates through the use of five job zones. A DOL overview of the job zones may be found at DOL Overview of O*NET Job Zones, *published on* AILA InfoNet at Doc. No. 05033016. O*NET, like DOT, however, should not be used as a verbatim source to describe a job or its requirements. *Matter of Marta Fashions Sportswear,* 95-INA-193 (BALCA Feb. 3, 1998), 1998 WL 83662 [for a position of Supervisor, Cutting Department, the DOL Certifying Officer was upheld in rejecting a labor certification where the job duties were copied verbatim from the DOT on grounds that requiring experience in all listed duties is not normal for the job].

1.b. Occupational Outlook Handbook (OOH)—specifies education and experience requirements for selected occupations.

1.c. The Specific Vocational Preparation (SVP)—The SVP is used to determine the minimum and maximum amount of training, experience, and education the DOL believes is necessary for each job. An SVP of 6 or greater is needed to avoid the "other worker" category. To a certain extent the SVP has now been replaced by the O*NET job zones discussed in ¶ 1.a (p. 882), *supra*. Job zones should also be consulted to determine the minimum amount of education, training, and experience required by DOL for a particular position, and specifically whether a baccalaureate degree may be required.

1.d. Labor Certification Standards—The DOL has provided a list of professional occupations for recruitment purposes for labor certifications that require a person to customarily hold a bachelors or higher degree. *See* 69 Fed. Reg. 77325, 77377–84 (Dec. 27, 2004). *See* **Appendix A**, *infra.* DOL has explicitly stated that the list is solely to determine the type of recruitment that must be utilized in labor certification cases, 69 Fed. Reg. at 77346 (Dec. 27, 2004). BALCA has agreed, finding that professional recruitment must be utilized if the position is listed, whether or not the employer requires a university degree. *EPI Limited Partnership,* 08-PER-4 (BALCA Apr. 28, 2008) [affirmed CO denial where employer required a high school degree but used SOC/O*NET property manager title, and did not conduct professional recruitment].

1.e. A person must have a U.S. degree or foreign degree equivalent as a professional to qualify for an EB-3 professional. 8 C.F.R. §204.5(*l*)(3)(ii)(C). If the applicant holds a foreign degree, he needs to have his degree analyzed to determine if it is equivalent to a U.S. degree. O.I. §204.4(d)(5). If a degree is listed in the *Adjudicator's Field Manual* then no further analysis is required. *See generally* AFM at Appendix 31-2. If the employee does not have a U.S. degree and has a foreign degree where he attended less than 4 years, CIS has asserted that if the employer lists the position as a bachelor's degree it will be treated as a professional position and the application will be denied unless he demonstrates that the foreign degree itself is equivalent to a U.S. degree. However, if the position is listed as a foreign degree *or its equivalent* then the position can be treated as a skilled worker position and evaluations showing a combination of educational degrees (rather than just one foreign degree) would suffice. *See e.g., Matter of ___,* SRC 07 174 51943 (TSC Dec. 18, 2007) *reprinted in* 13 No. 7 *Bender's Immigration Bulletin* 371, 410–12 (Apr. 1, 2008) [denied I-140 because employer listed the position solely as a bachelor's degree and USCIS determined that the 3 year program was not equivalent to a U.S. bachelor's degree despite petitioner's argument that this was for a skilled not a professional position]; *See also Snapnames.com v. Chertoff,* 2006 WL 3491005 (D. Or. 2006) [upholding USCIS position that bachelors degree or "foreign degree equivalent" for purposes of defining a professional or a person with advance degree means *one foreign degree* equivalent and *not* a combination of degrees. However, the court also found that for purposes of the skilled worker category a combination of *degrees* rather than one degree could meet the definition of bachelors degree or foreign degree equivalent].

D. *Definition of Professional*

1. See discussion on H-1Bs in Ch. 5, ¶ VII.C.2 (p.680), *supra.* The DOL has provided a list of professional occupations for recruitment purposes for labor certifications that require a person to customarily hold a bachelors or higher degree. *See* 69 Fed. Reg. 77326, 77377–84 (Dec. 27, 2004), *published on* AILA InfoNet at Doc. No. 04122312. *See* **Appendix A,** *infra.* See also 18 ALR Fed. 287, Immigration Examinations Handbook, Occupational and Professional Visas, Third Preference Petitions (June 1985); Staff, AAU, Third Preference Case Law Relating to the Professions (1985), *reprinted in* 62 *Interpreter Releases* 836 (Sept. 6, 1985); AFM at 22.2(m) [precedent decisions]. *But see EPI Limited Partnership,* 08-PER-4 (BALCA Apr. 28, 2008) [university education is not "mandatory" under Schedule A].

2. INA specifies, but does not limit definition of professionals to: architects, engineers, lawyers, physicians, surgeons and teachers in elementary or secondary schools, colleges, academies, or seminaries. INA §101(a)(32), 8 U.S.C. §1101(a)(32); *Matter of Shin*, 11 I&N Dec. 686 (DD 1966) [recognizes professions as constantly expanding with greater knowledge and specialized training].

   Can include specialized activities in journalism, finance and business administration. *Cf. Matter of Medina*, 13 I&N Dec. 506 (R.C. 1970); *Matter of Ling*, 13 I&N Dec. 35 (R.C. 1968); *Matter of Chu*, 11 I&N Dec. 881 (R.C. 1966). *But see Matter of Cantec Representatives, Inc.*, 19 I&N Dec. 241 (Comm. 1984).

3. USCIS requires degree. Cannot qualify as a "professional" under EB-3 if degree is based upon years of experience rather than education, 8 C.F.R. §204.5(*l*)(2). However, even if the professional criteria for EB-3 does not permit the use of experience in lieu of a degree or a combination of education and experience, the skilled worker category under EB-3 does and an I-140 should not be denied where the position permits an equivalency. *Grace Korean United Methodist Church v. Chertoff,* 437 F.Supp.2d 1174, 1177–79 (D. Or. 2005) [reversed denial of I-140 under skilled worker category because USCIS's claim that skilled worker category does not allow equivalency based on a combination of education and experience and only permits an equivalent foreign degree is contrary to the "plain meaning of the statute and regulations as well as the clear Congressional intent"]. *But see Snapnames.com v. Chertoff,* 2006 WL 3491005 (D. Or. 2006) [upholding USCIS position that bachelors degree or "foreign degree equivalent" for purposes of defining a professional or a person with advance degree means *one foreign degree* equivalent and *not* a combination of degrees. However, the court also found that for purposes of the skilled worker category a combination of *degrees* rather than one degree could meet the definition of bachelors degree or foreign degree equivalent even if a combination of education and experience was not permitted]. But even with a degree, educational background alone may be insufficient at the college level to be considered a professional. *Matter of Ling*, 13 I&N Dec. 35 (R.C. 1968) [general business administration degree without emphasis (such as finance or marketing) not *per se* entitled to former third preference].

4. Licensing—Unlike H-1 where license to practice in state needed immediately, may not be necessary for approval in light of treatment of former third preference petition. O.I. §204.4(d)(4). An applicant should show, however, that beneficiary intends to pursue license at place of intended employment. *See Matter of Maher*, 12 I&N Dec. 680 (R.C. 1968) [dentist]; *Matter of Semerjan*, 11 I&N Dec. 751 (R.C. 1966) [engineer]; *Matter of Naufahu*, 11 I&N Dec. 904 (R.C. 1966) [lawyers].

E. *Procedural Issues*

Whether someone is a professional or skilled worker no longer matters practically as both are in the same "pot" of visas. The only distinction arises with "other workers" which includes all workers who have less than 2 years training or experience. This category was specifically limited to 10,000 visas per year and has resulted in significant backlogs in the past. NACARA will backlog other workers even further by cutting the visa numbers by 5,000 beginning the fiscal year after all those who have approved petitions receive their visas. A judicial challenge to the reallocation and limitation of visas to the "other worker" category has been rejected. *Aliens for Better Immigration Laws v. U.S.*, 871 F.Supp. 182 (S.D.N.Y. 1994) [rejecting due process challenge by housekeepers and childcare workers].

V. FOURTH PREFERENCE—SPECIAL IMMIGRANTS—INA §§101(a)(27), 203(b)(4), 8 U.S.C. §§1101(a)(27), 1153(b)(4)

A. *Generally*

1. Part of the numerical limitation system (7.1% of worldwide visas per year) except for returning residents and persons seeking reacquisition of citizenship. INA §203(b)(4), 8 U.S.C. §1153(b)(4).
2. File visa (or adjustment) application with supporting documentation demonstrating eligibility. A preliminary visa petition is required on Form I-360. However, special immigrants may petition without an employer. INA §204(a)(1)(E).

B. *Categories:*

1. Person seeking reacquisition of citizenship/and returning resident.
2. Religious Workers—INA §101(a)(27)(C), 8 U.S.C. §1101(a)(27)(C); H.R. 723(I), 101st Cong.2d Sess, 1990 U.S.C.C.A.N. 6710, 6755; 8 C.F.R. §204.5(m); 22 C.F.R. §42.32(d)(1)(ii)

   2.a. Requirements:

   (1) For at least 2 years immediately preceding the time of the application, the person "has been a member of a religious denomination having a *bona fide*, nonprofit, religious organization in the United States," *and*

   (2) S/he seeks to enter the U.S.:

      (a) solely to carry on his or her vocation as a *minister; or*

      (b) if *before* Oct. 1, 2008 (PL 108-99) s/he seeks to work in a professional capacity in a religious vocation or occupation *or* to work for an organization or §501(c)(3) affiliate in a religious vocation or occupation; and

   (3) S/he has been carrying on such vocation, professional work or other work continuously for at least a 2-year period. However, INS does not regard voluntary service as meeting the 2-year requirement. The applicant must have been remunerated for his work. *Matter of ___*, EAC 98-075-53938 (AAO Jan. 10, 2000) *reported in* 20 *AILA Monthly Mailing* 23-24 (Jan./Feb.2001)

      (a) The 2-year period may have been in the U.S. 8 C.F.R. §204.5(m)(1). Moreover, studying in the U.S. under F-1 may be considered carrying on the vocation "if it can be demonstrated that such study is consistent with the ... ministerial vocation and provided that the [minister] continues to perform the duties of a minister of religion." Letter, Weinig, Acting Ass. Comm. Adjudications CO 204.26-C (May 8, 1992), *reprinted in* 69 No. 28 *Interpreter Releases* 905, 925 (July 27, 1992); *Matter of Roman Catholic Bishop of Sacramento*, WAC 93 041 50514 (AAU Jan. 13, 1994). A break in employment if significant is only allowed if it was beyond the person's control. Letter, Weinig (May 8, 1992), *supra*. The religious work must be continuous but need not be full-time for the requisite 2-year period. *Matter of ___*, EAC 93 056 50872 (AAU Sept. 15, 1993); *Matter of Greater Emanuel Temple, Inc.*, EAC 93 100 51628 (AAU Oct. 27, 1993). However, AAO unpublished decisions maintain that volunteer work does not satisfy the two year prior work experience requirement. *Matter of __*, EAC 97 205 52385 (AAO Sept. 1, 1999) *reprinted in* 19 *AILA Monthly Mailing* 149 (Mar. 2000); *Matter of ___* (AAO Sept. 30, 2003) (Vermont Service Center) [where W-2 was only for one year preceding the application and was for less than the claimed wage applicant failed to show he had 2 years of experience despite his submission indicating that he worked after the date of submission of the application] *reported in* 81 No. 11 *Interpreter Releases* 349–50 (Mar. 15, 2004). *But see Soltane v. DOJ,* 381 F.3d 143, 150 (3d Cir. 2004) [rejected AAO ruling that position must be paid as contrary to the regulations because the "agency explicitly stated" that the regulations had been "revised to account more clearly for uncompensated volunteers, whose services are engaged but who are not technically employees." 56 Fed. Reg. 66965 (Dec. 27, 1991)]. AAO decisions further indicate that the work must be for the two years immediately preceding the application. *Matter of* ___ (AAO Sept. 30 2003) (Vermont Service Center) [religious work in Brazil is not relevant because applicant was in the U.S. for more than two years after entering as a B-2 and he needs to show that he engaged in religious work for 2 years immediately preceding his application] *reported in* 81 No. 11 *Interpreter Releases* 349 (Mar. 15, 2004).

2.b. Includes spouses and children accompanying or following to join.

2.c. Definitions, 8 C.F.R. §204.5(m)(2):

(1) A minister is defined as an individual duly authorized by a recognized religious denomination to conduct religious worship and to perform other duties usually performed by authorized members of the clergy. A minister is not a lay preacher; a minister must be ordained to conduct religious worship and perform other duties performed by an ordained pastor/ clergymen of the denomination. 22 C.F.R. §42.32(d)(1), *Matter of Rhee*, 16 I&N Dec. 607 (BIA 1978). A minister must be full-time. *Matter of Faith Assembly Church*, 19 I&N Dec. 391 (Comm. 1986).

(2) A religious organization in the U.S. is defined as an IRC §501(c)(3) organization as it relates to religious organizations or one that never sought such exemption but can prove it would be eligible for it. 8 C.F.R. §204.5(m)(2). Under the IRS code, organizations that are classified or classifiable as "churches" pursuant to IRC §§509(a)(1) and 170(b)(1)(A)(i) are generally considered religious organizations. Letter, Kleczek, Assoc. Counsel, Chief, Adjudications Law Division, USCIS (Mar. 9, 2004), *published on* AILA InfoNet at Doc. No. 04031710. Other organizations classified under IRC §170(b)(1)(A) may qualify as religious organizations and USCIS field officers are "instructed to review, in addition to IRS documentation, evidence which establishes the religious nature and purpose of the organization." *Id.* Other definitions of religious organization are found at: *Lindenberg v. INS*, 657 F.Supp. 154 (D.D.C. 1987) [broad definition of religious organization]; *Unification Church v. INS*, 547 F.Supp. 623 (D.D.C. 1982) [implicitly rejects INS factors test as fraught with constitutional problems]; *Matter of N*, 5 I&N Dec. 173 (Comm. 1953) [15 factors]; *Matter of Sinha*, 10 I&N Dec. 758 (R.C. 1964); 9 FAM 41.58.

(3) Professional capacity means an activity in a religious vocation or occupation for which the minimum of a BA or a foreign equivalent is required.

(4) Religious denomination means a religious group or community of believers having some form of ecclesiastical government, a creed, or statement of faith, some form of worship, discipline, services and ceremonies or comparable indicia.

(5) Religious occupation means an activity which relates to traditional religious functions such as liturgical workers, religious instructors or counselors. 8 C.F.R. §204.5(m)(2). For a definition in the legislative history of religious "vocation or occupation" *see* H.R. Rep. No. 723 pt.1, 101st Cong. 2d Sess. 75 (1990).

Does not include lay members of religious organization who intend to engage in lay work, such as "immigrants engaging in administrative and other support functions." H. Rept. 723(I), 101st Cong., 2d Sess., reprinted in 1990 U.S.C.C.A.N. 6710, 6755. The job must involve "skill, training and experience related to religious objectives." *Matter of Blaich*, 15 I&N Dec. 304 (R.C. 1975); *Avena v. INS,* 989 F.Supp.1 (D.D.C. 1997) [upholding INS denial that Cradle Roll teacher who was also a deaconess and personal ministries secretary for Seventh Day Adventist Church was not a religious worker]. *But see Soltane v. DOJ,* 381 F.3d 143, 149–50 (3d Cir. 2004) [rejected narrow interpretation by AAO of regulation and found that position can be both secular and religious]; *Lindenberg v. INS*, 657 F.Supp. 154, 160 (D.D.C. 1987) [court said INS interpretation that applicant must perform religious work is inconsistent with the regulations]; *Matter of* ___ WAC 03 122 53068 (AAO Mar. 7, 2005), 2005 WL 2159872 [Christian book editor involved in content of publications, religious plays, newspapers is a qualifying religious occupation]. *See also* AFM at 22.3(b)(8) for a discussion by USCIS of precedent decisions.

USCIS now asserts that a person in a religious occupation must have formal training established by the governing body of the denomination. *Matter of* ___ (AAO Oct. 8, 2003) [finding that religious vocalist was not a religious occupation because applicant did not need specialized religious training only the ability to sing] *reported in* 81 No. 11 *Interpreter Releases* 347–48 (Mar. 15, 2004). *But see Perez v. Ashcroft,* 236 F.Supp.2d 899 (N.D. Ill. 2002) [refused to give effect to "formal training" requirement because it represents a substantive change not accompanied by notice and comment rule making].

(6) Religious vocation means a calling to religious life such as taking vows as exists for nuns, monks and religious brothers and sisters.

(7) Change in location of employment (to different congregation) within same religious denomination does not affect the validity of the petition. Letter, Skerrett, Chief, Immigration Branch, Adjudications HQ 204.26-C (May 6, 1994), *reprinted in* 13 *AILA Monthly Mailing* 511 (July/Aug. 1994), *published on* AILA InfoNet at Doc. No. 94051390 (May 13, 1994).

2.d. Evidence—8 C.F.R. §204.5(m)(3), (g)(2). Applicant must submit evidence that the organization is a 501(c)(3) organization or qualifies for the status as well as a letter from an authorized official of the U.S. organization establishing that the applicant has the 2 years of experience and that the person qualifies as a minister, religious professional or religious vocation or occupation. The authorized official must also explain how the person will be solely working in the religious capacity, how he will be remunerated, and the religious organization's ability to pay the salary. *Avena, supra* [upholding INS denial for failure to demonstrate ability to pay salary]. Application made on Form I-360 and must be approved in U.S. then sent to the post. Cannot file I-485 until I-360 approved. Memo, Puleo, Assoc. Comm. Adjudications CO 204.26-C (June 10, 1992), *reprinted in* 69 No. 25 *Interpreter Releases* 801, 813–22 (July 6, 1992).

(1) To meet the requirements of 8 C.F.R. §§204.5(m)(2) and (m)(3)(i) in regard to nonprofit status the following documents should be submitted:

(a) A signed letter from IRS showing §501(c)(3) status as a religious organization *or* an IRS group 501(c)(3) letter recognizing the group as an organization described under IRC 509(a)(1) where the religious organization is going under the group tax exemption *or* the documents required to be submitted for tax exempt religious status by IRS.

i) The organization does not need to have tax exemption it "merely has to establish that it is eligible for such exemption." AFM at 22.3(b)(3) note 1. This can include documents from the affiliated religious organization and a letter from the authorized official explaining how the affiliation exists

and

(b) Documents which establish the religious nature and purpose of the organization that include: (i) IRS Form 1023; (ii) Schedule A supplement where applicable; (iii) Articles of Incorporation or organizing document that contains IRS dissolution clause and specifies purpose of organization; and (iv) brochures, calendars, flyers and other literature describing the religious purpose and nature of the organization's activities. Memo, Yates, Assoc. Dir. Operations, USCIS HQ70/8 (Dec. 17, 2003), *published on* AILA InfoNet at Doc. No. 04011211.

2.e. Limitation of Five Thousand—There is an annual limit of five thousand (5,000) religious worker special immigrants. Ministers are not included in the limitation. INA §101(a)(27)(C)(ii)(1).

3. U.S. employee abroad or employee of American Institute in Taiwan for 15 years—For U.S. employee abroad, Principal office of Foreign Service must cite exceptional circumstances justifying grant of status. Requires petition to Secy. of State rather than AG. Must file petition within one year of notification from Secy. of State. 22 C.F.R. §42.32(d)(2). The 15 years of service may be obtained by employment abroad with more than one U.S. government agency. Cable, DOS, 91-State-352215 (Oct. 25, 1991), *reprinted in* 68 No. 44 *Interpreter Releases* 1662, 1663 (Nov. 18, 1991).

4. Panama Canal Treaty employees and their spouses and children. 22 C.F.R. §42.32(d)(3); AFM at 22.3(n)

5. FMGs—Foreign medical graduates if entered U.S. on H/J visa, licensed to practice or practicing medicine in a state as of Jan. 1, 1978 and continued to practice and been continuously present since date of entry. Visa qualifying medical exam is not a requirement. 22 C.F.R. §42.32(d)(4).

6. Commuters from border—*Saxbe v. Bustos*, 419 U.S. 65 (1974). 8 C.F.R. §211.5. To maintain resident status commuter's only requirement is to show he has not been unemployed in the U.S. for 6 continuous months or has worked a minimum of 90 days the past year.

7. G-4—Retired G-4 officer and his spouse or unmarried son or daughter or widow (if G-4 deceased) of employee or retired employee of an international organization described in INA §101(a)(15)(G)(i) who has maintained a G-4 or N status and who applies within 6 months of retirement. INA §101(a)(27)((I), 8 U.S.C. §1101(a)(27)(I). Application process at 8 C.F.R. §§101.5, 1101.5. Can file application for adjustment with I-360. Applications under this category may only be filed with the Nebraska Service Center. 69 Fed. Reg. 3380 (Jan. 23, 2004); Memo, Yates, Assoc Dir. Operations, USCIS, Concurrent Filing for Section 101(a)(27)(I) Special Immigrants (Jan. 23, 2004), *published on* AILA InfoNet Doc. No. 04020641 (Feb. 6, 2004).

8. Returning resident—INA §101(a)(27)(A), 8 U.S.C. §1101(a)(27)(A); *See* "Abandonment of Residency" in Ch. 6, section XIII.E (p.859); *Chavez-Ramirez v. INS*, 792 F.2d 932 (9th Cir. 1986).

9. Court Dependents—INA §101(a)(27)(J), 8 U.S.C. §1101(a)(27)(J), PL 105-119 §113, 111 Stat. 2440 (Nov. 26, 1997 Amendments), 143 Cong. Rec. H10809-01 (Nov. 13, 1997), 8 C.F.R. §204.11, 58 Fed. Reg. 42843–51 (Aug. 12, 1993); AFM at 22.3(q). Covers a child declared dependent by a juvenile court in U.S. *or* who that court has committed to the custody of a state agency or department *and* who has been deemed eligible by that court for long term foster care due to abuse, neglect or abandonment. The statute also requires that a judicial or administrative proceeding determine it is in the child's best interest not to be returned to his country or his parent's country. Finally, state juvenile courts were divested of jurisdiction to determine custody when the child is "in the actual or constructive custody of the Attorney General unless the Attorney General [now DHS] "specifically consents" to the State court's jurisdiction and "expressly consents" to the dependency order. In the case of juveniles in custody due to their immigration status (either by ICE or ORR), the specific consent to the court's jurisdiction must be obtained before there are dependency proceedings or the court's order is invalid. Memo, Yates, Assoc. Dir. Operations, USCIS, HQADN 70/23 (May 27, 2004), *published on* AILA InfoNet at Doc. No. 04062168. But if the child is not in the custody of DHS and not subject to an order of removal, the juvenile court can determine custody. *Matter of Saint Preux,* A97 634 322 (AAO June 5, 2007) (Miami) *reported in* 12 No. 17 *Bender's Immigration Bulletin* 1193, 1217 (Sept. 1, 2007) [AAO approved special immigrant status where juvenile court entered custody order where the 18 year old was not in DHS custody or subject to a removal order]. In addition, whether a child is in the "constructive custody" of ICE is a factual matter that may turn on the current practices of ICE. *Matter of Perez Quintanilla*, A 97 383 010 (AAO June 7, 2007)) *reprinted in* 84 No. 33 *Interpreter Releases* 2009-19 (Aug. 27, 2007) [finding that the policy of ICE at the time was that a child who was released from ICE custody during the removal process was *not* in the constructive custody of ICE for purposes of the Special Immigrant statute and therefore the state juvenile court did *not* need ICE's consent to enter the dependency order]. *See also Zheng v. Pogash,* 416 F.3d 550, 557–61 (S.D. Tex. 2006) [DHS erred in not giving specific consent to dependency court to adjudicate the claim of a Chinese minor who was abandoned by his father after refusal to repay the Snakeheads]; *Gao v. Jenifer,* 185 F.3d 548 (6th Cir. 1999). The 1997 amendments requiring the DHS's consent should not be applied retroactively to children declared dependent prior to the amendments. *Yu v. Brown,* 92 F.Supp.2d 1236 (D.N.M. 2000).

Pursuant to §462(a)–(c) of the Homeland Security Act of 2002, PL 107-296, 116 Stat. 2153 (Nov. 25, 2002), the Office of Refugee Resettlement within HHS now directs immigration functions related to "the care of unaccompanied alien children." HSA §462(a), 6 U.S.C. §279(a). However, DHS officials were left with the right to adjudicate immigration benefits under the section. HSA §462(c), 6 U.S.C. §279(c). DHS has entered into an agreement with ORR to retain the right to decide whether a juvenile should be placed in court proceedings. Statement of Principles Between DHS & ORR: Unaccompanied Alien Children Program (Apr. 6, 2004), *reprinted in* 81

No. 15 *Interpreter Releases* 494, 497–98 (Apr. 12, 2004); *F.L. v. Thompson,* 293 F.Supp.2d 86 (D.D.C. 2003) [court determined DHS was the appropriate authority regarding consent to the jurisdiction of the state court].

Eligibility—A child is deemed eligible for long term foster care if s/he is under 21 (although most jurisdictions invoke proceedings only for children under 18) and a juvenile court determines that family reunification is no longer viable. Some states that maintain 18 as a limit may have a provision that allows them to extend their jurisdiction beyond the child's 18th birthday. In that case the juvenile will continue to meet the definition. *Matter of Perez Quintanilla,* A97 383 010 (AAO June 7, 2007) *reprinted in* 84 No. 33 *Interpreter Releases* 2009-19 (Aug. 27, 2007) [applicant continued to meet the eligibility criteria for juvenile status set forth in 8 C.F.R. §204.11(c)(5) where the court continued to extend its jurisdiction over the case beyond the juvenile's 18th birthday pursuant to Fla. Stat. §39.013(2)]. An adopted child or one placed in guardianship will still be deemed to be eligible for long term foster care. 8 C.F.R. §204.11(a). A juvenile may be eligible even if the court does not expressly state the child is dependent on the court where a guardian was appointed. *Matter of Menjivar*, Case No. A70 117 167 (AAU Dec. 27, 1994). The applicant must also be under 21 and unmarried at the time he adjusts status as a special immigrant 8 C.F.R. §204.11(c). USCIS must provide a process to expedite cases so children do not "age out." Memo, Yates, Assoc. Dir. Operations, USCIS, HQADN 70/23 (May 27, 2004), *published on* AILA InfoNet at Doc. No. 04062168. No natural or *prior* adopting parent can obtain residency by virtue of such parentage. INA §101(a)(27)(J)(iii)(II). Certain grounds of inadmissibility are waived (public charge, labor certification, documentation). INA §245(h)((1); 8 C.F.R. §245.1(e)(2)(vi)(B)(3), 1245.1(e)(2)(vi)(B)(3). A waiver of most other noncriminal and nonsecurity grounds is available. A child cannot apply for admission into the U.S. as a court dependent. Miscellaneous and Technical Immigration and Naturalization Amendments of 1991 §301(d)(2). Procedures for filing, eligibility and grounds for revocation are specified at 8 C.F.R. §204.11. The applicant must submit orders from the juvenile court that s/he is dependent and eligible for long term foster care as well as evidence of a determination in judicial or administrative proceeding that it would not be in the juvenile's best interest to return to his or her country. 8 C.F.R. §204.11(d). An approval may be revoked if prior to adjustment or entry as a special immigrant the beneficiary reaches the age of 21, s/he marries, s/he ceases to be dependent or eligible for long-term foster care; or judicial or administrative proceedings determine it is in the juvenile's best interest to be returned to his or her country or his or her parents. 8 C.F.R. §205.1(a)(3)(iii).

Procedure—Application submitted on I-360 form. The I-360 must be supported by: (1) a court order declaring dependency; (2) a court order deeming the juvenile eligible for long-term foster care due to abuse, neglect, and abandonment; (3) a determination from an administrative or judicial proceeding that it is in the juvenile's best interest not to be returned to his or his parents' country of nationality; and (4) proof of the juvenile's age. Memo, Yates, Assoc. Dir. Operations, USCIS, HQADN 70/23 (May 27, 2004), *published on* AILA InfoNet at Doc. No. 04062168. Can file I-360 with AOS application. Can adjust even if out-of-status or EWI. 8 C.F.R. §§245.1(e)(2)(vi)(B)(3), 1245.1(e)(2)(vi)(B)(3). Can also adjust if paroled into U.S., but not if in INS custody unless INS paroles person to custody of state welfare authority or other entity that can petition a state juvenile court. Legal Opinion, Martin, General Counsel, INS, HQ COU 70.6.1.7-P, 50/10.9-P (May 30, 1997), *reprinted in* 74 No. 23 *Interpreter Releases* 964, 978–80 (June 16, 1997). Does not need prior approval of I-360 form to file AOS as is the case for most other special immigrants and, in fact, DHS encourages applicants to file the I-485 with the I-360. Memo, Yates (May 27, 2004), *supra.* In order to obtain the "express consent" of DHS, the USCIS District Director must determine that the dependency process was not to obtain LPR status but to obtain relief from abuse, neglect or abandonment. The most effective method for obtaining the "express consent" of USCIS is for the court to make detailed findings of fact in regard to dependency and the reasons why the juvenile cannot return to his country. Memo, Yates, Assoc. Dir. Operations, USCIS, HQADN 70/23 (May 27, 2004), *published on* AILA InfoNet at Doc. No. 04062168. In the absence of detailed finding the adjudicator must seek to review the transcript of the juvenile proceedings or obtain an affidavit from the court. *Id.* During the adjudication of the petition and during DHS determination of specific and express consent, the juvenile shall not be compelled by DHS to contact a parent who abused him (or family member of the alleged abuser). INA §287(h).

Judicial Review—The decision of the AG to withhold consent from a state court to hold a dependency hearing is subject to judicial review. *Yeboah v. DOJ,* 345 F.3d 216, 220–21 (3d Cir. 2003) [court does have jurisdiction to determine whether the Service should have permitted a state juvenile dependency hearing to establish special immigrant status, but the Service did not abuse its discretion when it chose not to institute proceedings in state court]; *M.B. v. Quarantillo,* 301 F.3d 109, 111–14 (3d Cir. 2002) [rejected INS claim that the matter was committed to agency discretion by law but found on the merits that the DD did not abuse his discretion when he considered whether the person who was under 21 was eligible to be treated as a juvenile under state law]; *Zheng v. Pogash,* 416 F.3d 550, 554–57 (S.D. Tex. 2006) [judicial review was not precluded by INA §242(a)(2)(B)(ii) because the claim is not reviewed under Subchapter II, and review is permitted under APA because there is law to apply in the form of DHS memos about when DHS should grant the state court jurisdiction for a dependency proceeding] *See also F.L.M. v. Florida Department of Children and Families,* 912 So.2d 1264 (Fla. App. 4th 2005) [DHS consent was unnecessary when the child was never in their custody].

10. Person who served honorably for 12 years in Armed Services on active duty—INA §101(a)(27)(K), 8 U.S.C. §1101(a)(27)(K); 8 C.F.R. §§204.9, 245.8(c), 1245.8(c). AFM at 22.3(r).

  10.a. Service must be after Oct. 15, 1978; enlistment must have been lawful enlistment outside of the U.S. under a treaty or agreement in effect on the date of enactment of the law (*i.e.*, with the Philippines, Micronesia, Marshall Islands, or Palau). Can also include person who has served for 6 years who is on active duty and has re-enlisted for 6 more years. 8 C.F.R. §204.9(b)(2)(ii).

  10.b. Includes spouse and children.

  10.c. Permits adjustment.

11. NATO civilian employees—INA §101(a)(27)(L), 8 U.S.C. §1101 (a) (27) (L); 22 C.F.R. §42.32(d)(5). Persons classified under NATO-6 who are: (1) Members of a civil component accompanying a force entering in accordance with the provision of NATO Status-of-Forces Agreement; (2) Members of a civilian component attached to or employed by an Allied Headquarters under the Protocol of the Status of International Military Headquarters. The provision includes spouses and children, and has identical eligibility requirements as G-4 nonimmigrants. Memo, Pearson, Ex. Assoc. Comm. Field Operations, (70/23.1, 70/6.2.22) (Feb.8, 1999), *reprinted in* 76 No. 11 *Interpreter Releases* 452, 463–65 (Mar. 22, 1999).

12. BBG—Broadcasters entering the U.S. to work for the International Broadcasting Bureau of the Broadcasting Board of Governors (BBG) or for a grantee of the Broadcasting Board. INA §101(a)(27)(M), 8 U.S.C. §1101(a)(27)(M); 22 C.F.R. §42.32(d)(8); 8 C.F.R. §204.13, 66 Fed. Reg. 51819–21 (Oct. 11, 2001). The section includes accompanying spouse and children.

  12.a. Applicable Petitioners: BBG or a grantee of the BBG which is Radio Free Asia, Inc or Radio Free Europe/Radio Liberty Inc.

  12.b. Broadcaster Defined as: reporter, writer, translator, editor, producer or announcer for news broadcasts; hosts for news broadcasts, news analysis, editorial and other broadcast features or a new analysis specialist. It does not include person performing purely technical or support services. 8 C.F.R. §204.13(a).

  12.c. Numerical Limitation. 100 visas per fiscal year.

  12.d. Procedure: I-360 petition accompanied by information that includes: (1) the job title and a full description of the job to be performed; and (2) the broadcasting expertise held by the beneficiary including how long he has been performing duties that relate to the prospective position or a statement on how he possesses the necessary skills qualifying him for the position.

13. Translators with the U.S. Armed Forces—National Defense Authorization Act for Fiscal Year 2006, PL 109-163, 119 Stat. 3136 (Jan. 6, 2006), Title X, Subtitle F, §1059; PL 110-36, 121 Stat. 227 (June 15, 2007).

  13.a. Provides that nationals of Iraq or Afghanistan are eligible for special immigrant status if: (1) they worked directly with U.S. Armed Forces or Chief of Mission as a translator or interpreter for a period of at least 12 months; (2) obtained a favorable written recommendation from the chief of mission, or a general or flag officer in the chain of command; (3) cleared a background check and screening as determined by the chief of mission, general or flag officer before filing the petition; and (4) they are otherwise admissible except for 212(a)(4) (public charge).

13.b. Procedure—Must file an I-360. There are 500 visas available per year. Spouse and children may accompany or follow to join. Unauthorized employment and an applicant's out-of-status under INA §245(c) are waived by virtue of PL 110-36. Certain naturalization periods also waived.

14. Iraqis Providing Faithful and Valuable Service to U.S., PL 110-181 (HR 4986), Title XII, Subtitle C §1244, 122 Stat. 3 (Jan. 28, 2008)

14.a. Provides that Iraqi citizens or nationals who: (1) were employed by or on behalf of the U.S. in Iraq after Mar. 20, 2003 for not less than one year; (2) provided faithful and valuable service to the U.S. which is documented in a positive recommendation or evaluation by the employees' senior supervisor and approved by the Chief of Mission; (3) have experienced or are experiencing ongoing serious threats as a consequence of employment by the U.S.; (4) are otherwise eligible to receive an IV; (5) are otherwise admissible except for public charge; and (6) submit an I-360 petition are eligible for residency as special immigrants.

14.b. Spouse and children are included who accompany or follow to join. Also includes surviving spouse or children who had an approved petition that was revoked on the death of the principal if the petition would have been approved.

14.c. 5000 visas per year.

14.d. Existence of another IR or preference petition is not a basis to deny special immigrant status.

VI. FIFTH PREFERENCE—EMPLOYMENT CREATION (INVESTORS)—INA §203(b)(5), 8 U.S.C. §1153(b)(5); 8 C.F.R. §204.6; *AFM* at 22.4; 21st Century Department of Justice Appropriations Authorization Act, PL 107-273, Div. C, Title I, Subtitle B, §§11031-37, 116 Stat. 1758 (Nov. 2, 2002).

A. *Generally*—Allows for conditional residency for persons who, after Nov. 29, 1990, invest $1,000,000 (or under certain circumstances $500,000) in a new commercial enterprise that employs 10 USCs or authorized immigrant workers full-time and engage in the business through day-to-day management or policy formation. 7.1% of worldwide visas per year of which 3,000 are set aside for "targeted employment areas."

B. *Person must invest in a new commercial enterprise*

1. Commercial enterprise includes a broad spectrum of business relationships including limited partnerships, holding companies and their wholly-owned subsidiaries, provided they are all for profit business operations.

2. An investor no longer has to "establish" the commercial enterprise. He satisfies the statute if he "invests" in a new commercial enterprise. INA §§203(b)(5)(A)(i), 216A(d)(1)(A). Although INS took the position that the participation in a partnership that was already in existence at the time of the partner's participation is not a new commercial enterprise because the investor did not "establish" the new enterprise *Matter of Izummi,* 22 I&N Dec. 169, 197–99 (Assoc. Comm. 1998), Congress abolished the "establishment" requirement and now a person who invests in a new commercial enterprise can apply for EB-5 even if he did not establish the business. INA §203(b)(5)(A)(i).

3. A *new* commercial enterprise 8 C.F.R. §204.6(h) includes:

3.a. A company formed after Nov. 29, 1990—The investor is not required to "establish" a new commercial enterprise but for the enterprise to be "new" the investment must be in a company that was formed after Nov. 29, 1990. 8 C.F.R. §204.6(e). Memo, Yates, Acting Assoc. Director, Operations USCIS, HQ40/6.1.3 (June 10, 2003), *published on* AILA InfoNet at Doc. No. 03061744.

3.b. A company formed before Nov. 29, 1990—A commercial enterprise in existence prior to Nov. 29, 1990 will be considered "new" for purposes of the law if: (a) it has been restructured or reorganized so that a new commercial enterprise results; or (b) it has been expanded so that a substantial change in the net worth or number of employees has occurred. Memo, Yates, Acting Assoc. Director, Operations BUSCIS, HQ40/6.1.3 (June 10, 2003), *published on* AILA InfoNet at Doc. No. 03061744.

(1) The mere change in decor and implementation of a new business plan is not sufficient restructuring to result in a new commercial enterprise. *Matter of Soffici,* 22 I&N Dec. 158, 165–66 (Assoc. Comm. 1998) [purchase of a 24-year-old Howard Johnson motel]. If the basis is due to restructuring, the petitioner may not create a net loss of employment. *Matter of Hsiung,* 22 I&N Dec. 201 (Assoc. Comm. 1998).

(2) Substantial change means a 40% increase in either the net worth or the number of employees. The expansion of an existing business so that its net worth or employees increases by 40% is addressed at 8 C.F.R. §204.6(h). The investor still needs to show the minimum financial investment. However, the 40% increase can be reached by counting all the capital contributed by other investors even investors who are USCs/ LPRs and/or not desirous of applying for status. Memo, Aleinikoff, General Counsel, INS, HQ 204.27-C (Jan. 31, 1995), *reprinted in* 73 No. 44 *Interpreter Releases* 1617, 1625–29 (Nov. 18, 1996).

C. *Investments (Amount)*—INA §203(b)(5)(C); 8 C.F.R. §204.6(f):

1. Invests (after Nov. 29, 1990) *or* is actively in the process of investing, capital of $1,000,000; or

2. Invests (after Nov. 29, 1990) or is in process of investing, $500,000 if the investment is in a targeted employment area (*i.e.*, a rural area of less than 20,000 population or an area which has experienced high unemployment of at least 150% of the national average).

3. Investment can be cash, equipment, inventory, other tangible property, cash equivalents, and indebtedness secured by assets owned by the entrepreneur, provided that the entrepreneur is personally and primarily liable and that the assets of the new commercial enterprise are not used to secure any of the indebtedness. A loan to the commercial enterprise or any other debt arrangement between the entrepreneur and the new commercial enterprise does *not* constitute an investment. 8 C.F.R. §204.6(e); *Matter of Soffici,* 22 I&N Dec. 158, 162–63 (Assoc. Comm. 1998) [loans to business do not constitute investment]. Retained earning are also not considered to be an investment. *Kenkhuis v. INS,* 2003 WL 22124059 (W.D.Tex. Mar. 7, 2003). Payment of partnership expenses does *not* constitute an investment because it is not "for the purpose of generating a return on the capital placed at risk." *Matter of Izummi,* 22 I&N Dec. 169, 176–80 (Assoc. Comm. 1998). [distinguishing between direct investment and expenses in employment generating enterprise and indirect investment through company whose purpose is solely to attract investors].

4. All capital is valued in U.S. dollars and at fair market value. 8 C.F.R. §204.6(e). Fair market value of a note is determined by factors such as the fair market value of the assets securing the note, the extent to which the assets are amendable to seizure, and the present value of the note. *Matter of Hsiung,* 22 I&N Dec. 201 (Assoc. Comm. 1998); *Matter of Izummi,* 22 I&N Dec. 169, 191–94 (Assoc. Comm. 1998) [fair market value is determined by whether note is adequately secured and the terms of the note including the payment schedule].

5. Investment can come from funds in joint account owned by petitioner and spouse. Memo, Weinig, Acting Asst. Comm. Adjudications (Aug. 5, 1992), *reprinted in* 11 *AILA Monthly Mailing* 776 (Oct. 1992). This does not extend to joint accounts by other family members. *Matter of Soffici,* 22 I&N Dec. 158, 164 (Assoc. Comm. 1998) [joint account of father and son cannot be attributed solely to investor]. Petitioner must establish that the investment comes from accounts under his name. *Matter of Ho,* 22 I&N Dec. 206 (Assoc. Comm. 1998) [unidentified account].

6. The investment must be in only one commercial enterprise and an investor cannot meet the requirements for the removal of conditions by combining investments in multiple commercial enterprises. Memo, Yates, Acting Assoc. Director, Operations BUSCIS, HQ40/6.1.3 (June 10, 2003), *published on* AILA InfoNet at Doc. No. 03061744.

D. *Investment (At Risk)*—8 C.F.R. §204.6(j)(2)

1. Promissory Notes—8 C.F.R. §204.6(j)(2)(v)

1.a. An unsecured promissory note is not an investment of capital. A petitioner must demonstrate that the note is secured by his or her property. *Matter of Hsiung,* 22 I&N Dec. 201 (Assoc. Comm. 1998) [where petitioner failed to demonstrate that property securing note was his the petition was denied]. The fair market value of the promissory note and not the face value govern the amount of the investment. Fair market value is determined from the time of filing through the period of conditional residency. Fair market value is determined by factors such as the fair market value of the assets securing the note, the extent to which the assets are amenable to seizure, the present value of the note, the terms of the note, the discounted amount of the cost for seizing the security interest if necessary, and the discounted value of the note. *Matter of Hsiung,* 22 I&N Dec. 201 (Assoc. Comm. 1998); *Matter of Izummi,* 22 I&N Dec. 169, 191–94 (Assoc. Comm. 1998).

1.b. Petitioner must "substantially complete" his payments on a signed valid promissory note prior to the end of the 2-year conditional residency period. *Matter of Izummi,* 22 I&N Dec. 169, 193–94 (Assoc. Comm. 1998) [five annual payments of $18,000 with balloon of $290,000 plus a completed payment of $120,000 are insufficient when reduced to present value and are outside the 2-year period]; 8 C.F.R. §216.6(c)(1)(ii), (iii) [requires investor to have "substantially met" the capital investment requirement].

1.c. Promissory Notes Secured by Foreign Property—PRC national cannot secure note by property, because it is not enforceable in PRC. Memo, Adjudications, INS, HQ 70/8.5-P (Oct. 20, 1997), *published on* AILA InfoNet at Doc. No. 97102091. *See also* 75 No. 1 *Interpreter Releases* 14-16, 27-33 (Jan. 5, 1998). The extent to which the assets securing the note are amendable to seizure is also a consideration of the note's fair market value. *Matter of Hsiung,* 22 I&N Dec. 201 (Assoc. Comm. 1998).

2. Trusts—Must ensure that funds are fully available from any trust agreement.

3. Guaranteed Interest Payments and Guaranteed Returns—Where promissory notes guarantee interest payments, these arrangements may be considered unqualifying "loans" or other debt arrangements, and not a contribution of qualifying "capital." Similarly, guaranteed annual returns that are used to meet part of the investors required payment is impermissible. *Matter of Izummi,* 22 I&N Dec. 169, 180–82 (Assoc. Comm. 1998).

4. Redemption Agreements—Prior to completing all cash payments under a promissory note, an investor may not enter into an agreement granting him the right to sell his interest back to the partnership. Also, the investor cannot enter into such an agreement prior to the end of the two-year period as a CR. *Matter of Izummi,* 22 I&N Dec. 169, 185–87 (Assoc. Comm. 1998).

5. Secured Loans—A loan taken from a bank with the investment as security (*e.g.*, mortgage and security agreement) is not an investment. *Matter of Sofici,* 22 I&N Dec. 158, 162–63 (Assoc. Comm. 1998) [bank loan secured by hotel property is not an investment even where the investor is also personally liable on the loan because the bank is not obligated to proceed against the investor].

6. Reserves—Funds that are set aside as reserves and are not available to the job-creating enterprise cannot be considered part of the capital contribution. *Matter of Izummi,* 22 I&N Dec. 169, 188–91 (Assoc. Comm. 1998).

7. Sole owner or person who exercises sole control over business cannot meet the at risk requirement by simply putting the funds into the company account, because s/he can withdraw it at will. *Matter of Ho,* 22 I&N Dec. 206 (Assoc. Comm. 1998). [must present some evidence of concrete business activity, not simply generalized plans].

8. INS General Counsel has challenged most of the investor plans that minimize investor risk finding that they can be revoked if previously granted. This includes investment plans that involve guaranteed interest payments, buy and sell options at a fixed price other than fair market value, and limitations on the amount of capital actually available for the job creating enterprise. Memo, Martin, G.C., HQ COU 70/6.1.8 and 70/9.-P (Dec. 19, 1997), *reprinted in* 75 No. 9 *Interpreter Releases* 332–49 (Mar. 9, 1998).

E. *Source of Funds*—Petitioner must show the source of funds and that they are legitimate. *Matter of Soffici,* 22 I&N Dec. 158, 164–65 (Assoc. Comm. 1998); *Matter of Izummi,* 22 I&N Dec. 169, 194–95 (Assoc. Comm. 1998).

F. *Multiple Investors/Partnerships*—8 C.F.R. §204.6(g).

1. Multiple Investors—8 C.F.R. §204.6(g). Can have multiple investors including nonpetitioners (*e.g.*, USCs). Each investor who wishes to qualify must independently meet the capital and employee requirements. All full-time employee positions, however, may be credited to the qualifying investors.
2. Partnerships—A limited partnership is considered a commercial enterprise under the law. INA §§203(b)(5)(A)(i), 216A(f), 8 U.S.C. §§1153(b)(5)(A)(i), 1186b(f). To qualify an investor may join the partnership after its formation because an investor is no longer required to "establish" a commercial enterprise but rather to "invest" in one. INA §203(b)(5)(A)(i). If there is a limited partnership agreement it must provide investor with rights, powers and duties under the Unified Limited Partnership Act. If the limited partnership is an investment fund investing in unrelated companies, then investor's management is related to the fund, not the companies. Letter, Weinig, Acting Asst. Comm. CO 204.27-C (Aug. 5, 1992), *reprinted in* 69 No. 43 *Interpreter Releases* 1440, 1452–53 (Nov. 9, 1992).

G. *Employment Creation*—8 C.F.R. §204.6(e). Must create full-time employment for at least 10 qualifying USC or immigrant workers (other than applicant or his or her immediate family) within the 2-year CR period.

1. Independent contractors are *not* considered employees. 8 C.F.R. §204.6(e).
2. Employment is defined in terms of the position not the person requiring full-time (35 hours/week) employment. INA §203(b)(5)(D), 8 U.S.C. §1153(b)(5)(D). Thus, investors in such industries as the construction industry can qualify even where individual workers are changed if the position continues.
3. U.S. worker includes USC, LPR, CR, temporary resident, asylee, refugee, grantee of suspension of deportation or cancellation of removal. It does not include NIV holders or family members of the investor. 8 C.F.R. §204.6(e).
4. Where investment only sustains current employees but does not create new full time jobs, it does *not* meet the jobs requirement unless investment is in a "troubled business" (net loss for 1 or 2 years exceeding 20% of net worth). Legal Opinion, Virtue, Acting General Counsel, CO 204.6 (Sept. 10, 1993), *reprinted in* 72 No. 34 *Interpreter Releases* 1191, 1220–31 (Sept. 1, 1995). 8 C.F.R. §§204.6(e), 204.6(j)(4)(ii).
5. Investment with regional center enables petitioner to count indirect job creation. 8 C.F.R. §204.6(j)(4)(iii).

H. *Evidence Required*—8 C.F.R. §204.6(j)

1. Regarding the enterprise [8 C.F.R. §204.6(j)(1)]
   - 1.a. Articles of incorporation or business organization documents; or
   - 1.b. Authorization to do business in state or municipality.
2. Regarding the Investment [8 C.F.R. §204.6(j)(2)]
   - 2.a. Documents evidencing investment which may include bank statements, evidence of purchased assets; evidence of property transferred from abroad; stock certificates given for investment; or loan or mortgage agreements.
3. Regarding obtaining the capital through lawful means [8 C.F.R. §204.6(j)(3)]
   - 3.a. Foreign business registration records;
   - 3.b. Corporate, partnership and personal tax returns filed within 5 years;
   - 3.c. Evidence identifying other sources of capital; or

3.d. Certified copies of any judgments or evidence of all pending governmental civil or criminal actions, administrative actions, and any private civil actions involving monetary judgments within the past 15 years.

3.e. Where source of funds are from sale of house or business, investor needs to provide sales contracts or deeds. *Matter of Soffici,* 22 I&N Dec. 158, 164–65 (BIA 1998).

3.f. Petitioner's level of income during the previous years. *Matter of Izummi,* 22 I&N Dec. 169, 195 (Assoc. Comm. 1998).

4. Job creation of 10 jobs [8 C.F.R. §204.6(j)(4)]

4.a. I-9s, tax records if employees already hired, including proof that they are working full time, *Matter of Ho,* 22 I&N Dec. 206 (Assoc. Comm. 1998) [where I-9s but not pay stubs and payroll records were produced, petition denied]; or

4.b. A copy of a comprehensive business plan demonstrating where the 10 employees will be hired and giving approximate dates within the next 2 years.

(1) A comprehensive business plan should contain, at a minimum: (1) a description of the business, its products and/or services, and its objectives; (2) a market analysis, including the names of competing businesses and their relative strengths and weaknesses, a comparison of the competition's products and pricing structures, and a new description of the target market/prospective customers of the new commercial enterprise; (3) a list of the required permits and licenses obtained; (4) a description of the manufacturing or production process, including the material required and the supply sources if appropriate; (5) a marketing strategy, including pricing, advertising and servicing; (6) the organizational structure and its personnel's experience; (7) the staffing requirements and a timetable for hiring, including job descriptions for all positions; and (8) sales, cost, and income projections and detail the bases for them. *Matter of Ho,* 22 I&N Dec. 206, 212–13 (Assoc. Comm. 1998) [rejected four page business plan].

4.c. If the enterprise is a "troubled business" (having lost 20% of its net worth) it must provide a comprehensive business plan and proof that the existing employees will be retained.

4.d. Jobs must be created in the targeted employment area if petitioner is relying on the reduced $500,000 investment. *Matter of Izummi,* 22 I&N Dec. 169, 173–74 (Assoc. Comm. 1998) [where business established in targeted area but the business is to give loans to companies who employ persons outside the area, the job creation requirement is not met].

5. Petitioner will be engaging in business on day-to-day basis or through policy formation [8 C.F.R. §204.6(j)(5)]

5.a. Title and description of his or her job duties;

5.b. Evidence that s/he is corporate officer and director; or

5.c. If partnership, the partners management or policy making activities consistent with rights, powers and duties normally granted limited partners under the Uniform Limited Partnership Act, 8 C.F.R. §204.6(j)(5)(iii).

6. Targeted Employment Area (where applicable) [8 C.F.R. §204.6(j)(6)]

6.a. Evidence of statistical area;

6.b. Letter meeting requirements from state agency that area is high unemployment. 8 C.F.R. §204.6(i). Letter or statistical information must be current. *Matter of Soffici,* 22 I&N Dec. 158, 159–60 (Assoc. Comm. 1998).

I. *Application Process (I-526)*—8 C.F.R. §§204.6(a)–(d). Priority date established on filing. EB-5 petitions (I-526) as well removal of conditions applications (I-829) must be filed at the California or Texas Service Centers. 63 Fed. Reg. 67135 (Dec. 4, 1998), *reprinted in* 75 No. 47 *Interpreter Releases* 1695, 1710 (Dec. 14, 1998).

J. *Conditional Grant*—Similar to CR status for marriages. INA §216A(a); 8 C.F.R. §216; 59 Fed. Reg. 26587 (May 23, 1994). Can remove condition after 2 years.

K. *Investor Must Petition for Removal of CR Status*—Must petition within 90 days before 2nd anniversary. File request on I-829. Petitioner need not be physically present in U.S. to file. 8 C.F.R. §§216.6(a)(1), (3). AFM at 25.2; Memo, Pearson, Ex. Assoc. Comm., Office of Field Operations (Mar. 3, 2000), *published on* AILA InfoNet at Doc. No. 00060702.

1. Petition must contain facts and information demonstrating that, 8 C.F.R. §216.6(a)(4):

 1.a. the conditional resident invested or was actively investing the required capital;

 1.b. the conditional resident sustained the enterprise and investment (*e.g.*, bank statements, invoices, receipts, contracts, business licenses, and tax returns, including quarterly statements) requirements, *i.e.*, "substantially met the capital investment requirement of the statute"; AFM at 25.2(e)(4)(C)

 1.c. the conditional resident "created or can be expected to create within a reasonable period of time 10 full-time jobs for qualifying employees" AFM at 25.2(e)(4)(D).

2. AG must make determination within 90 days of filing *or* interview (whichever is later). 8 C.F.R. §216.6(c). However, INS extended the period to one year to process the removal petition, Memo, Redman, Acting Asst. Comm., Adjudications, HQ 70/23.12-P (Oct. 9, 1997), *reprinted in* 74 No. 43 *Interpreter Releases* 1714, 1732 (Nov. 7, 1997). When application is timely filed at a service center, the director may approve it, may request additional evidence, may refer the applicant for an interview at a district office or may deny the I-829 if the eligibility requirements have not been met. AFM at 25.2(e).

3. Travel During Pendency of I-829 and Extension of I-829—USCIS is required to continue to document CR status until CR status has been removed or the I-829 is denied. Memo, Yates, Assoc. Dir. Operations, USCIS and Cuddihy, Director, Office of Refugee, Asylum and International Operations, USCIS, "Extension of Status for Conditional Residents with Pending or Denied Form I-829, Petitions Subject to Public Law 107-273," (Jan. 18, 2005), *published on* AILA InfoNet at Doc. No. 05012167. Even if USCIS denies I-829 it must still provide a temporary I-551 in CR's passport or Form I-94 with a temporary I-551 pending a final order of removal. AFM §25.2(g); Memo, Pearson, Ex. Assoc. Comm., Office of Field Operations (Mar. 3, 2000), *published on* AILA InfoNet at Doc. No. 00060702; Memo, Redman, Acting Asst. Comm., Adjudications, INS, HQ 70/23.13-C (Oct. 9, 1997), *reprinted in* 74 No. 43 *Interpreter Releases* 1714, 1731 (Nov. 7, 1997). Persons who are overseas with an expired I-551 may be admitted by obtaining a transportation letter at the consulate. Yates & Cuddihy, *supra.* A CR who presents an expired I-551 with a receipt issued within the past six months for an I-829 may be admitted pursuant to 8 C.F.R. §211.1(a)(5) if he seeks admission after a temporary absence of less than one year.

4. Erroneously approved or subsequently invalidated I-526—USCIS took the position that where it or INS approved I-526s and granted conditional resident status where the petition was not approvable based on subsequent interim decisions (*e.g.*, *Matter of Izummi*), it had no statutory authority to approve the removal of conditional residency (I-829). Letter, Dixon, Deputy Gen. Counsel (HQCOU 70/11.1-C) (Sept. 10, 1998) at p.3, *reprinted in* 75 No. 37 *Interpreter Releases* 1335, 1344–55 (Sept. 28, 1998); AFM at §25.2(f)(9)(A) (2005). [This is true even if the Service granted the original I-526 petition in error and the petitioner has complied with the investment plan outlined in Form I-526] *But see Chang v. U.S.*, 327 F.3d 911 (9th Cir. 2003) [under *Montgomery Ward v. FTC,* 691 F.2d 1322 (9th Cir. 1982) INS may not retroactively apply *Izummi* and it progeny to deny pending I-829 petitions]. The specific language in the AFM was removed Dec. 21, 2006 and now simply states: "USCIS lacks authority to grant a Form I-829 if the petition does not meet the statutory and regulatory requirements. If the service center director determines that the conditional resident has not established eligibility to have the conditions removed under the statute and regulations, the petition must be denied." AFM at 25.2(e)(6)(A)(i). *See also* AFM at 25.2(g)(8)(A)(i) [denial by field office director].

L. *Termination of Status*

1. If AG, during 2-year period, determines that it was not a qualifying investment under INA §216A(b)(1)(B)(i) because:

 1.a. Enterprise established solely to evade immigration laws;

1.b. No commercial enterprise was established;

1.c. Investor did not invest or was not in process of actively investing;

1.d. The funds for investment were obtained other than through legal means. 8 C.F.R. §216.3(a).

1.e. Investor was not sustaining investment as commercial enterprise; *or*

1.f. Investor was not otherwise conforming to investor status.

2. If petition not filed within the 90-day period, unless good cause and extenuating circumstances shown. INA §216A(d)(2).
3. If alien does not appear for interview, unless there is good cause shown. INA §216A(c)(2)(A)(ii).
4. If AG, after interview, determines that the facts in the petition are untrue.
5. District Director is empowered to hold I-829 denial and give conditional resident opportunity to file a new I-526. Memo, Pearson (Mar. 3, 2000), *supra.*
6. Children/Spouse—If the principal investor is terminated, spouse and children are terminated if they obtained visa on conditional basis. INA §216A(c)(2)(A). If child becomes 21 (or marries) or the spouse obtains a divorce after conditional basis is granted, the condition may be removed by filing I-829 jointly or separately from principal and if approved the "child" or ex-spouse remain LPRs. 8 C.F.R. §216.6(a). In addition, if entrepreneur dies during the 2-year period, spouse and children may become LPRs upon a showing that investment and other conditions were met. 8 C.F.R. §216.6(a)(6).

M. *Removal Proceedings*

1. Investor can be deported under INA §237(a)(1)(D)(i), 8 U.S.C. §1227(a)(1)(D)(i), if status terminated. If status terminated because AG, during 2-year conditional residence period or after an interview at the end of the 2-year period, found applicant ineligible, the burden is on the AG by a preponderance of the evidence. INA §§216A(b)(2), (c)(3)(D). However, if the investor fails to appear without valid cause at the interview, or fails to file petition removing condition, the burden is on the investor to establish eligibility. INA §216A(c)(2)(B).
2. Stay of Deportation—AG may stay the deportation proceeding to give an investor an opportunity to file petition to remove CR where s/he failed to file within 90-day period.

N. *Naturalization*

1. Conditional permanent residents enjoy the same rights, privileges, responsibilities and duties" as LPRs including the right to apply for naturalization. 8 C.F.R. §216.1. The EB-5 statute specifically provides that a conditional resident for purposes of naturalization "shall be considered to have been admitted" as an LPR. INA §216A(e), 8 U.S.C. §1186b(e). In *Abghari, et al. v. Gonzales,* ___F.Supp.2d ___, Case No. CV 05-1210 FMC (PLAx) (C.D. Cal. Feb. 15, 2006) the court rejected the government's claim that the statute only provided that a CR could apply for naturalization but could not get approved until his conditional residence status was lifted as he was made an LPR. The court ordered the government to adjudicate the N-400 within 120 days whether or not the CR status had been removed.

O. *Immigrant Investor Pilot Program*

1. Section 610 of the Appropriations Act, PL 102-395, 106 Stat. 1828 (Oct. 6, 1992); 58 Fed. Reg. 44606–08 (Aug. 24, 1993); 8 C.F.R. §204.6(m), established a pilot program for immigrant investors that would permit investment through regional centers that would relax the job creation requirements for employment creation visas. Section 11037, 21st Century DOJ Appropriations Authorization Act, PL 107-273, 116 Stat. 1758 (Nov. 2, 2002) amended the pilot program. The program is limited to 3000 visas per year and has been extended to Oct. 1, 2008 [PL 108-156, 117 Stat. 1944 (Dec. 3, 2003), *reprinted in* 80 No. 47 *Interpreter Releases* 1675 (Dec. 15, 2003)]. The program is designated by USCIS based upon a "general proposal." USCIS has established a separate Investor and Regional Center Unit within the Business and Trade Branch, OPRD at USCIS. Memo, Yates, Assoc. Dir. Operations, USCIS, HQPRD 70/6.2.8 (Jan. 19, 2005), *published on* AILA InfoNet at Doc. No. 05012663.

2. A regional center wishing to participate must demonstrate how "it will promote economic growth through increased export sales, improved regional productivity, job creation, or increased domestic capital investment." An application should be approved if the regional center bases its demonstration on "a general prediction" of certain conditions including direct or indirect job creation, positive economic impacts and the kinds of commercial enterprises that will attract investors. Section 11037, 21st Century Department of Justice Appropriations Authorization Act, PL 107-273, 116 Stat. 1758 (Nov. 2, 2002).

3. The investor must meet all criteria of employment-creation investors, except s/he can demonstrate that investment in the regional center will create jobs indirectly beyond the commercial enterprise. 8 C.F.R. §204.6(m)(7).

4. A listing of the regional centers can be found in **Appendix K,** *infra.*

P. *Litigation Concerning the Investor Program*—A number of cases are litigating various issues under the Investor Program as a result of the *Matter of Izummi* decision and its progeny and the General Counsel's December, 1997 memorandum.

Failure to Approve I-526. In *R.L. Investment Limited Partners and Wanxuan Zou v. INS,* 86 F.Supp.2d 1014 (D.C. Hawaii 2000), *aff'd* 273 F.3d 874 (9th Cir. 2001), the district court granted summary judgment for the government and denied plaintiffs' challenge to the denial of an I-526 petition that was virtually identical to others approved before *Izummi* on APA (notice and comment and arbitrary and capricious conduct) and estoppel grounds. In *Spencer Enterprises, Inc. v. U.S.,* 345 F.3d 683 (9th Cir. 2003), the Court determined that there was jurisdiction, notwithstanding INA §242(a)(2)(B)(ii), to review the denial of an immigrant investor (I-526) petition, but that there was substantial evidence for the AAO's determination that the investor's business plan was not credible enough to demonstrate the need for 10 full-time workers.

Failure to approve I-829. In *Chang v. U.S.,* 327 F.3d 911 (9th Cir. 2003) the district court determined under the retroactivity analysis in *Montgomery Ward v. FTC,* 691 F.2d 1322 (9th Cir. 1982) that INS may not retroactively apply *Izummi* and it progeny to pending I-829 petitions. The Court also ruled that legislation permitting I-829 applicants to submit new applications where post-*Izummi* standards would apply did not moot plaintiffs retroactivity claim.

Criminal proceedings have been successfully brought against the persons who organized the Interbank investment program on the grounds of immigration and wire fraud and money laundering. *U.S. v. O'Connor,* 158 F.Supp.2d 697 (E.D. Va. 2001).

Legal Malpractice. Where plaintiff's lawyer failed to disclose his longstanding business relationship with the owners of the corporation his client was investing in and failed to disclose to the client the small chance of success and substantial requirements under the E-5 program prior to plaintiff's investment, a cause of action could be maintained for legal malpractice. *Serova v. Teplen,* Case No. 05 CIV. 6748 (HB) (S.D.N.Y. Feb. 16, 2006) [retained legal malpractice claim but dismissed claims for breach of fiduciary duty, securities fraud and other causes of action].

Q. *Special Legislation for Certain Investors with CR Status or Approved I-526 Petitions*—The 21st Century DOJ Appropriations Authorization Act provides benefits, including the right to reapply for permanent residency to investors: (1) who filed their I-526 petitions and had them approved by the INS between Jan. 1, 1995 and Aug. 31, 1998; (2) who obtained conditional residence status and (3) who, before Nov. 2, 2002 (the date of enactment) filed an I-829 to remove their CR status. If they qualify and their I-829 has been denied, they must file motions to reopen the I-829 within 60 days of Nov. 2, 2002. If they have a final order of removal their cases shall be reopened as long as they file a motion to reopen within that time period. If they are outside the U.S. the USCIS must parole them back into the country. Unless there was a material misrepresentation, USCIS must reopen and decide whether the investor met the 10 job creating/preserving requirement and the financial investment requirement. USCIS must make the same determinations for those I-829s that are pending if the investor had an approved I-526 between Jan. 1, 1995 and Aug. 31, 1998. The investor has a choice as to which date the USCIS will use to determine the jobs/investment requirements: (1) the date the I-829 was filed; (2) six months after the I-829 was filed; or (3) the date USCIS makes its determination. If the I-829 is denied because of a material misrepresentation, jobs, or investment, the investor is first given an opportunity to rebut the decision and may thereafter appeal to the BIA and then the circuit court under INA §242(a)(1). If the application is denied because of jobs/investment, the investor is also given an additional two years to file a new investment if s/he wishes to do so. The investor will be credited with the jobs preserved and the investment made on the first investment. The "new" investment could have occurred before or after the determination on the first I-829. If the first or second I-829 is denied the person may also seek review before an IJ in a removal proceeding. Children of investors will continue to be treated as such if they were under 21 at time they were granted CR status.

Similar procedures are established for EB-5 investors: (1) who had I-526 petitions that were approved between Jan. 1, 1995 and Aug. 31, 1998; (2) who timely filed for an IV or AOS before Nov. 2, 2002; (3) who never became CRs; and (4) who are otherwise admissible. If the I-526 petition was revoked because of failure to comply with the capital investment requirement, it is automatically reinstated. If the AOS or IV is no longer pending because the investor departed the U.S. without advance parole or s/he was determined not to qualify because of the capital investment requirement, the case is automatically reopened unless there was a material misrepresentation. If the investor applied for AOS but is now overseas, USCIS will establish a procedure to allow him or her to be paroled into the U.S. The applicant must within 2 years file an I-829 and will be given credit for funds invested and jobs created or saved prior to and after the date of enactment. The investor may measure his compliance with the jobs/investment requirements by the date s/he filed the AOS application or the date USCIS adjudicates the I-829 petition.

Until regulations are promulgated the USCIS may not deny an I-829, AOS application or proceed with or place someone in removal proceedings.

The law also defines full time employment as a position requiring 35 hours per week, even if the employees (such as those in the construction industry) are interchangeable. The requirement that an investor "establish" a new commercial enterprise is eliminated and it is replaced only with a requirement that a person "invest" in a commercial enterprise. The legislation also specifically recognizes limited partnerships as commercial enterprises. The legislation also liberalizes requirements of the pilot immigration program by allowing for the approval of such programs based upon "general predictions contained in the proposal, concerning the kinds of commercial enterprises that will receive capital from aliens, the jobs that will be created directly or indirectly as a result of such capital investments, and the other positive economic effects such capital investments will have." It also changes the law to clarify that increased exports is not necessarily a requirement to approve a pilot program.

VII. COMMON ISSUES IN EMPLOYMENT-BASED IMMIGRATION

A. *Petition Process*

1. Employment-based immigration (with the exception of special immigrants, persons of extraordinary ability, national interest waiver cases, and investors) will require the employer or prospective employer (or in the national interest waiver case the beneficiary in lieu of an employer) to submit a petition. INA §204(b), 8 U.S.C. §1154(b), 8 C.F.R. §204.5(c), O.I. §204.4. The first three categories of employment-based applications (including persons of extraordinary ability) are filed on an I-140 (which can be submitted electronically, *see* Ch. 5, section II.J (p.628), *supra*). Application for special immigrants are filed on Form I-360. Investor applications are filed on Form I-526. 8 C.F.R. §§204.5(a), 204.6(a). To determine where petitions are filed in the ever-changing strategies of USCIS it is imperative that the instructions to the *current* petition are thoroughly reviewed. To review the SOPs of USCIS in regard to I-140 petitions *see* USCIS, I-140 Immigrant Petition for Alien Worker, SOPs *published on* AILA InfoNet at Doc. No. 07083067. Copies may be submitted instead of original documents except for the LC. 8 C.F.R. §204.5(g)(1). The employer-petitioner must be doing business in U.S. *Matter of A. Dow Steam Specialties, Ltd.*, 19 I&N Dec. 389 (Comm. 1986) [foreign parent company of L-1 transferee cannot file I-140 where it has no presence in U.S.]. The employer in the petition must also demonstrate that it has the "financial ability to pay the wage offered and that the employee beneficiary meets the minimum requirements to perform the job satisfactorily." *Chang v. Thornburgh*, 719 F.Supp. 532, 536 (N.D. Tex. 1989). The employee must intend to accept the employment pursuant to the terms and conditions of the LC and I-140. *Matter of* ___ (AAO Mar. 13, 2003) [denied adjustment of status because employee was currently working as a document control analyst for $50,000 and it was not reasonable to believe she would quit the job to accept the LC/I-140 position as a live-in housekeeper for $11,378 when she had not worked for the employer during the 12 years in the U.S.] *reported in* 80 No. 43 *Interpreter Releases* 1554–55 (Nov. 10, 2003).

1.a. Where the employee is terminated subsequent to the submission of the I-140 petition, the employer is *not* obligated to inform USCIS that the employee is terminated. Letter, Simmons, Branch Chief, Business and Trade Services, HQ/70/ 6.1.3 (Oct. 20, 1999), *reprinted in* 77 No. 18 *Interpreter Releases* 610 (May 8, 2000).

1.b. In order for the petition to be invalidated USCIS must demonstrate that the offered position no longer exists. *Matter of* ___ EAC 99 011 52474 (AAO Mar. 7, 2001) [where employer applied for position of tutor but two of the three children were already college students, AAO reversed the DD's denial because he did not establish that the offered position was no longer available].

2. Post-Submission Changes to a Petition—The AAO has determined that an unapprovable petition cannot be cured by post-submission changes. *Matter of Izummi,* 22 I&N Dec 169, 175 (Assoc. Comm. 1998) [prohibited post-submission changes in employment creation petition]. The Service's current interpretation is that "the standard for amending a petition is ...whether the petition was approvable on the date it was filed. Any amendment based on facts (such as changes to a business plan or new investment agreements) that come into existence after the filing date, must be made in a new petition with a new filing and priority date." Letter, Dixon, Deputy Gen. Counsel (HQCOU 70/11.1-C) (Sept. 10, 1998) at p.6, *reprinted in* 75 No. 37 *Interpreter Releases* 1335, 1344–55 (Sept. 28, 1998); *Matter of Izummi,* 22 I&N Dec. 169, 175 (1998); *Matter of Katigbak,* 14 I&N Dec. 45 (Reg. Com. 1971); AFM at 22.2(b)(3)(B)

3. USCIS Does Not Pre-Adjudicate Cases—Where INS officers provided a model investor petition and approved cases, it did not bind INS. *Matter of Izummi,* 22 I&N Dec. 169, 196 (Assoc. Comm. 1998).

4. I-140 petition submitted with forms ETA 9089 certified by Department of Labor (DOL) or under blanket certification (designated Schedule A at 20 C.F.R. §656.15). In light of USCIS's ever changing position concerning where to send petitions, the applicant should consult the latest edition of the application *and* USCIS website to ensure that the application is sent to the correct petition center. The labor certification is obtained from the DOL after testing the labor market for U.S. workers. A U.S. worker is defined as a U.S.C, U.S. national, or an alien who is legally permitted to work permanently within the U.S. 20 C.F.R. §655.200(c). Labor certification must establish that the alien will not displace U.S. workers or adversely affect the wages or working conditions of U.S. workers. This is established by demonstrating that no minimally qualified and willing U.S. worker can be found. 20 C.F.R. §656.2. Alternatively, a position may be precertified if the DOL has determined that there are insufficient USC/LPR workers in the field. This is accomplished through a list of precertified jobs designated as Schedule A by the DOL. 20 C.F.R. §656.10.

5. Approval—Priority Date Issues Under Current Law:

5.a. Priority date for I-140 is the date of filing labor certification application or if it is a blanket certification (Schedule A) the date of the filing of the I-140 petition. 8 C.F.R. §204.5(c), 22 C.F.R. §42.53(a); AFM at 22.2(b)(5)(A). These priority dates are in effect even for labor certifications filed before Oct. 1, 1991. Cable, DOS 95-State-070016 (Mar. 22, 1995), *reprinted in* 72 No. 14 *Interpreter Releases* 500–01 (Apr. 10, 1995); Memo, Puleo, Exec. Assoc. Comm., Programs HQ 204.24-P, 204.25-P (Apr. 4, 1995), *reprinted in* 72 No. 14 *Interpreter Releases* 500, 515–16 (Apr. 10, 1995). Where applications for labor certifications were changed from traditional to RIR processing, the original filing date when the SWA accepted the application for processing of the traditional application remains the priority date. PERM FAQs No. 3 (May 4, 2005), *published on* AILA InfoNet at Doc. No. 05050960 (May 9, 2005). When LCs are re-filed under PERM after a withdrawal of the ETA-750, USCIS will utilize the priority date specified by DOL in Section "O" of the ETA 9089. AFM at 22.2(b)(5)(A) [following DOL's requirement that to preserve the original priority date of the ETA-750 all of the elements relating to the job opportunity and the alien beneficiary on the newly filed ETA 9089 must be "identical" to the elements specified on the ETA-750]. Special immigrant priority dates are measured by the date of filing I-360. Investors priority date is the date of filing the I-526.

5.b. Portability / Effect of changed employment on priority date—8 C.F.R. §204.5(e). For I-140 filed under INA §§203(b)(1), (2) or (3), the priority date of the approved petition is preserved for any subsequently filed petition under these sections. AFM at 22.2(d). If unskilled worker subsequently gets new approval under skilled worker category, s/he would get the benefit of the earlier priority date. Moreover, an adjustment of status application pending more than 180 days that is based upon a first preference (outstanding researcher/professor or multinational transferee) or second or third preference employment-based petition can be used for a new job offer without filing any further petitions as long as the job is in the same or similar occupational classification. This portability provision allows an employee to change jobs if the adjustment application is pending more than 180 days because the adjustment "shall remain valid with respect to a new job if the individual changes jobs or employers if the new job is in the same or a similar occupational classification as the job for which the petition was filed." INA §204(j) (referring to INA §204(a)(1)(F)), §212(a)(5)(A)(iv). The underlying I-140 petition need not be approved but, according to a USCIS interpretation, should have been approvable when filed, Memo, Yates, Assoc. Dir. Operations, USCIS, HQOPRD 70/6.2.8-P (May 12, 2005) at Q. 13, *published on* AILA InfoNet at Doc. No. 05051810 (May 18, 2005). If the currently filed I-140 is not approved and it is discovered that the beneficiary has ported off of the unapproved I-140, the USCIS should review the petition and approve it or issue RFE and if satisfied subsequently approve it. Memo, Yates, Assoc. Dir. Operations, USCIS, HQPRD 70/6.2.8-P (Dec. 27, 2005), *published on* AILA InfoNet at Doc. No. 06092763 (Sept. 27, 2006). If the employee is in a removal proceeding, the BIA has stated, however, that the IJ has no jurisdiction over the visa petition pursuant to INA §204(j) and therefore cannot decide to adjust the respondent. *Matter of Perez Vargas,* 23 I&N Dec. 829 (BIA 2005). But *Perez-Vargas* was *vacated Perez-Vargas v. Gonzales,* 478 F.3d 191 (4th Cir. 2007) [the BIA's decision that the IJ has no jurisdiction to decide the continuing validity of an employment-based petition under INA §204(j) was reversed because 8 C.F.R. §1245.2(a)(1) provides IJs with exclusive jurisdiction to adjust applicants in removal proceedings and a determination under INA §204(j) is simply an act of fact finding incidental to AOS]. *See also Sung v. Keisler,* 505 F.3d 372 (5th Cir. 2007) [adopted reasoning of *Perez-Vargas v. Gonzales* and found that IJ does have jurisdiction over portability determination because it is incidental to AOS]; *Matovski v. Gonzales,* 492 F.3d 722 (6th Cir. 2007) [court reversed IJ's refusal to consider adjustment of status for person who "ported" because 8 C.F.R. §245.2(a)(5)(ii) made the portability issue irrelevant as the IJ had authority to adjust a person if he was eligible to adjust at the time he filed with the USCIS director and because there was no regulation that barred the IJ from considering portability].

5.c. Effect on labor certification—DOL will honor labor certification if new location within same Standard Metropolitan Statistical Area (SMSA) or commuting area. Technical Assistance Guide, No. 656, p.104, A-11. Appendix defines area of intended employment as area of normal commuting distance within the SMSA. *Seibel & Stern*, Case Nos. 90-INA-86, 90-INA-116 through 90-INA-129, 90-INA-144 through 90-INA-168 (BALCA 1990) [MSA defined as "a county or group of counties which contain at least one central city of at least 50,000 inhabitants or a central urbanized area of at least 100,000"].

5.d. I-140 cannot automatically be denied when H-2 and EB third preference petition are for the same position. *North American Industries, Inc. v. Feldman*, 722 F.2d 893 (1st Cir. 1983).

6. Successor in Interest—Employer must file new I-140 petition, but the LC remains valid (if filed originally with an I-140 within 180 days of its approval), when it: (a) is a successor in interest because it has been bought out, merged or had a significant change in ownership; (b) has changed its name; or (c) has moved (even within the same SMSA). A successor must submit documentation that it has assumed the rights, duties, obligations and assets of the original employer and that it continues to operate same type of business. Letter, Hernandez, Director, Business and Trade Services, INS HQ 70/6.1.3 (Oct. 17, 2001), *reprinted in* 78 No. 42 *Interpreter Releases* 1684, 1692–95 (Oct. 29, 2001); Memo, Puleo, Acting Exec. Assoc. Comm. HQ 204.24-P, HQ 204.25-P (Dec. 10, 1993), *reprinted in* 70 No. 48 *Interpreter Releases* 1676, 1692–93 (Dec. 20, 1993). But a more current version of the *Adjudicator's Field Manual* takes a different view finding that "a mere change in a Company's name or physical location without other organizational changes might not require the filling of a new or amended petition." AFM at 22.2(b)(5). However, if the move is beyond the metropolitan statistical area (MSA) the LC may no longer be valid, a successor in interest petition cannot be filed, and the employer must check with ETA. *Id.*

7. Portability/Subsequent Employer—An AOS application based upon a first preference (outstanding researchers/professors or multinational transferees) or a second or third preference employment-based petition that is pending more than 180 days "shall remain valid with respect to a new job if

the individual changes jobs or employers if the new job is in the same or a similar occupational classification as the job for which the petition was filed." INA §204(j) (referring to INA §204(a)(1)(F)), §212(a)(5)(A)(iv). AC21 §106(c); AFM at 20.2(c). Memo, Cronin, Acting Ex. Assoc. Comm. Program, HQPGM 70/6.2.8 (June 19, 2001) at ¶II F, *reprinted in* 78 No. 25 *Interpreter Releases* 1069, 1108–17 (July 2, 2001). If the I-140 petition is withdrawn before 180 days or USCIS denies or revokes the approval at any time, the portability provision does not apply. *But see Mawalla v. Chertoff,* 468 F.Supp.2d 177, 181–83 (D.D.C. 2007) [the 180 days is measured from the date previous employment is terminated and not from the pendency of the I-140, and the court rejected the application of 8 C.F.R. §205.1(a)(3)(iii)(C) to AC21 because it would allow I-140s to be revoked from the date they were filed thereby rending AC21 a nullity]. If the I-140 is still pending after 180 days because the I-485 was concurrently filed with it, and the I-140 remains unadjudicated, USCIS officers are required to determine first whether the I-140 is or would have been approvable had it been adjudicated within 180 days. If the petition is approvable but for an ability to pay issue or any other issue relating to a time after the filing of the petition, USCIS officers are directed to approve the petition and then determine whether the new position is the same or similar occupational classification for I-140 portability purposes. Memo, Yates, Assoc. Dir. Operations, USCIS, HQOPRD 70/6.2.8-P (May 12, 2005), *published on* AILA InfoNet at Doc. No. 05051810 (May 18, 2005); *reissued* Memo, Yates, Assoc. Dir. Operations, USCIS, HQPRD 70/6.2.8-P (Dec. 27, 2005), *published on* AILA InfoNet at Doc. No. 06092763 (Sept. 27, 2006). If the petition is not approvable, however, portability is not permitted even if the petition is denied more than 180 days after the filing of the I-485. *Matter of* ___, (AAO Jan. 12, 2005), *published on* AILA InfoNet at Doc. No. 05102761 (and adopted as a decision by USCIS, Divine (Oct. 18, 2005)). If the I-140 has been approved and the I-485 is on file 180 days, one can port by presenting to USCIS a letter from the new employer describing the same/similar occupation (that is, no new I-140 is needed). Memo, Yates, Asst. Dir. Operations, USCIS, HQBUSCIS 70/6.2.8-P (Aug. 4, 2003), *published on* AILA InfoNet Doc. No. 03081114.

There is no requirement in the statute that during the 180 days or any time thereafter until permanent residence is authorized that the beneficiary must be employed by the petitioner. AFM at 20.2(c); Memo, Yates, Acting Assoc. Dir. for Operations, BUSCIS, HQBUSCIS 70/6.2.8-P (Aug. 4, 2003), *published on* AILA InfoNet at Doc. No. 03081114. Nor is there a requirement that he could not continue to be employed by the employer he wishes to leave until he receives his LPR status. *Matter of* ____(AAO Mar. 22, 2004) *reported* in 81 No. 42 *Interpreter Releases* 1533, 1544–45 (Nov. 1, 2004) [reversed DD who denied petition because adjustment applicant was not working for company he sought to port to]. If the employee is in a removal proceeding, the BIA has stated, however, that the IJ has no jurisdiction over the visa petition pursuant to INA §204(j) and therefore cannot decide to adjust the respondent. *Matter of Perez Vargas,* 23 I&N Dec. 829 (BIA 2005) *vacated Perez-Vargas v. Gonzales,* 478 F.3d 191 (4th Cir. 2007) [the BIA's decision that the IJ has no jurisdiction to decide the continuing validity of an employment-based petition under INA §204(j) was reversed because 8 C.F.R. §1245.2(a)(1) provides IJs with exclusive jurisdiction to adjust applicants in removal proceedings and a determination under INA §204(j) is simply an act of fact finding incidental to AOS]. *See also Sung v. Keisler,* 505 F.3d 372 (5th Cir. 2007) [adopted reasoning of *Perez-Vargas v. Gonzales* and found that IJ does have jurisdiction over portability determination because it is incidental to AOS]; *Matovski v. Gonzales,* 492 F.3d 722 (6th Cir. 2007) [court reversed IJ's refusal to consider adjustment of status for person who "ported" because 8 C.F.R. §245.2(a)(5)(ii) made the portability issue irrelevant as the IJ had authority to adjust a person if he was eligible to adjust at the time he filed with the USCIS director and because there was no regulation that barred the IJ from considering portability].

7.a. Definition of Same or Similar Occupation Classification—In order to port from one employer to the other the beneficiary of the pending AOS application must demonstrate that the new employment is in the "same or similar" occupational classification. To make that determination, USCIS officers are directed to consider the following: (1) the description of the job duties contained in the ETA 750A (or now the ETA 9089) or the initial I-140 and the job duties of the new employment; (2) DOT and/or SOC code for I-140 and new position; and (3) Discrepancy between the previous and new wage (but a discrepancy in the wage alone is not a basis to deny). Whether or not the positions are in the same geographic area is not relevant. Nor is the new employer's ability to pay relevant. Memo, Yates, Assoc. Dir. Operations,

USCIS, HQOPRD 70/6.2.8-P (May 12, 2005) at pp. 4-5, *published on* AILA InfoNet at Doc. No. 05051810. In addition, there is no requirement that a new LC be obtained or that the applicant left the I-140 employment before the I-485 was pending 180 days. *Id.* at p. 6.

7.b. Multinational Transferees Under EB-1—A multinational manager or executive can port even to an unrelated company but USCIS still reviews the case to determine whether the new job duties are not in the same or similar occupational classification. Memo, Yates, Assoc. Dir. Operations, USCIS, HQOPRD 70/6.2.8-P (May 12, 2005) at p. 5, *published on* AILA InfoNet at Doc. No. 05051810 (May 18, 2005).

7.c. Self-Employment—An employee can port to self-employment. Memo, Yates, Assoc. Dir. Operations, USCIS, HQOPRD 70/6.2.8-P (May 12, 2005) at p. 5, *published on* AILA InfoNet at Doc. No. 05051810 (May 18, 2005). USCIS will look at whether: (1) The employment is in a "same or similar" occupational classification; (2) The new employer and the job offer are legitimate; (3) The I-140 petition represented a true employment opportunity; and (4) The intent of the beneficiary when the labor certification was filed. *Id.*

7.d. Accrual of 180 days—The 180 days that the I-485 is pending can be due to lack of visa availability. Memo, Yates (May 12, 2005), *supra* at p. 7.

8. Professional Athletes—INA §204(i), 8 U.S.C. §1154(i). An I-140 remains valid even if athlete goes to another team if the new employer is a team in the same sport (including minor league team) and the team is part of an association that has at least 6 teams and combined revenues in excess of $10,000,000.

9. Embargoed Countries.

9.a. Where U.S. has embargo it may be a violation of foreign assets laws to offer employment to nationals of that country. Therefore, an LC or I-140 may not be filed.

9.b. Iran—Cannot obtain E-2, H-1B, or L under terms of the embargo against Iran if the person is coming to the U.S. to work as an agent, employee or contractor of the government of Iran or a business entity or other organization in Iran. Cable, DOS, 99-State-128375 (July 8, 1999), *reprinted in* 76 No. 28 *Interpreter Releases* 1124–25 (July 26, 1999).

10. Expedited Processing of Cases—USCIS Service Centers do accept requests to expedite cases separate and apart from Premium Processing. They will accept expedite requests based on the following criteria: (1) Severe financial loss to the company or individual; (2) Extreme emergent situation; (3) Humanitarian situation; (4) DOD or National Interest Situation (Note: Request must come from U.S. government entity and explain why delay would be detrimental); and (5) USCIS error. Memo, Ohata, 70/1 (Apr. 20, 2001), *reprinted in* 78 No. 25 *Interpreter Releases* 1072, 1118 (July 2, 2001) [provides telephone and fax numbers to make requests at Service Centers].There is also a general number for information at all Service Centers. 1-800-375-5283.

11. Adjustment of Status:

11.a. An application for AOS (I-485) may be submitted with an I-140 petition in any employment-based category (INA §203(b)) that has a current priority date. 8 C.F.R. §§245.2(a)(2)(i), 1245.2(a)(2)(i). If the I-140 is pending but has not yet been approved, an adjustment application may be filed with proof of payment and a I-797 receipt notice. 8 C.F.R. §§245.2(a)(2)(i)(C)(3), 1245.2(a)(2)(i)(C)(3). The former requirement that the I-140 had to be approved before filing adjustment has been abandoned. If the I-140 petition is denied, the I-485 and the employment and parole requests should also be denied. Memo, Yates, Deputy Ex. Assoc. Comm., ISD, BUSCIS, HQADN 70/23.1 (Feb. 28, 2003), *published on* AILA InfoNet at Doc. No. 03030644. The service center accepting both the I-140 petition and I-485 application may simultaneously issue RFEs on both the petition and the application and failure to respond timely to either will result in a denial of that petition or application. Memo, Ohata, Director of Service Center Operations, 90/16.45 (Mar. 31, 2004), *published on* AILA InfoNet at Doc. No. 04041668. If the I-140 petition is pending more than 180 days then the beneficiary can use the portability provision of AC21 §106(c), change jobs or job offer, and retain the I-140 and the AOS if the new job is in the same or similar occupational classification. *But see Mawalla v. Chertoff,* 468 F.Supp.2d 177, 181–83 (D.D.C. 2007) [the 180 days is measured from the date previous employment is terminated and not from the pendency of the

I-140, and the court rejected the application of 8 C.F.R. §205.1(a)(3)(iii)(C) to AC21 because it would allow I-140s to be revoked from the date they were filed thereby rending AC21 a nullity]. *See in this section* "Portability/Subsequent Employer," ¶ 7 (p.900), *supra.*

(1) Non–Interview Cases. USCIS has determined that certain employment-based cases generally do not require interviews to obtain approvals if: (1) the principal applicant is employed by the same petitioner who submitted the I-140; (2) the applicant has been approved as a person of extraordinary or exceptional ability; (3) the applicant has been approved as an outstanding professor or researcher or a multinational executive/manager and has a continuing offer of employment from the same petitioner; or (4) an applicant with a national interest waiver based on performing medical care in medically-underserved area who intends to continue in work. Memo, Yates, Assoc. Dir. Operations, USCIS (Jan. 5, 2005), *published on* AILA InfoNet at Doc. No. 05030262 [listing criteria for transfer of cases to district offices for interviews].

12. Revocation of Petitions—The Secretary of DHS has the authority to revoke any petition for "good and sufficient cause" under 8 U.S.C. §1255.

12.a. Automatic revocation of petition if: (8 C.F.R. §§205.1(a), 1205.1(a))

(1) Invalidation of labor certification—USCIS can only invalidate where there is a showing of fraud or misrepresentation. 20 C.F.R. §636.30(d). A salary increase alone during the course of the petitioning process does not invalidate the labor certification. Letter, Weinig, Deputy Asst. Comm. Adjudications CO 204.8-C (Feb. 5, 1990), *reprinted in* 67 No. 17 *Interpreter Releases* 512, 525 (Apr. 30, 1990).

(2) Death of petitioner or beneficiary. *Mahabir v. Ashcroft,* 387 F.3d 32 (1st Cir. 2004) [upheld final removal order where DHS revoked home health attendant's I-140 when person attended to died and attendant was placed in removal proceeding]. However, where there is a surviving spouse and the petition for a home health attendant was filed by the other spouse who now died the petition remains valid even if the surviving spouse did not sign the petition. Letter, Skerrett, Chief, Immigr. Branch, Adjudications, HQ 204.25-C (May 10, 1995), *reprinted in* 72 No. 27 *Interpreter Releases* 952, 970–71 (July 17, 1995).

(3) Formal notice of withdrawal by the petitioner or self-petitioner of I-140. *Longwood Village Restaurant Ltd. v. Ashcroft,* 157 F.Supp.2d 61, 68–69 (D.D.C. 2001) [where beneficiary, not petitioner, initiated revocation court invalidated INS's automatic termination].

(4) Termination of employer's business—Successor corporation may continue labor certification, if petitioner can prove that predecessor corporation had financial resources at time of petition to pay beneficiary. *Matter of Dial Auto Repair Shop, Inc.*, 19 I&N Dec. 481 (Comm. 1986).

12.b. Revocation on Notice 8 C.F.R. §§205.2, 1205.2. The AG provides written notification of his intention to revoke and the petitioner or self-petitioner is given an opportunity to respond. The AG decision in this regard may be unreviewable because IIRIRA precludes review of discretionary decisions. *Systronics Corp. v. INS*, 153 F.Supp.2d 7, 11–13 (D.D.C. 2001) [no jurisdiction to review decision to revoke I-140 petition under INA §242(a)(2)(B)(ii) because the "good and sufficient cause" standard is discretionary];

13. State Department Revocation—Consular posts must obtain an advisory opinion before they can cancel a labor certification or deny a person admission under INA §212(a)(5)(A). Cable, DOS, 97-State-228477, *reprinted in* 75 No. 17 *Interpreter Releases* 624 (May 4, 1998); 9 FAM 40.51 N.10 & 10.1.

14. Consular Officer Return of Visa Petition to USCIS—On occasion a consular officer, rather than deny a visa under INA §221(g) will return the petition to USCIS to request reconsideration and revocation. DOS's position is that returning petitions to USCIS should be used judiciously since the process is lengthy and the evidentiary standard to revoke the petition is high. "Posts should not use the revocation request process as a means of disposing of problematic cases in which fraud, misrepresentation or ineligibility for status is only suspected but cannot be clearly established." Cable, DOS, 01-State-121801 (July 13, 2001), *reprinted in* 78 No. 30 *Interpreter Releases* 1276–77 (Aug. 6, 2001); 9 FAM 42.43 and N.1–N.3.

B. *USCIS Review of DOL Certification*

1. USCIS is required to consult with DOL during petition process, INA §204(b), 8 U.S.C. §1154(b), but it usually does not.

2. DOL is required to establish a procedure in each region to inform USCIS where a beneficiary on an ETA 750 appears to be out of status or presently employed without appropriate USCIS authorization. Technical Assistance Guide No. 757 p.133; Letter, Farmer, DOL Administrator for Regional Management (Jan. 28, 1993), *reported in* 12 *AILA Monthly Mailing* 277 (Apr. 1993).

3. Typical areas of inquiry by USCIS:

   3.a. Alien's qualification for position—The alien must have all the education, training and experience specified in the job offer as of the time of first filing the labor certification application or immigrant visa petition where no labor certification is required. *Matter of Katigbak*, 14 I&N Dec. 45 (R.C. 1971). Only submission of affidavits are necessary to prove alien meets requirements for the job. *Lu-Ann Bakery Shop, Inc. v. Nelson*, 705 F.Supp. 7 (D.D.C. 1988) [where INS required contemporaneous documentary evidence which was above and beyond the affidavits required in the regulation district court reversed denial]. USCIS can request consul overseas to do investigation of experience.

   3.b. Alien's fulfillment of minimum requirements for job.

   3.c. Employer's ability to pay wage—8 C.F.R. §204.5(g)(2) [the demonstration of financial ability must be from "the time the priority date is established and continuing until the beneficiary obtained lawful permanent residency"]. *Matter of Great Wall*, 16 I&N Dec. 142 (R.C. 1977); *Matter of Sonegawa*, 12 I&N Dec. 612 (R.C. 1967); *Masonry Masters, Inc. v. Thornburgh*, 875 F.2d 898 (D.C. Cir. 1989) [INS should consider employee's ability to generate income when determining employer's ability to pay salary. In determining employer's ability to pay INS should consider prevailing wage at time of submission of the application and not at the time of certification]. The employer is required to produce initial evidence in the form of its annual report, tax return *or* audited financial statement. 8 C.F.R. §204.5(g)(2). USCIS can also accept in its discretion a financial statement in lieu of initial evidence and/or: (1) profit/loss statements, (b) bank account records, or (3) personnel records. *Id.*; Memo, Yates, Assoc. Dir. Of Operations, USCIS, HQOPRD 90/16.45 (May 4, 2004), *published on* AILA InfoNet at Doc. No. 04051262 (May 12, 2004). USCIS can rely on net income, net assets, or employer's current or previous payment of the wage to the beneficiary to determine the company's ability to pay the salary. Memo, Yates, Assoc. Dir. Of Operations, USCIS, HQOPRD 90/16.45 (May 4, 2004), *published on* AILA InfoNet at Doc. No. 04051262 (May 12, 2004); *Chang v. Thornburgh*, 719 F.Supp. 532 (N.D. Tex. 1989); *Elatos Restaurant Corp. v. Sava*, 632 F.Supp. 1049 (S.D.N.Y. 1986). IRS quarterly wage reports showing person was actually paid during year when labor certification was filed can be source of proof. *Matter of ___*, CSC, WAC 02-208-52485 (AAO Aug. 6, 2003) [records demonstrated that wage in excess of proffered wage was paid] *reported in* 9 No. 4 *Bender's Immigration Bulletin* 218 (Feb. 15, 2004); *Matter of Quintero-Martinez*, Case No. A29 928 323 (AAU Aug. 4, 1992), *discussed in* 70 No. 8 *Interpreter Releases* 252–53 (Mar. 1, 1993). USCIS must also consider the normal accounting practices of the company even if the ability to pay is not reflected in the tax returns. *Matter of ___*, VSC, EAC 01-018-50413 (AAO Jan. 31, 2003) [where sole shareholder of medical corporation routinely minimizes taxable income by taking it as compensation to avoid double taxation, the net profit on the return should not control] *reported in* 8 No. 18 *Bender's Immigration Bulletin* 1528-29 (Sept. 15, 2003). USCIS must also consider other sources of income pledged to employer. *Full Gospel Portland Church v. Thornburgh*, 730 F.Supp. 441, 449 (D.D.C. 1988) [where national church pledged resources to maintain local church music program INS must consider it]. Where the employer is a sole proprietorship, the individual's assets should be considered in determining whether the employer has the ability to pay the proffered wage. *Ranchito Coletero,* 02-INA-105 (BALCA Jan. 8, 2004) (*en banc*). AAO has also taken, at times, a "totality of the circumstances" approach to determine ability to pay the proffered wage. *Matter of ___*,WAC 02 246 52330 (AAO Sept. 16, 2005) [looked at totality of financial circumstances including sole proprietor's access to a personal home equity line of credit and the company's history of financial stability] *reported in* 11 No. 17 *Bender's Immigration Bulletin* 1015, 1041 (Sept. 1, 2006); *Matter of ___*,WAC

03 158 53192 (AAO Nov. 10, 2005) [look at the totality of the company's financial circumstances including its continuing growth in number of employees, gross receipts, and total wages paid over a sustained period of time] *reported in* 11 No. 15 *Bender's Immigration Bulletin* 855, 996 (Aug. 1, 2006); *Matter of* __,EAC 03 048 51297 (AAO Nov. 10, 2005) [in recounting totality of the financial circumstances AAO looked to the steadily increasing gross receipts, total income during the company's 8 year existence, and its executive compensation] *reported in* 11 No. 15 *Bender's Immigration Bulletin* 855, 996 (Aug. 1, 2006); *Matter of* ___, (AAO July 7, 2004) [despite petitioner's inability to show sufficient assets for several years to pay the proffered wage because it had negative net assets, the AAO determined that based upon the totality of the circumstances, including the company's history, its gross income of over $2 million annually, and the fact it paid over a $1 million in wages in each of the previous 5 years, it demonstrated its financial strength and reversed the denial] *reported in* 82 No. 35 *Interpreter Releases* 1437, 1449 (Sept. 12, 2005). Pursuant to 8 C.F.R. §204.5(g)(2), USCIS may accept simply "a statement from a financial officer" of the employer to demonstrate it can pay the proffered wage where the petitioner employs 100 or more employees.

USCIS also recognizes that: "Sometimes companies will operate at a loss for a period of time to improve their business position in the long run. In those instances the documentation should fully explain the sources of funding for the entity (or unit) and the expected profit potential." AFM at 22.2(c).

USCIS should make a *positive* determination, without issuing an RFE or NOID, where the initial evidence reflects that: (1) the petitioner's net income is equal to or greater than the proffered wage; (2) the petitioner's net current assets are equal to or greater than the proffered wage; or (3) there is credible verifiable evidence that the petitioner not only is employing the beneficiary but also has paid or currently is paying the proffered wage. Memo, Yates, Assoc. Dir. of Operations, USCIS, HQOPRD 90/16.45 (May 4, 2004), *published on* AILA InfoNet at Doc. No. 04051262 (May 12, 2004). For more information of RFEs and NOIDs, *see* Ch. 5, ¶ III.N.4 (p.635), *supra*.

The employer's ability to pay must be a figure "reasonably determined to have been the prevailing wage." *Masonry Masters, Inc. v. Thornburgh*, 742 F.Supp. 682 (D.D.C. 1990) [where prevailing wage was less than wage offered, ability to pay is based on prevailing wage]. DOL regulations also reflect that the employer must have the ability to pay the proffered wage. 20 C.F.R. §656.10(c)(1). *The Whislers,* 90-INA-569 (BALCA Jan. 31, 1992). Also, note that the employer is not required to pay the offered wage until after permanent residence is granted. 20 C.F.R. §656.10(c)(4).

3.d. Alien's intent to work at job—*Spyropolos v. INS*, 590 F.2d 1 (1st Cir. 1978) [no intent to report for work found where beneficiary turned up in another job in another state shortly after entering]; *Yui Sing Tse v. INS*, 596 F.2d 831 (9th Cir. 1979) [where alien obtained labor certification as specialty cook and enrolled in dental school without giving up his employment, court reversed denial of adjustment].

3.e. Employer's intent to hold job open.

4. Issuance of Request for Evidence (RFE) or Notice of Intent to Deny (NOID)—When an application/petition is not being denied for clear ineligibility or approved because the record is complete and the applicant/petitioner met the appropriate evidentiary standard, USCIS may issue either an RFE or NOID. For a discussion of each, see Ch. 5, ¶ III.N.4 (p.635), *supra*.

5. Originals vs. Copies. Petitioner must submit originals of the application or petition and the documents issued to support them such as a labor certification, Form DS-2019, medical examinations, affidavits, formal consultations, letters of current employment and all other documents needed to support the benefit sought unless it is an document issued by USCIS or the legacy INS. 8 C.F.R. §§103.2(b)(4). The agency may request that other originals be submitted as well and failure to submit them by the deadline may result in denial or revocation. 8 C.F.R. §103.2(b)(5). Documentary requirements for petitioner's lawful status are found at 8 C.F.R. §103.2(b)(17). USCIS will continue to accept copies of a labor certification, even if expired, if it is filed with an amended or duplicate Form 1-140 where the original approved LC was filed in support of a previously filed petition during the time the LC was valid. AFM at 22.2(f). This type of filing may occur when a

new petition is required because there is a successor-in-interest, where the previously I-140 was lost, or where the amended petition is requesting a different visa category.

6. Question as to USCIS authority to reconsider DOL decision—The DOL decides the test of the labor market. USCIS decides if alien has the credentials for the job and if employer has the ability to provide job. *Hoosier Care, Inc. v. Chertoff,* 482 F.3d 987 (7th Cir. 2007) [as recognized in 8 C.F.R. §204.5(*l*)(4), it is the DOL and not USCIS that determines the requirements for the job and where USCIS denied application because job requirements were inappropriate the court reversed]; *Singh v. Attorney General*, 510 F.Supp. 351 (D.D.C. 1980), *aff'd*, 672 F.2d 894 (D.C. Cir. 1981) [solely job of DOL to decide job content]; *Ubeda v. Palmer*, 539 F.Supp. 647 (N.D. Ill. 1982) [INS had right to inquire into employer's ability to pay alien]; *Madany v. Smith*, 696 F.2d 1008 (D.C. Cir. 1983) [absent fraud or willful misrepresentation DOL's decision as to contents of labor certification not subject to INS review]; *Denver Tofu Co. v. District Director*, 525 F.Supp. 254 (D. Colo. 1981) [INS should not take mechanical approach in deciding alien's qualifications].

7. Discretionary Decisions on I-140s May Be Barred from Judicial Review—Pursuant to the REAL ID Act, PL 109-13, 119 Stat. 231 (May 11, 2005), Div. B §101(f), the discretionary decision bar applies to nonremoval decisions as well as removal cases because INA §242(a)(2)(B) is now applicable in all matters "regardless of whether the judgment, decision, or action is made in removal proceedings." INA §242(a)(2)(B), 8 U.S.C. §1252(a)(2)(B). However, courts disagree over the scope of the bar. *Compare Jilin Pharmaceutical USA, Inc. v. Chertoff,* 447 F.3d 196 (3d Cir. 2006) [distinguished *Soltane* regarding denial of visa petitions and found that there was no jurisdiction to review a revocation of an I-140 petition because it was a discretionary decision barred by INA §242(a)(2)(B)(ii)] and *El-Khader v. Monica,* 366 F.3d 562, 565–67 (7th Cir. 2004) [quoting *Samirah v. O'Connell* and finding that the discretionary decision bar under INA §242(a)(2)(B)(ii) is *not* limited solely to matters arising in removal, deportation, or exclusion proceeding thereby barring judicial review of the revocation of a visa petition]; *Systronics Corp. v. INS*, 153 F.Supp.2d 7 (D.D.C. 2001) [no jurisdiction, but even if there was jurisdiction the standard of review is highly deferential] *with Ana International Inc. v. Way,* 393 F.3d 886, 893–95 (9th Cir. 2005) [following *Spencer* and holding that INA §242(a)(2)(B)(ii) does not bar judicial review of an I-140 visa revocation of an EB-1 decision under 8 U.S.C. §1155 because the "good and sufficient cause" language of the statute provides a legal standard, as does the "managerial capacity" criteria of EB-1]; *Spencer Enterprises, Inc. v. U.S.*, 345 F.3d 683, 689 (9th Cir. 2003) [defining narrowly the discretionary decision bar]; *Soltane v. DOJ,* 381 F.3d 143, 146–48 (3d Cir. 2004) [followed *Spencer* in regard to special immigrant/religious worker case and found that Congress did not intend a broad construction of the discretionary decision bar]. If there is review, then the abuse of discretion test has been traditionally applied to the judgment to deny an employment-based petition. *Elatos Restaurant Corp. v. Sava*, 632 F.Supp. 1049 (S.D.N.Y. 1986). Inconsistent decisions by INS considered an abuse of discretion. *Omni Packaging, Inc. v. INS*, 733 F.Supp. 500 (D.P.R. 1990) [where INS approved L-1 petitions it was abuse of discretion to deny third preference application]. The substantial-evidence test may also be applied to review the factual finding of INS in denying the petition. *Chan v. INS*, 631 F.2d 978 (D.C. Cir. 1980); *Omni Packaging, Inc., supra*; *Full Gospel Portland Church v. Thornburgh*, 730 F.Supp. 441, 445 (D.D.C. 1988) [visa revocation]. The bar to review, if it exists, generally does not preclude mandamus actions to compel the government to make a decision. *Raduga USA Corp. v. DOS,* 440 F.Supp.2d 1140, 1143–48 (S.D. Cal. 2005) [employer had standing to bring mandamus action due to its own injury to compel consular officer to make a decision on employee's IV over government's objection that once the I-140 was approved the employer had no further interest].

C. *Work Authorization*—Labor certification does not confer employment authorization, *Matter of Raol*, 16 I&N Dec. 466 (BIA 1978). Alien may not apply for authorization solely because an I-140 is approved unless an application for adjustment of status has been filed. 8 C.F.R. §§274a.12(c)(9), 1274a.12(c)(9). Beneficiary may work if s/he has unexpired H, L, E or other employment authorization consistent with 8 C.F.R. §§274a.12–.14, 1274a.12–.14.

VIII. LABOR CERTIFICATION

A. *Requirements*

1. Originates in prior INA §212(a)(14), 8 U.S.C. §1182(a)(14). Now set forth in INA §§212(a)(5)(A) & (p), 8 U.S.C. §§1182(a)(5)(A) & (p); 20 C.F.R. pt. 656. H.R. Rep No. 1365, 82nd Cong. 2d Sess. (1952); 1952 U.S.C.C.A.N. 1653, 1705; S. Rep. No. 748, 89th Cong. 1st Sess. (1965), *reprinted in* 1965 U.S.C.C.A.N. 3328, *as amended* by H. Rep. No. 1553, 94th Cong. 2d Sess. 11 (Sept. 15, 1976); 122 Cong. Rec. Part 128 p33633 (Sept. 29, 1976); *as further amended* by IMMACT90 §§162 & 601 and MTINA §302(e)(6); *as further amended* by ACWIA, PL 105-277, 112 Stat. 2681; *as further amended* by §423 of the Consolidated Appropriations Act of 2005, PL 108-447, 118 Stat. 2809 (Dec. 8, 2004); The PERM regulations are found at 69 Fed. Reg. 77325–77421 (Dec. 27, 2004), 72 Fed. Reg. 27904–47 (May 17, 2007). For earlier history *see also Pesikoff v. Secy. of Labor*, 501 F.2d 757 (D.C. Cir.), *cert. denied* 419 U.S. 1038 (1974); *Mastroyanis v. DOL,* Case No. A88-089 Civ (D. Alaska May 5, 1989). Inadmissible if seeking entry to perform skilled/ unskilled labor unless Secy. of Labor has certified to Secy. of State and AG that:
   - 1.a. Not sufficient workers able, willing and qualified at the time and place of alien entry. Permanent U.S. workers include USCs and LPRs.
   - 1.b. Employment—Not adversely affect wages and working conditions of U.S. workers.
2. Only applicable to second/third employment-based categories and H-2 applicants. The labor certification for H-2s, however, is not binding on USCIS as are the other certifications. If DOL denies LC in the H-2 context, the employer may still seek approval of the I-129 through USCIS.
3. Regulations at 20 C.F.R. §656, 69 Fed. Reg. 77325–77421 (Dec. 27, 2004), *published on* AILA InfoNet at Doc. No. 04122312. The Certifying Officer (CO) determines whether a labor certification should be issued or revoked. The CO is required to interpret the law based on the regulations, the General Administration Letters (GAL), now called Training and Employment Guidance Letters (TEGLs), the DOL Technical Assistance Guide, No. 656 (TAG), and the decisions of the Board of Alien Labor Certification Appeals (BALCA), all of which are considered precedents. The TAG, however, "is only a manual" and not binding on BALCA. *Solectron Corp.,* 03-INA-143 (BALCA Aug. 12, 2004) and GALs "have been eliminated as an advisory series" although active GALs remain in the system. Memo, Flynn, Administrator, Office of Policy Development and Research, "General Administration Letter (GAL) Checklist" (Nov. 5, 2004), *published on* AILA InfoNet at Doc. No. 04113062. DOL now uses TEGLs instead.

B. *Method of Certification*

1. PERM, Reduction in Recruitment (RIR) and Traditional Recruitment (TR)—On Mar. 28, 2005 the Department of Labor initiated the Program Electronic Review Management System (PERM), 69 Fed. Reg. 77325–421 (Dec. 27, 2004), *published on* AILA InfoNet at Doc. No. 04122312 prior proposed regulations at 67 Fed. Reg. 30465 (May 6, 2002), *published on* AILA InfoNet at Doc. No. 02050740 (May 7, 2002). PERM created a new system for processing labor certification applications. Although the process and some criteria for determining labor certifications have changed, the basic criteria—whether the employer has met the procedural requirements of the regulations, whether there are insufficient U.S. workers who are able, willing, qualified, and available, and whether the employment of the alien will have an adverse effect on the wages and working conditions of U.S. workers similarly employed—remain the same. 69 Fed. Reg. 77325, 77327. Prior to PERM, the DOL utilized two different methods of recruitment to test the labor market for the availability of U.S. workers. The initial labor certification process, commonly called traditional recruitment (TR), had been in existence for approximately 25 years. It required the filing of an application (ETA 750A & B) with the state employment agency which would then direct the recruitment process and forward all documentation to a regional Certifying Officer (CO) employed by the DOL who would make a final determination as to the validity of the labor certification (LC). In 1996 the DOL began a process called Reduction in Recruitment as an alternative method for expediting cases. Generally, this process called for recruitment *prior* to filing the traditional application for alien labor certification (ETA-750A & B). Both of these processes are still in effect for applications filed prior to Mar. 28, 2005 where the employer has not chosen to refile under PERM. For greater details regarding TR and RIR, *see in this part* section C.10 (p.946), *infra*.

2. Individual job offer—20 C.F.R. §656.17

   Test labor market through the PERM process or through the traditional LC process or RIR for cases pending before Mar. 28, 2005.

3. Precertification (Schedule A)—20 C.F.R. §§656.5 & 656.15

   3.a. DOL designated job classifications that will not adversely affect U.S. workers. Schedule A includes nurses and physical therapists (Group I) and persons of exceptional ability in the sciences and arts and now in the performing arts (Group II).

   3.b. Under Schedule A an application (ETA Form 9089) is filed with supporting documentation directly with DHS when the I-140 application is filed. There is no recruitment process that involves a test of the labor market.

4. Schedule B Occupation—Prior to PERM, the DOL determined that there were enough U.S. workers in certain unskilled occupations to fill the demand and that employment of foreign workers in these categories would adversely affect U.S. workers. Schedule B, however, has now been eliminated and an unskilled position may be certified under PERM. 69 Fed. Reg. 77325, 77336 (Dec. 27, 2004).

5. Optional Special Recruitment for College and University Teachers—20 C.F.R. §656.18. The former special handling provisions have been eliminated and they have been replaced by an optional process of recruitment. Under these provisions an employer may opt to use the basic labor certification process under §656.17 as an alternative. §656.18(d).

6. Professional Athletes—The processing of athletes to be employed in professional team sports are not affected by PERM. The existing special procedures and the use of ETA 750 forms are retained. 69 Fed. Reg. 77325, 77328 (Dec. 27, 2004).

7. PERM (Program Electronic Review Management)—Proposed regulations, 67 Fed. Reg. 30465 (May 6, 2002), *published on* AILA InfoNet at Doc. No. 02050740 (May 7, 2002), and final regulations, 69 Fed. Reg. 77325 (Dec. 27, 2004), *published on* AILA InfoNet at Doc. No. 04122312.

   The PERM process represents a departure from the system utilized for 25 years to recruit U.S. workers. Under PERM, Schedule B and special handling procedures are eliminated, although there are special procedures for college and university teachers [20 C.F.R. §656.18] and for professional athletes. Schedule A is retained for nurses, physical therapists, persons of exceptional ability in the sciences and arts and persons of exceptional ability in the *performing* arts. 20 C.F.R. §§656.5 & 15. A worker who was subject to layoff within the past 6 months of filing the LC must be notified and considered first for the position if it is the same occupation or a related occupation to the one where the LC is being sought, and in the same geographical area. §656.17(k), 69 Fed. Reg. 77325, 77354–56 (Dec. 27, 2004). Also, U.S. workers may not be rejected even if they do not meet all job requirements, if within a reasonable period of time they can receive job training for those skills, or if they are able to perform the job duties in a normally acceptable manner given their backgrounds. §656.17(g)(2). The role of the local job service (SWA) is eliminated except to provide the prevailing wage. The employer would have to pay the prevailing wage, and the former 5% differential is eliminated. The Davis-Bacon Act and the McNamara-O'Hara Act (Service Contract Act or SCA) are no longer mandatory but could be asserted by the employer. §656.40(b)(4), 69 Fed. Reg. 77325, 77365–66 (Dec. 27, 2004). The employer no longer has to prove to DOL that it could pay the wage, as that is now left to USCIS to determine. 69 Fed. Reg. 77325, 77356 (Dec. 27, 2004). The recruitment process and the method of determining labor certifications is also altered. The recruitment process is completed *prior* to filing Form ETA-9089, which is now submitted electronically or, if necessary, by mail but not by fax to the National Processing Center in Atlanta (*PLC.Atlanta@dol.gov*). In a move toward more specialization, Atlanta will now take both mail-in and electronic PERM applications, including PERM applications for professional athletes. Chicago will accepts all D-1 attestations, H-1B, H-1B1 and E-3 LCAs, H-1C attestations, H-2A and H-2B labor certifications; and SWAs in Austin, New York and Sacramento will continue taking H-2B entertainers. 73 Fed. Reg. 11954–56 (Mar. 5, 2008). There is a distinction made between the processing of professional and nonprofessional positions, with professional positions being defined as those requiring a bachelor's or higher degree. The recruitment of professionals requires substantially greater recruitment efforts than nonprofessionals. *Compare* §656.17(e)(1) and §656.17(e)(2). Newspaper advertisements may now contain less information than in the traditional or RIR recruitment process, and they may contain "real-world wording" as long as the job opportunity is clearly identifiable. The ads must contain the employer's name, but need not contain the salary offered. §656.17(f). The employer does not have to produce the documents evidencing its recruitment or the results, but is subject to audit which would arise either randomly or by investigation. Notices of Findings (NOFs) are eliminated. The employer has 30 days to respond to the audit request. §656.20. This streamlined process should result in a quick determination on the application. If there is an audit and the materials requested are not provided within the 30 days, the application is denied. The denial may not be appealed, and the failure to provide documentation may result in attendant penalties including a "supervised" recruitment process for future filings. §§656.20 (a)(3) & (b). Applications are now filed on a new LC application (ETA-9089). If there is an appeal of the denial of a LC only the employer can appeal to BALCA. §656.26(a).

8. Refiling under PERM—20 C.F.R. §656.17(d), 69 Fed. Reg. at 77341–42. An employer who had a pending LC application under the reduction in recruitment (RIR) process or the basic LC process prior to Mar. 28, 2005, can refile under PERM and retain the original priority date if a job order has not been placed by SWA *and* (1) the application being submitted is "for an identical job opportunity" and (2) the prior application is being withdrawn. A job order placed by the employer as a recruitment step in an RIR application would not bar the employer from refiling because it is not treated as a job order being placed by SWA. PERM FAQs No. 1 ("Refiling") (Mar. 7, 2005), *published on* AILA InfoNet at Doc. No. 05030861. Filing the new application will automatically withdraw the pre–Mar. 28, 2005 application even if the PERM case is subsequently denied. Refiling under the new procedure must be made within 210 days of the withdrawal of the pre–Mar. 28, 2005 LC application. A job opportunity shall be considered identical if "the employer, alien, job title, job location, job requirements and job description are the same as those stated in the original application…" 20 C.F.R. §656.17(d)(4). Having a different prevailing wage would not bar refilling. PERM FAQs No. 1 ("Refiling") (Mar. 7, 2005), *published on* AILA InfoNet at Doc. No. 05030861. *See also http://www.foreignlaborcert.doleta.gov/perm.cfm.*

C. *Individual Certification under PERM*

1. Basic Procedure

   1.a. Employer Must Register—Only an employee or owner of the employer entity (not its lawyer or agent) may register to use the Permanent Online System for electronic filing of labor certification applications (ETA 9089). To register the employer must go to *www.plc.doleta.gov.* The registration must be submitted by an individual with actual hiring authority for the employer and the person with actual hiring authority must be listed under the Employer Contact Information section of the registration page. During the registration process, the employer may create sub-accounts for attorneys or agents to permit them to file applications in their name. However, an employer cannot establish sub-accounts for its own subsidiaries if they have different Federal Employer Identification Numbers (FEINs). PERM FAQs No. 4 ("Filing") (June 1, 2005), *published on* AILA InfoNet at Doc. No. 05060364. Registrations submitted by nonemployers will be canceled or denied. PERM FAQs No. 2 ("Registration") (Apr. 7, 2005), *published on* AILA InfoNet at Doc. No. 05041463.

   1.b. Employer Must File Form ETA 9089. Form ETA 9089 is filed electronically with an ETA application processing center. To file the application electronically, the employer, attorney or agent goes to *www.plc.doleta.gov.*

   (1) Multiple Applications Prohibited—An employer may only have one Form 9089 pending and in process for a beneficiary for the same job opportunity at one time as multiple, simultaneous, applications for the same beneficiary for the same job opportunity are prohibited. FAQs Revision to Question 12, *published on* AILA InfoNet at Doc. No. 05122160. In filling out the application the employer is required to submit an NAICS (North-American Industry Classification System) code that can be found at *www.naics.com/search.htm*. The employer is also required to submit the Standard Occupational Classification (SOC) code specific to the occupation that can be found at *www.bls.gov/soc*.

   (2) Employer Must Have Federal Employer Identification Number (FEIN) to file proper application—Employers, even households seeking to file an LC, must have a FEIN. *Maria*

Gonzalez, 07-PERM-24 (BALCA Apr. 25, 2007) [failure to provide a FEIN on ETA Form 9089 section C-7 is a violation of §656.17(a) because the FEIN is used to determine whether an employer is a bona fide business as the regulatory comments noted 69 Fed. Reg. 77329, 77329 (Dec. 27, 2004)]

(3) Errors Including Typoos Are Fatal/No Corrections—The employer must also place a correct federal employer identification number (FEIN) in section C-7 on the form. *Debra and Daniel Alpert,* 07-PER-109 (BALCA Dec. 17, 2007) [denial of LC upheld where employer did not submit a valid FEIN under section C-7); *Maria Gonzalez,* 07-PER-24 (BALCA Apr. 25, 2007) [employer can not use a Social Security number as a substitute for a FEIN when completing section C-7 on Form 9089]; *Lori Discolo,* 07-PERM-108 (BALCA Dec. 17, 2007) [same]. Once the application is filed it cannot be corrected. Revised PERM FAQs (Aug. 8, 2005), *published on* AILA InfoNet at Doc. No. 05082540. If the application is incomplete it will be denied. If the employer receives a certification that contains an error made by the employer, the ETA 9089 cannot be corrected and may only be withdrawn. Round 2, Fraud Rule PERM FAQs (Mar. 2008), *published on* AILA InfoNet at Doc. No. 08040234. Where the SWA presented a prevailing wage determination (PWD) with errors such as an incorrect SOC code or validity period, it is the employer's responsibility to ensure that the PWD obtained from the SWA is complete and in compliance with PERM and DOL will deny requests to correct the PWD information. PERM FAQs No. 6 (Feb. 21, 2006), *published on* AILA InfoNet at Doc. No. 06022474. It is also the employer's responsibility to ensure that all items on the Form 9089 are fully completed. *Subhashini Software Solutions,* 07-PER-39, 41, 42, 52, 53 (BALCA Dec. 10, 2007) [failure to respond to questions H-8 and H-10A on Form 9089]; *Best Manufacturing, Inc.*, 07-PER-80 (BALCA Dec. 19, 2007) [employer checked off box H-6 regarding experience but failed to complete H-6A regarding the months of experience]. However, the DOL's right to determine that a simple typographical error on the ETA 9089 form cannot be corrected has been called into question in *HealthAmerica,* 06-PER-1 (BALCA July 16, 2006) (*en banc*) [BALCA returned the case to the CO that denied certification where an employer made a typographical error on Form 9089 and rejected an answer to FAQ #5 where the ETA stated no typographical errors would be permitted holding that FAQs do not have the force of law and that FAQ#5 was unsupported by the regulations]. But the DOL has determined that after July 16, 2007 an error that results from an employer's disregard of system prompts or other direct instructions will result in a denial and the CO will not reconsider the determination. Round 2, Fraud Rule PERM FAQs (Mar. 2008), *published on* AILA InfoNet at Doc. No. 08040234.

(4) Employer/Attorney/Beneficiary Must Sign After Certification—If the ETA Form 9089 is certified electronically the employer, alien, and if applicable the preparer, upon receipt, must sign the form immediately in order for it to be valid. PERM FAQs No. 1 (Mar. 7, 2005), *published on* AILA InfoNet at Doc. No. 05030861. An excellent guide to filling out the ETA 9089 can be found at Clark, "Anatomy of Form ETA 9089, *The David Stanton Manual on Labor Certification* (AILA 2005) at 105–44.

(5) Applications by Mail—Applications may also be submitted by mail (but not by fax) and must contain the original signatures of the employer, the beneficiary, and counsel if applicable. 20 C.F.R. §656.17(a). An application by mail is submitted to the DOL National Processing Center (NPC) [now Atlanta]. *See* PERM FAQs No. 1 (Mar. 7, 2005), *published on* AILA InfoNet at Doc. No. 05030861 for mailing addresses. However, an application that is mailed to the NPC is simply re-recorded on the electronic ETA Form 9089 and reviewed in an identical manner. PERM FAQs No. 4 ("Filing") (June 1, 2005), *published on* AILA InfoNet at Doc. No. 05060364. The DOL interpretation that the Form 9089 if submitted by mail must contain the DOL logo was rejected as not grounded in any regulation or interpretation of the statute and a violation of fundamental fairness. *Subhashini Software Solutions,* 07-PER-43, 44, 46 (BALCA Dec. 18, 2007) [reversed denial of LC where because FORM 9089 did not contain the official DOL logo]

(6) Application Under Penalty of Perjury—The employer must attest, under penalty of perjury, to certain matters on the ETA 9089 form including that he will pay the prevailing wage, that the position is not vacant due to a labor dispute, that he has sufficient funds to

pay the wage and that he will be able to place the applicant on the payroll on or before the date of the applicant's entrance into the U.S. 20 C.F.R. §656.10(c).

(7) Supporting Docs Not Filed with ETA 9089—No supporting documentation is filed with the ETA 9089. PERM FAQs No. 1 (Mar. 7, 2005), *published on* AILA InfoNet at Doc. No. 05030861. The employer however must maintain the documentation for a period of five years from the filing of the ETA 9089, 20 C.F.R. §656.10(f), and must furnish the documentation when requested by the CO, generally pursuant to an audit. 20 C.F.R. §656.20

1.c. State Workforce Agency (SWA)—Before submitting the ETA 9089 to the processing center, the employer must get a prevailing wage determination from the SWA having jurisdiction over the proposed area of intended employment. The document evidencing the prevailing wage determination by the SWA must be physically kept by the employer in the event of an audit and the information regarding the prevailing wage must be entered on the ETA 9089 before submission. 20 C.F.R. §656.40(a). An employer may contest or offer alternative sources and alternative proof to establish the correct prevailing wage determination (PWD). 20 C.F.R. §656.40(b)-(h). The validity period for the PWD by the SWA may vary between 90 days and one year and the ETA 9089 must be filed or the required recruitment initiated during that period. 20 C.F.R. §656.40(c).

1.d. Recruitment Process—The recruitment process must occur *prior to filing* the ETA 9089. But it may begin before receiving the prevailing wage determination from the SWA. PERM FAQs No. 1 ("Prevailing Wage") (Mar. 7, 2005), *published on* AILA InfoNet at Doc. No. 05030861. Recruitment methods differ between professional and nonprofessional occupations. 20 C.F.R. §§656.17(e)(1) & (e)(2). For legal issues that arise in the recruitment process, *see in this section* ¶ 9 (p.940), *infra*.

(1) Recruitment for Professional Occupations. 20 C.F.R. §656.17(e)(1). The DOL has set forth a list of professional occupations that require specialized recruitment. The professional occupations are listed in Appendix A to the Preamble to the regulations, but the employer is not barred from asserting other occupations as professional. 69 Fed. Reg. 77325, 77345–46 and Appendix A (Dec. 27, 2004), *published on* AILA InfoNet at Doc. No. 04122312. *See* **Appendix A** to this book**,** *infra.* BALCA has held that professional recruitment must be utilized if the position is listed on Appendix A, whether or not the employer requires a university degree. *EPI Limited Partnership,* 08-PER-4 (BALCA Apr. 28, 2008) [affirmed CO denial where employer required a high school degree but used SOC/O*NET property manager title and did not conduct professional recruitment]. *See also Perrault Landscape Contracting, LLC,* 07-PER-08 (BALCA Apr. 6, 2007) [CO denial upheld for failure to engage in professional recruitment for landscape design position where the position was listed as landscape architect (an Appendix A position) and there were several indications that a landscape designer and landscape architect were the equivalent positions]. The employer may accept work experience in lieu of a degree but it must state so on the ETA-9089 and must apply the experience in lieu of a degree to U.S. applicants. The employer may also accept an equivalent foreign degree as long as it is clearly stated on the ETA-9089. PERM FAQs No. 1 ("Alien Experience") (Mar. 7, 2005), *published on* AILA InfoNet at Doc. No. 05030861.

The employer must conduct recruitment within the 6-month period prior to filing the ETA-9089. A posting notice to employees, a job order, and two print advertisements are mandatory and must be placed at least 30 days but no more than 180 days before filing the ETA 9089. The job order must be open with the SWA for a period of 30 calendar days and *completed* 30 days *prior* to filing the ETA 9089. *See* 67 Fed. Reg. 30466, 30471 (May 6, 2002) [ETA Proposed Rule]; *Construction Pros Corp.,* 07-PERM-77 (BALCA Dec. 18, 2007) [where ETA 9089 showed an end date for the SWA job order that was only 7 days prior to filing the ETA 9089, the application was properly denied because under 20 C.F.R. §656.17(e) the SWA job order must have been completed 30 days before filing the application]; *Luyon Corp.,* 07-PERM-27 (BALCA June 12, 2007); *Dr. Afshin Abdollahi DMD, Inc.,* 08-PERM-9 (BALCA Dec. 17, 2007) [CO denial affirmed where employer failed to enter the dates of the SWA job order on the ETA 9089]; *cf. Lam Garden*

Chinese Restaurant, 08-PER-14 (BALCA Dec. 17, 2007) [where the 30 day placement with the SWA was not met due to an error by the SWA, not the employer, (because Feb. had only 28 days), BALCA reversed the denial and ordered the LC to be granted]. The two advertisements must be placed on two different Sundays in a "newspaper of general circulation" in the area of intended employment most appropriate to the occupation and the workers likely to apply and most likely to bring responses from U.S. workers. An employer may substitute a professional journal for one of the two ads if the job requires experience and an advanced degree and a professional journal normally would be used to advertise the job opportunity. However, the employer may not use an electronic national professional journal but only a print journal. PERM FAQS No. 2 ("Recruitment/Advertising") (Apr. 7, 2005), *published on* AILA InfoNet at Doc. No. 05041463. Although the employer may not use an electronic national professional journal to satisfy the requirements of 20 C.F.R. §656.17(e)(1)(i)(B)(4) [permitting the use of a journal in lieu of one of the mandatory Sunday ads for professional positions], it may use it to satisfy the additional recruitment required for professionals found at 20 C.F.R. §656.17(e)(1)(ii)(E). PERM FAQs No. 9 (Nov. 29, 2006), *published on* AILA InfoNet at Doc. No. 06120460. If the job opportunity is located in a rural area without a Sunday edition, the newspaper with the widest circulation in the area may be used. However, if it is in a suburban area, the employer must publish in the most appropriate city newspaper that services the area. PERM FAQs No. 1 ("Recruitment/Advertisement/Time Frames") (Mar. 7, 2005), *published on* AILA InfoNet at Doc. No. 05030861.

In addition to the mandatory steps the employer must take three of the following 10 additional steps to recruit:

(a) Job fairs;

(b) Employer's website;

(c) Job search website other than the employer's.

  i) The job search website criteria cannot be satisfied by submission to an electronic national job bank (*e.g.,* formerly America's Job Bank) *if* the SWA's typical placement procedure is to put the ad in the cite. PERM FAQs No. 1 ("Recruitment/Professional/Non-Professional") (Mar. 7, 2005), *published on* AILA InfoNet at Doc. No. 05030861. The traditional e-national job bank was America's Job Bank, but it has been phased out. DeRocco, Asst. Sec, ETA, Notice 27-06 (Apr. 3, 2007), *published on* AILA InfoNet at Doc. No. 07040390. [noting other ETA-sponsored national e-tools such as CareerOneStop, Career Voyages, America's Career Information Network and America's Service Locator).

(d) On-campus recruiting;

  i) Can use this option even if the job requires experience in addition to a degree. Round 10, PERM FAQs, DOL, *published on* AILA InfoNet at Doc. No. 07051160.

(e) Trade or professional organizations;

(f) Private employment firms;

(g) Employee referral program with incentives;

(h) Campus placement offices;

(i) Local and ethnic newspapers;

(j) Radio and television advertisements.

These steps cannot be duplicated nor can one step be used to satisfy two requirements (*e.g.*, employer cannot count two advertisements in a local and/or ethnic newspaper or two postings on a website as two steps or count the use of a professional journal in lieu of a second Sunday ad as also meeting the "trade or professional organizations' advertising requirement). PERM FAQs No. 1 ("Recruitment/Professional/Non Professional") (Mar. 7, 2005), *published on* AILA InfoNet at Doc. No. 05030861. Nor can the posting of the notice of filing on in-house media be counted as an additional recruitment step. PERM

FAQS No. 2 ("Recruitment/Notice of Filing") (Apr. 7, 2005), *published on* AILA InfoNet at Doc. No. 05041463. Also, an employer may not use other forms of media (*e.g.*, ads in movie theaters) that are not provided on the list of alternative steps. PERM FAQs No. 4 ("Recruitment/Professional/Nonprofessional") (June 1, 2005), *published on* AILA InfoNet at Doc. No. 05060364.

(k) Thirty (30) and One Hundred Eighty (180) Day Requirements

i) Thirty Day—All recruitment must also take place within 30 and 180 days prior to filing the ETA 9089. This means that the last advertising must be closed 30 days prior to filing and placement with SWA must be completed 30 days prior to filing the ETA 9089. If the ETA 9089 is filed less than 30 days before completion of the SWA placement or of advertising, the failure is a basis for denial. *Golden Bridge Restaurant LLC,* 07-PER-99 (BALCA Dec. 18, 2007) [labor certification denied because ETA 9089 was filed less than 30 days after the end of the job order placed with SWA]. However, one of the three additional steps required for professional occupations may take place within 30 days of filing. PERM FAQs No. 1 ("Recruitment/Advertisement/Time Frames") (Mar. 7, 2005), *published on* AILA InfoNet at Doc. No. 05030861.

ii) One Hundred Eighty Day—Similarly, the first advertisements cannot run more than 180 days before the ETA 9089. If the application is submitted electronically then it is the date of submission. However, if it is mailed to the NPC, it is date the ETA is date stamped at the NPC that controls and not the date it was placed in the mail. *Café Vallarta,* 07-PER-29, -33 (BALCA June 12, 2007) [NPC's receipt stamp of the ETA that was more than 180 days beyond the first advertisement rendered the application invalid]; *Richmond Printing LLC,* 07-PER-35 (BALCA June 12, 2007) [rejected employer's fundamental fairness argument based upon *HealthAmerica* in its failure to file the ETA 9089 electronically within NPC due to timing out of the system].

(2) Recruitment for Nonprofessional Occupations 20 C.F.R. §656.17(e)(2)

Same mandatory requirements of a job order with the SWA and advertisements on two different Sundays. *See supra.* The job order must be open with the SWA for a period of 30 calendar days and *completed* 30 days *prior* to filing the ETA 9089. *See* 67 Fed. Reg. 30466, 30471 (May 6, 2002) [ETA Proposed Rule]; *Construction Pros Corp.,* 07-PERM-77 (BALCA Dec. 18, 2007) [where ETA 9089 showed an end date for the SWA job order that was only 7 days prior to filing the ETA 9089, the application was properly denied because under 20 C.F.R. §656.17(e) the SWA job order must have been completed 30 days before filing the application]; *Ameyovi J. Oyassan,* 07-PERM-69 (BALCA Dec. 18, 2007) [application for barber was properly denied where job order with SWA was filed, maintained for thirty days, and then ETA 9089 was filed without waiting 30 days from *completion* of job order]; *Luyon Corp,* 07-PERM-27 (BALCA June 12, 2007); *Beck AG Operations Inc.,* 08-PERM-5 (BALCA Dec. 18, 2007) [employer's lack of awareness that job order needed to be placed with SWA is insufficient justification to overcome denial by CO]; There is an exception for rural areas but no exception for professional journals. There are no nonmandatory requirements.

(3) Advertising Requirements. The advertisement is no longer required to enumerate "every job duty, job requirement, and condition of employment" and "lengthy, detailed advertisements are not required by the regulation." 69 Fed. Reg. 77325, 77347 (Dec. 27, 2004). It also does not require the employer to include his street address as resumes may be sent to a post office box. *Id.* at 77349.And the final rule eliminates "the requirement that the wage offer must be included in the advertisement." *Id.* at 77348. If the employer decides to advertise the wage, it may advertise it with a wage range as long as the bottom of the range is not less than the prevailing wage. PERM FAQS No. 2 ("Prevailing Wage") (Apr. 7, 2005), *published on* AILA InfoNet at Doc. No. 05041463

The advertisement must only do the following: (1) Name the employer; (2) Direct applicants to report or send resumes, as appropriate for the occupation, to the employer; (3) Provide a description of the vacancy specific enough to apprise the U.S. workers of the job opportunity; (4) Indicate the geographic area of employment with enough specificity to apprise applicants of any travel requirements or where they have to reside; (5) Not contain a wage rate lower than the prevailing wage if a wage is put in the ad; (6) Not contain any job requirements or duties which exceed the job requirements or duties listed on the ETA Form 9089; and (7) Not contain wages or terms and conditions of employment less favorable than those offered to the alien. If the employer wishes to include additional information such as the minimum education and experience requirements or specific job duties, she may do so provided these requirements also appear in the ETA 9089. PERM FAQs No. 1 ("Recruitment/Advertisement/Advertisement Content") (Mar. 7, 2005), *published on* AILA InfoNet at Doc. No. 05030861. Employers are not required to specify the job site unless it is unclear because the employee must report to a location other than the job site or the employer has multiple job sites. *Id.* Employers are also not required to give their address but may designate a central office or post office box to receive resumes. *Id.* Multiple positions may be advertised. *Id.* Advertising can be documented by saving copies of the pages where the ads appear in the newspaper or obtaining proof of publication by the newspaper and journal.

Name Change. Where the employer's name changed between the advertising and the submission of the ETA Form 9089, the employer is obligated to put the new name on the form and to provide documentation regarding the successor in interest/merger. Round 10, PERM FAQs, DOL, *published on* AILA InfoNet at Doc. No. 07051160.

(4) Counting the Time Periods and the Timelines. PERM FAQs No. 9 (Nov. 29, 2006), *published on* AILA InfoNet at Doc. No. 06120460. The DOL distinguishes between *timelines*, (which calculate the number of days prior to or after an event such as verifying that ads did not run less than 30 days nor more than 180 days from the date of filing) and *time periods* (which verify the number of days an activity took place such as verifying that a job order ran for 30 days)

(a) Calculating Timelines. The day the event occurred is not counted. The next day is counted as day one and the last day of the event is included in the count. For example, to calculate the 30 day period prior to filing the ETA 9089 after completing the job order, if the last day of the job order was Mar. 2nd the count for the 30 day period would begin on Mar.3rd and include the last day which would be April 1st.

(b) Calculating Time Periods. When calculating a time period, both the start date and the end date are included in the count. Thus, if the job order is placed on March 2, the 30-day period ends March 31.

1.e. Notice to Bargaining Representatives or Posting Notice to Employees—20 C.F.R. §656.10(d)

Notice To Bargaining Representative. The employer must provide notice to the bargaining representative (if any) of the *employer's employees* in the occupational classification and area for which aliens are sought. Notice to the bargaining representative in the area requires notice to each representative where there is more than one work site in the area. 56 Fed. Reg. 54920, 54924 (Oct. 23, 1991); or

Posting Notice to Employees. If no bargaining representative, employer must post the notice for 10 consecutive days in a conspicuous location at the facility. In addition, the employer must publish the notice in all in-house media, whether electronic or printed, in accordance with normal recruitment procedures, if it normally uses in-house media to recruit. The notice must: (1) state it is being provided as a result of filing a LC; (2) state that any person may provide documentary evidence bearing on the application to the CO; (3) provide the address of the CO; and (4) be posted between 30 and 180 days before filing the application. 20 C.F.R. §656.10(d)(3). When providing the address of the CO the employer is now on notice that the appropriate CO's office to list is the National Processing Center in Atlanta because it will be processing all permanent LCs. *Cf. Brooklyn Amity School*, 07-PER-64 (BALCA Sept. 19, 2007) [allowing in the unusual facts of the case to list the former New York CO office but recognizing that all future case must list the appropriate National Processing Center]. The notice must also contain the information required for advertisements under the basic labor certification process under §656.17(f) (*see in this section* "Advertising Requirements," ¶ 1.d(3) (p.913), *supra*), and the rate of pay. 20 C.F.R. §656.10(d)(4). When publishing the notice of filing in its in-house media, the employer must publish it for 10 consecutive business days or for a length of time consistent with its normal practice, whichever is longer. PERM FAQS No. 2 ("Recruitment/Notice of Filing") (Apr. 7, 2005), *published on* AILA InfoNet at Doc. No. 05041463. The last day of posting must be at least 30 days prior to filing the ETA 9089. PERM FAQs No. 1 ("Recruitment/Notice of Filing") (Mar. 7, 2005), *published on* AILA InfoNet at Doc. No. 05030861. The electronic in-house notice does not have to be identical to the physical in-house notice but it must meet the minimum requirements above and state the rate of pay. Round 10, PERM FAQs, DOL, *published on* AILA InfoNet at Doc. No. 07051160.

Posting the Wage. The wage must be placed in the notice even if it is not in the advertisement. 69 Fed. Reg. 77325, 77338 (Dec. 27, 2004). A wage range may be offered in the notice as long as the bottom of the range is no less than the prevailing wage at the time the recruitment was conducted. TAG at 114; 69 Fed. Reg. 77325, 77338 (Dec. 27, 2004). The employer must provide the address of the appropriate Certifying Officer for the area of intended employment on the notice. PERM FAQs No. 1 ("Recruitment/Notice of Filing") (Mar. 7, 2005), *published on* AILA InfoNet at Doc. No. 05030861.

Posting Notice For Roving Employees. The employer must post the notice at the work-site(s) where the employee will perform the work *and* publish the notice internally using in-house media according to normal internal procedures. If the employer does not know where the employee will be placed it must post at the work-site(s) of all current clients. If the work-site(s) are unknown and the staffing agency has no clients, the application would be denied as lacking a bona fide job offer. PERM FAQs No. 7 (Feb. 24, 2006), *published on* AILA InfoNet at Doc. No. 06022473.

The notice or posting requirement applies to Schedule A, College and University Teachers, Supervised Recruitment as well as the Basic Recruitment process. For college and university teachers, the notices of filing may be posted to employees or provided to the bargaining representative *after* the selection process has been completed as long as they are posted/provided between 30 and 180 days prior to the submission of the ETA 9089. PERM FAQs No. 1 ("Recruitment/Notice of Filing") (Mar. 7, 2005), *published on* AILA InfoNet at Doc. No. 05030861. The notice for college and university teachers does not have to contain the rate of pay. PERM FAQs No. 2 ("Recruitment/Notice of Filing") (Apr. 7, 2005), *published on* AILA InfoNet at Doc. No. 05041463. An employer may use the posting sample of a Notice of Filing issued by USCIS and DOL will honor it as long as it contains the employer's name. Round 10, PERM FAQs, DOL, *published on* AILA InfoNet at Doc. No. 07051160.

1.f. Recruitment Report—20 C.F.R. §656.17(g). The employer must prepare, but is not required to provide to the CO unless requested through an audit or otherwise, a recruitment report signed by the employer or his representative. It must describe the recruitment steps undertaken and the results achieved, the number of hires and, if applicable, the number of U.S. workers rejected, categorized by the lawful job related reasons for such rejections. The report need not identify each individual worker who applied for the job opportunity but was rejected. 69 Fed. Reg. at 77373 (Dec. 27, 2004). The CO may request the workers' resumes or applications sorted by the reason for their rejections. The employer must retain all documentation for a period of 5 years from the date the LC is filed. 20 C.F.R. §656.10(f).

1.g. Request for Audit—20 C.F.R. §656.20. A request for an audit may arise because of the need to review an individual LC application or due to a random request for quality control purposes. An audit letter will not be a "fishing expedition" and "will only request information necessary to make a determination on a specific case or to monitor the system effectively." 69 Fed. Reg. 77325, 77359 (Dec. 27, 2004). If the employer is sent an audit letter, s/he has 30 days to respond. The CO may grant one 30-day extension. Failure to produce the documents in a timely manner results in a denial and is treated as a failure to exhaust administrative remedies, thereby barring BALCA review. §656.20(a)(3)(ii). If the employer engages in a substantial failure to provide the required documentation, the LC will be denied by the CO under §656.24 and it may result in requiring the employer to conduct supervised recruitment under §656.21 for all future LCs for a period of two years. Before making a final determination, however, the CO may request supplemental information and/or documentation or may require the employer to conduct supervised recruitment for the LC. The employer may provide alternative evidence in the absence of primary evidence in response to the audit request. Round 10, PERM FAQs, DOL, *published on* AILA InfoNet at Doc. No. 07051160. An employer cannot avoid an audit by withdrawing the application. PERM FAQs No. 4 ("Audit") (June 1, 2005), *published on* AILA InfoNet at Doc. No. 05060364

(1) The traditional BALCA decisions regarding the sufficiency of the employer's documented responses will be relevant to audits. *See e.g., Gencorp,* 87-INA-659 (BALCA Jan. 13, 1988) (*en banc*) [the CO may request a document that has a direct bearing on the resolution of an issue and the employer's written assertions that are "reasonably specific and indicate their sources or bases" constitute "documentation"]; *Chatila Diamond Corporation d/b/a Blue and White,* 05-INA-145 (BALCA Sept. 29, 2006) [denial of LC upheld where current employer refused to provide information regarding employees prior employers who hired employee without authorization]. *See also South Valley Drywall Inc.,* 07-INA-272 (BALCA Jan. 16, 2008) [employer's letter stating he had 380 active employees and website indicated he had been in business almost 30 years was insufficient rebuttal when he should have produced tax records, unemployment insurance records, and payroll records to demonstrate he had funds to pay wage]; *Twin Industries,* 07-INA-270 (BALCA Jan. 16, 2008) [CO properly rejected rebuttal regarding landscape gardener's position where accountant provided cursory letter and employer improperly submitted clarifying letters to BALCA that were not in the record, but neither provided payroll and other primary records]; *Unique General Auto Repairs,* 03-INA-255 (BALCA Sept. 9, 2004) [employer's statement that 10 out of 12 domestic employees were rejected because they had procured other employment without any documentation to support it or reason for the failure to produce documentation was insufficient and RIR denial was upheld]; *Carlos Uy III,* 97-INA-304 (BALCA Mar. 3, 1999) (*en banc*) [employer's bare assertion without either supporting reasoning or evidence is generally insufficient to carry employer's burden of proof]; *Modular Container Systems, Inc.,* 89-INA-228 (BALCA July 16, 1991) (*en banc*) [lawyer's assertions on behalf of employer are not evidence].

(2) The 30-day deadline to respond to audit may not be jurisdictional and may be tolled. Under pre-PERM cases, a lawyer's incompetence could toll the time period for a NOF. *Compare Bloom,* 88-INA-152 (BALCA Oct. 13, 1989) [where attorney quit the practice of law and did not inform employer of the deadline, the 35-day time period to respond to NOF was waived because manifest injustice would otherwise result] *Nolhak Inc.,* 05-INA-114 (BALCA Aug. 2, 2006) [where employer demonstrated through Fed-X records it sent response timely and that response was received timely it was manifest injustice to deny application on that basis] *with Park Woodworking, Inc.,* 90-INA-93 (BALCA Jan. 29, 1992) (*en banc*) [calling for a narrow interpretation of *Bloom* and deciding that attorney negligence in failing to file is not manifest injustice].

1.h. Supervised Recruitment—20 C.F.R. §656.21. The use of supervised recruitment will "usually be based upon labor market information." 69 Fed. Reg. 77325, 77361 (Dec. 27, 2004). It is designed to maintain controls on the manner that recruitment is conducted by the employer and "is similar to the current regulations for recruitment under basic processing." *Id.* at 77328 However, "the CO should notify the employer of all appropriate recruitment sources at the outset of the recruitment process, so employers will not be required to go through multiple rounds of recruitment." *Id.* at 77361.

1.i. Payment of Fees In L.C. Case—20 C.F.R. §656.12(b).The employee is no longer permitted to pay his own fees and costs in the L.C. process if the attorney represents both the employer and employee. 72 Fed. Reg. 27904, 27919–24 (May17, 2007). The prohibition exists even if the attorney is representing the employer *pro bono.* FAQs on Substitutions Plus Final Rule, DOL, *published on* AILA InfoNet at Doc. No. 07071675. The employer must not seek or receive payment of any kind for any activity related to obtaining the L.C., including payment of the employer's attorneys' fees whether as an incentive or inducement to file or a reimbursement for costs incurred in preparing or filing the L.C. The only exception is the payment by a person or entity who would benefit by the beneficiary's work due to the established relationship between the person or entity and the employer. Applies to Schedule A cases as well.

Round 2, Fraud Rule PERM FAQs (Mar. 2008), *published on* AILA InfoNet at Doc. No. 08040234.

(1) Any activity is defined as recruitment activity, the use of legal services, and any other action associated with the "preparation, filing or pursuit of an application." FAQs on Substitutions Plus Final Rule, DOL, *published on* AILA InfoNet at Doc. No. 07071675.

(2) Effective Date. This provision is effective July 16, 2007 and therefore fees that accrued (even if not yet paid) before that date are exempt from the bar on fees and counsel may collect that fee after July 16, 2007. FAQs on Substitutions Plus Final Rule, DOL, *published on* AILA InfoNet at Doc. No. 07071675.

1.j. Investigation and Suspension of Application Process—20 C.F.R. §656.31(a). The LC application process may be suspended when the CO suspects or discovers fraud or willful misrepresentation in the process. The CO refers the matter to DOJ, DHS or other government agency for investigation with a copy of the referral to the Office of Inspector General (OIG) of the DOL. If 180 days pass without the filing of a criminal indictment or information, or receipt of a notification from DHS, OIG or another appropriate authority that an investigation is being conducted, the CO may continue to process the application. 20 C.F.R. §656.31(b)(2).

1.k. Debarment—20 C.F.R. §656.31(f). If an employer, attorney, or agent has participated in or facilitated: (i) the sale, barter or purchase of a L.C.; (ii) willful provision or assistance in the provision of false or inaccurate information in applying for an L.C.; (iii) a pattern and practice of failing to comply with the terms of the L.C. applications; (iv) a pattern or practice of failing to comply with the audit process or, (v) supervised recruitment or (vi) conduct resulting in a determination by a court, DHS or DOS of fraud or willful misrepresentation involving the LC application as referenced in §656.31(e), he or she may be disbarred for a period of six years. Where the attorney or agent has been found to be involved in fraud or misrepresentation, the employer will be notified and given 30 days to inform DOL whether he will continue with the same counsel while debarment proceedings are conducted in which case the application process will be suspended. §656.31(e)(3).

1.l. Final decision by CO—20 C.F.R. §656.24 The CO may grant, deny or in a special or unique case refer a LC to the Chief, Division of Foreign Labor Certification. If a LC is granted the CO must send the certified application to the employer or, if appropriate, to the employer's agent or attorney. If it is denied, the Final Determination must state the reasons for the denial, quote the BALCA review procedure and the 30-day deadline to request review, and advise the employer that a new LC may be filed at any time if there is no request for review but that a new LC may not be filed while a request for review is pending at BALCA. In addition, the CO may require supervised recruitment for future LCs for two years from the date of the Final Determination.

(1) Notice of CO Decision Under PERM. 20 C.F.R. §656.24(b)

(a) In making its determination the CO must decide whether or not: (1) the employer has met the requirements of the regulations; (2) there is in the U.S. a worker able, willing, qualified and available for and at the place of the job opportunity; and (3) the employment of the person will not have an adverse effect upon the wages and working conditions of U.S. workers similarly employed.

(2) Notice and Adequacy of CO Decision Under Pre-PERM Law

(a) Where CO based denial on issue raised for the first time in the final determination and where further delay in circumstances would be unfair, BALCA reversed and ordered CO to issue certification. *Clarkston Medical Group*, 87-INA-718 (BALCA 1988); *Little Mermaid Restaurant*, 87-INA-675 (BALCA 1988); and DOL Field Memorandum No. 61-89, reprinted in 8 AILA Monthly Mailing 343 (June, 1989); *Standard Oil Co.*, 88-INA-77 (BALCA 1988); *Shaw's Crab House*, 87-INA-714 (BALCA 1988). CO may not deny a labor certification for a reason that was raised for the first time in a final determination. *Cotton L.A.*, 00-INA-313 (BALCA Sept. 25, 2001) [raising issue for first time in final decision rather than in NOF "deprives the Employer of due process"]; *Tarmac Roadstone (USA), Inc.*, 87-INA-701

(BALCA 1989). A labor cert. cannot be denied where CO never raised ground to deny certification. *Vander Sterre*, 95-INA-511 (BALCA July 28, 1997) [where CO never disputed issue that employer unlawfully rejected qualified applicants, BALCA could not deny LC on that ground].

(b) Employer's offer to readvertise after CO denial of certification "comes too late." *Agha Khan Gems Corp.*, 88-INA-66 (BALCA 1989). However, when NOF was ambiguous evidence submitted after the final determination will be permitted. *Hsieh*, 88-INA-540 (BALCA 1989).

(c) CO's bare conclusion that there were qualified and available U.S. workers who were improperly rejected is insufficient to give the employer notice and fair opportunity to rebut. *Exxon Chemical Co.*, 87-INA-615 (BALCA 1988); *Hennessey's Tavern*, 88-INA-531 (BALCA 1989) [CO's notice of findings inadequate where it only identified issues but did not explain why the employer's application was deficient]; *Downey Orthopedic Medical Group*, 87-INA-674 (BALCA 1988) (*en banc*); *Seibel & Stern*, 90-INA-86 (BALCA 1990) [CO failed to inform petitioner in regard to burden on prevailing wage issue]. CO should not rely excessively on boilerplate language, but should provide a detailed and clear statement of the reason for denial. *Sizzler Restaurants, Inc.*, 88-INA-123 (BALCA 1989). Where CO asserts that a combination of education and training is sufficient in a case where applicants did not meet one of the stated job requirements, the CO has burden of proof under 20 C.F.R. §656.24(b)(2)(ii). *Community Hospital of the Monterey Peninsula,* 97-INA-331 (BALCA June 30, 1998).

(d) CO is not required to investigate another proffered reason for rejecting an applicant where employer first rejected the applicant for an unlawful reason. *Shogun Enterprises, Inc d/b/a I Love Sushi Restaurant,* 02-INA-294 (BALCA Jan. 9, 2004) [where the employer cited the applicant's failure to pass a test which was an unstated requirement, the CO was not obligated to entertain an entirely different proffered reason for the denial].

(3) Use of Hearsay—Hearsay evidence admissible, but must have probative value, meet minimum requirements of admissibility and bear indicia of reliability. *Cathay Carpet Mills, Inc.*, 87-INA-161 (BALCA 1988) [CO questionnaire sent to rejected applicants outweighed by employer's own statements to the contrary]. This is less of a problem currently as DOL has eliminated applicant questionnaires. GAL 1-97, Farmer, Admin. for Regional Management, DOL (Oct. 1, 1996), *reprinted in* 73 No. 40 *Interpreter Releases* 1458, 1476–82, 1480 (Oct. 21, 1996), *modified* May 4, 1999, *reprinted in* 76 No. 19 *Interpreter Releases* 759, 780–82 (May 17, 1999)

(4) Employer's Efforts in Pre-PERM cases.

(a) CO abused its discretion when it denied application where employer had agreed to readvertise, had requested a new job order number and had stated it would report the results of second recruitment but had been unable to complete recruitment within the 35-day period. *Alabama Reweaving Co.*, 89-INA-294 (BALCA 1989) ["Where legitimate efforts are being made to take corrective action, it has been held an abuse of discretion to deny an extension"]. *See also Friedman*, 89-INA-220 (BALCA 1990) [CO reversed for refusing to give employer who was making legitimate efforts to obtain letter proving experience sufficient time to do so].

(b) CO must also allow employer "two bites at the apple" by allowing the employer to cure the defect with arguments or documentation and, if the attempt fails, to have the additional right to readvertise the job opportunity. *O'Mara*, 96-INA-113 (BALCA Dec. 11, 1997) (*en banc*) [employer had right to rebut NOF that job requirements were unduly restrictive, and if unsuccessful, to readvertise without special requirements]; *Cottonwood Home,* 04-INA-2 (BALCA Mar. 11, 2005) [followed *O'Mara* and required CO to allow employer to cure defect by proffering business necessity and if unsuccessful to readvertise]; *Atlanta Oriental Food Wholesale Co.,* 08-INA-46 (BALCA Feb. 11, 2008) [followed *O'Mara* and *Cottonwood Home* and required remand to readvertise]; *Yurkevitch*, 90-INA-4 (BALCA 1990) [CO reversed where employer not given opportunity to readvertise because he sought to wait until CO resolved business necessity issue].

1.m. Validity of the Labor Certification—20 C.F.R. §656.30(b). An LC is no longer valid indefinitely. An approve LC *expires* if not filed in support of an I-40 petition with DHS within *180 calendar days* of the date it was granted by DOL. For LCs granted prior to July 16, 2007 (the effective date of the regulations), they had to be filed no later than 180 days from July 16, 2007. 72 Fed. Reg. 27904 (May 17, 2007). DOL may revoke a LC at any time for fraud and willful misrepresentations, obvious errors or for grounds or issues associated with the LC process. 69 Fed. Reg. at 77365. USCIS will continue to accept copies of a labor certification, even if expired, if it is filed with an amended or duplicate Form 1-140 where the original approved LC was filed in support of a previously filed petition during the time the LC was valid. AFM at 22.2(f). This type of filing may occur when a new petition is required because there is a successor-in-interest, where the previously I-140 was lost, or where the amended petition is requesting a different visa category.

1.n. Duplicate LC—20 C.F.R. §656.30(e)(2); AFM at 22.2(b)(8)–(10). An employer, beneficiary or her attorney or agent may request that the CO issue a duplicate approved LC (ETA-9089) to a consular or immigration officer. The request must be directed to the CO who issued the LC and must include documentary evidence that the visa application or petition has been filed and a tracking number for the consular officer or DHS. The DOL will not send the duplicate LC to the employer or his attorney but only to USCIS or a consular officer. PERM FAQs No. 8 (Procedure for Requesting Duplicate Labor Certification), *published on* AILA InfoNet at Doc. No. 06032716. If requesting a duplicate ETA-750 (as distinguished from a PERM ETA-9089) the duplicate can *only* be requested by USCIS and the employer must therefore file the I-140 (without the I-485) and note that the LC is lost or misplaced while requesting that USCIS secure a duplicate from DOL. *Id.*

1.o. No Expediting Cases for Aging-Out Children—The DOL adheres to a policy that cases will not be expedited, to assist aging-out children, preventing deportation, receiving medical treatment or for other reasons where it requires that the case be taken out of date order. Memo, Carlson, Chief Division of Foreign Labor Certification, "Expedite Policy," (Sept. 21, 2004), *published on* AILA InfoNet at Doc. No. 04100410.

1.p. Substitution of Beneficiary—The DOL no longer permits substitution of beneficiaries. 20 C.F.R. §656.11. The LC is only valid for the beneficiary named on the LC. Any substitution that was *approved* by DOL or DHS or in progress prior to July 16, 2007 are not effected by the elimination of the substitution rule. 72 Fed. Reg. 27904, 27906–07 (May 17 2007). *But see Medellin v. Bustos,* 854 F.2d 795 (5th Cir. 1988) [challenging whether DOL can revoke an L.C. because of substitution]. The nonsubstitution rule applies to Schedule A cases. Round 2, Fraud Rule PERM FAQs (Mar. 2008), *published on* AILA InfoNet at Doc. No. 08040234.

1.q. Substitution of employer—Substitutions or modifications of L.C. are no longer permitted. 20 C.F.R. §656.11 and although the regulation addresses changes to the identity of the beneficiary on the application, it also states that any requests for modification of the L.C. "will not be accepted. §656.11(b). Under pre-PERM law, DOL would permit the substitution of a *successor* employer if it occurred before a final determination where the particular job opportunity was preserved in the same area of intended employment consistent with 20 C.F.R. §656.30(c)(2). *Horizon Science Academy,* 06-INA-46 (BALCA Mar. 8, 2007) [under pre-PERM law cannot substitute employers "unless the alien is working in the exact same position, performing the same duties, in the same area of intended employment, and for the same wages"]; *American Chick Sexing Ass'n & Accu. Co.*, 89-INA-320 (BALCA Mar. 12, 1991) [substitution made before final rebuttal to CO]; *Int'l Contractors, Inc. & Technical Programming Services, Inc.*, 89-INA-278 (BALCA June 13, 1990). *But see American Chick Sexing Ass'n*, 89-INA-145 (BALCA Dec. 22, 1989); *Joram Rosenfeld*, 99-INA-158 (BALCA Jan. 6, 2000) [wife could not succeed husband on application for live-in cook because a personal application as opposed to a corporate one does not survive the death of the employer]. DOL would also allow a *new employer* to substitute where it is the same job opportunity in the same area of intended employment. *Law Offices of Jean-Pierre Karnos,* 03-INA-18 (BALCA May 20, 2004) [where there was a *new* employer who took over the law practice of Karnos on his death, a new LC does not have to be filed for an accountant applicant where it is the same job opportunity in the same area of intended employment including the same job duties and wages].

1.r. Modification of L.C.—20 C.F.R. §656.11. Modifications of L.C. are no longer permitted and will not be accepted. 72 Fed. Reg. 27904, 27916–18 (May17, 2007) [emphasizing the basis for the no-modification rule even for minor typographical errors].

1.s. Sale, Barter or Purchase of L.C., 8 C.F.R. §656.12(a)—LCs are not articles of commerce and may not be sold, bartered or purchased by individuals or entities. A violation of the section can result in a denial, revocation, debarment, or any combination of these actions.

(1) DOL defines the terms as follows: A "sale" means an agreement between a seller and a buyer to transfer ownership of an LC in consideration of monetary payment or promise to pay. "Barter" means the transfer by voluntary act or agreement in exchange for a commodity, service, property, or other valuable consideration. "Purchase" means the voluntary agreement to transfer ownership of a labor certification from one person to another based on valuable consideration. 20 C.F.R. §656.3; FAQs on Substitutions Plus Final Rule, DOL, *published on* AILA InfoNet at Doc. No. 07071675.

(2) Applies to Schedule A LCs as well. Round 2, Fraud Rule PERM FAQs (Mar. 2008), *published on* AILA InfoNet at Doc. No. 08040234.

1.t. Special Substitution Rule for Professional Athletes—INA §212(a)(5)(A)(iii), 8 U.S.C. §1182(a)(5)(A)(iii). LC is valid for professional athlete even if he changes employer if the new employer is a team in the same sport and the team is part of an association of 6 or more teams with combined revenues in excess of $10,000,000. This includes minor league teams affiliated with the association.

1.u. Amending LC Application—PERM was designed to preclude amendment of an application once filed; the only way to amend is to withdraw the application and refile. PERM FAQs No. 6 (Feb. 24, 2006), *published on* AILA InfoNet at Doc. No. 06022474. However, to refile, all recruitment must still be in place.

1.v. Revocation/Invalidation of Labor Certification. 20 C.F.R. §656.32

(1) Who May Revoke. The CO in consultation with the Chief, Division of Foreign Labor Certification. An LC may also be invalidated by DHS or DOS under 20 C.F.R. §656.30(d).

(2) Basis For Revocation. The CO may revoke *at any time* if s/he finds that the certification was *not justified.* There is no time limitation placed upon the authority of the CO to revoke. 69 Fed. Reg. 77325, 77364–65 (Dec. 27, 2004). The DOS and DHS may also invalidate an LC for fraud or material misrepresentation.

(3) Procedure. CO sends a notice of intent to revoke to the employer which contains a detailed statement of the grounds for revocation. The employer has 30 days *from receipt of the notice* to submit evidence in rebuttal. If the CO determines that the LC should be revoked, the employer may file an appeal to BALCA within 30 days of the date of the decision.

1.w. Denial/Appeal Process. 20 C.F.R. §§656.24–.27

(1) If CO denies the application and the employer does not appeal a new LC may be filed at any time. §656.24(e)(5). If the denial is appealed to BALCA, a new LC cannot be filed while review is pending at BALCA. §656.24(e)(6). Where the employer withdraws an application, he does not have to wait to reapply.

(2) Motion to Reconsider. After CO denial an employer can file a motion to reconsider. 20 C.F.R. §656.24(g)(1). The request for reconsideration may not include evidence not previously submitted unless it is documentation that the employer did not have an opportunity to present but that existed at the time the L.C. was filed and was maintained by the employer to support the application. 20 C.F.R. §656.24(g)(2). The CO may, at her discretion, treat the motion as an appeal to BALCA. Under pre-PERM law, the CO was not required to provide a statement for the reasons the motion was denied where it merely let stand a prior decision. *Richard Clarke Assoc.*, 90-INA-80 (BALCA May 13, 1992) (*en banc*). The CO may not deny a motion to reconsider without considering applicant's

claim. *Sotiangco Group of Companies,* 99-INA-194 (BALCA Sept. 7, 1999) [where the final determination is based on untimely rebuttal, it is an abuse of discretion for the CO not to reconsider the matter]. Under pre-PERM law, BALCA had the authority to remand cases and would do so where the CO failed to consider new evidence on reconsideration not available during the rebuttal period. *Madni, Inc. t/a Silver and Watch Palace,* 04-INA-75 (Mar. 3, 2005) [employer presented in motion to reconsider new, previously unavailable, financial information demonstrating employer's ability to pay salary]. For more details regarding motions to reconsider, *see in this chapter* ¶ IX.B.2 (p.950), *infra.*

(3) BALCA Appeal. 20 C.F.R. §§656.26–.27. If CO denies application, employer (only) can appeal within 30 days to the Board of Alien Labor Certification Appeals (BALCA), which is the administrative appellate body consisting of all ALJs assigned to labor certification matters. BALCA will only consider evidence in the record from the CO. *Western Waterproofing Co.*, 88-INA-514 (BALCA 1989); 20 C.F.R. §656.26(a)(2). Under PERM, BALCA no longer has no authority to remand cases to the CO. *See in this chapter* ¶ IX.B.7 (p.951), *infra.*

(4) If appeal denied by BALCA, employer or alien can seek review in federal court. *Reddy v. DOL*, 492 F.2d 538 (5th Cir. 1974). BALCA will entertain motions to reconsider its decision. *Edelweiss Mfg. Co.*, 87-INA-562 (BALCA 1988) [inherent authority where request grounded on oversight, omission or inadvertence]. But the motion can only be brought by the employer. An alien cannot bring the motion on her own. *K Super KQ-1541 A.M.*, 88-INA-397 (BALCA 1989).

1.x. Withdrawal— An employer may withdraw a certified PERM application at any time but must do so in writing, not electronically. A written request must be mailed to the appropriate NPC (Georgia or Chicago) and contain the application number, the employer's name and EIN number, the beneficiary's name and the name and title of the person requesting the withdrawal. If the application is withdrawn *after* an audit letter is received by the employer, the employer must still comply with the audit. A new application may not be filed after withdrawal until the PERM system shows the status changed from "in process" to "withdrawn" or until the employer receives confirmation by mail or e-mail. If the application is denied, the employer may not file a new application until the online status is changed to "denied." PERM FAQs No. 9 (Nov. 29, 2006), *published on* AILA InfoNet at Doc. No. 06120460. Under pre-PERM law if an application was denied the employer had to wait 6 months before reapplying. However, if the application was withdrawn prior to the issuance of a decision the employer could refile a new application without waiting 6 months. 12 *AILA Monthly Mailing* 185 (Mar. 1993). An applicant could also refile immediately even after a Notice of Findings (NOF) was issued, under pre-PERM law, if it was denied "solely because the wage or salary offered was below the prevailing wage." Memo, Farmer, Administrator for Regional Management Division of Foreign Labor Certification, DOL, Field Memo No. 48-94 (May 16, 1994), *published on* AILA InfoNet at Doc. No. 94052390.

1.y. Harmless Error—BALCA, under pre-PERM rules, recognized that errors by employer in process may simply be inadvertent and harmless. *Computech Int'l*, 94-INA-43 (BALCA Feb. 26, 1996) [directing that resumes on posted notice be sent to state agency as well as employer was harmless]; *Ritz Carlton*, 95-INA-265 (BALCA Jan. 29, 1997) [failing to put equivalency along with degree requirement on LC application where advertised properly]. Whether the harmless error doctrine will survive PERM is an unsettled proposition at this time.

2. Basic contested requirements

2.a. Minimum requirements—20 C.F.R. §§656.17(h) and (i).

(1) Job must be offered only with requirements that are "actual minimum" necessary to perform job satisfactorily. The employer could not have hired workers with less training or experience for jobs substantially comparable to that involved in the job opportunity. Applicant cannot count training or experience while working for the employer, including worked as a contract employee, unless the experience was obtained in a position not substantially comparable to the position on the application, or unless it is no longer feasible to train a worker for the position. 20 C.F.R. §656.17(i)(3). "Substantially comparable"

means "a job or position requiring performance of the same job duties more than 50 percent of the time." §656.17(i)(5)(ii).

(2) The job cannot be tailored to the alien, *e.g.*, a B.A. in horticulture cannot be required for a gardener. Job requirements must be normal for the occupation, unless justified by business necessity. Requirements cannot exceed Specific Vocational Preparation (SVP) level assigned to the occupation as shown in the O*NET Job Zones. 20 C.F.R. §656.17(h).

(3) Must be full time employee, permanent employment that is not self-employment. 20 C.F.R. §656.3 (Employment defined).

(4) Must be an employer and not seeking to subcontract. 20 C.F.R. §656.3 (Employer defined in subsection 1); 69 Fed. Reg. at 77331 (Dec. 27, 2004); *Emily Walder,* 03-INA-134 (BALCA June 18, 2004) [although the employee is "leased" to employer through a contract personnel agency which would normally preclude an employer relationship as a "shared employee contract," the unique facts of the case including that the employee was hired before the employer retained the agency's services, the employer remains liable for all wages, taxes, and benefits, the employer supervises and manages the employee and determines the amount of wages and benefits and the personnel agency's agreement with the employee states that it is the W-2 employer for purposes of recordkeeping only warrant a finding that Walder is the employer]; *V&R Construction Inc.,* 02-INA-153 (BALCA Feb. 7, 2003) [where employer could not demonstrate that the persons working for him were employees rather than independent contractors LC denied because he had no employees]. Persons who are temporarily in the U.S., including but not limited to A-1s, L-1s, F-1s, J-1s, B-1 or B-2s or I visa holders, cannot be LC employers. §656.3 (Employer defined in subsection 2).

(5) All job duties and requirements must be known to give U.S. worker an opportunity to compete. *Latin American Enterprises, Inc. d/b/a Telelink Inc.,* 08-INA-82 (BALCA Mar. 3, 2008) [knowledge requirements for IT director's position were not so obvious or inherent in job that the employer could decide not to list them on the ETA 750A and job ads]; *Vincent Trimarco, Jr.* 03-INA-293 (BALCA Sept. 27, 2004) [rejection of applicant for bookkeeper-accounts manager because he lived too far away when no distance to work was listed as a requirement is not a lawful reason for rejection]; *Ron Arthur,* 02-INA-54 (BALCA Oct. 24, 2002) [cannot accept applicant for position as domestic cook who meets alternative requirements (as hotel cook) for job when the alternative requirements were never listed or advertised]

(6) Inherent Job Requirements Not Stated on Form.

  (a) Proficiency in English, even if not listed as a requirement, is deemed to be so. *Ashbrook-Simon-Hartley v. McLaughlin*, 863 F.2d 410, 415 (5th Cir. 1989). *But see Express Line Corporation*, 07-INA-263 (BALCA Mar. 25, 2008) [lack of fluency or heavily accented speech is insufficient grounds to reject U.S. applicant, absent adequate explanation of how poor communication skills bear on job performance]; *Chicago Laser Systems*, 88-INA-10 (BALCA 1988) [record failed to show that software engineer who had no client contact could not be understood]; *Arcadia Enterprises*, 87-INA-692 (BALCA 1988) [poor grammar in cover letter insufficient to refuse to interview fashion importer].

  (b) Bad References. *Alfredo's Restaurant #2*, 90-INA-70 (BALCA June 12, 1991) [upheld rejection of U.S. worker where references said he was undependable even though reference requirements were not listed]. In *Alfredo's*, BALCA found "there are some qualifications that are so self-evidently requisites for a job that they are inherent and need not be expressly stated on the job description and yet provide a valid reason for rejecting a U.S. applicant."

  (c) Inability to verify work history. *Petit Jean Poultry*, 94-INA-318, 372 (BALCA Aug. 15, 1996) [where verification of, or inability to verify, shows applicant is not reliable it can be used as criteria].

  (d) Trustworthiness can be job requirement. *Roque*, 88-INA-4 (BALCA 1988).

  (e) Prior demonstrated inability to perform job with employer. *SAV on Drug*, 95-INA-596, 96-INA-121 (BALCA Apr. 3, 1997) [prior incompetent employee rejected].

  (f) Nonsmoking requirement. *Sandler*, 89-INA-316 (BALCA Feb. 11, 1991) (*en banc*).

(g) Performance Test. Employer may require a performance test even if not stated. It is not *per se* unlawful. However, employer must document, in detail, its reasons for rejecting U.S. applicants based on their performance test. *Franco Wood Crafting, Inc.*, 98-INA-131 (BALCA Dec. 22, 1998). A performance test cannot be used as a pretext to exclude U.S. workers and must be shown to have been a standardized test given to all employees for the position. *Advance Blinds Corp.*, 02-INA-302 (BALCA Feb. 10, 2004); *H.R. Shaikh & Co., LLP*, 06-INA-57 (BALCA Dec. 18, 2006) [challenged questionnaire provided to prospective employee accountants where some questions did not appear to be fair and there was no record of how questions were asked and whether they related to the "employer's needs" and "core duties" of the job].

(h) Demonstrable Incompetence At Interview. *The Madison School,* 00-INA-52 (BALCA Mar. 30, 2000) [where applicant for a teacher's position were unable to communicate effectively and one was repeatedly tardy for interview appointments the CO's denial was reversed].

(i) Conflict. Where prospective employee has his own business that s/he refuses to relinquish and that may conflict with employer's business. *Lafond,* 01-INA-154 (BALCA July 25, 2002) [prospective employee has own catering business that might be in conflict with schedule as cook]. *But see Fashions From India, Inc.*, 92-INA-26 (BALCA Feb. 4, 1993); *Roger Bowman Upholstering,* 91-INA-163 (BALCA May 18, 1992).

(7) Foreign Degree Equivalent. Must state on ETA 9089 that a "foreign degree equivalent" is acceptable if applicant wishes to rely on it. *Analysts International Corp.*, 95-INA-62 (Dec. 23, 1996).

(8) Licensure Requirements. Where a license is required, the applicant need not have the license at time LC granted, as long as s/he is able to obtain the license within a short period of time from entry into the U.S. and through a relatively ministerial process. *Aspire Public Schools,* 03-INA-254 (BALCA Sept. 9, 2004) [where teacher needed to successfully complete an exam to be licensed, the requirement was not ministerial and LC properly denied]; *Anthony T. Lee, M.D.*, 02-INA-274 (BALCA May 26, 2004) [where the position of Social Worker Medical required a state license and applicant did not have one, LC properly denied]; *Perla-Tate*, 90-INA-175 (BALCA Dec. 4, 1992) (*en banc*), *aff'd on recon.* (Feb. 10, 1992) [where doctors needed to have residency to obtain license in state, not eligible for LC]; *Glendale Family Medical Center*, 95-INA-40 (BALCA Oct. 3, 1996) [CO can require employer to inquire as to state licensure].

2.b. DOL challenge usually involves:

(1) Requirements on ETA 9089 exceed the SVP specified by O*NET job zones. DOL will no longer rely on the Dictionary of Occupational Titles (DOT). 69 Fed. Reg. 77325, 77332 (Dec. 27, 2004). The O*NET job zones can be found at *http://online.onetcenter.org* and a DOL Overview may be found at DOL Overview of O*NET Job Zones, *published on* AILA InfoNet at Doc. No. 05033016. *But see Greg's Collision Center, Inc.* 05-INA-121 (BALCA Aug. 10, 2006) [holding that the O*NET did *not* apply to pre-PERM cases and that under the DOT the employer could require two years of experience even if O*NET provided for only one year].

(2) Alien did not have specified minimum qualifications when s/he started or job cannot require the experience because on-the-job training was given or is reasonable. 20 C.F.R. §§656.17(g)(2), (i).

(a) Alien obtained experience through on-the-job training. Employer cannot require experience in job where it previously gave on-the-job training. 20 C.F.R. §656.17(i)(4). *Pancho Villa Rest. v. DOL*, 796 F.2d 596 (2d Cir. 1986) [where employer could not demonstrate why its changed circumstances required experienced cook when it had previously trained cooks on-the-job, labor certification denied]; *See also Brent-Wood Products, Inc.*, 88-INA-259 (BALCA 1989) (*en banc*); *Loews Anatole Hotel*, 89-

INA-230 (BALCA June 12, 1990) [where applicant on the record appeared to be trained on the job, even for different position initially, certification may be denied].

(b) Employer cannot require experience or skills necessary to perform the duties where a U.S. worker can acquire those skills "in the occupation during a reasonable period of on-the-job training." 20 C.F.R. §656.17(g)(2). A "reasonable period" will vary with the occupation, industry and job opportunity. 69 Fed. Reg. at 77350–51 (Dec. 27, 2004).

(c) In general, cannot count alien's on-the-job experience with the same employer as required experience, including contract employment with the employer. 20 C.F.R. §656.17(i)(3);*Iwasaki Images of America*, 87-INA-656 (BALCA 1988) [where employer hired alien with less experience than he now requires for replica maker's position, employer cannot require experience and employee cannot use experience learned on-the-job]. Employer includes contract employer to discount the experience, but the same employer is defined as having the same Federal Employer Identification Number (FEIN). There are, however, exceptions to the law:

i) On-the-job experience can be considered if it is infeasible to train a new worker due to unavailability of qualified personnel to train new workers or due to other objective business circumstances. 20 C.F.R. §656.17(i)(3)(ii). For example, where the expense to train new person for medical research position would be prohibitive given resources, employer can count on-the-job experience. *Cimmaron Realty Trust*, 81-INA-71 (DOL 1981); *Washington University Dept. of Biological Chemistry*, 81-INA-312 (DOL 1981). Or where the position involved newly developing technology. *Vac-Tec Systems, Inc.* 88-INA-353 (BALCA Aug. 2, 1989). Or where due to economic circumstances and layoffs there was a lack of trainers *Lutheran Medical Center,* 91-INA-302 (BALCA May 26, 1993), *Avicom International,* 90-INA-284 (BALCA July 31, 1991); or the trainer quit *Steel, Tool & Engineering Co,* 04-INA-45 (BALCA Nov. 16, 1994); or the trainer was dismissed. *Johnson, Johnson and Roy, Inc.*, 94-INA-504 (BALCA July 13, 1994). Alternatively, if employer can show business expansion making it infeasible to train someone as they previously had, employer can require trained or experienced person for the job. *M & R Plating Corp.*, 87-INA-355 (DOL 1987). *But see Johnny's Famous Reef Restaurant*, 96-INA-135 (BALCA Oct. 27, 1997) [a substantial growth in volume without staff increase was *not* a basis to allow on-the-job experience. Panel said increased training capability is presumed to accompany growth]; *G.C. Construction Corp.*, 88-INA-20 (BALCA 1988) [notwithstanding increased business volume, employer now has more trained staff]; *BSN Industries*, 88-INA-53 (BALCA 1988) [inefficiency of training new staff not basis for exception]; *Brazilian Portuguese Pavilion*, 87-INA-606 (BALCA 1987) [if employer trained alien when had 2 cooks, can train U.S. worker now that it has 4 cooks].

ii) On-the-job experience can be counted if the new job is a different job than the position that the alien gained her on-the-job experience. DOL has rejected the *Delitizer* standard discussed below as "unnecessarily complex and in practice difficult to administer," *see* 69 Fed. Reg. at 77354, and replaced it with regulatory criteria that allow for the use of prior on-the-job experience where the position was "not substantially comparable to the position for which certification is being sought." 20 C.F.R. §656.17(i)(3)(i). A "substantially comparable" position is defined as one which requires "performance of the same job duties more than 50 percent of the time" which can be documented by "furnishing position descriptions, the percentage of time spent on the various duties, organization charts, and payroll records." §656.17(i)(5)(ii). Prior to PERM, BALCA, in *Delitizer of Newton*, 88-INA-482 (BALCA 1990) (*en banc*), established guidelines to determine job similarity. They rejected the use of DOT codes and different job duties alone as sufficient to establish that jobs are dissimilar. Instead, they found that job duties are one of a number of criteria to determine whether jobs are dissimilar. The criteria includes: "relative job duties and supervisory responsibilities, job requirements, the positions of the jobs in the employer's job hierarchy, whether and by whom the position was filled previously, whether the position is newly created, the prior employment practices of the employer regarding the relative positions, the amount or percentage of time spent performing each job duty in each job and the job salaries." *Delitizer* at 9–10. The Board in *Delitizer* also noted that *de minimis* supervisory responsibilities standing alone would not establish dissimilar positions. This view has been adopted in subsequent cases to deny labor certification. *See Yamasho, Inc.*, 89-INA-203 (BALCA 1990) [found jobs similar even where there was additional training and supervising as service manager]. Traditionally, where a person goes from a nonsupervisory to a supervisory role, the jobs are generally regarded as dissimilar. *Sanchez Elvina, Inc. d/b/a Ely-Lyn House of Beauty,* 04-INA-8 (BALCA Feb. 25, 2005) [differences in responsibility and salary between RIR position as Beauty Salon Manager and former position as hair stylist/beautician]; *Paradise Produce, Inc.*, 90-INA-463 (BALCA Apr. 30, 1992) [salesman to sales manager]; *Deloitte and Touche,* 90-INA-493 (BALCA Feb. 7, 1992) [difference found between associate consultant and senior consultant]; *Coopers & Lybrand,* 92-INA-240 (BALCA July 26, 1993) [difference found between senior associate and associate]; *Duthie Electronic Corp.*, 89-INA-182 (BALCA 1989) [generator mechanic and assistant generator mechanic dissimilar]; *EIMCO Process Equipment Co.*, 88-INA-216 (BALCA 1989) [technician and development engineer dissimilar]; *Conde, Inc.*, 87-INA-598 (BALCA 1987) [change to senior level planner responsible for plans and supervision of draftsmen]; *Cosmetic Specialties, Inc.*, 93-INA-161 (BALCA June 2, 1994) (*en banc*); *New England Nuclear Corp.*, 80-INA-272 (DOL 1981). *But see JBR Gourmet Food,* 03-INA-279 (BALCA Nov. 18, 2004) [employer failed to demonstrate that position of master roaster regarding gourmet coffees was sufficiently dissimilar from coffee roaster]; *Emerald Terrace Convalescent Hospital,* 03-INA-17 (BALCA June 17, 2004) [Nurse Assistant and Licensed Vocational Nurse were not demonstrated to be dissimilar]; *L.A. Rubber Co.*, 89-INA-58 (BALCA 1989) [assistant fabricator and fabricator not sufficiently dissimilar]; *Kurt Salmon Assoc., Inc.*, 87-INA-636 (BALCA 1988) [senior consultant and consultant not sufficiently dissimilar].

iii) Exception if it is educational development where educational expenses were paid for solely by employee and the degrees were applied to fill a distinct position. Minutes, AILA-DOL Liaison Meeting, Item 5B (Jan. 17, 1990), *reprinted in* 67 No. 28 *Interpreter Releases* 830, 851 (July 30, 1990) *or* if employer paid for the education or training if the employer offers similar training to domestic worker applicants.

(d) Same Employer. DOL has provided a regulatory definition in 20 C.F.R. §656.3 and 656.17(i)(5)(i), to determine when two entities are the same employer for purposes of discounting on-the-job experience. To determine whether they are the same employers they must be entities "with the same Federal Employer Identification Number (FEIN) provided they meet the definition of an employer under §656.3. Alternative definitions, including that expressed in *Haden, Inc.* 88-INA-245 (BALCA Aug. 30, 1988) have been rejected. 69 Fed. Reg. at 77354 (Dec. 27, 2004). Prior definitions under pre-PERM regulations include: (1) Experience gained from one employer who had virtually identical shareholders and corporate officers of petitioning Employer was construed as on-the-job experience for petitioning employers. *Harvest Office Services, Inc t/a The Catalyst Group*, 05-INA-111 (BALCA Dec. 7, 2006) [ownership of law firm where beneficiary worked and consulting company that applied had same owners and addresses and experience therefore was not with independent employer]; *Best Western (Sutter House),* 03-INA-123 (BALCA June 8, 2004) [where applicant acquired her knowledge and experience with the Nova reservation system at another Best Western, it was considered acquired knowledge and experience with the same employer]; *Salad Bowl Restaurants*, 90-INA-200 (BALCA

1991); *Boulevard Cafe*, 96-INA-33 (BALCA Sept. 30, 1997); (2) Experience gained in working for a foreign parent corporation counted as on-the-job experience for purposes of the U.S. employer, at least where affiliate corporations do similar business and U.S. corporation is wholly owned subsidiary of parent corporation. *Inmos Corp.,* 88-INA-326 (BALCA 1990) (*en banc*) [denial of LC upheld where U.S. employer required experience that employee gained from foreign parent corporation]; *IBM Corp.,* 04-INA-12 (BALCA Mar. 4, 2005) [IBM Canada and IBM Corp. of Vermont considered same employer]. In *Reiter Corp.,* 2000-INA-193 (BALCA 2000), the *Inmos* test was relaxed in view of globalization of the marketplace. Employer should be permitted to show "distinct operational independence" to be able to use experience gained at affiliate abroad.

Where business is sole proprietorship, the previous owner's training is not imputed to the current owner. *Urrutia,* 98-INA-98 (BALCA May 28, 1999).

(e) Where applicant had completed course work and requirements for a degree but had not yet received diploma, BALCA reversed CO denial finding that there is no difference between receiving degree and completing all requirements. *Productivity Improvements, Inc.*, 86-INA-671 (BALCA 1988). *But see Affinitec Corp.*, 87-INA-516 (BALCA 1987) [minimum requirements not met where alien met course work, but not other degree requirements when hired].

(f) Alien's experience gained in a parent or relative's home cannot be regarded as a *bona fide* employer-employee relationship even if alien received salary. *Phelps*, 88-INA-214 (BALCA 1989) (*en banc*).

(g) Alien's unpaid or "under-the-table" experience. Experience which is unpaid or experience where someone is paid "off-the-books" or "under-the-table" can be qualifying experience. *B&B Residential Facility,* 01-INA-146 (BALCA July 16, 2002). However, there are serious proof problems and an affidavit from the applicant alone is insufficient. *Id.*

(h) Illegal employment may be counted toward the experience requirements. And the CO should not reject a LC because a former employer is reluctant to document the illegal employment. *Lendy Muller,* 98-INA-237 (BALCA Sept. 17, 1999) [whenever CO challenges proof of prior employment, it should consider alternatives to a letter from the employer because "previous employers might be reluctant to document that an alien was illegally employed."]. *But see Anabelo and Dorothy Borja,* 06-INA-54 (BALCA Mar. 13, 2007) [employer's refusal to come into compliance with federal and state tax law on the grounds that the beneficiary will report her own income in the future was insufficient to make the position lawful under former §656.20(c)(7)]; *Annie and Ronald Baldwin,* 05-INA-64 (BALCA Dec. 14, 2006) [BALCA, raised credibility issues in the context of whether the job specified ("head housekeeper") really existed where the employer's credibility was called into question due to her employment of the undocumented prospective employee].

(i) Alien does not have requisite experience in job. In determining whether alien has experience, CO should look to job duties of previous employment, not just job titles. *Maple Derby, Inc.*, 89-INA-185 (BALCA 1991) (*en banc*).

(j) In determining minimum requirements must look to job duties as well as job requirements. *Ashbrook-Simon-Hartley v. McLaughlin*, 863 F.2d 410 (5th Cir. 1989) [where job duties required experience but job requirements did not, it was abuse of discretion to deny labor cert. where other applicants had no experience]. Job requirements may be implied from duties, even though not expressly stated as requirements because DOL cannot "ignore the job duties listed by the employer when determining whether the employer has a job-related reason for rejecting a domestic applicant." *Ron Hartgrove, Inc.*, 88-INA-302 (BALCA 1989) [following *Ashbrook*, BALCA remanded case to determine if applicant was experienced in job duties even though he met job requirements]. *But see Metro Bank, N.A.,* 04-INA-20 (BALCA Nov. 30, 2004) [where there is no knowledge or experience listed as a requirement *Ashrook* does not apply]. Under PERM, 20 C.F.R. §656.24(b)(2)(i) establishes that a

U.S. worker is qualified if s/he can perform duties. Employer, therefore, cannot reject an applicant who has experience in job duties even if his or her job title was different. *National Institute for Petroleum & Energy Research*, 88-INA-535 (BALCA 1989); *Omega Contractor, Inc.*, 88-INA-37 (BALCA 1989) [following *Ashbrook-Simon-Hartley, supra*]. *But see Petrossian, Inc.*, 92-INA-41 (BALCA Sept. 1, 1993) [applicant need not qualify for the job duties when job of stock clerk "was not in a highly specialized area"; BALCA seeking to narrow *Ashbrook-Simon-Hartley*]; *Bell Communications Research, Inc.*, 88-INA-26 (BALCA 1988) [employer is to use items #14 and #15 to notify CO of minimum requirements, and CO is not expected to infer requirements from job description].

(k) Changing Job Requirements After Denial—Where employer sought to change the job requirements after denial while case was on appeal to obtain a remand under new criteria, the denial by the CO was affirmed. *Century Wilshire Hotel,* 07-INA-22 (BALCA Oct. 15, 2007) (en banc) [where employer first advertised position as 2 years experience as Hotel Manager and after denial then changed it to 2 years as clerk and this "fundamental change" was untimely].

3. Unduly restrictive

3.a. Defined: DOL regulations provide that the "job opportunity's requirements, unless adequately documented as arising from business necessity, must be those normally required for the occupation and must not exceed the Specific Vocation Preparation level assigned to the occupation as shown in the O*NET Job Zones." 20 C.F.R. §656.17(h)(1). A DOL overview of the job zones may be found at DOL Overview of O*NET Job Zones, *published on* AILA InfoNet at Doc. No. 05033016. The regulatory provisions that deal with unduly restrictive requirements and business necessity "also apply to unduly restrictive job duties." 69 Fed. Reg. at 77351 (Dec. 27, 2004); TAG at 46. [if requirements "demand skills, knowledge, abilities, and conditions of employment which are not normally required to satisfactorily perform work in the occupation."]. Under BALCA decisions, a job is not considered "unduly restrictive" when the job requirements: (1) Are those "normally required for the job in the U.S."; (2) Are those defined as part of the job in O*NET including those for subclasses of jobs; and (3) Do not contain a language requirement "other than English." All three conditions must be met for a job not to be considered unduly restrictive. *Martin Kaplan,* 00-INA-23 (BALCA July 2, 2001) (*en banc*) et al. ["The three elements for determining whether a job requirement is unduly restrictive are to be read conjunctively."]; *Jeffries & Co.*, 02-INA-48 (Mar. 14, 2002) [requirements of an MBA and two or three years experience for investment banker position were not unduly restrictive]. "Unduly restrictivc" relates to requirements for the job, not whether employer can request job. *Chang*, 88-INA-536 (BALCA 1989) [CO reversed where he challenged job requiring tutor in Mandarin Chinese and Taiwanese].

(1) Look to O*NET designations of the specific vocational preparation (SVP) for the job. Requirements beyond SVP definitions considered unduly restrictive. 20 C.F.R. §656.17(h)(1). *Interior Developers, Inc. v. Chao,* 521 F.Supp.2d 145 (D.P.R. 2007) [construction inspector's position that included requirements such as a demonstrated ability in certain software applications were not in the DOT definition and plaintiff could not establish under *Information Industries* that the requirements were essential to the performance of the duties]. However, if job requirements are within SVP it is generally not unduly restrictive. *Lebanese Arak Corp.*, 87-INA-683 (BALCA 1989) (*en banc*); *PC Club,* 99-INA-189 (BALCA 1999); *Annar Mangalji*, 88-INA-177 (BALCA 1988). But note that educational or experience requirements may be within SVP and still be challenged as beyond that normally required for the position. *Marta Fashions Sportswear,* 95-INA-193 (BALCA Feb. 3, 1998) [where job duties were copied verbatim from the DOT, CO's denial was affirmed because listing all job duties in DOT does not normally reflect supervisor's job]; *Sharp Printing,* 98-INA-21 (BALCA Aug. 119, 1998) [BA requirement for printing shop supervisor was within an SVP of 8, but was denied as unduly restrictive]; *Sidhu Assoc.*, 95-INA-182 (BALCA Jan. 2, 1997) [although request of master's degree still placed mechanical engineer position within SVP, it was rejected because the em-

ployer failed to show a master's degree was normally required for the position pursuant to 20 C.F.R. §656.21(b)(2)];

(a) SVP Determinations

i) For Education Purposes, in determining the SVP count as follows:

- Regard 30 hours of high school shop or commercial training as equivalent to about 15 hours of on-the-job training;
- Regard the average 4-year college curriculum (except for liberal arts) as equivalent to 2 years of specific vocational preparation. *Garland Community Hosp.*, 89-INA-271 (BALCA 1991); Memo, Farmer, Admin. for Regional Management, Div. of Foreign Labor Certification (Oct. 6, 1993), *reprinted in* 71 No. 11 *Interpreter Releases* 392, 402–03 (Mar. 21, 1994). Regard 2 years of junior or community college as 2 years of SVP only if it prepares an individual for a specific job, otherwise it does not count at all toward the SVP. Memo, Farmer, supra, but see «Matter of Sidhu Assoc., 95-INA-182 (BALCA Jan. 2, 1997) [suggesting that when counting an M.A. in SVP you count the B.A. as 4 years]; and
- Regard a master's degree as equivalent to 4 (2+2) years and a doctorate as 7 (2+2+3) years. Field Memorandum No. 48-94, Policy Guidance on Labor Certification Issues (PM) (May 16, 1994), *referred to in* 69 Fed. Reg. 77325, 77332 (Dec. 27, 2004), *published on* AILA InfoNet at Doc. No. 04122312. Thus, regard each year of graduate schooling as a year of specific vocational preparation. Handbook of Analyzing Jobs, at 209 n.1 (1972). This means generally that an M.A. would count as 2 years and a Ph.D. as 3 years. Memo, Farmer (Oct. 6, 1993), *supra*. However, USCIS takes a different view. It requires 5 years of experience for a master's degree. 8 C.F.R. §§204.5(k)(3)(i)(B), 214.2(h)(4)(iii)(D)(5).

ii) References to days and months. When the SVP refers to 30 days or 3 months, determine the time in months not by counting days because lapsed time is not the same as work time and the SVP refers to lapsed time. 20 C.F.R. §656.3 (Specific Vocational Preparation defined).

iii) SVP Levels and Time: (1) Short demonstration; (2) Anything beyond a short demonstration up to and including 30 days; (3) Over 30 days up to and including 3 months; (4) Over 3 months up to and including 6 months; (5) Over 6 months up to and including 1 year; (6) Over one year up to and including 2 years; (7) Over 2 years up to and including 4 years; (8) Over 4 years up to and including 10 years; and (9) Over 10 years.

(2) Language other than English is generally considered unduly restrictive, but may qualify as a business necessity under PERM. 20 C.F.R. §656.17(h)(2). *See in this section* ¶ 3.b(3)(d)i) (p.931), *infra*. *Posadas de Puerto Rico Assoc., Inc. v. Secy. of Labor*, 698 F.Supp. 396 (D.P.R. 1988) [upheld pre-PERM denial of LC because of language requirement]; *JN Distributor,* 03-INA-242 (BALCA Nov. 30, 2004) [LC denied, pre-PERM, where employer could not prove business necessity for a trilingual wholesaler]; *Eduardo Velez, M.D.,* 99-INA-302 (BALCA June 7, 2000) [proof that a sufficient number of employer's customers speak a foreign language was ruled (pre-PERM) insufficient to meet business necessity without showing the nexus between the customers' use of the language and the job to be performed].

(3) Combination of occupations that are unrealistic or abnormal considered unduly restrictive, *e.g.*, a mechanic/pilot. 20 C.F.R. §656.17(h)(3).

(a) To overcome unduly restrictive determination must show/document: (1) that employer has normally employed persons for combination of occupations; and/or (2) that workers customarily perform the combination of occupations in the area of intended employment; and/or (3) that there is other business necessity. *e.g.*, size of business or portions of work too small for separate employees). *David Razo Gardening Service,* 02-INA-129 (BALCA Apr. 23, 2003) [DOT is a guide that should not be applied mechanically and where landscape gardener customarily installed irrigation system and O*NET and OOH indicated it was part of position certification was appropriate]. The Board has rejected the use of the *Information Industries, Inc.* test for business necessity in this context finding that in cases involving a combination of job duties a more stringent test should be applied. *Robert L. Lippert Theatres*, 88-INA-433 (BALCA 1990) (*en banc*) [adopted business necessity test requiring "a showing of such a level of impracticability as to make the employment of two workers infeasible"]. Such documentation is not required when the DOT definition contemplates such combination. *Gulliver Preparatory School*, 87-INA-549 (BALCA 1988) [teacher expected to coach as well as teach substantive course].

(b) Documenting Combination of Occupations. 20 C.F.R. §656.17(h)(3). Combinations of occupations can be documented by position descriptions and relevant payroll records and/or letters from other employers in the area. An employer may also employ expert opinions to demonstrate that in the particular job or field a combination of job duties is justified. *Take One Computer*, 01-INA-66 (BALCA, Sept. 19, 2001), *published on* AILA InfoNet at Doc. No. 01121331 [BALCA reversed CO's determination that accountant's expert opinion regarding job duties should be discounted because he was known to work for immigration attorneys and determined that accounting and internal auditing is considered one position in small businesses].

(4) Live-at-work—20 C.F.R. §§656.17(j)(2) & 656.19: *See in this section* "Business Necessity," ¶ 3.b (p.930), *infra*.

(5) Work Schedules—Work schedule may be considered unduly restrictive where it is not the normal schedule for the position. *Summerville At Garden Manor,* 03-INA-257 (BALCA Sept. 9, 2004) [Nurse Aide required to work three different shifts per week considered unduly restrictive].

Knowledge of Company's Product Line May Be Unduly Restrictive—When experience requirements exceed the SVP and employer argued that it was necessary to develop sufficient knowledge of company's product line, the court rejected business necessity argument by saying it is tantamount to requiring 2 years of experience with the employer. *Coastal Pipeline Production of New York v. Gonzales,* Case No. 04 Civ 8252 (DF) (S.D.N.Y Feb. 27, 2006) [upheld CO and BALCA's rejection of business necessity for crane operator].

(6) Physical Requirements—A requirement that an applicant have certain physical capabilities without demonstrating they are normally required for the position is unduly restrictive. *Woodland Hills Fireplace Shop,* 03-INA-169 (BALCA Aug. 11, 2004) [a requirement that a sales manager for a barbeque/fireplace company be able to lift boxes over 100 pounds, was unduly restrictive in the absence of demonstrating it was the norm for the industry].

(7) Alternative Experience Requirements—20 C.F.R. §656.17(h)(4). An application may contain alternate experience requirements for the job where the alternatives are "substantially equivalent" to the primary requirements. If the beneficiary is already employed by the applicant-employer, the alternative experience requirements will not be permitted if the beneficiary only qualifies under the alternative requirements and does not meet the primary requirements *unless* the application states that *any* suitable combination (not just the primary or alternative requirements) of education, training, or experience is acceptable. DOL claims to have adopted the BALCA standard under *Francis Kellogg.* 69 Fed. Reg. at 77352–53 (Dec. 27, 2004), and BALCA has adhered to that view. *Demos Consulting Group, Ltd,* 07-PER-20 (BALCA May 16, 2007) [finding §656.17(b)(4)(ii) was clearly intended to implement *Francis Kellogg* and holding that employer's failure to state that any suitable combination of education, training, or experience properly resulted in denial by the CO]. Although the *Kellogg* standard has been adopted, it is worth noting that there is a potential discrepancy between the regulatory standard and the holding in *Kellogg*, because *Kellogg* addresses the situation where the primary and alternative requirements are *not* substantially equivalent, whereas the regulation asserts that they always must be equivalent. *Compare* §656.17(h)(4) *and Francis Kellogg*, 94-INA-465

(BALCA Feb. 8, 1998) (*en banc*). [both the primary and alternative requirement must be normal for the job. Where the applicant does not meet the primary job requirements but only potentially qualifies for the job because the employer has chosen to list alternative job requirements, the alternative job requirements are unlawfully tailored to the applicant's qualifications in violation of the regulation unless that employer has indicated that applicants with "any suitable combinations of education, training or experience are acceptable." *Id.* Thus, a job for a cook with 2 years' experience, where the applicant meets only the alternative requirement of housekeeping with some cooking duties, will be rejected. *Id.*]; *Accord Armand Bouzaglou,* 99-INA-152 (BALCA Aug. 30, 2001) [where technologist position had alternative requirements involving use of equipment or experience and the noncitizen applicant qualified only because of the alternative experience, BALCA found that alternative requirement restrictive]; *Maryland Parkway Building,* 97-INA-119 (BALCA Sept. 4, 1998) [alternative requirement of CPA or foreign CPA was unduly restrictive]; *Animal Crackers Café,* 99-INA-257 (BALCA Aug. 3, 2000) [a job offer for a cook that required 2 years in the job offered or, alternatively, 2 years as a kitchen helper was unduly restrictive]. The right of the employer to utilize alternative business requirements in PERM was maintained in the final regulations and BALCA has adhered to the *Francis Kellogg* standard. *Demos Consulting Group, Ltd.,* 07-PER-20 (BALCA May 16, 2007) [upheld denial by CO where review lead BALCA to conclude that beneficiary only qualified because of alternative experience and employer's application failed to state that any suitable combination of education, training or experience was acceptable]. In several cases, however, BALCA has upheld the denial of an LC where the employer failed to complete sections H-8 and/or H-10A of the ETA 9089 regarding alternate experience because both question areas are tied to §§656.17(h)(4)(i) and (ii) and the CO cannot determine if alternate experience requirements are equivalent to the primary requirements under §656.17(i)(I). *Alpine Store Inc,* 07-PER-40 (BALCA June 27, 2007)[applicants failed to answer question H-10A and H-8]; *Subhashini Software Solutions*, 07-PER-39 (BALCA Dec. 10, 2007) [upheld denial of 5 applications for failure to complete question H-8].

3.b. Business necessity: 20 C.F.R. §656.17(h)(1)

(1) Even if a requirement is in excess of normal job duties or is a foreign language, it is permissible if it arises from business necessity.

(2) Business necessity defined

(a) To establish business necessity, the employer must demonstrate that "the job duties and requirements bear a reasonable relationship to the occupation in the context of the employer's business and are essential to perform the job in a reasonable manner." §656.17(h)(1); 69 Fed. Reg. at 77351–52 (Dec. 27, 2004). DOL adopted the BALCA standard in *Information Industries, Inc.*, 88-INA-82 (BALCA 1989) (*en banc*).

(b) Former definitions

i) DOL: "overriding" and "essential" to the safety and operation of business. Not just preference or convenience. [TAG at 46]. *Diaz v. Pan American World Airways, Inc.*, 442 F.2d 385 (5th Cir. 1971); *or*

ii) *Crystal Shamrock, Inc.*, 81-INA-180 (1981) test: "if reasonable and tend to contribute to or enhance the efficiency and quality of the business." *See also Ratnayake v. Mack*, 499 F.2d 1207 (8th Cir. 1974); *Johnson, Lane & Gallagher v. Secy. of Labor*, ___ F.Supp. ___ (W.D. Wash. 1985) [New Zealand lawyer]; *Tracor Westronics*, 86-INA-429 (BALCA 1986) [knowledge of specific type of computer is business necessity]; *Marion General Hospital*, 86-INA-37 (BALCA 1986) [requirement that applicant have BS degrees in both chemistry and medical technology considered business necessity]; *Inspirational Coal, Inc.*, 86-INA-827 (1986) [BS in engineering and certificate as professional].

(3) Business necessity applied

(a) In determining business necessity, may use customer's preference as basis to support necessity. *Alwya Computer Co.*, 88-INA-218 (BALCA 1989) [necessity for requiring financial controller to speak Chinese based on customer's preference].

(b) Business necessity cannot be imposed on the need for the job itself, only on the requirements. The only issue related to the desire for the job is that it must be full time and permanent. *Lin*, 89-INA-28 (BALCA 1990) [CO cannot challenge employer's desire to employ a child tutor familiar with Chinese language and culture]; *accord Shinn Shyng Chang*, 88-INA-536 (BALCA 1989); *Vander Sterre*, 95-INA-511 (BALCA July 28, 1997) [rejected CO requirement that family demonstrate desire for cook's position arose out of business necessity]. But child monitor must have formal training for, *e.g.*, special language requirement. *Akhtar Rahnama*, 93-INA-27 (BALCA Jan. 24, 1994) [cert. denied to person teaching children Farsi who had no formal training].

(c) Business necessity based upon expansion of business (*e.g.*, director of international marketing who speaks foreign language) is permissible and business necessity is not limited to a demonstration of how the employer would lose business. *Remington Products, Inc.*, 89-INA-173 (BALCA 1991) (*en banc*); *Time Energy Systems, Inc.*, 92-INA-220 (BALCA Feb. 3, 1994) [cert. granted to company that was expanding business to Bulgaria, Russia and Eastern Europe and needed Russian/Bulgarian language fluency]; *Mouren-Laurens Oil Co., Inc.*, 91-INA-236 (BALCA Aug. 11, 1992) [employer need only make a reasonable showing of its intent to undergo significant expansion]. However, the documentation concerning employer's expansion and the need for the requirement will be subject to strict scrutiny and employer must document business plans thoroughly. *Advanced Digital Corp.*, 90-INA-137 (BALCA 1991). *Accord Cable Car Photo & Electronics*, 90-INA-141 (BALCA 1991).

(d) Business necessity has been found in cases where job requirements include:

i) *Foreign languages*—To demonstrate business necessity for a foreign language, the employer must demonstrate that it is either part of the nature of the occupation (*e.g.*, a translator) or that there is a need to communicate with a *large majority* of the employer's customers, contractors, or employees who cannot communicate effectively in English. The latter must be documented by furnishing the number and proportion of such people and/or a detailed plan to market products or services in a foreign country, with a detailed explanation of why the job requires frequent contact with non-English speaking people and why they cannot communicate in English. 20 C.F.R. §656.17(h)(2). Communicating with non-English speaking coworkers or employees may be justified where there are safety considerations in the work environment. 69 Fed. Reg. at 77352 (Dec. 27, 2004). *See also Townecraft, Inc.* 01-INA-7 (BALCA Feb. 4, 2002) [where job was for sales manager to develop a door-to-door sales organization which deals solely with Hispanics]; *Super Dental Care,* 00-INA-78 (BALCA Dec. 20, 2001) [trilingual dentist where employer showed 25% of patients were Spanish speaking, 50% were Persian speaking and because it was a walk-in clinic it was not possible to know who would show up]; *PC Club,* 99-INA-189 (BALCA 1999) [knowledge of bilingual software and capacity to program software that reads and writes Chinese permissible]; *Orient Hotel Group, Inc.*, 95-INA-496 (BALCA July 22, 1997) [reversed CO denial where employer demonstrated that corp. liaison director required to communicate in Chinese where 60% of work would be in Chinese]; *Sysco Intermountain Food Services*, 88-INA-138 (BALCA 1989) (*en banc*) [CO denial reversed where employer stated virtually all of its restaurant clients speak Chinese and many do not speak English]; *Kachina Country Day School,* 98-INA-14 (BALCA Aug. 19, 1998) [reversed CO denial of French and German requirement for language teacher]; *Alwya Computer Corp.*, 88-INA-218 (BALCA 1989) [CO denial reversed where employer's clients chose to speak Chinese]; However, the documentation proving the claim must be translated into English. *Amami International, Inc.* 96-INA-477 (BALCA May 19, 1998) [despite the production of "voluminous" documentation certification was denied because documents not translated into English];

ii) *Additional education—Quincy School Community Council*, 88-INA-81 (BALCA 1989) (*en banc*) [upheld need for master's degree for teacher];

iii) *Additional experience—Alan Bergman Photography*, 88-INA-404 (BALCA 1989) [employer's requirement of 2 years experience in "Latino settings" not restrictive];

iv) *Live-ins*—20 C.F.R. §656.19. A live-in must be provided private room and board at no cost. §656.19(b)(2)(ix). *TCM Elderly Camino Ramon Home Care,* 03-INA-166 (Aug. 23, 2004) [employer's response indicated that applicant would share a room thereby violating the regulation]. In *Graham*, 88-INA-102 (BALCA 1990) (*en banc*), BALCA stated the criteria used to determine a live-in requirement includes "the employer's occupation or commercial activities outside the home, the circumstances of the household itself, and any other extenuating circumstances." These criteria are used to determine the business necessary for live-ins under 20 C.F.R. §656.19(b). The relevant "business" is running the household or managing one's personal affairs and not the employer's business outside the home. The employer must provide detailed written proof (not just assertions) to determine whether there are cost effective alternatives to a live-in and whether the need is genuine. For example, a claim based on travel should be bolstered by travel vouchers and written estimates of costs. *See generally Wehba*, 87-INA-512 (DOL 1987); *Laurenzo*, 87-INA-603 (BALCA 1988). A live-in must provide proof of "total paid experience...equal to one full year's employment on a full-time basis." 20 C.F.R. §656.19(b)(3). A live-in cannot meet the one year experience requirement through work for the petitioning employer. *Lawrence Weinstein and Toni Albanese,* 05-INA-00009 (BALCA 2006) [reaffirmed *Roger and Denny Phelps,* 88-INA-214 (BALCA 2006)].

v) *Cooks*—Kosher domestic cook experience requirement is unduly restrictive. *Martin Kaplan*, 2000-INA-23 (BALCA July 2, 2001) (*en banc*) et. al. ["[W]e hold that all cooking specializations for domestic cooks are unduly restrictive job requirements ... and must be justified by business necessity."]. Indian dairy and vegetarian style cook rejected. *M. Balachandran & V.G. Veerubhotla,* 03-INA-136 (BALCA Sept. 13, 2004). However, for cooks to get above an SVP 5 (6 months to one year of experience) they must be preparing specialty foreign food or demonstrate the need for sophisticated skills. *Red Hot & Blue,* 01-INA-31 (Feb. 7, 2002) [two-year experience requirement as fast food cook or hotel and restaurant cook is unduly restrictive]; *Roberto's Taco Shop,* 01-INA-142 (Feb. 15, 2002) [two year requirement rejected for cook in Mexican restaurant where sophisticated cooking skill not required]; *Rosa Pizza,* 01-INA-164 (BALCA Apr. 9, 2002) [same because of "limited menu"].

vi) *Other special requirements—Texas A&M University*, 88-INA-162 (BALCA 1989) (*en banc*) [upheld special skills in chemical methods]; *Blenkhorn*, 91-INA-61 (BALCA May 21, 1992) [child monitor must know how to swim].

vii) *Knowledge Requirements*—An employer may require knowledge of a specific discipline and such a requirement is not impermissibly vague. *Avanti Restaurant & Club*, 93-INA-328 (BALCA Sept. 27, 1994) [mastery and knowledge of middle eastern cooking permissible].

(e) Business Necessity and Adverse Wage Effect. 20 C.F.R. §656.1(a)(2). Where employer asserts a business necessity for the requirement the CO cannot base a denial solely on the grounds that it would adversely affect the wages and working conditions of U.S. workers under 20 C.F.R. §656.1(a)(2) unless it is addressed "with great specificity and with a precise explanation of why the alleged deficiency would adversely affect wages and working conditions of workers similarly employed." *Cardenas Market, Inc.*, 02-INA-292, 02-INA-306, 03-INA-005 (BALCA Sept. 3,

2003) [remanded CO denial where employer asserted rotating shift was a business necessity and CO relied on adverse wage and working conditions effect for denial].

3.c. Procedure by DOL for Unduly Restrictive Requirements and Business Necessity. At the present time there appears no definite procedure, other than an audit, to address issues of business necessity or unduly restrictive requirements. Listing job requirements in excess of the SVP is likely to trigger an audit because it may be the only mechanism for airing the issue.

4. *Prevailing wage*—INA §§212(p)(3) & (4), 8 U.S.C. §§1182(p)(3) & (4), 20 C.F.R. § 656.40; TAG at 111–23; *www.flcdatacenter.com* (provides Online Wage Library). The prevailing wage is determined by looking to workers "similarly employed" in the "area of intended employment." 20 C.F.R. §656.40(b). Pursuant to the Consolidated Appropriations Act of 2005, PL 108-447, 118 Stat. 2809 §423 (Dec. 8, 2004), Congress amended the prevailing wage requirements to mandate that an employer must pay 100% of the stated wage, not 95% as the law previously provided. The law also requires the Secretary of Labor to establish government surveys providing for a prevailing wage that is divided into 4 levels of wages in each job category (instead of 2 levels) commensurate with experience, education and the level of supervision.

4.a. Procedure for Prevailing Wage Determination (PWD) under PERM—The employer obtains the PWD from SWA having jurisdiction over the proposed area of intended employment. The SWA provides the determination on its own form and sends it to the Employer. The regulations impose no time limit on SWA to provide the PWD. 69 Fed. Reg. at 77365 (Dec. 27, 2004). The SWA must specify the validity of the prevailing wage which in no event may be less than 90 days or more than one year from the date of the determination. 20 C.F.R. §656.40(c). If the Employer does not appeal the PWD under 20 C.F.R. §656.41(a) it files the ETA 9089 with the PWD information and retains the original in the event of an audit. The SWA determines the PWD as follows: (1) Collective Bargaining Agreement (CBA); (2) If no CBA then it uses the "arithmetic mean" of the wages of workers "similarly employed" in "the area of intended employment" by relying on the Occupational Employment Statistics Survey (OES) of the DOL *unless* (3) the employer provides an acceptable survey which may include the median rather than the arithmetic mean of wages or the employer relies on the Davis Bacon Act or McNamara-O'Hara Service Contract Act. 20 C.F.R. §656.40(b). Memo, DeRocco, Asst. Sec. ETA, "Prevailing Wage Guidance" (May 17, 2005), *published on* AILA InfoNet at Doc No. 05052066 (May 20, 2005); New FAQs on Prevailing Wage (Aug. 1, 2005), *published on* AILA InfoNet at Doc. No. 05081067. The parties are also encouraged to use the DOL's Online Wage Library and the comments to the regulations also recognize the validity of Bureau of Labor Statistics surveys even where they involve one skill level and use a median wage. 69 Fed. Reg. at 77368–72 (Dec. 27, 2004). The SWA must consider a survey or wage information provided by the Employer before or after it makes its PWD. If the employer submits a survey or other wage data it must: (1) provide information regarding the survey methodology used; (2) proof the publication of the survey was within 24 months on the date submitted to the SWA or (3) if an employer conducted her own survey that the information collected was within 24 months. The DOL has outlined appropriate criteria for employer-provided wage surveys. Memo, DeRocco, ETA, "Prevailing Wage Guidance," Appendix F (May 17, 2005), *published on* AILA InfoNet at Doc. No. 05052066 (May 20, 2005); New FAQs on Prevailing Wage ("Sec. VIII. Employer-Provided Wage Surveys") (Aug. 1, 2005), *published on* AILA InfoNet at Doc. No. 05081067. If the SWA rejects the employer's survey, the employer may file supplemental information and the SWA must consider one supplemental submission. The employer is afforded only one opportunity to submit supplemental information to the SWA. PERM FAQs No. 1 ("Prevailing Wage") (Mar. 7, 2005), *published on* AILA InfoNet at Doc. No. 05030861 An employer seeking review of a PWD determination by the SWA may appeal it to the CO. The appeal must be made within 30 days of the decision by the SWA. The 30 days to appeal to the CO run from the final decision by the SWA or if the employer submits supplemental information (as permitted one time) the 30 days run from the time the SWA considers and makes a final decision on the supplemental information. PERM FAQs No. 2 ("Certifying Officer Review and BALCA") (Apr. 7, 2005), *published on* AILA InfoNet at Doc. No. 05041463. An employer has one further review to BALCA from the CO's decision. 20 C.F.R. §656.41.

(1) Davis Bacon Act (DBA) and McNamara-O'Hara Service Contract Act (SCA). The DBA and SCA may be asserted by the employer, but are no longer binding. Although DBA and CSA are no longer mandatory, the employer may rely on them to argue the appropriate PWD. §656.40(b). The DBA and SCA rates are applicable to an occupation, not a particular employer, and can therefore apply even if employer does not do government contracting. *Standard Drywall*, 88-INA-99 (BALCA 1988). They are also applicable even if the employer's business as a whole is not in the construction field. *Brad Bartholomay Landscape Design & Consultation*, 88-INA-332 (BALCA 1989) (*en banc*). However, the position must be comparable to a position covered under the SCA or DBA for the acts to apply. *Sofia's Ristorante Italiano*, 98-INA-238 (BALCA May 21, 1999) [reversed CO's application of SCA where the position covered under that Act–Cook II–was not comparable to position of Cook, Specialty Foreign Food applied for in LC] and BALCA has jurisdiction to determine whether the CO properly applied the SCA wage. *El Rio Grande,* 98-INA-133 (BALCA, Feb. 4, 2000) (en banc) *aff'd upon reconsideration El Rio Grande,* 98-INA-133 (BALCA Feb. 4, 2000) (*en banc*) [upheld use of "slotting" technique in wage determination which allows comparing different occupations, but only where CO explains why slotting was used, what occupations were compared, and whether it was reasonable].The DOL has determined that employees who are highly skilled in computer systems analysis, programming and software engineering are *not* subject to wage determinations under McNamara-O'Hara. Memo, Farmer, Adm. for Regional Management DOL (Oct. 1, 1993), *reprinted in* 12 *AILA Monthly Mailing* 829 (Nov. 1993).

(2) One Hundred Percent (100%) of Wage Offered. INA §212(p)(3), 8 U.S.C. §1182(p)(3). In the H-1B Visa Reform Act (Div. J, Tit. IV, subtit. B of Consolidated Appropriations Act of 2005, PL 108-447, 118 Stat. 2809) (Dec. 8, 2004), *published on* AILA InfoNet at Doc. No. 04112366. Congress required that 100% of the prevailing wage be paid to an employee thereby ending prior regulations that permitted the employer to pay 95% of the prevailing wage.

(3) Prevailing Wage at Time of Filing and Payment above Stated Wage. The wage offered and advertised that the beneficiary received when initially hired can be used when filing ETA even if he or she earns higher wage at time ETA is filed as long as wage offered meets or exceeds the prevailing wage. *University of North Carolina*, 90-INA-422 (BALCA June 9, 1992) [interpreting former 20 C.F.R. §656.21(g)(8) as *not* requiring that advertising be the wage beneficiary is currently being paid]. Also, the employer can pay above prevailing wage as a result of raises given while the case is pending. Salary increase alone during petitioning process does not invalidate labor certification. Letter, Weinig, Deputy Asst. Commissioner, Adjudications CO 204.8C (Feb. 5, 1990), *reprinted in* 67 *Interpreter Releases* 525 (Apr. 30, 1990).

(4) Range of Wage. Can offer a salary range so long as the bottom end of the range is not below the prevailing wage, and ETA-9089 now reflects the employer's right to state a range. 69 Fed. Reg. 77325, 77333 (Dec. 27, 2004); *Sterling Mgmt. Systems*, 89-INA-216 (BALCA 1991). Positions advertised may use DOQ (Depending on Qualifications) or DOE (Depending on Experience). 8 *AILA Monthly Mailing* 519 (Sept. 1989).

(5) Fringe Benefits. Wage offered must not be based on commissions, bonuses or other incentives, unless the employer guarantees a wage. *Former* 20 C.F.R. §656.20(c)(3). But employer may count fringe benefits. *Kids "R" Us*, 89-INA-311 (BALCA Jan. 28, 1991) (*en banc*) [employer bears heavy burden when it seeks to include value of fringe benefits]. . However, in counting fringe benefits the Employer must establish the value of the fringe benefits and show that they are not common to comparable jobs. *Graphite Metalizing Corp., supra,* and *Kids "R" Us, supra.*

(6) Burden of Proof. Where the prevailing wage is in dispute, the certifying officer must provide copies of relevant portions of source for determination and a reasonable explanation of how the wage was determined. However, the burden remains on the employer to dispute the certifying officer's determination by showing it is erroneous *and* by showing its offer is at or above correct prevailing wage. *John Lehne & Sons*, 89-INA-267, 89-

INA-313 (BALCA May 1, 1992) (*en banc*). The Board's review of the prevailing wage determination is based upon the record that existed at the time of denial and any subsequent statement or position can not be considered. *Plaza Express Car & Limo Service,* 07-INA-8 (BALCA Dec. 10, 2007) The employer may satisfy his burden of proof even if he relies on his own *ad hoc* survey and even if the methodology of the DOL is not followed where he can demonstrate his survey is both accurate and relevant. *Ren-Mar Studios,* 90-INA-205 (BALCA Sept. 30, 1992). Employer can successfully challenge CO's wage determination by providing its own more accurate survey. *Pal-Mil Enterprises, d/b/a McDonald's,* 89-INA-251 (BALCA Mar. 29, 1991); *Phillip Maxwell & Julia Martelli,* 96-INA-291 (BALCA Dec. 30, 1998). The employer may also challenge the classification used under the OES/SOC code. Guidance Letter No. 5-02, DeRocco, Asst. Sec. ETA (Aug. 7, 2002) at ¶18, *published on* AILA InfoNet at Doc. No. 02081440. More recently, the DOL has outlined appropriate criteria for employer-provided wage surveys. Memo, DeRocco, Assistant Sec. ETA, "Prevailing Wage Guidance," Appendix F (May 17, 2005), *published on* AILA InfoNet at Doc No. 05052066 (May 20, 2005).

(7) Error By SWA on PWD. Where the SWA presented a PWD with errors such as an incorrect SOC code or validity period, it is the employer's responsibility to ensure that the PWD obtained from the SWA is complete and in compliance with PERM and DOL will deny requests to correct the PWD information. PERM FAQs No. 6 (Feb. 21, 2006), *published on* AILA InfoNet at Doc. No. 06022474.

(8) For pre-PERM analysis of prevailing wage determinations generally *see* Guidance Letter No. 5-02, DeRocco, Asst. Sec. ETA (Aug. 7, 2002), *published on* AILA InfoNet at Doc. No. 02081440 [clarifies Level I and Level II Positions Regarding Prevailing Wage as Discussed in GAL No. 2-98]; GAL No. 1-00, Jacobs-Simmons, Deputy Asst. Sec., ETA (May 16, 2000), *reprinted in* 77 No. 21 *Interpreter Releases* 694, 706–15 (May 26, 2000) [addresses employer surveys and discusses access to OES data which is now broken down into ALC data for most industries and EDU data for nonprofits/educational institutions]; GAL No. 2-98, McConnell, Acting Admin. of Regional Management (Oct. 31, 1997), *reprinted in* 74 No. 43 *Interpreter Releases* 1712, 1716–27 (Nov. 7, 1997) [providing criteria to be used if employer wishes private wage survey]; GAL No. 4-95, Farmer, Admin. for Regional Management (May 18, 1995), *reprinted in* 72 No. 24 *Interpreter Releases* 838, 848–55 (June 26, 1995), *published on* AILA InfoNet at Doc. No 95060690 (June 6, 1995).

4.b. Determination of Prevailing Wage Is Established By Analyzing Similarly Employed Persons In the Area of Intended Employment

(1) Similarly Employed Defined. 20 C.F.R. §656.40(e). Similarly employed means having a "substantially comparable job in the occupational category" unless a sufficient sample cannot be obtained in the area of intended employment. If there is an insufficient sample then similarly employed means having a job requiring a "similar level of skill" *or* having a substantial comparable job outside the area of intended employment.

(2) Area of Intended Employment Defined. The area of intended employment is "the area within normal commuting distance of the place (address) of intended employment." This area is defined as the Metropolitan Statistical Area [MSA] and the narrower Primary Metropolitan Statistical Area [PMSA]. *Rubie's Costume Company, Inc.* 00-INA-285 (BALCA Jan. 7, 2002) [rejected survey provided by employer that covered 11 states rather than PMSA]. If the place of intended employment is within a Metropolitan Statistical Area (MSA) or a Primary Metropolitan Statistical Area (PMSA) any place within either is deemed to be within normal commuting distance. Not all locations within the Consolidated Metropolitan Statistical Area, however, will be deemed automatically to be within normal commuting distance. But an area outside the MSA or PMSA may be within normal commuting distance if, for example, it is on the border of the MSA or PMSA. 20 C.F.R. §656.3 (Area of Intended Employment defined). The use of the CMSA to obtain a PWD may be appropriate if it was not possible to obtain a representative sample at the MSA or PMSA level. 69 Fed. Reg. at 77369 (Dec. 27, 2004). If the place of

employment does not fall in these areas, it will fall into the "Balance of State" area for purpose of the prevailing wage. GAL No. 2-98, McConnell, Acting Admin. of Regional Management (Oct. 31, 1997), *reprinted in* 74 No. 43 *Interpreter Releases* 1712, 1716–27 (Nov. 7, 1997) [providing criteria to be used if employer wishes private wage survey] at 3.

For pre-PERM authority *see Heritage Bindery*, 89-INA-351 (BALCA 1990) [use of national average listed in Occupational Outlook Handbook is improper; must use wage in local area]; *Seibel & Stern*, 90-INA-86 (BALCA 1990) [Bureau of Labor Standards survey for mid-Atlantic states was inappropriate to determine prevailing wage in rural area and wage for starting workers as it only measured median wage].

4.c. Skill Level in Determining Wage—The H-1B Visa Reform Act (Div. J, Tit. IV, subtit. B of Consolidated Appropriations Act of 2005, PL 108-447, 118 Stat. 2809) (Dec. 8, 2004), *published on* AILA InfoNet at Doc. No. 04112366 ended the former two level system of wage determinations and mandated a four level system. Under the Act, if an existing government survey has only two levels, two additional intermediate levels can be created by dividing by three the difference between the two levels offered and then adding the quotient obtained to the first level and subtracting it from the second. INA §212(p)(4), 8 U.S.C. §1182(p)(4). DOL has issued guidance on the 4 level wage system. Memo, DeRocco, Asst. Sec., ETA, "Prevailing Wage Guidance" (May 17, 2005), *published on* AILA InfoNet at Doc No. 05052066 (May 20, 2005). The DOL guidance divides the wages levels into: Entry (Level 1), Qualified (Level II), Experienced (Level III) and Fully Competent (Level IV). The prevailing wage determination begins with a level one (entry) analysis regardless of the inherent skill level of the occupation and then progresses to a wage within the occupation that is commensurate with that of a qualified, experienced, or fully competent worker only after considering the experience, education and skill requirements of the job. *DeRocco, Id.* When determining educational requirements for professionals, the SWA should rely on the list of educational requirements for professional positions listed in the appendix to the PERM regulations and DOL guidance rather than the O*NET Job Zone, unless it is an occupation not listed in the appendix. *See* Memo, DeRocco, Asst. Sec., ETA, "Prevailing Wage Guidance" (May 17, 2005), *published on* AILA InfoNet at Doc No. 05052066 (May 20, 2005) at Appendix A, Step 3 and Appendix D. *See also* New FAQs on Prevailing Wage ("Questions 5-6") (Aug. 1, 2005), *published on* AILA InfoNet at Doc. No. 05081067.

4.d. Prevailing Wage for Employees of Institutions of Higher Education and Research Entities—20 C.F.R. §656.40(e) The prevailing wage for institutions of higher education or an affiliated or related nonprofit entity, a nonprofit research organization or a Governmental research organization is determined by taking into account wage levels of employees only at such institutions and organizations in the area of intended employment. *See also* GAL No. 1-00, Jacobs-Simmons, Deputy Asst. Sec., ETA (May 16, 2000), *reprinted in* 77 No. 21 *Interpreter Releases* 694, 706–15 (May 26, 2000) [addressing separate OES determinations for nonprofits (EDU) and all other industries (ALC)].

4.e. Prevailing Wage for Professional Athletes—If the job opportunity is covered by professional sports league rules, the wage prescribed by those rules shall be considered the prevailing wage. INA §§212(p)(1), 212(a)(5)(A)(iii)(II); 20 C.F.R. §656.40(f)

5. *Bona fide* job offer—20 C.F.R. §656.17(*l*).

5.a. Employer has burden when asked to show that a valid employment relationship exists, and that a *bona fide* job opportunity is available to U.S. workers. *Amger Corp.*, 87-INA-545 (BALCA 1987). A relationship invalidating a bona fide job offer may arise where the beneficiary is related by "blood" or it may "be financial, by marriage, or through friendship." *Summart 374,* 00-INA-93 (BALCA May 15, 2000). Where company owned by person applying for position it is not *bona fide* offer. *Bulk Farms, Inc. v. Martin*, 963 F.2d 1286 (9th Cir. 1992) [president, sole shareholder and chief cheese-maker denied LC even where no person qualified for position applied]; *Pasadena Typewriter v. DOL*, ___ F.Supp. ___ (C.D. Cal. 1984) *referenced in* 66 No. 22 *Interpreter Releases* 623 (June 6, 1989); *Kiyomi's Fitting Room*, 86-INA-469 (BALCA 1986). Same is true where family owns majority. *Hall v. McLaughlin*, 864 F.2d 868 (D.C. Cir. 1989) [where husband sold 490 of 500 shares 2 weeks before labor certification filed and where wife still retained her 500 shares giving husband

and wife controlling interest, and where husband was president of company, no *bona fide* offer]. In *Lignomat USA, Ltd.*, 88-INA-276 (BALCA 1989) BALCA found that where applicant and wife each owned 24.5% of the shares that it was not a *bona fide* job offer. BALCA applied the two pronged analysis in *Hall*: (a) whether in light of the alien's ownership or interest the corporation is a sham and a scheme for obtaining the labor certification (sham test); or (b) whether the corporation has come to rely heavily upon the alien's skills and contacts so that, were it not for the alien, the corporation would probably cease to exist (inseparability test); *Capelli Antiques Furniture Restoration,* 03-INA-98 (BALCA Aug. 5, 2004) [where company had three officers who were all members of the same family, no employees, and the applicant was the nephew of the owner, the LC was denied under the totality of the circumstances test]; *Cleanex House Cleaning Service, Inc.*, 03-INA-208 (BALCA Sept. 7, 2004) [sister applying for Supervisor of Janitorial Service where there were at least 5 qualified applicants with requisite experience; *Paris Bakery* distinguished]. A family relationship does not preclude *per se* a *bona fide* job offer as BALCA has granted a labor certification where an owner applied for his brother as a French baker. *Paris Bakery Corp.*, 88-INA-337 (BALCA 1990) (*en banc*). *See also Silver Dragon Chinese Restaurant*, 19 I&N Dec. 401 (Comm. 1986) [I-140 may be filed for prospective employee who is also a shareholder of the petitioner; however where beneficiary of labor certification did not reveal ownership interest labor certification invalidated by INS pursuant to 20 C.F.R. §656.30(d)]. DOL has also stated that evidence that an employer, agent or attorney required the alien to pay costs of the LC process could be used in determining whether the position is open to U.S. workers under 20 C.F.R. §656.10(c)(8). 69 Fed. Reg. 77325, 77336 (Dec. 27, 2004).

5.b. In *Modular Container Systems, Inc.*, 89-INA-228 (BALCA July 16, 1991) (*en banc*), BALCA applied a "totality of the circumstances" test to determine whether there is a *bona fide* job offer. The factors it now considers include whether the alien: (a) is in the position to control or influence hiring decisions regarding the job for which labor certification is sought; (b) is related to the corporate directors, officers or employees; (c) was an incorporator or founder of the company; (d) has an ownership interest in the company; (e) is involved in the management of the company; (f) is on the board of directors; (g) is one of a small number of employees; (h) has qualifications for the job that are identical to specialized or unusual job duties and requirements stated in the application; and (i) is so inseparable from the sponsoring employer because of his or her pervasive presence and personal attributes that the employer would be unlikely to continue in operation without the alien. Relying on *Modular Container*, certification has been denied where person was the 100% owner of the company and held an E-1. *ATI Consultores,* 07-INA-64 (BALCA Feb. 11, 2008). Certification has also been denied even where the beneficiary owns no interest in the company but was the manager and sole employee. *Beximco USA, Ltd.*, 90-INA-302 (BALCA Apr. 15, 1992). Certification has also been denied to an E-2 who had no ownership interest in the company, but held an important executive position. *Driessen Aircraft Interior Systems*, 93-INA-82 (BALCA Jan. 11, 1995).

The approach in *Modular Container Systems* has been adopted by DOL. 69 Fed. Reg. 77325, 77356 (Dec. 27, 2004) ["In determining whether the job is subject to the alien's influence and control, we will evaluate the totality of the employer's circumstances using the *Modular Container Systems* criteria listed in the preamble to the proposed rule"]. Under 20 C.F.R. §656.17(*l*), the employer, in a closely held corporation or partnership in which the alien has an ownership interest or has a familial relationship with the stockholders, corporate officers, incorporators or partners *or* is one of a small number of employees, must provide the following documentation when requested: (1) Evidence of the business entity; (2) List of corporate officers and shareholders and their relationship to each other and the alien; (3) Financial history of the company and the amount each investor including the alien invested in the company; (4) Names and positions of business officials responsible for hiring and the LC process; and (5) Evidence of familial relationship between the alien and other employees if company has 10 or fewer employees.

The "totality of the circumstances" approach has also been used in cases involving domestic cooks. *Carlos Uy III,* 97-INA-304 (BALCA Mar. 3, 1999) (*en banc*) When case involves domestic cook the *bona fide* nature of job offer is raised because few families can afford the luxury of hiring someone simply to cook. The totality of the circumstances approach includes: (1) determining the wage offered in relationship to the family's income; (2) whether family had retained cooks in the past; (3) objective evidence to support dietary requirements such as a physician's letter; (4) whether the employee will be engaged in cooking duties for a substantial part of day; (5) whether employee will be required to perform child care or other duties; (6) training or experience as a cook. *Carlos Uy III, supra.; Enrique and Adriana Viano,* 98-INA-4 (BALCA May 25, 1999) [denied certification of domestic cook]. *But see Diane Simon,* 02-INA-44 (BALCA Aug. 28, 2002) [following totality of circumstances approach in *Carlos Uy III* and finding cook's position was bona fide].

5.c. Employer Not Contractor— 20 C.F.R. §656.3 (employer defined); 69 Fed. Reg. 77325, 77331 (Dec. 27, 2004) [an LC cannot be granted if filed on behalf of an independent contractor]; *V&R Construction Inc.,* 02-INA-153 (BALCA Feb. 7, 2003) [where employer could not demonstrate that the persons working for him were employees rather than independent contractors LC denied because he had no employees].

5.d. Employer cannot divert qualified U.S. applicant to other jobs—*Engineering Technology, Inc.*, 89-INA-10 (BALCA 1990) [where U.S. applicant was given a more senior position, LC for lesser position was denied because employer cannot divert applicants]; *Sam's Exxon*, 91-INA-362 (BALCA Dec. 11, 1992) [same].

5.e. New Job—Where the position did not exist before applicant was hired, it may still be considered a *bona fide* job offer. 69 Fed. Reg. 77325, 77356 (Dec. 27, 2004) [declining to adopt in final PERM regulations the criteria that a job that did not exist before the alien was offered the position is not open to U.S. workers]. *But see* GAL 1-97, Farmer, Admin. for Regional Management, DOL (Oct. 1, 1996), *reprinted in* 73 No. 40 *Interpreter Releases* 1458, 1476–83 (Oct. 21 1996) [where position did not exist before alien it will not be considered a *bona fide* job offer "unless the employer can clearly demonstrate that a major change in the business operation caused the position to be created after the alien was hired"]; *Neven Skalko Reproductions,* 00-INA-38 (BALCA May 2, 2000) [employer justified change from independent contractor to full time employee].

5.f. Ability to pay the salary—The employer must attest to his ability to pay the salary and will be able to place the alien on the payroll on or before the date of his proposed entrance to the U.S. 20 C.F.R. §656.10(c)(3),(4). Documentation can be requested. 69 Fed. Reg. 77325, 77356 (Dec. 27, 2004). It is not considered a bona fide job offer if the employer cannot produce documentation (*e.g.*, tax returns or other financial statements) demonstrating that the business has the financial ability to pay. *South Valley Drywall, Inc.* 07-INA-272 (BALCA Jan. 16, 2008) [CO had right to inquire into ability to pay as a function of whether job offer was bona fide and 8 C.F.R. §204.5(g)(2) regarding the production of financial records for I-140 petitions does not mean that only USCIS can make an inquiry]; *Gene R. McHam,* 08-INA-44 (BALCA Feb. 11, 2008) [employer failed to produce tax return to verify residential address and establish ability to page the wage for a day worker]; *Arkadia,* 98-INA-107 (BALCA Oct. 13, 1998) [where tax returns showed a net loss one year of $1,378 and a net profit of $1,537 the next year there was insufficient evidence to establish a bona fid job offer]. *The Whislers,* 90-INA-569 (BALCA Jan. 31, 1992). Where the employer is a sole proprietorship, the individual's assets should be considered in determining whether the employer has the ability to pay the proffered wage. *Ranchito Coletero,* 02-INA-105 (BALCA Jan. 8, 2004) (*en banc*). However, note that the employer is not required to pay the offered wage until after permanent residence is granted. 20 C.F.R. §656.10(c)(4). Amount paid employee at time application filed is relevant to determine if employer is able to pay the wage in the future. *Matter of Silver Spring Jewelers Mfg. Co.*, Case No. A21 409 743 (Comm. Dec. 8, 1983), *reported in* 3 *AILA Monthly Mailing* 4 (Jan. 1984). However, the fact that a person may be paid a lower wage, even below the prevailing wage, up until the time they take up the certified employment, is not a basis to deny the application. *Maysa, Inc.*, 98-INA-259 (BALCA May 21, 1999) [where the employer was paying person below the prevailing wage while employee was in H-1B status even during the adjustment of status process cannot be basis to deny certification because the prevailing wage must be paid "when the alien begins work" under former 20 C.F.R. §656.20(c)(2)]. Also it is the prevailing wage that must be used to determine employer's ability to pay, not the salary offered even if it is higher than the prevailing wage. *Masonry Masters, Inc. v. Thornburgh*, 742 F.Supp. 682 (D.D.C. 1990) [rejected INS claim where employer could afford to pay prevailing wage, which was lower than wage offered].

5.g. Virtual Office—The creation of an office in a remote location with no real work at the location can not be validated by an employer on the theory that in a computer driven age the office is a virtual office and can be located anywhere. *PR Consultants Inc.,* 07-INA-66 (BALCA Jan. 16, 2008) [where Cheyenne, Wyoming "branch" office was a small office with no signage and solely one desk and one bookcase and the employee was living in NJ, BALCA concluded this was not an actual place of work but merely for the purpose of obtaining a LC]. *See also eBusiness Applications Solutions, Inc.* 05-INA-87 (BALCA Dec. 6, 2006) [computer company did not offer a bona fide job to 10 applicants where it created a "virtual office" in Delaware to which workers were assigned but in fact the workers did not live in the area, they reported to a manager in California, and they were without support staff in Delaware where there was no business justification for the office].

5.h. Position Cannot Be Out of U.S.—A LC cannot be issued for a job opportunity consisting solely of job duties performed totally out of the U.S. 20 C.F.R. §656.3 (Employment defined).

6. Full-time and Permanent.

6.a. Job offer must be for permanent, full-time position. 20 C.F.R. §§656.3, 656.10(c)(10). The focus of 656.3 is on whether the job is permanent versus temporary.

(1) Work Week and Full Time Employment. Where employer is offering work week with hours customary for a full-time employee in the industry LC cannot be denied on grounds that workers duties do not require "constant work for the entire work day." *Daisy Schimoler,* 97-INA-218 (BALCA Mar. 3, 1999) (*en banc*) [denial of Domestic Cook, Cuban style food on grounds that job is not full time was incorrect analysis; instead it should be whether job was bona fide under 656.20(c)). Full-time teachers are considered to be in full-time employment. *Dearborn Public Schools*, 91-INA-222 (BALCA Dec. 7, 1993) (*en banc*); Job is full-time where position requires 35 hours per week. Memo, Farmer, Admin. for Regional Management, Div. of Foreign Labor Certification, DOL Field Memo No. 48-94 (May 16, 1994), *reprinted in* 13 *AILA Monthly Mailing* 544 (July/Aug. 1994), *published on* AILA InfoNet at Doc. No. 94052390 (May 23, 1994) [35 or 40 hrs/week in full-time]; *Walters*, 94-INA-7 (ALJ Nov. 30, 1994) [30 hours as cook not full-time]; *Central Korean Evangelical Church*, 88-INA-336 (BALCA 1988) [37 hours]; *Marrero*, 86-INA-470 (BALCA 1986) [absent contrary evidence, employer's claim of full-time employment will be accepted]; *Capossela*, 86-INA-342 (BALCA 1986) [irrelevant that household could function with part-time help]; *But see Open Evangelical Church,* 03-INA-225 (BALCA Sept. 7, 2004) [under the totality of the circumstances approach of *Carlos Uy III,* 97-INA-304 (BALCA Mar. 3, 1999) (*en banc*) the job of choir director did not involve full time employment where the church had a very small membership and where the lease permit for the facility only allowed use of the facility for 12 ½ hrs per week]; *Auerbach*, 88-INA-103 (BALCA 1988) [no full-time job where alien previously filled same job on half-time basis].

(2) Seasonal or Permanent Job. *Vito Volpe Landscaping*, 91-INA-300 (BALCA Sept. 29, 1993) (*en banc*) [landscape gardeners, lawn service workers are not considered full-time when they are not working during winter months because job performed on a seasonal basis]; *Crawford & Sons,* 01-INA-121 (BALCA Jan. 9, 2004) (*en banc*) [reaffirmed *Vito Volpe* and denied LC for landscape gardener who despite working for employer for seven years and being paid over the course of an entire year did not work for 2 ½ months during the winter]; *Rankin Landscaping, Inc.* 07-INA-57 (BALCA Jan. 16, 2008) [BALCA totaled hours that employee worked for the whole year and concluded that at 40 hours per week the employee engaged in full time employment for less than 39 weeks]; *Good Earth Gardens Centers,* 03-INA-284 (BALCA Nov. 5, 2004) [although winter break is only 4-6 weeks and is used as vacation break for gardeners, job was not full time because gardening could not be performed year round due to the weather].

(3) Temporary Employment. Where construction employees hired as independent contractors for temporary employment projects, the employer failed to demonstrate that job is permanent position. *Future Construction,* 03-INA-243 (BALCA Nov. 30, 2004).

(4) Staffing Companies. *Professional Staffing Services of America,* 04-INA-7 (BALCA Mar. 7. 2005) [where professional staffing company failed to provide documentation that it has staffing contracts with other companies sufficient to constitute a full-time, permanent position for an accountant, LC denied].

6.b. Worker must be able, qualified and available. 20 C.F.R. §656.1(a)(1). Overqualified workers who are able to perform in a normally acceptable manner the duties involved are deemed to be able, qualified and available. *Air Products & Chemicals, Inc.*, 89-INA-76 (BALCA 1990) and cannot be rejected simply because they are overqualified. *Metroplex Distributors,* 88-INA-249 (May 22, 1989) (*en banc*); *Southpoint Seafood Market,* 87-INA-614 (BALCA Jan. 20, 1988) BALCA held that the employer could not simply determine that the applicant was overqualified and would not remain on the job without making further efforts to contact him]; *Lico's Tree Service,* 01-INA-124 (BALCA 2002).

6.c. The job opportunity must not be vacant because the former occupant is on strike or locked out in the course of a labor dispute involving a work stoppage or at issue in a labor dispute involving a work stoppage. 20 C.F.R. §656.10(c)(6). *Elastic Stop Nut of America*, 90-INA-301 (BALCA Apr. 15, 1993) [labor dispute and work stoppage broadly defined].

6.d. The job terms, conditions and occupational environment are not contrary to federal, state or local law. 20 C.F.R. §656.10(c)(7); *Wallace*, 91-INA-389 (BALCA May 12, 1993) [failure of employer to document compliance with California law requiring payment of unemployment and disability insurance for domestic worker already employed].

7. *Layoffs*—20 C.F.R. §656.17 (k). If there has been a layoff within 6 months of filing the ETA 9089 in the same or "related occupation," the employer must notify and consider all potentially qualified laid off U.S. workers and document the results. A layoff is considered any involuntary separation without cause or prejudice. A "related occupation" for purposes of this section is any occupation that requires workers "to perform a majority of the essential duties" involved in the LC occupation. Although the employer need only notify and consider an applicant in a related occupation and not necessarily select her for the position, a U.S. worker will be deemed qualified if by education, training, experience or a combination thereof she is able to perform the position in the normally accepted manner *or* if she can acquire the skills during a reasonable period of on-the-job training. 69 Fed. Reg. 77325, 77355 (Dec. 27, 2004).

7.a. In RIR cases a CO does not abuse his discretion in denying an employer's RIR request where there is evidence of layoffs occurring subsequent to the filing of the labor certification application. *Solectron Corp.,* 03-INA-143 (BALCA Aug. 12, 2004). But where the CO grants RIR and denies the application because of layoffs, she must remand it back to the job service or SWA for regular processing. *Sprint United Management Company,* 6-INA-6-8, 10–12 (BALCA Aug. 21, 2006); *Oracle USA Inc.* 6-INA-26, 29 to 33 (BALCA Aug. 21, 2006).

8. *Location of Job*—The ETA 9089 form requests that the employer only list the primary site or location where work will be performed. Under a pre-PERM agency memorandum, the employer would have submitted a statement indicating whether there would be other locations and if unknown that the other locations could not anticipated at the time of filing. *See* Memo, Farmer, Admin. for Regional Management, Div. of Foreign Labor Certification, DOL Field Memo No. 48-94 (May 16, 1994), *reprinted in* 13 *AILA Monthly Mailing* 544 (July/Aug. 1994), *published on* AILA InfoNet at Doc. No. 94052390 (May 23, 1994). PERM however makes no provision for noting additional locations and the employer is forced to put the address of the company's headquarters or main office when there is uncertainty as to the location for the work.

9. *Recruitment program*

9.a. The PERM recruitment process is detailed above. *See in this section* ¶ 1 (p.909), *supra*. The process includes the following:

(1) Posting—must provide notice to collective bargaining representative if there is one, and if not, must post notice of position's availability at the place of business for 10 consecutive working days. In addition, the employer must publish the notice in all in-house media, whether electronic or printed, in accordance with normal recruitment procedures. For requirements of notice see 20 C.F.R. §656.10(d)(1)(ii).

(a) Failure to post or provide proof of posting is basis to deny labor certification. *Import S.H.K. Enterprises, Inc.*, 88-INA-52 (BALCA 1989).

(b) Including state agency as place to send resumes in one place of notice and employer in another place in the notice (instead of stating only employer) was harmless error. *Computech International*, 94-INA-43 (BALCA Feb. 26, 1996).

(2) Advertisements.

(a) Position Must Be Advertised in Two Different Sunday Editions in a newspaper of general circulation in the area of intended employment. An advertisement in a professional journal may be substituted for one Sunday advertisement for recruitment involving professionals. 20 C.F.R. §656.17(e)(1), (e)(2), (f).

i) Always On A Sunday—BALCA rejected claim that advertising from Monday through Friday met Sunday requirement because Friday's edition remained available on the newsstands through the weekend. *Virginia General Services, Inc.,* 07-PER-22 (BALCA Apr. 24, 2007).

ii) Placement of the Advertisement—The employer cannot seek to bury the ad by putting it an inappropriate heading or job title. 69 Fed. Reg. 77325, 77348–49 (Dec. 27, 2004) ["[P]lacement of the employer's advertisement under an inappropriate heading or keyword would be considered a failure to make good-faith efforts to recruit U.S. workers. See *H.C. LaMarche Enterprises Inc.,* 87-INA-607 (BALCA Oct. 27, 1988); *Wailua Associates,* 88-INA-533 (BALCA June 14, 1989); *Quality Rebuilders Corp.,* 93-INA-144 (BALCA June 28, 1994)"]

iii) CO Has Burden On Choice of Publication—Where employer makes prima facie case as to publishing in a particular journal and the CO objects to method of advertising, CO has burden to explain why employer's choice of publication did not test the labor market and why CO's suggestion would enhance the recruitment. *Hillel Hebrew Academy*, 90-INA-572 (BALCA Mar. 4, 1992); *Florida Ordnance, Inc.*, 89-INA-106 (BALCA Feb. 14, 1990); *Pater Noster H.S.*, 88-INA-131 (BALCA 1988); *Alpine Electronics of America, Inc.*, 88-INA-107 (BALCA 1989). However, where CO meets that burden, the employer's claim that it was directed by the state employment agency to publish in a certain magazine or journal at substantial cost is not a defense. *Peking Gourmet*, 88-INA-323 (BALCA 1989). Moreover, where the advertising is remedial due to prior problem the CO needs less rationale for selecting one newspaper over another. *Computech International*, 94-INA-43 (BALCA Feb. 26, 1996) [upheld directive by CO to advertise in Washington Post where employer chose Washington Times].

iv) Prior Regulation requiring advertising upheld. *Productions Tool Corp. v. Employment & Training Admin.*, 688 F.2d 1161 (7th Cir. 1982).

v) Under pre-PERM authority, readvertising if necessary was only for one day on Sunday in appropriate newspaper of general circulation. GAL 1-97, Farmer, Admin. for Regional Management, DOL (Oct. 1, 1996), *reprinted in* 73 No. 40 *Interpreter Releases* 1458, 1476–82, 1480 (Oct. 21, 1996) *modified* May 4, 1999, *reprinted in* 76 No. 19 *Interpreter Releases* 759, 780–82 (May 17, 1999). Although supervised recruitment may now required more extensive readvertising and recruitment. 20 C.F.R. §656.21.

(3) Concurrent placement by local employment office into statewide network (job bank). 20 C.F.R. §§656.17(e)(1)(i)(A), (e)(2)(i).

(4) Other Recruitment Steps for Professionals. DOL now requires employers recruiting for professional positions to engage in 3 additional steps from a menu of 10 possible alternatives. *See* 20 C.F.R. §656.17(e)(1)(ii) and discussion above. *Big Apple Educational Center,* 07-PER-26 (BALCA May 16, 2007) [CO denial upheld where employer failed to take 3 additional steps].

(5) CO has authority to require supervised recruitment subsequent to an audit. 20 C.F.R. §656.21. This procedure is similar to the basic LC recruitment procedure and results in more direct supervision over the employer during the process. This may include a requirement that employer recruit through a union where CO has determined that the union is an additional source of U.S. workers and that it is willing to refer workers. *David Howard of California*, 90-INA-241 (BALCA May 12, 1992) (*en banc*).

9.b. Interview applicants and state "lawful job related reasons" for denial. 20 C.F.R. §656.17(g). Must be *bona fide* interview.

(1) Alien or his or her attorney cannot participate in the interview process. 20 C.F.R. §656.10(b)(2)(i). Alien's participation is a *per se* violation rendering the selection process invalid. *Verdugo,* 03-INA-158 (BALCA 20004) [sending return receipts to alien's representative is a violation of the regulation]; *Master Video Productions, Inc.*, 88-INA-419 (BALCA 1989), *reprinted in* 66 No. 42 *Interpreter Releases* 1205, 1239–40 (Oct. 30, 1989). *But see Rojas*, 87-INA-685 (BALCA 1988) [attorney could sit in as interpreter-advisor where he represented employer in substance and not merely incidental to representation of alien]. The use of the attorney's or immigration consultant's address as the return address for the job applicant does not alone, however, invalidate the recruitment process. *Tom O'Brien Nissan, Inc.*, 97-INA-435 (BALCA Mar. 18, 1999). Where attorney has filed G-28 on behalf of employer, resumes of applicants for LC and other documentation, must be forwarded by the job service to the attorney. 20 C.F.R. §656.10(b)(1); Letter, Panati, Certifying Officer Reg. III, DOL III-TGTC-Rep. C/G (June 24, 1994), *reprinted in* 71 No. 26 *Interpreter Releases* 900, 915 (July 11, 1994). An LC application may not be denied solely because the employer's attorney signed the rebuttal. *Morici Bros. Fresh Fish Daily,* 03-INA-149 (BALCA Aug. 13, 2004) [reversed CO denial based upon attorney's signature on the rebuttal].

(2) Denial for Unlawful Reasons Bars Consideration of Lawful Reason. Where an employer has rejected a qualified applicant for an unlawful reason, the CO is not required to investigate the legitimacy of a totally independent reason for rejection that is offered by an employer in response to a NOF (or under PERM an audit letter). *Featherland Farms, Inc.*, 03-INA-6 (Mar. 29, 2004) [where employer unlawfully rejected applicant for an unstated requirement of travel, he could not assert the U.S. worker's degree as a basis].

(3) Labor Union Referrals. Where CO required the employer to contact a labor union as a source of recruitment and the employer demurred, the denial of the LC was upheld. *R.E. Drywall Contracting, Inc.* 03-INA-223 (BALCA Aug. 18, 2004) [CO referred employer to Drywall Lathers union for Drywall Applicator position].

(4) Not necessary to interview applicants if they don't meet the minimum qualifications. *Anonymous Mgmt.*, 87-INA-672 (BALCA 1988). *But see* 20 C.F.R. §656.17(g) [under PERM, employer cannot reject U.S. applicant "if the worker can acquire the skills necessary to perform the duties involved in the occupation during a reasonable period of on-the-job training."]. Employer can reject applicant on resume alone because "were we to find otherwise, we would be requiring an employer to interview every applicant who sends in a resume...." *Eny Textiles, Inc.*, 87-INA-641 (BALCA 1988) [rejected applicant solely on resume that said he had experience in knit sweaters, but did not state he was an importer of textiles]; *Nancy, Ltd. v. Dole*, No. 89-2257-Civ-Scott (S.D. Fla. Aug. 8, 1990), *aff'd per curiam*, No. 90-5857 (11th Cir. 1991) [reversing BALCA where resume did not meet minimum requirement]; *Mejico Express,* 02-INA-56 (BALCA July 16, 2002) [where applicant's resume was vague and sparse and he was uncooperative in providing additional information employer had no obligation to investigate further]. It is also not necessary for employer to accept a U.S. worker who does not meet the minimum requirements as stated but may meet them if employer combines U.S. worker's education, training, and experience. *Bronx Med. & Dental Clinic*, 90-INA-479 (BALCA Oct. 30, 1992) (*en banc*) [plurality opinion held that the CO may not rely on 20 C.F.R. §656.24(b)(2)(ii) to find applicant qualified based on combination of his education, training and experience when s/he does not meet minimum requirements as stated]. Employer's rejection will be upheld even if it was for reasons based on unstated re-

quirements where the rejection was also based on applicant's failure to meet stated minimum requirements. *Univ. of N. Carolina*, 90-INA-422 (BALCA June 9, 1992).

(5) Where applicant's resume indicates a broad range of experience, education, and training required for the position, the employer has the duty to inquire further to determine if U.S. worker meets all requirements. *Gorchev & Gorchev Graphic Design*, 89-INA-118 (BALCA Nov. 29, 1990) (*en banc*); *Takeo Kawamura, M.D. & Assoc.*, 04-INA-31 (BALCA Dec. 6, 2004); *Suma Fruit Int'l USA, Inc.*, 91-INA-47 (BALCA Feb. 3, 1993); *Quality Inn Rainbow Bridge at the Falls*, 93-INA-7 (BALCA Apr. 6, 1994). *But see Bloomberg, L.P.*, 94-INA-619 (BALCA July 30, 1996) [reversed CO denial where U.S. applicant had A.A. degree and a number of years experience, where job called for B.A. degree in journalism]. Employer improperly rejected applicant with supervisory as well as required technical experience, even though he failed to meet one of several subsidiary requirements, because CO may direct employer to interview applicants whose qualifications are comparable to employer's requirements, and employer must allow qualified applicants a reasonable amount of time on-the-job to learn specifics of the position. *Unisys*, 87-INA-555 (BALCA 1988).

(6) Employer must interview, or at least call applicant to resolve ambiguity in resume. *Norwest Bank Minneapolis, N.A.*, 87-INA-658 (BALCA 1988) [employer could not speculate applicant would lack experience in loan work and debt restructuring on the basis that the applicant's experience was only in personal banking]. This can also be accomplished by a letter stating the basis for rejection and asking applicant to call if resume was misinterpreted. *Harris Corp.*, 88-INA-293 (BALCA 1989). Failure of U.S. worker to follow up employer's request to provide validation in light of vague resume is basis to reject applicant. *Mejico Express*, 02-INA-56 (BALCA July 16, 2002). Reliance on resume is appropriate unless disputed by relevant information from other sources. *Aelry-Mart, Inc.*, 88-INA-243 (BALCA 1989). Cover letter asserting that the person is qualified is not "relevant information" when his resume shows he is not qualified. *New Consumer Products*, 87-INA-706 (BALCA 1988).

(7) Employer must make efforts to interview applicant to establish if applicant's credentials are justified. *El Jalisco Mexican Restaurant*, 07-INA-10 (BALCA Dec.10, 2007) [one-minute telephone interview as demonstrated by telephone records was insufficient]; *Ukay Trucking and Delivery*, 03-INA-137 (BALCA May 25, 2004) [BALCA rejects "passive recruitment" whereby employer simply makes one effort to contact applicant (telephone call in this case) without trying multiple good faith efforts to make contact]; *Precon Products, Ltd.*, 02-INA-123 (BALCA May 20, 2003) [where employer claims to have called 2 times and written applicant and applicant in follow up questionnaire said he was never contacted, certification was denied because employer did not have certified return receipt letter and only had his "repeated bare assertions" and a copy of a letter addressed to the applicant]; *Carpet Mall, Inc.*, 87-INA-166 (DOL 1987) [where employer sought to contact U.S./LPR applicant by call on 5 or 6 afternoons after normal working hours recruitment defective. Needed to write letters and call at other times]; *Bay Area Women's Resource Center*, 88-INA-379 (BALCA 1989) [need to write applicant when unable to contact by telephone]; *Cotton L.A.*, 00-INA-313 (BALCA Sept. 25, 2001) [employer fulfilled recruiting obligation where s/he sent certified letter and confirmed it was delivered because applicants' failure to respond, given the large number of applicants, cannot be basis to deny certification]. BALCA has urged employers to use certified return receipt mail to demonstrate proof that a prospective employee was contacted because it is a "useful device for documenting recruitment efforts." *M.N. Auto Electric Corp.*, 00-INA-165 (BALCA Aug. 8, 2001) (*en banc*). But certified return receipt letters alone may be insufficient. *M.N. Auto Electric Corp.* and *Pirco Dry Cleaning Inc.*, 00-INA-175 (Aug. 8, 2001) (*en banc*) [Board citing previous cases such as *Sierra Canyon School*, 90-INA-410 (BALCA Jan. 16, 1992) noted that sending out certified return receipt letters, particularly where there is a small group of potential applicants, and receiving no responses may *not* constitute sufficient recruitment efforts]; *Omar Construction*, 05-INA-135 (BALCA Dec. 18, 2006) [one attempt to contact applicant by certified return receipt mail which was returned undelivered is insufficient]. Employer must also *thoroughly* document all efforts to contact applicant, including when and how many times it attempted to contact appli-

cant, where the contacts were made and who messages were left with at business or home, and whether alternate means of communication, such as letters, were used. *Yaron Development Co., Inc.*, 89-INA-178 (BALCA 1991) (*en banc*). The employer's documentation must also include "at a minimum, ... reasonably detailed notes of the conversation (*e.g.*, when the call was made, how long it lasted, whether there was successful contact with the applicant, the substance of the conversation. Prepared checklists may be helpful in documenting what was discussed with the applicants). Where available, phone records showing the time and duration of the phone contacts should be submitted by Employer." *M.N. Auto Electric Corp.*, 00-INA-165 (BALCA Aug. 8, 2001); *Karina's Bakery,* 03-INA-199 (BALCA Aug. 4, 2004) [upheld CO denial where employer asserted but failed to document its telephone contacts with U.S. workers];/ *Tammy Taylor Nails, Inc.* 02-INA-218 (BALCA Sept. 9, 2003) [relying on language in *M.N Auto Electric* and finding the employer's bare assertions were not enough to overcome applicant's claim that he was not contacted and employer's unsuccessful effort to contact applicant by telephone if believed were insufficient]. As the test is whether the employer made reasonable efforts to contact applicants, the CO erred in denying certification simply because the employer failed to send certified return receipt letters. *Empire Bookbinding, Inc.* 00-INA-283 (BALCA Jan. 15, 2002). Where interviews were set and applicant failed to appear, employer has no obligation to recontact applicant. *Dynatech/U-Z, Inc.*, 88-INA-230 (BALCA 1989). However, employer cannot reject applicant who failed to appear at interview at considerable personal expense, when employer could have conducted interview by telephone or at its own expense, but refused to do so. *Warmtex Enterprises v. Martin*, 953 F.2d 1133 (9th Cir. 1992).

Although the employer has an obligation to document thoroughly its recruitment efforts, the CO cannot "blindside" the employer with a documentary requirement that reasonably could not have been anticipated because pre-NOF the employer was not on notice by either the state job service or the DOL. *Joyful Manor,* 01-INA-157 (BALCA Mar. 27, 2002); *PJM Bookkeeping and Tax Services,* 02-INA-156 (BALCA Oct. 3, 2002); *Walnut Home Care,* 01-INA-156 (BALCA Oct. 3, 2003). *Accord Norma Diamond,* 02-INA-122 (BALCA Sept. 4, 2003).

(8) Employer cannot unduly delay contacting applicants. The employer must contact applicants "as soon as possible." *Loma Linda Foods, Inc.*, 89-INA-289 (BALCA 1991) (*en banc*). How quickly an employer can examine credentials will include: (a) whether the position requires extensive or minimal credentials; (b) whether recruitment is local or nonlocal; and (c) whether many or few persons apply for the position. *Id. See Creative Cabinet & Store Fixture*, 89-INA-181 (BALCA 1990) (*en banc*) [failure to contact applicants for nonprofessional jobs within 30 days was not in good faith]. In *Creative Cabinet* BALCA rejected the position that the 45-day period for recruitment is an absolute defense to delay. BALCA determined the CO must look to the facts and circumstances in each case. In *Bobby McGee's*, 91-INA-39 (BALCA Apr. 15, 1992) the Board held that an unexplained failure to contact applicants within 13 days of receipt of applications, absent a complex job, was unreasonable and denial of LC was upheld. In *Prince Yeboah,* 00-INA-5 (BALCA Jan. 19, 2000) the Board applied similar rules to interviewing and not simply contacting applicant. Thus, a delay of 13 to 23 days in scheduling interviews of the applicants *after* contacting them was sufficient to deny certification even where the employer proffered that he had scheduled a purchasing trip for his business. Moreover, the employer cannot excuse contacting the applicant because he is out-of-the-country when he could have delegated recruitment responsibilities in the interim. *Bistany's Oriental Rug Dealers, Inc.,* 07-INA-9 (BALCA Dec. 10, 2007) [where prospective employee expressed interest in position and employer waited over a month and 20 days to contact applicant and did not contact applicant for the first 14 days after returning from overseas, LC was properly denied].

(9) Employer cannot put up unreasonable barriers to conduct an interview of a facially qualified applicant. Employer cannot send out letter requesting interview just several days later where there is a likelihood that U.S. worker will get letter after interview date. *Drywall Systems, Inc.,* 03-INA-148 (BALCA Apr. 29, 2004) [employer did not engage in

good faith recruiting where none of the U.S. workers responded to requests for interviews but the letters of invitation were sent on July 2 for July 6 interviews and others were dated July 10 for July 13 interviews]. Employer cannot require applicant to fill out an employment application after receipt of facially valid resume which is sent with a discouraging letter. *VIP Express, Inc.* 02-INA-289 (BALCA Jan. 22, 2004); *Sunview Properties,* 02-INA-80 (BALCA Oct. 11, 2002). Employer cannot require detailed letters verifying references prior to interview. *Gaynor Gardens Homes, Inc.* 07-INA-269 (BALCA Mar. 24, 2008). Employer's failure to mitigate hardship of applicant traveling to interview was deemed to be a means to reject U.S. workers. *CTS*, 91-INA-175 (BALCA June 19, 1992). Employer that insists on in person interview must offer reimbursement for travel expenses, at least where position is professional or executive level. *Hotel Group of America*, 89-INA-195 (BALCA Mar. 10, 1992).

(10) Employer's contact with wife of applicant (or other third party) instead of applicant to determine his or her interest in the job is insufficient recruitment. *Dove Homes, Inc.*, 87-INA-680 (BALCA 1988); *All American Computers,* 97-INA-143 (BALCA 1998).

(11) Employer's efforts to re-contact applicant subsequent to the recruitment period to cure previous failure not permissible. However, employer can show that at time of recruitment applicant was uninterested or unavailable. *Nancy, Ltd.*, 88-INA-358 (BALCA 1989), *rev'd on other grounds*, *Nancy, Ltd. v. Dole*, ___ F.Supp. ___, Case No. 89-2257-Civ-Scott (S.D. Fla. Aug. 8, 1990), *aff'd per curiam*, Case No. 90-5857 (11th Cir. 1991); WSB ¶13,566 c.851. *Accord Bada Apparels*, 87-INA-712 (BALCA 1988).

(12) Employer does not have to but should contact applicant by return receipt mail. Where employer sent copies of letters as well as photocopies of the outside of the metered stamped envelope as proof of its efforts, the CO could not assume it was invalid simply because applicant denied contact. *Ambras Trading Corp.*, 97-INA-406 (BALCA July 27, 1998) [BALCA "does not operate under a preconception that employers routinely engage in fraud or other willful misconduct in attempting to obtain labor certifications."]. However, in *M.N. Auto Electric Corp.*, 00-INA-165 (BALCA Aug. 8, 2001) (*en banc*) and *Pirco Dry Cleaning Inc.*, 00-INA-175 (Aug. 8, 2001) (*en banc*) the Board strongly urged employers to use certified return receipt mail noting that: "Without such documentation, an employer may have a difficult time responding to questions about date of mailing or an assertion by a U.S. applicant that he or she was never contacted." The Board further noted that "an employer who relies only on a declaration that the letter was timely mailed may find itself on shaky ground" and urged employers "at a minimum" to "obtain a Certificate of Mailing receipt from the Postal Service." In addition the Board citing previous cases such as *Sierra Canyon Sch.*, 90-INA-410 (BALCA Jan. 16, 1992) noted that sending out certified return receipt letters, particularly where there is a small group of potential applicants, and receiving no responses may *not* constitute sufficient recruitment efforts.

(13) Employer must offer job at salary and have job *rejected* by U.S. worker. Simply ascertaining that U.S. worker wants a higher salary is not sufficient. *Unique Chemtek, Inc.*, 88-INA-552 (BALCA Nov. 16, 1990). However, business judgment does apply and if an applicant states that he will not take less than a wage considerably more than is offered and the employer subsequently in writing offers the job at the stated wage, the applicant's failure to respond can be reasonably understood as a rejection of the job offer. *Four Season Garment Cutting,* 96-INA-443 (BALCA Sept. 14, 1999). But the rejection of a U.S. worker because she is already employed and cannot start immediately is not sufficient where she would have been ready to take the job in two weeks. *Murphy*, 91-INA-281 (BALCA Aug. 17, 1992).

(14) Employer cannot reject applicant who meets minimum requirements as stated in labor certification, but who fails to meet unstated requirement. 20 C.F.R. §656.21(b)(6); *Chromato Chem*, 88-INA-8 (BALCA Jan. 12, 1989) (*en banc*); *Houston Music Institute,* 07-INA-271 (BALCA Jan. 16, 2008) [in the case involving a music instructor: "A mere suspicion that the job does not match a U.S. applicant's long-term career goals...does not establish lawful grounds for rejecting that applicant"]; *Vincent Trimarco, Jr.* 03-INA-293 (BALCA Sept. 27, 2004) [rejection of applicant for bookkeeper/accounts manager be-

cause he lived too far away when no distance to work was listed as a requirement is not a lawful reason for rejection]; *Professional Staffing Services of America,* 03-INA-46 (BALCA Apr. 12, 2004) [where employer required travel between facilities for Social Service Director but requirement was not stated on ETA 750A or advertisement, it was unlawful]; *Jhaveri Diamond Corp.*, 94-INA-621 (BALCA Apr. 12, 1996) [speculation that hiring might affect business because applicant is an employee of customer was insufficient for rejection]; *Cantarero*, 92-INA-70 (BALCA Mar. 31, 1993) [where employer failed to document rejection because person had "too strong" personality, CO denial upheld]. *But see Sandler*, 89-INA-316 (BALCA Feb. 11, 1991) (*en banc*) [under facts of case employer's denial of applicant because of unstated nonsmoker requirement is permissible]; *Petit Jean Poultry*, 94-INA-318, 372 (BALCA Aug. 15, 1996) [unreliability of worker arising from verification or inability to verify]; *Alfredo's Restaurant #2*, 90-INA-70 (BALCA June 12, 1991) [following *Sandler*, employer could refuse to hire U.S. worker where reference stated that he was not reliable to show up for work, even though neither job description nor advertisement included requirement of reliability]; *Evens*, 92-INA-341 (BALCA June 3, 1993) [rejection of child monitor because she had two small children who would accompany her to work as full care monitor, even though requirement not listed]; *Hines*, 88-INA-510 (BALCA Apr. 9, 1990) [where employer documented that applicant had a "bad attitude" applicant could be rejected for this subjective, not listed, criterion].

(15) Employer cannot reject applicant because s/he refused to give permanent commitment. *Beth & David Dassa,* 03-INA-251 (BALCA Sept. 8, 2004) [employer could not reject domestic applicant because he stated his long-term goal was to do other work]; *World Bazaar,* 88-INA-54 (BALCA June 14, 1989) (*en banc*) [it was impermissible to reject U.S. worker solely based upon his statement that he would not commit beyond 6 months].

(16) Employer cannot request Social Security number or authorization to work in U.S. during recruitment process and cannot deny a U.S. worker for his or her refusal to provide that information. *Bliss Smulian,* 03-INA-171 (BALCA June 16, 2004) [it is unlawful to reject an applicant for his failure to provide his Social Security number and the request to verify employment authorization to work in the U.S. cannot be used to discourage applicants].

(17) Employer can request applicant to furnish references even if it was not a stated requirement. *Kam Kuo Foods Corp.*, 92-INA-395 (BALCA Oct. 23, 1993); *Sunee Kim's Enterprises*, 87-INA-713 (BALCA July 22, 1988). And it may reject the applicant for failure to provide the verification, *Sunee, supra*, or for receiving unfavorable references. *Broadway Baptist Child Dev. Ctr.*, 92-INA-405 (BALCA Sept. 30, 1993).

10. *Traditional Recruitment (TR) and Reduction in Recruitment (RIR)*—Prior to PERM, DOL relied upon a basic TR process and, more recently, through RIR. Both of these methods are still in effect for applications filed prior to Mar. 28, 2005, if the employer has chosen not to convert those applications to the PERM process. The applications were awaiting approval, denial, or additional recruitment at 2 Backlog Elimination Centers (BECs) (f/k/a Backlog Reduction Centers or Backlog Processing Centers) in Philadelphia and Dallas, established by DOL to address these "old" applications. These centers have now been closed. Round 7 Backlog FAQs, DOL (Oct. 2007), *published on* AILA InfoNet at Doc. No. 07110633. To further investigate pending cases DOL established a Backlog Public Disclosure System (PDS) at *http://pds.pbls.doleta.gov* and all disposition questions can be directed to the Chicago NPC at *bec.chicago@dol.gov*. FOIA requests are sent to the ETA national office and information regarding FOIA is found at *www.doleta.gov/foia*. Round 8, Backlog FAQs, DOL Q. 10, *published on* AILA InfoNet at Doc. No. 07121864. The DOL has encouraged through regulation the conversion of TR cases to RIR by extending the RIR eligibility date. 71 Fed. Reg. 59336 (Oct. 6, 2006)

10.a. RIR Issues—Under RIR, if the process is denied by the CO, the CO is supposed to remand the case back to the SWA for further processing under basic recruitment. *Sun Microsystems, Inc.*, 04-INA-271 through 274 (BALCA Nov. 18, 2004) [remanding case to CO to permit basic LC process and referencing "Ziegler memo" (GAL 1-97, Change 1) as basis for decision]; *Compaq Computer Corp.,* 02-INA-249 (BALCA Sept. 3, 2003). The CO can not avoid a remand to allow an employer to conduct supervised recruitment under *Compaq Computer* by granting the RIR and then denying the application based upon a defect in the recruitment. *Ex-*

press Photo, 05-INA-128 (BALCA May 16, 2007) (*en banc*) [CO denial was remanded where it granted the RIR but denied the application because the employer refused improperly to consider an overqualified applicant. BALCA rejected the CO contentions and found that all deficient pre-application recruitment efforts that were not adequate under DOL criteria for acceptable recruitment were a basis for remand for supervised recruitment]; *Oracle USA, Inc.*, 06-INA-26, 29, 30–33 (BALCA Aug. 21, 2006) [although CO was correct in investigating layoffs and whether there was a bona fide job offer, it erred in denying the RIR case outright instead of remanding it for supervised recruitment]. But where the LC application is so fundamentally flawed that a remand would not assist the process because there is no bona fide job offer, *Rigo Industries*, 07-INA-20 (BALCA Sept. 18, 2007) [where employer did not confess error that the position was unduly restrictive and instead argued that it was not feasible to train an employee, CO affirmed], *Professional Staffing Services of America*, 07-INA-58 (BALCA Jan. 23, 2008) [where employee did not qualify for position and employer did not offer to delete experience requirement, remand not necessary], *Beith Aharon,* 03-INA-300 (BALCA Nov. 18, 2004) or the employer refuses or fails to agree to cure an obvious defect, *Smith Group Inc.,* 05-INA-39 (BALCA Nov. 27, 2006) [refusal or failure to agree to amend offered wage to prevailing wage rate] a remand is not necessary. Where employer failed to timely respond to NOF, CO properly denied the application and remand for basic LC processing was also unnecessary. *Houston's Restaurant,* 03-INA-237 (BALCA Sept. 27, 2004).

10.b. Improper Denial from BEC—Although currently there is no formal process to reopen an improperly denied RIR or TR case where the BEC has erroneously closed the case, a letter or document-styled motion to reopen may be filed with proof that a response to the CRNL, Corrections List, and/or Selection of Continuation Letter was timely filed or was never received.

10.c. Delays in adjudication. The substantial backlog of LCs (estimated at over 350,000 cases) resulted in years of delay in adjudicating LCs. Often, by the time, the CO adjudicated a case the employer was out of business. The delay, however, could not be used as a defense to a CO denial under 20 C.F.R. §656.20(c)(8) that no bona fide job offer existed. *Camelback Wedding Center,* 08-INA-12 (BALCA Jan. 23, 2008) [LC was properly denied where it was filed in 2001 and the certifying officer's NOF was issued in May 2007 which was several years after the company was out of business].

D. *Schedule A, Teachers, Live-Ins, and Other Cases*

1. All cases have a posting requirement, except private households that do not employ any U.S. workers. 20 C.F.R. §656.10(d). Notice must go to bargaining representative under the collective bargaining agreement or, if no representative, then notice must be posted at the facility or location of employment and through in-house electronic or print media. The content of the notice is found at §656.10(d)(3). For additional guidelines for the timing and form of the notice *see* Field Memo, Kulick, Admin. for Regional Mgmt., Memo No. 76-92 (July 23, 1992), *reprinted in* 70 No. 13 *Interpreter Releases* 461, 481–82 (Apr. 5, 1993).

2. College/university teachers

2.a. Need to show only that alien is "more qualified." 20 C.F.R. §656.18(b); INA §212(a)(5)(A)(ii). Minimum requirements are inapplicable.

2.b. Recruitment Process—20 C.F.R. §656.18(b)

(1) The recruitment process requires that the college or university "document the alien was selected for the job opportunity in a competitive recruitment and selection process" pursuant to the procedures established under §656.18(b).

(2) Employer must document competitive selection process and file ETA Form 9089 within 18 months of the completion of the selection process (if 18 months pass, may reopen selection process or use normal recruitment procedure). Advertising for the job opportunity in a national professional journal must be placed during the recruitment period and university or college must obtain from the SWA the prevailing wage for the position. PERM FAQs No. 3 (May 4, 2005), *published on* AILA InfoNet at Doc. No. 05050960. The employer may not use an electronic national professional journal to satisfy the requirements of 20 C.F.R. §656.18(b)(3). PERM FAQs No. 9 (Nov. 29, 2006), *published on* AILA InfoNet

at Doc. No. 06120460. The notices of filing may be posted to employees or provided to the bargaining representative *after* the selection process has been completed as long as they are posted/provided between 30 and 180 days prior to the submission of the ETA 9089. PERM FAQs No. 1 ("Recruitment/Notice of Filing") (Mar. 7, 2005), *published on* AILA InfoNet at Doc. No. 05030861. The 18 months is measured from the validity date of an H-1B petition, where no other formal selection date is indicated. *Montgomery College,* 94-INA-584 and 585 (BALCA July 18, 1996). However, *Montgomery College* did not require that a person could not be legally selected until he was employment-authorized, and where the facts were clear that an offer was extended prior to that time, the earlier date prevailed. *Middlebury College,* 01-INA-136 (BALCA Jan. 24, 2002).

(3) A university or college employer may opt to use the basic labor certification process under §656.17 as an alternative to the process designated under §656.18. *See* 20 C.F.R. §656.18(d).

(4) Only for Teachers. Only applies to teachers not other university personnel, such as librarians or researchers. 69 Fed. Reg. 77325, 77357 (Dec. 27, 2004).

(5) May fit under Schedule A Group II blanket certification (persons of exceptional ability) in which case traditional LC is not necessary.

2.c. Not Limited to University Teachers. BALCA has found that Congress never intended to limit this category to college/university teachers, and therefore it applied it to teachers at any level. It decided, however, that it did not have the authority to determine that the DOL rule is inconsistent with the statute. *Dearborn Pub. Sch.*, 91-INA-222 (BALCA Dec. 7, 1993) (*en banc*); *See also Mastroyanis v. DOL,* No. A88-089 Civ (D. Alaska May 5, 1989) and discussion in PERM regulations at 69 Fed. Reg. 77325, 77357–58 (Dec. 27, 2004).

3. Professional Athletes—INA §212(a)(5)(A)(iii), 8 U.S.C. §1182(a)(5)(A)(iii).

3.a. LCs for professional athletes remain valid even if the athlete goes to another team (including the minor league) if the new employer is a team in the same sport and the team is a member of an association with 6 or more teams with total combined revenue in excess of $10 million. The I-140 petition also remains valid if the player changes teams. INA §204(i).

4. Live-In Household Domestic Service Workers—20 C.F.R. §656.19; *see also in this part* ¶ C.3.b(3)(d)iv) (p.932), *supra.*

4.a. Applications processed through the labor certification process for nonprofessionals under 20 C.F.R. §656.17(e)(2).

4.b. Additional documentation requirements including: (1) a statement describing the household living accommodations; (2) two copies of the employment contract that includes a statement that private room and board will be provided at no cost to the worker; (3) documentation of the applicant's paid experience demonstrating that the total paid experience is equal to one full year's employment on a full-time basis. That one-year experience requirement cannot be met by employment with applicant's own family, *Roger & Denny Phelps,* 88-INA-214 (BALCA 2006), or through work for the petitioning employer. *Lawrence Weinstein & Toni Albanese,* 05-INA-00009 (BALCA 2006) [reaffirmed *Phelps*)].

5. Cases Processed Directly in the National Office—The DOL has at times designated certain cases, including athletes in many sports, to be handled directly in the ETA National Office. *See former* 20 C.F.R. §656.24; TAG 656.24, n.2.

6. Schedule A pre-certification

6.a. Blanket determination that alien will not adversely effect U.S. labor force.

(1) The decision as to what occupation is given a blanket determination is made by Employment and Training Administration of the DOL. However, individual determinations of a particular person's qualification for Schedule A are made by USCIS. The application for Schedule A is therefore filed, in duplicate, with the appropriate USCIS office. PERM FAQs No. 1 ("Schedule A") (Mar. 7, 2005), *published on* AILA InfoNet at Doc. No. 05030861. USCIS requires: (1) I-140; (2) Uncertified ETA 9089 signed in the original by authorized official, alien and representative, if any; (3) A wage determination issued by SWA; (4) A

copy of the posted notice; (5) Copies of any and all in-house media, whether electronic or printed normally used for recruitment; (6) Licensure consistent with requirements for nurses or physical therapists. AFM at 22.2(b)(3)(C) and 22.2(b)(7) [detailing requirements for Schedule A cases as stated in DOL regulations including use of in-house media for posting notice and licensure requirements]. *See also* USCIS Revision of Adjudicator's Field Manual, *published on* AILA InfoNet at Doc. No. 06021661(Feb. 16, 2006).

(2) Schedule A cases have a *posting* requirement [*see in this section* ¶ 1 (p.947), *supra,* and 20 C.F.R. §656.10(d)] and a prevailing wage requirement, which must be obtained from the SWA. PERM FAQs No. 1 ("Schedule A") (Mar. 7, 2005), *published on* AILA InfoNet at Doc. No. 05030861.

(3) Schedule A labor certification is valid throughout the U.S. unless the certification contains a geographical limitation. 20 C.F.R. §656.30(c)(1). Thus, if employer changed location a new petition would be unnecessary. Letter, Weinig, Deputy Asst. Comm. Adjudications CO 1803-C (Feb. 6, 1992), *reprinted in* 69 No. 22 *Interpreter Releases* 709, 726 (June 8, 1992).

(4) Under the REAL ID Act, PL 109-13, 119 Stat. 231 (May 11, 2005) §502, Congress has provided for the recapture of unused employment-based visas for the fiscal years 2001–04 up to 50,000 visas to be used for Schedule A occupations.

6.b. Group I—certain medical personnel—20 C.F.R. §656.15(c).

(1) Physical therapists. 20 C.F.R. §656.15(c)(1)

(a) Need to show qualified to be state licensed. Do not actually need license. *Matter of Naufahu*, 11 I&N Dec. 904 (R.C. 1966); WSB ¶13,562 a.22. Need to obtain letters signed by state licensing official stating person is eligible to take exam. 20 C.F.R. §656.15(c)(1).

(2) Nurses—20 C.F.R. §§656.10, 656.15(c)(2).

(a) Need to show employed as professional nurse;

(b) Need to show that s/he received a Certificate from CGFNS, holds a full and unrestricted permanent license to practice in the state of intended employment *or* has passed the NCLEX-RN.

(3) No individual LC for Schedule A Nurses and Physical Therapists. If a Schedule A application for a nurse or physical therapist is denied an employer may *not* file an application under the basic process of 20 C.F.R. §656.17. PERM FAQs No. 1 ("Schedule A") (Mar. 7, 2005), *published on* AILA InfoNet at Doc. No. 05030861

6.c. Group II—persons of exceptional ability—20 C.F.R. §656.15(d).

(1) Persons in science or arts (except performing arts) and university teachers. 20 C.F.R. §656.15(d)(1)

(a) Exceptional ability—Must show "widespread acclaim and international recognition accorded by recognized experts in the field." *Matter of Medical University of South Carolina*, 17 I&N Dec. 266 (R.C. 1978) ["Far above average in their field"]; *Matter of Tagawa*, 13 I&N Dec. 13 (DD 1967). It contemplates "some rare or unusual talent ... or extraordinary ability in a calling which, of itself, requires talent or skill." *Matter of Frank*, 11 I&N Dec. 657 (DD 1966).

(b) Who have practiced in field for previous year and intends to practice in same field and that practice will require "exceptional ability."

(c) Documentary requirements from two of seven categories must be submitted that include: (1) receipt of internationally recognized prizes or awards for excellence in the field; (2) membership in international associations which required outstanding achievement as judged by recognized international experts; (3) published material in professional publications about the applicant; (4) participation on a panel or individually as a judge of the work of others; (5) original scientific or scholarly research contributions of major significance; (6) authorship of published scientific or scholarly articles in the field; (7) display of the applicant's work at artistic exhibitions in more than one country.

(2) Person of Exceptional Ability in the Performing Arts

(a) Person's work experience during the past 12 months did require and her intended work will require exceptional ability.

(b) Must submit documentation to show exceptional ability such as: (1) attestations of current widespread acclaim and international recognition; (2) internationally recognized prizes or awards for excellence; (3) published material by or about the applicant; (4) evidence of earnings commensurate with the claimed level of ability; (5) playbills and star billings; (6) attestations to the outstanding reputation of the places where applicant has performed or is scheduled to appear; and (7) attestation to the outstanding reputation as to theaters or groups that the applicant has performed during the past year.

IX. ADMINISTRATIVE APPEAL / REVIEW BY BALCA

A. *Generally*—The Board of Alien Labor Certification Appeals (BALCA) reviews denials or revocations of labor certifications by the Certifying Officer and challenges to prevailing wage determinations by the State Workforce Agency and the Certifying Officer. 20 C.F.R. §§656.26, 656.27 & 656.41(e). It was previously authorized to hear appeals in the H-1A nurses' program regarding denials to health care facilities or appeals of approvals (by interested third parties) of attestations to the health care facilities. For BALCA's address *see* **Appendix J**, *infra*.

B. *Procedure*

1. Review must be sought by employer—The regulations provide that only the employer may request review of a CO decision. 20 C.F.R. §656.26(a)(1). Where an attorney submits a G-28 solely for an employee, the appeal is not deemed timely. *Pat's Pizza Ristorante,* 97-INA-396 (BALCA Feb. 24, 1998).

2. Motion to Reconsider—The employer may file a motion to reconsider with the CO who denied the application within 30 days of the date of the determination. 20 C.F.R. §656.24(g). Under 20 C.F.R. §656.24(g)(2), the employer may not submit new evidence but may include in a motion for reconsideration documentation that the employer did not have an opportunity to present but existed at the time the L.C. was filed and was maintained in the employer's file to support the L.C. in compliance with §656.10(f). The CO may entertain the motion to reconsider or may treat it as a request for review to BALCA. Prior to the regulation permitting consideration of evidence in the employer's file pursuant to §656.24(g)(2), BALCA addressed this question in *HealthAmerica,* 06-PER-1 (BALCA July 16, 2006) (*en banc*) and rejected the CO's interpretation of "new evidence" under the former §656.24(g)(2). In *HeathAmerica* the Board, using a *Mathews v. Eldridge* analysis returned the case to the CO that denied certification where an employer made a typographical error on Form 9089 but could demonstrate through tearsheets that advertisements were submitted for two Sundays as required. The Board rejected an answer to FAQ #5 where the ETA stated no typographical errors would be permitted holding that FAQs do not have the force of law and that FAQ#5 was unsupported by the regulations. *Cf. Shogun at Bey Lea,* 06-PER-59 (BALCA Oct. 10, 2006) [where tearsheet evidence on reconsideration referred to a publication not listed on the Form 9089 and demonstrated that the ad was beyond the 180 day period, the CO's denial was affirmed]; *Best Park, LLC,* 07-PER-55 (BALCA Sept 10, 2007) [upheld CO denial where employer erroneously argued that there were no typographical errors in its motion to reconsider]. The DOL has also determined that after July 16, 2007 an error that results from an employer's disregard of system prompts or other direct instructions will result in a denial and the CO will not reconsider the determination. Round 2, Fraud Rule PERM FAQs (Mar. 2008), *published on* AILA InfoNet at Doc. No. 08040234. Under prior BALCA decisions a timely motion for reconsideration of the CO's decision stayed the period for appeal and the employer could appeal within the appropriate period (the 35 days, now 30 days) from a final decision on the motion to reconsider by the CO. *Meriko Tamaki Wong*, 90-INA-407 (BALCA Jan. 27, 1992).

3. Appeal to BALCA. The employer may appeal the CO's decision to BALCA without requesting a motion to reconsider. 20 C.F.R. §656.26(a)(1). The appeal is filed within 30 days of the CO's decision and is sent in writing to CO. The appeal must clearly identify the particular LC determination for which review is sought and the particular grounds for the request. A copy of the Final Determination must be attached. 20 C.F.R. §§656.26(a)(1)(i)–(iii). Upon a request for review to BALCA, the Certifying Officer must prepare an appeal file and send the original to BALCA and a copy to the employer. 20 C.F.R. §656.26(b). The employer has a right to supplement the appeal file if documentation is missing. 20 C.F.R. §656.26(b)(3).
4. Review is limited to the record below and legal argument—20 C.F.R. §656.26(a)(2); *Coastal Pipeline Production of New York v. Gonzales,* Case No. 04 Civ 8252 (DF) (S.D.N.Y. Feb. 27, 2006) [BALCA could not review evidence of business necessity where employer failed to present the evidence to the CO before the Final Determination and thereafter sought to introduce it to BALCA through the employer's request for review]
5. Parties are given 30 days to submit briefs—20 C.F.R. §656.27(b)
6. BALCA decisions are rendered by three judge panels or *en banc*
7. In the review of a denial of a LC under 20 C.F.R. §656.24 or a revocation of a LC under 20 C.F.R. §656.32 or an affirmation of a prevailing wage determination under 20 C.F.R. §656.41, BALCA can no longer remand cases back to the CO. 69 Fed. Reg. 77325, 77362–63 (Dec. 27, 2004), *published on* AILA InfoNet at Doc. No. 041122312 (Dec. 27, 2004). Rather, it may only: (1) affirm the denial or revocation of the LC or affirm the prevailing wage determination; (2) direct the CO to grant the certification, overrule the revocation or overrule the prevailing wage determination; or (3) direct that hearing be held. 20 C.F.R. §656.27(c). *But see HealthAmerica,* 06-PER-1 (BALCA July 16, 2006) (*en banc*) [the Board may return a PERM labor certification application for further processing where it finds that the CO should have granted reconsideration of an application rejected without a formal audit or other detailed review]. BALCA has determined it does not have jurisdiction to rule on the validity of DOL regulations even if they are inconsistent with the statute. *Dearborn Public Schools*, 91-INA-222 (BALCA Dec. 7, 1993) (*en banc*).

C. *Interlocutory Appeals*—BALCA may not be foreclosed from reviewing interlocutory appeals, although such appeals are disfavored. *Siemens Energy and Automation, Inc.,* 05-INA-1 through 5 (BALCA Feb. 11, 2005) [case did not warrant interlocutory appeal where denial of RIR processing could later be reviewed in denial of LC through regular processing].

D. *Order to Show Cause*—BALCA also has inherent authority to issue an OSC directed toward employers and their representatives (including attorneys) requiring them to respond to allegations of willful misrepresentation and fraud. *Miroslaw Kusmirek,* 2000-INA-116 (BALCA 2001), *published on* AILA InfoNet at Doc. No. 01110901 [required employer and counsel to show cause why the allegations of fraud and willful misconduct regarding the LC should not be referred to INS for investigation].

E. *Discipline Lawyers*—BALCA also has authority to discipline lawyers/agents for engaging in unprofessional conduct. *Kucharski,* 2000-INA-116 (BALCA Sept. 18, 2002) [agent suspended for six months because of "reckless negligence in maintaining a willful ignorance about the details of [a fraudulent] application and in relying solely on a third party intermediary for communication with his client"].

F. *Appeals to AAO*—Schedule A denials of employment-based preference petitions are appealed to the Administrative Appeals Office of USCIS.

X. FEDERAL JUDICIAL REVIEW

A. *Standing*—Alien by virtue of APA can challenge action even if employer does not join. *De Jesus Ramirez v. Reich,* 156 F.3d 1273 (D.C. Cir. 1998) [beneficiary had standing but case was dismissed where employer failed as indispensable party to appeal to BALCA and the federal court]; *Taneja v. Smith*, 795 F.2d 355 (4th Cir. 1986) [beneficiary of sixth preference petition had standing]; *Gladysz v. Donovan*, 595 F.Supp. 50 (N.D. Ill. 1984) [to extent 20 C.F.R. §656.26 is inconsistent w/APA it is invalid]; *Stenographic Mach., Inc. v. Regional Administrator*, 577 F.2d 521, 528 (7th Cir. 1978). However, a person denied position falsely as an unqualified U.S. worker has no standing to sue under the INA or the False Claims Act. *U.S. v. Richard Datter Architects*, 972 F.Supp. 738 (S.D.N.Y. 1997) [in H-2B context].

B. *Abuse-of-Discretion Standard Applicable*—*Seo v. DOL,* 523 F.2d 10 (9th Cir. 1975); *Digilab v. U.S. Secy. of Labor*, 495 F.2d 323 (1st Cir. 1974); *Posadas de Puerto Rico Assoc., Inc. v. Secy. of Labor*, 698 F.Supp. 396 (D.P.R. 1988); *Johnson, Lane & Gallagher v. Secy. of Labor*, ___ F.Supp. ___ (W.D. Wash. 1985); *See Gladysz, supra. But see Pesikoff v. Secy. of Labor*, 501 F.2d 757 (D.C. Cir. 1974); *Chang v. Thornburgh*, 719 F.Supp. 532 (N.D. Tex. 1989) [although *Chang* states abuse of discretion standard, it applies substantial-evidence test to facts].

C. *Litigation to Expedite DOL Proceeding*—In light of the substantial delays in processing LCs, the DOL has been sued by persons concerned that they will violate the 3/10 year bar. *Lauretta v. Herman*, Case No. CV 97-4479 WJR (C.D. Cal. Aug. 6, 1997), *reported in* 74 No. 39 *Interpreter Releases* 1245 (Aug. 18, 1997) [the court granted a preliminary injunction requiring DOL to expedite process of applications but denying an injunction against the enforcement of GAL 1-97 by the DOL]. *But see Office 36, Inc. v. Herman*, Case No. CV 97-4200 SVW (C.D. Cal. Sept. 10, 1997), *reported in* 74 No. 39 *Interpreter Releases* 1548–49 (Oct. 10, 1997) [denied request for preliminary injunction because delay is self-inflicted due to applicants illegal stay in U.S. and because expediting DOL process would not resolve 3-year-bar problem and would require more than mandamus relief requiring by expediting case in front of others before it].

D. *Attorneys Fees*—No attorneys fees under EAJA permissible for appeal of labor certification denial. *Larry Douglas, Ltd.*, 88-INA-130 (BALCA 1988) [relying on *Smedberg v. Donovan*, 730 F.2d 1089 (7th Cir. 1984), claiming no adversary adjudication].

CHAPTER 8
RELIEF FROM REMOVAL

CHAPTER 8
RELIEF FROM REMOVAL

I. OVERVIEW

A. *Forms of Relief*—A person seeking relief from removal may be eligible for several forms of relief including: voluntary departure, cancellation of removal (formerly §212(c) relief and suspension of deportation), adjustment of status, asylum, withholding of removal, protection under CAT, certain waivers of removability or inadmissibility, *nunc pro tunc* permission to reapply after removal, estoppel, collateral attack on a previous removal order, deferred action, and private legislation.

B. *Withdrawal of Relief Under IIRIRA*—IIRIRA imposed a 10-year bar to certain forms of relief (voluntary departure, cancellation, AOS, registry and change of status) following an order of removal for persons who: (a) fail to appear at a removal hearing after receiving oral notice (in his *native language or a language he understands*) unless there are exceptional circumstances, INA §240(b)(7), 8 U.S.C. §1229a(b)(7); (b) fail to depart after a grant of voluntary departure, INA §240B(d)(1), 8 U.S.C. §1229c(d)(1) [no exception for exceptional circumstances]; or (c) re-enter the U.S. illegally after removal, INA §241(a)(5), 8 U.S.C. §1231(a)(5) [applies to *all* forms of relief]. The bar to relief may apply even if a person is successful in reopening her removal proceeding. *Chedad v. Gonzales,* 497 F.3d 57 (1st Cir. 2007) [a timely filed motion to reopen does not stay the running of the VD period and if the motion is granted after VD has expired the respondent is barred from seeking relief §1229c(d)(1)]; *Singh v. Gonzales,* 468 F.3d 135 (2d Cir. 2006) [respondent could not adjust status based upon his marriage notwithstanding the IJ's grant of a motion to reopen proceedings. The granting of a motion to reopen proceedings by an IJ does *not* vacate the effect of prior noncompliance with a voluntary departure order that now bars respondent's adjustment of status]; *Dacosta v. Gonzales,* 449 F.3d 45 (1st Cir. 2006) [BIA properly denied adjustment after granting motion to reopen because granting a motion to reopen where applicant had previously stayed beyond the voluntary departure period without a stay did not expunge the previous violation]; *Banda-Ortiz v. Gonzales,* 445 F.3d 387, 391 (5th Cir. 2006). *But see Orichitch v. Gonzales,* 421 F.3d 595 (7th Cir. 2005). For a detailed discussion on the consequences of failing to voluntary depart, including the effect of filing a motion to reopen, and stays of voluntary departure, *see in this chapter* "Civil Penalty and Denial of Other Relief for Failure to Depart," ¶ III.B.6 (p.966), *infra.*

C. *Withdrawal of Relief Pre-IIRIRA*—The same provision denying relief for failure to appear existed under pre-IIRIRA law but for a period of 5 years. Former INA §242B(e). The former provisions however, contained an exception for "exceptional circumstances" in all situations including voluntary departure. *Matter of Powell*, 21 I&N Dec. 81 (BIA 1995) [notice given by IJ bars relief even if there was appeal to BIA and BIA did not provide additional notice]; *Matter of Ali*, 21 I&N Dec. 1058 (BIA 1997) [neither pre-existing minor illness nor allegations of serious illness of others, including family members, is an exceptional circumstance excusing VD overstay]; *Magala v. Gonzales,* 434 F.3d 523 (7th Cir. 2005) [remanding to BIA to consider whether ineffective assistance of counsel qualifies as an exceptional circumstance justifying failure to depart]; *Barker v. Ashcroft,* 382 F.3d 313, 316–17 (3d Cir. 2003) [failure to provide any exceptional circumstance for overstaying VD bars AOS]; *Stewart v. INS*, 181 F.3d 587, 595–96 (4th Cir. 1999) [failure to raise ineffective assistance of counsel claim before BIA barred finding of "exceptional circumstances" under former INA §242B(e)(2)(A)]; *Matter of Shaar*, 21 I&N Dec. 541 (BIA 1997) *aff'd Shaar v. INS*, 141 F.3d 953 (9th Cir. 1998) [motion to reopen for suspension denied where person did not depart voluntarily within time given before IJ ruled on motion]; *Bhiski v. Ashcroft,* 373 F.3d 363, 370–72 (3d Cir. 2004) [INS opposition to motion to reopen not based on *Matter of Arthur* upheld where respondent failed to depart upon expiration of VD under *Matter of Shaar*]; *Rojas-Reynoso v. INS,* 235 F.3d 26, 29–30 & n.3 (1st Cir. 2000) [filing a motion to extend VD and waiting beyond VD period for response is not an exceptional circumstance]; *Mardones v. McElroy,* 197 F.3d 619 (2d Cir. 1999) [finding that neither the passage of §245(i) nor INS's failure to respond to a request for extension of VD are exceptional circumstances]. *But see Barrios v. Att'y Gen. of the U.S.,* 399 F.3d 272 (3d Cir. 2005) [rejecting *Matter of Shaar* for *pre*-IIRIRA cases, and holding that a timely filed motion to reopen prevents the BIA/IJ from applying the bar to adjustment under INA §242B(e)(2)(A) because failure to adjudicate the motion within the VD period is an "exceptional circumstance"]; *Velezmoro v. Ashcroft,* 362 F.3d 1231 (9th Cir. 2004) [where person remained in the U.S. more than five years beyond the VD period, s/he may now be eligible to adjust because five years had elapsed]; *Ordonez v. INS,* 345 F.3d 777, 783–84 (9th Cir. 2003) [under former INA §242B(e), IJ was required to give oral and written notice of consequences of failing to depart and where IJ did not specifically list the forms of relief that would be lost, the denial of the right to suspension was reversed].

D. *Withdrawal of Relief for Violation of Protective Order*—All discretionary forms of relief must be withdrawn if a person violates a protective order when a document is submitted under seal. DOJ has established procedures before the IJ for the submission of documents/information under seal with a protective order which, if disclosed would "harm the national security...or law enforcement interests of the United States." 8 C.F.R. §1003.46. National security is defined under INA §219(c)(2), 8 U.S.C. §1189(c)(2) to include "the national defense, foreign relations, or economic interests of the United States." If a respondent or his attorney or accredited representative discloses information in violation of the protective order s/he becomes ineligible for "all forms of discretionary relief, except bond, unless the respondent fully cooperates with the Service or other law enforcement agencies in any investigation relating to noncompliance...and establishes by clear and convincing evidence either that extraordinary and extremely unusual circumstances exist or that failure to comply...was beyond the control of the respondent and his or her attorney or accredited representative." 8 C.F.R. §1003.46(i); *Matter of R-S-H-,* 23 I&N Dec. 629 (BIA 2003) [denying asylum, withholding and VD because of breach of protective order where respondent and counsel cooperated in the investigation of the breach, but did not show extraordinary circumstances or that failure to comply was beyond their control].

E. *Timing in Request for Relief*—A party may request discretionary relief at any time before the IJ enters a final order, *Zamora-Morel v. INS*, 905 F.2d 833, 839 (5th Cir. 1990) [reversing IJ denial of request for relief as "untimely" where IJ had not entered a final order], or thereafter in a motion to reopen. Relief often involves the weighing of equities. At least one court, in another context, has criticized the Service's parsimonious approach to equity. *U.S. v. Johnson*, 773 F.Supp. 114, 116 (N.D. Ill. 1991), *aff'd on other grounds*, 962 F.2d 579 (7th Cir. 1992) ["[m]uch of what the government's responsive memorandum states on the subject of fairness or equity...reflects the kind of small-mindedness that in recent years has become identified with too much of the INS's activities"]. An IJ cannot refuse to consider discretionary relief where the respondent is facially eligible and has not been charged with the specific grounds that make him/her ineligible. *Matter of Ching*, 12 I&N Dec. 710 (BIA 1968) [respondent eligible for 10-year suspension even though convicted of drug offense where INS did not charge him as deportable under drug provision]; *Matter of T*, 5 I&N Dec. 459 (BIA 1953) [reversing the denial of VD where IJ's decision rested on a ground that was not the basis of the deportation charge]. *See also Mullen-Cofee v. INS*, 976 F.2d 1375, 1378–79 (11th Cir. 1992) *amended on denial of reh'g* 986 F.2d 1364 (11th Cir. 1993). [distinguishing *Matter of T*].

F. *Burden and Standard of Proof after the REAL ID Act*—Section 101(d) of the REAL ID Act of 2005 [PL 109-13, 119 Stat. 231], amended INA §240(c) to clarify that applicants for relief or protection from removal have the burden of establishing: (1) satisfaction of the applicable eligibility requirements; and (2) that a favorable exercise of discretion (where relevant) is warranted. INA §240(c)(4)(A). The applicant must comply with the applicable information or documentary requirements specified by law, regulation and application instructions. Credibility determinations will be made under the same totality of the circumstances test as asylum under INA §208(b)(1)(B)(iii). INA §240(c)(4)(C). The IJ must weigh the applicant's credible testimony along with other evidence and can require corroboration unless the applicant does not have the evidence and cannot reasonably obtain it. INA §240(c)(4)(B). The AG's decision to require corroboration may only be reversed if "a reasonable trier of fact is compelled to conclude that such corroborating evidence is unavailable." INA §242(b)(4), 8 U.S.C. §1252(b)(4). Although the IJ's corroboration requirements are effective only for cases filed on or after May 11, 2005, the federal review provision under INA §242(b)(4) is effective for all final orders issued before, on or after May 11, 2005. *Matter of S-B-,* 24 I&N Dec. 42 (BIA

2006) [where asylum application was initially filed with asylum office before May 11, 2005 but with IJ after, new standards on credibility do not apply]. *Hor v. Gonzales,* 421 F.3d 497, 500–01 (7th Cir. 2005) [reversing IJ's corroboration findings because "[a]ll that this (new provision) means is that an immigration judge's determination…is entitled to reasonable deference (but that) the precondition to deference is that the immigration judge explain (unless it is obvious) why he thinks corroborating evidence, if it existed, would have been available to the alien"], *accord. Zhang v. Gonzales,* 434 F.3d 993, 998–99 (7th Cir. 2006) [quoting *Hor* and reversing IJ's demand for corroboration]. *But see Chen v. Gonzales,* 434 F.3d 212, 217–20 (3d Cir. 2005) [upholding denial of post-REAL ID asylum even where the IJ did not make a valid credibility assessment, because even a credible applicant may be required to produce corroborative evidence and respondent failed to do so]; *Zheng v. Gonzales,* 417 F.3d 379, 383 n.2 (3d Cir. 2005) [IJ's requirement to corroborate records is subject to the "compelling" review standard which is "effective immediately" including cases begun before May 11, 2005]. However, the standard may not apply to motions to reopen before the BIA because it applies only to review of a decision by the "trier of fact" (which is the IJ, not the BIA) and does not, by its terms, apply to the provision on motions to reopen at INA §240(c)(7), 8 U.S.C. §1229a(c)(7). *Fessehaye v. Gonzales,* 414 F.3d 746, 752–53 (7th Cir. 2005) .

G. *Fundamentally Fair Hearing*—A hearing on discretionary relief must be conducted in a fundamentally fair manner. *Cunanan v. INS,* 856 F.2d 1373 (9th Cir. 1988). Hearsay will not be admitted where it is prejudicial and the opposing party was prevented from cross-examining witnesses. *Id.*; *Alexandrov v. Gonzales,* 442 F.3d 395, 404–07 (6th Cir. 2006) [IJ violated due process by relying on unreliable hearsay memoranda from the U.S. Embassy in Sofia in concluding that asylum applicant's documents were fraudulent and asylum claim was frivolous]; *Ezeagwuna v. Ashcroft,* 325 F.3d 396, 405–08 (3d Cir. 2003) [reliance on double and triple hearsay letter from DOS to undermine credibility of documentary evidence in asylum claim violated due process]; *Zhen Nan Lin v. DOJ,* 459 F.3d 255, 268–72 (2d Cir. 2006) [BIA's adverse credibility finding based on a consular report that a document was forged was reversed where the hearsay report was found to be inherently unreliable]; *Corovic v. Mukasey,* 519 F.3d 90, 95–96 (2d Cir. 2008) [same, following *Zhen Nan Lin*]. Nevertheless, documents such as police reports are admissible in discretionary relief cases, *Matter of Grijalva,* 19 I&N Dec. 713 (BIA 1988), unless the reports involved matters that were not the subject of prosecution and were therefore not probative. *Sierra-Reyes v. INS*, 585 F.2d 762, 764 n.3 (5th Cir. 1978). *But see Doumbia v. Gonzales,* 472 F.3d 957, 962–63 (7th Cir. 2007) [admission of Embassy report in asylum hearing on validity of summonses in Côte d'Ivoire court was not prejudicial or fundamentally unfair under 8 U.S.C. §1229a(b)(4)]; *Paredes-Urrestarazu v. INS*, 36 F.3d 801 (9th Cir. 1994).

H. *Criminal and Other Conduct Affecting Discretionary Cases*—In discretionary relief cases, the IJ may consider criminal conduct either as a discretionary matter when considering relief or to determine whether relief is barred due to a mandatory criminal bar such as an aggravated felony. Under 8 C.F.R. §1240.8(d), the applicant always has the burden to establish that he is eligible for relief, but need overcome a mandatory denial only after "the evidence indicates" ineligibility. *See generally Matter of R-S-H-,* 23 I&N Dec. 629 (BIA 2003). The BIA and the courts have often ignored the subtleties of the burden of proof under §1240.8(d) and have relied on information concerning criminal activity in a variety of contexts. The Board has relied on alleged criminal activity even if there is no conviction for immigration purposes. *Matter of Thomas*, 21 I&N Dec. 20 (BIA 1995) [IJ allowed to consider a "conviction" pending appeal in determining discretionary relief even if it is not a final conviction for immigration purposes]; *Wallace v. Gonzales,* 463 F.3d 135, 138–40 (2d Cir. 2006) [IJ may consider Youthful Offender Adjudication in the exercise of discretion even though it is not a conviction]. However, the reliance on an arrest to deny relief where there was not a conviction may be error. *Matter of Arreguin*, 21 I&N Dec. 38 (BIA 1995). *But see Schroeck v. Gonzales,* 429 F.3d 947 (10th Cir. 2005) [IJ's consideration of a dismissed criminal case did not violate respondent's constitutional right to avoid double jeopardy or right to due process by requiring him to prove his innocence]. Proof of a conviction barring relief may also be relaxed. *Rosales-Pineda v. Gonzales,* 452 F.3d 627 (7th Cir. 2006) [distinguishing *Francis v. Gonzales,* 442 F.3d 131, 141–45 (2d Cir. 2006), and relying on the broad language of 8 C.F.R. §1003.41(d) in finding that an FBI rap sheet could be used as evidence of a conviction where there was other supporting evidence and the issue was discretionary eligibility, not removability by clear and convincing evidence]. In determining the weight accorded to a drug conviction as a discretionary factor, a guilty plea does "not constitute an admission that the petitioner possessed...any particular amount of [the drug]..." and the IJ cannot ignore evidence concerning the quantity which contradicts the amount stated in the indictment. *Martinez-Benitez v. INS*, 956 F.2d 1053 (11th Cir. 1992). In addition, a person may be barred from relief for a conviction even if s/he was not charged in the NTA under that ground of removal. *Salviejo-Fernandez v. Gonzales,* 455 F.3d 1063, 1065–66 (9th Cir. 2006) [due process was not violated where ICE did not charge respondent with an aggravated felony in the NTA but used the conviction to find respondent ineligible for cancellation]; *Taylor v. U.S.,* 396 F.3d 1322, 1329–30 (11th Cir. 2005) [upholding decision to bar §212(c) relief where respondent was not charged in NTA as an aggravated felon but where "conduct actually constituted an aggravated felony"]; *Brown v. Ashcroft,* 360 F.3d 346, 351–53 (2d Cir. 2004) [distinguishing *Matter of Fortiz* on grounds it applied only to AEDPA and finding that DHS was free to use an aggravated felony conviction to bar §212(c) relief even if it had not charged the felony in the NTA]. When the applicant is seeking relief such as cancellation the burden shifts to him by a preponderance of the evidence that he has not committed an aggravated felony or some other disqualifying act. The burden is met by establishing the crime does not fit under the categorical approach and it was *inconclusive* under the modified categorical approach. *Sandoval-Lua v. Gonzales,* 499 F.3d 1121, 1129–32 (9th Cir. 2007) [when respondent produced an *inconclusive* record of conviction on drug trafficking, he has met his burden that under the modified categorical approach he was not convicted of an aggravated felony]. At least one court has taken the view that overt abuse of the immigration laws alone is sufficient to deny discretionary relief. *Hamdan v. Gonzales,* 425 F.3d 1051, 1059–60 (7th Cir. 2005) [upholding denial of AOS where person abused student visa process].

I. *Constitutional Protection for Due Process Violations when Seeking Relief*—In *Arevalo v. Ashcroft,* 344 F.3d 1, 14–15 (1st Cir. 2003) the court found that INA §241(a)(5) (reinstatement of deportation order) could not be applied retroactively to bar an adjustment of status application filed prior to IIRIRA's effective date because adjustment was a vested right even if the relief itself was discretionary. Citing *Accardi v. Shaughnessy*, 347 U.S. 260 (1954), and other cases the court stated that "an alien is not precluded from having a vested right in a form of relief merely because the relief itself is ultimately at the discretion of the Executive Branch." *See also INS v. St. Cyr,* 533 U.S. 289, 307–08 (2001) ["[t]raditionally, courts recognized a distinction between eligibility for discretionary relief, on the one hand, and the favorable exercise of discretion, on the other hand. Eligibility that was 'governed by specific statutory standards' provided 'a right to a ruling on an applicant's eligibility,' even though the actual granting of relief was 'not a matter of right under any circumstances, but rather is in all cases a matter of grace'"]; *Succar v. Ashcroft,* 394 F.3d 8, 10 (1st Cir. 2005) [striking down regulation as ultra vires but holding, "[t]he mere fact that a statute gives the Attorney General discretion as to whether to grant relief after application does not by itself give the Attorney General the discretion to define eligibility for such relief"]; *Alcaraz v. INS,* 384 F.3d 1150, 1162–63 (9th Cir. 2004) [internal policies under the *Accardi* principle have binding effect on agency, although court remanded to BIA to determine whether various memoranda were sufficient to establish policy in regard to repapering]; *U.S. v. Copeland,* 376 F.3d 61, 72 (2d Cir. 2004) ["[t]he decisions holding that a failure to inform an alien about Section 212(c) relief cannot be a fundamental error … incorrectly assume that, because the grant of Section 212(c) relief is itself discretionary, the denial of a Section 212(c) hearing cannot be a fundamental procedural error"]; *Gutierrez v. Ashcroft,* 289 F.Supp.2d 555, 567–68 (D.N.J. 2003) [rejecting claim that because respondent has no due process right to obtain §212(c) relief he has no due process claim to seek relief]; *Mayers v. Reno,* 175 F.3d 1289, 1301 n.15 (11th Cir. 1999); *Rabiu v. INS,* 41 F.3d 879, 883 (2d Cir. 1994). *But see Guled v. Mukasey,* 515 F.3d 872, 879–80 (8th Cir. 2008) [cancellation of removal is roughly equivalent to executive clemency and there is no protected liberty interest permitting a claim for violation of due process rights]; *Garcia-Mateo v. Keisler,* 503 F.3d 698 (8th Cir. 2007) [no due process violation for IJ failure to inform respondent of post-VD relief because there is no property or liberty interest in VD as it is discretionary]; *Dekoladenu v. Gonzales,* 459 F.3d 500, 502–08 (4th Cir. 2006) [no due process violation in refusing to toll VD period during a timely filed motion to reopen because motions to reopen and adjustment are purely discretionary and there is no property or liberty interest at stake]; *Hernandez v. Gonzales,* 437 F.3d 341, 345–46 & n.7 (3d Cir. 2006) [no due process right to seek repealed suspension because there is no liberty interest to obtain relief from deportation or to be found ineligible for it]; *Hamdan v. Gonzales,* 425 F.3d 1051, 1060–61 (7th Cir. 2005) [rejecting due process argument regarding IJ's conduct in reviewing adjustment application because adjustment is discretionary]; *Nguyen v. District Director,* 400 F.3d 255, 259 (5th Cir. 2005) [no due process right to §212(c) discretionary relief]; *Guerra-Soto v. Ashcroft,* 397 F.3d 637, 641 (8th Cir. 2005) [affirming BIA denial of reopening on ground that when ineffective assistance of counsel touches upon respondent's chance to seek discretionary relief, there is no due process issue];

Jupiter v. Ashcroft, 396 F.3d 487, 492–93 (1st Cir. 2005) [rejecting due process claim where motion to reopen for AOS was denied for remaining beyond VD deadline on grounds that there is no property interest in VD or AOS because they are discretionary]; *Ali v. Ashcroft,* 395 F.3d 722, 732 (7th Cir. 2005) [no due process violation in applying *Pickering* to use vacated conviction for removal and to bar cancellation because there is no liberty or property interest in discretionary relief]; *Obleshchenko v. Ashcroft,* 392 F.3d 970, 971–72 (8th Cir. 2004) [no due process right regarding ineffective assistance of counsel in asylum claim because there is no liberty or property interest in discretionary relief]; *U.S. v. Torres,* 383 F.3d 92, 104–06 (3d Cir. 2004) [removal proceeding was not fundamentally unfair where IJ did not inform respondent of the right to seek §212(c) relief because grant of relief was speculative and a matter of "grace"]; *Assaad v. Ashcroft,* 378 F.3d 471, 475–76 (5th Cir. 2004) [no due process violation and therefore no circuit court jurisdiction where counsel's ineffective assistance involved the failure to receive a discretionary waiver of conditional residency]; *Dave v. Ashcroft,* 363 F.3d 649, 652–53 (7th Cir. 2004) [rejecting constitutional challenge to streamlining and ineffective assistance of counsel as to cancellation claim because there is no liberty or property interest in discretionary relief]; *U.S. v. Aguirre-Tello,* 353 F.3d 1199, 1204–05 (10th Cir. 2004) (en banc) [no constitutional right to be informed of discretionary relief that might be available such as §212(c)]; *Mireles-Valdez v. Ashcroft,* 349 F.3d 213, 219 (5th Cir. 2003) [no due process violation in regard to VD because eligibility for discretionary relief is not a liberty or property interest]; *Nativi-Gomez v. Ashcroft,* 344 F.3d 805 (8th Cir. 2003) [statutory relief such as AOS and §212(h) that are subject to the "unfettered discretion" of a governmental authority cannot provide the liberty interest necessary to give rise to a procedural due process claim]; *U.S. v. Wilson,* 316 F.3d 506, 510–11 (4th Cir. 2003) [proceedings not fundamentally unfair where BIA denied pre-*St. Cyr* §212(c) relief because there is no liberty or property interest in discretionary relief]; *U.S. v. Lopez-Ortiz,* 313 F.3d 225 (5th Cir. 2002) [failure to inform defendant of §212(c) eligibility does not rise to the level of fundamental unfairness and therefore does not affect the conviction because §212(c) relief is not a liberty or property interest warranting due process protection]; *Balogun v. U.S., Att'y Gen.,* 304 F.3d 1303, 1311 (11th Cir. 2002) [suspension applicant "has no constitutionally-protected right to discretionary relief or to be eligible for discretionary relief"]; *Smith v. Ashcroft,* 295 F.3d 425, 429–31 (4th Cir. 2002) [no due process right to challenge reinstatement order arising out of denial of §212(c) because there is no property or liberty interest in discretionary statute]; *Oguejiofor v. Att'y Gen.,* 277 F.3d 1305, 1309 (11th Cir. 2002) [rejecting argument that retroactive application of IIRIRA's repeal of §212(c) raises a substantial constitutional question]; *Ashki v. INS,* 233 F.3d 913, 921 (6th Cir. 2000) [no constitutionally protected liberty interest in obtaining discretionary relief from deportation]; *Tefel v. Reno,* 180 F.3d 1286, 1298–1305 (11th Cir. 1999) [rejecting due process claim on grounds that suspension is a matter of grace and therefore no liberty interest following *Conn. Bd. of Pardons v. Dumschat,* 452 U.S. 458, 464–67 (1981); *Appiah v. INS,* 202 F.3d 704 (4th Cir. 2000) [same].

J. *Equitable Tolling When Seeking Relief*—There may not be equitable tolling for persons seeking relief with defined deadlines. *Carrillo-Gonzalez v. INS,* 353 F.3d 1077 (9th Cir. 2003) [equitable tolling not applicable to person who had not adjusted before one-year period under DV lottery]; *Munoz v. Ashcroft,* 339 F.3d 950, 956–57 (9th Cir. 2003) [rejecting view that NACARA deadlines could be equitably tolled for person who was a minor when mother failed to apply for *ABC* or asylum benefits; distinguishing between statutes of limitations which may be equitably tolled and statutes of repose which may not be tolled because they are fixed, statutory cut-off dates independent of any variable such as a child's awareness]. *See also Romero-Rodriguez v Gonzales,* 488 F.3d 672, 677–80 (5th Cir. 2007) [court did not have authority to grant *nunc pro tunc* review to correct BIA's original error in denying INA §212(c) relief resulting in applicant's subsequent ineligibility because 5 years of incarceration accrued; however BIA had authority to grant *nunc pro tunc* review and court remanded the case to the BIA for its consideration]. *But see Ramirez-Canales v. Mukasey,* 517 F.3d 904, 910–11 (6th Cir. 2008 [followed *Matter of Briones* and upheld denial of AOS where person is barred from entering the U.S. for 10 years under INA §212(a)(9)(C)((i)(I), but remanded the case to determine whether *nunc pro tunc* relief was available]; *Albillo-De Leon v. Gonzales,* 410 F.3d 1090 (9th Cir. 2005) [where respondent was defrauded by person who posed as a lawyer, the time period for filing a motion to reopen under NACARA §203(c) and 8 C.F.R. §1003.43(e)(1) was tolled until the date that the current attorney found out that the motion was not filed]. Alternatively, a court may use the equitable device of *nunc pro tunc* relief. *Edwards v. INS,* 393 F.3d 299 (2d Cir. 2004) [granting *nunc pro tunc* equitable relief to allow persons to file for §212(c) relief who were eligible for the relief at the time of the IJ's error but are no longer eligible because they have been incarcerated for 5 years. *Nunc pro tunc* relief can be applied even in the absence of a constitutional violation or proof that respondent would obtain relief; respondent need only demonstrate that s/he was erroneously denied the opportunity to apply when s/he was eligible].

K. *Security Checks*—After Apr. 1, 2005, all persons seeking asylum and various forms of relief from removal, except voluntary departure, must comply with security clearance procedures. 8 C.F.R. §1003.47; Memo, Yates, Assoc. Dir. Operations, USCIS, "Executive Office for Immigration Review (EOIR) Processing," (Mar. 31, 2005), *published on* AILA InfoNet at Doc. No. 05051164. Failure to file the necessary documentation, and comply with the requirements to provide biometrics and other biographical information within the time allowed by the IJ's order constitutes "abandonment of the application and the immigration judge may enter an appropriate order dismissing the application unless the applicant demonstrates that such failure was the result of good cause." 8 C.F.R. §1003.47(c) & (d). *See also* 8 C.F.R. §103.2(b)(13)(ii). An IJ may not grant an application for relief until DHS has reported to the IJ that the investigation is complete and results have been reported to the IJ. 8 C.F.R. §1003.47(g). For a detailed analysis of the IJ's procedures, *see* Memo [Interim OPPM 05-03], Creppy, Chief IJ, EOIR, (Mar. 28, 2005), *published on* AILA InfoNet at Doc. No. 05041565. *See also* Ch. 3, ¶ X.S.7.1 (p.361), *supra*.

II. GOOD MORAL CHARACTER

In two of the most common forms of relief—voluntary departure and cancellation of removal for non-LPRs—the applicant must show, among other things, that s/he has been a person of good moral character for the requisite period of time for the relief requested. A finding of good moral character is both a statutory [INA §101(f); 8 U.S.C. §1101(f)] and a discretionary matter. *See Matter of Turcotte*, 12 I&N Dec. 206 (BIA 1967) [where specific conduct does not result in statutory ineligibility for GMC, the IJ may still consider it as a discretionary matter]. *See also Matter of Rojas*, 15 I&N Dec. 492 (BIA 1975) [entry with smuggler outweighs equity of LPR sister]. DHS's interpretation of statutory and discretionary issues is found at INS Interpretations §§316.1(e)–(g). The Board has "long held that good moral character does not mean moral excellence and that it is not destroyed by 'a single incident.'" *Matter of Sanchez-Linn*, 20 I&N Dec. 362 (BIA 1991).

A. *Statutory Ineligibility*—Under INA §101(f), 8 U.S.C. §1101(f), a person shall not be deemed a person of good moral character if, during the requisite period for the relevant form of relief, s/he is or was:

1. A habitual drunkard. INA §101(f)(1).
2. A member of one or more classes of persons described in INA §212(a)(10)(A) [practicing polygamist]; §212(a)(2)(D) [prostitute]; and §212(a)(6)(E) [smugglers]; or a person convicted of a crime of moral turpitude, multiple crimes (whether or not crimes of moral turpitude) or a drug crime (except a single offense of simple possession of 30 grams or less of marijuana). INA §101(f)(3). *Matter of Moncada,* 24 I&N Dec. 62, 65 & n.4 (BIA 2007) [parallel deportability exception for simple possession of less than 30 grams does not include a conviction for possession of less than 30 grams of marijuana *in prison*]; *Matter of Martinez-Zapata,* 24 I&N Dec. 424 (BIA 2007) [possession of marijuana in a drug-free zone is not simple possession of less than 30 grams of marijuana]; *Amador-Palomares v. Ashcroft,* 382 F.3d 864, 867 (8th Cir. 2004) [a single act of attempting to solicit a prostitute rendered respondent statutorily ineligible for suspension/good moral character]. The admission of such crimes will also bar a finding of good moral character. INA §101(f)(3). However, the facts admitted must constitute criminal behavior. *Mabugat v. INS*, 937 F.2d 426, 431–33 (9th Cir. 1991). A crime of moral turpitude that falls within the petty offense or juvenile exception under INA §212(a)(2)(A)(ii) will not preclude a finding of good moral character. *Matter of Garcia-Hernandez,* 23 I&N Dec. 590, 592–93 (BIA 2003). Similarly, the political offense exception may be considered. *Mabugat*, 937 F.2d at 431–33. [where applicant for VD did not admit *mens rea* and where testimony indicates crime was political, BIA erred in finding statutory ineligibility]. *See also Moran v. Ashcroft,* 395 F.3d 1089 (9th Cir. 2005) [where applicant smuggled woman who later became his wife, the smuggling waiver was inapplicable and he was therefore barred from good moral character].

   2.a. Conviction of a crime within the relevant statutory period for good moral character does not preclude a finding of good moral character where the crime was *committed* outside the statutory period. *Matter of Awaijane*, 14 I&N Dec. 117 (BIA 1972). *But see Matter of Lozada*, 19 I&N Dec. 637 (BIA 1988) [the period necessary for good moral character is measured from the date of conviction, not from the commission of the crime].

2.b. If a person has a judicial recommendation against deportation, s/he may not be precluded from establishing good moral character because of the conviction, but the IJ can consider the conviction as a matter of discretion. *Matter of Gonzalez*, 16 I&N Dec. 134 (BIA 1977). *See also Delgado-Chavez v. INS*, 765 F.2d 868 (9th Cir. 1985). *But see Giambanco v. INS*, 531 F.2d 141 (3d Cir. 1976) [JRAD bars use of conviction in discretionary relief]. Similarly, a pardon which eliminates the crime for deportation purposes cannot be used to establish statutory ineligibility for good moral character. *Matter of H*, 7 I&N Dec. 249 (BIA 1956).

2.c. A plea to a charge resulting in something less than a conviction is not an admission of a crime for purposes of the statutory bar. *Matter of Seda*, 17 I&N Dec. 550 (BIA 1980). *But see Matter of Roldan*, 22 I&N Dec. 512 (BIA 1999) [IIRIRA substantially broadened the definition of a conviction].

2.d. At least one court has held that a §212(h) waiver cannot be used to cure a statutory good moral character bar. *Miller v. INS*, 762 F.2d 21 (3d Cir. 1985).

2.e. For an extensive discussion of crimes involving moral turpitude, *see* Ch. 3, ¶ III.C.1 (p.69), *supra*.

3. A person whose income is derived principally from illegal gambling, INA §101(f)(4), or who has been convicted of two or more gambling offenses. INA §101(f)(5).

4. A person who has given false testimony for purposes of obtaining any benefit under the INA. INA §101(f)(6). Does not require materiality. *Kungys v. U.S.*, 485 U.S. 759, 780 (1988); *Matter of Haniatakis*, 376 F.2d 728 (3d Cir. 1967). The statement must be made under oath and DHS must prove it was false to be conclusive. *Matter of R-S-J,* 22 I&N Dec. 863 (BIA 1999) [remanding to determine whether asylum officer took statement under oath]. False testimony arising in a variety of administrative procedures can result in a GMC bar. *See e.g., Bernal v. INS,* 154 F.3d 1020 (9th Cir. 1998) [naturalization interview]; *Medina v. Gonzales,* 404 F.3d 628, 633–37 (2d Cir. 2005) [suspension applicant lacked good moral character due to false statement to an asylum officer]; *Ramos v. INS,* 246 F.3d 1264, 1265–66 (9th Cir. 2001); *Matter of R-S-J,* 22 I&N Dec. 863 (BIA 1999) [false oral statement under oath to asylum officer]; *Matter of Namio,* 14 I&N Dec. 412, 414 (BIA 1973) [false statement under oath to border patrol agent]; *Matter of Ngan,* 10 I&N Dec. 725 (BIA 1964) [false testimony to INS officer in processing a visa application]; *Opere v. INS,* 267 F.3d 10 (1st Cir. 2001) [false testimony at adjustment interview]. False statements made in the course of a removal proceeding before an IJ are also a bar to good moral character but a finding that testimony lacked credibility is not conclusive that false testimony was given. *Rodriguez-Gutierrez v. INS*, 59 F.3d 504, 507–08 (5th Cir. 1995). *But see Akinwande v. Ashcroft,* 380 F.3d 517, 523 (1st Cir. 2004) [inconsistencies in testimony and contradictions between petitioner's and his ex-wife's testimony provided substantial evidence to conclude petitioner provided false testimony]. False statements made in an application for immigration benefits are not a bar to good moral character because INA §101(f)(6) only encompasses oral statements. *Kungys,* 485 U.S. at 806; *Beltran-Resendez v. INS,* 207 F.3d 284 (5th Cir. 2000) [false statement on I-9 is not a bar to GMC]; *Matter of L-D-E-,* 8 I&N Dec. 399 (BIA 1959). A voluntary and timely retraction of a false statement will not bar good moral character. *Matter of M-,* 9 I&N Dec. 118 (BIA 1960). False testimony under this section must be accompanied by dishonesty; willful misrepresentations made for reasons other than immigration benefit such as embarrassment, fear or a desire for privacy are not sufficient to find statutory ineligibility. *Kungys,* 485 U.S. at 780; *Gonzalez-Maldonado v. Gonzales,* 487 F.3d 975 (5th Cir. 2007) [where applicant listed attorney's address as his on asylum application at attorney's request and orally swore to it, the false statement was not made to obtain an immigration benefit and the refusal to consider cancellation or VD for lacking good moral character is reversed]; *Plewa v. INS,* 77 F.Supp.2d 905 (N.D. Ill. 1999) [reversing natz denial for lack of good moral character where applicant failed to list arrest because of erroneous advice by an experienced immigration counselor].

5. A person who has been confined, as a result of any conviction, to a penal institution for an aggregate period of 180 days or more. INA §101(f)(7); *Arreguin-Moreno v. Mukasey,* 511 F.3d 1229, 1232–

33 (9th Cir. 2008) [pretrial detention later credited as time served counts as part of the 180 days of confinement]; *Gomez-Lopez v. Ashcroft,* 393 F.3d 882, 885–86 (9th Cir. 2005) [incarceration in county jail following vehicular manslaughter conviction falls within §101(f)(7)]; *Fonseca-Leite v. INS*, 961 F.2d 60, 62 (5th Cir. 1992) [upholding constitutionality of provision]; *Rivera-Zurita v. INS*, 946 F.2d 118, 122 (10th Cir. 1991) [recognizing that 180-day incarceration period may be aggregated]; *Matter of Zangwill*, 18 I&N Dec. 22 (BIA 1981).

6. A person who at *any time* has been convicted of an aggravated felony, INA §101(f)(8), where the *conviction* was entered on or after Nov. 29, 1990. IMMACT90 §509; *Matter of Reyes*, 20 I&N Dec. 789 (BIA 1994). May not be applied retroactively to convictions entered before Nov. 29, 1990. *Lopez-Castellanos v. Gonzales,* 437 F.3d 848, 851 (9th Cir. 2006); *U.S. v. Hovsepian,* 359 F.3d 1144, 1165–69 (9th Cir. 2004) (en banc) In determining the date of conviction, the court looks to the date of sentencing and not the date of the guilty plea. *Puello v. Bureau of USCIS,* 511 F.3d 324 (2d Cir. 2007) [applicant barred from GMC because he was convicted of an aggravated felony and sentenced "on or after" Nov. 29, 1990, even though he pleaded guilty before].

7. A person who *at any time* has engaged in conduct described in §212(a)(3)(E) [relating to assistance in Nazi persecution, participation in genocide, or commission of acts of torture or extrajudicial killings] or §212(a)(2)(G) [relating to severe violations of religious freedom].

8. A person who falsely claims U.S. citizenship or registers to vote or votes in violation of restrictions is *not* barred from good moral character if: (1) each parent is or was a USC; (2) the person permanently resided in the U.S. prior to age 16; and (3) the person reasonably believed at the time of the statement, claim or violation that s/he was a USC. INA §101(f).

9. *Catchall Provision*— "The fact that any person is not within any of the foregoing classes shall not preclude a finding that for other reasons such person is or was not of good moral character." INA §101(f).

10. *Standard of Review*—Review of factual determinations regarding good moral character are subject to substantial-evidence test. *Omagah v. Ashcroft,* 288 F.3d 254, 258 (5th Cir. 2002) [upholding BIA determination that conviction for conspiracy to possess illegal immigration documents with intent to defraud the government demonstrates a lack of good moral character].

B. *Discretionary Ineligibility*—Discretionary determinations denying good moral character may be based on criminal behavior not leading to an automatic bar. *Ikenokwalu-White v. INS,* 316 F.3d 798, 804–05 (8th Cir. 2003) [BIA may consider past conduct including expunged convictions beyond the statutory period because it may inform it of applicant's current character regarding issues such as rehabilitation or reform]; *Matter of Seda*, 17 I&N Dec. 550 (BIA 1980); *Matter of Turcotte*, 12 I&N Dec. 206 (BIA 1967). Thus, a person's nonfinal conviction for immigration purposes (*i.e.,* the conviction is on first-level appeal) may be considered in denying discretionary relief. *Matter of Thomas*, 21 I&N Dec. 20 (BIA 1995); *Parcham v. INS*, 769 F.2d 1001 (4th Cir. 1985). The applicant's general conduct, including the manner of entry into the country, may be a factor in determining lack of good moral character. *Matter of Carbajal*, 17 I&N Dec. 272 (Comm. 1978) [four illegal entries, without more, was insufficient to bar finding of good moral character]; *Matter of T*, 1 I&N Dec. 158 (BIA 1941). The possession of false documents should be placed in context. *See e.g., Matter of Pula*, 19 I&N Dec. 467 (BIA 1987). Knowingly providing fraudulent information on an income tax return may also preclude a finding of good moral character. *Matter of Locicero,* 11 I&N Dec. 805 (BIA 1966) [gross underreporting of income for purpose of avoiding payment of "substantial" sum in taxes precludes finding of good moral character]. The IJ, however, must consider all countervailing positive factors supporting the applicant's claim where there is no statutory bar to good moral character. *Torres-Guzman v. INS*, 804 F.2d 531 (9th Cir. 1986) [reversing BIA where it did not consider positive factor warranting a finding of good moral character].

III. VOLUNTARY DEPARTURE

A. *Prehearing Voluntary Departure by DHS*

1. *Generally*—INA §240B(a), 8 U.S.C. §1229c(a), 8 C.F.R. §240.25. DHS may grant voluntary departure, including *all extensions* up to a total of 120 days, to a person who agrees to depart the U.S. at her/his own expense in lieu of being subject to proceedings. This authority may only be

exercised by certain DHS authorities. 8 C.F.R. §240.25(a). DHS may attach any conditions including the posting of a bond, continued detention pending departure, and departure under safeguards. 8 C.F.R. §240.25(b). Aggravated felons and persons engaged in terrorist activities under INA §237(a)(4)(B), 8 U.S.C. §1227a(a)(4)(B) are ineligible for prehearing VD. Prehearing VD is not available to someone who is stopped at the border, but DHS may allow such a person to withdraw his application for admission pursuant to INA §235(a)(4). If proceedings have commenced, DHS can ask the IJ to terminate proceedings and then grant 120 days. 8 C.F.R. §240.25(d)(1). If a person fails to depart, s/he is subject to the sanctions under INA §240B(d); 8 C.F.R. §1240.26(a) [ineligible for relief for 10 years and subject to civil penalties].

2. *Visa Waiver Medical Problem*—Under INA §240B(a)(2)(B), a person who entered on the visa waiver program, who needs to remain in the U.S. to receive medical treatment beyond the 120 days that DHS may grant, may apply for a waiver to remain in the U.S. The applicant must provide a detailed diagnosis from the physician, a statement from the health care facility that the treatment is not being paid through any Federal or State public health assistance, and evidence of financial ability to support day-to-day expenses.

B. *Voluntary Departure in Removal Proceedings*—INA §240B, 8 U.S.C. §1229c; 8 C.F.R. §§1240.11(b), 1240.26. The immigration judge may grant VD before the completion of proceedings under INA §240B(a) or at the conclusion of proceedings under INA §240B(b).

1. *Voluntary Departure Prior to Completion of Proceedings*—INA §240B(a). The IJ may grant VD up to 120 days if respondent: (a) requests VD prior to or at the master calendar hearing at which the case is initially set for a merits hearing; (b) requests no other relief; (c) concedes removability; (d) waives appeal, *Matter of Ocampo,* 22 I&N Dec. 1301 (BIA 2000); and (e) has not been convicted of an aggravated felony and is not deportable under the security and related provisions of INA §237(a)(4). 8 C.F.R. §1240.26(b). *Hashish v. Gonzales,* 442 F.3d 572, 577–79 (7th Cir. 2006) [IJ did not err in failing to consider VD at start of proceedings because respondent never withdrew his request for other relief and never waived appeal]. *But see Matter of Cordova,* 22 I&N Dec. 966, 969–70 (BIA 1999) [where respondent inquires about cancellation but takes no further action, his failure to formally withdraw the request and his appeal of the IJ's erroneous denial of VD do not bar VD]. The requirement that respondent waive appeal does not, in the view of one circuit, violate due process. *Cervantes-Ascencio v. INS,* 326 F.3d 83, 86–87 (2d Cir. 2003). Good moral character and the financial means to depart are not required. *Matter of Arguelles*, 22 I&N Dec. at 817; *Matter of Cordova, supra.*

1.a. *IJ Ruling*—The IJ must rule on the VD request within 30 days. 8 C.F.R. §1240.26(b)(1)(ii). The 30 days may be extended by stipulation or where DHS is conducting a security check even though VD is not covered by the Background and Security Investigations Rule. *See* Memo [Interim OPPM 05-03], Creppy, Chief IJ, EOIR (Mar. 28, 2005), *published on* AILA InfoNet at Doc. No. 05041565.

1.b. *"Master Calendar Hearing"*—Neither the Act nor the regulations define "master calendar hearing" for purposes of §240B(a). The BIA has interpreted it to be "a preliminary stage of the proceedings at which, even though little or no testimony is taken, the Immigration Judge has great flexibility to identify issues, make preliminary determinations of possible eligibility for relief, resolve uncontested matters and schedule further hearings." *Matter of Cordova*, 22 I&N Dec. at 968.

1.c. *Notice*—The IJ may give notice of the date of VD orally, and failure to provide it in writing may not give rise to constitutional or statutory claims. Although the IJ must notify the person of the right to seek prehearing VD, failure to do so will not result in reversal without a showing of prejudice. *Matter of R-S-H-,* 23 I&N Dec. 629, 644 (BIA 2003) [where respondents applied for asylum and withholding there was no reason to believe they would have given up those claims to seek VD only].

1.d. *Travel Documents*—If travel documentation is not immediately available, the IJ may grant 120 days VD on the condition that the applicant secure travel documents and present them to DHS within 60 days. Failure to produce the documents within the 60-day period, or within any extension of time granted by DHS, results in VD being vacated and the alternate order of removal taking effect. 8 C.F.R. §1240.26(b)(3)(ii).

2. *By Stipulation*—At any time prior to the completion of the final hearing, parties can stipulate to 120 days VD. 8 C.F.R. §1240.26(b)(2).

3. *At Conclusion of Removal Hearing*—INA §240B(b), 8 C.F.R. §1240.26(c).

   3.a. *Eligibility*—The IJ may grant no more than 60 days VD at the conclusion of proceedings for individuals (whether inadmissible or deportable) who meet the following conditions:

      (1) Must be physically present in the U.S. for at least one year prior to service of the NTA;

      (2) Must be a person of good moral character for at least 5 years *preceding* the VD application. *Griffiths v. INS,* 243 F.3d 45, 56 (1st Cir. 2001) [cannot accrue 5 years after requesting VD during pendency of proceedings, because statute requires 5 years preceding the VD application]. *See* INA §101(f), 8 U.S.C. §1101(f); *Li Wang v. INS*, 872 F.2d 685 (5th Cir. 1989) for statutory grounds and *Matter of Seda*, 17 I&N Dec. 550 (BIA 1980) for discretionary grounds.

      (3) Must not be deportable as an aggravated felon or terrorist. The aggravated felony bar for cases initiated before Apr. 1, 1997 only applies to convictions on or after Nov. 18, 1988. 8 C.F.R. §1240.56. *Matter of Reyes*, 20 I&N Dec. 789 (BIA 1994); and

      (4) Must establish by clear and convincing evidence, the ability to leave at own expense and the intent to do so. *Cuadras v. INS*, 910 F.2d 567, 572 (9th Cir. 1990) [in asylum context, where applicant would not agree to leave U.S. voluntarily, VD denied as well].

      (5) Must have the financial ability to post a bond designated by the IJ within 5 days of the IJ's order. A bond is required "in an amount necessary to ensure that the alien will depart," INA §240B(b)(3), but in no case less than $500. 8 C.F.R. §1240.26(c)(3).

   3.b. *Prior Voluntary Departure Grant*—A person who has previously been granted VD after having been found inadmissible under INA §212(a)(6)(A) is ineligible for VD under INA §240B(b). Applies only to previous grants of VD under §240B and not to previous grants of VD under former INA §244(e). *Matter of Arguelles,* 22 I&N Dec. 811 at 819.

4. *Voluntary Departure is Discretionary*—Although VD under both statutory provisions is discretionary, "an Immigration Judge has broader authority to grant voluntary departure in discretion under section 240B(a) than under section 240B(b)". *Matter of Arguelles*, 22 I&N Dec. 811, 817 (BIA 1999). Factors pertinent to the exercise of discretion include the applicant's immigration and criminal history, length of residence and ties to the U.S., the existence of any USC/LPR family members and humanitarian factors. *Matter of Gamboa,* 14 I&N Dec. 244 (BIA 1972); *Matter of Seda*, 17 I&N Dec. 550 (BIA 1980).

5. *Expiration of Voluntary Departure Period*—The regulations provide no guidance as to whether the VD period expires if it ends on a weekend, and a motion to reconsider with the BIA or a motion to stay in federal court was filed the following Monday. *But see Barroso v. Gonzales,* 429 F.3d 1195, 1202–04 (9th Cir. 2005) [where the deadline for filing a motion to reconsider falls on the same day as the expiration of the VD period, which is a weekend, and BIA regulations allow the motion to reconsider to be filed on the first business day after the weekend, the motion will be treated as if it was filed within the VD period even if the regulations do not automatically extend VD to the next business day]; *Salvador-Calleros v. Ashcroft,* 389 F.3d 959, 963–65 (9th Cir. 2004) [where a motion to stay was filed on Monday following the Saturday when VD expired, the court, citing Fed. R. App. P. 26(a), held that the motion to stay would also be construed as a motion for VD and that the Monday filing was timely to preserve VD].

6. *Civil Penalty and Denial of Other Relief for Failure to Depart*—INA §240B(d)(1), 8 U.S.C. §1229c(d)(1). If person fails to depart within the time period specified for VD s/he is: (1) subject to a civil penalty of $1,000 to $5,000; and (2) ineligible for a period of 10 years for any further relief of VD, adjustment, cancellation of removal, C/S or registry. There is no exceptional circumstance exception under INA §240B(d). *Lubale v. Gonzales,* 484 F.3d 1078, 1080–81 (8th Cir. 2007) [BIA lacks authority to apply an exceptional circumstances test for post-IIRIRA failure to voluntarily depart]. *See e.g., Tapia-Martinez v. Gonzales*, 482 F.3d 417, 424–25 (6th Cir. 2007) [failure to voluntarily depart barred cancellation]. *But see Matter of Zmijewska,* 24 I&N Dec. 87, 92–93 (BIA 2007) [no failure to VD where person, through no fault of his or her own, was unaware of the VD order or was physically unable to depart]. The same provision denying relief ex-

isted under pre-IIRIRA law, although it barred the relief for 5 years. Former INA §242B(e). *See in this chapter* section I.C (p.957), *supra*.

6.a. *Effect of Motions to Reopen/Reconsider—Chedad v. Gonzales,* 497 F.3d 57 (1st Cir. 2007) [a timely filed motion to reopen does not stay the running of the VD period and if the motion is granted after VD has expired the respondent is barred from seeking relief §1229c(d)(1)]; *Naeem v. Gonzales,* 469 F.3d 33 (1st Cir. 2006) [where LPR wife became USC and her I-130 petition was approved for her husband during the VD period, but husband's motion to reopen, although filed within 90 days of the BIA's decision, was filed after the end of the VD period, BIA was correct in finding husband statutorily ineligible for AOS]; *Roberts v. Gonzales,* 422 F.3d 33, 35–36 (1st Cir. 2005) [MTR filed after statutory ineligibility period in attempt to avoid penalty for overstaying VD denied as untimely]; *Guerra-Soto v. Ashcroft,* 397 F.3d 637 (8th Cir. 2005) [MTR for cancellation filed after VD expired denied because petitioner failed to comply with VD order; although compliance with VD would have prohibited relief, failure to depart barred relief]; *Jupiter v. Ashcroft,* 396 F.3d 487, 491–92 (1st Cir. 2005) [affirming denial of MTR for failure to depart under VD because petitioner was simply unwilling to depart, not unable to depart]; *De Martinez v. Ashcroft,* 363 F.3d 1022 *amended by* 374 F.3d 759 (9th Cir. 2004) [MTR for AOS, although timely filed, denied due to VD overstay]. Where motion is filed before the expiration of VD, some courts are willing to "toll" the VD period pending review of the merits. *See Ugokwe v. U.S. Att'y Gen.,* 453 F.3d 1325 (11th Cir. 2006) [timely filed MTR tolls VD period and prohibits the application of *Matter of Shaar* to bar consideration of the merits]; *Barroso v. Gonzales,* 429 F.3d 1195, 1202–08 (9th Cir. 2005) [motion to reconsider filed within the VD period automatically tolls VD]; *Kanivets v. Gonzales,* 424 F.3d 330, 334–36 (3d Cir. 2005) [timely filed MTR for AOS tolls VD and allows the BIA to consider the motion]; *Sidikhouya v. Gonzales,* 407 F.3d 950 (8th Cir. 2005) [BIA abused its discretion in denying MTR for AOS based on *Matter of Shaar*, where motion was filed prior to VD expiration, but VD expired before BIA ruled]; *Azarte v. Ashcroft,* 394 F.3d 1278 (9th Cir. 2005) [finding *Shaar* does not apply to *post*-IIRIRA cases and determining that where a MTR is filed during the VD period and a stay of removal or VD is requested, the VD period is tolled while the BIA considers the motion]; *Barroso v. Gonzales,* 429 F.3d 1195, 1202–04 (9th Cir. 2005) [where the deadline for filing a motion to reconsider falls on a weekend and is the same day as the expiration of VD, and BIA regulations allow the motion to be filed on the first business day after the weekend, the motion will be treated as if it was filed within the VD period]. *But see Dekoladenu v. Gonzales,* 459 F.3d 500, 502–08 (4th Cir. 2006) [timely filed MTR does not toll VD].

6.b. *Reopened Proceedings*—The bar to relief may apply even if a person is successful in reopening proceedings. *Chedad v. Gonzales,* 497 F.3d 57 (1st Cir. 2007) [a timely filed motion to reopen does not stay the running of the VD period and if the motion is granted after VD has expired the respondent is barred from seeking relief §1229c(d)(1)]; *Singh v. Gonzales,* 468 F.3d 135 (2d Cir. 2006) [IJ's granting of MTR does *not* vacate the effect of prior noncompliance with a VD order that now bars respondent's adjustment of status]; *Dacosta v. Gonzales,* 449 F.3d 45 (1st Cir. 2006) [BIA properly denied adjustment after granting motion to reopen because granting a motion to reopen where applicant had previously remained beyond the voluntary departure period without a stay did not expunge the previous violation for purposes of barring adjustment]; *Banda-Ortiz v. Gonzales,* 445 F.3d 387, 391 (5th Cir. 2006) [BIA's decision to reopen does not cure respondent's failure to depart during VD period and respondent is therefore ineligible for cancellation]. *But see Orichitch v. Gonzales,* 421 F.3d 595 (7th Cir. 2005) [in granting petitioner's joint MTR for AOS, the BIA permanently "disposed of" the VD order and thus eliminated the §240B(d) issue]. The IJ or BIA may reinstate VD in a removal proceeding that has been reopened. If granted, the maximum cannot exceed the 120 (or 60 day) limitation. 8 C.F.R. §1240.26(h).

6.c. *Conditions of VD Must Be Met*—The withdrawal of relief for failure to voluntarily depart arises only if all conditions for VD are met including the payment of bond. *Matter of Diaz-Ruacho,* 24 I&N Dec. 47 (BIA 2006) [granting MTR because respondent's failure to post $500 bond resulted in VD order being vacated automatically under 8 C.F.R. §1240.26(c)(3)].

6.d. *VAWA Self-Petitioners*—VAWA self-petitioners who fail to voluntarily depart remain eligible for cancellation, adjustment of status, special rule cancellation and suspension for battered spouses and children if the extreme cruelty or battery was "at least one central reason for the alien's overstaying the grant of voluntary departure." INA §240B(d)(2).

7. *Additional Conditions*—The AG by regulation may limit eligibility for VD for any class or classes of persons and no court may review any regulation issued. INA §240B(e), 8 U.S.C. §1229c(e).

8. *Change in Voluntary Departure from Previous Law*—IIRIRA changed VD before IJs as follows:
   - Limited VD to 60 days (120 days for pre-hearing VD or by stipulation only);
   - Required physical presence in U.S. for one year prior to the application;
   - Raised the burden of proof to clear and convincing evidence of intention and financial ability to depart;
   - Required a $500 bond as a condition of VD which *must* be posted within *5 days of the order* to preserve VD on appeal. *Matter of A-M-,* 23 I&N Dec. 737, 744 n.8 (BIA 2005);
   - Imposed $1,000 to $5,000 penalty for failure to depart;
   - Made VD available to persons in removal proceedings who are inadmissible;
   - Made persons who previously received VD after having been found inadmissible under INA §212(a)(6)(A) ineligible;
   - Allowed AG by regulation to exclude categories of persons from VD; and
   - Withdrew judicial review of IJ's (but not DD's) denial of VD.

9. *Effectives Dates*—The changes to the VD provisions apply to persons placed in proceedings on or after Apr. 1, 1997.

C. *Procedural Issues*

1. *Extensions*—The DD has sole authority to extend VD granted by an IJ, *Matter of Ozcan*, 15 I&N Dec. 301 (BIA 1975); 8 C.F.R. §§244.2, 1244.2; 52 Fed. Reg. 24982; *Ademi v. INS*, 31 F.3d 517, 521 (7th Cir. 1994) [BIA may not extend VD], unless a case has been reopened by the IJ for some other purpose. An extension of VD may be given for good cause, but it may not exceed the 60 or 120-day limit. 8 C.F.R. §1240.26(f). In granting or denying extensions of VD, the DD must personally serve its decision. 8 C.F.R. §103.5a; Legal Opinion, Aleinikoff, General Counsel INS HQ 244-P (Jan. 10, 1995), *reprinted in* 72 No. 15 *Interpreter Releases*, 528, 534 (Apr. 17, 1995) [distinguishing pre-hearing voluntary departure which does *not* require personal service]. If no extension is granted, and the alien departs after VD period has lapsed, departure will be considered a self-deportation. 8 C.F.R. §§241.7, 1241.7. The DD's failure to consider VD may be reviewable in district court. *Sibanda v. District Director, INS*, 881 F.Supp. 1494 (D. Colo. 1995) [reversing denial of VD extension when DD failed to adequately address issues raised in request]. *But see* INA §240B(f) [eliminating judicial review of IJ's determination of VD].

2. *Hearsay Evidence*—VD cannot be denied on hearsay documents when doing so would be fundamentally unfair. *Cunanan v. INS*, 856 F.2d 1373 (9th Cir. 1988) [where INS used wife's affidavit to establish sham marriage without giving VD applicant the right to cross-examine, it could not be used as a basis to deny VD]. *But see Felzcerek v. INS*, 75 F.3d 112 (2d Cir. 1996); *Matter of Lemhammad*, 20 I&N Dec. 316 (BIA 1991) [BIA allowed affidavit where counsel waived the right to cross-examine the agent who prepared the document].

3. Testimony at VD hearing cannot be used for purposes of confirming or establishing alienage. *Matter of Bulos*, 15 I&N Dec. 645 (BIA 1976).

4. *BIA and Voluntary Departure*—The BIA will reinstate the VD period granted by the IJ that expired during appeal unless: (1) the respondent failed to post the necessary $500 bond *within 5 days of the IJ's* order on VD; or (2) there are specific reasons not to reinstate the IJ's order such as a frivolous appeal or one filed for delay. *Matter of A-M-,* 23 I&N Dec. 737, 742–44 (BIA 2005) [BIA will reinstate VD for up to 60 days if IJ gave 60 days but cannot give a greater time than IJ ordered if $500 bond was posted within 5 days of the IJ's order]; *Matter of Chouliaris*, 16 I&N Dec. 169 (BIA 1977) [pre-IIRIRA law providing for reinstatement of 30 days if VD had run during appeal]; *Matter of Patel*, 19 I&N Dec. 394 (BIA 1986) [no reinstatement where appeal is frivolous]; *Matter of R-P-*, 20 I&N Dec. 230 (BIA 1990) [reinstatement of VD denied where IJ

granted 6 months and no other relief was requested]. When the BIA issues an AWO opinion, it does not have the authority to lower the period of VD. *Padilla-Padilla v. Gonzales,* 463 F.3d 972, 980–82 (9th Cir. 2006) [reversing AWO that decreased the IJ's grant of VD from 60 to 30 days because BIA under AWO may only affirm the IJ's result]. Where the BIA reverses the IJ for a reason that undercuts the basis for the IJ's denial of VD, the Board must address whether VD should be granted. *Patel v. Gonzales,* 470 F.3d 216, 220–21 (6th Cir. 2006) [where BIA reversed IJ's determination that respondent was a persecutor of others and that finding was the basis to deny VD, the BIA failed to exercise its discretion when it did not address VD or remand the issue for a new hearing]. Where the IJ gave a greater amount of time than permitted, the BIA, following *Matter of A-M-* may reduced the time for VD. *Rivera v. Mukasey,* 508 F.3d 1271, 1276–78 (9th Cir. 2007) [where IJ incorrectly granted 90 days VD instead of 60, the BIA did not err in reducing the VD period to 30 days because *Matter of A-M-* permits the BIA to change the VD period if there are "specific reasons not to reinstate IJ's order"].

5. *Circuit Courts and Voluntary Departure*—Where VD granted and person appeals to federal court, virtually all circuits, post-IIRIRA, have held that they do not have the authority to reinstate VD. *Iouri v. Ashcroft,* 487 F.3d 76, 82–87 (2d Cir. 2007) [no authority to extend or stay VD when motion to stay deportation was filed but no motion to stay VD was filed until after the VD period]; *Bocova v. Gonzales,* 412 F.3d 257, 264–70 (1st Cir. 2005) [same]; *Mullai v. Ashcroft,* 385 F.3d 635, 639–40 (6th Cir. 2004) [court may not reinstate VD where the VD period granted by the BIA expires; however a petitioner may seek a stay of VD if it has not yet expired]; *Harchenko v. INS,* 379 F.3d 405, 411–13 (6th Cir. 2004) [court will not reinstate VD where applicant filed, and BIA denied, an untimely motion to reopen to reinstate VD]; *Boudaguian v. Ashcroft,* 376 F.3d 825, 829 (8th Cir. 2004) [questioning whether court has jurisdiction to reinstate VD but would not reinstate where petitioner failed to timely request a stay of VD]; *Ngarurih v. Ashcroft,* 371 F.3d 182, 191–95 (4th Cir. 2004) [court has no jurisdiction to reinstate VD directly or through stay motion]; *Reynoso-Lopez v. Ashcroft,* 369 F.3d 275, 279–84 (3d Cir. 2004) [court lacks power to reinstate VD where it expired before completion of review]; *Sviridov v. Ashcroft,* 358 F.3d 722, 731 (10th Cir. 2004) [rejecting motion to grant VD *nunc pro tunc* where motion was filed after expiration of VD granted by BIA]; *Zazueta-Carrillo v. Ashcroft,* 322 F.3d 1166, 1170–75 (9th Cir. 2003) [finding that *Contreras-Aragon v. INS*, 852 F.2d 1088 (9th Cir. 1988) (en banc) was no longer good law after IIRIRA and that filing a petition for review does not extend the period of VD granted by the BIA]; *Faddoul v. INS*, 37 F.3d 185, 191–92 (5th Cir. 1994) [refusing to reinstate VD where appeal filed one day late]; *Castaneda v. INS*, 23 F.3d 1576, 1578–83 (10th Cir. 1994) [no jurisdiction to reinstate VD]; *Nkacoang v. INS*, 83 F.3d 353 (11th Cir. 1996) [following *Castaneda*]; *Kaczmarczyk v. INS*, 933 F.2d 588, 597–98 (7th Cir. 1991) [court has no authority to extend VD unless denial of VD is for purpose of discouraging judicial review]. *But see Loulou v. Ashcroft,* 354 F.3d 706, 710 (8th Cir. 2003) [to preserve VD, court vacated order of deportation and reinstated respondent's previous grant of VD].

5.a. *Pre-IIRIRA and Transition Rule Cases*—Prior to IIRIRA, courts routinely reinstated VD in deciding petitions for review. *Liu v. DOJ*, 13 F.3d 1175 (8th Cir. 1994) [reinstating VD of 6 months given by IJ rather than BIA's 30 days]; *Ramsay v. INS*, 14 F.3d 206 (4th Cir. 1994) [following *Umanzor-Alvarado* and adding *Kaczmanczyk* condition that it would reinstate VD if INS refuses to grant it solely to deter judicial review]. The Ninth Circuit applied the same reasoning and found that VD would be reinstated automatically in all transition rule cases. *Elian v. Ashcroft,* 370 F.3d 897 (9th Cir. 2004). However, *post*-REAL ID Act, reinstatement may be barred even for transition rule cases because those cases are now subject to the jurisdictional rules under INA §242, 8 U.S.C. §1252. *Onikoyi v. Gonzales,* 454 F.3d 1, 4–5 (1st Cir. 2006) [section 106(d) of REAL ID Act provided that transition rule cases should be treated as appeals under §242 and therefore, court cannot reinstate VD for a transition case where no stay of VD was requested before it expired].

5.b. *Stay of Voluntary Departure*—However, even if a circuit court cannot extend VD, it can grant a stay of VD granted by the BIA, thereby preserving it. A respondent seeking review in federal court may seek a stay of the VD period until the petition for review is decided. *Vidal v. Gonzales,* 491 F.3d 250 (5th Cir. 2007) [agreeing with most circuits that it has the power to stay VD but denying it in specific case where petitioner could not show a likelihood of success on the merits of the underlying case]; *Iouri v. Ashcroft,* 487 F.3d 76, 82–89 (2d Cir.

2007) [motion to stay VD is permissible but must be filed before expiration of VD and must be separate request from motion to stay removal; court rejected *nunc pro tunc* filing]; *Obale v. Attorney General of the U.S.*, 453 F.3d 151, 154–57 (3d Cir. 2006) [court has inherent equitable powers to grant stay]; *Bocova v. Gonzales,* 412 F.3d 257, 264–70 (1st Cir. 2005) [court allowed motion to stay VD without exhausting administrative remedies if the motion is filed before the expiration of VD and is for the specific purpose of staying VD, not simply a motion to stay removal]; *Lopez-Chavez v. Ashcroft,* 383 F.3d 650 (7th Cir. 2004) [court has jurisdiction to grant stay filed before VD expires, but denied stay because of no likelihood of success]; *Rife v. Ashcroft,* 374 F.3d 606, 614–16 (8th Cir. 2004) [where appellant files a motion to stay removal before VD expires it will be construed as a timely motion to stay VD]; *Nwakanma v. Ashcroft,* 352 F.3d 325 (6th Cir. 2003); *El Himri v. Ashcroft,* 344 F.3d 1261 (9th Cir. 2003) [granting a stay does not conflict with the en banc decision in *Zazueta-Carillo* prohibiting a circuit court from extending VD].

5.c. *Standard for Stay of VD*—The standard for granting a stay of VD is the same as granting a stay of removal. *See e.g., Bocova, supra. But see Iouri v. Ashcroft,* 487 F.3d 76, 86–87 (2d Cir. 2007) [finding "equities" may differ between the stays and cited cases to that effect]. The court can only grant VD for the period remaining on the day the stay of removal and/or stay of VD is filed. *See e.g., Macotaj v. Gonzales,* 424 F.3d 464 (6th Cir. 2005) [following *Desta* and holding that where motion to stay was filed with 9 days VD remaining, the grant of the stay also stays VD but the court cannot reinstate or extend the VD beyond the 9 days left from the issuance of the mandate]; *Desta v. Ashcroft,* 365 F.3d 741, 747 (9th Cir. 2004) [court may stay VD but only for whatever period remains; motion to stay removal will be construed as including a motion to stay VD if brought within VD period]. *See also Salvador-Calleros v. Ashcroft,* 389 F.3d 959, 963–65 (9th Cir. 2004) [where motion to stay was filed on Monday following the Saturday when VD expired, the court, citing Fed. R. App. P. 26(a), held that the motion to stay would also be construed as a motion for VD and that the Monday filing was timely to preserve VD]. However, the court has no authority to grant a stay of VD if the request for the stay is brought beyond the VD period. *Bocova v. Gonzales,* 412 F.3d 257, 264–70 (1st Cir. 2005); *Molathwa v. Ashcroft,* 374 F.3d 661 (8th Cir. 2004); *Obleshchenko v. Ashcroft,* 374 F.3d 654 (8th Cir. 2004); *Garcia v. Ashcroft,* 368 F.3d 1157 (9th Cir. 2004). *See also Boudaguian v. Ashcroft,* 376 F.3d 825, 829 (8th Cir. 2004) [questioning whether court has jurisdiction to reinstate VD but will not where petitioner failed to submit a timely request for a stay of VD]. *But see Ngarurih v. Ashcroft,* 371 F.3d 182, 191–95 (4th Cir. 2004) [court has no jurisdiction to reinstate VD directly or through stay motion].

5.d. *Stay of Removal vs. Stay of Voluntary Departure*—Some courts have held that a stay of removal is not a stay of VD and does not automatically stay VD. *Iouri v. Ashcroft,* 487 F.3d 76, 82–87 (2d Cir. 2007) [must file separate motion to stay VD and standards are different in granting stays]; *Bocova v. Gonzales,* 412 F.3d 257, 264–70 (1st Cir. 2005) [filing a motion to stay removal within VD period will *not* be construed as a motion to stay VD]; *Alimi v. Ashcroft,* 391 F.3d 888, 891–93 (7th Cir. 2004) [granting a stay of removal does not automatically stay VD]. *But see Macotaj v. Gonzales,* 424 F.3d 464 (6th Cir. 2005) [following *Desta* and holding that motion to stay filed within VD period will also be considered a motion to stay VD]; *Salvador-Calleros v. Ashcroft,* 389 F.3d 959, 963–65 (9th Cir. 2004) [where motion to stay was filed on Monday following the Saturday when VD expired, the court, citing Fed. R. App. P. 26(a), held that the motion to stay would also be construed as a motion for VD and that the Monday filing was timely to preserve VD]; *Desta v. Ashcroft,* 365 F.3d 741, 747 (9th Cir. 2004) [motion to stay removal will be construed as including a motion to stay VD if brought within VD period].

5.e. *No Exhaustion of Administrative Remedies*—Generally, a person requesting a stay of VD from the court need not exhaust administrative remedies by first asking DHS. *Bocova v. Gonzales,* 412 F.3d 257, 269 (1st Cir. 2005) [no purpose would be served in requiring exhaustion because DHS can only grant an additional 60 days and the briefing and decision making time would exceed that period]. *But see Alimi v. Ashcroft,* 391 F.3d 888, 893 (7th Cir. 2004) [suggesting exhaustion may be required before filing motion to stay VD].

6. *Three- and Ten-Year Bar and VD*—The grant of VD does not cure the 3/10 year bar upon return under INA §212(a)(9)(B), 8 U.S.C. §1182(a)(9)(B). In addition, if a person is granted VD and then fails to depart they are barred from virtually all forms of relief until 10 years after departure.

D. ***Administrative Review***—8 C.F.R. §1240.26(g). No appeal shall lie regarding the length of time given for VD as opposed to whether to grant VD.

E. ***Judicial Review***—Under IIRIRA §304(a), Congress sought to eliminate judicial review for VD issues before IJ under INA §240B(e)–(f), 8 U.S.C. §1229c(e)–(f) as follows:

1. *Limitations on Judicial Review*—No judicial review of a denial of a request for VD made pursuant to §240B(b) (at the conclusion of proceedings). *Carcamo v. DOJ,* 498 F.3d 94, 97–98 (2d Cir. 2007) [lack jurisdiction to review denial of VD where petitioner does not allege a colorable due process claim]; *Kandamar v. Gonzales,* 464 F.3d 65, 69–70 (1st Cir. 2006) [no jurisdiction under INA §§240B(f) or 242(a)(2)(B)(i) where government seized passport and court denied VD because respondent did not have his passport; no due process claim because VD is a privilege, not a right]; *Abu-Khaliel v. Gonzales,* 436 F.3d 627, 630 (6th Cir. 2006) [INA §242(a)(2)(B)(i) bars jurisdiction over the IJ's denial of VD]; *Karim v. Gonzales,* 424 F.3d 109, 112 (1st Cir. 2005) [court lacks authority to review a refusal to allow VD]; *Gomez-Lopez v. Ashcroft,* 393 F.3d 882, 883–84 (9th Cir. 2005) [no review of denial of VD]; *Sofinet v. INS,* 196 F.3d 742, 748 (7th Cir. 1999) [section 240B(f) bars review and the decision lies solely within the AG's discretionary authority]; *Eyoum v. INS*, 125 F.3d 889, 891 (5th Cir. 1997) [referring to INA §§242(a)(2)(B) and 240B]. No review of denial of extension of VD, *Tutu v. Blackman,* 9 F.Supp.2d 534 (E.D. Pa. 1998). No review of VD denial under IIRIRA §309(c)(4)(E), transition rules. *Ali v. Ashcroft,* 366 F.3d 407, 412 (6th Cir. 2004); *Regalado-Garcia v. INS,* 305 F.3d 784, 786 n.2 (8th Cir. 2002); *Tamas-Mercea v. Reno,* 222 F.3d 417, 427 (7th Cir. 2000); *Antonio-Cruz v. INS,* 147 F.3d 1129 (9th Cir. 1998) [same, but court can entertain constitutional due process claim]. *But see Zazueta-Carrillo v. Ashcroft,* 322 F.3d 1166, 1169–70 (9th Cir. 2003) [section 240B(f) does not eliminate judicial review of nondiscretionary decisions regarding VD and jurisdiction exists to review the BIA's denial of a motion to reopen for AOS filed within 90 days but beyond the 30-day VD period]. *But see Tovar-Landon v. Ashcroft,* 361 F.3d 1164, 1166 (9th Cir. 2004). No court shall order a stay of person's removal pending consideration of a claim with respect to VD. *But see Zazueta-Carrillo v. Ashcroft,* 322 F.3d 1166, 1175–78 (9th Cir. 2003) (Berzon, J. concurring) [if court grants stay pending appeal as an equitable matter, then person's VD should be stayed as well]. For further discussion of stays of voluntary departure, *see in this part* ¶¶ C.5.b–5.d (p.969), *supra*. No court may review any regulation by the AG limiting the class or classes of persons eligible for VD.

2. *Abuse of Discretion Standard*—Decisions concerning VD, when they were reviewable, were reviewed under an abuse of discretion standard. *Campos-Granillo v. INS*, 12 F.3d 849 (9th Cir. 1993) [reversing IJ denial of VD because positive factors not weighed]; *Tarvand v. INS*, 937 F.2d 973, 975–76 (4th Cir. 1991) [affirming denial of VD where there was a past deportation proceeding and where applicant forum shopped for student visa]; *Garcia-Lopez v. INS*, 923 F.2d 72 (7th Cir. 1991) [affirming denial where applicant had a history of violating immigration laws]; *Oluyemi v. INS*, 902 F.2d 1032 (1st Cir. 1990) [VD denial affirmed where applicant married a USC but had poor immigration record]; *Platero-Reymundo v. INS*, 807 F.2d 865 (9th Cir. 1987) [upholding denial of motion to reopen for VD based on marriage where no explanation for failure to depart]; *Villanueva-Franco v. INS*, 802 F.2d 327 (9th Cir. 1986) [following *Rios-Pineda*, evidence of acts beyond statutory period can be considered to deny VD on discretionary grounds]; *Parcham v. INS*, 769 F.2d 1001 (4th Cir. 1985) [affirming denial of VD where assault charge was pending and prior conviction for disorderly conduct; evidence without a conviction may be considered]; *Ajurulloski v. INS*, 688 F.Supp. 1272, 1276–77 (N.D. Ill. 1988) [VD denial where person seeks VD to pursue worker's compensation claim or for medical treatment not an abuse of discretion]. The court must decide whether or not DHS "considered the appropriate factors and came to a decision that has any rational basis." *Felzcerek v. INS*, 75 F.3d 112, 117 (2d Cir. 1996) [quoting *Dhine v. Slattery*].

IV. CANCELLATION OF REMOVAL

A. *Elimination of Suspension of Deportation and INA §212(c)*—Under IIRIRA §304, Congress eliminated INA §212(c) relief and suspension of deportation and replaced it with (1) cancellation of removal for LPRs [INA §240A(a)]; and (2) cancellation of removal for non-LPRs [INA §240A(b)].

B. *Cancellation of Removal for LPRs*—INA §240A(a), 8 U.S.C. §1229b(a), 8 C.F.R. §§1240.11(a), 1240.20.

1. *Eligibility*—The AG may cancel the removal of an LPR if s/he:

1.a. Has been "lawfully admitted for permanent residence" for 5 years;

(1) Persons adjusted under the Cuban Refugee Adjustment Act of 1966 are given 30 months retroactive residency from the date of their applications. The 5-year period, based on prior decisions would run from the beginning of the 30-month period. *Matter of Rivera-Rioseco*, 19 I&N Dec. 833 (BIA 1988).

(2) A person who obtained LPR status by fraud or mistake is deemed to have not been "lawfully admitted for permanent residence" and is thus, ineligible for cancellation. *Matter of Koloamatangi*, 23 I&N Dec. 548 (BIA 2003) [where LPR status fraudulently obtained through bigamous marriage, respondent ineligible for cancellation]. *See also Mejia-Orellana v. Gonzales,* 502 F.3d 13 (1st Cir. 2007) [upheld *Koloamatangi* under *Chevron*]; *De La Rosa v. DHS,* 489 F.3d 551 (2d Cir. 2007) [affirmed analysis by BIA in *Koloamatangi* under second step of *Chevron* as to INA §212(c) case]; *Savoury v. U.S. Att'y Gen.,* 449 F.3d 1307, 1313–17 (11th Cir. 2006) [where petitioner fully disclosed his prior drug conviction but DHS granted AOS by mistake, BIA correctly concluded he was not an LPR for purposes of §212(c) relief because LPR status acquired by fraud *or* mistake nullifies the status]; *Arellano-Garcia v. Gonzales,* 429 F.3d 1183 (8th Cir. 2005) [LPR status obtained by fraud or negligent mistake of the agency renders one ineligible for §212(c) relief]; *Monet v. INS*, 791 F.2d 752 (9th Cir. 1986) [LPR status which was procured through failure to disclose foreign conviction that would have barred LPR status deemed invalid for §212(c) purposes]; *but see Matter of Sosa-Hernandez*, 20 I&N Dec. 758 (BIA 1993) [waiver of deportability under former INA §241(f) waives the underlying fraud or misrepresentation and grants LPR status retroactive to date person became LPR, thus eligible for §212(c) relief]. However, even if the former LPR is ineligible for LPR cancellation, he may be eligible for non-LPR cancellation under INA §240A(b). *Obioha v. Gonzales,* 431 F.3d 400, 408–10 (4th Cir. 2005) [upholding denial of remand to apply for non-LPR cancellation where former LPR obtained LPR status by fraud, but failed to timely apply for non-LPR cancellation].

(3) Parent's Residence Not Imputed. The BIA has held that a parent's LPR status may not be imputed to his or her child to give the child the necessary five years of LPR status to qualify for cancellation. *Matter of Escobar,* 24 I&N Dec. 231 (BIA 2007) [court distinguished *Cuevas-Gaspar v. Gonzales,* 430 F.3d 1013 (9th Cir. 2005) and found that applicant's conviction cut off the five year period]. *See also Augustin v. Attorney General of U.S.*, 520 F.3d 264 (3d Cir. 2008) [affirming under the second step of *Chevron* the same view that a parent's residence may not be imputed to his or her minor child for purposes of the 7-year residence provision of cancellation].

1.b. Has resided in the U.S. continuously for 7 years after having been admitted in any status;

(1) Continuous residence not required where the person has served in an active duty status in the Armed Forces for a minimum of 24 months and if separated, was honorably discharged, and was in the U.S. at the time of his or her enlistment or induction.

(2) Admission in "any status" includes admission as a temporary resident, *Matter of Perez,* 22 I&N Dec. 689, 692 (BIA 1999), a nonimmigrant *Matter of Blancas,* 23 I&N Dec. 458 (BIA 2002) [Mexican entering on border crossing card], or a person who was admitted into the family unity program even if he was never technically "admitted" at the border. *Garcia-Quintero v. Gonzales,* 455 F.3d 1006, 1015–19 (9th Cir. 2006) [admission into family unity program is sufficient to qualify as an admission for purposes of cancellation and

LPR in removal proceeding had the necessary seven years based upon his acceptance into the family unity program while in the US].

(3) Parent's Residence May Be Imputed. A parent's admission for permanent resident status may be imputed to the unemancipated minor children residing with the parent for purposes of accruing 7 years. *Cuevas-Gaspar v. Gonzales,* 430 F.3d 1013, 1021–29 (9th Cir. 2005) [respondent acquired 7 years for cancellation when his mother became an LPR in 1990 because he resided with her at that time and her status was imputed to him]. *But see Augustin v. Attorney General of U.S.*, 520 F.3d 264 (3d Cir. 2008) [affirming under the second step of *Chevron* the view adopted in an unpublished BIA decision that a parent's residence may not be imputed to his or her minor child for purposes of the 7- year residence provision of cancellation]; *Matter of Escobar,* 24 I&N Dec. 231 (BIA 2007).

1.c. Has not been convicted of an aggravated felony. *Garcia-Jimenez v. Gonzales,* 488 F.3d 1082 (9th Cir. 2007) [where IJ granted INA §212(c) relief for pre-IIRIRA convictions, it could not grant cancellation for a post-IIRIRA conviction]; *Peralta-Taveras v. Attorney General,* 488 F.3d 580 (2d Cir. 2007) [cannot file INA §212(c) and cancellation applications simultaneously to cure pre- and post-IIRIRA convictions where pre-IIRIRA convictions was an aggravated felony]; *Becker v. Gonzales,* 473 F.3d 1000, 1002 (9th Cir. 2007) [applicant ineligible for cancellation even if he has not been charged or found removable on that ground and he is not eligible for cancellation even if he qualifies for §212(c) relief]; *Amouzadeh v. Winfrey,* 467 F.3d 451, 458–59 (5th Cir. 2006) [a grant of §212(c) relief for a prior drug conviction still bars cancellation for a separate CIMT because §212(c) does not waive an aggravated felony conviction for cancellation]; *Munoz-Yepez v. Gonzales,* 465 F.3d 347 (8th Cir. 2006) [where respondent *could* receive §212(c) relief for first *pre*-1996 aggravated felony, he would still be denied cancellation for second post-1996 non–aggravated felony because the aggravated felony barred cancellation]; *Manzueta v. Ashcroft,* 206 F.Supp.2d 386 (W.D.N.Y. 2002). *See also Da Rosa Silva v. INS,* 263 F.Supp.2d 1005, 1013–15 (E.D. Pa. 2003) [a person eligible for §212(c) relief under *St. Cyr* is entitled to apply even if a waiver would be fruitless due to subsequent convictions which would bar cancellation]; and

1.d. Warrants a favorable exercise of discretion. *See in this section*, "Discretionary Eligibility for Cancellation of Removal," ¶ 8 (p.985), *infra*.

2. *Ineligible for LPR Cancellation*—INA §240A(c):

2.a. Crewman who entered subsequent to June 30, 1964;

2.b. Persons admitted on J to receive graduate medical training whether or not s/he received a waiver, or admitted on J with 2-year foreign residency requirement and never fulfilled the requirement or received a waiver;

2.c. Persons inadmissible under INA §212(a)(3) or deportable under INA §237(a)(4) for security reasons; *Hussain v. Mukasey,* 518 F.3d 534, 537–38 (7th Cir. 2008) [although statute stretches the definition of terrorism, it defines it—and in denying petitioner's request for cancellation, it is not relevant that the MQM-H in Pakistan did not have a political agenda and was not hostile to the U.S.];

2.d. Persons determined to have persecuted others, INA §241(b)(3)(B)(i);

2.e. Persons previously granted cancellation, suspension or §212(c) relief or who wish to simultaneously file applications—INA §240A(c)(6), 8 U.S.C. §1229b(c)(6) bars a respondent from obtaining cancellation if she has ever received a waiver of deportation even if the waiver was granted in the same proceeding. It has been interpreted to bar simultaneous filings as well. *Garcia-Jimenez v. Gonzales,* 488 F.3d 1082 (9th Cir. 2007) [where IJ granted INA §212(c) relief for pre-IIRIRA convictions, it could not grant cancellation for a post-IIRIRA conviction]; *Peralta-Taveras v. Attorney General,* 488 F.3d 580 (2d Cir. 2007) [cannot file INA §212(c) and cancellation applications simultaneously to cure pre- and post-IIRIRA convictions where pre-IIRIRA conviction was an aggravated felony]; *Amouzadeh v. Winfrey,* 467 F.3d 451, 458–59 (5th Cir. 2006) [a grant of §212(c) relief for a prior drug conviction still bars cancellation for a separate CIMT because §212(c) does not waive an aggravated felony conviction for cancellation]; *Munoz-Yepez v. Gonzales,* 465 F.3d 347 (8th Cir. 2006) [where respondent *could* receive §212(c) relief for first *pre*-1996 aggravated felony, he would still be denied cancellation for second post-1996 non–aggravated felony because the aggravated felony barred cancellation];*Mai v. Gonzales,* 473 F.3d 162, 165–67 (5th Cir. 2007) [lawyer ineffective where he admitted two grounds of removal where one required a §212(c) waiver and the second a waiver under §240A because once §212(c) granted for the first ground §240A is unavailable]; *Maldonado-Galindo v. Gonzales,* 456 F.3d 1064 (9th Cir. 2006) [statute was not impermissibly retroactive when it barred cancellation to person previously granted §212(c) relief].

3. *Continuous Residence and the Stop-Time Rule*—INA §240A(d)(1). The stop-time rule only applies to the seven (7) year continuous residence issue and "does not apply to the five-year requirement" *Sinotes-Cruz v. Gonzales,* 468 F.3d 1190, 1197 (9th Cir. 2006) and "has no bearing on the other requirements for cancellation of removal, including the issues of qualifying relatives, hardship, or good moral character." *Matter of Bautista Gomez,* 23 I&N Dec. 893, 895 (BIA 2006).

3.a. *Service of NTA*—Under INA §240A(d)(1)(A), continuous residence for purposes of cancellation of removal is deemed to end upon service of a notice to appear. *Matter of Nolasco,* 22 I&N Dec. 632 (BIA 1999); *Dababneh v. Gonzales,* 471 F.3d 806, 810 (7th Cir. 2006) [where DHS served NTA without date and time but Immigration Court subsequently sent a notice of hearing, the stop-time rule applied from the notice of hearing]. In the suspension context, it has been held that a person may not accrue a new 7 years subsequent to the service of the NTA. *Matter of Mendoza-Sandino,* 22 I&N Dec. 1236 (BIA 2000); *Casillas-Figueroa v. Gonzales,* 419 F.3d 447 (6th Cir. 2005) [rejecting position that 7 years may accrue after service of OSC]; *Al Najjar v. Ashcroft,* 257 F.3d 1262, 1299–1300 (11th Cir. 2001) [BIA view that 7 years may not accrue subsequent to service of OSC is supported by the statute]; *Iyamba v. INS,* 244 F.3d 606, 608 (8th Cir. 2001) [rejecting claim that 7 years could start anew after service of OSC]; *Ram v. INS,* 243 F.3d 510, 517–18 (9th Cir. 2001) [same]; *McBride v. INS,* 238 F.3d 371 (5th Cir. 2000) [same]. *But see Matter of Cisneros,* 23 I&N Dec. 668 (BIA 2004) [where person departs U.S. after service of OSC he may accrue 10-year period for cancellation upon his return if placed in a subsequent removal proceeding].

3.b. *Commission of Certain Crimes*—Under INA §240A(d)(1)(B), continuous residence is deemed to end upon the commission of an inadmissible offense under INA §212(a)(2), or a removable offense under INA §§237(a)(2) or 237(a)(4). The time period is measured from the commission of the crime, not the conviction, *Matter of Perez,* 22 I&N Dec. 689 (BIA 1999); *Matter of Robles,* 24 I&N Dec. 22, 27–28 (BIA 2006); *Reid v. Gonzales,* 478 F.3d 510, 512 (2d Cir. 2007) [*Matter of Perez* applied to foreclose cancellation for LPR], and the BIA has found that a conviction is not even necessary. *Matter of Jurado,* 24 I&N Dec. 29, 31 (BIA 2007) [applicant need not actually be convicted as admission is sufficient]. Continuous residence is not stopped by commission of an offense that is not "referred to in section 212(a)(2)." *Matter of Campos-Torres,* 22 I&N Dec. 1289 (BIA 2000) [firearm offense]. However, the time period is not stopped by the commission of a petty offense, even if a subsequent conviction for a CIMT would render the petty offense exception ineligible. *Matter of Deanda-Romo,* 23 I&N Dec. 597 (BIA 2003) ["stop-time" rule does not apply until the second conviction where the first conviction was a petty offense]. *But see Briseno-Flores v. Att'y Gen. of the U.S.,* 492 F.3d 226, 229–31 (3d Cir. 2007) [respondent's conviction in 1985 for petty offense stopped the time for calculating the seven years needed for suspension]. *See also Torres De La Cruz v. Maurer,* 483 F.3d 1013, 1019–22 (10th Cir. 2007) [upholding stop-time rule against due process and equal protection challenges]. A person may also not accrue a new 7 years subsequent to the commission of a crime. *Matter of Mendoza-Sandino,* 22 I&N Dec. 1236, 1241 (BIA 2000); *Briseno-Flores v. Att'y Gen. of the U.S.,* 492 F.3d 226, 229–31 (3d Cir. 2007) [respondent's conviction in 1985 stopped the time for calculating the seven years needed for suspension; nor did a new seven year period begin from that point; *Okeke distinguished*]. *But see Okeke v. Gonzales,* 407 F.3d 585 (3d Cir. 2005) [in non-LPR cancellation case, a conviction does not bar the clock from restarting to allow accrual of a new 10-year residence period where applicant left the U.S. and reentered lawfully].

3.c. *Retroactivity of Criminal Stop-Time Rule*—The criminal stop-time rule although not explicitly made retroactive may be applied retroactively to pre-IIRIRA crimes, where proceedings were begun post-IIRIRA. *Matter of Jurado,* 24 I&N Dec. 29, 32 (BIA 2007) [following *Mat-*

ter of Perez and *Matter of Robles*, the Board held the stop-time rule may be applied retroactively and applies even if the commission of the offense preceded IIRIRA]; *Zuluaga-Martinez v. Mukasey,* __ F.3d ___ (2d Cir. 2008), 2008 WL 1808290 (Apr. 23, 2008) [held that it was not impermissibly retroactive for petitioner's 1995 commission of a criminal offense to terminate his period of continuous residence, because commission of the crime immediately placed him in a category of persons eligible for deportation upon conviction]; *Briseno-Flores v. Att'y Gen. of the U.S.,* 492 F.3d 226, 229–31 (3d Cir. 2007) [respondent's conviction in 1985 stopped the time for calculating the seven years needed for suspension; nor did a new seven year period begin from that point; *Okeke distinguished*]; *Heaven v. Gonzales,* 473 F.3d 167 (5th Cir. 2006) [seven year continuous residence cut off cancellation application post-IIRIRA where conviction was pre-IIRIRA]; *Tablie v. Gonzales,* 471 F.3d 60 (2d Cir. 2006) [INA §240A(d)(1)(B), barring suspension for persons who commit crimes during the period of continuous residence applies retroactively]; *Valencia-Alvarez v. Gonzales,* 469 F.3d 1319, 1324–31 (9th Cir. 2006) [where applicant was not eligible for discretionary relief at the time he committed the offense, at the time he was convicted, or when IIRIRA became effective, the application of the stop-time rule was not impermissibly retroactive; *Sinotes-Cruz* distinguished because applicant in that case was eligible for relief before IIRIRA's effective date]; *Peralta v. Gonzales,* 441 F.3d 23 (1st Cir. 2006) [respondent ineligible for suspension because criminal stop-time provision applies retroactively, and his conviction for marriage fraud was a CIMT committed during the necessary 10-year period]; *Hernandez v. Gonzales,* 437 F.3d 341, 346–53 (3d Cir. 2006) [rejecting retroactivity argument for person seeking suspension who committed crime before IIRIRA on ground that he was still ineligible after plea because he could not establish 10 years of good moral character]; *Matter of Perez,* 22 I&N Dec. 689 (BIA 1999); *Matter of Robles,* 24 I&N Dec. 22, 27–28 (BIA 2006) [finding no retroactivity issue where the stop-time rule was applied to a respondent who committed a pre-IIRIRA crime; *Matter of Perez* reaffirmed]; *Worrell v. Ashcroft,* 207 F.Supp.2d 61, 67 (W.D.N.Y. 2002). *But see Sinotes-Cruz v. Gonzales,* 468 F.3d 1190, 1197–1203 (9th Cir. 2006) [the stop-time rule, regarding the commission of criminal offenses, can not be applied retroactively under the second step of *Landgraf* to bar LPR's cancellation of removal where respondent was eligible for relief prior to IIRIRA]; *Generi v. Ashcroft,* 2004 U.S. Dist. LEXIS 6396 (W.D. Mich. 2004).

3.d. *Other Challenges to the Application of the Stop-Time Rule—Aoun v. INS,* 342 F.3d 503 (6th Cir. 2003) [where BIA continued respondent's appeal for one reason or another for 12 years during which time the stop-time rule was enacted, the court declined to impose the rule on the applicant]; *Otarola v. INS,* 270 F.3d 1272 (9th Cir. 2001) [the stop-time rule should not apply where IJ granted suspension and INS took a frivolous appeal to permit the stop-time rule to be applied]; *Guadalupe-Cruz v. INS,* 240 F.3d 1209 (9th Cir. 2001) *opinion corrected* 250 F.3d 1271 (9th Cir. 2001) [where IIRIRA was not in effect and IJ erroneously applied stop time rule, decision was reversed and IJ ordered to apply pre-IIRIRA law but with current facts]; *Tang v. INS,* 223 F.3d 713 (8th Cir. 2000) [where petitioner and INS stipulated to a date for the service of the OSC beyond the 7 years, no bar to suspension]; *Arrozal v. INS,* 159 F.3d 429, 434 & n.2 (9th Cir. 1998) [stop-time rule does not apply to motion to reopen where final order was obtained prior to Apr. 1, 1997 and possibly by applicant accruing more than seven years since the OSC]; *But see Raffington v. Cangemi,* 399 F.3d 900, 902–03 (8th Cir. 2005) [rejecting *Otarola* and holding that even if the government had filed a frivolous, but ultimately successful appeal, it would not constitute affirmative misconduct to estop the government].

4. *Application*—Cancellation of Removal application is submitted on Form EOIR-42 if before the IJ, Form I-191 if before the DD. Must submit fee when filing in conjunction with removal proceeding. 8 C.F.R. §1240.20(a). Can only file with IJ if NTA filed. 8 C.F.R. §1240.20(b).

5. *Cancellation is Indefinite*—If cancellation is granted, it is granted indefinitely, 8 C.F.R. §§212.3(d), 1212.3(d), and returns the person to same LPR status previously held. *Matter of Przygocki*, 17 I&N Dec. 361 (BIA 1980). Once waiver granted, absent fraud or error, it cannot be revoked. *Matter of Gordon*, 20 I&N Dec. 52 (BIA 1989).

6. *Changes from Waiver Under Former* INA §212(c)—Former INA §212(c) provided for the waiver of inadmissibility or deportability for LPRs who had been lawfully domiciled in the U.S. for 7 consecutive years and who had not served an aggregate of more than 5 years imprisonment for an aggravated felony or felonies.

   6.a. *Effective Date*—The effective date of the changes from INA §212(c) to cancellation of removal for LPRs is Apr. 1, 1997. IIRIRA §309(a), (c). This effective date does not bar §212(c) relief for certain pre-IIRIRA convictions. *INS v. St. Cyr,* 533 U.S. 289 (2001). In addition, individuals who were in "deportation" proceedings commenced before April 24, 1996 (AEDPA enactment date) are eligible for §212(c) relief without regard to AEDPA or IIRIRA amendments. *See* 8 C.F.R. §1003.44.

   6.b. *LPR vs. "Lawfully Domiciled"*—The requirement that a person have been an LPR for 5 years before becoming eligible for cancellation resolved an issue in dispute under §212(c). *Compare Matter of Anwo*, 16 I&N Dec. 293, 298 (BIA 1977), *aff'd*, *Anwo v. INS*, 607 F.2d 435 (D.C. Cir. 1975) [requiring LPR status for 7 years], *with Kolster v. Ashcroft,* 188 F.Supp.2d 60 (D. Mass. 2002) [7 years of "lawful domicile" not LPR status is standard for §212(c) relief]; *Ortega de Robles v. INS,* 58 F.3d 1355 (9th Cir. 1995) ["lawful domicile" for purposes of §212(c) began when person first became a "temporary" resident under amnesty program]; *Castellon-Contreras v. INS*, 45 F.3d 149 (7th Cir. 1995) [lawful domicile and lawful permanent residence are separate criteria thus 7 years as LPR not required]; *White v. INS*, 75 F.3d 213 (5th Cir. 1996); 8 C.F.R. §212.3(f)(2). *But see Bonhometre v. Ashcroft,* 414 F.3d 442, 448–50 (3d Cir. 2005) [temporary resident ineligible for §212(c) relief].

   6.c. *Commencement of Residence*—The determination as to when continuous residence begins to run was resolved because the statute provides that the 7-year residence may accrue "after having been admitted in any status." INA §240A(a)(2). *Matter of Perez,* 22 I&N Dec. 689 (BIA 1999). Prior to IIRIRA, the entry status was often determinative of whether residence could be established. *See Melian v. INS*, 987 F.2d 1521 (11th Cir. 1993) [B-2 cannot have lawful intent to remain]; *Graham v. INS*, 998 F.2d 194 (3d Cir. 1993) [H-2A farmworker cannot establish lawful intent to remain]; *Prichard-Ciriza v. INS*, 978 F.2d 219, 223–24 (5th Cir. 1992) [person in unlawful status cannot establish intent to remain]; *Madrid-Tavarez v. INS*, 999 F.2d 111 (5th Cir. 1993) [EWI cannot establish intent to remain]. However, for purposes of §212(c), domicile for an unemancipated minor was determined to be the same domicile as the custodial parent. *Rosario v. INS*, 962 F.2d 220, 224 (2d Cir. 1992) [finding minor eligible for §212(c) relief even though he physically entered the U.S. less than 7 years prior, where his custodial parent was previously domiciled in the U.S.]. *See also Lepe-Guitron v. INS*, 16 F.3d 1021 (9th Cir. 1994). Residence could also accrue while the LPR was outside the U.S. *Matter of Hinojosa*, 17 I&N Dec. 34 (BIA 1979).

   6.d. *Aggravated Felony Bar to Cancellation*—Persons convicted of aggravated felonies are ineligible for cancellation. Prior to AEDPA, which barred §212(c) relief for virtually anyone convicted of a deportable offense, aggravated felons were ineligible for §212(c) relief only if they had been incarcerated for 5 years or more. Given the drastic expansion of "aggravated felony" to include virtually every felony and some misdemeanors, the cancellation provision will be useless in the vast majority of cases. In *Matter of Fortiz,* 21 I&N Dec. 1199 (BIA 1998), the BIA held that a person convicted of an aggravated felony is not barred from §212(c) relief where s/he was not charged with deportability as an aggravated felon. *But see Salviejo-Fernandez v. Gonzales,* 455 F.3d 1063, 1065–66 (9th Cir. 2006) [due process was not violated where ICE did not charge respondent with an aggravated felony in the NTA but used the conviction to find respondent ineligible for cancellation]; *Brown v. Ashcroft,* 360 F.3d 346, 351–53 (2d Cir. 2004) [distinguishing *Matter of Fortiz* on grounds it applied only to AEDPA and finding that DHS was free to use an aggravated felony conviction to bar §212(c) relief even if it had not charged the felony in the NTA]. *See also Matter of Jurado,* 24 I&N Dec. 29, 30–32 (BIA 2007) [finding that a cancellation applicant need not be charged or found inadmissible on a ground specified in INA §240A(d)(1)(B) for the stop-time rule to apply]. In addition, it has been found that the grant of §212(c) relief for an aggravated felon waives only the finding of deportability, not the conviction itself and that therefore, the bar to cancellation remains. *Rodriguez-Munoz v. Gonzales,* 419 F.3d 245 (3d Cir. 2005) [upholding denial of re-papering, because even if cancellation was available, it would not help respondent as the grant of §212(c) relief did not affect the aggravated felony bar to cancellation]; *Amouzadeh v. Winfrey,* 467 F.3d 451, 458–59 (5th Cir. 2006) [a prior grant of §212(c) relief for an aggravated felony still bars cancellation for a separate CIMT because §212(c) does not waive an aggravated felony for cancellation purposes].

A question remains as to whether the aggravated felony bar to cancellation applies retroactively to persons whose crime did not constitute an aggravated felony at the time of conviction. The effective date of the definition of aggravated felony under IIRIRA §321(b) appears to be retroactive for all aggravated felonies ["[n]otwithstanding any other provision of law (including any effective date), the term applies regardless of whether the conviction was entered before, on, or after the date of enactment of this paragraph."]. For a further discussion of aggravated felonies and their effective dates, *see* Ch. 3, ¶ V.G.3 (p.166), *supra.* In the context of §212(c), the BIA has determined that the bar applies to aggravated felons convicted prior to 1988. *Matter of Gomez-Giraldo*, 20 I&N Dec. 957 (BIA 1995) [rejecting retroactivity and *ex post facto* challenge]; *Matter of A-A-*, 20 I&N Dec. 492 (BIA 1992); *Sena v. Gonzales,* 428 F.3d 50, 51–53 (1st Cir. 2005) [retroactive application of alien smuggling provisions under §101(a)(43)(N) that results in barring §212(c) relief on lack of a comparable ground of inadmissibility has a rational basis and does not violate due process]; *Scheidemann v. INS*, 83 F.3d 1517 (3d Cir. 1996); *Asencio v. INS*, 37 F.3d 614 (11th Cir. 1994); *Campos v. INS*, 16 F.3d 118 (6th Cir. 1994); *De Osorio v. INS*, 10 F.3d 1034 (4th Cir. 1993) [following *Matter of A-A*]; *Buitrago-Cuesta v. INS*, 7 F.3d 291 (2d Cir. 1993); *Barreiro v. INS*, 989 F.2d 62 (1st Cir. 1993).

6.e. *Creation of Removal Proceedings*—The cancellation provision and the creation of one unified "removal" proceeding, eliminated the controversy over whether §212(c) relief is available in deportation proceedings where there is no comparable ground of exclusion. *See Matter of Hernandez-Casillas*, 20 I&N Dec. 262 (AG 1991); *Matter of Esposito*, 21 I&N Dec. 1 (BIA 1995); *Matter of Gabryelsky*, 20 I&N Dec. 750 (BIA 1993); *Farquharson v. U.S. Att'y Gen.,* 246 F.3d 1317, 1322–26 (11th Cir. 2001) [section 212(c) unavailable to person charged with EWI]; *Reid v. INS,* 203 F.Supp.2d 47 (D. Mass. 2002) [firearms conviction barred §212(c) relief]. However, this issue remains alive in cases in which persons seek §212(c) relief to waive pre-1996 aggravated felony and firearm convictions. *See in this section*, "Pre-AEDPA/IIRIRA Convictions & *St. Cyr*," ¶ 7.b (p.978), *infra.*

6.f. *Tolling of Residence Period*—Under INA §212(c) the 7-year period of lawful domicile was tolled when the order of deportation was administratively final. *Jaramillo v. INS*, 1 F.3d 1149 (11th Cir. 1993) (en banc). However, the 7 years for cancellation now tolls upon service of an NTA, *Matter of Nolasco,* 22 I&N Dec. 632 (BIA 1999), or when an applicant commits certain criminal offenses. INA §240A(d)(1). For further discussion of the stop-time rule and its retroactive application, *see in this section*, "Continuous Residence and the Stop-Time Rule," ¶ 3 (p.974), *supra*.

6.g. *Motions to Reopen*—Unlike former INA §212(c), motions to reopen for cancellation are unlikely because the person had to qualify prior to service of an NTA.

7. *Continuing Availability of §212(c) Relief*

7.a. *Proceedings Commenced Before Apr. 1, 1997*—Relief under former INA §212(c) remains available to individuals who were placed in deportation proceedings prior to Apr. 1, 1997 or who were in exclusion proceedings. *Matter of Fuentes-Campos*, 21 I&N Dec. 905 (BIA 1997) [§212(c) relief available for persons in exclusion proceedings initiated prior to Apr. 1, 1997]. Moreover, AEDPA §440(d)'s restrictions on §212(c) eligibility for aggravated felons do not apply to persons who were in proceedings before Apr. 24, 1996. 8 C.F.R. §§212.3(g), 1212(3)(g). Service of an OSC along with the filing of a detainer has been found sufficient to support the conclusion that proceedings had commenced. *Alanis-Bustamonte v. Reno,* 201 F.3d 1303 (11th Cir. 2000) [concluding that proceedings had commenced in 1995, when INS served an OSC and lodged a detainer, even though the OSC was not filed with the immigration court until June 1997]. *Accord Wallace v. Reno,* 194 F.3d 279 (1st Cir. 1999) [service of OSC was sufficient to demonstrate pendency of proceedings when AEDPA enacted]; *Cunningham v. U.S. Att'y Gen.,* 335 F.3d 1262 (11th Cir. 2003) [following *Alanis-Bustamante* and allowing §212(c) relief even where no detainer was lodged when INS never intended to lodge detainer]. *But see Thom v. Ashcroft,* 369 F.3d 158 (2d Cir. 2004) [detainer alone is not sufficient to find deportation proceedings commenced]; *Dipeppe v. Quarantillo,* 337 F.3d 326 (3d Cir. 2003) [delay between the service of OSC in 1992 and the filing of NTA in 2000 did not justify application of pre-AEDPA/IIRIRA law because OSC was never filed and proceedings commence only with the filing of the NTA]; *Armendariz-Montova v. Sonchik,* 291 F.3d 1116 (9th Cir. 2002) [rejecting both *Alanis-Bustamante* and *Wallace*]; *Deleon-Holguin v. Ashcroft,* 253 F.3d 811 (5th Cir. 2001); [proceedings have not commenced where OSC is served but not filed and thereafter INS serves and files NTA]; *Asad v. Reno,* 242 F.3d 702 (6th Cir. 2001) [all requiring filing of charging document with the immigration court to find proceedings commenced]; *Morales-Ramirez v. Reno,* 209 F.3d 977 (7th Cir. 2000) [finding that a person served with an exclusion notice but not put into proceedings until after IIRIRA is barred from §212(c) because proceeding only commenced under 8 C.F.R. §§1003.14 and 1240.30 after INS filed the NTA with the court].

7.b. *Pre-AEDPA/IIRIRA Convictions & St. Cyr*—In *INS v. St. Cyr,* 533 U.S. 289 (2001), the Supreme Court held that neither IIRIRA §304, nor AEDPA §440(d), may apply retroactively to bar §212(c) relief to persons who pled guilty to charges prior to AEDPA/IIRIRA and that "§212(c) relief remains available for aliens...whose convictions were obtained through plea agreements [prior to Apr. 24, 1996] and who, notwithstanding those convictions, would have been eligible for §212(c) relief at the time of their plea under the law then in effect." The relevant date for determining continued §212(c) eligibility is the date of the plea, not the date that the judgment of conviction was entered. *Alvarez-Hernandez v. Acosta,* 401 F.3d 327 (5th Cir. 2005); *cf. Perez v. Elwood,* 294 F.3d 552, 561–62 (3d Cir. 2002) [§212(c) relief not available to a person found guilty by jury pre-IIRIRA, but not sentenced until post-IIRIRA because the "formal judgment of guilt" is defined by reference to Fed. R. Crim. P. 32(d)(1), which occurs at the time of sentence].

(1) *"Under the Law Then in Effect"*—Circuit courts have relied on *St. Cyr's* language to provide even broader coverage. For example, a person who had not obtained 7 years of LPR status until after his plea, but would have continued to accrue time in such status under prior law may still be protected. *See Alvarez-Hernandez v. Acosta,* 401 F.3d 327, 329–32 (5th Cir. 2005) [under pre-*St. Cyr* law, 7 years could be accrued after the entry of the guilty plea]. *See also* 8 C.F.R. §1.1(p) [LPR status terminates only "upon entry of a final administrative order of exclusion or deportation]; 8 C.F.R. §1003.2(c)(1) [a motion to reopen for §212(c) relief "may be granted if the alien demonstrates that he or she was statutorily eligible for such relief prior to the entry of the administratively final order of deportation"]; 8 C.F.R. §1003.44(b)(3) and 69 Fed. Reg. 57826, 57831 (Sept. 28, 2004) [rejecting position that §212(c) is unavailable unless person had 7 years domicile at time plea was entered]. However, where a conviction was entered prior to AEDPA, but was subsequently vacated and petitioner re-pleaded after IIRIRA, §212(c) may not be available. *Lawrence v. Gonzales,* 446 F.3d 221, 225 (1st Cir. 2006) [rejecting petitioner's claim that his 1995 conviction should fix the pertinent date for §212(c) and not the vacatur and superseding 1998 conviction which was done for strategic purposes to avoid the expanded aggravated felony definition]. Similarly, INA §212(c) is not available if respondent was criminally charged before IIRIRA but absconded and pled guilty after IIRIRA. *Cespedes-Acquino v. Att'y Gen. of the U.S.,* 498 F.3d 221 (3d Cir. 2007).

(2) *Conviction by Trial*—An individual who did not plead guilty (*e.g.,* was convicted after trial) but gave up the right to apply for §212(c) relief affirmatively before AEDPA/IIRIRA in reliance on the later availability of such relief may also be protected. *Walcott v. Chertoff,* 517 F.3d 149 (2d Cir. 2008) [petitioner could make a *Restrepo* argument despite his jury conviction being on appeal after the passage of AEDPA because he could have waived appeal and applied for §212(c) relief before AEDPA]; *Carranza-De Salinas v. Gonzales,* 477 F.3d 200 (5th Cir. 2007) [relying on the second circuit opinion in *Restrepo*, the court held that IIRIRA's abolition of §212(c) would not be applied retroactively if the respondent demonstrated actual reliance by choosing not to apply for §212(c) relief immediately after his trial and instead waiting until deportation proceedings were initiated to bolster his claim for rehabilitation]; *Restrepo v. McElroy,* 369 F.3d 627, 632–40 (2d Cir. 2004) [recognizing that the repeal of §212(c) has an impermissible

retroactive effect on a person who gave up the right to submit an affirmative §212(c) application when such relief was available, in order to later present a stronger case of rehabilitation; court cited second prong of *Landgraf* concerning "fair notice, reasonable reliance and settled expectations"]. *See also Wilson v. Gonzales,* 471 F.3d 111, 117–23 (2d Cir. 2006) [following *Rankine* and rejecting the categorical approach for all persons found guilty after trial, but remanding case to BIA for an individualized showing of reliance]; *Thaqi v. Jenifer,* 377 F.3d 500 (6th Cir. 2004) [*St. Cyr* retroactivity analysis applies where a person was deportable for the commission of two crimes and he was convicted by jury trial of first crime but pleaded guilty to the second crime prior to AEDPA]; *Ponnapula v. Ashcroft,* 373 F.3d 480 (3d Cir. 2004) [where defendant went to trial prior to AEDPA/IIRIRA on reliance that he would still be eligible for §212(c) relief because he would not be sentenced to five years and was not, relief should not be retroactively barred]. Personal reliance may not be necessary to get the benefit of §212(c). *Atkinson v. Att'y Gen. of the U.S.,* 479 F.3d 222 (3d Cir. 2007) [person convicted before AEDPA/IIRIRA did *not* have to demonstrate a *quid pro quo* to obtain §212(c) relief because personal reliance is not a factor; the issue is whether the enactment of a new law has created a new disability following *Landgraf, Hughes* and *Hadix*]; *Hem v. Maurer,* 458 F.3d 1185 (10th Cir. 2006) [rejected subjective/actual reliance in favor of objective reasonable reliance of prior law, where respondent went to trial and did not appeal his conviction]. *But see Rankine v. Reno,* 319 F.3d 93 (2d Cir. 2003) [*St. Cyr* and *Landgraf* analysis do not extend to a conviction after a trial]; *Saravia-Paguada v. Gonzales,* 488 F.3d 1122, 1129–35 (9th Cir. 2007) [followed *Armendariz* and found that provision barring §212(c) relief to someone who was incarcerated for 5 years was not barred retroactively to a conviction prior to 1990 because the conviction was obtained after trial by jury and not through a plea]; *Mbea v. Gonzales,* 482 F.3d 276, 280–82 (4th Cir. 2007) [following *Chambers* and finding no impermissible retroactive effect where person went to trial]; *Alexandre v. U.S. Att'y Gen.,* 452 F.3d 1204, 1207 (11th Cir. 2006) [finding a petitioner ineligible for §212(c) relief who was found guilty after trial in 1989]; *Hernandez-Castillo v. Moore,* 436 F.3d 516, 519–20 & n.3 (5th Cir. 2006) [following *Rankine* and *Chambers* and rejecting §212(c) relief for LPR who was found guilty after 1989 trial, despite assertion that he gave up plea agreement believing §212(c) relief would be available]; *Thom v. Ashcroft,* 369 F.3d 158, 161–64 (2d Cir. 2004) [following *Rankine*, and determining that 1982 trial for second-degree murder did not implicate *St. Cyr.* retroactivity]; *Montenegro v. INS,* 245 F.Supp.2d 936, 937–39 (C.D. Ill. 2003) [where aggravated felon was convicted after trial, *St. Cyr* does not apply]; *Dias v. INS,* 311 F.3d 456 (1st Cir. 2002); *Chambers v. Reno,* 307 F.3d 284 (4th Cir. 2002) [where person was convicted by trial IIRIRA §304(b) applied retroactively to bar §212(c) relief notwithstanding *St. Cyr*]; *Armendariz-Montoya v. Sonchik,* 291 F.3d 1116 (9th Cir. 2002) [where LPR did not plead but was convicted of aggravated felony *St. Cyr* is inapplicable]; *but see also Brooks v. Ashcroft,* 283 F.3d 1268 (11th Cir. 2002) [rejecting equal protection challenge to distinction between LPRs who are convicted after trial and those who pleaded guilty, and finding that INA §242(a)(2)(C) stripped the court of jurisdiction to review the purely statutory question of retroactivity]. *See also Hernandez de Anderson v. Gonzales,* 497 F.3d 927, 937–44 (9th Cir. 2007) [the BIA erred in impermissibly repealing suspension of deportation where person was convicted after trial and was placed in removal proceedings after seeking naturalization one year before the passage of IIRIRA that eliminated suspension].

7.c. *Adjustment of Status & §212(c)*—Courts are now free to allow for a *Gabryelsky* AOS in conjunction with a §212(c) application where the criminal conviction occurred before AEDPA/IIRIRA. *Matter of Azurin,* 23 I&N Dec. 695 (BIA 2005) [reaffirming *Rainford* and *Gabryelsky* for pre-AEDPA/IIRIRA convictions and finding §212(c) relief available in conjunction with an adjustment application even if the ground of deportation (gun charge) could not be waived because it did not have an equivalent ground of inadmissibility]; *Drax v. Reno,* 338 F.3d 98 (2d Cir. 2003) [finding that person with drug conviction and attempted weapons conviction was eligible for *Gabryelsky* relief even where a visa was not immediately available because the IJ could have granted a continuance]; *Nolasco v. U.S.,* 358 F.Supp. 224, 230–31

(S.D.N.Y. 2004) [applying *St. Cyr* and *Drax* where respondent illegally reentered following deportation prior to either decision].

7.d. *Regulations Following St. Cyr*—DHS adopted rules to comply with *St. Cyr.* An aggravated felon who has served less than 5 years may apply for §212(c) relief if a plea agreement was made before Apr. 24, 1996. 8 C.F.R. §1212.3(f)(i). Aggravated felons who served more than 5 years are eligible if their plea agreements were made before Nov. 29, 1990. 8 C.F.R. §1212.3(f)(4)(ii). If the plea was made after Apr. 24, 1996 but before Apr. 1, 1997, an applicant would be eligible if he complies with AEDPA §440(d) and was not an aggravated felon. A person is ineligible for §212(c) relief if the plea was made after Apr. 1, 1997, the ground of deportation or removal does not have a statutory counterpart in INA §212, or the person is inadmissible for security, terrorism, foreign policy, Nazism or international child abduction grounds. *See* INA §§212(a)(3)(A)(B)(C)(E) and (10)(C); 8 C.F.R. §§1212.3(f)(3)–(5), (h)(3). The date of the plea agreement is the date it was agreed to by the parties, 8 C.F.R. §1212.3(h), not the date the judgment of conviction was entered. *Alvarez-Hernandez v. Acosta,* 401 F.3d 327, 332–34 (5th Cir. 2005) [rejecting the government's argument that it is the date of the entry of judgment and not the date of the plea that governs §212(c) eligibility]. The regulations do not cover a person who was found guilty after trial. *Alexandre v. U.S. Att'y Gen.,* 452 F.3d 1204, 1207 (11th Cir. 2006) [following 1212.3(f)(4)(ii), and determining that a person was not eligible for §212(c) relief who was found guilty after trial in 1989].

7.e. *Special Motions to Reopen for §212(c) Relief*—DHS has also issued regulations permitting motions to reopen to apply for §212(c) relief in limited circumstances. 8 C.F.R. §1003.44(h), 69 Fed. Reg. 57826–35 (Sept. 28, 2004). The applicant must establish that s/he: (1) was an LPR and is now subject to a final order of deportation or removal; (2) agreed to plead guilty or *nolo contendere* pursuant to plea agreement made before Apr. 1, 1997; (3) had 7 consecutive years of lawful unrelinquished domicile in the U.S. prior to the date of the final order; and (4) is otherwise eligible to apply for §212(c) relief under standards in effect at time of the plea, regardless of when plea was entered by the court. 8 C.F.R. §1003.44(b). The motion to reopen had to be filed prior to Apr. 26, 2005. *Johnson v. Gonzales,* 478 F.3d 795 (7th Cir. 2007) [rejecting due process, ultra vires, equitable tolling, and retroactivity arguments to deadline for filing the motion to reopen]. A person was eligible to file a special motion to reopen irrespective of the time and number limitations on motions to reopen, but the case could not be reopened if a prior §212(c) motion was denied on discretionary grounds or under *St. Cyr.* Applicants were required to submit a completed Form I-191 with supporting documentation. 8 C.F.R. §1003.44(f). The provision does not apply to persons who departed the U.S., to persons who had final orders and illegally returned, or to persons who were not admitted or paroled. 8 C.F.R. §1003.44(k). *Avila-Sanchez v. Mukasey,* 509 F.3d 1037, 1041 (9th Cir. 2007) [regulation does not violate equal protection or due process]; *Robledo-Gonzales v. Ashcroft,* 342 F.3d 667, 681–83 (7th Cir. 2003) [rejecting equal protection challenge under rational basis test to 8 C.F.R. §1003.44(k)]. It also does not apply to a person who is ineligible because the conviction is not a ground of inadmissibility. *Cyrus v. Keisler,* 505 F.3d 197, 201–02 (2d Cir. 2007) [respondent with gun conviction is not eligible for INA §212(c) relief and therefore not eligible to reopen under §1003.44].

7.f. *IMMACT90 Considerations*—Section 511 of IMMACT90 barred §212(c) relief to aggravated felons who had been incarcerated for 5 years or more, and applied to "admissions [to the U.S.] occurring after the date of enactment." IMMACT90 §511(b). *Leon-Davila v. INS*, 19 F.3d 1370 (11th Cir. 1994); *Matter of Ramirez-Somera*, 20 I&N Dec. 564 (BIA 1992) [relief under §212(c) is barred to any alien who has been convicted of an aggravated felony or felonies and who "has served," not merely been sentenced to, a term of imprisonment of at least 5 years for such felony or felonies]; *Romero-Rodriguez v Gonzales,* 488 F.3d 672 (5th Cir. 2007) [deferring to BIA's position pursuant to *Chevron* that the 5 year period runs from the date of the BIA's subsequent denial of an appeal following a prior reopening of the case but holding that the BIA, but not the court, may grant *nunc pro tunc* relief]; *Elia v. Gonzales,* 431 F.3d 268, 275–76 (6th Cir. 2005) [no substantive or procedural due process violation for failure to give incarcerated respondent a hearing within 5 years so he could apply for §212(c) relief]; *Dipeppe v. Quarantillo,* 337 F.3d 326, 332–35 (3d Cir. 2003) [no §212(c) relief for applicant who pled guilty knowing she would serve more than 5 years]. These individuals remain ineligible post-AEDPA/IIRIRA, even in light of *St. Cyr.* 8 C.F.R. §1212.3(f)(4)(i). *See also Velez-Lotero v. Achim,* 414 F.3d 776 (7th Cir. 2005) [person who served more than 5 years in prison after pleading guilty to a controlled substance violation in 1995 was properly denied §212(c) relief]; *Alexandre v. U.S. Att'y Gen.,* 452 F.3d 1204, 1207 (11th Cir. 2006) [petitioner was not eligible for §212(c) relief because she served 5 years before applying for relief in 1994]; *Gomes v. Ashcroft,* 311 F.3d 43, 45–46 (1st Cir. 2002) [the term "admission" in §511(b) refers not only to the original admission into the U.S. but also to whenever the applicant applies for §212(c); IMMACT90 bar applies]; *Mezrioui v. INS,* 154 F.Supp.2d 274 (D. Conn. 2001) [five years may be accrued at any time before IJ renders her decision on §212(c) relief]. At least one court has found that pre-AEDPA aggravated felony convictions where a person cumulatively spent more than 5 years in jail would not bar §212(c) relief. *Paulino-Jimenez v. INS,* 279 F.Supp.2d 313, 317–19 (S.D.N.Y. 2003) [person who pled guilty to two aggravated felonies prior to AEDPA would be eligible for §212(c) relief as he served less than 5 years for each one]; *Toledo-Hernandez v. Ashcroft,* 280 F.Supp.2d 112 (S.D.N.Y. 2003) [finding §212(c) relief available to person who pled guilty before AEDPA but not before IMMACT90 §511, notwithstanding aggregate time served of more than 5 years].

(a) Counting the Five Years—*Spina v. DHS,* 470 F.3d 116, 125–30 (2d Cir. 2006) [time spent in pre-conviction detention when credited is counted toward the five years and the court rejected the idea that the time should only be accrued at the end of a person's sentence as a matter of fairness regarding INA §212(c) eligibility]; *Saravia-Paguada v. Gonzales,* 488 F.3d 1122 (9th Cir. 2007) [time spent as recidivist counted toward 5 years and court rejected retroactivity argument because unlike in *Toia* respondent was convicted after trial in 1988]; *Moreno-Cebrero v. Gonzales,* 485 F.3d 395 (7th Cir. 2007) [time spent in pretrial detention counted toward the 5-year period]; *Torres-Rascon v. Heston,* 339 F.3d 633 (8th Cir. 2003) [rejecting the argument that time served after a guilty plea could not be counted toward the 5 year period for §212(c) purposes]; *Gordon v. Ashcroft,* 283 F.Supp.2d 435 (D. Mass. 2003) [pre-trial detention period is included in the 5-year period].

Pre-IMMACT90 Convictions— However, a person remains eligible for §212(c) relief even if he is an aggravated felon who served a five year sentence if his plea agreement was entered before Nov. 29, 1990, the date that the 5-year incarceration bar became effective. 8 C.F.R. §1212.3(f)(4)(ii); *Toia v. Fasano,* 334 F.3d 917 (9th Cir. 2003) [IMMACT90 §511 may not be applied retroactively under *St. Cyr* to bar relief for a person who was convicted by guilty plea before Nov. 29, 1990]; *De Cardenas v. Reno,* 278 F.Supp.2d 284 (D. Conn. 2003) [same and distinguishing *Buitrago-Cuesta* where the argument that the statute was meant to be retroactive because of its effective date was rejected in *St. Cyr*]. *See also Edwards v. INS,* 393 F.3d 299 (2d Cir. 2004) [awarding *nunc pro tunc* relief where petitioners accrued more than 5 years imprisonment subsequent to the legally erroneous denial of §212(c)]; *Hartman v. Elwood,* 255 F.Supp.2d 510 (E.D. Pa. 2003) [where imprisonment of 5 years accrued due to IJ's erroneous reliance on *Matter of Soriano* respondent still eligible for §212(c) relief]; *Falconi v. INS,* 240 F.Supp.2d 215 (E.D.N.Y. 2002) [same]. *But see Singh v. Mukasey,* 520 F.3d 119 (2d Cir. 2008) [person who confessed to crime before Nov. 29, 1990, but pled guilty after, was barred from INA §212(c) relief]; *Saravia-Paguada v. Gonzales,* 488 F.3d 1122 (9th Cir. 2007) [time spent as recidivist counted toward 5 years and court rejected retroactivity argument because unlike in *Toia* respondent was convicted after trial in 1988]; *Romero-Rodriguez v Gonzales,* 488 F.3d 672 (5th Cir. 2007) [deferring to BIA's position pursuant to *Chevron* that the 5 year period runs from the date of the BIA's subsequent denial of an appeal following a prior reopening of the case but holding that the BIA, but not the court, may grant *nunc pro tunc* relief]; *Alexandre v. U.S. Att'y Gen.,* 452 F.3d 1204, 1207 (11th Cir. 2006) [following 8 C.F.R. §1212.3(f)(4)(ii), the court rejected petitioner's retroactivity argument and found him ineligible for §212(c) relief because he was found guilty after trial]; *Fernandes-Pereira v. Gonzales,* 417 F.3d 38 (1st Cir. 2005) [declining to follow Second Circuit decision in *Edwards* granting *nunc pro tunc* relief]; *Melo v. Ashcroft,* 364 F.Supp.2d 183 (D.R.I. 2005) [finding that IMMACT90 applied retroactively to bar §212(c) relief for respondent who had aggregate time in prison of 5 years where some time was before and some after IMMACT90]; *Reid v. Holmes,* 323 F.3d 187 (2d Cir. 2003) [rejecting retroactivity argument regarding §511 for pre-1990 conviction]; *Clavis v. Ashcroft,* 281 F.Supp.2d 490, 493–97 (E.D.N.Y. 2003) [rejecting §212(c) for person with more than 5 years of incarceration without addressing retroactivity argument]; *Greenidge v. INS,* 263 F.Supp.2d 696 (S.D.N.Y. 2003) [five years accrues while case on appeal to BIA even if IJ made erroneous ruling on §212(c)]; *Gomes v. Ashcroft,* 311 F.3d 43, 45 (1st Cir. 2002) [where person served less than 5 years at time IJ misapplied law retroactively, he was still barred from §212(c) relief once 5 years had passed]; *Buitrago-Cuesta v. INS*, 7 F.3d 291, 295–96 (2d Cir. 1993); *Giusto v. INS*, 9 F.3d 8 (2d Cir. 1993).

7.g. *Possible Ineligibility for* INA §212(c) *Relief Post–St. Cyr*

(1) *Conviction by Jury*—Post–*St. Cyr*, DHS and some courts have been unwilling to extend §212(c) relief to persons convicted after trial rather than through a guilty plea. 8 C.F.R. §1212.3(f) and 69 Fed. Reg. 57826, 57828 (Sept. 28, 2004). *See in this section,* ¶ 7.b(2) (p.978), *supra*.

(2) *Deportation vs. Exclusion & AEDPA §440(d)*—In *Matter of Fuentes-Campos*, 21 I&N Dec. 905 (BIA 1997), the BIA held that AEDPA §440(d), which barred §212(c) relief to persons "deportable" for having committed certain criminal offenses, did not similarly bar such "excludable" persons. Post–*Fuentes-Campos*, courts have been unwilling to conclude that AEDPA §440(d)'s limitation of the §212(c) bar to persons in deportation proceedings violates equal protection. *Chuang v. U.S. Att'y Gen.,* 382 F.3d 1299, 1303–04 (11th Cir. 2004) [no equal protection violation because rational basis for distinction]; *Domond v. INS,* 244 F.3d 81, 83–87 (2d Cir. 2001) [equal protection not violated by distinction permitting excludable but not deportable persons to apply for §212(c) relief]; *Mohammed v. Reno,* 309 F.3d 95, 102–03 (2d Cir. 2002) [affirming *Domond* post–*St. Cyr* in decision to deny stay pending appeal]; *Almon v. Reno,* 192 F.3d 28 (1st Cir. 1999) [equal protection not violated and *Francis* distinguished]; *Requena-Rodriguez v. Pasquarell,* 190 F.3d 299, 308–09 (5th Cir. 1999) [same]; *DeSousa v. Reno,* 190 F.3d 175, 183–85 (3d Cir. 1999) [same]; *Jurado-Gutierrez v. Greene,* 190 F.3d 1135, 1152 (10th Cir. 1999) [no equal protection violation]; *Turkhan v. Perryman,* 188 F.3d 814, 828–29 (7th Cir. 1999); *LaGuerre v. Reno,* 164 F.3d 1035, 1041 (7th Cir. 1998) [in *dicta* finding no equal protection violation]; *Asad v. Reno,* 67 F.Supp.2d 886, 892–93 (M.D. Tenn. 1999) *aff'd, Asad v. Reno,* 242 F.3d 702 (6th Cir. 2001) [no equal protection violation]. In *U.S. v. Estrada-Torres*, 179 F.3d 776 (9th Cir. 1999), *overruled on other grounds*, *U.S. v. Rivera-Sanchez*, 247 F.3d 905, 909 (9th Cir. 2001) (en banc), the Ninth Circuit disagreed with *Fuentes-Campos* and concluded that despite the plain language of §440(d), it applies equally to exclusion and deportation proceedings. *See also Armendariz-Montoya v. Sonchik,* 291 F.3d 1116, 1122–23 (9th Cir. 2002) [no equal protection violation because excludable persons given right to apply for §212(c) relief]. *But see Servin-Espinoza v. Ashcroft,* 309 F.3d 1193 (9th Cir. 2002) [distinguishing *Estrada-Torres* and finding equal protection violation post *Fuentes-Campos*].

(3) *Post AEDPA/Pre-IIRIRA Convictions*—Some courts have found that a person convicted after AEDPA but before IIRIRA is barred from relief. *Morgan v. Keisler,* 507 F.3d 1053 (6th Cir. 2007) [because AEDPA barred persons with aggravated felonies from receiving INA §212(c), and IIRIRA §321 made the definition of aggravated felonies retroactive, a person whose conviction became an aggravated felony retroactively under INA §321 is ineligible for INA §212(c) relief where his plea was entered after the passage of AEDPA on April 24, 1996 and before IIRIRA's effective date of April 1, 1997]; *Cruz-Bucheli v. Gonzales* 463 F.3d 105 (1st Cir. 2006) [respondent not eligible for §212(c) relief because he pled guilty after AEDPA and had no expectation following *St Cyr* that relief would be available to him]; *Garcia-Echaverria v. U.S.,* 376 F.3d 507, 515–16 (6th Cir. 2004) [guilty plea entered after AEDPA but before IIRIRA nevertheless means that there was no reliance]; *U.S. v. Velasco-Medina,* 305 F.3d 839 (9th Cir. 2002) [in criminal proceeding for re-entry, court rejected defense that IJ should have informed defendant of his eligibility for §212(c) relief where guilty plea taken after passage of AEDPA]; *Oguejiofor v. Att'y Gen.,* 277 F.3d 1305, 1309–10 (11th Cir. 2002) [in *dicta* court found that guilty pleas taken after AEDPA barred retroactivity claim]; *Khan v. Ashcroft,* 352 F.3d 521 (2d Cir. 2003) [affirming *Mohammed* and *Domond* and finding no retroactivity issue in re-

gard to respondent who committed a crime before AEDPA but pled guilty after AEDPA and before IIRIRA]. However, DHS regulations allow persons who made a plea agreement after Apr. 24, 1996 and before Apr. 1, 1997 to apply for §212(c) relief as amended by AEDPA §440(d). 8 C.F.R. §1212.3 (h)(2).

(4) *Pre-AEDPA/IIRIRA Conduct, Post-AEDPA/IIRIRA Conviction*—Persons who committed a crime prior to AEDPA/IIRIRA but pled afterwards may not be eligible for §212(c) under a retroactivity analysis. *U.S. v. Zuñiga-Guerrero,* 460 F.3d 733, 735–39 (6th Cir. 2006) [no retroactivity concern for person who committed crime and turned down plea agreement before AEDPA but accepted plea after AEDPA]; *James v. Riley,* 329 F.Supp.2d 570 (E.D. Pa. 2004) [rejecting extension of *Ponnapula* to cover person who committed crimes before AEDPA/IIRIRA but pled afterwards]. *But see Garcia-Plaxcencia v. Ashcroft,* No. CV 04-1067-PA (D. Or. 2004) [the date of the offense, rather than the date of the plea or conviction, is the relevant date for retroactivity analysis]. Also, where a conviction was entered prior to AEDPA but it was vacated and the defendant re-pleaded after IIRIRA, §212(c) may be barred. *Lawrence v. Gonzales,* 446 F.3d 221, 225 (1st Cir. 2006) [rejecting petitioner's claim that his 1995 conviction should fix the pertinent date for §212(c) and not the vacatur and superseding 1998 conviction which was done for strategic purposes to avoid the expanded aggravated felony definition]. Similarly, INA §212(c) is not available if respondent was criminally charged before IIRIRA but absconded and pled guilty after IIRIRA. *Cespedes-Acquino v. Att'y Gen. of the U.S.,* 498 F.3d 221 (3d Cir. 2007).

(5) *Reinstatement Under* INA §241(a)(5)—It has been held that persons retroactively deprived of §212(c) relief have no due process liberty or property interest to challenge a prior order of removal in the context of reinstatement under INA §241(a)(5). *Smith v. Ashcroft,* 295 F.3d 425, 429–31 (4th Cir. 2002). *See also Alvarenga-Villalobos v. Ashcroft,* 271 F.3d 1169, 1172–73 (9th Cir. 2001) [rejecting claim that person subject to reinstatement should be allowed to reopen his case in light of *Magana-Pizano*, as that decision occurred after the first deportation order].

(6) *Terrorism*—At least one court has held that the bar to §212(c) relief may be retroactively applied to terrorist charges, because there is no reliance on legal status when committing a terrorist act. *Kelava v. Gonzales,* 434 F.3d 1120, 1124 (9th Cir. 2006).

(7) *Departure from U.S. Prior to Change in Law*—In addition, a person who left the U.S. or was deported prior to the change in law may be barred from re-opening if they seek to return or actually return. 8 C.F.R. §1003.44(k); *Avila-Sanchez v. Mukasey,* 509 F.3d 1037, 1041 (9th Cir. 2007) [regulation does not violate equal protection or due process]; *Pena-Muriel v. Gonzales,* 489 F.3d 438 (1st Cir. 2007) [due process was not violated where the BIA refused to allow respondent, who was outside the United States, to reopen his deportation proceeding because his conviction was vacated]; *Patel v. U.S. Att'y Gen.,* 334 F.3d 1259 (11th Cir. 2003) [no jurisdiction under INA §242(a)(2)(C) to review the denial of motion to reopen under 8 C.F.R. §1003.2(d), where the person was out of the country; district court lacked habeas jurisdiction because the person was no longer in custody]; *Mansour v. Gonzales,* 470 F.3d 1194 (6th Cir. 2007) [when person departed for brief trip to Mexico, his order of removal was executed and case could not be reopened]; *Robledo-Gonzales v. Ashcroft,* 342 F.3d 667, 681–83 (7th Cir. 2003) [rejecting equal protection challenge under rational basis test to 8 C.F.R. §1003.44(k)]. *But see William v. Gonzales,* 499 F.3d 329 (4th Cir. 2007) [the prohibition in 8 C.F.R. §1003.2(d) to motions to reopen where the person is outside the U.S. is contrary to INA §240(c)(7)(A), 8 U.S.C. §1229a(c)(7)(A) permitting one motion to reopen without limitation and the regulation is therefore invalid]; *Contreras-Rodriguez v. U.S. Att'y Gen.,* 462 F.3d 1314 (11th Cir. 2006) [although respondent was physically removed after *in absentia* order, he was not barred from filing a motion to reopen for lack of notice because §1003.23(b)(4)(ii) allows motion regarding lack of notice to be filed at "any time."]; *Cardoso-Tlaseca v. Gonzales,* 460 F.3d 1102 (9th Cir. 2006) [where respondent's conviction was vacated after removal, court reversed BIA for denying motion to reopen because conviction was a "key part" of removal proceeding]; *Leitao v. Reno,* 311 F.3d 453 (1st Cir. 2002) [where habeas denial

was appealed and person was deported during pendency of appeal, claim is not moot because he may be permanently barred].

(8) *Ineligibility Under IMMACT90*—Aggravated felons who served a term of imprisonment of 5 years or more were ineligible for §212(c) under pre-AEDPA/IIRIRA law and remain ineligible post-AEDPA/IIRIRA, even in light of *St. Cyr*, unless the plea agreement was entered before Nov. 29, 1990. 8 C.F.R. §1212.3(f)(4)(i). *See in this section*, ¶ 7.f (p.980), *supra*.

(9) *Statutory Counterpart Rule*—Prior to the institution of unified "removal" proceedings, §212(c) relief was not available in deportation proceedings where there was no comparable ground of exclusion. *See Matter of Hernandez-Casillas*, 20 I&N Dec. 262 (AG 1991); *Matter of Esposito*, 21 I&N Dec. 1 (BIA 1995); *Matter of Gabryelsky*, 20 I&N Dec. 750 (BIA 1993); *Farquharson v. U.S. Att'y Gen.*, 246 F.3d 1317, 1322–26 (11th Cir. 2001) [§212(c) unavailable to person charged with EWI]; *Reid v. INS,* 203 F.Supp.2d 47 (D. Mass. 2002) [firearms conviction barred §212(c) relief]. The statutory counterpart rule has since been promulgated by regulation. 8 C.F.R. §1212.3(f)(5); 69 Fed. Reg. 57826 (Sept. 28, 2004) [to be eligible for §212(c) relief, the applicant must be charged with a ground of deportability that has a statutory counterpart ground of inadmissibility]. *See also Cyrus v. Keisler,* 505 F.3d 197, 201–02 (2d Cir. 2007) [respondent with gun conviction is not eligible for INA §212(c) relief and therefore not eligible to reopen under §1003.44]. Whether there is a statutory counterpart between an aggravated felony and a ground of inadmissibility, turns on whether Congress employed similar language to describe substantially equivalent categories of offenses. The mere overlap between the aggravated felony and crimes of moral turpitude, for example, is insufficient to demonstrate that the provisions were statutory counterparts. *Matter of Brieva,* 23 I&N Dec. 766, 770–73 (BIA 2005) *aff'd Brieva-Perez v. Gonzales,* 482 F.3d 356 (5th Cir. 2007) [where respondent is charged with removal for the unauthorized use of a vehicle under Texas law, he was ineligible for §212(c) relief because there is only an "incidental overlap" between INA §101(a)(43)(F) (crime of violence) and §212(a)(2)(A)(i)(I) (CIMT)]; *Matter of Blake,* 23 I&N Dec. 722 (2005), *rev'd, Blake v. Carbone,* 489 F.3d 88 (2d Cir. 2007) [the BIA in *Blake* has held that a person who is removable because of an aggravated felony conviction for sexual abuse of a minor is not eligible for §212(c) relief even if there is overlap with CIMT, because there is no statutory counterpart that employs similar language in the grounds of inadmissibility]; *Zamora-Mallari v. Mukasey,* 514 F.3d 679, 689–93 (7th Cir. 2008) [in a case involving an aggravated felony for sexual abuse the court rejected retroactivity and equal protection challenges to *Matter of Blake* and 8 C.F.R. §1212.3(f)(5) recognizing that the regulation and *Blake* reflected existing law and also rejected Eighth Amendment challenge]; *Vue v. Gonzales,* 496 F.3d 858 (8th Cir. 2007) [following its brief opinion in *Soriano v. Gonzales,* 489 F.3d 909, the court upheld the BIA's position in *Matter of Blake* and rejected an equal protection challenge to the denial of INA §212(c) to a person convicted of first degree assault where the ground of removal was both an aggravated felony and CIMT]; *Abebe v. Gonzales,* 493 F.3d 1092 (9th Cir. 2007) *petition for reh'g granted* [upheld *Blake/Brieva* in the face of equal protection, due process, retroactivity and statutory challenges]; *Dalombo Fontes v. Gonzales,* 483 F.3d 115, 120–23 (1st Cir. 2007) [adopting BIA approach in *Blake* and *Brieva* in case involving sexual assault and rejecting equal protection, regulatory and comparability arguments]; *Vo v. Gonzales,* 482 F.3d 363 (5th Cir. 2007) [same in context of TX unauthorized use of a motor vehicle statute]; *Caroleo v. Gonzales,* 476 F.3d 158 (3d Cir. 2007) [respondent convicted in state court of attempted murder, burglary, and unlawful possession of a weapon for an unlawful purpose, he could not seek INA §212(c) relief, following *Brieva* and *Blake*, where his removal was sought as a "crime of violence" because there is a distinction between the underlying crime being a CIMT and a statutory counterpart for purposes of §212(c)]; *Valere v. Gonzales,* 473 F.3d 757 (7th Cir. 2007) [upheld *Blake* in the face of retroactivity and equal protection challenges]; *Kim v. Gonzales,* 468 F.3d 58 (1st Cir. 2006) [respondent convicted of manslaughter which was designated a COV and therefore no comparable §212(c) ground under *Brieva*]; *Sena v. Gonzales,* 428 F.3d 50, 53–54 (1st Cir. 2005) [no statutory counterpart ground of inadmissibility to aggravated felony of inducing and encouraging illegal alien to remain in

U.S., because alien smuggling under INA §212(a)(6)(E) does not apply to inducing or encouraging]. *But see Blake v. Carbone,* 489 F.3d 88 (2d Cir. 2007) [reversed *Matter of Blake* and determined that it would violate equal protection to focus on the ground of deportation rather than the particular offense]; *Matter of Meza,* 20 I&N Dec. 257 (BIA 1991) [finding §212(c) available where aggravated felony of illicit trafficking in drugs had a counterpart ground of inadmissibility for a drug conviction].

8. *Discretionary Eligibility for Cancellation of Removal*—To establish discretionary eligibility for cancellation, the criteria utilized in §212(c) cases under *Matter of Marin*, 16 I&N Dec. 581 (BIA 1978) and *Matter of Wadud*, 19 I&N Dec. 182 (BIA 1984) should be utilized. *Matter of C-V-T-*, 22 I&N Dec.7 (BIA 1998). These criteria include:

8.a. Positive Factors

- Family ties within the U.S.;
- Residency of long duration in the U.S.;
- Evidence of hardship to the respondent and family if deportation occurs;
- Service in Armed Forces;
- History of employment;
- Existence of property or business ties;
- Existence of value and service to the community;
- Proof of genuine rehabilitation if a criminal record exists;
- Evidence attesting to a respondent's good character.

8.b. Negative Factors

- Nature and underlying circumstances of grounds of removal;
- Additional significant immigration violations;
- Existence of criminal record;
- Other evidence of bad character or undesirability.

8.c. *Other Factors*—The IJ should also consider factors such as the potential or actual pregnancy of applicant or applicant's partner. *Drobny v. INS*, 947 F.2d 241, 246 (7th Cir. 1991) [denial of §212(c) reversed where girlfriend's pregnancy not considered]. The IJ, however, may *not* consider as a negative factor, children born out-of-wedlock or private sexual conduct between consenting adults. *Yepes-Prado v. INS*, 10 F.3d 1363, 1370 (9th Cir. 1993). In determining questions of family relationships, DHS cannot rely on state law but should maintain a uniform federal standard. *Kahn v. INS*, 36 F.3d 1412 (9th Cir. 1994) [reversing BIA rejection of family relationship because CA is not a common law marriage state]. The IJ should also consider the likelihood of persecution in determining hardship. *Bastanipour v. INS*, 980 F.2d 1129 (7th Cir. 1992) [Iranian's persecution for conversion to Christianity should be considered in §212(c) because "death is a hardship"]. *But see Matter of D-*, 20 I&N Dec. 915 (BIA 1994) [IJ did not err in refusing to consider asylum affidavits in adjudicating a §212(c) case; IJ may consider evidence of general country conditions in determining hardship for §212(c) purposes, but should not determine whether someone has a "well-founded fear"]. Other positive equities include long residence in U.S. and the existence of USC minor children. *Matter of Arreguin*, 21 I&N Dec. 38 (BIA 1995).

8.d. *Outstanding and Unusual Equities No Longer Applicable*—In light of the "aggravated felony" bar to cancellation, the BIA has rejected the use of an "outstanding and unusual equities" requirement as a threshold for relief and instead has found that the IJ should weigh the favorable and adverse factors to determine whether the "totality of the evidence" on balance indicates that a favorable exercise of discretion is warranted. *Matter of Sotelo,* 23 I&N Dec. 201, 204 (BIA 2001). *But see Chalas-Zapata v. Ashcroft,* 305 F.Supp.2d 333, 339 (S.D.N.Y. 2004) [affirming use of outstanding and unusual equities approach]. Prior case law utilizing the "outstanding and unusual equities" analysis may still be instructive: *Matter of Edwards*, 20 I&N Dec. 191 (BIA 1990); *Hazzard v. INS*, 951 F.2d 435, 438 (1st Cir. 1991) [IJ and BIA must weigh all facts and circumstances, must make a complete review of the favorable factors in the case]; *Diaz-Resendez v. INS*, 960 F.2d 493 (5th Cir. 1992) [reversing §212(c) denial and finding that IJ must actually consider and meaningfully address the positive equities and favorable evidence in its decision]; *Cortes-Castillo v. INS*, 997 F.2d 1199 (7th Cir. 1993) [where BIA summarily dismissed equities and did not provide reasons for its conclusions, §212(c) denial was reversed]; *Tipu v. INS*, 20 F.3d 580 (3d Cir. 1994) [BIA's failure to adequately explain factors it discredited and failure to consider other factors warranted reversal]; *Georgiu v. INS*, 90 F.3d 374 (9th Cir. 1996) [reversing BIA denial where it failed to address positive equities]; *Akinyemi v. INS*, 969 F.2d 285, 288 (7th Cir. 1992) [BIA must consider rehabilitation]. The IJ cannot rely on speculation unsupported by the record. *Espinoza v. INS*, 991 F.2d 1294 (7th Cir. 1993) [lack of rehabilitation]. *But see White v. INS*, 17 F.3d 475 (1st Cir. 1994) [where BIA erred in treating criminal charge as conviction, it was harmless error]. *See also Matter of Buscemi*, 19 I&N Dec. 628 (BIA 1988); *Maashio v. INS*, 45 F.3d 1235, 1239–40 (8th Cir. 1995); *Groza v. INS*, 30 F.3d 814, 820 (7th Cir. 1994); *Gouveia v. INS*, 980 F.2d 814, 817 (1st Cir. 1980); *Matter of Burbano*, 20 I&N Dec. 872 (BIA 1994); *Yepes-Prado v. INS*, 10 F.3d 1363, 1370 (9th Cir. 1993). The BIA has been criticized for simply denying all §212(c) drug cases. *Id.*; *Gonzalez v. INS*, 996 F.2d 804, 810–11 (6th Cir. 1993).

8.e. *Diminished Weight of Positive Factors*—The BIA and at least one court have found, however, that equities that accrue after a final order or after knowledge of potential deportation are diminished. *Matter of Correa*, 19 I&N Dec. 130, 134 (BIA 1984); *Ghassan v. INS*, 972 F.2d 631, 635 (5th Cir. 1992) [marriage while in deportation proceedings given less weight]. The BIA may give less weight to a record of employment, where employment was unauthorized, and long residence in the U.S., where status was undocumented. *Varela-Blanco v. INS*, 18 F.3d 584, 586–87 (8th Cir. 1994). Also, while the courts will not assume matters not addressed by the BIA, *Anderson v. McElroy*, 953 F.2d 803, 806 (2d Cir. 1992), it will not reverse the BIA where it fails to explicitly consider scant evidence of a positive equity. *Douglas v. INS*, 28 F.3d 241, 244 (2d Cir. 1994).

8.f. *Rehabilitation*—Rehabilitation, while an important factor, is not a prerequisite to obtaining a waiver, *Edwards*, *supra*, except where the conviction is recent and serious. *Matter of Roberts*, 20 I&N Dec. 294 (BIA 1991). A trial attorney's stipulation as to rehabilitation and relief is binding on IJ. *Rarogal v. INS*, 42 F.3d 570 (9th Cir. 1994). A person may be confined and still show rehabilitation. *Matter of Salmon*, 16 I&N Dec. 734 (BIA 1978); *Matter of Arreguin*, 21 I&N Dec. 38, 40 (BIA 1995) [noting that judge lowered sentence because person admitted culpability can establish rehabilitation even if s/he is still in custody]. However, DHS is not obligated to give a potential applicant time after release to show rehabilitation. *Chavez-Arreaga v. INS*, 952 F.2d 952 (7th Cir. 1991); *Matter of Silva-Rodriguez*, 20 I&N Dec. 448 (BIA 1992). Factors indicating rehabilitation include: the lack of commission of any additional crimes, enrollment in and attendance at rehabilitation programs, statements of remorse, and letters of good character. *Yepes-Prado v. INS*, 10 F.3d 1363, 1372 n.19 (9th Cir. 1993); *Georgiu v. INS*, 90 F.3d 374 (9th Cir. 1996). Moreover, the BIA cannot conclude that a person is not rehabilitated *solely* because s/he refuses to acknowledge guilt regarding her/his convictions. *Guillen-Garcia v. INS*, 999 F.2d 199 (7th Cir. 1993).

8.g. *Circumstances Surrounding the Crime*—While the IJ may inquire into the circumstances surrounding the commission of the crime in order to determine whether a favorable exercise of discretion is warranted, "it is impermissible to go behind a record of conviction to reassess an alien's ultimate guilt or innocence." *Matter of Roberts*, 20 I&N Dec. 294 (BIA 1991). *Accord Gouveia v. INS*, 980 F.2d at 817. The IJ cannot take a plea of guilty in a drug case as an admission that the person possessed any particular amount of the drug, nor can the IJ ignore facts which dispute the quantity stated in the indictment. *Martinez-Benitez v. INS*, 956 F.2d 1053, 1055 (11th Cir. 1992); *Yepes-Prado v. INS*, 10 F.3d 1363, 1371 (9th Cir. 1993) [general discussion of harmful effect of drugs instead of specific nature of person's conviction is abuse of discretion]. At least one court has found that the IJ may rely on an applicant's past conduct (*e.g.,* arrest) even if state law prevents the use of such information. *Paredes-Urrestarazu v. INS*, 36 F.3d 801 (9th Cir. 1994) [notwithstanding CA deferred adjudication statute, IJ could ask about arrest]; *but see Sierra-Reyes v. INS*, 585 F.2d 762, 764 n.2 (5th Cir. 1978). However, the reliance on an arrest where there was no conviction as a basis to deny relief is error. *Matter of Arreguin*, 21 I&N Dec. 38 (BIA 1995). *But see Henry v. INS*, 74 F.3d 1, 5–7 (1st Cir. 1996).

C. ***Cancellation of Removal and Adjustment of Status for Non-LPRs***—INA §240A(b); 8 U.S.C. §1229a(b); 8 C.F.R. §§1240.11(a), 1240.20.

1. *Eligibility*—The AG may cancel the removal and adjust the status of a non-LPR who is inadmissible or deportable if s/he:

   1.a. Has been physically present in the U.S. for a continuous period of not less than 10 years immediately preceding the date of such application;

      (1) The continuous physical presence requirement is not applicable to a person who has served at least 24 months in active duty status in the Armed Forces and if separated, received an honorable discharge and was in the U.S. at the time of her/his enlistment or induction.

      (2) Under INA §240A(d)(1), continuous physical presence for purposes of cancellation of removal is deemed to end upon service of a notice to appear, or upon commission of certain criminal acts. *See in this section*, "Continuous Physical Presence and the Stop-Time Rule," ¶ 3 (p.988), *infra*.

      (3) The review of whether a person has met the 10-year requirement is subject to the substantial-evidence test. *Santana-Albarran v. Ashcroft,* 393 F.3d 699, 705–06 (6th Cir. 2005) [applying substantial evidence standard to uphold denial of cancellation for failure to prove 10-year period where respondent submitted only oral testimony and no contemporaneously filed tax returns]; *Garcia-Melendez v. Ashcroft,* 351 F.3d 657, 661–63 (5th Cir. 2003) [applying substantial-evidence test and upholding IJ's determination that applicant did not have the requisite 10 years physical presence]. *But see Lopez-Alvarado v. Ashcroft,* 381 F.3d 847, 854 (9th Cir. 2004) [reversing IJ's decision for lack of substantial evidence where respondent's credibility was accepted but court erroneously found that substantial documentary evidence was required].

   1.b. Has been a person of good moral character for 10 years;

      (1) For good moral character criteria, *see in this chapter* part II (p.962), *supra*.

      (2) The 10-year period is calculated backward from the date on which the application is finally resolved before the IJ or BIA. *Matter of Ortega-Cabrera,* 23 I&N Dec. 793 (BIA 2005) [where alien smuggling committed in 1991 but IJ did not render cancellation decision until 2003, smuggling could not be used to demonstrate lack of good moral character].

   1.c. Has not been convicted of an offense under INA §§212(a), 237(a)(2) or 237(a)(3); and

      (1) A petty offense involving moral turpitude does not render an applicant ineligible for cancellation. *Matter of Garcia-Hernandez,* 23 I&N Dec. 590, 592–93 (BIA 2003). Nor does the conviction of a second crime along with the "petty offense" if the second crime was not a CIMT. *Id.* at 594–95.

      (2) The cancellation statute bars a convicted person described under the relevant deportation sections irrespective of the manner in which he was charged. *Gonzalez-Gonzalez v. Ashcroft,* 390 F.3d 649 (9th Cir. 2004) [respondent, who was convicted of domestic battery is barred from cancellation despite the fact that there is no domestic violence ground of inadmissibility]. However, the person must be convicted under the statute. *Matter of Gonzalez-Silva*, 24 I&N Dec. 218 (BIA 2007) [conviction which predated the effective date of INA §237(a)(2)(E) does not bar cancellation]. A conviction under IL law for reckless discharge of a rifle on New Year's Eve was sufficient to bar cancellation. *Lemus-Rodriguez v. Ashcroft,* 350 F.3d 652, 655–56 (7th Cir. 2003). Conviction for malicious punishment of a child under MN law bars cancellation because it can be considered child abuse under INA §237(a)(2)(E)(i). *Lopez-Dominguez v. Gonzales,* 428 F.3d 1156 (8th Cir. 2005).

   1.d. Establishes that removal would result in exceptional and extremely unusual hardship to his/her USC or LPR spouse, parent, or child.

      (1) While the applicant's hardship is generally not relevant, "factors that relate only to the respondent may be considered to the extent that they affect the potential level of hardship to her qualifying relatives." *Matter of Recinas,* 23 I&N Dec. 467, 471 (BIA 2002). A

son/daughter's hardship may not be considered. *Montero-Martinez v. Ashcroft,* 277 F.3d 1137, 1144–45 (9th Cir. 2002) [finding that definition of "child" does not include son/daughter who is 21 or over for purposes of §240A(b)(1)(D)]. Nor may hardship to a non-USC/LPR parent, *Molina-Estrada v. INS,* 293 F.3d 1089, 1093–94 (9th Cir. 2002), a grandchild or de facto child, *Moreno-Morante v. Gonzales,* 490 F.3d 1172 (9th Cir. 2007) [grandchild, even one in legal custody and guardianship of grandfather, can not be considered a "child" unless adopted for purposes of cancellation; nor can he be considered a "de facto child" by virtue of his sole loving relationship to grandfather], or a non-relative be considered. *Angamarca v. Gonzales,* 415 F.3d 897, 901 n.2 (8th Cir. 2005) [hardship to girlfriend's autistic son cannot be considered]. However, the existence of nonqualifying relatives may increase the hardship to a qualifying relative so they "cannot be ignored." *Matter of Recinas,* 23 I&N Dec. at 472.

(2) The BIA's interpretation of the hardship standard has been upheld in the face of a: (1) due process challenge, *Ramirez-Perez v. Ashcroft,* 336 F.3d 1001, 1005–07 (9th Cir. 2003); (2) international law challenge. *Oliva v. DOJ,* 433 F.3d 229 (2d Cir. 2005) [denying cancellation claim by the father of a USC child under Articles 3(1) and 7(1) of the United Nations Convention on the Rights of the Child because cancellation is a specific statutory provision governing the criteria to remain in the U.S. which trumps any claim based on customary international law]; *Cabrera-Alvarez v. Gonzales,* 423 F.3d 1006, 1009–13 (9th Cir. 2005) [denying claim that UN Convention on the Rights of the Child, even assuming it has attained the status of customary international law, is violated or inconsistent with the cancellation statute because Article 9(4) recognizes the potential for parents to be deported and cancellation weighs the hardship to the child]; and (3) a challenge under the Religious Freedom Restoration Act. *Fernandez v. Mukasey,* 512 F.3d 553 (9th Cir. 2008) [rejected claim that child requirement of cancellation burdens religious freedom under the RFRA where religious Catholics cannot conceive and refuse in vitro fertilization]. *See in this section,* ¶ 9 (p.993), *infra*; and

1.e. Warrants a favorable exercise of discretion.

1.f. *Eligible for Non-LPR Cancellation if LPR Status Obtained by Fraud or Mistake*—A person may apply for non-LPR cancellation, even if s/he was barred from LPR cancellation because s/he obtained LPR status by fraud or mistake. *See e.g., Obioha v. Gonzales,* 431 F.3d 400, 408–10 (4th Cir. 2005) [upholding denial of remand to apply for non-LPR cancellation where LPR status was obtained by fraud, but applicant failed to timely apply for non-LPR cancellation]. *See also Matter of Koloamatangi*, 23 I&N Dec. 548 (BIA 2003).

2. *Ineligible for Non-LPR Cancellation*—INA §240A(c):

2.a. Entered as a crewman subsequent to June 30, 1964;

2.b. Was admitted on J to receive graduate medical training whether or not s/he received a waiver, or was on J with 2-year foreign residency requirement and never fulfilled the requirement or received a waiver;

2.c. Inadmissible under INA §212(a)(3) or deportable under INA §237(a)(4) [security grounds]; *Hussain v. Mukasey,* 518 F.3d 534, 537–38 (7th Cir. 2008) [although statute stretches the definition of terrorism, it defines it—and in denying petitioner's request for cancellation, it is not relevant that the MQM-H in Pakistan did not have a political agenda and was not hostile to the U.S.];

2.d. Persecuted others under INA §241(b)(3)(B)(i);

2.e. Previously received suspension, §212(c) relief, or cancellation of removal, *Maldonado-Galindo v. Gonzales,* 456 F.3d 1064 (9th Cir. 2006) [statute barring cancellation to person previously granted §212(c) relief not impermissibly retroactive];

3. *Continuous Physical Presence and the Stop-Time Rule*—INA §240A(d)(1). The stop-time rule only applies to residence issues and "has no bearing on the other requirements for cancellation of removal, including the issues of qualifying relatives, hardship, or good moral character." *Matter of Bautista Gomez,* 23 I&N Dec. 893, 895 (BIA 2006). The constitutionality of the 10-year provision

and the stop-time rule have been upheld. *Padilla-Padilla v. Gonzales,* 463 F.3d 972, 978–79 (9th Cir. 2006) [Congress has broad powers to legislate eligibility requirements for cancellation].

3.a. *Service of NTA*—Under INA §240A(d)(1)(A), continuous physical presence for purposes of cancellation of removal is deemed to end upon service of a notice to appear. *Lagandaon v. Ashcroft,* 383 F.3d 983 (9th Cir. 2004) [stop-time rule cuts off physical presence *when* an NTA is served and therefore the 10-year period of physical presence includes the day the NTA is served]. The stop-time rule also applies where a final administrative order was issued prior to the passage of IIRIRA. *Suassuna v. INS,* 342 F.3d 578 (6th Cir. 2003) [continuous physical presence ends upon the service of an OSC even if issued prior to IIRIRA]; *Afful v. Ashcroft,* 380 F.3d 1, 6–7 (1st Cir. 2004) [same and citing cases from other circuits]; *Matter of Nolasco,* 22 I&N Dec. 632 (BIA 1999); *Rivera-Jimenez v. INS,* 214 F.3d 1213 (10th Cir. 2000). This provision (as applied to suspension) has been found to prohibit the accrual of a new (7 year) time for physical presence after service of the OSC. *Matter of Mendoza-Sandino,* 22 I&N Dec. 1236 (BIA 2000); *Casillas-Figueroa v. Gonzales,* 419 F.3d 447 (6th Cir. 2005) [rejecting position that 7 years may accrue after service of OSC]; *Al Najjar v. Ashcroft,* 257 F.3d 1262, 1299–1300 (11th Cir. 2001) [finding BIA view that seven years may not accrue subsequent to service of OSC is supported by the statute]; *Iyamba v. INS,* 244 F.3d 606, 608 (8th Cir. 2001) [rejecting claim that 7 years could start anew after service of OSC]; *Ram v. INS,* 243 F.3d 510, 517–18 (9th Cir. 2001) [same]; *McBride v. INS,* 238 F.3d 371 (5th Cir. 2000) [same]. *But see Matter of Cisneros,* 23 I&N Dec. 668 (BIA 2004) [where person departs U.S. after service of OSC he may accrue 10-year period for cancellation upon his return if placed in a subsequent removal proceeding].

3.b. *Commission of Certain Crimes*—Under INA §240A(d)(1)(B), continuous physical presence is deemed to end upon the commission of an inadmissible offense under INA §212(a)(2), or a removable offense under INA §§237(a)(2) or 237(a)(4). The 10-year period is cut off by the commission of the crime not the conviction. *Matter of Perez,* 22 I&N Dec. 689 (BIA 1999); *Matter of Robles,* 24 I&N Dec. 22, 27–28 (BIA 2006) [finding no retroactivity issue where the stop-time rule is applied to a respondent who committed the crime prior to IIRIRA but was convicted after. *Matter of Perez* reaffirmed]. The applicant need not be charged in the NTA nor found removable for a designated crime under INA §240A(d)(1)(B) for the rule to apply. *Matter of Jurado,* 24 I&N Dec. 29, 30–32 (BIA 2007) [stop-time rule applied where the CIMT was not charged in the NTA and respondent was not found removable for it]. Continuous residence is not stopped by commission of an offense that is not "referred to in section 212(a)(2)." *Matter of Campos-Torres,* 22 I&N Dec. 1289 (BIA 2000) [firearm offense]. It is also not stopped by the commission of a petty offense, even if a subsequent conviction for a CIMT would render the petty offense exception unavailable. *Matter of Deanda-Romo,* 23 I&N Dec. 597 (BIA 2003) [stop-time rule does not apply until the second conviction where the first conviction was a petty offense]. *See also Torres De La Cruz v. Maurer,* 483 F.3d 1013, 1019–22 (10th Cir. 2007) [upholding stop-time rule against due process and equal protection challenges]. A person may also not accrue a new 7 years subsequent to the commission of a crime. *Matter of Mendoza-Sandino,* 22 I&N Dec. 1236, 1241 (BIA 2000). *But see Okeke v. Gonzales,* 407 F.3d 585 (3d Cir. 2005) [in non-LPR cancellation case, a conviction does not bar the clock from restarting to allow accrual of a new 10-year residence period where applicant left the U.S. and reentered lawfully].

3.c. *Retroactivity of Criminal Stop-Time Rule*—The criminal stop-time rule although not made explicitly retroactive regarding criminal issues has been applied retroactively to pre-IIRIRA crimes, where proceedings were begun post-IIRIRA. *Briseno-Flores v. Att'y Gen. of the U.S.,* 492 F.3d 226, 229–31 (3d Cir. 2007) [respondent's conviction in 1985 stopped the time for calculating the seven years needed for suspension; nor did a new seven year period begin from that point; *Okeke distinguished*]; *Heaven v. Gonzales,* 473 F.3d 167 (5th Cir. 2006) [seven year continuous residence cut off cancellation application post-IIRIRA where conviction was pre-IIRIRA]; *Tablie v. Gonzales,* 471 F.3d 60 (2d Cir. 2006) [INA §240A(d)(1)(B), barring suspension for persons who commit crimes during the period of continuous residence applies retroactively]; *Valencia-Alvarez v. Gonzales,* 469 F.3d 1319, 1324–31 (9th Cir. 2006) [where applicant was not eligible for discretionary relief at the time he committed the offense, at the time he was convicted, or when IIRIRA became effective, the application of the stop-time rule was not impermissibly retroactive; *Sinotes-Cruz* distinguished because applicant in that case was eligible for relief before IIRIRA's effective date]; *Peralta v. Gonzales,* 441 F.3d 23, (1st Cir. 2006) [respondent ineligible for suspension because criminal stop-time provision applies retroactively, and his conviction for marriage fraud was a CIMT committed during the necessary 10-year period]; *Hernandez v. Gonzales,* 437 F.3d 341, 346–53 (3d Cir. 2006) [rejecting retroactivity argument for person seeking suspension who committed crime before IIRIRA on ground that he was still ineligible after plea because he could not establish 10 years of good moral character]; *Matter of Jurado,* 24 I&N Dec. 29, 32 (BIA 2007) [following *Matter of Perez,* 22 I&N Dec. 689 (BIA 1999) and *Matter of Robles,* 24 I&N Dec. 22 (BIA 2006),the stop-time rule may be applied retroactively even if the commission of the offense preceded IIRIRA]. *But see Sinotes-Cruz v. Gonzales,* 468 F.3d 1190, 1197–1203 (9th Cir. 2006) [the stop-time rule, regarding the commission of criminal offenses, can not be applied retroactively under the second step of *Landgraf* to bar LPR's cancellation of removal]; *Generi v. Ashcroft,* 2004 U.S. Dist. LEXIS 6396 (W.D. Mich. 2004).

3.d. *Other Challenges to the Application of the Stop-Time Rule—Aoun v. INS,* 342 F.3d 503 (6th Cir. 2003) [where BIA continued respondent's appeal for one reason or another for 12 years during which time the stop-time rule was enacted, the court declined to impose the rule on the applicant]; *Otarola v. INS,* 270 F.3d 1272 (9th Cir. 2001) [the stop-time rule should not apply where IJ granted suspension and INS took a frivolous appeal to permit the stop-time rule to be applied]; *Guadalupe-Cruz v. INS,* 240 F.3d 1209 (9th Cir. 2001) *opinion corrected* 250 F.3d 1271 (9th Cir. 2001) [where IIRIRA was not in effect and IJ erroneously applied stop- time rule, decision was reversed and IJ ordered to apply pre-IIRIRA law but with current facts]; *Tang v. INS,* 223 F.3d 713 (8th Cir. 2000) [where petitioner and INS stipulated to a date for the service of the OSC beyond the 7 years, no bar to suspension]; *Arrozal v. INS,* 159 F.3d 429, 434 & n.2 (9th Cir. 1998) [stop-time rule does not apply to motion to reopen where final order was obtained prior to Apr. 1, 1997 and possibly by applicant accruing more than seven years since the OSC]; *But see Raffington v. Cangemi,* 399 F.3d 900, 902–03 (8th Cir. 2005) [rejecting *Otarola* and holding that even if the government had filed a frivolous, but ultimately successful appeal, it would not constitute affirmative misconduct to estop the government].

4. *Certain Breaks in Continuous Physical Presence*—Physical presence shall be broken if an individual departs the U.S. for any period in excess of 90 days or for any periods in the aggregate exceeding 180 days during the ten-year period INA §240A(d)(2), 8 U.S.C. §1229b(d)(2). *Acevedo-Aguilar v. Mukasey,* 517 F.3d 8 (1st Cir. 2008) [cancellation denied because respondent departed the U.S. for more than 90 days]; *Sabido Valdivia v. Gonzales,* 423 F.3d 1144, 1149 (10th Cir. 2005) [same]; *Garcia-Ramirez v. Gonzales,* 423 F.3d 935, 938–47 (9th Cir. 2005) [the 90/180 day provision applies retroactively to person who departed for five months before IIRIRA; but majority questioned prior precedent]. A departure under a grant of voluntary departure also breaks physical presence, even if for less than 90 days. *Matter of Romalez-Alcaide,* 23 I&N Dec. 423 (BIA 2002) [a departure under threat of deportation breaks physical presence for purposes of cancellation]; *Palomino v. Ashcroft,* 354 F.3d 942 (8th Cir. 2004) [departure for 90/180 days is not the exclusive means to cut off the requisite 10-year period]; *Vasquez-Lopez v. Ashcroft,* 315 F.3d 1201 (9th Cir. 2003) [departure under VD broke the continuous physical presence and petitioner was served with an NTA within 10 years of his return]; *Mireles-Valdez v. Ashcroft,* 349 F.3d 213, 217–19 (5th Cir. 2003) [adopting *Matter of Romalez-Alcaide*]. One court has held that the act of withdrawing an application for admission at the border breaks continuous physical presence. *Mendez-Reyes v. Att'y Gen. of the U.S.,* 428 F.3d 187 (3d Cir. 2005). In *Matter of Avilez-Nava,* 23 I&N Dec. 799, 805–06 (BIA 2005), the BIA distinguished *Romalez-Alcaide* and found that a person turned away at the border who has been out of the U.S. for less than 90/180 days will not break continuous physical presence "unless there is evidence that the alien was formally excluded or made subject to an order of expedited removal, was offered and accepted the opportunity to withdraw his or her application for admission, or was subjected to any other formal, documented process pursuant to which the alien was determined to be inadmissible to the U.S." *See also Ibarra-Flores v. Gonzales,* 439 F.3d 614, 618–20 (9th Cir. 2006) [reversing IJ because there was no substantial evidence that respondent knowingly and voluntarily accepted administrative VD]; *Reyes-Vasquez v. Ashcroft,* 395 F.3d 903, 907–09 (8th Cir. 2005) [10-year period not broken because applicant, who was not out of the country more than 90 days, was not granted VD, but was

simply turned away at the border]; *Morales-Morales v. Ashcroft,* 384 F.3d 418 (7th Cir. 2004) [same]; *Tapia v. Gonzales,* 430 F.3d 997 (9th Cir. 2005) [physical presence not broken where applicant turned away at border and his photograph and fingerprints were taken by border officers, but no formal written agreement was made specifying the terms of departure; *Avilez* distinguished on issue of documented process]; *Ortiz-Cornejo v. Gonzales,* 400 F.3d 610 (8th Cir. 2005) [where immigration officers stopped person at border on two occasions but there is no evidence that his departure occurred under the threat of deportation or removal proceedings, the record does not support a break in physical presence]. However, a person who departs the U.S. through expedited removal severs continuous residence, *Juarez-Ramos v. Gonzales,* 485 F.3d 509 (9th Cir. 2007), as does a prior order of exclusion, deportation, or removal, *Landin-Zavala v. Gonzales,* 488 F.3d 1150 (9th Cir. 2007) (prior exclusion order).

5. *VWP Entrant*—Although no case has addressed the question of whether a visa waiver program (VWP) entrant is eligible for cancellation, the Tenth Circuit found a VWP entrant ineligible for suspension because in exchange for the streamlined entry procedure, the nonimmigrant agrees to waive the right to contest a removal order, other than on the basis of an application for asylum. *Itaeva v. INS,* 314 F.3d 1238, 1241–43 (10th Cir. 2003).

6. *Special Rule Cancellation for Battered Spouse or Child*—PL 106-386 §1504(a)(2)(A)(II), 114 Stat. 1464 (2000) *codified at* INA §240A(b)(2), 8 U.S.C. §1229b(b)(2).

6.a. The AG may grant cancellation of removal if: (i) a person has been battered or subjected to extreme cruelty by a spouse or parent who is or was a USC or LPR (or is the parent of a child of a USC or LPR and the child has been battered or subject to extreme cruelty by the USC or LPR); (ii) the person has been physically present in the U.S. for a continuous period of not less than 3 years immediately preceding the date of the application; (iii) the person is of good moral character during the 3 years; (iv) the person is not inadmissible under §§212(a)(2) or (3), is not deportable under §§237(a)(1)(G), (2), (3), or (4), and has not been convicted of an aggravated felony; and (v) the removal would result in extreme hardship to the person, the person's child or the person's parents. The 3-year period is not cut off by the filing of an NTA/OSC but rather by the filing of the suspension/cancellation application.

6.b. Special extreme hardship factors tailored to domestic violence apply. 8 C.F.R. §§1240.58(c), 1240.20.

6.c. The extreme cruelty standard may be subject to judicial review. *Hernandez v. Ashcroft,* 345 F.3d 824, 833–35 (9th Cir. 2003) [analyzing extreme cruelty standard and finding that despite the word "extreme," a determination of extreme cruelty is not a discretionary decision similar to extreme hardship; it is subject to judicial review because it is a matter of fact that can be ascertained on an objective basis]. *See also Angamarca v. Gonzales,* 415 F.3d 897, 901 (8th Cir. 2005) [reviewing denial of cancellation for substantial evidence but upholding denial of claim]. *But see Perales-Cumpean v. Gonzales,* 429 F.3d 977, 982–84 (10th Cir. 2005) [rejecting *Hernandez* and finding that a determination of extreme cruelty or credibility issues in determining special rule cancellation are barred from judicial review by INA §242(a)(2)(B)(i)]; *Wilmore v. Gonzales,* 455 F.3d 524 (5th Cir. 2006) [followed *Perales-Cumpean* and determined that REAL ID Act did not afford greater jurisdiction under INA §242(a)(2)(D)].

6.d. The AG may consider any credible evidence and the determination of credible evidence and the weight to given it is solely in the discretion of the AG. *But see Lopez-Umanzor v. Gonzales,* 405 F.3d 1049 (9th Cir. 2005) [finding due process violation where IJ refused to permit expert testimony regarding domestic violence where it could have affected IJ's view of respondent's credibility].

6.e. A battered spouse or child is ineligible for relief if s/he were out of the U.S. more than 90 days at one time or 180 days in the aggregate during the 3-year period. However, no absence will count toward the 90/180 days if there is a connection between the absence and the battering/extreme cruelty. INA §240A(b)(2)(B).

6.f. Section 101(f) shall not be a bar to good moral character if the AG determines that the act or conviction was connected to the person having been battered or subjected to extreme cruelty and a waiver is otherwise warranted. INA §240A(b)(2)(C). At least one circuit has found under the former suspension provision for battered spouses that the BIA may consider actions which occurred outside of the three year period, including expunged convictions, to inform the court of the rehabilitation and reform of the applicant. *Ikenokwalu-White v. INS,* 316 F.3d 798, 804–06 (8th Cir. 2003).

6.g. The child of a person granted cancellation/suspension or the parent of a child granted cancellation/suspension may be paroled into the U.S. until his or her status is adjusted. INA §240A(b)(4), 8 U.S.C. §1229b(b)(4).

7. *Limitation on Grant of Cancellation and Adjustment of Status*—The Act limits the number of people whose removal may be cancelled and who may adjust status to 4,000 per fiscal year. INA §240A(e)(1). This cap applies only to non-LPR cancellation and suspension of deportation. *Id.* Conditional grants of cancellation or suspension pending the availability of a numerical allocation are not permitted for persons after FY 1998. 8 C.F.R. §1240.21(c)(1). If the person applies for and is granted other forms of relief, such as asylum or withholding, the suspension or cancellation application shall be denied as a matter of discretion. 8 C.F.R. §1240.21(c)(2). Persons previously granted conditional suspension or cancellation maintain their conditional status until the numerical limitation is reached, and may travel during the conditional period. 8 C.F.R. §§1240.21(b)(3), (5). However, there is no limit on the number of grants under NACARA. INA §240A(e)(3).

8. *Changes from Suspension of Deportation Under Former* INA §§244(a)(1) and (2). Suspension of deportation under former INA §§244(a)(1) and (2) was available to persons who had been continuously present in the U.S. for 7 or 10 years, could establish good moral character and show that their deportation would cause extreme hardship (for 7-year provision) or exceptional and extremely unusual hardship (for 10-year provision) to themselves, or their USC/LPR spouse, parent or child.

8.a. *Generally*—Seven-year suspension was removed from the INA by IIRIRA and the standard under the former 10-year suspension provision—exceptional and extremely unusual hardship—is now the standard for cancellation. However, while 10-year suspension was available to persons who committed certain crimes, cancellation is not available to persons convicted of an offense under INA §§212(a)(2), 237(a)(2) or 237(a)(3). In addition, cancellation is only available upon a showing of hardship to a USC/LPR spouse, parent or child; hardship to the applicant is no longer sufficient. Congress clearly intended to make the standards for cancellation more restrictive than those for suspension. H.R. Conf. Rep. 104-828, 104th Cong., 2d Sess. (1996) at 213–14.

8.b. *Cancellation is Available to Inadmissible and Deportable Persons*—Cancellation, unlike suspension, is now available to persons formerly in exclusion proceedings, because it applies to persons who are inadmissible as well as deportable. INA §240A(b)(1).

8.c. *Tolling of Physical Presence*—The 10-year time period no longer runs until there is a final administrative order. Physical presence is now tolled by the service of an NTA or the commission of certain criminal offenses. Compare INA §240A(d)(1) *with Cipriano v. INS*, 24 F.3d 763 (5th Cir. 1994). *See in this section*, ¶ 3 (p.988), *supra*.

8.d. *Breaks in Physical Presence*—The "brief, casual and innocent" standard for determining when there has been a break in physical presence is replaced by a rule that terminates physical presence if a person is outside the U.S. for 90 days or 180 days in the aggregate during the 10-year period. INA §240A(d)(2). It also terminates if the applicant previously departed through voluntary departure even if less than 90 days, *Matter of Romalez-Alcaide,* 23 I&N Dec. 423 (BIA 2002), but does not terminate if the person was simply turned away at the border. *Matter of Avilez-Nava,* 23 I&N Dec. 799, 805–06 (BIA 2005). One court has held that the act of withdrawing an application for admission terminates physical presence. *Mendez-Reyes v. Att'y Gen. of the U.S.,* 428 F.3d 187 (3d Cir. 2005). A person who departs the U.S. through expedited removal procedures also severs physical presence. *Juarez-Ramos v. Gonzales,* 485 F.3d 509 (9th Cir. 2007). *See in this section* ¶ 4 (p.990), *supra.*

8.e. *Retroactivity*—The government may not apply IIRIRA's repeal of suspension of deportation retroactively. *Hernandez de Anderson v. Gonzales,* 497 F.3d 927, 937–44 (9th Cir. 2007) [the BIA erred in impermissibly repealing suspension of deportation where person was convicted after trial and was placed in removal proceedings after seeking naturalization one year before the passage of IIRIRA]; *Lopez-Castellanos v. Gonzales,* 437 F.3d 848, 851–54 (9th Cir. 2006) [following *St. Cyr,* suspension was not barred to a person who pre-IIRIRA, pled guilty to a crime that barred him from cancellation]. *But see Hernandez v. Gonzales,* 437 F.3d 341, 346–53 (3d Cir. 2006) [rejecting retroactivity argument for person seeking repealed 10-year suspension, who committed criminal conduct before IIRIRA on ground that after he entered plea he was still ineligible for lack of 10 years of good moral character].

9. *Criteria for Establishing Hardship*—The criteria for establishing hardship has been changed from "extreme hardship" to "exceptional and extremely unusual hardship." *Matter of Monreal,* 23 I&N Dec. 56 (BIA 2001) [must show more than extreme hardship but need not show that hardship would be unconscionable; denying relief because respondent was in good health and able to support USC family in Mexico]. In making the change and applying the stricter standard, Congress clearly intended to narrow the scope of persons eligible for relief. H.R. Conf. Rep. 104-828, 104th Cong., 2d Sess. (1996) at 213–14. However, the BIA has noted that "the hardship standard is not so restrictive that only a handful of applicants, such as those who have a qualifying relative with a serious medical condition, will qualify for relief." *Matter of Recinas,* 23 I&N Dec. 467, 470 (BIA 2002). In granting relief in *Recinas*, the BIA considered: (1) USC children do not know any other way of life than in U.S. and do not read or write in the language of country of deportation, and do not speak that language well; (2) USC children entirely dependent upon respondent for financial and emotional support because parents divorced and father not involved; (3) Respondent's ability to care for children if deported will be substantially hampered where she has LPR mother assisting her in U.S. and no family in country of deportation; (4) Strong family system in U.S. which has provided financial and emotional support without which respondent's hardship would increase and would effect hardship of USC children; (5) Respondent's prospects of immigrating are unrealistic due to backlog of visa availability. *Matter of Recinas*, 23 I&N Dec. at 469–72. *But see Matter of Andazola,* 23 I&N Dec. 319 (BIA 2002) [reversing IJ grant to single mother of 2 young USC children where children would be denied educational benefits but not deprived of schooling, would suffer some economic hardship but had father's support, had extended family in U.S. but family was illegal, and the mother had accumulated savings, owned a house and had two vehicles which could ease transition].

The former criteria concerning extreme hardship are instructive to the extent they relate to persons other than the respondent. *Matter of Monreal, supra* at 63.

9.a. *Generally*—Age of the subject; family ties in the U.S. and abroad; length of residency in the U.S.; health/medical conditions; conditions in country of removal—economic and political; financial status—business and occupation; the possibility of other means of legalizing status; immigration history; and position in/ties to the community. *Matter of Anderson*, 16 I&N Dec. 596 (BIA 1978). In *Matter of Ige*, 20 I&N Dec. 880, 882 (BIA 1994), the BIA found that "relevant factors though not extreme in themselves, must be considered in the aggregate in determining whether extreme hardship exists." *See also Matter of O-J-O-*, 21 I&N Dec. 381 (BIA 1996) and citations to all previous BIA decisions on extreme hardship in opinion of Member Holmes, D. In *Matter of Pilch*, 21 I&N Dec. 627 (BIA 1996), the BIA looked at substantial economic, family, emotional, medical, educational and other factors where there were 3 young USC children and where the father had a successful business and determined that individually or collectively there was no extreme hardship]. *But see Matter of Kao & Lin,* 23 I&N Dec. 45, 51 (BIA 2001) [finding extreme hardship to 15-year-old USC daughter; distinguishing *Pilch* because children in *Pilch* were younger and spoke the language of the parent's country]. The BIA has found that birth of USC child or "second class" medical facilities in a foreign country are not *per se* extreme hardship. *Matter of Correa*, 19 I&N Dec. 130 (BIA 1984).

9.b. *Family Separation*—Separation from family may be "[t]he most important single [hardship] factor." *Salcido-Salcido v. INS*, 138 F.3d 1292 (9th Cir. 1998); *Arrozal v. INS,* 159 F.3d 429, 433 (9th Cir. 1998); *Opoka v. INS*, 94 F.3d 392 (7th Cir. 1996) [where wife granted suspension after husband's application was denied, the denial was reversed]; *Babai v. INS*, 985 F.2d 252 (6th Cir. 1993) [failure to consider hardship to USC child if he remained is reversible error]; *Ramos v. INS*, 695 F.2d 181 (5th Cir. 1983); *Mejia-Carrillo v. INS*, 656 F.2d 520 (6th Cir. 1981); *Cerrillo-Perez v. INS*, 809 F.2d 1419 (9th Cir. 1987); *Matter of Kao & Lin,* 23 I&N Dec. 45, 50 (BIA 2001) [hardship to children is "an important fact that must receive close attention in evaluating a suspension claim"]. The BIA has held that the test is the hardship to the USC child if taken to the respondent's country, and in the absence of such hardship, the decision to permit the child to remain in U.S. is a personal decision of the parents. *Matter of Ige*, 20 I&N Dec. 880 (BIA 1994). Further, to give any weight to the claim of separation, the respondent parent must submit an affidavit stating it is their intention for the child to remain in the U.S., accompanied by evidence that reasonable provision will be made for child's care and support. *Id. Perez v. INS*, 96 F.3d 390, 393 (9th Cir. 1996) [affirming BIA's denial but questioning the interpretation that separation is really parental choice, not deportation]. Also, hardship can only be to qualifying family members under the statute. *INS v. Hector*, 479 U.S. 85 (1986) [hardship to niece cannot be considered].

9.c. *Economic Hardship*—Economic hardship may be sufficient where there is complete inability to find work, *Urban v. INS*, 123 F.3d 644, 648 (7th Cir. 1997); *Carrette-Michel v. INS*, 749 F.2d 490 (8th Cir. 1984); *but see Luna-Rodriguez v. INS*, 104 F.3d 313, 315 (10th Cir. 1997) [inability to find work without more is insufficient], or where coupled with other factors such as a disabled USC father, *Matter of Louie*, 10 I&N Dec. 223 (BIA 1963), or where the loss of employment created psychological problems because it severely frustrates the person's life plan to support her/his family. *Tukhowinich v. INS*, 64 F.3d 460 (9th Cir. 1995) [can consider noneconomic hardship that flows from economic concerns].

9.d. *Psychiatric and Medical Concerns*—Psychiatric information must be considered. *Ravancho v. INS*, 658 F.2d 169 (3d Cir. 1981). Medical hardship must also be considered. *Biggs v. INS*, 55 F.3d 1398 (9th Cir. 1995) [where applicant made *prima facie* showing of medical hardship it was abuse of discretion for IJ and BIA to preclude development of record].

9.e. *Lack of Enforcement of a Final Order*—DHS's intentional lack of enforcement of a final order may be considered in establishing "extreme hardship." *Matter of Pena-Diaz*, 20 I&N Dec. 841 (BIA 1994).

9.f. *Persecution*—Persecution may evidence extreme hardship but the BIA has not accorded it great weight. *Gebremichael v. INS*, 10 F.3d 28, 40 (1st Cir. 1993). However, "violence and threats that fail to establish the political, religious, or ethnic motivation necessary for asylum may nonetheless be probative of extreme hardship qualifying for suspension." *Blanco v. INS*, 68 F.3d 642, 646 (2d Cir. 1995). Moreover, once the IJ/BIA makes the decision to consider persecution in the context of a suspension claim, "the five asylum grounds become irrelevant" *Ordonez v. INS,* 137 F.3d 1120 (9th Cir. 1998).

9.g. *Community Ties and Acculturation*—Community assistance is a factor in determining whether there is extreme hardship. *Urbina-Osejo v. INS*, 124 F.3d 1314, 1319 (9th Cir. 1997) [volunteering to do AIDS work]; *Salameda v. INS*, 70 F.3d 447, 450 (7th Cir. 1995). Acculturation is a factor in determining hardship. *Urbina-Osejo v. INS*, 124 F.3d 1314, 1318 (9th Cir. 1997); *Matter of O-J-O-*, 21 I&N Dec. 381 (BIA 1996).

9.h. *Must Consider Each Factor*—DHS can only consider factors which can be taken into account, and cannot ignore factors which must be taken into account. *Rodriguez-Lariz v. INS,* 282 F.3d 1218, 1227 (9th Cir. 2002) [reversing BIA denial of motion to reopen for suspension where Board "merely repeated petitioners' claims and summarily dismissed them…[and] "did not give careful and individualized consideration to the hardship"]. IJ/BIA must consider all relevant facts bearing on extreme hardship, *Ordonez v. INS*, 137 F.3d 1120 (9th Cir. 1998) [failed to consider persecution]; *Gutierrez-Centeno v. INS*, 99 F.3d 1529 (9th Cir. 1996) [BIA failed to consider evidence of hardship]; *Watkins v. INS*, 63 F.3d 844 (9th Cir. 1995) [BIA failed to consider all factors and their cumulative effect]; *Salameda v. INS*, 70 F.3d 447 (7th Cir. 1995) [failed to consider community service]; *Cerrillo-Perez v. INS*, 809 F.2d 1419 (9th Cir. 1987), and must articulate the reasons for denying suspension. *Dulane v. INS*, 46 F.3d 988, 994–96 (10th Cir. 1995) [where BIA gave no indication it actually considered all relevant evidence, denial of motion to reopen for suspension reversed]; *Turri v. INS*, 997 F.2d 1306 (10th Cir. 1993) [reversing denial of suspension for person who had performed substantial work in the community for failure to "actually consider" all relevant factors]; *Jara-Navarrette v. INS*, 813 F.2d 1340 (9th Cir. 1986); *Ravancho v. INS*, 658 F.2d 169 (3d Cir. 1981). "Relevant factors, though not extreme in themselves, must be considered in the aggregate in determining whether extreme hardship exists." *Matter of Ige*, 20 I&N Dec. 880 (BIA

1994). The BIA also abuses its discretion where it mistakenly refers to material not considered by the IJ, relies on an IJ's opinion that lacks consideration of all relevant factors, and fails to support its conclusions with reasoned explanations. *Tukhowinich v. INS*, 64 F.3d 460 (9th Cir. 1995). At least one court has emphasized "many times before, that witnesses' testimony and other evidence may not be rejected on credibility grounds without a specific finding accompanied by a clear and direct explanation of persuasive reasons for such rejection." *Vera-Villegas v. INS,* 330 F.3d 1222, 1225 (9th Cir. 2003) [IJ's finding that applicant failed to establish physical presence was supported by speculation and conjecture and not substantial evidence].

9.i. *Equities*—In balancing equities for suspension or voluntary departure, equities which are acquired after a final deportation order (*i.e.*, birth of USC child) are entitled to less weight. Additionally, DHS may consider a person's immigration history or history with the agency, (*i.e.*, did s/he abscond). *Matter of Correa*, 19 I&N Dec. 130 (BIA 1984).

9.j. *Current Hardship Information*—The applicant has the right to update information before IJ and decision must be based on current information. *Jara-Navarette, supra*; *Figueroa-Rincon v. INS*, 770 F.2d 766 (9th Cir. 1985).

10. *Application*—Application must be made at a removal hearing, 8 C.F.R. §§1240.11(a)(1), 1240.20, on Form EOIR-42B with fee in accordance with 8 C.F.R. §1240.20(a) [citing to §103.7(b)(1)]. Where person is apparently eligible, IJ must inform him or her of right to apply. *Duran v. INS*, 756 F.2d 1338 (9th Cir. 1985).

11. *Effective Date for Cancellation and the Status of Suspension Applications Currently Pending*—The effective date for the changes from suspension of deportation under former INA §244(a) to non-LPR cancellation of removal under INA §240A is Apr. 1, 1997. IIRIRA §309(a), (c). Thus, a person who was in deportation proceedings before Apr. 1, 1997, can continue to apply for suspension under the old standards if s/he qualifies. Persons placed in removal proceedings on or after Apr. 1, 1997 must apply for cancellation of removal. However, if deportation proceedings had commenced prior to Apr. 1, 1997, but an evidentiary hearing had not been conducted, the AG could elect to proceed under removal proceedings where only cancellation would be available. IIRIRA §309(c)(2). Moreover, if an evidentiary hearing had been conducted before Apr. 1, 1997, the AG could terminate proceedings and begin again under the new procedures. IIRIRA §309(c)(3). Thus, a person would have to be eligible for cancellation if the AG decided to begin proceedings anew under the removal statute.

12. *Suspension of Deportation Under NACARA §203*—Congress exempted certain Salvadorans, Guatemalans and Eastern Europeans from the harsh consequences of the retroactive application of IIRIRA §309(c)(5) thereby permitting them to apply for suspension of deportation or special rule cancellation of removal if they meet the "old" suspension requirements (7 years, good moral character, extreme hardship; or 10 years, good moral character, exceptional and extremely unusual hardship). However, special rule cancellation is more generous than the former suspension because good moral character under the statute's language relates only to the seven years immediately preceding the application. *Cuadra v. Gonzales,* 417 F.3d 947, 950–52 (8th Cir. 2005) [events that demonstrate lack of good moral character after the application is filed are not relevant and cannot bar relief]; NACARA §203; 8 C.F.R. §240.66(b). *But see Matter of Garcia,* 24 I&N Dec. 179 (BIA 2007) [rejecting *Cuadra* and determining that special rule cancellation applications are continuing for both moral character and the 7 year residence requirement and that 7 years can accrue after application is filed]. The 4,000 cap in grants does not apply to cancellation or suspension under NACARA. INA §240A(e)(3), 8 U.S.C. §1229b(e)(3). DHS regulations are found at 8 C.F.R. §§240.58, 1240.58 *et seq.*

12.a. *Salvadorans*—Are eligible for cancellation under former suspension rules if not convicted of an aggravated felony and:

(1) Not apprehended after Dec. 19, 1990 at the time of entry and (a) first entered the U.S. on or before Sept. 19, 1990 and (b) registered for benefits pursuant to the settlement agreement in *American Baptist Churches v. Thornburgh*, 760 F.Supp. 796 (N.D. Cal. 1991) on or before Oct. 31, 1991, or applied for TPS on or before Oct. 31, 1991; or

(2) Filed an application for asylum on or before Apr. 1, 1990 *Hernandez-Mezquita v. Ashcroft,* 293 F.3d 1161 (9th Cir. 2002) [due process and equal protection were not violated by requiring the Apr. 1, 1990 filing date for asylum applications];

(3) Spouse and children are covered and sons/daughters are covered if the son/daughter entered the U.S. on or before Oct. 1, 1990. However, if the primary spouse was *granted* NACARA relief, the 7 years may begin after Oct. 1, 1990. IIRIRA §309(c)(5)(C)(i)(III). *See generally Matter of Garcia,* 24 I&N Dec. 179 (BIA 2007) [spouse of Salvadoran husband granted NACARA entered the U.S. in 1997 and BIA agreed the 7 years accrue at any time after that date before a final order is issued].

(4) Not convicted of certain crimes that would result in deportation. A crime that would result in deportation does not apply to a special rule cancellation case where the person is inadmissible and not deportable. Memo, Langlois, Chief, Asylum Division, USCIS, HQRIAO 120/15.22 (Sept. 6, 2007), *published on* AILA InfoNet at Doc. No. 07092562 [declining to apply *Gonzalez-Gonzalez v. Ashcroft,* 390 F.3d 649 (9th Cir. 2004) to special rule cases and determining that an applicant convicted of domestic violence, stalking or child abuse as described in INA §237(a)(2)(E)(i) after Sept. 30, 1996 who is inadmissible cannot be barred for that reason because it is not a ground of inadmissibility, but may be used to determine good moral character].

12.b. *Guatemalans*—Same rules as Salvadorans except they had to have entered the U.S. on or before Oct. 1, 1990 and have registered for benefits under *ABC* before Dec. 31, 1991.

12.c. *ABC Class Members Include*:

(1) Nationals of El Salvador who submitted an *ABC* registration form to the Service on or before Oct. 31, 1991, or applied for TPS on or before Oct. 31, 1991.

(2) Nationals of Guatemala who submitted an *ABC* registration form to the Service on or before Dec. 31, 1991.

(3) Individuals who are *ABC* class members but who did not file for asylum by a certain date (Feb. 16, 1996 for Salvadorans and Jan. 3, 1995 for Guatemalans) are still eligible for NACARA benefits and entitled to the presumption of hardship, 8 C.F.R. §§240.61(a)(1) & (2), 240.64(d)(1), 1240.61(a)(1) & (2), 1240.64(d)(1). However, the asylum office does not have jurisdiction over these applications. 8 C.F.R. §§240.62, 1240.62.

12.d. *Eastern Europeans*:

(1) Entered the U.S. on or before Dec. 31, 1990;

(2) Filed an application for asylum on or before Dec. 31, 1991;

(3) At the time of filing asylum was a national of the Soviet Union, Russia, any republic of the former Soviet Union, Latvia, Estonia, Lithuania, Poland, Czechoslovakia, Romania, Hungary, Bulgaria, Albania, East Germany, Yugoslavia, or any state of the former Yugoslavia;

(4) Not convicted of an aggravated felony.

12.e. *Asylum Office Jurisdiction*—Asylum officers have jurisdiction to consider the suspension claim if the asylum application *is still pending* with the asylum office and the person is a qualified: (1) Salvadoran *ABC* class member who filed a completed asylum application before Jan. 31, 1996 (with an administrative grace period extended to Feb. 16, 1996); (2) Guatemalan *ABC* class member who filed a completed asylum application on or before Jan. 3, 1995; (3) Salvadoran or Guatemalan who filed for asylum on or before Apr. 1, 1990; (4) Eastern European as defined in 8 C.F.R. §1240.61(a)(3), who filed for asylum on or before Dec. 31, 1991; or (5) spouse, child, or unmarried son/daughter under 8 C.F.R. §§240.61(a)(4) & (5), 1240.61(a)(4) & (5) whose parent or spouse has an application pending for suspension or has been granted relief. 8 C.F.R. §§240.62(a), 1240.62(a). The applicant must provide his or her own interpreter for interviews conducted at the asylum office. The interview shall be conducted in a nonadversarial manner; applicants may present witnesses, affidavits of witnesses and other evidence. 8 C.F.R. §§240.67(b), 1240.67(b). If the applicant fails to appear at the interview without prior authorization or fails to appear for fingerprint processing without reasonable excuse, his or her case may be dismissed. 8 C.F.R. §§240.68,

1240.68. If the DHS grants cancellation or suspension, the person is adjusted to LPR status as of the date of the grant. 8 C.F.R. §§240.70(b), (c), 1240.70(b), (c). If the asylum officer denies both cancellation and asylum, the case is referred to immigration court. §§240.70(d), 1240.70(d).

12.f. *IJ Jurisdiction*—The immigration court has jurisdiction if the person has been served with an OSC or NTA *after* the document has been filed with the court. 8 C.F.R. §240.62(b), §1240.62(b). The only exceptions to IJ jurisdiction are: (1) *ABC* class members whose cases have been administratively closed or continued (including those with final orders who filed and were granted motions to reopen) and who have not yet had a *de novo* asylum interview pursuant to the *ABC* settlement agreement, 8 C.F.R. §§240.62(b)(1), (2), 1240.62(b)(1); (2) the spouses, children, and unmarried sons/daughters of any qualified applicants where the principal applicants' IJ proceedings have been administratively closed (or BIA proceedings continued) to permit the principal applicant to file with DHS. If the spouse, child, or unmarried son/daughter of a qualified NACARA applicant is in proceedings, s/he may seek a continuance until the spouse or parent's cancellation application is decided. EOIR and legacy INS have set forth standards for determining whether continuances will be granted and when INS will join in a motion to continue. Memo, Creppy, Chief IJ, EOIR (May 13, 1998), *published on* AILA InfoNet at Doc. No. 98051391; and Memo, Virtue, G.C. (HQCOU 90/20-P) (May 28, 1998), *reprinted in* 75 No 24 *Interpreter Releases* 885, 897–99 (June 29, 1998).

12.g. *Application*—The application must be filed on form I-881. If an applicant submitted form EOIR-40 with EOIR before June 21, 1999 and later qualifies to submit the application to DHS, s/he may submit form EOIR-40 with the first page of the I-881. After June 21, 1999, form I-881 is required whether the filing is with EOIR or DHS. 8 C.F.R. §1240.63(b).

12.h. *Eligibility*—8 C.F.R. §§1240.64–.66. An applicant must be continuously physically presence in the U.S. for 7 years. Service of the NTA or OSC will not stop the accrual of physical presence. Absences of less than 90 days or 180 days in the aggregate do not break physical presence. However, voluntary departure under threat of deportation/removal does break physical presence, even if less than 90 days. 8 C.F.R. §1240.64(b)(3). The determination of whether any period in excess of the 90/180 days will be considered brief will be evaluated on "a case-by-case" basis. 8 C.F.R. §1240.64(b)(1). An applicant is not eligible if s/he has been convicted of an aggravated felony, was involved in Nazi persecution, or was barred from eligibility by former §242B(e) relating to *in absentia* orders. 8 C.F.R. §1240.65(a).

12.i. *Proving the Claim*—The criteria to prove a claim under this program is the same as proving a suspension claim with the exception of the special presumption for Salvadorans and Guatemalans and special provisions for battered spouses and children. DHS has listed numerous factors for an examiner to consider at 8 C.F.R. §1240.58, noting in the commentary that it is a "non-exclusive and broadly worded list." 64 Fed. Reg. 27856, 27867 (May 21, 1999).

12.j. *Special Presumption of Extreme Hardship for Salvadorans and Guatemalans*—DHS regulations provide that an *ABC* class member or a Salvadoran or Guatemalan who filed for asylum during the relevant periods "shall be presumed to have established that deportation or removal from the United States would result in extreme hardship." 8 C.F.R. §1240.64(d)(1). Under 8 C.F.R. §1240.64(d)(2) the presumption "shall be rebutted" if the evidence in the record establishes that it is more likely than not that neither the applicant nor a qualified relative would suffer extreme hardship after considering the relevant hardship factors established in 8 C.F.R. §1240.58. However, the commentary to the regulations provide a narrower reading regarding rebutting the presumption: "Generally, the presumption will be overcome only under two circumstances. First,...where there is no evidence of factors associated with extreme hardship (for example, an applicant who has no family in the United States, no work history, and no ties to the community). Second, evidence contained in the record could significantly undermine the basic assumptions on which the presumption is based. For example, if an individual has acquired significant resources or property in his or her home country, the individual and his or her qualified family members may be able to return without experiencing extreme hardship, in the absence of other hardship factors in the case (such as serious medical treatment for which there is no treatment in the home country)." 64 Fed. Reg. 27856, 27866 (May 21, 1999).

12.k. *Motions to Reopen*—If a Salvadoran, Guatemalan or Eastern European had a final order of deportation or removal, s/he had to file a motion to reopen between Jan. 16, 1998 and Sept. 11, 1998. The motion to reopen could have been supplemented with a suspension application and supporting documents no later than Nov. 18, 1999. 8 C.F.R. §1003.43(c)(2). Failure to timely file may be fatal to a claim. *Aguilar De Polanco v. DOJ,* 398 F.3d 199 (2d Cir. 2005) [rejecting equal protection challenge where LIFE amendment allowed persons subject to §241(a)(5) to file a motion to reopen but denied Salvadoran the right to file a second motion to reopen, after first was untimely]; *Useinovic v. INS,* 313 F.3d 1025, 1033–35 (7th Cir. 2002) [failure to timely file motion to reopen precluded remand to seek NACARA benefits]. Dependents must also meet filing deadlines but their cases will be reopened if DHS finds that they or the principal are *prima facie* eligible. DHS has agreed to consider joining motions to reopen in certain cases where the NACARA applicant was *prima facie* eligible for relief as of Sept. 11, 1998 if s/he can establish a valid reason for failing to timely submit a motion to reopen. 64 Fed. Reg. 27856, 27872 (May 21, 1999). However, persons may not apply for NACARA benefits relating to suspension if the stop-time rule did not affect their ability to seek suspension. *Buzdygan v. INS,* 259 F.3d 891 (7th Cir. 2001) [where Polish national was denied suspension for failure to establish extreme hardship NACARA §203(c) does not provide him with an additional avenue for seeking relief]. Persons in exclusion proceedings are ineligible to reopen their cases under NACARA because historically a person could not apply for suspension in exclusion proceedings. *Tanov v. INS,* 443 F.3d 195 (2d Cir. 2006); *Simeonov v. Ashcroft,* 371 F.3d 532 (9th Cir. 2004); *Fieran v. INS,* 268 F.3d 340 (6th Cir. 2001); *Sherifi v. INS,* 260 F.3d 737 (7th Cir. 2001).

Equitable Tolling—NACARA filing deadlines may be subject to equitable tolling. *Albillo-De Leon v. Gonzales,* 410 F.3d 1090 (9th Cir. 2005) [distinguishing *Munoz*; the time period for filing a motion to reopen under NACARA §203(c) was tolled until the current lawyer's discovery that the nonlawyer previously representing respondent committed fraud in failing to file the motion to reopen]. However, the Ninth Circuit rejected the view that the NACARA filing deadline could be equitably tolled for a minor whose mother should have, but did not, apply for *ABC* or asylum benefits. *Munoz v. Ashcroft,* 339 F.3d 950, 956–57 (9th Cir. 2003) [distinguishing between statutes of limitations, which may be equitably tolled, and statutes of repose, which may not be tolled because they are fixed, statutory cut-off dates independent of any variable such as a child's awareness].

12.l. *Circuit Court Authority*—The Ninth Circuit granted a 90-day stay of removal to allow the petitioner the opportunity to apply for NACARA benefits. *Aguilar-Escobar v. INS*, 136 F.3d 1240 (9th Cir. 1998). Moreover, if a person is prima facie eligible for NACARA as an applicant or derivative, the court may stay the decision on asylum pending a NACARA determination. *Ardon-Matute v. INS,* 157 F.3d 696 (9th Cir. 1998). However, where the issue of eligibility was not raised before the BIA, the circuit court lacks jurisdiction to consider the claim. *Ortiz v. INS,* 179 F.3d 1148, 1152 (9th Cir. 1999) [appellants must file separate motion to reopen with the BIA].

12.m. *Reinstatement of Removal Under INA §241(a)(5)*—The LIFE Act and Amendments §1505(c) provide that persons otherwise eligible for special rule cancellation under NACARA are not barred from such relief due to INA §241(a)(5). Under DHS regulations an immigration officer may not reinstate the prior order unless and until a final decision to deny the application for NACARA benefits has been made. 8 C.F.R. §1241.8(d). *See also* Memo, Pearson HQASY120/12/11 (Feb. 23, 2001), *reprinted in* 78 No. 9 *Interpreter Releases* 444, 455–64 (Mar. 5, 2001). A motion to reopen to file for special rule cancellation may be made on or before Oct. 16, 2001 but only if it is based upon the denial of prior benefits due to INA §241(a)(5). 8 C.F.R. §1003.43.

13. *Administrative Review*—The IJ's factual findings, including credibility determinations, in a cancellation case are subject to a "clearly erroneous" standard. All other matters remain subject to *de novo* review by the Board. 8 C.F.R. §1003.1(d)(3). Thus in a cancellation case "those facts that a respondent claims make up 'exceptional and extremely unusual hardship' to a respondent's qualifying relative, and whether the relative is actually a qualifying relative, will be reviewed by the BIA only to determine if the IJ's determination was clearly erroneous. Whether those facts...amount to 'excep-

tional and extremely unusual hardship' under act maybe reviewed *de novo.*" 67 Fed. Reg. 54890 (Aug. 26, 2002). *See also Matter of Andaloza,* 23 I&N Dec. 319 (BIA 2002).

14. *Judicial Review*—Pursuant to the transition rules for appellate review, "there shall be no appeal of any discretionary decision under section 212(c), 212(h), 212(i), 244 or 245 of the INA." IIRIRA §309(c)(4)(E). *Valenzuela-Alcantar v. INS,* 309 F.3d 946, 949–50 (6th Cir. 2002) (and cases cited therein) [no jurisdiction to review extreme hardship determination regarding suspension]. Subsequent to the transition, the statute now provides: "Notwithstanding any other provision of law, no court shall have jurisdiction to review...any judgment regarding the granting of relief under section 1182(h), 1182(i), 1229b, 1229c, or 1255 of this title, or any other decision or action of the Attorney General the authority for which is specified under this chapter to be in the discretion of the Attorney General, other than the granting of relief under section 1158(a) [asylum] of this title." INA §242(a)(2)(B)(i), (ii), 8 U.S.C. §1252(a)(2)(B)(i), (ii).

14.a. *Cases Finding No Judicial Review*—Federal courts lack jurisdiction to review the BIA's determination regarding whether an applicant for cancellation has established "exceptional and extremely unusual hardship." *Barco-Sandoval v. Gonzales,* 516 F.3d 35 (2d Cir. 2008) [finding that *Chen v. U.S. DOJ,* 471 F.3d 315 did not alter *De La Vega* where respondent's claim that the wrong legal standard was applied was not colorable and merely sought to address a factual question as to extreme hardship under cancellation]; *Martinez v. U.S. Att'y Gen.,* 446 F.3d 1219 (11th Cir. 2006) [INA §242(a)(2)(D) does not restore jurisdiction to review exceptional and extremely unusual hardship]; *Martinez-Maldonado v. Gonzales,* 437 F.3d 679, 682–84 (7th Cir. 2006) [no jurisdiction to review denial of motion to reopen for cancellation where the denial was based upon failure to establish hardship]; *Merza-Reyes v. Gonzales,* 436 F.3d 842 (8th Cir. 2006) [notwithstanding INA §242(a)(2)(D), respondent cannot obtain jurisdiction simply by cloaking an abuse of discretion argument in constitutional terms]; *De La Vega v. Gonzales,* 436 F.3d 141 (2d Cir. 2006) [INA §242(a)(2)(D) does not extend jurisdiction to review hardship determination for cancellation]; *Martinez-Rosas v. Gonzales,* 424 F.3d 926, 929–30 (9th Cir. 2005) [review of the discretionary hardship determination for cancellation is barred by INA §242(a)(2)(B)(i), notwithstanding INA §242(a)(2)(D)]; *Alvarez-Delmuro v. Ashcroft,* 360 F.3d 1254 (10th Cir. 2004) [no jurisdiction to review challenge to cancellation standard as applied to USC children]; *Morales Ventura v. Ashcroft,* 348 F.3d 1259, 1261–63 (10th Cir. 2003) [decision on hardship may not be reviewed and respondent failed to present a substantial constitutional question]; *Bravo v. Ashcroft,* 341 F.3d 590, 593 (5th Cir. 2003) [same]; *Mendez-Moranchel v. Ashcroft,* 338 F.3d 176 (3d Cir. 2003) [following *Montero-Martinez* and finding that "judgment" under the statute only applies to discretionary matters and there was no jurisdiction to review the IJ's discretionary finding that the applicant did not establish hardship]; *Kharkhan v. Ashcroft,* 336 F.3d 601, 604 (7th Cir. 2003) [no jurisdiction to review IJ's denial of special rule cancellation]; *Romero-Torres v. Ashcroft,* 327 F.3d 887 (9th Cir. 2003) [finding §242(a)(2)(B)(i) bars review]; *Gonzalez-Oropeza v. U.S. Att'y Gen.,* 321 F.3d 1331, 1332–33 (11th Cir. 2003) [same]. *See also Martinez Ortiz v. Ashcroft,* 361 F.3d 480 (8th Cir. 2004) [no jurisdiction to review extreme hardship decision under former suspension statute]; *Halabi v. Ashcroft,* 316 F.3d 807, 808–09 (8th Cir. 2003) [where BIA denied cancellation for failure to establish physical presence and/or extreme hardship there is no judicial review because of the preclusion statute and the failure of appellant to raise objections to BIA/IJ's rulings in his brief]. At least one court has also held that the courts lack judicial review over whether someone has 10 years of continuous residence, as it is a fact question barred by 242(a)(2)(B)(i) and not excepted under 242(a)(2)(D). *Cevilla v. Gonzales,* 446 F.3d 658 (7th Cir. 2006) [where IJ erred in concluding that applicant was not in the U.S. for the 10 years necessary for cancellation, review of the motion to reopen on those grounds was denied because the court lacked jurisdiction as no statutory or constitutional error occurred].

The courts may also lack jurisdiction under INA §242(a)(2)(C) to review ineligibility for cancellation and §212(c) due to abandonment of residency because it is fact intensive. *Alaka v. Att'y Gen. of the U.S.,* 456 F.3d 88, 102–03 (3d Cir. 2006) [no jurisdiction to review fact intensive inquiry whether person with conviction was ineligible for §212(c) relief or cancellation because he intended to abandoned his residency by departing for 21 months]. The courts also lack jurisdiction to review the IJ/BIA's denial of INA §212(c) relief in the exercise of their discretion. *Marquez-Marquez v. Gonzales,* 455 F.3d 548, 560–61 (5th Cir. 2006)

Some courts have taken the position that there is no review of constitutional claims of cancellation decisions because they are purely discretionary and there is no protected liberty interest to support a due process claims. *See in this chapter* "Constitutional Protection for Due Process Violations when Seeking Relief," section I.I (p.960), *supra.*

14.b. *Cases Supporting Judicial Review*—The preclusion of review does not extend to nondiscretionary issues involving cancellation, nor does it extend to constitutional challenges to the BIA's application of the rules. *Sepulveda v. Gonzales,* 407 F.3d 59 (2d Cir. 2005) [the §242(a)(2)(B)(i) bar to judicial review does not extend to the nondiscretionary decision whether person is unable to establish good moral character as a matter of law]; *Guerra-Soto v. Ashcroft,* 397 F.3d 637, 639–40 (8th Cir. 2005) [finding jurisdiction to review BIA denial of motion to reopen for cancellation because discretionary decision regarding cancellation not at issue]; *Reyes-Vasquez v. Ashcroft,* 395 F.3d 903, 906 (8th Cir. 2005) [finding jurisdiction to determine whether applicant's trip abroad stopped physical presence for cancellation]; *Santana-Albarran v. Ashcroft,* 393 F.3d 699, 703 (6th Cir. 2005) [finding jurisdiction to review whether respondent met physical presence requirement]; *Gomez-Lopez v. Ashcroft,* 393 F.3d 882, 883–84 (9th Cir. 2005) [finding jurisdiction to review the application of INA §101(f)(7) regarding good moral character for purposes of cancellation]; *Lopez-Alvarado v. Ashcroft,* 381 F.3d 847, 850–51 (9th Cir. 2004) [finding jurisdiction to review IJ's finding that cancellation applicant failed to establish the requisite 10 years]; *Lagandaon v. Ashcroft,* 383 F.3d 983, 986–87 (9th Cir. 2004 [jurisdiction to review when 10 years ceases as a matter of law]; *Mireles-Valdez v. Ashcroft,* 349 F.3d 213, 215–16 (5th Cir. 2003) [finding jurisdiction to determine whether voluntary departure breaks the 10-year physical present requirement for cancellation]; *Reyes-Melendez v. INS,* 342 F.3d 1001 (9th Cir. 2003) [IJ's extreme hardship determination in a suspension case may be challenged where the IJ violated due process by abandoning her role as a neutral fact-finder]; *Ramirez-Perez v. Ashcroft,* 336 F.3d 1001, 1005–07 (9th Cir. 2003) [court had authority to review claim that BIA's application of the exceptional and extremely unusual hardship standard violated due process].

14.c. *Judicial Review For Battered Spouse Cases.* There is a circuit split in regard to whether courts may review for certain issues concerning cancellation for battered spouses. *Compare Hernandez v. Ashcroft,* 345 F.3d 824, 833–35 (9th Cir. 2003) [finding that despite the word extreme, a determination of extreme cruelty is not a discretionary decision similar to extreme hardship; it is subject to judicial review because it is a matter of fact that can be ascertained on an objective basis]; *Angamarca v. Gonzales,* 415 F.3d 897, 901 (8th Cir. 2005) [reviewing denial of cancellation under substantial evidence review but upholding denial], *with Perales-Cumpean v. Gonzales,* 429 F.3d 977, 982–84 (10th Cir. 2005) [rejecting *Hernandez* and finding that a determination of extreme cruelty or credibility issues in the determination of cancellation for a battered spouse are barred from judicial review by INA §242(a)(2)(B)(i)].

14.d. *NACARA*—Judicial review may also be limited for decisions under NACARA. *See* Ch. 6, part VI (p. 1000), *supra*, and Ch. 10, ¶ I.D.13 (p.1077), *infra.*

15. *Suspension of Deportation Under Former Provisions*—Previously available under INA §244(a), 8 U.S.C. §1254(a)—There was a 7- and a 10-year suspension provision, which remains applicable to certain Salvadorans, Guatemalans, Eastern Europeans and persons who had applied for suspension prior to Apr. 1, 1997, who were not served with an OSC or committed certain crimes prior to being physically present in the U.S. for 7 (or 10) years. INA §240A(d)(1). It may also remain available on retroactivity grounds to persons who pled guilty or were found guilty after trial but prior to IIRIRA, and because of their plea are not now eligible for cancellation. *Hernandez de Anderson v. Gonzales,* 497 F.3d 927, 937–44 (9th Cir. 2007) [the BIA erred in impermissibly repealing suspension of deportation where person was convicted after trial and was placed in removal proceedings after seeking naturalization one year before the passage of IIRIRA that eliminated suspension]; *Lopez-Castellanos v. Gonzales,* 437 F.3d 848, 851–54 (9th Cir. 2007). *But see Hernandez v. Gonzales,* 437 F.3d 341, 346–53 (3d Cir. 2006) [rejecting retroactivity argument for person who committed criminal conduct before IIRIRA on ground that after he entered plea he was still ineligible for suspension for lack of good moral character].

15.a. *Seven-year Suspension*—INA §244(a)(1), 8 U.S.C. §1254(a)(1).

(1) *Seven Years of Continuous Physical Presence. Vera-Villegas v. INS,* 330 F.3d 1222 (9th Cir. 2003) [reversing IJ's denial of suspension for failure to establish 7 years where denial was based on speculation and conjecture rather than substantial evidence in making credibility determinations and where IJ noted failure to provide tax returns and other recommended but not required documents]. A brief, casual and innocent departure from the U.S. that is not "meaningfully interruptive" did not break physical presence. Former INA §244(b)(2), 8 U.S.C. §1254(b)(2); [IRCA statute reversed *INS v. Phinpathya*, 464 U.S. 183 (1984)]; *Matter of Cervantes*, 21 I&N Dec. 351 (BIA 1996) [readmission of temporary resident does not bar suspension where departed during deportation hearing]; *Rodriguez-Gutierrez v. INS*, 59 F.3d 504, 507 (5th Cir. 1995) [short trips outside U.S. while deportation proceedings are pending do not interrupt status]; *Castrejon-Garcia v. INS*, 60 F.3d 1359 (9th Cir. 1995) [reversing BIA's narrow definition of "casual"]. This provision was applied retroactively to cases arising before IRCA in 1986. *DeGurules v. INS*, 833 F.2d 861 (9th Cir. 1987) [applying standard for retroactive application in *Bradley v. School Bd. of City of Richmond*, 416 U.S. 696 (1974)]. A brief departure may be as long as 30 days or longer. *Kamheangpatiyooth v. INS*, 597 F.2d 1253 (9th Cir. 1979). *But see Tapia v. Ashcroft,* 351 F.3d 795, 798–99 (7th Cir. 2003) [*Fleuti* doctrine cannot be relied upon post-IIRIRA to assist respondent who claims he had 7 years of physical presence that were not interrupted because his 6½-month trip abroad was brief, casual and innocent]; *Rubio-Rubio v. INS*, 23 F.3d 273 (10th Cir. 1994) [no brief or casual departure where applicant went live in home country for 9 months].

(i) *90/180 Day Rule*—Under IIRIRA, the 90/180 day rule for cancellation under INA §240A(d)(2), 8 U.S.C. §1229b(d)(2) is now applied retroactively to all suspension cases where the OSC was issued before, on, or after Nov. 19, 1997. IIRIRA §309(c)(5)(A) *as amended by* NACARA. Thus, a person who had an absence of more than 90 days or aggregate absences of more than 180 days is no longer eligible for suspension. *Mendiola-Sanchez v. Ashcroft,* 381 F.3d 937 (9th Cir. 2004) [applying same analysis as "stop-time" rule and barring suspension despite the nonexistence of legislative history on the 90/180 day absences].

(ii) *Stop-Time Rule* – Physical presence is cut off upon service of an OSC or commission of certain criminal offenses. INA §240A(d)(1). *See in this section* ¶15.d (p.1002), *infra*.

(iii) *Accrual of Time During Appeal*—Under prior law an applicant could not reach the 7-year requirement through frivolous appeals. *INS v. Rios-Pineda*, 471 U.S. 444 (1985). However, where the appeal was not baseless, the time accrued during its pendency was counted toward the 7 years. *Cipriano v. INS*, 24 F.3d 763 (5th Cir. 1994); *Sida v. INS*, 783 F.2d 947 (9th Cir. 1986). *But see Flores v. INS*, 68 F.3d 1069 (9th Cir. 1995) [distinguishing *Sida* and finding that the statute prohibits counting any time toward the 7-year residency or good moral character requirements after the application is filed even if it is a nonfrivolous appeal].

(2) *Application Must Arise in Deportation Hearing*—An affirmative application for suspension before the District Director is not valid and if person is subsequently served with an NTA s/he has no right to have suspension application heard. *Karageorgious v. Ashcroft,* 374 F.3d 152 (2d Cir. 2004) [rejecting suspension applicant's retroactivity, due process, and statutory right to seek suspension arguments where applicant made affirmative application before he was served with NTA]; *Ramirez-Zavala v. Ashcroft,* 336 F.3d 872 (9th Cir. 2003) [person who filed suspension application with DD before Apr. 1, 1997, but was placed in removal proceedings after that date is not eligible for suspension]; *Jimenez-Angeles v. Ashcroft,* 291 F.3d 594, 602 (9th Cir. 2002) [placing affirmative applicant for suspension in removal proceedings and cutting off right to seek suspension does not have an impermissible retroactive effect because giving up a right to live illegally is not a right].

(3) *Good Moral Character is Required for Full 7-year Period—Amador-Palomares v. Ashcroft,* 382 F.3d 864, 867 (8th Cir. 2004) [single act of attempt to solicit a prostitute

rendered respondent statutorily barred from establishing good moral character under INA §101(f)(3)]. *See in this chapter*, "Good Moral Character," part II (p.962), *supra.*

(4) *Extreme Hardship*—Deportation must cause extreme hardship to the applicant or to his/her USC/LPR spouse, parent or child. *Matter of Anderson*, 16 I&N Dec. 596 (BIA 1978); *Babai v. INS*, 985 F.2d 252 (6th Cir. 1993) [reversing BIA denial when it failed to consider hardship to USC child]; *INS v. Hector*, 479 U.S. 85 (1986) [hardship to niece cannot be considered hardship to child]. But IJ may consider hardship to applicant due to separation from nonqualifying relatives. *Contreras-Buenfil v. INS*, 712 F.2d 401 (9th Cir. 1983). Also, a minor child who is not an LPR or USC may be entitled to have the hardship to him or her considered as if s/he had been a formal party to the proceedings. *Salameda v. INS*, 70 F.3d 447, 451–52 (7th Cir. 1995). Extreme hardship is often narrowly defined. *INS v. Wang*, 450 U.S. 139 (1981) [upholding a restrictive reading of hardship]. *See also Mejia-Rodriguez v. Reno,* 178 F.3d 1139 (11th Cir. 1999) [suspension is a matter of grace and denial of such relief cannot give rise to a liberty interest]; *Hernandez-Cordero v. INS*, 819 F.2d 558 (5th Cir. 1987) (en banc) [AG has "unfettered" discretion to determine extreme hardship]. *But see Matter of L-O-G-*, 21 I&N Dec. 413 (BIA 1996) [rejecting narrow interpretation]. *See also in this section*, ¶ 9 (p.993), *supra.*

15.b. *Ineligible Persons*—J visa holders and crewmembers are ineligible under former INA §244(f), 8 U.S.C. §1254(f), Nazis and terrorists under former INA §241(a)(4)(B) and (D), and, in the view of one court, persons in exclusion proceedings. *Patel v. McElroy*, 143 F.3d 56 (2d Cir. 1998). *See also Skelly v. INS,* 168 F.3d 88 (2d Cir. 1999) [rejecting *Francis* rationale and equal protection challenge to denial of suspension to excludable persons].

15.c. *Ten-Year Suspension*—Former INA §244(a)(2), 8 U.S.C. §1254(a)(2). Allowed suspension for more serious crimes including those involving moral turpitude and narcotics. However, if deportation is not sought under these more serious charges, alien can apply under former INA §244(a)(1), 8 U.S.C. §1255(a)(1). *Matter of Ching*, 12 I&N Dec. 710 (BIA 1968) [person with narcotics conviction who was not charged with deportability on those grounds was eligible for INA §244(a)(1) relief]. *But see Mullen-Cofee v. INS*, 976 F.2d 1375 (11th Cir. 1992) *amended on denial of reh'g* 986 F.2d 1364 (11th Cir. 1993). Need 10 years of good moral character from date of conviction (not commission of crime). *Matter of Lozada*, 19 I&N Dec. 637 (BIA 1988). Must establish "exceptional and extremely unusual hardship," not just "extreme hardship" as in 7-year suspension provision. There is no constitutionally protected right to 10-year suspension because it is discretionary. *Balogun v. U.S. Att'y Gen.,* 304 F.3d 1303, 1311 (11th Cir. 2002) [no constitutional right to discretionary relief or to be eligible for discretionary relief].

15.d. *Application of the Stop-Time Rule to Suspension Cases.*

(1) *Service of OSC*—An applicant is ineligible for relief if s/he was served with an OSC prior to the accrual of the 7 years. INA §240A(d)(1); *Matter of Nolasco,* 22 I&N Dec. 632 (BIA 1999); *Sibanda v. INS,* 282 F.3d 1330 (10th Cir. 2002) [rejecting retroactivity analysis post–*St. Cyr* based on claim that he accrued 7 years through affirmative asylum claim]; *Rivera-Jimenez v. INS,* 214 F.3d 1213 (10th Cir. 2000) [same and cases cited therein]. The stop-time rule also applies where the final administrative order pursuant to an OSC was issued prior to the passage of IIRIRA. *Suassuna v. INS,* 342 F.3d 578 (6th Cir. 2003); *Afful v. Ashcroft,* 380 F.3d 1, 6–7 (1st Cir. 2004) [same and citing cases from other circuits]. *See also Escudero-Corona v. INS,* 244 F.3d 608, 614 (8th Cir. 2001) [rejecting due process and equal protection claims based on retroactivity argument]; *Pinho v. INS,* 249 F.3d 183 (3d Cir. 2001) [rejecting due process and equal protection challenges]; *Sad v. INS,* 246 F.3d 811 (6th Cir. 2001) [recognizing possible statutory argument limiting NACARA but deferring to BIA under *Chevron* and rejecting due process and equal protection claims]; *Rojas-Reyes v. INS,* 235 F.3d 115, 122–24 (2d Cir. 2000) [rejecting substantive and procedural due process claims under rational basis standard]; *Angel-Ramos v. Reno,* 227 F.3d 942 (7th Cir. 2000) [rejecting equal protection and due process challenges]; *Ayoub v. INS,* 222 F.3d 214 (5th Cir. 2000) [NACARA codified stop time rule to bar suspension]; *Afolayan v. INS,* 219 F.3d 784, 789 (8th Cir. 2000) [rejecting due process and equal protection challenge]; *Tefel v. Reno*, 180 F.3d 1286, 1298–

1305 (11th Cir. 1999) [rejecting due process claim on grounds that suspension is a matter of grace; no equal protection violation]; *Appiah v. INS,* 202 F.3d 704 (4th Cir. 2000) [same]. An applicant may not accrue the 7 or 10 years necessary for suspension after the service of the OSC. *Matter of Mendoza-Sandino,* 22 I&N Dec. 1236 (BIA 2000); *Casillas-Figueroa v. Gonzales,* 419 F.3d 447 (6th Cir. 2005) [distinguishing *Aoun* and rejecting position that 7 years may accrue after service of OSC]; *Al Najjar v. Ashcroft,* 257 F.3d 1262, 1299–1300 (11th Cir. 2001) [finding BIA view that 7 years may not accrue subsequent to service of OSC is supported by the statute]; *Iyamba v. INS,* 244 F.3d 606, 608 (8th Cir. 2001) [rejecting claim that 7 years could start anew after service of OSC]; *Ram v. INS,* 243 F.3d 510, 517–18 (9th Cir. 2001) [same]; *McBride v. INS,* 238 F.3d 371 (5th Cir. 2000) [same]. *But see Matter of Cisneros,* 23 I&N Dec. 668 (BIA 2004) [where person departs U.S. after service of OSC he may accrue 10-year period for cancellation upon his return if placed in a subsequent removal proceeding].

(2) *Commission of Crime*—Under INA §240A(d)(1)(B), 8 U.S.C. §1229b(d)(1)(B), the commission of certain offenses also breaks the continuous residence requirement for cancellation. This section, although not explicitly made retroactive has been found to apply retroactively even to pre-IIRIRA crimes where action brought post-IIRIRA. *Briseno-Flores v. Att'y Gen. of the U.S.,* 492 F.3d 226, 229–31 (3d Cir. 2007) [respondent's conviction in 1985 stopped the time for calculating the seven years needed for suspension; nor did a new seven year period begin from that point; *Okeke distinguished*]; *Heaven v. Gonzales,* 473 F.3d 167 (5th Cir. 2006) [seven year continuous residence cuts off cancellation application post-IIRIRA where conviction was pre-IIRIRA]; *Tablie v. Gonzales,* 471 F.3d 60 (2d Cir. 2006) [INA §240A(d)(1)(B), which bars suspension for persons who commit crimes during the period of continuous residence, applies retroactively]; *Peralta v. Gonzales,* 441 F.3d 23, (1st Cir. 2006) [respondent ineligible for suspension because his conviction for marriage fraud was a CIMT committed during the necessary 7-year period and therefore cut off eligibility]; *Hernandez v. Gonzales,* 437 F.3d 341, 346–53 (3d Cir. 2006) [rejecting retroactivity argument for person seeking suspension under 10-year provision who committed criminal conduct before IIRIRA on ground that could not establish 10 years of good moral character]; *Arenas-Yeses v. Gonzales,* 421 F.3d 111, 1117 (2d Cir. 2005) [rejecting retroactivity argument to application of stop-time rule in absence of claim that petitioner relied on the existence of suspension and would have acted differently]. *But see Okeke v. Gonzales,* 407 F.3d 585 (3d Cir. 2005) [a conviction under §240A(d)(1)(B) does not bar the clock from restarting so that applicant can accrue a new 10-year period of continuous residence where applicant left the U.S. and re-entered lawfully].

(3) *Other Challenges to the Application of the Stop-Time Rule*—*Aoun v. INS,* 342 F.3d 503 (6th Cir. 2003) [where BIA continued respondent's appeal for one reason or another for 12 years during which time the stop-time rule was enacted, the court declined to impose the rule on the applicant]; *Otarola v. INS,* 270 F.3d 1272 (9th Cir. 2001) [the stop-time rule should not apply where IJ granted suspension and INS took a frivolous appeal to permit the stop-time rule to be applied]; *Guadalupe-Cruz v. INS,* 240 F.3d 1209 (9th Cir. 2001) *opinion corrected* 250 F.3d 1271 (9th Cir. 2001) [where IIRIRA was not in effect and IJ erroneously applied stop time rule, decision was reversed and IJ ordered to apply pre-IIRIRA law but with current facts]; *Tang v. INS,* 223 F.3d 713 (8th Cir. 2000) [where petitioner and INS stipulated to a date for the service of the OSC beyond the 7 years, no bar to suspension]; *Arrozal v. INS,* 159 F.3d 429, 434 & n.2 (9th Cir. 1998) [stop-time rule does not apply to motion to reopen where final order was obtained prior to Apr. 1, 1997 and possibly by applicant accruing more than seven years since the OSC]; *But see Raffington v. Cangemi,* 399 F.3d 900, 902–03 (8th Cir. 2005) [rejecting *Otarola* and holding that even if the government had filed a frivolous, but ultimately successful appeal, it would not constitute affirmative misconduct to estop the government].

15.e. *Battered Spouse or Child*—Former INA §244(a)(3), 8 U.S.C. §1254(a)(3). Permits battered spouses, children or parent of battered child (who is the child of the LPR/USC engaged in the battery), to apply for suspension if s/he was placed in proceedings before April 1, 1997, and if s/he is: subject to battery or extreme cruelty in the U.S., physically present in U.S. for 3 years, a person of good moral character during that 3-year period, and his or her deportation would result in extreme hardship to her, her child or her parents. Special extreme hardship factors tailored to domestic violence apply. 8 C.F.R. §1240.58(c). Ineligible if deportable due to marriage fraud or any of the criminal grounds specified in the 10-year provision. Victims of Trafficking and Violence Protection Act of 2000, PL 106-386, 114 Stat. 1464 (Oct. 28, 2000). Section 1506 also added a provision that exempted battered spouses/children from the stop-time rule and created a special motion to reopen with no time deadline. *See Hernandez v. Ashcroft,* 345 F.3d 824, 832–41 (9th Cir. 2003) [interpreting the extreme cruelty standard and finding that it occurred within U.S. even if husband's physical battery of wife occurred solely abroad]. The VAWA provision differs from "regular" cancellation in that:

(1) There is no "stop-time" rule [the service of the NTA does not cut off the accrual of the 3 years required for physical presence], INA §240A(b)(2)(A)(i)(III);

(2) The IJ may consider hardship to the applicants themselves. INA §240A(b)(2)(A)(v);

(3) The "extreme hardship" standard, not the "exceptional and extremely unusual hardship" applies. INA §240A(b)(2)(A)(v);

(4) Exceptions to the physical presence and good moral character requirements may apply if there is a connection between the act/absence and the abuse. INA §240A(b)(2)(B), (C).

15.f. *Barahona Settlement*—In *Barahona-Gomez v. Ashcroft,* 243 F.Supp.2d 1029 (N.D. Cal. 2002), the court entered a settlement agreement that permitted eligible immigrants to apply for suspension as it existed pre-IIRIRA. Persons are eligible if they "have had (or would have had) suspension of deportation hearings conducted before Apr. 1, 1997 [the effective date of IIRIRA] within the jurisdiction of the Ninth Circuit Court of Appeals" but for the memo of the Chief Immigration Judge directing IJs to reserve granting of suspension or the Chairman of the BIA directing that suspension decisions or motions to reopen or remand for suspension be withheld. *Navarro v. Mukasey,* 518 F.3d 729 (9th Cir. 2008) [court interpreted settlement to include respondents whose hearings were rescheduled to (as distinguished from after) April 1, 1997, and therefore would otherwise have been barred]. *But see Sotelo v. Gonzales,* 430 F.3d 968 (9th Cir. 2005) [petitioners did not meet class definition and therefore could not avail themselves of the settlement].

D. ***Repapering***—The DHS/BIA have established a procedure to administratively close cases and recharge someone in removal proceedings to allow that person to benefit from cancellation of removal. The process, called "repapering" may be used where the person: (1) would have been eligible for §212(c) relief but for AEDPA; and (2) is eligible for cancellation and is not otherwise barred by §240A(d)(1). DHS will not agree to reopen a case on this basis but once reopened, DHS is generally required to agree to administratively close the case absent unusual circumstances. Memo, Cooper, G.C. (HQCOU 90/16.1-P) (Dec. 7, 1999), *reprinted in* 77 No. 2 *Interpreter Releases*, 39, 57–58 (Jan. 10, 2000). The BIA also agreed to administratively close files where repapering was available. Memo, Scialabba, BIA Vice Chair (Mar. 14, 2000), available at *www.usdoj.gov/eoir/chip6.pdf* and Memo, Schmidt, BIA Chairman (Aug. 20, 2000), available at *www.usdoj.gov/eoir/vll/genifo/streamimplem.pdf. See Alcaraz v. INS,* 384 F.3d 1150 (9th Cir. 2004) [finding jurisdiction to review the denial of administrative closure to repaper and remanding to the BIA to determine whether repapering policy had been violated]. *But see Rodriguez-Munoz v. Gonzales,* 419 F.3d 245 (3d Cir. 2005) [upholding denial of repapering, because even if respondent could apply for cancellation and §212(c) simultaneously, the grant of §212(c) would not waive the aggravated felony bar to cancellation]; *Rojas-Reyes v. INS,* 235 F.3d 115, 125–6 (2d Cir. 2000) [failure to promulgate repapering regulations did not create due process, equal protection, or estoppel claims]; *Checknan v. McElroy,* 313 F.Supp.2d 270, 274–76 (S.D.N.Y. 2004) [cannot compel repapering by mandamus].

Without "repapering" IIRIRA §309(c)(5) may bar suspension. As originally written, §309(c)(5) provided that the stop-time rule under INA §240A(d)(1), applied to NTA's issued before, on or after IIRIRA's date of enactment. In *Matter of N-J-B-*, 22 I&N Dec. 1057 (BIA 1997), the BIA interpreted the statute and found that the stop-time rule applied retroactively to all cases that were not resolved on Sept. 30, 1996. However, that decision was vacated by the AG. *Id.* (AG July 10, 1997). Thereafter, Congress passed NACARA which clarified that the stop-time rule would be applied to NTAs and OSCs issued, before, on, or after IIRIRA's date of the enactment. Thus, even if a person filed for suspension before Apr. 1, 1997, her/his suspension application would be pretermitted if s/he was served with an OSC at any time before the seven/ten years needed for suspension accrued. *Matter of Nolasco,* 22 I&N Dec. 632 (BIA 1999); *Lockett v. INS,* 245 F.3d 1126 (10th Cir. 2001) *and cases cited therein. See in this part* ¶ C.3 (p.988), *supra*, for a discussion of the stop-time rule as applied in suspension cases.

V. ASYLUM, WITHHOLDING OF REMOVAL & PROTECTION UNDER CAT

See Chapter 4 (p. 429), *supra.*

VI. ADJUSTMENT OF STATUS

A. ***Eligibility***—Under INA §245(a), the AG may, in his or her discretion, adjust the status of an approved VAWA self-petitioner or of an alien who was inspected and admitted or paroled into the U.S. to LPR who (1) makes an application for adjustment; (2) is eligible to receive an immigrant visa and is admissible, *Matter of Torres-Varela,* 23 I&N Dec. 78, 80 (BIA 2001) [aggravated felony conviction does not, by itself, render one ineligible for adjustment because an aggravated felony is a ground of deportation not inadmissibility]; and (3) where an immigrant visa is immediately available. *See also* 8 C.F.R. §§1240.11(a)(1), 245.2(a)(1), 1245.2(a)(1). If DHS denies AOS, the application may be renewed in a removal proceeding if the person is not an arriving alien. *Compare* 8 C.F.R. §245.2(a)(5)(ii) *with* 8 C.F.R. §1245.2(a)(1). *But see Chambers v. Mukasey,* 520 F.3d 445, 450–51 (5th Cir. 2008) [IJ had no jurisdiction to address an AOS application that was filed 3 years after advance parole and was not the original denied AOS application, because the regulation only permits IJ review of a previously filed application]. At the time of the renewal of the application for AOS before the IJ, "an applicant does not need to meet the statutory requirement of section 245(c) of the Act [*e.g.*, not working without authorization] or §245.1(g) [immediate availability of an immigrant visa], if, in fact, those requirements were met at the time the renewed application was initially filed with the director." 8 C.F.R. §245.2(a)(5)(ii). *Accord, Matovski v. Gonzales,* 492 F.3d 722 (6th Cir. 2007) [court reversed IJ's refusal to consider adjustment of status for person who "ported" because 8 C.F.R. §245.2(a)(5)(ii) made the portability issue irrelevant as the IJ had authority to adjust a person if he was eligible to adjust at the time he filed with the USCIS director and because there was no regulation that barred the IJ from considering portability]. In removal proceedings, the applicant for AOS has the burden to establish both statutory eligibility and that s/he merits a favorable exercise of discretion. *Matovski, supra.* Also a person who might otherwise be ineligible for AOS under INA §245(a) or (c), may be eligible under INA §245(i). *See generally* Ch. 6, ¶ XII.C.2 (p.844), *supra.* Conditional residents under INA §216 are ineligible to adjust, unless such status has been terminated, *Matter of Stockwell,* 20 I&N Dec. 309 (BIA 1991), as are all K entrants seeking to adjust through a marriage to anyone other than the USC who filed the petition. INA §245(d). Persons who married during administrative or judicial proceedings are ineligible unless they can overcome the presumption that the marriage is not valid, or meet other requirements under 8 C.F.R. §245.1(c)(9)(iii). Adjustment may be denied as a matter of discretion. *Wallace v. Gonzales,* 463 F.3d 135, 138–40 (2d Cir. 2006) [IJ may consider Youthful Offender Adjudication in discretionary exercise of adjustment even though it is not a conviction]; *Mamoka v. INS*, 43 F.3d 184 (5th Cir. 1995) [denying AOS for violation of immigration laws]; *Matter of Ibrahim,* 18 I&N Dec. 55 (BIA 1981); *Matter of Cavazos*, 17 I&N Dec. 215 (BIA 1980); *Matter of Arai*, 13 I&N Dec. 494 (BIA 1970); *Matter of Huey*, 13 I&N Dec. 5 (BIA 1968). *But see Rashtabadi v. INS*, 23 F.3d 1562 (9th Cir. 1994). Adjustment under INA §245(i) is also discretionary. *Usmani v. Att'y Gen. of the U.S.,* 483 F.3d 1147 (11th Cir. 2007) [rejecting argument that §245(i) was mandatory if person qualified]. For a discussion of §245(i) adjustment, *see* Ch. 6, ¶ XII.C.2 (p.844), *supra.*

B. ***All Grounds of Inadmissibility Apply***—When seeking adjustment all grounds of inadmissibility apply and the IJ may address those, even if they were not pled in the notice to appear. *Matovski v. Gonzales,* 492 F.3d 722, 737–39 (6th Cir. 2007) [due process not violated where ground of inadmissibility—§212(a)(6)(C)(i)—is raised in relief phase of case although not charged as the ground of deportability because the IJ may rule on any ground of inadmissibility that arises during the course of proceedings].

C. ***Continuances for Adjustment of Status***—Where a visa petition/adjustment application is filed, the IJ cannot deny a continuance solely because the petition has not been approved. *Haswanee v. U.S. Att'y Gen.,* 471 F.3d 1212 (11th Cir. 2006) [where LC was approved, I-140 pending, and visa immediately available, but no I-485 filed, it was an abuse of discretion to deny continuance]; *Ahmed v. Gonzales,* 465 F.3d 806 (7th Cir. 2006) [IJ erred in not granting continuance to §245(i) eligible respondent with approved fourth preference petition who sought continuance to file labor certification to speed up process]; *Merchant v. U.S. Att'y Gen.,* 461 F.3d 1375 (11th Cir. 2006) [where LC approved and I-140 and I-485 filed with DHS, IJ abused discretion in denying a continuance. *Bull* supported and *Zafar* distinguished]; *Benslimane v. Gonzales,* 430 F.3d 828 (7th Cir. 2005) [IJ made legal error in denying continuance where respondent had filed I-130 and I-485 as part of a marriage-based adjustment but had not filed adjustment with IJ]; *Subhan v. Ashcroft,* 383 F.3d 591 (7th Cir. 2004) [IJ's denial of a continuance to finalize labor certification without a reason consistent with §245(i) violated that statute]; *Bull v. INS,* 790 F.2d 869 (11th Cir. 1986). *But see Ilic-Lee v. Mukasey,* 507 F.3d 1044, 1047–48 (6th Cir. 2007) [BIA did not abuse its discretion in upholding IJ's denial of a continuance to allow USCIS to decide motion to reopen I-130 that had been pending 14 months]; *Elbahja v. Keisler,* 505 F.3d 125 (2d Cir. 2007) [IJ did not abuse his discretion in denying continuance pending approval of labor certification]; *Vargas-Hernandez v. Gonzales,* 497 F.3d 919, 923 (9th Cir. 2007) [IJ did not abuse his discretion in denying continuance to respondent who sought to file I-130 petition and AOS at final removal hearing, where the respondent was married to the USC petitioner for 7 years and could have filed AOS after wife became USC 5 years prior to final hearing]; *Pedreros v. Keisler,* 503 F.3d 162 (2d Cir. 2007) [IJ did not err in denying continuance where I-130 had been denied and was on appeal to BIA and no argument or evidence was advanced addressing DD's error in denying the I-130]; *Lendo v. Gonzales,* 493 F.3d 439 (4th Cir. 2007) [respondent's rights were not violated when IJ refused to continue case pending wife's labor certification so they could adjust under INA §245(i)]; *Zafar v. U.S. Att'y Gen.,* 461 F.3d 1357, 1362–67 (11th Cir. 2006) *reh'g en banc denied* 473 F.3d 1350 (2007) [finding no abuse of discretion, due process or equal protection violation in denying a continuance to permit approval of a labor certification for §245(i) eligibility because no visa was immediately available and, as a constitutional matter, adjustment is discretionary]; *Khan v. Att'y Gen. of the U.S.,* 448 F.3d 226, 233–36 (3d Cir. 2006) [IJ did not abuse discretion by denying continuance where wife's labor certification was pending and therefore a visa was not immediately available]; *Ahmed v. Gonzales,* 447 F.3d 433, 439–40 (5th Cir. 2006) [followed *Zafar* and found no statutory, due process or equal protection violation in denying continuance where labor certification was filed but no visa immediately available]; *Morgan v. Gonzales,* 445 F.3d 549 (2d Cir. 2006) [IJ did not abuse his discretion or deny due process when he denied continuance to permit the adjudication of an I-130 stemming from a marriage that had previously been determined to lack *bona fides*]; *Pede v. Gonzales,* 442 F.3d 570 (7th Cir. 2006) [distinguishing *Subhan* and *Benslimane* in that IJ gave a reason for denying a continuance, which was the ultimate hopelessness of the adjustment application]; *Ali v. Gonzales,* 440 F.3d 678, 680–81 (5th Cir. 2006) [IJ did not abuse his discretion when he denied eighth continuance where respondent failed to provide proof that his LC was filed before Apr. 30, 2001 making him eligible for §245(i)]; *Abu-Khaliel v. Gonzales,* 436 F.3d 627, 634 (6th Cir. 2006) [IJ did not abuse her discretion in denying continuance where I-130 was filed by second wife who married respondent 5 days before the hearing, given the length of the previous continuance and the fact that respondent had prior criminal violations]; *Matter of Kotte,* 16 I&N Dec. 449 (BIA 1978).

D. ***Motions to Reopen for Adjustment of Status***—Persons with final orders of removal may seek to reopen proceedings for adjustment. Under DHS regulations, a motion to reopen must be filed within 90 days of the IJ or BIA's decision and only one motion may be filed. 8 C.F.R. §1003.2(c)(2). However, if the 90-day period has passed or one motion has already been filed, DHS can agree to reopen. 8 C.F.R. §1003.2(c)(3)(iii). *Bolshakov v. INS,* 133 F.3d 1279, 1281–82 (9th Cir. 1998) [agreement of parties to reopening is not an administrative remedy that requires exhaustion]. DHS's policy of consenting to reopen "only under exceptional and compelling circumstances," *see* Memo, Martin, General Counsel, INS, HQ COU 90/16.11-P (Dec. 23, 1997), *reprinted in* 75 No. 7 *Interpreter Releases,* 259, 275–77 (Feb. 23, 1998), has been modified for persons moving to reopen for adjustment of status. General Counsel has decided that DHS may join in a motion to reopen for adjustment "if such adjustment of status was not available to the respondent at the former hearing, the alien is statutorily eligible…and the respondent merits a favorable exercise of discretion." Memo, Cooper, Gen. Counsel, HQCOU 90/16.22.1 (May 17, 2001), *published on* AILA InfoNet at Doc. No. 01070333.

In *Matter of Garcia,* 16 I&N Dec. 653, 656 (BIA 1978), the BIA found that motions to reopen for AOS should generally be granted, even where the application was accompanied by an unadjudicated visa petition, unless the applicant was clearly ineligible for the preference classification requested. However, the BIA parted from the *Garcia* presumption, refusing to grant motions to reopen for adjustment with an unadjudicated visa petition, in cases falling within the ambit of INA §§204(g) and 245(e) (restricting AOS based on a marriage entered into during proceedings). *Matter of Arthur*, 20 I&N Dec. 475 (BIA 1992). *See also Matter of H-A-*, 22 I&N Dec. 728 (BIA 1999); *Rezai v. INS*, 62 F.3d 1286, 1289–92 (10th Cir. 1995) [upholding change from *Garcia* to *Arthur*]; *Dielmann v. INS*, 34 F.3d 851 (9th Cir. 1994) [same]. In *Matter of Velarde-Pacheco,* 23 I&N Dec. 253 (BIA 2002), the BIA modified *Matter of Arthur* and *Matter of H-A-* to allow motions to reopen that are timely filed, not numerically barred, not barred by *Matter of Shaar, infra*, or barred on any other procedural ground, where clear and convincing evidence supports the bona fides of the marriage, and the Service either does not oppose the motion or bases its opposition solely on *Matter of Arthur. See also Melnitsenko v. Mukasey,* 517 F.3d 42, 48–52 (2d Cir. 2008) [BIA cannot deny a motion under *Velarde-Pacheco* where petitioner meets all five criteria solely on the fact of DHS's opposition]; *Ssali v. Gonzales,* 424 F.3d 556, 562–64 (7th Cir. 2005) [vacating BIA's denial of motion to reopen for AOS and criticizing government's analysis of *Matter of Arthur*]; *Singh v. Gonzales,* 404 F.3d 1024, 1027–29 (7th Cir. 2005) [where I-130 had been approved, the BIA's reliance on *Matter of Velarde-Pacheco* to deny motion to reconsider was error because *Velarde* involved an unadjudicated I-130; however under facts of case error was harmless]; *Singh v. Quarantillo,* 92 F.Supp.2d 386 (D.N.J. 2000) [releasing applicant, tolling VD until INS approved I-130 that had been pending for 2 years and adopting dissent in *Matter of H-A-*]. *Cf. Miah v. Mukasey,* 519 F.3d 784, 789–90 (8th Cir. 2008) [denied motion to reopen under *Velarde* on insufficiency of the evidence, and distinguished *Velarde* because motion was filed after BIA ruled]; *Ilic-Lee v. Mukasey,* 507 F.3d 1044, 1049–53 (6th Cir. 2007) [BIA was correct to deny motion to reopen proceedings for AOS under *Velarde* where there was some evidence of a legal marriage but the weight of the evidence was slight and the government opposed reopening]; *Sarr v. Gonzales,* 485 F.3d 354, 362–64 (6th Cir. 2007) [upholding BIA denial of motion to remand under *Velarde* where applicant had testified falsely at asylum hearing and never filed waiver with *Velarde* motion]; *Ramchandani v. Gonzales,* 434 F.3d 337, 340–41 (5th Cir. 2005) [upholding BIA denial of motion to reopen under *Velarde* where DHS opposed motion because applicant didn't submit affidavit of support].

E. *Voluntary Departure and Adjustment of Status*—In *Matter of Shaar,* 21 I&N Dec. 541 (BIA 1996), the BIA found that a person who files a motion to reopen for relief from deportation prior to the expiration of the VD period, but subsequently overstays the VD period pending adjudication of the motion, is statutorily ineligible for the relief sought under former INA §242B(e)(2)(A). Some circuits have found that the *Matter of Shaar* limitation on adjustment is no longer good law in that a post-IIRIRA timely filed motion to reopen tolls the voluntary departure period, thus permitting consideration of the merits of the motion. *See Ugokwe v. U.S. Att'y Gen.,* 453 F.3d 1325 (11th Cir. 2006); *Azarte v. Ashcroft,* 394 F.3d 1278 (9th Cir. 2005); *Barroso v. Gonzales,* 429 F.3d 1195, 1202–08 (9th Cir. 2005); *Kanivets v. Gonzales,* 424 F.3d 330, 334–36 (3d Cir. 2005); *Sidikhouya v. Gonzales,* 407 F.3d 950 (8th Cir. 2005). *See also Barrios v. Att'y Gen. of U.S.,* 399 F.3d 272 (3d Cir. 2005) [rejecting *Matter of Shaar* for *pre*-IIRIRA cases, and holding that a timely filed motion to reopen prevents the BIA/IJ from applying the bar to adjustment under former INA §242B(e)(2)(A) because the failure of the BIA/IJ to adjudicate the motion within the VD period is an "exceptional circumstance"]. *Cf. De Martinez v. Ashcroft,* 363 F.3d 1022 *amended on reh'g* 374 F.3d 759 (9th Cir. 2004) [where motion to reopen for AOS was filed within the 90-day time limit but after VD expired, person was ineligible to adjust]. *But see Chedad v. Gonzales,* 497 F.3d 57 (1st Cir. 2007) [a timely filed motion to reopen does not stay the running of the VD period and if the motion is granted after VD has expired the respondent is barred from seeking relief §1229c(d)(1)]; *Dekoladenu v. Gonzales,* 459 F.3d 500, 502–08 (4th Cir. 2006) [timely filed motion to reopen does not toll the VD period]; *Banda-Ortiz v. Gonzales,* 445 F.3d 387, 391 (5th Cir. 2006). *See in this chapter*, "Civil Penalty and Denial of Other Relief for Failure to Depart," ¶ III.B.6 (p.966), *infra*.

F. *Deportability Generally Does Not Bar Adjustment*—Persons deportable but not inadmissible under INA §212(a) may adjust status. *Matter of Rainford*, 20 I&N Dec. 598 (BIA 1992) [person subject to deportation on a gun charge is eligible to adjust]; *Matter of Azurin,* 23 I&N Dec. 695 (BIA 2005) [reaffirming *Rainford* and *Gabryelsky* and determining that §212(c) was available for pre-AEDPA conviction in conjunction with AOS even if the ground of deportation (gun charge) could not be waived because it did not have an equivalent ground of inadmissibility].

G. ***IJ Must Adjudicate Adjustment or Conditionally Terminate Proceedings***—If the application is before the IJ, the adjustment must be adjudicated by the IJ and cannot be remanded to CIS unless ICE counsel agrees. *Matter of Roussis*, 18 I&N Dec. 256 (BIA 1982). IJs have conditionally terminated proceeding to allow DDs to decide applications with the DD's agreement under an I-471C motion. IJs have jurisdiction to consider §245(i) adjustment applications. *Matter of Grinberg*, 20 I&N Dec. 911 (BIA 1994). The grounds for ICE counsel's agreement as a matter of prosecutorial discretion are set forth in Ch. 3, ¶ X.S.2 (p.311), *supra*.

H. ***Adjustment of Status Unavailable for Certain Individuals***—IIRIRA withdrew the right to seek adjustment for a period of 10 years after entry of an order of removal for persons who: (a) fail to appear at a removal hearing after receiving oral notice unless there are extraordinary circumstances, INA §240(b)(7), 8 U.S.C. §1229a(b)(7); (b) fail to depart after a grant of voluntary departure, INA §240B(d), 8 U.S.C. §1229c(d) [no exceptional circumstances exception]; or (c) re-enter U.S. illegally after being removed, INA §241(a)(5), 8 U.S.C. §1231(a)(5) [applying to *all* forms of relief]. For discussion regarding pre- and post-IIRIRA withdrawal of relief, *see in this chapter* sections I.B & C (p.957), *supra*.

I. ***Adjustment of Status of Arriving Aliens***—As a result of regulatory changes arising from nationwide litigation an arriving alien may seek to adjust status before the USCIS. *See* Ch. 6, ¶ XII.C.5.g (p.853), *supra*.

J. ***Waiver***—An individual who is eligible for adjustment but inadmissible because of a criminal conviction may nevertheless seek to adjust before an IJ by filing a waiver. *Matter of Mendez,* 21 I&N Dec. 296, 298 (BIA 1996). An LPR who has been lawfully residing in the U.S. for 7 years prior to initiation of proceedings, and who is not an aggravated felon, may seek to readjust with a §212(h) waiver to avoid removal for a criminal conviction. Similarly, an aggravated felon may adjust status with an §212(h) waiver if s/he was never an LPR. A person may also adjust using a §212(i) waiver for fraud or misrepresentation. *See in this chapter* part XII (p.1013), *infra*. A person who was deported and reentered prior to the time permitted under law, may seek an I-212 waiver in proceedings. 8 C.F.R. §212.2(e); *Lopez-Flores v. DHS,* 376 F.3d 793, 795 n.2 (8th Cir. 2004) [reversing decision to place person in reinstatement process under INA §241 because it would retroactively bar adjustment with I-212 waiver]. In former §212(c) cases where there was no comparable ground of exclusion, the BIA had allowed the use of the §212(c) waiver, in conjunction with an adjustment application to waive multiple grounds of deportability. *Matter of Azurin,* 23 I&N Dec. 695 (BIA 2005) [for pre-AEDPA convictions, the Board reaffirmed *Rainford* and *Gabryelsky* and determined that a §212(c) waiver was available in conjunction with an application for adjustment even if the ground of deportation (gun charge) could not be waived because it did not have an equivalent ground of inadmissibility]; *Matter of Gabryelsky*, 20 I&N Dec. 750 (BIA 1993); *Matter of Rodarte, supra*. The use of concurrent waivers to overcome exclusion grounds in adjustment cases before the IJ is permitted. 8 C.F.R. §§245.1(f), 1245.1(f).

K. ***Security Check/Name Check***—The IJ must comply with certain security check procedures before an AOS can be granted. *See* Ch. 3, ¶ X.S.7.1 (p.361), *supra*.

L. ***Readjustment of LPRs***—An LPR in removal proceedings is not barred from readjustment. *Matter of Mendez*, 21 I&N Dec. 296, 298 (BIA 1996) (and cases cited therein); *Matter of Rodarte,* 21 I&N Dec. 150 (BIA 1995) [INA §§212(c) & 245 applications may be filed concurrently]; *Matter of Gabryelsky*, 20 I&N Dec. 750 (BIA 1993) [adjustment with INA §212(c) waiver]. However, an LPR who is an arriving alien may not need an adjustment application because a waiver alone may be sufficient. *Matter of Abosi,* 24 I&N Dec. 204 (2007) [IJ erred in determining that a returning LPR placed in removal proceedings was required to file an AOS application in conjunction with a 212(h) waiver].

M. ***Refugee or Asylee Adjustment of Status***—A refugee or asylee placed in removal proceedings may apply for adjustment of status under INA §209 and may apply for a waiver of inadmissibility under INA §209(c). However, the may be barred from readjusting as refugees/asylee. *See* Ch. 4, part XIV (p.609), *supra*.

VII. WAIVERS OF REMOVAL

A. *INA §237(a)(1)(H), Waiver for Certain Misrepresentations*

1. *Generally*—INA §237(a)(1)(H), 8 U.S.C. §1227(a)(1)(H) waives removal of persons who were inadmissible at the time of entry or AOS because of fraud or misrepresentation, whether willful or innocent, in the procurement of a visa, other documentation or admission into the U.S. under INA §212(a)(6)(C)(i). 8 C.F.R. §1240.11(d). The AG has discretion to waive the inadmissibility of the spouse, parent, son or daughter of a USC/LPR, who was in possession of an immigrant visa or equivalent document and was otherwise admissible to the U.S. except for INA §§212(a)(5)(A) & (a)(7)(A). *Matter of Fu,* 23 I&N Dec. 985 (BIA 2006). A spouse or child battered or subjected to extreme cruelty and eligible to self-petition is also covered. An applicant who commits marriage fraud and is placed in removal proceedings may obtain a §237(a)(1)(H) waiver, notwithstanding INA §204(c), if he is otherwise admissible. *Virk v. INS,* 295 F.3d 1055 (9th Cir. 2002); *Matter of Manchisi,* 12 I&N Dec. 132 (BIA 1967), *overruled by Matter of Diniz but reinstated by Matter of Da Lomba,* 16 I&N Dec. 616 (BIA 1978). *But see Dallo v. INS,* 765 F.2d 581, 588 (6th Cir. 1985) [suggesting that *Da Lomba* is not controlling law in light of change in waiver from nondiscretionary to discretionary]. A fraudulent marriage, however, cannot be used to form the necessary family relationship to obtain relief. *Matter of Matti*, 19 I&N Dec. 43 (BIA 1984). The section is inapplicable to persons who are removable as Nazis under INA §237(a)(4)(D).
2. *Initial Fraud as a Discretionary Factor*—Following *INS v. Yang*, 519 U.S. 26 (1996) [finding that the statute does not require an "initial fraud" exception and that INS's discretion is "unfettered"], both DHS and the BIA take the view that the initial fraud is a factor to be considered in determining whether someone should be denied the waiver. *Matter of Tijam,* 22 I&N Dec. 408 (1998). The BIA, over dissent, has now incorporated a *Matter of Marin* type analysis in determining these cases where the "question whether to exercise discretion favorably necessitates a balancing of an alien's undesirability as a permanent resident with the social and humane considerations present." *Id* at 412.

   2.a. The adverse factors may include:
   - The nature and underlying circumstances of the fraud or misrepresentation involved;
   - The nature, seriousness, and recency of any criminal record;
   - Other evidence of bad character or undesirability as an LPR.

   2.b. The favorable factors may include:
   - Family ties in the U.S.;
   - Residence of long duration in this country, particularly where it commenced when the alien was young;
   - Evidence of hardship to alien or family if deportation occurs;
   - A stable employment history;
   - The existence of property or business ties;
   - Evidence of value and service to the community;
   - Other evidence of the alien's good character.

   Where the BIA did not consider all equities, denial was reversed. *Virk v. INS,* 295 F.3d 1055, 1059–61 (9th Cir. 2002) [BIA's discretion is not limitless; it must take into account all relevant factors, both positive and negative]; *Casem v. INS*, 8 F.3d 700 (9th Cir. 1993) [although statute does not specify equities, failure to consider USC child's hardship was reversible]. However, post-IIRIRA, federal courts may have no jurisdiction to review the discretionary denial of a waiver. *Singh v. Gonzales,* 451 F.3d 400, 410–11 [no jurisdiction to review discretionary denial of a §237(a)(1)(H) waiver]; *San Pedro v. Ashcroft,* 395 F.3d 1156, 1157–58 (9th Cir. 2005) [where IJ determined that respondent was statutorily ineligible for the waiver but was also ineligible as a matter of discretion in the alternative, the court would have no jurisdiction over the discretionary determination].

B. *Waiver Under Predecessor Statute, INA §241(f)*—Under INA §241(f), a person could not waive fraud committed during adjustment, *Matter of Connelly*, 19 I&N Dec. 156 (BIA 1984), to defend against rescission, *Matter of Pereira*, 19 I&N Dec. 169 (BIA 1984), EWI, *Reid v. INS*, 420 U.S. 619 (1975), termination of conditional residency, *Matter of Gawaran*, 20 I&N Dec. 938 (BIA 1995), or where the applicant was not otherwise admissible. *Matter of Roman*, 19 I&N Dec. 855 (BIA 1988) [INA §241(f) only waives inadmissibility under former INA §§212(a)(14), (20), and (21), not INA §212(a)(17)]. *But see Matter of Sosa-Hernandez*, 20 I&N Dec. 758 (BIA 1993) [INA §241(f) waiver retroactively validated LPR status thereby giving respondent the 7 years necessary for §212(c) relief]. A §241(f) waiver was also unavailable where the applicant made a nonfraudulent misrepresentation, *Matter of Raqueno*, 17 I&N Dec. 10 (BIA 1979); where basis for eligibility is a sham marriage, *Matter of Matti*, 19 I&N Dec. 43 (BIA 1984); or where person entered as nonimmigrant. *Matter of Mangabat*, 14 I&N Dec. 75 (BIA 1972); *Caddali v. INS*, 975 F.2d 1428 (9th Cir. 1992). However, it was not necessary that the applicant be charged under former INA §212(a)(19) [now INA §212(a)(6)(C)(i)] to obtain the benefit of the waiver. *Matter of Agustin*, 17 I&N Dec. 14 (BIA 1979) [waiver available even if charged under former INA §212(a)(20) [now INA §212(a)(7)(A)] where there was fraud]. *See generally INS v. Errico*, 385 U.S. 214 (1966); *Reid v. INS*, 420 U.S. 619 (1975) [purpose of former INA §241(f) was a humanitarian gesture to preserve families].

C. *INA §237(a)(1)(E)(iii), Waiver for Smuggling*—Allows the AG to exercise discretion to waive deportability for smuggling "for humanitarian purposes, to assure family unity, or when it is otherwise in the public interest." Waiver is only available in connection with smuggling an individual who "at the time of the offense was the applicant's spouse, parent, son or daughter (and no other individual)." IJ can grant it in deportation proceedings. 8 C.F.R. §1240.11(d).

VIII. NUNC PRO TUNC PERMISSION TO REAPPLY

The use of *nunc pro tunc* permission to reapply pre-dates the 1952 Act. *Matter of S-N-*, 6 I&N Dec. 73, 76 (AG 1954). The BIA or IJ may grant permission to reapply for admission retroactively when appropriate and necessary to the disposition of a case. *Matter of Sosa-Hernandez*, 20 I&N Dec. 758 (BIA 1993); *Matter of Ng*, 17 I&N Dec. 63 (BIA 1979); *Matter of Ducret*, 15 I&N Dec. 620 (BIA 1976). Several situations have been identified in which the power may be exercised:

(1) Where the only ground of deportability or inadmissibility would thereby be eliminated; and

(2) Where the alien would receive a grant of adjustment of status in conjunction with the grant of any appropriate waivers of inadmissibility.

Matter of Roman, supra [no *nunc pro tunc* relief for former INA §212(a)(17) charge where a former INA §212(a)(20) charge would remain]; *Perez-Rodriguez v. INS*, 3 F.3d 1074, 1079–80 (7th Cir. 1993) [no *nunc pro tunc* relief where person was deportable because of re-entry in violation of INA §212(a)(9)(A) *and* 212(a)(7)(A)(i)(I)]. Moreover, *nunc pro tunc* relief is unavailable under INA §212(h) where person did not leave U.S. subsequent to the original act and return unless s/he is applying for waiver for adjustment of status. *Matter of Balao*, 20 I&N Dec. 440 (BIA 1992); *Matter of Alarcon*, 20 I&N Dec. 557 (BIA 1992). A *nunc pro tunc* waiver is also not available where granting it to allow a person to reapply for admission would only then make him or her eligible for a second (former INA §212(c)) waiver. *Matter of Garcia*, 21 I&N Dec. 254 (BIA 1996). *But see Matter of Sosa-Hernandez*, 20 I&N Dec. 758 (BIA 1993) [combining INA §§241(f) and 212(c) relief]; *Matter of Farinas*, 12 I&N Dec. 467 (BIA 1967).

Nunc pro tunc has also been used as an equitable remedy to cure errors by the IJ/BIA. *Edwards v. INS,* 393 F.3d 299, 308–12 (2d Cir. 2004) [granting the right to seek §212(c) relief to persons who, despite having been convicted of an aggravated felony after 1990 and accruing 5 years in prison, were erroneously deprived of the right to seek §212(c) relief at a time when they had not accrued 5 years; rejecting the idea that *nunc pro tunc* equitable relief could only be applied where there was a constitutional violation or where respondent could prove that he would definitively obtain the relief and finding that respondents need only demonstrate they were erroneously denied the opportunity to apply when they were eligible]. *See also Castillo-Perez v. INS,* 212 F.3d 518 (9th Cir. 2000) [remanding case requiring application of law as it existed prior to ineffective assistance of counsel]; *Snajder v. INS,* 29 F.3d 1203 (7th Cir. 1994) [where right to counsel was violated, court applied *nunc pro tunc* doctrine to permit §212(c) relief for respondent who had already served 5 years imprisonment]: *Batanic v. INS,* 12 I&N Dec. 962, 967 (7th Cir. 1993) [granting *nunc pro tunc* relief due to denial of right to counsel]. *See also Ramirez-Canales v. Mukasey,* 517 F.3d 904, 910–11 (6th Cir. 2008 [followed *Matter of Briones* and upheld denial of AOS where person was barred from entering the U.S. for 10 years under INA

§212(a)(9)(C)((i)(I), but remanded the case to determine whether *nunc pro tunc* relief was available]; *But see Romero-Rodriguez v Gonzales,* 488 F.3d 672, 677–80 (5th Cir. 2007) [court did not have authority to grant *nunc pro tunc* review to correct BIA's original error in denying INA §212(c) relief resulting in applicant's subsequent ineligibility because 5 years of incarceration accrued; however BIA had authority to grant *nunc pro tunc* review and court remanded the case to the BIA for its consideration]; *Iouri v. Ashcroft,* 487 F.3d 76, 87–88 (2d Cir. 2007) [*nunc pro tunc* relief not warranted in seeking stay of VD from circuit court because errors by agency did not put respondent in a worse position, as he could have sought VD from DD on his own]; *Fernandes Pereira v. Gonzales,* 417 F.3d 38, 46–48 (1st Cir. 2005) [rejecting *nunc pro tunc* relief as well as constitutional claim where respondent was not statutorily eligible for §212(c) relief due to erroneous decisions by IJ/BIA on retroactivity, later reversed by the Supreme Court in *St. Cyr*].

IX. ESTOPPEL

A. ***Affirmative Misconduct Required***—Must establish affirmative misconduct on the part of the government. *INS v. Miranda*, 459 U.S. 14 (1982); *INS v. Hibi*, 414 U.S. 5 (1973); *Shin v. Mukasey,* 519 F.3d 901, 906–07 (9th Cir. 2008) [where respondent unknowingly obtained her "green card" through fraud by a DHS official, estoppel is inapplicable because the government is not bound by unauthorized acts of its agents]; *Morgan v. Gonzales,* 495 F.3d 1084, 1091–92 (9th Cir. 2007) [convicted drug dealer who was allowed to remain in U.S. for many years while cooperating with the government was not entitled to estoppel based upon government's affirmative misconduct where there was only extreme delay in removing him and no duty by the government not to do so]; *Andrade v. Gonzales,* 459 F.3d 538, 545 n.2 (5th Cir. 2006) [absent affirmative misconduct, DHS is not equitably estopped from bringing removal proceedings based on convictions that were presented to USCIS before granting adjustment]; *Mudric v. Att'y Gen. of the U.S.,* 469 F.3d 94, 99–100 (3d Cir. 2006) [respondent cannot claim equitable estoppel because prejudicial delay in adjudicating asylum and adjustment applications is not affirmative misconduct]; *Savoury v. U.S. Att'y Gen.,* 449 F.3d 1307, 1318–19 (11th Cir. 2006) [DHS is not estopped from denying LPR status to a person who was granted AOS and had his conditional status removed despite fully disclosing a drug conviction that rendered him ineligible without a showing of affirmative misconduct]; *Raffington v. Cangemi,* 399 F.3d 900, 902–03 (8th Cir. 2005) [even if the government filed a frivolous, but ultimately successful appeal, it would not constitute affirmative misconduct to estop the government]; *Varela v. Ashcroft,* 368 F.3d 864 (8th Cir. 2004) [no affirmative misconduct in denial of adjustment and placing respondent in removal proceedings].

B. ***Inattention, Failure to Act, or Neglect not Sufficient***—*Elia v. Gonzales,* 431 F.3d 268, 276 (6th Cir. 2005) [no affirmative misconduct in failing to hold removal hearing within 5 years so incarcerated respondent could apply for §212(c) relief]; *Tovar-Alvarez,* 427 F.3d 1350, 1353–54 (11th Cir. 2005) [no affirmative misconduct in two-year delay in naturalization decision following interview]; *Kowalczyk v. INS,* 245 F.3d 1143, 1149–51 (10th Cir. 2001) [9-year delay in asylum adjudication where country conditions changed does not warrant estoppel]; *Socop-Gonzalez v. INS,* 272 F.3d 1176, 1183–85 (9th Cir. 2001) (*en banc*) [no affirmative misconduct where INS negligently misinformed respondent that he could withdraw the appeal of his deportation order before the BIA and file an adjustment application with INS]; *Cortez-Felipe v. INS,* 245 F.3d 1054, 1057 (9th Cir. 2001) [no equitable estoppel where INS failed to file OSC with court after service and later filed NTA thereby preventing suspension claim]; *Costa v. INS,* 233 F.3d 31, 37–38 (1st Cir. 2000) [same]; *Rojas-Reyes v. INS,* 235 F.3d 115, 126 (2d Cir. 2000) [failure to promulgate repapering regulations to permit cancellation does not permit estoppel]; *Sulit v. Schiltgen,* 213 F.3d 449, 454 (9th Cir. 2000) [no affirmative misconduct where petitioner was misinformed and had not lost any rights]; *Westover v. Reno,* 202 F.3d 475, 481 (1st Cir. 2000) [no affirmative misconduct where person stopped on re-entry after government advised her that she could leave and apply for a new visa]; *Moosa v. INS,* 171 F.3d 994, 1003–06 (5th Cir. 1999) [improper dismissal of an appeal as untimely and failure to comply with circuit precedent does not warrant estoppel]; *Tefel v. Reno,* 180 F.3d 1286, 1302–04 (11th Cir. 1999) [where INS continued to accept suspension applications where there was a *possibility* Congress would amend the statute to pretermit such applications there is no estoppel]; *Santamaria-Ames v. INS,* 104 F.3d 1127, 1133 (9th Cir. 1996) [delay insufficient to warrant estoppel]; *Wang v. Meese*, 823 F.2d 1273 (8th Cir. 1987) [no estoppel where INS lost documents resulting in prejudice to the applicant due to long delay]; *Sachdev v. INS*, 788 F.2d 912 (2d Cir. 1986); *Jaa v. INS*, 779 F.2d 569 (9th Cir. 1986); *Clavis v. Ashcroft,* 281 F.Supp.2d 490, 497 (E.D.N.Y. 2003) [no affirmative misconduct in unexplained 13-year delay in completing removal proceedings, resulting in the deprivation of §212(c) relief]; *Diallo v. Reno,* 61 F.Supp.2d 1361, 1369–71 (N.D. Ga. 1999) [no affirmative misconduct in processing lottery adjustment]; *Omni Packaging, Inc. v. INS*, 930 F.Supp. 28, 33–36 (D.P.R. 1996) [INS not estopped from denying third preference petition on ground that applicant is not a manager or executive, notwithstanding previous L-1 approvals]; *Eskite v. District Director*, 901 F.Supp. 530, 538 (E.D.N.Y. 1995) [no estoppel to deport Haitian who had been screened in, detained for 18 months at Guantanamo and who was only brought to U.S. after litigation]. *But see Salgado-Diaz v. Ashcroft,* 395 F.3d 1158, 1165–68 (9th Cir. 2005) [government would be estopped from asserting fraudulent re-entry by respondent as a basis for removing him if respondent could prove that legacy INS improperly deported him while his deportation hearing was pending]; *Harriott v. Ashcroft,* 277 F.Supp.2d 538, 542–45 (E.D. Pa. 2003) [ordering DHS to approve certificate of citizenship and pay attorney's fees under equitable estoppel theory where certificate was denied because child turned 18 during delay and delay was 14 times longer than the 60 days normally contemplated]; *Otarola v. INS,* 270 F.3d 1272 (9th Cir. 2001) [government estopped from applying the stop-time rule where IJ granted suspension and INS took a frivolous appeal]; *Corniel-Rodriguez v. INS*, 532 F.2d 301 (2d Cir. 1976) [failure to notify second preference applicant about consequences of marriage estopped INS from revoking residency and deporting applicant]; *Fano v. O'Neill*, 806 F.2d 1262 (5th Cir. 1987).

C. *Public Policy Considerations*—Equitable relief cannot override "a public policy established by Congress." *INS v. Pangilinan*, 486 U.S. 875 (1988) [federal court has no equitable authority to naturalize a person even assuming affirmative misconduct, where statute does not permit Filipino war veterans to be naturalized after a certain date]; *Mustanich v. Mukasey,* 518 F.3d 1084, 1087–90 (9th Cir. 2008) [followed *Pangilinan*, distinguished non–citizenship estoppel cases, and found estoppel could not be used to prevent removal where legacy INS failed to accept or act on adults' requests to naturalize petitioner before his 18th birthday]; *Rios v. Ziglar*, 398 F.3d 1201, 1208–10 (10th Cir. 2005) [where deadline had passed for NACARA application but government told applicant to file and kept the fee, the government's actions, even if affirmative misconduct, would not warrant estoppel because application was submitted beyond the filing deadline]; *But see Perales v. Thornburgh*, 967 F.2d 798, 811–14 (2d Cir. 1992), *vacated and remanded sub nom. Reno v. Perales*, 113 S.Ct. 3027 (1993) [*Pangilinan* does not prevent ordering injunctive relief consistent with congressional purpose that extends filing deadline]; *Catholic Social Services v. Thornburgh, and LULAC v. INS*, 956 F.2d 914 (9th Cir. 1992), *vacated on other grounds sub nom. Reno v. Catholic Social Services*, 509 U.S. 43 (1993) [distinguishing *Pangilinan* and upholding court's injunction extending the date for filing amnesty]; *Matter of Thornburgh*, 869 F.2d 1503, 1512 (D.C. Cir. 1989) [*Pangilinan* does not rule out due process challenges, constructive filing dates or other forms of lesser relief such as temporary stays of deportation which may be available in the legalization context]; *Wauchope v. DOS*, 985 F.2d 1407, 1416–18 (9th Cir. 1993) [rejecting application of *Pangilinan* to constitutional challenge to naturalization statute].

D. *Parents of Minor Child*—In the view of some courts, the government is not estopped from deporting the parents of a minor USC child on the ground that such deportation would be a *de facto* deportation of the child. *Acosta v. Gaffney*, 558 F.2d 1153 (3d Cir. 1977); *Matter of Anaya*, 14 I&N Dec. 488 (BIA 1973); *Matter of A-K-,* 24 I&N Dec. 275 (BIA 2007) [parent cannot establish ground for asylum solely on fear of FGM to child and cannot derivatively apply through them]; *Niang v. Gonzales,* 492 F.3d 505, 510–14 (4th Cir. 2007) [affirmed asylum denial where mother asserted derivative claim because USC daughter would be subject to FGM if she accompanied her to Senegal and because mother would suffer psychological harm if daughter accompanies her].

E. *Estoppel Against Government Funds*—No estoppel against the government requiring it to expend funds. *Office of Personnel Management v. Richmond*, 496 U.S. 414 (1990) [Appropriateness Clause Art. 1 §9 cl.7 prevents any expenditures].

F. *BIA Has No Estoppel Authority*—The BIA is "without authority to apply the doctrine of equitable estoppel against the Service...." *Matter of Hernandez-Puente,* 20 I&N Dec. 335 (BIA 1991); *Matter of United Airlines Flight UA802,* 22 I&N Dec. 777, 783 (BIA 1999) [no laches defense]. *But see Matter of Truong,* 22 I&N Dec. 1090 (BIA 1999) [finding INS did not engage in affirmative misconduct when it erroneously placed respondent in exclusion proceedings].

G. *Equitable Estoppel and Equitable Tolling Distinguished*—Courts have recognized that there is a distinction between equitable tolling which "focuses on the plaintiff's excusable ignorance of limitations period and on lack of prejudice to the defendant," and equitable estoppel which "focuses on the actions of the defendant." *Socop-Gonzalez v. INS,* 272 F.3d 1176, 1184 (9th Cir. 2001) (en banc) *quoting Naton v. Bank of California,* 649 F.2d 691, 696 (9th Cir. 1981). In *Socop-Gonzalez* the Court found that the doctrine of equitable tolling applied to require the BIA to reopen respondent's asylum claim even though INS's actions did not amount to equitable estoppel. *See also Bowen v. City of New York,* 476 U.S. 467 (1986).

X. COLLATERAL ATTACK ON PRIOR DEPORTATION ORDER

A person may collaterally attack a final order of removal in a subsequent proceeding where the prior order resulted in a gross miscarriage of justice. *Pupek v. INS*, 47 F.3d 899, 902 (7th Cir. 1995); *Ponce-Gonzalez v. INS*, 775 F.2d 1342 (5th Cir. 1985); *Ramirez-Juarez v. INS*, 633 F.2d 174 (9th Cir. 1980); *Hernandez-Almanza v. INS*, 547 F.2d 100 (9th Cir. 1976); *Matter of Roman*, 19 I&N Dec. 855 (BIA 1988); *Matter of Farinas,* 12 I&N Dec. 467 (BIA 1967); *Matter of Malone*, 11 I&N Dec. 730 (BIA 1966). *But see Lara v. Trominski,* 216 F.3d 487, 493 & n.5 (5th Cir. 2000). However, under INA §241(a)(5), 8 U.S.C. §1231(a)(5), and 8 C.F.R. §§241.8, 1241.8, where the AG finds that where a person who was removed or who voluntarily departed under an order of removal re-enters the U.S. illegally, DHS can reinstate the prior order of removal. The BIA has held that it has no jurisdiction to consider a challenge to a reinstated removal order. *Matter of G-N-C-,* 22 I&N Dec. 281, 286–88 (BIA 1998) [no prejudice where INS violated its regulations and terminated removal proceedings to institute proceedings under §241(a)(5) instead of seeking termination from the court]. The constitutionality of the reinstatement procedure has been upheld, *U.S. v. Martinez-Vitela,* 193 F.3d 1047, 1052–53 (9th Cir. 1999) [reinstatement proceeding complies with due process under *Mathews* analysis], as has its retroactive application. *Fernandez-Vargas v. Gonzales,* 126 S.Ct. 2422 (2006). A person who is subject to reinstatement still retains the right to seek withholding of removal and a CAT claim. 8 C.F.R. §§208.31, 241.8(d), 1208.31, 1241.8(d).

XI. DEFERRED ACTION

A. *Discretionary*—Deferred action is a discretionary act through the recommendation of a DD and approval of the Regional Commissioner, not to prosecute or deport a particular alien. It cannot be granted by the IJ. *Johnson v. INS*, 962 F.2d 579 (7th Cir. 1992). Deferred Action is "an act of administrative choice to give some cases lower priority and in no way an entitlement ...." Former O.I. §242.1(a)(22). Although the operations instructions for deferred action have been withdrawn, the relief is still available. *See Standard Operating Procedures for Enforcement Officers: Arrest, Detention, Processing, and Removal (Standard Operating Procedures),* Part X.; Meissner, Comm., Memo, HQOPP 50/4 (Nov. 17, 2000), *published on* AILA InfoNet at Doc. No. 00112702.

Among the factors that may be considered are:

- The likelihood of removal;
- The presence of sympathetic factors;
- The likelihood that because of sympathetic factors, a large amount of adverse publicity will be generated;
- The person's continued presence is desired by law enforcement for an ongoing investigation or review;
- Whether the individual is a member of a class of deportable aliens whose removal has been given high enforcement priority (*e.g.,* terrorists, drug traffickers).

B. *Preclusion of Review*—Some cases addressing deferred action include: *Pasquini v. Morris*, 700 F.2d 658 (11th Cir. 1983); *Nicholas v. INS*, 590 F.2d 802 (9th Cir. 1979); *David v. INS*, 548 F.2d 219 (8th Cir. 1977); *Lennon v. INS*, 527 F.2d 187 (2d Cir. 1975). The Supreme Court in *Reno v. American-Arab Anti-Discrimination Comm.*, 525 U.S. 471 (1999), has interpreted INA §242(g) as precluding judicial review of deferred action decisions.

XII. WAIVERS UNDER INA §§212(g), (h), (i), (k), 209(c), and 213

A. *Generally*—These waivers may be granted *nunc pro tunc* in removal proceedings where an alien was inadmissible at entry or is applying for adjustment. *Patel v. Gonzales,* 432 F.3d 685, 692–95 (6th Cir. 2005) [reversing IJ's determination that she did not have authority to grant *nunc pro tunc* waiver under former version of INA §212(i), but finding respondent ineligible]; *Matter of Ulloa,* 22 I&N Dec. 725

(BIA 1999) [respondent, who was inadmissible as a public charge and therefore ineligible for adjustment, had the right to be informed by the IJ of the availability of a §213 waiver and the IJ had jurisdiction to issue a waiver]. *Matter of Michel*, 21 I&N Dec. 1101 (BIA 1998) [aggravated felon with approved I-130 is eligible for AOS with a §212(h) waiver because he had not previously been an LPR]; *Matter of Alarcon*, 20 I&N Dec. 557 (BIA 1992); *Matter of Sanchez*, 17 I&N Dec. 218 (BIA 1980); *Matter of Parodi*, 17 I&N Dec. 608 (BIA 1980). However, an NIV waiver under INA §212(d)(3)(B) cannot be granted *nunc pro tunc* in removal proceedings. *Matter of Fueyo*, 20 I&N Dec. 84 (BIA 1989). The regulations allow waivers to be filed concurrently, 8 C.F.R. §§245.1(f), 1245.1(f), and the BIA has recognized that two waivers of inadmissibility may be granted simultaneously. *Matter of Millard*, 11 I&N Dec. 175 (BIA 1965) [INA §§212(h) and 212(i)]; *Matter of Sosa-Hernandez*, 20 I&N Dec. 758 (BIA 1993) [INA §§241(f) and 212(c) waivers]. *See also Perez-Gonzalez v. Ashcroft,* 379 F.3d 783 (9th Cir. 2004) [USCIS may waive §§212(a)(6)(C) and §212(a)(9)(A)–(C) in context of §245(i) adjustment and I-212 waiver; but opinion vacated in certain respects by *Gonzales v. DHS,* 508 F.3d 1227 (9th Cir. 2007)]; *Matter of Farinas*, 12 I&N Dec. 467 (BIA 1967); 8 C.F.R. §§212.2(d), 1212.2(d). *But see Matter of Roman*, 19 I&N Dec. 855 (BIA 1988). Waivers are also available in removal proceedings in connection with an adjustment of status application. 8 C.F.R. §245.1(f), 1245.1(f). For a more detailed discussion of each of the waivers of inadmissibility, *see* Ch. 3, section III.I (p. 113), *supra.*

B. ***INA §212(g) Waiver***—Section 212(g) waives inadmissibility on health-related grounds. *See* Ch. 3, ¶ III.I.12 (p.123), *supra.*

C. ***INA §212(c) and Cancellation***—Although the BIA has traditionally recognized that waivers may be filed simultaneously, *supra,* the BIA and the courts have declined to permit §212(c) and cancellation applications to be filed simultaneously to cure pre- and post-IIRIRA convictions. *Garcia-Jimenez v. Gonzales,* 488 F.3d 1082 (9th Cir. 2007) [where IJ granted INA §212(c) relief for pre-IIRIRA convictions, it could not grant cancellation for a post-IIRIRA conviction]; *Peralta-Taveras v. Attorney General,* 488 F.3d 580 (2d Cir. 2007) [cannot file INA §212(c) and cancellation applications simultaneously to cure pre- and post-IIRIRA convictions where pre-IIRIRA convictions was an aggravated felony]; *Amouzadeh v. Winfrey,* 467 F.3d 451, 458–59 (5th Cir. 2006) [a grant of §212(c) relief for a prior drug conviction still bars cancellation for a separate CIMT because §212(c) does not waive an aggravated felony conviction for cancellation]; *Munoz-Yepez v. Gonzales,* 465 F.3d 347 (8th Cir. 2006) [where respondent *could* receive §212(c) relief for first *pre*-1996 aggravated felony, he would still be denied cancellation for second *post*-1996 non–aggravated felony because the aggravated felony barred cancellation];*Mai v. Gonzales,* 473 F.3d 162, 165–67 (5th Cir. 2007) [lawyer ineffective where he admitted two grounds of removal where one required a §212(c) waiver and the second a waiver under §240A because once §212(c) granted for the first ground §240A is unavailable].

D. ***INA §§212(h), (i) Waivers***—Section 212(h) waives certain criminal grounds of inadmissibility but is unavailable as a waiver of deportation where person did not leave the U.S. and is not applying for adjustment of status. *Matter of Balao*, 20 I&N Dec. 440 (BIA 1992); *Klementanovsky v. Gonzales,* 501 F.3d 788 (7th Cir. 2007) [equal protection is not violated under a facially legitimate and bona fide standard by denying the use of a 212(h) waiver to defeat deportation while permitting it use to challenge inadmissibility; *Yeung* rejected]. *But see Yeung v. INS*, 76 F.3d 337 (11th Cir. 1995) [finding INA §212(h) applicable in deportation proceedings for person who never left the U.S. under the *Francis* rationale]. Section 212(i) waives inadmissibility due to fraud or willful misrepresentation, but cannot waive inadmissibility under §212(a)(6)(F), due to document fraud under §274C. Circuit courts have determined that applying the changes in §212(i) to pending cases is not impermissibly retroactive. *Okpa v. INS,* 266 F.3d 313, 318–19 (4th Cir. 2001); *Cervantes-Gonzales v. INS,* 244 F.3d 1001, 1005–06 (9th Cir. 2001). For a thorough discussion of INA §§212(h) and 212(i) waivers *see* Ch. 3, ¶¶ III.I.13 & 14 (pp.124 & 126), *supra.*

E. ***INA §212(k) Waiver***—A §212(k) waiver is available for a person with an immigrant visa who is inadmissible under INA §212(a)(5)(A) as a skilled or unskilled worker without a labor certification or under INA §212(a)(7)(A)(i) for lack of required documents or whose immigrant visa was not issued in compliance with law, if the AG is satisfied that the person did not know, nor could have known by exercise of reasonable diligence, that she was inadmissible at time of entry; 8 C.F.R. §§212.10, 1212.10. IJ can adjudicate a §212(k) waiver even if DD has not made a determination on the application. *Matter of Aurelio*, 19 I&N Dec. 458 (BIA 1987); *Mayo v. Ashcroft,* 317 F.3d 867, 873–74 (8th

Cir. 2003). A parent's knowledge of inadmissibility may be imputed to a child. *Senica v. INS*, 16 F.3d 1013 (9th Cir. 1994). *See* Ch. 3, ¶ III.I.15 (p.127), *supra.*

F. *INA §209(c) Waiver*—A refugee or asylee in removal proceedings may apply for AOS under INA §209 and may apply for a waiver of inadmissibility under INA §209(c). *Matter of K-A-,* 23 I&N Dec. 661 (BIA 2004) [finding that the IJ possessed original jurisdiction over §209 AOS and waiver, that the IJ had the authority but was not compelled to terminate asylee status because of applicant's aggravated felony conviction, and that if respondent is an aggravated felon it is only in "those rare situations" where "compelling countervailing equities" exist that AOS and waiver should be granted]; *Matter of H-N-,* 22 I&N Dec. 1039 (BIA 1999); 8 C.F.R. §§209.2(c), 1209.2(c), 1240.11(a)(2). However, a waiver for serious ("violent or dangerous") crimes will almost never be granted absent extraordinary circumstances such as those involving national security or foreign policy considerations or where the denial would result in exceptional and extremely unusual hardship. *Matter of Jean,* 23 I&N Dec. 373, 381–84 (AG 2002) *affirmed Jean v. Gonzales,* 452 F.3d 392, 396–98 (5th Cir. 2006) [denying adjustment to person convicted of second degree manslaughter in the death of a baby and reversing BIA where the focus was on the family's hardship without considering the nature of the criminal offense; on appeal court rejected argument that AG's standard was *ultra vires*]; *Ali v. Achim,* 468 F.3d 462, 465–67 (7th Cir. 2006) *cert. dismissed* 128 S.Ct. 828 (2007) [AG did not exceed his authority when he articulated the heightened waiver standard in *Matter of Jean*]. *But see Rivas-Gomez v. Gonzales,* 441 F.3d 1072, 1074–79 (9th Cir. 2006) [reversing IJ for denying §209(c) waiver where respondent was convicted of an aggravated felony (statutory rape) and IJ determined there was insufficient hardship without first determining that the crime was a violent or dangerous felony]. Also, a refugee/asylee who became an LPR and was then placed in removal proceedings who seeks to readjust as a refugee/asylee may be barred by INA §209(a)(1)(C). *Matter of S-I-K-,* 24 I&N Dec. 324, 330 (BIA 2007); *Saintha v. Mukasey,* 516 F.3d 243, 251–53 (4th Cir. 2008) [upheld BIA view under *Chevron* deference that refugee could not readjust in IJ proceedings because of INA §209(a)(1)(C)]. *See* Ch. 3, ¶ III.I.3 (p.120), *supra.*

G. *INA §213 Waiver*—Waives health-related grounds of inadmissibility. *See* Ch. 3, ¶ III.I.16 (p.127), *supra.*

H. *Judicial Review*—For a discussion concerning the limitations on judicial review of waivers, *see, generally,* Chapter 10 (p.1071), *infra*; *see also* "Review of Discretionary Waivers" in Ch. 10, ¶ V.F.3.h(5) (p.1175), *infra.*

XIII. PRIVATE LEGISLATION

A. When strong equities exist and other relief is not possible, it may be feasible to obtain relief through private congressional legislation. Any member of Congress can introduce private legislation but it is generally used as a last resort because only a small percentage of bills are actually passed. DHS does not give an automatic stay unless a congressional subcommittee asks DHS for report. O.I. §107.1(c). Congress has stringent criteria usually requiring extreme hardship, and is generally unwilling to assist in drug cases. The Senate and House rules are reprinted in 70 No. 11 *Interpreter Releases*, 591, 597–602 (May 3, 1993). An updated version of the House rules is reprinted in AILA's annually produced *Immigration & Nationality Act*. For a new comprehensive book on the topic, see Gallagher, *AILA's Focus on Private Bills and Pardons in Immigration* (AILA 2008). For a thorough review of the history all private bills through Congress until 1997, *see* Maguire, *Public Legislation and Private Bills* (University Press 1997).

CHAPTER 9
ADMINISTRATIVE REVIEW

XII. REVIEW BY EXCHANGE VISITOR WAIVER REVIEW BOARD

XIII. MOTION TO REOPEN OR RECONSIDER BEFORE EOIR

CHAPTER 9
ADMINISTRATIVE REVIEW

I. REVIEW BY BOARD OF IMMIGRATION APPEALS (BIA)

A. *Generally*—The Board of Immigration Appeals (BIA) is the appellate body designated to review decisions of the immigration court and, in some instances, of DHS. The BIA is part of the Executive Office for Immigration Review (EOIR) which also contains an Office of the Chief Immigration Judge. 8 C.F.R. §§1003.0, 1003.9–.10. The EOIR is within the U.S. Department of Justice.

B. *Jurisdiction*—The BIA has appellate jurisdiction under 8 C.F.R. §1003.1(b) over:

1. Final decisions of IJs in former exclusion cases, except the length of time of VD.
2. Final decisions of IJs in removal cases except: (1) where the sole ground is the length of time of VD; (2) where there is an *in absentia* order under former INA §242B(c), *see Matter of Gonzalez-Lopez*, 20 I&N Dec. 644 (BIA 1993) [remedy is a motion to reopen]; or (3) where there is an *in absentia* order under INA §240(b)(5). INA §240(b)(5)(C). *See also in this chapter*, "BIA's Authority to Enter Final Order of Removal," section V.B (p.1032), *infra*.
3. Decisions on cancellation of removal, adjustment of status, and decisions under former INA §212(c) and waivers in removal proceedings, but not INA §212(c), AOS or other decisions denying relief rendered by USCIS.
4. Decisions involving fines, penalties, and mitigation of fines or penalties.
5. Decisions on preference petitions (except employment-based and orphan petitions), and revalidation and revocation of petitions. However, jurisdiction extends only to discretionary revocation and the BIA has no authority to review automatic revocation. 8 C.F.R. §§205.1(a), 1205.1(a). *Matter of Zaidan*, 19 I&N Dec. 297 (BIA 1985). The BIA may only consider appeals brought by the petitioner. *Matter of Sano*, 19 I&N Dec. 299 (BIA 1985); *Joseph v. Landon*, 679 F.2d 113 (7th Cir. 1982). Courts, however, have found that beneficiaries do have standing. *Taneja v. Smith*, 795 F.2d 355 (4th Cir. 1986); *Ali v. INS*, 661 F.Supp. 1234 (D. Mass. 1986); *Sanchez-Trujillo v. INS*, 620 F.Supp. 1361 (W.D.N.C. 1985).
6. Decisions on waivers of inadmissibility for nonimmigrants under INA §212(d)(3), 8 U.S.C. §1182(d)(3).
7. Determinations relating to bond and detention in removal cases, except for persons deemed inadmissible or subject to mandatory detention (unless imposition of mandatory detention is challenged), and determinations relating to bond and detention in deportation, but not exclusion cases. 8 C.F.R. §§236.1(d)(3), 1236.1(d)(3).
8. Determinations made by an IJ to continue detention beyond removal period under 8 C.F.R. §§241.14, 1241.14. *Matter of Saelee,* 22 I&N Dec. 1258, 1261–62 (BIA 2000) [review may be permitted even if ICE *sua sponte* reviews detention where no request was initiated].
9. Decisions by the IJ on rescission of adjustment of status under INA §246, 8 U.S.C. §1246.
10. Decisions of IJs relating to asylum or TPS.
11. Decisions of IJs relating to the LIFE Act in accordance with 8 C.F.R. §§245.13, 1245.13.
12. The BIA has *no jurisdiction* to review decisions to reinstate removal/deportation/exclusion orders pursuant to INA §241(a)(5). *Matter of G-N-C-*, 22 I&N Dec. 281 (BIA 1998).

C. *Board Procedure*—The AG has drastically revised the procedures for the adjudication of cases before the BIA. 67 Fed. Reg. 54878–54905 (Aug. 26, 2002). The procedures call for the disposition of most cases by a single member of the BIA and referrals to a 3-member panel in only limited circumstances. Cases are initially screened for summary dismissal in accordance with 8 C.F.R. §1003.1(d)(2). 8 C.F.R. §1003.1(e)(1). In numerous memos the BIA set forth the criteria for streamlined, decision-making, including AWO cases. These memos are *published on* AILA InfoNet at Doc. Nos. 07011663-1 to 17.

1. *Three-Member Panel*—8 C.F.R. §1003.1(e)(6). A case may only be assigned to a three-member panel for adjudication on the merits if there is a need: (i) to settle inconsistencies among the rulings of different IJs; (ii) to establish a precedent construing the meaning of laws, regulations or procedures; (iii) to review a decision by an IJ or DHS that is not in conformity with the law or with applicable precedents; (iv) to resolve a case or controversy of major national import; (v) to review a clearly erroneous factual determination by an IJ; or (vi) to reverse the decision of an IJ or DHS other than by the procedure for a brief order by a single Board member.

2. *Single Member*—8 C.F.R. §§1003.1(e)(2)–(5). Most cases are decided by a single member of the BIA. A single Board member may summarily dismiss an appeal, affirm an IJ decision without opinion, or issue an abbreviated decision affirming, modifying, or remanding to an IJ. A single Board member may also reverse an IJ "if such reversal is plainly consistent with and required by intervening Board or judicial precedent, by an intervening Act of Congress, or by an intervening final regulation." 8 C.F.R. §1003.1(e)(5). In other cases, it may refer the matter to a three-member panel. For example, if the single BIA member "believes that the decision of an immigration judge should be reversed because of a clearly erroneous factual determination or an error in law, or one of the other reasons specified [for panel review], the member should refer the case to a three-member panel." 67 Fed. Reg. at 54887. At least one court has rejected a challenge to the single member process based on retroactivity. *Khattak v. Ashcroft,* 332 F.3d 250 (4th Cir. 2003) [the single member process is not an impermissible retroactive application of the law because it is a procedural change that does not alter legal standards]. Another court has found that the conflict between former 8 C.F.R. §1003.1(a)(7), which does not provide for the issuance of an abbreviated order by a single judge, and 8 C.F.R. §1003.1(e)(5), which does provide for such an order should be resolved by permitting such orders. *Settenda v. Ashcroft,* 377 F.3d 89, 96–98 (1st Cir. 2004) [BIA member may write an abbreviated order instead of issuing an AWO]. *See also Jarad v. Gonzales,* 461 F.3d 867, 871 (7th Cir. 2006) [finding no legal difference that one judge as opposed to a panel was assigned to the case]; *Gutnik v Gonzales,* 469 F.3d 683, 690–92 (7th Cir. 2006) [single judge under §1003.1(e)(5) is not required to send novel question to three-judge panel].

3. Affirmance Without Opinion (AWO)—8 C.F.R. §§1003.1(e)(4).

   3.a. *Generally*—A single member of the BIA may affirm an IJ without an opinion where s/he determines: (a) that the result reached by the IJ was correct; (b) that any errors were harmless or not material; *and* that (c) the issues on appeal are squarely controlled by existing BIA or federal court precedent and do not involve the application of precedent to a novel factual situation; *or* (d) the factual and legal issues raised are not so substantial that the case warrants the issuance of a written opinion.

   3.b. *Constitutional Challenges to AWO Procedures*—The AWO procedures have been upheld in virtually all circuits. *Martinez v. Mukasey,* 508 F.3d 255, 260 (5th Cir. 2007) [relying on *Garcia-Melendez v. Ashcroft,* 351 F.3d 657, 662–63 (5th Cir. 2003) it is unnecessary for the BIA to engage in a full review because the federal court has the IJ's opinion to review]; *Dia v. Ashcroft,* 353 F.3d 228, 234–45 (3d Cir. 2003) (en banc) [AWO procedure does not violate the INA or due process]; *Blanco De Belbruno v. Ashcroft,* 362 F.3d 272 (4th Cir. 2004) [same]; *Zhang v. DOJ,* 362 F.3d 155 (2d Cir. 2004) [same]; *Yuk v. Ashcroft,* 355 F.3d 1222, 1228–32 (10th Cir. 2004) [same]; *Loulou v. Ashcroft,* 354 F.3d 706, 708–09 (8th Cir. 2003) [same]; *Denko v. INS,* 351 F.3d 717, 725–32 (6th Cir. 2003) [same]; *Lonyem v. U.S. Att'y Gen.,* 352 F.3d 1338, 1342 (11th Cir. 2003) [respondent not entitled *per se* to full BIA opinion]; *Falcon Carriche v. Ashcroft,* 350 F.3d 845 (9th Cir. 2003) [streamlining does not violate due process and does not restrict right to obtain review in federal court]; *Mendoza v. U.S. Att'y Gen.,* 327 F.3d 1283, 1288–89 (11th Cir. 2003) [one-sentence summary affirmance procedure upheld because there is no constitutional or statutory right to an administrative appeal; there is no regulatory entitlement to a full opinion by the BIA; and the court will continue to have the IJ's decision and the record to review]; *Georgis v. Ashcroft,* 328 F.3d 962, 966–67 & n.4 (7th Cir. 2003) [no due process violation where issue is whether the record supports substantial evidence, because of the court's ability to conduct a full and fair appraisal of the case]; *Soadjede v. Ashcroft,* 324 F.3d 830 (5th Cir. 2003) [following *Albathani's* reasoning that administrative agencies should be free to fashion their own rules, and finding no due process violation in the procedure]; *Gonzalez-Oropeza v. U.S. Att'y Gen.,* 321 F.3d 1331, 1333 (11th Cir. 2003) [same]; *Albathani v. INS,* 318 F.3d 365, 375–77 (1st Cir. 2003) [same]; *Capital Area Immigrants' Rights Coalition v. DOJ,* 264 F.Supp.2d 14 (D.D.C. 2003) [rejecting APA challenge to streamlining regulations].

3.c. *Exhaustion*—In AWO cases or decisions in which the Board cites to *Matter of Burbano,* 20 I&N Dec. 872 (BIA 1994) exhaustion is not necessary if the issue was raised before the IJ because the BIA is presumed to have reviewed the entire record and adopted the IJ's position. *Arreguin-Moreno v. Mukasey,* 511 F.3d 1229, 1232 (9th Cir. 2008) [petitioner need not exhaust issues before the BIA that were raised before the IJ because in *Burbano* the BIA adopts the IJ's decision in its entirety and all issues are deemed presented to the BIA]; *Pasha v. Gonzales,* 433 F.3d 530, 532–34 (7th Cir. 2005) [exhaustion is not an issue where BIA issues AWO decision, because an AWO decision is assumed to be a resolution of the merits of all the issues absent waiver through a specific notice of appeal or the filing of a brief on a particular issue or failure to raise the issue before the IJ]. *But see Zara v. Ashcroft,* 383 F.3d 927 (9th Cir. 2004) [finding exhaustion doctrine applies to AWO/streamlined decisions].

3.d. *Voluntary Departure and AWO*—As the AWO procedure affirms the IJ's decision, the BIA does not have the authority to lower the VD period. *Padilla-Padilla v. Gonzales,* 463 F.3d 972, 980–82 (9th Cir. 2006) [reversing AWO that decreased the IJ's grant of VD from 60 to 30 days].

3.e. *Judicial Review of Streamlining Decision*—The decision to AWO or streamline a particular case is subject to review and may be reversed. *Montes-Lopez v. Gonzales,* 486 F.3d 1163 (9th Cir. 2007) [where BIA issued an AWO and failed to address respondent's statutory and constitutional claim that he had been denied the right to counsel and forced to proceed *pro se* when IJ refused to continue case despite counsel's temporary suspension, court reversed]; *Purveegiin v. Gonzales,* 448 F.3d 684 (3d Cir. 2006) [court has jurisdiction to review decision by single Board member to AWO a case instead of referring it to a three-member panel and where single Board member, contrary to 8 C.F.R. §1003.1(e)(5), reverses the IJ instead of "affirming, modifying, or remanding" the case, he erred in not referring the matter to a three-member panel]; *San Pedro v. Ashcroft,* 395 F.3d 1156 (9th Cir. 2005) (and cases cited therein) [where INA §237(a)(1)(H) waiver was denied by IJ on both statutory and discretionary grounds and BIA issued AWO, court reversed because the alternative holdings made it impossible to determine BIA's basis for decision]; *Cuellar Lopez v. Gonzales,* 427 F.3d 492, 495–99 (7th Cir. 2005) [where an IJ gives a reason for denial that can be reviewed by circuit court (physical presence requirement for cancellation) along with a reason that cannot be reviewed (discretionary good moral character finding), and the BIA issues an AWO, the court will remand the case back to the BIA to clarify the basis for its decision]; *Lanza v. Ashcroft,* 389 F.3d 917, 924–32 (9th Cir. 2004) [where IJ denied asylum as untimely and on the merits and the BIA issued an AWO, due process required remand because the merits are reviewable by the court but the one year filing deadline is not]; *Smriko v. Ashcroft,* 387 F.3d 279, 288–97 (3d Cir. 2004) [where respondent raised a novel question regarding whether a refugee may be deported without first revoking refugee status, it was arbitrary and capricious for the BIA to AWO]; *Zhu v. Ashcroft,* 382 F.3d 521, 526–27 (5th Cir. 2004) [where IJ suggests multiple grounds for denying relief, including the untimely filing of an asylum application that is not reviewable, the BIA's use of AWO creates a jurisdictional problem]; *Chong Shin Chen v. Ashcroft,* 378 F.3d 1081, 1086–88 (9th Cir. 2004) [challenge to denial of AOS of Chinese student who entered EWI but was granted protection under CSPA should not have been streamlined because it was a novel issue and not insubstantial]; *Batalova v. Ashcroft,* 355 F.3d 1246, 1253 (10th Cir. 2004) [decision not to send case to three-judge panel is not committed to agency discretion]; *Haoud v. Ashcroft,* 350 F.3d 201 (1st Cir. 2003) [AWO decision denying asylum remanded where substantially similar nonprecedent BIA decision granted asylum; AWO gave no guidance as to whether it affirmed on the nonreviewable one-year filing requirement or on the reviewable merits determination]; *cf. Vasha v. Gonzales,* 410 F.3d 863, 875–76 (6th Cir. 2005) [reviewing BIA decision to streamline but finding that respondent failed to demonstrate that three judge panel review appropriate]; *Kasnecovic v. Gonzales,* 400 F.3d 812, 814–15 (9th Cir. 2005) [distinguishing *Lanza* and reviewing asylum matter rather than remanding to BIA because the posture of the case required the court to review the IJ's adverse credibility determination on other issues, and it would have decided the asylum claim anyway]; *Vukmirovic v. Ashcroft,* 362 F.3d 1247, 1253 (9th Cir. 2004) [finding authority to review summary affirmance as a violation of due process but deciding issue was moot]. Some circuits have also explicitly applied the substantial evidence standard of review where streamlining was used. *Moin v. Ashcroft,* 335 F.3d 415, 418 (5th Cir. 2003) [upholding BIA's AWO decision finding LPR abandoned her residency based on substantial evidence]; *Albathani v. INS,* 318 F.3d 365 (1st Cir. 2003). *See also Kumar v. Gonzales,* 439 F.3d 520 (9th Cir. 2006) [applying harmless error rule to clear violation of AWO regulation where BIA issued AWO with a footnote disavowing the IJ's credibility finding]; *Shi v. BIA,* 374 F.3d 64, 66 (2d Cir. 2004) [BIA did not abuse its discretion because IJ's decision contained sufficient reasoning]; *Denko v. INS,* 351 F.3d 717, 731–32 (6th Cir. 2003) [finding AWO decisions are subject to judicial review and not exclusively committed to agency discretion, but finding AWO decision appropriate]; *Camponesco-Montejo,* 384 F.3d 814 (9th Cir. 2004) [same].

3.f. *No Judicial Review of Streamlining Decision*—One circuit presumes that "BIA members do their job thoroughly," *Batalova v. Ashcroft,* 355 F.3d 1246, 1252 (10th Cir. 2004), and has determined that the decision and manner in which the BIA streamlines is *not* subject to judicial review because it is "committed to agency discretion." *Tsegay v. Ashcroft,* 386 F.3d 1347, 1353–58 (10th Cir. 2004) [the decision to AWO is not reviewable because there was no jurisdiction to review the one-year asylum deadline, review of AWO decision is not review of a final order, and AWO is committed to agency discretion; distinguishing *Batalova*]. *See also Ibragimov v. Gonzales,* 476 F.3d 125, 138–39 (2d Cir. 2007) [no jurisdiction to review a single Board member's decision to affirm rather than refer to a 3-member panel, but leaving open the question of authority to review summary affirmance under the regulations]; *Jarad v. Gonzales,* 461 F.3d 867, 871 (7th Cir. 2006) [finding no legal difference whether BIA properly or improperly streamlined, because if there was no error in the IJ's decision it would be irrelevant, and if there was an error, the court has authority to remand to the IJ, which is all that the BIA would do]; *Kambolli v. Gonzales,* 449 F.3d 454 (2d Cir. 2006) [no jurisdiction to review BIA decision to AWO rather than refer appeal to three-member panel]; *Guyadin v. Gonzales,* 449 F.3d 465, 469–70 (2d Cir. 2006) [same]; *Martinez-Maldonado v. Gonzales,* 437 F.3d 679, 682–84 (7th Cir. 2006) [AWO was not reviewable because the IJ's decision to deny cancellation based on lack of hardship was not reviewable under INA §242(a)(2)(B)(i)]; *Ngure v. Ashcroft,* 367 F.3d 975, 980–88 (8th Cir. 2004) [whether BIA streamlining was proper is not reviewable because it is not possible to devise a meaningful and adequate standard of review]; *Hasalla v. Ashcroft,* 367 F.3d 799, 803–04 (8th Cir. 2004) [where respondent challenged streamlining on ground that it did not comport with the regulation, the court held that there is no constitutional, statutory, or regulatory right to a full BIA opinion]; *Reyes-Vasquez v. Ashcroft,* 395 F.3d 903, 905–06 (8th Cir. 2005) [rejecting separation of powers challenge to streamlining regulation]. A failure to properly streamline a case may be moot where the circuit court reviews the IJ's decision. *Hamdan v. Gonzales,* 425 F.3d 1051, 1057–58 (7th Cir. 2005) ["[i]t makes no practical difference whether the BIA properly or improperly streamlined review" where IJ's decision is reviewed]; *Mekhoukh v. Ashcroft,* 358 F.3d 118, 130 (1st Cir. 2004) [where court reviewed IJ's decision and found no reversible error, the issue of whether the case was appropriately streamlined was moot]. In the view of one circuit, the BIA's decision to AWO where the IJ has offered some reasons that would be jurisdictionally barred from review and others that would not, does not raise constitutional issues. *Ekasinta v. Gonzales,* 415 F.3d 1188, 1191–95 (10th Cir. 2005) [disagreeing with *Lanza* and finding no statutory or due process violation where AWO decision fails to state that it affirmed on discretionary or nondiscretionary grounds].

3.g. *Miscellaneous Dispositions*—A single BIA member is also given the authority to issue rulings on unopposed motions, motions to withdraw an appeal, DHS motions to remand an appeal from decisions of DHS officers, and motions to remand based on defective or missing transcripts or other procedural or ministerial issues. 8 C.F.R. §1003.1(e)(2).

3.h. *Motion to Reopen*—A single BIA member may adjudicate a motion to reopen from his or her decision. 8 C.F.R. §1003.1(e)(5).

4. *En Banc Decisions*—The BIA still retains the right to decide cases en banc, although en banc adjudications are "not favored" and will only be used to address issues of particular importance or to maintain consistency of BIA decisions. 8 C.F.R. §1003.1(a)(5).

5. *Clearly Erroneous Rule Established*—8 C.F.R. §1003.1(d)(3). The BIA will no longer engage in *de novo* review of findings of fact, including IJ credibility decisions in all cases filed after Sept. 24, 2002. *Matter of T-Z-,* 24 I&N Dec. 163, 166 (BIA 2007) [upheld IJ's determination that Chinese asylum seeker was credible under clearly erroneous standard]; *Matter of Adamiak,* 23 I&N Dec. 878, 880 (BIA 2006); *Wang v. Ashcroft,* 368 F.3d 347, 349 (3d Cir. 2004). Instead, the BIA will apply a clearly erroneous standard to the review of the IJ's findings of fact. *Matter of V-F-D-,* 23 I&N Dec. 859 n.1 (BIA 2006). However, *de novo* review of decisions of DHS officers remains and the BIA may review *de novo* mixed questions of fact and law including the possibility of a result in the future such as the likelihood that respondent will be tortured or whether s/he will be persecuted or whether a certain level of hardship exists. *Matter of V-K-,* 24 I&N Dec. 500 (May 8, 2008) [reversing IJ's mixed question of fact and law regarding the torture Ukrainian would suffer and denying CAT relief]. *See in this chapter*, "Scope of Review," part VIII (p.1035), *infra*.

6. *Review by the Attorney General*—The AG may review a BIA decision upon request from the BIA, the DHS Director, or the AG himself. 8 C.F.R. §§1003.1(h)(1)(i)–(iii). *Matter of Leon-Orosco & Rodriguez-Colas*, 19 I&N Dec. 136 (AG 1984). If a BIA decision has been certified to the AG, it is "neither final nor effective during the pendency of the Attorney General's review." *Matter of E-L-H-,* 23 I&N Dec. 700 (AG 2004) [overturning BIA, but recognizing that IJ's decision is not in force during pendency of AG review, that the respondent may seek relief from the automatic stay due to unfairness or hardship, and that the stay does not result in automatic re-incarceration of the respondent]. However, on remand from the AG, the BIA has taken the position that only nonprecedent decisions are not in force during the AG's review and unless the AG specifically vacates the BIA's decision, all precedent decisions of the BIA remain in force during review by the AG. *Matter of E-L-H-,* 23 I&N Dec. 814 (BIA 2005). Where the AG overrules, reverses, or vacates part of a precedent decision, the remainder retains its precedential value. *Matter of Robles*, 24 I&N Dec. 22 (BIA 2006). Notwithstanding the clearly erroneous rule and the BIA's limited review, the AG believes his review of BIA decisions is *de novo* and not confined to review of legal or factual error. *Matter of J-F-F-,* 23 I&N Dec. 912, 913 (AG 2006) [AG reserves the right to "receive additional information and to make de novo factual determinations"]; *Matter of A-H-,* 23 I&N Dec. 774, 779 n.4 (AG 2005); *Matter of D-J-,* 23 I&N Dec. 572, 575 (AG 2003); *Matter of Jean,* 23 I&N Dec. 373 (AG 2002); *Matter of Y-L-, A-G-, R-S-R-,* 23 I&N Dec. 270 (AG 2002).

D. *Certification*—The DHS Secretary or any other duly authorized DHS officer, an IJ, or the BIA itself may certify a case to the Board. 8 C.F.R. §§1003.1(c). For the Board to exercise its certification authority, it must be a matter within its jurisdiction under 8 C.F.R. §1003.1(b). *Matter of Sano,* 19 I&N Dec. 299 (BIA 1985). If the BIA accepts certification, it must provide proper notice to the parties. 8 C.F.R. §1003.7; *Chong v. District Director, INS,* 264 F.3d 378, 388–91 (3d Cir. 2001) [IJ violated former 8 C.F.R. §3.7 by not informing respondent of right to make representations, oral argument, and briefing before BIA on certification, but court found no prejudice]; *Waldron v. INS*, 17 F.3d 511, 516–17 (2d Cir. 1994). Pursuant to 8 C.F.R. §1240.1(a)(2), the IJ may request certification only if it involves an unusually complex or novel question of law or fact.

E. *Acquiescence to Circuit Court Decisions*—The BIA has traditionally acquiesced to the decisions of a circuit court, at least within that circuit. *Matter of Olivares,* 23 I&N Dec. 148 (BIA 2001) [applying 5th Cir. law in sentencing context to override BIA decision in *Matter of Puente*, 22 I&N Dec. 1006 (BIA 1999) that aggravated DUI is a crime of violence, even though BIA itself has taken the position that sentencing decisions and INS decisions are distinct]; *Matter of Cazares*, 21 I&N Dec. 188 (BIA 1996); *Matter of L-G-,* 21 I&N Dec. 89 (BIA 1995); *Matter of Anselmo*, 20 I&N Dec. 25 (BIA 1989); *Matter of Bowe*, 17 I&N Dec. 488 (BIA 1980). *See also Ladha v. INS,* 215 F.3d 889, 896 (9th Cir. 2000) [BIA "must" follow the decisions of the circuit court]. *But see Matter of Mangabat*, 14 I&N Dec. 75 (BIA 1972), *aff'd sub nom. Cabuco-Flores v. INS*, 477 F.2d 108 (9th Cir. 1973) [refusing to follow 9th Cir. ruling related to an application of former INA §241(f) which the Solicitor General was considering taking to the Supreme Court]. Where different circuits have different interpretations of the law, the BIA will follow the law within the relevant circuit. *Matter of Ramos,* 23 I&N Dec. 336, 346–47 (BIA 2002) [interpretation of "crime of violence"]. Where the BIA disagrees with a relevant circuit decision, it has not acquiesced outside the circuit. *Id.* However, where it agreed with the circuit's decision it has at times applied the principle nationwide. *Matter of Yanez-Garcia,* 23 I&N Dec. 390 (BIA 2002) [deferring to majority of circuits on standard for defining state drug offense as aggravated felony and overruling *Matter of K-V-D-*]; *Matter of Silva*, 16 I&N Dec. 26 (BIA 1976) [applying nationwide ruling in *Francis v. INS* that INA §212(c) is applicable in deportation proceedings]. BIA does not acquiesce to district court decisions and does not regard them as binding even within that district. *Matter of K-S-*, 20 I&N Dec. 715 (BIA 1993) [overruling *Matter of Amado & Monteiro*, 13 I&N Dec. 179 (BIA 1969)]. Because the Ninth Circuit hears about half of all immigration cases in the U.S., *Stroe v. INS,* 256 F.3d 498, 505 (7th Cir. 2001) (Wood, J., concurring), there is a question as to whether DHS should follow Ninth Circuit precedent more often.

F. *Undue Influence*—The BIA may not be subject to political influence. *Accardi v. Shaughnessy*, 347 U.S. 260 (1954); *Shaughnessy v. Accardi*, 349 U.S. 280 (1955); *Yi v. Reno*, 925 F.Supp. 320 (M.D. Pa. 1996).

II. INTERLOCUTORY JURISDICTION OF THE BIA

The BIA will entertain an interlocutory appeal where a significant issue is raised that affects the administration of the immigration laws. *Matter of M-D-,* 24 I&N Dec. 138, 139 (BIA 2007) [recurring questions regarding jurisdiction when a proceeding is remanded to an IJ for security checks]; *Matter of Dobere*, 20 I&N Dec. 188 (BIA 1990) [change of venue by IJ in exclusion proceedings]; *Matter of Victorino*, 18 I&N Dec. 259 (BIA 1982) [determination of commencement of deportation proceedings]. *But see Matter of Ruiz-Campuzano*, 17 I&N Dec. 108 (BIA 1979). The Board can grant a stay of proceedings while an interlocutory appeal is pending. *Matter of K-*, 20 I&N Dec. 418 (BIA 1991). Interlocutory appeals are rarely granted by the BIA.

III. APPEAL PROCEDURE

A. *In Removal Proceedings*—The procedure for appeals is now uniform for removal cases. 8 C.F.R. §§1240.15, 1240.53(a) [for deportation/exclusion]; 8 C.F.R. §1003.3. Both DHS and the respondent have the right to appeal.

1. *Timeliness of Appeal*—Appeal must be filed on Form EOIR-26 within 30 days of service of the IJ's decision. 8 C.F.R. §§1003.38(b), 1240.15. The 30 days begins to run from the *mailing* of the IJ's written decision, or from the stating of an oral decision. *Id.* If the filing deadline falls on a Saturday, Sunday, or legal holiday, it is extended to the next business day. 8 C.F.R. §1003.38(b). *Receipt of Appeal By BIA*—An appeal is not properly filed unless *received* by the BIA with all required documents and fees, or fee waiver request, within the time specified. 8 C.F.R. §§1003.3(a)(1), 1003.38(c), 1240.15, 1240.53(a). The BIA's *Practice Manual* notes that postal or delivery delays do not affect existing deadlines including the failure of a courier or overnight delivery service to deliver the appeal timely. §3.1(a)-(b). As a result of the Supreme Court's decision in *Eberhart v. U.S.,* 546 U.S. 12 (2005) and *Bowles v. Russell,* 127 S.Ct. 2360 (2007) the circuit courts have debated whether the 30-day deadline is jurisdictional and/or mandatory. If jurisdictional, it may not be waived. If mandatory, it may, under certain highly limited circumstances, be waived. The Supreme Court, in *Eberhart*, recognized that certain mandatory time limit are regarded as "claims-processing" rules, which are not jurisdictional and therefore may be waived under certain circumstances. In contrast, *Bowles* addressed the circumstance in which deadlines for filing cases in the lower federal courts are prescribed by statute and are therefore truly jurisdictional and may never be waived. Most circuit courts that have addressed the issue have found that the 30-day deadline is *not* jurisdictional. *See Huerta v. Gonzales,* 443 F.3d 753 (10th Cir. 2006) [holding that 30-day filing period is not jurisdictional but a mandatory, claims-processing rule, citing to *Eberhart*, and therefore where BIA accepted an appeal one day late it did not lose jurisdiction over the case]; *Khan v. DOJ,* 494 F.3d 255, 257–59 (2d Cir. 2007) [where the DHL courier delivered the notice of appeal one day late to the BIA, *Bowles* did not bar petitioner from providing extraordinary or unique circumstances for the failure to timely appeal]; *Liadov v. Mukasey,* 518 F.3d 1003, 1007-09 (8th Cir. 2008) [30-day deadline is not jurisdictional, but is mandatory, and the BIA did not abuse its discretion when it declined to accept an appeal filed one day late

when it was provided to a courier service 2 days before the deadline]. *But see Magtanong v. Gonzales,* 494 F.3d 1190 (9th Cir. 2007) [court upheld BIA denial of appeal where notice of appeal sent by DHL arrived on 31st day, citing to *Bowles v. Russell,* 127 S.Ct. 2360 (2007), which found no exceptions to the 30-day time limit to appeal civil judgments].

2. *Appeal Dismissed For Failing to Timely File—Holder v. Gonzales,* 499 F.3d 825 (8th Cir. 2007) [court affirmed BIA dismissal of appeal filed by Federal Express with incorrect zip code that arrived one day late and rejected due process and equal protection challenges]; *Ibarra-Terrazas v. Gonzales,* 461 F.3d 1046 (8th Cir. 2006) [BIA properly dismissed appeal filed one day late]; *Matter of Liadov,* 23 I&N Dec. 990 (BIA 2006), *aff'd, Liadov v. Mukasey,* 518 F.3d 1003 (8th Cir. 2008) [appeal filed one day late due to courier company error does not forgive the jurisdictional requirement]; *Malak v. Gonzales,* 419 F.3d 533 (6th Cir. 2005) [upholding dismissal of appeal where counsel timely mailed appeal through express service but did not discover for 21 months that it had never been received by BIA]; *Laboski v. Ashcroft,* 387 F.3d 628 (7th Cir. 2004) [upholding denial of motion to reconsider dismissal of appeal as untimely filed where respondent offered no affidavits or other proof regarding the date of service or receipt of the IJs order]; *Matter of Jean,* 23 I&N Dec. 373, 378–80 (AG 2002) [where IJ issued two post-remand decisions denying different claims in each, only the second decision was a final order requiring a notice of appeal]; *Anssari-Gharachedaghy v. INS,* 246 F.3d 512 (6th Cir. 2000) [notice received by BIA one day late, despite representation by post office that certified mail will be received on time, does not waive deadline]; *Da Cruz v. INS,* 4 F.3d 721 (9th Cir. 1993) [INS failure to file notice timely nullified BIA decision]; *Matter of Gawaran,* 20 I&N Dec. 938 (BIA 1995) [dismissing INS appeal filed one day late following *Da Cruz*].

   Appeal Not Dismissed—Vasquez Salazar v. Mukasey, 514 F.3d 643 (6th Cir. 2008) [where notice of appeal was sent by Federal Express 2 days before the Aug. 17th, deadline, but was not received until Aug. 23, court reversed denial of motion to reconsider]; *Sun v. DOJ,* 421 F.3d 105 (2d Cir. 2005) [where lawyer sent appeal notice by Airborne Express one day before appeal was due and Airborne failed to timely deliver it, motion to reconsider was granted and BIA must determine whether facts constituted exceptional circumstances tolling the 30-day period]; *Guzman-Andrade v. Gonzales,* 407 F.3d 1073, 1080 (9th Cir. 2005) [where LAU appeal was timely filed but the fee was returned, the denial of the appeal as untimely was an abuse of discretion]; *Oh v. Gonzales,* 406 F.3d 611 (9th Cir. 2005) [where Airborne Express delivered appeal notice well beyond the 30-day deadline through error and the BIA's manual named Airborne as an overnight carrier and provided for late filing in "rare circumstances" (BIA Practice Manual Ch. 3(b) p.28), the court reversed and remanded to the BIA].

   Ineffective Assistance of Counsel Because of Untimely Appeal—Siong v. INS, 376 F.3d 1030, 1037 (9th Cir. 2004) [BIA's denial of motion to reopen reversed because: "Failure to file a timely notice of appeal is obvious ineffective assistance of counsel....[and] [p]rejudice is ordinarily presumed in immigration proceedings when counsel's error 'deprives the alien of the appellate proceeding entirely'" although the presumption may be rebutted if the appellant has no plausible grounds for relief]; *Cf. Sswajje v. Ashcroft,* 350 F.3d 528, 532–33 (6th Cir. 2003) [counsel's malpractice in mailing notice of appeal one day late is not an "extraordinary circumstance"].

   Detained Persons, Appearing Pro Se, Are Required to Meet 30 Day Deadline—Matter of J-J-, 21 I&N Dec. 976, 982–84 (BIA 1997) [rejecting Supreme Court precedent that for detained persons, filing occurs when they give the document to prison authorities]. *Accord Smith v. Conner,* 250 F.3d 277 (5th Cir. 2001) [mailbox rule in *Houston v. Lack*, 487 U.S. 266 (1988) is not applicable to INS]. *But see Huang v. INS*, 47 F.3d 615 (3d Cir. 1995) [finding former §3.38(b) ambiguous and subject to interpretation that an additional 3 days are given if *respondent mails* the notice]; *Naderpour v. INS*, 52 F.3d 731 (8th Cir. 1995) [same].

   BIA Can Reissue Decision to Avoid Injustice—If the decision was not properly mailed to respondent, the BIA has vacated and reissued the decision so that the 30-day period for appeal runs anew. *Firmansjah v. Ashcroft,* 347 F.3d 625 (7th Cir. 2003) [BIA reissued final order at respondent's request who had not received notice and the circuit court permitted appeal within 30 days of reissued BIA decision]; *Lonyem v. U.S. Att'y Gen.,* 352 F.3d 1338, 1340 n.3 (11th Cir. 2003).

3. *Waiver of Appeal*—The IJ will ask the respondent if s/he waives appeal. If respondent waives appeal, the BIA will not hear the appeal even if a notice of appeal is timely filed. *Matter of Shih,* 20

I&N Dec. 697 (BIA 1993); 8 C.F.R. §§1003.38(b), 1003.39. The BIA and courts look to determine whether the waiver was knowingly and intelligently made. *Matter of Patino,* 23 I&N Dec. 74 (BIA 2001)*; U.S. v. Zarate-Martinez*, 133 F.3d 1194, 1197–98 (9th Cir. 1998) [waiver of appeal must be "considered and intelligent. Otherwise the deportee is deprived of judicial review in violation of due process"]; *U.S. v. Andrade-Partida,* 110 F.Supp.2d 1260 (N.D. Cal. 2000) [respondent did not knowingly and intelligently waive appeal where he was not informed of §212(c) relief]. The fact that a respondent has a lawyer does not necessarily mean that he has knowingly and intelligently waived his appeal. *U.S. v. Calderon,* 391 F.3d 370, 374–76 (2d Cir. 2004) [where IJ and counsel both advised respondent that he could not apply for §212(c) relief, he did not knowingly and intelligently waive his right to a BIA appeal]. A waiver that is not knowingly and intelligently made cannot be a jurisdictional bar to federal court review. *Biwot v. Gonzales,* 403 F.3d 1094, 1097–98 (9th Cir. 2005) [where respondent was denied the right to counsel and as a result, was under the impression that he had no choice but to waive appeal, court retained jurisdiction on the denial of counsel claim]. The IJ is responsible for providing notice to the respondent of the right to appeal, 8 C.F.R. §§1003.3, 1003.38(b), and the failure to notify a *pro se* respondent will not deprive him of the right to appeal. *Berhe v. Gonzales,* 464 F.3d 74, 88 (1st Cir. 2006) [where IJ failed to inform a *pro se* respondent of right to appeal, the untimely filing of a notice did not waive appeal rights because respondent did not "knowingly and intelligently" waive his appeal]. A pro se respondent who accepts an IJ's decision as "final" does not waive appeal where the IJ failed to make clear that acceptance as "final" constitutes an irrevocable waiver of appeal. *Matter of Rodriguez-Diaz,* 22 I&N Dec. 1320 (BIA 2000). At least one court has held that asking the lawyer whether he accepts the decision as final does not waive appeal for the respondent. *U.S. v. Ubaldo-Figueroa,* 364 F.3d 1042, 1048 (9th Cir. 2004). A party wishing to challenge the validity of his or her waiver of appeal may file either a motion to reconsider with the IJ or a timely notice of appeal to the BIA. *U.S. v. Mendoza Lopez,* 481 U.S. 828 (1987); *Matter of Patino,* 23 I&N Dec. 74 (BIA 2001).

4. *Form of Appeal*—The notice of appeal must be filed on Form EOIR-26 and must specify *in detail* the factual and legal grounds for the appeal. 8 C.F.R. §1003.3(b). In addition, the notice of appeal must identify, if appropriate, the specific legal or factual reasons that the case should be considered by a three-member BIA panel. *Id.* The notice of appeal must be accompanied by the lawyer's EOIR-27 and a certificate of service with a complete address demonstrating service on DHS. 8 C.F.R. §1003.3(a)(1). The EOIR-27 must be from the individual lawyer, not a law firm, and if another lawyer in the same firm files a document in the case, s/he must have a separate EOIR-27. *BIA Practice Manual* §2.3(f). Although a party may file a brief, the regulations do not require it. *Bhiski v. Ashcroft,* 373 F.3d 363, 367–68 (3d Cir. 2004) [failure to file a brief is not a failure to exhaust administrative remedies]. When a brief is filed, there is a presumption of regularity that the BIA will consider it. *Rashiah v. Ashcroft,* 388 F.3d 1126, 1130 (7th Cir. 2004) [BIA's failure to list brief in its order is an insufficient basis to assume BIA did not consider it in light of the presumption of regularity].

5. *Briefing Schedule*—In nondetained cases, the appellant may file a brief within 21 days of receipt of the transcript or schedule set by the BIA. Reply briefs are due within 21 days of receipt of opposing briefs. There is no provision to file a responsive brief to appellee's reply brief in nondetained cases. In detained cases, the parties must simultaneously file their briefs, and reply briefs are not permitted except by leave of court. 8 C.F.R. §1003.3(c)(1). The BIA may extend the time for filing briefs. 8 C.F.R. §1003.3(c). Generally, a person may obtain one extension of the 21-day period by filing a motion *prior to* the due date. Detained persons and government counsel may collectively only get one extension for 21 days per *detained case* (without regard to which party makes the request) as the briefs are simultaneously filed. 71 Fed. Reg. 51856 (Aug. 31, 2006). However, in the absence of an order granting an extension, the brief remains due on the *original* date. *See BIA Practice Manual* §4.7(c)(ii) (Sept. 25, 2002). In nondetained cases, if the extension is granted, the brief is due 21 days from the date the brief was *originally* due, not 21 days from the date of the order granting the extension. *Id.* Failure to grant a briefing extension does not violate due process. *Huicochea-Gomez v. INS,* 237 F.3d 696, 700–01 (6th Cir. 2001) [rejecting brief not served on opposing party as out-of-time]; *Anwar v. INS,* 116 F.3d 140, 144 (5th Cir. 1997); 8 C.F.R. §1003.3(c). *But see Hossain v. Ashcroft,* 381 F.3d 29 (1st Cir. 2004) [where transcript and briefing schedule mailed to incorrect address and brief never filed, basic fairness required that BIA's denial of motion to reconsider be reversed]; *Singh v. INS,* 362 F.3d 1164 (9th Cir. 2004)

[due process violated where BIA sent transcript and briefing schedule to wrong address and then refused to allow respondent the opportunity to file a brief beyond the scheduled time]. The BIA may accept late-filed briefs absent prejudice to the opposing party. *Getachew v. INS*, 25 F.3d 841, 845 (9th Cir. 1994); *Garcia Gomez v. Gonzales,* 498 F.3d 1050 (9th Cir. 2007) [followed *Gutierrez-Almazan* and found that BIA's one-sentence order denying a late-filed brief did not indicate how they arrived at their conclusion]; *Gutierrez-Almazan v. Gonzales,* 491 F.3d 341 (7th Cir. 2007) [reversed BIA denial of *pro se* petitioner's request to file brief late where the court could not tell from BIA's one sentence order whether the BIA "heard and thought" or "merely reacted" in denying request]. *But see Abdelwase v. Gonzales,* 496 F.3d 904 (8th Cir. 2007) [BIA's refusal to accept late-filed brief was not prejudicial because BIA entered AWO and court reviewed IJ's decision]. The brief must be filed with a certificate of service on opposing counsel. 8 C.F.R. §1003.3(c). A brief should *not* be bound on the side, should be hole-punched at the top, and should have a cover page consistent with BIA practice. *BIA Practice Manual* §3.3(c)(viii) [binding] and Appendix F [sample brief cover].

6. *Appeal from Decisions of a DHS Officer*—An appeal from a DHS decision within the jurisdiction of the BIA (*e.g.*, I-130 petition denials) must be filed on Form EOIR-29 within 30 days of the decision. The appeal is filed with the DHS office rendering the decision and not with the BIA. 8 C.F.R. §1003.3(a)(2). Both the petitioner and DHS are provided 21 days in which to file a brief, unless a shorter period is specified. 8 C.F.R. §1003.3(c)(2).

B. *Summary Dismissal of Appeal*—Appellant must provide detailed and precise reasons for the appeal on Form EOIR-26, filed in triplicate. 8 C.F.R. §1003.3(b). Under 8 C.F.R. §1003.1(d)(2) [formerly (1-a)]; 57 Fed. Reg. 11568–75 (Apr. 6, 1992), 59 Fed. Reg. 1896 (Jan. 13, 1994); IMMACT90 §545(a), the BIA may summarily dismiss any appeal in which:

1. The party concerned fails to specify the reasons for appeal on Form EOIR-26 or the reasons provided are not sufficiently specific. *Rojas-Garcia v. Ashcroft,* 339 F.3d 814, 819–22 (9th Cir. 2003) [upholding summary dismissal where appeal notice did not articulate how the IJ violated the pretrial order, what evidence was erroneously admitted as hearsay, did not provide supporting authority to legal conclusions, and counsel did not file a brief]; *Bayro v. Reno*, 142 F.3d 1377 (11th Cir. 1998) [notice stating that IJ abused his discretion in denying asylum and applied "reasonable man" standard inappropriately was insufficient where no brief was filed]; *Nazakat v. INS*, 981 F.2d 1146 (10th Cir. 1992) [affirming BIA dismissal of *pro se* appeal where notice was inadequate because appellant's English was flawed]; *Toquero v. INS*, 956 F.2d 193 (9th Cir. 1992) [statement that IJ erred in denying suspension because the evidence showed respondent would suffer extreme hardship if deported was not deemed sufficient where no brief filed]; *Athehortua-Vanegas v. INS*, 876 F.2d 238 (1st Cir. 1989); *Lozada v. INS*, 857 F.2d 10 (1st Cir. 1988); *Bonne-Annee v. INS*, 810 F.2d 1077 (11th Cir. 1987) [dismissal appropriate where *pro se* alien stated reasons in general form]; *Townsend v. INS*, 799 F.2d 179 (5th Cir. 1986) [dismissal upheld where statements on notice were conclusory and no brief was filed]; *Martinez-Zelaya v. INS*, 841 F.2d 294 (9th Cir. 1988). *See also Matter of Jean,* 23 I&N Dec. 373, 378–80 (AG 2002) [where notice of appeal addressed errors in the IJ's first post-remand order but not in the second post-remand order, AG would not review the denial of CAT claim in the second IJ order]; *Matter of Perez-Andrade*, 19 I&N Dec. 433 (BIA 1987); *Matter of Valencia*, 19 I&N Dec. 354 (BIA 1986); *Matter of Lodge*, 19 I&N Dec. 500 (BIA 1987) [appeal will be dismissed even where oral argument is requested]. *But see Escobar-Ramos v. INS*, 927 F.2d 482 (9th Cir. 1991) [addressing inadequacy of Form I-290A to provide notice and finding that where counsel failed to file brief and BIA made no independent review, summary dismissal was improper]; *Singh v. Swan*, 908 F.Supp. 634 (E.D. Wis. 1995) [reversing summary dismissal under abuse of discretion standard]. Failure to give the appellant notice of summary dismissal may violate due process. *Vargas-Garcia v. INS,* 287 F.3d 882 (9th Cir. 2002) [addressing the inadequacy of EOIR-26 for *pro se* respondent when coupled with the BIA's standards of specificity and lack of notice in dismissing appeal]; *Castillo-Manzanarez v. INS*, 65 F.3d 793 (9th Cir. 1995); *Padilla-Agustin v. INS*, 21 F.3d 970 (9th Cir. 1994).
2. The only reasons specified for the appeal involve findings of fact or conclusions of law which were conceded by appellants at the prior proceeding.
3. The appeal is from an order that granted the party the relief s/he requested.

4. The BIA is satisfied from a review of the record that the appeal is filed for an improper purpose, such as to cause unnecessary delay, or that the appeal lacks an arguable basis in law or fact unless the BIA determines that it is supported by a good faith argument for extension, modification or reversal of existing law.

5. The appealing party indicates s/he will file a brief or statement but does not do so and does not reasonably explain the failure to do so within deadline set for filing. *Kokar v. Gonzales,* 478 F.3d 803 (7th Cir. 2007) [rejecting due process claim and argument in *Esponda, infra* that regulations are confusing when read in *pari materia*]; *Singh v. Gonzales,* 416 F.3d 1006 (9th Cir. 2005) [due process not violated where counsel failed to file brief and failed to adequately specify the grounds for appeal]; *Singh v. Ashcroft*, 361 F.3d 1152 (9th Cir. 2004) [summary dismissal where notice of appeal insufficiently detailed and no brief was filed]; *Awe v. Ashcroft,* 324 F.3d 509 (7th Cir. 2003) [BIA appropriately dismissed appeal where respondent failed to file a brief]; *Rioja v. Ashcroft,* 317 F.3d 514 (5th Cir. 2003) [where appellant discharged lawyer and failed to seek any relief from BIA in regard to time for filing brief, the failure to file was sufficient basis for summary dismissal]. *But see Esponda v. U.S. Att'y Gen.,* 453 F.3d 1319 (11th Cir. 2006) [BIA abused its discretion in dismissing appeal for failure to file brief without first determining whether the Notice of Appeal adequately set forth the basis for the appeal]; *Garcia-Cortez v. Ashcroft,* 366 F.3d 749 (9th Cir. 2004) [due process denied where BIA summarily dismissed appeal for failure to file a brief when petitioners' notice of appeal was sufficiently detailed and brief filed late]; *Casas-Chavez v. INS,* 300 F.3d 1088 (9th Cir. 2002) [notice of appeal sufficiently detailed without brief]; *Medrano-Villatoro v. INS*, 866 F.2d 132 (5th Cir. 1989) [summary dismissal improper where party specified reasons for appeal without filing a brief]. *But see Rioja v. Ashcroft,* 317 F.3d 514 (5th Cir. 2003) [indicating *Medrano-Villatoro* superseded by amendment to regulations that provides for summary dismissal where party says it will file a brief and does not].

   5.a. Prior to the new regulations, at least one court found that summary dismissal for failure to file a brief may be rebutted by a showing of extraordinary circumstances. *Escobar-Ramos v. INS*, 927 F.2d 482, 485–86 (9th Cir. 1991) [applying case law under FRAP 31].

   5.b. The failure to file a brief does not necessarily bar review of a respondent's claim for failure to exhaust administrative remedies. *Bhiski v. Ashcroft,* 373 F.3d 363, 367–68 (3d Cir. 2004) [issue was not so complex that appeal required brief and the regulations do not require a brief but only that issues be identified with particularity. 8 C.F.R. §1003.3(b)].

6. The appeal does not fall with the Board's jurisdiction, is untimely, or is barred because the party clearly waived his or her right to appeal on the record; *or*

7. The appeal fails to meet essential statutory or regulatory requirements or is expressly excluded by statute or regulation.

8. The DHS files a motion arguing that the appeal should be summarily dismissed and the appellant fails to respond or fails to rebut DHS's arguments.

C. ***Rebuttal of Summary Dismissal***—When faced with a motion for summary dismissal, a respondent can: (i) argue that the statement in the Notice of Appeal adequately sets forth the reasons for the appeal; (ii) elaborate on the statements in the Notice to clarify and meaningfully identify the issues on appeal; (iii) submit a brief on the merits in response to the motion; and/or (iv) explain why there are unusual circumstances that bar an adequate response until a transcript is prepared. *Matter of Cespedes*, 19 I&N Dec. 730 (BIA 1988). *See also Matter of Torre*, 19 I&N Dec. 18 (BIA 1984).

D. ***Disciplinary Consequences***—The filing of an appeal that is summarily dismissed may be deemed frivolous behavior subjecting lawyers to sanctions. 8 C.F.R. §§1003.1(d)(2)(iii), 1292.3(a)(1).

E. ***Three-Member Panel Disposition***—As most decisions of the BIA will be decided by one Board member, 8 C.F.R. §1003.1(e), an appellant must explain in detail in the notice of appeal, the "specific factual or legal basis" in support of the claim that the case is appropriate for a full decision by a three-member panel. 8 C.F.R. §1003.3(b). Appellant must demonstrate why the case meets one or more of the six criteria for three-member review specified in 8 C.F.R. §1003.1(e)(6). *See in this chapter*, ¶ I.C.1 (p.1020), *supra*.

F. ***Automatic and Requested Stays***—An automatic stay of removal is issued upon timely filing of a BIA appeal. 8 C.F.R. §1003.6(a). *Pupo-Tordecilla v. Sava*, 704 F.Supp. 55 (S.D.N.Y. 1989). *See also*

Dalis v. Brady, 766 F.Supp. 901, 907 (D. Colo. 1991). However, there is no automatic stay of execution if an appeal is taken from a denial of a motion to reopen, reconsider, or stay of deportation, unless a stay is specifically granted by the IJ or the BIA. 8 C.F.R. §1003.6(b). Nor does the filing of a motion to reopen or reconsider automatically stay removal. 8 C.F.R. §§1003.2(f), 1003.23(b)(1)(v); *Patel v. Ashcroft,* 378 F.3d 610, 612 (7th Cir. 2004). The BIA will not act on a request for a discretionary stay unless it has jurisdiction *and* the applicant is in DHS custody. *See* 70 No. 19 *Interpreter Releases*, 652, 672–76 (May 17, 1993); *Anderson v. McElroy*, 953 F.2d 803 (2d Cir. 1992) [BIA abused its discretion in denying a stay pending motion to reopen for §212(c) relief]. The BIA may grant a stay where a change in law affects the respondent's removability. *Matter of Herrera,* 23 I&N Dec. 43 (BIA 2001) [stay granted pending consideration of motion to reopen where circuit court issued a decision which would reverse previous IJ finding that DUI is an aggravated felony].

G. ***Denial of Oral Argument***—The applicant must request oral argument in the notice of appeal. However, the BIA may deny oral argument granting it only in its discretion. 8 C.F.R. §1003.1(e)(7).

H. ***BIA May Permit Untimely Appeal***—*Matter of Keyte*, 20 I&N Dec. 158 (BIA 1990); *Matter of Ruiz*, 20 I&N Dec. 91 (BIA 1989); *Matter of Rodriguez-Esteban*, 20 I&N Dec. 88 (BIA 1989); *Matter of Iberia Airlines Flight No. 1B951*, 19 I&N Dec. 768 (BIA 1988); *Matter of Rivera*, 19 I&N Dec. 688 (BIA 1988); *Tarvand v. INS*, 937 F.2d 973, 977 (4th Cir. 1991); *Garcia v. Bolden*, 691 F.2d 1172, 1182 n.17 (5th Cir. 1982). *See also Lonyem v. U.S. Att'y Gen.*, 352 F.3d 1338, 1340 n.3 (11th Cir. 2003); *Hrubec v. INS*, 828 F.Supp. 251 (S.D.N.Y. 1993) [reinstating 30-day appeal period in bond breach case].

I. ***Notice of BIA Decision and Reinstatement of Decision.*** The BIA is required to serve its decision in writing. 8 C.F.R. §1003.1(f). Where respondent did not receive the BIA decision, and the time period to file appeal in the circuit court has run, the BIA may reinstate its order to provide for a timely appeal. *Firmansjah v. Ashcroft,* 347 F.3d 625 (7th Cir. 2003) [BIA reissued final order at respondent's request who had not received notice and the circuit court permitted appeal within 30 days of reissued BIA decision]. A motion to reissue will be treated as a motion to reopen. *Jahjaga v. Att'y Gen. of the U.S.,* 512 F.3d 80, 82 (3d Cir. 2008). The circuits are currently split on what would be considered sufficient notice of a BIA decision under §1003.1(f), to warrant reopening of the case and reinstatement of the order. *Compare Gaberov v. Mukasey,* 516 F.3d 590 (7th Cir. 2008) [applying equitable tolling to four year old order despite lack of affidavits by petitioner where he erroneously received another person's final order, inquired, and was told his case was still pending]; *Jahjaga v. Att'y Gen. of the U.S.*, 512 F.3d 80 (3d Cir. 2008) [agreeing with *Singh* and ordering the case remanded to the BIA to determine whether submission of affidavits of nonreceipt are sufficient to overcome BIA's indication of mailing]; *Singh v. Gonzales,* 494 F.3d 1170 (9th Cir. 2007) [reversed and remanded BIA denial of motion to reopen where respondent and counsel filed affidavits of nonreceipt of BIA decision and BIA did not explain how it properly served its decision] *with Chen v. U.S. Att'y Gen.*, 502 F.3d 73 (2d Cir. 2007) [motion to reinstate is treated as a motion to reopen but where BIA has proof it sent notice, the respondent's nonreceipt is irrelevant]. *See in this part*, "Timeliness of Appeal," ¶ A.1 (p.1024), *supra.*

J. ***Withdrawal of Appeal***—A party may withdraw his or her appeal under 8 C.F.R. §1003.4. However, once withdrawn, the BIA has no authority to reinstate the appeal. *Panchevre v. DOJ*, 922 F.2d 1229 (5th Cir. 1991). *But see Matter of Rodriguez-Diaz,* 22 I&N Dec. 1320 (BIA 2000).

K. ***Criticism of BIA Procedures and Decisions***—The quality of transcripts, the delay in rendering decisions, and the legal quality of BIA decisions all have been criticized. One circuit court has written that "the adjudication of these cases at the administrative level has fallen below the minimum standards of legal justice." *Benslimane v. Gonzales,* 430 F.3d 828, 830 (7th Cir. 2005) [reversing removal order where IJ refused to grant continuance when I-130 was pending and lawyer was under mistaken belief that he could not file I-485 with IJ]. *See also Ahmed v. Ashcroft,* 388 F.3d 247, 248 (7th Cir. 2004) [BIA's explanation for denying a petition for reconsideration "appears to be a piece of boilerplate mindlessly affixed to a case to which it's irrelevant"]; *Mamedov v. Ashcroft,* 387 F.3d 918, 919–20 (7th Cir. 2004) [criticizing the policy of allowing IJs to correct their opinions after a notice of appeal is filed]; *Berishaj v. Ashcroft,* 378 F.3d 314, 326–28 (3d Cir. 2004) [criticizing the BIA's streamlining process as not a license to say that it is "not our problem" when it comes to ensuring that the circuit court has an up-to-date record regarding country conditions in asylum cases]; *Njuguna v. Ashcroft,* 374 F.3d 765, 771 n.4 (9th Cir. 2004) [finding it "disturbing" that three Kenyans were granted asylum but a fourth was not involving the same incident because "it is a foundation of the rule of law that similarly situated individuals be treated similarly"]; *Guchshenkov v. Ashcroft,* 366 F.3d 554 (7th Cir. 2004) [criticizing and removing IJs from asylum cases where they did not present a reasoned decision]; *Niam v. Ashcroft,* 354 F.3d 652, 653–54 (7th Cir. 2004) [finding "a pattern of serious misapplications by the board and the immigration judges of elementary principles of adjudication"]; *Wang v. Ashcroft,* 341 F.3d 1015, 1019 n.2 (9th Cir. 2003) [where counsel for INS argued that there was nothing wrong in BIA decision granting asylum to husband based on wife's forced abortion claim but denying asylum to wife, the court "wonder[ed] how any rational system could tolerate such inconsistent treatment"]; *Ramirez-Alejandre v. Ashcroft,* 320 F.3d 858, 860–61 (9th Cir. 2003) (en banc) [comparing BIA treatment of suspension cases to a game without rules that "morphed without any consistency from fact-finding to pure appellate review of a fixed record" thereby violating due process]; *Yadegar-Sargis v. INS,* 297 F.3d 596 (7th Cir. 2002) [delay in rendering decision created substantial hardship on widow who turned 71 years old and INS should take steps to avoid returning her to court]; *Meghani v. INS,* 236 F.3d 843, 848 (7th Cir. 2001) ["[w]e re-express our disesteem for the delays that plague INS proceedings" in case where BIA took 7 years to decide asylum appeal]; *Rodriguez-Barajas v. INS*, 992 F.2d 94, 98 (7th Cir. 1993) ["[u]nconscionable delay" in rendering decision]; *Galina v. INS,* 213 F.3d 955, 958–59 (7th Cir. 2000) [finding the Board's analysis "woefully inadequate" and stating that "[t]he elementary principles of administrative law, the rules of logic, and common sense seem to have eluded the Board in this as in other cases"]; *Marquez v. INS*, 105 F.3d 374, 378 (7th Cir. 1997) ["[b]y laying a coat of confusion on top of the Immigration Judge's more intelligible opinion, the BIA undermines our confidence in it"]; *Stankovic v. INS*, 94 F.3d 1117, 1120 (7th Cir. 1996) ["[t]he Board's own discussion of the case strongly suggests that it had not read, or was confused about, the record or the Immigration Judge's decision"], *Yepes-Prado v. INS*, 10 F.3d 1363, 1367 (9th Cir. 1993) [criticizing BIA's failure to set standard of review in §212(c) case as irresponsible, astonishing and incoherent]; *Osorio v. INS*, 18 F.3d 1017, 1030 (2d Cir. 1994) [BIA's decision reveals a complete lack of understanding of the political dynamics in Guatemala]; *Osmani v. INS*, 14 F.3d 13, 14 (7th Cir. 1994) [finding BIA's analysis in asylum deficient because "the Board seems unaware of the elementary facts of contemporary history, even those that bear vitally on its mission"]; *Ortiz-Salas v. INS*, 992 F.2d 105 (7th Cir. 1993) [criticizing failure to prepare adequate transcript and failure to announce what standard of review the BIA applies]; *Rivas-Martinez v. INS*, 997 F.2d 1143, 1147 (5th Cir. 1993) [describing BIA's reasoning in denying asylum as a "flawed syllogism" and "non sequitur"]; *Montecino v. INS*, 915 F.2d 518, 521 (9th Cir. 1990). The BIA has also been chastised for the insufficient time given to submit briefs following the provision of transcripts, *Escobar-Ramos v. INS*, 927 F.2d 482, 484–85 (9th Cir. 1991) [granting less than 15 days to write a brief when EOIR took two years to produce transcripts]; the failure to provide notice as to the time for filing a brief, *Chike v. INS*, 948 F.2d 961 (5th Cir. 1991) [reversing final order where respondent not notified of briefing schedule]; and the failure to provide notice of its decision, *Reid v. INS*, 949 F.2d 287 (9th Cir. 1991) [failure to provide written notice constitutes reversible error]. *But see* BIA delay in deciding appeal may not be a due process violation, *Maghsoudi v. INS,* 181 F.3d 8, 11 n.8 (1st Cir. 1999) [6-year delay in processing appeal was not violation of due process] or grounds for estoppel. *Kowalczyk v. INS,* 245 F.3d 1143, 1149–51 (10th Cir. 2001) [nine-year delay in asylum decision where country conditions changed does not warrant estoppel].

IV. DEPARTURE DURING APPEAL

A. *Removal/Deportation Proceedings*—Departure from the U.S. during the pendency of an appeal constitutes withdrawal. 8 C.F.R. §1003.4; *Aguilera-Ruiz v. Ashcroft,* 348 F.3d 835 (9th Cir. 2003) [rejecting argument that 8 C.F.R. §1003.4 is without statutory basis, conflicts with INA §101(a)(20) and 8 C.F.R. §1.1(p) and runs counter to *Fleuti*]; *Mejias-Ruiz v. INS*, 51 F.3d 358, 363–65 (2d Cir. 1995) [upholding former 8 C.F.R. §3.4 from APA and *Fleuti* attack and relying on INA §101(g)]; *U.S. v. Blaize*, 959 F.2d 850 (9th Cir. 1992). *See also Aleman-Fiero v. INS,* 481 F.2d 601 (5th Cir. 1973). One court has determined that even an accidental departure may constitute a withdrawal of appeal. *Long v. Gonzales,* 420 F.3d 516 (5th Cir. 2005) [no exception for involuntary departure where respondent was a passenger in a car that mistakenly entered Mexico; respondent's conduct in going near the border and not paying attention constituted a waiver]. *But see Martinez-De Bojorquez v. Ashcroft,* 365 F.3d 800 (9th Cir. 2004) [application of 8 C.F.R. §1003.4 to person who briefly entered Mexico for medical treatment without being notified of consequence of departure, violated due process]. However, the departure of a respondent does not withdraw a DHS appeal. *Matter of Luis-Rodriguez,* 22 I&N Dec.

747 (BIA 1999) [LPR's departure during INS appeal does not render appeal withdrawn or require dismissal for mootness]. Departure of a person subject to removal proceedings prior to appeal likewise constitutes waiver of appeal. 8 C.F.R. §1003.3(e). Withdrawal or self-deportation generally does not occur where person left after OSC had issued but before deportation hearing occurred. *Mrvica v. Esperdy*, 376 U.S. 560, 563 (1964). However, the IJ may enter an order *in absentia*. *Joo v. INS*, 813 F.2d 211 (9th Cir. 1987). 8 C.F.R. §1003.2(d) bars only persons who depart *after* removal proceedings have been instituted. *Singh v. Gonzales,* 412 F.3d 1117, 1120–21 (9th Cir. 2005) [person who departs before removal proceedings are initiated and seeks motion to reopen to vacate *in absentia* order is not barred by §1003.2(d)]. *See also William v. Gonzales,* 499 F.3d 329 (4th Cir. 2007) [the prohibition in 8 C.F.R. §1003.2(d) to motions to reopen where the person is outside the U.S. is contrary to INA §240(c)(7)(A), 8 U.S.C. §1229a(c)(7)(A) permitting one motion to reopen without limitation and the regulation is therefore invalid]; *Contreras-Rodriguez v. U.S. Att'y Gen.,* 462 F.3d 1314 (11th Cir. 2006) [although respondent was physically removed after *in absentia* order, he is not barred from filing a motion to reopen for lack of notice because §1003.23(b)(4)(ii) allows motion regarding lack of notice to be filed at "any time." *Patel* distinguished]. *See also in this chapter*, "Departure from the U.S. During Pendency of Motion," section XIII.F (p.1050), *infra.*

1. *Exclusion Proceedings*—The BIA takes a different view in former exclusion proceedings. *Matter of Keyte*, 20 I&N Dec. 158 (BIA 1990); *Matter of Kennedy*, 13 I&N Dec. 242 (BIA 1969). In *Keyte*, the BIA held that the departure of an applicant while the exclusion order was on appeal does not constitute withdrawal and does not moot the appeal. *See also Matter of Morales*, 21 I&N Dec. 130 (BIA 1996) (*on reh'g*) [declining to vacate as moot an interlocutory decision that was made after excludable person was deported]. In addition, departure does not moot a request for §212(c) relief even in deportation, *Matter of Brown*, 18 I&N Dec. 324 (BIA 1982), or where DHS seeks review of an order finding respondent not deportable. *Matter of Luis-Rodriguez,* 22 I&N Dec. 747 (BIA 1999). *But see Matter of Okoh*, 20 I&N Dec. 864 (BIA 1994) [BIA has no jurisdiction to decide motion to reconsider after applicant was excluded and deported].

V. REINSTATEMENT OF VOLUNTARY DEPARTURE AND AUTHORITY TO ENTER FINAL ORDER

A. *VD Order Generally*—The BIA will reinstate VD that expired during the course of a respondent's appeal unless: (1) the respondent failed to post the necessary $500 bond *within 5 days of the IJ's* order; or (2) there are specific reasons not to reinstate the IJ's order, such as a frivolous appeal or one filed for the purpose of delay. *Matter of A-M-,* 23 I&N Dec. 737, 742–44 (BIA 2005) [BIA will reinstate VD for up to 60 days if IJ gave 60 days, but cannot give a greater time than IJ ordered and VD will be reinstated only if respondent posted the $500 required within 5 days of the IJ's order]; *Matter of Chouliaris*, 16 I&N Dec. 169 (BIA 1977); *Matter of Patel*, 19 I&N Dec. 394 (BIA 1986) [no reinstatement where appeal is frivolous]; *Matter of R-P-*, 20 I&N Dec. 230 (BIA 1990) [reinstatement of VD denied where respondent was granted 6 months VD and no other relief requested].

1. *Tolling of Voluntary Departure Period Pending Motion*—The circuit courts are divided as to whether a respondent whose case the BIA reopens has violated a VD order by failing to depart during the VD period. *Compare Azarte v. Ashcroft,* 394 F.3d 1278, 1288–89 (9th Cir. 2005) [motion to reopen filed within the VD period, coupled with a request for a stay of removal, tolls the VD period so that respondent is not barred from relief for failure to depart]; *Ugokwe v. U.S. Att'y Gen.,* 453 F.3d 1325 (11th Cir. 2006) [a timely filed motion to reopen tolls the VD period and prohibits the application of *Matter of Shaar* to bar consideration of the merits of the motion]; *Kanivets v. Gonzales,* 424 F.3d 330 (3d Cir. 2005) [agreeing with *Azarte*]; and *Sidikhouya v. Gonzales,* 407 F.3d 950 (8th Cir. 2005) [same], with *Chedad v. Gonzales,* 497 F.3d 57 (1st Cir. 2007) [a timely filed motion to reopen does not stay the running of the VD period and if the motion is granted after VD has expired, the respondent is barred from seeking relief INA §240B(d)(1), 8 U.S.C. §1229c(d)(1)]; *Dekoladenu v. Gonzales,* 459 F.3d 500, 502–08 (4th Cir. 2006) [a timely filed motion to reopen does not toll the VD period]; *Banda-Ortiz v. Gonzales,* 445 F.3d 387, 391 (5th Cir. 2006) [BIA's decision to reopen case does not cure respondent's failure to depart during the VD period]. *See* "Civil Penalty and Denial of Other Relief for Failure to Voluntarily Depart" in Ch. 8, ¶ III.B.6 (p.966), *supra.*

2. *Exercising Discretion on VD*— Where the BIA reverses the IJ for a reason that undercuts the basis for the IJ's denial of VD, the Board must address whether VD should be granted. *Patel v. Gonzales,* 470 F.3d 216, 220–21 (6th Cir. 2006) [where BIA reversed IJ's determination that respondent was a persecutor of others and that finding was the basis to deny VD, the BIA failed to properly exercise its discretion when it did not either address VD or remand the issue for a new hearing].

B. ***BIA's Authority to Enter Final Order of Removal***— It is open to dispute whether the BIA may enter a final order in the first instance after reversing the IJ, or whether it is required to remand the case to the IJ for entry of a final order that would then be subject to federal court review. *Lolong v. Gonzales,* 484 F.3d 1173, 1175–78 (9th Cir. 2007) (en banc) [reversing *Molina-Camacho v. Ashcroft,* 393 F.3d 937 (9th Cir. 2004) in light of the REAL ID Act and finding jurisdiction to review a BIA order that reversed the IJ's grant of relief]; *Cruz-Camey v. Gonzales,* 504 F.3d 28 (1st Cir. 2007) [following *Lolong* and other circuits and finding that the BIA can enter final order when reversing a grant of relief]; *Guevara v. Gonzales,* 477 F.3d 456, 460–61 (7th Cir. 2007) [where BIA reverses INA §212(c) relief, it is leaving intact the IJ's finding of removability when it enters a final order]; *Lazo v. Gonzales,* 462 F.3d 53 (2d Cir. 2006) [disagreeing with *Molina-Camacho* and agreeing with *Delgado-Reynua, Solano-Chicas,* and *Del Pilar* and finding that the BIA does have the authority to enter final orders]; *Delgado-Reynua v. Gonzales,* 450 F.3d 596, 601 (5th Cir. 2006) [where IJ entered order of removal but granted relief which was reversed, BIA had right to enter final order]; *Solano-Chicas v. Gonzales,* 440 F.3d 1050, 1053–54 (8th Cir. 2006) [same]; *Del Pilar v. U.S. Att'y Gen.,* 326 F.3d 1154, 1156 (11th Cir. 2003) [same]. *But see Rhodes-Bradford v. Keisler,* 507 F.3d 77 (2d Cir. 2007) [where IJ finds that the respondent is not subject to removal and BIA reverses, the Board is without authority to enter a final order; the court distinguished *Lazo* as a case where the IJ found removability and the BIA was not entering a final order but simply removing an impediment to it]; *Sosa-Valenzuela v. Gonzales,* 483 F.3d 1140 (10th Cir. 2007) [where IJ granted §212(c) relief without entering order of removal and BIA reversed, BIA had no authority to enter final order]; *Avilez-Granados v. Gonzales,* 481 F.3d 869, 872–73 (5th Cir. 2007) [although respondent never sought AOS before BIA, the Board was required to remand the case to the IJ to entertain that relief after the BIA reversed the IJ's grant of §212(c) relief]; *James v. Gonzales,* 464 F.3d 505, 512–14 (5th Cir. 2006) [where IJ found respondent not removable, the BIA did not have independent authority to order removal and instead had to remand to IJ for entry of final order. *Delgado-Reynua* distinguished]; *Noriega-Lopez v. Ashcroft,* 335 F.3d 874, 882–85 (9th Cir. 2003) [where IJ ruled for respondent on insufficiency of the evidence, the BIA may reverse and remand but cannot enter a final order of removal]. Also, when the BIA reverses the IJ and remands the case to the IJ, the court has no jurisdiction. *Cordes v. Mukasey,* 517 F.3d 1094 (9th Cir. 2008) [majority distinguished *Lolong* and found that were IJ is reversed and case is remanded back to her, the circuit court is stripped of jurisdiction].

The BIA has *no jurisdiction* to review decisions to reinstate removal/deportation/exclusion orders pursuant to INA §241(a)(5). *Matter of G-N-C-,* 22 I&N Dec. 281 (BIA 1998).

VI. MOTIONS PRACTICE BEFORE THE BIA

A. ***Generally***—Regulations governing motions practice in cases over which the BIA last exercised jurisdiction are found at 8 C.F.R. §1003.2. Motions are filed directly with the BIA, 8 C.F.R. §1003.2(g)(2), unless case involves a matter initially adjudicated by a service officer (*e.g.,* I-130), in which case, the motion shall be filed with the office having control over the record. 8 C.F.R. §1003.2(g)(2)(ii). All motions must include Form EOIR-27, even if counsel previously filed one for the appeal. 8 C.F.R. §1003.2(g)(1). A brief may be filed with the motion and the opposing party has 13 days from the date of service to respond. 8 C.F.R. §1003.2(g)(3). The motion is deemed unopposed unless a timely response is made. *Id. Husssain v. Gonzales,* 477 F.3d 153, 156 (4th Cir. 2007) [where respondent filed motion to remand and DHS did not file a response, the motion is deemed unopposed]. The movant may also request oral argument. 8 C.F.R. §1003.2(h). The BIA must provide notice of its decision. 8 C.F.R. §1003.2(i). *Reid v. INS*, 949 F.2d 287 (9th Cir. 1991) [BIA violated its own rule when it failed to notify party that motion to reopen was granted]. *See in this chapter*, "Motion to Reopen or Reconsider Before EOIR," part XIII (p.1046), *infra*.

1. *Remands*—Either party may request that a case be remanded to the IJ. In *Matter of Coelho*, 20 I&N Dec. 464, 473 (BIA 1992), the BIA found that a motion to reconsider/remand must conform to the same standards as a motion to reopen, where the respondent presents new evidence, but will

only be granted if the new evidence "would likely change the result in the case." *Accord Fadiga v. Attorney General USA,* 488 F.3d 142, 145 & n.5 (3d Cir. 2007) [treating motion to remand under the motion to reopen standard and reversing denial of motion for asylum from Guinea where BIA applied a clear probability or more-likely-than-not standard, instead of applying a "reasonable likelihood" standard]; *Hussain v. Gonzales,* 477 F.3d 153 (4th Cir. 2007) [where respondent was ineligible for AOS because he entered EWI, the court denied motion to remand even where it was clear that BIA erred in failing to address the issue]; *Sanusi v. Gonzales,* 445 F.3d 193, 200–01 (2d Cir. 2006) [motion to remand properly denied because any new evidence that applicant would have submitted concerning CAT claim would not have changed the decision]; *Falae v. Gonzales,* 411 F.3d 11, 14–15 (1st Cir. 2005) [BIA properly treated motion to remand for adjustment based on new marriage as a motion to reopen]; *Olujoke v. Gonzales,* 411 F.3d 16, 23–24 (1st Cir. 2005) [where motion to remand offered expert psychological testimony addressing respondent's credibility, the BIA properly treated it as a motion to reopen]; *Al Najjar v. Ashcroft,* 257 F.3d 1262, 1302 (11th Cir. 2001). *But see Ahmed v. Mukasey,* 519 F.3d 579 (6th Cir. 2008) [BIA's failure to consider or address petitioner's documentation indicating he timely filed an AOS before his 21st birthday was abuse of discretion]; *Uriostegui v. Gonzales,* 415 F.3d 660, 664–65 (7th Cir. 2005) [where BIA issued AWO on *in absentia* order but never addressed motion to remand, court reversed noting that the BIA may not have the authority to AWO a motion to remand]; *Cao v. DOJ,* 421 F.3d 149, 156–58 (2d Cir. 2005) [reversing BIA's denial of motion to remand where Chinese asylum applicant presented new evidence]. A motion to remand to the BIA may be filed when an appeal is pending and does not trigger either the single motion or 90-day time limitation under 8 C.F.R. §1003.2(c). *Akhtar v. Gonzales,* 406 F.3d 399, 408–09 (6th Cir. 2005) [reversing BIA denial of motion to reopen based on one motion rule because prior motion to remand filed in the absence of a final administrative decision is not subject to the one motion rule]; *Chowdhury v. Ashcroft,* 241 F.3d 848, 852–54 (7th Cir. 2001). Similarly, a motion to reopen or reconsider will be treated as a motion to remand by the BIA if it was pending at the time an appeal was filed or if it was filed after an appeal was taken. 8 C.F.R. §§1003.2(b)(1), 1003.2(c)(4). A motion to remand that is filed during the pendency of an appeal from the IJ's denial of a motion to reopen may be treated as a supplement to the motion to reopen rather than as a second motion which would be numerically barred. *Guzman v. INS,* 318 F.3d 911 (9th Cir. 2003) [BIA has the discretion to treat a motion to remand as something other than a numerically-barred second motion to reopen]. However, a motion to remand filed after the BIA has issued a final order will be treated the same as a motion to reopen and is therefore subject to the constraints of 8 C.F.R. §1003.2(c). *Matter of Oparah,* 23 I&N Dec. 1 (BIA 2000) [motion to remand filed during pendency of appeal of a denial of a motion to reopen is treated as a motion to reopen for purposes of the 90-day/one-motion rules]; *Matter of L-V-K-,* 22 I&N Dec. 976 (BIA 1999) *rev'd on other grounds Konstantinova v. INS,* 195 F.3d 528 (9th Cir. 1999) [BIA has no jurisdiction over a motion to remand for AOS filed more than 90 days after a *final order*, while appeal of denial of motion to reopen was pending with the BIA]; *Krougliak v. INS,* 289 F.3d 457 (7th Cir. 2002) [upholding BIA's denial of motion to remand as untimely where motion was filed more than 90 days after entry of the final order]; *Wang v. Ashcroft,* 260 F.3d 448, 450–52 (5th Cir. 2001) [motion to remand treated as motion to reopen and deemed untimely where it is filed more than 90 days after the BIA's decision; distinguishing a motion to remand filed while appeal is pending, because there is no final order]. The AG has *sua sponte* authority to remand a case for additional fact-finding. *Matter of A-H-,* 23 I&N Dec. 774, 790–91 (AG 2005) [AG has concluded that he has authority to remand for additional fact finding as he deems necessary and appropriate, including the authority to override DHS's stipulation that respondent's life or freedom would be threatened if returned to his home country].

1.a. *Abuse of Discretion Standard of Review*—The BIA's decision on a motion to remand is reviewed under the abuse of discretion standard. *Ahmed v. Mukasey,* 519 F.3d 579 (6th Cir. 2008) [BIA's failure to consider or address petitioner's documentation indicating he timely filed an AOS before his 21st birthday was abuse of discretion]; *Narayan v. Ashcroft,* 384 F.3d 1065, 1068–69 (9th Cir. 2004) [BIA abused its discretion in failing to address motion to remand to consider new evidence of worsened country conditions]; *Patel v. Ashcroft,* 375 F.3d 693 (8th Cir. 2004) [BIA abused its discretion in denying remand for marriage-based AOS and requiring additional evidence of *bona fides* where an approved petition was submitted]; *Matter of Velarde-Pacheco,* 23 I&N Dec. 253 (BIA 2002) [regarding marriage case]. *But see Vargas-Hernandez v. Gonzales,* 497 F.3d 919, 923–25 (9th Cir. 2007) [BIA did not abuse its discretion in denying motion to remand for AOS where applicant needed a waiver with adjustment and IJ had already determined that his equities did not outweigh his serious conviction at 16 for voluntary manslaughter]; *Sarr v. Gonzales,* 485 F.3d 354, 362–64 (6th Cir. 2007) [upholding BIA denial of motion to remand under *Velarde* where applicant testified falsely at asylum hearing and did not file waiver with motion]; *Falae v. Gonzales,* 411 F.3d 11, 14–15 (1st Cir. 2005) [although motion to remand contained prima facie eligibility for marriage-based AOS and the BIA made no finding of a "sham marriage," the BIA did not abuse its discretion in refusing to remand where respondent had persistently used fraudulent documents, had a checkered previous marital history that indicated fraud, and lacked credibility]; *Malhi v. INS,* 336 F.3d 989, 993–95 (9th Cir. 2003) [no abuse of discretion to deny motion to remand based on marriage during removal proceeding where clear and convincing evidence of a bona fide marriage and *Matter of Velarde-Pacheco* were not produced]. The BIA's refusal to remand when a respondent became eligible for §212(c) relief during appeal was an abuse of discretion where the remand was requested by both parties and the BIA did not explore respondent's equities. *Anderson v. McElroy*, 953 F.2d 803, 806 (2d Cir. 1992). Similarly, the BIA's refusal to remand an asylum case where new material evidence is produced is an abuse of discretion. *Ubau-Marenco v. INS*, 67 F.3d 750, 755–60 (9th Cir. 1995). *See also Yang v. McElroy,* 277 F.3d 158 (2d Cir. 2002) [where there was a four-year delay between the BIA decision and the IJ decision which relied on a five year old DOS country report, the court remanded the case to the BIA for more current reports]. *But see Berte v. Ashcroft,* 396 F.3d 993, 997 (8th Cir. 2005) [no abuse of discretion in BIA's denial of remand to provide additional country reports and other documentary evidence in support of asylum claim because the BIA need not remand a case unless it "would likely change the result"]. Remand is also warranted where the Service fails to adequately explain its views consistent with 8 C.F.R. §§103.3(a)(1), 1103.3(a)(1), and the record was inadequate for BIA review. *Matter of Air India, Flight No. 101,* 21 I&N Dec. 890 (BIA 1997). Remand should also be granted where a person becomes eligible for AOS and DHS does not oppose, even if respondent fails to meet all procedural requirements. *Konstantinova v. INS,* 195 F.3d 528 (9th Cir. 1999) [reversing BIA's denial of remand where INS did not oppose, but respondent failed to file I-485 with motion]. *See also Matter of Yeondwosen,* 21 I&N Dec. 1025 (BIA 1997) [where INS affirmatively joins motion, technical defect may be waived]. In addition, where the BIA reverses an IJ grant of relief, the BIA should remand to the IJ to consider additional relief even if the respondent did not request it. *Avilez-Granados v. Gonzales,* 481 F.3d 869, 872–73 (5th Cir. 2007) [although respondent never sought AOS before BIA, the Board was required to remand to the IJ to entertain that relief after reversing the IJ's grant of §212(c)]. However, the BIA's denial of remand was affirmed where applicant did not file and was not prima facie eligible for AOS. *Onyeme v. INS,* 146 F.3d 227, 233–34 (4th Cir. 1998).

1.b. *Substantial Evidence Standard of Review*—The BIA's factual determinations in a motion to remand are reviewed for substantial evidence. *Korytnyuk v. Ashcroft,* 396 F.3d 272, 282–86 (3d Cir. 2005) [where BIA denied remand for AOS under *Abudu* theory that one may "leap ahead" and deny application on discretionary grounds, the factual basis for discretion is subject to substantial evidence review and the circuit court reversed the denial because the claim that respondent was involved in criminal activity was not supported by the record].

1.c. *No Jurisdiction to Review Remand*—In cases involving petitioners with criminal convictions, the court may be without jurisdiction to review a denial of a request to remand where the denial is based solely on factual issues and no legal or constitutional issues raised. *Zamora-Mallari v. Mukasey,* 514 F.3d 679, 696–97 (7th Cir. 2008) [court had no jurisdiction due to INA §242(a)(2)(C) to reverse a denial of remand for AOS of aggravated felon where no statutory or constitutional issues pursuant to INA §242(a)(2)(D) were raised].

1.d. *DHS Denied Remand*—DHS may not obtain remand where it had a prior opportunity to try an issue but failed to do so. *Matter of Kasinga,* 21 I&N Dec. 357, 363 (BIA 1996); *Matter of Guevara,* 20 I&N Dec. 238, 249 (BIA 1991). Nor may it obtain remand where it seeks to base a hearing on evidence that was previously available. *Johnson v. Ashcroft,* 378 F.3d 164 (2d Cir. 2004) [legacy INS not entitled to remand to retry a removal proceeding based on criminal charges that existed and were known to the government prior to the appeal].

1.e. *Remand Where Relief Previously Available*—A remand may not be granted where the relief requested was previously available and the respondent waived his right to apply for it before the immigration judge under 8 C.F.R. §1003.31(c). *Matter of A-K-,* 24 I&N Dec. 275, 281 (BIA 2007) [rejected remand to IJ to apply for asylum because respondent was given opportunity at hearing and he declined, instead applying for withholding and CAT, and thereby waiving his right to apply].

1.f. *Jurisdiction on Remand*—When the BIA remands a case, it divests itself of jurisdiction unless it expressly retains it, and "unless the Board qualifies or limits the remand for a specific purpose, the remand is effective for the stated purpose and for consideration of any and all matters which the [IJ] deems appropriate in the exercise of his administrative discretion or which are brought to his attention in compliance with the appropriate regulations." *Matter of Patel,* 16 I&N Dec. 600, 601 (BIA 1978). *See also BIA Appeals Practice Manual* §5.2(a)(iii)(B). *Patel* applies even if the remand is only for security checks. *Matter of M-D-,* 24 I&N Dec. 138, 141 (BIA 2007) [BIA remand for security check does not preclude IJ from considering motion to reopen based on marriage to a USC]. The BIA's decision to retain jurisdiction or to narrow the issues that the IJ may consider must be expressly stated and cannot be inferred. *Johnson v. Ashcroft,* 286 F.3d 696 (3d Cir. 2002) [reversing BIA decision that IJ did not have discretion to consider asylum claim after BIA reopened for CAT]. *But see Zhang v. Gonzales,* 434 F.3d 993, 996–98 (7th Cir. 2006) [absent exceptional circumstances, such as a change in the law, new evidence, or compelling circumstances, a new IJ assigned to a case on remand should not make rulings inconsistent with the prior IJ based merely on differing impressions of credibility].

VII. APPEAL FROM DECISIONS OF A DHS OFFICER

A. An appeal from a DHS decision that is within the jurisdiction of the BIA (*e.g.*, I-130 petition denials) must be filed on Form EOIR-29 within 30 days of the decision. The appeal is filed with the DHS office rendering the decision and not with the BIA. 8 C.F.R. §1003.3(a)(2). Both the petitioner and DHS are provided 21 days in which to file a brief, unless a shorter period is specified. 8 C.F.R. §1003.3(c)(2).

VIII. SCOPE OF REVIEW

A. *Limitations on De Novo Review*—The BIA traditionally maintained *de novo* review over all legal and factual matters decided by an IJ. *Charlesworth v. INS*, 966 F.2d 1323, 1325 (9th Cir. 1992); *Hazzard v. INS*, 951 F.2d 435, 440 n.4 (1st Cir. 1991); *Castillo-Rodriguez v. INS*, 929 F.2d 181 (5th Cir. 1991); *Cordoba-Chaves v. INS*, 946 F.2d 1244 (7th Cir. 1991); *Cardoza-Fonseca v. INS*, 767 F.2d 1448 (9th Cir.), *aff'd on other grounds*, 480 U.S. 421 (1987); *Dwomoh v. Sava*, 696 F.Supp. 970, 973 (S.D.N.Y. 1988); *Matter of Edwards*, 20 I&N Dec. 191 (BIA 1990). The Board was criticized, however, for its inability to decide whether and when to apply *de novo* review and when to apply an abuse of discretion standard. *Yepes-Prado v. INS*, 10 F.3d 1363, 1367, 1372 n.18 (9th Cir. 1993) [describing BIA's practice as "schizophrenic"]; *Ortiz-Salas v. INS*, 992 F.2d 105, 107–08 (7th Cir. 1993). *But see Matter of Burbano*, 20 I&N Dec. 872 (BIA 1994) [clarifying BIA's position by stating it does not apply an abuse of discretion standard but rather applies its "independent judgment"].

The scope of review has been altered by regulation, and the BIA will no longer engage in *de novo* review of findings of fact, including IJ credibility decisions in all cases filed on or after Sept. 25, 2002. 8 C.F.R. §1003.1(d)(3); *Wang v. Ashcroft,* 368 F.3d 347, 349 (3d Cir. 2004) [upholding BIA's findings and its decision to conduct *de novo* review in appeal filed by legacy INS before Sept. 25, 2002]. *But see Matter of J-F-F-,* 23 I&N Dec. 912, 913 (AG 2006) [AG reserves the right to "receive additional information and to make *de novo* factual determinations"]. Instead, the BIA reviews the facts, including credibility findings, under the "clearly erroneous" rule. 8 C.F.R. §1003.1(d)(3)(i); *Matter of V-F-D-,* 23 I&N Dec. 859 n.1 (BIA 2006). The Board does, however, retain *de novo* review over "questions of law, discretion, and judgment and all other issues in appeals from decisions" of IJs. 8 C.F.R. §1003.1(d)(3)(ii). *See Wood v. Mukasey,* 516 F.3d 564, 568–70 (7th Cir. 2008) [BIA has authority in the first instance to pass on whether AOS should be granted as a matter of discretion instead of remanding it back to the IJ because §1003.1(d) allows *de novo* review of discretionary issues that were actually decided or that might have been, but were not, decided by the IJ]; *Wallace v. Gonzales,* 463

F.3d 135, 140–41 (2nd Cir. 2006) [rejecting petitioner's claim that the BIA erred in reversing the IJ's grant of adjustment without making a clearly erroneous finding, because the BIA had *de novo* review over the AOS denial]. The BIA also retains *de novo* review on all matters of fact and law on appeal from decisions by DHS. 8 C.F.R. §1003.1(d)(3)(iii).

B. *Clearly Erroneous Rule*—An IJ's finding of fact is clearly erroneous "when, although there is evidence to support it, the reviewing Board member or panel is left with the definite and firm conviction that a mistake has been committed." 67 Fed. Reg. 54878 at 54889. The Board will not disturb an IJ's adverse credibility finding that is "supported by specific and cogent reasons with respect to inconsistencies and omissions with respect to a respondent's claim, observations of the respondent's demeanor, and reasonable inferences from those indicia…*Matter of A-S-,* [21 I&N Dec. 1106 (BIA 1998)]." 67 Fed. Reg. at 54889. *See Matter of T-Z-,* 24 I&N Dec. 163, 166 (BIA 2007) [upholding IJ's determination that Chinese asylum seeker was credible under clearly erroneous standard]; *Matter of R-S-H-,* 23 I&N Dec. 629, 637 & 641 (BIA 2003) [applying the clearly erroneous standard to the IJ's adverse credibility determination in an asylum/withholding case]; *Matter of S-H-,* 23 I&N Dec. 462 (BIA 2002) [reversing and remanding asylum case because IJ failed to make detailed findings that would enable BIA to review under clearly erroneous standard]. When the clearly erroneous rule applies, it is often difficult to ascertain. In asylum claims, the rule may apply to "what happened" but is not applicable to determinations whether the same facts demonstrate persecution or whether the claims meet other standards such as "on account of" a protected ground. 67 Fed. Reg. 54878 at 54890. Similarly in cancellation of removal cases, facts supporting the hardship claim are reviewed under the clearly erroneous standard, but whether the facts amount to "exceptional and extremely unusual hardship" is a question for *de novo* review. *Id.* In *Matter of V-K-,* 24 I&N Dec. 500 (BIA 2008) [reversing IJ's mixed question of fact and law regarding the torture Ukrainian would suffer and denying CAT relief] the BIA addressed the limits to the clearly erroneous rule and determined that it may review *de novo* mixed questions of fact and law including the possibility of a result in the future, such as the likelihood that respondent will be tortured or whether s/he will be persecuted or whether a certain level of hardship exists. In *Matter of A-S-B-,* 24 I&N Dec. 493 (BIA 2008) the Board, in affirming its denial of asylum and withholding, went further stating that its interpretation of the clearly erroneous rule allowed it to re-weigh evidence in a manner different than the IJ to determine whether a legal standard, such as the well-founded fear standard, was met. Citing to the comments to the Federal Register establishing and interpreting the clearly erroneous standard of review for the BIA (67 Fed. Reg. at 54,888–90), the Board determined that: "The clearly erroneous standard therefore does not apply to the application of legal standards, such as whether the facts established by an alien 'amount to past persecution or a well-founded fear of persecution.' " However, when the clearly erroneous rule applies and the BIA fails to adhere to it, the decision will be reversed. *Nabulwala v. Gonzales,* 481 F.3d 1115, 1118–19 (8th Cir. 2007) [to the extent the IJ made no factual findings on whether the government was unable or unwilling to control persecutors, the BIA may not supply such facts]; *Ramirez-Peyro v. Gonzales,* 477 F.3d 637 (8th Cir. 2007) [BIA factfinding that threat to U.S. drug informant from Mexico would only be limited to the northern part of Mexico violated BIA procedure under the clearly erroneous standard]; *Chen v. BUSCIS,* 470 F.3d 509 (2d Cir. 2006) [where BIA did not point to any misstatements of fact, errors in analysis, flawed reasoning or improper application of law, but simply started anew in its analysis of respondent's asylum claim, the court reversed]. *Cf. Rotinsulu v. Mukasey,* 515 F.3d 68 (1st Cir. 2008) [rejecting clearly erroneous challenge to withholding claim]; *Noble v. Keisler,* 505 F.3d 73 (7th Cir. 2007) [rejecting clearly erroneous challenge to INA §212(c) denial finding that BIA's reversal of IJ grant of relief was solely based upon weighing equities]; *Guevara v. Gonzales,* 477 F.3d 456, 458–60 (7th Cir. 2007) [same]. However, the clearly erroneous standard only applies in cases where an appeal was filed after September 25, 2002. 8 C.F.R. §1003.3(f); *Chavarria v. Gonzales,* 446 F.3d 508, 516–17 (3d Cir. 2007) [rejecting claim that clearly erroneous standard applied to the BIA where appeal was filed prior to Sept. 25, 2002].

C. *No Factfinding*—Traditionally, the BIA did not consider evidence first offered on appeal. *Matter of S-A-,* 22 I&N Dec. 1328, 1328–29 (BIA 2000); *Matter of Soriano*, 19 I&N Dec. 764 (BIA 1988); *Matter of Obaigbena*, 19 I&N Dec. 533 (BIA 1988). *But see Matter of Li*, 21 I&N Dec. 13, 18 (BIA 1995); *Matter of Godfrey*, 13 I&N Dec. 790, 791 n.1 (BIA 1971); *Matter of SS Captain Demosthenes*, 13 I&N Dec. 345, 346 n.1 (BIA 1969). However, the Board has been upheld both when it decided to consider new evidence, *Hazzard v. INS*, 951 F.2d 435, 440 (1st Cir. 1991), and when it decided not to consider new evidence; *Ghassan*, 972 F.2d 631at 638 (5th Cir. 1992). The Board has also been upheld when it reviewed record evidence that neither party objected to. *Ghassan v. INS*, 972 F.2d 631, 635 (5th Cir. 1992). The BIA's lack of procedures for treating new evidence that arose during appeal was found to violate due process. *Ramirez-Alejandre v. Ashcroft,* 320 F.3d 858 (9th Cir. 2003) (en banc).

Presently, however, the Board "will not engage in factfinding in the course of deciding appeals." *Matter of Adamiak,* 23 I&N Dec. 878, 880 (BIA 2006) [where respondent's conviction was vacated but there was a new plea while case was before the BIA, the BIA remanded to the IJ to determine whether respondent's new plea bars him from relief as an aggravated felon because the BIA has "limited review authority" that "precludes [it] from engaging in fact-finding in the course of deciding appeals"]. The Board retains the right to take administrative notice "of commonly known facts such as current events or the contents of official documents." 8 C.F.R. §1003.1(d)(3)(iv). However, administrative notice cannot be taken where facts are contested. *Argaw v. Ashcroft,* 395 F.3d 521, 525 (4th Cir. 2005) [BIA rebuffed in effort to take administrative notice that "khat" was a controlled substance subjecting respondent to removal]. The BIA will remand a case to the IJ where it "remain[s] uncertain, after examining the record...whether the Immigration Judge made a finding...and, if so, whether appropriate weight was afforded such a finding." *Matter of Tijam,* 22 I&N Dec. 408, 414 (BIA 1998) [remanding for clarification on findings regarding §241(a)(1)(H) waiver]. The BIA will also remand a case if the IJ has not provided a complete record to review. *Matter of Kelly*, 24 I&N Dec. 446 (BIA 2008) [remanding case where IJ's opinion references attachments but does not specify them to establish a complete record]; In cases where a party believes the Board cannot properly resolve the matter without additional factfinding, the respondent must file a motion to remand. 8 C.F.R. §1003.1(d)(3)(iv). The BIA has raised the standard for such a motion and will only grant it if the new evidence would change the outcome of the case. *Matter of Coelho*, 20 I&N Dec. 464 (BIA 1992). The AG has also concluded that he has *sua sponte* authority to remand a case for additional fact-finding. *Matter of A-H-,* 23 I&N Dec. 774, 790–91 (AG 2005) [AG may remand for additional fact-finding as he deems necessary and appropriate and has authority to override DHS's stipulation that respondent's life or freedom would be threatened if returned to his home country].

D. *Credibility Determinations*

1. *Review of Record—Matter of R-S-H-,* 23 I&N Dec. 629, 637 & 641 (BIA 2003). In order to make a credibility determination, the BIA must have a complete administrative record. *Matter of S-S-*, 21 I&N Dec. 121 (BIA 1995). However, where there is documentary material in the record from which the BIA can evaluate the credibility determination without a transcript or detailed written interview, it will do so. *Matter of M-S-*, 21 I&N Dec. 125 (BIA 1995). The BIA should not resolve credibility determinations by resorting to matters outside the record. *Jiang v. Houseman*, 904 F.Supp. 971, 981 (D. Minn. 1995). Moreover, where the IJ failed to make a credibility determination, the BIA should not make an adverse credibility finding without notice and an opportunity to respond. *Mendoza Manimbao v. Ashcroft,* 329 F.3d 655, 660 (9th Cir. 2003).
2. *Clearly Erroneous Standard*—The IJ's credibility determinations will be reviewed only to determine whether they are "clearly erroneous." 8 C.F.R. §1003.1(d)(3)(i). Historically, an IJ's credibility finding was upheld unless it was based on speculation and conjecture. *Vera-Villegas v. INS,* 330 F.3d 1222, 1225 (9th Cir. 2003) [IJ's finding on lack of physical presence was based on speculation and conjecture]; *Secaida-Rosales v. INS,* 331 F.3d 297, 307–12 (2d Cir. 2003) [quoting *Gao v. Ashcroft,* 299 F.3d 266, 272 (3d Cir. 2002) and reversing BIA]. Credibility determinations must be "based on specific, cogent reasons that bear a legitimate nexus to the finding." *Zahedi v. INS,* 222 F.3d 1157, 1165 (9th Cir. 2000). The IJ "must have a legitimate articulable basis to question the petitioner's credibility, and must offer a specific, cogent reason for any stated disbelief." *Gui v. INS,* 280 F.3d 1217, 1225 (9th Cir. 2002) [quoting *Hartooni v. INS,* 21 F.3d 336, 342 (9th Cir. 1994)]; *Mayo v. Ashcroft,* 317 F.3d 867 (8th Cir. 2003) [where IJ made credibility determination in respondent's favor, the BIA failed to set forth "cogent and articulate reasons for rejecting" it]. Where the BIA and IJ have disagreed on a factual question involving credibility, the appellate court have given substantial weight to IJ's findings. *Gonzalez-Rivera v. INS*, 22 F.3d 1441, 1445 (9th Cir. 1994) [vacating BIA decision on suppression that reversed IJ's decision]. *But see Ozdemir v. INS*, 46 F.3d 6, 8 (5th Cir. 1995) [if BIA and IJ credibility determinations conflict, court may consider both].
3. *Former Substantial Evidence Standard*—Pre-REAL ID, the IJ's credibility findings were entitled to considerable deference, but were reviewable for lack of substantial evidence. *He v. Ashcroft,*

328 F.3d 593 (9th Cir. 2003) [reversing BIA's adverse credibility determination under a substantial evidence standard]; *Pop v. INS,* 270 F.3d 527 (7th Cir. 2001) [affirming IJ's adverse credibility finding]; *Bandari v. INS,* 227 F.3d 1160, 1165–68 (9th Cir. 2000) [inconsistencies that reveal nothing about credibility, where IJ or BIA fail to explain significance, are insufficient for negative credibility determination]; *Matter of Y-B-*, 21 I&N Dec. 1136 (BIA 1998); *Osorio v. INS*, 99 F.3d 928, 932 (9th Cir. 1996) [inconsistencies between poorly filled-out application and statements do not support adverse credibility finding]; *Lopez-Reyes v. INS*, 79 F.3d 908 (9th Cir. 1996) [adverse credibility finding based on applicant's failure to file completed asylum application, failure to file corroborating affidavits, and IJ's own personal conjecture on likely guerrilla action was not supported by substantial evidence]; *Mosa v. Rogers*, 89 F.3d 601 (9th Cir. 1996); *Garcia v. INS*, 31 F.3d 441, 444–45 (7th Cir. 1994); *Cardoza-Fonseca v. INS*, 767 F.2d 1448 (9th Cir.), *aff'd on other grounds*, 480 U.S. 421 (1987); *Castillo-Rodriguez v. INS,* 929 F.2d 181 (5th Cir. 1991).

4. *Totality of the Circumstances Under REAL ID*—Post–May 11, 2005 asylum, withholding and CAT cases have new, specific standards for credibility. Credibility is now determined by the "totality of the circumstances and all relevant factors." The trier of fact may base credibility on "demeanor, candor, or responsiveness of the applicant or witness, the inherent plausibility of the applicant's or witness's account, the consistency between the applicant's or witness's written and oral statements (whenever made and whether or not under oath, and considering the circumstances under which the statements were made), the internal consistency of each such statement, the consistency of such statements with other evidence of record (including DOS country reports) and any inaccuracies or falsehoods in such statements, without regard to whether an inconsistency, inaccuracy, or falsehood goes to the heart of the applicant's claim, or any other relevant factor." INA §208(b)(1)(B)(iii); *Chen v. U.S. Att'y Gen.,* 463 F.3d 1228, 1230–32 (11th Cir. 2006) [adverse credibility finding under REAL ID need not be based on the heart of the claim; rejecting respondent's argument that an adverse credibility determination could not be based on "trivial" issues or issues "irrelevant to the dispositive issues"]. There is no presumption of credibility, but the applicant has a rebuttable presumption on appeal if no adverse credibility determination is explicitly made. INA §§208(b)(1)(B)(iii), 240(c)(4)(C), 241(b)(3)(C), 8 U.S.C. §§1158(b)(1)(B)(ii), 1230(c)(4)(C), 1231(b)(3)(C).

4.a. *Demeanor*—Deference should be accorded the IJ's credibility determination particularly where it is based on demeanor and sincerity. *Matter of A-H-,* 23 I&N Dec. 774, 786–87 (AG 2005) [where IJ's adverse credibility determination was based on the applicant's demeanor and sincerity as well as omissions and discrepancies, BIA erred in reversing]; *Paredes-Urrestarazu v. INS*, 36 F.3d 801, 817–20 (9th Cir. 1994) [demeanor based credibility findings are entitled to special deference]. *But see* Ch. 4, ¶ XII.B.2.g(8) (p.548), *supra.*

4.b. *Plausibility*—*Matter of B-*, 21 I&N Dec. 66 (BIA 1995) [where asylum applicant's testimony was plausible, detailed, internally consistent, consistent with asylum application and unembellished during probing cross-examination, the IJ's adverse credibility finding was reversed].

4.c. *Inconsistencies and Omissions*—Except to the extent superseded by the new standards, the BIA will defer to an adverse credibility determination based on inconsistencies and omissions regarding events central to an alien's asylum claim where a review of the record reveals that (1) the discrepancies and omissions described by the IJ are actually present in the record; (2) such discrepancies and omissions provide specific and cogent reasons to conclude that the alien provided incredible testimony; and (3) the alien has failed to provide a convincing explanation for the discrepancies and omissions." *Matter of A-S-,* 21 I&N Dec. 1106, 1109 (BIA 1998). *See also Matter of S-A-,* 22 I&N Dec. 1328, 1331 (BIA 2000) [reversing IJ and relying on test established in *Matter of A-S-*]. *See also Georgis v. Ashcroft,* 328 F.3d 962, 967–70 (7th Cir. 2003) [denial of asylum reversed under *Elias-Zacarias* standard where minor inconsistencies concerning dates and actions were easily resolved by other facts in evidence and explained by improperly excluded evidence]; *Singh v. Ashcroft,* 301 F.3d 1109 (9th Cir. 2002) [an omitted detail in a corroborative medical letter does not create inconsistency, nor does a minor discrepancy or unidentified unresponsiveness make the asylee's account not credible].

5. *No IJ Credibility Finding*—The BIA may not make an adverse credibility finding in the first instance. *Mendoza Manimbao v. Ashcroft,* 329 F.3d 655 (9th Cir. 2003) [where IJ does not expressly

make an adverse credibility determination, the BIA may not imply such a finding without violating the applicant's due process right to notice]; *Stoyanov v. INS,* 172 F.3d 731, 735 (9th Cir. 1999) [due process violated where BIA denied asylum on credibility grounds where IJ found respondent credible and respondent afforded no opportunity to rebut BIA's finding]; *Campos-Sanchez v. INS,* 164 F.3d 448 (9th Cir. 1999) [same]. *See also Mayo v. Ashcroft,* 317 F.3d 867 (8th Cir. 2003) [where IJ made favorable credibility determination, BIA failed to accord it sufficient deference]. *But see Pal v. INS,* 204 F.3d 935, 938–39 (9th Cir. 2000) [narrowing *Campos-Sanchez* where BIA credibility findings include IJs]; INA §208(b)(1)(B)(iii) [REAL ID Act provides that there is no longer a presumption of credibility if the IJ makes no finding; but applicant has rebuttable presumption of credibility on appeal].

6. *Remand on Credibility*—When the BIA is reversed in a case where it expressly abstained from ruling on credibility, the case may be remanded to the Board for a credibility finding. *Kayembe v. Ashcroft,* 334 F.3d 231, 237–39 (3d Cir. 2003) [where the BIA did not address credibility and did not point to anything in the record that refuted asylum claim, the denial of asylum was reversed]; *Briones v. INS,* 175 F.3d 727, 730 (9th Cir. 1999) (en banc) [where IJ made adverse credibility finding but BIA expressly declined to rule on that issue and denied asylum on another basis, the court reversed on the legal issue and remanded for credibility finding]. However, there are circumstances where the reversal of the BIA's credibility finding does not necessitate a remand. In *He v. Ashcroft,* 328 F.3d 593, 603–04 (9th Cir. 2003), the court found that where forced sterilization required asylum under INA §101(a)(42), there was no need to remand for additional investigation or explanation after reversing the adverse credibility finding. *Accord Zheng v. Ashcroft,* 397 F.3d 1139, 1147–48 (9th Cir. 2005) [remanding case after reversing adverse credibility determination but where respondent is automatically eligible for asylum, *Ventura* remand to determine eligibility is not required]; *Zhao v. Gonzales,* 404 F.3d 295, 310–11 (5th Cir. 2005) [*Ventura* remand unnecessary where government acknowledged no changed circumstances in China regarding Falun Gong claim]; *Edwards v. INS,* 393 F.3d 299, 312 (2d Cir. 2004) [remand for fact finding on §212(c) was unnecessary where IJ/BIA previously agreed that respondent was eligible for the relief and it was only their erroneous application of legal principles that required a reversal; BIA ordered to grant relief]; *Ghebremedhin v. Ashcroft,* 392 F.3d 241 (7th Cir. 2004) [limiting *Ventura* to circumstances where a factual issue is in dispute but remanding to BIA to exercise discretion]; *Wang v. Ashcroft,* 341 F.3d 1015, 1023 (9th Cir. 2003) [*Ventura* remand is unnecessary because if the adverse credibility determination is reversed the forced abortion claim is sufficient to warrant grant of asylum and withholding]; *Ding v. Ashcroft,* 387 F.3d 1131, 1140 (9th Cir. 2004) [remand unnecessary in forced abortion case because the applicant is necessarily eligible for asylum under correct standard].

7. *Credibility of Documents*—The standard for credibility of documents should be the same as credibility of testimony and therefore any adverse decision must be "based on specific, cogent reasons that bear a legitimate nexus to the finding." *Zahedi v. INS,* 222 F.3d 1157, 1165 (9th Cir. 2000) [reversing IJ's decision that documents lacked credibility based on ambiguous decision from INS Forensics Lab].

E. *Waiver of Issues Not Objected to or Raised Before IJ*—The BIA has found that if a matter was not objected to or raised before the IJ it is waived. *Matter of J-Y-C-,* 24 I&N Dec. 260, 261 n.1 (BIA 2007) [asylum applicant's failure to raise forced sterilization claim before IJ where his claim was based upon religious persecution as a Christian resulted in waiver of issue]; *Matter of R-S-H-,* 23 I&N Dec. 629, 638 (BIA 2003) [failure to object to presence of DOJ attorneys at hearing waived issue on appeal]; *Matter of Garcia-Reyes,* 19 I&N Dec. 830, 832 (BIA 1988) [objections should be made on the record to preserve issue for appeal]. *See also Pinos-Gonzalez v. Mukasey,* 519 F.3d 436, 440 (8th Cir. 2008) [upheld decision of BIA not to consider legal argument that a conviction would not bar cancellation because it was a petty-offense where it was not raised before the IJ]; *Torres De La Cruz v. Maurer,* 483 F.3d 1013, 1022–23 (10th Cir. 2007) [Article 36 Vienna Convention claim deemed waived and court refused to hear it for failure to exhaust where respondent failed to raise the claim before the IJ]. However, waiver owing to government error involving underlying action, like estoppel, may be difficult to assert. *Savoury v. U.S. Att'y Gen.,* 449 F.3d 1307, 1318–19 (11th Cir. 2006) [where DHS granted AOS and removed conditions despite respondent fully disclosing his ineligibility due to a drug conviction, government did not waive the right to assert the conviction in removal proceedings or to deny LPR status for purposes of §212(c) relief].

F. *BIA Decision*—In rendering a decision, the BIA may not make specific findings of fact and is only allowed to make a decision based on the record developed by the IJ. *Abdulai v. Ashcroft*, 239 F.3d 542, 549–50 (3d Cir. 2001); *Alleyne v. INS*, 879 F.2d 1177, 1183 (3d Cir. 1989).

1. *No Boilerplate Decisions*—With the exception of AWO under 8 C.F.R. §1003.1(e)(4), the Board cannot issue decisions based solely on boilerplate language. *Khan v. DOJ,* 494 F.3d 255, 259–60 (2d Cir. 2007) [court reversed BIA where its refusal to allow a party to file his notice of appeal one day late was not accompanied by any indication in its opinion that the BIA considered any exception to the 30 day deadline]; *Filja v. Gonzales,* 447 F.3d 241, 256–58 (3d Cir. 2006) [reversing BIA where it merely stated it had "carefully reviewed the record" but its one paragraph statement devoted to ineffective assistance of counsel evidenced no analysis of the record]; *Chavarria v. Gonzales,* 446 F.3d 508, 521 (3d Cir. 2007) [finding BIA's one sentence dismissal of applicant's future persecution claim was "both grossly inadequate and erroneous"]; *Paramasamy v. Ashcroft,* 295 F.3d 1047, 1048–52 (9th Cir. 2002) [reversing BIA for relying on credibility finding in asylum case based on boilerplate demeanor observations by the IJ]; *De La Llana-Castellon v. INS*, 16 F.3d 1093, 1098 (10th Cir. 1994) [where BIA decision consisted entirely of boilerplate language, the BIA's consideration was so deficient as to deprive respondent of due process]; *Rhoa-Zamora v. INS*, 971 F.2d 26, 36–37 (7th Cir. 1992); *Castillo v. INS*, 951 F.2d 1117, 1121 (9th Cir. 1991). Nor can the Board simply give a "bare conclusion" for its decision not to exercise discretion unless the ground or argument it rejects is frivolous. *Garcia Gomez v. Gonzales,* 498 F.3d 1050 (9th Cir. 2007) [followed *Gutierrez-Almazan* and held that BIA's one-sentence order denying a late-filed brief did not indicate how BIA arrived at its conclusion]; *Gutierrez-Almazan v. Gonzales,* 491 F.3d 341 (7th Cir. 2007) [reversing BIA denial of *pro se* petitioner's request to file brief late where the court could not tell from BIA's one sentence order whether the BIA "heard and thought" or "merely reacted" in denying request]; *Ssali v. Gonzales,* 424 F.3d 556, 564–66 (7th Cir. 2005) [in denying a motion to reopen for marriage-based adjustment, the BIA failed to indicate its reasoning in a manner sufficient for review]; *Bastanipour v. INS*, 980 F.2d 1129, 1131 (7th Cir. 1992) [reversing BIA for giving only a bare conclusion in denying discretionary asylum]. *Accord Halo v. Gonzales,* 419 F.3d 15, 18–19 (1st Cir. 2005) [where BIA decision stated only that asylee had not made a showing of persecution justifying relief and record suggested otherwise, case remanded to BIA for elaboration]; *Awolesi v. Ashcroft,* 341 F.3d 227 (3d Cir. 2003) [where IJ granted asylum to Nigerian and BIA reversed by stating only that "the evidence was insufficient" and that the arguments made by INS on appeal were "persuasive," the court was unable to tell the basis for the decision, and accordingly reversed and remanded]; *Butros v. INS*, 804 F.Supp. 1336, 1339 (D. Or. 1991) [reversing BIA for its "merely conclusory" decision to deny a stay pending motion to reopen]. The BIA's "failure to explain a decision adequately provides grounds for reversal." *Zhao v. DOJ,* 265 F.3d 83, 96–97 (2d Cir. 2001) [where BIA addressed and denied petitioner's new evidence in motion to reopen in two sentences it created "controversy and confusion" compelling reversal]; *Mekhael v. Mukasey,* 509 F.3d 326 (7th Cir. 2007) [BIA did not provide reasoned decision for denying motion to reopen for Lebanese Christian who presented evidence relating to the war between Israel and Hezbollah that began after IJ decision].

2. *Summary Affirmance*—The BIA may summarily affirm so long as the IJ's decision contains sufficient reasoning and evidence to permit review by a federal court. *Chen v. INS*, 87 F.3d 5 (1st Cir. 1996); *Arango-Aradondo v. INS*, 13 F.3d 610, 613 (2d Cir. 1994); *Panrit v. INS*, 19 F.3d 544 (10th Cir. 1994) [permitting BIA per curiam affirmance]; *Safaie v. INS*, 25 F.3d 636, 641 (8th Cir. 1994) [no abuse of discretion where BIA adopted IJ's findings and added its own "*de novo*" footnotes]; *Prado-Gonzalez v. INS*, 75 F.3d 631 (11th Cir. 1996) [BIA need not write a lengthy opinion merely repeating the IJ's decision and may affirm for reasons stated in the IJ's opinion]. In the view of some courts, the Board need not address specifically each claim or each piece of evidence where it has given reasoned consideration to the petition and made adequate findings. *Kamara v. Att'y Gen. of the U.S.,* 420 F.3d 202, 211–12 (3d Cir. 2005) [BIA decision that sets forth its reasoning with sufficient clarity to allow a reviewing court to discern the basis for the decision, even if not a model of clarity, does not violate due process or the APA]; *Morales v. INS,* 208 F.3d 323, 328 (1st Cir. 2000). *Accord Wang v. BIA,* 437 F.3d 270, 274–76 (2d Cir. 2006) [denying motion to reopen based on changed country conditions and noting that while the BIA must consider all evidence, it can do so in a summary fashion]; *Rhoa-Zamora v. INS,* 971 F.2d 26, 34–36 (7th Cir. 1992). *But see Mezvrishvili v. U.S. Att'y Gen.,* 467 F.3d 1292, 1294–97 (11th Cir. 2006) [BIA did not provide a reasoned decision in affirming IJ's denial of asylum]; *Babai v. INS,* 985 F.2d 252,

255 (6th Cir. 1993) [BIA's consideration of issue "must be careful and individualized"]; *Diaz-Resendez v. INS*, 960 F.2d 493, 497 (5th Cir. 1992) [BIA must actually consider and meaningfully address relevant factors]. The Board's failure to provide detailed analysis may not result in reversal where the moving party failed to provide a written brief. *INS v. Aguirre-Aguirre,* 526 U.S. 415 (1999). An error by the IJ may be harmless if corrected by the BIA. *Balazoski v. INS*, 932 F.2d 638, 640 (7th Cir. 1991); *Elnager v. INS*, 930 F.2d 784, 787 (9th Cir. 1991).

G. *Court Review of BIA or IJ Decision*

1. *BIA Separate Opinion*—If the BIA writes a separate decision, the court will review the BIA's decision, not the IJ's decision. *Huang v. U.S. Att'y Gen.,* 429 F.3d 1002, 1008 (11th Cir. 2005) [court will review only the BIA's decision except to the extent it expressly adopts the IJ's opinion]; *Zheng v. Gonzales,* 409 F.3d 804, 809 (7th Cir. 2005) [where BIA did not accept IJ's credibility determination and instead evaluated case on the ground that the respondent was credible, the court reviewed the BIA decision only]; *Voci v. Gonzales,* 409 F.3d 607, 612–13 (3d Cir. 2005) [where BIA agreed with IJ decision to deny asylum but did not adopt, reference or defer to the IJ's findings and expressed disagreement with the IJ's credibility determination, the court reviewed the BIA's determination]; *Liu v. Ashcroft,* 380 F.3d 307, 311–12 (7th Cir. 2004) [where BIA's decision rested on grounds that were alternative to those used by the IJ, the court will review the BIA's decision]; *Kayembe v. Ashcroft,* 334 F.3d 231, 237–39 (3d Cir. 2003) [where the BIA did not address IJ's negative credibility finding and did not point to anything in the record that refuted the asylum claim, the denial of asylum was reversed notwithstanding DOS country report that provided substantial evidence to deny claim based on ethnic persecution]; *Abdulai v. Ashcroft,* 239 F.3d 542, 548–49 (3d Cir. 2001) [final order review is from the BIA decision]; *Iyamba v. INS,* 244 F.3d 606, 607 (8th Cir. 2001) [respondent's arguments regarding IJ decision are misdirected where it is the BIA's decision that is being reviewed]; *Balazoski v. INS*, 932 F.2d 638, 640 (7th Cir. 1991); *Elnager v. INS*, 930 F.2d 784, 787 (9th Cir. 1991); *Castillo-Rodriguez v. INS*, 929 F.2d 181 (5th Cir. 1991).

   Where the BIA affirms the IJ's decision *per curiam* under the AWO provision of 8 C.F.R. §1003.1(e)(4), the court will review the IJ's decision. *Gandarillas-Zambrana v. BIA*, 44 F.3d 1251, 1255 (4th Cir. 1995). However, where the BIA's opinion is not clear and it did not summarily affirm, the court may look to the IJ's decision to determine whether it provides an adequate basis for review. *Cruz-Funez v. Gonzales,* 406 F.3d 1187, 1190–91 (10th Cir. 2005) [where BIA's opinion was muddled but IJ's decision provided adequate basis for review of asylum case, court reviewed IJ's decision]. In addition, where the BIA enters an order by a single member pursuant to the "brief order" provision of 8 C.F.R. §1003.1(e)(5) the situation is more complicated. In the view of one circuit, it will not affirm a decision from a "brief order" on a ground raised by the IJ unless it was also relied upon by the BIA. But where the BIA does rely on the same ground as the IJ it may consult the IJ's more complete explanation of that ground. *Uanreroro v. Gonzales,* 443 F.3d 1197, 1203–04 (10th Cir. 2006)

2. *Summary Affirmance*—Where the BIA summarily affirms the IJ's decision, 8 C.F.R. §1003.1(e)(4), courts will review the IJ's decision as if it were the Board's. *Falcon Carriche v. Ashcroft,* 350 F.3d 845, 855 (9th Cir. 2003) [where BIA streamlines, the IJ's decision becomes the final agency decision]; *Sepulveda v. U.S. Att'y Gen.,* 401 F.3d 1226, 1230 (11th Cir. 2005); *Al Najjar v. Ashcroft,* 257 F.3d 1262, 1284 (11th Cir. 2001); *Lata v. INS,* 204 F.3d 1241, 1244 (9th Cir. 2000); *Mousa v. INS,* 223 F.3d 425, 428 (7th Cir. 2000). However, the court should be confined to the reasons offered by the IJ and should not search the record for alternative reasons to affirm the BIA's decision. *Pang v. BUSCIS,* 448 F.3d 102, 107 (2d Cir. 2006); *Secaida-Rosales v. INS,* 331 F.3d 297, 305 (2d Cir. 2003) [reversing IJ's credibility findings and remanding for new hearing]. *Accord Gandarillas-Zambrana v. BIA,* 44 F.3d 1251, 1255 (4th Cir. 1995); *Cuevas v. INS,* 43 F.3d 1167, 1170 (7th Cir. 1995); *Panrit v. INS,* 19 F.3d 544, 546 (10th Cir. 1994).

3. *Review of Both IJ and BIA Decisions*—Where the BIA substantially relies on an IJ's decision but supplements the IJs findings and makes some of its own findings, typically pursuant to 8 C.F.R. §1003.1(e)(5), the court will review both the IJ and BIA decisions. *Savoury v. U.S. Att'y Gen.,* 449 F.3d 1307, 1312 (11th Cir. 2006) [where the BIA adopted the IJ's decision but made a few additions, the court will review the IJ's decision as supplemented by the Board]; *Giday v. Gonzales,* 434 F.3d 543, 547 (7th Cir. 2006) [where the BIA affirmed and adopted the IJ's decision and also appended a ruling on respondent's due process claim and added its own statement regard credibil-

ity and likelihood of future persecution, the court reviewed both the IJ decision and the additional reasoning of the BIA]; *Guan v. Gonzales,* 432 F.3d 391, 394 (2d Cir. 2005) [where the BIA agrees with the IJ's conclusion that petitioner is not credible and, without rejecting any of the IJ's grounds for decision, emphasizes particular aspects of that decision, the court reviews both opinions and relies on the portions of the IJ's decision not explicitly discussed by the BIA]; *Chacon-Botero v. U.S. Att'y Gen.,* 427 F.3d 954, 956 (11th Cir. 2005) [where the BIA expressly adopts the IJ's reasoning and briefly articulates its reasons for doing so, the court will review both the IJ and BIA decisions]; *Ssali v. Gonzales,* 424 F.3d 556, 561 (7th Cir. 2005) [finding the IJ's opinion as supplemented by the BIA's opinion the basis for review]; *Eta-Ndu v. Gonzales,* 411 F.3d 977, 982 (8th Cir. 2005) [where BIA adopted IJ's opinion on asylum and withholding but added some of its own reasoning, court reviewed both decisions]; *Korytnyuk v. Ashcroft,* 396 F.3d 272, 286–87 (3d Cir. 2005) [where BIA denied motion to remand for adjustment but adopted IJ's factual determination in doing so, the court reviewed the IJ's factual determination and the BIA's denial on discretionary grounds]; *He Chun Chen v. Ashcroft,* 376 F.3d 215, 222 (3d Cir. 2004) [in forced sterilization case, where IJ and BIA both made credibility findings but BIA's decision rested largely on IJ's, the court reviewed both). At least one circuit has recognized that determining what parts of the IJ order is being adopted by the BIA is a delicate process and the court will only review the IJ's opinion where the BIA has incorporated the IJ's reasoning expressly or by implication. *Sarr v. Gonzales,* 474 F.3d 783, 789–93 (10th Cir. 2007) [where BIA determined that respondent's statements regarding Mauritanian citizenship were inconsistent and IJ determined citizenship was improbable, court reviewed only BIA's inconsistency claim and reversed denial of asylum]; *Uanreroro v. Gonzales,* 443 F.3d 1197, 1203–04 (10th Cir. 2006) Where the BIA adopts portions of the IJ's opinion, those portions are reviewed along with the BIA's opinion on other issues. *Romilus v. Ashcroft,* 385 F.3d 1, 5 (1st Cir. 2004); *Najjar v. Ashcroft,* 257 F.3d 1262, 1284 (11th Cir. 2001) [court will review only the BIA's decision except to the extent that it expressly adopts the IJ's opinion]. But to the degree the BIA adopts the IJ's decision it "must be charged with whatever flaws or inadequacies" the court discerns and the court will not uphold the decision because "the Board might have been able to eliminate the flaws and come to the same conclusion." *Angoucheva v. INS,* 106 F.3d 781, 789 (7th Cir. 1997). The IJ's opinion will be given deference only where it "announces its decision in terms sufficient to enable a reviewing court to perceive that it has heard and thought and not merely reacted." *Sosnovskaia v. Gonzales,* 421 F.3d 589, 592–94 (7th Cir. 2005) [reversing IJ's determination where "the procedure that the IJ employed…is an affront to [the applicant's] right to be heard" on her claim involving anti-Semitism in the Ukraine]. Moreover, the court's review may be more searching when the IJ and the BIA determinations differ. *Laipenieks v. INS,* 750 F.2d 1427, 1429–30 (9th Cir. 1985) [although substantial-evidence test is applied, "where the hearing examiner and the Agency have reached opposite results the appellate court's reviewing eye may be more searching"].

4. *Abuse of Discretion*—Where the BIA does not engage in *de novo* review, but rather reviews IJ's decision for abuse of discretion, the BIA's decision is subject to review for abuse of discretion. *Yepes-Prado v. INS,* 10 F.3d 1363, 1367 (9th Cir. 1993).

H. *Precedent Decisions, Constitutional Claims, and Application of the Law*

1. *Precedent vs. Non-Precedent Decisions*—DHS is bound by decisions designated as precedent by the Board. 8 C.F.R. §1003.1(g); *Martinez-Montoya v. INS,* 904 F.2d 1018 (5th Cir. 1990) [rejecting LAU decision in *Matter of M* as contrary to *Ozkok*]. However, the BIA is not bound to follow precedent decisions of the Service, *Matter of Tijam,* 22 I&N Dec. 408, 416 (BIA 1998); *Matter of Fueyo*, 20 I&N Dec. 84 (BIA 1989), or DHS policy memoranda that have not been incorporated into regulations. *Matter of Briones,* 24 I&N Dec. 355, 365 n.7 (BIA 2007). Non-precedent decisions have been recognized as expressing the BIA's position. *Shardar v. Att'y Gen. of the U.S.,* 503 F.3d 308, 314–16 (3d Cir. 2007) [BIA's claim it did not have to follow unpublished decision missed the mark because "by reaching an exactly contrary decision on a materially indistinguishable set of facts, the Board acted arbitrarily"]; *Davila-Bardales v. INS,* 27 F.3d 1, 5–6 (1st Cir. 1994) ["[p]ut bluntly, we see no earthly reason why the mere fact of nonpublication should permit an agency to take a view of the law in one case that is flatly contrary to the view it set out in earlier (yet contemporary) cases without explaining why it is doing so"]. *But see Ajdin v. USCIS,* 437 F.3d 261, 264–65 (2d Cir. 2006) [BIA did not abuse its discretion by failing to adhere to an unpublished decision]; *Ang v. Gonzales,* 430 F.3d 50, 58 (1st Cir. 2005) [single unpublished decision

has no precedential force and will not bind the BIA]; *Guillen-Garcia v. INS*, 60 F.3d 340, 345–46 (7th Cir. 1995) [unpublished BIA decisions have no precedential value], *Douglas v. INS*, 28 F.3d 241, 245 (2d Cir. 1994) [unpublished BIA decisions should not be relied on as binding precedent in unrelated matters]. *See also Avena v. INS*, 989 F.Supp.1 (D.D.C. 1997) [contrary unpublished INS decisions by appellate unit are not binding on AAO nor are DOS regulations]; *Matter of Izummi,* 22 I&N Dec. 169, 188 (BIA 1998) [General Counsel's memos not binding on INS adjudicating bodies such as Service Centers and AAO].

2. *Constitutional Claims*—BIA will generally not rule on the constitutionality of the statute/regulations that it administers, *Matter of U-M-*, 20 I&N Dec. 327 (BIA 1991) [BIA will not rule on whether deportation is double jeopardy]; *Matter of L*, 4 I&N Dec. 556 (BIA 1951), and it does not have the authority to ignore or disregard regulations established by the AG. *Matter of Anselmo*, 20 I&N Dec. 25 (BIA 1989); *Matter of Fede*, 20 I&N Dec. 35 (BIA 1989). The Board has therefore concluded that it cannot grant equitable estoppel because it does not have the authority to exceed the regulations. *Matter of Hernandez-Puente*, 20 I&N Dec. 335 (BIA 1991) [no authority to grant adjustment to person who was no longer eligible as a result of INS error]; *Matter of United Airlines Flight UA802,* 22 I&N Dec. 777, 782 (BIA 1999) [same]. The BIA may entertain due process and fundamental fairness challenges to procedures as applied, *Matter of Toro*, 17 I&N Dec. 340 (1980), and it can entertain procedural due process challenges that it can correct administratively. *Alleyne v. INS*, 879 F.2d 1177, 1183 n.10 (3d Cir. 1989). It will not consider a collateral attack on prior order unless there was a gross miscarriage of justice. *Matter of Malone*, 11 I&N Dec. 730 (BIA 1966); *see also Lara v. Trominski,* 216 F.3d 487, 493–94 (5th Cir. 2000) [where gross miscarriage of justice not found BIA need not consider collateral attack].

3. *Law Applied at Time of Review*—The BIA "will apply the law existing at the time of its review," even where such application has negative consequences. *Matter of Alarcon*, 20 I&N Dec. 557 (BIA 1992) [amendment to §212(h) applied on appeal]; *Matter of A-A-*, 20 I&N Dec. 492 (BIA 1992) [applying §212(c) bar retroactively even though not in effect at time of IJ decision]; *Matter of U-M-*, 20 I&N Dec. 327 (BIA 1991) [applying Congress' determination that aggravated felonies were particularly serious crimes to deny asylum, even though asylum application was filed prior to IMMACT90].

I. *Administrative Notice*—The BIA may take administrative notice of "commonly known facts such as current events or the contents of official documents." 8 C.F.R. §1003.1(d)(3)(iv). However, the BIA is not required to take administrative notice. *Meghani v. INS,* 236 F.3d 843, 848 (7th Cir. 2001) [rejecting claim that BIA was required to *sua sponte* take administrative notice of reports reflecting changed conditions in Pakistan in light of 7-year delay in deciding case].

1. *Country Conditions*—"Official documents" under 8 C.F.R. §1003.1(d)(3)(iv) include "country condition reports prepared by the Department of State, including its foreign policy expertise, analysis and opinion." 67 Fed. Reg. 54892 (Aug. 26, 2002). Courts generally take the view that the BIA may take administrative notice of changed political conditions in a country subject to an abuse of discretion standard. *Useinovic v. INS,* 313 F.3d 1025, 1030–31 (7th Cir. 2002) [affirming BIA denial where Yugoslavian government was no longer in power]; *Francois v. INS,* 283 F.3d 926, 933–34 (8th Cir. 2002) [although not given notice of BIA's reliance on changed conditions in Eritrea, court found no prejudice]. *But see Fergiste v. INS,* 138 F.3d 14, 17–19 (1st Cir. 1998) [rejecting simple administrative notice and citation to *Matter of E-P-*, 21 I&N Dec. 860, as a basis to rebut past persecution where applicant presented evidence of continuing problems in Haiti]; *Getachew v. INS,* 25 F.3d 841 (9th Cir. 1994) [reversing BIA where INS raised issue of changed circumstances because regulations do not clearly permit respondent the right to present new evidence before the BIA]; *Kowalczyk v. INS,* 245 F.3d 1143 (10th Cir. 2001) [finding abuse of discretion to take administrative notice of changed political conditions in Poland nine years after brief submitted]. The BIA may not take notice of adjudicative facts without giving an opportunity to respond. *Burger v. Gonzales,* 498 F.3d 131 (2d Cir. 2007) [following the Ninth and Tenth Circuits the failure to give an asylum applicant from the former Yugoslavia the opportunity to respond to administrative findings of changed conditions in Serbia-Montenegro *before* making those finding is a violation of due process and is not cured by a motion to reopen]; *Chhetry v. DOJ,* 490 F.3d 196 (2d Cir. 2007) [although BIA could take administrative notice of new developments, it violated due process when it denied motion to reopen based on changed conditions in Nepal by

citing to recent sources that indicated positive developments in Nepal after motion was filed without giving applicant an opportunity to respond]; *Circu v. Gonzales,* 450 F.3d 990 (9th Cir. 2006) (*en banc*) [failure to give asylum applicant the right to rebut DOS report violated due process]; *Castillo-Villagra v. INS*, 972 F.2d 1017 (9th Cir. 1992). *See also Lorisme v. INS*, 129 F.3d 1441, 1445 (11th Cir. 1997); *Gonzalez v. INS*, 82 F.3d 903, 910–12 (9th Cir. 1996); *Janusiak v. INS*, 947 F.2d 46, 48 n.1 (3d Cir. 1991); *Kaczmarczyk v. INS*, 933 F.2d 588, 593–97 (7th Cir. 1991); *Baka v. INS*, 963 F.2d 1376, 1379 (10th Cir. 1992); *Wojcik v. INS*, 951 F.2d 172, 173 (8th Cir. 1991).

2. *Commonly Known Facts and Opinions*—The Board may take official notice of commonly acknowledged legislative facts and technical or scientific facts that are within the agency's area of expertise. *Rivera-Cruz v. INS*, 948 F.2d 962 (5th Cir. 1991). The BIA may not take administrative notice of opinions. *Galina v. INS,* 213 F.3d 955, 958–59 (7th Cir. 2000).

3. *Challenging Administrative Notice*—Administrative notice may be challenged if factually incorrect. *Argaw v. Ashcroft,* 395 F.3d 521, 525 (4th Cir. 2005) [BIA rebuffed in effort to take administrative notice that "khat" was a controlled substance subjecting respondent to removal]. Some courts have found that a motion to reopen is the mechanism for challenging the BIA's administrative notice. *Toptchev v. INS,* 295 F.3d 714, 723–24 (7th Cir. 2002) [lawyer for applicants could not have been surprised by use of Country Reports by BIA in light of their frequent use and he nevertheless could have filed a motion to reopen]; *Gutierrez-Roque v. INS*, 954 F.2d 769, 773 (D.C. Cir. 1992); *Rivera-Cruz*, 948 F.2d 962 (5th Cir. 1991); *Kaczmarczyk v. INS,* 933 F.2d 588, 593–97 (7th Cir. 1991); *Baka v. INS,* 963 F.2d 1376, 1379 (10th Cir. 1992). The AG supports this view and believes "that a compelling case is made for a liberal interpretation" of the rule regarding reopening or reconsideration and that a party "should have the opportunity to challenge" the facts that have been administratively considered. 67 Fed. Reg. 54878 at 54892–93 (Aug. 26, 2002). DOJ's interpretation is that "the 'not available' and 'could not have been discovered' requirements of section [100]3.2(c)" are not applicable in this scenario. *Id.* Other courts believe the proper remedy is to remand the case to permit the agency to hold a hearing. *Burger v. Gonzales,* 498 F.3d 131 (2d Cir. 2007) [following the Ninth and Tenth Circuits the failure to give an asylum applicant from the former Yugoslavia the opportunity to respond to administrative findings of changed conditions in Serbia-Montenegro *before* making those finding is a violation of due process and is not cured by a motion to reopen]; *De La Llana-Castellon v. INS*, 16 F.3d 1093 (10th Cir. 1994) [violation of due process for BIA to reverse IJ without any opportunity to respond]; *Castillo-Villagra v. INS*, 972 F.2d 1017, 1025–31 (9th Cir. 1992) [rejecting requirement that applicant subject to administrative notice file a motion to reopen]; *Osaghae v. INS*, 942 F.2d 1160 (7th Cir. 1991); *Desir v. Ilchert*, 840 F.2d 723, 730 (9th Cir. 1988). Failure to grant an automatic stay pending a motion to reopen to challenge administrative notice would raise a "significant due process concern." *Gutierrez-Roque*, 954 F.2d at 773. *But see Acewicz v. INS*, 984 F.2d 1056, 1059–61 (9th Cir. 1993) [distinguishing *Castillo-Villagra* and permitting administrative notice without a new hearing where issue could have been addressed before the IJ]; *Matter of H-M-*, 20 I&N Dec. 683 (BIA 1993) [following *Acewicz*]. The denial of a motion to reopen is improper if based on administrative notice of facts first raised in the denial. *Gebremichael v. INS*, 10 F.3d 28, 37–39 (1st Cir. 1993).

4. *Administrative Notice Taken By Court*—The court has taken judicial notice of changed circumstances where events are "troubling" and "well publicized," *Gafoor v. INS,* 231 F.3d 645, 654–57 (9th Cir. 2000) [court took judicial notice of recent coup in Fiji that was not reflected in the record], or where the BIA's adverse credibility finding was based on a failure to recognize an undisputed fact. *Singh v. Ashcroft,* 393 F.3d 903 (9th Cir. 2004) [where BIA made adverse credibility finding because asylum applicant did not prove the existence of the Indian intelligence service (RAW), the court reversed, citing Fed. R. Evid. 201, and rejected the government's argument that the court could not take notice of such an obvious fact as "nonsense"]. *But see INS v. Ventura,* 537 U.S. 12 (2002) [reversing 9th Cir. for making finding on changed circumstances where BIA had not reached the issue because the appropriate procedure required a remand to the agency]; *Gonzales v. Thomas,* 547 U.S. 183 (2006) [vacating 9th Cir. *en banc* decision that defined a social group before giving the BIA the opportunity to determine whether "the members of a family can and do constitute a 'particular social group' within the meaning of the Act"]. *See also Ezeagwuna v. Ashcroft,* 325 F.3d 396, 398 & 411 (3d Cir. 2003) [on rehearing, vacating previous grant of asylum and withholding after determining it misapplied credibility issues; remanding to IJ to make those decisions].

IX. REVIEW BY AAO / REGIONAL COMMISSIONER

A. ***Jurisdiction***—The Associate Commissioner for Examinations through the AAO, under 8 C.F.R. §§103.3(a)(1)(ii), 1103.3(a)(1)(ii), AFM at 3.5(c), has jurisdiction over decisions concerning: (i) bond breaches; (ii) I-140 preference petitions (including Hong Kong, special immigrants, and entrepreneur petitions), except when the denial of the petition is based on lack of labor certification; (iii) Indochinese applications for AOS; (iv) revocation of approved petitions under 8 C.F.R. §§205.2, 1205.2; (v) applications for permission to reapply for admission into the U.S. after deportation or removal as provided in §212.2; (vi) applications for waiver of certain grounds of inadmissibility under INA §§212(h) & (i); (vii) 8 U.S.C. §1182e waivers; (ix) petitions for approval of schools or the decisions of IJs to withdraw school approval; (x) petitions for temporary workers or trainees and fiancé(e)s; (xi) applications for re-entry permits under 8 C.F.R. §223.1; (xii) applications for refugee travel documents; (xiii) applications for AOS of certain diplomats under §13 of the Act of Sept. 11, 1957; (xiv) applications for adjustment of certain LPRs to nonimmigrants; (xv-xx) applications related to naturalization; (xxi) applications by organizations to be listed for free legal service; (xxii) Amerasian petitions; (xxiii) revocation of nonimmigrant petitions; (xxiv–xxv) orphan petitions; (xxvi) invalidation of temporary labor certifications from Guam; (xxvii–xxxiii) applications concerning temporary or permanent residence under IRCA; (xxxv) petitions for special immigrant juveniles; and (xxxvi) applications for AOS based on the *bona fide* marriage exception in INA §245(e) concerning 2-year foreign residency. All of these matters are reviewed by the AAO within the Office of the Associate Commissioner for Examinations, except legalization matters under IRCA which are decided by the Legalization Appeals Unit (LAU). 8 C.F.R. §245a.2(p). The AAO does not review denied I-130 petition as those are reviewed by the BIA. Selected decisions of the AAO or other decisions of the DHS Secretary may be published only after approval by the AG. 8 C.F.R. §1003.1(i). The AAO has been likened to an appellate court not bound by the decisions of the Service Centers. *Louisiana Philharmonic Orchestra v. INS*, 2000 WL 282785 (E.D. La. Mar. 15, 2000). The record before the AAO, absent bad faith, inadequacy, or improper behavior can generally not be supplemented. *Balaton, Inc. v. Reno,* 93 F.Supp.2d 61 (D.D.C. 2000) [refusing to allow petitioner to supplement record based on claim that AAO continuously pursued an unlawful policy to deny L-1 extensions to small business petitioners]. There is no review of the denial of an extension of stay or change of nonimmigrant status.

B. ***Notice of Appeal and Brief***

1. *Timeliness of Appeal*—The appellant has 30 days after service of the decision to file a notice of appeal to the AAO/RC, 8 C.F.R. §103.3(a)(2)(i), 1103.3(a)(2)(i). Three days are added if notice is served by mail. 8 C.F.R. §103.5a(b). Appellant may file a brief with the notice of appeal. Notice is on Form I-290B. 8 C.F.R. §§103.3(a)(2)(vi), 1103.3(a)(2)(vi). Must make request for oral argument, if desired, in the notice of appeal. 8 C.F.R. §§103.3(b), 1103.3(b). Extensions for filing the brief may be granted for good cause. 8 C.F.R. §§103.3(a)(2)(vii), 1103.3(a)(2)(vii). Where appellant did not receive decision or notice of right to appeal, the district court reinstated 30-day appeal period to give petitioner the right to appeal bond breach. *Hrubec v. INS*, 828 F.Supp. 251 (S.D.N.Y. 1993).

2. *Motions to Reopen and Appeals*—The AAO may treat a properly and timely filed appeal as a motion to reopen or reconsider and take favorable action. 8 C.F.R. §103.3(a)(2)(iii). An *untimely* appeal that meets the requirements of a motion to reopen under §103.5(a)(2) or a motion to reconsider under §103.5(a)(3) *must be* treated as a motion and a decision must be made on the merits. 8 C.F.R. §103.3(a)(2)(v)(B)(2). A field officer decision made on a motion may be appealed to the AAO if the original decision was appealable to the AAO. 8 C.F.R. §103.5(a)(6). Procedures for motions to reopen or reconsider before USCIS are governed by 8 C.F.R. §103.5. Each Service Center maintains its own detailed procedures on appeals and motions to reopen/reconsider. *See e.g.,* Way, Director, Nebraska Service Center, NSC Motions and Appeals Processes for other than Special Agricultural Worker and Legalization Cases, NSC 70/41.1.1 (Feb. 10, 2004), *published on* AILA InfoNet at Doc. No. 04021763.

3. *Standing to Appeal*—The petitioner, not the beneficiary, can appeal. 8 C.F.R. §§103.3(a)(1)(iii)(B), 1103.3(a)(1)(iii)(B). The obligor on bond, not bonded alien can appeal. A notice of appeal must be accompanied by the appropriate fee as specified in 8 C.F.R. §103.7 and a properly executed G-28 by the petitioner.

4. *Unlawful Presence Accrues During Appeal*—An appeal to the AAO does not toll unlawful presence under INA §212(a)(9). A person appealing an I-129 C/S or E/S denial, must depart the U.S. or risk triggering the 3/10 year bar. The appellant may not work unless he is otherwise authorized. An L-1, for example, who filed an extension may continue to work even if the extension is denied if the I-94 endorsed for employment is still valid.

X. REVIEW BY BALCA

A. *Generally*—The Board of Alien Labor Certification Appeals (BALCA) reviews denials or revocations of labor certifications by the Certifying Officer and challenges to prevailing wage determinations by the State Workforce Agency and the CO. 20 C.F.R. §§656.26, 656.27 & 656.41(e). BALCA was previously authorized to hear H-1A appeals regarding denials to health care facilities or approvals (by interested third parties) of attestations to health care facilities. For BALCA's address, *see* **Appendix J**. For a full discussion of the BALCA appeal process, *see* Ch. 7, part IX (p.950), *supra*.

XI. REVIEW BY OCAHO

A. *Generally*—The Office of Chief Administrative Hearing Officer (OCAHO) oversees administrative law judge (ALJ) proceedings in Unfair Immigration Related Employment Practices, employer sanctions cases, and fine proceedings under INA §274C, 8 U.S.C. §1324c. 28 C.F.R. §0.118.

B. *Appeals*—There is no administrative appeal over Unfair Immigration Related Employment Practice cases and no appeal of right over employer sanctions cases. 28 C.F.R. §68.54(a). OCAHO may review employer sanctions cases if deemed appropriate, even if a party has not requested review. 28 C.F.R. §68.54(a)(2). Any party may request OCAHO review within 10 days of the ALJ's decision. 28 C.F.R. §68.54(a)(1). Legal arguments should accompany the request. Within 30 days, OCAHO may issue an order adopting, affirming, modifying, or vacating the ALJ's decision. 28 C.F.R. §68.52(d)(1).

XII. REVIEW BY EXCHANGE VISITOR WAIVER REVIEW BOARD

A. *Provides for Review of INA §212(e) Waivers*—22 C.F.R. §§41.63(b)–(e), (g)

B. *Composition*—The Board is composed of officials within DOS and allows for review at the request of the Chief, Waiver Review Division of the Visa Office. Traditionally, the cases heard by the Board involved:

1. Requests of interested government agencies where waiver review branch's recommendation was unfavorable;
2. A federal agency has submitted a written opposition to a waiver that was recommended by the waiver review branch;
3. Where the J-1 was given a "no objection" letter by his or her government, the U.S. financed the program for $2,000 or less and waiver review branch gave unfavorable recommendation;
4. Persecution case where waiver review branch gave favorable recommendation but BHRHA gave negative opinion; and
5. Cases in which, for any reason, the waiver review branch requests review of its decision.

XIII. MOTION TO REOPEN OR RECONSIDER BEFORE EOIR

A. *Generally*—A motion to reopen or reconsider may be filed with the BIA, 8 C.F.R. §1003.2, or the IJ, 8 C.F.R. §1003.23. A motion to reopen must be filed no later than 90 days from "the date on which the final administrative decision was rendered." 8 C.F.R. §1003.2(c)(2). A motion to reconsider must be filed "within 30 days after the mailing of the Board decision." 8 C.F.R. §1003.2(b)(2). The same deadlines apply for motions before the IJ. 8 C.F.R. §1003.23(b)(1). A motion to reopen may not be filed with an IJ once an appeal of the IJ's decision is pending with the BIA. *Ilic-Lee v. Mukasey,* 507 F.3d 1044, 1049 (6th Cir. 2007) [BIA was correct to dismiss appeal of IJ's denial of motion to reopen because respondent had appealed IJ's underlying order and the IJ did not have jurisdiction to entertain the motion to reopen once the notice of appeal to the BIA was filed]. A motion to reopen granted by an IJ may be reconsidered and denied by another IJ who received the transferred case. *Singh-Bhathal v.*

INS, 170 F.3d 943 (9th Cir. 1999). A motion to rescind an *in absentia* order, may be filed only with the IJ and must be filed within 180 days if claiming exceptional circumstances, but there is no time limit for failure to receive notice. *Singh v. Gonzales,* 436 F.3d 484 (5th Cir. 2006) [upholding BIA decision that motion to reopen/rescind *in absentia* order could only be filed with the IJ]. The motion must contain English translations for all documents, a notice of representation form, the appropriate fee and proof of service. 8 C.F.R. §§1003.2(g). Motions to the Board are filed directly with the BIA, 8 C.F.R. §1003.2(g)(2), unless it was from a decision of a DHS officer in which case it is filed with the officer. 8 C.F.R. §1003.2(g)(2)(iii). If a petition for review has been filed, the BIA does *not* need the circuit court's permission to reopen. *Gao v. Gonzales,* 464 F.3d 728 (7th Cir. 2006). The filing of a petition for review *does not* toll the time for filing a motion to reconsider or reopen. *Randhawa v. Gonzales,* 474 F.3d 918 (6th Cir. 2007). The filing of a motion to reopen or reconsider does not automatically stay removal. 8 C.F.R. §1003.2(f).

B. *Motion to Reconsider*—A motion to reconsider is a "request that the Board reexamine its decision in light of additional legal arguments, a change of law, or perhaps an argument or aspect of the case which was overlooked." *Matter of Ramos,* 23 I&N Dec. 336, 338 (BIA 2002) [quoting *Matter of Cerna*]; *Khan v. Gonzales,* 495 F.3d 31, 36–37 (2d Cir. 2007) [where the respondent merely repeats the arguments previously raised, the BIA does not abuse its discretion in denying the motion]; *Asemota v. Gonzales,* 420 F.3d 32, 33–34 (1st Cir. 2005) [upholding BIA denial of motion to reconsider its decision upholding IJ's denial of continuance because it failed to meet *Matter of Cerna* standards]. Under 8 C.F.R. §1003.2(b), a motion to reconsider must contain: (1) an allegation of material factual or legal error in the Board's decision that is supported by pertinent authority; (2) if the Board issued an AWO, a showing that the alleged errors and legal arguments were previously raised on appeal and a statement explaining how the Board erred in utilizing AWO; or (3) if there has been a change in law, a reference to the relevant statute, regulation, or precedent and an explanation of how the BIA's decision is materially affected. *Matter of O-S-G-,* 24 I&N Dec. 56, 60 (BIA 2006) [where respondent's motion to reconsider raised a new asylum theory related to membership in a particular social group, motion to reconsider was inappropriate]. A motion to reconsider may be made even if the case was dismissed for lack of jurisdiction where the dismissal was due to an untimely appeal. *Matter of Lopez,* 22 I&N Dec. 16 (BIA 1998); *but see Chen v. Gonzales,* 436 F.3d 76 (2d Cir. 2006) [where respondent characterized his motion as one to "reconsider or reopen" after his appeal was filed late, the court reversed the BIA for treating it as an untimely motion to reconsider instead of a timely motion to reopen]. A motion to reconsider may also be made where the BIA has decided to remand the case to the IJ. *Matter of Perez Vargas,* 23 I&N Dec. 829 at n.1 (BIA 2005). A motion to reconsider may not be used as a substitute for a motion to reopen where the party does not meet the standard for a motion to reopen. *Mungongo v. Gonzales,* 479 F.3d 531, 535 (7th Cir. 2007) [new evidence may not be submitted in a motion to reconsider]; *Alizoti v. Gonzales,* 477 F.3d 440, 452–53 (6th Cir. 2007) [where BIA denied motion to reopen proceeding based upon marriage and respondent filed a motion to reconsider and attached the newly approved I-130 petition, the court upheld the denial of the motion to reconsider on the grounds that it was a second motion to reopen that was numerically barred]; *Sinistaj v. Ashcroft,* 376 F.3d 516 (6th Cir. 2004) [where evidence was available at time of original hearing and there was no identification of errors in fact or law, the BIA correctly denied motion to reopen or in the alternative reconsider because neither standard was met]; *Walters v. Ashcroft.* 291 F.Supp.2d 237, 244–47 (S.D.N.Y. 2003) [where INS sought to introduce facts concerning respondent's incarceration for more than 5 years to invalidate §212(c) relief, it was a violation of due process to try to add such facts through a motion to reconsider when a motion to reopen could not demonstrate that these were new facts unknown to the government during the appeal]. Similarly, a motion to reopen for ineffective assistance of counsel should not be characterized as a motion to reconsider. *Siong v. INS,* 376 F.3d 1030, 1036 (9th Cir. 2004); *Singh v. Ashcroft,* 367 F.3d 1182 (9th Cir. 2004) [where respondent learned of the BIA's final order after 30 days and learned that his appeal was summarily dismissed for failure to file a brief, his motion to reopen was improperly treated as a motion to reconsider]; *Iturribarria v. INS,* 321 F.3d 889, 894–97 (9th Cir. 2003) [BIA abused its discretion when it treated IAC claim as a motion to reconsider instead of a motion to reopen]. A motion to reconsider a denied motion to reopen will be granted where the BIA improperly denied the motion to reopen. *Yeghiazaryan v. Gonzales,* 439 F.3d 994 (9th Cir. 2006). The court, therefore, must look at the validity of the order denying the motion to reopen to determine whether there is any basis for the motion to reconsider. *Aneyoue v. Gonzales,* 478 F.3d 905, 907 (8th Cir. 2007) [motion to reconsider properly denied because motion to reopen was properly denied where evidence was previously available]. A motion to reconsider will be granted where the BIA plainly misreads a DOS Report ignoring substantial evidence that supports a respondent's claim. *Dawoud v. Gonzales,* 424 F.3d 608, 611–12 (7th Cir. 2005) [BIA misread DOS report supporting asylum claim of Coptic from Egypt]. The grant of a motion to reconsider and the subsequent affirmance of the original order may not affect the finality of the original order for purposes of appeal. *Jaggernauth v. U.S. Att'y Gen.,* 432 F.3d 1346, 1350–52 (11th Cir. 2005) [the granting of a motion to reconsider and the reaffirmance of the original order did not affect the finality of the order and the court therefore had jurisdiction to review the matter when petitioner appealed the original order within 30 days]; *Plasencia-Ayala v. Mukasey,* 516 F.3d 738, 744–46 (9th Cir. 2008) [same]. *But see Mu Ju Li v. Mukasey,* 515 F.3d 575, 578–80 (6th Cir. 2008) [when the BIA grants a motion to reconsider and renders a new decision addressing the arguments raised, the original order has been vacated, a new order has been entered in its place, and a new appeal must be filed]. A motion to reconsider may also be entertained even if more than one motion to reconsider has been filed because the numerical limitation under 8 C.F.R. §1003.2(b)(2) applies to each "decision" made during a removal proceeding and not solely to the respondent's immigration case as a whole. *Calle v. U.S. Att'y Gen.,* 504 F.3d 1324 (11th Cir. 2007) [where applicant for asylum/withholding from Colombia filed a motion to reconsider with the BIA, then a motion to reopen, and then a motion to reconsider the denial of the motion to reopen, the last motion to reconsider was not numerically barred].

C. *Motion to Reopen*—In a motion to reopen before the BIA or the IJ, the applicant must show that the evidence is: (1) material; (2) unavailable at time of original hearing; and (3) could not have been discovered or presented at the original hearing. 8 C.F.R. §1003.2(c)(1). *Kaur v. BIA,* 413 F.3d 232, 234 (2d Cir. 2005) [motion to reopen properly denied where the "new" evidence was not material because it did not rebut the adverse credibility finding that was the basis for the IJ's asylum denial]; *Gebremaria v. Ashcroft,* 378 F.3d 734, 737–39 (8th Cir. 2004) [BIA correctly denied motion to reopen asylum case where applicant's HIV status was known to her at time of IJ hearing]; *Sinistaj v. Ashcroft,* 376 F.3d 516, 519 (6th Cir. 2004). It is error, however, for the BIA to make credibility determinations on motions to reopen. *Bhasin v. Gonzales,* 423 F.3d 977, 986 (9th Cir. 2005) [BIA improperly discounted respondent's affidavit as self-serving in Indian social group claim]; *Ghadessi v. INS,* 797 F.3d 804, 806 (9th Cir. 1986). One court has found that a respondent is not entitled to the hearing rights under INA §240(b)(4) when filing a motion to reopen. *Altamirano-Lopez v. Gonzales,* 435 F.3d 547, 550–51 (5th Cir. 2006) [IJ's decision to hold a hearing on a motion to reopen did not give the respondent the statutory rights of a removal proceeding and he had no constitutional due process right because the decision to grant or deny the motion is discretionary]. Motions to reopen have been analogized to motions for relief from judgment under Fed. R. Civ. P. 60(b). *Stone v. INS,* 514 U.S. 386 (1995). Motions to reopen based on vacating or overturning a conviction are deemed appropriate. *DeFaria v. INS,* 13 F.3d 422, 423 (1st Cir. 1993)

1. *Supporting Documentation and Fees*—A motion to reopen must be supported by affidavits or other evidentiary materials. 8 C.F.R. §§1003.2(c)(1), 103.5(a)(2). A motion to reopen seeking relief or a benefit *must* be accompanied by the application and all supporting documents. *Palma-Mazariegos v. Keisler,* 504 F.3d 144 (1st Cir. 2007) [*Matter of Velarde-Pacheco* does not forgive the requirement that a completed I-485 application must be submitted with motion]; *Waggoner v. Gonzales,* 488 F.3d 632, 638–39 (5th Cir. 2007) [BIA did not err in denying reopening to applicant from Fiji who was arguing changed circumstances but failed to submit an application for asylum/withholding]. At least one court has found, however, that 8 C.F.R. §1003.2(c)(1) does not require that the supporting documentation be filed simultaneously with the motion as long as the documentation is filed within the 90-day period. *Yeghiazaryan v. Gonzales,* 439 F.3d 994 (9th Cir. 2006) [where counsel filed a timely motion to reopen and stated that supporting briefs would follow, the BIA improperly denied the motion within the 90-day period because counsel did not simultaneously file the briefs]. Where ineffective assistance of counsel is raised, the BIA has not required the production of new evidence to reopen. *Matter of N-K- & V-S-,* 21 I&N Dec. 879, 880 (BIA 1977); *Matter of Lozada,* 19 I&N Dec. 637, 639 (BIA), *aff'd,* 857 F.2d 10 (1st Cir. 1988); *Osei v. INS,* 305 F.3d 1205 (10th Cir. 2002) [BIA reversed where it required the production of new evidence for a motion based upon IAC]. The fee for a motion to reopen must be paid when filing the motion except when it is to reopen an *in absentia* order. The movant must only pay for the motion, and if successful will thereafter pay the separate fee, if required, for the relief requested. 8 C.F.R. §§103.7(b)(1), 1103.7(b)(1).

2. *Ineffective Assistance of Counsel*—A motion regarding ineffective assistance of counsel should be treated as a motion to reopen and not a motion to reconsider. *Siong v. INS,* 376 F.3d 1030, 1036 (9th Cir. 2004); *Singh v. Ashcroft,* 367 F.3d 1182 (9th Cir. 2004) [where respondent learned of the BIA's final order after 30 days and learned that his appeal was summarily dismissed for failure to file a brief, motion to reopen was improperly treated as a motion to reconsider]; *Iturribarria v. INS,* 321 F.3d 889, 894–97 (9th Cir. 2003) [BIA abused its discretion when it treated IAC claim as a motion to reconsider]. However, the movant must still show prejudice by counsel's ineffectiveness. *Canaveral v. Ashcroft,* 385 F.3d 40, 46 (1st Cir. 2004) [claim against nonlawyer who committed fraud even if deemed ineffective was insufficient because there was no showing of prejudice]. Failure of counsel to raise an asylum/CAT/withholding claim before the IJ or BIA may waive the right and prevent a motion to reopen from being granted even if ineffective assistance is raised. *Maindrond v. Ashcroft,* 385 F.3d 98, 100–01 (1st Cir. 2004) [denial of motion to reopen for CAT upheld where movant was represented by counsel before IJ and BIA]. But a respondent is not required to show that he would win his case in order to have it reopened; he need only show that the representation was so inadequate that it may have affected the outcome. *Maravilla Maravilla v. Ashcroft,* 381 F.3d 855, 858 (9th Cir. 2004) [reversing BIA denial of motion to reopen for IAC where they improperly analyzed the standard. In the 9th Cir., the analysis of IAC requires the BIA to consider: (1) whether competent counsel would have acted otherwise; and (2) whether counsel's performance was so inadequate that it may have affected the outcome of proceedings]. Moreover, the BIA cannot dismiss an ineffective assistance claim simply by stating it was a strategic decision. *Mai v. Gonzales,* 473 F.3d 162, 165–67 (5th Cir. 2007) [reversed BIA denial of motion to reopen for ineffective assistance despite BIA's claim that the lawyer made a strategic decision when he admitted two grounds of removal where one required a §212(c) waiver and the second a waiver under §240A because once §212(c) granted for the first ground §240A was unavailable for the second].

3. *Grant of Motion to Reopen and Finality of Order*—The *grant* of the motion to reopen vacates the previous order and reinstates the removal proceeding. *Verano-Velasco v. U.S. Att'y Gen.,* 456 F.3d 1372, 1373 n.1 (11th Cir. 2006) [where court reversed BIA's denial of motion to reopen, "the effect of [the] reversal is that the entire case [was] remanded for further proceedings and reconsideration"]; *Orichitch v. Gonzales,* 421 F.3d 595 (7th Cir. 2005) [where BIA reversed IJ denial of motion to reopen to adjust, case was reopened for all purposes]. *But see Gomes v. Gonzales,* 429 F.3d 1264, 1267 (9th Cir. 2005) [grant of a motion to reopen because of changed circumstances addresses issues concerning future persecution and applicant's failure to appeal original order of removal regarding past persecution could not be included in new appeal].

D. *Motions Filed while Appeal Pending*—A motion to reopen or reconsider that is filed with the BIA when an appeal is pending with the BIA will be treated as a motion to remand and may be consolidated with the underlying appeal. 8 C.F.R. §§1003.2(b)(1), 1003.2(c)(4). Notwithstanding the procedures for motions to reopen and remand, the BIA's determination that it was precluded as a matter of law from considering new evidence while appeal was pending violated due process when it was not based on a procedural defect. *Ramirez-Alejandre v. Ashcroft,* 320 F.3d 858 (9th Cir. 2003) (en banc) [due process was violated where the BIA had inconsistent procedures for treating evidence that arose during the appeal process in suspension cases that often continued for years]. A motion to reopen may not be filed with an IJ once an appeal of the IJ's decision is pending with the BIA. *Ilic-Lee v. Mukasey,* 507 F.3d 1044, 1049 (6th Cir. 2007) [BIA was correct to dismiss appeal of IJ's denial of motion to reopen because respondent had appealed IJ's underlying order and the IJ did not have jurisdiction to entertain the motion to reopen once the notice of appeal to the BIA was filed].

E. *BIA May Deny Reopening*—Under *INS v. Abudu*, 485 U.S. 94 (1988), the BIA may deny reopening under three circumstances: (1) failure of applicant to make *prima facie* case; (2) failure to reasonably explain under 8 C.F.R. §§1003.2, 103.5, and if asylum, 8 C.F.R. §§208.17, 1208.17 why information was not available sooner; and (3) as a matter of discretion. *INS v. Rios-Pineda*, 471 U.S. 444 (1985). *Accord INS v. Doherty*, 502 U.S. 314 (1992); *Fesseha v. Ashcroft,* 333 F.3d 13, 20–21 (1st Cir. 2003) [applying *Abudu* and finding no abuse of discretion for failure of Ethiopian to establish a prima facie case of asylum]. The BIA has described a *prima facie* case as one in which "the evidence reveals a reasonable likelihood that the statutory requirements for relief have been satisfied." *Matter of S-V-,* 22 I&N Dec. 1306, 1308 (BIA 2000). The BIA does *not* require a conclusive showing that relief would be granted because it is not ruling on the merits in deciding whether reopening is warranted. *Matter of L-O-*

G-, 21 I&N Dec. 413 (BIA 1996); *Guo v. Ashcroft,* 386 F.3d 556, 563–66 (3d Cir. 2004) [BIA erred in denying reopening based on fear of future persecution due to U.S.-born children because third-party expert affidavit provided sufficient evidence to meet *prima facie* case]. The grant of a motion to reopen will turn in part "upon the likelihood that the applicant will be granted the relief sought [asylum, suspension, §212(c), etc.] if reopening is permitted." *Matter of Rodriguez-Vera*, 17 I&N Dec. 105 (BIA 1979). *See also Matter of C-C-,* 23 I&N Dec. 899 (BIA 2006) [denying motion to reopen based on U.S.-born children, finding insufficient evidence to establish prima facie eligibility that respondent would be persecuted in China; distinguishing *Guo v. Ashcroft*]; *Ordonez v. INS,* 345 F.3d 777, 784–87 (9th Cir. 2003) [reversing BIA denial of motion to reopen where BIA failed to accept respondent's declaration as true and impermissibly made an adverse credibility finding because part, but not all, of the evidence could have been produced previously].

The BIA may deny reopening even in the absence of opposition or response from DHS. *Limsico v. INS*, 951 F.2d 210 (9th Cir. 1991). The IJ and the BIA must clearly and fully explain the reason for denial. *Matter of M-P-*, 20 I&N Dec. 786 (BIA 1994) [reversing denial of motion where IJ did not articulate reasons]; *Mickeviciute v. INS,* 327 F.3d 1159 (10th Cir. 2003) [reversing BIA where it failed to articulate which of the three *Abudu* grounds it relied on in denying motion to reopen]. The applicant, however, has a "heavy burden" to succeed on a motion to reopen. A motion to reopen may not be filed with an IJ once an appeal of the IJ's decision is pending with the BIA. *Ilic-Lee v. Mukasey,* 507 F.3d 1044, 1049–53 (6th Cir. 2007) [BIA was correct to deny motion to reopen proceedings for AOS based upon marriage where there was some evidence of a legal marriage but the weight of the evidence was slight]; *Al Najjar v. Ashcroft,* 257 F.3d 1262, 1302 (11th Cir. 2001) [upholding BIA denial of motion to reopen for CAT]. But the BIA cannot summarily deny reopening based on cursory, irrational or speculative determinations. *Bhasin v. Gonzales,* 423 F.3d 977, 986 (9th Cir. 2005) [reversing denial of motion to reopen where BIA discounted mother's affidavit as self-serving thereby improperly making an adverse credibility determination, improperly relied on the fugitive disentitlement doctrine, and where the new evidence was highly probative of her family persecution claim]; *Zhao v. Gonzales,* 404 F.3d 295, 304–06 (5th Cir. 2005) [BIA abused its discretion in denying motion to reopen to admit DOS reports on China where reports supported persecution of Falun Gong]; *Zhao v. DOJ,* 265 F.3d 83, 95–97 (2d Cir. 2001) [reversing denial of reopening in forced sterilization claim where BIA appeared to acknowledge that IJ determined sterilization had occurred but refused to allow additional proof regarding it]. The BIA's discretionary denial is subject to review for abuse of discretion and for lack of substantial evidence where fact finding is involved. *Melnitsenko v. Mukasey,* 517 F.3d 42, 48–52 (2d Cir. 2008) [BIA cannot deny a motion under *Velarde-Pacheco* where petitioner meets all five criteria solely on the basis of DHS's opposition]; *Korytnyuk v. Ashcroft,* 396 F.3d 272, 282–86 (3d Cir. 2005) [where BIA denied motion to remand for adjustment as a matter of discretion, the factual basis for discretion is subject to substantial evidence review].

F. *Departure from the U.S. During Pendency of Motion*—Departure from the U.S. while a motion to reopen or reconsider is pending, including by deportation, removal, or exclusion, constitutes abandonment. And a person is prohibited from filing a motion to reopen if s/he is outside the U.S. 8 C.F.R. §§1003.2(d), 1003.23(b)(1). *Matter of Yih-Hsiung Wang*, 17 I&N Dec. 565 (BIA 1980); *Aguilar v. Gonzales,* 475 F.3d 415, 417–18 (1st Cir. 2007) [respondent's voluntary departure effected a withdrawal of his motion to reopen]; *Pena-Muriel v. Gonzales,* 489 F.3d 438 (1st Cir. 2007) [due process was not violated and the regulation was upheld where respondent, who was out of the country for five years, had vacated his conviction and sought to reopen proceedings]; *Mansour v. Gonzales,* 470 F.3d 1194 (6th Cir. 2007) [brief trip to Mexico executed the order of removal and barred reopening]; *Navarro-Miranda v. Ashcroft,* 330 F.3d 672 (5th Cir. 2003) [finding 8 C.F.R. §1003.2(d) a reasonable construction and not in conflict with 8 C.F.R. §1003.2(a) allowing for *sua sponte* reopening]. *See also Patel v. U.S. Att'y Gen.,* 334 F.3d 1259 (11th Cir. 2003) [INA §242(a)(2)(C) barred jurisdiction to review the denial of motion to reopen where petitioner was out of the country; no district court habeas jurisdiction because petitioner was no longer in custody]. *But see William v. Gonzales,* 499 F.3d 329 (4th Cir. 2007) [the prohibition in 8 C.F.R. §1003.2(d) to motions to reopen where the person is outside the U.S. is contrary to INA §240(c)(7)(A), 8 U.S.C. §1229a(c)(7)(A) permitting one motion to reopen without limitation and the regulation is therefore invalid]. However, 8 C.F.R. §1003.2(d) only bars motions to reopen for persons who depart *after* removal proceedings begin. *Singh v. Gonzales,* 412 F.3d 1117, 1120–21 (9th Cir. 2005) [person who departs before removal proceedings are initiated and seeks motion to reopen to vacate *in absentia* order is not barred by §1003.2(d)]. *See also Contreras-Rodriguez v. U.S. Att'y Gen.,* 462 F.3d 1314 (11th Cir. 2006) [respondent who was physically removed after *in absentia* order is not barred from filing a motion to reopen for lack of notice because such a motion may be filed at "any time," distinguishing *Patel*]; *Mendez-Alcaraz v. Gonzales,* 464 F.3d 842, 844 (9th Cir. 2006) [finding jurisdiction to review denial of motion to reconsider filed 14 months after respondent's removal from the U.S.]; *Cardoso-Tlaseca v. Gonzales,* 460 F.3d 1102 (9th Cir. 2006) [reversing BIA denial of motion to reopen where respondent's conviction was vacated after physical removal because conviction was a "key part" of removal proceeding]; *Wiedersperg v. INS*, 896 F.2d 1179 (9th Cir. 1990) [motion to reopen improperly denied where respondent's conviction was vacated after he left the U.S. under deportation order].

G. *Reopening or Reconsideration Barred*—A motion to reopen or reconsider before the IJ or BIA is barred by the following:

1. *Time & Numerical Limitations*—A motion to reopen must be filed no later than 90 days after the issuance of the final administrative order, and absent certain exceptions discussed below (*see in this part* section H (p.1055), *infra*), a second motion to reopen is barred if a prior motion to reopen has been filed. INA §240(c)(7), 8 U.S.C. §1229a(c)(7), 8 C.F.R. §§1003.2(c)(2), 1003.23(b)(1). Similarly, a motion to reconsider must be filed no more than 30 days after the IJ's decision or after the mailing of the BIA decision, and a second motion to reconsider is barred if a prior motion to reconsider has been filed. INA §240(c)(6), 8 U.S.C. §1229a(c)(6), 8 C.F.R. §§1003.2(b)(2), 1003.23(b).

   1.a. *Time Barred—Abdi v. U.S. Att'y Gen.,* 430 F.3d 1148 (11th Cir. 2005) [failure to file motion to reopen within 90 days is jurisdictional; no equitable tolling for IAC]; *Roberts v. Gonzales,* 422 F.3d 33, 35–36 (1st Cir. 2005); *Ajose v. Gonzales,* 408 F.3d 393 (7th Cir. 2005) [where counsel did not inform BIA of new address after partnership dissolved and did not inquire until after the 90-day period, failure to obtain notice of decision is attributed to client and reopening is barred]; *Radkov v. Ashcroft,* 375 F.3d 96 (1st Cir. 2004) [BIA did not abuse its discretion in refusing to reopen where it provided proof that the notice of decision was mailed to counsel but returned because counsel had moved and did not submit a change of address until after the 90 days expired]; *Matter of C-W-L-,* 24 I&N Dec. 346 (BIA 2007) [denied untimely motion to reopen where respondent claimed that he could file a successive asylum claim based upon changed personal circumstances and did not have to file motion to reopen]. The 90 day period runs from the date of the BIA order (or the IJ order if it is final), not from any decision in a federal proceeding. *Matter of Susma,* 22 I&N Dec. 947 (BIA 1999) [appeal filed within 90 days of court's denial of rehearing was untimely]. At least one court has found that the 90-day period runs from date of the removal order and not from an order reconsidering the removal order. *William v. INS,* 217 F.3d 340 (5th Cir. 2000) [motion to reopen a denial of a motion to reconsider where it was beyond 90 days from the removal order is untimely]. An IJ's order is final for purposes of the 90-day rule when it is entered, not from the completion or extension of voluntary departure. *Matter of Goolcharan,* 23 I&N Dec. 5 (BIA 2001). "Filing" for purposes of the 90-day rule means receipt by the BIA. *Matter of J-J-*, 21 I&N Dec. 976 (BIA 1997) [declining to follow Supreme Court precedent that "filing" for detained person means giving it to the jailer]. *See also Ekimian v. INS,* 303 F.3d 1153, 1155–56 (9th Cir. 2002) [motion to reopen for adjustment filed outside the 90-day period was properly denied; 90-day statutory limitation does not conflict with AOS and visa petition statutes]; *Foroglou v. Reno,* 241 F.3d 111, 113 (1st Cir. 2001) [upholding BIA's refusal to consider CAT claim not filed within time proscribed for reopening by §208.18(b)(2)]. *Mejia-Rodriguez v. Reno,* 178 F.3d 1139 (11th Cir. 1999) [upholding 90-day time limitation as not raising a constitutional concern even if person suffered a constitutional violation]. Where a motion to reopen is pending and 90 days have passed, an applicant may supplement the pending motion rather than file a separate one. *Wang v. Ashcroft,* 260 F.3d 448, 452 (5th Cir. 2001) [request to treat second motion as supplement to motion to reopen thereby avoiding the 90-day bar was denied where applicant made no reference to it as a supplement]. The BIA is not obligated to reopen proceedings outside the 90-day period due to a favorable change in the law. *Joumaa v. Gonzales,* 446 F.3d 244 (1st Cir. 2006) [upholding BIA denial of motion to reopen to permit AOS based on *Succar* for TWOV because Congress did not provide an exception to the 90-day requirement based on a new decision of law]. The 90-day deadline may not be stayed when the court grants a motion to stay removal. *Keo Chan v. Gonzales,*

413 F.3d 161 (1st Cir. 2005). However, the 90-day period may not be a jurisdictional limitation and is therefore subject to equitable tolling. *See in this part* ¶ H.5.a (p.1059), *infra*.

1.b. *Numerically Barred*

Motions to Reopen—Yang v. Mukasey, 510 F.3d 793 (8th Cir. 2007) [second motion to reopen that finally contained appropriate documents for AOS was properly denied as numerically barred]; *Lemus v. Gonzales,* 489 F.3d 399 (1st Cir. 2007) [respondent's fifth motion to reopen was denied]; *Chen v. Gonzales,* 415 F.3d 151, 153–54 (1st Cir. 2005) [in Chinese family planning case, a second motion to reopen based on IAC was numerically barred, not subject to equitable tolling, nor based on changed circumstances]; *Jupiter v. Ashcroft,* 396 F.3d 487, 489–91 (1st Cir. 2005) [affirming denial of second motion to reopen where first motion was denied without prejudice to pursue *Lozada* claim and second motion was unrelated and based on AOS]; *Pilch v. Ashcroft,* 353 F.3d 585, 586 (7th Cir. 2003) [second motion to request *sua sponte* reopening still violates the one-motion rule]; *Saiyid v. INS,* 132 F.3d 1380, 1385 n.6 (11th Cir. 1998) [raising, but not deciding, whether multiple motions are barred only if the first motion is filed after Apr. 29, 1996, the effective date of the regulation]. The limitation on one motion to reopen does not include motions to remand made while the case is on appeal to the BIA. *Chowdhury v. Ashcroft,* 241 F.3d 848 (7th Cir. 2001). However, the BIA has held that a motion to remand before the BIA when an appeal of a denial of a motion to reopen is pending is treated as a motion to reopen for purposes of the 90-day/one-motion rules. *Matter of Oparah,* 23 I&N Dec. 1 (BIA 2000). *But see Guzman v. INS,* 318 F.3d 911 (9th Cir. 2003) [motion to remand that is filed while the case is before the BIA on appeal from the IJ denial of a motion to reopen may be treated as a supplement to the motion to reopen rather than a second motion that would be barred by the regulations]. The numerical limitation will also not apply to motions to reopen for *in absentia* proceedings in deportation. 8 C.F.R. §1003.23(b)(4)(iii)(D); *Saakian v. INS,* 252 F.3d 21, 25 (1st Cir. 2001) but do apply in removal *Luntungan v. Att'y Gen. of the U.S.,* 449 F.3d 551, 555–57 (3d Cir. 2006) [finding numerical limit does apply to *in absentia* orders in removal under 8 C.F.R. §1003.23(b)(4)(ii) as distinguished from *in absentia* deportation orders and holding that equitable tolling did not apply to third motion to reopen]. *But see Montano Cisneros v. U.S. Att'y Gen.,* 514 F.3d 1224 (11th Cir. 2008) [numerical bar does not apply in removal proceedings to the case as a whole, but to each removal order, and where first motion to reopen was granted, respondent is not numerically barred from filing a motion to reopen second removal order]. The one-motion rule is also subject to equitable tolling. *See in this part,* Section H.5.c (p.1061), *infra*.

Motion to Reconsider—A motion to reconsider is also numerically limited to one motion to reconsider "a decision" that the person is removable from the U.S. 8 C.F.R. §1003.2(b)(2). The numerical limitation applies to each decision and not to the respondent's immigration case as a whole. *Calle v. U.S. Att'y Gen.,* 504 F.3d 1324 (11th Cir. 2007) [where applicant for asylum/withholding from Colombia filed a motion to reconsider with the BIA, then a motion to reopen, and then a motion to reconsider the denial of the motion to reopen, the last motion to reconsider was not numerically barred].

2. *Motion Seeks Relief That is Barred*—A motion to reopen will be denied if it seeks relief which is barred under INA §240(b)(7) [failure to appear], §240B(d) [failure to voluntarily depart] or 241(a)(5) [reinstatement of removal]. *Matter of Shaar,* 21 I&N Dec. 541 (BIA 1997) *aff'd Shaar v. INS,* 141 F.3d 953 (9th Cir. 1998) [motion to reopen for suspension denied where person failed to voluntarily depart within time given before IJ ruled on motion to reopen]; *Chedad v. Gonzales,* 497 F.3d 57 (1st Cir. 2007) [a timely filed motion to reopen does not stay the running of the VD period and if the motion is granted after VD has expired the respondent is barred from seeking relief §1229c(d)(1)]; *Dekoladenu v. Gonzales,* 459 F.3d 500, 502–08 (4th Cir. 2006) [timely filed motion to reopen does not toll VD period]; *Banda-Ortiz v. Gonzales,* 445 F.3d 387, 391 (5th Cir. 2006) [BIA's decision to reopen does not cure failure to depart during the VD period]; *Bhiski v. Ashcroft,* 373 F.3d 363, 370–72 (3d Cir. 2004) [INS opposition to motion to reopen upheld where respondent failed to depart upon expiration of VD under *Matter of Shaar*]; *De Martinez v. Ashcroft,* 363 F.3d 1022 *amended on reh'g* 374 F.3d 759 (9th Cir. 2004) [denying motion to reopen for AOS filed within the 90-day time limit but after VD expired]. *But see Ugokwe v. U.S. Att'y Gen.,* 453 F.3d 1325 (11th Cir. 2006) [a timely filed motion to reopen tolls VD period and prohibits the application of *Matter of Shaar* to bar consideration of the merits]; *Magala v. Gonza-*

les, 434 F.3d 523 (7th Cir. 2005) [remanding to BIA to consider whether IAC would qualify as an exceptional circumstance of the pre-IIRIRA 5-year bar for failure to depart]; *Barroso v. Gonzales,* 429 F.3d 1195, 1202–08 (9th Cir. 2005) [filing a motion to reconsider within the VD period automatically tolls VD]; *Ssali v. Gonzales,* 424 F.3d 556, 562–64 (7th Cir. 2005) [vacating BIA's denial of motion to reopen for marriage adjustment and criticizing government's analysis of *Matter of Arthur*]; *Kanivets v. Gonzales,* 424 F.3d 330, 334–36 (3d Cir. 2005) [distinguishing *Bhiski* and finding that *post*-IIRIRA, a timely filed motion to reopen tolls VD period and allows the BIA to consider the motion]; *Orichitch v. Gonzales,* 421 F.3d 595 (7th Cir. 2005) [where BIA granted motion to reopen after IJ denied motion to reopen to adjust because respondent was barred by INA §240B(d) for failure to voluntarily depart, case was reopened for all purposes and respondent was eligible to adjust]; *Sidikhouya v. Gonzales,* 407 F.3d 950 (8th Cir. 2005) [where motion to reopen for AOS was filed within VD period, it was an abuse of discretion *post*-IIRIRA for the BIA to deny reopening based on *Matter of Shaar* when VD expired before BIA ruled]; *Barrios v. Att'y Gen. of U.S.,* 399 F.3d 272 (3d Cir. 2005) [rejecting *Matter of Shaar* for *pre*-IIRIRA cases, and holding that a timely filed motion to reopen prevents the BIA/IJ from applying the bar to adjustment under former INA §242B(e)(2)(A) because the failure of the BIA/IJ to adjudicate the motion within the VD period is an "exceptional circumstance"]; *Azarte v. Ashcroft,* 394 F.3d 1278 (9th Cir. 2005) [rejecting *Shaar* post-IIRIRA and finding that where a motion to reopen is filed during the VD period and a stay of removal or VD is requested, the VD period is tolled while the BIA considers the motion]. The failure by the IJ to comply with the notice requirements for the 10-year bar under INA §240(b)(7) to apply does not automatically result in the grant of a motion to reopen, because the movant must still comply with the time, numerical, or other requirements to reopen. *Aragon-Munoz v. Mukasey,* 520 F.3d 82, 86-87 (1st Cir. 2008) [the IJ's failure to provide oral warnings in petitioner's own language pursuant to INA §240(b)(7) did not require automatic reopening where petitioner otherwise failed to establish a basis, through lack of notice, to reopen his *in absentia* order].

3. *Prior Opportunity to Apply for Benefits*—A motion seeking leave to apply for cancellation, adjustment, creation of record of lawful admission, or asylum will be denied if the right to apply for these benefits was fully explained at the original hearing, and the alien was given the opportunity to apply, unless there are new circumstances. *Matter of G-Q-*, 9 I&N Dec. 376 (BIA 1961); 8 C.F.R. §1003.2(c)(1).

4. *Application for Relief Must Be Attached*—A motion to reopen will be denied if the application for the requested relief (*e.g.*, adjustment, suspension) with supporting documentation is not attached to a motion before the IJ. 8 C.F.R. §§1003.2(c), 1003.23(b)(3). Failure to submit supporting documentation would not bar reopening before the BIA where DHS does not oppose reopening. *Matter of Yewondwosen*, 21 I&N Dec. 1025 (BIA 1997); *Konstantinova v. INS,* 195 F.3d 528 (9th Cir. 1999).

5. *Ineligible for Relief*—A motion will be denied if the applicant is no longer eligible for relief. *Matter of Cerna*, 20 I&N Dec. 399 (BIA 1991) [LPR seeking §212(c) relief denied motion to reopen where he was no longer eligible because a final order of deportation deprived him of LPR status which is required for statutory eligibility]. *Accord Wright v. Ouellette,* 171 F.3d 8 (1st Cir. 1999) [AEDPA §440(d) bars motion to reopen denial of §212(c) relief where the BIA originally reviewed the application]; *Nwolise v. INS*, 4 F.3d 306 (4th Cir. 1993); *Katsis v. INS*, 997 F.2d 1067 (3d Cir. 1993); *Ghassan v. INS*, 972 F.2d 631, 637–38 (5th Cir. 1992). *But see Goncalves v. INS*, 6 F.3d 830 (1st Cir. 1993); *Henry v. INS*, 8 F.3d 426 (7th Cir. 1993) [rejecting BIA's reliance on 7th Cir. in *Cerna*]; *Butros v. INS*, 990 F.2d 1142 (9th Cir. 1993) (en banc); *Vargas v. INS*, 938 F.2d 358 (2d Cir. 1991); *Maxwell v. INS,* 331 F.Supp.2d 599, 604–05 (N.D. Ohio 2004).

6. *Inadequate Support for Legal Argument*—A motion to reconsider may be denied if it is solely supported by nonprecedent decisions and there is no adequate explanation for failure to raise the legal argument before. *Matter of Medrano*, 20 I&N Dec. 216 (BIA 1990).

7. *Appeal Pending*—A motion to reopen before the IJ will be denied for lack of jurisdiction where an appeal to the BIA has been filed. *Marrero v. INS*, 990 F.2d 772, 777–78 (3d Cir. 1993).

8. *Marriage-Based Visa Petition Not Yet Approved*—A motion to reopen based on marriage entered into after deportation proceedings commenced may be denied if the visa petition has not yet been

approved. *Matter of Arthur*, 20 I&N Dec. 475 (BIA 1992); *Matter of H-A-*, 22 I&N Dec. 728 (BIA 1999) [reaffirming *Matter of Arthur* notwithstanding regulations at former 8 C.F.R. §3.2(c) giving a party only 90 days to reopen]. *But see Matter of Velarde-Pacheco,* 23 I&N Dec. 253 (BIA 2002) [*Matter of Arthur* and *Matter of H-A-* modified to allow motions to reopen where the I-485/I-130 are filed within 90 days, the motion is not barred numerically, is not barred by *Matter of Shaar* or by any other procedural ground, the motion presents clear and convincing evidence that the marriage is *bona fide*, and DHS does not oppose the motion or bases its opposition solely on *Matter of Arthur*]; *Melnitsenko v. Mukasey,* 517 F.3d 42, 48–52 (2d Cir. 2008) [BIA cannot deny a motion under *Velarde-Pacheco* where petitioner meets all five criteria solely on the fact of DHS's opposition]; *Conteh v. Gonzales,* 461 F.3d 45, 64–65 (1st Cir. 2006) [*Velarde* standard did not apply where a visa was not immediately available because spouse was only an LPR]; *De Martinez v. Ashcroft,* 363 F.3d 1022 *amended on reh'g* 374 F.3d 759 (9th Cir. 2004) [where motion to reopen for AOS was filed within the 90-day time limit but after VD expired, adjustment barred notwithstanding *Matter of Velarde-Pacheco*]; *Rezai v. INS*, 62 F.3d 1286, 1289–92 (10th Cir. 1995); *Dielmann v. INS*, 34 F.3d 851 (9th Cir. 1994). *But see Palma-Mazariegos v. Keisler,* 504 F.3d 144 (1st Cir. 2007) [*Matter of Velarde-Pacheco* does not forgive the requirement that a completed I-485 application must be submitted with motion]; *Benslimane v. Gonzales,* 430 F.3d 828 (7th Cir. 2005) [IJ made legal error in denying continuance where respondent had filed I-130 and I-485 as part of marriage based adjustment but had not filed adjustment with IJ]; *Bull v. INS*, 790 F.2d 869 (11th Cir. 1986); *Ssali v. Gonzales,* 424 F.3d 556, 562–64 (7th Cir. 2005) [vacating BIA's denial of motion to reopen for marriage adjustment and criticizing government's analysis of *Matter of Arthur*]; *Singh v. Gonzales,* 404 F.3d 1024, 1027–29 (7th Cir. 2005) [where I-130 was approved, the BIA's reliance on *Velarde* to deny motion was error because *Velarde* involved an unadjudicated I-130; however, error was harmless]. *Cf. Miah v. Mukasey,* 519 F.3d 784, 789–90 (8th Cir. 2008) [denied motion to reopen under *Velarde* on insufficiency of the evidence and distinguished *Velarde* because motion was filed after BIA ruled]; *Ilic-Lee v. Mukasey,* 507 F.3d 1044, 1049–53 (6th Cir. 2007) [BIA was correct to deny motion to reopen proceedings for AOS under *Velarde* where there was some evidence of a legal marriage but the weight of the evidence was slight and the government opposed reopening]; *Ramchandani v. Gonzales,* 434 F.3d 337, 340–41 (5th Cir. 2005) [upholding BIA denial of motion to reopen under *Velarde* where DHS opposed motion because applicant didn't submit affidavit of support].

The BIA has broad discretion to deny a motion to reopen where it believes the applicant has not met the "clear and convincing standard" in a marriage during removal proceedings or where it believes there was a history of recurrent marriage fraud. *Krazoun v. Ashcroft,* 350 F.3d 208 (1st Cir. 2003) [where respondent had two previous marriages that BIA deemed fraudulent it was within discretion to deny reopening]. However, it may not refuse to consider an adjustment for lack of evidence where the I-130 has been approved. *Patel v. Ashcroft,* 375 F.3d 693 (8th Cir. 2004) [BIA abused its discretion in denying remand for marriage-based AOS and requiring the production of additional evidence of bona fides where the I-130 was approved].

9. *Motion Abandoned*—A motion is deemed abandoned where the applicant is physically removed, deported, or departs the U.S. prior to or during the pendency of the motion. 8 C.F.R. §§1003.2(d), 1003.23(b)(1). This section bars persons who depart *after* removal proceedings begin. *Singh v. Gonzales*, 412 F.3d 1117, 1120–21 (9th Cir. 2005) [person who departs before removal proceedings are initiated and seeks motion to reopen to vacate in absentia order is not barred by §1003.2(d)]. It also bars persons who are outside the U.S. when they file the motion. *Pena-Muriel v. Gonzales,* 489 F.3d 438 (1st Cir. 2007) [due process was not violated where the BIA refused to allow respondent, who was outside the United States, to reopen his deportation proceeding because his conviction was vacated]. *But see William v. Gonzales,* 499 F.3d 329 (4th Cir. 2007) [the prohibition in 8 C.F.R. §1003.2(d) to motions to reopen where the person is outside the U.S. is contrary to INA §240(c)(7)(A), 8 U.S.C. §1229a(c)(7)(A) permitting one motion to reopen without limitation and the regulation is therefore invalid]; *Contreras-Rodriguez v. U.S. Att'y Gen.*, 462 F.3d 1314 (11th Cir. 2006) [holding that noncitizen outside of U.S. may file motion to reopen *in absentia* order because Congress used language "at any time" which does not include any geographical limitation]. In the view of one court, §1003.23(b)(1) does *not* bar a person who is deported, then returns illegally, and then files a motion to reopen the original removal order. *Lin v. Gonzales,* 473 F.3d 979 (9th Cir. 2007) [resolving ambiguities in favor of the respondent, the court read the "abandonment" regulation as not including persons who return illegally after a final

order]. *Accord. Reynoso-Cisneros v. Gonzales,* 491 F.3d 1001 (9th Cir. 2007) [person in exclusion proceedings who was deported and then re-entered is not barred by 8 C.F.R. §1003.2(d) from filing a motion to reopen before BIA]. *See also in this part,* "Departure From the U.S. During Pendency of Motion," Section F (p.1050), *supra.*

10. *Motion Filed During Judicial Proceedings*—A motion filed during judicial proceedings without complying with 8 C.F.R. §1003.2(e) will be denied. In addition, some courts will not stay the mandate to allow for a motion to reopen. *Valderrama v. INS,* 260 F.3d 1083, 1086 (9th Cir. 2001) [staying the mandate to allow motion to reopen because of marriage to USC would be inappropriate].

11. *Motion Challenges BIA Streamlining*—A motion to reconsider based solely on the argument that he case should not have been affirmed without opinion by a single board member or a three-judge panel is barred. 8 C.F.R. §1003.2(b)(3).

H. *Exceptions to Rule Barring Motions to Reopen*—The BIA at 8 C.F.R. §§1003.2(a) and (c)(3) and the IJ at 8 C.F.R. §1003.23(b)(4) recognize that a motion to reopen may be entertained even if it does not meet the time or numerical limitations where:

1. *Sua Sponte Reopening by BIA*—The BIA may *sua sponte* reopen proceedings. 8 C.F.R. §1003.2(a). *Sua sponte* reopening may only be used in exceptional circumstances and is not meant to cure filing defects or circumvent the regulations. *Matter of J-J-,* 21 I&N Dec. 976 (BIA 1997); *Matter of Beckford,* 22 I&N Dec. 1216 (BIA 2000) [burden is on movant to show exceptional circumstances]; *Matter of G-D-,* 22 I&N Dec. 1132 (BIA 1999) [declining *sua sponte* reconsideration because the change in the law under *Matter of O-Z- & I-Z-* was not sufficiently compelling to warrant extraordinary intervention]; *Matter of G-L-C-,* 23 I&N Dec. 359 (BIA 2002) [overruling *Matter of X-G-W-,* 22 I&N Dec. 71 (BIA 1998) regarding reopening in coercive population control cases on grounds that "the interest of finality in immigration proceedings now takes precedence" over asylum claims]; *Navarro-Miranda v. Ashcroft,* 330 F.3d 672 (5th Cir. 2003) [finding §1003.2(d) regarding dismissal of petition where person is removed or otherwise out of the country to be a reasonable construction of the statute and not in conflict with §1003.2(a) allowing for *sua sponte* reopening]. Failure to seek *sua sponte* review may be a failure to exhaust administrative remedies. *Padilla v. Gonzales,* 470 F.3d 1209, 1212–15 (7th Cir. 2006) [where respondent's convictions were vacated after BIA appeal and counsel never sought *sua sponte* review after government refused to file joint motion, the court found that counsel failed to exhaust administrative remedies and dismissed the petition for review]; *Wang v. Ashcroft,* 260 F.3d 448, 452–53 (5th Cir. 2001) [must raise issue before BIA to exhaust remedies for purposes of judicial review].

   The BIA's decision to invoke §1003.2(a) is "nonreviewable" in the view of most circuits. *Cyrus v. Keisler,* 505 F.3d 197, 203 (2d Cir. 2007) [no jurisdiction to review *sua sponte* denial by BIA of a motion to reopen]; *Johnson v. Gonzales,* 478 F.3d 795, 799 (7th Cir. 2007) [refusal of the BIA to reopen *sua sponte* is a nonreviewable discretionary decision]; *Zhang v. Gonzales,* 469 F.3d 51 (1st Cir. 2006) [where respondent filed out-of-time motion to reopen for *sua sponte* consideration court lacked jurisdiction to review denial]; *Ali v. Gonzales,* 448 F.3d 515, 517–19 (2d Cir. 2006) [citing other circuits, court lacked jurisdiction to review *sua sponte* denial]; *Harchenko v. INS,* 379 F.3d 405, 410–11 (6th Cir. 2004) [decision is committed to unfettered discretion of the BIA and is therefore not subject to review]; *Belay-Gebru v. INS,* 327 F.3d 998, 1000–01 (10th Cir. 2003) [BIA's decision to reopen *sua sponte* under "exceptional circumstances" provides no meaningful standard of review]; *Calle-Vujiles v. Ashcroft,* 320 F.3d 472 (3d Cir. 2003) [same]; *Ekimian v. INS,* 303 F.3d 1153, 1157–59 (9th Cir. 2002) [same]; *Abassi v. INS,* 305 F.3d 1028, 1032 (9th Cir. 2002) [following *Ekimian*]; *Anin v. Reno,* 188 F.3d 1273, 1279 (11th Cir. 1999); *Luis v. INS,* 196 F.3d 36, 40–41 (1st Cir. 1999); *Prado v. Reno,* 198 F.3d 286, 292 (1st Cir. 1999). *But see Tamenut v. Gonzales,* 477 F.3d 580 (8th Cir. 2007) [circuit law compels review of denial of motion to reopen BIA proceedings *sua sponte* but court found no abuse where respondent was married to USC before AWO and did not file motion at that time]; *Cruz v. Att'y Gen. of the U.S.,* 452 F.3d 240, 249–50 (3d Cir. 2006) [BIA decision to deny *sua sponte* reopening for person with vacated conviction can be reviewed where the denial was not discretionary but was rather based on the BIA position, contrary to all previous cases, that a respondent with a vacated conviction has not shown an exceptional situation]; *See also Mejia Rodriguez v. Reno,* 178 F.3d 1139, 1145 n.5 (11th Cir. 1999) [reviewing a decision under former §3.2(a)]. Similarly, there is no review of the IJ's *sua sponte* authority to reopen under 8 C.F.R. §1003.23(b). *Enriquez-Alvarado v. Ashcroft,* 371 F.3d 246 (5th Cir. 2004) [relying on cases finding that the BIA's *sua sponte* authority to reopen is nonreviewable].

In the view of one circuit a motion for *sua sponte* relief may not be permissible because it would then not be *sua sponte. Pilch v. Ashcroft,* 353 F.3d 585, 586 (7th Cir. 2003). *But see Roberts v. Gonzales,* 422 F.3d 33, 37 (1st Cir. 2005) [there may be BIA jurisdiction to request remand to IJ to exercise her *sua sponte* authority where case never appealed to BIA].

2. *Agreement to Reopen*—The parties may agree to reopen under 8 C.F.R. §§1003.2(c)(3)(iii), 1003.23(b)(4)(iv); *Bolshakov v. INS,* 133 F.3d 1279, 1281–82 (9th Cir. 1998) [no exhaustion requirement because agreement of parties to reopen is not a remedy].

2.a. *Agreement in Non-Adjustment Cases*—Legacy INS General Counsel has stated that consent should be given "only under exceptional and compelling circumstances." Memo, Martin, General Counsel, INS, HQ COU 90/16.11-P (Dec. 23, 1997), *reprinted in* 75 No. 7 *Interpreter Releases*, 259, 275–77 (Feb. 23, 1998). Factors to be considered in nonadjustment cases are: (a) whether there is new, material evidence that was not previously available; (b) eligibility for relief; (c) whether a favorable exercise of discretion is warranted; (d) the hardship to the person and LPR/USC family members; (e) criminal history; (f) number and severity of immigration violations; (g) whether the person is cooperating with the U.S. and his/her presence is necessary for that purpose; and (h) whether removal is consistent with Service objectives. Memo, Martin (Dec. 23, 1997), *supra.* At least one court has ruled that review of INS's decision not to agree to reopening is barred by INA §242(g) and principles of justiciability. *Prado v. Reno,* 198 F.3d 286, 292 (1st Cir. 1999). *But see Aguilera v. Kirkpatrick,* 241 F.3d 1286 (10th Cir. 2001) [INA §242(g) does not bar jurisdiction; upholding the regulation because there is no constitutionally protected interest where the government has "unfettered discretion" to deny reopening].

2.b. *Agreement in Adjustment Cases*—The Service modified its position regarding "exceptional and compelling circumstances" in addressing motions to reopen for adjustment. General Counsel decided that the government may join in a motion to reopen for consideration of AOS "if such adjustment of status was not available to the respondent at the former hearing, the alien is statutorily eligible...and the respondent merits a favorable exercise of discretion." Memo, Cooper, Gen. Counsel, HQCOU 90/16.22.1 (May 17, 2001), *published on* AILA InfoNet at Doc. No. 01070333. Statutory ineligibility would include persons who have final *in absentia* orders unless the respondent, under former provisions, was not provided written notice in English and in Spanish and with oral notice in his or her native language of the consequences of failing to appear under former INA §242B(c)(1). The same is true for determining statutory ineligibility under removal proceedings, INA §240(b)(5)(A). In determining whether to favorably exercise discretion the factors to be considered include but are not limited to: (1) the hardship to the person and USC/LPR family members if required to consular process including the applicability of the 3/10 year bar; (2) criminal history; (3) the number and severity of immigration violations; (4) whether the person has cooperated with law enforcement agencies; and (5) whether his or her removal is consistent with Service objectives.

3. *Changed Country Conditions*—Asylum, withholding or CAT claims based on changed circumstances in the country of nationality where there is material evidence that could not have been discovered or presented before. INA §240(c)(7)(C)(ii); 8 C.F.R. §§1003.2(c)(3)(ii), 1003.23(b)(4)(i); The provision applies to *in absentia* orders as well even in the absence of reasonable cause for failing to appear. *Matter of A-N- & R-M-N-,* 22 I&N Dec. 953 (BIA 1999) [Afghan citizen did not have reasonable cause for failing to appear but could reopen *in absentia* order based on changed circumstances]. There is a question as to what standard to apply in seeking to file successive applications for asylum or after the one year deadline if a final order of removal has been entered. Prior to a final order, an applicant may seeking to file an asylum application if he can show changed circumstances (in regard to successive applications) or changed or extraordinary circumstances (if beyond the one year deadline) pursuant to §1158(a)(2)(D). However, if there is a final order, some courts have found that the applicant may only file the application through a motion to reopen and only under the "changed country condition" standards of §1229a(c)(7)(C)(ii). *Zheng v. Mukasey,* 509 F.3d 869 (8th Cir. 2007) [there is no conflict between §1158(a)(2)(D) which allows for changed circumstances when filing successive applications for asylum and §1229a(c)(7)(C)(ii)

which permits successive applications in a motion to reopen only for changed country conditions when there is a final order of removal]; *Chen v. Gonzales,* 498 F.3d 758 (7th Cir. 2007) [notwithstanding §208(a)(2)(D), an applicant's subsequent marriage and birth of two children cannot be a basis to reopen proceedings for fear of sterilization in China because the changed contemplated under INA §240(c)(7)(C)(ii) relates to changed country conditions not personal circumstances]; *Matter of C-W-L-,* 24 I&N Dec. 346 (BIA 2007) [denied untimely motion to reopen where only "changed personal circumstances" and not changed country conditions were alleged]. The BIA standards for filing motions to reopen based upon changed country conditions are set forth in: *Matter of S-Y-G-,* 24 I&N Dec. 247 (BIA 2007) [Chinese applicant did not overcome heavy burden to show changed country conditions that would result in her persecution because of second child born in U.S. and BIA noted it was not inclined to favorably exercise its discretion to reopen where applicant was previously found to have offered incredible testimony]; *Matter of J-J-,* 21 I&N Dec. 976 (BIA 1997) [setting standard for motion but finding no changed circumstances warranting reopening].

3.a. *Motion to Reopen Granted—Mekhael v. Mukasey,* 509 F.3d 326 (7th Cir. 2007) [BIA did not provide reasoned decision for denying motion to reopen for Lebanese Christian who presented evidence relating to the war between Israel and Hezbollah that began after IJ decision]; *Shardar v. Att'y Gen. of the U.S.,* 503 F.3d 308, 314–16 (3d Cir. 2007) [re-emergence of BNP political party in Bangladesh constituted changed circumstances for member of the Jatiya Party]; *Li v. U.S. Att'y Gen.,* 488 F.3d 1371, 1374–76 (11th Cir. 2007) [BIA abused its discretion in not granting motion to reopen where Chinese applicant demonstrated that local government officials have intensified their punishment against those who violate the one child policy]; *Gebreeyesus v. Gonzales,* 482 F.3d 952, 954–46 (7th Cir. 2007) [reversing BIA denial of motion to reopen by Amharan from Ethiopia that was not based on a reasoned explanation]; *Kebe v. Gonzales,* 473 F.3d 855 (7th Cir. 2007) [BIA abused its discretion in not granting motion to reopen due to changed country conditions where Ethiopian citizen and member of the Oromo Liberation Front (OLF) provided evidence that before the 2005 elections conditions worsened]; *Guo v. Gonzales,* 463 F.3d 109, 114–15 (2d Cir. 2006) [BIA erred in failing to reopen where evidence was submitted after close of proceedings demonstrating that local authorities in Changle City did consider a child born abroad to be in violation of one child policy]; *Norani v. Gonzales,* 451 F.3d 292, 294 n.3 (2d Cir. 2006) [BIA abused its discretion in not reopening case of Iranian Jews where new evidence of changed circumstances arose after the IJ's decision but before the BIA decision]; *Paul v. Gonzales,* 444 F.3d 148, 153–55 (2d Cir. 2006) [Christian from Pakistan was granted motion to reopen based upon changed circumstances, despite IJ's prior adverse credibility finding, because he may prevail on a theory of future persecution as long as the factual predicate for the claim is independent of the testimony the IJ found not credible]; *Poradisova v. Gonzales,* 420 F.3d 70, 81–82 (2d Cir. 2005) [where Jewish applicants from Belarus submitted reports from DOS and international organizations that demonstrated that hostility to Jews had worsened since IJ/BIA decision, the BIA abused its discretion in not reopening]; *Malty v. Ashcroft,* 381 F.3d 942, 945–48 (9th Cir. 2005) [reversing BIA denial of motion to reopen as untimely/numerically barred for Egyptian Coptic Christian based on changed circumstances supported by respondent's affidavit and a report from Freedom House]. A party may reopen under this provision even if unable to demonstrate reasonable cause for failing to appear and an *in absentia* order was entered. *Matter of A-N- & R-M-N,* 22 I&N Dec. 953 (BIA 1999) [Afghani did not have reasonable cause for failing to appear at exclusion hearing but could reopen *in absentia* order based on changed circumstances].

3.b. *Motion to Reopen Denied—Alemu v. Mukasey,* 509 F.3d 907 (8th Cir. 2007) [Ethiopian denied reopening on basis of an academic article that was not relevant]; *He v. Gonzales,* 501 F.3d 1128 (9th Cir. 2007) [birth of a child outside the country of nationality is insufficient, on its own, to establish changed circumstances within the meaning of 8 C.F.R. §1003.2(c)(3)(ii)]; *Chen v. Gonzales,* 498 F.3d 758 (7th Cir. 2007) [notwithstanding §208(a)(2)(D), an applicant's subsequent marriage and birth of two children cannot be a basis to reopen proceedings for fear of sterilization in China because the changed contemplated under 8 U.S.C. §1229a(c)(7)(C)(ii) relates to changed country conditions not personal circumstances];*Poniman v. Gonzales,* 481 F.3d 1008 (8th Cir. 2007) [where motion based on changed conditions did not address IJ's concern regarding safe relocation within Indonesia of Christian, the petition was denied]; *Habchy v. Gonzales,* 471 F.3d 858, 867–68 (8th Cir. 2006) [conditions did not change sufficiently in 2003 in Lebanon, but court left open a successive motion based on 2006 events]; *Zhao v. Gonzales,* 440 F.3d 405, 407 (7th Cir. 2006) [BIA properly denied motion to reopen where cumulative evidence that conditions in original application have persisted because no evidence of *changed* circumstances]; *Alam v. Gonzales,* 438 F.3d 184 (2d Cir. 2006) [where BIA erroneously failed to consider changed circumstances in motion to reopen but did so in applicant's subsequent motion to reconsider, court upheld denial of motion to reconsider]; *Wang v. BIA*, 437 F.3d 270, 274–76 (2d Cir. 2006) [denying motion where evidence of changed circumstances in China was insufficient and included an affidavit which was not prepared specifically for petitioner and was not particularized as to his circumstances]; *Haddad v. Gonzales,* 437 F.3d 515 (6th Cir. 2006) [changed circumstances for purposes of a motion to reopen does not include divorce because the change must relate to the country, but it may be a basis for spouse to file a separate asylum application beyond the one-year period]; *Ghasemimehr v. Gonzales,* 427 F.3d 1160, 1162 (8th Cir. 2005 [denying motion to reopen where it would not be "unreasonable to deduce" alleged facts regarding Iranian government and respondent failed to provide proof through affidavits and evidence as to his harm]; *Maryam v. Gonzales,* 421 F.3d 60 (1st Cir. 2005) [moderate Muslim from Indonesia failed to demonstrate changed circumstances]; *Zheng v. DOJ,* 416 F.3d 129, 130–31 (2d Cir. 2005) [changed circumstances in U.S. due to arrival of wife who was pregnant with second child is not changed circumstances in the PRC]; *Chen v. Gonzales,* 415 F.3d 151, 153–54 (1st Cir. 2005) [changed circumstances do not include ineffectiveness of counsel]; *Harchenko v. INS,* 379 F.3d 405, 410 (6th Cir. 2004) [upholding BIA denial where Ukrainian unsuccessfully argued changed circumstances]; *Betouche v. Ashcroft,* 357 F.3d 147, 152 (1st Cir. 2004); *Matter of S-Y-G-,* 24 I&N Dec. 247 (BIA 2007) [Chinese applicant did not overcome heavy burden to show changed country conditions that would result in her persecution because of second child born in U.S. and BIA noted it was not inclined to favorably exercise its discretion to reopen where applicant was previously found to have offered incredible testimony].

3.c. *Previous Hearing/Proceeding Refers to IJ not BIA*—The statutory and regulatory language signifying changed country conditions since the "previous hearing," or "previous proceeding" refer to the IJ proceeding, not the BIA. *Norani v. Gonzales,* 451 F.3d 292, 294 n.3 (2d Cir. 2006) [BIA abused its discretion in not reopening case for Iranian Jews whose new evidence of changed circumstances arose after the IJ's decision but before the BIA decision]; *Filja v. Gonzales,* 447 F.3d 241, 251–56 (3d Cir. 2006) [reversing BIA denial of motion to reopen based on changed circumstances as untimely because the change occurred while the case was pending before the BIA; the BIA could not entertain new evidence and the relevant hearing/proceeding is the IJ's hearing].

3.d. *Change in U.S. Law Not a Basis for Changed Conditions*—*Shi Liang Lin v. DOJ,* 494 F.3d 296, 314 (2d Cir. 2007) (*en banc*) [rejecting *Matter of C-Y-Z-* regarding automatic refugee status to spouses, partners and fiancées of persons subject to forced abortion or sterilization but noting that the change in law is not a basis to reopen cases already granted]; *Azanor v. Ashcroft,* 364 F.3d 1013, 1022 (9th Cir. 2004) [change in U.S. law as changed conditions is an improper expansion of §1003.2(c)(3)(ii)]; *Matter of G-C-L-,* 23 I&N Dec. 359 (BIA 2002) [overruling *Matter of X-G-W-,* 22 I&N Dec. 71 (BIA 1998) regarding reopening in coercive population control cases on grounds that "the interest of finality in immigration proceedings now takes precedence" over asylum claims]. *See also Joumaa v. Gonzales,* 446 F.3d 244 (1st Cir. 2006) [upholding BIA denial of reopening for AOS based on *Succar* for TWOV because Congress did not provide an exception to the 90-day rule based on a new decision of law issued after the 90-day period].

3.e. *Change in U.S. Conditions Not a Basis for Changed Conditions*—*Chen v. Gonzales,* 498 F.3d 758 (7th Cir. 2007) [notwithstanding §208(a)(2)(D), an applicant's subsequent marriage and birth of two children cannot be a basis to reopen proceedings for fear of sterilization in China because the changed contemplated under 8 U.S.C. §1229a(c)(7)(C)(ii) relates to changed country conditions not personal circumstances];*Zheng v. DOJ,* 416 F.3d 129, 130–31 (2d Cir.

2005) [changed circumstances in U.S. due to arrival of wife who was pregnant with second child is not a changed circumstance in the PRC].

3.f. *Judicial Review*—Although circuit courts might normally be barred from reviewing a motion to reopen that was denied as untimely, the court can review a late-filed motion alleging changed circumstances because the regulations contemplate that the motion may be filed outside the 90-day period. *Panjwani v. Ashcroft,* 401 F.3d 626, 628–32 (5th Cir. 2005) [IIRIRA's transitional rules permit review where untimely motion is based on changed conditions]. *See also Filja v. Gonzales,* 447 F.3d 241, 251–56 (3d Cir. 2006) [reversing BIA denial of motion to reopen based on changed circumstances as untimely because the change occurred while the case was pending before the BIA; the BIA could not entertain new evidence and the relevant hearing/proceeding is the IJ hearing, not the BIA appeal].

4. *Exceptional Circumstances/Failure to Receive Notice for In Absentia Orders*—8 C.F.R. §1003.23(b)(4). *See* Ch. 3, ¶ X.S.7.w (p.383), *supra*.

5. Equitable Tolling.

5.a. *Ninety-Day Period*—If the 90-day limitation is not jurisdictional equitable tolling applies. *Gaberov v. Mukasey,* 516 F.3d 590 (7th Cir. 2008) [granting motion to reopen order denying asylum by applying equitable tolling, despite lack of affidavits, regarding four year old order, where petitioner erroneously received another person's final order, inquired, and was told his case was still pending]; *Ghahremani v. Gonzales*, 498 F.3d 993, 999–1001 (9th Cir. 2007) [reversing BIA denial of motion to reopen for equitable tolling, where respondent used due diligence in hiring several lawyers]; *Zhao v. INS,* 452 F.3d 154 (2d Cir. 2006) [reversing denial of first motion to reopen regarding numerical and time limits where second counsel did not timely file motion to reopen but argued that first counsel was ineffective and respondent was diligent in hiring second and third counsel]; *Socop-Gonzalez v. INS,* 272 F.3d 1176, 1187–93 (9th Cir. 2001) (en banc) [90-day period is not jurisdictional and equitable tolling applies where BIA refused to reopen asylum case after respondent was told he should dismiss appeal to pursue adjustment]; *Ray v. Gonzales,* 439 F.3d 582, 588–92 (9th Cir. 2006) [numerical and time limitations on motions to reopen should be tolled where two attorneys failed to properly file motions to reopen and their performance was so poor that there was a presumption of prejudice because they prevented respondent from reasonably presenting his case]; *Singh v. Gonzales,* 416 F.3d 1006, 1015 (9th Cir. 2005) [allowing equitable tolling of deadline and remanding to BIA where lawyer failed to file brief or specify grounds for appeal on form]; *Joshi v. Ashcroft,* 389 F.3d 732, 734–35 (7th Cir. 2004) [deadlines that govern transitions from one court to another such as from the BIA to the circuit court are jurisdictional but other deadlines such as the number or time limitation on motions to reopen are not]; *Singh v. Ashcroft,* 367 F.3d 1182, 1185–86 (9th Cir. 2004) [where respondent filed motion to reopen on 91st day, the time limit for filing was equitably tolled due to former counsel's ineffective assistance in not filing brief resulting in summary dismissal]; *Iturribarria v. INS,* 321 F.3d 889, 897–99 (9th Cir. 2003) [90-day period was equitably tolled until respondent met with new counsel and became aware of previous counsel's ineffectiveness]; *Iavorski v. INS,* 232 F.3d 124 (2d Cir. 2000) [90-day time limitation may be equitably tolled because it is not jurisdictional but denying tolling on facts where counsel never filed appeal for lack of due diligence]. The limitations period is tolled until the respondent "definitively learns" of counsel's ineffectiveness or fraud. *Albillo-De Leon v. Gonzales,* 410 F.3d 1090, 1100 (9th Cir. 2005) [where respondent was defrauded by nonlawyer, the time period for filing a motion to reopen under NACARA §203(c) and 8 C.F.R. §1003.43(e)(1) was tolled until date that current attorney found out that motion was not filed].

No Tolling for Lack of Due Diligence— Most circuit courts will engage in a two-step analysis to determine tolling for ineffective assistance of counsel. First, the court must determine whether and when the ineffective assistance was or should have been discovered by a reasonable person. Second, the court must determine whether the person exercised due diligence in filing the motion to reopen after discovering the ineffective representation. *Wang v. Board of Immigration Appeals,* 508 F.3d 710, 715 (2d Cir. 2007) [upheld denial of motion to reopen where petitioner waited 8 months after learning of ineffective assistance and 5 months after complying with *Lozada* to file motion]. *See also Yuan Gao v. Mukasey,* 519 F.3d 376 (7th

Cir. 2008) [a 75-day wait to file motion to reopen was deemed to be lack of due diligence]; *Singh v. Gonzales,* 491 F.3d 1090, 1096–97 (9th Cir. 2007) [upheld lack of due diligence where respondent waited approximately six months to take any action with a new lawyer after he became suspicious]; *Singh v. Gonzales,* 491 F.3d 1090, 1096–97 (9th Cir. 2007) [upheld lack of due diligence where respondent waited approximately six months to take any action with a new lawyer after he became suspicious]; *Valeriano v. Gonzales,* 474 F.3d 669 (9th Cir. 2007) [no equitable tolling where respondent's new counsel waited approximately 7 months, after filing *Lozada* complaint, to try and get district counsel to agree to joint motion to reopen]; *Habchy v. Gonzales,* 471 F.3d 858, 864–66 (8th Cir. 2006) [no equitable tolling where respondent argued that he lost the opportunity to reopen his case because of his own *pro se* initial motion to reopen]; *Mendez-Alcaraz v. Gonzales,* 464 F.3d 842, 844 (9th Cir. 2006) [90 day period was not equitably tolled where respondent waited 14 months to reopen his case after removal to Mexico, where he had counsel at hearing, IJ cautioned him, and the internet and law libraries are available in Mexico]; *Ali v. Gonzales,* 448 F.3d 515, 517 (2d Cir. 2006) [respondent's wait of seven years to file motion to reopen lacked due diligence]; *Patel v. Gonzales,* 442 F.3d 1011 (7th Cir. 2006) [upholding BIA decision not to allow equitable tolling where respondent family failed to exercise due diligence as they waited almost 2 years to file motion to reopen, based on ineffective assistance]; *Cekic v. INS,* 435 F.3d 167 (2d Cir. 2006) [declining to toll deadline for filing motion to reopen due to IAC where respondent failed to exercise due diligence by waiting two years beyond the time they should have known for filing motion]; *See also Galvez Pineda v. Gonzales,* 427 F.3d 833, 838–39 (10th Cir. 2005) [although equitable tolling was appropriate for ineffective assistance, the motion to reopen was properly denied for lack of due diligence when it was not filed within 90 days of receipt of the administrative record]; *Mahmood v. Gonzales,* 427 F.3d 248 (3d Cir. 2005) [recognizing equitable tolling for ineffective assistance in failing to notify client about prior order thereby missing the time for filing a motion to reopen, but denying petition for lack of due diligence]; *Hernandez-Moran v. Gonzales,* 408 F.3d 496 (8th Cir. 2005) [declining to toll 90-day period for motion to reopen where respondent failed to comply with *Lozada* and there was no showing of extraordinary circumstances beyond his control]; *Mejia-Rodriguez v. Reno,* 178 F.3d 1139 (11th Cir. 1999) [upholding 90-day time limitation as not raising a constitutional concern even if person suffered a constitutional violation].

No Tolling Because Filing Period Is Jurisdictional—Only the Eleventh circuit has adhered to the view that there is no equitable tolling for ineffective assistance of counsel on the theory that the 90/180 day period is jurisdictional. *Abidi v. U.S. Att'y Gen.,* 430 F.3d 1148 (11th Cir. 2005) [followed *Anin* and found that 90-day period to reopen could not be equitably tolled for ineffective assistance of counsel and failure to file motion to reopen within 90 days was jurisdictional]; *Dakane v. U.S. Att'y Gen.,* 399 F.3d 1269, 1272–73 n.3 (11th Cir. 2005) [no equitable tolling for ineffective counsel's failure to file appeal timely as issue is jurisdictional]; *Anin v. Reno,* 188 F.3d 1273, 1278–79 (11th Cir. 1999) *affirming Matter of A-A-,* 22 I&N Dec. 140 (BIA 1998) [the exceptional circumstance claim based upon counsel's failure to inform client of deportation hearing may not be heard because it was not brought within the 180-day period and that period is jurisdictional]. *But see generally Huerta v. Gonzales,* 443 F.3d 753 (10th Cir. 2006) [following *Eberhart v. U.S.,* 546 U.S. 12 (2005), and discussing difference between jurisdictional rules and mandatory claim-processing rules including the 30 day appeal period to the BIA which the court did not regard as jurisdictional]. There may also be a weakening of the 11th Circuit position. *Pereira v. U.S. Attorney General,* 258 Fed. Appx. 277, 279-80 (11th Cir. 2007) [in unpublished decision seeking to distinguish *Anin* and *Abidi* as *dicta*].

5.b. *180 Period In Absentia Proceedings*—*Pervaiz v. Gonzales,* 405 F.3d 488, 490 (7th Cir. 2005) [180-day period to reopen an *in absentia* order is a statute of limitations, not jurisdictional, and may be tolled for IAC where counsel failed to distinguish between the adequacy of notice and the failure to receive notice of a hearing change. Although second lawyer's motion for ineffective assistance was not filed within 180 days, the court remanded to BIA to determine tolling given the fact that appeal was still pending on original denial and respondent's difficulty in navigating U.S. law]; *Borges v. Gonzales,* 402 F.3d 398 (3d Cir. 2005) [if notary working with lawyer committed fraud then 180 period is tolled, motion to reopen is timely filed, and ineffectiveness of counsel would constitute an exceptional circumstance to rescind order; *Bejar* distinguished]; *Fajardo v. INS,* 300 F.3d 1018 (9th Cir. 2002).

5.c. *Numerical Limitation—Zhao v. INS,* 452 F.3d 154 (2d Cir. 2006) [reversing denial of first motion to reopen where second counsel did not timely file motion to reopen but argued that first counsel was ineffective and respondent was diligent in hiring second and third counsel]; *Ray v. Gonzales,* 439 F.3d 582, 588–92 (9th Cir. 2006) [numerical and time limitations should be tolled where two attorneys failed to properly file motions to reopen and their performances were so poor that they prevented respondent from reasonably presenting his case]; *Joshi v. Ashcroft,* 389 F.3d 732, 734–35 (7th Cir. 2004) [time and numerical limitations are not jurisdictional and court could review BIA's denial of fourth motion to reopen *in absentia order*]; *Rodriguez-Lariz v. INS,* 282 F.3d 1218, 1223–26 (9th Cir. 2002) [numerical limitation where ineffective assistance of counsel in failure to file for suspension]; *Varela v. INS,* 204 F.3d 1237 (9th Cir. 2000) [equitably tolling one-motion rule where second motion was filed after person was defrauded by notary purporting to provide legal representation]. *But see Tapia-Martinez v. Gonzales,* 482 F.3d 417, 423–24 (6th Cir. 2007) [equitable tolling does not apply to numerical limitations where respondent failed to exercise due diligence and file motions regarding her former lawyers]; *Chen v. Gonzales,* 415 F.3d 151, 153–54 (1st Cir. 2005) [refusing to toll in Chinese family planning case where BIA found that respondent's could have, but failed to raise ineffective assistance in first motion to reopen and therefore failed to exercise due diligence].

6. *Motions to Reopen/Rescind In Absentia Orders*—8 C.F.R. §§1003.2(c)(3)(i), 1003.23(b)(4)(ii), (iii). A 180-day period applies and one motion to reopen is permitted where the issue is exceptional circumstances for failing to appear. There is no time limitation where respondent demonstrates lack of notice. Because there is no time limitation on a motion for lack of notice, the motion may be made even if the person is physically removed from the U.S. *Contreras-Rodriguez v. U.S. Att'y Gen.,* 462 F.3d 1314 (11th Cir. 2006) [respondent who was physically removed after *in absentia* order, is not barred from filing a motion to reopen for lack of notice because §1003.23(b)(4)(ii) allows such a motion to be filed at "any time"]. The motion, in the view of one circuit, can only be made to an IJ, not the BIA. *Singh v. Gonzales,* 436 F.3d 484 (5th Cir. 2006) [upholding BIA decision that motion to reopen to rescind *in absentia* order could only be filed with the IJ]. The time and numerical restrictions on motions to reopen *in absentia* orders are not applicable to exclusion proceedings, *Matter of N-B-,* 22 I&N Dec. 590 (BIA 1999), or deportation hearings that occurred prior to June 13, 1992. *Matter of Cruz-Garcia,* 22 I&N Dec. 1155 (BIA 1999). Persons in deportation proceedings subject to *in absentia* orders by regulation have 180 days to reopen but are not restricted by any numerical limitation. 8 C.F.R. §1003.23(b)(4)(iii)(A), (D). *Saakian v. INS,* 252 F.3d 21, 25 (1st Cir. 2001) [reversing BIA for not considering *Lozada* claim that was not perfected before IJ when regulations permit more than one motion to reopen before IJ in an *in absentia* proceeding]. However, the numerical restriction applies to *in absentia* orders in removal. *Luntungan v. Att'y Gen. of the U.S.,* 449 F.3d 551, 555–57 (3d Cir. 2006) [finding numerical limit does apply to *in absentia* orders in removal under 8 C.F.R. §1003.23(b)(4)(ii) as distinguished from *in absentia* deportation orders and holding that equitable tolling did not apply to third motion to reopen where second motion was not numerically barred or denied due to incompetence of second counsel].

7. *Motion For Battered Spouse, Parent, or Child*—A battered spouse, parent or child seeking to reopen proceedings as a self-petitioner or to seek cancellation of removal may file within one year of the entry of a final order as long as the applicant is physically present in the U.S. The AG in his or her discretion may waive the one-year requirement if the applicant demonstrates extraordinary circumstances or extreme hardship to his or her child. INA §240(c)(7)(C)(iv), 8 U.S.C. §1229a(c)(6)(C)(iv). The one-motion rule does not apply to battered spouse, parent or child cases. INA §240(c)(7)(A). If the motion to reopen is for suspension or adjustment as a self-petitioner and the person is in deportation (not removal) proceedings, there is no time limit for the filing of the motion and one motion may be filed notwithstanding the numerical limitation. Sec. 825(b) of PL 109-162, 119 Stat. 2960, Violence Against Women and Department of Justice Reauthorization Act of 2005.

I. ***A Motion to Reopen or Reconsider Does Not Result in a Stay***—The filing of a motion to reopen or reconsider does not automatically stay removal. 8 C.F.R. §§1003.2(f), 103.5(a)(1)(iv), 1003.23(b)(1)(v). *Patel v. Ashcroft,* 378 F.3d 610, 612 (7th Cir. 2004) [filing of a motion to reconsider does not stay removal]; *Baria v. Reno,* 180 F.3d 1111, 1113 (9th Cir. 1999) [filing of motion does not stay rescission of LPR status]. *But see* INA §240(b)(5)(C), 8 U.S.C. §1229(b)(5)(C) [filing of motion to reopen for failure to receive notice where *in absentia* order entered stays deportation]; 8 C.F.R. §1003.23(b)(4)(ii); In at least one circuit, a stay to permit consideration of a motion to reopen or reconsider cannot be granted by the DD when the movant is in exclusion proceedings. *Zardui-Quintana v. Richard*, 768 F.2d 1213 (11th Cir. 1985). However, the failure to grant a stay pending a determination on a motion to reopen may in some instances, raise constitutional concerns. *Castaneda-Suarez v. INS*, 993 F.2d 142, 145 (7th Cir. 1993); *Gutierrez-Roque v. INS*, 954 F.2d 769 (D.C. Cir. 1992) [BIA's decision to take administrative notice of changed political conditions, would raise "significant due process concern[s]" if a stay was not automatically granted while a party challenges the administrative notice determination].

J. *Appeal of Motion to Reopen Does Not Provide Automatic Stay*—In general, the appeal of a denial of a motion to reopen does not automatically stay deportation; a stay must be granted by the IJ or the BIA. 8 C.F.R. §1003.6(b), or DHS. However, removal will be automatically stayed pending appeal of a motion to rescind an *in absentia* order and reopen proceedings. *Id.* The grant of a motion to reopen is not appealable because it is an interlocutory order, unless there is a pattern of improper conduct by the IJ. *Matter of Correa*, 19 I&N Dec. 130 (BIA 1984).

K. *Unavailability Issue*—8 C.F.R. §1003.23(b)(3). If documents were available or should have reasonably been available at the time of the original hearing, the IJ will not grant a motion to reopen. *Parvez v. Keisler,* 506 F.3d 93, 96–97 (1st Cir. 2007) [upheld BIA denial of motion to reopen where uncle's death one year prior to BIA's decision was not new evidence, previously unavailable, in cancellation case]; *Goel v. Gonzales,* 490 F.3d 735 (9th Cir. 2007) [motion to reopen asylum case to submit polygraph evidence regarding applicant's torture was denied because evidence was not unavailable during prior hearing as applicant was not incarcerated and could have taken test previously]; *Ivanov v. Gonzales,* 487 F.3d 635 (8th Cir. 2007) [where DHS sought to reopen proceedings because birth certificate in asylum case was allegedly fraudulent, the IJ/BIA grant of the motion to reopen was reversed because DHS failed to show that the document was unavailable and undiscoverable at the time of the prior hearing; however, DHS could bring new proceeding to revoke asylum based upon fraud]; *Maghradze v. Gonzales,* 462 F.3d 150, 155–56 (2d Cir. 2006) [IJ/BIA may deny reopening for Georgian who sought CAT where evidence was previously available even if respondent establishes prima facie case]; *Hailemichael v. Gonzales,* 454 F.3d 878 (8th Cir. 2006) [reversed reopening for asylum fraud where no showing by DHS that evidence was new and previously unavailable and rejected argument that DHS was exempt from unavailability requirements even if it was exempt from time and numerical limitations]; *Zeng v. Gonzales,* 436 F.3d 26, 29–30 (1st Cir. 2006) [evidence of wife's sterilization was available at time of hearing and was not material because IJ did not question sterilization but whether it was coerced]; *Lin v. Gonzales,* 435 F.3d 708, 711 (7th Cir. 2006) [upholding denial of motion to reopen because expert's affidavit on China could have been submitted before IJ or while case was at the BIA]; *Fongwo v. Gonzales,* 430 F.3d 944, 947 (8th Cir. 2005) [failure to provide identification documents at the prior hearing because of advice of counsel did not make them unavailable]; *Sukhov v. Gonzales,* 403 F.3d 568, 570 (8th Cir. 2005) [BIA did not abuse its discretion when it declined to reopen case on claim that "new fact" was the "imminent filing of a work visa"]; *Strato v. Ashcroft,* 388 F.3d 651, 654–55 (8th Cir. 2004) [where evidence was available but excluded at asylum hearing, the applicant should have sought a motion to reconsider instead of a motion to reopen]; *Mabikas v. INS,* 358 F.3d 146, 149 (1st Cir. 2004) [upholding BIA denial of motion to reopen for asylum from the Republic of the Congo where applicant could have but failed to present father's asylum approval in France]; *Ramon-Sepulveda v. INS*, 743 F.2d 1307 (9th Cir. 1984) [reversing grant of motion to reopen by INS where INS could have obtained the foreign birth certificate it sought to introduce at the time of the original hearing]. When seeking reopening before the BIA, the issue is not whether the information was available before the BIA but whether it was available at the time of the hearing before the IJ rendered a final decision. *Verano-Velasco v. U.S. Att'y Gen.,* 456 F.3d 1372, 1377 (11th Cir. 2006) [where new evidence might have been available while case was pending before BIA but was unavailable at the time of the final IJ hearing, "unavailability" has been met]; *Bhasin v. Gonzales,* 423 F.3d 977, 987 (9th Cir. 2005) [although information submitted in affidavit to BIA could have been presented while case was initially pending before the BIA, both the regulation 8 C.F.R §1003.2(c)(1) and the statute 8 U.S.C. §1229a(c)(6)(B) refer to evidence that was unavailable before the IJ]. *But see Haile v. Gonzales,* 421 F.3d 493, 497 (7th Cir. 2005) [where Human Rights Watch report on persecution of Eritreans in Ethiopia was available before BIA rendered its decision, the motion to reopen was properly denied]; *Gando-Coello v. INS*, 888 F.2d 197 (1st Cir. 1989) [where respondent could have sought §212(c) relief at initial deportation hearing, his failure to do so on grounds he lacked counsel is insufficient to support reopening].

L. *Untimely Opposition*—A motion to reopen or reconsider "shall be deemed unopposed unless timely response is made." 8 C.F.R. §1003.23(b)(1)(iv); *Wellington v. INS*, 108 F.3d 631, 634, 637 (5th Cir. 1997) [IJ erred in not treating motion to reopen as unopposed where INS filed untimely response].

M. *Due Process*—Due process violations require that motions to reopen be granted even where new evidence was not presented. *Cano-Merida v. INS,* 311 F.3d 960, 964–65 (9th Cir. 2002) [where *pro se* respondent withdrew asylum claim after IJ informed him off-record that he had no basis for asylum before testimony or documents were presented, due process full and fair hearing and neutral judge requirements were violated].

N. *Discretionary Denials*

1. *Deferential Abuse of Discretion Standard*— In *INS v. Rios-Pineda*, 471 U.S. 444 (1985), the AG (and BIA) were given great deference in exercising their discretion to refuse to reopen deportation proceedings. "Even assuming that respondent's motion to reopen made out a *prima facie* case of eligibility for suspension of deportation the Attorney General had discretion to deny the motion". 471 U.S. at 449. *Accord INS v. Wang*, 450 U.S. 139 (1981). If the AG decides not to grant the relief as a matter of discretion, he need not discuss statutory eligibility. *Rios-Pineda* also suggests that the AG can consider the method of illegal status (*e.g.*, overstay vs. EWI), and of illegal entry (*e.g.*, by smuggler), when determining exercise of discretion, as well as matters not expressly within the immigration laws. Substantial deference is extended to EOIR in their decisions on motions to reopen for asylum, *INS v. Abudu*, 485 U.S. 94 (1988); *M.A. v. INS*, 899 F.2d 304 (4th Cir. 1990) (en banc); *Fesseha v. Ashcroft,* 333 F.3d 13, 20–21 (1st Cir. 2003) [applying *Abudu* standards and finding no abuse of discretion for failure of Ethiopian to establish a prima facie case of asylum]; withholding, *INS v. Doherty*, 502 U.S. 314 (1992); adjustment of status, *Manzano-Garcia v. Gonzales,* 413 F.3d 462, 469–71 (5th Cir. 2005) [no abuse of discretion where BIA declined to grant additional continuance because applicant did not file I-140 petition despite opportunity to do so for several months], *Medina-Morales v. Ashcroft,* 371 F.3d 520, 529–31 (9th Cir. 2004) [BIA could rely on grant of VD as discretionary factor in determining whether to reopen for adjustment but reversing BIA on legal issue for its decision to consider strength of (rather than simply the fact of) step-parent relationship], *Williams v. INS*, 773 F.2d 8 (1st Cir. 1985) [denying reopening even where statutorily eligible because petitioner "overstayed by many years," "repeatedly ignored grants of voluntary departure," and "most recent admission was gained by failure to disclose"]; suspension, *Saiyid v. INS*, 132 F.3d 1380 (11th Cir. 1998) [failure to show *prima facie* case of extreme hardship sufficient for BIA to deny reopening]; *Guan v. INS*, 49 F.3d 1259 (7th Cir. 1995) [can deny reopening even where statutorily eligible], *Vasquez v. INS*, 767 F.2d 598 (9th Cir. 1985) [same], *but see Dill v. INS*, 773 F.2d 25 (3d Cir. 1985); §212(c) relief, *Borokinni v. INS*, 974 F.2d 442 (4th Cir. 1992) [no reopening where frivolous appeal filed to reach 7 years]; denials of stay, *Vasquez v. Ilchert*, 614 F.Supp. 538 (N.D. Cal. 1985); and even ineffective assistance of counsel, *Maindrond v. Ashcroft,* 385 F.3d 98, 100–01 (1st Cir. 2004) [denial of motion to reopen for CAT upheld where movant was represented by counsel before IJ and BIA and ineffectiveness raised in motion]; *Lara v. Trominski,* 216 F.3d 487, 496 (5th Cir. 2000) [regulations authorize but do not require reopening; highly deferential abuse of discretion standard is applied]. However, even broad deference has its limits. *Korytnyuk v. Ashcroft,* 396 F.3d 272, 282–86 (3d Cir. 2005) [where BIA denied motion to remand for adjustment under *Abudu* theory that one may "leap ahead" and deny application on discretionary grounds, the factual basis for discretion is subject to substantial evidence review; reversing the denial because the claim that respondent was involved in criminal activity was not supported by the record]; *Kay v. Ashcroft,* 387 F.3d 664, 673–75 (7th Cir. 2004) [where evidence established *prima facie* CAT claim and BIA's cursory denial was made without a rational explanation, court reversed]; *Mickeviciute v. INS,* 327 F.3d 1159 (10th Cir. 2003) [reversing BIA where it failed to articulate which of the three *Abudu* grounds it relied on in denying respondent's motion to reopen]; *Watkins v. INS*, 63 F.3d 844, 850 (9th Cir. 1995) [notwithstanding *Rios-Pineda*, court reversed where BIA's actions were irrational].
2. *Marriage During Removal Proceedings*—The BIA is given broad discretion to deny a motion to reopen where it believes the applicant has not met the "clear and convincing standard" in a mar-

riage during removal proceedings or where it believes there was a history of recurrent marriage fraud. *Krazoun v. Ashcroft,* 350 F.3d 208 (1st Cir. 2003) [where respondent had two previous marriages that BIA deemed fraudulent it was within its discretion to deny reopening]. However, the BIA may not refuse to remand a case for consideration of adjustment for lack of evidence where the I-130 petition has been approved. *Patel v. Ashcroft,* 375 F.3d 693 (8th Cir. 2004) [BIA abused its discretion in denying remand for marriage-based AOS and requiring the production of additional evidence that the marriage was bona fide where the I-130 was approved].

3. *Denial Must be Reasoned, Not Arbitrary*—The BIA must give a reasoned decision in its denial of a motion to reopen, unlike a streamlined case where it can simply review the IJ's decision. *Franco-Rosendo v. Gonzales,* 454 F.3d 965 (9th Cir. 2006) [BIA's failure to evaluate favorable factors and new evidence regarding motion to reopen for cancellation while assuming eligibility, was error because it focused solely on her misconduct in failing to depart after grant of VD]; *Movsisian v. Ashcroft,* 395 F.3d 1095, 1097–98 (9th Cir. 2005) [BIA abused its discretion where it streamlined denial by giving a one sentence decision ("The motion to reopen is denied") that failed to articulate any reasoned basis for the denial]; *Fuentes v. INS,* 765 F.2d 886, 889 (9th Cir. 1985) *vacated on other grounds* 844 F.2d 699 (9th Cir. 1988) [AG's discretion could not be "unreasonable or arbitrary"]. It is also inappropriate for the BIA to make credibility determinations on motions to reopen. *Bhasin v. Gonzales,* 423 F.3d 977, 986 (9th Cir. 2005) [BIA improperly discounted affidavit in Indian mother's social group claim as self-serving].

4. *Fugitive Disentitlement Doctrine*—In *Matter of Barocio*, 19 I&N Dec. 255 (BIA 1985), the BIA held that a person who fails to report for deportation pursuant to a "bag and baggage letter" does not merit a favorable exercise of discretion for reopening. *Barocio* followed the principle established in *Molinaro v. New Jersey*, 396 U.S. 365 (1970), that a person who fails to comply with a court order cannot utilize the courts for his own purposes. *Sequeira-Solano v. INS*, 104 F.3d 278 (9th Cir. 1997) [affirming BIA denial based on *Barocio*]; *Arana v. INS*, 673 F.2d 75 (3d Cir. 1982) [no appeal for alien who concealed whereabouts and failed to report to INS after issuance of bench warrant]; *Wittgenstein v. INS*, 124 F.3d 1244, 1245 (10th Cir. 1997) [no violation of due process for BIA to refuse to review IJ's order when respondent was a fugitive from justice]. *But see Bhasin v. Gonzales,* 423 F.3d 977, 987–89 (9th Cir. 2005) [where notice to respondent to report for removal was clearly deficient, it was inappropriate for the BIA to invoke the fugitive disentitlement doctrine to bar motion to reopen]; *Arrozal v. INS,* 159 F.3d 429, 433–34 (9th Cir. 1998) [*Barocio* does not establish a *per se* rule to limit BIA's discretion to consider factors]; *Esposito v. INS*, 987 F.2d 108, 110 (2d Cir. 1993) [failure to surrender for 4 years after receipt of bag and baggage letter is insufficient basis to deny appeal]; *Matter of A-N- & R-M-N-,* 22 I&N Dec. 953 (BIA 1999) [*Barocio* does not bar reopening for asylum/withholding under changed circumstances where person remained in U.S. after issuance of deportation order]; *Matter of Pena-Diaz*, 20 I&N Dec. 841 (BIA 1994) [INS grant of deferred action or refusal to enforce deportation order may favor subsequent motion to reopen for suspension]. IMMACT90 [former INA §242B(e)] barred most forms of relief to persons who failed to report for deportation after receipt of a bag and baggage letter. INA §§240(b)(7), 241(a)(5), 240B(d) bars relief for failure to appear at a hearing and failure to depart after receiving voluntary departure. The former provision under INA §242B was repealed. IIRIRA §308(b)(6).

5. *Consideration of Motion to Reopen Factors*—BIA must consider all appropriate factors and not consider inappropriate factors. *Norani v. Gonzales,* 451 F.3d 292 (2d Cir. 2006) [BIA abused its discretion in not reopening case of Iranian Jews who failed to proceed on their original asylum claim but presented substantial evidence of worsened conditions in Iran, especially for Jews]; *Bhasin v. Gonzales,* 423 F.3d 977, 985–89 (9th Cir. 2005) [reversing denial of motion to reopen where BIA discounted mother's affidavit as self-serving thereby improperly making a credibility determination, improperly relying on the fugitive disentitlement doctrine, and where the new evidence was highly probative of her family persecution claim]; *Twum v. INS,* 411 F.3d 54 (2d Cir. 2005) [reversing and remanding where IJ misconstrued *in absentia* motion as an ineffective assistance of counsel claim under *Lozada* rather than a claim that security guards barred his entry to the court]; *Medina-Morales v. Ashcroft,* 371 F.3d 520, 531–32 (9th Cir. 2004) [reversing BIA denial of motion to reopen where IJ, contrary to precedent, relied on the strength of a step-parent relationship in consideration of motion to reopen for adjustment; however BIA could rely on grant of VD as discretionary factor in determining whether to reopen]; *Virk v. INS,* 295 F.3d 1055 (9th Cir. 2002) [reversing BIA denial of

motion to reopen for former INA §241(f) relief where it departed from precedent, failed to consider all relevant factors and improperly considered an irrelevant factor]; *Rodriguez-Lariz v. INS,* 282 F.3d 1218, 1227 (9th Cir. 2002) [reversing BIA denial of motion to reopen for suspension where Board "merely repeated petitioners' claims and summarily dismissed them without even purporting to engage in any substantive analysis or articulating any reasons for its decision...[and] did not give careful and individualized consideration to the hardship"]; *Watkins v. INS*, 63 F.3d 844 (9th Cir. 1995) [reversing BIA denial of suspension where "it did not consider all relevant factors before ruling, it did not consider the cumulative effect of the factors it did consider, and it did not provide a reasoned explanation for its conclusions"]; *Rodriguez-Gutierrez v. INS*, 59 F.3d 504, 508–09 (5th Cir. 1995) [reversing denial of motion to reopen for adjustment where BIA failed to meaningfully address positive equities and mischaracterized negative ones]; *Dulane v. INS*, 46 F.3d 988, 994–96 (10th Cir. 1995) [failing to consider all facts on motion to reopen for suspension]; *Delmundo v. INS*, 43 F.3d 436 (9th Cir. 1994) [even if BIA had authority under *Rios-Pineda* to skip over eligibility issues, its denial on discretionary grounds cannot be supported by improper criteria]. BIA must consider facts as they presently exist. *Opoka v. INS*, 94 F.3d 392 (7th Cir. 1996) [where wife granted suspension after husband's denial, court took judicial notice and reversed denial]; *Ng v. INS*, 804 F.2d 534 (9th Cir. 1986) [reversing BIA denial of reopening where BIA relied on misconduct of another]; *Luna v. INS*, 709 F.2d 126 (1st Cir. 1983) [failure to consider meaningful facts reversible]; *Chookhae v. INS*, 756 F.2d 1350 (9th Cir. 1985) [BIA should not have reviewed facts as they existed in 1977, but rather as it had case before it in 1982]; *Figueroa-Rincon v. INS*, 770 F.2d 766 (9th Cir. 1985). BIA must consider new facts in the totality of the circumstances. *Turri v. INS*, 997 F.2d 1306 (10th Cir. 1993); *Ravancho v. INS*, 658 F.2d 169 (3d Cir. 1981) [BIA erred in failing to consider new psychiatric report in light of the totality of the circumstances]. *See also Ordonez v. INS,* 345 F.3d 777, 784–87 (9th Cir. 2003) [reversing BIA denial of motion to reopen because it failed to accept respondent's declaration as true and impermissibly made an adverse credibility finding because some, but not all, of the evidence could have been produced previously]; *Gonzalez-Batoon v. INS*, 767 F.2d 1302, n.2 (9th Cir. 1985), *aff'd en banc*, 791 F.2d 681 (9th Cir. 1986) [reversing where BIA failed to properly consider psychiatric evaluations]. Moreover, an agency must accept facts as true unless "inherently unbelievable." *Limsico v. INS*, 951 F.2d 210, 213 (9th Cir. 1991); *Haftlang v. INS*, 790 F.2d 140 (D.C. Cir. 1986); *Mattis v. INS*, 774 F.2d 965, 968 (9th Cir. 1985); *Matter of L-O-G-*, 21 I&N Dec. 413 (BIA 1996) [reopening suspension application where *prima facie* case established]. *But see Caruncho v. INS*, 68 F.3d 356, 361–62 (9th Cir. 1995) [marriage subsequent to final deportation order entitled to little weight]; *M.A. v. INS*, 899 F.2d 304, 310 (4th Cir. 1990) (en banc). However, the BIA may consider prior testimony which rebuts affidavits submitted. *Limsico*, 951 F.2d 210 at 213–14.

XIV. MOTION TO REOPEN OR RECONSIDER BEFORE REGIONAL SERVICE CENTERS

A motion to reopen shall state new facts supported by affidavits or other evidentiary material. Where an application has been denied for failure to respond to an RFE, a motion to reopen must include evidence that the RFE was sent to an incorrect address, the requested evidence was not material or the reply was properly submitted. 8 C.F.R. §103.5(a)(2). A motion to reconsider must be supported by precedent that establishes that the decision was based on an incorrect application of law or USCIS policy. A motion must be filed within 30 days of the decision unless, in regard to a motion to reopen, the delay was reasonable and beyond the control of the applicant or petitioner. 8 C.F.R. §103.5(a)(1)(i). The motion is submitted on Form I-290B or separately as a motion to reopen or both. Each Service Center maintains its own detailed procedures on how to treat appeals, motions to reopen and reconsider. *See e.g.* Way, Director, Nebraska Service Center, NSC Motions and Appeals Processes for other than Special Agricultural Worker and Legalization Cases, NSC 70/41.1.1 (Feb. 10, 2004), *published on* AILA InfoNet at Doc. No. 04021763. The reviewing official may treat a properly and timely filed appeal as a motion to reopen or reconsider and take favorable action. 8 C.F.R. §103.3(a)(2)(iii). An *untimely* appeal that meets the requirements of a motion to reopen under §103.5(a)(2) or a motion to reconsider under §103.5(a)(3) *must be* treated as a motion and a decision must be made on the merits. 8 C.F.R. §103.3(a)(2)(v)(B)(2). A field officer decision may be appealed to the AAO if the original decision was appealable to the AAO. 8 C.F.R. §103.5(a)(6).

CHAPTER 10
FEDERAL JUDICIAL REVIEW

CHAPTER 10
FEDERAL JUDICIAL REVIEW

I. OVERVIEW

A. *Generally*—Judicial review of all exclusion, deportation and removal orders, as a result of section 106(d) of the REAL ID Act of 2005, PL 109-13, 119 Stat. 231 (May 11, 2005), Div. B §106 are now governed by INA §242, 8 U.S.C. §1252 and the former transition rules for appeals under former INA §106, 8 U.S.C. §1105a established under the Illegal Immigration Reform and Immigrant Responsibility Act (IIRIRA) §309(c)(4) have been eliminated. Section 242 of the INA requires that all appeals go to the court of appeals and that procedures under INA §242 govern all cases. *See e.g., Elia v. Gonzales,* 431 F.3d 268, 272–73 (6th Cir. 2005) [Transition Rule case treated as a case filed under INA §242]; *Joseph v. Att'y Gen. of the U.S.,* 421 F.3d 224, 229 (3d Cir. 2005) [where nationality claim would have been governed by former INA §106(a), court determined that as a result of REAL ID Act §106(d), the procedures under INA §242 applied and not the transition rules]. Procedures under INA §242 include that a petition must be filed within 30 days of the date of the final order and that there are no automatic stays of removal pending appeal.

Under IIRIRA Congress sought to abolish many forms of judicial review of immigration decisions. In a dramatic reversal of existing law and procedure the Congress eliminated INA §106, 8 U.S.C. §1105a, and replaced it with INA §242, 8 U.S.C. §1242. As a further restriction the REAL ID Act eliminated habeas corpus review, mandamus and All Writs Act jurisdiction in the district court regarding "an order of removal entered or issued under any provision of this Act," INA §242(a)(5). Some courts have found that this limitation does not violate the Suspension Clause. *Mohamed v. Gonzales,* 477 F.3d 522, 525–26 (8th Cir. 2006) [upheld validity of REAL ID Act's removal of habeas in as-applied constitutional challenge where respondent claimed that evidence outside the administrative record could not be considered and therefore review limited to the circuit courts was not an adequate or effective remedy under *Swain v. Pressley,* 430 U.S. 372 (1977)]; *Puri v. Gonzales,* 464 F.3d 1038, 1041–42 (9th Cir. 2006) [the lack of an evidentiary hearing in habeas does not mean the Suspension Clause is violated because judicial review of agency action is an adequate and effective remedy]; *Alexandere v. U.S. Att'y Gen.,* 452 F.3d 1204, 1205–07 (11th Cir. 2006) [suspension Clause not violated because constitutional and statutory review that existed in habeas still preserved in the courts of appeal provides an adequate and effective remedy to the elimination of habeas in the district court]. In addition all habeas cases pending on the date of the REAL ID Act, May 11, 2005, are transferred to the circuit court of appeals where the petition could have been *properly* filed under INA §242(b)(2), and the transferred case shall be reviewed as a petition for review even if it was not filed within the 30-day deadline. REAL ID Act §106(c). *Jaber v. Gonzales,* 486 F.3d 223 (6th Cir. 2007) [court could not hear transferred habeas case on issuing involving motions to reopen that had not yet been decided by the BIA because they could not have been properly filed with the circuit court until the BIA rendered a decision]; *Ishak v. Gonzales,* 422 F.3d 22, 29–30 (1st Cir. 2005) [where appeal of a denied habeas petition was pending in the circuit court at the time of the passage of the REAL ID Act, the case will be treated as a petition for review and the 30-day provision for petitions for review is waived]; *Dorisme v. Gonzales,* 410 F.Supp.2d 79 (D. Conn. 2006) [includes transfers of CAT claims]. However, habeas cases filed incorrectly after May 11, 2006 may simply be dismissed rather than transferred. *In the Matter of Lawrence,* 448 F.Supp.2d 572 (S.D.N.Y. 2006); *Iasu v. Chertoff,* 426 F.Supp.2d 1124 (S.D. Cal. 2006) [where petition was filed in district court before May 11, 2006 but was amended after that date to add a challenge to removal based upon citizenship, court dismissed habeas and found no violation of the Suspension Clause even if petitioner could not pursue claim in circuit court]. But if a habeas case was not filed before May 11, 2005 (because there was no time limit on filing habeas petitions) and an appeal was not appropriate because of jurisdictional issues, the failure to file before May 11, 2005 if fatal would violate the Suspension Clause. *Kolkevich v. Att'y Gen. of the U.S.*, 501 F.3d 323 (3d Cir. 2007) [it would violate the Suspension Clause not to provide any avenue of review where respondent did not file habeas before May 11, 2005 and could not file petition for review after May 11, 2005 because the 30 days had passed; therefore, a party would be given 30 days from May 11, 2005 to file a petition for review]; *See also Ruiz-Martinez v. Mukasey,* 516 F.3d 102, 112–17 (2d Cir. 2008) [petitioner who filed habeas two days after May 11th and within 30 days of the removal order would have habeas treated as properly filed petition for review]. *But see Iasu v. Smith,* 511 F.3d 881 (9th Cir. 2007). In *Iasu* petitioner filed a habeas petition before May 11, 2005 regarding his detention and then added a challenge to his removal order *after* May 11, 2005 on the grounds that he was a citizen. The removal order had been final far more than 30 days at the time the habeas was amended. The court determined that the claim to citizenship could not be heard in the district court because the case was transferred to the circuit court under REAL ID and could not be heard in the circuit court because the transferred petition was not valid as to claims made after May 11, 2005. The court determined that the Suspension Clause issue could be alleviated by filing a motion to reopen before the BIA and seeking appeal of that order, notwithstanding the petitioner's claim that there was no basis for a motion to reopen because the evidence as to his citizenship was available at the time of the removal hearing.

Congress preserved in the court of appeals constitutional claims and questions of law in a petition for review, notwithstanding any preclusion statute that would otherwise bar review in the circuit court. INA §242(a)(2)(D). *Liu v. INS,* 508 F.3d 716, 720–22 (2d Cir. 2007) [recognizing that questions of law could include applying the wrong standard or making an unambiguous factual error, but finding that it did not occur in the denial of asylum under the one-year filing deadline]; *Jean-Pierre v. U.S. Att'y Gen.,* 500 F.3d 1315, 1320–22 (11th Cir. 2007) [the court's jurisdiction to review questions of law extends to the review of undisputed or historical facts to a legal standard]; *Khan v. Gonzales,* 495 F.3d 31, 34–36 (2d Cir. 2007) [following *Chen* a claim that an IJ based his decision on an "unambiguous misstatement of pertinent facts in the record" is a question of law reviewable under INA §242(a)(2)(D), but denying claim for failure to exhaust]; *Ghahremani v. Gonzales*, 498 F.3d 993, 998-99 (9th Cir. 2007) [followed *Ramadan* in equitable tolling case regarding factual issue concerning due diligence]; *Ramadan v. Gonzales,* 479 F.3d 646, 648–54 (9th Cir. 2007), *reh'g en banc denied*, 504 F.3d 973 (2007) [questions of law includes not only pure issues of statutory interpretation but mixed questions of law and fact where the court is applying undisputed facts to statutory and regulatory questions]; *Chen v. DOJ,* 471 F.3d 315, 323–32 (2d Cir. 2006) [finding that "questions of law" should be read, consistent with the legislative history at H.R. Rep. No. 109-72 at 175, 2005 U.S.C.C.A.N. at 300, to include "those issues that were historically reviewable in habeas"]; *Berhe v. Gonzales,* 464 F.3d 74, 86–87 (1st Cir. 2006) [the adequacy of the BIA's reasoning is a legal question where the IJ offered two reasons for granting withholding and the BIA addressed only one in reversing the decision]; *Abiodun v. Gonzales,* 461 F.3d 1210, 1214–15(10th Cir. 2006) [in light of section 242(a)(2)(D) respondent's aggravated felony convictions did not, under INA §242(a)(2)(C), bar his legal claim regarding U.S. citizenship]; *Ramirez-Molina v. Ziglar,* 436 F.3d 508, 513–14 (5th Cir. 2006) [jurisdiction under INA §242(a)(2)(D) to review legal challenge to reinstated removal order notwithstanding preclusion provision of INA §241(a)(5)]; *Schroeck v. Gonzales,* 429 F.3d 947, 950–51 (10th Cir. 2005) [notwithstanding preclusion of review of 212(h) petitions, INA §242(a)(2)(D) permits jurisdiction to review respondent's constitutional claim that the IJ should not have heard and considered evidence regarding a dismissed criminal case]; *Cabrera-Alvarez v. Gonzales,* 423 F.3d 1006, 1009 (9th Cir. 2005) [whether the BIA interpreted the exceptional and extremely unusual hardship provision of cancellation consistent with international law is a legal question reviewable under INA §242(a)(2)(D)] *Ramos v. Gonzales,* 414 F.3d 800, 802–04 (7th Cir. 2005) [Congress added §242(a)(2)(D) to consider all constitutional and statutory claims in review of a final order]; *Papageorgiou v. Gonzales,* 413 F.3d 356, 357–58 (3d Cir. 2005) [Section 242(a)(2)(D) restores jurisdiction to the circuit court for persons who previously were barred from such review under 242(a)(2)(C) because of criminal convictions and makes the restoration retroactive by applying it to any order issued before, on or after May 11, 2005]; *Fernandez-Ruiz v. Gonzales,* 468 F.3d 1159, 1163 (9th Cir. 2006) [same].

However, INA §242(a)(2)(D) may have no application to INA §242(g). *Mohammad Hussain v. Keisler,* 505 F.3d 779, 783–85 (7th Cir. 2007) [INA §242(g) precludes *constitutional* challenges because the language in INA §242(a)(2)(D) stating that it applies "other than this section" means that the constitutional and statutory review under §242(a)(2)(D) does not apply to INA §242(g) and therefore the court lacks jurisdiction to hear petitioner's constitutional challenge to the decision to commence proceedings through NSEERS in violation of equal protection]. It may also be inapplicable to review of expedited removal proceedings under INA §235(b)(1), 8 U.S.C. §1225(b)(1) because INA §242(a)(2)(D) does not "override the jurisdictional bar of §1252(a)(2)(A)(i)." *Turgerel v. Mukasey,* 513 F.3d 1202, 1205–06 (10th Cir. 2008) [no jurisdiction to review *constitutional* claims in petitioner's current removal proceeding where she sought AOS based upon her marriage to a U.S. citizen because the court determined that she was barred from collaterally attacking on constitutional grounds a prior expedited removal proceeding, notwithstanding INA §242(a)(2)(D), where she was subject to a life-time ban, without waiver, for making a false claim to U.S. citizenship].

The legislative history of the REAL ID Act also provides that it "will not preclude habeas review over challenges to detention that are independent of challenges to removal orders. Instead, the bill would eliminate habeas review only over challenges to removal orders." Joint Explanatory Statement of the Committee of Conference, H.R. Conf. Rep. No. 109-72 at 175, 151 Cong. Rec. H2836, 2873 (May 3, 2005). *See also Kellici v. Gonzales,* 472 F.3d 416 (6th Cir. 2007) [right of habeas upheld where challenge only to arrest and detention and not to hearing before IJ/BIA or final order]; *Hernandez v. Gonzales,* 424 F.3d 42 (1st Cir. 2005) [remanding habeas detention challenge by Mariel Cuban back to district court because habeas may be brought post–REAL ID Act when it is a challenge to detention]; *Ali v. Gonzales,* 421 F.3d 795, 797 n.1 (9th Cir. 2005) [the REAL ID Act does not apply to matters outside of challenges to removal orders and the court declined to transfer a habeas case to the circuit court where petitioners challenged solely their physical removal]; *Bonhometre v. Ashcroft,* 414 F.3d 442, 446 n.4 (3d Cir. 2005); *Moallin v. Cangemi,* 427 F.Supp.2d 908, 918–21 (D. Minn. 2006) [citing the REAL ID Act legislative history a Somalian detained subsequent to his removal order can challenge his custody as violative of the constitution]; *Abdulle v. Gonzales,* 422 F.Supp.2d 774, 776 (W.D. Tex. 2006) [REAL ID does not preclude habeas related to detention only]. *But see Deljevic v. Baker,* 463 F.Supp.2d 699 (E.D. Mich. 2006) [no habeas jurisdiction to review detention where there is final order of removal and detention is challenged on ground that final order was improper]. As a result habeas, mandamus and All Writs Act review is eliminated for matters subject to a petition for review, but judicial review is restored, at least in the courts of appeals for constitutional and statutory claims because of INA §242(a)(2)(D), notwithstanding many preclusion statutes restricting judicial review. *See e.g., Ramirez-Molina v. Ziglar,* 436 F.3d 508, 513–14 (5th Cir. 2006) [jurisdiction under INA §242(a)(2)(D) to review legal challenge to reinstated removal order notwithstanding preclusion provision of INA §241(a)(5)].

Non–Final Order. Of course, a matter which is not deemed to be a review of a removal order may still be addressed in habeas or otherwise in the district court. *See Singh v. Gonzales,* 499 F.3d 969, 976–81 (9th Cir. 2007) [claim that ineffective assistance of counsel resulted in failure to file a timely appeal to the circuit court was not a review of a final order and district court jurisdiction was not precluded by INA §§242(a)(5) & (b)(9)]; *Ikenokwalu-White v. Gonzales,* 495 F.3d 919, 924–26 (8th Cir. 2007) [review of revocation of I-130, despite it potentially affecting mother's removal, was not part of a removal order and the case had to be pursued in the district, not circuit, court]; *Hamilton v. Gonzales,* 485 F.3d 564 (10th Cir. 2007) [notwithstanding INA §242(a)(2)(D) revocation of I-130/adoption petition that was affirmed by BIA is not reviewable in circuit court because it is not part of a final order and 242(a)(2)(D) applies only to final orders, the APA is not an independent jurisdictional ground, and it is precluded by INA §242(a)(2)(B)]; *Nnadika v. Att'y Gen. of the U.S.,* 484 F.3d 626 (3d Cir. 2007) [court of appeals remanded to the district court a claim for injunctive and declaratory relief seeking review of a denied I-730 because it was not a final order for purposes of INA §242 review]; *Fonseca-Sanchez v. Gonzales,* 484 F.3d 439 (7th Cir. 2007) [where respondent sought review of a U visa denial that arose subsequent to a final administrative removal order, the court lacked jurisdiction under INA §242 and the proper remedy was habeas]; *Sandher v. Gonzales,* 481 F.3d 108 (2d Cir. 2007) [court dismissed habeas that was transferred to it improperly under REAL ID Act where habeas only challenged the validity of petitioner's conviction and not his removal order]; *Kellici v. Gonzales,* 472 F.3d 416 (6th Cir. 2007) [challenge only to arrest and detention and not to hearing before IJ/BIA or final order]; *Madu v. U.S. Att'y Gen.,* 470 F.3d 1362, 1366–67 (11th Cir. 2006) [where respondent claims he voluntarily departed and reentered, and therefore does not have a removal order, habeas was appropriate and circuit court dismissed and remanded it to district court]; *Kumarasamy v. Att'y Gen. of the U.S.,* 453 F.3d 169, 172 (3d Cir. 2006) [a person who claims his deportation was illegal because there was no order of removal is not barred by the REAL ID Act from bringing a habeas petition]; *Ballesteros v. Ashcroft,* 452 F.3d 1153, 1160 (10th Cir. 2006) [constitutional claim regarding warrantless arrest is not part of final order despite claim that it improperly resulted in a final order]; *Khouzam v. Hogan,* 497 F.Supp.2d 615, 623 (M.D. Pa. 2007) [denied motion to dismiss habeas where petitioner's deferral of removal under CAT was revoked by DHS]. *But see Rafaelano v. Wilson,* 471 F.3d 1091

(9th Cir. 2006) [treating habeas as a petition for review pursuant to REAL ID Act but remanding the case to the BIA for a factual record]. *See also Rhodes-Bradford v. Keisler,* 507 F.3d 77, 81–82 (2d Cir. 2007) [where court found BIA could not enter a final order of removal and the government argued the court therefore could not review the matter because there was no final order from the BIA, the court held it could review to avoid serious due process concerns].

B. *Scope of Review*—The scope of review for questions of law is the same as it was for habeas. *Liu v. INS,* 508 F.3d 716, 720–22 (2d Cir. 2007) [recognizing that questions of law could include applying the wrong standard or making an unambiguous factual error, but finding that it did not occur in the denial of asylum under the one-year filing deadline]; *Jean-Pierre v. U.S. Att'y Gen.,* 500 F.3d 1315, 1320–22 (11th Cir. 2007) [the court's jurisdiction to review questions of law extends to the review of undisputed or historical facts to a legal standard and "offers the same scope of review as a habeas remedy"]; *Khan v. Gonzales,* 495 F.3d 31, 34–36 (2d Cir. 2007) [following *Chen* a claim that an IJ based his decision on an "unambiguous misstatement of pertinent facts in the record" is a question of law reviewable under INA §242(a)(2)(D), but denying claim for failure to exhaust]; *Chen v. U.S. DOJ,* 471 F.3d 315, 323–32 (2d Cir. 2006) [finding that "questions of law" should be read, consistent with the legislative history at H.R. Rep. No. 109-72 at 175, 2005 U.S.C.C.A.N. at 300, to include "those issues that were historically reviewable in habeas"]; *Kamara v. Att'y Gen. of the U.S.,* 420 F.3d 202, 210–11 (3d Cir. 2005) [the standard is the same as in habeas and court will limit review to pure questions of law and to issues of application of law to fact, where the facts are undisputed and not the subject of challenge]; *Oyebanji v. Gonzales,* 418 F.3d 260, 262 n.3 (3d Cir. 2005) [same]. But there must be a record to review. *Rafaelano v. Wilson,* 471 F.3d 1091 (9th Cir. 2006) [treating habeas as a petition for review pursuant to REAL ID Act but remanding the case to the BIA for a factual record]. However, the REAL ID Act of 2005, by enacting INA §242(a)(2)(D), may not have extended circuit court review in such cases to:

1. A challenge based solely upon substantial evidence, *Conteh v. Gonzales,* 461 F.3d 45, 62–63 (1st Cir. 2006) [court had no authority to engage in substantial evidence review of a withholding of removal claim for a applicant who was convicted of an aggravated felony]; *Boakai v. Gonzales,* 447 F.3d 1 (1st Cir. 2006) [the BIA's determination that the petitioner did not act with due diligence to support equitable tolling for an ineffective assistance of counsel claim is a nonreviewable factual question]; *Hamid v. Gonzales,* 417 F.3d 642, 647 (7th Cir. 2005) [because respondent is an aggravated felon the court declined to consider whether the IJ's factual conclusions in the denial of a CAT claim are supported by substantial evidence because such challenge fails to raise either a constitutional or statutory claim under INA §242(a)(2)(D)]; *but see Ibarra-Flores v. Gonzales,* 439 F.3d 614, 618 (9th Cir. 2006) [reviewed for substantial evidence IJ's nondiscretionary factual determination that respondent was ineligible for cancellation because he was given VD];

2. Discretionary or factual determinations—*Saintha v. Mukasey,* 516 F.3d 243, 248–51 (4th Cir. 2008) [BIA determinations regarding deferral of removal that the court would ordinarily review under the substantial evidence standard are necessarily factual in nature and beyond review]; *Barco-Sandoval v. Gonzales,* 516 F.3d 35 (2d Cir. 2008) [finding that *Chen v. U.S. DOJ,* 471 F.3d 315 did not alter *De La Vega* where respondent's claim that the wrong legal standard was applied was not colorable and merely sought to address a factual question as to extreme hardship under cancellation]; *Pepaj v. Mukasey,* 509 F.3d 725, 727–28 (6th Cir. 2007) [followed *Almuhtaseb* and held no review for abuse of discretion regarding solely factual questions in denying motion to reopen for changed country conditions]; *Arias v. U.S. Att'y Gen.*, 482 F.3d 1281 (11th Cir. 2007) [finding s not supported by the record, failure to properly weight factors, and mischaracterization of the record by the IJ in §212(c) case were not constitutional claims permitting review]; *Almuhtaseb v. Gonzales,* 453 F.3d 743, 746–49 (6th Cir. 2006) [in the review of the bar to filing asylum beyond one year, the court narrowly construed constitutional questions as only claims brought pursuant to a specific provision of the constitution and narrowly construed statutory questions as those regarding the construction of a statute; the court declined to consider factual questions regarding the changed circumstances exception to the one year filing deadline]; *Haman v. Gonzales,* 449 F.3d 834 (8th Cir. 2006) [review of CAT denial regarding Pashtun returning to Afghanistan is factual question not subject to court's jurisdiction]; *Boakai v. Gonzales,* 447 F.3d 1 (1st Cir. 2006) [the BIA's determination that the petitioner did not act with due diligence to support equitable tolling for an ineffective assistance of counsel claim is a nonreviewable factual question]; *Avendano-Espejo v. DHS,* 448 F.3d 503 (2d Cir. 2006) ["dressing up" the IJ's exercise of discretion in

denying INA §212(c) with the language of "due process" or "erroneous legal standard" did not alter the decision's nonreviewable status]; *Martinez v. U.S. Att'y Gen.,* 446 F.3d 1219 (11th Cir. 2006) [INA §242(a)(2)(D) does not restore jurisdiction to review exceptional and extremely unusual hardship]; *Bygayong v. INS,* 442 F.3d 67 (2d Cir. 2006)[INA §242(a)(2)(D) does not overcome the discretionary decision bar under §242(a)(2)(B)(i) for a §212(h) waiver even if there was a finding of extreme hardship because the ultimate decision to grant the waiver is discretionary]; *Elysee v. Gonzales,* 437 F.3d 221 (1st Cir. 2006) [INA §242(a)(2)(D) is not applicable because respondent did not raise a statutory or colorable constitutional claim to the denial of cancellation]; *De La Vega v. Gonzales,* 436 F.3d 141 (2d Cir. 2006) [INA §242(a)(2)(D) did not extend jurisdiction to review the denial of cancellation based upon exceptional and extremely unusual hardship which review is barred by INA §242(a)(2)(B)(i)]; *Jean v. Gonzales,* 435 F.3d 475, 480–81 (4th Cir. 2005) [no jurisdiction to review that aspect of a motion to reconsider that seeks reconsideration of a discretionary denial of INA §212(h) because the discretionary denial was not reviewable in the first place under INA §242(a)(2)(B), but whether respondent was precluded from establishing good moral character was a legal issue that was reviewable]; *Sukwanputra v. Gonzales,* 434 F.3d 627, 633–35 (3d Cir. 2006) [changed circumstances affecting one year deadline for filing asylum is not reviewable under INA §242(a)(2)(D) because it does not raise a statutory or constitutional claim]; *Higuit v. Gonzales,* 433 F.3d 417, 419–20 (4th Cir. 2006) [court lacked jurisdiction to review the discretionary decision to deny adjustment of status to a person involved in the persecution of others]; *Mehilli v. Gonzales,* 433 F.3d 86, 92–94 (1st Cir. 2005) [followed *Vasile* and other circuits in a *post*–REAL ID Act case and determined that issues regarding untimeliness in filing an asylum claim were factual and discretionary and therefore could not be reviewed in the court of appeals under INA §242(a)(2)(D)]; *Ignatova v. Gonzales,* 430 F.3d 1209, 1213–14 (8th Cir. 2005) [*Post*–REAL ID Act, the court found no jurisdiction to review determinations concerning exceptions to the one year filing deadline for asylum because they are discretionary decisions not questions of law under §1252(a)(2)(D)]; *Chacon-Botero v. U.S. Att'y Gen.,* 427 F.3d 954, 957 (11th Cir. 2005) [followed *Vasile* and found that the issue of timely filing an asylum claim was not reviewable because it was not a constitutional claim or question of law covered under INA §242(a)(2)(D)]; *Martinez-Rosas v. Gonzales,* 424 F.3d 926, 929–30 (9th Cir. 2005) [notwithstanding section INA §242(a)(2)(D) pursuant to the REAL ID Act, the court still has no jurisdiction to review the discretionary determination of hardship under cancellation because INA §242(a)(2)(B)(i) precludes review]; *Grass v. Gonzales,* 418 F.3d 876, 878–89 (8th Cir. 2005) [the REAL ID Act of 2005 did not alter that lack of jurisdiction over discretionary decisions under §242(a)(2)(B)(ii) such as the denial of a continuance to await an approved I-130 petition]; *Vasile v. Gonzales,* 417 F.3d 766, 768 (7th Cir. 2005) [REAL ID Act of 2005 under 8 U.S.C. §1252(a)(2)(D) allowing for constitutional and statutory claims did not alter the bar to the review of the failure to file within one year or that there were no extraordinary circumstances permitting review because these are factual and discretionary issues].

But see Liu v. INS, 508 F.3d 716, 720–22 (2d Cir. 2007) [recognizing that questions of law could include applying the wrong standard or making an unambiguous factual error, but finding that it did not occur in the denial of asylum under the one-year filing deadline]; *Jean-Pierre v. U.S. Att'y Gen.,* 500 F.3d 1315, 1320–22 (11th Cir. 2007) [in case involving whether a particular fact patter amounts to torture, the court's jurisdiction to review questions of law extends to the review of undisputed or historical facts to a legal standard and "offers the same scope of review as a habeas remedy"]; *Khan v. Gonzales,* 495 F.3d 31, 34–36 (2d Cir. 2007) [following *Chen* a claim that an IJ based his decision on an "unambiguous misstatement of pertinent facts in the record" is a question of law reviewable under INA §242(a)(2)(D) but denying claim for failure to exhaust]; *Ghahremani v. Gonzales*, 498 F.3d 993, 998-99 (9th Cir. 2007) [followed *Ramadan* in equitable tolling case regarding factual issue concerning due diligence]; *Ramadan v. Gonzales,* 479 F.3d 646, 648–54 (9th Cir. 2007) *reh'g en banc denied* 504 F.3d 973 (2007) [questions of law includes not only pure issues of statutory interpretation but mixed questions of law and fact where the court is applying undisputed facts to statutory and regulatory questions and therefore the court can review the issue of the failure to file asylum within one year due to "changed circumstances"]; *Chen v. DOJ,* 471 F.3d 315, 323–32 (2d Cir. 2006) [although broadly reading "questions of law," the court ultimately determined it did not have jurisdiction to review respondent's claim that the IJ abused his discretion when determining that respondent failed to demonstrate changed or extraordinary circumstances to waive the one year deadline for filing asylum]; *Mabasa v. Gonzales,* 455

F.3d 740, 744 (7th Cir. 2006) [where IJ relied on changed circumstances to deny right to file asylum claim beyond one year but BIA confused changed circumstances with exceptional circumstances, there was review under INA §242(a)(2)(D).

C. *Restriction Under INA §242 Regarding the Judicial Review of a Final Order of Removal*

1. The AG's decisions regarding summary removal (§235(b)(1)) except in extraordinarily limited circumstances. INA §242(a)(2)(A), 8 U.S.C. §1252(a)(2)(A); INA §242(e), 8 U.S.C. §1252(e); *Sissoko v. Rocha,* 509 F.3d 947 (9th Cir. 2007) [*Bivens* action challenging unlawful detention of a person government claimed was an alien subject to summary removal was barred by INA §242(g) in the limited circumstance where the plaintiff could have challenged his detention by habeas corpus under INA §242(e)(2)];
2. The AG's judgment regarding the granting of relief under INA §§212(h), 212(i), cancellation of removal (§240A), voluntary departure (§240B), and adjustment of status (§245). INA §242(a)(2)(B)(i), 8 U.S.C. §1252(a)(2)(B)(i);
3. The AG's decision regarding "any other decision or action ... the authority for which is specified under this subchapter [§§1151–1378] to be in the discretion of the Attorney General" other than asylum. INA §242(a)(2)(B)(ii), 8 U.S.C. §1252(a)(2)(B)(ii);
4. Any final order of removal against a person who is removable because of having committed a criminal offense under INA §212(a)(2), §237(a)(2)(A)(iii) (aggravated felony), §237(a)(2)(B) (drugs), §237(a)(2)(C) (firearms offenses), §237(a)(2)(D) (miscellaneous offenses) or §237(a)(2)(A)(ii) (where there are two crimes of moral turpitude for which a sentence of one year or longer may be imposed on each). INA §242(a)(2)(C), 8 U.S.C. §1252(a)(2)(C);
5. Any removal decision by an immigration judge based solely on a medical certification under INA §240(c)(1)(B), §1229a(c)(1)(B). INA §242(a)(3), 8 U.S.C. §1252(a)(3);
6. Collateral attacks on removal orders—INA §235(b)(1)(D), 8 U.S.C. §1225(b)(1)(D) and §242(a)(7)(A), 8 U.S.C. §1252(a)(7)(A);
7. Injunctive relief (except direct petition in the U.S. Supreme Court) enjoining the operation of removal proceedings (all matters under Title II, Chapter 4 of the INA) unless it is in an individual case and only then can removal be enjoined if there is a showing by clear and convincing evidence that the entry or execution of such order is prohibited as a matter of law. INA §242(f), 8 U.S.C. §1252(f);
8. The AG's decision or action "to commence proceedings, adjudicate cases, or execute removal orders against any alien under this Act." INA §242(g), 8 U.S.C. §1252(g); *Reno v. American-Arab Anti-Discrimination Committee,* 525 U.S. 471 (1999);

D. *Restriction on Judicial Review in Other Areas*

1. The AG's/DHS's decision to grant or deny a waiver under INA §212(i), 8 U.S.C. §1182(i);
2. The AG's/DHS's decision or action regarding a waiver of INA §212(a)(9)(B) inadmissibility, INA §212(a)(9)(B)(v), 8 U.S.C. §1182(a)(9)(B)(v);
3. Suits against the U.S. or its agencies or officers under INA §279 except those initiated by the government. INA §279, 8 U.S.C. §1329;
4. Review of the denial of the right to seek asylum because the applicant: (a) can go to a safe third country; (2) was previously denied asylum; (3) did not file the asylum application within one year of entry; (4) is deemed to be a terrorist or (5) because the AG determined there were no changed circumstances warranting an exception to the one-year deadline. INA §208(a)(3), (b)(2)(D), 8 U.S.C. §1158(a)(3), (b)(2)(D);
5. Review of regulations implementing the Torture Convention or determinations with respect to U.S. policy under the Torture Convention are restricted: FARA §2242(d) ["Notwithstanding any other provision of law ... no court shall have jurisdiction to review the regulations adopted to implement [the Convention Against Torture] or any other determination made with respect to the application of the policy [regarding expelling, extraditing or otherwise involuntarily returning someone] except as part of the review of a final order of removal pursuant to section 242 of the [INA]]. In addition, under the REAL ID Act of 2005, habeas, mandamus, and the All Writs Act are elimi-

nated as a source of jurisdiction to review Convention Against Torture claims and the courts of appeal "shall be the sole and exclusive means for judicial review of any cause or claim under" CAT. INA §242(a)(4);

6. Review of reinstated removal orders under INA §241(a)(5) because such order "is not subject to being reopened or reviewed";
7. The AG's/DHS's discretionary decisions regarding detention or release, including the grant, revocation or denial of bond or parole. INA §236(e), 8 U.S.C. §1226(e);
8. The AG's/DHS's decisions regarding voluntary departure. INA §240B(e), (f), 8 U.S.C. §1229c(e), (f);
9. The AG's/DHS's decision to grant or deny a waiver under INA §212(d)(12), 8 U.S.C. §1182(d)(12) or INA §237(a)(3)(C)(ii), 8 U.S.C. §1227(a)(3)(C)(ii), for being inadmissible or deportable because of a final order under INA §274C
10. The AG's/DHS decision to grant or deny a waiver under INA §212(h), 8 U.S.C. §1182 (h).
11. The AG's decision to require corroboration in asylum or other relief from removal may only be reversed if "a reasonable trier of fact is compelled to conclude that such corroborating evidence is unavailable." INA §242(b)(4), 8 U.S.C. §1252(b)(4);
12. The AG's/DHS's discretionary decisions in all matters "regardless of whether the judgment, decision, or action is made in removal proceedings." INA §242(a)(2)(B), 8 U.S.C. §1252(a)(2)(B).
13. The AG's determination "as to whether the status of any alien should be adjusted under [NACARA] is final and shall not be subject to review by any court." NACARA §202(f);
14. The Secretary of State or consular officer's decision to revoke an immigrant visa or NIV under INA §221(i) is not reviewable in habeas, mandamus, or All Writs Act except the decision may be reviewed in the context of a removal proceeding and only then if the revocation provides the sole ground for removal under INA §237(a)(1)(B). *Bolante v. Achim,* 457 F.Supp.2d 896 (E.D. Wis. 2006) [no habeas jurisdiction to review claim that revocation was improper under 22 C.F.R. §41.122(a)].

Restrictions on judicial review are therefore divided between limitations on review in the courts of appeals through petitions for review which are governed by INA §242, and other statutes that specifically preclude review of certain immigration matters whether in the district court or court of appeals. The provisions having the broadest impact under IIRIRA with respect to the elimination of judicial review have been INA §236(e) [review of bond], §242(a)(2)(B) [discretionary decisions of the AG], §242(a)(2)(C) [review involving criminal aliens], §242(b)(7) [consolidation of all questions] and §242(g) [bar to challenging AG's authority to commence proceedings, adjudicate cases, or execute removal orders against any alien]. Consistent with long-standing principles of judicial construction, however, the courts have read these judicial preclusion statutes narrowly. *See, e.g., Reno v. American-Arab Anti-Discrimination Committee,* 525 U.S. 471 (1999) [narrowly construing the preclusion provisions of INA §242(g)]. However, even when the courts have construed these provisions to restrict judicial review, they have preserved review through other means to avoid a constitutional problem. *Compare Calcano-Martinez v. INS,* 533 U.S. 348 (2001) [INA §242(a)(2)(C) restricting judicial review for persons with certain criminal convictions] *with INS v. St. Cyr,* 533 U.S. 289, 297–315 (2001) [habeas jurisdiction for the same criminal deportees remains and it is not affected by provisions restrict review such as INA §242(a)(2)(C)]. The limitation of review in the court of appeals and even in the district court therefore, did not mean that all review was precluded. Habeas corpus review under 28 U.S.C. §2241 remained. *Demore v. Kim*, 538 U.S. 510, 517 (2003) ["Section 1226(e) contains no explicit provision barring habeas review and we think that its clear text does not bar respondent's constitutional challenge to the legislation authorizing his detention without bail"]; *INS v. St. Cyr,* 533 U.S. 289, 297–315, 121 S.Ct. 2271, 2278–87 (2001); *Zadvydas v. Davis,* 533 U.S. 678, 687–88, 121 S.Ct. 2491, 2497–98 (2001).

But Congress under the REAL ID Act of 2005, PL 109-13, 119 Stat. 231 (May 11, 2005), Div. B §106 eliminated habeas corpus review, mandamus and All Writs Act jurisdiction in the district court regarding "an order of removal entered or issued under any provision of this Act." INA §242(a)(5). However, to avoid the constitutional problem that would arise by the elimination of all review, the REAL ID Act preserves, in the court of appeals, constitutional claims and questions of law in a petition for review notwithstanding preclusion provisions under §242. INA §242(a)(2)(D). *Ghahremani v. Gonzales*, 498 F.3d 993, 998-99 (9th Cir. 2007) [followed *Ramadan* in equitable tolling case regarding factual issue concerning due diligence]; *Ramadan v. Gonzales,* 479 F.3d 646, 648–54 (9th Cir. 2007), *reh'g en banc denied* 504 F.3d 973 (2007) [questions of law includes not only pure issues of statutory interpretation but mixed questions of law and fact where the court is applying undisputed facts to statutory and regulatory questions and therefore the court can review the issue of the failure to file asylum within one year due to "changed circumstances"]; *Nakimbugwe v. Gonzales,* 475 F.3d 281 (5th Cir. 2007) [court found there was jurisdiction to reverse IJ's determination that one year asylum bar applied where person mailed application within the one year but EOIR did not received it until after the year]; *Chen v. U.S. DOJ,* 471 F.3d 315, 323–32 (2d Cir. 2006) [finding that "questions of law" should be read, consistent with the legislative history at H.R. Rep. No. 109-72 at 175, 2005 U.S.C.C.A.N. at 300, to include "those issues that were historically reviewable in habeas"]; *Diallo v. Gonzales,* 447 F.3d 1274, 1281–82 (10th Cir. 2006) [in the case of a asylee whose status was revoked there was jurisdiction to interpret that the one year period to apply for asylum should run from the time of revocation and not last entry; cited legislative history of REAL ID Act for proposition that constitutional and statutory issues historically reviewable in habeas are covered]; *Jean v. Gonzales,* 435 F.3d 475, 480–81 (4th Cir. 2005) [whether respondent was precluded from establishing good moral character under INA §212(h) was a legal issue that was reviewable notwithstanding the bar under INA §242(a)(2)(B)]; *Cabrera-Alvarez v. Gonzales,* 423 F.3d 1006, 1009 (9th Cir. 2005) [whether the BIA interpreted the exceptional and extremely unusual hardship provision of cancellation consistent with international law is a legal question reviewable under INA §242(a)(2)(D)]; *Kamara v. Att'y Gen. of the U.S.,* 420 F.3d 202, 210–11 (3d Cir. 2005) [the court reviews pure questions of law and issues regarding the application of law to fact, and found that the BIA applied the wrong quantum of proof required for a CAT claim]; *Ramos v. Gonzales,* 414 F.3d 800, 802–04 (7th Cir. 2005) [Congress added §242(a)(2)(D) to consider all constitutional and statutory claims in review of a final order even if otherwise barred by INA §242(a)(2)(C)]; *Papageorgiou v. Gonzales,* 413 F.3d 356, 357–58 (3d Cir. 2005) [Section 242(a)(2)(D) restores jurisdiction to the circuit court for persons who previously were barred from such review under 242(a)(2)(C) because of criminal convictions and makes the restoration retroactive by applying it to any order issued before, on or after May 11, 2005]; *Fernandez-Ruiz v. Gonzales,* 468 F.3d 1159, 1163 (9th Cir. 2006) [same]. But INA §242(a)(2)(D) may not overcome the bar to review only final orders of removal. *Hamilton v. Gonzales,* 485 F.3d 564 (10th Cir. 2007) [revocation of I-130/adoption petition that was affirmed by BIA is not reviewable in circuit court because it is not part of a final order, the APA is not an independent jurisdictional ground, and it is precluded by INA §242(a)(2)(B)]. Or the bar to the review of factual or discretionary matters. *Barco-Sandoval v. Gonzales,* 516 F.3d 35 (2d Cir. 2008) [finding that *Chen v. U.S. DOJ,* 471 F.3d 315 did not alter *De La Vega* where respondent's claim that the wrong legal standard was applied was not colorable and merely sought to address a factual question as to extreme hardship under cancellation]; *Pepaj v. Mukasey,* 509 F.3d 725, 727–28 (6th Cir. 2007) [followed *Almuhtaseb* and held no review for abuse of discretion regarding solely factual questions in denying motion to reopen for changed country conditions]; *Almuhtaseb v. Gonzales,* 453 F.3d 743, 746–49 (6th Cir. 2006) [in the review of the bar to filing asylum beyond one year, the court narrowly construed constitutional questions as only claims brought pursuant to a specific provision of the constitution and narrowly construed statutory questions as those regarding the construction of a statute; the court declined to consider factual questions regarding the changed circumstances exception to the one year filing deadline]; *Boakai v. Gonzales,* 447 F.3d 1 (1st Cir. 2006) [the BIA's determination that the petitioner did not act with due diligence to support equitable tolling for an ineffective assistance of counsel claim is a nonreviewable factual question]; *Martinez v. U.S. Att'y Gen.*, 446 F.3d 1219 (11th Cir. 2006) [INA §242(a)(2)(D) does not restore jurisdiction to review exceptional and extremely unusual hardship]; *Sukwanputra v. Gonzales,* 434 F.3d 627, 633–35 (3d Cir. 2006) [changed circumstances affecting one year deadline for filing asylum is not reviewable under INA §242(a)(2)(D) because it does not raise a statutory or constitutional claim]; *De La Vega v. Gonzales,* 436 F.3d 141 (2d Cir. 2006) [INA §242(a)(2)(D) did not extend jurisdiction to review the denial of cancellation based upon exceptional and extremely unusual hardship which review is barred by INA §242(a)(2)(B)(i)]; *Higuit v. Gonzales,* 433 F.3d 417, 419–20 (4th Cir. 2006) [court lacked jurisdiction to review the discretionary decision to deny adjustment of status to a person involved in the persecution of others]; *Mehilli v. Gonzales,* 433 F.3d 86, 92–94 (1st Cir. 2005) [followed *Vasile* and other circuits in a *post*–REAL ID Act case and determined that issues regarding untimeliness in filing an asylum claim were factual and discretionary and therefore could not be reviewed in the court of appeals under INA §242(a)(2)(D)]; *Chacon-Botero v. U.S. Att'y Gen.*, 427 F.3d 954, 957 (11th Cir. 2005) [followed *Vasile* and found that the issue of timely filing an asylum claim was not reviewable because it was not a constitutional claim or question of law covered under INA §242(a)(2)(D)]; *Hamid v. Gonzales,* 417 F.3d 642, 647 (7th Cir. 2005) [because respondent is an aggravated felon the court declined to consider whether the IJ's factual conclusions in the denial of a CAT claim are supported by substantial evidence because such challenge fails to raise either a constitutional or statutory claim under INA §242(a)(2)(D)]; *Vasile v. Gonzales,* 417 F.3d 766, 768 (7th Cir. 2005) [REAL ID Act of 2005 under 8 U.S.C. §1252(a)(2)(D) allowing for constitutional and statutory claims did not alter the bar to the review of the failure to file within one year or that there were no extraordinary circumstances permitting review because these are factual and discretionary issues]. *But see Ibarra-Flores v. Gonzales,* 439 F.3d 614, 618 (9th Cir. 2006) [reviewed for substantial evidence IJ's nondiscretionary factual determination that respondent was ineligible for cancellation because he was given VD].

At least one court has found that the elimination of habeas corpus review in the district court does not violate the Supremacy Clause *Alexandere v. U.S. Att'y Gen.*, 452 F.3d 1204, 1205–07 (11th Cir. 2006) [Supremacy Clause not violated because constitutional and statutory review that existed in habeas still preserved in the courts of appeal provides an adequate and effective remedy to the elimination of habeas in the district court].

The REAL ID Act also does not bar review in the district court of a matter that is not considered the review of a removal order. *See Singh v. Gonzales,* 499 F.3d 969, 976–81 (9th Cir. 2007) [claim that ineffective assistance of counsel resulted in failure to file a timely appeal to the circuit court was not a review of a final order and district court jurisdiction was not precluded by INA §§242(a)(5) & (b)(9)]; *Ikenokwalu-White v. Gonzales,* 495 F.3d 919, 924–26 (8th Cir. 2007) [review of revocation of I-130, despite it potentially affecting mother's removal, was not part of a removal order and the case had to be pursued in the district, not circuit, court]; *Nnadika v. Att'y Gen. of the U.S.,* 484 F.3d 626 (3d Cir. 2007) [court of appeals remanded to the district court a claim for injunctive and declaratory relief seeking review of a denied I-730 because it was not a final order for purposes of INA §242 review]; *Fonseca-Sanchez v. Gonzales,* 484 F.3d 439 (7th Cir. 2007) [where respondent sought review of a U visa denial that arose subsequent to a final administrative removal order, the court lacked jurisdiction under INA §242 and the proper remedy was habeas]; *Sandher v. Gonzales,* 481 F.3d 108 (2d Cir. 2007) [court dismissed habeas that was transferred to it improperly under REAL ID Act where habeas only challenged the validity of petitioner's conviction and not his removal order]; *Madu v. U.S. Att'y Gen.,* 470 F.3d 1362, 1366–67 (11th Cir. 2006) [where respondent claims he voluntarily departed and reentered, and therefore does not have a removal order, habeas was appropriate and circuit court dismissed and remanded it to district court]; *Kumarasamy v. Att'y Gen. of the U.S.,* 453 F.3d 169, 172 (3d Cir. 2006) [a person who claims his deportation was illegal because there was no order of removal is not barred by the REAL ID Act from bringing a habeas petition]; *Khouzam v. Hogan,* 497 F.Supp.2d 615, 623 (M.D. Pa. 2007) [denied motion to dismiss habeas where petitioner's deferral of removal under CAT was revoked by DHS].

In addition to the REAL ID Act of 2005, the courts of appeal did not previously bar, in a petition for review, constitutional claims even where there were preclusion provisions. *Moore v. Ashcroft,* 251 F.3d 919, 923–24 (11th Cir. 2001) [claim that INA §212(h) violated equal protection was reviewable in appellate court]; *Singh v. Reno,* 182 F.3d 504 (7th Cir. 1999) [claim that INS improperly delayed a deportation hearing in violation of due process may still be raised in the Court of Appeals]. *Tefel v. Reno,* 972 F.Supp. 608, 612–17 (S.D. Fla. 1997) *rev'd on other grounds Tefel v. Reno,* 180 F.3d 1286 (11th Cir. 1999), *cert. denied,* 120 S.Ct. 2657 (2000). Review in the court of appeals on a petition for review also remains to determine whether the person removed is an alien and whether s/he is deportable on the specific criminal grounds raised, *Moore v. Ashcroft,* 251 F.3d 919, 923–25 (11th Cir. 2001); *Coronado-Durazo v. INS,* 123 F.3d 1322 (9th Cir. 1997); *Choeum v. INS,* 129 F.3d 29 (1st Cir. 1997); *Anwar v. INS,* 116 F.3d 140 (5th Cir. 1997); *Yang v. INS,* 109 F.3d 1185 (7th Cir. 1997), *cert. denied sub nom. Katsoulis v. INS,* 522 U.S. 1027 (1997).

In addition to the provisions insulating federal agencies from judicial review, IIRIRA and the REAL ID Act of 2005 also substantially altered the procedures concerning review. Automatic stays of deportation orders are removed. INA §242(b)(3)(B), 8 U.S.C. §1252(b)(3)(B). Venue is restricted to the court of appeals for the judicial circuit where the immigration judge completed the proceedings, thereby eliminating the right to appeal in the circuit where the respondent resides. INA §242(b)(2), 8 U.S.C. §1252(b)(2). *Georcely v. Ashcroft,* 375 F.3d 45, 47–49 (1st Cir. 2004) [discussing the complexity of venue questions where the hearing is in the Virgin Islands which is governed by the 3d circuit but the court for the Virgin Islands is in Puerto Rico which is governed by the 1st circuit]. The standard and scope of review are substantially narrowed and administrative findings of fact are conclusive "unless any reasonable adjudicator would be compelled to conclude to the contrary." INA §242(b)(4)(B), 8 U.S.C. §1252(b)(4)(B); *Dia v. Ashcroft,* 353 F.3d 228, 248 (3d Cir. 2003) (*en banc*) [finding that 242(b)(4)(B) codified *Elias-Zacarias* thereby maintaining the traditional substantial evidence standard]; *Castellano-Chacon v. INS,* 341 F.3d 533, 551–52 (6th Cir. 2003) [upheld denial of CAT claim under §1252(b)(4) because decision was not "manifestly contrary to the law"]; *Fahim v. U.S. Att'y Gen.,* 278 F.3d 1216, 1218 (11th Cir. 2002) [affirmed BIA's denial of withholding and CAT claim following *Elias-Zacarias* and INA §§242(b)(4)(A)–(B)]. And this narrow standard of review under the REAL ID Act §101(e) is applied to the decision to require corroborative evidence. In addition, procedures for review are more expedited and more restrictive than former provisions. INA §242(b)–(d), 8 U.S.C. §1252(b)–(d).

The major statutory sources for judicial review of actions in the immigration field that remain are found at INA §242, habeas corpus jurisdiction pursuant to 28 U.S.C. §2241 for detention decisions, and mandamus jurisdiction under 28 U.S.C. §1361 for nonremoval issues. Although the Administrative Procedure Act, 5 U.S.C. §702, is a separate source of judicial review of certain aspects of the immigration agency's actions (*i.e.,* denial of an I-129 petition for H-1B/L-1, etc.), it is not a separate source of general jurisdiction. *Califano v. Sanders,* 430 U.S. 99 (1977). An aggrieved party must allege an independent jurisdictional basis in federal court such as federal question jurisdiction, 28 U.S.C. §1331.

II. INA §242 REVIEW

A. ***Review is Limited to Review of Final Orders of Removal***—INA §242(a)–(b), 8 U.S.C. §§1252(a)–(b) and 1101(a)(47)(B). The prior section, INA §106, has been repealed in its entirety. IIRIRA §306(b). The legislative history of INA §242 is found at H.R. Conf. Rep. 828, 104th Cong. 2d Sess. at 219–21 (1996). The legislative history of former INA §106 may be found in H.R. Rep. No. 1086, 87th Cong. 1st Sess. (1961); U.S.C.C.A.N. 2950, 2967. Review under INA §242(a), (b) is the review of a final order of the Board of Immigration Appeals. The term "final order" now includes not only the final orders of immigration judges, but orders of administrative officers who have been delegated the responsibility for determining whether the person is deportable (*e.g.,* summary removal for nonresident aggravated felons, visa waiver program removal). It also includes orders in which an IJ merely determines that an person is removable and issues a contingent order of removal as in voluntary departure. *Thapa v. Gonzales,* 460 F.3d 323, 332–34 (2d Cir. 2006) [a voluntary departure order with an alternate order of removal is a "final order" under 8 U.S.C. §1101(a)(47)(B) and the DHS interpretation of 8 C.F.R. §1241.1(f) as not including VD in a final order is inconsistent with the statute]; *Obale v. Att'y Gen. of the U.S.,* 453 F.3d 151, 157–60 (3d Cir. 2006) [same]. It also includes reinstated orders under INA §241(a)(5). *Castro-Cortez v. INS,* 239 F.3d 1037, 1043–47 (9th Cir. 2001). However, there may be circumstances were there is an insufficient record to review requiring remand. *Rafaelano v. Wilson,* 471 F.3d 1091 (9th Cir. 2006) [treating habeas as a petition for review pursuant to REAL ID Act but remanding the case to the BIA for a factual record]. An order becomes final upon a determination by the BIA or where the time lapsed to seek review with the BIA. INA §101(a)(47), 8 U.S.C. §1101(a)(47). If an action is part of a final order of review, the district court is now clearly barred from reviewing the action as only review in the courts of appeals is permitted. INA §242(a)(5), 8 U.S.C. §1252(a)(5) ["Notwithstanding any other provision of law (statutory or nonstatutory), including [habeas, mandamus, and All Writs Act]...a petition for review filed with an appropriate court of appeals...shall be the sole and exclusive means for juridical review of an order of removal entered or issued under any provision of this Act...].

Remands May Not be Final Orders—A remand is generally not considered a final order but may encompass matters that are final orders. *See in this chapter* "Remands Unnecessary," ¶ VI.M.2 (p.1198), *infra*.

B. However, where the action is not encompassed within a final order, the circuit court lacks jurisdiction and district court review under the APA or habeas may be the only remedy. *Singh v. Gonzales,* 499 F.3d 969, 976–81 (9th Cir. 2007) [claim that ineffective assistance of counsel resulted in failure to file a timely appeal to the circuit court was not a review of a final order and district court jurisdiction was not precluded by INA §§242(a)(5) & (b)(9)]; *Ikenokwalu-White v. Gonzales,* 495 F.3d 919, 924–26 (8th Cir. 2007) [review of revocation of I-130, despite it potentially affecting mother's removal, was not part of a removal order and the case had to be pursued in the district, not circuit, court]; *Nnadika v. Att'y Gen. of the U.S.,* 484 F.3d 626 (3d Cir. 2007) [court of appeals remanded to the district court a claim for injunctive and declaratory relief seeking review of a denied I-730 because it was not a final order for purposes of INA §242 review]; *Fonseca-Sanchez v. Gonzales,* 484 F.3d 439 (7th Cir. 2007) [where respondent sought review of a U visa denial that arose subsequent to a final administrative removal order, the court lacked jurisdiction under INA §242 because the U visa denial was not part of a final order and the proper remedy was to seek relief in district court].

C. ***Statutory Standard Under INA §242(b)(9), 8 U.S.C. §1252(b)(9)***—Congress has determined that all questions of law or fact "arising from any action taken or proceeding brought to remove" a person from the U.S. is available only through the review of a final order in the court of appeals. It is unclear whether this provision effects *INS v. Chadha*, 462 U.S. 919, 937–39 (1983) and the interpretation of what constitutes a final order. However, the Supreme Court in addressing the reach of INA §242(g) in *Reno v. American-Arab Anti-Discrimination Committee,* 119 S.Ct. 936, 943 (1999) took the opportunity to address this question. It described this provision as a "zipper" clause "that those specified decisions and actions, which...some courts had held *not* to be included within the non–final-order review prohibition of §1105a, *are* covered by the 'zipper' clause of §1252(b)(9)." The broad reach of the "zipper clause" in defining what questions are encompassed within a final order of removal may now affect habeas corpus jurisdiction for ancillary matters that might be included with INA §242. The REAL ID Act of 2005 has precluded habeas review, mandamus and All Writs Act jurisdiction for all matters encompassed with INA §242, including INA §242(b)(9) and legal questions, such as those raised in *INS v. St. Cyr,* 533 U.S. 289, 313–15, 121 S.Ct. 2271, 2285–87 (2001), may now only be raised in a petition for review. Although *St. Cyr* held that judicial review and habeas review "have historically distinct meanings" and that INA §242(b)(9) "simply provides for the consolidation of issues to be brought in petitions for judicial review," the passage of the REAL ID Act of 2005 precludes a statutory habeas claim, although it may not preclude a claim based upon the Suspension Clause. Prior to The REAL ID Act of 2005 other courts followed *St. Cyr, see Saint Fort v. Ashcroft,* 329 F.3d 191, 201 (1st Cir. 2003) [judicial review and habeas review are distinct processes]; *Lopez-Ruiz v. Ashcroft,* 298 F.3d 886 (9th Cir. 2002) [court may entertain review of any ground which was raised before the BIA originally or on reopening]; *Bejacmar v. Ashcroft,* 291 F.3d 735 (11th Cir. 2002) [abandoning its reasoning in *Richardson v. Reno* and finding that "*St. Cyr* removes the last statutory pillar supporting our circuit's earlier conclusion that IIRIRA repealed district court jurisdiction in habeas cases."]; *Al Jabari v. Chertoff,* 536 F.Supp.2d 1029 (D. Minn. 2008) [In action to compel DHS to complete the security check involving the grant by an IJ of a marriage hardship waiver to lift conditional residence under 8 U.S.C. §1186a(c)(4), the court determined that the APA permitted injunctive relief and was not barred by INA §242(b)(9) because it only applies to review of orders of removal]; *But see De La Teja v. U.S.,* 321 F.3d 1357, 1365–66 (11th Cir. 2003) [under INA §242(b)(9) the district court could not hear challenge to removal proceeding prior to final order]. One court has also rejected the legal argument that INA §242(b)(9) expands jurisdiction to include all questions of law and fact including ones barred by other jurisdiction limiting provisions. *Leyva v. Ashcroft,* 380 F.3d 303, 306–07 (7th Cir. 2004) [rejected claim that notwithstanding the limitation on review of cancellation under §242(a)(2)(B)(i), the court could hear law and fact claims under §242(b)(9)]. And notwithstanding the REAL ID Act removal of habeas jurisdiction, §242(b)(9) does not bar habeas where the applicant contends there is no removal order. *Singh v. Gonzales,* 499 F.3d 969, 976–81 (9th Cir. 2007) [claim that ineffective assistance of counsel resulted in failure to file a timely appeal to the circuit court was not a review of a final order and district court jurisdiction was not precluded by INA §§242(a)(5) & (b)(9)]; *Madu v. U.S. Att'y Gen.,* 470 F.3d 1362, 1367 (11th Cir. 2006) [where respondent claims he voluntarily departed and reentered, and therefore does not have a removal order, §242(b)(9) did not bar habeas review because it only applies with respect to an order of removal].

D. ***Pre-IIRIRA Definition of Final Order***—Prior to IIRIRA and INA §242(b)(9), the determination of what actions were final orders spawned substantial litigation. The scope of matters included within the meaning of a "final order" prior to IIRIRA included "all determinations made during and incident to the administrative proceeding." *Foti v. INS*, 375 U.S. 217, 229 (1963); *Cheng Fan Kwok v. INS*, 392 U.S. 206 (1968). Under this standard, stays of deportation were not reviewable in the courts of appeal because they were not made "during" or "incident to" the deportation hearing. *Mapoy v. Carroll,* 185 F.3d 224, 230 (4th Cir. 1999) [post-IIRIRA finding that request for a stay was not reviewable under INA §242, but INA §242(g) precluded district court review because the request for a stay involved the "execution" of a final order]; *Cheng Fan Kwok, supra*; *Akrap v. INS*, 966 F.2d 267, 270 (7th Cir. 1992) [denial of stay by BIA is not reviewable in circuit court]; *Vlassis v. INS*, 963 F.2d 547 (2d Cir. 1992) [same]; *Reynolds v. INS*, 846 F.2d 1288 (11th Cir. 1988) [same]; *Reid v. INS*, 766 F.2d 113 (3d Cir. 1985) [same]; *Abedi-Tajrishi v. INS*, 752 F.2d 441 (9th Cir. 1985); *Gando-Coello v. INS*, 857 F.2d 25, 26 (1st Cir. 1988) [and cases cited therein]. Distinctions were made between the denial of a stay by an IJ and the BIA on the one hand, and the denial of stay by a DD on the other. *Dibi v. Moyer*, 801 F.Supp. 214 (E.D. Wis. 1992); *Saleh v. Meese*, 669 F.Supp. 885 (N.D. Ill. 1987) [denial by IJ and BIA of stay is within exclusive jurisdiction of circuit court but only after ruling on denial of motion to reopen. There is district court jurisdiction, however, over a denial of a stay by the DD]; *Garay v. Slattery*, 23 F.3d 744 (2d Cir. 1994) [review of IJ denial of stay only available in circuit court in context of motion to reopen]. *But see Butros v. INS*, 804 F.Supp. 1336, 1339 (D. Or. 1991) [district court has jurisdiction over both]; *Lemos-Garcia v. Weiss*, 797 F.Supp. 126, 128–29 (D. Conn. 1991) [where denial of stay by BIA and IJ raise identical issues, district court has jurisdiction over BIA's denial].

Motions to reopen, *Giova v. Rosenberg*, 379 U.S. 18 (1964) (*per curiam*); *Jahjaga v. Att'y Gen. of the U.S.*, 512 F.3d 80, 82 (3d Cir. 2008) [denial of motion to reopen is a final order]; *Maynard v. INS*, 129 F.3d 438 (8th Cir. 1997); *Williams v. INS*, 795 F.2d 738 (9th Cir. 1986) [motion to reopen to reinstate voluntary departure is within the term "final order"], and requests for relief from deportation, such as suspension, *Foti, supra*; *Sbeih v. EOIR*, 982 F.Supp. 596 (N.D. Ill. 1997) [same], and asylum, *Perkovic v. INS*, 33 F.3d 615, 618–20 (6th Cir. 1994) [appeal of BIA reversal of grant of asylum], were considered to be within the meaning of a final order and were reviewable in the circuit courts of appeal.

E. *Chadha*—In *INS v. Chadha*, 462 U.S. 919, 937–39 (1983), the Supreme Court determined that a final order includes, "all matters in which the validity of the final order is contingent rather than only those determinations actually made at a hearing." The lower courts have treated the *Chadha* language in different ways. The most detailed analysis has come from the Sixth Circuit in *Ghaelian v. INS*, 717 F.2d 950 (6th Cir. 1983). The court interpreted *Chadha* as establishing two tests for the "contingency" standard:

- Whether the deportation order can "stand or fall on the validity of the challenged issue"; and
- Whether the relief sought is "plainly inconsistent with the deportation order"

Ghaelian v. INS, 717 F.2d 950, 952 (6th Cir. 1983) [denial of F-1 extension of stay by DD is not within a "final order"].

Applying *Chadha* in other circumstances, the Ninth Circuit has found that there is no jurisdiction to review a denial of an F-1 school transfer under former INA §106(a). *Mohammadi-Motlagh v. INS*, 727 F.2d 1450 (9th Cir. 1984). In more recent applications of *Chadha*, the First Circuit found that legalization decisions are matters over which the validity of the final order is contingent, *Ruginski v. INS*, 942 F.2d 13, 15–16 (1st Cir. 1991), and the Third Circuit concluded that a challenge to the standard applied to Chinese sterilization cases in *Matter of Chaig* is part of a final order of exclusion, thereby precluding separate review. *Yi v. Maugans*, 24 F.3d 500, 505 (3d Cir. 1994). *But see Gottesman v. INS*, 33 F.3d 383 (4th Cir. 1994) [finding that a DD decision rescinding LPR status was not part of final order under *Chadha*].

F. *District Director Decisions*—The vast majority of courts prior to IIRIRA recognized that unless the issue was specifically encompassed within a final order, no jurisdiction existed in the circuit courts of appeal. Thus, decisions by the DD regarding denials of stays of deportation, extensions of stay, or adjustment of status are not contemplated within the meaning of a final order. *Ikenokwalu-White v. Gonzales*, 495 F.3d 919, 924–26 (8th Cir. 2007) [post-IIRIRA, review of revocation of I-130, despite it potentially affecting mother's removal, was not part of a removal order and the case had to be pursued in the district, not circuit, court]; *Fatehi v. INS*, 729 F.2d 1086 (6th Cir. 1984) [the court of appeals lacked jurisdiction to review the DD's decision to deny an extension of stay]; *Che-Li Shen v. INS*, 749 F.2d 1469 (10th Cir. 1984) [no jurisdiction under former INA §106 to review a denial by the DD of adjustment of status]; *Shahla v. INS*, 749 F.2d 561 (9th Cir. 1984) [neither INS requirement that NIV student has permission to transfer schools nor an INS decision to press deportation charges is final reviewable order under former INA §106]; *Kavasji v. INS*, 675 F.2d 236 (7th Cir. 1982) [no jurisdiction over DD denial of extension of stay]. Courts have also found no jurisdiction to review denials of visa petitions, *Elbez v. INS*, 767 F.2d 1313 (9th Cir. 1985); *De Figueroa v. INS*, 501 F.2d 191, 194 (7th Cir. 1974), waivers, *Ibrahim v. INS*, 821 F.2d 1547 (11th Cir. 1987) [no jurisdiction to review denial of

INA §212(e) application], or denials of work authorization, even where unlawful employment is the basis of the deportation charge. *Olaniyan v. District Director*, 796 F.2d 373 (10th Cir. 1986). Circuit courts also lacked jurisdiction to review bond determinations, *Young v. DOJ*, 759 F.2d 450 (5th Cir.), *cert. denied,* 474 U.S. 996 (1985), or to review refusal to permit paroled alien to seek suspension of deportation at exclusion hearing. *Delgado-Carrera v. INS*, 773 F.2d 629 (5th Cir. 1985). Similarly, the courts of appeal may not have jurisdiction over the decision of the DD to review rescission orders. *Gottesman v. INS*, 33 F.3d 383 (4th Cir. 1994); *Kuh v. INS*, 758 F.2d 370 (9th Cir. 1985); *Bachelier v. INS*, 548 F.2d 1157 (5th Cir. 1977). However, once there is a final order, court can review rescission. *Bachelier v. INS*, 625 F.2d 902 (9th Cir. 1980). *But see Gottesman, supra.*

G. *Pendent Review*—Under former INA §106, courts recognized that in certain circumstances there may be review of collateral determinations which are pendent to claims that can be reviewed. *Adame-Hernandez v. INS*, 769 F.2d 1387, 1388 (9th Cir. 1985) [circuit court can review selective prosecution claim if reviewing deportation order]; *Mahammadi-Motlagh v. INS, supra*; *Wall v. INS*, 722 F.2d 1442 (9th Cir. 1984). Pendent jurisdiction will be applied only if the action or decision at issue underlies the deportation order, if there is a factual record to decide the question and if it involves a purely legal question. *Abedi-Tajrishi v. INS*, 752 F.2d 441, 443–44 (9th Cir. 1985). Pendent review may also exist in other contexts, including review of issues "inextricably intertwined" with the issue appealed, such as whether there is a constitutional or statutory basis for a *Bivens* action when the government has appealed the denial of qualified immunity. *Kwai Fun Wong v. U.S.*, 373 F.3d 952, 960–66 (9th Cir. 2004) [*Bivens* action by religious figure claiming unconstitutional and RFRA violations].

III. OTHER JURISDICTIONAL BASES

A. *Federal Question, 28 U.S.C. §1331 Review*

1. The fact that no jurisdiction may exist under INA §242 does not mean that no action can be brought at all. If the action does not directly challenge the validity of a final order, is not required to be channeled to the court of appeals through INA §§242(a)(5) or (b)(9), is not otherwise precluded from review by one of the preclusion statutes noted above, or if the preclusion of such action would raise serious constitutional questions, *McNary v. Haitian Refugee Center, Inc.*, 498 U.S. 479 (1991); *Webster v. Doe*, 486 U.S. 592 (1988); *Pinho v. Gonzales,* 432 F.3d 193, 200–04 (3d Cir. 2005) [neither INA §242(a)(2)(B), nor principles of exhaustion, barred the district court under the APA from reviewing a legal determination as to whether a person with a substantive vacated conviction could adjust status]; *Succar v. Ashcroft,* 394 F.3d 8, 19–20 (1st Cir. 2005) [there is §1331 jurisdiction because respondent's challenge regarding AOS is to the invalidity of a DHS regulation as contrary to the statute and it is therefore not a discretionary decision barred under INA §242(a)(2)(B)(i) but a pure legal question];*Wang v. Reno*, 81 F.3d 808 (9th Cir. 1996), jurisdiction may continue to exist under federal question jurisdiction, 28 U.S.C. §1331. *Soneji v. DHS,* 525 F.Supp.2d 1151 (N.D. Cal. 2007) [court denied motion to dismiss action under §1331 pursuant to section 555(b) of the APA and mandamus to compel DHS to adjudicate an AOS application pending for 38 months]; *Kim v. Ashcroft,* 340 F.Supp.2d 384 (S.D.N.Y. 2004) [same 42 months]; *M.B. v. Quarantillo,* 301 F.3d 109, 111–14 (3d Cir. 2002) [APA review of DD's decision regarding special immigrant juvenile status]; *Sabhari v. Reno,* 197 F.3d 938, 941–43 (8th Cir. 1999) [post-IIRIRA, neither §242(g) nor the change in §1329 barred jurisdiction under §1331 to review the denial of an I-130 or adjustment of status application]; *Martinez v. DHS,* 502 F.Supp.2d 631, 634–36 (E.D. Mich. 2007) [followed *Pinho v. Gonzales* and held that INA §242(a)(2)(B)(1) nor principles of exhaustion barred a district court under the APA from reviewing whether a petitioner qualified for the benefits of CSPA when he was denied adjustment]; *Singh v. Still*, 470 F.Supp.2d 1064 (N.D. Cal. 2007) [where asylum AOS has been pending seven years and marriage AOS for four, mandamus or APA/1331 was appropriate to compel decision]; *Calexico Warehouse, Inc. v. Neufeld,* 259 F.Supp.2d 1067, 1072–75 (S.D. Cal. 2002) [jurisdiction under §1331 remains to review revocation of L-1 petition because 242(a)(2)(B) may only apply to matters in removal proceedings]; *Bartolini v. Ashcroft,* 226 F.Supp.2d 350 (D. Conn. 2002) [jurisdiction under §1331 exists to review claim under §555(b) of the APA that INS unlawfully delayed adjudication of adjustment of status application; court found gov't conduct reasonable]; *Nair v. Coultice,* 162 F.Supp.2d 1209 (S.D. Cal. 2001) [jurisdiction under §1331 to challenge INS's erroneous interpretation that time spent out of U.S. counts toward 6-year H-1B bar]; *Mart v. Beebe,*

94 F.Supp.2d 1120 (D. Or. 2000) [district court had jurisdiction over denial of adjustment and INA §242(a)(2)(B) only precluded judicial review of adjustment applications in removal proceedings]. Under the former statutory scheme, matters such as a denial of an extension of stay, denial of a labor certification, denial of visa petition, and denial of an extension of voluntary departure, could be challenged independently in federal court under the APA and by virtue of federal question jurisdiction, 28 U.S.C. §1331. *Ortiz v. Meissner,* 179 F.3d 718 (9th Cir. 1999) [jurisdiction under §1331 remained to review denial of employment authorization to persons appealing legalization denials]; *Baria v. Reno*, 94 F.3d 1335, 1337–40 (9th Cir. 1996) [review permissible in district court of BIA's rescission order under former §1329 while deportation proceedings are pending and before final order of deportation entered]; *Salehi v. District Director*, 796 F.2d 1286 (10th Cir. 1986) [jurisdiction under 28 U.S.C. §1331 to review challenge to procedures on motion to reopen asylum claims and DD's denial of a stay where not attacking deportation order]; *Jaa v. INS*, 779 F.2d 569 (9th Cir. 1986) [DD's denial of adjustment of status subject to district court review]; *Karmali v. INS*, 707 F.2d 408 (9th Cir. 1983) [review of NIV petition]; *Shanti, Inc. v. Reno,* 36 F.Supp.2d 1151, 1157–61 (D. Minn. 1999) [post-IIRIRA finding jurisdiction under §1331 remains to review denial of H-1B petition]; *Velazquez v. INS*, 876 F.Supp. 1071, 1075 (D. Minn. 1995) [DD denial of hardship waiver for conditional resident, like denial of adjustment, is reviewable separately]; *Ijoma v. INS*, 854 F.Supp. 612 (D. Neb. 1993) [DD denial of adjustment not part of final deportation order and reviewable in district court]; *Carrillo v. Mohrman*, 832 F.Supp. 1412, 1415–16 (D. Idaho 1989) [DD refusal to extend V.D. is reviewable]; *Erbas v. Parra*, 1988 WL 22815 (S.D. Tex. Mar. 8, 1988) [review of denial of adjustment of status because of alleged unauthorized employment]; *Gurbisz v. INS*, 675 F.Supp. 436 (N.D. Ill. 1987) [review of denial of EVD to Polish nationals]; *Ali v. INS*, 661 F.Supp. 1234 (D. Mass. 1986) [review of INS procedures for marriage petitions]; *Chung v. INS*, 662 F.Supp. 474 (W.D. Wash. 1987) [remand where INS denied extension of stay to E-2]; *Giraldo-Hernandez v. INS*, 1989 WL 39684 (S.D.N.Y. Apr. 12, 1989); WSB ¶13, 101.94 [INS abused discretion in denying stay where the denial would have resulted in foreclosing judicial review]; *Anyanwu v. INS*, 645 F.Supp. 266 (D.N.J. 1986) [granting stay pending motion to reopen]; *Lopez-Alegria v. Ilchert*, 632 F.Supp. 932 (N.D. Cal. 1986) [granting stay of deportation to provide alien review of motion to reopen before BIA]; *Villegas v. O'Neill*, 626 F.Supp. 1241 (S.D. Tex. 1986) [review of denial of stay in District Court]; *Emmanuel v. INS*, 579 F.Supp. 1541 (D.C.V.I. 1984) [same]; *Padula v. INS*, 537 F.Supp. 563 (D. Conn. 1982); *Piper v. Crosland*, 519 F.Supp. 962 (E.D.N.Y. 1981).

The fact that a legal challenge under §1331 may be by aliens outside of the U.S. does not necessarily bar the claim. The Supreme Court's decision in *Rasul v. Bush,* 542 U.S. 466 (2004) may have dramatically altered the right to bring such actions on behalf of persons outside of the U.S. In *Rasul,* the Court found that there was habeas jurisdiction to review the physical custody of aliens being held at the military base in Guantanamo, Cuba. The Court distinguished *Johnson v. Eisentrager,* found that habeas applies extraterritorially to aliens, that aliens like U.S. citizens can invoke federal court authority, and that the presence of the detainee in the territorial jurisdiction of a federal court is not a jurisdictional requirement for habeas as long as there is jurisdiction over the custodian. The Court also found that jurisdiction existed under 28 U.S.C. §1331 (General Federal Question jurisdiction) and §1350 (Alien Tort Claims Act) for aliens outside the U.S. and noted that: "The courts of the United States have traditionally been open to nonresident aliens." *Rasul,* 124 S.Ct. at 2698–99. *See also Abu Ali v. Ashcroft,* 350 F.Supp.2d 28, 39–57 (D.D.C. 2004) [denied motion to dismiss habeas petition brought by a U.S. citizen being held in Saudi Arabia at the direction of the U.S.].

2. In addition, under prior and current law, even if there are matters which might be encompassed within a "final order," the courts will allow independent district court action that is not a review of an individual proceeding if the action is not otherwise precluded, where there are allegations of widespread abuses, improper policy determinations by immigration officials, constitutional challenges to regulations or across-the-board procedures that are deficient. *McNary v. Haitian Refugee Center, Inc.*, 498 U.S. 479 (1991) [affirmed pattern and practice challenge to constitutional violations in SAW program, finding that "Because respondent's action does not seek review on the merits of a denial of a particular application, the District Court's general federal question jurisdiction under 28 U.S.C. §1331 to hear the action remains unimpaired"]; *Barahona-Gomez v. Reno,* 236 F.3d 1115 (9th Cir. 2001) [injunctive relief regarding EOIR directive that IJs not adjudicate suspension claims because numerical cap may be reached]; *Ortiz v. Meissner,* 179 F.3d 718 (9th

Cir. 1999) [jurisdiction under §1331 remained to review denial of employment authorization to persons appealing legalization denials because work authorization was collateral to proceeding]; *Walters v. Reno,* 145 F.3d 1032, 1051–53 (9th Cir. 1998), *cert. denied, Reno v. Walters,* 526 U.S. 1003 (1999) [injunction against deportation proceedings where INA §274C notice was inadequate]; *El Rescate Legal Services v. EOIR*, 959 F.2d 742 (9th Cir. 1992) (*on reh'g*) [jurisdiction to hear competency of translators]; *Morales v. Yeutter*, 952 F.2d 954, 956–57 (7th Cir. 1991) [jurisdiction following *McNary* for rule challenge]; *Campos v. Nail*, 940 F.2d 495 (9th Cir. 1991) [jurisdiction to hear challenge to IJ who engaged in pattern of denying change of venue], *reported in* 68 No. 48 *Interpreter Releases* 1848 (Dec. 20, 1991); *Montes v. Thornburgh*, 919 F.2d 531, 537 (9th Cir. 1990) [applying *HRC v. Smith* rationale to EAJA claim involving the actions of a single IJ]; *National Center for Immigrants Rights, Inc. v. INS*, 913 F.2d 1350, 1352 (9th Cir. 1990), *rev'd on other grounds*, 502 U.S. 183 (1991); *Jean v. Nelson*, 727 F.2d 957, 979–81 (11th Cir. 1984) (*en banc*), *aff'd on other grounds*, 472 U.S. 846 (1985) [detention of Haitian nationals]; *Haitian Refugee Center v. Smith*, 676 F.2d 1023, 1033 (5th Cir. 1982) [right to apply for asylum]; *Doe v. Nelson*, 703 F.Supp. 713 (N.D. Ill. 1988) [legalization regulation]; *Orantes-Hernandez v. Meese*, 685 F.Supp. 1488 (C.D. Cal. 1988), *aff'd*, 919 F.2d 549 (9th Cir. 1990). *Campos v. INS,* 32 F.Supp.2d 1337, 1341–42 (S.D. Fla. 1999) [challenging naturalization practices post-IIRIRA]. *But see Reno v. Catholic Social Services,* 509 U.S. 43 (1993) [a challenge to the application of a regulation was not ripe for review as the application may be denied on other grounds]; *Aguilar v. ICE,* 510 F.3d 1, 6–18 (1st Cir. 2007) [INA §242(b)(9) precluded a pattern and practice class-wide claim challenging ICE raids that resulted in detaining and transferring petitioners out of state thus depriving them of counsel]; *Yi v. Maugans*, 24 F.3d 500 (3d Cir. 1994) [Sections 1105a(b) and 1105a(c) preclude nationwide class concerning challenge to *Matter of Chang* as challenge is substantive not collateral or procedural and can be addressed in separate habeas challenges]; *Xiao v. Barr*, 979 F.2d 151 (9th Cir. 1992) [no jurisdiction in district court to hear challenge to IJ jurisdiction to hear exclusion hearing as that may be raised at hearing].

B. *APA Review*

1. The APA governs the review of agency action where a person has suffered a "legal wrong" or has been "adversely affected or aggrieved" by agency action 5 U.S.C. §702. The APA allows challenges to agency action that include agency action that is "arbitrary, capricious, an abuse of discretion, or otherwise not in accordance with law." 5 U.S.C. §706(2)(A). For legislative history concerning §702 and its waiver of sovereign immunity see H.R. Rep. No. 1656, 94th Cong. 2d Sess.1-5 (1976), *reprinted in* 1976 U.S.C.C.A.N. 6121; *Presbyterian Church (USA) v. U.S.*, 870 F.2d 518, 523 (9th Cir. 1989). The agency action must be "final," but this term is liberally construed. *Pinho v. Gonzales,* 432 F.3d 193, 200–04 (3d Cir. 2005) [APA challenge to DHS's denial of adjustment on grounds that vacated conviction for ineffective assistance was nevertheless a conviction was final even if agency might put plaintiff in removal proceedings]; *Hubbard Richard Community Council v. City of Detroit*, 901 F.Supp. 1255, 1259–61 (E.D. Mich. 1995). *But see Transport Robert (1973) Ltée v. INS*, 940 F.Supp. 338 (D.D.C. 1996) [letter from INS Associate Commissioner on issue is not final agency action]. The APA is not a separate ground for jurisdiction in federal court *Califano v. Sanders,* 430 U.S. 99 (1977); *Hamilton v. Gonzales,* 485 F.3d 564, 568–69 (10th Cir. 2007) [the APA is not a separate jurisdictional provision to challenge the revocation of an I-130/adoption petition that is precluded from review by §242(a)(2)(B)]. Although the APA does not apply to deportation hearings, *Ardestani v. INS*, 502 U.S. 129, 112 S.Ct. 515 (1991); *Marcello v. Bonds*, 349 U.S. 302, 305–10 (1955) *reh'g denied* 350 U.S. 856 (1955); *Silveyra v. Moschorak*, 989 F.2d 1012, 1015 (9th Cir. 1993) [APA inapplicable to compel a deportation hearing], it has been used:

1.a. to challenge a variety of actions by DHS, DOS, and DOL, including their failure to properly promulgate regulations, *Air India v. Brien,* 261 F.Supp.2d 134, 140–42 (E.D.N.Y. 2003) [struck down on notice and comment grounds the application of 8 C.F.R. §211.1 resulting in fines to air carriers for the failure of special immigrants to provide proof on re-entry]; *Perez v. Ashcroft,* 236 F.Supp.2d 899 (N.D. Ill. 2002) [refused to give effect to "formal training" requirement for religious occupations because it represents a substantive change not accompanied by notice and comment rule making and not entitled to deference under *Mead*]; *Iyengar v. Barnhart,* 233 F.Supp.2d 5, 13–15 (D.D.C. 2002) [SSA's change in position without notice and comment that no longer permits unauthorized workers to obtain a SSN number is unlawful]; *United Farmworkers of America, AFL-CIO v. Chao,* 227 F.Supp.2d 102 (D.D.C. 2002) [where DOL sought to change the time of year it published its adverse effect wage rate for H-2A workers without prior publication it violated the notice and comment provisions of the APA]; *Dia Navigation Corp. Ltd. v. Pomeroy*, 34 F.3d 1255 (3d Cir. 1994) [INS policy of charging carriers for detention of stowaways seeking asylum violated APA notice and comment provision]; *Kooritzky v. Reich*, 17 F.3d 1509 (D.C. Cir. 1994) [where interim final rule regarding substitution on labor certification was never open for public comment APA was violated]; *DeBraun v. Meissner*, 958 F.Supp. 227 (E.D. Pa. 1997) [improper promulgation of regulation requiring fingerprint companies to be in nonmobile facilities]; *National Ass'n of Manufacturers v. DOL*, 1996 WL 420868 (D.D.C. July 22, 1996) [successful challenge on notice and comment grounds of some DOL regulations regarding labor attestations]; *Louis v. Nelson*, 544 F.Supp. 973 (S.D. Fla. 1982), *aff'd on other grounds*, 105 S.Ct. 2992 (1985) [APA challenge to detention regulations]; *Sannon v. U.S.*, 460 F.Supp. 458 (S.D. Fla. 1978) [violation of notice and comment provisions in publication of asylum regulations]; *but see L.A. Closeout, Inc. v. DHS,* 513 F.3d 940, 942 (9th Cir. 2007) [Pearson memo determining the validity of a c/s from B-2 to H-1B in light of the H-1B cap was an "interpretive" rule regarding 8 C.F.R. §248.1 not requiring notice and comment rulemaking under the APA]; *Martinez-Garcia v. Ashcroft,* 366 F.3d 732, 734–35 (9th Cir. 2004) [Chief IJ's directive that court would not accept any OSCs filed after Mar. 31, 1997 did not require APA rulemaking]; *Public Citizen v. DOS,* 276 F.3d 634, 640–41 (D.C. Cir. 2002) [DOS policy cutting off FOIA response at date request made was a procedural rule not subject to notice and comment]; *Jeanty v. Bulger,* 204 F.Supp.2d 1366, 1382–83 (S.D. Fla. 2002) *aff'd sub nom. Moise v. Bulger,* 321 F.3d 1336 (11th Cir.), *cert denied*, 540 U.S. 1016 (2003) [notice and comment provisions did not apply to decision to deny parole to Haitians seeking asylum because it was general statement of policy]; *R.L. Investment Limited Partners and Wanxuan Zou v. INS*, 86 F.Supp.2d 1014 (D.C. Hawaii 2000), *aff'd* 273 F.3d 874 (9th Cir. 2001) [notice and comment provision of APA inapplicable in investor context where agency simply corrected a "mistake"];

1.b. to challenge INS policies violating the INA. *Pinho v. Gonzales,* 432 F.3d 193, 200–04 (3d Cir. 2005) [the court under the APA could review the legal determination as to whether a person with a substantive vacated conviction for ineffective assistance of counsel could adjust status]; *ILWU v. Meese*, 891 F.2d 1374 (9th Cir. 1989) [union challenged INS policy permitting on-board crane operators to work as alien crewmen]; *Campos v. INS,* 32 F.Supp.2d 1337, 1344–45 (S.D. Fla. 1999) [challenge to INS policies regarding disability waivers in naturalization applications]; *Haitian Centers Council, Inc. v. Sale*, 823 F.Supp. 1028, 1045–49 (E.D.N.Y. 1993) [improper detention of HIV positive asylees]; *Abreu v. U.S.*, 796 F.Supp. 50 (D.R.I. 1992) [failure to provide incarcerated persons a prompt deportation hearing];

1.c. to review agency action for abuse of discretion. *Bangura v. Hansen,* 434 F.3d 487, 500–03 (6th Cir. 2006) [USCIS did not abuse its discretion by denying I-130 petition for marriage fraud]; *Kamara v. Att'y Gen. of the U.S.,* 420 F.3d 202, 211–12 (3d Cir. 2005) [a BIA decision that sets forth its reasoning with sufficient clarity so a reviewing court can discern the basis for the decision, even if not a model of clarity, does not violate due process or the APA]; *Hanif v. DHS,* 472 F.Supp.2d 914, 920–22 (E.D. Mich. 2007) [court has jurisdiction to review denial of I-130 petition under the APA but there is no final agency action by the BIA so the petition must be dismissed]; *Fred 26 Importers, Inc. v. DHS,* 445 F.Supp.2d 1174, 1180–81 (C.D. Cal. 2006) [court reversed AAO where it failed to address expert and other evidence that a human resource manager position in a small export/import company required duties which were specialized and complex and, instead, simply asserted that small company did not require specialized and complex duties];*Capital Area Immigrants' Rights Coalition v. DOJ,* 264 F.Supp.2d 14, 25–39 (D.D.C. 2003) [DOJ made reasoned decisions in expanding streamlining at the BIA, in reducing the BIA's size, and in setting a time limit to reduce backlog of cases]; *M.B. v. Quarantillo,* 301 F.3d 109, 111–14 (3d Cir. 2002) [APA review of DD's decision regarding special immigrant juvenile status but DD's conduct was not arbitrary]; *Air India v. Brien,* 261 F.Supp.2d 134, 138–40 (E.D.N.Y. 2003) [INS decision to apply provision for special immigrants resulting in fines to air carriers after 22 years was arbitrary and capricious]

1.d. to review the Secretary of State's duty not to extradite a person facing torture under the Convention Against Torture, *Cornejo-Barreto v. Seifert,* 218 F.3d 1004 (9th Cir. 2000).

1.e. to enforce Executive Orders against an agency's failure to act where the Executive Order has the force of law. *Dong v. Slattery*, 84 F.3d 82, 85–86 (2d Cir. 1996) [Executive Order did not have force of law and therefore APA not applicable]; and

1.f. to compel agency action unlawfully withheld or unreasonably delayed. 5 U.S.C. §§555(b), 706(1). *Ceken v. Chertoff,* 544 F.Supp.2d 211 (D. Conn. 2008) [mandamus and APA claim to adjudicate AOS application pending for 5 years]; *Al Jabari v. Chertoff,* 536 F.Supp.2d 1029 (D. Minn. 2008) [In action to compel DHS to complete the security check involving the grant by an IJ of a marriage hardship waiver to lift conditional residence under 8 U.S.C. §1186a(c)(4), the court determined that although mandamus was unavailable because the statute does not impose a nondiscretionary duty, the APA permitted injunctive relief]; *Shirmohamadali v. Heinauer,* 533 F.Supp.2d 1059 (E.D. Cal. 2008) [more than 4 year wait for AOS was unreasonable]; *Aslam v. Mukasey,* 531 F.Supp.2d 736 (E.D. Va. 2008) [granted summary judgment for 12-year wait for AOS where USCIS had a duty to adjudicate within a reasonable time and ordered them to instruct the FBI to expedite the name check]; *Lindems v. Mukasey,* 530 F.Supp.2d 1044 (E.D. Wis. 2008) [INA §242(a)(2)(B)(ii) did not bar APA or Mandamus action for AOS pending 5 years]; *Soneji v. DHS,* 525 F.Supp.2d 1151 (N.D. Cal. 2007) [court denied motion to dismiss action under §1331 pursuant to section 555(b) of the APA and mandamus to compel DHS to adjudicate an AOS application pending for 38 months]; *Zhu v. Chertoff,* 525 F.Supp.2d 1098 (W.D. Mo. 2007) [four year delay in AOS unreasonable and summary judgment was granted]; *Belegradek v. Gonzales,* 523 F.Supp.2d 1364 (N.D. Ga. 2007) [court denied motion to dismiss APA claim for adjudication of adjustment application within reasonable time]; *Saleem v. Keisler,* 520 F.Supp.2d 1048, 1057–61 (W.D. Wis. 2007) [a five-year delay in adjudicating an AOS was unreasonable delay under APA §555(b) and court granted summary judgment]; *Alkeylani v. DHS,* 514 F.Supp.2d 258 (D. Conn. 2007) [three year delay in adjudicating I-485 is actionable and mandamus and federal question jurisdiction apply and are not barred by INA §242(a)(2)(B)(ii)]; *Dong v. Chertoff,* 513 F.Supp.2d 1158, 1166–68 (N.D. Cal. 2007) [8 C.F.R. §103.2(b)(18) limits the discretion of USCIS to continue/withhold the adjudication of an I-485 pending two-and-a-half years and therefore the demand that the I-485 be adjudicated *is subject* to judicial review under mandamus and APA §706(1) and is not precluded by INA §242(a)(2)(B)(ii)]; *Liu v. Novak,* 509 F.Supp.2d 1 (D.D.C. 2007) [summary judgment granted to petitioner waiting 4 years on AOS and neither INA §242(a)(2)(B), nor INA §242(g) precluded mandamus and §1331 jurisdiction pursuant to APA §555(b) because adjudication was "unreasonably withheld"]; *Han Cao v. Upchurch,* 496 F.Supp.2d 569, 574–77 (E.D. Pa. 2007) [court granted motion for summary judgment under mandamus and the APA to compel USCIS to make a decision on an I-485 pending more than 3 years]; *Tang v. Chertoff,* 493 F.Supp.2d 148 (D. Mass. 2007) [followed *Spencer* and determined that §§242(a)(2)(B)(i) & (ii) do not bar action to compel adjudication of AOS pending for 4 years and that there is jurisdiction under mandamus to enforce APA §§555(b) and 706(1)]; *Linville v. Barrows,* 489 F.Supp. 2d 1278 (W.D. Okla.2007) [government has ministerial nondiscretionary duty to adjudicate I-485, court denied motion to dismiss, and court discussed factors to use in determining whether there is a violation of §555(b)]; *Kaplan v. Chertoff,* 481 F.Supp. 2d 370, 398–404 (E.D. Pa. 2007) [cause of action under APA for USCIS and FBI delay in granting LPR status]; *Singh v. Still,* 470 F.Supp.2d 1064 (N.D. Cal. 2007) [where asylum AOS has been pending seven years and marriage AOS for four, mandamus or APA/1331 was appropriate to compel decision]; *Saleh v. Ridge,* 367 F.Supp.2d 508, 511–14 (S.D.N.Y. 2005) [where adjustment of status application as a refugee was pending for five years there was §1331 jurisdiction pursuant to APA §555(b), although court found delay was not unreasonable on the merits given the waiting times for refugee adjustment]; *Bartolini v. Ashcroft,* 226 F.Supp.2d 350 (D. Conn. 2002) [jurisdiction under §1331 exists to review claim under §555(b) of the APA that INS unlawfully delayed adjudication of AOS application; court found gov't conduct reasonable]; *Yu v. Brown,* 36 F.Supp.2d 922, 928 (D. N.Mex. 1999). *But see Ibrahim v. Chertoff,* 529 F.Supp.2d 611 (E.D.N.C. 2007) [where naturalization applicant did not have his interview for 3½ years, APA claim was denied because there was no clear right to have application adjudicated within a certain period of time];*Orlov v. Howard,* 523 F.Supp.2d 30 (D.D.C. 2007) [INA §242(a)(2)(B)(ii) precludes jurisdiction to compel adjudication of AOS pending 4 years and neither APA §555(b), nor mandamus, are a source of jurisdiction]; *Tao Luo v. Keisler,* 521 F.Supp.2d 72 (D.D.C. 2007) [same following *Grinberg* and *Safadi*]; *Omar v. Mueller,* 501 F.Supp.2d 636, 640–41 (D.N.J. 2007) [a 4 year delay in interviewing applicant for naturalization and concluding fingerprint checks does not violate the APA because there is no set time required by law]; *Shen v. Chertoff,* 494 F.Supp.2d 592 (E.D. Mich. 2007) [no cause of action for mandamus or APA for delay of 50 months in deciding AOS because of security checks because there is no nondiscretionary duty under mandamus and it is committed to agency discretion under the APA]; *Takkallapalli v. Chertoff,* 487 F.Supp.2d 1094, 1097–98 (W.D. Mo. 2007) [delay of 3 years in adjudicating AOS because of security checks is not agency action unlawfully withheld or unreasonably delayed under the circumstances]; *Linville v. Barrows,* 489 F.Supp. 2d 1278 (W.D. Okla.2007) [government has ministerial nondiscretionary duty to adjudicate I-485, court denied motion to dismiss, and court discussed factors to use in determining whether there is a violation of §555(b)]; *Qiu v. Chertoff,* 486 F.Supp.2d 412, 420–21 (D.N.J. 2007)[no APA jurisdiction to obtain answer on I-485 because regulation at §103.2(b)(18) confers discretion to withhold adjudication pending an investigation]; *Li v. Chertoff,* 482 F.Supp.2d 1172, 1178–79 (S.D. Cal. 2007) [where USCIS has no regulatory time period to complete I-485, no APA claim]; *Grinberg v. Swancia,* 478 F.Supp.2d 1350 (S.D. Fla. 2007) [following *Safadi v. Howard,*, 466 F.Supp.2d 696 (E.D. Va. 2006) and finding that *post*-REAL ID Act INA §242(a)(2)(B)(ii) bars mandamus for adjustment under mandamus statute and 555(b) of the APA because it bars pace of "actions" as well as decisions]; *Keane v. Chertoff,* 419 F.Supp. 2d 597 (S.D.N.Y. 2006) [petitioner's request that USCIS reopen AOS that was erroneously denied for abandonment and reschedule interview was committed to agency discretion under the APA and not subject to mandamus].

2. Unlike regulations, USCIS's *Adjudicator's Field Manual* (AFM), CBP's *Inspector's Field Manual* (IFM), and EOIR's *Operating Policy and Procedural Memoranda* (OPPMs), as well as the now-superseded *Operations Instructions* (OI) from legacy INS, may fall within 5 U.S.C. §553(b)(1)(A)'s exception for internal directives, however, and thus may not require compliance with the APA publication requirements. *Loa-Herrera v. Trominski,* 231 F.3d 984, 989 (5th Cir. 2000) [declining to enforce INS memorandum regarding procedure when confiscating a green card]; *Haitian Refugee Center, Inc. v. Baker*, 953 F.2d 1498, 1511 (11th Cir. 1992), *cert. denied*, 502 U.S. 1112, 112 S.Ct. 1245 (1992) [INS Guidelines in interdiction program creates no substantive right that can be judicially enforced]; *Romeiro De Silva v. Smith*, 773 F.2d 1021 (9th Cir. 1985) [deferred action, O.I. §103.1(a)(1)(ii), did not require publication]. But no *per se* rule applies to OIs. Mada *Luna v. Fitzpatrick*, 813 F.2d 1006, 1012 n.6 (9th Cir. 1987) [modifies broad language of *DeSilva*, but finds that deferred action O.I. is a general statement of policy and does not require APA notice and comment]; *Si v. Slattery*, 864 F.Supp. 397, 403–05 (S.D.N.Y. 1994). APA publication requirement under 5 U.S.C. §552(a)(1) may not be advanced where O.I. "clearly does not create substantive rights" and therefore "the failure to publish does not adversely effect the public." *Mada-Luna*, *supra* at 1018. However, some courts have enforced OIs and even INS statements on the ground that they confer procedural rights even if they do not confer substantive rights. *Pasquini v. Morris*, 700 F.2d 658 (11th Cir. 1983); *Zhang v. Slattery*, 840 F.Supp. 292 (S.D.N.Y. 1994). *See also Morton v. Ruiz*, 415 U.S. 199, 235 (1974). General statements of policy, however, are exempt from the APA notice and comment requirements. *Chen Zhou Chai v. Carroll*, 48 F.3d 1331, 1340–41 (4th Cir. 1995). Similarly, "it is doubtful" that operating policies and procedures stated in a memorandum "could confer substantive legal benefits upon aliens and bind the INS." *Prokopenko v. Ashcroft,* 372 F.3d 941, 944 (8th Cir. 2004) [discussing but not deciding the issue regarding asylum applicant's enforceable right based upon memorandum to prevent asylum officer's assessment of his application].

C. *Habeas Corpus Jurisdiction*

1. The Writ of Habeas Corpus—The "Great Writ" has a pre-eminent role in our constitutional system and "is the fundamental instrument for safeguarding individual freedom against arbitrary and lawless state action." *Harris v. Nelson*, 394 U.S. 286, 290 (1969); "The writ of habeas corpus has played a great role in the history of human freedom." *Blackledge v. Allison,* 431 U.S. 63, 72 (1977), *quoting Price v. Johnston,* 334 U.S. 266, 269 (1948); U.S. Const. Art. I §9 cl.2. *See also*

Rasul v. Bush, 542 U.S. 466 (2004) [habeas corpus confers a right to judicial review of the legality of Executive detention of aliens in a territory over which the U.S. exercises plenary and exclusive jurisdiction but not ultimate sovereignty]; *Peyton v. Rowe*, 391 U.S. 54 (1968); *Townsend v. Sain*, 372 U.S. 293 (1963); *Fay v. Noia*, 372 U.S. 391 (1963). "At its historical core, the writ of habeas corpus has served as a means of reviewing the legality of Executive detention and it is in that context that its protections have been strongest." *INS v. St. Cyr,* 121 S.Ct. 2271, 2280 (2001); *See also Reno v. Flores*, 507 U.S. 292 (1993). It "has been recognized by countless generations as one of the bulwarks of liberty under the Anglo-American system of government." *Hermanowski v. Farquharson,* 39 F.Supp.2d 148, 153 (D.R.I. 1999). The Federalists encouraged the passage of the Writ arguing that it should be "provided for, in the most ample manner." *The Federalist,* No. 83 at 499 (Alexander Hamilton) (Clinton Rossiter ed., 1961). The power of the court to inquire in habeas "is plenary." *Townsend*, 372 U.S. at 312 (1963). The writ is codified at 28 U.S.C. §2241.

2. Habeas Review after AEDPA, IIRIRA and the REAL ID Act—Federal courts formerly had jurisdiction to review deportation matters in habeas corpus under INA §106(a)(10), 8 U.S.C. §1105a(a)(10), H.R. Rep. No. 1086, 87th Cong., 1st Sess. (1961), *reprinted in* 1961 U.S.C.C.A.N. 2950, 2973. The immigration habeas provision of INA §106(a)(10) was repealed in AEDPA §401(e). In light of this change and the changes as a result of AEDPA §440(a) and IIRIRA §306 (amending INA §242 and adding §242(g)) withdrawing judicial review from virtually all immigration decisions and §242(b)(9) consolidating all claims in a petition for review), a question remained as to whether 28 U.S.C. §2241 habeas remained to review immigration matters. The Supreme Court in *Felker v. Turpin*, 518 U.S. 651, 116 S.Ct. 2333, 2338 (1996), relying on *Ex Parte Yerger,* 75 U.S. (8 Wall.) 85, 105 (1868), interpreted another court stripping provision of AEDPA and found that where Congress had not explicitly repealed habeas corpus jurisdiction that such jurisdiction could not be repealed "by implication." Following *Felker* and general provisions regarding the presumption of judicial review for constitutional issues and for other matters absent clear congressional intent to the contrary, the Supreme Court determined that habeas corpus had not been abolished under AEDPA or IIRIRA to review constitutional and statutory immigration claims and that habeas applies to review the "legal validity" of a final order of removal even in the face of preclusion statutes. *INS v. St. Cyr,* 121 S.Ct. 2271, 2278–88 (2001) [habeas review and judicial review are separate and Congress did not preclude habeas review of pure questions of law that arise during the removal proceeding]. The Supreme Court also reaffirmed the supremacy of habeas corpus in the review of Executive detention in *Demore v. Kim*, 538 U.S. 510, 517 (2003) ["Section 1226(e) contains no explicit provision barring habeas review and we think that its clear text does not bar respondent's constitutional challenge to the legislation authorizing his detention without bail] and in *Zadvydas v. Davis,* 533 U.S. 678, 687–88 (2001) ["We conclude that §2241 habeas corpus proceedings remain available as a forum for statutory and constitutional challenges to post–removal-period detention"]. In *St. Cyr,* 533 U.S. at 311 and reinforced in *Demore,* 538 U.S. at 534–35 (O'Connor, J. concurring in part), the Supreme Court held that "judicial review" under INA §242 and habeas corpus under §2241 are distinct processes. *Accord Saint Fort v. Ashcroft,* 329 F.3d 191, 197–201 (1st Cir. 2003) [rejecting the government's preclusion of review argument and holding that habeas and judicial review are distinct processes]; *Kuhali v. Reno,* 266 F.3d 93, 99–101 (2d Cir. 2001) [post–*St. Cyr* rejection of INS argument that habeas precluded until a determination is made under INA §242(a)(2)(C) that no direct review is possible for a person with a conviction; court raises but does not address procedural default rule]; *Jeanty v. Bulger,* 204 F.Supp.2d 1366, 1373–75 (S.D. Fla. 2002) *aff'd sub nom. Moise v. Bulger,* 321 F.3d 1336 (11th Cir.), *cert. denied,* 540 U.S. 1016 (2003) [preclusion statute barring review of discretionary decisions under INA §242(a)(2)(B)(ii) did not bar habeas jurisdiction to review parole decisions].

REAL ID Act of 2005. With the passage of the REAL ID Act of 2005, PL 109-13, 119 Stat. 231, Div. B §106 (May 11, 2005), Congress unequivocally sought to eliminate habeas, mandamus and All Writs jurisdiction in the district courts in regard to "judicial review of an order of removal entered or issued under any provision of this Act." INA §242(a)(5), 8 U.S.C. §1252(a)(5) ["Notwithstanding any other provision of law (statutory or nonstatutory), including [habeas, mandamus, and All Writs Act]...a petition for review filed with an appropriate court of appeals...shall be the sole and exclusive means for juridical review of an order of removal entered or issued under any provision of this Act...]. Habeas, mandamus and All Writs Act jurisdiction was also eliminated as a source of jurisdiction to review Convention Against Torture claims and the courts of appeals "shall be the sole and exclusive means for judicial review of any cause or claim under" CAT. INA §242(a)(4), 8 U.S.C. §1252(a)(4). *Haman v. Gonzales,* 449 F.3d 834 (8th Cir. 2006) [CAT claim transferred to circuit court but review of the claim was denied for Pashtun returning to Afghanistan on grounds he sought review of only factual issues]; *Dorisme v. Gonzales,* 410 F.Supp.2d 79 (D. Conn. 2006) [includes transfers of CAT claims]. The Congress also reemphasized the elimination of habeas, mandamus and All Writs Act review even if the statute otherwise precluded review. *See e.g.,* INA §§242(a)(2)(B), (a)(2)(C) & (g), 8 U.S.C. §1252(a)(2)(B), (a)(2)(C) & (g). The REAL ID Act, however, no longer bars the court of appeals from considering constitutional claims or questions of law in a petition for review even where other sections (*e.g.,* criminal aliens, discretionary decision, §242(g)) would bar or limit review. *Ramirez-Molina v. Ziglar,* 436 F.3d 508, 513–14 (5th Cir. 2006) [jurisdiction under INA §242(a)(2)(D) to review legal challenge to reinstated removal order notwithstanding preclusion provision of INA §241(a)(5)]; *Kamara v. Att'y Gen. of the U.S.,* 420 F.3d 202, 210–11 (3d Cir. 2005) [the court reviews pure questions of law and issues regarding the application of law to fact, and found that the BIA applied the wrong quantum of proof required for a CAT claim]; *Ramos v. Gonzales,* 414 F.3d 800, 802–04 (7th Cir. 2005) [Congress added §242(a)(2)(D) to consider all constitutional and statutory claims in review of a final order]; *Papageorgiou v. Gonzales,* 413 F.3d 356, 357–58 (3d Cir. 2005) [Section 242(a)(2)(D) restores jurisdiction to the circuit court for persons who previously were barred from such review under 242(a)(2)(C) because of criminal convictions and makes the restoration retroactive by applying it to any order issued before, on or after May 11, 2005]; *Fernandez-Ruiz v. Gonzales,* 468 F.3d 1159, 1163 (9th Cir. 2006) [same].

At least one court has found that the elimination of habeas corpus review in the district court does not violate the Supremacy Clause *Alexandere v. U.S. Att'y Gen.,* 452 F.3d 1204, 1205–07 (11th Cir. 2006) [Supremacy Clause not violated because constitutional and statutory review that existed in habeas still preserved in the courts of appeal provides an adequate and effective remedy to the elimination of habeas in the district court].

The legislative history of the REAL ID Act also provides that it "will not preclude habeas review over challenges to detention that are independent of challenges to removal orders. Instead, the bill would eliminate habeas review only over challenges to removal orders." Joint Explanatory Statement of the Committee of Conference, H.R. Cong. Rep. No 109-72 at 175, 151 Cong. Rec. H2836, 2873 (May 3, 2005). *Singh v. Gonzales,* 499 F.3d 969, 976–81 (9th Cir. 2007) [claim that ineffective assistance of counsel resulted in failure to file a timely appeal to the circuit court was not a review of a final order and district court jurisdiction was not precluded by INA §§242(a)(5) & (b)(9)]; *Hernandez v. Gonzales,* 424 F.3d 42 (1st Cir. 2005) [remanding habeas detention challenge by Mariel Cuban back to district court because habeas may be brought post–REAL ID Act when it is a challenge to detention]; *Bonhometre v. Ashcroft,* 414 F.3d 442, 446 n.4 (3d Cir. 2005); *Moallin v. Cangemi,* 427 F.Supp.2d 908, 918–21 (D. Minn. 2006) [citing the REAL ID Act legislative history a Somalian detained subsequent to his removal order can challenge his custody as violative of the constitution]; *Abdulle v. Gonzales,* 422 F.Supp.2d 774, 776 (W.D. Tex. 2006) [REAL ID does not preclude habeas related to detention only]. *But see Deljevic v. Baker,* 463 F.Supp.2d 699 (E.D. Mich. 2006) [no habeas jurisdiction to review detention where there is final order of removal and detention is challenged on ground that final order was improper]. And the transfer provision and elimination of habeas *does not* apply to review of or challenges to matters that are not part of removal orders. *Nnadika v. Att'y Gen. of the U.S.,* 484 F.3d 626 (3d Cir. 2007) [court of appeals remanded to the district court a claim for injunctive and declaratory relief seeking review of a denied I-730 because it was not a final order for purposes of INA §242 review]; *Fonseca-Sanchez v. Gonzales,* 484 F.3d 439 (7th Cir. 2007) [where respondent sought review of a U visa denial that arose subsequent to a final administrative removal order, the court lacked jurisdiction under INA §242 and the proper remedy was habeas]; *Sandher v. Gonzales,* 481 F.3d 108 (2d Cir. 2007) [court dismissed habeas that was transferred to it improperly under REAL ID Act where habeas only challenged the validity of petitioner's conviction and not his removal order]; *Madu v. U.S. Att'y Gen.,* 470 F.3d 1362, 1366–67 (11th Cir. 2006) [where respondent claims he voluntarily departed and reentered, and therefore does not have a removal order, habeas was appropriate and circuit court dismissed and remanded it to district court]; *Kumarasamy v. Att'y Gen. of the U.S.,* 453 F.3d 169, 172 (3d Cir. 2006) [a person who claims his deportation was illegal because there was no order of removal is not barred by the REAL ID Act from bringing a habeas petition];*Hernandez v. Gonzales,* 424 F.3d 42 (1st Cir. 2005) [remanding habeas detention challenge by Mariel Cuban back to district court because habeas may be brought post–REAL ID Act when it is a challenge to detention]; *Ali v. Gonzales,* 421 F.3d 795, 797 n.1 (9th Cir. 2005) [declined to transfer case to circuit court where petitioners challenge their physical removal]; *Lin v. Chertoff,* 522 F.Supp.2d 1309 (D. Colo. 2007) [habeas jurisdiction existed to compel, through mandamus, the adjudication of an I-601 waiver, where USCIS refused to grant an AOS due to prior misrepresentations].

The REAL ID Act §106(c) also orders the transfer of all habeas cases pending in the district courts to the circuit courts and shall treat the cases as if they had been filed pursuant to a petition for review, except that the 30-day time limitation for filing a petition for review shall not apply. *Medellin-Reyes v. Gonzales,* 435 F.3d 721, 723–24 (7th Cir. 2006) [habeas petition filed outside of 30-day period for review of underlying removal order does not bar review in circuit court after case is transferred pursuant to REAL ID Act]; *De Araujo v. Gonzales,* 457 F.3d 146, 152 (1st Cir. 2006) [same]; *Ishak v. Gonzales,* 422 F.3d 22, 29 (1st Cir. 2005) [same]; *Dorisme v. Gonzales,* 410 F.Supp.2d 79 (D. Conn. 2006) [includes transfers of CAT claims]. But if a habeas case was not filed before May 11, 2005 (because there was no time limit on filing habeas petitions) and an appeal was not appropriate because of jurisdictional issues, the failure to file before May 11, 2005 if fatal would violate the Suspension Clause. *Kolkevich v. Att'y Gen. of the U.S.,* 501 F.3d 323 (3d Cir. 2007) [it would violate the Suspension Clause not to provide any avenue of review where respondent did not file habeas before May 11, 2005 and could not file petition for review after May 11, 2005 because the 30 days had passed; therefore, all parties would be given 30 days from May 11, 2005 to file a petition for review]; *See also Ruiz-Martinez v. Mukasey,* 516 F.3d 102, 112–17 (2d Cir. 2008) [petitioner who filed habeas two days after May 11th and within 30 days off the removal order would have habeas treated as properly filed petition for review]. *But see Iasu v. Smith,* 511 F.3d 881 (9th Cir. 2007). However, if a habeas was filed more than 30 days after May 11, 2005, it would simply be dismissed. *Wang v. DHS,* 484 F.3d 615 (2d Cir. 2007) [petition transferred to circuit court pursuant to REAL ID Act was dismissed where petition was filed in the district court more than a year after the REAL ID Act and more than 30 days beyond the time for appeal]; *Chen v. Gonzales,* 435 F.3d 788, 790 (7th Cir. 2006) [no jurisdiction in the circuit court to review transferred habeas filed after May 11, 2005]; *Okeezie v. Chertoff,* 462 F.Supp.2d 731 (W.D. Tex. 2006) [where petitioner did not file a petition for review or timely file a habeas, the habeas was dismissed]; *In the Matter of Lawrence,* 448 F.Supp.2d 572 (S.D.N.Y. 2006) [dismissed rather than transfer case filed after May 11, 2006]; *but see Wahab v. U.S. Att'y Gen.,* 373 F.Supp.2d 524 (E.D. Pa. 2005) [habeas case filed post–May 11, 2005 transferred to circuit court]. The transfer of the case raises the question whether the circuit court can ignore the district court's decision and render a new decision without reviewing the lower court order. *See e.g., Padilla v. Gonzales,* 470 F.3d 1209, 1213 (7th Cir. 2006) [construing habeas as petition for review and dismissing for failure to exhaust remedies]; *Hernandez v. Gonzales,* 437 F.3d 341, 344–45 (3d Cir. 2006) [vacating the district court opinion and addressing the claims as if they were presented on appeal for the first time]; *Ramirez-Molina v. Ziglar,* 436 F.3d 508, 512–13 (5th Cir. 2006) [reversed district court's findings in habeas and treated habeas appeal as a petition for review]; *Bonhometre v. Gonzales,* 414 F.3d 442, 446 (3d Cir. 2005) [treating the habeas court's decision as "nonexistent" and dismissing the petition for review for failure to exhaust administrative remedies regarding petitioner's procedural due process claim]. Similarly, the circuit court must decide whether to accept a petition for review when the habeas petition was filed within its jurisdiction but the removal hearing was not, thereby establishing the venue in another circuit. *Compare Amunikoro v. Secy. of DHS,* 432 F.3d 383 (2d Cir. 2005) [where respondent agreed that venue was properly in the Third Circuit because the removal hearing arose there, the appeal of the habeas petitioner, filed in the Second Circuit, was converted to a petition for review and transferred to the Third Circuit. The Second Circuit declined to decide whether it was compelled jurisdictionally to transfer the case to the Third Circuit] *with Moreno-Bravo v. Gonzales,* 463 F.3d 253, 257–63 (2d Cir. 2006) [INA §242(b)(2) is not jurisdictional and where IJ proceeding was completed in Louisiana and a habeas action was filed in the second circuit, the second circuit retained jurisdiction because respondent had been in government custody for three and a half years, the district court had rendered a thorough opinion, and the case had been thoroughly briefed on the merits in the second circuit] and *Wilson v. Gonzales,* 471 F.3d 111, 116–17 (2d Cir. 2006). *See also Jama v. Gonzales,* 431 F.3d 230, 233 (5th Cir. 2005) [maintaining the case in the Fifth Circuit despite improper venue because of the unfairness in relitigating the case anew in another forum]; *Bonhome-*

tre v. Gonzales, 414 F.3d 442, 446 n.5 (3d Cir. 2005) [although the case was not properly before the court as a converted petition for review because the removal hearing arose in the First Circuit, it would be manifest injustice not to decide the case as it was thoroughly briefed and argued and petitioner had waited a long time for its resolution]. The circuit courts must also decide how they will treat an appeal of a habeas petition that was pending in the circuit court on May 11, 2005. Some courts have treated the appeal of a habeas pending on May 11, 2005 as a petition for review notwithstanding the statute's language. *See e.g., Gonzalez-Gonzalez v. Weber,* 472 F.3d 1198, 1199 (10th Cir. 2006) [habeas appeal converted to petition for review]; *Francois v. Gonzales,* 448 F.3d 645, 648 (3d Cir. 2006) [the appropriate way to treat an appeal from the district court's habeas decision is to vacate and disregard the opinion]; *Gittens v. Menifee,* 428 F.3d 382, 384–87 (2d Cir. 2005) [habeas appealed to circuit will be treated as a petition for review]; *Kamara v. Att'y Gen. of the U.S.,* 420 F.3d 202, 209–10 (3d Cir. 2005) [appeal of habeas pending in circuit court would be converted to a petition for review and district court's habeas decision will be disregarded]; *Martinez-Rosas v. Gonzales,* 424 F.3d 926, 928–31 (9th Cir. 2005) [habeas appeals pending in the circuit court on May 11, 2005 that were challenging final removal orders shall be treated *de novo* as petitions for review]; *Rosales v. ICE,* 426 F.3d 733, 736 (5th Cir. 2005) [treating appeal of habeas pending on May 11, 2005 as a petition for review]. *But see Alvarez-Barajas v. Gonzales,* 418 F.3d 1050, 1053 and n.3 (9th Cir. 2005) [reading the REAL ID Act of 2005 to allow for review of habeas cases already pending in the circuit court is consistent with the Act but rendering no opinion on whether there would be jurisdiction if the case had to be remanded for additional fact finding].

3. Scope of Habeas, Review Permitted—If habeas corpus does apply notwithstanding preclusion statutes, the scope of habeas becomes important in defining what matters may be reviewed. The U.S. Supreme Court in *INS v. St. Cyr,* 533 U.S. 289, 121 S.Ct. 2271, 2282–83 (2001) has determined that the Writ may been used to "challenge[] the Executive interpretations of the immigration laws" including "questions of law that arose in the context of discretionary relief." *Id.* at 2283. *St. Cyr* also stated that the writ may be used to challenge "detentions based on errors of law, including the erroneous application or interpretation of statutes..." *St. Cyr,* 533 U.S. at 302, 121 S.Ct at 2280 *See also Gegiow v. Uhl,* 239 U.S. 3 (1915); *Mahler v. Eby,* 264 U.S. 32 (1924), *Kessler v. Strecker*, 307 U.S. 22 (1939); *Delgadillo v. Carmichael*, 332 U.S. 388 (1947); *Fong Haw Tan v. Phelan,* 333 U.S. 6 (1948); *Wong Yang Sung v. McGrath,* 339 U.S. 33 (1950); *Carlson v. Landon*, 342 U.S. 524 (1952); and *Kwong Hai Chew v. Colding,* 344 U.S. 590 (1953); *Auguste v. Ridge,* 395 F.3d 123, 137–38 (3d Cir. 2005) [in a case involving the review of the legal definition of torture, the court found that the scope of review is "limited to constitutional issues and errors of law, including both statutory interpretation and application of law to undisputed facts or adjudicated facts, but does not include review of administrative fact findings or the exercise of discretion"]; *Cadet v. Bulger,* 377 F.3d 1173, 1183–85, 1192 (11th Cir. 2004) [same]; *Ogbudimkpa v. Ashcroft,* 342 F.3d 207, 222 (3d Cir. 2003) [habeas includes review of the application of the law to the undisputed facts]; *Singh v. Ashcroft,* 351 F.3d 435, 441–42 (9th Cir. 2003) [in the context of a review of a CAT claim, the court determined, following *St. Cyr* and *Wang* (2d Cir), that habeas extends to the "erroneous application or interpretation of statutes" and that it can review the application of the Convention to the facts of the case; The scope of habeas is therefore not limited solely to "legal questions of statutory construction"]; *Nolan v. Holmes,* 334 F.3d 189, 194 (2d Cir. 2003) [naturalization applicant seeking interpretation whether good moral character is a requirement for person seeking citizenship through military service raises a legal issue subject to review]; *Saint Fort v. Ashcroft,* 329 F.3d 191, 203–04 (1st Cir. 2003) ["Habeas also encompasses colorable claims that an alien's statutory rights have been violated.... Included in this category are issues of the proper construction of a statute, which is an issue of law.... As a result, if a statute makes an alien eligible to be considered for a certain form of relief, he may raise on habeas the refusal of the agency to even consider him."]; *Wang v. Ashcroft,* 320 F.3d 130, 142–43 (2d Cir. 2003) [habeas review of the application of the particular facts of a CAT claim to the relevant law (§208.16) falls within the permissible scope of habeas because review extends "to claims of erroneous *application* or interpretation of statutes"].

Habeas has also been used "to attack deportation proceedings when some essential finding of fact is unsupported by the evidence." *Taylor v. U.S.,* 396 F.3d 1322, 1328 n.5 (11th Cir. 2005) [although challenge was dismissed for failure to exhaust, the court cited *U.S. ex rel. Bilokumsky v. Tod,* 163 U.S. 149 (1923) for the proposition that essential facts may be reviewed for error].

Before *St. Cyr* many circuit courts addressed the scope of habeas corpus under IIRIRA. *Mahadeo v. Reno,* 226 F.3d 3 (1st Cir. 2000), *cert. denied* 121 S.Ct. 2590 (2001) [habeas not barred under IIRIRA permanent provisions including statutory claims regarding retroactivity]; *Flores-Miramontes v. INS,* 212 F.3d 1133, 1141–43 (9th Cir. 2000) [habeas review of statutory as well as constitutional claims under the permanent rules]; *Mayers v. Reno,* 175 F.3d 1289, 1296 n.7, 1300–01 (11th Cir. 1999) [habeas permits review of statutory claims]; *Sandoval v. Reno,* 166 F.3d 225 (3d Cir. 1999); *Henderson v. INS,* 157 F.3d 106, 119–22 (2d Cir. 1998); *Goncalves v. Reno,* 144 F.3d 110, 123–24 (1st Cir.), *cert. denied,* 119 S.Ct. 1141 (1999). *See also* Neuman, "The Constitutional Requirement of 'Some Evidence,' " 25 *San Diego L. Rev.* 631 (1988); Benson, "Back to the Future: Congress Attacks the Right to Judicial Review of Immigration Proceedings," 29 *Conn. L. Rev.* 1411 (1997).

Scope of Habeas, Review Denied. *Moussa v. Jenifer,* 389 F.3d 550, 554–55 (6th Cir. 2004) [although habeas petitioner raised statutory and constitutional claims regarding the denial of motion to stay before ICE they were nothing more than an effort to review the nonreviewable discretionary decision of the DD to execute an order of removal barred by INA §242(g)]; *Duamutef v. INS,* 386 F.3d 172, 181–82 (2d Cir. 2004) [the district court lacked habeas jurisdiction to compel ICE to take custody over state prisoner and to execute order of removal because this was discretionary act and did not implicate a constitutional or statutory right]; *Bakhtriger v. Elwood,* 360 F.3d 414, 410 (3d Cir. 2004) [because habeas proceedings are "confined to questions of constitutional and statutory law" and "do not embrace review of the exercise of discretion or the sufficiency of the evidence" a challenge to the denial of asylum because the factual findings were incorrect or the BIA abused its discretion were dismissed]; *Gutierrez-Chavez v. INS,* 298 F.3d 824 (9th Cir. 2002) *amended on denial of reh'g* 337 F.3d 1023 (9th Cir. 2003) [habeas is limited to claims of constitutional or statutory error, including that the agency failed to exercise discretion in accordance with federal law and the constitution or where there is manifest injustice, but petitioner cannot use §2241 to obtain review of the equitable balance in denying a INA §212(c) waiver]; *Sol v. INS,* 274 F.3d 648 (2d Cir. 2001), *cert. denied,* 536 U.S. 941 (2002) [*Post–St. Cyr* habeas review does not extend to review purely discretionary determinations by the BIA such as whether the IJ's decision to deny INA §212(c) was supported by the record]; *Cervantes De Hernandez v. Chertoff,* 368 F.Supp.2d 896, 904–09 (E.D. Wis. 2005) [claims that the evidence was insufficient to find a material misrepresentation on an I-485 or that the IJ erroneously refused to waive inadmissibility were precluded from habeas review]; *Giap v. INS,* 311 F.Supp.2d 438 (S.D.N.Y. 2004) [habeas does not extend to the review of denial of CAT claim where challenge is to factual or discretionary determinations]; *Reyes-Sanchez v. Ashcroft,* 261 F.Supp.2d 276, 288 (S.D.N.Y. 2003) [habeas review of withholding and CAT claims does not extend to BIA's discretionary decisions regarding whether the applicant met the "extraordinary and compelling circumstances" exception to a finding that a crime was particularly serious or that he is "more likely than not" to be tortured on return to his country]; *Millian-Zamora v. Ashcroft,* 228 F.Supp.2d 272, 275–76 (E.D.N.Y. 2002) [*Post–St. Cyr* habeas review does not extend to review of discretionary decision to deny CAT withholding claim but can review procedural fairness claim]; *U.S. ex rel. Kovalev v. Ashcroft,* 223 F.Supp.2d 688 (E.D .Pa. 2002) [no review in habeas of Service's discretionary decision to deny motion to reopen for NACARA where person appeared facially eligible].

The REAL ID Act of 2005, §106, now requires review in the circuit courts of appeal, the constitutional questions and questions of law, that historically were reviewed under a habeas scope of review. INA §242(a)(2)(D). *Ramos v. Gonzales,* 414 F.3d 800, 802–04 (7th Cir. 2005) [Congress added §242(a)(2)(D) to consider all constitutional and statutory claims in review of a final order].

4. Habeas Actions and Bail Determinations—At least one circuit has determined that federal courts in habeas proceedings have authority to set bail for detained noncitizens where setting bail is necessary to make the habeas remedy effective. *Mapp v. Reno,* 241 F.3d 221 (2d Cir. 2001) [district courts have inherent authority to grant bail while habeas petition is pending where to do so is "necessary to make the habeas remedy effective"]. The Second Circuit following *Mapp* has also determined it has the inherent authority to grant bond while a petition for review is pending in the circuit court where petitioner has presented a substantial claim and there are extraordinary circumstances that make the grant of bail necessary to make the petition for review remedy effective. *Elkimya v. DHS,* 484 F.3d 151 (2d Cir. 2007) [finding court has inherent authority to grant bail pending resolution of a petition for review of returning LPR who has been out of the U.S. for 4

years, but concluding there were no extraordinary circumstances permitting bail); *but see Bolante v. Keisler,* 506 F.3d 618 (7th Cir. 2007) [admitting a person to bail while challenging admission is contrary to the INA and the inherent authority to admit persons to bail does not extend to persons deemed inadmissible at the border].

5. Habeas Not Available to Review Matters Within and Not Precluded by INA §242—Although the lower courts previously debated whether matters within INA §242 may be challenged in habeas, *compare Lee v. Gonzales,* 410 F.3d 778 (5th Cir. 2005) [no habeas jurisdiction when issue of whether crime was CIMT could have been raised in circuit court]; *with Olatunji v. Ashcroft,* 387 F.3d 383, 386–88 (4th Cir. 2004) [the preclusion provision of INA §242(a)(2)(C) is an absolute bar to a petition for review and therefore habeas action was not improperly brought], the REAL ID Act of 2005, §106, clearly precludes district court jurisdiction in habeas, mandamus, or under the All Writs Act for any "judicial review of an order of removal entered or issued under any provision of this Act." INA §242(a)(5). At least one court has found that the elimination of habeas corpus review in the district court to review removal orders does not violate the Supremacy Clause *Alexandere v. U.S. Att'y Gen.,* 452 F.3d 1204, 1205–07 (11th Cir. 2006) [Supremacy Clause not violated because constitutional and statutory review that existed in habeas still preserved in the courts of appeal provides an adequate and effective remedy to the elimination of habeas in the district court]. Of course, a matter which is not deemed to be a review of a removal order may still be addressed in habeas. *See Singh v. Gonzales,* 499 F.3d 969, 976–81 (9th Cir. 2007) [claim that ineffective assistance of counsel resulted in failure to file a timely appeal to the circuit court was not a review of a final order and district court jurisdiction was not precluded by INA §§242(a)(5) & (b)(9)]; *Nnadika v. Att'y Gen. of the U.S.,* 484 F.3d 626 (3d Cir. 2007) [court of appeals remanded to the district court a claim for injunctive and declaratory relief seeking review of a denied I-730 because it was not a final order for purposes of INA §242 review]; *Fonseca-Sanchez v. Gonzales,* 484 F.3d 439 (7th Cir. 2007) [where respondent sought review of a U visa denial that arose subsequent to a final administrative removal order, the court lacked jurisdiction under INA §242 and the proper remedy was habeas]; *Sandher v. Gonzales,* 481 F.3d 108 (2d Cir. 2007) [court dismissed habeas that was transferred to it improperly under REAL ID Act where habeas only challenged the validity of petitioner's conviction and not his removal order]; *Madu v. U.S. Att'y Gen.,* 470 F.3d 1362, 1366–67 (11th Cir. 2006) [where respondent claims he voluntarily departed and reentered, and therefore does not have a removal order, habeas was appropriate and circuit court dismissed and remanded it to district court]; *Kumarasamy v. Att'y Gen. of the U.S.,* 453 F.3d 169, 172 (3d Cir. 2006) [a person who claims his deportation was illegal because there was no order of removal is not barred by the REAL ID Act from bringing a habeas petition]; *Khouzam v. Hogan,* 497 F.Supp.2d 615, 623 (M.D. Pa. 2007) [denied motion to dismiss habeas where petitioner's deferral of removal under CAT was revoked by DHS]; *Tejada v. Cabral,* 424 F.Supp.2d 296 (D. Mass. 2006) [where person with final order of removal brought challenge to his underlying state conviction the court had jurisdiction to review validity of state conviction; however it could not issue a stay of removal because that is within a removal order].

6. Habeas Not Available to Review Revocation of Visas—The Secretary of State or consular officer's decision to revoke an immigrant visa or NIV under INA §221(i) is not reviewable in habeas, mandamus, or All Writs Act except the decision may be reviewed in the context of a removal proceeding and only then if the revocation provides the sole ground for removal under INA §237(a)(1)(B). *Bolante v. Achim,* 457 F.Supp.2d 896 (E.D. Wis. 2006) [no habeas jurisdiction to review claim that revocation was improper under 22 C.F.R. §41.122(a)].

7. The Meaning of "In Custody" for Habeas—The meaning of "in custody" is often relevant to whether a habeas corpus petition may proceed. Generally, the federal courts have recognized that an expanded concept of custody under *Hensley v. Municipal Court,* 411 U.S. 345, 348–49 (1973) and *Jones v. Cunningham,* 371 U.S. 236, 240–43 (1963) results in coverage even where a person is not physically detained by INS. *Rumsfeld v. Padilla,* 542 U.S. 426, 124 S.Ct. 2711, 2719 (2004) ["[O]ur understanding of custody has broadened to include restraints short of physical confinement"]; *Rosales v. ICE,* 426 F.3d 733, 734–36 (5th Cir. 2005) [upon remand from the Supreme Court, the Fifth Circuit joined the Second, Sixth, Ninth and Tenth Circuits and held that a person subject to a final order of removal is in custody for habeas purposes]; *Garcia-Echaverria v. U.S.,* 376 F.3d 507, 510–11 (6th Cir. 2004) [person in state custody in Kentucky was "in custody" for §2241 purposes where legacy INS had reinstated prior final order of removal]; *Zalawadia v.*

Ashcroft, 371 F.3d 292, 296–98 (5th Cir. 2004) [person deported after habeas filed is still "in custody" because that determination is made at the time the petition is filed]; *Simmonds v. INS,* 326 F.3d 351, 354–56 (2d Cir. 2003) [where respondent who is in state custody serving an indefinite sentence had his removal hearing while in prison he is "in custody" for purposes of habeas review but there were issues of ripeness]; *Aguilera v. Kirkpatrick,* 241 F.3d 1286, 1291 (10th Cir. 2001) [in custody for purposes of challenging denial of motion to reopen]; *Park v. California,* 202 F.3d 1146, 1148 (9th Cir. 2000) [release from prison does not moot person's habeas petition where he still faces deportation]; *Gutierrez v. Ashcroft,* 289 F.Supp.2d 555 (D.N.J. 2003) [where counsel affirmatively misrepresented that he had filed a habeas petition challenging the denial of the right to seek former INA §212(c) before respondent was physically removed but had not filed petition, his actions violated due process and permitted the court to find equitable tolling and accept the habeas *nunc pro tunc* to the time before respondent was physically removed from the U.S.]; *Kanivets v. Riley,* 286 F.Supp.2d 460, 463–64 (E.D. Pa. 2003) [notice to surrender for removal is sufficient to establish custody for habeas review]; *Galaviz-Medina v. Wooten*, 27 F.3d 487, 492–93 (10th Cir. 1994), *cert. denied,* 513 U.S. 1086 (1995) [in custody includes someone in criminal custody if they have a detainer *and* a final order of deportation]; *Fuller v. INS,* 144 F.Supp.2d 72, 83–87 (D. Conn. 2000) [in custody includes person deported where petition was filed prior to physical removal from U.S.]; *Williams v. INS*, 795 F.2d 738, 744 (9th Cir. 1986) [challenge to denial of voluntary departure where person not in custody]; *Umanzor v. Lambert, supra* [airline custody is in custody]; *Gurbisz, supra*; *Salehi v. District Director*, 796 F.2d 1286 (10th Cir. 1986) [in custody includes person in deportation with a bond]; *Guti v. INS*, 908 F.2d 495 (9th Cir. 1990) [in custody includes placement of detainer]; *Vargas v. Swan*, 854 F.2d 1028 (7th Cir. 1988) [same]; *Lemeshko v. Wrona,* 325 F.Supp.2d 778, 782–83 (E.D Mich. 2004) [person in custody where DHS placed detainer and state detainee already has final order of deportation even if not in DHS physical custody]; *Ceballos de Leon v. Reno,* 58 F.Supp.2d 463, 469 n.14 (D.N.J. 1999) [LPR subject to final order but not in physical custody still meets custody requirement for §2241]; *Mendonca v. INS,* 52 F.Supp.2d 155, 159 (D. Mass.), *aff'd,* 201 F.3d 427 (1st Cir. 1999) ["In custody" for §2241 includes persons subject to a final order of deportation even if they are not in physical custody]; *Eltayeb v. Ingham*, 950 F.Supp. 95, 99 (S.D.N.Y. 1997); *Sharma v. Reno*, 902 F.Supp. 1130, 1135 (N.D. Cal. 1995) [persons seeking review of denial of adjustment while under final order of exclusion]; *Sibanda v. District Director, INS*, 881 F.Supp. 1494, 1495 (D. Colo. 1995) [letter advising respondent he would receive notice of when and where to report for deportation met custody requirement]; *Fragedela v. Thornburgh*, 761 F.Supp. 1252, 1253–54 (W.D. La. 1991) [in custody includes person paroled]; *Ajurulloski v. INS*, 688 F.Supp. 1272 (N.D. Ill. 1988).

The Narrow Construction of In Custody. In contrast to the broad "in custody" definition, certain federal courts have suggested that "in custody" can only include persons who are physically detained by immigration authorities. *Perez v. Greiner,* 296 F.3d 123 (2d Cir. 2002) [claim was moot when the petitioner was deported after habeas denial was appealed notwithstanding "collateral consequences' doctrine because there was an independent conviction for drug trafficking which would have barred petitioner's return even if he was successful in habeas]; *Chavez v. Superior Court of California,* 194 F.Supp.2d 1037 (C.D. Cal. 2002) [person deported to Mexico seeking to challenge his California state convictions is not in either California custody or INS custody and therefore court has no jurisdiction]; *Digrado v. Ashcroft,* 184 F.Supp.2d 227, 231–33 (N.D.N.Y. 2002) [no habeas jurisdiction for person held by U.S. Marshals for prosecution on re-entry who is challenging original denial of §212(c) relief because he is not in INS custody]; *Ramirez-Centeno v. Wallis*, 957 F.Supp. 1267, 1271 (S.D. Fla. 1997); *Isaraphanich v. Sava*, 663 F.Supp. 120 (S.D.N.Y. 1987) [person who posts bond not in custody]; *Campillo v. Sullivan*, 853 F.2d 593 (8th Cir. 1988), *cert. denied,* 490 U.S. 1082 (1989) [no habeas jurisdiction to lift INS detainer because alien not in INS custody]; *Accord* following *Campillo. Zolicoffer v. DOJ,* 315 F.3d 538 (5th Cir. 2003); *Garcia v. Taylor*, 40 F.3d 299 (9th Cir. 1994); *Santana v. Chandler*, 961 F.2d 514 (5th Cir. 1992); *Prieto v. Gluch*, 913 F.2d 1159 (6th Cir. 1990), *cert. denied*, 111 S.Ct. 976 (1991); *Orozco v. INS*, 911 F.2d 539 (11th Cir. 1990); *Bell v. INS,* 292 F.Supp.2d 370, 373–74 (D. Conn. 2003); *Topazov v. INS*, 929 F.Supp. 479, 483 (D.D.C. 1996). Some courts have found that a person who has been removed cannot proceed in habeas because s/he is no longer "in custody." *Kumarasamy v. Att'y Gen. of the U.S.*, 453 F.3d 169 (3d Cir. 2006) [a person is not "in custody" for purposes of §2241 if the habeas petition was filed after deportation]; *Patel v. U.S. Att'y Gen.,* 334 F.3d 1259,

1263–64 (11th Cir. 2003) [the court of appeals refused to transfer the review of a denial of a motion to reopen to the district court where the person had been deported because the district court lacked habeas jurisdiction as the person was no longer in custody]; *Miranda v. Reno,* 238 F.3d 1156 (9th Cir. 2001), *cert. denied, Miranda v. Ashcroft* 534 U.S. 1018 (2001) [person removed to Mexico not "in custody" for habeas purposes and case was dismissed for lack of jurisdiction]; *Terrado v. Moyer,* 820 F.2d 920 (7th Cir. 1987) [no jurisdiction where stay denied and person deported]. Similarly, a person who is out of the U.S. at the time DHS or another government agency takes an adverse action that prevents his return may not challenge the action by habeas. *Samirah v. O'Connell,* 335 F.3d 545 (7th Cir. 2003) [district court lacked jurisdiction to review revocation of advance parole while person out of the U.S. because INA §242(a)(2)(B)(ii) precludes review of discretionary decisions and because habeas jurisdiction was unavailable to someone outside the U.S. who is not in custody and is unable to have personal service over a custodian]; *Sadhyani v. Chertoff,* 460 F.Supp.2d 114 (D.D.C. 2006) [person who was deported was not in custody for habeas purposes and REAL ID Act and INA §242(g) divest the court of jurisdiction]; *El-Hadad v. U.S.,* 377 F.Supp.2d 42 (D.D.C. 2005) [no habeas or other jurisdiction to review denial of B-1/B-2 visa or advance parole for person who wishes to return to U.S. to pursue litigation because he is not in custody]. There is also no habeas jurisdiction

8. Transfer of Person after Habeas Filed—Under the expanded concept of custody, once the habeas petition is properly filed, jurisdiction is maintained even if the petitioner is transferred out of the jurisdiction or removed from the United States. *Ex Parte Mitsuye Endo,* 323 U.S. 283, 304, 65 S.Ct. 208 (1944) [subsequent removal of Japanese American to internment camp outside of habeas court's jurisdiction did not divest court of jurisdiction];*Rumsfeld v. Padilla,* 124 S.Ct. 2711, 2721 (2004) [dismissing Padilla's habeas petition for failure to name the "immediate custodian" as the respondent but recognizing the *Endo* exception where the immediate custodian was properly named but detainee was moved]; *Handa v. Clark,* 401 F.3d 1129, 1132 (9th Cir. 2005) [in visa waiver removal case, habeas jurisdiction was not lost were respondent was removed after petition was filed because of collateral consequences]; *Johnson v. Ashcroft,* 378 F.3d 164, 168 (2d Cir. 2004) [respondent deported after habeas filed and habeas subsequently denied, but circuit court reversed]; *Zalawadia v. Ashcroft,* 371 F.3d 292, 296–98 (5th Cir. 2004) [person deported after habeas filed is still "in custody" because that determination is made at the time the petition is filed]; *Swaby v. Ashcroft,* 357 F.3d 156, 159–60 (2d Cir. 2004) [where habeas petitioner was deported during pendency of appeal case was not moot because of permanent bar due to aggravated felony conviction]; *Noriega-Lopez v. Ashcroft,* 335 F.3d 874, 878 (9th Cir. 2003) [court had jurisdiction to review habeas denial when person deported after habeas denied]; *Zegarra-Gomez v. INS,* 314 F.3d 1124 (9th Cir. 2003) [where habeas petitioner is deported *after* filing petition, the petition is not moot where there are collateral consequences arising from the deportation such as the inability to return]; *Smith v. Ashcroft,* 295 F.3d 425, 428 (4th Cir. 2002) [if person was in custody at time habeas was filed jurisdiction remains even if s/he is removed from the U.S.]; *Chong v. District Director, INS,* 264 F.3d 378, 382–83 (3d Cir. 2001) [where person was deported after habeas was filed, the "in custody" requirement was met in *post–St. Cyr* case]; *Steele v. Blackman,* 236 F.3d 130, 134 n.4 (3d Cir. 2001) [continued jurisdiction after person deported because of collateral consequences following *Sibron v. New York,* 392 U.S. 40, 55–56 (1968) regarding collateral consequences of habeas petitioners not in custody]; *Goodman v. Keohane*, 663 F.2d 1044, 1047 (11th Cir. 1981); *Jones v. DHS,* 325 F.Supp.2d 551, 554 (E.D.Pa. 2004) [petitioner in custody where he was deported after he filed petition challenging removal on grounds of citizenship]; *Atem v. Ashcroft,* 312 F.Supp.2d 792, 796 (E.D. Va. 2004) [where person placed in criminal custody after habeas is filed there is still jurisdiction to review noncustodial issues]; *Osses v. McElroy,* 287 F.Supp.2d 199, 203–04 (W.D.N.Y. 2003) [jurisdiction retained where detainee transferred from Western District of NY to Penn after he filed habeas petition]; *Reyes-Sanchez v. Ashcroft,* 261 F.Supp.2d 276, 282–84 (S.D.N.Y. 2003) [where person was deported while case was pending in court of appeals and that court determined jurisdiction was in the district court in habeas, the district court's jurisdiction was not moot by virtue of petitioner's removal prior to transfer of case to district court]; *So v. Reno,* 251 F.Supp.2d 1112, 1120 (E.D.N.Y. 2003) [the "in custody" requirement is satisfied if petitioner files habeas before being deported]; *Chavez-Rivas v. Olsen,* 194 F.Supp.2d 368 (D.N.J. 2002) [distinguishing *Yi v. Maugans* and finding the AG is custodian and there is personal jurisdiction over the AG where transfer of person after habeas filed would deprive court of jurisdiction]; *Matter of Mariel Cubans*, 822 F.Supp. 192, 194 (M.D. Pa. 1993);

Ramos v. Thornburgh, 761 F.Supp. 1258, 1260 n.2 (W.D. La. 1991); *Gonzalo v. Thornburgh*, 761 F.Supp. 1264, 1265 n.3 (W.D. La. 1991), or even if the person is on airplane when the action is filed. *Ledesma-Valdes v. Sava*, 604 F.Supp. 675, 679–80 (S.D.N.Y. 1985).

Equitable Tolling. *Gutierrez v. Ashcroft,* 289 F.Supp.2d 555 (D.N.J. 2003) [where counsel affirmatively misrepresented that he had filed a habeas petition challenging the denial of the right to seek former INA §212(c) before respondent was physically removed but had not filed petition, his actions violated due process and permitted the court to accept the habeas *nunc pro tunc* to the time before respondent was physically removed from the U.S.].

9. Personal Jurisdiction, Personal Service, and Venue.

Habeas for Persons in the U.S. In *Rumsfeld v. Padilla,* 124 S.Ct. 2711 (2004) the Supreme Court addressed the issue of who is the proper respondent in a habeas corpus petition. Distinguishing *Braden v. 30th Judicial Circuit Court*, 410 U.S. 484, 494–95 (1973) [habeas not limited to place of petitioner's confinement but only to court's jurisdiction over custodian] and *Strait v. Laird,* 406 U.S. 341, 345 (1972) [habeas jurisdiction is proper even if custodian is not physically present in the district as long as the custodian is within reach of the court's process under *International Shoe* standards] and recognizing exceptions to the rule (such as in *Endo, supra*), a majority of the Court, nevertheless determined that a habeas corpus action must be brought against the "immediate custodian" of the person detained and must be filed in the district court whose territorial jurisdiction includes the place where the custodian is located. The Court found the "immediate custodian" rule applicable in cases that involved challenges to physical detention (which it described as "core" cases), but declined to decide whether the rule would apply to persons in immigration custody "pending deportation." *Rumsfeld,* 121 S.Ct. at 2718 n.8. The Court's decision also noted the split in the circuits on the immediate custodian rule in immigration matters. *Id. Compare Ali v. Ashcroft,* 346 F.3d 873, 887–88 (9th Cir. 2003); and *Nolasco v. U.S.*, 358 F.Supp.2d 224, 231–34 (S.D.N.Y. 2004) [post-*Padilla*, the court determined that the AG or Secy. of DHS was the proper respondent and that the government waived objection to personal jurisdiction]; *Somir v. U.S.,* 354 F.Supp.2d 215, 216–18 (E.D.N.Y. 2005 [post-*Padilla,* the AG remains the proper custodian]; *Mandarino v. Ashcroft,* 318 F.Supp.2d 13, 16–17 (D. Conn. 2003 [AG is proper custodian for habeas purposes] *with Kholyavskiy v. Achim,* 443 F.3d 946 (7th Cir. 2006) [post-*Padilla,* neither the AG, the DHS Secretary, nor the ICE Field Director are the proper custodians and the habeas petition should be directed to the warden of the state jail where the person is detained]; *Robledo-Gonzales v. Ashcroft,* 342 F.3d 667, 672–76 (7th Cir. 2003) [where petitioner was in custody of Bureau of Prisons awaiting trial on illegal re-entry charge, his failure to name prison officials in habeas petition resulted in dismissal of his immigration claims]; *Roman v. Ashcroft,* 340 F.3d 314 (6th Cir. 2003) [DD is the immediate custodian and immediate custodian rule applies absent extraordinary circumstances]; *Samirah v. O'Connell,* 335 F.3d 545 (7th Cir. 2003) [district court lacked jurisdiction to review revocation of advance parole because habeas jurisdiction is unavailable where petitioner cannot obtain personal service over a custodian because there is none]; *Vasquez v. Reno,* 233 F.3d 688 (1st Cir. 2000), *cert. denied,* 534 U.S. 816 (2001) [AG is not subject to nationwide habeas and immediate custodian is the head of the detention facility]; *Yi v. Maugans*, 24 F.3d 500, 507 (3d Cir. 1994) [limited habeas to persons the DD had actual custody over and declined to include those he had constructive custody over and therefore could release, but who were not physically in the district]; *Excellent v. Ashcroft,* 359 F.Supp.2d 333, 335–36 (S.D.N.Y. 2005) [reading *Padilla* strictly to require naming of immediate custodian where petitioner was in Louisiana at time he filed petition in S.D.N.Y.]; *Diallo v. Holmes,* 288 F.Supp.2d 442 (E.D.N.Y. 2003) [where respondent was in detention in Batavia, N.Y. as a result of the ICE district director's decision, his transfer to Western District is appropriate]; *Andrade v. Ashcroft,* 270 F.Supp.2d 344 (E.D.N.Y. 2003) [on review of denied adjustment application, venue is properly in Oakdale where petitioner is detained because although his family resides in New York, they have not entered into a lease for property in N.Y. and the fact that case is on appeal to BIA is not persuasive where BIA remand or reversal will place case before IJ in Louisiana]. *Valdivia v. INS,* 80 F.Supp.2d 326, 332–33 (D.N.J. 2000) [no personal jurisdiction where custodian not within jurisdiction; but court transferred case under 28 U.S.C. §1631 rather than dismiss action]; *Wang v. Reno*, 862 F.Supp. 801, 811–13 (E.D.N.Y. 1994) [no habeas unless there is personal service over custodian]; *Chukwurah v. U.S.,* 813 F.Supp. 161, 168 (E.D.N.Y. 1993); *Peon v. Thornburgh*, 765

F.Supp. 155 (S.D.N.Y. 1991). For a general discussion of the service of process in habeas against the AG *see Henderson v. INS,* 157 F.3d 106, 122–28 (2d Cir. 1998).

Immediate Custodian Is DHS or Local Warden. Even if one assumed that the immediate custodian is not the Attorney General, a question remains post-*Padilla* whether the immediate custodian is a DHS or ICE official or the local warden of a county, state or federal prison where the respondent is detained. *See e.g., Campbell v. Ganter,* 353 F.Supp.2d 332, 336–38 (E.D.N.Y. 2004) [following *Padilla* and finding that because jurisdiction in a habeas case is not limited in a territorial sense but is a matter of venue and personal jurisdiction, the Field Director of ICE whose office is in the Southern District of New York may nevertheless be sued in the Eastern District of New York]. *Somir v. U.S.,* 354 F.Supp.2d 215, 218–19 (E.D.N.Y. 2005 [post-*Padilla,* venue was proper in the E.D.N.Y despite petitioner's detention in New Jersey]. *But see Kholyavskiy v. Achim,* 443 F.3d 946 (7th Cir. 2006) [post-*Padilla,* neither the AG, the DHS Secretary, nor the ICE Field Director are the proper custodians and the habeas petition should be directed to the warden of the state jail where the person is detained]; *Galaviz-Medina v. Wooten*, 27 F.3d 487, 493–94 (10th Cir. 1994), *cert. denied,* 513 U.S. 1086 (1995) [habeas jurisdiction found where the custodian is a federal warden and not the Service because the Supreme Court has recognized that a challenge to future confinement is actionable and a warden acts as a Service agent where there is a detainer *and* a final deportation order].

Immediate Custodian Is USCIS or ICE. If the AG is not named, a person seeking to challenge his removal order should name the Field Office Director (FOD) of ICE, and not the District Director for USCIS, because ICE has custody over a person subject to removal. *Campbell v. Ganter,* 353 F.Supp.2d 332, 335–36 (E.D.N.Y. 2004). *But see Kholyavskiy v. Achim,* 443 F.3d 946 (7th Cir. 2006) [post-*Padilla,* neither the AG, the DHS Secretary nor the ICE Field Director are the proper custodians and the habeas petition should be directed to the warden of the state jail where the person is detained].

Venue, Not Subject-Matter Jurisdiction, Is the Criterion. The concurring opinion in *Padilla* written by Justice Kennedy and necessary for a majority expressly held that the immediate custodian rule is not a matter of subject-matter jurisdiction, but of venue and personal jurisdiction. *Padilla,* 124 S.Ct. at 2728. In *So v. Reno,* 251 F.Supp.2d 1112, 1126–27 (E.D.N.Y. 2003) the district court, citing *Braden* and *Mojica v. Reno,* 970 F.Supp. 130, 167–68 (E.D.N.Y. 1997) stated that because no venue statute exists for habeas, the court must rely on the traditional considerations for determining venue including: (1) the location where the material events took place, (2) where records and witnesses pertinent to the claim are likely to be found, (3) the convenience of the forum for respondent and petitioner, and (4) the familiarity of the court with the applicable law." *So* at 1126. Based on these general considerations a number of courts have agreed that venue is proper outside of the district where the person is detained. *Campbell v. Ganter,* 353 F.Supp.2d 332, 336–38 (E.D.N.Y. 2004) [following *Padilla* and finding that because jurisdiction in a habeas case is not limited in a territorial sense but is a matter of venue and personal jurisdiction, the Field Director of ICE whose office is in the Southern District of New York may nevertheless be sued in the Eastern District of New York]. *Somir v. U.S.,* 354 F.Supp.2d 215, 218–19 (E.D.N.Y. 2005 [post-*Padilla,* venue was proper in the E.D.N.Y despite petitioner's detention in New Jersey]; *Walters v. Ashcroft,* 291 F.Supp.2d 237, 241–44 (S.D.N.Y. 2003) [AG is the proper custodian and venue is proper in NY despite respondent's detention in Florida because crimes were committed in NY and the hearing where §212(c) relief was granted was in NY]; *Clavis v. Ashcroft,* 281 F.Supp.2d 490, 492–93 (E.D.N.Y. 2003) [in the absence of a venue statute for habeas, general venue principles apply and petitioner's detention in Oakdale, La. does not bar venue in Eastern District of New York where issue does not involve personal appearance]; *Chavez-Rivas v. Olsen,* 194 F.Supp.2d 368 (D.N.J. 2002) [distinguishing *Yi v. Maugans* and finding the AG is custodian and there is personal jurisdiction over the AG where transfer of person after habeas filed would deprive court of jurisdiction]; *Barton v. Ashcroft,* 152 F.Supp.2d 235 (D. Conn. 2001) [AG was proper custodian for purposes of habeas jurisdiction in Conn. for detainee at Oakdale and venue was also proper in Conn.]; *Barnaby v. Reno,* 127 F.Supp.2d 322, 324–25 (D. Conn. 2001) [venue proper in Conn. where removal proceeding started there and person transferred to Oakdale, La]; *Santos-Gonzalez v. Reno,* 93 F.Supp.2d 286, 291–93 (E.D. N.Y. 2000) [where person held in Buffalo and custodian could be served under Fed. R. Civ. P. 4(e)(1) venue was proper in Eastern District of N.Y.]; *Pottinger v. Reno,* 51 F.Supp.2d 349, 356–57 (E.D.N.Y. 1999) *aff'd* 242 F.3d 367 (2d Cir. 2000) [jurisdiction in Eastern District of N.Y., where district director is in New Orleans]; *Eltayeb v. Ingham*, 950 F.Supp. 95, 99 (S.D.N.Y. 1997) [custodian not in district but subject to jurisdiction under NY service of process statute]; *Nwankwo v. Reno*, 828 F.Supp. 171 (E.D.N.Y. 1993) [there is nothing in §2443 which expressly prohibits habeas brought against the AG where personal service (through state long-arm statute) can be brought against AG and there are policy reasons for not deferring to Western District of Louisiana].

10. Habeas for Persons Outside the U.S.—In *Rasul v. Bush,* 542 U.S. 466 (2004) the Court found that there was habeas jurisdiction to review the physical custody of aliens being held at the military base in Guantanamo, Cuba. The Court distinguished *Johnson v. Eisentrager,* found that habeas applies extraterritorially to aliens, that aliens like U.S. citizens can invoke federal court authority, and that the presence of the detainee in the territorial jurisdiction of a federal court is not a jurisdictional requirement for habeas as long as there is jurisdiction over the custodian. The Court also found that jurisdiction existed under 28 U.S.C. §1331 (General Federal Question jurisdiction) and §1350 (Alien Tort Claims Act). *Rasul,* 124 S.Ct. at 2698–99. Where a person is confined oversees and therefore outside the territory of any district court, the habeas petition should be brought against the respondent official (such as the AG) in the district in which s/he resides which is typically Washington DC. *Rumsfeld v. Padilla,* 124 S.Ct. 2711, 2725 n.16 (2004) [the immediate custodian rule is relaxed where the person is outside the U.S. and therefore the AG or another government official may be the respondent, but the petition must be brought in the place of residence of the respondent official]; *Gherebi v. Bush,* 374 F.3d 727, 739 (9th Cir. 2004) [following *Padilla* in action regarding Guantanamo detainees brought in Central District of California, court transferred venue to D.C. where Bush resides]; *Gherebi v. Bush,* 338 F.Supp.2d 91 (D.D.C. 2004) [after transfer district court held it had jurisdiction]; *Abu Ali v. Ashcroft,* 350 F.Supp.2d 28, 39–57 (D.D.C. 2004) [denied motion to dismiss habeas petition brought by a U.S. citizen being held in Saudi Arabia at the direction of the U.S.]. *But see e.g., El-Hadad v. U.S.,* 377 F.Supp.2d 42 (D.D.C. 2005) [no habeas or other jurisdiction to review denial of B-1/B-2 visa or advance parole to return to pursue litigation of person outside the U.S.].

11. Exhaustion of Administrative Remedies Under 8 U.S.C. §1252(d)(1) or Otherwise Associated with a Petition for Review Prior to Filing a Habeas Petition—In light of the Supreme Court's distinction in *INS v. St. Cyr,* 533 U.S. 289, 311–12 (2001) between petitions for review and habeas corpus, there is a question as to whether a petitioner must exhaust administrative remedies normally associated with a petition for review. *Compare Ali v. Ashcroft,* 346 F.3d 873, 877–78 (9th Cir. 2003) [statutory and prudential exhaustion unnecessary in habeas pattern and practice claim, unrelated to removal hearing, where habeas petitioners challenge whether government can remove person to a country, Somalia, that is unable to accept them]; *Arango Marquez v. INS,* 346 F.3d 892, 896–97 (9th Cir. 2003) [exhaustion in habeas is a prudential not a statutory matter]; *Pequeno-Martinez v. Tominski,* 281 F.Supp.2d 902, 911–12 (S.D. Tex. 2003) [Section 1252(d)(2) should not be interpreted to require exhaustion of petition for review in circuit court before filing habeas]; *Jankowski v. INS,* 138 F.Supp.2d 269, 273–76 (D. Conn. 2001) *rev'd on other grounds* 291 F.3d 172 (2d Cir. 2002) [constitutional issues in habeas not applicable to 1252(d)]; *Ying Fong v. Ashcroft,* 317 F.Supp.2d 398, 406–07 (S.D.N.Y. 2004) [post-*Theodoropoulos/Beharry* habeas should not be dismissed for failure to exhaust the administrative remedy of filing a motion to reopen an *in absentia* order for lack of notice where respondent was deported before he could effect motion to reopen], *with Taylor v. U.S.,* 396 F.3d 1322, 1326–28 (11th Cir. 2005) [applying *Sundar* to factual finding and determining that habeas court lacked jurisdiction where issue as to date of entry was not raised in *pro se* appeal to the BIA; Court distinguished between isolated statement in brief versus making an argument]; *Sayyah v. Farquharson,* 382 F.3d 20 (1st Cir. 2004) [exhaustion of administrative remedies is required in habeas under §1252(d)(1)]; *Laing v. Ashcroft,* 370 F.3d 994 (9th Cir. 2004) [habeas court lacked jurisdiction because §2241 petition was filed more than 30 days after BIA decision and petitioner failed to timely file a petition for review in the circuit court thereby failing to exhaust judicial remedies]; *Sun v. Ashcroft,* 370 F.3d 932, 935–44 (9th Cir. 2004) [same]; *Theodoropoulos v. INS,* 358 F.3d 162, 167–74 (2d Cir. 2004) [the statutory exhaustion requirement under §1252(d)(1) bars habeas review even where petitioner claims futility]; *Duvall v. Elwood,* 336 F.3d 228 (3d Cir. 2003) [habeas review is barred under §1252(d)(1) where there was no final order of removal]; *Beharry v. Ashcroft,* 329 F.3d 51 (2d Cir. 2003) [finding judicial exhaustion required but not deciding whether statutory exhaustion would be required in habeas notwithstanding *St. Cyr*]; *Sundar v. INS,* 328 F.3d 1320 (11th Cir.) *cert. denied* 124 S.Ct. 531

(2003) [finding that 8 U.S.C. §1252(d)(1) applies to §2241 habeas proceedings and dismissed petition for failure to seek BIA review even if there was perceived futility]; *De La Teja v. U.S.,* 321 F.3d 1357, 1366 (11th Cir. 2003) [failure to raise CAT claim issue to BIA deprived habeas court of jurisdiction under INA §242(d)(2)]; *Kurfees v. INS,* 275 F.3d 332 (4th Cir. 2001) [exhaustion requirement under former 8 U.S.C. §1105a(c) applied in habeas]; *Boz v. U.S.* 248 F.3d 1299 (11th Cir. 2001) [habeas corpus properly dismissed where petitioner did not exhaust INS procedure for review after 90-day period]; *DeJesus Corona v. Derosa,* 325 F.Supp.2d 516, 523–25 (D.N.J. 2004) [where petitioner had several previous opportunities to raise claim of citizenship before IJ or federal judge in criminal re-entry case and failed to do so, habeas barred to review USC claim]; *Jordan v. Ashcroft,* 296 F.Supp.2d 249, 251–53 (D. Conn. 2003) [where counsel conceded deportability and never raised legal issue, his client was barred from litigating whether offense was an aggravated felony]; *Brzuszek, et. al v. McElroy,* 275 F.Supp.2d 442, 447–48 (S.D.N.Y. 2003) [absent a substantial constitutional question, habeas petitioner must exhaust administrative remedies under INA §242(d) when raising an INA §212(c) retroactivity claim].

However, even if statutory exhaustion applies pursuant to INA §242(d)(1) to habeas petitions, the traditional exceptions to exhaustion would apply; *see in this chapter* section IV.B (p.1133), *infra*. The Second Circuit has also recognized that *issue* exhaustion is *not* jurisdictional under INA §242(d)(1) and may be waived. *Zhong v. DOJ,* 480 F.3d 104, 116–25 (2d Cir. 2007) [court distinguished between exhaustion of claims which is jurisdictional and exhaustion of issues which is not jurisdiction and therefore may be waived by the government. The waiver argument has even greater force in streamlining cases].

The doctrine of exhaustion of administrative remedies should not be confused with the doctrine requiring direct appeal instead of habeas where direct appeal is available. *Latu v. Ashcroft,* 375 F.3d 1012, 1017 (10th Cir. 2004) [criticizing the government for confusing exhaustion of administrative remedies and the need for direct review when seeking to dismiss a habeas petition on the grounds that the case should have been brought in the court of appeals].

12. Law of the Case/Res Judicata—A district court in habeas proceedings will be bound by findings of the Court of Appeals under the law of the case doctrine (or res judicata) where it finds it has no jurisdiction because the appellant committed an aggravated felony. *Nunes v. Ashcroft,* 348 F.3d 815 (9th Cir. 2003) *rehearing en banc denied* 375 F.3d 810 (9th Cir. 2004) [where circuit court dismissed appeal on jurisdictional grounds because respondent was convicted of aggravated felony he could not seek habeas review on whether conviction was for aggravated felony because res judicata/law of case barred the claim]; *Gavilan-Cuate v. Yetter,* 276 F.3d 418, 419–20 (8th Cir. 2002) [dismissal in court of appeals on jurisdictional grounds because appellant was convicted of an aggravated felony barred reconsideration of aggravated felony status in district court on habeas]; *Santos v. Reno,* 228 F.3d 591, 597 (5th Cir. 2000) [same]; *Beshli v. DHS,* 272 F.Supp.2d 514, 519–22 (E.D. Pa. 2003) [the law of the case doctrine barred the district court from reviewing whether petitioner committed an aggravated felony resulting in expedited removal where the court of appeals in dismissing petitioner's former appeal concluded he had committed an aggravated felony]; *Digrado v. Ashcroft,* 184 F.Supp.2d 227, 233–34 (N.D.N.Y. 2002) [denial of INA §212(c) relief even if erroneous bars habeas action challenging denial again in light of *St. Cyr*]. But the Court will not resolve jurisdictional issues based upon dicta in a Court of Appeals suggestion that the district court had jurisdiction. *Ogbudimkpa v. Ashcroft,* 342 F.3d 207, 210 n.7 (3d Cir. 2003).

13. Habeas Must be Filed in District Court—To seek habeas relief must first go to district court, not court of appeals. *Emejulu v. INS*, 989 F.2d 771 (5th Cir. 1993) [recognizing problems caused by Oakdale and flood of habeas petitions in Western District of Louisiana, but finding habeas must first be made in district court]. The federal transfer statute, 28 U.S.C. §1631, allows a case to be transferred from the circuit court to the district court and vice-versa, if the appropriate criteria are met. *Dragenice v. Ridge,* 389 F.3d 92 (4th Cir. 2004) [where respondent sought release from detention on theory he was a national of U.S., the circuit court, notwithstanding 242(b)(5) was barred from considering the nationality claim because of 242(a)(2)(C) and case should be re-transferred under §1631 to the district court in habeas];*Yanez-Garcia v. Ashcroft,* 388 F.3d 280, 284 (7th Cir. 2004) [where circuit court's jurisdiction was barred by INA §242(a)(2)(C) case was transferred to district court for habeas proceeding]; *Olaguez-Garcia v. INS,* 152 F.3d 1005 (7th Cir. 1998) [habeas petition filed in circuit court was transferred to district court]. And a court of

appeals pursuant to 28 U.S.C. §1631 may transfer an action to the district court even if the circuit court has no jurisdiction. *Cruz-Aguilera v. INS,* 245 F.3d 1070 (9th Cir. 2001) [where §242(a)(2)(C) barred circuit court review case was transferred to the district court for habeas review]. It also allows transfer from one district court to another. *Simpson v. Ashcroft,* 321 F.Supp.2d 13 (D.D.C. 2004) [ordered transfer from DC to NY where petitioner was detained prior to transfer to Oakdale]. *But see Acevedo-Carranza v. Ashcroft,* 371 F.3d 539, 542–43 (9th Cir. 2004) [habeas dismissed because case could not be transferred to circuit court under 28 U.S.C. §1631 where habeas was not filed within 30 days of BIA decision and court therefore lacked jurisdiction]. The court may also transfer a habeas proceeding to the circuit court. *Salazar-Regino v. Gonzales,* 415 F.3d 436, 444–46 (5th Cir. 2005) [where case should have been brought in the circuit court but there was confusion over jurisdictional issues when a respondent asserted he was not convicted, court waived failure to file in circuit court and had habeas transferred to it under §1631]. *But see Puri v. Gonzales,* 464 F.3d 1038, 1042–43 (9th Cir. 2006) [transfer denied because it was not in "the interest of justice" to transfer a habeas case that was improperly filed in the district court subsequent to REAL ID Act of 2005 and was filed to circumvent prior order of dismissal].

14. Discovery in Habeas Proceeding under 28 U.S.C. §2241—Although review is generally limited to the administrative record "the district court may, if necessary, conduct a hearing to take evidence concerning illegal action that is not reflected in the record." *Johns v. DOJ,* 653 F.2d 884, 896 (5th Cir. 1981); *Marczak v. Greene,* 971 F.2d 510, 518–19 (10th Cir. 1992); *Jean v. Nelson,* 472 U.S. 846 (1985). This is particularly so where constitutional questions are raised or the record is obviously deficient. *Bracy v. Gramley,* 117 S.Ct. 1793, 1796–98 (1997); *Harris v. Nelson,* 394 U.S. 286 (1969); *Townsend v. Sain,* 372 U.S. 293, 312 (1963) [power of court to inquire is plenary]. The Court is not limited to accepting the government's view about the scope of inquiry. *Zadvydas v. Davis,* 533 U.S. 678, 687–88, 699 121 S.Ct. 2491, 2503 (2001). Rule 6(a) of Rules Governing 28 U.S.C. §2254 cases provides for discovery in habeas under 28 U.S.C. §2254.

15. Stay or Delay in Hearing Habeas Proceedings—District courts must "summarily" hear and determine habeas petitions. 28 U.S.C. §2243. A trial court must act within a reasonable time and any stay of proceedings will be reversed where there is no set time to hear the petition. *Yong v. INS,* 208 F.3d 1116 (9th Cir. 2000) [reversed district court's stay of habeas proceedings pending a determination in the circuit court that would clarify the law].

16. Habeas May Not Be Permissible for Collateral Attack—Habeas may not be used against INS for the purpose of collaterally attacking an expired state court conviction. *Resendiz v. Kovensky,* 416 F.3d 952, 960–61 (9th Cir. 2005) [post-AEDPA and post-IIRIRA respondent cannot collaterally attack in a §2241 habeas his state-court conviction that forms the basis for his DHS custody]; *Taylor v. U.S.,* 396 F.3d 1322, 1330 (11th Cir. 2005) [barred collateral challenge to validity of state court conviction in habeas seeking review of removal order]; *Broomes v. Ashcroft,* 358 F.3d 1251, 1255 (10th Cir. 2004) [cannot challenge expired state court conviction under §2241]; *Drakes v. INS,* 330 F.3d 600 (3d Cir.), *cert. denied,* 124 S.Ct. 541 (2003) [following S.Ct. decisions in *Coss and Daniels* the court determined that petitioner could not challenge, through a §2241 action against INS, the constitutionality of his state court conviction that resulted in his removal]; *Contreras v. Schiltgen,* 122 F.3d 30 (9th Cir. 1997); *Martinez v. Lockyer,* 453 F.Supp.2d 1150 (C.D. Cal. 2006) [cannot collaterally attack a state conviction in a federal coram nobis proceeding challenging removal because there is not jurisdiction and respondent is no longer "in custody" in regard to his state conviction for habeas corpus purposes]; *Neyor v. INS,* 155 F.Supp.2d 127 (D.N.J. 2001) [following S.Ct. decisions in *Coss and Daniels* court determined that petitioner could not challenge through §2254 or §2241 a state court conviction by suing INS]; *Plummer v. Ashcroft,* 258 F.Supp.2d 43, 45–46 (D. Conn. 2003); It may also not be used to attack a purely discretionary decision such as the INS decision to refuse to exercise discretion in instituting deportation proceedings. *Carranza v. INS,* 277 F.3d 65 (1st Cir. 2002) [no subject-matter jurisdiction in habeas to challenge INS's refusal to exercise discretion in instituting removal proceeding].

17. Successive Applications and Fee Requirements for Habeas Petitions—The fee requirements of the Prison Litigation Reform Act of 1996, PL 104-134, 100 Stat. 1321 (1996) do not apply to habeas petitions or petitions for review filed by persons who are incarcerated and facing deportation because they are not deemed to be "prisoners" for purposes of the act. *Agyeman v. INS,* 296 F.3d

871, 885–86 (9th Cir. 2002); *LaFontant v. INS,* 135 F.3d 158, 165 (D.C. Cir. 1998); *Ojo v. INS,* 106 F.3d 680, 683 (5th Cir. 1997). Similarly, habeas petitions filed under 28 U.S.C. §2241 in immigration proceedings are not subject to the prohibition under 28 U.S.C. §§2244(a), 2244(b), 2255 ¶8 against successive habeas petitions filed under 28 U.S.C. §§2254 or 2255.*Zayas v. INS,* 311 F.3d 247, 253–5 (3d Cir. 2002) [agreeing with *Barapind* and *Valona* and holding that the "gate keeping" regime of §2244(b) does not apply to immigration petitions filed under §2241 but also holding that the "abuse of writ" doctrine does apply]; *Barapind v. Reno,* 225 F.3d 1100, 1110–12 (9th Cir. 2000) [reversed dismissal of suit challenging BIA decision to stay asylum consideration while extradition pending because the successive bar doctrine only applies under §2244(a) and (b) to judgments of a court and not the BIA]; *Valona v. U.S.,* 138 F.3d 693, 694 (7th Cir. 1998). *See also Grullon v. Ashcroft,* 374 F.3d 137 (2d Cir. 2004) [where another §2241 petition is pending a subsequently filed petition will be treated as an amendment to the first petition]; *Lema v. INS,* 341 F.3d 853, 857 n.9 (9th Cir. 2003). However, the "abuse of writ" doctrine under *McCleskey v. Zant,* 499 U.S. 467, 111 S.Ct. 1454 (1991) may apply to bar successive petitions. *Zayas v. INS,* 311 F.3d 247, 256–58 (3d Cir. 2002) [dismissing habeas by *pro se* litigant challenging denial of INA §212(c) on abuse of writ theory]; *Esposito v. Ashcroft,* 288 F.Supp.2d 292 (E.D.N.Y. 2003) [court dismissed habeas on grounds that it was an abuse of writ to bring successive habeas action raising the same issues as were dismissed six years earlier]. Similarly, 8 U.S.C. §1252(d) bars a subsequent court from deciding a case where another court has decided the matter unless the prior proceeding "was inadequate or ineffective." *Filsaime v. Ashcroft,* 393 F.3d 315 (2d Cir. 2004) [remanded case to district court to determine whether habeas proceeding in the W.D. La. was inadequate or ineffective in disposing of respondent's CAT claim]. Even if the successive petition doctrine applies an intervening change in the law provides an exception to barring review. *Rosales-Garcia v. Holland,* 322 F.3d 386, 398–400 (6th Cir. 2003) [doctrine does not apply to persons not in custody due to conviction and if it did under prior law petitioner has established that *Zadvydas* and IIRIRA are intervening changes]. Also, principles of *res judicata* generally have no application to successive habeas corpus cases. *Sanders v. U.S.,* 373 U.S. 1, 8 (1963); *Fernandez Luiz v. Luttrell,* 46 F.Supp.2d 754, 756 (W.D. Tex. 1999). However, *res judicata* may apply in certain circumstances in habeas cases. *Nunes v. Ashcroft,* 348 F.3d 815 (9th Cir. 2003) *rehearing en banc denied* 375 F.3d 810 (9th Cir. 2004) [where circuit court dismissed appeal on jurisdictional grounds because respondent was convicted of aggravated felony he could not seek habeas review on whether conviction was for aggravated felony]; *Digrado v. Ashcroft,* 184 F.Supp.2d 227, 233–34 (N.D.N.Y. 2002) [finding doctrine of *res judicata* applicable in habeas action challenging denial of INA §212(c) relief].

18. Habeas Proceeding Reviewing Summary Removal Under INA §235(b)(1)—Judicial review of summary exclusion orders are limited to habeas proceedings and only to determine (1) whether the petitioner is an alien; (2) whether s/he was ordered removed; *and* (3) whether s/he can prove by a preponderance of the evidence that s/he is an LPR, granted refugee status or granted asylum. *Brumme v. INS,* 275 F.3d 443 (5th Cir. 2001) [cannot review whether person subject to summary removal was admissible or entitled to relief]. *But see American-Arab Anti-Discrimination Comm. v. Ashcroft,* 272 F.Supp.2d 650 (E.D. Mich. 2003) [habeas jurisdiction exists to determine whether expedited removal statute was lawfully applied to the petitioner and where person was paroled into the U.S. it was inappropriate to apply summary removal]. No declaratory, injunctive or other equitable relief may be brought and no class action. INA §242(e)(1) and (2). The only other challenge is one made to the validity of the summary exclusion "determination" under §235(b) and its implementation. Constitutional challenges and challenges to regulations may only be brought in the District of Columbia and must be filed no later than 60 days after statute's or regulation's effect. INA §242(e)(3). Even if the court determines there is a problem, the only relief is a new hearing. INA §242(e)(4). Habeas review may not apply where the person is subject to summary removal, re-enters, and this is subject to reinstatement of removal under INA §241(a)(5).*Ochoa-Carrillo v. Gonzales,* 446 F.3d 781 (8th Cir. 2006) [cannot obtain habeas review over reinstatement of removal under INA §241(a)(5) even if original order was expedited removal where habeas review was permissible].

19. Procedural Requirements—Any habeas petition reviewing a final order of removal must: (1) attach a copy of the order; and (2) state whether a court has upheld the validity of the order and if so, state the name of the court, the date, and the nature of the proceeding. INA §242(e), 8 U.S.C. §1252(e). The petition must also meet all the requirements of 28 U.S.C. §§2242 and 2243 includ-

ing alleging the name of the person who has custody over the petitioner and by virtue of what claim or authority if known. 28 U.S.C. §2242 ¶2; *Robledo-Gonzales v. Ashcroft,* 342 F.3d 667, 672–76 (7th Cir. 2003) [where petitioner was in custody of Bureau of Prisons awaiting trial on illegal re-entry charge, his failure to name prison officials in habeas petition resulted in dismissal of his immigration claims].

20. Sanctions Against Counsel—The counsel for a habeas petitioner may be sanctioned by the court for failing to disclose that s/he has also filed and pursued a petition for review regarding the respondent before the circuit court. *Ndreko v. Ridge,* 351 F.Supp.2d 904, 909–11 (D. Minn. 2004) [where lawyer filed emergency habeas for a client who was removed from the U.S. to have him returned to the country, but did not disclose that a circuit court petition for review was pending in the case and that the circuit court had denied a stay, the district court imposed sanctions against counsel for failure to disclose the information].

D. *Mandamus*

1. Mandamus jurisdiction is invoked under 28 U.S.C. §1361 to compel an officer or employee of the INS or another government agency to perform a nondiscretionary duty owed to a party. To be entitled to mandamus a party must establish: (1) a clear and certain claim; (2) that the duty owed is ministerial and so plainly prescribed as to be free from doubt; and (3) that no other adequate remedy is available. *Belegradek v. Gonzales,* 523 F.Supp.2d 1364 (N.D. Ga. 2007) [court denied motion to dismiss APA claim under §555(b) for adjudication of adjustment application within reasonable time because agency had nondiscretionary duty to do so]. *See also Ceken v. Chertoff,* 544 F.Supp.2d 211 (D. Conn. 2008) [mandamus and APA claim to adjudicate AOS application pending for 5 years was not barred]; *Shirmohamadali v. Heinauer,* 533 F.Supp.2d 1059 (E.D. Cal. 2008) [more than 4-year wait for AOS was unreasonable]; *Aslam v. Mukasey,* 531 F.Supp.2d 736 (E.D. Va. 2008) [granted summary judgment for 12-year wait for AOS where USCIS had a duty to adjudicate within a reasonable time and ordered them to instruct the FBI to expedite the name check]; *Lindems v. Mukasey,* 530 F.Supp.2d 1044 (E.D. Wis. 2008) [INA §242(a)(2)(B)(ii) did not bar APA or Mandamus action for AOS pending 5 years]; *Soneji v. DHS,* 525 F.Supp.2d 1151 (N.D. Cal. 2007) [court denied motion to dismiss action under §1331 pursuant to §555(b) of the APA and mandamus to compel DHS to adjudicate an AOS application pending for 38 months]; *Zhu v. Chertoff,* 525 F.Supp.2d 1098 (W.D. Mo. 2007) [four year delay in AOS unreasonable and summary judgment was granted]; *He v. Chertoff,* 528 F.Supp.2d 879 (N.D. Ill. 2008) [denied motion to dismiss mandamus/APA claim regarding AOS applications pending two years despite government's national security, jurisdictional (INA §242(a)(2)(B)) and precedent (*Iddir v. INS*) claims]; *Lin v. Chertoff,* 522 F.Supp.2d 1309 (D. Colo. 2007) [habeas jurisdiction existed to compel, through mandamus, the adjudication of an I-601 waiver, despite petitioner's final order or removal, where USCIS refused to grant an AOS due to prior misrepresentations]; *Ahmadi v. Chertoff,* 522 F.Supp.2d 816 (N.D. Tex. 2007) [court denied USCIS's motion to dismiss mandamus to compel adjudication of AOS and rejected the claim that the time that USCIS *and* the FBI take to complete the name check process is *per se* reasonable]; *Saleem v. Keisler,* 520 F.Supp.2d 1048, 1057–61 (W.D. Wis. 2007) [a five-year delay in adjudicating an AOS was unreasonable delay under APA §555(b) and mandamus was a source of jurisdiction because the government's failure to act is not discretionary; summary judgment was granted for petitioner]; *Alkeylani v. DHS,* 514 F.Supp.2d 258 (D. Conn. 2007) [3 year delay in adjudicating I-485 is actionable and mandamus and federal question jurisdiction apply and are not barred by INA §242(a)(2)(B)(ii)]; *Dong v. Chertoff,* 513 F.Supp.2d 1158, 1166–68 (N.D. Cal. 2007) [8 C.F.R. §103.2(b)(18) limits the discretion of USCIS to continue/withhold the adjudication of an I-485 pending two-and-a-half years and therefore the demand that the I-485 be adjudicated *is subject* to judicial review under mandamus and APA §706(1) and is not precluded by INA §242(a)(2)(B)(ii)]; *Tang v. Chertoff,* 493 F.Supp.2d 148 (D. Mass. 2007) [followed *Spencer* and determined that §§242(a)(2)(B)(i) & (ii) do not bar action to compel adjudication of AOS pending for 4 years and that there is jurisdiction under mandamus to enforce APA §§555(b) and 706(1)]; *Singh v. Still,* 470 F.Supp.2d 1064 (N.D. Cal. 2007) [where asylum AOS has been pending seven years and marriage AOS for four, mandamus or APA/1331 was appropriate]; *Yu v. Brown,* 36 F.Supp.2d 922, 933–34 (D.N.M. 1999) [mandamus available where juvenile required to wait 2½ years for adjudication of special immigrant petition including one year after it was returned to him for additional fingerprints]; *Raduga USA Corp. v. DOS,* 440 F.Supp.2d 1140, 1143–48 (S.D. Cal. 2005) [employer had standing to

bring mandamus action due to its own injury to compel consular officer to make a decision on employee's IV over government's objection that once the I-140 was approved the employer had no further interest]; *Przhebelskaya v. U.S. Bureau of Citizenship and Immigration Services,* 338 F.Supp.2d 399 (E.D.N.Y. 2004) [mandamus action to compel INS to adjust lottery applicant before the end of the fiscal year and if INS fails to do so the court had continuing jurisdiction to compel grant]; *Paunescu v. INS* 76 F.Supp.2d 896 (N.D. Ill. 1999) [same]; *But see Castillo v. Ridge,* 445 F.3d 1057 (8th Cir. 2006) [where applicant for AOS needed a waiver and he was only waiting six months for adjudication from time waiver was necessary, mandamus was not appropriate]; *Taylor v. Barnhart,* 399 F.3d 891, 897–98 (8th Cir. 2005) [no clear duty to provide disability benefits to applicant whose lawful status was in question]; *Iddir v. INS,* 301 F.3d 492, 499–501 (7th Cir. 2002) [denying mandamus relief because INS does not have a clear duty to adjudicate petitions and in fact lacks the statutory authority to award diversity visas beyond the fiscal year]; *Ahmed v. DHS,* 328 F.3d 383 (7th Cir. 2003) [following *Iddir* the Court held that mandamus should be denied not on jurisdictional grounds but on the grounds that no relief could be granted]; *Ibrahim v. Chertoff,* 529 F.Supp.2d 611 (E.D.N.C. 2007) [where naturalization applicant did not have his interview mandamus was denied because there was no clear right to have application adjudicated within a certain period of time]; *Orlov v. Howard,* 523 F.Supp.2d 30 (D.D.C. 2007) [INA §242(a)(2)(B)(ii) precludes jurisdiction to compel adjudication of AOS pending 4 years and neither APA §555(b), nor mandamus, are a source of jurisdiction]; *Morgovsky v. DHS,* 517 F.Supp.2d 581 (D. Mass. 2007) [no requirement that USCIS act immediately, or even promptly, on an appeal of a preliminary denial of naturalization that has been pending only 16 months]; *Omar v. Mueller,* 501 F.Supp.2d 636, 639–40 (D.N.J. 2007) [a 4 year delay in interviewing applicant for naturalization and concluding fingerprint checks does not compel mandamus because there is no duty to conduct an interview within a certain period of time in contrast to the duty to complete a case in 120 days once an interview has been conducted]; *Takkallapalli v. Chertoff,* 487 F.Supp.2d 1094, 1099 (W.D. Mo. 2007) [delay of 3 years in adjudicating AOS is not so extraordinary as to require court intervention]; *Dridi v. Chertoff,* 412 F.Supp.2d 465, 468 (E.D. Pa. 2006) [in dicta court found that actions of immigration authorities with respect to the timeliness of decisions on immigration petitions are discretionary not mandatory and therefore, where I-129F petition for fiancée was pending for two years, it was not subject to mandamus]; *Espin v. Gantner,* 381 F.Supp.2d 261 (S.D.N.Y. 2005) [mandamus cannot be used to compel DHS to issue a favorable decision on adjustment of status]; *Checknan v. McElroy,* 313 F.Supp.2d 270, 274–76 (S.D.N.Y. 2004) [cannot mandamus Service to repaper applicant];*Bell v. INS,* 292 F.Supp.2d 370, 372–73 (D. Conn. 2003) [no clear right to the remedy of release from state custody for person serving a criminal sentence who has an immigration detainer preventing his early release]; *Afsharzadehyadzi v. Perryman,* 214 F.Supp.2d 884 (N.D. Ill. 2002) [no jurisdiction under mandamus due to INA §242(a)(2)(B)(i) and failure to exhaust before IJ to consider denial of AOS application for "aged-out" child]; *Luo v. Coultice,* 178 F.Supp.2d 1135 (C.D. Cal. 2001) [no jurisdiction because there was no enforceable right requiring the time period that INS may have for readjudicating a returned visa petition]; *Holasek v. DOJ,* 123 F.Supp.2d 1126, 1129 (N.D. Ill. 2000) [no mandamus because applicant can raise claim before IJ and its precluded under INA §242(a)(2)(B)(i)]; *Sadowski v. INS,* 107 F.Supp.2d 451, 453 (S.D.N.Y. 2000) [no mandamus jurisdiction where "aged-out" child sought to compel adjustment]. *But see Pierre v. McElroy,* 200 F.Supp.2d 251 (S.D.N.Y. 2001) [where person "aged out" of eligibility for special immigrant status as juvenile, court granted mandamus under theory that PATRIOT ACT intended to protect persons who aged out in light of Sept. 11, 2001].

2. Mandamus petitions are typically filed against DHS to compel them to adjudicate petitions. *Liu v. Novak,* 509 F.Supp.2d 1 (D.D.C. 2007) [summary judgment granted to petitioner waiting four years on AOS and neither INA §242(a)(2)(B), nor INA §242(g) precluded mandamus and §1331 jurisdiction pursuant to APA §555(b) because adjudication was unreasonably withheld]; *Jefrey v. INS*, 710 F.Supp. 486 (S.D.N.Y. 1989). Mandamus may also lie against consular officers for their failure to make a decision on a visa application. *Patel v. Reno*, 134 F.3d 929 (9th Cir. 1997) [while no jurisdiction may exist to review the correctness of the decision, 22 C.F.R. §42.81 requires consular officers to issue a decision]; *Han Cao v. Upchurch,* 496 F.Supp. 2d 569, 574–77 (E.D. Pa. 2007) [court granted motion for summary judgment under mandamus and the APA to compel USCIS to make a decision on an I-485 pending more than 3 years]; *American Academy of Religion v. Chertoff,* 463 F.Supp.2d 400, 420–22 (S.D.N.Y. 2006) [mandamus available to obtain deci-

sion on B visa for Islamic scholar in light of section 6 of the APA, 5 U.S.C. §555(b), and in light of 21 C.F.R. §§41.106, 41.121 requiring prompt adjudication of visas]. As only discretionary acts are precluded from review under 8 U.S.C. §1252(a)(2)(B)(ii), mandamus may be useful in the future. Mandamus has also been applied in other immigration related contexts. *Garcia v. Taylor*, 40 F.3d 299 (9th Cir. 1994) [to compel deportation hearing pursuant to expedited deportation provision]; *Abreu v. U.S.*, 796 F.Supp. 50 (D.R.I. 1992) [claim that incarcerated person was denied prompt deportation hearing under 8 U.S.C. §1252(i)]; *Piledrivers Local Union No. 2375 v. Smith*, 695 F.2d 390 (9th Cir. 1982) [compelling INS to enforce INA on outer continental shelf]; *Diaz v. Reno,* 40 F.Supp.2d 984 (N.D. Ill. 1999) [person claiming to be USC who was deported sought return of his documentation establishing U.S. citizenship]; *Clow v. Nelson*, 579 F.Supp. 981 (W.D.N.Y. 1984) [requiring INS to consider petition for remission and mitigation in forfeiture proceeding].

3. However, mandamus does not lie

3.a. where it involves judicial review "of an order of removal entered or issued under any provision" of the Immigration and Nationality Act. INA §242(a)(5); *Bhatt v. BIA,* 328 F.3d 912 (7th Cir. 2003) [filing petition in district court to compel BIA to hear motion to reconsider that it dismissed as untimely is precluded by exclusive jurisdiction in the court of appeal under §1252];

3.b. where the courts have no jurisdiction to compel DHS. The REAL ID Act of 2005, PL 109-13, 119 Stat. 231 (May 11, 2005), Div. B §106 eliminated habeas corpus review, mandamus and All Writs Act jurisdiction in the district court regarding "an order of removal entered or issued under any provision of this Act." *Tao Luo v. Keisler,* 521 F.Supp.2d 72 (D.D.C. 2007) [same following *Grinberg* and *Safadi* mandamus to compel adjustment decision barred by INA §242(a)(2)(B)(ii)]; *Bugulu v. Gonzales,* 490 F.Supp.2d 965 (W.D. Wis. 2007) [same]; *Grinberg v. Swancia,* 478 F.Supp.2d 1350 (S.D. Fla. 2007) [following *Safadi v. Howard,*, 466 F.Supp.2d 696 (E.D. Va. 2006) and finding that *post*-REAL ID Act INA §242(a)(2)(B)(ii) bars mandamus for adjustment under mandamus statute and 555(b) of the APA because it bars pace of "actions" as well as decisions]; *Afsharzadehyadzi v. Perryman,* 214 F.Supp.2d 884 (N.D. Ill. 2002) [no jurisdiction under mandamus due to INA §242(a)(2)(B)(i) and failure to exhaust before IJ to consider denial of AOS application for "aged-out" child]; *Holasek v. DOJ*, 123 F.Supp.2d 1126 (N.D. Ill. 2000) [mandamus precluded by INA §242(a)(2)(B)(i)]. However, to avoid the constitutional problem that would arise by the elimination of all review, the REAL ID Act of 2005 preserves, in the court of appeals, constitutional claims and questions of law in a petition for review notwithstanding preclusion provisions under §242. INA §§242(a)(2)(D), (a)(5). *Fernandez-Ruiz v. Gonzales,* 468 F.3d 1159, 1163 (9th Cir. 2006) [Section 242(a)(2)(D) restores jurisdiction to the circuit court for persons who previously were barred from such review under 242(a)(2)(C) because of criminal convictions and makes the restoration retroactive by applying it to any order issued before, on or after May 11, 2005]. Similarly, the REAL ID Act of 2005, eliminated habeas, mandamus, and the All Writs Act as sources of jurisdiction to review Convention Against Torture claims and the courts of appeal "shall be the sole and exclusive means for judicial review of any cause or claim under" CAT. INA §242(a)(4). For other district court jurisdictional hurdles *see Duamutef v. INS,* 386 F.3d 172, 180–81 (2d Cir. 2004) [the district court lacked mandamus jurisdiction due to INA §242(g) to compel ICE to take custody over state prisoner and to execute order of removal]; *Chapinski v. Ziglar,* 278 F.3d 718 (7th Cir. 2002) [mandamus to compel INS to place person in removal proceedings is barred by INA §242(g)]; *Alvidres-Reyes v. Reno,* 180 F.3d 199 (5th Cir. 1999) [no jurisdiction under INA §242(g) to challenge refusal of DD to place person in removal proceedings to obtain benefit of former suspension provisions]; *Danilov v. Aguirre,* 370 F.Supp.2d 441, 444–45 (E.D. Va. 2005) [where naturalization statute, INA §336(b), 8 U.S.C. §1447, provides for federal jurisdiction only where naturalization application has not been decided within 120 days after process, applicant could not bring mandamus action before the 120-day period has run because the naturalization statute trumps the more general mandamus statute]; *Diallo v. Reno,* 61 F.Supp.2d 1361, 1366–67 (N.D. Ga. 1999) [mandamus jurisdiction is precluded in action to review denial of visa lottery adjustment because INA §242(a)(2)(B)(i) precludes review of any judgment involving adjustment]; *Ray v. Reno,* 3 F.Supp.2d 1249 (D. Utah 1998) [INA §242(g)]; *Gerrero v. Moyer*,

738 F.Supp. 1164 (N.D. Ill. 1990) [cannot mandamus DD to adjudicate asylum claim when proceeding is before the IJ]; *But see Paunescu v. INS* 76 F.Supp.2d 896, 899–900 (N.D. Ill. 1999) [neither INA §242(g), nor INA §242(a)(2)(B) bar jurisdiction over mandamus to compel adjudication of diversity visa]; *Yu v. Brown,* 36 F.Supp.2d 922, 933–34 (D. New Mexico 1999) [INA §242(g) only effects removal proceedings and does not bar mandamus to compel adjudication of special immigrant juvenile petition]; *Asare v. Ferro,* 999 F.Supp. 657 (D. Md. 1998).

3.c. where the duty is discretionary, *Farag v. USCIS,* 531 F.Supp.2d 602, 608–09 (S.D.N.Y. 2008) [USCIS had no duty to back date a misfiled application by asylee would wanted to petition within the 2-year deadline permitted by the I-730]; *In Re Freeman,* 489 F.3d 966 (9th Cir. 2007) [where circuit court remanded case back for an adjustment interview and DHS still denied AOS, the denial did not implicate the law of the case and the discretionary decision to deny was not reviewable in mandamus]; *Rios v. Ziglar,* 398 F.3d 1201, 1206–08 (10th Cir. 2005) [no clear right to have improperly filed NACARA application treated as timely filed where regulation is to the contrary and where return of all fees left material questions unanswered]; *Esteves Gonzales v. Embajada de la Republica Dominicana,* 497 F.Supp.2d 279 (D. Puerto Rico 2007) [dismissed mandamus brought against petitioner's ambassador to direct him to help petitioner in dispute at prison because mandamus does not apply to foreign officials and ambassador has no legal duty to assist]; *Shen v. Chertoff,* 494 F.Supp.2d 592 (E.D. Mich. 2007) [no cause of action for mandamus or APA for delay of 50 months in deciding AOS because of security checks because there is no nondiscretionary duty under mandamus and it is committed to agency discretion under the APA]; *Kaur v. Chertoff,* 489 F.Supp.2d 52 (D.D.C. 2007) [mandamus could not compel adjustment in light of failure to voluntarily depart, nor approval of earlier filed I-130 to obtain §245(i) benefits as neither request was a nondiscretionary duty requiring an extraordinary remedy];*Qiu v. Chertoff,* 486 F.Supp.2d 412, 420–21 (D.N.J. 2007) [no mandamus jurisdiction to obtain answer on I-485 because regulation at §103.2(b)(18) confers discretion to withhold adjudication pending an investigation]; *Li v. Chertoff,* 482 F.Supp.2d 1172, 1176–78 (S.D. Cal. 2007) [mandamus does not lie because as long as USCIS is making efforts to adjudicate the I-485, the pace of the adjudication is committed to its discretion]; *Rodney v. INS*, 462 F.Supp.2d 285, 287–89 (D. Conn. 2006) [no clear right to deportation prior to the expiration of term of incarceration and INS has no obligation to remove respondent prior to release from state custody, *see* 8 U.S.C. §§ 1228(a)(3)(B), 1231(a)(1)(B)(iii)]; *Keane v. Chertoff,* 419 F.Supp. 2d 597 (S.D.N.Y. 2006) [petitioner's request that USCIS reopen AOS that was erroneously denied for abandonment and reschedule interview was committed to agency discretion under the APA and not subject to mandamus]; *Espin v. Gantner,* 381 F.Supp.2d 261 (S.D.N.Y. 2005) [mandamus cannot be used to compel DHS to issue a favorable decision on adjustment of status]; *Saleh v. Ridge,* 347 F.Supp.2d 508, 511 (S.D.N.Y. 2005) [because adjustment of status is discretionary mandamus does not lie to compel decision on AOS application pending for five years, although action may be brought under §1331 pursuant to APA §555]; *Ferris v. INS,* 303 F.Supp.2d 103, 107–08 (D. Conn. 2004) [no right to compel DHS to provide a removal hearing or lift a detainer]; *Zheng v. Reno,* 166 F.Supp.2d 875 (S.D. N.Y. 2001) [no mandamus jurisdiction to schedule adjustment interview because adjustment is discretionary]; *Diallo v. Reno,* 61 F.Supp.2d 1361, 1368 (N.D. Ga. 1999) [the decision how to handle and investigate a lottery adjustment and the application's denial are discretionary]; *Silveyra v. Moschorak*, 989 F.2d 1012 (9th Cir. 1993); *Maldonado-Coronel v. McElroy*, 943 F.Supp. 376, 381 (S.D.N.Y. 1996) [no duty to schedule adjustment for derivative beneficiary who will reach 21]; *Rahman v. McElroy*, 884 F.Supp. 782, 786–87 (S.D.N.Y. 1995) [no duty to schedule adjustment interview for visa lottery winners]; *Robertson v. Attorney General*, 957 F.Supp. 1035 (N.D. Ill. 1997) [90-day time limit to adjudicate removal of conditional residency not mandatory];

3.d. where there are alternative adequate remedies, *Shah v. Wilco Systems, Inc.*, 126 F.Supp.2d 641, 653–55 (S.D.N.Y. 2000). [no mandamus to enforce either 1182(n) regarding LCAs or unfair employment practices under 1324b];

3.e. where decision cannot affect rights because of mootness, *Mohamed v. Gonzales,* 436 F.3d 79 (3d Cir. 2006) [court is without authority to hear claim that is now moot because the Service lacks the statutory authority to issue a DV visa beyond the fiscal year]; *Nyaga v. Ashcroft,* 323 F.3d 906 (11th Cir. 2003) [mandamus action to compel diversity visa issuance dismissed as moot where claim was filed after the end of the fiscal year because court cannot compel issuance of visas after fiscal year ended]; *Gebre v. Rice,* 462 F.Supp.2d 186 (D. Mass. 2006) [same]; *But see Raduga USA Corp. v. DOS,* 440 F.Supp.2d 1140, 1143–48 (S.D. Cal. 2005) [employer had standing to bring mandamus action due to its own injury to compel consular officer to make a decision on employee's IV over government's objection that once the I-140 was approved the employer had no further interest]. Or where decision may become moot through other action by DHS. *Hanif v. Gantner,* 369 F.Supp.2d 502, 507–08 (S.D.N.Y. 2005) [cannot compel USCIS to adjudicate adjustment application before DHS removes respondent who has existing deportation order];

3.f. where an incarcerated respondent is seeking to compel swift adjudication of his deportability. *Hernandez-Avalos v. INS*, 50 F.3d 842 (10th Cir. 1995); *Giddings v. Chandler*, 979 F.2d 1104 (5th Cir. 1992)

E. *Injunctive Relief*

1. Traditionally, district courts have broad discretionary power to fashion equitable relief. *Orantes-Hernandez v. Thornburgh*, 919 F.2d 549, 558 (9th Cir. 1990); *Haitian Refugee Center v. Nelson*, 694 F.Supp. 864, 881 (S.D. Fla. 1988), *aff'd*, 872 F.2d 1555 (11th Cir. 1989), *aff'd sub nom. McNary v. HRC, Inc.*, 498 U.S. 479 (1991); *Chau v. DOS*, 891 F.Supp. 650 (D.D.C. 1995). This principle is particularly applicable to remedy constitutional violations. *Swann v. Charlotte-Mecklenburg Board of Education*, 402 U.S. 1 (1971). Equity relief also contemplates granting complete relief including ancillary relief necessary to accomplish complete justice. *Xiao v. Reno*, 930 F.Supp. 1377 (N.D. Cal. 1996) [ordering INS to provide documents necessary to allow Xiao to remain lawfully and work in U.S.]. However, where injury is speculative irreparable harm cannot be found. *Tenacre Foundation v. INS*, 892 F.Supp. 289 (D.D.C. 1995), *aff'd,* 78 F.3d 693 (D.C. Cir. 1996). And the courts may also vacate or modify injunctive relief when appropriate. *Orantes-Hernandez v. Gonzales,* 504 F.Supp.2d 825 (C.D. Cal. 2007) [modified original injunction in *Orantes-Hernandez* by eliminating paragraphs 10 (administrative segregation) and12 (legal presentations) of the injunction].

2. Bar to Injunctive Relief, INA §242(f)(1); 8 U.S.C. §1252(f)(1)—Under INA §242(f)(1), no court (except the Supreme Court) shall have the jurisdiction or authority to enjoin or restrain the operation of the provisions of Title II, Chapter 4, other than in any individual case. *Van Dinh v. Reno,* 197 F.3d 427, 433 (10th Cir. 1999) [*Bivens* class action concerning the transfer of detained persons is barred by 242(f) and 242(a)(2)(B)(ii)]; *But see Gonzales v. DHS,* 508 F.3d 1227, 1232–33 (9th Cir. 2007) [class action challenge to denial of adjustment, although collaterally effecting reinstate or removal provision under chapter 4, is not barred because adjustment is not within chapter 4]; *Ali v. Ashcroft,* 346 F.3d 873, 886–87 (9th Cir. 2003) [class-wide injunction barring removal to country without a functioning government (Somalia) is not prohibited by 242(f)(1) because action does not seek to enjoin the *operation* of the statute and also involves policies and practice and constitutional issues]; *Barahona-Gomez v. Reno,* 236 F.3d 1115, 1121–22 (9th Cir. 2001) [section does not apply to deportation/exclusion proceedings]; *Catholic Social Services v. INS,* 232 F.3d 1139, 1149–50 (9th Cir. 2000) (en banc) [this section does not bar class wide injunctive relief under Chapter V pertaining to adjustment of status].

3. Bar to Injunctive Relief, INA §242(f)(2), 8 U.S.C. §1252(f)(2)—No court may enjoin the removal of any person pursuant to a final order under this section unless the person shows by clear and convincing evidence that the entry or execution of such order is prohibited as a matter of law. INA §242(f)(2). INA §242(f)(2) does not bar federal courts from issuing a stay of removal pending appeal from the denial of a habeas petition challenging the merits of a removal order. *Andreiu v. Ashcroft,* 253 F.3d 477 (9th Cir. 2001) (en banc); *Douglas v. Ashcroft,* 374 F.3d 230, 233–34 (3d Cir. 2004) [following the First, Second and Sixth Circuits that the proper standard for a stay is the traditional four-part test for preliminary injunctions and rejected the "clear and convincing evidence" standard]; *Arevalo v. Ashcroft,* 344 F.3d 1, 6–9 (1st Cir. 2003) [following the majority of circuits and rejecting the Eleventh Circuit view in *Weng* "that would require courts invariably to construe all immigration statutes in the most draconian manner that their words conceivably could support"]; *Maharaj v. Ashcroft,* 295 F.3d 963 (9th Cir. 2002) [followed reasoning in *Andreiu* and *American-Arab*]. INA §242(f)(2) does not bar the court of appeals from issuing a stay pending appeal. *Mohammed v. Reno,* 309 F.3d 95, 98–100 (2d Cir. 2002); *Bejjani v. INS,* 271 F.3d

670, 687–89 (6th Cir. 2001); *See also Kahn v. Elwood,* 232 F.Supp.2d 344 (M.D. Pa. 2002) [the standards under 242(f)(2) do not apply to district court stay orders where the action was initiated in the district court]; *But see Weng v. U.S. Att'y Gen.,* 287 F.3d 1335, 1337–40 (11th Cir. 2002) [INA §242(f)(2) does prevent the court of appeals from issuing a stay pending appeal unless there is clear and convincing evidence that the execution of the order is prohibited as a matter of law]; *Dorelien v. U.S. Att'y Gen.,* 317 F.3d 1314 (11th Cir. 2003) [denial of *en banc* review regarding changing *Weng* standard for issuance of a stay]. The split in the circuits regarding application of INA §242(f)(2) to individual stay applications has now been recognized by Justice Kennedy who suggested the Supreme Court may wish to consider the matter. *Kenyeres v. Ashcroft,* 538 U.S. 1301, 123 S.Ct.1386 (2003).

F. *Declaratory Judgment Action*—The Declaratory Judgment Act permits federal court litigants to seek a judgment from the federal courts to declare an action unconstitutional or illegal. 28 U.S.C. §2201 ["In a case of actual controversy within its jurisdiction....any court of the United States, upon the filing of an appropriate pleading, may declare the rights and other legal relations of any interested party seeking such declaration, whether or not further relief is or could be sought. Any such declaration shall have the force and effect of a final judgment or decree and shall be reviewable as such."] However, some courts take the view that the Declaratory Judgment Act does not confer jurisdiction but rather provides an additional remedy where jurisdiction already exists. *Li v. Chertoff,* 482 F.Supp.2d 1172, 1179 (S.D. Cal. 2007) [Declaratory Judgment Act does not confer jurisdiction to compel adjudication of I-485]; *Baez-Fernandez v. INS,* 385 F.Supp.2d 292, 295 (S.D.N.Y. 2005) [where court does not have jurisdiction under §§1441(c), 1447(b) to review naturalization applications, there is no jurisdiction for declaration that person in removal proceedings is prima facie eligible for naturalization]; *Holasek v. DOJ,* 123 F.Supp.2d 1126, 1129 (N.D. Ill. 2000) [no jurisdiction under 2201 to obtain review of denial of adjustment under diversity visa]; *Amoakowaa v. Reno,* 94 F.Supp.2d 903, 906 (N.D. Ill. 2000) [same]. Also, the declaratory judgment act cannot be used to render an advisory opinion. *Transport Robert (1973) Ltée v. INS,* 195 F.Supp.2d 136 (D.D.C. 2002) [where Canadian transport companies sought declaration that INS practices were illegal in a series of hypothetical circumstances court would not render advisory opinion].

IV. BAR TO JUDICIAL REVIEW

A. *Preclusion of Review*—A major bar to judicial review is congressional enactments that specifically bar review of certain matters in federal courts. *Heckler v. Ringer*, 466 U.S. 602 (1984). Under IIRIRA, Congress has sought to eliminate federal jurisdiction over a broad range of issues previously reviewable in federal court. INA §242, 8 U.S.C. §1252; H.R. Conf. Rep. 104-828, 104th Cong., 2d Sess. at 219–21 (1996). In determining the scope of the preclusion statutes some courts have found that it is not limited solely to matters arising in removal, deportation and exclusion proceedings even where the preclusion statute falls within INA §242. *El-Khader v. Monica,* 366 F.3d 562, 565–67 (7th Cir. 2004) [quoting *Samirah v. O'Connell* and finding that prior to the REAL ID Act the discretionary decision bar under INA §242(a)(2)(B)(ii) was *not* limited solely to matters arising in removal, deportation, or exclusion proceeding thereby barring judicial review of the revocation of a visa petition]. The Congress has sought to eliminate judicial review in the following areas:

1. Review of AG's discretionary decisions regarding detention or release, including the grant, revocation, or denial of bond or parole—INA §236(e); 8 U.S.C. §1226(e); Congress under INA §236(e) barred federal courts from reviewing discretionary decisions regarding parole and bond "under this section." Review is only prohibited for "discretionary" decisions regarding bond or parole. *Pisciotta v. Ashcroft,* 311 F.Supp.2d 445, 453 (D.N.J. 2004) [the decision of ICE to redetain petitioner without bond or revoke his previous status because his removal hearing was reopened, notwithstanding a previous $12,000 bond, is not reviewable]. *But see U.S. v. Grand China, Inc.,* 376 F.Supp.2d 1150 (D.N.M. 2005) [reviews denial of bond by ICE but upholds denial]. It does not apply to issue of statutory construction or constitutional claims such as mandatory detention under the statutory writ of habeas corpus, 28 U.S.C. §2241 or to post-removal detention under INA §241. *Demore v. Kim*, 538 U.S. 510, 517 (2003) [INA §236(e) does not bar habeas jurisdiction in absence of specific provision barring habeas and because petitioner lodged a constitutional challenge to mandatory detention legislation]; *Zadvydas v. Davis,* 533 U.S. 678, 687–88, 121 S.Ct. 2491, 2497–98 (2001) [INA §§236(e), 242(a)(2)(B)(ii), 242(a)(2)(C), 242(g) did not bar habeas jurisdiction for challenge to post removal detention and indefinite detention]; *Gonzalez v.*

O'Connell, 355 F.3d 1010, 1014–15 (7th Cir. 2004) [habeas jurisdiction to challenge mandatory detention even where the predicate issue to the constitutional claim was a statutory claim]; *Doan v. INS,* 311 F.3d 1160, 1162 (9th Cir. 2002) [noting that petitioner may bring a challenge regarding the reasonableness of the amount of the bond if it has the effect of preventing release]; *Waffi v. Loiselle,* 527 F.Supp.2d 480, 483–85 (E.D. Va. 2007) [INA §236(e) does not bar habeas jurisdiction to determine statutory question whether person released from criminal custody can be subject to mandatory detention]; *Campbell v. Chadbourne,* 505 F.Supp.2d 191, 195–97 (D. Mass. 2007) [INA §236(e) does not bar constitutional challenge to detention where refugee claims he was detained for refusing to apply for AOS]; *Aguilar v. Lewis,* 50 F.Supp.2d 539, 542–42 (E.D. Va. 1999) [INA §236(e) bars discretionary decisions not statutory interpretation]. Moreover, INA §242(g) does not bar review of detention decisions; nor does INA §242(b)(9). *Zhislin v. Reno,* 195 F.3d 810 (6th Cir. 1999) [INA §242(g) as interpreted by *American-Arab* does not bar review of challenge to indefinite detention]; *Parra v. Perryman,* 172 F.3d 954 (7th Cir. 1999) [in light of *American-Arab* INA §242(g) does not bar habeas to review detention issue]; *Bouayad v. Holmes,* 74 F.Supp.2d 471, 473–74 (E.D. Pa. 1999) [government conceded that habeas jurisdiction existed to challenge mandatory detention and the court determined that neither INA §236(e) nor INA §242(b)(9) preclude jurisdiction over detention]; *Kiareldeen v. Reno,* 71 F.Supp.2d 402, 405–07 (D.N.J. 1999) [neither INA §236(e), nor §242(g) bars habeas jurisdiction to review detention based upon secret evidence]; *Alikhani v. Fasano,* 70 F.Supp.2d 1124, 1126–30 (S.D. Cal. 1999) [INA §§242(g), 242(b)(9) and 236(e) do not bar challenge to statutory and constitutional challenge to mandatory detention]; *Pastor-Camarena v. Smith*, 977 F.Supp. 1415, 1416–17 (W.D. Wash. 1997) [section does not apply to transition custody decisions]; *But see Loa-Herrera v. Trominski,* 231 F.3d 984, 990–91 (5th Cir. 2000) [no jurisdiction by district court to require DD to permit parole hearing for LPR stopped at the border]; *Galvez v. Lewis,* 56 F.Supp.2d 637 (E.D. Va. 1999) [no jurisdiction to review IJ's decision to apply 236(c) and refuse bond hearing because INA §236(e) bars jurisdiction over the application of §236(c)].

2. Review of Decisions Regarding Persons with Convictions—Under INA §242(a)(2)(C), 8 U.S.C. §1252(a)(2)(C) there is no jurisdiction to review any final order of removal against a person who is removable because of having committed a criminal offense under INA §§212(a)(2), 237(a)(2)(A)(iii) (aggravated felony), §237(a)(2)(B) (drugs), §237(a)(2)(C) (firearms offenses), §237(a)(2)(D) (miscellaneous offenses) or §237(a)(2)(A)(ii) (where there are two crimes of moral turpitude for which a sentence of one year or longer may be imposed on each). *Alvarez Acosta v. U.S. Attorney General,* ___F.3d ___ (11th Cir. Apr. 16, 2008) 2008 WL 1733208 [conviction for drug paraphernalia barred consideration of denial of continuance under *Bull v. INS* because there was no constitutional or statutory claim]; *Ali v. Achim,* 468 F.3d 462, 465–66, 470 (7th Cir. 2006) *cert. dismissed* 128 S.Ct. 828 (2007) [jurisdiction to review whether proper standard was applied to determine a particularly serious crime but there was no jurisdiction to review BIA's exercise of discretion under the proper legal standard including whether it misapplied its own precedent]; *Conteh v. Gonzales,* 461 F.3d 45, 62–63 (1st Cir. 2006) [post–REAL ID Act, the court had no authority to engage in substantial evidence review of a withholding of removal claim for a applicant who was convicted of an aggravated felony because the review was neither a constitutional question nor a question of law]; *Alaka v. Att'y Gen. of the U.S.,* 456 F.3d 88, 102–03 (3d Cir. 2006) [no jurisdiction to review fact intensive inquiry whether person with conviction was ineligible for §212(c) relief or cancellation because he intended to abandoned his residency by departing for 21 months]; *Lopez-Molina v. Ashcroft,* 368 F.3d 1206 (9th Cir. 2004) [no jurisdiction to review removal order based upon inadmissibility arising from reason to believe charge]; *Oguejiofor v. Attorney General,* 277 F.3d 1305, 1308–09 (11th Cir. 2002) [no jurisdiction to review *St. Cyr* retroactivity claim on direct appeal]; *Zhang v. INS,* 274 F.3d 103, 106–08 (2d Cir. 2001) [post-*Calcano* rejected claim that 242(a)(2)(C) applies only to aggravated felons who commit crimes after admission].

The bar to review may also apply to review of motions to reopen and to remand. *Zamora-Mallari v. Mukasey,* 514 F.3d 679, 696–97 (7th Cir. 2008) [court had no jurisdiction to reverse a denial of remand for AOS of aggravated felon where no statutory or constitutional issues were raised]; *De Araujo v. Ashcroft,* 399 F.3d 84, 88–89 (1st Cir. 2005) [review of designation as aggravated felon is barred because respondent did not appeal BIA's final decision on that issue and appeal of a denial of respondent's motion to reopen for INA §212(c) relief is also barred because

INA §242(a)(2)(C) bars review of all claims of an aggravated felon]; *Durant v. INS,* 393 F.3d 113, 114–15 (2d Cir. 2004) [permitting review of a motion to reopen where person would be barred under INA §242(a)(2)(C) would provide an improper backdoor method of challenging the removal order]; *Patel v. U.S. Att'y Gen.,* 334 F.3d 1259, 1261–63 (11th Cir. 2003) [joining the Seventh and Ninth Circuits in *Chow v. INS,* and *Sarmadi v. INS* and finding the bar applies to review of motions to reopen of final orders as well as final orders]. The bar to review under the predecessor to INA §242(a)(2)(C) [AEDPA §440(a)] also applied to motions to reopen and to reconsider. *Beltran-Leon v. INS*, 134 F.3d 1379 (9th Cir. 1998) [no review regarding BIA decision to deny reopening because writ of *audita querela* was ineffective]; *Choeum v. INS*, 129 F.3d 29 (1st Cir. 1997); *Sarmadi v. INS*, 121 F.3d 1319 (9th Cir. 1997); *Chow v. INS*, 113 F.3d 659, 664 (7th Cir. 1997). *But see Arrozal v. INS,* 159 F.3d 429, 431–32 (9th Cir. 1998) [permitting review of motion to reopen to seek suspension as not being barred by IIRIRA §309(c)(4)(E) and distinguished *Sarmadi* as relating to person with deportation order based on crime]. *See also Cruz v. Att'y Gen. of the U.S.,* 452 F.3d 240, 246–48 (3d Cir. 2006) [BIA decision to deny untimely request for reopening *sua sponte* of person with vacated conviction may be reviewed notwithstanding §242(a)(2)(C) but only if he is not removable for having a conviction under *Pickering*]. The bar may also include the denial of a motion to reconsider a denial of a motion to reopen. *Santos-Salazar v. DOJ,* 400 F.3d 99, 102–04 (2d Cir. 2005).

REAL ID Act of 2005 Requires Review in Circuit Court. Notwithstanding the bar to review under INA §242(a)(2)(C), the REAL ID Act of 2005, PL 109-13, 119 Stat. 231 (May 11, 2005), Div. B, §106 preserves in the court of appeals constitutional claims and questions of law through a petition for review while eliminating habeas corpus as an alternative to the petition for review. INA §§242(a)(2)(D), (a)(5); *Hanan v. Mukasey,* 519 F.3d 760, 763–64 (8th Cir. 2008) [found jurisdiction to review due process claims in motion to reopen notwithstanding conviction, but denied claims on the merits]; *Bosede v. Mukasey,* 512 F.3d 946, 950–51 (7th Cir. 2008) [IJ violated fundamental due process in failing to consider evidence rebutting the AG's presumption that petitioner committed a particularly serious crime and the court therefore had jurisdiction under INA §242(a)(2)(D) notwithstanding INA §242(a)(2)(C)]; *Abiodun v. Gonzales,* 461 F.3d 1210, 1214–15 (10th Cir. 2006) [in light of section 242(a)(2)(D) respondent's aggravated felony convictions did not, under INA §242(a)(2)(C), bar his legal claim regarding U.S. citizenship]; *Balogun v. U.S. Att'y Gen.,* 425 F.3d 1356, 1359–60 (11th Cir. 2005) [notwithstanding the bar under INA §242(a)(2)(C), the court could review respondent's claim that he was not convicted of an aggravated felony and therefore not barred from 212(h) relief]; *Flores-Ledezma v. Gonzales,* 415 F.3d 375, 379–81 (5th Cir. 2005) [the REAL ID Act of 2005 enacting INA §242(a)(2)(D) preserved constitutional review and the review of questions of law for summary removal proceedings under INA §238(b) notwithstanding §242(a)(2)(C) or §242(g)]; *Ramos v. Gonzales,* 414 F.3d 800, 802–04 (7th Cir. 2005) [Congress added §242(a)(2)(D) to consider all constitutional and statutory claims in review of a final order notwithstanding INA §242(a)(2)(C)]; *Papageorgiou v. Gonzales,* 413 F.3d 356, 357–58 (3d Cir. 2005) [Section 242(a)(2)(D) restores jurisdiction to the circuit court for persons who previously were barred from such review under 242(a)(2)(C) because of criminal convictions and makes the restoration retroactive by applying it to any order issued before, on or after May 11, 2005]; *Fernandez-Ruiz v. Gonzales,* 468 F.3d 1159, 1163 (9th Cir. 2006) [same]. The REAL ID Act of 2005, by enacting INA §242(a)(2)(D), however, may not have extended circuit court review in such cases to a challenge based solely upon substantial evidence. *Haman v. Gonzales,* 449 F.3d 834 (8th Cir. 2006) [CAT claim transferred to circuit court but review of the claim was denied for Pashtun returning to Afghanistan on grounds he sought review of only factual issues]; *Hamid v. Gonzales,* 417 F.3d 642, 647 (7th Cir. 2005) [because respondent is an aggravated felon the court declined to consider in the denial of a CAT claim whether the IJ's factual conclusions are supported by substantial evidence because such challenge fails to raise either a constitutional or statutory claim under INA §242(a)(2)(D)]; *Arias v. U.S. Att'y Gen.*, 482 F.3d 1281 (11th Cir. 2007) [finding s not supported by the record, failure to properly weigh factors, and mischaracterization of the record by the IJ in §212(c) case were not constitutional claims permitting review]; *Conteh v. Gonzales,* 461 F.3d 45, 62–63 (1st Cir. 2006) [court had no authority to engage in substantial evidence review of a withholding of removal claim for a applicant who was convicted of an aggravated felony]; *but see Ibarra-Flores v. Gonzales,* 439 F.3d 614, 618 (9th Cir. 2006) [reviewed for substantial evidence IJ's nondiscretionary factual determination that respondent was ineligible for cancellation because he was given VD].

Review of CAT Claims. At least one circuit has taken the position that a denial of deferral of removal may be reviewed in the circuit court, even if respondent was charged in the NTA and ordered deported based upon his criminal conviction. *Lemus-Galvan v. Mukasey,* 518 F.3d 1081 (9th Cir. 2008) [court had jurisdiction to review the denial of deferral of removal on the merits].

Even without the REAL ID Act of 2005, the circuit courts always retained jurisdiction to review whether the appellant was properly removable by determining whether s/he is: (a) an alien and (b) removable for (c) committing a crime covered under the section. *Leocal v. Ashcroft,* 543 U.S. 1, 125 S.Ct. 377, 379–80 n.3 (2004) [notwithstanding INA §242(a)(2)(C), the Court reviewed the Eleventh Circuit's dismissal of jurisdiction after the circuit court considered whether petitioner was removable for his conviction]; *Munoz-Yepez v. Gonzales,* 465 F.3d 347, 350–51 (8th Cir. 2006) [conviction for domestic violence is not covered under INA §242(a)(2)(C) and therefore jurisdiction is not barred]; *Brissett v. Ashcroft,* 363 F.3d 130, 133 (2d Cir. 2004) [court retains jurisdiction to determine whether respondent with aggravated felony conviction was a derivative citizen through mother's naturalization]; *Valansi v. Ashcroft,* 278 F.3d 203, 207–08 (3d Cir. 2002) [post–*Calcano-Martinez v. INS* finding that court had jurisdiction because person was not deportable as aggravated felon]; *Zavaleta-Gallegos v. INS,* 261 F.3d 951, 954 & n.3 (9th Cir. 2001) [finding jurisdiction over these threshold factual inquires *post-Calcano*]; *Nehme v. INS,* 252 F.3d 415, 421 (5th Cir. 2001) [in claim of citizenship court has jurisdiction to determine whether person is an alien and whether the jurisdiction stripping provisions are being applied constitutionally]; *Fierro v. Reno,* 217 F.3d 1, 3 (1st Cir. 2000) [no bar to review if that person is a citizen]; *Lewis v. INS,* 194 F.3d 539, 541–43 (4th Cir. 1999) [reviewed issue of statutory construction to determine whether aggravated felony conviction that occurred *prior* to 1988 is a deportable offense]; *Xiong v. INS,* 173 F.3d 601, 604 (7th Cir. 1999) [court reversed BIA on grounds that person was not an aggravated felon finding that it had jurisdiction to determine whether person was actually convicted notwithstanding INA §242(a)(2)(C)].

The bar also may not be applicable where the petitioner was not deported for a crime barring review even if the record would support a deportation on a ground that would bar jurisdiction. *McAllister v. Att'y Gen. of the U.S.,* 444 F.3d 178, 183–85 (3d Cir. 2006) [where respondent was convicted of conspiracy to murder and malicious wounding with intent to do grievous bodily harm to a police officer in Northern Ireland but his deportation charge was for solely for terrorist activity, he is not barred under 242(a)(2)(C) from review]; *Unuakhaulu v. Gonzales,* 416 F.3d 931 (9th Cir. 2005) [court was not stripped of jurisdiction where the respondent was not removed based upon his aggravated felony conviction *and* the BIA did not predicate its denial of withholding or CAT on respondent's aggravated felony conviction or on a discretionary decision]; *Hernandez-Barrera v. Ashcroft,* 373 F.3d 9, 16–20 (1st Cir. 2004) [IIRIRA §309(c)(4)(G) does not deprive the court of jurisdiction where respondent admits committing an aggravated felony but was not charged or found deportable for it; *Ruckbi* distinguished]; *Lemus-Rodriguez v. Ashcroft,* 350 F.3d 652, 654 (7th Cir. 2003) [where respondent was charged with being undocumented his appeal was not barred because he was also convicted of a crime]; *Alvarez-Santos v. INS,* 332 F.3d 1245, 1249–53 (9th Cir. 2003) [citing the strong presumption of judicial review and due process concerns the court determined that a person who was not found removable by the IJ by reason of having committed an offense under the statute was not barred from judicial review in the court of appeals]; *Yousefi v. INS,* 260 F.3d 318, 324–25 (4th Cir. 2001) [followed *Choeum* finding that applicant could not be deprived of review where the INS did not charge him as an aggravated felony]; *Pondoc Hernaez v. INS,* 244 F.3d 752 (9th Cir. 2001) [where person was drug addict and was not charged with criminal offense, the Court of Appeals has jurisdiction to review decision]; *Hernandez-Montiel v. INS,* 225 F.3d 1084, 1090 (9th Cir. 2000) [mere allegation that person committed crime without charging person in OSC does not bar jurisdiction]; *Choeum v. INS,* 129 F.3d 29, 35–40 (1st Cir. 1997) [INS cannot, consistent with due process and the statutory and regulatory requirements governing its own proceedings, substitute new grounds for deportation at this stage in the proceedings solely for the purposes of depriving the federal courts of jurisdiction]; *Yousefi v. INS,* 260 F.3d 318, 324–25 (4th Cir. 2001) [followed *Choeum*]. *But see Zaidi v. Ashcroft,* 374 F.3d 357, 359 & n.2 (5th Cir. 2004) [where person placed in summary removal as aggravated felon, court has no jurisdiction to review decision following *Lopez-Elias,* 209 F.3d 781, 793 even if the wrong ground for aggravated felony was asserted because court determined respondent was deportable as aggravated felon]; *Garcia v. Att'y Gen. of the U.S.,* 329 F.3d 1217, 1220–22 (11th Cir. 2003) [jurisdictional bar applies where respondent was charged with CIMT that is not covered by IIRIRA §309(c)(4)(G) but was found ineligible for relief on the CIMT which is a ground of inadmissibility under INA §212(a)(2) covered by §309(c)(4)(G)]; *Renteria-Gonzalez v. INS,* 322 F.3d 804, 810 (5th Cir. 2002) [language of statute—"is deportable"—does not require that person be deported for having committed aggravated felony only that he could be deported for it]; *Ruckbi v. INS,* 159 F.3d 18, 19–21 (1st Cir. 1998) [court divested of jurisdiction where person was charged on deportation grounds that did not trigger bar but at a hearing on adjustment admitted committing act covered under INA §212(a)(2) which is covered by the bar]. *Fernandez-Bernal v. Att'y Gen. of the U.S.,* 257 F.3d 1304, 1308–11 (11th Cir. 2001) [no jurisdiction to review claim that BIA improperly found that the person was convicted of a crime because the record revealed he acknowledged the commission of the crime and §242(a)(2)(C) bars review if a person "committed" a crime even if not charged with commission as distinct from conviction].

Habeas Corpus. Even if the bar prevents circuit court review and the REAL ID Act of 2005 prevents habeas review of removal orders, matters involving issues other than removal orders, such as bond, may still be available in habeas in the district court under 28 U.S.C. §2241. *See e.g.,* Joint Explanatory Statement of the Committee of Conference, H.R. Conf. Rep. No. 109-72 at 175, 151 Cong. Rec. H2836, 2873 (May 3, 2005) [regarding preservation of habeas to review bond]; *Hernandez v. Gonzales,* 424 F.3d 42 (1st Cir. 2005) [remanding habeas detention challenge by Mariel Cuban back to district court because habeas may be brought post–REAL ID Act when it is a challenge to detention]; *INS v. St. Cyr,* 121 S.Ct. 2271, 2278–87 (2001) [judicial review under §242 and habeas review "have historically distinct meanings"]; *Saint Fort v. Ashcroft,* 329 F.3d 191, 197–204 (1st Cir. 2003) [same]; *Moallin v. Cangemi,* 427 F.Supp.2d 908, 918–21 (D. Minn. 2006) [citing the REAL ID Act legislative history a Somalian detained subsequent to his removal order can challenge his custody as violative of the constitution]; *Abdulle v. Gonzales,* 422 F.Supp.2d 774, 776 (W.D. Tex. 2006) [REAL ID does not preclude habeas related to detention only]. *But see Deljevic v. Baker,* 463 F.Supp.2d 699 (E.D. Mich. 2006) [no habeas jurisdiction to review detention where there is final order of removal and detention is challenged on ground that final order was improper].

3. *The Discretionary Decision Bars*—INA §242(a)(2)(B)(ii), 8 U.S.C. §1252(a)(2)(B)(ii) provides that "Notwithstanding any other provision of law, no court shall have jurisdiction to review...any other decision or action of the Attorney General the authority for which is specified under this subchapter [§§1151–1378] to be in the discretion of the Attorney General" other than granting asylum.). Pursuant to the REAL ID Act of 2005, PL 109-13, 119 Stat. 231 (May 11, 2005), Div. B §101(f), the discretionary decision bar applies to nonremoval decisions as well as removal cases because INA §242(a)(2)(B) is now applicable in all matters "regardless of whether the judgment, decision, or action is made in removal proceedings." INA §242(a)(2)(B), 8 U.S.C. §1252(a)(2)(B). *Hamdan v. Gonzales,* 425 F.3d 1051, 1056–57 (7th Cir. 2005) [notwithstanding REAL ID Act, respondent could raise res judicata and constitutional challenges to IJ's decision to deny adjustment of status].

3.a. Finding No Review

First Circuit. *Onikoyi v. Gonzales,* 454 F.3d 1, 2–4 (1st Cir. 2006) [no jurisdiction to review discretionary determinations regarding the denial of adjustment or waiver]; *Bencosme De Rodriguez v. Gonzales,* 433 F.3d 163, 164 (1st Cir. 2005) [no jurisdiction to review exceptional and extremely unusual hardship determination in cancellation case]; *Maine State Building and Construction Trades Council, AFL-CIO v. Chao,* 265 F.Supp.2d 105, 110–11 (D. Me. 2003) [dismissed complaint by Union against INS for issuance of I-129 petitions approving H-2Bs]; *Ginters v. Cangemi,* 419 F.Supp.2d 1124, 1128–31 (D. Mass. 2006) [no habeas jurisdiction to review denial of I-130 because the requirement under 8 C.F.R. §204.2(a)(1)(ii) regarding the USCIS director's determination of whether there is "substantial and probative evidence" of immigration fraud in previous marriage is a discretionary decision].

Second Circuit. *Atsilov v. Gonzales,* 468 F.3d 112, 116 (2d Cir. 2006) [INA §242(a)(2)(B)(ii) bars review of the AG's decision to deny a waiver under 8 U.S.C. §1186a(c)(4) as a matter of discretion]; *Avendano-Espejo v. DHS,* 448 F.3d 503 (2d Cir. 2006) ["dressing up" the IJ's exercise of discretion in denying INA §212(c) with the language of "due process" or "erroneous legal standard" did not alter the decision's nonreviewable status]; *Saloum v. USCIS,* 437 F.3d 238 (2d Cir. 2006) [*Post*–REAL ID Act, no jurisdiction to review a denial of a INA §212(d)(11) waiver on discretionary grounds]; *Sol v. INS,* 274 F.3d 648 (2d Cir. 2001), *cert. denied,* 536 U.S. 941(2002) [post–*St. Cyr* habeas review does not extend to review purely discretionary determinations by the BIA such as whether the IJ's decision to deny INA §212(c) was supported by the record]; *Blacher v. Ridge,* 436 F.Supp.2d 602 (S.D.N.Y. 2006) [notwithstanding employer's claim that USCIS violated its due process rights by erroneously interpreting the definition of specialty occupation under the H-1B category when it determined that a professional travel manager was not a professional position, the court held that 8 U.S.C. §1184(a)(1) regarding the admission of nonimmigrants leaves the decision to USCIS's discretion and therefore bars review under INA §242(a)(2)(B)(ii); the court also found that venue was not proper because neither defendants nor plaintiffs resided in the Southern District and the decision was made in Vermont]; *Avramenkov v. INS,* 99 F.Supp.2d 210, 213–15 (D. Conn. 2000) [no jurisdiction to contest transfer under 242(a)(2)(B)(ii) and no due process violation on interference with counsel or hindering witness absent factual showing];

Third Circuit. *Jilin Pharmaceutical USA, Inc. v. Chertoff,* 447 F.3d 196 (3d Cir. 2006) [distinguished *Soltane* regarding denial of visa petitions and found that there was no jurisdiction to review a revocation of an I-140 petition because it was a discretionary decision barred by INA §242(a)(2)(B)(ii)]; *Urena-Tavarez v. Ashcroft,* 367 F.3d 154, 157–61 (3d Cir. 2004), [no jurisdiction to review IJ's denial of a waiver of conditional residency]; *U.S. ex rel. Kovalev v. Ashcroft,* 223 F.Supp.2d 688 (E.D. Pa. 2002) [no review in habeas of Service's discretionary decision to deny motion to reopen for NACARA where person appeared facially eligible]; *Curri v. Reno,* 86 F.Supp.2d 413 (D.N.J. 2000) [habeas petition seeking review of parole decision denied because section repeals §2241];

Fourth Circuit. *Zhang v. Chertoff,* 491 F.Supp.2d 590 (W.D. Va. 2007) [no jurisdiction to compel USCIS to adjudicate I-485 within specified period of time]; *Rodas v. Chertoff,* 399 F.Supp.2d 697, 704–06 (E.D. Va. 2005) [INA §242(a)(2)(B)(ii) bars review of the denial of an individual's application for TPS];

Fifth Circuit. *Ghanem v. Upchurch,* 481 F.3d 222 (5th Cir. 2007) [revocation of I-130 petition is not reviewable]; *Assaad v. Ashcroft,* 378 F.3d 471, 475 (5th Cir. 2004) [following *Urena-Tavarez* and finding no jurisdiction to review good-faith marriage waiver under 8 U.S.C. §1186a(c)(4)(B) even in context of motion to reopen]; *Eastern Carpet House, Inc. v. DHS,* 430 F.Supp.2d 672, 674–75 (S.D. Tex. 2006) [no review of AAO denial of L-1 extension because 8 U.S.C. §1184 provides that the admission of a nonimmigrant is discretionary and 8 U.S.C. §1252(a)(2)(B)(ii) bars review of discretionary decisions];

Sixth Circuit. *Singh v. Gonzales,* 451 F.3d 400, 410–11 (6th Cir. 2006) [no jurisdiction to review the discretionary aspects of the denial of an INA §237(a)(1)(H) waiver]; *CDI Information Services, Inc. v. Reno,* 278 F.3d 616 (6th Cir. 2002) [no jurisdiction to review a denial of an H-1B extension]; *Hanif v. DHS,* 472 F.Supp.2d 914 (E.D. Mich. 2007) [no jurisdiction to review revocation of I-130 petition]; *Global Export/Import Link v. U.S. Bureau of Citizenship and Immigration Services,* 423 F.Supp.2d 703 (E.D. Mich. 2006) [where USCIS denied I-129 petition for L-1A classification in its authority under 8 U.S.C. §1184(c), the decision is not reviewable because it is a discretionary decision barred from review under INA §242(a)(2)(B)(ii)];

Seventh Circuit. *Wood v. Mukasey,* 516 F.3d 564 (7th Cir. 2008) [no jurisdiction following *Ali* to review IJ's denial of a continuance to await approval of I-130]; *Iqbal Ali v. Gonzales,* 502 F.3d 659, 660–65 (7th Cir. 2007) [INA §242(a)(2)(B)(i) & (ii) bar jurisdiction to review continuances because when underlying matter is not reviewable anything leading up to it is not reviewable; rejected argument that continuances are regulatory and therefore not barred; *Subhan* distinguished]; *Holy Virgin Protection Cathedral v. Chertoff,* 499 F.3d 658 (7th Cir. 2007) [no jurisdiction to review revocation of religious worker petition]; *Ali v. Achim,* 468 F.3d 462, 465–66, 470 (7th Cir. 2006) *cert. dismissed* 128 S.Ct. 828 (2007) [jurisdiction to review whether proper standard was applied to determine a particularly serious crime but there was no jurisdiction to review BIA's exercise of discretion under the proper legal standard including whether it misapplied its own precedent]; *El-Khader v. Monica,* 366 F.3d 562 (7th Cir. 2004) [no jurisdiction to review revocation of employment-based visa petition under §1155 because of previous marriage fraud. Citing *Samirah v. O'Connell* the court rejected the claims that the discretionary decision bar is limited to removal, deportation and exclusion proceedings and that marriage fraud is not discretionary]; *Samirah v. O'Connell,* 335 F.3d 545 (7th Cir. 2003) [district court lacked jurisdiction to review revocation of advance parole because INA §242(a)(2)(B)(ii) precludes review of discretionary decisions and because habeas jurisdiction was unavailable to someone outside the U.S. who is not in custody and is unable to have personal service over a custodian]; *Sharif v. Chertoff,* 497 F.Supp.2d 928 (N.D. Ill. 2007) [requiring the approval of the 129F petition for a K-1 visa or seeking to compel the adjudication of the petition is barred by INA §242(a)(2)(B)(ii)].

Eighth Circuit. *Ebrahim v. Gonzales,* 471 F.3d 880, 883–84 (8th Cir. 2006) [no jurisdiction to review good faith marriage exception under INA §216(c)(4)(B), 8 U.S.C. §1186a(c)(4)(B)]; *Suvorov v. Gonzales,* 441 F.3d 618, 621–22 (8th Cir. 2006) [no jurisdiction to review good-faith marriage exception under 8 U.S.C. §1186a(c)(4)(B)]; *Ignatova v. Gonzales,* 430 F.3d 1209, 1212–13 (8th Cir. 2005) [post–REAL ID Act, the court found no jurisdiction following *Urena-Tavarez* to review hardship waiver under §1186a(c)(4)(A)]; *Grass v. Gonzales,* 418 F.3d 876, 878–89 (8th Cir. 2005) [the court lacked jurisdiction to hear a challenge to the denial of a continuance to wait approval of an I-130 petition and the REAL ID Act of 2005 did not alter that lack of jurisdiction because the decision to grant a continuance was discretionary and not a question of law]; *Onyinkwa v. Ashcroft,* 376 F.3d 797 (8th Cir. 2004) [no jurisdiction under INA §242(a)(2)(B)(ii) to review discretionary decision by IJ to deny continuance pending approval of IV petition]; *Bah v. Cangemi,* 489 F.Supp.2d 905, 912–14 (D. Minn. 207) [court had no jurisdiction to review AAO decision to withdraw Liberian's TPS on the grounds that his vacated conviction for second-degree criminal sexual conduct under *Matter of Pickering* was still a conviction and therefore he was ineligible for TPS].

Ninth Circuit. *San Pedro v. Ashcroft,* 395 F.3d 1156 (9th Cir. 2005).[where IJ determined that respondent was not statutorily eligible for a 237(a)(1)(H) waiver, but also stated in the alternative that as a discretionary matter he would not grant it, the circuit court would normally not have jurisdiction over the discretionary determination]; *Avendano-Ramirez v. Ashcroft,* 365 F.3d 813, 819 (9th Cir. 2004) [no jurisdiction to review IJ decision to deny withdrawal of application for admission or no jurisdiction to review summary removal order by petition for review]; *Singh v. Ashcroft,* 351 F.3d 435, 438–40 (9th Cir. 2003) [following *Matsuk,* there is no jurisdiction to review BIA's exercise of discretion that respondent committed a particularly serious crime that bars withholding, although jurisdiction exists over CAT claim]; *Molina-Estrada v. INS,* 293 F.3d 1089, 1093 (9th Cir. 2002) [no jurisdiction to review the discretionary decision to deny cancellation]; *Matsuk v. INS,* 247 F.3d 999, 1002 (9th Cir. 2001) [circuit court barred from reviewing decision to deny withholding based upon determination whether crime is particularly serious barring withholding];

Tenth Circuit. *Hamilton v. Gonzales,* 485 F.3d 564 (10th Cir. 2007) [revocation of I-130/adoption petition that was affirmed by BIA is not reviewable in circuit court because it is not part of a final order, the APA is not an independent jurisdictional ground, and it is precluded by INA §242(a)(2)(B)]; *Ballesteros v. Ashcroft,* 452 F.3d 1153, 1159–60 (10th Cir. 2006) [no jurisdiction to review change of venue claim where respondent argued that DHS reorganization should not preclude him from obtaining review in the Ninth Circuit]; *Yerkovich v. Ashcroft,* 381 F.3d 990 (10th Cir. 2004) [no jurisdiction to review an IJ's decision to deny a continuance due to pending IV petition]; *Van Dinh v. Reno,* 197 F.3d 427, 431–32 (10th Cir. 1999) [section bars *Bivens* under 28 U.S.C. §1331 seeking to restrain transfers of detained persons];

Eleventh Circuit. *Arias v. U.S. Att'y Gen.***,** 482 F.3d 1281 (11th Cir. 2007) [finding s not supported by the record, failure to properly weight factors, and mischaracterization of the record by the IJ in §212(c) case were not constitutional claims permitting review]; *Grinberg v. Swancia,* 478 F.Supp.2d 1350 (S.D. Fla. 2007) [following *Safadi v. Howard,*, 466 F.Supp.2d 696 (E.D. Va. 2006) and finding that post–REAL ID Act INA §242(a)(2)(B)(ii) bars mandamus for adjustment under mandamus statute and 555(b) of the APA because it bars pace of "actions" as well as decisions];

D.C. Circuit. *Zhu v. Gonzales,* 411 F.3d 292 (D.C. Cir. 2005) [rejecting analysis relied upon in *Spencer* and holding that review of national interest waivers of medical researchers is barred]; *Systronics Corp. v. INS*, 153 F.Supp.2d 7, 11–13 (D.D.C. 2001) [no jurisdiction to review decision to revoke I-140 petition because "good and sufficient cause" standard is discretionary]; *Orlov v. Howard,* 523 F.Supp.2d 30 (D.D.C. 2007) [INA §242(a)(2)(B)(ii) precludes jurisdiction to compel adjudication of AOS pending 4 years and neither APA §555(b), nor mandamus, are a source of jurisdiction]; *Tao Luo v. Keisler,* 521 F.Supp.2d 72 (D.D.C. 2007) [same following *Grinberg* and *Safadi*].

3.b. *Narrow Construction Permitting Review*—However, some courts have taken the view that INA §242(a)(2)(B)(ii) should be narrowly construed. The Supreme Court in *INS v. St. Cyr,* 121 S.Ct. 2271, 2283 (2001) for example, determined that it does not bar the writ of habeas corpus under 28 U.S.C. §2241 to challenge, within the context of a final order of removal, constitutional questions or questions of law including those arising in the context of discretionary relief. In *Spencer Enterprises, Inc. v. U.S.,* 345 F.3d 683, 689 (9th Cir. 2003), the Ninth Circuit, finding there was review of the denial of an EB-5 investor petition, narrowly construed the section to include only "acts the *authority* for which is *specified* under the INA to be discretionary" and not simply any discretionary decision. The court found that the section includes only acts that are matters of "pure discretion" and not "discretion guided by legal standards." *Id* at 690. *See also Ayanbadejo v. Chertoff,* 517 F.3d 273, 276–78 (5th Cir. 2008) [jurisdiction exists to review denial of I-130 petition and regulatory language that may suggest it is a discretionary decision cannot bind the court because Congress precluded review only of decisions described as discretionary under the *statute*]; *Jahjaga v. Att'y Gen. of the U.S.,* 512 F.3d 80, 82–83 (3d Cir. 2008) [following *Khan* and the strong presumption of judicial review, the denial of motion to reissue an opinion is not a discretionary act specified in designated subchapter]; *Alsamhouri v. Gonzales,* 484 F.3d 117, 122 (1st Cir. 2007) [adopting narrow construction of *Spencer* in context of review of denial of continuance]; *Zafar v. U.S. Att'y Gen.,* 461 F.3d 1357, 1360–62 (11th Cir. 2006) *reh'g en banc denied* 473 F.3d 1350 (2007) [review of the denials of respondents' requests for continuance were not precluded by INA §242(a)(2)(B)(ii) because that section applies only to statutes and continuances are governed by regulation]; *Khan v. Att'y Gen. of the U.S.,* 448 F.3d 226, 229–33 (3d Cir. 2006) [same]; *Ahmed v. Gonzales,* 447 F.3d 433, 436–37 (5th Cir. 2006) [same]; *Alaka v. Att'y Gen. of the U.S.,* 456 F.3d 88, 95–102 (3d Cir. 2006) [following reasoning in *Spencer* and determining that discretionary bar does not apply to determination of particularly serious crime exception to withholding of removal]; *Sanusi v. Gonzales,* 445 F.3d 193, 198–99 (2d Cir. 2006) [continuances are not even mentioned in the subchapter referred to (subchapter II of Chapter 12) by 242(a)(2)(B)(ii)]; *Abu-Khaliel v. Gonzales,* 436 F.3d 627, 631–34 (6th Cir. 2006) [INA §242(a)(2)(B)(ii) does not bar jurisdiction over the IJ's denial of a continuance because that section refers to matters in the discretion of the Attorney General and continuances are part of the removal hearing which Congress has specified under INA §240(a)(1) are conducted by IJs]; *Manzano-Garcia v. Gonzales,* 413 F.3d 462, 465–66 (5th Cir. 2005) [following *Zhao* and finding that review of motions to reopen are not barred because the discretion emanates from a regulation not a statute]; *Oropeza-Wong v. Gonzales,* 406 F.3d 1135, 1141–49 (9th Cir. 2005) [following *Spencer* and *Medina-Morales,* the court determined that §1252(a)(2)(B)(ii) did not bar the court's jurisdiction to review whether a conditional resident in removal proceedings qualified for good faith marriage waiver under §1186a(c)(4)(B), that the court also had jurisdiction over the removal order, but that there was substantial evidence to support the IJ's denial of the good faith waiver on the merits]; *Zhao v. Gonzales,* 404 F.3d 295, 301–04 (5th Cir. 2005) [following *Medina-Morales* and holding that because the statute on motions to reopen does not specify that the matter is within the discretion of the AG, there is no bar to judicial review even if DHS regulations establish the AG's discretion]; *Ana International Inc. v. Way,* 393 F.3d 886, 893–95 (9th Cir. 2005) [following *Spencer* and holding that INA §242(a)(2)(B)(ii) does not bar judicial review of an I-140 visa revocation of an EB-1 decision under 8 U.S.C. §1155 because the "good and sufficient cause" language of the statute provides a legal standard, as does the "managerial capacity" criteria of EB-1]; *Soltane v. DOJ,* 381 F.3d 143, 146–48 (3d Cir. 2004) [followed *Spencer* in regard to special immigrant/religious worker case]; *Kwai Fun Wong v. U.S.,* 373 F.3d 952, 962–63 (9th Cir. 2004) [*Bivens* action is not precluded because a violation of the Constitution cannot be discretionary and because there is no authority that specifies discretion following *Spencer Enterprises*]; *Medina-Morales v. Ashcroft,* 371 F.3d 520, 528–29 (9th Cir. 2004) [following *Spencer Enterprises* there is jurisdiction to review the denial of a motion to reopen for adjustment because the statutory provision for motions to reopen do not specify the AG's discretionary authority]; *Nakamoto v. Ashcroft,* 363 F.3d 874, 878–81 (9th Cir. 2004) [court's jurisdiction was not precluded by INA §242(a)(2)(B)(ii) to review AG's decision to deport for marriage fraud under INA §237(a)(1)(G)(ii)]; *Aslam v. Mukasey,* 531 F.Supp.2d 736, 739–42 (E.D. Va. 2008) [followed *Spencer* and recognized that INA §242(a)(2)(B)(i) was not implicated because there was no decision]; *Tang v. Chertoff,* 493 F.Supp.2d 148, 151–54 (D. Mass. 2007) [followed *Spencer* and determined that §§242(a)(2)(B)(i) & (ii) do not bar action to compel adjudication of AOS pending for 4 years]; *National Collegiate Recreation Services v. Chertoff,* 447 F.Supp.2d 527 (D. S.C. 2006) [followed *Spencer Enterprises Inc.* and held that INA §242(a)(2)(B)(ii) did not bar judicial review of denial of Q-1 because neither the statute nor the regulations specifically state that the decision is in the discretion of DHS].

Courts have narrowly interpreted the bar by declaring that the subject matter at issue does not fall under Subchapter II of the INA, and therefore there is no bar to judicial review. *Zheng v. Pogash,* 416 F.3d 550, 554–57 (S.D. Tex. 2006) [judicial review was not precluded by INA §242(a)(2)(B)(ii) because the REAL ID Act only barred review of matters within Subchapter II in the INA, and the review of whether DHS should have granted specific consent to allow a juvenile dependency proceeding is within Subchapter I].

3.c. Additional Cases Providing for Review

The discretionary bar is also limited in other respects.

First Circuit. *Aguilar v. ICE,* 510 F.3d 1, 18–24 (1st Cir. 2007) [INA §242(a)(2)(B)(ii) does not preclude a substantive due process challenge to detention but the court found that ICE raids which interfered with a parent's ability to provide care, custody and control of their children does not violate substantive due process]; *Cho v. Gonzales,* 404 F.3d 96, 98–102 (1st Cir. 2005) [court had authority to review whether conditional resident in removal proceedings qualified for good faith marriage waiver under §1186a(c)(4)(B) and reversed BIA for lack of substantial evidence]; *Prado v. Reno,* 198 F.3d 286, 288, 290–91 (1st Cir. 1999) [review of BIA's decision not to reopen case *sua sponte* is not barred by INA §242(a)(2)(B)]; *Mendes v. INS,* 197 F.3d 6, 12–13 (1st Cir. 1999) [review of IJ denial of petition to remove conditional residence]; *Bernal-Vallejo v. INS,* 195 F.3d 56 (1st Cir. 1999) [jurisdiction precluded "only where (1) the agency decision as to which review is sought is a 'decision under' one of the enumerated sections, and (2) the agency decision rests on a ground that is committed to agency discretion."]. In *Bernal-Vallejo,* the Court ruled that an appeal challenging the finding of extreme hardship was precluded but that the constitutional due process claim arising out of ineffective assistance of counsel was not. *See also Luis v. INS,* 196 F.3d 36, 39–41 (1st Cir. 1999) [review of BIA's decision to deny motion to reconsider on timeliness grounds is not barred from review];

Second Circuit. *Firstland Int'l Inc. v. INS,* 377 F.3d 127, 130–31 (2d Cir. 2004) [no bar to review of AG's nondiscretionary decision to revoke I-140 petition where person is in U.S., because it raises a pure legal question of whether §1155 permits revocation where beneficiary is in the U.S.]; *Nolan v. Holmes,* 334 F.3d 189, 194 (2d Cir. 2003) [challenge to whether good moral character can be a requirement for naturalization for someone in military service is not a challenge to prosecutorial decision to continue with removal proceeding]; *Ceken v. Chertoff,* 544 F.Supp.2d 211 (D. Conn. 2008) [mandamus and APA claim to adjudicate AOS application pending for 5 years was not barred].

Third Circuit. *Okeke v. Gonzales,* 407 F.3d 585, 588 n.4 (3d Cir. 2005) [the interpretation of the "stop-time" rule is not subject to the discretionary bar];

Fourth Circuit. *Stewart v. INS,* 181 F.3d 587, 594–95 (4th Cir. 1999) [a denial of a motion to reopen for adjustment of status under §245 was *not* covered by this provision because the denial was based on the failure to show exceptional circumstances under former INA §242B(e)(2)(A)];

Fifth Circuit. *Ayanbadejo v. Chertoff,* 517 F.3d 273, 276–78 (5th Cir. 2008) [jurisdiction to review denial of I-130 petition]; *Zhao v. Gonzales,* 404 F.3d 295, 301–04 (5th Cir. 2005) [following *Medina-Morales* and holding that because the statute on motions to reopen does not specify that the matter is within the discretion of the AG, there is no bar to judicial review even if DHS regulations establish the AG's discretion];

Sixth Circuit. *Sillah v. Davis,* 252 F.Supp.2d 589, 593–97 (W.D. Tenn. 2003) [INA §242(a)(2)(B)(ii) does not preclude habeas jurisdiction to challenge revocation of parole];

Seventh Circuit. *Boyanivskyy v. Gonzales,* 450 F.3d 286, 291–92 (7th Cir. 2006) [followed *Benslimane* and *Subhan* and found that where IJ denied continuance to allow witnesses to testify in asylum case, INA §242(a)(2)(B)(ii) does not apply because to apply it will "nullify some statutory right" or "lead[] inescapably to a substantive adverse decision on the merits"]; *Benslimane v. Gonzales,* 430 F.3d 828, (7th Cir. 2005) [rejected preclusion of review pursuant to INA §242(a)(2)(B) because case involved a legal interpretation and found that IJ made a legal error in denying a continuance where respondent had filed an I-130 and I-485 as part of a marriage based adjustment but had not filed adjustment with the IJ]; *Singh v. Gonzales,* 404 F.3d 1024, 1026–27 (7th Cir. 2005) [following *Medina-Morales* and *Infanzon* and finding that INA §242(a)(2)(B)(ii) does not bar review of denial of motion to reopen for adjustment]; *Subhan v. Ashcroft,* 3 83 F.3d 591 (7th Cir. 2004) [INA §242(a)(2)(B)(ii) does not bar review of a denial of a continuance to submit a §245(i) application because Congress did not intend to interpret 242(a)(2)(B)(ii) in a manner to permit a procedural issue to frustrate a statutory claim to adjustment]; *Paunescu v. INS,* 76 F.Supp.2d 896, 899–900 (N.D. Ill. 1999) [compelling completion of diversity visa adjustment through mandamus is not seeking judicial review of any judgment regarding adjustment]; *Ogbolumani v. USCIS,* 523 F.Supp.2d 864, 871–78 (N.D. Ill. 2007) [denial of I-130 petition is not a discretionary decision and unlike revocation of a petition is reviewable].

Eighth Circuit. *Al Jabari v. Chertoff,* 536 F.Supp.2d 1029 (D. Minn. 2008) [In action to compel DHS to complete the security check involving the grant by an IJ of a marriage hardship waiver to lift conditional residence under 8 U.S.C. §1186a(c)(4), the court determined that APA action was not barred by INA §242(a)(2)(B)];

Ninth Circuit. *Morales v. Gonzales,* 478 F.3d 972, 978–81 (9th Cir. 2007) [jurisdiction to hear: asylum claim; what IJ may refer to in deciding whether a prior offense is a particularly serious crime for withholding; and the IJ's application of the wrong legal standard for CAT]; *Nath v. Gonzales,* 467 F.3d 1185, 1188 (9th Cir. 2007) [court has jurisdiction to review a denial of a motion to reopen removal proceedings where conviction was vacated]; *Freeman v. Gonzales,* 444 F.3d 1031, 1037–43 (9th Cir. 2006) [INA §242(a)(2)(B) does not bar review of the purely legal question whether a widow remains a spouse for purposes of 8 U.S.C. §1151(b)(2)(A)(i)]; *Afridi v. Gonzales,* 442 F.3d 1212, 1217–19 (9th Cir. 2006) [distinguishing its own precedent in *Unuakhaulu v. Gonzales,* 416 F.3d 931 (9th Cir. 2005), the court held that INA §242(a)(2)(B)(ii) did not bar review of the BIA's determination that respondent committed a particularly serious crime because respondent challenged the failure to apply the proper legal standard under *Frentescu*]; *Cabrera-Alvarez v. Gonzales,* 423 F.3d 1006, 1009 (9th Cir. 2005) [whether the BIA interpreted the exceptional and extremely unusual hardship provision of cancellation consistent with international law is a legal question reviewable under INA §242(a)(2)(D)]; *Reyes-Melendez v. INS,* 342 F.3d 1001 (9th Cir. 2003) [an IJ's extreme hardship determination in a suspension case may be challenged where the IJ in making the decision violated due process by abandoning her role as a neutral fact-finder]; *Dillingham v. INS,* 267 F.3d 996, 1003 (9th Cir. 2001) [discretionary bar does not prevent review of denial of adjustment of status application that was based upon statutory ineligibility because BIA treated foreign expungement as conviction]; *Beltran-Tirado v. INS,* 213 F.3d 1179, 1182–83 n.4 (9th Cir. 2000) [discretionary bar does not cover registry applicant]; *Lafarga v. INS,* 170 F.3d 1213, 1215 (9th Cir. 1999) [statutory eligibility for voluntary departure is not a discretionary decision]; *Arrozal v. INS,* 159 F.3d 429, 431–32 (9th Cir. 1998) [motion to reopen to apply for suspension not barred]; *Shirmohamadali v. Heinauer,* 533 F.Supp.2d 1059 (E.D. Cal. 2008) [more than 4-year wait for AOS was unreasonable]; *Dong v. Chertoff,* 513 F.Supp.2d 1158, 1166–68 (N.D. Cal. 2007) [8 C.F.R. §103.2(b)(18) limits the discretion of USCIS to continue/withhold the adjudication of an I-485 pending two-and-a-half years and therefore the demand that the I-485 be adjudicated *is subject* to judicial review under mandamus and APA §706(1) and is not precluded by INA §242(a)(2)(B)(ii)]; *Fred 26 Importers, Inc. v. DHS,* 445 F.Supp.2d 1174, 1178–79 (C.D. Cal. 2006)[jurisdiction under the APA, 5 U.S.C. §706(2)(A), to review AAO decision where it denied H-1B]; *Del Toro-Chacon v. Chertoff,* 431 F.Supp.2d 1135, 1140–42 (W.D. Wash. 2006) [court had jurisdiction to entertain constitutional challenge to denial of bond hearing because it was not a matter of discretion]; *Mart v. Beebe,* 94 F.Supp.2d 1120 (D. Or. 2000) [rejecting preclusion statute's application to prevent the review of adjustment of status applications that are not in removal proceedings];

Tenth Circuit. *Infanzon v. Ashcroft,* 386 F.3d 1359 (10th Cir. 2004) [review of a motion to reopen is not barred unless underlying BIA order was not reviewable]; *Sierra v. INS,* 258 F.3d 1213 (10th Cir. 2001) [habeas jurisdiction regarding withdrawal of parole to Mariel Cuban];

Eleventh Circuit. *Jeanty v. Bulger,* 204 F.Supp.2d 1366, 1373–75 (S.D. Fla. 2002), *aff'd sub nom. Moise v. Bulger,* 321 F.3d 1336 (11th Cir.), *cert. denied*, 540 U.S. 1016 (2003) [habeas jurisdiction exists to review INS parole determinations];

D.C. Circuit. *Liu v. Novak,* 509 F.Supp.2d 1 (D.D.C. 2007) [summary judgment granted to petitioner waiting four years on AOS and neither INA §242(a)(2)(B), nor INA §242(g) precluded mandamus and §1331 jurisdiction pursuant to APA §555(b)].

3.d. *Preclusion Not Limited Solely to Removal Proceedings*—The REAL ID Act of 2005, PL 109-13, 119 Stat. 231 (May 11, 2005), Div. B §101(f), extended the discretionary preclusions to all matters "regardless of whether the judgment, decision, or action is made in removal proceedings." INA §242(a)(2)(B), 8 U.S.C. §1252(a)(2)(B). Prior to the REAL ID Act of 2005, some courts took the view that the jurisdictional bar under INA §242(a)(2)(B)(ii) related solely to review in removal proceedings. *Grinberg v. Swancia,* 478 F.Supp.2d 1350 (S.D. Fla. 2007) [following *Safadi v. Howard,*, 466 F.Supp.2d 696 (E.D. Va. 2006) and finding that *post*–REAL ID Act INA §242(a)(2)(B)(ii) bars mandamus for adjustment under mandamus statute and APA §555(b) because it bars pace of "actions" as well as decisions]; *Evangelical Lutheran Church in America v. INS,* 288 F.Supp.2d 32, 40–42 (D.D.C. 2003); *Calexico Warehouse, Inc. v. Neufeld,* 259 F.Supp.2d 1067, 1072–75 (S.D. Cal. 2002); *Mart v. Beebe,* 94 F.Supp.2d 1120, 1124 (D. Or. 2000); *Shanti, Inc. v. Reno,* 36 F.Supp.2d 1151, 1157–61 (D. Minn. 1999).

3.e. Review Barred under INA §242(a)(2)(B)(i)

Judicial review is also barred under INA §242(a)(2)(B)(i), 8 U.S.C. §1252(a)(2)(B)(i). The bar provides that: "Notwithstanding any other provision of law, no court shall have jurisdiction to review...any judgment regarding the granting of relief under section 1182(h), 1182(i), 1229b, 1229c, or 1255 of this title..." .

Second Circuit. *Barco-Sandoval v. Gonzales,* 516 F.3d 35 (2d Cir. 2008) [finding that *Chen v. DOJ,* 471 F.3d 315 did not alter *De La Vega* where respondent's claim that the wrong legal standard was applied was not colorable and merely sought to address a factual question as to extreme hardship under cancellation]; *Camara v. DHS,* 497 F.3d 121 (2d Cir. 2007) [INA §242(a)(2)(B)(i) bars review of extreme hardship decision in denying INA §212(i) waiver]; *Barnaby-King v. DHS,* 485 F.3d 684 (2d Cir. 2007) [same as *Camara*]; *Zhang v. Gonzales,* 457 F.3d 172 (2d Cir. 2006) [post–REAL ID Act, INA §242(a)(2)(B)(i) bars review of the discretionary decision of extreme hardship under INA §212(i)]; *Bygayong v. INS,* 442 F.3d 67 (2d Cir. 2006) [INA §242(a)(2)(D) does not overcome the discretionary decision bar under §242(a)(2)(B)(i) for a §212(h) waiver even if there was a finding of extreme hardship because the ultimate decision to grant the waiver is discretionary]; *De La Vega v. Gonzales,* 436 F.3d 141 (2d Cir. 2006) [INA §242(a)(2)(D) did not extend jurisdiction to review the denial of cancellation based upon exceptional and extremely unusual hardship which review is barred by INA §242(a)(2)(B)(i)]; *Santos-Salazar v. DOJ,* 400 F.3d 99, 104 (2d Cir. 2005) [no jurisdiction to review BIA's order denying respondent the opportunity to apply for discretionary relief from removal];

Third Circuit. *Mendez-Moranchel v. Ashcroft,* 338 F.3d 176 (3d Cir. 2003) [following *Montero-Martinez* and finding that "judgment" under the statute only applies to discretionary matters and there was no jurisdiction to review the discretionary finding of the IJ that the applicant did not establish sufficient hardship];

Fifth Circuit. *Said v. Gonzales,* 488 F.3d 668 (5th Cir. 2007) [no review of extreme hardship decision in 212(i) waiver]; *Bravo v. Ashcroft,* 341 F.3d 590, 593 (5th Cir. 2003) [decision on exceptional and extremely unusual hardship may not be reviewed and respondent failed to present a substantial constitutional question];

Seventh Circuit. *Leguizamo-Medina v. Gonzales,* 493 F.3d 772 (7th Cir. 2007) [no jurisdiction to review denial of cancellation for lack of good moral character]; *Jarad v. Gonzales,* 461 F.3d 867 (7th Cir. 2006) [court lacked jurisdiction to review denial of motion to reopen to adjust status under INA §245(i) for applicant married to USC where the IJ cited discretionary factors]; *Cevilla v. Gonzales,* 446 F.3d 658 (7th Cir. 2006) [where IJ erred in concluding that applicant was not in the U.S. for the 10 years necessary for cancellation, review of the motion to reopen on those grounds was denied because the court lacked jurisdiction under 242(a)(2)(B)(i) as no statutory or constitutional error occurred]; *Sokolov v. Gonzales,* 442 F.3d 566, 568–70 (7th Cir. 2006) [where IJ denied AOS in his discretion because he believe applicant was dishonest review is barred]; *Martinez-Maldonado v. Gonzales,* 437 F.3d 679, 682–84 (7th Cir. 2006) [no jurisdiction to review the motion to reopen or the decision to AWO respondent's case regarding the denial of cancellation where the denial was based upon the failure to establish hardship]; *Mireles v. Gonzales,* 433 F.3d 965, 968 (7th Cir. 2006) [no review of discretionary decision to deny cancellation whether the argument is abuse of discretion or failure to conduct a thorough review of the record]; *Kharkhan v. Ashcroft,* 336 F.3d 601, 604 (7th Cir. 2003) [no jurisdiction to review special rule cancellation denial by IJ];

Eighth Circuit. *Merza-Reyes v. Gonzales,* 436 F.3d 842 (8th Cir. 2006) [notwithstanding INA §242(a)(2)(D), respondent cannot obtain jurisdiction simply by cloaking an abuse of discretion argument in constitutional terms where he seeks review of the IJ's determination regarding extraordinary and extremely unusual hardship under cancellation of removal];

Ninth Circuit. *Mejia v. Gonzales,* 499 F.3d 991, 995–99 (9th Cir. 2007) [court had jurisdiction to review validity of AG's regulation at §212.7(d) for a §212(h) waiver, but rejected challenge to the application of the regulation to respondent's rehabilitation]; *Fernandez v. Gonzales,* 439 F.3d 592 (9th Cir. 2006) [the court has no jurisdiction to review the denial of a motion to reopen where the motion seeks to submit additional evidence of hardship after there has been a merits denial of cancellation on discretionary grounds; *Medina-Morales* distinguished as applying to motions to reopen where relief is sought for the first time in the motion]; *Martinez-Rosas v. Gonzales,* 424 F.3d 926, 929–30 (9th Cir. 2005) [same]; *Romero-Torres v. Ashcroft,* 327 F.3d 887 (9th Cir. 2003) [finding §242(a)(2)(B)(i) bars review of exceptional and extremely unusual hardship];

Tenth Circuit. *Perales-Cumpean v. Gonzales,* 429 F.3d 977, 982–84 (10th Cir. 2005) [a determination of extreme cruelty or credibility issues in the determination of cancellation for a battered spouse are barred from judicial review by INA §242(a)(2)(B)(i)]; *Ekasinta v. Gonzales,* 415 F.3d 1188, 1189–91 (10th Cir. 2005) [where IJ determined that person was ineligible for cancellation and adjustment both as a legal matter and on discretionary grounds, jurisdiction was barred]; *Alvarez-Delmuro v. Ashcroft,* 360 F.3d 1254 (10th Cir. 2004) [no jurisdiction to review cancellation even where respondents raise constitutional challenge to cancellation standard as applied to USC children]; *Morales Ventura v. Ashcroft,* 348 F.3d 1259, 1261–63 (10th Cir. 2003) [decision on exceptional and extremely unusual hardship may not be reviewed and respondent failed to present a substantial constitutional question];

Eleventh Circuit. *Gonzalez-Oropeza v. U.S. Att'y Gen.,* 321 F.3d 1331, 1332–33 (11th Cir. 2003) [bars review of exceptional and extremely unusual hardship].

The bar, in the view of one court, extends to constitutional challenges. *Leyva v. Ashcroft,* 380 F.3d 303, 305–06 (7th Cir. 2004) [no jurisdiction to entertain Fifth Amendment challenge to standards for cancellation]; *Dave v. Ashcroft,* 363 F.3d 649, 652–53 (7th Cir. 2004) [rejected constitutional challenge to BIA streamlining cancellation claim because there is no liberty or property interest in discretionary relief and because INA §242(a)(2)(B)(i) bars review of discretionary decisions]. Review of discretionary decision granting VD may also be barred. *Eyoum v. INS*, 125 F.3d 889, 891 (5th Cir. 1997), *Tutu v. Blackman,* 9 F.Supp.2d 534 (E.D. Pa. 1998).

3.f. <u>Jurisdiction Notwithstanding INA §242(a)(2)(B)(i)</u>

First Circuit. *Singh v. Gonzales,* 413 F.3d 156, 160 n.4 (1st Cir. 2005) [whether someone is ineligible for INA §245(i) because he is inadmissible is not a discretionary denial barred from review]; *Succar v. Ashcroft,* 394 F.3d 8, 19–20 (1st Cir. 2005) [there is §1331 jurisdiction because respondent's challenge regarding AOS is to the invalidity of a DHS regulation as contrary to the statute and it is therefore not a discretionary decision barred under INA §242(a)(2)(B)(i) but a pure legal question];

Second Circuit. *Sepulveda v. Gonzales,* 407 F.3d 59 (2d Cir. 2005) [the §242(a)(2)(B)(i) bar to cancellation and adjustment does not extend to the nondiscretionary decision whether a person is unable to establish good moral character as a matter of law or to statutory eligibility for adjustment under §245(i) even if they arise in the context of the review of motions to reopen or reconsider];

Fourth Circuit. *Jean v. Gonzales,* 435 F.3d 475, 480–81 (4th Cir. 2005) [no jurisdiction to review that aspect of a motion to reconsider that seeks reconsideration of a discretionary denial of INA §212(h) because the discretionary denial was not reviewable in the first place under INA §242(a)(2)(B), but whether respondent was precluded from establishing good moral character was a legal issue that was reviewable]; *Obioha v. Gonzales,* 431 F.3d 400, 404–08 (4th Cir. 2005) [BIA denial of motion to remand for cancellation did not result in a review of a denial of cancellation and therefore review is not barred];

Fifth Circuit. *Manzano-Garcia v. Gonzales,* 413 F.3d 462, 466–69 (5th Cir. 2005) [distinguished *Rodriguez v. Ashcroft,* 253 F.3d 797 (5th Cir. 2001) and determined that where IJ/BIA's did not make a discretionary determination regarding adjustment or VD, but rather denied continuance because evidence was previously available, the review of his motion to reopen is not barred]; *Mireles-Valdez v. Ashcroft,* 349 F.3d 213, 215–16 (5th Cir. 2003) [jurisdiction is not barred to determine whether voluntary departure breaks the 10-year physical present requirement for cancellation and the court read "judgment" under the permanent statute to mean discretionary decisions in keeping with other circuit decisions];

Sixth Circuit. *Santana-Albarran v. Ashcroft,* 393 F.3d 699, 703 (6th Cir. 2005) [jurisdiction to review whether respondent had the requisite continuous physical presence for cancellation]; *Pilica v. Ashcroft,* 388 F.3d 941, 945–48 (6th Cir. 2004) [motion to remand for adjustment of status was not barred]; *Martinez v. DHS,* 502 F.Supp.2d 631, 634–36 (E.D. Mich. 2007) [followed *Pinho v. Gonzales* and held that INA §242(a)(2)(B)(1) nor principles of exhaustion barred a district court under the APA from reviewing whether a petitioner qualified for the benefits of CSPA when he was denied adjustment];

Seventh Circuit. *Subhan v. Ashcroft,* 383 F.3d 591 (7th Cir. 2004) [neither INA §242(a)(2)(B)(i) nor (ii) bars review of a denial of a continuance to submit a §245(i) application because it is not a review of a final denial of adjustment under INA §242(a)(2)(B)(i) and Congress did not intend to interpret §242(a)(2)(B)(ii) in a manner to permit a procedural issue to frustrate a statutory claim to adjustment]; *But see Wood v. Mukasey,* 516 F.3d 564 (7th Cir. 2008) [no jurisdiction following *Ali* to review IJ's denial of a continuance to await approval of I-130]; *Iqbal Ali v. Gonzales,* 502 F.3d 659, 660–65 (7th Cir. 2007) [INA §§242(a)(2)(B)(i)–(ii) bar jurisdiction to review continuances because underlying matter of adjustment is nonreviewable and rejected argument that continuances are regulatory and therefore not barred];

Eighth Circuit. *Guerra-Soto v. Ashcroft,* 397 F.3d 637, 639–40 (8th Cir. 2005) [jurisdiction to review BIA denial of motion to reopen seeking cancellation because discretionary decision regarding cancellation not at issue]; *Reyes-Vasquez v. Ashcroft,* 395 F.3d 903, 906 (8th Cir. 2005) [jurisdiction to determine whether applicant's trip abroad stopped his 10-year continuous residence needed for cancellation];

Ninth Circuit. *Mejia v. Gonzales,* 499 F.3d 991, 995–99 (9th Cir. 2007) [court had jurisdiction to review validity of AG's regulation at §212.7(d) for a §212(h) waiver, but rejected challenge to the application of the regulation to respondent's rehabilitation]; *Nath v. Gonzales,* 467 F.3d 1185, 1188 (9th Cir. 2007) [court has jurisdiction to review a denial of a motion to reopen removal proceedings where conviction was vacated]; *Gomez-Lopez v. Ashcroft,* 393 F.3d 882, 883–84 (9th Cir. 2005) [although there is no review of the denial of VD, where there was a legal question as to the application of 1101(f)(7) regarding good moral character for purposes of cancellation , the court had jurisdiction]; *Lagandaon v. Ashcroft,* 383 F.3d 983, 986–87 (9th Cir. 2004) [jurisdiction to review when 10 years ceases as a matter of law]; *Perez-Gonzalez v. Ashcroft,* 379 F.3d 783, 788–89 (9th Cir. 2004) *motion to r'consd denied* 403 F.3d 1116 (2005) [review of a denial of an I-212 waiver in the context of adjustment is reviewable where the basis for denial was the purely legal question of whether a waiver was available to someone physically in the U.S.; opinion vacated in other respects by *Gonzales v. DHS,* 508 F.3d 1227 (9th Cir. 2007)]; *Medina-Morales v. Ashcroft,* 371 F.3d 520, 526–27 (9th Cir. 2004) [there is no judicial bar to a petition for review of a motion to reopen for adjustment under INA §242(a)(2)((B)(i) because the petition is reviewing the denial of the reopening and not adjustment or any other section enumerated under 242(a)(2)(B)(i)]; *Lopez-Alvarado v. Ashcroft,* 381 F.3d 847, 850–51 (9th Cir. 2004) [jurisdiction is not barred to review IJ's improper finding that applicant for cancellation had failed to establish the requisite 10 years]; *Hernandez v. Ashcroft,* 345 F.3d 824 (9th Cir. 2003) [jurisdiction to review extreme cruelty in determination of cancellation for a battered spouse in transition case]; *Ramirez-Perez v. Ashcroft,* 336 F.3d 1001, 1005–07 (9th Cir. 2003) [court had authority to review claim that BIA's application of the exceptional and extremely unusual hardship standard in cancellation of removal cases violated due process, although finding no violation]; *Zazueta-Carrillo v. Ashcroft,* 322 F.3d 1166, 1169–70 (9th Cir. 2003) [upheld judicial review for nondiscretionary decisions regarding voluntary departure and jurisdiction existed to review the BIA's determination that a motion to reopen for adjustment filed within 90 days but beyond the 30-day V.D. period precluded reopening]. *Montero-Martinez v. Ashcroft,* 277 F.3d 1137, 1140–44 (9th Cir. 2002) [finding that "judgment regarding the granting of relief" refers to "any decision involving the exercise of discretion" and the court therefore had jurisdiction to determine whether a son/daughter could be a qualifying relative for cancellation];

Tenth Circuit. *Schroeck v. Gonzales,* 429 F.3d 947, 950–51 (10th Cir. 2005) [notwithstanding preclusion of review of 212(h) petitions, INA §242(a)(2)(D) permits jurisdiction to review respondent's constitutional claim that the IJ should not have heard and considered evidence regarding a dismissed criminal case]; *Sabido Valdivia v. Gonzales,* 423 F.3d 1144 (10th Cir. 2005) [nondiscretionary decisions regarding cancellation such as required physical presence are reviewable];

3.g. Review of Adjustment of Status

No Review of Adjustment Because of INA §§242(a)(2)(B)(i) & (ii). *Ayanbadejo v. Chertoff,* 517 F.3d 273, 276–78 (5th Cir. 2008) [no jurisdiction to review denial of I-485 petition but there is jurisdiction to review the denial of an I-130 petition]; *Ling Yang v. Mukasey,* 514 F.3d 278 (2d Cir. 2008) [denial of AOS purely on discretionary grounds is not reviewable]; *Bazua-Cota v. Gonzales,* 466 F.3d 747 (9th Cir. 2006) [no jurisdiction to review an abuse of discretion argument regarding denial of adjustment even if it is couched as a due process claim]; *Jarad v. Gonzales,* 461 F.3d 867 (7th Cir. 2006) [court lacked jurisdiction to review denial of motion to reopen to adjust status under INA §245(i) for applicant married to USC where the IJ cited discretionary factors]; *Guyadin v. Gonzales,* 449 F.3d 465 (2d Cir. 2006) [where IJ denied adjustment as a matter of discretion for respondent's failure to pay taxes, an assertion that the IJ misread, misunderstood, or misapplied the law does not convert the decision into a legal question]; *Sokolov v. Gonzales,* 442 F.3d 566, 568–70 (7th Cir. 2006) [where IJ denied AOS in his discretion because he believe applicant was dishonest review is barred]; *Higuit v. Gonzales,* 433 F.3d 417, 419–20 (4th Cir. 2006) [*Post*–REAL ID Act, the court lacked jurisdiction, notwithstanding INA §242(a)(2)(D), to review the discretionary decision to deny adjustment of status to a person involved in the persecution of others]; *McBrearty v. Perryman,* 212 F.3d 985 (7th Cir. 2000) [no jurisdiction to review denial of visa lottery adjustment where no constitutional issue raised and because of failure to exhaust removal process]; *Singh v. Enzer,* 528 F.Supp.2d 38 , 40-41 (D. Conn. 2007) [no jurisdiction to review abuse of discretion argument regarding denial of AOS, I-212 and I-601 waivers]; *Ogbolumani v. USCIS,* 523 F.Supp.2d 864, 871 (N.D. Ill. 2007) [no jurisdiction to review IR adjustment under §§242(a)(2)(B)(i) & (ii)]; *Bugulu v. Gonzales,* 490 F.Supp.2d 965 (W.D. Wis. 2007) [mandamus to compel adjustment decision barred by INA §242(a)(2)(B)(ii)]; *Grinberg v. Swancia,* 478 F.Supp.2d 1350 (S.D. Fla. 2007) [following *Safadi v. Howard,*, 466 F.Supp.2d 696 (E.D. Va. 2006) and finding that post–REAL ID Act INA §242(a)(2)(B)(ii) bars mandamus for adjustment under mandamus statute and APA §555(b) because it bars pace of "actions" as well as decisions]; *Rivera-Durmaz v. Chertoff,* 456 F.Supp.2d 943 (N.D. Ill. 2006) [no jurisdiction to review discretionary denial of 212(i) waiver in adjustment and respondent failed to exhaust administrative remedies by not completing removal hearing where adjustment may be raised]; *Hope v. Immigration Service (ICE),* 349 F.Supp.2d 490, 494–95

(E.D.N.Y. 2004) [no jurisdiction to review IJ's factual and discretionary decision to deny adjustment]; *Cedeno v. Ridge,* 336 F.Supp.2d 147, 150–52 (D.P.R. 2004) [jurisdiction over adjustment to review INA §204(c) determination because it is nondiscretionary, but review is in circuit court not district court]; *Afsharzadehyadzi v. Perryman,* 214 F.Supp.2d 884 (N.D. Ill. 2002) [no jurisdiction under mandamus due to INA §242(a)(2)(B)(i) and failure to exhaust before IJ to consider denial of AOS application for "aged-out" child]; *Holasek v. DOJ,* 123 F.Supp.2d 1126 (N.D. Ill. 2000) [followed *McBrearty*]; *Amoakowaa v. Reno,* 94 F.Supp.2d 903, 905 (N.D. Ill. 2000) [jurisdiction to challenge adjustment barred by INA §242(a)(2)(B)(i) absent constitutional claim]. **Transition Rule Cases:** Congress established a similar transitional rule under IIRIRA §309(c)(4)(E) to bar review of discretionary decisions that arose from former deportation and exclusion proceedings. *Mariuta v. Gonzales,* 411 F.3d 361 (2d Cir. 2005) [IIRIRA §309(c)(4)(E) bars jurisdiction over a motion to reopen for adjustment where the denial was unequivocally on discretionary grounds because the BIA denied reopening after weighing the applicant's equities against her false asylum testimony]; *Ali v. Ashcroft,* 366 F.3d 407, 412 (6th Cir. 2004) [no jurisdiction under §309(c)(4)(E) to review denial of VD]; *Valenzuela-Alcantar v. INS,* 309 F.3d 946, 949–50 (6th Cir. 2002) (and cases cite therein) [no jurisdiction to review extreme hardship determination regarding suspension]; *Regalado-Garcia v. INS,* 305 F.3d 784, 786 n.2 (8th Cir. 2002) [no jurisdiction to review denial of VD]; *Kalkouli v. Ashcroft,* 282 F.3d 202 (2d Cir. 2002) [review of extreme hardship determination in suspension is barred]; *Beslic v. INS,* 265 F.3d 568 (7th Cir. 2001) [void for vagueness challenge to denial of adjustment of status did not raise sufficient constitutional question to avoid bar to review]; *Rodriguez v. Ashcroft,* 253 F.3d 797 (5th Cir. 2001) [no review of motion to reopen on extreme hardship issue involving suspension]; *Torres-Aguilar v. INS,* 246 F.3d 1267 (9th Cir. 2001) [cannot circumvent bar to review of discretionary decision by characterizing them as constitutional violations; must have at least a colorable constitutional claim]; *Westover v. Reno,* 202 F.3d 475, 482 (1st Cir. 2000) [discretionary denial of AOS cannot be reviewed]. *Moosa v. INS,* 171 F.3d 994, 110–13 (5th Cir. 1999) [no review of extreme hardship decision in suspension case]; *Antonio-Cruz v. INS,* 147 F.3d 1129 (9th Cir. 1998) [no review of VD, but may review constitutional due process claim]; *Skutnik v. INS,* 128 F.3d 512 (7th Cir. 1997) [same]; *Mendonca v. INS,* 52 F.Supp.2d 155, 161 (D. Mass.), *aff'd,* 201 F.3d 427 (1st Cir. 1999) [no review of discretionary act to deny AOS]; *Lerma de Garcia v. INS*, 141 F.3d 215 (5th Cir. 1998) [no jurisdiction in the circuit court to hear constitutional claims although no bar to habeas in district court].

Review of Adjustment Permitted. *Pinho v. Gonzales,* 432 F.3d 193, 200–04 (3d Cir. 2005) [neither INA §242(a)(2)(B), nor principles of exhaustion, barred the district court under the APA from reviewing a legal determination as to whether a person with a substantive vacated conviction could adjust status]; *Benslimane v. Gonzales,* 430 F.3d 828 (7th Cir. 2005) [rejected preclusion of review pursuant to INA §242(a)(2)(B) because case involved a legal interpretation and found that IJ made a legal error in denying a continuance where respondent had filed an I-130 and I-485 as part of a marriage based adjustment but had not filed adjustment with the IJ]; *Sepulveda v. Gonzales,* 407 F.3d 59 (2d Cir. 2005) [the §242(a)(2)(B)(i) bar to adjustment does not extend to the nondiscretionary decision whether a person is eligible as a matter of law for adjustment under §245(i) even if it arises in the context of the review of a motion to reopen or reconsider]; *Subhan v. Ashcroft,* 383 F.3d 591 (7th Cir. 2004) [neither INA §242(a)(2)(B)(i) nor (ii) bars review of a denial of a continuance to submit a §245(i) application because it is not a review of a final denial of adjustment under INA §242(a)(2)(B)(i) and Congress did not intend to interpret §242(a)(2)(B)(ii) in a manner to permit a procedural issue to frustrate a statutory claim to adjustment]; *Succar v. Ashcroft,* 394 F.3d 8, 19–20 (1st Cir. 2005) [there is §1331 jurisdiction because respondent's challenge regarding AOS is to the invalidity of a DHS regulation as contrary to the statute and it is therefore not a discretionary decision barred under INA §242(a)(2)(B)(i) but a pure legal question];*Billeke-Tolosa v. Ashcroft,* 385 F.3d 708 (6th Cir. 2004) [court free to review nondiscretionary legal error where IJ looked behind the applicant's conviction to deny adjustment based upon a police report]; *Medina-Morales v. Ashcroft,* 371 F.3d 520, 526–27 (9th Cir. 2004) [there is no judicial bar to a petition for review of a motion to reopen for adjustment under INA §242(a)(2)((B)(i) because the petition is reviewing the denial of the reopening and not adjustment or any other section enumerated under 242(a)(2)(B)(i)];*Hernandez v. Ashcroft,*

tors to adjudicate cases or to refer them to IJs for hearing"]; *Catholic Social Services v. INS,* 232 F.3d 1139, 1150 (9th Cir. 2000) (en banc) [INA §242(g) does not bar class wide injunctive relief under amnesty program]; *Barapind v. Reno,* 225 F.3d 1100, 1110 (9th Cir. 2000) [INA §242(g) does not bar habeas petition challenging BIA stay of asylum consideration pending extradition]; *Ho v. Greene,* 204 F.3d 1045, 1050–52 (10th Cir. 2000) [post-IIRIRA and post-*AADC,* no bar to habeas jurisdiction to challenge indefinite detention]; *Sabhari v. Reno,* 197 F.3d 938, 941–43 (8th Cir. 1999) [post-IIRIRA and post-*AADC,* no bar under §1331 to review denial of I-130 or adjustment of status]; *Zhislin v. Reno,* 195 F.3d 810 (6th Cir. 1999) [INA §242(g) as interpreted by *American-Arab* does not bar review of challenge to indefinite detention]; *Wallace v. Reno,* 194 F.3d 279, 285 (1st Cir. 1999) [*American-Arab* does not bar retroactivity challenge simply because of ancillary request to stay deportation]; *Stewart v. INS,* 181 F.3d 587, 593–94 (4th Cir. 1999) [INA §242(g) does not cover motions to reopen]. *Tefel v. Reno,* 180 F.3d 1286, 1298 (11th Cir. 1999) [action for injunctive relief regarding stop-time rule is not precluded by 242(g)]; *Baria v. Reno,* 180 F.3d 1111, 1113 (9th Cir. 1999) [INA §242(g) does not bar district court review of rescission proceedings]; *Mustata v. DOJ,* 179 F.3d 1017 (6th Cir. 1999) [INA §242(g) does not bar habeas challenge to ineffective assistance of counsel]; *Selgeka v. Carroll,* 184 F.3d 337, 341–42 (4th Cir. 1999) [challenge to procedure used for stowaways seeking asylum does not challenge the AG's authority to adjudicate cases under *American-Arab*]; *Shah v. Reno,* 184 F.3d 719 (8th Cir. 1999); *Mayers v. Reno,* 175 F.3d 1289, 1297 (11th Cir. 1999) [finding INA §242(g) "eliminate[s] review of certain interim, discretionary decisions the INS may take" but does not apply to nondiscretionary issues of statutory interpretation involving review of final orders]; *Humphries v. Various Federal INS Employees,* 164 F.3d 936, 944 (5th Cir. 1999) [detention has no more than a "remote relationship" to the Attorney General's decision to execute removal orders under INA §242(g)]; *Al Jabari v. Chertoff,* 536 F.Supp.2d 1029 (D. Minn. 2008) [In action to compel DHS to complete the security check involving the grant by an IJ of a marriage hardship waiver to lift conditional residence under 8 U.S.C. §1186a(c)(4), the court determined that the APA permitted injunctive relief and was not barred by INA §242(g)]; *Khouzam v. Hogan,* 497 F.Supp.2d 615, 623–24 (M.D. Pa. 2007) [denied DHS motion to dismiss habeas under INA §242(g) because 242(g) only implicates selective prosecution and here petitioner challenged DHS revocation of deferral of removal under CAT at 8 C.F.R. §1208.18(c) on grounds that DHS failed to comply with its own regulations]; *Coleman v. U.S.,* 454 F.Supp.2d 757, 765–66 (N.D. Ill. 2006) [USC son who brought action enjoining mom's removal was not barred by INA §242(g) because claim was by USC and not "by or on behalf of any alien"]; *F.L. v. Thompson,* 293 F.Supp.2d 86, 92 (D.D.C. 2003) [following *M.B. v. Quarantilla* the court found INA §242(g) does not bar review of DHS's refusal to issue consent to unaccompanied minors to apply for court dependency]; *Evangelical Lutheran Church in America v. INS,* 288 F.Supp.2d 32, 42–43 (D.D.C. 2003) [INA §242(g) does not bar review of a denial of an H-1B extension of stay]; *Digrado v. Ashcroft,* 184 F.Supp.2d 227, 230–31 (N.D.N.Y. 2002) [challenge to pretermission of INA §212(c) to person who has now re-entered U.S. and subject to 241(a)(5) is not barred on theory that he is seeking a stay of removal]; *Medina v. U.S.,* 92 F.Supp.2d 545 (E.D. Va. 2000) [INA §242(g) does not bar FTCA action suing over unlawful detention where removal proceeding was terminated]; *Paunescu v. INS,* 76 F.Supp.2d 896, 899 (N.D. Ill. 1999) [post–*American-Arab,* INA §242(g) does not bar mandamus action to compel grant of diversity visa]; *Rogan v. Reno,* 75 F.Supp.2d 63, 65–66 (E.D. N.Y. 1999) [INA §242(g) does not bar review of denial of individual family/ orphan petition because it relates solely to removal proceedings]; *Garcia-Guzman v. Reno,* 65 F.Supp.2d 1077, 1082–84 (N.D. Cal. 1999) [court finds habeas jurisdiction over denial of change of venue and deprivation of counsel in post–*American-Arab* case and rejects INS broad reading of statute] *Moro v. INS,* 58 F.Supp.2d 854 (N.D. Ill. 1999) [*American-Arab* interpretation of INA §242(g) as including execution of removal orders does not bar review of post–final order detention].

Cases Barring Jurisdiction—This provision has resulted in the dismissal of a variety of immigration cases on the grounds that the courts no longer have jurisdiction. *Sissoko v. Rocha,* 509 F.3d 947 (9th Cir. 2007) [*Bivens* action challenging unlawful detention of a temporary resident government claimed was subject to summary removal was barred by INA §242(g) in the limited circumstance where the plaintiff could have challenged his detention by habeas corpus under INA §242(e)(2)]; *Iqbal Ali v. Gonzales,* 502 F.3d 659, 665 (7th Cir. 2007) [following *Hadayat* INA §242(g) bars jurisdiction to hear constitutional challenges to NSEERS]; *Hadayat v. Gonzales,* 458 F.3d 659, 664–65 (7th Cir. 2006) [where respondent argued that NSEERS registration violated equal protection resulting in removal proceedings, the court held INA §242(g), pursuant to *American-Arab*, barred federal court review of the reasons for the issuance of an NTA]; *Grass v. Gonzales,* 418 F.3d 876, 877 (8th Cir. 2005) [the court lacked jurisdiction to hear a challenge to the initiation of removal proceedings against someone who was INA §245(i) eligible]; *Moussa v. Jenifer,* 389 F.3d 550, 554–55 (6th Cir. 2004) [although habeas petitioner raised statutory and constitutional claims regarding the denial of motion to stay before ICE they were nothing more than an effort to review the nonreviewable discretionary decision of the DD to execute an order of removal barred by INA §242(g)]; *Duamutef v. INS,* 386 F.3d 172, 180–81 (2d Cir. 2004) [the district court lacked mandamus jurisdiction to compel ICE to take custody over state prisoner and to execute order of removal]; *S-Cheng v. Ashcroft,* 380 F.3d 320, 324–25 (8th Cir. 2004) [decision to forgo exclusion proceeding and initiate removal proceeding is not reviewable]; *Latu v. Ashcroft,* 375 F.3d 1012, 1019 (10th Cir. 2004) [action challenging the decision to commence removal proceedings in one venue versus another is barred by INA §242(g)]; *De La Teja v. U.S.,* 321 F.3d 1357, 1365 (11th Cir. 2003) [action to stop initiation of removal proceedings after prior judicial order vacated is barred by INA §242(g)]; *Wigglesworth v. INS,* 319 F.3d 951, 960–61 (7th Cir. 2003) [where person subject to VWP seeks an order that INS recommence deportation proceedings so she can apply for suspension, action is barred]; *Jimenez-Angeles v. Ashcroft*, 291 F.3d 594, 598–99 (9th Cir. 2002) [no jurisdiction to address argument that INS should have put respondent in removal proceedings before Apr. 1, 1997 to obtain benefit of suspension]; *Sharif ex. rel. Sharif v. Ashcroft,* 280 F.3d 786 (7th Cir. 2002) [post–*St. Cyr* the court determined that INA §242(g) barred habeas petition seeking a stay of deportation]; *Chapinski v. Ziglar,* 278 F.3d 718 (7th Cir. 2002) [mandamus, declaratory and injunctive relief to compel INS to place person in removal proceedings to obtain benefit as NACARA spouse is barred by INA §242(g)]; *Cardoso v. Reno,* 216 F.3d 512 (5th Cir. 2000) [review of denial of adjustment of status is barred where petition is "end-run" around final removal order]; *Bhatt v. Reno,* 204 F.3d 744 (7th Cir. 2000) [INA §242(g) barred habeas action by noncriminal requesting a stay pending a motion to reopen before the BIA because there was a final order]; *Prado v. Reno,* 198 F.3d 286, 292 (1st Cir. 1999) [review of INS decision not to join in motion to reopen is barred post *American-Arab* by INA §242(g)]; *Fedorca v. Perryman,* 197 F.3d 236 (7th Cir. 1999) [post–*American-Arab* there is no district court review even in habeas over denial of stay]; *Botezatu v. INS,* 195 F.3d 311 (7th Cir. 1999) [same]; *Mapoy v. Carroll,* 185 F.3d 224 (4th Cir. 1999) [district court lacks habeas jurisdiction to review denial of motion to stay deportation pending BIA decision on motion to reopen]; *Alvidres-Reyes v. Reno,* 180 F.3d 199 (5th Cir. 1999) [an action to compel the AG to adjudicate suspension applications was in effect an effort to compel AG to put persons in deportation proceedings and is therefore barred by 242(g)]; *Auguste v. Reno,* 152 F.3d 1325 (11th Cir. 1998) [finding no jurisdiction to review the visa waiver pilot program]; *Jean-Baptiste v. Reno,* 144 F.3d 212 (2d Cir. 1998) [finding no jurisdiction under 28 U.S.C. §1331 for LPRs challenging due process violations in deportation hearing]; *Ramallo v. Reno*, 114 F.3d 1210 (D.C. Cir. 1997) [vacated district court order pursuant to 28 U.S.C. §1331 enforcing government's promise not to deport plaintiff]; *Sadhyani v. Chertoff,* 460 F.Supp.2d 114 (D.D.C. 2006) [person who was deported was not in custody for habeas purposes and REAL ID Act and INA §242(g) divest the court of jurisdiction]; *Somir v. U.S.,* 354 F.Supp.2d 215, 220 (E.D.N.Y. 2005) [a *res judicata* challenge cannot be brought in federal court until the IJ/BIA makes a decision because INA §242(g) bar habeas review challenging initiation of proceedings]; *Roudnahal v. Ridge,* 310 F.Supp.2d 884, 890–92 (N.D. Ohio 2003), [seeking to enjoin removal proceedings because of discriminatory practices violates 242(g)]; *Hatami v. Ridge,* 270 F.Supp.2d 763 (E.D. Va. 2003) [habeas seeking stay of removal pending state habeas to vacate conviction dismissed under INA §242(g)]; *Espinal v. Pere,* 144 F.Supp.2d 53 (D.P.R. 2001) [injunction to prevent removal proceeding because applicant believes he is eligible under LIFE act is barred under *American-Arab*]; *Reverdes v. Reno,* 95 F.Supp.2d 22, 26–27 (D. Mass. 2000) [*American-Arab* bars claim against AG for delay in the commencement of removal proceedings resulting in harm to respondent]; *Barca v. Holmes,* 73 F.Supp.2d 484 (M.D. Pa. 1999) [*American-Arab* precludes challenge to decision to invoke reinstatement under INA §241(a)(5)]; *Naidoo v. INS,* 39 F.Supp.2d 755 (W.D.La. 1999) [*American-Arab* precludes review of stays of deportation].

In addition, INA §242(g) may be limited to decisions that arise in removal proceedings only *Walters v. Reno,* 145 F.3d 1032, 1051–53 (9th Cir. 1998), *cert. denied, Reno v. Walters,* 526 U.S. 1003 (1999) [INA §242(g) does not preclude challenge to notice provided in INA §274C proceedings even if court enjoins deportation of class members]; *Medina v. U.S.,* 92 F.Supp.2d 545 (E.D. Va. 2000) [INA §242(g) does not bar FTCA action suing over unlawful detention where removal proceedings were terminated]; *Rogan v. Reno,* 75 F.Supp.2d 63, 65–66 (E.D. N.Y. 1999) [INA §242(g) does not bar review of denial of individual family/orphan petition that is not part of the removal hearing]; *Moro v. INS,* 58 F.Supp.2d 854 (N.D. Ill. 1999) [*American-Arab* interpretation of INA §242(g) as including execution of removal orders does not bar review of post–final order detention]; *Shanti, Inc. v. Reno,* 36 F.Supp.2d 1151, 1157–61 (D. Minn. 1999) [jurisdiction is not barred for review of denial of H-1B petition because it is not within a removal proceeding]; *Morisath v. Smith,* 988 F.Supp. 1333 (W.D. Wash. 1997) [finding jurisdiction to review challenges to deportation as well as denial of bond]; *Xiao v. Reno,* 963 F.Supp. 874 (N.D. Cal. 1997) [jurisdiction stripping provision of §242(g) only applies to Chapter 12 of Title 8 and does not effect action under due process clause]; *Yu v. Brown,* 36 F.Supp.2d 922, 933–34 (D. New Mexico 1999) [INA §242(g) only effects removal proceedings and does not bar mandamus to compel adjudication of special immigrant juvenile petition]. INA §242(g) may also be limited to the decisions directly made by the AG and, in any event, could not be interpreted to bar review of constitutional claims. *Tefel v. Reno,* 972 F.Supp. 608, 612–13 (S.D. Fla. 1997) *rev'd on other grounds,* 180 F.3d 1286 (11th Cir. 1999), *cert. denied,* 120 S.Ct. 2657 (2000). *But see Foster v. Townsley,* 243 F.3d 210 (5th Cir. 2001) [finding INA §242(g) bars *Bivens* action for wrongful deportation].

5. Review of AG or DHS's decisions regarding voluntary departure. INA §240B(e), (f), 8 U.S.C. §1229c(e), (f); *see* Ch. 8, part III (p.964), *supra*; *Zazueta-Carrillo v. Ashcroft,* 322 F.3d 1166, 1169–70 (9th Cir. 2003) [§1229c(f) does not eliminate judicial review for nondiscretionary decisions regarding voluntary departure and jurisdiction existed to review the BIA's determination that a motion to reopen for adjustment filed within 90 days but beyond the 30-day VD period precluded reopening]. *But see Kandamar v. Gonzales,* 464 F.3d 65, 69–70 (1st Cir. 2006) [no jurisdiction under INA §§240B(f) or 242(a)(2)(B)(i) where government seized passport and court denied VD because respondent did not have his passport; no due process review because VD is a privilege not a right].

6. Review of DHS of AG's judgment regarding the granting of relief under INA §§212(h), 212(i), cancellation of removal (§240A), voluntary departure (§240B), INA §242(a)(2)(B)(i), 8 U.S.C. §1252(a)(2)(B)(i). *Romero-Torres v. Ashcroft,* 327 F.3d 887 (9th Cir. 2003) [finding §242(a)(2)(B)(i) bars review of BIA's determination regarding "exceptional and extremely unusual hardship" in cancellation claim]; *Gonzalez-Oropeza v. U.S. Att'y Gen.,* 321 F.3d 1331, 1332–33 (11th Cir. 2003) [same]; *Eyoum v. INS,* 125 F.3d 889, 891 (5th Cir. 1997), *Tutu v. Blackman,* 9 F.Supp.2d 534 (E.D. Pa. 1998); and adjustment of status (§245); *Sabhari v. Reno,* 197 F.3d 938, 941–43 (8th Cir. 1999) [post-IIRIRA, neither §242(g) nor the change in §1329 barred jurisdiction under §1331 to review the denial of an I-130 or adjustment of status application]; *Stewart v. INS,* 181 F.3d 587, 594–95 (4th Cir. 1999) [a denial of a motion to reopen for adjustment of status under §245 was *not* covered by this provision because the denial was based on the failure to show exceptional circumstances under former INA §242B(e)(2)(A)]

7. Review of DHS's decisions regarding summary exclusion (§235(b)(1)), except in extraordinarily limited circumstances. INA §242(a)(2)(A), 8 U.S.C. §1252(a)(2)(A); INA §242(e), 8 U.S.C. §1252(e). *Turgerel v. Mukasey,* 513 F.3d 1202, 1205–06 (10th Cir. 2008) [no jurisdiction to review *constitutional* claims in petitioner's current removal proceeding where she sought AOS based upon her marriage to a U.S. citizen because the court determined that she was barred from collaterally attacking on constitutional grounds a prior expedited removal proceeding, notwithstanding INA §242(a)(2)(D), where she was subject to a life-time ban, without waiver, for making a false claim to U.S. citizenship]. *But see Sissoko v. Rocha,* 509 F.3d 947 (9th Cir. 2007) [*Bivens* action challenging unlawful detention of a temporary resident government claimed was subject to summary removal was barred by INA §242(g) in the limited circumstance where the plaintiff could have challenged his detention by habeas corpus under INA §242(e)(2)]; *Diaz v. Reno,* 40 F.Supp.2d 984 (N.D. Ill. 1999) [INA §242(e)(1)(A) restricting review of summary exclusion inapplicable to person claiming U.S. citizenship]

8. Review of DHS's decision to grant or deny a waiver under INA §212(d)(12), 8 U.S.C. §1182(d)(12) or INA §237(a)(3)(C)(ii), 8 U.S.C. §1227(a)(3)(C)(ii) for being inadmissible or deportable for having a final order under INA §274C;

9. Review of DHS or AG's decision to grant or deny a waiver under INA §212(h), 8 U.S.C. §1182(h); *Rodrigues-Nascimento v. Gonzales,* 485 F.3d 60 (1st Cir. 2007) [no judicial review of discretionary denial of 212(h) relief];

10. Review of DHS's or AG's decision to grant or deny a waiver under INA §212(i), 8 U.S.C. §1182(i), *Zhang v. Gonzales,* 457 F.3d 172 (2d Cir. 2006) [post-REAL ID Act, INA §242(a)(2)(B)(i) bars review of the discretionary decision of extreme hardship]; *Okpa v. INS,* 266 F.3d 313, 318–19 (4th Cir. 2001) [after finding that statutory changes were not impermissibly retroactive, court determined it had no jurisdiction to review the BIA's discretionary decision denying the waiver]; *Cervantes-Gonzales v. INS,* 244 F.3d 1001, 1005–06 (9th Cir. 2001) [same].

11. Review of DHS or AG's decision or action regarding a waiver of INA §212(a)(9)(B) inadmissibility. INA §212(a)(9)(B)(v), 8 U.S.C. §1182(a)(9)(B)(v);

12. Review of any removal decision by an immigration judge based solely on a medical certification under §240(c)(1)(B). INA §242(a)(3), 8 U.S.C. §1252(a)(3);

13. Collateral attacks on removal orders. INA §235(b)(1)(D), 8 U.S.C. §1225(b)(1)(D) and INA §242(b)(7)(A), 8 U.S.C. §1252(b)(7)(A);

14. Suits against the U.S. or its agencies or officers under INA §279 except those initiated by the government. INA §279, 8 U.S.C. §1329; *Diallo v. Reno,* 61 F.Supp.2d 1361, 1366 (N.D. Ga. 1999) [Section 1329 only limited to right of government to bring action];

15. The Secretary of State or consular officer's decision to revoke an immigrant visa or NIV under INA §221(i) is not reviewable in habeas, mandamus, or All Writs Act except the decision may be reviewed in the context of a removal proceeding and only then if the revocation provides the sole ground for removal under INA §237(a)(1)(B). *Bolante v. Achim,* 457 F.Supp.2d 896 (E.D. Wis. 2006) [no habeas jurisdiction to review claim that revocation was improper under 22 C.F.R. §41.122(a)];

16. *Asylum Review*—Review of the denial of the right to seek asylum because the applicant: (1) can go to a safe third country; (2) was previously denied asylum; (3) did not file the asylum application within one year of entry; (4) is deemed to be a terrorist or (5) because the AG determined there were no changed circumstances warranting an exception to the one-year deadline. INA §208(a)(3), (b)(2)(D), 8 U.S.C. §1158(a)(3), (b)(2)(D). *Sillah v. Mukasey,* 519 F.3d 1042, 1043–44 (9th Cir. 2008) [no judicial review because it was not simply the application of the law to undisputed facts regarding the one-year period to file for asylum, but rather a factual dispute as to when respondent entered the country and could have filed for asylum]; *Viracacha v. Mukasey,* 518 F.3d 511, 514–16 (7th Cir. 2008) [INA §242(a)(2)(D) only encompasses pure questions of law not the application of the law to the facts and therefore there was no judicial review of petitioner's claim that he deliberately refrained from filing within one year]; *Zine v. Mukasey,* 517 F.3d 535, 539 (8th Cir. 2008) [no review of timeliness or extraordinary circumstances issue]; *Pepaj v. Mukasey,* 509 F.3d 725, 727–28 (6th Cir. 2007) [followed *Almuhtaseb* and held no review for abuse of discretion regarding solely factual questions in denying motion to reopen for changed country conditions]; *Zhu v. Gonzales,* 493 F.3d 588, 594–96 (5th Cir. 2007) [where applicant filed asylum six months after B-2 stay expired, the definition of whether that was a reasonable time was fact intensive and therefore not a question of law reviewable under INA §242(a)(2)(D)]; *Mouawad v. Gonzales,* 485 F.3d 405, 411–12 (8th Cir. 2007) [REAL ID Act and 242(a)(2)(D) did not alter bar to review of one year filing deadline]; *Chen v. U.S. DOJ,* 471 F.3d 315, 323–32 (2d Cir. 2006) [finding that "questions of law" should be read, consistent with the legislative history at H.R. Rep. No. 109-72 at 175, U.S.C.C.A.N. 2005 at p.300 to include "those issues that were historically reviewable in habeas"]; *Almuhtaseb v. Gonzales,* 453 F.3d 743, 746–49 (6th Cir. 2006) [REAL ID Act §106 adding §1252(a)(2)(D) does not alter bar to review of changed circumstances to the degree it is a factual question but questions of law or constitutional questions may be reviewed];*Sukwanputra v. Gonzales,* 434 F.3d 627, 633–35 (3d Cir. 2006) [changed circumstances affecting one year deadline for filing asylum is not reviewable under INA §242(a)(2)(D) because it does not raise a statutory or constitutional claim]; *Mehilli v. Gonzales,* 433 F.3d 86, 92–94 (1st Cir. 2005) [issues regarding untimeliness in filing an asylum claim were factual and discretionary and therefore could not be reviewed in the court of appeals under INA §242(a)(2)(D) and jurisdiction was not granted by reviewing a motion to reconsider rather than original decision on untime-

liness]; *Ignatova v. Gonzales,* 430 F.3d 1209, 1213–14 (8th Cir. 2005) [*Post*–REAL ID Act, the court found no jurisdiction to review determinations concerning exceptions to the one year filing deadline for asylum]; *Chacon-Botero v. U.S. Att'y Gen.,* 427 F.3d 954, 957 (11th Cir. 2005) [followed *Vasile* and found that the issue of timely filing an asylum claim was not reviewable because it was not a constitutional claim or question of law covered under INA §242(a)(2)(D)]; *Vasile v. Gonzales,* 417 F.3d 766, 768 (7th Cir. 2005) [REAL ID Act of 2005 under INA §242(a)(2)(D), 8 U.S.C. §1252(a)(2)(D) allowing for review of constitutional and statutory claims did not alter the bar to the review of the failure to file within one year or that there were no extraordinary circumstances permitting review because these are factual and discretionary issues]; *Sharari v. Gonzales,* 407 F.3d 467, 473 (1st Cir. 2005) [no jurisdiction to review whether asylum application was filed within one year deadline and if not, whether there were exceptional circumstances warranting delay]; *Vladimirova v. Ashcroft,* 377 F.3d 690, 695–96 (7th Cir. 2004) [following *Zaidi* and finding no jurisdiction over whether there were "extraordinary circumstances" overcoming the one year filing deadline]; *Zaidi v. Ashcroft,* 377 F.3d 678, 680–81 (7th Cir. 2004) [joining other circuits in holding it has no jurisdiction to review IJ decision that asylum application was untimely because it was not filed within one year of entry]; *Bellout v. Ashcroft,* 363 F.3d 975, 977 (9th Cir. 2004) [no jurisdiction to review finding that applicant for asylum is ineligible due to terrorism];*Castellano-Chacon v. INS,* 341 F.3d 533, 541–44 (6th Cir. 2003) [no jurisdiction to review failure to file within one year due to changed circumstances]; *Tarrawally v. Ashcroft,* 338 F.3d 180, 184–86 (3d Cir. 2003) [no jurisdiction to review compliance with one-year filing requirement for asylum *or* establishment of extraordinary circumstances that would excuse untimely filing]; *Mendoza v. U.S. Att'y Gen.,* 327 F.3d 1283, 1286–87 (11th Cir. 2003) [same]; *Tsevegmid v. Ashcroft,* 336 F.3d 1231, 1234–35 (10th Cir. 2003) [same]; *Fahim v. U.S. Att'y Gen.,* 278 F.3d 1216 (11th Cir. 2002) [same]; *Hakeem v. INS,* 273 F.3d 812, 815–16 (9th Cir. 2001) [no jurisdiction to review IJ denial of asylum for failure to file within year although separate habeas action may not be precluded]; *Izmailov v. Reno,* 263 F.3d 851 (8th Cir. 2001) [no jurisdiction to review denial of asylum for failing to file within one year under INA §208(a)(3) notwithstanding contrary suggestion in 242(a)(2)(B)(ii) and 242(b)(4)(D)]. *But see Ramadan v. Gonzales,* 479 F.3d 646, 648–54 (9th Cir. 2007) *reh'g en banc denied* 504 F.3d 973 (2007) [questions of law includes not only pure issues of statutory interpretation but mixed questions of law and fact where the court is applying undisputed facts to statutory and regulatory questions and therefore the court can review the issue of the failure to file asylum within one year due to "changed circumstances"]. The bar to judicial review regarding the one year filing deadline was not unconstitutional under the due process clause. *Hana v. Gonzales,* 503 F.3d 39, 43–44 (1st Cir. 2007) [applicant who had nervous breakdown when he entered U.S. that prevented his filing for asylum unsuccessfully challenged the constitutionality of the preclusion statute].

Although there is no review of the one year bar, there may be review regarding the interpretation of the regulation governing the bar, *Nakimbugwe v. Gonzales,* 475 F.3d 281 (5th Cir. 2007) [court found there was jurisdiction to reverse IJ's determination that bar applied where person mailed application within the one year but EOIR did not received it until after the year]; *Diallo v. Gonzales,* 447 F.3d 1274, 1281–82 (10th Cir. 2006) [in the case of a asylee whose status was revoked there was jurisdiction to interpret that the one year period to apply for asylum should run from the time of revocation and not last entry]. There is also jurisdiction to review a due process claim regarding submission of evidence of exceptional or changed circumstances, *Somakoko v. Gonzales,* 399 F.3d 882 (8th Cir. 2005) [entertained but rejected a due process challenge to IJ's alleged refusal to hear evidence regarding exceptional circumstances]; *Kanivets v. Riley,* 320 F.Supp.2d 297, 300 (E.D. Pa. 2004) and 286 F.Supp.2d 460, 468 (E.D. Pa. 2003) [habeas jurisdiction to review whether there are changed circumstances that warranted extension of one-year time bar], or to review whether the application of the law results in a reasoned decision. *Gjyzi v. Ashcroft,* 386 F.3d 710, 713–14 (6th Cir. 2004) [where the BIA reversed the IJ's adverse credibility finding that was the basis for finding the application was filed beyond one year, but still upheld the IJ's decision, a due process issue is raised for lack of a reasoned decision and the court vacated the order]. *See also Mabasa v. Gonzales,* 455 F.3d 740, 744 (7th Cir. 2006) [where IJ relied on changed circumstances to deny right to file asylum claim beyond one year but BIA confused changed circumstances with exceptional circumstances, there was review under INA §242(a)(2)(D)]. One circuit has also determined that there is jurisdiction to review the IJ/BIA failure to address a properly raised extraordinary circumstances claim to the one year bar. *Sagaydak v. Gonzales,* 405 F.3d 1035, 1039–41 (9th Cir. 2005) [where petitioner alleges failure to file in one year was due to extraordinary circumstances and both the IJ and the BIA failed to address whether the exception applies, the court has jurisdiction to review the failure to make the determination].

The AG's decision to require corroboration in asylum or other relief from removal may only be reversed if "a reasonable trier of fact is compelled to conclude that such corroborating evidence is unavailable." INA §242(b)(4), 8 U.S.C. §1252(b)(4); *Hor v. Gonzales,* 421 F.3d 497, 500–01 (7th Cir. 2005) [reversing IJ's corroboration findings because "All that this (INA §242(b)(4) provision) means is that an immigration judge's determination ... is entitled to reasonable deference (but that) the precondition to deference is that the immigration judge explain (unless it is obvious) why he thinks corroborating evidence, if it existed, would have been available to the alien"]. *Accord. Zhang v. Gonzales,* 434 F.3d 993, 998–99 (7th Cir. 2006) [quoting *Hor* and reversing IJ's demand for corroboration]. *But see Chen v. Gonzales,* 434 F.3d 212, 217–20 (3d Cir. 2005) [in case decided under new review standard *post*–REAL ID Act, the court upheld the denial of asylum even where the IJ did not make a valid credibility assessment because even a credible applicant may be required to produce corroborative evidence and respondent failed to do so in this case]; *Zheng v. Gonzales,* 417 F.3d 379, 383 n.2 (3d Cir. 2005) [finding that the IJ's requirement to corroborate what may be speculative records is subject to the "compelling" review standard which is "effective immediately" including cases begun before May 11, 2005]. However, the standard may not apply to motions to reopen before the BIA because it applies only to review of a decision by the "trier of fact" (which is the IJ not the BIA) and does not, by its terms, apply to the provision on motions to reopen at INA §240(c)(7), 8 U.S.C. §1229a(c)(7), *Fessehaye v. Gonzales,* 414 F.3d 746, 752–53 (7th Cir. 2005).

17. *Judicial Review of CAT Claims*—

17.a. CAT Claims Regarding Withholding of Removal Not Involving Criminal Issues. CAT claims not involving persons within convictions who are otherwise precluded by INA §242(a)(2)(C) are generally reviewable under the substantial evidence standard consistent with 8 U.S.C. §1252(b)(4). *Ferry v. Gonzales,* 457 F.3d 1117, 1130–31 (10th Cir. 2006) [IRA member on death list of Northern Irish loyalists could not demonstrate UK government acquiesced in torture under substantial evidence standard]; *Lanza v. Ashcroft,* 389 F.3d 917, 936 (9th Cir. 2004) [upholding denial of CAT for applicant from Argentina because no reasonable fact finder would be compelled to conclude a contrary result]; *Castellano-Chacon v. INS,* 341 F.3d 533, 551–52 (6th Cir. 2003) [upholding denial of CAT claim under §1252(b)(4) because decision was not "manifestly contrary to the law"]; *cf. Nigussie v. Ashcroft,* 383 F.3d 531, 534 (7th Cir. 2004) [review is under substantial evidence standard]. They are also reviewed for errors of law. *Enwonwu v. Gonzales,* 438 F.3d 22, 34–35 (1st Cir. 2006) [where BIA failed to address one of IJ's reasons for granting CAT relief, court reversed because BIA opinion was insufficient as a matter of law]; *Mihalev v. Ashcroft,* 388 F.3d 722, 731 (9th Cir. 2004) [remanding IJ's decision because it failed to address respondent's CAT claim, and if his opinion is read to mean that his asylum analysis is applicable to the CAT claim, he erred because the standards are different].

17.b. CAT Claims For Persons With Criminal Records Addressing Deferral of Removal

(1) *REAL ID Act of 2005 & CAT*—Prior to the REAL ID Act of 2005, certain respondents with criminal records were barred completely from judicial review in the circuit courts under INA §242(a)(2)(C), former §106(a)(10) as amended by AEDPA §440 and IIRIRA §309(c)(4)(G). *Balogun v. Ashcroft,* 270 F.3d 274 (5th Cir. 2001) [once determined that INA §242(a)(2)(C) applied, that section barred review of CAT claim], *Diakite v. INS,* 179 F.3d 553 (7th Cir. 1999). Those persons could only seek habeas review in the district courts to bring constitutional challenges or challenges involving errors of law, including both statutory interpretations and application of law to undisputed facts or adjudicated facts. A habeas challenge did not permit, however, the review of administrative fact finding or the exercise of discretion. *Auguste v. Ridge,* 395 F.3d 123, 137–38 (3d Cir. 2005); *Cadet v. Bulger,* 377 F.3d 1173, 1181–83 (11th Cir. 2004) [reviewing the administrative denial of respondent's CAT claim for the incorrect application of the legal standard for torture to the facts]. The REAL ID Act of 2005, however, abolished habeas, mandamus, and All Writs Act review for CAT claims and the courts of appeal "shall be the sole and

exclusive means for judicial review of any cause or claim under" CAT. INA §242(a)(4). Although the REAL ID Act of 2005 abolished habeas and other district court review, it restored judicial review of constitutional questions and questions of law in the circuit court, notwithstanding the judicial bar under INA §242(a)(2)(C) and other sections. *See* INA §242(a)(2)(D); *Jean-Pierre v. U.S. Att'y Gen.,* 500 F.3d 1315, 1320–22 (11th Cir. 2007) [the court's jurisdiction to review questions of law extends to the review of undisputed or historical facts to a legal standard and "offers the same scope of review as a habeas remedy"]; *Kamara v. Att'y Gen. of the U.S.,* 420 F.3d 202, 210–11 (3d Cir. 2005) [under INA §242(a)(2)(D), the court reviews pure questions of law and issues regarding the application of law to fact, and found that the BIA applied the wrong quantum of proof required for a CAT claim]; *Ramos v. Gonzales,* 414 F.3d 800, 802–04 (7th Cir. 2005) [Congress added §242(a)(2)(D) to consider all constitutional and statutory claims in review of a final order]; *Papageorgiou v. Gonzales,* 413 F.3d 356, 357–58 (3d Cir. 2005) [section 242(a)(2)(D) restores jurisdiction to the circuit court for persons who previously were barred from such review under 242(a)(2)(C) because of criminal convictions and makes the restoration retroactive by applying it to any order issued before, on or after May 11, 2005]; *Fernandez-Ruiz v. Gonzales,* 468 F.3d 1159, 1163 (9th Cir. 2006) [same]. Although the court of appeals pursuant to INA §242(a)(2)(D) may review constitutional or statutory claims regarding a CAT claim even if a person is otherwise barred under INA §242(a)(2)(C), the REAL ID Act of 2005, by enacting INA §242(a)(2)(D), did not extend circuit court review in such cases to a challenge based solely upon substantial evidence in the denial of a CAT claim. *Saintha v. Mukasey,* 516 F.3d 243, 248–51 (4th Cir. 2008) [BIA determinations regarding deferral of removal that the court would ordinarily review under the substantial evidence standard are necessarily factual in nature and beyond review]; *Haman v. Gonzales,* 449 F.3d 834 (8th Cir. 2006) [CAT claim transferred to circuit court but review of the claim was denied for Pashtun returning to Afghanistan on grounds he sought review of only factual issues]; *Hamid v. Gonzales,* 417 F.3d 642, 647 (7th Cir. 2005) [because respondent is an aggravated felon the court declined to consider whether the IJ's factual conclusions are supported by substantial evidence because this fails to raise either a constitutional or statutory claim under INA §242(a)(2)(D). *But see Lemus-Galvan v. Mukasey,* 518 F.3d 1081 (9th Cir. 2008) [court had jurisdiction to review the denial of deferral of removal on the merits, even where respondent was ordered removed based upon his criminal conviction]; *Morales v. Gonzales,* 478 F.3d 972 (9th Cir. 2007) [none of the jurisdiction-stripping provisions apply to bar review of legal standard underpinning a CAT denial, even if there is an aggravated felony where the aggravated felony was not the basis for the denial of the CAT claim]. The district court, however, may have jurisdiction to review at CAT related claim that does not implicate a final order of removal. *Khouzam v. Hogan,* 497 F.Supp.2d 615 (M.D. Pa. 2007) [denied DHS motion to dismiss habeas under REAL ID Act, INA §242(g) and political question doctrine where petitioner challenged DHS revocation of deferral of removal under CAT at 8 C.F.R. §1208.18(c) on grounds that DHS failed to comply with its own regulations, violated procedural and substantive due process, and violated CAT as implemented by FARRA].

17.c. Judicial Review of CAT Regulations—Congress in §2242(d) of FARRA barred challenges to the regulations adopted to implement CAT, or any other decision made with respect to the application of CAT, except as part of the review of a final order under INA §242. *See also* 8 C.F.R. §§208.18(e), 1208.18(e). While some courts have found that CAT is not self-executing and therefore does not provide a source of independent enforceable rights, FARRA regulations are enforceable in federal court, including (pre-REAL ID) in habeas proceedings.

18. Reinstatement of Removal Order Review—Review of the underlying removal/deportation order in reinstated removal cases may be precluded under INA §241(a)(5) because such order "is not subject to being reopened or reviewed." *Garcia-Marrufo v. Ashcroft,* 376 F.3d 1061, 1063–64 (10th Cir. 2004) [rejected challenge under *Mendoza-Lopez* and found that there was no jurisdiction to review underlying deportation order even where the criminal conviction that was the basis for the order had been vacated]; *Avila-Macias v. Ashcroft,* 328 F.3d 108, 115 (3d Cir. 2003) [review of underlying deportation order precluded in court of appeals]. However, the reinstatement order may be challenged

by petition for review on the grounds that the respondent is a USC. *Batista v. Ashcroft,* 270 F.3d 8 (1st Cir. 2001). And the circuit courts have jurisdiction to review the lawfulness of the application of INA §241(a)(5) even if they cannot collaterally review the original removal/deportation order. *Duran-Hernandez v. Ashcroft,* 348 F.3d 1158 (10th Cir. 2003) [habeas case transferred to circuit court because jurisdiction only in circuit court]; *Arevalo v. Ashcroft,* 344 F.3d 1, 9 (1st Cir. 2003) [recognizing that it may not revisit the validity of the original deportation order but having the authority "to determine the appropriateness of its resurrection"]; *Ojeda-Terrazas v. Ashcroft,* 290 F.3d 292, 295 (5th Cir. 2002); *Velasquez-Gabriel v. Crocetti,* 263 F.3d 102, 105 (4th Cir. 2001) [same] *Bejjani v. INS,* 271 F.3d 670, 674 (6th Cir. 2001) [same] *Castro-Cortez v. INS,* 239 F.3d 1037, 1043–45 (9th Cir. 2001) [same]. However, the REAL ID Act now permits, pursuant to INA §242(a)(2)(D), review of legal and constitutional challenges to a reinstated removal order, including a challenge to the underlying deportation/removal order. *Ramirez-Molina v. Ziglar,* 436 F.3d 508, 513–14 (5th Cir. 2006) [jurisdiction under INA §242(a)(2)(D) to review legal challenge to reinstated removal order notwithstanding preclusion provision of INA §241(a)(5), although court found no miscarriage of justice warranting collateral attack on removal order]. *See also Debeato v. U.S. Attorney General,* 505 F.3d 231 (3d Cir. 2007) [same].

19. Prior Bars to Review—In addition to these areas precluding review, the federal courts have previously found that certain immigration matters are precluded from federal review. *Quezada-Gomez v. INS*, 723 F.Supp. 1396 (D. Nev. 1989) [no jurisdiction to review amnesty denial by LAU in district court]. Some courts have suggested that 8 U.S.C. §1329 precludes review by federal courts unless the matter falls within Title II of the INA. *Chung v. Smith*, 640 F.Supp. 1065 (S.D.N.Y. 1986) [review of denial of work authorization precluded because it was not within Title II of the INA]; *Chaun-Fa v. Kiley*, 459 F.Supp. 762 (S.D.N.Y. 1978) [same]. At least one court has also found that the INA precludes judicial review under the APA of claims concerning the procedures used to adjudicate or screen interdicted Haitian refugees who are beyond the physical boundaries of the U.S. *Haitian Refugee Center, Inc. v. Baker*, 953 F.2d 1498, 1505–08 (11th Cir.), *cert. denied*, 112 S.Ct. 1245 (1992). *But see Rasul v. Bush,* 542 U.S. 466 (2004) [the Court found that there was habeas jurisdiction to review the physical custody of aliens being held at the military base in Guantanamo, Cuba and that jurisdiction existed under 28 U.S.C. §1331 (General Federal Question jurisdiction) and §1350 (Alien Tort Claims Act)]; *Abu Ali v. Ashcroft,* 350 F.Supp.2d 28, 39–57 (D.D.C. 2004) [denied motion to dismiss habeas petition brought by a U.S. citizen being held in Saudi Arabia at the direction of the U.S.]. The preclusion doctrine also bars actions by persons requesting a review of the AG's decision not to deport. *Chiles v. U.S.*, 874 F.Supp. 1334, 1339–41 (S.D. Fla. 1994).

20. Strong Presumption of Review—There is, however, a strong presumption in favor of review. *INS v. St. Cyr,* 121 S.Ct. 2271, 2278 (2001) [in finding that habeas remained to review statutory and constitutional claims to final removal order, the Court stated that "[f]or the INS to prevail it must overcome both the strong presumption in favor of judicial review of administrative actions and the longstanding rule requiring a clear statement of congressional intent to repeal habeas jurisdiction."]; *McNary v. Haitian Refugee Center, Inc.*, 498 U.S. 479 (1991) [pattern and practice class action litigation in U.S. district court not precluded by SAW statute]; *Bowen v. Michigan Academy of Family Physicians*, 476 U.S. 667, 670 (1986); *Lindahl v. Office of Personnel Mangement*, 470 U.S. 768 (1985); *Dunlop v. Bachowski*, 421 U.S. 560, 571 (1975); *Barlow v. Collins*, 397 U.S. 159, 166–67 (1970); *Abbott Laboratories v. Gardner*, 387 U.S. 136 (1967); *Traynor v. Turnage*, 108 S.Ct. 1372, 1378 (1988); *Zafar v. U.S. Att'y Gen.,* 461 F.3d 1357, 1361–62 (11th Cir. 2006) *reh'g en banc denied* 473 F.3d 1350 (2007) [recognizing the "strong presumption of judicial review" and finding that review of the denial of continuances was not barred by INA §242(a)(2)(B)(ii) because that section applies only to statutes and continuances are governed by regulation]; *Jahjaga v. Att'y Gen. of the U.S.,* 512 F.3d 80, 82 (3d Cir. 2008) ["in the absence of statutory authority prescribing the BIA's discretionary authority, there is a strong presumption in favor of judicial review of the administrative action"]; *Perez-Martin v. Ashcroft,* 394 F.3d 752, 757 (9th Cir. 2005) [citing the strong presumption of judicial review in *McNary* and *St. Cyr* and concluding that there is jurisdiction in the circuit courts to review SAW denials]; *Montero-Martinez v. Ashcroft,* 277 F.3d 1137, 1141 (9th Cir. 2002) [finding there is a strong presumption of judicial review and a longstanding principle of construing ambiguities in deportation statutes in favor of aliens thus leading to a narrow construction of preclusion statutes]; *Alvarez-Santos v. INS,* 332 F.3d 1245, 1249–53 (9th Cir. 2003) [citing the strong presumption of judicial review and due

process concerns the court determined that a person who was not found removable by the IJ by reason of having committed an offense covered under 8 U.S.C. §1252(a)(2)(C) was not barred from judicial review in the court of appeals under that statute]; *Haitian Refugee Center v. Smith*, 676 F.2d 1023 (5th Cir. Unit B 1982); *Graham v. Caston*, 568 F.2d 1092, 1096–97 (5th Cir. 1978). Judicial review "is the rule, and non-reviewability an exception which must be demonstrated," *Barlow,* 397 U.S. at 166–67, and that nonreviewability can only be demonstrated by "clear and convincing evidence of a contrary legislative intent." *Abbott Laboratories*, 387 U.S. at 141; *Rusk v. Cort*, 369 U.S. 367, 379–80 (1962). "In the absence of judicial review, grave injustices could take place for which our government and our people would have to bear moral responsibility." *Rodriguez-Roman v. INS*, 98 F.3d 416, 433 (9th Cir. 1996); *Shanti, Inc. v. Reno,* 36 F.Supp.2d 1151, 1157–58 (D. Minn. 1999) [in light of strong presumption of judicial review jurisdiction in post-IIRIRA case is not barred under §1331 because of repeal of §1329 jurisdiction].

Review of Constitutional Claims. The presumption of reviewability has particular force when seeking review of constitutional claims. *Zadvydas v. Davis,* 533 U.S. 678, 121 S.Ct. 2491 (2001); *McNary v. Haitian Refugee Center, Inc.*, 498 U.S. 479 (1991); *Webster v. Doe*, 486 U.S. 592 (1988) [where statute precludes judicial review it does not, by itself, establish the "heightened showing" necessary for preclusion of constitutional claims]; *Estep v. U.S.*, 327 U.S. 114, 120–23 (1946); *Johnson v. Robinson*, 415 U.S. 361, 367–74 (1974); *Shaughnessy v. Pedreiro*, 349 U.S. 48, 52 (1955); *Oestereich v. Selective Service Systems Local Board No. 11*, 393 U.S. 233, 237–38 (1968); *Walters v. Reno,* 145 F.3d 1032, 1051–52 (9th Cir. 1998), *cert. denied Reno v. Walters,* 526 U.S. 1003 (1999) [constitutional attack on notice in INA §274C proceeding]; *Gete v. INS*, 121 F.3d 1285 (9th Cir. 1997) [bar to review of the merits of a forfeiture decision does not bar constitutional attack on forfeiture scheme]; *Doe v. Nelson*, 703 F.Supp. 713 (N.D. Ill. 1988) [statutory preclusion in legalization under §1255a(f)(2) does not bar review of constitutional claims]. *But see Aguilar v. ICE,* 510 F.3d 1, 6–18 (1st Cir. 2007) [INA §242(b)(9) precluded a pattern and practice class-wide claim challenging ICE raids that resulted in detaining and transferring petitioners out of state thus depriving them of counsel].

21. Clear Statement Rule—Where the Congress intends to abolish review and thereby create a potentially significant constitutional issue, it must make a clear statement of its intent. *INS v. St. Cyr,* 121 S.Ct. 2271, 2279 (2001) [finding the writ of habeas corpus was preserved absent a clear statement to the contrary, the court stated that "when a particular interpretation of a statute invokes the outer limits of Congress' power, we expect a clear indication that Congress intended that result."]

22. Maintaining the Writ of Habeas Corpus—Congress in restricting judicial review may have eliminated statutory habeas corpus jurisdiction under 28 U.S.C. §2241 for removal orders under the REAL ID Act of 2005, but it could not eliminate the Great Writ (Suspension Clause) in the U.S. Const. Art. I, §9, Cl. 2. *But see Enwonwu v. Gonzales,* 438 F.3d 22 (1st Cir. 2006) [where case presented only purely legal issues reviewable pursuant to INA §242(a)(2)(D), the court concluded that "there is no possible claim that the REAL ID Act violates the Suspension Clause].

B. *Exhaustion Requirement*

1. Statutory Failure to Exhaust—One bar to judicial review that is typically asserted by the government is the statutory failure to exhaust administrative remedies under 8 U.S.C. §1252(d)(1) ["A court may review a final order of removal only if the alien has exhausted all administrative remedies available to the alien as of right"]. In light of the Supreme Court's decision in *Bowles v. Russell,* 127 S.Ct. 2360 (2007) one circuit has determined that §1252(d)(1) is "jurisdictional" and that the "manifest injustice" exception to exhaustion is no longer valid. *Grullon v. Mukasey,* 509 F.3d 107 (2d Cir. 2007) [dismissed appeal for failure to exhaust and rejected futility and manifest injustice arguments]; *Sayyah v. Farquharson,* 382 F.3d 20 (1st Cir. 2004); *Ramani v. Ashcroft,* 378 F.3d 554, 558–59 (6th Cir. 2004) [the improper use of some evidence and the failure to consider other evidence was not reviewable because respondent did not raise them before the BIA]; *Theodoropoulos v. INS,* 358 F.3d 162, 167–74 (2d Cir. 2004) [the statutory exhaustion requirement under §1252(d)(1) bars habeas review even where petitioner claims futility in INA §212(c) challenge after *Matter of Soriano*]; *Duvall v. Elwood,* 336 F.3d 228 (3d Cir. 2003) [habeas review is barred under §1252(d)(1) where there was no final order of removal]; *Abdulrahman v. Ashcroft,* 330 F.3d 587, 594–95 (3d Cir. 2003) [failure to raise appropriate burden of proof standard in asy-

lum case before BIA waived issue]; *Sundar v. INS,* 328 F.3d 1320 (11th Cir. 2003) *cert. denied* 124 S.Ct. 531 (2003) [finding that 8 U.S.C. §1252(d)(1) applies to §2241 habeas proceedings and dismissed petition for failure to seek BIA review even if there was perceived futility pre–*St. Cyr* for aggravated felon seeking INA §212(c) relief]. One court has even held that where the petitioner failed to raise the issue before the BIA, there was no jurisdiction even when the BIA reviewed the issue *sua sponte. Amaya-Artunduaga v. U.S. Att'y Gen.,* 463 F.3d 1247, 1249–51 (11th Cir. 2006) [where adverse credibility determination was not challenged before the BIA by Colombian asylum seeker, but the BIA addressed the issue *sua sponte,* the court, nevertheless, determined that it had no jurisdiction to review the issue]; *but see Sidabutar v. Gonzales,* 503 F.3d 1116, 1119–23 (10th Cir. 2007) [rejecting *Amaya-Artunduaga* where BIA *sua sponte* considered CAT claim of Christian Indonesian and agreeing with ninth circuit in *Socop-Gonzales*]. Another court found that respondent failed to exhaust his administrative remedies where he included in his BIA brief a title that stated the issue but he did not fully develop it in his brief. *Silva v. Gonzales,* 463 F.3d 68, 72 (1st Cir. 2006) [Colombian asylum applicant who titled a section of his brief that "the IJ failed in finding that respondent had not suffered past persecution" was denied circuit court review of IJ's factual determinations concerning past persecution because he failed to fully develop the argument in the brief]. Or where he included it in the notice of appeal but did not brief the issue. *Zhuang v. Gonzales,* 471 F.3d 884, 888 (8th Cir. 2006) [no review of respondent's due process deprivation due to improper translation where his notice of appeal stated the "interpreter was not competent" but nothing was briefed]. Or where he raised it before the BIA but not the IJ, and the BIA affirmed without opinion. *Ghebrehiwot v. Att'y Gen. of the U.S.,* 467 F.3d 344, 357 (3d Cir. 2006) [where respondent failed to raise social group asylum claim before IJ, but raised it for the first time before the BIA, the court would not review the issue where BIA affirmed without opinion; however it light of remand on other issues respondent could reassert it on remand]. Or where the general issue was raised but not a specific aspect of it. *Morales-Alegria v. Gonzales,* 449 F.3d 1051, 1058–59 (9th Cir. 2006) [where respondent raised issue whether forgery conviction under California law was an aggravated felony before the BIA, but did not raise the specific claim of whether his conviction was for a year or more before the BIA, his claim was not considered by the court]; Or where he raised it in his notice of appeal but the case was summarily dismissed, *De Araujo v. Gonzales,* 457 F.3d 146, 153 (1st Cir. 2006) [rejected appellant's attempt to address merits of whether he was an aggravated felon without challenging the basis for summary dismissal by the BIA because he believed the merits issue was raised in the notice of appeal to the BIA].

But some courts liberally interpret the exhaustion requirement so that if an immigration petitioner "makes some effort, however insufficient to place the Board on notice of a straightforward issue being raised on appeal," s/he is deemed to have exhausted her remedies. *Wu v. Ashcroft,* 393 F.3d 418, 422–23 (3d Cir. 2005) [where notice of appeal stated that IJ's decision was not supported by substantial evidence, it was sufficient to put BIA on notice that there was a claim of error that might address the improper reliance on respondent's airport interview]; *Kaganovich v. Gonzales,* 470 F.3d 894, 896–97 (9th Cir. 2006) [where respondent in notice of appeal to BIA stated that IJ erred in disregarding his refugee status, it was sufficient, without briefing, to raise claim that his refugee status had to be terminated prior to removal]; *Karaj v. Gonzales,* 462 F.3d 113, 117–18 (2d Cir. 2006) [respondent's recitation of the correct standard for asylum and citation to *Cardoza-Fonsecai* was sufficient to put BIA on notice that IJ improperly utilized a heightened burden for asylum]; *Abebe v. Gonzales,* 432 F.3d 1037, 1040–41 (9th Cir. 2005) (*en banc*) [where respondents did not signify the issue in the notice of appeal but had one line in their brief regarding female genital mutilation and the BIA cited *Matter of Burbano* stating that it had conducted an independent review of the record and agreed with the IJ, the FGM issue was sufficiently raised]; *Singh v. Gonzales,* 413 F.3d 156, 160 n.3 (1st Cir. 2005) [challenged raised in perfunctory manner to BIA sufficient]; *Zhang v. Ashcroft,* 388 F.3d 713, 721 (9th Cir. 2004) [applicant's request in his brief that BIA reverse CAT denial was sufficient to put BIA on notice and nothing more is required for exhaustion]. *See also Gill v. INS,* 420 F.3d 82, 85–89 (2d Cir. 2005) [where respondent challenged his conviction as a CIMT and raised the general issue of *mens rea,* but did not raise certain specific legal arguments, the court limited *Beharry* and *Theodoropoulos*, found that the statutory and judicial exhaustion doctrine did not bar consideration of the issue, and held "that §1252(d)(1) bars the consideration of bases for relief that were not raised below, and of general issues that were not raised below, but not of specific, subsidiary legal arguments or arguments by extension that were not made below"]. Similarly, where a second appeal is a mere formality because the BIA ruled previously in the same case on the identical issue, exhaustion was not required. *Popal v. Gonzales,* 416 F.3d 249, 252–53 (3d Cir. 2005) [where petitioner raised only one claim and that claim was heard before the BIA, petitioner's appeal from the IJ's order instead of a second BIA appeal was not barred by exhaustion]. And in the view of some courts a party need not file a brief before the BIA to exhaust administrative remedies. *Bhiski v. Ashcroft,* 373 F.3d 363, 367–68 (3d Cir. 2004) [the regulations do not mandate the filing of a brief before the BIA]. *But see Korsunskty v. Gonzales,* 461 F.3d 847, 849 (7th Cir. 2006) [appearing before the IJ *pro se* was not a basis alone to waive exhaustion requirements]; *Xu v. Gonzales,* 424 F.3d 45, 48–49 (1st Cir. 2005) [respondent waived argument regarding past persecution where he appealed future persecution denial to BIA but did not specify past persecution]; *Alyas v. Gonzales,* 419 F.3d 756, 761–62 (8th Cir. 2005) [although respondent argued to the BIA that the interpreter was ineffective at his hearing, his failure to raise before the BIA his due process challenge to the translation foreclosed his appeal]; *Taylor v. U.S.,* 396 F.3d 1322, 1327 n.4 (11th Cir. 2005) [in denying habeas for lack of exhaustion by *pro se* petitioner, the court distinguished between isolated statement in brief versus making an argument]; *Ramani v. Ashcroft,* 378 F.3d 554 (6th Cir. 2004) [where specific issue was not addressed in his brief in the manner it is now addressed before the court, the general statements in the notice of appeal to the BIA were insufficient to constitute exhaustion of administrative remedies]; *Hasan v. Ashcroft,* 397 F.3d 417, 420 (6th Cir. 2005) [following *Ramani* and relying on dicta in that case to deny review on lack of exhaustion grounds because "even if an issue is raised by the alien in his notice of appeal to the BIA, we will consider it waived if it is not argued in the brief filed with the BIA"].

2. Issue and Claims Exhaustion Distinguished. The Second Circuit has also recognized that *issue* exhaustion is *not* jurisdictional under INA §242(d)(1) and may be waived. *Zhong v. DOJ,* 480 F.3d 104, 116–25 (2d Cir. 2007) [court distinguished between exhaustion of claims which is jurisdictional and exhaustion of issues which is not jurisdiction and therefore may be waived by the government]. The court in *Zhong* found that the basis for waiver of issue exhaustion has more force in light of streamlining and that failure to raise certain issues should be treated as an affirmative defense and not as a jurisdictional issue. But in *Melnitsenko v. Mukasey,* 517 F.3d 42, 47 n.6 (2d Cir. 2008) the same circuit required exhaustion on a claim that evidence in removal proceeding should be suppressed because of widespread Fourth Amendment violations on the grounds that the claim was fact-intensive and should have been addressed by the IJ]. *See also Zine v. Mukasey,* 517 F.3d 535, 539–40 (8th Cir. 2008) [noting the claims versus issue exhaustion as an intra- and inter-circuit issue but not resolving it in this case except to note that lawyers must appeal the denial of withholding when appealing denial of asylum].

3. Prudential Failure to Exhaust—Other courts have also determined that as a prudential matter a party must exhaust remedies even where it is not a statutory requirement. *Acevedo-Carranza v. Ashcroft,* 371 F.3d 539 (9th Cir. 2004) [habeas dismissed because issue as to whether respondent's conviction was an aggravated felony could have been raised through a petition for review].

4. Waiver Before BIA as Basis for Failure to Exhaust—At least one court has taken the position that failure to raise an issue before the IJ results in waiver before the BIA and the court may not address the issue for lack of administrative exhaustion. *Torres De La Cruz v. Maurer,* , 1022-23 (10th Cir. 2007) [where respondent failed to raise Article 36 notification under the Vienna Convention before the IJ, the BIA determined it was waived and the court refused to hear it because of failure to exhaust administrative remedies].

5. Exhaustion of Constitutional Issues—Apart from IIRIRA courts have found that exhaustion was required in various circumstances, including due process constitutional challenges that could have been raised administratively. *Singh v. DHS,* 517 F.3d 638, 642–43 (2d Cir. 2008) [court found that petitioner failed to exhaust his administrative remedies when he failed to raise his due process claim before BIA that the NTA lacked specificity and therefore did not provide him with adequate notice of the charges]; *Sharashidze v. Gonzales,* 480 F.3d 566, 569–70 (7th Cir. 2007) [failure to raise due process claim that IJ denied respondent opportunity to present evidence under *Matter of K-A-* should have been presented to BIA]; *Zhuang v. Gonzales,* 471 F.3d 884, 888 (8th Cir. 2006) [no review of respondent's due process deprivation due to improper translation where his notice of appeal stated the "interpreter was not competent" but nothing was briefed]; *Pjetri v. Gonzales,* 468

F.3d 478 (7th Cir. 2006) [IJs violations of regulations and due process could not be addressed because they were not presented to the BIA]; *Amaya-Artunduaga v. U.S. Att'y Gen.,* 463 F.3d 1247, 1251 (11th Cir. 2006) [where respondent raised a due process objection to the heavy sarcasm and hostility of the IJ in a Colombian asylum hearing, the court dismissed the claim on jurisdictional grounds because this type of due process challenge could have been raised before the BIA]; *Valbrun v. Hogan,* 439 F.3d 136 (2d Cir. 2006) [where procedural errors could have been addressed by BIA claiming due process will not avoid exhaustion requirement]; *Bencosme De Rodriguez v. Gonzales,* 433 F.3d 163, 164 (1st Cir. 2005) [court declined to review due process challenge to improper conduct by IJ because it was not raised to BIA]; *Alyas v. Gonzales,* 419 F.3d 756, 761–62 (8th Cir. 2005) [although respondent argued to the BIA that interpreter was ineffective at his hearing, his failure to raise before the BIA his due process challenge to the translation foreclosed his appeal]; *Bonhometre v. Ashcroft,* 414 F.3d 442, 446–48 (3d Cir. 2005) [court dismissed due process claim for failure to exhaust administrative remedies where IJ failed to inform the respondent of eligibility for relief when the issue could have been raised before the BIA and the BIA was capable of granting relief]; *Barron v. Ashcroft,* 358 F.3d 674 (9th Cir. 2004) [due process challenge regarding prejudice due to lack of counsel at IJ hearing had to be raised before BIA]; *Kurfees v. INS,* 275 F.3d 332, 337 (4th Cir. 2001) [habeas dismissed because respondent failed to appeal motion to reopen to BIA and constitutional claim regarding evidence could have been raised at BIA]; *Mendes v. INS,* 197 F.3d 6, 11–12 (1st Cir. 1999) [the IJ's impermissibly placing the burden on the respondent in a removal of conditional residence case is the kind of due process argument that could have been raised before the BIA]; *Sayaxing v. INS,* 179 F.3d 515, 522–23 (7th Cir. 1999) [court declined to review due process issue regarding IJ's conduct because it involved procedural issues correctable by the BIA]; *Liu v. Waters*, 55 F.3d 421 (9th Cir. 1995) [court found failure to exhaust remedies, even when the issue on review was a due process question concerning ineffective assistance of counsel, when it could have been resolved by the agency]; *Castaneda-Suarez v. INS*, 993 F.2d 142, 144–45 (7th Cir. 1993) [same]. *But see Bosede v. Mukasey,* 512 F.3d 946, 950–51 (7th Cir. 2008) [where the IJ violated fundamental due process in not considering evidence, stated that petitioner might not have problems because he could bribe his way out of jail, and "applied whatever rationale he could muster to justify a predetermined outcome" exhaustion was not required]; *Colaianni v. INS,* 490 F.3d 185, 187 (2d Cir. 2007) [exhaustion not required for equal protection challenge regarding derivative citizenship because BIA lacked the authority to address it]; *Saravia-Paguada v. Gonzales,* 488 F.3d 1122, 1129–30 (9th Cir. 2007) [exhaustion not required where retroactivity argument concerning relief from removal raised due process considerations];*Hadayat v. Gonzales,* 458 F.3d 659, 664–65 (7th Cir. 2006) [where respondent argued that NSEERS registration violated equal protection resulting in removal proceedings, the court noted this was the type of fundamental constitutional claim the BIA does not address]; *Geach v. Chertoff,* 444 F.3d 940, 945–46 (8th Cir. 2006) [equal protection challenge to denial of suspension to person granted advance parole is not subject to exhaustion because constitutional challenges unrelated to procedural errors need not be exhausted because BIA has no jurisdiction to adjudicate them];

Under former INA §106(a) at least one court found that the congressional scheme required exhaustion of administrative remedies even if the agency could not have addressed the constitutional claim where that claim could have eventually been addressed in the court of appeals. *Massieu v. Reno,* 91 F.3d 416 (3d Cir.) [relying on *Thunder Basin Coal Co. v. Reich,* 510 U.S. 200 (1944) the court determined that Congress intended that a constitutional question that was not collateral to the removal proceeding required exhaustion before the IJ and BIA before seeking review in the court of appeals]. *See also Yang v. U.S. Att'y Gen.,* 494 F.3d 1311, 1316 (11th Cir. 2007) [declining to entertain Equal Protection challenge to BIA's position that traditional marriages in China should not be given the same status as legal marriages for purposes of persecution of spouses under the forced abortion provision].

Following the Supreme Court's decision in *Booth v. Churner,* 532 U.S. 731 (2001), the Second Circuit determined that the failure to raise the administrative right to INA §212(h) relief even where the statute clearly foreclosed it, barred the district court from considering constitutional and international law challenges because *Booth* requires exhaustion except "where the relevant administrative procedure lacks authority to provide any relief or to take any action whatsoever in response to a complaint [*Booth*] at 736." *Beharry v. Ashcroft,* 329 F.3d 51, 58 (2d Cir. 2003) [where applicant failed to raise the right to INA §212(h) relief based on international law principles before IJ or BIA his claim could not be heard in federal court for failure on judicial grounds to exhaust administrative remedies even if the IJ or BIA would not decide his international law claim]; *Grullon v. Mukasey,* 409 F.3d 107, 112–14 (2d Cir. 2007) [reading *Booth* to require exhaustion before the BIA notwithstanding BIA's on-point precedent decision because the BIA has the authority to change its opinion in an *en banc* decision]; *but see Gill v. INS,* 420 F.3d 82, 87 (2d Cir. 2005) [distinguished *Booth* and *Beharry* and found no judicial exhaustion bar where the issue of whether a NY Penal Law was legally incoherent was purely legal and fell outside the INS's traditional area of expertise]. *See also Sundar v. INS,* 328 F.3d 1320 (11th Cir. 2003) *cert. denied* 124 S.Ct. 531 (2003) [finding that 8 U.S.C. §1252(d)(1) applies to §2241 habeas proceedings and dismissed petition for failure to seek BIA review even if there was perceived futility pre–*St. Cyr* for aggravated felon seeking INA §212(c) relief]. *But see Gonzalez v. O'Connell,* 355 F.3d 1010, 1015–18 (7th Cir. 2004) [habeas petitioner did not have to exhaust constitutional challenge to mandatory detention even though the predicate for the challenge was a statutory interpretation where the BIA had spoken on the statutory issue and it would have been futile].

6. Exhaustion of Nonconstitutional Claims Required

6.a. **First Circuit.** *Ouk v. Gonzales,* 464 F.3d 108, 111–12 (1st Cir. 2006) [court without jurisdiction to hear PTSD claim in withholding where Cambodian applicant failed to raise it before BIA]; *Silva v. Gonzales,* 463 F.3d 68, 72 (1st Cir. 2006) [Colombian asylum applicant who titled a section of his brief that "the IJ failed in finding that respondent had not suffered past persecution" was denied circuit court review of IJ's factual determinations concerning past persecution because he failed to fully develop the argument in the brief]; *Bollanos v. Gonzales,* 461 F.3d 82, 87 (1st Cir. 2006) [failure to address country of deportation to BIA waived issue]; *Berrio-Barrera v. Gonzales,* 460 F.3d 163, 167–68 (1st Cir. 2006) [failure to raise particular social group claim before BIA, waived it]; *Joumaa v. Gonzales,* 446 F.3d 244, 246 (1st Cir. 2006) [failure to argue equitable tolling to BIA waived it]; *Estrada-Canales v. Gonzales,* 437 F.3d 208, 218 (1st Cir. 2006) [failure to raise *Fleuti* brief, casual and innocent argument before BIA waived issue on appeal]; *Roberts v. Gonzales,* 422 F.3d 33, 36–37 (1st Cir. 2005) [where respondent in motion to reopen to BIA failed to request remand to IJ to reopen marriage case *sua sponte*, issue waived on appeal]; *Ishak v. Gonzales,* 422 F.3d 22, 31 (1st Cir. 2005) [where respondent did not raise IJ's failure to address credibility issues before BIA, they were waived]; *Njenga v. Ashcroft,* 386 F.3d 335, 338 (1st Cir. 2004) [failure to raise issue regarding validity of signatory on NTA was waived]; *Oliva-Muralles v. Ashcroft,* 328 F.3d 25, 26 (1st Cir. 2003) [failure to raise CAT claim before IJ/BIA barred claim in Court]; *Prado v. Reno,* 198 F.3d 286, 292 (1st Cir. 1999) [failure to raise in motion to reopen or appeal of denial of motion the request that BIA reopen case *sua sponte*]; *Bernal-Vallejo v. INS,* 195 F.3d 56, 63–65 (1st Cir. 1999) [failure to raise ineffective assistance of counsel by way of motion to reopen barred claim]; *Ravindran v. INS,* 976 F.2d 754, 761–62 (1st Cir. 1992) [failure to raise asylum based on a particular social group was waived, even where political asylum was raised]; *Alvarez-Flores v. INS,* 909 F.2d 1, 8 (1st Cir. 1990) [where one of several theories as a basis for asylum was not raised before the BIA, applicant failed to exhaust as to that theory]; *Espinal v. Pere,* 144 F.Supp.2d 53 (D.P.R. 2001) [exhaustion required where arriving alien placed in removal proceedings after DD denied adjustment under LIFE Acts]; *Bajwa v. Cobb*, 727 F.Supp. 53, 56 (D. Mass. 1989) [concession of excludability and failure to raise issue before BIA deprives the court of jurisdiction];

6.b. **Second Circuit**. *Grullon v. Mukasey,* 409 F.3d 107, 112–14 (2d Cir. 2007) [reading §1252(d)(1) in light of *Bowles v. Russell* to be a jurisdictional statute where neither futility (in light of *Booth v .Churner*) nor manifest injustice can be exceptions to exhaustion]; *Khan v. Gonzales,* 495 F.3d 31, 36 (2d Cir. 2007) [where IJ made an "unambiguous misstatement of pertinent facts in the record" regarding respondent's conviction record, but respondent failed to raise it with the BIA, court lacked jurisdiction]; *Steevenez v. Gonzales,* 476 F.3d 114 (2d Cir. 2007) [respondent failed to exhaust administrative remedies regarding his claim for asylum by failing to address the issue of "safe relocation" on the theory that it was addressed in his argument that the government failed to establish changed country conditions]; *Foster v. INS,* 376 F.3d 75, 77–78 (2d Cir. 2004) [*Pro se* respondent's failure to raise issue whether his criminal conviction was an aggravated felony before the IJ precluded review]; *Arango-Aradondo v. INS*, 13 F.3d 610, 614–15 (2d Cir. 1994) [where ineffective assistance of counsel and inadequate record not raised to BIA petitioner must exhaust by filing motion to reopen with the BIA]; *But see U.S. v. Sosa,* 387 F.3d 131, 136–37 (2d Cir. 2004) [where *pro se* respondent was not informed of INA §212(c) relief the failure to exhaust "must be excused" where it arises from an invalid waiver of the right to administrative appeal because it was not knowingly and intelligently made]; *Kendall v. Mooney,* 273 F.Supp.2d 216, 219–20 (E.D.N.Y. 2003) [where *pro se* appellant raised lack of severity of crime on appeal to BIA but BIA only addressed finality of conviction, appellant did exhaust his remedies for purposes of asserting he was not convicted of an aggravated felony]; *Lleo-Fernandez v. INS,* 989 F.Supp. 518 (S.D.N.Y. 1998) [failure to obtain DD's decision on release before habeas action foreclosed review]; *Nsukami v. INS,* 890 F.Supp. 170, 174–75 (E.D.N.Y. 1995) [same as to improper translators]; *Yeung v. Reno,* 868 F.Supp. 53 (S.D.N.Y. 1994) [no review of adjustment application in district court]; *Bak v. INS,* 682 F.2d 441 (2d Cir. 1982) [where respondent failed to appeal denial of motion to reopen to BIA, circuit court had no jurisdiction]; *Henriquez v. Ashcroft,* 269 F.Supp.2d 106, 108 (E.D.N.Y. 2003) [dismissed habeas where denied applicant for certificate of citizenship failed to exhaust his administrative appeal of the denial before the AAO]; *Chung v. Smith,* 640 F.Supp. 1065 (S.D.N.Y. 1986);

6.c. **Third Circuit**. *Barker v. Ashcroft,* 382 F.3d 313, 317 (3d Cir. 2003) [failure to raise in a motion to reopen the lack of adequate and sufficient oral notice of the consequences of failing to depart voluntarily barred respondent from seeking judicial review of that issue]; *Alleyne v. INS,* 879 F.2d 1177, 1182–86 (3d Cir. 1989) [where errors asserted were never even arguably raised before BIA, the circuit court is barred from reviewing them under 8 U.S.C. §1105a(c), even if they raise constitutional concerns that were procedural because BIA can correct such procedural errors]; *Mentor v. INS,* 834 F.Supp. 133, 137–38 (E.D. Pa. 1993) [failure to raise incompetent translation before BIA barred district court review];

6.d. **Fourth Circuit**. *Asika v. Ashcroft,* 362 F.3d 264, 267 n.3 (4th Cir. 2004) [claim that IJ erred in determining respondent was not eligible for AOS because he was inadmissible could not be raised for failure to exhaust]; *but see Tarvand v. INS,* 937 F.2d 973, 976–77 (4th Cir. 1991) [where INS briefed issue on appeal to BIA issue preserved even if respondent failed to do so];

6.e. **Fifth Circuit**. *Falek v. Gonzales,* 475 F.3d 285 (5th Cir. 2007) [failure to raise retroactivity of INA §101(a)(13)(C) before BIA barred federal review]; *Goonsuwan v. Ashcroft,* 252 F.3d 383 (5th Cir. 2001) [habeas dismissed because ineffective assistance of counsel claim had to be raised by motion to reopen before BIA in transitional rule case governed by 106(c) exhaustion requirement]; *Cardoso v. Reno,* 216 F.3d 512, 517–18 (5th Cir. 2000) [denial of adjustment must first be reviewed in removal]; *Pierre v. INS,* 932 F.2d 418, 421 (5th Cir. 1991) [procedural challenges to deportation order will not be addressed by circuit court where they were not raised before the BIA]; *Vargas v. INS,* 826 F.2d 1394, 1399 (5th Cir. 1987) [failure to raise issue concerning extreme hardship before BIA is failure to exhaust and need not be addressed in circuit court]; *Youssefinia v. INS,* 784 F.2d 1254 (5th Cir. 1986) [where deportation order not appealed to BIA, not reviewable in circuit court, notwithstanding grant of motion to reopen solely for discretionary relief of asylum/suspension].

6.f. **Sixth Circuit.** *Csekinek v. INS,* 391 F.3d 819, 822–23 (6th Cir. 2004) [failure to raise claim that conviction predated IIRIRA barred court's consideration]; *Dokic v. INS,* 899 F.2d 530 (6th Cir. 1990) [where ineffective assistance of counsel and inadequate record not raised to BIA petitioner must exhaust by filing motion to reopen with the BIA];

6.g. **Seventh Circuit.** *Margos v. Gonzales,* 443 F.3d 593, 598–99 (7th Cir. 2006) [no exhaustion where there was a failure to raise claim for persecution before the BIA based upon status as Assyrian Christian in Iraq]; *Awad v. Ashcroft,* 328 F.3d 336, 340 (7th Cir. 2003) [failure to raise stop-time issue before BIA barred claim]; *Toptchev v. INS,* 295 F.3d 714, 721 (7th Cir. 2002) [respondent failed to specifically enumerate to the BIA the errors in the IJ's findings that resulted in the denial of asylum and therefore a challenge to these findings could not be raised in the circuit court]; *McBrearty v. Perryman,* 212 F.3d 985 (7th Cir. 2000) [failure to first seek review of nonconstitutional claims regarding denial of adjustment in removal proceeding bars district court action]; *But see Gonzalez v. O'Connell,* 355 F.3d 1010, 1015–18 (7th Cir. 2004) [habeas petitioner did not have to exhaust constitutional challenge to mandatory detention even though the predicate for the challenge was a statutory interpretation where the BIA had spoken on the statutory issue and it would have been futile]; *Kashani v. Nelson*, 793 F.2d 818 (7th Cir. 1986) [no review in district court of DD's denial of asylum until remedies before IJ are exhausted]; *Bothyo v. INS*, 783 F.2d 74 (7th Cir. 1986) [cannot seek benefit of automatic-stay provision of §1105a(a) in circuit court where BIA has not yet decided motion to reopen]; *Gallego v. INS*, 674 F.Supp. 280 (W.D. Wis. 1987) [failure of alien to seek appeal of exclusion order barred district court action seeking parole];

6.h. **Eighth Circuit.** *Frango v. Gonzales,* 437 F.3d 726 (8th Cir. 2006) [failure to raise law-of-the-case issue before IJ or BIA constituted failure to exhaust]; *Etchu-Njang v. Gonzales,* 403 F.3d 577, 581–85 (8th Cir. 2005) [appellant was required to exhaust administrative remedies before raising ineffective assistance and no due process claim where ineffective assistance arose out of failure to seek discretionary relief of cancellation]; *Ateka v. Ashcroft,* 384 F.3d 954, 956–57 (8th Cir. 2004) [declining to rule, for failure to exhaust administrative remedies, on whether a false statement on an I-9 in private employment is a ground of inadmissibility under the bar for a false claim to citizenship]; *Ruston v. DOS,* 29 F.Supp.2d 518, 522 (S.D. Ark. 1998), *aff'd* 187 F.3d 643 (8th Cir. 1999) [challenge to revocation of L-1 status requires exhaustion through INS prior to suit];

6.i. **Ninth Circuit.** *Rendon v. Mukasey,* __F.3d ___(9th Cir. Mar. 19, 2008) 2008 WL 726354 [failed to exhaust claim that Utah conviction was not a basis for removal because he never raised the conviction with the BIA]; *Puga v. Chertoff,* 488 F.3d 812 (9th Cir. 2007) [court would not address ineffective assistance of counsel claim because respondent failed to raise it in a motion to reopen before the BIA]; *Almaghzar v. Gonzales,* 457 F.3d 915, 920–21 (9th Cir. 2006) [respondent failed to exhaust claim that the frivolous bar in asylum was inapplicable to his case because his application was filed before the effective date of the provision]; *Morales-Alegria v. Gonzales,* 449 F.3d 1051, 1058–59 (9th Cir. 2006) [where respondent raised issue whether forgery conviction under California law was an aggravated felony before the BIA, but did not raise the specific claim of whether his conviction was for a year or more before the BIA, the court would not consider the issue]; *Ontiveros-Lopez v. INS,* 213 F.3d 1121, 1124 (9th Cir. 2000) [requiring a person who argues ineffective assistance of counsel to first present the issue to the BIA]; *Lata v. INS,* 204 F.3d 1241, 1245–46 (9th Cir. 2000) [ineffective assistance of counsel claim cannot be raised in court of appeals for first time where *Lozada* not followed below]; *Ortiz v. INS,* 179 F.3d 1148, 1152 (9th Cir. 1999) [appellants must file a motion to reopen with the BIA to raise NACARA or Torture Convention claim before circuit court will review them]; *Rashtabadi v. INS,* 23 F.3d 1562, 1567 (9th Cir. 1994) [must exhaust by motion to reopen even where incompetent counsel represented person on appeal]; *Xiao v. Barr,* 979 F.2d 151 (9th Cir. 1992) [no jurisdiction in district court to challenge of immigration court's jurisdiction over exclusion hearing when issue could be raised at exclusion hearing]; *Vargas v. INS,* 831 F.2d 906, 908 (9th Cir. 1987) [where errors asserted were never even arguably raised before BIA, the circuit court is barred from reviewing them under 8 U.S.C. §1105a(c), even if they raise constitutional concerns that were procedural because BIA can correct such procedural errors]; *Joo v. INS,* 813 F.2d 211 (9th Cir. 1987) [where respondent departed after OSC issued but before hearing, BIA denied jurisdiction for appeal and circuit court held it had no jurisdiction because no exhaustion of remedies]; *Florez de Solis v. INS,* 796 F.2d 330 (9th Cir. 1986) [failure to raise inaudible transcript issue to BIA waived for nonexhaustion];

6.j. **Tenth Circuit**. *Ismaiel v. Mukasey,* 516 F.3d 1198, 1206–07 (10th Cir. 2008) [failure to raise claim that BIA did not consider that membership in the Muslim Brotherhood in Syria leads to persecution]; *Mahamat v. Gonzales,* 430 F.3d 1281 (10th Cir. 2005) [failure to raise equitable tolling before BIA bars review in circuit court]; *Galvez Pineda v. Gonzales,* 427 F.3d 833, 837–38 (10th Cir. 2005) [where respondent timely appealed BIA's summary dismissal for failure to file brief and argued ineffective assistance of counsel, the court found the issue was not exhausted and respondent had to file a timely motion to reopen pursuant to *Lozada* and allow the BIA to rule]; *Vatulev v. Ashcroft,* 354 F.3d 1207, 1211 (10th Cir. 2003) [failure to file BIA appeal of denial of motion to reconsider barred federal appeal of issue]; *Akinwunmi v. INS,* 194 F.3d 1340 (10th Cir. 1999) [failure to raise ineffective assistance of counsel by motion to reopen barred claim]; *Rivera-Zurita v. INS,* 946 F.2d 118, 120 n.2 (10th Cir. 1991) [failure to raise hardship issue before BIA constitutes failure to exhaust remedies];

6.k. **Eleventh Circuit.** *Amaya-Artunduaga v. U.S. Att'y Gen.*, 463 F.3d 1247, 1249–51 (11th Cir. 2006) [where adverse credibility determination was not challenged before the BIA by a Colombian asylum seeker but the BIA *sua sponte* address the matter, the court, nevertheless, determined it had no jurisdiction to review the issue]; *Melian v. INS*, 987 F.2d 1521 (11th Cir. 1993) [failure to raise issue of termination of domicile for INA §212(c) purposes before BIA precluded appeal];

Motions to Reopen—Although the circuit courts might be barred from reviewing a motion to reopen that was denied as untimely because of failure to exhaust administrative remedies, such a motion, when based upon "changed country conditions," can be judicially reviewed because the regulations contemplate that the motion may be filed outside of the 90-day period. *Panjwani v. Ashcroft,* 401 F.3d 626, 628–32 (5th Cir. 2005) [transition rules under IIRIRA permit review where it is untimely motion based upon changed country conditions].

Failure to Exhaust Where Evidence Not Presented—One court has even found that the failure to present evidence to the IJ or BIA forecloses an appeal on exhaustion grounds despite raising the legal issue before the IJ and the BIA. *Bosede v. Ashcroft,* 309 F.3d 441 (7th Cir. 2002) [although petitioner raised the legal issue of the denial of the right to seek withholding before the BIA, he failed to exhaust his administrative remedies when his less-than-competent counsel failed to present the appropriate records of conviction that would have proven his argument].

Failure to exhaust may also arise even if person is deported before an opportunity to appeal. *Bejar v. Ashcroft,* 324 F.3d 127, 132–33 (3d Cir. 2003) [where respondent ordered deported *in absentia* was physically removed from the U.S. within the 30-day period allotted to appeal denial of motion to reopen, he failed to exhaust administrative remedies].

7. Exhaustion Does Not Apply

No Exhaustion Where No Adequate Procedure to Exhaust—The exhaustion doctrine, of course, does not apply where the agency has not provided any review procedures or any adequate review procedures for their determination. *Alcaraz v. INS,* 384 F.3d 1150, 1160 (9th Cir. 2004) [where there is no *statutory* right to review respondent's repapering argument, the failure to exhaust a discretionary remedy, even if regulatory, such as a motion to reopen is not jurisdictional]; *Chang v. U.S.*, 327 F.3d 911, 919–20, 922–24 (9th Cir. 2003) [where an IJ in removal proceedings could not address APA, estoppel and constitutional claims and where statutes now limit the scope of removal proceedings, plaintiffs did not have to exhaust removal proceeding to seek review of the retroactive application of administrative decisions to the investor's application]; *Castro-Cortez v. INS,* 239 F.3d 1037, 1044–45 (9th Cir. 2001) [INA §241(a)(5) regarding reinstatement of prior removal order has no administrative remedy as of right and therefore exhaustion unnecessary]; *Jean v. Nelson*, 727 F.2d 957, 980 (11th Cir. 1984), *aff'd as to judgment only on other grounds*, 472 U.S. 846 (1985) [review of DD's failure to provide notice of right to claim political asylum]; *Haitian Refugee Center v. Smith*, 676 F.2d 1023 (5th Cir. 1982) [review of DD's procedures in denying asylum]; *Edwards v. Johnson,* 209 F.3d 772, 777 (5th Cir. 2000) [exhaustion was not required to bring Bivens action against federal officers because federal detention centers have no procedure to grant monetary relief]; *Martinez v. DHS,* 502 F.Supp.2d 631, 634–36 (E.D. Mich. 2007) [plaintiff's challenge to DHS's determination that the CSPA did not apply to his adjustment application was subject to review because the denial of AOS was final and the review procedure, in a removal proceeding, is exclusively in the control of DHS]; *Basova v. Ashcroft,* 373 F.Supp.2d 192, 196–97 (E.D.N.Y. 2005) [no administrative remedy to exhaust for action compelling adjustment under visa lottery because it is not a denial of residency in context of removal hearing]; *Ying Fong v. Ashcroft,* 317 F.Supp.2d 398, 406–07 (S.D.N.Y. 2004) [post-*Theodoropoulos/Beharry* habeas should not be dismissed for failure to exhaust the administrative remedy of filing a motion to reopen an *in absentia* order for lack of notice where respondent was deported before he could effect motion to reopen]; *Milosevic v. Ridge,* 301 F.Supp.2d 337, 345 (M.D. Pa. 2003) [exhaustion not required of ineffective assistance of counsel claim that surfaced after motion to reopen before BIA was denied and motion for *sua sponte* reopening by the BIA is discretionary]; *Phan v. Reno,* 56 F.Supp.2d 1149 (W.D. Wash. 1999) (en banc) [exhaustion not required because there is no administrative procedure to a constitutional challenge to indefinite detention]; *Dalis v. Brady*, 766 F.Supp. 901, 903 (D. Colo. 1991) [exhaustion not required to obtain bond when former 8 C.F.R. §242.2(d) does not provide for appeal of bond decision where there is a final deportation order] or where the party was not timely notified of the review procedures. *Shirkhani v. Greene*, 790

F.Supp. 1065 (D. Colo. 1992) [where INS did not advise person of 10-day appeal time to challenge bond, court entertained habeas].

No Exhaustion in Detention Cases—Exhaustion also does not apply where a petition challenges immigration detention. *Soberanes v. Comfort,* 388 F.3d 1305, 1310 (10th Cir. 2004) *Welch v. Reno,* 101 F.Supp.2d 347, 351 (D. Md. 2000) [statutory exhaustion only for review of final orders of removal]; *Alikhani v. Fasano,* 70 F.Supp.2d 1124, 1129–30 (S.D. Cal. 1999); *Aguilar v. Lewis,* 50 F.Supp.2d 539, 541 (E.D. Va. 1999) [no federal statute imposes an exhaustion requirement concerning bond]; *Rowe v. INS,* 45 F.Supp.2d 144, 145–46 (D. Mass. 1999) (and cases cited therein); *Pastor-Camarena v. Smith*, 977 F.Supp. 1415, 1417 (W.D. Wash. 1997) (and cases cited therein); *Montero v. Cobb*, 937 F.Supp. 88, 90–91 (D. Mass. 1996). *But see Boz v. U.S.* 248 F.3d 1299 (11th Cir. 2001) [habeas corpus properly dismissed where petitioner did not exhaust INS procedure for review after 90-day period]; *Al-Siddiqi v. Nehls,* 521 F.Supp.2d 870 (E.D. Wis. 2007) [where ICE refused to accept bond and conditions changed because FBI raised national security issues and the BIA directed petitioner to seek a new bond hearing before the IJ, petitioner had to exhaust his administrative remedies as a discretionary matter before seeking review]; *Campbell v. Chadbourne,* 505 F.Supp.2d 191 (D. Mass. 2007) [constitutional challenge by refugee to detention because of his failure to apply for adjustment should as a discretionary matter be exhausted]; *Bui v. INS,* 80 F.Supp.2d 1123 (D. Or. 1999).

No Exhaustion In Certain Ineffective Assistance of Counsel Claims—Where ineffective assistance of counsel rises to the level of a due process violation because the proceeding was so fundamentally unfair that the respondent was unable to present his case. *Granados-Oseguera v. Gonzales,* 464 F.3d 993, 996–99 (9th Cir. 2006) [where ineffective counsel represented the respondent through the entire proceeding and failed to get an extension of VD or ask that the case be reopened within the VD period, and subsequent counsel was numerically barred by first counsel's motion to reopen outside the VD period, subsequent counsel did not have to file a motion to reopen but could instead file a petition for review].

No Exhaustion Where Review Procedure Is Not Mandatory—Exhaustion is also not required where a review procedure exists but it is not mandated by statute or agency regulations. *Darby v. Cisneros*, 113 S.Ct. 2539 (1993) [where regulation provided that ALJ's determination shall be final unless the Secy. of HUD, in his discretion, decides to review the decision after request of a party, such regulation does not provide for mandatory review and plaintiff could file suit without making request to Sec.]; *Padilla-Padilla v. Gonzales,* 463 F.3d 972, 978 (9th Cir. 2006) [failure to file a discretionary motion to reconsider to BIA to challenge reduction of VD does not deprive court of jurisdiction]; *Bangura v. Hansen,* 434 F.3d 487, 498–99 (6th Cir. 2006) [plaintiffs not required to exhaust APA challenge to denial of I-130 petition because of INA §204(c) because they are not required to appeal to the BIA, but the taking of the appeal to the BIA rendered the decision nonfinal]; *Pinho v. Gonzales,* 432 F.3d 193, 200–04 (3d Cir. 2005) [the district court under the APA was not barred on exhaustion grounds from reviewing a legal determination as to whether a person with a substantive vacated conviction could adjust status simply because there might be further review of the adjustment in a removal proceeding]; *Alcaraz v. INS,* 384 F.3d 1150, 1160 and n.4 (9th Cir. 2004) [where there is no *statutory* right to review respondent's repapering argument, the failure to exhaust a discretionary remedy, even if regulatory, such as a motion to reopen is not jurisdictional. The court noted that *INS v. Doherty*, 502 U.S. 314, 323 recognized motions to reopen as discretionary]; *Noriega-Lopez v. Ashcroft,* 335 F.3d 874, 880–82 (9th Cir. 2003) [failure to file a motion to reconsider BIA decision is neither statutorily required under INA §242(d)(1) nor prudentially required]; *Chang v. U.S.,* 327 F.3d 911, 922–24 (9th Cir. 2003) [where investor was not required to seek a removal proceeding to review denied petition and where IJ in removal could not address APA, estoppel and constitutional claims and where statutes now limit the scope of removal proceedings, plaintiffs did not have to exhaust removal proceeding]; *Castro-Cortez v. INS,* 239 F.3d 1037, 1045 (9th Cir. 2001) [opportunity to make a statement contesting reinstatement of removal "is not an 'administrative remedy available to the alien as of right,' because the government is not required to reconsider its prior decision"]; *Air Espana v. Brien,* 165 F.3d 148, 151 (2d Cir. 1999) [district court could not impose exhaustion requirement where statutory scheme did not mandate exhaustion for fine proceedings before INS; however ripeness considerations exist]; *Abboud v. INS,* 140 F.3d 843, 847 (9th Cir. 1998) [beneficiary need not exhaust denial of visa petition]; *Young v. Reno*, 114 F.3d 879, 881–83 (9th Cir. 1997) [not required to appeal visa revocation because appeal to BIA discretionary]; *Castillo-Villagra v. INS*, 972 F.2d 1017, 1024–25 (9th Cir. 1992) [failure to file motion to reopen not jurisdictional]; *Rhoa-Zamora v. INS*, 971 F.2d 26, 31–32 (7th Cir. 1992), *cert. denied*, 113 S.Ct. 2331 (1993) [same]; *Wong v. DOS*, 789 F.2d 1380, 1384 (9th Cir. 1986) [failure to seek reconsideration of a visa revocation does not bar review]; *Louis-Martin v. Ridge,* 322 F.Supp.2d 556, 558–59 (M.D.Pa. 2004) [not required to exhaust potential remedy of a motion to reopen because it is completely discretionary and not a remedy available as a right]; *Schaeuble v. Reno,* 87 F.Supp.2d 383, 387–90 (D.N.J. 2000) [exhaustion under Privacy Act is not statutorily mandated and provides no time to complete administrative process]; *Hermanowski v. Farquharson,* 39 F.Supp.2d 148, 154 (D.R.I. 1999) [Congress has not created an exhaustion requirement for judicial review of custody claims]; *Zhang v. Reno,* 27 F.Supp.2d 476, 477 (S.D.N.Y. 1998) [filing a motion to reopen not required because exhaustion doctrine only applies to those remedies available as a matter of right]. *But see generally Padilla v. Gonzales,* 470 F.3d 1209, 1212–15 (7th Cir. 2006) [where respondent vacated convictions after BIA appeal and counsel never sought *sua sponte* review from BIA after government refused to file joint motion, the court determined that counsel failed to exhaust administrative remedies and dismissed the petition for review]; *Howell v. INS,* 72 F.3d 288, 293–94 (2d Cir. 1995) [distinguished *Darby* in adjustment of status case]; *Garcia-Mir v. Smith*, 766 F.2d 1478, 1489 n.13 (11th Cir. 1985), *cert. denied sub nom. Marquez-Medina v. Meese,* 475 U.S. 1022 (1986) [must at least present claim to agency. Failure to do so is jurisdictional under former 8 U.S.C. §1105a(c) when matter is within competence of agency]. Similarly, exhaustion does not apply where there may be an alternative form of relief but no review over the matter. *Ajurulloski v. INS*, 688 F.Supp. 1272, 1275–76 (N.D. Ill. 1988) [where denial of voluntary departure applicant did not have to seek stay from DD to challenge denial in federal court]; *Hanif v. DHS,* 472 F.Supp.2d 914, 920–22 (E.D. Mich. 2007) [court has jurisdiction to review denial of I-130 petition under the APA but there is no final agency action by the BIA so the petition must be dismissed].

*No Exhaustion in AWO/*Burbano *Cases*—In AWO cases or decisions in which the Board cites to *Matter of Burbano,* 20 I&N Dec. 872 (BIA 1994) exhaustion is not necessary if the issue was raised before the IJ because the BIA is presumed to have reviewed the entire record and adopted the IJ's position. *Arreguin-Moreno v. Mukasey,* 511 F.3d 1229, 1232 (9th Cir. 2008) [petitioner need not exhaust issues before the BIA that were raised before the IJ because in *Burbano* the BIA adopts the IJ's decision in its entirety and all issues are deemed presented to the BIA]; *Pasha v. Gonzales,* 433 F.3d 530, 532–34 (7th Cir. 2005) [exhaustion is not an issue where BIA issues AWO decision, because an AWO decision is assumed to be a resolution of the merits of all the issues absent waiver through a specific notice of appeal or the filing of a brief on a particular issue or failure to raise the issue before the IJ]. *But see Zara v. Ashcroft,* 383 F.3d 927 (9th Cir. 2004) [finding exhaustion doctrine applies to AWO/streamlined decisions].

Exhaustion May Be Prudential Not Jurisdictional—Moreover, the exhaustion requirement is often not a jurisdictional prerequisite but a matter committed to the "sound discretion of the trial court." *Haitian Refugee Center, Inc.*, 676 F.2d 1023, 1034 (5th Cir. 1982); *See NLRB v. Industrial Union of Marine and Shipbuilding Workers*, 391 U.S. 418, 426 n.8 (1968). The exhaustion requirement may thus be waived when its imposition fails to serve underlying policy considerations or where it may lead to an unjust result. *Padilla-Padilla v. Gonzales,* 463 F.3d 972, 978 (9th Cir. 2006) [exhaustion as a prudential matter in a constitutional challenge to cancellation and a statutory challenge to reduction of VD was not appropriate because the record was developed, respondent did not deliberately bypass the administrative scheme and the agency could not correct its error as the time for a motion to reconsider had passed]; *Mohammad v. Slattery*, 842 F.Supp. 1553, 1557–58 (S.D.N.Y. 1994) [reversed denial of motion to reopen for asylum after *in absentia* order]; *Grant v. Zemski,* 54 F.Supp.2d 437, 441–42 (E.D. Pa. 1999) [where person detained on balance he should not be required to exhaust]. Where Congress has not clearly required exhaustion, it is left to the sound discretion of the court. *McCarthy v. Madigan,* 112 S.Ct. 1081, 1086 (1992) [*Bivens* action did not require exhaustion notwithstanding prison procedure for prompt resolution of complaints]; *Bangura v. Hansen,* 434 F.3d 487, 493–94 (6th Cir. 2006) [exhaustion was prudential where no statute or regulation required exhaustion and there were substantive due process claims that could not be exhausted administratively]. And "administrative remedies need not be pursued if the litigant's interests in immediate judicial review outweigh the government's interests in the efficiency or administrative autonomy that the exhaustion doctrine is designed to further." *Madigan, supra* at 1087. The decision is "intensely practical" and "attention is directed to both the nature of the claim presented and the characteristics of the particular administrative procedure provided." *Id.* The Supreme Court has recognized three broad set of circumstances in which the interests of the individual weigh heavily against requiring administrative exhaustion: (1) Where there is undue prejudice because there is an unreasonable or indefinite time frame for administrative action or the person will suffer irreparable harm even it is completed in a reasonable time; (2) Where there is some doubt as to the agency's empowerment to grant effective relief; or (3) Where the administrative body is biased or has otherwise predetermined the issue so that administrative review would be futile. *Madigan* at 1087–88.

No Exhaustion If Not Part of Removal Proceeding—Even if there is a requirement by statute that claims are exhausted, 8 U.S.C. §1252(d)(1), those claims may be confined solely to removal (formerly deportation or exclusion) matters and to matters concerning aliens and not nationals or citizens, and may not extend to habeas corpus proceedings. *Ali v. Ashcroft,* 346 F.3d 873, 877–78 (9th Cir. 2003) [statutory and prudential exhaustion unnecessary in habeas pattern and practice claim, unrelated to removal hearing, where habeas petitioners challenge whether government can remove person to a country, Somalia, that is unable to accept them]; *National Center for Immigrants Rights, Inc. v. INS*, 791 F.2d 1351 (9th Cir. 1986), *vacated on other grounds*, 481 U.S. 1009 (1987), *reaff'd*, 913 F.2d 1350 (9th Cir. 1990), *vacated on other grounds*, 502 U.S. 183 (1991) [inapplicable to bond conditions]; *Rowe v. INS,* 45 F.Supp.2d 144, 145–46 (D. Mass. 1999) [does not apply to challenge to bond]; *Morisath v. Smith*, 988 F.Supp. 1333 (W.D. Wash. 1997) [same].

No Exhaustion For Citizenship Claims—A nationality claim in removal proceedings need not be exhausted because the government has no power to deport citizens. *Minasyan v. Gonzales,* 401 F.3d 1069, 1074–75 (9th Cir. 2005) [citing *Rivera v. Ashcroft,* 394 F.3d 1129 (9th Cir. 2005)]. *See also Theagene v. Gonzales,* 411 F.3d 1107, 1110–12 (9th Cir. 2005) [a nationality claim in the circuit court under INA §242(b)(5) is not subject to the exhaustion requirement of INA §242(d)(1)]; *Rivera v. Ashcroft,* 394 F.3d 1129 (9th Cir. 2005) [a habeas action to establish a nonfrivolous claim of U.S. citizenship cannot be barred even if respondent failed to exhaust his remedies because the Fifth and Fourteenth amendments are implicated; *Taniguchi* distinguished as frivolous claim]; *Moussa v. INS,* 302 F.3d 823, 825 (8th Cir. 2002) [in challenge to BIA's reversal of IJ's determination that person was citizen through naturalization of his father, the court had jurisdiction to determine whether applicant was an alien in order to decide whether statutory exhaustion under §1252(d)(1) even applied]. *But see Theodoropoulos v. INS,* 358 F.3d 162, 167–74 (2d Cir. 2004) [the statutory exhaustion requirement under §1252(d)(1) bars habeas review even where petitioner claims futility]; *Duvall v. Elwood,* 336 F.3d 228 (3d Cir. 2003) [habeas review is barred under §1252(d)(1) where there was no final order of removal]; *Taniguchi v. Schultz,* 303 F.3d 950, 955–56 (9th Cir. 2002) [under INA §242(b)(5) a claim of U.S. nationality had to be brought in the circuit court and failure to exhaust administrative remedies barred claim in circuit court under INA §242(d)(1) where motion to reopen based upon citizenship claim was denied as untimely because it was filed beyond the 90-day period].

No Exhaustion Where BIA Raises the Issue *Sua Sponte*—Respondent has jurisdiction in federal court to challenge the denial of issues not raised by the applicant if the BIA considered them *sua sponte. Sidabutar v. Gonzales,* 503 F.3d 1116, 1119–23 (10th Cir. 2007) [because the BIA addressed the CAT issue regarding a Christian Indonesian *sua sponte*, the circuit court had jurisdiction even if the respondent failed to raise the issue before the BIA. The court rejected the eleventh circuit decision in *Amaya-Artunduaga* and agreed with the ninth circuit decision in *Socop-Gonzales*].

The predecessor to §1252(d)(1), §1105a(c), because it was co-extensive with §1105a(a), did not require exhaustion where the party was not attacking a final order of exclusion or deportation or where the court was enforcing its own order even if it had an effect on deportation proceedings. *U.S. v. Yacoubian*, 24 F.3d 1, 5–6 (9th Cir. 1994) [district court enjoined deportation hearing when it enforced JRAD]. Moreover, even 8 U.S.C. §1105a(c) did not impose an absolute, unwaivable limitation on judicial review. *Rafeedie v. INS*, 880 F.2d 506, 525 (D.C. Cir. 1989) (Ginsburg, R. J. concurring) [distinguishes *Weinberger v. Salfi*, 422 U.S. 749 (1975) in light of the subsequent decisions in *Mathews v. Eldridge*, 424 U.S. 319 (1976) and *Bowen v. City of New York*, 476 U.S. 467 (1986) in context of returning LPR who challenges the application to him of summary proceedings under INA §235(c)]. Further, 8 U.S.C. §1105a(c) could not be invoked where review did not and could not have taken place prior to current judicial proceeding. *Nakaranurack v. U.S.*, 68 F.3d 290, 293–94 (9th Cir. 1995) [habeas permitted where circuit court review was not sought because respondent never received BIA decision within 30-day period for appeal].

8. Other Exceptions to Exhaustion—The courts have also recognized many other exceptions to the exhaustion doctrine.

8.a. Exhaustion is not required where there would be manifest injustice in doing so. *Gill v. INS,* 420 F.3d 82, 87–88 (2d Cir. 2005) [it would be manifest injustice if the crime which went to the basis of respondent's deportation and was legally incoherent could not be reviewed given respondent's long history and ties in the U.S. and the fact that the issue was not apparent when the N.Y. statute was first challenged as not involving a CIMT]; *Marrero Pichardo v. Ashcroft,* 374 F.3d 46, 52–54 (2d Cir. 2004) [where respondent appeared *pro se* in removal proceedings, where he was a resident of long duration with strong ties to the U.S. and no ties abroad, where his claim refers to deportability and not a collateral matter because his DUI conviction is not an aggravated felony under the law in the Second Circuit, and where the government did not raise the issue of exhaustion until the court of appeal, it would be manifestly unjust to dismiss the habeas]. The Second Circuit, however, has overruled these cases in light of *Bowles v. Russell,* 127 S.Ct. 2360 (2007) finding that §1252(d)(1) is jurisdictional and may not be waived for manifest injustice. *Grullon v. Mukasey,* 409 F.3d 107, 114–16 (2d Cir. 2007) [in light of *Bowles* the court held there is no longer a manifest injustice exception].

8.b. Exhaustion is not required where "legal issues based on events that occur *after* briefing to the BIA has been completed." *Alcaraz v. INS,* 384 F.3d 1150, 1158–59 (9th Cir. 2004) [where the memos supporting respondent's claim regarding administrative closure and repapering of his case arose *after* BIA briefs were filed there was no exhaustion requirement]; Or where the issue had been raised and rejected by the BIA in the first appeal but not raised in subsequent appeals in the same case. *Miguel-Miguel v. Gonzales,* 500 F.3d 941, 944–45 (9th Cir. 2007) [there is no requirement that petitioners exhaust an argument before the BIA more than once].

8.c. Exhaustion may not be required where the issue raised is a pure question of law, including a challenge to the legality of a regulation. *Momin v. Gonzales,* 447 F.3d 447 (5th Cir. 2006) *vacated on other grounds* 462 F.3d 497 (5th Cir. 2006); *Huerta-Guevara v. Ashcroft,* 321 F.3d 883 (9th Cir. 2003) [*pro se* concession as to conviction did not prevent court from addressing legal issue of whether conviction was an aggravated felony, where there was no prejudice to the government].

8.d. Exhaustion is not required "where an agency's exercise of authority is clearly at odds with the specific language of the statute." *McClendon v. Jackson Television Inc.*, 603 F.2d 1174, 1177 (5th Cir. 1979);

8.e. A constitutional challenge to administrative action also does not require exhaustion. *Mathews,* 424 U.S. at 328–30; *Bosede v. Mukasey,* 512 F.3d 946, 950–51 (7th Cir. 2008) [where the IJ violated fundamental due process in not considering evidence, stated that petitioner might not have problems because he could bribe his way out of jail, and "applied whatever rationale he could muster to justify a predetermined outcome" exhaustion was not required];*Morgan v. Gonzales,* 495 F.3d 1084, 1089–90 (9th Cir. 2007) [substantive due process and equitable estoppel claims need not be exhausted where challenge was to unlawful removal because of government promise or reliance that he would not be deported]; *Colaianni v. INS,* 490 F.3d 185, 187 (2d Cir. 2007) [exhaustion not required for equal protection challenge regarding derivative citizenship because BIA lacked the authority to address it]; *Padilla-Padilla v. Gonzales,* 463 F.3d 972, 976–77 (9th Cir. 2006) [constitutional and international law challenges to 10 year and stop-time limitations on cancellation did not require exhaustion]; *Hadayat v. Gonzales,* 458 F.3d 659, 664–65 (7th Cir. 2006) [where respondent argued that NSEERS registration violated equal protection resulting in removal proceedings, the court noted this was the type of fundamental constitutional claim the BIA does not address]; *Geach v. Chertoff,* 444 F.3d 940, 945–46 (8th Cir. 2006) [equal protection challenge to denial of suspension to person granted advance parole is not subject to exhaustion because constitutional challenges unrelated to procedural errors need not be exhausted because BIA has no jurisdiction to adjudicate them]; *Bangura v. Hansen,* 434 F.3d 487, 493–94 (6th Cir. 2006) [substantive and procedural due process challenges to INA §204(c) barring the approval of a subsequent I-130 petition when the beneficiary previously engaged in marriage fraud]; *Singh v. Reno,* 182 F.3d 504, 511 (7th Cir. 1999) [due process challenge based on INS's failure to promptly put person in deportation proceedings thus subjecting him to removal]; *Anwar v. INS*, 116 F.3d 140, 144 n.4 (5th Cir. 1997) [where due process challenge to regulations regarding submission of briefs]; *Wang v. Reno*, 81 F.3d 808, 813–16 (9th Cir. 1996) [exhaustion not required to enjoin exclusion proceeding where due process claim does not implicate INA]; *Garberding v. INS*, 30 F.3d 1187, 1188 n.1 (9th Cir. 1994) [although a party may be required to exhaust a procedural due process claim that could be remedied by the IJ, an equal protection claim that the IJ/BIA cannot decide does not require exhaustion]; *Rafeedie v. INS*, 880 F.2d 506 (D.C. Cir. 1989) [constitutional challenge to INA §235(c)]; *Mandarino v. Ashcroft,* 318 F.Supp.2d 13, 16 (D. Conn. 2003) [constitutional retroactivity argument did not require exhaustion by appeal to BIA]; *Milosevic v. Ridge,* 301 F.Supp.2d 337 (M.D. Pa. 2003) [constitutional challenge to BIA policy of refusing to toll VD while motion to reopen is pending before it did not have to be presented to BIA]; *Ashley v. Ridge,* 288 F.Supp.2d 662, 666–67 (D.N.J. 2003) [need not exhaust administrative remedies where constitutionality of automatic-stay provision under 8 C.F.R. §1003.19(i)(2) cannot be addressed administratively before BIA]; *Hodel v. Aguirre,* 260 F.Supp.2d 695, 698–99 (N.D. Ill. 2003) [due process challenge to detention after deportation does not require exhaustion although court found no due process violation because person in detention less than 90 days]; *Kelly v. Farquharson,* 256 F.Supp.2d 93, 99–100 (D. Mass. 2003) [access to court claim in habeas did not have to be raised with IJ/BIA]; *Jankowski v. INS,* 138 F.Supp.2d 269, 273–76 (D. Conn. 2001) *rev'd on other grounds* 291 F.3d 172 (2d Cir. 2002) [equal protection challenge does not require exhaustion]; *Saba v. INS,* 52 F.Supp.2d 1117, 1124–25 (N.D. Cal. 1999) [exhaustion not required where pervasive ineffective assistance of counsel that cannot be corrected through agency and constitutes a due process violation]; *Ali v. INS*, 661 F.Supp. 1234 (D. Mass. 1986) [challenging constitutionality of marriage interview procedures];

8.f. A challenge to the agency's regulations that are binding on its officers and employees. *Momin v. Gonzales,* 447 F.3d 447 (5th Cir. 2006) *vacated on other grounds* 462 F.3d 497 (5th Cir. 2006) [challenge to the legality of arriving alien adjustment regulation which was not considered by the BIA was not waived as it was a pure issue of law and BIA followed the regulations in unpublished decisions]; *Espinoza-Gutierrez v. Smith*, 94 F.3d 1270, 1273 (9th Cir. 1996) *reh'g denied* 109 F.3d 551 (9th Cir. 1997) ["Exhaustion doctrine does not bar review of a question concerning the validity of an INS regulation because of conflict with a statute"].

8.g. Administrative remedies also need not be exhausted where they would be futile. *Arce-Vences v. Mukasey,* 512 F.3d 167, 172–72 (5th Cir. 2007) [where fifth circuit law was clearly binding on the BIA, no purpose would be served in raising the issue before the BIA]; *Gonzalez v. O'Connell,* 355 F.3d 1010, 1015–18 (7th Cir. 2004) [habeas petitioner did not have to exhaust constitutional challenge to mandatory detention even though the predicate for the challenge was an issue of statutory interpretation controlled by *Matter of Roldan* and therefore would be futile]; *Iddir v. INS,* 301 F.3d 492, 498 (7th Cir. 2002) [BIA had predetermined statutory issue]; *Pastor-Camarena v. Smith*, 977 F.Supp. 1415 (W.D. Wash. 1997) [no exhaustion necessary where BIA decided bond issue *en banc*]; *Selgeka v. Carroll,* 184 F.3d 337, 345 (4th Cir. 1999) [where BIA's position was clearly against right of stowaway to seek asylum before IJ the petitioner need not exhaust]; *American-Arab Anti-Discrimination Comm. v. Reno*, 70 F.3d 1045, 1058 (9th Cir. 1995) *rev'd on other grounds* 525 U.S. 471 (1999) [futile where agency does not have authority and where its position is fixed]; *Castillo-Villagra v. INS*, 972 F.2d 1017, 1024 (9th Cir. 1992) [where BIA unlikely to change its position prudential exhaustion through motion to reopen not required]; *Fuller v. INS,* 144 F.Supp.2d 72, 80–83 (D. Conn. 2000) [deported person under transition rules was not required to exhaust because BIA's position on retroactivity of §212(c) bar was clear]; *Grant v. Zemski,* 54 F.Supp.2d 437 (E.D. Pa. 1999) [exhaustion was futile where BIA had "predetermined" the issue]; *American Baptist Churches v. Meese*, 712 F.Supp. 756 (N.D. Cal. 1989) [allegations of low approval rates for Salvadorans and persecution that awaits plaintiffs were sufficient on futility grounds to withstand a motion to dismiss for failure to exhaust remedies]; *Full Gospel Portland Church v. Thornburgh*, 730 F.Supp. 441, 444–45 (D.D.C. 1988) [unreasonable delay on adjudication of 3d/ 6th preference]; *Beltre v. Kiley*, 470 F.Supp. 87 (S.D.N.Y. 1979); *Deldago v. INS*, 473

F.Supp. 1343 (S.D.N.Y. 1979); *Rhodes v. U.S.*, 574 F.2d 1179, 1181 (5th Cir. 1978). *But see Bowles v. Russell,* 127 S.Ct. 2360, 2366 (2007) [futility is not an exception to statutorily mandated exhaustion requirements]; *Booth v. Churner,* 532 U.S. 731, 741 n.6 (2001) [where Congress has provided for a statutory exhaustion process "we will not read futility or other exceptions into statutory exhaustion requirements"]; *Bah v. Mukasey,* 521 F.3d 857, 859–60 (8th Cir. 2008) [citing *Bowles v. Russell,* 127 S.Ct. 2360 (2007), and holding that petitioner's failure to exhaust appeal to AAO, even if futile, barred court's exercise of jurisdiction]; *Grullon v. Mukasey,* 409 F.3d 107, 112–14 (2d Cir. 2007) [reading *Booth* to require exhaustion before the BIA notwithstanding BIA's on-point precedent decision because the BIA has the authority to change its opinion in an *en banc* decision]; *Popal v. Gonzales,* 416 F.3d 249, 252 (3d Cir. 2005) [agreeing in *dicta* with *Theodoropoulas* that futility is not a exception to the statutory exhaustion requirement]; *Theodoropoulos v. INS,* 358 F.3d 162, 167–74 (2d Cir. 2004) [statutory exhaustion requirement under §1252(d)(1) bars habeas review even where petitioner claims futility in INA §212(c) challenge after *Matter of Soriano* on the ground that "futility–is simply not available when the exhaustion requirement is statutory"]; *Beharry v. Ashcroft,* 329 F.3d 51, 57–58 (2d Cir. 2003) [following *Booth* the Court determined that respondent was required to exhaust as a judicial matter (rather than as a statutory matter) administrative remedies before the IJ/BIA on the application of INA §212(h) under international law to an LPR with an aggravated felony conviction even if his chances of prevailing were remote and the IJ/ BIA were not empowered to interpret 212(h) in light of international law]; *Sundar v. INS,* 328 F.3d 1320 (11th Cir. 2003) *cert. denied* 124 S.Ct. 531 (2003) [finding that 8 U.S.C. §1252(d)(1) applies to §2241 habeas proceedings and dismissed petition for failure to seek BIA review even if there was perceived futility pre–*St. Cyr* for aggravated felon seeking INA §212(c) relief]; *Ramirez-Osorio v. INS*, 745 F.2d 937 (5th Cir. 1984).

8.h. Exhaustion is not required for estoppel claims—*Morgan v. Gonzales,* 495 F.3d 1084, 1089–90 (9th Cir. 2007) [substantive due process and equitable estoppel claims need not be exhausted where challenge was to unlawful removal because of government promise or reliance that he would not be deported]; *Chang v. U.S.,* 327 F.3d 911, 919–20, 922–24 (9th Cir. 2003) [where an IJ in removal proceedings could not address APA, estoppel and constitutional claims and where statutes now limit the scope of removal proceedings, plaintiffs did not have to exhaust removal proceeding to seek review of the retroactive application of administrative decisions to the investor's application].

8.i. Exhaustion is not required where there is a clear showing of irreparable harm. *Mathews v. Eldridge,* 424 U.S. 319, 330 (1975) [exhaustion not required where plaintiff raised colorable claim that because of physical condition and dependency upon the disability benefits, erroneous termination of disability benefits would damage plaintiff in a way not recompensable through retroactive payments]; *Kelly v. U.S. Postal Service*, 492 F.Supp. 121, 127 (S.D. Ohio 1980);

8.j. Where the agency failed to inform the applicant of the right to relief notwithstanding an obligation to do so. *U.S. v. Sosa,* 387 F.3d 131, 136–37 (2d Cir. 2004) [where *pro se* respondent was not informed of INA §212(c) relief the failure to exhaust "must be excused" where it arises from an invalid waiver of the right to administrative appeal because it was not knowingly and intelligently made]; *Asani v. INS,* 154 F.3d 719, 727–29 (7th Cir. 1998) [IJ violated regulation in failing to inform applicant of right to suspension]; *Kossov v. INS,* 132 F.3d 405 (7th Cir. 1998) [IJ failed to advise applicant of right to apply for withholding of deportation]; *Duran v. INS,* 756 F.2d 1338 (9th Cir. 1985) [IJ failed to inform applicant of suspension];

8.k. Where the law does not bind the agency to any definite time frame for administrative action. *Iddir v. INS,* 301 F.3d 492, 498–99 (7th Cir. 2002) [where INS acknowledged that it had no idea when, if ever, it would institute removal proceedings so that appellants could obtain review of their denied diversity visa applications it was not necessary to exhaust review in removal proceedings]; *Schaeuble v. Reno,* 87 F.Supp.2d 383, 389 (D.N.J. 2000) [plaintiff not required to exhaust Privacy Act claim to amend records where law does not require agency to make a final response within any period of time];

8.l. Where issue was fairly raised even if not precisely articulated in manner now argued before the federal court. *Restrepo v. McElroy,* 369 F.3d 627, 633 n.10 (2d Cir. 2004) [where retroactivity argument was based upon alternative theory and BIA considered retroactivity issue was fairly raised]; *Walcott v. Chertoff,* 517 F.3d 149, 153 (2d Cir. 2008) [followed *Restrepo* claiming that general challenge was sufficient]; *Moussa v. INS,* 302 F.3d 823, 825–26 (8th Cir. 2002) [where IJ ruled in favor of respondent on his derivative naturalization claim and BIA reversed, respondent's argument in the circuit court that his parents were not remarried under the INA definition of spouse and therefore were legal separated for purposes of derivative naturalization was not barred].

8.m. Where the issue was fairly raised but not on appeal but through a motion to reopen where the administrative agency (BIA) had the opportunity to review the issue. *U.S. v. Copeland,* 376 F.3d 61, 67 (2d Cir. 2004) [where respondent filed motion to reopen his deportation hearing instead of filing direct appeal, but then appealed the denial of the motion to reopen he exhausted his administrative remedies].

8.n. Where certain claims are "intimately intertwined" with other claims which need not be exhausted so "as to make the application of the exhaustion requirement improvident." *Haitian Refugee Center v. Civiletti*, 503 F.Supp. 442, 468 (S.D. Fla. 1980), *aff'd sub nom. Haitian Refugee Center v. Smith*, 676 F.2d 1023 (5th Cir. 1982);

8.o. Where the waiver of appeal was not knowingly, intelligently and voluntarily made. *Biwot v. Gonzales,* 403 F.3d 1094, 1097–98 (9th Cir. 2005) [where respondent denied counsel and because of it he labored under the impression that he had no choice but to waive BIA appeal, court retained jurisdiction on the denial of counsel claim]; *U.S. v. Sosa,* 387 F.3d 131, 136–37 (2d Cir. 2004) [where *pro se* respondent was not informed of INA §212(c) relief the failure to exhaust "must be excused" where it arises from an invalid waiver of the right to administrative appeal because it was not knowingly and intelligently made]; *Selgeka v. Carroll,* 184 F.3d 337, 345 (4th Cir. 1999) [applicant was represented by accredited representative who was law graduate but not lawyer and there is nothing in record indicating his knowledge of due process or failure to raise constitutional claim before agency].

9. *Pro Se* Applicants—Court will apply a more lenient standard in determining whether *pro se* applicants have sufficient exhausted their administrative remedies. Such claims are construed liberally. *Estelle v. Gamble,* 429 U.S. 97, 106 (1976); *Agyeman v. INS,* 296 F.3d 871, 877–78 (9th Cir. 2002)

10. Nonfinal Orders—The courts distinguish between exhaustion and nonfinal orders. Even where a party does not have to exhaust administrative remedies, his or her decision to do so prevents a federal court from reviewing the action until the agency makes a final decision. *M.A. v. Reno*, 114 F.3d 128 (9th Cir. 1997) [dismissed case because decision by agency is not final]. *But see Popal v. Gonzales,* 416 F.3d 249 (3d Cir. 2005) [a claim that has been fully and fairly litigated by the parties, before the IJ, and the BIA, has been exhausted for finality purposes].

11. Government Waiver—The government may waive an exhaustion argument by arguing the issue on the merits and waiting until oral argument to raise the claim. *Abdelqadar v. Gonzales,* 413 F.3d 668, 670–71 (7th Cir. 2005).

C. *Other Article III Questions*

1. In addition to exhaustion and statutory preclusion, an alien's efforts to seek review in the federal courts may be barred by constitutional and prudential Article III concerns. These concerns may be expressed as lack of subject-matter jurisdiction, lack of standing, ripeness, mootness, and the political question doctrine. These and other bars to judicial review must be addressed prior to addressing the merits of a party's claims. *Steel Co. v. Citizens for a Better Environment,* 523 U.S. 83, 93–95 (1998) [a court cannot hypothesize jurisdiction to reach the merits of the case but must first determine its jurisdiction].

2. Subject-Matter Jurisdiction

2.a. At least some courts have found that there is no subject-matter jurisdiction to review consular decisions. *Saavedra Bruno v. Albright,* 197 F.3d 1153 (D.C. Cir. 1999) [distinguished *Abourezk* and finding no review of decision to grant or to revoke a visa; noting that traditionally these were matters for diplomatic protest]; *Centeno v. Shultz*, 817 F.2d 1212 (5th Cir. 1987), *cert. denied*, 484 U.S. 1005 (1988) [no power to review consular denial of B visa]; *Li Hing of Hong Kong, Inc. v. Levin*, 800 F.2d 970 (9th Cir. 1986); *Ventura-Escamilla v. INS*, 647 F.2d 28 (9th Cir. 1981) [no power to substitute judgment where regulation valid and consul exercising discretion]; *Rivera de Gomez v. Kissinger*, 534 F.2d 518 (2d Cir. 1976), *cert. denied*, 429 U.S. 897 (1976); *Burrafato v. DOS*, 523 F.2d 554 (2d Cir. 1975), *cert. denied*, 424 U.S. 910 (1976) [no review even where DOS fails to follow own regs]; *El-Hadad v. U.S.*, 377 F.Supp.2d 42 (D.D.C. 2005) [no habeas or other jurisdiction to review denial of B-1/B-2 visa or advance parole to return to pursue litigation]; *Chun v. Powell,* 223 F.Supp.2d 204, 206–07 (D.D.C. 2002) [no jurisdiction to review by declaratory judgment whether consular officer has weighed all factors in denying on §214(b) grounds a B-2 visa to plaintiff's sister]; *Mansur v. Albright,* 130 F.Supp.2d 59 (D.D.C. 2001) [when the Deputy Assistant Secy. of State for Visa Services revokes a visa under 8 U.S.C. §1201(i), it is committed to agency discretion and is not reviewable]; *Ruston v. DOS,* 29 F.Supp.2d 518, 523 (E.D. Ark. 1998) [no review of revocation of visa by consular officer because notice of intent to revoke is not mandatory]; *Reznik v. DOJ, INS*, 901 F.Supp. 188, 191 (E.D. Pa. 1995) [no jurisdiction to review denial of waiver under §1157 for refugees]; *Encuentro Del Canto Popular v. Christopher*, 944 F.Supp. 805 (N.D. Cal. 1996); *Romero v. Consulate of the U.S. in Barranquilla, Colombia*, 860 F.Supp. 319 (E.D. Va. 1994) [no jurisdiction in denial of NIV on "reason to believe" ground]; *Shen v. U.S. Consulate General at Shanghai, China*, 866 F.Supp. 779 (S.D.N.Y. 1994) [no jurisdiction to force consulate to issue visas to persons subpoenaed]; *Garcia v. Baker*, 765 F.Supp. 426 (N.D. Ill. 1990); *Hermina-Sague v. U.S.*, 416 F.Supp. 217 (D.P.R. 1976); *Pena v. Kissinger*, 409 F.Supp. 1182 (S.D.N.Y. 1976) [where LPR spouse sought review of consular's denial of an IV for husband court affirmed on ground there is no jurisdiction]. This has also been characterized as a lack of standing. *Saavedra Bruno v. Albright,* 197 F.3d 1153, 1163–64 (D.C. Cir. 1999); *Adams v. Baker*, 909 F.2d 643, 647 n.3 (1st Cir. 1990).

There is jurisdiction, however, to review claims by USCs challenging visa denials. *Kleindienst v. Mandel*, 408 U.S. 753 (1972); *Adams v. Baker*, 909 F.2d 643, 647 n.3 (1st Cir. 1990); *Abourezk v. Reagan*, 785 F.2d 1043, 1051 n.6 (D.C. Cir. 1986), *aff'd per curiam by equally divided court*, 108 S.Ct. 252 (1987) [jurisdiction to review denial of visa]; *American Academy of Religion v. Chertoff,* 463 F.Supp.2d 400, 416–19 (S.D.N.Y. 2006) [First Amendment challenge by academic organizations to refusal/revocation of visa to Islamic scholar is not subject to consular nonreviewability because it involves a constitutional issue and the DHS and other agencies involved in security advisory opinions are involved in the decision-making process]. *See also Raduga USA Corp. v. DOS,* 440 F.Supp.2d 1140, 1149–52 (S.D. Cal. 2006) [allowed plaintiff to amend mandamus complaint to encompass review of consulate's bad faith denial of employee's IV after court ordered mandamus]. There is also jurisdiction to review revocation of visas, *Wong v. DOS*, 789 F.2d 1380, 1382 (9th Cir. 1986), whether or not the person challenging the revocation was in the U.S. *Shimizu v. DOS*, No. CV 89-2741-WMB [unpublished] (C.D. Cal. May 31, 1990). There is also mandamus jurisdiction to compel a consular officer to make a decision on a visa application. *Patel v. Reno*, 134 F.3d 929 (9th Cir. 1997); *American Academy of Religion v. Chertoff,* 463 F.Supp.2d 400, 420–22 (S.D.N.Y. 2006) [mandamus available to obtain decision on B visa for Islamic scholar in light of section 6 of the APA, 5 U.S.C. §555(b), and 21 C.F.R. §§41.106, 41.121 requiring prompt adjudication of visas]. However, the Secretary of State or consular officer's decision to revoke an immigrant visa or NIV under INA §221(i) is not reviewable in habeas, mandamus, or All Writs Act except the decision may be reviewed in the context of a removal proceeding and only then if the revocation provides the sole ground for removal under INA §237(a)(1)(B). *Bolante v. Achim,* 457 F.Supp.2d 896 (E.D. Wis. 2006) [no habeas jurisdiction to review claim that revocation was improper under 22 C.F.R. §41.122(a)].

2.b. Extending this doctrine, the Eleventh Circuit has found that there is no subject-matter jurisdiction to review the use of improper procedures to screen Haitian refugees under the U.S. government interdiction program when acts occur outside the physical territory of the U.S. *Haitian Refugee Center, Inc. v. Baker*, 953 F.2d 1498 (11th Cir.), *cert. denied*, 502 U.S. 1112, 112 S.Ct. 1245 (1992). They have also determined that neither the constitution nor the INA extend to refugees on Guantanamo. *Cuban American Bar Ass'n, Inc. v. Christopher*, 43 F.3d 1412 (11th Cir. 1995), *cert. denied,* 515 U.S. 1145 (1995). The Supreme Court has determined that former INA §243(h) and the U.N. Convention Relating to the Status of Refugees do not apply outside the physical territory of the U.S. in regard to the U.S. interdiction program. *Sale v. Haitian Centers Council, Inc.*, 509 U.S. 155 (1993). The doctrine of consular nonreviewability has been extended to a decision by an INS officers abroad to deny a refugee waiver. *Doan v. INS,* 160 F.3d 508 (8th Cir. 1998). *See also* Legal Opinion, Virtue, G.C. to Meissner, Comm. (HQCOU 90/15) (Sept. 1, 1998), *reprinted in* 76 No. 13 *Interpreter Releases* 529, 536–45 (Apr. 2, 1999) [finding INS had no authority to operate Guantanamo because it was outside U.S.].

2.c. The Supreme Court's decision in *Rasul v. Bush,* 542 U.S. 466 (2004) may have dramatically altered these doctrines. In *Rasul,* the Court found that there was habeas jurisdiction to review the physical custody of aliens being held at the military base in Guantanamo, Cuba. The Court distinguished *Johnson v. Eisentrager,* found that habeas applies extraterritorially to aliens, that aliens like U.S. citizens can invoke federal court authority, and that the presence of the detainee in the territorial jurisdiction of a federal court is not a jurisdictional requirement for habeas as long as there is jurisdiction over the custodian. The Court also found that jurisdiction existed under 28 U.S.C. §1331 (General Federal Question jurisdiction) and §1350 (Alien Tort Claims Act) for aliens outside the U.S. and noted that: "[t]he courts of the United States have traditionally been open to nonresident aliens." *Rasul,* 124 S.Ct. at 2698–99. *See also Abu Ali v. Ashcroft,* 350 F.Supp.2d 28, 39–57 (D.D.C. 2004) [denied motion to dismiss habeas petition brought by a USC being held in Saudi Arabia at the direction of the U.S.].

2.d. Federal courts, however, have jurisdiction to review the validity of INS or DOS regulations or Operations Instructions. *McNary v. Haitian Refugee Center, Inc.*, 498 U.S. 479, 491–94 (1991) [jurisdiction to review action alleging a pattern and practice of procedural violations in the administration of the SAW program]; *Mulligan v. Schultz*, 848 F.2d 655 (5th Cir. 1988) [review of decision of DOS to designate certain dates to accept NP-5 applications]; *International Union of Bricklayers & Allied Craftsman v. Meese*, 761 F.2d 798 (D.C. Cir. 1985) [court has subject-matter jurisdiction over INS O.I. that provides for issuance of B-1]; *North American Industries Inc. v. Feldman*, 722 F.2d 893 (lst Cir. 1983) [federal court may review INS O.I. to determine whether it is consistent with Act]; *Rahim v. McNary*, 827 F.Supp. 224, 228–29 (S.D.N.Y. 1993), *aff'd*, 24 F.3d 440 (2d Cir. 1994) [court had subject-matter jurisdiction to review validity of SAW regulations]; *Friedberger v. Schultz*, 616 F.Supp. 1315 (D.C. Pa. 1985) [fiancé(e) had right to challenge regulation of Secy. of State resulting in denial of K visa because of INA §212(e)]. The same courts, however, may have no authority to enforce operations instructions. *Romeiro De Silva v. Smith*, 773 F.2d 1021 (9th Cir. 1985) [O.I. in regard to deferred action, O.I. §103.1(a)(1)(ii), does not give rise to action, because it does not confer substantive benefit]. *Compare Pasquini v. Morris*, 700 F.2d 658 (11th Cir. 1983) [confers no substantive right, but a procedural right to be considered]; *Zhang v. Slattery*, 840 F.Supp. 292 (S.D.N.Y. 1994). There is also no subject-matter jurisdiction to enforce an INS discretionary policy. *Maldonado-Coronel v. McElroy*, 943 F.Supp. 376 (S.D.N.Y. 1996) [INS decision not to expedite child's case when he became 21].

3. Standing

3.a. To obtain standing a party must show: (1) that it has actual injury or will suffer actual injury as a result of defendant's actions; (2) that the injury "fairly can be traced to the challenged actions; and (3) "is likely to be redressed by a favorable decision." *Valley Forge Christian College v. Americans United for Separation of Church and State, Inc.*, 454 U.S. 464, 472 (1982); *Presbyterian Church (USA) v. U.S.*, 870 F.2d 518, 521 (9th Cir. 1989); *see also Clarke v. Securities Industry Assoc.*, 479 U.S. 388, 396 (1987); *Coleman v. U.S.,* 454 F.Supp.2d 757, 762–65 (N.D. Ill. 2006) [USC son who brought action enjoining mom's removal had an injury-in-fact because he is forced to self-deport or remain without his mother]. In addition to these constitutional criteria, there are prudential considerations governing standing. *Etuk v. Slattery*, 936 F.2d 1433, 1440–41 (2d Cir. 1991) [LPRs denied temporary proof of employment authorization had standing]. These include the need for plaintiff to assert his own rights and that generalized grievances affecting a large population may not warrant standing. *Id.* Prudential standing also requires that the interest sought to be protected by the complainant must be "arguably within the zone of interests to be protected or regulated by the statute...in question." *National Credit Union Administration v. First National Bank and Trust Co.*, 118 S.Ct. 927, 933 (1998) [quoting *Data Processing*]. This requirement cannot be interpreted to require the would-be plaintiff to prove the statute was passed for his benefit. *Id.* at 935.

3.b. Where the party initiating litigation has no injury in fact or fails to meet the traceability or redressability criteria, it has no standing and the case will be dismissed. *Valley Forge Christian College, supra*; *Garcia-Echaverria v. U.S.,* 376 F.3d 507, 514–15 (6th Cir. 2004) [no standing to raise equal protection challenge regarding §212(h) waiver where respondent would have been ineligible for §212(h) in any event because he possesses more than 30 grams of marijuana]; *Hosein v. Gonzales,* 452 F.3d 401 (5th Cir. 2006) [parent who sought an injunction to obtain a *nunc pro tunc* order for an earlier naturalization date to benefit her son through derivative naturalization had no injury and therefore no standing]; *NAACP v. U.S. Sugar*, 84 F.3d 1432, 1438 (D.C. Cir. 1996) [no standing where DOL cannot get growers to redress past foreign workers certification errors]; *Lozano v. City of Hazleton,* 496 F.Supp.2d 477, 490–92 (M.D. Pa. 2007) [although plaintiff business owner was injured by illegal ordinances, the closure of the business defeats standing because the injury can no longer be redressed]; *Arden Wood, Inc. v. USCIS,* 480 F.Supp.2d 141, 148 (D.D.C. 2007) [neither petitioner, nor beneficiary had standing once I-360 petition was approved]; *Movimiento Democracia, Inc. v. Chertoff,* 417 F.Supp. 2d 1350 (S.D. Fla. 2006) [neither relatives of repatriated Cubans nor associations had standing to represent repatriated Cubans challenging government "wet-foot/dry-foot" policy]; *Hanif v. Gantner* 369 F.Supp.2d 502, 505–07 (S.D.N.Y. 2005) [no standing to bring §1331 action requesting injunction to adjudicate adjustment of status application before executing 12 year-old deportation order because respondent failed to demonstrate action within zone-of-interest of INA]; *Sadowski v. Bush,* 293 F.Supp.2d 15, 18–19 (D.D.C. 2003) [relative of persons who died in September 11 attack had no standing to sue Bush and others for failing to properly enforce the immigration laws]; *Panas v. Reno,* 114 F.Supp.2d 283, 286–88 (S.D.N.Y. 2000) [where Polish citizens bring due process challenge to regulation favoring Guatemalans and Salvadorans in granting special cancellation presumption, they lack standing because their alleged injury before having a removal hearing is not concrete, actual or imminent]; *Garcia v. Yeutter*, 756 F.Supp. 581 (D.D.C. 1990) [Farmworkers and AFL/CIO lacked standing to challenge RAW regulations and determinations because they had no injury]; *Lopez v. Garriga*, 917 F.2d 63 (1st Cir. 1990) [where plaintiff lost on his damages claim before a jury he had no standing to continue to seek injunctive relief]; *FAIR v. Reno*, 93 F.3d 897 (D.C. Cir. 1996) [FAIR's members' claimed injuries of school overcrowding and other associated problems are not traceable to US-Cuba migratory agreement]; *U.S. v. Richard Dattner Architects*, 972 F.Supp. 738, 742–47 (S.D.N.Y. 1997) [USC has no standing to assert claim that employer made false LC and deprived him of position]; *Garrison v. OCK Construction Ltd.*, 864 F.Supp. 134 (D. Guam 1993) [where prospective employee sued, case dismissed because H-2 had not yet been granted to third party]; *Association of Immigration Attorneys v. INS*, 675 F.Supp. 781 (S.D.N.Y. 1987) [attorneys' group lacks standing to challenge change in I-130 form]; *FAIR v. Meese*, 643 F.Supp. 983 (S.D. Fla. 1986) [FAIR lacked injury and not within zone of interest to challenge Cuban-Refugee Adjustment Act]. Similarly, where a person or organization does not fall within the zone of interest the statute was designed to protect s/he or it lacks standing. *INS v. Legalization Project of Los Angeles*, 114 S.Ct. 422 (1993) (O'Connor, J.) [granting stay application]; *Ayuda, Inc. v. Reno*, 7 F.3d 246, 250 (D.C. Cir. 1993) *reh'g denied,* 14 F.3d 61 (D.C. Cir. 1994), *cert. denied,* 513 U.S. 815 (1994); *Giddings v. Chandler*, 979 F.2d 1104 (5th Cir. 1992). *See generally Clarke v. Securities Industry Assoc.*, 479 U.S. 388, 396 (1987). *But see F.L. v. Thompson,* 293 F.Supp.2d 86, 92 (D.D.C. 2003) [plaintiff trying to obtain decision that federal government will grant him court dependency rights had standing to sue].

Union Standing. Unions have standing to assert claims of members where challenging an INS Operations Instruction that affects its members, *International Union of Bricklayers & Allied Craftsmen v. Meese*, 761 F.2d 798 (D.C. Cir. 1985), or challenging INS practice, *Hotel & Restaurant Emp. Union v. Attorney General*, 804 F.2d 1256 (D.C. Cir. 1986), *vacated*, 808 F.2d 847 (D.C. Cir. 1987), or challenging INS policy. *American Federation of Labor v. Chertoff,* Case No. C 07-04472 CRB (N.D. Cal. Oct. 10, 2007), 2007 WL 2972952 [plaintiffs Unions and employer organizations had standing to challenge publication of DHS "no-match" regulations]; *ILWU v. Meese*, 891 F.2d 1374 (9th Cir. 1989); *Comite De Apoyo Para Los Trabajadores Agricolas (CATA) v. Dole*, 731 F.Supp. 541, 543–44 (D.D.C. 1990). Similarly, churches have standing to contest INS actions violating their First Amendment rights, *Presbyterian Church (USA) v. U.S.*, 870 F.2d 518 (9th Cir. 1989) [injunction sought to stop INS undercover investigation concerning sanctuary movement].

Other Organizational Standing. Organizational standing in other contexts is also recognized. *Havens Realty Corp. v. Coleman*, 455 U.S. 363 (1982) [organization that gave counseling to low and moderate income home seekers had standing to challenge discriminatory housing policies]; *League of United Latin American Citizens (LULAC) v. Bredesen,* 500 F.3d 523, 527–30 (6th Cir. 2007) [LULAC had standing to represent its members in challenge to Tennessee law regarding vehicular licenses and the named plaintiffs were members of LULAC]; *California Rural Legal Asst. v. Legal Services*, 917 F.2d 1171, 1174–75 (9th Cir. 1990) [challenge to legal services regulation]; *Lozano v. City of Hazleton,* 496 F.Supp.2d 477, 491–96 (M.D. Pa. 2007) [business owners and Hispanic business organization had standing to challenge local ordinance regarding employment and tenancy of undocumented]. *See generally National Credit Union Administration v. First National Bank & Trust Co.,* 118 S.Ct. 927, 933–38 (1998); I*nternational Union UAW v. Brock*, 477 U.S. 274, 288–90 (1986). *But see Air Transport Ass'n of America v. Reno*, 80 F.3d 477, 483–84 (D.C. Cir. 1996) [air transport association had standing to bring injunctive relief but not damages for its members]; *Arizona Contractors Ass'n Inc. v. Napolitano,* 526 F.Supp.2d 968 (D. Ariz. 2007) [plaintiff organizations had no standing to challenge the Legal Arizona Workers Act, Ariz. Rev. Stat. §§23-211 to 214, that ties licensing of business to authorized employment because no plaintiff is employing unauthorized persons, there is no imminent threat of enforcement, and the wrong defendants were sued because only country attorneys can enforce the law]; *Parinejad v. ICE,* 501 F.Supp.2d 280 (D. Mass. 2007) [Political Asylum/Immigration Representation Project and Catholic Legal Immigration Network, Inc. did not have standing in *habeas* where individual petitioners' cases were moot and no showing that third party representation was required]; *INS v. Legalization Assistance Project of Los Angeles, supra*; *AILA v. Reno,* 18 F.Supp.2d 38, 47–52 (D.D.C. 1998) [organizational plaintiffs alleging loss of clients and diversion of resources lacked standing to challenge expedited removal regulations because such claims were speculative].

3.c. Standing exists where there is a threatened injury. *Loa-Herrera v. Trominski,* 231 F.3d 984, 987–88 (5th Cir. 2000) [policy of seizing green cards and providing temporary documents results in sufficient injury because "green cards play a significant role in the day-to-day lives of LPRs"]; *Equal Access Education v. Merten,* 305 F.Supp.2d 585, 594–600 (E.D. Va. 2004) [students who were challenging Virginia's policy of denying admission to undocumented aliens seeking to enroll in post-secondary institutions had standing because they have applied to the institutions].

3.d. Statutory Standing. Where Congress enacts statutes creating legal rights, the invasion of those rights creates standing even though no injury would exist without the statute. *Linda R.S. v. Richard D.,* 410 U.S. 614, 617 n.3 (1973); *Warth v. Seldin,* 422 U.S. 490, 514 (1975); *Zivotofsky ex rel. Ari Z v. Secretary of State,* 444 F.3d 614, 617–19 (D.C. Cir. 2006) [three-year-old child born in Jerusalem who is seeking to enforce section 214(d) of the Foreign Relations Authorization Act, Fiscal Year 2003, PL 107-228, 116 Stat. 1350, 1365–66 (2002), which mandates that, upon request, the Secretary of State "shall" register the child's birth as Israel if born in Jerusalem had "statutory" standing because his individual right was violated when the Secretary refused to designate Israel on his U.S. passport].

3.e. In injunction cases plaintiffs have the additional burden of showing they will be subject to recurring violations of statutory or constitutional rights to have standing to obtain prospective injunctive relief *City of Los Angeles v. Lyons*, 461 U.S. 95 (1983). *But see Hodgers-Durgin v. De La Vina,* 199 F.3d 1037 (9th Cir. 1999) (en banc) [found there was Article III standing for Hispanic motorists challenging police practices but denying equitable relief on grounds that there was no showing of immediate irreparable harm]; *Hernandez v. Cremer*, 913 F.2d 230, 233–35 (5th Cir. 1990) [distinguishing *City of Los Angeles v. Lyons*, 461 U.S. 95 (1983)]; *Presbyterian Church*, 870 F.2d at 523; *LaDuke v. Nelson*, 762 F.2d 1318, 1323 (9th Cir. 1985); *Nicacio v. INS*, 797 F.2d 700 (9th Cir. 1985) [*Lyons* distinguished]; *American Federation of Labor v. Chertoff,* Case No. C 07-04472 CRB (N.D. Cal. Oct. 10, 2007), 2007 WL

2972952 [employer organization had standing to seek to enjoin effect of DHS's no-match regulations because under *Lyons* it is clear that the harm will be recurring]. In addition, "injunctions against the INS have focused ... upon the important role of the federal courts in constraining misconduct by federal agents" and the prudential limitations circumscribing federal court intervention in state law enforcement matters involved in *Lyons* is inapplicable to oversight of federal actions. *Orantes-Hernandez v. Thornburgh*, 919 F.2d 549, 558 (9th Cir. 1990). And the courts may also vacate or modify injunctive relief when appropriate. *Orantes-Hernandez v. Gonzales,* 504 F.Supp.2d 825 (C.D. Cal. 2007) [modified original injunction in *Orantes-Hernandez* by eliminating paragraphs 10 (administrative segregation) and12 (legal presentations) of the injunction].

3.f. Petitioners seeking immigrant visas for beneficiaries outside the U.S. have standing. *Patel v. Reno*, 134 F.3d 929, 932 n.1 (9th Cir. 1997) [mandamus petition granted to compel decision on I-130]; *Academy of Religion v. Chertoff,* 463 F.Supp.2d 400, 411–13 (S.D.N.Y. 2006) [First Amendment challenge by academic organizations to refusal/revocation of visa to Islamic scholar is justiciable because organizations have standing in their own right to assert First Amendment claims]; *Legal Assistance for Vietnamese Asylum Seekers v. DOS*, 45 F.3d 469, 475 (D.C. Cir. 1995), *remanded on other grounds*, 117 S.Ct. 318 (1996) [standing where DOS conduct prolongs the separation of petitioners from their immediate family members outside the U.S.]; *Raduga USA Corp. v. DOS,* 440 F.Supp.2d 1140, 1143–48 (S.D. Cal. 2005) [employer had standing to bring mandamus action due to its own injury to compel consular officer to make a decision on employee's IV over government's objection that once the I-140 was approved the employer had no further interest]; *Chau v. DOS*, 891 F.Supp. 650 (D.D.C. 1995) [same]. *But see Saavedra Bruno v. Albright,* 197 F.3d 1153 (D.C. Cir. 1999) [U.S. company that submitted subsequently approved L-1 petition has no standing in regard to beneficiary's denial of the visa by consular officer];

Person claiming derivative citizenship has standing. *Miller v. Albright,* 118 S.Ct. 1428 (1998) [standing found in some opinions of the Justices even where transmitting parent did not petition]; *Breyer v. Meissner,* 214 F.3d 416, 423–26 (3d Cir. 2000) [beneficiary of derivative citizenship claim had standing to assert mother's claim of discriminatory transmission of citizenship solely by fathers]; *U.S. v. Ahumada-Aguilar,* 189 F.3d 1121, 1126 (9th Cir. 1999) *judgment vacated on other grounds* 533 U.S. 913 (2001) [third party standing by beneficiary son where father deceased]. Persons subject to denaturalization having standing to make facial challenge to AG's authority without awaiting procedures.

Beneficiaries of immigrant visa petitions may also have standing. *Abboud v. INS*, 140 F.3d 843, 847 (9th Cir. 1998); *Ghaly v. INS*, 58 F.3d 1425, 1434 n.6 (9th Cir. 1995) [beneficiary had standing to contest revocation of visa petition]; *Lockhart v. Chertoff,* Case No. 1:07CV823 (N.D. Ohio Jan. 7, 2008), 2008 WL 80225 [spouse of deceased husband seeking validity of I-130 although no married for two years had standing]; *Oddo v. Reno,* 17 F.Supp.2d 529, 531 (E.D. Va. 1998) [same]; *Sanchez-Trujillo v. INS*, 620 F.Supp. 1361 (W.D.N.C. 1985) [beneficiary of 2d preference petition had standing to sue for approval of deceased father's petition]; *Taneja v. Smith*, 795 F.2d 355 (4th Cir. 1986) [beneficiary of 6th preference petition has standing]. *But see* 8 C.F.R. §§103.2(a)(3), 103.3(a)(1)(iii)(B) [a beneficiary of a petition is not a recognized party in such a proceeding and does not have standing]; *Blacher v. Ridge,* 436 F.Supp.2d 602, 606 n.3 (S.D.N.Y. 2006) [beneficiary of H-1B petition did not have standing to challenge denial]; *Chun v. Powell,* 223 F.Supp.2d 204, 207–08 (D.D.C. 2002) [person denied B-2 visa abroad or brother of person denied do not have standing].

Beneficiaries of labor certifications also have standing. *De Jesus Ramirez v. Reich,* 156 F.3d 1273, 1276 (D.C. Cir. 1998). [where beneficiaries of LCs sued DOL they had standing; however, case was dismissed because employer never pursued BALCA or federal court and was an indispensable party to LC process];

3.g. For questions concerning congressional and state standing in the immigration context. *See Chiles v. Thornburgh*, 865 F.2d 1197, 1205–11 (11th Cir. 1988).

3.h. The doctrine of *jus tertii* (third party standing) may be invoked to permit any party to represent the interests of others. *Craig v. Boren*, 429 U.S. 190 (1976) [holder of liquor license asserts rights of males ages 18-20 to drink beer]; *Singleton v. Wulff,* 428 U.S. 106 (1976) [doctor sought injunction on behalf of pregnant women of Missouri statute denying Medicaid benefits to persons seeking abortion]. *See also Powers v. Ohio,* 499 U.S. 400, 410–11 (1990) [requiring a showing of potential injury in fact, a close relationship, and "some hindrance to the third party's ability to protect his or her own interest"]. In order to assert third party standing, the plaintiff must also have an injury, *Craig, supra*, or the third party must be incapable of asserting a claim because of mootness or fear of protecting interest. *Singleton, supra.* If it is based on organizational standing, the organization must demonstrate standing of the persons it seeks to represent or at least that there are obstacles that prevent those persons from asserting their own right. *Equal Access Education v. Merten,* 305 F.Supp.2d 585, 599–600 (E.D. Va. 2004) [following *Warth* and *Hunt* standards educational organization had standing to represent undocumented students seeking admission into post-secondary schools where Virginia's policy was to bar undocumented persons]; *Capital Area Immigrants' Rights Coalition v. DOJ,* 264 F.Supp.2d 14, 20–22 (D.D.C. 2003) [applying the standard in *Hunt v. Washington State Apple Advertising Comm'n,* 432 U.S. 333 (1977) and determining that organization had standing to file APA challenge to BIA streamlining regulations because: (1) its members had standing in their own right; (2) the interests it seeks to protect are germane to the organization's purpose; and (3) neither the claim asserted nor the relief requested requires the participation of individual members in the lawsuit]; *AILA v. Reno*, 199 F.3d 1352, 1357–64 (D.C. Cir. 2000) [finding no organizational standing on prudential grounds where individuals did not have obstacles preventing them from challenging summary removal]. A parent has the right to assert constitutional and international law claims that his removal will affect his U.S. citizen child. *Payne-Barahona v. Gonzales,* 474 F.3d 1 (1st Cir. 2006) [parent had *jus tertii* standing but denied claims on the merits]. Similarly, children denied citizenship had standing to assert equal protection claim of their mothers who were denied the right to transmit citizenship under pre-1934 statute. *Breyer v. Meissner,* 214 F.3d 416, 423–26 (3d Cir. 2000) [beneficiary of derivative citizenship claim had standing to assert mother's claim of discriminatory transmission of citizenship solely by fathers]; *Wauchope v. DOS*, 985 F.2d 1407, 1410–11 (9th Cir. 1993). Where lawyers association had no injury of its own and its clients were not deterred from complaining about revised I-130 form, third party standing could not be invoked. *Association of Immigration Attorneys v. INS*, 675 F.Supp. 781 (S.D.N.Y. 1987). And where injury to association members was too speculative, there was no associational standing. *AILA v. Reno,* 199 F.3d 1352, 1356–57 (D.C. Cir. 2000) [upholding district court determination on prudential grounds that injury to association's members whose clients might be injured by summary removal was too speculative]; *Movimiento Democracia, Inc. v. Chertoff,* 417 F.Supp.2d 1350 (S.D. Fla. 2006) [neither relatives of repatriated Cubans nor associations had third party standing to represent repatriated Cubans challenging government "wet-foot/dry-foot" policy]. Similarly, where associational standing is sought to initiate a broad policy attack on an agency, the claim is not justiciable. *Arden Wood, Inc. v. USCIS,* 480 F.Supp.2d 141, 147–50 (D.D.C. 2007) [case dismissed for lack of associational standing where Christian Science nursing association sought to challenge the policies and procedures of USCIS in regard to I-360 petitions].

Where the participation of individual members of an association is required in the litigation (*e.g.,* to prove damages) the association's *jus tertii* claim must be dismissed. *American Baptist Churches v. Meese*, 712 F.Supp. 756 (N.D. Cal. 1989) [association dismissed where individual members are needed to prove claims of persecution].

In habeas petitions third party standing may exist where party acts as "next friend." *Lenhard v. Wolff,* 443 U.S. 1306 (1979) [stay of execution granted where petition brought by public defenders and not defendant]. *But see Coalition of Clergy, Lawyers & Professors v. Bush,* 310 F.3d 1153 (9th Cir. 2002), *cert. denied,* 123 S.Ct. 2073 (2003) [persons bringing the action as a coalition did not have the right as "next friends" to invoke the writ of habeas corpus on behalf of Taliban incarcerated at Guantanamo]; *Parinejad v. ICE,* 501 F.Supp.2d 280 (D. Mass. 2007) [Political Asylum/Immigration Representation Project and Catholic Legal Immigration Network, Inc. did not have standing in *habeas* where individual petitioners' cases were moot and no showing that third party representation was required].

4. Ripeness

4.a. A person's claims may also be dismissed where the court determines they are not yet ripe for review. A case may be declared unripe because there is no jurisdiction under the Constitution unless there is a case or controversy; Or it may be declared unripe as a matter of judicial prudence. *Reno v. Catholic Social Services*, 509 U.S. 43, 57 n.18 (1993) [where promulgated regulations under the amnesty program that are challenged impose no penalty but rather limit access to a benefit, the appellants' challenge was not ripe because there were several grounds other than the regulation which the applicants had to prove in the review process before obtaining the benefit]; *Davis v. U.S.,* 499 F.3d 590 (6th Cir. 2007) [court dismissed declaratory judgment action by legally separated U.S. husband to determine amount owed to wife and step-sons under I-864 after wife obtained support ruling in state court because it was not ripe as to step-sons, there was no standing as to USCIS, and no subject-matter jurisdiction]; *Hoxha v. Levi,* 465 F.3d 554, 563–65 (3d Cir. 2006) [decision on whether a party subject to extradition may not be returned to his country if he would be tortured was not ripe for review; although the magistrate ordered extradition the Secy. of State must make that decision under CAT independent of the extradition proceeding]; *Simmonds v. INS,* 326 F.3d 351, 356–61 (2d Cir. 2003) [person with final order who is serving indefinite state sentence does not have ripe claim at the moment as a matter of judicial prudence; must wait until he is closer in time to his release to immigration authorities]; *Aparicio v. Blakeway,* 302 F.3d 437 (5th Cir. 2002) [challenge to INS reliance upon SAW confidential information in denying naturalization was not ripe]; *Naranjo-Aguilera v. INS*, 30 F.3d 1106 (9th Cir. 1994) [same]; *Ayuda, Inc. v. Reno*, 7 F.3d 246 (D.C. Cir. 1993) *reh'g denied*, 14 F.3d 61 (D.C. Cir. 1994), *cert. denied,* 513 U.S. 815 (1994) [same]; *Air Espana v. Brien,* 165 F.3d 148, 151–53 (2d Cir. 1999) [claims by airlines that regulation requiring fines even where INS gave waivers is not ripe because airlines did not obtain "final agency action" by the BIA]; *American-Arab Anti-Discrimination Comm. v. Reno*, 70 F.3d 1045, 1057, 1060–62 (9th Cir. 1995) *rev'd on other grounds* 119 S.Ct. 936 (1999) [where agency proceeding insufficient to address selective enforcement prudential ripeness exists and question not at issue]; *Perales v. Reno*, 48 F.3d 1305, 1312–13 (2d Cir. 1995) [challenge to INS dissemination of unlawful regulations not ripe because it is pre-enforcement challenge]; *American-Arab Anti Discrimination Comm. v. Nelson*, 940 F.2d 445, 453–54 (9th Cir. 1991) [challenge to INS statute that may be applied to supporters of the PFLP is not ripe]; *Randall v. Meese*, 854 F.2d 472 (D.C. Cir. 1988) [review of DD decision to deny adjustment not ripe where IJ denied adjustment and case can be reviewed in circuit court after BIA decision]; *Ali v. Barlow,* 446 F.Supp.2d 604, 609–10 (E.D. Va. 2006) [where respondent has not been in custody for six months subsequent to final order, his *Zadvydas* claim for release is not yet ripe]; *Lemeshko v. Wrona,* 325 F.Supp.2d 778, 786 (E.D Mich. 2004) [claim that legacy INS will detain person with final order indefinitely is not ripe while person is still in state custody serving sentence]; *Panas v. Reno,* 114 F.Supp.2d 283, 286–88 (S.D.N.Y. 2000) [where Polish citizens bring due process challenge to regulation favoring Guatemalans and Salvadorans in granting special cancellation presumption, the challenge was not ripe because plaintiffs had not yet had their removal hearings]; *Transport Robert (1973) Ltée v. INS*, 940 F.Supp. 338 (D.D.C. 1996) [letter from Assoc. Comm. is not final action]; *National Ass'n of Manufacturers v. DOL*, 1996 WL 420868 (D.D.C. July 22, 1996) [found certain pre-enforcement challenges to DOL H-1B attestation regulations not ripe]; *Wang v. Reno*, 862 F.Supp. 801, 810–11 (E.D.N.Y. 1994) [following *Catholic Social Services* and finding limiting access to a benefit (asylum) is not sufficient harm to establish ripeness]; *Roshan v. Smith*, 615 F.Supp. 901 (D.D.C. 1985) [no imminent injury where no showing that government has as yet affirmatively interfered in the attorney-client relationship when it built the Oakdale facility]; *Louis v. Meissner*, 532 F.Supp. 881 (S.D. Fla. 1982) [denial of counsel was not a ripe issue].

4.b. Cases Where Ripeness Found—*Quezada-Luna v. Gonzales,* 439 F.3d 403 (7th Cir. 2006) [where petitioner conceded removability for a firearms offense but disputed that the offense was a crime of violence, the case was ripe because resolution would determine the length of petitioner's future inadmissibility]; *Chang v. U.S.,* 327 F.3d 911, 921–22 (9th Cir. 2003) [relying on Justice O'Connor's "firm prediction rule" in her concurring opinion in *CSS,* 509 U.S. at 69 the Court found that an investor's claim that his I-829 conditional residence petition would be denied rendered the case ripe and there was no need to wait for INS's denial];

Immigrant Assistance Project of the Los Angeles County Federation of Labor (AFL-CIO) v. INS, 306 F.3d 842, 859–62 (9th Cir. 2002) [an applicant for legalization who filed his claim but had not yet been rejected presented a ripe controversy because one could "firmly predict" that the application would be denied]; *Academy of Religion v. Chertoff,* 463 F.Supp.2d 400, 416–19 (S.D.N.Y. 2006) [First Amendment challenge by academic organizations to refusal/revocation of visa to Islamic scholar was ripe despite government's claim they had not yet adjudicated scholar's visa because the First Amendment rights of the organizations were continually violated by a refusal to decide on the visa]; *Olajide v. ICE,* 402 F.Supp.2d 688, 691–93 (E.D. Va. 2005) [habeas seeking release from detention post-removal order was ripe because petitioner had been in detention for more than six months at the time the court was adjudicating the matter even though the petition had been filed prior to six months]; *F.L. v. Thompson,* 293 F.Supp.2d 86, 93 (D.D.C. 2003) [where agencies had not decided which would be responsible for allowing unaccompanied minors to court, the case was ripe because right to receive a decision is thwarted]; *United Farmworkers of America, AFL-CIO v. Chao,* 227 F.Supp.2d 102, 107 (D.D.C. 2002) [where DOL changed its position in regard to the publication date each year for the AEWR for H-2A workers plaintiffs APA notice and comment challenge was ripe]; *Perales, supra* [challenge to dissemination of inaccurate eligibility requirements in amnesty program that contravened INS practices was ripe because it does not require a decision as to whether the substance of the INS policies accord with the statute]; *Rahim v. McNary*, 827 F.Supp. 224, 228–29 (S.D.N.Y. 1993), *aff'd*, 24 F.3d 440 (2d Cir. 1994) [subsequent to *Catholic Social Services*, court found challenge to SAW regulation denying motions to reopen was ripe]; *Barmo v. Reno*, 899 F.Supp. 1375, 1378–80 (E.D. Pa. 1995) [constitutional challenge to INA §204(c) was ripe even where petition was not yet denied]; *Gurbisz v. INS*, 675 F.Supp. 436 (N.D. Ill. 1987) [APA §704 does not bar claim against AG for denial of EVD on ripeness grounds because matter became ripe when final order of deportation was issued]; *Ali v. INS*, 661 F.Supp. 1234 (D. Mass. 1986) [challenge to marriage interview procedures was ripe even where I-130 petition had not been decided]; *Saywack v. INS*, 1993 WL 205121 (S.D.N.Y. June 8, 1993), *reported in* 7 *Immigration Policy and Law* No. 10 at 3–4 (June 29, 1993) [BIA's 5-year delay in adjusting appeal constitutes final agency action under the APA]

5. Mootness

5.a. The federal courts will also decline to review a claim if they determine it is moot and no longer at issue. *Abdala v. INS,* 488 F.3d 1061 (9the Cir. 2007) [although physical removal from the U.S. pursuant to an order does not, by itself, result in mootness, this case was moot because the basis of the habeas petition was to challenge the length of petitioner's detention]; *Qureshi v. Gonzales,* 442 F.3d 985, 988–90 (7th Cir. 2006) [where USCIS denied I-130 petition after circuit court review was sought, respondent's claim that IJ erred in denying continuance until I-130 was decided was moot]; *Ali v. Cangemi,* 419 F.3d 722 (8th Cir. 2005) [habeas action challenging respondent's custody was moot on prudential grounds where respondent was released even where the release was allegedly in error]; *Khotesouvan v. Morones,* 384 F.3d 1046, 1047–48 (9th Cir. 2004) [habeas petition challenging right to hold person in custody is moot upon his release]; *Nyaga v. Ashcroft,* 323 F.3d 906 (11th Cir. 2003) [mandamus action to compel diversity visa was dismissed as moot where claim was filed after the end of the fiscal year because court cannot affect the rights of the litigants as it cannot compel issuance of visas after fiscal year ended]; *Iddir v. INS,* 301 F.3d 492, 501–02 (7th Cir. 2002) (Flaum, J. Concurring) [because INS lacks capability to issue diversity visa before year deadline its claim is moot]; *Soliman v. U.S.,* 296 F.3d 1237 (11th Cir. 2002) [challenges to prolonged detention after final order and forced feeding were moot when respondent was deported]; *Perez v. Greiner,* 296 F.3d 123 (2d Cir. 2002) [claim was moot when the petitioner was deported after habeas denial was appealed notwithstanding "collateral consequences' doctrine because there was an independent conviction for drug trafficking which would have barred petitioner's return even if he was successful in habeas] *Liu v. INS,* 274 F.3d 533 (D.C. Cir. 2001) [challenge to denial of EB-2 application is moot where INS approved EB-1 petition while appeal was pending]; *Al Najjar v. Ashcroft,* 273 F.3d 1330 (11th Cir. 2001) [claim for bond is moot where federal court upheld final order of removal and therefore detention may now occur pursuant to a different INS provision]; *Humphries v. Various Federal INS*

Employees, 164 F.3d 936, 941–42 (5th Cir. 1999) [claims seeking *injunctive* relief regarding detention and retaliatory exclusion are moot when plaintiff departed country]; *NAACP v. U.S. Sugar Corp.*, 84 F.3d 1432 (D.C. Cir. 1996) [likelihood that DOL's improper application of foreign worker regulations is too remote]; *Chou v. INS*, 774 F.2d 1318 (5th Cir. 1985) [appeal of denial of a grant of voluntary departure in excess of 60 days is moot where appeal process resulted in stay in excess of 2 years]; *Etape v. Chertoff,* 446 F.Supp.2d 408 (D. Md. 2006) [if USCIS rules on the naturalization application, the lawsuit under §1447(b) becomes moot and respondent must seek review separately under §1421(c)]; *Basova v. Ashcroft,* 383 F.Supp.2d 390 (E.D.N.Y. 2005) [where government provided statistics demonstrating that all visa numbers had been used for the diversity lottery, court reversed former opinion and entered order dismissing case as moot against applicants who brought their claims prior to the end of the fiscal year]; *Excellent v. Ashcroft,* 359 F.Supp.2d 333, 335 (S.D.N.Y. 2005) [where BIA reopened case habeas challenge to deportation order was moot]; *Ticheva v. Ashcroft,* 241 F.Supp.2d 1115 (D. Nev. 2002) [as INS is without power to grant diversity visa beyond the fiscal year, injunctive action is dismissed as moot]; *Sadowski v. INS,* 107 F.Supp.2d 451, 454 (S.D.N.Y. 2000) [aged-out child's mandamus action for adjustment is moot]; *Zapata v. INS,* 93 F.Supp.2d 355 (S.D.N.Y. 2000) [court declined to issue order preserving right to obtain visa where visa lottery had ended for the year].

Courts are generally reluctant to find mootness. *Mingkid v. U.S. Att'y Gen.,* 468 F.3d 763, 768–69 (11th Cir. 2006) [IJ's determination that untimely asylum claim was frivolous is not moot even if denied as untimely because of permanent consequences of frivolous finding]; *Alwan v. Ashcroft,* 388 F.3d 507, 510–11 (5th Cir. 2004) [petitioner's deportation does not moot his appeal because of the collateral consequence of permanent inadmissibility]; *Dailide v. U.S. Att'y Gen.,* 387 F.3d 1335, 1336 n.1 (11th Cir. 2004) [where court denied stay and respondent fled the country so that order of removal was never executed, the petition was nevertheless not moot because 1252(b)(2) does not "expressly preclude" review under the circumstances, the government "acknowledges that the petition may be reviewed" and the denial of Social Security benefits is "clearly a collateral consequence of the order of removal"]; *Kamagate v. Ashcroft,* 385 F.3d 144, 149–51 (2d Cir. 2004) [removal from U.S. while case on appeal from denial of habeas is not moot because aggravated felony finding resulting in a lifetime bar is a collateral consequence]; *Marrero Pichardo v. Ashcroft,* 374 F.3d 46, 51–52 (2d Cir. 2004) [habeas not moot where there were convictions, other than the one on appeal, that would have resulted in removal, but the government failed to furnish tangible evidence they existed]; *Swaby v. Ashcroft,* 357 F.3d 156, 159–60 (2d Cir. 2004) [where habeas petitioner was deported during pendency of appeal, case was not moot because of permanent bar due to aggravated felony conviction]; *Chang v. U.S.,* 327 F.3d 911, 918–19 (9th Cir. 2003) [legislation allowing EB-5 investors to re-open their denials and reapply under new criteria did not moot their case challenging the retroactive application of the new criteria to their existing investments]; *Rosales-Garcia v. Holland,* 322 F.3d 386, 394–97 (6th Cir. 2003) [release of Cuban parolee from detention does not moot appeal]; *Zegarra-Gomez v. INS,* 314 F.3d 1124 (9th Cir. 2003) [where habeas petitioner is deported *after* filing petition, the petition is not moot where there are collateral consequences arising from the deportation such as the inability to return]; *U.S. v. Gonzalez-Roque,* 301 F.3d 39, 44–45 (2d Cir. 2002) [dismissal of indictment for re-entry after deportation and defendant's subsequent removal by INS did not moot appeal of dismissal because defendant/respondent would be subject to arrest and imprisonment if he sought re-entry in the future]; *Chong v. District Director, INS,* 264 F.3d 378, 384–86 (3d Cir. 2001) [removal does not moot claim of withholding because of collateral consequence of 10-year deportation bar]; *Moore v. Ashcroft*, 251 F.3d 919, 922 (11th Cir. 2001) [removal does not moot claims where person put in proceedings post Apr. 1, 1997 under IIRIRA permanent rules because of removal consequences to future admissibility]; *Tapia-Garcia v. INS,* 237 F.3d 1216, 1217–18 (10th Cir. 2001) [removal does not moot case of aggravated felon who would be subject to permanent bar]; *Steele v. Blackman,* 236 F.3d 130, 134 n.4 (3d Cir. 2001) [same]; *Max-George v. Reno,* 205 F.3d 194, 196 (5th Cir. 2000) *vacated on other grounds* 121 S.Ct. 2585 (2001) [same]. *Legal Assistance for Vietnamese Asylum Seekers v. DOS*, 74 F.3d 1308, 1311–12 (D.C. Cir. 1996) [DOS cannot escape litigation in visa denial case by giving in to plaintiff's individual claim without renouncing challenged policy]; *Etuk v. Slattery*, 936 F.2d 1433, 1441–42 (2d Cir. 1991) [grant of employment authorization to some class members and issuance of ambiguous INS memo for prospective cases does not moot case]; *Ukrainian-American Bar Ass'n, Inc. v. Baker*, 893 F.2d 1374, 1377–78 (D.C. Cir. 1990) [where plaintiff attacks the government's policy, case is not moot even if individual subject to policy deported]; *Fano v. O'Neill*, 806 F.2d 1262, 1266 n.2 (5th Cir. 1987) [case not moot even if INS promises not to deport alien pending visa because alien's status restricts his ability to live and work in U.S.]; *Umanzor v. Lambert*, 782 F.2d 1299 (5th Cir. 1986) [case not moot where alien physically deported because of future collateral consequences under INA §212(a)(17)]; *Elaasar v. Mueller,* 522 F.Supp.2d 932 (N.D. Ohio 2007) [denied mootness claim on grounds that USCIS had denied petition because §1447(b) jurisdiction vests district court with authority to decide naturalization petition and USCIS's decision is irrelevant]; *Santillan v. Gonzales,* 388 F.Supp.2d 1065, 1075 (N.D. Cal. 2005) [issuance of new regulations regarding security clearances for persons in proceedings being relief by an IJ did not "completely and irrevocably eradicate[] the effects of the alleged violation"]; *Castracani v. Chertoff,* 377 F.Supp.2d 71 (D.D.C. 2005) [where USCIS did not adjudicate naturalization within 120 days of interview, it lost jurisdiction over the case once a petition was filed in federal court and the subsequent grant of naturalization did not moot the case]; *Catholic Social Services v. Ashcroft,* 268 F.Supp.2d 1172, 1184–88 (E.D. Cal. 2002) [finding that the LIFE Act did not moot claims under IRCA's legalization program because "the avenue of relief provided by section 1104 of LIFE Act is clearly not intended to supersede that available under IRCA"]. *Reyes-Sanchez v. Ashcroft,* 261 F.Supp.2d 276, 282–84 (S.D.N.Y. 2003) [where person was deported while case was pending in court of appeals and that court determined jurisdiction was in the district court in habeas, the district court's jurisdiction was not moot by virtue of petitioner's removal prior to transfer of case to district court]; *So v. Reno,* 251 F.Supp.2d 1112, 1120–24 (E.D.N.Y. 2003) [finding a "wealth and severity" of collateral consequences to deportation, habeas petitioner's claims after deportation were not moot]; *Longwood Village Restaurant, Ltd. v. Ashcroft,* 157 F.Supp.2d 61, 66–67 (D.D.C. 2001) [where I-140 petitioner challenged refusal of INS to provide earlier priority date case was not moot even though later priority date became current]; *Singh v. Ilchert*, 784 F.Supp. 759, 762 (N.D. Cal. 1992) [although INS approved all employment applications it is likely that the same plaintiffs will seek extensions of work authorization]; *American Bictech, Inc. v. INS*, CIV-2-88-262 (E.D. Tenn. Mar. 27, 1989), *reported in* 66 No. 23 *Interpreter Releases* 653–55 (June 19, 1989) [subsequent approval of H-1 petition for another position with the same company does not moot out erroneous denial of original petition for another position]. Moreover, the moving party bears a "heavy burden" to establish mootness. *Etuk v. Slattery, supra.* Compliance with enforcement of a subpoena does not moot out appeal challenging subpoena. *Church of Scientology v. U.S.*, 113 S.Ct. 447, 449 (1992); *U.S. v. Florida Azalea Specialists*, 19 F.3d 620 (11th Cir. 1994) *reh'g en banc denied* 26 F.3d 1123 (11th Cir. 1994).

5.b. There are generally four exceptions to the mootness doctrine even where a case might otherwise be moot: (1) A class action is not moot simply because the named plaintiffs claims are moot. *Sosna v. Iowa,* 419 U.S. 393, 399 (1975); (2) The wrongful act is likely to reoccur notwithstanding voluntary cessation, *U.S. v. W.T. Grant Co.*, 345 U.S. 629 (1958); (3) The defendant's conduct is capable of repetition yet evading review. *Sosna v. Iowa*, 419 U.S. 393 (1975); *Martinez v. Reich*, 934 F.Supp. 232, 235–36 (S.D. Tex. 1996) [challenge to H-2A program]; (4) The defendant's conduct has left the plaintiff with a collateral injury even if the primary injury cannot be remedied. *Peralta-Cabrera v. Gonzales,* 501 F.3d 837, 841–43 (7th Cir. 2007) [respondent's unlawful removal pre-IIRIRA did not render his case moot because he would still be subject to a bar to return to the U.S. which is a collateral consequence];*Dulal-Whiteway v. DHS,* 501 F.3d 116, 120–21 (2d Cir. 2007) [where court found respondent subject to removal based upon firearms charge, it nevertheless analyzed whether respondent's second conviction was an aggravated felony, because it would effect respondent's ability to reenter the U.S. in the future making the issue a live case or controversy]; *Alwan v. Ashcroft,* 388 F.3d 507, 510–11 (5th Cir. 2004) [petitioner's deportation does not moot his appeal because of the collateral consequence of permanent inadmissibility]; *So v. Reno,* 251 F.Supp.2d 1112, 1120–24 (E.D.N.Y. 2003) [finding a "wealth and severity" of collateral consequences to deportation, habeas petitioner's claims after deportation were not moot]; *But see Zapata v. INS,* 93 F.Supp.2d 355, 359 (S.D.N.Y. 2000) [finding no collateral injury and upholding claim as moot where time had expired for visa lottery].

5.c. Effect of Mootness—When the court determines that an appeal is moot it may vacate the district court's order as well because this practice "clears the path for future relitigation of the issues between the parties and eliminates a judgment, review of which was prevented through happenstance." *Soliman v. U.S.,* 296 F.3d 1237, 1243–44 (11th Cir. 2002) [following *U.S. v. Munsingwear,* 340 U.S. 36, 40 (1950) appellate court vacated district court order when dismissing appeal as moot]; *See also Shokeh v. Thompson,* 375 F.3d 351 (5th Cir. 2004) [in bond case were respondent was released court vacated its order, vacated district court's order and dismissed the action pursuant to *Munsingwear*]; *Motta v. District Director,* 61 F.3d 117 (1st Cir. 1995) [where parties settled matter on appeal, controversy was moot and court vacated lower court decision]. *But see U.S. Bancorp Mortgage Co. v. Bonner Mall Partnership,* 513 U.S. 18, 115 S.Ct. 386 (1994) [prohibition against vacatur where through settlement party relinquishing its right to it].

6. Attenuation—A court may refuse to entertain a suit which is not moot but which has become so attenuated that considerations of prudence and comity "counsel nonintervention." *Ukrainian-American Bar Ass'n, Inc. v. Baker*, 893 F.2d 1374, 1378 (D.C. Cir. 1990) [case not considered attenuated where plaintiff challenges government policy].

7. Laches—To assert laches a party must demonstrate that there was inexcusable delay in asserting a known right and that the delay caused the moving party prejudice. *Elia v. Gonzales,* 431 F.3d 268 (6th Cir. 2005) [rejecting claim that laches prevented the government from benefiting from the purported delay in scheduling petitioner's deportation hearing]; *Thom v. Ashcroft,* 369 F.3d 158, 165–67 (2d Cir. 2004) [no lack of diligence or inexcusable delay where respondent was convicted in 1982 and legacy INS did not institute proceedings until 3 years before his 20-year minimum sentence thus depriving him of INA §212(c) rights]; *Wauchope v. DOS,* 985 F.2d 1407, 1411–12 (9th Cir. 1993) [no inexcusable delay and no prejudice in asserting that a pre-1934 statute was unconstitutional].

8. Political Question—Simply because a claim implicates important government policy does not mean the judiciary is barred from hearing it. *Ukrainian-American Bar Ass'n, Inc. v. Baker,* 893 F.2d 1374 (D.C. Cir. 1990) [political question doctrine does not bar first amend. challenge to INS policy of refusing to notify potential asylees of organization's services]. The political question doctrine does not preclude the district court's review of INS's failure to notify Salvadorans about their right to seek asylum or about political conditions in another country. *Orantes-Hernandez v. Meese*, 685 F.Supp. 1488, 1503 (C.D. Cal. 1988), *aff'd*, 919 F.2d 549 (9th Cir. 1990) [evidence of political conditions important in determining the interest affected by any deprivation of rights and to demonstrate availability of evidence]; *Haitian Refugee Center v. Smith*, 676 F.2d 1023, 1042 [same]. Courts are not precluded under the political question doctrine from determining the validity of INS's detention and parole policies under applicable statutes, regulations and the U.S. Constitution, *Chiles v. Thornburgh*, 865 F.2d 1197, 1215–16 (11th Cir. 1988), or enjoining the return of a witness who fears persecution upon his return to China and alleges the U.S. violated his substantive due process rights. *Xiao v. Reno*, 837 F.Supp. 1506, 1546–47 (N.D. Cal. 1993), *aff'd sub nom. Wang v. Reno*, 81 F.3d 808 (9th Cir. 1996). Nor does the doctrine bar a challenge to an immigration agreement between the U.S. and Cuba where the agreement may be in violation of U.S. immigration law. *FAIR v. Reno*, 897 F.Supp. 595, 601–03 (D.D.C.), *aff'd on other grounds*, 93 F.3d 897 (D.C. Cir. 1996). The doctrine also does not bar review of the constitutionality of the Secy. of State's authority to request deportation because of the foreign policy interests of the U.S. *Massieu v. Reno*, 915 F.Supp. 681 (D.N.J. 1996) *rev'd on other grounds* 91 F.3d 416 (3d Cir. 1996) [district court lacked jurisdiction because petitioner failed to exhaust administrative remedies and seek review of constitutional claim in court of appeals]. And it does not bar a statutory and constitutional challenge to DHS's revocation of CAT under 1208.18(c) in violation of its own regulations. *Khouzam v. Hogan,* 497 F.Supp.2d 615, 624–25 (M.D. Pa. 2007) [denied DHS motion to dismiss habeas under political question doctrine where petitioner challenged DHS revocation of deferral of removal under CAT at 8 C.F.R. §1208.18(c) on grounds that DHS failed to comply with its own regulations, violated procedural and substantive due process, and violated CAT as implemented by FARRA]. However, the doctrine may bar actions by states and state groups to require the federal government to provide Medicaid and AFDC to illegal aliens and to require the federal government to control illegal aliens in the state. *State of California v. U.S.*, 104 F.3d 1086, 1090–91 (9th Cir. 1997); *Padavan v. U.S.*, 82 F.3d 23 (2d Cir. 1996); *State*

of Texas v. U.S., 106 F.3d 661 (5th Cir. 1997); *Chiles v. U.S.*, 69 F.3d 1094 (11th Cir. 1995). Similarly, at least one court has concluded that general policy challenges to the manner in which immigration law are enforced are nonjusticiable political questions. *Sadowski v. Bush,* 293 F.Supp.2d 15, 19–20 (D.D.C. 2003).

9. Proper Party Defendant—Where a plaintiff sues the United States, various U.S. agencies related to immigration cannot conclude that they are not parties to the action for purposes of relief. *Paunescu v. INS,* 76 F.Supp.2d 896, 903 n.2 (N.D. Ill. 1999).

D. *Waiver of Review*

1. Escape from federal custody is inconsistent with pursuing judicial remedies and constitutes a voluntary waiver. *Hussien v. INS*, 817 F.2d 63 (9th Cir. 1986).

2. Fugitive Disentitlement Doctrine—A fugitive during the ongoing appellate process may forfeit his right to appeal. *Martin v. Mukasey,* 517 F.3d 1201 (10th Cir. 2008) [applied fugitive disentitlement doctrine to dismiss appeal where petitioner failed to appear]; *Giri v. Keisler,* 507 F.3d 833 (5th Cir. 2007) [court dismissed appeal and held that fugitive disentitlement doctrine applies in the immigration context when the petitioner fails to comply with a removal order by failing to report to ICE after a stay of removal was denied]; *Gao v. Gonzales,* 481 F.3d 173 (2d Cir. 2007) [applied fugitive disentitlement doctrine to bar review of motion to reopen asylum claim based upon changed circumstances where applicant refused to report for custody throughout appeal]; *Garcia-Flores v. Gonzales,* 477 F.3d 439 (6th Cir. 2007) [court dismissed appeal where petitioner refused to report for removal]; *Sapoundjiev v. Ashcroft,* 376 F.3d 727 *reh'ing denied* 384 F.3d 916 (7th Cir. 2004) [fugitive disentitlement doctrine is applicable to petitions for review and the court vacated its stay of deportation and dismissed the appeal where appellants refused to appear to be taken into custody]; *Armentero v. INS,* 412 F.3d 1088 (9th Cir. 2005) [fugitive disentitlement doctrine applicable to habeas corpus appeals]; *Antonio-Martinez v. INS,* 317 F.3d 1089 (9th Cir. 2003) and cases cited therein [court dismissed the appeal under the fugitive disentitlement doctrine of an immigration appellate who could not be located]; *Bar-Levy v. DOJ*, 990 F.2d 33, 35 (2d Cir. 1995) [dismissing appeal of BIA deportation order by alien who refused to surrender]. *But see Hassan v. Gonzales,* 484 F.3d 513, 515 (8th Cir. 2007) [fugitive disentitlement doctrine does not apply to person denied asylum who voluntarily departs to Canada under VD order]; *Dailide v. U.S. Att'y Gen.,* 387 F.3d 1335, 1336 n.1 (11th Cir. 2004) [where court denied stay and respondent fled the country so that order of removal was never executed, the petition was nevertheless not moot because 1252(b)(2) does not "expressly preclude" review under the circumstances, the government "acknowledges that the petition may be reviewed" and the denial of Social Security benefits is "clearly a collateral consequence of the order of removal"]; *Degen v. U.S.,* 116 S.Ct. 1777 (1996) [fugitive disentitlement doctrine inapplicable in forfeiture]; *Ali v. Gonzales,* 486 F.Supp.2d 1197, 1204 (W.D. Wash. 2007) [fugitive disentitlement doctrine inapplicable to prevailing party status for purpose of EAJA fees]. However, where a person is a fugitive but is returned to custody before appellate jurisdiction is invoked he may pursue appeal. *Ortega-Rodriguez v. U.S.*, 507 U.S. 234 (1993). The judicial review of a criminal conviction, though, may not be waived simply because appellant was deported. *See e.g., Swaby v. Ashcroft,* 357 F.3d 156, 159–60 (2d Cir. 2004) [where habeas petitioner was deported during pendency of appeal case was not moot because of permanent bar due to aggravated felony conviction]. *See also in this chapter* section VI.D (p.1193), *infra.*

3. The courts have also declined to review an order of deportation where the person concealed his whereabouts from immigration authorities and failed to comply with a bench warrant. *Arana v. INS*, 673 F.2d 75, 76–77 (3d Cir. 1982). The courts have also declined to grant a stay unless the person was in custody. *Ofosu v. McElroy*, 98 F.3d 694 (2d Cir. 1996). However, where the respondent did not escape custody and did not conceal his whereabouts and the INS never requested a bench warrant the appeal would proceed even if the respondent failed to surrender for 4 years after receiving a notice to surrender (bag and baggage letter). *Esposito v. INS*, 987 F.2d 108, 110 (2d Cir. 1993).

4. Where appellant raises issues for first time at oral argument, they are waived. *Patel v. Gonzales,* 470 F.3d 216, 218–19 (6th Cir. 2006) [where IJ denied asylum on discretionary and nondiscretionary grounds, the respondent waived any argument that the decision on discretionary grounds was in error by failing to raise it]; *Galvez Pineda v. Gonzales,* 427 F.3d 833, 837 (10th Cir. 2005) [where

respondent raised for the first time at oral argument in the appeal of a BIA summary dismissal that the BIA improperly imposed a briefing requirement, the court considered it waived]; *Zheng v. Gonzales,* 409 F.3d 804, 809 (7th Cir. 2005) [petitioner waived CAT claim when she failed to raise issue in her opening brief]; *Szczesny v. Ashcroft,* 358 F.3d 464 (7th Cir. 2004) [failure to raise prejudice from DD's lack of notice of rescission was waived]. Or where s/he failed to object to evidentiary ruling below, s/he now waives issue on appeal. *Ocasio v. Ashcroft,* 375 F.3d 105 (1st Cir. 2004) [where IJ admitted affidavit of spouse regarding sham marriage, respondent/beneficiary wife waived issue because she did not raised the claim that DHS failed to make reasonable efforts to secure spouse's appearance]. Waiver also occurs if a petitioner raises an issue but does not actually argue or present any analysis on the issue. *Wang v. Mukasey,* 508 F.3d 80, 85 (1st Cir. 2007) [petitioner's request to remand the case to the BIA based upon second circuit cases regarding changed circumstances was waived where petitioner did not file a motion to reopen with the BIA and failed to explain what the circuit court's authority was to remand]; *Berrio-Barrera v. Gonzales,* 460 F.3d 163, 168 & n.2 (1st Cir. 2006) [CAT claim waived where petitioner asserted that IJ erred but never argue issue or presented analysis]. However, an appellant does not waive review because s/he cited an incorrect standard for review. *Ndom v. Ashcroft,* 384 F.3d 743, 750 (9th Cir. 2004); *Mejia v. Ashcroft,* 298 F.3d 873, 876–77 (9th Cir. 2002).

5. Incorporation by cross-reference issues raised in a habeas proceeding or other proceeding in the district court without specifically briefing the issues on appeal may be waived. . *Lawrence v. Gonzales,* 446 F.3d 221, 226 (1st Cir. 2006) [efforts to cross-reference claims made in a district court proceeding rather than presenting them in an appellate brief may result in their being summarily disregarded].

6. Waiving a Waiver—The government can waive the issue of the respondent's waiver by failing to assert it. *Tokatly v. Ashcroft,* 371 F.3d 613, 618 (9th Cir. 2004) [where the government argued in the circuit court that respondent waived his argument that testimony may not be used to establish the record of conviction, the court held that the government had waived this waiver argument by not raising the issue of waiver before the BIA but rather addressing the issue on the merits when respondent argued to the BIA that the testimony was impermissible].

7. Manifest Injustice/Exceptional Circumstance—Where manifest injustice or exceptional circumstance will result in failing to review an issue, the court will decide an issue not raised in appellant's opening brief. *Haxhiu v. Mukasey,* 519 F.3d 685, 691–92 (7th Cir. 2008) [petitioner failure to adequately address the government involvement in his persecution or their unwillingness or inability to stop it does not constitute waiver, because it would be manifest injustice to do so in light of IJ's statement that petitioner would be killed upon return to Albania]; *Bona v. Gonzales,* 425 F.3d 663, 667 n.4 (9th Cir. 2005) [court considered legal argument raised for the first time in a 28(j) letter where the parties argued the issue, where they were given a subsequent opportunity to brief it, and where the opposing party will not be prejudiced]; *Bagot v. Ashcroft,* 398 F.3d 252, 256 (2d Cir. 2005) [exceptional circumstance permitted review where pure legal question concerning derivative citizenship was close to legal issues raised in district court]; *Alcaraz v. INS,* 384 F.3d 1150, 1161 (9th Cir. 2004) [court would hear repapering issue despite appellant's failure to raise it in his opening brief because the government is not prejudiced and manifest injustice would result].

E. *Prior Adjudication*—Under INA §242(d)(2), 8 U.S.C. §1252(d)(2), an issue will not be considered by the court if previously determined in civil or criminal proceedings unless the petition presents grounds which could not have been presented in prior proceedings or proceedings were inadequate or ineffective to test the validity of the order. *Gutierrez-Morales v. Homan,* 461 F.3d 605, 608–09 (5th Cir. 2006) [third petition for review did not bar claim of ineffective assistance where on first petition he was represented by ineffective counsel and on second he failed to timely file claim so there was no decision on the merits]; *Filsaime v. Ashcroft,* 393 F.3d 315 (2d Cir. 2004) [remanded case to district court to determine whether habeas proceeding in the W.D. La. was inadequate or ineffective in disposing of respondent's CAT claim]; *Variamparambil v. INS,* 831 F.2d 1362 (7th Cir. 1987) [previous appeal to circuit court on finding of deportability not a bar to review of denial of motion to reopen where issue concerning the tolling of the seven-year period for INA §212(c) was raised for the first time]. *But see Santos v. Reno,* 228 F.3d 591, 597 (5th Cir. 2000) [under transitional rules issue in habeas could have been (and was) raised in prior appeal].

F. ***Departure from U.S.***—Prior to IIRIRA, under 8 U.S.C. §1105a(c), "an order of deportation or exclusion shall not be reviewed if the alien ... has departed from the United States after the issuance of the order." *Kon v. Gonzales,* 400 F.3d 1225 (9th Cir. 2005) [applicant for asylum who departed U.S. after denial of asylum was summarily affirmed by BIA deprived circuit court of review under transitional rules]; *Robledo-Gonzales v. Ashcroft,* 342 F.3d 667, 674–76 n.4 (7th Cir. 2003) [habeas petitioner lacked jurisdiction to seek reopening of deportation case to obtain INA §212(c) relief where petition was filed subsequent to his illegal re-entry after deportation]; *Baez v. INS,* 41 F.3d 19 (1st Cir. 1994), *cert. denied,* 515 U.S. 1158 (1995) [rejecting analysis in *Mendez* and finding no jurisdiction where person deported without proper notice to counsel]. This provision was removed from the new jurisdictional statute pursuant to IIRIRA §306. INA §242(a). Therefore, post-IIRIRA the departure of a person ordered removed no longer moots his or her appeal. *Spina v. DHS,* 470 F.3d 116, 124–25 (2d Cir. 2006) [court retained jurisdiction over appeal of statutory ineligibility to apply for INA §212(c) relief despite applicant's request to be deported while preserving his rights, and his removal to Italy]; *Mendez-Alcaraz v. Gonzales,* 464 F.3d 842, 844 (9th Cir. 2006) [court had jurisdiction to review denial of motion to reconsider filed 14 months after respondent's removal from the U.S.]; *Handa v. Clark,* 401 F.3d 1129, 1132 (9th Cir. 2005) [in visa waiver removal case, habeas jurisdiction was not lost where petitioner was removed after habeas petition was filed because of collateral consequences]; *Alwan v. Ashcroft,* 388 F.3d 507, 510–11 (5th Cir. 2004) [petitioner's deportation does not moot his appeal because of the collateral consequence of permanent inadmissibility]; *Dailide v. U.S. Att'y Gen.,* 387 F.3d 1335, 1336 n.1 (11th Cir. 2004) [where court denied stay and petitioner fled the country so that order of removal was never executed, the petition was nevertheless not moot because 1252(b)(2) does not "expressly preclude" review under the circumstances, the government "acknowledges that the petition may be reviewed" and the denial of Social Security benefits is "clearly a collateral consequence of the order of removal"]; *Kamagate v. Ashcroft,* 385 F.3d 144, 149–51 (2d Cir. 2004) [removal from U.S. while case on appeal from denial of habeas is not moot because aggravated felony finding resulting in a lifetime bar is a collateral consequence]; *Ghounem v. Ashcroft,* 378 F.3d 740 (8th Cir. 2004) [court ordered the reopening of *in absentia* removal order because of lack of notice where petitioner's stay had been denied and he had been deported to Egypt]; *Johnson v. Ashcroft,* 378 F.3d 164, 168 (2d Cir. 2004) [petitioner deported after habeas filed and habeas subsequently denied, but circuit court reversed]; *Zalawadia v. Ashcroft,* 371 F.3d 292, 296–98 (5th Cir. 2004) [person deported after habeas filed is still "in custody" and habeas is still viable because the "in custody" determination is made at the time the petition is filed]; *Reynoso-Lopez v. Ashcroft,* 369 F.3d 275, 281–82 (3d Cir. 2004) [appellant free to depart and still pursue appeal]; *Swaby v. Ashcroft,* 357 F.3d 156, 159–61 (2d Cir. 2004) [where habeas petitioner was deported during pendency of appeal case was not moot because of permanent bar due to aggravated felony conviction]; *Noriega-Lopez v. Ashcroft,* 335 F.3d 874, 878 (9th Cir. 2003) [court had jurisdiction to review habeas denial when person deported after habeas denied]; *Zegarra-Gomez v. INS,* 314 F.3d 1124 (9th Cir. 2003) [where habeas petitioner is deported after filing petition, the petition is not moot where there are collateral consequences arising from the deportation such as the inability to return]; *Moore v. Ashcroft,* 251 F.3d 919, 922 (11th Cir. 2001) [proceeding commenced post Apr. 1, 1997 are governed by IIRIRA permanent rules that do not contain a statutory bar to review and claim is not moot because there are consequences to future admissibility by removal]; *Chong v. District Director, INS,* 264 F.3d 378, 385 (3d Cir. 2001) [same]; *Tapia-Garcia v. INS,* 237 F.3d 1216, 1217 (10th Cir. 2001) [same]; *Steele v. Blackman,* 236 F.3d 130, 134 n.4 (3d Cir. 2001) [same]; *Max-George v. Reno,* 205 F.3d 194, 196 (5th Cir. 2000) *vacated on other grounds* 121 S.Ct. 2585 (2001) [same]; *Smith v. Ashcroft,* 295 F.3d 425, 428 (4th Cir. 2002) [if person was in custody at time habeas was filed jurisdiction remains even if s/he is removed from the U.S.]; *Ying Fong v. Ashcroft,* 317 F.Supp.2d 398, 404–05 (S.D.N.Y. 2004) [habeas court ordered government to return respondent from abroad to the U.S. after government had illegally deported him]; *Reyes-Sanchez v. Ashcroft,* 261 F.Supp.2d 276, 282–84 (S.D.N.Y. 2003) [where person was deported while case was pending in court of appeals and that court determined jurisdiction was in the district court in habeas, the district court's jurisdiction was not moot by virtue of petitioner's removal prior to transfer of case to district court]; *So v. Reno,* 251 F.Supp.2d 1112, 1120–24 (E.D.N.Y. 2003) [case not rendered moot by petitioner's removal where habeas filed before removal]. *But see Abdala v. INS,* 488 F.3d 1061 (9the Cir. 2007) [although physical removal from the U.S. pursuant to an order does not, by itself, result in mootness, this case was moot because the basis of the habeas petition was to challenge the length of petitioner's detention]; *Perez v. Greiner,* 296 F.3d 123 (2d Cir. 2002) [claim was moot when the petitioner was deported after habeas denial was appealed notwithstanding "collateral consequences' doctrine because there was an independent conviction for drug trafficking which would have barred petitioner's return even if he was successful in habeas]; *Sadhyani v. Chertoff,* 460 F.Supp.2d 114 (D.D.C. 2006) [person who was deported was not in custody for habeas purposes and REAL ID Act and INA §242(g) divest the court of jurisdiction].

Equitable Tolling May Permit Jurisdiction Even if Habeas Is Filed After Person Is Deported. *Gutierrez v. Ashcroft,* 289 F.Supp.2d 555 (D.N.J. 2003) [where counsel affirmatively misrepresented that he had filed a habeas petition challenging the denial of the right to seek former INA §212(c) before respondent was physically removed but had not filed petition, his actions violated due process and permitted the court to accept the habeas *nunc pro tunc* to the time before petitioner was physically removed from the U.S.].

In addition, the law prior to IIRIRA permitted courts of appeal to review deportation orders where departure was due to wrongful deportation. *Peralta-Cabrera v. Gonzales,* 501 F.3d 837, 841–43 (7th Cir. 2007) [pre-IIRIRA respondent was deported despite filing petition for review that gave him automatic stay]; *Singh v. Waters*, 87 F.3d 346 (9th Cir. 1996); *Wiedersperg v. INS*, 896 F.2d 1179 (9th Cir. 1990) [where conviction vacated after petitioner deported, former INA §106 is not a bar]; *Zepeda-Melendez v. INS*, 741 F.2d 285, 287 (9th Cir. 1984) [deportation of LPR without notice to counsel]; *Juarez v. INS*, 732 F.2d 58, 59–60 (6th Cir. 1984); *Martinez-Cabrera v. Thornburgh*, ___ F.Supp. ___, Case No. B-19-126 (S.D. Tex. Oct. 5, 1986), *reprinted in* 66 No. 42 *Interpreter Releases* 1202–03 (Oct. 30, 1989); *Mendez v. INS*, 563 F.2d 956 (9th Cir. 1977) [deportation of LPR without notice to counsel may be reviewed]. Some circuits also held they had jurisdiction to review the order of a person already deported where "the record reveals a colorable due process claim." *Camacho-Bordes v. INS,* 33 F.3d 26 (8th Cir. 1993); *Marrero v. INS*, 990 F.2d 772, 773 (3d Cir. 1993) [same]; *Fuller v. INS,* 144 F.Supp.2d 72, 80–83 (D. Conn. 2000) [Section 1105a(c) is not a bar to review under transitional rules where person deported but court would have granted stay but for mishaps in the clerk's office in docketing case]; Similarly, if a person departed the U.S. before he was aware that the circuit court reconsidered his case *sua sponte en banc,* that court retained jurisdiction. *Contreras-Aragon v. INS*, 852 F.2d 1088 (9th Cir. 1988) (*en banc*). Also, departure from the U.S. in compliance with an order of deportation does not constitute an abandonment of the claim against the DD for improper denial of a J-1 hardship waiver. *Chang v. Reno*, 986 F.Supp. 19, 25–26 (D.D.C. 1997). A person deported in violation of a stay order may also obtain review if the failure to adhere to the order was deliberate. *Patel v. Ashcroft,* 378 F.3d 610, 613 (7th Cir. 2004) [under transition rule, IIRIRA §309(c)(4) the court lost jurisdiction after person deported unless there was a deliberate violation of court's stay order, but no deliberate violation occurred].

Motions to reopen filed after a person's removal, however, may be treated differently. *Pena-Muriel v. Gonzales,* 489 F.3d 438 (1st Cir. 2007) [due process was not violated where the BIA refused to allow respondent, who was outside the United States, to reopen his deportation proceeding because his conviction was vacated]; *Patel v. U.S. Att'y Gen.,* 334 F.3d 1259, 1261–63 (11th Cir. 2003) [court of appeals lacked jurisdiction because of the criminal alien bar under INA §242(a)(2)(C) to review the denial of motion to reopen under 8 C.F.R. §1003.2(d) where the person was out of the country and the district court lacked habeas jurisdiction because the person was no longer in custody]. *But see William v. Gonzales,* 499 F.3d 329 (4th Cir. 2007) [the prohibition in 8 C.F.R. §1003.2(d) to motions to reopen where the person is outside the U.S. is contrary to INA §240(c)(7)(A), 8 U.S.C. §1229a(c)(7)(A) permitting one motion to reopen without limitation and the regulation is therefore invalid]; *Mendez-Alcaraz v. Gonzales,* 464 F.3d 842, 844 (9th Cir. 2006) [court had jurisdiction to review denial of motion to reconsider filed 14 months after respondent's removal from the U.S.]; *Contreras-Rodriguez v. U.S. Att'y Gen.,* 462 F.3d 1314 (11th Cir. 2006) [although respondent was physically removed after *in absentia* order, he is not barred from filing a motion to reopen for lack of notice because §1003.23(b)(4)(ii) allows motion regarding lack of notice to be filed at "any time." *Patel* distinguished]; *Cardoso-Tlaseca v. Gonzales,* 460 F.3d 1102 (9th Cir. 2006) [where respondent's conviction is vacated after physical removal, court reversed BIA for denying motion to reopen because conviction was a "key part" of removal proceeding].

G. *Venue*—Venue for federal proceedings is addressed at 28 U.S.C. §§1391(b), (e). A federal prisoner's residence for purpose of venue is not necessarily where s/he is incarcerated but rather, his or her residence prior to his or her involvement in the criminal justice system. *Abreu v. U.S.*, 796 F.Supp. 50, 52 (D.R.I. 1992). Venue for circuit courts under INA §242 is in "the judicial circuit in which the immigration judge completes the proceedings." INA §242(b)(2). *See in this chapter* section VI.F (p.1194), *infra.* *Nwaokolo v. INS,* 314 F.3d 303, 305–06 (7th Cir. 2002) [pre–Oct. 30, 1996 rules applied for venue purposes where the IJ's order was finalized before that date even though review was sought of a motion to reopen filed after that date]. Venue in habeas matters is often more complex. *See in this chapter* ¶ III.C.9 (p.1097), *supra*. Venue regarding the review of the denial of immigrant or nonimmigrant petitions arises under 28 U.S.C. §1391(e). *Blacher v. Ridge,* 436 F.Supp.2d 602 (S.D.N.Y. 2006) [in action by employer to review the denial of an I-129 petition for an H-1B position, the court found that venue was not proper in the Southern District of New York because neither defendants, nor plaintiffs resided in the Southern District and the decision was made in Vermont].

V. SCOPE OF REVIEW

A. *Plenary Review*—When federal jurisdiction exists, courts must determine scope of review to be applied in reviewing agency action. All agency decisions or interpretations that are based upon errors of law are subject to plenary review by the courts. *INS v. Cardoza-Fonseca*, 480 U.S. 421 (1987) [reversed agency's application of an incorrect standard of proof in asylum determinations]; *Rosenberg v. Fleuti*, 374 U.S. 449 (1963); *Jordan v. De George*, 341 U.S. 223 (1951); *Fernandez v. Keisler,* 502 F.3d 337, 342–48 (4th Cir. 2007) [there is *de novo* review of all legal questions regarding naturalization, however, it does not preclude *Chevron* deference]; *Larin-Ulloa v. Gonzales,* 462 F.3d 456, 461 & n.7 (5th Cir. 2006) [notwithstanding any deference the court owes the BIA under *Chevron,* it reviews *de novo* whether a state criminal statute constitutes an aggravated felony under the INA]; *Le v. U.S. Att'y Gen.,* 196 F.3d 1352 (11th Cir. 1999) [*De novo* review but will defer to the BIA's determination if it is reasonable]; *Coronado-Durazo v. INS*, 123 F.3d 1322 (9th Cir. 1997) [*Chevron* deference inappropriate in determining whether a given crime is a deportable offense]; *Albillo-Figueroa v. INS,* 221 F.3d 1070, 1072 (9th Cir. 2000) [same]; *Padilla-Caldera v. Gonzales,* 453 F.3d 1237, 1241 (10th Cir. 2006) [reversed IJ/BIA under *de novo* review standard where IJ barred §245(i) adjustment to a person subject to inadmissibility under INA §212(a)(9)(C)(i)(I) where statute and legislative history was to the contrary]; *Innab v. Reno,* 204 F.3d 1318, 1320 (11th Cir. 2000) [issues involving subject-matter jurisdiction are reviewed *de novo*]; *Mikhael v. INS*, 115 F.3d 299 (5th Cir. 1997) [BIA reversed where they applied improper standard to asylum claim]; *Hamdan v. INS*, 98 F.3d 183, 185 (5th Cir. 1996) [whether crime constitutes CIMT for purposes of deportation]; *Goldeshtein v. INS*, 8 F.3d 645 (9th Cir. 1993) [reversed *de novo* determination that money laundering is CIMT]. This includes procedural errors arising from the violation of regulations, statutes, treaties or the constitution. *Accardi v. Shaughnessy*, 347 U.S. 260 (1954); *ILWU v. Meese*, 891 F.2d 1374 (9th Cir. 1989); *Rios-Berrios v. INS*, 776 F.2d 859 (9th Cir. 1985) [denial of counsel]; *Kaho v. Ilchert*, 765 F.2d 877, 881 (9th Cir. 1985) [review of INS interpretation of foreign law]. This plenary or *de novo* review may also extend to mixed questions of law and fact. *Blancada v. Turnage*, 891 F.2d 688 (9th Cir. 1989) [review of order denying stay]; *Colindres-Aguilar v. INS*, 819 F.2d 259 (9th Cir. 1987) [review of deprivation of counsel]; *Bodeux v. INS*, 668 F.Supp. 1452 (D. Kan. 1987) [failure to follow H-1 extension regulations]. *De novo* review is also appropriate where a court of appeals reviews the decision of a district court reviewing the BIA's decision. *Sotelo-Aquije v. Slattery*, 17 F.3d 33, 35 (2d Cir. 1994).

B. *Committed to Agency Discretion*—Contrarily, there are some matters which are simply not reviewable in the federal courts because they are "committed to agency discretion." 5 U.S.C. §701(a)(2). This is a narrow exception to the general principle that agency action is reviewable. *Heckler v. Chaney*, 470 U.S. 821 (1985) [5 U.S.C. §701(a)(2) "is applicable in those rare instances where statutes are drawn in such broad terms that in a given case there is no law to apply"; it applies in situations where there is "no meaningful standard against which to judge the agency's exercise of discretion" and thus "it is impossible to evaluate agency action for abuse of discretion"); *Socop-Gonzalez v. INS,* 208 F.3d 838, 844 (9th Cir. 2000) [regulations or agency practice can provide a standard against which to judge the agency's exercise of discretion].

Several district and circuit courts have found that the denial of a waiver pursuant to INA §212(e) by the USIA is just such an action committed to agency discretion. *Korvah v. Brown*, 66 F.3d 809 (6th Cir. 1995); *Singh v. Moyer*, 867 F.2d 1035 (7th Cir. 1989); *Slyper v. Attorney General*, 827 F.2d 821 (D.C. Cir. 1987), *cert. denied,* 485 U.S. 941 (1988) [same]; *Dina v. Attorney General*, 793 F.2d 473 (2d Cir. 1986); *Abdelhamid v. Ilchert*, 774 F.2d 1447 (9th Cir. 1985); *Mansur v. Albright,* 130 F.Supp.2d 59 (D.D.C. 2001) [when the Deputy Assistant Secy. of State for Visa Services revokes a visa under 8 U.S.C. §1201(i), it is committed to agency discretion and is not reviewable]; *But see Chong v. Director, USIA*, 821 F.2d 171 (3d Cir. 1987). Similarly, the decision of the AG not to deport someone to the country they designate "is essentially unreviewable." *Doherty v. Meese*, 808 F.2d 938, 943–44 (2d Cir. 1986).

Other areas have been found to be committed to agency discretion or not justiciable. *Harchenko v. INS,* 379 F.3d 405, 410–11 (6th Cir. 2004) [decision of BIA to reopen case *sua sponte* is committed to unfettered discretion of the BIA and therefore not subject to review]; *Ngure v. Ashcroft,* 367 F.3d 975, 980–88 (8th Cir. 2004) [whether the BIA properly applied the streamlining regulations/AWO procedure is not reviewable because it is not possible to devise a meaningful and adequate standard of review]; *but see Camposeco-Montejo v. Ashcroft,* 384 F.3d 814, 821–22 (9th Cir. 2004). *See also Zhang v. Gonzales,* 469 F.3d 51 (1st Cir. 2006) [where respondent filed out-of-time motion to reopen for *sua sponte* consideration court lacked jurisdiction to review denial]; *Belay-Gebru v. INS,* 327 F.3d 998, 1000–01 (10th Cir. 2003) [the BIA's decision to reopen *sua sponte* under "exceptional circumstances" provides no meaningful standard for review]; *Calle-Vujiles v. Ashcroft,* 320 F.3d 472 (3d Cir. 2003) (and cases cited therein) [same]; *State of California v. U.S.*, 104 F.3d 1086, 1093 (9th Cir. 1996), *cert. denied,* 522 U.S. 806 (1997) [AG's decision regarding allocation of money to state is committed to agency discretion]; *Chiles v. U.S.*, 69 F.3d 1094, 1096 (11th Cir. 1995) [whether AG is adequately guarding the border is committed to agency discretion]; *Shen v. Chertoff,* 494 F.Supp.2d 592 (E.D. Mich. 2007) [no cause of action for mandamus or APA for delay of 50 months in deciding AOS because of security checks because there is no nondiscretionary duty under mandamus and it is committed to agency discretion under the APA]; *Keane v. Chertoff*, 419 F.Supp. 2d 597 (S.D.N.Y. 2006) [petitioner's request that USCIS reopen AOS that was erroneously denied for abandonment and reschedule interview was committed to agency discretion under the APA and not subject to mandamus]; *Saccoh v. INS,* 24 F.Supp.2d 406, 409–10 (E.D. Pa. 1998) [DD's denial of extension of VD is not reviewable because there are no standards to apply]. The doctrine has also been applied to bar review of denials of employment authorization and prehearing voluntary departure for the beneficiaries of approved visa petitions. *Perales v. Casillas*, 903 F.2d 1043 (5th Cir. 1990) [no statutory or regulatory standard to apply]; *Lalani v. Perryman*, 105 F.3d 334, 337–38 (7th Cir. 1997) [DD decision denying administrative VD is unreviewable]; *Uzuegbu v. Caplinger*, 745 F.Supp. 1200, 1216 (E.D. La. 1990) [extending principle to denial of employment authorization for person in deportation hearing]; *Gomez-Arauz v. McNary*, 779 F.Supp. 1308 (W.D. Okl. 1991) [same]. And on certain consular decisions. *Legal Assistance for Vietnamese Asylum Seekers v. DOS*, 104 F.3d 1349, 1352–53 (D.C. Cir. 1997) [consular venue policy of Secy. of State is unreviewable]. This doctrine may also apply to preclude review of decisions concerning the remission or mitigation of fines. *McCoy v. U.S.*, 758 F.Supp. 299, 302 (E.D. Pa. 1991). One court has also applied the "committed to agency discretion" doctrine to bar the review of the propriety of screening decisions made by INS officers of interdicted Haitians outside the physical territory of the U.S. *Haitian Refugee Center, Inc. v. Baker*, 953 F.2d 1498, 1508 (11th Cir.), *cert. denied*, 502 U.S. 1112, 112 S.Ct. 1245 (1992).

Courts have rejected the "committed to agency discretion" doctrine in other immigration contexts. *Alcaraz v. INS,* 384 F.3d 1150, 1161 (9th Cir. 2004) [despite IIRIRA §309(c)(3) broad discretion by AG to grant repapering, the discretion has been legally circumscribed and therefore justiciable by various memos through which INS implemented its repapering policy]; *Haoud v. Ashcroft,* 350 F.3d 201, 206 (1st Cir. 2003) [the BIA decision to streamline a case is not committed to agency discretion as 8 C.F.R. §1003.1(e)(4) sets out substantial law to apply]; *Denko v. INS,* 351 F.3d 717, 731–32 (6th Cir. 2003) [finding that streamlining/AWO decisions are in principle subject to judicial review and not committed to agency discretion but determining that the AWO decision in this case was appropriate]; *Mendez-Gutierrez v. Ashcroft,* 340 F.3d 865, 868–69 (9th Cir. 2003) [IJ/BIA's decision not to reinstate a withdrawn asylum application is not committed to agency discretion because the criteria governing motions to reopen may be applied]; *Evangelical Lutheran Church in America v. INS,* 288 F.Supp.2d 32, 43–45 (D.D.C. 2003) [the doctrine does not apply to review of the denial of an untimely filed H-1B extension because the review of whether there were "extraordinary circumstances" warranting a waiver of the filing deadline is not committed to agency discretion by law]; *Capital Area Immigrants' Rights Coalition v. DOJ,* 264 F.Supp.2d 14, 22–24 (D.D.C. 2003) [regulatory changes to BIA involving streamlining, reduction in Board members, and time deadlines were not committed to agency discretion]; *M.B. v. Quarantillo,* 301 F.3d 109, 111–14 (3d Cir. 2002) [regulations *and* memorandum do supply "some law to apply" and therefore whether INS abused its discretion in denying to transfer a case to state court to permit a determination that an individual was a juvenile and eligible for special status was not committed to agency discretion by law]; *Cornejo-Barreto v. Seifert,* 218 F.3d 1004, 1013–14 (9th Cir. 2000) [Secy. of State's decisions regarding extradition of a fugitive who claims he will be tortured if returned are not committed to agency discretion]; *Gurbisz v. INS*, 675 F.Supp. 436, 443–44 (N.D. Ill. 1987) [rejecting applicability of *Heckler v. Chaney*, 470 U.S. 821 (1985) to AG denial of extended voluntary departure because initiation of deportation proceedings involves affirmative government action]; *Carrillo v. Mohrman*, 832 F.Supp. 1412, 1416–19 (D. Idaho 1989) [DD denial of request to extend V.D. is *not* committed to agency action].

C. *De Novo Review*—When actions are subject to review, they may be subject to different levels of scrutiny and different standards of review. In determining the applicable standard, the court must first determine the scope of its review power. Questions of law, including issues of statutory interpretation and constitutional issues, are reviewed de novo. *McNary v. Haitian Refugee Center,* 498 U.S. 479, 493 (1991); *Larin-Ulloa v. Gonzales,* 462 F.3d 456, 461 & n.7 (5th Cir. 2006) [notwithstanding any deference the court owes the BIA under *Chevron,* it reviews *de novo* whether a state criminal statute constitutes an aggravated felony under the INA]. In reviewing an agency's findings of fact, courts are generally limited to a review of the agency's record and may not decide factual questions *de novo.* Under INA §242(b)(4)(A), the court of appeals reviewing a final order of removal "shall decide the petition only on the administrative record on which the order is based." *Lukowski v. INS,* 279 F.3d 644, 646 (8th Cir. 2002) [where conviction was vacated and respondent now convicted of misdemeanor court of appeals could not consider it because it was not in the administrative record]; *Pollgreen v. Morris*, 770 F.2d 1536 (11th Cir. 1985) ["Factual questions may not be decided *de novo* by the district court unless (1) the agency's fact finding procedures are inadequate, or (2) when issues not before the agency are raised to enforce certain agency actions]; *Camp v. Pitts*, 411 U.S. 138, 141–42 (1973); *Citizens to Preserve Overton Park, Inc. v. Volpe*, 401 U.S. 402 (1971)."] *U.S. v. Von Harten*, 825 F.2d 1493 (11th Cir. 1987) [following *Pollgreen* and rejecting *de novo* review in final proceedings absent inadequacy in procedure or failure of agency to review issue]. *Crespo-Gomez v. Richard*, 780 F.2d 932 (11th Cir. 1986) [nothing in the statute or regulations require detailed findings in a decision by BIA on discretionary issues, if the administrative record sets out clearly the ground which forms the basis for the denial so that the court can review it for abuse of discretion]. *But see Rafaelano v. Wilson,* 471 F.3d 1091 (9th Cir. 2006) [where ICE's record was nonexistent on issue whether respondent voluntarily departed and was not subject to reinstatement, the court remanded the case to the BIA for a factual record]. Federal courts may receive testimony for a preliminary injunction, but cannot use it for the merits determination. *See Pollgreen, supra.*

D. *Post Hoc Review Prohibited*—An agency in federal court is also limited to the record it established at the time of its action, INA §242(b)(4)(A), and may not utilize *post hoc* rationalizations for its prior action; nor may the courts supply such reasons. *Citizens to Preserve Overton Park, Inc. v. Volpe*, 401 U.S. 402 (1971). *See also Bowen v. Georgetown Univ. Hosp.,* 488 U.S. 204, 212–13 (1988) [no deference given to agency's counsel's litigation position]; *Florida Power and Light Co. v. Lorion,* 470 U.S. 729, 744 (1985); *Federal Power Comm. v. Texaco, Inc.*, 417 U.S. 380, 397 (1974); *SEC v. Chenery Corp.*, 318 U.S. 80, 87 (1943); *Wala v. Mukasey,* 511 F.3d 102, 106 n.3 (2d Cir. 2007) [government was precluded from arguing that all convictions for burglary with intent to deprive a person of her property, whether the deprivation was temporary or permanent, was a CIMT because the BIA order expressly reference permanent taking]; *Badwan v. Gonzales,* 494 F.3d 566, 570–71 (6th Cir. 2007) [court rejected government's attempt to supply new reasons for IJ's improper denial of a continuance that were not addressed or discussed by the IJ in his denial]; *Galvez-Vergara v. Gonzales,* 484 F.3d 798, 803 n.6 (5th Cir. 2007) [reversed BIA for failure to follow *Matter of Grijalva* and declined DHS's invitation to affirm the decision on a ground not provided by the agency]; *Chukwu v. Att'y Gen. of the U.S.,* 484 F.3d 185, 193 (3d Cir. 2007) [where BIA did not rely on IJ's theory that beating of asylum applicant did not rise to persecution, the court could not rely on that rationale]; *Gebreeyesus v. Gonzales,* 482 F.3d 952, 955–56 (7th Cir. 2007) [reversed BIA denial of motion to reopen by Amharan from Ethiopia based upon changed country conditions where BIA did not supply reasoned decision and government sought to do so in violation of *Chenery*]; *Mouawad v. Gonzales,* 485 F.3d 405, 413–14 (8th Cir. 2007) [under *Chenery* the failure of the IJ to address acquiescence of Lebanese government to violence of Hezbollah did not permit review and CAT decision reversed]; *Singh v. DOJ,* 461 F.3d 290, 294 and n.3 (2d Cir. 2006) [finding that the BIA could not offer INA §204(c) as a reason for refusing to reopen the denial of a hardship waiver filed under an I-751, when the BIA itself failed to refer to it in denying the motion to reopen]; *Banks v. Gonzales,* 453 F.3d 449, 451 (7th Cir. 2006) [federal judges following *Chenery* cannot resolve administrative litigation on grounds that the agency ignored and a remand was appropriate where neither the IJ nor the BIA denied asylum to a Liberian of the Krahn tribe because Charles Taylor's repressive government was no longer in power]; *Lin v. Gonzales,* 445 F.3d 127, 136 (2d Cir. 2006) [court will not rely on purported inconsistencies in asylum testimony suggested by the government that the IJ did not consider]; *Wu v. INS,* 436 F.3d 157 (2d Cir. 2006) ["It is not the function of a reviewing court in an immigration case to scour the record to find reasons why a BIA decision should be affirmed. Rather, we take the Board's decision as we find it, and if the reasoning it advances for denying a petitioner's claim cannot support the result, we will vacate the decision"]; *Altamirano v. Gonzales,* 427 F.3d 586, 595 (9th Cir. 2005) ["*Chenery* requires that an agency's discretionary order be upheld, if at all, on the same basis articulated in the order by the agency itself…"]; *Zheng v. Gonzales,* 422 F.3d 98, 121–22 (3d Cir. 2005) [where BIA explicitly rejected AOS application because applicant was an arriving alien, the government could not argue other reasons for denying applicant a second opportunity to adjust]; *Lin v. DOJ,* 416 F.3d 184 (2d Cir. 2005) [rejecting government suggestion that court may simply supply its own rationale for the BIA's decision in *Matter of C-Y-Z-* and then act accordingly]; *Li v. Att'y Gen. of the U.S.,* 400 F.3d 157, 163–64 (3d Cir. 2005) [under *Chenery*, the court could not affirm or review BIA's decision on lack of credibility when the BIA did not rely on that ground in its decision]; *Uriostegui v. Gonzales,* 415 F.3d 660, 664–65 (7th Cir. 2005) [where BIA issued AWO on in absentia order but never addressed motion to remand court reversed noting that where there was no evidence of what the agency really intended and government counsel could not supply the reasons]; *Comollari v. Ashcroft,* 378 F.3d 694, 696–70 (7th Cir. 2004) [under *Chenery* doctrine rejected OIL's proffered reasons for denying CAT claim not offered by IJ/BIA]; *Berishaj v. Ashcroft,* 378 F.3d 314, 328–32 (3d Cir. 2004) [following *Chenery* and holding that the circuit could not take judicial notice of changed country conditions through DOS reports or otherwise as does the Seventh Circuit (*Pelinkovic*) because it violates the principle of resting the decision on the administrative record]. *Miljkovic v. Ashcroft,* 376 F.3d 754, 757 (7th Cir. 2004) [criticizing government lawyers for violating *Chenery Corp* doctrine for arguing that an asylum claim should be denied for reasons not considered by the IJ/BIA]; *Mengistu v. Ashcroft,* 355 F.3d 1044, 1046–47 (7th Cir. 2004) [government lawyer offering reasons for denial of motion to reopen Eritreans' case not provided by BIA violates *Chenery* doctrine]; *Rodriguez-Barajas v. INS*, 992 F.2d 94, 97–98 (7th Cir. 1993) ["In reversing administrative orders we review the agency's stated reasons, not counsel's rationalizations"]; *Osaghae v. INS*, 942 F.2d 1160 (7th Cir. 1991) [cannot supply new grounds for BIA's decision in court of appeals]; *Vargas v. INS*, 938 F.2d 358, 363 (2d Cir. 1991) [finding abuse of discretion]; *Mayo v. Schiltgen*, 921 F.2d 177 (8th Cir. 1990) [reversed exclusion finding where habeas judge relied upon theory/ facts not relied upon by agency]; *Shahandeh-Pey v. INS*, 831 F.2d 1384 (7th Cir. 1987) [court cannot review determination to deny asylum where BIA did not articulate reasons]; *Choi v. INS*, 798 F.2d 1189, 1192 (8th Cir. 1986) [remanded where applicant on E visa not given opportunity to respond to reasons on appeal given for denial]; *Bull v. INS*, 790 F.2d 869, 873 n.3 (11th Cir. 1986) [claim that alien not entitled to INA §212(h) waiver will not be considered where BIA/IJ did not articulate this as reason for their decision]; *Moret v. Karn*, 746 F.2d 989, 992 (3d Cir. 1984) [DD's decision to revoke parole may not be explained by *post hoc* rationalizations outside of the record]; *Tongatapu Woodcraft Hawaii, Ltd. v. Feldman*, 736 F.2d 1305 (9th Cir. 1984) [court can only judge agency's actions solely on grounds invoked by agency]; *Evangelical Lutheran Church in America v. INS,* 288 F.Supp.2d 32, 48 n.9 (D.D.C. 2003) [the post hoc rationalization of government counsel for the denial of an untimely extension of stay for an H-1B cannot substitute for the former INS's own lack of clarity in denying the application]; *Guirola-Beeche v. DOJ*, 662 F.Supp. 1414 (S.D. Fla. 1987) [in bond breach case, Court cannot supply reasoned basis for decision that agency did not articulate]; *Matter of Pradieu*, 19 I&N Dec. 419 (BIA 1986) [in the DD's decision denying a relative visa petition the record should contain all evidence submitted by petitioner as well as INS]. The same is true of the nongovernmental party. *The Sweet Life v. Dole*, 876 F.2d 402 (5th Cir. 1989) [court of appeals cannot consider decision not part of original record simply because it is appended to petitioner's brief]; *K.C.P. Food Co. v. Sava*, 623 F.Supp. 1080 (S.D.N.Y. 1985) [petitioner precluded from offering additional nonrecord evidence in district court]. *cf. Flores-Garza v. Reno,* 369 F.Supp.2d 894, 896–98 (S.D. Tex. 2005) [*Chenery* doctrine does not preclude a court from stating its own legal preference in reaching a result that does not reject the result reached by the agency].

E. ***Agency Record***—The agency also has a clear definition of its administrative record. 8 C.F.R. §1240.9. *Okoroha v. INS*, 715 F.2d 380, 383–84 (8th Cir. 1983); *Choi v. INS*, 798 F.2d 1189 (8th Cir. 1986) [remanded where decision not based on consideration of the full record]. Where the record is inadequate, the case will be remanded. *Recinos De Leon v. Gonzales,* 400 F.3d 1185 (9th Cir. 2005) [where IJ wrote incoherent opinion and BIA entered a streamlined affirmed order, the court held that:

"When the agency's only explanation of its final action is incoherent, we may not substantively review it without violating basic principles of judicial review"]; *Yang v. McElroy,* 277 F.3d 158 (2d Cir. 2002) [where there was a four-year delay between the BIA decision and the IJ decision which relied on a five-year-old State Department Country report the Court remanded the case back to the BIA for more current reports]; *Osaghae v. INS,* 942 F.2d 1160 (7th Cir. 1991) [remand where asylum applicant claimed there was new evidence the BIA should consider]. The IJ has the obligation to mark documents for identification so the court may review them. *Ladha v. INS,* 215 F.3d 889, 903–05 (9th Cir. 2000). The agency has a "duty to prepare a reasonably accurate, reasonably complete transcript." *Garza-Moreno v. Gonzales,* 489 F.3d 239, 241–42 (6th Cir. 2007) [although "due process demands a reasonable accurate and complete transcript to allow for meaningful appellate review" the BIA's decision was not reversed despite 67 "indiscernible" notations in the transcript because there was no showing of prejudice]; *Ortiz-Salas v. INS,* 992 F.2d 105, 106 (7th Cir. 1993) [where testimony that was not transcribed was not shown to be material or affect outcome BIA affirmed]; *Kheireddine v. Gonzales,* 427 F.3d 80 (1st Cir. 2005) [finding that IJ/BIA had duty to provide accurate transcript but where respondent failed to show specific prejudice to perfect appeal the court will not remand or reverse the decision]. *See also Teng v. Mukasey,* 516 F.3d 12, 18 (1st Cir. 2008) [no due process violation because to succeed on a claim for inadequate or inaccurate translation the party must show specific prejudice that hindered the ability to appeal]; *Chickwendu v. Gonzales,* 415 F.3d 142 (1st Cir. 2005) [IJ's reconstruction of two witnesses testimony after forgetting to tape record them was not a due process violation where counsel participated and did not object to the reconstruction, where there were affidavits from the witnesses in evidence and where there was no showing of prejudice]; *but see Khan v. Mukasey,* 517 F.3d 513, 518–19 (7th Cir. 2008) [IJ's off-the-record discussion regarding wife's testimony did not prevent petitioner from receiving a fair hearing, despite Chief IJ's memorandum requiring discussion to be on the record, where IJ stated he would have denied waiver anyway]; *Mathews v. INS,* 170 F.Supp.2d 99 (D. Mass. 2001) [respondent not provided transcript of IJ's oral decision did not suffer prejudice because he is only entitled to IJ's order and was not prevented from making all arguments to BIA].

Argument of counsel in brief to BIA is not evidence for court of appeals to consider. *Tang v. INS,* 223 F.3d 713, 720 (8th Cir. 2000).

The court of appeals is generally limited by statute to the administrative record (unless the appeal involves a citizenship claim). INA §242(b)(4)(A), 8 U.S.C. §1252(b)(4)(A). Under INA §242(b)(4)(A), the court of appeals reviewing a final order of removal "shall decide the petition only on the administrative record on which the order is based." *Ocha-Carillo v. Gonzales,* 2006 U.S. App. LEXIS 3513 (8th Cir 2006) [review of reinstatement order is "limited to the agency's certified administrative record," *citing* INA §242(b)(4)(A) and *Grass v. Gonzales,* 418 F.3d 876, 879 (8th Cir. 2005)]; *Castro-Cortez v. INS,* 239 F.3d 1037, 1040 n.2 (9th Cir. 2001) ["We may decide [these direct appeals] only on the administrative record on which the INS based its decision"]; *Al-Fara v. Gonzales,* 404 F.3d 733, 743–44 (3d Cir. 2005) [court would not consider new evidence outside the record in asylum case as respondent should file motion to reopen with BIA regarding new country conditions]; *Lukowski v. INS,* 279 F.3d 644, 646 (8th Cir. 2002) [where conviction was vacated and respondent now convicted of misdemeanor court of appeals could not consider it because it was not in the administrative record]. *See also Infanzon v. Ashcroft,* 386 F.3d 1359, 1363 (10th Cir. 2004) [rejected respondent's attempt to add information to asylum claim before circuit court or to bolster *Lozada* claim by providing proof that Bar charge was filed]; *Berishaj v. Ashcroft,* 378 F.3d 314, 317 (3d Cir. 2004) [noting that administrative records in asylum cases are "grossly out-of-date" and calling upon Congress and the Executive Branch to restructure the process]. Citizenship claims are not necessarily bound by the record. 8 U.S.C. §1252(b)(5); *Batista v. Ashcroft,* 270 F.3d 8, 12–15 (1st Cir. 2001) [permitting consideration of documents outside of the administrative record as in summary judgment under Fed. R. Civ. P. 56 where citizenship claim is raised]. A petitioner may also be permitted to present evidence on appeal that is outside the record of proceedings in the immigration court "in order to show that he was prejudiced by the lack of a full and fair hearing." *Colmenar v. INS,* 210 F.3d 967, 972 n.5 (9th Cir. 2000). The record may also be supplemented and discovery permitted in the district court where there is a strong showing of bad faith or improper behavior. *Citizens to Preserve Overton Park, Inc. v. Volpe,* 401 U.S. 402, 420 (1971). *But see Balaton, Inc. v. Reno,* 93 F.Supp.2d 61 (D.D.C. 2000) [claim that AAU always affirms denials of small company L-1s is not a basis for discovery to supplement administrative record]. Where the record is inadequate a remand is appropriate. *Rafaelano v. Wilson,* 471 F.3d 1091 (9th Cir. 2006) [where ICE's record was nonexistent on issue whether respondent voluntarily departed and was not subject to reinstatement, the court remanded the case to the BIA for a factual record]. The agency opinion must also be specific and must state with sufficient particularity and clarity the reasons for denial. Boilerplate opinions are insufficient. *Paramasamy v. Ashcroft,* 295 F.3d 1047, 1048–52 (9th Cir. 2002) [BIA reversed for relying on credibility finding in asylum case based upon boilerplate demeanor observations by the IJ]; *De La Llana-Castellon v. INS*, 16 F.3d 1093, 1098 (10th Cir. 1994); *Rhoa-Zamora v. INS*, 971 F.2d 26, 36–37 (7th Cir. 1992), *cert. denied*, 113 S.Ct. 2331 (1993) [where opinion entirely boilerplate it must be reversed]; *Castillo v. INS*, 951 F.2d 1117, 1121 (9th Cir. 1991). Bare conclusions for refusing to exercise discretion are also insufficient absent a frivolous argument. *Bastanipour v. INS*, 980 F.2d 1129, 1131 (7th Cir. 1992). Under a writ of habeas corpus other evidence may be permitted. *Townsend v. Sain*, 372 U.S. 293 (1963); *Amanullah v. Nelson*, 811 F.2d 1, 16 (1st Cir. 1987); *Nguyen Da Yen v. Kissinger*, 528 F.2d 1194, 1202–04 (9th Cir. 1975); *Ahmad v. Russell*, ___ F.Supp. ___, Case No. 88-2-984 (D. Colo. Mar. 6, 1989). *But see Haghi v. Russell*, 744 F.Supp. 249 (D. Colo. 1990) [court in habeas will not consider alien's vacation of conviction because it was not part of admin. record].

F. *Standards of Review*—There are many matters that were reviewable prior to IIRIRA that are now precluded from judicial review. *See in this chapter* section IV.A (p.1108), *supra*. Where judicial review has not been precluded, and where matters are not subject to *de novo* or plenary review different standards will be applied that relate to the nature of the matter being reviewed if there is jurisdiction to review them:

1. Facially Legitimate and *Bona Fide*. *Kleindienst v. Mandel*, 408 U.S. 753 (1972); *Fiallo v. Bell*, 430 U.S. 787 (1977) [regarding questions of admission]; *Noh v. INS*, 248 F.3d 938 (9th Cir. 2001) [applied standard to the decision of the Asst. Secy. of State to revoke a visa]; *Miller v. Christopher*, 96 F.3d 1467, 1470–71 (D.C. Cir. 1996) [applying standard to citizenship claim]; *Ablang v. Reno*, 52 F.3d 801 (9th Cir. 1995) [same]; *Price v. INS*, 962 F.2d 836 (9th Cir. 1992) [applying standard to validate questions on naturalization application]; *Garcia-Mir v. Smith*, 766 F.2d 1478 (11th Cir. 1985), *cert. denied sub nom. Marquez-Medina v. Meese,* 475 U.S. 1022 (1986) [utilizing the facially legitimate and *bona fide* standard in reviewing parole determinations]. *But see Jean v. Nelson*, 472 U.S. 846 (1985) [adopting less deferential standard in matters concerning parole based on race or national origin]; *Marczak v. Greene*, 971 F.2d 510, 515–17 (10th Cir. 1992) [arguing that there is no practical difference between facially legitimate and abuse of discretion standards]. The "facially legitimate and bona fide" standard has also been used in the context of an Equal Protection challenge. *Fiallo v. Bell,* 430 U.S. 787 (1977). In this context, some courts have equated the "facially legitimate and bona fide standard" with rational basis review. *Ablang v. Reno,* 52 F.3d 801, 804 (9th Cir. 1995); *Wauchope v. DOS,* 985 F.2d 1407, 1414 n.3 (9th Cir. 1993).
2. Manifestly Contrary to Law—INA §242(b)(4) now applies a "manifestly contrary to law" standard in reviewing a decision as to a person's eligibility for admission and the AG's discretionary judgment concerning whether to grant asylum. A decision regarding eligibility for admission is conclusive unless manifestly contrary to law. INA §242(b)(4)(C). The discretionary judgment of the AG in asylum cases is conclusive unless manifestly contrary to law and an abuse of discretion. INA §242(b)(4)(D). *Huang v. INS,* 436 F.3d 89, 96–102 (2d Cir. 2006) [IJ acted manifestly contrary to law under INA §242(b)(4)(D) in denying asylum as a matter of discretion where he failed to examine the totality of the circumstances and focused solely on the embellishment of peripheral testimony and the applicant's payment to a smuggler].
3. Abuse of Discretion Test

   3.a. *Wong Wing Hang v. INS*, 360 F.2d 715, 718–19 (2d Cir. 1966) states classic test ["If it was made without a rational explanation, inexplicably departed from established procedures, or rested on an impermissible basis such as an invidious discrimination against a particular race or group or other considerations that Congress could not have intended to make relevant"]. When determining whether the agency's action was arbitrary, irrational or not in accordance with law, the courts "engage in a substantial inquiry ... a thorough probing, in-depth review of [the] discretionary agency action." *Citizens to Preserve Overton Park, Inc. v. Volpe*, 401 U.S. 402, 416 (1971); *Diaz-Resendez v. INS*, 960 F.2d 493, 495 (5th Cir. 1992) [same]. Abuse of discretion can occur by courts "neglecting to consider a significant factor that appropriately bears on the discretionary decision, by attaching weight to a factor that does not appropriately bear on the decision, or by assaying all the proper factors and no improper ones, but nonetheless making a clear judgmental error in weighing them." *Henry v. INS*, 74 F.3d 1, 4 (1st Cir. 1996) [rejected abuse of discretion argument in AOS]. *See also Twum v. INS,* 411 F.3d 54 (2d Cir. 2005) [where IJ misconstrued *in absentia* motion to reopen as an ineffective assistance of counsel claim under *Lozada* rather than a claim that security guards barred his entry to the court, the circuit court reversed and remanded]. The agency will also abuse its discretion if it does not make a careful *and* individualized determination, *Stankovic v. INS*, 94 F.3d 1117 (7th Cir. 1996) [reversed BIA where its legal reasoning has no applicability to facts of the case]; *Babai v. INS*, 985 F.2d 252, 255 (6th Cir. 1993), or fails to articulate its reasons for its decision. *Rodriguez-Matamoros v. INS*, 86 F.3d 158, 161 (9th Cir. 1996) [asylum claim]; *Tukhowinich v. INS*, 64 F.3d 460 (9th Cir. 1995).

The agency also abuses its discretion when it inexplicably departs from prior precedent, departs from its own regulations, fails to consider all relevant factors, or considers irrelevant factors. *Melnitsenko v. Mukasey,* 517 F.3d 42, 48–52 (2d Cir. 2008) [BIA cannot deny a motion under *Velarde-Pacheco* where petitioner meets all five criteria solely on the basis of DHS's opposition]; *Shardar v. Att'y Gen. of the U.S.,* 503 F.3d 308, 314–16 (3d Cir. 2007) [BIA's claim it did not have to follow unpublished decision missed the mark because "by reaching an exactly contrary decision on a materially indistinguishable set of facts, the Board acted arbitrarily"]; *Galvez-Vergara v. Gonzales,* 484 F.3d 798 (5th Cir. 2007) [reversed BIA in *in absentia* proceeding for failure to give any explanation for not following *Matter of Grijalva* where respondent argued exceptional circumstances due to ineffective assistance of counsel]; *Singh v. DOJ,* 461 F.3d 290, 295–97 (2d Cir. 2006) [failure of BIA to follow its regulation regarding acceptance of evidence concerning hardship that occurred after conditional residency is terminated was an abuse of discretion]; *Nadarajah v. Gonzales,* 443 F.3d 1069 (9th Cir. 2006) [ICE abused its discretion in denying parole under INA §212(d)(5)(A) in part by ignoring evidence of the detention's deleterious effect on petitioner's health]; *Osei v. INS,* 305 F.3d 1205 (10th Cir. 2002) [BIA reversed where it departed from its consistent interpretation of the motion to reopen provision, former 8 C.F.R. §3.2(c)(1), that a motion based upon ineffective assistance of counsel was not required to show new evidence]; *Virk v. INS,* 295 F.3d 1055 (9th Cir. 2002) [reversed BIA's denial of motion to reopen to apply for INA §241(f) relief where it departed from former precedent under INA §241(f) and where it failed to consider all relevant factors and improperly considered an irrelevant factor]; *Johnson v. Ashcroft,* 286 F.3d 696 (3d Cir. 2002) [finding that the BIA had inexplicably departed from *Matter of Patel,* 16 I&N Dec. 600, 601 (BIA 1978) regarding what an IJ may consider on remand, the court reversed BIA's decision that IJ did not have discretion to consider asylum claim after BIA reopened case for CAT claim]. *Lal v. INS,* 255 F.3d 998, 1006–07 (9th Cir. 2001) *amended on reh'g* 268 F.3d 1148 (9th Cir. 2001) [BIA's interpretation adding new criteria to obtain asylum through past persecution flatly contradicts previous BIA decisions without a reasoned explanation for the departure]; *Arrozal v. INS,* 159 F.3d 429, 433–34 (9th Cir. 1998) [failure to consider all factors when it superficially mentions them in denial of motion to reopen for suspension]; *Urbina-Osejo v. INS*, 124 F.3d 1314, 1318–19 (9th Cir. 1997) [BIA failed to consider all relevant factors in denying suspension]; *Urban v. INS*, 123 F.3d 644 (7th Cir. 1997) [same]; *Watkins v. INS*, 63 F.3d 844, 850 (9th Cir. 1995) [reversed denial of motion to reopen for suspension for failing to consider all relevant factors and the cumulative effect of the factors and recognized that the INS abuses its discretion "no less by arriving at plausible decisions in an arbitrary fashion than by reaching unreasonable results."]; *Rodriguez-Gutierrez v. INS*, 59 F.3d 504 (5th Cir. 1995) [BIA failed to consider positive factors and mischaracterized negative ones]; *Delmundo v. INS*, 43 F.3d 436 (9th Cir. 1994) [reversed denial of INA §212(i) waiver for considering impermissible factors and failing to consider other factors]; *Margalli-Olvera v. INS*, 43 F.3d 345 (8th Cir. 1994) [BIA abused discretion by changing its position without explanation as to the tolling period for INA §212(c)]; *Yepes-Prado v. INS*, 10 F.3d 1363, 1372 (9th Cir. 1993) [inexplicably departed from *Edwards*]; *Braun v. INS*, 992 F.2d 1016 (9th Cir. 1993) [considered irrelevant factor in denying INA §241(f)]; *Espinoza v. INS*, 991 F.2d 1294 (7th Cir. 1993) [denial of former INA §212(c) based on speculation unsupported by the record vacated]; *Akinyemi v. INS*, 969 F.2d 285 (7th Cir. 1992) [denial of INA §212(c) where BIA inexplicably departed from precedent and failed to consider positive equities]; *Vargas v. INS*, 938 F.2d 358 (2d Cir. 1991) [abuse of discretion by BIA to deny INA §212(c) applicants the right to file motions to reopen where agency's sole support is an inapplicable case, where other BIA decisions are inconsistent, where a regulation conflicts with the decision, and where the decision has no logical foundation]; *Lauvik v. INS*, 910 F.2d 658 (9th Cir. 1990) [where denial of E-2 extension is based on "evidence so slight and so thoroughly outweighed by contrary evidence" it is an abuse of discretion]; *Hall v. McLaughlin*, 864 F.2d 868, 872 (D.C. Cir. 1989) [*quoting Greater Boston Television Corp. v. FCC*, 444 F.2d 841 (D.C. Cir. 1970), abuse where agency "glosses over or swerves from prior precedent"]; *Kabongo v. INS*, 837 F.2d 753, 756 (6th Cir. 1988) [abuse of discretion where court "has definite and firm conviction that the court below committed a clear error of judgment in the conclusion it reached upon the weighing of the relevant factors"]; *Gonzalez-Batoon v. INS*, 791 F.2d 681, 685 (9th Cir. 1986) (*en banc*) [BIA abused its discretion when it gave no reason for its deviation from past practice]; *Achacoso-Sanchez v. INS*, 779 F.2d 1260 (7th Cir. 1985) [applies *Wong Wing* standard]; *Salehpour v. INS*, 761 F.2d 1442 (9th Cir. 1985) [abuse of discretion where the agency's interpretation is inconsistent with its own regulations and is not reasonable or where it adds additional requirements not specified in regulations when alien has met the regulation's requirements]; *Fred 26 Importers, Inc. v. DHS,* 445 F.Supp.2d 1174, 1178–79 (C.D. Cal. 2006) [court reversed AAO denial of an H-1B petition where it failed to address expert and other evidence that a human resource manager position in a small export/import company required duties which were specialized and complex and, instead, simply asserted that a small company did not require specialized and complex duties]; *The Button Depot, Inc. v. DHS,* 386 F.Supp.2d 1140 (C.D. Cal. 2005) [reversed denial of H-1B petition for accountant where DHS abused its discretion by failing to apply the relevant standards regarding an equivalent foreign degree, by failing to consider evidence, and by relying on unrelated factors]; *Peppercorn, Inc. v. Ridge,* ___ F.Supp.2d ___, Case No. 04-20667-CIV-HIGHSMITH (S.D.Fla. May 10, 2005) [denied DHS motion for summary judgment where DHS had denied an H-1B petition for a management analyst after approving one with the same evaluation for another company]; *Camarena v. Meissner,* 78 F.Supp.2d 1044 (N.D. Cal. 1999) [INS abused its discretion in denying extension of family unity benefits by relying on information that was rebutted and shown to be demonstrably false]; *Bodeux v. INS*, 668 F.Supp. 1452 (D. Kan. 1987) [same in H-1 context]; *Israel v. INS*, 785 F.2d 738 (9th Cir. 1986) [BIA reversed for abuse of discretion where it failed to follow its own precedent in marriage cases]; *Babai v. INS*, 985 F.2d 252 (6th Cir. 1993) [agency must consider all relevant factors]; *Cerrillo-Perez v. INS*, 809 F.2d 1419 (9th Cir. 1987) [same]; *Unical Aviation, Inc. v. INS,* 248 F.Supp.2d 931 (C.D. Cal. 2002) [reversed AAO denial of H-1B extension where company submitted sufficient evidence to show that position of senior market analyst required person with specialized study]; *Louisiana Philharmonic Orchestra v. INS,* 44 F.Supp.2d 800 (E.D.La. 1999) [where H-1B denied on unexplained change by AAU after approving other applications]; *Singh v. Swan*, 908 F.Supp. 634 (E.D. Wis. 1995) [BIA abused discretion in summarily dismissing appeal]; *Buletini v. INS*, 860 F.Supp. 1222 (E.D. Mich. 1994) [incorrect application of regulations for priority worker of exceptional ability]; *Grijalva v. Ilchert*, 815 F.Supp. 328 (N.D. Cal. 1993) [application of frivolous standard inconsistent with INS own policies]; *Masonry Masters, Inc. v. Thornburgh*, 742 F.Supp. 682 (D.D.C. 1990) [inconsistent adjudications on 2 employer I-140 petitions for same position for 2 employees not entitled to deference]; *Omni Packaging, Inc. v. INS*, 733 F.Supp. 500 (D.P.R. 1990) [INS reversed for abuse of discretion where it failed to apply standards consistently in approving L-1 petitions and denying 3d preference petition]; *National Collegiate Recreation Services v. Powell,* Case No. 9:02cv02676 (D.S.C. Nov. 26, 2002), *reported in* 80 No. 7 *Interpreter Releases* 244–46 (Feb. 19, 2003) [revocation of American Hospitality Academy's J-1 program designation was arbitrary and capricious because the DOS imposed the harshest penalty without basis and its fact finding was deficient]; *But see Rust v. Sullivan*, 111 S.Ct. 1759, 1768–69 (1991) [a revised interpretation deserves deference where there is a reasoned analysis]; *Ajdin v. USCIS,* 437 F.3d 261, 264–65 (2d Cir. 2006) [BIA did not abuse its discretion by failing to adhere to an unpublished decision]; *AFL-CIO v. Dole*, 923 F.2d 182, 186 (D.C. Cir. 1991) [it is not an abuse of discretion where agency substantially changes its policy but provides a detailed and reasonable explanation]; *Karapetian v. INS*, 162 F.3d 933 (7th Cir. 1998) [different treatment of family members regarding asylum did not compel grant to family member denied asylum]; *Q Data Consulting*

Inc. v. INS, 293 F.Supp.2d 25, 29–30 (D.D.C. 2003) [INS did not abuse its discretion in its denial of EB-1 managerial position when it approved an L-1A petition subsequent to the denial for the same managerial position]; *Louisiana Philharmonic Orchestra v. INS*, 2000 WL 282785 (E.D. La. Mar. 15, 2000) [service center's prior decisions are not binding on the AAO]; *Matter of Burbano*, 20 I&N Dec. 872, 873 (BIA 1994) ["Differing decisions may be reached based on essentially identical facts"].

3.b. It is an abuse of discretion also to fail to exercise discretion. *Accardi v. Shaughnessy*, 347 U.S. 260 (1954). The abuse of discretion test, however, does not permit the Court to encroach upon the INS's decisions in weighing various factors. *London Typographers Inc. v. Sava*, 628 F.Supp. 570, 577 (S.D.N.Y. 1986) [agency may prefer another interpretation of the statute]; *INS v. Wang*, 450 U.S. 139, 144 (1981); *INS v. Rios-Pineda*, 471 U.S. 444 (1985); *INS v. Bagamasbad*, 429 U.S. 24 (1976). *See also Jay v. Boyd*, 351 U.S. 345 (1956).

3.c. Unfettered Discretion—Even where the agency's discretion is unfettered at the outset it may abuse its discretion. In *INS v. Yueh-Shaio Yang,* 519 U.S. 26, 117 S.Ct. 350, 353 (1996) the Court recognized that: "Though the agency's discretion is unfettered at the outset, if it announces and follows—by rule or by settled course of adjudication—a general policy by which its exercise of discretion will be governed, an irrational departure from the policy (as opposed to an avowed alteration of it) could constitute action that must be overturned as 'arbitrary, capricious, [or] an abuse of discretion' within the meaning of the Administrative Procedure Act, 5 U.S.C. §706(1)(A)."

3.d. Extreme Hardship—Review of "extreme hardship" decisions (including both suspension of deportation cases and cancellation of removal cases) is restricted by section 309(c)(4)(H) of AEDPA, which was enacted in April 1996 and INA §242(a)(2)(B)(i), which was enacted as part of IIRIRA in September 1996. *See in this chapter* ¶ IV.A.3 (p.1112), *supra*. Prior to AEDPA and IIRIRA, review of "extreme hardship" decisions in suspension cases, although narrow, was subject to scrutiny. *Ordonez v. INS,* 137 F.3d 1120 (9th Cir. 1998) [failure to properly evaluate fear of persecution in suspension]; *Salameda v. INS*, 70 F.3d 447 (7th Cir. 1995) [failure to consider community services]; *Blanco v. INS*, 68 F.3d 642 (2d Cir. 1995) [reversed BIA denial of motion to reopen for failure to consider violence in El Salvador]; *Tukhowinich v. INS*, 64 F.3d 460 (9th Cir. 1995) [where BIA opinion did not articulate reasons for denial]; *Biggs v. INS*, 55 F.3d 1398, 1401–02 (9th Cir. 1995) [abuse of discretion to prevent applicant from fully developing record of medical hardship]; *Turri v. INS*, 997 F.2d 1306 (10th Cir. 1993) [effect of community service on extreme hardship]; *Babai v. INS*, 985 F.2d 252 (6th Cir. 1993) [reversed BIA where it failed to consider hardship to USC child if he remained in U.S.]; *Hernandez-Patino v. INS*, 831 F.2d 750, 752 (7th Cir. 1987). *But see Hernandez-Cordero v. INS*, 819 F.2d 558, 563 (5th Cir. 1987) (*en banc*) ["We are entitled to find that the BIA abused its discretion only in a case where the hardship is uniquely extreme, at or closely approaching the outer limits of the most severe hardship the alien could suffer and so severe that any reasonable person would necessarily conclude that the hardship is extreme"].

3.e. Motions to Reopen—On motions to reopen, the Supreme Court and the lower federal courts have given great deference to the agency when making those determinations. *INS v. Rios-Pineda*, 471 U.S. 444 (1985) [agency can consider factors outside of the statutes in determining motions to reopen without being arbitrary and capricious. For example, the INS may consider the "flagrancy and nature" of aliens' immigration violations so long as the concerns are legitimate concerns about the administration of immigration laws].

(1) In *INS v. Abudu*, 485 U.S. 94 (1988), the Court articulated three grounds for denying motions to reopen. First, failure to make out a *prima facie* case for the underlying substantive relief. Second, failure to explain under 8 C.F.R. §1003.2, 8 C.F.R. §103.5, 8 C.F.R. §1003.23, or in asylum, 8 C.F.R. §§208.17, 1208.17 why the movant did not file originally. Third, in the case of matters concerning discretionary relief such as asylum and suspension, as distinguished from withholding, the agency exercises its discretion under *Rios-Pineda* irrespective of eligibility on the first two grounds. The latter two criteria are reviewed under an abuse of discretion test. *INS v. Wang*, 450 U.S. 139 (1981); *Fesseha v. Ashcroft,* 333 F.3d 13, 20–21 (1st Cir. 2003) [applying *Abudu* standards and finding no abuse of discretion for failure of Ethiopian to establish a prima facie case of asylum]. The

abuse of discretion standard has not been lessened by the codification of motions to reopen in IIRIRA. *Fessehaye v. Gonzales,* 414 F.3d 746, 752 and n.5 (7th Cir. 2005) [rejected asylum claimant's argument that the statutory recognition of motions to reopen under IIRIRA lessened the degree of deference owed the BIA].

(2) Cases Finding Abuse of Discretion. *Melnitsenko v. Mukasey,* 517 F.3d 42, 48–52 (2d Cir. 2008) [BIA cannot deny a motion under *Velarde-Pacheco* where petitioner meets all five criteria solely on the basis of DHS's opposition]; *Mai v. Gonzales,* 473 F.3d 162, 165–67 (5th Cir. 2007) [reversed BIA denial of motion to reopen for ineffective assistance despite BIA's claim that the lawyer made a strategic decision when he admitted two grounds of removal where one required a §212(c) waiver and the second a waiver under §240A because once §212(c) granted for the first ground §240A was unavailable for the second];*Larin-Ulloa v. Gonzales,* 462 F.3d 456 (5th Cir. 2006) [BIA abused its discretion where it denied a motion to reopen based upon an error of law in its interpretation that a Kansas aggravated battery statute was an aggravated felony]; *Norani v. Gonzales,* 451 F.3d 292 (2d Cir. 2006) [BIA abused its discretion when it failed to consider motion to reopen by Iranian Jews for asylum/withholding/CAT based upon changed circumstances and instead issued a three-sentence order that was devoid of reasoning and denied the motion because applicants had not filed previously]; *Bhasin v. Gonzales,* 423 F.3d 977, 986 (9th Cir. 2005) [Indian mother's social group claim, based upon her family, submitted an affidavit that other family members were missing and the BIA improperly discounted the affidavit as self-serving]; *Fessehaye v. Gonzales,* 414 F.3d 746, 754–56 (7th Cir. 2005) [where applicant relied on her own affidavit to reopen for asylum due to religious persecution as a Jehovah Witness in Ethiopia, the BIA abused its discretion in not articulating why her evidence was insufficient in light of law permitting asylum to person who does not present corroborating evidence]; *Zhao v. Gonzales,* 404 F.3d 295, 304–06 (5th Cir. 2005) [the BIA abused its discretion in refusing to grant a motion to reopen to admit the 2002 International Religious Freedom Report and the 2002 Country Report on China from the DOS because both reports supported respondent's contention that Falun Gong members were persecuted]; *Movsisian v. Ashcroft,* 395 F.3d 1095, 1097–98 (9th Cir. 2005) [BIA decision was reversed as an abuse of discretion where it sought to streamline its denial by giving a one sentence decision (The motion to reopen is denied) that failed to articulate any reasoned basis for denying the motion]; *Zhao v. DOJ,* 265 F.3d 83, 95–97 (2d Cir. 2001) [reversed denial of reopening in forced sterilization asylum case where BIA relied on cursory and speculative statements that simultaneously appeared to acknowledge that IJ determined that sterilization had occurred but refused to allow reopening to present proof regarding it]; *Mickeviciute v. INS,* 327 F.3d 1159 (10th Cir. 2003) [reversed BIA where it failed to articulate which of the 3 *Abudu* grounds it relied upon in denying respondent's motion to reopen]; *Arrozal v. INS,* 159 F.3d 429, 433–34 (9th Cir. 1998) [BIA reversed where it superficially mentioned factors but failed to address them in suspension context]; *Watkins v. INS*, 63 F.3d 844 (9th Cir. 1995) [reversed denial of motion to reopen by BIA where it failed to consider all factors and their cumulative effect in suspension]; *Rodriguez-Gutierrez v. INS*, 59 F.3d 504, 508–09 (5th Cir. 1995) [reversed denial of motion to reopen for adjustment where failed to consider positive factors and mischaracterized negative ones]; *Dulane v. INS*, 46 F.3d 988, 994–96 (10th Cir. 1995) [failure to consider all relevant factors in denying motion to reopen for suspension is reversed]; *Shin v. INS*, 750 F.2d 122 (D.C. Cir. 1984); *Osuchukwu v. INS*, 744 F.2d 1136 (5th Cir. 1984); *Yahkpua v. INS*, 770 F.2d 1317 (5th Cir. 1985) [*Rios* extended to adjustment of status]; *Hernandez-Ortiz v. INS*, 777 F.2d 509 (9th Cir. 1985) [there are limits to *Rios-Pineda* where the agency must grant relief such as INA §243(h) or where disqualifying equities written into regulations and statutes such as INA §208]; *Mattis v. INS*, 774 F.2d 965 (9th Cir. 1985) [*Rios-Pineda* may not be extended to include impermissible factors such as last minute marriages]. The question of whether a party has established a prima facie case is also subject to an abuse of discretion standard in the view of some circuits. *Limsico v. INS*, 951 F.2d 210, 213 (9th Cir. 1991); *M.A. v. INS*, 899 F.2d 304, 307–10 (4th Cir. 1990) (*en banc*).

(3) Procedural Problems On Review. For purposes of judicial review, all decisions on motions to reopen or reconsider an administrative order must be consolidated with that order

in the federal appeal. INA §242(b)(6), 8 U.S.C. §1252(b)(6). In *Stone v. INS*, 514 U.S. 386, 398–401, 405–06, 115 S.Ct. 1537 (1995), the Supreme Court interpreted this section (under former INA §106) as *not* requiring the tolling of the underlying time period for an appeal so that the finality of the removal order is not affected by the filing of a motion to reopen. *Accord Tchuinga v. Gonzales,* 454 F.3d 54, 60–61 (1st Cir. 2006) [court lacked jurisdiction to review IJ's determination that respondent's asylum application was frivolous where finding was not appealed and respondent sought to raise it on appeal of denial of motion to reopen]; *Gomes v. Gonzales,* 429 F.3d 1264, 1267 (9th Cir. 2005) [the grant of a motion to reopen because of changed circumstances in an asylum case addresses issues concerning future persecution and applicant's failure to appeal original order of removal regarding past persecution could not be included in new appeal of denial of future persecution]; *Membreno v. Gonzales,* 425 F.3d 1227 (9th Cir. 2005) (*en banc*) [where petition for review was filed within 30 days of denial of motion to reopen but almost one year after the underlying removal order, the court had no jurisdiction to review the underlying removal order]; *De Araujo v. Ashcroft,* 399 F.3d 84, 88–89 (1st Cir. 2005) [review of designation as aggravated felon is barred because respondent did not appeal BIA's final decision and appeal of a denial of motion to reopen for INA §212(c) relief is also barred because INA §242(a)(2)(C) bars review of all claims of an aggravated felon]; *Ahmed v. Ashcroft,* 388 F.3d 247 (7th Cir. 2004) [motion for reconsideration does not toll time on original BIA order and therefore the court could only review the propriety of the denial of the request to reopen]; *Boudaguian v. Ashcroft,* 376 F.3d 825, 827 (8th Cir. 2004) [court lacks jurisdiction to review BIA's original order because the appeal was filed within 30 days of the motion to reopen and not the original BIA decision]; *Dakane v. U.S. Attornet General,* 399 F.3d 1269, 1272–73 n.3 (11th Cir. 2005) [the 30-day filing deadline for the appeal is not tolled by filing a motion to reopen]; *Zhang v. INS,* 348 F.3d 289 (1st Cir. 2003) [appeal of issues regarding credibility and IJ/BIA application of the well-founded fear standard were untimely because the appeal notice was filed beyond 30 days and the pendency of the motion to reopen did not stop time for filing appeal]; *Raffington v. INS,* 340 F.3d 720, 724 (8th Cir. 2003) [where respondent in her motion to reopen never raised the impropriety of the stop-time rule and never appealed the underlying removal order, she could not now raise the issue in her appeal to the denial of her motion to reopen]; *Nascimento v. INS,* 274 F.3d 26, 27 (1st Cir. 2001) [court will not review underlying BIA decision where appellant only timely appealed denial of motion to reconsider]. If a respondent files a petition for review of the underlying order but does not file for review of a denied motion to reopen addressing the same issue, s/he is not barred by the doctrine of res judicata from pursuing the same issue on appeal. *Desta v. Ashcroft,* 329 F.3d 1179, 1183–84 (10th Cir. 2003).

(4) Motion to reopen while judicial proceedings are pending. In order to file a motion to reopen while judicial proceedings are pending, the applicant must comply with the requirements of 8 C.F.R. §1003.2(e), which requires a description of pending civil proceeding. When the BIA reopens proceedings while a petition for review is pending, the parties are advised to notify the court as reopening usurps the court's jurisdiction by eliminating the final order which was the subject of the petition for review. *Timbreza v. Gonzales,* 410 F.3d 1082 (9th Cir. 2005).. The filing of a petition for review *does not* toll the time for filing a motion to reopen or reconsider. *Zhao Quan Chen v. Gonzales,* 492 F.3d 153, 155 (2d Cir. 2007) [the time for filing a motion to reopen was not tolled by filing a petition for review, nor can it be considered equitably tolled]; *Randhawa v. Gonzales,* 474 F.3d 918 (6th Cir. 2007) [motion for reconsideration was untimely filed with BIA because petition for review of the BIA's original decision did not toll the time for filing the motion to reconsider].

(5) INS May Abuse Its Discretion in Motions to Reopen Where Equitable Tolling Should be Granted. In *Socop-Gonzalez v. INS,* 272 F.3d 1176, 1187–97 (9th Cir. 2001) (en banc) the court found that the BIA abused its discretion in failing to reopen a case and recognize equitable tolling as a result of misinformation provided to an adjustment applicant that he should withdraw his asylum appeal and file an adjustment application with the INS. *See also e.g., Pervaiz v. Gonzales,* 405 F.3d 488 (7th Cir. 2005) [holding the

180-day deadline for motions to reopen *in absentia* proceedings, INA §240(b)(5)(C)(ii) is "merely a statute of limitations and is therefore subject to equitable tolling" based on a claim that prior counsel rendered ineffective assistance]; *Albillo-De Leon v. Gonzales,* 410 F.3d 1090 (9th Cir. 2005) [where respondent was defrauded by nonlawyer who posed as a lawyer, the time period for filing a motion to reopen under NACARA §203(c) and 8 C.F.R. §1003.43(e)(1) was tolled until date that current attorney found out that motion was not filed].

3.f. Motions to Reconsider—An appeal of a motion to reconsider is not barred by failure to appeal the underlying order. *Esenwah v. Ashcroft,* 378 F.3d 763, 764–66 (8th Cir. 2004) [court rejected DHS argument that failure to file appeal of initial decision forecloses review of a motion to reconsider because the motion to reconsider raises the same issues as the underlying appeal].

3.g. Motions to Remand—*Ahmed v. Mukasey,* 519 F.3d 579 (6th Cir. 2008) [BIA's failure to consider or address petitioner's documentation indicating he timely filed an AOS before his 21st birthday was abuse of discretion]; *Ubau-Marenco v. INS*, 67 F.3d 750 (9th Cir. 1995) [BIA abused its discretion where it refused to remand case in light of new asylum facts] *overruled on other grounds by Fisher v. INS,* 79 F.3d 955 (9th Cir. 1996) (*en banc*); *Thomas v. INS*, 976 F.2d 786, 789 (1st Cir. 1992) [same abuse of discretion standard as applied to motions to reopen].

3.h. Review of Other Agency Actions

(1) Voluntary Departure. Judicial review of discretionary decisions concerning voluntary departure is restricted by INA §240B(f) and may also be restricted by INA §242(a)(2)(B)(i) and (ii), although INA §242(a)(2)(D) provides for continuing review for questions of law and constitutional questions. Prior to INA §240B(f), discretionary decisions on voluntary departure were reviewed for abuse of discretion. *Campos-Granillo v. INS*, 12 F.3d 849 (9th Cir. 1993) [abuse of discretion where IJ failed to weigh positive factors]; *Parcham v. INS*, 769 F.2d 1001, 1003 (4th Cir. 1985); *Carnejo-Molina v. INS*, 649 F.2d 1145, 1151 (5th Cir. 1981); *Cuevas-Ortega v. INS*, 588 F.2d 1274, 1278 (9th Cir. 1979); *Fernandez-Gonzalez v. INS*, 347 F.2d 737, 740 (7th Cir. 1965); *Sibanda v. District Director, INS*, 881 F.Supp. 1494 (D. Col. 1995) [reversed DD's refusal to grant request for extension of VD].

(2) Review of Denial of Stay By DD and BIA. Judicial review of a district director's discretionary denial of a stay of removal is prohibited by INA §242(g), although questions of law and constitutional questions may still be reviewed in connection with a denial of a stay by virtue of INA §242(a)(2)(D). Prior to INA §242(g), decisions regarding a stay of deportation were reviewed for abuse of discretion. *Anderson v. McElroy*, 953 F.2d 803 (2d Cir. 1992) [BIA abused its discretion when it refused to stay proceedings pending consideration of motion to reopen under INA §212(c)]; *Blancada v. Turnage*, 891 F.2d 688 (9th Cir. 1989) [abuse of discretion to deny stay where applicant establishes a nonfrivolous legal issue not yet decided by circuit court or the Supreme Court]; *Castro-Carvache v. INS*, 911 F.Supp. 843 (E.D. Pa. 1995) [in habeas proceeding, reversed DD denial of stay where motion to reopen filed with BIA based on ineffective assistance of counsel]; *Villegas-Ulloa v. Radcliffe*, 902 F.Supp. 1196 (D. Hawaii 1995) [reversed DD for failing to grant a stay pending motion to reopen where he did not consider claim of ineffective assistance of counsel, hardship to respondent's children, or that she did not consent to a telephonic hearing deciding the merits of her deportation case]; *Suarez-Rodriguez v. Epperson*, 878 F.Supp. 61 (E.D. La. 1994) [reversed DD denial of motion to stay that he perfunctorily addressed even though it would take two years to decide motion to reopen]; *Butros v. INS*, 804 F.Supp. 1336 (D. Or. 1991) [reversed denial of stay by BIA pending motion to reopen where its decision was conclusory. However, affirmed DD denial where person asserted right to stay pending decision on legal malpractice and disciplinary proceedings]; *Anyanwu v. INS*, 645 F.Supp. 266 (D.N.J. 1986) [abused discretion when denied stay to person who sought to reopen for asylum even where alien waited until last minute to file asylum]. *But see Garay v. Slattery*, 23 F.3d 744 (2d Cir. 1994) [no jurisdiction in district court to review IJ denial of a stay; only DD denial]; *Bal*

v. Moyer, 883 F.2d 45 (7th Cir. 1989) [apply *Achacoso-Sanchez* test in upholding denial of a stay of deportation]; *Khalaj v. Cole*, 46 F.3d 828 (8th Cir. 1995) (DD and BIA did not abuse their discretion]; *Moore v. District Director*, 956 F.Supp. 878, 882 (D. Neb. 1997) [DD did not abuse discretion in denying stay where applicant barred from actual relief of AOS].

(3) Asylum (Discretion to Grant/Deny)

(a) The AG discretionary judgment to grant or deny relief under INA §208(a) "shall be conclusive unless manifestly contrary to law and an abuse of discretion." INA §242(b)(4)(D). *Huang v. INS,* 436 F.3d 89, 96–102 (2d Cir. 2006) [IJ acted manifestly contrary to law under INA §242(b)(4)(D) in denying asylum as a matter of discretion where he failed to examine the totality of the circumstances and focused solely on the embellishment of peripheral testimony and the applicant's payment to a smuggler].

(4) Review of IV/NIV Denials

(a) IV Petition Denials. *Q Data Consulting Inc. v. INS,* 293 F.Supp.2d 25 (D.D.C. 2003) [where former position as Senior Software Consultant was only 60 to 65% managerial and where prospective position as Team Manager over 5 to 14 employees was not primarily managerial, INS did not abuse its discretion in denying EB-1 petition even if it had previously granted L-1A petitions]; *Buletini v. INS*, 860 F.Supp. 1222 (E.D. Mich. 1994) [reversed denial of first preference petition]; *Gipson v. INS,* 284 F.3d 913 (8th Cir. 2002) [upheld denial of I-130 where husband submitted to INS many different identities and INS claimed fraud].

(b) NIV Petition Denials. *Lauvik v. INS*, 910 F.2d 658 (9th Cir. 1990); *Fred 26 Importers, Inc. v. DHS,* 445 F.Supp.2d 1174, 1178–79 (C.D. Cal. 2006)[jurisdiction under the APA, 5 U.S.C. §706(2)(A), to review AAO decision where it denied H-1B]; *The Button Depot, Inc. v. DHS,* 386 F.Supp.2d 1140 (C.D. Cal. 2005) [reversed denial of H-1B petition for accountant where DHS abused its discretion by failing to apply the relevant standards regarding an equivalent foreign degree, by failing to consider evidence, and by relying on unrelated factors]; *Louisiana Philharmonic Orchestra v. INS,* 44 F.Supp.2d 800 (E.D. La. 1999); [H-1B for musician]; *Hird/Blaker v. Sava,* 712 F.Supp. 1095 (S.D.N.Y. 1989), *final judgment*, 764 F.Supp. 872 (S.D.N.Y. 1991); *London Typographers, Inc. v. Sava*, 628 F.Supp. 570 (S.D.N.Y. 1986).

(c) NIV revocations. *Calexico Warehouse, Inc. v. Neufeld,* 259 F.Supp.2d 1067, 1075–80 (S.D. Cal. 2002) [failure to provide the Service with the company's stock ledger, organizational chart, and further evidence of managerial/executive duties was sufficient under the abuse of discretion standard to affirm revocation of the petition].

(5) Review of Discretionary Waivers

(a) Under IIRIRA, judicial review of the denials of discretionary waivers may be precluded. INA §212(h) ["No court shall have jurisdiction to review a decision of the Attorney General to grant or deny a waiver under this subsection"]; INA §212(i)(2) ["No court shall have jurisdiction to review a decision or action of the Attorney General regarding a waiver under paragraph (i)"]; INA §212(a)(9)(B)(v) ["No court shall have jurisdiction to review a decision or action of the Attorney General regarding a waiver under this clause"]; INA §212(a)(2)(B)(i) and (ii) [no court shall have jurisdiction to review ... any judgment regarding the granting of relief under section 212(h), 212(i), 240A, 240B, or 245, or...any other decision or action of the Attorney General the authority for which is specified under this title to be in the discretion of the Attorney General). *See also in this chapter,* generally, part I (p.1071), *supra.* However, the nondiscretionary aspects of the discretionary decision are still subject to judicial review. *Hernandez v. Ashcroft,* 345 F.3d 824 (9th Cir. 2003); *Medina-Morales v. Ashcroft,* 371 F.3d 520, 531–32 (9th Cir. 2004).

(b) Prior to IIRIRA, courts reviewed denials of discretionary waivers under an abuse of discretion standard. *Virk v. INS,* 295 F.3d 1055 (9th Cir. 2002) [reversed BIA's denial of motion to reopen to apply for INA §241(f) relief where it departed from former precedent under INA §241(f) and where it failed to consider all relevant factors and improperly considered an irrelevant factor]; *Arrozal v. INS,* 159 F.3d 429, 433–34 (9th Cir. 1998) [reversed denial of motion to reopen for suspension where BIA only superficially mentioned equities]; *Urban v.* INS, 123 F.3d 644 (7th Cir. 1997) [reversed denial of suspension]; *Salameda v. INS*, 70 F.3d 447 (7th Cir. 1995) [same]; *Blanco v. INS*, 68 F.3d 642 (2d Cir. 1995) [reversed denial of motion to reopen for suspension]; *Tukhowinich v. INS*, 64 F.3d 460 (9th Cir. 1995) [reversed denial of suspension]; *Watkins v. INS*, 63 F.3d 844 (9th Cir. 1995) [reversed denial of motion to reopen for suspension]; *Rodriguez-Gutierrez v. INS*, 59 F.3d 504, 508–09 (Reversed denial of motion to reopen for adjustment]; *Delmundo v. INS*, 43 F.3d 436 (9th Cir. 1994) [reversed INA §212(i) denial]; *Yepes-Prado v. INS*, 10 F.3d 1363 (9th Cir. 1993) [reversed INA §212(c) denial]; *Cortes-Castillo v. INS*, 997 F.2d 1199 (7th Cir. 1993) [reversed INA §212(c) denial finding that BIA abuses its discretion "when it fails to weigh important factors or neglects to state its reasons for denying relief"]; *Braun v. INS*, 992 F.2d 1016 (9th Cir. 1993) [reversed denial of INA §241(f)]; *Espinoza v. INS*, 991 F.2d 1294 (7th Cir. 1993) [denial of INA §212(c) based on speculation unsupported by the record is vacated]; *Babai v. INS*, 985 F.2d 252 (6th Cir. 1993) [reversed denial of suspension]; *Akinyemi v. INS*, 969 F.2d 285 (7th Cir. 1992) [reversed INA §212(c) denial for failure to consider all factors]; *Diaz-Resendez v. INS*, 960 F.2d 493 (5th Cir. 1992) [same]; *Vergara-Molina v. INS*, 956 F.2d 682 (7th Cir. 1992) [denial of INA §212(c) reviewed under arbitrary, capricious and abuse of discretion]; *Hazzard v. INS*, 951 F.2d 435, 438 (1st Cir. 1991) [same]; *McLean v. INS*, 901 F.2d 204 (1st Cir. 1990) [same].

(6) Review of Denial of Employment Authorization

(a) *Grijalva v. Ilchert*, 815 F.Supp. 328 (N.D. Cal. 1993); *Gomez-Arauz v. McNary*, 746 F.Supp. 1071, 1073 (W.D. Okl. 1990).

(7) Review of Bond

(a) Under IIRIRA, judicial review of the discretionary judgments regarding bond decisions made under INA §236 are not subject to judicial review. INA §236(e). However, review of constitutional and statutory claims are not precluded. *Demore v. Kim,* 538 U.S. 510 (2003). But if the habeas action requires review of the removal order when deciding to grant bond, at least one court has determined that such review is precluded by the REAL ID Act. *Deljevic v. Baker,* 463 F.Supp.2d 699 (E.D. Mich. 2006) [no habeas jurisdiction to review detention where there is final order of removal and detention is challenged on ground that final order was improper].

(b) Prior to IIRIRA, bond determinations were reviewed for abuse of discretion. *Shirkhani v. Greene*, 790 F.Supp. 1065 (D. Colo. 1992) [ordering petitioner's release notwithstanding final administrative order].

(8) Review of Adjustment of Status

(a) Judicial review of denials of adjustment of status is restricted under INA §242(a)(2)(B)(i). Review of nondiscretionary aspects of the exercise of discretion are subject to review, and the denial will be reversed if the decision is "contrary to law." *Hernandez v. Ashcroft,* 345 F.3d 824 (9th Cir. 2003); *Medina-Morales v. Ashcroft,* 371 F.3d 520, 531–32 (9th Cir. 2004). *See in this chapter* ¶ IV.A.3.g (p.1121), *supra*.

(b) Prior to IIRIRA, denials of adjustment of status were reviewed for abuse of discretion. *Rashtabadi v. INS*, 23 F.3d 1562 (9th Cir. 1994) [reversed where INS denied validity of JRAD in adjustment and failed to consider other equities].

(9) Review of Family Unity Benefits. *Camarena v. Meissner,* 78 F.Supp.2d 1044 (N.D. Cal. 1999) [INS abused its discretion in denying extension of family unity benefits by relying on information that was rebutted and shown to be demonstrably false].

(10) Review of License Revocation. *National Collegiate Recreation Services v. Powell,* Case No. 9:02cv02676 (D.S.C. Nov. 26, 2002), *reported in* 80 No. 7 *Interpreter Releases* 244–

46 (Feb. 19, 2003) [revocation of American Hospitality Academy's J-1 program designation was arbitrary and capricious because the DOS imposed the harshest penalty without basis and its fact finding was deficient].

4. Substantial-Evidence Test

4.a. Statutory Review of Removal Order—The substantial-evidence test is applicable by statute to review removal decisions. INA §242(b)(4)(B), 8 U.S.C. §1252(b)(4)(B). *Santana-Albarran v. Ashcroft,* 393 F.3d 699, 705–06 (6th Cir. 2005) [applying statutory standard to uphold denial of cancellation for failure to establish 10-year physical presence where respondent submitted no contemporaneously filed tax returns as proof]; *Dia v. Ashcroft,* 353 F.3d 228, 248–61 (3d Cir. 2003) (*en banc*) [finding that 242(b)(4)(B) codified *Elias-Zacarias* thereby maintaining the traditional substantial evidence standard and reversed the IJs credibility finding]; *Fahim v. U.S. Att'y Gen.,* 278 F.3d 1216, 1218 (11th Cir. 2002) [affirmed BIA's denial of withholding and CAT claim following *Elias-Zacarias* and INA §§242(b)(4)(A)–(B)]; *Dashto v. INS*, 59 F.3d 697, 701–02 (7th Cir. 1995) [reversed deportation order based on clerk of court's certified statement]; *Murphy v. INS*, 54 F.3d 605 (9th Cir. 1995) [reversed deportation order]; *Pinto-Vidal v. Attorney General*, 680 F.Supp. 861 (S.D. Tex. 1987). The "substantial-evidence test" requires that there must be substantial evidence on the record as a whole to support the particular finding. The scope of substantial evidence review when reviewing whether the government has established clear and convincing evidence under *Woodby* is at issue. *Compare Adefemi v. Ashcroft,* 386 F.3d 1022, 1029 (11th Cir. 2004) (*en banc*) [relying on a highly deferential view of the substantial-evidence test, the court affirmed the use of a City Court of Atlanta document that contains several ambiguities to establish deportability for a firearms offense by clear and convincing evidence because the court under the substantial-evidence test "must affirm the agency's decision unless there is no reasonable basis for that decision"] *with Francis v. Gonzales,* 442 F.3d 131, 138–39 (2d Cir. 2006) [joining the Sixth and Ninth Circuits the court determined that the substantial-evidence test required reversal where the government did not establish deportability by clear and convincing evidence (*i.e.*, "any rational trier of fact would be compelled to conclude that the proof did not rise to the level of clear and convincing evidence) and not as the Eleventh Circuit found that reversible occurs only where there is no reasonable basis for the decision] and *Castaneda-Castillo v. Gonzales,* 488 F.3d 17, 22–26 (1st Cir. 2007) (*en banc*) [reversed adverse credibility determination and the *en banc* court noted that the language in 8 U.S.C. §1252(b)(4)(B) regarding reversal only if evidence "compels" reversal reflects a "gloss by the Supreme Court" and does not "eliminate[] the conventional requirement that an administrative agency's explanation be rational"]. *But see also Bigler v. U.S. Att'y Gen.,* 451 F.3d 728, 732–33 (11th Cir. 2006) [substantial-evidence test used to establish that the government presented clear and convincing evidence that respondent abandoned his LPR status]

4.b. The substantial-evidence test traditionally has required that the agency rely on more than a "scintilla" of evidence and that it must be "such relevant evidence as a reasonable mind might accept as adequate to support a conclusion." *Consolidated Edison Co. v. NLRB*, 305 U.S. 197, 229 (1938). *See also Richardson v. Perales,* 402 U.S. 389, 401 (1971); *Ibarra-Flores v. Gonzales,* 439 F.3d 614, 618 (9th Cir. 2006) [reviewed for substantial evidence IJ's nondiscretionary factual determination that respondent was ineligible for cancellation because during 10-year period he was given VD]; *Ding v. Ashcroft,* 387 F.3d 1131, 1136 (9th Cir. 2004) [IJ reversed in Chinese forced-abortion case, because his credibility finding was not supported by substantial evidence, as it was based upon speculation, conjecture, and an inappropriate legal standard]; *Alvarado-Carillo v. INS,* 251 F.3d 44, 49 (2d Cir. 2001) [reversed BIA denial of asylum, noting that more than a mere scintilla of evidence was necessary]. In *Universal Camera Corp. v. NLRB*, 340 U.S. 474, 488 (1961), the court defined the test further to mean that the evidence must be substantial after taking into account "whatever in the record detracts from its weight." In *Palavra v. INS,* 287 F.3d 690 (8th Cir. 2002) the court relied on the standard in *Universal Camera Corp.* and *SEC v. Chenery Corp.,* 318 U.S. 80 (1943) and reversed the finding of removal for failure to consider evidence in the record regarding citizenship in a third country].

The substantial-evidence standard in the asylum, withholding, and CAT context allows reversal only where the reviewing court finds that the evidence not only supports a contrary conclusion, "but compels it." *INS v. Elias-Zacarias*, 112 S.Ct. 812, 815 n.1 (1992). The *Elias-Zacarias* standard has been written into the INA by IIRIRA §306(a), INA §242(b)(4)(B) ["The administrative findings of fact are conclusive unless any reasonable adjudicator would be compelled to conclude to the contrary"]. For case citations, *see* Ch. 4, ¶¶ XII.C.4.h (p.597), 4.i (p.600), and 4.j (p.604), *supra*.

4.c. Review of Factual Determinations and Nondiscretionary Grants. This less deferential substantial-evidence test applies to review factual evidence considered by an IJ. *Ibarra-Flores v. Gonzales,* 439 F.3d 614, 618 (9th Cir. 2006) [reviewed for substantial evidence IJ's nondiscretionary factual determination that respondent was ineligible for cancellation because during 10-year period he was given VD]; *Cheema v. Ashcroft,* 383 F.3d 848, 856–59 (9th Cir. 2004) [substantial evidence did not support BIA's conclusion that wife engaged in terrorist activities with Sikh militants, but evidence did support conclusion against husband]; *Uwase v. Ashcroft,* 349 F.3d 1039 (7th Cir. 2003) [in persecution based upon mixed Hutu-Tutsi claim court reversed IJ determination not based upon substantial evidence and where undue weight was given to lack of corroborating testimony]; *Qui v. Ashcroft,* 329 F.3d 140 (2d Cir. 2003) [denial of asylum reversed where BIA confused vague testimony with testimony that lacked detailed but would qualify applicant, failed to support its findings by substantial evidence and failed to consider key elements in the record]; *Lukwago v. Ashcroft,* 329 F.3d 157, 180 (3d Cir. 2003) [reversed BIA determination that there is no factual basis for future persecution claim of child soldier who escaped guerrillas group in Uganda because he is in no greater danger than general population]; *Georgis v. Ashcroft,* 328 F.3d 962, 967–70 (7th Cir. 2003) [denial of asylum reversed under *Elias-Zacarias* standard where minor inconsistencies concerning dates and actions are easily resolved by other facts in evidence and explained by improperly excluded evidence]; *He v. Ashcroft,* 328 F.3d 593 (9th Cir. 2003) [reversed BIA's adverse credibility determination under a substantial evidence standard]; *Palavra v. INS,* 287 F.3d 690 (8th Cir. 2002) [reversed BIA denial of Bosnian asylum application where BIA determined respondents were Croatian citizens without considering all evidence]; *Begzatowski v. INS,* 278 F.3d 665, 668–69 (7th Cir. 2002) [reversed BIA denial of asylum without reference to *Elias-Zacarias* and by reciting more lenient substantial evidence standard]; *Senathirajah v. INS,* 157 F.3d 210, 216–21 (3d Cir. 1998) [reversed denial of asylum where lack of credibility determination was not supported by the record]; *Gailius v. INS,* 147 F.3d 34, 44 (1st Cir. 1998) [IJ reversed where he failed to address corroborative documentary evidence that supported claim for asylum]; *Stoyanov v. INS,* 149 F.3d 1226 (9th Cir. 1998) [BIA reversed where it relied in part on a factual error in denying asylum]; *Ardestani v. DOJ*, 904 F.2d 1505 (11th Cir.), *aff'd on other grounds*, 112 S.Ct. 515 (1991). The less deferential substantial-evidence test also applies to former INA §243(h) claims, *Melendez v. DOJ*, 926 F.2d 211, 216–19 (2d Cir. 1991); *Vilorio-Lopez v. INS*, 852 F.2d 1137 (9th Cir. 1988) [substantial-evidence test to review IJ's determination as to applicant's credibility in asylum and INA §243(h)]; *Chavarria v. DOJ*, 722 F.2d 666 (11th Cir. 1984); *Del Valle v. INS*, 776 F.2d 1407 (9th Cir. 1985), to the factual determinations concerning political asylum under INA §208. *Lorisme v. INS*, 129 F.3d 1441 (11th Cir. 1997); *Kapcia v. INS*, 944 F.2d 702, 707 (10th Cir. 1991); *Melendez, supra*; *Zamora-Morel v. INS*, 905 F.2d 833, 837–38 (5th Cir. 1990); *Zalega v. INS*, 916 F.2d 1257, 1259 (7th Cir. 1990); *Novoa-Umania v. INS*, 896 F.2d 1 (1st Cir. 1990); *Perlera-Escobar v. EOIR*, 894 F.2d 1292, 1296 (11th Cir. 1990); *Carvajal-Munoz v. INS*, 743 F.2d 562 (7th Cir. 1984); *Bolanos-Hernandez v. INS*, 749 F.2d 1316 (9th Cir. 1984); *Rasool v. INS*, 758 F.Supp. 188 (S.D.N.Y. 1991); *Sarkis v. Nelson*, 585 F.Supp. 235 (E.D.N.Y. 1984), and the determination of statutory eligibility. *Dulane v. INS*, 46 F.3d 988, 996–99 (10th Cir. 1995) [reversed asylum denial based on erroneous view that applicant needed to establish his nationality]; *Cordero-Trejo v. INS*, 40 F.3d 482 (1st Cir. 1994) [reversed denial of eligibility for asylum based upon negative credibility findings unsupported by the record]; *Shirazi-Parsa v. INS*, 14 F.3d 1424 (9th Cir. 1994) [reversed denial of eligibility for asylum because no substantial evidence] *overruled on other grounds by Fisher v. INS,* 79 F.3d 955 (9th Cir. 1996) (*en banc*); *Gebremichael v. INS*, 10 F.3d 28, 34 n.17 (1st Cir. 1993) [reversed BIA finding of ineligibility for asylum in denial of motion to reopen].

It is also used to review factual determinations upon which the agency exercises its discretion in other contexts. *Khodagholian v. Ashcroft,* 335 F.3d 1003 (9th Cir. 2003) [under the substantial evidence standard the IJ was reversed where LPR, who made three trips out of U.S. and the last trip exceeded one year, did not abandon his residency]; *Moin v. Ashcroft,* 335 F.3d 415, 418 (5th Cir. 2003) [upholding IJ decision after AWO on substantial evidence review regarding decision finding an LPR abandoned her residency]; *Vera-Villegas v. INS,* 330 F.3d 1222, 1225 (9th Cir. 2003) [in suspension of deportation context court found that IJ's finding that applicant failed to establish 7 years of continuous physical presence was supported only by speculation and conjecture and not substantial evidence]; *Alarcon-Serrano v. INS,* 220 F.3d 1116, 1119 (9th Cir. 2000) [affirming exclusion on reason to believe charge]. *Rodriguez-Barajas v. INS*, 992 F.2d 94, 97 (7th Cir. 1993) [registry case]; *Martinez v. INS*, 970 F.2d 973 (1st Cir. 1992) [findings regarding INA §212(c)]; *Diaz-Resendez v. INS*, 960 F.2d 493, 495 (5th Cir. 1992) [INA §212(c)]; *Jarecha v. INS*, 417 F.2d 220 (5th Cir. 1969). It is also applied to review the factual basis to determine statutory eligibility for a benefit. *Braun v. INS*, 992 F.2d 1016 (9th Cir. 1993) [reversed BIA's determination that respondent ineligible for INA §241(f) relief because he committed bigamy]; *Rivera-Zurita v. INS*, 946 F.2d 118, 120 (10th Cir. 1991).

4.d. Review of Decisions Regarding Corroboration—The AG's decision to require corroboration in asylum or other relief from removal may only be reversed if "a reasonable trier of fact is compelled to conclude that such corroborating evidence is unavailable." INA §242(b)(4), 8 U.S.C. §1252(b)(4) (REAL ID Act §101(e)). Although the IJ's corroboration requirements/standards set forth in the REAL ID Act are effective only for cases filed on or after May 11, 2005, the federal review provision under INA §242(b)(4) is effective for all final orders concerning asylum, withholding, and others form of relief or protection from removal issued before, on or after May 11, 2005. REAL ID Act §101(h)(3), 119 Stat. at 305–06; *Hor v. Gonzales,* 421 F.3d 497, 500–01 (7th Cir. 2005) [reversing IJ's corroboration findings because "All that this (new provision) means is that an immigration judge's determination … is entitled to reasonable deference (but that) the precondition to deference is that the immigration judge explain (unless it is obvious) why he thinks corroborating evidence, if it existed, would have been available to the alien"]. *Accord, Zhang v. Gonzales,* 434 F.3d 993, 998–99 (7th Cir. 2006) [quoting *Hor* and reversing IJ's demand for corroboration]. *But see Chen v. Gonzales,* 434 F.3d 212, 217–20 (3d Cir. 2005) [in case decided under new review standard *post*–REAL ID Act, the court upheld the denial of asylum even where the IJ did not make a valid credibility assessment because even a credible applicant may be required to produce corroborative evidence and respondent failed to do so in this case]; *Zheng v. Gonzales,* 417 F.3d 379, 383 n.2 (3d Cir. 2005) [finding that the IJ's requirement to corroborate what may be speculative records is subject to the "compelling" review standard which is "effective immediately" including cases begun before May 11, 2005]. However, the standard may not apply to motions to reopen before the BIA because it applies only to review of a decision by the "trier of fact" (which is the IJ not the BIA) and does not, by its terms, apply to the provision on motions to reopen at INA §240(c)(7), 8 U.S.C. §1229a(c)(7). *Fessehaye v. Gonzales,* 414 F.3d 746, 752–53 (7th Cir. 2005).

4.e. Review of Factual Finding in Suspension/Cancellation—Although the grant of suspension in the exercise of discretion is subject to an abuse of discretion standard, *Saldana v. INS,* 762 F.2d 824 (9th Cir. 1985); *Sanchez v. INS,* 755 F.2d 1158 (5th Cir. 1985), review of the findings of fact of the BIA as to statutory ineligibility is conducted under the substantial-evidence test. *Ibarra-Flores v. Gonzales,* 439 F.3d 614, 618 (9th Cir. 2006) [reviewed, for substantial evidence, IJ's nondiscretionary factual determination that respondent was ineligible for cancellation because during 10-year period he was given VD]; *Vera-Villegas v. INS,* 330 F.3d 1222, 1225 (9th Cir. 2003) [in suspension of deportation context court found that IJ's finding that applicant failed to establish 7 years of continuous physical presence was supported only by speculation and conjecture and not substantial evidence]; *Hernandez-Luis v. INS,* 869 F.2d 496 (9th Cir. 1989) [factual determinations concerning eligibility for suspension of deportation reviewed under substantial-evidence test].

4.f. Revocation of Visas and Visa Denials—*Tongatapu Woodcraft Hawaii, Ltd. v. Feldman,* 736 F.2d 1305 (9th Cir. 1984) [revocation of visa]; *Konishi v. INS*, 661 F.2d 818 (9th Cir.

1981) [denial of visa]; *Omni Packaging, Inc. v. INS*, 733 F.Supp. 500 (D.P.R. 1990) [applied substantial-evidence test to facts and abuse of discretion to judgment in denial of 3d preference petition]; *Full Gospel Portland Church v. Thornburgh*, 730 F.Supp. 441, 445 (D.D.C. 1988) [visa revocation]. *But see Knoetze v. DOS*, 634 F.2d 207 (5th Cir. 1981), *cert. denied,* 454 U.S. 823 (1981) [applied abuse of discretion test to decision to revoke visa].

4.g. Employer Sanctions Cases—Findings are subject to substantial evidence standard. *Maka v. INS*, 904 F.2d 1351, 1355 (9th Cir. 1990) *amended* 932 F.2d 1352 (9th Cir. 1991) [discussing test where ALJ and CAHO decisions differ]; *Mester Mfg. Co. v. INS*, 879 F.2d 561 (9th Cir. 1989); *Garcia v. Secy. of Labor*, 10 F.3d 276 (5th Cir. 1993) [pre–employer sanctions case where Sec. was reversed for fining farm contractor for employment of illegal workers under MSAWPA].

4.h. Rescission—Findings are subject to substantial evidence standard. *Baria v. Reno*, 94 F.3d 1335, 1340 (9th Cir. 1996), *aff'd on other grounds,* 180 F.3d 1111 (9th Cir. 1999).

4.i. Registry—*Manzo-Fontes v. INS*, 53 F.3d 280, 282 (9th Cir. 1995).

4.j. Good Moral Character—Review of factual determinations are subject to substantial-evidence test. *Omagah v. Ashcroft,* 288 F.3d 254, 258 (5th Cir. 2002) [upholding BIA's determination that conviction for conspiracy to possess illegal immigration documents with intent to defraud government demonstrates a lack of good moral character].

4.k. Terrorist Determination Under INA §212(a)(3)(B)—*McAllister v. Gonzales,* 444 F.3d 176 (3d Cir. 2006) [the IJ/BIA finding that petitioner was removable for having engaged in terrorist activity under INA §237(a)(4)(B) reviewed for substantial evidence]; *Cheema v. Ashcroft,* 383 F.3d 848, 856–59 (9th Cir. 2004) [two donations by wife to unspecified widows and orphans in India with no evidence linking it to specific group is not a terrorist activity and BIA reversed under substantial evidence standard. However, husband's fundraising did reach terrorist organizations and unfavorable inferences can be drawn against him from his telephone calls to Sikh militants supporting BIA's findings].

4.l. AWO/Streamlined Opinions—Generally, the courts of appeal will not review the Board's decision to streamline, but rather the IJ's decision on the merits. *Moin v. Ashcroft,* 335 F.3d 415, 418 (5th Cir. 2003) [upholding IJ decision after AWO on substantial evidence review regarding decision finding an LPR abandoned her residency]; *Georgis v. Ashcroft,* 328 F.3d 962 (7th Cir. 2003); However, the courts have reviewed streamlining decisions or remanded cases when due process or other issues are implicated. *Purveegiin v. Gonzales,* 448 F.3d 684 (3d Cir. 2006) [court has jurisdiction to review decision by single Board member to AWO a case instead of referring it to a three-member panel and where single Board member, contrary to 8 C.F.R. §1003.1(e)(5) reverses the IJ, instead of "affirming, modifying, or remanding" the case, he erred in not referring the matter to a three-member panel]; *Lanza v. Ashcroft,* 389 F.3d 917, 924–32 (9th Cir. 2004 [where IJ denied asylum based upon failure to file within one year and on the merits and the BIA affirmed without opinion, due process requires that the case is remanded for clarification because the merits are reviewable by the court but the one year deadline is not]; *Smriko v. Ashcroft,* 387 F.3d 279, 288–97 (3d Cir. 2004) [where respondent raised a novel question regarding whether a refugee may be deported without first revoking refugee status, it was arbitrary and capricious for the BIA to AWO the decision and the decision to streamline is subject to judicial review and not committed to agency discretion]; *Zhu v. Ashcroft,* 382 F.3d 521, 526–27 (5th Cir. 2004) [where IJ suggested multiple grounds for denying relief including an untimely filing of an asylum application which is not reviewable in the circuit court, the BIA's use of AWO created a jurisdictional problem]; *Haoud v. Ashcroft,* 350 F.3d 201 (1st Cir. 2003) [BIA decision remanded where substantially similar nonprecedent BIA decision granted asylum in contrast to AWO for respondent. Also the decision gave no guidance as to whether it affirmed on nonreviewable one year filing requirement or on reviewable merits determination]. *But see Ekasinta v. Gonzales,* 415 F.3d 1188, 1191–95 (10th Cir. 2005) [disagreed with the Ninth Circuit's decision in *Lanza* and finding no statutory or due process violation where an AWO decision fails to state that it affirmed on discretionary or nondiscretionary grounds]; *Kasnecovic v. Gonzales,* 400 F.3d 812, 814–15 (9th Cir. 2005) [distinguished *Lanza* and reviewed asylum matter rather than remanding to BIA because the posture of the case required the court to review the IJ's adverse credibility determination on other issues and therefore it would have decided the asylum claim anyway].

5. Harmless Error Doctrine—Federal courts view the harmless error doctrine differently depending upon the circuit and the issue at stake. *Compare Waldron v. INS*, 17 F.3d 511 (2d Cir. 1994), *cert. denied,* 513 U.S. 1014 (1994) [failure to follow regulations where fundamental right is not at issue is not reversible error *per se*]; *Montilla v. INS*, 926 F.2d 162 (2d Cir. 1991) [failure to follow regulation regarding counsel is reversible *per se*]; and *Rios-Berrios v. INS*, 776 F.2d 859 (9th Cir. 1985) [rejecting BIA decision in *Santos* applying the harmless error doctrine to right to counsel issues] *with Mullen-Cofee v. INS*, 976 F.2d 1375, 1380 n.12 (11th Cir. 1992) *amended on denial of reh'g* 986 F.2d 1364 (11th Cir. 1993) [where IJ failed to follow regulations in not advising respondent of his right to counsel no redress absent substantial prejudice in outcome]; *Avila-Murrieta v. INS*, 762 F.2d 733 (9th Cir. 1985) [adopting harmless error rule where there was no showing that exclusion of parts of the record resulted in prejudice]; *Li Wang v. INS*, 872 F.2d 685 (5th Cir. 1989) [where agency erred in considering the original fraud as a basis to deny former INA §241(f) relief, the court did not reverse because there was sufficient evidence to deny the relief].

6. Doctrine of Agency Deference

6.a. Where Congress has explicitly or implicitly left a gap in the statute to be filled by the agency, the courts should defer to the agency determination unless it is irrational or clearly in error. *Chevron USA v. Natural Resources Defense Council*, 467 U.S. 837, 843–44 (1984); *INS v. Aguirre-Aguirre,* 526 U.S. 415, 425, 119 S.Ct. 1439, 1445–46 (1999) [the "BIA should be accorded *Chevron* deference as it gives ambiguous statutory terms concrete meaning through a process of case-by-case adjudication." Deference appropriate on whether the statutory conditions for withholding of deportation have been met under former §243(h)(1)(2)]. The *Chevron* analysis is in 2 parts: First, the court must determine "whether Congress has directly spoken to the precise question at issue." *Chevron,* 467 U.S. at 842. If the statute or the intent of Congress is clear, "that is the end of the matter, for the court, as well as the agency must give effect to the unambiguously expressed intent of Congress." *Id.* at 842–43. If the statute, however, is ambiguous or the matter is not directly addressed, the second step of the analysis requires the court to inquire "whether the agency's [position/regulation] is based on a permissible construction of the statute." *Id.* at 843. If it is based upon a permissible construction, even if it is one that the court may not agree with, the court is generally obligated with the exceptions noted below, to defer to the agency's construction. The same rules of deference generally apply to an agency's interpretation of its own ambiguous regulation. *Auer v. Robbins,* 519 U.S. 452 (1997). It also applies even if the court has a contrary prior judicial precedent where the prior judicial decision rested upon resolving an ambiguity in the statute and the agency's subsequent resolution of the ambiguity resulted in a different decision. *National Cable and Telecommunications Ass'n v. Brand X Internet Services,* 545 U.S. 967, 982–83 (2005) [a court's prior judicial construction of a statute trumps an agency construction otherwise entitled to *Chevron* deference only if the prior court decision holds that its construction follows from the unambiguous terms of the statute and thus leaves no room for agency discretion]. However, the Supreme Court has noted that "*Chevron* deference...is not accorded merely because the statute is ambiguous and an administrative official is involved." *Gonzales v. Oregon*, 546 U.S. 243, 258 (2005) [AG rule interpreting the Controlled Substances Act in regard to physician assisted suicide not entitled to *Chevron* or *Skidmore* deference].

6.b. Deference Granted—*Ali v. Mukasey,* 521 F.3d 737 (7th Cir. 2008) [following *Matter of Babaisakov* and reinterpreting its own precedent post–*Brand X Internet Services,* the circuit court concluded the BIA could rely on the presentence investigation report to establish whether crime is a CIMT]; *Kosak v. Aguirre,* 519 F.3d 210 (3d Cir. 2008) [upheld holding in *Matter of Li* that an adopted child cannot petition for biological siblings]; *Yusupov v. Att'y Gen. of the U.S.,* 518 F.3d 185 (3d Cir. 2008) [affirming on *Chevron* grounds the AG's interpretation of INA §241(b)(3)(B)(iv) in *Matter of A-H-*, except the part stating that the government need only show that the respondent "may" be a danger rather than "is" a danger to the security of the U.S.]; *Saintha v. Mukasey,* 516 F.3d 243, 251–53 (4th Cir. 2008) [upheld BIA view under *Chevron* deference that refugee could not readjust as a refugee/asylee in IJ proceedings because of BIA's interpretation of INA §209(a)(1)(C)]; *Scheerer v. U.S. Att'y Gen.,*

513 F.3d 1244 (11th Cir. 2008) [AG regulation, 8 C.F.R. §1245.2(a)(1), limiting arriving aliens' adjustment to USCIS was valid under *Chevron* because it did not eliminate adjustment but merely limited the forum for it]; *L.A. Closeout, Inc. v. DHS,* 513 F.3d 940 (9th Cir. 2007) [USCIS memo interpreting 8 C.F.R. §248.1 to allow a change of status from B-2 to H-1B only if the applicant maintains her current B-2 status until the new H-1B status is operative upheld under *Auer* deference]; *Gonzales v. DHS,* 508 F.3d 1227, 1235–42 (9th Cir. 2007) [court followed *National Cable and Telecommunications Ass'n v. Brand X Internet Services,* 545 U.S. 967, 982–83 (2005) and reversed its prior opinion in *Perez-Gonzalez v. Ashcroft,* 379 F.3d 783 because the BIA's subsequent decision in *Matter of Torres-Garcia* that barred a retroactive I-212 waiver for a person subject to inadmissibility under INA §212(a)(9)(C)(i)(II), was entitled to *Chevron* deference]; *Fernandez v. Keisler,* 502 F.3d 337, 342–48 (4th Cir. 2007) [*Chevron* deference applies to naturalization interpretations notwithstanding INA §242(b)(5) and circuit's previous opinion under *U.S. v. Morin*]; *Camins v. Gonzales,* 500 F.3d 872 (9th Cir. 2007) [under *Chevron* deference following *Matter of Collado-Munoz,* the court determined that IIRIRA's passage of INA §101(a)(13)(C) abrogated the *Fleuti* doctrine]; *Mejia v. Gonzales,* 499 F.3d 991, 995–97 (9th Cir. 2007) [deferred to agency under second step of *Chevron* regarding AG's regulation tightening restrictions for a 212(h) in 8 C.F.R. §212.7(d)]; *Sun Wen Chen v. Att'y Gen. of the U.S.,* 491 F.3d 100, 105–09 (3d Cir. 2007) [upholding BIA analysis that spouse under forced abortion/sterilization statute qualifies for asylum under step two of *Chevron*]; *De La Rosa v. DHS,* 489 F.3d 551 (2d Cir. 2007) [affirmed analysis by BIA in *Koloamatangi* under second step of *Chevron* as to INA §212(c) case where the applicant for relief, who obtained residency by fraud, was found ineligible for relief where the relief was based upon the fraudulent residency]; *Morales-Izquierdo v. Gonzales,* 486 F.3d 484, 489–94 (9th Cir. 2007) (en banc) [upheld AG regulation allowing reinstatement of removal before DHS officer instead of IJ under second step of *Chevron* analysis and finding change of long standing policy not invalid]; *Briseno-Flores v. Att'y Gen. of the U.S.,* 492 F.3d 226, 229–31 (3d Cir. 2007) [deference granted to BIA's interpretation of the stop-time rule in *Matter of Mendoza-Sandino* that precluded restarting the continuous physical presence after a stop-time event]; *Perez-Enriquez v. Gonzales,* 463 F.3d 1007, 1012–14 (9th Cir. 2006) (en banc) [*Chevron* deference was appropriate where BIA previously determined that SAW applicant could not be denied LPR status for acts he committed after he obtained his temporary residence]; *Rumierz v. Gonzales,* 456 F.3d 31 (1st Cir. 2006) [deference given to BIA determination that the respondent has the burden on a motion to reopen to demonstrate compliance with the *Pickering* standard when the conviction is vacated or modified after a final order of removal have been entered]; *Romanishyn v. Attorney General of the U.S.*, 455 F.3d 175, 180–85 (3d Cir. 2006) [deference given to BIA decision in *Matter of Smriko* permitting removal proceedings without first terminating refugee status]; *Damko v. INS,* 430 F.3d 626 (2d Cir. 2005) [followed *Acosta's* standard for economic deprivation under *Chevron* deference and determined that Albanian's economic deprivation did not threaten his life or freedom under substantial evidence review]; *Balogun v. U.S. Att'y Gen.,* 425 F.3d 1356, 1360–61 (11th Cir. 2005) [*Chevron* deference given to interpretation of aggravated felony section regarding fraud crimes where the IJ/BIA interpreted the word "victim" under the statute to include the government]; *Lopez v. Henley,* 416 F.3d 455, 457–58 (5th Cir. 2005) [DHS regulation that person seeking citizenship through military service must still establish good moral character is entitled to *Chevron* deference]; *Mortera-Cruz v. Gonzales,* 409 F.3d 246 (5th Cir. 2005) [*Chevron* deference granted to BIA's determination that a person inadmissible under INA §212(a)(9)(C)(i) may not adjust under INA §245(i)]; *Medina v. Gonzales,* 404 F.3d 628, 633–37 (2d Cir. 2005) [permissible construction under *Chevron* to hold that false statements under oath to an asylum officer is testimony for purposes of determining lack of good moral character under INA §101(f)(6)]; *U.S. v. Jean-Baptiste*, 395 F.3d 1190, 1194 (11th Cir. 2005) [in a denaturalization case the court granted *Chevron* deference to 8 C.F.R. §316.10(b)(3)(iii) broadly construing lack of good moral character to include the *commission*, rather than the conviction or admission, of unlawful acts]; *Ali v. Ashcroft,* 395 F.3d 722, 728–29 (7th Cir. 2005) [upholding under *Chevron*, the BIA's decision in *Matter of Pickering* that allows vacated convictions to be treated as conviction for immigration purposes]; *Auguste v. Ridge,* 395 F.3d 123, 144–45 (3d Cir. 2005) [gave *Chevron* deference to BIA's determination in *Matter of J-E-* that "specific intent" to torture is required to establish a CAT claim and

quoted *Tineo* for the proposition that "there is no longer any question that the BIA should be accorded *Chevron* deference for its interpretations of the immigration laws"]; *Hernandez-Guadarrama v. Ashcroft,* 394 F.3d 674, 678–79 (9th Cir. 2005) [*Chevron* deference accorded BIA interpretation of alien smuggling removal statute to encompass more than direct participation in smuggling at the border]; *Knapik v. Ashcroft*, 384 F.3d 84, 88–90 (3d Cir. 2004) [under *Chevron* deference court determined that BIA's longstanding position is that crimes involving recklessness may be CIMTs]; *Lattab v. Ashcroft,* 384 F.3d 8, 17–20 (1st Cir. 2004) [under *Chevron* deference regulations permitting reinstituting removal without a hearing before IJ are not inconsistent with 241(a)(5)]; *Chen v. Ashcroft,* 381 F.3d 221 (3d Cir. 2004) [under *Chevron*, deferred to agency interpretation in *Matter of C-Y-Z-*, limiting forced abortion/sterilization to person subject to practice and his or her spouse and denied asylum and withholding to fiancée]; *Asika v. Ashcroft,* 362 F.3d 264 (4th Cir. 2004) [under *Chevron* deference the 5-year statutory limit on rescission does not prohibit removal proceedings where LPR status was obtained in error]; *Tineo v. Ashcroft,* 350 F.3d 382, 396–97 (3d Cir. 2003) [Congress intended to alter *Fleuti* when it enacted INA §101(a)(13)(C) but even if it was questionable *Chevron* requires we accept the agency interpretation pursuant to *Matter of* Collado]; *Acosta v. Ashcroft,* 341 F.3d 218 (3d Cir. 2003) [BIA's decision to treat what would be state convictions under the Federal First Offender Act as convictions is entitled to *Chevron* deference]; *Nolan v. Holmes,* 334 F.3d 189 (2d Cir. 2003) [where INA §329, regarding naturalization through military service, is ambiguous as to whether good moral character under INA §316 is a requirement, the BIA's interpretation that it is required is reasonable under *Chevron*]; *Griffiths v. INS,* 243 F.3d 45 (1st Cir. 2001) [deferring to BIA interpretation that Massachusetts "on file" procedure is a conviction and meets finality requirements post-IIRIRA]; *Gonzalez v. Reno,* 212 F.3d 1338 (11th Cir. 2000) [upheld rejection by INS of unadmitted 6-year-old's application for asylum notwithstanding the right to apply for asylum under §1158 on theory that the agency had the right to fill in the gap of what the word "apply" for asylum meant and their gap-filling was not "totally unreasonable"]. *Lettman v. Reno,* 207 F.3d 1368 (11th Cir. 2000) [upheld BIA interpretation of IMMACT90 to permit deportability for an aggravated felony prior to the definition of aggravated felony as reasonable]; *Michel v. INS,* 206 F.3d 253, 262–66 (2d Cir. 2000) [*Chevron* deference accorded to INS interpretation of moral turpitude under INA but not to construction of a state penal code]; *Young v. Reno*, 114 F.3d 879 (9th Cir. 1997) [upheld *Matter of Li* regarding denial of benefits to natural siblings of adopted sister]; *Yang v. INS*, 79 F.3d 932 (9th Cir. 1996) [upheld regulatory bar to asylum for firm resettlement]; *Hamama v. INS*, 78 F.3d 233 (6th Cir. 1996) [upheld INS interpretation barring withholding of deportation]; *Ahmetovic v. INS*, 62 F.3d 48 (2d Cir. 1995) [regulation barring asylum]; *Jaramillo v. INS*, 1 F.3d 1149 (11th Cir. 1993) (*en banc*); *Akindemowo v. INS*, 61 F.3d 282 (4th Cir. 1995).

6.c. The principle of deference is not applicable where the language of the statute is clear on its face or the congressional intent is clearly discernible. *INS v. Cardoza-Fonseca*, 480 U.S. 421, 446 (1987); *INS v. St. Cyr,* 121 S.Ct. 2271, 2290 n.45 (2001) ["We only defer...to agency interpretations of statutes that, applying the normal 'tools of statutory construction,' are ambiguous."]; *National Cable and Telecommunications Ass'n v. Brand X Internet Services,* 545 U.S. 967, 982–83 (2005) [a court's prior judicial construction of a statute trumps an agency construction otherwise entitled to *Chevron* deference only if the prior court decision holds that its construction follows from the unambiguous terms of the statute and thus leaves no room for agency discretion]; *Robinson v. Shell Oil Co.*, 519 U.S. 337, 340 (1997); *Martinez v. Mukasey,* 519 F.3d 532, 542-45 (5th Cir. 2008) [under the first prong of *Chevron* and under longstanding principles construing statutes in favor of persons facing removal, the court concluded that the term "admitted" as used in INA §212(h) does not bar LPRs convicted of aggravated felonies who were adjusted from applying for relief]; *Shi Liang Lin v. DOJ,* 494 F.3d 296 (2d Cir. 2007) (*en banc*) [BIA not accorded *Chevron* deference and the court rejected the decision in *Matter of C-Y-Z-*, finding that the unambiguous language of IIRIRA §601(a) does *not* extend automatic refugee status to spouses or unmarried partners of persons protected under the statute]; *Waggoner v. Gonzales,* 488 F.3d 632, 634–38 (5th Cir. 2007) [deference not accorded to BIA's interpretation of the extreme hardship waiver for a conditional resident under INA §216(c)(4)(A) because the statute plainly provides for the waiver even if the marriage was not in good faith]; *Knutsen v. Gonzales,* 429 F.3d 733, 740 (7th Cir.

2005) [DHS's contention that relevant conduct for sentencing purposes should be considered in determining whether someone was convicted of fraud in excess of $10,000 for purposes of the aggravated felony statute is not entitled to deference because the statute is clear that only a conviction counts]; *Succar v. Ashcroft,* 394 F.3d 8, 20–34 (1st Cir. 2005) [court invoked the first prong of *Chevron*—clear statutory language—to invalidate DHS regulation prohibiting parolees from AOS]; *Akhtar v. Burzynski,* 384 F.3d 1193 (9th Cir. 2004) [struck down 8 C.F.R. §214.15(g) that prevented extension of V-2/V-3 status beyond child's 20th birthday finding that *Chevron* deference did not apply because regulation was contrary to congressional intent and frustrated congressional policy]; *Firstland International, Inc. v. INS,* 377 F.3d 127, 131–32 (2d Cir. 2004) [where 8 U.S.C. §1155 regarding revocation of petition is not ambiguous *Chevron* deference inapplicable]; *Valansi v. Ashcroft,* 278 F.3d 203, 208–14 (3d Cir. 2002) [followed *Cardoza-Fonseca* and *St. Cyr* and found embezzlement was not agg. felony for fraud or deceit after referring to language of criminal statute 18 U.S.C. §656, the specific context the language was used, and the broader context of the statute as a whole]; *Bejjani v. INS,* 271 F.3d 670, 676–80 (6th Cir. 2001) [*Chevron* deference not applicable to retroactivity analysis]; *Lujan-Armendariz v. INS,* 222 F.3d 728, 748–49 (9th Cir. 2000) [when the use of general rules of statutory construction resolves the matter (regarding the definition of a conviction for immigration purposes) there is no ambiguity and therefore no deference to the agency is required]; *Dillingham v. INS,* 267 F.3d 996, 1011 (9th Cir. 2001) [same]; *Chowdhury v. INS,* 249 F.3d 970, 972–74 (9th Cir. 2001) [definition of aggravated felony statute was clear on its face]; *Gorbach v. Reno,* 219 F.3d 1087, 1093 (9th Cir. 2000) (en banc) [*Chevron* deference not accorded in striking down INS authority to revoke naturalization by regulation because Congress has not "explicitly left a gap for the agency to fill" or made an "implicit" delegation to it]; *Innab v. Reno,* 204 F.3d 1318, 1321 n.6. (11th Cir. 2000); *Robison Fruit Ranch, Inc. v. U.S.,* 147 F.3d 798, 802 (9th Cir. 1998) [discriminatory intent required for document abuse charge under Unfair Immigration Employment Practices statute]; *Coronado-Durazo v. INS*, 123 F.3d 1322, 1324–26 (9th Cir. 1997); *Goncalves v. Reno,* 144 F.3d 110, 127 (1st Cir. 1998), *cert. denied,* 119 S.Ct. 1140 (1999) [congressional intent to not apply section 440(d) of AEDPA retroactively was clear]; *Pak v. Reno,* 196 F.3d 666, 675 & n.10 (6th Cir. 1999) [same]; *Shah v. Reno,* 184 F.3d 719, 724 (8th Cir. 1999); *Chang v. INS*, 119 F.3d 1055, 1062 (3d Cir. 1997) [BIA's interpretation of asylum, withholding law as inapplicable to the enforcement of a law of general applicability (*e.g.*, exit visa/state security law) is not based on a permissible construction of the statute]; *Hernandez v. Reno,* 91 F.3d 776, 780–81 (5th Cir. 1996) [where statute requires only that qualifying relationship exist on May 5, 1988 for Family Unity purposes, the regulation preventing continued benefits due to subsequent marriage is contrary to the statute and not deserving *Chevron* deference]; *Legal Assistance for Vietnamese Asylum Seekers v. DOS*, 45 F.3d 469, 473 (D.C. Cir. 1995), *remanded*, 117 S.Ct. 378 (1996), *remanded*, 104 F.3d 1349 (1997), based upon IIRIRA §633 amending INA §202(a)(1)(B) [where statutory language unambiguously requires no discrimination in the issuance of visa, *Chevron* deference inapplicable]. *Castellon-Contreras v. INS*, 45 F.3d 149, 152–53 (7th Cir. 1995) [equating lawful domicile with LPR status is incorrect statutory interpretation given plain meaning of "domicile"]; *Kahn v. INS*, 36 F.3d 1412 (9th Cir. 1994) [relying on state law as conclusive measure of family ties was erroneous]; *Almero v. INS*, 18 F.3d 757, 763 (9th Cir. 1994) [deference is no abdication and court must first try to determine congressional intent using traditional tools of statutory construction]; *Ali v. Smith,* 39 F.Supp.2d 1254 (W.D. Wash. 1999) [where regulation is clearly inconsistent with statutory language regarding qualifications for naturalization *Chevron* deference is inappropriate]; *Gee v. INS*, 875 F.Supp. 666 (N.D. Cal. 1994).

6.d. *Chevron* deference is also not applicable where Congress did not delegate authority to the agency generally to make rules carrying the force of law or the agency interpretation claiming deference was not promulgated in the exercise of that authority. *U.S. v. Mead Corp.,* 121 S.Ct. 2164, 2171–74 (2001); *Christensen v. Harris County,* 529 U.S. 576, 587 (2000). Thus, where the agency did not promulgate its rules under the APA, the "rules" were merely interpretive, or there was no delegation by Congress of the specific issue, the courts have found that *Chevron* deference does no t apply. *U.S. v. Mead Corp.,* 121 S.Ct. 2164 (2001) [where Custom's classification ruling letters are issued by 46 different offices and in excess of 10,000 per year, *Chevron* deference inapplicable]; *Christensen v. Harris County,* 529 U.S.

576 (2000) [interpretations do not warrant *Chevron*-style deference]; *Gonzales v. Oregon,* 546 U.S. 243 (2005) [AG's interpretative rule indicating that physicians who assisted suicide of terminally ill patients pursuant to Oregon statute would be violating the Controlled Substances Act was not entitled to *Chevron* or *Skidmore* deference]; *Rotimi v. Gonzales,* 473 F.3d 55, 57–58 (2d Cir. 2007) [nonprecedent decision by single member of BIA is not entitled to *Chevron* deference because there is no indication it was promulgated to make rules carrying the force of law]; *Ucelo-Gomez v. Gonzales,* 464 F.3d 163, 168–69 (2d Cir. 2006) [*Chevron* deference not accorded IJ's decision on social group that was summarily affirmed by BIA in Guatemalan asylum case]; *Garcia-Quintero v. Gonzales,* 455 F.3d 1006, 1011–15 (9th Cir. 2006) [unpublished disposition issued by a single Board member which does not bind third parties does not carry the force of law]; *Miranda Alvarado v. Gonzales,* 449 F.3d 915, 920–24 (9th Cir. 2006) [*Chevron* deference is not appropriate for an IJ's statutory interpretation because it cannot be an agency's interpretation]; *NG v. Att'y Gen. of the U.S.*, 436 F.3d 392, 395 n.4 (3d Cir. 2006) [where BIA affirms without opinion there is a question as to whether the IJ's decision is entitled to *Chevron* deference when the BIA is free to depart from it]; *Padilla-Caldera v. Gonzales,* 453 F.3d 1237, 1244 (10th Cir. 2006) [*Chevron* deference not accorded to conclusive language in Crocetti memo of May 1, 1997 barring INA §245(i) adjustment to a person subject to inadmissibility under INA §212(a)(9)(C)(i)(I) where statute, legislative history and other memo are to the contrary]; *Perez-Gonzalez v. Ashcroft,* 379 F.3d 783, 792–95 (9th Cir. 2004) *motion to r'consd denied* 403 F.3d 1116 (2005) [USCIS memo barring §245(i) adjustment for persons previously removed under §212(a)(9)(A)–(C) was not entitled to *Chevron* deference and was contradicted by a DHS regulation at §212.2, which provides for a waiver; opinion vacated in some respects by *Gonzales v. DHS,* 508 F.3d 1227 (9th Cir. 2007)]; *Hernandez v. Ashcroft,* 345 F.3d 824, 839 n.13 (9th Cir. 2003) [a nonprecedent decision of the BIA is not entitled to *Chevron* deference]; *Scales v. INS,* 232 F.3d 1159, 1166 (9th Cir. 2000) [an interpretation which lacks the force of law does not warrant *Chevron*-style deference]; *Bussian v. RJR Nabisco, Inc.*, 223 F.3d 286, 296–97 (5th Cir. 2000) [*Chevron* deference inapplicable notwithstanding notice provided to Federal Register where regulations not promulgated in final form]; *Southern Utah Wilderness Alliance v. Dabney,* 222 F.3d 819, 828–30 (10th Cir. 2000) [*Chevron* deference inapplicable even where agency published draft policies in the Federal Register and gave the public an opportunity to comment but no final rules]; *Orr v. Hawk,* 156 F.3d 651, 655 (6th Cir. 1998) [*Chevron* deference inapplicable to interim rule because "it is not the product of a notice and comment rulemaking process."]; *Accord Ngwanyia v. Ashcroft,* 302 F.Supp.2d 1076, 1081–83 (D. Minn. 2004) [finding *Chevron* deference inapplicable to DHS's interpretation and refusal to recapture numbers for adjustment of asylees that are not used by end of fiscal year because it is neither a regulation nor an interpretation of an ambiguous regulation but rather a "sort of sub-regulatory policy"]; *F.L. v. Thompson,* 293 F.Supp.2d 86, 93–98 (D.D.C. 2003) [where DHS and ORR have correspondence regarding which agency would decide case, *Chevron* deference is unwarranted]; *Perez v. Ashcroft,* 236 F.Supp.2d 899 (N.D. Ill. 2002) [refused to give effect to "formal training" requirement for religious occupations because it represents a substantive change not accompanied by notice and comment rule making and not entitled to deference under *Mead*]. *HealthAmerica,* 06-PER-1 (BALCA July 16, 2006) (en banc) [the ETA publication of frequently asked questions and the agency's response (FAQs) are not entitled to *Chevron* deference and FAQ #5 relating to harsh penalties for typographical errors in PERM processing on Form 9089 does not withstand *Skidmore* deference]. However, deference may apply where agency interpretation is arrived at through formal adjudication. *Mazariegos v. INS,* 241 F.3d 1320, 1327 n.4 (11th Cir. 2001). *See also Augustin v. Attorney General of U.S.*, 520 F.3d 264 (3d Cir. 2008) [affirming under the second step of *Chevron* the view adopted in an *unpublished* BIA decision that a parent's residence may not be imputed to his or her minor child for purposes of the 7- year residence provision of cancellation].

Moreover, the fact that *Chevron* deference is inapplicable does not mean that the agency is not given any deference. *U.S. v. Mead, supra.* Under *Skidmore v. Swift & Co.* 323 U.S. 134 (1944) an agency decision may merit some deference given its specialized experience and the value of uniformity. *Skidmore* factors include "the thoroughness evident in [the agency's] consideration, the validity of its reasoning, its consistency with earlier and later pronouncements, and all those factors which give it power to persuade." 323 U.S. at 140. *See e.g., Auer v. Robbins,* 519 U.S. 452, 461, 117 S.Ct. 905, 911 (1997) [deferred to Secy. of Labor's interpretation of its own regulation absent the interpretation being "plainly erroneous or inconsistent with the regulation"]. *But see Miranda Alvarado v. Gonzales,* 449 F.3d 915, 924 n.6 (9th Cir. 2006) [*Skidmore* deference not accorded where IJ gave a brief and conclusory decision which referred to none of the relevant BIA or federal caselaw].

6.e. Deference is also inappropriate in regard to retroactivity analysis. *INS v. St. Cyr,* 121 S.Ct. 2271, 2290 n.45 (2001) [*Chevron* deference inappropriate in retroactivity analysis]; *Hem v. Maurer,* 458 F.3d 1185, 1189 (10th Cir. 2006) [same and cases cited therein].

6.f. Deference is also inappropriate where:

(1) the agency does not have a permissible construction of the statute and there are compelling indications that the agency is wrong, *Espinoza v. Farah Mfg. Co.*, 414 U.S. 86, 94–95 (1973); *Amir v. Gonzales,* 467 F.3d 921, 926–27 (6th Cir. 2006) [accepted willful blindness standard for CAT claims and rejected *Matter of S-V* as manifestly contrary to the statute]; *Aremu v. DHS,* 450 F.3d 578 (4th Cir. 2006) [reversing *Matter of Shanu,* finding §101(a)(13)(A) is clear and that admission applies to lawful entry and not to AOS, and determining that DHS regulation §245.11(h) is contrary to the statute]; *Singh v. Gonzales,* 451 F.3d 400 (6th Cir. 2006) [the court invoked the second prong of *Chevron* and determined that imputing fraudulent conduct of parents to their minor children was not a reasonable extension of caselaw]; *Scheerer v. U.S. Att'y Gen.,* 445 F.3d 1311, 1318–22 (11th Cir. 2006) [finding that former 8 C.F.R. §1245.1(c)(8) barring arriving aliens/parolees from adjusting status is not based upon a permissible construction of 8 U.S.C. §1255 the statute regarding adjustment of status]; *Freeman v. Gonzales,* 444 F.3d 1031, 1037–43 (9th Cir. 2006) [the text, structure and context of 8 U.S.C. §1151(b)(2)(A)(i) and DHS willingness to adjust spouses regardless of the marriage's duration, demonstrate that USCIS's interpretation barring widows who have already applied for adjustment to adjust because they are no longer "spouses" is unwarranted]; *Zheng v. Gonzales,* 422 F.3d 98, 114–18 (3d Cir. 2005) [court invoked second prong of *Chevron* in invalidating former 8 C.F.R. §1245.1(c)(8) prohibiting adjustment of status for arriving aliens and found that the clear legislative intent under INA §245 was to allow adjustment for parolees]; *Iavorski v. INS,* 232 F.3d 124, 133 (2d Cir. 2000) [BIA's claim that 90-day period for reopening is jurisdictional and therefore equitable tolling does not apply does not meet minimum rationality standard]; *Osorio v. INS*, 18 F.3d 1017, 1022–23 (2d Cir. 1994) [BIA's definition of political asylum contrary to the statute]; *Tenacre Foundation v. INS*, 892 F.Supp. 289, 293–94 (D.D.C. 1995), *aff'd,* 78 F.3d 693 (D.C. Cir. 1996) [INS interpretation regarding R-1 visa is erroneous]; *Linea Area Nacional de Chile S.A. v. Sale*, 865 F.Supp. 971, 985–87 (E.D.N.Y. 1994), *aff'd*, 65 F.3d 1034 (2d Cir. 1995) [INS interpretation of user fee statute was unreasonable];

(2) where it is simply a matter of statutory construction, *INS v. St. Cyr,* 121 S.Ct. 2271, 2290 n.45 (2001) [principle of nonretroactive application of statute is not ambiguous and therefore *Chevron* inapplicable]; *INS v. Cardoza-Fonseca*, 480 U.S. 421, 446–47 (1987); *Arevalo v. Ashcroft,* 344 F.3d 1, 9–10 (1st Cir. 2003) [whether statute should be interpreted retrospectively or prospectively is not a matter of *Chevron* deference]; *Bejjani v. INS,* 271 F.3d 670, 676–80 (6th Cir. 2001) [*Chevron* deference not applicable to retroactivity analysis]; *Bankers Trust New York Corp. v. U.S.,* 225 F.3d 1368 (Fed. Cir. 2000) [no deference to subsequent agency regulation under *Chevron* where there were previous court interpretations of same issue]; *Iavorski v. INS,* 232 F.3d 124, 132–33 (2d Cir. 2000) [whether a limitations period creates a jurisdictional bar is a question purely of statutory construction]; *Canas-Segovia v. INS*, 902 F.2d 717, 721 n.6 (9th Cir. 1990), *aff'd after remand*, 970 F.2d 599 (9th Cir. 1992); *Ali v. Smith,* 39 F.Supp.2d 1254 (W.D. Wash. 1999);

(3) where the agency acts contrary to governing regulations, *Morton v. Ruiz,* 415 U.S. 199 (1974); *Lin v. DOJ,* 459 F.3d 255, 260–64 (2d Cir. 2006) [in a Chinese asylum case, the BIA's interpretation of 8 C.F.R. §208.6 (now §1208.6) that the nondisclosure of information contained in an asylum application only pertains to "sensitive" information in the application is inconsistent with the plain language of the regulation and with the government's prior interpretations]; *Nair v. Coultice,* 162 F.Supp.2d 1209 (S.D. Cal. 2001) [INS

regulation that prevents renewal of H-1B for person who spent six years in the U.S. cannot be interpreted contrary to the regulation to include time person spent abroad]; *Masonry Masters, Inc. v. Thornburgh*, 742 F.Supp. 682 (D.D.C. 1990) [where INS ignored DOL regulations regarding prevailing wage, INS not entitled to deference in its interpretation];

(4) where a higher court has clearly resolved the ambiguity. *Tran v. Mukasey,* 515 F.3d 478, 484 (5th Cir 2008) [*Chevron* deference is inappropriate to 8 C.F.R. §241.14 authorizing indefinite detention of person whose mental illness is a threat to the public because the Supreme Court in *Zadvydas* resolved the ambiguity of the length of time that a person may be detained];

(5) where the agency has no particular expertise on the issue, *Leocal v. Ashcroft,* 543 U.S. 1 (2004) [finding BIA interpretation of criminal statute not entitled to deference]; *Young Wong Park v. Attorney General of the U.S.*, 472 F.3d 66, 70–71 (3d Cir. 2007) [AG has no particular expertise in defining whether a particular offense is an aggravated felony]; *Rodriguez v. Gonzales,* 451 F.3d 60, 63 (2d Cir. 2006) [BIA's interpretation of federal criminal statute not entitled to deference because "BIA has no particular expertise in construing federal and state criminal statutes"]; *NG v. Att'y Gen. of the U.S.,* 436 F.3d 392, 395 (3d Cir. 2006) [BIA's interpretation of crimes of violence under 18 U.S.C. §16 is not entitled to deference because the statute is not within the INA and lies beyond the BIA's special expertise]; *Patel v. Ashcroft,* 401 F.3d 400, 407 (6th Cir. 2005) [interpreting federal and state statutes to determine whether crime is an aggravated felony is subject to *de novo* review and not *Chevron* deference because it is unrelated to immigration]; *Singh v. Ashcroft*, 386 F.3d 1228, 1230–31 (9th Cir. 2004) [interpretation of state and federal criminal laws is not subject to agency deference where court determined that Oregon harassment statute was not a domestic violence statute]; *Abimbola v. Ashcroft,* 378 F.3d 173, 175–76 (2d Cir. 2004) [determining that *Chevron* deference does not apply to the BIA's interpretation of state criminal laws because it is "not charged with the administration of these laws;" it is the court's decision whether the crime is a theft offense and an aggravated felony]; *Omar v. INS,* 298 F.3d 710, 714–15 (8th Cir. 2002) [INS interpretation of criminal statutes that it does not administer is not entitled to deference]; *Francis v. Reno,* 269 F.3d 162, 168 (3d Cir. 2001) [BIA does not have expertise in construing 18 U.S.C. §16 to determine an aggravated felony]; *Sandoval v. Reno,* 166 F.3d 225 (3d Cir. 1999) [determining a statute's temporal reach is not an issue that implicates agency's expertise]; *Bamidele v. INS,* 99 F.3d 557, 561–62 (3d Cir. 1996); *Tovar v. U.S. Postal Service*, 3 F.3d 1271, 1276 (9th Cir. 1993).

(6) where its current interpretation conflicts with previous interpretations, *INS v. Cardoza-Fonseca*, 480 U.S. 421, 446 n.30 (1987); *Good Samaritan Hosp. v. Shalala,* 508 U.S. 402, 417 (1993) ["The consistency of an agency's position is a factor in assessing the weight that position is due"]; *Lal v. INS,* 255 F.3d 998, 1006–07 (9th Cir. 2001) *amended on reh'g* 268 F.3d 1148 (9th Cir. 2001) [BIA's interpretation regarding past persecution is at odds with previous decisions]; *Robison Fruit Ranch, Inc. v. U.S.,* 147 F.3d 798, 802 (9th Cir. 1998); *Batanic v. INS,* 12 F.3d 662 (7th Cir. 1993); *Nair v. Coultice,* 162 F.Supp.2d 1209 (S.D. Cal. 2001) [INS's previous interpretation did not count time spent outside of the U.S. by an H-1B visa holder toward the 6-year maximum period and therefore it was impermissible to apply that analysis now]; *Gee v. INS,* 875 F.Supp. 666 (N.D. Cal. 1994); *Masonry Masters, supra*; *Sun Moon Star Advanced Power, Inc. v. Chappell*, 773 F.Supp. 1373 (N.D. Cal. 1990) [struck down INS interpretation of affiliate for L-1 purposes], *but see Rust v. Sullivan*, 111 S.Ct. 1759, 1768–69 (1991) [a revised interpretation deserved deference where there is a reasoned analysis], *Morales-Izquierdo v. Gonzales,* 486 F.3d 484, 493–94 (9th Cir. 2007) (en banc) [deference not accorded only in rare instances where the agency provides no explanation for its change or it is so unclear or contradictory as to doubt it reasoning]; *Wilson v. INS*, 43 F.3d 211, 216 (5th Cir. 1995);

(7) where its interpretation is unreasonable, *Cuevas-Gaspar v. Gonzales,* 430 F.3d 1021–27 (9th Cir. 2005) [BIA was unreasonable when it refused to impute the residency status of

parents to their unemancipated minor children for purposes of meeting the seven year continuous residence requirement of cancellation under INA §240A(a)]; *Immigrant Assistance Project of the Los Angeles County Federation of Labor (AFL-CIO) v. INS,* 306 F.3d 842, 870–73 (9th Cir. 2002) [determined that INS's interpretation prior to and in *Matter of H* that legalization applicant's failure to file quarterly address reports resulting in unlawful status could not be imputed to the government was unreasonable] and leads to an unconstitutional result, *Batanic, supra*;

(8) where a regulation is not a construction or interpretation of a statute but simply an exercise of authority pursuant to the statute, *Tovar, supra* at 1276;

(9) where the issue involves the interpretation of a regulation but the regulation is not ambiguous and therefore does not require interpretation. *Restrepo v. McElroy,* 369 F.3d 627, 638–9 n.19 (2d Cir. 2004) [where regulation regarding the right to affirmatively apply for §212(c) relief was unambiguous, a letter from the Acting Assistant Commissioner of Adjudications at the legacy INS could not defeat the clear language of the regulation];

(10) where a substantial constitutional question is raised by the agency's interpretation. *Flores-Chavez v. Ashcroft,* 362 F.3d 1150, 1162–63 (9th Cir. 2004) [reversed *in absentia* order against 15-year-old who was served with OSC pursuant to 8 C.F.R. §103.5a but no service was provided to adult custodian. Court found that reading the statute to permit service solely on minor was not entitled to *Chevron* deference because it raised serious constitutional questions].; *Ma v. Reno,* 208 F.3d 815 (9th Cir. 2000) [interpreting detention statute governing post-removal proceedings to avoid a constitutional question];

(11) where the matter is not consigned to INS discretion in the first place because it is traditionally a matter for the courts to decide. *O'Sullivan v. USCIS,* 453 F.3d 809, 811–12 (7th Cir. 2006) [where district court proceeding is brought to review *de novo* denial of naturalization pursuant to 8 U.S.C. §1421(c), *Chevron* deference in inapplicable]; *Francis v. Reno,* 269 F.3d 162, 168 (3d Cir. 2001) [BIA does not have expertise in construing 18 U.S.C. §16 to determine an aggravated felony]; *Albillo-Figueroa v. INS,* 221 F.3d 1070, 1072 (9th Cir. 2000) [whether a conviction under federal law is a deportable offense is a matter consigned to federal courts not the agency];

(12) where the agency's position is a mere litigation position, *Bowen v. Georgetown Univ. Hosp.,* 488 U.S. 204, 212–13 (1988);

(13) where the agency is interpreting state or federal criminal laws. *Leocal v. Ashcroft,* 543 U.S. 1 (2004) [finding BIA interpretation of criminal statute not entitled to deference]; *Plasencia-Ayala v. Mukasey,* 516 F.3d 738, 743–44 (9th Cir. 2008) [BIA given no deference in interpreting whether state statute is a CIMT because it has "done nothing to particularize the meaning of the term" and "it is not a statute which the BIA administers or has any particular expertise in interpreting"]; *Dulal-Whiteway v. DHS,* 501 F.3d 116, 120 (2d Cir. 2007) ["We do not extend *Chevron* deference to the BIA's or an IJ's construction of federal criminal laws"]; *Gill v. INS,* 420 F.3d 82, 89 (2d Cir. 2005) [BIA is given deference on how to construe the term moral turpitude, but it has no expertise in construing federal or state criminal statutes and so the court reviews *de novo* whether respondent's conviction contains elements that are found to be CIMTs]; *Partyka v. Attorney General,* 417 F.3d 408, 411 (3d Cir. 2005) [the court owes "no deference to the IJ's interpretation of a state criminal statute"]; *Sui v. INS,* 250 F.3d 105, 112–13 (2d Cir. 2001) [where agency is determining whether conviction meets the BIA's interpretation the answer is not entitled to *Chevron* deference]; *Sutherland v. Reno,* 228 F.3d 171 (2d Cir. 2000) [to the extent the court is interpreting Massachusetts or federal criminal laws, they are reviewed *de novo*]; *Dalton v. Ashcroft,* 257 F.3d 200, 203–04 (2d Cir. 2001). [felony DUI under N.Y. Vehicle & Traffic Law §1192.3 is not aggravated felony].

6.g. IJ Decision with AWO by the BIA May Not be Accorded *Chevron* Deference. *See Dulal-Whiteway v. DHS,* 501 F.3d 116, 120 (2d Cir. 2007) ["We do not extend *Chevron* deference to any statutory construction of the INA set forth in a summarily affirmed IJ opinion"]; *Ucelo-Gomez v. Gonzales,* 464 F.3d 163, 168–69 (2d Cir. 2006) [followed *Lin* and found that *Chevron* deference is not accorded IJ's decision on social group that was summarily affirmed by BIA in Guatemalan asylum case]; *Miranda Alvarado v. Gonzales,* 449 F.3d 915, 924 (9th Cir. 2006) [declined to extend *Chevron* deference to summary affirmance by BIA]; *Zhang v. Gonzales,* 426 F.3d 540, 543–44 (2d Cir. 2005) [followed *Lin* and found *Chevron* deference inapplicable to AWO cases]; *Lin v. DOJ,* 416 F.3d 184, 189–91 (2d Cir. 2005) [IJ's summarily affirmed decision is not entitled to *Chevron* deference but may be entitled to the lesser form of deference established in *Skidmore* and *Meade*]; *Smriko v. Ashcroft,* 387 F.3d 279, 289 n.6 (3d Cir. 2004) [although *Aquirre-Aguirre* determined that the BIA's case-by-case decision-making should be accorded *Chevron* deference, the AWO procedure only affirms the result].

6.h. Rule of Lenity and *Chevron* Deference. *Ruiz-Almanzar v. Ridge,* 485 F.3d 193, 198–99 (2d Cir. 2007) [Rule of Lenity cannot be applied whenever there is an ambiguity in a statute or *Chevron* deference would be meaningless; it is only applied when other cannons of statutory construction are not capable of resolving the statute's meaning and the BIA has not offered a reasonable interpretation].

VI. PROCEDURES FOR REVIEW OF REMOVAL DECISIONS

A. *Removal Proceedings*—The traditional distinction between review of exclusion orders in district court and deportation orders in circuit court has been repealed. IIRIRA §306(b). Although IIRIRA provided for special procedures on appeal for transition case regarding final orders of *exclusion* and *deportation* entered before or after Oct. 30, 1996 under IIRIRA §309, the 2005 REAL ID Act §106(d) eliminated these special procedures and now requires all appeals to be treated as appeals under INA §242. The law provides for one uniform procedure for the review of removal orders, including reinstatement orders under INA §241(a)(5). These orders are now reviewed exclusively in the circuit courts of appeal. A petition for review must be filed within 30 days of the final order of removal. INA §242(b)(1), 8 U.S.C. §1252(b)(1). *Ruiz-Martinez v. Mukasey,* 516 F.3d 102, 117–19 (2d Cir. 2008) [following the Court's decision in *Bowles v. Russell,* 127 S.Ct. 2360 (2007) the court determined that the 30 day limit was jurisdictional and could not be waived]; *Wang v. DHS,* 484 F.3d 615 (2d Cir. 2007) [petition transferred to circuit court pursuant to REAL ID Act was dismissed where petition was filed in the district court more than a year after the REAL ID Act and more than 30 days beyond the time for appeal]; *Dalombo Fontes v. Gonzales,* 483 F.3d 115, 118–20 (1st Cir.) *reh'g denied* 498 F.3d 1 (2007) [failure to file appeal within 30 days was not excused by lack of appeal rights for criminal aliens at the time and Suspension Clause issue was not addressed on rehearing because it was not previously raised]; *Asere v. Gonzales,* 439 F.3d 378 (7th Cir. 2006) [where appeal was filed beyond 30 days because respondent's counsel was waiting for a decision on the motion to reconsider, the court had no jurisdiction over the original order and the respondent waived review of the motion to reconsider by addressing only the underlying removal order in his brief]; *Dakane v. U.S. Att'y Gen.,* 399 F.3d 1269, 1272–73 n.3 (11th Cir. 2005) [no equitable tolling for ineffective counsel's failure to file appeal timely as issue is jurisdictional]; *Ven v. Ashcroft,* 386 F.3d 357, 359–60 (1st Cir. 2004) [no review of BIA decision because the motion to reopen did not toll the 30-day time period to review the original order]; *Ponta-Garca v. Ashcroft,* 386 F.3d 341 (1st Cir. 2004) [petition for review was dismissed because the 30-day period also applies to orders of reinstatement entered pursuant to INA §241(a)(5) and the petitioner's response to DHS of the order does not toll the 30 days]; *Prekaj v. INS,* 384 F.3d 265, 267–68 (6th Cir. 2004) [timely appeal of motion to reopen does not include appeal for underlying order]; *Sankarapillai v. Ashcroft,* 330 F.3d 1004 (7th Cir. 2003) ["Filed" under 242(b)(1) means "received" and a petition for review mailed within 30 days but not received by the court within 30 days is not timely; appeal dismissed on jurisdictional grounds]; *Navarro-Miranda v. Ashcroft,* 330 F.3d 672, 676–77 (5th Cir. 2003) [same in regard to review of denial of motion to reconsider]; *Nahatchevska v. Ashcroft,* 317 F.3d 1226 (10th Cir. 2003) [the 30 days are not extended by Fed. R. App. P. 26(c), which provides for an additional 3 days in another context after a paper is served on a party]; *Singh v. INS,* 315 F.3d 1186 (9th Cir. 2003) [where counsel failed to file notice of appearance and consequently no petition for review was filed for 10 months, jurisdiction was barred in the circuit court]; *Malvoisin v. INS,* 268 F.3d 74 (2d Cir. 2001) [the 30-day period is jurisdictional even for detainee who was not informed by his counsel of appeal date]; *Sheviakov v. INS,* 237 F.3d 1144 (9th Cir. 2001) [appeal timely filed when the clerk's office obtained express mail notice but did not pick up package until after 30 days]; *Ibrik v. INS,* 108 F.3d 596 (5th Cir. 1997). The date of issuance of the final order is considered in some circuits to be the date of mailing to the correct address. *Martinez-Serrano v. INS,* 94 F.3d 1256, 1258–59 (9th Cir. 1996), *cert. denied,* 118 S.Ct. 49 (1997); *Zaluski v. INS,* 37 F.3d 72,

73 (2d Cir. 1994); *Quedraogo v. INS*, 864 F.2d 376, 378 (5th Cir. 1989). *But see Nowak v. INS*, 94 F.3d 390, 391 (7th Cir. 1996) [time begins to run from issuance not mailing and burden is on counsel to periodically check with BIA]. And where the BIA decides to reissue their decision because notice of the original decision was never received the circuit court may treat the 30-day clock as beginning from the reissuance of the decision. *Firmansjah v. Ashcroft,* 347 F.3d 625 (7th Cir. 2003) [BIA reissued final order at respondent's request who had not received notice and the circuit court permitted appeal within 30 days of reissued BIA decision]. *cf. Singh v. Gonzales,* 494 F.3d 1170 (9th Cir. 2007) [reversed and remanded BIA denial of motion to reopen where respondent and counsel filed affidavits of nonreceipt of BIA decision and BIA did not explain how it properly served its decision]; *Roy v. Ashcroft,* 389 F.3d 132, 135–36 (5th Cir. 2004) [where BIA because of mismailing reissued opinion for equitable reasons to allow respondent to comply with VD and respondent filed a timely appeal on the first final order, circuit court was not divested of jurisdiction]. However, the BIA's decision to reissue its decision is discretionary and where there was proper service of the decision, the respondent's nonreceipt is not relevant. *Chen v. U.S. Att'y Gen.,* 502 F.3d 73 (2d Cir. 2007) [motion to reinstate is treated as a motion to reopen but where BIA has proof it sent notice, the respondent's nonreceipt is irrelevant]. The petitioner's failure to appeal the initial decision within 30 days does not foreclose his timely appeal of a motion to reopen that might raise the same issues. *Esenwah v. Ashcroft,* 378 F.3d 763, 764–66 (8th Cir. 2004) [court rejected DHS argument that failure to file appeal of initial decision forecloses review of a motion to reconsider because the motion to reconsider raises the same issues as the underlying appeal]; *cf. Asere v. Gonzales,* 439 F.3d 378 (7th Cir. 2006) [where appeal was filed beyond 30 days because respondent's counsel was waiting for a decision on the motion to reconsider, the court had no jurisdiction over the original order and the respondent waived review of the motion to reconsider by addressing only the underlying removal order in his brief]; *Liu v. Gonzales,* 439 F.3d 109 (2d Cir. 2006) [although respondent appealed the denial of his motion to reconsider, his brief discussed the underlying merits of the asylum claim which was not before the court but failed to address the only issue before the court which was why the BIA abused its discretion in not reconsidering its original decision].

However, a respondent is not required to appeal interlocutory orders and if a final order is timely appealed those orders are included in the appeal. *Boykov v. Ashcroft,* 383 F.3d 526 (7th Cir. 2004) [where BIA issued decision rescinding its previous order and stated that a decision will be forthcoming and respondent timely appealed the subsequent decision, he was not required to appeal the interlocutory order]. The grant of a motion to reconsider and the affirmance of the original order may not affect the finality of the original order for purposes of appeal. *Jaggernauth v. U.S. Atty. General,* 432 F.3d 1346, 1350–52 (11th Cir. 2005) [the granting of a motion to reconsider and the reaffirmance of the original final order did not affect the finality of the original order and the court therefore had jurisdiction to review the matter when petitioner appealed the original order within 30 days]; *Plasencia-Ayala v. Mukasey,* 516 F.3d 738, 744–46 (9th Cir. 2008) [same]. *But see Mu Ju Li v. Mukasey,* 515 F.3d 575, 578–80 (6th Cir. 2008) [when the BIA grants a motion to reconsider and renders a new decision addressing the arguments raised, the original order has been vacated, a new order has been entered in its place, and a new appeal must be filed].

The 30-day provision is suspended for cases that were brought in the district court as habeas, mandamus or All Writs Act claims and must be transferred to the circuit court of appeals, pursuant to the REAL ID Act §106(c), in the circuit where the case would have been brought under INA §242(b)(2). *See e.g., Medellin-Reyes v. Gonzales,* 435 F.3d 721, 723–24 (7th Cir. 2006) [habeas petition filed outside of 30-day period for review of underlying removal order does not bar review in circuit court after case is transferred pursuant to REAL ID Act §106(c), in the circuit where the case would have been properly filed under INA §242(b)(2)]; *Ishak v. Gonzales,* 422 F.3d 22, 29 (1st Cir. 2005) [same]; *Marquez-Almanzar v. INS,* 418 F.3d 210, 215 (2d Cir. 2005) [same]. To determine where the case would have been brought, *see in this chapter* "Venue," section VI.F (p.1194), *infra*.

The petitioner must attach a copy of the order of removal and must state in the petition whether any court has upheld the validity of the order and if so, the name of the court and the date and nature of the proceeding. INA §242(c). In addition to the BIA order some circuits require the parties to submit the IJ's order where the BIA affirmed without opinion. The petition must contain the names of all petitioners and must appeal the appropriate administrative orders (*e.g.,* BIA merits decision and/or motion to reopen) or s/he may inadvertently waive appeal. *But see Marrero Pichardo v. Ashcroft,* 374 F.3d 46, 54–55 (2d Cir. 2004) [court excused failure to file appeal from habeas court's denial of motion to reopen where error was due to lawyer's poor representation and where it was clear that respondent raised the correct issue]; *Miljkovic v. Ashcroft,* 366 F.3d 580 (7th Cir. 2004) [granted motion to amend notice of appeal to include spouse of asylum applicant where her name appeared on asylum *application* but she appeared not to be in removal proceeding with her spouse]; *Bace v. Ashcroft,* 332 F.3d 1133, 1137 (7th Cir. 2003) [where husband's name inadvertently left off timely filed petition for review, court considered asylum appeal because husband would be eligible to join on wife's appeal if she was successful]. The respondent is the AG of the U.S. and the petition must be served on the AG and the DD in the district where the final order of removal was entered. INA §242(b)(3)(A). The petitioner's brief must be filed within 40 days after the date on which the administrative record is available and may serve and file a reply within 14 days after service of the AG's brief. INA §242(b)(3)(C). The court may not extend the deadline for filing briefs except upon motion for good cause shown. Failure to file a brief within the time period results in dismissal unless manifest injustice would result. INA §242(b)(3)(C). *Recinos De Leon v. Gonzales,* 400 F.3d 821 (9th Cir. 2005) [court struck government brief that was not timely filed]. A *pro se* petitioner had the right to rely on a BIA member's dissent as his brief. *Lorisme v. INS,* 129 F.3d 1441, 1444 n.3 (11th Cir. 1997).

B. *No Automatic Stay*—In removal proceedings there is no longer an automatic stay upon the filing of any petition for review. INA §242(b)(3)(B). A request for a stay should be treated as a request for a stay or injunction on appeal, requiring the applicant to show the traditional criteria for such a stay: (1) a likelihood of success on the merits; (2) that irreparable harm would occur if a stay is not granted; (3) that the potential harm to the movant outweighs the harm to the opposing party if a stay is not granted; and (4) that the granting of a stay would serve the public interest. *Tesfamichael v. Gonzales,* 411 F.3d 169 (5th Cir. 2005) [rejecting Eleventh Circuit standard in *Weng,* adopting the traditional standard for a stay and granting stay in asylum case]. *See also Koutcher v. Gonzales,* 494 F.3d 1133 (7th Cir. 2007) [declined to grant a bare-bones motion that did not address the four points supporting a stay and did not conform to Fed. R. App. P. 18(a)(2)(B)]; *Nwaokolo v. INS,* 314 F.3d 303, 307–11 (7th Cir. 2002) [stay granted on BIA denial of motion to reopen under CAT where *USC daughter* might suffer female genital mutilation]; *Sofinet v. INS,* 188 F.3d 703, 706 (7th Cir. 1999) [stay granted and court acknowledged that in the stay process there are "some differences between discretionary stays of deportation and the ordinary stay or injunction pending appeal" and that "the lack of an adequate remedy at law is always present"]; *Lim v. Ashcroft,* 375 F.3d 1011 (10th Cir. 2004) [stay denied despite DHS's agreement where stay criteria were not met, petition was not in proper form, and the IJ/BIA orders were not attached]; *Lucacela v. Reno,* 161 F.3d 1055 (7th Cir. 1998) [stay denied where movant failed to show likelihood of success and failed to meet other three criteria]; *Ofosu v. McElroy,* 98 F.3d 694 (2d Cir. 1996) [stay conditioned on fugitive presenting himself]; *Ignacio, supra*; *Zardui-Quintana v. Richard,* 768 F.2d 1213, 1215 n.7 (11th Cir. 1985), *see also Zheng v. Mukasey,* 507 F.3d 1074 (7th Cir. 2007) [stay denied where petitioner failed to allege sufficient facts to meet the standard]; *Stepanovic v. Mukasey,* 511 F.3d 653 (7th Cir. 2007) [same]. *But see Dorelien v. U.S. Att'y Gen.,* 317 F.3d 1314 (11th Cir. 2003) [the standard articulated in *Zardui-Quintana* is no longer applicable in light of IIRIRA] and *Weng v. U.S. Att'y Gen.,* 287 F.3d 1335, 1337–40 (11th Cir. 2002) [INA §242(f)(2) does prevent the court of appeals from issuing a stay pending appeal unless there is clear and convincing evidence that the execution of the order is prohibited as a matter of law].

The Ninth Circuit's test is slightly less onerous and only requires "either (1) a probability of success on the merits and the possibility of irreparable injury, or (2) that serious legal questions are raised and the balance of hardships tips sharply in the petitioner's favor." *Abbassi v. INS,* 143 F.3d 513, 514 (9th Cir. 1998); *Andreiu v. Ashcroft,* 253 F.3d 477 (9th Cir. 2001) (en banc). The Second Circuit uses the traditional criteria for a stay but suggests that hardship not likelihood of success is the most important criteria. *Mohammed v. Reno,* 309 F.3d 95, 100–02 (2d Cir. 2002). *See also Douglas v. Ashcroft,* 374 F.3d 230, 233–34 (3d Cir. 2004) [following the First, Second and Sixth Circuits that the proper standard for a stay is the traditional four-part test for preliminary injunctions and rejected the "clear and convincing evidence" standard]; *Bejjani v. INS,* 271 F.3d 670, 687–89 (6th Cir. 2001) [adopting an injunction standard but not distinguishing between *Sofinet* and *Andreiu*]. Under Fed. R. App. P. 18, a movant for a stay may first have to seek a stay with the BIA or show why obtaining a stay is not practical. But the INS has acknowledged that there is "nothing in the INA's provisions or the immigration regulations that conferred authority on the INS to grant a stay of deportation pending the outcome of review in the court of appeals." *Sofinet v. INS,* 188 F.3d 703, 706–07 (7th Cir. 1999). The Ninth Circuit has established a special procedure for such requests because of the large volume of cases. *DeLeon v. INS,* 115 F.3d 643 (9th Cir. 1997) [filing for stay will stay deportation until court can rule].

Circuit courts have also rejected the Service's argument that INA §242(f)(2), 8 U.S.C. §1252(f)(2) limits the power of federal courts to grant a stay of removal. *Tesfamichael v. Gonzales,* 411 F.3d 169 (5th Cir. 2005) [rejecting Eleventh Circuit standard in *Weng,* adopting the traditional standard for a stay and granting stay in asylum case]; *Douglas v. Ashcroft,* 374 F.3d 230, 233–34 (3d Cir. 2004) [following the First, Second and Sixth Circuits that the proper standard for a stay is the traditional four-part test for preliminary injunctions and rejected the "clear and convincing evidence" standard]; *Arevalo v. Ashcroft,* 344 F.3d 1, 6–9 (1st Cir. 2003) [following *Andreiu* and the majority of circuits and rejecting the Eleventh Circuit's approach in *Weng* the Court determined that the appropriate standard to apply for a stay pending appeal is the traditional preliminary injunction standard and not the clear and convincing standard under INA §242(f)(2)]; *Maharaj v. Ashcroft,* 295 F.3d 963 (9th Cir. 2002) [followed reasoning in *Andreiu* and *American-Arab* and finding that INA §242(f)(2) does not bar federal courts from issuing a stay of removal pending appeal from the denial of a habeas petition challenging the merits of a removal order]; *Mohammed v. Reno,* 309 F.3d 95, 98–100 (2d Cir. 2002) [agreeing with *Andreiu* and finding that INA §242(f)(2) does not bar the entry of a temporary stay pending appeal in the district or circuit court and that the standard is the traditional standard for a stay pending appeal]; *Bejjani v. INS,* 271 F.3d 670, 687–89 (6th Cir. 2001) [agreeing with *Andreiu* analysis that section does not apply]; *Andreiu v. Ashcroft,* 253 F.3d 477 (9th Cir. 2001) (en banc) [the term "enjoin" in 1252(f)(2) does not encompass stay orders]; *Kanivets v. Riley,* 286 F.Supp.2d 460, 464–65 (E.D. Pa. 2003) [the standards under 242(f)(2) do not apply to district court stay orders where the action was initiated in the district court]; *Kahn v. Elwood,* 232 F.Supp.2d 344 (M.D. Pa. 2002) [same]; *But see Weng v. U.S. Att'y Gen.,* 287 F.3d 1335, 1337–40 (11th Cir. 2002) [INA §242(f)(2) does prevent the court of appeals from issuing a stay pending appeal unless there is clear and convincing evidence that the execution of the order is prohibited as a matter of law]; *Dorelien v. U.S. Att'y Gen.,* 317 F.3d 1314 (11th Cir. 2003) [denial of *en banc* review regarding standard for issuance of a stay and noting that the standard articulated in *Zardui-Quintana* is no longer applicable in light of IIRIRA]. The split in the circuits has now been recognized by Justice Kennedy who suggested the Supreme Court may wish to consider the matter. *Kenyeres v. Ashcroft,* 123 S.Ct.1386 (2003).

1. *Contempt for Violating the Stay*. Failure to stay removal when court has ordered stay may result in contempt against the government. *Dimitrov v. Ashcroft,* 368 F.3d 960 (7th Cir. 2004) [issued order to show cause but declined to issue contempt in light of government procedural changes and fact that person was not physically removed]. But if the government has no actual or constructive notice of the court's order a person would not be considered to be deported in violation of the order. *U.S. v. Garcia-Echaverria,* 374 F.3d 440, 449–50 (6th Cir. 2004) [government unaware of stay order issued by the Southern District of New York before it deported respondent whose habeas case had been transferred to the Western District of Louisiana].

2. *Vacating Stay*. A stay of removal will not be vacated until the mandate is issued in the court of appeals. *Mariscal-Sandoval v. Ashcroft,* 370 F.3d 851, 856 (9th Cir. 2004) [although court denied the petition for review, it maintained the stay in effect until the mandate issues].

3. *Stay of Removal Is Not a Stay of VD*. A stay of removal is not a stay of voluntary departure and may not automatically stay VD. *Compare Iouri v. Ashcroft,* 487 F.3d 76, 82–87 (2d Cir. 2007) [filing a motion to stay removal within VD period will *not* be construed as a motion to stay VD]; *Bocova v. Gonzales,* 412 F.3d 257, 264–70 (1st Cir. 2005) [same] and *Alimi v. Ashcroft,* 391 F.3d 888, 891–93 (7th Cir. 2004) [granting a stay of removal does not automatically stay VD] *with Desta v. Ashcroft,* 365 F.3d 741, 747 (9th Cir. 2004) [court has equitable power to stay voluntary departure but only for whatever period remains and petitioner's motion to stay removal will be construed as including a motion to stay voluntary departure if brought within voluntary departure period];*Macotaj v. Gonzales,* 424 F.3d 464 (6th Cir. 2005) [followed *Desta* and held that motion to stay filed within VD period will also be considered a motion to stay VD]. *See also Salvador-Calleros v. Ashcroft,* 389 F.3d 959, 963–65 (9th Cir. 2004) [where motion to stay was filed on Monday following the Saturday when VD expired, the court, citing Fed. R. App. P. 26(a), held that the motion to stay would also be construed as a motion for VD and that the Monday filing was timely to preserve VD].

4. *Stay of Removal Does Not Stay Time Period to File Motion to Reopen*. The 90-day deadline to file a motion to reopen is not stayed when the court grants a motion to stay removal. *Keo Chan v. Gonzales,* 413 F.3d 161 (1st Cir. 2005).

5. *District Court Stay Pending Appeal.* At least one court has determined it is barred by INA §242(g) from entering a stay of removal pending appeal of its decision. *Cervantes De Hernandez v. Chertoff,* 368 F.Supp.2d 909 (E.D. Wis. 2005) [court denied relief, denied stay and when asked to stay removal pending appeal, held it was barred by INA §242(g)].

C. *Bond/Bail Pending Petition for Review*—At least one circuit court has also determined it has the inherent authority to grant bond while a petition for review is pending in the circuit court where petitioner has presented a substantial claim and there are extraordinary circumstances that make the grant of bail necessary to make the petition for review remedy effective. *Elkimya v. DHS,* 484 F.3d 151 (2d Cir. 2007) [finding court has inherent authority to grant bail pending resolution of a petition for review of returning LPR who has been out of the U.S. for 4 years, but concluding there were no extraordinary circumstances permitting bail); *Mapp v. Reno,* 241 F.3d 221 (2d Cir. 2001) [district courts have inherent authority to grant bail while habeas petition is pending where to do so is "necessary to make the habeas remedy effective"]; *but see Bolante v. Keisler,* 506 F.3d 618 (7th Cir. 2007) [admitting a person to bail while challenging admission is contrary to the INA and the inherent authority to admit persons to bail does not extend to persons deemed inadmissible at the border].

D. *Departure Does Not Bar Review*—Even if a request for a stay is denied and the person deported, the court may still hear the case as a result of the removal of former section 8 U.S.C. §1105a(c). *Hor v. Gonzales,* 421 F.3d 497 (7th Cir. 2005) [one panel of court denied a stay but the merits panel on rehearing granted the petition without knowing whether respondent had been removed from the country stating "it makes no difference" because the "alien's departure no longer moots his challenge to a removal order"]. *See also Spina v. DHS,* 470 F.3d 116, 124–25 (2d Cir. 2006) [court retained jurisdiction over appeal of statutory ineligibility to apply for INA §212(c) relief despite applicant's request to be deported while preserving his rights, and his removal to Italy]; *Dailide v. U.S. Att'y Gen.,* 387 F.3d 1335, 1336 n.1 (11th Cir. 2004) [where court denied stay and respondent fled the country so that order of removal was never executed, the petition was nevertheless not moot because 1252(b)(2) does not "expressly preclude" review under the circumstances, the government "acknowledges that the petition may be reviewed" and the denial of Social Security benefits is "clearly a collateral consequence of the order of removal"]; *Ghounem v. Ashcroft,* 378 F.3d 740 (8th Cir. 2004) [court ordered the reopening of *in absentia* removal order because of lack of notice where petitioner's stay had been denied and he had been deported to Egypt]; *Johnson v. Ashcroft,* 378 F.3d 164, 168 (2d Cir. 2004) [applicant deported after habeas filed and stay granted, but circuit court ruled for applicant and reversed district judge]; *Swaby v. Ashcroft,* 357 F.3d 156, 159–60 (2d Cir. 2004) [where habeas petitioner was deported during pendency of appeal case was not moot because of permanent bar due to aggravated felony conviction]; *Noriega-Lopez v. Ashcroft,* 335 F.3d 874, 878 (9th Cir. 2003) [court had jurisdiction to review habeas denial when person deported after habeas denied]; *Zegarra-Gomez v. INS*, 314 F.3d 1124 (9th Cir. 2003) [where habeas petitioner is deported after filing petition, the petition is not moot where there are collateral consequences arising from the deportation such as the inability to return]; *Moore v. Ashcroft,* 251 F.3d 919, 922 (11th Cir. 2001) [proceeding commenced post–Apr. 1, 1997 are governed by IIRIRA permanent rules that do not contain a statutory bar to review and claim is not moot because of removal consequences to future admissibility]; *Chong v. District Director, INS,* 264 F.3d 378, 385 (3d Cir. 2001) [same]; *Weng v. U.S. Att'y Gen., supra.* [same in regard to removal of asylum applicant]; *Tapia-Garcia v. INS,* 237 F.3d 1216, 1217 (10th Cir. 2001) [same]; *Steele v. Blackman,* 236 F.3d 130, 134 n.4 (3d Cir. 2001) [same]; *Max-George v. Reno,* 205 F.3d 194, 196 (5th Cir. 2000) *vacated on other grounds* 121 S.Ct. 2585 (2001) [same]; *Ying Fong v. Ashcroft,* 317 F.Supp.2d 398, 404–05 (S.D.N.Y. 2004) [habeas court ordered government to return respondent from abroad to the U.S. after government had illegally deported him]; *Gutierrez v. Ashcroft,* 289 F.Supp.2d 555 (D.N.J. 2003) [where counsel affirmatively misrepresented that he had filed a habeas petition challenging the denial of the right to seek relief under former INA §212(c) before respondent was physically removed but had not filed petition, his actions violated due process and permitted the court to accept the habeas *nunc pro tunc* to the time before petitioner was physically removed from the U.S.]; *Fuller v. INS,* 144 F.Supp.2d 72, 80–83 (D. Conn. 2000) [former INA §106(c) is not a bar under transitional rules to review where person deported but court would have granted stay but for mishaps in the clerk's office in docketing case]. *But see Abdala v. INS,* 488 F.3d 1061 (9the Cir. 2007) [although physical removal from the U.S. pursuant to an order does not, by itself, result in mootness, this case was moot because the basis of the habeas petition was to challenge the length of petitioner's detention]; *Perez v. Greiner,* 296 F.3d 123 (2d Cir. 2002) [claim was moot when the petitioner was deported after habeas denial was appealed notwithstanding "collateral consequences" doctrine because there was an independent conviction for drug trafficking which would have barred petitioner's return even if he was successful in habeas].

E. ***Stay of Voluntary Departure***—In addition to seeking a stay of removal pending a petition for review, a respondent who was granted voluntary departure may seek a stay of the voluntary departure period pending a decision on the petition for review. *Falaja v. Gonzales,* 418 F.3d 889, 899–900 (8th Cir. 2005) [where appellant filed stay of VD one day before it expired, court granted one day from issuance of mandate to depart]; *Lopez-Chavez v. Ashcroft,* 383 F.3d 650 (7th Cir. 2004) [court has jurisdiction to grant stay filed before stay expires, but denied stay because of no likelihood of success]; *Rife v. Ashcroft,* 374 F.3d 606, 614–16 (8th Cir. 2004) [where appellant files a motion to stay removal before VD expires it will be construed as a timely motion to stay VD]; *Nwakanma v. Ashcroft,* 352 F.3d 325 (6th Cir. 2003); *El Himri v. Ashcroft,* 344 F.3d 1261 (9th Cir. 2003). In the Ninth Circuit, the standard for granting a stay of removal is the same as for a stay of voluntary departure and the filing of a stay of removal will be construed as a request for a stay of voluntary departure. However, the court can only grant VD for the period remaining on the day the stay of removal and/or stay of VD is filed. *Desta v. Ashcroft,* 365 F.3d 741, 747 (9th Cir. 2004) [court has equitable power to stay voluntary departure but only for whatever period remains and petitioner's motion to stay removal will be construed as including a motion to stay voluntary departure if brought within voluntary departure period]. However, the court has no authority to grant stay of voluntary departure if the request for the stay is brought beyond the voluntary departure period. *Garcia v. Ashcroft,* 368 F.3d 1157 (9th Cir. 2004); *cf. Salvador-Calleros v. Ashcroft,* 389 F.3d 959, 963–65 (9th Cir. 2004) [where motion to stay was filed on Monday following the Saturday when VD expired, the court, citing Fed. R. App. P. 26(a), held that the motion to stay would also be construed as a motion for VD and that the Monday filing was timely to preserve VD]. *See also Boudaguian v. Ashcroft,* 376 F.3d 825, 829 (8th Cir. 2004) [court questioned whether it had jurisdiction to reinstate VD but would not in this case where respondent failed to submit a timely request for a stay of VD]; *but see Ngarurih v. Ashcroft,* 371 F.3d 182, 191–95 (4th Cir. 2004) [court has no jurisdiction to reinstate VD directly or through stay motion].

F. ***Venue***—Venue is now restricted to the court of appeals for the judicial circuit where the immigration judge completed the proceedings, thereby eliminating the right to appeal in the circuit where the respondent resides. INA §242(b)(2), 8 U.S.C. §1252(b)(2). Prior to IIRIRA, venue could lie in the circuit where the petitioner resided. *Nwaokolo v. INS,* 314 F.3d 303, 305–06 (7th Cir. 2002) [pre–Oct. 30, 1996 rules applied for venue purposes where the IJ's order was finalized before that date even though review was sought of a motion to reopen filed after that date]. The prior "choice of law" questions are therefore unlikely. However, what happens if the hearing is conducted telephonically or through teleconference and the respondent is in the jurisdiction of one circuit, his lawyer in another and the IJ in a third? Or what happens if the hearing is in one location (Virgin Islands) but the court with administrative control where papers are filed is in another location (Puerto Rico) and the motion to reopen is docketed and filed in the second (Puerto Rico) location? The EOIR has required IJs to specifically state on the record the location of the hearing. For example, an IJ sitting in Chicago but conducting a hearing with a respondent in Kansas City, Mo., must state on the record that the location of the hearing is Kansas City so that review will be in the Eighth Circuit instead of the Seventh Circuit (Chicago). Memo [OPPM 04-06], Creppy, Chief IJ, EOIR, (Aug. 18, 2004), *published on* AILA InfoNet at Doc. No. 04081891 (superseding Memo 04-04, Creppy, Chief, I.J. EOIR, (July 22, 2004), *published on* AILA InfoNet at Doc. No. 04080166). The Seventh Circuit has held, however, that jurisdiction remains with the IJ's home office. *Ramos v. Ashcroft,* 371 F.3d 948 (7th Cir. 2004) [jurisdiction remained in Seventh Circuit because Chicago was IJ's home office]; *Ramos v. Gonzales,* 414 F.3d 800, 803 (7th Cir. 2005) [rejected government's invitation, based upon the law of the case, to follow the Chief IJ Creppy memo that hearings for venue purposes will be presumed to be where the parties and lawyers are located and not where the IJ sits]. *See also Georcely v. Ashcroft,* 375 F.3d 45, 47–49 (1st Cir. 2004) [discussing the complexity of venue questions where the hearing is in the Virgin Islands which is governed by the Third Circuit but the court for the Virgin Islands is in Puerto Rico which is governed by the First Circuit and finding that the party waived objection to the First Circuit]. A party may also waive venue because it is not a jurisdictional issue. *Georcely v. Ashcroft,* 375 F.3d 45, 47–49 (1st Cir. 2004) [finding waiver by respondent who did not object to transfer].

But the venue provision is not jurisdictional and therefore a court of appeals may retain jurisdiction over the case even if the IJ's proceeding was completed in another circuit. *Moreno-Bravo v. Gonzales,*

463 F.3d 253, 257–63 (2d Cir. 2006) [where IJ proceeding was completed in Louisiana and a habeas action was filed in the second circuit, the second circuit retained jurisdiction because respondent had been in government custody for three and a half years, the district court had rendered a thorough opinion, and the case had been thoroughly briefed on the merits in the second circuit]; *Jama v. Gonzales,* 431 F.3d 230, 233 (5th Cir. 2005) [maintaining the case in the Fifth Circuit despite improper venue because of the unfairness in re-litigating the case anew in another forum]; *Bonhometre v. Gonzales,* 414 F.3d 442, 446 n.5 (3d Cir. 2005) [although the case was not properly before the court as a converted petition for review because the removal hearing arose in the First Circuit, it would be manifest injustice not to decide the case as it was thoroughly briefed and argued and petitioner had waited a long time for its resolution].

If the petition for review is filed in the wrong court, it may also be transferred pursuant to 28 U.S.C. §1631, and the proper circuit court may accept the appeal even if it is out of time. *Rodriguez-Roman v. INS,* 98 F.3d 416, 421–22 (9th Cir. 1996). *Cf. Lucaj v. Gonzales,* 425 F.3d 203 (2d Cir. 2005) [where there was insufficient proof that Second Circuit case was originally timely filed in Fifth Circuit, court lacked jurisdiction and case was dismissed]. For example, if a citizenship claim is filed in habeas in district court, the case should be transferred to the court of appeals. *Baeta v. Sonchik,* 273 F.3d 1261, 1263–65 (9th Cir. 2001); *Martinez-Piedras v. INS,* 354 F.Supp.2d 1149, 1152–55 (S.D.Cal. 2005) [followed *Baeta* and transferred habeas to circuit court to hear citizenship claim even though habeas had been filed prior to the final order of deportation]. Similarly, if a motion or habeas petition is filed in the district court within the 30-day time limit for a petition for review and it meets all the requirements of a petition for review, it will be treated as a petition and transferred to the court of appeals. *Salazar-Regino v. Gonzales,* 415 F.3d 436, 444–46 (5th Cir. 2005) [where case should have been brought in the circuit court but there was confusion over jurisdictional issues when a petitioner asserted he was not convicted, court waived failure to file in circuit court and had habeas transferred to it under §1631]; *Paul v. INS,* 348 F.3d 43 (2d Cir. 2003); *Lopez v. Heinauer,* 332 F.3d 507, 510–11 (8th Cir. 2003) [transferring habeas action seeking review of a reinstatement order to court of appeals because, without transfer, "the petitioner will have lost his opportunity to present the merits of the claim due to a statute of limitations bar"]; *Castro-Cortez v. INS,* 239 F.3d 1037, 1046–47 (9th Cir. 2001) [transferring habeas action seeking review of a reinstatement order to the court of appeals where "petitioners had good reason to believe that direct review was not available and that a habeas corpus petition was their avenue to secure judicial review"]. *But see Rivera-Martinez v. Ashcroft,* 389 F.3d 207 (1st Cir. 2004) [dismissed habeas and declined to transfer citizenship claim to circuit court where habeas was filed out of time]; *Acevedo-Carranza v. Ashcroft,* 371 F.3d 539, 542–43 (9th Cir. 2004) [habeas dismissed because case could not be transferred to circuit court under 28 U.S.C. §1631 where habeas was not filed within 30 days of BIA decision and court therefore lacked jurisdiction]; *Taniguchi v. Schultz,* 303 F.3d 950, 956 (9th Cir. 2002) [transfer from habeas court to circuit court not permitted where the court of appeals could not have exercised jurisdiction on the date habeas was filed because habeas was filed beyond the 30-day period and because respondent never raised her citizenship argument before the BIA and therefore failed to exhaust remedies].

G. *Standard of Review*—Review is substantially narrowed and administrative findings of fact are conclusive "unless any reasonable adjudicator would be compelled to conclude to the contrary." INA §242(b)(4)(B), 8 U.S.C. §1252(b)(4)(B); *Dia v. Ashcroft,* 353 F.3d 228, 248–61 (3d Cir. 2003) (*en banc*) [finding that 242(b)(4)(B) codified *Elias-Zacarias* thereby maintaining the traditional substantial evidence standard and reversed the IJs credibility finding in asylum claim]; *Castellano-Chacon v. INS,* 341 F.3d 533, 551–52 (6th Cir. 2003) [upheld denial of CAT claim under §1252(b)(4) because decision was not "manifestly contrary to the law" and contrary decision not compelled]; *Fahim v. U.S. Att'y Gen.,* 278 F.3d 1216, 1218 (11th Cir. 2002) [affirmed BIA's denial of withholding and CAT claim following *Elias-Zacarias* and INA §§242(b)(4)(A)–(B)]. Also, finding of fact by an IJ/BIA in regard to the need for corroborative evidence in asylum, withholding, and other forms of relief are conclusive unless "a reasonable trier of fact is compelled to conclude that such corroborating evidence is unavailable." INA §242(b)(4). *Cf. Castaneda-Castillo v. Gonzales,* 488 F.3d 17, 22–26 (1st Cir. 2007) (*en banc*) [reversed adverse credibility findings and the *en banc* court noted that the language in 8 U.S.C. §1252(b)(4)(B) regarding reversal only if evidence "compels" reversal reflects a "gloss by the Supreme Court" and does not "eliminate[] the conventional requirement that an administrative agency's explanation be rational"].

H. *Motions to Reopen/Reconsider*—Any review of a motion to reopen or reconsider must be consolidated with the review of the underlying order. INA §242(b)(6). The filing of a motion to reopen does not toll the running of the 30-day appeal period. *Stone v. INS*, 115 S.Ct. 1537 (1995) [where a timely motion to reopen was filed before the expiration of the time period to file a petition for review of the underlying order, it did not toll the period of time to file the appeal of the underlying order and failure to do so meant the underlying order was not reviewable]; *Potdar v. Keisler,* 505 F.3d 680, 683–85 (7th Cir. 2007) [BIA's erroneous grant of a motion to reopen and subsequent reversal of that grant did not allow petitioner to address underlying issues initially decided by the BIA on appeal as petitioner failed to appeal original removal order]; *Nwogu v. Gonzales,* 491 F.3d 80 (2d Cir. 2007) [petition for review filed within 30 days of BIA denial of motion to reconsider does not permit review of the BIA's decision on the merits]; *Gomes v. Gonzales,* 429 F.3d 1264, 1267 (9th Cir. 2005) [the grant of a motion to reopen because of changed circumstances addresses issues concerning future persecution and applicant's failure to appeal original order of removal regarding past persecution could not be included in new appeal of denial of future persecution]; *Membreno v. Gonzales,* 425 F.3d 1227 (9th Cir. 2005) (*en banc*) [where petition for review was filed within 30 days of denial of motion to reopen but almost one year after the underlying removal order, the court had no jurisdiction to review the underlying removal order]; *De Araujo v. Ashcroft,* 399 F.3d 84, 88–89 (1st Cir. 2005) [review of designation as aggravated felon is barred because respondent did not appeal BIA's final decision and appeal of a denial of respondent's motion to reopen for INA §212(c) relief is also barred because INA §242(a)(2)(C) bars review of all claims of an aggravated felon]; *Simtion v. Ashcroft,* 393 F.3d 733, 735–36 (7th Cir. 2004) [although court had jurisdiction over timely filed appeal of denial of motion to reopen for asylum, it had no jurisdiction to review denial of adjustment in the underlying order that was not addressed in the motion to reopen]; *Zhang v. INS,* 348 F.3d 289 (1st Cir. 2003) [appeal of issues regarding credibility and IJ/BIA application of the well-founded fear standard were untimely because the appeal notice was filed beyond 30 days and the pendency of motion to reopen did not stop time for filing appeal]; *Raffington v. INS,* 340 F.3d 720, 724 (8th Cir. 2003) [where respondent in her motion to reopen never raised the impropriety of the stop-time rule and never appealed the underlying removal order, she could not now raise the issue in her appeal to the denial of her motion to reopen]; *Nascimento v. INS,* 274 F.3d 26, 27 (1st Cir. 2001) [court will not review underlying BIA decision where appellant only timely appealed denial of motion to reconsider]. Conversely, the filing of a petition for review does not toll the time for filing a motion to reopen or reconsider. *Randhawa v. Gonzales,* 474 F.3d 918 (6th Cir. 2007) [motion for reconsideration was untimely filed with BIA because petition for review of the BIA's original decision did not toll the time for filing the motion to reconsider] The failure to file a petition for review of a denied motion to reopen where review was properly sought of the final order, does not prevent review of the issue that is pending, under the doctrine of res judicata, by virtue of the timely review of the underlying order. *Desta v. Ashcroft,* 329 F.3d 1179, 1183–84 (10th Cir. 2003) [where petitioner sought review of the denial of asylum on firm resettlement grounds, but failed to seek review of a motion to reopen on the same grounds, the doctrine of res judicata did not bar review of the firm resettlement issue]. The grant of a motion to reopen vacates the previous order and reinstates the previously terminated immigration proceedings and allow the original proceedings to go forward as if there had never been a final order. *Bronisz v. Ashcroft,* 378 F.3d 632, 636–37 (7th Cir. 2004) [review occurs under transition rules and not old rules because the final order under the old rules was vacated once the motion to reopen was granted]. But the grant of a motion to reconsider and the affirmance of the original order may not affect the finality of the original order for purposes of appeal. *Jaggernauth v. U.S. Atty. General,* 432 F.3d 1346, 1350–52 (11th Cir. 2005) [the granting of a motion to reconsider and the reaffirmance of the original final order did not affect the finality of the original order and the court therefore had jurisdiction to review the matter when petitioner appealed the original order within 30 days]; *Plasencia-Ayala v. Mukasey,* 516 F.3d 738, 744–46 (9th Cir. 2008) [same]. *But see Mu Ju Li v. Mukasey,* 515 F.3d 575, 578–80 (6th Cir. 2008) [when the BIA grants a motion to reconsider and renders a new decision addressing the arguments raised, the original order has been vacated, a new order has been entered in its place, and a new appeal must be filed].

I. *Treatment of Nationality Claims*—INA §242(b)(5). If a petitioner makes a claim to be a U.S. national, the court of appeals may decide the matter if they find there is no genuine issue of material fact. If they find that there is such an issue, the matter shall be transferred to the district court. *Agosto v. INS,* 436 U.S. 748, 754–57, 98 S.Ct. 2081 (1978) [reversed circuit court finding there was a genuine issue of material fact and remanded case to be sent to district court for a *de novo* hearing]; *Joseph v. Att'y Gen. of the U.S.,* 421 F.3d 224 (3d Cir. 2005) [Haitian entitled to *de novo* hearing before district court because there is genuine material issue of fact]. There is no original jurisdiction in the district court to hear the nationality claim. *Giap v. INS,* 311 F.Supp.2d 438, 440 (S.D.N.Y. 2004); *Alvarez-Garcia v. INS,* 234 F.Supp.2d 283, 289–90 (S.D.N.Y. 2002); *U.S. v. Lawrence,* 991 F.Supp. 149 (W.D.N.Y. 1998). If citizenship claim is filed in habeas in district court, the case should be transferred to the court of appeals. *Baeta v. Sonchik*, 273 F.3d 1261, 1263–65 (9th Cir. 2001); *Martinez-Piedras v. INS,* 354 F.Supp.2d 1149, 1152–55 (S.D. Cal. 2005) [followed *Baeta* and transferred habeas to circuit court to hear citizenship claim even though habeas had been filed prior to the final order of deportation]. *But see Atem v. Ashcroft,* 312 F.Supp.2d 792, 796–99 (E.D. Va. 2004) [where citizenship challenge was filed in habeas in the district court, but petitioner failed to appeal nationality issue to BIA, the case could not be transferred to circuit court because of failure to exhaust administrative remedies].

J. *Consolidation of Issues for Review*—INA §242(b)(9). Judicial review of all questions of law and fact, including interpretation and application of constitutional and statutory provisions arising from any action taken or proceeding brought to remove a person from the U.S. shall be available only in the judicial review of a final order. The Supreme Court in addressing the reach of INA §242(g) in *Reno v. American-Arab Anti-Discrimination Committee,* 525 U.S. 471, 119 S.Ct. 936, 943 (1999) described INA §242(b)(9) as a "zipper" clause and "that those specified decisions and actions, which...some courts had held *not* to be included within the non–final-order review prohibition of §1105a, *are* covered by the 'zipper' clause of §1252(b)(9)." Although prior to the REAL ID Act a number of courts, including the Supreme Court in *St. Cyr,* narrowly read INA §242(b)(9) to continue to permit habeas review in the district court, *INS v. St. Cyr* 121 S.Ct. 2271, 2286–87 (2001) [finding the section did not bar habeas review because it only applied to review of an order of removal under section 242(a)(1) and not habeas review], although *St. Cyr* was prior to the REAL ID Act. *See also Bejacmar v. Ashcroft,* 291 F.3d 735 (11th Cir. 2002) [finding that *Richardson v. Reno,* 180 F.3d 1311 (11th Cir. 1998) *cert. denied,* 120 S.Ct. 1529 no longer good law in light of *St.* Cyr]; *Mahadeo v. Reno,* 226 F.3d 3 (1st Cir. 2000), *cert. denied, Ashcroft v. Mahadeo,* 121 S.Ct. 2590 [habeas not barred under IIRIRA permanent provisions including §242(b)(9) from entertaining both statutory and constitutional claims]; *Flores-Miramontes v. INS,* 212 F.3d 1133, 1139–41 (9th Cir. 2000) [habeas jurisdiction is not barred because §242(b)(9) only applies to consolidation of APA/petition for review claims]; *Liang v. INS,* 206 F.3d 308, 317–20 (3d Cir. 2000), *cert. denied sub nom. Rodriguez v. INS,* 533 U.S. 949 (2001) [INA §242(b)(9) does not bar habeas review in the district court. Rejected *Richardson* and *Manx-George*]; *Bouayad v. Holmes,* 74 F.Supp.2d 471, 473–74 (E.D. Pa. 1999) [the language of INA §242(b)(9) does not preclude habeas jurisdiction over detention], some courts read the statute more broadly. *Max-George v. Reno,* 205 F.3d 194 (5th Cir. 2000), *vacated on other grounds* 121 S.Ct. 2585 (2001); *Barca v. Holmes,* 73 F.Supp.2d 484 (M.D. Pa. 1999) [INA §242(b)(9) barred a district court action challenging INS's decision to invoke INA §241(a)(5)]. In the post-REAL ID Act era, at least one circuit has interpreted the statute quite broadly to preclude even pattern and practice claims unless wholly independent of or collateral to a removal proceedings. *Aguilar v. ICE,* 510 F.3d 1, 6–18 (1st Cir. 2007) [INA §242(b)(9) precluded a pattern and practice class-wide claim challenging ICE raids that resulted in detaining and transferring petitioners out of state thus depriving them of counsel];

K. *Circuit Courts Are Concerned with Dilatory or Frivolous Appeals*—The Second Circuit has assessed costs and damages to an appellant and his counsel for frivolous appeals. *Muigai v. INS*, 682 F.2d 334 (2d Cir. 1982); *Acevedo v. INS*, 538 F.2d 918 (2d Cir. 1976). *See also Pillay v. INS*, 45 F.3d 14 (2d Cir. 1995) [dismissed INA §212(c) appeal as frivolous]; *Osuch v. INS*, 970 F.2d 394 (7th Cir. 1992); *Calderon-Ontiveros v. INS*, 809 F.2d 1050 (5th Cir. 1986) [double costs taxed against attorney who raised due process issue because of INS actions]. The circuit courts may also sanction lawyers for what they perceive as procedural errors in preparing the record on appeal. *McBrearty v. Perryman*, 212 F.3d 985, 986 (7th Cir. 2000); *Guentchev v. INS*, 77 F.3d 1036 (7th Cir. 1996). The Seventh Circuit has warned counsel not to file petitions for review in "thin" asylum cases or face sanctions. *Gramatikov v. INS*, 128 F.3d 619, 620 (7th Cir. 1997). Lawyers may also be sanctioned under 28 U.S.C. §1927 for baseless district court litigation. *Bowler v. INS*, 901 F.Supp. 597 (S.D.N.Y. 1995) or for filing motions untimely and in lieu of timely filed briefs. *Ramos v. Ashcroft,* 371 F.3d 948, 949–50 (7th Cir. 2004) [court chastised government for failing to file motion to transfer before respondent was required to file his brief]. A lawyer for a habeas petitioner was also sanctioned for failing to disclose that s/he has also filed and pursued a petition for review regarding the petitioner before the circuit court. *Ndreko v. Ridge,* 351 F.Supp.2d 904, 909–11 (D. Minn. 2004) [where lawyer filed emergency habeas for a client who was removed from the U.S. to have him returned to the country, but did not disclose that a circuit court petition for review was pending in the case and that the circuit court had denied a stay, the district court imposed sanctions against counsel for failure to disclose the information].

L. *Record on Appeal*

1. Record governed by Fed. R. App. P. 10(a).
2. Where documents are attached as an appendix to a brief, but are not in the original record, the court of appeals cannot consider them. *The Sweet Life v. Dole*, 876 F.2d 402 (5th Cir. 1989).
3. A petitioner may be permitted to present evidence in the appellate court that is outside the record of proceedings in the immigration court "in order to show that he was prejudiced by the lack of a full and fair hearing." *Colmenar v. INS,* 210 F.3d 967, 972 n.5 (9th Cir. 2000).

M. *Remands*

1. *General Principles*—"Well established principles of administrative law" require the courts of appeal to remand cases to the agency for fact finding rather than make those determinations at the appellate level except in rare circumstances. *INS v. Ventura,* 537 U.S. 12, 123 S.Ct. 353, 355 (2002) [reversed the Ninth Circuit for addressing changed circumstances in an asylum case where the BIA had not reached the issue]. It is up to the BIA in the first instance on remand, and not the federal courts, to decide what might constitute a cognizable social group. *Gonzales v. Thomas,* 547 U.S. 183 (2006) [Court vacated *en banc* decision of the Ninth Circuit that defined a particular social group before giving the BIA the opportunity to determine whether "the members of a family can and do constitute a 'particular social group' within the meaning of the Act]; *Gonzales v. Tchoukhrova,* __S.Ct.___(2006) [vacated social group finding of disabled children in light of *Thomas*]. *See also Velazquez-Herrera v. Gonzales,* 466 F.3d 781 (9th Cir. 2006) [remanded case to BIA to clarify whether a conviction under Washington state's fourth-degree assault statute, Wash. Rev. Code §9A.36.041 constitutes child abuse]; *Jian Hui Shao v. Board of Immigration Appeals,* 465 F.3d 497, 501–03 (2d Cir. 2006) [under *Thomas* case remanded to BIA to determine whether having two children in China is sufficient grounds *per se* for a well-founded fear of future persecution]; *Ucelo-Gomez v. Gonzales,* 464 F.3d 163, 167–72 (2d Cir. 2006) [remand mandated by *Thomas* to address whether affluent Guatemalans are a social group]; *Esponda v. U.S. Att'y Gen.,* 453 F.3d 1319, 1322–23 (11th Cir. 2006) [case remanded to BIA to determine in first instance whether notice of appeal adequately apprised the BIA of the grounds for appeal notwithstanding appellant's failure to file a brief]; *Cruz v. Att'y Gen. of the U.S.,* 452 F.3d 240, 248 (3d Cir. 2006) [BIA decision to deny untimely request for reopening *sua sponte* of person with vacated conviction should be remanded to determine the status of the conviction under *Pickering*]; *Chen v. DOJ,* 426 F.3d 104, 116–17 (2d Cir. 2005) [criticizing 9th Cir. approach in *He* and remanding case even after reversing IJ's credibility determination]; *Zalawadia v. Ashcroft,* 371 F.3d 292, 296 (5th Cir. 2004) [in habeas proceeding the government agreed with petitioner that it was error for the habeas judge in light of *Ventura* to consider the merits of eligibility for relief under INA §212(c) instead of remanding the proceedings to the BIA]; *Silva-Calderon v. Ashcroft,* 371 F.3d 1135 (9th Cir. 2004) [remanded cases to BIA to correct administrative record and to decide issues on corrected record]; *Ezeagwuna v. Ashcroft,* 325 F.3d 396, 398 & 411 (3d Cir. 2003) [following rehearing the court vacated its previous grant of asylum and withholding after determining court misapplied credibility issues and remanded case back to IJ to make those decisions].
2. *Remand Unnecessary*—*Xiu Fen Xia v. Mukasey,* 510 F.3d 162 (2d Cir. 2007) [remand denied where petitioner should present evidence to BIA in a motion to reopen and where the new BIA decision (*Matter of T-Z-*), representing a change in law, does not represent a change in policy]; *Akio Kawashima v. Gonzales,* 503 F.3d 997, 1004 n.7 (9th Cir. 2007) [rejected government request to remand under *Ventura* to obtain additional documents to prove loss in excess of $10,000 to establish an aggravated felony under 101(a)(43)(M)(i)]; *Ruiz-Vidal v. Gonzales,* 473 F.3d 1072, 1079–80 (9th Cir. 2007) [government's failure to prove deportability by producing records that indicate the drug that subjects a person to removal is not a basis to remand under *Ventura*]; *Zhu v. Gonzales,* 493 F.3d 588, 5601–02 (5th Cir. 2007) [unnecessary to remand to develop a further factual or legal record regarding withholding where government failed to present evidence for eight years and where BIA previously determined that there are no changed circumstances in China with respect to forced abortion]; *Calle v. U.S. Att'y Gen.,* 504 F.3d 1324, 1329–31 (11th Cir. 2007) [BIA's denial of second motion to reconsider on erroneous belief that it was numerically

barred should not result in remand because case presents the "rare circumstance" under *Ventura* where legal issue was clear that petitioner did not meet legal standard for motion to reconsider]; *Fedunyak v. Gonzales,* 477 F.3d 1126, 1130–31 (9th Cir. 2007) [remand under *Ventura* to give the government the opportunity to address changed country conditions for asylum and withholding was unnecessary where BIA agreed that applicant was eligible for CAT relief which covers a higher burden]; *Hussain v. Gonzales,* 477 F.3d 153, 157–58 (4th Cir. 2007) [court entered final order in "rare circumstance" where remand would be nothing more than a mere formality because respondent doesn't qualify for AOS as he was EWI]; *Fernandez-Ruiz v. Gonzales,* 466 F.3d 1121, 1132–35 (9th Cir. 2006) (en banc) [remand pursuant to *Ventura* was unnecessary where court determined that misdemeanor domestic violence assault under Ariz. Rev. Stat. §§13-1203 and 13-3601 were not crimes of violence under the categorical approach because they permitted convictions for something short of intentional conduct and the government failed to produce documents that would have demonstrated crimes of violence under the modified categorical approach]; *Perez-Enriquez v. Gonzales,* 463 F.3d 1007, 1014–15 (9th Cir. 2006) (en banc) [remand to BIA on whether SAW applicant could be denied LPR status because he pled guilty to possession for sale of a controlled substance after he obtained his temporary residence was unnecessary as BIA previously had clearly addressed the issue and determined that it could not]; *Pickering v. Gonzales,* 465 F.3d 263, 270–71 (6th Cir. 2006) [no authority to remand for additional evidence where the government failed to meet its burden of clear, convincing and unequivocal evidence in seeking removal]; *Zheng v. Ashcroft,* 397 F.3d 1139, 1147–48 (9th Cir. 2005) [remanded case after reversing adverse credibility determination but where the person is automatically eligible for asylum it is not a remand under *Ventura* to determine eligibility]; *Smolniakova v. Gonzales,* 422 F.3d 1037, 1051–53 (9th Cir. 2005) [*Ventura* remand unnecessary in asylum case regarding Jewish persecution in Russia where IJ ruled on changed country conditions and the court can review that determination for substantial evidence]; *Zhao v. Gonzales,* 404 F.3d 295, 310–11 (5th Cir. 2005) [it was unnecessary to remand under *Ventura* where government acknowledged there were not changed circumstances in China regarding Falun Gong claim]; *Ali v. Ashcroft,* 394 F.3d 780, 787–88 (9th Cir. 2005) [remand to BIA under *Ventura* on factual issues concerning asylum is unnecessary where BIA streamlined case and made no findings]; *Edwards v. INS,* 393 F.3d 299, 312 (2d Cir. 2004) [remand for fact finding on INA §212(c) was unnecessary where IJ/BIA previously agreed that respondent was eligible for the relief and it was only their erroneous application of legal principles that required a reversal and BIA was ordered to grant relief]; *Ghebremedhin v. Ashcroft,* 392 F.3d 241 (7th Cir. 2004) [limited *Ventura* to circumstance where a factual issue is in dispute but remanded back to BIA to exercise discretion]; *Ding v. Ashcroft,* 387 F.3d 1131, 1140 (9th Cir. 2004) [remand unnecessary in forced abortion case because the applicant is necessarily eligible for asylum under correct standard]; *Khup v. Ashcroft,* 376 F.3d 898, 904–06 (9th Cir. 2004) [remand unnecessary under *Ventura* because there was no adverse credibility determination and future persecution was established]; *Wang v. Ashcroft,* 341 F.3d 1015, 1023 (9th Cir. 2003) [remand pursuant to *Ventura* is unnecessary because if the adverse credibility determination is reversed the forced abortion claim is sufficient to warrant asylum and withholding]; *Baballah v. Ashcroft,* 335 F.3d 981, 992 (9th Cir. 2003) *amended* 367 F.3d 1067 (9th Cir. 2004) [remand unnecessary under *Ventura* to present changed country conditions where INS failed to present evidence of changed conditions and it did not argue that changed conditions would eliminate applicant's fear]; *He v. Ashcroft,* 328 F.3d 593, 603–04 (9th Cir. 2003) [remand for additional investigation regarding eligibility for withholding and asylum is not necessary in statutory sterilization case where court reversed BIA's credibility finding and such action is not contrary to *Ventura*]; *Mayo v. Ashcroft,* 317 F.3d 867, 874–75 (8th Cir. 2003) [where BIA took 8 years to issue opinion, where 12 years have elapsed since the court issued its prior opinion in the same case, and where respondent spent 22 months in detention, the case presents the "rare" circumstance where remand to BIA is unnecessary and IJ's order should be carried out]; *Fergiste v. INS,* 138 F.3d 14 (1st Cir. 1998) [reversal and not remand appropriate where remand would allow INS to argue its case for a second time after BIA failed to comply with its own regulation]. Although the circuit courts under *Ventura* may generally only remand to the IJ, they have suggested that a different hearing officer be assigned to the case. *Muhur v. Ashcroft,* 355 F.3d 958, 961 (7th Cir. 2004) [in view of IJ's "mishandling" of asylum claim by applying an incorrect standard, BIA urged to remand to a different IJ]; *Bace v. Ashcroft,* 352 F.3d 1133, 1141 (7th Cir. 2003) [suggested new hearing officer where circuit court thought IJ made numerous errors].

3. *Evidence and Remands*—Courts of appeals traditionally had authority in immigration appeals to consider new evidence brought to its attention and to remand to the BIA to consider the new evidence. 28 U.S.C. §2347(c); *Feleke v. INS*, 118 F.3d 594, 599 (8th Cir. 1997) [remand to BIA to consider newly discovered evidence]; *Makonnen v. INS*, 44 F.3d 1378, 1384–86 (8th Cir. 1995); *Bernal-Garcia v. INS*, 852 F.2d 144 (5th Cir. 1988); *Young v. DOJ*, 759 F.2d 450, 456 (5th Cir.), *cert. denied,* 474 U.S. 996 (1985); *Coriolan v. INS*, 559 F.2d 993 (5th Cir. 1977); *Dolores v. INS*, 772 F.2d 223 (6th Cir. 1985); *Fleurinor v. INS*, 585 F.2d 129 (5th Cir. 1978); *Alsheweikh v. INS*, 990 F.2d 1025, 1027 (8th Cir. 1993). However, the Congress under IIRIRA §306(a) (and the transitional rules under 309(c)(4)(B)) has barred courts reviewing final orders of removal from taking additional evidence under 28 U.S.C. §2347(c). INA §242(a)(1). *Gebremaria v. Ashcroft,* 378 F.3d 734, 737 (8th Cir. 2004) [following *Al Najjar* the court cannot supplement the record under §2347(c) or remand for additional evidence]; *Al Najjar v. Ashcroft,* 257 F.3d 1262, 1278–83 (11th Cir. 2001); *Altawil v. INS,* 179 F.3d 791, 792–93 (9th Cir. 1999). However, in *Gallo-Alvarez v. Ashcroft,* 266 F.3d 1123, 1129 (9th Cir. 2001), the Ninth Circuit transferred a petition for review to the district court for factual development under 28 U.S.C. §2347(b)(3). The case involved a reinstatement of removal under INA §241(a)(5). There was no "hearing" that would prevent the application of §2347(b)(3), because the regulations at 8 C.F.R. §241.8 purport to eliminate the right to an IJ hearing. *See also Morgan v. Gonzales,* 495 F.3d 1084, 1090 (9th Cir. 2007) [recognizing the availability but not utilizing §2347(b)(3) where petitioner did not raise "colorable claims" to due process and estoppel]. In *Lin v. DOJ,* 473 F.3d 48 (2d Cir. 2007) another circuit recognized that in light of IIRIRA and the prohibition against the use of §2347(c) it could not remand a case based upon petitioner's request, but nevertheless remanded the case based upon the "gravity" of the asylum claim, its inherent powers to remand and the government's agreement. However, in *Xiao Xing Ni v. Gonzales,* 494 F.3d 260, 263–72 (2d Cir. 2007) the Second Circuit severely restricted its inherent powers to remand for more evidence under *Lin* and held that its inherent power, in light of the removal of §2347(c), should not be exercised where: (i) the basis for the remand is to consider evidence that was *not* in the record before the BIA and (ii) the agency has regulations, as does the BIA, to reopen cases for the taking of additional evidence.*Xiao Xing Ni,* 494 F.3d at 269. The Supreme Court has also not hesitated to accept evidence of the vacation of a conviction which alters the validity of the decision below. The Supreme Court, over the objection of the Solicitor General that the court should not consider the vacation of petitioner's criminal conviction which occurred after the decision of the court of appeals, vacated the circuit court's decision and remanded the case back to it "for further consideration" in light of the intervening state court decision vacating the criminal conviction. *Chew-Villasana v. INS*, 113 S.Ct. 313 (1992). *See also Yang v. McElroy,* 277 F.3d 158 (2d Cir. 2002) [where there was a four-year delay between the BIA decision and the IJ decision which relied on a five-year-old State Department Country report the Court remanded the case back to the BIA for more current reports]; *Cardenas-Uriarte v. INS,* 227 F.3d 1132, 1138 (9th Cir. 2000) [remand to district court for additional evidence to determine whether person qualified for Federal First Offender treatment does not violate IIRIRA because evidence necessary to determine Court's jurisdiction].

4. *Scope of Remand*—Where the circuit court remands a case to the BIA for one purpose, it may allow remand on other issues. *Ghebrehiwot v. Att'y Gen. of the U.S.,* 467 F.3d 344, 357 (3d Cir. 2006) [where court remanded case on evidentiary issues concerning asylum, it permitted respondent to assert a social group claim on remand despite previously failing to exhaust administrative remedies]. However, where the scope of the circuit court's remand is clear, the BIA/IJ has no power to expand the remand beyond the boundary ordered by the court. *Mendez-Gutierrez v. Gonzales,* 444 F.3d 1168 (9th Cir. 2006) [upheld BIA decision not to consider validity of NTA on remand because it was not a part of the remand order]. At least one circuit court takes the view that remanding a case where a motion to reopen had been filed before the BIA might violate former 8 C.F.R. §3.2(c) (now 8 C.F.R. §1003.2(c)). *Saiyid v. INS*, 132 F.3d 1380, 1386 n.9 (11th Cir. 1998). Another circuit has determined that the Convention Against Torture does not require a remand to the BIA. *Khourassany v. INS,* 208 F.3d 1096 (9th Cir. 2000) [denying motion to remand but agreeing to stay mandate for 90 days to allow application to BIA to reopen].

5. *Applicable Law on Remand*—The law to apply in a remand may be the law that was in force at the time the violation occurred. In *Otarola v. INS,* 270 F.3d 1272 (9th Cir. 2001) the Court held that INS should not benefit from a frivolous appeal to the BIA that provided post-IIRIRA changes regarding the stop-time rule for suspension to take effect. If INS had not appealed, the law at the

time of the IJ's decision granting suspension under pre-IIRIRA law (no stop-time rule) would have stood. The court determined that in light of INS's frivolous appeal, pre-IIRIRA law should apply. In *Castillo-Perez v. INS,* 212 F.3d 518, 528 (9th Cir. 2000) the Court determined that the appropriate remedy for an ineffective assistance claim was to remand the case to the BIA with instructions that the agency apply the law in existence at the time the suspension claim should have been made but for the ineffective assistance. *See also Guadalupe-Cruz v. INS,* 240 F.3d 1209 (9th Cir. 2001) *opinion corrected,* 250 F.3d 1271 (9th Cir. 2001) [where IIRIRA was not in effect and IJ erroneously applied stop time rule, decision is reversed and IJ ordered to apply pre-IIRIRA law but with current facts].

6. *Stipulations and Remands*—Where the parties stipulate to a remand they will be bound by the terms of the stipulation. *Belortaja v. Gonzales,* 484 F.3d 619 (2d Cir. 2007) [where the parties stipulated to a remand to the BIA, the BIA was free to make an adverse credibility finding and resolve the case without further remand to the IJ because the case arose under the pre-clearly erroneous rules established by the AG in 2002 and the BIA could engage in *de novo* review].

7. *Government Request for Remand*—A decision by the U.S. Attorney's Office to agree to or to request a remand back to the BIA should be directed to the local ICE Chief Counsel Office where the IJ proceeding was held with an explanation of why a remand is sought. Memo, Appellate Counsel, Office of the Principal Legal Advisor, ICE (May 10, 2005), *published on* AILA InfoNet at Doc. No. 06050519. A requested remand by OIL has a different procedure. OIL has set guidelines to its attorneys as to the following circumstances where a request for remand would be appropriate assuming the court has jurisdiction: (1) the agency's decision contains material errors of fact or law; (2) it is contrary to circuit law; (3) the agency has committed material procedural error; (4) there are material and unexplained discrepancies between the IJ and BIA decisions or there was a failure to address a determination required by law; (5) sustaining the decision would violate the *Chenery* doctrine or *INS v. Ventura*; (6) the administrative record is stale; (7) defending the case would risk significant agency policies or programs; or (8) defense of the case would be patently inappropriate. Memo, Hussey, Director, OIL (Dec. 8, 2004), *published on* AILA InfoNet at Doc. No. 06050518. The procedure for a remand for OIL requires an internal memorandum to the Director and thereafter concurrence with DHS and/or EOIR but OIL may still remand absent their consent. Memo, Hussey (Dec. 8, 2004), *supra.* The government may also request that the circuit court remand a case to the BIA without necessarily confessing error. *Ren v. Gonzales,* 440 F.3d 446 (7th Cir. 2006).

8. *Remand as a Final Order*—For purposes of remand there is also a question of whether a BIA remand constitutes a final order that may be appealed to the circuit courts. *Compare Vakker v. Attorney General of U.S.,* 518 F.3d 143, 146–48 (3d Cir. 2008) [BIA's order upholding grant of withholding, remanding case for security checks and denying petitioner's remand for AOS, did not become final until security checks were complete]; *Singh v. Gonzales,* 432 F.3d 533, 537 n.4 (3d Cir. 2006) [finding that BIA's first order affirming removability but remanding to allow petitioner to pursue relief from removal was not final for purposes of judicial review until remand proceedings were completed and the BIA ruled on the second appeal] *with Viracacha v. Mukasey,* 518 F.3d 511,513–14 (7th Cir. 2008) [IJ remand for security checks but denial of asylum for failure to file within one year was a final order allowing petition for review]; *Yusupov v. Attorney General of U.S.,* 518 F.3d 185, 195-96 (3d Cir. 2008) [although BIA upheld deferral of removal under CAT and therefore remanded case to IJ, it denied withholding and because the withholding order was final it was subject to review]; *Del Pilar v. U.S. Att'y Gen.*, 326 F.3d 1154, 1156–57 (11th Cir. 2003) [BIA's reversal of §212(c) relief and remand to IJ to give respondent opportunity to designate country of deportation is a final appealable order]; *Castrejon-Garcia v. INS,* 60 F.3d 1359, 13651–62 (9th Cir. 1995) [reversing IJ grant of suspension and remanding for determination of VD is a final reviewable order]; *Perkovic v. INS,* 33 F.3d 615, 618–19 (6th Cir. 1994) [reversal of IJ grant of asylum and remand was reviewable final order].

N. *Judicial Notice*—Pursuant to Fed. R. Evid. 201(f), a court may take judicial notice at any stage of a proceeding. In *Opoka v. INS*, 94 F.3d 392 (7th Cir. 1996), the court took judicial notice that the wife had been granted suspension after husband was denied and reversed and remanded in light of wife's grant. A circuit court may also take judicial notice of changed political conditions in asylum cases. *Namo v. Gonzales,* 401 F.3d 453, 458–59 (6th Cir. 2005) [although court would have granted CAT relief to Iraqi based on the administrative record, it took judicial notice of changed conditions in Iraq due to the demise of Saddam Hussein regime and remanded case to the BIA]; *Gafoor v. INS,* 231 F.3d 645, 654–57 (9th Cir. 2000) [court took judicial notice of new, more recent, coup in Fiji that was not reflected in the record because events were "so troubling" and "so well publicized"]; *Ivezaj v. INS,* 84 F.3d 215, 218–19 (6th Cir. 1996). Judicial notice is also appropriate where the BIA's adverse credibility finding was based upon a failure to recognize a fact that is beyond dispute. *Singh v. Ashcroft,* 393 F.3d 903 (9th Cir. 2004) [where BIA made adverse credibility finding because asylum applicant did not prove the existence of the Indian intelligence service (RAW), the court reversed, cited Fed. R. Evid. 201, and rejected the government's argument that the court could not take notice of such an obvious fact as "nonsense"].

O. ***All Writs Act***—Courts of appeal on occasion have relied on the All Writs Act to stay the deportation of an appellant who is not otherwise eligible for an automatic stay. *Michael v. INS,* 48 F.3d 657 (2d Cir. 1995) [stayed deportation pending BIA review of IJ's denial of motion to reopen and Second Circuit review thereafter]; *Reid v. INS,* 766 F.2d 113, 116 n.9 (3d Cir. 1985); *Daborne v. Karn,* 763 F.2d 593, 597 n.2 (3d Cir. 1985); *Ying Fong v. Ashcroft,* 317 F.Supp.2d 398, 404–05 (S.D.N.Y. 2004) [pursuant to authority under All Writs Act, the habeas court ordered government to return respondent from abroad to the U.S. after government had illegally deported him]. *But see* REAL ID Act §106 [eliminating review in district court under the All Writs Act for the judicial review "of an order of removal entered or issued under any provision of this Act"]; INA §242(a)(5).

P. ***Stay of the Mandate***—Courts of appeal have, on occasion, stayed the issuance of their mandate and remanded to INS to permit additional evidence or to permit alien to apply for other relief. *Dokic v. INS,* 899 F.2d 530 (6th Cir. 1990) [stay to permit petitioner to exhaust administrative remedies by filing motion to reopen]; *Becerra-Jimenez v. INS,* 829 F.2d 996 (10th Cir. 1987) [stay of mandate and remand to permit IJ to consider additional factors after voluntary departure had been denied] or *Sida v. INS,* 783 F.2d 947 (9th Cir. 1986); *Shahla v. INS,* 749 F.2d 561, 564 (9th Cir. 1984). But Court of Appeals lacks power to issue a general stay of deportation. *Larimi v. INS,* 782 F.2d 1494, 1497 (9th Cir. 1986). Court may also be in violation of Dept. of Justice regulations regarding one motion to reopen if it remands case. *Saiyid v. INS,* 132 F.3d 1380, 1386 (11th Cir. 1998)

Q. ***Scope***—Court of Appeals cannot grant remand for agency determination of issue it has no power to review (*e.g.,* cannot remand to DD for consideration of deferred action). *Luciano-Vicente v. INS,* 786 F.2d 706, 709 (5th Cir. 1986).

VII. REVIEW OF SUMMARY REMOVAL ORDERS—INA §242(e), 8 U.S.C. §1252(e)

The Congress has determined that except for challenges to the statute or regulations concerning summary removal which must be brought in the District of Columbia within 60 days of their effective dates, INA §242(e)(3), the only review of summary exclusion orders shall be by habeas corpus proceedings.*Avendano-Ramirez v. Ashcroft,* 365 F.3d 813, 816–19 (9th Cir. 2004) [statute does not permit review of summary removal through a petition for review]. However, judicial review in habeas is limited to: (1) whether the petitioner is an alien; (2) whether the petitioner was ordered removed under §235(b)(1); and (3) whether the petitioner can prove by a preponderance of the evidence that s/he is an LPR, or a person granted and having refugee or asylum status. INA §242(e)(2). If a person successfully demonstrates that they are entitled to a writ, "the court may order no remedy or relief other than to require that the petitioner [have a removal hearing]." In determining whether the person was ordered removed, the court's inquiry is limited to whether there is such an order and the court cannot review whether the petitioner is actually inadmissible or entitled to relief. The legislative history suggests that determinations as to credible fear and whether persons may be removed in the case of individual applicants is not reviewable. H.R. Conf. Rep. 104-828, 104th Cong., 2d Sess. at 220 (1996).

VIII. CLASS TREATMENT

A. ***Generally***—Class treatment is appropriate where challenging the policy or procedure of INS in regard to a class of persons. *McNary v. Haitian Refugee Center, Inc.*, 498 U.S. 479 (1991) [policies and unconstitutional practices concerning the treatment of SAW applicants challenged in a class action]; *Jean v. Nelson,* 472 U.S. 846 (1985) [class treatment concerning parole]; *Walters v. Reno,* 145 F.3d 1032, 1045–47 (9th Cir. 1998), *cert. denied, Reno v. Walters,* 526 U.S. 1003 (1999) [challenge to

INS form concerning INA §274C]; *Franklin v. Barry*, 909 F.Supp. 21, 29–31 (D.D.C. 1995) [challenge to unconstitutional effect of detainer policy]. However, class treatment may be inappropriate where suit addresses questions concerning individual treatment regarding asylum claims, *Garcia-Mir v. Smith*, 766 F.2d 1478, 1488 n.11 (11th Cir. 1985), *cert. denied sub nom. Marquez-Medina v. Meese,* 475 U.S. 1022 (1986), or work authorization, *John Doe I v. Meese*, 690 F.Supp. 1572 (S.D. Tex. 1988) [no commonality to review work authorization denials in asylum context because decision must be on case-by-case basis]. *See also International Molders & Allied Workers Local 164 v. Nelson*, 102 F.R.D. 457 (N.D. Cal. 1983). The burden for class certification is on the movant. *Murillo v. Musegades*, 809 F.Supp. 487, 501 (W.D. Tex. 1992). Class actions may be barred in injunctive relief cases. Injunctive relief is not permitted (except direct petition in the U.S. Supreme Court) to enjoin the operation of removal proceedings (all matters under Title II, Chapter 4 of the INA) unless it is with respect to an individual against whom proceedings have commenced and only then can removal be enjoined if there is a showing by clear and convincing evidence that the entry or execution of such order is prohibited as a matter of law. INA §242(f), 8 U.S.C. §1252(f). *Van Dinh v. Reno,* 197 F.3d 427, 433 (10th Cir. 1999) [*Bivens* class action concerning the transfer of detained persons is barred by 242(f) and 242(a)(2)(B)(ii)]; *But see Barahona-Gomez v. Reno,* 236 F.3d 1115, 1121–22 (9th Cir. 2001) [section does not apply to deportation/exclusion proceedings]; *Catholic Social Services v. INS,* 232 F.3d 1139, 1149–50 (9th Cir. 2000) (en banc) [this section does not bar class wide injunctive relief under Chapter V pertaining to adjustment of status].

B. *Subclasses*—The court may decide that a class action should be divided into subclasses. *Santillan v. Gonzales,* 388 F.Supp.2d 1065, 1073–74 (N.D. Cal. 2005) [creating subclasses in action challenging government's policy regarding temporary documentation to persons awarded relief by an IJ].

C. *Class Treatment and Habeas*—Class-wide relief is allowed in habeas cases, *Ali v. Ashcroft,* 346 F.3d 873, 887–91 (9th Cir. 2003) [nationwide class of persons seeking to enjoin removal to country without functioning government upheld notwithstanding challenges to standing or inapplicability of Fed. R. Civ. P. 23, because all persons affected need not be plaintiffs and there is a procedure in habeas analogous to Rule 23]; *Nguyen Da Yen v. Kissinger*, 528 F.2d 1194, 1202 (9th Cir. 1975), but is not compelled. *Yi v. Maugans*, 24 F.3d 500, 507 (3d Cir. 1994) [district court did not abuse its discretion in denying habeas class]; *Wang v. Reno*, 862 F.Supp. 801, 810–12 (E.D.N.Y. 1994) [no habeas class where no personal jurisdiction over custodian, where no jurisdiction over subject matter for failure to exhaust and where individual considerations on Chinese asylum claims were still required].

D. *Summary Exclusions under §235(b)(1)*—Class treatment is barred by statute in cases seeking review of summary exclusion decisions under INA §235(b)(1), 8 U.S.C. §1252(e)(1)(B).

E. *Specificity*—Class treatment requires more than mere general allegations of numerosity. *John Doe I v. Meese, supra* [denied class certification where plaintiffs alleged class was too numerous to make joinder practical but could only identify less than 60 denials].

F. *Class Treatment and Statutes of Limitation*—The commencement of a class action suspends the applicable statute of limitations as to all asserted members of the class who would have been parties had the suit been permitted to continue as a class action. *American Pipe and Construction Co. v. Utah,* 414 U.S. 538, 554 (1974); *Catholic Social Services v. INS,* 232 F.3d 1139, 1145–49 (9th Cir. 2000) (en banc). Thus, individual plaintiffs are not time barred from filing claims that were part of class claims. However there is a split in the circuits as to whether a first class action can toll the statute for a second. *CSS, Inc., supra* [second class action not barred]. *But see Basch v. Ground Round, Inc.,* 139 F.3d 6, 11 (1st Cir. 1998); *Griffin v. Singletary,* 17 F.3d 356, 359 (11th Cir. 1994); *Andrews v. Orr,* 851 F.2d 146, 149 (6th Cir. 1988); *Korwek v. Hunt,* 827 F.2d 874, 879 (2d Cir. 1987); *Salazar-Calderon v. Presidio Valley Farmers Ass'n,* 765 F.2d 1334, 1351 (5th Cir. 1985), *cert. denied,* 475 U.S. 1035 (1986). The Ninth Circuit has also applied the relation back doctrine to a second amended complaint involving class action allegations that was filed beyond the six-year statute of limitations period. *Immigrant Assistance Project of the Los Angeles County Federation of Labor (AFL-CIO) v. INS,* 306 F.3d 842, 855–59 (9th Cir. 2002) [case can proceed as class action on theory that it relates back to first class action complaint].

G. *Class Treatment and Individual Representatives*—A class representative Plaintiff whose claim is denied or whose case is on appeal or moot may still pursue claims on behalf of the class. *Martinez-Mendoza v. Champion Intern. Corp.,* 340 F.3d 1200, 1215–16 (11th Cir. 2003). In *Martinez v. Mecca Farms, Inc.,* 213 F.R.D. 601, 606–07 (S.D. Fla. 2002), [rejected employer's claim that undocumented worker could not adequately represent class because he is subject to deportation and would be preoccupied with that defense].

H. ***Class Treatment and Pro Se Litigants***—A *pro se* litigant may not represent or be an adequate representative of a class. *Sillah v. Davis,* 252 F.Supp.2d 589, 597 (W.D. Tenn. 2003).

IX. APPEALABLE ORDER

Kaho v. Ilchert, 765 F.2d 877, 880 (9th Cir. 1985). District court order *remanding* case back to agency for further proceeding is appealable order under 28 U.S.C. §1291. *But see Kuh v. INS*, 758 F.2d 370 (9th Cir. 1985); *Shahla v. INS*, 749 F.2d 561 (9th Cir. 1984); *Bachelier v. INS*, 548 F.2d 1157, 1158 (5th Cir. 1977); *Heitland v. INS*, 551 F.2d 495, 499 (2d Cir.), *cert. denied*, 434 U.S. 819 (1977).

X. RULES OF STATUTORY CONSTRUCTION IN IMMIGRATION

A. ***Clarity of Statutory Language***—Where the language of a statute is clear on its face, there is no need to inquire into congressional intent. *INS v. Phinpathya*, 464 U.S. 183 (1984); *Shaar v. INS,* 141 F.3d 953, 956 (9th Cir. 1998); *Matter of Barrientos,* 24 I&N Dec. 100, 102 (BIA 2007) [plain language of the statute provided IJ jurisdiction to engage in *de novo* review of eligibility for TPS even if AAO has denied claim]; *Matter of Lemhammad*, 20 I&N Dec. 316 (BIA 1991). Similarly, the plain meaning of the language in a statute or regulation governs unless its interpretation would lead to an absurd result. *Barroso v. Gonzales,* 429 F.3d 1195, 1206–08 (9th Cir. 2005) [interpreting 8 C.F.R. §1003.2(f) to require that a person filing a motion to reconsider within the VD period must also file a request for a stay in order to stay VD would lead to an absurd result]; *Azarte v. Ashcroft,* 394 F.3d 1278, 1288–89 (9th Cir. 2005) [finding *Matter of Shaar* no longer good law for post-IIRIRA cases and determining that it would be absurd to interpret the motion to reopen and VD statutes in a way that would allow people to file motions to reopen but deny them a hearing because the VD period had passed before the BIA could hear them]; *Andreiu v. Ashcroft,* 253 F.3d 477, 482 (9th Cir. 2001) [allowing 1252(f)(2) to bar circuit courts from granting stays pending appeal unless there was clear and convincing evidence would lead to an absurd result because it would require a higher standard on a stay than on the merits]; *Areyalo v. Ashcroft,* 344 F.3d 1, 8 (1st Cir. 2003) [same, citing to *U.S. v. Wilson,* 503 U.S. 329, 334 (1992)]; *Cardenas-Uriarte v. INS,* 227 F.3d 1132, 1137 (9th Cir. 2000) [interpreting Federal First Offender Statute not to apply to possession of drug paraphernalia but to more serious offense leads to absurd result]; *Coronado-Durazo v. INS*, 123 F.3d 1322 (9th Cir. 1997); *Santamaria-Ames v. INS*, 104 F.3d 1127, 1130 (9th Cir. 1996); *Matter of Masri,* 22 I&N Dec. 1145, 1147–48 (BIA 1999).

The Supreme Court, however, has also recognized "the tyranny of literalness" where serious constitutional questions would be raised. *U.S. v. Witkovich*, 353 U.S. 194, 199 (1957). Where the language is susceptible to more than one interpretation or where the legislative history in "rare and exceptional circumstances" is clearly contrary to the clear language of the statute, the congressional intent controls. *INS v. Cardoza-Fonseca*, 480 U.S. 421 (1987).

When there is ambiguity in the text, the title of the statute or section can aid in resolving any ambiguities. *INS v. National Ctr. for Immigrants Rights, Inc.*, 502 U.S. 183 (1991); *Almendarez-Torres v. U.S.,* 118 S.Ct. 1219, 1226 (1998) [heading of a section is relevant in determining its meaning]; *Singh v. Gonzales,* 499 F.3d 969, 977–78 (9th Cir. 2007). However, the title alone is not controlling and where it is contrary to the text, the text is controlling. *INS v. St. Cyr*, 121 S.Ct. 2271, 2284 (2001) [finding title to preclusion statute under AEDPA §401(e) not controlling where language of statute did not explicitly preclude habeas]; *Pennsylvania Dept. of Corrections v. Yeskey,* 118 S.Ct. 1952, 1956 (1998) [title cannot limit plain meaning; its use is to resolve ambiguities]; *Jogi v. Voges,* 480 F.3d 822, 834 (7th Cir. 2007) [general language in the preamble of a treaty—Vienna Convention on Consular Relations—cannot be used to create an ambiguity in specific treaty text where none exists]; *Drax v. Reno,* 338 F.3d 98, 110 (2d Cir. 2003) [in determining that statute was retroactive the title suggesting it was only a technical correction would not affect the clear retroactive application of INTCA §203 amendments]; *CDI Information Services, Inc. v. Reno,* 278 F.3d 616, 619 (6th Cir. 2002) [title of statute cannot be used to constrict the plain language of the statute which bars judicial review]; *Matter of Anifowoshe,* 24 I&N Dec. 442, 443–44 (BIA 2008) [where statute is clear in regard to adoption of siblings, title in the legislation, but not in codified law, that conflicts is not controlling].

In reviewing statutes a legislature is presumed not to use any superfluous language. *Bailey v. U.S.*, 516 U.S. 137, 145 (1995). The courts will not read statutes to render language in the statute superfluous. *Pennsylvania Department of Public Welfare v. Davenport,* 495 U.S. 552, 562, 110 S.Ct. 2126 (1990) ["Our cases express a deep reluctance to interpret a statutory provision so as to render superfluous other provisions in the same enactment."]. "[S]tatutes should be interpreted, whenever possible, to give every word and phrase some operative effect. *See Walters v. Metro. Educ. Enters.,* 519 U.S. 202, 209, 117 S.Ct. 660, 136 L.Ed 2d 644 (1997) (explaining this point)..." *Schneider v. Chertoff,* 450 F.3d 944, 954 (9th Cir. 2006) [certain regulations regarding foreign medical graduates would render provisions of the Nursing Relief Act meaningless]; *Arevalo v. Ashcroft,* 344 F.3d 1, 7 (1st Cir. 2003) [distinguishing language to "enjoin" and to "restrain" and concluding that Congress did not intend in INA §242(f)(2) to limit the right of a court of appeals to issue a stay of removal under traditional standards]; *Azarte v. Ashcroft,* 394 F.3d 1278, 1287–88 (9th Cir. 2005) [finding *Matter of Shaar* no longer good law as the BIA's interpretation of the motion to reopen and the VD statutes eliminates the availability of motions to reopen for persons granted VD thereby impermissibly reading out motions to reopen under the statutory scheme];*Padash v. INS,* 358 F.3d 1161, 1167–74 (9th Cir. 2004) [court read the first provision of section 8 of the CSPA to include appeals pending before the federal courts because DHS's reading of the statute would have made that section redundant with another section that limited CSPA cases to ones pending before the agencies on Aug. 6, 2002].

The legislature is also presumed to be familiar with background of existing law when it legislates. *Cannon v. Univ. of Chicago,* 441 U.S. 677, 699 (1979); *Duvall v. Att'y Gen. of the U.S.,* 436 F.3d 382, 387 (3d Cir. 2006) [finding that the doctrine of collateral estoppel applies in removal proceedings in the absence on a clear reference in the INA because Congress legislates against the backdrop of well-established common law principles]; *Etchu-Njang v. Gonzales,* 403 F.3d 577, 582–83 (8th Cir. 2005) [quoting *Sutherland* that: "The legislature is presumed to know the prior construction of the original act"]; *Valansi v. Ashcroft,* 278 F.3d 203, 212 (3d Cir. 2002); *Matter of Gomez-Giraldo,* 20 I&N Dec. 957, 964 n.3 (BIA 1995) [Congress is "presumed to be cognizant of existing law pertinent to the legislation it enacts."]. Where "Congress adopts a new law incorporating sections of a prior law, Congress normally can be presumed to have had knowledge of the interpretation given to the incorporated law, at least insofar as it affects the new statute." *Lorillard v. Pons,* 434 U.S. 575, 581 (1978). In addition, "Congress is presumed to be aware of an administrative or judicial interpretation of a statute and to adopt that interpretation when it re-enacts a statute without change." *Lorillard, supra* at 580–81 (and cases cited therein).

The Last Antecedent Rule. "A limiting clause or phrase...should ordinarily be read as modifying only the noun or phrase that it immediately follows."*Jama v. ICE,* 543 U.S. 335, ___ (2005) [quoting *Barnhart v. Thomas,* 540 U.S. 20, 26 (2003) the Court determined that the limiting language under 8 U.S.C. §1231(b)(2)(E)(vii) that required a receiving country's consent for deportation did not apply to other methods for determining the country of removal in §1231(b)(2)(E)(i)–(vi) because it only modified the last phrase in that provision]. *But see Nobelman v. American Savings Bank,* 508 U.S. 324, 330–31 (1993); *U.S. v. Bass,* 404 U.S. 336, 340 n.6 (1971); *U.S. v. Standard Brewery,* 251 U.S. 210, 218 (1920) finding that rule can be overcome by other indicia of meaning.

Once the Supreme Court has given a definitive interpretation of a statute, it is an authoritative statement as to the meaning of the statute. *Rivers v. Roadway Express, Inc.,* 511 U.S. 298, 312–13 (1994) [it is (the Supreme Court's) responsibility to say what a statute means, and once the Court has spoken, it is the duty of other courts to respect that understanding of the governing rule of law. A judicial construction of a statute is an authoritative statement of what the statute means].

B. *Omission/Inclusion of Language*—"Where Congress includes particular language in one section of a statute but omits it in another section of the same Act, it is generally presumed that Congress acts intentionally and purposefully in the disparate inclusion or exclusion." *INS v. Cardoza-Fonseca*, 480 U.S. 421, 432 (1987); *Andreiu v. Ashcroft,* 253 F.3d 477 (9th Cir. 2001) (en banc) [Congress used the language enjoin in regard to injunctions in 1252(f)(2) and not stays on appeal]; *Gee v. INS*, 875 F.Supp. 666, 671 (N.D. Cal. 1994); *Alanis-Bustamante v. Reno,* 201 F.3d 1303 (11th Cir. 2000).

Where Congress uses the same word or phrase in the same statute, Congress generally intends the word or phrase to mean the same thing each time it uses it. *Commissioner v. Keystone Consolidated Industries Inc.,* 508 U.S. 152, 159 (1993); *Sale v. Haitian Centers Council,* 509 U.S. 155, 203 n.12 (1993); *Moosa v. INS,* 171 F.3d 994, 1007 (5th Cir. 1999). *But see Atlantic Cleaners & Dyers, Inc. v. U.S.*, 286 U.S. 427,

433 (1932) ["Where the subject matter to which the words refer is not the same in the several places where they are used, or the conditions are different, or the scope of the legislative power exercised in one case is broader than that exercise in another, the meaning well may vary to meet the purposes of the law..."]; *U.S. v. Pornes-Garcia,* 171 F.3d 142, 147 (2d Cir. 1999) [definition of aggravated felony for sentencing guidelines and INA are different although the former relies on the latter].

When "one interpretation of a statute or regulation obviously could have been conveyed more clearly with different phrasing, the fact that the authors eschewed that phrasing suggests, *ceteris paribus*, that they in fact intended a different interpretation." *U.S. v. Ibarra-Galindo,* 206 F.3d 1337, 1339 (9th Cir. 2000), *cert. denied,* 121 S.Ct. 837 (2001) [Congress did not use the term "punishable as felonies under the Controlled Substances Act" but instead "felony punishable under the Controlled Substances Act" thereby rejecting the first interpretation].

C. *Deportation Statutes*—Deportation statutes must be narrowly construed in favor of aliens. *Leocal v. Ashcroft,* 543 U.S. 1, 125 S.Ct. 377, 384 n.8 (2004) [applied the rule of lenity as an alternative basis in its interpretation of why negligent acts would not constitute a crime of violence and therefore not an aggravated felony under 18 U.S.C. §16]; *INS v. St. Cyr,* 121 S.Ct. 2271, 2290 (2001) [recognizing the rule of lenity and "the longstanding principle of construing any lingering ambiguities in deportation statutes in favor of the alien"]; *Fong Haw Tan v. Phelan*, 333 U.S. 6 (1948) [matters of doubt should be resolved in favor of the alien in deportation proceedings]; *INS v. Cardoza-Fonseca*, 480 U.S. 421, 449 (1987); *INS v. Errico*, 385 U.S. 214, 225 (1966) [applying rule to provisions relating to relief]; *Rosenberg v. Fleuti*, 374 U.S. 449, 459 (1963); *Bonetti v. Rogers*, 356 U.S. 691, 699 (1958); *Barber v. Gonzalez*, 347 U.S. 637, 642–43 (1954); *Martinez v. Mukasey,* 519 F.3d 532, 542-45 (5th Cir. 2008) [under the first prong of *Chevron* and under longstanding principles construing statutes in favor of persons facing removal, the court concluded that the term "admitted" as used in INA §212(h) does not bar LPRs who were convicted of aggravated felonies from obtaining relief if they obtained LPR status through adjustment because they were not "admitted"]; *Lin v. Gonzales,* 473 F.3d 979 (9th Cir. 2007) [resolving ambiguities in favor of the respondent because it is a "well-established canon that ambiguities in deportation statutes should be construed in favor of the alien," the court read the regulation prohibiting motions to reopen for persons who are deported as not including persons who return illegally after a final order]; *Esponda v. U.S. Att'y Gen.,* 453 F.3d 1319, 1322 (11th Cir. 2006) [the "longstanding principle" that deportation laws should be construed in favor of the alien barred summary dismissal of BIA appeal for failure to file a brief where another regulation provided that notice of appeal might be sufficient]; *Azarte v. Ashcroft,* 394 F.3d 1278, 1289 (9th Cir. 2005) [finding *Matter of Shaar* no longer good law for post-IIRIRA cases and reasoning that the motion to reopen statute and the VD statute must be read to toll the VD period while the motion to reopen is pending because *inter alia* deportation statutes should be construed in favor of the alien]; *Hernandez v. Ashcroft,* 345 F.3d 824, 840 (9th Cir. 2003) [in context of interpreting VAWA, the court stated "the general rule of construction that when the legislature enacts an ameliorative rule designed to forestall harsh results, the rule will be interpreted and applied in an ameliorative fashion...This is particularly so in the immigration context where doubts are to be resolved in favor of the alien"]; *Francis v. Reno,* 269 F.3d 162, 170–71 (3d Cir. 2001) [applying rule of lenity to narrow interpretation of aggravated felony]; *Lennon v. INS*, 527 F.2d 187, 193 (2d Cir. 1975); *Pottinger v. Reno,* 51 F.Supp.2d 349, 363 (E.D.N.Y. 1999) *aff'd* 242 F.3d 367 (2d Cir. 2000) [applying rule of lenity in conjunction with *Landgraf* analysis]; *Homayun v. Cravener,* 39 F.Supp.2d 837, 850 (S.D. Tex. 1999); *Matter of Tiwari*, 19 I&N Dec. 875 (BIA 1989); *Matter of Hou*, 20 I&N Dec. 513, 520 (BIA 1992); *Matter of Chartier*, 16 I&N Dec. 284, 287 (BIA 1977); *Matter of G*, 9 I&N Dec. 159, 164 (AG 1961). Similarly, where the immigration statutes are ameliorative doubts should be resolved in favor of aliens. *U.S. v. Sanchez-Guzman*, 744 F.Supp. 997, 1002 (E.D. Wash. 1990). The courts have also repeatedly recognized the complexity of immigration laws as having an effect on persons in INS proceedings. *Montilla v. INS*, 926 F.2d 162 (2d Cir. 1991); *Castro-O'Ryan v. INS*, 847 F.2d 1307, 1312 (9th Cir. 1987); *Doug Sik Kwon v. INS*, 646 F.2d 909, 919 (5th Cir. 1981); *Lok v. INS*, 548 F.2d 37, 38 (2d Cir. 1977). But the Rule of Lenity does not apply where the language of the statute is plain. *Puello v. USCIS* 511 F.3d 324, 334 (2d Cir. 2007) [in defining conviction, the plain language of the statute requires that a judgment be entered and therefore Rule of Lenity was inapplicable]; *Ruiz-Almanzar v. Ridge,* 485 F.3d 193, 198–99 (2d Cir. 2007) [Rule of Lenity cannot be applied whenever there is an ambiguity in a statute or *Chevron* deference would be meaningless; it is only applied when other cannons of statutory construction are not capable of resolving the statute's meaning and the BIA has not offered a reasonable interpretation]; *Spina v. DHS,* 470 F.3d 116, 129–30 (2d Cir. 2006) [where traditional rules of statutory construction permit the court to conclude that the statute is not ambiguous, the rule does not apply]. *See* "Rule of Lenity and Rule Granting Presumption to Alien" in Ch. 3, ¶ X.S.7.q(6) (p.378), *supra.*

D. ***Agency Deference***—*See in this chapter* ¶ V.F.6 (p.1181), *supra.*

E. ***Principles Concerning More than One Statute***—Where there is no clear intention otherwise, a specific statute will not be controlled or nullified by a general one, regardless of the priority of enactment. *Morton v. Mancari*, 417 U.S. 535, 550–51 (1974); *Ardestani v. DOJ*, 904 F.2d 1505, 1513 (11th Cir.), *aff'd on other grounds*, 112 S.Ct. 515 (1991). The latter statute will not be considered to repeal a former statute by implication unless they are irreconcilable, *Morton, supra*, and the latter act covered the whole subject of the earlier one and was clearly intended as a substitute, *Radzanower v. Touche Ross & Co.,* 426 U.S. 148, 154 (1976); *Lujan-Armendariz v. INS,* 222 F.3d 728, 743–46 (9th Cir. 2000) [finding First Offender Act is not repealed directly or by implication by new definition of conviction under IIRIRA] because repeal by implication is not favored. *Radzanower, supra; Matter of Q-T-M-T-*, 21 I&N Dec. 639, 647–48 (BIA 1996); *Matter of Grinberg*, 20 I&N Dec. 911 (BIA 1994). A later enacted statute may also nullifies an existing treaty if they are in conflict. *Breard v. Greene,* 523 U.S. 371, 376 (1998) ["We have held that an Act of Congress....is on a full parity with a treaty, and that when a statute which is subsequent in time is inconsistent with a treaty, the statute, to the extent of conflict, renders the treaty null."]. The principle applies equally to regulations. *Settenda v. Ashcroft,* 377 F.3d 89, 97–98 (1st Cir. 2004) [when there is a conflict between regulations regarding when a three member BIA panel must be invoked under streamlining, the more recent, specific enactment supersedes the older, more generous one]; *Flores-Chavez v. Ashcroft,* 362 F.3d 1150, 1158 (9th Cir. 2004) [specific regulation pertaining to custodial care and responsibility for minor, trumped more general notice regulation thereby requiring that notice of removal proceedings be provided to guardian of minor]. Also, where Congress deliberately selects language in the later act that differs from that used in earlier acts, it can indicate "that a change of law was intended." *Brewster v. Gage,* 280 U.S. 327, 337 (1930). However, even where statutes are in irreconcilable conflict, the rule that the later statute applies does not automatically "preclude consideration of … [t]he circumstances of the enactment of particular legislation," *Watt v. Alaska,* 451 U.S. 259, 266, 101 S.Ct. 1673 (1981) and the court can look to the legislative history, *Padilla-Caldera v. Gonzales,* 453 F.3d 1237, 1242 (10th Cir. 2006) [citing rule in *Watt* and looking at legislative history to resolve conflict between INA §245(i) permitting adjustment to a person who was EWI and INA §212(a)(9)(C)(i)(I) barring entry to person who was in U.S. illegally for one year in the aggregated and entered EWI], or the manner or interpretation of the statute in the context of the legislation. *Fernandez-Vargas v. Gonzales,* 126 S.Ct. 2422, 2429 (2006) [interpreting the removal of language from the former version of INA §241(a)(5) as affecting people who remained after the new law's effective date would be a "strange" result].

A specific statutory provision controls a more general one. *Dekoladenu v. Gonzales,* 459 F.3d 500, 505 (4th Cir. 2006) [a timely filed motion to reopen does not toll the VD period because the VD statute is more specific than the more general right to file a motion to reopen].

Rules governing redundancy. In *Spencer Enterprises, Inc. v. U.S.,* 345 F.3d 683, 690–91 (9th Cir. 2003), the court addressed the possibility that its narrow interpretation of the statute barring review of certain discretionary matters (INA §242(a)(2)(B)(ii)) would be redundant of the committed to agency discretion by law interpretation found in the APA. Rejecting the view that the interpretation would be redundant the Court wrote: "Although 'the rule against redundancy' is only 'one rule of construction among many,' and 'does not necessarily have the strength to turn a tide of good cause to come out the other way,' *Gutierrez v. Ada,* 528 U.S. 250, 258 (2000), it is nonetheless a 'cardinal rule of statutory interpretation that no provision should be construed to be entirely redundant,' *Kungys v. U.S.,* 485 U.S. 759, 778 (1988)."

F. ***Avoidance of Serious Constitutional Questions***—Statutes must be interpreted to avoid serious constitutional questions. *Zadvydas v. Davis,* 533 U.S. 678, 688–702 121 S.Ct. 2491, 2498–2505 (2001) [interpreting post–final order immigration detention statute to avoid unconstitutionality raised by possible indefinite detention]; *Clark v. Martinez,* 543 U.S. 371, 125 S.Ct. 716 (2005) [construing same statute as *Zadvydas* as applied to inadmissible persons]; *U.S. v. Witkovich*, 353 U.S. 194, 199 (1957). *Accord DeBartolo v. Florida Gulf Coast Bldg. & Constr. Trades Council*, 108 S.Ct. 1392, 1397 (1988); *NLRB v. Catholic Bishop of Chicago*, 440 U.S. 490, 500 (1979). Moreover, "[p]rior to reaching any constitutional questions, federal courts must consider nonconstitutional grounds for decision." *Jean v. Nelson,* 472 U.S. 846, 854 (1985) *quoting Gulf Oil Co. v. Bernard,* 452 U.S. 89, 99 (1981).

Accord Mobile v. Bolden, 446 U.S. 55, 60 (1980) and *Kolender v. Lawson,* 461 U.S. 352, 361 n.10 (1983) citing *Ashwander v. TVA,* 297 U.S. 288, 347 (1936) (Brandeis, J., concurring). Addressing statutory issues before reaching constitutional ones is a "fundamental rule of judicial restraint." *Three Affiliated Tribes of Berthold Reservation v. Wold Engineering,* 467 U.S. 138, 157–58 (1984).

G. ***Congressional Intent***—In determining congressional intent the "report of a conference committee is one of the more reliable forms of legislative history." *Cevilla v. Gonzales,* 446 F.3d 658, 661 (7th Cir. 2006). But in determining legislative history the Court does not rely on statements that were made by persons other than Members of Congress or were not included in official Senate and House Reports. *Kelly v. Robinson,* 479 U.S. 36, 51 n.13, 107 S.Ct. 353 (1986) ["[N]one of those statements was made by a Member of Congress, nor were they included in the official Senate and House Reports. We decline to accord any significance to these statements."]; *Circuit City Stores v. Adams,* 121 S.Ct. 1302, 1311 (2001) [citing quote from *Kelly*]. Moreover, the statements by members of Congress in a subsequent Congress as to the meaning of legislation that was adopted in the past is not helpful. *Pierce v. Underwood,* 108 S.Ct. 2541 (1988).

H. ***Avoidance of Violation of International Law***—Congressional legislation should be construed to avoid violating international law. *Weinberger v. Rossi,* 456 U.S. 25, 34 (1982) [citing *Murray v. The Schooner Charming Betsy,* 6 U.S. (2 Cranch) 64, 117–18 (1804)]; *Cabrera-Alvarez v. Gonzales,* 423 F.3d 1006, 1009–13 (9th Cir. 2005) [reading the cancellation statute as consistent with the UN Convention on the Rights of the Child even assuming the Convention has attained the status of customary international law]; *Cornejo-Barreto v. Seifert,* 218 F.3d 1004, 1014 (9th Cir. 2000) [interpreting U.S. obligations under the Convention Against Torture to be consistent with international obligations]; *Ma v. Reno,* 208 F.3d 815, 829–30 (9th Cir. 2000) [if 8 U.S.C. §1231(a)(6) is interpreted to permit indefinite detention post–removal order then it would violate international law against arbitrary and prolonged detention]; *Beharry v. Reno,* 183 F.Supp.2d 584 (E.D.N.Y. 2002), *rev'd on jurisdictional grounds,* 329 F.3d 51 (2d Cir. 2003) [reversed on jurisdictional grounds the grant of INA §212(h) relief to LPRs who committed crimes prior to AEDPA/IIRIRA but were convicted after passage of the acts because it violates the International Covenant on Civil and Political Rights and customary international law in that it results in separation from USC children]. *But see Padilla-Padilla v. Gonzales,* 463 F.3d 972, 979–80 (9th Cir. 2006) [the International Convention on Civil and Political Rights do not impose obligation on the U.S. that would be violated by the application of the 10 year and stop-time rules of cancellation]; *Oliva v. DOJ,* 433 F.3d 229 (2d Cir. 2005) [denied claim preventing the removal of the father of a USC child under Articles 3(1) and 7(1) of the United Nations Convention on the Rights of the Child because cancellation of removal as a specific statutory provision governing the criteria to remain in the U.S. trumps any claim based upon customary international law]; *Arellano-Garcia v. Gonzales,* 429 F.3d 1183, 1187–88 (8th Cir. 2005) [same in regard to preventing deportation due to harm to child]; *Guaylupo-Moya v. Gonzales,* 423 F.3d 121, 132–37 (2d Cir. 2005) [finding *Beharry's* international law analysis inappropriate because Congress clearly intended to bar LPRs with aggravated felonies from obtaining the benefit of INA §212(h) and *Beharry* relied on Congress' ambiguity]. At least one court has also determined that a guardian ad litem need not be appointed for a 15-year-old Nicaraguan boy in deportation proceedings. *Calero v. INS*, 957 F.2d 50 (2d Cir. 1992).

I. ***Foreign Convictions***—Foreign convictions may not be relevant in a statutory scheme unless Congress specifically legislates that they are included. In *Small v. U.S.,* 125 S.Ct. 1752 (2005), the Supreme Court held that the language "convicted in any court" as an element of a felon-in-possession-of-a-firearm did not include a foreign conviction because Congress generally legislates with domestic concerns in mind and because foreign convictions differ from domestic convictions in important ways. However, the Court did mention that in certain circumstances such as immigration or terrorism "one could argue that foreign convictions would seem especially relevant." 125 S.Ct. at ____.

J. ***Retroactive Application***

1. Analytic Framework—In the absence of clear congressional intent favoring the retroactive application of a statute and where such application would offend elementary principles of fairness, courts should not apply statutes retroactively. *Landgraf v. USI Film Products*, 511 U.S. 244, 265, 114 S.Ct. 1483, 1497 (1994) [the presumption against retroactivity has roots as far back as the English common law and is reflected in our Constitution]. The analytic framework for deciding retroactivity requires the court to first determine "whether Congress has expressly prescribed the

statute's proper reach" and if not, "the court must decide whether the new statute would have retroactive effect, *i.e.,* whether it would impair rights a party possessed when he acted, increase a party's liability for past conduct, or impose new duties with respect to transactions already completed." *Landgraf,* 114 S.Ct. at 1505. A statute is not given retroactive effect "unless such construction is required by explicit language or by necessary implication." *Fernandez-Vargas v. Gonzales,* 126 S.Ct. 2422, 2428(2006) [quoting *United States v. St. Louis, S.F. & T.R Co.,* 270 U.S. 1, 3 (1926). If Congress has expressly prescribed the statute's temporal scope then the intent of Congress controls. If it has not done so, then the court is required to determine the statute's retroactive effect. In determining the first prong of the *Landgraf* analysis as to the intent of Congress a court should employ the traditional rules of statutory construction. *Lindh v. Murphy*, 521 U.S. 320 (1997). This means that the court must first decide whether the language is clear on its face. *See e.g., Guaylupo-Moya v. Gonzales,* 423 F.3d 121, 128–32 (2d Cir. 2005) [under step one of the *Landgraf* analysis Congress clearly intended that IIRIRA §321(a) regarding the retroactive definition of aggravated felonies and IIRIRA §§348(a) & (b) regarding the elimination of §212(h) for aggravated felons apply retroactively]. If not, then the court must examine the text, structure and history of the legislation to determine Congress' intent. *See, e.g., Fernandez-Vargas v. Gonzales,* 1266 S.Ct. 2422, ___ (2006) [the better reading of INA §241(a)(5) is that Congress intended it to apply to persons who reentered the U.S. before the effective date of IIRIRA]; *Bejjani v. INS,* 271 F.3d 670, 676–87 (6th Cir. 2001) [finding Congress did not intend INA §241(a)(5) to apply retroactively]. If Congress' intent cannot be ascertained then the court must engage in the second prong of the analysis to determine whether applying the statute retroactively "would impair rights a party possessed when he acted, increase a party's liability for past conduct, or impose new duties with respect to transactions already completed." Under the *Landgraf* analysis: "When determining whether a new statute operates retroactively, it is not enough to attach a label (*e.g.,* 'procedural,' 'collateral') to the statute; we must ask whether the statute operates retroactively." *Martin v. Hadix,* 119 S.Ct. 1998, 2006 (1999). The *Landgraf* analysis has been used to deny retroactive effect to statutes that change a cause of action or eliminate a defense. *Hughes Aircraft Co. v. U.S. ex rel. Schumer*, 117 S.Ct. 1871 (1997). *See also e.g., Alvarez-Portillo v. Ashcroft*, 280 F.3d 858, 866–68 (8th Cir. 2002) [applying the Court's analysis in *Hughes Aircraft Co.* and determining that INS may not interpret INA §241(a)(5) to apply retroactively to bar relief].

Reliance May Not Be Element of Retroactivity. There is also a question as to whether a retroactive analysis under *Landgraf* and its progeny requires any form of reliance before a statute or regulation will be denied retroactive effect. *Compare Hernandez de Anderson v. Gonzales,* 497 F.3d 927, 937–44 (9th Cir. 2007) [in step-two of *Landgraf* the issue is whether reliance on the law at the time is objectively reasonable and not a matter of personal reliance by the individual]; *Atkinson v. Att'y Gen. of the U.S.,* 479 F.3d 222 (3d Cir. 2007) [a person convicted before AEDPA/IIRIRA did *not* have to demonstrate a *quid pro quo* to obtain §212(c) relief because personal reliance is not a factor; rather the issue is whether the enactment of a new law has created a new disability following *Landgraf, Hughes and Hadix. Distinguished Fernandez-Vargas*]; *Hem v. Maurer,* 458 F.3d 1185 (10th Cir. 2006) [rejected subjective/actual reliance in favor of objective reasonable reliance of prior law, where respondent went to trial and did not appeal his conviction]; *Dinnall v. Gonzales,* 421 F.3d 247 (3d Cir. 2005) [statute may not be retroactively applied to person who re-entered illegally before IIRIRA, married a USC and is eligible for VD even if he failed to show any previous personal reliance]; *Olatunji v. Ashcroft,* 387 F.3d 383, 388–96 (4th Cir. 2004) [finding that "reliance, in any form, is irrelevant to the retroactivity inquiry" and holding that IIRIRA's change in the *Fleuti* doctrine could not be retroactively applied to a person who pled guilty prior to its enactment] and *Ponnapula v. Ashcroft,* 373 F.3d 480, 489–93 (3d Cir. 2004) [criticizing other circuits for their incorrect analysis of the *Landgraf* line of cases in that they failed to emphasize the presumption against retroactivity and that there is no requirement of actual reliance on the facts but rather reasonable reliance by a category of persons] *with Rankine v. Reno,* 319 F.3d 93, 99 (2d Cir. 2003) [barred the use of INA §212(c) relief to person who pled guilty prior to IIRIRA because *St. Cyr* required reliance].

2. Regulations—"Under general rules of statutory construction, a substantive, noncurative, adverse change in administrative rules is not to be applied retroactively unless the language of both the administrative rule and the statute authorizing the rule requires such a result." *Uzuegbu v. Caplinger*, 745 F.Supp. 1200, 1215 (E.D. La. 1990). *See also Kankamalage v. INS,* 335 F.3d 858

(9th Cir. 2003) [although the regulation at 8 C.F.R. §208.13(c)(2) barring person who commit particularly serious crimes states that it applies to asylum applications filed before Apr. 1, 1997, the court, following *St. Cyr,* held it may not be applied retroactively to a person whose conviction arose before that date]; *Montgomery Ward v. FTC,* 691 F.2d 1322, 1333 (9th Cir. 1982). *But see Mejia v. Gonzales,* 499 F.3d 991, 995–99 (9th Cir. 2007) [court rejected challenge to the retroactive application of 8 C.F.R. §212.7(d) tightening restrictions by the AG on the use of a INA §212(h) waiver].

3. Denying Retroactive Application—*INS v. St. Cyr,* 121 S.Ct. 2271, 2287–93 (2001) [finding bar to discretionary relief under INA §212(c) may not be retroactively applied and quoting Scalia, J. in *Kaiser* and stating that "[This] presumption against retroactive legislation is deeply rooted in our jurisprudence, and embodies a legal doctrine centuries older than our Republic." at 2288]; *Chew Hoeng v. U.S.,* 112 U.S. 536 (1884); *American Trucking Assoc., Inc. v. Smith*, 110 S.Ct. 2323 (1990); *Kaiser Aluminum & Chemical Corp. v. Bonjorno*, 493 U.S. 974 (1990); *Bowen v. Georgetown Univ. Hosp.*, 488 U.S. 204 (1988); *Chevron Oil v. Huson*, 404 U.S. 97 (1971); *Greene v. U.S.*, 376 U.S. 149 (1964); *Camins v. Gonzales,* 500 F.3d 872, 880–85 (9th Cir. 2007) [abrogation of *Fleuti* doctrine by IIRIRA's passage of 101(a)(13)(C) cannot be applied retroactively to guilty plea prior to IIRIRA]; *Miguel-Miguel v. Gonzales,* 500 F.3d 941, 950–53 (9th Cir. 2007) [AG's regulatory presumption regarding particularly serious crimes announced in *Matter of Y-L-* may not be applied retroactively under *Montgomery Ward*]; *Hernandez de Anderson v. Gonzales,* 497 F.3d 927, 937–44 (9th Cir. 2007) [the BIA erred in impermissibly repealing suspension of deportation where person was convicted after trial and was placed in removal proceedings after seeking naturalization one year before the passage of IIRIRA that eliminated suspension]; *Valdez-Sanchez v. Gonzales,* 485 F.3d 1084 (10th Cir. 2007) [the Tenth Circuit addressed the issue left open in *Fernandez-Vargas* and found that where a person married and adjusted status to that of a conditional resident before IIRIRA, the application of INA §241(a)(5) to respondent was impermissibly retroactive.]; *Atkinson v. Att'y Gen. of the U.S.,* 479 F.3d 222 (3d Cir. 2007) [a person convicted before AEDPA/IIRIRA did *not* have to demonstrate a *quid pro quo* to obtain §212(c) relief because personal reliance is not a factor; rather the issue is whether the enactment of a new law has created a new disability following *Landgraf, Hughes and Hadix*]; *Sinotes-Cruz v. Gonzales,* 468 F.3d 1190, 1197–1203 (9th Cir. 2006) [the stop-time rule, regarding the commission of criminal offenses, can not be applied retroactively under the second step of *Landgraf* to bar LPR's cancellation of removal]; *Hem v. Maurer,* 458 F.3d 1185 (10th Cir. 2006) [rejected subjective/actual reliance in favor of objective reasonable reliance of prior law, where respondent went to trial and did not appeal his conviction]; *Lopez-Castellanos v. Gonzales,* 437 F.3d 848, 851–54 (9th Cir. 2006) [following *St. Cyr,* the elimination of suspension of deportation was not applied retroactively to bar person who pled guilty prior to IIRIRA to a crime that would now bar him from cancellation]; *Dinnall v. Gonzales,* 421 F.3d 247 (3d Cir. 2005) [INA §241(a)(5) may not be retroactively applied to person who re-entered illegally before IIRIRA and had reasonable expectation of being able to apply for VD before the change in law without showing any previous personal reliance]; *Faiz-Mohammad v. Ashcroft,* 395 F.3d 799, 809–10 (7th Cir. 2005) [reinstatement of removal provision under INA §241(a)(5) may not retroactively bar relief where person entered and applied for relief/AOS before Apr. 1, 1997]; *Olatunji v. Ashcroft,* 387 F.3d 383, 388–96 (4th Cir. 2004) [finding that "reliance, in any form, is irrelevant to the retroactivity inquiry" and holding that IIRIRA's change in the *Fleuti* doctrine could not be retroactively applied to a person who pled guilty prior to its enactment]; *Sarmiento Cisneros v. U.S. Att'y Gen.,* 381 F.3d 1277 (11th Cir. 2004) [finding that INA §241(a)(5) may not be retroactively applied to person who re-entered and applied for relief prior to the effective date of IIRIRA and relied on the fact that when statute is ambiguous it is construed to be "unambiguously prospective"]; *Ponnapula v. Ashcroft,* 373 F.3d 480, 489–93 (3d Cir. 2004) [may not apply elimination of discretionary relief under INA §212(c) retroactively to person who went to trial and was convicted of an aggravated felony prior to IIRIRA/AEDPA where he chose trial over plea because he believed he would still have relief available]; *Toia v. Fasano,* 334 F.3d 917 (9th Cir. 2003) [IMMACT90 §511 which was enacted on Nov. 29, 1990 barring INA §212(c) relief to persons who served a term of imprisonment of more than five years for an aggravated felony may not be applied retroactively under *St. Cyr* and if the conviction arose before Nov. 29, 1990 such person is eligible for §212(c) relief]; *Chang v. U.S.,* 327 F.3d 911, 924–30 (9th Cir. 2003) [following *Montgomery Ward & Co.,* 691 F.2d 1322 (9th Cir. 1982), the court determined that INS could not retroactively apply precedent decisions to

investors granted conditional residence when adjudicating the removal of the conditional residence in an I-829 petition]; *Bejjani v. INS,* 271 F.3d 670, 676–87 (6th Cir. 2001) [finding Congress did not intend INA §241(a)(5) to apply retroactively]; *Magana-Pizano v. INS,* 200 F.3d 603 (9th Cir. 1999) [post-*American-Arab*]; *Cox v. Schweiker*, 684 F.2d 310, 318–19 (5th Cir. 1982); *Pak v. Reno,* 196 F.3d 666, 674–76 (6th Cir. 1999) [post-*American-Arab*]; *Mayers v. Reno,* 175 F.3d 1289, 1301–04 (11th Cir. 1999); *Goncalves v. Reno,* 144 F.3d 110, 126–33 (1st Cir. 1998), *cert. denied,* 119 S.Ct. 1140 (1999); *De Cardenas v. Reno,* 278 F.Supp.2d 284 (D. Conn. 2003) [using *Landgraf* analysis the Court found that someone who pled guilty before IMMACT90 could not be barred from §212(c) relief due to 5-year bar under §511 of IMMACT90 and Court distinguished *Buitrago-Cuesta* and *Reid*]; *Matter of Gomez-Giraldo*, 20 I&N Dec. 957 (BIA 1995); *Yu v. Brown,* 92 F.Supp.2d 1236 (D.N.M. 2000) [amendments to juvenile special immigrants do not apply retroactively]; *Pottinger v. Reno,* 51 F.Supp.2d 349, 357–63 (E.D.N.Y. 1999) *aff'd* 242 F.3d 367 (2d Cir. 2000); *Ranglin v. Reno,* 27 F.Supp.2d 262 (D. Mass. 1998); *Mojica v. Reno*, 970 F.Supp. 130, 180 (E.D.N.Y. 1997); *Yesil v. Reno*, 958 F.Supp. 828, 836–40 (S.D.N.Y. 1997), *reconsideration denied* 973 F.Supp. 372 (S.D.N.Y. 1997); Sutherland, Statutory Construction §41.02-41.04 (4th Ed.).

4. Permitting Retroactivity—*Republic of Austria v. Altmann,* 544 U.S. 677, 124 S.Ct. 2240 (2004) [FSIA applied retroactively to prevent Austria to bar suit for complicity in expropriating property of Jewish citizens]; *James B. Beam Distilling Co. v. Georgia*, 501 U.S. 529 (1991); *Silva Rosa v. Gonzales,* 490 F.3d 403 (5th Cir. 2007) [INA §241(a)(5) was not impermissibly retroactive where person married LPR before IIRIRA and had approved I-130 before that date, but a visa number was not available and respondent did not file AOS until *after* IIRIRA's effective date]; *Saravia-Paguada v. Gonzales,* 488 F.3d 1122, 1129–35 (9th Cir. 2007) [followed *Armendariz-Montoya* and found that provision barring §212(c) relief to someone who was incarcerated for 5 years could be applied retroactively to a conviction prior to 1990 because the conviction was obtained after trial by jury and not through a plea]; *Heaven v. Gonzales,* 473 F.3d 167 (5th Cir. 2006) [retroactively applying stop-time rule to pre-IIRIRA convictions where proceeding was post-IIRIRA]; *Tablie v. Gonzales,* 471 F.3d 60 (2d Cir. 2006) [the stop-time rule, INA §240A(d)(1)(B), barring suspension for persons who commit crimes during the period of continuous residence applies retroactively]; *Maldonado-Galindo v. Gonzales,* 456 F.3d 1064 (9th Cir. 2006) [INA §240A(c)(6) was not impermissibly retroactive when it barred cancellation to person previously granted INA §212(c) relief];*Peralta v. Gonzales,* 441 F.3d 23, (1st Cir. 2006) [respondent ineligible for suspension because criminal stop-time provision applies retroactively, his conviction for marriage fraud was a CIMT committed during the necessary 10-year period, and his eligibility was therefore cut off]; *Alexandre v. U.S. Att'y Gen.,* 452 F.3d 1204, 1207 (11th Cir. 2006) [following 8 C.F.R. §§1003.44(a), 1212.3(f)(4)(ii), the court determined that a person was not eligible for INA §212(c) relief because of retroactivity concerns who was found guilty after trial in 1989 and who served 5 years before applying for relief in 1994]; *Hernandez v. Gonzales,* 437 F.3d 341, 346–53 (3d Cir. 2006) [found that the repeal of suspension of deportation under former INA §244 could be applied retroactively because petitioner had no reasonable expectation of applying for suspension immediately after he entered his guilty plea because the statute at former INA §244(a)(2) precluded him from making the requisite showing of 10 years' continuous physical presence and good moral character following a deportable act. *St.Cyr/Ponnapula* distinguished]; *U.S. v. Gonzalez,* 429 F.3d 1252 (9th Cir. 2005 [the bar to INA §212(h) relief under INA §238(b)(5), which barred all discretionary relief for a person subject to expedited removal who was a non-LPR aggravated felon, could be retroactively applied]; *Garcia-Ramirez v. Gonzales,* 423 F.3d 935, 938–47 (9th Cir. 2005) [the 90/180 day provision under INA §240A(d)(2) barring cancellation applies retroactively to person who departed for five months before enactment of statute; but majority questioned prior precedent]; *Guaylupo-Moya v. Gonzales,* 423 F.3d 121, 128–32 (2d Cir. 2005) [under step one of the *Landgraf* analysis Congress clearly intended that IIRIRA §321(a) regarding the retroactive definition of aggravated felonies and IIRIRA §§348(a) & (b) regarding the elimination of §212(h) for aggravated felons apply retroactively]; *Labojewski v. Gonzales,* 407 F.3d 814 (7th Cir. 2005) [reinstatement of removal is not impermissibly retroactive when applied to person who re-entered before IIRIRA but applied for AOS after]; *Lattab v. Ashcroft,* 384 F.3d 8 (1st Cir. 2004) [same]; *Karageorgious v. Ashcroft,* 374 F.3d 152, 155–56 (2d Cir. 2004) [followed *Jimenez-Angeles* and found that IIRIRA's bar to suspension is not impermissibly retroactive]; *Drax v. Reno,* 338 F.3d 98 108–10 (2d Cir. 2003) [Congress intended the amendments to the firearms statute under INTCA §203 that included "attempts" to ap-

ply retroactively]; *Khattak v. Ashcroft,* 332 F.3d 250 (4th Cir. 2003) [the use of a single member decision making process at the BIA is not an impermissible retroactive application of the law under *Landgraf* because it is a procedural change that does not alter legal standards]; *Jimenez-Angeles v. Ashcroft,* 291 F.3d 594, 600–02 (9th Cir. 2002) [there was no "settled expectation" in respondent giving up her living in an illegal status undetected by INS and her decision to surface to obtain a benefit did not trigger the impermissible retroactive application of the permanent rules under IIRIRA pursuant to *Landgraf* and *St. Cyr*]; *Wright v. Ouellette,* 171 F.3d 8 (1st Cir. 1999). [applied AEDPA §440(d) to bar motions to reopen for INA §212(c)]; *Turkhan v. Perryman,* 188 F.3d 814, 825–27 (7th Cir. 1999) [upholding retroactive application barring INA §212(c)]; *Hamama v. INS*, 78 F.3d 233 (6th Cir. 1996) [upholding retroactive application of deportation statute to prior gun charge]; *Berlanga v. Reno,* 56 F.Supp.2d 751, 767–68 (S.D. Tex. 1999) [dicta]; *U.S. v. Yacoubian*, 24 F.3d 1, 7–9 (9th Cir. 1994) [new deportation ground applied retroactively notwithstanding JRAD]; *De Osorio v. INS*, 10 F.3d 1034 (4th Cir. 1993) [definition of aggravated felony to applies to crimes before statute passed]; *Buitrago-Cuesta v. INS*, 7 F.3d 291 (2d Cir. 1993); *Molina v. INS*, 981 F.2d 14, 22–23 (1st Cir. 1992); *Matter of Yanez-Garcia,* 23 I&N Dec. 390, 401 & n.10 (BIA 2002) [relied on *NLRB v. Wayne Transport,* 776 F.2d 745 (7th Cir. 1985), reversed precedent, and adopted different definition for state conviction as aggravated felony].

5. Constitutional concerns—Applying a law retroactively such that it results in manifest injustice violates the Due Process Clause. *Jideonwo v. INS,* 224 F.3d 692 (7th Cir. 2000) [relying on *Bradley v. School Bd. of City of Richmond*, 416 U.S. 696 (1974) and finding that the retroactive application of AEDPA to bar INA §212(c) where plea relied on belief that relief was still available]. *See also U.S. v. Ubaldo-Figueroa,* 364 F.3d 1042 (9th Cir. 2004) [retroactively applying the expanded definition of aggravated felony to encompass an attempted burglary conviction that arose prior to 1996 would plausibly violate due process (Pergerson, concurring opinion]; *Hamama v. INS*, 78 F.3d 233, 236 (6th Cir. 1996); *U.S. v. Yacoubian*, 24 F.3d 1 (9th Cir. 1994); *Maria v. McElroy,* 68 F.Supp.2d 206, 222 (E.D.N.Y. 1999). *But see Pedroza-Padilla v. Gonzales,* 486 F.3d 1362, 1364 (9th Cir. 2007) [application of stop-time rule to application for suspension on the facts of the case did not have an unconstitutional retroactive effect]; *Sena v. Gonzales,* 428 F.3d 50, 51–53 (1st Cir. 2005) [retroactive application of alien smuggling provisions under §101(a)(43)(N) has a rational basis and does not violated due process]; *Salazar-Regino v. Gonzales,* 415 F.3d 436, 448–51 (5th Cir. 2005) [the retroactive application of BIA (*Roldan*) and judicial opinions (*Hernandez-Avalos*) to persons who pled guilty to possession charges before the opinions were issued and now find they are subject to removal for drugs and as aggravated felons does not offend due process]; *Lopez De Jesus v. INS,* 312 F.3d 155, 161–64 (5th Cir. 2002) [found retroactive application of IIRIRA §351 amendment limiting waiver for alien smuggling constitutional]. Changing the quantum of evidence necessary to prove a criminal violation is impermissible under the *ex post facto* clause. *Carmell v. Texas,* 120 S.Ct. 1620 (2000).

K. *Summary Judgment*—Criteria for summary judgment under Fed. R. Civ. P. 56 are discussed in *Lujan v. National Wildlife Federation,* 110 S.Ct. 3177 (1990); *Anderson v. Liberty Lobby, Inc.*, 477 U.S. 242 (1986); and *Celotex Corp. v. Catrett*, 477 U.S. 317 (1986). *See also Ruiz-Rivera v. Moyer*, 874 F.Supp. 870 (N.D. Ill. 1995); *Presbyterian Church (USA) v. U.S.*, 752 F.Supp. 1505, 1508–09 (D. Ariz. 1990). Before summary judgment may be entered the court must give notice and an opportunity to respond. *Baria v. Reno,* 94 F.3d 1335 (9th Cir. 1996) [summary judgment reversed where district court did not give petitioner 10 days notice required by Rule 56(c)]; *Balogun v. INS*, 9 F.3d 347, 351–52 (5th Cir. 1993) [reversed and remanded habeas denial where detainee not given notice of summary judgment]. Moreover, the party opposing summary judgment should be given an adequate opportunity to complete discovery prior to the court considering the motion. *Jones v. City of Columbus, GA*, 120 F.3d 248, 253 (11th Cir. 1997).

L. *Pleading to Avoid Motion to Dismiss under Rule 12(b)(6)*—The traditional standard of notice pleading to avoid dismissal under Fed. R. Civ. P. 12(b)(6) set forth in *Conley v. Gibson,* 355 U.S. 41, 45–46 (1957) has been modified by *Bell Atlantic Corp. v. Twombly,* __U.S.___, 127 S.Ct. 1955, 1974 (2007). Under the *Bell Atlantic* standard a 12(b)(6) motion will be granted if the party does not plead "enough facts to state a claim to relief that is plausible on its face" and Fed. R. Civ. P. 8(a)(2) "still requires a 'showing' rather than a blanket assertion, of entitlement to relief." 127 S.Ct. at 1965 n.3. In effect, the Court abrogated the old standard under *Conley v. Gibson* requiring that a motion to dismiss may not be granted unless there is "no set of facts" that would allow a cause of action and they have replaced it with one that requires a pleading to be "plausible on its face" or be subject to dismissal. 127 S.Ct. at 1968, 1974.

M. *Sovereign Immunity*—Waivers of sovereign immunity are to be strictly construed in favor of the U.S. *Library of Congress v. Shaw*, 478 U.S. 310 (1986). However, once a waiver is found the court should not "assume the authority to narrow the waiver that Congress intended." *U.S. v. Kubrick*, 444 U.S. 111, 118 (1979). Moreover, the waiver should be construed to follow congressional purpose. *Irwin v. U.S. Dep't of Veterans Affairs*, 111 S.Ct. 453, 457 (1990) [applied equitable tolling against government]; *Sullivan v. Hudson*, 490 U.S. 877, 109 S.Ct. 2248 (1989) [fees under EAJA available for administrative proceedings on remand as integral part of civil action].

N. *Void for Vagueness*—If a statute's provisions are not clearly defined, court must invalidate the provision. *Grayned v. City of Rockford*, 408 U.S. 104 (1972); *Jordan v. DeGeorge*, 341 U.S. 223, 231–32 (1951); *Massieu v. Reno*, 915 F.Supp. 681, 699–703 (D.N.J.) [former INA §241(a)(4)(C)(i) regarding Secy. of State's authority to determine person's presence contrary to foreign policy is void for vagueness] *rev'd on other grounds* 91 F.3d 416 (3d Cir. 1996) [district court lacked jurisdiction because petitioner failed to exhaust administrative remedies and seek review in court of appeals]; *Rafeedie v. INS*, 795 F.Supp. 13, 23 (D.D.C. 1992) [court struck down former INA §212(a)(27)(F)]. *But see Miguel-Miguel v. Gonzales,* 500 F.3d 941, 950 (9th Cir. 2007) [rejected void for vagueness challenge to AG's decision in *Matter of Y-L-*]; *Rojas-Garcia v. Ashcroft,* 339 F.3d 814, 822–24 (9th Cir. 2003) [rejecting void for vagueness challenge to "reason to believe" standard as applied to a person convicted of purchasing five kilograms of cocaine, but does not decide whether "reason to believe" standard may be void for vagueness as applied to a person who sold an ounce of marijuana to a roommate]; *Beslic v. INS,* 265 F.3d 568, 571 (7th Cir. 2001) [finding void for vagueness standard has no application in challenge to statutes regarding bar to admissibility as an export violator].

O. *Rulemaking vs. Adjudication*—In administrative law, parties often raise the claim that the agency must *announce* a new rule through rulemaking and not adjudication. *NLRB v. Bell Aerospace Co. Div. of Textron, Inc.*, 416 U.S. 267, 294 (1974); *But see Negrete-Rodriguez v. Mukasey,* 518 F.3d 497, 503 (7th Cir. 2008) [agency is not precluded from announcing new principles in an adjudicative proceeding]; *Miguel-Miguel v. Gonzales,* 500 F.3d 941, 950 (9th Cir. 2007) [AG's authority to announce a new rule in *Matter of Y-L-* through adjudication was permissible]; *Siu Ling Chen v. Gonzales,* 489 F.3d 861, 863 (7th Cir. 2007 [recognizing that the BIA's decision in *Matter of C-C-* is functionally equivalent to rulemaking]; *Yanez-Popp v. INS*, 998 F.2d 231 (4th Cir. 1993) [upheld *Ozkok* claiming that IJ or BIA could announce rule through adjudication without rulemaking].

XI. EFFECTIVE DATES

The effective date of the judicial review provisions under INA §242 and the repeal of former INA §106 are governed by IIRIRA §306(c). Section 306 provides that the effective date stated in IIRIRA §309 will apply except as to INA §242(g). The effective date under IIRIRA §309(a) is Apr. 1, 1997. However, if a person is in exclusion or deportation proceedings on Apr. 1, 1997 "the amendments made by [Title II] shall not apply and the proceedings (including judicial review thereof) shall continue to be conducted without regard to such amendments." IIRIRA §309(c)(1)(B). The Supreme Court determined that INA §242(g) does apply to pending deportation or exclusion cases. *Reno v. American-Arab Anti-Discrimination Committee,* 525 U.S. 471 (1999); *See also Auguste v. Reno,* 152 F.3d 1325 (11th Cir. 1998) *reh'g denied* 162 F.3d 1179 (11th Cir. 1998). If an evidentiary hearing has not begun before Apr. 1, 1997 the AG may elect to proceed under the new statutes (presumably including judicial review). The AG may also elect to terminate proceedings that are not completed and begin again. IIRIRA §§309(c)(2) & (3).

The statute (IIRIRA §309(c)(4)) also provides for transitional changes in judicial review where a final order of exclusion or deportation is entered more than 30 days after Sept. 30, 1996. Under these circumstances the following rules apply: (1) exclusion orders may only be reviewed by the circuit court of appeals; (2) a circuit court of appeals may not take additional evidence under 28 U.S.C. §2347(c); (3) the petition for judicial review in both exclusion and deportation must be filed within 30 days of the final administrative order; (4) the petition can only be filed in the circuit where the IJ proceedings was completed; (5) there is no appeal of any discretionary decision under INA §§212(c), 212(h), 212(i), 244, or 245; (6) no automatic stay of deportation while the case is pending in the circuit court of appeals; and (7) no appeal permitted in the case of someone who is inadmissible or deportable by reason of having committed a criminal offense covered in INA §212(a)(2) or sections pertaining to aggravated felons (§237(a)(2)(B)(iii)), drugs (§237(a)(2)(B)), firearms (§237(a)(2)(C)), miscellaneous crimes such as violating the Cuban embargo or the Selective Service laws (§237(a)(2)(D)) or any multiple criminal conviction under §237(a)(2)(A)(ii) for which both predicate offenses are, without regard to their date of commission, otherwise considered a crime of moral turpitude for which a sentence of one year or longer may be imposed under §237(a)(2)(A)(i).

As a result of an amendment to the statute on Oct. 11, 1996, PL 104-302, 110 Stat. 3656, making technical corrections to IIRIRA, INA §242(g) became immediately effective. INA §242(g) became effective on Apr. 1, 1997 and on that date applied "without limitation to claims arising from all past, pending, or future exclusion, deportation, or removal proceedings under such Act." IIRIRA §306(c)(1). *Reno v. American-Arab Anti-Discrimination Committee,* 119 S.Ct. 936 (1999).

It is important to note that if (former) INA §106 applies, it applies as amended by AEDPA, PL 104-132. INA §106(a)(10) as amended by AEDPA and then by IIRIRA §306(d), bars judicial review for persons in deportation who have committed any of the crimes mentioned above in the transition rule, except for INA §212(a)(2).

Further amendments to the judicial review of all exclusion, deportation and removal orders were made under §106(d) of the REAL ID Act of 2005, PL 109-13, 119 Stat. 231 (May 11, 2005). As of May 11, 2005 the former transition rules discussed above for appeals under former INA §106, 8 U.S.C. §1105a established under the Illegal Immigration Reform and Immigrant Responsibility Act (IIRIRA) §309(c)(4) have been eliminated. Section 242 of the INA now requires that all appeals go to the court of appeals and that procedures under INA §242 govern all cases.

CHAPTER 11
ACTIONS AGAINST GOVERNMENT OFFICIALS

CHAPTER 11
ACTIONS AGAINST GOVERNMENT OFFICIALS

I. CIVIL RIGHTS STATUTES

A. ***42 U.S.C. §1983***—Creates a private right of action against "persons" who, acting under color of state law, violate federal constitutional or statutory rights. Local governing bodies and local officials acting in their official capacities are "persons" for purposes of §1983. *Monell v. Dep't of Social Services*, 436 U.S. 658 (1978). While neither states nor state officials acting in their official capacities may be sued for damages for past acts under §1983, a state official may be sued for injunctive relief. *Will v. Michigan Dept. of State Police*, 491 U.S. 58 (1989). State officials may also be sued in their "individual capacity" for actions taken under color of state law. *Hafer v. Melo*, 502 U.S. 21 (1991). Section 1983 does not cover suits against U.S. territories. *Ngiraingas v. Sanchez*, 495 U.S. 182, 192 (1990) [territory of Guam is not a "person" under §1983]; *DeNieva v. Reyes*, 966 F.2d 480 (9th Cir. 1992) [Commonwealth of the Northern Mariana Islands is not a "person" under §1983]. Section 1983 protects the rights of U.S. citizens or "person[s] within the jurisdiction thereof," and therefore, covers constitutional violations against LPRs by local police. *Mena v. City of Simi Valley,* 332 F.3d 1255, 1264–66 (9th Cir. 2003). To seek redress under §1983, a plaintiff must assert the violation of a federal *right*, not merely a violation of federal law. *Blessing v. Freestone*, 520 U.S. 329 (1997). Section 1983 may extend to federal officials if "there is proof of a joint conspiracy with state officials." *Peck v. U.S.*, 470 F.Supp. 1003 (S.D.N.Y. 1979). May also extend to the enforcement of international treaty rights against state officials. *Jogi v. Voges*, 480 F.3d 822 (7th Cir. 2007) [allowing noncitizen convicted of aggravated battery and deported to bring §1983 claim for failure of state officials to notify him of the right to consular assistance under Article 36 ¶1(b) of the Vienna Convention]; *Standt v. City of New York,* 153 F.Supp.2d 417 (S.D.N.Y. 2001) [allowing §1983 claim against NY police for violation of the right to consular notification following arrest as provided by the Vienna Convention]. *But see Cornejo v. County of San Diego,* 504 F.3d 853 (9th Cir. 2007) [Article 36 does not create an independent enforceable right under §1983 for Mexican nationals who were not advised on their consular rights]; *Bieregu v. Ashcroft,* 259 F.Supp.2d 342, 352–54 (D.N.J. 2003) [no ATCA claim for violation of Article 36 because there is no tort]. To bring a §1983 lawsuit challenging conditions of confinement, the petitioner must show that each defendant was personally involved in subjecting him to the conditions and that there was deliberate indifference on the part of those responsible. *Despaigne v. Crolew,* 89 F.Supp.2d 582 (E.D. Pa. 2000) [summary judgment granted in favor of defendants in suit alleging failure to protect and denial of medical care brought by INS detainee in county prison on ground that petitioner failed to show deliberative indifference on part of prison officials]. *See also Jama v. U.S.*, 343 F.Supp.2d 338 (D.N.J. 2004) [permitting damages action by prisoners under the ATCA against Esmor, one of the companies running immigration detention centers]; *Edwards v. Johnson*, 209 F.3d 772, 776 (5th Cir. 2000) [alien detainees awaiting deportation failed to demonstrate that officials acted with deliberate indifference, where he was punished with administrative segregation].

B. ***42 U.S.C. §1981***—Prohibits discrimination in the enforcement and making of contracts. Protects individuals from "non-governmental discrimination" and impairment of rights "under color of State law." 42 U.S.C. §1981(c). Might be relied on by a USC denied employment by an employer seeking LC for an intending immigrant. *U.S. v. Richard Dattner Architects*, 972 F.Supp. 738, 747–48 (S.D.N.Y. 1997). An action under §1981 may also be brought by noncitizens alleging discrimination based on alienage. *Anderson v. Conboy,* 156 F.3d 167 (2d Cir. 1998); *Lozano v. City of Hazleton,* 496 F.Supp.2d 477, 546–48 (M.D. Pa. 2007) [illegal aliens are persons under §1981 and the city's ordinance prohibiting undocumented persons from entering into leases violates §1981]. *But see Bhandari v. First Bank of Commerce*, 829 F.2d 1343 (5th Cir. 1987) (en banc), *reinstated after remand*, 887 F.2d 609 (5th Cir. 1989) (en banc) [section 1981 does not extend to prohibit alienage discrimination by private persons]. The Supreme Court has found that §1981 protects identifiable classes of persons who are subjected to intentional discrimination based on their ancestry or ethnic characteristics. *St. Francis College v. Al-Khazraji*, 481 U.S. 604 (1987) [remanding suit by college professor of Arab ancestry denied tenure]. *See also Donaire v. NME Hospital, Inc.*, 27 F.3d 507 (11th Cir. 1994) [concluding that persons of Philippine ancestry are a protected class under §1981]. However, a foreign state may not sue in *parens patriae* under §1981, to protect its citizens or their American descendants against discrimination by a private employer. *Estados Unidos Mexicanos v. Decoster,* 59 F.Supp.2d 120 (D. Me. 1999) [dismissing Mexico's claims for lack of standing].

C. *42 U.S.C. §§ 1985 & 1986*—Section 1985 prohibits the conspiracy to interfere with civil rights. Applies to conspiracies under color of state law as well as private conspiracies. *Griffin v. Breckenridge*, 403 U.S. 88 (1971). Where a §1985 claim exists, a state official who is not part of the conspiracy may still be liable for refusing to stop harm under §1986. *Park v. City of Atlanta*, 120 F.3d 1157 (11th Cir. 1997). In the immigration context, "recent immigrants including undocumented persons" were found not to be a class protected by §1985. *Zavala v. Wal-Mart Stores, Inc.*, 393 F.Supp.2d 295 (D.N.J. 2005).

II. FEDERAL TORT CLAIMS ACT (FTCA)

A. *Generally*—Waives sovereign immunity against the U.S. for certain torts committed by federal employees. 28 U.S.C. §§2671–80. Holds U.S. liable for persons acting on its behalf to same extent as a private individual under like circumstances. 28 U.S.C. §2674; *Logue v. U.S.*, 412 U.S. 521, 526–27 (1973). In determining whether a private individual would be liable under like circumstances, courts must apply the law of the state where the act or omission occurred, including federal law. *Rhoden v. U.S.*, 55 F.3d 428, 430–31 (9th Cir. 1995) [reversing dismissal of FTCA claim where district court found state law did not cover federal agents]. Claimant must first file administrative claim within 2 years of the accrual of the action. 28 U.S.C. §2401(b); *Lacey v. U.S.,* 74 F.Supp.2d 13 (D.D.C. 1999) [administrative claim must contain both a description of the injury and the amount claimed]; *Mazur v. INS*, 957 F.Supp. 1041 (N.D. Ill. 1997) [dismissing suit for INS failure to timely process DV application because administrative claim not filed within 2 years]. Action must then be filed within 6 months of the administrative denial. 28 U.S.C. §2401(b); 28 C.F.R. §14.2; *Papa v. U.S.,* 281 F.3d 1004, 1011 (9th Cir. 2002) [finding FTCA claim filed by family of person killed in INS detention untimely and rejecting equitable tolling where plaintiffs could not obtain U.S. visas]. However, an administrative claim will be deemed denied if the agency does not issue its final disposition within 6 months, in which case a plaintiff may sue at any time after the six months have elapsed from the filing of the administrative claim, but not more than 6 years after the claim has accrued. 28 U.S.C. §2675(a); *Jama v. INS,* 22 F.Supp.2d 353, 366 (D.N.J. 1998). Notice to the agency is jurisdictional, *Alkatabi v. DOJ,* 777 F.Supp. 271 (S.D.N.Y. 1991), and a claimant must demand a sum certain on form SF-95. *Dalrymple v. U.S.,* 460 F.3d 1318, 1324–26 (11th Cir. 2006) [upholding dismissal for failure to list sum certain on claim form against INS during Elian Gonzales raid]. *But see Bernard v. Calejo,* 17 F.Supp.2d 1311, 1315–18 (S.D. Fla. 1998) [where plaintiff put government on notice of damages and suit, the "sum certain" requirement was liberally construed to allow plaintiff to proceed]. In 1988, Congress enacted the Federal Employees Liability Reform and Tort Compensation Act, PL 100-694, 102 Stat. 4563, which required that the U.S. be substituted as the defendant in any action brought against an individual federal employee if the AG certifies that the individual acted within the scope of his employment. 28 U.S.C. §§2679(b)(1), (d)(1). The act formalized the decision of the Supreme Court in *Westfall v. Erwin,* 484 U.S. 292 (1988) that found that a federal official was immune from state tort liability if the act was discretionary in nature and fell within the scope of official duties. The test is still applied to determine whether non–governmental employees enjoy immunity. *Murray v. Northrop Grumman Information Technology, Inc.* 444 F.3d 169 (2d Cir. 2006) [the program administrator (a private company Northrop) was absolutely immune from suit in conveying possible national security issues regarding the petitioners to DOS and DHS]. The action must therefore be brought against the U.S. and not the individual employee. *Chiang v. Skeirik,* 529 F.Supp.2d 166, 172 (D. Mass. 2007) [negligence claim against DHS and DOS employees for failure to properly process K-1 visa was dismissed because proper party was the U.S.]; *Ramirez v. U.S.*, 998 F.Supp. 425, 432–33 (D.N.J. 1998).

B. *Jurisdiction in the Immigration Context*—At least one court has rejected the argument that INA §242(g) bars federal courts from hearing FTCA claims. *Medina v. U.S.,* 92 F.Supp.2d 545 (E.D. Va. 2000) [INA §242(g) does not bar FTCA action over unlawful detention where removal proceedings were terminated].

C. *Exception: Intentional Torts*—28 U.S.C. §2680 sets forth 13 exceptions to U.S. liability under the FTCA, including assault and battery, false imprisonment and other intentional torts. For example, seizure of property by border patrol agents may be immune from suit under 28 U.S.C. §2680(c). *Ysasi v. Rivkind*, 856 F.2d 1520 (Fed. Cir. 1988). However, the intentional tort exception may be waived and an action can exist where the federal official is deemed a law enforcement officer. 28 U.S.C. §2680(h); *Arevalo v. Woods*, 811 F.2d 487 (9th Cir. 1987) [false imprisonment, battery]; *Caban v. INS*, 671 F.2d 1230 (2d Cir. 1982) [INS officers considered law enforcement officials and therefore liable for intentional torts]; *Ramirez v. U.S.*, 998 F.Supp. 425, 433 (D.N.J. 1998) [allowing a claim against INS agents for false imprisonment]; *Sanchez v. Rowe*, 651 F.Supp. 571 (N.D. Tex. 1986) [finding U.S. liable for actual damages resulting from assault and battery by INS agent]. *But see Irving v. U.S.,* 162 F.3d 154, 160 (1st Cir. 1998) (*en banc*)

D. *Exception: Discretionary Acts*—Under 28 U.S.C. §2680(a), the U.S. has no liability under the FTCA for "discretionary" acts. Moreover, where the tortious conduct involves a discretionary function, a plaintiff may not be permitted to maintain an FTCA claim, even if the conduct also constitutes an intentional tort by a law enforcement official under §2680(h). *Medina v. U.S.,* 259 F.3d 220 (4th Cir. 2001) [finding no claim for false arrest where INS agents brought a removal charge that was terminated because the actions were considered discretionary]; *Adras v. Nelson*, 917 F.2d 1552 (11th Cir. 1990) [incarceration of Haitian nationals seeking asylum is a discretionary function even where plaintiffs asserted race and national origin discrimination]. *But see Garcia v. U.S.*, 826 F.2d 806 (9th Cir. 1987) [border patrol officer's arrest and use of force not discretionary under FTCA]. *Penn v. U.S.*, 1987 WL 10833 (E.D.N.Y. 1987) [decision to turn alien over to airline custody not discretionary function. The discretionary function exception does not preclude liability for all acts arising out of an agency's regulatory programs, but insulates from liability only those governmental actions that involve an element of judgment or choice and that are based on public policy considerations. *Berkowitz v. U.S.*, 486 U.S. 531 (1988). *See also U.S. v. Varig Airlines*, 467 U.S. 797 (1984); *Dalehite v. U.S.*, 346 U.S. 15 (1953). The U.S. has been held liable for wrongful deportation where it failed to follow its own regulations and instructions. *Kim v. U.S.*, No. C90-1163 WD (W.D. Wash. 1993) [discretionary function exception rejected where persons eligible for legalization were wrongfully deported; court awarded $283,000 in damages], *reported in* 70 No. 22 *Interpreter Releases* 744 (June 7, 1993). *See also Adedeji v. U.S.*, 782 F.Supp. 688 (D. Mass. 1992) [awarding damages for past and future pain and suffering and psychiatric care arising from false imprisonment at airport]; *Rhoden v. U.S.*, 55 F.3d 428, 431–32 (9th Cir. 1995) [prolonged incarceration of returning LPR at airport].

E. *Actions Outside the U.S.*—FTCA does not apply to claims arising from actions outside the U.S. 28 U.S.C. §2680(k); *Sosa v. Alvarez-Machain,* 542 U.S. 692 (2004) [finding that the FTCA's foreign country exception "bars all claims based on any injury suffered in a foreign country, regardless of where the tortious act or omission occurred"]. *But see* 21 U.S.C. §904 making exception for DEA actions abroad.

F. *Privilege*—No FTCA liability if action is privileged under state law. *Caban v. INS*, 728 F.2d 68 (2d Cir. 1984) [where NY law permits reference to federal law in determining whether actions were privileged, detention of plaintiff at NY airport was privileged because INS agents acted in conformance with federal standards regarding applicants for admission]; *Gallegos v. Haggerty*, 689 F.Supp. 93 (N.D.N.Y. 1988) [no privilege under *Caban* where INS agents did not act in conformance with federal standards]; *Araujo v. U.S.*, 301 F.Supp.2d 1095, 1099 (N.D. Cal. 2004) [whether the INS lawfully deported plaintiff under reinstatement provision and whether agents acted with "lawful privilege" are the same question]. But the U.S. may not invoke state immunity rules in analyzing the scope of FTCA liability because to do so would conflict with Congress's "private person" liability under 28 U.S.C. §2674. *Crider v. U.S.*, 885 F.2d 294, 296–97 (5th Cir. 1989).

G. *Reasonableness*—No FTCA liability if DHS officers' actions in detaining LPR at the border were found to be reasonable. *Ramirez v. U.S.,* 81 F.Supp.2d 532 (D.N.J. 2000). INS use of tear gas, rather than pepper spray as required by their own internal policies was reasonable and did not create a cause of action because it was not independently tortious under applicable state law. *Dalrymple v. U.S.,* 460 F.3d 1318, 1326–28 (11th Cir. 2006).

H. *Damages*—Compensatory damages are available; punitive damages are not. FTCA does not permit jury trials. Liability of the U.S. or its agencies may be limited by the amount of loss stated in the administrative claim first presented to the agency. *Salcedo-Albanez v. U.S.,* 149 F.Supp.2d 1240 (S.D. Cal. 2001) [plaintiff limited to damages stated in original administrative claim even though injury became worse, because Plaintiff's worsening injury was reasonably foreseeable]. Attorney's fees are limited to 20% of the monetary award if the case is settled administratively, or 25% of the judgment or settlement after the case is filed in federal court. 28 U.S.C. §2678.

III. ACTIONS ARISING UNDER THE CONSTITUTION

A. *Bivens Claims Generally*—*Bivens* actions may be brought directly against a federal officer in his private capacity for the violation of an individual's constitutional rights. *Bivens v. Six Unknown Named Agents of the Federal Bureau of Narcotics*, 403 U.S. 388 (1971). *Bivens* involved a Fourth Amendment claim against federal agents for unlawful seizure. *Bivens* actions were expanded to protect Fifth Amendment due process and equal protection guarantees in *Davis v. Passman*, 442 U.S. 228 (1979); Eighth Amendment guarantees against cruel and unusual punishment in *Carlson v. Green*, 446 U.S. 14 (1980); First Amendment rights in *Garcia v. U.S.*, 666 F.2d 960 (5th Cir. 1982); Sixth Amendment rights in *Wounded Knee Legal Defense/Offense Comm. v. FBI*, 507 F.2d 1281 (8th Cir. 1974); and Fourth Amendment guarantees against malicious prosecution in *Uboh v. Reno,* 141 F.3d 1000 (11th Cir. 1998). To assert a *Bivens* action, a party must demonstrate

- the violation of a clearly established, constitutionally protected right;
- that plaintiff has no effective means other than the judiciary to enforce his or her right; and
- that there are no congressional directives that specifically deny recovery, nor any "special factors counseling hesitation" of a claim.

Davis, 442 U.S. at 242–48. In filing a *Bivens* action, plaintiff must meet all venue [28 U.S.C. §1391(b)], jurisdiction and service of process requirements. *Pollack v. Meese*, 737 F.Supp. 663 (D.D.C. 1990) [dismissing action brought in DC for matters arising in Missouri]. Although federal law determines when a *Bivens* claim accrues, the law of the forum state determines the statute of limitations for such action. *Papa v. U.S.,* 281 F.3d 1004, 1009 (9th Cir. 2002) [dismissing claims of adults as untimely under CA statute of limitations, but claims of minors found valid until adulthood]. A *Bivens* action may be brought only against individual officers, not the U.S. or its agencies. Supervisory officials are generally not liable for the unconstitutional acts of their subordinates under theories of respondeat superior or vicarious liability. *Gonzalez v. Reno,* 325 F.3d 1228, 1234–35 (11th Cir. 2003) [AG and high ranking DOJ officials not responsible for Fourth Amendment violations during raid without facts demonstrating personal participation or a causal connection between their actions and the violation]. A *Bivens* action may not be brought against private entities acting under color of federal law that engage in constitutional deprivations. *Correctional Services Corp. v. Malesko,* 534 U.S. 61 (2001). *See also Christopher v. Harbury,* 536 U.S. 403 (2002) [dismissing *Bivens* claim for denial of access to courts for failure to state a cause of action in case involving alleged government conspiracy in husband's death by Guatemalan military]; *Rasul v. Myers,* 512 F.3d 644 (D.C. Cir. 2008) [no *Bivens* action under the 5th and 8th amendment for people detained at Guantanamo because nonresident aliens outside the U.S. have no constitutional rights].

B. *Bivens Actions Against DHS*—*Bivens* actions have been successfully brought against DHS officials. *See Martinez-Aguero v. Gonzales,* 459 F.3d 618 (5th Cir. 2006) [noncitizen could prosecute *Bivens* claim against INS agent for false imprisonment and excessive force at port-of-entry]; *Kwai Fun Wong v. U.S.,* 373 F.3d 952, 968–75 (9th Cir. 2004) [finding *Bivens* claim for discrimination regarding the revocation of parole and rejection of AOS actionable]; *Papa v. U.S.,* 281 F.3d 1004, 1010–11 (9th Cir. 2002) [allowing constitutional claims by family of INS detainee regarding his death in detention]; *Castaneda v. U.S.,* __ F.Supp.2d __, 2008 WL 704073 (C.D. Cal. Mar. 11, 2008) [detainee could allege Eighth Amendment violation when PHS officials failed to provide basic medical treatment (penile biopsy) that resulted in castration and death from metastatic cancer and 42 U.S.C. §233(a) did not preclude a *Bivens* claim]; *Ramirez v. Webb*, 719 F.Supp. 610 (W.D. Mich. 1989) [improper detention and excessive force]; *Ysasi v. Rivkind*, 856 F.2d 1520 (Fed. Cir. 1988) [deprivation of property without due process when INS seized plaintiff's vehicle]; *Guerra v. Sutton*, 783 F.2d 1371 (9th Cir. 1986) [warrantless search of home and arrest of occupants]; *Sanchez v. Rowe*, 651 F.Supp. 571 (N.D. Tex. 1986) [arrest, detention and beating by border patrol]. *But see Sissoko v. Rocha,* 509 F.3d 947 (9th Cir. 2007

[*Bivens* claim under the Fourth Amendment for improper detention of temporary resident in summary removal is barred by INA §242(g) in the limited circumstance where the temporary resident could have challenged his detention in habeas under INA §242(e)(2)]; *Habeeb v. Castloo,* 434 F.Supp.2d 899 (D. Mont. 2006) [where refugee disembarked on train 50 miles from Canadian border it was not a Fourth Amendment violation to stop or arrest him at the train station (the arrest based upon his not carrying his original I-94 as required by 8 U.S.C. §1304(e) and his failure to comply with NSEERS) nor a Fifth Amendment violation because it did not violate his due process or equal protection rights]; *Arar v. Ashcroft,* 414 F.Supp.2d 250, 266–87 (E.D.N.Y. 2006) [dismissing *Bivens* claim for violation of Fifth Amendment due process rights where plaintiff was removed to Syria and subjected to torture, coercive interrogation and arbitrary and indefinite detention, citing foreign policy and national security concerns]; *Gonzalez v. Reno,* 325 F.3d 1228 (11th Cir. 2003) [finding no supervisory liability by AG and other officials for INS raid, despite conclusory allegations that they directed officers' Fourth Amendment violations]; *Dalrymple v. Reno,* 334 F.3d 991 (11th Cir. 2003) [same]; *Edwards v. Johnson,* 209 F.3d 772 (5th Cir. 2000) [finding no First Amendment violation where INS detainee was given 15-day disciplinary segregation for speaking with and handing a note to prison visitors about conditions at Oakdale]; *Chiang v. Skeirik,* 529 F.Supp.2d 166, 172–73 (D. Mass. 2007) [denied TRO and PI where petitioner argued that consular officials unconstitutionally seized K-1 beneficiaries documents]; *Fares v. INS,* 29 F.Supp.2d 259 (W.D.N.C. 1998) [finding *Bivens* claim unavailable where challenge is to: (1) action covered by Privacy Act; (2) tampering of adjustment application; or (3) *ex parte* and other irregularities in exclusion proceedings]; *Ramirez v. U.S.,* 998 F.Supp. 425 (D.N.J. 1998) [dismissing *Bivens* claims against Commissioner and DD for failure to train, and against INS as a federal agency]; *Marshall v. Reno*, 915 F.Supp. 426 (D.D.C. 1996) [no constitutional violation in refusing to transfer plaintiff to Canadian prison under treaty, nor in refusing to expeditiously deport or release him]. *Franco de Jerez v. Burgos*, 876 F.2d 1038 (1st Cir. 1989) [no *Bivens* action for alien's detention because excludable alien had no constitutional right].

C. *Jurisdiction over Bivens Claims in the Immigration Context*—*Bivens* actions have not been barred by immigration jurisdiction preclusion statutes such as INA §§242(a)(2)(A), 242(e)(3), 242(g). *Kwai Fun Wong v. U.S.,* 373 F.3d 952, 968–75 (9th Cir. 2004) [finding that a *Bivens* claim for discrimination regarding the revocation of parole and rejection of adjustment of status were actionable because the entry fiction applies to a narrow class of procedural rights and does not apply to all constitutional claims of nonadmitted persons, but granting qualified immunity]; *Arar v. Ashcroft,* 414 F.Supp.2d 250, 266–87 (E.D.N.Y. 2006) [*Bivens* action against DHS officials not barred by INA §§242(b)(9), 242(g), 242(a)(2)(B)(ii) or FARRA §2242(d)]; *Martinez-Aguero v. Gonzales,* 459 F.3d 618 (5th Cir. 2006 [entry fiction did not bar *Bivens* claim for false imprisonment and excessive force at port of entry]. *But see Sissoko v. Rocha,* 509 F.3d 947 (9th Cir. 2007) [*Bivens* claim under the Fourth Amendment for improper detention of temporary resident in summary removal is barred by INA §242(g) in the limited circumstance where the temporary resident could have challenged his detention in habeas under INA §242(e)(2)]; *Foster v. Townsley,* 243 F.3d 210 (5th Cir. 2001) [finding INA §242(g) bars *Bivens* action for wrongful deportation]; *Humphries v. Various Federal U.S. INS Employees,* 164 F.3d 936, 945 (5th Cir. 1999) [finding INA §242(g) bars *Bivens* claims concerning exclusion in retaliation for exercising First Amendment rights, but allowing claims for involuntary servitude and mistreatment while in detention].

D. *Damages Under Bivens*—Punitive damages are available in a *Bivens* action. *Carlson v. Green*, 446 U.S. at 21–22. Under 28 U.S.C. §2676, a judgment against the U.S. under the FTCA precludes a *Bivens* action against a federal employee where the conduct alleged under *Bivens* is the same conduct which resulted in the judgment against the U.S. *Arevalo v. Woods*, 811 F.2d 487 (9th Cir. 1987). *But see Hallock v. Bonner,* 281 F.Supp.2d 425 (N.D.N.Y. 2003) [dismissal of FTCA claim for lack of subject-matter jurisdiction does not bar *Bivens* claim].

E. *Actions Under Fifth Amendment Takings Clause*—*Russian Volunteer Fleet v. U.S.,* 282 U.S. 481 (1931) [permitting Russian company that was assignee of certain contracts for construction of vessels to challenge eminent domain action by U.S.]. At least one court has said, however, that a Fifth Amendment takings clause claim may not be asserted by a nonresident alien. *Hoffmann v. U.S.,* 53 F.Supp.2d 483, 490–91 (D.D.C. 1999) [dismissing Fifth Amendment claims by nonresident successors-in interest in their effort to recover photographic archive seized from Nazi Germany by U.S. Army due to lack of "substantial connections" to the U.S.].

IV. PRIVACY ACT —5 U.S.C. §552a(g)

An action may be brought against an agency for improper disclosure of information. *Quinn v. Stone,* 978 F.2d 126 (3d Cir. 1992); *Waters v. Thornburgh*, 888 F.2d 870 (D.C. Cir. 1989). The action must be brought within two years of the disclosure or if there was a misrepresentation, within two years of discovery of the misrepresentation. *Lacey v. U.S.*, 74 F.Supp.2d 13 (D.D.C. 1999). The elements of a Privacy Act claim are: (1) agency disclosure; (2) to an individual or another agency; (3) of a "record" contained "in a system of records;" (4) which is unauthorized by the individual; (5) is not within an exception; (6) has an adverse effect on the individual; and (7) that the agency action was intentional or willful. *Orekoya v. Mooney,* 330 F.3d 1, 5–6 (1st Cir. 2003). The unauthorized release of one agency's information by another agency to a third party is actionable. *Orekoya,* 330 F.3d at 5–7 [finding actionable the unauthorized release of INS information to an individual's employer by the Secret Service]. An aggrieved person is entitled to actual damages, statutory minimum damages of $1,000 and attorney's fees. *Id.* A Privacy Act action may be brought against the INS, FBI and other federal agencies to amend their records. 5 U.S.C. §552a(g)(2)(A); *Schaeuble v. Reno,* 87 F.Supp.2d 383 (D.N.J. 2000) [ordering FBI and INS to amend records to show that LPR's conviction had been vacated].

V. ALIEN TORT CLAIMS ACT (ATCA)

The Alien Tort Claims Act, 28 U.S.C. §1350, was enacted in 1789 and grants "original jurisdiction of any and all action by an alien for a tort only, committed in violation of the law of nations or a treaty of the U.S." Therefore, the ATCA allows foreign victims of serious violations of international human rights laws to sue the perpetrators in U.S. court. *See Filartiga v. Pena-Irala*, 630 F.2d 876, (2d Cir. 1980).

A. *Pre-Sosa ATCA Case Law*—Under *Filartiga*, the "law of nations" or customary international law "may be ascertained by consulting the works of jurists, writing professedly on public law; or by the general usage and practice of nations; or by judicial decisions recognizing and enforcing that law." *Filartiga,* 630 F.2d at 880. Any ATCA suit under *Filartiga* "must interpret international law…as it has evolved and exists among the nations of the world today." *Id.* at 881. Following *Filartiga*, courts found liability in a number of ATCA actions. *See Doe v. Saravia,* 348 F.Supp.2d 1112, 1144, 1153 (E.D.Cal. 2004) [finding liability for the extrajudicial killing of Archbishop Romero in El Salvador as a crime against humanity under the ATCA]; *Estate of Rodriquez v. Drummond Co. Inc.,* 256 F.Supp.2d 1250, 1262–64 (N.D. Ala. 2003) [right to associate and organize are norms of international law for purposes of an ATCA action]; *Iwanowa v. Ford Motor Co.,* 67 F.Supp.2d 424 (D.N.J. 1999) [finding that Ford subsidiary during Nazi regime was a *de facto* state actor involved in a joint venture that utilized slave labor, but dismissing case on other grounds]; *Jama v. INS,* 22 F.Supp.2d 353, 361–66 (D.N.J. 1998) [inhumane and degrading treatment of asylum seekers by INS and contract prison officials found to violate international human rights norms under the ATCA]; *Hilao v. Estate of Marcos*, 103 F.3d 767, 773–75 (9th Cir. 1997) [cause of action under ATCA not abated by death of Marcos]; *Abebe-Jira v. Negewo*, 72 F.3d 844 (11th Cir. 1996) [affirming district court judgment awarding damages to victims of torture by Ethiopian official and concluding that ATCA not only confers jurisdiction but also gives federal courts power to "fashion domestic common law remedies to give effect to violations of customary international law"]; *Kadic v. Karadzic*, 70 F.3d 232 (2d Cir. 1995) [conduct can violate law of nations whether undertaken by those acting under the auspices of a state or as private individuals.] *Forti v. Suarez-Mason*, 672 F.Supp. 1531 (N.D. Cal. 1987) [denying motion to dismiss and finding ATCA jurisdiction in suit against former Argentine general]. *But see Argentine Republic v. Amerada Hess Shipping Corp.* 488 U.S. 428 (1989) [Foreign Sovereign Immunities Act bars ATCA suit against a foreign state]; *Flores v. Southern Peru Copper Corp.*, 414 F.3d 233 (2d Cir. 2003) [ATCA claims do not extend to international polluters because there is no rule of customary international law regarding international pollution]; *Aldana v. Fresh Del Monte Produce, Inc.* 305 F.Supp.2d 1285, 1296–99 (S.D.Fla. 2003) [right to associate and organize is not a universally recognized norm of international law]; *Doe v. Islamic Salvation Front,* 257 F.Supp.2d 115, 119–20 (D.D.C. 2003) [organizations do not have associational standing under ATCA where seeking money damages]; *Bao Ge v. Li Peng,* 201 F.Supp.2d 14, 22–23 (D.D.C. 2000) [finding no liability for Adidas under ATCA because "forced prison labor" is not a state practice proscribed by international law]. *Beanal v. Freeport-McMoran, Inc.*, 197 F.3d 161 (5th Cir. 1999) [ATCA does not encompass environmental torts or cultural genocide]; *Tel-Oren v. Libyan Arab Republic*, 726 F.2d 774 (D.D.C. 1984) [affirming dismissal of ATCA claim for lack of subject-matter jurisdiction].

B. *Post-Sosa ATCA Case Law*—In *Sosa v. Alvarez-Machain,* 542 U.S. 692 (2004), the Supreme Court substantially narrowed the scope of claims that may be brought under the ATCA for violation of the law of nations, holding that the ATCA confers jurisdiction, but does not create a cause of action, except in limited circumstances. The Court urged that "great caution" should be used when considering new causes of action under the ATCA and that "federal courts should not recognize private claims under federal common law for violations of any international law norm with less definite content and acceptance among civilized nations than the historical paradigms familiar when §1350 was enacted." The Court rejected the idea that sources of law such as the International Covenant on Civil and Political Rights created obligations in federal court and that unless it was a clear norm of international law, it may not be enforced. *See Vietnam Association for Victims of Agent Orange v. Dow Chemical Company,* 517 F.3d 104, 114–23 (2d Cir. 2008) [because Agent Orange was intended to be used as a defoliant and for destruction of crops only, its use did not violate international norms]; *Cisneros v. Aragon*, 485 F.3d 1226, 1228–31 (10th Cir. 2007) [statutory rape and sexual assault does not violate the law of nations simply because it is criminalized, even if criminalized by all civilized nations, like auto theft]; *Aldana v. Del Monte Fresh Produce, N.A., Inc.*, 416 F.3d 1242, 1246–50 (11th Cir. 2005) [post-*Sosa* finding that brief detention and kidnapping does not rise to a violation of the ATCA as cruel, inhuman and degrading treatment]; *Tachiona v. U.S.,* 386 F.3d 205 (2d Cir. 2004) [diplomatic immunity under Vienna Convention and UN Convention on Privileges and Immunities prevented service of process and judgment under ATCA against President Mugabe]; *Adamu v. Pfizer,* 399 F.Supp.2d 495 (S.D.N.Y. 2005) [improper drug testing on Nigerian children resulting in their death not actionable under ATCA because there was neither a treaty violation nor a clear violation of customary international law]; *Ibrahim v. Titan Corp.* 391 F.Supp.2d 10, 13–15 (D.D.C. 2005) [ATCA does not extend to purely private actors not acting under color of law in DC Cir.]; *But see Khulumani v. Barclay Nat. Bank Ltd.*, 504 F.3d 254 (2d Cir. 2007) [major U.S. and foreign corporations doing business in South Africa during apartheid may be liable under ATCA under an aiding and abetting theory]; *Arias v. Dyncorp,* 517 F.Supp.2d 221 (D.D.C. 2007) [upheld ATCA claim for aerial herbicide spraying that harmed humans and property in Ecuador in violation of international treaties, and neither national security claims, nor claim by private contractor that no state action existed were sufficient to defeat claim]; *John Roe I v. Bridgestone Corp.*, 492 F.Supp.2d 988, 1019–22 (S.D. Ind. 2007) [worst forms of child labor abuses of children 6, 7 and 10 year-olds does violate international norms]; *Almog v. Arab Bank, PLC,* 471 F.Supp.2d 257, 269–84 (E.D.N.Y. 2007) [bank's aiding and abetting terrorists through funding and providing bank accounts for terrorists]; *Sarei v. Rio Tinto, PLC,* 487 F.3d 1193 (9th Cir. 2007) [international mining company can be held vicariously liable for violations of *jus cogens* norms committed at its behest by the army of Papua New Guinea; rejecting the argument that the claims were nonjusticiable under the political question doctrine, the act of state doctrine, international comity, and exhaustion of domestic remedies].

C. *Torture Victims Protection Act*—In 1991, Congress passed the Torture Victims Protection Act, PL 102-256, 106 Stat. 73 (1991); 28 U.S.C. §1350 note §1(a) (TVPA), which added to the ATCA, the right to bring a claim for damages against persons who committed acts of torture.

1. *Generally*—Unlike the ATCA, which is limited to actions brought by aliens, the TVPA allows U.S. citizens to sue as well. *Chavez v. Carranza,* 413 F.Supp.2d 891, 899 (W.D. Tenn. 2005). It also allows a legal representative/claimant in a wrongful death action involving extrajudicial killing to bring an action. TVPA §2(a)(2). Under the doctrine of "command responsibility," the TVPA allows actions against commanders of persons who committed acts in violation of the statute. *Ford v. Garcia,* 289 F.3d 1283, 1286 (11th Cir. 2002) [for liability to attach, must prove that commander had effective control over his troops]. It also permits an action for conspiracy and accomplice liability. *Doe v. Saravia,* 348 F.Supp.2d 1112, 1145–51 (E.D.Cal. 2004) [allowing action for accomplice liability in extrajudicial killing of Archbishop Romero in El Salvador]; *Cabello Barrueto v. Fernandez Lario,* 205 F.Supp.2d 1325, 1331–33 (S.D. Fla. 2002). The 10-year statute of limitations for TVPA claims may be equitably tolled. *Jean v. Dorelien,* 431 F.3d 776 (11th Cir. 2005) [where torturer remained in power and did not come to the U.S., statute was tolled]; *Doe,*

348 F.Supp.2d at 1146–48 [TVPA statute tolled until filing of complaint because person could not receive justice in Salvadoran courts and reasonably feared retaliation if suit was brought]; *Cabello Barrueto*, 205 F.Supp.2d at 1330–31 [statute tolled where persecutor concealed victim's body and cause of death]. It may also be tolled where the foreign state was immune from suit. *Collett v. Socialist People's Libyan Arab Jamahiriya,* 362 F.Supp.2d 230, 242 (D.D.C. 2005); *Chavez v. Carranza*, 413 F.2d 891, 899 (W.D. Tenn. 2005).

2. *Relationship Between ATCA and TVPA*—The relationship between the ATCA and TVPA is not entirely clear. *See e.g., Enahoro v. Abubakar,* 408 F.3d 877, 886–93 (7th Cir. 2005) (Cudahy, J. dissenting) [discussing whether TVPA precludes or restricts action under ATCA]. *But see Aldana v. Del Monte Fresh Produce, N.A., Inc.*, 416 F.3d 1242, 1250–51 (11th Cir. 2005) [ATCA and TVPA provide for separate claims for torture as they define torture differently]. In determining the statute of limitations for ATCA cases, some courts have borrowed the 10-year statute of limitations from the TVPA rather than a shorter state statute. *Papa v. U.S.*, 281 F.3d 1004, 1012–13 (9th Cir. 2002).

D. ***Actual or Apparent Authority/Color of Law***—There must be a finding that the person acted under actual or apparent authority or color of law in committing or abetting the act. *Doe v. Saravia,* 348 F.Supp. 2d 1112, 1149–50 (E.D. Cal. 2004) [accomplice acting under apparent authority and color of law of Salvadoran government in extrajudicial killing of Archbishop Romero]; *Presbyterian Church of Sudan v. Talisman Energy, Inc.*, 374 F.Supp.2d 331, 337–38 (S.D.N.Y. 2005) [aiding and abetting liability exists and is not altered post-*Sosa*]. *But see Khulumani v. Barclay Nat. Bank Ltd.*, 504 F.3d 254 (2d Cir. 2007) [dismissed aiding and abetting claim where plaintiffs could not link corporations to state aid or the conduct of state officials during apartheid in South Africa].

E. ***Corporate Liability***—A corporation may be liable under the ATCA for violations of *jus cogens* norms, such as genocide, torture, slavery, crimes against humanity and extrajudicial killings. *Sarei v. Rio Tinto, PLC,* 487 F.3d 1193 (9th Cir. 2007) [international mining company liable for violations committed at its behest by Papua New Guinea army]; *Presbyterian Church of Sudan v. Talisman Energy, Inc.,* 244 F.Supp.2d 289, 319 (S.D.N.Y. 2003). However, selling products to a government does not make the seller a participant in that government's international law violations. *Corrie v. Caterpillar, Inc.*, 403 F.Supp.2d 1019, 1024–25 (W.D. Wash. 2005) [dismissing claim against company for selling tractors to Israel that killed a USC and Palestinians when a home was bulldozed]. *See also Khulumani v. Barclay Nat. Bank Ltd.*, 504 F.3d 254 (2d Cir. 2007) [dismissed aiding and abetting claim where plaintiffs could not link corporations to state aid or the conduct of state officials during apartheid in South Africa].

F. ***Extraordinary Rendition Claim***—The TVPA does not cover U.S. officials engaged in extraordinary rendition of persons to third countries to be tortured, because it applies only to persons acting under actual or apparent authority or color of law of "any foreign nation," and FARRA indicates that no private right of action was contemplated for individuals improperly sent to third countries practicing torture. *Arar v. Ashcroft,* 414 F.Supp.2d 250, 259–66 (E.D.N.Y. 2006) [Canadian/Syrian citizen could not bring TVPA claim against the U.S. when it conspired to send him to Syria to be tortured after he stopped in the U.S. while in transit from Switzerland to Canada].

G. ***Jurisdiction and Service of Process***—In ATCA cases, as in all federal cases, there must be service of process and personal jurisdiction. *Omni Capital Int'l Ltd. v. Rudolf Wolff & Co.,* 484 U.S. 97 (1987). *See also Sisso v. Islamic Republic of Iran,* 448 F.Supp.2d 76, 87–88 (D.D.C. 2006) [Hamas was subject to personal jurisdiction in the District of Columbia under Fed. R. Civ. P. 4(k)(2)]. Personal service may be obtained by publication and personal jurisdiction may be obtained where the defendants directed malignant actions felt in the U.S. and the defendants could reasonably expect to be "hailed into court." *Mwani v. Bin Laden,* 417 F.3d 1, 8–14 (D.C. Cir. 2005).

H. ***Exhaustion of Domestic Remedies under ATCA and TVPA***—Exhaustion is not required under the ATCA and is an affirmative defense that must be pleaded and proven under TVPA. *Jean v. Dorelien,* 431 F.3d 776, 781–83 (11th Cir. 2005); *Sarei v. Rio Tinto, PLC,* 487 F.3d 1193, 1213–23 (9th Cir. 2007); *Enahoro v. Abubakar,* 408 F.3d 877, 886 (7th Cir. 2005) [remanding case to district court to review exhaustion under TVPA]; *Abiola v. Abubakar,* 435 F.Supp.2d 830 (N.D. Ill. 2006) [exhaustion unnecessary under TVPA because Nigerian remedies would be futile].

I. ***Political Question Doctrine***—Suit for damages for torture and other human rights abuses under the ATCA and the TVPA against former Secretary of State and National Security Advisor for actions taken in support of Pinochet military junta was dismissed under political question doctrine. *Gonzalez-Vera v. Kissinger,* 449 F.3d 1260 (D.C. Cir. 2006) [following *Schneider v. Kissinger,* 412 F.3d 190 (D.C. Cir. 2005), court could not evaluate the legal validity of policy measures].

VI. INTERNATIONAL TERRORISM STATUTES—18 U.S.C. §2331 *et seq.*

Enacted as part of the 1991 Anti-Terrorism Act, 18 U.S.C. §2333(a) provides that, "[a]ny national of the United States, injured in his or her person, property, or business by reason of an act of international terrorism, or his or her estate, survivors, or heirs, may sue therefore in any appropriate district court of the United States and shall recover three-fold the damages he or she sustains and the cost of the suit, including attorney's fees." The statute does not permit a civil action against "a foreign state, an agency of a foreign state, or an officer or employee of a foreign state or an agency thereof acting within his or her official capacity or under color of legal authority." 18 U.S.C. §2337(2); *Ungar v. PLO*, 402 F.3d 274, 282–92 (1st Cir. 2005) [neither the Palestine Authority, nor the PLO are a foreign state for purposes of sovereign immunity that would prevent suit under the ATA]. The statute does not cover claims by corporations for property damage brought against a foreign state or persons in an official capacity. *Pugh v. Socialist People's Libyan Arab Jamahiriya*, 290 F.Supp.2d 54, 60–61 (D.D.C. 2003). However, it does cover claims *against* corporate defendants. *Almog v. Arab Bank, PLC,* 471 F.Supp.2d 257, 266–69 (E.D.N.Y. 2007) [bank's aiding and abetting terrorists through funding and providing bank accounts for terrorists]. It also covers claims against organizations that fund and support terrorism, but there must be an evidentiary showing that the conduct of the organization, by either direct or indirect support of the terrorist group/organization/individual was a casual link (at any stage) that brought about the specific terrorist attack that is the subject of the litigation. *Boim v. Holy Land Foundation for Relief and Development,* 511 F.3d 707 (7th Cir. 2007). The district courts have jurisdiction. 18 U.S.C. §2338. Personal jurisdiction exists if there are minimum contacts with the U.S., *Estates of Ungar v. The Palestinian Authority,* 153 F.Supp.2d 76, 86–95 (D.R.I. 2001), and service of process is "made in any district where the defendant resides, is found, or has an agent." 18 U.S.C. §2334(a).

VII. TUCKER ACT

The Tucker Act assigns to the court of federal claims, jurisdiction to render judgment upon any claim against the U.S. founded upon the Constitution, an act of Congress, executive regulation or upon an express or implied contract with the U.S. for liquidated or nonliquidated damages. 28 U.S.C. §1491(a)(1). *Aerolineas Argentinas v. U.S.*, 77 F.3d 1564 (Fed. Cir. 1996) [airlines entitled to recover money that INS required them to pay to detain TWOVs claiming asylum]. *But see Humphries v. Various Federal USINS Employees,* 164 F.3d 936, 941 (5th Cir. 1999) [upholding district court dismissal of $65,000 claim against INS and other federal employees for breach of contract because the Court of Claims has exclusive jurisdiction over Tucker Act claims in excess of $10,000]; *Roudnahal v. Ridge,* 310 F.Supp.2d 884, 894–96 (N.D. Ohio 2003) [no Tucker Act jurisdiction on implied contract theory or "unlawful taking" under the Fifth Amendment where INS accepted I-485 fee because sovereign immunity was not waived and "unlawful taking" has not been extended to government service fees].

VIII. FOREIGN SOVEREIGN IMMUNITIES ACT (FSIA)

A. ***Sole Basis for Jurisdiction***—The FSIA was enacted in 1976 and is the sole basis for jurisdiction in any action where a foreign state is a defendant in a lawsuit in U.S. district court. 28 U.S.C. §§1602–11. Generally, FSIA grants immunity to foreign sovereigns, ministries of foreign sovereigns, and officials acting on behalf of foreign sovereigns, unless there is an exception to the FSIA under section 1605 or the government has waived immunity. *Matar v. Dichter,* 500 F.Supp.2d 284 (S.D.N.Y. 2007) [former head of Israeli General Security Service had immunity under FSIA as a government official in putative class action brought on behalf of citizens injured or killed in Gaza because no exception to the FSIA applied]; *Doe I v. State of Israel,* 400 F.Supp.2d 86, 104–08 (D.D.C. 2005). Once a defendant has established that it qualifies as a foreign state under FSIA, it is presumed to be immune from suit and the burden shifts to the plaintiff to prove an exception. *See* 28 U.S.C. §1605. *Argentine Republic v. Ame-*

rada Hess Shipping Co., 488 U.S. 428, 109 S. Ct. 683, 690 (1989); *Dominican Energy Ltd., Inc. v. Dominican Rep*, 903 F.Supp. 1507 (M.D. Fla. 1995). The FSIA is inapplicable to individual defendants unless they were acting in their official capacity. *Enahoro v. Abubakar,* 408 F.3d 877, 880–83 (7th Cir. 2005) [FSIA does not give immunity to Gen. Abubakar in suit brought by relatives of persons who were tortured and killed while he was part of a committee governing Nigeria].

B. *Service of Process*—Service on a foreign state or its subdivision, agency or instrumentality is governed by 18 U.S.C. §1608. Service may be obtained in descending order: (1) by special arrangement between the plaintiff and the foreign state; (2) in accordance with applicable international conventions; (3) by requesting the clerk of the court to dispatch to the head of the ministry of foreign affairs of the foreign state, with translation, all documents by mail requiring a return receipt; or (4) by requesting the clerk of the court send two sets of the documents to the Secretary of State who then shall transmit one copy of the papers through diplomatic channels to the foreign state and provide a certified copy of the diplomatic note that indicated when the papers were transmitted. *O'Bryan v. Holy See,* 490 F.Supp. 2d 826 (W.D. Ky. 2005) [service of process must be strictly adhered to and plaintiffs need to refile]; *Sisso v. Islamic Republic of Iran,* 448 F.Supp.2d 76, 83–86 (D.D.C. 2006) [service perfected on Iran by diplomatic means]. In *Nikbin v. Islamic Republic of Iran*, 471 F.Supp.2d 53, 63–67 (D.D.C. 2007), the court found that an officer of an entity that is considered a foreign state under the core-function test should be treated as a state for purposes of service of process].

C. *Suits Against State Sponsors of Terrorism*—In 1996, the FSIA was amended to allow U.S. victims of terrorism to file suit against foreign states that are designated state sponsors of terrorism (Cuba, Syria, Iran, Sudan, and North Korea) for acts of, or provision of material support for, torture, extrajudicial killing, aircraft sabotage, or hostage taking, which resulted in personal injury or death, if officials, agents or employees of the government engaged in such activities in the scope of their employment or agency. 28 U.S.C. §1605(a)(7). Applies only if the foreign state was a designated state sponsor of terrorism at the time of the act, or as a result of the act. 28 U.S.C. §1605(a)(7)(A); *Belhas v. Ya'alon,* 515 F.3d 1279 (D.C. Cir. 2008) [FSIA prevents suit against former general of Israeli Army Intelligence for bombing in Southern Lebanon as no exception applies]; *Kilburn v. The Republic of Iran*, 441 F.Supp.2d 74 (D.D.C. 2006) [where Libya was removed from list of states sponsoring terrorism, but was on list at the time of the events, the plain language of the statute provided for liability]. In addition, the claimant or victim must have been a "national" of the U.S. as defined by 28 U.S.C. §1605(a)(7)(B)(ii), at the time the act took place. *Oveissi v. Islamic Republic of Iran,* 498 F.supp.2d 268, 278–79 (D.D.C. 2007) [despite plaintiff-grandson's U.S. citizenship, court lacked jurisdiction to hear wrongful-death claim where decedent was neither a national or citizen of the U.S.]. The National Defense Authorization Act for Fiscal Year 2008, PL 110-181, Title X, Subtitle F §1083(c) (HR 4986), 122 Stat 3 (Jan. 28, 2008), has now added 28 U.S.C. §1605A(c), which allows employees and contractors, as well as U.S. citizens and nationals to bring suit. A third-party cause of action by a family member is allowed only if the victim is unable to bring suit on his or her own. *Reed v. Islamic Republic of Iran,* 439 F.Supp.2d 53, 62–63 (D.D.C. 2006) [dismissing cause of action by son on behalf of his father where father could and did bring his own action]. The foreign state must also have been given a reasonable opportunity to arbitrate the claim if the act occurred within its territory. 28 U.S.C. §1605(a)(7)(B)(i). Liability extends to vicarious acts. *Haim v. Islamic Republic of Iran,* 425 F.Supp.2d 56, 68–70 (D.D.C. 2006) [Iran held vicariously liable for conspiracy its intelligence service engaged in with Palestine Islamic Jihad that resulted in severe injury to plaintiff in bus bombing in Israel]. If the §1605(a)(7) exception does not apply (*e.g.*, the claimant is not a U.S. national), immunity will not be deemed implicitly waived under §1605(a)(1) by virtue of the commission of terrorist acts. *Abur v. Republic of Sudan,* 437 F.Supp.2d 166, 177–78 (D.D.C. 2006); *Prevatt v. Islamic Republic of Iran,* 421 F.Supp.2d 152, 159–60 (D.D.C. 2006). The 10-year statute of limitations may be equitably tolled. 28 U.S.C. §1605(f); *Vine v. Republic of Iraq,* 459 F.Supp.2d 10, 20–25 (D.D.C. 2006) [no equitable tolling where persons took no action for several years and did not diligently pursue claims]. A lawsuit under §1605(a)(7) is not barred by the Act of State Doctrine or as a "political question" beyond the court's competence. *Owens v. Republic of Sudan,* 374 F.Supp.2d 1, 26–28 (D.D.C. 2005).

1. *The Flatow Amendment*—Created a right of action against officials, employees, and agents of a foreign state while acting within the scope of their office, employment or agency. 28 U.S.C. §1605 note; Omnibus Consolidated Appropriations Act of 1997, PL 104-208, Div. A, tit. I, §101(c); 110 Stat. 3009-172. Allows for a wrongful death action where plaintiff demonstrates that

defendant caused a person's wrongful death. *Flatow v. Islamic Republic of Iran,* 999 F.Supp. 1, 27 (D.D.C. 1998).

2. *No Private Cause of Action*—The DC Circuit has held that neither 28 U.S.C. §1605(a)(7), nor the Flatow Amendment create a private right of action against a foreign state, but merely waive sovereign immunity and provide for jurisdiction in federal court. *Cicippio-Puleo v. Islamic Republic of Iran,* 353 F.3d 1024 (D.C. Cir. 2004). A cause of action, however, may arise out of another source of law such as state law under 28 U.S.C. §1606, *Estate of Bayani v. Islamic Republic of Iran,* 530 F.Supp.2d 40, 45–46 (D.D.C. 2007) [action recognized under California law for assault, battery, false imprisonment and intentional infliction of emotional distress]; *Levin v. Islamic Republic of Iran,* 529 F.Supp.2d 1, 16–19 (D.D.C. 2007) [claims of common law of D.C. for false imprisonment, battery, assault, intentional infliction of emotional distress, negligence and loss of consortium]; *Beaty v. Republic of Iraq*, 480 F.Supp.2d 80, 90–99 (D.D.C. 2007) [plaintiff may have a cause of action under FL or OK law for intentional infliction of emotional distress, even if she was not physically present at the time the hostage taking and possible torture took place]; *Bodoff v. Islamic Republic of Iran,* 424 F.Supp.2d 74, 84–85 (D.D.C. 2006) [DC law provides basis for wrongful death and intentional infliction of emotional distress]; *Salazar v. Islamic Republic of Iran,* 370 F.Supp.2d 105, 113–15 (D.D.C. 2005) [cause of action for wrongful death and intentional infliction of emotional distress under IL law] *or* federal law. *Rux v. Republic of Sudan,* 495 F.Supp.2d 541, 559–65 (E.D. Va. 2007) [certain family members of servicemen killed on the U.S.S. Cole could bring suit under the Death on the High Seas Act]. Generic common law torts do not provide a source of law sufficient for a cause of action. *Acree v. Republic of Iraq,* 370 F.3d 41, 58–60 (D.C. Cir. 2004) [reversing $959 million default judgment and dismissing a case where plaintiffs were unable to articulate a cause of action grounded in a concrete source of law].

   But the National Defense Authorization Act for Fiscal Year 2008, PL 110-181, tit. X, subtit. F §1083(c) (HR 4986), 122 Stat 3 (Jan. 28, 2008) has now established a private cause of action not only for traditional personal injury claims but also for reasonable foreseeable property lost and loss claims under life and property insurance policies.

3. *Scope of Conduct: Material Support*—The underlying purpose of §1605(a)(7) supports a generous and expansive reading of what constitutes material support or resources to terrorists. *Rux v. Republic of Sudan,* 461 F.3d 461, 465–71 (4th Cir. 2006) [broadly defining "safehouse" to include Sudan's grant of safe haven to Al-Qaeda]; *Kilburn v. Socialist People's Libyan Arab Jamahiriya,* 376 F.3d 1123, 1127–28 (D.C. Cir. 2004) [for purposes of defeating a motion to dismiss plaintiff need only show "proximate cause," and not that the support provided was used specifically to harm plaintiff].

4. *Torture or Hostage Taking*—To prevail on a claim of "torture" or "hostage taking" under the FSIA, the torture must be "severe" and the hostage taking must be in the form of a *quid pro quo*. *Price v. Socialist People's Libyan Arab Jamahiriya,* 294 F.3d 82, 91–95 (D.C. Cir. 2002) [no allegation that defendant's conduct "rose to such a level of depravity and caused them such intense pain and suffering" to constitute torture, nor was any *quid pro quo* alleged as a basis for the hostage taking claim]. Hostage taking has been broadly defined to include a government order denying U.S. citizens the right to leave the country, even if they were not physically detained by the regime. *Vine v. Republic of Iraq,* 459 F.Supp.2d 10, 16–19 (D.D.C. 2006) [Iraqi government order prohibiting USCs from leaving Iraq or Kuwait constitutes "hostage taking" whether they were detained or not]. *See also Simpson v. Socialist People's Libyan Arab Jamahiriya*, 470 F.3d 356 (D.C. Cir. 2006) [addressing criteria for hostage taking and rejecting the requirement that a plaintiff must demonstrate that the hostage taker communicated the purpose of the hostage taking to a third party].

5. *Damages*—For persons suffering personal injury, the statute permits recovery under traditional principles such as proof that the consequences of the damage are "reasonably certain" and proof of damages by "reasonable estimate." *Hill v. Republic of Iraq,* 328 F.3d 680 (D.C. Cir. 2003). The law also allows for "solatium" damages (*i.e.,* mental anguish for loss) by siblings and unmarried companions. *Eisenfeld v. Islamic Republic of Iran,* 172 F.Supp.2d 1, 10–11 (D.D.C. 2000); *Surette v. Islamic Republic of Iran,* 231 F.Supp.2d 260, 267, 269–73 (D.D.C. 2002). *See also Dammarell v. Islamic Republic of Iran,* 404 F.Supp.2d 261 (D.D.C. 2005) [extensive discussion of damages

arising from wrongful death claims including mental suffering, intentional infliction of emotional distress, and physical pain and suffering based upon causes of action under different state laws]. The statute permits punitive damages, but only against agencies or instrumentalities of a foreign state. 28 U.S.C. §1606. *See supra* National Defense Authorization Act regarding damages.

D. *Retroactive/Extraterritorial Application*—The FSIA applies retroactively. *Republic of Austria v. Altmann,* 541 U.S. 677 (2004) [allowing retroactive application of 28 U.S.C. §1605(a)(3), to allow suit against Austria for complicity in expropriating property of Jewish citizens]; *Jenco v. Islamic Republic of Iran,* 154 F.Supp.2d 27, 32–33 n.5 (D.D.C. 2001); *Flatow v. Islamic Republic of Iran,* 999 F.Supp. 1 (D.D.C. 1998) [allowing retroactive application of §1605(a)(7) and holding Iran liable for bombing by Islamic Jihad which occurred prior to 1996]. Some courts have also found that FSIA provisions apply extraterritorially and that they are not unconstitutional. *Rein v. Socialist People's Libyan Arab Jamahiriya,* 162 F.3d 748 (2d Cir. 1998) [rejecting ex post facto, bill of attainder and unconstitutional delegation arguments relating to §1605(a)(7) claim by survivors of persons killed on Pan Am flight 103]. *But see Moore v. United Kingdom*, 384 F.3d 1079 (9th Cir. 2004) [FSIA is limited by NATO-SOFA agreement and bars action against British servicemen for bar brawl in U.S.]; *Roeder v. Islamic Republic of Iran,* 333 F.3d 228 (D.C. Cir. 2003) [suits arising out of Iranian hostage taking barred by Algiers Accords that provides for extinguishment of claims and binding arbitration against Iran].

E. *Head of State Immunity Not Eliminated*—The FSIA does not apply to heads-of-state and decisions relating to head-of-state immunity are vested with the Executive Branch. Notwithstanding the TVPA and subsequent legislation, head-of-state immunity and the UN Convention on Privileges and Immunities still protect foreign heads-of-state from suit. *Ye v. Zemin,* 383 F.3d 620 (7th Cir. 2004) [rejecting plaintiff's argument that under customary international law, the executive branch cannot provide immunity to the President of PRC who was accused of violating *jus cogens* norms]; *Doe v. Roman Catholic Diocese of Galveston-Houston*, 408 F.Supp.2d 272 (S.D. Tex. 2005) [Pope entitled to head-of-state immunity for acts allegedly committed before he was Pope in suit for abuses by Catholic priest and alleged cover-up]; *Doe v. State of Israel,* 400 F.Supp.2d 86, 110–11 (D.D.C. 2005) [where Executive Branch recognizes that a head-of-state is entitled to immunity, that determination is conclusive on U.S. courts]; *Abiola v. Abubakar,* 267 F.Supp.2d 907 (N.D. Ill. 2003) [dismissing part of claim against Abubakar for time he was head-of-state]; *Tachiona v. Mugabe,* 169 F.Supp.2d 259 (S.D.N.Y. 2001) [dismissing action against Mugabe as head-of-state and country's foreign minister under UN Convention]; *Lafontant v. Aristide,* 844 F.Supp.128 (S.D.N.Y. 1994) [enactment of FSIA did not alter the role or binding effect of DOS's suggestions of immunity for foreign heads-of-state].

IX. INTER-AMERICAN COMMISSION ON HUMAN RIGHTS

The Charter of the Organization of American States authorized the creation of the Inter-American Commission on Human Rights, "whose principal function shall be to promote the observance and protection of human rights and to serve as a consultative organ of the Organization in these matters." OAS Charter, Article 112, 21 U.S.T. 607. The Commission hears cases of victims of alleged human rights violations. After reaching a decision, the Commission calls upon the offending state to take corrective action, but there is no mechanism for enforcing its decisions. In a case of first impression, the Seventh Circuit held that the decisions of the Commission are not binding on U.S. courts. *Garza v. Lappin,* 253 F.3d 918 (7th Cir. 2001) [Commission's decision that Petitioner's death sentence violated international human rights norms because the trial court admitted evidence of other murders for which he was never indicted or tried, could not be enforced in U.S. court].

X. TRAFFICKING VICTIMS CIVIL ACTION

Trafficking victims may bring a civil action against the perpetrator in U.S. district court for a violation of 18 U.S.C. §§1589–91 and may recover attorney's fees. 18 U.S.C. §1595.

XI. PRIVATE RIGHT OF ACTION UNDER INA/TREATIES

It has been found that the Vienna Convention on Consular Relations may confer a private right of action for civil damages and injunctive relief. *Jogi v. Voges,* 480 F.3d 822 (7th Cir. 2007) [allowed noncitizen convicted of aggravated battery and deported to bring civil rights claim under §1983 for failure of state officials to notify him of the right to consular assistance under Article 36 ¶1(b)]; *Standt v. City of New York,* 153 F.Supp.2d 417 (S.D.N.Y. 2001) [private right permissible]. *But see Cornejo v. County of San Diego,* 504 F.3d 853 (9th Cir. 2007) [Article 36 does not create an independent enforceable right under §1983 for Mexican nationals who were not advised on their consular rights]; *Bieregu v. Ashcroft,* 259 F.Supp.2d 342, 352–54 (D.N.J. 2003) [no ATCA claim for violation of Article 36 because there is no tort]. Courts have been less willing, however, to find a private right of action under the INA. *See Urbina-Mauricio v. INS*, 989 F.2d 1085, 1088 (9th Cir. 1993) [no private right of action for expedited deportation hearing]; *Prieto v. Gluch*, 913 F.2d 1159 (6th Cir. 1990) [same]; *Gonzalez v. INS*, 867 F.2d 1108 (8th Cir. 1989) [same]; *Chairez v. Van Buren,* 790 F.2d 544 (6th Cir. 1986) [no implied private right of action under INA §287(a) to allow persons deprived of procedural protections in the statute to sue INS for damages]; *Ortega v. Rowe*, 796 F.2d 765 (5th Cir. 1986) [no private right of action for detained aliens complaining of conditions under 18 U.S.C. §4002]; *Shah v. Wilco Systems, Inc.*, 126 F.Supp.2d 641, 646–48 (S.D.N.Y. 2000) [no private right of action to enforce LCA violations under INA §212(n) or unfair immigration employment practices under INA §274B]; *Alamprese v. MNSH, Inc.*, 9 OCAHO no. 1094 (2003) [no private right of action under INA §274A to enforce a claim against a company for hiring undocumented workers].

XII. DOCTRINE OF IMMUNITY

A. *Qualified Immunity*—Under civil rights statutes and *Bivens*, a government officer, sued in his individual capacity, is entitled to qualified immunity for actions taken in the course of duty unless his conduct violated a "clearly established statutory or constitutional right of which a reasonable person would have known." *Harlow v. Fitzgerald*, 457 U.S. 800, 818 (1982); *Anderson v. Creighton*, 483 U.S. 635 (1987). The Supreme Court in *Saucier v. Katz,* 533 U.S. 194 (2001) fashioned a two part test for qualified immunity. First, the court must determine whether the facts "taken in the light most favorable to the party asserting the injury...show the officer's conduct violated a constitutional right." If a constitutional right would have been violated under the plaintiff's version of the facts, the court must then determine "whether the right was clearly established." *Id.* Qualified immunity will not be granted in situations where "various courts have agreed that certain conduct is a constitutional violation under facts not distinguishable in a fair way from the facts presented in the case at hand." *Id.* at 202. However, courts cannot require that the party opposing immunity demonstrate that the facts in the case are "materially" or "fundamentally" similar to previous cases, because qualified immunity also depends on whether the law gave the officer fair warning of his unconstitutional conduct. *Hope v. Pelzer,* 536 U.S. 730 (2002) [reversing finding of qualified immunity because a reasonable officer would have known that tying an inmate to a hitching post who no longer posed an immediate threat was unlawful].

The court must look to the "objective reasonableness" of the officer's conduct. *Severino v. Negron*, 996 F.2d 1439 (2d Cir. 1993) [state correctional officers who revoked work release after INS filed detainer were entitled to qualified immunity because plaintiff's due process right not to be reincarcerated was not drawn with clarity]; *Adras v. Nelson*, 917 F.2d 1552 (11th Cir. 1990) [qualified immunity applies where excludable aliens, who are entitled to limited constitutional protections, claim ill treatment but not gross physical abuse or malicious infliction of cruel treatment]; *Presbyterian Church v. U.S.*, 870 F.2d 518 (9th Cir. 1989) [qualified immunity upheld in INS undercover investigation of sanctuary movement]; *Luna v. Ridge,* 436 F.Supp.2d 1163 (S.D. Cal. 2006) [no violation of Fourth Amendment where Border Patrol officer's gun accidentally discharged while arresting plaintiff]; *Tungwarara v. U.S.*, 400 F.Supp.2d 1213 (N.D. Cal. 2005) [qualified immunity granted to INS inspector because the right of nonadmitted person to be free from strip searches and discriminatory treatment were not clearly established Fourth and Fifth Amendment rights until the court's later decision in *Wong*]; *Ramirez v. U.S.,* 81 F.Supp.2d 532 (D.N.J. 2000) [detention and arrest of returning LPR was not unreasonable under Fourth Amendment]; *Lopez v. Aran*, 699 F.Supp. 365 (D.P.R. 1988) [claim for qualified immunity upheld where two INS officers detained USC]. *But see Martinez-Aguero v. Gonzales,* 459 F.3d 618, 622–25 (5th Cir. 2006) [Fourth Amendment right to be free from unlawful detention and excessive force at the border was clearly established under *Lynch*]; *Lynch v. Cannatella*, 810 F.2d 1363 (5th Cir. 1987) [officers who mistreated excludable detained aliens cannot assert entry fiction doctrine to claim the aliens had no constitutional rights]; *Guerra v. Sutton*, 783 F.2d 1371 (9th Cir. 1986) [INS officers not entitled to qualified immunity where they failed to inquire as to the nature and scope of a warrant allegedly issued by a state officer before a joint state-federal raid]; *Gallegos v. Haggerty*, 689 F.Supp. 93 (N.D.N.Y. 1988) [rejecting INS's claim for dismissal based on qualified immunity where plaintiffs' facts, if true, could result in finding that agents' actions were unreasonable]. Qualified immunity is applicable solely to individual officers, not governmental entities. Supervisors may be entitled to qualified immunity because *Bivens* does not permit liability based upon respondeat superior or vicarious liability. *Gonzalez v. Reno,* 325 F.3d 1228 (11th Cir. 2003) [qualified immunity granted to AG and other high-ranking DOJ officials for raid alleged to be in violation of Fourth Amendment due to excessive force, where there were only conclusory allegations that AG and others had a causal connection to the violations].

Qualified immunity should be resolved at the earliest possible stage of litigation. *Hunter v. Bryant,* 502 U.S. 224, 227 (1991); *Anderson v. Creighton,* 483 U.S. 635 n.5 (1987). Where immunity is never asserted, it is wrong to give summary judgment to defendant. *Franco de Jerez v. Burgos,* 876 F.2d 1038 (1st Cir. 1989). Moreover, in a motive-based case, plaintiff is not required to prove the officer acted with unconstitutional intent by "clear and convincing evidence." *Crawford-El v. Britton,* 523 U.S. 574 (1998) [in a case claiming retaliation by a government official, the plaintiff need not rebut qualified immunity or prove his case by "clear and convincing evidence"].

B. *Absolute Immunity*—The grant of absolute immunity to an official "is determined by the nature of the function performed, not the identity of the actor who performed it..." *Buckley v. Fitzsimmons,* 509 U.S. 259 (1993) [rejecting absolute immunity for prosecutor where acts were administrative, not prosecutorial]. There may be absolute immunity for IJs because they perform functions "closely associated with the judicial process." *Hernandez-Ortez v. Godinez,* 1988 WL 129997, Case No. 88-C-5925 (J. Kocoras) (N.D. Ill. Nov. 30, 1988) [relying on *Cleavinger v. Saxner,* 474 U.S. 193 (1985) and *Butz v. Economou,* 438 U.S. 478 (1978)]. One federal court has determined that INS trial attorneys have absolute immunity. *Fares v. INS,* 29 F.Supp.2d 259, 262–63 (W.D.N.C. 1998). *See also Murray v. Northrop Grumman Information Technology, Inc.* 444 F.3d 169 (2d Cir. 2006) [the program administrator of the Irish Peace Process Cultural and Training Program (a private company Northrop) was absolutely immune from suit in conveying possible national security issues regarding the program participants to DOS and DHS].

XIII. ATTORNEY'S FEES

A. *The Equal Access to Justice Act (EAJA)*

1. *Legislative History*—The EAJA was enacted in 1981 [PL 96-481; 94 Stat. 2321, 96th Cong. 2d Sess. (Oct. 21, 1980), H.R. Rep. No. 1418, 96 Cong., 2d Sess. (1980), *reported in* 1980 U.S.C.C.A.N. 4984 (1980); H.R. Rep. No. 96-1431, 1980 U.S.C.C.A.N. 5003, S. Rept. 253, 96 Cong., 1st Sess. (1979)], and was amended and made permanent in 1985 [PL 99-80; 99 Stat. 183 *reported in* 1985 U.S.C.C.A.N. 132 (1985)]. Its provisions are codified at 28 U.S.C. §2412(d); 5 U.S.C. §504 *et seq.* The legislative history plainly provides for a broad and liberal construction of the waiver of sovereign immunity to benefit persons litigating against the U.S. H. Rep. 120(I), 99th Cong., 1st Sess. 4-14 (1985); H.R. Supp. Rep No. 99-120(II) (1985); S. Rep. 98-586 (1984). The Act's clearly stated objective is to eliminate financial disincentives for those who would defend against unjustified governmental action, thereby deterring the unreasonable exercise of government authority. *Ardestani v. INS,* 502 U.S. 129 (1991); *Commissioner, INS v. Jean,* 496 U.S. 154, 163–64 (1990). EAJA's purpose is not only to "provide relief to victims of abusive governmental conduct," but also to "induce [government] administrators to behave more responsibly in the future" and "to foster greater precision, efficiency and fairness...in the formulation and enforcement of governmental regulations." *Spencer v. NLRB,* 712 F.2d 539, 550 (D.C. Cir. 1983). The legislative history also clearly provides that "at a minimum, the United States should be held to the same standards in litigating as private parties." H.R. Rep. No. 96-1418, at 9 (1980) *quoted in Scarborough v. Principi,* 541 U.S. 401 n.9 (2004).

2. *Common Law Bad Faith Exception* —Under EAJA, a party can recover against the U.S. to the same extent that a party would be liable under common law or under the terms of any statute which specifically provides for an award. 28 U.S.C. §2412(b). An exception to the common law "American Rule" that each party must pay its own attorney's fees, is the "bad faith" exception, which allows a party to recover fees if it is determined that the opposing party litigated in bad faith. *Alyeska Pipeline Service Co. v. Wilderness Society,* 421 U.S. 240, 258–59 (1975); *American Hospital v. Sullivan,* 938 F.2d 216, 220 (D.C. Cir. 1991); *Kreager v. Solomon & Flanagan P.A.,* 775 F.2d 1541 (11th Cir. 1985). According to the Fifth Circuit, the "bad faith" determination is made by examining the government's response to a substantive claim, not by examining the gov-

ernment's conduct underlying the basis for the claim itself. *Sanchez v. Rowe*, 870 F.2d 291 (5th Cir. 1989). Bad faith may arise where INS continues to disregard its own regulations over a year into litigation or where it agrees to change its policy, but takes no action. *Perales v. Casillas*, 950 F.2d 1066, 1072 (5th Cir. 1992). It may also arise during the course of the litigation where the agency fails to provide the entire administrative record. *Maritime Management, Inc. v. U.S.*, 242 F.3d 1326 (11th Cir. 2001). Awarding fees under the bad faith exception is punitive and should only arise in exceptional cases. *Espinoza-Gutierrez v. Smith*, 94 F.3d 1270, 1279 (9th Cir. 1996).

3. *Eligibility for Attorney's Fees Under EAJA* – 28 U.S.C. §2412(d)(1)(A)-(B)

The EAJA also provides for the award of attorney's fees in litigation against the U.S. when an eligible party is the "prevailing party" before an administrative agency or in federal court, unless the deciding body finds that the position of the U.S. was substantially justified or that special circumstances make an award unjust. 28 U.S.C. §2412(d)(1)(A).

3.a. *Jurisdiction*—The court must have jurisdiction over the underlying action before it can award fees. 28 U.S.C. §2412(d)(1)(A). *Zambrano v. INS,* 282 F.3d 1145 (9th Cir. 2002) *amended by* 302 F.3d 909 (9th Cir. 2002) [where district court dismissed underlying action for lack of jurisdiction, it also lacked jurisdiction under EAJA]; *Montes v. Thornburgh*, 919 F.2d 531 (9th Cir. 1990) [rejecting government claim that district court did not have jurisdiction on the merits and upholding award of fees].

3.b. *Eligible Parties*—To obtain attorney's fees, a petitioning party must establish that s/he is an eligible party under EAJA. "Eligibility" under the statute includes an individual whose net worth did not exceed $2,000,000 at the time the action was filed; or a corporation, association or partnership whose net worth did not exceed $7,000,000 (or a §501(c)(3) tax-exempt organization) with less than 500 employees. 28 U.S.C. §2412(d)(2)(B). *Unification Church v. INS*, 762 F.2d 1077, 1083–92 (D.C. Cir. 1985) [denying fees to a §501(c)(3) organization with the resources to meet the essential needs of thousands of employees]. Where a party's application fails to make a showing of eligibility, it may be dismissed with prejudice. *U.S. v. Hopkins Dodge Sales, Inc.*, 707 F.Supp. 1078 (D. Minn. 1989). In determining eligibility, the DC Circuit has looked to the real party in interest. *Unification Church*, 762 F.2d at 1082; *American Ass'n of Retired Persons v. EEOC*, 873 F.2d 402 (D.C. Cir. 1989). *But see Nail v. Martinez,* 391 F.3d 678 (5th Cir. 2004) [disagreeing with the DC Circuit's analysis and finding that the statutory language does not permit a real party in interest analysis]. However, the DC Circuit has declined to apply the real party in interest analysis to adopt a *per se* rule that an association suing on behalf of its members is only eligible for attorney's fees if both the association and its members are statutorily eligible. *National Ass'n of Mfrs. v. DOL,* 159 F.3d 597, 600–05 (D.C. Cir. 1998) [statute's plain language looks to net worth of association and not the aggregate wealth of its members to determine eligibility]. Pro se litigants, including attorneys, may not be eligible for fees under EAJA. *Kooritzky v. Herman,* 178 F.3d 1315 (D.C. Cir. 1999) [overruling *Jones v. Lujan*, 883 F.2d 1031 (D.C. Cir. 1989) in light of *Kay v. Ehrler*, 499 U.S. 432 (1991)]; *Krecioch v. U.S.,* 316 F.3d 684, 688 (7th Cir. 2003); *SEC v. Waterhouse,* 41 F.3d 805 (2d Cir. 1994); *Celeste v. Sullivan*, 988 F.2d 1069 (11th Cir. 1992) (and cases cited therein). However, pro bono counsel is not precluded from receiving fees. *American Ass'n of Retired Persons v. EEOC,* 873 F.2d 402, 406 (D.C. Cir. 1989).

3.c. *Prevailing Parties.*

(1) *Catalyst Theory*—EAJA's "prevailing party" language was originally construed broadly to include persons whose actions served as a "catalyst" to legal remedies without a court ordered judgment. *Bradley v. Heckler*, 785 F.2d 954 (11th Cir. 1986) [plaintiff was "prevailing party," where litigation resulted in termination of SS benefits, because plaintiff had requested an appealable decision from the Secy. of HHS]; *Martin v. Heckler*, 773 F.2d 1145 (11th Cir. 1985) (en banc) [plaintiff was prevailing party where action mooted by defendant's remedial action subsequent to suit]; *Kopunec v. Nelson*, 801 F.2d 1226 (10th Cir. 1986) [avoidance of deportation was a substantial victory].

(2) *Rejection of Catalyst Theory in Buckhannon*—In *Buckhannon Bd. and Care Home, Inc. v. W. Va. Dep't of Health & Human Res.*, 532 U.S. 598, 610 (2001), the Supreme Court

rejected the catalyst theory as a viable means of awarding attorney's fees under the Fair Housing Amendments Act and the Americans with Disabilities Act. A number of courts have since found that *Buckhannon* applies to EAJA cases, and have similarly rejected the catalyst theory. *See Morillo-Cedron v. District Director,* 452 F.3d 1254 (11th Cir. 2006); *Brickwood Contrs., Inc. v. U.S.*, 288 F.3d 1371 (Fed. Cir. 2002); *Perez-Arellano v. Smith,* 279 F.3d 791 (9th Cir. 2002); *Goldstein v. Moatz,* 445 F.3d 747, 752 (4th Cir. 2006); *Marshall v. Comm'r of Soc. Sec.*, 444 F.3d 837, 840 (6th Cir. 2006); *Thomas v. NSF,* 330 F.3d 486, 492 n.1 (D.C. Cir. 2003); *Babel v. DHS,* 321 F.Supp.2d 963, 966–67 (N.D. Ill. 2004). Under *Buckhannon,* prevailing party status is obtained whenever there is a "court ordered chang[e] [in] the legal relationship between [the plaintiff] and the defendant" or a "material alteration of the legal relationship of the parties." *Buckhannon*, 532 U.S. at 604. The Court held that "judgments on the merits" and "court-ordered consent decrees" materially alter the parties' legal relationship, thus permitting an award. *Id.* Some courts have found that these were simply examples, and have granted prevailing party status to plaintiffs whose cases were resolved by other means. *Li v. Keisler,* 505 F.3d 913, 917–18 (9th Cir. 2007) [order by a circuit mediator granting an unopposed motion to remand satisfies prevailing party standard under *Buckhannon*]; *Carbonell v. INS,* 429 F.3d 894 (9th Cir. 2005) [plaintiff is a prevailing party where court order incorporated a voluntary stipulation between parties that stayed plaintiff's removal until the BIA ruled on his motion to reconsider]; *Vacchio v. Ashcroft,* 404 F.3d 663, 672–74 (2d Cir. 2005) [finding petitioner to be the prevailing party because the court order releasing him from detention pending appeal was a sufficient change in the legal relationship, but denying EAJA fees on substantial justification grounds]; *Lord v. Chertoff,* 526 F.Supp.2d 435, 437–38 (S.D.N.Y. 2007) [consent agreement to approve naturalization petition and to swear person in within 30 days created prevailing party status]; *Ali v. Gonzales*, 486 F.Supp.2d 1197 (W.D. Wash. 2007) [petitioners granted injunctive relief under *Zadvydas* were prevailing parties even though relief is temporary and their situation may change in the future]; *Berishev v. Chertoff,* 486 F.Supp.2d 202, 204–06 (D. Mass. 2007) [petitioner is a prevailing party where the court entered a conciliatory order to remand a case for adjudication of naturalization application and where naturalization was promptly granted]; *Aboushaban v. Mueller*, 475 F.Supp.2d 943, 945–47 (N.D. Cal. 2007) [petitioner in mandamus action for adjustment of status was prevailing party where court granted summary judgment, ordered USCIS to adjudicate the application and retained jurisdiction]; *Kholyavskiy v. Schlecht,* 479 F.Supp.2d 897, 908–09 (E.D. Wis. 2007) [petitioner was prevailing party for EAJA purposes where court instructed respondent to make final decision regarding release and petitioner was then released]. A settlement where the court retains jurisdiction to enforce the agreement is considered the equivalent of a consent decree, thus permitting the plaintiff to be characterized as the prevailing party. *Smalbein v. City of Daytona Beach,* 353 F.3d 901 (11th Cir. 2003); *American Disability Ass'n Inc. v. Chmielarz,* 289 F.3d 1315, 1317 (11th Cir. 2002).

(3) *Remands*—In *Shalala v. Schaefer*, 509 U.S. 292, 300–02 (1993), the Supreme Court determined that a remand for further proceedings in the Social Security context constituted a final judgment because the remand terminated the litigation in favor of the claimant. The claimant, therefore, is the prevailing party for EAJA purposes. The Ninth Circuit later applied *Shalala* in the immigration context and found that a petition for review that is granted and remanded to the BIA is a final action conferring prevailing party status on the petitioner. *Rueda-Menicucci v. INS*, 132 F.3d 493 (9th Cir. 1997). *See also Li v. Keisler,* 505 F.3d 913, 917–18 (9th Cir. 2007) [order by a circuit mediator granting an unopposed motion to remand satisfies prevailing party standard under *Buckhannon*]; *Johnson v. Gonzales,* 416 F.3d 205, 208–10 (3d Cir. 2005); *Muhur v. Ashcroft,* 382 F.3d 653, 654–55 (7th Cir. 2004) [petitioner was a prevailing party where case was remanded for reconsideration of asylum]; *Salem v. INS,* 122 F.Supp.2d 980, 983–84 (C.D. Ill. 2000) [natz applicant was prevailing party where case remanded for further evidentiary consideration]; *Berishev v. Chertoff,* 486 F.Supp.2d 202, 204–06 (D. Mass. 2007) [petitioner is a prevailing party where the court entered a conciliatory order to remand a case for adjudication of naturalization and where naturalization was promptly granted]. *But see Bernal-Garcia v. INS*, 852 F.2d 144, 147 (5th Cir. 1988) [petitioner can not yet be con-

sidered prevailing party where case was remanded for consideration of additional evidence]; *Rico-Sorio v. INS*, 552 F.Supp. 965 (D. Or. 1982) [TRO to prevent deportation does not give alien prevailing party status when court refused to extend it]; *Maduka v. Meissner*, 114 F.3d 1240 (D.C. Cir. 1997) [plaintiff was not prevailing party where he could not show that the lawsuit induced INS to act favorably on his petition]. A plaintiff may not be a prevailing party when the case is remanded, but later affirmed. *Omni Packaging v. INS*, 940 F.Supp. 42, 45–46 (D.P.R. 1996). A party also does not prevail where it obtains a settlement requiring INS to obey the law, when there was no evidence that INS had violated it. *Cervantez v. Whitfield*, 776 F.2d 556 (5th Cir. 1985).

(4) *Party Need Not Obtain Relief on Every Claim to Prevail*—In the context of the civil rights attorney's fee statute, 42 U.S.C. §1988, the Supreme Court adopted a broad test for prevailing party status by finding that a party need prevail only on "any significant issue in litigation which achieve[d] some of the benefit the parties sought in bringing suit." *Texas State Teachers Ass'n v. Garland Independent School Dist.*, 489 U.S. 782 (1989). This test has been adopted in EAJA cases. *Sullivan v. Hudson*, 490 U.S. 877 (1989); *Achaval-Bianco v. Gustafson*, 736 F.Supp. 214 (C.D. Cal. 1989) [EAJA fees warranted in mandamus action resulting in adjudication of AOS applications]; *Dabone v. Thornburgh*, 734 F.Supp. 195, 197–98 (E.D. Pa. 1990); *Jean v. Nelson*, 863 F.2d 759, 766 (11th Cir. 1988).

(5) Where a party elects to take recovery under a statute that does not permit EAJA fees (FTCA), he cannot select a different remedy (*Bivens*) to collect the fees. *Sanchez v. Rowe*, 870 F.2d 291, 293 (5th Cir. 1989).

(6) Prevailing party language means that fees go to the client, not the attorney. *Panola Land Buying Ass'n v. Clark*, 844 F.2d 1506 (11th Cir. 1988) [attorney had no right to intervene to challenge settlement between former client and government where settlement did not include attorney's fees].

3.d. *Substantial Justification.*

(1) *Generally*—In order for fees to be awarded, the "position of the United States" must not have been "substantially justified." 28 U.S.C. §2412(d)(1)(B). The government must make a "strong showing" to demonstrate substantial justification. *S&H Riggers & Rectors, Inc. v. Occupational Safety and Health Review Commission*, 672 F.2d 426, 430 (5th Cir. 1982); *Vitale v. Secy. of HHS*, 673 F.Supp. 1171 (N.D.N.Y 1987). The government cannot rely solely on its legal position when there was underlying agency action that was unreasonable. *Commission, INS v. Jean*, 496 U.S. 154, 159 n.7, 110 S.Ct. 2316 (1990). Substantial justification is a threshold consideration and is not to be made again at successive stages of the litigation. *Commissioner, INS v. Jean*, 496 U.S. 154 (1990). The government bears the burden of establishing that its position was substantially justified in both law and fact. *Jean*, 496 U.S. at 158 n.6. The "position of the United States" includes both the government's legal position and "the action or failure to act by the agency upon which the civil action is based." 28 U.S.C. §2412(d)(2)(D); H.R. Rep. No. 120 (I) at 11, 99th Cong., 1st Sess. 11, *reprinted in* 1985 U.S.C.C.A.N. 132, 140. *Thangaraja v. Gonzales,* 428 F.3d 870, 873–74 (9th Cir. 2005) [the position of the U.S. includes both DHS's litigating position and the underlying decisions of the IJ or BIA]. Thus, only one threshold determination is to be made for the entire action, and the government cannot rely solely on its legal position where the underlying agency action was unreasonable. *Jean,* 496 U.S. at 159 n.7; *Thangaraja*, 428 F.3d at 875 n.2 [a subsequent litigating position cannot cure an underlying agency action that is not substantially justified]; *Bruland v. Howerton*, 742 F.Supp. 629, 634–35 (S.D. Fla. 1990). Even if the government was substantially justified in some aspects of the case, if the legal and factual issues are intertwined with those claims in which the government was not substantially justified, the prevailing party "should be fully compensated." *Haitian Refugee Center v. Meese*, 791 F.2d 1489, 1500 (11th Cir. 1986). Moreover, if the court of appeals denies fees for an appeal, a district court can still determine that the government's position at *trial* was not substantially justified. *U.S. v. Jones*, 125 F.3d 1418, 1426 (11th Cir. 1997). The court can

also separate defendants for purposes of determining substantial justification. *Montes v. Meese*, ___ F.Supp. ___ (C.D. Cal. 1987), *reported in* 65 No.1 *Interpreter Releases* (Jan. 4, 1988), *aff'd sub nom. Montes v. Thornburgh*, 919 F.2d 531 (9th Cir. 1990) [IJ who prevented applicants from filing for asylum was not substantially justified, but AG and EOIR were because they took prompt action to correct it]. The government's legal position includes not only the DHS position before the circuit courts but also the IJ's, BIA's and DOJ's position. *Singh v. Gonzales,* 502 F.3d 1128, 1129 (9th Cir. 2007) [rejecting DHS that only their legal position is relevant].

(2) *Reasonableness*—In order to establish substantial justification, the government must show that its position was "[j]ustified in substance or in the main—that is justified to a degree that could satisfy a reasonable person." *Pierce v. Underwood*, 487 U.S. 552 (1988). In determining whether the government's position was reasonable, courts can consider, but are not limited to:

(a) The state in which litigation was resolved;

(b) Views expressed by other courts on the merits;

(c) The legal merits of the government's position;

(d) The clarity of the governing law;

(e) The foreseeable length and complexity of the litigation; and

(f) The consistency of the government's position.

Jean v. Nelson, 863 F.2d 759, 767 (11th Cir. 1988). However, in determining substantial justification, courts will not re-litigate the merits because that would put the court in the position of assessing legal questions that are not before it. *Id.* at 768. While "[a] string of losses...[or] even more so a string of successes" may be indicative of whether the government's position was substantially justified, *Pierce*, 487 U.S. at 569, a lack of adverse precedent does not necessarily insulate an agency from a fee award. *Ramon-Sepulveda v. INS*, 863 F.2d 1458, 1459 (9th Cir. 1988). In addition, the government's failure to timely respond to a fee petition may be considered as a concession that the government's position was not substantially justified or that it failed to meet its burden of proof. *Gwaduri v. INS,* 362 F.3d 1144 (9th Cir. 2004). Where the circuit's position on an issue is clear, the BIA cannot argue it was substantially justified by reference to the law in another circuit. *Ratnam v. INS,* 177 F.3d 742, 743 n.1 (9th Cir. 1999). Moreover, a court's ruling in favor of the government does not preclude fees where the ruling was reversed on appeal. *U.S. v. One 1984 Ford Van*, 873 F.2d 1281 (9th Cir. 1989).

(3) *The Government's Legal Position*—Where the BIA's decision is contrary to agency and circuit precedent and INS regulations, it is not substantially justified. *Singh v. Gonzales,* 502 F.3d 1128 (9th Cir. 2007) [it is not acceptable to repeat an argument already rejected without acknowledging the case that rejected it, particularly where the DOJ was involved in the previous case]; *Rueda-Menicucci v. INS*, 132 F.3d 493, 495 (9th Cir. 1997); *Haitian Refugee Center v. Meese*, 791 F.2d 1489, 1497 (11th Cir. 1986). Moreover, a court finding that there was a lack of substantial evidence to support the agency's decision, may indicate that government lacked substantial justification. *Thangaraja v. Gonzales,* 428 F.3d 870, 873–74 (9th Cir. 2005). *But see Welter v. Sullivan*, 941 F.2d 674, 676 (8th Cir. 1991) [claimant's attempt to equate the substantial evidence and substantial justification standards thereby making a fee award automatic is misplaced]; *Broussard v. Bowen*, 828 F.2d 310, 311–12 (5th Cir. 1987) [the substantial evidence standard and the substantial justification standard are neither semantic nor legal equivalents]. An agency's conduct which is determined to be arbitrary and capricious will usually be deemed to lack substantial justification except where there are "the most extraordinary circumstances." *Hong Kong TV v. Ilchert*, 685 F.Supp. 712 (N.D. Cal. 1988]. Where a case was originally remanded because the decision was arbitrary, no EAJA award was granted where INS clarified and affirmed. *Omni Packaging v. INS*, 940 F.Supp. 42, 46–47 (D.P.R. 1996).

(4) *No Substantial Justification Found*—The government's position was not substantially justified in the following cases: *Tchemkou v. Mukasey,* 517 F.3d 506, 509–10 (7th Cir. 2008) [Cameroon asylum case where government defense was either not argued originally or without support including its claim that persecution should not be viewed cumulatively]; *Floroiu v. Gonzales,* 498 F.3d 746, 748–49 (7th Cir. 2007) [government was not substantially justified in arguing the merits of petitioner's asylum claim on appeal when the issue was the IJ's conduct making a fair hearing not possible]; *Thangaraja v. Gonzales,* 428 F.3d 870, 873–74 (9th Cir. 2005) [IJ's decision denying asylum not supported by substantial evidence]; *Johnson v. Gonzales,* 416 F.3d 205, 210–13 (3d Cir. 2005) [government continued to argue against asylum where respondent was credible and evidence demonstrated fear was due to imputed political opinion]; *Muhur v. Ashcroft,* 382 F.3d 653, 655 (7th Cir. 2004) [DOJ committed clear error by stating that Jehovah's Witness could return to Eritrea without fear of persecution if she practiced her religion covertly]; *Bui v. INS*, 76 F.3d 268, 271 (9th Cir. 1996) [IJ failed to permit respondent to designate country of deportation]; *Sotelo-Aquije v. Slattery*, 62 F.3d 54 (2d Cir. 1995) [BIA denial of asylum]; *Jean v. Nelson*, 863 F.2d 759, 767 (11th Cir. 1988) [incarceration of Haitian refugees]; *LaDuke v. Nelson*, 762 F.2d 1318 (9th Cir. 1985) [search without probable cause]; *Berishev v. Chertoff*, 486 F.Supp.2d 202, 20–07 (D. Mass. 2007) [DHS not substantially justified in delaying naturalization adjudication 15 months]; *Kholyavskiy v. Schlecht*, 479 F.Supp.2d 897, 908–09 (E.D. Wis. 2007) [ICE position in reading *Zadvydas* to permit 6 months detention even if removal is not reasonably foreseeable was not substantially justified]; *Aboushaban v. Mueller*, 475 F.Supp.2d 943, 947–49 (N.D. Cal. 2007) [USCIS was not substantially justified in failing for years to adjudicate asylee's adjustment application and in its litigation position that it had no duty to adjudicate the application within any period of time]; *Harriott v. Ashcroft,* 277 F.Supp.2d 538, 545–46 (E.D. Pa. 2003) [long delay in processing certificate of citizenship such that child turned 18 and became ineligible for benefit]; *Salem v. INS,* 122 F.Supp.2d 980, 984–85 (C.D. Ill. 2000) [INS substantially delayed adjudicating petition and refused to allow an amendment to the petition]; *U.S. v. One 48 Ft. White Colored Sailboat,* 59 F.Supp.2d 362, 365–66 (D.P.R. 1999) [forfeiture]; *Kooritzky v. Herman,* 6 F.Supp.2d 1, 4 (D.D.C. 1997) *rev'd on other grounds* 178 F.3d 1315 (D.C. Cir. 1999) [challenge to DOL rule denying substitution of employee on labor cert. was sustained in court of appeals]; *U.S. v. Eleven Vehicles*, 966 F.Supp. 361 (E.D. Pa. 1997) [forfeiture]; *Reid v. INS*, 897 F.Supp. 798, 801 (S.D.N.Y. 1995) [undue delay in processing residency petition]; *Bullfrog Films, Inc. v. Catto*, 815 F.Supp. 338, 341–42 (C.D. Cal. 1993) [USIA promulgating regulations treating educational materials as propaganda]; *Douglas v. Baker*, 809 F.Supp. 131, 134 (D.D.C. 1992) [government fighting case despite substantial evidence of plaintiffs' U.S. citizenship]; *Dabone v. Thornburgh*, 734 F.Supp. 195, 201 (E.D. Pa. 1990) [19-month delay in processing unopposed motion to reopen]; *Nadler v. INS*, 737 F.Supp. 658, 660–61 (D.D.C. 1989) [two-year processing delay for AOS where average processing time was 130 days]; *Jefrey v. INS*, 710 F.Supp. 486 (S.D.N.Y. 1989) [government could not locate file for 16 months until mandamus filed and plaintiff's counsel agreed to discontinue action]; *U.S. v. One 1984 Chevrolet Truck*, 701 F.Supp. 213 (N.D. Ga. 1988) [government not substantially justified in seizure where transportation did not bear a "direct or substantial relationship" to the alien's continued presence in the U.S.].

(5) *Substantial Justification Found*—The government's position was substantially justified in the following cases: *Vacchio v. Ashcroft,* 404 F.3d 663, 674–77 (2d Cir. 2005) [government's unsuccessful resistance to respondent's release from detention on grounds that procedure was constitutional and that respondent was an aggravated felon]; *Al-Harbi v. INS,* 284 F.3d 1080, 1084–85 (9th Cir. 2002) [although BIA's asylum denial was reversed as lacking in "reasonable, substantial, and probative evidence," government's position on appeal was substantially justified]; *Kiareldeen v. Ashcroft,* 273 F.3d 542 (3d Cir. 2001) [government defense of the constitutionality of INA §240(b)(4)(B) which restricts release of national security information]; *Zapon v. DOJ,* 53 F.3d 283 (9th Cir. 1995) [INS opposition to stay of deportation where petitioner was a fugitive]; *Aguilar-Ayala v. Ruiz*, 973 F.2d 411 (5th Cir. 1992) [government defense of challenge to treat-

ment of alien witnesses]; *Mester Mfg. Co. v. INS*, 900 F.2d 201, 204 (9th Cir. 1990) [in employer sanctions case, government had a reasonable basis in law and fact for the charges]; *De Allende v. Baker*, 891 F.2d 7 (1st Cir. 1989) [government substantially justified where case raised issues of first impression]; *Hallman v. INS*, 879 F.2d 1244 (5th Cir. 1989) [INS finding Salvadoran asylum request frivolous because applicant did not fit under any of the five grounds of persecution, even where decision later reversed in light of new evidence]; *U.S. v. B&M Used Cars*, 860 F.2d 121 (4th Cir. 1988) [initiation of forfeiture justified even where forfeiture later dismissed]; *Ramos v. Haig*, 716 F.2d 471 (7th Cir. 1983) [indefinite detention of Mariel Cuban]; *Lord v. Chertoff*, 526 F.Supp.2d 435, 438–40 (S.D.N.Y. 2007) [six month delay in adjudicating naturalization application and initial denial were substantially justified]; *Babel v. DHS*, 321 F.Supp.2d 963, 967–68 (N.D. Ill. 2004) [DHS prolonged adjudication where it needed to complete extensive background check]; *Reeves v. Reno*, 61 F.Supp.2d 661, 667 (E.D. Mich. 1999) [INS arguing that AEDPA was retroactive and barred §212(c) relief when Sixth Circuit had not decided the issue]; *Toutounjian v. INS*, 2 F.Supp.2d 374, 377–78 (W.D.N.Y. 1998) [INS determination that it was bound by the Canadian courts on issues of moral turpitude where Second Circuit law was unsettled]; *Gomez-Arauz v. McNary*, 779 F.Supp. 1308 (W.D. Okl. 1991) [INS interpretation of EAD regulation, although incorrect, was substantially justified].

(6) *Voluntary Remands and Substantial Justification*—Where the government seeks a remand because the record indicates that the BIA's prior action was not consistent with clearly established law at the time the case was before it, then the government's position would not be substantially justified. *Li v. Keisler*, 505 F.3d 913, 918–21 (9th Cir. 2007) [where government asks for remand to reevaluate the prior proceedings due to a misapplication of, or failure to apply, controlling law and where there is no new law or claims of new facts, the government was not substantially justified]

(7) *Standard of Review*—The correct standard of appellate review of whether the government was substantially justified is the "abuse of discretion" standard, not *de novo* review. *Pierce v. Underwood*, 487 U.S. 552 (1988).

3.e. *Special Circumstances*—Even if the government's position was not substantially justified, a court may deny attorney's fees if "special circumstances make an award unjust." 28 U.S.C. §2412(d)(1)(A). Special circumstances include the government advancing in good faith, novel but credible extensions and interpretations of the law. H.R. Rep. No. 1418 at 11, 96th Cong., *reprinted in* 1980 U.S.C.C.A.N. 4984, 4990. This provision is to be narrowly construed so as not to interfere with or defeat Congress' purpose in passing the statute. *Martin v. Heckler*, 773 F.2d 1145 (11th Cir. 1985). The "special circumstances" defense was not intended to be applied across-the-board to an entire class of cases, but rather to prevent injustice on a case-by-case basis. *National Ass'n of Mfrs. v. DOL*, 159 F.3d 597, 606 (D.C. Cir. 1998). An alien's notorious and repeated violation of the immigration laws has been deemed a special circumstance. *Oguachuba v. INS*, 706 F.2d 93 (2d Cir. 1983). Special circumstances were also found in *Gomez-Arauz v. McNary*, 779 F.Supp. 1308, 1312–13 (W.D. Okl. 1991), where, although the court ordered INS to grant plaintiff's EAD application, the application was filed "during a brief window of time when a short-lived and apparently unintended regulatory amendment stripped the District Director of discretion to deny" EADs and the applicant would have been otherwise ineligible.

4. *Proceedings Covered Under EAJA*

4.a. *Federal Litigation*—Attorney's fees are recoverable for "civil actions" under EAJA. 28 U.S.C. §2412(d)(1)(A). For purposes of the statute, federal litigation may include habeas corpus actions in immigration proceedings. *Kholyavskiy v. Schlecht*, 479 F.Supp.2d 897, 901 (E.D. Wis. 2007) [civil habeas is included under EAJA]; *Vacchio v. Ashcroft*, 404 F.3d 663, 667–72 (2d Cir. 2005) [finding that immigration habeas cases are civil actions for purposes of EAJA]; *Diaz-Magana v. Rogers*, 81 F.3d 167 (9th Cir. 1996); *Petition of Hill*, 775 F.2d 1037 (9th Cir. 1985); *Toutounjian v. INS*, 2 F.Supp.2d 374 (W.D.N.Y. 1998). *But see O'Brien v. Moore*, 395 F.3d 499 (4th Cir. 2005) [rejecting Bureau of Prison habeas petition as a civil action under EAJA].

4.b. *Administrative Proceedings*—While EAJA fees are recoverable for certain adversarial administrative proceedings, 5 U.S.C. §§504(a)(1), the Supreme Court has held that EAJA does not apply to administrative deportation proceedings. *Ardestani v. INS*, 502 U.S. 129 (1991). *See also Matter of Anselmo*, 20 I&N Dec. 25 (BIA 1989); *Matter of Fede*, 20 I&N Dec. 35 (BIA 1989). However, the Supreme Court has recognized that fees for administrative proceedings may be awarded when the administrative work is related to the federal litigation. *Sullivan v. Hudson*, 490 U.S. 877, 887 (1989) ["where administrative proceedings are intimately tied to the resolution of the judicial action and necessary to the attainment of the results Congress sought to promote by providing for fees, they should be considered part and parcel of the action for which fees may be awarded"]; *Pollgreen v. Morris*, 911 F.2d 527, 534–36 (11th Cir. 1990) [allowing recovery of fees for administrative fine proceeding intertwined with federal litigation]; *Tacas-Juan v. Eddy*, No. 95-0493-CV-HRH (D. Alaska 1997). *But see Shalala v. Schaefer*, 509 U.S. 292 (1993) [may only recover fees for administrative work where district court retains jurisdiction pending completion of administrative proceeding]; *Full Gospel Portland Church v. Thornburgh*, 927 F.2d 628 (D.C. Cir. 1991) [no fees for pre- or post-litigation administrative work where district court reversed INS denial of I-140 petition]; *Douglas v. Baker*, 809 F.Supp. 131, 136–37 (D.D.C. 1992) [no fees for passports applications at U.S. consulate before litigation or DOS after litigation]. There may still remain an issue as to whether EAJA fees are available for work before the BIA. *See* 28 C.F.R. §24.101 *et seq.* (1988).

4.c. *Naturalization/Citizenship Claims*—Federal courts have awarded EAJA fees in naturalization petitions in federal court on motions to calendar over the government's objection that they are *ex parte* actions and that therefore, fees are not recoverable. *Abela v. Gustafson*, 888 F.2d 1258 (9th Cir. 1989) [when government actively opposes petition EAJA fees appropriate]; *Matter of Narcisco y Digamon*, Case No. K-87-1818 (D. Md. 1988), *reported in* 65 No. 35 *Interpreter Releases* 942 (Sept. 12, 1988) and *Matter of Calcagno*, Case No. K-87-1819 (D. Md. 1988), *reported in* 65 No. 35 *Interpreter Releases* 942–43 (Sept. 12, 1988). EAJA fees have also been awarded in actions seeking declaratory judgment affirming U.S. citizenship. *Douglas v. Baker*, 809 F.Supp. 131 (D.D.C. 1992).

4.d. *Criminal Proceedings*—At least one court has refused to grant fees for successfully opposing deportation during a criminal sentencing on the ground that EAJA fees are not available for criminal proceedings. *U.S. v. Soueiti,* 154 F.3d 1018 (9th Cir. 1998).

4.e. *Labor Certification*—It has been held that labor certification appeals are not adversary adjudications permitting an award of fees. *Smedberg Machine & Tool, Inc. v. Donovan*, 730 F.2d 1089 (7th Cir. 1984). *See also Matter of Larry Douglas, Ltd.*, 88-INA-130 (BALCA 1988).

4.f. *Employer Sanctions*—Employer sanctions cases are adversary proceedings within the meaning of the APA and fees are recoverable. 5 U.S.C. §§504(a)(1) & (b)(1)(C); *Mester Mfg. Co. v. INS*, 900 F.2d 201 (9th Cir. 1990).

5. *Submitting the EAJA Fee Application.*

5.a. *Filing Deadline*—Fee applications must be filed within 30 days of final judgment ("judgment that is final and not appealable, including an order of settlement." 28 U.S.C. §§2412(d)(1)(B), (d)(2)(G); *Haitian Refugee Center v. Meese*, 791 F.2d 1489 (11th Cir. 1986); *Bruland v. Howerton*, 742 F.Supp. 629, 632 (S.D. Fla. 1990) [final judgment means "the date on which a party's case has met its final demise (such) that there is nothing further the party can do to give it life"]; *Omni Packaging v. INS*, 940 F.Supp. 42, 47 (D.P.R. 1996); *Illinois Migrant Council v. Pilliod*, 672 F.Supp. 1072 (N.D. Ill. 1987). The filing deadline is 30 days from the date a decision becomes final, or 90 days from a district court order (*i.e.,* order + 60 days to appeal + 30 days); and 120 days from an appellate order (*i.e.,* court of appeals decision + 90 days to petition for certiorari + 30 days). *Al-Harbi v. INS,* 284 F.3d 1080, 1082–84 (9th Cir. 2002) [the filing deadline for attorney's fees in appeal of BIA decision to circuit court is 30 days from the expiration of period for filing petition for certiorari]; *Singleton v. Apfel,* 231 F.3d 853, 855 n.4 (11th 2000); *Kolman v. Shalala,* 39 F.3d 173, 175 (7th Cir. 1994); *Federal Election Comm'n v. Political Contributions Data,* 995 F.2d 383, 385–86 (2d Cir. 1993);

Taylor v. U.S., 749 F.2d 171, 175 (3d Cir. 1984); *Youngdale & Sons Constr. Co. v. U.S.,* 31 Fed. Cl. 167, 175 (Ct. Cl. 1994). The 120-day period from the appellate court decision begins running from the issuance of the opinion, not the issuance of the mandate. *Zheng v. Ashcroft,* 383 F.3d 919 (9th Cir. 2004). A petition for rehearing tolls the time period for filing the writ of certiorari. *Arulampalam v. Gonzales,* 399 F.3d 1087 (9th Cir. 2005) [where final judgment was rendered 90 days after rehearing denied, the fee petition was untimely where it was mailed, but not filed 30 days later]. The filing deadline following a voluntary dismissal is 30 days from the date of dismissal, because there is no appeal. *Briseno v. Ashcroft,* 291 F.3d 377 (5th Cir. 2002). In cases involving remands to the agency, the 30 days begin from the end of the period permitted for appeal. *Shalala v. Schaefer*, 509 U.S. 292 (1993) [court order remanding case back to agency is a judgment which, if not appealed, begins the 30-day period even if proceedings continue before the agency]. The Ninth Circuit has determined that the 30 day time period begins to run *after* the 90 days to appeal (*i.e.*, for a petition for certiorari) has expired. *Li v. Keisler,* 505 F.3d 913, 916–17 (9th Cir. 2007) [the 30-day EAJA fee application period does not begin to run until 90 days after an order remanding and immigration matter to the BIA, even if such order is at the request of the government].

5.b. *Equitable Tolling of Filing Deadline*—The 30-day filing period is not jurisdictional and may be equitably tolled. *Townsend v. Comm'r of Social Security,* 415 F.3d 578 (6th Cir. 2005). The relation back doctrine is also applicable to EAJA cases. *Scarborough v. Principi,* 541 U.S. 401, 410 (2004) [allowing an amendment to EAJA petition that the government was not substantially justified, filed after the 30-day filing period, to relate back to the filing of the complaint].

5.c. *The Fee Application*—Fee applications must allege and make a showing on all essential elements under 28 U.S.C. §2412(d)(1)(B): (1) that the party is a prevailing party; (2) that the party is eligible to receive an award; (3) the amount sought, including an itemized statement from any attorney or expert witness; and (4) that the position of the U.S. was not substantially justified. Failure to allege all statutory requirements may not be fatal. *Scarborough v. Principi,* 541 U.S. 401 (2004) [where applicant failed to allege that government's position was not substantially justified, application could be amended to cure defect]; *Singleton v. Apfel,* 231 F.3d 853, 857–58 (11th Cir. 2000) [failure to allege that net worth did not exceed $2 million was not basis to dismiss because Petitioner could amend petition within the 30-day period]; *Dunn v. U.S.,* 775 F.2d 99, 103 (3d Cir. 1985) [where application filed within the 30-day time limit but failed to state the amount sought or to include an itemized statement, applicant could supplement the petition unless the government was prejudiced by the defect].

6. *Calculating EAJA Fees.*

6.a. *Generally*—Congress allows for the recovery of reasonable attorney's fees and other expenses including expert witness fees and the cost of any study, analysis, report, or test. 28 U.S.C. §2412(d)(2)(A). "[F]ees awarded...shall be based upon prevailing market rates for the kind and quality of the services furnished," except that attorney's fees are limited to $125 an hour "unless the court determines that an increase in the cost of living or a special factor such as the limited availability of qualified attorneys for the proceedings involved" permits a higher hourly fee. *Id.*; *Jean v. Nelson*, 863 F.2d 759, 773 (11th Cir. 1988). Fee requests must be well documented. *Kooritzky v. Herman,* 6 F.Supp.2d 1, 11–13 (D.D.C. 1997), *rev'd on other grounds,* 178 F.3d 1315 (D.C. Cir. 1999) [attorney's fees denied in part where attorney submitted generalized affidavit without detailing the specific work performed and the time and date of each task]. The hours expended must be reasonable. *Tchemkou v. Mukasey,* 517 F.3d 506, 510–12 (7th Cir. 2008) [it was reasonable for counsel to spend 150 hours on his opening brief, 40 hours on the reply and 20 hours on internal and external communications with a total of 247.5 hours on the appeal].

6.b. *Cost of Living*:

(1) In determining the cost of living, the majority of courts today rely on the CPI-U (Consumer Price Index for All Urban Consumers). *U.S. v. 22249 Dolorosa St.,* 190 F.3d 977, 984 (9th Cir. 1999); *Masonry Masters, Inc. v. Nelson*, 105 F.3d 708, 710 (D.C. Cir. 1997); *Jones v. Espy*, 10 F.3d 690, 692–93 (9th Cir. 1993); *Harris v. Sullivan*, 968 F.2d 263 (2d Cir. 1992); *DeWalt v. Sullivan*, 963 F.2d 27 (3d Cir. 1992); *Sullivan v. Sullivan*,

958 F.2d 574 (4th Cir. 1992); *Chen v. Slattery*, 842 F.Supp. 597 (D.D.C. 1994); *Uskokovic v. Sullivan*, 772 F.Supp. 387 (N.D. Ill. 1991); *Ramon-Sepulveda v. INS*, 863 F.2d 1458, 1463 (9th Cir. 1988); *Dabone v. Thornburgh*, 734 F.Supp. 195, 204 (E.D. Pa. 1990); *Douglas v. Baker*, 809 F.Supp. 131, 134–35 (D.D.C. 1992). Surveys from the Bureau of Labor Statistics might also be relied on to yield a higher cost of living. *See www.bls.gov*.

(2) The cost-of-living adjustment for inflation is measured as of March 1996, when the rate of attorney compensation was raised to $125/hour. Although historically, the cost of living was measured at the time the fee was sought, *Garcia v. Schweiker*, 829 F.2d 396 (3d Cir. 1987), a majority of the courts have concluded that the cost of living adjustment must be made on a year-by-year basis, according to when the work was done. *See e.g., Tchemkou v. Mukasey,* 517 F.3d 506, 512 (7th Cir. 2008) [granted cost of living increase for year 2006 to $161.85 per hour]; *Sorenson v. Mink,* 239 F.3d 1140, 1148 (9th Cir. 2001); *Masonry Masters, Inc. v. Nelson*, 105 F.3d 708, 710 (D.C. Cir. 1997); *Marcus v. Shalala*, 17 F.3d 1033 (7th Cir. 1994); *Perales v. Casillas*, 950 F.2d 1066, 1074–77 (5th Cir. 1992); *Chiu v. U.S.*, 948 F.2d 711, 719–22 (Fed. Cir. 1991).

6.c. Special Factors.

(1) *Limited Availability of Qualified Attorneys*—In determining whether an increase above $125/hr is warranted, courts may also consider "special factors" such as the "limited availability of qualified attorneys." 28 U.S.C. §2412(d)(2)(A)(ii). This provision is generally limited to attorneys "having some distinctive knowledge or specialized skill needful for the litigation in question." *Pierce v. Underwood*, 487 U.S. 552 (1988). Immigration law has been found to be a specialized skill. *Floroiu v. Gonzales,* 498 F.3d 746, 749–50 (7th Cir. 2007) [immigration lawyers may receive an enhanced fee but counsel's conclusory statements about his experience and the complexity of the case were insufficient because counsel must provide: (1) sufficient information regarding the particular qualifications of the attorney involved; (2) the manner in which those qualifications were brought to bear on this litigation; and (3) information regarding the availability of attorneys with qualifications to pursue the case]; *Muhur v. Ashcroft,* 382 F.3d 653, 656 (7th Cir. 2004) [although immigration lawyers may not *per se* be entitled to fees above the cap, where they bring relevant expertise to a case "such as knowledge of foreign cultures or of particular, esoteric nooks and crannies of immigration law, in which expertise is needed," they can exceed the cap]; *Jean v. Nelson*, 863 F.2d 759, 774 (11th Cir. 1988) [specialized skill needful for litigation includes immigration law as narrow legal specialty]; *Montes v. Meese*, ___ F.Supp. ___ (C.D. Cal. 1987), *reported in* 65 No. 1 *Interpreter Releases* 5 (Jan. 4, 1988) *aff'd sub nom. Montes v. Thornburgh*, 919 F.2d 531 (9th Cir. 1990) [awarding $135/hour based on immigration expertise, nonavailability of counsel and inflation]; *Harriott v. Ashcroft,* 277 F.Supp.2d 538, 546–47 (E.D. Pa. 2003) [awarding $300/ hour in certificate of citizenship case because of lawyer's specialized knowledge in immigration law]; *Douglas v. Baker*, 809 F.Supp. 131, 135 (D.D.C. 1992) [awarding $150/hour based on paucity of available counsel and immigration specialty, but rejecting this rate for time spent litigating fees for fees]; *Bamondi v. INS*, ___ F.Supp. ___, Case No. 88-1410-EBG (CM) (S.D. Cal. Aug. 16, 1990), *reported in*, 67 No. 33 *Interpreter Releases* 974 (Aug. 31, 1990) [awarding $200 per hour where immigration law considered "distinctive knowledge or specialized skill needed for the litigation"]; *United Farm Workers of America v. INS,* ___ F.Supp. ___, Case No. Civ-S-87-1064-JPM (LKK) (E.D. Cal. Sept. 18, 1990), *reported in* 67 No. 36 *Interpreter Releases* 1068 (Sept. 24, 1990) [specialties in immigration and farmworker law permitting upward adjustment]; *Lyden v. Howerton*, 731 F.Supp. 1545, 1556 (S.D. Fla. 1990) [awarding $200/hr based on shortage of immigration lawyers]; *Nadler v. INS*, 737 F.Supp. 658, 662 (D.D.C. 1989) [immigration is legal specialty requiring upward adjustment]. *But see Aboushaban v. Mueller*, 475 F.Supp.2d 943, 950 (N.D. Cal. 2007) [although counsel possessed special skills in immigration, the case was a straight-forward mandamus action that did not demand specialized knowledge or skill]; *Johnson v. Gonzales,* 416 F.3d 205, 213–14 (3d Cir. 2005) [although counsel was an experienced immigration specialist, the case was

straightforward and did not require research into little known areas of immigration law]; *Perales v. Casillas*, 950 F.2d 1066, 1077–79 (5th Cir. 1992) [no evidence of limited availability of qualified immigration attorneys]; *Rueda-Menicucci v. INS*, 132 F.3d 493, 496 (9th Cir. 1997) [specialty in immigration law not needed]; Limited availability of counsel must be proven by fee petitioners. *Ramon-Sepulveda*, 863 F.2d at 1463 [no shortage of attorneys in LA to handle deportation cases].

(2) *Other Special Factors*—An unusual delay in the award of fees that is not attributable to negligence or improper conduct by the prevailing party may be regarded as a special factor justifying a fee increase. *Wilkett v. ICC*, 844 F.2d 867, 876 (D.C. Cir. 1988). *See also Pollgreen v. Morris*, 911 F.2d 527, 537–38 (11th Cir. 1990) [government's excessive or bad faith delay in litigation might constitute a special factor]. *But see Library of Congress v. Shaw*, 478 U.S. 310 (1986) [compensation for delay impermissible in Title VII action against the U.S. government]. The government's unduly litigious prosecution may also be a special factor. *Jean v. Nelson*, 863 F.2d 759, 776 (11th Cir. 1988). Special factors cannot include those of broad and general application such as "Johnson factors" normally used to compute a fee application under 42 U.S.C. §1988. *See Pierce v. Underwood*, 487 U.S. 552 (1988); *Johnson v. Georgia Highway Express*, 488 F.2d 714 (5th Cir. 1974). Nor can the contingent nature or the risk of the case be used as a special factor. *Id.* The *pro bono publico* nature of the case, the vindication of public rights, and the emotional hardship to counsel are not special factors permitting enhancement. *Jean*, 863 F.2d at 775.

6.d. *Interest*—A party is entitled to interest "if the U.S. appeals an award of costs or fees and other expenses...and the award is affirmed in whole or in part." 28 U.S.C. §2412(f). Interest is paid on the amount of the award as affirmed. *Id.*

6.e. *Fees for Fees*—Where the government was not substantially justified in the merits litigation, a second "substantial justification" finding is not required before fees are awarded for the fee litigation itself. *Commissioner, INS v. Jean*, 496 U.S. 154, 158–66 (1990). Thereafter, the court may increase or decrease the fee award for litigating fees by determining what a "reasonable" fee would be as described in *Hensley v. Eckerhart*, 461 U.S. 424 (1983). *Jean*, 496 U.S. at 161; *Douglas v. Baker*, 809 F.Supp. 131, 136–38 (D.D.C. 1992).

6.f. *Fees for Certain Activities*—Fees may be obtained for consultation with *amici* and contact with the press. *Bullfrog Films, Inc. v. Catto*, 815 F.Supp. 338, 343–44 (C.D. Cal. 1993).

6.g. *Costs and Expenses*—Some courts have broadly construed expense provisions under EAJA. *Tchemkou v. Mukasey,* 517 F.3d 506, 512–13 (7th Cir. 2008) [costs include computerized legal research, postage, telephone calls and delivery charges]; *Jean v. Nelson*, 863 F.2d 759, 776–78 (11th Cir. 1988) [costs include telephone, reasonable travel, postage, computerized research and certain paralegal work]; *Holden v. Bowen*, 668 F.Supp. 1042, 1053 (N.D. Ohio 1986) [long-distance telephone, messengers, computer-assisted legal research, travel compensation]. Costs, as distinguished from expenses, are recoverable under 28 U.S.C. §1920, as they would be against any party to litigation.

6.h. *Standard of Review*—The amount of the fee is reviewed under an abuse of discretion standard. *Pierce v. Underwood*, 487 U.S. 552 (1988).

B. *Attorney's Fees under Other Statutes*

1. 42 U.S.C. §1988—Provides for attorney's fees for actions brought under the civil rights statutes, 42 U.S.C. §§1981–86. While this provision does not provide for fees in a *Bivens* action, *Hall v. U.S.*, 773 F.2d 703 (6th Cir. 1985); *Unification Church v. INS*, 762 F.2d 1077 (D.C. Cir. 1985), it may permit recovery where there was an independent claim against a federal officer under the civil rights statutes. *Bergman v. U.S.*, 844 F.2d 353 (6th Cir. 1988); *Knights of the Ku Klux Klan v. East Baton Rouge Parish School Bd.*, 735 F.2d 895 (5th Cir. 1984). However, at least one court has found that where state and federal defendants are sued, fees are governed by EAJA for the federal defendants and §1988 for the state defendants. *Jones v. Espy*, 10 F.3d 690 (9th Cir. 1993). Expert witness fees can be recovered in civil rights cases under §1988 as part of the attorney's fees. Pro se attorneys cannot recover attorney's fees. *Kay v. Ehrler*, 499 U.S. 432 (1991).

2. *FTCA*—Permits attorney's fees up to 20% of the recovery if the case is settled at the administrative stage, and 25% of the settlement or judgment after suit is filed. 28 U.S.C. §2678. It has been suggested that where EAJA applies, the 25% cap is not a bar to a court-ordered fee award exceeding that amount. *Stive v. U.S.,* 366 F.3d 520, 523–24 (7th Cir. 2004).

3. *Bivens*—Fees for *Bivens* actions are left to contractual arrangements with counsel consistent with the relevant state bar's canons of ethics. The EAJA, however, does not permit an award of attorney's fees in a *Bivens* action. *Kreines v. U.S.*, 33 F.3d 1105 (9th Cir. 1994).

4. *FOIA*—Provides for attorney's fees if a party has "substantially prevailed." *Union of Needletrades, Industrial and Textile Employees, AFL-CIO v. INS,* 336 F.3d 200 (2d Cir. 2003) [applied *Buckhannon* to "substantially prevailed" language in FOIA and determined that absent a consent decree or judgment on the merits, petitioner could not obtain attorney's fees where it agreed to dismiss the case after obtaining most documents it sought]. In determining fee awards, courts look to criteria such as the nature of plaintiff's interest in the records, the public benefit derived from the litigation and whether the government's basis for withholding the records was reasonable. *Union of Concerned Scientists v. U.S. NRC,* 824 F.2d 1219 (D.C. Cir. 1987); *Aviation Data Service v. FAA*, 687 F.2d 1319 (8th Cir. 1982); *Stein v. DOJ*, 662 F.2d 1245 (7th Cir. 1981). In *Arevalo-Franco v. INS*, 772 F.Supp. 959 (W.D. Tex. 1991), the court denied fees finding that where INS did not disclose documents due to administrative problems, and where there is no showing that the lawsuit caused disclosure, fees are not warranted. At least one court has determined that a pro se attorney was not entitled to attorney's fees under FOIA, and that he was limited in his recovery of expert witness fees to $40 per day as provided by the federal court taxing statute. *Ray v. DOJ*, 856 F.Supp. 1576 (S.D. Fla. 1994), *aff'd on other grounds*, 87 F.3d 1250 (11th Cir. 1996).

5. Fees are permitted for employer sanctions and for unfair immigration employment proceedings. *See* Chapter 12.

6. Trafficking victims who sue in district court under 18 U.S.C. §§1589–91 may recover attorney's fees under 18 U.S.C. §1595.

CHAPTER 12
EMPLOYER SANCTIONS, UNFAIR IMMIGRATION-RELATED EMPLOYMENT PRACTICES, AND LEGALIZATION

IX. ADMINISTRATIVE AND JUDICIAL REVIEW

X. EMPLOYMENT AUTHORIZATION

XI. EMPLOYMENT / LABOR RIGHTS

XII. UNFAIR IMMIGRATION-RELATED EMPLOYMENT PRACTICES

XIII. LEGALIZATION UNDER INA §245A

XV. LEGALIZATION FOR SPECIAL AGRICULTURAL WORKERS (SAWs)

CHAPTER 12
EMPLOYER SANCTIONS, UNFAIR IMMIGRATION-RELATED EMPLOYMENT PRACTICES, AND LEGALIZATION

I. EMPLOYER SANCTIONS—INA §274A, 8 U.S.C. §1324a. Legislative history found at H.R. Rep. No. 99-682 (I), reprinted in 1986 U.S.C.C.A.N. 5649.

A. *Generally*—It is unlawful to hire, recruit or refer for a fee, a person who is not authorized to work in the U.S. INA §274A(a)(1), 8 U.S.C. §1324a(a)(1).

1. *Authorized to Work*— All employees must be authorized to work either automatically (USC/LPR) or by USCIS. If employment authorization expires then a person is no longer authorized to work. Employment authorization is automatically extended 240 days upon filing a timely application to extend A-3, E-1/E-2, G-5, H-1, H-2A/B, H-3, I, J-1, L-1, O-1/O-2, P-1/P-2/P-3, R, or TN status under INA §214(e) (NAFTA). 8 C.F.R. §§274a.12(b)(20), 1274a.12(b)(20). An H-1B holder may change jobs upon the filing of a new petition as long as s/he is in lawful status and has not engaged in unauthorized employment since her last lawful admission. An extension on any other basis or a request to change status to one permitting employment does not accord employment authorization while pending.

2. *Hire, Recruit or Refer For a Fee*—"Hiring" means actual commencement of employment "for wages or other remuneration," and includes the use of a contract, subcontract or exchange to obtain the labor of a person knowing that person is not authorized to work 8 C.F.R. §§274a.1(c), 274a.5, 1274a.1(c), 1274a.5. Also includes renegotiated or extended contracts or subcontracts. "Referring or recruiting for a fee" does not include union hiring halls. 8 C.F.R. §§274a.1(d), 1274a.1(d).

3. *Employees*—An "employee" is "an individual who provides services or labor for an employer for wages or other remuneration," and does not include casual hires or independent contractors. 8 C.F.R. §§274a.1(f), 1274a.1(f). Does not include volunteers who do work "without any expectation of compensation...." 66 No. 41 *Interpreter Releases* 1173–74, 1186–89 (Oct. 23, 1989). If remuneration is outside the U.S., the person is still regarded as an employee for I-9 purposes. Letter, Carpenter, Assoc. General Counsel, INS, HQ COU 90/10.10-C (Sept. 17, 1996), *reprinted in* 73 No. 44 *Interpreter Releases* 1624, 1637–39 (Nov. 18, 1996).

   3.a. *Casual Hires*—Limited to domestic employment that is sporadic, irregular, or intermittent. 8 C.F.R. §§274a.1(f), (h), 1274a.1(f), (h). Domestic employment has been interpreted to include upkeep and maintenance around the home, but not home construction work. *Jenkins v. INS*, 108 F.3d 195, 199–201 (9th Cir. 1997) [suggesting domestic exception may be *ultra vires* to the statute].

   3.b. *Independent Contractors*—Includes "individual entities who carry on independent business, contract to do a piece of work according to their own means and methods, and are subject to control only as to results." Indicia of independence include: (1) who supplies tools/materials; (2) whether services are available to the public; (3) whether work is done for other clients; (4) whether there is an opportunity for profit or loss as a result of the labor; (5) whether there is an investment in the facilities for work; and (6) who determines order, sequence, and time work is done. 8 C.F.R. §§274a.1(j), 1274a.1(j). The government's position is that an employer need not complete verification forms for an independent contractor, but if the employer has "knowledge" the contractor is undocumented, the employer cannot continue using their services.

4. *Employers*—Covers both natural persons and entities.

   4.a. *Agent/Individual Liability*—"Employer" also includes "an agent or anyone acting directly or indirectly in the interest" of a person or entity "who engages the services or labor of an employee...for wages or other remuneration." 8 C.F.R. §§274a.1(g), 1274a.1(g). This regulation was upheld in *U.S. v. Wrangler's Country Cafe*, 1 OCAHO no. 138 (Mar. 6, 1990), *aff'd sub nom. Steiben v. INS*, 932 F.2d 1225 (8th Cir. 1991) [rejecting the argument that the president of a corporation is protected from liability by the corporate entity]; *U.S. v. Mr. Z Enterprises, Inc.*, 1 OCAHO no. 288 (Jan. 11, 1991) [president of company *and* company held liable but for different counts]. *But see U.S. v. Mexico Bakery, Inc.*, 2 OCAHO no. 315 (Apr. 12, 1991) [refusing to enter default against shareholders of company where there was considerable doubt that they acted for the employer, as they neither worked at nor managed the bakery].

   4.b. *Agricultural Associations and Contractors*—IMMACT90 explicitly made agricultural associations "employers" *and* farm labor contractors liable for reporting requirements (I-9s) when hiring, recruiting or referring for a fee. INA §274A(a)(1)(B)(ii), 8 U.S.C. §1324a(a)(1)(B)(ii). The Act exempted all other recruiters or persons who refer others for a fee from the reporting requirements, but they may still be liable for knowingly hiring or referring an undocumented worker.

   4.c. *Successor Employers*—Successor employers who retain part or all of the prior employer's staff are responsible for verification requirements. *U.S. v. Nevada Lifestyles, Inc., d/b/a Commercial Drapery Cleaners*, 3 OCAHO no. 518 (May 10, 1993) [successor employer is not required to execute all new I-9s but is responsible for predecessor's failure to complete or defective completion of I-9s]. *But see U.S. v. Marnul*, 3 OCAHO no. 441 (July 21, 1992) [successor employer *was* required to execute new I-9s because the rehired employees were deemed new hires]. In determining successor liability, courts will rely on: (1) the continuity of ownership; (2) the time lapse between dissolution of the first company and formation of the second; (3) the continuation of the business; and (4) the assumption of liabilities. *U.S. v. Spring & Soon Fashion, Inc.* 8 OCAHO no. 1003 (1998) [finding successor liable]; *U.S. v. Wailolo, Inc.* __OCAHO no. __ (1999), *reprinted in* 76 No. 34 *Interpreter Releases* 1313 (Sept. 3, 1999) [successor responsible for second tier penalty where previous violation was almost identical, the same individuals served as officers, directors and manager, and the address and trade name remained the same]. Must show transfer of assets from predecessor to successor as a prerequisite for liability. *U.S. v. WSC Plumbing,* 8 OCAHO no. 1045 (2000) [INS failed to show a transfer of assets and sufficient facts to demonstrate continuity of ownership from predecessor to successor].

   4.d. *Federal Government*—IIRIRA amended the definition of "entity" to make employer sanctions applicable to "any branch of the federal government." INA §274A(a)(7), 8 U.S.C. §1324a(a)(7).

   4.e. *State Workforce Agencies* (SWA) are required both to complete and retain I-9s when potential employee appears in person at their offices because they recruit and refer H-2As and H-2Bs and to E-Verify the status of potential employees who they are recruiting. TEGL No. 11-07, Change 1 (Nov. 14, 2007), *published on* AILA InfoNet at Doc. No. 07111560; Memo, Jacob, Solicitor of Labor, DOL (Mar. 14, 2008), *published on* AILA InfoNet at Doc. No. 08040762; Round 1, H-2As TEGL 11-07, Change 1, DOL FAQs (Feb. 5, 2008), *reprinted in* 85 No. 7 *Interpreter Releases* 417, 465–75 (Feb. 11, 2008); TEGL 11-07, Change 1, Questions from SWA Training Webinars-Round 3, *published on* AILA InfoNet at Doc. No. 08050163.

5. *Pre-Enactment Employees*—Employer sanctions and I-9 requirements do not apply to employees hired before Nov. 7, 1986. An employee hired prior to Nov. 7, 1986 loses their "pre-enactment status" if the employee quits, is terminated (including seasonal work), is excluded, deported or departs under an order of voluntary departure, or is no longer continuing in employment or does not have a reasonable expectation of employment at all times. 8 C.F.R. §§274a.7, 1274a.7.

B. *Verification System (Form I-9)*—INA §274A(b), 8 U.S.C. §1324a(b)

1. *Who is Subject to Verification?*

   1.a. All employees hired after Nov. 6, 1986, and still employed on June 1, 1987.

   1.b. Employees who left employment and are rehired must be reverified by completing a new I-9, if rehired more than three years after the original hire date.

2. *Who is Not Subject to Verification?*

2.a. Casual hires.

2.b. Employees of independent contractors.

2.c. B-1 domestic servants. Memo, Schroeder, Asst. Comm. CO 1738-C (Sept. 16, 1988), *reprinted in* 65 No. 45 *Interpreter Releases* 1231–32 (Nov. 21, 1988).

2.d. B-1 trainees on short term training program. Letter, Bednarz, Chief, NIV Adjudications CO 214b-C (June 1, 1994), *reprinted in* 71 No. 29 *Interpreter Releases* 992, 1007 (Aug. 1, 1994).

2.e. Pre-Enactment employees (employees hired before Nov. 7, 1986), unless continuity of employment is broken.

3. *What Must the Employer Do?*

3.a. *Generally*—Employer must review a prospective employee's documents and attest under penalty of perjury on Form I-9 that employee produced documents establishing both employment authorization and identity. The attestation may be done by either hand-written or electronic signature. 71 Fed. Reg. 34510 (June 15, 2006) [establishing the electronic verification system with an electronic signature]. Employer may complete verification forms through an agent. 52 Fed. Reg. 16216 at 16218; 8 C.F.R. §§274a.1(g), 274a.2(b)(1)(iv), 1274a.1(g), 1274a.2(b)(1)(iv). Employer must "within three business days of hire" examine employee's employment and identity documents and provide verification of those documents on Form I-9. 8 C.F.R. §§274a.2(b)(1)(i), (ii), 1274a.2(b)(1)(i), (ii). If person is hired for less than 3 days, the employer must comply "at the time of hire." 8 C.F.R. §§274a.2(b)(1)(iii), 1274a.2(b)(1)(iii). The employer, not the employee, is liable for any defects in the completion of section 1 of Form I-9 and defects in the completion and accuracy of section 2 of Form I-9. *Mester Mfg. Co., Inc. v. INS*, 879 F.2d 561 (9th Cir. 1989); 8 C.F.R. §§274a.2(b)(1)(i)(A), 1274a.2(b)(1)(i)(A) [employer is obligated to ensure employee correctly completes section 1 of Form I-9]. Regulations specifically require the employer to note the identification number and expiration date (if any) of any document provided by employee. 8 C.F.R. §§274a.2(b)(1)(v), 1274a.2(b)(1)(v).

3.b. *Receipt Evidencing Application for Replacement Documents*—If the employee cannot produce documents within the required 3 days, s/he may submit a receipt for an application for replacement document, and have up to 90 days to submit the replacement document. 8 C.F.R. §§274a.2(b)(1)(vi), 1274a.2(b)(1)(vi); *Getahun v. OCAHO*, 124 F.3d 591, 595–96 (3d Cir. 1997) [employee fired within 90 days after providing receipt has unfair immigration employment practice claim]. The receipt must be for a replacement document that evidences existing employment authorization; a receipt of an application to *apply* for employment authorization is not acceptable (*i.e.*, receipt for replacement EAD card is acceptable; receipt for original EAD application is not). Letter, Scialabba, Deputy General Counsel, INS (June 17, 1996), *published on* AILA InfoNet at Doc. No. 96061790. Provision also applies to reverification. 62 Fed. Reg. 51001 at 51004. Provision does not apply to persons working less than 3 days. 55 Fed. Reg. 25928 at 25929 n.11 (June 25, 1990). Employer may also accept as a receipt: (1) I-94 evidencing LPR status (with I-551 stamp) for the validity period of the receipt or if no validity period within one year of issuance date; or (2) I-94 evidencing refugee status for first 90 days of receipt.

3.c. *Copies of Documents*—Employer may, but is not required to, copy the employee's documents. 8 C.F.R. §§274a.2(b)(3), 1274a.2(b)(3). However, the employer is not relieved of its responsibility to complete the I-9 simply by attaching copies of documents. Copying the documents only of employees of certain nationalities or citizenship may be an Unfair Immigration Related Employment Practice. *Id.*

3.d. *Good Faith Defense/Reasonableness*—The employer is not liable for technical or procedural failure to meet the verification requirements if it acted in good faith. INA §274A(b)(6)(A), 8 U.S.C. §1324a(b)(6)(A). *U.S. v. Anthony Borrelli and Sons, Inc.*, 8 OCAHO no. 1027 (1999) [denying motion to strike good faith affirmative defense as premature and disfavored]. The employer does not attest to the legitimacy of the document(s) (or the person) but rather that s/he has reviewed the original document and "it reasonably *appears* to him or her, upon reasonable inspection of its features and the information it contains, to be genuine and to relate to the employee...." Employer Information Bulletin 103, Office of Business Liaison, DHS, I-9 Document Review (Sept. 25, 2003), *reprinted in* 80 No. 43 *Interpreter Releases* 1554, 1562–63 (Nov. 10, 2003). However, an employer is liable where it failed to correct Form I-9 after notice. INA §274A(b)(6)(B). *See also U.S. v. Big Bear Market*, 1 OCAHO no. 48 (Mar. 30, 1989), *aff'd*, *Big Bear Market 3 v. INS*, 913 F.2d 754 (9th Cir. 1990) [statute imposes a continuing duty on company to prepare and make I-9 forms available]. The good faith defense is also inapplicable to an employer who engaged in pattern and practice of violations. INA §274A(b)(6)(C).

3.e. *Employer Cannot Require Specific Documents*—Employer cannot require or specify which documents an individual is to present. 8 C.F.R. §§274a.2(b)(1)(v), 1274a.2(b)(1)(v). To do so violates the Unfair Immigration Employment Practices if there is discriminatory intent. INA §274B(a)(6), 8 U.S.C. §1324b(a)(6); IIRIRA §421; *Robison Fruit Ranch, Inc. v. U.S.*, 147 F.3d 798 (9th Cir. 1998).

3.f. *Documents Evidencing Employment & Identity*—INA §274A(b)(1)(B), 8 U.S.C. §1324a(b)(1)(B), 8 C.F.R. §§274a.2(b)(1)(v)(A), 1274a.2(b)(1)(v)(A). Documents evidencing employment and identity (List A) were reduced by regulation, 72 Fed. Reg. 65974–80 (Nov. 26, 2007):

- U.S. passport (unexpired or expired);
- Resident alien ("green") card, alien registration card (I-551);
- A unexpired foreign passport with I-551 stamp;
- An unexpired EAD with photo;
- An unexpired foreign passport with an unexpired I-94 bearing the same name as the passport and containing an NIV endorsement if it authorizes the holder to work; or
- Other document designated by the AG if: (a) it contains a photo and other personal identification as AG finds sufficient; (b) is evidence of employment authorization; and (c) contains security features.

3.g. *Documents Evidencing Employment Authorization*—INA §274A(b)(1)(C), 8 U.S.C. §1324a(b)(1)(C), 8 C.F.R. §§274a.2(b)(1)(v)(C), 1274a.2(b)(1)(v)(C)

- Social Security card (not including cards "not authorized for employment" or "valid for work only with USCIS authorization" unless, in the latter case, the employee has USCIS authorization);
- Certification of Birth Abroad issued by DOS
- Original or certified copy of a birth certificate issued by a state, county, municipal authority or outlying possession of the U.S. bearing an official seal
- A Native American tribal document
- U.S. Citizen ID Card (I-197)
- ID Card for us of Resident Citizen of the U.S. (I-179)
- An unexpired EAD issued by DHS; or
- Other documentation evidencing authorization of employment in the U.S. which the AG finds acceptable.

Note:

(1) DHS may by notice, extend expired EADs until a new one may be obtained. For example, an employer may rely on an expired EAD for a TPS beneficiary as authorized by DHS. 67 Fed. Reg. 22451 (May 6, 2002) [permitting employer to rely on expired EAD of Honduran or Nicaraguan in TPS program and cautioning not to request additional documents or proof of nationality]. DHS issued an Interim Final Rule permitting certain F-1 students an opportunity to automatically extend OPT if they are the beneficiary of an H-1B petition and timely filed a C/S so that there is no "gap" between the time their OPT would have expired and the Oct. 1 start-up date for the H-1B. 73 Fed. Reg. 18944 (Apr. 8, 2008), 8 C.F.R. §§214.2(f)(5)(vi)(A), 214.2(f)(10)(C)(2). *See also* **Appendix M**, *infra*.

(2) Persons granted asylum or refugee status, like LPRs, are authorized to work incident to their status, need not apply for employment authorization, and therefore need not present an EAD. However, they must still present documents sufficient to meet the identity and

employment criteria (*e.g.,* driver's license and Social Security card). Letter, Friedman, Special Policy Counsel, Civil Rights Division, DOJ (Oct. 18, 2002), *reprinted in* 79 No. 43 *Interpreter Releases* 1640–41, 1653–54 (Nov. 4, 2002)

3.h. *Documents Establishing Identity*—INA §274A(b)(1)(D), 8 U.S.C. §1324a(b)(1)(D), 8 C.F.R. §§274a.2(b)(1)(v)(B), 1274a.2(b)(1)(v)(B):

- Drivers license or similar document issued for the purpose of identification by a state. If document does not contain a photo it must have identifying information; DHS has now promulgated final regulations to standardize driver's licenses. 6 C.F.R. §37; 73 Fed. Reg. 5272–5340 (Jan. 29, 2008).
- ID card issued by federal, state or local government agencies or entities, provided it contains a photograph or information such as name, date of birth, gender, height, eye color, and address
- School ID card with a photograph
- Voter's registration card
- U.S. Military card or draft record
- Military dependent's ID card
- U.S. Coast Guard Merchant Mariner Card
- Native American tribal document
- Driver's license issued by a Canadian government authority

3.i. For persons under 16, AG will accept as ID document:

- School record or report card;
- Clinic, doctor or hospital record;
- Daycare or nursery school record.

Parent of minor is authorized to sign I-9. 8 C.F.R. §§274a.2(b)(1)(v)(B)(3)(i), 1274a.2(b)(1)(v)(B)(3)(i). Provisions also apply to handicapped persons. 8 C.F.R. §§274a.2(b)(1)(v)(B)(4), 1274a.2(b)(1)(v)(B)(4).

3.j. *Collective Bargaining Units*—An employer who is a member of a collective bargaining association where another employer has verified the employee, need not also verify the employee within 3 years or the time the employee authorized to work, whichever is less. INA §274A(a)(6), 8 U.S.C. §1324a(a)(6).

4. *Employee Attestation*—Employee must also attest either by a hand-written or electronic signature that s/he is a USC, LPR or authorized to work on Form I-9. INA §274A(b)(2), 8 U.S.C. §1324a(b)(2). Employee must complete the attestation on date of hire, but has three days to provide documentation of the right to work, unless employment is for less than three days. 8 C.F.R. §274a.2(b)(1)((i)(A).

5. *Retention of I-9 Forms*

5.a. I-9s must be retained throughout the period of employment. After employee's termination, I-9 must be retained for either 3 years after the date of hire or 1 year after the date of termination, whichever is later. INA §274A(b)(3)(B), 8 U.S.C. §1324a(b)(3)(B)

5.b. Recruiters/Referrers must retain I-9s for 3 years after referral date. INA §274A(b)(3)(A), 8 U.S.C. §1324a(b)(3)(A)

5.c. ICE and DOL must provide at least 3 days' notice prior to inspection of I-9s. 8 C.F.R. §§274a.2(b)(2)(ii), 1274a.2(b)(2)(ii). No subpoena or warrant is required. Employer must make I-9 available and can provide I-9s on microfilm or microfiche. 8 C.F.R. §§274a.2(b)(2)(ii)–(iii), 1274a.2(b)(2)(ii)–(iii).

C. *Reverification of I-9 Forms*

1. *Generally*—If an employee's work authorization expires or DHS informs employer that authorization is not sufficient, the employer must re-verify the I-9 or terminate employee. 8 C.F.R. §§274a.2(b)(1)(vii), 1274a.2(b)(1)(vii); *U.S. v. C&D Plastics, Inc.*, 1 OCAHO no. 240 (Sept. 24,

1990); *U.S. v. Buckingham Limited Partnership*, 1 OCAHO no. 151 (Apr. 6, 1990). While it is not necessary to re-verify an LPR's status upon expiration of I-551, employer must re-verify a temporary I-551 placed in a passport. Letter, Aleinikoff, General Counsel, INS (Aug. 2, 1994), *reprinted in* 71 No. 33 *Interpreter Releases* 1152 (Aug. 29, 1994). Employer can re-verify directly on existing I-9 by noting document's ID number and expiration dates in section 3 or it may complete a new I-9.

2. *Continuing in Employment*—The employer will not be deemed to have "hired" an individual, and therefore need not reverify an employee's eligibility if s/he is "continuing in employment" and has a reasonable expectation of employment at all times. 8 C.F.R. §§274a.2(b)(1)(viii), 1274a.2(b)(1)(viii). "Continuing employment" under 8 C.F.R. §§274a.2(b)(1)(viii)(A), 1274a.2(b)(1)(viii)(A) includes, but is not limited to:

   2.a. Leave related to normal employment relationship such as illness, vacation, maternity/paternity leave, union business or other temporary leave approved by employer;

   2.b. Promotion/demotion, layoff, or strike;

   2.c. Reinstatement after wrongful discharge;

   2.d. Transfer from one distinct unit of employer to another unit of employer;

   2.e. Employee continues employment for related, merged, successor or reorganized employer or same employer at different location;

   2.f. Employee's work in same bargaining unit for another employer in multi-employer association;

   2.g. An individual is engaged in seasonal employment; or

   2.h. Employee in A-3, E-1/E-2, G-5, H-1, H-2, H-3, I, J-1, L-1, O-1/O-2, P-1/P-2/P-3, R, or TN status who timely files for extension of stay obtains 240 days from application date. 8 C.F.R. §§274a.12(b)(20), 1274a.12(b)(20).

3. *Reasonable Expectation of Employment*—The employer claiming continuing employment must also establish that the individual expected to continue in employment and that such expectation is reasonable. 8 C.F.R. §§274a.2(b)(1)(viii)(B), 1274a.2(b)(1)(viii)(B). Factors include:

   3.a. Prior employment on a regular and substantial basis;

   3.b. Employee's compliance with employer's established and published policy regarding absence;

   3.c. Employer's past history of recalling employees;

   3.d. Former position not taken permanently by another employee;

   3.e. Employee did not obtain benefits from employer inconsistent with expectation of returning to work (*e.g.*, retirement benefits);

   3.f. Employer's financial condition permits resumption of employment; and

   3.g. Oral and written communication between employer and person indicating return.

4. *Rehiring*—Where person is rehired and is still eligible to work, the employer may simply update the I-9, by providing the new date of hire in section 3 of the I-9, if rehire is within 3 years of the date of initial execution of the I-9. 8 C.F.R. §§274a.2(c)(1)(i), 1274a.2(c)(1)(i).

D. *Employer Violations*—An employer violates the Act where:

1. It employs an alien knowing that s/he is not authorized to be employed under the INA or by the AG. INA §§274A(a)(1)(A) and (h)(3), 8 U.S.C. §§1324a(a)(1)(A) and (h)(3).

2. It continues to employ an alien knowing the alien has become unauthorized. Where employer is informed that employee is or may be unauthorized to work by INS, it is on constructive notice and must inquire further. Whether employer receives information orally or in writing from the government is not relevant. *Mester Mfg. Co. v. INS*, 879 F.2d 561, 566–67 (9th Cir. 1989).

   2.a. *Time Frame for Firing*—There is no set time limit for firing unauthorized alien after learning of his/her status, but it has been found that failure to fire within 2 weeks was sufficient for sanctions. *Mester*, 879 F.2d at 567. To determine whether employer fired employee within a reasonable time, courts may look to certain factors, including:

(1) The number of days that the employee continued to work after notice;

(2) The certainty of information that the employee is illegal;

(3) The steps taken by employer to confirm employee's illegality.

Mester, 879 F.2d at 568 n.9.

2.b. *"Knowing" Requirement*—The regulations adopt a broad definition of "knowing" which includes "constructive" knowledge—"not only actual knowledge, but also knowledge which may fairly be inferred through notice of certain facts and circumstances which would lead a person, through the exercise of reasonable care, to know about a certain condition." 8 C.F.R. §§274a.1(*l*)(1), 1274a.1(*l*)(1). *See also Mester Mfg. Co. v. INS,* 879 F.2d 561, 566–67 (9th Cir. 1989) [INS demonstrated that Meister had knowledge where he failed to take corrective action after he received "specific information that several of his employees were likely to be unauthorized"]; *U.S. v. New El Rey Sausage Co.*, 1 OCAHO no. 66 (July 7, 1989), *aff'd*, 925 F.2d 1153 (9th Cir. 1991) ["knowing" includes an employer in possession of information that would lead a person exercising reasonable care to acquire knowledge of the fact in question...or to infer, on the basis of reliable INS warnings, that officially questioned employees are not authorized to work]. The "should have known" standard also applied to establish liability where the employer failed to reverify the employee's status. *U.S. v. Buckingham Limited Partnership,* 1 OCAHO no. 151 (Apr. 6, 1990). Notwithstanding the broad regulations, liability under a "knowing" standard normally requires *mens rea*. One court found that the ALJ's interpretation of the knowing language was too broad and that constructive knowledge cannot arise where a person is hired (but does not start work) without review of the documents or because the employer did not verify the back of the person's Social Security card. *Collins Food International, Inc. v. INS*, 948 F.2d 549 (9th Cir. 1991) [rejecting broad interpretation of knowledge as contrary to statute, EEOC guidelines, regulations and legislative history]; *U.S. v. American Terrazzo*, 6 OCAHO no. 828 (Dec. 13, 1995) [questioning constructive knowledge doctrine].

2.c. *Constructive Knowledge*— Constructive knowledge can be ascertained from the "totality of relevant circumstances." 8 C.F.R. §274a.1(*l*)(1); 72 Fed. Reg. 45611, 45615–16 [quoting Black's Law Dictionary and citing to several Supreme Court cases regarding constructive knowledge]. *But see Collins Food Int'l v. INS,* 948 F.2d 549 (9th Cir. 1991). The regulations specify the following circumstances where an employer may be viewed as having constructive knowledge that his employee is not authorized to be employed because he: (1) fails to complete or improperly completes the I-9: *but see U.S. v. Walden Station, Inc. d/b/a Walden Grille,* 8 OCAHO no. 1053 (2000) [an incorrect or incomplete I-9 by itself is not sufficient to establish respondent's knowledge of unauthorized employment]; (2) acts with reckless and wanton disregard for the legal consequences of permitting another individual to introduce an unauthorized person into the work force or to act on his behalf; (3) fails to take "reasonable steps after receiving information" that the employee may not be employment authorized such as: (a) an employee's request that the employer file a labor certification or employment-based visa; *but see U.S. v. Jonel, Inc.* 7 OCAHO no. 967 (1997); *U.S. v. Valenca Bar and Liquors, Inc.* 7 OCAHO no. 995 (1998); 72 Fed. Reg. 45611, 45618 ["not all situations involving such a request will be evidence of constructive knowledge—for example, employers may have work-authorized employees who are seeking permanent residency"] (b) a no-match letter from the Social Security Administration; or (c) written notice from DHS that the employment authorization/status document presented for the I-9 is assigned to another person or that DHS has no agency record that the document has been assigned to any person. 8 C.F.R §274a.1(*l*)(1)(i)–(iii).

(1) *No-Match Social Security Numbers*

(a) Pre-Regulatory Position of DHS/INS. Prior to the current regulations, 72 Fed. Reg. 45611–24 (Aug. 15, 2007), DHS and legacy INS maintained that a no-match letter from SSA stating that the Social Security number did not match the person using it, did not, standing alone, provide notice to the employer that his employee is working without authorization. Letter, Virtue, General Counsel, INS HQCOU 90/10.15-C (Apr. 12, 1999), *reported in* 20 *AILA Monthly Mailing* 357 (July/Aug. 2001), *published on* AILA InfoNet Doc. No. 01061431 (June 14, 2001). *See also* Memo, Martin, Gen. Counsel INS (Dec. 23, 1997), *reprinted in* 75 No. 6 *Interpreter Releases* 203 (Feb. 9, 1998). However, it held the view that subsequent action (or inaction) by the employer after receiving the letter, as well as the letter itself, would be considered in determining whether under the "totality of circumstances" the employer had "constructive knowledge" that the employee was working without authorization. Memo, Virtue, Gen. Counsel INS (Apr. 12, 1999), *supra*.

(b) Post–August 15, 2007, Regulations. On August 15, 2007 DHS issued final regulations that included the no-match provision referenced *supra.* The regulations provide that receipt by the *employer* (not the employee) of the no-match letter or notice from DHS triggers constructive knowledge, 72 Fed. Reg. 45611, 45617. The regulation contained a "safe-harbor" provision, *see infra,* but did not immunize the employer who followed the "safe-harbor" provisions where the employer had actual knowledge or there was evidence of other constructive knowledge. 72 Fed. Reg. 45611 45614, 45616. However, a preliminary injunction was issued against the enforcement of the regulation in *American Federation of Labor v. Chertoff,* No. C 07-04472 CRB (N.D. Cal. Oct. 10, 2007), 2007 WL 2972952 [plaintiffs have raised serious questions as to the validity of the regulation because the DHS changed its position without a rational explanation, it invaded the province of the Special Counsel's office of DOJ in enforcing the Unfair Immigration Employment Practices, and it violated the Regulatory Flexibility Act]. DHS responded to the court order by issuing a proposed rule that sought to address the court's three objections. 73 Fed. Reg. 15944–55 (Mar. 26, 2008]. As of the date of publication, the final outcome of the regulation remains unresolved.

(2) Safe-Harbor Provision—DHS established a "safe-harbor" provision for employers who receive a no-match letter from SSA or notice from DHS.

(a) After Non-Match Letter—If an employer receives a no-match letter, the letter will not be used as evidence of constructive knowledge if the employer takes the following steps: (i) checks its records to determine whether the discrepancy results from a typographical, transcription, or similar clerical error, corrects the error, verifies the correction with SSA to ensure a "match", and updates or creates a new I-9 form within 30 days (but the employer should not perform a new verification), 8 C.F.R. §274a.1(*l*)(2)(i)(A); or (ii) determines that the error is not due to its own records, requests that the employee confirm the name and SS account number, and if the employee provides correct information, the employer must verify with SSA, update or create a new I-9 (but do not initiate a new verification); if the employee states the information he provided is correct, he is given 90 days to correct the discrepancy with SSA but if he is unable to correct it the employer only has three (3) additional days thereafter to complete a new verification process *without reliance* on the documents creating the mismatch or a receipt for a replacement for such document. 8 C.F.R. §§274a.1(*l*)(2)(i)(B)–(C), (iii)(A)(2). The employee must present a document that contains a photograph to establish identity or identity and employment. §274a.1(*l*)(2)(iii)(A)(3). The "new" I-9 that is generated will be retained for the same period as the original I-9. 72 Fed. Reg. 45611, 45619 (Aug. 15, 2007).

(b) After DHS Notice—If DHS provides notice that the I-9 is improper, the notice will not be used to establish constructive notice against the employer if the employer takes the following steps: (i) contacts DHS to resolve the discrepancy within 30 days and (ii) if unable to do so the employer has 90 days from the original notification to resolve the matter and within an additional three days (after the 90 days) must verify the employee's status in the same manner as the no-match verification. 8 C.F.R. §§274a.1(*l*)(2)(ii)(A)–(B).

(c) Safe-Harbor is Not a Complete Defense—The comments to DHS's regulations provide that the safe-harbor provisions are not defenses to employer sanction violations where there is other evidence that the employer had actual knowledge or constructive knowledge. 72 Fed. Reg. 45611 45614["The regulation would not preclude DHS from finding that the employer had *actual* knowledge that an employee was an unauthorized alien…Further, DHS may find that the employer had constructive notice from other sources."] at 45616 ["If, in the totality of the circumstances, other independent evidence exists to prove the employer has constructive knowledge, the employer may still face liability."]. However, DHS also acknowledged that finding constructive knowledge from the totality of the circumstances "could be unusual…in the situation where an employer carefully follows the safe-harbor procedures provided in this regulation and has no information suggesting that the employee is using another person's identity." at 45616. Moreover, the safe-harbor provisions do not apply to information that the employer may receive through other DHS programs such as EEV (Electronic Verification), IMAGE (ICE Mutual Agreement between Government and Employers) and SAVE (Systematic Alien Verification for Entitlements) or where SSA provides SSN verification through other methods. But "[a]ll of these good faith efforts militate against…sanctions" and DHS "may exercise its prosecutorial discretion favorably for employers who take [these] other affirmative steps." 45617-18

(d) Employee's Status During the Safe-Harbor Procedure. Does the employer have to fire the employee as soon as there is a no-match letter or a notice from DHS. The answer is a qualified no according to DHS. "If the employer does not obtain actual knowledge during the safe-harbor process, and instead merely has information that could lead to a finding of constructive knowledge from the no-match letter, the employer may continue to employ the individual until all of the steps in the safe-harbor procedure are completed. This, of course …does not speak to what actions an employer could or should take under its own internal personnel policies…" 72 Fed. Reg. 45611, 45617 (Aug. 15, 2007).

(3) Foreign Appearance or Accent. Constructive knowledge cannot be inferred from an employee's foreign appearance or accent. 8 C.F.R. §§274a.1(*l*)(3).

(4) Authorization to Work Incident to Status. An employer cannot be charged with knowingly continuing to hire a person unauthorized to work where the person is authorized to work incident to status but fails to obtain or present an EAD. Memo, Carpenter, Chief Employer Sanctions, G.C. INS, HQCOU 90/10.15-C (Nov. 10, 1998), *reprinted in* 76 No. 16 *Interpreter Releases* 632, 659–60 (Apr. 26, 1999).

3. *Employer Fails to Comply with Verification System*—INA §274A(a)(1)(B), 8 U.S.C. §1324a(a)(1)(B). Persons who refer or recruit others for a fee, except in agricultural employment, are not obligated to comply with the verification requirements. INA §274A(a)(1)(B)(i), 8 U.S.C. §1324a(a)(1)(B)(i).

4. *False Statements on Form I-9*—False attestations on Form I-9 is a separate criminal offense, 18 U.S.C. §1546(b), and is also an offense under 18 U.S.C. §1001, regarding material misrepresentations to federal officers. It may also result in inadmissibility or deportability because of a false claim to U.S. citizenship. *Rodriguez v. Mukasey,* 519 F.3d 773, 776–78 (8th Cir. 2008) [A noncitizen who marks the "citizen or national of the United States" box on Form I-9 for the purpose of falsely representing himself as a citizen (as distinguished from a national) to secure private employment is inadmissible under §1182(a)(6)(C)((ii)(I)]; *Kechkar v. Gonzales,* 500 F.3d 1080 (10th Cir. 2007) [where the respondent checked off the box on the I-9 that stated he was a "citizen *or* national" the court upheld the BIA's determination that he falsely claimed citizenship and that doing so for private employment is not a defense because it was done for the purpose of evading the employer sanctions statute]; *Ateka v. Ashcroft,* 384 F.3d 954, 956–57 (8th Cir. 2004) [upheld on substantial evidence grounds IJ finding of ineligibility for AOS but declined to rule, due to failure to exhaust administrative remedies, on whether a false statement on an I-9 in private employment is a bar to residency]; *Njai v. U.S.,* 484 F.Supp.2d 1040, 1048 & n.11 (D. Ariz. 2007) [person pled to 18 U.S.C. §911 and then IJ asserted removability for signing I-9]. *But see U.S. v. Karaouni,* 379 F.3d 1139 (9th Cir. 2004) [where defendant checked off I-9 box that stated he was a citizen *or* national of the U.S., he could not be convicted under §911 that makes it a crime only to make a false claim to citizenship]. However, it is not a statutory bar to good moral character

under INA §101(f)(6) because that section only applies to oral statements. *Beltran-Resendez v. INS,* 207 F.3d 284 (5th Cir. 2000).

E. *Compliance Programs*

1. *E-Verify (Electronic Verification) Program*—The EEV, E-Verify or Electronic Verification system originated in 1996 as the "Basic Pilot" system. It is a program in which employment eligibility of all newly hired employees will be confirmed electronically by access to SSA's and DHS's databases. DHS and SSA have established an MOU to be signed by those agencies and the employer setting forth mutual obligations. MOU Between SSA, DHS, and Employers Regarding Employer Participation in E-Verify (July 18, 2007), *published on* AILA InfoNet at Doc. No. 07122862. An MOU has also been created for other government agencies (*e.g.,* State Workforce Agencies who need to now verify employment eligibility for H-2A & H-2B workers) with DHS/SSA, *published on* AILA InfoNet at Doc. No. 08040763 *and* Doc. No. 08040764. *See also* TEGL No. 11-07, Change 1 (Nov. 14, 2007), *published on* AILA InfoNet at Doc. No. 07111560; Memo, Jacob, Solicitor of Labor, DOL (Mar. 14, 2008), *published on* AILA InfoNet at Doc. No. 08040762; Round 1, H-2As TEGL 11-07, Change 1, DOL FAQs (Feb. 5, 2008), *reprinted in* 85 No. 7 *Interpreter Releases* 417, 465–75 (Feb. 11, 2008). SWAs are not only required to E-Verify, they are also required to maintain I-9s for persons if they are referring those workers to a job, Round 1 at Qs 4–18, *supra.* They are also required to complete I-9s for persons who seek employment in person at their offices. TEGL 11-07, Change 1, Questions from SWA Training Webinars—Round 3, *posted on* AILA InfoNet at Doc. No. 08050163 E-Verify has also begun testing a photo screening tool enhancement that allows an employer to check a DHS-issued document being presented to it against a document in the E-Verify database. Fact Sheet, E-Verify (Sept. 25, 2007), *reprinted in* 84 No.38 *Interpreter Releases* 2241, 2254, 2292 (Oct. 1, 2007). The E-Verify program began as a pilot program between INS and SSA. *See* 76 No. 45 *Interpreter Releases* 1693, 1698–1705 (Nov. 22, 1999); Basic Pilot Program Extension and Expansion Act of 2003, PL 108-156, 117 Stat. 1944 (Dec. 3, 2003) [expanded the programs to all states by Dec. 1, 2004]. For government information regarding E-Verify call 1-888 464-4218.

   1.a. Verification under E-Verify System. The system verification process differs slightly for persons who claim to be U.S. citizens and persons who claim to be foreign nationals. For persons claiming to be U.S. citizens, approximately 96% of inquires result in an immediate authorized finding and only 4% are tentative nonconfirmations. For foreign nationals, only 68% result in immediate authorization finding. Approximately 15% are tentative nonconfirmations; 17% result in further analysis by a status verifier that takes approximately 24 hours. Workers issued a tentative nonconfirmation may contest the finding, and, if they do not contest it they will be issued an immediate final nonconfirmation. For foreign nationals, E-Verify compares data entered from Form I-9 to the SSA database. If the data matches, E-Verify then compares the data to USCIS's databases. TEGL 11-07, Change 1, Questions from SWA Training Webinars—Round 3 ¶12-15, *published on* AILA InfoNet at Doc. No. 08050163

2. *IMAGE*—ICE has initiated a program ICE Mutual Agreement between Government and Employers ("IMAGE") designed to "assist employers in building legal workforces" and "to build cooperative relationships between government and industry to reduce the unlawful employment of illegal aliens through strengthened employment practices and enhanced training of employees." As part of the program ICE "will provide education and training on proper hiring procedures, fraudulent document detention, use of the E-Verify employment eligibility verification program and anti-discrimination safe-guards." *www.ice.gov/image.* Worksite Enforcement Advisory (Feb. 2008), *published on* AILA InfoNet at Doc. No. 08020770.

3. *SAVE (Systematic Alien Verification for Entitlements)*—The SAVE program is a database that has been in existence for many years, although it is plagued by many errors. The system is generally used to verify eligibility for benefits, but DHS specifically discusses the SAVE program in its "No-Match regulations" as an appropriate source of information that an employer may rely on in seeking information regarding the immigration status of its employees. 72 Fed. Reg. 45611, 45616–18 (Aug. 15, 2007). The use of SAVE, however, to verify workers may constitute discrimination and document abuse on the basis of citizenship, because it only provides information on noncitizens. TEGL 11-07, Change 1, Questions From SWA Training Webinars—Round 3 ¶17, *published on* AILA InfoNet at Doc. No. 08050163.

II. INVESTIGATION OF EMPLOYER SANCTIONS CASES

A. *ICE Needs Leads and Articulable Facts*

1. *Generally*—To conduct an investigation, ICE must have a lead and articulable facts concerning employer violations. Articulable facts cannot be based solely on an employee's ancestry. *U.S. v. Brignoni-Ponce*, 422 U.S. 873 (1975). However, articulable facts may include race or alienage when coupled with other aspects, such as the employer's history of hiring undocumented workers and the ICE agent's observation of persons entering or leaving the place of business. *Matter of King & Yang*, 16 I&N Dec. 502 (BIA 1978). Articulable facts forming the basis of a reasonable suspicion are "measured against an objective reasonable man standard, not by the subjective impressions of a particular officer," *Nicacio v. INS*, 797 F.2d 700 (9th Cir. 1985), and may be based on an anonymous tip. *U.S. v. Widow Brown's Inn*, 3 OCAHO no. 399 (Jan. 15, 1992).

2. The Employer Sanctions Field Manual identifies articulable facts as including:

   2.a. Officer's knowledge of high concentration of illegal aliens in the area;

   2.b. The industry or type of employment involved;

   2.c. Employee's excessive nervousness or studied nonchalance around INS officials;

   2.d. Inability to speak English.

B. *Random Audits*—ICE conducts I-9 compliance audits through the use of statistical methods that are supposed to ensure random selection of employers. This program is called the General Inspection Program. Revised Immigration Officer's Field Manual for Employer Sanctions, INS Pub. No. M-278 (Nov. 1987) (INS Field Manual) at Sec. IV-B. The program also provides a subset of randomly selected employers within industries known to employ undocumented workers. This program is called the Special Emphasis Inspections Program. INS Field Manual, *supra*, at Sec. IV-B-1-c. *See also* MOU, DOL-INS on Labor Standards and Employer Sanctions, *reported in* 75 No. 47 *Interpreter Releases* 1696 (Dec. 14, 1998) and Memo, McNary, Commissioner INS (Jan. 2, 1992), *reprinted in* 69 No. 8 *Interpreter Releases* 253 (Mar. 2, 1992). Under policy guidelines, ICE has accelerated its enforcement strategy and will focus on lead driven investigations instead of random audits. ICE will no longer maintain an educational visit or contact as a prerequisite for instituting a fine proceeding. Memo, McNary, Comm., CO-274A-P (Apr. 5, 1991), *reprinted in* 68 No. 14 *Interpreter Releases* 429, 445, 446, 449 (Apr. 15, 1991).

III. NOTICE OF INSPECTION (NOI)

A. *Generally*—ICE, DOL, and Office of Special Counsel can inspect I-9s. ICE and DOL have entered into a memorandum of understanding regarding their joint roles. MOU, Meissner, Comm. INS and Anderson, Asst. Sec. ESA (Nov. 23, 1998), *reprinted in* 75 No. 47 *Interpreter Releases* 1696, 1711–21 (Dec. 14, 1998). By regulation, ICE must provide at least three days notice to the employer prior to inspection. 8 C.F.R. §§274a.2(b)(2)(ii), 1274a.2(b)(2)(ii). Inspection is usually initiated by a Notice of Inspection (NOI) delivered personally or by certified return receipt mail. Failure to properly notify an employer may not implicate the due process clause because, unlike the Notice of Intent to Fine, the NOI does not lead to the employer's final deprivation of property. *Maka v. INS*, 904 F.2d 1351, 1357 (9th Cir. 1990) *amended* 932 F.2d 1352 (9th Cir. 1991). DHS regulations provide that no subpoena or warrant is required for an inspection and that "any refusal or delay in presentation of the Form I-9 for inspection is a violation of the retention requirements as set forth in §274A(b)(3) of the Act." 8 C.F.R. §§274a.2(b)(2)(ii), 1274a.2(b)(2)(ii). There is serious doubt as to the constitutionality of penalizing the employer when ICE does not obtain a warrant or subpoena that may be judicially challenged. *McLaughlin v. Kings Island*, 849 F.2d 990 (6th Cir. 1988); *Brock v. Emerson Elec. Co.*, 834 F.2d 994 (11th Cir. 1987). *But see McLaughlin v. A.B. Chance Co.*, 842 F.2d 724 (4th Cir. 1988). If a person or entity does not comply with the request for I-9s, the officer may compel production by issuing a subpoena. 8 C.F.R. §§274a.2(b)(2)(ii), 1274a.2(b)(2)(ii).

B. *Administrative Subpoenas and Enforcement*—If ICE seeks an administrative subpoena, it may do so pursuant to INA §274A(e)(2)(C), 8 U.S.C. §1324a(e)(2)(C). This subpoena may only be issued by ICE officers designated by the ICE Commissioner and only prior to filing a complaint. The subpoena can compel attendance and production of documents. *See U.S. v. DeBooth*, 915 F.2d 697 (11th Cir.

1990). ICE may issue a subpoena providing for less than 3 days notice. Memo, Virtue, G.C. HQCOU 90/15-P (Dec. 21, 1998), *reprinted in* 76 No. 16 *Interpreter Releases* 632, 661–64 (Apr. 26, 1999). If an administrative subpoena is issued, the employer has the right to challenge its reasonableness in district court before compliance. *Donovan v. Lone Steer, Inc.*, 464 U.S. 408 (1984). U.S. district courts, however, may be without authority to quash subpoenas issued by ICE where the agency does not seek the subpoena's enforcement in federal court. *Matter of Subpoena of Gilbert Ramirez*, 905 F.2d 97 (5th Cir. 1990). In *U.S. v. Moore*, ___ F.Supp. ___, Case No. 89A (E.D. Va. Mar. 10, 1989), *reprinted in* 8 *AILA Monthly Mailing* 411 (July 1989), the court upheld INS subpoena authority under INA §235(a), subject to Fifth Amendment protection against self-incrimination which applies to persons including sole-proprietorships and documents that unlike I-9s, are not required to be maintained by law. Corporations do not enjoy the same protection. *But see U.S. v. Minker*, 350 U.S. 179 (1956) [limiting subpoena power].

C. *Civil Search Warrants*—Under *See v. City of Seattle*, 387 U.S. 541 (1967) and *Marshall v. Barlow's Inc.*, 436 U.S. 307 (1978), ICE may not make a warrantless inspection of business premises. The only exception to the warrant requirement arises where there is a "pervasively regulated industry" and where "the privacy interests of the owner are weakened and the government interests in regulating particular businesses are concomitantly heightened." *New York v. Burger*, 482 U.S. 691, 702 (1987). Under *Camara v. Municipal Court of City and County of San Francisco*, 387 U.S. 523 (1967), however, a less than probable cause standard may be sufficient to issue a warrant where area-wide inspections of buildings are initiated to determine owner compliance. *See also Blackie's House of Beef, Inc. v. Castillo*, 659 F.2d 1211 (D.C. Cir. 1981). In *Camara*, the court determined in an OSHA search, that an employer's Fourth Amendment right would be protected and that probable cause for a warrant was sufficiently established where the search was conducted on the basis of a general administrative plan which was derived from neutral sources. In challenging a warrant based on a *Camara* inspection, the court applies a two-part test: (1) whether the plan pursuant to which the warrant was issued was based on specific, neutral criteria; and (2) whether the warrant application clearly and adequately established that the particular company was selected pursuant to an application of the plan's neutral criteria. *Matter of Trinity Industries*, 876 F.2d 1485 (11th Cir. 1989). Some courts, however, have distinguished between warrants of inspection to search and warrants to seize, finding that the less than probable cause standard does not apply to open-ended seizure warrants. *International Molders and Allied Workers Local 164 v. Nelson*, 799 F.2d 547 (9th Cir. 1986); *Gallegos v. Haggerty*, 689 F.Supp. 93 (N.D.N.Y. 1988).

D. *Warrantless Searches*—Without a warrant, ICE officers have no right to enter premises and speak with employees. ICE officers' conduct is governed by Fourth Amendment standards. *U.S. v. Widow Brown's Inn*, 3 OCAHO no. 399 (Jan. 15, 1992).

IV. NOTICE OF INTENT TO FINE (NIF)

After investigation, ICE may issue a warning notice, 8 C.F.R. §§274a.9(c), 1274a.9(c) or a Notice of Intent to Fine. The NIF contains the basis for the notice, a designation of the charges against the employer, the statutory provisions alleged to have been violated, and the penalty imposed. 8 C.F.R. §§274a.9(d)(1), 1274a.9(d)(1). Although the NIF should be personally served pursuant to 8 C.F.R. §103.5a(a)(3), one ALJ has held that personal service is not required by statute or regulation. *U.S. v. Big Bear Market*, Case No. 88-100038 (OCAHO Apr. 12, 1989). To preserve its right to a hearing before an ALJ, the employer must file a written request for a hearing within 30 days of receiving the NIF or 35 days if it received the NIF by ordinary mail. 8 C.F.R. §§274a.9(e), 1274a.9(e). The response must be received by ICE within the appropriate period. *Id.*; *KPMG Peat Marwick of Puerto Rico v. INS*, 943 F.2d 91 (1st Cir. 1991) [petition dismissed for lack of jurisdiction where INS did not *receive* request for a hearing within 30 days]. A response to each allegation in the NIF may be filed, but is not required. 8 C.F.R. §§274a.9(e), 1274a.9(e). If no request for a hearing is filed within the deadline, the NIF becomes a final, nonappealable order. No motion to reopen is permitted. 8 C.F.R. §§103.5(a)(1)(i), 274a.9(f), 1274a.9(f).

Under IIRIRA §411, codified at INA §274A(b)(6), with respect to investigations conducted after Sept. 30, 1996, ICE should defer issuance of an NIF until the employer is given notice of the technical or procedural I-9 violations and is provided at least 10 business days to cure the deficiencies. *See* INS Interim Guidelines, Section A.2, B.4 issued in March 1997 by the INS published in 74 No. 16 *Interpreter Releases* 706 (Apr. 28, 1997). In *U.S. v. WSC Plumbing,* 9 OCAHO no. 1071 (June 4, 2001), the

ALJ held that the Interim Guidelines have the force and effect of law, and that the remedy for ICE's failure to follow the Guidelines is to compel it to drop from its complaint charges regarded as procedural or technical verification failures pursuant to its own guidelines.

V. HEARING PROCEDURES—54 Fed. Reg. 48593 (Nov. 24, 1989); 56 Fed. Reg. 50049 (Oct. 3, 1991), 57 Fed. Reg. 57669–73 (Dec. 7, 1992), 64 Fed. Reg. 7066 (Feb. 12, 1999), 64 Fed. Reg. 49659 (Sept. 14, 1999), codified at 28 C.F.R. pt. 68.

A. *Initiation of Proceedings*

1. *Complaint & Answer*—A proceeding to enforce employer sanctions, unfair immigration employment practices and document fraud cases is heard before an ALJ and is governed by rules similar to those in federal court, 28 C.F.R. §68 *et seq.*, although the Federal Rules of Civil Procedure are used only as "general guidelines." 28 C.F.R. §68.1. Enforcement proceedings require the government to file a detailed and specific complaint. 28 C.F.R. §68.7(b). The employer is given 30 days after the service of the complaint to file an answer. No additional time is given for service by mail as the 30 day period runs from the time of actual receipt. 28 C.F.R. §§68.3(b), 68.8(c)(2), 68.9(a). The complaint may be served on counsel who responded to the NIF. 28 C.F.R. §§68.3(a)(3). Where counsel does not file answer and does not move to withdraw, but claims that he does not represent client, a default judgment may be entered. *U.S. v. Medina*, 3 OCAHO no. 485 (Feb. 5, 1993). A party may file affirmative defenses in addition to an answer. 28 C.F.R. §68.9(d). A party may also file a motion to dismiss, but the filing of a motion to dismiss does *not* stay the time period to answer. 28 C.F.R. §68.10. A document is deemed filed only when it is received. 28 C.F.R. §68.8(b).
2. *Dismissal of Counts*—The ALJ has authority to dismiss counts where the substance of the charge does not match the statutory violations cited in the NIF. *Mester Mfg. Co. v. INS*, *supra* [where employer failed to present I-9 the court dismissed certain counts based on INA §274A(b)(1) because the charge should have been brought under INA §274A(b)(3)].
3. *Default*—The ALJ also has authority to enter a default judgment if the party fails to timely answer. *Kirk v. INS*, 927 F.2d 1106 (9th Cir. 1991). In the view of at least one court, Fed. R. Civ. P. 60(b) cannot be used to vacate a default judgment. *Kirk*, 927 F.2d at 1108.
4. *Effect of Bankruptcy*—OCAHO takes the position that sanctions hearings fall under an exception to the automatic-stay provision in bankruptcy, 11 U.S.C. §362(a) [permitting the agency to enforce its regulatory/police authority], and therefore ICE may proceed to get a judgment, even if the employer has filed for bankruptcy. *U.S. v. United Pottery Manuf. & Accessories, Inc.*, 1 OCAHO no. 57 (May 19, 1989), *reprinted in* 8 *AILA Monthly Mailing* 413 (July/Aug. 1989).

B. *Discovery*

1. *Generally*—Broad discovery is permitted consistent with the Federal Rules, which allow discovery regarding any matter not privileged that is relevant to the subject matter involved in the proceeding. 28 C.F.R. §68.18(b). Discovery should include requests for various ICE worksheets (G-123, G-123A, G-166, G-166C), as well as statements (I-213) or affidavits (I-215) taken from the alien. As in the Federal Rules, a party may seek a protective order to prevent certain discovery. 28 C.F.R. §68.18(c). The ALJ is given broad discretion to determine the frequency and methods of discovery that may be used. 28 C.F.R. §68.18(a). The rules provide for interrogatories, 28 C.F.R. §68.19, requests for production, 28 C.F.R. §68.20, requests for admissions, 28 C.F.R. §68.21, and depositions, 28 C.F.R. §68.22. At least 10 days' written notice must be given before a deposition is taken if it is in the U.S., 20 days written notice if it is taken outside the continental U.S. 28 C.F.R. §68.22(b). A party may assert the Fifth Amendment in refusing to answer deposition questions. *U.S. v. Mark Carter*, 6 OCAHO no. 897 (Oct. 29, 1996). Parties disagreeing over discovery may also file motions to compel. 28 C.F.R. §68.23. The ALJ may impose sanctions such as drawing adverse inferences for failure to comply with discovery, 28 C.F.R. §68.23(c), but cannot impose monetary sanctions. *U.S. v. Nu Look Cleaners of Pembroke Pines, Inc.*, 1 OCAHO no. 274 (Dec. 5, 1990).
2. *Subpoenas*—ALJs are expressly authorized by INA §274A(e)(2)(B), 8 U.S.C. §1324a(e)(2)(B), and 28 C.F.R. §68.25, to issue subpoenas requiring the appearance of persons and the production

of evidence. If a party does not wish to comply with a subpoena, s/he must petition the ALJ to revoke or modify the subpoena within 10 days after service of the subpoena. 28 C.F.R. §68.25(e). The ALJ does not have contempt power, and failure to honor a subpoena can only be addressed by filing a contempt proceeding in federal court. 28 C.F.R. §68.25(d). The ALJ can impose other sanctions, such as drawing adverse inferences, when a party fails to comply with a subpoena. *U.S. v. Nu Look Cleaners of Pembroke Pines, Inc.*, 1 OCAHO no. 274 (Dec. 5, 1990). A party has standing to challenge a subpoena to a nonparty if the party can claim a personal right or privilege in the discovery sought. 28 C.F.R. §68.25(d).

3. *Motion for Summary Decision*—In an effort to avoid lengthy discovery, a party may file a motion for summary decision. 28 C.F.R. §68.38. The standards governing summary decisions are the same as those governing summary judgment under Fed. R. Civ. P. 56(c). *Getahun v. OCAHO*, 124 F.3d 591, 594 (3d Cir. 1997); *Alvarez v. Interstate Highway Construction*, 1 OCAHO no. 430 (1992). *See also U.S. v. Chen,* 9 OCAHO no. 1092 (2003) [ALJ applied collateral estoppel against employer where he had pled guilty to criminal violation of employer sanctions provisions]. A summary decision will not be granted where there are disputed issues of fact, *U.S. v. American Terrazzo*, 6 OCAHO no. 828 (Dec. 13, 1995), and where there are issues concerning the state of mind of a party regarding constructive knowledge. *Id.*

C. *The Hearing*

1. *Generally*—Parties at an administrative hearing have the right to be represented by counsel. 28 C.F.R. §68.33. A hearing will not normally be set without 30 days notice. 28 C.F.R. §68.5. Hearings in employer sanctions cases must be held at the nearest practical location to the place where the employer resides or where the alleged violation occurred. 28 C.F.R. §68.5(b). The ALJ or any party may request a prehearing conference. 28 C.F.R. §68.13. Parties may request a continuance based on prior judicial commitments, undue hardship or a showing of other good cause. 28 C.F.R. §68.27(a).

2. *Evidence*—The Federal Rules of Evidence are a general guide to all proceedings. 28 C.F.R. §68.40(a). The ALJ will admit all relevant material and reliable evidence, but may exclude material if its probative value is substantially outweighed by unfair prejudice or confusion of the issues, or by consideration of undue delay, waste of time, immateriality or needless presentation of cumulative evidence. 28 C.F.R. §68.40. Hearsay evidence is not automatically excluded if it is considered relevant, material and reliable. In *U.S. v. Cafe Camino Real, Inc.*, 1 OCAHO no. 224 (Aug. 28, 1990), the ALJ found INS forms and videotaped statements admissible under the APA, 5 U.S.C. §556(d) and Fed. R. Evid. 803(8), where the documents were mutually consistent and a person knowledgeable about the documents was available. *U.S. v. Jenkins*, 5 OCAHO no. 743 (Mar. 24, 1995), *aff'd*, *Jenkins v. U.S.*, 108 F.3d 195 (9th Cir. 1997) [I-213 is admissible].

3. *Record of Proceedings*—A verbatim written record of all hearings must be kept. 28 C.F.R. §68.48(a). Once the record is closed no additional evidence is accepted except upon a showing that new and material evidence has become available which was not readily available prior to the closing of the record. 28 C.F.R. §68.49(c).

4. *No Private Right of Action*—No private right of action to enforce a claim against a company for hiring undocumented aliens in violation of INA §274A, 8 U.S.C. §1324a. *Alampreses v. MNSH, Inc.*, 9 OCAHO no. 1094 (2003).

5. *Attorney Sanctions*—An ALJ cannot impose monetary sanctions under Fed. R. Civ. P. 11 or other sanctions against an attorney, because the regulations do not provide for such sanctions. *U.S. v. Nu Look Cleaners of Pembroke Pines, Inc.*, 1 OCAHO no. 274 (Dec. 5, 1990).

6. *Attorney Conflict*

   6.a. *In Testimony*—An attorney may testify on behalf of his client and continue to represent him at proceedings, where counsel's testimony is regarding an important issue and may be the only available testimony. *U.S. v. Scandia Interiors, Inc.*, 1 OCAHO no. 271 (Nov. 28, 1990) [attorney permitted to testify if s/he has other counsel present during testimony]. The decision to permit counsel to testify is with the sound discretion of the ALJ. *Id.*

   6.b. *In Representation*—The issue of conflict is particularly acute in employer sanction cases where counsel seeks to represent the undocumented employee, who is often arrested by ICE, and the employer, who may be subject to sanctions. One method of addressing this problem is to obtain in writing from *both* parties a signed statement recognizing but waiving any possible conflict.

VI. DEFENSES

A. *Good Faith and Substantial Compliance*—Good faith and substantial compliance are distinct affirmative defenses that must be separately pled and proven. *U.S. v. Carter*, 6 OCAHO no. 865 (May 23, 1996).

1. *Good Faith Defense to Unauthorized Hiring*—Good-faith compliance with the verification system is an affirmative defense to sanctions for unauthorized hiring. INA §274A(a)(3), 8 U.S.C. §1324a(a)(3); 8 C.F.R. §§274a.4, 1274a.4. Where the documents are facially genuine or where there is a referral from a state agency, the employer has retained the referral notice and the referral documents indicate state compliance, good faith may be properly asserted. 8 C.F.R. §§274a.6, 1274a.6. The standard in reviewing the prospective employee's documents is "reasonableness." The employer does not attest to the legitimacy of the person but rather that s/he has reviewed the original documents and "it reasonably *appears* to him or her, upon reasonable inspection of its features and the information it contains, to be genuine and to relate to the employee..." Employer Information Bulletin 103, Office of Business Liaison, DHS, I-9 Document Review (Sept. 25, 2003), *reprinted in* 80 No. 43 *Interpreter Releases* 1554, 1562–63 (Nov. 10, 2003). However, a good faith defense may not be available to a charge of violating INA §274A(a)(2) [continuing to employ unauthorized aliens], even if the employer complied with the verification system under INA §274A(b), where the employer had notice, or gained the requisite knowledge, of unlawful status of the alien. *Mester Mfg. Co.*, 879 F.2d at 569 n.11.

2. *Good Faith Defense to Paperwork Violations*—Although not previously a defense to paperwork violations, IIRIRA §411(b) specifically amended the statute to allow a good faith defense for technical and procedural violations, unless the employer failed to correct errors within 10 business days after notice or was engaged in a pattern and practice of violations. INA §274A(b)(6). Under previous authority, a good faith defense was used to mitigate fines. *Mester Mfg. Co., supra. Accord Big Bear Supermarket No. 3 v. INS*, 913 F.2d 754, 757 (9th Cir. 1990). DHS has defined, for purposes of the good faith defense, what it regards as a technical error as distinguished from a substantive error (which is not covered by good faith) on the I-9. Memo, Virtue, Acting Exec. Comm., Programs, HQ IRT 50/5.12 (Mar. 6, 1997), *reprinted in* 74 No. 16 *Interpreter Releases* 706, 720–31 (Apr. 28, 1997). In *U.S. v. WSC Plumbing, Inc.* 9 OCAHO no. 1061 (Nov.29, 2000) the ALJ determined that it was not a "technical or procedural" violation where: (1) the I-9 forms should have been completed before Sept. 30, 1996 [IIRIRA date adding the good faith defense]; (2) the I-9 forms did not include the employees document identification numbers and the employer did not attach legible copies of the documents; (3) the employer failed to produce I-9s; and (4) the employer failed to require employees to attest to their immigration status in section 1 of the I-9. However, the ALJ did rule that failure to complete an attestation date in section 2 of the I-9 was a technical or procedural violation.

3. *Substantial Compliance Defense to Paperwork Violations*—Substantial compliance is also a defense to paperwork violations. The defense was not previously available where the employer attached the employee's documents to the I-9 but did not have the employee's attestations in Part 1, *U.S. v. J.J.L.C., Inc.*, 1 OCAHO no. 154 (Apr. 13, 1990), or where the employer attached the documents but failed to complete the part of the I-9 regarding the document's ID number. *U.S. v. Corporate Loss Prevention Associates*, 6 OCAHO no. 908 (Feb. 5, 1997) [discussing criteria for substantial compliance defense to paperwork violations].

4. An error due to high employee turnover is not a defense and would "vitiate the purpose of the employment eligibility verification program." *U.S. v. Great Bend Packing Co., Inc.*, 6 OCAHO no. 835 (Feb. 13, 1996). Also, curing a timeliness violation prior to an inspection is not an affirmative defense. *U.S. v. WSC Plumbing Inc.*, 9 OCAHO no. 1061 (Sept. 7, 2000).

B. *Independent Contractor*—A person is not considered an "employee" for purposes of employer sanctions if s/he is an independent contractor as defined under 8 C.F.R. §§274a.1(j), 1274a.1(j). *U.S. v. ABC Roofing & Waterproofing, Inc.*, 1 OCAHO no. 247 (July 25, 1991), *aff'd*, 2 OCAHO no. 358 (Aug. 26, 1991). Factors to be considered in the determination of independent contractor status include whether the individual or entity supplies his/its own tools or materials, makes its services available to the general public, works for a number of clients at the same time, directs the order or sequence in which the work is to be done and determines the hours during which the work is to be done. Additional common law factors include: (1) the relationship with the employer including the amount of supervision and the manner in which the work relationship is terminated; (2) whether the rate of pay is by hour or by the number and quality of jobs; (3) whether the job requires low level or high level skills (job requiring low level skill is rarely independent); (4) employer/employee intent and local and industry practice; and (5) provision of certain benefits (*e.g.,* annual leave, retirement, Social Security). *U.S. v. Bakovic*, 3 OCAHO no. 482 (Jan. 15, 1993). In urging this defense, counsel should also look to IRS Guidelines, Pub. No. 539 (rev. Nov. 1986), Restatement (Second) of Agency, §220(2) (1958), and state law definitions. An employer may also request a determination as to whether a person is an independent contractor by submitting Form SS-8 to the IRS. However, an IRS determination on exemption does not prevent a separate and different determination for employer sanctions purposes. *Bakovic, supra* [IRS determination that maritime crews are generally independent contractors not binding]. The independent contractor defense is not available where a person or entity knowingly uses a contract or subcontract to obtain labor or services of an unauthorized alien. 8 C.F.R. §§274a.5, 1274a.5.

C. *Casual Hires*—Domestic employment that is sporadic, irregular, or intermittent is not subject to sanctions. 8 C.F.R. §§274a.1(f) and (h), 1274a.1(f) and (h). This may include gardeners, *U.S. v. ABC Roofing & Waterproofing, Inc.*, 1 OCAHO no. 247 (July 25, 1991), *aff'd*, 2 OCAHO no. 358 (Aug. 26, 1991), but does not include construction work at the curtilage of a person's home. *U.S. v. Jenkins*, 5 OCAHO no. 743 (Mar. 24, 1995), *aff'd*, *Jenkins v. U.S.*, 108 F.3d 195 (9th Cir. 1997).

D. *Statute of Limitations*—The statute of limitations under 28 U.S.C. §2462 may bar any claim that is commenced five years or more after the claim accrued. *U.S. v. WSC Plumbing,* 9 OCAHO no. 1061 (Sept 7, 2000) [statute of limitations could apply to violations of the requirement that portions of the I-9 be completed within a specific time after hiring]; *U.S. v. Carran Engineering Co., Inc.* 7 OCAHO no. 975 (1997) [the filing of the complaint with the ALJ, not the issuance of the NIF, is the event which tolls the statute of limitations].

E. *Improper Statutory Charge*—Where the substance of the charge does not match the statutory violation cited, the charge is improper. *U.S. v. Mester Mfg. Co.*, 1 OCAHO no. 18 (June 17, 1988).

F. *Employer in Multi-Employer Bargaining Unit*—If an employer of a multi-employer bargaining group employs a person who has previously been verified by another employer in the group, the new employer shall be deemed to have complied and "shall not be liable" for civil penalties if the employment arose within 3 years or employment was authorized, whichever is less. However, if an employer hires someone who is not authorized, there is a reasonable presumption that the employer knew the person was unauthorized. INA §274A(a)(6), 8 U.S.C. §1324a(a)(6).

G. *Grandfathered Employee*

1. If an employee began work before Nov. 7, 1986, and is continuing his or her employment, the employer cannot be sanctioned. 8 C.F.R. §§274a.7(a), 1274a.7(a). A grandfathered employee includes persons defined as continuing in employment under 8 C.F.R. §§274a.2(b)(1)(viii)(A)–(B), 1274a.2(b)(1)(viii)(A)–(B) [*see in this chapter* ¶ I.C.3 (p. 1250), *supra*], except persons who are seasonal workers or who work for a different employer within a multi-employer association. A person who quits, is terminated or is excluded, deported or voluntarily departs is not grandfathered. 8 C.F.R. §§274a.7(b), 1274a.7(b).
2. A determination that an employee was grandfathered was reversed where OCAHO found that an employee was terminated. *U.S. v. Maka's Akamia Serv.*, 1 OCAHO no. 36 (Dec. 15, 1988), *aff'd*, *Maka v. INS*, 904 F.2d 1351 (9th Cir. 1990) *amended* 932 F.2d 1352 (9th Cir. 1991).

H. *Ultra Vires Regulations*—The ALJ has authority to entertain challenges to the validity of regulations adopted by the AG *U.S. v. WSC Plumbing, Inc.* 9 OCAHO no. 1061 at 18 (Sept. 7, 2000) [challenging employer sanctions regulations].

I. *Constitutional Challenges*—An employer may challenge the ICE audit procedure on constitutional grounds. The employer may argue that the General Inspection Program or the Special Employers Inspection Program for selecting employers for audit is not random, and therefore violates the Fourth Amendment. The employer may also challenge on Fifth Amendment equal protection grounds, the selective enforcement of employer sanctions, particularly where race or national origin discrimination is raised. *Yick Wo v. Hopkins*, 118 U.S. 356 (1886); *U.S. v. ABC Roofing & Waterproofing, Inc.*, 1 OCAHO no. 247 (July 25, 1991) [recognizing but rejecting discriminatory and selective enforcement defense]; *Seven Star, Inc. v. U.S.*, 933 F.2d 791 (9th Cir. 1991) [rejecting selective prosecution claim where INS obtained a lead from a newspaper article and not because company filed H-2 petitions].

VII. DECISION/ORDER OF ALJ

A. *Final Order*—The ALJ may enter a final order based on the evidence before the court and shall do so within 60 days of receipt of the hearing transcript, unless an extension is given by the Chief Administrative Hearing Officer. 28 C.F.R. §68.52(b). If the ALJ determines that a person has violated the unlawful hiring provisions, the order "shall require the person or entity to cease and desist from such violations and to pay a civil penalty...." 28 C.F.R. §68.52(c)(1).

B. *Settlement*—If a party settles and asks the court to dismiss the case, the ALJ may do so. *Matter of Sea, Inc.*, 19 I&N Dec. 817 (Comm. 1988). Alternatively, the government may request a consent order and the ALJ must then enter an order which contains the consent findings and agreement by the parties. 28 C.F.R. §68.14. The Service reversed its position that all settlement agreements must contain admissions of all allegations in the NIF. Memo, Rees, General Counsel (Nov. 2, 1992), *reprinted in* 70 No. 2 *Interpreter Releases* 61, 68–70 (Jan. 11, 1993). ICE may not issue a final order unless and until the ALJ approves the settlement and dismisses the case. *U.S. v. Turner's Japanese Auto Repair,* 8 OCAHO no. 1009 (1998). Parties may also seek alternative dispute resolution procedures before a settlement judge. 29 C.F.R. §18.9.

C. *Penalty Imposed*—The ALJ may impose a greater penalty than that requested by ICE. *U.S. v. Aid Maintenance Company, Inc.,* 8 OCAHO no. 1023 (1999).

VIII. PENALTIES

A. *Generally*—ALJ may issue penalties under INA §274A(e)(4), 8 U.S.C. §1234a(e)(4); 28 C.F.R. §68.52:

1. Cease and desist orders;
2. Civil penalties for each offense of employing unauthorized aliens (not including paperwork violations):
   - First offense—$375 to $3,200 for each alien.
   - Second offense—$3,200 to $6,500 for each alien.
   - Third or more offenses—$4,300 to $16,000 for each alien
   - For offenses which occurred before March 27, 2008 the penalties are less.

   73 Fed. Reg. 10130–37 (Feb. 26, 2008).
3. Paperwork violations (failure to correctly complete and maintain I-9s) $110 to $1,100 for each I-9. Paperwork violations may not include failure to file, correct or supplement I-9s where "continuing to employ" unlawful person is an issue. *Compare* INA §274A(a)(1)(B) *and* INA §274A(a)(2). Because INA §274A(a)(2) does not mention paperwork violations, failure to correct an I-9 for someone whose valid H-1B expired may not result in a paperwork violation. *But see* 8 C.F.R. §§274a.2(b)(1)(vii), 1274a.2(b)(1)(vii) [requiring reverification by the employer].
4. *Compliance and Remedial Orders*—The ALJ may require the employer to comply with INA §274A(b) for 3 years and take other remedial actions.

B. *Enforcement of the Final Decision and Order*

1. If the employer fails to comply with a final order, the AG can seek enforcement by filing suit in U.S. district court. However, the validity of the order cannot be reviewed.
2. The filing of bankruptcy does not automatically stay sanctions proceedings. *U.S. v. United Pottery Mfg. and Accessories, Inc.*, 1 OCAHO no. 57 (May 19, 1989).

C. *Circumstances Warranting Mitigation or Aggravation of Damages*—INA §274A(e)(5), 8 U.S.C. §1324a(e)(5); 8 C.F.R. §§274a.10(b)(2), 1274a.10(b)(2).

1. *Size of Employer*—Criteria include business revenue or income, amount of payroll, number of salaried employees, nature of ownership, length of time in business and nature and scope of facilities. *U.S. v. Felipe,* 1 OCAHO no. 93 (Oct. 11, 1989). A small business may include those with over 100 employees. *U.S. v. Vogue Pleating, Stitching & Embroidery Corp.*, 5 OCAHO no. 782 at 3–4 (July 18, 1995).

2. *Good Faith of Employer*—Employer acts in good faith where s/he is "careless" as opposed to demonstrating "disdain or gross disregard." *U.S. v. Big Bear Market*, 1 OCAHO no. 48 (Apr. 12, 1989). *But see U.S. v. Felipe, Inc., supra* [good faith requires "honest intention to exercise reasonable care and diligence to ascertain what IRCA requires and to act in accordance with it"]. Good faith is determined by the company's actions at the time the violations occurred and not willingness to cooperate subsequent to investigation. *U.S. v. Great Bend Packing Co., Inc.*, 6 OCAHO no. 835 (Feb. 13, 1996) at 5. Paperwork violations alone cannot be used to demonstrate lack of good faith. *U.S. v. Taco Plus, Inc.*, 5 OCAHO no. 775 (June 20, 1995); *U.S. v. Karnival Fashion, Inc.*, 5 OCAHO no. 783 (Aug. 21, 1995).

3. *Seriousness of Violation*—Established on a continuum from: (1) intentional falsification of I-9; (2) deliberate refusal to prepare I-9; (3) negligent failure to prepare I-9; (4) preparing I-9 in part but employer or employee failing to sign; (5) failure of employer to sign; and (6) not checking boxes correctly on verification. *U.S. v. Felipe, Inc., supra.*

4. *Employee Authorized to Work*—To aggravate the civil penalty, documentation of the employee's unauthorized status is sufficient. The government need not show that the employer had knowledge that the employee was unauthorized. *U.S. v. Chef Rayko, Inc.*, 5 OCAHO no. 794 (Sept. 29, 1995). Cannot seek to enhance penalty based on other unauthorized employees for whom employer sanctions charges were not brought. *U.S. v. Irma Hernandez,* 8 OCAHO no. 1043 (2000).

5. *History of Violations*

D. *Calculating Fines for Paperwork Violations*

1. *OCAHO Formula*—In *U.S. v. Felipe,* 1 OCAHO no. 93 (Oct. 11, 1989), the ALJ established a formula to determine the extent a fine may be mitigated for paperwork violations. The ALJ determined that each factor is equivalent to $180 representing the difference between the maximum and minimum fines. ($1,000 – $100 = $900) divided by the five factors. This mathematical approach is in contrast to the more judgmental approach in *U.S. v. Big Bear Market*, 1 OCAHO no. 48 (Apr. 12, 1989), and other cases where the ALJ attempts to relate the penalty to the employer's fault in the matter. The mathematical approach has been adopted by ICE in initially setting fines. Guidelines for Employer Sanctions, Civil Money Penalties, McNary, Comm. CO 274A-P (Aug. 30, 1991), *reprinted in* 69 No. 8 *Interpreter Releases* 253, 267 (Mar. 2, 1992).

2. *ICE Approach*—The ICE Field Manual, *supra,* and Guidelines, *supra*, include these and other factors which the officer may consider. Under ICE Guidelines, the baseline for an initial penalty is the statutory minimum. The baseline for a subsequent penalty is the statutory maximum. These will be adjusted according to aggravating and mitigating factors. Among the factors considered are:

    2.a. Whether the violation or type of violation had previously been brought to the employer's attention;

    2.b. Whether the violation involved failure to complete the I-9, or failure to complete it accurately or in a timely manner. For paperwork violations occurring after Sept. 30, 1996 which are viewed as merely technical, ICE may not fine an employer unless the deficiencies are not corrected within 10 days after receipt of a notice of deficiencies;

    2.c. Whether the I-9 was altered, backdated or completed after notice of inspection;

    2.d. Whether the violation appeared to be a reflection of the employer's overall practice;

    2.e. Whether there is evidence the employer assisted employees with concealing unlawful status;

    2.f. Whether the violation occurred subsequent or prior to an educational visit;

2.g. Whether the employer used all personnel and financial resources to comply with the law;

2.h. Whether an increased penalty would enhance the probability of compliance;

2.i. Whether the employer exercised reasonable care and diligence to ascertain what the law requires and to act in accordance with it;

2.j. Whether and to what degree a paperwork violation materially affects the purpose of the verification process; and

2.k. Whether the paperwork violation involved an undocumented person.

E. ***Indemnity Bond Penalty***—INA §274A(g). It is illegal for an employer to require an employee to post bond for the purpose of providing a financial indemnity against any liability relating to hiring, recruiting or referring of the employee. However, the employer may have an indemnity bond as part of a performance clause between parties, *e.g.*, independent contractors. An administrative proceeding may be conducted to determine if an employer violated §274A(g). An employer may be subject to a civil penalty of $1,100 for each violation. For offenses which occurred on or before Sept. 29, 1999, the amounts are 10% less. The employer may be required to return the money to the employee.

F. ***Debarment under Executive Order***—Pursuant to Executive Order 12989 (Feb. 13, 1996), 61 *Federal Register* 6091, *reprinted in* 73 No. 8 *Interpreter Releases* 225, 242 (Feb. 26, 1996), the President can preclude the federal government from procuring goods and services from an employer who violates employer sanctions. It permits debarment for one year with the ability to extend in one year increments. 48 C.F.R. §§9.406-2(b)(2), 9.406-4(b). According to ICE, there is no constitutional, statutory or regulatory requirement to notify the employer that it may be subject to debarment when it issues an NIF. Legal Opinion, Martin, Gen. Counsel, 97-4 (Mar. 26, 1997), *reprinted in* 75 No. 17 *Interpreter Releases* 638 (May 4, 1998).

G. ***Criminal Penalties***

1. *Pattern and Practice Violations*—8 C.F.R. §§274a.10, 1274a.10.

1.a. Standard of pattern and practice found in: *Cooper v. Fed. Reserve Bank of Richmond*, 467 U.S. 867 (1984); *International Brotherhood of Teamsters v. U.S.*, 431 U.S. 324 (1977); *U.S. v. Mayton*, 335 F.2d 153 (5th Cir. 1964); 42 U.S.C. §1971 (Voting Rights Act); 42 U.S.C. §3601 (Fair Housing Act); 42 U.S.C. §2000e (Civil Rights Act). "Pattern and practice" defined as "regular, repeated, *and* intentional activities, but does not include isolated, sporadic, or accidental acts." 8 C.F.R. §§274a.1(k), 1274a.1(k); *U.S. v. Calhelha,* 456 F.Supp.2d 350, 363 (D. Conn. 2006) [facts sufficient to allege pattern and practice for person who arranged employees from Portugal to work at franchise stores].

1.b. Criminal violations are reserved "for serious and repeat offenders who have clearly demonstrated an intention to evade the law." H. Conf. Rep. No. 1000, 99th Cong. 2d Sess. 86 (1986), *reprinted in* 1986 U.S.C.C.A.N. 5840 at 5841.

2. Employer may face penalty of $3,000 and/or 6 months in jail.

3. AG may seek an injunction in U.S. district court to prevent continued criminal violations.

4. *Criminal Cases*—*U.S. v. Tyson Food, Inc.*, 258 F.Supp.2d 809 (E.D. Tenn. 2003) [company and three managers were acquitted of all counts in a 36-count indictment that alleged that they participated in, but sought to circumvent, the Employment Eligibility Verification Program (EVP) by paying recruiters who they knew hired workers not authorized and by aiding and abetting persons to falsely represent Social Security numbers]; *U.S. v. DavCo Food, Inc.*, Case No. 88-00253-A (E.D. Va. 1988) [pattern and practice charged where 17 employees arrested in two of 106 Wendy's restaurants owned by company]; *U.S. v. Chauvin*, Case No. 88-00236-A (E.D. Va. Oct. 4, 1988) [including counts against company officials under 18 U.S.C. §1546(b) and against attorney on strict liability theory of INA §210(b)(7)(A)(ii)].

5. Under INA §274(a)(3)(A), 8 U.S.C. §1324(a)(3)(A), it is a criminal offense carrying a penalty of up to 5 years, for "any person who during a 12-month period knowingly hires for employment at least 10 individuals with actual knowledge" that the individuals are not authorized to work *and* were brought to the U.S. in violation of 18 U.S.C. §1324. The legislative history of IIRIRA §203(b) clearly provides that "in order to be liable under this provision, the employer must have

actual knowledge both of the alien's unauthorized status and of the fact that the alien was brought into the United States illegally."

6. Under INA §274(a)(1)(A), 8 U.S.C. §1324(a)(1)(A), it is a criminal offense for any employer to smuggle, transport or harbor undocumented workers or to engage in a conspiracy to do so. *See* "Convictions Under INA §274" in Ch. 3, section VIII.C (p.239), *supra*.
7. Under 18 U.S.C. §1957, an employer can be convicted of money laundering for engaging in a financial transaction with proceeds of specified unlawful activity, including harboring, attempting to harbor, aiding and abetting harboring, and conspiracy to harbor. The maximum penalty for each violation is 10 years imprisonment.
8. Upon conviction of any federal felony, under the Criminal Asset Forfeiture statute, 18 U.S.C. §982(a)(6)(a), a jury may authorize seizure of all assets used in the commission of the crime and all proceeds of the crime.
9. *Double Jeopardy*—ICE takes the view that double jeopardy does not attach to civil fine proceedings. Memo, Virtue, G.C. (HQCOU 90/10.6-P: 90/5/5-P), *reprinted in* 76 No. 32 *Interpreter Releases* 1259, 1279–83 (Aug. 23, 1999); *Hudson v. U.S.,* 522 U.S. 93 (1997).

H. ***Defining Entity for Penalty Purposes***—Where the respondent is composed of distinct, physically separate subdivisions which do its own hiring, recruiting or referring for a fee for employment (without reference to the practices of, and under the control of, or common control with another subdivision), the subdivision shall be considered a separate person or entity. 8 U.S.C. §1324a(a)(4), 8 C.F.R. §§274a.10(b)(3), 1274a.10(b)(3). *U.S. v. Furr's/Bishop's Cafeterias, a limited partnership, d/b/a Furr's Cafeterias*, 2 OCAHO no. 330 (May 28, 1991), *aff'd*, *Furr's/Bishop's Cafeterias, L.P. v. INS*, 976 F.2d 1366 (10th Cir. 1992) [where cafeteria does not independently hire and is part of the same subsidiary under which another cafeteria was previously fined, and is part of the same regional management team that can countermand hiring decisions, it was treated as one entity for fine purposes].

IX. ADMINISTRATIVE AND JUDICIAL REVIEW

A. ***Administrative Review***—Administrative review is discretionary with the Chief Administrative Hearing Officer. A party may seek an interlocutory appeal if requested within 10 days of the entry of the interlocutory order. 28 C.F.R. §68.53(a)(2). A party may file a request for final review with the CAHO within 10 days of the ALJ order, although CAHO is not required to respond or enter any order. 28 C.F.R. §68.54(a). CAHO may modify or vacate the ALJ's order, 28 C.F.R. §68.54(d); *Maka v. INS*, 904 F.2d 1351 (9th Cir. 1990) *amended* 932 F.2d 1352 (9th Cir. 1991), but must do so *within 30 days of the ALJ* decision or the order is final. INA §274A(e)(7), 8 U.S.C. §1324a(e)(7). When CAHO rejects the credibility findings of the ALJ it must state its reasons for doing so. *Id.* at 1355. CAHO exercises *de novo* review consistent with the APA. 5 U.S.C. §557(b); *Maka v. INS*, *supra* at 1356 [rejecting vagueness challenge to 28 C.F.R. §68.52 on the grounds CAHO review is subject to APA]; *Mester Mfg. Co. v. INS*, 900 F.2d 201, 203–04 (9th Cir. 1990). The order of the ALJ becomes administratively final after 30 days if not modified or vacated. INA §274A(e)(7). The AG may also review an ALJ or CAHO decision *sua sponte* or at the request of the Commissioner. 28 C.F.R. §68.55.

B. ***Judicial Review***—Within 45 days of the date of a final order from the administrative agency, a party may file a petition for review in the court of appeals. 28 C.F.R. §68.56. The 45-day period begins when the order is issued under 28 C.F.R. §68.2, that is, 30 days after the ALJ enters his order if no administrative appeal was made. *A-Plus Roofing, Inc. v. INS*, 929 F.2d 489 (9th Cir. 1991). An order is deemed entered when the ALJ signs the order. 28 C.F.R. §68.2(i). The court of appeals will apply the substantial evidence standard in reviewing factual questions and will review questions of law *de novo*. *Maka v. INS*, 904 F.2d 1351, 1355 (9th Cir. 1990) *amended* 932 F.2d 1352 (9th Cir. 1991); *Mester Mfg. Co. v. INS*, 879 F.2d 561, 565 (9th Cir. 1989).

C. ***Attorney's Fees***—Employer sanctions hearings are conducted in accordance with the requirements of §554 of Title 5 of the APA; and attorneys fees are available under EAJA, 5 U.S.C. §§504(a)(1), 504(b)(1)(C). *Mester Mfg. Co. v. INS*, 900 F.2d 201, 202–03 (9th Cir. 1990). However, in order to obtain fees, a party must plead and prove all statutory requirements under 5 U.S.C. §§504(a)(2), (b)(1)(B). *U.S. v. Charo's Corp. d/b/a Charo's Restaurant*, 3 OCAHO no. 467 (Oct. 27, 1992) [failure to plead that there were less than 500 employees was fatal].

D. ***Preemption***—All state and local civil and criminal laws (except through licensing and other similar laws) are preempted. For a more extensive discussion of preemption, *see* Ch. 2, ¶ III.A.1 (p.38), *supra.*

E. ***Constitutionality***—Statute upheld in face of substantive and procedural due process challenge and claim that it is null and void as contrary to the Presentment Clause. *Mester Mfg. v. INS*, 879 F.2d 561, 569–71 (9th Cir. 1989). First Amendment challenge based on free exercise of religion and establishment clause was also rejected, *American Friends Service Comm. v. Thornburgh*, 961 F.2d 1405 (9th Cir. 1992); *Intercommunity Center for Justice & Peace v. INS*, 910 F.2d 42 (2d Cir. 1990), as was a challenge on vagueness grounds. *Big Bear Supermarket No. 3 v. INS*, 913 F.2d 754, 757 (9th Cir. 1990) [record keeping provision not void].

F. ***Effective Dates***

1. For the change for treatment (and nonpunishment) of technical I-9 errors, the effective date is all failures occurring on or after Sept. 30, 1996. IIRIRA §411(b).
2. The multi-employer defense applies to persons hired on or after 60 days from Sept. 30, 1996.
3. The addition of federal employees to employer sanctions applies to hirings occurring before, on or after Sept. 30, 1996; however, no penalty may be imposed for hiring before Sept. 30, 1996.

X. EMPLOYMENT AUTHORIZATION

A. ***Generally***—Originally governed by 8 C.F.R. §109; replaced with 8 C.F.R. §§274a.12–.14, 1274a.12–.14. Further amendments were made on June 25, 1990, 55 Fed. Reg. 25928, Aug. 23, 1991, 56 Fed. Reg. 41767 and July 30, 2004, 69 Fed. Reg. 45555. The regulations establish three categories of persons eligible for employment authorization: (1) persons authorized for employment incident to status; (2) persons authorized to work for a specific employer incident to status; and (3) persons who must apply for permission to work. Persons in the first (with certain exceptions enumerated below) and third categories must apply for an Employment Authorization Document (EAD) on Form I-765. *See* USCIS Office of Business Liaison, Employer Information Bulletin 1 (Dec. 8, 2004), *reprinted in* 82 No. 4 *Interpreter Releases* 189, 198, 214–23 (Jan. 24, 2005) [list of NIV categories and whether employment is authorized and EAD required].

B. ***Persons Authorized for Employment Incident to Status***—8 C.F.R. §§274a.12(a), 1274a.12(a). With the exception of LPRs, temporary residents, persons granted asylum, K-3 or child of K-3, T-1 and U-1, spouses of Es and L-2 all of whom have employment authorization incident to their status, all other individuals in the §274a.12(a) category who are authorized to work incident to their status must nevertheless apply on an I-765 for an EAD as *evidence* of their authorization to work. 8 C.F.R. §274a.13. USCIS may, in its discretion, determine the validity period of the EAD. 8 C.F.R. §§274a.12(a), 1274a.12(a).

C. ***Persons Authorized for Employment with a Specific Employer Incident to Status***—8 C.F.R. §§274a.12(b), 1274a.12(b). No EAD required; I-94 authorizes employment.

1. Working visas—H, I, L, E, O, P, Q-1, and R;
2. Government visas—A (foreign government officials and their employees), G (representatives of international organizations and their employees), C (in transit);
3. F-1 students if seeking (i) part-time employment on campus when school is in session or full-time when school is not in session; or (ii) curricular practical training;
4. J-1 exchange visitors, if program permits;
5. NATO representatives, officials, staff and their attendants, servants and personal employees; and
6. TNs—Canadian and Mexican professionals under INA §214(e) (NAFTA).

D. ***Persons Who Must Apply for Employment Authorization***—8 C.F.R. §§274a.12(c), 1274a.12(c). The approval of such applications [except for asylum applicants under 8 C.F.R. §§274a.12(c)(8), 1274a.12(c)(8)] is within the discretion of DHS. 8 C.F.R. §§274a.13(a)(1), 1274a.13(a)(1). USCIS may, in its discretion, establish a specific validity period for an EAD, which may include any period when an administrative appeal or judicial review of an application is pending. 8 C.F.R. §§274.12(c), 1274a.12(c). The following persons must apply for EA:

1. Persons Under Certain Categories of §274a.12(a):
   - 1.a. Refugee admitted pursuant to INA §207; Refugee paroled into U.S.
   - 1.b. K-1 or K-2
   - 1.c. N-8 or N-9
   - 1.d. Citizen of Federated States of Micronesia or Marshall Islands
   - 1.e. Person granted Withholding of deportation or removal
   - 1.f. Person granted EVD or TPS
   - 1.g. Person granted VD under Family Unity; Person granted Family Unity benefits under LIFE
   - 1.h. V status
   - 1.i. Family members of U visa holder (U-2 to U-5)
2. All categories of persons under §274a.12(c).

E. ***Battered Spouses and Children***—All approved VAWA self-petitioners not in proceedings are eligible for deferred action and work authorization. INA §§204(a)(1)(D)(i)(II), (IV); Memo, Cronin, Acting Assoc. Comm., Office of Programs, HQ204-P (Dec. 22, 1998). VAWA self-petitions and deferred action requests are filed with the Vermont Service Center. Memo, Cronin, Acting Ex. Assoc. Comm., Office of Programs, HQ/AND/70/6.1P (Sept. 8, 2000). VAWA 2005 created INA §204(a)(1)(K), which grants employment authorization to self-petitioners incident to status. Battered spouses of A, E-3, G and H nonimmigrants are eligible for work authorization. INA §106.

F. ***Nonimmigrant Extensions/Change of Employer/Change of Status***—Nonimmigrants in valid A-3, E-1, E-2, G-5, H-1, H-2A/B, H-3, I, J-1, L-1, O-1, O-2, P-1, P-2, P-3, R or TN status who timely file for an extension of status with the same employer are automatically granted authorization to work for 240 days beyond the expiration of status. 8 C.F.R. §§274a.12(b)(20), 1274a.12(b)(20). Under the H-1B portability provisions, an H-1B worker may change employers upon the filing of a new petition, as long as the individual is in lawful status and has not engaged in unauthorized employment since his/her last lawful admission. AC21 §1015. However, when requesting change from a nonemployment category (F-2) to an employment category (H-1), employment is not authorized until approved. Letter, Puleo, Asst. Comm., Examinations (Dec. 7, 1987), *reprinted in* 64 No. 48 *Interpreter Releases* 1400, 1410 (Dec. 21, 1987). *But see Salehpour v. INS*, 761 F.2d 1442 (9th Cir. 1985) [holding that INS's interpretation that employment pending adjudication of a prima facie approvable H-1 petition constitutes "unauthorized employment," thus rendering the petitioner statutorily ineligible for adjustment, is unreasonable and inconsistent with the regulations]; *Erbas v. Parra*, 1988 WL 22815 (S.D. Tex. Mar. 8, 1988).

G. ***Professional Athletes***—O-1 and P-1 professional athletes who are traded may continue employment with their new team without interruption as long as a new petition is filed within 30 days of the trade. 8 C.F.R. §§274a.12(b)(13) and (14), 1274a.12(b)(13) and (14).

H. ***Asylum and Employment Authorization***—*See* Ch. 4, ¶ XII.A.9 (p.521), *supra*.

I. ***Students***—No EAD required for on-campus employment and curricular practical training. EAD required for employment due to severe economic hardship, employment with an international organization or optional practical training for a maximum period of 12 months. 8 C.F.R. §214.2(f)(11).

J. ***Persons in Proceedings, Ordered Removed***—DHS has no authority to grant employment authorization to persons in proceedings, except for LPRs or persons who would otherwise be eligible for employment authorization [such as asylum applicants under 8 C.F.R. §274a.12(c)(8)]. INA §236(a)(3), 8 U.S.C. §1226(a)(3). No person ordered removed shall be eligible for EAD, unless the person cannot be removed or removal is otherwise impracticable or contrary to the public interest. INA §241(a)(7), 8 U.S.C. §1231(a)(7). EAD is granted in the district director's discretion upon consideration of factors including: economic necessity, existence of dependents and length of time before removal. 8 C.F.R.

§§274a.12(c)(18), 1274a.12(c)(18). Persons granted voluntary departure are not eligible for work authorization. 8 C.F.R. §274a.12(c)(12).

K. ***NIW Physicians***—Physicians working in medically underserved areas who have a pending adjustment of status based on an approved National Interest Waiver are eligible for discretionary employment authorization under 8 C.F.R. §274a.12(c)(9). NIW physicians may be required to show evidence of "meaningful progress toward completing the NIW employment obligation or of plans to use the EAD for the purpose of completing the medical service obligation." Memo, Aytes, Assoc. Dir., Domestic Operations, HQ70/6.2, AD06-46 (Jan. 23, 2007).

L. ***Procedure for Obtaining Employment Authorization Document (EAD)***

1. *Form I-765*—Where EAD is required, the applicant must file Form 1-765. No fee is required for initial EADs for refugees, asylees, N-8/N-9 nonimmigrants, citizens of Palau, persons granted withholding of removal, deferred enforced departure, asylum applicants (except those filing under special *ABC* procedures), T-1 nonimmigrants, and dependents of certain foreign government, international organization and NATO personnel. No fee for renewal EADs for citizens of Palau, persons granted withholding of removal, deferred enforced departure and dependents of certain foreign government, international organization and NATO personnel.

2. *Economic Necessity*—Applicants for deferred action [8 C.F.R. §§274a.12(c)(14), 1274a.12(c)(14)] and persons with a final order of removal under supervision [8 C.F.R. §§274a.12(c)(18), 1274a.12(c)(18)] must establish economic necessity to obtain employment authorization. The poverty guidelines are used as the basic criteria and the applicant must submit a list of assets, income, and expenses. 8 C.F.R. §§274a.12(d), 274a.13(a)(1), 1274a.12(d), 1274a.13(a)(1).

3. *Adjudication/Interim EADs*—Except for initial applications by asylum applicants [*see* 8 C.F.R. §§274a.13(a)(2), 1274a.13(a)(2)], and certain Nicaraguan, Cuban and Haitian AOS applicants [*see* 8 C.F.R. §§245.13(j), 245.15(n)], DHS must adjudicate EAD within 90 days of receipt or applicant is automatically eligible for interim employment authorization for 240 days. 8 C.F.R. §§274a.13(d), 1274a.13(d). If EAD is denied, interim authorization is automatically terminated. USCIS's position that it has 90 days to adjudicate an EAD application without penalty has been upheld, notwithstanding §555(b) of the APA. *Singh v. Ilchert*, 784 F.Supp. 759, 762–65 (N.D. Cal. 1992).

4. *Validity Period*—DHS may, in its discretion, determine the validity period of EADs issued to different classes of applicants. 8 C.F.R. §§274a.12(a), (a)(5) & (c), 1274a.12(a), (a)(5) & (c).

5. *Denial*—If application for EAD is denied, applicant shall be notified in writing. There is no appeal. 8 C.F.R. §§274a.13(c), 1274a.13(c). Written denial may not require detailed findings. *John Doe I v. Meese*, 690 F.Supp. 1572, 1577 (S.D. Tex. 1988). In view of some courts, no judicial review of denial of EAD because such action is "committed to agency discretion." *Perales v. Casillas*, 903 F.2d 1043 (5th Cir. 1990); *Uzuegbu v. Caplinger*, 745 F.Supp. 1200, 1216 (E.D. La. 1990); *Gomez-Arauz v. McNary*, 779 F.Supp. 1308 (W.D. Okla. 1991).

M. ***Termination and Revocation of Employment Authorization***

1. *Automatic Termination*—For individuals required to obtain EAD under 8 C.F.R. §274a.12(c), employment authorization is automatically terminated upon expiration of the EAD, upon commencement of proceedings or upon grant of voluntary departure. 8 C.F.R. §§274a.14(a)(1), 1274a.14(a)(1). Automatic termination does not preclude reapplication for employment authorization. 8 C.F.R. §§274a.14(a)(2), 1274a.14(a)(2).

2. *Revocation*—Employment authorization under 8 C.F.R. §274a.12(c) may be revoked if conditions upon which it was granted have not been met, for good cause shown or upon discovery of false information in the application. 8 C.F.R. §§ 274a.14(b)(1), 1274a.14(b)(1). Revocation of work authorization normally requires notice and compliance with the APA. *National Council of Churches v. Egan*, Case No. 79-2959-Civ-WMH (S.D. Fla. Aug. 29, 1979); *Augustin v. Harrison*, Case No. 86-0882-Civ-Marcus (S.D. Fla. Sept. 29, 1986). The individual is given 15 days from the date of service of the notice of intent to revoke to submit countervailing evidence. 8 C.F.R. §§274a.14(b)(2), 1274a.14(b)(2).

N. ***Employment Authorization as a Constitutional Right***—In *McNary v. Haitian Refugee Center, Inc.*, 498 U.S. 479 (1991), the Supreme Court stated that where employment authorization was to be granted upon the filing of a nonfrivolous SAW application, "[t]he impact of a denial on the opportunity to obtain gainful employment is plainly sufficient to mandate constitutionally fair procedures in the application process." This view has significant implications for the treatment accorded to EAD applicants.

XI. EMPLOYMENT / LABOR RIGHTS

A. ***Protection Under the National Labor Relations Act***—Undocumented and nonimmigrant workers are considered employees under the NLRA. *Hoffman Plastic Compounds, Inc. v. NLRB*, 535 U.S. 137, 144–45 (2002); *Sure-Tan, Inc. v. NLRB*, 467 U.S. 883, 892 (1984) [undocumented workers]; *Agri Processor Co., Inc. v. NLRB,* 514 F.3d 1 (D.C. Cir. 2008) [undocumented workers were employees and allowed to vote in election to unionize]; *WJA Realty Ltd. Partnership v. Nelson*, 708 F. Supp. 1268, 1277 (S.D. Fla. 1989) [NIV workers]. However, NLRA protection may not extend to employees working temporarily outside the U.S. for U.S. employers. *Asplundh Expert Co. v. NLRB*, 365 F.3d 168 (3d Cir. 2004) [employees cutting trees in Ottawa temporarily are not covered by NLRA]. Statutory employees enjoy protection from unfair labor practices, including unlawful discharge, and the right to vote in NLRB elections, regardless of immigration status. Memo, Rosenfeld, General Counsel of NLRB, GC 02-06 (July 19, 2002), *reprinted in* 79 No. 33 *Interpreter Releases* 1237-39, 1265–71 (Aug. 19, 2002). An employer may not submit evidence of an employee's unlawful status during an unfair labor practice proceeding and may only do so at the compliance stage. *Id. See also Matter of Regal Recycling*, 329 NLRB 355 (Sept. 30, 1999) [concluding that a sudden request for EADs during representation battle is an unfair labor practice]. However, the INA does not preclude deportation of an undocumented worker based on evidence obtained during a labor dispute. *Montero v. INS*, 124 F.3d 381 (2d Cir. 1997) [cannot exclude evidence of a person's unlawful status where such evidence was obtained as a result of an unfair labor practice].

1. *Backpay under NLRA*—Prior to *Hoffman Plastic*, the NLRB awarded a limited backpay remedy (that is compensation for lost work due to ULP) to unlawfully discharged undocumented workers who the employer hired knowing of their unlawful status. *APRA Fuel Oil Buyers Group*, 320 NLRB 408 (1995), *enforced*, 134 F.3d 50 (2d Cir. 1997). Under *Hoffman Plastic Compounds, Inc. v. NLRB*, 535 U.S. 137 (2002), the Supreme Court held that the NLRB may not award backpay as a remedy for NLRA violations for undocumented workers, because such awards conflict with the goals and policies of IRCA. Following *Hoffman Plastic*, the General Counsel of the NLRB issued a memorandum stating: (1) backpay may not be awarded even where the employer knowingly hired undocumented workers; (2) compensation for work previously performed by undocumented workers under unlawfully imposed conditions remains available; (3) backpay for unlawful demotion may remain available; and (4) other remedies such as contempt sanctions and requiring the employer to continue with efforts to legalize the status of the employee remain available. Memo, Rosenfeld, (July 19, 2002), *supra*.

2. *State Labor Laws*—Prior to *Hoffman Plastic*, the California Agricultural Labor Relations Board determined that the state has the right to order backpay and reinstatement for undocumented workers. *Philip Bertelsen, Inc. v. Agricultural Labor Relations Board*, 29 Cal. Rptr.2d 204 (Cal.App.5 Dist. 1994). The AG of New York issued an opinion stating that *Hoffman Plastic* does not preclude enforcement of state wage payment laws on behalf of undocumented workers. Spitzer, A.G. New York, Legal Opinion No. 2003-F3 (Oct. 21, 2003), *reported in* 9 No. 1 *Bender's Immigration Bulletin* 40-50 (Jan. 1, 2004). *See also Incalza v. Fendi North America, Inc.*, 479 F.3d 1005 (9th Cir. 2007) [IRCA did not preempt California labor law and require that employee be fired where employer was seeking H-1B for employee, could have taken action other than discharge, and did not fired employee because of his unauthorized status]; *Reyes v. Van Elk, Ltd,* 148 Cal. App.4th 604 (C.A. Cal. 4th 2007) [reversed summary judgment against undocumented workers who sought prevailing wages and found that neither *Hoffman* nor IRCA barred or preempted their right to recovery]; *Pineda v. Kel-Tech Construction, Inc.*, 2007 NY Slip Op. 27015 (NY 2007) [denying summary judgment and allowing undocumented workers who used false documents to obtain employment, to proceed with lawsuit for wages allegedly withheld as part of money laundering scheme].

3. *Strikes and Labor Disputes*—Regulations govern the effect of a strike on persons in F status (8 C.F.R. §214.2(f)(14)), H status (8 C.F.R. § 214.2(h)(17)), O status (8 C.F.R. §214.2(o)(14)), and P status (8 C.F.R. §214.2(p)(16)), or seeking to enter under NAFTA (INA §214(j)(1), 8 U.S.C. §1184(j)(1), 8 C.F.R. §214.6(k), 8 C.F.R. §214.2(e)(22), 8 C.F.R. §214.2(*l*)(18)) or the U.S.-Chile or U.S.-Singapore Free Trade Agreements (INA §214(j)(2)). Cable, INS HQ 214L-P/HQ, 1815-P/HQ, 214E-P (Oct. 17, 1994), *reprinted in* 71 No. 44 *Interpreter Releases* 1516, 1517 (Nov. 14, 1994). The USCIS's general policy is to not arrest undocumented workers while on the picket line (Special Agent Field Manual, §33.14(h)) and to avoid involvement in labor disputes. Memo, Aleinikoff and Slattery, HQ, INV 50/1.1.2-P (Dec. 20, 1996), *reprinted in* 74 No. 4 *Interpreter Releases* 188, 189–201 (Jan. 27, 1997); *Matter of Herrera-Priego* (EOIR, Lamb, IJ, New York July 10, 2003), *reported in* 8 No. 24 *Bender's Immigration Bulletin* 1887 (Dec. 15, 2003) [IJ terminated proceedings where INS issued NTA during labor dispute].

4. *Fine Proceedings*—Evidence obtained as a result of an unfair labor practice under the NLRA is not barred in fine proceedings under INA §274C. *Velasquez-Tabir v. INS*, 127 F.3d 456 (5th Cir. 1997) ["even if the INS's evidence was obtained in violation of the NLRA, the congressional intent of the INA would be abrogated if such evidence were excluded"].

B. *Protection under FLSA and Migrant and Seasonal Agricultural Worker Protection Act*

1. *Undocumented Workers Protected*—Undocumented workers are protected under the FLSA, which allows unpaid or underpaid workers to recover wages for past work performed. *Patel v. Quality Inn South*, 846 F.2d 700 (11th Cir. 1988). *See also Antenor v. D&S Farms*, 88 F.3d 925 (11th Cir. 1996) [finding grower and labor contractor joint employers of agricultural workers]. FLSA also applies to H-2B workers. *Rivera v. Brickman Group Ltd.*, __ F.Supp.2d __ (E.D. Pa. Jan. 7, 2008) 2008 WL 81570 [H-2B landscapers entitled to receive transportation, visa, and payments to recruiters as costs under the FLSA] *Castellanos-Contreras v. Decatur Hotels, L.L.C.*, 488 F.Supp.2d 565, 572 n.5 (E.D. La. 2007) [finding that the FLSA applies to H-2B workers and suggesting that hotel workers may have a claim for reimbursement for travel, visa, recruitment and other expenses incurred in migrating to the U.S.]. The AWPA provides protection to seasonal and agricultural workers. Plaintiffs in FLSA/AWPA cases do not need to divulge their alienage or citizenship, as those matters are irrelevant with regard to recovery. *Matter of Reyes*, 814 F.2d 168 (5th Cir. 1987). FLSA protection extends to payment for transportation of farm workers to the U.S., immigration fees, and pre-employment expenses that primarily benefit the grower. *Arriaga v. Florida Pacific Farms, L.L.C.*, 305 F.3d 1228 (11th Cir. 2002). FLSA also includes protection from retaliation. *Contreras v. Corinthian Vigor Ins. Brokerage, Inc.*, 103 F.Supp.2d 1180 (N.D. Cal 2000). *But see Alvarado-Guevara v. INS*, 902 F.2d 394 (5th Cir. 1990) [detained alien has no right under FLSA to receive more than $1/day for work performed in detention because s/he is not an employee]; *Channer v. Hall*, 112 F.3d 214 (5th Cir. 1997) [requiring detainees to work at Oakdale Detention Center does not violate the 13th Amendment].

2. *FLSA/AWPA Claims for Undocumented Workers Remain Post-*Hoffman Plastic—*Chellen v. John Pickle Co.*, 446 F.Supp. 2d 1247 (N.D. Okla. 2006) [*Hoffman Plastic* does not bar FLSA reward for past work performed by B-1/B-2 visitors, not authorized to work]; *Zavala v. Wal-Mart Stores, Inc.*, 393 F.Supp.2d 295, 320–32 (D.N.J. 2005) [*Hoffman Plastic* does not bar FLSA claim by undocumented janitors]; *Ulloa v. Al's All Tree Service, Inc.*, 768 N.Y.S.2d 556 (App. Div. 2003) [undocumented employee who did not tender false documents to procure employment is entitled to wages earned, but limited to minimum wages]; *Garcia v. Pasquareto*, 812 N.Y.S.2d 216 (N.Y. Sup. Ct. 2004) [criticizing *Ulloa*'s limitation of awards for undocumented workers to minimum wage]; *Flores v. Amigon*, 233 F.Supp.2d 462 (E.D.N.Y. 2002) [employee's immigration status is not relevant to back wage claim under FLSA]; *Singh v. Jutla & C.D. & R's Oil, Inc.*, 214 F.Supp.2d 1056 (N.D. Cal. 2002) [*Hoffman Plastic* does not preclude undocumented worker from pursuing retaliation claim against employer who reported him to DHS]; *Martinez v. Mecca Farms, Inc.*, 213 F.R.D. 601 (S.D. Fla. 2002) [*Hoffman Plastic* does not bar a claim by undocumented workers under the AWPA for payment for work already performed].

C. *Protection under State Workers' Compensation Laws*—Post-*Hoffman Plastic*, several courts have upheld the right of an undocumented worker to receive workers' compensation benefits. *See Farmers Bros. Coffee v. Workers Compensation Appeal Board*, 35 Cal.Rptr.3d 23 (2d Dist. 2005); *Continental PET Technologies, Inc. v. Palacias*, 604 S.E.2d 627 (Ga. Ct. App. 2004); *Rajeh v. Steel City Corp.*,

813 N.E.2d 697 (Ohio Ct. App. 2004); *Reinforced Earth Co. v. W.C.A.B.*, 570 Pa. 464, 810 A.2d 99 (Pa. 2002); *Correa v. Waymouth Farms, Inc.* 664 N.W. 2d 324 (Minn. 2003); *Safeharbor Employer Services I, Inc. v. Velasquez*, 2003 WL 22326966 (Fla. 1st DCA 2003).

D. *Protection under Title VII and State Anti-Discrimination Laws*

1. *Pre-Hoffman Plastic*—Prior to *Hoffman Plastic*, broad relief was available under Title VII. *EEOC v. Hacienda Hotel*, 881 F.2d 1504, 1516–17 (9th Cir. 1989) [undocumented workers are entitled to backpay under Title VII]; *Rios v. Enterprise Assoc. Steamfitters Local 638*, 860 F.2d 1168, 1170–73 (2d Cir. 1988) [undocumented workers eligible for backpay where claimants were never deported and award is pre-IRCA]; *EEOC v. Tortilleria "La Mejor,"* 758 F.Supp. 585 (E.D. Cal. 1991) [Title VII applicable to undocumented workers]. *But see Egbuna v. Time-Life Libraries, Inc.*, 153 F.3d 184 (4th Cir. 1998) (en banc) [Title VII does not cover an undocumented worker who resigned and was later refused reinstatement].
2. *Post-Hoffman Plastic*—Following *Hoffman Plastic*, the EEOC on June 27, 2002 rescinded its previous guidelines on remedies available to undocumented workers. *See* Rescission of Enforcement Guidance on Remedies Available to Undocumented Workers Under Federal Employment Discrimination Laws, No. 915.002 (EEOC June 27, 2002). In *Escobar v. Spartan Security Service*, 281 F.Supp.2d 895 (S.D. Tex. 2003), the court found that while *Hoffman* precluded backpay under Title VII, the employee was entitled to other remedies including reinstatement and front pay after he obtained permission to work. In *Rivera v. Nibco, Inc.*, 364 F.3d 1057 (9th Cir. 2004), the court affirmed a protective order preventing the defendant's lawyers from deposing the plaintiffs on their immigration status in a Title VII case and in dicta, distinguished *Hoffman Plastic*'s limit on backpay for undocumented workers, noting that the NLRA and Title VII are distinct remedial schemes. *But see Crespo v. Evergo Corp.*, 841 A.2d 471 (N.J. Sup. Ct. 2004) [post-*Hoffman Plastic* undocumented worker not eligible for economic or noneconomic damages under New Jersey's Law Against Discrimination].
3. *Non-USCs Working Outside the U.S.*—Title VII may not extend to non-USCs working outside the U.S. *Shekoyan v. Sibley Intern Corp.*, 217 F.Supp.2d 59, 64–69 (D.D.C. 2002), *aff'd* 409 F.3d 414 (DC Dir. 2005) [Title VII does not apply to LPRs working outside the U.S.]; *Chaudry v. Mobil Oil Corp.*, 186 F.3d 502 (4th Cir. 1999) [Title VII does not protect a foreign national of a U.S. company working overseas who seeks to transfer to the U.S. but does not have the proper documentation to become authorized for employment in the U.S.]. *But see Olvera-Morales v. Sterling Onions, Inc.*, 322 F.Supp.2d 211, 219–22 (N.D.N.Y. 2004) [court declined to dismiss Title VII discrimination claim by H-2 worker despite defendant's assertion that the law did not apply to the plaintiff who was undocumented and outside the U.S. at the time she applied].
4. *DHS Employees*—Hostile work environment claim denied where DHS employee claimed she was raped by coworker. *Lapka v. Chertoff,* 517 F.3d 974 (7th Cir. 2008).
5. *Wrongful Termination Under State Law—Incalza v. Fendi North America, Inc.,* 479 F.3d 1005 (9th Cir. 2006) [where E-1 Italian national was fired after company changed from Italian to French ownership, employee's award of damages for wrongful termination under CA law was upheld because company could have requested H-1B status or placed him on temporary unpaid leave until he married a USC instead of terminating him].

**E. *Protection under the Age Discrimination in Employment Act of 1967*—*O'Laughlin v. The Pritchard Corp.*, 972 F.Supp. 1352, 1363–64 (D. Kan. 1997) [finding that the ADEA in general protects noncitizens in the U.S. from unlawful discrimination, but does not apply to noncitizens working abroad]. *Reyes-Gaona v. North Carolina Growers Ass'n, Inc.*, 250 F.3d 861 (4th Cir. 2001) [ADEA does not apply to seasonal workers who were interviewed outside the U.S. and denied employment because of their age].

F. *Right to Lost Wages in Civil Litigation*

1. *Pre-Hoffman Plastic*—Prior to *Hoffman Plastic*, documented and undocumented workers were entitled to recover lost wages in the U.S. *Mischalski v. Ford Motor Co.*, 935 F.Supp. 203, 204–05 (E.D.N.Y 1996) [and cases cited therein]. *See also Hernandez v. M/V Rajaan*, 848 F.2d 498, 500 (5th Cir. 1988) [use of past wages to calculate future lost wages is proper for undocumented worker who intends to reside permanently in the U.S. and there is no evidence that he will be de-

ported]. In other cases, state courts found the employee's status irrelevant and inadmissible. *Sanchez v. Galey*, 112 Idaho 609, 733 P.2d 1234 (1986); *Peterson v. Neme*, 222 Va. 477, 281 S.E.2d 869 (1981). At least one court also rejected an "unclean hands" defense to discrimination and tort claims regarding sexual harassment where employee had fraudulent employment documents. *Murillo v. Rite Stuff Foods, Inc.*, 65 Cal. App. 4th 833 (2d Dist. 1998).

2. *Post-Hoffman Plastic*—Courts have found that *Hoffman Plastic* does not foreclose an undocumented worker's wage loss in civil litigation. *Balbuena v. IDR Realty LLC*, 2006 NY Slip Op. 01248 (N.Y. 2006) [in the absence of proof that plaintiffs used false documents to obtain employment, IRCA and *Hoffman Plastic* do not bar a claim for lost wages by an undocumented worker for injuries resulting from the employer's worksite violations under state labor laws]; *Madeira v. Affordable Hous. Found., Inc.*, 469 F.3d 219 (2d Cir. 2006) [federal immigration law does not clearly preempt NY state law allowing undocumented workers to recover lost earnings in personal injury action where the employer, not the worker, knowingly violated IRCA]; *Chopra v. U.S. Professionals, LLC*, 2005 WL 280346 (Tenn. App. Feb. 2, 2005) [breach of contract action for lost wages not affected by *Hoffman Plastic* where person entered lawfully on H-1B but was given nonprofessional work]; *Tyson Foods, Inc. v. Guzman*, 116 S.W.3d 233 (Tex. C.A. 2003) [upholding jury verdict that included past and future lost earnings because *Hoffman Plastic* "does not apply to common-law personal injury damages"]. *Hoffman Plastic* does not foreclose an undocumented immigrant's right to pursue civil litigation and obtain damages for pain and suffering. *Cano v. Mallory Mgmt.*, 760 N.Y.S.2d 816, 195 Misc.2d 666 (S.Ct. N.Y. 2003) [denying motion to dismiss undocumented worker's personal injury lawsuit based on *Hoffman Plastic* and finding that his status may not be presented to the jury on the issue of pain and suffering, but may be presented on the issue of lost wages]. An effort to recover lost wages from the Mexican government under the infamous Bracero program was permitted over sovereign immunity and Act of State objections. *Cruz v. U.S.* 387 F.Supp.2d 1057 (N.D. Cal. 2005).

G. *Discovery Issues Involving Undocumented Plaintiffs*—In a number of cases under both state and federal law, the issue of what discovery, if any, may a defendant pursue in regard to the plaintiff's immigration status. Many courts have been reluctant to allow discovery often viewing it as an act of intimidation against the plaintiff. *Gomez v. F&T Int'l LLC,* 842 N.Y.S.2d 298 (S.Ct. June 25, 2007) [employer precluded from requesting discovery regarding plaintiff's immigration status in action for damages arising out of injury]; *Galaviz-Zamora v. Brady Farms, Inc.,* 230 F.R.D. 499 (W.D. Mich. 2005) [precluding defendant in FLSA/AWPA case for backpay for obtaining information through interrogatories and requests for production of plaintiffs Social Security numbers, alien registration cards, and birth certificates]; *Flores v. Amigon,* 233 F.Supp.2d 462, 464–65 (E.D.N.Y. 2002) [same]; *EEOC v. City of Joliet,* 239 F.R.D. 490 (N.D. Ill. 2006) [defendants barred from insisting that plaintiffs suddenly fill out I-9 forms].

H. *Civil RICO Actions*—The Racketeer Influenced and Corrupt Organizations statute (RICO), 18 U.S.C. §1964(c) allows for civil actions to be brought against persons or entities that engage in a pattern of racketeering activity. Section 1962(c) makes it unlawful for any person to engage in, directly or indirectly, a pattern of racketeering activity on behalf of any entity. Section 1961(1) makes an act indictable under INA §274 (relating to bringing in and harboring certain aliens), §277 (relating to aiding and assisting certain aliens in entering the U.S.) and §278 (relating to importation of aliens for immoral purposes) if committed for financial gain, a RICO predicate crime. Immigration-related crimes under 18 U.S.C. §1028 (fraudulent identification documents), §1542 (false statement in application and use of passport), §1543 (forgery or false use of passport), §1544 (misuse of passport), and §1546 (fraud and misuse of visas, permits and other documents) are RICO predicate crimes regardless of financial gain. *See Williams v. Mohawk Industries, Inc.* 465 F.3d 1277 (11th Cir. 2007) [on remand from the Supreme Court, affirming district court's denial of defendant's motion to dismiss federal and state RICO claims by class of employees for depressing wages due to hiring and harboring undocumented workers]. *See also Trollinger v. Tyson Foods, Inc.*, 370 F.3d 602 (6th Cir. 2004), No. 4:02-CV-23 (E.D. Tenn. 2006) [granting class certification]; *Mendoza v. Zirkle Fruit Co.*, 301 F.3d 1163 (9th Cir. 2002). In *Commercial Cleaning Services, LLC v. Colin Service Systems, Inc.*, 271 F.3d 374 (2d. Cir. 2001), a company's action against its competitor in a civil case for hiring undocumented workers and violating INA §274 stated a cause of action under RICO. *But see Zavala v. Wal-Mart Stores, Inc.*, 393 F.Supp.2d 295, 302–17 (D.N.J. 2005) [RICO claim dismissed because plaintiffs, who were undocumented workers, did not allege sufficient facts for predicate immigration violations of transporting, harboring, encouraging, and bringing aliens into U.S.].

XII. UNFAIR IMMIGRATION-RELATED EMPLOYMENT PRACTICES—INA §274B, 8 U.S.C. §1324b

A. *Scope and Purpose*

1. *Who is Protected?*—The statute is designed to protect individuals from national origin discrimination and "protected" individuals from citizenship discrimination by an employer in hiring, recruitment, referral or discharge. Protected individuals include:

   1.a. Citizens or nationals of the United States—INA §274B(a)(3)(A), 8 U.S.C. §1324b(a)(3)(A), including naturalized USCs, *Nickman v. Mesa Air Group,* 9 OCAHO no. 1113 (2004) [naturalized USC has right to assert claim of discrimination in favor of native-born USC].

   1.b. LPRs, refugees, asylees, temporary residents who apply for naturalization within 6 months of eligibility. S/he must thereafter become naturalized within 2 years or be actively pursuing it. INA §274B(a)(3)(B), 8 U.S.C. §1324b(a)(3)(B), 28 C.F.R. §§44.101(c)(1) and (2). USCIS processing time is not counted toward the 2-year period. 28 C.F.R. §44.101(c)(2)(ii). *Dhillon v. Regents of the University of California*, 3 OCAHO no. 497 (Mar. 10, 1993). "Actively pursuing citizenship" may include withdrawing an application for naturalization and enrolling in class to improve English. *U.S. v. Southwest Marine Corp.*, 3 OCAHO no. 429 (May 15, 1992).

2. *Employer*—INA §274B(g)(2)(D), 8 U.S.C. §1324b(g)(2)(D). Where there is a distinct, physically separate subdivision that does its own hiring (not under a unified contract), the subdivision is treated as a separate employer.

3. *What is Prohibited?*—The statute prohibits discrimination against an employee because of national origin or citizenship in hiring, recruitment, referral or discharge. *LULAC v. Pasadena School Dist.*, 662 F.Supp. 443 (S.D. Tex. 1987) [discharge of workers for false Social Security numbers is discriminatory based on citizenship when applied to legalization applicants]. "Employment" is defined in case law as the "common law agency test." *U.S. v. General Dynamics Corp.*, 3 OCAHO no. 517 at 27–30 (May 6, 1993) [relying on Age Discrimination in Employment Act (ADEA) as guideline]. The statute may also cover a person or entity who is not in the position to hire the applicant, but "interfered with the individual's employment opportunities with another employer." *Elhajomar v. City and County of Honolulu*, 1 OCAHO no. 246 (Oct. 4, 1990) [state job service may be covered]. Refusing to reemploy someone in a layoff is considered "hiring" for purpose of the statute. *U.S. v. Southwest Marine Corp.*, 3 OCAHO no. 429 (May 15, 1992). "Hiring" also includes contract extensions and renewals. *General Dynamics Corp.*, *supra* at 35. Knowing discrimination includes failure to exercise reasonable care to acquire knowledge of legal significance of immigration related documents and to conduct employment practices in a fair and consistent manner. *U.S. v. Lasa Marketing Firms*, 1 OCAHO no. 106 (Nov. 27, 1989), *reported in* 67 No. 1 *Interpreter Releases* 10–11 (Jan. 1, 1990).

   3.a. *Retaliation*—The Act also protects against intimidation or retaliation against those who file charges or assert rights under the Act. INA §274B(a)(5); 28 C.F.R. §44.200(a)(2); 52 Fed. Reg. 37402 (Oct. 6, 1987). A protected individual can bring a claim for retaliation when allegedly fired for opposing the employer's discriminatory failure to hire a third party. *Diarrassouba v. Medallion Financial Corp.,* 9 OCAHO no. 1076 (Nov. 28, 2001). A claim for retaliation may survive rejection of the underlying claim of discrimination. *McNeir v. San Francisco State Univ.,* 9 OCAHO no. 1074 (Sept. 17, 2001) (dictum).

   3.b. *Conditions of Employment Not Covered*—The Office of Special Counsel, charged with enforcement of the statute, does not extend coverage to terms and conditions of employment. 65 No. 37 *Interpreter Releases* 991 (Sept. 26, 1988). However, it is arguable that conditions of employment could constitute "constructive discharge" if they are intolerable, and "hiring" could include terms and conditions of employment that existed at the time of hire.

   3.c. *National Origin/Citizenship Discrimination*— Applicants who were rejected in an H-2B or H-2A program may have a cause of action for citizenship discrimination if they were rejected for discriminatory reasons. *U.S. v. McDonnell Douglas*, 2 OCAHO no. 351 at 1–14 (1991) [H-2B]; *Matter of Investigation of Carolina Employers Ass'n, Inc.*, 3 OCAHO no. 455 (1992) [H-2A]. Applicants who were rejected in labor certification process are also covered. *Ironworkers Local 455 v. Lake Construction & Development*, 7 OCAHO no. 964 (Sept. 12, 1997). A naturalized citizen alleging discrimination in favor of native born USCs has cause of action. *Nickman v. Mesa Air Group,* 9 OCAHO no. 1113 (2004).

3.d. *Document Abuse*—The Act also covers discrimination due to "document abuse" where the employer, in seeking to comply with I-9 requirements, asks for more or different documents than required, or refuses to accept documents which are genuine on their face with the intent to discriminate. INA §274B(a)(6), 8 U.S.C. §1324b(a)(6), 28 C.F.R. §44.200(a)(3). Document abuse arising out of national origin discrimination is within the exclusive jurisdiction of OCAHO and Unfair Immigration Related Employment Practices, notwithstanding Title VII's exclusive claim to national origin discrimination when the business exceeds 14 employees. *Ondina-Mendez v. Sugar Creek Packing Co.,* 9 OCAHO no. 1085 (2002). Discriminatory document requests or refusals are actionable only under §274B(a)(6) and cannot support a claim of citizenship status discrimination under §274B(a)(1) (discrimination in hiring process). *U.S. v. Swift & Co.,* 9 OCAHO no. 1068 (May 7, 2001).

(1) *Pre-IIRIRA Document Abuse Cases*—Prior to the amendments made by IIRIRA §421 requiring a finding of discriminatory intent, one federal court found that document abuse required at least some form of discrimination for a violation to occur. *Robison Fruit Ranch, Inc. v. U.S.,* 147 F.3d 798 (9th Cir. 1998). *See also Getahun v. OCAHO*, 124 F.3d 591 (3d Cir. 1997) [document abuse found where employer fired asylee whose employment authorization was automatically extended and who filed for an EAD and obtained a receipt]; *U.S. v. Acosta, Inc.*, 7 OCAHO no. 961 (Aug. 28, 1997) [refusal to accept valid I-94]; *U.S. v. Beverly Center*, 5 OCAHO no. 762 (May 19, 1995) [document abuse found where employer rejected an applicant because his work authorization had a future expiration date; Handbook for Employers, 56 Fed. Reg. 41767, 41772 (Aug. 23, 1991)]; *U.S. v. Strano*, 5 OCAHO no. 748 (Mar. 28, 1995) [fine in excess of $100,000]; *U.S. v. Louis Padnos Iron & Metal Co.*, 3 OCAHO no. 414 (1992) [document abuse found where employer required applicant to produce INS document notwithstanding employee's Social Security card and drivers license]. *But see U.S. v. Zabala Vineyards*, 6 OCAHO no. 844 (Dec. 13, 1995) [no document abuse where employer asks everyone for a green card but does not deny employment to persons who have other documentation]; *Toussaint v. Tekwood Assoc., Inc.*, 6 OCAHO no. 892 (Sept. 12, 1996) [no document abuse in requesting a Social Security number].

(2) *Post-IIRIRA Document Abuse Cases*—As a result of IIRIRA §421, document abuse cases now require a finding of discriminatory intent, not simply discriminatory impact, thereby eliminating document abuse as a strict liability offense. *U.S. v. Diversified Technology & Services of Virginia, Inc.* 9 OCAHO no. 1095 (2003) [document abuse after the 1996 amendments is no longer a strict liability offense and therefore intentional discrimination under the traditional tests must be applied]. *See generally Diaz v. Pacific Maritime Ass'n,* 9 OCAHO no. 1108 (2004) [no document abuse because no discriminatory intent]; *Simon v. Ingram Micro, Inc.,* 9 OCAHO no. 1088 (Jan. 27, 2003) [where person worked illegally for five years, lied on their I-9, and presented a new Social Security card after obtaining lawful status, she was lawfully fired for violation of the company's honesty policy; no document abuse]; *U.S. v. Patrol & Guard Enterprises, Inc.*, 8 OCAHO no. 1040 (2000) [no document abuse where employer requested a green card because state law requires security guards to be citizens or LPRs].

(3) *Pre-Hiring Document Abuse*—In *U.S. v. Swift & Co.,* 9 OCAHO no. 1068 (May 7, 2001), the ALJ found that document abuse can arise when a verification-related document request or refusal occurs *before* hiring In *Swift*, the ALJ declined to follow *Harris v. Hawaii Dep't of Education,* 6 OCAHO no. 922, 1214 (1997) and *Huesca v. Rojas Bakery,* 4 OCAHO no. 654 at 5 (1994), which held that the employer cannot be liable for document abuse unless the challenged practice occurred *after* hiring and noted that the rulings of other ALJ's were "persuasive" but not binding. *Id.*

4. *The Statute Does Not Cover*:

4.a. Undocumented workers—8 U.S.C. §1324b(a)(3). Cannot maintain document abuse claim if not authorized to work. *Brown v. Baltimore City Public Schools*, 3 OCAHO no. 480 at 4 (June 4, 1992); *U.S. v. Hyatt Regency Lake Tahoe*, 6 OCAHO no. 879 (May 16, 1996).

4.b. Employer with 3 or less employees—28 C.F.R. §44.200(b)(1)(i), 52 Fed. Reg. 37402 (Oct. 6, 1987).

4.c. National origin cases where discrimination is covered by Title VII—(*i.e.*, where the employer is engaged in industry affecting commerce and employs 15 or more employees for 20 weeks in either the current or previous calendar years). *U.S. v. General Dynamic Corp.*, 3 OCAHO no. 517 at 20 n.28 (May 6, 1993). *But see Ondina-Mendez v. Sugar Creek Packing Co.*, 9 OCAHO no. 1085 (2002) [document abuse arising out of national origin discrimination is within the exclusive jurisdiction of OCAHO and Unfair Immigration Related Employment Practices, notwithstanding Title VII's exclusive claim to national origin discrimination when the business exceeds 14 employees].

Number of Employees—For purposes of determining whether there are sufficient employees (3) to meet jurisdictional concerns for citizenship discrimination, or less than 15 employees for national origin discrimination "courts generally do not count part-time employees who did not work each day of the working week." *Nickman v. Mesa Air Group,* 9 OCAHO no. 1113 (2004) [dismissing national origin complaint because employer had more than 15 full-time employees]. However, unlike Title VII, there is no 20 week durational requirement to determine 3 or more employees and OSC will look to all part-time and full-time employees employed on the date the alleged discrimination occurred. 52 Fed. Reg. 37402 (Oct. 6, 1987); *Sanchez v. Leobardo and Carmen Ocanas D/B/A Leo Ocanas Farm,* 9 OCAHO no. 115 (2005) [dismissing the complaint because the employer had one employee on the date the alleged discrimination occurred].

4.d. Where citizenship discrimination is required by:

(1) Law, regulation or executive order—INA §274B(a)(2)(C), 8 U.S.C. §1324b(a)(2)(C), *Murtano v. C.R. England, Inc.,* 9 OCAHO no. 1116 (2005) [dismissing complaint against employer for only hiring USCs where DOT interim regulations permitted only USCs to be issued hazardous material endorsements for a commercial driver's license]; *U.S. v. Patrol and Guard Enterprises, Inc.,* 8 OCAHO no. 1040 (2000) [no document abuse in requesting green card where NY law requires security guards to be USC or LPR]; *Sosa v. U.S. Postal Service*, 1 OCAHO no. 115 (Dec. 15, 1989) [rejecting lawful temporary resident based on postal regulations accepting only USC/LPR]. *But see Tovar v. U.S. Postal Service*, 3 F.3d 1271 (9th Cir. 1993) [rejecting claim that postal regulation barring temporary residents is contrary to IRCA, but finding that the regulation exceeded statutory authority based on the reasons advanced]; *U.S. v. Southwest Marine Corp.*, 3 OCAHO no. 429 at 22 (1992) [regulation not followed in practice cannot be used as defense].

(2) Federal, state, or local government contract—*Seaver v. BAE Systems,* 9 OCAHO no. 1111 (2004) [motion to dismiss claim by LPR granted where position required USC due to secret security clearance as part of a federal government contract]; or

(3) AG's determination that it is essential for employer to do business with "federal, state, local government"—28 C.F.R. §44.200(b)(1)(iii).

4.e. Where USC and alien are equally qualified—Although this could raise Title VII national origin problems for the employer, it only applies where the employer actually makes a one-to-one comparison between the citizen and the alien. 8 U.S.C. §1324b(a)(4); *Mesa Airlines*, 1 OCAHO no. 74 (1989) at 29 and 45.

4.f. Where discrimination is based on citizenship and employee is not a protected individual as defined in the Act.

4.g. Where discrimination arises out of disparate impact alone without a showing of intentional discrimination—28 C.F.R. §44.200(a) [comments to final rules adhere to this position but note that it would be illegal to have facially neutral policies (*e.g.*, English only) which are intended to discriminate]. Disparate impact was also removed as a basis for liability in document abuse cases. INA §274B(a)(6), 8 U.S.C. §1324b(a)(6); *U.S. v. Diversified Technology & Services of Virginia, Inc.* 9 OCAHO no. 1095 (2003) [document abuse after IIRIRA is no longer a strict liability offense and therefore intentional discrimination under the traditional tests must be applied].

B. *Procedures*

1. *Filing a Charge*

1.a. *Who May File*—28 C.F.R. §44.300(a)

(1) Any person directly adversely affected or his or her representative.

(2) Any USCIS officer.

(3) Private organizations, including labor unions, community organizations, etc.

1.b. *Office of Special Counsel (OSC)*

(1) Charge is filed at Office of Special Counsel for Immigration Related Unfair Employment Practices, 950 Pennsylvania Avenue, N.W., Washington D.C. 20530, 1-800-255-7688, (202) 616-5594, (202) 616-5509 (fax).

(2) OSC investigates charges and issues complaints before ALJ within 120 days.

(a) OSC may subpoena documents and witnesses during course of investigation prior to issuance of complaint. *U.S. v. Florida Azalea Specialists*, 19 F.3d 620 (11th Cir. 1994); *Whitney, Bailey, Cox & Magnani*, Case No. JFM 88-3456 (D. Md. 1988), *reprinted in* 66 No. 7 *Interpreter Releases* 182–83 (Feb. 13, 1989); *In re Tropicana Casino & Resort,* 9 OCAHO no. 1064 (2000) [denying request by employer to revoke or modify subpoena that asked for documents beyond the 180-day period]. OSC may also issue subpoenas to answer interrogatories. *In Re Investigation of Strano Farms,* 3 OCAHO no. 521 (1993). *But see In Re Investigation of Charge of Swift and Company,* 9 OCAHO no. 1058 at 8 (2000) [subpoenas limited to production of documents].

(b) OSC may bring "pattern and practice" complaints against an employer even if charge involves only one person. *U.S. v. Mesa Airlines*, 1 OCAHO no. 74 (OCAHO no. 1989) [OSC or private persons under INA §274B(d)(2) can bring pattern and practice cases].

(c) The 120-day rule is not always a strict guideline and a relatively minor delay may be excusable. *U.S. v. IBP, Inc.*, 7 OCAHO no. 949 (June 1, 1995). Moreover, the rule is an impetus to government action and should not be construed as barring suit in the absence of prejudice. *U.S. v. Agripac,* 8 OCAHO no. 1028 (1999) [OSC permitted to amend charge beyond the 120-day period where there was an absence of prejudice].

(d) Complainant's failure to check off "citizenship status discrimination" in OSC charge form does not preclude that claim in his or her subsequent OCAHO complaint for document abuse. *Guzman v. Yakima Fruit and Cold Storage,* 9 OCAHO no. 1066 (Apr. 12, 2001). *See also Nickman v. Mesa Air Group,* 9 OCAHO no. 1113 (2004) [failure to check box for citizenship discrimination in OSC charge does not preclude it in complaint where it was like or related to the original charges].

1.c. *Time Limitations*—Charge must be filed with OSC within 180 days of occurrence. 8 U.S.C. §1324b(d)(3). Equitable tolling may apply in appropriate cases. Letter, OSC (Feb. 23, 1988), *reprinted in* 7 AILA Monthly Mailing 542 (Nov. 1988).

(1) Where there are continuing violations (as distinguished from continuing impact), 180 days does not apply. *U.S. v. Southwest Marine Corp.*, Case No. 88-200036 (OCAHO no. 1989), *reported in* 66 No. 25 *Interpreter Releases* 709 (July 3, 1989) [employer continued to refuse to rehire person because he was a noncitizen]; *U.S. v. Fairfield Jersey, Inc.* 9 OCAHO no. 1069 (May 9, 2001) [applying the "continuing violation doctrine" and tolling the 180-day time limit in pattern and practice suit]. *But see Sodhi v. Maricopa Country Special Health Care District,* 9 OCAHO 1124 at 7–10 (Nov. 28, 2007) [citing

Ledbetter v. Goodyear Tire & Rubber Co., 127 S.Ct. 2162 (2007) and *National Railroad Passenger Corp. v. Morgan,* 536 U.S. 101 (2002) the ALJ recognized that the continuing violation position, *post-Ledbetter* and *Morgan,* had little vitality and because "each discrete discriminatory or retaliatory act starts a new clock" the claims for discriminatory evaluations and denial of leave were time barred].

(2) The 180 period begins to run at the time the employee becomes aware of the discrimination, *Mesa Airlines, supra, Sabol v. Northern Michigan University,* 9 OCAHO no. 1107 (2004) or when s/he should have been aware of it. *U.S. v. Weld County School District,* Case No. 90-200097 (OCAHO May 14, 1991).

(3) OSC and EEOC agree to appoint each other as agent for receipt of charges under Title VII and IRCA. 54 Fed. Reg. 32499, 32509 (Aug. 8, 1989). However, the charge must have been filed with EEOC within the time period for unfair immigration related employment practices (*i.e.,* 180 days) to be considered timely for the OSC. *Toussaint v. Tekwood Associates, Inc.*, 6 OCAHO no. 892 (Sept. 12, 1996) [general discussion of tolling].

1.d. *Private Action*

(1) If OSC fails to file complaint before ALJ within 120 days, it shall notify the charging party, who can file his or her own charge with ALJ. 28 C.F.R. §44.303(c). The OSC may continue to investigate the charge for an additional 90-day period and may bring the charge within that period if deemed appropriate. INA §274B(d)(2), 28 C.F.R. §§44.303(d), 68.4.

(2) Complaint to ALJ by private party must be brought within 90 days of *receipt* of OSC's notice that it does not intend to file charges. 8 U.S.C. §1324b(d)(2); 28 C.F.R. §§44.303(b), (c), 68.4. The 90 days may be equitably tolled. *Uthaiwan Wong-Opasi v. Tennessee Board of Regents,* 8 OCAHO no. 1037 (1999) [equitable tolling allowed where complaint was mailed on 83rd day but due to misdelivery, did not arrive for more than 90 days].

1.e. *EEOC Overlap*—The OSC will not consider a charge involving only national origin if the same charge based on identical facts is filed with EEOC, and vice versa unless the case is dismissed as outside of the scope of jurisdiction of EEOC/SC. *Romo v. Todd Corp.*, 1 OCAHO no. 25 (Aug. 19, 1988), *aff'd, U.S. v. Todd*, 900 F.2d 164 (9th Cir. 1990). If a claim raises discrimination based on both citizenship and national origin, and assuming that the employer is covered by Title VII, both agencies can and will assert their respective jurisdiction. *U.S. v. Marcel Watch Corp.*, 1 OCAHO no. 169 (1990) [same conduct can constitute national origin and citizenship discrimination; EEOC and SC have concurrent jurisdiction]. *But see Ondina-Mendez v. Sugar Creek Packing Co.*, 9 OCAHO no. 1085 (2002) [document abuse arising out of national origin discrimination is within the exclusive jurisdiction of OCAHO, notwithstanding Title VII's exclusive claim to national origin discrimination when the business exceeds 14 employees].

2. *Hearing*—INA §274B(e), 8 U.S.C. §1324b(e); 28 C.F.R. §68 (same as employer sanctions discussed above, except there is no review by the CAHO)

2.a. ALJ proceeding.

2.b. Any complaining party is party to proceeding.

2.c. ALJ may allow any other person to intervene.

2.d. Representation. A person may proceed *pro se* or with counsel and a corporation, partnership or unincorporated association may be represented by a nonlawyer. 28 C.F.R. §68.33(c)(3)(iv); *Daniel Ojeda-Ojeda v. Booth Farms, L.P.,* Case No. 06E00021 (Sept. 26, 2006)

2.e. *Default*—Complaint must be answered in 30 days or default may be entered. 28 C.F.R. §68.9(b). Default can be vacated upon showing of good cause. *Nickman v. Mesa Air Group,* 9 OCAHO no. 1106 (2004) [in determining good cause court should consider whether there was culpable or willful conduct; whether adversary was prejudiced; whether there is meritorious defense to the action].

2.f. *Motion to Dismiss*—Although OCAHO rules do not provide for a motion to dismiss for lack of subject-matter jurisdiction, ALJs have incorporated Fed. R. Civ. P. 12. *Seaver v. BAE Systems,* 9 OCAHO no. 1111 (2004) [granting motion to dismiss because on the face of the complaint the petitioner was not a protected individual]. However, the rules do provide for a motion to dismiss for failure to state a claim much akin to Fed. R. Civ. P. 12(b)(6). *Nickman v. Mesa Air Group,* 9 OCAHO no. 1113 (2004) [motion to dismiss national origin discrimination claim because company has more that 15 full-time employees]. A motion to dismiss has also been granted to enforce an oral settlement agreement. *Aziz Aityahia v. Sabena Airline Training Center, Inc.,* 9 OCAHO no. 1122 (Nov. 20, 2006) [oral settlement agreement is enforceable and case is dismissed].

2.g. *Subpoena Power*—ALJ has subpoena power (no contempt)—INA §274B(f)(2), 8 U.S.C. §1324b(f)(2). The scope of documents deemed relevant is very broad. *Matter of Investigation of Carolina Employers Ass'n, Inc.*, 3 OCAHO no. 455 (1992) [following *EEOC v. Shell Oil Co.*, 466 U.S. 54, 68–69 (1984)]. A subpoena was upheld against Miccosukee Resort and Convention Center notwithstanding claim that OSC and OCAHO lacked jurisdiction over a Native American tribe. *In re: Miccousukee Resort and Convention Center,* 9 OCAHO no. 1114 (Dec. 10, 2004).

2.h. *Standard of Review*—Preponderance of evidence.

2.i. *Full Discovery*—As in any civil action, full discovery is allowed. 28 C.F.R. §68.18–.24

(1) Sanctions for failure to comply with discovery including dismissal. *Rodriquez v. Tyson Foods, Inc.,* 9 OCAHO no. 1109 (2004) [dismissing case where *pro se* petitioner failed to respond to discovery]. *See also Dinko Sefic v. Marconi Wireless,* 9 OCAHO no. 1123 (Feb. 15, 2007) [motion to compel granted in part and denied in part].

(2) Ex parte communication with current employees of respondent company who are at a managerial or supervisory level and whose acts and omissions may bind the employer is not permitted. *U.S. v. Select Temporaries, Inc.* 9 OCAHO no. 1079 (2002).

2.j. *Hearsay Admissible*—Federal Rules of Evidence may be used, 28 C.F.R. §68.40, but do not bar hearsay under certain circumstances. *Diaz v. Pacific Maritime Ass'n,* 9 OCAHO no. 1108 (2004) [hearsay evidence may be included in affidavit where affiant is competent to testify to the matter, 20 C.F.R §68.38(b)].

2.k. *Summary Decision*—Similar to Fed. R. Civ. P. 56, allows for summary dismissal where there is no genuine issue of any material fact. 28 C.F.R. §68.38(c). *Diaz v. Pacific Maritime Ass'n,* 9 OCAHO no. 1108 (2004) [granting summary decision for employer on document abuse and citizenship status discrimination].

2.l. *Dismissal for Abandonment*—28 C.F.R. §68.37(b); *Rodriquez v. Tyson Foods, Inc.,* 9 OCAHO no. 1109 (2004) [dismissing case where *pro se* complainant abandoned claim by failing to respond to ALJ's orders including discovery].

2.m. *Alternative Dispute Resolution*—May be sought before a settlement judge. 29 C.F.R. §18.9 or settled between the parties.

(1) Settlement May Be Oral. *Aziz Aityahia v. Sabena Airline Training Center, Inc.,* 9 OCAHO no. 1122 (Nov. 20, 2006) [oral settlement agreement is enforceable and case is dismissed].

3. *Types of Relief*—INA §274B(g), 8 U.S.C. §1324b(g)

3.a. Cease and desist.

3.b. Compliance for 3 years.

3.c. Retain records for 3 years of persons applying.

3.d. Backpay, Frontpay and rehire; *Martinez v. Ray's Bar-B-Que,* Case No. 04B00054 (Dec. 19, 2005) *reported in* 12 No. 20 *Bender's Immigration Bulletin* 1419, 1469 (Oct. 15, 2007) [frontpay and backpay granted to USC whose hours were decreased when unauthorized worker returned and who was eventually terminated].

(1) Limited to 2 years prior to filing charge with ALJ.

(2) Interim earnings or amounts earnable by reasonable diligence deducted.

(3) No backpay or rehire if employment refused for any reason other than discrimination.

3.e. *Civil Fines*—Analogous to employer sanctions. Also provides for a separate civil fine from $100 to $1,000 if fine arises out of employer questioning of individual's documents. A civil penalty may be assessed for each type of violation. *U.S. v. A.J. Bart*, 3 OCAHO no. 538 (July 15, 1993) at 13–15 [separate penalties for document abuse and citizenship discrimination].

3.f. NLRB type remedies include posting notices, educating personnel, removing false performance reviews from file and ordering the lifting of any restrictions on the employee's work.

3.g. Debarment pursuant to Executive Order No. 12989 (Feb. 16, 1996), 61 Fed. Reg. 6091.

3.h. A list of violators through 2000 and the fines they paid is available at *www.cis.org*.

4. *Applicable Law*—The ALJ will apply the law in the circuit where the parties are located, if they are located in the same circuit. 28 C.F.R. §68.57 (2003).

5. *Burden of Proof*

5.a. *Generally*—ALJs have used Title VII law as a model to establish the shifting burdens of proof. *Hsieh v. PMC-Sierra, Inc.*, 9 OCAHO no. 1100 (2003); *U.S. v. Sargetis (Castle Valley Sales)*, 3 OCAHO no. 407 at 14–16 (1992); *U.S. v. Marcel Watch Corp., supra*. The test for determining whether the employee has established a *prima facie* case is set forth in *McDonnell Douglas Corp. v. Green*, 411 U.S. 792 (1973). *See also St. Mary's Honor Center v. Hicks*, 113 S.Ct. 2742 (1993) [where employer offers nondiscriminatory reason, even an unbelievable one, he meets his burden of rebuttal and plaintiff still has burden of going forward]; *Cooper v. Fed. Reserve Bank of Richmond*, 467 U.S. 867 (1984); *Texas Dept. of Community Affairs v. Burdine*, 450 U.S. 248 (1981). Pattern and practice cases also rely on Title VII law. *Dinko Sefic v. Marconi Wire*

5.b. *less*, 9 OCAHO no. 1125 (Nov. 29, 2007) [summary decision for employer defendant was granted where plaintiff could not demonstrate that his firing was due to his United States citizenship or as retaliation]; *U.S. v. General Dynamics Corp.*, 3 OCAHO no. 517 at 39–45 (May 6, 1993).

5.c. *Mixed Motive Cases*—In mixed motive cases, it is sufficient for a plaintiff to establish that race, color, religion, sex or national origin was a motivating factor for any employment practice, "even though other factors also motivated the practice." 42 U.S.C. §2000e-2(m). An employer has a limited affirmative defense that it would have taken the same action in the absence of impermissible motivating factors but rather than absolve it of liability, this defense only "restricts the remedies available to a plaintiff [to] ... declaratory relief, certain types of injunctive relief, and attorney's fees and costs. 42 U.S.C. §2000e-5(g)(2)(B)." *Desert Palace, Inc. v. Costa*, 539 U.S. 90, 94 (2003). Under *Desert Palace, Inc.* a plaintiff is not required to prove mixed-motive by direct evidence and the court rejected the contrary implication in *Price Waterhouse v. Hopkins*, 490 U.S. 228, 275 (1989). *Accord Dare v. Wal-Mart Stores, Inc.*, 267 F.Supp.2d 987 (D. Minn. 2003) [explaining change in burden post–*Desert Palace, Inc.*].

5.d. *Disparate Treatment Cases*—Disparate treatment cases require proof that a similarly situated nonprotected person was treated differently under "nearly identical" circumstances. *Bendig v. Conoco, Inc.*, 9 OCAHO no. 1065 (Mar. 8, 2001). The shifting burden analysis of *McDonald/Burdines* is unnecessary where there is direct evidence of discrimination. *Trans World Airlines, Inc. v. Thurston*, 469 U.S. 111 (1985). For purposes of the *McDonald Douglas* test, the fact that the person accorded preferential treatment has the "wrong type of visa" or is not authorized to work does not make him or her unqualified for the job. *Bendig v. Conoco, Inc.*, 9 OCAHO no. 1077 (Mar. 8, 2001). However, to prevent summary decision, there must be sufficient evidence of pretext. *Id.* Moreover, it is not necessary to show that discrimination is motivated by animus. *U.S. v. Southwest Marine Corp.*, 3 OCAHO no. 429 at 14–20 (1992). Cases involving discrimination based on disparate treatment (as opposed to disparate impact) also include *U.S. Postal Service Board of Governors v. Aikens*, 460 U.S. 711 (1983); *Furnco Construction Corp. v. Waters*, 438 U.S. 567 (1978).

5.e. *Document Abuse Cases*—Must prove discriminatory intent. *U.S. v. Diversified Technology & Services of Virginia, Inc.* 9 OCAHO no. 1095 (2003) [document abuse after IIRIRA is no longer a strict liability offense and therefore intentional discrimination under the traditional tests must be proven]; *Diaz v. Pacific Maritime Ass'n,* 9 OCAHO no. 1108 (2004) [no document abuse because no discriminatory purpose or intent]. *See also Simon v. Ingram Micro, Inc.* 9 OCAHO no. 1088 (2003); *Robison Fruit Ranch, Inc. v. U.S.,* 147 F.3d 798, 801–02 (9th Cir. 1998).

6. *Defenses*

6.a. *Sovereign Immunity*—State immunity under the Eleventh Amendment and sovereign immunity of the U.S. have been held to bar suit. *Hensel v. OCAHO,* 38 F.3d 505 (10th Cir. 1994); *Santos v. U.S. Postal Service,* 9 OCAHO no. 1105 (Apr. 7, 2004) [USPS may assert sovereign immunity]; *Massala Prince Reffell v. Prairie View A&M University,* OCAHO no. 1057 (2000); *Elhaj-Chehade v. University of Texas S.W. Medical School,* 8 OCAHO no. 1022 (1999). *But see Iwuchukwu v. City of Grand Prairie, TX,* 6 OCAHO no. 915 (Feb. 25, 1997) [home rule municipality is not accorded sovereign immunity]; *Mir v. Federal Bureau of Prisons,* 3 OCAHO no. 510 (Apr. 20, 1993); *McNier v. San Francisco State University College of Business,* 8 OCAHO no. 1030 (1999) [state officials not individually protected by the Eleventh Amendment can be sued in their official capacities for injunctive relief only]; *McNier v. San Francisco State Univ.* 9 OCAHO no. 1074, 2001 WL 1400366 (Sept. 17, 2001).

6.b. *Statute of Limitations*—Failure to file complaint within 90 days of receipt of 120-day notice from OSC bars the action. Failure of OSC to provide notice to complainant within 120 days does not necessarily bar the action. *U.S. v. Workrite Uniform Company,* 5 OCAHO no. 736 (Mar. 2, 1995).

6.c. *Reduction in Force (RIF)*—In *Bendig v. Conoco, Inc.,* 9 OCAHO no. 1065 (Mar. 8, 2001), the ALJ denied OSC's motion for summary decision finding, under Fifth Circuit law in RIF cases, that OSC failed to prove a prima facie case of intent to discriminate in giving preferential treatment to noncitizens in carrying out an RIF in 1999. *See also Hsieh v. PMC-Sierra, Inc.,* 9 OCAHO no. 1100 (2003) [accepting RIF and complainant's job performance as legitimate nondiscriminatory reasons]; *Santiglia v. Sun Microsystems, Inc.,* 9 OCAHO no. 1110 (2004) [granting summary decision to Sun in RIF case].

6.d. *Outsourcing*—Some courts have held that outsourcing cannot constitute discrimination because under *McDonnell Douglas* the employer is not "replacing" the discriminated worker, but is rather contracting the work to another company. *Humphries v. Palm, Inc.,* 9 OCAHO no 1112 (2004) [software employee could not establish prima facie case of citizenship discrimination because outsourced independent contractors in India were not replacement employees]. *See also Mitchell v. Worldwide Underwriter Ins. Co.,* 967 F.2d 565 (11th Cir. 1992).

6.e. *Good Faith*—There is no good faith affirmative defense to liability for citizenship discrimination. *U.S. v. Fairfield Jersey, Inc.,* 9 OCAHO no. 1072 (May 9, 2001) [rejecting employer's argument that it was motivated by a good-faith attempt to comply with §274A]. *But see U.S. v. Diversified Technology & Services of Virginia, Inc.* 9 OCAHO no. 1095 (2003) [refusing to strike "good faith" defense in a document abuse case where defendant essentially asserted compliance with the law]; *U.S. v. Desert Palace, Inc.,* 9 OCAHO no. 1067 (May 1, 2001) [refusing to strike in document abuse case affirmative defense of good faith].

6.f. *Honesty Policy*—Terminating an employee for falsifying employment information is a legitimate nondiscriminatory reason. *Simon v. Ingram Micro, Inc.* 9 OCAHO no. 1088 (Jan. 27, 2003) [where person worked illegally for five years, lied on their I-9, and presented a new Social Security card after obtaining lawful status, she was fired for violation of the company's honesty policy]; *Contreras v. Cascade Fruit Company,* 9 OCAHO no. 1090 (Feb. 4, 2003) [it is lawful to terminate an employee who presented fraudulent documents but subsequently obtained and presented valid documents].

6.g. *Collateral Estoppel*—State unemployment board determination did not have collateral estoppel effect in citizenship discrimination case. *Diarrassouba v. Medallion Financial Corp.,* 9 OCAHO no. 1076 (Nov. 28, 2001). *See generally Iron Workers Local 455 v. Lake Construction and*

Development Corp., 7 OCAHO no. 964 at 17–18 (1997) [doctrine applicable to administrative adjudications and proponent of collateral estoppel has burden to show that issue in prior proceeding was identical and decisive]; *McNier v. San Francisco State Univ.*, 9 OCAHO no. 1074 (Sept. 17, 2001) [state court's finding of race discrimination does not have collateral estoppel effect on issue of citizenship discrimination in OCAHO proceeding].

6.h. *Arbitration—Hiseh v. PMC-Sierra, Inc.*, 9 OCAHO no. 1096 (2003) [rejecting employer's claim that case should be dismissed and sent to arbitration].

7. *Constitutional Issues*—ALJ cannot rule on the constitutionality of a statute or regulation. *Elhajomar v. City and County of Honolulu*, 1 OCAHO no. 246 (Oct. 4, 1990) [declining to rule on the constitutionality of a state statute prohibiting referral for employment of non-USCs or LPRs]. However, the ALJ may be free to rule on the constitutionality of various due process questions such as selective prosecution and Fourth or Fifth Amendment violations. *U.S. v. Law Offices of Manulkin, Glaser & Bennett*, 1 OCAHO no. 100 (Oct. 27, 1989).

8. *Judicial Review*—INA §274B(i), 8 U.S.C. §1324b(i).

8.a. *Circuit Court of Appeals*—An appeal must be filed (received) within 60 days after entry of the ALJ's order to the court of appeal where the violation allegedly occurred or where the employer resides or transacts business. 28 C.F.R. §68.57; *Curuta v. OCAHO,* 398 F.3d 329 (5th Cir. 2005) [dismissing appeal where it was received by court one day late]. The 60 day period runs from the time the ALJ signs the order, not when it is served. *Mesa Airlines v. U.S.*, 951 F.2d 1186 (10th Cir. 1991). The time limitation is jurisdictional, no extensions may be granted, and the provision has been narrowly construed. *Id.* If the court upholds the ALJ's order, it has the power to enforce it.

8.b. *District Court*—If the order is not appealed to the circuit court, the OSC or person who filed the charge may seek enforcement of a final administrative order in district court where the discrimination occurred or employer resides. However, the ALJ's order is not subject to review in U.S. district court.

8.c. *Attorney's Fees*—The prevailing party, other than the U.S., may recover reasonable attorney's fees if the losing party's argument was without reasonable foundation in law and fact. INA §274B(h), 8 U.S.C. §1324b(h). The rule in *Christianburg Garment Co. v. EEOC*, 434 U.S. 412 (1978), that defendants cannot recover attorney's fees unless plaintiff's action was frivolous, unreasonable or without foundation, is applicable. *Daniel Ojeda-Ojeda v. Booth Farms, L.P.*, Case No. 06E00021 (Sept. 26, 2006); *U.S. v. General Dynamics Corp.*, 3 OCAHO no. 517 at 43–44 (May 6, 1993); *Kalil v. Utica City School District,* 9 OCAHO no. 1103 (2003) [where complainant's case was dismissed with prejudice for willfully and deliberately abusing the litigation process and defying the court's orders, attorney's fees were awarded to the respondent]; *Williamson v. Autorama, Inc.*, 1 OCAHO no. 174 (May 16, 1990); *Jones v. DeWitt Nursing Home*, 1 OCAHO no. 189 (June 29, 1990), *reported in* 67 *Interpreter Releases* 885 (Aug. 13, 1990) [fees awarded to plaintiff prevailing party where defendant's position was without foundation]. Attorneys fees cannot be awarded against the U.S. *General Dynamics, supra*; *U.S. v. Great Earth Cos.*, 9 OCAHO no. 1070 (June 1, 2001) [employer could not recover fees against OSC because there is no waiver of sovereign immunity]. The charging party in an ALJ proceeding based on an OSC complaint can have no liability for attorney's fees unless the OSC withdraws. *U.S. v. Great Earth Co.*, 9 OCAHO no. 1070 (June 1, 2001). Costs are never recoverable. *Id.* Attorneys employed by nonprofit organization are entitled to attorney's fees at market rate. *Ordonez v. Educational Employment Enterprise*, 1 OCAHO no. 293 (Feb. 1, 1991).

8.d. *Attorney's Conduct—Hseih v. PMC-Sierra, Inc.*, 9 OCAHO no. 1100 (2003) [describing the conduct of the employer's attorneys as "objectionable and unprofessional" and skirting "on the very edge of unethical conduct"].

8.e. *Private Right of Action*—Several courts have determined that there is no private right of action to enforce the provisions of §1324b pertaining to the unfair immigration employment decisions. *Shah v. Wilco Systems, Inc.*, 126 F.Supp.2d 641, 646–51 (S.D.N.Y. 2000) and *cases cited therein.* [no private right of action to enforce 1182(n) violations or violations under §1324b].

XIII. LEGALIZATION UNDER INA §245A

A. *Scope and Coverage*—An applicant for legalization must first apply for temporary residence under INA §245A(a), 8 U.S.C. §1255a(a). If successful, s/he may thereafter apply for permanent residency. INA §245A(b), 8 U.S.C. §1255a(b).

1. *Requirements for Temporary Residence*:

1.a. Must have entered U.S. before Jan. 1, 1982.

1.b. Must have resided continuously in U.S. in unlawful status since Jan. 1, 1982, and through the date of the application.

(1) *Unlawful Status*—Includes failure to file quarterly and annual reports pursuant to INA §265. *Matter of H-*, 20 I&N Dec. 693 (A.C. 1993), *overturned on other grounds Immigrant Assistance Project v. INS,* 306 F.3d 842, 871 (9th Cir. 2002). "Unlawful status" also includes persons whose entry was not lawful and begins from the date of entry. *Matter of S*, 19 I&N Dec. 851 (Comm. 1988) [person who entered under 2nd preference who was married at time was in unlawful status from that date].

(2) *Continuous Residence*

(a) *Prolonged Absence from U.S.*—Continuous unlawful residence is broken if absent from U.S. more than 45 days on any one trip or 180 days total since Jan. 1, 1982, unless return could not be accomplished due to emergent reasons. "Emergent reasons" has been defined as "coming unexpectedly into being." *Matter of C*, 19 I&N Dec. 808 (AC 1988) [letter containing funds for applicant's return not timely delivered]. Departure on I-512 does not break continuity of residence. 8 C.F.R. §245a.1(c)(1). In *Ruginski v. INS*, 942 F.2d 13 (1st Cir. 1991), the court upheld INS's determination that person who gave birth abroad and remained beyond the 45 days was not eligible for legalization.

(b) *Departure Under Deportation Order*—Continuous unlawful residence is broken where person departs "under an order of deportation." INA §245A(g)(2)(B)(i). INS's policy of denying legalization applications on the basis of an alleged prior deportation without affording an opportunity to file a waiver and without affording an opportunity to collaterally attack the prior deportation was successfully challenged in *Proyecto San Pablo v. INS*, 784 F.Supp. 738 (D. Ariz. 1991), *vacated in part and aff'd in part on jurisdictional grounds,* 189 F.3d 1130 (9th Cir. 1999). As a result of the litigation, USCIS is required to reopen class member's cases upon request so that they may submit I-690 waiver applications, and obtain FOIA materials that may be helpful in bringing a collateral attack. *Proyecto San Pablo v. INS,* Case No. 89-456-WDP (D. Ariz. Mar. 27, 2001). *See* 68 Fed. Reg. 37508 (June 24, 2003). After USCIS failed to comply, the district court issued another order requiring USCIS to reopen the applications a second time and readjudicate them in accordance with the proper procedures. *See also Proyecto San Pablo v. DHS,* No. CV 89-456-TUC-RCC (D. Ariz. June 6, 2007), *appeal pending* [ordering DHS to produce a complete copy of the deportation files including a copy of the tapes and/or transcripts of the prior deportation hearings]. *But see Pedroza-Padilla v. Gonzales,* 486 F.3d 1362, 1364–65 (9th Cir. 2007) [interpreting *Projecto San Pablo* as only applying to issues of inadmissibility arising from deportation and finding that deportation does break the continuous residence requirement where person was out more than 180 days].

(c) Continuous unlawful residence not broken where person went stateside criteria, not granted visa and returned to U.S. Legalization Wire No. 25, Everson, Deputy Comm. CO 1588-C (July 14, 1987), *reprinted in* 64 No. 28 *Interpreter Releases* 870 (July 27, 1987). 8 C.F.R. §245a.1(c)(1).

(d) *Effect of Fraudulent Return to U.S.*—Continuous unlawful residence is not broken even where the applicant returned as a nonimmigrant subsequent to Jan. 1, 1982, so long as s/he was in unlawful status prior to Jan. 1, 1982, and returned to unlawful residence in U.S. which includes entering the U.S. through the commission of visa fraud or fraud at entry. 8 C.F.R. §245a.2(b)(9); *LULAC v. INS*, 956 F.2d 914 (9th

Cir. 1992). Must obtain a waiver if committed visa fraud upon reentry (INA §212(a)(6)(C)). 8 C.F.R. §245a.2(b)(10). *Matter of P*, 19 I&N Dec. 823 (Comm. 1988). Continuous unlawful status not broken where out-of-status student obtained reinstatement through fraudulent means. *Matter of N*, 19 I&N Dec. 760 (Comm. 1988), holding affirmed in *Immigration Assistance Project v. INS*, 709 F.Supp. 998 (W.D. Wash. 1989), *aff'd sub nom. Legalization Assistance Project v. INS*, 976 F.2d 1198, 1213–15 (9th Cir. 1992), *vacated on other grounds INS v. Legalization Assistance Project of Los Angeles County Federation of Labor,* 510 U.S. 1007 (1993), *on remand* 50 F.3d 789 (9th Cir. 1995), *reinstated* 306 F.3d 842 (9th Cir. 2002).

1.c. If applicant entered as a nonimmigrant:

(1) Authorized stay expired before Jan. 1, 1982 through passage of time, or:

(a) *F-1 Duration of Status*—An F-1 with duration of status who proves s/he completed full course of study plus 30 days before Jan. 1, 1982, is covered. Legalization Wire No. 26, Everson, Deputy Comm., CO 1588-C (July 14, 1987), *reprinted in* 64 No. 28 *Interpreter Releases* 870 (July 27, 1987); 8 C.F.R. §245a.2(b)(12). Effective Feb. 23, 1981, later changed to Mar. 30, 1981, every such D/S F-1 student was automatically converted into a "date certain" status. The date certain for NIV expiration was the expected graduation date from the student's I-20 form. This conversion occurred automatically, whether or not INS made a notation on the student's visa or I-94. 8 C.F.R. §214.2(f)(5), 46 Fed. Reg. 7268 (Jan. 23, 1981), 1090 (Feb. 5, 1981). *See also* 58 *Interpreter Releases* 47 (Feb. 2, 1981). INS returned to its policy of issuing D/S student visas after Aug. 1, 1983, *See* 48 Fed. Reg. 14575 (Apr. 5, 1983), 60 *Interpreter Releases* 290 (Apr. 11, 1983). Thus, as of Jan. 1, 1982 all D/S student visas were considered by INS regulation to be date certain visas, with an expiration date as indicated on the Form I-20. If the date indicated on the I-20 was before 1982, then the student's visa expired through the passage of time and the student need not show that his or her unlawful status was known to the government, unless there had been a valid extension.

(b) *A or G Duration of Status*—A or G visa holders under D/S where employment terminated or otherwise ceased to be recognized by DOS. Legalization Wire No. 36, Everson, Deputy Comm., CO 1588-C (Aug. 25, 1987), *reprinted in* 64 No. 34 *Interpreter Releases* 1027 (Sept. 4, 1987); 8 C.F.R. §245a.2(b)(11). *Orquera v. Ashcroft,* 357 F.3d 413 (4th Cir. 2003) [upholding INS interpretation in regulation and denying amnesty for failure to provide proof that A-2 employment terminated or that DOS withdrew recognition]. In *Immigration Assistance Project of Los Angeles County v. INS*, 709 F.Supp. 998, 1003 (W.D. Wash. 1989), *aff'd sub nom. Legalization Assistance Project etc. v. INS*, 976 F.2d 1198, 1210–13 (9th Cir. 1992) *vacated on other grounds INS v. Legalization Assistance Project of Los Angeles County Federation of Labor,* 510 U.S. 1007 (1993) *on remand* 50 F.3d 789 (9th Cir. 1995), the court determined that distinctions between A, G and F visa holders who had completed their status (A/G) or their studies (F-1) before Jan. 1, 1982 and F-1 on D/S or H or L who were out of status before Jan. 1, 1982 is irrational. All should be treated as "out of status and known to the government"; *See also Immigrant Assistance Project of the Los Angeles County Federation of Labor (AFL-CIO) v. INS,* 306 F.3d 842, 870–73 (9th Cir. 2002) [reaffirming original preliminary injunction].

(c) *Silva-Levi* cases, 8 C.F.R. §245a.2(b)(13); or

(d) Asylum applicants who filed before Jan. 1, 1982, and whose claims were denied or not adjudicated. 8 C.F.R. §245a.2(b)(14); Legalization Wire No. 35, Everson, Deputy Comm., CO 1588-C (Aug. 19, 1987), *reprinted in* 64 No. 32 *Interpreter Releases* 970 (Aug. 24, 1987).

(2) Unlawful status known to the government before Jan. 1, 1982:

(a) *Known to the Government*—Means known to any federal agency. 8 C.F.R. §245a.1(d). For history of litigation, *see Immigrant Assistance Project of the Los*

Angeles County Federation of Labor (AFL-CIO) v. INS, 306 F.3d 842, 848–53 (9th Cir. 2002) and *Ayuda, Inc. v. Reno*, 7 F.3d 246 (D.C. Cir. 1993); *Farzad v. Chandler*, 670 F.Supp. 690 (N.D. Tex. 1987); *Matter of P*, 19 I&N Dec. 823 (Comm. 1988) [where applicant worked without authorization, obtained Social Security card and paid taxes he is "known to the government"].

(b) If school provides documentation or affidavit to INS clearly indicating that student had violated status prior to Jan. 1, 1982, and student was not reinstated subsequently, unlawful status was "known to the government." 8 C.F.R. §245a.1(d)(4).

(c) If applicant willfully failed to provide INS yearly or quarterly address updates under INA §265, unlawful status was known to the government. *Immigrant Assistance Project of the Los Angeles County Federation of Labor (AFL-CIO) v. INS,* 306 F.3d 842, 871–72 (9th Cir. 2002) [reaffirming original preliminary injunction and overturning *Matter of H-,* 20 I&N Dec. 693 (Comm. 1993)], *proceeding sub nom. Northwest Immigrants Rights Project v. INS*, 709 F.Supp. 998 *amended in part* 717 F.Supp. 1444 (W.D. Wash. 1989).

(d) There is a rebuttable presumption that all violations of status are known to the government. *Immigrant Assistance Project, supra.* For example, if a student or employee violated status in a manner that the school or employer was required to report to the INS, there is a rebuttable presumption that the school or employer did so. *Id.* INS document retention protocols make it unlikely that such information would have been retained, particularly if there was no A-file in existence at the time of the possible report.

1.d. Must have been continuously physically present since the date of enactment (Nov. 6, 1986).

(1) If re-entered before May 1, 1987, and applicant meets continuous residence requirement, s/he is eligible. 8 C.F.R. §245a.1(f).

(2) *Advance Parole*—Permits brief, casual and innocent trips after May 1, 1987 (and prior to temporary residency), if on I-512 for legitimate emergency or humanitarian purpose unless DD granted more time or stay out of U.S. was beyond the applicant's control. 8 C.F.R. §245a.2(*l*)(2); 8 C.F.R. §245a.1(g). In *Catholic Social Services v. Meese*, 685 F.Supp. 1149 (E.D. Cal. 1988), *aff'd sub nom. Catholic Social Services v. Thornburgh*, 956 F.2d 914 (9th Cir. 1992), *vacated and remanded on jurisdictional grounds sub nom. Reno v. Catholic Social Services*, 509 U.S. 43 (1993), the court struck down the regulation as inconsistent with the statute which was not limited to authorized departures under an I-512. In *Catholic Social Services v. INS,* 232 F.3d 1139 (9th Cir. 2000) (en banc), the court upheld a new class action for people who were "front desked" and for persons who were unable to present applications due to INS's interpretation of the brief, casual and innocent policy. *See also Catholic Social Services v. Ashcroft,* 268 F.Supp.2d 1172, 1177–87 (E.D. Cal. 2002) [reviewing the history of the case, recounting three new subclasses of legalization/LIFE applicants who departed the U.S. without advance parole, affirming that the court's finding in 1988 that 8 C.F.R. §245a.1(g) was invalid under IRCA, and finding that LIFE Act did not moot claims under IRCA's legalization program]. *Accord DeOliviera v. INS*, 873 F.Supp. 338 (C.D. Cal. 1994); *Bailey v. Brooks*, 688 F.Supp. 575 (W.D. Wash. 1986); *Gutierrez v. Ilchert*, 682 F.Supp. 467, 473–75 (N.D. Cal. 1988). *But see Matter of Singh*, 21 I&N Dec. 427 (BIA 1996) [IJ has no authority to terminate exclusion proceeding of CSS class member who proceeded abroad without I-512]; *Kasbati v. District Director*, 805 F.Supp. 619 (N.D. Ill. 1992) [finding trip abroad without advance parole resulted in new entry subjecting person to exclusion].

1.e. Must be otherwise eligible, 8 C.F.R. §245a.1(c)

(1) *Crimes*—Must not have been convicted of any felony or three or more misdemeanors committed in U.S. Felony means a crime committed in U.S. punishable by imprisonment of more than one year, regardless of the term actually served. Misdemeanor is defined as a crime carrying a sentence of more than 5 days, less than one year. 8 C.F.R. §§245a.1(o), (p). Where a state defines a conviction as a misdemeanor and the sentence actually imposed is less than one year, it will be considered a misdemeanor. *Matter of M,*

19 I&N Dec. 861 (Comm. 1989) [defining conviction and expungement for legalization purposes]. *Matter of M* criteria is harsher than *Matter of Ozkok*, 19 I&N Dec. 546 (Comm. 1988). *But see Martinez-Montoya v. INS*, 904 F.2d 1018 (5th Cir. 1990) [rejecting *Matter of M* as contrary to *Ozkok*]. Conviction requires only a finding of guilt or plea and that the judge ordered some form of punishment or penalty including, but not limited to, fine or probation. JRAD will not nullify a conviction, *reported in* 65 No. 16 *Interpreter Releases* 437, 443–46 (Apr. 25, 1988).

(2) Must not have assisted in the persecution of others.

(3) Must have registered for Selective Service if required to do so.

(4) *Must be Otherwise Admissible*—Inadmissible if: public charge (unless applicant can demonstrate history of employment, without public assistance); certain crimes; drugs (except 30 grams possession of marijuana); or on political and security grounds.

(a) *Public Charge*—Public charge determination includes many factors, not just whether the person is employed. *Matter of A-*, 19 I&N Dec. 867 (Comm. 1988) [reversing public charge finding where person was young and able to work despite current unemployment]; *Zambrano v. INS* (C.D. Cal. 1989), *vacated* 509 U.S. 918 (1993) [must use totality of the circumstances test]. Court in *Zambrano* gave applicants who were discouraged by INS rule limiting grounds to rebut public charge until Dec. 31, 1989 to apply. *Accord Perales v. Thornburgh*, 967 F.2d 798 (2d Cir. 1992), *vacated and remanded sub nom. Reno v. Perales*, 113 S.Ct. 3027 (1993) [extending filing deadline where INS had improperly determined that public charge included family members receipt of benefits and had failed to publicize the correct application of the rule].

Rebuttal of Public Charge Determination—An applicant may rebut a public charge finding under the special rule by demonstrating history of employment without public cash assistance. 8 C.F.R. §245a.2(d)(4). Public cash assistance does not include food stamps, public housing, other noncash benefits, unemployment, Medicare, Medicaid, or other treatment in the interest of public health. Letter, Slattery, Asst. Comm., Legalization, *reprinted in* 65 No. 10 *Interpreter Releases* 234, 235 (Mar. 14, 1988). Also does not include AFDC or SSI that went to children unless family relies on the benefits as its sole means of support. 65 No. 16 *Interpreter Releases* 438, 447–51 (Apr. 25, 1988). Includes SSI or needs based monetary assistance received directly by alien. Also includes funds for foster care. However, even where public cash assistance was received, INS may weigh a consistent history of employment, in determining eligibility under former INA §212(a)(15). 8 C.F.R. §245a.2(k)(4).

(b) *Waivers of Inadmissibility*—INA §245A(d), 8 U.S.C. §1255a(d).

i) No waiver for §§212(a)(2)(A) & (B) (crimes); §212(a)(2)(C) (drug offenses, except single offense of simple possession of 30 grams or less of marijuana); §212(a)(3) (security and related grounds). May obtain waiver of public charge provision to obtain temporary residence and may obtain waiver of public charge for permanent residence if SSI eligible (*i.e.,* blind, elderly, disabled). INA §245A(d)(2)(B)(ii), 8 U.S.C. §1255a(d)(2)(B)(ii).

ii) Automatic waivers for INA §§212(a)(5) and (7)(A), 8 U.S.C. §1182(a)(5) and (7)(A).

iii) Discretionary waivers for rest of §212(a) including HIV waiver if humanitarian purpose, to assure family unity or when it is otherwise in public interest. *Matter of P*, 19 I&N Dec. 823 (Comm. 1988). "In most cases, denials of legalization on the basis of the waivable exclusions should only occur when the applicant also falls within one of the specified nonwaiverable grounds of exclusion." *Id.* This is one of the most generous waiver standards in the INA.

a) "Family unity" defined as "maintaining the family group without deviation." Limited to spouse, unmarried children under 18, parents. 8 C.F.R. §245a.1(m).

b) Criteria for waiver not as limited or strict as INA §§212(h) and (i). (*e.g.*, family relations need not be as close). Public interest provision interpreted broadly (*e.g.*, there is a shortage of workers).

iv) INS must inform applicant of right to apply for a waiver. 8 C.F.R. §245a.2(k)(2); *Matter of A-*, 19 I&N Dec. 867 (Comm. 1988).

(5) *Application Must be Timely Filed*—Application must be filed within one year of period beginning May 5, 1987. If OSC issued between May 5, 1987 and April 4, 1988, application must be filed within 30 days of issuance of the OSC. Where OSC issued between April 5, 1988 and May 4, 1988, must file no later than May 4, 1988. 8 C.F.R. §§245a.2(a), 245a.2(c)(6). Three court cases have extended the time for filing legalization applications beyond May 4, 1988, in limited circumstances. *LULAC v. INS*, 956 F.2d 914 (9th Cir. 1992) [persons who were illegally in U.S. before Jan. 1, 1982, and re-entered with fraudulently obtained visa]; *Catholic Social Services v. Meese*, Case No. 86-1343-LKK (E.D. Cal. Apr. 1988) [persons who were illegally in the U.S. before Jan. 1, 1982, but who made a brief, casual and innocent trip outside U.S. between May 1, 1987 and May 4, 1988]; *Immigrant Assistance Project of the Los Angeles County Federation of Labor (IAP)*, 306 F.3d 842 (9th Cir. 2002) [persons who entered the U.S. before Jan. 1, 1982 on a nonimmigrant visa and who violated their status prior to Jan. 1, 1982, in a manner that was "known to the government," or who were reinstated to status or obtained some other benefit that apparently provided lawful immigration status]. In these cases the applicant must show that he was misled or discouraged from applying before May 5, 1988. *CSS* and *LULAC* were affirmed by the Ninth Circuit on Feb. 13, 1992, in consolidated appeals. *Catholic Social Services v. Thornburgh* and *League of United Latin American Citizens v. INS*, 956 F.2d 914 (9th Cir. 1992). The Supreme Court, however, found that applicants' claims were not ripe, except those who were turned away and could not submit their applications to the legalization officer ["front desked cases"]. *Reno v. Catholic Social Services*, 509 U.S. 43 (1993). Subsequent to the Supreme Court's decision, Congress in IIRIRA §377 and then in the LIFE Act §1104(c)(8) and (f), withdrew and then reinstated judicial review over certain legalization claims. *Catholic Social Services v. Ashcroft,* 268 F.Supp.2d 1172, 1177–87 (E.D. Cal. 2002) [reviewing the history of the case, recounting 3 new subclasses of legalization/LIFE applicants who departed the U.S. without advance parole, and finding that the LIFE Act did not moot claims under IRCA's legalization program]. In addition, the Ninth Circuit in *IAP* determined that several of the named plaintiffs (both individuals whose applications were timely filed and then denied, and also individuals whose applications were "front-desked" and not accepted for filing) have ripe claims and permitted an amended complaint to proceed challenging INS's definition of "known to the government."

LULAC/Newman and CSS Settlement—The parties reached a settlement in the *CSS* and *LULAC/Newman* cases that gave class members until Dec. 31, 2005 to apply for legalization under the 1986 IRCA. 80 No. 46 *Interpreter Releases* 1635, 1666–67 (Dec. 8, 2003); 81 No. 9 *Interpreter Releases* 275–77 (Mar. 1, 2004). Under the *LULAC/Newman* settlement, the following persons are covered: (1) persons who (or whose parent or spouse) are otherwise prima facie eligible for legalization under INA §245A who attempted to file a completed application and fee with INS or a QDE during the period May 5, 1987 to May 4, 1988 but had the application and fee refused because they traveled outside the U.S. and returned with a visa or travel document; (2) persons who filed for class membership under *Newman,* met the same characteristics as *LULAC*, and were denied or turned away because of the travel and the facially valid visa rule. Under *CSS* the settlement covers: (1) persons similar to *LULAC* but who traveled outside the U.S. after Nov. 6, 1986 without advance parole; (2) class members under *CSS* who met the same characteristics as (1) above, and who, because they (or their parent or spouse) were told they were ineligible or unable to obtain the required application forms, were not able to complete or timely file an application. The settlement agreement in these cases is separate and in addition to any application that may be made under LIFE.

IAP/NWIRP Settlement—The parties filed a settlement agreement with the district court on Aug. 24, 2007, that is still pending final approval as of this writing. *Northwest*

Immigrant Rights Project v. USCIS, No. 88-379R (Aug. 24, 2007). The settlement agreement covers both individuals who attempted to file applications during the application period but who were turned away or discouraged from filing by INS, and also individuals who filed timely legalization applications and were denied, or whose applications are still pending. Under the agreement, USCIS will adopt a new and more generous standard for determining whether a person's violation of status was "known to the government."

(6) Persons paroled into U.S. before Jan. 1, 1982, but parole not terminated until after that date are ineligible. 8 C.F.R. §245a.2(c)(8).

1.f. J-1s must still obtain INA §212(e) waiver.

1.g. Applicants in voluntary departure, extended voluntary departure, or deferred action or whose parole terminated prior to Jan. 1, 1982, are eligible. 8 C.F.R. §245a.2(b)(5).

1.h. Entries subsequent to Jan. 1, 1982, not documented on I-94 do not bar residency. 8 C.F.R. §245a.2(b)(8).

B. *Application Procedures*

1. Submit application to DHS or qualified designated entities (QDE). Government access to aliens' files at QDEs is restricted.

2. *Documentation/Preponderance of the Evidence*—Must show proof of identification, proof of residence and proof of financial responsibility. A voluminous submission is unnecessary; need not document every day of person's life. Cable, Norton, Assoc. Comm., Examinations, CO-1588 (July 7, 1987), *reprinted in* 64 No. 27 *Interpreter Releases* 846 (July 20, 1987). Must establish requirements by a preponderance of the evidence. *Matter of E-M-*, 20 I&N Dec. 77 (Comm. 1989) [defining preponderance of the evidence as "probably true"]. The form required to obtain or correct a Social Security number (SS-5) is not required as part of a legalization or SAW application. Cable, Landon (June 9, 1987), *reprinted in* 64 No. 23 *Interpreter Releases* 741 (June 15, 1987).

3. *Confidentiality*—INA §245A(c), 8 U.S.C. §1255a(c). Neither the AG, nor any official or employee of DOJ or bureau or agency thereof can use information submitted except for criminal purposes. Cannot use information for deportation proceedings. Criminal penalties for disclosure. IRS will not require information about legalization applicants. 6 *AILA Monthly Mailing* 1023 (July 1987).

3.a. *Fraud in Application*—Information on fraudulent application can be used to deport. 8 C.F.R. §245a.2(t)(4). *But see* INA §245A(c)(5)(A)(i) [can only use information to make a determination on amnesty applications]. However, INS will not issue an OSC where U.S. Attorney declines to prosecute in SAW/legalization cases. Legalization Wire No. 54. Provision may not bar inquiry by INS officers at port of entry concerning possible fraud in underlying application. *Lopez v. Ezell*, 716 F.Supp. 443 (S.D. Cal. 1989). Can use information even at removal proceeding if it was not furnished to the INS by the applicant. *Perez v. INS*, 72 F.3d 256 (2d Cir. 1995). However, information that was furnished by the respondent may not be used in a rescission proceeding. *Matter of Masri,* 22 I&N Dec. 1145 (BIA 1999) [information may only be used to determine eligibility for temporary status, to terminate temporary status, or for criminal purposes].

3.b. *Criminal Proceedings*—Confidentiality provision does *not* prevent the government from disclosing the applicant's name or the contents of the application in a criminal proceeding, even where the criminal proceeding is unrelated to IRCA. *U.S. v. Hernandez*, 913 F.2d 1506 (10th Cir. 1990). *But see U.S. v. Bajaj,* No. A92-174-CR (D. Alaska Apr. 8, 1993) [cannot breach confidentiality provision to charge someone for violation of 18 U.S.C. §1001 even if you could where the charge is under 8 U.S.C. §1255a(c)(6)]. Congress now requires the AG to provide legalization and SAW information: (a) to a duly recognized law enforcement entity in connection with a criminal investigation or prosecution when requested in writing; or (b) to an official coroner for identification purposes. INA §245A(c)(5)(B).

3.c. *Discovery*—Confidentiality provision does not bar disclosure of files in discovery in litigation brought on behalf of applicant, *Matter of Nelson*, 873 F.2d 1396 (11th Cir. 1989), or to discover class plaintiffs' names. *Zambrano v. INS*, 972 F.2d 1122, 1125–26 (9th Cir. 1992), *vacated and remanded, INS v. Zambrano*, 113 S.Ct. 3028 (1993).

3.d. Confidentiality provision may not prohibit INS from checking the file to verify deportability after person disclosed information to INS. *Arreola-Arellano v. INS,* 223 F.3d 653 (7th Cir. 2000).

4. *Fraudulent Application*—INA §245A(c)(6), 8 U.S.C. §1255a(c)(6)—5-year sentence and fine.

5. Work authorization and travel permitted during application period. INA §245A(b)(3), 8 U.S.C. §1255a(b)(3).

5.a. *Travel*—Regulation at 8 C.F.R. §245a.2(m)(1) requiring applicants for temporary residence to travel only on advance parole was invalidated in *Espinoza-Gutierrez v. Smith*, 94 F.3d 1270 (9th Cir. 1996). *But see Assa'ad v. U.S. Att'y Gen.,* 332 F.3d 1321 (11th Cir. 2003) [finding that INA §245A(a)(3)(B), permitting "brief, casual, and innocent" trips abroad as maintaining physical presence for purposes of legalization did not alter the entry doctrine and legalization applicant who was denied adjustment could be put in exclusion rather than deportation proceeding]. Where temporary resident status is approved, applicant can travel not more than 30 days on one trip and 90 days in the aggregate until s/he becomes an LPR. 8 C.F.R. §245a.2(m)(2). This restriction may be waived where absence was a brief trip due to emergent or extenuating circumstances beyond the alien's control. 8 C.F.R. §245a.2(m)(3).

5.b. *Employment Authorization*—Prior to grant of temporary residence, employment authorization granted in 1-year intervals. 8 C.F.R. §245a.2(n)(2). INS is not obligated to grant authorization to denied applicants during judicial review of their claims. *Ortiz v. Meissner,* 179 F.3d 718, 723–25 (9th Cir. 1999). After grant of temporary residence, employment authorization is continuous.

6. *Stay of Deportation*—Is available if applicant can establish prima facie eligibility for temporary residence until application is adjudicated. INA §245A(e), 8 U.S.C. §1255a(e). No deportation even if final order of BIA is affirmed on appeal. *Lopez-Rayas v. INS*, 828 F.2d 1134 (5th Cir. 1987). Moreover, INS cannot deport a person granted temporary residency without first revoking and terminating the temporary residency. *Matter of Medrano*, 20 I&N Dec. 216 (BIA 1990).

7. *Adjustment Date*—temporary resident adjustment date is date on fee receipt. 8 C.F.R. §245a.2(s).

8. *Proof of Temporary Residence*—I-688 card provides proof of temporary resident status and may be replaced if lost, stolen, destroyed, mutilated or requiring a change due to name or biographic data. 8 C.F.R. §264.1(c) [application made on I-695].

9. *Termination of Temporary Residence*—Temporary residence may be terminated under circumstances which would make the applicant ineligible for LPR status such as a felony conviction. 8 C.F.R. §245a.2(u); *Guzman-Andrade v. Gonzales,* 407 F.3d 1073, 1077–80 (9th Cir. 2005) [finding abuse of discretion where LAU denied adjustment of status on ground that petitioner's temporary residence was terminated where notice to LAU was timely filed, but fee was not perfected]. Service of notice of termination must be made by certified return receipt mail, although personal service may be deemed sufficient. *Eze v. Gonzales,* 478 F.3d 46 (1st Cir. 2007).

10. *May Not Petition for Family Members*—A temporary resident is ineligible to petition for family members for residency. 8 C.F.R. §245a.2(v).

11. *No Motions to Reopen/Reconsider*—Motions to reopen/reconsider are not permitted under INA §§210, 245A, 8 C.F.R. §103.5(b). *Rahim v. McNary*, 24 F.3d 440 (2d Cir. 1994) [upholding regulation denying motion to reopen in SAW cases]. However, an applicant may seek *sua sponte* reopening with a demonstration of "manifest injustice." *Matter of O-,* 19 I&N Dec. 871 (Comm. 1988); *Matter of S-,* 19 I&N Dec. 851 (Comm. 1988). Examples of such injustice include INS error or subsequent changes in the law.

C. *Administrative and Judicial Review*

1. *Administrative Appeal*:

1.a. To Legalization Appeals Unit (LAU) within 30 days. 8 C.F.R. §245a.2(p).

1.b. Appeal is based on the administrative record and upon such additional and newly discovered evidence not available at time of determination.

1.c. Notice and procedures provided for at 8 C.F.R. §§103.3(a), 1103.3(a).

1.d. No review for late filing.

2. *Judicial Review*

2.a. *Generally*—IRCA provided for judicial review only in review of an order of deportation under former INA §106. INA §245A(f)(4), 8 U.S.C. §1255a(f)(4). Therefore, judicial review of the two administrative appellate decisions (LAU and BIA) in the court of appeals under the same procedures was available. IIRIRA amended the statute to provide that the review was under INA §106 as it existed prior to IIRIRA's effective date. Since persons with denied amnesty cases would likely be placed in removal, rather than deportation proceedings, the effort to continue judicial review as before is at odds with the limitation to §106 deportation hearing review. Post-IIRIRA BIA decisions on removal are pursuant to INA §242, not former INA §106. In *Orquera v. Ashcroft,* 357 F.3d 413, 418–23 (4th Cir. 2003), the court found that INA §245A(f)(4)(A), regarding judicial review of individual orders, permits review under §242 despite the language limiting it to §106. *See also Guzman-Andrade v. Gonzales,* 407 F.3d 1073, 1075–77 (9th Cir. 2005) [following *Perez-Martin* and *Orquera* and finding jurisdiction in removal proceedings to review an amnesty application]; *Perez-Martin v. Ashcroft,* 394 F.3d 752 (9th Cir. 2005) [adopting *Orquera* for SAW cases under 8 U.S.C. §1160(e)(3)(A)]. *Orquera* left unresolved which venue provision applies, whether the automatic-stay provision of former INA §106 applies, and whether the jurisdictional limitations of §242 apply to BIA review, *e.g.,* limitations on review of cancellation decisions.

2.b. *Standard of Review*—Abuse of discretion or clear and convincing standard contained on record as a whole. *Guzman-Andrade v. Gonzales,* 407 F.3d 1073, 1077–80 (9th Cir. 2005) [finding abuse of discretion where LAU denied appeal where applicant provided necessary records of his convictions where available]; *Ruginski v. INS*, 942 F.2d 13 (1st Cir. 1991) ["[t]he Act provides for only very limited judicial review"].

2.c. *Injunction*—May seek injunction solely to effectuate appellate process. *Kalaw v. Ferro*, 651 F.Supp. 1163 (W.D.N.Y. 1987).

2.d. *District Court*—Judicial review in district court exists independently to permit a challenge to INS procedures in a pattern and practice claim. *McNary v. Haitian Refugee Center, Inc.*, 498 U.S. 479 (1991); *Immigrant Assistance Project of the Los Angeles County Federation of Labor (AFL-CIO) v. INS,* 306 F.3d 842, 862–64 (9th Cir. 2002) [following *McNary* and finding that a challenge to the burden of proof was a procedural challenge and that jurisdiction was therefore not barred]; *Catholic Social Services v. INS,* 232 F.3d 1139 (9th Cir. 2000) (en banc) [rejecting §242(f) and §242(g) challenges to jurisdiction]; *Abdullah v. INS*, 184 F.3d 158, 162–65 (2d Cir. 1999) [reaffirming *McNary*]; *Morales v. Yeutter*, 952 F.2d 954 (7th Cir. 1991); *Doe v. Nelson*, 703 F.Supp. 713, 720–22 (N.D. Ill. 1988). *But see Reno v. Catholic Social Services*, 509 U.S. 43 (1993) [reaffirming *McNary* but dismissing challenge to regulations on ripeness grounds]; *Aparicio v. Blakeway,* 302 F.3d 437 (5th Cir. 2002) [challenge to INS reliance on confidential SAW information in denying naturalization was not ripe]; *Espinoza-Gutierrez v. Smith*, 94 F.3d 1270, 1278 (9th Cir. 1996) [no jurisdiction to review LAU denial in exclusion proceeding]; *Waldei v. INS*, 938 F.Supp. 362 (E.D. La. 1996) [same]; *Naranjo-Aguilera v. INS*, 30 F.3d 1106 (9th Cir. 1994); *Ayuda, Inc. v. Reno*, 7 F.3d 246 (D.C. Cir. 1993); *Khan v. Meissner*, 921 F.Supp. 2 (D.D.C. 1995) [no review of termination of SAW temporary resident status; must go through exclusion or deportation]. The Ninth Circuit takes the view that district court jurisdiction remains to challenge INS practices and procedures following *McNary,* but that challenges to INS interpretation or application of IRCA's substantive eligibility criteria is permissible only on direct review. *Proyecto San Pablo v. INS,* 189 F.3d 1130 (9th Cir. 1999) [jurisdiction remains to review inadequate access to prior deportation files, refusal to accept IRCA waivers, and termination of employment authorization but not for interpretation of the scope of the waiver and pretext denials that may be reviewed in a final order].

2.e. *IIRIRA/LIFE Act Amendments*—IIRIRA §377 abolished this form of judicial review for *LULAC* and *CSS* cases by providing that no court shall have jurisdiction unless the person filed his or her amnesty application within the original deadline under the amnesty law or unless s/he was improperly turned away ("front-desked") at that time. INA §245A(f)(4)(C), 8 U.S.C. §1255a(f)(4)(C). *But see Catholic Social Services v. INS*, 232 F.3d 1139 (9th Cir. 2000) (en banc) [permitting litigation challenging §377]. Under the LIFE Act this provision was modified and effectively repealed for persons who, before Oct. 1, 2000, filed with the AG a written claim for class membership in either CSS or LULAC. *See also Catholic Social Services v. Ashcroft,* 268 F.Supp.2d 1172, 1177–87 (E.D. Cal. 2002) [reviewing the history and jurisdiction of the case, recounting three new subclasses of legalization/LIFE applicants who departed the U.S. without advance parole, and finding that the LIFE Act did not moot claims under IRCA's legalization program]. In *Immigrant Assistance Project of the Los Angeles County Federation of Labor (AFL-CIO) v. INS,* 306 F.3d 842, 865–67 (9th Cir. 2002) the court determined that some named plaintiffs should be given the opportunity to replead their compliance with §245A(f)(4)(C) in light of their failure to specifically detail that they actually tendered an application and fee or attempted to do so.

D. *Family Unity Program*—8 C.F.R. §236.10—236.18 [formerly 8 C.F.R. §242.6, 57 Fed. Reg. 6457 (Feb. 25, 1992)]. Provides for automatic stay of deportation and EAD for spouse and unmarried children of person granted temporary or permanent residence status as SAW, Amnesty, or Cuban/Haitian entrant.

1. *Requirements*

1.a. Family relationship existed as of May 5, 1988 for legalization, or Dec. 1, 1988, for SAW and has not terminated through death or divorce. Common law marriages where recognized are valid for family unity. An unmarried child who becomes 21 does not lose family unity benefits. 8 C.F.R. §236.12(a)(2).

1.b. Family member must have entered before May 5, 1988, or Dec. 1, 1988 in SAW cases, and have resided continuously in U.S. since that date. 8 C.F.R. §236.12(a)(1).

1.c. Family member must not have been convicted of a felony or 3 or more misdemeanors, be a person described in INA §241(b)(3)(B) or have committed an act of juvenile delinquency which if committed by an adult would be a felony involving violence or substantial risk that physical force may be used, 8 C.F.R. §236.13(b)–(d)

1.d. Family member may not be excludable or deportable under one of the criminal, foreign policy or security grounds of deportation or exclusion or the public charge provision. 8 C.F.R. §236.13(a).

(1) *No Stay of Deportation*—Does not protect families of persons whose applications are pending but not yet approved; does not provide a blanket stay of deportation for those who are denied or are subject to deportation on criminal and public charge grounds.

(2) *Smuggling Exemption*—The law provides an exemption from exclusion or deportation arising under the smuggling provision if applicant for family unity smuggled his spouse, parent, son or daughter prior to May 5, 1988. INA §§212(a)(6)(E)(ii), 237(a)(1)(E)(ii).

2. Termination of Family Unity Benefits—8 C.F.R. §236.18:

2.a. Unmarried son/daughter marries, spouse and the marriage terminates. *But see Hernandez v. Reno,* 91 F.3d 776, 780–81 (5th Cir. 1996) [where statute requires only that the qualifying relationship exist on May 5, 1988, the prior regulation preventing continued benefits due to a subsequent marriage is contrary to the statute and not deserving *Chevron* deference].

2.b. Final order of deportation is issued on a ground which would have made him or her ineligible for Family Unity.

2.c. Family Unity beneficiary becomes ineligible or inadmissible.

2.d. Family member loses status.

2.e. Family Unity was gained through fraud or willful misrepresentation of a material fact.

2.f. *Notice of Termination*—8 C.F.R. §236.18(b). Applicant has 30 days to respond.

2.g. Family unity benefits are not lost if the legalized family member becomes a citizen. 8 C.F.R. §236.11(3).

2.h. *Unlawful Presence*—Authorized stay pursuant to 8 C.F.R. §236.15(c) begins from the date Form I-817 is filed and continues until Family Unity benefits are terminated. Unlawful presence begins from the denial of I-817 and is in addition to any unlawful presence accrued before the I-817 was filed. Memo, Williams, Ex. Assoc. Comm., Field Operations, HQADN 70/10.19 (Jan. 27, 2003), *published on* AILA InfoNet at Doc. No. 03013042.

3. *Procedures*

3.a. *Form I-817*—Filed at service center of applicant's residence. A separate application for each family member is required. 8 C.F.R. §236.14.

3.b. *Approval*—Applicant is given VD for 2 years and can apply for EAD. *Escutia v. Reno,* Case No. SA CV 00-841 (C.D. Cal. Oct. 28, 2002) [settlement of class action requiring processing *inter alia* of employment authorizations within 90 days for family unity applicants].

3.c. *Advance Parole*—Where Family Unity beneficiary reenters on advance parole, s/he will be re-admitted in same status and will not lose eligibility for suspension. Miscellaneous and Technical Immigration and Naturalization Amendments of 1991, PL 102-232, 105 Stat. 1733, Sec. 304(c)(1); 8 C.F.R. §236.16.

3.d. *Extensions*—File new I-817. USCIS cannot deny an extension merely because it receives contrary information that is demonstrably false. *Camarena v. Meissner,* 78 F.Supp.2d 1044 (N.D. Cal. 1999).

3.e. *Denials*—No appeal, but can reapply if applicant has overcome denial. 8 C.F.R. §236.14(b).

4. *Permanent Residency for Family Members*—Section 112 of IMMACT90 provided special immigrant visa numbers in FY 92-94 for spouses and children of legalized persons, even if relationship arose after the date the petitioner became an LPR. 8 C.F.R. §204.2(d). Temporary resident can also seek permanent residence through regular immigrant visa categories. Letter, Norton, Assoc. Comm., Examinations, *reprinted in* 65 No. 23 *Interpreter Releases* 615, 631 (June 13, 1988).

5. *Eligibility for Cancellation of Removal* A family unity member is "admitted in any status" for purposes of LPR cancellation and therefore may qualify for relief. *Garcia-Quintero v. Gonzales,* 455 F.3d 1006, 1015–19 (9th Cir. 2006) [admission into family unity program is sufficient to qualify as an admission for purposes of cancellation and LPR in removal proceeding had the necessary seven years based upon his acceptance into the family unity program while in the US].

E. ***Second Stage of Legalization: Permanent Residency***—Final regulations published in 66 No. 27 *Interpreter Releases* 768, 780–83 (July 17, 1989).

1. *Eligibility*—8 C.F.R. §245a.3(a) and (b).

1.a. Applicant must apply within 43 months after temporary residence is granted. 8 C.F.R. §245a.3(a)(2). If applicant does not apply, legalization benefits are lost illegal status is restored.

(1) Application for permanent residence may be submitted at any time after receiving temporary residence. 8 C.F.R. §245a.3(a)(1). The application will not be processed until the beginning of the 19th month from the date of the fee receipt for the application for temporary residence. 8 C.F.R. §§245a.3(a), 245a.2(s).

(2) IMMACT90 amended INA §245A(b) to allow a temporary resident an additional year to file for permanent residence. If temporary resident is encountered by INS and has not been a temporary resident for 42 months or more, INS must advise him/her of the time s/he has left to apply for permanent residence. IMMACT90 Wire No. 16, McNary, Comm., CO-1588-L (Dec. 20, 1990).

1.b. *Continuous Residence*—Must establish continuous residence since temporary resident status. Absence not exceeding 30 days on one trip and 90 in the aggregate does not break continuous residence. A single absence exceeding these limits can be waived upon a showing that the person did not abandon residency. 8 C.F.R. §245a.3(b)(2).

1.c. *Admissibility*—Must not have any conviction of a felony or 3 misdemeanors and must be otherwise admissible. 8 C.F.R. §245a.3(b)(3).

(1) INA §§212(a)(5) and (7)(A) are automatically waived.

(2) Other sections may be waived except: INA §§212(a)(2)(A), (2)(B), (2)(C) and (3) (except subparagraph D);

(3) Public charge exclusion may be waived for persons who qualify for SSI. 8 C.F.R. §245a.3(g)(3)(ii). An applicant may also prove that he is not a public charge by reference to the special rule under 8 C.F.R. §245a.3(g)(4)(iii), permitting a showing of a consistent employment history.

(4) HIV test is necessary for eligibility if the test was not previously taken. 8 C.F.R. §245a.3(d)(4). HIV is a bar to admissibility, but may be waived.

1.d. *Knowledge of English, History, Civics*—Must meet the requirements of INA §312 (minimal understanding of English, history and U.S. government) or must be "satisfactorily pursuing" a course of study recognized by the AG. 8 C.F.R. §245a.1(s).

(1) Not applicable to those under 16 or over 65, or over 50 who have lived in U.S. for 20 years. 8 C.F.R. §245a.3(b)(4)(ii).

(2) "Satisfactorily pursuing," 8 C.F.R. §245a.1(s), includes:

(a) 40 hours of a minimum 60 hour course in English/government;

(b) High school diploma/GED if English proficiency test passed;

(c) One-year attendance at state recognized, accredited learning institution;

(d) Attending INS certified course given by employers or social, community or private groups;

(e) Passed proficiency test.

2. *Application Process*

2.a. I-698 with documents and filing fee to service center.

2.b. Interview conducted at LO or INS office.

2.c. Denials may be appealed to LAU.

3. *Residency Date for Naturalization*—The adjustment date is "the date of filing of the application for permanent residence or the eligibility date, whichever is later." 8 C.F.R. §245a.3(m). Continuous residence for naturalization begins from the adjustment date. *Id.*

XIV. LIFE ACT ADJUSTMENT— Legal Immigration Family Equity Act, PL 106-553, 114 Stat. 2762, Title XI of H.R. 5548 (Dec. 21, 2000), H. Rep. No. 106-1005 and LIFE Act Amendments, PL 106-554, 114 Stat. 2763, Title XV, Div. B of H.R. 5666 (Dec. 21, 2000), H. Rep. No. 106-1033, 146 Cong. Rec. S11850-52 (daily ed. Dec. 15, 2000, Senators Joint Memorandum); 8 C.F.R. §§245a.10–.37; 66 Fed. Reg. 29661–82 (June 1, 2001); 67 Fed. Reg. 38341–52 (June 4, 2002).

A. *Requirements for Adjustment*

1. *Class Membership*—Class members in *Catholic Social Services v. Meese, LULAC v. INS,* or *Zambrano v. INS* who filed a written claim for class membership with the AG before Oct. 1, 2000. 8 C.F.R. §245a.10; *and*

2. *Continuous Unlawful Residence*—Entered the U.S. before Jan. 1, 1982 and resided continuously in the U.S. in unlawful status since that date, through May 4, 1988. 8 C.F.R. §245a.11(b). In determining continuous residence: (i) no single absence may exceed 45 days and aggregate absences may not exceed 180 days, unless applicant shows "emergent reasons"; (ii) must have been maintaining a residence during the relevant period; (iii) no departure under an order of deportation.

8 C.F.R. §245a.15(c)(1). Unlawful status is defined in a manner similar to legalization. 8 C.F.R. §245a.15(d). The criteria used in regulations pursuant to INA §245A(g) shall apply and NIVs whose lawful status expired before Jan. 1, 1982 as well as Cuban-Haitian entrants are qualified. J-1 visa holders required to meet the 2-year foreign residence requirement are barred.

3. *Continuous Physical Presence*—Applicant must establish continuous physical presence in the U.S. from Nov. 6, 1986, to May 4, 1988. 8 C.F.R. §245a.11(c). Brief, casual and innocent absences from the U.S. (even without advance parole) do not break the physical presence requirement. A single absence of 30 days and aggregate absences of 90 days are deemed brief casual and innocent. 8 C.F.R. §245a.16(b).

4. *Admissibility and Other Requirements*—Applicants must establish: (i) admissibility except as to INA §§212(a)(5), (7)(A), (9)(A) & (C) and certain other grounds that the AG may waive under INA §245A(d)(2)(B); (ii) no felony conviction or 3 or more misdemeanors; (iii) that they have not assisted in the persecution of others; (iv) registration with Selective Service, if required; (v) that they meet the English, history and government requirements generally reserved for citizens or that they are satisfactorily pursuing a course of study. 8 C.F.R. §§245a.11(d), (e), 245a.18. AG may waive the English and history/government requirements for someone who is 65 or older or developmentally disabled. 8 C.F.R. §245a.17(c).

5. *Application Period*—Applicants must file (postmark) the application on or before June 4, 2003. If postmark is illegible or missing and it was mailed within the U.S., it is timely filed if received on or before June 9, 2003. If mailed from abroad with an illegible or missing postmark, it is timely filed if received on or before June 18, 2003. 8 C.F.R. §245a.12. The Missouri Service Center has jurisdiction over all applications. 8 C.F.R. §245a.12(b). If the person is in exclusion, deportation or removal proceedings, s/he may seek administrative closure of the case by presenting prima facie documents supporting the claim to INS. If INS concurs the IJ/BIA "shall" close the proceedings. 8 C.F.R. §245a.12(b)(1). If proceedings have already been administratively closed or there is a final order, the applicant may apply directly to INS. 8 C.F.R. §245a.12(b)(3). The filing of a LIFE legalization application after June 1, 2001 and before June 4, 2003 stays the execution of a final order of exclusion, deportation or removal until there is a final decision on the application. 8 C.F.R. §245a.13(f).

6. *Application and Documentation*—A LIFE legalization application must include, under 8 C.F.R. §245a.12(d):
   - Forms I-485, G-325A, medical, 2 photos, filing fee and fingerprint fee;
   - Evidence of identity;
   - Proof of class membership in *CSS, LULAC,* or *Zambrano. See* 8 C.F.R. §245a.14;
   - Proof of continuous residence in unlawful status prior to Jan. 1, 1982 until May 4, 1988;
   - Proof of continuous physical presence from Nov. 6, 1986 through May 4, 1988.
     [Although an application cannot be denied solely on the ground that only affidavits were submitted to establish physical presence, affidavits alone will not always be sufficient to support the applicant's claim. Memo, Carpenter, Acting Principal Legal Advisor, USCIS, HQCOU 70/10.14 (Dec. 5, 2003), *reprinted in* 80 No. 47 *Interpreter Releases* 1685–87 (Dec. 15, 2003).]
   - Proof of Citizenship Skills.
     [Citizenship skills are similar to legalization and includes complying with naturalization requirements; having a high school diploma or GED where English and U.S. history requirements were met; or having attended or attending a state recognized accredited learning institution that takes attendance for English and U.S. history and government.]

   8 C.F.R. §245a.17.

6.a. *Waivers of Inadmissibility*—Form I-690 for INA §§212(a)(9)(A) & (C). 8 C.F.R. §245a.18(c)(1). Waivers may be granted for most grounds of inadmissibility for "humanitarian purposes, to ensure family unity, or when the granting of such a waiver is otherwise in the public interest." 8 C.F.R. §245a.18(c). Special rule for public charge waiver applies. 8 C.F.R. §245a.18(d).

6.b. *Former Applications*—Information contained in Form I-687 amnesty application may be used in a subsequent LIFE application. Memo, Carpenter, Acting Principal Legal Advisor, USCIS,

HQCOU 70/ 10.14 (Dec. 5, 2003), *reprinted in* 80 No. 47 *Interpreter Releases* 1685–87 (Dec. 15, 2003).

6.c. *Burden of Proof*—Applicant's burden of proof may be met through the production of secondary evidence. §245a.12(e), (f).

7. *Effect of Pending Application*—While application is pending, the applicant (1) may not be removed or deported; (2) can obtain advance parole; and (3) can obtain employment authorization. 8 C.F.R. §245a.13. INS distinguishes between granting advance parole, permission to be paroled at the border even if inadmissible (*e.g.,* a person with a final order who obtains an I-512 may still be paroled when he returns to the U.S.), and being approved under the LIFE legalization program. A person may be paroled with a final order, but the final order would preclude him or her from being admitted and granted adjustment of status. Memo, Pearson, Ex. Assoc. Comm. Field Operations, HQADN 70/23.1 (May 30, 2001), *reprinted in* 78 No. 22 *Interpreter Releases* 914, 965–68 (June 4, 2001).

7.a. LIFE legalization applicants who apply for admission are not subject to the 3/10 year bar. 8 C.F.R. §245a.13(e)(4).

7.b. If LIFE legalization applicant is denied admission, s/he may still pursue the application for AOS abroad. 8 C.F.R. §245a.13(e)(5).

8. *Administrative and Judicial Review*—The provisions of the amnesty program regarding administrative and judicial review shall generally apply. A denied application may be appealed to the AAO on I-290B. 8 C.F.R. §245a.20(b). The notice of appeal is filed with the service center that issued the decision, and must be *received,* with the appropriate fee, within 30 days after service of the notice of denial. 8 C.F.R. §§245a.20(a)(2), (b)(1). If the applicant is outside the U.S. and the notice of denial was mailed to a foreign address, the appeal must be *received* within 60 days. 8 C.F.R. §245a.20(b)(2). An appellant may renew employment authorization until a final decision by the AAO. 8 C.F.R. §245a.20(a)(2).

9. *Family Unity*—Eligible family members may apply for Family Unity benefits. 8 C.F.R. §236.14(a). Form I-817 is filed at the Missouri Service Center. 8 C.F.R. §245a.33(a), (b). A person is eligible for Family Unity benefits if: (1) s/he is the spouse or unmarried child under 21 of an eligible applicant at the time the I-817 is adjudicated; (2) s/he entered the U.S. before Dec. 1, 1988 and resided in the U.S. on such date; *and* (3) if applying for Family Unity benefits on or after June 5, 2003, s/he is the spouse/unmarried child under 21 of a LIFE Legalization applicant who has filed an I-485. 8 C.F.R. §245a.31. Persons ineligible for Family Unity include: (a) persons convicted of a felony or 3 or more misdemeanors; (b) persons who have ordered, incited, assisted or otherwise participated in the persecution of others; (c) persons who have been convicted of a particularly serious crime and who are a danger to the U.S.; (d) persons who the AG has serious reasons to believe have committed a serious nonpolitical crime outside the U.S.; *or* (e) persons who the AG has reasonable grounds to believe are a danger to U.S. security. 8 C.F.R. §245a.32. Removal proceedings may be instituted on any grounds except INA §§237(a)(1)(A)–(C) and 237(a)(3)(A). §245a.34(a). Persons granted Family Unity benefits are authorized to be employed and are not subject to the 3/10 year bar. 8 C.F.R. §§245a.34(c), (d). Family Unity beneficiary may also obtain advance parole and if not inadmissible under criminal or security grounds, will be paroled into the U.S. upon return. 8 C.F.R. §245a.35(b). Family Unity benefits may be terminated if: (1) the benefits were obtained by fraud or willful misrepresentation of a material fact; (2) the beneficiary commits an act that renders him ineligible for Family Unity; (3) the principal LIFE Legalization applicant fails to apply before May 31, 2002; or (4) the qualifying basis for the relationship with the principal applicant no longer exists (*e.g.,* spouse and principal divorce). 8 C.F.R. §245a.37(a). Before benefits are terminated, a notice of intent to terminate is issued, allowing 30 days to respond. 8 C.F.R. §245a.37(b).

10. *Confidentiality*—The confidentiality provisions of the amnesty program under INA §245A apply. 8 C.F.R. §245a.21; Memo, Carpenter, Acting Principal Legal Advisor, USCIS, HQCOU 70/10.14 (Dec. 5, 2003), *reprinted in* 80 No. 47 *Interpreter Releases* 1685–87 (Dec. 15, 2003) [DHS may not use or disclose information in LIFE application except to adjudicate the application itself or for law enforcement or fraud proceedings].

XV. LEGALIZATION FOR SPECIAL AGRICULTURAL WORKERS (SAW)—INA §210

A. *Scope and Coverage*—Temporary residency then permanent residency.

1. *Temporary Residence*

   1.a. Resided in U.S.

   1.b. Performed "seasonal agricultural services" in U.S. for at least 90 "man days" between May 1, 1985 to May 1, 1986.

   (1) "Man day" includes not less than one hour of qualifying work for wages. Can include work for more than one employer in one day, but is counted as one man day. 8 C.F.R. §210.1(j). Piece work included. Requires only work for the time required to do piece work. *Id.*

   (2) "Seasonal Agricultural Services" means the performance of field work relating to planting, cultural practices, cultivating, growing and harvesting fruits and vegetables of every kind and other perishable commodities as defined by Secy. of Agriculture.

   (a) *Perishable Commodities*—Defined at 7 C.F.R. §1(d), 52 Fed. Reg. 20372. Does not include sugar cane, livestock or poultry. See also *National Cotton Council of America v. Lyng*, ___ F.Supp. ___ (N.D. Tex. 1988); 65 No. 7 *Interpreter Releases* 153 (Feb. 22, 1988); Legalization Wire No. 58 [cotton is a fruit for purposes of the statute]; *Matter of* ___, (LAU Feb. 8, 1988); 65 No. 14 *Interpreter Releases* 410–11 (Apr. 18, 1988) [corn, whether or not for human consumption is included]; *Wint v. Yeutter*, 902 F.2d 76 (D.C. Cir. 1990) [sugar cane is not a perishable commodity or vegetable]; *Morales v. Yeutter*, 952 F.2d 954 (7th Cir. 1991) [sod is not a perishable commodity]; *Texas Farm Bureau v. Lyng*, 697 F.Supp. 935 (E.D. Tex. 1988) [hay is not a perishable commodity].

   (b) *Field Work*—Defined as employment on agricultural land. Includes stripping, grading, drying, or packing performed in or adjacent to the field where produce is grown. Legalization Wire No. 23 (June 5, 1987), *reprinted in* 64 No. 24 *Interpreter Releases* 777 (June 29, 1987). If work is performed at a remote site, it can still be considered field work if 85% of produce was grown by growers/employer. Legalization Wire No. 33, Norton, Assoc. Comm., Examinations, CO-1988-C (Aug. 14, 1987), *reprinted in* 64 No. 32 *Interpreter Releases* 971 (Aug. 24, 1987).

   1.c. Must be otherwise admissible. Same waivers as legalization. INA §210(c)(2).

   1.d. Must have filed a timely application for temporary residence during 18-month period beginning June 1, 1987.

B. *Procedures for SAW Status*

1. *Filing*—Applications filed in U.S. (with AG or designated entities) or at consular office abroad.

   1.a. INS moved the date a SAW worker could file from before May 1, 1987 to entry before June 27, 1987. 8 C.F.R. §210.2(c)(1). Date further extended through court action. *Vargas v. Meese*, 682 F.Supp. 591 (D.D.C. 1987) [H-2 could file under SAW even if they entered after June 27, 1987].

   1.b. Applicants outside U.S. can apply at consulate without documentation, and provide qualifying documentation within 90 days of entry. 8 C.F.R. §210.2 (c)(4)(iii). Legalization Wire No. 27, Everson, Deputy Comm., CO 1588 (July 1, 1987), *reprinted in* 64 No. 26 *Interpreter Releases* 824 (July 13, 1987).

2. *Proof of Eligibility*—INA §210(b)(3), 8 U.S.C. §1160(b)(3).

   2.a. Through employment records and "such other reliable documentation."

   2.b. *Burden of Proof*—Preponderance of evidence met if: (1) farm labor contractor or employer kept proper records; or (2) alien produced sufficient evidence to infer the extent of employment. Burden then shifts to government. *Haitian Refugee Center v. Nelson*, 694 F.Supp. 864 (S.D. Fla. 1988), *aff'd*, 111 S.Ct. 888 (1991) [reversing INS denial of approximately 22,000 applications where an incorrect standard was applied]; *United Farmworkers of America v.*

INS, Case No. Cv. S-87-1064-JFJ (E.D. Cal. June 15, 1989), *reported in* 66 No. 16 *Interpreter Releases* 452 (Apr. 24, 1989) [proposed settlement] and 66 No. 25 *Interpreter Releases* 712 (July 3, 1989) [approval of settlement reopening 25,000 SAW denials to ensure that farmworkers were allowed to carry their burden of proof of 90 days of farm work as a matter of "just and reasonable" inference].

2.c. Must submit proof of identity, residence, financial ability as well as eligibility. 8 C.F.R. §210.3.

2.d. Applicant has right to present witnesses and the government must provide competent translators at the interview. *Haitian Refugee Center v. Nelson,* 872 F.2d 1555 (11th Cir. 1989), *aff'd,* 111 S.Ct. 888 (1991). INS agents also required to keep particularized account of evidence on I-696 interview sheets so that reviewing courts have record to review. *Id.*

3. *Confidentiality*—INA §210(b)(6), 8 U.S.C. §1160(b)(6)—Same as the confidentiality provision for legalization. *See in this chapter,* ¶ XIII.B.3 (p.1286), *supra.*

4. Penalties (5 years and fine) for false statements in application.

C. *Procedures for Permanent Residence*

1. *Automatic Adjustment*—SAW temporary residents are automatically adjusted to permanent residency under INA §210(a)(2), 8 U.S.C. §1160. Applicants were divided into two groups:
   a. *Group One*—Automatically adjusted to LPR status on Dec. 1, 1989.
      (1) Worked 90 man-days for each of 3 years ending May 1, 1984, 1985, 1986.
      (2) "Shall" adjust the later of one year after temporary residence or after Jan. 1, 1990. However, the AG may deny adjustment if he finds by a preponderance of the evidence that temporary resident status was the result of fraud or willful misrepresentation or the applicant committed an act making him inadmissible except as provided in the Act for waivers of excludability.
      (3) Only first 350,000 eligible in Group One.
   b. *Group Two*—Automatically adjusted to LPR status on Dec. 1, 1990.
      (1) All other SAWS (those who did not work for 3-year period and those beyond the 350,000)
      (2) "Shall" adjust the later of 2 years after temporary residence or after Jan. 1, 1991. The AG may deny the application for reasons set forth above under Group 1.
2. *Proof of Permanent Residence*—A green card is obtained by filing an I-90 at the service center where the temporary resident resides. 56 Fed. Reg. 482 (Jan. 7, 1991). Date of registration for adjustment is date fee paid on temporary residence application. 8 C.F.R. §210.4(a). At least one circuit has determined that admissibility is determined as of the date of admission as a temporary resident and cannot be redetermined as of the date of adjustment to permanent residency. *Perez-Enriquez v. Gonzales,* 463 F.3d 1007 (9th Cir. 2006) (en banc) [SAW applicant could not be denied LPR status because he pled guilty to possession for sale of a controlled substance after he obtained temporary residence].

D. *Travel and Employment*—Unlike INA §245A, temporary residents under SAW can travel without restriction. 8 C.F.R. §210.4(b)(3). INS permits travel once employment card issued. Letter, Norton, Assoc. Comm. Adjudications CO 235-C (June 15, 1987), *reprinted in* 64 No. 26 *Interpreter Releases* 827 (July 13, 1987). Employment obtained upon filing nonfrivolous application.

E. *Termination of Status*—INS may terminate temporary SAW status if proceedings are instituted before the person becomes eligible for AOS, the temporary resident is notified and given an opportunity to object, and termination is being sought because of: (1) fraud; (2) commission of an inadmissible act; or (3) conviction of a felony or 3 or more misdemeanors. 8 C.F.R. §210.4(d). For statutory language see PL 101-238, §4, 103 Stat. 2099, 2103. The one-felony / three-misdemeanor disqualification was not initially part of the statute, but was added after the application period closed. PL 101-238, 103 Stat. 2099 (Dec. 18, 1989). A district court held that the regulations were impermissibly retroactive as applied to convictions prior to the change, but the Ninth Circuit vacated the decision on jurisdictional grounds. *Naranjo-Aguilera v. INS,* 30 F.3d 1106 (9th Cir. 1994). The issue remains alive for litigation in the context of an individual petition for review.

F. *Removal Proceedings*—The rescission procedure is not exclusive and deportation proceedings may be brought independently. *Francis v. Gonzales,* 442 F.3d 131, 134 n.4 (2d Cir. 2006). However, DHS may not deport someone who has filed a nonfrivolous application until a final determination is made. INA §210(d)(2)(A), 8 U.S.C. §1160(d)(2)(A); 8 C.F.R. §210.2(c)(4)(iv). *Yao v. INS*, 2 F.3d 317 (9th Cir. 1993) [upholding statute permitting deportation proceedings in face of equal protection challenge that other legalization applicants are not subject to proceedings]. Denial of the right to request a motion to reopen has been upheld. *Rahim v. McNary*, 24 F.3d 440 (2d Cir. 1994).

G. *Apprehension*—If person entered U.S. between Nov. 6, 1986, and June 1, 1987 and was apprehended by INS, s/he is not eligible. *But see Catholic Social Services v. Meese*, 664 F.Supp. 1378 (E.D. Cal. 1987), *aff'd sub nom. Catholic Social Services v. Thornburgh*, 956 F.2d 914 (9th Cir. 1992), *vacated on other jurisdictional grounds sub nom. Reno v. Catholic Social Services*, 509 U.S. 43 (1993).

H. *Administrative and Judicial Review*—Same as legalization except for 8 U.S.C. §1255a(f)(4)(C) which places jurisdictional limitations on certain cases. Review is to the circuit courts upon a final order of removal. *Perez-Martin v. Ashcroft,* 394 F.3d 752 (9th Cir. 2005) [INA §242 permits review of a final LAU determination pursuant to 8 U.S.C. §1160(e)(3)(A) without requiring review of the SAW determination by the BIA and without relying on review under former INA §106a]. In certain circumstances there may also be review of aspects of the SAW program in the district courts. *McNary v. Haitian Refugee Center, Inc.*, 498 U.S. 479 (1991); *Abdullah v. INS*, 184 F.3d 158, 162–64 (2d Cir. 1999). *But see Naranjo-Aguilera v. INS*, 30 F.3d 1106 (9th Cir. 1994) [no jurisdiction to challenge substantive SAW regulations in light of *Reno v. CSS*]. *Rios v. Aguirre,* 276 F.Supp.2d 1195 (D. Kansas 2003) [no mandamus jurisdiction to challenge refusal to issue decision on motion to reconsider denial of SAW status and no §1331 jurisdiction over SAW denial because challenge is on substantive grounds]; *Khan v. Meissner*, 921 F.Supp. 2 (D.D.C. 1995) [no jurisdiction to review termination of SAW status; must seek review through deportation proceedings].

CHAPTER 13
NATURALIZATION AND CITIZENSHIP

CHAPTER 13
NATURALIZATION AND CITIZENSHIP

I. ELIGIBILITY FOR CITIZENSHIP

The INA grants U.S. citizenship at birth based on: (1) birth in the U.S. [INA §§301(a), (b) and (f)] or certain other places [INA §§302, 304–07]; (2) the citizenship of one or both parents [INA §§301(c), (d), (g) and (h)]; and (3) a combination of location and parental citizenship [INA §§301(e) and 303]. U.S. citizenship is also granted to persons after their birth based on a combination of parental citizenship and later residence [INA §§320 and 322] and by naturalization [INA §316]. U.S. noncitizen national status is granted based on the birth location in certain other places [INA §§308(1) and (3)], and the U.S. national status of one or both parents [INA §308(2) and (4)].

A. *Birth in the U.S. or Certain Incorporated Territories*—Under the Fourteenth Amendment "all persons born or naturalized in the United States...are citizens of the United States." We adhere to the doctrine of citizenship based on *jus soli*—birth in the U.S. *U.S. v. Wong Kim Ark,* 169 U.S. 649 (1898) [child born in U.S. to Chinese citizen parents is a USC, not subject to Chinese Exclusion Act]*; Matter of Cantu,* 17 I&N Dec. 190, 207 (AG 1979) [person born in the U.S. is a USC even where U.S. exercises no control over the territory because of boundary confusion]; INA §301(a) and (b), 8 U.S.C. §1401(a) and (b). Citizenship by birth also includes persons born in certain territories under U.S. control. INA §§302 and 304-307, 8 U.S.C. §§1402 and 1404–07. *But see Dred Scott v. Sandford,* 60 U.S. (19 How.) 393 (1856) [African-Americans not citizens because slaves were not part of the "political body," overturned by Fourteenth Amendment]. Persons born in territories "incorporated" into the U.S. are USCs at birth. *Boyd v. Nebraska,* 143 U.S. 135 (1892). Persons born in unincorporated territories are not USCs at birth. *Friend v. Reno,* 172 F.3d 638 (9th Cir. 1999) [person born and residing in the Philippines when it was a U.S. possession is not considered residing "in the United States" for purposes of citizenship]; *Valmonte v. INS,* 136 F.3d 914 (2d Cir. 1998) [person born in unincorporated U.S. territory is not born in the U.S. under the Fourteenth Amendment]; *Rabang v. INS,* 35 F.3d 1449 (9th Cir. 1994) [same]; *Lacap v. INS,* 138 F.3d 518 (3d Cir. 1998) [same]. Historically, Congress naturalized groups of persons who were born in certain unincorporated territories during certain periods of time in Alaska, Puerto Rico, Virgin Islands, Guam, and the trust territories of the Northern Mariana Islands. INA §§302, 304, 306, 307, 8 U.S.C. §§1402, 1406, 1407. Act of Mar. 24, 1976. PL 94-241, 301, 90 Stat. 263; Sec. 2. Presidential Proclamation No. 5564, Nov. 3, 1986, 51 Fed. Reg. 40399. Persons born in the Commonwealth of the Northern Mariana Islands after Jan. 9, 1978 are USCs by virtue of a covenant between the U.S. and the CNMI. *Sabangan v. Powell,* 375 F.3d 212 (9th Cir. 2004). Sons and daughters of diplomats do not acquire citizenship if born in the U.S. because they are not "subject to the jurisdiction of the United States" under the Fourteenth Amendment. *Wong Kim Ark,* 169 U.S. at 682.

Proof of Birth in U.S.—The absence of an official birth certificate is not decisive as to whether a person was born in the U.S. *U.S. v. Breyer,* 841 F.Supp. 679, 684 (E.D. Pa. 1993). *But see DeBrown v. DOJ,* 18 F.3d 774 (9th Cir. 1994). A person of unknown parentage found in the U.S. while under the age of five is considered a USC by birth unless proven not to have been born in the U.S. prior to the age of 21. INA §301(f), 8 U.S.C. §1401(f).

B. *By Acquisition at Birth*

1. *Generally*—A child born outside the U.S. where one or both parents are USCs may acquire U.S. citizenship at birth. INA §301(c)–(e), (g)–(h), 8 U.S.C. §1401(c)–(e), (g)–(h). Acquisition of citi-

zenship for a child born out-of-wedlock is also provided for under INA §309, 8 U.S.C. §1409. The latter provision requires the mother to be physically present in the U.S. for only *one year* to transmit citizenship. INA §309(c). A child who acquires citizenship is a citizen at the moment of birth and does not need a certificate of citizenship. *U.S. v. Smith-Baltiher,* 424 F.3d 913, 920–21 (9th Cir. 2005) [in illegal re-entry case, the court rejected the government's contention that defendant could not assert his *derivative* citizenship because he did not have a certificate and because only the AG/Secy. of DHS can determine acquisition at birth]. **Appendix B**, *infra*, provides charts demonstrating when and under what circumstances a child born in or out-of-wedlock can acquire citizenship.

2. *Residence or Physical Presence of the USC Parent*—The congressional acts providing for acquisition of citizenship require the USC parent to reside or be physically present in the U.S. for certain time periods prior to the birth of the child so that he or she may "transmit" citizenship. The transmission requirements are established by the law in effect at the time of the child's birth. *U.S. v. Flores-Villar,* 497 F.Supp.2d 1160, 1163 (S.D. Cal. 2007) [father could not transmit citizenship because the law at the time of his son's birth required him to be in the U.S. 10 years, not 5]. Residence has been defined as "the principal dwelling place of a person" without regard to intent. *Savorgnan v. U.S.,* 338 U.S. 491 (1950); *Alcarez-Garcia v. Ashcroft,* 293 F.3d 1155 (9th Cir. 2002) [where Mexican farmworker worked and lived in U.S. for 9 months each year and only left to visit family during vacation months, he resided in U.S. for transmission purposes]. For purposes of physical presence, the time period need not be counted to the minute and a parent who was in the U.S. for a sufficient number of years may transmit citizenship even if the "exact months, days, or hours are unknown." 7 FAM 1133.3-4(b). If the parent is a naturalized USC, the time both *before* and after naturalization can be counted in determining transmission by the parent. 7 FAM 1133.3-3(a)(2); *Matter of M-,* 7 I&N Dec. 643 (Reg. Comm. 1958); *Matter of ___,* 2005 WL 2271372 (AAO Jan. 12, 2005) A parent cannot argue constructive physical presence for purposes of transmission of citizenship where the parent was prevented from coming to the U.S. due to financial constraints, war, or imprisonment. *Tullius v. Albright,* 240 F.3d 1317 (11th Cir. 2001) [following *Drozd* and rejecting constructive physical presence]; *Drozd v. INS,* 155 F.3d 81, 85–87 (2d Cir. 1998). On the other hand, constructive physical presence has been applied where U.S. government officials prevented a parent from entering the U.S. because of an erroneous interpretation of the law. *Matter of Navarrete,* 12 I&N Dec 138 (BIA 1967). *See also Matter of Farley,* 11 I&N Dec. 51 (BIA 1965); *Matter of Yanez-Carrillo,* 10 I&N Dec. 366 (BIA 1963).

3. *Elimination of Retention Requirement*—The requirement that the child had to reside in the U.S. for certain time periods to retain citizenship under former statutes was eliminated by §103 of the Immigration and Nationality Technical Corrections Act of 1994, PL 103-416, 108 Stat. 4305, 4307–08 (Oct. 25, 1994). Thus, a person born after Oct. 10, 1952 is not divested of citizenship by retention requirements. In addition, a USC born before Oct. 10, 1952 who lost citizenship for failure to comply with the retention requirement may now have their citizenship restored. INA §324(d); 22 C.F.R. §50.30(d).

4. *Children Born Out of Wedlock*—The requirements for a child born out of wedlock to acquire citizenship through his father are particularly onerous. *O'Donovan-Conlin v. DOS,* 255 F.Supp.2d 1075, 1081–86 (N.D. Cal. 2003) [where father provided child support to child while under 18 but did not agree to it in writing as required by 8 U.S.C. §1409(a)(3), the child could not acquire citizenship]. However, Congress may constitutionally impose limitations on acquisition of citizenship at birth abroad. *Nguyen v. INS,* 533 U.S. 53 (2001) [relying on the heightened standard in gender discrimination cases, the Court found that §1409(a)(4) requiring fathers to acknowledge paternity does not violate equal protection]; *Rogers v. Bellei*, 401 U.S. 815 (1971); *U.S. v. Viramontes-Alvarado,* 149 F.3d 912 (9th Cir. 1998) [upholding requirement that applicant physically reside with father for purposes of legitimation under CA law]. *But see Breyer v. Meissner,* 214 F.3d 416 423–26 (3d Cir. 2000) [former §1993, granting derivative citizenship through USC fathers but not USC mothers, is unconstitutional because it perpetuated gender discrimination]; *Wauchope v. DOS*, 985 F.2d 1407 (9th Cir. 1993) [striking down on equal protection grounds the pre-1934 provision of §1401 that provided acquisition of citizenship only through fathers]; *Lebrun v. Thornburgh*, 777 F.Supp. 1204 (D.N.J. 1991) [striking down retention requirements as they apply to children born out-of-wedlock as a violation of equal protection]. Congress amended the law to allow mothers to transmit citizenship to children born before noon on May 24, 1934. INA

§301(h), 8 C.F.R. §301.1(a). For cases involving children considered not born-out-of-wedlock where the USC was *not* their biological parent, *see Scales v. INS,* 232 F.3d 1159 (9th Cir. 2000) [child treated as legitimate by court]; *Solis-Espinoza v. Gonzales,* 401 F.3d 1090 (9th Cir. 2005) [same].

5. *Adopted Children.* In *Marquez-Marquez v. Gonzales,* 455 F.3d 548 (5th Cir. 2006) the court determined that an adopted child could not benefit from the provisions of INA §301(g) although he or she may be eligible to benefit under INA §322. *See also Colaianni v. INS,* 490 F.3d 185, 197–89 (2d Cir. 2007) [rejected claim that former INA §301(a)(3) regarding birth abroad to USC parents applied to adopted children and denied equal protection claim by adopted child for citizenship under former INA §320-322].

6. *Procedures and Burden of Proof,* 8 C.F.R. pt. 301—There is a presumption of alienage for persons born abroad. *Matter of Tijerina-Villarreal,* 13 I&N Dec. 327, 330 (BIA 1969), *citing Matter of A.M.*, 7 I&N Dec. 332, 336 (BIA 1956) and *U.S. ex rel. Rongetti v. Neely*, 207 F.2d 281, 284 (7th Cir. 1953); 8 C.F.R. §341.2(c) [burden on petitioner by a preponderance of the evidence]. Although the burden of producing evidence to rebut the presumption of alienage is on the petitioner, *see e.g., Chau v. DHS,* 424 F.Supp.2d 1159 (D. Ariz. 2006) [where applicant could not prove that father was a USC and that he lived in the U.S. for the requisite transmission period, or that applicant was legitimated by father, he cannot be a derivative citizen], if the presumption is overcome the burden of proof may shift to the government, but the ultimate burden always remains with the petitioner. *Matter of Tijerina-Villarreal*; *see also* Fed. R. Evid. 301 [in all civil actions, a presumption imposes a burden of going forward with evidence to rebut it, but the burden of proof remains with the original party]. *Accord Leal Santos v. Gonzales,* 495 F.Supp.2d 180, 184–85 (D. Mass. 2007) [accepting framework for burden of proof established in *Tijerina-Villarreal* and rejecting respondent's claim that the government has the burden by clear and convincing evidence]. There is no such presumption if the respondent denies birth abroad. *Murphy v. INS*, 54 F.3d 605 (9th Cir. 1995). Absent discrepancies in the evidence, where a claim of derivative citizenship has "reasonable support," it will not be rejected. *Id.* In *Matter of Tijerina-Villarreal*, such discrepancies were found where the respondent's father had consistently stated in citizenship applications for five of his older children (where presence in the U.S. had not been at issue) that he was in Mexico during a certain time period. Under such circumstances, his testimony that he was actually in the U.S. during the critical time period did not provide credible evidence to support the citizenship claim of the respondent. There is also no presumption of citizenship if the person immigrated under the Amerasian Immigration Act, and nothing in that Act precludes INS from contesting a petitioner's claim that s/he is the child of a USC and parental residency requirements. *Chau v. INS,* 247 F.3d 1026, 1030–32 (9th Cir. 2001).

C. *By Derivation Through the Naturalization or U.S. Birth of One Parent*—A child born outside the U.S. may become a USC as a matter of law by virtue of his or her parent or parents' birth or naturalization. INA §320, 8 U.S.C. §1431; 8 C.F.R. §320, 66 Fed. Reg. 32138, 32166 (June 13, 2001).

1. *Former Law*—Prior to the Child Citizenship Act, a child could be a derivative USC when one parent became naturalized while the child was under 18 and the child was residing in the U.S. after lawful admission for permanent residence at the time of the parent's naturalization *or* began to reside permanently in the U.S. under the age of 18 *and* was in the legal custody of that parent. The law required: (1) the naturalization of both parents; (2) the naturalization of the surviving parent if one of the parents was deceased; or (3) the naturalization of the parent having legal custody of the child when there was a legal separation of the parents *or* the naturalization of the mother if the child was born out of wedlock and the paternity of the child had not been established by legitimation. *Matter of Rowe,* 23 I&N Dec. 962 (BIA 2006) [respondent was born out of wedlock in Guyana and was never legitimated and therefore was eligible for naturalization through mother]. Under this law, if the petitioning child was a "child" as defined under the INA, and the parents were separated, the petitioner would need to show that the parents were previously married and that they were now legally separated or divorced, that the child was in the USC parent's sole lawful custody and that all events occurred before the child was 18. Former INA §321(a), 8 U.S.C. §1432(a). The Board has held that the provision raising the age limits for derivation under INA

§321(a) from 16 to 18 applies retroactively such that a child who was under 18 at the time the parent(s) naturalized would obtain naturalization even if s/he was over 18 at any time since enactment of the INA. *Matter of Fuentes*, 21 I&N Dec 893 (BIA 1997). DOS agreed. Passport Bulletin—96-18 (Nov. 6, 1996). *See also Jahed v. Acri,* 468 F.3d 230 (4th Cir. 2006) [where parents were both physically present in Pakistan for the divorce and both consented, the divorce was not valid for derivative citizenship papers under *Matter of Ma* because they were never citizens of Pakistan and were never domiciled there]; *Afeta v. Gonzales,* 467 F.3d 402 (4th Cir. 2006) [legal separation under USCIS's interpretation means an order entered by the court and a written separation, a "voluntary separation agreement," even if consistent with state law, was insufficient]; *Bustamante-Barrera v. Gonzales,* 447 F.3d 388, 395–402 (5th Cir. 2006) [petitioner was not in his mother's sole legal custody at the time she naturalized because there was a joint custody order; the state court's effort to remedy this with a *nunc pro tunc* order granting the mother sole custody is not binding under federal law]; *Morgan v. Att'y Gen. of the U.S.,* 432 F.3d 226 (3d Cir. 2005) [respondent was not a derivative citizen because parents were not legally separated under the law of PA or Jamaica at the time mother naturalized]; *Minasyan v. Gonzales,* 401 F.3d 1069, 1075–80 (9th Cir. 2005) [under CA law, parents were legally separated for purposes of derivative naturalization]; *Bagot v. Ashcroft,* 398 F.3d 252 (3d Cir. 2005) [under BIA standard in *Matter of M-*, the respondent was in his father's sole custody at 14 before his father naturalized]; *Langhorne v. Ashcroft,* 377 F.3d 175 (2d Cir. 2004) [where father naturalized when respondent was 15 but mother never naturalized and did not separate from husband until respondent was 19, he was ineligible for derivative status]; *Brissett v. Ashcroft,* 363 F.3d 130 (2d Cir. 2004) [NY state court support and protective orders were not sufficient formal acts establishing legal separation]; *Moussa v. INS,* 302 F.3d 823, 826–27 (8th Cir. 2002) [where parents were divorced and were only remarried by proxy but marriage was not consummated at time father, who had son in his custody, was naturalized, the son was a derivative citizen]; *Batista v. Ashcroft,* 270 F.3d 8 (1st Cir. 2001); *Fierro v. Reno,* 217 F.3d 1 (1st Cir. 2000) [custody must be at the time of naturalization and court would not allow *nunc pro tunc* change of custody]. The legal separation, in the view of one circuit, had to occur prior to the custodial parent's naturalization. *Jordan v. Att'y Gen. of the U.S.,* 424 F.3d 320, 329–30 (3d Cir. 2005) [where mother was not legally separated from father until after she was naturalized, she could not transmit derivative citizenship]. But the Board has rejected this view finding that the child did not have to be in the parent's legal custody before the parent naturalized as long as s/he was in the parent's legal custody before s/he was 18. *Matter of Baires,* 24 I&N Dec. 467 (BIA 2008). *Accord,* AFM at 71.1(d)(2) (Feb. 2008). Also, the former provision regarding the requirement that adopted children had to reside in the U.S. at the time of the naturalization of his or her adoptive parent(s) was upheld in the face of an equal protection challenge. *Smart v. Ashcroft,* 401 F.3d 119, 121–23 (2d Cir. 2005). For the child to be eligible based on residency, s/he did not need to be an LPR but must have actually resided in the U.S. before s/he was 18. Having the intention without actual residence before 18 was insufficient. *Ashton v. Gonzales,* 431 F.3d 95 (2d Cir. 2005).

2. *Child Citizenship Act*—As a result of the Child Citizenship Act of 2000, PL 106-395 §101, 114 Stat. 1631 (2000), H. Rep. No. 852, 106th Cong., 2d Sess. 8, 146 Cong. Rec. H7774-78 (Sept. 19, 2000), INA §320(a), 8 C.F.R. §320, 66 Fed. Reg. 32138–66 (June 13, 2001), a child no longer needs to prove that his or her parents were legally separated or divorced if s/he is in the custody of one parent as s/he did under prior law. Under the present version of INA §320(a) a child derives citizenship as long as: (1) one parent is a citizen by birth or naturalization; (2) the child is under 18; (3) the child is an LPR; and (4) the child is residing in the U.S. in the legal and physical custody of the citizen parent. INA §320(b) explicitly extends the provisions to adopted children. This law means that orphans who were *adopted abroad prior* to issuance of the IV (IR-3 classification) become USCs upon their admittance to the U.S. as LPRs. Cable, DOS, 01-State-105804 (June 16, 2001), *reprinted in* 78 No. 25 *Interpreter Releases* 1077–78 (July 2, 2001).

2.a. *Definition of Residing in the U.S.*—The child, on or after Feb. 27, 2001, was admitted as an LPR and is living in the U.S., or the child was admitted previously as an LPR, was absent from the U.S. on Feb. 27, 2001, but returned and was readmitted as an LPR after that date. 66 Fed. Reg. at 32139. Because the statute requires residence in the U.S., it does not apply to children who go to the U.S. solely to naturalize and then reside outside the U.S. Cable, DOS, 05-State-050940 (Mar. 22, 2005), *published on* AILA InfoNet at Doc. No. 05090766. Residence for this purpose relies on the statutory definition under INA §101(a)(33), 8 U.S.C.

§1101(a)(33) and "mere statements of intent to establish residence in the United States will not be sufficient to meet this burden. *See* 9 FAM 40.41 N.6." Cable (Mar. 22, 2005), *supra*. However children of U.S. military or U.S. government employees, even if living abroad will be considered to be residing in the U.S. for purposes of INA §320 under 9 FAM 42.22 N.9. Cable (Mar. 22, 2005), *supra.*

2.b. *Definition of Legal Custody*—There is a presumption of custody by the USC parent, absent contrary evidence where: (a) the biological child currently resides with both natural parents who are living in marital union and not separated; (b) the biological child currently resides with a surviving natural parent where the other is deceased; or (c) the biological child born out-of-wedlock has been legitimated and currently resides with the natural parent. In the case of an adopted child, legal custody will be based on the existence of a final adoption decree. In the case of divorced or legally separated parents, the INS looks to the award of a court of law of the primary care, control, and maintenance of the child. The INS will consider a USC parent who has been awarded "joint custody" to have legal custody. 8 C.F.R. §320.1.

2.c. *Children Born Out of Wedlock*—Children born out-of-wedlock who have not been legitimated are eligible for derivative citizenship when the mother becomes a naturalized citizen. Memo, Yates, Acting Assoc. Director, BUSCIS, HQ 70/34.2-P (Sept. 26, 2003), *published on* AILA InfoNet at Doc. No. 03100241. In order to determine eligibility for derivative status, like citizenship by acquisition, it is necessary to review which act of Congress is applicable; *See* **Appendix B**, *infra*. For out-of-wedlock children claiming through a father, the claim may be based on the legitimation laws of any jurisdiction where the father or the child resided or was domiciled between the date of the child's birth to his or her 18th birthday. *See* 7 FAM 1133, Exhibit 1133.4-2a, Summary of Legitimation Laws.

2.d. *Step-Children*—Are not covered because they are not deemed to be children for purposes of Title III of the INA. Letter, Lacot, Acting Director, Business Process and Re-engineering, Immigration Services Division, HQ 70/33 (Aug. 8, 2001), *reprinted in* 78 No. 32 *Interpreter Releases* 1350, 1369–70 (Aug. 20, 2001). *Compare* INA §101(b)(1) [defining "child" for purposes of Titles I and II] *with* INA §101(c)(1) [defining "child" for purposes of Title III].

2.e. *Certificate of Citizenship*—An application for a certificate of citizenship is made on Form N-600. Evidence includes: (a) child's birth certificate; (b) marriage certificate of child's parents if applicable; (c) proof of termination of previous marriages; (4) U.S. citizenship of parent; (5) verifying legitimation according to the laws of the child's or father's residence or domicile if child born out-of-wedlock; (6) documentation of legal custody in case of divorce, legal separation or adoption; (7) LPR card or stamp for child; (8) full adoption decree if adopted; (9) legal name changes; and (10) any additional documentation INS requires to make a decision. 8 C.F.R. §320.3(b).

2.f. *Passport*—A USC by derivation may also apply directly for a U.S. passport, without obtaining or requiring a certificate of citizenship. 22 C.F.R. §51.44(b)(2).

2.g. *Effective Date*—The law came into effect on Feb. 27, 2001. The BIA and most circuit courts have rejected claims that its benefits may be retroactive. *Jordan v. Att'y Gen. of U.S.,* 424 F.3d 320, 328 (3d Cir. 2005) [CCA does not apply to derivate claims that arose prior to its effective date]; *Ali v. Ashcroft,* 395 F.3d 722, 725–26 (7th Cir. 2005) [person was over 18 at passage of Act and therefore not a USC; followed *Dave v. Ashcroft,* 363 F.3d 649, 654 and *Gomez-Diaz v. Ashcroft,* 324 F.3d 913, 915–16]; *Drakes v. Ashcroft,* 323 F.3d 189 (2d Cir. 2003); *U.S. v. Arbelo,* 288 F.3d 1262 (11th Cir. 2002) (per curiam); *Hughes v. Ashcroft,* 255 F.3d 752, 758–60 (9th Cir. 2001); *Nehme v. INS,* 252 F.3d 415, 430–33 (5th Cir. 2001); *Matter of Rodriguez-Tejedor,* 23 I&N Dec. 153 (BIA 2001). Thus, a child who was over 18 before Feb. 27, 2001, would also have to demonstrate that his or her parents were legally separated or divorced if one parent had custody. Former INA §321(a)(5), 8 U.S.C. §1432(a)(5) (statute repealed by CCA). *See e.g., Lewis v. Gonzales,* 481 F.3d 125 (2d Cir. 2007) [where parents were never legally separated, no derivative citizenship]. The constitutionality of the former statute has been upheld. *Barthelemy v. Ashcroft,* 329 F.3d 1062–68 (9th Cir. 2003) [upholding constitutionality of §321(a)(3) despite equal protection challenges based on gender and marital status]; *Wedderburn v. INS,* 215 F.3d 795 (7th Cir. 2000) [finding no constitutional claim based upon distinction] as has the distinction between pre- and post–Feb. 27, 2001, cases. *Nehme,* 252 F.3d at 433 n.21.

D. *Certificate of Citizenship under INA §322*—8 U.S.C. §1433, 8 C.F.R. §322; 66 Fed. Reg. 32138–42 (June 13, 2001).

1. *Generally*—Children of USCs who did not acquire citizenship at birth abroad or derive it through naturalization of their parent(s) may still obtain a certificate of citizenship upon application of the USC parent if: (1) one parent is a USC; (2) the child is temporarily physically present in the U.S. pursuant to lawful admission and is in status; (3) the child is under 18; and (4) the child is residing outside the U.S. in the legal and physical custody of the USC parent who has been in the U.S. five years, two of which were after her/his 14th birthday. Time periods for parents are waived when the parent is in the Armed Forces stationed abroad. A child may obtain a certificate if his or her parent is no longer alive if the citizen parent died within five years of filing the application and there is a citizen grandparent or legal guardian. If the child is adopted, the child must have been adopted prior to 16 (unless the child was a natural sibling of an adopted child and was adopted while under 18 pursuant to PL 106-139) and must meet all of the requirements for an adopted child or orphan. A child born out of wedlock who has not been legitimated is also eligible for a certificate when the mother becomes a naturalized citizen. Memo, Yates, Acting Assoc. Director, BUSCIS, HQ 70/34.2-P (Sept. 26, 2003), *published on* AILA InfoNet at Doc. No. 03100241. A citizen parent who has not been physically present in the U.S. for five years, two of which were after his or her 14th birthday, may also obtain a certificate for her/his child if: (a) the child is under 18, is presently in the U.S. pursuant to lawful admission, and is an LPR; or (b) the child is under 18, is present in the U.S. pursuant to lawful admission, and a *grandparent* (parent of the USC parent) has been physically present in the U.S. for five years, two of which are after the grandparent's 14th birthday. INA §322, 8 U.S.C. §1433; 8 C.F.R. §322, 66 Fed. Reg. 32138–42 (June 13, 2001). The child remains eligible through a grandparent even if the grandparent is deceased if the child met all other requirements of §322 and the grandparent met the physical presence requirement at the time of death. Memo, Yates, Acting Assoc. Director, BUSCIS (Apr. 17, 2003), *published on* AILA InfoNet at Doc. No. 03042240. However, the child must reside *outside the U.S.* and be present in the U.S. only temporarily. *Matter of* ___(AAO Jan. 10, 2005), 2005 WL 2374241, Phoenix, AZ and *Matter of* ___(Jan. 10, 2005), 2005 WL 2374242, Phoenix, AZ [children who entered U.S. on K-4s and resided with the USC parent since entry did not qualify as residing outside the U.S.]; *Matter of* ___, (AAO Jan. 12, 2005), 2005 WL 23742443, Chicago, IL and *Matter of* ____, (AAO Jan 12, 2005), 2005 WL 23742453, Chicago, IL [children in the U.S. on L-2 visas until their father's assignment was complete were residing in the U.S. using criteria under *Matter of Jalil,* 19 I&N Dec. 679 (BIA 1980) (residence for registry)]. The child must have also made a lawful "admission"; DOS does not consider a child paroled into the U.S. to be eligible for a certificate of citizenship. 9 FAM 41.31 N14.6-4.

2. *Procedures For Certificate*—Application filed on Form N-600K. *See generally* INS Field Office cables dated July 7, 1995, *reprinted in* 72 No. 31 *Interpreter Releases* 1,089-91 (Aug. 14, 1995) and Mar. 9, 1998, *reported in* 75 No. 9 *Interpreter Releases* 328 (Mar. 9, 1998).

   2.a. Definition of "lawful admission" is the same as INA §101(a)(13).

   2.b. Definition of "legal custody" is the same as under INA §320 and includes the concept of "joint custody." *See* 8 C.F.R. §322.1.

   2.c. Required documentation is similar to INA §320, except applicant need only prove lawful admission (I-94), not LPR status. 8 C.F.R. §322.3(b)(1)(viii). Note that B-2 visa entrants are *not* exempt from the nonimmigrant-intent requirements of INA §214(b).

   2.d. If approved, applicant is scheduled for naturalization interview.

   2.e. If denied, applicant may appeal to the AAO. 8 C.F.R. §322.5(b). Failure to exhaust this avenue of appeal may be a bar to judicial review. *Henriquez v. Ashcroft,* 269 F.Supp.2d 106, 108 (E.D.N.Y. 2003) [dismissing habeas where applicant for certificate failed to exhaust administrative appeal before AAO]. Although the child must be under 18 when the certificate is issued, the government may be equitably estopped if the child reached 18 due to USCIS delays. *Harriott v. Ashcroft,* 277 F.Supp.2d 538, 542–45 (E.D. Pa. 2003) [ordering USCIS to approve petition and pay attorney's fees where delay was 14 times longer than the 60 days normally contemplated for certificate].

E. *By Naturalization*—A person who is 18 years or older, who meets certain requirements, including residence, presence, good moral character, and legal status, may file an application for naturalization. INA §316, 8 U.S.C. §1427. All federal district courts and virtually all state courts have jurisdiction to naturalize persons. INA §310(b)(5), 8 U.S.C. §1421(b)(5). The court's power stems from federal legislation consistent with Art. I, §8, cl.4 of the Constitution directing Congress to make a uniform rule of naturalization. Congress has broad powers to act. *Schneiderman v. U.S.*, 320 U.S. 118 (1943).

II. ELIGIBILITY FOR NATURALIZATION BY APPLICATION

A. *Criteria for Naturalization*—Congress has the constitutional duty to "establish a uniform Rule of Naturalization." Art. I, §8, cl. 4. To qualify for naturalization, an applicant:

1. *Must Be a Lawful Permanent Resident*—INA §318, 8 U.S.C. §1429.

   1.a. *Conditional Permanent Resident*—May be eligible for citizenship if s/he has accrued the requisite residence period even if s/he has not had the condition on residency lifted. INA §§216(e), 216A(e), 8 U.S.C. §§1186a(e), 1186b(e); 8 C.F.R. §§216.1, 1216.1. *Abghari v. Gonzales,* Case No. CV 05-1210-FMC (PLAx) (C.D. Cal. Feb. 15, 2006).

   1.b. *Military Duty*—Where person honorably served in time of war or declared hostilities during a period designated by the President through Executive Order, LPR status is *not* required and applicant may, therefore, be in undocumented status to obtain citizenship. INA §329(a), 8 U.S.C. §1440(a). In *Reyes v. INS*, 910 F.2d 611 (9th Cir. 1990), the court struck down an executive order permitting persons serving in Grenada to benefit from this provision on the ground that the President does not have authority to make area restrictions under this statute, only time restrictions. But in *Singh v. Gantner,* 503 F.Supp.2d 592 (E.D.N.Y. 2007) the court upheld the denial of petitioner's naturalization application because his service in Kosovo was not named in an Executive Order except an order for IRS purposes. Posthumous citizenship may be granted to persons who die in active duty during a period of hostility and whose family petition within two years of his or her death. Form N-644. However, family members cannot benefit from the award of posthumous citizenship. INA §329A, 8 U.S.C. §1140-1. The application is filed on Form N-644. Fees are waived. For general information, *see* Fact Sheet, Naturalization Through Military Service, USCIS, *published on* AILA InfoNet at Doc. No. 08012866

2. *Must be 18 Years or Older*—INA §334(b), 8 U.S.C. §1445(b), unless age requirement is waived due to military involvement under INA §329(a), 8 U.S.C. §1440(a).

3. *Must Meet Continuous Residence and Physical Presence Requirements*

   3.a. *Continuous Residence Following LPR Status*—Must generally be a continuous resident for 5 years subsequent to LPR status. INA §316(a), 8 U.S.C. §1427(a)(1); 8 C.F.R. §316.5. *Valerio v. INS,* 86 F.Supp.2d 1009 (D. Hawaii 1999) [rejecting INS claim that daughter had not lawfully entered U.S. and was ineligible for USC where she received residency through mother whose own citizenship may have been unlawfully obtained but was not revoked].

      (1) *Marriage to a USC*—If married to a USC the residency requirement is 3 years if: (i) the USC spouse is a USC for three years; and (ii) the parties have been "living in marital union" for 3 years. 8 C.F.R. §319.1(a)(3). A divorce, legal separation, or even an informal separation may signify dissolution of the marital union. 8 C.F.R. §319.1(b)(2). "Living in marital union" has been interpreted to mean actually residing together. *U.S. v. Moses*, 94 F.3d 182 (5th Cir. 1996); *U.S. v. Maduno*, 40 F.3d 1212 (11th Cir. 1994). A spouse is only required to be living in marital union for the 3 years "immediately preceding the date of filing the application." 8 U.S.C. §1430(a). Although the applicant is not required to live with the USC spouse after filing the application, they still must be married at the time of naturalization. *Ali v. Smith,* 39 F.Supp.2d 1254 (W.D. Wash. 1999) [8 C.F.R. §319.1(a)(3) requiring the applicant spouse to be living with the USC for three years

prior to *examination* is in conflict with the statute which only requires three years prior to filing application]. 8 C.F.R. §319.1(b)(2)(ii)(C) sets forth an exception to the marital union requirement for "involuntary separation." *U.S. v. Onabanjo,* 351 F.3d 1064 (11th Cir. 2003) [reversing loss of citizenship where district court failed to consider exception to 3-year requirement].

(2) *Battered Spouse/Child*—A spouse or child who obtained LPR status because of battering or extreme cruelty may also apply for citizenship within a 3-year period under INA §319(a), 8 U.S.C. §1430(a). The 3-year marital union requirement is waived. The requirement that a child be defined as a "child" under the INA at the time s/he became an LPR is also waived, but the requirement that the child be at least 18 to petition is not waived. Memo, Yates, Deputy Ex. Assoc. Comm., Field Operations, HQISD 70/33 (Oct. 15, 2002), *published on* AILA InfoNet at Doc. No. 02103143.

3.b. *Must Have Resided for at Least Three Months in the State Where the Application is Filed*—INA §§316(a)(1), 319(a), 8 U.S.C. §§1427(a)(1), 1430(a). Residence is defined at INA §101(a)(33), 8 U.S.C. §1101(a)(33).

3.c. *Must Meet Physical Presence Requirements*—Must be physically present in the U.S. for at least one-half of the 5 years (or one-half of 3 years if the applicant is the spouse of a USC). INA §316(a), 8 U.S.C. §1427(a).

3.d. *Must Reside Continuously in the U.S. From the Date of Filing the Application to Admission to Citizenship*—INA §316(a)(2), 8 U.S.C. §1427(a)(2); 8 C.F.R. 316.2(a)(6).

3.e. *Disruption of Continuity of Residence*—An absence between 6 months and 1 year raises a rebuttable presumption that continuity of residence has been interrupted. INA §316(b), 8 U.S.C. §1427(b), 8 C.F.R. §316.5(c)(1)(i); *Li v. Chertoff,* 490 F.Supp.2d 130 (D. Mass. 2007) [study abroad did not result in abandonment of residency]; *Matter of Vafaei Makhsoos*, 597 F.Supp. 499 (D. Minn. 1984). *Abdul-Khalek v. Jenifer*, 890 F.Supp. 666 (E.D. Mich. 1995) [11-month absence between date of application and interview deemed abandonment of residency]. *Alvear v. Kirk,* 87 F.Supp.2d 1241 (D.N.M. 2000) [prolonged departure resulted in failure to meet residency requirement]. Factors which may establish continuity of residence include: (a) not terminating employment in U.S.; (b) presence of immediate family in U.S.; (c) retention of full access to U.S. home; and (d) not obtaining employment abroad. 8 C.F.R. §316.5(c)(1)(i)(A)–(D). An absence of 1 year or more "shall" disrupt the continuity of residence 8 C.F.R. §316.5(c)(1)(ii). However, there are certain statutory exemptions from disqualification for a 1-year continuous absence:

(1) *Military Service Abroad*—INA §328, 8 U.S.C. §1439; Also the time spent abroad by the spouse and child of a member of the Armed Forces residing with their husband and father is deemed to be time in the U.S.

(2) *Employees Working Abroad*—INA §§316(b), (c), 8 U.S.C. §§1427(b), (c). Employees who work for the U.S. government, an American research institute, a U.S. firm engaged in the development of foreign trade and commerce, or a public international organization of which the U.S. is a member, who obtain approval to preserve their residency by filing Form N-470. A U.S. firm includes a subsidiary where more than 50% of stock is owned by a U.S. firm or corporation. It also includes a publicly held corporation that is incorporated in the U.S. and trades stock exclusively on U.S. exchanges. *Matter of Chawathe,* A74 254 994 (AAO Jan. 11, 2006) [adopting the definition of U.S. companies that are publicly traded for purposes of INA §316(b)]; AFM at Appendix 74-14. If the company does not trade exclusively on the U.S. stock market, the nationality of the firm is determined by who owns 51% of the stock. AFM at Appendix 74-14; *Matter of Warrach,* 17 I&N Dec. 285, 286–87 (Reg. Comm. 1979). This section requires one year of physical presence after LPR status, and it is strictly construed. *Matter of Copeland*, 19 I&N Dec. 788 (Comm. 1988); AFM at Appendix 74-14.

(3) *LPR Spouses of USCs Working Abroad for a U.S. Company*—INA §319(b). The physical presence and residence requirements are waived in limited circumstances for applicants whose USC spouse is employed abroad by: the U.S. government, a public international organization in which the U.S. participates by treaty or statute, an American institution of re-

search recognized by DHS (8 C.F.R. §316.20), a religious organization ministering or doing missionary work, or an American firm, or a subsidiary thereof, engaged in whole or in part in the development of foreign trade and U.S. commerce. INA §319(b), 8 U.S.C. §1430(b). Legal Opinion, Rees, General Counsel, HQ 319-C (Feb. 23, 1993), *reprinted in* 72 No. 33 *Interpreter Releases* 1154, 1178–83 (Aug. 28, 1995) [providing a broad reading to term "trade and commerce"]. The "nationality" of the company must be more than 50% U.S. Legal Opinion, Martin, General Counsel, HQ 319-P (Sept. 14, 1995), *reprinted in* 73 No. 14 *Interpreter Releases* 437, 449–53 (Apr. 8, 1996). With the exception of religious organizations, all of the above categories may also waive the bar to citizenship that arises from an absence of 1 year or more from the U.S. that breaks the continuity of residence. INA §316(b), 8 U.S.C. §1427(b).

(4) Spouse, child or parent of USC who died in combat or spouse of person granted USC posthumously.

3.f. *Reapplication*—A person whose continuous residence has been broken may reapply 4 years and 1 day following the date of her or his return to U.S. to resume residency. If the statutory 3-year period is involved, then it is 2 years and 1 day following return. 8 C.F.R. §316.5(c)(1)(ii).

4. *Must Meet the Good Moral Character Requirements*—Must be a person of good moral character for 5 years (or for a spouse of a USC, 3 years, or for person in the military, 1 year) prior to filing and up to the time of admission. INA §§316(a)(3), 319(a)(1), 8 U.S.C. §§1427(a)(3), 1430(a)(1); 8 C.F.R. §§316.2(a)(7), 316.10, 329.2(d). Statutory ineligibility for good moral character is defined at INA §101(f), 8 U.S.C. §1101(f). For detailed discussion on good moral character, *see* Ch. 8, Part II (p.962), *supra.*

4.a. *False Testimony*—INA §101(f)(6), 8 C.F.R. §316.10(b)(2)(vi); *Azziz v. Chertoff,* 527 F.Supp.2d 188 (D. Mass. 2007) [upheld denial of naturalization for lack of good moral character where applicant falsely represented that she and former husband were living together on their joint I-751 petition and that she had no children when in fact she had children by another man]; *Aboud v. INS*, 876 F.Supp. 938 (S.D. Ohio 1994) [false testimony even if immaterial is statutory bar to GMC]. *But see U.S. v. Hovsepian,* 422 F.3d 883, 887–89 (9th Cir. 2005) (en banc) [false testimony must be given with the subjective intent of obtaining an immigration benefit; upholding district court's decision that inaccurate statements on naturalization application or in testimony were not intentional or made to secure an immigration benefit]; *Cacho v. Ashcroft,* 403 F.Supp.2d 991 (D. Hawaii 2004) [granting naturalization where there were discrepancies between applicant's account and police report regarding 15-year-old event, because it did not amount to false testimony to obtain an immigration benefit].

4.b. *Crimes*—*Zaranska v. DHS*, 400 F.Supp.2d 500, 504–05 (E.D.N.Y. 2005) [assaulting a police officer pursuant to N.Y. Penal Law §120.15(3) was not a CIMT]; *Plewa v. INS,* 77 F.Supp.2d 905 (N.D. Ill. 1999) [reversing denial of naturalization for lack of GMC where applicant failed to list arrest because of erroneous advice given to her by an experienced immigration counselor]; INS Interpretations §316.1(e)(1) [moral standard of average citizen applied]; *Matter of Gantus-Bobadilla*, 13 I&N Dec. 777 (BIA 1971). A person convicted of a petty offense will not be barred from a finding of GMC unless sentenced to a term of imprisonment in excess of 6 months (regardless of whether the sentence is suspended). *Laryea v. U.S.,* 300 F.Supp.2d 404 (E.D. Va. 2004) [conviction for petty larceny during required period barred GMC where 9 months of an 11-month sentence was suspended]. A person who has been convicted of murder *at any time* is *permanently* barred from establishing GMC. 8 C.F.R. §316.10(b)(1)(i)–(ii); *Castiglia v. INS*, 108 F.3d 1101, 1103 (9th Cir. 1997). The permanent bar also applies to persons convicted of an aggravated felony *after* Nov. 29, 1990, even if §212(c) relief was granted, Letter, Miller, Acting Asst. Comm. Adjudications HQ 316-C (May 5, 1993), *reprinted in* 70 No. 22 *Interpreter Releases* 752, 769–70 (June 7, 1993) and even if it was *not* an aggravated felony at the time of conviction. *Chan v. Gantner,* 464 F.3d 289, 292–94 (2d Cir. 2006) [applying INA §§101(a)(43)(N) & (U) retroactively such that a conviction for conspiracy to commit alien smuggling barred citizenship for lack of GMC despite grant of §212(c) relief]. In determining the date of conviction, the court looks to the date of sentencing, not the date of the guilty plea. *Puello v. Bureau of USCIS,* 511 F.3d 324 (2d Cir. 2007) [applicant barred from GMC finding because he was convicted of an aggravated felony "on or after" Nov. 29, 1990 as he was sentenced after that date, even if he pleaded guilty before it].

(1) *Admission vs. Conviction*—A person must be denied citizenship not only if he is convicted, but if he admits facts that constitute certain crimes. 8 C.F.R. §316.10(b)(2)(iv); INA §101(f)(3); *Deluca v. Ashcroft,* 203 F.Supp.2d 1276, 1279 (M.D. Ala. 2002) [admission of theft with a youthful adjudication and no conviction bars naturalization on the grounds that she admitted to a CIMT during the statutory period].

(2) *Expunged Convictions*—In the assessment of GMC, DHS may use expunged convictions. *U.S. v. Hovsepian* 359 F.3d 1144, 1158–59 (9th Cir. 2004) (en banc) [facts underlying expunged convictions are relevant to a GMC determination].

(3) *Criminal Records*—DHS may request all criminal records but should not do so if the arrest and/or conviction is outside the statutory period, will not result in issuing an NTA, and would not reflect on matters that occurred within the statutory period. Memo, Pearson, Ex. Assoc. Comm. Field Operations, HQ 70/33-C (Apr. 27, 2001), *reprinted in* 78 No. 20 *Interpreter Releases* 848, 863–65 (May 21, 2001).

4.c. *Voting Unlawfully and False Claim to USC*—The CCA of 2000 added a narrow exception to the grounds of removal for false claims to U.S. citizenship and unlawful voting, and added the parallel last clause to INA §101(f), which provides that a person will not be statutorily barred from GMC even if he voted unlawfully or made a false claim to USC if: (1) each natural or adoptive parent is or was a USC; (2) the applicant permanently resided in the U.S. prior to 16; and (3) s/he reasonably believed at the time of such statement, claim, or violation that s/he was a USC. However, a person may be barred from GMC if convicted under 18 U.S.C. §1015(f) for making a false claim to USC to vote or register to vote, or 18 U.S.C. §611 for voting in a federal election as a noncitizen. An officer adjudicating a naturalization application must therefore make the following determinations: (1) whether the applicant is precluded from establishing GMC pursuant to §101(f)(1)–(8); (2) whether the unlawful conduct warrants a discretionary denial after balancing the equities; and (3) whether the applicant qualifies for the exception under §101(f). If the person is not statutorily barred and removal proceedings are not initiated because the respondent is not removable or as a matter of prosecutorial discretion, the officer must then consider the totality of the circumstances in determining whether naturalization should be denied as a matter of discretion. An officer may balance the unlawful voting or false claim to USC against: (1) family ties and background; (2) the absence or presence of other criminal history; (3) education and school records; (4) employment history; (5) other law-abiding behavior such as paying taxes, child support; (6) community involvement; (7) credibility of the applicant; and (8) length of time in the U.S. Memo, Yates, Deputy Exe. Assoc. Comm. Operations, USCIS, HQ 70/33 (May 7, 2002), *published on* AILA InfoNet at Doc. No. 05030768.

4.d. *Discretionary GMC Determination*—Nonstatutory grounds have been used to support a finding of lack of good moral character as a matter of discretion, unless the applicant can establish extenuating circumstances, 8 C.F.R. §316.10(b)(3), former INS Interpretations 316.1(f):

(1) Nonsupport of dependents. 8 C.F.R. §316.10(b)(3)(i); *Matter of Dobric,* 189 F.Supp. 638 (D. Minn. 1960). *But see Matter of Valad,* 465 F.Supp. 120 (E.D. Va. 1979).

(2) Adultery tending to destroy a marriage. 8 C.F.R. §316.10(b)(3)(ii); INS Interpretations §316.1(g).

(3) Commission of unlawful acts that adversely reflect upon the applicant's moral character. 8 C.F.R. §316.10(b)(3)(iii). *U.S. v. Dang,* 488 F.3d 1135 (9th Cir. 2007) [court rejected *ultra vires,* void-for-vagueness, overbreadth, and Uniformity Clause challenge to regulation in the context of denaturalization for illegal procurement where petitioner committed crimes of arson, willful injury to a child and others prior to being naturalized]; *U.S. v. Jean-Baptiste,* 395 F.3d 1190 (11th Cir. 2005) [relying on the "catch-all" provision of INA §101(f) and *Chevron* deference to 8 C.F.R. §316.10(b)(3)(iii) that broadly construes lack of GMC to include the *commission* of unlawful acts, the court denaturalized a person

who had a minor role in one incident of cocaine trafficking but was not arrested, charged, or indicted until *after* he became a citizen]; *U.S. v. Lekarczyk,* 354 F.Supp.2d 883 (W.D. Wis. 2005) [followed *Jean-Baptiste* where bank fraud, forgery-uttering and bail jumping all occurred before but were not charged until after citizenship obtained]; *U.S. v. Ekpin,* 214 F.Supp.2d 707, 713–15 (S.D. Tex. 2002) [charge of illegal procurement sustained where applicant admitted to committing aggravated felony during statutory period but conviction was subsequent to naturalization]; *Meyersiek v. USCIS,* 445 F.Supp.2d 202 (D. R.I. 2006) [where applicant suffered from a debilitating medical condition but USCIS claimed he was untruthful in his medical claim to UNUM, court upheld denial under §316.10(b)(3)(iii)].

(4) Homosexuality. *Matter of Longstaff,* 716 F.2d 1439 (5th Cir. 1983). *But see* INS Interpretations §316.1(f)(7) [homosexuality is not a basis *per se* for denying naturalization]; *Nemetz v. INS*, 647 F.2d 432 (4th Cir. 1981) [conviction under VA law making consensual sodomy a crime would not bar naturalization].

(5) Failure to register with the Selective Service. Knowingly and willfully failing to register with the Selective Service between 18 and 26 years of age during the statutory GMC period may result in an adverse moral character determination. If the person is under 26 he may also be denied on the basis that he refuses to bear arms pursuant to INA §337(a)(5)(A) or that he is not disposed to the good order and happiness of the U.S. INA §316(a)(3). Memo, Virtue, G.C. to Penca, Eastern Reg. Counsel (HQCOU 90/15-P, HQCOU 70/33-P) (Apr. 27, 1998), *reprinted in* 76 No. 14 *Interpreter Releases* 562, 573–75 (Apr. 12, 1999). A person is not ineligible for failure to register if: (a) he was not in the U.S. between the ages of 18 and 26; (b) he was in a lawful nonimmigrant status between 18 and 26; or (c) he was born after Mar. 29, 1957 and before Dec. 31, 1959. An applicant is not *permanently* barred even if he knowingly and intentionally failed to register with Selective Service between the ages of 18 and 26. If he is over 31, the failure *Matter of V-K-,* 24 I&N Dec. 500 (May 8, 2008) [reversing IJ's mixed question of fact and law regarding the torture Ukrainian would suffer and denying CAT relief] falls outside the 5-year statutory GMC period and the person "should ordinarily be found eligible for naturalization." Memo, Yates, Deputy Exec. Assoc. Comm., Field Operations (June 18, 1999), *published on* AILA InfoNet at Doc. No. 99010740.

(6) Driving Under the Influence. Where an applicant had one DUI during the statutory period, but five DUIs over the past 10 years, a statutory rape conviction outside of the five year period, and lacked candor in responding to a number of questions, the court upheld the naturalization denial. *Rico v. INS,* 262 F.Supp.2d 6 (E.D.N.Y. 2003).

4.e. *Military Applicants*—Nothing in INA §329 requires the applicant to show GMC, but 8 C.F.R. §329.2(e), in the view of some circuits, reasonably adopts the GMC requirements of §316. *Lopez v. Henley,* 416 F.3d 455, 457–58 (5th Cir. 2005) [upholding DHS interpretation of 8 C.F.R. §329.2(e) to require that a person seeking citizenship through military service must establish GMC]; *Nolan v. Holmes,* 334 F.3d 189 (2d Cir. 2003) [BIA properly dismissed appeal from IJ decision that respondent failed to establish prima facie eligibility for naturalization under §316 because of conviction. Although nothing in §329 requires a showing of GMC, *Chevron* deference applied]. *Accord Castiglia v. INS,* 108 F.3d 1101, 1102 (9th Cir. 1997); *Cacho v. Ashcroft,* 325 F.Supp.2d 1140, 1144 (D. Hawaii 2004) [petitioner must meet the one-year GMC requirement]; 8 C.F.R. §329.2(d). *See in this part* ¶ B.1.a (p.1313), *infra*.

4.f. *No Limitation on GMC Inquiry*—The inquiry into a person's moral character is not limited to the 5- or 3-year period and DHS may, by statute and regulation, inquire into time periods beyond the 5- or 3-year period. INA §316(e), 8 U.S.C. §1427(e); 8 C.F.R. §316.10(a)(2); *U.S. v. Hovespian,* 359 F.3d 1144, 1166–67 (9th Cir. 2004) (en banc) [in determining whether a person possesses GMC, the court or agency can look beyond the statutory period]; *Tieri v. INS,* 457 F.2d 391 (2d Cir. 1972). However, it is impermissible to rely solely on acts outside the statutory period and such reliance must be tied into current conduct. *Gatcliffe v. Reno,* 23 F.Supp.2d 581, 585 (D.V.I. 1998). Acts beyond the statutory period should be considered only if the conduct during the statutory period does not indicate reform from the earlier period *or* if the earlier conduct "appears" relevant to the applicant's present moral character. 8 C.F.R. §316.10(a)(2). But note that if the applicant demonstrates exemplary conduct during the statutory period, his application cannot be denied based solely on his prior criminal record. *Santamaria-Ames v. INS,* 104 F.3d 1127, 1132 (9th Cir. 1996) *See also U.S. v. Hovsepian,* 422 F.3d 883 (9th Cir. 2005) (en banc). The government can, however, initiate removal proceedings if past conduct is a ground of deportation.

4.g. *Effect of Removal Proceedings*—Under INA §318, 8 U.S.C. §1429, no application for naturalization shall be considered by the AG if removal proceedings are pending against the applicant. *See also* INS Interpretation 318.2(c)(1)(iii). Therefore, where a *removable* crime does not result in a statutory bar to good moral character (*e.g.*, an aggravated felony occurring before Nov. 29, 1990), DHS can stay the naturalization procedure pending completion of removal proceedings or simply issue an NTA and deny naturalization because removal proceedings are pending. INA §318, 8 U.S.C. §1429, 8 C.F.R. §318.1. Legal Opinion, Martin, General Counsel (Dec. 3, 1996), *reprinted in* 74 No. 38 *Interpreter Releases* 530–32 (Oct. 6, 1997). While the IJ has the authority to terminate proceedings if the respondent is *prima facie* eligible for naturalization, 8 C.F.R. §1239.2(f), based on humanitarian or "exceptionally appealing" factors, the BIA has stated that this is permissible only if DHS affirmatively communicates *prima facie* eligibility. *Matter of Acosta Hidalgo,* 24 I&N Dec. 103 (BIA 2007) [DHS *denial* of naturalization cannot be taken as a communication that respondent is *prima facie* eligible].

If USCIS has denied naturalization, pending removal proceedings do not divest the district court of jurisdiction to review the denial. *Abiodun v. Gonzales,* 461 F.3d 1210, 1216–17 (10th Cir. 2006) [distinguishing between review of a claim that one is a citizen under INA §242(b)(5) and review of a denial of naturalization under 8 U.S.C. §1421(c)]; *De Lara Bellajaro v. Schiltgen,* 378 F.3d 1042 (9th Cir. 2004) [notwithstanding §1429, courts can review a naturalization denial under §1421(c) for whatever reason the application was denied including whether §1429 was properly invoked]; *Farghaly v. Frazier,* 404 F.Supp.2d 1125 (D. Minn. 2005)[court can review whether §1429 was properly invoked to deny petition because removal proceedings were pending but cannot review it for any substantive reason]; *O'Sullivan v. USCIS,* 372 F.Supp.2d 1097, 1098–1100 (N.D. Ill. 2005) *affirmed on other grounds* 453 F.3d 809 (7th Cir. 2006) [section 1429 does not apply to wartime veteran cases by its own language]; *Ngwana v. Att'y Gen. of U.S.,* 40 F.Supp.2d 319 (D. Md. 1999) [court retains jurisdiction to review denial of naturalization even where there were subsequent pending removal proceedings]; *Gatcliffe v. Reno,* 23 F.Supp.2d 581, 585 (D.V.I. 1998) [court retains power under §1421(c) to review denial of naturalization based on GMC notwithstanding pendency of removal proceedings and §1429]; *but see Zayed v. U.S.,* 368 F.3d 902 (6th Cir. 2004) [amended §1429 does not divest district court of jurisdiction under §1421(c) but precludes court from granting naturalization while removal proceeding is pending. However, court could grant declaratory relief that applicant is eligible]; *Baez-Fernandez v. INS,* 385 F.Supp.2d 292, 295 (S.D.N.Y. 2005) [no jurisdiction for declaratory judgment that applicant is prima facie eligible for naturalization where court lacks jurisdiction to review naturalization application of person in removal proceeding because under §1441(c) applicant failed to exhaust his administrative remedies as to his first application and under §1447(b) USCIS refused to grant an interview as to his second application]; *Mosleh v. Strapp,* 992 F.Supp. 874, 876 (N.D. Tex. 1998).

5. *Must be Attached to the Principles of the Constitution and Well Disposed to the Good Order and Happiness of the U.S.*—INA §316(a)(3), 8 U.S.C. §1427(a)(3); 8 C.F.R. §316.11. Applicant must reveal all organizations of which s/he has been a member, regardless of relevance to qualifications for citizenship. *Price v. INS*, 962 F.2d 836 (9th Cir. 1992) [requirement does not violate First Amendment]. Applicant must take an oath of allegiance to the U.S. or modified oath based on deeply held religious or moral beliefs regarding his or her willingness to bear arms. AFM at App. 72-1(5)(b); INS Interpretations §316.1(h). The section should be construed "not in opposition to, but in accordance with, the theory and practice of our government in relation to freedom of conscience." *Schneiderman v. U.S.*, 320 U.S. 118, 135 (1943) (*quoting* Hughes, C.J. in *U.S. v. Macintosh*, 283 U.S. 605 (1931)) [reversing cancellation of certificate of citizenship]. Under INA §340(c), 8 U.S.C. §1451(c), if a naturalized USC joins a communist, anarchist or subversive or-

ganization within the definition of INA §313 within 5 years of obtaining citizenship, it is prima facie proof of nonattachment and a basis for revocation of citizenship.

6. *Must be Willing to Bear Arms, Perform Noncombatant Service or Work of National Importance*—Must be willing to "(A) bear arms on behalf of the United States when required by the law, or (B) to perform noncombatant service in the Armed Forces of the United States when required by the law, or (C) to perform work of national importance under civilian direction when required by the law." INA §337(a)(5)(A)–(C), 8 U.S.C. §1448(a)(5)(A)–(C). This section has been interpreted as consistent with selective service law. *Petition for Naturalization of Mahmoud Kassas*, 788 F.Supp. 993 (M.D. Tenn. 1992) [denying petitioner who would bear arms in certain cases but not others pursuant to his Islamic beliefs]; *Welsh v. U.S.*, 398 U.S. 333, 339–40 (1970) ["[i]f an individual deeply and sincerely holds beliefs that are purely ethical or moral in source and content but that nevertheless impose upon him a duty of conscience to refrain from participating in any war at any time, those beliefs certainly occupy in the life of that individual "a place parallel to that filed by...'God' in traditionally religious persons"].

7. *Must Not Otherwise be Barred as a*:

   7.a. Subversive. INA §§313–16(f), 8 U.S.C. §§1424–27(f), 8 C.F.R. §313.1;

   7.b. Member of the communist party, INA §313(a), 8 U.S.C. §1424(a), where such membership is meaningful, *Rowoldt v. Perfetto*, 355 U.S. 115 (1957), and not involuntary or otherwise excusable under INA §313(d), 8 U.S.C. §1424(d); 8 C.F.R. §313.3;

   7.c. Deserter during war time who was convicted by court martial or civil court, INA §314, 8 U.S.C. §1425, unless s/he had received a pardon or general amnesty. INS Interpretations §316.1(h);

   7.d. Person against whom removal proceedings are pending, or who has an outstanding and final order of deportation, INA §318, 8 U.S.C. §1429, unless eligible for naturalization due to military service under INA §§328–29, 8 U.S.C. §§1439–40. *See U.S. v. Ali*, 757 F.Supp. 710 (W.D. Va. 1991); *but see* 8 C.F.R. §1239.2(f) [IJ may terminate proceedings to allow naturalization]; *but see Matter of Acosta Hidalgo,* 24 I&N Dec. 103 (BIA 2007) [IJ or BIA may terminate proceedings only if DHS affirmatively communicates that respondent is *prima facie* eligible. DHS *denial* of naturalization cannot be taken as a communication that respondent is *prima facie* eligible]; or

   7.e. Person who applied for and received relief from the Selective Service system based on his or her alienage. INA §315(a), 8 U.S.C. §1426(a). *But see Astrup v. INS,* 402 U.S. 509 (1971) [excepting applicant from the bar to citizenship where he obtained exemption but was inducted and therefore there was no *quid pro quo* preventing his naturalization]; *Moser v. United States,* 341 U.S. 41 (1951) [where applicant did not knowingly and intelligently waive his right to citizenship due to misleading statements, he was still eligible for naturalization];*Gallarde v. INS,* 486 F.3d 1136 (9th Cir. 2007) [applicant not barred from naturalization who is discharged from *voluntary* training and service in the armed forces]; *Fuchs v. District Director, INS,* 329 F.2d 114 (1st Cir. 1964) [where person received exemption from military service without signing Selective Service form acknowledging that he would lose right to be a citizen, right to citizenship not waived]. An applicant is not ineligible for citizenship "because of an exemption from training or service in the Armed Forces of the United States pursuant to the exercise of rights under a treaty, if before the time of the exercise of such rights the alien served in the Armed Forces of a foreign country which the alien was a national." INA §315(c), 8 U.S.C. §1426(c); 8 C.F.R. §315.

8. *Must Demonstrate Knowledge of English Language, U.S. History and Government*

   8.a. Requires elementary-level reading, writing and understanding of the English language, INA §312(a)(1), 8 U.S.C. §1423(a)(1); 8 C.F.R. §312.1, *and*

   8.b. A knowledge and understanding of the fundamentals of U.S. history and government. INA §312(a), 8 U.S.C. §1423(a); 8 C.F.R. §312.2.

8.c. For persons who became LPRs through amnesty, these requirements are already satisfied and no retest is required. INA §245A(b)(1)(D)(iii), 8 U.S.C. §1255a(b)(1)(D)(iii); 8 C.F.R. §312.3(b). The civics and reading/writing English requirements are also met if the applicant passes a standardized citizenship test within one year preceding the submission of the naturalization application or at any time prior to a final determination on the application. 8 C.F.R. §312.3. The applicant must still demonstrate his or her ability to speak and understand English. 8 C.F.R. §312.3(a)(2). If the applicant has passed a standardized exam, s/he cannot be re-examined unless the examiner has reason to believe the examination was passed by fraud or misrepresentation. 8 C.F.R. §312.3(a)(3). Standardized exams are not currently offered.

8.d. An applicant who fails the English or civics test will be offered a second test within 90 days. 8 C.F.R. §312.5.

8.e. *Age/LPR Status Exception*—The English language requirement shall not apply to (1) persons who are over 50 and have lived in U.S. for 20 years in LPR status; or (2) persons who are over 55 and have lived in U.S. for 15 years in LPR status. INA §312(b)(2), 8 U.S.C. §1423(b)(2). The AG shall also give special consideration in civics knowledge to persons over 65 with 20 years as LPR. INA §312(b)(3). Special consideration has been determined to be a test of 10 out of 25 civics questions in the person's language where they need only answer 6 correctly. Memo, Crocetti, Assoc. Comm., Adjudication, CO 70/33.2-P (Dec. 22, 1995), *reprinted in* 73 No. 3 *Interpreter Releases* 66, 86 (Jan. 16, 1996).

8.f. *Medical Disability Waiver*—Persons who are physically or developmentally disabled or have a mental impairment are exempt from the English language and history and government requirements. INA §312(b)(1), 8 U.S.C. §1423(b)(1); 8 C.F.R. §312.1(b)(3); 8 C.F.R. §312.2(b)(1); 62 Fed. Reg. 12915, 12923 (Mar. 19, 1997); AFM at 72.2(d)(5). This may include elderly persons who suffer from Alzheimer's, Parkinson's disease, senile dementia or a related disease. Policy Memorandum No. 47, Pearson, Ex. Assoc. Comm., Field Operations (HQ 70/33-P) (Apr. 7, 1999), *reprinted in* 76 No. 17 *Interpreter Releases* 677, 693–711 (May 3, 1999), *published on* AILA InfoNet at Doc. No. 99041420. A medical doctor, osteopath, or clinical psychologist "experienced in diagnosing" these disabilities must complete an N-648 to be filed with the N-400. 8 C.F.R. §312.2(b)(2). The applicant must still meet the moral character, residence, and oath requirements. Policy Memorandum No. 47, Pearson (Apr. 7, 1999), *supra.* However, the AG is authorized separately to waive the oath if the applicant is unable to understand or communicate the meaning of it, INA §337(a), and requiring an oath may violate the Rehabilitation Act of 1973. AFM at 72.2(d)(5)(H); *Galvez-Letona v. Kirkpatrick,* 54 F.Supp.2d 1218 (D. Utah 1999); Memo, Cooper, G.C. INS (Mar. 13, 2002), *reprinted in* 80 No. 16 *Interpreter Releases* 570, 592–96 (Apr. 21, 2003), *published on* AILA InfoNet at Doc. No. 03060641 [Rehabilitation Act of 1973 is applicable and disabled person may have guardian or other proxy regarding oath]. USCIS has determined that a designated representative of a person who is developmentally or physically disabled or suffering from a mental impairment may complete the N-400 examination (including the oath), by attesting orally and through affidavit and submission of documentary evidence that the person qualifies for naturalization. The designated representative may be a legal guardian or court recognized surrogate or, in the absence of a guardian or surrogate, a USC spouse, parent, adult son or daughter or adult brother or sister. A licensed medical or osteopathic doctor or a licensed clinical psychologist must provide an evaluation attesting to the severity of the applicant's impairment and how it affects his or her ability to take the oath. Memo, Yates, Acting Assoc. Director, BUSCIS, HQISD 70/33 (June 30, 2003), *published on* AILA InfoNet at Doc. No. 03071544. The N-648 may be submitted with the N-400, as a supplement to the N-400, or at the time of the interview. However, if it is submitted at the time of the interview, the examination may be continued. AFM at 72.2(d)(5)(E).

Application for Medical Disability Waiver—The N-648 must be certified by the physician or psychologist under penalty of perjury and must contain: (1) a full and complete description of the doctor's medical diagnosis, including, if applicable, the most recent Diagnostic Statistical Code which is the *Diagnostic and Statistical Manual of Mental Disorders*, 4th Edition, better known as the DSM-IV; (2) an explanation of how the disability or impairment affects the applicant and prevents him or her from learning or demonstrating knowledge of English and/or U.S. history and government; and (3) the doctor's conclusion whether the applicant is able to learn or demonstrate knowledge of English and/or U.S. history and government. The adjudicator must ensure that the Form N-648 also contains: (1) a documented explanation of the origin, nature, and extent of the medical condition including the tests employed; (2) how the medical condition or impairment severely affects the applicant in regard to the required tests; (3) an attestation that the disability has lasted or is expected to last 12 months or longer: and (4) an attestation that the disability is not the direct effect of illegal drug use. Memo, Neufeld, Acting Deputy Assoc. Dir., Domestic Operations, USCIS, HQRPM 70/33-P at ¶3B (Sept. 18, 2007), *published on* AILA InfoNet at Doc. No. 07092061. The "adjudicator however is not a physician and should not be placed in the position of making a medical determination" Memo, Neufeld (Sept. 18, 2007), *supra*, at ¶3C, and the diagnosis of the medical professional will be presumed valid in the absence of significant discrepancies or credible doubt. AFM at 72.2(d)(5)(D)(3). In addition the "adjudicator should not presume the existence of fraud merely based on the number of applicants who seek a medical examination from a particular medical professional." Memo, Neufeld (Sept. 18, 2007), *supra*, ¶3E. However, the officer "reserves the right" to request documentation if the interview raises questions about the extent of the disability. Memo, Yates, HQISD 70/33 (June 30, 2003), *supra, published on* AILA InfoNet at Doc. No. 03071544 and the officer may refer the applicant to another authorized medial specialist. AFM at 72.2(d)(5)(E)(5)(c). If the Form N-648 does not provide a sufficiently thorough explanation, the officer can request the underlying medical records. AFM at 72.2(d)(5)(D). The focal point should be the nexus between the disability and the applicant's ability to learn or demonstrate knowledge of English, U.S. history and government. The INS may not "second guess" the medical determination made on the waiver. *Campos v. INS,* 70 F.Supp.2d 1296 (S.D. Fla. 1998) [granting injunction where INS denied waivers by second guessing doctors without obtaining medical records or referral to second medical professional in violation of 8 C.F.R. §312.2(b)]. The application should be filed at the time the N-400 is filed but the N-400 cannot be denied simply because it filed later. Memo, Neufeld (Sept. 18, 2007), *supra*, at ¶3A.

8.g. *Reasonable Accommodations Under Section 504 of the Rehabilitation Act of 1973*—The Rehabilitation Act requires USCIS adjudicators to make accommodations for people taking the examinations. An accommodation is not a waiver but rather modifies the manner in which the applicant demonstrates that she meets the requirements. For example, a person who is physical disability does not enable him to write because he physically can not hold a pen or pencil, can take the U.S. history and government test orally. AFM at 72.2(d)(5)(G).

B. *Other Naturalization Programs*

1. *Veterans/Military Service*

1.a. *Military Service for One Year*—Applicant served in the Armed Forces for an aggregate period of one year (and if separated from service, the separation was honorable), and the application is filed during service or within 6 months of separation. Residency and physical presence requirements are inapplicable. If person files application after 6 months of separation from service, he must be an LPR at the time of the naturalization application. INA §328, 8 U.S.C. §1439. If applicant is in active duty the application must be filed with the Nebraska Service Center. 8 C.F.R. §328, 64 Fed. Reg. 67323–24 (Dec. 1, 1999); *See www.uscis.gov/military.*

1.b. *Military Service During Hostilities*—Applicant served in the Armed Forces during hostilities and continues to be in Armed Forces or was honorably discharged. If the person was inducted in the U.S. or certain other territories, *e.g.,* American Samoa, s/he need not be an LPR to obtain naturalization. The provision also covers persons who are in the Selected Reserve of the Ready Reserve. Physical presence and residency requirements are inapplicable. INA §329, 8 U.S.C. §1440. On July 3, 2002, President George W. Bush designated the period beginning Sept. 11, 2001, to the present as a period in which the Armed Forces were engaged in hostility for purposes of permitting expedited naturalization under INA §329. Executive Order 13269, Bush (July 3, 2002), 67 Fed. Reg. 45287 (July 8, 2002), *published on* AILA InfoNet at Doc. No. 02070843. A person is covered under the Executive Order if he served honorably or was honorably discharged after Sept. 11, 2001, even if he is not an LPR. Memo, Yates, Deputy

Ex. Assoc. Comm., Field Operations HQISD 70/33 (July 17, 2002), *published on* AILA InfoNet at Doc. No. 02080946; Fact Sheet, Military Naturalizations, USCIS (Jan. 26, 2005), *reprinted in* 82 No. 7 *Interpreter Releases* 317, 322, 343–45 (Feb. 14, 2005).

1.c. *Revocation*—Naturalization under INA §§328, 329 may be revoked if a person is dishonorably discharged from the Armed Forces before the s/he has served honorably for a period or periods aggregating 5 years. This provision applies to citizenship granted after Nov. 24, 2003.

1.d. *Fees Waived*—All fees for naturalization or for a certificate of naturalization are waived.

1.e. *Good Moral Character*—There is an issue as to whether and to what extent the good moral character criteria applies to veterans under these provisions. *Compare* INA §329, 8 U.S.C. §1440 [no GMC requirement] *with* 8 C.F.R. §329.2(d) [requiring GMC for at least one year prior to filing natz application]; *O'Sullivan v. USCIS,* 453 F.3d 809 (7th Cir. 2006) [both the GMC requirement and the aggravated felony bar under 8 U.S.C. §1101(f)(8) apply to veterans seeking naturalization under §329]; *Boatswain v. Ashcroft,* 414 F.3d 413 (2d. Cir. 2005) [following *Nolan* and finding that §329 contains a GMC requirement, that the provisions of INA §101(f), including the permanent bar for aggravated felons, apply, and that §101(f)(8) regarding aggravated felonies is not retroactive as to petitioner]. *See in this part* ¶ A.4.e (p.1309), *supra.*

2. *Filipino War Veterans*—In 1997 Congress amended INA §329, 8 U.S.C. §1440 note (a)(1)(B)(ii) to permit Filipino war veterans to become naturalized USCs if they were WWII veterans of recognized guerilla units that appeared on the final roster prepared by the Guerilla Affairs Division of the U.S. Army. *Valle v. INS*, 80 Fed. Appx. 947, 2003 WL 22803509 (9th Cir. 2003) [unpublished opinion that denied naturalization to person who served in guerilla unit that did not appear on GAD list]. Prior to the 1997 amendment, Filipino war veterans could naturalize even if they were not on the GAD list. *Almero v. INS*, 18 F.3d 757 (9th Cir. 1994) [veterans not required to prove military service solely by certificate from U.S. Army].

3. *Persian Gulf Veterans*—If served honorably in active duty status between Aug. 2, 1990 and Apr. 11, 1991, eligible for naturalization. White House Press Release, Nov. 22, 1994, *published on* AILA InfoNet at Doc. No. 94112290.

4. *Hmong Veterans' Naturalization Act*—PL 106-207, 114 Stat. 316 (May 26, 2000). Facilitated the naturalization of persons from the Hmong tribe who served with special guerrilla units/irregular forces in Laos at any time from February 1961 through September 1978. Also includes widows of such veterans. The filing deadline for veterans and their spouses was May 26, 2003. The deadline for qualified widows was Nov. 1, 2003.

5. *Extraordinary Contributions to National Security*—If the CIA Director, the AG, and the INS Commissioner determine that an applicant eligible for naturalization has made an extraordinary contribution to U.S. national security or to the conduct of U.S. intelligence activities, the person may be naturalized without regard to the residence and physical presence requirements, the prohibitions for support of totalitarianism/communism, or residence within a particular state. However, if the person falls under one of the grounds for mandatory denial of asylum under INA §208(b)(2)(A) (except firm resettlement), s/he is ineligible for citizenship under this section. INA §316(f), 8 U.S.C. §1427(f).

III. APPLICATION PROCEDURE

A. *Administrative Naturalization*

1. *AG and Court Authority*—IMMACT90 vested the AG with exclusive authority to naturalize. INA §310(a); 8 U.S.C. §1421(a). However, courts may have exclusive authority to administer oaths of allegiance, if they provide sufficient notification to the AG. INA §310(b)(1)(B), 8 U.S.C. §1421(b)(1)(B). *See also* INA §§334–35, 8 U.S.C. §§1445–46. Prior to 1990, only district courts could administer the oath. *Sebastian-Soler v. U.S. Att'y Gen.,* 409 F.3d 1280, 1283–85 (11th Cir. 2005) [LPR was not naturalized in 1988 when he signed the oath before an INS officer because the requirement at that time was that a final hearing must be held in open court]. The applicant may choose to have the oath of allegiance administered by USCIS, U.S. district court, or any state court, INA §310(b), 8 U.S.C. §1421(b), unless the court establishes its exclusive authority.

8 C.F.R. §310.3. Even if the court does not exercise exclusive jurisdiction to administer the oath, USCIS does not have administrative authority to grant a name change, so a person will need to go to court if s/he wishes his or her name changed. INA §336(e), 8 U.S.C. §1447(e).

2. *District Court Review of Naturalization Denial*—District courts have jurisdiction to review *de novo* an administrative decision to deny naturalization. INA §§310(c), 336, 8 U.S.C. §§1421(c), 1447. *Tieri v. INS*, 457 F.2d 391 (2d Cir. 1972). A denied applicant must be informed of the available judicial remedies. INA §335(b), 8 U.S.C. §1446(b). The applicant must exhaust administrative remedies before seeking court review. *Aparicio v. Blakeway,* 302 F.3d 437 (5th Cir. 2002) [class action challenge to INS reliance on SAW confidential information in denying naturalization was not ripe for class members not yet denied and court lacked jurisdiction if there was a denial because §1421(c) provided the exclusive mechanism for review].

B. ***Filing of Application***

1. *N-400*—Applicant must submit a naturalization application (N-400), a photocopy of resident card (if available), two color photos and all other supporting documents prior to examination. A G-325 is not required and the applicant will be called in separately to have fingerprints taken. A waiver of the fingerprint requirement is available to persons who, due to a permanent disability, are unable to be fingerprinted. Memo, Pearson, Ex. Assoc. Comm. Field Operations, HQISD 70/28 (July 20, 2001), *reprinted in* 78 No. 31 *Interpreter Releases* 1308, 1330–34 (Aug. 13, 2001) [waiver applies to all benefit applications]. Applicant is interviewed under oath by USCIS officers. INA §335, 8 U.S.C. §1446; 8 C.F.R. §335.2(c).

2. *Timing of Application*—Applications can be filed up to 3 months before the continuous residence requirements are met. INA §334(a), 8 U.S.C. §1445(a). *Compare* 8 C.F.R. §334.2(b) (90 days includes 3-month state residence requirement). Applications filed after June 29, 1999, are screened to determine whether they were filed prematurely. Memo, Yates, Deputy Exec. Assoc. Comm., Field Operations, (June 29, 1999), *published on* AILA InfoNet at Doc. No. 99070140.

3. *Family Grouping of Applications*—USCIS will no longer group family naturalization applications unless there is a specific request to do so. 83 No. 5 *Interpreter Releases* 201, 205–06 (Jan. 30, 2006).

4. *Substitute Filing and Place of Oath*—A person may file an application other than in the AG's office and an oath may be administered other than in a public ceremony before the AG if the person has a permanent illness or disability which is sufficiently serious to prevent his or her appearance *or* the illness is of a nature which so incapacitates him or her as to prevent him or her from appearing personally. INA §334(e), 8 U.S.C. §1445(e), 8 C.F.R. §334.4.

5. *Withdrawal*—Once the application is filed, it cannot be withdrawn without AG's consent. If the AG does not consent, the application shall be determined on the merits. If the applicant fails to appear when requested, the AG may dismiss the application for lack of prosecution. INA §335(e), 8 U.S.C. §1446(e).

6. *Interview/FBI Name Checks*—The initial examination of an N-400 applicant can only occur "after the Service has received a definitive response from the Federal Bureau of Investigation that a full criminal background check of an applicant has been completed." 8 C.F.R. §335.2(b). A name-check by the FBI is valid for 15 months. Memo, Aytes, Assoc. Dir. Domestic Operations, USCIS (Dec. 21, 2006), *published on* AILA InfoNet at Doc. No. 07022660.

7. *120-Day Decision Period*—If INS fails to make a decision on a naturalization application within 120 days after interview, the applicant may appeal to the U.S. district court for relief. INA §336(b); 8 U.S.C. §1447(b). USCIS has sought to minimize litigation over the 120 day deadline by refusing to schedule interviews until all background checks are complete. Memo, Aytes, Acting Assoc. Director, Domestic Operations (Apr. 25, 2006), *published on* AILA InfoNet at Doc. No. 06051164. The 120 day period may also be waived by the applicant. *Raufi v. Chertoff,* 434 F.Supp.2d 813 (S.D. Cal. 2006) [after naturalization applicant signed waiver the 120 day period did not begin again until he withdrew waiver]. For judicial review, *see in this chapter* ¶ VI.B.2 (p.1325), *infra*.

8. *Change of Address*—As part of its general telephone service, USCIS now allows an applicant to notify it of a change of address. The telephone number is 1-800-375-5283 x1 x2. If a person has more than one address and resides in multiple states, the address on her income tax return is considered the residence address for purposes of determining the appropriate place for filing the application. 8 C.F.R. §316.5(b)(4).

9. *Rescheduling Naturalization Interview and Denial for Abandonment*—USCIS may deem a naturalization application abandoned where the individual fails to appear for the examination and fails to notify USCIS of the reason for not appearing in writing (with a request to reschedule) within 30 days of the scheduled exam. 8 C.F.R. §335.6(a). An applicant may reopen an administratively closed application by submitting a written request to USCIS within one year from the date the application was closed. The date of the reopening request shall be the date of filing for naturalization purposes. 8 C.F.R. §335.6(b). A denial due to abandonment after one year may not be appealed but a motion to reopen may be filed, 8 C.F.R. §103.2(b)(15), if the applicant demonstrates that a request providing good cause to reschedule was postmarked, faxed, or received telephonically before the date and time of the scheduled interview or a notification of a change of address was received prior to adjudication of the application. AFM at 15.1(d)(3)(B).

10. *Re-examination*—Applicant may request or obtain one re-examination—8 C.F.R. §335.3(b). If unsuccessful on the second try, a new N-400 must be filed.

11. *Removal Proceedings*—A person in removal proceedings is not necessarily barred from naturalization. *See in this chapter* ¶ II.A.4.g (p.1310), *supra*.

12. *Nondiscretionary Grant*—If the applicant complies with the naturalization requirements, USCIS *shall* grant the application and may not exercise its discretion to deny naturalization. 8 C.F.R. §335.3(a).

C. *Expedited Processing for Naturalization of Children of USCs*—INS has established expedited procedures to process these applications (including adopted/orphan children) when they are close to age 18. INA §322; Cable, INS (Dec. 22, 1995), *reprinted in* 73 No. 3 *Interpreter Releases* 66–70 (Jan. 16, 1996).

D. *Oath of Allegiance*—In some jurisdictions, the applicant can have oath administered by DHS instead of the court. 8 C.F.R. §337.2. If the applicant fails to appear, s/he will be renotified. 8 C.F.R. §337.10. Failure to appear a second time is deemed an abandonment of the application. If the public oath is not taken, the applicant may not be considered a citizen even if they previously signed the N-400 and swore allegiance to the U.S. *Tovar-Alvarez v. U.S. Att'y Gen.,* 427 F.3d 1350, 1352–53 (11th Cir. 2005) [a person is not a USC if they signed the oath of allegiance to the U.S. but did not take the oath at a public ceremony]; *Abiodun v. Gonzales,* 461 F.3d 1210, 1215–16 (10th Cir. 2006) [same];

E. *Expedited Oath*—An applicant may seek to expedite the administration of the oath if certain conditions are met. 8 C.F.R. §337.3. Special circumstances warranting an expedited oath include a serious illness of the applicant or a family member or urgent or compelling circumstances related to travel or employment. Request must be in writing and may be made to the court or USCIS. 8 C.F.R. §337.3(c).

F. *Correcting Certificate*—Clerical errors on a naturalization certificate may be corrected on Form N-565. 8 C.F.R. §334.16. However, an applicant cannot change his or her name or date of birth where s/he stated that it was correct on the original application, absent a name change by a court. 8 C.F.R. §334.16(b); *Matter of* ___ (AAO Feb. 27, 2003), *reported in* 80 No. 21 *Interpreter Releases* 750 (May 23, 2003) [denying appeal where applicant sought certificate with different birth date than he filed on his adjustment and naturalization applications]. *But see Kouanchao v. USCIS,* 358 F.Supp.2d 837 & 840 (D. Minn. 2005) [allowing amendment to birth date on certificate]; *Varghai v. INS*, 932 F.Supp. 1245 (D. Or. 1996) [change approved where applicant obtained incorrect birth date from officials of his own country].

G. *Obtaining a Passport*

1. *Generally*—A USC or U.S. national is eligible for a U.S. passport and may apply for one directly to the passport office without submitting an application for certificate of citizenship. 22 C.F.R. §§51.20–.26, 51.42–.43 If a passport is granted, it is conclusive (not just *prima facie*) proof of U.S. citizenship and is not subject to collateral attack in an administrative proceeding. 22 U.S.C. §2705 (1982); *Matter of Villanueva*, 19 I&N Dec. 101 (BIA 1984).

2. *Passport for a Child*—All persons, including children under 14, must appear in person to obtain a passport unless the appearance is waived. Both parents must consent to issuance of a passport for their child. 22 C.F.R. §51.28.

3. *Passports to Enter the U.S. and Passport Cards*—It is unlawful for any U.S. citizen to depart or enter the U.S. without a passport, unless he or she:
   - participates in the NEXUS, SENTRI or FAST Program;
   - is a Native American holder of Tribal Documents or Native American Tribal Cards;
   - is a child under 16 or traveling in a group;
   - presents an enhanced driver's license;
   - is returning from military duty;
   - is traveling on a cruise ship within the Western Hemisphere and boarded ship in U.S.;
   - is traveling on a Merchant Marine Document; or
   - has been granted a waiver.

   INA §215(b), 8 U.S.C. §1185(b); 8 C.F.R. §235.1(b) ; 22 C.F.R. §§53.1, 53.2 [exemptions and waivers of passport requirement]. CBP officers are now prohibited from accepting oral declarations at land borders and USCs must provide documentary evidence of citizenship. 72 Fed. Reg. 72744–45 (Dec. 21, 2007). In the future no USC will be able to travel outside the U.S. or return to the U.S. without a passport, passport card, a military ID with official travel orders, a U.S. Merchant Mariner document, or a valid trusted traveler program card (FAST, NEXUS or SENTRI). Western Hemisphere Travel Initiative (WHTI) FAQs, *published on* AILA InfoNet at Doc. No. 08032765. The DOS has established a procedure to get a passport card in lieu of a passport. U.S. Passport Card *published on* AILA InfoNet at Doc. No. 08011132.

4. DOS may issue electronic passports in the future with machine readable chips. 22 C.F.R. §51.1(j) [defining electronic passport]; 70 Fed. Reg. 61553–55 (Oct. 25, 2005) [adopting the use of electronic passports notwithstanding security and privacy concerns raised by the commentators].

H. *Cancellation of Passport*—The Secy. of State is authorized to cancel any U.S. passport or Consular Report of Birth if it appears that such document was illegally, fraudulently, or erroneously obtained or was created through illegality or fraud. INA §361(a), 8 U.S.C. §1504(a); 22 C.F.R. §51.80 to .89. The cancellation or revocation of a passport may be challenged in a declaratory action under 28 U.S.C. §2201 in federal court pursuant to INA §360(a), 8 U.S.C. §1503(a). In *Magnuson v. Baker*, 911 F.2d 330 (9th Cir. 1990), the court held that a passport could not be revoked unless the holder had a pre-deprivation hearing and that the basis for revocation was limited to "exceptional grounds such as fraud and misrepresentation." The court invalidated 22 C.F.R. §51.80 as in conflict with 22 U.S.C. §2705 because the latter requires a process similar to 8 U.S.C. §1453. Revocation of a passport where loss of citizenship is not implicated is valid if post-deprivation hearing is begun with 60 days. *Kelso v. DOS,* 13 F.Supp.2d 12 (D.D.C. 1998) [finding 22 C.F.R. §51.80 constitutional where revocation arose over holder's criminal acts and not because his citizenship was doubted; however DOS enjoined for failing to begin post-deprivation hearing within 60 days]. *But see Atem v. Ashcroft,* 312 F.Supp.2d 792, 799–801 (E.D. Va. 2004) [post-deprivation hearing not necessary on claim that passport was improperly taken from alleged USC where petitioner had removal proceeding where issue of citizenship was addressed].

I. *Invalidity, Revocation and Refusal to Issue Passport*—22 C.F.R. §§51.4(f), 51.60–74; 72 Fed. Reg. 64930–39 (Nov. 19, 2007). The Secy. of State may invalidate a passport, or refuse to issue or revoke a passport for other than lack of citizenship where an applicant:

1. Is subject to an outstanding federal warrant, 22 C.F.R. §51.60(b)(1);
2. Is subject to a criminal court order, condition of probation or parole which forbids departure; §51.60(b)(2)
3. Is subject to a court order committing him or her to a mental institution; §51.60(b)(3)
4. Has been legally declared incompetent, §51.60(b)(4)

5. Is subject of a request for extradition or provisional arrest for extradition which has been presented to the government of a foreign country; §51.60(b)(5)
6. Is subject of a subpoena issued pursuant to 28 U.S.C. §1783 in a matter involving a federal prosecution or grand jury investigation; §51.60(b)(6)
7. Is a minor and the passport may be denied under 22 C.F.R. §51.28, §51.60(b)(7);
8. Is subject to an order of restraint or apprehension issued by the U.S. Armed Forces pursuant to Title 10, Subchapter 47, §51.60(b)(8);
9. Is subject to an outstanding state or local warrant of arrest for a felony, §51.60(b)(9);
10. The applicant is the subject of a request for extradition submitted to the U.S. by a foreign country, §51.60(b)(10);
11. Has not repaid a loan received from the U.S. as prescribed under 28 U.S.C. §2670(j) or §2671(b)(2)(A) and (B); §51.60(c)(1)
12. Is in default on a loan from the U.S. to effectuate his or her return from a foreign country; §51.60(a)(1)
13. Is the subject of a warrant of arrest for a felony after being informed by a foreign government authority or international organization, §51.60(d);
14. The applicant's activities abroad are causing or are likely to cause serious damage to the national security or the foreign policy of the U.S., §51.60(d)(4);
15. Has been certified by the Secy. of HHS to be in arrears in child support in an amount exceeding $2,500. 22 C.F.R. §51.60(a)(2); *Eunique v. Powell,* 302 F.3d 971 (9th Cir. 2002) [upholding constitutionality of statute and regulation authorizing denial of passport]; *Weinstein v. Albright,* 261 F.3d 127 (2d Cir. 2001) [upholding revocation and refusal to renew passport from due process challenge because there is an opportunity to contest arrears before state agency].
16. Is convicted of a federal or state drug charge where he or she used a U.S. passport or crossed an international border in the commission of a crime. 22 C.F.R. §61.51See Omnibus Anti-Drug Abuse Act of 1988, PL 100-690, title VII, subtitle J, §4603; 102 Stat. 4181 (Nov. 18, 1988); 1988 U.S.C.C.A.N. 5937.
17. Other grounds for refusal to issue or revoke a passport include a determination by the Secy. of State that "the national's activities abroad are causing, or are likely to cause serious damage to the national security or the foreign policy of the United States." 22 C.F.R. §51.70(b)(4).
18. A passport is deemed to be invalid if it is: (a) revoked; and (b) registered by the DOS as lost or stolen. 22 C.F.R. §51.4(f).

J. *Amending and Replacing Passports*

1. *Amending*—DOS has abolished to the right to seek amendment of a passport and they will not be amended except at the convenience of the government. 22 C.F.R. §51.9.
2. *Replacing*—The passport office may issue a replacement passport to: (1) correct an error or rectify a mistake; (2) reflect a name change; (3) provide a new document where law enforcement or the judiciary has seized the previous passport for evidentiary purposes; or (4) provide a new electronic passport because the previous one had a damaged chip. 22 C.F.R. §§51.10, 51.54.

K. *Noncitizen Nationals of the U.S.*—INA §308 provides for noncitizen nationality based on birth or parentage in unincorporated outlying possessions of the U.S. Nationals are not citizens, but have special rights with regard to naturalization under INA §325.

IV. DUAL CITIZENSHIP

The U.S. government has generally looked with disfavor upon USCs maintaining dual nationality. *Rogers v. Bellei*, 401 U.S. 815, 831–32 (1971) ["Congress has an appropriate concern with problems attendant to dual nationality"]; *Kennedy v. Mendoza-Martinez*, 372 U.S. 144, 187 (1963) (Brennan, J. concurring) ["[w]e have recognized the entanglements which may stem from dual allegiances"]; *Kawakita v. U.S.*, 343 U.S. 717, 733 (1952) ["[o]ne who has a dual nationality will be subject to claims from both nations, claims which at times may be competing and conflicting"]. However, the court has also recognized that dual nationality is "a status long recognized in the law" and "the mere fact that he asserts the rights of one citizenship does not without more mean that he renounces the other." *Kawakita, supra*. A USC is not precluded from dual nationality that is obtained:

(1) Through naturalization in the U.S. when the foreign state does not divest its citizens of their citizenship upon naturalization in a foreign country;

(2) Through birth in the U.S. to nationals of a country that follows principles of *jus sanguinis*; or

(3) Through naturalization of a USC in a foreign state that does not require the USC to renounce his or her U.S. citizenship or where the USC was found not to expatriate him or herself.

Moreover, there is no requirement that the dual national choose one nationality or the other when s/he becomes an adult. *Mandoli v. Acheson*, 344 U.S. 133 (1952). A dual national should use his or her U.S. passport to enter and leave the U.S. INA §215(b), 8 U.S.C. §1185(b).

For a listing of countries that support or reject dual nationality as of 2001, see *Citizenship Laws of the World* (OPM 2001), available at *www.opm.gov/extra/investigate/IS-01.pdf.*

V. LOSS OF CITIZENSHIP

A. *Voluntary Relinquishment*—A native born or naturalized USC may lose his or her U.S. citizenship by voluntarily relinquishing it through an act of expatriation. *See Afroyim v. Rusk*, 387 U.S. 253 (1967).

B. *Grounds for Denaturalization*—A naturalized USC may lose his or her citizenship by revocation of naturalization often referred to as denaturalization. However, denaturalization should not be presumed and citizenship should only be taken away where there is clear, unequivocal and convincing evidence that leaves the issue of illegality free of doubt. *Fedorenko v. U.S.,* 449 U.S. 490, 506 (1981).

1. *Membership in Certain Organizations; Prima Facie Evidence*—INA §340(c), 8 U.S.C. §1451(c). Membership or affiliation with a subversive, communist, or anarchist organization under INA §313, 8 U.S.C. §1424, within 5 years of naturalization is considered prima facie evidence that the applicant was not attached to the principles of the U.S. Constitution and was not well-disposed to the good order and happiness of the U.S. at the time of naturalization. INA §340(c), 8 U.S.C. §1451(c).

2. *Concealment of Material Evidence or Willful Misrepresentation*—INA §340(a), 8 U.S.C. §1451(a). In *Kungys v. U.S.*, 485 U.S. 759 (1988) the Court cast aside the previous standard defining material misrepresentation for denaturalization purposes in *Chaunt v. U.S.*, 364 U.S. 350 (1960) and determined that "the test of whether...concealments or misrepresentations were material [under 8 U.S.C. §1451(a)] is whether they had a natural tendency to influence the decision of the INS." The Court recognized that denaturalization based on a material misrepresentation requires four independent elements: "the naturalized citizen must have misrepresented or concealed some fact, the misrepresentation or concealment must have been willful, the fact must have been material, and the naturalized citizen must have procured citizenship as a result of the misrepresentation or concealment." *Id.* at 767. Determination of materiality is therefore a mixed question of law and fact. *U.S. v. Gaudin*, 115 S.Ct. 2310, 2319 (1995). The government must establish a factual case proving that the naturalized citizen procured the naturalization decision by unlawful conduct. *U.S. v. Stelmokas*, 100 F.3d 302, 337–42 (3d Cir. 1996). If the government establishes materiality, the respondent has the right to rebut the presumption of denaturalization by demonstrating that he nevertheless met the statutory requirements. *Kungys,* 485 U.S. at 777; *Monter v. Gonzales,* 430 F.3d 546, 554 (2d Cir. 2005) [applying *Kungys* test to material misrepresentation in I-751 context and reversing removal where respondent was denied the opportunity to overcome the presumption]. *See also U.S. v. Nunez-Garcia,* 262 F.Supp.2d 1073, 1084–85 (C.D. Cal. 2003) [defendant's claim that he told the notary the correct information was rejected because defendant read and spoke English and signed document]; *U.S. v. Damrah,* 412 F.3d 618, 625–28 (6th Cir. 2005) [upholding conviction under 1425(a) and (b) and automatic denaturalization under 1451(e) of Moslem cleric on grounds that he was a member and assisted organizations that persecuted others]; *U.S. v. Ekpin,* 214 F.Supp.2d 707, 715–17 (S.D. Tex. 2002) [applicant made willful and ma-

terial misrepresentation when he answered "no" to whether he had ever committed a crime for which he had not been arrested after he had sexually abused his daughter during the 5-year period for GMC].

3. *Illegal Procurement*—INA §340(a), 8 U.S.C. §1451(a). In *Fedorenko v. U.S.*, 449 U.S. 490 (1981), the Court addressed the meaning of "illegally procured" under INA §340(a) and determined that because naturalization under INA §§316(a), 318; 8 U.S.C. §§1427(a), 1429 requires the applicant to be lawfully admitted to the U.S., Fedorenko's citizenship was illegally procured where misrepresentations on his original application for admission rendered his admission unlawful. The Court, therefore, read the illegal procurement provision to permit denaturalization based on misconduct not arising out of the naturalization application itself. *Accord. U.S. v. Firishchak,* 468 F.3d 1015, 1025 (7th Cir. 2006) [member of Ukrainian Auxiliary Police illegally procured his citizenship even if he was not personally involved in atrocities on Nazi's behalf]; *U.S. v. Wittje,* 422 F.3d 479 (7th Cir. 2005) [rejecting equal protection argument against denaturalization and involuntary argument against DPA]; *U.S. v. Friedrich,* 402 F.3d 842 (8th Cir. 2005) [working as a guard at Nazi concentration camp was sufficient, without more, to establish assisting in persecution for purposes of denaturalization based on illegal procurement]; *U.S. v. Demjanjuk,* 367 F.3d 623, 636–37 (6th Cir. 2004) [voluntarily providing assistance in the persecution of others is not an element for denaturalization based on illegal procurement of residency through the DPA]; *U.S. v. Reimer,* 356 F.3d 456 (2d Cir. 2004) [naturalized citizen who assisted Nazis in the persecution of Jews illegally procured his citizenship]; *U.S. v. Dailide,* 316 F.3d 611, 618 (6th Cir. 2003) [revoking citizenship of former member of Lithuanian special unit that persecuted Jews during WWII based on illegal procurement because, notwithstanding his compliance with all administrative procedures for naturalization, he was statutorily ineligible to receive a visa in the first place because of his Nazi past]; *U.S. v. Nunez-Garcia,* 262 F.Supp.2d 1073, 1081–83 (C.D. Cal. 2003) [person who committed aggravated felony prior to the five year period and a CIMT for lewd conduct in public during the five year period illegally procured his citizenship]; *U.S. v. Samaei,* 260 F.Supp.2d 1223 (M.D. Fla. 2003) [person who committed second petty theft before swearing-in ceremony but after interview illegally procured citizenship because he lacked GMC]. Illegal procurement has been extended to encompass illegal acts reflecting on a person's GMC which arose before naturalization, but for which the person was not arrested, charged or convicted until *after* he became a citizen. *U.S. v. Dang,* 488 F.3d 1135 (9th Cir. 2007) [court rejected *ultra vires,* void-for-vagueness, overbreadth, and Uniformity Clause challenge to GMC regulation at 8 C.F.R. §316.10(b)(3)(iii) in the context of denaturalization for illegal procurement where petitioner committed crimes of arson, willful injury to a child and others prior to being naturalized]; *U.S. v. Jean-Baptiste*, 395 F.3d 1190 (11th Cir. 2005) [relying on the "catch-all" provision of INA §101(f) and *Chevron* deference to 8 C.F.R. §316.10(b)(3)(iii) that broadly construes lack of GMC to include the *commission* of unlawful acts, the court denaturalized a person who had a minor role in one incident of cocaine trafficking but was not arrested, charged, or indicted until *after* he became a citizen]; *U.S. v. Lekarczyk,* 354 F.Supp.2d 883 (W.D. Wis. 2005) [followed *Jean-Baptiste* where bank fraud, forgery-uttering and bail jumping all occurred before but were not charged until after citizenship obtained]; *U.S. v. Ekpin,* 214 F.Supp.2d 707, 713–15 (S.D. Tex. 2002) [charge of illegal procurement sustained where applicant admitted to committing aggravated felony during statutory period but conviction was subsequent to naturalization]. A conviction under 18 U.S.C. §1425 for knowingly procuring naturalization in violation of law is a grounds for automatic denaturalization. INA §340(e), 8 U.S.C. §1451(e).

4. *Subversive Activities*—INA §340(a), 8 U.S.C. §1451(a). Refusing to testify before a congressional committee regarding one's pre-naturalization subversive activities not revealed in the application is a ground for revocation where the person has been convicted of contempt for such refusal and where it occurs within 10 years following naturalization.

5. *Military Service Denaturalization*—Naturalization under INA §§328, 329 may be revoked if the person is separated from the Armed Forces under other than honorable conditions before the person has served honorably for a period or periods aggregating 5 years. Applies to citizenship granted after Nov. 24, 2003.

C. *Denaturalization Procedure*—Denaturalization may occur: (1) through a court proceeding; (2) through an administrative proceeding; or (3) as a result of a criminal conviction for knowingly procuring naturalization by fraud under 18 U.S.C. §1425, where the sentencing judge strips the person of his or her citizenship.

1. *Court Proceedings*—Revocation of naturalization by a court under INA §340(a), 8 U.S.C. §1451(a), must be initiated by action in a state or federal court competent to hear naturalization matters under INA §310, 8 U.S.C. §1421. The action, initiated by a U.S. Attorney, is "for the purpose of revoking and setting aside the order admitting such person to citizenship." INA §340(a), 8 U.S.C. §1451(a). The basis for the revocation is that the order and certificate were procured illegally *or* were procured by the concealment of a material fact or by willful misrepresentation. *Id. See, e.g., U.S. v. Szehinskyj,* 277 F.3d 331 (3d Cir. 2002) [finding that a material misrepresentation is not a necessary element to revoke naturalization as it is sufficient to demonstrate person did not qualify for the Displaced Persons' Act visa because he persecuted others]; *U.S. v. Tittjung,* 235 F.3d 330, 340–42 (7th Cir. 2000) [persecutor's ineligibility for DPA visa even where there was no material misrepresentation renders naturalization invalid]; *U.S. v. Kiang,* 175 F.Supp.2d 942 (E.D. Mich. 2001) [naturalization revoked because conviction for sexual misconduct under pre-1994 Michigan statute is a CIMT barring naturalization during statutory GMC period]; *U.S. v. Tarango-Pena,* 173 F.Supp.2d 588 (E.D. Tex. 2001) [naturalization revoked where LPR status was procured by fraud because petitioning wife was not USC]; *U.S. v. Wasylyk,* 162 F.Supp.2d 86, 87–89 (N.D.N.Y. 2001) [Nazi denaturalization case where LPR status illegally procured because respondent was a war criminal]. The action generally must be brought in the judicial district where the naturalized citizen resides. In the denaturalization proceeding, the government must comply with the *Brady* rule and provide all exculpatory evidence when denaturalization is based alleged criminal activities. *Demjanjuk v. Petrovsky,* 10 F.3d 338, 353 (6th Cir. 1993). At least one circuit has granted denaturalization on summary judgment. *U.S. v. Dailide,* 227 F.3d 385, 388–90 (6th Cir. 2000). *But see U.S. v. Singh,* 94 F.Supp.2d 540 (W.D. Pa. 1999) [where naturalized citizen pled guilty to a crime that antedated his application, INS was denied revocation by summary judgment because citizen's failure to note on his naturalization application that he had committed a crime for which he was not arrested was a factual question].

1.a. *Burden of Proof*—The government "carries a heavy burden of proof in a proceeding to divest a naturalized citizen of his citizenship." *Fedorenko v. U.S.,* 449 U.S. 490, 505 (1981) [quoting *Costello v. U.S.,* 395 U.S. 265, 269 (1961)]. The government must prove its case by "clear, unequivocal, and convincing" evidence that does not leave "the issue in doubt." *Fedorenko,* 449 U.S. at 505. The standard is informed by the recognition that the loss of citizenship "can have severe and unsettling consequences." *Id.*

1.b. *Memorandum of Understanding*—USCIS, OIL, and the U.S. Attorneys offices have entered into a memorandum of understanding that allows OIL by "delegation and acquiescence" of the local U.S. Attorney offices to file denaturalization suits and litigate actions under 8 U.S.C. §1451(a). USCIS will still recommend whether there should be civil or criminal prosecutions and the U.S. Attorney offices will still decide whether to prosecute criminally. "Memorandum of Understanding Between the United States Attorneys Offices, the Immigration and Naturalization Service and the Civil Division—Office of Immigration Litigation Regarding Actions to Revoke Naturalization," *reprinted in* 77 No. 30 *Interpreter Releases* 1130, 1144–50 (Aug. 7, 2000).

1.c. *Defenses to Denaturalization*—Laches, waiver, statute of limitations, or equitable estoppel may not be defenses to denaturalization proceedings. *INS v. Pangilinan,* 486 U.S. 875, 883–84 (1988); *U.S. v. Mandycz,* 447 F.3d 951, 964–66 (6th Cir. 2006) [when government acts in its sovereign capacity laches does not apply]; *U.S. v. Robelo,* 358 F.Supp.2d 400, 407–13 (D.N.J. 2005) [general statute of limitations for penalties and forfeitures under 28 U.S.C. §2462 is inapplicable to denaturalization proceeding]; *U.S. v. Reve,* 241 F.Supp.2d 470, 478 (D.N.J. 2003) [denaturalization for material misrepresentation may not be fought through equitable defenses such as waiver, laches or estoppel]; *U.S. v. Koreh*, 856 F.Supp. 891, 893 n.3 (D.N.J. 1994). Incompetence, in the view of one court, is also not a defense because denaturalizing an incompetent does not violate due process. *U.S. v. Mandycz,* 447 F.3d 951, 961–64 (6th Cir. 2006). *But see U.S. v. Wang,* 404 F.Supp.2d 1155 (N.D. Cal. 2005) [rejecting a statute of limitations and laches defense, but allowing an estoppel claim where citizen asserted that government was aware of his criminal background prior to naturalization. However, the court ultimately rejected the estoppel defense because there was no showing that the government engaged in affirmative misconduct].

2. *Administrative Revocation*—INA §340(h). The AG has the authority administratively "to correct, reopen, alter, modify, or vacate an order naturalizing [a] person." INA §340(h), 8 U.S.C. §1451(h). The courts interpreting the prior statute that permitted court revocation, narrowly construed the AG's authority. *Matter of Campbell,* 326 F.2d 101 (2d Cir. 1964); *Matter of Arevalo,* 352 F.Supp. 215 (D. Haw. 1972). INS has since promulgated regulations regarding the revocation of naturalization through the AG. 8 C.F.R. §340.1, 61 Fed. Reg. 55551–55 (Oct. 15, 1996); 65 Fed. Reg. 17127–28 (Mar. 31, 2000). The government's burden of proof is clear, convincing, and unequivocal evidence. 8 C.F.R. §340.1(b)(6). However, at least one circuit has found that the statute does not give the AG the power to revoke naturalization and that such power remains expressly with the federal courts. *Gorbach v. Reno,* 219 F.3d 1087 (9th Cir. 2000) (en banc) [treating INA §340(h) as a savings clause that permits the AG to retain the power to cancel certificates under INA §342 but not to grant new authority to revoke naturalization]. Following the Ninth Circuit's *en banc* decision, the district court issued a nationwide permanent injunction preventing INS from invoking the administrative denaturalization provision under 8 C.F.R. §340.1. *Gorbach v. Reno,* Case No. C-98-0278R (W.D. Wash. Feb. 14, 2001), *discussed at* 78 No. 9 *Interpreter Releases* 442–43 (Mar. 5, 2001).

2.a. *DHS Basis to Reopen Naturalization*—8 C.F.R. §340.1(a); *but see Gorbach v. Reno,* No. C-98-0278R (W.D. Wash. Feb. 14, 2001), *discussed at* 78 No. 9 *Interpreter Releases* 442–43 (Mar. 5, 2001). The government must obtain credible and probative evidence that will establish:

(1) Application granted in error. If person not qualified, courts do not have discretion to waive a requirement. *INS v. Pangilinan,* 486 U.S. 875, 884 (1988); *Friend v. Reno,* 172 F.3d 638, 646–47 (9th Cir. 1999).

(2) Evidence was not known *at time naturalization granted* that (a) would have a material effect on the outcome of the original naturalization; and (b) would have proven that the application was based on fraud or misrepresentation or concealment of a material fact or that the applicant was ineligible.

2.b. *Procedure*—8 C.F.R. §340.1(b); 65 Fed. Reg. 17127–28 (Mar. 31, 2000), 61 Fed. Reg. 55551–54 (Oct. 15, 1996); *but see Gorbach supra.*

(1) Notice of intent to reopen (NIR) must be served no later than 2 years after person is USC.

(2) NIR must be served in accordance with 8 C.F.R. §103.5a(a)(2), and if unsuccessful must be re-served with other method described by regulation. The NIR "shall include all evidence which the district director believes warrants reopening." 8 C.F.R. §340.1(b)(2)(i).

(3) Applicant has 60 days to respond. May submit evidence or may request a hearing in writing with an additional statement or evidence. Failure to respond results in final order.

(4) Right to counsel. 8 C.F.R. §340.1(b)(5).

(5) The government has burden of proof that grounds for reopening in NIR have been met. 8 C.F.R. §340.1(b)(6).

(6) DD "shall render" a decision where practicable within 180 days of service of the NIR or refer it to district court where there are genuine issues of fact in dispute.

(7) Appeal to AAO within 30 days on Form I-290B.

(8) Within 45 days of notice of appeal, DD may *sua sponte* reconsider his or her decision.

2.c. *INS Internal Guidelines*—Set forth in Standards for Issuance of Notice of Intent to Reopen Naturalization Proceeding and Revoke Naturalization, *reprinted in* 74 No. 12 *Interpreter Releases* 533, 555, 558 (Mar. 28 1997) [requiring INS to have "clear case" where evidence should be "clear, unequivocal and convincing"].

2.d. *Judicial Review*—If AAO decision is adverse, judicial review may be sought in accordance with INA §310. 8 C.F.R. §340.1(f).

3. *Revocation after Conviction for Naturalization Fraud*—8 U.S.C. §1451(e). If a person was convicted of knowingly procuring naturalization by fraud, the court where the conviction occurred shall revoke the person's naturalization. *U.S. v. Inocencio,* 215 F.Supp.2d 1095 (D. Hawaii 2002) [no prior notice needed for revocation as it is automatic under §1451(e)] *aff'd U.S. v. Inocencio,* 328 F.3d 1207 (9th Cir. 2003) [revocation of naturalization as a result of a conviction for fraudulently obtaining citizenship under 18 U.S.C. §1425(b) five years after sentencing does not violate due process]; *U.S. v. Damrah,* 412 F.3d 618, 625–28 (6th Cir. 2005) [upholding conviction under §§1425(a) and (b) and automatic denaturalization under §1451(e) of Moslem cleric on grounds that he was a member and assisted organizations that persecuted others]; *U.S. v. Maduno,* 40 F.3d 1212, 1217 (11th Cir. 1994) [filing notice of appeal of criminal conviction does not divest the court of authority under 8 U.S.C. §1451(e) to revoke naturalization].

4. *Effect on Family Members of Denaturalization*—Denaturalization based on concealment or material misrepresentation causes any person who claimed citizenship through the denaturalized parent or spouse to lose their citizenship. INA §340(d), 8 U.S.C. §1451(d).

5. *Cancellation of Certificate*—The AG may also seek to cancel a certificate of citizenship when the document was obtained illegally or fraudulently. The cancellation of the document does not affect the citizenship status of the person. INA §342, 8 U.S.C. §1453.

D. *Loss of U.S. Citizenship*

1. *Generally*—Pursuant to INA §349(a), 8 U.S.C. §1481(a), a native born or naturalized USC may lose his or her citizenship by voluntarily performing any of the following acts with the intention of relinquishing citizenship:

1.a. Obtaining naturalization in or taking an oath of allegiance to a foreign state after attaining the age of 18;

1.b. Entering or serving in the armed forces of a foreign state engaged in hostilities against the U.S. or serving in any foreign army as a commissioned or noncommissioned officer;

1.c. Accepting, serving in or performing duties of any office, post or employment of a foreign government;

1.d. Making a formal renunciation of U.S. citizenship before a diplomatic or consular officer on a DOS form or making a formal written renunciation whenever the U.S. is in a state of war; or

1.e. Committing an act of treason against, or attempting by force to overthrow, or bearing arms against the U.S.

2. *Burden of Proof*—The statute places the burden of demonstrating the loss of citizenship on the U.S. by a preponderance of the evidence but also provides that the expatriating acts listed in INA §349(a) were presumed to be done voluntarily, but such presumption "may be rebutted." INA §349(b), 8 U.S.C. §1481(b).

3. *Relinquishment Voluntary and Intentional*—Naturalization, lawfully obtained, cannot be lost without a determination by DOS under INA §358 that citizenship was voluntarily relinquished. *Afroyim v. Rusk*, 387 U.S. 253 (1967) [statute expatriating citizen due to voting in foreign election violative of the Fourteenth Amendment]. Expatriation is only constitutionally permissible where the government can prove that a party not only voluntarily engaged in the expatriating acts, but that in doing so s/he intended to relinquish citizenship. *Vance v. Terrazas*, 444 U.S. 252 (1980); *Breyer v. Ashcroft,* 350 F.3d 327 (3d Cir. 2003) [continued military service in the Waffen SS after the age of 18 did not, under the totality of the circumstances, demonstrate intent to relinquish citizenship]; *Action S.A. v. Marc Rich & Co., Inc.*, 951 F.2d 504, 506–07 (2d Cir. 1991); *U.S. v. Schiffer*, 831 F.Supp. 1166, 1186–96 (E.D. Pa. 1993) [citizenship relinquished by serving in Romanian Army and Nazi SS]. *Compare Kahane v. Shultz*, 653 F.Supp. 1486 (E.D.N.Y. 1987) [citizenship not relinquished merely by taking seat in foreign parliament without evidence of intention

to relinquish] with *Kahane v. Secy. of State*, 700 F.Supp. 1162 (D.D.C. 1988) [relinquishment found where renunciation made at U.S. consulate].

4. *Presumption Against Expatriation*—In *Matter of Kekich*, 19 I&N Dec. 198 (BIA 1984), the BIA read *Terrazas* as permitting the government to satisfy its evidentiary burden in light of the statute's presumption of voluntariness simply by demonstrating by a preponderance of the evidence under INA §349(b) that the USC committed one of the intentional expatriating acts enunciated in INA §349(a). However, under a new evidentiary standard established by DOS, a person committing certain expatriating acts is *presumed to retain* his or her citizenship unless his or her conduct "is so inconsistent with obligations to the United States as to compel the conclusion that the intent to relinquish was present (we envision cases in this category would be quite rare and would involve fact situations substantially beyond *pro forma* disavowals of allegiance to the U.S.) or where an individual...formally advises the consular officer in writing that his or her intent was to relinquish U.S. nationality." *Matter of CMS*, Decision No. 90-12 (Board of Appellate Review July 5, 1990), *reported in* 67 No. 27 *Interpreter Releases* 799–800 (July 23, 1990). The presumption against expatriation by certain acts is now in DOS regulations at 22 C.F.R. §50.40(a), (b), and applies to cases where a person is:

 4.a. Naturalized in a foreign country;

 4.b. Takes a routine oath of allegiance; or

 4.c. Accepts non–policy level employment with a foreign government.

 The presumption is applicable retroactively to cases previously denied. However, the presumption is *not* applicable where someone:

 4.d. Formally renounces U.S. citizenship before a consular officer;

 4.e. Takes a policy level position in a foreign state;

 4.f. Is convicted of treason; or

 4.g. Performs an act made potentially expatriating by statute accompanied by conduct which is so inconsistent with retention of U.S. citizenship that it compels a conclusion that the individual intended to relinquish U.S. citizenship.

 Statement about possible loss of U.S. citizenship and dual nationality, DOS, *reprinted in* 67 No. 37 *Interpreter Releases* 1092 (Oct. 1, 1990). *See generally* Office of Legal Counsel, DOJ, *Survey of the Law of Expatriation* (June 12, 2002), *www.usdoj.gov/olc/expatriation.htm*.

5. *Loss of Citizenship and LPR Status*—*Costello v. INS,* 376 U.S. 120 (1964) [denaturalized USC cannot be deported for two CIMTs when he was convicted of the crimes while he was a citizen]; *Matter of Vielma-Ortiz*, 11 I&N Dec. 415 (BIA 1965) [loss of citizenship does not result in automatic loss of LPR status]. *But see Matter of Gonzalez-Muro,* 24 I&N Dec. 472 (BIA 2008) [reaffirmed *Matter of Rossi,* 11 I&N Dec. 514 (BIA 1966) and distinguished *Costello* and held that respondent could be removed for crimes he was convicted of while a citizen, because he *committed* the crimes while he was an LPR, had his citizenship revoked because he committed the crimes before naturalization, and obtained his citizenship by concealing his activity]

VI. ADMINISTRATIVE AND JUDICIAL REVIEW

A. *Administrative Review*

1. *Appeal of Naturalization Denial*—Denial of a naturalization application may be appealed to an immigration officer. INA §336(a), 8 U.S.C. §1447(a). The appeal may involve an evidentiary hearing including the right to subpoena witnesses. INA §§336(c) and (d), 8 U.S.C. §§1447(c) and (d), 8 C.F.R. §336.2.

2. *Loss of Nationality/Passport Denial, Revocation, Restriction*—Administrative review of the Bureau of Consular Affairs' issuance of a certificate of loss of nationality or any administrative decision to deny, revoke, restrict or invalidate a passport under 22 C.F.R. §§51.70–.71, is conducted through the DOS Board of Appellate Review. 22 C.F.R. §7.1 *et seq.* A person who has been issued a certificate of loss of nationality has one year to appeal the decision. 22 C.F.R. §§7.5(b)(1), 50.51. *Matter of M-J-F,* Case No. 96-4 (BAR Oct. 15, 1996), *reprinted in* 73 No. 44 *Interpreter*

Releases 1616–17 (Nov. 18, 1996) [where 16 years had passed after DOJ determined appellant had expatriated himself, appeal barred]. An aggrieved party to an administrative decision revoking, restricting, denying, or invalidating a passport can appeal the decision to the Board of Appellate Review within 60 days. 22 C.F.R. §§7.5(b)(2), 51.89. However, the appeal provision is not applicable to denials based upon lack of U.S. citizenship. 22 C.F.R. §51.80(a)(1). A party may submit briefs and request a hearing before the Board. 22 C.F.R. §7.5(d) and (e). In cases reviewing certificates of loss of nationality, the Board may also take evidence and allow discovery through depositions and interrogatories. 22 C.F.R. §7.5(h). DOS, however, may vacate a certificate of loss of nationality even if the Board affirmed it. 22 C.F.R. §7.2(b). In passport cases, the Board is limited to the review of the record created at the hearing under 22 C.F.R. §§51.81–.89 which is accorded an aggrieved person whose passport is denied, revoked, restricted or invalidated. 22 C.F.R. §7.7. In addition, an applicant for admission at a port of entry may seek a hearing before an IJ to prove U.S. citizenship. The procedure used to deny admission must comport with due process. *Hernandez v. Cremer*, 913 F.2d 230 (5th Cir. 1990).

B. *Judicial Review*

1. *Naturalization Application*—An applicant can obtain *de novo* review in U.S. district court of a denial of a naturalization application. INA §310(c), 8 U.S.C. §1421(c). Such review must be in accordance with the APA. INA §310(c), 8 U.S.C. §1421(c). *Gatcliffe v. Reno,* 23 F.Supp.2d 581, 585 (D.V.I. 1998); *Aparicio v. Blakeway,* 302 F.3d 437 (5th Cir. 2002) [class action challenge to INS reliance on SAW confidential information in denying naturalization was not ripe if there was no denial and court lacked jurisdiction if there was a denial because §1421(c) provided the exclusive mechanism for review]. Under DHS regulations review must be filed within 120 days of the DHS denial. 8 C.F.R. §336.9(b). However, as the action is governed by the APA, the regulatory time limit for initiating litigation is probably invalid. *Nagahi v. INS,* 219 F.3d 1166 (10th Cir. 2000) [INS regulation §336.9(b) cannot limit the jurisdiction of federal courts to a 120-day period]. If an applicant seeks judicial review of a naturalization denial, the court must review the matter and cannot remand the case to the agency as it could under INA §336(b), 8 U.S.C. §1447(b). *Epie v. Caterisano,* 402 F.Supp.2d 589 (D. Md. 2005) [court lacked jurisdiction to remand and was required to decide the case *de novo*]. However, where USCIS vacates its denial during the pendency of the district court proceedings, the court may lose jurisdiction. *Gizzo v. INS,* 510 F.Supp.2d 210 (S.D.N.Y. 2007) [court dismissed case brought under INA §310(c) when USCIS vacated its denial of petitioner's N-400].

2. *Court Intervention Where USCIS Fails to Act*—An applicant can also seek district court review of the failure of USCIS to act within 120 days after a naturalization examination. INA §336(b), 8 U.S.C. §1447(b); 8 C.F.R. §§310.5, 336.9. *Walji v. Gonzales,* 500 F.3d 432 (5th Cir. 2007) [rejected government's argument that the 120 day period did not run until the mandatory FBI security investigation was complete and instead found the 120 days begin from the time the naturalization examination was conducted]; *Nagahi v. INS,* 219 F.3d 1166 (10th Cir. 2000); *Imran v. Keisler,* 516 F.Supp.2d 967 (S.D. Iowa 2007) [court had jurisdiction but remanded case to agency to make decision expeditiously]; *Ahmed v. Gonzales,* 509 F.Supp.2d 556 (E.D. Va. 2007) [same]; *Hussain v. Chertoff,* 486 F.Supp. 196 (D. Mass. 2007) [granting naturalization]; *Castracani v. Chertoff,* 377 F.Supp.2d 71, 74 & n.8 (D.D.C. 2005) [waiting for FBI clearance was not a satisfactory basis to refuse to adjudicate naturalization application within 120 days of interview and USCIS lost jurisdiction over the case once a petition was filed in federal court such that its subsequent grant of naturalization did not moot action]; *See also Abuhadba v. Gonzales,* 512 F.Supp.2d 1347 (N.D. Ga. 2007) [court has jurisdiction and will grant limited discovery on USCIS claim that the FBI background check was requested and that it has not yet been received]; *Al-Farisi v. Mueller,* 492 F.Supp.2d 335 (S.D.N.Y.2007) [the 120 day period runs from the initial examination not the FBI/USCIS background check and the case is remanded to FBI to do name check within 30 days and USCIS to decide application 30 days after that]; *Andron v. Gonzales,* 487 F.Supp.2d 1089 (W.D. Mo. 2007) [same but remanded to USCIS for a decision in 60 days]; *Issa v. Mueller,* 486 F.Supp.2d 668 (E.D. Mich. 2007) [USCIS/FBI background check does not toll the 120 day period because 8 C.F.R. §335.2(b) requires the check *before* the interview; court remanded to USCIS for determination]; *Silebi De Donado v. Swacina,* 486 F.Supp.2d 1360, 1363 (S.D. Fla.

2007) [same]; *Lin v. Secy. of DHS,* 485 F.Supp.2d 263 (W.D.N.Y. 2007) [same]; *Khelifa v. Chertoff,* 433 F.Supp.2d 836, 840–42 (E.D. Mich. 2006) [same]; *Hussein v. Gonzales,* 474 F.Supp. 1265 (M.D. Fla. 2007) [same]; *Manzoor v. Chertoff,* 472 F.Supp.2d 801 (E.D. Va. 2007) [same]; *Shalan v. Chertoff,* No. 05-CV-10980, 2006 WL 42143 *1 (D.C. Mass. Jan. 6, 2006); *El Doour v. Chertoff,* 417 F.Supp.2d 679 (W.D. Pa. 2005); *Al-Kudsi v. Gonzales,* No. CV.05-1584-PK (D. Or. Mar. 22, 2006) [rejecting reasoning in *Danilov*]. *But see Lahrar v. Gonzales,* 485 F.Supp.2d 705 (E.D. Va. 2007) [following *Danilov*]; *Martinez v. Gonzales,* 463 F.Supp.2d 569 (E.D. Va. 2006) [following *Danilov*]; *Danilov v. Aguirre,* 370 F.Supp.2d 441 (E.D. Va. 2005) [the 120-day period does not run from the interview but from the completion of the USCIS process, which also includes the results of the FBI investigation].

Exclusive Jurisdiction in District Court, Not at USCIS—Once an action is filed under §1447(b), the court, not the agency, has exclusive jurisdiction over the matter and it may either determine the matter or remand it to USCIS for a decision. INA §336(b), 8 U.S.C. §1447(b). *Etape v. Chertoff,* 497 F.3d 379 (4th Cir. 2007) [once §1447(b) jurisdiction vests, USCIS had no authority to enter a decision on the merits of the naturalization case and its decision is vacated and the case is remanded to the district court to determine whether it will decide the naturalization matter or remand it to USCIS]; *Hovsepian v. U.S.,* 359 F.3d 1144, 1159–64 (9th Cir. 2004) (en banc) [district court under §1447(b) has exclusive authority to decide the naturalization application once the application has been pending more than 120 days and may thus decide the merits after denial]; *Elaasar v. Mueller,* 522 F.Supp.2d 932 (N.D. Ohio 2007) [denied mootness claim on grounds that USCIS had denied petition because §1447(b) jurisdiction vests district court with authority to decide naturalization petition and USCIS's decision is irrelevant]; *Zaranska v. DHS,* 400 F.Supp.2d 500, 501–04 (E.D.N.Y. 2005) [denying DHS's motion to dismiss the §1447(b) complaint more than 120 days after the interview but before DHS had denied naturalization; finding the applicant eligible for naturalization and denying the government's motion for summary judgment]. *But see Bustamante v. Chertoff,* 533 F.Supp.2d 373 (S.D.N.Y. 2008) [where USCIS denied petition while §1447(b) action was pending, the issue was moot because USCIS had concurrent jurisdiction with the court]; *Pichardo-Martinez v. Ashcroft,* 399 F.Supp.2d 1043 (D. Ariz. 2005) [where action brought under §1447(b) but petitioner requested only a determination on prima facie eligibility so he could terminate his removal proceeding, USCIS had jurisdiction to deny the application]; *Perry v. Gonzales,* 472 F.Supp.2d 623 (D.N.J. 2007) [both the court and USCIS have concurrent jurisdiction over 1447(b) petition and USCIS may grant naturalization while the petition is pending]. *See also Miller v. INS,* ___ F.Supp.2d ___, Civ. No. 7:01CV00178 (W.D. Va. May 28, 2001), *reported in* 78 No. 34 *Interpreter Releases* 1412 (Aug. 31, 2001) [district court found that INS could not delay adjudicating a naturalization application beyond 120 days because it wanted to wait for the outcome of a criminal indictment against the applicant].

Applicant in Removal Proceedings—If removal proceedings are pending 8 U.S.C. §1429 prohibits the DHS from considering the application and therefore §1447(b) review may be prohibited. *Saba-Bakare v. Chertoff,* 507 F.3d 337, 340–41 (5th Cir. 2007)

3. *Cancellation or Revocation of a Passport*—If DOS refuses to renew or issue a passport, any person within the U.S. may bring an action for a declaratory judgment that s/he is a U.S. national or USC and is entitled to a passport or any other document associated with citizenship. INA §360(a), 8 U.S.C. §1503(a). The court reviews the matter *de novo. Patel v. Rice,* 403 F.Supp.2d 560, 562 (N.D. Tex. 2005) [upholding denial of passport].

4. *Denaturalization Cases*—Denaturalization is initiated by the U.S. Attorney in the district where the naturalized citizen resides. INA §340(a), 8 U.S.C. §1451(a). The USC is given 60 days to answer. INA §340(b). A party also may seek review of the DD's decision under INA §340(h) to revoke naturalization. The case will then be litigated in district court. A party may raise the defense that s/he is a citizen by birth in §340(a) proceeding, even if s/he failed to timely challenge a previous loss of citizenship. *U.S. v. Schiffer*, 798 F.Supp. 1128, 1134–37 (E.D. Pa. 1992).

5. *Denial of Certificate of Citizenship*—A party also may seek review in U.S. district court under INA §360 of the INS's refusal to issue a certificate of citizenship.

6. *Loss of Citizenship*—The district court has jurisdiction to entertain an action for declaratory relief where a person within the U.S. claims citizenship and is "denied such right or privilege by any department or independent agency, or official thereof ..." INA §360(a), 8 U.S.C. §1503(a); *Cartier v.*

Secy. of State, 506 F.2d 191 (D.C. Cir. 1974) [declaratory relief under INA §360, not mandamus, is the appropriate remedy]. An action under this statute must generally be brought within 5 years. There is a split in the circuits as to whether the 5 years runs from the issuance of the Certificate of Loss of Nationality by DOS, *Heuer v. U.S. Secy. of State*, 20 F.3d 424 (11th Cir. 1994), or from the date the citizen's passport is denied. *Whitehead v. Haig*, 794 F.2d 115 (3d Cir. 1986). The split may have been resolved, however, by the amendment to INA §358 in the Immigration and Nationality Technical Corrections Act of 1994, PL 103-416, 108 Stat. 4305, §106, which defined a final administrative decision for purposes of INA §360(b) as the approval by the Secy. of State of the Loss of Nationality Certificate. No action under this section may be brought if it arose by reason of, or in connection with, or is an issue in, a removal/deportation/exclusion proceeding. *Rios-Valenzuela v. DHS,* 506 F.3d 393 (5th Cir. 2007) [dismissed action brought under §360(a) seeking review of a denied N-600 application because §360(a)(1) provides that no action may be brought that arose by reason of, or in connection with, a removal proceeding, and the N-600 was a response to removal proceedings against the petitioner]; *DeBrown v. DOJ*, 18 F.3d 774 (9th Cir. 1994) [upholding district court's refusal to grant *de novo* review in habeas on ground that review limited to exclusion proceeding and petitioner could not get *de novo* review of Declaratory Judgment Act due to bar under INA §360(a)]; *Austin v. INS,* 308 F.Supp.2d 125 (E.D.N.Y. 2004) [transferring case to circuit court under 28 U.S.C. §1631 because there was no jurisdiction to hear a declaratory action regarding nationality despite §360 where petitioner is in removal proceedings]. A declaratory judgment action under §360(a) may not be brought in the district court "in any case if the issue of such person's status as a national of the United States (1) arose by reason of, or in connection with any removal proceeding ... or (2) is in issue in any such removal proceeding." *Geronimo v. Mukasey,* 535 F.Supp.2d 808 (W.D. Tex. 2008) [declaratory judgment action in district court was dismissed because the petitioner had a removal hearing and an independent action is now barred, although court transferred the case to the Fifth Circuit]; *Said v. Eddy,* 87 F.Supp.2d 937 (D. Alaska 2000) [no jurisdiction under §360(a) where citizenship issue had been raised in removal proceedings and proceeding was resolved by granting withholding of removal].

Party Outside the U.S.—If a party is outside the U.S. and is denied citizenship s/he must request a certificate of identity from a consular officer so that s/he may travel to a U.S. port of entry and apply for admission. INA §360(b). If the consular officer denies the certificate, s/he may appeal the decision to the Secy. of State. 22 C.F.R. §50.11. Denial of the appeal may be reviewable in mandamus in the district court. *Compare Wong Bick Ling v. Pulles*, 119 F.Supp. 513 (D.D.C. 1954) [no jurisdiction], *with Way v. Acheson*, 110 F.Supp. 64 (D.C. Cal. 1953) [jurisdiction to entertain mandamus]. There is also independent review under the APA for an aggrieved party, 5 U.S.C. §702, so that a declaratory judgment may be brought by a person outside the U.S. contesting his or her loss of citizenship. *Rusk v. Cort*, 369 U.S. 367 (1962).

7. *Claim of Citizenship Arising in Review of Removal Proceeding*—INA §242(b)(5), 8 U.S.C. §1252(b)(5). If the court of appeals believes there is a genuine issue of material fact as to a litigant's U.S. citizenship, it may remand the case to the district court for a hearing. INA §242(b)(5)(B). *Batista v. Ashcroft,* 270 F.3d 8 (1st Cir. 2001) [court will consider evidence outside the administrative record where there is an explanation for failure to raise it previously]; *Alexander v. INS*, 74 F.3d 367 (1st Cir. 1996). Traditional summary judgment standards apply and therefore a court of appeals cannot refuse to allow *de novo* review of citizenship in district court where the applicant would be entitled to a trial if such evidence were presented in opposition to a summary judgment motion. *Chau v. INS,* 247 F.3d 1026, 1029 (9th Cir. 2001). There is no jurisdiction in the district court to review a citizenship claim under INA §242(b)(5). *Rivera-Martinez v. Ashcroft,* 389 F.3d 207 (1st Cir. 2004) [dismissing habeas and declining to transfer citizenship claim to circuit court where habeas was filed beyond the time limit for circuit court review]; *Benjamin v. Bureau of Customs,* 401 F.Supp.2d 184 (D. Conn. 2005) [habeas filed two years after final order was dismissed]. *But see Dragenice v. Ridge,* 389 F.3d 92 (4th Cir. 2004) [where respondent sought release from detention on theory he was a U.S. national, the circuit court, notwithstanding §242(b)(5), was barred from considering the nationality claim because of §242(a)(2)(C), and case should be re-transferred under §1631 to the district court in habeas]. This holding, however, may now be altered as a result of the REAL ID Act, 8 U.S.C. §1252(a)(5) requirement that

virtually all issues raised in habeas must now be heard in the circuit court notwithstanding INA §242(a)(2)(C) and other jurisdictional bars.

7.a. *Exhaustion*—A citizenship claim may not be barred for failing to exhaust administrative remedies pursuant to 8 U.S.C. §1252(d)(1). *Theagene v. Gonzales,* 411 F.3d 1107, 1110–12 (9th Cir. 2005) [distinguishing *Taniguchi* and finding that a nationality claim in circuit court under INA §242(b)(5) is not subject to the exhaustion requirement of INA §242(d)(1)]; *Rivera v. Ashcroft,* 394 F.3d 1129 (9th Cir. 2005) [habeas action to establish a nonfrivolous claim of U.S. citizenship cannot be barred even if respondent failed to exhaust his remedies because the Fifth and Fourteenth amendments are implicated; *Taniguchi* distinguished as frivolous claim]; *Moussa v. INS,* 302 F.3d 823, 825 (8th Cir. 2002) [in challenge to BIA's reversal of IJ's determination that person was citizen through naturalization of his father, the court had jurisdiction to determine whether applicant was an alien in order to decide whether statutory exhaustion under §1252(d)(1) applied]. *But see Taniguchi v. Schultz,* 303 F.3d 950, 955–56 (9th Cir. 2002) [under INA §242(b)(5), a claim of U.S. nationality had to be brought in the circuit court and failure to exhaust administrative remedies barred claim under INA §242(d)(1) where motion to reopen based on citizenship claim was denied as untimely]; *Boyd v. ICE,* 344 F.Supp.2d 869 (E.D.N.Y. 2004) [dismissing habeas challenging reinstatement order on grounds that respondent failed to exhaust his administrative remedies in regard to his citizenship claim where he did not present citizenship claim to IJ, did not appeal IJ's decision and did not seek review in circuit court]; *Giap v. INS,* 311 F.Supp.2d 438, 440 (S.D.N.Y. 2004).

7.b. *Transfer to Circuit Court*—If citizenship claim is filed in habeas in district court, the case can be transferred to the court of appeals. *Baeta v. Sonchik*, 273 F.3d 1261, 1263–65 (9th Cir. 2001); *Martinez-Piedras v. INS,* 354 F.Supp.2d 1149, 1152–55 (S.D.Cal. 2005) [following *Baeta* and transferring habeas to circuit court to hear citizenship claim even though habeas had been filed prior to the final order of deportation]; *Jones v. DHS,* 325 F.Supp.2d 551 (E.D. Pa. 2004) [habeas raising nationality claim should be transferred to circuit court even where person has been deported]. *But see Rivera-Martinez v. Ashcroft,* 389 F.3d 207 (1st Cir. 2004) [dismissing habeas and declining to transfer citizenship claim to circuit court where habeas was filed beyond the time limit for circuit court review]; *DeJesus Corona v. Derosa,* 325 F.Supp.2d 516, 523–25 (D.N.J. 2004) [where petitioner had several previous opportunities to raise citizenship claim before IJ or federal judge in criminal re-entry case and failed to do so, habeas barred to review USC claim]; *Atem v. Ashcroft,* 312 F.Supp.2d 792, 796–99 (E.D. Va. 2004) [where citizenship challenge was filed in habeas in district court, but petitioner failed to appeal nationality issue to BIA, the case could not be transferred to circuit court because of failure to exhaust]. A declaratory judgment action may also be transferred to circuit court where person is in removal proceedings. *Austin v. INS,* 308 F.Supp.2d 125 (E.D.N.Y. 2004) [transferring case to circuit court pursuant to 28 U.S.C. §1631 because there was no jurisdiction to hear a declaratory action on nationality despite 8 U.S.C. §1503 where petitioner is in removal proceedings].

7.c. *Bar under INA §336(b)*—An action may be brought under INA §336(b), 8 U.S.C. §1447(b) to obtain review of an application pending more than 120 days after interview. However, if removal proceedings are pending 8 U.S.C. §1429 prohibits the DHS from considering the application and therefore §1447(b) review may be prohibited. *Saba-Bakare v. Chertoff,* 507 F.3d 337, 340–41 (5th Cir. 2007).

7.d. *Bar under INA §360(a)*—An action may be brought in district court seeking review of the denial of a person's citizenship by any department or agency of the U.S. by initiating a action under 28 U.S.C. §2201. However, the provision permitting this review, INA §360(a), 8 U.S.C. §1503(a) does not permit an action if the issue of the applicant's citizenship: (1) arose "by reason of, or in connection with any removal proceeding" or (2) "is in issue in any removal proceeding." *Rios-Valenzuela v. DHS,* 506 F.3d 393 (5th Cir. 2007) [dismissed action brought under §360(a) seeking review of a denied N-600 application because §360(a)(1) provides that no action may be brought that arose by reason of, or in connection with, a removal proceeding, and the N-600 was a response to removal proceedings against the petitioner].

VII. CRIMINAL MATTERS RELATED TO CITIZENSHIP

A. ***Procuring Naturalization In Violation of Law***—Under 18 U.S.C. §1425 a person may be convicted for knowingly procuring or attempting to procure, contrary to law, the naturalization of any person. *U.S. v. Pasillas-Gaytan,* 192 F.3d 864 (9th Cir. 1994) [*Mens rea* required; not a strict liability crime]; *U.S. v. Moses*, 94 F.3d 182 (5th Cir. 1996) ["living in marital union" for purposes of INA §319(a) means actually residing with citizen spouse]; *U.S. v. Maduno*, 40 F.3d 1212 (11th Cir. 1994) [same]; *U.S. v. Castro-Vasquez,* 481 F.Supp.2d 664, 671–73 (W.D. Tex. 2006) [statute not void for vagueness]. *But See U.S. v. Onabanjo,* 351 F.3d 1064 (11th Cir. 2003) [reversing where court failed to consider exceptions to actual residence in same home]. The statute of limitations is 10 years. 18 U.S.C. §3291. *U.S. v. Alameh,* 341 F.3d 167, 171–72 (2d Cir. 2003) [where criminal charge was based on illegally obtaining LPR status which has a 5-year statute of limitations, the 10-year limitation for 18 U.S.C. §1425(a) still applied]. To obtain a conviction, the government must establish that there was a knowing attempt to acquire citizenship *and* that the defendant knew he was not eligible for naturalization or knowingly misrepresented his eligibility on the application or during the interview. *U.S. v. Alameh,* 341 F.3d 167, 175 (2d Cir. 2003). False statements on a naturalization application which are not material, however, cannot support a conviction even if they could be the basis for a lack of good moral character. *U.S. v. Alferahin,* 433 F.3d 1148 (9th Cir. 2006) [reversing conviction for failure to give instruction regarding materiality; following *Puerta*]; *U.S. v. Puerta*, 982 F.2d 1297 (9th Cir. 1992) [failure to list alias and stating person had never left the country when he had left cannot be basis for conviction absent showing of ineligibility]. *But see U.S. v. Biheiri,* 293 F.Supp.2d 656 (E.D. Va. 2003) [materiality is not an element necessary for a conviction]; *U.S. v. Rogers*, 908 F.Supp. 219 (S.D.N.Y. 1995) [same]. A defense of selective prosecution is available, but there must be some evidence of discriminatory motive before discovery will be permitted. *U.S. v. Alameh,* 341 F.3d 167, 172–75 (2d Cir. 2003) [upholding district court decision to deny discovery because most of the investigation against defendant occurred before Sept. 11, 2001, notwithstanding evidence that after Sept. 11, prosecution of persons from the Middle East for this and related crimes increased from 15% to 85% of the defendants in the Southern and Eastern Districts of NY]. If convicted, a person may be subject to removal for a CIMT. *Amouzadeh v. Winfrey,* 467 F.3d 451, 455 (5th Cir. 2006) [conviction of 18 U.S.C. §1425(a) for unlawful procurement of naturalization is a CIMT because it requires proof of a culpable mind].

B. ***Criminal Penalty For False Claim To U.S. Citizenship***—A person who "falsely and willfully represents himself to be a citizen of the United States" shall be fined or imprisoned. 18 U.S.C. §911. The three elements of the crime are (1) a false claim; (2) a willful misrepresentation; and (3) a misrepresentation to someone with good reason to inquire into the defendant's citizenship. *U.S. v. Romero-Avila,* 210 F.3d 1017 (9th Cir. 2000) [rejecting the defense that the exact identity of the person lied to is an element of the offense]. But §911 does not include a person who makes a false claim to U.S. *nationality. U.S. v. Karaouni,* 379 F.3d 1139 (9th Cir. 2004) [where defendant checked off I-9 box that stated he was a citizen *or* national of the U.S., he could not be convicted under §911 that makes it a crime only to make a false claim to citizenship]. To establish a willful violation the government must prove that the defendant acted with knowledge that his conduct was unlawful. *U.S. v. Ramirez,* 495 F.Supp.2d 92, 118–20 (D. Me. 2007) [quoting *Bryan v. United States* and finding that Cuban national willfully made a false claim to citizenship when purchasing a firearm]. A knowingly false statement or claim that a person is or at any time has been a citizen or national of the U.S. with the intent to obtain for himself or another a federal or state benefit or the right to vote is also a crime. 18 U.S.C. §1015(e), (f). It is also a crime to knowingly make any false statement under oath, in any case, proceeding, or matter relating to any law regarding naturalization, citizenship or registry of aliens. 18 U.S.C. §1015(a). This statute, in the view of one circuit, does not require materiality. *U.S. v. Abuagla,* 326 F.3d 277 (4th Cir. 2003). The Eleventh Circuit has held that there is no "exculpatory no" defense in 18 U.S.C. §1001 cases to false claims of U.S. citizenship. *U.S. v. Lopez-Iraeta*, 129 F.3d 1206 (11th Cir. 1997) [rejecting defense that person merely answered a question during interrogation rather than affirmatively misrepresented his citizenship]. *See also Brogan v. U.S.*, 522 U.S. 398 (1998). The statute has also withstood an over breadth attack under the First Amendment. *U.S. v. Esparza-Ponce,* 193 F.3d 1133, 1137–38 (9th Cir. 1999).

C. *Other Criminal Offenses Related to Citizenship*

1. *Identification Document Fraud*—18 U.S.C. §1546(b). Use of an identification document knowing that the document was not issued lawfully or is false, or submission a false attestation for purposes of satisfying the requirements for I-9/employer verification purposes.

2. *Fraud and Related Activity in Connection with Identification Documents*—18 U.S.C. §1028. Includes knowingly and without lawful authority producing, transferring, possessing or possessing with intent to use an identification document or false identification document which appears to be issued by or under the authority of the U.S., a state, foreign government or international governmental or generic governmental organization.

3. *Knowing and Willful Use of a False Passport*—18 U.S.C. §1543. Permits the prosecution of a person carrying a false passport from any country, not just the U.S. *U.S. v. Dangdee,* 616 F.2d 1118, 1119 (9th Cir. 1980).

4. *Knowing and Willful False Statement to Obtain U.S. Passport*—18 U.S.C. §1542. Includes securing a passport through a false statement and making a false statement in an application for a passport.

5. F*ailure to Disclose Role as Document Preparer*—INA §274C(e), 8 U.S.C. §1324c(e). It is a crime punishable by up to 5 years in prison to knowingly and willfully fail to disclose, conceal or cover up the fact that a person has prepared or assisted in the preparation of a falsely made application for immigration benefits for a fee or other remuneration.

6. *Aggravated Identity Theft in Conjunction with Immigration Crimes*—18 U.S.C. §1028A. A person who uses the identity of another person during the commission of various felonies including failure to depart, failure to register, or alien smuggling will receive an enhanced penal of 2 years and if related to terrorism 5 years.

7. *Criminal Penalty for Voting by Alien in Federal Election*—18 U.S.C. §611, §1015(f). It is unlawful for an alien to vote in a federal election. This section does not apply if the defendant's: (1) parents were or are USCs; (2) the person permanently resided in the U.S. prior to age 16; and (3) the person reasonably believed at the time of voting that s/he was a USC. The exception is applies retroactively and applies to persons prosecuted on or after Sept. 30, 1996 unless criminal proceedings were concluded before Oct. 30, 2000. One circuit has found this to be a general, not a specific intent, crime. *U.S. v. Knight,* 490 F.3d 1268 (11th Cir. 2007).

APPENDICES

Appendix A

Appendix A to Preamble of PERM Regulation

Professional Recruitment Occupations
Education and Training Categories by O*NET-SOC Occupation

69 Fed. Reg. 77325, at 77377 (Dec. 27, 2004) [AILA InfoNet Doc. No. 04122312]

O*NET-SOC Code	O*NET-SOC Title	Educ. & training category code
21-2011.00	Clergy	1
23-1011.00	Lawyers	1
29-1011.00	Chiropractors	1
29-1021.00	Dentists, General	1
29-1022.00	Oral and Maxillofacial Surgeons	1
29-1023.00	Orthodontists	1
29-1024.00	Prosthodontists	1
29-1041.00	Optometrists	1
29-1051.00	Pharmacists	1
29-1061.00	Anesthesiologists	1
29-1062.00	Family and General Practitioners	1
29-1063.00	Internists, General	1
29-1064.00	Obstetricians and Gynecologists	1
29-1065.00	Pediatricians, General	1
29-1066.00	Psychiatrists	1
29-1067.00	Surgeons	1
29-1081.00	Podiatrists	1
29-1131.00	Veterinarians	1
15-1011.00	Computer and Information Scientists, Research	2
19-1021.01	Biochemists	2
19-1021.02	Biophysicists	2
19-1022.00	Microbiologists	2
19-1042.00	Medical Scientists, Except Epidemiologists	2
19-2011.00	Astronomers	2
19-2012.00	Physicists	2
19-3031.00	Clinical, counseling, and school psychologists	2
19-3031.01	Educational Psychologists	2
19-3031.02	Clinical Psychologists	2
19-3031.03	Counseling Psychologists	2
25-1021.00	Computer Science Teachers, Postsecondary	2
25-1022.00	Mathematical Science Teachers, Postsecondary	2
25-1032.00	Engineering Teachers, Postsecondary	2
25-1041.00	Agricultural Sciences Teachers, Postsecondary	2
25-1042.00	Biological Science Teachers, Postsecondary	2
25-1043.00	Forestry and Conservation Science Teachers, Postsecondary	2
25-1052.00	Chemistry Teachers, Postsecondary	2
25-1054.00	Physics Teachers, Postsecondary	2
25-1071.00	Health Specialties Teachers, Postsecondary	2
25-1072.00	Nursing Instructors and Teachers, Postsecondary	2
25-1121.00	Art, Drama, and Music Teachers, Postsecondary	2
25-1191.00	Graduate Teaching Assistants	2
15-2021.00	Mathematicians	3
15-2031.00	Operations Research Analysts	3
15-2041.00	Statisticians	3
19-1041.00	Epidemiologists	3
19-2041.00	Environmental Scientists and Specialists, Including Health	3
19-2042.00	Geoscientists, Except Hydrologists and Geographers	3
19-2042.01	Geologists	3
19-2043.00	Hydrologists	3
19-3011.00	Economists	3
19-3021.00	Market Research Analysts	3
19-3022.00	Survey Researchers	3
19-3032.00	Industrial-Organizational Psychologists	3
19-3041.00	Sociologists	3
19-3051.00	Urban and Regional Planners	3
19-3091.01	Anthropologists	3
19-3091.02	Archeologists	3
19-3092.00	Geographers	3
19-3093.00	Historians	3
19-3094.00	Political Scientists	3
21-1011.00	Substance Abuse and Behavioral Disorder Counselors	3
21-1012.00	Educational, Vocational, and School Counselors	3
21-1013.00	Marriage and Family Therapists	3
21-1014.00	Mental Health Counselors	3
21-1015.00	Rehabilitation Counselors	3
21-1023.00	Mental Health and Substance Abuse Social Workers	3
21-1091.00	Health Educators	3
25-4011.00	Archivists	3
25-4012.00	Curators	3
25-4021.00	Librarians	3
25-9031.00	Instructional Coordinators	3
29-1121.00	Audiologists	3

O*NET-SOC Code	O*NET-SOC Title	Educ. & training category code
29-1123.00	Physical Therapists	3
29-1127.00	Speech-Language Pathologists	3
11-1011.00	Chief Executives	4
11-1011.01	Government Service Executives	4
11-1011.02	Private Sector Executives	4
11-1021.00	General and Operations Managers	4
11-2011.00	Advertising and Promotions Managers	4
11-2021.00	Marketing Managers	4
11-2022.00	Sales Managers	4
11-2031.00	Public Relations Managers	4
11-3011.00	Administrative Services Managers	4
11-3021.00	Computer and Information Systems Managers	4
11-3031.00	Financial Managers	4
11-3031.01	Treasurers, Controllers, and Chief Financial Officers	4
11-3031.02	Financial Managers, Branch or Department	4
11-3040.00	Human Resources Managers	4
11-3041.00	Compensation and Benefits Managers	4
11-3042.00	Training and Development Managers	4
11-3061.00	Purchasing Managers	4
11-9011.00	Farm, Ranch and Other Agricultural Managers	4
11-9011.01	Nursery and Greenhouse Managers	4
11-9011.02	Agricultural Crop Farm Managers	4
11-9011.03	Fish Hatchery Managers	4
11-9031.00	Education Administrators, Preschool and Child Care Center/Program	4
11-9032.00	Education Administrators, Elementary and Secondary School	4
11-9033.00	Education Administrators, Postsecondary	4
11-9041.00	Engineering Managers	4
11-9111.00	Medical and Healthy Services Managers	4
11-9121.00	Natural Sciences Managers	4
13-1011.00	Agents and Business Managers of Artists, Performers, and Athletes	4
13-1111.00	Management Analysts	4
15-2011.00	Actuaries	4
23-1021.00	Administrative Law Judges, Adjudicators, and Hearing Officers	4
23-1022.00	Arbitrators, Mediators, and Conciliators	4
23-1023.00	Judges, Magistrate Judges, and Magistrates	4
25-2023.00	Vocational Education Teachers, Middle School	4
25-2032.00	Vocational Education Teachers, Secondary School	4
27-1011.00	Art Directors	4
27-2012.00	Producers and Directors	4
27-2012.01	Producers	4
27-2012.02	Directors- Stage, Motion Pictures, Television, and Radio	4
27-2012.03	Program Directors	4
27-2012.04	Talent Directors	4
27-2012.05	Technical Directors/Managers	4
27-2041.00	Music Directors and Composers	4
27-2041.01	Music Directors	4
27-2041.02	Music Arrangers and Orchestrators	4
27-2041.03	Composers	4
27-3020.00	New analysts, reporters and correspondents	4
27-3021.00	Broadcast News Analysts	4
27-3022.00	Reporters and Correspondents	4
11-3051.00	Industrial Production Managers	5
11-9021.00	Construction Managers	5
11-9141.00	Property, Real Estate, and Community Association Managers	5
11-9151.00	Social and Community Service Managers	5
13-1071.00	Employment, Recruitment, and Placement Specialists	5
13-1071.01	Employment Interviewers, Private or Public Employment Service	5
13-1071.02	Personnel Recruiters	5
13-1072.00	Compensation, Benefits, and Job Analysis Specialists	5
13-1073.00	Training and Development Specialists	5
13-1121.00	Meeting and Convention Planners	5
13-2011.01	Accountants	5
13-2011.02	Auditors	5
13-2031.00	Budget Analysts	5
13-2041.00	Credit Analysts	5
13-2051.00	Financial Analysts	5
13-2052.00	Personal Financial Advisors	5
13-2053.00	Insurance Underwriters	5
13-2061.00	Financial Examiners	5
13-2071.00	Loan Counselors	5
13-2072.00	Loan Officers	5
13-2081.00	Tax Examiners, Collectors, and Revenue Agents	5
15-1021.00	Computer Programmers	5
15-1031.00	Computer Software Engineers, Applications	5
15-1032.00	Computer Software Engineers, Systems Software	5
15-1051.00	Computer Systems Analysts	5
15-1061.00	Database Administrators	5
15-1071.00	Network and Computer Systems Administrators	5
15-1071.01	Computer Security Specialists	5
15-1081.00	Network Systems and Data Communications Analysts	5
17-1011.00	Architects, Except Landscape and Naval	5
17-1012.00	Landscape Architects	5
17-1021.00	Cartographers and Photogrammetrists	5
17-1022.00	Surveyors	5

O*NET-SOC Code	O*NET-SOC Title	Educ. & training category code
17-2011.00	Aerospace Engineers	5
17-2021.00	Agricultural Engineers	5
17-2031.00	Biomedical Engineers	5
17-2041.00	Chemical Engineers	5
17-2051.00	Civil Engineers	5
17-2061.00	Computer Hardware Engineers	5
17-2071.00	Electrical Engineers	5
17-2072.00	Electronics Engineers, Except Computer	5
17-2081.00	Environmental Engineers	5
17-2111.00	Health and Safety Engineers, Except Mining Safety Engineers and Inspectors	5
17-2111.01	Industrial Safety and Healthy Engineers	5
17-2111.02	Fire-Prevention and Protection Engineers	5
17-2111.03	Product Safety Engineers	5
17-2112.00	Industrial Engineers	5
17-2121.00	Marine Engineers and Naval Architects	5
17-2121.01	Marine Engineers	5
17-2121.02	Marine Architects	5
17-2131.00	Materials Engineers	5
17-2141.00	Mechanical Engineers	5
17-2151.00	Mining and Geological Engineers, Including Mining Safety Engineers	5
17-2161.00	Nuclear Engineers	5
17-2171.00	Petroleum Engineers	5
19-1010.00	Agricultural and food scientists	5
19-1011.00	Animal Scientists	5
19-1012.00	Food Scientists and Technologists	5
19-1013.01	Plant Scientists	5
19-1013.02	Soil Scientists	5
19-1020.00	Biological Scientists	5
19-1020.01	Biologists	5
19-1023.00	Zoologists and Wildlife Biologists	5
19-1031.00	Conservation Scientists	5
19-1031.01	Soil Conservationists	5
19-1031.02	Range Managers	5
19-1031.03	Park Naturalists	5
19-1032.00	Foresters	5
19-2021.00	Atmospheric and Space Scientists	5
19-2031.00	Chemists	5
19-2032.00	Materials Scientists	5
21-1021.00	Child, Family, and School Social Workers	5
21-1022.00	Medical and Public Health Social Workers	5
21-1092.00	Probation Officers and Correctional Treatment Sp	5
21-2021.00	Directors, Religious Activities and Education	5
23-2092.00	Law Clerks	5
25-2012.00	Kindergarten Teachers, Except Special Education	5
25-2021.00	Elementary School Teachers, Except Special Education	5
25-2022.00	Middle School Teachers, Except Special and Vocational Education	5
25-2031.00	Secondary School Teachers, Except Special and Vocational Education	5
25-2041.00	Special Education Teachers, Preschool, Kindergarten and Elementary	5
25-2042.00	Special Education Teachers, Middle School	5
25-2043.00	Special Education Teachers, Secondary School	5
25-3011.00	Adult Literacy, Remedial Education, and GED Teachers and Instructors	5
25.4013.00	Museum Technicians and Conservators	5
25-9021.00	Farm and Home Management Advisors	5
27-1014.00	Multi-Media Artists and Animators	5
27-1021.00	Commercial and Industrial Designers	5
27-1022.00	Fashion Designers	5
27-1024.00	Graphic Designers	5
27-1025.00	Interior Designers	5
27-1027.00	Set and Exhibit Designers	5
27-1027.01	Set Designers	5
27-1027.02	Exhibit Designers	5
27-3031.00	Public Relations Specialists	5
27-3041.00	Editors	5
27-3042.00	Technical Writers	5
27-3043.00	Writers and Authors	5
27-4032.00	Film and Video Editors	5
29-1031.00	Dietitians and Nutritionists	5
29-1071.00	Physician Assistants	5
29-1122.00	Occupational Therapists	5
29-1125.00	Recreational Therapists	5
29-2011.00	Medical and Clinical Laboratory Technologists	5
29-2091.00	Orthotists and Prosthetists	5
29-9010.00	Occupational health and safety specialists and technicians	5
29-9091.00	Athletic Trainers	5
33-3021.03	Criminal Investigators and Special Agents	5
39-9032.00	Recreation Workers	5
41-3021.00	Insurance Sales Agents	5
41-3031.01	Sales Agents, Securities and Commodities	5
41-3031.02	Sales Agents, Financial Services	5
41-9031.00	Sales Engineers	5
53-2011.00	Airline Pilots, Copilots, and Flight Engineers	5

APPENDIX B

NATURALIZATION CHARTS

AUTOMATIC ACQUISITION OF CITIZENSHIP UNDER THE CHILD CITIZENSHIP ACT OF 2000

Effective Date of Act*	Eligibility Requirements**	Age Limit	Date of Automatic Acquisition	Law Applicable
2/27/01	At least one parent is U.S. citizen by birth or naturalization. Child residing in U.S. in the legal and physical custody of citizen parent pursuant to a lawful admission for permanent residence.	Under 18	Date last condition fulfilled	INA §320, as amended by P.L. 106-395

* Law is not retroactive, *i.e.*, acquisition can only occur on or after 2/27/01 and only for children under 18 after 2/27/01.
** Applies to adopted child if child has met requirements applicable to adopted children under INA §101(b)(1)(E) or (F).

EXPEDITED NATURALIZATION OF CHILDREN

Effective Date of Act*	Eligibility Requirements	Age Limit	Date of Acquisition	Law Applicable
2/27/01	At least one parent is U.S. citizen by birth or naturalization at time of filing N-600K. If citizen parent deceased during preceding 5 years, citizen grandparent or citizen legal guardian may file N-600K. Prior to filing, citizen parent has been physically present in U.S. for at least 5 years, at least 2 after age 14, or citizen parent has a citizen parent who has been physically present in U.S. for 5 years, at least 2 after age 14. Child is currently residing outside U.S. in legal and physical custody of citizen parent, or if citizen parent deceased, an individual who does not object to the application. Child is temporarily present in U.S. pursuant to a lawful admission and maintaining lawful status.	Under 18	Date of Issuance of Certificate	INA §322, as amended by P.L. 106-395 & by P. L. 107-273

* Applies to adopted children under 18 if child has met requirements applicable to adopted children under INA §101(b) (1)(E) or (F)

These charts and tables are intended for use only as a helpful generalized reference guide, and not to make determinations or to be cited in any case. Information current as of May 2008.

Courtesy of Mr. Carmen DiPlacido, of Arlington, Virginia

AUTOMATIC ACQUISITION OF CITIZENSHIP THROUGH NATURALIZATION OF PARENT(S)

Date Parent(s) Naturalized	Who Naturalized	Age Limit*	Date of Automatic Acquisition		Law Applicable
			If Residing in U.S.	If Residing Abroad	
Prior to 3/2/07	Either parent	Under 21	Date of naturalization of parent	Date child lawfully admitted U.S. for permanent residence	§2172, R.S. (Act 4/14/1802)
3/2/07 to noon EST, 5/24/34	Either parent	Under 21	Date of naturalization of parent	Date child lawfully admitted U.S. for permanent residence	§2172, R.S. Sec. 5, Act 3/2/07
noon EST, 5/24/34, to 1/13/41	One parent, other remaining alien	Under 21 when admitted U.S.	Upon completion 5 yrs. residence in U.S. including residence completed after age 21 and after 1/13/41		§5, Act 3/2/07, as amended by Sec. 2 Act 5/24/34
	Alien parent (other being citizen); surviving parent; or parent having custody in divorce	Under 21	Date of naturalization of parent	Date child lawfully admitted U.S. for permanent residence	§2172, R.S.
1/13/41 to 12/24/52	Alien parent other being citizen from child's birth	Under 18	Date of naturalization of parent	Date child lawfully admitted U.S. for permanent residence	§313, 1940 Act
	Both parents; surviving parent; or parent having custody in legal separation	Under 18	Date of naturalization of parent	Date child lawfully admitted U.S. for permanent residence	§314, 1940 Act
Subsequent to 12/24/52 but before 2/27/01	**Alien parent, other being citizen from child's birth	Under 18	Date last condition fulfilled	Date child lawfully admitted U.S. for permanent residence	INA §320, as amended by P.L. 95-417. Repealed by P.L. 106-395
	**Both parents; surviving parent; parent having custody in legal separation; or mother of child out of wedlock	Under 18	Date last condition fulfilled	Date child lawfully admitted U.S. for permanent residence	INA §321, as amended by P.L. 95-417. Repealed by P.L. 106-395

* The date of the parent(s) naturalization and the date of the lawful admittance of the child must occur before the age shown in the age limit column.

** Applies to an adopted child if the child is residing in the U.S. at the time of naturalization of such adopted parent or parents, in the custody of his adoptive parent or parents, pursuant to a lawful admission for permanent residence.

ADJUDICATING CITIZENSHIP BASED ON BIRTH OUT OF WEDLOCK TO A U.S. FATHER

Determining Whether to Use "New" or "Old" INA §309(a)

Date of Birth	Applicable Statute	Age Before Which "Legitimation" Must Occur*	Date Before Which "Legitimation" Must Occur*	Statement of Support Required?
Before **Nov. 14, 1968**	Old Section 309(a)	21	11/14/89	No
On or after **Nov. 14, 1968** *but before* **Nov. 14, 1971**	Old Section 309(a)	21	11/14/92	No
	New Section 309(a)	18	11/14/89	Yes
On or after **Nov. 14, 1971** *but before* **Nov. 14, 1986**	Old Section 309(a)	15	11/14/86	No
	New Section 309(a)	18	11/14/04	Yes
On or after **Nov. 14, 1986**	New Section 309(a)	18	None	Yes

* Note that under **New Section 309(a),** the citizen father can, in lieu of legitimation, acknowledge paternity in writing and under oath, or paternity of the child can be established by adjudication of a competent court. Any one of the three methods of establishing paternity must occur before the child's 18th birthday.

Tables of Transmission Requirements Over Time for Citizenship for Certain Individuals Born Abroad

Note—Governing Statute: Acquisition of U.S. citizenship **at birth abroad** to a U.S. citizen parent(s) is governed by federal statute. The governing law in the case of a person born abroad who claims U.S. citizenship through a U.S. citizen parent(s) is **the law in effect on the date of the claimant's birth,** unless a subsequent law specifically by its language in the statute applies retroactively to persons who had not already become citizens by the provisions of the prior law. At times, a new law will merely renumber an old law without changing the requirements or provisions. As such, it will read, *e.g.*, "§301(a)(7), now §301(g) INA."

When pertinent law requires specific conditions on the part of the U.S. citizen parent(s), the conditions must be met prior to the child's birth unless otherwise stated in the statute.

Residence or physical presence transmission requirements can be met while the transmitting parent is not a citizen.

Birth Abroad to U.S. Citizen Parent and Alien Parent

Date of Birth	Transmission Requirements	Reference	Retention Requirements	Reference
Before **May 24, 1934** (noon EST)*	Either U.S. citizen father or mother could transmit. U.S. citizen parent resided in U.S. before child's birth.	§1993, Revised Statutes (RS); 7 FAM 1135; §301(h) INA; P.L. 103-416.	None	
On or after **May 24, 1934** (noon EST),* *but before* **Jan. 13, 1941**	Either U.S. citizen father or mother could transmit. U.S. citizen parent resided in U.S. before child's birth.	§1993, RS as amended in 1934; 7 FAM 1135.1, 11.35.2.	Persons failing to fulfill below requirements may have citizenship restored upon taking oath of allegiance. (1) 5 years residence between the ages 13-21 if begun before 12/24/52; or (2) 2 years continuous physical presence between ages 14–28;[1] or (3) 5 years continuous physical presence between ages 14–28 if begun before 10/27/72.[2] (4) None if parent employed certain occupation.[3] (5) None if alien parent naturalized and child began to reside permanently in U.S. while under age 18.	§324(d)(1) Immigration and Nationality Act of 1952 (INA), §101 P.L. 103-416; 7 FAM 1133.5-15. (1) §201(g) and (h) Nationality Act of 1940 (NA), 54 Stat. 1137; 7 FAM 1134.6-3 (2) Former §301(b), (c) INA; 7 FAM 1133.5-7, 5-8 (3) Former §301(b), (d) INA; 7 FAM 1133.5-2, 1133.5–9 (4) §201(g) INA; 7 FAM 1134.6-2 (5) Former §301(b) INA; 7 FAM 1133.5-7, 1133.5-11

* *Sic.* The statute refers to "Eastern Standard Time"; however, Daylight Savings Time was in effect on May 24, 1934.

[1] Absences of less than 60 days in aggregate during 2 year period do not break continuity.

[2] Absences of less than one year in aggregate during 5 year period do not break continuity.

[3] U.S. Government, American education, scientific, philanthropic, religious, commercial, or financial organization or an International Agency in which the U.S. takes part. Note: residence or physical presence of parent must take place *before* child's birth.

Date of Birth	Transmission Requirements	Reference	Retention Requirements	Reference
On or after **Jan. 13, 1941**, *but before* **Dec. 24, 1952**	Citizen parent resided in U.S. or possession 10 years prior to child's birth, five of which after the age of 16.	§201(g) NA; 7 FAM 1134.2, 1134.3	Persons failing to fulfill below requirements may have citizenship restored upon taking oath of allegiance. (1) 2 years continuous physical presence between ages 14–28;[1] or (2) 5 years continuous physical presence between ages 14–28 if begun before 10/27/72.[2] (3) None if parent employed in certain occupation.[3] (4) None if child born on or after 10/10/52; (5) None if alien parent naturalized and child began to reside permanently in U.S. while under age 18.	§324(d)(1) INA, §101 P.L. 103-416; 7 FAM 1133.5-15 (1) Former §301(b), (c) INA; 7 FAM 1133.5-7, 5-8 (2) Former §301(b), (d) INA; 7 FAM 1133.5-2, 1133.5-9 (3) §201(g) NA; 7 FAM 1134.6-2 (4) P.L. 95-432; 7 FAM 1133.5-13 (5) Former §301(b) INA; 7 FAM 1133.5-7, 1133.5-11
	Citizen parent in U.S. military 12/7/41 to 12/31/46 and resided in U.S. or possession 10 years prior to child's birth, five of which after age 12.	§201(i) NA; 7 FAM 1134.2, 1134.4	Persons failing to fulfill below requirements may have citizenship restored upon taking oath of allegiance. (1) 2 years continuous physical presence between ages 14-28;[1] or (2) 5 years continuous physical presence between ages 14-28 if begun before 10/27/72.[2] (3) None if child born on or after 10/10/52. (4) None if alien parent naturalized and child began to reside permanently in U.S. while under age 18.	§324(d)(1) INA, §101 P.L. 103-416; 7 FAM 1133.5-15 (1) Former §301(b) INA; 7 FAM 1134.4e, 1133.5 (2) Former §301(b), (d) INA; 7 FAM 1133.5-2, 1133.5-9 (3) P.L. 95-432; 7 FAM 1133.5-15 (4) Former §301(b) INA; 7 FAM 1133.5-7, 1133.5-11

[1] Absences of less than 60 days in aggregate during 2 year period do not break continuity.
[2] Absences of less than one year in aggregate during 5 year period do not break continuity.
[3] U.S. Government, American education, scientific, philanthropic, religious, commercial, or financial organization or an International Agency in which the U.S. takes part. Note: residence or physical presence of parent must take place *before* child's birth.

Date of Birth	Transmission Requirements	Reference	Retention Requirements	Reference
(on or after Jan 13, 1941, but before Dec. 24, 1952—cont'd)	Citizen parent in U.S. military 1/1/47 to 12/24/52 and physically present in U.S. or possession 10 years prior to child's birth, five of which after age 14, and who did not qualify under either provision above.	§301(a)(7), now §301(g) INA; 7 FAM 1134.4f	Persons failing to fulfill below requirements may have citizenship restored upon taking oath of allegiance. (1) 2 years continuous physical presence between ages 14–28;[1] or (2) 5 years continuous physical presence between ages 14–28 if begun before 10/27/72.[2] (3) None if child born on or after 10/10/52. (4) None if alien parent naturalized and child began to reside permanently in U.S. while under age 18.	§324(d)(1) INA; P.L. 103-416; 7 FAM 1133.5-15 (1) Former §301(b) INA; 7 FAM 1133.5-7, 5-8 (2) Former §301(b), (d) INA; 7 FAM 1133.5-2, 1133.5-9 (3) P.L. 95-432; 7 FAM 1133.5-13 (4) Former §301(b) INA; 7 FAM 1133.5-7, 1133.5-11
On or after **Dec. 24, 1952**, *but before* **Nov. 14, 1986**	Citizen parent physically present in U.S. or possession 10 years prior to child's birth, five of which after age 14. Honorable U.S. military service, employment with U.S. government or intergovernmental international organization, or as dependent unmarried son or daughter and member of the household of a parent in such service or employment, may be included.	§301(a)(7), now §301(g) INA; 7 FAM 1133.2-2, 1133.3-3	None	
On or after **Nov. 14, 1986**	Citizen parent physically present in U.S. or possession 5 years prior to child's birth, two of which after age 14. Honorable U.S. military service, employment with U.S. government or intergovernmental international organization, or as dependent unmarried son or daughter and member of the household of a parent in such service or employment, may be included.	§301(g) INA; P.L. 99-653, P.L. 100-525; 7 FAM 1133.2-1	None	

[1] Absences of less than 60 days in aggregate during 2 year period do not break continuity.
[2] Absences of less than one year in aggregate during 5 year period do not break continuity.
[3] U.S. Government, American education, scientific, philanthropic, religious, commercial, or financial organization or an International Agency in which the U.S. takes part. Note: residence or physical presence of parent must take place *before* child's birth.

Birth Abroad to Two U.S. Citizen Parents

Date of Birth	Transmission Requirements (Parents' Residence)	Applicable Laws	Reference
Before **May 24, 1934** (noon, EST)*	One parent resided in the U.S.	§1993, Revised Statutes (RS); §301(h) INA; §101 P.L. 103-416	7 FAM 1135.1
On or after **May 24, 1934** (noon, EST),* *but before* **Jan. 13, 1941**	One parent resided in the U.S.	§1993, RS as amended by Act of 5/24/34	7 FAM 1135.6-1
On or after **Jan. 13, 1941**, *but before* **Dec. 24, 1952**	One parent resided in the U.S. or possession.	§201(c) NA	7 FAM 1134.2, 1134.3-1, 1134.3-2
On or after **Dec. 24, 1952**	One parent resided in the U.S. or possession.	§301(a)(3), now §301(c) INA	7 FAM 1133.2-1a, 1133.3-1a

Notes: (1) In all cases, residence must take place prior to the child's birth; (2) the law does not define how long residence must be; and (3) children born to two U.S. citizen parents never had retention requirements.

Child Born Out of Wedlock to U.S. Citizen Mother

Date of Birth	Transmission Requirements (Parents' Residence)	Applicable Laws	Reference
Before **May 24, 1934** (noon, EST)*	Mother resided in the U.S. or possession prior to child's birth; child not legitimated by alien father before 1/13/41.	§205, paragraph 2, NA	7 FAM 1135.3-2
On or after **May 24, 1934** (noon, EST),* *but before* **Jan. 13, 1941**	Mother resided in U.S. or possession prior to child's birth.	§1993, RS as amended by Act of 5/24/34; §205, paragraph 2, NA	7 FAM 1135.7-2
On or after **Jan. 13, 1941**, *but before* **Dec, 24, 1952**	Mother resided in U.S. or possession prior to child's birth.	§205, paragraph 2, NA	7 FAM 1134.5-4
On or after **Dec. 24, 1952**	Mother physically present in U.S. or possession continuously 12 months prior to child's birth.	§309(c), INA	7 FAM 1133.4-3

Note: Children born out of wedlock to a U.S. citizen mother never had retention requirements.

Child Born Out of Wedlock to U.S. Citizen Father and Alien Mother

Date of Birth	Transmission and Legal Relationship Requirements	Reference	Retention Requirements	Reference
Before **May 24, 1934** (noon, EST)*	Legitimated under law of father's U.S. or foreign domicile. Father resided in U.S. before child's birth.	§1993, RS; 7 FAM 1135.3-1	None	
On or after **May 24, 1934** (noon EST),* *but before* **Jan. 13, 1941**	Legitimated under law of father's U.S. or foreign domicile. Father resided in U.S. before child's birth.	§1993, RS as amended in 1934; 7 FAM 1135.7-1	Persons failing to fulfill below requirements may have citizenship restored upon taking oath of allegiance. (1) 5 years residence between ages 13-21 if begun before 12/24/52; or (2) 2 years continuous physical presence between ages 14–28;[1] or (3) 5 years continuous physical presence between ages 14–28 if begun before 10/27/72.[2] (4) None if parent employed certain occupation.[3] (5) None if alien parent naturalized and child began to reside permanently in U.S. while under age 18.	§324(d)(1) INA; §101 P.L. 103-416 1133.5-15 (1) §201(g) and (h) NA; 7 FAM 1133.6-3 (2) Former §301(b), (c) INA; 7 FAM 1133.5-7, 1133.5-8 (3) Former §301(b), (d) INA; 7 FAM 1133.5-2, 1133.5-9 (4) §201(g) NA; 7 FAM 1134.6-2 (5) Former §301(b) INA; 7 FAM 1133.5-7, 1133.5-11

* *Sic.* The statute refers to "Eastern Standard Time"; however, Daylight Savings Time was in effect on May 24, 1934.

[1] Absences of less than 60 days in aggregate during 2 year period do not break continuity.

[2] Absences of less than one year in aggregate during 5 year period do not break continuity.

[3] U.S. government, American educational, scientific, philanthropic, religious, commercial, or financial organization or an international agency in which the U.S. takes part.

Note: Residence or physical presences of parent must take place before child's birth. Section 301(h) of INA took effect Oct. 25, 1994, and is retroactive to 1790. Section 324(d) of INA took effect March 1, 1995, and is applicable to anyone who failed to retain citizenship regardless of date citizenship ceased.

Date of Birth	Transmission Requirements	Reference	Retention Requirements	Reference
On or after **Jan. 13, 1941,** *but before* **Dec. 24, 1952.**	(1a) Father physically present in U.S. or possession 10 years prior to child's birth, 5 of which after the age of 14. Honor-able U.S. military service, employment with U.S. government or intergovernmental international organization, or as dependent unmarried son or daughter and member of the household of a parent in such service or employment may be included; and (1b) Paternity established fore age 21 by the legitimation law of father's or child's residence/domicile; *or* (2a) Father resided in U.S. or possession 10 years prior to child's birth, five of which after the age of 16 years; and (2b) Paternity established during minority by legitimation or court adjudication before 12/24/52.	§301(a)(7) INA; 7 FAM 1133.3-3 §309(b) INA §201(g) NA §205 NA; 7 FAM 1134.5-2	Persons failing to fulfill below requirements may have citizenship restored upon taking oath of allegiance. (1) 2 years continuous physical presence between ages 14-18;[1] (2) 5 years continuous physical presence between ages 14-28 if begun before 10/27/72.[2] (3) None if parent employed in certain occupation.[3] (4) None if child born on or after 10/10/52. (5) None if alien parent naturalized and child began to reside permanently in U.S. while under age 18.	§324(d)(1) INA; §101 P.L. 103-416; 7 FAM 1133.5-15 (1) Former §301(b), (c) INA; 7 FAM 1133.5-7, 5-8 (2) Former §301(b), (d) INA; 7 FAM 1133.5-2, 1133.5-9 (3) 201(g) NA; 7 FAM 1134.6-2 (4) P.L. 95-432; 7 FAM 1133.5-13 (5) Former §301(b) INA; 7 FAM 1133.5-7, 1133.5-11
On or after **Dec. 24, 1952,** *through* **Nov. 14, 1968**	(1) Father physically present in U.S. or possession 10 years prior to child's birth, five of which after age 14. Honorable U.S. military service, employment with U.S. government or intergovernmental international organization, or as dependent unmarried son or daughter and member of the household of a parent in such service or employment, may be included; and (2) Paternity established under age 21 by legitimation law of father's or child's residence/domicile.	§301(a)(7) INA §309(a) INA as originally enacted	None	

Note: INA §301(h) took effect 10/25/94 and is retroactive to 1790. INA §324(d) took effect 3/1/95 and is applicable to anyone who failed to retain citizenship regardless of date citizenship ceased.

[1] Absences of less than 60 days in aggregate during 2 year period do not break continuity.
[2] Absences of less than one year in aggregate during 5 year period do not break continuity.
[3] U.S. government, American educational, scientific, philanthropic, religious, commercial, or financial organization or an international agency in which the U.S. takes part.
Note: Residence or physical presences of parent must take place before child's birth. Section 301(h) of INA took effect Oct. 25, 1994, and is retroactive to 1790. Section 324(d) of INA took effect March 1, 1995, and is applicable to anyone who failed to retain citizenship regardless of date citizenship ceased.

Date of Birth	Transmission Requirements	Reference	Retention Requirements	Reference
After **Nov. 14, 1968,** *through* **Nov. 14, 1971**	(1) Father physically present in U.S. or possession 10 years prior to child's birth, five of which after age 14. Honorable U.S. military service, employment with U.S. government or intergovernmental international organization, or as dependent unmarried son or daughter and member of the household of a parent in such service or employment, may be included; and	§301(a)(7) INA	None	
	(2a) Blood relationship established between father and child, father a U.S. citizen at time of child's birth, father (unless deceased) agrees in writing to support child until 18 years, and while child is under 18 years: (i) child is legitimated, (ii) father acknowledges paternity, or (iii) paternity established by court adjudication, or	§309(a) INA as amended 11/14/86, 102 Stat. 2619; 7 FAM 1133.4-2		
	(2b) Paternity is established under age 21 by the legitimation law of father's or child's residence/domicile.	§309(a) INA, as originally enacted		

[1] Absences of less than 60 days in aggregate during 2 year period do not break continuity.
[2] Absences of less than one year in aggregate during 5 year period do not break continuity.
[3] U.S. government, American educational, scientific, philanthropic, religious, commercial, or financial organization or an international agency in which the U.S. takes part.
Note: Residence or physical presences of parent must take place before child's birth. Section 301(h) of INA took effect Oct. 25, 1994, and is retroactive to 1790. Section 324(d) of INA took effect March 1, 1995, and is applicable to anyone who failed to retain citizenship regardless of date citizenship ceased.

Date of Birth	Transmission Requirements	Reference	Retention Requirements	Reference
After **Nov. 11, 1971**, *but before* **Nov. 14, 1986**	(1) Father physically present in U.S. or possession 10 years prior to child's birth, five of which after age 14. Honorable U.S. military service, employment with U.S. government or intergovernmental international organization, or as dependent unmarried son or daughter and member of the household of a parent in such service or employment, may be included; and (2) Blood relationship established between father and child, father a U.S. citizen at time of child's birth, father (unless deceased) agrees in writing to support child until 18 years, and while child is under 18 years (i) child is legitimated, (ii) father acknowledges paternity, or (iii) paternity established by court adjudication.	§301(a)(7) INA §309(a) INA, as amended 11/14/86; 102 Stat. 2619; 7 FAM 1133.4-2	None	
On or after **Nov. 14, 1986**	(1) Father physically present in U.S. or possession five years prior to child's birth, two of which after age 14. Honorable U.S. military service, employment with U.S. government or intergovernmental international organization, or as dependent unmarried son or daughter and member of the household of a parent in such service or employment, may be included; and (2) Blood relationship established between father and child, father a U.S. citizen at time of child's birth, father (unless deceased) agrees in writing to support child until 18 years, and while child is under 18 years: (i) child is legitimated, (ii) father acknowledges paternity, or (iii) paternity established by court adjudication.	§301(g) INA; 7 FAM 1133.3-3 §309(a) INA as amended 11/14/86; 102 Stat. 2619; 7 FAM 1133.4-2		

[1] Absences of less than 60 days in aggregate during 2 year period do not break continuity.
[2] Absences of less than one year in aggregate during 5 year period do not break continuity.
[3] U.S. government, American educational, scientific, philanthropic, religious, commercial, or financial organization or an international agency in which the U.S. takes part.

Note: Residence or physical presences of parent must take place before child's birth. Section 301(h) of INA took effect Oct. 25, 1994, and is retroactive to 1790. Section 324(d) of INA took effect March 1, 1995, and is applicable to anyone who failed to retain citizenship regardless of date citizenship ceased.

APPENDIX C

EXECUTIVE OFFICE FOR IMMIGRATION REVIEW (EOIR)

5107 Leesburg Pike, Falls Church, VA 22041
Kevin A. Ohlson, *Director*

OFFICE OF THE GENERAL COUNSEL

Acting General Counsel
John N. Blum

Senior Associate General Counsel
Cecelia M. Espenoza
Gustavo D. Villageliu

Suite 2600 — (703) 305-0470

FOIA Requests: (703) 605-1297

Law Library & Immigration Research Center
(703) 605-1103

Coordinator, Legal Orientation & Pro Bono Program
Steven C. Lang

Associate General Counsel
Scott Anderson
Jennifer J. Barnes
Heidi Brissette
Lisa Ann Compagno
JuanCarlos M. Hunt
Barbara Joan Leen
C. Lockhart Nimick
Carolyn M. Piccotti
Sharon J. Pomeranz
Sandy Reinfurt
Marta Rothwarf
Sue B. Sheehan
Charles F. Smith

BOARD OF IMMIGRATION APPEALS (BIA)

Chairman (Acting)
Juan P. Osuna, (703) 305-1194

Office of the Chief Clerk, Suite 2000

Mailing Address:
Clerk's Office
P.O. Box 8530
Falls Church, VA 22041

Board Members
Patricia A. Cole
Lauri S. Filppu
Edward R. Grant
Frederick D. Hess
David B. Holmes
Neil P. Miller
Roger Pauley

Clerk's Office Information: (703) 605-1007; *Case Information:* 1-800-898-7180

OFFICE OF THE CHIEF ADMINISTRATIVE HEARING OFFICER (OCAHO)

Chief Administrative Hearing Officer
Michael J. Creppy

Suite 2519 — (703) 305-0864

Deputy Chief Administrative Hearing Officer
Louis J. Ruffino

Administrative Law Judge (ALJ)
Ellen K. Thomas

OFFICE OF THE CHIEF IMMIGRATION JUDGE (OCIJ)

Chief Immigration Judge
David L. Neal

Suite 2500 — (703) 305-1247

Counsel to the Chief Immigration Judge
Brooke Grandle
Edward F. Kelly, *Special Counsel*
Scott M. Rosen, *Special Counsel*

Assistant Chief Immigration Judges
Richard J. Bartolomei
Sarah M. Burr
Larry R. Dean
Thomas Y.K. Fong
Anne J. Greer
Stephen S. Griswold
MaryBeth Keller
Michael C. McGoings
Gary W. Smith
Elisa M. Sukkar
Phillip T. Williams

DEADLINES

This table is provided for general guidance *only*. To determinate the particular deadlines in a given case, parties *must* consult the text of the *Immigration Court Practice Manual.*[1] IJs have discretion to set deadlines for pre-decision filings. Moreover, the *Practice Manual's* deadlines for filings submitted while proceedings are pending before the immigration court **apply only to cases involving nondetained respondents**. For cases involving detained respondents, "filing deadlines are as specified by the Immigration Court." *Practice Manual,* Chap. 3.1(b)(i)(B), 3.1(b)(ii)(B).

Type of filing		Must be filed within[2]	Chapter[1]
Changes of address or phone number	alien	5 days after alien's change of address or phone number	2.2(c)
	representative	promptly	2.3(h)
Filing in advance of master calendar hearing	filings	15 days before hearing, if requesting a ruling[3]	3.1(b)(i)
	responses	10 days after filing is received by immigration court[3]	
Filings in advance of individual calendar hearings	filings	30 days before hearing, if requesting a ruling[3]	3.1(b)(ii)
	responses	15 days after filing is received by immigration court[3]	
Asylum applications	defensive applications	at master calendar hearing[4]	3.1(b)(iii)(A)
	affirmative applications	referred to immigration court by DHS[4]	3.1(b)(iii)(B)
Post-decision motions	motions to reopen	90 days after final administrative order by immigration judge, with certain exceptions	5.7(c)
	motions to reconsider	30 days after final administrative order by immigration judge	5.8(c)
	motions to reopen *in absentia* removal order	180 days after *in absentia* order, if based on exceptional circumstances	5.9(d)(ii)(A)
Appeals to BIA		30 days after decision was mailed or rendered orally	6.2

[1] The new *EOIR Practice Manual*, which went into effect July 1, 2008, is available at *www.usdoj.gov/eoir*.

[2] All filing deadlines are calculated in calendar days. *Practice Manual* Chap. 3.1(c)(i).

[3] If alien is detained, deadline is determined by immigration court

[4] Subject to one-year filing rule. *See* INA §208(a)(2)(B), 8 C.F.R. §1208.4(a)(2).

BIA MAILING INFORMATION

If sending by:	Use this address:	Remember:
courier hand delivery overnight or express delivery (including USPS Express Mail)	Board of Immigration Appeals Clerk's Office 5107 Leesburg Pike, Ste. 2000 Falls Church, VA 22041	Deliveries *must be received* during normal window hours (8:00 am to 4:30 pm (ET), Mon. to Fri., except holidays). Phone: (703) 605-1007.
If sending by:	**Use this address:**	**Remember:**
USPS (any class except Express Mail) priority mail certified mail registered mail return-receipt requested mail	Board of Immigration Appeals Clerk's Office P.O. Box 8530 Falls Church, VA 22041	Use caution when there is a filing deadline. Deadlines are determined by when the mailing is *received* by the Clerk's Office. When there is a filing deadline, try to use a delivery method from the row above.

When the intended recipient of correspondence is a particular person or office within the Board, the sender should label the envelope or packaging to the attention of that person or office. *Example*: "ATTN: Oral Argument Coordinator"

IMMIGRATION COURTS

[including Administrative Control Court (ACC) responsibilities]*

ARIZONA

Eloy, AZ 85231
1705 E. Hanna Rd., Suite 366
(520) 466-3671

Immigration Judges
John W. Davis
James Alan DeVitto
Thomas M. O'Leary
Stephen M. Ruhle
Linda Inez Spencer-Walters

Administrator
Victoria Padilla

ACC Assigned Responsibility
Eloy Detention Center (DHS detainees)

Florence, AZ 85232
3260 N. Pinal Parkway Ave.
(520) 868-3341

Immigration Judges
Bruce A. Taylor
Scott M. Jefferies

Administrator
Lizbeth L. Patterson

ACC Assigned Responsibility
Florence Detention Center (DHS detainees)
AZ Dep't of Corrections, Florence

Other Hearing Locations
[Clerical transfers allowed]
AZ Dep't of Corrections, Florence

Phoenix, AZ 85012
200 E. Mitchell Dr., Ste 200
(602) 640-2747

Immigration Judges
LaMonte S. Freerks
Wendell Hollis
John W. Richardson

Administrator
Lizbeth L. Patterson

ACC Assigned Responsibility
DHS District Office, Phoenix (incl. any suboffices except San Luis (AZ) POE and Tucson)
AZ Dep't of Corrections (Perryville and Phoenix West)
Lewis Prison (Buckeye, AZ) (IHP)

Other Hearing Locations
[Clerical transfers allowed]
AZ State Prison Complex—Perryville, Goodyear, AZ
AZ State Prison—Phoenix West
Lewis Prison, Buckeye, AZ (IHP)

Tucson, AZ 85701
160 N. Stone Ave., Suite 300
(520) 670-5212

Immigration Judges
Sean H. Keenan

Administrator
Corey Graff

ACC Assigned Responsibility
DHS Suboffice, Tucson
AZ Dep't of Corrections (Tucson)

Other Hearing Locations
AZ Dep't of Corrections—Wilmont, Tucson

CALIFORNIA

East Mesa
[San Diego, CA 92158]
East Mesa CCA
446 Alta Rd.
(619) 661-3327

Immigration Judge
C. Zsa Zsa De Paolo

Administrator
Brent L. Perkins

ACC Assigned Responsibility
DHS Detention Facility

El Centro, CA 92243
1115 North Imperial Ave.
(760) 353-2328

Immigration Judge
Jack H. Weil

Administrator
David R. Dixon

ACC Assigned Responsibility
El Centro SPC (incl. Yuma, AZ, Sector and San Luis, AZ, POE) (DHS detainees)

Other Hearing Locations
[Clerical transfers allowed]

Imperial, CA 92251
2409 La Brucherie Rd.
(760) 355-0070

Immigration Judges
Dennis R. James
Jack W. Staton

Administrator
David R. Dixon

ACC Assigned Responsibility
CA Dep't of Corr. (Calipatria & Centinela) (nondetainees)

Other Hearing Locations
[Clerical transfers allowed]
Calipatria (CA) State Prison
Centinela (CA) State Prison

Lancaster, CA 93536
Mira Loma Facility
45100 N. 60th St. West
(661) 942-8633

Immigration Judges
William J. Nickerson, Jr.
Robert O. Vicars, Jr.

Administrator
Graciela Sosa

ACC Assigned Responsibility
DHS District Office, Los Angeles (incl. any suboffices)

Other Hearing Locations
[Clerical transfers allowed]
FCI—Lompoc, CA
Mira Loma Detention Facility, Lancaster, CA

Los Angeles, CA 90014
606 S. Olive St., 15th Floor
(213) 894-2811

Immigration Judges
David C. Anderson
Ira E. Bank
Lori Bass
Christine A. Bither
Isabel A. Bronzina
Alison Daw
Philip L. DiMarzio
Dorothy Dunkel-Bradley
Thomas Y.K. Fong, *Ass't Chf. IJ*
Gilbert T. Gembacz
Anthony T. Giattina

*An administrative control court (ACC) is one that creates and maintains records of proceedings for immigration courts within an assigned geographic area. *See* 8 C.F.R. §1003.11. It may have jurisdiction over charging documents issued by DHS district offices or suboffices, or over charging documents relating to aliens in custody at detention facilities or service processing centers (SPCs) or to incarcerated alien inmates in the custody of state departments of corrections.

Anna Ho
Jan D. Latimore
William J. Martin, Jr.
Lorraine J. Munoz
Lourdes Rodriquez de Jongh
Stephen L. Sholomson
Christine E. Stancill
A. Ashley Tabaddor
Frank Travieso
Mimi Tsankov
Gita Vahid-Tehrani
John F. Walsh
Richard D. Walton

Administrator
Stephen P. Perkins

ACC Assigned Responsibility
DHS District Office, Los Angeles (incl. any suboffices)

San Diego, CA 92101
401 West A St., Suite 800
(619) 557-6052

Immigration Judges
Anthony Atenaide
Kenneth A. Bagley
Richard J. Bartolomei, Jr., *Ass't Chief IJ*
Ignacio P. Fernandez
Henry Ipema, Jr.
Renee L. Renner
John C. Williams

Administrator
Brent L. Perkins

ACC Assigned Responsibility
DHS District Office, San Diego (incl. any suboffices except East Mesa POE)
Donovan CA State Prison

Other Hearing Locations
[Clerical transfers allowed]
Federal Building, San Diego
Donovan CA State Prison, San Diego

San Francisco, CA 94104
120 Montgomery St., Suite 800
(415) 705-4415

Immigration Judges
Jeffrey J. Bernstein
Lawrence N. DiCostanzo
Loreto Geisse
Stephen Griswold, *Ass't Chief IJ*
Miriam R. Hayward
Carol A. King
Dana Leigh Marks
Anthony S. Murry
Tue Phan-Quang
Laura L. Ramirez
Brian H. Simpson
Bette Kane Stockton
Marilyn J. Teeter
Polly A. Webber
Michael J. Yamaguchi
Robert Yeargin

Administrator
Maria Jauregui

ACC Assigned Responsibility
DHS District Office, San Francisco (incl. any suboffices)
FCI—Pleasanton

Other Hearing Locations
FCI—Pleasanton, Dublin, CA

San Pedro, CA
[Los Angeles, CA 90014]
606 S. Olive St., 15th Floor
(213) 894-2811

[San Pedro operations are temporarily located in the L.A. facility]

Immigration Judges
Rose C. Peters
D.D. Sitgraves

Administrator
Daisy Barrero

ACC Assigned Responsibility
San Pedro SPC

Other Hearing Locations
[Clerical transfers allowed]

COLORADO

Denver, CO 80294
Byron G. Rogers Federal Bldg.
1961 Stout St., Room 1403
(303) 844-5815

Immigration Judges
David J. Cordova
Donn L. Livingston
James P. Vandello

Administrator
Alec Revelle

ACC Assigned Responsibility
DHS District Office, Denver (incl. any suboffices)
Departments of Corrections for CO and WY
GEO Detention Facility, Aurora, CO

Other Hearing Locations
CO Territorial Corr. Facility, Canon City
Denver Detention Facility, Aurora
WY State Penitentiary, Rawlins

CONNECTICUT

Hartford, CT 06103
A.A. Ribicoff Building
450 Main St., Room 509
(860) 240-3881

Immigration Judge
Michael W. Straus

Administrator
Philip Verrillo

ACC Assigned Responsibility
DHS Suboffice, Hartford
CT Dep't of Corrections
FCI—Danbury

Other Hearing Locations
CT Dep't of Corr., Suffield, CT
FCI—Danbury, Danbury, CT
York Corr. Ctr., Niantic, CT
Wyatt Detention Ctr., Central Falls, RI

FLORIDA

Krome
[Miami, FL 33194]
18201 SW 12th St., Bldg. 1, Ste. C
(305) 530-7196

Mailing address:
P.O. Box 940998
Miami, FL 33194

Immigration Judges
Rex J. Ford
Kenneth S. Hurewitz
Denise N. Slavin

Administrator
Mark Russelburg

ACC Assigned Responsibility
Krome North SPC
Broward Transitional Center
Monroe Co. Jail (female detainees)

Other Hearing Locations
[Clerical transfers allowed]

Miami, FL 33130
One Riverview Square
333 S. Miami Ave., Suite 700
(305) 789-4221

Immigration Judges
Scott G. Alexander
Kevin G. Bradley
Teofilo Chapa
J. Daniel Dowell
Mahlon F. Hanson
Rodger C. Harris
Carey Holliday
Michael C. Horn
Denise A. Marks Lane
Stephen E. Mander

Nancy R. McCormack
Pedro A. Miranda
Adam Opaciuch
John Opaciuch
Charles J. Sanders
Bruce W. Solow
Elisa M. Sukkar, *Ass't Chief IJ*
Lilliana Torreh-Bayouth

Administrator
James Griffin

ACC Assigned Responsibility
DHS District Office, Miami (incl. any suboffices except Orlando)
Central FL Reception Ctr.
North FL Reception Ctr.
South FL Reception Ctr.
Broward Correctional Inst.
Charlotte Correctional Inst.
Dade County Corrections
Washington Correctional Inst.

Other Hearing Locations
[Clerical transfers allowed]
Central FL Recep. Ctr., Orlando
South FL Recep. Ctr., Miami
North FL Recep. Ctr., Lake Butler
Turner Guilford Knight Correctional Ctr., Miami
Broward Correctional Inst., Pembroke Pines, FL
Washington Correctional Inst., Chipley, FL
Charlotte Correctional Inst., Punta Gorda, FL

Orlando, FL 32801
80 N. Hughey Ave., Ste. 203
(407) 648-6565

Immigration Judges
Kevin J. Chapman
Victoria L. Ghartey
Daniel Lippman
Rafael B. Ortiz-Segura
Earle Wilson

Administrator
George A. Spreyne

ACC Assigned Responsibility
DHS Suboffice, Orlando

GEORGIA

Atlanta, GA 30303
180 Spring Street, SW, Ste. 241
(404) 331-0907

Immigration Judges
William A. Cassidy
Wayne K. Houser, Jr.
J. Dan Pelletier, Sr.
Grace A. Sease

Administrator
Cynthia Long

ACC Assigned Responsibility
DHS District Office, Atlanta (incl. any suboffices)
Departments of Corrections for AL, GA, NC, and SC

Other Hearing Locations
Kilby Correctional Facility, Mt. Meigs, AL
Diagnostic Center, Jackson, GA
Central Prison, Raleigh, NC
Broad River Reception & Evaluation Center, Columbia, SC

HAWAII

Honolulu, HI 96850
PJKK Federal Bldg.
300 Ala Moana Blvd., Rm. 8-112
(808) 541-1870

Immigration Judge
Dayna Beamer

Administrator
Beverly Takemoto

ACC Assigned Responsibility
DHS District Office, Honolulu (incl. Hagatna, GU, and any suboffices)
FDC—Honolulu
HI Dep't of Public Safety

Other Hearing Locations
Immigration Court, Haganta, GU

ILLINOIS

Chicago, IL 60603
55 East Monroe St.
Suite 1900
(312) 353-7313

Immigration Judges
Glen Bower
Carlos Cuevas
James R. Fujimoto
Jennie L. Giambastiani
Robert D. Vinikoor
Craig M. Zerbe

Administrator
Christine Epstein

ACC Assigned Responsibility
DHS district offices—Chicago (incl. any suboffices), Kansas City, MO (incl. any suboffices), and Omaha
Departments of Corrections for IL, IN, IA, KS, NE, and WI

Other Hearing Locations
Immigration courts—Chicago (detained), Kansas City, and Omaha
Indiana Youth Center, Plainfield
Statesville Correctional Center, Joliet, IL
Waupun Correctional Institution, Waupun, WI
KS State Penitentiary, Lansing
IA Medical & Classification Center, Oakdale
NE Penitentiary, Lincoln

Chicago, IL 60605 [Detained]
536 Clark St., Rm. B1330/1320
(312) 353-1387

Immigration Judge
George Katsivalas

Administrator
Christine Epstein

LOUISIANA

New Orleans, LA 70130
One Canal Place
365 Canal St., Suite 2450
(504) 589-3992

Immigration Judge
William Stogner

Administrator
Lynda C. Mobley

ACC Assigned Responsibility
DHS District Office, New Orleans (incl. any suboffices except Memphis)

Other Hearing Locations
New Orleans Detention

Oakdale, LA 71463
1900 East Whatley Rd.
(318) 335-0365

Immigration Judges
John A. Duck, Jr.
James Nugent
Agnelis L. Reese

Administrator
Melba J. Bennett

ACC Assigned Responsibility
FCI—Oakdale
FDC—Oakdale
LA Dep't of Public Safety and Corrections
MS Dep't of Corrections
MO Dep't of Corrections and Human Resources

Other Hearing Locations
Immigration Court, St. Louis
FDC—Oakdale 2, Oakdale, LA
FCI—Oakdale 1, Oakdale, LA
Allen Corr. Ctr., Kinder, LA
Rankin Co. Corr. Facility, Pearl, MS
MO Dep't of Corrections, Mineral Point, MO

MARYLAND

Baltimore, MD 21201
George H. Fallon Federal Bldg.
31 Hopkins Plaza, Room 440
(410) 962-3092

Immigration Judges
Bruce M. Barrett
Lisa Dornell
Jill H. Dufresne
John F. Gossart, Jr.
Elizabeth A. Kessler

Administrator
Brenda Cook

ACC Assigned Responsibility
Baltimore DHS District Office (incl. any suboffices)
MD Dep't of Public Safety and Correctional Service

Other Hearing Locations (non-IHP cases)
Wicomico Co. Det. Ctr., Salisbury
MD Corr. Inst., Hagerstown
MD Dep't of Corrections, Jessup

MASSACHUSETTS

Boston, MA 02203
John F. Kennedy Federal Bldg.
15 New Sudbury St., Room 320
(617) 565-3080

Immigration Judges
Francis L. Cramer
Matthew J. D'Angelo
Robin Feder
Paul M. Gagnon
Eliza C. Klein
Leonard I. Shapiro

Administrator
Robert Halpin

ACC Assigned Responsibility
DHS district offices—Boston (incl. any suboffices except Hartford) and Portland, ME (incl. any suboffices)
Departments of Corrections for ME, MA, NH, RI, and VT
Bristol, Essex, and Suffolk Co. Jails

Other Hearing Locations
Bristol Co. (MA) Corr. Facility, N. Dartmouth
Essex Co. (MA) House of Corr., Middletown
ME State Prison, Thomaston
MA Dep't of Corr., MC 1, Concord, MA
NH State Prison Complex, Concord
Plymouth Co. (MA) Correctional Facility, Plymouth
RI Dep't of Corr., Cranston
Suffolk Co. House of Corrections, Boston
Chittenden (VT) Corr. Ctr., South Burlington
Wyatt (RI) Det. Ctr., Central Falls
DHS DRO Office, Portland, ME

MICHIGAN

Detroit, MI 48226
P.V. McNamara Federal Building
477 Michigan Ave., Ste. 440
(313) 226-2603

Immigration Judges
Elizabeth A. Hacker
Marsha K. Nettles
Robert D. Newberry

Administrator
Sandra L. Roberts

ACC Assigned Responsibility
DHS District Office, Detroit (incl. any suboffices)
MI Department of Corrections

Other Hearing Locations
MI State Prison, Jackson

Televideo Sites:
MI Dep't of Corrections
Calhoun Co. Sheriff's Dep't, Battle Creek
Monroe Co. Sheriff's Dep't, Monroe

MINNESOTA

Bloomington, MN 55425
7850 Metro Pkwy, Suite 320
(612) 725-3765

Immigration Judges
Joseph R. Dierkes
Kristin W. Olmanson

Administrator
Daniel Ponce de Leon

ACC Assigned Responsibility
DHS District Office, St. Paul (incl. ND and SD IHP)
MN Dep't of Corrections

Other Hearing Locations
MN Dep't of Corr., Stillwater
ND State Prison, Bismarck
SD Penitentiary, Sioux Falls

NEVADA

Las Vegas, NV 89120
3365 Pepper Lane, Suite 200
(702) 458-0227

Immigration Judges
Harry L. Gastley
Ronald L. Mullins
Irene Weiss

Administrator
Rachel Newsome

ACC Assigned Responsibility
DHS district offices (incl. any suboffices)—Los Angeles and Reno

Other Hearing Locations
NV State Prison, Carson City
DHS Remote Site, Reno
Southern Desert Correctional Ctr., Indian Springs, NV

NEW JERSEY

Elizabeth, NJ 07201
625 Evans St., Room 148A
(973) 693-4113

Immigration Judges
Dorothy Harbeck
Mirlande Tadal

Administrator
Yolanda English

ACC Assigned Responsibility
DHS Detention Facility

Other Hearing Locations
[Clerical transfers allowed]

Newark, NJ 07102
970 Broad St., Room 1135
(973) 645-3524

Immigration Judges
Henry S. Dogin
Annie S. Garcy
Frederick G. Leeds
Eugene Pugliese
Margaret R. Reichenberg
Alberto J. Riefkohl
Susan Girardo Roy

Administrator
Charlene McLaughlin

ACC Assigned Responsibility
DHS District Office, Newark (incl. any suboffices)
Hudon Co. Jail
Middlesex Co. Jail
NJ Dep't of Corrections

Other Hearing Locations
[Clerical transfers allowed]

NEW YORK

Batavia, NY 14020
4250 Federal Dr., Room F108
(585) 345-4300

Immigration Judge
John B. Reid

Administrator
Gary M. Somerville

ACC Assigned Responsibility
DHS District Office, Buffalo (incl. any suboffices)
Batavia Detention Facility

Other Hearing Locations
[Clerical transfers allowed]

Buffalo, NY 14202
130 Delaware Ave., Suite 410
(716) 551-3442

Immigration Judges
Philip J. Montante, Jr.
Michaelangelo Rocco

Administrator
Gary M. Somerville

ACC Assigned Responsibility
DHS District Office, Buffalo (incl. any suboffices)
Batavia Detention Facility

Other Hearing Locations
[Clerical transfers allowed]

Fishkill, NY 12524
Downstate Correctional Facility
121 Red Schoolhouse Rd.
(845) 831-3657

Immigration Judge
Roger Sagerman

Administrator
Thomas J. Bonita III

ACC Assigned Responsibility
NY State Dep't of Corr. Servs.

Other Hearing Locations
[Clerical transfers allowed]
Bedford Hills (NY) Corr. Facility

New York, NY 10278
26 Federal Plaza
12th Floor, Room 1237
(917) 454-1040

Immigration Judges
Steven R. Abrams
Terry A. Bain
Javier Balasquide
Noël A. Brennan
Joanna M. Bukszpan
Sarah M. Burr, *Ass't Chief IJ*
George T. Chew
Paul A. DeFonzo
Annette S. Elstein
Noel Anne Ferris
Vivienne E. Gordon-Uruakpa
Theresa Holmes-Simmons
Sandy K. Hom
Brigitte Laforest
Elizabeth A. Lamb
Margaret McManus
Philip L. Morace
Thomas Mulligan
Barbara A. Nelson
Patricia A. Rohan
Douglas B. Schoppert
Helen Sichel
William P. Van Wyke
Gabriel C. Videla
Robert D. Weisel

Administrator
Star B. Pacitto

ACC Assigned Responsibility
DHS District Office, New York, NY (incl. any suboffices)

Other Hearing Locations
[Clerical transfers allowed]

Ulster
[Napanoch, NY 12458]
Ulster Correctional Facility
Berme Rd.
P.O. Box 800
(845) 647-5506

Immigration Judge
Roger Sagerman

Administrator
Thomas J. Bonita III

ACC Assigned Responsibility
NY State Dep't of Corr. Servs.

Other Hearing Locations
[Clerical transfers allowed]

Varick Street
[New York, NY 10014]
201 Varick St., Room 1140
(212) 620-6279

Immigration Judges
Alan L. Page
Alan A. Vomacka

Administrator
Thomas J. Bonita III

ACC Assigned Responsibility
Varick Street SPC
Passaic Co. (NJ) Jail
Bergen Co. (NJ) Jail
Monmouth Co. (NJ) Jail
Sussex Co. (NJ) Jail

Other Hearing Locations
[Clerical transfers allowed]

OHIO

Cleveland, OH 44113
801 W. Superior Ave., Ste. 13-100
(216) 802-1100

Immigration Judges
D. William Evans Jr.
[Vacant (2)]

Administrator
James W. Roder

ACC Assigned Responsibility
DHS District Office, Cleveland (incl. any suboffices) (excl. cases south of I-70, and Montgomery Co./Dayton, but incl. Franklin Co. and Columbus)
OH Department of Corrections

Ohio Televideo Sites
Seneca County Jail, Tiffin, OH (CLE-CLD)
Immigration Court, Cleveland (CLE-CEL)
Correctional Reception Center, Orient, OH (CLE-ORI)

OREGON

Portland, OR 97204
1220 SW Third Ave., Suite 218
(503) 326-6341

Immigration Judge
Michael H. Bennett

Administrator
Joseph A. Neifert

ACC Assigned Responsibility
DHS district offices (incl. any suboffices)—Anchorage, Helena, Portland, OR
DHS Suboffice, Boise
Departments of Corrections for AK, ID, and MT
Eastern OR Corrections (Pendleton)
Marion Co. Corr. Facility
OR State Penitentiary (Salem)

Other Hearing Locations
Immigration Court, DHS Detention Ctr., Portland, OR
DHS district offices—Anchorage and Helena
DHS Suboffice, Boise
Marion Co. (OR) Corr. Ctr.
Eastern OR Corr. Inst., Pendleton
OR State Penitentiary, Salem

PENNSYLVANIA

Philadelphia, PA 19130
1600 Callowhill St., Suite 400
(215) 656-7000

Immigration Judges
Charles M. Honeyman
Rosalind K. Malloy
Miriam Mills

Administrator
R. Elliott Edwards

ACC Assigned Responsibility
DHS District Office, Philadelphia (incl. WV and any suboffices)
DHS Suboffice, Pittsburgh
DE Dep't of Corrections

Other Hearing Locations
Immigration Court, Pittsburgh

York, PA 17402
3400 Concord Rd., Suite #2
(717) 755-7555

Mailing Address:
P.O. Box 20370
York, PA 17402

Immigration Judge
Andrew R. Arthur
Walter A. Durling
Jeffrey L. Romig

Administrator
Tina Barrow

ACC Assigned Responsibility
DHS District Office, Philadelphia (incl. any suboffices)
York Co. Prison
PA Dep't of Corrections
Moshanon Valley Corr. Facility

Other Hearing Locations
Berks Co. Det. Ctr., Leesport, PA
PA Dep't of Corr., Camp Hill
FCI—Allenwood, Whitedeer, PA

PUERTO RICO

San Juan
[Guaynabo, PR 00968]
San Patricio Office Center
#7 Tabonuco St., Room 401
(787) 749-4386

Immigration Judge
Irma Lopez-Defillo

Administrator
Milagros Torres

ACC Assigned Responsibility
DHS District Office, San Juan (incl. St. Croix and St. Thomas, VI, and any suboffices)

Other Hearing Locations
Immigration courts—St. Thomas, VI, and St. Croix, VI

TENNESSEE

Memphis, TN 38103
Clifford B. Davis Federal Bldg.
167 North Main St., Room 460
(901)544-3818

Immigration Judges
Lawrence O. Burman
Charles E. Pazar

Administrator
J. Thomas Davis

ACC Assigned Responsibility
DHS suboffices—Memphis (AR, MS (north of Jackson), and TN) and Louisville
AR Dep't of Corrections

Other Hearing Locations
AR Dep't of Corrections, Pine Bluff, AR
Louisville, KY

TEXAS

Dallas, TX 75242
1100 Commerce St., Suite 404
(214) 767-1814

Immigration Judges
D. Anthony Rogers
Deitrich H. Sims

Administrator
Barbara Baker

ACC Assigned Responsibility
DHS District Office, Dallas (incl. any suboffices)
DHS Suboffice, Oklahoma City
Big Spring Correctional Center
OK Department of Corrections
Eden Detention Center

Other Hearing Locations
Immigration courts—Dallas (detained), Eden, TX, Oklahoma City, and Oklahoma City (detained)
Big Spring Corr. Ctr. (Airpark), Big Spring, TX
Rolling Plains Det.ention Ctr., Haskell, TX

El Paso, TX 79901
Richard C. White Federal Bldg.
700 E. San Antonio Ave., Ste. 750
(915) 534-6020

Immigration Judges
Robert Hough
Thomas Roepke

Administrator
Theresa N. Baeza

ACC Assigned Responsibility
DHS District Office, El Paso (incl. any suboffices)
FCI—LaTuna
Penitentiary of NM, Santa Fe
Reeves Co. Detention Center
Southern NM Corr. Facility

Other Hearing Locations
[Clerical Transfers Allowed]
Immigration Court, Paso Del Norte, El Paso
FCI—LaTuna, Anthony, TX
Penitentiary of NM, Santa Fe
Southern NM Correctional Facility, Las Cruces, NM
Reeves Co. Detention Center, Pecos, TX

El Paso, TX 79925
[Detailed]
Service Processing Center
8915 Montana Ave., Suite 100
(915) 225-0750

Immigration Judge
William L. Abbott
Richard R. Ozmun

Administrator
Theresa N. Baeza

ACC Assigned Responsibility
El Paso Service Processing Ctr.

Other Hearing Locations
[Clerical Transfers Allowed]
Regional Corrections Center, Albuquerque
Otero Co. Prison Facility, Chaparral, NM

Harlingen, TX 78550
2009 W. Jefferson Ave., Ste. 300
(956) 427-8580

Immigration Judges
Howard Achtsam
David Ayala
Margaret D. Burkhart
William C. Peterson
Eleazar Tovar

Administrator
Celeste G. Garza

ACC Assigned Responsibility
DHS District Office, Harlingen (incl. any suboffices, and Brownsville POE)

Other Hearing Locations
[Clerical Transfers Allowed]
Hidalgo (TX) POE (once per month)
Willacy Detention Center, Raymondville, TX

Houston, TX 77004
2320 LaBranch St., Room 2235
(713) 718-3870

Immigration Judges
Chris A. Brisack
Phillip S. Law
Mimi S. Yam
Clarease Rankin Yates
William K. Zimmer

Administrator
Dina P. Sherman

ACC Assigned Responsibility
DHS District Office, Houston (incl. any suboffices)
Huntsville Dep't of Corrections
Bokenkamp Children's Center

Other Hearing Locations
[Clerical Transfers Allowed]
Polk Co. Detention Center

Houston, TX 77032
[Detained]
5520 Greens Rd.
(281) 987-2112

Immigration Judges
Jimmie L. Benton
Howard Rose

Administrator
Dina P. Sherman

ACC Assigned Responsibility
Houston SPC

Other Hearing Locations
[Clerical Transfers Allowed]

Port Isabel
[Los Fresnos, TX 78566]
27991 Buena Vista Blvd., Bldg. 37
(956) 547-1789

Mailing address:
2009 W. Jefferson Ave., Ste. 300
Harlingen, TX 78550

Administrator
Celeste G. Garza

ACC Assigned Responsibility
Port Isabel SPC

Other Hearing Locations
[Clerical Transfers Allowed]

San Antonio, TX 78207
800 Dolorosa St., Suite 300
(210) 472-6637

Immigration Judges
Gary D. Burkholder
John D. Carté
Susan E. Castro
Larry R. Dean, *Ass't Chief IJ*
Glenn P. McPhaul
Bertha A. Zuniga

Administrator
Marion Hicks

ACC Assigned Responsibility
DHS District Office, San Antonio (incl. any suboffices)
Laredo Detention Facility
Laredo Port of Entry
Pearsall Detention Facility

Other Hearing Locations
Immigration courts—Laredo Detention Facility, Laredo POE, Pearsall Detention Facility, Hutto Residential Facility (Taylor, TX)

UTAH

Salt Lake City, UT 84116
5500 W. Amelia Earhart Drive
Suite 160
(801) 524-3000

Immigration Judge
William Nixon
Dustin B. Pead

Administrator
Jon J. Hill

ACC Assigned Responsibility
UT Dep't of Corrections

Other Hearing Locations
Immigration Court, Salt Lake City
UT State Prison—South Point, Draper, UT

VIRGINIA

Arlington, VA 22203
901 N. Stuart St., Suite 1300
(703) 235-2307

Immigration Judges
John M. Bryant
Wayne R. Iskra
Garry Malphrus
Brian M. O'Leary
Paul W. Schmidt
Thomas G. Snow

Administrator
Joseph Egozcue

ACC Assigned Responsibility
DHS District Office, Arlington, VA (incl. any suboffices)
DHS Suboffice, Cincinnati (excl. all cases north of I -70 and Franklin Co. (Columbus), but incl. all of Montgomery Co. (Dayton))
Departments of Corrections for DC, VA, and OH

Other Hearing Locations
Powhatan Correctional Center, State Farm, VA

Televideo Sites
Hampton Roads Regional Jail, Portsmouth, VA
Piedmont Regional Jail, Farmville, VA
Pamunkey Regional Jail, Hanover, VA
Rappahannock Regional Jail, Stafford, VA
Riverside Regional Jail, Hopewell, VA
Immigration Court, Cincinnati (CIN Hearing Location)

Note: Arlington is no longer receiving new charging documents for Cleveland. All new charging documents for Cleveland will be filed at the Cleveland Immigration Court.

Falls Church, VA 22041
[EOIR Headquarters]
5107 Leesburg Pike, Suite 1850
(703) 305-0273

Immigration Judges
Charles Adkins-Blanch
Quynh Vu Bain
Roxanne C. Hladylowycz
Robert P. Owens

Administrator
Sheridan Butler

WASHINGTON

Seattle, WA 98104
1000 Second Ave., Suite 2500
(206) 553-5953

Immigration Judges
Kenneth Josephson
Edward Kandler

Administrator
Joseph A. Neifert

ACC Assigned Responsibility
DHS District Office, Seattle (incl. any suboffices)
Airway Heights Corr. Ctr.
WA Dep't of Corrections (Monroe & Walla Walla)

Other Hearing Locations
Airway Heights (WA) Corr. Ctr.
Peace Arch POE
Monroe (WA) Corr. Complex
WA State Pen., Walla Walla

Tacoma, WA 98421
1623 East J Street, Suite 3
(206) 553-5953

Immigration Judges
Tammy L. Fitting

Administrator
Joseph A. Neifert

ACC Assigned Responsibility
DHS District Office, Seattle (incl. any suboffices)
Northwest Detention Center

Other Hearing Locations
Northwest Detention Ctr., Tacoma

APPENDIX D

180-DAY ASYLUM CLOCK MATRIX *

for post–Jan. 4, 1995 Asylum Cases

Event	Impact on Asylum Clock
USCIS receives **complete** I-589	**Day 1**. 180-day clock starts as of filing date with Service Center. [Incomplete I-589s are rejected and clock does not start.]
AO interview notice sent	No impact.
Asylum Office interview	No impact. Generally occurs on **Day 43** for vast majority of cases at local Asylum Offices. [USCIS maintains a rigid adherence to timely processing of the I-589 at both the Service Centers and the Asylum Offices. Most I-589s filed at the Service Centers are automatically scheduled for interviews 43 days after acceptance of the complete I-589 (scheduling for cases interviewed on circuit rides varies). Generally, applications filed on the same day and interviewed at local AOs will be scheduled for interviews on the same date forward. To avoid scheduling conflicts, it is best to limit and stagger the number of I-589s submitted to the Service Centers on any one day.]
Interview cancelled by USCIS	No impact. (Rescheduled interviews are given first priority for any available reschedule interview slots. Interviews are generally 21 days from date of cancelled interview. Note this includes applicant-generated requests to re-schedule.) [If a notice of a new interview is not received after 30 days, a request to expedite the interview can be submitted to the local Asylum Office director.]
Interview cancelled by applicant	**Stops Clock**. Restarts on date of next interview, if the applicant appears. (Request of applicant can include: (a) request to reschedule prior to or during the interview due to illness or accident, unavailability of representative/interpreter or witness; (b) awaiting documentation; (c) interpreter incompetent; or (d) any other type of request made by the applicant.) [If a notice of a new interview is not received after 30 days, a request to expedite the interview can be submitted to the local Asylum Office director.]
Applicant fails to appear for interview	**Stops Clock**. Restarts only if applicant establishes exceptional circumstances for failure to appear or improper notice provided. If failure to appear is excused, Clock restarts on date of next interview. If referred to EOIR, subsequent clock action is controlled by EOIR. [Employment authorization may not be granted to an applicant who fails to appear for a scheduled interview or hearing, unless applicant demonstrates that failure to appears was the result of exceptional circumstances. 8 C.F.R. §§208(a)(4), 1208(a)(4).]
Applicant fails to appear for pick-up of decision, or otherwise causes delay.	**Stops Clock**. Subsequent Clock activities controlled by EOIR. Only the applicant can pick up asylum decision—no agent can pick up—unless applicant is under 14 years old. [Applicant-caused delays may include failure without good cause to follow requirements for fingerprint processing. 8 C.F.R. §§208.7(a)(2), 1208.7(a)(2).]
AO administratively closes I-589	**Stops Clock**. *Examples*: The case is already before EOIR, withdrawal, lack of prosecution, or bad address.
AO reopens I-589	**Restarts Clock on new interview day**, if the applicant appears. Generally does not affect post-reform cases.

* *Adapted from 180-Day Clock Matrix Draft (AILA InfoNet Doc. No. 01031905) and other sources. Special thanks to Dan Kesselbrenner of NLG's National Immigration Project.* ***Note:*** *Information reflects policy as characterized by EOIR or the Asylum Office; unless specifically noted, it is not necessarily statutory or regulatory law.*

Event	Impact on Asylum Clock
Asylum officer requests additional documents	**Clock is *not* tolled**. [This relates to short extensions of time prior to pick-up. In rare cases where document is critical to decision and would take longer than two weeks to obtain, applicant may choose to request further extension, which would stop Clock.]
Applicant requests additional time to submit documents	**Clock stops**. Restarts when taken from HOLD in RAPS. [This is considered to be an applicant request to re-schedule.]
AO approves asylum status	No impact. [Applicant may apply for an EAD upon receipt of the recommended approval notice or final grant.]
AO refers I-589 to IJ	No impact. Generally occurs by **Day 60** for reform cases at local AOs.
AO rejects I-589 (application is referred to IJ)	No impact.
AO denies asylum status (final denial)	**Clock stops**. This applies to in-status applicants. [If an applicant who is in status at the time of the interview falls out of status before the final decision is made, the case is referred, and the Clock does not stop.]
IJ determines, for case referred to EOIR, that applicant created delay*	**Adjudication clock stops** until next EOIR hearing.
EOIR denies asylum status (prior to Day 180)	**Clock stops**.

* The clock will stop until the next hearing if the immigration judge adjourns or reschedules the hearing for any of the following reasons:

- to permit respondent to seek representation
- to allow respondent or his or her attorney/representative time to prepare the case
- to allow respondent to file an asylum application with the immigration court
- to allow respondent to file another application for relief with the immigration court, other than asylum
- to permit DHS to adjudicate the respondent's application (*e.g.*, I-130 or I-140)
- to allow naturalization of respondent's petitioning relative
- because respondent or respondent's attorney/representative did not appear, unless reason for nonappearance was incorrect notice or DHS oversight
- at the request of respondent, or respondent's attorney/representative, for a reason not specifically included in the existing list
- to allow respondent time to supplement request for asylum.
- adjourned and respondent did not accept earliest asylum date available
- because respondent withdrew the asylum application
- because respondent requested an in-person hearing instead of televideo hearing
- to allow the immigration court to consolidate the case under lead family member's A-number
- to allow respondent time to complete paperwork for a biometrics check
- due to legitimate illness of respondent or respondent's attorney/representative
- due to legitimate illness of material witness or expert [although not mentioned in codes, this would presumably have to be respondent's witness or expert]
- because respondent requested a forensics evaluation
- at the joint request of both parties
- because respondent contests charges
- because respondent claims to be a U.S. citizen
- because respondent filed an appeal to BIA that divests immigration judge of jurisdiction over case

See OPPM 05-07 (June 16, 2005), Definitions and Use of Adjournment, Call-up and Case Identification Codes (*published on* AILA InfoNet at Doc. No. 05070660; also available at *www.usdoj.gov/eoir/efoia/ocij/oppm05/05-07.pdf*), which specifies that certain codes that immigration judges use will stop the asylum clock until the next hearing. For a detailed description of these codes, see AILF Practice Advisory, "Employment Authorization and Asylum: Strategies to Avoid Stopping the Asylum Clock" (Feb. 26, 2006), *published on* AILA InfoNet at Doc. No. 06030260; also available at: *www.ailf.org/lac/pa/lac_pa_022806.pdf.*

NOTES

8 C.F.R. §§208.7(a)(1) and 1208.7(a)(1) provide:

- Incomplete I-589 applications do not start the clock. Only the filing of a complete I-589 application will start the 180-day clock. (*See* 8 C.F.R. §§208.7(a)(2), 1208.7(a)(2)—first sentence.)
- I-589 applications denied within 150-day period by either the Asylum Office or the Immigration Court are NOT eligible to apply for EAD.
- If the I-589 is denied prior to 180-days the EAD is denied (e.g. I-765 submitted day 150 and the I-589 is denied by the IJ on day 179—the I-765 is denied.)
- Persons with recommended approvals may apply for EAD upon receipt of the notice of the recommended approval.

Attorney/Representative Schedule Conflicts. Asylum Office policy is to make all reasonable accommodations for applicants who are present at the Asylum Office but whose representative (and/or interpreter) is in another interview. While the burden is technically on the applicant to be ready to proceed with the scheduled interview, AOs will try to make all reasonable accommodations for this situation, provided the applicant has notified the AO of the situation. Where possible and when the AO has been notified by the representative, the AO will try to stagger interviews during the course of the day for representatives who have more than one client being interviewed on the same day.

However, the AO also cautions that representatives and interpreters should be realistic about the ability to represent more than one or two clients for asylum interviews on any given day.

APPENDIX E
USCIS ASYLUM OFFICES

USCIS REFUGEE, ASYLUM, AND INTERNATIONAL OPERATIONS DIRECTORATE

20 Massachusetts Ave. NW, Ste. 3300, Washington, DC 20529 • (202) 272-1663; (202) 272-1681 (fax)

Asylum Division
Joseph Langlois, *Director*

ARLINGTON, VA

1525 Wilson Blvd., Suite 300
Arlington, VA 22209
(703) 525-8141 x1308
(703) 812-8455 (fax)

Ann Palmer, *Director*

Jurisdiction: AL; DC; GA;* MD; NC; western PA†; SC; VA; WV

* except Atlanta expedited removal and stowaways cases, which are handled by NY

† Allegheny, Armstrong, Beaver, Bedford, Blair, Bradford, Butler, Cambria, Clarion, Clearfield, Crawford, Elk, Erie, Fayette, Forest, Greene, Indiana, Jefferson, Lawrence, McKean, Mercer, Somerset, Venango, Warren, Washington, and Westmoreland counties

Circuit rides to Atlanta (will now include applicants who reside in South Carolina, Georgia and Alabama).

CHICAGO

401 S. LaSalle St., 8th Floor
Chicago, IL 60605
(312) 353-9607; 9608; 9609; 9610
(312) 886-0204 (fax)

Kenneth Madsen, *Director*

Jurisdiction: ID; IL; IN; IO; KS; KY; MI; MN; MO; MT; NE; ND; OH; SD; WI.

Circuit rides to Cleveland, St. Paul, Kansas City, Omaha, Louisville, St. Louis, and Helena

All asylum and NACARA 203 applicants who reside in the Columbus, Toledo, Mansfield, Cincinnati, Dayton, Chilicothe, and Lima, Ohio, areas; and in Indiana zip code areas 47000 to 47099 will have their interviews conducted in the Chicago Asylum Office. All asylum and NACARA §203 applicants who reside in the Zanesville and Athens, Ohio, area will have their interviews conducted at the USCIS District Office in Cleveland. All asylum and NACARA §203 applicants who reside in Louisville and Cincinnati areas will have their interviews conducted in the Chicago Asylum Office.

69 Fed. Reg. 17437 (Apr. 2, 2004; effective May 3, 2004).

HOUSTON

16630 Imperial Valley Dr., Suite 200
Houston, TX 77060

Mailing Address:
P.O. Box 670626, Houston, TX 77267-0626
(281) 774-4830
(281) 774-5823 (fax)

Marie Hummert, *Director*

Jurisdiction: AR; CO; LA; MS; OK; NM; TN; TX; UT; WY

Circuit rides to Denver, El Paso, Salt Lake City, and Memphis

All asylum and NACARA 203 applicants who reside within the jurisdiction of the USCIS District Office in Harlingen, Texas, will have their asylum and/or NACARA 203 interviews conducted at the Houston Asylum Office. Also, all asylum and NACARA 203 applicants who reside within the jurisdiction of the USCIS District Office in New Orleans—except residents of Arkansas, Tennessee, and Mississippi (who currently interview in Memphis)—will have their interviews conducted at the Houston Asylum Office. The Houston Asylum Office will no longer circuit ride to Harlingen or New Orleans.

69 Fed. Reg. 17437 (Apr. 2, 2004; effective May 3, 2004).

LOS ANGELES

1585 S. Manchester Ave
Anaheim, CA 92802

Mailing Address:
P.O. Box 65015
Anaheim, CA 92815-5015
(714) 808-8206
(714) 635-8707 (fax)

George S. Mihalko, *Director*
David Radel, *Deputy Director*

Jurisdiction: AZ; southern CA*; GU; HI; southern NV†

* Los Angeles, Orange, Riverside, San Bernardino, San Luis Obispo, Santa Barbara, Ventura, Imperial, and San Diego counties

† within the jurisdiction of the Las Vegas suboffice

Circuit rides to Phoenix; Honolulu; and Agana, Guam.

MIAMI

77 SE Fifth Street, 3rd Floor
Miami, FL 33131
(305) 960-8600
(305) 530- 6071 (fax)

Erich J. Cauller, *Director*
Erin Fatica, Deputy *Director*

Jurisdiction: FL; PR; VI

Circuit rides to San Juan and Jacksonville.

NEW YORK (ROSEDALE)

One Cross Island Plaza, 3rd Fl.
Rosedale, NY 11422
(718) 723-5954 x1002
(718) 723-1121 (fax)

Patricia Jackson, *Director*
Mick Dedvukaj, *Deputy Director*

Jurisdiction: NY (excluding counties under jurisdiction of Newark Office)

Circuit rides: No circuit rides.

NEWARK

1200 Wall Street West, 4th Floor
Lyndhurst, NJ 07071
(201) 531-0555
(201) 531-1877 (fax)

Susan Raufer, *Director*
Astor Zeleke, *Deputy Director*

Jurisdiction: CT; DE; ME; MA; NH; NJ; portions of NY*; eastern/central PA†; RI; VT

* Albany, Allegany, Bronx, Broome, Cattaraugus, Cayuga, Chautauqua, Chemung, Chenango, Clinton, Columbia, Cortland, Delaware, Erie, Essex, Franklin, Fulton, Genesee, Greene, Hamilton, Herkimer, Jefferson, Lewis, Livingston, Madison, Monroe, Montgomery, New York (Manhattan), Niagara, Oneida, Onondaga, Ontario, Orleans, Oswego, Otsego, Rensselaer, Saint Lawrence, Saratoga, Schenectady, Schoharie, Schuyler, Seneca, Steuben, Tioga, Tompkins, Warren, Washington, Wayne, Wyoming, and Yates counties

† Adams, Berks, Bucks, Cameron, Carbon, Centre, Chester, Clinton, Columbia, Cumberland, Dauphin, Delaware, Franklin, Fulton, Huntingdon, Juniata, Lackawanna, Lancaster, Lebanon, Lehigh, Luzerne, Lycoming, Mifflin, Monroe, Montgomery, Montour, Northampton, Northumberland, Perry, Philadelphia, Pike, Potter, Schuylkill, Snyder, Sullivan, Susquehanna, Tioga, Union, Wayne, Wyoming, and York counties

Circuit rides to Portland, ME; Buffalo; St. Albans, VT; and Boston

SAN FRANCISCO

75 Hawthorne St., #303 S
San Francisco, CA 94105

Mailing Address:
PO Box 77530
San Francisco, CA 94107
(415) 293-1234
(415) 293-1234 (fax)

Emilia Bardini, *Director*
Calton Yue, *Deputy Director*

Jurisdiction: AK; northern CA*; northern NV†; OR; WA

* Alameda, Alpine, Amador, Butte, Calaveras, Colusa, Contra Costa, Del Norte, El Dorado, Fresno, Glenn, Humboldt, Inyo, Kern, Kings, Lake, Lassen, Madera, Marin, Mariposa, Mendocino, Merced, Modoc, Mono, Monterey, Napa, Nevada, Placer, Plumas, Sacramento, San Benito, San Francisco, San Joaquin, San Mateo, Santa Clara, Santa Cruz, Shasta, Sierra, Siskiyou, Solano, Sonoma, Stanislaus, Sutter, Tehama, Trinity, Tulare, Tuolumne, Yolo, and Yuba counties

† Carson City, Churchill, Douglas, Elko, Eureka, Humboldt, Lander, Lyon, Mineral, Pershing, Storey, Wash, White Pine

Circuit rides to Reno; Seattle; Portland, OR; and Anchorage

APPENDIX F

IMMIGRATION ELIGIBILITY FOR FEDERAL PUBLIC BENEFITS*

PROGRAM	"QUALIFIED" IMMIGRANTS WHO ENTERED THE U.S. BEFORE AUG. 22, 1996	"QUALIFIED" IMMIGRANTS WHO ENTERED THE U.S. ON OR AFTER AUG. 22, 1996	"NOT QUALIFIED" IMMIGRANTS
Supplemental Security Income (SSI)	*Eligible only if:* ▪ Receiving SSI (or application pending) on Aug. 22, 1996 ▪ Qualify as disabled and were lawfully residing in the U.S. on Aug. 22, 19961 ▪ Lawful permanent resident with credit for 40 quarters of work[1,2] ▪ Were granted refugee or asylum status or withholding of deportation/removal, Cuban/Haitian entrant, or Amerasian immigrant, but only during first 7 years after getting status ▪ Veteran, active duty military; spouse, unremarried surviving spouse, or child[1] ▪ Certain American Indians born abroad	*Eligible only if:* ▪ Lawful permanent resident with credit for 40 quarters of work[2] (but must wait until 5 years after entry before applying) ▪ Were granted refugee or asylum status or withholding of deportation/removal, Cuban/Haitian entrant, or Amerasian immigrant, but only during first 7 years after getting status ▪ Veteran, active duty military; spouse, unremarried surviving spouse, or child[1] ▪ Certain American Indians born abroad	*Eligible only if:* ▪ Receiving SSI (or application pending) on Aug. 22, 1996 ▪ Certain American Indians born abroad ▪ Victims of trafficking and their derivative beneficiaries
Food Stamps[3]	*Eligible only if:* ▪ Are under age 183 ▪ Were granted refugee or asylum status or withholding of deportation/removal, Cuban/Haitian entrant, or Amerasian immigrant ▪ Have been in "qualified" immigrant status for 5 years[1] ▪ Are receiving disability-related assistance[1,4] ▪ Lawful permanent resident with credit for 40 quarters of work ▪ Were 65 years or older and were lawfully residing in the U.S. on Aug. 22, 1996[1] ▪ Veteran, active duty military; spouse, unremarried surviving spouse, or child[1] ▪ Member of Hmong or Laotian tribe during the Vietnam era, when tribe militarily assisted the U.S.; spouse, surviving spouse, or child of tribe member[1] ▪ Certain American Indians born abroad	*Eligible only if:* ▪ Are under age 183 ▪ Were granted refugee or asylum status or withholding of deportation/removal, Cuban/Haitian entrant, or Amerasian immigrant ▪ Have been in "qualified" immigrant status for 5 years[1] ▪ Are receiving disability-related assistance[1,4] ▪ Lawful permanent resident with credit for 40 quarters of work ▪ Veteran, active duty military; spouse, unremarried surviving spouse, or child[1] ▪ Member of Hmong or Laotian tribe during the Vietnam era, when the tribe militarily assisted the U.S.; spouse, surviving spouse, or child of tribe member[1] ▪ Certain American Indians born abroad	*Eligible only if:* ▪ Member of Hmong or Laotian tribe during the Vietnam era, when the tribe militarily assisted the U.S., spouse, surviving spouse or child of tribe member, who is lawfully present in the U.S. ▪ Certain American Indians born abroad ▪ Victims of trafficking and their derivative beneficiaries
Temporary Assistance for Needy Families (TANF)	Eligible[1]	*Eligible only if:* ▪ Were granted refugee or asylum status or withholding of deportation/removal, Cuban/Haitian entrant, or Amerasian immigrant[5] ▪ Veteran, active duty military; spouse, unremarried surviving spouse, or child[1] ▪ Have been in "qualified" immigrant status for 5 years or more[1,5]	*Eligible only if:* ▪ Victims of trafficking and their derivative beneficiaries

* This table provides an overview of immigrant eligibility for the major federal public assistance programs. Some states provide assistance to immigrants who are not eligible for federally funded services.

PROGRAM	"QUALIFIED" IMMIGRANTS WHO ENTERED THE U.S. BEFORE AUG. 22, 1996	"QUALIFIED" IMMIGRANTS WHO ENTERED THE U.S. ON OR AFTER AUG. 22, 1996	"NOT QUALIFIED" IMMIGRANTS
Emergency Medicaid (includes labor and delivery)	Eligible	Eligible	Eligible
Full-Scope Medicaid	Eligible[6]	*Eligible only if:* ▪ Were granted refugee or asylum status or withholding of deportation/removal, Cuban/Haitian entrant, or Amerasian immigrant[7] ▪ Veteran, active duty military; spouse, unremarried surviving spouse, or child[1] ▪ Have been in "qualified" immigrant status for 5 years or more[1,7]	*Eligible only if:* ▪ Were receiving SSI on Aug. 22, 1996 (in states that link Medicaid to SSI eligibility) ▪ Certain American Indians born abroad ▪ Victims of trafficking and their derivative beneficiaries
State Children's Health Insurance Program (SCHIP)[8]	Eligible	*Eligible only if:* ▪ Were granted refugee or asylum status or withholding of deportation/removal, Cuban/Haitian entrant, or Amerasian immigrant ▪ Veteran, active duty military; spouse, unremarried surviving spouse, or child[1] ▪ Have been in "qualified" immigrant status for 5 years or more[1]	*Eligible only if:* ▪ Victims of trafficking and their derivative beneficiaries
Medicare "Premium Free" Part A (hospitalization) (eligibility based on work history)	Eligible	Eligible	*Eligible only if:* ▪ Lawfully present, and eligibility for assistance is based on authorized employment
Premium "Buy-in" Medicare	*Eligible only if:* ▪ Lawful permanent resident who has resided continuously in the U.S. for at least 5 years	*Eligible only if:* ▪ Lawful permanent resident who has resided continuously in the U.S. for at least 5 years	Not Eligible
HUD Public Housing and Section 8 Programs	*Eligible except:* ▪ Certain Cuban/Haitian entrants and "qualified" abused spouses and children Note: If at least one member of the household is eligible based on immigration status, the family may reside in the housing, but the subsidy will be pro-rated.	*Eligible except:* ▪ Certain Cuban/Haitian entrants and "qualified" abused spouses and children Note: If at least one member of the household is eligible based on immigration status, the family may reside in the housing, but the subsidy will be pro-rated.	*Eligible only if:* ▪ Temporary resident under IRCA general amnesty, or paroled into the U.S. for less than 1 year ▪ Victims of trafficking and their derivative beneficiaries ▪ Citizens of Micronesia, the Marshall Islands, and Palau Note: For other immigrants, eligibility may depend on the date the family began receiving housing assistance, the immigration status of other household members, and the household composition. Also note: If at least one member of the household is eligible based on immigration status, the family may reside in the housing, but the subsidy will be pro-rated.
Title XX Block Grants	Eligible	Eligible	Eligible only if: ▪ Victims of trafficking and their derivative beneficiaries ▪ Program or service funded by the block grant is exempt from the welfare law's restrictions
Social Security	Eligible[9]	Eligible[9]	*Eligible only if:* ▪ Lawfully present[9] ▪ Were receiving assistance based on an application filed before Dec. 1, 1996 ▪ Eligibility required by certain international agreements

PROGRAM	"QUALIFIED" IMMIGRANTS WHO ENTERED THE U.S. BEFORE AUG. 22, 1996	"QUALIFIED" IMMIGRANTS WHO ENTERED THE U.S. ON OR AFTER AUG. 22, 1996	"NOT QUALIFIED" IMMIGRANTS
Other Federal Public Benefits Subject to welfare law's restrictions	Eligible	Eligible	*Eligible only if:* ▪ Victims of trafficking and their derivative beneficiaries
Benefits Exempt from welfare law's restrictions	Eligible	Eligible	Eligible

KEY TERMS USED IN TABLE

"Qualified" immigrants are: (1) lawful permanent residents (LPRs); (2) refugees, asylees, persons granted withholding of deportation/removal, conditional entry (in effect prior to Apr. 1, 1980), or paroled into the U.S. for at least one year; (3) Cuban/Haitian entrants; and (4) battered spouses and children with a pending or approved (a) self-petition for an immigrant visa, or (b) immigrant visa filed for a spouse or child by a U.S. citizen or LPR, or (c) application for cancellation of removal/suspension of deportation, whose need for benefits has a substantial connection to the battery or cruelty. Parent/child of such battered child/spouse are also "qualified." Victims of trafficking (who are not included in the "qualified" immigrant definition) and their derivative beneficiaries are eligible for benefits funded or administered by federal agencies, without regard to their immigration status.

"Not qualified" immigrants include all noncitizens who do not fall under the "qualified" immigrant categories.

ENDNOTES

[1] Eligibility may be affected by deeming: a sponsor's income/resources may be added to the immigrant's in determining eligibility. Exemptions from deeming may apply.

[2] LPRs are eligible if they have worked 40 qualifying quarters in the U.S. Immigrants also get credit toward their 40 quarters for work performed (1) by parents when the immigrant was under 18; and (2) by spouse during the marriage (unless the marriage ended in divorce or annulment). No credit is given for a quarter worked after Dec. 31, 1996, if a federal means-tested public benefit (SSI, food stamps, TANF, Medicaid, or SCHIP) was received in that quarter.

[3] Children are not subject to sponsor deeming in the food stamp program.

[4] Disability-related benefits include SSI, Social Security disability, state disability or retirement pension, railroad retirement disability, veteran's disability, disability-based Medicaid, and disability-related General Assistance if the disability determination uses criteria as stringent as those used by federal SSI.

[5] In Indiana, Mississippi, Ohio, South Carolina, and Texas, TANF is available only to immigrants who entered the U.S. on or after Aug. 22, 1996, who are: (1) LPRs credited with 40 quarters of work; (2) veterans, active duty military (and their spouse, unremarried surviving spouse, or child); or (3) refugees, asylees, persons granted withholding of deportation/removal, Cuban/Haitian entrants, and Amerasian immigrants during the five years after obtaining this status. Indiana provides TANF to "refugees" listed in (3) regardless of the date they obtained that status. Mississippi does not address eligibility for Cuban/Haitian entrants or Amerasian immigrants.

[6] In Wyoming, only LPRs with 40 quarters of work credit, abused immigrants, parolees, veterans, active duty military (and their spouse, unremarried surviving spouse, or child), refugees, asylees, persons granted withholding of deportation/removal, Cuban/Haitian entrants, and Amerasian immigrants who entered the U.S. prior to Aug. 22, 1996, are eligible for full-scope Medicaid.

[7] In Alabama, Mississippi, North Dakota, Ohio, Texas, Virginia, and Wyoming, full-scope Medicaid is available only to immigrants who entered the U.S. on or after Aug. 22, 1996, who are: (1) LPRs credited with 40 quarters of work; (2) veterans, active duty military (and their spouse, unremarried surviving spouse, or child); or (3) refugees, asylees, persons granted withholding of deportation/removal, Cuban/Haitian entrants, and Amerasian immigrants during the seven years after obtaining this status. Wyoming provides full-scope Medicaid to "qualified" abused immigrants and persons paroled into the U.S., regardless of their date of entry. In Texas, Amerasian immigrants are eligible only during the five years after obtaining this status; Mississippi, and North Dakota do not address eligibility for Cuban/Haitian entrants or Amerasian immigrants.

[8] In states that opt to cover fetuses, SCHIP provides prenatal care regardless of the mother's immigration status. The scope of coverage depends in part on how the option is implemented.

[9] For applications based on Social Security numbers issued on or after Jan. 1, 2004: must have been assigned a Social Security number that was, at the time assigned or at any later time, valid for work purposes. Alternatively, must have been admitted to the U.S. temporarily for business or as a crewman when the relevant work quarters were earned.

APPENDIX G

U.S. TAX TREATIES IN FORCE AS OF JANUARY 1, 2008

Country	Income	Estate	Gift	GST*	TIEA*
Antigua & Barbuda					x
Aruba					x
Armenia[2]	x				
Australia[1]	x	x	x		
Austria	x	x	x	x	
Azerbaijan[2]	x				
Bahamas					x
Barbados	x				x
Belarus[2]	x				
Belgium	x				
Bermuda	x				x
British Virgin Islands					x
Canada	x				
Cayman Islands					x
China	x				
Costa Rica					x
Cyprus	x				
Czech Republic	x				
Denmark	x	x	x	x	
Dominica					x
Dominican Republic					x
Egypt	x				
Estonia	x				
Finland	x	x			
France	x	x	x	x	
Georgia[2]	x				
Germany	x	x	x	x	
Greece	x	x			
Grenada					x
Guernsey					x
Guyana					x
Honduras					x
Hungary	x				
Iceland	x				
India	x				
Indonesia	x				
Ireland	x	x			
Isle of Man					x
Israel	x				
Italy	x	x			
Jamaica	x				x
Japan	x	x	x		
Jersey	x				x
Kazakhstan	x				
Korea	x				
Kyrgyzstan[2]	x				
Latvia	x				
Lithuania	x				
Luxembourg	x				
Marshall Islands					x
Mexico	x				x
Moldova[2]	x				
Morocco	x				
Netherlands	x	x			
Netherlands Antilles[3]	x				x
New Zealand	x				
Norway	x	x			
Pakistan	x				
Peru					x
Philippines	x				
Poland	x				
Portugal	x				
Romania	x				
Russia	x				
St. Lucia					x
Slovak Republic	x				
Slovenia	x				
South Africa	x	x			
Spain	x				
Sri Lanka	x				
Sweden	x	x			
Switzerland	x	x			
Tajikistan[2]	x				
Thailand	x				
Trinidad & Tobago	x				x
Tunisia	x				
Turkey	x				
Turkmenistan[2]	x				
Ukraine	x				
United Kingdom	x	x	x	x	
Uzbekistan[2]	x				
Venezuela	x				

* GST = Generation Skipping Transfer Tax;
TIEA = Tax & Information Exchange Agreement

Courtesy of Mr. Leslie A. Share, of Packman Neuwahl & Rosenberg, Miami.

1 Only Australia has a separate gift tax treaty.

2 The former US-USSR income tax treaty apparently applies to all Commonwealth of Independent States member countries on an interim basis until new individual treaties replace it.

3 This treaty and a related treaty with Aruba were generally terminated in two separate steps effective as of Jan. 1, 1988, and Dec. 30, 1996.

APPENDIX H

RESEARCH RESOURCES

GOVERNMENT AGENCIES, NGOs, AND OTHER SITES

GENERAL LEGAL RESEARCH SITES

All Law: *www.alllaw.com*
American Law Sources: *www.lawsource.com/also*
CataLaw: *www.catalaw.com*
Cornell University's Legal Information Institute (LII): *www.law.cornell.edu*
FedLaw: *www.thecre.com/fedlaw*
FindLaw: *www.findlaw.com*
Global Legal Information Network: *www.glin.gov*
Hieros Gamos: *www.hg.org*
IndexMaster: *www.indexmaster.com*
Internet Legal Research Group: *www.ilrg.com*
Law.com: *www.law.com*
LawInfo.com: *www.lawinfo.com*
LawResearch: *www.lawresearch.com*
Meta-Index for Legal Research: *http://gsulaw.gsu.edu/metaindex*
Prarienet—Statutes & Legislation: *www.prairienet.org/~scruffy/f.htm*
University of Michigan Law School Refugee Case Law Site: *www.refugeecaselaw.org*
Virtual Law Library: *http://vlib.org/Law*
WashLaw Legal Research on the Web: *www.washlaw.edu*
WebLaw1: *www.Weblaw1.com*

STATUTES & CODES

Public & Private Laws (GPO) [from 104th Cong. (1995) to date]: *www.gpoaccess.gov/plaws*
U.S. Code: *www.law.cornell.edu/uscode* | *http://uscode.house.gov* | *www.gpoaccess.gov/uscode*
Federal Register: *www.gpoaccess.gov/fr*
CFR: *http://ecfr.gpoaccess.gov* | *www.gpoaccess.gov/cfr*

FEDERAL COURTS & JUDICIAL INFORMATION

[for Administrative Courts, see "Selected Federal Government Sites" (p.1368), infra]

Generally (including links to alternative sites): *www.law.cornell.edu/federal/opinions.html* | *http://www.law.emory.edu/law-library/research/federal-courts-finder.html*
U.S. Supreme Court: *www.supremecourtus.gov* | *http://supct.law.cornell.edu/supct* | *www.findlaw.com/casecode/supreme.html* | *www.oyez.org*
U.S. Courts of Appeals & District Courts: *www.uscourts.gov/links.html*
Administrative Office of the U.S. Courts: *www.uscourts.gov/adminoff.html*
Federal District Court Civil Trials Database: *http://teddy.law.cornell.edu:8090/questtr2.htm*
Federal Rules: *www.law.cornell.edu/rules*

FEDERAL LEGISLATIVE RESEARCH

Committee Reports and Materials: *www.gpoaccess.gov/serialset/creports* | *www.gpoaccess.gov/congress* | *http://thomas.loc.gov/cp110/cp110query.html*
Congressional Documents: *www.gpoaccess.gov/serialset/cdocuments*
Congressional Hearings: *www.gpoaccess.gov/chearings*
Congressional Record: *www.gpoaccess.gov/cri* | *http://thomas.loc.gov/home/r110query.html*
Government Accountability Office (GAO): *www.gao.gov*
GPO Access: *www.gpoaccess.gov/multidb.html*
History of Bills: *www.gpoaccess.gov/hob*
House of Representatives: *www.house.gov*
  Members of the House: *www.house.gov/house/MemberWWW.html*
  Committee on the Judiciary: *http://judiciary.house.gov*
Internet Resources: *http://thomas.loc.gov/links*
Senate: *www.senate.gov*
  Members of the Senate: *www.senate.gov/general/contact_information/senators_cfm.cfm*
  Committee on the Judiciary: *www.judiciary.senate.gov*
  Subcommittee on Immigration, Border Security, and Citizenship: *www.judiciary.senate.gov/subcommittees/110/immigration110.cfm*
Thomas (Library of Congress): *http://thomas.loc.gov*

SELECTED FEDERAL GOVERNMENT SITES

Department of Justice (DOJ)

DOJ Home Page Home Page: *www.usdoj.gov*
Office of the Attorney General (OAG): *www.usdoj.gov/ag*
Office of Special Counsel for Immigration-Related Unfair Employment Practices (OSC): *www.usdoj.gov/crt/osc*

EOIR (Executive Office for Immigration Review) (*www.usdoj.gov/eoir*)
BIA / AG precedent decisions: *www.usdoj.gov/eoir/vll/intdec/lib_indecitnet.html*
Forms: *www.usdoj.gov/eoir/formspage.htm*
Freedom of Information Act (FOIA): *www.usdoj.gov/eoir/efoia/foiainfo.htm*
Immigration Court Practice Manual: *www.usdoj.gov/eoir/vll/OCIJPracManual/ocij_page1.htm*
OCAHO (including index and link to decisions): *www.usdoj.gov/eoir/OcahoMain/ocahosibpage.htm*
Operating Policies & Procedures Memoranda (OPPMs): *www.usdoj.gov/eoir/efoia/ocij/OPPMLG2.htm*
Virtual Law Library: *www.usdoj.gov/eoir/vll/libindex.html*

Department of State (DOS)

Home Page: *www.state.gov*
Bureau of Consular Affairs: *http://travel.state.gov*
Bureau of Democracy, Human Rights, & Labor: *www.state.gov/g/drl*
Country Reports on Human Rights Practices: *http://www.state.gov/g/drl/rls/hrrpt*
Bureau of Educational & Cultural Affairs: *http://exchanges.state.gov*
Bureau of Population, Refugees, and Migration: *www.state.gov/g/prm*
Consulates, Embassies, and Diplomatic Missions (U.S.): *http://usembassy.state.gov*
Diversity Visa Program Information: *http://travel.state.gov/visa/immigrants_types_diversity.html*
Registration: *http://dvlottery.state.gov* (registration)
Exchange Visitor (J Visa) Program: *http://exchanges.state.gov/education/jexchanges*
Skills List: *http://exchanges.state.gov/education/jexchanges/participation/skills_list.pdf*
Foreign Affairs Manual: *www.state.gov/m/a/dir/regs*
Foreign Terrorist Organization list : *www.state.gov/s/ct/rls/fs/37191.htm*
Forms: *www.state.gov/m/a/dir/forms* | *https://evisaforms.state.gov*
International Information Programs: *http://usinfo.state.gov www.america.gov*
J Visa Waiver Status: *http://travel.state.gov/visa/temp/info/info_1296.html*
Visa Appointment Reservation System: *www.nvars.com*
Visa Bulletin: *http://travel.state.gov/visa/frvi/bulletin/bulletin_1360.html*
Visa Policy and Procedures: *www.unitedstatesvisas.gov*
Visa Reciprocity Tables: *www.travel.state.gov/visa/reciprocity*

Department of Homeland Security (DHS)

Home Pages: *www.dhs.gov* | *www.uscis.gov* | *www.ice.gov* | *www.cbp.gov*
Office of Immigration Statistics: *www.dhs.gov/ximgtn/statistics*
Traveler Redress Inquiry Program: *www.dhs.gov/trip*
US-VISIT: *www.dhs.gov/usvisit*

USICS
Asylum Information: *www.uscis.gov/asylum*
Case Status Search: *https://egov.uscis.gov/cris/jsps*
Civil Surgeons: *www.uscis.gov/civilsurgeons* | *www.cdc.gov/ncidod/dq/technica.htm*
E-filing: *www.uscis.gov/e-filing* (general information) | *https://efiling.uscis.dhs.gov/efile* (log-in)
Forms: *www.uscis.gov/forms*
INFOPASS: *http://infopass.uscis.gov*
Premium Processing Information: *www.uscis.gov/premiumprocessing*

ICE
Detention Operations Manual: *www.ice.gov/partners/dro/opsmanual*
Family Residential Standards: *www.ice.gov/pi/familyresidential*
Student and Exchange Visitor Information System (SEVIS): *www.ice.gov/sevis*

Department of Labor (DOL)

Home Page: *www.dol.gov*
Employment Standards Administration: *www.dol.gov/esa*

Office of Administrative Law Judges (*www.oalj.dol.gov*)
Dictionary of Occupational Titles (DOT): *www.oalj.dol.gov/libdot.htm*
Law library immigration collection, including decisions: *www.oalj.dol.gov/LIBINA.HTM*

Employment & Training Administration (*www.doleta.gov*)
Analyst Resource Center: *www.almisdb.org*
Backlog Public Disclosure System: *http://pds.pbls.doleta.gov*
Foreign Labor Certification Data Center:
O*NET: *www.onetcenter.org* | *www.doleta.gov/programs/onet*
Office of Foreign Labor Certification: *www.foreignlaborcert.doleta.gov*

Bureau of Labor Statistics (*http://stats.bls.gov*)
Occupational Employment Statistics: *www.bls.gov/oes*
Occupational Outlook Handbook: *www.bls.gov/oco*
Standard Occupational Classification System: *www.bls.gov/soc*

Department of Commerce / Census Bureau

Bureau of Economic Analysis: *www.bea.gov*
Economic Development Administration: *www.eda.gov*
FedWorld Information Network: *www.fedworld.gov*
Metropolitan Statistical Areas: *www.census.gov/population/www/estimates/metroarea.html*
NAICS: *www.census.gov/epcd/www/naics.html*
STAT-USA: *www.stat-usa.gov*

Department of Health & Human Services (HHS)

Office of Refugee Resettlement: *www.acf.hhs.gov/programs/orr*
Poverty Guidelines: *http://aspe.hhs.gov/poverty/index.shtml*

White House

White House: *www.whitehouse.gov*
Executive Orders: *www.whitehouse.gov/news/orders*
Office of Management and Budget: *www.whitehouse.gov/omb*
Presidential Documents, Weekly: *www.gpoaccess.gov/wcomp*
Statements of Administration Policy: *www.whitehouse.gov/omb/legislative/sap*

Other Departments & Agencies

CIA's World Factbook: *https://www.cia.gov/library/publications/the-world-factbook*
Office of Migrant Education (Dep't of Education): *www.ed.gov/about/offices/list/oese/ome/aboutus.html*
Social Security Administration, Immigration Issues: *www.ssa.gov/immigration*
U.S. Sentencing Commission: *www.ussc.gov*

PRIVATE WAGE & OCCUPATIONAL SURVEYS AND INFORMATION

Abbot, Langer & Associates: *www.abbott-langer.com*
Bay Area Compensation Association: *www.baca-online.org*
College & University Professional Association for Human Resources: *www.cupahr.org*
DataMasters (Computer Industry): *www.datamasters.com*
Economic Research Institute: *www.erieri.com*
HomeFair.Com International Salary Calculator: *www.homefair.com/find_a_place/calculators/salarycalc*
JobStar Central: *http://jobsmart.org/tools/salary/sal-prof.htm*
KForce Professional Staffing Salary Wizard: *www.kforce.com/SiteMap.aspx*
Labor Market Information Training Institute: *www.lmi-net.org*
Occupation profiles, America's Career InfoNet: *www.acinet.org/acinet/occ_rep.asp*
SalariesReview.com: *www.salariesreview.com*
Watson Wyatt Worldwise: *www.watsonwyatt.com*

STATE & LOCAL GOVERNMENT SITES & RESOURCES

See also "State-Specific Sites"(p.1375), infra

Generally [including links]: *www.loc.gov/rr/news/stategov/stategov.html* | *www.law.cornell.edu/states/listing.htm* | *www.findlaw.com/11stategov*
Council of State Governments: *www.csg.org*
Courts.net: *www.courts.net*
International City/County Management Association: *www.icma.org/main/sc.asp?t=0*
Local Government Institute: *www.lgi.org/local_govt__institute.htm*
Model Codes: *www.law.upenn.edu/library/ulc/ulc.htm* | *www.law.cornell.edu/statutes.html* | *www.lawsource.com/also/usa.cgi?usm*
Municipal Codes Online: *www.municode.com* | *www.generalcode.com/webcode2.html*
National Association of Counties: *www.naco.org*
National Association of State Budget Officers: *www.nasbo.org*
National Center for State Courts: *www.ncsconline.org*
National Conference of State Legislators: *www.ncsl.org*
National Governors Association: *www.nga.org*
National League of Cities: *www.nlc.org*
State and Local Government on the Net: *www.statelocalgov.net*
U.S. Conference of Mayors: *www.usmayors.org*
Uniform Codes: *www.law.upenn.edu/library/ulc/ulc.htm* | *www.law.cornell.edu/statutes.ht*

INTERNATIONAL SITES & RESOURCES

Foreign Consulates & Embassies

Embassies: *www.embassy.org*
Foreign Consulates: *www.infoplease.com/ipa/a0004582.html*

International Organizations

Bank for International Settlements: *www.bis.org*
Council of Europe: *www.coe.int/DefaultEN.asp*
Electronic Frontier Foundation (EFF): *www.eff.org*
European Union (EU): *http://europa.eu/index_en.htm*
Inter-American Development Bank (IADB): *www.iadb.org*
International Committee of the Red Cross: *www.icrc.org*
Coalition for the International Criminal Court: *www.iccnow.org*
International Labour Organization (ILO): *www.ilo.org*
International Maritime Organization (IMO): *www.imo.org*
International Monetary Fund (IMF): *www.imf.org*
North Atlantic Treaty Organization (NATO): *www.nato.int*
Organization of American States (OAS): *www.oas.org*
Organization for Economic Co-operation & Development (OECD): *www.oecd.org*
Pan-American Health Organization (PAHO): *www.paho.org*
World Bank (IBRD/IDA): *www.worldbank.org*
World Health Organization (WHO): *www.who.int*
World Intellectual Property Organization (WIPO): *www.wipo.int*

United Nations (*www.un.org*)

See also substantive headings, below

Human Rights, generally: *www.un.org/rights*
Humanitarian Affairs: *www.un.org/ha*
International Court of Justice: *www.icj-cij.org*
International Law: *www.un.org/law*
Official Document System: *http://documents.un.org*
U.N. Development Programme (UNDP): *www.undp.org*
U.N. Educational, Scientific & Cultural Organization (UNESCO): *www.unesco.org*

IMMIGRATION POLICY, ASYLUM & REFUGEE RIGHTS, AND RELATED SITES

See also "Region-Specific Sites" (p.1373) and "Theme-Specific Sites" (p.1374), infra

ACLU Immigrant Rights: *www.aclu.org/immigrants*
American Immigration Law Foundation: *www.ailf.org*
Americans for Better Borders (U.S. Chamber of Commerce): *www.uschamber.org/coalitions/abb*
Asylumlaw.org: *www.asylumlaw.org*
Center for Immigration Studies (CIS) [Restrictionists]: *www.cis.org*
Center for International & European Law on Immigration & Asylum: *http://migration.uni-konstanz.de*
Center for Migration Studies of New York: *www.cmsny.org*
Central American Resource Center (DC): *www.carecendc.org*
Central American Resource Center (Los Angeles): *www.carecen-la.org*
Country of Origin Research (Immig. & Refugee Bd. of Canada): *www.irb-cisr.gc.ca/en/research/origin_e.htm*
Expedited Removal Study (U.C. Hastings College of Law): *http://w3.uchastings.edu/ers*
Federation for American Immigration Reform (FAIR) [Restrictionists]: *www.fairus.org*
Forced Migration Projects: *www.forcedmigration.org*
Georgetown U. Asylum Research: *www.ll.georgetown.edu/intl/guides/CALSAsylumLawResearchGuide.cfm*
Immigrant Legal Resource Center: *www.ilrc.org*
Immigration Policy Center (AILF): *www.immigrationpolicy.org*
International Center for Migration, Ethnicity & Citizenship (ICMEC): *www.newschool.edu/icmec*
International Organization for Migration: *www.iom.int*
Massachusetts Immigrant Health Access Coalition: *http://hcfa.org*
Massachusetts Immigrant and Refugee Advocacy Coalition: *www.miracoalition.org*
Migration Policy Group (MPG): *www.migpolgroup.com*
Migration Policy Institute (MPI) Data Hub: *www.migrationinformation.org/datahub*
N.Y. State Defenders Association Criminal Defense Immigration Project: *www.nysda.org/idp*
National Immigration Forum: *www.immigrationforum.org*
National Immigration Project (National Lawyer's Guild): *www.NationalImmigrationProject.org*
National Network for Immigrant & Refugee Rights: *www.nnirr.org*
Political Asylum Research and Documentation Service: *www.refugeelaw.org*
Refugee Caselaw Site, U. Michigan Law School (comparative asylum law): *www.refugeecaselaw.org*
Refugee Studies Centre: *www.rsc.ox.ac.uk*
Refugees International: *www.refintl.org*
Transactional Records Access Clearinghouse—Immigration: *http://trac.syr.edu/immigration*
U.S. Committee for Refugees and Immigrants: *www.refugees.org*
U.N. High Commission for Refugees (UNHCR): *www.unhcr.org*
  RefWorld: *www.refworld.org*
  Universal Declaration of Human Rights: *www.unhchr.ch/udhr*
Univ. of Calif. Migration Dialogue: *http://migration.ucdavis.edu*
Univ. of Minn. Asylum and Refugee resources: *www1.umn.edu/humanrts/center/asylum/refugee_index.html*

GENERAL HUMAN RIGHTS, EQUAL JUSTICE, TORTURE VICTIM, AND RELATED SITES

See also "Region-Specific Sites" (p.1373) and "Theme-Specific Sites" (p.1374), infra

Alliance for Justice: *www.afj.org*
American Civil Liberties Union: *www.aclu.org*
American Friends Service Committee: *www.afsc.org*
Americans for Legal Reform: *www.halt.org*
Amnesty International: *www.amnesty.org* | *www.amnestyusa.org*
Center for Human Rights & Constitutional Law: *www.centerforhumanrights.org*
Center for Victims of Torture (CVT): *www.cvt.org*
Center for World Indigenous Studies (CWIS)—Fourth World Documentation Project: *www.cwis.org*
Citizens Commission on Civil Rights: *www.cccr.org*
Columbia University Center for the Study of Human Rights: *http://hrcolumbia.org*
Come Back Alive: *http://comebackalive.com*
Cultural Survival: *www.cs.org*
Derechos Human Rights: *www.derechos.org*
Detained Torture Survivor Legal Support Network (LIRS): *www.lirs.org/What/programs/torturesurvivor.htm*
Detention Watch Network: *www.detentionwatchnetwork.org*
DIANA—International Human Rights Database: *www.yale.edu/lawweb/avalon/diana*
Equal Rights Advocates: *www.equalrights.org*

Freedom House: *www.freedomhouse.org*
Global Rights Partners for Justice: *www.globalrights.org*
Human rights documents, Kresge Law Library, U. Notre Dame: *www.nd.edu/~lawlib/find/human_rights.html*
Human Rights First (formerly, Lawyers Committee for Human Rights): *www.humanrightsfirst.org*
Human Rights Interactive Network: *www.webcom.com/hrin*
Human Rights Internet: *www.hri.ca*
Human Rights Resource Center: *www.hrusa.org*
Human Rights Search Engine: *www.hurisearch.org*
Human Rights Watch: *www.hrw.org*
Human Rights Web: *www.hrWeb.org*
INCORE, Conflict Data Service: *www.incore.ulst.ac.uk/services/cds/countries*
Institute for Civil Justice—RAND: *www.rand.org/icj*
Institute for Justice: *www.instituteforjustice.org*
International Centre for Human Rights & Democratic Development: *www.ichrdd.ca*
International Commission of Jurists: *www.icj.org*
International League for Human Rights: *www.ilhr.org*
International Rescue Committee: *www.theirc.org*
Justice at Stake Campaign: *www.faircourts.org*
Kovler Center for the Treatment of Survivors of Torture: *www.heartlandalliance.org/kovler*
Lawyers Committee for Civil Rights: *www.lawyerscommittee.org*
Leadership Conference on Civil Rights: *www.civilrights.org*
Minnesota Advocates for Human Rights: *www.mnadvocates.org*
Minority Rights Group, International: *www.minorityrights.org*
National Equal Justice Library: *https://proxy.wcl.american.edu/login*
National Health Law Program, Inc.: *www.healthlaw.org*
National Urban League: *www.nul.org*
Netherlands Institute of Human Rights: *www.law.uu.nl/english/sim*
Open Society Institute: *www.soros.org*
Partners in Human Rights Education: *http://www1.umn.edu/humanrts/education/pihre*
Peace Brigades International: *www.peacebrigades.org*
Physicians for Human Rights: *http://physiciansforhumanrights.org*
Project Disappeared: *www.desaparecidos.org*
Public Justice (formerly, Trial Lawyers for Public Justice): *www.tlpj.org*
ReliefWeb: *www.reliefWeb.int*
Rural Opportunities, Inc.: *www.ruralinc.org*
The Sentencing Project: *www.sentencingproject.org*
Survival International: *www.survival-international.org*
Survivors International: *www.survivorsintl.org*
Survivors of Torture, International: *www.notorture.org*
Sweatshop Watch: *www.sweatshopwatch.org*
University of Minnesota Human Rights Library: *http://www1.umn.edu/humanrts*
U.N. Voluntary Fund for Victims of Torture: *www.unhchr.ch/html/menu2/i2civftr.htm*
Witness Program: *www.witness.org*
World Organisation Against Torture: *www.omct.org*

LEGAL SERVICES

California Rural Legal Assistance Foundation: *www.crlaf.org*
Catholic Charities Immigration & Refugee Services: *www.catholiccharitiesla.org/immigration.html*
Catholic Legal Immigration Network (CLINIC): *www.cliniclegal.org*
Christian Legal Society: *www.clsnet.org*
Hebrew Immigrant Aid Society: *www.hias.org*
Immigration Counseling Service: *www.immigrationcounseling.org*
Lutheran Immigration and Refugee Services: *www.lirs.org/what/programs/LegalServices.htm*
Mexican American Legal Defense & Educational Fund (MALDEF): *www.maldef.org*
Political Asylum/Immigration Representation Project: *www.pairproject.org*
Public Counsel Law Center: *www.publiccounsel.org*
Washington Legal Foundation: *www.wlf.org*

REGION-SPECIFIC SITES

Africa
African Commission on Human and People's Rights: *www.achpr.org*
African Human Rights Resource Center: *http://www1.umn.edu/humanrts*
African Union: *www.africa-union.org*
allAfrica.com: *http://allafrica.com*
Human Rights Watch/Africa: *http://hrw.org/doc/?t=africa*

Americas
Americas Program: *http://americas.irc-online.org*
Centro Presente: *www.cpresente.org*
Council on Hemispheric Affairs: *www.coha.org*
Human Rights Documentation Exchange: *www.handplant.com/mockups/hrde*
Human Rights Watch, Americas: *http://hrw.org/doc/?t=americas*
Inter-American Commission on Human Rights (OAS): *www.cidh.org*
Inter-American Court of Human Rights (OAS): *www.corteidh.or.cr*
Inter-American Institute of Human Rights: *www.iidh.ed.cr*
N. American Congress on Latin America: *www.nacla.org*
Washington Office on Latin America: *www.wola.org*

El Salvador

El Rescate: *www.elrescate.org*

Guatemala

Guatemala Human Rights Commission/USA: *www.ghrc-usa.org*
Network in Solidarity with the People of Guatemala: *www.nisgua.org*

Haiti

Haiti Action Committee: *www.haitiaction.net*
Haiti Asylum Information Project: *www.ijdh.org/HAIP.htm*
Haiti Democracy Project: *www.haitipolicy.org*
Haiti Reborn: *www.haitireborn.org*
Haiti Support Group: *http://haitisupport.gn.apc.org*
Index of Documentation for Haitian Asylum Seekers: *www.gbls.org/immigration/Index_Of_Documentation.htm*

Europe
Center for Int'l & European Law on Immigr. & Asylum: *http://migration.uni-konstanz.de/index.php?lang=en*
Council of Europe, Human Rights: *www.coe.int/T/E/Human_rights*
European Council on Refugees & Exiles (ECRE): *www.ecre.org*
European Court of Human Rights: *www.echr.coe.int* | *cmiskp.echr.coe.int* (Search Portal)
European Research Centre on Migration and Ethnic Relations: *www.ercomer.org*
Human Rights Watch, Europe & Central Asia: *http://hrw.org/doc/?t=europe*

Mideast
Al-Haq: *www.alhaq.org*
Arab Organization for Human Rights: *www.aohr.org*
DEBKAfile: *www.debka.com*
Institute Kurde de Paris: *www.institutkurde.org/en*
Iranian Refugees Alliance, Inc.: *www.irainc.org*
Kurdish Human Rights Project: *www.khrp.org*
Palestine Center for Human Rights: *www.pchrgaza.org*
U.N. Relief and Works Agency for Palestinian Refugees: *www.un.org/unrwa*

Tibet
International Campaign for Tibet: *www.savetibet.org*
The Office of Tibet: *www.tibetoffice.org/en*
Tibet Justice Center: *www.tibetjustice.org/asylum*

Soviet Jews
Union of Councils for Soviet Jews: *www.fsumonitor.com*

THEME-SPECIFIC SITES

Children's Rights

Child Rights Information Network: *www.crin.org*
U.N. Children's Fund (UNICEF): *www.unicef.org*

Farmworkers

Association of Farmworker Opportunity Programs: *www.afop.org*
HUD's Migrant Farmworkers Page: *www.hud.gov/offices/odoc/swbr/index.cfm*
National Center for Farmworker Health, Inc.: *www.ncfh.org*
USDA Chief Economist's Office (H-2A Workers): *www.usda.gov/oce/labor*

Gender and Women

Asista (includes VAWA updates and experts): *www.asistaonline.org*
Battered Immigrant Women's Rights Project: http://endabuse.org/programs/immigrant
Center for Gender & Refugee Studies: *http://cgrs.uchastings.edu*
Women's Commission for Refugee Women & Children: *www.womenscommission.org*
Women's Human Rights Resources: *www.law-lib.utoronto.ca/diana*

LGBT and HIV Status

Asylumlaw.org guide: *www.asylumlaw.org/legal_tools/index.cfm?fuseaction=&countryID=233*
International Gay and Lesbian Human Rights Commission: *www.iglhrc.org*
Lesbian, Gay, Bisexual, Transgender, and HIV-Positive Immigration Rts.: *www.immigrationequality.org*
National Asylum Partnership on Sexual Orientation:
www.immigrantjustice.org/client/programs/asylumseekers/lgbt.html
National Center for Lesbian Rights Immigration Page: *www.nclrights.org/immigration*

ETHNIC & CULTURAL ORGANIZATIONS

American-Arab Anti-Discrimination Committee: *www.adc.org*
American Jewish Committee: *www.ajc.org*
Anti-Defamation League: *www.adl.org*
Asian American Justice Center (NAPALC): *www.advancingequality.org*
Asian Community Online Network (ACON): *www.acon.org*
Association of Asian Pacific Community Health Organizations: *www.aapcho.org*
Bahá'í International Community: *www.bahai.org*
Conference on Asian Pacific American Leadership: *www.capal.org*
Cuban American National Council, Inc.: *www.cnc.org*
Indian American Center for Political Awareness: *www.iacfpa.org*
Intercultural Mutual Assistance Association: *www.imaa.net*
Japanese American Citizens League: *www.jacl.org*
League of United Latin American Citizens: *www.lulac.org*
National Association for the Advancement of Colored People (NAACP): *www.naacp.org*
National Coalition for Asian Pacific American Community Development: *www.nationalcapacd.org*
National Council of Churches USA: *www.ncccusa.org*
National Council of La Raza: *www.nclr.org*
National Federation of Filipino American Associations: *www.naffaa.org*
National Italian American Foundation: *www.niaf.org*
National Korean American Service & Education Consortium: *www.nakasec.org*
Organization of Chinese Americans: *www.ocanatl.org*
Simon Wiesenthal Center: *www.wiesenthal.com*
Southeast Asia Resource Action Center: *www.searac.org*

LEGAL ASSOCIATIONS

American Association for Justice (formerly Association of Trial Lawyers of America): *www.justice.org*
American Bar Association (ABA): *www.abanet.org*
  ABA Legal Technology Resource Center: *www.abanet.org/tech*
  Commission on Immigration: *www.abanet.org/publicserv/immigration/home.html*
  Section of Int'l Law, Immigr. & Naturalization Comm.: *www.abanet.org/dch/committee.cfm?com=IC925000*
    Subcommittee on International Refugee Law, *www.abanet.org/dch/committee.cfm?com=IC925000*
  Model Rules of Professional Conduct: *www.abanet.org/cpr/mrpc/mrpc_home.html*
American Immigration Lawyers Association (AILA): *www.aila.org*
American Society of International Law: *www.asil.org*
Hispanic National Bar Association: *www.hnba.com*
NAFSA: Association of International Educators: *www.nafsa.org*
National Lawyers Guild: *www.nlg.org*

STATE-SPECIFIC SITES

Alabama: *www.alabama.gov*
  Courts: *www.judicial.state.al.us*
  Dep't of Labor: *www.alalabor.state.al.us*
  Bar Association: *www.alabar.org*
Alaska: *www.state.ak.us*
  Bar Association: *www.alaskabar.org*
  Court System: *www.state.ak.us/courts*
  Foreign Labor Cert.: *http://labor.state.ak.us/alien*
Arizona: *www.az.gov/webapp/portal*
  Courts: *www.supreme.state.az.us*
  Industrial Commission: *www.ica.state.az.us*
  Bar Association: *www.azbar.org*
Arkansas: *www.state.ar.us*
  Courts: *http://courts.state.ar.us/courts/acs.html*
  Dep't of Labor: *www.arkansas.gov/labor*
California: *www.ca.gov*
  Courts: *www.courtinfo.ca.gov*
  Labor Market Info: *www.labormarketinfo.edd.ca.gov*
  Labor Statistics & Research: *www.dir.ca.gov/DLSR*
  State Bar: *www.calbar.ca.gov*
Colorado: *www.colorado.gov*
  Courts: *www.courts.state.co.us*
  Labor & Employment: *www.coworkforce.com*
  Bar Association: *www.cobar.org*
Connecticut: *www.ct.gov*
  Dep't of Labor: *www.ctdol.state.ct.us*
  Courts: *www.jud.state.ct.us*
  Bar Association: *www.ctbar.org*
Delaware: *http://delaware.gov*
  Courts: *http://courts.delaware.gov/Courts*
  Dep't of Labor: *www.delawareworks.com*
  Bar Association: *www.dsba.org*
District of Columbia: *www.dc.gov*
  Dep't of Employment Services: *www.does.dc.gov*
  Courts: *www.dccourts.gov/dccourts*
  Labor-Management Programs: *http://olmp.dc.gov*
  Bar Association: *www.dcbar.org*
Florida: *www.myflorida.com*
  Workforce Innovation: *www.floridajobs.org*
  Courts: *www.flcourts.org*
  Bar Association: *www.flabar.org*
Georgia: *www.georgia.gov*
  Dep't of Labor: *www.dol.state.ga.us*
  Supreme Court: *www.gasupreme.us*
  Bar Association: *www.gabar.org*
Hawaii: *www.hawaii.gov/portal*
  Courts: *www.courts.state.hi.us*
  State Bar Association: *http://64.29.92.27*
  Labor & Industrial Relations: *http://hawaii.gov/labor*
Idaho: *www.state.id.us*
  Courts: *www.isc.idaho.gov*
  Bar Association: *http://www2.state.id.us/isb*
  Labor & Commerce: *http://cl.idaho.gov/portal*
Illinois: *www.illinois.gov*
  Dep't of Employment Security: *www.ides.state.il.us*
  Courts: *www.state.il.us/court*
  Bar Association: *www.illinoisbar.org*
Indiana: *www.in.gov*
  Dep't of Workforce Development: *www.in.gov/dwd*
  Courts: *www.in.gov/judiciary*
  Bar Association: *www.inbar.org*
Iowa: *www.iowa.gov/state/main*
  Courts: *www.judicial.state.ia.us*
  Workforce Development: *www.iowaworkforce.org*
  Bar Association: *www.iowabar.org*
Kansas: *www.kansas.gov*
  Courts: *www.kscourts.org*
  Dep't of Labor: *www.dol.ks.gov*
  Bar Association: *www.ksbar.org*
Kentucky: *http://kentucky.gov*
  Office of Employment and Training: *www.oet.ky.gov*
  Courts: *http://courts.ky.gov*
  Bar Association: *www.kybar.org*
  Dep't of Labor: *http://labor.ky.gov*
Louisiana: *www.louisiana.gov*
  Supreme Court: *www.lasc.org*
  Dep't of Labor: *www.laworks.net*
  Bar Association: *www.lsba.org*
Maine: *www.maine.gov*
  Dep't of Labor: *www.maine.gov/labor*
  Courts: *www.courts.state.me.us*
  Bar Association: *www.mainebar.org*
Maryland: *www.maryland.gov*
  Labor, Licensing & Regulation: *www.dllr.state.md.us*
  Courts: *http://mdcourts.gov*
  Bar Association: *www.msba.org*
Massachusetts: *www.mass.gov*
  Courts: *www.mass.gov/courts*
  Workforce Development: *www.mass.gov/eolwd*
  Bar Association: *www.massbar.org*

Michigan: *www.michigan.gov*
- Career, Educ., & Workplace: *www.michigan.gov/mdcd*
- Courts: *www.icle.org/michlaw*
- Bar Association: *www.michbar.org*

Minnesota: *www.state.mn.us*
- Courts: *www.courts.state.mn.us*
- Bar Association: *www.mnbar.org*
- Dep't of Empl. Security: *www.deed.state.mn.us*

Mississippi: *www.ms.gov*
- Courts: *www.mssc.state.ms.us*
- Bar Association: *www.msbar.org*

Missouri: *www.mo.gov*
- Courts: *www.courts.mo.gov*
- Economic Development: *http://ded.mo.gov*
- Bar Association: *www.mobar.org*

Montana: *http://mt.gov*
- Dep't of Labor & Industry: *http://dli.mt.gov*
- Research & Analysis: *http://ourfactsyourfuture.mt.gov*
- Courts: *www.montanacourts.org*
- Bar Association: *www.montanabar.org*

Nebraska: *www.nebraska.gov*
- Workforce Development: *www.dol.state.ne.us*
- Courts: *http://court.nol.org*
- Bar Association: *www.nebar.com*

Nevada: *www.nv.gov*
- Empl., Training & Rehab: *http://detr.state.nv.us*
- Courts: *www.nvsupremecourt.us*
- State Bar: *www.nvbar.org*

New Hampshire: *www.nh.gov*
- Employment Security: *www.nhes.state.nh.us*
- Courts: *www.courts.state.nh.us*
- Bar Association: *www.nhbar.org*

New Jersey: *www.state.nj.us*
- Courts: *www.judiciary.state.nj.us*
- Labor & Workforce Dev't: *www.state.nj.us/labor*
- Bar Association: *www.njsba.com*

New Mexico: *www.newmexico.gov*
- Courts: *www.nmcourts.com*
- Dep't of Labor: *www.dol.state.nm.us*
- Bar Association: *www.nmbar.org*

New York: *www.ny.gov*
- Courts: *www.courts.state.ny.us*
- Dep't of Labor: *www.labor.state.ny.us*
- Workforce Dev't: *www.workforcenewyork.org*
- Bar Association: *www.nysba.org*

North Carolina: *www.ncgov.com*
- Courts: *www.nccourts.org*
- Employment Security Commission: *www.ncesc.com*
- Dep't of Labor: *www.nclabor.com*
- Bar Association: *www.ncbar.com*

North Dakota: *www.nd.gov*
- Job Service: *www.jobsnd.com*
- Supreme Court: *www.court.state.nd.us*
- Dep't of Labor: *www.nd.gov/labor*
- Bar Association: *www.sband.org/Foundation*

Ohio: *http://ohio.gov*
- Job & Family Services Online: *http://jfs.ohio.gov*
- Supreme Court: *www.sconet.state.oh.us*
- Bar Association: *www.ohiobar.org*

Oklahoma: *www.ok.gov*
- Employment Security Comm'n: *www.oesc.state.ok.us*
- Public Legal Research: *http://oklegal.onenet.net*
- Courts Network: *www.oscn.net*
- Bar Association: *www.okbar.org*

Oregon: *www.oregon.gov*
- Foreign Labor Certification: *www.oregon.gov/EMPLOY/ES/BUS/foreign_labor_cert.shtml*
- Oregon Labor Market Information System (OLMIS): *www.qualityinfo.org/olmisj/OlmisZine*
- Courts: *www.ojd.state.or.us*
- Bar Association: *www.osbar.org*

Pennsylvania: *www.state.pa.us*
- Courts: *www.courts.state.pa.us*
- Dep't of Labor & Industry: *www.dli.state.pa.us*
- Bar Association: *www.pabar.org*

Rhode Island: *www.ri.gov*
- Dep't of Labor & Training: *www.dlt.ri.gov*
- Courts: *www.courts.ri.gov*
- Bar Association: *www.ribar.com*

South Carolina: *http://sc.gov*
- Employment Security Commission: *www.sces.org*
- Courts: *www.judicial.state.sc.us*
- Dep't of Labor: *www.llr.state.sc.us*
- Bar Association: *www.scbar.org*

South Dakota: *www.state.sd.us*
- Labor Dep't: *www.state.sd.us/applications/LD01DOL*
- Courts: *www.sdjudicial.com*
- Bar Association: *www.sdbar.org*

Tennessee: *www.tennessee.gov*
- Admin. Office of the Courts: *www.tsc.state.tn.us*
- Labor & Wkforce Dev't: *www.tennessee.gov/labor-wfd*
- Bar Association: *www.tba.org*

Texas: *www.state.tx.us*
- Workforce Commission: *www.twc.state.tx.us*
- Courts: *www.courts.state.tx.us*
- Bar Association: *www.texasbar.com*

Utah: *www.utah.gov*
- Courts: *www.utah.gov/government/judicial.html*
- Dep't of Workforce Services: *http://jobs.utah.gov*
- Bar Association: *www.utahbar.org*

Vermont: *http://vermont.gov*
- Dep't of Labor: *http://labor.vermont.gov*
- Courts: *www.vermontjudiciary.org*
- Bar Association: *www.vtbar.org*

Virginia: *www.virginia.gov*
- Courts: *www.courts.state.va.us*
- Workforce Connection: *www.vaworkconnect.com*
- Dep't of Labor and Industry: *www.dli.state.va.us*
- Bar Association: *www.vsb.org*

Washington: *http://access.wa.gov*
- Labor Market Information: *www.wa.gov/esd/lmea*
- State Courts: *www.courts.wa.gov*
- Dep't of Labor and Industries: *www.lni.wa.gov*
- Bar Association: *www.wsba.org*

West Virginia: *www.wv.gov*
- Labor market information: *www.wvbep.org/bep/LMI*
- Supreme Court of Appeals: *www.state.wv.us/wvsca*
- Division of Labor: *www.labor.state.wv.us*
- Courts: *www.state.wv.us/wvsca/wvsystem.htm*
- Bar Association: *www.wvbar.org*

Wisconsin: *www.wisconsin.gov*
- Workforce Development: *www.dwd.state.wi.us*
- Courts: *www.wicourts.gov*
- State Bar: *www.wisbar.org*

Wyoming: *http://wyoming.gov*
- Courts: *http://courts.state.wy.us*
- Workforce Services: *www.wyomingworkforce.org*
- Bar Association: *www.wyomingbar.org*

APPENDIX I
DETENTION FACILITIES

For additional information or updates, see *www.ice.gov/pi/dro/facilities.htm*

Federally Owned Facilities*

BATAVIA

Batavia FDF
4250 Federal Drive
Batavia, NY 14020
(585) 343-0814
Officer-in-Charge
Charles Mule

EL CENTRO

El Centro SPC
1115 North Imperial Ave.
El Centro, CA 92243-1739
(760) 353-2170
Acting Assistant Officer-in-Charge
Johnny N. Williams, Jr.

EL PASO

El Paso SPC
8915 Montana Avenue
El Paso, TX 79925
(915) 225-1941
Officer-in-Charge
Alfredo Campos

LOS FRESNOS

Port Isabel SPC
Buena Vista Road
Route 3, Box 341
Los Fresnos, TX 78566
(956) 547-1700
Officer-in-Charge
Aaron L. Cabrera

MIAMI

Krome North SPC
18201 SW 12th Street
Miami, FL 33194
(305) 552-1845
Officer-in-Charge
Wesley Lee

NEW YORK

Varick Street SPC
201 Varick Street
New York, NY 10014
(212) 620-3441 / 3442
Detainee message service
(212) 242-9893

OAKDALE, LA

Oakdale II FDC
P.O. Box 5060
Oakdale, LA 71463
(318) 335-4466

PHOENIX

Florence SPC
3250 N. Pinal Parkway
Florence, AZ 85232
(520) 868-5862
Officer-in-Charge
David A. Kollus

SAN JUAN

Aguadilla SPC
505 Gun Road
Aguadilla, PR 00604
(787) 890-3600 / 3611
[mailing address]
P.O. Box 250480
Aguadilla, PR 00604
Officer-in-Charge
Linda Renz

SAN PEDRO

San Pedro SPC
2001 S. Seaside Ave.
Terminal Island
San Pedro, CA 90731
(310) 241-2300
Officer-in-Charge
Rudolph Garcia

TACOMA

[Correctional Service Corp.]
Detention and Removal Operations
Northwest Detention Center
1623 East J Street, Suite 2
Tacoma, WA 98421
(253) 779-6000

* All these facilities, except for Seattle and Oakdale, are ICE-owned and -operated service processing centers (SPCs) or federal detention facilities (FDFs). The Tacoma facility is federally owned, but contractor-operated. Oakdale is owned and operated by Bureau of Prisons (part of DOJ).

Contractor-Owned and -Operated Detention Facilities

DENVER

[Global Expertise Outsourcing (GEO)]
Aurora Contract Detention Facility
11901 E. 30th Avenue
Aurora, CO 80010
(303) 361-0701 (detainee information)
(303) 361-6612 (contacting detainees)

GEO Warden:
J. Alexander

ICE Supervisory Deportation Officer:
J. Good, (303) 361-0723

ELIZABETH DETENTION FACILITY

[Corrections Corp. of America]
Service Processing Center
625 Evans Street
Elizabeth, NJ 07201

Warden: C. Collins
Ass't Warden: T. Dickerson
(908) 352-3776

Field Office Director: S. Weber
Ass't Field Office Director: D. Henkel
(973) 622-7157

HOUSTON

[Corrections Corp. of America]
Houston Processing Center
15850 Export Plaza Dr.
Houston, TX 77032
(281) 449-1481

Officer-in-Charge
James L. Heathman

Warden
Jimmy Cook

PHOENIX

[Corrections Corp. of America]
Eloy Detention Center *
1705 East Hanna Road
Eloy, AZ 85231
(520) 466-2000

ICE Officer-in-Charge
Mark Soukup (Acting)

Warden
Thomas A. Long

SAN ANTONIO

[Corrections Corp. of America]
Laredo Detention Facility
4702 E. Saunders
Laredo, TX 78041

(956) 727-4118

[ICE Office]
4602 E. Saunders
Laredo, TX 78041

Officer-in-Charge
Conrad Agagan, (956) 729-9620

Warden
Jose L. Hinojosa, (956) 727-4118

SAN DIEGO

[Corrections Corp. of America]
Otay Detention Facility
446 Alta Road, Suite 5400
San Diego, CA 92158
(619) 661-9119

[ICE Office]
P.O. Box 439020
San Diego, CA 92143-9020
(619) 710-8300

Officer-in-Charge
Hector Najera

* Operated with federal Bureau of Prisons.

APPENDIX J
BALCA / OFFICE OF ADMINISTRATIVE LAW JUDGES

NATIONAL HEADQUARTERS
www.oalj.dol.gov/HEADQUARTERS.HTM

Office of Administrative Law Judges
U.S. Department of Labor
800 K Street, NW, Suite 400 North
Washington, DC 20001-8002
(202) 693-7300
(202) 693-7365 (fax)

Board of Alien Labor Certification Appeals
John M. Vittone, *Chair*
Thomas M. Burke
Linda Chapman
Pamela Lakes Wood

Judges
John M. Vittone, *Chief Judge*
Linda Chapman
William Colwell
Paul C. Johnson, Jr.
Stuart A. Levin
Edward Terhune Miller
Stephen L. Purcell
Daniel Solomon
Richard T. Stansell-Gamm
Jeffrey Tureck
Pamela Lakes Wood

BOSTON DISTRICT OFFICE
www.oalj.dol.gov/BOSTON.HTM

U.S. Department of Labor
Office of Administrative Law Judges
O'Neill Federal Building, Room 411
10 Causeway St
Boston, MA 02222
(617) 223-9355
(617) 223-4254 (fax)

Judges
Daniel F. Sutton, *District Chief Judge*
Colleen A. Geraghty

CHERRY HILL (NJ) DISTRICT OFFICE
www.oalj.dol.gov/CHERRY_HILL.HTM

Office of Administrative Law Judges
U.S. Department of Labor
2 Executive Campus, Suite 450
Cherry Hill, NJ 08002
(856) 486-3800
(856) 486-3806 (fax)

Judges
Robert D. Kaplan, *District Chief Judge*
Janice K. Bullard
Adele H. Odegard
Ralph A. Romano

CINCINNATI DISTRICT OFFICE
www.oalj.dol.gov/CINCINNATI.HTM

Office of Administrative Law Judges
U.S. Department of Labor
36 E. 7th St., Suite 2525
Cincinnati, Ohio 45202
(513) 684-3252
(513) 684-6108 (fax)

Judges
Donald W. Mosser, *District Chief Judge*
Alice Craft
Joseph E. Kane
Larry S. Merck
Thomas F. Phalen, Jr.

COVINGTON, LA, DISTRICT OFFICE *www.oalj.dol.gov/COVINGTON.HTM*

Office of Administrative Law Judges
United States Department of Labor
St. Tammany Courthouse Annex
First Floor
428 E. Boston St.
Covington, LA 70433-2846
(985) 809-5173
(985) 893-7351 (fax)

Judges

Lee J. Romero, Jr., *District Chief Judge*
C. Richard Avery
Clement J. Kennington
Patrick Rosenow

NEWPORT NEWS (VA) DISTRICT OFFICE *www.oalj.dol.gov/NEWPORT_NEWS.HTM*

Office of Administrative Law Judges
U.S. Department of Labor
11870 Merchants Walk, Suite 204
Newport News, VA 23606
(757) 591-5140
(757) 591-5150 (fax)

Judges

Daniel A. Sarno, Jr., *District Chief Judge*
Alan L. Bergstrom
Kenneth A. Krantz
Richard K. Malamphy

PITTSBURGH DISTRICT OFFICE *www.oalj.dol.gov/PITTSBURGH.HTM*

Office of Administrative Law Judges
U.S. Department of Labor
7 Parkway Center, Suite 290
Pittsburgh, PA 15220
(412) 644-5754
(412) 644-5005 (fax)

Judges

Daniel L. Leland, *District Chief Judge*
Thomas M. Burke
Michael P. Lesniak
Richard A. Morgan

SAN FRANCISCO DISTRICT OFFICE *www.oalj.dol.gov/SAN_FRANCISCO.HTM*

U.S. Department of Labor
Office of Administrative Law Judges
90 Seventh Street, Suite 4-800
San Francisco, CA 94103-1516
(415) 625-2200
(415) 625-2201 (fax)

Judges

Jennifer Gee, *District Chief Judge*
Steven B. Berlin
William R. Dorsey
Gerald M. Etchingham
Russell D. Pulver
Anne Beytin Torkington

APPENDIX K

DESIGNATED REGIONAL CENTERS—IMMIGRANT INVESTOR PILOT PROGRAM

ALABAMA

Alabama Center for Foreign Investment
RSA Union
100 N. Union Street, Suite 682
Montgomery, AL 36104
(334) 954-3111
www.acfi-alabama.com/alabama.html

Mailing Address:
P.O. Box 5079
Montgomery, AL 36103

CALIFORNIA

California Consortium for Agricultural Export
333 S. Grand Avenue, 25th Floor
Los Angeles, CA 90017
(213) 892-6367
www.ccax.com

CMB Export LLC
Corona Professional Center
400 S. Ramona Ave., Ste. 212AA
Corona, CA 91719
1-800-238-8022
www.cmbeb5visa.com

Southeast Los Angeles Regional Center
David B. Brearley
2440 S. Hacienda Blvd., Ste. 223
Hacienda Heights, CA 91745
(626) 336-3408

Los Angeles Film Regional Center
c/o Thomas Rosenfeld
CanAm Enterprises, LLC
32 Court Street, Suite 1501
Brooklyn, NY 11201
(718) 624-7850

DISTRICT OF COLUMBIA

Capitol Area Regional Center
888 16th Street NW, Ste. 800
Washington, DC 20006
(202)349-9848
www.eb5dc.com

IOWA

Iowa Department of Economic Development
200 E. Grand Ave.
Des Moines, IA 50309
(515)242-4700
www.extension.iastate.edu/ag/staff/info/ianewfarmfamily.pdf

KANSAS

Kansas Biofuel Regional Center, LLC
915 Wilshire Boulevard, #2050
Los Angeles, CA 90017
(213) 380-2828

LOUISIANA

City of New Orleans
Mayor's Economic Development Department
1515 Poydras Street, Suite 1150
New Orleans, LA 70112
(504) 658-0919
www.nobleoutreach.com

NEVADA

[Reaffirmation Pending]
Unibex Global Corporation
1201 Eleanor Ave.
Las Vegas, NV 89106
(702) 646-7068

PENNSYLVANIA

Philadelphia Industrial Development Corporation
2600 Centre Square West
1500 Market St.
Philadelphia, PA 19102-2126
(215) 496-8020
www.canamenterprises.com

PA Dep't of Community & Econ. Dev't Regional Ctr.
Harrisburg, PA 17120
(718) 624-7850
www.newPA.com

SOUTH DAKOTA

SD International Business Institute
1200 S. Jay Street
Aberdeen, SD 57401-7198
(605) 626-3149
www.sd-exports.org/eb-5

TEXAS

Global Century Development Group I, LP
11205 Bellaire Blvd., Suite B-33
Houston, TX 77072-2545

TEXAS & OKLAHOMA

Southwest Biofuels Regional Center, LLC
915 Wilshire Boulevard, #2050
Los Angeles, CA 90017
(213) 380-2828

VERMONT

VT Agency of Commerce and Community Dev.
National Life Bldg., Drawer 20
Montpelier, VT 05620-0501
(802) 828-5202
www.eb5greencard.com

WISCONSIN

Metropolitan Milwaukee Association of Commerce
756 N. Milwaukee Street, Ste. 400
Milwaukee, WI 53202
(414) 287-4100
www.mmac.org/display/router.asp?DocID=1028

WASHINGTON

The Gateway Freedom Fund
Golden Rainbow Freedom Fund / American Life
18034 13th Street
Seattle, WA 98177
(206) 624-5622
www.amlife.us/visa.html

Whatcom Opportunities Regional Center, Inc.
1305 11th Street, Suite 304
Bellingham, WA 98225
(360) 201-3933
www.worc.biz

Mailing Address:
P.O. Box 2803
Bellingham, WA 98225

[Reaffirmation Pending]
Aero-Space Port International Group
512 Strander Blvd.
Tukwila, WA 98188
www.aspigroup.com
(206) 241-8000

Previously Designated Regional Center
Now Under Suspension

As of May 2008, based on a USCIS-issued "Intent to Terminate," with an open period of time in which to respond with evidence, data, and documentation necessary for reinstatement to avoid a final Action to Terminate

HAWAII

HI Dep't of Business, Economic Dev. & Tourism
No. 1 Capitol District Bldg.
5th Floor, Diamond Head Wing
250 South Hotel Street
Honolulu, HI 96813
(808) 586-2355 x3033
http://www.hawaii.gov/dbedt

APPENDIX L

TREATY TRADER AND TREATY INVESTOR COUNTRIES

Nations with treaties with United States. Current through March 31, 2006. For updates, see 9 FAM §41.51, Exhibit 1, www.state.gov/documents/organization/87221.pdf

Country	Visa	Entered into force
Albania	E-2	Jan. 4, 1998
Argentina	E-1 & E-2	Dec. 20, 1854
Armenia	E-2	Mar. 29, 1996
Australia[1]	E-1	Dec. 16, 1991
	E-2	Dec. 27, 1991
	E-3	Sept. 2, 2005
Austria	E-1 & E-2	May 27, 1931
Azerbaijan	E-2	Aug. 2, 2001
Bahrain	E-2	May 31, 2001
Bangladesh	E-2	July 25, 1989
Belgium	E-1 & E-2	Oct. 3, 1963
Bolivia	E-1	Nov. 9, 1862
	E-2	June 6, 2001
Bosnia & Herzegovina[15]	E-1 & E-2	Nov. 15, 1882
Brunei	E-1	July 11, 1853
Bulgaria	E-2	June 2, 1994
Cameroon	E-2	Apr. 6, 1989
Canada	E-1 & E-2	Jan. 1, 1993
Chile[2]	E-1, E-2, & H-1B1	Jan. 1, 2004
China (Taiwan)[3]	E-1 & E-2	Nov. 30, 1948
Colombia	E-1 & E-2	June 10, 1948
Congo (Brazzaville)	E-2	Aug. 13, 1994
Congo (Kinshasa)	E-2	July 28, 1989
Costa Rica	E-1 & E-2	May 26, 1852
Croatia[15]	E-1 & E-2	Nov. 15, 1882
Czech Republic[4]	E-2	Jan. 1, 1993
Denmark[5]	E-1	July 30, 1961
Ecuador	E-2	May 11, 1997
Egypt	E-2	June 27, 1992
Estonia	E-1	May 22, 1926
	E-2	Feb. 16, 1997
Ethiopia	E-1 & E-2	Oct. 8, 1953
Finland	E-1	Aug. 10, 1934
	E-2	Dec. 1, 1992
France[6]	E-1 & E-2	Dec. 21, 1960
Georgia	E-2	Aug. 17, 1997
Germany	E-1 & E-2	July 14, 1956
Greece	E-1	Oct. 13, 1954
Grenada	E-2	Mar. 3, 1989
Honduras	E-1 & E-2	July 19, 1928
Iran[7]	E-1 & E-2	June 16, 1957
Ireland	E-1	Sept. 14, 1950
	E-2	Nov. 18, 1992
Israel	E-1	Apr. 3, 1954
Italy	E-1 & E-2	July 26, 1949

Country	Visa	Entered into force
Jamaica	E-2	Mar. 7, 1997
Japan[8]	E-1 & E-2	Oct. 30, 1953
Jordan	E-1 & E-2	Dec. 17, 2001
Kazakhstan	E-2	Jan. 12, 1994
Korea (South)	E-1 & E-2	Nov. 7, 1957
Kyrgyzstan	E-2	Jan. 12, 1994
Latvia	E-1	July 25, 1928
	E-2	Dec. 26, 1996
Liberia	E-1 & E-2	Nov. 21, 1939
Lithuania	E-2	Nov. 22, 2001
Luxembourg	E-1 & E-2	Mar. 28, 1963
Macedonia[15]	E-1 & E-2	Nov. 15, 1882
Mexico	E-1 & E-2	Jan. 1, 1994
Moldova	E-2	Nov. 25, 1994
Mongolia	E-2	Jan. 1, 1997
Morocco	E-2	May 29, 1991
Netherlands[9]	E-1 & E-2	Dec. 5, 1957
Norway[10]	E-1 & E-2	Jan. 18, 1928
Oman	E-1 & E-2	June 11, 1960
Pakistan	E-1 & E-2	Feb. 12, 1961
Panama	E-2	May 30, 1991
Paraguay	E-1 & E-2	Mar. 7, 1860
Philippines	E-1 & E-2	Sept. 6, 1955
Poland	E-1 & E-2	Aug. 6, 1994
Romania	E-2	Jan. 15, 1994
Senegal	E-2	Oct. 25, 1990
Serbia & Montenegro[15]	E-1 & E-2	Nov. 15, 1882
Singapore[2]	E-1, E-2, & H-1B1	Jan. 1, 2004
Slovakia[4]	E-2	Jan. 1, 1993
Slovenia[15]	E-1 & E-2	Nov. 15, 1882
Spain[11]	E-1 & E-2	Apr. 14, 1903
Sri Lanka	E-2	May 1, 1993
Suriname[12]	E-1 & E-2	Feb. 10, 1963
Sweden	E-1 & E-2	Feb. 20, 1992
Switzerland	E-1 & E-2	Nov. 8, 1855
Thailand	E-1 & E-2	June 8, 1968
Togo	E-1 & E-2	Feb. 5, 1967
Trinidad & Tobago	E-2	Dec. 26, 1996
Tunisia	E-2	Feb. 7, 1993
Turkey	E-1	Feb. 15, 1933
	E-2	May 18, 1990
Ukraine	E-2	Nov. 16, 1996
Uruguay[13]	E-2	Nov. 1, 2006
United Kingdom[14]	E-1 & E-2	July 3, 1815
Yugoslavia[15]	E-1 & E-2	Nov. 15, 1882

NOTES

[1] **AUSTRALIA** The E-3 visa is for nationals of the Commonwealth of Australia who wish to enter the United States to perform services in a "specialty occupation." The term "specialty occupation" means an occupation that requires theoretical and practical application of a body of highly specialized knowledge, and attainment of a bachelor's or higher degree in the specific specialty (or its equivalent) as a minimum for entry into the occupation in the United States. The definition is the same as the Immigration and Nationality Act definition of an H-1B specialty occupation.

[2] **CHILE & SINGAPORE**. January 1, 2004, also is the effective date for implementation of the immigration provisions of two new Free Trade Agreements with the countries of Chile and Singapore. Under the immigration provisions of these agreements, as approved by Congress in Public Laws 108-77 and 108-78, a new H-1B1 nonimmigrant category has been created for professionals from Chile and Singapore.

[3] **CHINA (TAIWAN)**. Pursuant to Section 6 of the Taiwan Relations Act, Pub. L. 96-8, 93 Stat, 14, and Executive Order 12143, 44 F.R. 37191, this agreement which was concluded with the Taiwan authorities prior to January 1, 1979, is administered on a nongovernmental basis by the American Institute in Taiwan, a nonprofit District of Columbia corporation, and constitutes neither recognition of the Taiwan authorities nor the continuation of any official relationship with Taiwan.

[4] **CZECH REPUBLIC & SLOVAK REPUBLIC (Slovakia)**. The Treaty with the Czech and Slovak Federal Republics entered into force on December 19, 1992; entered into force for the Czech Republic and Slovak Republic as separate states on January 1, 1993.

[5] **DENMARK**. The Convention of 1826 does not apply to the Faroe Islands of Greenland. The Treaty which entered into force on July 30, 1961, does not apply to Greenland.

[6] **FRANCE**. The Treaty which entered into force on December 21, 1960, applies to the departments of Martinique, Guadeloupe, French Guiana and Reunion.

[7] **IRAN**. Treaty inoperative in relation to E-1 (but not E-2) because of Executive Orders preventing trade with Iran. *See* E.O. Nos. 12957 (3/15/95), 12959 (5/6/95), 13059 (8/19/97)

[8] **JAPAN**. The Treaty which entered into force on October 30, 1953, was made applicable to the Bonin Islands on June 26, 1968, and to the Ryukyu Islands on May 15, 1972.

[9] **NETHERLANDS**. The Treaty which entered into force on December 5, 1957, is applicable to Aruba and Netherlands Antilles.

[10] **NORWAY**. The Treaty which entered into force on September 13, 1932, does not apply to Svalbard (Spitzbergen and certain lesser islands).

[11] **SPAIN**. The Treaty which entered into force on April 14, 1903, is applicable to all territories.

[12] **SURINAME**. The Treaty with the Netherlands which entered into force December 5, 1957, was made applicable to Suriname on February 10, 1963.

[13] **URUGUAY**. A Bilateral Investment Treaty between the United States and Uruguay was signed on November 4, 2005, and entered into force November 1, 2006. The concomitant E-2 visa, however, is not yet noted on the State Department website.

[14] **UNITED KINGDOM**. The Convention, which entered into force on July 3, 1815, applies only to British territory in Europe (the British Isles (except the Republic of Ireland), the Channel Islands and Gibraltar) and to "inhabitants" of such territory. This term, as used in the Convention, means "one who resides actually and permanently in a given place, and has his domicile there." Also, in order to qualify for treaty trader or treaty investor status under this treaty, the alien must be a national of the United Kingdom. Individuals having the nationality of members of the Commonwealth other than the United Kingdom do not qualify for treaty trader or treaty investor status under this treaty.

[15] **YUGOSLAVIA**. The U.S. view is that the Socialist Federal Republic of Yugoslavia (SFRY) has dissolved. The successors that formerly made up the SFRY. Bosnia, Herzegovina, Croatia, the Former Yugoslav Republic of Macedonia, Slovenia, Serbia and Montenegro (formally the Federal Republic of Yugoslavia) continue to be bound by the treaty in force with the SFRY at the time of dissolution.

APPENDIX M
"STEM" DEGREES ELIGIBLE FOR OPT EXTENSION

*F-1 students with the following science, technology, engineering, and mathematics (STEM) degrees are eligible to extend the maximum period of optional practical training (OPT) from 12 to 29 months. Categorization based on Education Department's ''Classification of Instructional Programs'' (CIP). List is current through 6/1/08. See www.ice.gov/sevis.**

COMPUTER & INFORMATION SCIENCES AND SUPPORT SERVICES

Computer & Information Sciences, General (11.01)

11.0101 Computer & Information Sciences, General
11.0102 Artificial Intelligence & Robotics
11.0103 Information Technology

Computer Programming (11.02)

11.0201 Computer Programming/Programmer, General
11.0202 Computer Programming, Specific Applications
11.0203 Computer Programming, Vendor/Product Certif.

11.0301 Data Processing & DP Technology/Technician
11.0401 Information Science/Studies
11.0501 Computer Systems Analysis/Analyst
11.0701 Computer Science

Computer Software & Media Applications (11.08)

11.0801 Web Page, Digital/Multimedia, & Information Resources Design
11.0802 Data Modeling/Warehousing & Database Admin.
11.0803 Computer Graphics

11.0901 Computer Systems Networking & Telecommunications

Computer/Information Technology Administration and Management (11.10)

11.1001 System Administration/Administrator
11.1002 System, Networking, & LAN/WAN Management/Manager
11.1003 Computer & Information Systems Security
11.1004 Web/Multimedia Management & Webmaster

ENGINEERING

14.0101 Engineering, General
14.0201 Aerospace, Aeronautical & Astronautical Eng'g
14.0301 Agricultural/Biological Eng'g & Bioengineering
14.0401 Architectural Engineering
14.0501 Biomedical/Medical Engineering
14.0601 Ceramic Sciences and Engineering
14.0701 Chemical Engineering

Civil Engineering (14.08)

14.0801 Civil Engineering, General
14.0802 Geotechnical Engineering
14.0803 Structural Engineering
14.0804 Transportation and Highway Engineering
14.0805 Water Resources Engineering

Computer Engineering, General (14.09)

14.0901 Computer Engineering, General
14.0902 Computer Hardware Engineering
14.0903 Computer Software Engineering

14.1001 Electrical, Electronics & Communications Eng'g
14.1101 Engineering Mechanics
14.1201 Engineering Physics
14.1301 Engineering Science
14.1401 Environmental/Environmental Health Engineering
14.1801 Materials Engineering
14.1901 Mechanical Engineering
14.2001 Metallurgical Engineering
14.2101 Mining and Mineral Engineering
14.2201 Naval Architecture and Marine Engineering
14.2301 Nuclear Engineering
14.2401 Ocean Engineering
14.2501 Petroleum Engineering
14.2701 Systems Engineering
14.2801 Textile Sciences and Engineering
14.3101 Materials Science
14.3201 Polymer/Plastics Engineering
14.3301 Construction Engineering
14.3401 Forest Engineering
14.3501 Industrial Engineering
14.3601 Manufacturing Engineering
14.3701 Operations Research
14.3801 Surveying Engineering
14.3901 Geological/Geophysical Engineering

ENGINEERING TECHNOLOGY / TECHNICIANS

15.0000 Engineering Technology, General
15.0101 Architectural Engineering Technology/Technician
15.0201 Civil Engineering Technology/Technician

Electrical Engineering Technologies/Technicians (15.03)

15.0303 Electrical, Electronic & Communications Engineering Technology/Technician
15.0304 Laser and Optical Technology/Technician
15.0305 Telecommunications Technology/Technician

---

* Pursuant to 8 CFR §214.2(f)(10)(C)(2), as amended by ICE's Interim Final Rule at 73 FR 18944 (4/8/08), the most current STEM Designated Degree Program List is published at *www.ice.gov/sevis*.
For fuller descriptions of each degree, see *http://nces.ed.gov/pubs2002/cip2000/ciplist.asp*.

Electromechanical Instrumentation & Maintenance Technologies/Technicians (15.04)

15.0401 Biomedical Technology/Technician
15.0403 Electromechanical Technology / Electromechanical Engineering Technology
15.0404 Instrumentation Technology/Technician
15.0405 Robotics Technology/Technician

Environmental Control Technologies/Technicians (15.05)

15.0501 Heating, Air Conditioning & Refrigeration Technology/Technician (ACH/ACR/ACHR/HRAC/HVAC/AC Technology)
15.0503 Energy Mgmt. & Systems Technology/Technician
15.0505 Solar Energy Technology/Technician
15.0506 Water Quality & Wastewater Treatment Management and Recycling Technology/Technician
15.0507 Envtl. Eng'g Technology / Envtl. Technology
15.0508 Hazardous Materials Management & Waste Technology/Technician

Industrial Production Technologies/Technicians (15.06)

15.0607 Plastics Engineering Technology/Technician
15.0611 Metallurgical Technology/Technician
15.0612 Industrial Technology/Technician
15.0613 Manufacturing Technology/Technician

Quality Control and Safety Technologies/Technicians (15.07)

15.0701 Occupational Safety and Health Technology/Technician
15.0702 Quality Control Technology/Technician
15.0703 Industrial Safety Technology/Technician
15.0704 Hazardous Materials Information Systems Technology/Technician

Mechanical Engineering Related Technologies/Technicians (15.08)

15.0801 Aeronautical/Aerospace Engineering Technology/Technician
15.0803 Automotive Eng'g Technology/Technician
15.0805 Mechanical Engineering/Mechanical Technology/Technician

Mining & Petroleum Technologies/Technicians (15.09)

15.0901 Mining Technology/Technician
15.0903 Petroleum Technology/Technician

15.1001 Construction Eng'g Technology/Technician

Engineering-Related Technologies (15.11)

15.1102 Surveying Technology/Surveying
15.1103 Hydraulics & Fluid Power Technology/Technician

Computer Engineering Technologies/Technicians (15.12)

15.1201 Computer Engineering Technology/Technician
15.1202 Computer Technology / Computer Systenms Technology
15.1203 Computer Hardware Technology/Technician
15.1204 Computer Software Technology/Technician

Drafting / Design Engineering Technologies/Technicians (15.13)

15.1301 Drafting & Design Technology/Technician, Gen.
15.1302 CAD/CADD Drafting and/or Design Technology/Technician
15.1303 Architectural Drafting & Architectural CAD/CADD
15.1304 Civil Drafting & Civil Engineering CAD/CADD
15.1305 Electrical/Electronics Drafting & Electrical/Electronics CAD/CADD
15.1306 Mech. Drafting & Mech. Drafting CAD/CADD

15.1401 Nuclear Engineering Technology/Technician
15.1501 Engineering/Industrial Management

BIOLOGICAL AND BIOMEDICAL SCIENCES

Biology, General (26.01)

26.0101 Biology/Biological Sciences, General
26.0102 Biomedical Sciences, General

Biochemistry, Biophysics and Molecular Biology (26.02)

26.0202 Biochemistry
26.0203 Biophysics
26.0204 Molecular Biology
26.0205 Molecular Biochemistry
26.0206 Molecular Biophysics
26.0207 Structural Biology
26.0208 Photobiology
26.0209 Radiation Biology/Radiobiology
26.0210 Biochemistry/Biophysics and Molecular Biology

Botany/Plant Biology (26.03)

26.0301 Botany/Plant Biology
26.0305 Plant Pathology/Phytopathology
26.0307 Plant Physiology
26.0308 Plant Molecular Biology

Cell/Cellular Biology and Anatomical Sciences (26.04)

26.0401 Cell/Cellular Biology and Histology
26.0403 Anatomy
26.0404 Developmental Biology and Embryology
26.0405 Neuroanatomy
26.0406 Cell/Cellular and Molecular Biology
26.0407 Cell Biology and Anatomy

Microbiological Sciences and Immunology (26.05)

26.0502 Microbiology, General
26.0503 Medical Microbiology and Bacteriology
26.0504 Virology
26.0505 Parasitology
26.0506 Mycology
26.0507 Immunology

Zoology/Animal Biology (26.07)

26.0701 Zoology/Animal Biology
26.0702 Entomology
26.0707 Animal Physiology
26.0708 Animal Behavior and Ethology
26.0709 Wildlife Biology

Genetics (26.08)

26.0801 Genetics, General
26.0802 Molecular Genetics
26.0803 Microbial and Eukaryotic Genetics
26.0804 Animal Genetics
26.0805 Plant Genetics
26.0806 Human/Medical Genetics

Physiology, Pathology, and Related Sciences (26.09)

26.0901 Physiology, General
26.0902 Molecular Physiology
26.0903 Cell Physiology
26.0904 Endocrinology
26.0905 Reproductive Biology
26.0906 Neurobiology and Neurophysiology
26.0907 Cardiovascular Science
26.0908 Exercise Physiology
26.0909 Vision Science/Physiological Optics
26.0910 Pathology/Experimental Pathology
26.0911 Oncology and Cancer Biology

Pharmacology and Toxicology (26.10)

26.1001 Pharmacology
26.1002 Molecular Pharmacology
26.1003 Neuropharmacology
26.1004 Toxicology
26.1005 Molecular Toxicology
26.1006 Environmental Toxicology
26.1007 Pharmacology and Toxicology

Biomathematics and Bioinformatics (26.11)

26.1101 Biometry/Biometrics
26.1102 Biostatistics
26.1103 Bioinformatics

26.1201 Biotechnology

Ecology, Evolution, Systematics, and Population Biology (26.13)

26.1301 Ecology
26.1302 Marine Biology and Biological Oceanography
26.1303 Evolutionary Biology
26.1304 Aquatic Biology/Limnology
26.1305 Environmental Biology
26.1306 Population Biology
26.1307 Conservation Biology
26.1308 Systematic Biology/Biological Systematics
26.1309 Epidemiology

MATHEMATICS AND STATISTICS

Mathematics (27.01)

27.0101 Mathematics, General
27.0102 Algebra and Number Theory
27.0103 Analysis and Functional Analysis
27.0104 Geometry/Geometric Analysis
27.0105 Topology and Foundations

Applied Mathematics (27 .03)

27.0301 Applied Mathematics
27.0303 Computational Mathematics

Statistics (27.05)

27.0501 Statistics, General
27.0502 Mathematical Statistics and Probability

MILITARY TECHNOLOGIES

29.0101 Military Technologies

PHYSICAL SCIENCES

40.0101 Physical Sciences

Astronomy and Astrophysics (40.02)

40.0201 Astronomy
40.0202 Astrophysics
40.0203 Planetary Astronomy and Science

Atmospheric Sciences and Meteorology (40.04)

40.0401 Atmospheric Sciences and Meteorology, General
40.0402 Atmospheric Chemistry and Climatology
40.0403 Atmospheric Physics and Dynamics
40.0404 Meteorology

Chemistry (40.05)

40.0501 Chemistry, General
40.0502 Analytical Chemistry
40.0503 Inorganic Chemistry
40.0504 Organic Chemistry
40.0506 Physical and Theoretical Chemistry
40.0507 Polymer Chemistry
40.0508 Chemical Physics

Geological and Earth Sciences/Geosciences (40.06)

40.0601 Geology/Earth Science, General
40.0602 Geochemistry
40.0603 Geophysics and Seismology
40.0604 Paleontology
40.0605 Hydrology and Water Resources Science
40.0606 Geochemistry and Petrology
40.0607 Oceanography, Chemical and Physical

Physics (40.08)

40.0801 Physics, General
40.0802 Atomic/Molecular Physics
40.0804 Elementary Particle Physics
40.0805 Plasma and High-Temperature Physics
40.0806 Nuclear Physics
40.0807 Optics/Optical Sciences
40.0808 Solid State and Low-Temperature Physics
40.0809 Acoustics
40.0810 Theoretical and Mathematical Physics

SCIENCE TECHNOLOGIES/TECHNICIANS

41.0101 Biology Technician / Biotechnology Laboratory Technician

Nuclear and Industrial Radiologic Technologies/Technicians (41.02)

41.0204 Industrial Radiologic Technology/Technician
41.0205 Nuclear/Nuclear Power Technology/Technician

Physical Science Technologies/Technicians (41.03)

41.0301 Chemical Technology/Technician

HEALTH PROFESSIONS & RELATED CLINICAL SCIENCES

51.1401 Medical Scientist (MS, PhD)

BUSINESS, MANAGEMENT, MARKETING, & RELATED SUPPORT SERVICES

52.1304 Actuarial Science

Appendix N
Visa Classification Symbols

from 22 C.F.R. §§41.12 & 42.11, as revised (73 FR 14926, 3/20/08), and other sources

Nonimmigrants

Symbol	Description	Section of law*
A1	Ambassador, public minister, career diplomat or consular officer, or immediate family	101(a)(15)(A)(i)
A2	Other foreign government official or employee, or immediate family	101(a)(15)(A)(ii)
A3	Attendant, servant, or personal employee of A1 or A2, or immediate family	101(a)(15)(A)(iii)
B1	Temporary visitor for business	101(a)(15)(B)
B2	Temporary visitor for pleasure	101(a)(15)(B)
B1/B2	Temporary visitor for business & pleasure	101(a)(15)(B)
C1	Alien in transit	101(a)(15)(C)
C1/D	Combined transit and crewmember visa	101(a)(15)(C) & (D)
C2	Alien in transit to UN Headquarters District under §11.(3), (4), or (5) of Headquarters Agreement	101(a)(15)(C)
C3	Foreign gov't official, immediate family, attendant, servant or personal employee, in transit	212(d)(8)
D	Crewmember (sea or air)	101(a)(15)(D)
E1	Treaty trader, spouse or child	101(a)(15)(E)(i)
E2	Treaty investor, spouse or child	101(a)(15)(E)(ii)
E3	Australian treaty alien coming to U.S. solely to perform services in a specialty occupation	101(a)(15)(E)(iii)
E3D	Spouse or child of E3	101(a)(15)(E)(iii)
E3R	Returning E3	101(a)(15)(E)(iii)
F1	Student in an academic or language training program	101(a)(15)(F)(i)
F2	Spouse or child of F1	101(a)(15)(F)(ii)
F3	Canadian or Mexican national commuter student in an academic or language training program	101(a)(15)(F)(iii)
G1	Principal resident representative of recognized foreign gov't to international org., staff, or immediate family	101(a)(15)(G)(i)
G2	Other representative of recognized foreign member gov't to international organization, or immediate family	101(a)(15)(G)(ii)
G3	Representative of nonrecognized or nonmember foreign gov't to international org., or immediate family	101(a)(15)(G)(iii)
G4	International organization officer or employee, or immediate family	101(a)(15)(G)(iv)
G5	Attendant, servant, or personal employee of G1 through G4, or immediate family	101(a)(15)(G)(v)
H1B	Alien in a specialty occupation (profession)	101(a)(15)(H)(i)(b)
H1B1	Chilean or Singaporean national to work in a specialty occupation	101(a)(15)(H)(i)(b1)
H1C	Nurse in health professional shortage area	101(a)(15)(H)(i)(c)
H2A	Temporary worker performing agricultural services unavailable in the United States	101(a)(15)(H)(ii)(a)
H2B	Temporary worker performing other services unavailable in the United States	101(a)(15)(H)(ii)(b)
H3	Trainee	101(a)(15)(H)(iii)
H4	Spouse or child of alien classified H1B/B1/C, H2A/B/R, or H–3	101(a)(15)(H)(iv)
I	Representative of foreign information media, spouse and child	101(a)(15)(I)
J1	Exchange visitor	101(a)(15)(J)
J2	Spouse or child of J1	101(a)(15)(J)
K1	Fiancé(e) of U.S. citizen	101(a)(15)(K)(i)
K2	Child of fiancé(e) of U.S. citizen	101(a)(15)(K)(iii)
K3	Spouse of U.S. citizen awaiting availability of immigrant visa	101(a)(15)(K)(ii)
K4	Child of K3	101(a)(15)(K)(iii)
L1	Intracompany transferee (executive, managerial, and specialized knowledge personnel continuing employment with international firm or corporation)	101(a)(15)(L)
L2	Spouse or child of intracompany transferee	101(a)(15)(L)
M1	Vocational student or other nonacademic student	101(a)(15)(M)(i)
M2	Spouse or child of M1	101(a)(15)(M)(ii)
M3	Canadian or Mexican national commuter student (vocational student or other nonacademic student)	101(a)(15)(M)(iii)

* References are to the Immigration and Nationality Act (INA), as amended, unless otherwise noted.

N8	Parent of an alien classified SK3 or SN3	101(a)(15)(N)(i)
N9	Child of N8 or of SK1, SK2, SK4, SN1, SN2 or SN4	101(a)(15)(N)(ii)
NATO 1	Principal permanent representative of member state to NATO (including any of its subsidiary bodies) resident in U.S. and resident members of official staff; Secretary General, assistant secretaries general, and Executive Secretary of NATO; other permanent NATO officials of similar rank, or immediate family	Art. 12, 5 UST 1094; Art. 20, 5 UST 1098
NATO 2	Other representative of member state to NATO (including any of its subsidiary bodies) including representatives, advisers, and technical experts of delegations, or immediate family; dependents of member of a force entering in accordance with the provisions of the NATO Status-of-Forces Agreement or in accordance with the provisions of the "Protocol on the Status of International Military Headquarters"; members of such a force if issued visas	Art. 13, 5 UST 1094; Art. 1, 4 UST 1794; Art. 3, 4 UST 1796
NATO 3	Official clerical staff accompanying representative of member state to NATO (including any of its subsidiary bodies), or immediate family	Art. 14, 5 UST 1096
NATO 4	Official of NATO (other than those classifiable as NATO-1), or immediate family	Art. 18, 5 UST 1098
NATO 5	Experts, other than NATO officials classifiable under NATO4, employed in missions on behalf of NATO, and their dependents	Art. 21, 5 UST 1100
NATO 6	Member of a civilian component accompanying a force entering in accordance with the provisions of the NATO Status-of-Forces Agreement; member of a civilian component attached to or employed by an allied headquarters under the "Protocol on the Status of International Military Headquarters" set up pursuant to the North Atlantic Treaty; and their dependents	Art. 1, 4 UST 1794; Art. 3, 5 UST 877
NATO 7	Attendant, servant, or personal employee of NATO1, NATO2, NATO3, NATO4, NATO5, and NATO6 classes, or immediate family	Arts. 12–20, 5 UST 1094–1098
O1	Alien with extraordinary ability in sciences, arts, education, business or athletics	101(a)(15)(O)(i)
O2	Alien accompanying and assisting in the artistic or athletic performance by O1	101(a)(15)(O)(ii)
O3	Spouse or child of O1 or O2	101(a)(15)(O)(iii)
P1	Internationally recognized athlete or member of internationally recognized entertainment group	101(a)(15)(P)(i)
P2	Artist or entertainer in a reciprocal exchange program	101(a)(15)(P)(ii)
P3	Artist or entertainer in a culturally unique program	101(a)(15)(P)(iii)
P4	Spouse or child of P1, P2, or P3	101(a)(15)(P)(iv)
Q1	Participant in an international cultural exchange program	101(a)(15)(Q)(i)
Q2	Irish Peace Process Program participant	101(a)(15)(Q)(ii)(I)
Q3	Spouse or child of Q2	101(a)(15)(Q)(ii)(II)
R1	Alien in a religious occupation	101(a)(15)(R)
R2	Spouse or child of R1	101(a)(15)(R)
S5	Certain aliens supplying critical information relating to a criminal organization or enterprise	101(a)(15)(S)(i)
S6	Certain aliens supplying critical information relating to terrorism	101(a)(15)(S)(ii)
S7	Qualified family member of S5 or S6	101(a)(15)(S)
T1	Victim of a severe form of trafficking in persons	101(a)(15)(T)(i)
T2	Spouse of T1	101(a)(15)(T)(ii)
T3	Child of T1	101(a)(15)(T)(ii)
T4	Parent of T1 under 21 years of age	101(a)(15)(T)(ii)
T5	Unmarried sibling under age 18 of T1 under 21 years of age	101(a)(15)(T)(ii)
TN	NAFTA professional	214(e)(2)
TD	Spouse or child of NAFTA professional	214(e)(2)
U1	Victim of criminal activity	101(a)(15)(U)(i)
U2	Spouse of U1	101(a)(15)(U)(ii)
U3	Child of U1	101(a)(15)(U)(ii)
U4	Parent of U1 under 21 years of age	101(a)(15)(U)(ii)
U5	Unmarried sibling under age 18 of U1 under 21 years of age	101(a)(15)(U)(ii)
V1	Spouse of a lawful permanent resident alien awaiting availability of immigrant visa	101(a)(15)(V)(i) or (ii)
V2	Child of a lawful permanent resident alien awaiting availability of immigrant visa	101(a)(15)(V)(i) or (ii)
V3	Child of a V1 or V2	203(d) & 101(a)(15)(V)(i) or (ii)

IMMIGRANTS

IMMEDIATE RELATIVES

IR1	Spouse of U.S. citizen	201(b)
IR2	Child of U.S. citizen	201(b)
IR3	Orphan adopted abroad by U.S. citizen	201(b) & 101(b)(1)(F)
IH3	Child from Hague Convention country adopted abroad by U.S. citizen	201(b) & 101(b)(1)(G)
IR4	Orphan to be adopted in U.S. by U.S. citizen	201(b) & 101(b)(1)(F)
IH4	Child from Hague Convention country to be adopted in U.S. by U.S. citizen	201(b) & 101(b)(1)(G)
IR5	Parent of U.S. citizen at least 21 years of age	201(b)
CR1	Spouse of U.S. citizen (conditional status)	201(b) & 216
CR2	Child of U.S. citizen (conditional status)	201(b) & 216
IW1	Certain spouses of deceased U.S. citizens	201(b)
IW2	Child of IW1	201(b)
IB1	Self-petition spouse of U.S. citizen	204(a)(1)(A)(iii)
IB2	Self-petition child of U.S. citizen	204(a)(1)(A)(iv)
IB3	Child of IB1	204(a)(1)(A)(iii)
VI5	Parent of U.S. citizen who acquired permanent resident status under the Virgin Islands Nonimmigrant Alien Adjustment Act	201(b) & §2 of the Virgin Islands Nonimmigrant Alien Adjustment Act (PL 97–271)

VIETNAM AMERASIAN IMMIGRANTS

AM1	Vietnam Amerasian principal	§584(b)(1)(A) of Foreign Operations, Export Financing, and Related Programs Appropriations Act, 1988 (as contained in §101(e) of PL 100–102) as amended.
AM2	Spouse or child of AM1	§584(b)(1)(A) and (B) of Foreign Operations, Export Financing, and Related Programs Appropriations Act, 1988 (as contained in §101(e) of PL 100–102) as amended.
AM3	Natural mother of AM1 (and spouse or child of such mother) or person who has acted in effect as the mother, father, or next-of-kin of AM1 (and spouse or child of such person)	§584(b)(1)(A) and (C) of Foreign Operations, Export Financing, and Related Programs Appropriations Act, 1988 (as contained in §101(e) of PL 100–102) as amended.

CUBAN IMMIGRANTS

CU6	Cuban refugees	§1 of PL 89-732, as amended by PL 94-571
CU7	Non-Cuban spouse or child of alien classified as CU6	§1 of PL 89-732, as amended by PL 94-571

SPECIAL IMMIGRANTS

SB1	Returning resident	101(a)(27)(A)
SC1	Person who lost U.S. citizenship by marriage	101(a)(27)(B) & 324(a)
SC2	Person who lost U.S. citizenship by serving in foreign armed forces	101(a)(27)(B) & 327
SI1	Certain aliens employed by the U.S. government in Iraq or Afghanistan as translators or interpreters	§1059 of PL 109–163 as amended by PL 110–36
SI2	Spouse of SI1	§1059 of PL 109–163 as amended by PL 110–36
SI3	Child of SI1	§1059 of PL 109–163 as amended by PL 110–36
SM1	Alien recruited outside the U.S. who has served or is enlisted to serve in the U.S. Armed Forces for 12 Years	101(a)(27)(K)
SM2	Spouse of SM1	101(a)(27)(K)
SM3	Child of SM1	101(a)(27)(K)
SQ1	Certain Iraqis employed by or on behalf of U.S. government	§1244 of Public Law 110–181
SQ2	Spouse of SQ1	§1244 of Public Law 110–181
SQ3	Child of SQ1	§1244 of Public Law 110–181

FAMILY-SPONSORED PREFERENCES

Family 1st Preference

F11	Unmarried son or daughter of U.S. citizen	203(a)(1)
F12	Child of F11	203(d) & 203(a)(1)
B11	Self-petition unmarried son or daughter of U.S. citizen	204(a)(1)(A)(iv) & 203(a)(1)
B12	Child of B11	203(d), 204(a)(1)(A)(iv) & 203(a)(1)

Family 2nd Preference (Subject to Country Limitations)

F21	Spouse of lawful permanent resident	203(a)(2)(A)
F22	Child of lawful permanent resident	203(a)(2)(A)
F23	Child of F21 or F22	203(d) & 203(a)(2)(A)
F24	Unmarried son or daughter of lawful permanent resident	203(a)(2)(B)
F25	Child of F24	203(d) & 203(a)(2)(B)
C21	Spouse of lawful permanent resident (conditional)	203(a)(2)(A) & 216
C22	Child of alien resident (conditional)	203(a)(2)(A) & 216
C23	Child of C21 or C22 (conditional)	203(d) & 203(a)(2)(A) & 216
C24	Unmarried son or daughter of LPR (Conditional)	203(a)(2)(B) & 216
C25	Child of F24 (conditional)	203(d) & 203(a)(2)(B) & 216
B21	Self-petition spouse of lawful permanent resident	204(a)(1)(B)(ii)
B22	Self-petition child of lawful permanent resident	204(a)(1)(B)(iii)
B23	Child of B21 or B22	203(d) & 204(a)(1)(B)(ii)
B24	Self-petition unmarried son or daughter of LPR	204(a)(1)(B)(iii)
B25	Child of B24	203(d) & 204(a)(1)(B)(iii)

Family 2nd Preference (Exempt from Country Limitations)

FX1	Spouse of lawful permanent resident	202(a)(4)(A) & 203(a)(2)(A)
FX2	Child of lawful permanent resident	202(a)(4)(A) & 203(a)(2)(A)
FX3	Child of FX1 or FX2	202(a)(4)(A) & 203(a)(2)(A) & 203(d)
CX1	Spouse of lawful permanent resident (conditional)	202(a)(4)(A) & 203(a)(2)(A) & 216.
CX2	Child of lawful permanent resident (conditional)	202(a)(4)(A) & 203(a)(2)(A) & 216.
CX3	Child of CX1 or CX2 (conditional)	202(a)(4)(A) & 203(a)(2)(A) & 203(d) & 216.
BX1	Self-petition spouse of lawful permanent resident	204(a)(1)(B)(ii)
BX2	Self-petition child of lawful permanent resident	204(a)(1)(B)(iii)
BX3	Child of BX1 or BX2	204(a)(1)(B)(ii) & 203(d)

Family 3rd Preference

F31	Married son or daughter of U.S. citizen	203(a)(3)
F32	Spouse of F31	203(d) & 203(a)(3)
F33	Child of F31	203(d) & 203(a)(3)
C31	Married son or daughter of U.S. citizen (conditional)	203(a)(3) & 216.
C32	Spouse of C31 (conditional)	203(d) & 203(a)(3) & 216.
C33	Child of C31 (conditional)	203(d) & 203(a)(3) & 216.
B31	Self-petition married son or daughter of U.S. citizen	204(a)(1)(A)(iv) & 203(a)(3)
B32	Spouse of B31	203(d), 204(a)(1)(A)(iv) & 203(a)(3)
B33	Child of B31	203(d), 204(a)(1)(A)(iv) & 203(a)(3)

Family 4th Preference

F41	Brother or sister of U.S. citizen at least 21 years of age	203(a)(4)
F42	Spouse of F41	203(d) & 203(a)(4)
F43	Child of F41	203(d) & 203(a)(4)

EMPLOYMENT-BASED PREFERENCES

Employment 1st Preference (Priority Workers)

Code	Description	Section
E11	Alien with extraordinary ability	203(b)(1)(A)
E12	Outstanding professor or researcher	203(b)(1)(B)
E13	Multinational executive or manager	203(b)(1)(C)
E14	Spouse of E11, E12, or E13	203(d) & 203(b)(1)(A) & 203(b)(1)(B) & 203(b)(1)(C)
E15	Child of E11, E12, or E13	203(d) & 203(b)(1)(A) & 203(b)(1)(B) & 203(b)(1)(C)

Employment 2nd Preference (Professionals Holding Advanced Degrees or Persons of Exceptional Ability)

Code	Description	Section
E21	Professional holding advanced degree or alien of exceptional ability	203(b)(2)
E22	Spouse of E21	203(d) & 203(b)(2)
E23	Child of E21	203(d) & 203(b)(2)

Employment 3rd Preference (Skilled Workers, Professionals, and Other Workers)

Code	Description	Section
E31	Skilled worker	203(b)(3)(A)(i)
E32	Professional holding baccalaureate degree	203(b)(3)(A)(ii)
E34	Spouse of E31 or E32	203(d) & 203(b)(3)(A)(i) & 203(b)(3)(A)(ii)
E35	Child of E31 or E32	203(d) & 203(b)(3)(A)(i) & 203(b)(3)(A)(ii)
EW3	Other worker (subgroup numerical limit)	203(b)(3)(A)(iii)
EW4	Spouse of EW3	203(d) & 203(b)(3)(A)(iii)
EW5	Child of EW3	203(d) & 203(b)(3)(A)(iii)

Employment 4th Preference (Certain Special Immigrants)

Code	Description	Section
BC1	Broadcaster in U.S. employed by Int'l Broadcasting Bureau of Broadcasting Bd. of Governors, or a grantee of such organization	101(a)(27)(M) & 203(b)(4)
BC2	Accompanying spouse of BC1	101(a)(27)(M) & 203(b)(4)
BC3	Accompanying child of BC1	101(a)(27)(M) & 203(b)(4)
SD1	Minister of religion	101(a)(27)(C)(ii)(I) & 203(b)(4)
SD2	Spouse of SD1	101(a)(27)(C)(ii)(I) & 203(b)(4)
SD3	Child of SD1	101(a)(27)(C)(ii)(I) & 203(b)(4)
SE1	Certain employees or former employees of U.S. government abroad	101(a)(27)(D) & 203(b)(4)
SE2	Spouse of SE1	101(a)(27)(D) & 203(b)(4)
SE3	Child of SE1	101(a)(27)(D) & 203(b)(4)
SF1	Certain Former Employees of the Panama Canal Company or Canal Zone Government	101(a)(27)(E) & 203(b)(4)
SF2	Spouse or Child of SF1	101(a)(27)(E) & 203(b)(4)
SG1	Certain former employees of U.S. government in Panama Canal Zone	101(a)(27)(F) & 203(b)(4)
SG2	Spouse or child of SG1	101(a)(27)(F) & 203(b)(4)
SH1	Certain former employees of the Panama Canal Company or Canal Zone government on April 1, 1979	101(a)(27)(G) & 203(b)(4)
SH2	Spouse or child of SH1	101(a)(27)(G) & 203(b)(4)
SJ1	Certain foreign medical graduates (adjustments only)	101(a)(27)(H)
SJ2	Accompanying spouse or child of SJ1	101(a)(27)(H) & 203(b)(4)
SK1	Certain retired international organization employees	101(a)(27)(I)(iii) & 203(b)(4)
SK2	Spouse of SK1	101(a)(27)(I)(iv) & 203(b)(4)
SK3	Certain unmarried sons or daughters of an international organization employee	101(a)(27)(I)(i) & 203(b)(4)
SK4	Certain surviving spouses of a deceased international organization employee	101(a)(27)(I)(ii) & 203(b)(4)
SL1	Juvenile court dependent (adjustment only)	101(a)(27)(J) & 203(b)(4)
SN1	Certain retired NATO6 civilians	101(a)(27)(L) & 203(b)(4)
SN2	Spouse of SN1	101(a)(27)(L) & 203(b)(4)
SN3	Certain unmarried sons or daughters of NATO6 civilian employees	101(a)(27)(L) & 203(b)(4)
SN4	Certain surviving spouses of deceased NATO6 civilian employees	101(a)(27)(L) & 203(b)(4)

SP	Alien beneficiary of petition or labor certification application filed prior to Sept. 11, 2001, if petition or application was rendered void due to terrorist act of 9/11. Spouse, child of such alien, or grand-parent of child orphaned by a terrorist act of 9/11	§421 of PL 107–56.
SR1	Certain religious workers	101(a)(27)(C)(ii)(II) & (III) as amended, & 203(b)(4)
SR2	Spouse of SR1	101(a)(27)(C)(ii)(II) & (III) as amended, & 203(b)(4)
SR3	Child of SR1	101(a)(27)(C)(ii)(II) & (III) as amended, & 203(b)(4)

Employment 5th Preference (Employment Creation Conditional Status)

C51	Employment creation *outside* targeted areas	203(b)(5)(A)
C52	Spouse of C51	203(d) & 203(b)(5)(A)
C53	Child of C51	203(d) & 203(b)(5)(A)
T51	Employment creation *in* targeted rural / high-unemployment area	203(b)(5)(B)
T52	Spouse of T51	203(d) & 203(b)(5)(B)
T53	Child of T51	203(d) & 203(b)(5)(B)
R51	Investor Pilot Program, not in targeted area	203(b)(5) &.§610 of the Departments of Commerce, Justice, and State, the Judiciary and Related Agencies Appropriations Act, 1993 (PL 102–395), as amended.
R52	Spouse of R51	203(d) & 203(b)(5) & Sec. 610 of the Departments of Commerce, Justice, and State, the Judiciary and Related Agencies Appropriations Act, 1993 (PL 102–395), as amended.
R53	Child of R51	203(d) & 203(b)(5) & Sec. 610 of the Departments of Commerce, Justice, and State, the Judiciary and Related Agencies Appropriations Act, 1993 (PL 102–395), as amended.
I51	Investor Pilot Program, in targeted area	203(b)(5) & Sec. 610 of the Departments of Commerce, Justice, and State, the Judiciary and Related Agencies Appropriations Act, 1993 (PL 102–395), as amended.
I52	Spouse of I51	203(d) & 203(b)(5) & Sec. 610 of the Departments of Commerce, Justice, and State, the Judiciary and Related Agencies Appropriations Act, 1993 (PL 102–395), as amended.
I53	Child of I51	203(d) & 203(b)(5) & Sec. 610 of the Departments of Commerce, Justice, and State, the Judiciary and Related Agencies Appropriations Act, 1993 (PL 102–395), as amended.

OTHER NUMERICALLY LIMITED CATEGORIES

Diversity Immigrants

DV1	Diversity immigrant	203(c)
DV2	Spouse of DV1	203(d) & 203(c)
DV3	Child of DV1	203(d) & 203(c)

TABLES OF AUTHORITIES CITED

Federal Statutes Cited

Federal Regulations Cited

Federal Agency Documents Cited

Other Citations

IMMIGRATION & NATIONALITY ACT (INA)

References to Former INA Sections Listed Under Original Section Number

CONVERSION TABLE
8 U.S.C. TO INA

8 USC	INA
1101	101
1102	102
1103	103
1104	104
1105	105
1105a	106
1151	201
1152	202
1153	203
1154	204
1155	205
1156	206
1157	207
1158	208
1159	209
1160	210
1181	211
1182	212
1183	213
1183a	213A
1184	214
1185	215
1186a	216
1186b	216A
1187	217
1188	218
1189	219
1201	221
1202	222
1203	223
1204	224
1221	231
1222	232
1223	233
1224	234
1225	235
1225a	235A
1226	236
1227	237
1228	238
1229	239
1229a	240
1229b	240A
1229c	240B
1230	240C
1231	241
1252	242
1253	243
1254	244
1255	245
1255a	245A
1256	246
1257	247
1258	248
1259	249
1260	250
1281	251
1282	252
1283	253
1284	254
1285	255
1286	256
1287	257
1288	258
1301	261
1302	262
1303	263
1304	264
1305	265
1306	266
1321	271
1322	272
1323	273
1324	274
1324a	274A
1324b	274B
1324c	274C
1324d	274D
1325	275
1326	276
1327	277
1328	278
1329	279
1330	280
1351	281
1352	282
1353	283
1354	284
1355	285
1356	286
1357	287
1358	288
1359	289
1360	290
1361	291
1362	292
1363	293
1363a	294
1401	301
1402	302
1403	303
1404	304
1405	305
1406	306
1407	307
1408	308
1409	309
1421	310
1422	311
1423	312
1424	313
1425	314
1426	315
1427	316
1428	317
1429	318
1430	319
1431	320
1432	321
1433	322
1435	324
1436	325
1437	326
1438	327
1439	328
1440	329
1440-1	329A
1441	330
1442	331
1443	332
1444	333
1445	334
1446	335
1447	336
1448	337
1449	338
1450	339
1451	340
1452	341
1453	342
1454	343
1455	344
1455	345
1457	346
1458	347
1481	349
1483	351
1488	356
1489	357
1501	358
1502	359
1503	360
1504	361
1521	411
1522	412
1523	413
1524	414
1531	501
1532	502
1533	503
1534	504
1535	505
1536	506
1537	507

IMMACT90, IIRIRA, PATRIOT ACT, REAL ID ACT
AND OTHER PUBLIC LAWS

IMMACT 90 (PL 101-649)

IIRIRA (PL 104-208, DIV. C)

USA PATRIOT ACT (PL 107-56)

REAL ID ACT (PL 109-13)

OTHER PUBLIC LAWS

OTHER FEDERAL STATUTES

8 C.F.R. — ALIENS & NATIONALITY

References to Former CFR Sections Listed Under Original Section Number

20 C.F.R. — EMPLOYEES' BENEFITS

22 C.F.R. — FOREIGN RELATIONS

28 C.F.R. — JUDICIAL ADMINISTRATION

OTHER FEDERAL REGULATIONS

5 C.F.R.
(Administrative Personnel)

6 C.F.R.
(Domestic Security)

7 C.F.R. (Agriculture)

15 C.F.R.
(Commerce & Foreign Trade)

19 C.F.R.
(Customs Duties)

21 C.F.R.
(Food & Drugs)

26 C.F.R.
(Internal Revenue)

27 C.F.R.
(Alcohol, Tobacco, & Firearms)

29 C.F.R.
(Labor)

34, C.F.R.
(Education)

42 C.F.R.
(Public Health)

45 C.F.R.
(Public Welfare)

48 C.F.R.
(Federal Acquisition)

FEDERAL REGISTER CITATIONS

Agency Memos, Letters, Etc.

Legal Opinions; General Counsel Memos

Letters & Memos

Memoranda of Understanding

OTHER AGENCY DOCUMENTS

Adjudicator's Field Manual (AFM)

Inspector's Field Manual (IFM)

Immigration Court Practice Manual (EOIR)

EOIR Operating Policies & Procedures Memoranda (OPPMs)

ICE Directives

General Administration Letters (GALs)

Training & Employment Guidance Letters (TEGLs)

Technical Assistance Guide (TAG) No. 656

Operation Instructions (OIs)

DOS CABLES

FOREIGN AFFAIRS MANUAL

7 FAM

9 FAM

STATE STATUTES

NEW JERSEY

NEW MEXICO

NEW YORK

OHIO

OKLAHOMA

OREGON

PENNSYLVANIA

RHODE ISLAND

TEXAS

UTAH

VIRGINIA

WASHINGTON

WISCONSIN

Federal Rules

Rules of Civil Procedure

Rules of Evidence

Rules of Criminal Procedure

Rules of Appellate Procedure

Rules of Procedure, Alien Terrorist Removal Court

U.S. Constitution

TABLE OF CASES

Alphabetization is letter-by-letter (e.g., "Sango" precedes "San Juan")

A

B

C

D

E

F

G

H

I

J

K

L

M

N

O

P

Q

R

S

T

U

V

W

X

Y

Z

Abbreviations

A/S Adjustment of Status

AAO Administrative Appeals Office [f/k/a Administrative Appeals Unit]

ABC American Baptist Churches v. Thornburgh

AC Associate Commissioner (Legacy INS)

AC21 American Competitiveness in the 21st Century Act

ACC Administrative Control Court (EOIR)

ACE Accelerated Citizen Examination

ACWIA American Competitiveness and Workforce Improvement Act

ADD Assistant District Director. Also, ADDE (Examinations); ADDI (Investigations); ADDM (Management)

ADIT Alien Documentation, Identification and Telecommunications System

AEDPA Anti-Terrorism and Effective Death Penalty Act of 1996

AFACS A-Files Accountability and Control System

AFM Adjudicator's Field Manual

AG Attorney General of the United States

AMIS Asset Management Information System

AO Asylum Office(r)

AOS (1) Adjustment of Status (as used by USCIS and most immigration lawyers, as well as in this book); (2) Affidavit of Support (as used by the Department of State)

APA Administrative Procedures Act

ARC Alien Registration Card (also called Permanent Resident Card or "Green Card")

ASC Application Support Center

AWO Affirmance Without Opinion

BALCA Board of Alien Labor Certification Appeals

BAR Board of Appellate Review

BCBP U.S. Customs and Border Protection [now, more commonly, CBP]

BCC Border Crossing Card

BCIS U.S. Citizenship and Immigration Services [now, more commonly, USCIS]

BEC Backlog Elimination Center [f/k/a Backlog Reduction Center]

BIA Board of Immigration Appeals (DOJ/EOIR)

BICE U.S. Immigration and Customs Enforcement [now, more commonly, ICE]

BIT Bilateral Investment Treaty

BOP Bureau of Prisons (DOJ)

BP Border Patrol

BRC Backlog Reduction Center [now, Backlog Elimination Center]

C/S Change of Status

CAT U.N. Convention Against Torture and Other Cruel, Inhuman or Degrading Treatment or Punishment

CBP U.S. Customs and Border Protection (DHS)

CGFNS Commission on Graduates of Foreign Nursing Schools

CIJ Chief Immigration Judge

CIS (1) U.S. Citizenship and Immigration Services [more commonly, USCIS]; (2) "Center for Immigration Studies," a restrictionist group

CJA Criminal Justice Act

CLAIMS Computer Linked Application Information Management System

CLASS Consular Lookout and Support System

CLN Certificate of Loss of Nationality

CMT Crime of Moral Turpitude [also, CIMT]

CO Certifying Officer (DOL)

COV Crime of Violence

CPT Curricular Practical Training

CR Conditional Resident

CSA Controlled Substances Act, 21 U.S.C. §844(a)

CSC California Service Center

CSPA Child Status Protection Act of 2002

CSS *Catholic Social Services v. Thornburgh*

D/S Duration of Status

DD District Director

DED Deferred Enforced Departure

DHS Department of Homeland Security

DO (1) District Office; (2) Deportation Officer

DOD Department of Defense

DOE Date of Entry

DOJ Department of Justice

DOL Department of Labor

DOS Department of State

DOT Dictionary of Occupational Titles

DSO Designated School Official

DV Diversity Visa Lottery Program
E/S Extension of Status
EA Employment Authorization
EAC Eastern Adjudication Center [now, Vermont Service Center]
EAD Employment Authorization Document
EAJA Equal Access to Justice Act
EEV Electronic Employment Verification (E-Verify)
ENFORCE Enforcement Case Tracking System
EOIR Executive Office for Immigration Review (DOJ)
ER Expedited Removal
ETA Employment & Training Administration (DOL)
EVD Extended Voluntary Departure
EWI Entry Without Inspection
FAM Foreign Affairs Manual
FARES Fees and Applications Receipt and Entry System
FARRA Foreign Affairs Reform and Restructuring Act
FCCPT Foreign Credentialing Commission on Physical Therapy
FCI Federal Correctional Institution
FCN Treaty of Friendship, Commerce, and Navigation
FDC Federal Detention Center
FDF Federal Detention Facility
FFOA Federal First Offender Act
FGM Female Genital Mutilation
FMG Foreign Medical Graduate
FOIA Freedom of Information Act
FSN Foreign Service National
FSO Foreign Service Officer
FTO Foreign Terrorist Organization
GAL General Administration Letter (DOL)
GEMS General Counsel Management System
GPO Government Printing Office
H.R. House Report
HRIFA Haitian Refugee Immigration Fairness Act
HSA Homeland Security Act of 2002
IBIS Interagency Border Inspection System
ICE U.S. Immigration and Customs Enforcement (DHS)
ICMS Investigations Case Management System
IDENT Automated Fingerprint Identification System
IFM Inspector's Field Manual
IG Inspector General
IIO Immigration Information Officer
IIRIRA Illegal Immigration Reform & Immigrant Responsibility Act of 1996 (also IIRAIRA)
IJ Immigration Judge
ILT AILA's *Immigration Law Today*
IMFA Immigration Marriage Fraud Amendments Act of 1986
IMMACT90 Immigration Act of 1990
INA Immigration and Nationality Act
INS Immigration and Naturalization Service
INSPASS INS Passenger Accelerated Service System
INTCA Immigration and Nationality Technical Corrections Act of 1994
IO Immigration Officer
IR Immediate Relative
IRCA Immigration Reform and Control Act of 1986
ISD Immigrant Services Division
IV Immigrant Visa
JRAD Judicial Recommendation Against Deportation
KCC Kentucky Consular Center
LAU Legalization Appeals Unit
LAW Lawfully Authorized or Admitted Worker
LC Labor Certification
LCA Labor Condition Application
LIFE Legal Immigration and Family Equity Act of 2000
LIN Northern Service Center [now, Nebraska Service Center]
LPR Lawful Permanent Resident
MRD Machine Readable Document
MS&D Maintenance of Status and Departure bond
MSC Missouri Service Center
MTINA Miscellaneous & Technical Immigration & Nationality Act Amendments of 1991
NACARA Nicaraguan Adjustment and Central American Relief Act
NACS Naturalization Automated Casework System
NAFTA North American Free Trade Agreement
NAILS National Automated Immigration Lookout System
Natz Naturalization
NBC National Benefits Center
NBCOT National Board for Certification of Occupational Therapists
NBCOTA Noncitizen Benefit Clarification and Other Technical Amendments Act of 1998
NCIC National Crime Information Center
NIF Notice of Intent to Fine
NIV Nonimmigrant Visa
NIW National Interest Waiver

NOF Notice of Findings
NRC National Record Center
NSC Nebraska Service Center
NTA Notice to Appear
NVC National Visa Center
O*NET Occupational Information Network
O/S Out of Status, or Overstay
OARS Outlying Area Reporting Station
OCAHO Office of Chief Administration Hearing Officer
OCIJ Office of the Chief Immigration Judge
ODP Orderly Departure Program
OES Occupational Employment Statistics
OI Operations Instructions
OIC Officer-in-Charge
OIL Office of Immigration Litigation (DOJ)
OMB Office of Management and Budget
OOH *Occupational Outlook Handbook* (DOL)
OPPM Operating Policies and Procedures Memorandum (EOIR)
OPT Optional Practical Training
OSC Order to Show Cause
PERM Program Electronic Review Management System
PIMS Petition Information Management System
POE Port of Entry
PRC Permanent Resident Card (also called an Alien Registration Card or Green Card)
PT Practical Training
PTI Pretrial Intervention Program
QDE Qualified Designated Entity
RAW Replenishment Agricultural Worker
RC Regional Commissioner (Legacy INS)
RFE Request for Evidence
RIR Reduction in Recruitment
RN Registered Nurse
RO Responsible Officer (J-1 Exchange Visitor Program)
RSC Regional Service Center
RTD Refugee Travel Document
RVIS Remote Video Inspection System
S.R. Senate Report
SA Special Agent
SAO Security Advisory Opinion
SAO Supervisory Adjudication Officer
SAW Special Agricultural Worker
SC Service Center
SDAO Supervisory District Adjudications Officer
SENTRI Secure Electronic Network for Travelers Rapid Inspection
SEVIS Student & Exchange Visitor Information System
SEVP Student & Exchange Visitor Program
SK Specialized Knowledge (for L Visa)
SPC Service Processing Center
SRC Southern Regional Center [now, Texas Service Center]
STEM Scientific, Technical, Engineering, Mathematics
SVP Specific Vocational Preparation
SWA State Workforce Agency
TA Trial Attorney
TAG Technical Assistance Guide No. 656—Labor Certifications
TAL Technology Alert List
TCN Third Country National
TEGL Training and Employment Guidance Letter
TN Trade NAFTA
TPCR Transition Period Custody Rules
TPS Temporary Protected Status
TSA Transportation Security Administration.
TSC Texas Service Center
TWOV Transit Without Visa
U.S.C.C.A.N. U.S. Code Cong. & Admin. News
UNHCR United Nations High Commission for Refugees
UPL Unauthorized Practice of Law
USC or U.S.C. (1) U.S. Citizen *(abbreviated without periods herein)*; (2) U.S. Code *(abbreviated with periods herein)*
USCIS U.S. Citizenship and Immigration Services (DHS)
USSG U.S. Sentencing Guidelines
US-VISIT U.S. Visitor and Immigrant Status Indicator Technology Program
VAWA Violence Against Women Act
VD Voluntary Departure
VGTOF Violent Gang or Terrorist Organization File
VO Visa Office
VSC Vermont Service Center
VWP Visa Waiver Program [formerly, Visa Waiver Pilot Program (VWPP)]
WAC Western Adjudication Center [now, California Service Center]

SUBJECT MATTER INDEX

Alphabetization is word-by-word (e.g., "L Visas" precedes "Labor Certification")

A

B

C

D

E

F

G

H

I

J

K

L

M

P

Q

R

S

T

U

V

W